A LITERARY GAZETTEER
of ENGLAND

A LITER

Beere bay

ARY GAZETTEER
of ENGLAND

by Lois H. Fisher

The Globe

McGRAW-HILL BOOK COMPANY

New York   St. Louis   San Francisco   Auckland
Bogotá   Hamburg   Johannesburg   London
Madrid   Mexico   Montreal   New Delhi
Panama   São Paulo   Singapore
Sydney   Tokyo   Toronto

Library of Congress Cataloging in Publication Data

Fisher, Lois H, date.
   A literary gazetteer of England.

   Includes index.
   1. Literary landmarks—England. 2. England—
Gazetteers. I. Title.
PR109.F5   914.2′04′857   79-22776
ISBN 0-07-021098-5

1234567890   HAHA   89876543210

*The editors for this book were Robert A. Rosenbaum and Tobia L. Worth,
the designer was Naomi Auerbach, and the production supervisor
was Paul A. Malchow. It was set in Plantin
by University Graphics, Inc.*

Printed and bound by Halliday Lithograph Corporation.

To my husband

PREFACE

A Literary Gazetteer of England is a comprehensive survey of the "literary associations" of more than 500 English (and occasionally foreign) authors with more than 1,200 English localities. It is arranged alphabetically, by place name, and each entry appears as a distinct essay with as much history, geography, and archaeology as seems relevant to the literary material. The main focus of the book is on the localities, of course, and these include every English town, village, hamlet, river, mountain, or other area of significant literary interest. The separate essays range in size from fewer than 100 words to the London entry, which is well over 100,000 words, and they cover virtually every important writer in the general area of English literature from the Early English period until the 1970s. The associations documented are as extensive as the coverage and include all significant personal events in the lives of major writers, as well as much of their commentary as seems still interesting to a late-20th-century reader. Furthermore, and in this respect the *Literary Gazetteer* is unique among all other books in the field, there is extensive verbatim coverage of the literary associations in the literature ("Pickwick slept here") together with a large amount of quoted material in order to enliven and make clear the nature of the relationship between writer and locale.

My initial interest in the subject, during the 1960s, was that of a traveler trying to explore the principal literary sites in England, and as such I was frustrated by the lack of a single compilation of basic material. At that time, the most important published work was John Freeman's *Literature and Locality*, but that book was neither comprehensive (as a glance at any standard English guidebook will easily verify), nor, of course, up to date. I thought for a time of producing a guidebook, but that seemed a less rewarding project than the one which I actually undertook; and in any event, after I had finished my first draft of the *Literary Gazetteer*, early in 1977, Oxford University Press published *The Oxford Literary Guide to the British Isles*, edited by Dorothy Eagle and Hilary Carnell, which took the form of a guide-book to the considerably larger subject of the British Isles.

I began the *Literary Gazetteer* in late 1971 and spent the better part of eight years in the full-time task of collecting and collating (then writing) vastly more material on literary associations than has ever before been put into a single volume. After reviewing the many works on the subject, I felt that a new approach would be necessary. What I noticed almost immediately was that the greatest part of the information in these secondary sources was circulating from book to book without many fresh infusions, as, for example, could be obtained by digging into the more promising works of the authors or, of course, into the most recent biographies. Before writing a single word (other than sample material), I read through some 250 biographies, collect-ing and collating the material with that from the *Dictionary of National Biography*, *Encyclopaedia Britannica*, and the other stan-dard and well-known material in the "literary associations" genre; there were many revelations. That done, I collected quantities of direct material—passages from works, letters, and so on—and mate-rial from the standard guidebooks (of which there are many, usually of a city or county). This effort was achieved through reference to my bookseller and, more significantly, through access to the following libraries (in alphabetical order): the Bowes Museum (Bowes, York-shire), the British Museum, the Claremont Colleges (Claremont, Cal-ifornia), Concordia University (Montreal, Quebec), the University of Durham (County Durham), McGill University (Montreal, Quebec), North Carolina State University (Raleigh, North Carolina), and the University of California at Los Angeles.

The biggest problem I had in constructing this survey was in decid-ing which material to include of the considerable amount I had drawn together. I decided simply to write up what I had, with McGraw-Hill's concurrence, and to see what emerged. What emerged was about a million and a quarter words, and so I began the task of trimming somewhere around 400,000 words from a manuscript already described by one of McGraw-Hill's reviewers as "compact." A great deal of nonliterary material was scrapped (historical, etymological, etc.) and some minor literary figures shrank further into the back-ground, but on the whole the literary core of my first draft survived the bath of red ink which I gave the manuscript. One casualty of this editorial process was any extensive reference to modern writers (after 1950); however, some reference to good taste (Do I really have the right to reveal the addresses of extant literary figures?) and expedience (it is especially difficult to document the locations in the more recent works) also played a part in this decision.

There were other decisions made on the coverage of this book, some of them taken at the outset of the project. For one thing, we decided to limit our research to England (recall that the *Oxford Lit-erary Guide* covers the entire British Isles) on the grounds that under-taking any larger scope would necessitate publishing two volumes if the work were on the scale the subject seemed to require. After all, the *Oxford Guide*, which is by no means a small book, has about one-fifth of the English material of the *Literary Gazetteer* and wanders into areas which I would regard as nonliterary (even by stretching things a bit, I could not present Hester Lynch Thrale and Sir Robert Bruce Cotton as literary figures). Perhaps we may yet do the companion work to the *Literary Gazetteer*, and if we do, it would be just as long. For another thing, if we had actually undertaken a separate volume, it would have been on London, which if you look back in the book, runs over 150 pages in the final draft. Here our major problem was that most important literary figures had extensive London connections; these, then, stretched over the centuries, from the time London consisted of little more than the present City right down to modern London, as it has had incorporated into it many of the towns which were formerly a day's ride away. To deal with this problem, I elected to write an essay on each author, arranging the essays chronologically by birth date (whether they were born in London or not), and to write a historical/geographical sketch for each major period so that the location could be visualized more easily. In any case I made no attempt to provide a modern guide, although places still extant are so indicated. Of course, there is a *Guide to Literary London*, by George Williams, which does indeed provide such a guide, and I must express my considerable debt to that excellent and comprehensive compilation.

A gazetteer, of course, generally has maps and photographs, and mine are done with an eye both to illustrating and to locating the places of interest. Where possible, photographs of some of the more important literary sites are included, but here a lack of space has made the most severe inroads. It was, quite simply, not possible to provide visual and written documentation of the subject, and so the photographs were used mainly as supplements with the role of providing generally new information for the book. The maps, on the other hand, are an essential part of the book, and on these one can find many of the places referred to in the text along with as many of the most useful reference points as seemed essential. The careful reader will no doubt notice, at this point, that the older county designations, not those of recent redistricting, are used. The reason for this choice is that since I essentially terminated my subject at 1950 the older boundaries seemed appropriate; that is, both the lives and works of the authors reported here have meaning with reference to the older divisions, and so it shall remain, at least for the time being. It is, in any event, not difficult to find things on the newer maps. I should note, in this regard, that every place referred to in the book is given a precise location in terms of a standard reference point. This information appears at the beginning of each essay.

Perhaps the part of my work that I enjoyed the most was that involving the original literary material which was ultimately included in the text. I did have to trim my quotations somewhat when we cut down my first draft, but what remains is still substantial and makes, I hope, an effective counterbalance to the necessarily matter-of-fact material describing each author's connection with a particular location. Indeed, this dimension to the book certainly has helped the prose style along no end and, most importantly, provides an exact and verbatim description of the literary experience referred to. I trust those who, like myself, have suffered from vague guidebook references such as "Mary Shelley has an important association here" will appreciate the detail I have been permitted to put into my book. Of course, in this area, one should also note that I am not claiming anything like completeness in this respect, for that is impossible, and so my judgment as to what might please both the serious reader and the browser will itself have to be judged in the final analysis.

There are other features of the book which I should mention at this point. The first of these is that no attempt has been made to restrict the presentation to places which still exist or have ever existed. Thus, reference has been made to such areas as John Bunyan's "Delectable Mountains," and many localities which no longer exist are described in detail as they existed in the time of the literary figure. In some cases there is not even a plaque to stimulate the visitor, and in others meadows have given way to concrete, but even so, when the location has literary significance, it is included. Then, too, there is no list of those places which are under the care of the British National Trust or the Ministry of Works, and there is no collection of the opening and closing times of these or other places (although I have indicated when a private property is open to the public); numerous guidebooks provide this information.

I should like to thank all of those persons along the way who so patiently put up with me and my inquiries in the preparation of this book. Numerous archivists and librarians throughout England answered my queries with patience and often offered information beyond that which was requested. I have mentioned the libraries which I used, above, and my thanks go to their staffs and in particular to Jayne K. Finney, of the Claremont Colleges Library, and to the late Michael Kirkby of the Bowes Museum in Barnard Castle, Yorkshire, who put many of the museum's facilities at my disposal throughout 1971–1972. Also, both Barbara Haner and Jacqueline Lindauer made many helpful suggestions while I was putting my material together, and Drs. Paul D. Orr of Claremont, California, and Irving Yachnin of Montreal, Quebec, answered my many questions concerning the numerous specified and, especially, vague illnesses which overtook many of the writers considered here.

Finally, my thanks must go to my daughter, who helped in those of the more tiresome tasks as they arose, but most of all I wish to thank my husband, to whom this book is dedicated. His patience over these writing years was truly inexhaustible, and without his encouragement, help, and editorial advice this book would never have been written.

Lois H. Fisher

A LITERARY GAZETTEER
of ENGLAND

ABINGER, Surrey (pop. 1,458) Some of the finest views in southern England are from the Surrey North Downs; the view from the sandstone escarpment of Leith Hill is especially good. Abinger, 3½ miles southwest of Dorking, sitting halfway up the hill, is an old village with wooden stocks and a partly Norman church. Tradition maintains that the stocks have never been used except in Edward Bulwer-Lytton's *My Novel*, when Lenny Fairfield and then Dr. Riccabocca manage to get themselves shut into them:

> "But how on earth did you get into my new stocks?" asked the squire, scratching his head.
> "My dear sir, Pliny the elder got into the crater of Mount Etna."
> "Did he, and what for?"
> "To try what it was like, I suppose," answered Riccabocca.
> The squire burst out a laughing.
> "And so you got into the stocks to try what it was like. Well, I can't wonder,—it is a very handsome pair of stocks," continued the squire. . . .

The stocks stand outside the parish church.

About 1 mile north of the village and halfway to the hamlet of Abinger Hammer (so named because of the hammer ponds, the places where water for driving hammer mills is stored) is Crossways Farm, dating from 1601. One of the county's earliest gentleman's residences built specifically as a farm, it became the setting of George Meredith's novel *Diana of the Crossways;* this was an area that Meredith knew well since he lived at nearby Box Hill. Ridworth describes Crossways to Lady Dunstane:

> "She has often pointed out to me . . . where The Crossways lies. . . . The house has a small plantation of firs behind it, and a bit of river, rare for Sussex, to the right. An old straggling red brick house at Crossways, a stone's

throw from a fingerpost on a square of green; roads to Brasted, London, Wickford, Riddlehurst. I shall find it. . . ."

ACOL, Kent (pop. 270) On the chalky Isle of Thanet, 4 miles southwest of Margate, Acol (pronounced "ay'cole") is in a region which came into special favor in Victorian times because of its "miraculous air"; today it is popular both as a holiday site and as a sanatorium. Near the hamlet is a disused but formidable chalk pit, known as the Smuggler's Leap, about which a legend exists. It is said that an officer of the crown and the smuggler he was pursuing in a heavy fog fell over the precipice; they still haunt the spot. This is the basis for Richard Harris Barham's "The Smuggler's Leap: A Legend of Thanet" in *The Ingoldsby Legends:*

> You may hear old folks talk   Of that quarry of chalk;
> Or go over—it's rather too far for a walk,
> But a three-shilling drive will give you a peep
> At that fearful chalk-pit—so awfully deep,
> Which is call'd to this moment "The Smuggler's Leap!"

ACTON, Middlesex (pop. 68,670) Formerly a west suburb of London, 4½ miles west of Paddington Station, Acton is now officially in the new borough of Ealing. Most of the town's old buildings have disappeared, but in the 18th century Acton was a spa with its wells in Old Oak Lane and its assembly rooms and villas (both gone) for guests.

While the records here are scanty, Poyntz Park (now gone) John Aubrey claimed was where Sir Walter Ralegh stood "in a stand . . . [and] took a pipe of tobacco, which made the ladies quitt it till he had done." One important building with literary associations can still be found, though with difficulty; on Salisbury Street is Berrymead Priory, a 16th-century establishment of forty or so nuns that has been rebuilt a number of times and used for a myriad of purposes. It is now part of the premises of Nevill's bread factory. The priory was rebuilt during George II's reign and again in the early 19th century, when it took on its aspect of a battlemented medieval castle. The large baronial-style hall with a beamed roof is two stories high, and some parts of the hall are obviously incorporated from a previous structure. This was the home of Edward Bulwer-Lytton (Lord Lytton) in 1836, the year in which he and his wife agreed to a legal separation. His residence here was very short, and no evidence of his presence can be found.

ADDERBURY, Oxfordshire (pop. 1,336) The small village of Adderbury, about 3½ miles south of Banbury, is a charming place with one of the finest churches in Oxfordshire, thatch-roofed houses, and an old tithe barn. Around the church tower and under the parapet of both aisles is one of the most famous carved picture galleries in England, including a twin-tailed mermaid, a knotted-tailed dragon, a medieval orchestra, a dragon with two bodies, and, as the *pièce de résistance,* an archer whose aim at a horrible animal is so bad that he has struck an old woman in the knee and so frightened her that she clings to her cow.

Near the green is the gabled 17th-century Adderbury House (originally Adderbury Hall), the home of John Wilmot, 2d Earl of Rochester, a dissolute poet with peculiar interests. After his marriage to Elizabeth Malet, a wealthy heiress whom Samuel Pepys described as "the great beauty and fortune of the north," Adderbury Hall became their home. The hall later passed into the hands of the 2d Duke of Argyll, with whom Alexander Pope stayed in 1739; when in the duke's company, Pope wrote the flattering "Verses Left by Mr. Pope, on his lying in the same bed which . . . Rochester slept in," in which the ducal virtues are contrasted with the alleged vices of the earlier earl.

ADLESTROP, Gloucestershire (pop. 138) The valley of the Evenlode River, cut through by a spiderweb of small lanes, holds the lovely stone-built hamlet of Adlestrop, 6 miles west of Chipping Norton. The church here dates in part to the 14th century, and the Gothic-style Adlestrop Park and its gardens are especially attractive. Jane Austen was a visitor to the rectory in the summer of 1806, when her uncle held the living here. There is a more recent association with the 20th-century poet Edward Thomas, who traveled through the village, noting as the express went through that

No one left and no one came
On that bare platform. What I saw
Was Adlestrop, only the name.

ADSCOMBE, Somerset A tiny village in the Bridgwater Rural District 1 mile west of Over Stowey, Adscombe is central to the Quantocks, the hills loved so much by Samuel Taylor Coleridge and William Wordsworth; here wooded combes cut deeply into the sharp escarpment, and the upland areas are heather-covered. The two poets walked over the entire area and found considerable inspiration here, as *Lyrical*

Ballads shows. Coleridge was especially impressed by the ruined Norman chapel (gone) standing in a nearby open field; it was this which suggested part of the setting of "The Foster Mother's Tale." Here the baby "wrapped in mosses" was found by

. . . the huge round beam
Which props the hanging wall of the old chapel[.]

ADUR RIVER, Sussex Rising in the vicinity of Horsham, 26 miles northwest of Brighton, the Adur River flows 20 miles south to the English Channel at Shoreham-by-Sea. Having cut a gap through the downland, the Adur has formed a landscape of green pastures, woodlands, and leafy lanes on its journey to the sea. The name Adur supposedly came from the Roman Portus Adurni, which had been at the river's estuary, but in fact the name can be laid to Michael Drayton, who first wrote in the seventeenth song of *Poly-Olbion:*

$\mathbf{ff}$ And *Adur* coming on, to *Shoreham* softly said,
The Downes did very ill, poore Woods so to debase.

The corresponding illustrations explain his use:

This River that here falls into the Ocean might well bee understood in that *Port* of *Adur,* about this coast, the reliques whereof, learned *Camden* takes to be *Edrington,* or *Adrington,* a little from *Shoreham.* And the Author here so calls it *Adur.*

At low tide the river is yellow and unattractive, but at high tide it looks like a lake, especially near Shoreham. The river at sunset is described by Algernon Swinburne in "On the South Coast":

Skies fulfilled with the sundown, stilled and splendid, spread as a flower that spreads.
Pave with rarer device and fairer than heaven's the luminous oyster-beds,
Grass-embanked, and in square plots ranked, inlaid with gems that the sundown sheds.

Squares more bright and with lovelier light than heaven that kindled it shines with shine
Warm and soft as the dome aloft, but heavenlier yet than the sun's own shrine:
Heaven is high, but the water-sky lit here seems deeper and more divine.

Another late-19th-century poet, William Ernest Henley, makes good use of the river in his volume entitled *Hawthorn and Lavender:*

In Shoreham River, hurrying down
To the live sea,
By working, marrying, breeding Shoreham Town,
Breaking the sunset's wistful and solemn dream,
An old, black rotter of a boat
Past service to the labouring, tumbling flote,
Lay stranded in mid-stream:
With a horrid list, a frightening lapse from the line,
That made me think of legs and a broken spine:
Soon, all-too soon,
Ungainly and forlorn to lie
Full in the eye
Of the cynical, discomfortable moon
That, as I looked stared from the fading sky,
A clown's face flour'd for work. . . .
. . . .
The poor old hulk remained. . . .

AFFPUDDLE, Dorset (pop. 357) Southwest of Bere Regis on the Puddle River are three small villages with a *-puddle* suffix: Turnerspuddle, Briantspuddle, and Affpuddle. The last-named has a lovely mid-13th-century church that had its own vicar of Bray at the time of the dissolution of the monasteries. Located less than 8 miles from Dorchester, this is an area that Thomas Hardy knew well and used in *The Return of the Native*. In the novel Affpuddle becomes East Egdon, on the opposite side of the heath from Mrs. Yeobright's house, and here is located Alderworth (probably fictional), the cottage in which Clym and Eustacia live after their marriage. This is, as Hardy says, a location "almost as lonely as that of Eustacia's grandfather, but the fact that it stood near a heath was disguised by a belt of firs which almost enclosed the premises." As well as living at Alderworth, Eustacia and Clym are married in the old church here.

ALBURY, Surrey (pop, 1,172) The best approach to Albury is from the south, where the visitor can pass the impressive Roman ruins from which, it is said, the village takes its name. The Roman settlement was known of in John Aubrey's day, and he wrote of it in his *Perambulation of Surrey*, which was later included in Richard Rawlinson's *The Natural History and Antiquities of Surrey*. Albury, 4 miles east of Guildford, is known for its fantastic chimneys, sixty-three of which, all different and all twisted, are on Albury House.

It is the house and its park that are of greatest interest here. In the 17th century there was a 12-acre vineyard above the broad terrace. The present Queen Anne house was built after the original manor burned (it belonged to the Dukes of Northumberland in the 19th century), but in the 17th century the estate belonged to Thomas Howard, Earl of Arundel and later Duke of Norfolk, a friend of the diarist John Evelyn. Evelyn was frequently here, and, indeed, the gardens were laid out to his specifications. He visited the estate to observe the progress on September 23, 1670, and remarks in his diary:

> 23 to *Alburie* to see how that Garden proceeded, which I found exactly don according to the Designe & plot I had made, with the *Crypta* through the mountaine in the parke, which is 30 pearches in length, such a *Pausilippe* is no where in England besides: The Canals were now digging, & Vineyards planted.

Evelyn's visits continued even after Heneage Finch bought the property around 1687. Richard Gough in his additions to William Camden's *Britannia* notes the sale to Finch and the rebuilding that subsequently took place:

> Near Guildford on the same stream is *Aldbury*, the darling villa, as Mr. Evelyn calls it, of . . . Thomas Howard, earl of Arundel. . . . [I]t was purchased of his heir by the earl of Aylesford, who pulled down great part of this old building, and his brother, captain Finch, has built a new house. It is romantically situated in a bottom, shaded from the North and South by oaks, surrounded by a park, vineyards, and canals, and a road cut through a rock 30 perches in length.

Two centuries later William Cobbett had nothing but high praise for Albury Park in his *Rural Rides;* he asked the owner's permission, "having got into the park," to allow "me [to] go out of it on the side next to the Shire":

> He not only granted this request, but . . . permitted us to ride all about the park, and to see his gardens, which, without any exception, are, to my fancy, the prettiest in England; that is to say, that I ever saw in England. . . .
> The mansion-house, which is by no means magnificent, stands on a little flat by the side of the parish church, having a steep, but not lofty, hill rising on the south side of it. It looks right across the gardens, which lie on the slope of a hill which runs along at about a quarter of a mile distant from the front of the house.

He continues:

> At the back of . . . [the] garden, and facing the yew-tree row, is a wall probably ten feet high, which forms the breastwork of a *terrace;* and it is this terrace which is the most beautiful thing that I ever saw in the gardening way. . . . Take it altogether, this, certainly, is the prettiest garden that I ever beheld. There was taste and sound judgment at every step in the laying out of this place. Everywhere utility and convenience is combined with beauty.

A final note concerns the use Hilaire Belloc makes of the park and the yew walk in *The Four Men.* He has his pilgrims come this way, and a pilgrim path does pass just north of Albury.

ALCESTER, Warwickshire (pop. 2,259) A market town whose earliest history is Roman, Alcester (pronounced "ols'ter") lies at the confluence of the Alne and Arrow Rivers, 8 miles west of Stratford-on-Avon. It lies along Ryknild Street and the Ridgeway and flourished during Roman times as Aluna, but little remains of the old camp. Most of the old-world feeling in today's town comes from the timber-fronted houses, the town hall (rebuilt in the mid-17th century), and the extensive range of Georgian buildings near the church. The Old Malt House (ca. 1500) on Malt Mill Lane is well preserved, and the lane itself is one of the best Tudor streets in the county; here everything is authentic, and all the structures have been carefully preserved.

Beauchamps Court here was probably the birthplace of Sir Fulke Greville, the poet and intimate of Sir Philip Sidney, on October 3, 1554; this was one of the estates belonging to his paternal grandfather, also Sir Fulke, one of the largest property holders in Warwickshire. Not only did the grandfather own Beauchamps Court, but Henry VIII presented him with the old monastery (nothing remains) and many of the adjacent estates at the dissolution. There is, however, virtually no information about the younger Greville's life until he entered Shrewsbury School in 1564.

ALCONBURY, Huntingdonshire (pop. 523) Alconbury, one of several villages on Alconbury Brook, a tributary of the Ouse, is 4 miles northwest of Huntingdon and is divided into two distinct parts: the older, grouped around a triangular open space known as Maypole Square; and the newer eastern area, grouped along the green and the brook. It is the newer section of the village that is of literary interest. Matcham's Bridge has been submerged beneath the roadway of the A1, but it once stood at the junction of Woolley Road and contained the gibbet from which Gervase Matcham was hanged in August 1786. The story of Matcham, a sailor who had taken part in the robbery and brutal murder of a drummer boy in 1780, is told in *The Ingoldsby Legends* by Richard Harris Barham.

ALDBURY, Hertfordshire (pop. 519)   Set in an area of west Hertfordshire known for its thatched and half-timbered houses, Aldbury is on the Ash River 4½ miles northwest of Bishop's Stortford. A 16th-century manor house with latticed windows looks out on the green, which is surrounded by old cottages. The local almshouses are black-timbered cottages with thatched roofs; and the church, part of which dates from the 14th century, contains lovely treasures including medieval glass and a 1514 chalice.

Stocks was the home of Mrs. Humphry Ward (Mary Augusta Ward), author of *Robert Elsmere* and granddaughter of Dr. Thomas Arnold, from 1892 until 1920. It was here that she wrote many of her novels, including *The Story of Bessie Costrell, Sir George Tressady, Helbeck of Bannisdale, Eleanor, Lady Rose's Daughter,* and *Fenwick's Career.* During this period she was frequently in London, where she was actively engaged with children's recreational and educational centers, and partly on her account such facilities as special education centers were made mandatory in 1918. Among her many guests here were Henry James, George Bernard Shaw, and Julian and Aldous Huxley. Mrs. Ward died in London on March 24, 1920, and was buried in the churchyard here.

ALDEBURGH, Suffolk (pop. 2,793)   Aldeburgh today is a relatively quiet resort and festival town, but this was not always the case; in particular the town has suffered from the erosive powers of the gale-lashed North Sea. Slaughden, once a part of Aldeburgh and a wealthy fishing and shipbuilding center, saw its livelihood slip into the sea. In 1669 Samuel Pepys stood as the Member of Parliament for Aldeburgh, but his candidature did not prosper in spite of very powerful patronage. A great deal of the opposition raised—that he did not know the needs of the corporation and was a stranger to the area—was true enough and made sufficient inroads with the electors to cause his defeat.

It was in the old Aldeburgh that George Crabbe was born on December 24, 1754, in a small house at what was then the end of one of the two parallel and unpaved streets leading to the water's edge. Crabbe's father was a salt master, a collector of salt duties, and his early neighbors made their living from the sea. Crabbe lived here before going to school in Bungay and returned in 1777 to set up a singularly unsuccessful medical practice. His patients, seeing him bring back "handfuls of weeds" from his walks and not understanding his consuming interest in botany, felt that since "Dr. Crabbe got his medicines in the ditches, he could have little claim for payment." Two years later the sea took its due, and Crabbe's birthplace and ten other houses were swept out to sea. The following year, 1780, Crabbe gave up his practice and moved to London.

Advised and assisted by Edmund Burke, he took holy orders before returning briefly to Aldeburgh as a curate. *The Village,* though not completed until 1783, is the immediate result of his life in the town, and its success was enough to secure for him four small livings, at Muston, Leicestershire, Allington, Lincolnshire, and Sweffling and Great Glemham, Suffolk. *The Borough,* not finished until 1810, which was well after Crabbe left Aldeburgh, in its descriptions of the life in and around the town, the quay, and the river, and of Suffolk nature, presents the environment as it was earlier. It was one of the episodes in this poem that Benjamin Britten, another Suffolk native, used as the basis for the libretto of *Peter Grimes.* Some Aldeburgh inhabitants still maintain that on the nearby beaches the ghost of Peter Grimes can be seen as it traces "how sidelong crabs had scrawl'd their crooked race" or sadly listens "to the tuneless cry/Of fishing gull or the clanging golden-eye." Crabbe was, as Byron commented, "Nature's sternest painter, yet the best," and in his work he never shirked describing what was sordid and ugly in 18th-century village life. Curiously enough, lines from *The Borough* appear appropriate today if applied to the tremendous influx of people for the annual Aldeburgh Music Festival presentations:

> Soon as the season comes, and crowds arrive,
> To their superior rooms the wealthy drive.
> Others look round for lodging snug and small
> The brick-floored parlour which the butcher lets. . . .

There is a commemorative bust of Crabbe by Thomas Thurber in the Aldeburgh Church.

Aldeburgh was one of the small towns that Edward FitzGerald favored; he spent his summer holidays here as a child, and his interest grew because of his intimacy with the Crabbe family. When he came up from Woodbridge to collect sea lore from the fishermen, he stayed at Clare Cottage, fronting the sea, in "two little rooms, enough for me; [and] a civil woman pleased to have me in them." His schooner,

ALDEBURGH   The ghost of Peter Grimes, subject of Benjamin Britten's opera as drawn from a character in George Crabbe's *The Borough,* is still said to walk the beach here in Aldeburgh. Crabbe, a native of the town, was preoccupied with both Aldeburgh and the sea and drew heavily upon both in his works.

the *Scandal,* was often tied up here. FitzGerald, asking Tennyson's wife to send the poet up to join him, ended his missive by commenting that Aldeburgh is "where nobody scarce knows his name (don't be angry, Mrs. A. T.)." There is no record that Tennyson came.

Wilkie Collins was one of the first passengers to take the train here after the line was established in 1862. He was seeking a change of air and ideas for part of the setting for his novel *No Name.* He describes in detail Crag Path, the prehistoric rock promenade that has been partially destroyed by the action of the ocean and today is tarmacked over and flanked on one side by a retaining wall. Aldeburgh is the scene both of the battle of wits between Captain Wragge and Mrs. Lecount and of the suicide contemplated by Magdalen when her long-sought revenge is near; her lodgings have a clear view of the coast. One of the features of Suffolk and the coast that Collins describes vividly in *No Name* is the sense of isolation: to the east, "the horizon line invisibly melting into the monotonously misty sky"; to the south, cut off by the martello tower on the high grass mound; to the west, "a lurid streak of sunset"; and close by,

> the sullen flow of the tidal river Alde, ebbed noiselessly from the muddy banks; and nearer still, lonely and unprosperous by the bleak waterside, lay the lost little port of Slaughden; with its forlorn wharfs and warehouses of decaying wood, and its few scattered coasting vessels deserted on the oozy river shore.

When here, Collins stayed at Sea View.

Sir James Matthew Barrie and Sir Arthur Conan Doyle were here for a working holiday in early 1893 when Doyle helped Barrie with the libretto of a light opera, *Jane Annie.* During the late 19th and early 20th centuries two novelists of note frequented Aldeburgh. George Gissing, an admirer of Edward FitzGerald's, came here often in the late 19th century, both as a visitor and as a member of the Omar Khayyam Club. Gissing stayed with Edward Clodd, one of the founders of the club and a native of Aldeburgh, who lived at Strafford House. Gissing's mistress Gabrielle Fleury also visited here and delivered messages from Gissing to FitzGerald. Another of Edward Clodd's house guests was George Meredith, who spent a great deal of time in 1905 on the sea front talking with the local fishermen and wrote, "There is no element of charm there, only grandeur of sea and strengthening air."

ALDERBURY, Wiltshire (pop. 731) On one of the many English rivers called Avon, Alderbury lies 3 miles southeast of Salisbury and is the village nearest to the historic Forest of Clarendon; recent excavations have found a royal palace originally dating to Saxon times but made into a royal hunting box by the Normans. The palace is important because it is the first-known royal site not to have been fortified; that is, Clarendon Palace was used strictly for pleasure in times, presumably, when the early kingdom was peaceful. Henry III (r. 1216–1272) took a great interest in the palace, made many improvements in it, and probably directed the founding of a kiln for tiles here, the first to be established outside monastic walls. Thousands of tiles have been discovered, some with

lions rampant, griffins, and dragons and all with fleurs-de-lis on them.

The village itself stands on a hill and contains a gabled inn, the Green Dragon, said to have been known to Charles Dickens and used in *Martin Chuzzlewit* as the Blue Dragon Inn. Here the winds are rampant "and indeed, before Christmas, reared [the sign] clean out of its crazy frame." Alderbury is the "little Wiltshire village, within an easy journey of the fair old town of Salisbury." Dickens also describes the effect of autumn upon the village:

> The wet grass sparkled in the light; the scanty patches of verdure in the hedges—where a few green twigs yet stood together bravely, resisting to the last the tyranny of nipping winds and early frosts—took heart and brightened up; the stream, which had been dull and sullen all day long, broke out into a cheerful smile; the birds began to chirp and twitter on the naked boughs, as though the hopeful creatures half believed that winter had gone by, and spring had come already.

It should perhaps be noted that Amesbury and Winterslow also claim the distinction of being the intended "little Wiltshire village," but their claims are not nearly so strong as that of Alderbury.

ALDERLEY EDGE, Cheshire (pop. 3,112) Alderley Edge, 14 miles south of Manchester, is a quaint old residential town snuggled under the Edge, a fine vantage point for views of both Lancashire and Cheshire. There is a second town, Alderley, which is perched on the hillside itself, and the two towns are often referred to as one. Indeed, their population figures are combined above. The rectory in the old town was the birthplace of Arthur Stanley, the educator and dean of Westminster Abbey, in 1815.

In December 1870, George Gissing was sent with his brother to Lindow Grove School after the death of their father; it was at this time that Gissing began his study of Greek. His time here was not happy because of a reputed lack of intellectual companionship. Indeed, Gissing's sister Ellen commented modestly that his "intellectual ability . . . was much above average and . . . it set him apart from his natural associates." He left here in 1873, probably in December.

ALDERMASTON, Berkshire (pop. 2,186) Perfectly located on a wooded hillside on the south bank of the Kennet River 11 miles southwest of Reading, Aldermaston, an old village with a number of brick-and-tile cottages, is notable in that an atomic research establishment and its associated appendages have made virtually no impression on it. The manor house retains the 17th-century staircase and the Jacobean chimney.

The village and the manor have been traditionally associated with William Congreve and his play *The Old Bachelor.* It has been suggested that he began the work here when recovering from illness in 1689 or 1690; however, a similar claim has been presented by Stretton Hall. It is known that Congreve visited both estates, but there is no evidence regarding the play.

In June 1654 John Evelyn and his wife were here on a trip out of London. Evelyn noted in his diary that Sir Humphry Forster's estate had been "built *a-la-moderne*" but made no other comment about it.

ALDERTON, Suffolk (pop. 426) This tiny east Suffolk village, 6½ miles southeast of Woodbridge, has an especially fine location 1 mile from the East Anglia coast. The living here was presented to Giles Fletcher the Younger sometime around 1618 when he gave up his fellowship at Trinity College, Cambridge, and it is possible that Sir Francis Bacon was Fletcher's benefactor. According to Thomas Fuller, the parishioners, "clownish" and "low-parted," who had "nothing but their shoes high about them," had little respect for Fletcher, and their disregard led to the melancholia which brought about the poet's death sometime before the end of November 1623. He was buried in the Alderton church.

ALDINGTON, Kent (pop. 526) Situated on the edge of Romney Marsh 5½ miles west of Hythe, the small village of Aldington is best known for its connection, around 1525, with Elizabeth Barton, the "Holy Maid of Kent," whose prophetic visions and trances ultimately brought about her execution at Tyburn on April 20, 1534. Two centuries earlier, in 1365, John Gower, author of *Confessio Amantis* and a man of Kentish ancestry and means, secured Aldington Septvauns, a 14th-century manor, which he kept until 1373. Chaucer's "moral Gower" is said to have purchased the estate in 1365 under irregular conditions: the owner, Sir William Cobham's son and heir, was not of legal age in 1365 and could not enter into a contract; Gower was accused of having encouraged the youth to lie with respect to his age. But this fable does not conform with Gower's character, and he was probably slandered.

In 1509 Thomas Linacre was rector here and possibly spent some time at the rectory (now a farm), and two years later, after Linacre had become Henry VIII's physician, Erasmus became the rector. More recently Aldington Knoll was the home of Ford Madox Ford before Joseph Conrad took the house. Conrad had long had a particular affection for the county and moved here in the early months of 1909. Soon after he and his wife arrived, however, he seems to have taken a violent dislike to their house, and a letter to John Galsworthy contains the comment, "I want a change for this hole is growing more odious to me every day." "The Secret Sharer" was written in November of that year, and by January 1910 Conrad finished *Under Western Eyes.* Five months later the Conrads moved to Orlestone. H. G. Wells makes use of the Aldington area in *The Food of the Gods:* at Aldington Knoll, an ancient Roman beacon, the picnickers are dispersed by the giant wasps, and the puppy is killed in front of its horrified mistress.

ALDWINCLE, Northamptonshire (pop. 396) In the northern and more agricultural part of the shire 3 miles north of Thrapston, Aldwincle (often spelled Aldwinkle) is a hamlet made up of two parishes, Aldwincle St. Peter and Aldwincle All Saints. Aldwincle St. Peter, the more northerly parish, has a magnificent basically 14th-century church with a medieval font, a 13th-century piscina, and a 14th-century chancel arch. The parish register records the baptism of Thomas Fuller, author of *The History of the Worthies of England,* who was born in the rectory in June 1608. Fuller first attended a school run by the

Rev. Arthur Smith, but his father's dissatisfaction with the boy's progress occasioned his removal, and his father took over his instruction. Fuller went up to Queens' College, Cambridge, in 1621. Nothing is left of his birthplace here, but the church has a memorial to him in which he is referred to as "a scribe instructed into the kingdom of heaven."

Aldwincle All Saints is at the southern end of the street, which is lined with gray stone houses; the church, now disused, dates from the 13th to the 15th century and has a font dating from the 14th century. Facing the church is the old rectory, where, tradition states, John Dryden was born on August 9, 1631. His maternal grandfather, the Rev. Henry Pickering, was the rector here, and it is generally agreed that the poet was born and baptized here. Now called Dryden House, the rectory, with thatched gables, stands back from the road and is covered with purple clematis and wisteria; as a child Dryden frequently came here from his home in Titchmarsh.

ALFRETON, Derbyshire (pop. 22,200) An early coal-mining town and now in an intensely industrialized area, Alfreton is a market town 14 miles northeast of Derby and 10 miles south of Chesterfield. It is an area that D. H. Lawrence knew well, and he used it in *Sons and Lovers;* on their way to Wingfield (South Wingfield), Paul Morel, Miriam, and a few others break their journey here and visit the church:

> They were all rather timid of entering [the church], with their bags of food, for fear of being turned out. . . . The place was decorated for Easter. In the font hundreds of white narcissi seemed to be growing. The air was dim and coloured from the windows, and thrilled with a subtle scent of lilies and narcissi. In that atmosphere Miriam's soul came into a glow. Paul was afraid of the things he mustn't do; and he was sensitive to the feel of the place. Miriam turned to him. He answered. They were together. He would not go beyond the Communion-rail.

ALKERTON, Oxfordshire (pop. 84) Just 5 miles northwest of Banbury, Alkerton is a pleasant hillside village whose 13th-century church is of special architectural interest; because the church stands on a hill, there are three steps from the nave to the sanctuary. Also of interest is the Jacobean rectory built by Thomas Lydyat, whose life was markedly shortened by his generosity. He pledged himself for his brother's debts, and treated roughly in jail, he did not long survive. Lydyat reputedly was a brilliant scholar, especially in astronomy and chronology, and is remembered because Dr. Samuel Johnson inserts him in "The Vanity of Human Wishes":

> Yet hope not life from grief or danger free,
> Nor think the doom on man reversed for thee:
> Deign on the passing world to turn thine eyes,
> And pause awhile from letters, to be wise;
> There mark what ills the scholar's life assail,
> Toil, envy, want, the patron, and the jail.
> See nations slowly wise, and meanly just,
> To buried merit raise the tardy bust.
> If dreams yet flatter, once again attend,
> Hear Lydiat's life, and Galileo's end.

ALL CANNINGS, Wiltshire (pop. 379) Four miles due east of Devizes in the lovely Vale of Pewsey is the tiny village of All Cannings, whose 15th-century church has a tall turret and some fine specimens of early colored glass in its windows. One of the rectors of the parish, Anthony Methuen, was a friend of Samuel Taylor Coleridge, and the poet made his home here for a short time in 1817.

ALLINGTON, Kent On a lock in the Medway River, Allington, 1½ miles northwest of Maidstone, the county town, is in an area of rich orchard land, and in spring apple blossoms form a heavy scented canopy. The squat, moated Norman Allington Castle, now housing a colony of Carmelite nuns and open to the public in summer, was the birthplace of Sir Thomas Wyatt in 1503. The major story associated with Wyatt and his home is undoubtedly apocryphal. He is said to have raised a lion's whelp and an Irish greyhound together on the estate before the lion reverted to type in adulthood. On this occasion, instead of greeting Wyatt playfully, the lion turned on its owner; Wyatt, shielded by the more faithful dog, dispatched the lion with a rapier. It was here in 1527 that Wyatt translated Petrarch's *De remediis utriusque fortunae* for Queen Catherine. Following the execution of Thomas Cromwell in 1540, Wyatt returned to Allington from London and probably worked on his *Penitential Psalms*.

The weir at Allington is claimed to be the Cloisterham Weir of Charles Dickens's *The Mystery of Edwin Drood*. There are other claimants for this distinction, among them East Farleigh and Snodland, and while Snodland fits Dickens's description somewhat better than Allington, there is no weir there and no proof that there ever was one.

ALLINGTON, Lincolnshire (pop. 217) Situated near the border of Leicestershire and 4 miles northwest of Grantham, Allington, once the two small hamlets of East and West Allington, is now amalgamated. The village is set on a narrow limestone ridge known as the Lincoln Edge and contains two towerless churches. George Crabbe was presented with the living at West Allington in 1789; the partly 12th-century church has a Jacobean pulpit from which Crabbe would have preached on the infrequent occasions on which he came here. He held this living jointly with that of Muston, Leicestershire, and left a curate in charge here while he lived at the Muston parsonage. He retained this parish until 1814, when he went to Trowbridge, Wiltshire.

ALNWICK, Northumberland (pop. 6,988) Located near the mouth of the Aln River, Alnwick (pronounced "ann'ick") has long been the ducal and county seat of Northumberland. The town and the castle no doubt antedate the Norman Conquest, but no records of earlier inhabitants exist. A Saxon fortification possibly existed on the site of Alnwick Castle, but the earliest construction of the present impressive castle took place in the early 12th century under Yvo de Vescy, 1st Baron of Alnwick. By the end of the century the castle was substantially as it is now. The castle, lands, and barony remained in the de Vescy family until they came into the hands of the Percys on November 19, 1309. William de Vescy, the last of that family to hold the Northumbrian estates, died in 1297 and left only one minor illegitimate son, William de Vescy of Kildare, for whom Bishop Anthony Bek (Bec) of Durham was to administer the estates. Bek sold the estates to Henry de Percy, the family most strongly associated with the castle, with Warkworth, and with William Shakespeare. Shakespearean use of the Percy family in the histories generally revolves around Warkworth Castle, the Percys' main residence until the 18th century. Henry Percy, the 6th Earl of Northumberland (known as "The Unthrifty"), who lived here, is used in *Henry VIII* and is the earl who had fallen in love with Anne Boleyn and was ordered to arrest Thomas Cardinal Wolsey. Later the King repaid the earl cruelly by making him serve on the commission that tried the Queen.

The North Country is full of legend and folklore, including a northern King Arthur, and, indeed, the northern associations have been worked out in considerable detail. Sir Thomas Malory mentions Alnwick in *Le Morte d'Arthur* and says that Joyous Gard, Sir Launcelot's castle, may be located here. Knowledge that Malory's designations are sometimes historically accurate gives credence to this view; he states that "some men say it [the castle] was Anwick and some men say it was Bamborrow [Bamburgh]." One is tempted to speculate that a fortress of some sort did exist in Alnwick before the 12th century. Malory himself was here in December 1462; after his release from Newgate Prison in London, he accompanied the Earl of Warwick's expedition to Northumberland under the orders of Edward IV to suppress and defeat the forces from Scotland led by Queen Margaret.

Bishop Thomas Percy (who was not an Alnwick Percy) came to the castle in 1765 at the invitation of the 1st Duke of Northumberland. The castle had fallen into extreme disrepair during the previous three centuries, and in the 18th century, when the Percys decided to make this their seat, they undertook large-scale renovation that was essentially completed by the time the compiler of *Reliques of Ancient English Poetry* was invited. Bishop Percy left an extremely fine description of the Alnwick surroundings, especially of the 13th-century Hulne Priory, 3½ miles to the northwest, and the Cheviots:

> On a little hill on [the river's] margin, are seen . . . the fine remains of Hulne Abbey: more to the left are little swellings, the hollows of which are fringed with a chain of small, rough thickets. . . . Over these [the plains beyond] the eye gradually rises to where the vast mountains of Cheviot erect their huge conic heads. . . .

Percy left no record of his impression of the castle. Perhaps he found shortcomings, as did Sir Walter Scott, who visited the castle in the early 1820s. Scott noted that the exterior of Alnwick lacked variety and grandeur, a comment that probably helped influence the 4th Duke of Northumberland to add a high, dominating tower to the keep. The duke also renovated the inside of the castle in Italian Renaissance style.

The castle contains an extremely fine collection of paintings, including two Canalettos, one of Alnwick Castle and one of Northumberland House in London. The library is particularly good and contains a copy of the Sherborne Missal.

ALRESFORD, Hampshire (pop. 1,709) Located at the junction of the Arle and Itchen Rivers, Alresford (pronounced "als'ford") is properly designated New

Alresford but is hardly ever so called. The place is anything but new, for there was a village here in the 12th century, when Bishop Godfrey de Lucy rebuilt it on a rather large scale, and by the 14th century it was considered one of the ten greatest wool centers in the country. Two particularly devastating fires, one set ablaze by the Royalists after the Battle of Cheriton and one in 1689, explain why the village is now styled "an 18th-century town."

It was in a house (that is now marked with a plaque) on the west side of Broad Street that Mary Russell Mitford was born on December 16, 1787; she lived here until 1798, when her family won a £20,000 lottery. Information on this event is conflicting: either ten-year-old Mary won the money, which was turned over to her father because she was a minor, or Dr. Mitford won the money. A brief period of prosperity followed (Dr. Mitford seems to have had an unenviable reputation for uncontrollable extravagance), and the family moved to a large house in Reading. Alresford was probably the source of much of the inspiration for *Our Village: Sketches of Rural Life, Character and Scenery*, which Miss Mitford began in 1824.

In the 16th century John Leland visited both New Alresford and Old Alresford, a scattered village at the end of Broad Street, when researching his *Itinerary*. He left comments about the Arle River but nothing about the village itself:

> The river first beginnith with a great number of fair sylver springs a good mile above Alresford; and these resorting to a botom make a good brode lake, communely caullied Alsford Pond.

James Elroy Flecker spent occasional holidays here when he was at Oxford from 1902 to 1906.

ALSTONFIELD, Staffordshire (pop. 402) Set above the lovely Dove Valley on limestone uplands at the Derbyshire border, Alstonfield is 9 miles east of Leek and exudes history with six Bronze Age barrows as well as a number of Saxon and Norman remains. The church is a remarkable hodgepodge of several centuries, and the churchyard and porches hold treasures: Saxon remnants of the early church. Three medieval coffin lids can be seen, too. This was the church that Izaak Walton and Charles Cotton attended and on which Walton commented, "What have we here, a church? As I'm a honest man, a very pretty church!" Cotton's pew, 17th-century and canopied, is paneled and ornately carved.

Cotton lived nearby at Beresford Hall, where he had been born; and here Walton often stayed. They fished in the Dove, and here is the Pike Pool, which Walton describes in *The Compleat Angler*. In 1674 Cotton built the Fishing House (now difficult to reach), and above its doorway is a stone inscribed with their initials. Walton writes of the house:

> PISC. But look you, sir, . . . and the situation of my little fishing-house[.]
> VIAT. The house seems at this distance a neat building.
> PISC. Good enough for that purpose. . . . And now, sir, you are come to the door, pray walk in, and there we will sit and talk as long as you please.
> VIAT. Stay, what's here over the door? *PISCATORIBUS SACRUM.* . . . Has my master Walton ever been here to see it, for it seems new built?
> PISC. Yes, he saw it cut in the stone before it was set up;

but never in the posture it now stands; for the house was but building when he was last here, and not raised so high as the arch of the door.

The relationship between the men was somewhat unusual in that Walton was already an old man, the son of a linendraper of London, while Cotton was almost forty years younger, an aristocrat, well traveled, and sophisticated. But Cotton finished the second half of the book that guaranteed Walton's fame.

ALTON, Hampshire (pop. 7,693) The trunk road which crosses Hampshire, following the route of the medieval pilgrims from Winchester to Canterbury in the eastern part of the county, cuts through farming country in which beech-hung streams meander about. Alton, about 9 miles southwest of Farnham, is now almost a part of Holybourne but in other times was a cloth and brewery center in its own right. Indeed, both Watney Mann and Harp Lager have large establishments here on the main street across from the basically 15th-century church, which itself shows the scars of a Civil War battle; in addition, well-preserved Georgian houses line the long, winding main street.

Literary associations in Alton date to the 14th century, when William Langland mentioned the village in *Piers Plowman:*

> Ye, thorugh the pass of Aultone
> Poverte inyght pass
> Withouten peril of robbynge.

In 1590, 1 Amery Street (marked with a plaque) became the home of Edmund Spenser. The poet had returned from Ireland with Sir Walter Ralegh in November 1589, and since the license for the publication of "the fayre Queen dysposed into xij bookes" was granted in December and Spenser is known to have been in London in January, it seems that the only feasible time for his residence here was in the period when he was arranging for the publication of that work. He may also have been working on *Complaints, Containing Sundrie Small Poemes of the Worlds Vanitie* during his time here.

Alton's brewing fame was used by a later writer; William Makepeace Thackeray, whose *Vanity Fair* is set partly in this Hampshire area, has Joseph Sedley stop in Alton on his way to London after landing in Southampton:

> Having partaken of a copious breakfast, with fish, and rice, and hard eggs, at Southampton, he had so far rallied at Winchester as to think a glass of sherry necessary. At Alton he stepped out of the carriage, at his servant's request, and imbibed some of the ale for which the place is famous.

Thackeray also mentions the Bell Inn here, where Boniface is the landlord, in *Henry Esmond*. More recently, Sir Compton Mackenzie, who lived at Canadian Cottage (demolished) in Beech, 1½ miles to the east, from 1896 to 1900, uses Alton as Galton in *The Altar Steps, The Parson's Progress*, and *Buttercups and Daisies;* in the last-named work he draws on many local persons. In 1925 Mackenzie presented the manuscript of *Mabel in Queer Street* to the Curtis Museum here. Finally, John Henry Newman lived at Swarthmore, 59 High Street (marked with a plaque), when he was an Oxford undergraduate.

ALTON, Staffordshire (pop. 1,367) Seeming somewhat like a village from a fairy tale because of its setting among the pines in the Churnet Valley, the stone-built village of Alton is looked down upon from a precipitous rock on one side by a 19th-century convent (built where the Norman castle stood) and from a hill on the other side by Alton Towers, the now partially abandoned home of the Talbots. The estate came into the hands of the Talbots through the marriage to an heir of John Furnival in the 15th century. It is John Talbot, 1st Earl of Shrewsbury, captured by Joan of Arc at Patay, who becomes the "brave captain and victorious" lord in William Shakespeare's *Henry VI: Part I.* Alton Towers, badly damaged during the Civil War, was rebuilt by the 15th and 16th Earls and remained the Talbot seat until 1924, when the estate was sold and the house began to slide along its present course. Today the exterior remains intact, and the interior parts which have survived contain refreshment rooms and a model railroad, said to be the largest of its kind.

Aside from the Talbots and a visit in September 1835 by the poet Thomas Moore to Lady Shrewsbury, Alton's greatest literary importance is in Benjamin Disraeli's *Lothair,* where it becomes "the chief seat of his [Lothair's] race":

> Muriel Towers crowned a wooded steep, part of a wild and winding sylvan valley at the bottom of which rushed a foaming stream. On the other side of the castle the scene, though extensive, was not less striking, and was essentially romantic. A vast park spread in all directions . . . with much variety of character . . . everywhere, sometimes glittering and sometimes sullen, glimpses of the largest natural lake that inland England boasts, Muriel Mere, and in the extreme distance moors, and the first crest of mountains.

Lothair's extravagant coming-of-age party is staged here; over the grounds and Muriel Mere

> Fanciful barges and gondolas of various shapes and colours were waiting for Lothair and his party, to carry them over to the pavilion, where they found a repast which became the hour and the scene. . . . No sooner were they seated than the sound of music was heard, distant, but now nearer, till there came floating on the lake, until it rested before the pavilion, a gigantic shell, larger than the building itself, but holding in its golden and opal seats Signor Mardoni and all his orchestra.

ALVESTON, Warwickshire (pop. 1,034) One of an attractive group of villages near Stratford-on-Avon, 2½ miles to the southwest, Alveston is on the Avon River and boasts a beautiful but much neglected old chapel, a very old cottage, and a lovely inn on the river bank. The disused Norman church stands in a field off a side lane, and while the exterior is in desperate need of repair, the interior contains a lovely Jacobean pulpit and an effigy of Nicholas Lane, a man who must have known William Shakespeare, for he engaged in a bitter dispute with the playwright's father over a debt the latter had taken over from his brother-in-law.

Dante Gabriel Rossetti came here in 1853, when he was in one of the deepest depressions he had ever known. Contemplating suicide, he reached the old church and its ancient graves and found himself strangely soothed by the harmonizing of the landscape with his mood. The result was "The Hill Summit":

> And now that I have climbed and won this height,
>   I must tread downward through the sloping shade
> And travel the bewildered tracks till night.
>   Yet for this hour I still may here be stayed
>   And see the gold air and the silver fade
> And the last bird fly into the last light.

AMBERLEY, Gloucestershire (pop. 1,222) An old village in the Cotswold Hills 3 miles south of Stroud and near Minchinhampton Common, Amberley has some fine views from Rodborough. Dinah Mulock Craik lived in Rose Cottage, a gray stone house, and wrote much of *John Halifax, Gentleman* here.

AMBLESIDE, Westmorland (pop. 2,876) A resort area in the center of the Lake District, Ambleside is at the head of Lake Windermere, in a sheltered position under Wansfell Pike, where Stock Gill and Kirkstone Pass enter the Rothay Valley; the town lies 13 miles northwest of Kendal. There is extensive evidence of Roman habitation here; and the 17th-century Bridge House, which spans a stream, was once a summerhouse to Ambleside Hall. The 19th-century Church of St. Mary the Virgin, which still engages in the medieval custom of rush-bearing every July, contains the Wordsworth Memorial Chapel, a memorial window, and the poet's Bible, presented by Mrs. Wordsworth. It also has a memorial window to Matthew Arnold. None of the Lake poets ever lived in Ambleside, but there are many literary associations just the same.

The poets have described Ambleside and not always in flattering terms. In 1843 Wordsworth wrote of the town's pall of early-morning smoke:

> While beams of orient light shoot wide and high,
> Deep in the vale a little rural Town
> Breathes forth a cloud-like creature of its own,
> That mounts not toward the radiant morning sky,
> But, with a less ambitious sympathy,
> Hangs o'er its Parent waking to the cares
> Troubles and toils that every day prepares.

Years earlier Wordsworth's fame had drawn another poet to Ambleside when John Keats made a walking tour of this area in the late spring of 1818; he came here from Bowness-on-Windermere and wrote of the walk:

> We walked . . . along the border of Winandermere all beautiful with wooded shores and Islands—our road was a winding lane, wooded on each side, and green overhead, full of Foxgloves—every now and then a glimpse of the Lake, and all the while Kirkstone and other large hills nestled together in a sort of grey black mist.

He stayed over in Ambleside on May 24 and finished "Isabella." The following morning he journeyed to see the Ambleside waterfall and then went on to visit Wordsworth at Rydal Mount.

While none of the Lake poets had homes in the immediate area, other literary figures did live in Ambleside. In 1832 Dr. Thomas Arnold built a holiday home, Fox House, beside the Rothay River, about 1 mile northwest of Ambleside; here the young Matthew Arnold spent a great deal of time, and after the death of his father in 1842 he continued to return to the area. In 1844, with the final examination in classics coming up at Oxford, Arnold and Arthur Hugh Clough came here to read, but Arnold found the scenic distractions enormous and spent a great deal of time walking and fishing. Both Thomas Carlyle and Ralph Waldo Emerson were visitors to the Arnold home. Harriet Martineau, well known for her *Survey of the Lake District* and *History of England during the Thirty Years' Peace, 1816–46,* came to Ambleside in 1845 for reasons of health and built the Knoll, a still-existing house on the road to Rydal Mount. When she came to live in Ambleside, she had already been lionized in London, and though often ill, she continued to write; *Eastern Life* and a translation and condensation of Auguste Comte's *Cours de philosophie positive* are among the works she produced here. Miss Martineau had many visitors including Wordsworth, Charlotte Brontë, George Eliot, and Emerson. She died here on June 27, 1876, having suffered from heart trouble since 1854; she was buried in Birmingham. Finally, in 1847 John Ruskin came to Ambleside to try to recover from a fit of depression resulting from his unsuccessful courtship of Charlotte Lockhart, Sir Walter Scott's granddaughter. The area did not suit him, and he returned to London extremely ill.

AMESBURY, Wiltshire (pop. 1,530) Set on a bend in the Avon River, on the Salisbury Plain, Amesbury is often called "a little miniature capital of the Plain proper." The town was mentioned in the *Anglo-Saxon Chronicle* under the date 995, but the facts establish that there was an earlier community here, for just west of the river on the outskirts of Amesbury Park is an earthwork structure called Vespasian's Camp. This Roman general and future Emperor, who served under Claudius in A.D. 43, actually occupied a site that can be dated at least three centuries earlier, when the British probably constructed it. The Norman and Early English church here, incorporating relics of a 10th-century nunnery that survived the dissolution of the monastic establishments in the 16th century, is called the Cathedral of the Valley and retains the fragments of an old Saxon wheel cross and an old Norman font. A strange feature is found in the aisle roof, where a carved head shows Henry VIII as a cherub.

Both Daniel Defoe and William Cobbett visited Amesbury and the Avon Valley on their turns around England. Defoe was much impressed by a practice said to occur here in the 18th century and wrote of it in *A Tour thro' the Whole Island of Great Britain:*

> I was told that at this Town there was a Meadow on the Bank of the River *Avon,* . . . which was Let for 12 *l.* a Year *per* Acre for the Grass only: This I enquir'd particularly after, at the Place, and was assur'd by the Inhabitants as one Man, that the Fact was True, and was shew'd the Meadows; the Grass which grew on them was such as grew to the length of Ten or Twelve Foot, rising up to a good Height, and then taking Root again, and was of so rich a Nature as to answer very well such an extravagant Rent.

Cobbett found a great deal of pleasure in the Avon Valley; he comments in *Rural Rides:*

> . . . [from] the top of a very high part of the down . . . I first saw this *Valley of Avon;* and a most beautiful sight it was! Villages, hamlets, large farms, towers, steeples, fields,

meadows, orchards, and very fine timber trees, scattered all over the valley. . . . The farm-houses, mansions, villages, and hamlets are generally situated in that part of the arable land which comes nearest the meadows.

> Great as my expectations had been, they were more than fulfilled.

But literary associations with Amesbury go back to Geoffrey of Monmouth, who, in the 12th century, wrote in an extraordinarily muddled fashion of a monastery here when Aurelius was rebuilding a realm "which the fury of the enemy [the Saxon] had certainly not spared." Aurelius, according to the *Historia Regum Britanniae,*

> visited the monastery near Kaercaradduc, which is now called Salisbury. It was there that were buried the leaders and princes whom the infamous Hengist had betrayed. A monastery of three hundred brethren stood there, on Mount Ambrius, for it was Ambrius, so they say, who had founded the monastery years before. As Aurelius inspected the place in which the dead lay, he was moved to compassion and burst into tears. In the end . . . it was his opinion that the greensward covering so many noble men who had died for their fatherland was certainly worthy of some memorial.

Merlin was engaged to erect the monument, and this becomes Geoffrey's explanation of how Stonehenge appeared. Mount Ambrius is intended to mean Amesbury, but Geoffrey repeatedly confused Avebury, where there is a set of megaliths, Amesbury, and Stonehenge.

Arthurian legend is involved in other ways here. It is held that after King Arthur's death Queen Guinevere, to do penance for her transgressions, joined a nunnery in Amesbury. This is somewhat unlikely, for the monastic establishment of which there is a trace was not founded until 980. Nevertheless, Sir Thomas Malory made use of the tradition in *Le Morte d'Arthur,* in which Amesbury becomes Almesbury:

> And when Queen Guenever understood that King Arthur was slain, and all the noble knights, Sir Mordred and all the remnant, then the Queen stole away, and five ladies with her, and so she went to Almesbury; and there she let make herself a nun, and ware white clothes and black, and great penance she took, as ever did sinful lady in this land, and never creature could make her merry. . . .

Malory continues by relating how a dream vision appears to Sir Launcelot, now a priest, commanding him to hasten to the nunnery where Guinevere is dying and to bury her next to King Arthur in Glastonbury:

> Then Sir Launcelot took his seven fellows with him, and on foot they yede from Glastonbury to Almesbury, the which is little more than thirty mile. And thither they came within two days. . . . Queen Guenever died but half an hour afore.
>
> And the ladies told Sir Launcelot that Queen Guenever told them all " . . . I beseech Almighty God that I may never have power to see Sir Launcelot with my wordly eyen." "And thus," said all the ladies, "was ever her prayer these two days, till she was dead."

Following what was by then a literary tradition, Alfred, Lord Tennyson's *Idylls of the King* first tells how, before Arthur's death,

Queen Guinevere had fled the court, and sat
There in the holy house at Almesbury
Weeping, none with her save a little maid,
A novice. . . .

Then, Tennyson adds to the legend; Arthur arrives
at the nunnery:

A murmuring whisper through the nunnery ran,
Then on a sudden a cry, "The King!" She sat
Stiff-stricken, listening; but when armed feet
Thro' the long gallery from the outer doors
Rang coming, prone from off her seat she fell,
And grovell'd with her face against the floor. . . .

Finally, Tennyson changes his source. In Malory
Arthur condemns Guinevere to be burned to death
(she is rescued by Launcelot); here she

Was chosen abbess, there, an abbess, lived
For three brief years, and there, an abbess, past
To where beyond these voices there is peace.

After the dissolution the monastic buildings
passed to the Duke of Somerset, who pulled them
down. Eventually the property was acquired by the
Earl of Queensberry, who had a great house designed
and built for him by Inigo Jones. In the 18th century
the house, known as Amesbury Abbey, was the seat
of the Duchess of Queensberry (Catherine Hyde),
whose hospitality was extended to Alexander Pope,
James Thomson, Matthew Prior, and John Gay; indeed, it is the duchess whom Prior calls

Kitty beautiful and young,
And wild as cat untamed.

Here, with the generous support of the duke and
duchess, John Gay wrote *The Beggar's Opera* in a
stone room resembling a cave, known as the Diamond and overlooking the river. It was this 3d Duke
of Queensberry who carefully looked after Gay in his
later years; in fact, Gay spent most of his time at the
duke's home here or in London.

There is one other literary association: Joseph Addison, who was born in nearby Milston, had some of
his early schooling here under the Rev. Thomas
Naise; after a short period he went from Amesbury to
Salisbury. Amesbury, as well, claims to be the "little
Wiltshire village, within an easy journey of the fair
old town of Salisbury" of Charles Dickens's *Martin
Chuzzlewit;* however, Alderbury has a much stronger
case.

AMPTHILL, Bedfordshire (pop. 2,270) The area that
contains the town of Ampthill, 7 miles south of
Bedford, is sandstone, and partly as a consequence
the old stone-built market town is especially attractive. In the early 15th century Sir John Cornwall,
Lord Fanhope, built a castle here for his new bride,
the sister of Henry IV, and in due course his estates
came into the hands of Henry VIII. The King
hunted here in 1532, and Anne Boleyn gave him a
hunting horn, a greyhound, and the desire for a new
wife. The next year Catherine of Aragon was sent
here while divorce proceedings were being carried
out at nearby Dunstable. By the time the lands came
into the hands of John Ashburnham, a new house
was needed, and when the house and lands passed
into the hands of Lord Upper Ossory in the 18th
century, there was renewed interest in the ruined

castle. At the urging of Horace Walpole a cross was
erected to commemorate the original structure and
Queen Catherine's imprisonment. The Gothic cross
was inscribed with lines written by Walpole:

In days of old, here Ampthill's towers were seen,
The mournful refuge of an injured Queen.
Here flowed her pure and unavailing tears,
Here blinded zeal sustained her sinking years,
Yet Freedom hence her radiant banner waved,
And love avenged a realm by priests enslaved
From Katharine's wrongs a nation's bliss was spread,
And Luther's light from Henry's lawless bed.

ANNESLEY, Nottinghamshire (pop. 1,061) On the
border of Sherwood Forest near the old market town
of Mansfield and the ancient but presently industrial
city of Nottingham, Annesley is divided into two
distinct parts. In the older area Annesley Hall, standing in a park with a lake, has been the home of the
Chaworth-Musters family since the 18th century,
and it was with Mary, the daughter of the original
Chaworth family, that George Gordon, Lord Byron,
fell in love at the beginning of the 19th century. The
two were cousins; Mary was the heiress of William
Chaworth, who had been killed in a duel with the 5th
Baron Bryon, the poet's great-uncle. The later Lord
Byron often met Mary Chaworth, two years his senior,
in the park, and it was in the park that they parted—
an occasion recalled in *The Dream,* in which the
nearby hill (now known as Diadem Hill) is described
as "crowned with a peculiar diadem" of trees. Mary
was Byron's "star of Annesley," and after she told
him of her impending marriage to John Musters of
nearby Colwick Hall, Annesley lost its charm for
Byron:

Hills of Annesley, bleak and barren,
   Where my thoughtless childhood strayed,
How the northern tempests, warring,
   Howl above thy tufted shade.

Now no more, the hours beguiling,
   Former favourite haunts I see,
Now no more my Mary smiling
   Makes ye seem a heaven to me.

There are bullet marks in a door beneath the terrace where Byron engaged in target practice in the
summer of 1803.

The old church in Annesley Park where William
Chaworth is buried is now unsafe to visit, but D. H.
Lawrence, whose native county of Nottinghamshire
appears throughout his works, uses the old church in
The White Peacock; indeed, this is where the white
peacock appears. The road leading to the church is
still recognizable from Lawrence's description:

So I left the wild lands, and went along by the old red
wall of the kitchen garden, along the main road as far as
the mouldering church which stands high on a bank by
the roadside just where the trees tunnel the darkness and
the gloom of the highway startles the traveller at noon.
Great trees growing on the banks suddenly fold over
everything at this point in the swinging road, and in the
obscurity rots the Hall church, black and melancholy
above the shrinking head of the traveller.

ARBORFIELD, Berkshire (pop. 287) This small village near the Loddon River, 4 miles south of Reading, once contained a lovely old manor house, be-

longing to the Standens, and a medieval church. The hall is gone (only the 17th-century stables remain), and the medieval church is in ruins. Arborfield becomes Aberleigh in Mary Mitford's *Our Village,* in which she describes the old house as

> a beautiful structure of James the First's time, whose glassless windows and dilapidated doors form a melancholy contrast with the strength and entireness of the rich and massive front.

ARBURY, Warwickshire The northern part of Warwickshire is dominated by the sprawling industrial town of Birmingham; indeed, more than half of the county's approximate population of 2 million live in the greater metropolitan area. Nevertheless, Arbury, 2½ miles southwest of Nuneaton and 21 miles east of the center of Birmingham, has escaped most of the industrial pall. Arbury Hall has been the seat of the Newdegate family (the spelling varies) since the 16th century and was built on the site of an Augustinian priory. The property came into the possession of John Newdegate in 1586, and Sir Roger Newdigate converted the Elizabethan structure into the Gothic mansion known today as Arbury Hall. Also in the grounds of Arbury Park is South Farm, the birthplace of George Eliot (Mary Ann Evans) on November 22, 1819; her father, Robert Evans, was the land agent for Francis Parker Newdigate of Arbury Hall and for Col. Francis Newdegate. She was baptized in the parish church at Chilvers Coton and attended that church while she lived in this area. Her family moved to Griff House, another part of the Newdegate estate four months after her birth.

Arbury Hall enters Eliot's "Mr. Gilfil's Love Story" as Cheverel Manor, where the young Maynard Gilfil spends his vacations with his guardian. The rebuilding of the house, which took place thirteen years before George Eliot was born, was done exactly as she portrays it, and Sir Christopher Cheverel is Sir Roger. She writes:

> And a charming picture Cheverel Manor would have made that evening . . . the castellated house of gray-tinted stone, with the flickering sunbeams sending dashes of golden light across the many-shaped panes in the mullioned windows, and a great beech leaning athwart one of the flanking towers, and breaking, with its dark flattened boughs, the too formal symmetry of the front; the broad gravel-walk on the right, by a row of tall pines, alongside the pool—on the left branching out among swelling grassy mounds, surmounted by clumps of trees, where the red trunk of the Scotch fir glows in the descending sunlight against the bright green of limes and acacias. . . .

Sir Roger acted as his own architect most of the time, as described in the novel:

> I, who have seen Cheverel Manor as he bequeathed it to his heirs, rather attribute that unswerving architectural purpose of his, conceived and carried out through long years of systematic personal exertion, to something of the fervour of genius, as well as inflexibility of will. . . .

Most of the story is based on people living at Arbury Hall in the latter part of the 18th century; Sir Roger Newdigate, founder of the Newdigate Prize for Poetry at Oxford, was

> as fine a specimen of the old English gentleman as could well have been found. . . . I have felt that there dwelt in this old English baronet some of the sublime spirit which distinguishes art from luxury and worships beauty apart from self-indulgence.

Lady Newdigate as Lady Cheverel is not quite as accurately portrayed; while her "fine musical taste" and her "profound deference for Sir Christopher" were well known, the coldness of her nature was not. Caterina was Sarah (Sally) Shilton, a child who lived on on the estate and who had been brought to Arbury to live; she possessed a beautiful voice, and Sir Roger had hoped she would become a professional singer under the direction of Dominico Motto, the Newdigates' resident singing master. Charles Parker, Sir Roger's heir, becomes Captain Wybrow, but the love story of Caterina and the captain is one of the fictional elements of the story. The harpsichord belonging to Sally Shilton is at Arbury Hall, as are the embroidered chairs. The Rev. Maynard Gilfil is based on the Rev. B. G. Ebdell, resident vicar of Chilvers Coton and incumbent of Astley, who was Sir Roger's chaplain here. In *Daniel Deronda* Arbury becomes Mallinger Abbey.

ARDEN, FOREST OF, Warwickshire The southern part of the county of Warwickshire can be divided into the two areas of the Feldon and the Arden, the first south and the second north of Stratford-on-Avon. Arden, or more accurately the Forest of Arden, lies mainly between Stratford and Alcester, covering an area of 17 miles in length and 12 miles in breadth. None of the original forest remains, and the name is now used only as an area designation. Arden was surveyed for the Domesday Book (1086), and William Camden, the antiquarian and historian, surveyed the area for his *Britannia.* Michael Drayton, a native of the shire and the author of *Poly-Olbion,* writes extensively of this area in that work and characterizes it well; the Hermit of Arden

> . . . comes out of his homely Cell,
> Where from all rude resort he happily doth dwell:
> Who in the strength of youth, a man at Armes hath been;
> Or one who of this world the vilenesse having seene,
> Retyres him from it quite; and with a constant mind
> Mans beastliness so loathes, that flying humane kind,
> The black and darksome nights, the bright and gladsome
>   dayes

ARBURY Born at South Farm on this estate, George Eliot makes Arbury Hall, seat of the Newdigate [Newdegate] family since 1586, into Cheverel Manor ["Mr. Gilfil's Love Story"] and into Mallinger Abbey (*Daniel Deronda*). Its "exterior . . . was much defaced, maimed of finial and gurgoyle, the friable limestone broken and fretted, and lending its soft gray to a powdery dark lichen. . . ."

Indifferent are to him, his hope on God that staies.
Each little Village yeelds his short and homely fare:
To gather wind-falne sticks, his great'st and onely care;
Which every aged tree still yeeldeth to his fire.

Drayton continues:

Heere finds he on an Oake Rheume-purging Polipode;
And in some open place that to the Sunne doth lye,
He Fumitorie gets, and Eye-bright for the eye:
The Yarrow, where-with-all he stops the wound-made
    gore:
The healing Tutsan then, and Plantan for a sore.
And hard by them againe he holy Vervaine finds,
Which he about his head that hath the Megrim binds.

The most famous use of the area is William Shakespeare's. In his time the Arden district was scattered with farms and fields, and encroachments were being made steadily into its primitive nature. Enough was still retained when Shakespeare was a boy, though, for him to recall the beauty and freedom of the woodland in his works. Without doubt *Love's Labour's Lost* and *A Midsummer Night's Dream* draw much of their woodland scenery from Arden, and *As You Like It* (taken from Thomas Lodge's *Rosalynde: Euphues Golden Legacie,* itself set in the Forest of Arden between France and Belgium) is located mostly here. If a conclusion about the darkness of the forest can be drawn from this play, it would have to be that no enemy except the weather exists here:

Hath not old custom made this life more sweet
Than that of painted pomp? Are not these woods
More free from peril than the envious court?
Here feel we but the penalty of Adam,—
The seasons' difference: as the icy fang
And churlish chiding of the winter's wind,
Which when it bites and blows upon my body,
Even till I shrink with cold, I smile and say,
This is no flattery: these are counsellors
That feelingly persuade me what I am.

ARELEY KINGS, Worcestershire   A hamlet adjoining Stourport across the Severn River and 12 miles north of Worcester, Areley Kings has a hill setting that shows off its church, rectory, and half-timbered church house to advantage. The church, which was once Norman, was almost totally rebuilt in the 19th century; but the Norman part of the chancel and its deep-set window would have been familiar to the early Middle English poet and priest Layamon, author of the romance-chronicle *Brut;* this was the poet's church, and the Norman window now contains a fantasized picture of him in his priest's robes writing his book. The 19th-century rebuilding uncovered the door that Layamon would have used to enter the church; decayed beyond repair, it and its hinges were reproduced and put into the restored church.

For centuries a great deal of doubt surrounded the location of Layamon's church, for all that is known of him comes from his *Brut,* in which he notes:

There was a priest in the land;   Layamon was he
    called
He was Leovenath's son;   the Lord be gracious to him;
He dwelt at Ernley,   at a noble church,
Upon Severn shore,—good there he thought it,—
Quite near to Redstone;   he read there his service book.

However, the identification problems were removed

when a Latin inscription reading "In the time of St. Layamon" was found on the shaft and base of the old font, buried in the floor. The Redstone to which he refers is claimed to be the Redstone Rock along the riverbank; here Layamon probably lived as a hermit. The enormous rock is a labyrinth with its hewn-out chambers, including a dining hall, dormitories, and chimneys bored out to the top. There are also a chapel and a pulpit.

ARUNDEL, Sussex (pop. 2,489)   It is easy to pass over the old town of Arundel and to concentrate on its fairy-tale castle in a leafy setting, but the village, on the Arun River 5 miles from its mouth and 10 miles east of Chichester, itself is delightful. The source of its name, Arundel, has long been debated, and the strange etymologies that existed have been picked up in literature. Michael Drayton, however, did not accept the etymologies or even make one up himself in his *Poly-Olbion.* The illustrations to the seventeenth song discuss the name:

As Arun *which doth name the beutious* Arundel.

So it is conjectured, and is without controversie justifiable if that be the name of the River. Some, fable it from *Arundel,* the name of *Bevis* horse: It were so tolerable as *Bucephalon,* from *Alexanders* horse ... But *Bevis* was about the Conquest, and this Towne, is by name of *Erundele,* knowne in time of King *Alfred* who gave it with others to his Naphew *Athelm.*

The name probably derives from the Old English *hārhūne,* the plant called the "horehound," and *dell,* "a valley," and meant simply "the valley where the horehound grows."

The town was a major port for the Romans, and after their departure the whole Saxon Shore, as it was called, became an opening point for marauders. Mentioned first in 899 in Alfred the Great's will, Arundel came into importance shortly before the Norman Conquest.

After the conquest the combined rapes (administrative units) of Chichester and Arundel were given to Roger of Montgomery, 1st Earl of Arundel, and he began his work on the castle here around 1080. By 1097 it was in a sufficient state to offer hospitality to King William II when he was detained here by bad weather, and a few years later the 3d Earl, Robert of Belesme (Bellême), rebelled against Henry I in favor of Robert, Duke of Normandy, the King's brother, as the *Anglo-Saxon Chronicle* reports:

The king went and besieged the castle at Arundel, but when he could not take it quickly he had castles built before it and garrisoned them with his men; . . . he took that castle, and deprived earl Robert of his lands, and confiscated everything he possessed in England.

Exactly how much work Roger of Montgomery did on the castle is not known, but in 1135 it was given to Queen Adeliza, widow of Henry I. Three years later she married William de Albini, who was created 4th Earl of Arundel by virtue of possession of the castle; from the Albini family Arundel passed to the Fitzalans, who gained the earldom through possession, and then to Thomas Howard, 4th Duke of Norfolk and son of Henry Howard, Earl of Surrey, in the mid-16th century. The castle has since remained in the Howard family.

Across the lawns west of the castle is the 14th-century Protestant parish church dedicated to St. Nicholas with its Catholic chapel; the eastern part of the church, known as the Fitzalan Chapel, can be reached only through the castle precincts, while the parish church can be entered only from the High Street. The Catholic chapel, legally property of the Duke of Norfolk, was originally the Collegiate Church of the Holy Trinity, and the two churches are separated by a screen. The chapel contains many extraordinarily good monuments to the Fitzalans and the Howards. Just south of the collegiate church is a part of the former college founded by Richard Fitzalan about 1380; suppressed by Henry VIII, it was conveyed by patent to Henry Fitzalan in 1544, was allowed to fall into decay, and eventually passed to the Howards. The college is now occupied by a community of nuns, who are permitted the use of the chapel.

Literary associations here date to the 14th-century verse romance *Bevis of Hampton*. After many exploits and adventures, Bevis becomes warder of the gatehouse and every week eats a whole ox, drinks vast quantities of beer, and consumes an enormous amount of bread and mustard. When he feels that death is near, he throws his ax from the tower (now called Bevis Tower) to mark the site of his grave. Bevis is buried on that spot, the mound of Pugh Dean in the park, and his sword Morglay can be seen hanging on a wall in the armory of the castle. It should be noted that the sword is an obvious fraud. Not the weapon of a large man, it is a relatively small two-handed sword, smaller, indeed, than the Chinese execution sword hanging nearby.

ARUNDEL   Crowning a hilltop overlooking the Arun River, Arundel Castle was the home of the legendary figure Bevis of Hampton, who settled here as warder of the gatehouse after he had rescued Josian from the stake. The castle has been the seat of the Earls of Arundel for over 800 years.

Daniel Defoe's visit to the village and castle showed him how greatly everything had changed from its medieval prosperity. He notes in *A Tour thro' the Whole Island of Great Britain:*

> From hence we come to *Arundel*, a decay'd Town also; but standing near the Mouth of a good River, call'd *Arun*, which signifies, says Mr. *Cambden*, the swift, tho' the River it self is not such a Rapid Current as merits that Name. . . .
> The principal advantage to the Country from this River, is the Shipping of great quantities of large Timber here. . . .
> The River, and the old decay'd, *once famous* Castle at *Arundel*, which are still belonging to the Family of *Howards*, Earls of *Arundel*, a Branch of the *Norfolk* Family, is all that is remarkable here; except it be that in this River are catch'd the best *Mullets*, and the largest in *England*, a Fish very good in it self, and much valued by the Gentry round, and often sent up to *London*.

Around 1823 Edward Lear began to visit the village; staying with his sister Sarah, who had married Charles Street, the poet-artist made frequent trips here between 1823 and 1829. In the autumn of 1827 Mary Shelley arrived in Arundel with her child Percy and stayed either with or near some friends, the Misses Robinson, but there is very little information available about her stay here. In more recent times Hilaire Belloc lived in nearby Slindon and occasionally attended mass at St. Philip Neri.

ASH or ASH AND NORMANDY, Surrey (pop. 5,479)
The village of Ash and Normandy, 2 miles east of Aldershot, Hampshire, has become part of the spreading urban mass that runs along the Surrey-Hampshire border and has, as a result, lost not only its 19th-century rurality but its identity. In better days, in the early 1830s, William Cobbett, the outspoken author of *Rural Rides*, acquired a long lease on Normandy Farm here; he then gave up his seed farm at Kensington and the farm at Barn Elms and planned to retire here. But only four years later he died (on June 18, 1835) and was buried in Farnham, the village of his birth.

Ash is also traditionally associated with Edward Young, author of *Night Thoughts*. His brother-in-law held the living here in the 1740s, and Young visited Ash on numerous occasions, especially after the deaths of his wife, his stepdaughter, and her husband. It is assumed that much of *Night Thoughts* was composed here.

ASHBOURNE, Derbyshire (pop. 5,660)   An old market town standing at the gateway to the Peak District, Ashbourne is on the Henmore River 1¼ miles above its influx into the Dove and 13 miles northwest of Derby. The 14th- to 15th-century church of St. Oswald on Church Street has an impressive spire, with five tiers of windows and strings of more than 1,500 ball-flowers running up the walls. The font is 13th-century, and the monuments are outstanding, especially those to the Cokaynes and the 18th-century sculpture of the five-year-old child Penelope Boothby; the work is fragile and delicate with the child in a simple sashed dress, hands clasped, and feet one upon another. The only child of Sir Brooke Boothby and Lady Susannah, she was painted by Sir

Joshua Reynolds, and the effigy here was the inspiration for Sir Francis Chantrey's *Sleeping Children* at Lichfield Cathedral. There is a great deal of good old glass, including some of the 13th century in a lancet in the north transept. Some of the modern glass blends in well, but as John Ruskin said, a 19th-century depiction of David and Goliath would disgrace even a penny edition of *Jack the Giant Killer*.

On Church Street across from the gabled Elizabethan grammar school is the 17th-century red-brick house (now the headmaster's house) where Dr. John Taylor lived. It was to this house that Samuel Johnson frequently came to stay with his old schoolfellow; the visits were generally made in summer because Taylor spent winters in London as rector of St. Margaret's at Westminster and prebendary of Westminster Abbey. Johnson was here as early as 1739, and on one of his later trips James Boswell, who came twice with Dr. Johnson, found him trying to pole a dead cat over the dam in the Henmore Brook:

> Johnson, partly from a desire to see it [the water] play more freely, and partly from that inclination to activity which will animate, at times, the most inert and sluggish mortal, took a long pole which was lying on a bank, and pushed down several parcels of this wreck with painful assiduity, while I stood quietly by, wondering to behold the sage thus curiously employed, and smiling with an humorous satisfaction each time when he carried his point. He worked till he was quite out of breath; and having found a large dead cat so heavy that he could not move it after several efforts, "Come," said he (throwing down the pole,) "*you* shall take it now": which I accordingly did, and being a fresh man, soon made the cat tumble over the cascade.

Boswell (and it is thought Dr. Johnson, too) stayed at the Green Man and Blacks Head Inn just below the marketplace. This is where Boswell found the landlady, "a mighty civil gentlewoman," who "presented . . . [him] with an engraving of the sign of her house" which read in part:

> Would Mr. Boswell name the house to his extensive acquaintance, it would be a singular favour conferr'd on one who has it not in her power to make any other return but her most grateful thanks, and sincerest prayers for his happiness in time, and in a blessed eternity.

Mary Ann Evans (George Eliot) makes extensive use of Derbyshire as Stonyshire in *Adam Bede* with Ashbourne becoming Oakbourne. Here Hetty emerges from the coach on her flight to Windsor, and it is to this village that Adam comes in search of her:

> Adam walked much faster. . . .
> It seemed a very short walk, the ten miles to Oakbourne, that pretty town within sight of the blue hills, where he breakfasted. After this, the country grew barer and barer: no more rolling woods, no more wide-branching trees near frequent homesteads, no more bushy hedgerows; but gray stone walls intersecting the meagre pastures, and dismal wide-scattered gray stone houses on broken lands where mines had been and were no longer.

In more recent times D. H. Lawrence uses Ashbourne in *The Virgin and the Gipsy*.

ASHBURY, Berkshire (pop. 534) The village of Ashbury, high up on the Berkshire Downs looking toward Swindon, Wiltshire, 7 miles to the west, has a 15th-century manor house, built by the monks of Glastonbury, to whom the vast estate once belonged, and a lovely cruciform church, whose pride is the late Norman double-chevron south doorway. Above the village is the Ridgeway, a pre-Roman trackway that runs more than 20 miles along the crest of the Berkshire Downs. The path is thought to have been made by prehistoric pilgrims on their way to Avebury, Wiltshire. Here, as well as at Avebury, is a primitive temple, in this case a grouping of thirty-two stones with one great stone resting on five smaller ones; called Wayland's Smithy, it was once thought to be the underground chamber of a priest or chieftain. While this place is linked with the legend of Wayland the Smith, whose swords no one could resist, a local legend also grew up: it was said that if a traveler left money on the top stone and his horse nearby and if he did not return until the job was completed, Wayland would shoe the horse.

In *Tom Brown's School Days* Thomas Hughes refers to the cave as "a place of classic fame now" but justifies not describing it by saying,

> as Sir Walter has touched it, I may as well let it alone, and refer you to "Kenilworth" for the legend.

Indeed, Sir Walter Scott did stop once to view these beech-sheltered stones on the windswept downs and then incorporated them in *Kenilworth*. Richard Sludge and Tressilian "are at Wayland Smith's forge-door" when the legend is related:

> "Why," said Dickie, with a grin, "you must tie your horse to that upright stone that has the ring in't, and then you must whistle three times, and lay me down your silver groat on that other flat stone, walk out of the circle, sit down on the west side of that little thicket of bushes, and take heed you look neither to right nor to left for ten minutes, or so long as you shall hear the hammer clink, and whenever it ceases, say your prayers for the space you could tell a hundred, or count over a hundred, which will do as well,—and then come into the circle; you will find your money gone and your horse shod."

ASHBY-DE-LA-ZOUCH, Leicestershire (pop. 5,892) Situated 17 miles northwest of Leicester near the border of Derbyshire, this town is called Ashby locally. The full name of Ashby-de-la-Zouch was created to distinguish it from other places named Ashby. While the castle is now merely a remarkable ruin, the old kitchen tower, with a 14th-century vaulted roof, and the buttery are intact. The chapel still has four medieval windows, and nearby is the Solar, the room where Mary, Queen of Scots was kept for a short time. James I brought his court here for an extended visit, which, it is said, came close to impoverishing his host, the 5th Earl of Huntingdon; and both Charles I and Charles II stayed here. In 1607 an entertainment by John Marston, in honor of a visit to Lord and Lady Huntingdon by her mother, the Dowager Countess of Derby, was performed in the castle.

The parish church is remarkable in that it has a finger pillory, once used to subdue persons whose behavior in church was found offensive.

There was at one time a tournament field at Ashby, and it is still noted on ordnance survey maps as about 1½ miles north of the town. The field is used by Sir Walter Scott for "the gentle and Joyous Passage at Arms" that he describes in *Ivanhoe*. He calls the site for the tournament "singularly romantic":

On the verge of a wood, which approached to within a mile of the town of Ashby, was an extensive meadow, of the finest and most beautiful green turf, surrounded on one side by the forest, and fringed on the other by straggling oak-trees, some of which had grown to an immense size. The ground, as if fashioned on purpose for the martial display which was intended, sloped gradually down on all sides to a level bottom, which was enclosed for the lists with strong palisades, forming a space of a quarter of mile in length, and about half as broad. The form of the enclosure was an oblong square, save that the corners were considerably rounded off, in order to afford more convenience to the spectators.

Scott goes on to describe the spectator area, distinct from that where King John and his courtiers watch the Disinherited Knight successively unhorse Bois-Guilbert, Front-de-Boeuf, Malvoisin, De Grantmesnil, and Ralph de Vipont:

The exterior of the lists was in part occupied by temporary galleries, spread with tapestry and carpets, and accommodated with cushions for the convenience of those ladies and nobles who were expected to attend the tournament. A narrow space, betwixt these galleries and the lists, gave accommodation for yeomanry and spectators of a better degree than the mere vulgar, and might be compared to the pit of a theatre. The promiscuous multitude arranged themselves upon large banks of turf prepared for the purpose, which, aided by the natural elevation of the ground, enabled them to overlook the galleries, and obtain a fair view into the lists. Besides the accommodations which these stations afforded, many hundreds had perched themselves on the branches of the trees which surrounded the meadow; and even the steeple of a country church, at some distance, was crowded with spectators.

The country church referred to is at nearby Simsby.

ASHFORD, Kent (pop. 22,099) Central to all communications in Kent, Ashford, situated on the Stour River 14 miles southwest of Canterbury, is a rapidly growing community with numerous main roads and railways running through it. Chosen as one of the new rapid-growth areas under the Strategic Plan for the South East, the town is still a place of small shops, especially in the High Street, and despite a rapidly expanding industrial base, a good number of old Georgian buildings survive. The much-ridiculed Poet Laureate Alfred Austin died here on June 2, 1913; his popularity was such that *The Athenaeum* announced his death and commented that the laureateship was now actually vacant although it had been virtually so since Tennyson's death. Richard Harris Barham, author of *The Ingoldsby Legends,* was a curate here for a short time before taking the living of Snargate, in nearby Romney Marsh, of which he writes: "The world is divided into five parts, namely Europe, Asia, Africa, America and Romney Marsh." In more recent times H. G. Wells incorporates Ashford into *Tono-Bungay;* in the novel it becomes Ashborough, the town 8 miles from Bladesover.

ASHLEY COMBE, Somerset Facing Porlock Bay and bounded on the south by Exmoor Forest, Ashley Combe contains the manor belonging to Mary Caroline, Countess of Lovelace. Sir Hugh Walpole, whose strong friendship with Lady Lovelace had ensued immediately after Henry James introduced them, first came here in August 1909 after having been in Durham and was a frequent house guest afterward. Walpole said the manor "was the most beautiful house I've ever stayed in, built into the forest on the side of the hill with the sea at the bottom. The gardens are laid out wonderfully." He returned in the summer of 1910 and finished *Mr. Perrin and Mr. Traill* here on September 4. On another occasion, in May 1912, on his way back to London from Truro and St. Ives, he stopped off at Ashley Combe and found that John Buchan was a fellow guest; the two men enjoyed long walks on Exmoor at this time.

ASHOVER, Derbyshire (pop. 2,432) Near the river in the Amber Valley and 7 miles southwest of Chesterfield, Ashover is set in attractive moorland near the Peak District. Rocky hills, once worked for their lead by the Romans, surround the village, which has grown up around its medieval church. The 12th-century font of local lead has a series of twenty men in robes holding books and standing under pillared arches, and the chancel brasses are especially good. The literary association with Ashover is with the church, for here is buried Dorothy Matley (d. 1606), whose story John Bunyan includes in *The Life and Death of Mr. Badman.* Mr. Wiseman tells this tale of sudden judgment:

This Dorothy Matley . . . was noted by the people of the town to be a great swearer, and curser, and liar, and thief. . . . And the labour that she did usually follow, was to wash the rubbish that came forth of the lead mines, and there to get sparks of lead ore; and her usual way of asserting of things, was with these kind of imprecations: I would I might sink into the earth if it be not so; or, I would God would make the earth open and swallow me up. Now upon the 23rd of March, 1660, this Dorothy was washing of ore upon the top of a steep hill, about a quarter of a mile from Ashover, and was there taxed by a lad for taking of two single pence out of his pocket, for he had laid his breeches by, and was at work in his drawers; but she violently denied it; wishing, that the ground might swallow her up if she had them: she also used the same wicked words on several other occasions that day.

A child and one George Hodgkinson of the village were standing by Dorothy. Then the child was called, and the two walked away. Bunyan relates:

Behold, they had not gone above ten yards from Dorothy, but they heard her crying out for help; so, looking back, he saw the woman, and her tub and sieve, twisting round, and sinking into the ground. . . . So she and her tub twirled round and round, till they sunk about three yards into the earth, and then for a while stayed. Then . . . a great stone which appeared in the earth, fell upon her head, and broke her skull, and then the earth fell in upon her and covered her. She was afterwards digged up, and found about four yards within ground, with the boy's two single pence in her pocket. . . .

ASTLEY, Warwickshire (pop. 448) In the area of northern Warwickshire dominated by the heavy industry of Birmingham, Astley has retained some of its rural air; 3½ miles southwest of Nuneaton and almost across the road from Arbury, it has a relatively modern castle on a site which has a long history and an interesting old church. Astley Castle, 1½ miles south of the village, is scarcely of castle proportions; in fact, the present castle is the third one to stand on the site, and it is the last in the line which has literary interest. After a long and complicated series of ownerships and demolitions, Astley Castle eventually was purchased by Sir Richard Newdigate of neighboring Arbury Hall, where George Eliot (Mary Ann Evans) was born. She, of course, knew the area well and introduced Astley Castle and the adjacent church into "Mr. Gilfil's Love Story." Here the church becomes the Knebley Church, of which the Rev. B. G. Ebdell (Mr. Gilfil) is the incumbent; having preached in the morning at Shepperton,

> he mounted his horse and rode hastily with the other [sermon] in his pocket to Knebley, where he officiated in a wonderful little church, with a checkered pavement which had once rung to the iron tread of military monks, with coats of arms in clusters on the lofty roof, marble warriors and their wives without noses occupying a large proportion of the area, and the twelve apostles, with their heads very much on one side, holding didactic ribbons, painted in fresco on the walls.

The "wonderful little church" was the original choir of the 1343 church, whose spire crashed down in 1606 and demolished much of the structure. Eliot's twelve apostles are only nine on the north side of the nave, painted on the choir stalls, and each holds a scroll. The "marble warriors and their wives" refer to a group of three effigies (damaged) of Sir Edward Grey, Elizabeth Talbot, Viscountess Lisle (his daughter-in-law), and Lady Cecily, second wife of Sir Thomas Grey. George Eliot's parents were married in this church, and her father's first wife, Harriet Evans, is buried here. The moated Astley Castle, adjoining the church, and now a hotel, also enters the story as Knebley Abbey, where Mr. Gilfil at one time dined every Sunday, but "he had given up the habit . . . [because of] a very bitter quarrel with Mr. Oldinport, the cousin and predecessor of the Mr. Oldinport who flourished in the Rev. Amos Barton's time."

ASTON CANTLOW, Warwickshire (pop. 878) Fringed with willows, the Alne River meanders slowly through Aston Cantlow, a small village 6 miles northwest of Stratford-on-Avon. Its church has two unique distinctions. First, it is the only church in Warwickshire to have had an incumbent saint, Thomas de Cantelupe; and, second, the Church of St. John the Baptist is traditionally held to have been the scene of the marriage of John Shakespeare and Mary Arden, parents of the dramatist William Shakespeare. Mary Arden lived in Wilmcote, which is 2 miles closer to Stratford, and this was the parish church. There is no evidence of the ceremony, since they were married in 1557, and the church did not begin keeping records until 1561.

ASTON CLINTON, Buckinghamshire (pop. 2,791) The village of Aston Clinton, 5 miles southeast of Aylesbury, has suffered indignities because of its location beside a major road but has come through reasonably well. Aston Hill dominates the southern reaches of the village; the fields between Halton, 1½ miles to the south, and this village once contained Aston Clinton House, built in the early 1840s and bought in 1851 by Sir Anthony de Rothschild of the banking Rothschilds. Only the lodge gates remain. Here Lady de Rothschild often entertained eminent literary figures: Robert Browning, Thomas Babington Macaulay, Samuel Rogers, and Alfred, Lord Ten-

ASTON CANTLOW   The Church of St. John the Baptist, a building which is partly medieval, is the one in which William Shakespeare's parents are supposed to have been married.

nyson. One of the earliest and most frequent visitors was Matthew Arnold, who first met the Rothschilds in London, when, as inspector of education, he visited the Jewish schools established by Lady de Rothschild in London's East End. Another of the guests and the only one thought to have used her in his works was William Makepeace Thackeray, who describes Lady de Rothschild in *Pendennis*. Aston Clinton House was demolished in 1960. From 1925 to 1927 Evelyn Waugh was a schoolmaster here, and *Decline and Fall*, based on his previous experiences as a teacher in Flintshire, Wales, was begun here.

ASTON-CUM-AUGHTON, Yorkshire (pop. 4,489) Just about equidistant from Rotherham, to the north, and Sheffield, to the west, Aston-cum-Aughton is generally called Aston. Lying in a heavily industrialized part of Yorkshire, Aston has nevertheless retained a number of fine old buildings, including the Old Rectory, where William Mason lived from 1754 until his death in 1797. This was Thomas Gray's "Scroddles," and the poet was often a guest here at "an Elysium among the coal pits"; on one of his trips here he went on to visit the ruins of Roche Abbey, a 12th-century Cistercian foundation near Maltby. Horace Walpole, another of Mason's guests, also made the excursion to the abbey.

ATHELHAMPTON, Dorset (pop. 49) In the wild heathland of mid-Dorset, 6 miles northeast of Dorchester, the hamlet of Athelhampton is surrounded by bracken and wild flowers in its lonely site in the heath. Traditionally this is said to be the site of a castle built by King Athelstan (r. 924–940), and the present Tudor seat is said to stand on the castle site. The tiny "new" church here was built by the architect John Hicks while Thomas Hardy was his apprentice, and Hardy later uses the knowledge he gained of the hamlet in "The Dame of Athelhall":

> She homed as she came, at the dip of eve
>   On Athel Coomb
> Regaining the Hall she had sworn to leave . . .
> The house was soundless as a tomb,
> And she entered her chamber, there to grieve
>   Lone, kneeling, in the gloom.
>
> From the lawn without rose her husband's voice
>   To one his friend:
> "Another has her Love, another my choice,
> Her going is good. Our conditions mend;
> In a change of mates we shall both rejoice;
>   I hoped that it thus might end!"

The hall suffered a disastrous fire in 1863, and the "new rooms" to which Hardy refers in the poem were part of the rebuilding.

AUDLEY END, Essex   Audley End is not a village or a town but a house that has become known, quite rightly, as the greatest house in Essex. Located about 2 miles from Saffron Walden, the present house dates from the early 17th century. The land was originally occupied by Benedictine monks, and at the dissolution of the monasteries in the 16th century, Audley End became the property of Sir Thomas Audley for services rendered to the crown. He built an enormous house on the present site. As large as the house was then, it was insufficient for Audley's grandson, Thomas Howard, Earl of Suffolk and Lord Treasurer of England. It was he who built what was then the largest house in England (the house still standing is roughly half the size of the original) and caused James I to remark, "Too much for a King, but it might do very well for a Lord Treasurer."

Sir Philip Sidney came here in July 1578 to take leave of Elizabeth I, who was Sir Thomas's guest; Sidney was expecting to join an expedition for the Netherlands. In the winter of 1579 and 1580 Edmund Spenser, then a member of the Earl of Leicester's household, spent a profitable time here, talking about the state of English poetry with Sidney and Sir Edward Dyer. Writing to Gabriel Harvey in Saffron Walden, Spenser commented: "Minds were stirring: there was abundant material to hand, but the forms of English poetry needed to be modernised by discussion, experiment, and by that knowledge which is gained through making mistakes." John Evelyn was a later visitor to Audley End; in 1654 he noted that the house was "twixt antiq and modern" and that the gardens were "not in order." The gardens and park are pretty much as they were later planned by Lancelot Brown (Capability Brown).

AYLESBURY, Buckinghamshire (pop. 18,606)   To a gourmet Aylesbury might just as well be named after its duckling, which is generally considered the best in England and possibly a rival to the Rouen duckling of France, but actually this market and county town, 17 miles southeast of Buckingham and 38 miles northwest of London, is more of a printing and engineering center. The medieval King's Head Inn (established in 1386 but with the "head" today of Henry VIII), in a narrow passage off the market square, is owned by the National Trust, to which it was presented in 1926 by the Rothschild banking family. The building is approached through a medieval gateway, and the leaded windows in the lounge were old by Tudor times; the hall windows contain 15th-century glass and stretch almost from floor to ceiling.

There is an early association between Aylesbury and John Lyly, author of *Euphues;* the official Parliament lists of returns for members records "John Lillye, esq." in the company of Sir Thomas Weste, returned for Aylesbury in February 1593. "John Lyllye gent" was returned as one of the members for Appleby in September 1597 and again for Aylesbury in October 1601, as "John Lillie, esq." Lyly must have been here during the campaigning, but nothing specific is known. Otherwise, only the King's Head Inn figures in literary history and that only for Sir Walter Scott, who stayed there on his way to London in the spring of 1828.

AYLESFORD, Kent (pop. 3,113)   On the Medway River 3½ miles northwest of Maidstone, with a modernized 14th-century bridge spanning the river, Aylesford has had its tranquillity and attractiveness restored with the construction of the Maidstone bypass. A Carmelite friary founded in 1242 has been rebuilt, and the reestablished (1949) Carmelite community of monks and nuns is now noted for its pottery. The restored house, known as the Friars, incorporates parts of the original friary and is often claimed to be the birthplace of Sir Charles Sedley. There is no direct evidence to support this claim, but Sedley did inherit this estate after the death of his two brothers. The house, located beside the Medway and at one time in the hands of Sir John Banks, was the scene of an official visit by Samuel Pepys in March 1669; here on Admiralty business, Pepys recorded his impression of the Friars as "mighty finely placed by the river; and he [Sir John] keeps the grounds about it, and the walls and the house, very handsome."

The most important association of Aylesford with literature is through its use in Charles Dickens's *Pickwick Papers.* Nearby Cob Tree Hall (or Manor) in the grounds of the Maidstone Zoo is usually designated as the prototype of Manor Farm, although there is another claimant, Birling Place on the North Downs, and Aylesford is said to appear in disguise as Dingley Dell in the same work. The name Dingley is thought to be a combination of the terminal syllables of Boxley and Sandling, the parish and hamlet in which Dingley (Aylesford) is located. Dickens's description of Manor Farm closely corresponds to Cob Tree Hall at the time; additionally, the Wardles of the novel closely resemble the Spongs, owners of the hall. Indeed, in the 19th century the Spongs claimed to be the originals of the fictitious family and maintained that William Spong, commemorated in the Aylesford churchyard, was Mr. Wardle.

AYOT ST. LAWRENCE, Hertfordshire   Ayot St. Lawrence, a village of shady lanes and black-and-white timbered cottages, is 6 miles north of Hatfield. At the south end of the village is Shaw's Corner, originally called the New Rectory and the home of George Bernard Shaw from 1906 until his death in 1950. It has been said that he chose to live here after reading an inscription on a tombstone in the churchyard; the inscription, referring to the death of a seventy-year-old woman, simply stated: "Her Time Was Short." Shaw commented: "I knew that Ayot, where they call a life of 70 years a short one, was the place for me." Shaw renamed the building, not out of conceit, as is often said, but to avoid being confused with the rector of Ayot St. Lawrence. Among his many guests were Sean O'Casey and William Butler Yeats. *Pygmalion, The Doctor's Dilemma,* and *St. Joan* all were written here. In 1948 Shaw took part in a dedication service of the new wrought-iron gates at the Ayot St. Lawrence Church and gave, for an atheist, a surprising speech that concluded: "This is His house, this is His Gate, and this is His Way."

In September 1950, at the age of ninety-four, Shaw was pruning trees in the garden when, stepping back to admire his handiwork, he slipped on the uneven ground and broke his leg in the fall. He was taken to the hospital in Luton, where he remained until October 4, when his request to be allowed to return home was granted. He died at Shaw's Corner in the early morning of November 2, 1950; his body was cremated, and according to the dictates of his will, his ashes, mingled with those of his wife, were sprinkled in the garden here. He also directed that no public monument be erected to his memory. Shaw's Corner is now in the care of the National Trust and is open to the public; everything has been kept as it was in 1950, and on display are his books, his 1925 Nobel Prize, his enormous collection of hats, and his Bible. The well-known Augustus John portrait of Shaw and Rodin's bronze bust of the playwright are here as well.

BABLOCK HYTHE, Oxfordshire Hythes (landing places) were named either for the goods handled there—for example, Rotherhithe in London, where cattle were put ashore—or from the owner's name. Bablock Hythe, undoubtedly records the owner's name. This is a ferry on the Isis River (the Isis is the name given to the upper part of the Thames) 4 miles west of Oxford. Bablock Hythe is the ferry described by Matthew Arnold in *The Scholar-Gipsy;* the ferry is still plied by wire punt across the river:

> For most, I know, thou lov'st retirèd ground!
> Thee, at the ferry Oxford riders blithe,
>   Returning home on summer nights, have met
> Crossing the stripling Thames at Bablock-Hithe,
>   Trailing in the cool stream thy fingers wet,
>   As the punt's rope chops round;
> And leaning backward in a pensive dream,
>   And fostering in thy lap a heap of flowers
>   Plucked in shy fields and distant Wychwood bowers,
> And thine eyes resting on the moonlit stream.

BACTON, Norfolk A small coastal village with a coast guard and lifeboat station in northern Norfolk, 4½ miles northeast of North Walsham, Bacton has pleasant sands for bathing and is a minor resort area. It has, in the past, been unspoiled, but the creation of a North Sea gas terminal means that the area will be greatly affected no matter how careful planners are. About half a mile south of the village are the remains of the 12th-century Cluniac Bromholm Priory whose existence was marked by extreme poverty until 1223, when it "discovered" that it owned a piece of the true Cross. King Henry III made a pilgrimage here in 1233, and William Camden comments on the priory and the cross in *Britannia:*

> The cross was made of the true cross which used to be carried before the Greek emperor in battle by an English priest, who on the emperor's death brought it hither. It wrought many miracles. Here are considerable ruins of the priory, converted into a farm-house, and the gate.

One of the first literary allusions to the Rood of Bromholm occurs in "The Reeve's Tale" in Geoffrey Chaucer's *The Canterbury Tales.* The students who have been robbed by the Miller successfully shift sleeping partners, only to have the ruse uncovered at dawn. The Miller's wife has been sleeping soundly

> With John the clerk, that waked hadde al nyght,
> And with the fal out of hir sleep she breyde.
> "Help! hooly croys of Bromeholm," she seyde,
> *In manus tuas!* Lord, to thee I calle!

Not much later William Langland also used the Rood of Bromholm in *Piers Plowman,* when he has Covetousness speak:

> "But now I swear to break myself of these sins—no more selling short weight or swindling the customers. And I'll make a pilgrimage to Walsingham, with my wife as well, and pray to the Rood of Bromholm to get me out of debt."

There is one other association of note: John Paston, of an old Norfolk family, whose letters to his wife present a clear insight into the 15th century, died in London on May 21 or 22, 1466, and his body was brought to the priory here for burial. It was recorded that

> the reke of the torches of the dirge was so overpowering that the priory glazier had to remove two panes of glass so that the mourners should not be suffocated.

BAG ENDERBY, Lincolnshire Lying under Warden Hill in the Wolds 5 miles east of Horncastle, Bag Enderby is a village which Alfred, Lord Tennyson knew well as a child when his father held the joint livings of Somersby and Bag Enderby. This is one of the four hamlets referred to in *In Memoriam:*

> The time draws near the birth of Christ:
>   The moon is hid; the night is still;

The Christmas bells from hill to hill
Answer each other in the mist.

Four voices of four hamlets round,
From far and near, on mead and moor,
Swell out and fail, as if a door
Were shut between me and the sound.

BALDOCK, Hertfordshire (pop. 4,300) With the Great Northern Road becoming the main road through the village of Baldock, it could be expected that any old-world charm here would have been lost; but this is not the case, and the road is attractively tree-lined as it runs through the village. Near the 17th-century almshouses are numerous old cottages and inns, many with overhanging upper stories; and the main street contains some rather fine Georgian houses. The chiefly 14th-century church has a rich display of medieval masonwork, and the 15th-century screens are noteworthy.

The village has an association that only literati may know, for this was the home of the Rev. John Smith, the scholar who spent an estimated 10,000 hours at St. John's College, Cambridge, deciphering the six volumes of closely written shorthand in Samuel Pepys's *Diary*. Lord Grenville put the task to Smith, who was then an undergraduate of St. John's. Smith became rector of Baldock in 1832 and was buried here in 1870.

BAMBURGH, Northumberland (pop. 734) The history of Bamburgh and Bamburgh Castle, set high on rocks above the North Sea just south of Lindisfarne (Holy Island), goes back at least fourteen centuries. This town was the royal city of the Northumbrian kingdom: glorious, proud, and wealthy, it retained its royal status until the unification of the English kingdom. It was in 547 that the King of the Northumbrians, Ida the Flamebearer, began the fortifications on the whin sill rocks that rise 150 feet out of the North Sea. Like most primitive structures of the time, the first castle was wooden, even though Sir Walter Scott makes it stone in *Marmion:*

Thy tower proud Bamburgh, mark'd they there
King Ida's castle, huge and square,
From its tall rock look grimly down,
And on the swelling ocean frown....

The stone castle, with its tower and keep "huge and square," did not exist as such until the 13th century; this type of anachronism is not unusual with Scott.

The castle has also had a long association with Christianity. The town of Bamburgh, several other parishes, and Holy Island made up what was known as Bamburghshire, in many ways the cradle of English Christianity. The ancient ballad "The Battle of Otterburn" speaks of this county:

And they hae burnt the dales o' Tyne,
And part of Bamburghshire,
And three good towers on Redeswire fells,
They left them all on fire.

Bamburgh Castle is also part of the Arthurian legend; it is one of the two localities mentioned by Sir Thomas Malory as the site of Launcelot's castle Joyous Gard; the other is Alnwick. Malory comments, "Some men say it was Anwick and some say it was Bamborrow," when telling how Launcelot comes to Joyous Gard to die. This, then, is the site to which Launcelot elopes with Guinevere. In December 1462, Malory himself was here and at Alnwick with the Earl of Warwick's forces under Edward IV's orders. Released from Newgate Prison in London, he was a member of the expedition sent to quell and defeat the Scots forces under Queen Margaret.

BANBURY, Oxfordshire (pop. 22,070) Situated 22 miles north of Oxford on the Cherwell River, Banbury is a large industrial and market town noted for centuries for a lack of enthusiasm for its past. In the 17th century the town petitioned Parliament for permission to tear down the old castle so that the stone could be used to repair Civil War damage, and the petition was granted. Then, in the 18th century, rather than restore a lovely church (known as Banbury Cathedral because of its beauty) the townspeople blew it up. Nonetheless, some parts of the town retain the charm of their age. The bayed and gabled marketplace still contains mid-17th-century wooden gates leading to an old inn, and the Reindeer Inn, dating from the 16th century, has gates dated 1570.

Every child has heard of Banbury and its cross, and most children have been here in fancy at least. The new market cross, dating from 1859, is not the cross of nursery-rhyme fame; the lady on the white horse was most likely a member of the Fiennes family, whose residence was nearby Broughton Castle. The family still lives there. The ride to the cross is conjectured to have been some sort of May-morning cer-

BANBURY The original Banbury Cross to which one rode a horse to "see a fine lady upon a white horse" was destroyed by the Puritans in 1602; this replica was erected in 1859.

emony. The destruction of the original cross was only one small gesture by the zealous Puritans in Banbury, but this wanton act became the symbol of a town known throughout England for its many sanctimonious inhabitants. Thus, the term "Banbury man" as used by Ben Jonson and others was meant to be especially derogatory. In *Bartholomew Fair* Jonson creates the character of the Banbury baker Zeal-of-the-Land Busy, who gives up his trade because of his conscience: he can no longer contribute to "profane feasts." A now-obscure 17th-century writer, Richard Brathwaite, also comments on Banbury and its puritanical population; he first describes the town as "famous for twanging Ale, Zeal, Cakes and Cheese," and his *Barnabae Itinerarium (Drunken Barnaby's Four Journeys)* presents a picture of the population:

> To Banbury came I, o profane one,
> Where I saw a Puritane One
> Hanging of his cat on Monday
> For killing of a mouse on Sunday.

Banbury entered literature quite early because of Banbury cakes, which are made of flaky or puff pastry and filled with dried spiced fruit. Of the three original shops that made the cakes, one still exists and sells them. The cakes were first mentioned in 1615 in Gervase Markham's *The English Huswife* but are known to have been made in the 15th century. Banbury has also been noted in literature for its cheeses, although today these are not even known in the town. William Shakespeare obviously knew of them and writes of them in *The Merry Wives of Windsor.* The cheeses were extremely thin, and after Slender complains that Bardolph, Nym, and Pistol carried him "to the tavern, and made . . . [him] drunk, and afterwards picked . . . [his] pocket," he is referred to as "You Banbury cheese!"

BARBURY HILL, Wiltshire High up on the Wiltshire Downs above the Vale of the White Horse, Barbury Hill, 4 miles south of Swindon, holds the remains of a prehistoric camp. Michael Drayton includes Barbury Hill in the third song of *Poly-Olbion;* Salisbury Plain has spoken in defense of all plains, and Drayton says, "Those brothers *Barbury,* and *Badbury"* are among those who "did much applaud her speech." The hill is far better known because here Richard Jefferies wrote that his "heart looks into space to be away from earth." A great megalith stands on the hill, and a modern plaque has been put on the prehistoric stone to honor the poet:

> Richard Jefferies
> 1848–1887
>
> It is Eternity now.
> I am in the midst
> of it. It is about
> me in the sunshine.

BARDSEY CUM RIGHTON, Yorkshire (pop. 314) A tiny village in the West Riding of Yorkshire, 7 miles northeast of Leeds, Bardsey, as it is usually called, is known for its church with a Saxon tower and restored 14th-century chancel and as the birthplace of William Congreve, in February 1670. The manor house where he was born belonged to Sir John Lewis, his great-uncle, and Congreve was baptized in the old church on February 10. His father, an army officer, was posted to Ireland shortly after the dramatist's birth; Congreve had no other real association with Bardsey until after his graduation from Trinity College, Dublin, in 1688, when it is thought that he spent two years here before going to London.

BARN ELMS, Surrey Barn Elms, on the south bank of the Thames in northern Surrey, hardly exists in its own right anymore because of its proximity to the city of Barnes and to the western reaches of London. It is now in the grounds of the Ranelagh Club (Barn Elms Park), a fact that has helped to preserve at least some of its old-world atmosphere. In the 15th and 16th centuries this part of Surrey contained large and relatively rural estates, and the manor house that gave Barn Elms its name was the sometime home and political headquarters of Sir Philip Sidney, who married Frances, daughter of Sir Francis Walsingham, owner of Barn Elms, on September 21, 1583. Not much is known of Sidney's life here, but his man was one Poley, the same Poley who was present in the Deptford public house in which Christopher Marlowe was killed. A second literary figure, Abraham Cowley, lived at "a quiet old estate across the Thames" from 1663 to the spring of 1665; undoubtedly his residence was not the manor house but seems to have been near the present stable yard where old garden walls are still extant. One of Cowley's visitors was John Evelyn, who was living in Sayes Court in Deptford. The two men had probably known each other for some time, although such evidence is at best circumstantial, and by March 1663 Evelyn was supplying Cowley with seeds from his own garden. Evelyn's diary records two visits to Cowley, one on May 14, 1663, and one on January 2, 1664. Samuel Pepys was here numerous times and noted in his diary under the date May 26, 1667, his enjoyment in walking in the area and the "great pleasure [with which he] saw some gallant ladies and people come with their bottles, and baskets, and chairs, and form, to sup under the trees by the waterside, which was mighty pleasant."

BARNACK, Northamptonshire (pop. 542) Usually thought of until the recent redistricting as one of the most notable villages in the soke of Peterborough, the village of Barnack is surrounded by the "Hills and Holes," an area that provided the famous Barnack stone which built Ely Cathedral. The church here, dating to the 9th century with 13th-century additions, has an impressive Saxon tower of long-and-short work, and an effigy of Christ delivering a benediction discovered during some restoration work. The playwright George Gascoigne was probably buried here in the Whetstone family vault after his death in Stamford on October 7, 1577.

Just north of the church are the remains of a Norman manor house, and west of the church is the rectory, rebuilt in the 19th century but retaining some of its medieval parts. The rectory was the boyhood home of both Charles Kingsley, author of *The Water Babies* and *Hereward the Wake,* and of his brother Henry Kingsley, author of *Ravenshoe.* The Rev. Charles Kingsley, father of the two novelists, entered orders late and held the living here from 1824 to 1830 on a temporary basis. The fen area made an extreme impression on the young Charles, and he drew on his experiences here in *Hereward the Wake:*

For that fair land, like all things on earth, had its darker aspect. The foul exhalations of autumn called up fever and ague, crippling and enervating, and tempting, almost compelling, to that wild and desperate drinking which was the Scandinavian's special sin. Dark and sad were those short autumn days, when all the distances were shut off, and the air choked with foul brown fog and drenching rains from off the eastern sea; and pleasant the bursting forth of the keen northeast wind, with all its whirling snowstorms. For though it sent men hurrying out into the storm, to drive the cattle in from the fen and lift the sheep out of the snow-wreaths, and now and then never to return, lost in mist and mire, in ice and snow, yet all knew that after the snow would come the keen frost and bright sun and cloudless blue sky, and the fenman's yearly holiday, when, work being impossible, all gave themselves up to play, and swarmed upon the ice on skates and sledges....

Such was the Fenland.

Henry Kingsley was born here on January 2, 1830, just before his father took the living at Clovelly, Devon.

The village was also known to the poet John Clare; indeed, the road from Barnack to Helpston, 2 miles to the east, passes through several of the scenes described in *The Village Minstrel.*

BARNARD CASTLE, County Durham (pop. 5,465) A delightful market town set on a bank above the Tees River, Barnard Castle takes its name from the present Norman stronghold, built here in 1180. During the rebellion of the northern Earls of Westmorland and Northumberland, Barnard Castle was besieged, and under Sir George Bowes withstood the assault until December 12, 1569. A traditional ballad, "The Rising in the North," relates part of the attempt to keep Barnard Castle in the hands of the crown:

This barron [Sir George Bowes] did a castle then,
  Was made of lime and stone;
The vttermost walls were ese to be woon;
  The erles haue woon them anon.

But tho they woone the vttermost walls,
  Quickly and anon,
The innermust walles the cold not winn:
  The were made of a rocke of stone.

The castle's remains cover a little more than 6 acres and are accessible from the open Scar Top that overlooks the Tees. The massive stone keep in the inner ward still contains a stone stair that leads to the upper stories. It is the view of the river scenery from the windows of the keep that Sir Walter Scott describes in the second canto of *Rokeby:*

What prospects from his watch-tower high
Gleam gradual on the warder's eye!—
Far sweeping to the east, he sees
Down his deep woods the course of Tees,
And tracks his wanderings by the steam
Of summer vapors from the stream ...
These silver mists shall melt away
And dew the woods with glittering spray.
Then in broad lustre shall be shown
That mighty trench of living stone....

Scott's notes comment on "the rich and magnificent valley of Tees.... The banks ... very thickly wooded....the richness of woodland scenery." This is where Bertram takes aim at Mortham's son while Matilda tells Mortham's story to Wilfrid and Redmond; indeed, the tower between the keep and the river is known as Mortham's Tower. Scott also refers to local legend when he describes how Fairy Thorsgill was named; the general vicinity is known as Thorsgill Glen:

Beneath the shade the Northmen came,
Fixed on each dale a Runic name,
Rear'd high their altar's rugged stone,
And gave their gods the land they won.
....
Remember Thor's victorious fame,
And gave the dell the Thunderer's name.

In the 16th century John Leland visited Barnard

BARNARD CASTLE Set in a public park of 21 acres, the 19th-century Bowes Museum and Art Gallery is the repository for the original ledgers kept by the owner of the Bowes Academy, William Shaw, the man on whom Charles Dickens modeled Wackford Squeers in *Nicholas Nickleby.*

Castle and described it in his *Itinerary* as "standing stately upon the Tees." A few years after Scott, Charles Dickens came north from Gadshill, Kent, to gather material on northern boarding schools for boys. While staying at the Kings Head Inn (still there with the same name) in the marketplace, he is supposed to have called daily at the shop of Thomas Humphrey, a clockmaker, to get the time. Humphrey's shop was across from the inn and just below the cross at Amen Corner. The tradition is that Dickens saw here a clock whose pendulum was designed to ward off the effects of temperature upon its length and that he, naturally curious, inquired "Did you make that?" The clockmaker's answer, "No, it was my lad there," is supposed to have prompted the reply, "So that is Master Humphrey's Clock, is it?" and suggested the title of his next work. The clockmaker's shop was pulled down in 1933, and the original clock (taken to Old Hartlepool, County Durham, in 1839) is now in Lartington, Yorkshire.

The Bowes Museum and Art Gallery, begun in November 1869 and built in the Renaissance style of a French chateau (somewhat out of place in this landscape), has the original ledgers of William Shaw of the Bowes Academy in Bowes. The ledgers kept by Shaw, who was the model for Dickens's Squeers in *Nicholas Nickleby,* are still quite legible, although the later handwriting appears to be either of a different hand or quite enfeebled. The museum also has manuscript letters from Mary Bousfield, "Squeers's" granddaughter, relating to the "northern school protest" that resulted from the publication of Dickens's novel.

BARNESDALE FOREST, Yorkshire This woodland region in the West Riding of Yorkshire a little south of Pontefract is much diminished since it was one of the favorite haunts of England's most popular folk hero. Robin Hood, who is as difficult to locate accurately as he was elusive for the sheriff of Nottingham, is claimed by two wooded areas, Barnesdale Forest and Sherwood Forest in Nottinghamshire. Perhaps the best evidence points to Barnesdale, but popular tradition and belief point to Sherwood Forest. The earliest-known mention of a possible historical Robin Hood is in the Yorkshire section of the 1230 Pipe Roll, in which he is noted as "Robertus Hood *fugitivus.*" Another historical mention of a Robin Hood occurs about 1285, when note is made of the birth of a son to a Yorkshire forester; for aiding the Earl of Lancaster in the uprising against Edward II in 1322, this particular Robin Hood was banished. In all, seven Robin Hoods are traceable between Edward I and Edward III, a period of less than forty years. Some of these are unlikely candidates for the position of folk hero: one was a citizen of London and a supplier of beer to the King's household; another was born at Wakefield; a third lived at Throckelawe, Northumbria; a fourth was in Lostwithiel, Cornwall; and a fifth, of Howden, Yorkshire, was on the Patent Rolls Calendar. The first-known literary reference to Robin Hood occurs in William Langland's *Piers Plowman,* when Sloth is shouted awake by Repentance to finish his confession. Sloth comments on his inability to stay awake and says:

> I don't even know the Paternoster perfectly, not as a priest should really sing it. I know plenty of ballads about

Robin Hood and Randolph Earl of Chester, but I don't know a verse about our Lord or our Lady.

But the very first mention of Robin Hood and Barnesdale Forest, in the *Scotichronicon* by John of Fordun, written in the latter part of the 14th century, slightly predates Langland. Here is the first specific reference to "that most famous cut-throat" who was hearing mass in the forest when word was brought that his enemies were at hand. He insisted that mass be completed before he dispatched his foes.

Then, from the time of "A Gest of Robyn Hode" (16th century) until the present, he appears often in balladry and folklore. In the tradition of any mythologized hero, Robin Hood gave his name to places throughout the country, some places where he was unlikely to have been. He has been termed everything from a forest elf, a Scandinavian deity, a sun myth, and a god of witches to a real person with a peerage, Robert FitzOoth, Earl of Huntingdon. Robin Hood has also been associated with Robin o' the Wood, a close relation of Robin Goodfellow, and numerous wells, stones, and the like bear his name; he is also associated with the *silvatici,* the "salvage" men who abounded in the northern woods after the Norman Conquest. Similarly, he has been characterized as a very rude yeoman, a great Saxon warrior (one of the last to hold out against the Normans), a leader of peasant revolt, and a chivalric hero, perfectly evolved in the medieval tradition. His popularity appears to have been at its height in the Middle Ages, when bards and minstrels fashioned him into an avenger of wrongs and a securer of social justice. He was given all the medieval ideal traits: even as an outlaw, he was bound to the Virgin Mary and therefore was the champion of all women; he was God-fearing, and his disrespect for the greedy, lecherous, or usurious religious was a moral judgment that the chivalric code of the time upheld. Indeed, his sanctuary was the forest with the exceptions of Whitby Abbey and Kirklees Priory, the latter to his regret. With a band of as many as 100 men, Robin Hood successfully withstood all adversaries: priests and religious laymen, the official establishment, and especially the ubiquitous sheriff of Nottingham.

Barnesdale was once entirely covered by forest and afforded excellent coverage to those evading the law. Moreover, Watling Way or Street, which cut through the forest, was the most frequently traveled north-south road and offered easy prey to the numerous forest outlaws. In "Robin Hood and the Bishop of Hereford," Robin Hood expects the bishop to travel through the forest, has a deer killed in preparation for the ecclesiastic's dinner, dresses as a poor shepherd, and confesses to making "merry with the king's venison." Taken into the depths of the forest and relieved of £300 by Little John, the bishop is made to dance in his boots and say mass before being allowed to leave. Undoubtedly it was this ballad that suggested the scene in Sir Walter Scott's *Ivanhoe* between Locksley (another name for Robin Hood) and the prior of Jervaulx Abbey. It is also in this forest that Robin fights Guy of Gisborne, in the ballad of that name, and kills him, saying, "My name is Robin Hood of Barnesdale." "A Gest of Robyn Hode" describes Robin's intense longing to return to the forest of Barnesdale after being detained for a time at the court of the King:

"Me longeth sore to Bernysdale,
    I may not be therefro;
Barefode and wolward I have hyght
    Thyder for to go."

The ballad specifies many events in Barnesdale, and from the balladic evidence offered by Francis J. Child in *The English and Scottish Popular Ballads* and others it appears as if two Robin Hood cycles existed at one time, one with references relating to Barnesdale and the other to Sherwood Forest. The only extant relic of the legendary character in this area is Robin Hood's Well on the roadside near Castle Howard, where the parishes of Kirby-Smeaton and Burghwallis join. Even this is no longer within the remnants of Barnesdale Forest.

BARNINGHAM WINTER, Norfolk (pop. 30) Also called Barningham Town and not to be confused with nearby Barningham Norwood, this tiny village, 5 miles southeast of Holt, has a lovely park at its center, a partially ruined 14th-century church with a medieval mass dial in a meadow, and an early-17th-century manor house built by Sir Edward Paston of the family whose 15th-century letters have left a dynamic view of the economic, political, and social affairs of the time. Sir Edward's house stands where an earlier house known to Sir John Paston stood. The church contains a number of fine memorials to the family.

BARNSTAPLE, Devon (pop. 14,693) Located at the mouth of the Taw River near the Bristol Channel, Barnstaple along with neighboring Bideford has an interesting history going back to the days when the two ports vied for the maritime supremacy that is now Bideford's. Both towns built ships, and both supplied them generously to fight against the Armada; even today the competition has resulted in a confusion over whether map makers should label the silted-up Taw Estuary Barnstaple Bay or Bideford Bay; maps usually designate it as "Barnstaple *or* Bideford Bay." Barnstaple today is the larger of the two places, but Bideford is still an active port.

Barnstaple is one of the oldest towns in Britain and claims to be the capital of north Devon. Barum, as it was called at the time of the Roman occupation, was the Romans' port and a center for pottery, and pottery later supported refugee Huguenots. Public subscription built the arched stone bridge over the Taw, and the 13th-century letter requesting money says the river is full of "great, hugy, mighty, perylous, and dreadfull water which" has tides four times a day. A great deal of the present town is Georgian. Of especial interest is Queen Anne's Walk, a colonnade with the surviving Tome Stone, a flat-topped mushroomlike stone on which money for business transactions was placed.

Barnstaple was the birthplace of John Gay on June 30, 1685; the house in which he was born was a large one at the corner of Joy Street and the High Street. He was baptized at St. Peter's Church on September 16. When Gay's father died in 1694, his mother moved the family to a house on Ivy Street, where she died a few months later; an uncle, Thomas Gay, then raised the child. Gay attended Barnstaple Grammar School, which was housed in the small building known as St.

Anne's Chantry in back of the church; originally this was a chapel built over the charnel house of the parish cemetery. It then became the grammar school and is now a local museum. In 1702 Gay left his uncle's home for London, for an unsuccessful period as a mercer's apprentice, but was back in Barnstaple in 1706 living with a second uncle, the Rev. John Hanmer. Since this uncle was a Puritan, the two did not get on particularly well, and Gay left again for London in 1707 after his uncle's death.

BARTON-ON-THE-HEATH, Warwickshire (pop. 133) Situated 5 miles south of Shipston-on-Stour, Barton-on-the-Heath has the distinction of pioneering the Cotswolds Games on what is now known as Dover's Hill above Chipping Campden; they were begun by Capt. Robert Dover, who was master of the revels and an attorney at Barton. Ben Jonson, a friend of Dover's, came from London to see the games, and William Shakespeare is also said to have been here for them. Whether he did come or not, he must have known the village, for it was the home of his cousins, the Lamberts. The church here is Norman and has two windows of medieval glass; its most curious possession is a carved pig running across the chancel arch. It was in this church on June 18, 1581, that Sir Thomas Overbury, who was born in Ilmington, was baptized.

The most famous use of Barton-on-the-Heath in literature is William Shakespeare's; this was the home of the tinker Christopher Sly in *The Taming of the Shrew*:

What, would you make me mad? Am not I Christopher Sly, old Sly's son of Burton-heath; by birth a pedlar, by education a card-maker, by transmutation a bear-herd, and now by present profession a tinker?

BASSENTHWAITE, Cumberland (pop. 437) A parish and railway station on the west side of Bassenthwaite Lake (the third largest lake in Lakeland), 7½ miles northwest of Keswick, this community has in its view the mighty Skiddaw, a peak 3,053 feet high.

BARNSTAPLE The 13th-century bridge spanning the Taw River was built by a London merchant after seeing a woman drown trying to cross the river. Barnstaple was the birthplace and home of John Gay from 1685 to 1702.

The Norman church in Bassenthwaite, rebuilt in the 19th century, contains a memorial to James Spedding, known for his edition of Francis Bacon's *Life and Letters*. Spedding lived at nearby Mire House (Mirehouse); Thomas Carlyle was an early admirer of Spedding and his work and called the latter "the hugest and faithfullest bit of literary navvy work I ever met with in this generation." Carlyle's letters contain references to his visits here, including his first visit in 1818, when he was in Keswick. Carlyle was a relatively constant visitor for almost fifty years. Both Alfred, Lord Tennyson and Edward FitzGerald had known James Spedding at Cambridge and were here for a short visit in 1835; they discussed Tennyson's "Morte d'Arthur" as well as "The Day-Dream," "The Lord of Burleigh," "Dora," and "The Gardener's Daughter"; and Tennyson read to them from a little red-covered manuscript. FitzGerald wrote of the occasion:

> Spedding's father, . . . who was of a practical turn, and had seen enough of poets in Shelley and Coleridge (perhaps in Wordsworth also), whom he remembered about the Lakes, rather resented our making so serious a business of verse-making, though he was so wise and charitable as to tolerate everything and everybody, except poetry and poets.

BATCOMBE, Dorset (pop. 116) Above the hamlet of Batcombe, on the verge of lofty Batcombe Down, is a curiously shaped prehistoric pillar, well known to readers of Thomas Hardy as the Cross-in-Hand. Reached by climbing an unmarked road from Dogbury Gate to Evershot over Gore Hill (863 feet), the carved monolith is of a rock not known in local quarries. The accounts of its function and its history are at variance with each other. Some maintain that the stone simply marked a meeting place or a boundary line; some, that its original shape was that of a devotional cross of which only the base remains; and some, natives of the area, still steadfastly maintain that it was and is a wishing stone. The Cross-in-Hand forms the motif of Hardy's "The Lost Pyx" in *Poems of the Past and Present*, but it is far better known from *Tess of the D'Urbervilles* as the spot upon which Alec D'Urberville forces Tess to swear never to tempt him. Hardy describes the area:

> Of all spots on this bleached and desolate upland this was the most forlorn. . . . The place took its name from a stone pillar which stood there, a strange, rude monolith . . . on which was rudely carved a human hand.

There is, as Hardy says, "something sinister, or solemn" in its positioning on the down. "The Lost Pyx" relates another of the legendary stories of how the cross came about: losing the pyx on his way to shrive a dying man, the priest from Cernel's Abbey (Cerne Abbas) eventually finds the eucharistic vessel at this spot. Hardy then relates:

> And when by grace the priest won place,
>   And served the Abbey well,
> He reared this stone to mark where shone
>   That midnight miracle.

The hamlet of Batcombe itself contains yet another piece of Hardiana, for here lived the conjurer Mynterne, mentioned in *Tess* as one of the numerous Wessex sages consulted by local people for all manner of things. The squire of Batcombe, the original of the conjurer, is buried in the church here in an unorthodox manner, according to his directions, neither inside nor outside the church; his tomb is alleged to be the one projecting from the wall of the church into the churchyard.

BATH, Somerset (pop. 70,000) Bath, the oldest and largest city in Somerset and perhaps the oldest inhabited city in England, owes its origin and existence to the mineral waters that rise at King's Spring and pour forth, in three springs, about 500,000 gallons of water per day, all at a constant temperature of 120°F. In legendary terms Bath was founded by Bladud, the son of Hudibras and the father of Leir (Shakespeare's Lear). One account of the town's founding, related in Geoffrey of Monmouth's *Historia Regum Britanniae*:

> Bladud . . . built the town of Kaerbadum, which is now called Bath, and . . . constructed the hot baths there which are so suited to the needs of mortal men. He chose the goddess Minerva as the tutelary deity of the baths. In her temple he lit fires which never went out and which never fell away into ash, for the moment that they began to die down they were turned into balls of stone.

Geoffrey does not include the tradition that Bladud was a leper, banished from court; making his way as a swineherd, he was cured in a spring-filled swamp and regained his royal position. He eventually created a spa here and gave it his name. A second version of the founding places the town firmly in the Arthurian tradition; here the father of King Melwas of Goire had his capital, and here Melwas lived with his father.

BATH Called Aquae Sulis (the waters of Sul, a Celtic goddess), Bath was inhabited by the Romans as a resort in the 1st century A.D. The waters of the Roman Baths, towered over by Bath Abbey, still flow through a lead conduit laid down almost 2,000 years ago; these were the waters which Samuel Pepys found unclean because too "many bodies [go] together in the same water."

Undoubtedly the area was inhabited before the Romans arrived in the 1st century A.D. It was they who christened it Aquae Sulis after a Celtic goddess; the Romans were interested not in a military post here but in the waters. They built the magnificent Thermae, dedicated to Sul Minerva, and within a century visitors arrived here from all over the Roman world. Royal favors and patronage from the 7th through the 10th century elevated Bath and especially honored it in 973, when the town and its Saxon abbey of "wondrous workmanship" were chosen for the coronation of the first King of a united England, Edgar.

> In this year, Edgar, ruler of the English,
> Was consecrated king by a great assembly,
> In the ancient city of *Acemannesceaster,*
> Also called Bath by the inhabitants
> Of this island. On that blessed day,
> Called and named Whit Sunday by the children of men,
> There was great rejoicing by all. As I have heard,
> There was a great congregation of priests, and a goodly
>   company of monks,
> And wise men gathered together.

There had been no fixed ceremony for the crowning of a monarch, and the ceremony devised in Bath on this occasion is the one presently in use. An extensive fire that severely damaged the old cathedral in 1137 marked the beginning of the abbey's downward trend, and by the early 15th century, partly through corruption and neglect, the cathedral was "ruined to its foundation."

Meanwhile, the town itself rapidly became one of the West Country's leading manufacturing towns; Geoffrey Chaucer mentions Bath as a clothmaking center in the description of the Wife of Bath in the General Prologue to *The Canterbury Tales:*

> A good Wif was ther of biside Bathe,
> But she was somdel deef, and that was scathe.
> Of clooth-makyng she hadde swich an haunt,
> She passed hem of Ypres and of Gaunt.

The expression "of biside Bathe" undoubtedly refers to the parish of "St. Michael's juxta Bathon," a suburb known for its weaving, through which Chaucer probably passed on his way to North Petherton, where he served as forester from 1391 on. This prosperity was not reflected in all aspects of life, and the abbey was in a state of decay. Work on the new abbey, known today as the Lantern of the West, was interrupted by the dissolution of the monasteries, and the abbey property was sold in 1548 to Matthew Colthurst, a Member of Parliament for Bath, who began the restoration work; in 1572 his son Edmund gave the abbey and its grounds to the town. Two years later Queen Elizabeth was in Bath, granted it a royal charter, and arranged financial aid for finishing the restoration. This was the impetus needed to revitalize the town, and an influx of doctors and apothecaries, all intent on studying the healing powers of the waters, began. As invalids came from all over, buildings were erected for housing, new baths were opened, and existing ones were cleaned and made usable.

The curative nature of the waters was well established by the end of the 16th century, and the first-known literary and political figure to take the waters at Bath was Sir Walter Ralegh, in 1602. After his release from the Tower of London in 1616, he again stopped here before going on to his home in Sherborne. Ralegh is known to have stayed in the Hart Lodgings, where the Queen's Bath now stands, and to have eaten oysters there that he maintained were among the best he had ever tasted. It has been suggested that William Shakespeare was here in 1602, but there is no evidence to support this claim. A few years later, in May 1610, Sir Fulke Greville, Lord Brooke, moved to Bath for his health. He had been coming to the town for some years before his move, and he continued to divide his time between Bath and London, where he died in 1628. His residence here is not known. As the fame of the spa spread and the illustrious and the wealthy frequented the town, a number of large houses were built of Bath stone. Hart Lodgings, Abbey House, near the present Kingston Parade, Hetling House (the Abbey Church House), and West Gate were among the most notable. Michael Drayton, who was here to gather material for *Poly-Olbion,* writes of the curative powers and the legendary founder of Bath in the third song:

> Her, *Somerset* receives, with all the bounties blest
> That Nature can produce in that *Bathonian* Spring,
> Which from the Sulphury Mines her med'cinall force
>   doth bring;
> As Physick hath found out by colour, taste, and smell,
> Which taught the world at first the vertue of that Well;
> What quickliest it could cure: which men of knowledge
>   drew
> From that first minerall cause; but some that little knew
> (Yet felt the great effects continually it wrought)
> Ascrib'd it to that skill, which *Bladud* hither brought,
> As by that learned King the Bathese should be be-
>   gunne. . . .

A visit by Thomas Fuller, who was interested in the abbey and not in the waters, produced the mixed comment that Bath Abbey was "both spacious and specious, most lightsome as ever I beheld." John Evelyn had little to say about the abbey, although he was in Bath a number of times from 1639 on; he does say, "The *Faciate* . . . is remarkable for this Historical Carving . . ." (that is, the west front). Evelyn usually lodged at Hetling House on the Lower Borough Walls and bathed in the Cross Bath, which was used almost exclusively by the gentry. He seems to have enjoyed the "idle diversions of the Towne . . . intirely built of stone" only slightly and found "the streetes narrow, uneven & unpleasant. . . ." On a trip to the West Country in June 1668, Samuel Pepys, his wife, and Deb were in Bath for a number of days, but his diary contains no mention of their lodgings. He did frequent the baths, on June 13 using the Cross Bath, where he "stayed above two hours in the water, home to bed, sweating for an hour. . . ." Pepys found the town pleasant with its "many good streets and very fair stone-houses." His one unpleasant experience concerned Sunday-morning services at the abbey, where "a vain, pragmatical fellow preached a ridiculous affected sermon"; during the afternoon services, which he also attended, he "slept most of the sermon." He also had reservations about the water, commenting, "Methinks it cannot be clean to go so many bodies together in the same water."

By the beginning of the 18th century Bath was a preeminent resort; the baths were improved again, and Richard Nash, known as Beau Nash, appeared to reign as the "King of Bath." Nash was at once a social arbiter and the man who transformed Bath from a mere watering place into a center of fashionable society; he was also concerned with the establishment of a hospital for the treatment of rheumatic diseases and with tending and financing persons so ill that Bath was, indeed, their last resort. The town rapidly became a center for the arts and a meeting place for the popular wits, and even the cathedral bells pealed out a welcome to prominent guests. Daily the Pump Room was filled with persons drinking their prescribed three glasses of water, and at the King's Bath,

> 'Twas a glorious sight to behold the fair sex
> All wading with gentlemen up to their necks,
> And view them so prettily tumble and sprawl
> In a great smoking kettle as big as our hall;
> And today many persons of rank and condition
> Were boil'd by command of an able physician.

Sometime in the last quarter of the 17th century Daniel Defoe was in Bath to drink the waters, which were then touted as a guarantee against dysentery and scurvy, but it was his short stay here in the summer of 1705 that provoked this severe judgment: "It is more like a prison than a place of diversion, scarce gives the company room to converse out of the smell of their own excrements, and the very city itself may be said to stink like a general common-shore." Defoe had previously used Bath in *Moll Flanders*. Following the discovery in Virginia that she is living incestuously, Moll returns to England and takes "the diversion of going to Bath . . . a place of gallantry enough; expensive and full of snares." At about the time of Defoe's visit, William Congreve was in Bath for reasons of health; he suffered extremely with gout, and for nine weeks beginning in June 1704 he vainly sought a watery cure for that ailment and for the cataracts that eventually caused his blindness. Congreve also spent the 1722 (or 1723) and the 1728 seasons here in the company of John Gay. This last visit extended well into the autumn, and it was on the return trip to London in late autumn that the coach overturned and so severely injured Congreve that he did not recover.

Joseph Addison was another 18th-century writer who came to take the waters in the hope of benefiting his eyes. He arrived first in January 1711 and appears to have returned in August and September of that year. Addison intensely disliked the noise of the wrangling at cards and the gaming tables and thought it louder than the sound of ten cockpits. Sir Richard Steele, who had been ill in London, came to take the waters and recover his health in September 1723 and did not give up his lodgings until January 1724, when he was making plans to leave for Carmarthen, Wales. Whether or not Alexander Pope made his first trip to Bath in September 1714 to take the waters is not known, although it seems likely in view of his recurrent headaches. However, it was as a tourist that he explored Bath thoroughly, taking in the baths, the walks, and the promenade and making the rounds of the chocolate houses and the raffling shops. Here, too, he met Lady Sandwich, whom he called "the best thing this country has to boast of"; he returned yearly for some time, often in the company of Thomas Parnell and John Gay (*The Beggar's Opera* was performed here in 1732). Samuel Richardson was in Bath sometime before his first recorded visit in June 1742, but details of the earlier trip do not exist. In 1742 he was here, most likely, for three reasons: to consult his physician, Dr. Cheyne, who was in the town; to visit his wife's family; and to try the waters. He made a second trip in the late summer of 1753 after a severe illness that spring.

Bath is associated with Henry Fielding and *The History of Tom Jones*, which he probably wrote at nearby Widcombe. Fielding's first association with the town seems to have occurred in 1744, when he brought his first wife here; intermittently ill, she died "of a fever" on November 11 and was taken back to London for burial. Fielding suffered severely with gout in his later years and often could walk only with crutches. Ordered to Bath by his physician in August 1753 to effect a cure for his gout, he was unable to make the trip because of the demands of public service in London, where, as a magistrate, he was working on the problem of widespread crime and corruption and drawing up the initial plans for a city constabulary. Many of the characters in *Tom Jones* are based on people in Bath, and when Fielding was staying with Ralph Allen (the basis for Squire Allworthy) at nearby Widcombe and working on the novel, he had ample opportunity to see the town and the people who frequented the spa. Beau Nash receives special mention, and the marriage of the Fitzpatricks and its attendant consequences occur in Bath.

For Tobias Smollett, a displaced Scot and a misplaced doctor, Bath was an obvious place to try to establish a practice when London proved inhospitable; sometime after 1752 he arrived to set up his surgery, but his practice here also was unsuccessful. He gave up his lodgings on the South Parade and his practice in 1756 but returned for his own health in 1762 and in 1766, when he lived on Gay Street. The town, its people, and its amenities appear often in Smollett's work and especially in *The Expedition of Humphry Clinker*, which he may well have begun on the 1766 trip. Through the letters of Jeremy Melford, Bath and the lodgings taken by Matthew Bramble are vividly described; he writes:

> Three days ago we . . . took possession of the first floor of a lodging-house, on the South Parade; a situation which my uncle chose, for its being near the Bath, and remote from the noise of carriages.

Bramble is disturbed by "the Abbey bells [which] . . . rang so loud, that we could not hear one another speak." Perhaps echoing Smollett's own view, Bramble writes to Dr. Lewis:

> I find nothing but disappointment at Bath; which is so altered, that I can scarce believe it is the same place that I frequented about thirty years ago. . . . A national hospital it may be, but one would imagine that none but lunatics are admitted; and truly, I will give you leave to call me so, if I stay much longer at Bath. . . . The Square, though irregular, is, on the whole pretty well laid out, spacious, open, and airy; . . . but the avenues to it are mean, dirty, dangerous, and indirect.

Bath as a place for husband or wife hunting appears in another of Smollett's works, *The Adventures of Roderick Random*. After joining the French Army and fighting at Dettingen, Roderick, supported by Strap, appears at the spa looking for a rich wife.

A figure of passing interest here is Edmund Burke, whose physician, Dr. Nugent, invited an ailing Burke to stay with him at Circus House on the Circus. Burke's acceptance gained him not only his health but Nugent's daughter as his wife; they were married here in 1756. Forty years later, when his health was failing, he returned to Bath and lived at 11 North Parade in a house more closely associated with Oliver Goldsmith than with Burke. Goldsmith, first in Bath in 1762, when he was ill and was preparing a biography of Beau Nash, who had died that year, returned in 1771 and stayed with his friend and patron Lord Clare at 11 North Parade (marked with a plaque). This was the occasion of an incident concerning the Duke and Duchess of Cumberland which became the basis of the classic blunder in *She Stoops to Conquer*. The houses rented by the duke and Lord Clare were adjacent, and one morning Goldsmith walked into the Duke of Cumberland's dining room just as he and the duchess were about to breakfast. Sprawling on the sofa and appearing totally at ease, Goldsmith answered their questions about the day's news in Bath; realizing that Goldsmith was in a reverie, they conversed until breakfast was served and he was asked to join them. Only then did he realize his *faux pas*, and he left in a state of utter confusion after accepting their invitation to dinner.

Laurence Sterne was in Bath in late March and early April 1765, when he stayed at the Three Black Birds Inn, then in a passage between New Bond and North Gate Streets, had his portrait painted by Thomas Gainsborough (who lived here) in one sitting, and visited Ralph Allen at Prior Park. In 1766 Horace Walpole was sent to Bath by his physician and stayed at the northeast corner of Chapel Court (marked by a commemorative tablet). Intensely disliking the town from the start, he wrote, "I am tired to death of the place," but stayed for the cure. He commented as well that the buildings on the Royal Crescent were no better than "a collection of little hospitals." Richard Brinsley Sheridan first lived here with his father in 1770 at a house on King's Mead Street, and later that year they moved into 9 New King Street when they made the acquaintance of Thomas Linley, a composer and music teacher, and his daughters. Both Richard and his brother Charles fell in love with Elizabeth Linley, and the dramatist addressed his "Uncouth in this moss-covered grotto of stone" to her. A complication arose when Maj. Thomas Mathews pressed his attentions on Miss Linley and attempted, so Sheridan thought, to defame her character. When the two decided to flee to France (Miss Linley was planning to join a convent there), they escaped from Linley House, 11 Royal Crescent, in March 1772; their plans changed, and Sheridan and Miss Linley were married abroad just before the arrival of her extremely irate father. Sheridan's wife was taken back to the family home in Bath, and Sheridan returned to England to fight two duels with Mathews, the first in London and the second, in which Sheridan was injured, here at Kingsdown. Sheridan and his wife were eventually reunited after Sheridan recovered from his wounds at Waltham Holy Cross. The dramatist returned briefly to Bath in 1792 following his wife's death. The Pump Room society and its prescribed tonic inspired *The School for Scandal*, and Sheridan also set the final scene of *The Rivals* in Kingmead Field (long gone), near the center of the town.

Bath also served as the introduction to drama for the very young Sir Walter Scott, who was brought here by an aunt in 1775. From infancy Scott had suffered from a lame right leg, later discovered to be the result of poliomyelitis, and was here to take the waters at the age of four. Aunt and nephew stayed for a year, during which time the young boy learned to read and attended his first play, *As You Like It*. Dr. Samuel Johnson was here in 1776 with the Thrales, but where they stayed at this time is not known (it may have been the house on the North Parade where the Thrales later stayed). James Boswell joined them at Johnson's request and stayed at the Pelican Inn (demolished). Dr. Johnson himself was particularly fond of going with Mrs. Thrale to the Assembly Rooms, where he "contemplated humanity." Toward the end of 1789, having given up their school in Bristol, Hannah More and her sisters decided to divide their time between their house in Cowslip Green and Bath. They built a house at 76 Great Pulteney Street and became active in the formation of Sunday schools in small parishes outside Bath. Hannah More continued to live here until 1802, when she moved to Barley Wood in Wrington. Edward Gibbon, the historian, is one of the few well-known figures to have claimed a cure for taking the waters here; brought to Bath first at the age of twelve, having been extremely frail and sickly from birth, he asserted that he had been thoroughly cured during his many trips to the town. He lived at 10 Belvedere (marked with a plaque) before his death in 1794. William Cowper also spent a holiday in Bath.

As a child, from 1796 to 1799, Thomas De Quincey lived in Bath with his mother at 6 Green Park Buildings (the site is marked with a tablet). He was placed in the Bath Grammar School under Mr. Morgan and began a brilliant career in Greek and Latin that was terminated by an accident. One of the masters, in attempting to cane a boy, accidentally struck De Quincey on the head, injuring him seriously. The headmaster's apology for the affair contained such extreme flattery of the son that the "morally austere" Mrs. De Quincey, feeling such excessive praise would harm the boy, withdrew him. For a short time before being sent to Winkfield, Wiltshire, to continue his education, he was unsuccessfully tutored at home by a French *émigré*. Robert Southey spent some of his boyhood and young manhood here at the home of his mother's rather rich and imperious half sister at 108 Walcot Street; a tablet marks the house. Although only quiet games were permitted, there were compensations for the child, the most important of which were the aunt's extensive library and their frequent attendance at the theater. Here in 1793 Southey informed his mother of his intention of quitting Oxford and joining Coleridge in a pantisocratic scheme. Both his aunt and his mother disapproved of his "radical opinions," and his engagement in 1794 to Edith Fricker brought his expulsion from his aunt's household. Later, Southey returned frequently to Bath to visit Walter Savage Landor.

At the beginning of the 19th century Bath was no longer the place of fashion and cures, and the New Assembly Rooms and the lavish balls gave way to intimate at-homes and private parties. The rivalry of the new seaside resorts helped create the change, and

Bath now became a place to live in rather than to visit. It filled up with barristers and clergymen, widows, and retired service commanders, but it was still attractive to writers and painters. Fanny Burney made her first trip to Bath with the Thrales in 1780, when she stayed at 14 South Parade (marked with a commemorative tablet); she and Mrs. Thrale often amused themselves at the expense of the gout-ridden London gentlemen, and Miss Burney expressed extreme distaste for the showiness of those who frequented the Assembly Rooms. Nevertheless, after her marriage to Gen. Alexandre d'Arblay and a ten-year internment in France, she returned with her husband to Bath. In 1815 they first had lodgings on Rivers Street and shortly after moved to 23 Great Stanhope Street. On her death in 1840 she was buried in her son's grave in the Walcot churchyard here; the tomb is in the garden. Around 1800 young Lord Byron came to Bath with his mother; relatively little is known about the excursion except that mother and son attended a masquerade ball for which Byron was dressed as a Turkish boy.

But Bath is associated mostly with Jane Austen. Probably she was first here in November 1797, when she undoubtedly stayed with her uncle, James Leigh Parrot, and his family at 1 Paragon. By May 1799 her brother Edward and his family were established at 13 Queen Street, and Miss Austen was a frequent guest here until her father's retirement from the church at Steventon, Hampshire, in 1801. The Rev. George Austen had already determined that he and his family would return to Bath, with which the Austens had numerous connections.

The Austens took a three-year lease on 4 Sydney Terrace (now Sydney Place and marked with a plaque), on the Bathwick Estate across the Avon River at the far end of Pulteney Street. It was in this house that Jane Austen wrote *Lady Susan*, began *The Watsons* (never finished), and completed all revisions on *Northanger Abbey*, which she sold in 1803 for £10. Following the expiration of the Sydney Place lease in 1804, the Austens took possession of 27 Green Park Buildings, a house that had been rejected three years previously as unhealthy; with a lovely unspoilt view of the river and the countryside, it survived intact until World War II, when the east side of the building was demolished. The Reverend Mr. Austen died in January 1805, and on Lady Day his widow and daughters moved to 25 Gay Street, about halfway up that very steep street. They later moved to lodgings on Trim Street, and they finally left Bath for Clifton (Bristol) and Southampton in the summer of 1806. The last removal must have been a pleasant one for Jane Austen, who had complained at various times, "We do nothing but walk about."

The use of Bath in Jane Austen's novels is frequent. Many of her characters visit here: in *Emma* Mr. Elton comes to Bath in search of a wife, and in *Pride and Prejudice* Wickham is allowed to come here to find distraction from Lydia's behavior. Those who come in search of a cure include the Reverend Dr. Grant in *Mansfield Park* and the Palmers in *Sense and Sensibility*, who stay with friends "on the other side of Bath" when Marianne is ill. Part of the plot of *Lady Susan* concerns Mr. Johnson's removal to Bath, where, as his wife writes, "If the waters are favourable to his constitution and my wishes, he will be laid up with gout for many years." Others seek society and excitement here, and in *Northanger Abbey* and *Persuasion* Miss Austen records her own changing attitude toward Bath. In the first work the Allens bring the young Catherine Morland to Bath to endure "all the difficulties and dangers of a six weeks residence. . . ." They cross the Old Bridge, where the

BATH The fantastic Pulteney Bridge, designed and built by Robert Adam, is an enclosed structure with shops on either side; this is one of the many attractions that have brought numerous literary and other visitors to Bath over the centuries.

Churchill Bridge is now, and are driven up Stall Street to their hotel, probably the White Hart. They seek society in the Lower and Upper Rooms and the Pump Room, and in the Lower Rooms Catherine is introduced to Henry Tilney. The chase by Catherine and Isabella Thorpe of the two young men who stare at them in the Pump Room leads through the abbey churchyard, through the archway, across Cheap Street, up Union Passage, and onto Milsom Street. It is then only a short walk to the Edgar Buildings on George Street. Other walks are accurately described, among them the Sunday outing on Crescent Fields and the climb to Beechen Cliff, "that noble hill whose beautiful verdure and hanging coppice render it so striking an object from almost every opening in Bath."

In *Persuasion* Bath becomes a retirement place for officers, especially naval men. The arrogant Sir Walter Elliot and his daughters live overlooking the city on Camden Place (now Camden Crescent), "a lofty and dignified situation such as becomes a man of consequence." Lady Russell, the widow "extremely well provided for," has lodgings on Rivers Street; Lady Dalrymple and her daughters have "taken a house for three months in Laura Place and would be living in style"—this is the more exclusive Bathwick Estate. Colonel Wallis's furnished house is in the Marlborough Buildings, just west of the Royal Crescent; Mrs. Smith's lodgings are in the Westgate Buildings; and Admiral Croft and his wife have lodgings on Gay Street, the same street on which Miss Austenonce lived. Other places mentioned include the Octagon Room, where Captain Wentworth and Anne attend a concert and have a promising conversation; Bond Street, where Sir Walter "counted eighty-seven women go by, one after another, without there being a tolerable face among them"; the White Hart Hotel, where the Musgrove family stays; and the final scene on Union Street, where Anne and the Captain are "more exquisitely happy, perhaps, in their re-union, than when it had been first projected."

Another author connected closely with Bath is Walter Savage Landor, who first came to the city briefly in 1802 and returned in 1803. From that time until his marriage in 1811 Bath was basically the center of his life, although there are references to nearby Bristol and Clifton. For a time in 1808 he lived at Sidney House, and by 1809 he was at 9 South Parade and on Pulteney Street. His variety of residences is best explained in a letter of a later date to Robert Southey:

> You remind me of Bath! if not a delightful, a most easy place. I cannot bear brick houses and wet pavements. . . . The South Parade was always my residence in winter. Towards spring I removed into Pulteney Street—or rather towards summer; for there were formerly as many nightingales in the garden, and along the river opposite the South Parade, as ever there were in the bowers of Schiraz. The situation is unparalleled in beauty, and is surely the warmest in England.

Count Julian was written in the Pulteney Street lodgings in 1810–1811. Early in January 1811, attending a Bath ball, he first saw Julia Thuillier, of whom he is said to have exclaimed, "By heaven! that's the nicest girl in the room, and I'll marry her"—which he did on May 24 at St. James' Church. However, Landor was quarrelsome, and after sepa-

rating from "the nicest girl in the room" in 1835, he settled here two years later. In mid-November 1837 he came to 35 St. James's Square, and the town was to be his home until he was forced to leave England in 1857. Number 35 and Landor's other homes were to become important centers for visiting literary figures. Charles Dickens was one of the first to arrive (January 1840) and became a frequent guest. On January 29 of the first trip the idea of Little Nell for *The Old Curiosity Shop* arose at dinner in Landor's lodgings; Landor later commented that he regretted not having bought Number 35 and burned it to the ground "so that no meaner association should ever desecrate the birthplace of Little Nell."

The following year, when Dickens reappeared at his friend's residence, he had with him Henry Wadsworth Longfellow, who wanted to meet Landor. Landor was still making yearly summer trips to Warwick, and when he returned in September 1846, he moved to 42 St. James's Square. He became a friend of Louis Napoleon, who was there that summer for two months; in typical fashion Landor claims to have remarked to the exile that he "had escaped two great curses—a prison and a throne" and noted that Napoleon "smiled at this, but made no remark." Both his addresses in St. James's Square are marked with plaques. On March 24, 1849, he found that another removal was inevitable because "the people of my house are most impudent thieves—wine, umbrella, penknife—are carried off." He took 3 Rivers Street, where Thomas Carlyle visited him in July 1850, had an "elaborately simple" dinner with him, and in the evening made the usual stroll through the Royal Crescent and the park. Among Landor's other guests were Nathaniel Hawthorne and William Wordsworth.

Landor's health began to deteriorate rapidly in the mid-1850s, and in the same period the "awful Yescombe business" arose. Details concerning the libel, slander, and pilfering accusations and the authorship of the somewhat indelicate poems are at variance; in any case, Landor was an old man whose mental faculties, as he admitted, had become slow. The result was that after one court appearance and after a public recantation of his "libels," Landor's health broke completely. He was found unconscious in March and was said to have only a short time to live. He rallied, however, and by mid-April was thought to be fully recovered. A second suit was brought by the Yescombes in June 1857, and Landor, somewhat ill advised by his solicitor, left the country in July to avoid a possible £5,000 award and imprisonment.

George Crabbe often made the coach trip to Bath from Trowbridge, Wiltshire, where he was rector. He noted in his diary under the date of August 25, 1814, that he had been "elected of the Reading Society and New Room," a fact of which he was immensely proud. At 11 Pulteney Street, when he was sixty-two, Crabbe met Elizabeth Charter, with whom he was to form one of a series of semiromantic attachments that he carried on by letter. It was not this but his trips to Bath to attend concerts and balls that scandalized his parishioners. Percy Bysshe Shelley stayed at 3 Miles Buildings as a child, but his main association with the town occurred in September 1815, when he was here with Mary Wollstonecraft Godwin, who was to become his second wife. They lived first at 5 Abbey Churchyard (now the Roman Pavement) and then at 6 Queen Street until leaving for Hampstead in mid-December. William Beckford, the eccentric author of *Vathek*, came to Beckford House, Lansdown Crescent, in 1822 after extravagance forced him to sell the fantastic Fonthill Abbey in Fonthill Gifford. (The house is marked with a plaque.) Even though in reduced circumstances, he created a miniature Fonthill here and continued his passion of collecting *objets d'art* and books. In 1827 he built a tower on Lansdown Hill that was to serve as a personal memorial, and at his direction he was buried there after his death in Bath on May 2, 1844. The tower and its surrounding grounds were later given to the Bath Corporation by his daughter, the Duchess of Hamilton. Elizabeth Barrett (Browning) was here on one occasion when her father was moving from Hope End, Herefordshire, to Sidmouth, Devon, after declaring bankruptcy. By the time she arrived in Bath on August 23, 1832, she was in such poor health that she was unable to leave her room at the York Hotel; she commented on the town, ". . . take it altogether, marble and mountains, [it] is the most beautiful town I ever looked upon."

When Charles Dickens was here in 1840 to visit Landor, he stayed at York House, then the largest hotel in Bath. Five years earlier he was here to prepare a report of a political dinner given by Lord John Russell and stayed at the Saracen's Head, a small hotel on Broad Street. No bedrooms were available, and he was accommodated in a room over some outbuildings at the far end of the innyard. Not one of his favorite cities, Bath, "a city of the dead," is called "that grass-grown city of the ancients" in *Bleak House*. In January 1869, he writes:

> The place looks to me like a cemetery which the dead have succeeded in rising and taking. Having built streets of their old gravestones, they wander about scantly trying to "look alive." A dead failure.

A number of chapters of *Pickwick Papers* are devoted to Bath, the objective of Mr. Pickwick. Mr. Pickwick and the others stay at the White Hart run by Moses Pickwick; Sam Weller thinks the waters taste "like warm flat-irons," and Mr. Pickwick is taken to the Pump Room,

> a spacious saloon, ornamented with Corinthian pillars, and a music gallery, and a tompion clock, and a statue of Nash, and a golden inscription, to which all the water-drinkers should attend, for it appeals to them in the cause of a deserving charity. There is a large bar with a marble vase, out of which the pumper gets the water; and there are a number of yellow-looking tumblers, out of which the company get it; and it is a most edifying and satisfactory sight to behold the perseverance and gravity with which they swallow it. . . . There is another pump-room, into which infirm ladies and gentlemen are wheeled, in such an astonishing variety of chairs and chaises, that any adventurous individual who goes in with the regular number of toes is in imminent danger of coming out without them; and there is a third, into which the quiet people go, for it is less noisy than either. There is an immensity of promenading, on crutches and off, with sticks and without, and a great deal of conversation, and liveliness, and pleasantry.

BATH   The famous Royal Crescent, a Palladian terrace which overlooks much of this fashionable resort city on the Avon, was where Mr. Pickwick and his friends were staying when Mr. Winkle, who was mistakenly thought to be running off with Mrs. Dowler, "throwing off his slippers into the road, took to his heels and tore round the Crescent, hotly pursued by Dowler and the watchman."

In the evening Mr. Pickwick attends a ball in the Assembly Rooms, and the spot where he plays whist is still pointed out. He and his friends stay on the Royal Crescent (probably Number 15 or Number 16, the only two places that were let in that way). The Royal Hotel from which Mr. Winkle hastily departs for Bristol is possibly the Royal Hotel (demolished before Dickens's visits to Bath) or the York House Hotel, where numerous members of the royal family had stayed. The "small green-grocer's shop" to which Sam Weller is taken by Smauker for "a friendly swarry, consisting of a boiled leg of mutton with the usual trimmings," is now the Beaufort Arms on Prince's Street; 12 Queen's Square was the house of Angelo Cyrus Bantam, Esq., the master of ceremonies who "welcomed Mr. Pickwick to Ba—ath," and the houst next door has preserved a large screen with the name and date: Moses Pickwick, 1830.

William Wordsworth was in Bath on at least two occasions, the first in 1797 and the second in April 1841, when he stayed at 9 North Parade (marked with a plaque). He and his wife were here for the wedding of their daughter Dora to Edward Quillinan, but Wordsworth was unable to attend the service, and Dora was given away by her brother. In 1848 James Anthony Froude, the historian, lived at 16 Lansdown Place East, and in 1857 William Makepeace Thackeray (who earlier often stayed on the Circus with an aunt) resided in the same house. In 1859 Thomas Babington Macaulay stayed in a house at 2 Pulteney Street, which became the residence of Edward Bulwer-Lytton (Lord Lytton) in 1867 and 1872. In 1866 Bulwer-Lytton stayed at 9 Royal Crescent. In the spring of 1888 Virginia Stephen (Woolf) was sent here to convalesce after a severe bout of whooping cough, and W. H. Hudson lived at 22 King Street in 1898 and 1899.

Thomas Hardy made fairly extensive use of Bath, the town full of "great glass windows to the shops, and great clouds in in the sky, full of rain and old wooden trees in the country round," as Cainy Ball describes it in *Far from the Madding Crowd*. Ball has followed Bathsheba Everdene here on her trip to meet Sergeant Troy, and it is at the Church of St. Ambrose that she and Troy are married by the Rev. G. Mincing, B.A. In "The Marchioness of Stonehenge" (*A Group of Noble Dames*), Lady Caroline is secretly married in St. Michael's Church, and Bath Abbey is mentioned in *Two on a Tower*. The town is also mentioned in *The Mayor of Casterbridge, The Woodlanders*, "Lady Mottisfont" (*A Group of Noble Dames*), "The Melancholy Hussar" (*Wessex Tales*), and "Geographical Knowledge" (*Time's Laughingstocks and Other Poems*). In June and July 1873 Hardy spent ten days here when Emma Lavinia Gifford, the sister-in-law of the rector at St. Juliot, Cornwall, and the woman Hardy was to marry, was staying here with a Miss d'Arville, "a delightful old lady." His meeting Miss Gifford at the train,

She . . . with a travel-tired smile,
  Half scared by scene so strange;
. . . outworn by mile on mile,

occasioned the poem "The Change."

Bath retained much of its atmosphere well into the 20th century, but when World War II broke out, the Admiralty came to stay, and the town suffered rather severe bomb damage. After the war new office buildings were erected, and housing estates were developed on the "beautifully green and feathered hills" that Carlyle noted. The town also became more than ever a retirement center and a tourist attraction. George Saintsbury retired to 1 Royal Crescent in 1915, after twenty years as Professor of Rhetoric and English Literature at the University of Edinburgh. It was here that he wrote *Notes on a Cellar-Book* and *The Scrap Book* and died on January 28, 1933; he was buried in Southampton, Hampshire.

BATTLEFIELD, Shropshire (pop. 102) Usually considered a part of Shrewsbury, 3 miles to the south, Battlefield has a distinct place both in literature and in history, for here is Hatley Field, the site of the Battle of Shrewsbury (1403), dramatized by William Shakespeare in *Henry IV: Part I*. Here Henry is victorious over the northern barons and the Welsh "insurgents," and Hotspur is killed by the repentant Prince Hal on July 21. The King, hearing of the rebels' proposed meeting in Shrewsbury on July 11, plans to assemble the royal forces at nearby Bridgnorth:

On Wednesday next, Harry, you shall set forward;
On Thursday we ourselves will march;
Our meeting is Bridgenorth: and, Harry, you
Shall march through Glostershire; by which account,
Our business valued, some twelve days hence
Our general forces at Bridgenorth shall meet.

The march to battle is short, and the King's forces camp "near Shrewsbury." Henry's reference to "yon bosky hill" is to Haughmond Hill, east of Hatley Field. After the slaughter of the battle and while in command of the rebels, Henry built an impressive chantry with a new hammer-beam roof to commemorate the war dead.

BAWDESWELL, Norfolk A small Norfolk village 14 miles northwest of Norwich, Bawdeswell has some incidental literary fame, which local tradition holds to be far greater than the evidence supports. The fact is that Geoffrey Chaucer, who did have familial links with Norfolk, used Bawdeswell in *The Canterbury Tales*. The Reeve was of this town:

Of Northfolk was this Reve of which I telle,
Biside a toun men clepen Baldeswelle,
Tukked he was as is a frere aboute,
And evere he rood the hyndreste of oure route.

The description of the Reeve is specific, and it is thought that Chaucer had a particular person in mind. Bawdeswell once belonged to the Earls of Pembroke, and the poet may have served as deputy surveyor after some mismanagement by Sir William de Beauchamp, Chaucer's cousin. It is also said locally that the poet's uncle held the living here and that Chaucer's House on the main street was the old rectory where the poet probably stayed. It has never been established that the house dates from the 14th century.

BEACHY HEAD, Sussex A promontory on the south coast 3 miles southwest of Eastbourne, Beachy Head, soaring 534 feet above the sea on the South Downs, presents unparalleled views to Pevensey, Hastings, Dungeness, and the Isle of Wight. A popular spot with sightseers, Beachy Head is at its best in the off

BEACHY HEAD The tallest headland on the south coast at 534 feet, Beachy Head has always attracted visitors from nearby Eastbourne, and the walk here was one favored by Lewis Carroll when he was on his yearly holiday in that town.

season, when a walk along the cliffs at low tide is memorable. Richard Jefferies, the Wiltshire-born author of *Wild Life in a Southern County,* found such a walk inspiration for an essay:

> The sea seems higher than the spot where I stand, its surface on a higher level—raised like a green mound—as if it could burst in and occupy the space up to the foot of the cliff in a moment. It will not do so, I know; but there is an infinite possibility about the sea; it may do what it is not recorded to have done. . . .
>
> So the white spray rushes along the low broken wall of rocks, the sun gleams on the flying fragments of the wave, again it sinks, and the rhythmic motion holds the mind, as an invisible force holds back the tide.

Another writer, Algernon Swinburne, was inspired by Beachy Head and its wildlife in September 1886; the result was "To a Seamew":

> We, sons and sires of seamen,
>   Whose home is all the sea,
> What place man may, we claim it;
> But thine—whose thought may name it?
> Free birds live higher than freemen,
>   And gladlier ye than we—
> We, sons and sires of seamen,
>   Whose home is all the sea.

BEACONSFIELD, Buckinghamshire (pop. 6,000) Astride the A40 London to Oxford Road, 8 miles northwest of Uxbridge, Beaconsfield has become a market town with a split personality. The new town, across the railway, is a conglomerate small modern city that could be any undistinguished place in England, but at the roundabout a mile away is the old village, with a wide, tree-lined High Street, old inns, timbered cottages, and mellow Georgian buildings. The 17th-century parish church of St. Mary and All Saints, impressive on the outside, was ruthlessly restored in the 19th century, when the old timbered galleries and box pews were removed, but the adjoining

old rectory, begun in 1500 and completed in 1540, retains some of its upper timberwork.

Beaconsfield has a number of important literary associations beginning in the early 17th century, when the poet Edmund Waller, who was born in Coleshill, was brought here as a child by his family. The Wallers lived at Hall Barn (rebuilt), the estate that the poet inherited in 1624. Waller's early life is something of a mystery; however, after many adventures during the Commonwealth and long periods abroad, he settled here at Hall Barn in 1651. Called by John Evelyn "Waller's town box," the house sat just off the old road to Windsor; the entrance is marked by Little Hall Barn. Waller died here on October 21, 1687, and was buried in the churchyard of the parish church. The grave, under a walnut tree, is marked by a large black-and-white marble pyramid adorned with skulls.

Beaconsfield was also the home of Edmund Burke from 1768 until his death in 1797; in 1768 he bought the Gregories, an extensive estate that became his refuge from politics. He roamed the estate and visited many of the cottages of the farmhands before becoming ill in the summer of 1796. Growing progressively worse in the early part of the next year and said to have suffered from extensive internal abscesses, he died here just after midnight on July 9; on the day before his death, he spoke of his hatred of the "revolutionary spirit in France" and had a number of his favorite Addison essays read to him. Burke was buried in the parish church; there is a commemorative plaque on the wall, but the tablet for the grave is hidden under a hassock of one of the pews. One of Burke's visitors was George Crabbe after he petitioned Burke for support in 1781. Crabbe and Burke often strolled on the grounds while conversing, and on one occasion Crabbe met Sir Joshua Reynolds, who was also a guest. Crabbe appears to have stayed at the Gregories in the autumn of 1781 and to have returned to London for the winter. Among Burke's other guests were Richard Brinsley Sheridan and Dr. Samuel Johnson, who was brought by Mrs. Thrale.

In more modern times G. K. Chesterton made his home here. He and his wife moved to Beaconsfield from Battersea, London, in 1909 and first took a small house; later they built Overroads (marked by a plaque) on Grove Road, where Chesterton lived for the rest of his life. The house, of his own design, was composed of an enormous living room, used for all the family's entertaining, with a number of small but functional bedrooms attached. *The Innocence of Father Brown* (1911) was one of the first books Chesterton worked on at Beaconsfield, and it is said that at least part of it was written at the White Hart Inn, where a commemorative bust marks the author's favorite corner. Another local frequented by Chesterton was the Edwardian Earl of Beaconsfield, which was constructed to carry on the medieval tradition of the monks' hospice since the pub is connected to the local Roman Catholic church. This is the church which received Chesterton into the Catholic faith. A frequent visitor here was a longtime friend, Hilaire Belloc. Many of the Chesterton drawings for Belloc's satirical novels were done in the Earl of Beaconsfield after the two had lunch. Chesterton died in Beaconsfield on June 14, 1936, and was buried in the churchyard of St. Teresa of the Child Jesus, where there is a monument by Eric Gill.

BEAMINSTER, Dorset (pop. 1,651) With the southern range of the Dorset chalk hills to the southeast, the small town of Beaminster (pronounced "bem′mis-ter" or "bem′ster") has changed little in the last 150 years. Set amid steep farmland hills, this town of ancient lineage appears surprisingly modern, for wars and disastrous fires in 1644, 1684, and 1781 almost destroyed the old town. Beaminster has a fine pinnacled market cross and outstanding examples of large 18th-century merchants' houses constructed of a regional golden Ham Hill stone, which seems to mellow the town and to put a honeylike glaze over the market square.

Beaminster was a favorite of the early-19th-century Dorset dialect poet William Barnes, who wrote:

Sweet Be'mi'ster, that bist a-bound
By green an' woody hills all around
Wi' hedges, reachen up between
A thousan' vields o' zummer green
Where elems' lofty heads do drow
Their sheädes vor häy-meakers below,
An' wild hedge-flow'rs do charm the souls
O' maidens in their evenen strolls.

The vividly green wooded hills still come close to the town, and the hedges still bound the elm-shaded fields and bloom with elder blossoms and white eltrot in season.

Beaminster is very much a part of Thomas Hardy's Wessex; it becomes Emminster in "The Home-Coming," *Two on a Tower,* and *Tess of the D'Urbervilles,* where the location is used most frequently. Benvill Lane is the actual name of the road leading from the town to the author's Evershead (Evershot). Angel Clare makes his way to Emminster, "the hill surrounded little town," three weeks after his marriage to Tess; the red stone Tudor tower of the church of which Angel's father is parson is the parish church; and the vicarage where Angel stays a day or so with his family and to which Tess is determined to go to get news of him is still standing. Tess also travels on Benvill Lane, which leads up to "the edge of the basin in which Emminster and its vicarage lay."

BEARSTED, Kent (pop. 924) About 3 miles east of Maidstone, Bearsted is more famous for its cricket associations, as the site of one of the oldest playing fields in the country and the home of the redoubtable A. P. Freeman, than for its literary association. At the foot of the North Downs, just 1 mile outside the village to the east, is Rose Acre, the home of the poet Edward Thomas from 1901 on; to justify the cottage's original name, Thomas later planted the roses. The cottage was, in fact, disagreeably damp, dark, and dingy, and he and his family took a second house, also called Rose Acre, on the village green. Thomas left the village in 1904 for Sevenoaks; he was killed in Flanders in 1917. There is a second association with the American novelist Sinclair Lewis, who worked on *Babbitt* at Bell House in August and September 1921.

BEAULIEU, Hampshire (pop. 1,011) Taken from the French *beau lieu,* meaning "beautiful place," this name came to be pronounced "bew′ley"; the village, at the head of the tidal Beaulieu River, was the site of a Cistercian monastery founded in 1204 by King John. Beaulieu Abbey took on great importance during the 14th and 15th centuries when the order be-

came heavily involved in forestry and farming. Because of its extensive involvement in agriculture, the order here was one of a very few permitted to employ *conversi,* or lay brothers, men barred from taking holy orders who took vows of poverty, chastity, and obedience and lived within the monastic community. Within three months of the dissolution of the monasteries, the abbey and grounds were purchased by Thomas Wriothesley, one of Thomas Cromwell's principal henchmen and later 1st Earl of Southampton. It was Wriothesley's grandson Henry, the 3d Earl of Southampton, who was the patron of William Shakespeare. Although no biographical evidence supports the tradition, it is maintained that Shakespeare visited the home of his patron here.

Sir Arthur Conan Doyle, who knew southern England well and lived in this area for many years, used Beaulieu Abbey and the area west to Christchurch in *The White Company:*

Out of Beaulieu Abbey the horrified monks expelled big John of Hordle, all fist and grin. From Beaulieu, into a turbulent world he had never before seen, came young Alleyne Edricson, the student, of the old Saxon line. And [with Samkin Aylward] these three, along the road to adventure, met and swore friendship before they went to the wars under the five roses of Sir Nigel Loring.

Just south of Beaulieu is the bleak expanse of heath which William Cobbett in his *Rural Rides* describes as "as barren as it is possible for land to be"; heather stretches for miles without a tree to break the monotony, even though the area is part of the New Forest.

BEAUMANOR, Leicestershire On the east side of the lovely Charnwood Forest and almost 10 miles northwest of Leicester, Beaumanor is a seat and nothing more. The estate here was bought in 1598 by Sir William Herrick, uncle and legal guardian of the poet Robert Herrick. Although there is no absolute evidence that the young boy spent any time here, it has been traditionally assumed that he did.

BEAUVALE, Nottinghamshire Beauvale, 9 miles northwest of Nottingham, contains nothing but a ruin of the last priory founded in England. Originally established in 1343 by Nicholas de Cantelupe, soldier and friend to Edward III, this Carthusian priory was one of the first, if not the first, of the priories to be dissolved by Henry VIII. There is a farmhouse on the site of the old priory, and some of the farm outbuildings have incorporated parts of the monastic buildings, notably the prior's house. D. H. Lawrence makes use of the priory ruins in an early short story, "A Fragment of Stained Glass," originally entitled "Legend." The work was submitted to a Christmas competition held by the *Nottingham Gazette* in 1908 but was not the winning entry; another of Lawrence's manuscripts, "A Prelude," submitted by a friend under the name Rosalind, won. "A Fragment" recounts a local legend told by the "vicar of Beauvale" and contains a particularly effective description of the ruins:

These ruins lie in a still rich meadow at the foot of the last fold of woodland, through whose oaks shines a blue of hyacinths, like water, in Maytime. Of the abbey, there remains only the east wall of the chancel standing, a wild thick mass of ivy weighting one shoulder, while pigeons perch in the tracery of the lofty window.

Lawrence attended Beauvale School, just opposite the new Ram Inn. In *The White Peacock* he describes the original of the inn.

BECCLES, Suffolk (pop. 6,048)   The most notable aspect of the market town of Beccles on the Suffolk border is its location in the general area described as the Norfolk Broads, a triangular expanse of land and navigable waterways whose points of Lowestoft, Norwich, and Sea Palling offer easy access to the more than thirty Broads. The Waveney River, which flows through the town and then on a generally northerly course by Lowestoft to the sea at Great Yarmouth, is bordered here with numerous towpaths and mellow old houses that seem to turn their backs to the town. Beccles was the home of Sarah Elmy, who became the wife of George Crabbe. The courtship was quite a long one, but eventually the couple was married in December 1783 at the Church of St. Michael. Crabbe often made the almost 9-mile walk from Aldeburgh when he was courting; indeed, the first part of the poem *The Lover's Journey* describes in some detail the scenery of the trip, which ranged from the plush to the arid.

> "This neat low gorse," said he, "with golden bloom,
> Delights each sense, is beauty, is perfume;
> And this gay ling, with all its purple flowers,
> A man at leisure might admire for hours;
> This green-fringed cup-moss has a scarlet tip....
> And then how fine his herbage! men may say
> A heath is barren; nothing is so gay...."

BECKHAMPTON, Wiltshire   A hamlet on the Marlborough Downs 6 miles west of Marlborough, Beckhampton was long a stopping place on the coaching roads, and it is often argued that the inn near the

BECCLES   Seen from the Waveney River, the Church of St. Michael with its massive 14th-century detached bell tower was the scene of the marriage of George Crabbe and Sarah Elmy, the Mira of his poetry.

Marlborough Downs described by Charles Dickens in *Pickwick Papers* is the Waggon and Horses here:

> It was a strange old place, built of a kind of shingle, inlaid, as it were, with cross-beams, with gable-topped windows projecting completely over the pathway, and a low door with a dark porch, and a couple of steep steps leading down into the house instead of the modern fashion of half a dozen shallow ones leading up to it. It was a comfortable-looking place, though, for there was a strong cheerful light in the bar-window, which shed a bright ray across the road and even lighted up the hedge on the other side; and there was a red flickering light in the opposite window, one moment but faintly discernible, and the next gleaming strongly through the drawn curtains, which intimated that a rousing fire was blazing within. ...

BECKINGTON, Somerset (pop. 727)   Almost on the Wiltshire border 3 miles northeast of Frome, Beckington, once a prosperous cloth-weaving town, is quite attractive with its gabled and mullioned houses, Norman church tower, and Georgian Nonconformist chapel. The village is one of two places frequently mentioned as the birthplace in 1562 or 1563 of Samuel Daniel (the other is Norton St. Philip). Thomas Fuller maintained that the birthplace was Taunton, but Anthony à Wood stated that Daniel was born at or near "Philips Norton" or Beckington. The two villages are near each other, but neither contains a record of the birth. While baptism and marriage records of other Daniels exist at both places, Beckington seems the more likely choice, especially since Samuel Daniel retired here. The usual assumption from the reference in Daniel's will to "my house at Ridge"—that his house was called Ridge Farm—is in error; the house was simply in that area of the hamlet known now as Rudge. How long Daniel lived here is not known, nor is it known whether the Mrs. Daniell who was buried here on March 25, 1619, was his wife. Samuel Daniel died at his home in October of that year and was buried in the church on October 4. Lady Anne Clifford, Countess of Pembroke, for whom Daniel was a tutor, raised the monument to the poet. A document found in a castle held by the Cliffords in Appleby, Yorkshire, states that the poet "lyeth buried in the Chancell of the sayd [Beckington] Church. ..."

In June 1688 Samuel Pepys and his wife were on a trip to the West Country and came through Breckington, as he calls it, on the way from Salisbury to Bath. It was here that Mrs. Pepys and her maid Deborah Willett felt that they had returned to their native area and "where, stopping for something for the horses," writes Pepys, "we called two or three little boys to us, and pleased ourselves with their manner of speech, and did make one of them kiss Deb., and another say the Lord's Prayer (hallowed be thy kingdom come)." The party went on from here to Norton St. Philip.

BECKLEY, Oxfordshire (pop. 178)   The eastern part of Oxfordshire is a generally heavily cultivated and domesticated area, but it contains a geographic curiosity in the form of Ot Moor (Otmoor), a 6-mile-square tract of desolate moorland; here a modern road follows the old Roman road across the moor, and a ring road connects the scattered villages on the moor. Beckley, 5 miles northeast of Oxford, has a Norman to 15th-century church with a (probably) Saxon font and a stone reading desk; the splendid manor of Beckley Park is 1 mile north on the moor. Surrounded by three moats, this Tudor house with three gables was built by Lord Williams of Thame on the site of an earlier castle built by Richard, Earl of Cornwall, King of the Romans, and brother of Henry III. Beckley Park is often claimed to be the model for Crome in Aldous Huxley's *Crome Yellow.* Denis Stone approaches by bicycle:

> The road plunged down, steep and straight, into a considerable valley. There . . . stood Crome. . . . The facade with its three projecting towers rose precipitously from among the dark trees of the garden. The house basked in full sunlight; the old brick rosily glowed. How ripe and rich it was, how superbly mellow!

He looks at the house like an excavator "exploring a dead, deserted Pompeii":

> There was the long gallery, with its rows of respectable and . . . rather boring Italian primitives, its Chinese sculptures, its unobtrusive, dateless furniture. There was the panelled drawing-room . . . the morning-room, with its pale lemon walls . . . the library, cool, spacious, and dark, book-lined from floor to ceiling, rich in portentous folios. . . . the dining-room, solidly, portwinily English. . . .

There is a second modern association with Evelyn Waugh, who stayed at the Abingdon Arms here on two occasions; on the first of these visits he was working on *Rossetti: His Life and Works,* and on the second, in June 1928, he was on his honeymoon.

BEDFORD, Bedfordshire (pop. 65,370) Straddling the Great Ouse River, Bedford, the county town, is a thriving modern city with rather too many modern high rises but with the saving grace of having kept many of its ancient monuments. Near Batts Ford is the partly Saxon St. Paul's Church, where an early monastic settlement was established. The Normans erected a great castle on the north bank of the Ouse, and the walls and outer bailey reached the river. The castle was taken in the great siege of 1224 and destroyed; only a mound remains to mark its site. Medieval Bedford was a busy market town, and a very lovely and noticeable link with the town's early history is St. John House, where the religious community cared for the aged poor of the city. An interesting but deceptive building adjoins the modern town hall; behind its 18th-century facade is the original Tudor free school. Bedford has continued to prosper through the centuries, and when Daniel Defoe visited here in the 18th century, he was deeply impressed:

> *Bedford,* as I have said, is a large, populous, and thriving Town, and a pleasant well-built Place. . . . [I]t is full of very good Inns, and in particular we found very good Entertainment here.
> Here is the best Market for all Sorts of Provisions, that is to be seen at any Country Town in all these Parts of *England.* . . .
> Here is also a great Corn Market, and great Quantities of Corn are bought here, and carry'd down by Barges and other Boats to *Lynn,* where it is again shipp'd, and carry'd by Sea to *Holland:* The Soil hereabouts is exceeding rich and fertile, and particularly produces great Quantities of the best Wheat in *England.* . . .

The most important literary association with Bedford is that of John Bunyan. Although he lived in nearby Elstow, he probably attended Sir William Harpur's grammer school; in November 1644, aged sixteen, he joined the Parliamentary forces in Bedford, an event which he said was the turning point of his life. Some years later, in 1653, John Bunyan, received into the dissenting church by William Gifford, was baptized in the Ouse by total immersion. Actually the baptism (which undoubtedly took place at night in secret) occurred in an inlet of the Ouse, underneath an elm tree near the corner of Duck Mill Lane. Two years later Bunyan moved here from Elstow with his wife and two children; they took a house on the east side of what is now St. Cuthbert's Street. What is now pointed out and called Bunyan Cottage is most likely not the original, though of appropriate daub-and-wattle construction and on the same site. After the Restoration, repressive measures were revived against the Nonconformists; when Bunyan refused to agree to refrain from public preaching, he was imprisoned. For years it has been held that Bunyan was committed twice to jail, the first time from 1660 to 1672 in the old County Gaol, which stood at the corner of the High Street and Silver Street, and the second in 1675 and 1676 in the Bedford Bridge Town Prison, where he wrote *The Pilgrim's Progress.* New evidence shows rather conclusively that the sequence, place, and dates are somewhat different. A writ in the Aylesbury Museum, dated June 21, 1677, verifies that the second incarceration was actually of less than twelve months' duration, so that Bunyan could not have been in custody before the autumn of 1676. This leaves an unexplained gap of eighteen months in his life, during which time he was probably in hiding (there was a warrant dated March 4, 1675). It also appears that the second commitment was to the County Gaol, not to the Bridge Town Prison. It seems reasonable to assume that work on *The Pilgrim's Progress* began in 1666, during the first sentence, since Part I was recorded in Stationers' Hall Records on December 22, 1677, a date which allows only the unlikely period of six months for the writing of the final third of the work. The manuscript break, "So I awoke from my Dream," signifies the end of Bunyan's first jail term. He was to be held initially for three months but was ultimately held until May 17, 1672, when he was released as part of a general amnesty brought about when the Declaration of Indulgence toward Nonconformists and recusants was issued by the crown. During this first period in jail, Bunyan was occasionally allowed to be free during the day and would return at night. Indeed, he was released in the summer of 1666 but was rearrested in a few weeks because he had resumed preaching. Shortly after his release Bunyan was licensed as a preacher (May 9, 1672); in August a barn and an orchard on Mill Lane (now Mill Street) were purchased for £50 as a meetinghouse site; the Bunyan Meeting House and Museum stands on the site. The entrance to the chapel contains the heavy barred and grated doors of the County Gaol, and the room which contains copies of his works also holds his chair, a survival from the original vestry; the legs of the chair were shortened by one of his successors. There have been two notable 20th-century additions to this collection: the wooden belfry door from the Elstow Church and the pulpit from which Bunyan occasionally preached at Zoar

Chapel, Southwark, London. *The Pilgrim's Progress* makes use of Bedford; the den of the opening lines refers to the County Gaol, not the Bedford Bridge Town Prison:

> I lighted on a certain place where was a den, and I laid me down in that place to sleep, and as I slept I dreamed a dream.

Also used in the work was the home of the Rev. William Gifford, the rector of St. John's Church; this became the Interpreter's House, which Christian desires to reach, and the Interpreter is obviously Gifford. The house is still standing.

A later writer, greatly influenced by Bunyan, was a native of Bedford: William Hale White, better known as Mark Rutherford, was born in a house on the High Street on December 22, 1831, and was educated at the Bedford Modern School before attending the Countess of Huntingdon's college in Cheshunt, Hertfordshire. His was a dissenting family, and Rutherford's novels and autobiographical works often portray the Bedford dissenting community of the 19th century although he rarely returned to Bedford in later years.

Toward the end of the 19th century, Saki (H. H. Munro) attended the grammar school here.

BEDFORD PARK, Middlesex (pop. 8,379)   Right on the border of Acton and Chiswick, Bedford Park, a London suburb, was planned as a middle-class housing area in 1875. Trees from the old open estate were retained, and such buildings as the timbered and gabled Tabard Inn (the prototype of the "Olde Englysshe" inn) date from this period. Bedford Park became the home of the family of William Butler Yeats in 1887, just after Yeats abandoned an art career. The house here was, as Yeats later recalled,

> a red-brick house with several mantelpieces of wood, copied from marble mantelpieces designed by the brothers Adam, a balcony and a little garden shadowed by a great horse-chestnut tree.

At the time Bedford Park was also an artists' community (Yeats's father was a brilliant painter whose finances were greatly helped through magazine illustrations):

> Opposite our house lived an old artist who worked also for the illustrated papers for a living, but painted landscapes for his pleasure. . . . Three or four doors off on our side of the road lived a decorative artist in all the naïve confidence of popular ideals and the public approval. He was our daily comedy. "I myself and Sir Frederick Leighton are the greatest decorative artists of the age," was among his sayings. . . .

Nearby, "Some quarter of an hour's walk from Bedford Park, out on the high road to Richmond, lived W. E. Henley," under whom, Yeats said, "I, like many others, began . . . my education."

G. K. Chesterton poked fun at the area in *The Man Who Was Thursday*. Portraying the area as Saffron Park, he writes:

> The suburb of Saffron Park lay on the sunset side of London, as red and ragged as a cloud of sunset. It was built of a bright brick throughout; its sky-line was fantastic, and even its ground plan was wild. It had been the outburst of a speculative builder, faintly tinged with art, who called its architecture sometimes Elizabethan and sometimes Queen Anne, apparently under the impression that the two sovereigns were identical. It was described with some justice as an artistic colony, though it never in any definable way produced any art.

BEDHAMPTON, Hampshire (pop. 870)   In the rapidly growing south central coastal area, 1 mile west of Havant, Bedhampton actually has been fighting for its identity for at least half a century. While its church, with a 12th-century chancel arch, was fully restored in the 19th century and the manor house dates in part to the 17th, it is the many good 18th-century houses which create the village's attractiveness and charm. Much new building has occurred, but the old town is of special interest; here, near the church on Mill Lane, is Old Mill House (marked with a plaque), the home of Mr. and Mrs. John Snook, where John Keats and Charles Armitage Brown stayed in early 1819 after attending the consecration of a new chapel in Stanstead. "The Eve of St. Agnes," which describes the chapel's stained glass, was started in Chichester but finished here. Keats was again at the Old Mill House in September 1820 and spent his last night in England here when the *Maria Crowther* was storm-bound in Portsmouth Harbor.

BEDWORTH, Warwickshire (pop. 17,644)   Around Bedworth, midway between Nuneaton and Coventry, is the easternmost tip of the extensive Warwickshire coalfields, and mining was first recorded in the area in the 13th century. The mining industry has made Bedworth a dark, dingy, expanding town, and only the tower of the 15th-century church and a 17th-century bell remain. Mary Ann Evans (George Eliot), who was born in Arbury and spent most of her early life in this area (probably) used Bedworth under the guise of Sproxton in *Felix Holt, the Radical*. She describes the general 19th-century aspect of the mining town:

> The canal was only a branch of the grand trunk, and ended among the coal-pits, where Felix, crossing a network of black tram-roads, soon came to his destination— that public institute of Sproxton, known to its frequenters chiefly as Chubb's, but less familiarly as the Sugar Loaf, or the New Pits. . . . The other nucleus, known as the Old Pits, also supported its "public," but it had something of the forlorn air of an abandoned capital. . . .

BELTON, Leicestershire (pop. 588)   Six miles due west of Loughborough, Belton secured its place in history only after the founding of Grace Dieu Priory in the 13th century. The priory here was founded by Lady Roesia de Verdun (Rohese de Verdon) beside a little brook; its grounds were granted to one of Henry VIII's trusted commissioners, John Beaumont of Thringstone, at the dissolution of the monasteries. Beaumont built a magnificent Tudor home, also called Grace Dieu, which two generations later was probably the birthplace of Francis Beaumont, the dramatist. There are no baptismal records to confirm Grace Dieu as the place of birth, but it is possible that the christening took place in London, where the elder Beaumont had his chief residence. All that remains of Grace Dieu are the fragments of two towers, the chapel, and the walls, in approximately the condition that William Wordsworth described after his visit in the autumn of 1811 with Sir George Beaumont at Coleorton:

Beneath yon eastern ridge, the craggy bound,
Rugged and high, of Charnwood's forest ground,
Stand yet, but, Stranger! hidden from thy view,
The ivied Ruins of forlorn *Grace Dieu;*
Erst a religious House, which day and night
With hymns resounded, and the chanted rite:
And when those rites had ceased, the Spot gave birth
To honourable Men of various worth. . . .

An earlier guest of the Beaumont family was Michael Drayton, whose general memories of his visits here are included in the twenty-sixth song of *Poly-Olbion.* "Sharpley . . . and Cadmans aged rocks," from which Drayton viewed the Soar River, were only a few minutes' walk from the estate.

BELTON, Lincolnshire (pop. 145) Lincolnshire contains two villages of this name, and they are frequently confused; the larger of the two Beltons, with a population of 1,528, lies in the Isle of Axholme; the smaller village lies at the edge of Belton Park, 2 miles northeast of Grantham. Here, in the smaller village, gray limestone cottages are grouped around the village cross, and the adjacent great park, which contains Belton Park, covers nearly 700 acres. Great elm and lime avenues lead to lakes, and the sloping parkland is heavily wooded. The great house, in the form of an H, was designed by Sir Christopher Wren and later altered by James Wyatt; the church has a 13th-century tower, and the nave arcade and font are Norman.

Belton claims to be the original of the village of Willingham in Sir Walter Scott's *The Heart of Midlothian;* nearby Syston and Stainton, Nottinghamshire, make the same claim. In the company of Madge Wildfire, Jeanie Deans approaches the village on a Sunday:

They were now close by the village, one of those beautiful scenes which are so often found in merry England, where the cottages, instead of being built in two direct lines on each side of a dusty high-road, stand in detached groups, interspersed not only with large oaks and elms but with fruit-trees, so many of which were at this time in flourish, that the grove seemed enameled with their crimson and white blossoms. In the centre of the hamlet stood the parish church, and its little Gothic tower, from which at present was heard the Sunday chime of bells.

The church

was one of those old-fashioned Gothic parish churches which are frequent in England, the most cleanly, decent, and reverential places of worship that are perhaps, anywhere to be found in the Christian world.

After the disruption of the services, Jeanie is taken off to the rectory:

It was situated about four hundred yards from the village, and on a rising ground which sloped gently upward. . . . When they approached nearer to the house, a handsome gateway admitted them into a lawn, of narrow dimensions indeed. . . . The front of the house was irregular. Part of it seemed very old, and had, in fact, been the residence of the incumbent in Romish times. Successive occupants had made considerable additions and improvements, each in the taste of his own age, and without much regard to symmetry.

BELVOIR, Leicestershire (pop. 77) The tiny village of Belvoir (pronounced "bea'ver"), located high on an isolated spur of the Lincolnshire Wolds 7 miles southwest of Grantham, overlooks the Vale of Belvoir. The original grant of land was made by William the Conqueror to his standard-bearer, Robert de Todeni, who built the first castle here in the 11th century. Razed in the Civil War, the castle was rebuilt when Charles II restored the land to the Earl of Rutland. Although the original ground-floor plan was kept, the second floor was so altered by the insertion of an entire bedroom floor that the whole looked more like a house than a castle. More recent renovations further confused the structure.

Many of the literary figures for whom the Earls and Dukes of Rutland and their wives have been patrons visited here. Francis Beaumont, who lived at nearby Grace Dieu in Belton, Leicestershire, was undoubtedly a guest of the Countess of Rutland, to whom he wrote poetry. Indeed, he composed an "Elegy on the Death of the Virtuous Lady, Elizabeth, Countess of Rutland" (Sir Philip Sidney's daughter). Other frequent guests of the countess were Ben Jonson and Thomas Gray, who stopped at Belvoir on his northern tour in July 1754 and left a description of the castle in his notebooks. Later the Rev. George Crabbe came here as chaplain to the Duke of Rutland. Arriving in 1782, he found the life-style of the duke and duchess alien to his own. Nevertheless, he finshed *The Village* during his tenure; after marrying in December 1783, Crabbe and his wife settled here. In 1785 they moved to Stathern, where Crabbe had taken a curacy.

In July 1881 Francis Thompson visited Belvoir Castle and the Duke of Rutland on a break from his medical studies at Owens College, Manchester, and dedicated "a handful of pleasant rhymes" to the duke to repay his kindness:

My thoughts go back to last July
 Sweet happy thoughts and tender,
The bridal of the earth and sky,
 A day of noble splendour;
A day to make the saddest heart
 In joy a true believer;
When two good friends we roamed apart
 The shady walks of Belvoir.

Belvoir Castle appears in Benjamin Disraeli's *Coningsby* as Beaumanoir; the estate is described:

Beaumanoir was one of those Palladian palaces, vast and ornate, such as the genius of Kent and Campbell delighted in at the beginning of the eighteenth century. Placed on a noble elevation, . . . its sumptuous front . . . was the boast and pride of the midland counties. The surrounding gardens, equalling in extent the size of ordinary parks, were crowded with temples dedicated to abstract virtues and to departed friends. . . . Beyond the limits of this pleasance the hart and hind wandered in a wilderness abounding in ferny coverts and green and stately trees.

BEMERTON, Wiltshire (pop. 2,179) So close to Salisbury, 1½ miles to the east, as almost to be a part of it, Bemerton contains the lovely 14th-century Church of St. Andrew and a notable old rectory. In 1630 Bemerton became the home of George Herbert, who was presented with this living by Charles I at the behest of the 3d Earl of Pembroke. Basically a mystic, Herbert had served in the court of James I but, finding that neither court life nor university life agreed with him, entered the priesthood at the age of thirty-three:

Whereas my birth and spirit took
The way that takes the town,
Thou didst betray me to a ling'ring brook
And wrap me in a gown.

Herbert, in fact, was persuaded to take the post here by Archbishop William Laud's contention that it would be sinful to refuse the living. He settled here in the old rectory with his wife and twice weekly walked to Salisbury for cathedral services. His years here were notable, and he seems to have lived up to every rule of conduct he outlined in *A Priest to the Temple*. Izaak Walton, a visitor here and Herbert's biographer, writes that after his induction he lay

> prostrate on the ground before the altar; at which time and place (as he after told Mr. Woodnot) he set some rules to himself for the future manage of his life, and then and there made a vow to labor to keep them.

One of the most delightful works to originate in the parish here (and proof of Herbert's ability to get on well in this rural setting) is the collection of folk sayings in *Outlandish Proverbs*: "Laugh and a cough cannot be hid"; "Every path hath a puddle"; "He that lies with dogs, riseth with fleas"; "Better a snotty child, than his nose wiped off." The inscription on one of the exterior parsonage walls in Herbert's time was above the hall chimney:

TO MY SUCCESSOR

If thou chance for to find
A new house to thy mind
And built without thy Cost:
  Be good to the Poor,
  As God gives thee store,
And then, my Labour's not lost.

Herbert died here of tuberculosis on March 1, 1633, and was buried on March 3 beneath the altar of the church with only a simple inscription, "G. H. 1633," marking the grave. The Anglican services for the dead were performed, according to his wishes, by the men of Salisbury Cathedral. Shortly before his death, according to Walton, Herbert made arrangements with Edmund Duncon, of Gidden Hall in Huntingdonshire, to look after his poems:

> "Sir, I pray deliver this little book to my dear brother Ferrar, and tell him he shall find in it a picture of the many spiritual conflicts that have passed betwixt God and my soul[;] . . . desire him to read it, and then, if he can think it may turn to the advantage of any dejected poor soul, let it be made public; if not, let him burn it; for I and it are less than the least of God's mercies."

The book was *The Temple; or, Sacred Poems and Private Ejaculations*.

BENTWORTH, Hampshire (pop. 522) The country northeast of New and Old Alresford rises to the Hampshire Downs, an area of high arable land with villages set in gentle valleys; Bentworth, 3½ miles northwest of Alton, with its 13th-century church and a considerable number of large houses, may well be the most attractive of the villages. Bentworth was the birthplace of the poet and pamphleteer George Wither (Withers) on June 11, 1588; the eldest son of a prosperous farmer, Wither received his earliest education here from a cousin by marriage, Ralph Starkey, before attending a local school run by the vicar

of Coleman. Wither later referred to "Bentworth's beechy shadows" in his *Abuses Stripte and Whipt*.

BERE REGIS, Dorset (pop. 970) On the edge of the wild heathland of mid-Dorset, referred to in Thomas Hardy's novels as Egdon Heath, Bere Regis, as its name suggests, was once a royal residence. Elfrida, the stepmother of King Edward the Martyr (r. 975–978), had a house here. Later, King John was in Bere Regis on six occasions, probably to hunt; and by the mid-13th century half of the original manor was given to the Turberville family, which ultimately acquired the entire estate.

The literary interest of Bere Regis revolves around the Turberville family and the use made of its history by Thomas Hardy. Bere Regis becomes Kingsbere or Kingsbere-sub-Greenhill. It is on this Catholic family of Sir Pagan (Hardy's name) or Payne de Turberville that Hardy bases *Tess of the D'Urbervilles;* and the lovely Saxon church has become a place of pilgrimage for Hardiophiles, for this is where Tess is buried. The church, with a beautifully carved and painted roof, contains the Turberville family vault, their tombs and memorials, and a chapel dedicated to them in the south aisle; on a 15th-century window are the family armorial bearings.

Hardy also mentions Kingsbere in *The Return of the Native* (Tamsin returns here from Angelbury [Wareham] unmarried because of license problems), *The Trumpet-Major, The Mayor of Casterbridge, Far from the Madding Crowd,* "The Distracted Preacher" (*Wessex Tales*), "The Alarm" (*Wessex Poems*), and "The Well-Beloved" (*Poems of the Past and Present*). The nearby Iron Age rampart overlooking the village from the east, becomes Hardy's Greenhill. An extensive local autumnal fair was held here until the mid-12th century, with travelers coming from as far away as London and Birmingham; it was revived in the 18th century. Hardy describes the site in *Far from the Madding Crowd:*

> . . . the Nijni Novgorod of South Wessex, and the busiest, merriest, noisiest day of the whole statute number was the day of the sheep fair. This yearly gathering was upon the summit of a hill which retained in good preservation the remains of an ancient earthwork, consisting of a huge rampart and entrenchment of an oval form encircling the top of the hill. . . .

This is the fair to which Bathsheba goes before she is supposed to give Boldwood her conditional promise of marriage. Hardy himself attended the fair on September 21, 1873; this was the first day of the fair, a day set aside as "gentlefolks" day. He declared when writing the novel, "I always go to a place first before attempting to describe it. . . . I hate *word-painting*." The fair and its contiguous activities are also mentioned in *Tess of the D'Urbervilles, The Trumpet-Major,* and "The Fiddler of the Reels" (*Life's Little Ironies and a Few Crusted Characters*).

BERKELEY, Gloucestershire (pop. 790) Just off the busy Bristol to Gloucester Road and 17 miles northeast of Bristol, Berkeley (pronounced "bark'ley") is on the Avon River at the Severn Estuary. Berkeley Castle, notorious in history and the home of the Berkeleys continuously since the 12th century, stands on the high meadows above the Little Avon here.

Built of varicolored stone, the castle is well buttressed, and some of its walls are 14 feet thick. Two buildings around the inner courtyard, the chapel and the 61-foot hall, are 14th-century, and the keep (now only a shell) is Norman. The castle became a complete feudal stronghold and passed out of Berkeley control in 1485, when Lord William, seeking to become a marquess, conveyed this castle and other lands to Henry VII and his male heirs. With the death of Edward VI in 1553, the grant was returned to the Berkeleys.

In the 14th century the castle gained a special notoriety, which is remembered in literature, particularly in Christopher Marlowe's *Edward II*. King Edward II, deposed by his wife Isabella with the help of Roger de Mortimer, 1st Earl of March, was brought here in the summer of 1327 under the charge of Thomas de Gurnay and John Maltravers, two knights. We do not have all the facts as yet, but one theory claims that the following is what happened. It had probably been hoped that captivity itself would finish off the physically weak monarch, but neither captivity nor various barbaric acts perpetrated by his jailers worked. An ambiguous message then arrived, and Edward died by a red-hot rapier for lack of a comma in a sentence. What was intended was undoubtedly not a command to execute the King, but the addition of a comma, supplied by Gurnay and Maltravers after *fear*, made it appear so: "*To seek to shed King Edward's blood refuse to fear I think it good.*"

Daniel Defoe visited Berkeley Castle and wrote his impressions in *A Tour thro' the Whole Island of Great Britain*:

> Hence we kept on *North*, passing by *Durfley* to *Berkley-Castle*; the Antient Seat of the Earls of *Berkley*, a Noble tho' Antient Building, and a very fine Park about it. The Castle gives Title to the Earl, and the Town of *Durfly* to the Heir Apparent. . . . I say nothing of the dark Story of King *Edward* II. of *England;* who, all our learned Writers agree, was murther'd in this Castle: As *Richard* II. was in that of *Pontefract*, in *Yorkshire;* I say I take no more notice of it here, for History is not my present Business: 'Tis true, they show the Apartments where they say that King was kept a Prisoner: But they do not admit that he was kill'd there.

Adjacent to the castle is the church, which is unusual in that its bell tower is fully separate and stands at the opposite end of the churchyard. The church has a rare medieval rose window, and the nave is one of the outstanding examples of Early English work in the country. At the foot of a canopied recess in the chancel is the grave of Edward Jenner, who discovered vaccination; his first experiments were carried out in a hut on the grounds of the Chantry, as the vicarage is called.

There are a number of other scattered associations with Berkeley. Jonathan Swift entered the employ of the 2d Earl of Berkeley around 1699 and became a frequent visitor here; even after the marriage in 1706 of Lord Berkeley's daughter Lady Betty Germain, who was clearly an attraction to Swift, he kept coming. In the early 19th century Lord Byron stayed with Col. William Berkeley before going on to Cheltenham. In the 19th century, on the old coach route from Bristol to Birmingham, the coaches made their first stop at Berkeley Heath, just a few miles from the village; here was the Bell Inn (later converted into a private home), which Charles Dickens used in *Pickwick Papers;* Mr. Pickwick and his party lunch here. For years it was claimed by a signpost outside the Bell that Charles Dickens and his party also ate here, but this has not been confirmed.

BERKHAMSTED, Hertfordshire (pop. 16,000) The Grand Union Canal runs through Berkhamsted, as do the Bulbourne River and the main road from Aylesbury to Watford, which is 10 miles to the southeast. The town is a pleasant country town within easy commuting distance of London, 28 miles to the southeast, and is located in the Chiltern Valley. The 1-mile-long High Street is part of the original Roman Akeman Street, and remains of Grim's Dyke can be seen on the common. The Norman Berkhamsted Castle may have stood on the site of an earlier Saxon stronghold; in the 12th century it was rebuilt with a stone keep and curtain walls by Thomas à Becket when he was Henry II's Chancellor, and here Becket lived in state. The castle, a favorite of Henry III, was the scene of the wedding banquet for Henry's sister-in-law and Richard, Earl of Cornwall, his brother; indeed, the castle was given to the couple. A later owner of the castle was Piers Gaveston, the favorite of Edward II, although Christopher Marlowe makes no mention of this in *Edward II*. An association traditionally ascribed to the castle is that when Geoffrey Chaucer was appointed Clerk of Works around 1388, this castle fell under his jurisdiction. It has long been assumed that at some time during his clerkship Chaucer lived here, but there is no proof. The castle fell into complete ruin; a lawn now marks the 15,000-square-yard outer court, and some wall fragments remain.

On November 26, 1731 (New Style), the old rectory (now gone) in Berkhamsted was the birthplace of William Cowper, author of *The Task* and the *Olney Hymns;* the fourth child of the Rev. John Cowper and his wife, William was the first child to survive. With the death of his mother in childbirth in 1737, young William was sent to school in Hertford, where he spent an unhappy two years. At the age of ten he was sent to Westminster School in London, but Cowper frequently returned to Berkhamsted until his father's remarriage. The rectory comes into a later poem, "On the Receipt of My Mother's Picture out of Norfolk, the Gift of My Cousin, Ann Bodham":

> Where once we dwelt our name is heard no more,
> Children not thine have trod my nursery floor;
> And where the gardener Robin, day by day,
> Drew me to school along the public way,
> Delighted with my bauble coach, and wrapp'd
> In scarlet mantle warm, and velvet capp'd,
> 'Tis now become a history little known,
> That once we called the pastoral house our own.

A few of the *Delia* poems, including "Delia's Absence" and "Written after Leaving Her at New Burns," were written at Berkhamsted. Delia was Theodora Jane Cowper, the poet's cousin, whom Cowper had courted and won but was forbidden to marry by her father.

The cruciform St. Peter's Church, which Cowper attended and where his father preached, dates partly from the 13th century and is one of the largest churches in the county. The east window is a modern memorial (1872) to the poet; it depicts a series of biblical scenes, including the Resurrection; in one panel Cowper is seen at his prayer desk surrounded by his tame hares. A number of quotations from the *Olney Hymns* are inscribed on the glass. The church register contains Cowper's baptismal record.

Another literary figure, Sir James Matthew Barrie, came frequently to Berkhamsted to visit Arthur Llewellyn Davis and his family. Davis was the father of five sons, one of whom is thought to have been the model for Peter Pan.

A second native of Berkhamsted is the novelist Graham Greene, who was born on October 2, 1904, in the living quarters of the Berkhamsted School, where his father was headmaster; Greene's childhood was spent here, and he received his education at his father's school. Unhappiness with the contrast he perceived between his own home and the evil he saw in the classrooms caused him to run away, and he was placed under the care of a London psychologist.

BERWICK-UPON-TWEED, Northumberland (pop. 12,-060) A geographical description of the British Isles once divided the land into England, Ireland, Scotland, Wales, and Berwick-upon-Tweed; and the historical basis for such a division is rooted in Berwick's history as a frontier city. Indeed, Berwick (pronounced "ber'ick") changed hands between Scotland and England thirteen times in 300 years. Even today its position is anomalous: the city is politically and physically in England, but it is also one of the royal burghs of Scotland with full ancient rights, including arms, shield, and motto, which were restored in 1958. One interesting survival of the border warfare consists of more than 2 miles of great Elizabethan walls, which

BERWICK-UPON-TWEED On his tour of the British Isles, Daniel Defoe visited Berwick, noted the "noble, stately" bridge over the Tweed, and concluded, "As for the Town it self, it is old, decay'd, and neither populous nor rich; the chief Trade I found here was in Corn and Salmon."

can still be walked for a considerable length. The poem "The Freiris of Berwick," probably written by William Dunbar, describes the ancient city well:

For it is wallet weill about with stane,
And dowbil stankes cassin mony are;
And syn the castell is so strang and wicht,
With staitelie touris, and turatis he on hight,
With kernalis closit most craftelie of all,
The partculis must subtillie to fall,
That guken thay list to draw them vpon hicht,
Than it may be into na mannis might,
To win that hous by craft or subtiltie.

Virtually nothing is left of the 12th-century castle mentioned in the poem. Geoffrey Chaucer mentions Berwick in his description of the Pardoner in the Prologue to *The Canterbury Tales.* The Pardoner is, according to Chaucer, unique for

... of his craft from Berwyk into Ware,
Ne was ther swich another pardoner....

And Dr. Samuel Johnson, with James Boswell, passed through Berwick on his way to the Hebrides.

Both Robert Burns and Charles Dickens were in Berwick. Dickens, here on a northern reading tour, stayed at the King's Arms Hotel on Hide Hill but did not leave any impression of the town. Burns took a decided dislike to Berwick and its inhabitants, who were neither Scots enough nor English enough for his taste. George Borrow recalled passing through the town as a child; his father, a professional soldier, was posted to Edinburgh, and the family stopped in Berwick on their way. Years later, in *Lavengro,* Borrow remembers his awe at the Tweed River, whose name he did not know at the time:

The river was a noble one, the broadest that I had hitherto seen. Its waters, of a greenish tinge, poured with impetuosity beneath the narrow arches [of the bridge] to meet the sea.

After asking a local fisherman the name of the river and being asked "Did ye never hear of the Tweed, my bonny man?" young Borrow stated the impression the river had made upon him: "I never heard of it; but now I have seen it, I shall not soon forget it!"

BETHERSDEN, Kent (pop. 922) An old Kent village almost equidistant from Ashford and Tenterden, Bethersden was famous in the Middle Ages for its marble, which was used in the cathedrals of both Canterbury and Rochester. Located in the Weald, the village, with its weathered clapboard houses arranged around an encircling road, is typical of settlements in the area.

The family of the poet Richard Lovelace held the manor here from 1367 on, and he inherited this estate and those at Chart, Halden, Shadoxhurst, and Canterbury upon the death of his mother in 1633. Lovelace, who did not take possession here until he had taken part in the two Scottish expeditions led by George Goring (later Lord Goring), settled here and was chosen to deliver the Kentish Royalist petition of 1642 to Parliament; his reward was imprisonment on April 30 for his part in the proposal. Imprisoned again in 1648, supposedly for taking part in the Kentish riots and uprisings in June of that year, he no doubt spent some of the time between prison terms at Bethersden Manor. After his release in December

1648, he was forced to sell the manor here, and it passed from family hands.

BEWDLEY, Worcestershire (pop. 4,270) Just on the edge of the Wyre Forest, an area of trees and scrubland, 3 miles west of Kidderminster, Bewdley, once named Bealieu, is beautifully located on the steep hillside of the right bank of the Severn, and it has a wealth of well-preserved 17th- and 18th-century buildings. The Recorder's House on the High Street dates to 1610, and Wyre Court, a black-and-white house on the hill, was built about 1600.

After the Norman invasion, William the Conqueror granted the manor to Roger de Mortimer. Eventually the manor became crown property through Edward IV, a direct descendant of Mortimer. Prince Arthur married Catherine of Aragon here by proxy in 1499, and with the prince's death three years later, Catherine's fate was sealed when, in 1509, she became the wife of Henry VIII. Tickenhill House, still Tudor and Georgian, was greatly enlarged over the centuries, and it is said that by the time Henry VIII finished with it, the courtyard covered 2 acres.

In the mid-16th century Sir Henry Sidney, Lord President of the Marches of Wales, came to live at Tickenhill House, and he, too, improved the house, adding a water supply and a great fountain. Here the young Philip Sidney lived for a short while, and Mary, "Sidney's sister, Pembroke's mother," was born on October 27, 1561. Tickenhill remained in the hands of the Sidneys until Sir Henry's death, when it became the property of the crown.

BIDEFORD, Devon (pop. 9,442) On the west bank of the Torridge River, 4 miles from the sea Bideford (pronounced "bid′-e-ford") has long rivaled its neighbor, Barnstaple, for maritime supremacy. Both towns built and sailed ships, and both sent a large number to fight against the Armada. The rivalry was once a serious matter, and even today map makers use the legend "Barnstaple *or* Bideford Bay." During Elizabeth I's reign the Bideford fleet played an active role in the cod fishing off Newfoundland, and as late as the 19th century shipping and fishing activities supported the town. While Bideford remains an active port, discharging more than 200 ships yearly, it is still designated a subport of Barnstaple, a town that has virtually given up its shipping industry.

Erroneously, Charles Kingsley is often claimed as a native of Bideford, but in fact he was born in Holne, on the Dart River, more than 30 miles away. However, Kingsley did move in July 1854 to North Down House, Bideford, where he lived for a little more than a year; the house is now part of the Royal Hotel. The locality was convenient for Kingsley, and he took pleasure in observing the docks without the annoyances of what he termed "a resort of fashion." He was working on *Westward Ho!* and describes the setting of the old town and port in the novel:

> The little white town of Bideford, which slopes upward from its broad tide-river, paved with yellow sands, and many-arched old bridge where salmon wait for autumn floods, towards the pleasant upland on the west. Above the town the hills close in, cushioned with deep oak woods through which juts here and there a crag of fern-fringed slate; below they lower and open more and more in soft rounded knolls, and fertile squares of red and green till they sink into the wide expanse of hazy, flat, rich salt marshes and rolling sandhills. . . .

The bridge is the old twenty-four-arch span over the Torridge. Kingsley calls it "first an inspired bridge; a soul-saving bridge; an almsgiving bridge; an educational bridge [in 1761 the feoffees gave its revenue for the establishment of the Bideford Writing School]; a sentient bridge; and last, but not least, a dinner-giving bridge." The portrait of Sir Richard Grenville "in the streets of Bideford" is quite accurate, and Grenville's house was situated where the Castle Inn now stands. The Old Ship Tavern, on the quay, claims to stand on the original site where the Brotherhood of the Rose was founded. Kingsley and his family left here for Farley Court in Berkshire in the winter of 1855.

Both Charles Dickens and Wilkie Collins were in Bideford in November 1860 on a tour of the West Country to secure local color for a Christmas story for *Household Words*. Their experience in Bideford was unpleasant: they spent their first night in a "beastly hotel" (which they leave unnamed), "had stinking fish for dinner," and were unable to get any

BIDEFORD An ancient seaport in sailing days, Bideford was never a fashionable resort place, and for that reason Charles Kingsley came here when he was working on *Westward Ho!* A statue commemorating his stay stands at the north end of the promenade.

kind of a drink. Rudyard Kipling, who attended the United Services College in nearby Westward Ho! from 1878 to 1882, was confirmed in the Bideford Church by the Bishop of Exeter in 1878. James Anthony Froude, the historian and brother-in-law of Charles Kingsley, is thought to have begun his *History of England* here.

BIDFORD-ON-AVON, Warwickshire (pop. 1,698) A community since Roman times with a sample of Saxon burials, Bidford, 3½ miles south of Alcester, has a number of stone-and-timber cottages with neat gardens, a basically 15th-century church, and an old bridge that has drawn pilgrims for two centuries, ever since John Jordan put out his story concerning William Shakespeare's intemperance. A manuscript from about 1770 relates that Shakespeare and his companions, because of their reputations, were challenged to a drinking contest by men in Bidford "[W]ho boasted themselves Superior in the Science of drinking to any set of equal number in the Kingdom. . . ." Of the two groups of Bidford drinkers, the Topers had gone off to the Evesham Fair, but the Sippers were at work when Shakespeare and his companions arrived from Stratford. Jordan relates:

> Shakespr. and his compainions made a Scoff at their Opponents but for want of better Company they agreed to the Contest and in a little time our Bard and his Compainions got so intollerable intoxicated that they was not able to Contend any longer and acordingly set out on their return to Stratford But had not got above half a mile on the road e'er the found themselves unable to proceed any farther, and was obliged to lie down under a Crabtree which is still growing by the side of the road where they took up their repose till morning when some of the Company roused the poet and intreated him to return to Bidford and renew the Contest he declined it saying I have drank with—

> "Piping Pebworth, Dancing Marston,
> Haunted Hilborough, and Hungry Grafton,
> With Dadging Exhall, Papist Wixford,
> Beggarly Broom, and Drunken Bidford."

The story has survived, although there is considerable doubt as to its authenticity; the crab tree was marked on district maps, and a representative of it is still pointed out in a field. The inn frequented by Shakespeare and his "boon companions" was the Falcon, the west side of a stone-fronted and gabled old house on the north side of the church. Michael Drayton, author of *Poly-Olbion*, is held to have been one of Shakespeare's companions that day.

BILTON, Warwickshire (pop. 6,080) Bilton, just southwest of Rugby, is an old village with a good black-and-white house near the 14th-century church and a fine Jacobean manor, Bilton Hall. The hall, which stands on the brow of a small hill overlooking meadows and a stream, became Joseph Addison's home in 1712 in anticipation of his marriage to Charlotte, Dowager Countess of Warwick. The price of £8,000 included not only the house but 1,000 surrounding acres. He removed the Jacobean mullioned windows and replaced them with sash windows in the French style, built the south wing of the house, and laid out the gardens; he had the initials JA and CW entwined on the top of the iron gates leading to the Old Close; a seat at the bottom of the

garden is said to have been a favorite and a place where he frequently worked on his essays. The hall was the birthplace of Addison's only child, Charlotte, who was buried in the church here; a brass near the altar rails on the south side of the church reads:

> In memory of Charlotte, only child of Joseph Addison, Esq., Secretary of State, and Charlotte, Countess of Warwick, who died at Bilton Hall, A.D. 1797, aged 80 years.

Addison died when the child was two years old, and she lived on here after the death of the countess. Walter Savage Landor often walked to the estate from Rugby, and his impression of Addison's daughter as a fat old woman of weak intellect coincides with other stories to the effect that while Charlotte inherited her father's memory and could recite any part of his work with extreme accuracy, she was nevertheless incapable of writing or speaking coherently. On one of his walks Landor was inspired to compose "Dum per Biltonios errabam," the poem which describes a beautiful country girl as well as his beginning of understanding of the meaning of love.

BINFIELD, Berkshire (pop. 2,583) Situated in Windsor Forest, 3½ miles northeast of Wokingham, Binfield is surrounded by three smaller wooded parks, Allanby, Binfield, and Billingbear. The village is fortunate in being near the great Royal City of Windsor, within easy distance of London, and in one of the loveliest forest areas in England. The stone-and-flint Church of All Saints with its tiled roof has a chained copy of Erasmus's paraphrase of the New Testament and a medallion portrait of the historian and radical Catherine Sawbridge Macaulay, whom Dr. Samuel Johnson regarded as the ultimate of hypocrisy because of her view of equality. Upon hearing that she was interested in dress and society, Johnson is said to have remarked; "She is better employed at her toilet, than using her pen. It is better she should be reddening her own cheeks, than blackening other people's characters."

Binfield was one of the childhood homes of Alexander Pope. His father, a Roman Catholic linendraper, moved his family here around 1700, when the boy was about twelve years of age. Pope remembered this home as

> A little house with trees a-row
> And like its master very low. . . .

Pope's full height, 4 feet 6 inches, is the reason for the reference. Of his excursions into the forest Pope later noted that this was "where I sat down with an earnest desire of reading, and applied as constantly as I could to it for some years." The boy sang in the choir and is said to have had an excellent voice. His father encouraged him to write and rewrite verse, and Pope maintained that at the age of twelve he wrote "Ode to Solitude," which referred to the Binfield area:

> Happy the man whose wish and care
> A few paternal acres bound,
> Content to breath his native air
> On his own ground.

By the age of sixteen Pope had a severely deformed back, and he began to suffer from the recurrent headaches that were to afflict him for the rest of his life. It has now virtually been established that he suffered from Pott's Disease, a tubercular infection. Nicholas Rowe is known to have visited the Pope home in September 1713. Within a year of his father's death in late October 1717, Pope leased a villa in Twickenham.

A little more than a century later William Cobbett passed through Binfield on his way to Reading from London. On the morning of November 9, 1822, he

> stopped to breakfast, at a very nice country inn called the *Stag and Hounds*. Here you go along the north border of that villainous tract of country that I passed over in going from Oakingham to Egham.

William Wordsworth appears to have spent a few days in Binfield with his uncle, Dr. William Cookson, on his way to London in April 1812, most likely between April 20 and 22.

BIRCHINGTON, Kent (pop. 3,503) Located on the north coast of Kent, an area of excellent sand beaches, extremely safe bathing, and an enviably small annual rainfall, Birchington is an attractive residential and resort town on the Isle of Thanet 3½ miles southwest of Margate. The town has always been a popular spot for convalescence. In February 1882 Dante Gabriel Rossetti, who was very ill, came to stay at Westcliffe Bungalow. By now always wearing a black glove on his paralyzed hand, he had a nurse in constant attendance. Early in April, his brother William states, Rossetti was "barely capable of tottering a few steps, half blind and suffering a great deal of pain." On Good Friday the rector of Birchington visited at the poet's request, and on Easter Sunday, April 9, Rossetti died. The now-famous plaster casts of his face and hand were taken the next day; one full and undamaged set was still available for private purchase in England in 1973. On April 14 Rossetti was buried on the south side of the parish churchyard, near the porch where lilacs and laurustines bloom. The grave is marked by a Celtic cross designed by Ford Madox Brown. The church contains a commemorative window. It was about this time that Christina Rossetti, who had also been in constant attendance, wrote "Birchington Churchyard":

> A lovely hill which overlooks a flat,
>   Half sea, half countryside;
>   A flat-shored sea of low-voiced creeping tide
> Over a chalky weedy mat.
>
> A hill of hillocks, flowers and kept green
>   Round crosses raised for hope,
>   With many-tinted sunsets where the slope
> Faces the lingering western sheen.

BIRDOSWALD, Cumberland The hamlet of Birdoswald, 6½ miles northeast of Brampton, near the border with Northumberland, consists of about one farm and a few attendant buildings, but its location on the steep slopes above the gorge of the Irthing River is impressive. The cliffs are heavily wooded, and the view of the river is especially worthwhile. This location was part of the extensive northern Roman fortification known as Hadrian's Wall; the camp here was called Camboglanna and was the largest of the camps near the wall. Birdoswald is often said to have been the site of King Arthur's last battle at Camblan by those who hold him to be a North Country figure, but the case for the Strathclyde hero is not nearly so convincing as that of the West Country Arthur in Cornwall.

BIRMINGHAM, Warwickshire (pop. 1,086,400) The second largest city in England, Birmingham has had more than its share of growing pains through the centuries as well as far more than its share of damage during World War II. On the verge of coal and iron districts, it stands in the center of an upland plateau contained by the Avon, Trent, and Severn River Valleys. The lack of effective river transportation held back the city's growth for centuries; indeed, the medieval city of Birmingham had no maritime contacts, and the population remained under 15,000 until the late 17th century. Since then, however, the burgeoning population and rapid industrial expansion have pushed the greater metropolitan area into Worcestershire and made the city part of the Staffordshire Black Country. John Leland, Henry VIII's librarian and antiquarian, characterizes the town as a market town in his 16th-century *Itinerary:*

> The bewty of Bremischam, a good market towne in the extreme partes that way of Warwike-shire, is in one strete goynge up alonge almoste from the lefte ripe of the broke up a mene hille by the lengthe of a quartar of a mile.

The population explosion in Birmingham began with the industrial revolution, and by the end of the 18th century the population had risen to 70,000. The manufacture of guns expanded into the jewelry trade and other metalwork and eventually, in the 20th century, into the automotive industry. The 19th century brought railroad connections to London and Liverpool, and while living conditions here were bad, Birmingham had one of the most enlightened and efficient administrations in the country.

BIRMINGHAM While Birmingham is often portrayed in literature as a vulgar and modern city, the magnificent Victoria Square presents another facet.

The combination of early urban renewal and the destruction of World War II means that there are few old buildings of note; even the churches are relatively modern. The 1601 Stratford House retains many of its original features, and on the outskirts of Birmingham is Aston Hall (1618), now a museum, with fine carved fireplaces. The city has long had an interest in the arts and as the cultural center for a very wide area takes its responsibilities seriously. There are three professional theaters and an astonishingly large number of amateur companies; furthermore, the Corporation Art Gallery and Museum is one of the finest museums outside London and possesses an outstanding collection of English watercolors. The University of Birmingham has had enrollments in excess of 6,500 students since the early 1970s and has an outstanding medical school.

Literary associations with Birmingham are numerous but relatively recent. Samuel Johnson, often said to have made his first visit in 1732, was in fact here in 1719 on his first trip away from his Lichfield, Staffordshire, home. Then he stayed with two uncles, Nathaniel Ford, a clothier, and John Harrison, a saddler, for a little over two weeks; Harrison's shop was on the High Street next to the Castle Inn. On his second trip, in 1732, he came to see Edmund Hector, a former Lichfield schoolmate, after unpleasant experiences as an usher at the school in Market Bosworth, Leicestershire. Hector was lodging in the house of Thomas Warren, Birmingham's first bookseller, on the High Street by the Swan Inn; Johnson stayed with him for six weeks before taking lodgings of his own. Hector began *The Birmingham Journal* in November 1732, and Johnson contributed a number of essays to it; no issues of the paper have ever been found. Warren's role, however, was the more important one in that he urged Johnson to write. On one occasion Johnson mentioned that he had read Jerânimo Lobo's *A Voyage to Abyssinia* and felt an abridged translation would be useful; both men encouraged Johnson, and because the volume was unavailable in this city, Hector borrowed it for him from Pembroke College, Cambridge. Johnson got off to an excellent start, but as Boswell states, "his constitutional indolence soon prevailed, and the work was at a stand." Hector prodded futilely until he finally told the author that the printer and his family were suffering on this account:

> Johnson upon this exerted the powers of his mind, though his body was relaxed. He lay in bed with the book, which was a quarto, before him, and dictated while Hector wrote. Mr. Hector carried the sheets to the press, and corrected almost all the proof sheets, very few of which were ever seen by Johnson.

On this visit Johnson met Harry Porter, a mercer, and his wife Tetty, who was to become Johnson's wife after her husband's death in September 1734 (Johnson came from Lichfield to attend Porter in his last illness).

A favorite spot of Johnson's was the Swan Inn, where his favorite drink was a "bishop," a strange concoction of port, sugar, and a roasted orange. A visit from one of his Ford cousins, a known heavy drinker, prompted Johnson and Hector to try to split the evening's drinking at the Swan Inn with Hector taking the first part of the evening and Johnson the second. By the time Johnson arrived, three bottles of port had been drunk, and Hector was in no shape to go home; Johnson took a room at the inn for him and rejoined his cousin. However, Johnson had spent the first part of the evening drinking at the Porters' home, and by the time his half of the evening here was over, he wound up in the same bed as his friend.

Another 18th-century visitor to the city was William Beckford, who stopped here on his English tour of August–October 1779 to visit the Soho Engineering Works, where James Watt and Matthew Boulton had just perfected the first steam engine capable of raising power in a factory. Charles Lamb spent a fortnight here in the summer of 1789; he stayed at Bingley Hall, the home of Charles Lloyd.

In the 19th century Birmingham became the center of the activities of John Henry Newman, later Cardinal Newman. With the Pope's permission, he introduced the concept of an oratory to England and founded the Oratory of St. Philip Neri. Newman spent most of the rest of his life here and died at the oratory on August 11, 1890; he was buried at Rednall Hill. It was to the oratory that Gerard Manley Hopkins came in August 1866 to see Newman about his conversion to Catholicism, and arrangements were made for Hopkins to return in one month's time for reception into the church. In September 1867 he returned again at Newman's request for six months to teach Latin and Greek at the Oratory School and found that "Teaching is very burdensome.... I am always tired." When Hopkins left around Easter, 1868, he informed Newman of his intention to become a Jesuit. It was a realistic move for Hilaire Belloc to be sent to Birmingham for school in 1880 since his maternal grandfather, Joseph Parkes, lived here; Belloc was at the Oratory School from 1880 to 1887 and took part in the many Latin plays which Newman directed. Belloc left school just before his seventeenth birthday and enrolled at the Collège Stanislas in Paris.

Charles Dickens had a longtime association with Birmingham, beginning in 1838, when he came here from Wolverhampton; on one occasion he stayed at the old Hen and Chickens Inn, and his knowledge of the manufacturing center was used in *Pickwick Papers*. Mr. Pickwick travels here on a most delicate commission, mollifying Mr. Winkle, Sr., over his son's amatory escapade. Looking out of the windows of the coach, he sees the approach to Birmingham:

> The straggling cottages by the roadside, the dingy hue of every object visible, the murky atmosphere, the paths of cinders and brick-dust, the deep-red glow of furnace fires in the distance, the volumes of dense smoke issuing heavily forth from high toppling chimneys, blackening and obscuring everything around; the glare of distant lights, the ponderous waggons which toiled along the road, laden with clashing rods of iron or piled with heavy goods—all betokened their rapid approach to the great working town of Birmingham.

The party stay at the Old Royal Hotel on Temple Row, which survives in name only, and proceed to the task of seeing Mr. Winkle:

> About a quarter of a mile off, in a quiet, substantial-looking street, stood an old red-brick house with three steps before the door and a brass plate upon it, bearing, in fat Roman capitals, the words "Mr. Winkle." The steps were very white, and the bricks were very red, and the house was very clean....

The house is believed to be on Easy Row, near the Old Wharf, with white steps leading to the doorway, but there have been other claimants. Dickens also uses the city in *The Old Curiosity Shop:* Little Nell and her grandfather leave the canal boat at the Gas Street Bridge; the busy thoroughfare which they cross is Broad Street; and the winding lane down which they travel is St. Martin's Lane.

Dickens was again in the city in 1844, when he presided at a meeting of the Polytechnic Institution of Birmingham, and in 1857, when he was elected the first honorary member of the Birmingham and Midland Institute. He also gave a number of readings in the city throughout the 1860s.

After her death in Ambleside, Westmorland, on June 27, 1876, Harriet Martineau was buried in the old church cemetery in Birmingham beside her mother's grave. Only her name, age, and places of birth and death are on the tombstone. In the same decade Sir Arthur Conan Doyle came to the city as an assistant to Dr. Reginald Ratcliffe Hoare, who lived in Clifton House on Aston Road; Doyle was paid £2 a month for his services. He remained throughout the summer of 1879, and the arrangement evidently suited both men, for Doyle returned for another term after his service on the *Hope.* In the summer of 1903 he bought his first car here, a 10-horsepower dark blue Wolseley with red wheels, and promptly drove to Hindhead, Surrey, with Holden, his coachman, seated beside him; Doyle had never driven a car before, and the trip was eventful.

The 20th century saw Francis Brett Young spend a great deal of time in the city when his father decided that he take a degree in medicine at Birmingham University since Oxford was financially impossible. Young's entrance into the university in 1901 is related in *The Young Physician.* When taking his examinations, Young stayed with Miss Gertrude Dale at 5 Harborne Road, Edgbaston (then a Birmingham suburb), and qualified on November 4, 1907. Young and his future wife met for coffee at the Kardomah, had tea at the Grand Hotel, and took many walks in the Clent and Walton Hills. The view from the latter is described in both *The Dark Tower* and *Mr. Lucton's Freedom.* Following his qualification, Young took the post of medical officer aboard the 4,000-ton *Kintuck.*

There are a few other associations of note with Birmingham. J. M. Shorthouse, author of *John Inglesant*, was born on Great Charles Street on September 9, 1834, and attended a local Quaker school; he lived here all his life, at 6 Beaufort Street (gone) and at 60 Wellington Road from 1876 until his death on March 4, 1903. Shorthouse is buried in Old Edgbaston cemetery. Charles Reade's exposé of the English prison system, *It Is Never Too Late to Mend*, was motivated partly by the published accounts of the extreme cruelty practiced at the jail here. Thomas Hardy makes a brief mention of Birmingham in *A Pair of Blue Eyes*, and H. G. Wells uses the town in two of his works. In "The Story of the Late Mr. Elvesham" (*The Plattner Story and Others*), George Eden is brought up here by his journalist uncle; and at an inn near Birmingham Leadford stops to eat the night after his mother's death in *In the Days of the Comet.* John Drinkwater lived here beginning in 1901, when he was manager of the Pilgrim Players (later the Birmingham Repertory Theatre). In 1818 the American author Washington Irving wrote "Rip Van Winkle" here at a house (long gone) on Easy Row; it is thought that Aston Hall was the original of his Bracebridge Hall. Finally, from 1930 to 1935 the poet Louis MacNeice was a lecturer in classics at the University of Birmingham; his *Poems* was published before he left.

BIRSTALL, Yorkshire (pop. 6,401) This town in the West Riding of Yorkshire, 7 miles southwest of the industrial city of Leeds, has retained much of the atmosphere of the 19th century, when Charlotte and Emily Brontë attended Miss Wooler's School here. The area is important in Charlotte's life and works; sent here at the beginning of 1832, she was extremely homesick and in the manner of perfect Methodism would cry "quietly, as Wesley had bidden, in the long shadows of an alien school-room." She also often visited Red House, half a mile to the west, the home of the Taylors, but found the environment totally alien to that at Haworth. Both *Jane Eyre* and *Shirley* are full of local color; in *Jane Eyre* the exterior features of Thornfield Hall, Mr. Rochester's residence, are drawn partly from the Rydings. When Charlotte Brontë knew the house between 1832 and 1837, it belonged to Reuben Walker, the great-uncle of Ellen Nussey, her close friend. Since then it has become part of the Birstall Carpet Factory.

The novel *Shirley* is far more intimately concerned with the community: Birstall is the Briarfield of the novel, and the contiguous parish of Gomersal is included in Briarfield. The Red House is Briarmains, and nearby Oakwell Hall becomes Fieldhead (the name is obviously suggested by the nearby hamlet of the same name), the home of Shirley Keeldar, and the description of the building both inside and out is still accurate. This stone building, typical of structures in the West Riding, originally was a timber structure that was subsequently refaced in local stone (in 1583 in this case). The irregular gables at the front of the building and the long latticed windows between them are as Charlotte Brontë describes them, and the interior description is accurate even to the detail of the oak-paneled room that was painted "pinky white" by its owner, who gained the gratitude of the housemaids, whose duties were thereby considerably lightened. The dog gates undoubtedly suggested the episode concerning the visiting curates' escape from Shirley Keeldar's dog; and the curiously labeled Dairy (in perfect Yorkshire dialect, *diry*) made to comply with the window-tax exemptions during George III's reign caught her attention as well.

Birstall Church (only a tower remains) and a nearby house become Briarhead Church and Rectory. Charlotte Brontë's reference to the church spire is frequently considered an invention but Yorkshire people often use the term "spire" to mean tower, and this was undoubtedly her intent. The rectory where Caroline Helstone and her uncle live, while not the present rectory, is still there with its garden separated from the church by a low wall and a screen of trees. In *Shirley* Hallows Mill is located only a short distance from the church and the hall (between the hall and the village); however, the mill described is about 3 miles away in Hunsworth. The Rev. Patrick Brontë, Charlotte's father, was buried in the parish church here.

When John Dyer wrote *The Fleece* in 1757, he described the first "factory" built for the wool trade in the Vale of Calder. At the time the entire area was concerned with various stages in the manufacture of cloth and had achieved a relatively intensive degree of industrialization. Dyer continued his journey in a more pleasant way:

> . . . now an eastward course
> To the rich fields of Birstal. Wide around
> Hillock and valley, farm and village smile. . . .

BISHAM, Berkshire (pop. 875)   Between Reading and Windsor on the Thames River, Bisham has had historical importance that has drawn it into literature. While it was in the reign of Henry VI that the important events occurred, the story began earlier. The church of the 14th-century priory once held the remains of four Earls of Salisbury. The first, William de Montacute, was the founder of the priory. The second, who gained fame in the Battle of Poitiers (1356), was briefly married to Joan, the Fair Maid of Kent, before Edward the Black Prince established his royal prerogative. The third was a Wycliffite who was executed and who enters William Shakespeare's *Richard II*. Through the fourth, Thomas de Montacute, who died at the siege of Orléans (1428), the estate came into the hands of the Nevilles. Alice, Thomas de Montacute's daughter, married Richard Neville, and their son was the man often considered the outstanding figure in the Wars of the Roses, the Earl of Warwick. Shakespeare presents Warwick as a towering figure in the three parts of *Henry VI*. After

BISHAM   On the Thames River, the lovely old church in Bisham contains the grave of Dr. Robert Vansittart, whom readers of James Boswell's *The Life of Samuel Johnson* will recognize. He took seven or eight minutes, "in a plentitude of phrase," to relate "that the Counsel upon the circuit at Shrewsbury were much bitten by fleas" before Johnson blurted out, "It is a pity, Sir, that you have not seen a lion; for a flea has taken you such a time, that a lion must have served you a twelvemonth."

the Suppression Act and the acquisition of the estate by the Hobys, John Lyly was a guest at the manor house in August and September 1592.

In 1817 Percy Bysshe Shelley often sailed the river between Bisham and Great Marlow, Buckinghamshire, where he had taken Albion House. Jerome K. Jerome's *Three Men in a Boat* draws attention to Shelley and this area:

> Just before you come to the abbey, and right on the river's bank, is Bisham Church. . . . It was while floating in his boat under the Bisham beeches that Shelley . . . composed *The Revolt of Islam*.

BISHOP'S TACHBROOK, Warwickshire (pop. 552)   Situated 3 miles southeast of Warwick, Bishop's Tachbrook has been untouched by the urban Midlands centers, and the Avon Valley here is especially peaceful. The Church of St. Chad here is also from another time; its ancient roof is beamed, and the arches are 13th-century. As a child Walter Savage Landor lived in the old manor house, which is filled with old oak paneling but is not open to the public. The church contains a memorial tablet to Landor, who died in Florence on September 17, 1864, and the nave has the engraved stones of the Landor family vaults. Also of note is the east window in the chancel, which contains a memorial to the novelist Charles Kingsley's wife, Frances Elizabeth, who lived for a time at the Grove.

BISHOP'S WALTHAM, Hampshire (pop. 2,597)   The geological break in Hampshire between the extensive southern chalk hills and the relatively flat clay banks adjacent to the coast occurs in the neighborhood of Bishop's Waltham, 8 miles northeast of Southampton. The roads leading into the little town, modern surfacing aside, are much as they must have been in the 14th century: on the north, for example, the road plunges down sharply from Corhampton Down into the narrow streets. The name of the town suggests its place in history: the south side was the site of a bishop's palace begun by Bishop Henry of Blois in 1136. William of Wykeham, founder of Winchester College and New College, Oxford, built the Great Hall in the late 14th century and also undertook extensive rebuilding of the original structure before dying here in 1404. William Camden visited the Bishop's Palace prior to the compilation of his *Britannia* in 1607 and described it as "a right ample and goodly manor place moted about." But with the Civil War much of the palace was destroyed, and only remnants of the state apartments, a cloister, the great hall, and the four-story tower still exist.

The church here, on the opposite side of the town, dates partly from the 13th century. Although an extensive 19th-century renovation altered many of its best features, one of the most important survivals of earlier times is the canopied oak pulpit with side panels carved in Renaissance designs, which was presented to the church by Lancelot Andrewes, Bishop of Winchester, in 1626.

BISHOPSBOURNE, Kent (pop. 304)   The Stour Valley, where the village of Bishopsbourne lies, is a flat area of rich farmland, narrow and seldom-used roads, and old thatched and boarded cottages. In 1595 Queen Elizabeth I presented the living here to

Richard Hooker as a token of her admiration for the first four volumes of *Of the Lawes of Ecclesiasticall Politie.* Hooker had given up his fellowship at Oxford after contracting what proved to be a disastrous marriage and came here from Boscombe, Wiltshire. He completed the final volume of the *Ecclesiasticall Politie* in 1597 and died at his home (long gone) on November 2, 1600; he was buried in the chancel of the old church, where a monument contains the first-known reference to him as the "Judicious" Hooker.

Another literary figure, Joseph Conrad, made Oswalds (now the rectory) his home from early 1919 until 1924; he came to Bishopsbourne from Wye and was plagued by acute attacks of the gout and serious financial problems. Conrad died here of a heart attack on August 3, 1924, and was buried in the Roman Catholic portion of the Canterbury Cemetery. Alec Waugh lived at Oswalds for a brief period in the early 1930s.

BISHOPSTONE, Herefordshire (pop. 149)   In the fantastic Wye Valley 6½ miles northwest of Hereford, Bishopstone is set in some of the loveliest natural scenery in the South Midlands. William Wordsworth was a frequent visitor to the village when he was staying at nearby Brinsop Court, the home of his brother-in-law Thomas Hutchinson. On one of these occasions he wrote "Roman Antiquities Discovered at Bishopstone."

BISHOPTHORPE, Yorkshire (pop. 486)   On the Ouse River 2½ miles south of York, Bishopthorpe was an archepiscopal residence for the Archbishop of York, also styled Primate of England and second in power only to the Archbishop of Canterbury, styled Primate of All England. This diplomatic splitting of hairs was a 14th-century device and explains, at least in part, the important political role played by both archbishops throughout the 17th and 18th centuries. William Shakespeare sets two scenes of the *Henry IV* plays here. In Part I, Richard Scrope, Archbishop of York, voices his pessimism about the forthcoming Battle of Shrewsbury and reveals his view of the consequences. Part II contains the conference scene between the Archbishop, Hastings, Bardolph, and Mowbray, the Earl Marshal, prior to the encounter in Galtres Forest. Because of dramatic constraints Shakespeare has these men sentenced as traitors and taken "to the block of death" in that forest; in fact, Scrope was sentenced at Bishopthorpe and after beheading was buried in the cathedral at York.

BLACK BOURTON, Oxfordshire (pop. 3,640)   In rich meadow country 6 miles southwest of Witney, Black Bourton can boast one of the richest (and undefiled) medieval church art galleries in England. The paintings were actually obscured with whitewash by the Puritans, but recent restoration has displayed a treasure trove on the 13th-century nave walls. No less impressive is the rest of the clerestoried church, which contains a Norman arcade with scalloped capitals, a Norman baptismal font, an old scratch dial, and one of the very few medieval stone pulpits remaining in the country.

Black Bourton was the birthplace of Maria Edgeworth on January 1, 1767, and she spent her infancy here. Many of the stories associated with the village

and Miss Edgeworth—for example, that she was swung daily by the neck to increase her height and that she was dosed with tar-water to cure an eye inflammation—undoubtedly are local fabrications. The incident with the mechanical device to increase her height took place in London, and the tar-water episode in Anningsley, Surrey. Following her mother's death and her father's remarriage in 1773, the family left for Edgeworthstown, County Longford, Ireland.

BLACK DOWN, Sussex   Woodland still covers Black Down (2 miles south of Haslemere, Surrey) as it did centuries ago, but today the old Wealden oak, ash, birch, and chestnut are outnumbered by black fir and spruce. The relative isolation of the highest point in Sussex led Alfred, Lord Tennyson to establish a home called Aldworth here. This was his alternate home from 1868 until his death. Since the Isle of Wight was too crowded with summer visitors and curiosity seekers for his tastes, Tennyson found the land here, probably in early 1867, for in June his wife wrote of their agreement to purchase 35 acres (now 150 acres):

> It is a ledge on a hill nearly 1000 feet high, all copse and foxgloves almost, and a steep descent of wood and field below; the ledge looking over an immense plain, and backed by a hill slightly higher than itself.

The Tennyson family had already rented a farm, Greyshott, here in April 1867, and they spent the early summer familiarizing themselves with the area. The original plans called for a small house, which they planned to call Greenhill; what they ended up with was a much larger and more elaborate home. Tennyson laid the foundation stone on April 23, 1868, and while the building was going on, the project kept expanding; indeed, the architect, his friend and neighbor John Knowles, submitted the sketches for the arcaded porch, and Tennyson rebelled, saying that any more additions would ruin him, but the porch won out. Tennyson decided to plant the Italian cypresses along the terrace edge and commented that the area "wants nothing . . . but a great river looping along through the midst of it." The gables of the dormer windows, with one exception, contain stone shields; the one was left blank because Tennyson, not knowing what to do with it, was reminded of his own *Idylls*, when Merlin asks, "Who shall blazon it?—When and how?" and decided to leave the window as it was. He made a great point of having his favorite motto, "Gwyr ym erbyn y byd" ("Truth against the world") emblazoned in the mosaic at the threshold to the front door and in the pavement of the hall. In 1875, when a new sundial was placed in the garden, he had placed on it "Horas non numero nisi serenas" ("I count only the sunny hours").

Tennyson spent many hours walking and exploring the area; a favorite spot was Wegners, or Waggoners, Well near Hindhead, Surrey, only a few miles to the northwest, where he was inspired to write "Flower in the Crannied Wall"; another favorite area was the "Silent Pool," near Arbury beneath the Merrow Downs:

> The splendour and ripply play of light on the stream as it gushes from the chalk over the greensand bottom, the mackerel colours which flit about in the sunshine, and

the network of the current on the surface of the pool like crystal smoke.

He added: "The water itself was like what Keats says of Neptune's cave, the 'palace floor breath-air.'" Aldworth inspired the lines on honeysuckle in "Gareth and Lynette" in *Idylls of the King:*

Good lord, how sweetly smells the honeysuckle
In the hush'd night, as if the world were one
Of utter peace, and love, and gentleness.

Tennyson had many visitors here, including Prime Minister William Ewart Gladstone and his wife, Ivan Tourgueneff (Lady Tennyson's spelling), and Edward Lear, of whom his good friend Lady Tennyson wrote:

Mr. Lear came from Liphook: he liked our neighbourhood so much that he said we were to look out for some land for him hereabouts.

He told an excellent story about a misquotation of a passage in "You ask me, why." A friend of his remarked to him: "It is a well-known fact that Tennyson hates travelling." "Nonsense," answered Lear, "he loves it." "On the contrary," the friend retorted, "he hates it, and he says so himself somewhere:

'And I will *die* before I see
The palms and temples of the South.'"

Tennyson continued to reside at both Aldworth and the house in Farringford until his death at Aldworth on October 6, 1892. The attending physician, a Dr. Dabbs, issued a bulletin and description of the scene:

Nothing could have been more striking than the scene during the last few hours. On the bed a figure of breathing marble, flooded and bathed in the light of the full moon streaming through the oriel window; his hand clasping the Shakespeare which he had asked for but recently, and which he had kept by him to the end; the moonlight, the majestic figure as he lay there, "drawing thicker breath," irresistibly brought to our minds his own "Passing of Arthur."

The house is not open to the public, but the view from the gardens, where there is a fine commemorative bust of the poet, is dazzling in its panorama of the rolling countryside toward the sea.

Thomas Hardy also uses Black Down in "At Casterbridge Fair" (*Time's Laughingstocks and Other Poems*):

Black'on frowns east on Maidon,
And westward to the sea,
But on neither is his frown laden
With scorn, as his frown on me!

BLACKMOOR VALE, Dorset The Blackmoor Vale is the basis of the upper Stour Valley, an area of clay broken by limestone banks; the hills here are gently undulating, crowned with heavy woods, and the whole area is dotted with small fields. The rivers, Caundle Brook, the Lydden, and, especially, the Stour, give their names to the small towns and villages of the deep alluvial valley. Shaftesbury, originally called Shaston, has a commanding view of all of Blackmoor, and in *Jude the Obscure* Thomas Hardy describes its central vista as "a unique position on the summit of a steep and imposing scarp, rising on the north, south, and west sides of the borough out of the deep alluvial Vale of Blackmoor." This is the "Valley of the Little Dairies" (*Tess of the D'Urbervilles*), a

fertile and sheltered tract of country, in which the fields are never brown and the springs never dry, [and which] is bounded on the south by the bold chalk ridge that embraces the prominences of Hambledon Hill, Bulbarrow, Nettlecombe-Tout, Dogbury, High Stoy, and Bubb Down.

These chalk hills form the southern boundary of the vale, in which

the world seems to be constructed on a smaller and more delicate scale; the fields are mere paddocks, so reduced that from this height their hedge-rows appear a net-work of dark green threads overspreading the paler green of the grass.

Hardy uses Blackmoor in *The Woodlanders, The Mayor of Casterbridge, Far from the Madding Crowd,* "The First Countess of Wessex" (*A Group of Noble Dames*), "A Trampwoman's Tragedy" and "Geographical Knowledge" (*Time's Laughingstocks and Other Poems*), and "The Bullfinches" and "The Lost Pyx" (*Poems of the Past and Present*).

The legend of the alternative name of the vale and its woods (White Hart Vale and Forest of the White Hart) is told in *Tess* and *The Woodlanders:* during the reign (1216–1272) of Henry III, Thomas de la Lynd ran down and killed a beautiful white stag that Henry had previously pursued and caught but spared. The nobleman was brought before the King and summarily ordered to pay in expiation for his crime an annual fine that came to be known as White Hart Silver.

BLAKESLEY, Northamptonshire (pop. 432) Much of southern Northamptonshire was once part of the Whittlebury Forest, and the large expanses of woodland around Blakesley (4½ miles west of Towcester) serve as a reminder of its previously forested state. John Dryden lived in this village for a short time before he left for London after being at Trinity College, Cambridge; and, indeed, the family estate here, valued then at about £60 a year, became his on the death of his father in 1654. A tree on a farm near the church is still known as Dryden's Oak.

BLANDFORD FORUM, Dorset (pop. 3,800) The Ryves Almshouse in Salisbury Square and the Old House east of the Post Office are essentially all that remain of the ancient town of Blandford Forum; almost every other piece of antiquity was wiped out in 1731 by a fire, which destroyed the old church and the school that John Aubrey attended. The subsequent rebuilding of the town, Edward Gibbon said, resulted in a "pleasant and hospitable" Georgian town. Blandford Forum is generally referred to as Shottsford or Shottsford Forum in Thomas Hardy's Wessex although it is called "the Stour-bordered Forum" in "My Cicely" (*Wessex Poems*). Shottsford is mentioned in *Tess of the D'Urbervilles, The Trumpet-Major, Jude the Obscure,* and *The Woodlanders.* In *Far from the Madding Crowd,* Oake walks here from Dorchester on the London Road; and in *The Mayor of Casterbridge,* Michael Henchard buys the goldfinch here that is intended to reconcile him with Elizabeth-Jane. The town also appears in "Barbara of the House of Grebe" (*A Group of Noble Dames*) and in "The Three Strangers" (*Wessex Tales*), in which the third stranger has just come from

Shottsford, his home as well as the home of the doomed man.

Just outside Blandford Forum was a military training camp to which Rupert Brooke reported in November 1914 for more training after the Antwerp expedition. In the Royal Navy as a sublieutenant in charge of No. 3 Platoon, A Company, Hood Battalion, he spent almost three months here and began his famous five war sonnets, including "The Dead" ("These hearts were woven of human joys and cakes"). On February 27, 1915, Brooke and his men left to board the *Grantully Castle* for the Dardanelles.

BLEA TARN, Westmorland   Situated in Little Langdale 6 miles west of Ambleside, Blea Tarn is on the western edge of Lingmoor. Here is where "The Solitary" of William Wordsworth's *The Excursion* was found. Wordsworth noted:

> I suppose that the pedlar and I ascended from a plain country up the vale of Langdale, and struck off a good way above the chapel to the western side of the vale. We ascended the hill, and thence looked down upon the circular recess in which lies Blea Tarn, chosen by the Solitary for his retreat.

The hill is Lingmoor. The "tumultuous waste of high hill-tops" which were before them were the western range of Great End, Bowfell, Shelter Crags, Crinkle Crags, and Pike o' Blisco, the northern twin peaks of Langdale, and the southwestern range of Coniston, Wrynose, and Wetherlam. Wordsworth describes the summit walk:

> . . . when, all at once, behold!
> Beneath our feet, a little lowly vale,
> A lowly vale. . . .
> . . . .
> Urn-like it was in shape, deep as an urn;
> With rocks encompassed, save that to the south
> Was one small opening, where a heath-clad ridge
> Supplied a boundary less abrupt and close;
> A quiet treeless nook, with two green fields,
> A liquid pool that glittered in the sun,
> And one bare dwelling; one abode, no more!

Most of Wordsworth's references are readily identifiable: "a lowly little valley" is the head of Little Langdale; the "one small opening" is the path into Little Langdale; the "liquid pool" is Blea Tarn; the "one abode" is the cottage now called Blea Tarn House. Much of Book II of *The Excursion* concerns this area and its views; Wordsworth does, however, err when he writes:

> In genial mood,
> While at our pastoral banquet thus we sate
> Fronting the window of that little cell,
> I could not, ever and anon, forbear
> To glance an upward look on two huge Peaks,
> That from some other vale peered into this.

The "two huge Peaks," "those lusty twins," are the Langdale Pikes, and they are not visible from the upper room of the cottage where Wordsworth places the banquet.

BLEWBURY, Berkshire (pop. 1,126)   A village of half-timbered houses on the road between Reading and Wantage, Blewbury dates at least to the 11th century, when the town charter, describing the village as a "venerable place," was granted. There is an exceptional Saxon relic in the form of four long thatched wattle-and-daub walls, two of which form a winding alley leading between orchards to a stream; and the church has a lovely Norman vault on four arches and a vaulted chancel.

After retiring from the secretaryship of the Bank of England, Kenneth Grahame and his wife wanted a quiet place in which to settle, and at Christmas, 1909, after a 3½-year sojourn in Cookham Dean, he found Bohams, a Tudor brick farmhouse here. It had a thatched roof, two farm kitchens, a granary, an apple-loft, and its own trout stream. Grahame commented on the area in a letter:

> It is only about fifty-four miles from London, but fifty-four thousand years remote from it in every way. Alfred beat the Danes close by about 860 and nothing has really happened since.

Life here was quite enjoyable until on May 7, 1920, when Alastair, Grahame's only child, a student at Christ Church, Oxford, was killed by a train; an inquest verdict of accidental death was brought in. However, both Arthur Quiller-Couch and Grahame were convinced that the boy had actually committed suicide. Grahame and his wife were unable to continue living here and let the house in October.

Blewbury was also the home of the Reverend Morgan-Jones, whose miserly qualities won him immortality as Blewbury Jones in Charles Dickens's *Our Mutual Friend*. Jones is said to have lived on 1 crown a week, spending the money only on bread, bacon, and tea. He went to a farmhouse three times a week to get the bacon himself because each time he was asked to stay for a meal. From a stipend of £80 a year, he left an estate of £18,000.

BLIDWORTH, Nottinghamshire (pop. 2,003)   Approximately 9 miles north of Nottingham, Blidworth is in the heart of Sherwood Forest and thus in the domain of Robin Hood. While parallel legends exist for two forests, Sherwood and Barnesdale, the far more popular spot is in the Nottinghamshire woods. Tradition here holds that Blidworth was the home of Maid Marian and that Will Scarlet also was a local resident. Indeed, the grounds of the largely 18th-century Church of St. Mary contain the original local cemetery, which is now a "Garden of Rest." This rather somber area, which is in perpetual care, is alleged to contain the remains of Will Scarlet. Friar Tuck is said to have lived 1 mile west of Blidworth.

BLOXHAM, Oxfordshire (pop. 1,384)   Situated on twin hilltops 3½ miles southwest of Banbury, Bloxham has a splendid Norman church with a sheltered doorway of two-color stone. Just below the open quatrefoils around the spire is the earliest-known depiction of the nursery rhyme and folk song "John, John, the Grey Goose Is Gone": John is shown brandishing a cudgel, while his wife holds her distaff, and the fox is making off with the goose. More modern times saw the craftsmanship of William Morris, who created the lovely Te Deum east window.

BLUNDESTON, Suffolk (pop. 676)   Only 3½ miles northwest of the busy marine center of Lowestoft, Blundeston has been almost engulfed by that rapidly expanding city and is also threatened by the fast-growing resort activity of the Norfolk Broads. But a great deal of its 19th-century charm remains in Blundeston Hall, the rectory, the Plough Inn, and the church. In August 1848 Charles Dickens, on an excursion from nearby Somerleyton Hall, discovered this village, whose name he promptly altered to the more symbolic Blunderstone in *David Copperfield*. This is David's birthplace, and the Rookery, the Copperfield family home, is probably a combination of the rectory and Blundeston Hall. The former provides the external description,

> with the latticed bedroom windows standing open to let in the sweet-smelling air, and the ragged old rooks' nests still dangling in the elm-trees at the bottom of the front garden. Now I am in the garden at the back, beyond the yard where the empty pigeon-house and dog-kennel are—a very preserve of butterflies ... with a high fence, and a gate and padlock; where the fruit clusters on the trees. ...

But the description of the inside of the house fits that of the Hall with Peggotty's kitchen on the ground floor "opening into a back yard" and with the "long passage" that leads to the front door and has the "dark store-room" opening off it. Dickens also uses the church with its round tower and, more especially, the sundial that David Copperfield sees with "the red light shining on the sun-dial, and [I] think within myself: 'Is the sun-dial glad, I wonder, that it can tell the time again?'" Indeed, the church has been fully restored as a memorial to the author's faithful description of the town. The parish cemetery and the "village ale house" (frequented by Barkis) are easily identified, the latter as the Plough Inn.

In the 18th century Thomas Gray was an occasional visitor to the village.

BLUNHAM, Bedfordshire (pop. 603) Blunham is a village with some fine old houses, a lovely old sandstone church, and a rough manor house once used by the Earls of Kent. In April 1622 John Donne received the benefice here and placed a curate in charge. Thereafter Donne paid at least annual visits to the parish and always preached on these occasions. Tradition maintains that on these visits he stayed at the manor house, and he is known once to have returned to London with a load of cucumbers in his carriage. Present-day inhabitants also claim that Donne lived in the rectory (the present Victorian rectory stands on the original site) during his summer visits. In 1626 Dr. Donne presented the church with a chalice engraved "From Dr Donne Deane of Pauls, for Blunham Church," and he included his old parishioners in his will by leaving an endowment for the maintenance of the poor of the parish. His last-known visit was in August 1628.

BLUNTISHAM, Huntingdonshire (pop. 1,006) The old village of Bluntisham, on the Ouse River 3¾ miles northeast of St. Ives, no longer exists, and the extensive new building here has left a somewhat shapeless community in its wake. The basically 14th-century church, on the main road, is topped by a notable spire, and three of the chancel walls terminate externally in high gables. Across from the church and surrounded by trees is the 18th-century rectory, the longtime home of Dorothy Sayers. Her

family came here from Oxford in 1898, when her father took the living of this parish; going up to Somerville College, Oxford, on scholarship in 1912, she returned after graduation and was living in Bluntisham when *Op I* was published in 1916.

BOAR'S HILL, Berkshire Very likely the name of this hamlet, 4 miles north of Abingdon and very near Oxford, has nothing to do with boars. For more than twenty-five years this was the home of Robert Bridges; he and his family came here from Yattendon in 1907 and settled at Chilsworth House. Bridges's early years here were not very productive, but *The Testament of Beauty* (1929) was begun shortly after he moved here.

With the death in 1913 of the Poet Laureate Alfred Austin, Bridges was offered and accepted the laureateship. He and his family discovered that the appointment brought a constant flood of people seeking advice, self-aggrandizement, or nothing in particular. To regain some privacy, Bridges hired a stone-deaf village girl to answer the door; as he commented, "... that girl soon cured them. Now they leave us alone." *The Spirit of Man* and *October and Other Poems* were also written here. For the nine months preceding his death, Bridges suffered from internal hemorrhaging; he died on April 21, 1930, and was buried at the church in Yattendon. Among the many literary figures to visit Bridges were Hugh Walpole, who was here for the first time in November or December 1920 with John Masefield and his wife; and Virginia Woolf, who came in June 1926.

BOCKHAMPTON, Dorset This village is variously referred to and located on maps as Bockhampton, Higher Bockhampton, and Upper Bockhampton; even gazetteers and census records are sufficiently inconsistent to render a final identification hazardous. This Bockhampton is located on the edge of the heath 3 miles east of Dorchester in the heart of Thomas Hardy country. Still almost as secluded as in Hardy's day, many of the houses are thatched and hidden by beech and chestnut trees. Hardy was born in Bockhampton on June 2, 1840, and his birthplace has been taken over by the National Trust. The

BOCKHAMPTON The birthplace of Thomas Hardy on June 2, 1840, this is the cottage described in his earliest known poem, "Domicilium":
  It faces west, and round the back and sides
  High beeches, bending, hang a veil of boughs,
  And sweep against the roof ...

thatched cottage with its timbered, whitewashed rooms is easily recognized from its description in *Under the Greenwood Tree:*

> A little wicket admitted to the garden, and a path led up to the house. It was a long low cottage with a hipped roof of thatch, having dormer windows breaking up into the eaves, a chimney standing in the middle of the ridge and another at the further end. . . . The walls of the dwelling were for the most part covered with creepers. . . .

The interior with "the main room on the left . . . with a beam bisecting the ceiling" and the room in which Hardy wrote reflect the simplicity of which he was fond. His study looks out over the heath, "majestic, watchful, haggard Egdon," which he describes in the opening of *The Return of the Native.* His education, in a school kept by a Mrs. Martin, was started rather late because of his frail health, but after only a year he was sent to a private school in Dorchester. The Hardy family attended the parish church in Stinsford, less than a mile away. Only general influences of Bockhampton appear in Hardy's works; nothing is specifically set here, and the name undergoes no transformation to become an integral part of the author's Wessex.

BODMIN MOOR, Cornwall   One of three moorland areas on the southwestern peninsula of England, Bodmin Moor is the lowest, the most western, and considerably smaller (132 square miles) than either Dartmoor or Exmoor. A granite moor with a thin, acid soil and some peat, it consists of three divisions. Part of the upland area is heather and grass; another supports furze and whortleberries; and a third distinct division barely supports thorn and rowan trees, which have at best a precarious existence. Geographers call the weather on Bodmin, as well as on the other southwestern moors, sub-Arctic, the average temperature dropping 1°C for every 400 feet of elevation.

References to King Arthur are found all over Cornwall, and Arthurian associations are linked to the landscape. Bodmin Moor, for example, contains Arthur's Hall, a natural outcropping of stone, and Dozmary Pool, near Bolventor, into which Sir Bedivere is said to have thrown Excalibur. And it was across this moor (even though Geoffrey of Monmouth in his *Historia Regum Britanniae* fails to mention it by name) that Arthur pursues Mordred before their encounter at Slaughter Bridge on the Camel River at Camelford.

Bodmin itself, a small village on the edge of the moor, was the birthplace of Sir Arthur Quiller-Couch on November 21, 1863; he was born in a house (now gone) on Pool Street, but a freestanding commemorative column in Church Square (as the area is now known) marks the site of the house.

BOGNOR REGIS, Sussex (pop. 19,890)   Begun as a Saxon coastal town, 6¾ miles southeast of Chichester, Bognor became a relatively prosperous medieval fishing hamlet and in the 1790s, at the height of the bathing craze, developed into a fashionable but fairly quiet watering place. The town has 5 miles of sandy beaches and is a jumbled collection of houses and shops. "Regis" was added to Bognor early in the 20th century when George V was at Aldwick recovering

from pneumonia; one of the few persons invited to visit the King here was Rudyard Kipling.

Dante Gabriel Rossetti came to nearby Aldwick Lodge to be under the care of Dr. Thomas Gordon Hake in October 1875. Staying for nine months, he took long winter walks along Selsey Bay and arranged his affairs because of his conviction that he was dying. He refused to be buried at Highgate Cemetery, perhaps because of the exhumation of Elizabeth Siddal; he arranged for his cremation, and he adamantly forbade the taking of a death mask or a hand cast. But hand casts were nevertheless taken, and as recently as the spring of 1973 one of the original plaster casts of Rossetti's hands was offered for sale in Newcastle upon Tyne. Rossetti left Bognor for Cheyne Walk, London, in July 1876.

BOLAS MAGNA or Great Bolas, Shropshire (pop. 264)   Situated in northern Shropshire 6½ miles west of Newport, Bolas Magna has an idyllic location on the Tern River. An event here in 1791 prompted "The Lord of Burleigh," one of the lesser poems of Alfred, Lord Tennyson. In the summer of that year Sarah Hoggins, daughter of the miller, fell in love with his new apprentice, nicknamed Gentleman Harry; they were married in London that autumn and settled down to a quiet existence at the Burleigh Farm near Stamford. In 1793 the 9th Earl of Exeter died, and only on the trip to Burleigh House in Lincolnshire did Sarah discover that Gentleman Harry was the 10th Earl, who had earlier left his family home because of his own divorce. Tennyson turns the earl into a landscape painter and has the new marchioness deeply distresed by her sudden elevation:

> So she strove against her weakness,
>   Tho' at times her spirit sank:
> Shaped her heart with woman's meekness
>   To all duties of her rank;
> And a gentle consort made he,
>   And her gentle mind was such
> That she grew a noble lady,
>   And the people loved her much.
> But a trouble weigh'd upon her,
>   And perplex'd her, night and morn,
> With the burthen of an honour
>   Unto which she was not born.

Thomas Moore also had versified the story in "You Remember Ellen" but changed both the names and the ending.

BOLTON ABBEY, Yorkshire (pop. 186)   Mistakenly but firmly called an abbey, the 12th-century Bolton Priory stands in a rural setting on the Wharfe River almost 6 miles from Ilkley. In either 1151 or 1153 Cecilia de Romilée with her husband William FitzDuncan moved an Augustinian foundation to Bolton Priory from Embsay. The full-scale movement of a monastic order was not common, but the traditional reason in this particular case was that recorded by William Wordsworth in *The White Doe of Rylstone:*

> Her Son in Wharf's abysses drowned,
> The noble Boy of Egremound.
> From which affliction . . .
> A pious structure, fair to see,
> Rose up, this stately Priory!

The gorge in which the "noble Boy" died is the famous Strid, about 2 miles up the river from the priory, where the Wharfe is squeezed in a deceptive limestone channel; the ledges appear an easy matter to leap, and drowning fatalities are not uncommon even now. The legend of the formation of the priory and of the white doe was known to Wordsworth both from a visit to the area and from Dr. Thomas Dunham Whitaker's *The History and Antiquities of the Deanery of Craven*. After the dissolution of the priory in 1539, a white doe "continued to make a weekly pilgrimage from Rylstone over the fells of Bolton, and was constantly found in the Abbey Churchyard during divine service; after the close of which she returned home as regularly as the rest of the congregation." The poem tells the story of the Norton family and of the Rising in the North in 1569; Rylstone was the residence of the Nortons, who figured importantly in the uprising.

The priory has come through history and time quite well considering its vulnerability. Indeed, the nave is in very good condition, and underneath the Mauleverer chantry, which is enclosed by a screen at the end of the nave aisle, is the famous upright burial vault in which were interred the Claphams of Beamsley and the Mauleverers. Wordsworth says that looking down through a "chink in the fractured floor" is seen

> a griesly sight;
> A vault where the bodies are buried upright!
> There, face to face, and hand by hand,
> The Claphams and Mauleverers stand. . . .

Whether or not the "old monastic tower" from which Wordsworth has "The bells ring out with gladsome power" was ever built is not known; if it was, its date of destruction is also unknown. Wordsworth's poem "The Force of Prayer" also concerns the priory.

Samuel Rogers and Robert Collyer both visited Bolton Abbey, and it was known to be a favorite place of Mary Ann Evans (George Eliot).

BOLTON CASTLE, Yorkshire (pop. 138) Bolton Castle is located in the wide and heavily wooded Wensleydale, source of the cheese of that name. The valley is watered by the Ure River, and the castle and village of the same name are just a short distance from the magnificent Aysgarth Force. The castle was built in the 14th century by Richard, Lord Scrope, Richard II's Chancellor and father of the famous Richard Scrope, Archbishop of York. John Leland, Henry VIII's librarian and royal antiquarian, visited here and describes the castle in his *Itinerary*. The Scrope family inhabited the castle from the reign of Richard II until the time of the Long Parliament (1640–1660). It was from here, as "The Battle of Flodden Field" relates, that Lord Scrope gathered his men to join the fight at Flodden, near Branxton:

> Lord Scrope of Bolton, stern and stout,
>   On horseback who had not his peer;
> No Englishman Scots more did doubt—
>   With him did wend all Wensadale
> Lord Morton unto Mosedale Moor. . . .

BOLVENTOR, Cornwall (pop. 270) Located in the middle of Bodmin Moor on the A30, the only main road across the upland region, Bolventor is a tiny hamlet of a few houses; about equidistant from Launceston to the north and Bodmin to the south, it is the site of the Jamaica Inn used by Daphne du Maurier for the setting of her novel of that title (1936). The young Mary Yellan sees it first:

> Ahead of her, on the crest, and to the left . . . some sort of a building, standing back from the road. She could see tall chimneys, murky dim in the darkness. There was no other house, no other cottage. If this was Jamaica, it stood alone in glory, foursquare to the winds.

But long before Du Maurier, Bolventor was associated with literature, although with legend rather than fact. About 1½ miles southeast of the hamlet is Dozmary (Dozmare) Pool, a gloomy tarn at an elevation of 890 feet, famed in Arthurian and Cornish legends. In both legends the pool is said to be bottomless (a point that local people still accept as fact), even though as an upland tarn it is shallow and, indeed, has even been known to dry up. The Cornish legend, which far predates the Arthurian, tells of a giant, Jan Tregeagle, who was condemned to the never-ending task of emptying Dozmary with a limpet shell as a punishment for ordering his daughters to murder their husbands. The Arthurian legend concerns Sir Bedivere's disposal of King Arthur's sword. According to Sir Thomas Malory, following the battle with Mordred in which King Arthur is mortally wounded, he commands Bedivere to "take thou Excalibur, my good sword, and go with it to yonder water side, and when thou comest there, I charge thee throw my sword in that water, and come again and tell me what thou seest." Twice caught not having executed the command,

> Sir Bedivere departed, and went to the sword, and lightly took it up, and went to the water side; and there he bound the girdle about the hilts, and then he threw the sword as far into the water as he might; and there came an arm and an hand above the water and met it, and caught it, and so shook it thrice and brandished, and then vanished away the hand with the sword in the water.

Loe Bar near Helston also claims this part of the Arthurian legend.

BONCHURCH, Isle of Wight (pop. 501) The small village of Bonchurch, storybook in appearance, is situated in the midst of magnificent scenery on the southeast coast of the Isle of Wight. Thick limestone cliffs have been exposed by the slippage of greensand and gault into the sea, and on the ground below the cliffs ferns and trees proliferate. Steep, narrow zigzag steps lead down to the channel front through the woodlands from the cliffs above.

Algernon Swinburne retained his early love of this area all his life. Much of his childhood was spent in a house known as East Dene (now a guesthouse) on the sheltered Undercliff. He spent much time exploring this part of the island and describes with obvious pride his successful climb of the difficult Culver Cliff, although it appears from his description that he climbed the easier eastern face of the cliff and not the treacherous western face. Swinburne returned to Bonchurch and the Isle of Wight frequently as an adult, and following his death on April 10, 1909, in Putney, London, his body was brought to the cemetery of St. Boniface's Church for burial with the rest of his family.

Charles Dickens, another of the many Victorians

who visited the island, rented Winterbourne, an attractive Victorian villa, for six months in 1849 (the house is now a hotel containing Dickens memorabilia). The first part of his sojourn was extremely pleasant: he was working effectively on *David Copperfield*, and his children romped over the sands and swam with the young "golden-haired lad of the Swinburnes'." But then in "high summer," as he described it, Dickens found that the climate was not bracing enough for him to work; consequently, before his lease was up, he moved his family to Broadstairs, Kent. Among other visitors were William Makepeace Thackeray, and Thomas Babington Macaulay; the latter lived at Madeira Hall on the Ventnor-Bonchurch Road, but Thackeray's residence cannot be established.

BOOTLE, Cumberland (pop. 806) The Cumbrian coast, which stretches for 60 miles from Silloth to Millom, has large expanses of sandy beaches with rather spectacular views of the sea. Numerous valleys and rivers cut in from the sea, and on the southern coastal reaches the Cumbrian mountain chain virtually meets the water. Nine miles north of Millom, near the bracken-covered fells of the Annas River, is the ancient village of Bootle. In August 1811 William Wordsworth brought his wife and two of his children here for a holiday. For some reason the poet did not appreciate his seaside holiday in spite of being in the immediate vicinity of his beloved Lakeland mountains. He complained about the holiday in his "Epistle to Sir George Howland Beaumont, Bart., from the South-west Coast of Cumberland":

Far from our home by Grasmere's quiet Lake,
From the Vale's peace which all her fields partake,
Here on the bleakest point of Cumbria's shore
We sojourn stunned by Ocean's ceaseless roar....

It appears that Wordsworth was unfortunate in his choice of lodging and in the weather and that he was reacting to these and not to the "Ocean's ceaseless roar."

Just southeast of the village is Black Combe Peak, 1,969 feet high, which on a clear day presents an outstanding view of fourteen English and Scottish counties, the Isle of Man, Snowdon, and the Irish coast. Wordsworth includes the view from here in "Return" (Duddon River sonnet sequence) and, like many antiquaries, ascribed the nearby stone circle at Hardknott Pass to the druids; the "timorous flocks"

Slept amid that lone Camp on Hardknot's height,
Whose Guardians bent the knee to Jove and Mars:
Or near that mystic Round of Druid frame
Tardily sinking by its proper weight
Deep into patient Earth....

BORROWDALE, Cumberland Considered the most beautiful valley in Lakeland, Borrowdale stretches from near Glaramara Mountain north to Derwent Water, an area of about 5 miles. On the north end is Castle Crag, an early British fortification, and on the south the scenery is dominated by Great End, 2,984 feet high. Michael Drayton was one of the first to include Borrowdale in his writing. The last song in *Poly-Olbion* describes the area:

Whence soone the Muse proceeds, to find out fresher Springs,

Where *Darwent* her cleere Fount from *Borowdale* that brings,
Doth quickly cast her selfe into an ample Lake,
And with *Thurls* mighty Mere, between them two doe make
An Island, which the name from *Darwent* doth derive....

In 1770 Thomas Gray came to Cumbria. Reaching the natural gateway to the north end of the valley, the Jaws of Borrowdale, he turned back in fear of the "terrifying" mountains; he wrote a vignette of the scene just before entering the valley:

... the ground rising and covered with a glade of scattering trees and bushes on the very margin of the water, opens both ways the most delicious view, that my eyes ever beheld. Behind you are the magnificent heights of Walla Crag; opposite lie the thick hanging woods of Lord Egremont, and Newland Valley, with green and smiling fields embosomed in the dark cliffs; to the left the jaws of Borrowdale, with that turbulent chaos of mountain behind mountain rolled in confusion; beneath you, and stretching far away to the right, the shining purity of the lake, just ruffled with the breeze, enough to show it is alive, reflecting rocks, woods, fields, and inverted tops of mountains, with the white buildings of Keswick, Crossthwaite Church, and Skiddaw for a back-ground at a distance.

Ever since then Borrowdale's sublime beauty has attracted poets, novelists, and critics. William Wordsworth used Borrowdale extensively in his poetry; here on the hillside near Seathwaite, the wettest inhabited place in the country, are the yew trees,

... those fraternal Four of Borrowdale,
Joined in one solemn and capacious grove;
Huge trunks! and each particular trunk a growth
Of intertwisted fibres serpentine
Up-coiling, and inveterately convolved....

The "fraternal Four" stood untouched until a gale in December 1883, when one was uprooted and the main branches of the other three were damaged; however, the grove can still be identified. The poet also found inspiration in St. Herbert's Isle, named after the hermit who was a close friend of St. Cuthbert; the Venerable Bede tells the story of their desire to die on the same day in his *Historia Ecclesiastica Gentis Anglorum*.

Perhaps the best-known aspect of Borrowdale is its falls, and certainly the Lodore Falls live forever in the children's poem by Robert Southey:

The Cataract strong
Then plunges along,
Striking and raging
As if a war waging
Its caverns and rocks among:
Rising and leaping,
Sinking and creeping,
Swelling and sweeping,
Showering and springing,
Flying and flinging,
Writhing and ringing,
Eddying and whisking,
Spouting and frisking,
Turning and twisting,
Around and around
With endless rebound!
Smiting and fighting,
A sight to delight in;
Confounding, astounding,
Dizzying and deafening the ear with its sound.

In Southey's *Colloquies* Sir Thomas More is met in

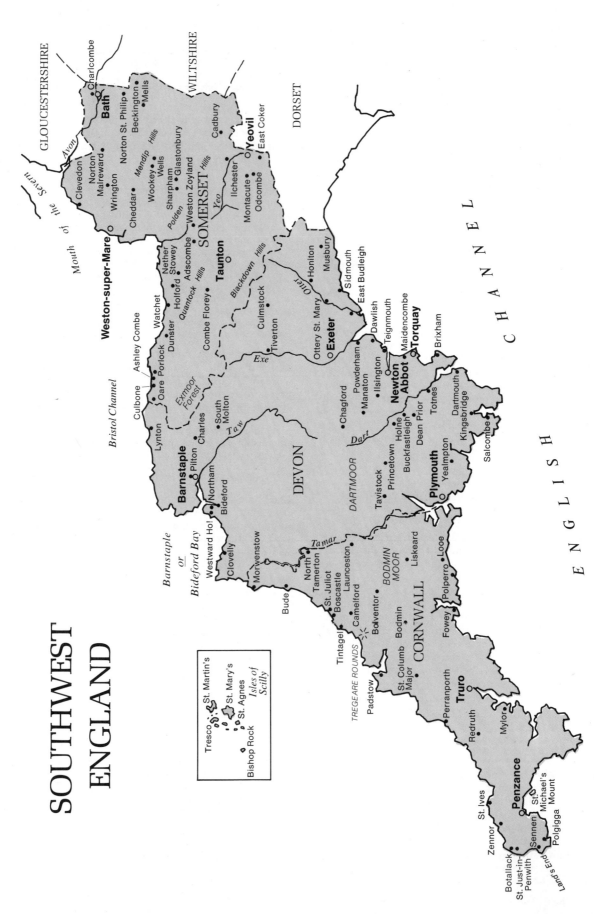

SOUTHWEST ENGLAND

GLOUCESTERSHIRE

WILTSHIRE

DORSET

Mouth of the Severn

Severn

Avon

Charlcombe

Bath

Norton St. Philip
Beckington
Mells

Cadbury

Yeovil
East Coker

Norton
Clevedon
Malreward
Wrington

Cheddar
Mendip Hills
Wookey
Wells
Sharpham
Glastonbury

Weston Zoyland

Ilchester
Montacute
Odcombe

Weston-super-Mare

SOMERSET
Yeo

Hills

Nether Stowey
Adscombe

Taunton

Blackdown Hills

Honiton
Musbury
Sidmouth
East Budleigh

Watchet
Dunster
Holford
Quantock Hills
Combe Florey

Culmstock

Otter

Ottery St. Mary

Exeter

Tiverton

Exe

Dawlish
Teignmouth
Maidencombe
Torquay
Brixham

Ashley Combe

Bristol Channel

Culbone
Oare Porlock
Exmoor Forest

Powderham
Ilsington
Manaton
Newton Abbot

Lynton
Charles

South Molton

Taw

Chagford

Dart

Dartmouth
Kingsbridge

Totnes
Holne
Buckfastleigh
Dean Prior

Salcombe

Princetown
Tavistock

Pilton

Barnstaple
Northam
Bideford

DEVON

DARTMOOR

Plymouth
Yealmpton

Barnstaple
or
Bideford Bay

Westward Ho!

Clovelly

Morwenstow

Tamar

North Tamerton

St. Juliot
Boscastle
Camelford

Launceston

BODMIN MOOR

Liskeard

Fowey
Polperro
Looe

Bude

ENGLISH CHANNEL

Tintagel

TREGEARE ROUNDS

Bolventor
Bodmin

CORNWALL

St. Columb
Major

Padstow

Perranporth

Truro

Redruth
Mylor

Tresco
St. Martin's
St. Mary's
St. Agnes
Isles of Scilly
Bishop Rock

Penzance
St. Michael's Mount
Polgigga

St. Ives

Zennor

Botallack
St. Just-in-Penwith
Land's End
Sennen

Borrowdale seated under an ash tree near the stream of Cat Ghyll, about halfway up that mountainside between Falcon and Walla Crags.

No doubt the writer who made the most extensive use of the area was Sir Hugh Walpole in the four novels of "The Herries Chronicles"; Walpole knew and loved the area well but was not accepted by the natives because he lacked the "Cumbrian blood." One of his best descriptions of this area occurs in *Judith Paris:*

> He had reached now the spot where Watendlath Beck tumbled into Lodore, and as always when he was here he must stop and breathe in deeply that perfect beauty. This was surely one of the loveliest places in all England—English, too, in its qualities of old imperturbable age, a kind of wistful tranquillity, a cosiness of beauty mingled with an almost fierce suggestion of force. . . . [T]he cataract (when the rains had fallen) would fling clouds of mist above the turning flower-like whiteness of the water that leapt and fell and leapt again between the thin brown stones. The dark bare stems of the larch and oak stood sentinel on either side, and exactly framed by the delicate pattern Derwentwater lay, in colour now snow upon steel, a thin shadow of stainless white hovering over the silver grey. Skiddaw and Blencathra seemed to sway under the changing passing cloud.

Judith Paris's longed-for farm is a farmhouse in Watendlath, and three places in Rosthwaite claim to be the original of Rogue Herries's farm.

In the summer of 1818, John Keats was in the Lake District on a walking tour, and among the places he visited was Borrowdale; a letter to his brother Thomas describes his excursion here; after breakfast

> we took a complete circuit of the Lake going about ten miles, and seeing on our way the Fall of Lowdore. I had an easy climb among the streams, about the fragments of Rocks, and should have got I think to the summit, but unfortunately I was damped by slipping one leg into a squashy hole. There is no great body of water, but the accompaniment is delightful; for it oozes out from a cleft in perpendicular Rocks, all fledged with Ash and other beautiful trees. . . . [T]he Mountains of Borrowdale are perhaps as fine as any thing we have seen.

Matthew Arnold explored the reaches of Borrowdale first with his father in 1831 and many times thereafter; they walked across the fells from Armboth to Watendlath, and later Arnold described the trip in "Resignation." When Lewis Carroll (Charles Lutwidge Dodgson) spent the Long Vacation from Oxford here in 1856, he climbed the 2,949-foot Great Gable, one of the highest and best-known mountains in the area. The mountain is a notorious challenge in wet weather, and Carroll made his climb during an icy gale.

BOSCASTLE, Cornwall Boscastle, a quaint village on the Atlantic coast of Cornwall, has an S-shaped harbor and is long and straggling with its oldest section on the slopes above the harbor. The High Street with an attractive collection of irregular houses drawn from different architectural periods is unusual even for coastal Cornwall. Among a number of good old inns in Boscastle are the Napoleon (named in 1807 during the Napoleonic Wars), the nearby Wellington, and the Ship. It was the Ship, now altered but retaining its original shape, in which the Rev. Robert Stephen Hawker stayed in 1825 when on a school holiday and of which he wrote a scathing account:

> We reached in safety our bourn for the night at the bottom of the hill. . . . Here we received a smiling welcome from the hostess, a ruddy-visaged widow. She then invited us to enter her "parrolar," a room rather cosy than magnificent; for when our landlady had followed in her two guests, . . . no one beside could have forced an entrance any more than a canon ball could cleave through a featherbed. . . . We . . . then went on to entreat that we might dine. She graciously agreed; but to all our questions as to our fare her sole response was, "Meat—meat and taties". "Some call 'em," she added in a scornful tone, " 'putraties,' but we always say 'taties' here." The specific differences between beef, mutton, veal, etc., seemed to be utterly or artfully ignored. . . .
>
> It is a wretched truth that by no effort could we ascertain what it was that was roasted for us that day by widow Treworgy, hostess of The Ship, and which we consumed. Was it a piece of Boscastle baby? . . . [T]he not unsavory taste was something like tender veal. It was not until years afterwards that light was thrown on our mysterious dinner that day by a passage which I accidently turned up in an ancient history of Cornwall. Therein I read "that the sillie people of Bouscastle and Boussiney do catch in the summer seas divers young soleys [seals], which, doubtful if they be fish or flesh, conynge housewives will nevertheless roast, and do make thereof very savoury meat."

The Ship is much improved now. One of Hawker's best-known ballads, "The Silent Tower of Bottreau," concerns the legend of the bells of St. Symphorian's Church (often called the Forrabury Church), high on the cliffs. The legend relates how the bells were being brought by sea to the church; as the ship approached land, the pilot thanked God for their safety, to which the captain retorted, "Thank God on land, but at sea thank a good captain and a fine ship." A fierce Atlantic storm came down on them suddenly, and the bells, ship, and crew except

BOSCASTLE The picturesque village of Boscastle in the Valency Valley is the Castle Bottreau of the Rev. Robert Stephen Hawker's ballad and the Castle Boterel of Thomas Hardy's Wessex.

for the pilot were lost; to this day the partly Norman church of St. Symphorian has no bells.

Boscastle is Castle Boterel, the westernmost point of Thomas Hardy's Wessex. In March 1870 Hardy was here for the first time. Working as an apprentice architect in the offices of John Hicks in Dorchester, he was sent to St. Juliot to work on the restoration of the parish church and was escorted around the Boscastle-Tintagel-Penpenthy area by Emma Lavinia Gifford, sister-in-law of the rector of St. Juliot. Hardy made frequent trips between Dorchester and St. Juliot, especially because of his interest in Miss Gifford, who was later to become his wife, and he spent almost all of August 1870 in Cornwall. "Often we walked to Boscastle Harbour," he wrote, "down the beautiful Valency Valley, where we had to jump over stones . . . to come out on great wide spaces . . . with a sparkling little brook . . . in which we once [August 19] lost a tiny picnic tumbler, and there it is to this day no doubt." This is the incident referred to first in "Under the Waterfall" and later in "Where the Picnic Was." "At Castle Boterel," which Hardy wrote after revisiting Cornwall in 1916, some four years after the death of his wife, reflects his intense emotion at the knowledge that

> Primaeval rocks form the road's steep border,
>   And much have they faced there, first and last,
> Of the transitory in Earth's long order;
>   But what they record in colour and cast
>   Is—that we two passed.

Hardy made the most extensive use of Castle Boterel in *A Pair of Blue Eyes;* most notable, perhaps, is the "One enormous sea-bord cliff," which he never specified. However, the cliff, the one from which Elfride Swancourt rescues Henry Knight by making a rope from her petticoats and which Hardy describes as "Grimness . . . in every feature, and to its very bowels the inimical shape was desolation," is undoubtedly the nearby Willapark Point. It matches the author's description perfectly:

> The crest of this terrible natural facade passed among the neighbouring inhabitants as being seven hundred feet above the water it overhung. It had been proved by actual measurement to be not a foot less than six hundred and fifty.

And, as Hardy notes, this cliff has a peculiar feature: "sheer perpendicularity from the half-tide level." The bay Hardy calls "Targen Bay, near West Endelstow," is modeled on Pentargen Cove here.

One other author has made use of Boscastle, but under its own name. H. G. Wells has Isbister stay here in *When the Sleeper Wakes;* it is here that the children stop and stare at him and here that he exchanges greetings with the boatman.

BOSCOMBE, Wiltshire (pop. 81) A small village 4 miles southeast of Amesbury and 6 miles northeast of Salisbury, Boscombe has an especially fine Perpendicular church containing a magnificent three-tier Jacobean pulpit with a tester. From 1591 to 1595 Richard Hooker was the vicar here; he had requested a country benefice so that he could investigate "the general principles involved in the position of the church of England. . . ." It was here that he began his massive treatise *Of the Lawes of Ecclesiasticall Politie;* the first four books, which appeared in 1594, were written in Boscombe. Hooker was responsible for the building of the north transept of the church in Boscombe before he received the living of Bishopsbourne, Kent, in 1595.

BOSHAM, Sussex (pop. 1,558) On a tiny peninsula between two tidal creeks, Bosham (pronounced "boz' zam") is 3½ miles west of Chichester. A village of soft-colored cottages, it has a Saxon church whose chancel arch rises from Roman-column bases that may have come from an early basilica. Roman tiles and bricks have been built into the walls of the church; the church itself appears to have been placed on the site of an early monastery founded by the Irish monk Dicul. The church here appears in the Bayeux Tapestry; it shows Harold, a hawk on his wrist, on his way to mass at the church before his voyage. By the steps to the crypt in the church is an old tomb where Herbert of Bosham is buried; he was Thomas à Becket's secretary, and if tradition is correct, he saw the saintly Archbishop murdered. Alfred, Lord Tennyson refers to the man and the village in his play *Becket.*

A modern association exists with Dylan Thomas. In 1944, when the Germans again began bombing London, Thomas brought his wife Caitlin and their baby to a cottage near here. They remained three months, although the poet hated the village intensely and went off to London at every opportunity. There was an especially revolting earth closet at the lower end of their garden, with a large rat population; even so, Thomas said the rats at the bottom did not annoy him half as much as the magpies halfway up. Later Thomas wrote:

> The Sussex months were beastly. When it wasn't wet, I was. Aeroplanes grazed the roofs, bombs came by night, police by day, there were furies at the bottom of my garden, with bayonets, and a floating dock like a kidney outside the window, and Canadians in the bushes, and Americans in the hair; it was a damned banned area altogether. They worshipped dogs there, too, and when a pom was born in one house the woman put out the Union Jack.

He kept pretty much to his studio on Monresa Road during his ordeal and then left here for a house near Beaconsfield.

BOSLEY, Cheshire (pop. 361) Set in the Cheshire hills 6 miles south of Macclesfield, Bosley is attractively dominated by its lakelike reservoir. This village is thought to have been the home of Raphael Holinshed, whose *Chronicles* William Shakespeare used. The evidence, though, is slight and is based on the known fact that a Holinshed family, thought to be that of the chronicler's uncle, resided here.

BOSTON, Lincolnshire (pop. 23,020) Boston, deep in the Lincolnshire Fens, is perhaps the second-best-known town in the county, and its church, the "Boston Stump," is one of England's most notable. An ancient town on the Witham River, it was a flourishing seaport as early as the 13th century. The name Boston is a contracted form of Botolph's Town, but very little is known of the association between that Saxon saint and the town other than that the town grew up around St. Botolph's Church, now called the Stump. The tower of the Church of St. Botolph is its

BOSTON St. Botolph's Church, whose tall tower is known throughout the Fens as the Boston Stump, contains a commemorative window to Anne Bradstreet and Jean Ingelow, both natives of the town.

pride; 272½ feet high, it has an octagonal lantern that has served for centuries as a guide for travelers. The tower foundations are 36 feet deep, and the tower walls are richly paneled.

Many old buildings survive here, most of them on the east side of the river; South Street contains the 15th-century hall of the Guild of St. Mary, which has retained the original glass in the stone-mullioned window of the west front. The hall is also of especial note for its iron-grated cells that once held William Brewster, William Bradford, and others who were to become the Pilgrim Fathers. Fydell House, built in 1726, belongs to the Boston Preservation Trust and has become the home of Pilgrim College, an adult education branch of the University of Nottingham; one room has been set aside for the use of visitors from Boston, Massachusetts. Boston has a series of noteworthy bridges, especially the oldest, the Grand Sluice Bridge, which was built in the 1760s.

Michael Drayton writes of Boston and its river in the twenty-fifth song of *Poly-Olbion:*

Delicious *Wytham* leads to holy *Botulphs* Towne,
Where proudly she puts in amongst the great resort,
That their appearance make in *Neptunes* watry Court.

In *A Tour thro' the Whole Island of Great Britain* Daniel Defoe is more deeply interested in the church:

Here we first saw *Boston,* a handsome well-built Sea Port Town, at the Mouth of the River *Wittham.* The Tower of this Church is, without question, the largest and highest in *England;* and, as it stands in a Country, which (they say) has no Bottom, nothing is more strange, than that they should find a Foundation for so noble and lofty a Structure; it has no Ornament, Spire, or Pinnacle

on the Top, but it is so very high, that few Spires in *England* can match it, and is not only beautiful by Land, but is very useful at Sea to guide Pilots into that Port, and even into the Mouth of the River *Ouse.* . . .

In 1830 William Cobbett offered a rather astonishing comment on the name of the town in his *Rural Rides:*

Boston (*bos* is Latin for *ox*) though not above a fourth or fifth part of the size of its *daughter* in New England, which got its name, I dare say, from some persecuted native of this place, who had quitted England and all her wealth . . . is, nevertheless, a very fine town. . . .

He continues, in his normal haranguing fashion, about the church:

The great pride and glory of the Bostonians is *their church* which is . . . both a landmark and a sea-mark. To describe the richness, the magnificence, the symmetry, the exquisite beauty of this pile is wholly out of my power. It is impossible to look at it without feeling, first, admiration and reverence and gratitude to the memory of our fathers who reared it; and next, indignation at those who do believe, that when this pile was reared the age was *dark,* the people rude and ignorant, and the country *destitute of wealth* and *thinly peopled.*

John Foxe, author of *The Book of Martyrs,* was born here in 1516; his birthplace appears to have been in the marketplace, quite possibly on the site presently occupied by the Rum Puncheon Inn. Much more is not known, and the statement that his early education took place here is debated. A second native of Boston, Jean Ingelow, known both as a poet and as a novelist, was born here on March 17, 1820; the house on South Square where she was born burned down in 1823, and her father, a banker, moved his business next door to the house now known as Ingelow House. Her father's bankruptcy a few years later caused the family to move. A great deal of Jean Ingelow's poetry is imbued with a sense of the Fenland, and even though she is little read now, her "High Tide on the Coast of Lincolnshire" is remembered. This poem relates the storm and flood of 1571, when Boston and the coastal area were devastated. The Boston bells sounded the warning:

The old Mayor climbed the belfry tower,
The ringers rang by two, by three;
"Pull, if ye never pulled before;
Good ringers, pull your best," quoth he.
"Play uppe, play uppe, O Boston bells!
Play all your changes, all your swells,
Play uppe 'The Brides of Enderby.'"

There was no "Brides of Enderby," and a tune by that name was later composed.

Two final associations here concern the poet Anne Bradstreet and her husband, who emigrated to Massachusetts in 1630 on the *Arabella* from Boston, and John Clare, the poet, who visited here in September 1828 at the request of Henry Brooke of the Boston *Gazette.*

BOTALLACK, Cornwall   Two miles north of St. Just-in-Penwith, in westernmost Cornwall, is the locality known as Botallack Head, at one time one of the greatest copper- and tin-producing areas in England. From 1721 until the late 19th century the mines were worked extensively seven days a week. The mine here, 1,200 feet deep, ran under the sea for a third of a mile.

In the summer of 1850 Wilkie Collins, on holiday in western Cornwall, descended this mine, going down the steep vertical ladders in miner's garb provided by the company, a suit several sizes too large because of Collins's 5-foot 6-inch frame. Collins, who actually went under the sea, was impressed by the mysterious sounds:

> At last, the Miner speaks again, and tells us that what we hear is the sound of the surf lashing the rocks a hundred and twenty feet above us, and of the waves that are breaking on the beach beyond. The tide is now at the flow, and the sea is in no extraordinary state of agitation: so the sound is low and distant. . . . But, when storms are at their height, when the ocean hurls mountain after mountain of water on the cliffs, then the noise is terrific; the roaring heard down here in the mine is so inexpressibly fierce and awful, that the boldest men at work are afraid to continue their labour.

BOTLEY, Hampshire (pop. 1,166) The navigable Hamble River rises north of Botley, a red-brick market town with a few old houses of interest on the main street, known primarily as the one-time home of William Cobbett, author of *Rural Rides*. Not exactly the most popular of men, he lived in a house now in the grounds of Botley Hill from 1804 to 1817, and his residence here was punctuated with the same sort of difficulties experienced elsewhere. He began publication of a weekly, the *Political Register*, in 1802, and by 1804 settled in Botley, where he carried out farm experiments and continued his writing, which included attacks on various established institutions. In 1810, he was again in trouble after publishing an article that criticized the practice of flogging in the Army. Tried and found guilty, he was sentenced to two years' imprisonment and a fine of £1,000. His two-year absence from Botley pleased at least one resident, the Rev. Richard Baker, whom Cobbett later called "the Botley Parson" and quarreled with heatedly and consistently. In *Rural Rides* there are a number of references to the Reverend Mr. Baker, including one following Cobbett's autumn 1826 ride through the village:

> I had not seen "the Botley Parson" for several years, and I wished to have a look at him now, but could not get sight of him, though we rode close before his house, at much about his breakfast time and though we gave him the strongest of invitation that could be expressed by hallooing, and by the cracking of whips.

After his absence Cobbett resettled in Botley, where he remained until 1817, when the Habeas Corpus Act was suspended. Rather shrewdly guessing that this would mean his reimprisonment, he left again for the United States for a two-year stay; when he returned to England, he lived in Surrey. A modern memorial to Cobbett on the main street of Botley was erected by the Hampshire members of the Institute of Journalists.

BOUGHTON MALHERBE, Kent (pop. 366) Appropriately termed a "forgotten village" by many geographers and topographers, Boughton Malherbe is set on a ridge of hills at the edge of the Kentish Weald 8 miles southwest of Maidstone. The hamlet, situated in a virtual cul-de-sac, is rarely visited. The family seat Boughton Hall (Bocton Hall in the old spelling) was the birthplace in 1568 of the diplomat Sir Henry Wotton, author of "The Character of a Happy Life," in *Reliquiae Wottonianae* (posthumously printed in 1651), and of the famous definition of an ambassador as one who is "an honest man, sent abroad to lie for the good of his country." In the introduction to his biography of Wotton, Isaak Walton describes Boughton Hall and its location:

> . . . an ancient and goodly structure, beautifying, and being beautified by the Parish Church of Bocton Malherbe adjoyning unto it; and both seated within a fair Park of the Wottons, on the brow of such a Hill, as gives the advantage of a large Prospect, and of equal pleasure to all Beholders.

BOULGE, Suffolk (pop. 76) In crowded Great Britain the citizens of Boulge, 3½ miles from Woodbridge, are fortunate in being spread over 545 acres of a largely rural area of the central plateau of Suffolk. The plateau was once heavily forested, but since the Middle Ages the woodlands, having steadily given way to agriculture, sometimes appear bleak. In 1835 Boulge Hall (demolished in 1956) was inhabited by the FitzGerald family, and for three years it was the home of Edward FitzGerald. In 1838 he removed himself to Boulge Cottage, a two-room building at the gates to Boulge Park, where he remained until 1853, when he returned to Woodbridge. FitzGerald wished to establish his own life tempo; one of his rooms functioned as a sitting room, generally in a state of complete disorder with a barrel of beer in one corner, and the other served as the bedroom. He began his work on the *Rubáiyát* here. Thomas Carlyle was one of FitzGerald's guests here in 1848, but FitzGerald found the visits trying because of Carlyle's gloominess and destructive wit. He often commented that he became "quite impatient" because of Carlyle's mental set and even wrote to a friend, "I really know not if I can stand another visit without telling him so." But they remained friends until death. The stables, which are still intact, contain Old Nelly, the clock whose chimes the poet called "lugubrious"; the clock is still in use. FitzGerald and his family attended the Church of St. Michael and the Archangels here; the church escaped Cromwellian destruction, and when FitzGerald knew it, the ceiling was "of a fine blue sprinkled with golden stars," and the internal roof supports were finely carved angels.

FitzGerald died on the night of June 13–14, 1883, in the rectory at Merton, Norfolk, on a visit to George Crabbe, the poet's grandson; FitzGerald had been working on his *Readings from Crabbe* and paid this visit to the Reverend Mr. Crabbe as a "loving duty." His body was brought here for burial in the churchyard; his grave, marked with a flat granite stone carved with a cross fleury, has on it a rosebush that is always noted as an offspring of the rosebush on Omar Khayyám's grave in Nishapur (Neyshabur). The story is that William Simpson, an artist and traveler, visited Omar Khayyám's grave and brought back the hips from which the bush on FitzGerald's grave was raised; the rosebush was planted on October 7, 1893, and replanted in 1932. However, Omar Khayyám's grave is alleged never to have had a rosebush on it. The stone on the grave, by FitzGerald's request, has inscribed on it, "It is He that hath made us, and not we ourselves."

Local lore strongly maintains the tradition of an Edward FitzGerald ghost, a bald-headed, tall figure of "sad though severe aspect" that can be seen walking on the lanes and across the field late at night.

BOURNE, Lincolnshire (pop. 4,889) To the east is fenland; to the west, wooded uplands; and Bourne has been settled at least since Roman times, when Car Dyke, 56 miles long, drained the hills and kept the low fenlands from flooding. The town, which was a Saxon stronghold under Morcar, Lord of Bourne, who was killed by the Danes at Threekingham in 870, gained importance throughout the Norman period, and an Augustinian abbey was founded here in 1138 either by Baldwin FitzGilbert or by Hugh de Wake. For a small place, Bourne has a number of noteworthy buildings, including the 17th-century Red Hall, the Elizabethan grammar school (founded 1603), and the Bull Inn, once a home and the birthplace of William Cecil, Lord Burghley.

Bourne was also the birthplace of the early medieval poet Robert Mannyng (Robert de Brunne) around 1279; what little is known of his life derives from his writings. A Gilbertine monk at Sempringham Priory, 6 miles north of Bourne, he began *Handlyng Synne* in 1303 by his own account; because he had to be twenty-four years old to enter the house, he must have been born by 1279 and not in 1283, as is usually stated. While Mannyng never wrote anything original, his *Handlyng Synne* is of importance because of its 14th-century social commentary and its influence in standardizing the English language.

Also associated with Bourne is Hereward the Wake (fl. 1070), who, legend says, was born here and from whom the Norman Wakes (who held the castle here) claimed descent. Hereward and a band of men joined a group of Danes and sacked Peterborough Abbey; the *Laud Chronicle* in the *Anglo-Saxon Chronicle* recorded the event under 1070:

Then, in this same year, king Swein came into the Humber from Denmark.... Englishmen from all the fenlands came to meet them, thinking that they were sure to conquer the whole land. Then the monks of Peterborough heard it said that their own men, namely Hereward and his band, wished to plunder the monastery, because they had heard it said that the king had given the abbacy to a French abbot called Turold, and that he was a very ferocious man....

Hereward and his men established themselves on the Isle of Ely, where King William attacked:

The outlaws surrendered to him, namely bishop Aethelwine and earl Morcar and all their followers, except Hereward alone and all who wished to follow him; and he courageously led their escape.

Charles Kingsley wrote of the Anglo-Saxon patriot in *Hereward the Wake* and made Bourne part of the setting of the story:

A pleasant place and a rich is Bourne now; and a pleasant place and rich must it have been in the old Anglo-Danish times, when the hall of Leofric, the great Earl of Mercia, stood where the Wakes' feudal castle stood in after years. To the south and west stretched, as now, the illimitable flat of fen, with the spires of Crowland gleaming bright between high trees upon the southern horizon; and to the north, from the very edge of the town fields, rose the great Bruneswald, the forest of oak, and ash, and elm which still covers many miles of Lincolnshire, as Bourne Wood, Grimsthorpe Park, and parks and woodlands without number. To the south-west it joined the great forest of Rockingham, in Northamptonshire. To the west it all but marched with Charnwood Forest in Leicestershire, and to the north-west with the great Sherwood, which covered Nottinghamshire, and reached over the borders of Yorkshire.

BOURNEMOUTH, Hampshire (pop. 154,000) Facing Poole Bay, Bournemouth is a very large town: the town proper covers more than 12,000 acres, of which more than 2,000 are parks and gardens. Looking at the city today, devoted as it is to the vacationer with every sort of entertainment, it is difficult if not impossible to realize that less than 200 years ago this was a wilderness of worthless common land. In the late 18th century Bournemouth became a very popular bathing resort, the rival of Bath, though it never reached the peak of fashion of the Somerset spa. As a popular watering place, Bournemouth has had its share of literary associations, with both writers and their works.

Thomas Hardy and his wife settled here for a short time in July 1875, and Hardy's reaction was to call the town a "Mediterranean lounging-place on the English Channel." A late poem, "We Sat at the Window" (1917), is a record of July 15, 1875, "when the rain came down." Bournemouth becomes Sandbourne in *The Hand of Ethelberta, Jude the Obscure, The Well-Beloved,* "A Tragedy of Two Ambitions" (*Life's Little Ironies*), and *Tess of the D'Urbervilles.* The description of Sandbourne in this last work is almost literal: "This fashionable watering-place, with its eastern and western stations, its piers, its groves of pines, its promenades, and its covered gardens, was ... like a fairy place suddenly created by the stroke of a wand, and allowed to get a little dusty." The Herons, the lodging house to which Angel traces Tess and in which the great tragedy of the novel occurs, is unidentifiable. What Hardy terms Sandbourne Moor in *The Hand of Ethelberta* is Poor's Common, a marshy heathlike meadow outside Bournemouth, which the author brings nearer to the town. On the moor beside a large pool stood "The Weir House," Hardy's "little square building not much larger inside than the Lord Mayor's coach." Upper Street is the location of Christopher Julian's house, and Wyndway House is "a country seat," located "three or four miles out of the town" and "overlooking a wide sheet of the sea." The description is not unlike that of nearby Upton House, just west of the town.

Robert Louis Stevenson lived in Bournemouth from 1884 to August 1887 and first lived in lodgings on the West Cliff. In the following spring he bought Sea View, a retired naval officer's villa, "secluded on the cliffs of Westbourne"; the place was perched on the brink of Alum Chine (on the present Alum Chine Road) with an acre of garden between the house and the cliff face. Stevenson stocked the dovecote, renamed the house Skerryvore, and placed a model lighthouse at the street entrance. Stevenson and his wife became close friends of Sir Percy Shelley, the son of Percy Bysshe Shelley, and his wife. From here Stevenson delivered "Markheim," *A Child's Garden of Verses, Kidnapped,* and *The Strange Case of Dr. Jek-*

yll and Mr. Hyde to his publishers. It is said he wrote *Dr. Jekyll and Mr. Hyde* in three days. After hearing his wife's criticism, he destroyed the manuscript, only to rewrite the novel immediately. W. E. Henley and his wife visited the Stevensons here shortly after their arrival and later were frequent guests at Skerryvore. Henry James was here in 1886, when he brought his sister down to regain her health; calling at the Stevensons' residence, James was mistaken by a servant for a tradesman who had come to apologize for an omission of part of a grocery order. The error was apparently a stiff blow to James's ego, but he stayed on. Stevenson and his family lived in Bournemouth for three years before embarking on a second trip to the United States. Skerryvore was destroyed in an air raid in 1940, but a memorial garden has been laid out on the site of the house.

It was in Bournemouth that Rupert Brooke discovered the beauty of poetry. His grandfather, formerly the rector of Bath, had retired to Granchester Dene, a house on Littledown Road about a quarter of a mile from the railway station. On holiday here in 1896 Brooke discovered Robert Browning's poetry, which, as he later recalled, was something other than nursery rhymes. Brooke spent many of his holidays in Bournemouth, which he found an especially conducive environment for reading heavy or new works, *De Profundis* in 1905 and a serious study of Baudelaire in 1906. John Galsworthy received part of his early education in Bournemouth at a school run by a Dr. Breckenbury; he arrived here in 1876 and remained until 1881, when he went to Harrow, Middlesex. While in school Galsworthy attended St. Swithun's Church and sang in the choir.

Mary Shelley, Percy Bysshe Shelley's second wife, was buried in the graveyard at St. Peter's Church in 1851; Sir Percy Shelley was buried in his mother's grave in 1889. After Percy Bysshe Shelley drowned near Spezia in Italy on July 8, 1822, his body was cremated and the ashes buried in the Protestant Cemetery in Rome. His heart was snatched from the flames by Trelawney before it was consumed (Leigh Hunt and Trelawney both describe the incident) and eventually was brought back here and interred in his son's grave. William Godwin and his wife Mary Wollstonecraft Godwin, the parents of Shelley's second wife, also are buried here; their graves were moved to Bournemouth from Old St. Pancras's churchyard in London in 1851 because of railway construction.

Finally, Bournemouth was the birthplace, in 1886, of the novelist (Marguerite) Radclyffe Hall, whose novel *The Well of Loneliness* (1928) created a scandal because of its treatment of lesbianism.

George William Russell, who wrote as "AE," spent his last years here, where he died on July 17, 1935.

BOURTON-ON-THE-HILL, Gloucestershire (pop. 363) A picture-book Cotswold village of bow-windowed stone cottages with terraced gardens, Bourton-on-the-Hill is 4½ miles north of Stow-on-the-Wold. Standing high on the hillside is a fine church dating in part to the 11th century. It preserves a number of early parish registers, one of which is endorsed with Sir Thomas Overbury's signature. Remembered for *Sir*

Thomas Overbury . . . New Newes and Divers More Characters as well as for his excruciating death in the Tower of London, Sir Thomas spent a great deal of his early life at the family home here.

BOWES, Yorkshire (pop. 655) High up in the bleak area of Stainmore, cut by an Ice Age glacier and left barren and remote, is the village of Bowes. Stainmore is a strategic area: the Romans cut a road to connect Brough, Westmorland, with their camp Lavatrae at Bowes; the Scots used the pass in many of their raids; and the modern motorist is provided with a good east-west route.

Bowes is especially infamous in literature as the result of a visit to the thriving 19th-century community (population, more than 2,000) by Charles Dickens in 1838; he came to the Unicorn Inn here from Barnard Castle, County Durham, with his illustrator, Phiz (Hablot Knight Browne). This was one of his northern Yorkshire stops "to see a schoolmaster or two." He visited William Shaw's Academy on the western extremity of town and had the door shut in his face. This rebuff, along with a visit to the local churchyard, where, as he wrote later, "The first gravestone I stumbled on . . . was over a boy who had died suddenly. I suppose his heart broke. He died in this wretched place, and I think his ghost put Smike into my mind on the spot." Shaw's Academy is, of course, Do-the-boys Hall in *Nicholas Nickleby,* and Bowes itself is "the delightful village of Dotheboys." The hall still looks "long and cold," and the stable and barn are still there. This is the school where a number of boys went blind from untreated ophthalmia; as the symptoms appeared, each child was placed in a cold stone washhouse near the desolate pump in the cobbled courtyard, which Dickens describes as the place where the boys performed their morning ablutions. Shaw was tried before a court of common pleas in two cases of blindness, found guilty in both instances, and fined £300 each time. Ruined by the publication of *Nicholas Nickleby,* Shaw closed down the school shortly after the novel appeared; Dickens asserted that Shaw was not Squeers, that "Mr. Squeers is the representative of a class and not an individual," but his protestations were mild and his purpose was served.

Hundreds of these unsavory north Yorkshire schools were forced to close as students were removed by their alarmed parents and guardians. The graves of Shaw and his wife are in the same graveyard as that of John Ashton Taylor, aged nineteen, the lad whose grave had made such an impression on Dickens. The local church has a commemorative window to William Shaw, placed there by Miss Bousfield, his granddaughter, at Whitsuntide, 1896, because she felt Shaw had been seriously maligned. It is often claimed locally that *Nicholas Nickleby* caused the ruin of the village, and its population dropped to fewer than 400 in 1850; however, it was the local people who first brought the academy to Dickens's attention; the community was overjoyed when the Bowes school was forced to close.

There is one other literary association in Bowes: the graveyard contains the graves of Rodger Wrightson and Martha Railton, the lovers whose death is related by David Mallet (Malloch) in the well-known ballad "Edwin and Emma." The entry in the parish register tells the story:

> He died in a Fever, and upon tolling his passing Bell she cry'd out, "My heart is broke," and in a Few hours expir'd purely thro' Love March 15, 1714.

The memorial stone was erected in 1848.

BOWNESS-ON-WINDERMERE, Westmorland (pop. 3,860)

Bowness is now usually combined with Windermere because both places are governed by the same urban council. Certainly the two communities are not visibly divided, although the center of Bowness is 1½ miles down the main road from Windermere. Situated on Lake Windermere with a good harbor, Bowness and the Bowness Inn were visited by John Keats in May 1818 on his way to Ambleside; here for dinner, he saw a man putting out in a small boat to fetch fish for the meal, and Keats accompanied him. Too many tourists, Keats claimed, were the reason for not staying over, and it is much the same today. Keats did ask a waiter here about William Wordsworth and was disgusted to find that the famous poet was electioneering on behalf of the Tories. Seven years later Storrs' Hall, which has been turned into a hotel, was the locale of the celebration of Sir Walter Scott's fifty-fourth birthday. John Gibson Lockhart, Scott's biographer and son-in-law, descries the event:

> The weather was as Elysian as the scenery. There were brilliant cavalcades through the woods in the mornings, and delicious boatings on the lake by moonlight; and the last day, "the Admiral of the Lake" presided over one of the most splendid regattas that ever enlivened Windermere. . . . The bards of the Lakes led the cheers that hailed Scott and Canning; and music and sunshine, flags, streamers, and gay dresses, the merry hum of voices, and the rapid splashing of innumerable oars, made up a dazzling mixture of sensations as the flotilla wound its way among the richly-foliaged islands, and along bays and promontories peopled with enthusiastic spectators.

Among the guests were William Wordsworth, Christopher North (John Wilson), Robert Southey, and George Canning, who was to become Prime Minister in 1827.

Wordsworth makes use of Bowness in his poetry, and Book II of *The Prelude* refers to the lake, the ferry here, and the inn:

> When summer came,
> Our pastime was, on bright half-holidays,
> To sweep along the plain of Windermere
> With rival oars; and the selected bourne
> Was now an Island musical with birds
> That sang and ceased not; now a Sister Isle
> Beneath the oaks' umbrageous covert, sown
> With lilies of the valley like a field;
> And now a third small Island, where survived
> In solitude the ruins of a shrine
> Once to Our Lady dedicate, and served
> Daily with chaunted rites.

It should also be noted that St. Martin's Church has often been claimed to be the one referred to in *The Excursion* as

> Not raised in nice proportions was the pile,
> But large and massy; for duration built:
> With pillars crowded, and the roof upheld

> By naked rafters intricately crossed,
> Like leafless under-boughs, in some thick grove,
> All withered by the depth of shade above.

The description, however, is far more appropriate to the church in Grasmere.

Other writers have visited Bowness, among them Harriet Martineau, who lived in nearby Ambleside; Ralph Waldo Emerson, who was disappointed in the natural scenery and claimed that he had seen better in Massachusetts; and Thomas De Quincey, who commented that the area was as one might expect "on Athos seen from Samothrace."

BOX HILL, Surrey

Rising 590 feet in the chalk downs and itself a down, Box Hill, 1½ miles northeast of Dorking, is one of the most popular scenic viewpoints in Surrey. John Evelyn came here on August 27, 1655, "to see those rare natural bowers, cabinets & shady walkes in the box-coppses; & went to view the *Swallow* famous for the diving of the river [Mole] of *Darking* [Dorking] there. . . ." The "swallows" of the Mole River at Box Hill are well known; at the foot of the hill the river contains numerous chalk holes through which the water disappears in summer, only to reappear about 3 miles downstream near Leatherhead. Evelyn also noted the evergreens here made it appear "to be summer all the winter." Some years later Daniel Defoe visited Box Hill and was outraged by the behavior of ladies and gentlemen from London, who, it seems, were supplied by an enterprising publican from the King's Head in Dorking. Others, even more puritan than Defoe, wrecked the improvised pub.

Box Hill is inextricably associated with George Meredith, who lived at Flint Cottage here from 1867 until his death in 1909. The cottage, situated a little way along the zigzag road at the bottom of the hill, is a small, square stone building, and the gardens and orchard, covering 3 acres, turn into a fir woodland that leads up the slopes. Meredith was a great walker and frequently was up at 5:30 A.M. to climb the down and enjoy "the fresh loveliness of the downs, the fields, the velvet shadows, sharp and thin, and the exquisite sky." His enjoyment of the walk frequently appears in his work:

> Happy, happy time, when the white star hovers
> Low over dim fields fresh with bloomy dew,
> Near the face of dawn, that draws athwart the darkness,
> Threading it with colour, like yewberries the yew.
> Thicker crowd the shades as the grave East deepens
> Glowing, and with crimson a lone cloud swells.

The Egoist, The Tragic Comedians, The Adventures of Harry Richmond, and *Diana of the Crossways* were all written here, and the publication of the last-named work in 1885 made Flint Cottage a place of literary pilgrimage. Earlier, the Meredith home was the scene of visits by many persons who later were to become famous writers themselves. Thomas Hardy, whose manuscript *The Poor Man and the Lady* Meredith had rejected in January 1869 for Chapman and Hall, often visited here, as did Robert Louis Stevenson from 1878 on. James Thomson, author of *The City of Dreadful Night,* was also a frequent guest.

In 1884 Meredith began having a great deal of

trouble walking, and the problem, *tabes dorsalis*, progressed slowly until about 1896 (following the breaking of a leg, which never healed properly), when he was confined to a wheelchair. The illness brought changes in Meredith's personality, and when Rudyard Kipling visited him in 1889, he was sickened and disillusioned by the "sulking child"; Kipling writes:

> He is full to a painful overflowing of elaborated epigrammatic speech which on the first fizz strikes one as deuced good. Five minutes later one cannot remember what on earth it was all about. And neither time, tide, Heaven nor Hell, nor the sanctities of five-o-clock tea seem to be able to stop that flow of talk. The raucous voice continues; the little old man balances himself on his toes like a Shanghai rooster to command attention, and that attention *must* be given or he sulks like a child.

Not everyone responded to him in this way. George Gissing, in whom Meredith had taken an interest from 1891 on, was often here and, in fact, virtually maintained a bedside vigil when the old poet was ill in 1898 and early 1899, but Meredith outlived Gissing.

Sir James Matthew Barrie, another of the young men who was encouraged by Meredith, repaid his debt with relatively consistent visits and was present for the celebration of Meredith's eightieth birthday. It was Barrie who brought Sir Arthur Conan Doyle here to meet Meredith in March 1892. Doyle returned in early 1893 from Aldeburgh, where he had been on a working holiday with Barrie, and found Meredith working in the summerhouse, a kind of Norwegian chalet. Meredith's "pestiferous pride," Doyle said, kept anyone from helping him walk and caused a great deal of anguish. Meredith persisted in climbing Box Hill and on this occasion fell on going up a steep path. Doyle, knowing how great the offense would be, offered no assistance and kept on walking. In the spring of 1896 Meredith met Alice Meynell, and a strong friendship began that lasted until his death on May 18, 1909. Meredith's ashes were buried in the Dorking Cemetery, where his wife had been buried in 1884, and commemorative services were held on the same day in Westminster Abbey.

BOXLEY, Kent (pop. 1,381) Near the village of Boxley, on the lower reaches of the Downs, 2 miles northeast of Maidstone, is a ruined Cistercian abbey, famous in medieval times for its Rood of Grace and for an image of St. Rumwold, the child saint. The Rood of Grace, an ingenious device, which Thomas Cromwell turned to his advantage and the Pope's disadvantage at the dissolution of the monasteries by displaying it in the Maidstone marketplace, was said to hold an image of Christ capable of movement and speech. It was discovered in 1538 that inside the rood were

> certain engines and old wire, with old rotten sticks in the back, which caused the eyes to move and stir in the head thereof, like unto a lively thing, and also the nether lip likewise to move as though it should speak, which was not a little strange to him and to others present.

It is possible that Boxley was the birthplace of John Lyly sometime between October 9, 1553, and October 8, 1554. Lyly states in *Euphues*, "I was born in

the Wylde of Kent," but the Weald applies to the whole valley between the North and South Downs and includes Tonbridge and Ashford, both of which are mentioned in *Mother Bombie*, as well as Maidstone. No parish information is extant in either Tonbridge or Ashford. The Maidstone Record Office, however, has recorded a dated lease for the manor of Boxley to one William Lylly, who may well have been the dramatist's father.

A second literary association is on surer ground. By 1841 Alfred, Lord Tennyson was living in the vicinity of nearby Park House, the home of the Lushingtons (Tennyson's sister and brother-in-law), and he was here through 1843, although he went off periodically on his "morose pilgrimages." Indeed, it is Park House that is portrayed at the opening of *The Princess:*

> . . . long we gazed, but satiated at length
> Came to the ruins. High-arch'd and ivy-claspt,
> Of finest Gothic lighter than a fire,
> Thro' one wide chasm of time and frost they gave
> The park, the crowd, the house; but all within
> The sward was trim as any garden lawn:
> And here we lit on Aunt Elizabeth,
> And Lilia with the rest, and lady friends
> From neighbour seats. . . .

Tennyson made frequent visits to his sister's home and in the summer of 1849 probably met Edward Lear, who was staying at Park House at the invitation of Frank Lushington.

BRACKNELL, Berkshire (pop. 49,050) On the edge of the Great Windsor Forest, Bracknell not long ago was a small village that mercifully had escaped the sprawl of Wokingham and Reading. Now Bracknell and Easthampstead have been amalgamated by the Development Corporation, and the goal is a community of 60,000 bound together by the Corporation's optimistic motto "Home, Industry, and Leisure." Old Bracknell had a few lovely old cottages, a 19th-century flint church, and a population of under 2,000. In July 1813, when Percy Bysshe Shelley rented High Elms, he fully intended to remain until the following spring; however, just as at many other times in his life, he was relatively unhappy and left after a few months for the Lake District and Windermere, which he also left promptly. Shelley, who had been here with his wife the first time, returned again by himself in 1814, when he stayed with the Bonville (De Boinville) family. It was then that Shelley is said to have attempted punting in a washerwoman's tub, unsuccessfully. Nevertheless, he found this a good spot for sailing his paper boats. Even on this return jaunt he was dissatisfied and wrote to Thomas Jefferson Hogg that he had fallen "into premature old age and exhaustion that renders me dead to everything."

BRADENHAM, Buckinghamshire (pop. 132) A valley village set among beech-clad hills 4 miles northwest of High Wycombe, Bradenham is signaled by an inn at the junction of the village road. Bradenham's church, which has two bells cast in 1300 and some of the earliest enameled (heraldic) glass in England, stands next to a 17th-century manor house that was once the property of Isaac D'Israeli and the boyhood home of his son Benjamin Disraeli. A year before the elder D'Israeli's death in 1848, Benjamin bought the nearby estate at Hughenden because he could not acquire Bradenham permanently. Disraeli's lifetime love of Buckinghamshire is obvious in a number of his works, and in *Endymion* Bradenham becomes Hurstley:

> At the foot of the Berkshire downs, and itself on a gentle elevation, there is an old hall with gable ends and lattice windows, standing in grounds which once were stately. . . . In front of the hall huge gates of iron, highly wrought, and bearing an ancient date as well as the shield of a noble house, opened on a village green, round which were clustered the cottages of the parish with only one exception, . . . the vicarage. . . . The church was contiguous to the hall, and had been raised by the lord on a portion of his domain. Behind the hall and its enclosure, the country was common land but picturesque.

Isaac D'Israeli, author himself of *Curiosities of Literature,* died here and is buried in the church, which has a simple memorial tablet on the north side of the chantry chancel.

BRADGATE PARK, Leicestershire (pop. 4) Only 5 miles northwest of the metropolitan area of Leicester, Bradgate Park and its hall, because they are situated in Charnwood Forest, have been able to maintain some of the open country atmosphere they must have had in the 16th century when the substantial manor was built. Even today one can walk across the bracken-covered hills and startle deer, rabbits, and other wildlife in this protected area. Bradgate Park was the birthplace of Lady Jane Grey, whom Roger Ascham visited in the summer of 1550 on his trip from Yorkshire to London to take up an appointment as secretary to Sir Richard Morison. In *The Scholemaster* Ascham describes how he found Lady Jane

> in her chamber, reading *Phaedon Platonis* in Greek, and that with as much delight as some gentleman would read a merry tale in Boccace. After salutation and duty done, with some other talk, I asked her why she would leese such pastime in the park. Smiling, she answered me, "I wiss, all their sport in the park is but a shadow to that pleasure I find in Plato. Alas! good folk, they never felt what true pleasure meant." "And how came you, madam," quoth I, "to this deep knowledge of pleasure[?] . . ." "I will tell you," quoth she, " . . . One of the greatest benefits that ever God gave me is that he sent me so sharp and severe parents, and so gentle a schoolmaster. For when I am in presence either of father or mother . . . [whatever I do must be as perfect] as God made the world; or else I am so sharply taunted, so cruelly threatened . . . that I think myself in hell, [but Mr. Elmer] teacheth me so gently, so pleasantly, with such fair allurements to learning, that I think all the time nothing whiles I am with him. . . . And thus my book hath been so much my pleasure. . . ."

BRADLEY, Derbyshire (pop. 241) Situated 2 miles east of Ashbourne, Bradley is in an area of winding lanes and lovely woodlands. The village is clustered about the old church and hall, which was converted from stables. This was the home of Dr. Samuel Johnson's Mrs. Meynell; he frequently came here from Ashbourne to visit her and her daughters when he was staying with his old schoolfellow Dr. John Taylor. Mrs. Meynell, as their correspondence indicates, was a great source of encouragement to Johnson.

BRAINTREE, Essex (pop. 20,970) Braintree, located on the main Roman road from Camulodunum (Colchester) to Verulamium (St. Albans), seems to have profited from its situation, since the town was important for its wool industry by 1500. After the wool trade declined, the community turned to silk, which is still an important local industry. Because of Braintree's lucrative trade the living here was rather highly coveted, and the post was even more desirable in that the vicar was allowed to serve *in absentia.* On September 26, 1537, Nicholas Udall, later famous as the author of *Ralph Roister Doister,* became vicar here. No evidence supports the belief that he visited his new parish, and, in fact, he was permitted to serve *in absentia,* for a royal dispensation in 1538 relieved him of the duty of residence.

Sometime in the autumn of 1454 Sir Thomas Malory was in lodgings here with a man named John Aleyn; Malory later took part in a series of house break-ins with Aleyn and was eventually apprehended and imprisoned in the castle at Colchester.

BRAMPTON, Cumberland (pop. 2,590) A town almost wholly built of sandstone, Brampton is set in the farmlands of the border area 9 miles northeast of Carlisle. Close by are the Roman wall (a few miles to the north) and Talkin Tarn and the Written Rock; the stone, more than 50 feet above the water, has a badly weathered inscription commemorating a 3d-century legionnaire. Alfred, Lord Tennyson came here to see the stone and was impressed by the pathetic reminder of the standard-bearer of the once-proud legion. He incorporates this into his story of "Gareth and Lynette" in *Idylls of the King:*

> Anon they past a narrow comb wherein
> Were slabs of rock with figures, knights on horse
> Sculptured, and deckt in slowly-waning hues.
> "Sir Knave, my knight, a hermit once was here,
> Whose holy hand hath fashioned on the rock
> The war of Time against the soul of man.
> And yon four fools have sucked their allegory
> From these damp walls, and taken but the form.
> Know ye not these?" and Gareth lookt and read—
> In letters like to those the vexillary
> Hath left crag-carven o'er the streaming Gelt—
> "PHOSPHORUS," then "MERIDIES"—
> "HESPERUS"—
> "NOX"—"MORS."

BRAMPTON, Huntingdonshire (pop. 3,068) Once a small, typically Huntingdonshire village, Brampton is well on its way to becoming a part of Huntingdon itself, 2 miles to the northeast. In recent years housing estates have sprung up on two sides, and the Royal Air Force has built a headquarters on a third side. Just outside the village, Hinchingbrooke House, the only proper stately home in the shire and now a sixth-form comprehensive school, is on the site of a medieval Benedictine nunnery that came into the hands of Sir Richard Cromwell, great-grandfather of Oliver. In 1627, when Oliver Cromwell sold the house to pay off massive debts, it came into the possession of Sir Sidney Montagu, who married Paulina Pepys, great-aunt of Samuel Pepys. The house stayed in the family until Victor Montagu relinquished the title of Earl of Sandwich in 1964 and sold the estate to the county council.

It is quite possible that as a youth Pepys knew this house well since his own family home is near Bell End in Brampton. Pepys was not born here, although guidebooks often state that he was, but his father did own a dusky-red and yellow yeoman farmer's residence; the timbered section is most likely 16th-century, and the brick portion is Georgian. Pepys often visited the village after his days at Trinity Hall and Magdalene College, Cambridge, and with these visits are associated numerous stories, the most famous of which involves the Dutch invasion of 1667. Pepys is said to have gone into a panic when the Dutch ships came up the Medway and sent his wife and father from London to Brampton to hide his money in the garden. The pair carried out Pepys's wish but, contrary to his instructions, performed the ceremony in broad daylight. His annoyance was increased when he discovered that they had forgotten where they buried the funds.

BRANCEPETH, County Durham (pop. 355) Just 4½ miles southwest of Durham, Brancepeth has only one main street lined with ivy-covered cottages and gives the impression of not having joined the 20th century. The castle, once the seat of the Neville family, is where the 16th-century Rising in the North is said to have started; it resulted in the forfeit of the castle by the Nevilles. William Wordsworth's *The White Doe of Rylstone* refers to the rebellion and the castle:

> From every side came noisy swarms
> Of Peasants in their homely gear;
> And, mixed with these, to Brancepeth came
> Grave Gentry of estate and name,
> And Captains known for worth in arms,
> And prayed the Earls in self-defence
> To rise, and prove their innocence.

BRANDON, Suffolk (pop. 2,462) On the Little Ouse River 6 miles west of Thetford, Brandon has been the center of a flint industry since Neolithic times. To the northwest is Grime's Graves, once theorized to be the remains of Roman or Danish encampments but now known to be Neolithic flint mines dug to a depth of more than 40 feet. It is highly unlikely that Thomas Dekker, the 16th-century dramatist, ever visited the village, but he did use one of its most illustrious native sons for a prominent role in *The Shoemaker's Holiday*. This was Simon Eyre, one-time lord mayor of London and the builder of the Leadenhall, who was born here. Eyre appears in the play under his own name.

BRANTHAM, Suffolk (pop. 960) Brantham is just north of the Stour River, near Manningtree, in an area where willows, elms, and poplars live along the waterway paths and ditches. This is the country where John Constable was raised, and Brantham has one of two area churches which contain a Constable original. In the 1520s Roger Ascham, author of *The Scholemaster*, was placed in the house of Sir Anthony Wingfield to be educated and raised with Wingfield's sons either at Bridge House or at Brantham Hall; while evidence is insufficient, the latter is more likely. Ascham always retained the highest regard for Wingfield, and it was Sir Anthony who

taught him archery, Ascham's favorite recreation; indeed, it may be said that without Sir Anthony's patronage and interest in archery *Toxophilus* would never have been written. Ascham remained here until 1530, when at fifteen he went up to St. John's College, Cambridge.

BRANXTON, Northumberland (pop. 184) Just a few hundred yards south of the village of Branxton, near Coldstream, is the site of one of the bloodiest battles ever fought on English soil: the Battle of Flodden Field, in which from 10,000 to 16,000 English and Scots soldiers lost their lives on Friday, September 9, 1513. The battle began at four o'clock in the afternoon, and by nightfall Flodden was history. In the summer of 1513 King James IV decided to invade England and marched to the border with pipes playing and drums rolling. Demolishing the castles of Wark, Norham, and Etal, James set up his headquarters at Ford Castle until leaving for Flodden Field. The English forces, including the Stanley Archers, the Percys, and the Bishop of Durham's standing army, simply outfought the Scots, and the commemorative monument on Piper's Hill near the church, inscribed "To the brave of both nations," is traditionally held to mark the spot where James fell.

For the modern reader the real and the literary have become inextricably mixed because of Sir Walter Scott's *Marmion;* his descriptions make an unforgettable impression:

> From Flodden Ridge
> The Scots beheld the English host
> Leave Barmore-Wood, their evening post
> And heedful watched them as they crossed
> The Till by Twisel Bridge.

Scott has James rush down immediately to engage Surrey's forces under the cover of the smoke from his own camp, but in fact the distance from Flodden Hill to the Twizel Bridge is 4 miles; James merely moved to Branxton Hill. The well where Clare ministers to the dying Marmion is near Branxton Church and has become known as Marmion's Well:

> A little fountain cell
> Where water, clear as diamond spark
> In a stone basin fell. . . .

The well, which is moss-covered, has had a variation of the inscription from the poem cut into it:

> Drink weary pilgrim, drink, and stay
> Rest by the well of Sybil Grey.

Scott, who was in Branxton on at least three occasions, brought his family here after the great success of *Marmion.* A local innkeeper, whose business had increased, expressed his sincere gratitude to the poet and asked to signpost the pub Scott's Head. Scott refused, commenting that the flowing tankard on the sign was more appropriate. The innkeeper replied: "I would fain have some thing more connected with the book that has brought me so much good custom" and, producing a well-worn copy of *Marmion,* implored Scott to find him a motto from the poem. Scott opened to the death scene, read out "Drink, weary, pilgrim, drink, and pray/For the kind soul of Sybil Grey" and asked, "What more would you have? You need but strike out one letter in the first of these lines. . . ." To Scott's great delight on his next trip to Branxton, he saw on the inn the legend "Drink, weary pilgrim, drink and pay."

BRAY, Berkshire (pop. 2,428)   Just 1½ miles southeast of Maidenhead, on the Thames, is the village of Bray, an important riverside town known for more than three centuries as the home of the Vicar of Bray, usually said to be one Simon Aleyn, Canon of Windsor and vicar here from 1540 to 1588. He was a papist under Henry VIII, a Protestant under Edward VI, a papist under Mary, and a Protestant under Elizabeth. Thomas Fuller records Aleyn's reply when taxed with being a religious "turncoat and inconstant changling": "Not so neither; for if I changed my religion, I am sure I kept true to my principle; which is, to live and die the Vicar of Bray." The story eventually gave rise to many references, such as that in Robert Southey's *Common Place Book;* Aleyn's doctrine was simple:

> And this is law, that I'll maintain
> Until my dying day, Sir,
> That whatsoever king shall reign
> I'll still be the Vicar of Bray, Sir.

It now seems that Aleyn was not really the vicar's prototype since Simon Symonds became vicar in 1522 and appears to have died about 1551. If this is the case, the story cannot refer to Aleyn and leaves the door open for other claimants if, indeed, the song refers to any particular person.

BREDE, Sussex (pop. 951)   Perched on a spur of land just north of the Brede River, this village, 5 miles northeast of Battle, has a Norman to 16th-century church that houses a number of remarkable treasures, including a rare copy of the Vinegar Bible (an authorized version, printed in 1716–1717 at Oxford, that contains the headline "The Parable of the Vinegar" in place of "The Parable of the Vineyard" for Luke 20) and Jonathan Swift's canopied cradle.

Brede is also noted for its modern associations, the most unusual of which involves Stephen Crane, the American novelist and short-story writer, who moved to Brede Place from Oxted, Surrey, in 1899. The partly 14th-century house is a brick-and-stone manor house that overlooks the river valley. At the turn of the 20th century it was a rambling, decaying property, unpopular on account of superstition. Henry James disliked the bohemian ménage, but Joseph Conrad befriended the then-ill novelist. Parties were the order of the day, and the turn-of-the-century party here was characteristic of the Cranes in its excess. There was to be a play, a ball, and a running house party for the fifty guests, and the fact that proper sleeping space was not available made no difference. The guests all had to bring their own bedding, but an omnibus met them at the station in Hastings to transport them here in style. Lewis Hind, one of the guests, recalled that

> H. G. Wells . . . invented a game of racing on broom-sticks over the polished floor, which I think would have staggered the local gentry if they had turned up.

The play, presented at the village hall, concerned the Brede ghost, and Crane enlisted the aid of Conrad, Rider Haggard, Henry James, and George Gissing, among others, in writing it.

When most of the guests had retired after the ball, Crane was taken quite ill in front of the living-room fire; H. G. Wells was summoned; finding Crane in the midst of a tubercular hemorrhage, he rode off by bicycle in the rain to get a Dr. Skinner from Rye. Wells later wrote to Crane, "I'll bet an even halo that haemorrhages aren't the way you will take out of this terrestial tumult"; but he was wrong, and Crane died in the following June in the Black Forest from his illness.

Early in the 20th century when Sir James Matthew Barrie visited Brede, he heard the story of the Rev. J. W. Mahler, a pirate turned preacher, and of a black-mailer named Smith. Mahler became the basis of Captain Hook in *Peter Pan*, and Smith became Smee. Finally, the modern novelist Sheila Kaye-Smith spent most of her life here and in St. Leonard's-on-Sea.

BREDFIELD, Suffolk (pop. 325)   Situated on an unclassified road 3 miles north of Woodbridge in the lovely Deben Valley, Bredfield is associated mainly with Edward FitzGerald, who was born here in Bredfield House, a "stately old Jacobean mansion," on March 31, 1809; the house is often erroneously referred to as Bredfield Hall because of FitzGerald's autobiographical poem "Bredfield Hall." The seventh child of the marriage of first cousins, FitzGerald had the same surname as his mother; his father, John Purcell, in a shadow personally and financially, had taken his wife's name at the marriage. FitzGerald lived in Bredfield until 1825, when the family moved to Wherstead Lodge, near Ipswich. In 1821 the young boy was sent to the King Edward VI Grammar School in Bury St. Edmunds, where he stayed until going up to Trinity College, Cambridge, in 1826.

The grandson of the poet George Crabbe held the living here for a time when FitzGerald was living in a cottage on the grounds of nearby Boulge Hall, in Boulge, and the Bredfield rectory, named by Crabbe The Cobblery, was often the scene of visits from FitzGerald, whose lifelong devotion to the Crabbe family can be seen in his *Readings from Crabbe* (1882). It was during this period of FitzGerald's life that he frequently helped Caroline Crabbe teach school here and that he helped Lucy Barton, daughter of the Quaker poet Bernard Barton and FitzGerald's future wife, teach Sunday school. FitzGerald had edited a volume of Barton's poetry. The FitzGerald birthplace was so severely damaged by bombs during World War II that no attempt at restoration was made.

BREDON HILL, Worcestershire   The Avon River twists its way around the 961-foot Bredon Hill, located midway between Tewkesbury and Evesham. Crowning the hill is a folly from which there is a spectacular view of at least eight counties on a clear day. This is the hill celebrated in A. E. Housman's poem "Bredon Hill":

> In summertime on Bredon
>   The bells they sound so clear;
> Round both the shires they ring them
>   In steeples far and near,
>   A happy noise to hear.

BREDON HILL
Here of a Sunday morning
My love and I would lie,
And see the coloured counties,
And hear the larks so high
About us in the sky.
A. E. Housman

There is no evidence that the poet knew the hill, and, indeed, his reference in the fourth stanza to "the springing thyme" suggests that he did not, at least, know it well since that plant does not grow here.

BREMHILL, Wiltshire (pop. 937) The northwest Wiltshire countryside is rural and low-lying, and the villages are often built of Bath limestone, a substance widely used here before the industrial revolution. Situated 4 miles east of Chippenham, Bremhill, which has a fine 13th-century church with a tower said to contain Saxon work, was the home for forty-six years of William Lisle Bowles, who was given the living here in 1804. One of his many diversions with the sheep he permitted to wander in front of the terrace of the rectory was to tune their bells in fourths and fifths. A very hospitable man, he numbered among his many guests William Wordsworth, Charles Lamb, and Thomas Moore. Bowles wrote many of the epitaphs in the churchyard, and for the sundial there he wrote:

So passes silent o'er the dead thy shade,
Brief Time; and hour by hour and day by day
The pleasing pictures of the present fade
And like the summer vapour steal away.

BRENTFORD, Middlesex (pop. 62,020 with Chiswick) For centuries the northern and western suburbs of London were heath and wood and rich farmland, which attracted the fashionable rich for hunting and pleasure. Now flyovers, factories, and urban-renewal high rises are the order, and such towns as Brentford are difficult to find. An old market town at the influx into the Thames of the Brent River, it was once considered the county town of Middlesex, but since the redistricting in 1965 it is officially in London and is incorporated in the borough of Hounslow. The Romans occupied this area; Offa, King of the Mercians, held a church council here in A.D. 780; in 1016 Brentford got its first mention in the *Anglo-Saxon Chronicle* when Edmund Ironside defeated the Danes here; and in 1642 Royalist forces defeated the Parliamentarians here in the Battle of Brentford.

Only one important literary figure has lived in Brentford, but many have included the town in their writings. Sarah Trimmer, the author of numerous children's stories and virtually unknown today, came here after her marriage in 1762 and lived in Brentford for the rest of her life. She taught Sunday school at St. George's, the small church next to the waterworks and, indeed, was instrumental in the establishment of Sunday schools. (St. George's is now a musical museum.) She also founded a school for girls that is no longer a school. Mrs. Trimmer died here on December 15, 1810, and was buried in Ealing.

The literary uses of Brentford are diverse and interesting. One of the first occurs in William Shakespeare's *The Merry Wives of Windsor*. Falstaff, with Mistress Ford, is told for a second time by Mistress Page that Ford is again searching for Sir John. Refusing the basket device again, Falstaff is induced to put on a disguise:

Mrs. Ford. How might we disguise him?
Mrs. Page. Alas the day, I know not. There is no woman's gown big enough for him; otherwise he might put on a hat, a muffler, and a kerchief, and so escape.
Fal. Good hearts, devise something: any extremity rather than a mischief.
Mrs. Ford. My maid's aunt, the fat woman of Brentford, has a gown above.
Mrs. Page. On my word, it will serve him; she's as big as he is: and there's her thrummed hat, and her muffler too. Run up, Sir John.

In the quarto edition of the play the "fat woman of Brentford" is "My maid's aunt, Gillian of Brentford," and Gillian (or Julian, as it is sometimes stated) was presumably a famous witch.

Another reference to Brentford occurs in Ben Jonson's *The Alchemist* (1610). Subtle, the alchemist, comments:

My fine flitter-mouse,
My bird o' the night! We'll tickle it at the Pigeons. . . .

The Three Pigeons here was an inn held by John Lowin of the Globe Theatre and, undoubtedly, a fellow member with Shakespeare. Ben Jonson and many of his London acquaintances made this their rendezvous, and it would seem likely that Shakespeare also knew it.

Another dramatist was associated with this inn. George Peele with four companions set out with £5 to have a good time and to bring back the money intact. The story of their cheating and conning is set forth in the *Merry Conceited Jests of George Peele, Sometime a Student in Oxford,* and into that work comes this inn. The Three Pigeons, at the corner of the High Street and the Market Square, was demolished in the mid-19th century.

John Gay mentions one then-famous aspect of Brentford in "An Epistle to the Right Honourable the Earl of Burlington." Long known for its dirtiness and enormous number of public houses, the town was castigated when he wrote:

Three dusty Miles reach *Brandford's* tedious Town,
For dirty Streets, and white leg'd Chicken known. . . .

Not long after Gay stigmatized Brentford, James Thomson portrayed the town in no better light in "The Castle of Indolence":

Even so through *Brentford* Town, a Town of Mud,
An Herd of bristly Swine is prick'd along;
The filthy Beasts, that never chew the Cud,
Still grunt and squeak, and sing their troublous Song,
And oft they plunge themselves the Mire among. . . .

William Cowper takes up Brentford in *The Task* when writing of the settee:

So sit two kings of Brentford on one throne;
And so two citizens who take the air
Close pack'd and smiling, in a chaise and one.

The two kings sitting on one throne with one bouquet between them has no foundation and merely refers to the 1671 play *The Rehearsal* by George Villiers, 2d Duke of Buckingham. Another legendary king of Brentford occurs in a delightful ballad by William Makepeace Thackeray. After recounting the virtues and defects of his children—Tom is overcautious and miserly, and Edward is a spendthrift—the king concludes:

"Wherefore my lease and copyholds,
   My lands and tenements,
My parks, my farms, and orchards,
   My houses and my rents,
My Dutch stock and my Spanish stock,
   My five and three per cents.,

I leave to you my Thomas—
   ("What all?" poor Edward said,
"Well, well, I should have spent them,
   And Tom's a prudent head.")
I leave to you, my Thomas—
   To you IN TRUST for Ned.

Oliver Goldsmith uses Brentford in *The Citizen of the World*. This is the account of the race to be "run on the road from London to a village called Brentford, between a turnip-cart, a dust-cart, and a dung-cart: each of the owners condescending to mount and be his own driver."

Another author to include the town in his works is Thomas Hood, who sets the scene of "The Duel" here:

In Brentford town, of old renown,
   There lived a Mister Bray,
Who fell in love with Lucy Bell,
   And so did Mr. Clay.

The duel is set to occur:

Now all was ready for the foes,
   But when they took their stands,
Fear made them tremble so they found
   They both were shaking hands.

Said Mr. C. to Mr. B.,
   Here one of use may fall,
And like St. Paul's Cathedral now,
   Be doom'd to have a ball.

Charges are withdrawn, and because of a concern that no shots would be heard,

. . . up into the harmless air
   Their bullets they did send;
And may all other duels have
   That upshot in the end!

One final note regarding Brentford should be made. James Boswell records that he and Dr. Samuel Johnson were engaged in a discussion on the beauty of Glasgow:

I once reminded him that when Dr. Adam Smith was expatiating on the beauty of Glasgow, he had cut him short by saying, "Pray, Sir, have you ever seen Brentford?" and I took the liberty to add, "My dear Sir, surely that was *shocking*."—"Why, then, Sir, (he replied,) YOU have never seen Brentford."

BRERETON-CUM-SMETHWICK, Cheshire (pop. 506) Occasionally called Brereton Green, Brereton-cum-Smethwick, situated 3 miles northeast of Sandbach, is well known for Brereton Hall, one of the finest 16th-century buildings in the county. Now a girls' school, the house, with its ornate internal wood paneling, two octagonal towers, and parkland setting, stands next to a good 15th-century church with finely constructed arcades. Michael Drayton writes of the Croc River here in the eleventh song of *Poly-Olbion*:

. . . and at last, as hee approacheth neere,
Dane, *Whelock* drawes, then *Crock*, from that black ominous Mere,
Accounted one of those that Englands wonders make;
Of neighbours, *Black-mere* nam'd, of strangers, *Breretons-Lake*;
Whose property seemes farre from Reasons way to stand:
For, neere before his death that's owner of the Land,
Shee sends up stocks of trees, that on the top doe float;
By which the world her first did for a wonder note.

BRIDGE CASTERTON, Rutland An area 3 miles northwest of Stamford, Bridge Casterton with its rich, green undulating hills has much in common with the wolds of Leicestershire. In 1817 the Northamptonshire peasant poet John Clare came here to work as a limeburner after being unable to find employment in his native Helpston. He found the countryside here pleasant and commented:

There are some beautiful spots on its banks toward the little village of Tickencote southward, where the bank on the field side rises very stunt in some places from the edge of the river, and may, by a fancy used to a flat country, be easily imagined into mountains. The whole prospect is diversified by gently-swelling slopes and easy-swimming valleys.

BRIDGNORTH, Shropshire (pop. 5,141) All around Bridgnorth are good farming country, clear, sparkling brooks, and lovely small woodlands. So pastoral is the landscape that it is difficult to believe that the area is only 14 miles west of the industrial sprawl of Wolverhampton, itself on the western edge of the industrial heart of the Midlands. Bridgnorth, which is an ancient market town, sits on a sandstone ridge and is divided by the Severn into two parts, the Low Town and the High Town, which are connected by a bridge. The High Town is reached by the winding main street, a steep but short cliff railway (with a gradient of 2 in 3), or the Stoneways Steps, so steep as to be almost useless. It is small wonder that a castle was placed on the cliff in Norman times. Henry II later besieged the castle, but the structure appears to have survived until the Civil War, when it was placed in grave danger by the determined Parliamentary forces, which tunneled to the powder room and threatened to destroy the whole place. Only the tower remains; 17 degrees out of line (the Leaning Tower of Pisa leans only 5 degrees), it is perfectly safe and has been in this state for more than 800 years. The old town hall has window portraits of fourteen English monarchs and a scene depicting the meeting between Henry IV, Prince Hal, and Sir Walter Blount (Blunt), a meeting presented in Part I of William Shakespeare's *Henry IV*.

The collector of the materials in the notable *Reliques of Ancient English Poetry*, Thomas Percy, later Bishop Percy, was born here on April 13, 1729. The house in which he was born is the oldest house in Bridgnorth. Built in 1580, it is a superb example of Tudor timberwork and stands near the bridge in Cartway Friars Street. The three-story house has three gables and an inscription on the porch:

Except the Lord built the Ouse
The labourers thereof avail nothing.

The son of a grocer, Percy was educated at the grammar school here before going up to Christ Church, Oxford, in 1746. The family name as recorded here was spelled both Pearcy and Piercy, and when the bishop tried to establish descent from the Percys of Northumberland through Sir Henry Percy, 2d Earl (who was, in fact, unmarried), the spelling of the grocer's name proved too great a stumbling block. Notwithstanding this irremediable inconsistency, the bishop did adopt the Northumberland spelling.

BRIDLINGTON, Yorkshire (pop. 21,720) The coastline of the East Riding of Yorkshire changes almost daily as the North Sea hacks away at the clay cliffs; indeed, anywhere from 2 to 7 feet of coast disappear yearly. Although Bridlington, 31 miles north of Hull and called Burlington well into the 19th century, is a modern and popular seaside resort with all of the usual amusements, its Old Town is entirely different, with the Priory Church (founded by Henry I and approached through Bayle Gate) and numerous Georgian houses and shops lining the High Street. Indeed, the resort which Charlotte Brontë first visited in September 1839, when she joined Ellen Nussey on a holiday, was quite unlike the modern version. The two had originally planned to stay here, but Henry Nussey arranged for his sister and Miss Brontë to lodge with friends at nearby Easton Farm House. They walked the 2-mile distance to Burlington; it was the first time Charlotte Brontë had seen the sea. A month later, so vivid was the impression that she writes:

Have you forgotten the sea by this time, E.? . . . Or can you still see it, dark, blue, and green, and foam-white, and hear it roaring roughly when the wind is high, or rushing softly when it is calm. . . .

The second week here was spent in the resort town in cliffside lodgings. Miss Brontë made a second trip to the town in 1849 after the death of her sister Anne; here she worked on *Shirley*.

BRIDPORT, Dorset (pop. 5,909) The town of Bridport, while not a port, is located 1½ miles from the mouth of the Brit River; even so, until the 20th century its principal economic activities were related to the sea. The town has a decided Georgian air with wide streets and spacious pavements, and most of its buildings date from the 18th century. By the early 13th century Bridport was noted for its rope making, and nearly all the flax that went into the ropes, as well as into twine and fishing nets, was locally grown. John Leland, the Tudor antiquary, comments on Bridport in his *Itinerary* and, describing its industry, says: "At Bridporth be made good daggers." This industry is noted by other writers, apparently using Leland as their source, but in fact there is no dagger industry here. Indeed, the phrase "to be stabbed by a Bridport dagger," used for centuries, was a euphemism for being hanged with Bridport rope. Daniel Defoe visited the town and notes in *A Tour thro' the Whole Island of Great Britain* that he watched boats "all the way on the Shore fishing for *Mackerell*" and was amazed at the ease of the operation:

They fix one End of the Net to a Pole, set deep into the Sand, then the Net being in a Boat, they row right out into the Water some Length, then turn, and row parallel with the Shore, vering out the Net all the while, till they have let go all the Net, except the Line at the End, and then the Boat rows on Shore, when the Men haling the Net to the Shore at both Ends, bring to Shore with it such Fish, as they surrounded in the little Way they rowed; this, at that Time, proved to be an incredible Number, insomuch, that the Men could hardly draw them on Shore. . . .

Bridport is part of Thomas Hardy's Wessex under the name Port Bredy; it is mentioned in *Tess of the D'Urbervilles*, *The Mayor of Casterbridge*, *The Woodlanders*, and "The Withered Arm" (*Wessex Tales*). The town takes on an important role in "Fellow Townsmen" from *Wessex Tales*. George Barnet and Downe drive into town, "past the little townhall, the Black Bull, and onward"; Barnet puts up at the Black Bull on his return to his native town. St. Mary's Church is the scene of the marriage of Lucy Savile to Charles Downe. Barnet is a trustee of the Town Savings Bank, and Port Bredy is well described:

The harbour-road soon began to justify its name. A gap appeared in the rampart of the hills which shut out the sea, and on the left of the opening rose a vertical cliff, coloured a burning orange by the sunlight, the companion cliff on the right being livid in shade. Between these cliffs, like the Libyan bay which sheltered the shipwrecked Trojans, was a little haven, seemingly a beginning made by Nature herself of a perfect harbour, which appealed to the passer-by as only requiring a little human industry to finish it and make it famous, the ground on each side as far back as the daisied slopes that bounded the interior valley being a mere layer of blown sand. . . . There were but few houses here: a rough pier, a few boats, some stores, an inn, a residence or two, a ketch unloading in the harbour, were the chief features of the settlement.

The Harbour Inn is where they debate taking the bodies of Mrs. Downe and Mrs. Barnet after their recovery from the sea. Finally, the Brit River becomes the Bride Stream in "My Cicely" (*Wessex Poems*) and appears under its own name in *Tess of the D'Urbervilles*.

BRIGHTON, Sussex (pop. 188,935) Now a town of spectacular contrasts with Georgian and late Victorian houses coexisting with the extravaganza of such places as the Royal Pavilion, with modern antique shops made from old stone fishermen's cottages in the Lanes, and with the 14th-century Church of St.

Nicholas competing with the monumental Victorian Church of St. Bartholomew, Brighton was once a tiny fishing hamlet with a farming settlement located on the high ground behind. Thomas Babington Macaulay describes the old fishing village in *The History of England from the Accession of James II:*

> Brighton was described as a place which had once been thriving, which had possessed many small fishing barks, and which had, when at the height of prosperity, contained above two thousand inhabitants, but which was sinking fast into decay. The sea was gradually gaining on the buildings, which at length almost entirely disappeared. Ninety years ago the ruins of an old fort were to be seen lying among the pebbles and seaweed on the beach; and ancient men could still point out the traces of foundations on a spot where a street of more than a hundred huts had been swallowed up by the waves. So desolate was the place after this calamity, that the vicarage was thought scarcely worth having.

The village existed when William the Conqueror invaded England, and it was recorded in the Domesday Book (1086) as Bristelmenstune; at a recent count, at least forty-five Saxon and medieval variants of the name exist, from Bryghmeston and Brighthempston to Brighthelmstone, the last being the most frequent until the beginning of the 18th century, when Brighton became a common alternative form. Indeed, Brighton appears to have become the popular and proper form at the beginning of the 19th century.

Ancient history did not involve Brighton, and, in fact, Brighton was still small and poor as late as the 18th century, by Daniel Defoe's account of his visit here in 1724. He mentions two severe storms, in 1703 and 1705, that wreaked havoc on the coast. Writing in *A Tour thro' the Whole Island of Great Britain,* Defoe notes:

> ... we ride ... to *Bright Helmston,* commonly call'd *Bredhemston,* a Poor fishing Town, Old built, and on the very edge of the Sea....
>   The Sea is very unkind to this Town, and has by its continual Encroachments, so gain'd upon them, that in a little time more they might reasonably expect it would eat up the whole Town, above 100 Houses having been devoured by the Water in a few Years past; they are now obliged to get a Brief granted them, to beg Money all over *England,* to raise Banks against the Water; the Expence of which, the Brief expressly says, will be Eight Thousand Pounds; which if one were to look on the Town, would seem to be more than all the Houses in it are worth.

The nature of the village changed in the mid-18th century when Dr. Richard Russell, a practitioner of Lewes, pronounced the salt water efficacious in a Latin treatise in which he advised both internal and external use of the water. An English translation of the study appeared in 1752, and in 1755 bottled Brighthelmston Water could be obtained in London. Dr. Russell bought land here and surrounded himself with a group of fashionable hypochondriacs to whom he promised results.

The resort prospered on this small scale until the Prince of Wales, the famous "Prinny" and son of George III, visited it in 1783; his patronage was extended almost immediately, and the modern town was born. Within a few years he built himself a villa and had the first Royal Pavilion constructed. Later

BRIGHTON   Considered by William Hazlitt to be the result of the genius of architecture having "at once the dropsy and the megrims," the Royal Pavilion has been likened to a bunch of turnips and their tops (by William Cobbett), "some sort of Chinese stables" (by Sir Walter Scott), and the dome of St. Paul's which "had come to the sea and pupped" (by Sydney Smith). The Royal Pavilion, commissioned by the Prince of Wales after his visit in 1783 and furnished lavishly by him, caused Lord Byron to write:
> Shut up—no, not the King, but the Pavilion,
> Or else twill cost us all another million.

John Nash added an onion-shaped main dome, minarets, and pinnacles and thus fashioned one of the most uselessly extravagant pieces of architecture in the country. At once Brighton became the leading resort in England amid some derision, and it expanded dramatically; the original town was bounded by North, West and East Streets—remaining are the Lanes (narrow alleys where the fishermen's cottages were located) and the parish church dedicated to St. Nicholas. In the churchyard is a gravestone to Phoebe Hessel, one of the most famous women in English military history. Determined to be near her lover, she dressed as a man and served in the British Army for seventeen years and was bayoneted in the arm at the Battle of Fontenoy in 1745 before retiring to Brighton in the same year; she died here in 1821 at the age of 108. For her service she received a pension from the King, and for her help in the conviction of highway robbers, a place in the poetry of Alfred, Lord Tennyson. It was she who gathered the necessary information that convicted Rooke and Howell while on her rounds of the area villages selling fish; Tennyson's manuscript note includes the following information:

> They [the mail robbers] were gibbeted on the spot where the robbery was committed, and there is an affecting story with the body of Rooke. When the elements had caused the clothes and flesh to decay, his aged mother, night after night, in all weathers, and the more tempestuous the weather the more frequent the visits, made a sacred pilgrimage to the lonely spot on the Downs, and it was noticed that on her return she always brought something away with her in her apron. Upon being watched it

was discovered that the bones of the hanging man were the objects of her search, and as the wind and rain scattered them on the ground she conveyed them to her home. There she kept them, and, when the gibbet was stripped of its horrid burden, in the dead silence of the night she interred them in the hallowed enclosure of Old Shoreham Churchyard.

"Rizpah," of course, was the poem.

In the late 1790s an extensive building program began, and the Royal Crescent came into being; two promenade piers beckon summer tourists, and the Palace Pier, which was the center of activity in Edwardian Brighton, in later times was used as the setting for *Oh! What a Lovely War*.

Brighton has been visited by many literary figures, and most of them left fairly extensive records of their time here: Dr. Samuel Johnson was one of the first literary greats to visit Brighton; staying with the Thrales on West Street (on the site of the Grand Concert Hall), he appeared in the summer of 1756 and continued to visit until 1779. He engaged in uncharacteristically strenuous physical activities here; he first bathed in 1756, and his dipper's comment, "Why, Sir, you must have been a stout-hearted gentleman forty years ago," pleased Johnson enormously. He acquired a sudden and quite amazing addiction to horses and even rode Mrs. Thrale's old hunter with "good firmness," as she generously said. He often followed the hounds for as much as 50 miles without seeming unduly tired. He comments:

> I have now learned by hunting to perceive that it is not a diversion at all. . . . It is very strange and melancholy that the paucity of human pleasures should persuade us ever to call hunting one of them.

He also notes:

> You hunt in the morning and crowd to the rooms at night, and call it *diversion;* when your heart knows it is perishing for poverty of pleasures and your wits get blunted for want of some other mind to sharpen them upon.

Johnson's visits were obviously inspired by the Thrales, for more than once Boswell recalls such comments as, "I was some weeks this autumn at Brighthelmstone. The place was very dull, and I was not well. . . ." Johnson also said: "I do not much like the place, but yet I shall go, and stay while my stay is desired."

Dr. Johnson and the Thrales attended services at the Church of St. Nicholas, where the Thrales had a family pew; a memorial tablet to Dr. Johnson has been placed on the windowsill in the nave. In 1782, a year after the death of Henry Thrale, Dr. Johnson accompanied the widow to Brighthelmstone, where they were joined by Fanny Burney; Johnson, totally out of humor except with his "little Burney," was cut off all invitation lists because of his ill temper. Like most of the visitors to the resort at that time, Miss Burney and Mrs. Thrale believed that the prudent did not bathe in the summer or after exercise when the pores were open; accordingly the two women and Mrs. Thrale's two eldest daughters bathed before dawn on a November morning. Miss Burney had first been here with the Thrales in 1779, and during her visits the group occasionally ate at the officers' mess

at the Old Ship Tavern and would walk out on the parade ground, where they enjoyed the informality and friendliness of the regimental mustering of the Sussex militia.

The poet William Cowper spent the summer and perhaps the spring of 1759 here; he viewed the resort as a "scene of idleness and luxury, music, dancing, cards, walking, riding, bathing, eating, drinking, coffee, tea, scandal, yawning, sleeping." Cowper returned in 1762. Sometime around 1782, after finishing the third volume of *The History of the Decline and Fall of the Roman Empire*, Edward Gibbon came to Brighton for a much-needed rest; he found the society congenial and the town conducive to work. He read and wrote in the morning and would either lounge on the Steine or hire horses for an excursion in the afternoon. A second holiday was not as successful; he considered his lodgings oppressively dark and the town almost always enveloped by fog. Gibbon had come here with the 1st Earl of Sheffield, who was then called to Canterbury on business; the historian, placed in the position of caring for Lady Sheffield, felt that his position was that of "the servile state of a married man" and counted the hours until he could return home. Horace Walpole, here on numerous occasions, was especially fond of attending the Lewes races; his 1784 trip was highlighted by a dinner party given by Lady Clermont in honor of the Duc de Chartres, who was later known as Philippe-Égalité. Also in the 18th century William Wordsworth was stranded here by unfavorable winds on his way to France for four days in November 1791. He was met and received graciously by the novelist Charlotte Smith, whose *Emmeline* had appeared in 1788.

The number of 19th-century visitors was also large. George Gordon, Lord Byron was frequently a visitor in Brighton during his second year at Trinity College, Cambridge; he spent his Saturday-to-Monday weekends here, most often in the company of Gentleman John Jackson, the champion boxer, who was also in Byron's company at the university. The two were a strange pair, Byron holding a couple of large dogs on a leash, limping, and dressed in pantaloons, while Jackson towered over the slight, dandified figure. Byron played hazard every night and kept a mistress in one of the houses opposite the Royal Pavilion; during the days he would box with Jackson, ride across the Downs, or go boating.

Jane Austen, who is also frequently associated with Bath and Winchester, visited Brighton before 1813, the date of the publication of *Pride and Prejudice,* and in that novel she caught some of the flavor of the early-19th-century city:

> In Lydia's imagination, a visit to Brighton comprised every possibility of earthly happiness. She saw with the creative eye of fancy, the streets of that gay bathing place covered with officers. She saw herself the object of attention, to tens and scores of them at present unknown. She saw all the glories of the camps—its tents stretched forth in beauteous uniformity of lines, crowded with the young and gay, and dazzling with scarlet; and, to complete the view, she saw herself seated beneath a tent, tenderly flirting with at least six officers at once.

Sir Walter Scott visited the town on at least two

occasions, once in 1815 and again in the spring of 1828; his impression was that the city had doubled in size in the thirteen-year interval, and he noted:

> It is a city of loiterers and invalids—a Vanity Fair for piping, dancing of bears, and for the feats of Mr. Punch.

He compared the famous pavilion to some "sort of Chinese stables." Scott's commentary was not the only one on the pavilion; one of the most famous and wittiest descriptions came from the cleric Sydney Smith, who stated that the dome of St. Paul's in London "had come to the sea and pupped." Smith also left a vivid description of Lieutenant Colonel Eld, the last master of ceremonies here:

> A gentleman attired *point device,* walking down the Parade, like Agag, "delicately." He pointed out his toes like a dancing-master; but carried his head like a potentate. . . . Sure that in following him, I was treading in the steps of greatness, I went on to the Pier, and there I was confirmed in my conviction of his eminence; for I observed him look first over the right side and then over the left, with an expression of serene satisfaction spreading over his countenance, which said, as plainly as if he had spoken to the sea aloud, "That is right. You are low-tide at present; but never mind, in a couple of hours I shall make you high-tide again."

Charles and Mary Lamb spent the summer of 1817 visiting here with Mrs. Morgan in sight of the sea, and one of their favorite pastimes, so Mary told Dorothy Wordsworth, was walking the Downs. Charles Lamb, though, found the town not to his liking, as he later recorded in "The Old Margate Hoy":

> We have been dull at Worthing one summer, duller at Brighton another, dullest at Eastbourne a third, and are at this moment doing dreary penance at—Hastings!—and all because we were happy many years ago for a brief week at—Margate.

William Cobbett, author of *Rural Rides,* quite naturally had a great deal to say about Brighton and the Royal Pavilion:

> Brighton is a very pleasant place. For a *wen* remarkably so. The *Kremlin,* the very name of which has so long been a subject of laughter all over the country, lies in the gorge of the valley, and amongst the old houses of the town. . . . As to the "palace" as the Brighton newspapers call it, . . . when you see the thing from a distance, you think you see a parcel of *cradle-spits,* of various dimensions, sticking up out of the mouths of so many enormous squat decanters. Take a square box, the sides of which are three feet and a half, and the height a foot and a half. Take a large Norfolk-turnip, cut off the green of the leaves, leave the stalks 9 inches long, tie these round with a string three inches from the top, and put the turnip on the middle of the top of the box. Then take four turnips of half the size, treat them in the same way, and put them on the corners of the box. Then take a considerable number of bulbs of the crown-imperial, the narcissus, the hyacinth, the tulip, the crocus, and others; let the leaves of each have sprouted to about an inch, more or less according to the size of the bulb; put all these, pretty promiscuously, but pretty thickly, on the top of the box. Then stand off and look at your architecture. There! That's "a *Kremlin!*" . . . As to what you ought to put *into* the box, that is a subject far above my cut.

A prevailing belief was that the pavilion had been built in imitation of the Moscow structure. Yet, no matter how much Cobbett was disgusted by the "shifty ugly-looking swarm" assembled here, he found some of the town's attractions:

> These vermin excepted, the people at Brighton make a very fine figure. The trades-people are very nice in all their concerns. The houses are excellent, built chiefly with a blue or purple brick; and bow-windows appear to be the general taste. I can easily believe this to be a very healthy place: the open downs on the one side and the open sea on the other. No inlet, cove, or river; and, of course, no swamps.

William Hazlitt visited Brighton on at least two occasions, on his way to and from France in 1824 and 1825. He had remarried before his arrival here, but it was a bigamous marriage because Scottish divorce law was not recognized in England. Arriving by coach in the evening, Hazlitt wrote:

> A lad offered to conduct us to an inn. "Did he think there was room?" He was sure of it. "Did he belong to the inn?" "No," he was from London. In fact, he was a young gentleman from town, who had been stopping some time at the White-horse Hotel, and who wished to employ his spare time . . . in serving the house, and relieving the perplexities of his fellow-travellers. No one but a Londoner would volunteer his assistance in this way.

Hazlitt considered the Royal Pavilion a collection of stone pumpkins and pepperboxes. "It seems to me," he wrote, "as if the genius of architecture had at once the dropsy and the megrims." *Notes of a Journey through France and Italy* describes this town vividly. Hazlitt left Brighton via Dieppe on September 1, 1824, and returned in October 1825 with the son by his first marriage; his second wife stayed behind in Switzerland and no doubt, having heard of the bigamous relationship, returned to Scotland alone. For ten years after 1829 Robert Smith Surtees, the creator of Jorrocks, hunted here, but he never became a member of the exclusive set of hunters and returned only rarely after 1838, when he settled in Hamsterley. He died here on March 16, 1864, and was buried in Ebchester, County Durham. Walter Savage Landor paid a short visit to Brighton in September 1832, when he came from London to visit Edward John Trelawny.

On Charles Dickens's first trip to Brighton in 1837 he stayed at the Old Ship Hotel, 38 Kings Road (not, as is often stated, at the newer hotel of the same name on Ship Street), and resumed work on *Oliver Twist.* Writing to John Forster, he talks of a terrible windstorm and of his rooms:

> It is a beautiful day and we have been taking advantage of it, but . . . . [o]n Wednesday it blew a perfect hurricane, breaking windows, knocking down shutters, carrying people off their legs, blowing the fires out, and causing universal consternation. The air was for some hours darkened with a shower of black hats (second-hand) which are supposed to have been blown off the heads of unwary passengers in remote parts of the town. . . . We have a beautiful bay-windowed sitting-room here, fronting the sea . . . and my notions of the place are . . . limited to the Pavilion, the Chain Pier, and the sea. The last is quite enough for me. . . .

For more than fifteen years Brighton was the novelist's favorite south coast resort. Here again in February 1841 and staying at the Old Ship Hotel, he worked on *Barnaby Rudge.* In 1847, several months after the birth of Sydney Smith Haldemand, Dickens and his wife lodged at 148 Kings Road, where he worked on *Dombey and Son;* and in March 1848 they spent three weeks at Junction House, where they were "very comfortably (not to say gorgeously) accommodated." In the spring of 1853, when Dickens was at work on *Bleak House,* he rented rooms at 1 Junction Parade. Perhaps the most famous of the Dickens lodgings here is the Bedford Hotel (marked by a plaque), where he first stayed in November 1848. A letter to the artist Frank Stone comments:

> I don't in the abstract approve of Brighton. I couldn't pass an autumn here, but it is a gay place for a week or so; and when one laughs or cries, and suffers the agitation that some men experience over their books, it's a bright change to look out of window, and see the gilt little toys on horseback going up and down before the mighty sea, and thinking nothing of it.

Just three months later Dickens experienced an event so unnerving that he was forced to flee to the Bedford; he had been in his lodgings for less than a week when both the landlord and his daughter went mad. Writing to Forster, Dickens says:

> If you could have heard the cursing and crying of the two; could have seen the physician and nurse quoited out into the passage by the madman at the hazard of their lives; could have seen Leech and me flying to the doctor's rescue; could have seen our wives pulling us back; could have seen the M.D. faint with fear; could have seen three other M.D.'s come to his aid; with an atmosphere of Mrs. Gamps, strait-waistcoats, struggling friends and servants, surrounding the whole; you would have said it was quite worthy of me, and quite in keeping with my usual proceedings.

Apart from Dickens's personal associations, the town has become important to his readers because of its role in *Dombey and Son.* It is to Brighton that young Paul is sent to be placed under the guiding hand of the "marvelous ill-favoured, ill conditioned lady," Mrs. Pipchin:

> The Castle of this ogress and child-queller was in a steep bye-street at Brighton; where the soil was more than usually chalky, flinty, and sterile, and the houses were more than usually brittle and thin; where the small front-gardens had the unaccountable property of producing nothing but marigolds, whatever was sown in them; and where snails were constantly discovered holding on to the street doors, and other public places they were not expected to ornament, with the tenacity of cupping-glasses. In the winter time the air couldn't be got out of the Castle, and in the summer time it couldn't be got in. There was such a continual reverberation of wind in it, that it sounded like a great shell, which the inhabitants were obliged to hold to their ears night and day, whether they liked it or no. It was not, naturally, a fresh-smelling house. . . .

Brighton also is the site of Dr. Blimber's "very expensive" establishment, "a great hot-house, in which there was a forcing apparatus incessantly at work." "The Doctor's," wrote Dickens,

> was a mighty fine house, fronting the sea. Not a joyful style of house within, but quite the contrary. Sad-coloured curtains, whose proportions were spare and lean, hid themselves despondently behind the windows. . . . [T]he dining-room seemed the last place in the world where any eating or drinking was likely to occur; there was no sound through all the house but the ticking of a great clock in the hall . . . and sometimes a dull cooing of young gentlemen at their lessons, like the murmurings of an assemblage of melancholy pigeons.

Dr. Blimber and his school really existed here; Dr. Blimber was based on a Doctor Everad, whose "seminary" was known locally as the "Young House of Lords" because of the aristocracy of the pupils. Blimber's school was probably what is now Chichester House; the building actually once served as a school. Mr. Dombey stays at the Bedford Hotel, and Major Bagstock dines there.

Another 19th-century novelist to visit and make use of Brighton was William Makepeace Thackeray; he was here several times, including an occasion when he was to deliver a lecture on "The Four Georges." The talk had been scheduled originally for the Royal Pavilion, but (the story varies) either Thackeray himself remarked or someone suggested that "it was not strictly etiquette to abuse a man in his own house," and the lecture was moved to the town hall. The novelist's most extensive use of Brighton is in *The Newcomes:*

> In Steyne Gardens, Brighton, the lodging houses are among the most frequented in that city of lodging houses. These mansions have bow windows in front, bulging out with gentle prominences, and ornamented with neat verandas, from which you can behold . . . that blue ocean over which Britannia is said to rule. . . . The chain-pier, as everybody knows, runs intrepidly into the sea, which sometimes, in fine weather, bathes its feet with laughing wavelets, and anon, on stormy days, dashes over its sides with roaring foam. Here, for the sum of twopence, you can go out to sea and pace this vast deck without need of a steward with a basin. . . . You behold a hundred bathing machines put to sea; and your naughty fancy depicts the beauties splashing under their white awnings. . . . One of the best physicians our city has ever known, is kind, cheerful, merry Doctor Brighton. Hail, thou purveyor of shrimps and honest prescriber of South Down mutton! There is no mutton so good as Brighton mutton; no flies so pleasant as Brighton Flies; nor any cliff so pleasant to ride on; no shops so beautiful to look at as the Brighton gimcrack shops, and the fruit shops, and the market.

Many of Thackeray's contributions to *Punch* contain references to Brighton, and some use is made of the town in *Vanity Fair,* for James Crawley tells his aunt he stopped at Tom Cribb's Inn here:

> "[W]hat 'otel, sir, shall Thomas fetch the luggage from?"
> "Oh, dam," said young James, starting up, as if in some alarm, "I'll go."
> "What!" said Miss Crawley.
> "The Tom Cribb's Arms," said James, blushing deeply.
> Miss Crawley burst out laughing at this title. Mr. Bowls gave one abrupt guffaw. . . .
> "I—I didn't know any better," said James, looking down. "I've never been here before; it was the coachman told me." The young story-teller!

One of the most difficult and disastrous 19th-century marriages got its start here; Edward FitzGerald, who married Lucy Barton on November 4, 1856, in Chichester, came here on his honeymoon and found himself disliking the town as much as he did his wife. The marriage had not been well thought out, for FitzGerald married the daughter of his friend Bernard Barton out of sheer sympathy, and the honeymoon was short. FitzGerald went to his bachelor lodgings at 31 Great Portland Street, London, while his wife went to Norfolk to look for a house.

Richard Jefferies, the Wiltshire poet, was here on numerous occasions—once at 5 (now 87) Lorma Road—and was a resident during his final illness in 1887. He comments, "There are more handsome women in Brighton than anywhere else in the world" and "Where all the flowers are roses you do not see a rose." Strangely enough, he was especially fond of the general treelessness in the town:

> Let nothing cloud the descent of those glorious beams of sunlight which fall at Brighton. Watch the pebbles on the beach; the foam runs up and wets them, almost before it can slip back, the sunshine has dried them again. So they are alternately wetted and dried. Bitter sea and glowing light, bright clear air, dry as dry—that describes the place.

Jefferies died in nearby Goring-by-Sea in 1887.

In September 1894 Oscar Wilde arrived in town with Lord Alfred Douglas; they first stayed at the Grand Hotel, but when their money ran short, they moved to lodgings at 20 Kings Road. Thomas Hughes, author of *Tom Brown's Schooldays,* was in failing health when he came to Brighton early in 1896 and died here on March 22; he was buried in the Brighton Cemetery. Also in Brighton at the end of the century was Virginia Stephen (Woolf); following the marriage of her half sister Stella in April 1897, Sir Leslie Stephen brought the family to 9 St. Aubyns in Hove. The house, the novelist considered a dismal place, the worst she had ever known, and she disliked Brighton as well, for it was full of "third rate actresses turned out in gorgeous clothes, tremendous hats, powder and rouge; and dreadful young men to escort them." The Stephen family spent a second holiday here in April 1899 and possibly a third at Easter, 1900.

A number of 20th-century authors have also been in Brighton. Rupert Brooke was here on a family holiday at Easter in 1900, when he met Lytton Strachey. Arnold Bennett arrived in Brighton on January 5, 1910, to begin work on *Clayhanger.* Bennett, who was still living in France, was unable to finish his novel here before leaving for Paris; he stayed at the Old Ship Hotel and characteristically spent full days at work on the book. This hotel becomes the Royal Sussex Hotel of *Clayhanger* when Edwin Clayhanger arrives in the town:

> When, in an astounding short space of time, he stood in the King's Road at Brighton, it seemed to him that he was in a dream; that he was not really at Brighton, that town which for so many years had been to him naught but a romantic name. . . . As for Brighton, it corresponded with no dream. It was vaster than any imagining of it. . . .
>
> The bricks and stucco which fronted the sea on the long embanked promenade never sank lower than a four-storey boarding-house, and were continually rising to the height of some gilt-lettered hotel, and at intervals rose sheer into the skies—six, eight, ten storeys—where a hotel, admittedly the grandest on any shore of ocean sent terra-cotta chimneys to lose themselves amid the pearly clouds. Nearly every building was a lodgment waiting for the rich. . . .

William Butler Yeats spent a small part of the winter of 1911–1912 in Brighton visiting H. T. Tucker, the brother of Yeats's friend Mrs. Olivia Shakespear. D. H. Lawrence spent almost a month here convalescing in early January 1912, when he began the second writing of *The Trespasser.* Hilaire Belloc spent a great deal of time making expeditions to the town with his children; they took in the theater on at least two occasions, seeing *Dick Whittington* and *Mother Goose.* Hugh Walpole spent some time here in August 1933, when he finished *Captain Nicholas* before going on to the Isle of Wight to visit J. B. Priestley.

Undoubtedly, the most famous modern use of Brighton occurs in Graham Greene's *Brighton Rock;* Greene admits in the Introduction to the novel that "The Brighton authorities proved a little sensitive to the picture . . . [he] had drawn of their city," and he adds:

> However the setting of this one book may in part belong to an imaginary geographic region. Though Nelson Place has been cleared away since the war, and the race gangs were to all intents quashed forever as a serious menace at Lewes Assizes a little before the date of my novel, and even Sherry's dance hall has vanished, they certainly did exist; there *was* a real slum called Nelson Place, and a man was kidnapped on Brighton front in broad daylight of the thirties, though not in the same circumstances as Hale, and his body was found somewhere out towards the Downs flung from a car. Colleoni, the gang leader, had his real prototype who had retired by 1938 and lived a gracious Catholic life in one of the Brighton crescents, although I found his name was still law, when I demanded entrance by virtue of it, at a little London nightclub called The Nest behind Regent Street. . . .
>
> All the same I must plead guilty to manufacturing this Brighton of mine. . . . There were no living models for these gangsters, nor for the bar-maid who so obstinately refused to come alive. . . .

The disclaimer, though, was insufficient, partly because of the atmosphere Greene evokes:

> It was a fine day for the races. People poured into Brighton by the first train. It was like Bank Holiday all over again, except that these people didn't spend their money; they harboured it. . . . By eleven o'clock it was impossible to get a seat on the buses going out to the course. A negro wearing a bright striped tie sat on a bench in the Pavilion garden and smoked a cigar. Some children played touch wood from seat to seat, and he called out to them hilariously. . . . A band came up the pavement through Old Steyne, a blind band playing drums and trumpets, walking in the gutter, feeling the kerb with the edge of their shoes, in Indian file. . . .
>
> In the public school grounds above the sea the girls trooped solemnly out to hockey: stout goal-keepers padded like armadillos; captains discussing tactics with their lieutenants; junior girls running amok in the bright day. Beyond the aristocratic turf, through the wrought-iron main gates they could see the plebian procession, those whom the buses wouldn't hold, plodding up the Down, kicking up the dust, eating buns out of paper bags.

Hale has a set program:

> . . . from ten till eleven Queen's Road and Castle Square, from eleven till twelve the Aquarium and Palace Pier, twelve till one the front between the Old Ship and West Pier, back for lunch between one and two in any restaurant he chose round the Castle Square, and after that he

had to make his way all down the parade to the West Pier and then to the station by the Hove Streets. These were the limits of his absurd and widely advertised sentry-go.

Rose lives in Nelson Place, and the boy's home is in Paradise Piece:

"This is better than going home," Rose said.
"Where's home?"
"Nelson Place. Do you know it?"
"Oh, I've passed through," he said airily, but he could have drawn its plan as accurately as a surveyor on the turf: the barred and battlemented Salvation Army gaff at the corner: his own home beyond in Paradise Piece: the houses which looked as if they had passed through an intensive bombardment, flapping gutters and glassless windows, an iron bedstead rusting in a front garden, the smashed and wasted ground in front where houses had been pulled down for model flats which had never gone up.

Among the other places mentioned in Brighton are the Old Ship, the Palace Pier, the Aquarium, the Grand Parade, Old Steyne, and the Pavilion:

He thought: that woman—how does she know anything—what's she doing asking questions? I didn't want to have Hale killed; it wouldn't be fair if I took the drop with the others; I told 'em not to do it. He came out into the sunlight and climbed back on to the parade. It'll be this way the bogies will come, he thought, if they know anything; they always reconstruct the crime. He took up his stand between the turnstile of the pier and the ladies' lavatory. There weren't many people about: he could spot the bogies easily enough—if they came. Over there was the Royal Albion; he could see all the way up the Grand Parade to Old Steyne; the pale green domes of the Pavilion floated above the dusty trees; he could see anyone in the hot empty mid-week afternoon who went down below the Aquarium, the white deck ready for dancing, to the little covered arcade where the cheap shops stood between the sea and the stone wall, selling Brighton rock.

BRINSLEY, Nottinghamshire (pop. 1,953) Set in the heart of the colliery district northwest of Nottingham, Brinsley comes to notice because of its associations with D. H. Lawrence. His grandfather was a Brinsley tailor who supplied pit trousers for the miners; Lawrence was a frequent visitor with his sister Ida and later recalled the great rolls of flannel in the shop "and the strange old sewing-machine, like nothing else on earth, which sewed the massive pit-trousers." Living also in Brinsley was his Aunt Sally, "the haughty wife of the sexton at New Brinsley Church," but visits to her were rare. "Odour of Chrysanthemums" is set here, and the small white cottage described in "The Widowing of Mrs. Holroyd" is here.

BRISTOL, Gloucestershire and Somerset (pop. 415,-500) Situated in both Gloucestershire and Somerset and since 1373 a county in its own right with its own assizes, Bristol is at the confluence of the Avon and Frome (pronounced "frume") Rivers, 6 miles up the Bristol Channel and about 120 miles west of London. The founding of Bristol is usually attributed to Brennus and Belinus, the sons of a "British" king, but Geoffrey of Monmouth, who chronicles the history of these two brothers in *Historia Regum Britanniae,* never mentions this tradition. There was a Roman settlement here as well, but it was dominated by nearby Bath.

By the 10th century there was a Saxon mint here, but it was not until after the Battle of Hastings in 1066 that Bristol's importance as a port was established. The apparent vulnerability of the town led to the building of a fortified castle (now recalled only in the name Castle Street, which is near the site) on a narrow part of a peninsula between the Avon and the Frome. The slave trade here was important in the 11th and 12th centuries, when Irish men and women were sold to the prospering merchants; Bristol was also deeply involved in the African slave trade in the 18th century. The commercial port, which had originated in the 10th century, flourished throughout the Middle Ages. Its importance was acknowledged in the 14th century, when Bristol was made a county in its own right with all attendant rights and privileges.

By the 15th century Bristol had an enormous overseas trade and was the taking-off point for explorers. John Cabot, who sailed from here, was the first man to set foot on continental North America, in 1497. Indeed, Bristolians are convinced that the name America came from Richard Ameryck, a local merchant and one of Cabot's financiers, and have erected a monument to him. Today the city is engaged in a variety of industries including the processing of tobacco, cocoa, and chocolate; the manufacture of furniture, glass, soap, aerospace products, and earthenware; and shipbuilding, tanning, and sugar refining. Probably the best-known product of the city is Harvey's Bristol Cream. It was because Bristol was such an important port that it was bombed so heavily during World War II; 1,299 persons were killed, 3,000 homes were destroyed, and 90,000 buildings were damaged. As a consequence, much of central Bristol is new.

The cathedral, which had its beginnings in an Augustinian abbey founded by Robert Fitzharding between 1140 and 1148, contains remarkable Norman work. While the cathedral itself is somewhat squat in appearance, the Chapter House is an outstanding piece of Norman construction. One of the most impressive pieces of sculpture in the cathedral was found under the floor of the Chapter House and is now in the south transept wall. Most likely a Saxon coffin lid, it portrays the Harrowing of Hell in deep relief. The misericords in the choir are marvelous in their comic depiction. One shows a woman on a turkey dueling with a man on a pig, both being armed with brooms; and another shows two foxes addressing a flock of geese from a pulpit. There are only a few literary associations with the cathedral, and the few visitors who commented on it disagreed about its merits. Daniel Defoe, in *A Tour thro' the Whole Island of Great Britain*, felt that it was a "(very mean) Cathedral, the reason of which, may be, it is but a very modern Bishoprick," while in 1766 Horace Walpole described it as "very neat." In the north choir aisle there is a commemorative bust of Robert Southey, who was born in Bristol, but the memorial inscription written by Walter Savage Landor is missing because the memorial committee was unable to agree on accepting the inscription.

The Church of St. Mary Redcliffe, often called Bristol's second cathedral, was built in what was once a separate township and, in fact, stands across the river from the original town of Bristol. With open parapets and flying buttresses, St. Mary's is one of

England's largest and grandest churches, and the ornately carved hexagonal North Porch is probably its outstanding feature. The interior is awe-inspiring: the 240-foot nave contains about 150 windows, while the stone roof over the nave and transepts holds 1,200 different bosses. The church has many more associations with literary figures than does the cathedral, although it is its connection with Thomas Chatterton that is most notable. Chatterton was born on November 20, 1752, in a house on Pile Street, was christened in St. Mary's in January, and spent almost all his life in Bristol. Sent to the Pile Street School as a child of five, he was dismissed by Stephen Love, the schoolmaster, as a dullard, "incapable of improvement"; but he became a voracious reader by the age of eight and that year was entered at Colston's School, a Blue-Coat school, where he was to receive commercial training. (Colston Hall now stands on the site of the school.) After school, he would read, draw heraldic emblems, castles, and churches, and write poetry in the lumber room at home; he would also haunt St. Mary's Church and read either by William Canynge's tomb or in the towers. Some of his books were procured from Mr. Goodall's Book Shop, Tower Lane, opposite Ciderhouse Passage; some may have been secured from Samuel Green's Circulating Library on Wine Street, at the corner of Dolphin Lane; but, contrary to popular belief, none came from the City Library on King Street.

In July 1767 Chatterton was apprenticed to John Lambert, an attorney, "to be educated as a scrivener." Lambert's office was at 37 Corn Street, where the Midland Bank now stands. Chatterton now gained access to the unguarded Muniment Room of St. Mary's Church, where he secured parchment from the old oak chests. By the age of eleven he had been writing "antique" poetry, and a local pewterer, George Catcott, who became the young boy's patron, sent the manuscript of *The Ryse of Peyncteynge in Englande* and other pieces to Horace Walpole, who kept the manuscripts but did nothing. In this period Chatterton invented Thomas Rowley, monk, to whom he attributed these compositions. The uniform of Colston's School and the obligatory tonsure may have provided the model for Rowley's attire. "Clifton" and "English Metamorphosis" both date from this period. "The Storie of William Canynge" (Canynge was selected as Rowley's patron) was only one of a number of "old" poems about St. Mary's Church; "Onn Oure Ladies Church" also concerns this structure, as does "The Parliamente of Sprytes."

Chatterton left Bristol for London in April 1770 and arrived in the capital by April 26. In complete poverty and in a state of frustration, he poisoned himself in his rooming house three months later and was buried in London in a pauper's grave. A few years later Dr. Samuel Johnson, accompanied by James Boswell, came to Bristol to inquire into the authenticity of Rowley's poetry; but even after a visit to the Muniment Room he remained unconvinced.

In addition to the cathedral, St. Mary's Redcliffe, and the twenty other churches, there are a number of noteworthy sites in Bristol. One significant part of Bristol's past is the Theatre Royal on King Street, which opened on May 30, 1766, with Richard Steele's *The Conscious Lovers.* A number of well-known actors played here, including Edmund Kean, William Macready, and Sarah Siddons, who, indeed, was artist in residence for four years. A new facade was built in 1903, but the theater itself is one of the oldest still in use in the country. Today the Bristol Old Vic is housed here along with its offspring, the Little Theatre, which is closely linked to the University of Bristol's department of drama. The university, founded in 1876, has been in harmony with the town, as J. B. Priestley notes in his *English Journey;* he was pleasantly surprised that Bristol was "not a dirty nineteenth-century hotch-potch, not merely an extended factory and warehouse, but a real city with a charm and dignity of its own." He goes on to characterize Bristol:

> I knew about Bristol, of course. I knew that the Cabots had set sail from there to discover the mainland of America; that Hakluyt had been one of its deans and Burke one of its members; that it has associations with all manner of literary folk, Chatterton, Savage, Hannah More, Coleridge and Southey. I knew it was a famous old port—or, if you like, a vintage port—and had its cathedral and its St. Mary Redcliff Church and its Merchant Venturers' Hall and other fine old buildings.

Priestley notes a literary heritage here, and indeed Bristol's part in English literary history was extensive from the earliest times on. William Langland is said to have had some connection with the town, and John Lydgate, the "monk of Bury," is often mentioned because of his conjectured authorship of the 15th-century poem "The Childe of Bristowe." The poem, regardless of who wrote it, does concern the town:

> Here at Bristow dwelleth on
> is held right a juste trew man,
> as y here now telle;
> his prentys will y be vij yer,
> his science truly for to lere
> and w^t hym will y dwelle.

The relationship with William Grocyn, the Reformation scholar and educator, is on firmer ground; it is now accepted that he was educated in this town before his admission at Winchester even though the details are lacking. Richard Hakluyt, author of *Divers Voyages Touching the Discoverie of America,* was a prebendary of Bristol Cathedral in the late 16th century after being appointed rector of Wetheringsett, Suffolk, in 1590. William Shakespeare set one scene of *Richard II* here: Act III, scene i, presents "Bolingbroke's camp at Bristol."

The early travel writers and diarists also left definite impressions of the area. John Leland, Henry VIII's antiquarian, carefully examined the situation of the town in his *Itinerary* before viewing the castle, of which nothing remains:

> In the castle be 2. cowrtes. In the utter courte, as in the northe west parte of it, is a great dungeon tower, made, as it is sayde, of stone browght out of Cane in Normandye by the redde Erle of Glocestar.
> A praty churche and muche longging in 2. area. On the southe syde of it a great gate, a stone bridge, and 3. bullewarks *in laeva ripa ad ostium Frai.*
> There be many towres yet standynge in bothe the cowrtes; but all tendithe to ruine.

Michael Drayton includes "Bristow" in the third song of *Poly-Olbion* and speaks lavishly of its "delicacies":

Even so this Citie doth; the prospect of which place
To her faire building addes an admirable grace;
Well fashioned as the best, and with a double wall,
As brave as any Towne; but yet excelling all
For easement, that to health is requisit and meete;
Her piled shores, to keepe her delicate and sweete:
Hereto, she hath her Tides; that when she is opprest
With heat or drought, still poure their floods upon her
   breast.

Samuel Pepys journeyed here in June 1668 from Bath; his *Diary* records his trip, accommodations, and impression of Bristol in the following terms:

... the way bad, but country good, where set down at the Horseshoe ... walked with my wife and people through the city, which is in every respect another London. ... So to the Three Crowns tavern I was directed; but when I came in the master told me that he had newly given over the selling of wine: it seems, grown rich. And so went to the Sun ... I to see the quay, which is a most large and noble place. ...

He seems to have been most deeply impressed by the meal provided by the Butts family, relations of "our girl Deb":

Then walked with Butts and my wife and company round the quay, and to the ship; and he ... brought us a back way by surprise to his house, where a substantial good house, and well furnished; and did give us good entertainment of strawberries, a whole venison pasty, cold, and plenty of brave wine, and above all Bristol milk. ...

Daniel Defoe includes Bristol in *A Tour thro' the Whole Island of Great Britain*. Commenting first on the richness of Bristolian trade and the attendant wealth of the merchants, he goes on to add:

The greatest Inconveniences of *Bristol*, are, its Situation, and the tenacious Folly of its Inhabitants; who by the general Infatuation, the Pretence of Freedoms and Priviledges, that Corporation-Tyranny, which prevents the Flourishing and Encrease of many a good Town in *England*, continue obstinately to forbid any, who are not Subjects of their City Soveranity, (that is to say, Freemen,) to Trade within the Chain of their own Liberties; were it not for this, the City of *Bristol*, would before now, have swell'd and encreas'd in Buildings and Inhabitants, perhaps to double the Magnitude it was formerly of.

In fact, Defoe came to Bristol for a few months in 1692 after declaring bankruptcy; he went out only cautiously at night or on Sunday, when he could not be arrested, and consequently became known as the Sunday Gentleman. Defoe returned to London after an agreement for repayment was reached; fortunately, this was not before he had met Alexander Selkirk, who had been brought to Bristol from Juan Fernández Island by a local sea captain named Woodes Rogers. Defoe is said to have had the idea for *Robinson Crusoe* from Selkirk, whom he met in Ye Llandoger Trow, a Jacobean half-timbered inn that faces King Street just below the Bristol Bridge.

In the 18th century there were many important visitors to Bristol; especially notable was Joseph Addison, whose mother was the sister of the Bishop of Bristol. Addison's presence in the town was fairly frequent, and it is traditionally held that some of the papers for *The Spectator* were written here in a summerhouse on the St. Anne's estate in Breslington. A verified association can be found for the year 1718,

when Addison had sufficiently recovered from illness by August to come to Bristol with his wife, the Dowager Countess of Warwick, to take the waters at Hot Well. They stayed until early October, when it was apparent that the course of treatment was not working; in addition, his wife had become pregnant, and they returned to London, where Addison died eight months later. Alexander Pope visited the town in 1739 and describes it in a letter to Martha Blount:

The streets are as crowded as London; but the best image I can give you of it is, it is as if Wapping and Southwark were ten times as big, or all their people ran into London.

Pope also described the glass cones as "twenty odd pyramids smoking over the town" and the docks as "a long street full of ships in the middle, with houses on each side, [which] looks like a dream." In a different vein was the visit of Richard Savage in the same year, on his way from London to Swansea. Not known for his financial acumen, he arrived without funds, although he had been given sufficient money for the entire journey and his first few months in Swansea. He stayed in Bristol for some time, haranguing his London friends for additional funds; eventually he made his way to Wales, somewhat bereft of friends, but returned here about a year later. He was tempted by what he thought were offers of hospitality to stay here before going to London to raise more money and, delaying his departure too long, was arrested on January 10, 1743, and sent to debtor's prison. Savage calls Bristol "Thou blank of sciences, thou dearth of arts," and while in prison wrote *London and Bristol Compar'd*, a satire published after his death. Savage died in prison here on August 1, 1743, and was buried the next day in St. Peter's churchyard at the expense of his jailer. The position of the grave is not known, and both churchyard and church were destroyed by bombs during World War II.

Hannah More came to Bristol around 1757 from nearby Stapleton, where she was born; at that time her eldest sister began a boarding school on Trinity Street, and her other sisters joined her there. Miss More continued her already-prodigious studies under the masters at the flourishing school, and the sisters built a new house on Park Street after the school's success was assured. All the Mores shared in the school, although Hannah gave up her interest in it in anticipation of marriage around 1767, an event that did not occur. She then divided her time between London, Blagdon, and Bristol. Many years later she returned from her Wrington, Somerset, home and died at Windsor Terrace on September 7, 1833. Through Miss More, Thomas Babington Macaulay, a former pupil's son whom she treated as a sort of protégé, knew Bristol and the Clifton section well; in 1832 he stayed at 16 Caledonia Place (marked with a plaque).

Perhaps the most notable of all the literary associations of Bristol collect around Robert Southey, who was born at 9 Wine Street on August 12, 1774. The son of a linendraper, he spent a childhood divided between here and Bath, where his mother's maiden half sister resided. He was first educated at Colston and then in the city school before going to Westminster in 1788. Southey settled here in 1794 after meeting Samuel Taylor Coleridge at Oxford and becoming a convert to the pantisocratic scheme. With a third member of the society, Robert Lovell, he took a house at 48 College Street and soon became acquainted with Joseph Cottle, the bookseller. In the meantime Coleridge, who also lodged on College Street, returned from Nether Stowey, Somerset, and all three men met Edith, Mary, and Sarah Fricker, three of the six daughters of an unsuccessful manufacturer. Southey became engaged to Edith, and Lovell soon married Mary, but Coleridge, who had contracted an engagement with Sarah long before October 1795, was estranged from her after a period in London. Southey and Cottle both felt that Coleridge should honor his engagement, and Southey followed Coleridge to London and successfully urged Coleridge to fulfill his commitment. Southey would later support the three sisters himself at Keswick. Coleridge was married in St. Mary Redcliffe on October 4, 1795. On November 14, Southey married Edith Fricker in the same church; next day he left his new bride for an extended trip to Lisbon with his uncle, the Rev. Herbert Hill; indeed, Edith Fricker Southey continued to use her maiden name until her husband's return in 1797.

Before Southey went abroad, William Wordsworth came here; arriving from London in August 1795, he stayed for five weeks with John Pinney at his house (now a furniture museum) at 7 Great George Street. Wordsworth first met Coleridge at this time, but the circumstances are a bit obscured by time: Wordsworth claimed that they met at some lodgings (probably Coleridge's on College Street), but the *Farington Diaries* say that they met after Wordsworth was speaking somewhere and Coleridge inquired of his identity. The latter is most unlikely; if anything, Coleridge would have been speaking. It would appear that Wordsworth worked on *The Prelude* and indeed wrote the first fifty-four lines here (the walk recorded in the Postpreamble of Book I seems to refer to the walk from Racedown to Bristol). Wordsworth returned in 1798, when he stayed with Cottle on Wine Street; finding Coleridge delaying their proposed trip to Germany, he went on to Wales and the Wye Valley, where he wrote "Tintern Abbey."

Following their honeymoon in Clevedon, Somerset, Coleridge and his bride returned to Bristol and tried to live with the bride's widowed mother before going to Nether Stowey on the invitation of Thomas Poole. They returned to Bristol early in 1796, when Coleridge began *The Watchman*, whose purpose was "to preserve Freedom and her Friends from the attacks of Robbers and Assassins!" and whose conception occurred in the Rummer Tavern. With the generally negative reaction to the month-late first issue, Coleridge turned to opium. His first son, David Hartley, was born here on September 19, 1796, and the family moved to Nether Stowey at the end of December.

In the meantime Southey's sojourn in Portugal had drawn to a close, and he returned to Bristol and his wife early in 1797; a former schoolfellow, Charles Watkin Williams Wynn, settled £160 a year on Southey, and the essayist determined to study law. He entered Gray's Inn in London on February 7, 1797, but his flirtation with the bar lasted only a little over a year.

Another literary figure lived in the Clifton area for a short time in the 1790s; Maria Edgeworth, the Anglo-Irish novelist, was here with her parents from December 1791 to the end of 1793, when they returned to Edgeworthstown, County Longford, Ireland. Two other 18th-century figures also visited Bristol. Horace Walpole, who came here from Bath in 1766, felt Bristol was

the dirtiest great shop I ever saw, with so foul a river, that, had I seen the least appearance of cleanliness, I should have concluded they washed all their linen in it, as they do at Paris.

Bristol held very bad memories for the dramatist Richard Brinsley Sheridan, who brought his wife here in 1792 to visit the Hot Well; already ravaged by tuberculosis, Elizabeth Linley Sheridan died here on June 28, 1792, and was buried in Wells at the cathedral.

Two 18th-century works contain marvelous satire on the Hot Well at Bristol. Tobias Smollett's *The Expedition of Humphry Clinker* is, no doubt, the better known of the two. Matthew Bramble's opening letter to Dr. Lewis, in which he complains that he "might as well swallow snow-balls to cool my veins," explains that he is setting "out to-morrow morning for the Hot Well at Bristol...." His nephew later comments:

My uncle was complaining of the stink, occasioned by the vast quantity of mud and slime, which the river leaves at low ebb under the windows of the Pump-room. He observed, that the exhalations arising from such a nuisance, could not but be prejudicial to the weak lungs of many consumptive patients, who came to drink the water. The Doctor overhearing this remark, made up to him, and assured him he was mistaken. He said, people in general were so misled by vulgar prejudices that philosophy was hardly sufficient to undeceive them.... [H]e had reason to believe that stercoraceous flavour, condemned by prejudice as a stink, was, in fact, more agreeable to the organs of smelling; for, that every person who pretended to nauseate the smell of another's excretions, snuffed up his own with particular complacency....

The doctor's discourse continued, says Melford, until he had offended the females in Bramble's company by

then addressing himself to my uncle, "Sir (said he) you seem to be of a dropsical habit, and probably will soon have a confirmed *ascites:* if I should be present when you are tapped, I will give you a convincing proof of what I assert, by drinking without hesitation the very water that comes out of your abdomen."—The ladies made wry faces at this declaration....

Fanny Burney's *Evelina* also contains a satire of the Hot Well.

A number of important literary figures stayed in Bristol in the 19th century, and one, Thomas Lovell Beddoes, was born here, at 3 Rodney Place, Clifton, on July 20, 1803. Beddoes, whose father died in 1808, had no further association with Bristol after his early schooling in Bath. Thomas De Quincey arrived in Bristol in August 1807 to visit a relative and called on Thomas Poole, the friend of Coleridge; De Quincey discovered that Coleridge was in Bridgwater and went there to meet him. In November of the same year De Quincey offered to escort Coleridge's family, from which he was partially estranged, to Greta Hall, Keswick, while Coleridge was lecturing in London. Harriet Martineau, whose early life in Norwich was made more difficult by anosmia, the inability to taste or smell, and deafness, was sent to Bristol in 1817 to be with her aunt Mrs. Kentish, who kept a school here. Finding warmth and understanding, Miss Martineau improved mentally and emotionally when harsh home discipline and derision of the five older children were removed. Although she was still in need of medical attention when she left Bristol in April 1819, the year and a half here, she later claimed, formed one of the happiest periods in her life.

Charles Kingsley, author of *Westward Ho!*, was sent to school in Clifton in 1831 and witnessed the August riots here; he recalled seeing Queen Square burning from his vantage point on Clifton Heights. Robert Southey, accompanied by his son Cuthbert, visited in the late 1830s to see the places of his childhood, and Walter Savage Landor, who joined the Southeys for most of their stay, found the city "beyond all comparison the most interesting and beautiful city in England." It is perhaps fair to note that Landor was usually more strongly impressed by his company than he was by the environment. In 1864 Thomas Edward Brown, the Manx poet, was persuaded by Dr. John Percival, one of the outstanding headmasters of the 19th century, to take the second mastership at Clifton College. As well as holding the post here, Brown was curate of St. Barnabas from 1884 to 1893. Brown was an extremely popular master; he died of a cerebral hemorrhage at the college on October 30, 1897, while lecturing to a group of students. He was buried as Redland Green, on the outskirts of the city. Sir Arthur Quiller-Couch attended Bristol College in the 1870s, and Anthony Trollope lived here for a short time after the Post Office transferred him from Ireland. Sir Arthur Conan Doyle also had a brief experience with Bristol after he qualified as a surgeon; an old friend, Dr. Budd, had a highly successful practice here and invited Doyle to share it. The relationship was a short one because Budd's opening of Doyle's letters from "Ma'am" (as Doyle called his mother) led him to believe Doyle was ruining the practice, and he asked him to leave.

It may be that the most famous use of Bristol in literature occurred in the 19th century in Charles Dickens's *Pickwick Papers*. Dickens had first been here in 1835, when he and Thomas Beard were sent to cover Lord John Russell's political speeches for the *Morning Chronicle*. Dickens lodged at the Bush Inn on Corn Street where Lloyd's Bank now stands, and this, of course, is where that "ill starred gentleman" Mr. Winkle stays in the novel. After registering, he

walked forth to view the city, which struck him as being a shade more dirty than any place he had ever seen. Having inspected the docks and shipping and viewed the cathedral, he inquired his way to Clifton, and being directed thither, took the route which was pointed out to him. But as the pavements of Bristol are not the widest or cleanest upon earth, so its streets are not altogether the straightest or least intricate. . . .

The house to which Arabella Allen is sent to spend a period with an old aunt is in Westbury, and Sam Weller, who discovers Winkle here, is the one who makes the memorable trip across the Downs to find Miss Allen:

Accordingly, next morning Sam Weller issued forth upon his quest . . . and away he walked, up one street and down another—we were going to say up one hill and down another, only it's all uphill at Clifton. . . .

Sam struggled across the Downs against a good high wind, wondering whether it was always necessary to hold your hat on with both hands in that part of the country, and came to a shady by-place about which were sprinkled several little villas of quiet and secluded appearance. Outside a stable-door at the bottom of a long back-lane without a thoroughfare, a groom in undress was idling about, apparently persuading himself that he was doing something with a spade and wheelbarrow.

Dickens was also in Bristol in 1858, 1866, and 1869 on his provincial reading tours.

A second use of Bristol occurs in the opening chapters of Robert Louis Stevenson's *Treasure Island*. Indeed, the ship is berthed in the Bristol Channel, and Jim Hawkins travels here by coach to go on as a cabin boy:

"Where are we?" I asked.
"Bristol," said Tom. "Get down."
Mr. Trelawney had taken up his residence at an inn far down the docks, to superintend the work upon the schooner. Thither we had now to walk, and our way, to my great delight, lay along the quays and beside the great multitude of ships of all sizes and rigs and nations. . . . Though I had lived by the shore all my life, I seemed never to have been near the sea till then. The smell of tar and salt was something new. I saw the most wonderful figureheads, that had all been far over the ocean. I saw, besides, many old sailors, with rings in their ears, and

BRISTOL   West of Bristol proper is the Clifton area with its downs, gorge, and Leigh Wood. It was the gorge which Thomas Edward Brown, the Manx poet, directed a friend to visit for him after his death; in "Epistola ad Dakyns" he writes:
And you shall start as from a dream,
While I, withdrawing down the stream,
Drift vaporous to the ancient sea,
A wraith, a film, a memory--

whiskers curled in ringlets, and tarry pigtails, and their swaggering, clumsy sea-walk; and if I had seen as many kings or archbishops I could not have been more delighted.

The "Spy Glass" Inn (not identifiable) was on the quay:

The squire gave me a note addressed to John Silver, at the sign of the "Spy-glass," and told me I should easily find the place by following the line of the docks, and keeping a bright lookout for a little tavern with a large brass telescope for sign. . . .
It was a bright enough little place of entertainment. The sign was newly painted; the windows had neat red curtains; the floor was cleanly sanded. There was a street on each side, and an open door on both, which made the large, low room pretty clear to see in, in spite of clouds of tobacco smoke.

A third but relatively minor use of Bristol is in the works of Thomas Hardy, where it appears under its own name in *The Mayor of Casterbridge, The Woodlanders, A Pair of Blue Eyes,* "The Distracted Preacher" (*Wessex Tales*), and "The Lady Icenway" and "The First Countess of Wessex" (*A Group of Noble Dames*). In the last-named story, the critically ill Squire Dornell rides from Falls Park (Mells) to Bristol to confront Reynard, his unwelcome son-in-law. Hardy also uses the city in *The Dynasts* when he has "the winter sun a-slanting over Baldwin Street as 'a used to do. . . ."

In the 20th century Joyce Cary was here for a period of three years beginning in the autumn of 1903, when he entered Clifton College, which was then a kind of middle-class school preparing boys for Sandhurst. Cary lived at Tait's House, a sports-oriented dormitory, where he was "as temperamentally suited to the place as a duck is to a desert." In the spring following his arrival, his stepmother, of whom he was very fond, died; and about this time he determined on the life of a painter. He spent the requisite three years here, leaving at the age of seventeen for Paris to study art.

During World War I, Hilaire Belloc lectured on the war at Colston Hall to an audience of more than 2,000; following the death of his wife in 1914, Belloc threw himself into the war effort and lectured all over England. In July 1917 John Galsworthy and his wife Ada arrived here for a fortnight's stay; they were at the Spa Hotel in Clifton—"a nice hotel, very," as Galsworthy writes—and now called the Avon Gorge Hotel. Ada Galsworthy was having radiant-heat baths for the treatment of her rheumatism, and one of the Galsworthys' excursions was to the now-famed Bristol Zoo with its unique pair of white tigers. It was here that Galsworthy wrote "The Brave Angel."

BRITFORD, Wiltshire (pop. 366) In the Avon Valley less than 2 miles southeast of Salisbury, Britford contains a Saxon church that is an architectural treasure. The walls contain Roman bricks, the molding is the earliest known, and the soffit of the north arch shows the first-known example of paneling. Nearby, in a park of more than 250 acres by the Avon River, is one of the finest homes in Wiltshire, Longford Castle, built at the end of the 16th century by Sir Henry Gorges. Sir Philip Sidney makes Longford into the Castle of Amphialus in *Arcadia:*

[They] brought the three Ladies (by that time the night seemed with her silence to conspire to their treason) to a castle about ten mile off from the lodges; where they were fain to take a boat which waited for them. For the castle stood in the midst of a great lake, upon a high rock, where partly by art, but principally by nature, it was by all men esteemed impregnable.

The castle has been much altered since Sidney's time, but with a little effort one can still discern the original triangular shape.

BRIXHAM, Devon (pop. 8,147) Noted for its lush, colorful vegetation (including palm trees) and the attractiveness of sand and sea, the south Devon coast draws hordes of holiday visitors, and most towns live solely on revenue from tourism. Brixham, however, because it is situated on two excellent harbors, supports a large maritime industry; here the old village crawls up the hillside with the harbor half a mile below. Brixham's place in history is secure since this was the landing site of William of Orange on November 5, 1688, an event which ended the Glorious Revolution. During the latter part of the 19th century Brixham's fishing fleet was the most prosperous on the south coast; it was a little after this era that Francis Brett Young came here to join a Dr. Quicke's medical practice at Cleveland House; he found the town

lovely beyond words. No big hotel, no pier, no pierrots or theatre, a small beautiful harbour with 250 trawlers with brown sails . . . warm enough in winter for hedges of fuchsia and magnolias and palms and peaches.

By October 1908 he was living at Cumbers and planned to take Cleveland House in the spring when Quicke vacated it. Brixham becomes the setting of *Deep Sea,* his first novel, which was written here; Young became critically ill in January 1914 with influenza and jaundice and was sent to Algiers to recover. He returned here for only a short time before moving to the Old Garden House in Berry Head, on the south side of Torquay Bay, just east of Brixham. In the early summer of 1920 George Bernard Shaw walked here from his coastal lodgings on Start Bay; Young writes,

. . . we took tea on the lawn sitting on the grass, G.B.S. removed his shoes and put his feet on the tablecloth. . . . My wife sang *lieder* of Hugo Wolf. . . . He [Shaw] was enraptured.

Flora Thompson, the novelist, lived here at Hearthstone, a thatched cottage in Higher Brixham, from 1940 until her death in 1947.

BROAD CHALKE, Wiltshire (pop. 661) Broad Chalke, 8 miles southwest of Salisbury, is sheltered by the downs and irrigated by the lovely Ebble River. Its 13th-century church stands on Saxon foundations and has a great stone 15th-century porch sculpted with strange monsters and enormous bunches of foliage. The village was for a time the home of John Aubrey, the antiquarian, who served as warden of the church for a number of years. A more modern literary association is with Maurice Hewlett, who lived here from 1914 until his death on June 15, 1923; it was during this period that he wrote *The Song of the Plow* and was visited by William Butler Yeats. Hewlett was buried in Broad Chalke, and the church has a brass plaque referring to the *Song*.

BROAD CLYST, Devon (pop. 2,043)   Close enough to Exeter (5¼ miles southwest) for convenience, yet removed sufficiently to retain its pastoral nature, Broad Clyst has an enviable position. For many years Eden Phillpotts, prolific author of West Country novels, made his home here, at Kerswell; Phillpotts died here, at the age of 98, on December 29, 1960.

BROADSTAIRS, Kent (pop. 13,230)   With good sandy beaches beneath chalk cliffs, long hours of sunshine, a low annual rainfall, and a location less than 80 miles from London, Broadstairs is a popular residential and resort area. The old town around the jetty retains a 19th-century appearance, and Broadstairs is full of odd corners and surprises such as the alley of flint cottages on Serene Place and the remains of the 16th-century York Gate at the base of Harbour Street. In many essential ways the town is little changed from the days when Charles Dickens frequented it, and he still appears to be its presiding deity. There is an annual mid-June Dickens Festival during which people dress up in top hats, crinolines, muttonchop whiskers, parasols, and embroidered waistcoats to take a turn around the gardens at Bleak House (a place that has nothing to do with the novel of that name).

Dickens's first visit to Broadstairs occurred in the autumn of 1837, and he returned every summer (excepting 1844 and 1846, when he was in Italy and Switzerland) until 1851. He first had lodgings at 12 (now 31) High Street, a small two-story tenement with a small parlor, all of which has been rebuilt since his tenancy. It was here that he wrote the final

pages of *Pickwick Papers*. In 1839 he lodged at 40 Albion Street (now part of the Royal Albion Hotel), where he wrote the concluding chapters of *Nicholas Nickleby;* the next year he was in Broadstairs twice, at Lawn House (now Archway House), while he was working on *The Old Curiosity Shop*. It appears from Dickens's later correspondence that this house was absorbed into the hotel by 1859 when he was here. Although ill and trying to prepare himself for a provincial reading tour, he entertained numerous friends. He had then penned a description of Broadstairs:

> A good sea—fresh breezes—fine sands—and pleasant walks—with all manner of fishing-boats, lighthouses, piers, bathing-machines, are its only attractions; but it is one of the freshest and freest little places in the world.

The August 2, 1861, issue of *Household Words* contained an essay entitled "Our Watering-Place" (later reprinted as "Our English Watering-Place"), in which he describes the beach at low tide when "The ocean lies winking in the sunlight like a drowsy lion" and

> Rusty cables and chains, ropes and rings, undermost parts of posts and piles, and confused timber-defences against the waves, lie strewn about, in a brown litter of tangled seaweed and fallen cliff. . . .

The medieval parish church he calls "a hideous temple of flint, like a great petrified haystack," possibly an apt description but surely an unfair one. His observations of the High Street are no longer accurate:

> You would hardly guess which is the main street of our watering-place, but you may know it by its being always stopped up with donkey-chaises. Whenever you come here, and see harnessed donkeys eating clover out of barrows drawn completely across a narrow thoroughfare, you may be quite sure you are in our High Street.

These donkeys serve as a reminder that a Miss Mary Strong, the original of Betsy Trotwood in *David Copperfield*, lived on Nuckell's Place, at the end of Victoria Parade on the seafront, and, like Betsy, was convinced that she had the right to stop the passage of the animals in front of her cottage.

In 1847 and 1848 Dickens had lodgings on Chandos Place; tired of the continual search for lodgings and the attendant discomforts, he tried to secure the castellated Fort House (later called Bleak House) but was unable to take possession until the autumn of 1850. In the meantime he leased Lawn House. Here he worked on *Barnaby Rudge*. When Dickens first took possession of Bleak House, formerly the home of the sea captains in charge of the forts guarding Broadstairs Harbor, it was a good deal smaller than it is now, but it had more than an acre of ground, a large carriage drive, and a rent of a little less than £100 per year. This was Dickens's "airy nest," where within a few years "Vagrant music," as he called it, forced him to leave. His study, where he wrote a great deal of *David Copperfield*, has been described as a "small, three-cornered slip, 'about the size of a warm bathroom,'" and it contained an expansive window overlooking sand beach and sea. Dickens's last sojourn at Bleak House was his longest, from early May to November 1851, but by now complaints sounded in an earlier letter forced him out:

BROADSTAIRS   Presided over by the spirit of Charles Dickens, the inhabitants of Broadstairs hold an annual mid-June Charles Dickens Festival and dress the part. The house here is Bleak House, where the novelist stayed from 1850 on; Elizabeth Bowen describes the house in *Eva Trout*.

Vagrant music is getting to that height here and is so impossible to be escaped from, that I fear Broadstairs and I must part company in time to come. Unless it pours rain, I cannot write half an hour without the most excruciating organs, fiddles, bells, or glee-singers. There is a violin of the most torturing kind under the window now (time, ten in the morning), and an Italian box of music on the steps, both in full blast.

Bleak House is now a Dickens museum.

Wilkie Collins also frequented Broadstairs but for a much shorter period of time. His first trip in August 1858 was made to recuperate from illness, and he so liked the town that he leased Church Hill Cottage for six weeks the next year. He was working on *The Woman in White* and had finished the first installment by the middle of August. In 1862 Collins decided to spend the entire summer here and made arrangements to lease Fort House. His holiday lasted four months, and under the influence of the sea air his health improved immeasurably. Collins became a firm believer in one of the local treatments: "I swear by tepid salt-water baths—they soothe while you are in there and they invigorate afterwards." Dickens, who was in Folkestone at the time, was Collins's guest on the August Bank Holiday weekend.

Four other writers had associations with Broadstairs. George Eliot (Mary Ann Evans) lived in the town for a short time in 1852, Edward Bulwer-Lytton spent a small part of his Long Vacation here in 1824 with his mother; Lionel Johnson was born here on March 15, 1867; and Harold Monro died here on March 16, 1952.

BROADWATER, Sussex (pop. 5,498) The parent village of Worthing, 1½ miles to the south and on the seaside, but now the smaller of the two, Broadwater was once located at the edge of a wide expanse of the sea that stretched inland beneath the Downs. In 1887, after his death in Goring-by-Sea, Richard Jefferies, the naturalist and poet, was buried in the cemetery here. W. H. Hudson, author of *Green Mansions*, was also buried in this cemetery after his death in London on August 18, 1922. Of interest, too, is the grave of Mary Hughes, the subject of "Mary had a little lamb"; her association with the rhyme is noted on the tombstone.

BROADWINDSOR, Dorset (pop. 901) Surrounded by rich dairy countryside but in a sparsely settled area, Broadwindsor, 3 miles northwest of Beaminster, is overlooked by Lewesdon Hill, and Pilsdon Pen, the highest point in the shire. The Norman to Perpendicular church, built of golden ashlar, contains a very good Jacobean pulpit from which the Rev. Thomas Fuller probably preached. He was given the living here around 1634 and arrived to take up the post in July; he did, though, keep his legal residence at Cambridge so as to receive his D.D. Fuller wrote *The Historie of the Holy Warre* and *The Holy State and the Profane State* here. He married in 1637 or 1638, but only his wife's Christian name, Ellen, is known; she died within six months of the birth of their child in 1641. Fuller, who was removed from this post for siding with the Royalists in the Civil War, refused to take back the living, in 1660 when he returned and heard John Pinney, the interim incumbent, preach. Fuller said he "would not deprive them [the parishioners] of such a man."

BROCKENHURST, Hampshire (pop. 2,159) Attractively situated in one of the most picturesque parts of the New Forest, Brockenhurst is a popular residential village almost equidistant from Lymington and Lyndhurst, the area where even now a wealth of flora and fauna flourish. The area had an obvious attraction for W. H. Hudson, who lodged at Royden Manor in Brockenhurst when he was writing *Hampshire Days*, which deals with local natural history and people.

BROKENBOROUGH, Wiltshire (pop. 332) Situated on the Gloucestershire-Wiltshire border 2 miles northwest of Malmesbury, Brokenborough is spread over several levels with the church on a hill and the Avon River winding its way slowly through the meadows below. In 1576 Thomas Campion was brought here by his mother after the death of his father; they lived here for almost a year before leaving for London.

BROMHALL, Berkshire A small hamlet near Sunninghill and the Surrey border, Bromhall contained a lovely old manor house that belonged to St. John's College, Oxford, a fact that Roger Ascham knew when he asked the master and fellows of the college to permit him to serve as steward here. His request of January 18, 1565, was granted the following November, and Ascham's rent, for a forty-year period from Michaelmas, 1574, was assessed at £7/6/8.

BROMHAM, Wiltshire (pop. 1,147) Situated 3½ miles northwest of Devizes, the village of Bromham can be dated to the time when the site was a Roman station. Wans House, in the park, stands on the earlier site. The village has a group of 17th-century almshouses with five gables and six doors, but its 15th-century church, which overlooks the village, is the outstanding attraction. The Irish poet Thomas Moore, author of *Lalla Rookh* and "The Harp That Once in Tara's Halls," is buried in the churchyard. He lived in the nearby hamlet of Chittoe for almost thirty-five years and died there on February 25, 1852. His grave is marked by an 18-foot Celtic cross with an inscription from Byron and one from his own works:

Dear Harp of my country in darkness I found thee,
The cold chain of silence had hung o'er thee long,
When proudly, my own Island Harp, I unbound thee,
And gave all thy chords to light, freedom, and song.

BROMLEY, Kent (pop. 60,377) The growth of the megalopolis of London has reached the point that suburbs have their own suburbs, and Bromley, which a century ago was a quiet, relatively rural environment, has joined the parade quickly enough. In the 16th century this was a beautiful area of palatial homes and of Bromley Palace, the home of the bishops of Rochester from 967 to 1846 and now a teachers training college. In 1578 Edmund Spenser was appointed secretary to Bishop John Young, and he worked on a great deal of *The Shepheardes Calender* before leaving by the summer of 1579. His work contains a rather clear reference to the salt Medway and repeated references to the shire and some of its worthies.

In June 1652, returning to London from Tunbridge Wells, John Evelyn was set upon here by two cutthroats; the men

> threw me downe, & immediately tooke my sword, & haled me into a deepe Thickett, some quarter of a mile from the high-way, where they might securely rob me, as they soone did; what they got of mony was not considerable, but they tooke two rings, the one an Emrald with diamonds, an (Onyx), & a pair of boucles set with rubies & diamonds which were of value, and after all, barbarously bound my hands behind me, & my feete . . . & then set me up against an Oake. . . .

Evelyn managed to free himself, and with the help of "two Country fellows . . . got downe a steepe bank, into the highway againe" and made his way to Colonel Blount, the local justice. The diarist eventually recovered his rings and buckles but not the silver-hilted sword.

William Cobbett visited Bromley in 1822 on his way from Kensington to Battle and comments that this is "a very ugly country." He notes that the land in the area is generally "a deep loam on a gravel," with "few trees except elm," and seems amazed that it is so poor that only a few acres of swedes (rutabagas) are being raised and that the hop fields and orchards are of extremely low quality.

A more consistent association with Bromley begins later in the century with the birth of H. G. Wells at 47 (now 170) High Street on September 21, 1866. The house, called Atlas House, was a small three-story row house facing the Market Square; here Wells's father maintained an unsuccessful china shop. At the age of five Wells was sent to a Dame School kept by a Mrs. Knott nearby at 8 South Street, and two years later he was entered in Bromley Academy, run by Thomas Morley, just a few doors along on the High Street. Young Wells also attended the Bromley Parish Church, on the High Street, where Tetty, the wife of Dr. Samuel Johnson, is buried. Wells is known to have returned here in 1885 to visit his father after going to Uppark, Sussex, with his mother. Bromley appears in at least two of Wells's works, *The War in the Air* and *The New Machiavelli*. In the first work Bromley is the home of the Smallways, and in the second it becomes Bromstead, a London suburb and Remington's birthplace. Wells recalls the Bromstead of years past with its "narrow irregular little street of thatched houses strung out on the London and Dover Road" and a population of less than 2,000 before describing the effects of "progress":

> The population doubled again and doubled again, and became particularly teeming in the prolific "working-class" district about the deep-rutted, muddy, coal-blackened roads between the gasworks, Blodgett's laundries, and the railway goods-yard. . . . A single national school in an inconvenient situation set itself inadequately to collect subscriptions and teach the swarming, sniffing, grimy offspring of this dingy new population to read.

The Ravensbourne River here, which Wells calls the Ravensbrook, was a "beautiful stream" that

> came into my world out of a mysterious Beyond, out of a garden, splashing brightly down a weir which had once been the weir of a mill. (Above the weir and inaccessible there were bulrushes growing in splendid clumps, and beyond that, pampas grass, yellow and crimson spikes of hollyhock, and blue suggestions of wonderland.) From the pool at the foot of this initial cascade it flowed in a leisurely fashion beside a footpath. . . . Yellow and purple loose-strife and ordinary rushes grew in clumps along the bank, and now and then a willow. On rare occasions of rapture one might see a rat cleaning his whiskers at the water's edge. The deep places were rich with tangled weeds, and in them fishes lurked—to me they were big fishes. . . .

This stream, changed by progress, Wells later describes as a "dump for old iron, rusty cans, abandoned boots and the like . . ." that turns into a polluted, inky rivulet when it rains heavily.

BROMPTON, Yorkshire (pop. 598) The two villages of Brompton in Yorkshire are often confused: one is quite near Northallerton while the other, the smaller of the two and often called Brompton-by-Sawdon, is just a few miles southwest of Scarborough. It was in the parish church of the latter village that William Wordsworth and Mary Hutchinson were married on October 4, 1802. Mary Hutchinson had been living on her brother's farm at nearby Gallow Hill.

BROMSGROVE, Worcestershire (pop. 23,540) An old market town and now an industrial center, Bromsgrove is almost equidistant from Worcester and Birmingham; even though the M5 Motorway bypasses the city, the urban sprawl from Birmingham threatens to engulf the town. Bromsgrove has preserved a number of fine old buildings, and the High Street has a series of good Georgian structures. The battlemented sandstone Church of St. John the Baptist has a prime location on a hill just west of the High Street with a commanding view of the town. Of interest in the church are a chained copy of Bishop John Jewel's *Apology* and two alabaster monuments, dated 1450 and 1550. The later monument is that to Sir John Talbot, and the earlier is that of the armored Sir Humphrey Stafford who appears in William Shakespeare's *Henry VI: Part II*.

William Camden visited Bromsgrove and notes in his *Britannia*:

> "The town of *Bromesgrove* is all in a manner of one street, very long, standing in a plaine ground. There is once a week a meetly good market. The heart of the town is meetly well paved. The town standeth something by clothing." It . . . has a charity-school, founded by Edward VI and a market.

The school to which Camden refers is the Bromsgrove School to the south of the town. The poet and classical scholar A. E. Housman was brought to the town by his parents from nearby Fockbury in 1860; his father, a solicitor, had offices here. The family lived at Perry Hall (now a hotel). In 1870 the boy was elected to a foundation scholarship at Bromsgrove School, where he remained until going up to Oxford in 1877; his level of scholarship here was quite high, and he won his first school prize at fourteen for a poem on Sir Walter Ralegh. Housman captured two more school prizes for "The Death of Socrates" and "Paul on Mars Hill." After he took his degree at Oxford, he took a temporary assignment teaching VIth form Greek and Latin here while studying at home for his Civil Service examinations.

BROOKSBY, Leicestershire (pop. 43) Just 9 miles northeast of Leicester on the Wreak River, the village contains a magnificent Elizabethan and later manor house and a church which is more a nobleman's chapel than a villager's church. The Hall was the birthplace in 1592 of George Villiers, later the 1st Duke of Buckingham. His father, Sir George Villiers, was married to Mary Beaumont, through whom Francis Beaumont, the dramatist, had an association with Brooksby. As a young man Beaumont often journeyed here from Belton, 13 miles to the west, to visit his younger cousins John, George, and Christopher.

BROUGHAM, Westmorland (pop. 253) Brougham (pronounced "bruff'am") is on the Eamont River 2 miles southeast of Penrith; the Romans had a camp here, and the small Saxon Church of St. Ninian is notable for its fine old woodwork. The Norman castle, once the home of the powerful Clifford family and of Lady Anne de Clifford, stands on the south bank of the Eamont and was one of the most nearly complete military strongholds in Westmorland. The story of how Lady Anne hid her two young sons from the Yorkist forces after the death of Lord de Clifford at Towton and of how they were kept in hiding in Yorkshire and Scotland learning to become shepherds is part of this castle's past. William Wordsworth celebrates this story in the "Song at the Feast of Brougham Castle":

Love had he found in huts where poor men lie;
His daily teachers had been woods and rills,
The silence that is in the starry sky,
The sleep that is among the lonely hills.

In him the savage virtue of the Race,
Revenge, and all ferocious thoughts were dead:
Nor did he change; but kept in lofty place
The wisdom which adversity had bred.

BROUGHTON, Staffordshire (pop. 351) Situated 10 miles southwest of Newcastle-under-Lyme and close to the Shropshire border, Broughton has a lovely 17th-century church and a fine Elizabethan hall. A story of high adventure concerns Blore Pipe House and the sober figure of Izaak Walton, who risked imprisonment in the Tower of London to help King Charles II. After the Battle of Worcester, Col. John Blague came here to hide with one of the crown jewels entrusted to his care by Charles; knowing that his capture was almost certain, he entrusted the stone to his host, George Barlow, left the house on foot, and was promptly captured. Walton, then aged fifty-eight, was in Stafford on one of his periodic visits when he learned of his friend's dilemma and came here to take the stone away. Not under suspicion by the Parliamentarians, he carried the gem to London and managed to return it to Blague after the colonel's escape from the tower.

BUCKDEN, Huntingdonshire (pop. 998) For centuries the bishops of Lincoln made their home here. Near the river and Huntingdon, 3 miles to the northeast, Buckden gave the churchmen excellent access to both London and Lincoln. In the Middle Ages this diocese had the largest area in Great Britain, and the strategic location of Buckden was ideal for its administration. John Leland, antiquarian and librarian to Henry VIII, visited Buckden and noted the palace and the surrounding area in his *Itinerary*. The bishops' palace was used until 1837, when the diocese was divided into more manageable portions; coming into secular hands, it was unroofed and dismantled, and little was left except half of the inner gatehouse and the tower. Daniel Defoe saw the estate in its original form:

The House and Garden surrounded by a very large and deep Moat of Water; the House is old, but pleasant, the Chappel very pretty, 'tho' small; there is an Organ painted against the Wall, but in a seeming Organ-loft, and so properly placed and well painted, that we at first believed it really to be an Organ.

It is because of the association with the Lincoln bishopric that there is literary interest in Buckden. Laurence Sterne, who entered holy orders on the advice of his uncle Jacques, a canon of the Cathedral of York, was ordained deacon here by Richard Reynolds, Bishop of Lincoln, on March 6, 1736, and appears also to have served as a curate here.

BUCKFASTLEIGH, Devon (pop. 2,264) Set between the Dart River to the west and the Asburn River to the east, the village of Buckfastleigh, 12 miles west of Torquay, is on the edge of the Dartmoor Forest. Henry II (r. 1154–1189) refounded a monastery that was originally Saxon; the buildings were only partially destroyed at the dissolution of the monasteries in the 16th century, and the old tithe barn is still intact. In 1882 the monastic ruins were bought for the refounding of a Benedictine colony, and the present abbey and church have been constructed by modern monks from Burgundy and Belgium. When George Bernard Shaw visited here from Torquay, he was much taken with the abbey and his guide, a scholarly Belgian monk. While touring the grounds, the two men debated the merits of the Authorized and Douai Versions of the Bible, with the monk arguing that the Authorized was by far the better. So deeply impressed was Shaw that when he departed, he stuffed the building fund box with treasury notes.

BUCKLEBURY, Berkshire (pop. 1,908) Situated in the lovely Pang Valley 5 miles northeast of Newbury, Bucklebury is a village of old cottages, a partly Norman church, and an enormous common. An outstanding feature of the common is a mile-long avenue of oaks planted in honor of Queen Anne when she came to the old manor house to visit Viscount Bolingbroke. The manor house once belonged to the Abbey of Reading and served as the abbot's country residence. At the dissolution of the monasteries in the 16th century the lands came to John Winchcombe, who began the Tudor residence. The estate passed to the St. John family with the marriage of Sir Henry Winchcombe's daughter to Viscount Bolingbroke. The St. John family was intimately connected with literature in the 18th century, and among Bolingbroke's frequent guests here were Alexander Pope, John Gay, and Jonathan Swift. Swift described the viscount's management of the estate in a letter to Stella: "He smoked tobacco with one or two neighbours; he enquired after wheat in such a field; he went to visit his hounds and knew all their names." The house was destroyed by fire in the 19th century.

BUDE, Cornwall (pop. 4,940) On the Atlantic coast, Bude was at one time an important port, but the treachery of the coastal rocks and the frequently severe storms ultimately brought an end to its harbor activities. From 1824 to 1874, for example, more than eighty ships were wrecked in the vicinity. The town is now a pleasant resort known for its bracing breezes and wide, sandy beaches; it also boasts the best surfing in Great Britain. The old part of the town along the canal has remained virtually untouched, and just west of the canal are St. Michael's Church and the vicarage, with its associations with the Rev. Robert Stephen Hawker, who spent many holidays in the area as a boy. The vicarage is an unusual building: none of the walls of its rooms join at right angles. It was here that Hawker, at the age of nineteen, successfully proposed to Charlotte I'Ans, who was forty-one; the marriage lasted for almost forty years. Bude was the scene of the prank perpetrated by Hawker on the superstitious inhabitants of the town in July 1826. Making his way to the rocks offshore, wearing a seaweed wig, and wrapped in an oilskin from the waist down, Hawker flashed "moonbeams" at the shore with a hand mirror and sang until the people noticed the "mermaid." Crowds appeared nightly; "she" sang, dived into the water, and disappeared. Hawker finally became too hoarse and cold to carry on, and the finale was fitting; "she" sang "God Save the King" and disappeared. It was years later, on a return visit, that he revealed the hoax.

Near St. Michael's Church west of the canal is the Falcon Hotel, where John Galsworthy stayed on his second visit to Bude in January 1915. He was here for a special reason, as his diary records under the date of January 25: "Walked by downs to Widemouth, thence to Markhamchurch and back by canal to Bude, looking for local colour for story Manna." He also spent the 1907 summer holidays in Devon and Cornwall, but mostly here, and was then undoubtedly working on *The Shadows,* later titled *Fraternity.*

BULKINGTON, Warwickshire (pop. 4,950) The small country roads wind about the village of Bulkington, 3½ miles southeast of Nuneaton, and are lined with a mixture of new houses and 16th- to 18th-century cottages. The church, which dates in part from the 12th century, has a remarkable marble font made by a local amateur sculptor, Richard Hayward, and other local artists have added their work to the building. Marston Hall here was the prototype for Garum Firs in *The Mill on the Floss* by George Eliot (Mary Ann Evans); as a child George Eliot often visited the Hall, where her mother's sister Elizabeth and her husband Richard Johnson lived. The Johnsons (he was a gentleman farmer) were the originals of the Pullets of the novel. Maggie and Tom arrive at the hall:

> . . . [T]his was only the beginning of beautiful sights at Garum Firs. All the farmyard life was wonderful there— bantams, speckled and top-knotted; Friesland hens, with their feathers all turned the wrong way; Guinea-fowls that flew and screamed and dropped their pretty-spotted feathers; pouter pigeons and a tame magpie; nay, a goat, and a wonderful brindled dog, half mastiff, half bull-dog, as large as a lion. Then there were white railings and white gates all about, and glittering weathercocks of various design, and garden-walks paved with pebbles in beautiful

patterns—nothing was quite common at Garum Firs: and Tom thought that the unusual size of the toads there was simply due to the general unusualness which characterized uncle Pullet's possessions as a gentleman farmer. Toads who paid rent were naturally leaner.

Elizabeth and Richard Johnson are buried in the Bulkington churchyard, near the south door of the church.

BUNGAY, Suffolk (pop. 3,103) At one time the Suffolk central plateau was heavily wooded, but now that it has been cleared, it is rich farming land; some of the present farms cover more than 2,500 acres, and villages tend to cluster around greens which date to medieval clearings. One such village is Bungay, on the Waveney River, at the north edge of the plateau, 6 miles west of Beccles (itself west of Lowestoft). It is an old town, and the castle ruins seen today date to Roger Bigod, 5th Earl of Norfolk and Marshal of England during the reign (1272–1307) of Edward I. The castle was actually Roger's crenellated house; at Bigod's death there was no issue, and the castle passed out of family hands and eventually into a ruinous state.

Holy Trinity Church dates in part from the early 12th century; the 15th-century St. Mary's Church, strange-looking because of its missing chancel, has the ruins of an old priory abutting its east side. West of the church's north porch is the 3-foot-high Bungay Stone, reportedly a druidical relic some 2,000 years old; until recently the village's children had a ritual of dancing around the stone twelve times and pretending to invoke the devil.

Some of the very little formal education that the poet George Crabbe received was here in Bungay; his father enrolled him in a school run by a Mr. Harvey where the discipline was extremely harsh if not sadistic. Crabbe disliked the school intensely and was eventually removed and sent to Stowmarket. *The Borough* describes some of his feelings.

At one time during his exile from France from 1793 to 1800, Vicomte François-René de Chateaubriand lived on Bridge Street and survived by teaching French privately and at Beccles College. Sir Henry Rider Haggard, who later lived in nearby Ditchingham, called Chateaubriand "Monsieur Shatterbrain."

BUNTINGFORD, Hertfordshire (pop. 1,559) Situated 7 miles south of Royston on the Rib River, Buntingford has a Roman road for its High Street and a goodly number of 16th- and 17th-century houses and inns lining the roadway. Nearby West Mill (Westmill Green) contains the cottage and garden that Charles Lamb owned from 1812 on; Lamb's godfather, Francis Fielde, died in August of that year and left all the property to his wife, who gave the cottage to Lamb in the same month. The cottage, which the essayist named Button Snap, is thatched and has diamond-paned windows; it is now in the hands of the Royal Society of Arts. Lamb never lived here. "My First Play" describes his feelings here:

> When I journeyed down to take possession, and planted foot on my own ground, the stately habits of the donor descended upon me, and I strode (shall I confess the vanity?) with larger paces over my allotment of three-quarters of an acre, with its commodious mansion in the midst,

with the feeling of an English freeholder that all betwixt sky and centre was my own. The estate has passed into more prudent hands, and nothing but an agrarian can restore it.

Thomas Babington Macaulay spent the years from 1814 to 1818 at a school at nearby Aspenden Hall run by a Mr. Preston, who recognized the young man's precocity.

BURFORD, Oxfordshire (pop. 1,453) There is frequent confusion over Burford Bridge, Surrey, and Burford, Oxfordshire, but this Cotswold Oxfordshire village is an ancient town, and it may be the location of a church assembly attended by the King of Mercia in 683. The long main street slopes down to the Windrush River and crosses the water over an old stone bridge with three arches. The streets are lined with numerous Tudor and Georgian houses, and two of the ancient inns are of note: the 15th-century Bear and the 16th-century Bull. Near the bridge is a long four-gable house that once belonged to Symeon Wysdom and was given to the local grammar school. It was here that John Wilmot, 2d Earl of Rochester, received his early education; he succeeded to the title in February 1658 at the age of ten, and in 1659 he went up to Wadham College, Oxford. The old priory, an Elizabethan mansion, became a private residence at the dissolution of the monasteries in the 16th century, when it came into the hands of Lawrence Tanfield, a distinguished lawyer. It is generally conceded that Michael Drayton was employed by Tanfield as a tutor to his daughter Elizabeth in 1596 or 1597 and lived here at that time. Drayton dedicated "The Epistle of William de la Pole and Margaret of Anjou" to Elizabeth, "my honoured mistresse," when she was approximately ten years of age.

BURFORD BRIDGE, Surrey Located in one of the most scenic English down and valley areas, Burford Bridge is the most popular approach to Box Hill in the lovely Mole Valley. Just over 1½ miles northeast of Dorking, the small community consists of nothing more than an old bridge and the Burford Bridge Hotel, which was originally a smaller establishment called the Fox and Hounds. That inn established a reputation for its accommodations and its vista by the late 18th century, and it was probably on the recommendation of William Hazlitt, who had been here earlier, that John Keats lodged at the inn in November and December 1817. Keats's room looked out on the 2-acre garden, which was half invaded by box and yews. His delight with Burford Bridge, heightened by his view of the Mole River and the walk up Box Hill, is shown in a letter: "I like this place very much. There is Hill & Dale and a little River—I went up Box Hill this Evening after the Moon—you a' seen the Moon—came down—and wrote some lines." The lines, most likely, were part of *Endymion,* which he finished after six months' work on November 28, and could even have been the following:

> Under the brow
> Of some steep mossy hill, where ivy dun
> Would hide us up, although spring leaves were none;
> And where dark yew trees as we rustle through,
> Will drop their scarlet berry cups of dew?
> O thou wouldst joy to live in such a place;
> Dusk for our loves, yet light enough to grace
> Those gentle limbs on mossy bed reclin'd

> For by one step the blue sky shouldst thou find,
> And by another, in deep dell below,
> See, through the trees, a little river go
> All in its midday gold and glimmering.

A later guest at the hotel was Robert Louis Stevenson, who stayed on four separate occasions at "the inn at Burford Bridge with its arbours and green gardens and silent, eddying river." In the 20th century the Burford Bridge Hotel was used by H. G. Wells in *The Research Magnificent,* in which Benham has lunch here on his walking tour. It also seems likely that Wells himself was here on one of his many escapes from Spade House, at Sandgate, or London. There is as well an interesting historical sidelight about the hotel. In a room adjacent to that occupied later by Keats, Lord Nelson stayed on his last night in England and said his farewell to Lady Hamilton.

BURGHLEY HOUSE, Northamptonshire A great house is not usually a geographical entity in England, but an exception has to be made for the home of a branch of the Cecil family, Burghley House, which is located on the south side of Stamford on the Welland River. The town, actually known properly as Stamford Barton St. Michael's Without, embraces three civil parishes, and to further the confusion, part of Stamford is in Lincolnshire, and part is in Northamptonshire. In the 10th century Burghley belonged to the Benedictine abbey at Peterborough, but it became prominent after the grounds came into the hands of David Cecil in 1526. It was his grandson, William Cecil, the 1st Baron Burghley and Elizabeth's Lord High Treasurer, who built the great house, which incorporated a smaller structure built by his father as part of the east wing. Burghley passed to his son Thomas Cecil, later 1st Earl of Exeter. The house is built on a courtyard plan with the longer axis running east to west. Frequently called the finest Elizabethan mansion in England, it has many rooms of exceptional beauty; the Great Hall has a double hammer-beam roof, the chapel that Queen Elizabeth attended has an altarpiece by Paolo Veronese, and the walls and ceiling of the Heaven Room are covered with the work of Antonio Verrio.

Daniel Defoe visited the house and park and describes them in lavish detail in *A Tour thro' the Whole Island of Great Britain:*

> But the Beauty of *Stamford* is ... call'd *Burleigh House.* . . .
> This House, built all of Free-stone, looks more like a Town than a House, at which Avenue soever you come to it; the Towers and the Pinnacles so high, and placed at such a Distance from one another, look like so many distant Parish-Churches in a great Town, and a large Spire cover'd with Lead, over the great Clock in the Center, looks like the Cathedral, or chief Church of the Town.

While Defoe does not catalog the paintings, he comments on the collection and shows a special interest in Verrio,

> of whose Work I need say no more than this, that the Earl kept him twelve Years in his Family, wholly employ'd in Painting those Cielings and Stair-Cases, &c. and allow'd him a Coach and Horses, and Equipage, a Table, and Servants, and a very considerable Pension.

N.B. "The Character this Gentleman left behind him at this Town, is, that he deserv'd it all for his Paintings; but for nothing else; his scandalous Life, and his unpaid Debts, it seems, causing him to be but very meanly spoken of in the Town of *Stamford*.

Sir Walter Scott also visited the house about a century later and writes:

The house is magnificent, in the style of James I's reign, and consequently in mixed Gothic. Of paintings I know nothing; so shall attempt to say nothing. But whether to connoisseurs, or to an ignorant admirer like myself, the Salvator Mundi, by Carlo Dolci, must seem worth a king's ransom.

John Dryden was a frequent guest of the Cecils and, in fact, worked on a great part, possibly the entire seventh book, of his translation of Virgil here. The house itself entered a poem by Alfred, Lord Tennyson; "The Lord of Burleigh" was based, said the author, on the true story of Sarah Hoggins, who married a landscape painter in 1791, only to find out he was heir to the estate:

And they speak in gentle murmur,
  When they answer to his call,
While he treads with footstep firmer,
  Leading on from hall to hall.
And, while now she wonders blindly,
  Nor the meaning can divine,
Proudly turns he round and kindly,
  "All of this is mine and thine."
Here he lives in state and bounty,
  Lord of Burleigh, fair and free,
Not a lord in all the county
  Is so great a lord as he.

The same story is told by Thomas Moore in "You Remember Ellen" and by William Hazlitt in the *New Monthly Magazine*.

Finally, Burghley Park seems to have played a role in the development of the Northamptonshire poet John Clare; in 1806 Clare bought a copy of James Thomson's *Seasons* for a shilling in Stamford and began reading it while on his walk back to Helpston. The thirteen-year-old reached Burghley Park, sat down among the lime trees, and wrote his first poem here.

BURITON, Hampshire (pop. 644) Buriton, on the edge of the Queen Elizabeth Forest, is much changed since Edward Gibbon knew it, but it is still a quiet village, and much of its 18th-century character remains, at least in the old part of the village. The church, rectory, cottages, and old manor house are very much as they were then; and the late Georgian manor house, just north of the church, is where Gibbon spent much of his early adulthood. Gibbon's father settled here after the death of his first wife, and Edward Gibbon joined him in 1759 after returning from the Continent. One of the more distasteful experiences of young Gibbon's life occurred at this time: he joined the local militia, in which he served as a captain. Gibbon's *Autobiography* describes the house as formerly "an old mansion in a state of decay," which had been renovated in the current style. The location, "not happily chosen," was that of the original owner: the original house, a long, low Elizabethan structure, was added to at various times in the 18th century. A large rectangular pond quite near the house is still a breeding ground and sanctuary for wild ducks.

BURNHAM, Buckinghamshire (pop. 4,113) The village of Burnham stands guard over the park, common, and beech woods of the 600-acre forest of Burnham Beeches; acquired by the City of London Corporation in 1879 and now in the hands of the National Trust, this area has maintained an air of rusticity even though it is close to London and to Maidenhead, 2½ miles to the southwest. Burnham had its first major settlement in 1265, when a nunnery was established here. In 1916 the original order, Anglican nuns of the Society of the Precious Blood, was reestablished in the original location; a massive wall surrounds the grounds and buildings, and since the order is a closed one, none of the ruins can be seen.

Thomas Gray was a frequent visitor to Burnham Grove, the home of his uncle, Robert Antrobus, and spent here a number of vacations from Cambridge, as in August 1736 and August 1737; the nearness to Stoke Poges afforded him the opportunity of visiting other relatives. In 1737 Thomas Southerne, author of *Oroonoko* and *The Fatal Marriage*, was in the vicinity and came here to see Gray; Southerne was then aged seventy-seven, and this was one of a number of contacts, continued when Gray later visited Southerne at his home. In the 19th century William Butler Yeats came here from Sligo, Ireland, to be with his father, an artist, who was working here.

BURNHAM The 600-acre forest of Burnham Beeches dominates the small village of Burnham, where the poet Thomas Gray spent many of his Cambridge vacations.

BURSLEM, Staffordshire (pop. 41,566) One of the famous Five Towns known as the Potteries, Burslem is 20 miles north of Stafford on the Grand Trunk Canal and stands above the Trent River. (The towns in fact number six—Burslem, Hanley, Longton, Tunstall, Fenton, and Stoke and are now loosely amalgamated into Stoke-on-Trent.) It was no accident that the pottery industry grew up here; indeed, archaeological evidence shows that pottery was made here as early as Neolithic times and that the Romans and the Saxons also worked the clay here. The introduction of tea to England in 1657, a taste which became fashionable among the rich, brought about a heavy demand for cups, saucers, teapots, and sugar bowls, and the industry was well set by the time Josiah Wedgwood was born here in 1730. The town grew rapidly without any sort of planning, and its aspect is rather dull, with a noticeable lack of symmetry.

Burslem and the Potteries are intimately associated with Arnold Bennett's life and his novels; his father, after being a potter, schoolmaster, and pawnbroker, decided to qualify as a solicitor and moved his family to the Dalehall area, St. John Street, from Hanley. The family fortunes were then low, and their four-room house here was set in a cul-de-sac of similar houses; the Bennetts were then offered 175 Newport Lane by Bennett's grandfather, and the family lived here until 1879, after the elder Bennett had passed his first law examination, when they moved to one of a group of terraced houses with stone ornamentation and iron balconies on Waterloo Road; it was Number 198. Two years later they built 205 Waterloo Road, a small red-brick house. Bennett first attended the Wesleyan Infants' School at Swan Bank and then went to the Burslem Endowed School in the Wedgwood Institute on Queen Street. The school was moved in 1880 to Longport Hall; and in May 1882 Bennett began attending the middle school in Newcastle-under-Lyme. He left Burslem for London in March 1889 but returned to spend a few holidays here (summer 1893 and Christmas 1903). After Bennett's death in March 1931, his ashes were brought here and placed in his mother's grave, which is marked by an obelisk and her family name of Longton. The museum on the south side of the town at Corbridge contains a good Bennett collection.

Bennett uses both the general area and Burslem extensively in his novels; Freehold Terrace, near the Bennetts' early Newport Lane home, becomes Freehold Villas in *Hilda Lessways:*

> The row was called Freehold Villas: a consciously proud name in a district where much of the land was copyhold. . . . Most of the dwellings were owned by their occupiers, who, each an absolute monarch of the soil, niggled in his sooty garden of an evening amid the flutter of drying shirts and towels. Freehold Villas symbolized the final triumph of Victorian economics, the apotheosis of the prudent and industrious artisan. . . . She saw in Freehold Villas nothing but narrowness (what long narrow strips of gardens, and what narrow homes all flattened together!), and uniformity, and brickiness, and polished brassiness, and righteousness, and an eternal laundry.

From her window

at the front of the house, Hilda looked westwards up toward the slopes of Chatterley Wood, where as a child she used to go with other children to pick the sparse bluebells that thrived on smoke. The bailiwick of Turnhill lay behind her; and all the murky district of the Five Towns, of which Turnhill is the northern outpost, lay to the south. At the foot of Chatterley Wood the canal wound in large curves on its way towards the undefiled plains of Cheshire and the sea. On the canal-side, exactly opposite to Hilda's window, was a flour-mill, that sometimes made nearly as much smoke as the kilns and chimneys closing the prospect on either hand. From the flour-mill a bricked path, which separated a considerable row of new cottages from their appurtenant gardens led straight into Lessways Street, in front of Mrs. Lessways' house.

Clayhanger and *Anna of the Five Towns* are the works most widely associated with Burslem; in the former, Edwin comes down into Bursley's Duck Square,

> one of the oldest, if the least imposing, of all the public places in Bursley. It had no traffic across it, being only a sloping rectangle, like a vacant lot, with Trafalgar Road and Wedgwood Street for its exterior sides, and no outlet on its inner sides. The buildings on those inner sides were low and humble, and, as it were, withdrawn from the world, the chief of them being the ancient Duck Inn, where the hand-bell-ringers used to meet. But Duck Square looked out upon the very birth of Trafalgar Road. . . . At the junction of Trafalgar Road and Aboukir Street stood the Dragon Hotel, once the great posting-house of the town, from which all roads started. Duck Square had watched coaches and waggons stop at and start from the Dragon Hotel for hundreds of years. It had seen the Dragon rebuilt in brick and stone, with fine bay windows on each storey, in early Georgian times, and it had seen even the new structure become old and assume the dignity of age.

Nearby Corbridge, where the Bennetts' last house is actually located, becomes Bleakridge in these works, and the house is intimately portrayed in *Clayhanger:*

> Towards six o'clock he [Edwin] was in his bedroom, an attic with a floor very much more spacious than its ceiling, and a window that commanded the slope of Trafalgar Road towards Bleakridge. It had been his room, his castle, his sanctuary, for at least ten years, since before his mother's death of cancer.

Trafalgar Road is Waterloo Road; this novel also supplies the details of Bennett's school days. The Stych Pottery in the novel is the Mill Pottery:

> Mr. Orgreave crossed the road and then stood still to gaze at the facade of the Stych Pottery. It was a long two-storey building, purest Georgian, of red brick with very elaborate stone facings which contrasted admirably with the austere simplicity of the walls. The porch was lofty, with a majestic flight of steps narrowing to the doors. The ironwork of the basement railings was unusually rich and impressive.

Most of the names here are local, including Leicester, the chemist; Pidduck and Beardmore, the ironmongers; Swinnerton, the caterers; Cliffs, the butcher; Calvert, the grocer; Norris, the wines and spirits merchant; Savage, the printer; Heaton, the solicitor; and Steele, the auctioneer.

In *Anna of the Five Towns*, Bursley,

> the ancient home of the potter, has an antiquity of a thousand years. It lies towards the north end of an exten-

sive valley, which must have been one of the fairest spots in Alfred's England, but which is now defaced by the activities of a quarter of a million people. Five contiguous towns—Turnhill, Bursley, Hanbridge, Knype, and Longshaw ... are mean and forbidding of aspect—sombre, hard-featured, uncouth; and the vaporous poison of their ovens and chimneys has soiled and shrivelled the surrounding country till there is no village lane within a league but what offers a gaunt and ludicrous travesty of rural charms.

Waterloo Road again becomes Trafalgar Road,

the long thoroughfare which, under many aliases, runs through the Five Towns from end to end, uniting them as a river might unite them.

Bennett continues and makes the social distinction:

Within the municipal limits Bleakridge was the pleasantest quarter of Bursley—Hillport, abode of the highest fashion, had its own government and authority—and to reside "at the top of Trafalgar Road" was still the final ambition of many citizens, though the natural growth of the town had robbed Bleakridge of some of that exclusive distinction which it once possessed.

The overpowering atmosphere of the Five Towns emerges later in the novel:

Probably no one in the Five Towns takes a conscious pride in the antiquity of the potter's craft, nor in its unique and intimate relation to human life, alike civilized and uncivilized. Man hardened clay into a bowl before he spun flax and made a garment, and the last lone man will want an earthen vessel after he has abandoned his ruined house for a cave, and his woven rags for an animal's skin. ... If no other relic of immemorial past is to be seen in these modernized sordid streets, there is at least the living legacy of that extraordinary kinship between workman and work, that instinctive mastery of clay which the past has bestowed upon the present. The horse is less to the Arab than clay is to the Bursley man. He exists in it and by it; it fills his lungs and blanches his cheek; it keeps him alive and it kills him. His fingers close round it as round the hand of a friend. He knows all its tricks and aptitudes; when to coax it and when to force it, when to rely on it and when to distrust it. ... A dozen decades of applied science have of course resulted in the interposition of elaborate machinery between the clay and the man; but no great vulgar handicraft has lost less of the human than potting. Clay is always clay. ...

Bennett attended the Swan Bank Methodist Church, which plays an important role in this novel under the guise of Duck Bank. Many of Bennett's other works also include Burslem; for example, his brother Frank's house appears in *Whom God Hath Joined* as the solicitor Fearn's house.

Other authors have used Burslem and the Potteries; H. G. Wells spent a holiday here with a friend who worked at the Potteries and later mentions a conjurer in Burslem at the beginning of *The Time Machine*. George Orwell (Eric Blair) includes a description of the area (and a comment about Bennett) in *The Road to Wigan Pier*:

The pottery towns are almost equally ugly in a prettier way. Right in among the rows of tiny blackened houses, part of the street as it were, are the "pot banks"—conical brick chimneys like gigantic burgundy bottles buried in the soil and belching their smoke almost in your face. You come upon monstrous clay chasms hundreds of feet across and almost as deep, with little rusty tubs creeping

on chain railways up one side, and on the other workmen clinging like samphire-gatherers and cutting into the face of the cliff with their picks. I passed that way in snowy weather, and even the snow was black. The best thing one can say for the pottery towns is that they are fairly small and stop abruptly.

The most critical view of the area is that of J. B. Priestley in his *English Journey;* he notes the amalgamation into Stoke-on-Trent and comments:

For what distinguishes this district to my eye and mind, is its universal littleness. ... You see no huge warehouses, no high public buildings. The houses, which stretch out in a ribbon development for miles and miles, are nearly all workmen's cottages, and if they are not actually small of their kind, they contrive to suggest they are. ...

It resembles no other industrial area I know. I was at once repelled and fascinated by its odd appearance. ... Here ... there was more smoke than I had ever seen before. ...

To begin with, it is extremely ugly. ... [T]he general impression is of an exceptionally mean, dingy provinciality, of Victorian industrialism in its dirtiest and most cynical aspect.

BURTON, Hampshire (pop. 637) The small village of Burton, located 1 mile northeast of Christchurch, is practically a part of the larger town although it has managed to retain its individuality. Robert Southey lived in a cottage here in the summer of 1797, when he was visited by Charles Lamb and Charles Lloyd, a mutual friend whose tangled love affair Lamb and Southey tried to sort out. Lamb and Lloyd stayed overnight, and Lamb wrote a letter from Burton dated August 24. Numerous cottages here claim to be the one leased by Southey; the best claimant appears to be Burton Cottage, on the south end of the green.

BURTON-IN-KENDAL, Westmorland (pop. 460) Burton-in-Kendal, at the southern tip of Westmorland on the Lancashire border 10 miles south of Kendal, is a mixture of old and new with some good 18th-century houses, a market cross with recesses cut for leg-irons, and a partly medieval church. John Keats was here in May 1818 on his walking tour through the Lake District; he stopped first at the Green Dragon Inn, where he was turned away by the landlord, of whom Keats says:

It was the Green Dragon himself, in the shape of a tall corpulent figure, with the largest face that ever man was blessed with, a face like a target, and one that a starving traveller would be tempted to shoot at.

He was finally able to secure food but not lodging at the King's Arms.

BURWASH, Sussex Spread along a ridge between the Rother and Dudwell Rivers, Burwash is an extremely attractive village 5½ miles east of Heathfield; the village consists of a single main street with the church at its eastern end. Just a short distance outside the village is a house that draws thousands of visitors yearly; standing in the valley with a wooded hill on one side and the village on the other is Bateman's, the home of Rudyard Kipling from 1902 until his death in London in 1936. Kipling moved here from Rottingdean, and he later told of the family's first visit to Bateman's:

> We had seen an advertisement of her, and we reached her down an enlarged rabbit-hole of a lane. At very first sight the Committee of Ways and Means said: "That's her! The Only She! Make an honest woman of her quick!" We entered and felt her Spirit—her Feng Shui—to be good.

He describes the house as "a grey stone lichened house—A.D. 1634 over the door—beamed, panelled, with old oak staircase, and all untouched and unflaked." He says that it was "a good and peaceable place standing in terraced lawns nigh to a walled garden of old red brick, and two fat-headed oasthouses with red brick stomachs, and an aged silver-grey dovecot on top."

At Bateman's Kipling wrote *Puck of Pook's Hill, Rewards and Fairies,* and his Sussex poems:

> Here through the strong and shadeless days
>   The tinkling silence thrills;
> Or little, lost, Down churches praise
>   The Lord who made the hills:
> But here the Old Gods guard their round,
>   And, in her secret heart,
> The heathen kingdom Wilfrid found
>   Dreams, as she dwells, apart.

Kipling's study on the first floor of the house is much as he left it, with the raised chair (because of his shortness) and his books lining the walls. From the bedroom across the hall Pook's Hill, a small dome-shaped hill, can be seen; here Puck appears before Dan and Una, and Dan states, "This is our field":

> "Is it?" said their visitor, sitting down. "Then what on Human Earth made you act *Midsummer Night's Dream* three times over, *on* Midsummer Eve, *in* the middle of a Ring, and under—right *under* one of my oldest hills in Old England? Pook's Hill—Puck's Hill—Pook's Hill! It's as plain as the nose on my face."
> He pointed to the bare, fern-covered slope of Pook's Hill that runs up from the far side of the mill-stream to a dark wood. Beyond that wood the ground rises and rises for five hundred feet, till at last you climb out on the bare top of Beacon Hill, to look over the Pevensey Levels and the Channel and half the naked South Downs.

Kipling planned the garden himself, and it leads down to the Dudwell, where the old mill is. Most of the trees on the 33-acre estate are oak, hawthorn, and ash, and hence "A Tree Song":

> *Of all the trees that grow so fair,*
>   *Old England to adorn,*
> *Greater are none beneath the Sun,*
>   *Than Oak, and Ash, and Thorn.*
> *Sing Oak, and Ash, and Thorn, good Sirs*
>   *(All of a Midsummer morn)!*
> *Surely we sing no little thing,*
>   *In Oak, and Ash, and Thorn!*

The Bull Inn, opposite the church, comes into "Hal o' the Draft" in *Puck of Pook's Hill,* as does St. Barnabas Church. The church plays a far larger role in "The Conversion of St. Wilfred" in *Rewards and Fairies,* and the long south aisle and the iron memorial are unmistakable:

> The Lady who practises the organ was speaking to the blower-boy behind the organ-screen. "We can't very well

BURWASH Set amid the "broad and brookless vales" of Sussex is Bateman's, the home of Rudyard Kipling for over thirty years. Here, in the Sussex he loved so much, he found inspiration for *Puck of Pook's Hill,* some of his best poetry, and the autobiographical fragment *Something of Myself.*

talk here," Puck whispered. "Let's go to Panama Corner."
> He led them to the end of the south aisle, where there is a slab of iron which says in queer, long-tailed letters: *Orate p. annema Jhone Coline.* The children always called it Panama Corner.

A tablet on the same south aisle commemorates Kipling's only son John, who was killed in October 1915 at the Battle of Loos.

Local names occur in every story; for example, mention is made of the family of Charles Frewen Maude, rector of the church for twenty-one years, in "Glorianna" (*Rewards and Fairies*), and the Courthope family comes into the same story. Bateman's was given to the National Trust by Kipling's widow after his death on January 18, 1936; the view from the house is the Weald, which Kipling knew and loved so well:

> God gives all men all earth to love,
>   But, since man's heart is small,
> Ordains for each one spot shall prove
>   Belovèd over all.
> Each to his choice, and I rejoice
>   The lot has fallen to me
> In a fair ground—in a fair ground—
>   Yea, Sussex by the sea!

BURY, Sussex (pop. 477) Bury is a secluded village on the Arun River 4 miles north of Arundel; it was once approached by a ferry from Amberley, and its chief attraction is its tall-spired 14th-century church. Two literary visitors here left some trace. The nonsense-verse poet and artist Edward Lear wrote of Bury Hill after an 1829 visit. Just at the foot of the South Downs is Manor Farm, where Hilaire Belloc was sent after dropping out of the Collège Stanislas in Paris in 1888. He spent just a little over one term at the college and came here to train as an estate agent. He lasted only a few months in this occupation and left in late July or early August of the same year.

Bury is most noted as the home of John Galsworthy; in 1926 Galsworthy bought Bury House, a fifteen-bedroom home where he was to live the rest of his life. It was a long three-story stone house (rebuilt in 1910) with formal gardens on both sides as well as a paddock, a fishpond, and a rookery; both Bury Hill (to the right of the house) and the Amberley Downs (to the left) add to the general pleasantness Galsworthy found here. He had a study at the top of the house and also did some writing in the billiards room. He spent a great deal of time traveling until 1930, when his health began to deteriorate; facial cancer was conquered through radium treatments, but he nevertheless lost his power of speech beginning in 1931, and he lost some control over one leg at about the same time. Indeed, he was unable to go to Stockholm to receive in person the Nobel Prize in Literature he had been awarded in November 1932; the £9,000 prize he made over to a trust fund for the P.E.N. Club, which he had founded. Increasingly failing health caused him to enter a Hampstead nursing home, where he died on January 31, 1933. Galsworthy was cremated, and his ashes were scattered on the top of Bury Hill on March 28.

Among Galsworthy's visitors at Bury House was Hugh Walpole, whose first visit was toward the end of July 1927; a second visit, which occurred at Whitsuntide, 1929, is described in Walpole's journal:

> I had a very amusing Whitsun at Galsworthy's—Bury near Pulborough, Sussex. A really lovely house, pearl-grey stone fronting lawns that run straight to the open fields. The house inside clean and shining like the inside of a nut, with the colour of his nephew's pictures which are all over the house. Everything artistic, Liberty fashion and a little beyond it. Very like a special edition of one of John's own books.

Galsworthy's nephew, of whom Walpole speaks, was Rudolf Sauter, who lived here with his wife during the time the novelist owned the home. During the same Whitsun holidays Arnold Bennett and his wife also were here.

BURY ST. EDMUNDS, Suffolk (pop. 16,890) Originally this busy market town was concentrated around an important Saxon monastic establishment founded by King Sigebercht in honor of the Virgin Mary in 637, but there is no real information about the town or the monastery until it gained fame and importance with the building of a large wooden church to contain the remains of the martyred Edmund (d. 870). The town that grew up around the church was called St. Edmundsbury, that is, the Town of St. Edmund. A new church was dedicated to St. Edmund, and with the miracles associated with the shrine St. Edmundsbury became an important stopping point for pilgrims; enormous prosperity came to the town. With the completion of this construction phase, finished in 1095, the cathedral joined the category of the really great ecclesiastic foundations of Glastonbury (a royal abbey), St. Albans, and Westminster. The abbots here were mitered abbots; that is, each held a parliamentary seat, the title of Lord, and absolute authority within a mile radius of the town limits. On St. Edmund's Day in 1214 before the high altar of the cathedral twenty-five feudal lords protested the tyranny and misgovernment of King John and pledged themselves to fight for a charter of civil liberties; seven months later the Magna Carta was signed at Runnymede.

Bury St. Edmunds also became an important seat of learning, and its clerics included some of the earliest writers in England, many of whom are important in the development of English literature. Magister Dionysius the Cellarer wrote the *Life of St. Edmund,* Simon of Walsingham wrote the Anglo-Norman *Life of St. Faith,* Jocelin de Brakelond wrote an account of the abbey under Abbot Samson, and Martin authored *The Fifteen Joys of Mary.* The most important cleric was John Lydgate, who entered the monastery as a novice about 1385 from nearby Lidgate. Although when young he seemed unsuited to a monastic life (perhaps because his boyish pranks have been recorded), he was admitted to minor orders in December 1389. Within eight years he was ordained a priest, and he spent almost his entire life here. Lydgate had at his disposal one of the finest libraries in the country; it contained more than 2,000 volumes and the first dictionary of literature ever compiled, *Registrum liborum Angliae.* He was away from St. Edmundsbury only once, from July 1423 to April 1434, when prior at Hatfield Regis (Hatfield Broad Oak); in 1439 he was given a comfortable pension from the crown and continued living in St. Edmundsbury. He died in 1449 or 1450 and was buried in the abbey with the epitaph

> Mortuus seclo superis superstas,
> Hic jacet Lidgat tumulatus urna
> Qui fuit quondam celebris Brittaniae fama Poesis.

Thomas Carlyle thought that Bury was a "prosperous, brisk town beautifully diversifying" and based part of *Past and Present* on the account of the abbey under Abbot Samson written by Jocelin de Brakelond.

The abbey itself is used by William Shakespeare in *Henry VI: Part II;* it is here that Parliament sits and the Duke of Gloucester is arrested for treason. The next scene is placed at "Bury; a room in the Palace," which is actually the same location, since the palace was merely the living quarters of the Archbishop; here Henry summons Gloucester for trial, hoping to prove his uncle's innocence, only to discover that Gloucester has been murdered in his sleep. The general area of Bury St. Edmunds is used in the last act of *King John;* two concurrent scenes take place here: the first is the French camp "near St. Edmund's Bury," and the second the English camp in the same general area from which King John, stricken with fever, departs for Swinstead Abbey (Swineshead, Lincolnshire).

Sir Thomas Browne, author of *Religio Medici,* was in the city in 1655 to testify at the trial of Rose Cullender and Amy Duny, who were accused of being practicing witches. Sir Matthew Hale presided over the trial; and Browne's testimony was instrumental in the condemnation and subsequent hanging of the two women, an event that probably took place in the marketplace. Cupola House, just off the market and parallel to Cornhill, contains a commemorative plaque over the entrance in honor of Daniel Defoe. The ambiguously worded marker could imply three different things: that he lived here, died here, or wrote *Robinson Crusoe* here. None of these assertions is true, but Defoe may well have lodged at the house in 1704, when he was sent to Bury by Robert Harley, then Secretary of State, to discover the "state of mind" of the nation outside London. He was not recuperating from his Newgate imprisonment, as is commonly believed, for he had been out of prison for more than a year. Defoe was taken by the town and observed that the "Beauty and healthiness of its Situation, was no doubt the Occasion which drew the Clergy to settle here, for they always chose the best Places in the Country. . . ." He was also favorably impressed by the "most agreeable Company" of people, natives and visitors. Another traveler who was favorably impressed was William Cobbett, who visited Bury and gave it a strong recommendation in his *Rural Rides,* calling it "the nicest town in the world." Other visitors include Richard Brinsley Sheridan and Samuel Taylor Coleridge.

Thomas Shadwell attended school here for one year before going up to Cambridge, and Edward FitzGerald attended the King Edward VI Grammar School here from 1821 to 1826. Under the tutelage of Dr. Benjamin Heath Malkin, the headmaster, he received a good grounding in the classics; he attended St. James's Church for Sunday services. Charles Dickens was in Bury St. Edmunds numerous times from 1835 on; he was first here when reporting on the election of that year. He always stayed at the Angel Inn, which faces the abbey gateway and actually has a grill room in one of the abbey vaults. This inn dates from 1779 and may incorporate some of the structure of an inn of 1452. Dickens had Room 11 in 1835, and when he was here on reading tours in the 1850s and 1860s he most probably had Room 15. The inn is mentioned as the principal coaching inn of West Suffolk in *Pickwick Papers.* In pursuit of Mr. Jingle, Mr. Pickwick and his friends arrive here in August before going on to Newmarket; it was at this hotel that Mr. Pickwick received the news of the beginning of Mrs. Bardell's breach-of-promise suit against him, but the room that he occupied cannot be distinguished from the account in the novel.

Marie Louise de la Ramée, better known as Ouida and author of *A Dog of Flanders,* was born in Bury St. Edmunds on January 1, 1839; the daughter of a French teacher, she received her education here. On the A143 to Haverhill there is a memorial column to Ouida erected by the subscription of readers of the *Daily Mirror.* The column rises from a water trough, and one of the mourning figures appropriately holds a small dog.

Bury St. Edmunds is the setting for Percy Bysshe Shelley's poem "St. Edmond's Eve"; the Black Canon arrives at the cathedral "to say the mass" that will "lay the wandering spirit" to rest. The canon "told his beads" before crossing the threshold; there the nun's

... spirit to penance this night was doomed,
'Till the Canon atoned the deed. . . .

Hark! a loud peal of thunder shakes the roof,
Round the altar bright lightnings play,
Speechless with horror the monks stand aloof,
And the storm dies sudden away—

The inscription was gone! a cross on the ground,
And a rosary shone through the gloom,
But never again was the Canon there found,
Or the Ghost on the black marble tomb.

BUSHBURY, Staffordshire (pop. 3,784) Wolverhampton, the "Capital of the Black Country," has expanded so much that its outlying districts to the north-

east have begun to encroach upon this small village. Nevertheless, Bushbury has a fine old church and the Elizabethan Mosley Hall, where Charles II hid after the Battle of Worcester in 1651, to distinguish it. The church is 14th-century with carved roof beams in the chancel; it was to this church that George Borrow and his gypsy friends came for services in 1825. Borrow describes the church and their experiences in *The Romany Rye:*

Before . . . we reached the churchyard the bells had ceased their melody. It was surrounded by lofty beech-trees of brilliant green foliage. We entered the gate, Mrs. Petulengro leading the way, and proceeded to a small door near the east end of the church. As we advanced, the sound of singing within the church rose upon our ears. Arrived at the small door, Mrs. Petulengro opened it and entered, followed by Tawno Chikno. I myself went last of all, following Mr. Petulengro, who, before I entered, turned round, and with a significant nod, advised me to take care how I behaved. The part of the church which we had entered was the chancel; on one side stood a number of venerable old men—probably the neighbouring poor—and on the other a number of poor girls belonging to the village school, dressed in white gowns and straw bonnets.

Borrow missed few details in the church; he especially noted the benches for the poor and the magnificent pew where the prayer book was engraved with an earl's coronet:

. . . [W]e were confronted by the sexton. . . [who] motioned towards the lower end of the church, where were certain benches, partly occupied by poor people and boys. Mrs. Petulengro, however, with a toss of her head, directed her course to a magnificent pew, which was unoccupied, which she opened and entered, followed closely by Tawno Chikno, Mr. Petulengro, and myself. . . . I took up a prayer-book, on which was engraved an earl's coronet.

BUXTON, Norfolk (pop. 511) An old water mill now stands beside the Bure River here in Buxton (4 miles southeast of Aylsham), and the village's 13th-century church looks across the green. About 2 miles north is Oxnead Hall, a former seat of the Pastons, the 15th-century family whose letters reveal much about Norfolk and England during the Wars of the Roses. Also here, across from the Black Lion, is Dudwick Hall, set in its own parkland. In the 19th century the hall belonged to relatives of Anna Sewell, and it is thought that Dudwick becomes Birtwick Place in *Black Beauty.* Anna Sewell also frequented Dudwick Farm here, the home of her grandparents, where she learned to ride.

BYFLEET, Surrey (pop. 4,173) Surrey has managed to absorb an enormous commuter population without the total sacrifice of its natural beauty, and the northern part of the county has even preserved a good deal of the heathland, woodlands, and wide commons that characterized it for centuries. The mostly 14th-century church stands in an open field and has a fine bell tower, and in the churchyard is the grave of George Smith, founder of the *Dictionary of National Biography.* Byfleet, 2½ miles west of Weybridge, was once a royal manor, and unsupported local tradition claims that much of Henry VIII's childhood was spent here. The best-known literary association with this village is traceable to the royal manor; in 1389

Geoffrey Chaucer was appointed Clerk of the King's Works, and Byfleet was one of the seven manors in his jurisdiction. It is assumed that Chaucer was here at least to inspect the manor, but of that there is no evidence.

A second association with Byfleet occurred in the 18th century when Stephen Duck, the "thresher poet," was appointed to the living here; the son of poor Wiltshire peasants, Duck found court support in the person of Queen Caroline. Indeed, she not only pensioned him but made him a yeoman of the guard in 1733. Not until 1746, at the age of forty-one, was he ordained a priest, and he was appointed here in January 1752. Three years later his *Caesar's Camp, or St. George's Hill,* an imitation of Sir John Denham's *Cooper's Hill,* appeared, and at about the same time he showed definite signs of madness. Duck, of whom Jonathan Swift had written

Thrice happy Duck! Employed in threashing stubble,
Thy toil is lessened, and thy profits double[,]

drowned himself on March 21, 1756, in Reading.

CAISTER NEXT YARMOUTH, Norfolk (pop. 2,346) A Roman port of more than 30 acres before becoming a *colonia*, Caister is a coastal village and lifeboat and coast guard station 3 miles north of Yarmouth. Near the village are the ruins of the old Church of St. Edmund and of Caister Castle, built by Sir John Fastolf after he had served at Patay and been governor of the Bastille. When Sir John died in 1459, Caister Castle was bequeathed (in a much-disputed will) to John Paston. John Mowbray, the 4th Duke of Norfolk, subsequently claimed that the castle had been given to his father, the 3rd Duke (and, in 1468, was sold to himself by two of Fastolf's executors), and in 1469 he set about to secure his rights by besieging the castle and the Pastons. More than 3,000 men were needed before the Pastons' garrison of twenty-eight were forced to surrender. The Pastons regained Caister Castle at Mowbray's death in 1476 and retained it until the 17th century. Many of the *Paston Letters*, which tell of 15th-century life here and in London, were written by Margaret Paston here. Sir John Fastolf was said to be Shakespeare's Sir John Falstaff, but the career coincidences are probably accidental.

CAISTOR, Lincolnshire (pop. 1,571) An old Roman town high in the Lincolnshire Wolds, Caistor, 12 miles southwest of Grimsby, was originally a walled Roman town encompassing 7 or 8 acres. The Church of SS. Peter and Paul is partly Saxon, and the tower is partly Norman. The large mansion on the town square was occupied for more than half a century by the Rev. Samuel Turner, rector of nearby Grasby and great-uncle of Alfred, Lord Tennyson. The Tennyson grandnephews were his favorites, and they were often here.

CALBOURNE, Isle of Wight (pop. 670) Calbourne is a lovely village, best known for Winkle Street, which has low stone cottages with thatched or tiled roofs. One likes to conjecture that Nicholas Udall lived in one of these cottages when he was appointed rector here in March 1553. The partly Norman church where Udall is known to have preached contains a particularly fine 14th-century brass. But Udall was rector here for only one year; with the accession of Queen Mary the living was given to someone else, and Udall left to become a schoolmaster in the household of Stephen Gardiner, Bishop of Winchester.

CALDER, VALE OF, Yorkshire The Calder River rises south of Burnley, Lancashire, and then flows 45 miles eastward through the West Riding of Yorkshire to join the Aire River at Castleford. This has always been sheep country; originally the wool industry was a cottage craft, with individual families shearing, carding, spinning, and weaving the wool into the often-beautiful Yorkshire cloth. With the beginning of mechanization in the 18th century, the Calder Vale industry was fortunate in that the transition from cottage to factory was an easy one. Indeed, one of the first integrated wool factories in England was built in the valley. The original factory, constructed as a parish workhouse, was especially successful in that role. John Dyer, author of *The Fleece*, which gives a full account of the British wool industry, was especially interested in this particular factory in the Vale of Calder:

Behold in Calder's Vale, . . .
. . . .
A spacious dome for this fair purpose rise.
. . . .
. . . By gentle steps
Upraised, from room to room we slowly walk,
And view with wonder and with silent joy
The sprightly scene; where many of busy hand,
Where spoles, cards, wheels, and looms, with motion quick
And ever-murmuring sound, the unwonted sense
Wrap in surprise.

CALNE, Wiltshire (pop. 5,760) Calne, the bacon-curing center of Wiltshire, lies in a sheltered valley 6 miles east of Chippenham; its early affluence, like that of many other northern Wiltshire towns, was derived from the cloth industry. Calne has always been an important coaching stop, and the Lansdowne Arms (rebuilt) is of medieval origin and has the original brewhouse intact in its courtyard. One of the most extraordinary events in Anglo-Saxon history occurred here during the 978 *witenagemot*, the Anglo-Saxon council meeting whose purpose was to guide the King's governmental acts. The *Anglo-Saxon Chronicle* relates the event:

> In this year the leading councillors of England fell down from an upper storey at Calne, all except the holy archbishop Dunstan, who alone remained standing on a beam; some were severely injured there, and some did not escape with their lives.

The heated debate was over celibacy, and Dunstan, who was holding for the church view against the secular view, was accused of having staged the "fall from grace."

For almost two years Samuel Taylor Coleridge lived here through the kindness of John Morgan while he finished the *Biographia Literaria* and worked on various plays. Coleridge left here for James Gillman's care in Highgate, London, in April 1816. That year Charles and Mary Lamb spent a month's holiday here; they also stayed with the Morgan family. Lamb took the opportunity to do a great deal of traveling and visited Bath, Bristol, Marlborough, and Chippenham; he also stayed at nearby Dalston, which was, as he wrote to William Wordsworth,

> about one mischievous boy's stone's throw off Kingsland Turnpike, one mile from Shoreditch church—thence we emanate in various directions to Hackney, Clapton, Totham, and such like romantic country.

CALVERLEY, Yorkshire Situated so close to Leeds as virtually to be a part of the city, Calverley Hall and its inhabitants supplied the plot for the Elizabethan play *A Yorkshire Tragedy,* published in 1608 and attributed on the title page to Shakespeare. The hall was the scene of a series of horrible murders committed by Walter Calverley, a man who had dissipated almost his entire estate. Brutally killing his two elder sons and his wife on April 23, 1605, he attempted to escape but was caught when his horse fell; at his trial in York he refused to plead and "suffered accordingly the 'peine forte et dure.'" In this one noble act, he was able to save the remainder of his estate for his third son, who was an infant and at nurse when Calverley butchered the rest of the family.

CAMBERLEY, Surrey Historically the large part of Surrey north of the Hog's Back up to Windsor Great Park has been a royal forest, and it is no doubt fitting that the land is still the crown's, only not for hunting; it now belongs to the Queen's Army. Here tanks come bolting over the countryside, red warning flags signal range practice, and wooden huts dot the heath. The onetime village of Camberley, 2½ miles southwest of Bagshot and part of a larger district, has succumbed to the urban sprawl common to locations along the A30 between London and Basingstoke. It

was far more rural at the turn of the twentieth century when Bret Harte, the Ameican author, was here visiting; he left the United States in 1878 for Krefeld, Germany, where he had taken a consulship and, indeed, held the same post in Glasgow, Scotland, within a few years. Retiring to England in 1885, he died here on May 5, 1902, and was buried in nearby Frimley.

CAMBRIDGE, Cambridgeshire (pop. 77,000) Its eminence as a university town in the English-speaking world challenged only by its namesake, Cambridge, Massachusetts, and by Oxford, Cambridge is situated on the east bank of the Cam (Granta) River 57 miles north of London and just south of the drained and reclaimed area known as the Fens. A distinguished recorded history began here when the Romans established Camboritum on the banks of the Granta River, where a previous British settlement had stood. After the Romans left in A.D. 411, the area was not again heavily populated until the 7th or 8th century, although there was a small settlement on Market Hill from the mid-5th century on. In Saxon times the remains of the old Roman city were amalgamated with this newer settlement, and the entity was renamed Grantanbrycge; the name further changed in the Domesday survey (1086) to Grantebrigge, in Chaucer to Cantebrigge, and through the variants of Cauntbrigge and Cawnbrigge became Cambridge.

The Danes harried the area and occupied it for a year in 875, as the *Parker Chronicle* of the *Anglo-Saxon Chronicle* reports, and, indeed, Cambridge was annexed to Denmark by the Treaty of Wedmore in 878. In the early 11th century it was burned by the Danes in retaliation for an open rebellion and later was pillaged by the Normans, especially by the infamous sheriff Roger Picot, who not only usurped land belonging to St. Etheldreda's Church but denied all knowledge of its saint. The town was much favored by the church, and numerous religious houses were established here from the 11th century on. The Augustinians settled near the castle in the 11th century and then moved on to Barnwell in the 12th, the Benedictine nunnery of St. Rhadegund was founded about 1132 and later made way for Jesus College, and there were establishments of Franciscans, Carmelites, and Friars of the Sack. Indeed, the scholastic leanings of these early religious orders were important in the development of Cambridge University.

Until the 12th century Englishmen had obtained their educations abroad; the turning point came when the French king Louis VII expelled all foreign students and visitors during a dispute with the academic community and when Henry II proclaimed that the English would no longer be permtted to go abroad for study. The flow of returning scholars and their tutors, who numbered in the thousands, was directed mostly to Oxford; but when two innocent Oxford clerks were hanged in 1209 by the townspeople for the murder of a local woman, 3,000 came here. Cambridge then had a population of less than 1,000, and the town was unable to provide for the students, many of whom were mere ruffians living "under no discipline, having no tutor, saving him who teacheth all mischief."

The university was then divided into a northern area, called the Boreales, and a southern, called the

Astrales; each was controlled by its own proctor. Warfare between the groups was common, and if they were not fighting each other, they were fighting the townspeople. The reasons for the town-and-gown conflict are many: discipline in the university was at best lax; housing was overcrowded or nonexistent; students frequently turned tradesmen and competed with the town proprietors; and students could not be brought to justice by the town. A chancellor's court, called "The Townsmen's Scourge," to which reference was made in 1246, allowed the university to exercise the right of "consuance" and to try its own students; the townsmen had no redress. When the Pope recognized Cambridge University as a *studium generale* and removed it from the Bishop of Ely's control, it became an overwhelmingly powerful force in the community. It licensed the alehouses, controlled grain and coal at the quayside, disallowed bearbaiting on Sundays and whenever sermons were being preached, and even had the right of entry into private homes.

One of the major problems faced by medieval Cambridge, a town of normal squalor, was the problem of the King's Ditch, a moat built in 1268 on Henry III's orders to keep out the Ely islanders. When its purpose was no longer necessary, the Ditch became infamous. The Ditch, essentially an open sewer, and its pollution were the source of a serious dispute between town and gown for more than 300 years. It must be remembered that Cambridge was in a low-lying area surrounded by marsh and river, and many stagnant, polluted ditches cut through the area and contaminated the water supply. Disease, including ague and the Black Death, was rampant. Household refuse and dung lay in the streets until washed away by rain, and university records show that in 1393 masters and students were overcome by the stench merely while walking on Trinity Lane, then appropriately called Foul Lane. The Ditch became worse and worse, and an ordinance in 1503 called for cleaning "the common sege" once every three years. Only in 1610 was an effective plan adopted; eventually a new conduit system was built to bring in fresh water; the refuse problem was dealt with separately.

The medieval university, despite inadequate funding and a bad location, grew rapidly in reputation and accomplishment. Here the student (once as young as fourteen on entrance) pursued a three-year course of the trivium (Latin grammar, rhetoric, and logic) toward the B.A. degree. Then, if he survived his oral disputation for the B.A., he went on as a commencing bachelor to the quadrivium, a four-year study of arithmetic, geometry, astronomy, and music; success here ensured that he himself was qualified to lecture. Further, a doctoral course could be pursued for another eight years; it was not until the 19th century that the disputation gave way to a written examination. Today, of course, as at Oxford, the M.A. is automatically awarded to all B.A.'s after a short qualifying period if they pay the fee.

There is no Cambridge University per se; *universitas* simply means an organized body of students: it has nothing to do with where they congregate. The colleges, specific entities in themselves, are loosely bound together by the university but themselves are not teaching communities; the colleges provide accommodations and supervision, while the university performs the teaching function. All this simply reflects the fact that the university is the legally constituted body through which degrees are conferred and members are disciplined. The colleges are independent bodies, each with a set of complex statutes by which it rules, and as a sign of this independence a student must gain admission to a specific college before he can enter the university. The early students were scattered about the town, and many were living in extreme poverty when the first college was introduced into Cambridge by Hugh de Balsham, Bishop of Ely. In 1280 he removed some of the clerks from their miserable hovels and lodged them, free of charge, at the Augustinian Hospital of St. John, but the experiment ended in failure after only four years. The bishop then moved the group to two houses near St. Peter's Church (now called St. Mary's the Less), where they were to live following the rules governing "the Oxford scholars of Merton." It is doubtful that his intent was to found a college even though he endowed it himself (and Peterhouse did not actually get its statutes until 1338). Almost half a century passed before Clare College was founded in 1326 by Richard Badew; it was later refounded by Lady Elizabeth de Clare, from whom it takes its name. Pembroke, originally the Hall of Valence-Marie, followed in 1347, and Gonville and Caius College was established in 1348 by Edmund Gonville and reformed in 1554 by John Caius. Other important colleges followed: Trinity Hall in 1350, Corpus Christi in 1352, King's in 1441, and the rest at various intervals through the centuries down to Churchill in 1960.

Curiously, early accounts do not correspond well with the facts set forth here; William Camden, for example, tells of the founding in his *Britannia:*

> Cantaber the Spaniard is said to have first founded this university 375 years before Christ, and Sigebert king of the East Angles to have restored it. Being ruined in the Danish invasion, it lay long neglected till the prospect began to clear under the Norman government. Houses of learning, inns, and halls for scholars were now founded, but without endowments.

While going on to state that the date of founding cannot be pushed "beyond the bounds of truth" into the time of the "foundation of Rome," he does allow an alternative date which drifts back into the reign of Henry I when he quotes an "account in the old appendix to Ingulphus by Peter Blesensis." Michael Drayton, too, picks up some of the same "historical facts" in the illustrations to the eleventh song of *Poly-Olbion;* he dismisses Sigebert, who "about the year DC.XXX . . . desiring to imitate what he had seen observable in France" founded a school for children, and then "Gurguntius with Cantaber" and the others until he arrives at Abbot Joffred

> of Growland, [who] with one *Gilbert* his Commoigne, and III. other Monkes came to his Mannor of *Cotenham*, as they used oftimes, to read; and thence daily going to *Cambridge*. . . .

As might be expected, there is much debate over the relative merits of Oxford and Cambridge, but one fact is indisputable: here there are many more literary figures who do not have a firm association with a college (or even with the university). Sometimes, of course, the lack of association is the result of the loss of historical information. Robert Mannyng was here around 1300 before going to Sempringham Priory about 1302, and John Lydgate was possibly sent here sometime after 1386 from the monastery at Bury St. Edmunds, but this proposition rests only on John Bale's assertion in his 16th-century biographical dictionary that Lydgate studied at both universities. Another essentially untraceable association is with John Skelton, who claimed to have studied at both Cambridge and Oxford; most likely, he is the "one Scheklton" who graduated with an M.A. here in 1484, and it is also likely that he had an earlier period here when he left without a degree and transferred to Oxford. It is known that in 1493 he was admitted by this university to the title "poet laureate," a title which suggested one who was skilled in rhetoric and letters and had nothing to do with poetry as such. A fourth early author with uncertain associations is Michael Drayton; he was here, obviously, but there is no evidence of an academic affiliation with either this university or Oxford. However, he writes of Cambridge as "my most beloved Towne" in the twenty-first song of *Poly-Olbion*:

> O noble *Cambridge* then, my most beloved Towne,
> In glory flourish still, to heighten thy renowne:
> In womans perfect shape, still be thy Embleme right,
> Whose one hand holds a Cup, the other beares a Light.

He seems to have known Cambridge better than Oxford, but his name appears on no matriculation list here. An association with some specific evidence exists with the dramatist John Lyly; he was at Magdalen College, Oxford, where he received a B.A. in 1573 and an M.A. in 1575. Sometime before 1579 he is assumed to have come to Cambridge, although his college affiliation is unknown. In any event, he received an M.A. here in 1579, and his attachment to the university and to Oxford clearly shows in *Euphues and His England*.

There is an early native son for Cambridge: Jeremy Taylor was the son of a local barber and was baptized at Trinity Church on April 15, 1613. Neither the date nor the place of his birth is known, although his birthplace now is traditionally said to have been a house known as the Black Bear, just across from the church, and not the Wrestler's Inn in Petty Cury. According to Taylor's own account, he was educated in grammar and mathematics by his father, but a note on the admissions book at Gonville and Caius College states that in 1626, his date of admission, he had been at Perse School here. A now-obscure 18th-century poet and, indeed, Poet Laureate from 1757 to 1785, William Whitehead, was born here early in 1715 and was baptized in St. Botolph's Church on February 12. Whitehead had some sort of education here before going on to Winchester College in 1729 and then entered Clare Hall (Clare College) here as a sizar in 1735.

There are a number of associations with St. Benedict's (St. Benet's) Church, a partly Saxon structure and the oldest building in the town. Thomas Hobson, the carrier, whose name has been assured fame in the expression "Hobson's choice," is buried here. His grave has no memorial, but John Milton's "On the University Carrier Who Sicken'd in the Time of His Vacancy, Being Forced to Go to *London*, by Reason of the Plague" has immortalized his name:

> Here lies old *Hobson*, Death hath broke his girt,
> And here, alas, hath laid him in the dirt,
> Or else the ways being foul, twenty to one,
> He's here stuck in a slough, and overthrown.
> 'Twas such a shifter, that if truth were known,
> Death was half glad when he had got him down;
> For he had any time this ten years full,
> Dodg'd with him, betwixt *Cambridge* and the Bull.

Hobson's funeral sermon was preached by Thomas Fuller, who had been appointed to the perpetual curacy of St. Benet's by Corpus Christi and had taken orders at the same time. Fuller, who earlier had been at Queens' College and Sidney Sussex College, held the curacy here until 1633.

Throughout the centuries many established literary figures arrived here for various reasons. Because of the references in "The Reeve's Tale" in *The Canterbury Tales*, Geoffrey Chaucer is believed to have known the area well, but there is no evidence to connect him with the university. Sir Thomas More was elected High Steward in 1525 and played an important role in the extensive pageantry here which attended the elevation of Henry Fitzroy, King Henry VIII's illegitimate son, as Duke of Richmond in June. The poet and divine John Donne is often stated to have moved here from Oxford in 1587 or 1588 from the evidence in Izaak Walton's *The Life of John Donne*:

> About the fourteenth year of his age he was transplanted from Oxford to Cambridge; where, that he might receive nourishment from both soils, he stayed till his seventeenth year . . . [when] he was removed to London.

The religious restrictions here were less stringent than those at Oxford, but the incompleteness of university records for the period leaves us no evidence for Walton's claim. Donne did, however, come here shortly after his ordination in the company of James I and Prince Charles as the King's Chaplain-in-Ordinary. During the visit the King signified his desire that an honorary D.D. be conferred upon his chaplain, but the Cambridge officials, for some reason (possibly Donne's early Catholicism), were opposed to the plan. The royal command, however, left them no alternative; even so, they granted the degree with the worst possible grace. They waited until the royal retinue had departed to grant the degree and then took great care that no mention be made of it in the university register. Another honorary degree was more generously given; the poet and courtier, Thomas Sackville, later 1st Earl of Dorset and Baron Buckhurst, was granted an honorary M.A. by the University in 1571.

A frequent visitor to Cambridge after his undergraduate days at Magdalene College was Samuel Pepys; on one occasion when his brother came up to Christ's College, the diarist spent an afternoon at the Rose in immoderate drinking. On another he brought his wife along and conducted her around some of the colleges. John Evelyn made a tour of the city and university in September 1654 and left an extensive account in his diary; St. John's, in his opinion, "is well built of brick," but, he continues, the Trinity College Quadrangle, said to be the finest in Europe, was "in truth far inferior to that of Christ-Church Oxford." Evelyn also describes the colleges; thus, the Chapel at King's is "altogether answerable to expectation," but "the Library is too narrow"; Peterhouse is "a pretty neate Coll," while Catharine Hall is a "meane structure." Jesus College, "one of the best built," is in a "melanchoy" situation while Christ College is "very ⟨nobly⟩ built." But Evelyn concludes:

. . . [T]he whole Towne situated in a low dirty unpleasant place, the streetes ill paved, the aire thick, as infested by the fenns; nor are its Churches (of which St. *Maries* is the best) anything considerable in compare to *Oxford* which is doubtlesse the noblest Universitie now in the whole World.

Among the 18th-century visitors was Dr. Samuel Johnson, who, said Boswell, "paid a short visit to the University of Cambridge, with his friend Mr. Beauclerk." The biographer, citing a letter from Dr. John Sharp, continues:

"Several persons got into his company the last evening at Trinity, where, about twelve, he began to be very great; stripped poor Mrs. Macaulay to the very skin, then gave her for his toast, and drank her in two bumpers."

Daniel Defoe visited Cambridge when gathering material for *A Tour thro' the Whole Island of Great Britain;* he does not describe either the college or the university structures (as he does for Oxford) because "they are so effectually and so largely treated of by other Authors, and are so foreign to the familiar Design of these Letters. . . ." Indeed, he refers his readers "to Mr. *Camden's Britannia,* and the Author of the Antiquities of *Cambridge,* and other such learned Writers, by whom they may be fully informed." Defoe, however, was much concerned with the town-and-gown problems, and while granting the "Tradesmen . . . get their Bread by the Colleges," he concludes:

Thus I say, Interest gives them Authority; and there are abundance of Reasons . . . why the University shou'd not differ to any Extremity with the Town; nor, *such is their prudence,* do they let any Disputes between them run up to any Extremities, if they can avoid it.

In the 19th century the number of visitors to Cambridge was considerable. Charles Lamb was here on at least three occasions, the first in mid-August of 1815 in the company of his sister Mary. Another visit occurred in August 1819, at which time he wrote "Written at Cambridge on the 15th August, 1819":

Yet can I fancy, wandering 'mid thy towers,
Myself a nursling, Granta, of thy lap;
My brow seems tightening with the Doctor's cap,
And I walk *gowned;* feel unusual powers.

In the summer of 1820, with Henry Crabb Robinson, he visited the chapel and grounds at Trinity College; they lodged with a Mrs. Smith, whom he used in the essay "The Gentle Giantess." She became the Widow Blackett, and Cambridge becomes Oxford. Probably on this visit, Lamb met Emma Isola at the house of a Miss Humphreys on Trumpington Street; Emma Isola, whom he later adopted and educated, was the daughter (orphaned) of Charles Isola, one of the bedells of the university. Sir Walter Scott stopped in Cambridge on his way to Waterloo; in the company of Alexander Pringle, Robert Bruce, and John Scott, he stayed at the Sun Inn, opposite Trinity

College, at the end of July 1815. Five years later both Cambridge and Oxford offered Sir Walter "the highest compliment which it was in their power to offer. . . ." John Lockhart, Scott's son-in-law and biographer, continues:

The Vice-Chancellors of Oxford and Cambridge communicated to him, in the same week, their request that he would attend at the approaching Commemorations, and accept the honorary degree of Doctor in Civil Law. It was impossible for him to leave Scotland again that season. . . .

George Eliot (Mary Ann Evans) and George Lewes came to Cambridge as the guests of William George Clark, tutor of Trinity College, and Oscar Browning and stayed at the Bull Hotel in the early 1870s; they made a return visit in May 1873. Finally, two 19th-century literary figures were elected Rede Lecturer: John Ruskin, in 1867, whose lecture was "The Relation of National Ethics to National Arts," and Matthew Arnold, in 1882, who spoke on "Literature and Science."

Much was written about Cambridge in the 19th century, but William Makepeace Thackeray (Trinity College), probably made the most extensive use of it in *The History of Henry Esmond, Esq., Lovel the Widower,* and, especially, *Pendennis;* in the last-named novel, the town and university become Oxbridge. This is the university attended by Pendennis; he and the major

entered at the wicket of the venerable ivy-mantled gate of the College. It is surmounted with an ancient dome almost covered with creepers, and adorned with the effigy of the Saint from whom the House takes its name, and many coats-of-arms of its royal and noble benefactors. . . .

. . . [A]nd the two gentlemen walked across the square, the main features of which were at once and for ever stamped in Pen's mind—the pretty fountain playing in the centre of the fair grass plats; the tall chapel windows and buttresses rising to the right; the hall, with its tapering lantern and oriel window. . . .

Thackeray goes on to talk of St. George's (St. John's) and St. Boniface (Trinity):

St. George's is the great College of the University of Oxbridge, with its four vast quadrangles, and its beautiful hall and gardens, and the Georgians, as the men are called, wear gowns of a peculiar cut, and give themselves no small airs of superiority over all other young men. Little St. Boniface is but a petty hermitage in comparison of the huge consecrated pile alongside of which it lies. But considering its size it has always kept an excellent name in the university. . . . [T]he college livings are remarkably good, the fellowships easy; the Boniface men had had more than their fair share of university honours; their boat was third upon the river; their chapel-choir is not inferior to Saint George's itself; and the Boniface ale the best in Oxbridge.

Thackeray does not disguise Trinity College and Cambridge in *The History of Henry Esmond, Esq.* and writes that Esmond

. . . was entered a pensioner of Trinity College in Cambridge, to which famous college my Lord had also in his youth belonged. . . . Tom Tusher, who was of Emanuel College, and was by this time a junior soph, came to wait upon my Lord, and to take Harry under his protection; . . . comfortable rooms [being] provided for him in the great court close by the gate, and near to the famous Mr. Newton's lodgings. . . .

Thomas Hardy also makes slight use of Cambridge in both *Desperate Remedies* and *Tess of the D'Urbervilles*. One of the best descriptions of Cambridge (and the eccentric Darwin family) after the turn of the century is in the delightful *Period Piece* by Gwen Darwin Raverat, who was born in 1885 at Newnham Grange, which now houses the graduate Darwin College.

Cambridge in the 20th century has had its share of distinguished visitors and lecturers; one of the earliest, Virginia Stephen Woolf, first came to recuperate from a breakdown in October 1904, when she stayed at the Porch with her aunt, Caroline Emma Stephen, and began helping Frederic Maitland with his biography of Sir Leslie Stephen. She returned again in December and on numerous other occasions including part of the summer of 1905, when she attended the Trinity College Ball. Virginia Woolf's most renowned time at Cambridge occurred more than twenty years later, in 1928, when she was invited to lecture on "Women and Fiction" at Newnham and Girton Colleges. Other literary figures lectured here as well. Hilaire Belloc held the post of Lees Knowles Lecturer in military history at Trinity College during the 1915–1916 academic year, and Sir Arthur Quiller-Couch, knighted in June 1912, was appointed King Edward VII Professor of English Literature and elected a fellow of Jesus College in January 1913. His fame was already established, and his inaugural lecture was so well attended that the audience could not be contained in the largest lecture hall of the university. During his time here Q had a large number of guests including Kenneth Grahame, who was invited for the Rustat Audit Feast at Jesus College on May 15, 1913, and A. E. Housman. Quiller-Couch's lectures here not only were extremely well prepared and well delivered but became a point of fashionable attendance; they were known for their insight and stimulation and in published form lost little of their delivered quality. His contributions at Cambridge were great: he freed undergraduates from the overemphasized and traditional philological approach to language and literature and presented them with a live model of a writer who believed "Literature is not a mere science, to be studied; but an art, to be practiced." While Q held the chair, he constantly commuted to his home in Fowey, Cornwall, where he died in 1944.

June 5, 1930, was one of the university's most memorable occasions: Stanley Baldwin was installed as chancellor, and John Galsworthy, Sir James Matthew Barrie, Albert Einstein, Max Planck, Lascelles Abercrombie, and the Duke of Gloucester were all awarded honorary degrees. In 1946, C. Day-Lewis became Clark Lecturer here; his lectures were published as *The Poetic Images*.

Christ's College Christ's College was founded either in 1506 or in 1442; at the earlier date God's House was founded by a London schoolmaster as a college for schoolmasters; its initial purpose was to supply teachers for a number of schools (mostly in the Midlands and the north) that had been closed by a scarcity of masters. God's House, often called the "puny infant" of Cambridge, stood opposite St. Andrew's Church, outside the Barnwell Gate; supposed to support a proctor and twenty-four postgraduate

scholars, it was an extremely impoverished foundation and in 1441 had no table in its dining hall and only thirteen books in its library. Against this background Lady Margaret Beaufort, Countess of Richmond and Derby and mother of Henry VII, founded Christ's College in 1506; widowed three times before taking a vow of celibacy, she relied on her friend and spiritual adviser, John Fisher, to help guide the direction of the new foundation. Fisher urged her to save God's House and enlarge it to include a master, twelve fellows, and as many as forty-seven scholars; pensioners were also admitted.

Some of the original college structure of God's House was well built and substantial, and Lady Margaret's first tasks were to establish a traditional quadrangle and to enlarge the modest gatehouse to the turreted Tudor construction standing today. She set on it the famous Beaufort arms with their seemingly strange antelopes; these apparently deformed animals are actually yales (jalls) and can be traced back some 4,000 years in Eastern culture to a time when the animal's "fore and aft" horns were trained so that one extended over its nose and one reached back to the tail. Other buildings followed, and the college chapel is one of the oldest in Cambridge. Lady Margaret instructed that "primary chambers for our own use" be built, and these were the first-floor rooms of the master's lodge. From there, according to Thomas Fuller, she observed the dean thrashing a student so soundly that she cried out, "Gently! Gently!"

Christ's College has had a number of literary men on its rolls. The first one known to have attended the college was John Leland, Henry VIII's antiquarian, who came here from St. Paul's School in London. He received his B.A. degree in 1522 and subsequently studied at All Souls' College, Oxford. Sir John Harington was here around 1575, and another early figure who attended Christ's College was Francis Quarles, author of *Emblems, Moral and Divine*. He graduated with a B.A. in 1608 before going to London to study law at Lincoln's Inn.

The most famous member of the college is John Milton, who was admitted on February 12, 1625, and matriculated on April 9 as a lesser-pensioner. The rooms traditionally thought to have been his, a first-floor set on the north side of the First Court, cannot be the ones he had in his first year. Then, most likely, he shared a room with two or three others in a temporary wooden building known as "The Little Building" or "Rat's Hall." If, in fact, the other, choicer rooms were Milton's, they were assigned after his first year. Known as "The Lady of Christ's" because of his extraordinary handsomeness, Milton evidently had some difficulty with his tutor, William Chappell, and in March 1626 the poet was rusticated and sent home for his failure to conform. The event prompted his "Elegia Prima," the work in which he confesses to Charles Diodati:

> I am in the city which the Thames washes with its tidal waters and I am willingly detained in my dear native place. At present I feel no concern about returning to the sedgy Cam and I am troubled by no nostalgia for my forbidden quarters there. . . . It is disgusting to be constantly subjected to the threats of a rough tutor and to other indignities which my spirit cannot endure.

Milton returned to Cambridge most likely on April

19, 1626, the beginning of Easter term, when Nathaniel Tovey became his new tutor. He worked through the summer of 1628, except for a short trip to Stowmarket, Suffolk, where he visited Andrew Gill, and he received his B.A. on March 26, 1629, listed fourth in the university honors list. Milton graduated with an M.A., cum laude, on July 3, 1632, and still planned to be ordained; he was, however, becoming disillusioned with the church and its doctrine, as he later confessed in *The Reason of Church-Government Urg'd against Prelaty,* in which he claimed to have been "church-outed by the prelates."

Milton did a great deal of writing here, including "On the Death of the Vice-Chancellor, a Physician," "Elegia Secunda," "On the Fifth of November," "At a Vacation Exercise in the College," and "On the Morning of Christ's Nativity." One of the major stories concerning Milton's residence here is apocryphal. It is held that he planted the mulberry tree in the Fellows' Garden. However, sixteen years before the poet came up to the university, the college had purchased 300 mulberry plants, which James I wanted cultivated, and they were placed "in a certeyn parcell of Grounde lying in the bakeside of the said Collegge." The land, originally hired from Jesus College, was later purchased; thus, Milton's tree is most likely the sole survivor of the 300. When William Wordsworth entered St. John's College in 1787, he visited Milton's rooms, which were occupied by a class fellow, one Edward Joseph Birkett, also from Hawkshead. *The Prelude* recalls visiting

> The very shell reputed of the abode
> Which he had tenanted. O temperate Bard!
> One afternoon, the first time I set foot
> In this thy innocent Nest and Oratory,
> Seated with others in a festive ring
> Of common-place convention, I to thee
> Pour'd out libations, to thy memory drank,
> Within my private thoughts, till my brain reel'd
> Never so clouded by the fumes of wine
> Before that hour, or since.

Another 17th-century literary figure whose deep affection for Edward King prompted an elegy upon his death was John Cleveland, who was here from 1627 to 1631; he then went over to St. John's, where he became a fellow in 1634.

Not until 1852 did another major literary figure attend this college; then Charles Stuart Calverley entered after being forced to withdraw from Balliol College, Oxford, because of numerous disciplinary infractions. He stayed on the safe side of the authorities here and soon gained a reputation for wit and charm. His academic successes at Christ's, including the Craven Scholarship, the Damden Medal, the Browne Medal, and a second in the classical tripos, are surprising in light of his lack of academic ardor; indeed, it was well known that his friends, concerned by his decided lack of concentration, would lock him in his rooms to force him to work. At Christmas, 1857, Calverley set the famous examination paper on *Pickwick Papers* while entertaining his voluntary candidates on oysters, beer, and milk punch; included among the questions were:

1. What are the components of dog's nose, and a red-faced Nixon?

2. Who, besides Mr. Pickwick, is recorded to have worn gaiters?

3. Mention any occasion in which it is specified that the Fat Boy was not asleep.

Walter Besant won the prize. In 1858 Calverley was elected a fellow, and *Verses and Translations* was published in 1862. Calverley then began to study law and was called to the bar in 1865, the year in which he gave up his fellowship because of his marriage.

Walter Besant came up to Christ's from King's College, London, in 1856, when he first met Calverley. In addition to taking Calverley's prize, he graduated with a B.A. in 1859 as eighteenth wrangler. He also gained the special bachelor's theological prize the same year. Besant wrote fondly of his university days, which, he recalled, began with a "good honest breakfast with cold pie and beer." After their four o'clock main meal in the hall, he continues, the

> men divided into little sets and went in turn to each other's rooms and drank port and sherry until six.

But the activities did not cease at six:

> It seems wonderful after all these years to relate that, at midnight, when the whist was knocked off, we always sat down to a great supper with copious beer, and after supper to milk punch, and talked till four. And yet some of us survived.

Life such as this has long vanished from the university, and Calverley wrote a fitting epitaph for the passing of the old ways:

> I go. Untaught and feeble is my pen:
>   But on one statement I may safely venture:
> That few of our most highly gifted men
>   Have more appreciation of the trencher.
> I go. One pound of English beer, and then
>   What Mr Swiveller called a "modest quencher";
> The home-returning, I may "soothly say,"
>   "Fate cannot touch me: I have dined today."

Clare College Clare College was founded in 1326 as University Hall by Richard Badew, chancellor of the university. Indeed, the university's decision to found a college of its own was probably encouraged by the success Oxford had had with its "great University Hall." After two fires the foundation was reformed as Clare House and then as Clare Hall (in 1338) and Clare College (in 1856). Somehow the Chancellor persuaded Lady Elizabeth de Clare to take on the task of refounding the college, and under her statutes socii appeared for the first time at Cambridge; Clare House was designed to consist of a master, nineteen fellows, and ten poor scholars, whose studies were to include grammar, logic, and singing. The fellows were empowered to elect the master and to fill the vacancies in their ranks—a practice then unheard of. Additionally, with a particularly secular view for the times, only six of the fellows and the master had to be in orders.

The original small and low quadrangle had fallen into total disrepair by Elizabethan times and was replaced over a period of eighty years by the present court, which is entered through a fan-vaulted entranceway surrounded by beautifully worked iron gates and railings. A path from the quadrangle leads to Grumbold's Bridge, a three-arch stone bridge which escaped the destructive force of Oliver Cromwell's troops.

Tradition has for centuries tried to associate Geoffrey Chaucer with Clare College in one way or another, but there is no evidence that he was ever in residence here, and the argument that Clare College should be identified as the "Soler Halle at Cantebrigge" of "The Reeve's Tale" is also without justification. One early scholar who was here was the dramatist and pamphleteer Robert Greene, who came here from St. John's sometime after receiving his B.A. in 1578 or 1579. He took the M.A. degree in 1583 but was not incorporated until July 1585. Greene was often abroad, but he probably was in residence in 1583, for the dedicatory epistle of the second part of *Mamillia: A Mirrour or Looking-glasse for the Ladies of England*, licensed on September 5, 1583, is dated "From my Studie in Clare Hall." Greene is thought to have given some consideration to the study of medicine since the end of his *Planetomachia* is signed "R. Greene, Master of Arts and Student in Phisicke," but in *The Repentance of Robert Greene Maister of Artes* he admitted his time was ill spent.

In 1735 the now-obscure Poet Laureate William Whitehead, a native of Cambridge, entered Clare College as a sizar. He received his B.A. in 1739 and his M.A. in 1743 and was elected a fellow of the college in 1742. The theologian Hugh Latimer was also a member of the college. In more modern times Siegfried Sassoon was a member of Clare College from 1904 to 1908 after attending Marlborough College.

Corpus Christi College   Between 1347 and 1352 four colleges were founded at Cambridge; the last of these, the House of Corpus Christi and the Blessed Virgin, was founded by the united city guilds of Corpus Christi and the Blessed Virgin as a place for the education of priests who could then serve the townspeople and sing mass for the departed souls of guild members. The causes of self-interest and of reconciliation of the differences between town and gown were served simultaneously in this way; indeed, members of the guild made over their houses and land on Luthburne or Lurthburgh (now Free School Lane) to the college, and this land, when cleared, is that on which the college now stands.

The college of chaplains (for such the students were intended to be) used St. Benet's Church, and the foundation grew in wealth even though the prosperity of the town declined. But the imposition of candle rents angered the townspeople, who rose in a body, destroyed a university bedell's house, and marched on their own college. Thomas Fuller writes:

> Here they brake open the College gates on the Saturday night . . . and . . . violently fell on the Master and Fellows therein. . . . Hence they advanced to the house of the Chancellor, threatening him and the University with fire and sword. . . .

The Bishop of Norwich, with a force of archers, intervened and, says Fuller, "seasonably suppressed their madness." The university, of course, had the sympathy of both Parliament and the King, and it was the mayor who was held responsible.

The 1630 visitation of the plague was particularly bad in Cambridge, and Dr. Henry Butts, Master of Corpus Christi and Vice Chancellor, remained here alone:

> Myself am alone, a destitute and forsaken man: not a Scholler with me in College, not a Scholler seen by me without. God, all-sufficient, I trust is with me; to whose most holy protection I humbly commend your Lordship.

In Cambridge 617 people died that year, 347 from the plague, and Dr. Butts hanged himself in his rooms.

The library at Corpus has an outstanding collection of manuscripts gathered after the dissolution of the monasteries by Matthew Parker, Archbishop of Canterbury during the early years of Elizabeth's reign. Here is the oldest copy of the *Anglo-Saxon Chronicle*, which Parker found open to the year 899, the year of King Alfred's death. The small holes in the parchment are not the wear of years or human abuse but are the work of ticks which once swarmed over Anglo-Saxon sheep. Other priceless volumes are St. Augustine's 6th-century Gospel book, the self-illustrated *Chronica* of Matthew Paris, a 5th-century Roman manuscript showing St. Luke in a toga, and an illuminated 12th-century Bible.

Of the two early literary figures associated with Corpus Christi College, one is thought to have been here and one is known to have taken his degree. It is assumed now that the dramatist John Fletcher was the "John Fletcher of London" who was admitted a pensioner of Benet's College (Corpus Christi) in 1591. It is also assumed that he was the one admitted as a Bible clerk in 1593, but there is no record of Fletcher's having taken a degree. Christopher Marlowe was admitted during the winter term of 1580 as the new Archbishop Parker scholar from the grammar school in Canterbury and planned to read divinity before taking orders. Marlowe's name is entered in the matriculation register simply as "Marlin." About three years older than the normal university entrant, he had no difficulty in living the ascetic life of the scholar here: the devoted students rose at four, prayed, listened to lectures, studied by candlelight in unheated rooms, and communicated only in Latin or Hebrew. The ground-floor room (once used as a storehouse) near the Old Court staircase was thought to have been Marlowe's, but this is now considered doubtful.

There is a memorial plaque to both Marlowe and Fletcher on the north side of the Old Court, and the dining hall contains a splendid set of portraits including one found in 1953 in a heap of rubble left by repairmen working on the master's lodge. The portrait, executed on boards and now authenticated as Elizabethan, is almost without a doubt a portrait of Marlowe. The work contains an inscription, "AEtatis suae 21 1585," followed by *Quod me nutrit me destruit* ("That which nourishes me, destroys me"). On Palm Sunday, 1584, Marlowe received his B.A., 199th in the class of 231; his M.A. was granted in 1587 only after a dispute with the authorities over his absences. Marlowe probably frequented the Eagle Inn on Benet Street, and it is usually assumed that *Dido, Queen of Carthage* was written during this time and that *Tamburlaine* was at least begun, if not finished, before he left Cambridge.

John Cowper Powys came up to Corpus Christi from Sherborne around 1890; he left with a second in history and became a lecturer in English in a girls' school in Brighton. His youngest brother, Llewelyn, also attended Corpus Christi.

Emmanuel College Emmanuel College, on the site of a 13th-century Dominican religious establishment, now stands in St. Andrew's Street surrounded by a well-kept garden. Founded by the staunchly Puritan Sir Walter Mildmay in 1584 during Elizabeth I's reign, the college anticipated a trend in England; its purposes were to proselytize and reform the Church of England and to produce doctors of divinity. No fellowship could be held for life. The college was enormously successful, especially during the Commonwealth, and in 1644 eighty-one candidates were admitted. Parts of the Dominican structure remained when Sir Walter took over the property, and he took obvious delight in transforming the Dominican refectory into a chapel which ran north and south, rather than the traditional east and west orientation; he also made the original chapel into the refectory. The chapel was not rebuilt on traditional lines for almost 100 years.

Emmanuel has had a distinguished list of religious alumni, including John Harvard, after whom the American university was named. There have also been two literary figures associated with the college, one in the 18th century and one in the 20th. Bishop Thomas Percy, collector of the *Reliques of Ancient English Poetry,* became D.D. here in 1770 after receiving both his B.A. and his M.A. from Christ Church, Oxford. More recently, Hugh Walpole came here from Durham School in 1903. The son of an Anglican clergyman, he had understood from early adolescence that he was to take orders and in 1906 took honors in historical tripos. Leaving Cambridge, he spent some time on the staff of the Mersey Mission for Seamen in Liverpool, Lancashire, before his lack of a vocational calling made itself clear.

Gonville and Caius College Caius (usually pronounced "keys"), more formally known as The College of Gonville and Caius founded in honour of the Annunciation of Blessed Mary the Virgin, had a founding almost as complicated as its name. Gonville Hall (as it was then known) on Free School Lane was originally established in 1348 by Edmund Gonville, who directed that the master and four fellows study the arts and theology. Upon Gonville's death, William Bateman, his executor and Bishop of Norfolk, moved the hall to the bottom of Foul Lane, opening onto Milne Street, and without any apparent concern for its original purpose, set up new statutes in which civil and canon law replaced the earlier emphasis on theology. The school was refounded in 1557 by John Caius, the great Norfolk physician who affected the Latinized form of Keys. Regarded in fact as a "cantankerous idealist," he refused to consider applications from those who were "deaf, dumb, deformed, lame, confirmed invalids or Welshmen"; his house rules were no less fussy, disciplinary offenders being put in stocks.

Caius used his wealth well here; he built in Tudor Gothic and had the Cambridge clunch (clay) faced with stone brought from the ruins of Ramsey Abbey; indeed, much of the early medieval walling can still be seen. Caius's hold on the college began to loosen when the Reformation arrived; the college accepted the changes, but he did not. Reports concerning Caius and the college reached the Archbishop of Canterbury: Caius himself was accused of keeping "copes, vestments, albs, crosses, tapers with all massing abominations" and of setting up "a crucifix and idols with the image of a doctor kneeling before them." A raid on the master's rooms was carried out, and all the offending articles were seized and burned or defaced by common consent. The doctor's greatest contribution was the development of the School of Medicine and Anatomy. At the time medicine was little more than a token school, and anatomy was nonexistent; but under Caius, with his great reputation and interest, both developed rapidly and even along scientific lines. At his death in 1573 Caius was buried in the chapel, and his monument has an ornate canopy over the gilded and colored sarcophagus.

One of the early scholars here was Jeremy Taylor, who entered as a sizar on August 18, 1626; a native of Cambridge, he was referred to in the admission book as "anno aetatis suae 15" and was designated as a former pupil at the local Perse School. Under Thomas Bachcroft's tutorage, Taylor matriculated in 1627, became a Perse scholar in 1628, and received his B.A. in 1631; elected a Perse Fellow around 1633, he took orders before 1634 and his M.A. that year. Another early figure to attend Caius was the future Poet Laureate Thomas Shadwell, who entered as a pensioner in 1656, "then aged 14"; how long he stayed is not known, but he left for the Middle Temple and then traveled abroad before settling on a literary career.

More modern members of Caius include Harold Monro, who took a third in the medieval and modern languages tripos in 1901, and James Elroy Flecker, who entered in May 1908 to study Oriental languages preparatory to joining the Consular Service. (He had already received his B.A. at Oxford in 1906.) Flecker had rooms on Jesus Lane, but he liked neither his rooms nor the university. Nevertheless, his two years here were successful, and with his examinations passed Flecker was sent in June 1910 to Constantinople, where his health broke down almost immediately.

Jesus College Jesus College of the University of Cambridge, as it is popularly known, is correctly titled The College of the Blessed Virgin Mary, St. John the Evangelist and the Glorious Virgin St. Rhadegund; founded in 1496 by Bishop John Alcock, Jesus is unique among the Cambridge schools in that it has made its home in a nunnery. Indeed, Bishop Alcock took over the partly ruined buildings of the 12th-century Benedictine nunnery of St. Rhadegund; his adaptation of the original buildings was very well done, and the resemblance to a monastery is striking. The present college hall was the nuns' refectory, the master's lodge was the prioress's lodging, the library was the nunnery guesthouse, the scholars' quarters were fashioned from the nuns' dormitory, and the chapel was fashioned from the nunnery church. Bishop James Stanley of Ely, Alcock's successor, determined that only one of the eight fellows and master had to be in holy orders (not necessarily the master), and he further decreed that only one man was required to study canon and civil law, while the others were permitted to branch out from theology as widely as they desired. His most important directive encouraged teaching within the college.

Two literary figures were here in the 16th century: Thomas Cranmer and Sir Fulke Greville. Cranmer, who later exchanged Canterbury for death at the stake, entered Jesus College in 1503 and spent eight years studying logic and philosophy before receiving his B.A. in 1512. He became an M.A. in 1515 and was elected a fellow shortly after his degree was conferred. All might have gone well for Cranmer had it not "chanced him to marry a wife"; he lodged her at the Dolphin Inn, where the innkeeper's wife was one of his wife's relatives. His frequent visits to the inn gave rise later to the story that Cranmer was a hostler. His marriage, of course, made him ineligible to hold the fellowship, and he secured an appointment as a common reader at Buckingham (now Magdalene) College. Reelected a fellow after the death of his wife, Cranmer received his D.D. degree and took a readership in divinity here, which he held until 1529 (when the plague was ravaging Cambridge). Sir Fulke Greville, the poet and friend of Sir Philip Sidney, came up to Jesus College from the Shrewsbury School as a fellow-commoner just short of the age of fourteen. Matriculating in the Easter term, 1568, he remained at the college until 1571, when he left without a degree.

In the 18th century, Laurence Sterne attended Jesus College. His uncle Jacques had been a scholar here, and his great-grandfather, Richard Sterne, Archbishop of York, had been master of Jesus in 1634 as well as its benefactor. Laurence Sterne entered as a sizar on July 6, 1733, at the very late age of twenty and in a year secured the exhibition instituted by his great-grandfather; he did not, however, matriculate until March 29, 1735. He had no capacity for mathematics, his study of formal logic ended only in jokes about its terminology, and some of his reading brought about his extreme dislike of pedantry and false erudition. He had few friends here, and one of his firmer friendships with a younger student, John Hall (later John Hall-Stevenson), was the result of the young man's delight in obscene literature. The two frequently sat in the inner court where the famous Jesus College walnut tree grew; Sterne wrote of the tree:

At Cambridge many years ago,
In Jesus was a walnut-tree;
The only thing it had to show,
The only thing folk went to see.

Being of such a size and mass,
And growing in so wise a college,
I wonder how it came to pass
It was not called the "Tree of Knowledge."

He received his B.A. in January 1736 and his M.A. in 1740 and left under difficult circumstances, for even with a generous allowance from his cousin Richard and the university allowance, Sterne had run up a considerable debt.

Another 18th-century alumnus of Jesus College was Samuel Taylor Coleridge, who entered as a sizar from Christ's Hospital on September 7, 1790. His admission plainly implied an informal obligation to take orders, but the decision against a life in the church came by 1792. He became a foundation scholar in 1793 and also had some funds from Rustat scholarships. In his first year he captured the Browne Medal for a Greek ode on the slave trade and in his second was one of four finalists for the Craven scholarship, which was won by Samuel Butler, later headmaster of Shrewsbury and the grandfather of the author of *Erewhon*. Two events in 1793 are said to have contributed to Coleridge's leaving the college. In the first instance he had his rooms furnished by a "polite upholsterer" over whom he exercised no authority; left to his own devices, the upholsterer arranged everything as he saw fit and at his own price. The bill was for a staggering amount, which Coleridge could not pay, and he was equally hurt by the tradesman's obvious self-interest. The second case concerned the Chancellor's Medal, the primary test of classical excellence in the 18th century. The competition was open only to wranglers and senior optimes, and Coleridge's inability to cope with mathematics made it likely that he probably would not even be qualified to compete. As a consequence of being twice "hurt by life," he fled from Jesus College on December 2, 1793, for London; two days later he enlisted in the 15th Dragoons under the name Silas Tomkyn Comberbacke. Coleridge was as inept a horseman as he was a mathematician, and after a fortnight he secured a discharge and returned to Cambridge on April 12. Admonished in front of the fellows and confined to the college for a month, he set off in June on a walking tour to Ottery St. Mary, Devon, via Oxford and Wales and so left Cambridge without a degree; "in an inauspicious hour I left the friendly cloisters and the happy grove of quiet, ever honoured Jesus College. . . ." A student prank here during Coleridge's time was stealing a portion of the tail of a scholar's gown, and this so frequently happened to the poet that the gown was shortened "to the length of a spencer." The master of Jesus apprehended Coleridge one day and asked, "Mr. Coleridge! Mr. Coleridge! when will you get rid of that shameful gown?" Coleridge, looking over his shoulder to see the length remaining, replied, "Why, Sir, I think I've got rid of the greatest part of it already."

Sir Arthur Quiller-Couch was elected a fellow of Jesus College when he became King Edward VII Professor of English Literature in 1912.

King's College Because of the apparent seclusion of university life, 15- and 16th-century Cambridge is frequently thought of as a haven in an age of squalor, filth, and contagion; but a more erroneous view is difficult to imagine. Even as late as 1574 Cambridge was especially filthy with streets so narrow and filled with debris that two wheelbarrows could not pass at the same time; water spilled onto the street (and passersby) from overhanging gables, and human waste was put out daily. As the plague frequently ravaged the town, the townsmen became increasingly resentful of their squalid surroundings and the attendant pestilence, especially when they observed the obvious contrast with the grandeur and magnificence of the academic foundations, which by then had surpassed the earlier religious foundations. This was the situation in 1441, when Henry VI, at the age of nineteen, determined to found a royal college, the

King's College of Our Lady and St. Nicholas; it was to occupy a broad strip of land that began at the river and almost reached the High Street. In the way stood part of Milne Street, two lanes leading to Market Hill from the river, and a number of houses, churches, businesses, and other buildings; as much as a third of the central part of the town was affected.

Henry's original ideas for the buildings were on a modest-enough scale, with one exception: King's College Chapel. This building is the glory of English architecture at Cambridge and is just as Henry planned it, not so much a chapel as a personal cathedral. Work on the chapel began in 1446, and Henry VIII completed it. The great windows are magnificent, and the woodwork scarcely less so; Tudor arms and badges abound, out of keeping with the founder's dislike of "cuirous werkes of entaille and besy molding." Perhaps most unfortunate is the lover's knot carved with the initials *H* and *A* for Henry and Anne Boleyn. John Ruskin saw the finished structure in a most peculiar light; it was "a piece of architectural juggling" akin to "a table upside down with its four legs in the air." Ruskin, though, is almost alone in this negative view; William Wordsworth first saw the chapel when he arrived to take up residence at St. John's College in 1787; he notes in *The Prelude*:

> It was a dreary morning when the Chaise
> Roll'd over the flat Plains of Huntingdon
> And, through the open windows, first I saw
> The long-back'd Chapel of King's College rear
> His pinnacles above the dusky groves.

Years later, probably during a visit in November and December 1820, he wrote "Inside of King's College Chapel, Cambridge":

> Give all thou canst; high Heaven rejects the lore
> Of nicely-calculated less or more;
> So deemed the man who fashioned for the sense
> These lofty pillars, spread that branching roof
> Self-poised, and scooped into ten thousand cells
> Where light and shade repose, where music dwells
> Lingering—and wandering on as loth to die;
> Like thoughts whose very sweetness yieldeth proof
> That they were born for immortality.

By 1443 Henry had changed his modest establishment and tied the college to his other foundation at Eton so that only Etonians had the right to attend King's College, and they proceeded, by right, to fellowships. The university had no control over this privilege, and the men of King's were allowed to proceed to their degrees without the normal examination process. The college buildings took centuries to complete, and fittingly the greatest damage King's has suffered throughout the years occurred in the 1960s, when the foot of a "night climber" went through some of the glass.

Literary associations here began in the mid-16th century, when Giles Fletcher the Elder was admitted as a scholar on August 27, 1565; coming up from Eton, he progressed quite normally, and he was admitted a fellow on August 28, 1568, and received his B.A. in 1569 and his M.A. in 1573. His career was not without incident, the most notable of which was his involvement in 1576 in the accusations of maladmin-

KING'S COLLEGE, CAMBRIDGE
What awful perspective! while from our sight
With gradual stealth the lateral windows hide
Their Portraitures, their stone-work glimmers, dyed
In the soft chequerings of a sleepy light.
          William Wordsworth, "Inside of
          King's College Chapel, Cambridge"

istration and infringement of the college statutes laid against the provost, Dr. Roger Goad. However, Fletcher appears not to have fallen too far from grace since he was named deputy orator at the university the following year and began a study of civil law at the request of the provost in 1579. During Fletcher's residence, Samuel Harsnett, author of *A Declaration of Egregious Popish Impostures* and later Archbishop of York, was admitted a sizar. He arrived on September 8, 1576, but there is no record of his having attended Eton; indeed, it is most likely that Harsnett attended the grammar school in his native Colchester. Harsnett went to Pembroke College after only a short time here. Phineas Fletcher, the elder son of Giles Fletcher, entered King's College from Eton on August 24, 1600; by the time he became B.D. in 1604 (M.A. in 1608), he had earned a reputation as a poet and in 1603 had contributed verse to the university's collection of poetry. Fletcher secured a fellowship in (probably) 1611, and remained at King's until the summer of 1616. The circumstances surrounding Fletcher's departure in 1616 are obscure, but it would seem that some sort of difficulty or some slight from the officials occurred; Fletcher alludes to this in his *Piscatorie Eclogs:*

> Not I my Chame, but me proud Chame refuses,
> His froward spites my strong affections sever;
> Else from his banks could I have parted never.

Another 17th-century literary figure to enter King's College was Edmund Waller, who was admitted a fellow commoner on March 22, 1620; he is thought to have had a relative for his tutor, but there are no records to support the assertion. In fact, there is no evidence that Waller even took a degree; he left King's before July 3, 1622, when he was admitted a member of Lincoln's Inn. Not until 1735 did another important literary figure come up to King's College; that year Horace Walpole, later 4th Earl of Orford, entered the same college his father had attended. Of Walpole's university days little is known; even the story that his blind mathematics professor told him that he was incapable of learning anything of the subject may well be apocryphal. Walpole was not very good in the classics; his greatest proficiency lay in French and Italian studies. He left in 1739 without a degree.

In 1906 Rupert Brooke entered King's on a classical scholarship. He had visited Cambridge the previous year with Geoffrey Keynes, son of John Neville Keynes and brother of John Maynard Keynes, and Brooke stayed in the Keynes's Harvey Road house. When Brooke came up to King's in October, his rooms were at the top of Staircase A in the Fellows' Building; the second year he moved to Room One on Staircase E, on the ground floor of Gibbs' Building. His early reaction to Cambridge lacked enthusiasm:

> I do not know if it's the climate or the people: most probably it's neither, but my cantankerous old self. But for some reason I find this place absolutely devoid of interest and amusement. I like nobody. They all seem dull, middle-aged, and ugly.

However, Brooke became involved in a large number of activities and even came to believe that Cambridge would become the vital center of the arts. He was a member of the Apostles and president of the Fabian Society, but, more important, he was one of the group of undergraduates who formed what was to become The Marlowe Dramatic Society. Their first production, Christopher Marlowe's *Dr. Faustus,* on November 11, 1907, was a great success, and the second production, Milton's *Comus,* on July 10, 1908, was performed before a private audience of fellows and their guests. In this audience were Alfred Austin, Poet Laureate, Thomas Hardy, Edmund Gosse, and Robert Bridges, who left early because of his impatience with the production. The next day Brooke was invited to breakfast at Charles Sayle's home at 8 Trumpington Street with Hardy, whom the young man found "incredibly shrivelled and ordinary and [who] made faintly pessimistic remarks about the toast." In June of the following year Brooke met Henry James at Sayle's home and took the novelist punting the next day. September 1910 brought some very good news for the young man when he learned that the Harkness Essay Prize had been awarded to his "Puritanism in the Early Drama." The award was a great step for him because of his disappointing performance in the tripos; Brooke was awarded a B.A. in 1909 and moved to the Old Vicarage in nearby Grantchester. He was elected a fellow of King's on March 8, 1912, and was admitted on March 19; he received his M.A. on April 25.

Magdalene College Magdalene (pronounced "maud'lin") College, the earliest of the colleges to stretch across the Cam, was an offshoot of the Benedictine Crowland Abbey and was originally a hostel for monks; at its inception it so closely resembled a normal college that it was known as Buckingham College (from the duke's patronage) long before the Reformation changed the character of the Cambridge establishment. The buildings are gabled with mullioned windows and clustered chimneys. Catching the winds of the dissolution of the monasteries, the student monks abandoned the college in 1539, and a few years later the first students entered; here the shift from religious to lay was easy. Thomas, Lord Audley, owner of Walden Abbey, took over as owner and decided to found the present college in 1542. Audley's death in 1544 left the college in a difficult financial position and with an administrative peculiarity: that the mastership, normally the result of an election by fellows, was to be the gift of the holder of the barony of Braybrooke. An early figure associated with Magdalene when it was still a Benedictine school was Thomas Cranmer, who was forced to resign his fellowship at Jesus College because of his marriage. He taught theology here while living with his wife at the Dolphin Inn; after her death in childbirth, he was reinstated in his fellowship at Jesus College.

Perhaps the most important treasure at Magdalene College is the personal library and the *Diary* of its most distinguished graduate, Samuel Pepys. Coming up from St. Paul's School in London, he was first admitted to Trinity Hall on June 21, 1650, and transferred to Magdalene on March 5, 1651, as a sizar. He was elected on the Spendluffe Foundation in April 1651 and took his B.A. in March 1654. In the preceding autumn Pepys and a companion had gotten into a serious situation for being "scandalously overserved with drink," and the two were "solemnly admonished" by Pepys's tutor "in the presence of the fellows then resident. . . ." Where he was so wickedly served is not known, but he did frequent a drinking establishment run by one Betty Aynsworth, a noted procuress who was eventually run out of town by the university authorities before setting up a shop at the Reindeer Inn in Bishop's Stortford. Pepys became an M.A. in June 1660; he returned many times to Cambridge and his college in later years, as the *Diary* relates, and frequented any number of pubs in the town. The Rose Tavern, where Rose Crescent is today, held fond memories:

> I went to the Rose, and there with Mr. Peachell, Sanchy, and others, sat and drank till night, and were very merry, only they tell me how high the old doctors are in the University over those they found there, though a great deal better scholars than themselves. . . .

He also went to the Three Tuns. Pepys made arrangements before his death that his library, including manuscripts, was to go to his nephew John Jackson for his life before being given to some college, preferably Magdalene; at Jackson's death in 1726, some 3,000 volumes went to Magdalene Library. Pepys prescribed the arrangement of the books in the presses he provided, and it is fitting that the central arch of the "new" library is inscribed "Bibliotheca Pepysiana 1724" and that his coat-of-arms is above the central window. The six shorthand volumes of the *Diary* lay in the library until 1819, when John Smith, a St. John's undergraduate, began his task, totaling 10,000 hours, of deciphering the symbols and gave the world its first glimpse of the work.

Charles Kingsley entered Magdalene in October 1838 and gained a scholarship at the end of his first year. He was known to be an average student and was deeply troubled by religious doubts; the debate over the Oxford movement added to his confusion. As a consequence, he threw himself into every activity other than academic that he could find. He found much delight in rowing, though he never made first boat, in fishing, especially in the Fens, in boxing, and in walking. Although he virtually abandoned his academic pursuits, his brilliance and early extensive reading helped him to prepare for his examinations in the last six months of his residence. He barely gained a first class degree in the classical tripos in 1842; he had the last position in the list. One of the stories which has come down from his undergraduate days concerns a question set in the Mechanics paper, which was to describe the pump, as invented by Samuel Morland. Kingsley, who had many abilities, had no knowledge of the inside workings of such a mechanism; consequently, his paper consisted of a drawing of a pump on a village green with a church in the background and a sign, "This pump locked during Divine Service." In May of 1860 Kingsley was elected Professor of Modern History and for the first three years kept a house here as well as one at Eversley, Hampshire, where he held the living. The expense proved too great, and he abandoned the Cambridge house. His tenure in the chair was not successful because history held no established place in the course of study. In January 1864 Kingsley entered into a serious controversy with John Henry Newman, to whom he attributed the statement "Truth for its own sake, had never been a virtue with the Roman catholic clergy." Never having made the comment, Newman took exception, and his *Apologia pro Vita Sua* was the

result. Kingsley ultimately apologized, rather unsatisfactorily, but his original argument was so confused and full of misunderstanding that Newman easily carried off the victory.

From 1954, following his election to the Chair of Medieval and Renaissance English, until his death in Oxford in 1963, C. S. Lewis was a fellow of Magdalene College.

Pembroke College Established during one of the periods of rapid growth of the university, from 1347 to 1352, with three other colleges, Pembroke is the third oldest foundation in the university. Dating from 1347 and officially the Hall of Valence-Marie, Pembroke was founded by a woman, Marie de St. Paul de Valence, the widow of Aymer de Valence, Earl of Pembroke. The countess requested and received papal permission in 1358 to build a private chapel for the school's master, fellows, and scholars, and so Pembroke became the first college to have its own chapel. The normal requirement of celibacy was imposed. The physical appearance of the college remained unimposing until Matthew Wren, master of Pembroke in 1663, had the new Italianate chapel known as Wren's Chapel built by his nephew Sir Christopher Wren. The chapel was, in fact, the nephew's first work. Almost two centuries later more building was undertaken under the guidance of Alfred Waterhouse, and the old master's lodging and old court were dynamited and a neo-Gothic building constructed. This has been called one of the great artistic misfortunes of Cambridge.

Pembroke has been very much the college of literary people, especially poets. Edmund Spenser, who entered Pembroke as a sizar in 1569, suffered from ill health and poverty while here, but he read widely and avidly in Latin and Greek literature and eventually in French and Italian literature. He came under the influence of Gabriel Harvey, who shared Spenser's tastes and poetry and encouraged the poet's use of Latin models for his verse. Spenser left the university in 1576, the year he received his M.A. His later works, with the exception of *The Faerie Queene*, have few references to Cambridge; there he writes:

> Thence doth [the Ouse] by Huntingdon and Cambridge flit,
> My mother Cambridge, whom as with a Crowne
> He doth adorne, and is adorn'd of it
> With many a gentle Muse, and many a learned wit.

As one of the most famous churchmen and sermonists of the late 16th and early 17th centuries, Lancelot Andrewes had a long and fruitful association with Pembroke; he first came here from the Merchant Taylors' School and was elected a fellow in 1576. Receiving a fellowship at Jesus College, he took orders in 1580 and became catechist here the same year. He was elected master of Pembroke around 1590 and retained the post until 1605. The period of Andrewes's mastership was a valuable one for the college, for he was able to change the college deficit to a surplus. Upon his resignation Samuel Harsnett succeeded to the post on November 9, 1605, and in 1606 became vice chancellor of the university. He ruled with rather a high hand and even as vice-chancellor kept control of Pembroke. His frequent absences coupled with alleged financial mismanagement and High Church practices inspired a great deal of animosity within the ranks of the fellows, although he was reelected vice chancellor in 1614. The situation worsened, and in 1616 the fellows of Pembroke took a series of fifty-seven accusations to King James I and requested Harsnett's removal. The master politely resigned and then stayed in favor in court.

On July 6, 1631, the poet Richard Crashaw became a pensioner of Pembroke; he matriculated on March 26, 1632. His special aptitude for languages was cultivated here, and he mastered Greek, Latin, Italian, Hebrew, and Spanish. Even during this period his religious fervor was apparent, and he spent hours every day at St. Mary's Church, where he prayed and composed religious verse. Crashaw received his B.A. in 1634, the same year that his *Epigrammatum Sacrorum Liber* appeared. In 1637 he moved to Peterhouse, where he was elected a fellow.

Another of Pembroke's noted literary figures was Thomas Gray, who had two experiences with the college. He first came here as a pensioner in 1734 but moved to Peterhouse, his uncle's college, the same year. After the fire incident there in February 1756, he returned and remained for the rest of his life, except for short periods in London. His chambers consisted of a large, low room at the western end of the Hitcham Building. In December 1757, upon the death of Colley Cibber, Gray declined the Poet-Laureateship even though the necessity to write birthday odes was removed. The opening of the British Museum in early 1759 induced Gray to move to London to carry on his research, and he did not return to Cambridge, except for occasional visits, until June 1761. In 1762 he applied unsuccessfully for the Chair of Modern History and Modern Languages. When the professorship fell vacant in 1768, it was then given to Gray and renamed the Chair of Modern Literature and Modern Languages. Gray, a recluse, had an extreme fear of fire, which was heightened when he narrowly escaped a fire that partially destroyed the college in 1768. Reticence was a progressive malady, and in later years he even refused to take his meals in the hall. He ventured into society only when necessary; to secure books from the circulating library, for example, Gray had to go to the Rainbow Coffee House, where he was the object of frequent stares from the curious. He could, though, find some gratification in that people fought over the honor of being a secondary user of his books. Gray's health was declining steadily, and on a trip to London in 1771 he became ill. Treated for a gastric ailment (then, erroneously, termed "stomach gout"), he deteriorated rapidly, and attended by his cousin Mary Antrobus, he died in his rooms on July 30, 1771. He was buried in Stoke Poges, Buckinghamshire, in the churchyard of his elegy.

While Gray was here, Christopher Smart was admitted as a sizar on October 20, 1739; relying mostly on the £40 sent to him annually by the Duchess of Cleveland, Smart had to struggle to survive, and the winning of the Watts Scholarship (worth £6 a year) in 1740 helped only a little. He received his B.A. in January 1743, third in his class. On July 3, 1745, he was elected a fellow of Pembroke College and in October was made praelector in philosophy. Until this time he had lived in Room 43, but in December he moved to a much larger room, Number 38, belonging to the

master. It is clear that he was living above his means; and this, along with his tavern excesses, caused Gray to note prophetically, ". . . all this, you see, must come to a jail or a bedlam." About the time he received his M.A. degree, on February 11, 1746, his creditors confined him to his rooms for a debt of over £350. While he won the Seatonian Prize in 1750, he appears to have left "silently" for London about this time and was confined for a short period in Bedlam (Bethlehem Hospital). His marriage to Anna Maria Carnan during this absence brought a measure of official displeasure, but it was not enough for the authorities to turn him out; it was agreed that if he continued writing for the Seatonian Prize, they would extend his fellowship. Shortly after, he left permanently for London. His feelings for Cambridge were of the utmost affection, and the *Jubilate Agno* is full of references to the university:

For I bless God in the behalf of TRINITY COLLEGE in CAMBRIDGE & the society of PURPLES in LONDON.

Peterhouse   Founded in 1280 as the House of Peter by Hugh de Balsham, Bishop of Ely, Peterhouse has stood at the Trumpington Street entrance to the university for almost 700 years; in 1284 the master of the House of St. Peter and its scholars were set up in two houses next to St. Peter's Church (now the Church of St. Mary's the Less), where they were to live "as scholars studying in the University of Cambridge" and to follow the rules governing "the Oxford scholars of Merton." The Hall was built from Balsham's endowment, and as the college grew, the south portion of the principal quadrangle took shape. The north and west sides, as well as the kitchen, date from 1424 to 1460, and much of the old work there can be traced. There was less religious regimen here than was usual, and the scholars were not required to take holy orders. On the other hand, they had to attend services at normal canonical hours, and they wore clerical habit (the prototype of the modern academic robe) and had a clerical tonsure.

The 1623 wood-paneled chapel with its classical west front is still lighted by candles, and the Flemish glass in an east window is said to be a Rubens design for the Crucifixion. The Hall, with a particularly fine gallery of portraits, has windows that may be without equal in Cambridge; designed and executed by William Morris, Sir Edward Burne-Jones, and Ford Madox Brown, they are richly colored and contain portraits of Balsham, Sir Isaac Newton, Thomas Gray, and Richard Crashaw.

Peterhouse is most likely the Cambridge college attended by John Skelton, and he probably arrived here around 1474, at the age of fourteen. Toward the end of his life the poet stated, ". . .it was Cambridge that first lovingly suckled me with her pap of wisdom," and it would seem that he was here before going to Oxford for his degree. A second early writer is now also thought to have studied at Peterhouse. Thomas Campion, poet and physician, came up from London in the summer of 1581 and was joined in the autumn by his stepbrother, Thomas Sisley. He stayed in residence over the vacations and shared a bedroom with his stepbrother, although each had his own study room. Campion left in 1584 without a degree and proceeded to London to study law. Whether a third author, Thomas Heywood, studied here is not certain, although internal evidence in his works suggests a time at the university. The view that it was here is based on William Cartwright's statement that Heywood "was a Fellow of *Peter*-house in Cambridge" when he went on to discuss the 1658 rededication of *An Apology for Actors*. But Cartwright's statement that the poem was written shortly before Heywood's death in 1641 discredits his argument since the poem was actually written before 1612.

Peterhouse has had at least one eminent alumnus, Thomas Gray, and a reasonable claim can be made for another, Richard Crashaw, who was here a full century before Gray. In 1637 Crashaw came over from Pembroke College; he was elected a fellow here that year and received his M.A. in 1638. Crashaw considered taking Anglican orders, but the increasing Puritanism in the Anglican Church and personal leanings toward Catholicism made the thought untenable. For some years Crashaw undertook the life of a scholar and writer here, but the 1653 sacking of the Peterhouse Chapel by the Parliamentarians and the requirement to subscribe to the Solemn League and Covenant settled his religious questions. Crashaw refused to take the oath and was ejected. He went to Oxford and then to London before leaving for Paris, where he lived in a state of extreme poverty and joined the Roman Catholic Church.

Thomas Gray's academic career began as a pensioner at Pembroke Hall in 1734, but he soon transferred to Peterhouse, the college of his uncle, Robert Antrobus. Gray left Peterhouse in September 1738 without a degree and went for some months to his father's house in London before accompanying Horace Walpole on a grand tour. Opinions of Gray did not vary greatly at this time: Walpole claims "he never was a boy," and Dr. Samuel Johnson describes him as "a dull fellow"; he and Boswell continue the conversation:

> BOSWELL. "I understand he was reserved, and might appear dull in company; but surely he was not dull in poetry." JOHNSON. "Sir, he was dull in company, dull in his closet, dull every where. He was dull in a new way, and that made people think him GREAT".

Gray returned to the college in November 1742 and took a degree in civil law. He disliked his stay at the university and also cared little for his studies; "Must I plunge into metaphysics?" he wrote:

> Alas, I cannot see in the dark: nature has not furnished me with the optics of a cat. Must I pore upon mathematics? Alas, I cannot see in too much light: I am no eagle. It is very possible that two and two make four, but I would not give two farthings to demonstrate this ever so clearly; and if this be the profits of life, give me the amusements of it.

Gray's room after 1742 was on the north side nearest the road on the second floor; it still has a fine view of Pembroke College, just a bit east on Trumpington Street. Of these first years of residence, much is conjectured; the 1749 death of his aunt, Mary Antrobus, in Stoke Poges acted as a stimulus for resuming work on the "Elegy," and tradition maintains that some of the stanzas were written among the tombstones at Grantchester. After his London house burned, Gray was particularly afraid of fire and was concerned that some of those in the lodgings here

would carry out their wine-induced threats to burn down the college. Gray incautiously let both his concern and his request for a rope ladder be known, and in February 1756 a group of undergraduates called out "Fire" beneath his window. Gray escaped down his rope ladder only to land in a tub of cold water placed there to receive him; feeling that the college officials had not treated the perpetrators with enough severity, he went over to Pembroke, where he remained until his death in 1771.

A far more modern association exists with the novelist Kingsley Amis, who was a fellow of Peterhouse from 1961 to 1963.

Queens' College   Queens' was the original conception of Andrew Doket, Rector of St. Botolph's and Principal of the Hostel of St. Bernard, who received royal consent in 1446 to build his college between the High Street and what finally became the end of Milne Street. The original plan for the College of St. Bernard called for a master and four fellows, but Doket simply did not have the funds to get the college going and in 1448 petitioned Margaret of Anjou to take over since there was "no collage founded by eny Quene of Englond hidertoward." St. Bernard's became Queen's College of St. Margaret and St. Bernard, and the Queen spirited away the King's master mason from King's College to aid the building program here. A second queen, Elizabeth Woodville, wife of Edward IV, refounded and endowed the college in 1465, and so the name was changed to Queens' College.

A tower on the southwest corner of the first court here is known as the Erasmus Tower, for Desiderius Erasmus is said to have lived in these rooms when he came to Cambridge as Professor of Greek. Even though these were supposedly the best rooms in the college, Erasmus complained about them constantly and about his study. He criticized student laxity in paying lecture fees, and he was even more upset over the "raw, smal and windy" beer which the college made available. Unable to find suitable wine, he wrote to a friend for help:

> If you can send me a barrel of Greek wine, the best which can be had, Erasmus will bless you; only take care it is not sweet. . . . I am being killed with thirst. Imagine the rest. Farewell.

Even so he met with defeat: the first cask was so small that it did not even last a few months, and the carriers drained off half the contents of the second cask and refilled it with water. While holding the Lady Margaret Chair of Divinity, he introduced Greek into the university, worked on his new Latin version of the New Testament, and stimulated critical thought.

In 1621, when his uncle Dr. John Davenant was President of Queens' and Lady Margaret Professor of Divinity, Thomas Fuller entered the college. Fuller received his B.A. in 1625 and his M.A. in 1628 but was unsuccessful in securing a fellowship here. He went on to Sidney Sussex College as a fellow commoner but again was unable to secure a fellowship. *The History of the University of Cambridge* was written in 1655.

St. Catharine's College   St. Catharine's College was founded in 1473 by Robert Woodlark (Wodelarke),

Provost of King's, and his original building, a small clunch-built court, has disappeared. The college was to have a master and ten fellows, all of whom were to study "philosophy and sacred theology," but with the Wars of the Roses the college dwindled to the master and three fellows. Its endowments also fell sharply, and the college, because of its relationship to King's, was referred to opprobriously as "a sucker thrown up by the parent stem." Today, St. Catharine's dominates King's and has the only three-sided court facing Trumpington Street which is open to passersby.

By and large, literary figures have not been in residence here; indeed, only one literary figure in the 17th century studied at St. Catharine's, and of him there are no records. The dramatist James Shirley came here from St. John's College, Oxford, sometime after 1612; his reasons for the transfer may well have been related to Archibishop William Laud's attempt to dissuade him from holy orders because of a physical disfigurement, a mole on his left cheek. He graduated with a B.A. about 1618, and sometime after 1619 he took holy orders and received his M.A. From Cambridge he took a living near St. Albans and later became master of the Edward VI Grammar School there.

The only other literary figure to attend St. Catharine's did not appear until 1929; Malcolm Lowry came here after a stint as a cabin boy on a China-bound freighter. He had been educated at the nearby Leys School; Lowry's rooms were on Bateman Street, and he could frequently be found drinking at the Red Cow and the Bath. *Ultramarine* was written here and, in fact, was accepted in place of his thesis for graduation.

St. John's College   The transpontine St. John's College shares its founder with Christ's College, but the story of St. John's actually began long before Lady Margaret Beaufort's interest in it. Around 1135 Henry Frost founded a small hospital for the sick which was to be run by Augustinian friars on the same site as the present college, and Hugh de Balsham, Bishop of Ely, tried unsuccessfully to establish a college here in 1280. His experiment failed in 1284; the hospital continued to minister to the sick until the 16th century, when Lady Margaret decided to do with the hospital what she had done with God's House when she refounded it as Christ's. Lady Margaret died in 1509, and her executor, John Fisher, took on the task of dissolving the hospital and in 1511, with far scantier endowments than Lady Margaret had imagined, founded the College of St. John the Evangelist, although it did not actually open until 1516. In the 1860s, unfortunately, a building mania swept Cambridge, and the surviving parts of the hospital as well as the original chapel were swept away. Only the original magnificent Tudor gateway has survived. Over the archway is a great stone panel holding the French and English arms, supported by the Beauforts' heraldic yales (jalls), which look very much like deformed antelopes. Below the shield is the Tudor rose. A third, Carolean court added in the 17th century took the college down to the riverbank, where two bridges now give access to the other side; the most famous of these is the Bridge of Sighs, reached through an archway on the cloistered west end of the quadrangle. The bridge gives the impression of an exquisitely carved stone screen with iron grills filling the window tracery. Besides the bridge, St. John's is justly proud of its Combination Room, a typical Tudor gallery with an exquisite plaster ceiling and paneled walls.

Cambridge has been the home of many poets, and St. John's and Trinity are the undisputed leaders of the colleges. Sir Thomas Wyatt, who entered the college at the age of twelve at an undetermined date, graduated with a B.A. in 1518 and received his M.A. in 1520. While here, he met another early student, John Leland, Henry VIII's antiquarian. Roger Ascham came here in 1530 under the auspices of his patron, Sir Anthony Wingfield, and appears to have developed his special aptitude for Greek at this time. He had the highest regard for his tutors at St. John's and later writes of them in *The Scholemaster*, stating:

> By their only example of excellency in learning, of godliness in living, of diligency in studying, of counsel in exhorting, of good order in all things, [they] did breed up so many learned men in that one college of St. John's at one time, as I believe the whole university of Louvain in many years was never able to afford.

Although Greek appears to have been Ascham's main interest, he also mastered almost all the extant literature in Latin, studied mathematics, and acquired some musical skills. He became a B.A. on February 18, 1534, and was admitted a fellow of St. John's in March. He received his M.A. in early June 1537 after paying the usual grace of 5 shillings and became a reader in Greek around 1538. This post served his interests well, and in a short time, it is said, Greek writers became at least as familiar as the Latin ones had been. He unsuccessfully sought a lectureship in mathematics in 1539, at which time he left Cambridge for a short visit to his family in Kirby Wiske, Yorkshire. His return to the university was postponed for two years because of malarial fever. When the Archbishop of Winchester forbade the new pronunciation of Greek that Ascham favored, he threw himself into the writing of *Toxophilus* in 1543 and 1544 and dedicated it to Henry VIII. He succeeded Sir John Cheke as public orator in 1546 and became Princess Elizabeth's tutor in 1548, when he took up residence at Cheshunt, Hertfordshire.

About thirty years later, the pamphleteer and dramatist Robert Greene matriculated as a sizar. He became a B.A. in 1578 or 1579 and left St. John's, according to *The Repentance of Robert Greene, Maister of Artes,* and went to the Continent before he transferred to Clare College, where he took the M.A. degree in 1583. In *Repentance* Greene comments that the university had a deleterious effect on his character. In October 1582 Thomas Nashe (Nash) matriculated as a sizar here and possibly had been in residence a year or two before his matriculation; in any event, he graduated with a B.A. degree in 1586 and referred to his stay here in *Have with You to Saffron-Walden.* Nashe's claim that he could have become a fellow here aroused his bitter enemy, Gabriel Harvey, who asserted that not only had Nashe left without his M.A. degree but that his insulting character was such "that to this day [they] call every untoward scholar of whom there is great hope 'a very Nashe.'" Harvey himself is to be doubted here, but Nashe did not obtain the M.A.

In the early 17th century Robert Herrick entered St. John's as a fellow commoner; he seems to have had a taste for spending money and a proportionate distaste for studying. There are numerous letters from the poet to his uncle, Sir William Herrick, asking for funds even though he had a share of his father's estate (about £340) and had £10 a term for expenses. It was perhaps for reasons of economy that Herrick left St. John's for Trinity Hall in 1616. After graduating from Christ's College in 1631, John Cleveland came here and was elected a fellow in 1634 before receiving his M.A. in 1635. Matthew Prior came here on scholarship in 1682 from Westminster School. He attracted no especial notice at St. John's and took his B.A. in 1686; he completed his first literary work, a reply to John Dryden's *The Hind and the Panther*, in the following year. In April 1688 he obtained a fellowship and wrote St. John's annual tribute to the Earl of Exeter, a benefactor of the college. The result was the offer of the post of tutor to Exeter's sons, and Prior left the university to take it. In 1720 he stood for Parliament after the death of Dr. Pasch but withdrew without contesting the seat. His affection for St. John's did not diminish over the years, and he left his books and the manuscript of his *Poems on Several Occasions* to the college.

On October 30, 1787, the most famous Johnian of all, William Wordsworth, came up as a sizar from Hawkshead. His rooms, among the cheapest available, were high up on the south side of the first court above the college kitchens. The window of the keeping room (study) had a view to Trinity College Chapel, but his bedroom was closetlike and windowless. This cheerless room was the source of the "unlovely cell" in *The Prelude:*

> The Evangelist St. John my patron was:
> Three Gothic courts are his, and in the first
> Was my abiding-place, a nook obscure;
> Right underneath, the College kitchens made
> A humming sound, less tuneable than bees,
> . . . .
> Near me hung Trinity's loquacious clock,
> Who never let the quarter, night or day,
> Slip by him unproclaimed. . . .

Wordsworth's career was undistinguished; he refused to take some examinations, notably in mathematics, and exhibited great scorn and distaste for the competitiveness of the system and a lack of proper reverence for the dons. Left to his own devices by his tutors, he ignored mathematics in order to study Italian with Charles Isola, father of Emma Isola, the girl later adopted by Charles Lamb. Wordsworth's reading program in his second and third years was a mixture of the miscellaneous and the deliberate:

> . . . many books
> Were skimmed, devoured, or studiously perused,
> But with no settled plan. I was detached
> Internally from academic cares;
> Yet independent study seemed a course
> Of hardy disobedience toward friends
> And kindred, proud rebellion and unkind.

But, he says, "This spurious virtue" then "encouraged me to turn" even from personal "restraints and bonds."

Perhaps no better picture of 18th-century Cambridge exists than in *The Prelude*. Wordsworth and the coach passengers approached on "a dreary morning" until

> first we saw
> The long-roofed chapel of King's College. . . .

ST. JOHN'S COLLEGE, CAMBRIDGE
**I could not print
Ground where the grass had yielded to the steps
Of generations of illustrious men,
Unmoved. I could not always lightly pass
Through the same gateways, sleep where they had slept,
Wake where they waked, range that in closure old,
That garden of great intellects, undisturbed.**
William Wordsworth, *The Prelude*

Passing "a student clothed in gown and tasselled cap," they

> . . . drove beneath the Castle; caught,
> While crossing Magdalene Bridge, a glimpse of Cam:
> And at the *Hoop* alighted, famous Inn.

The Hoop is gone, and so is the academic dress. Wordsworth's attitude toward the competitive system, especially the examinations, is clearly put forth:

> Examinations, when the man was weighed
> As in a balance! of excessive hopes,
> Tremblings withal and commendable fears,
> Small jealousies, and triumphs good or bad,
> Let others that know more speak as they know.
> Such glory was but little sought by me,
> And little won.

Another of his most irksome restraints, compulsory chapel, comes in for its share of criticism:

> Was ever known
> The witless shepherd who persists to drive
> A flock that thirsts not to a pool disliked?
> A weight must surely hang on days begun
> And ended with such mockery. Be wise
> Ye Presidents and Deans, and, till the spirit
> Of ancient times revive, and youth be trained
> At home in pious service, to your bells
> Give seasonable rest, for 'tis a sound
> Hollow as ever vexed the tranquil air;
> And your officious doings bring disgrace
> On the plain steeples of our English Church. . . .

The dons do not escape his censure, but here he seems almost to exhibit the usual undergraduate misconceptions:

> Nor wanted we rich pastime of this kind,
> Found everywhere, but chiefly in the ring

Of the grave Elders, men unscoured, grotesque
In character, tricked out like aged trees
Which through the lapse of their infirmity
Give ready place to any random seed
That chooses to be reared upon their trunks.

In his second and third years, especially, Wordsworth took frequent walks beside the Cam:

Lofty elms,
Inviting shades of opportune recess,
Bestowed composure on a neighbourhood
Unpeaceful in itself. A single tree
With sinuous trunk, boughs exquisitely wreathed,
Grew there; an ash which Winter for himself
Decked as in pride, and with outlandish grace:
Up for the ground, and almost to the top,
The trunk and every master branch were green
With clustering ivy, and the lightsome twigs
And outer spray profusely tipped with seeds
That hung in yellow tassels, while the air
Stirred them, not voiceless. Often have I stood
Foot-bound uplooking at this lovely tree
Beneath a frosty moon.

Wordsworth took his B.A. on January 27, 1791, and went straight to London but returned in August at his uncle's insistence to study Oriental languages. He had left again by November, when he was on his way to France. He did not return to Cambridge or St. John's until his brother Christopher was appointed to the mastership of Trinity College in the autumn of 1820.

Two notable 19th-century literary figures had associations with St. John's. William Barnes placed his name on the register of St. John's on March 2, 1837, but did not actually take up residence until his summer holiday from teaching in 1847. In the ten-year interval, Barnes, who was teaching in his own school in Dorchester, published a great deal and appears to have read widely. In January 1847 he was ordained deacon by the Bishop of Salisbury and became a B.D. here in 1850. In October 1854 the novelist Samuel Butler entered the college of his forebears. He received so firm a grounding in the classics that he was able, while an undergraduate, to write "The Shield of Achilles, an Homeric Picture of Cambridge Life," a burlesque which gained enormous popularity throughout the university. His time here was in many ways the happiest of his life; he found freedom and privacy, and the strong influence of his father was felt only partially. He graduated twelfth in the classical tripos in 1858 and went to London as a lay assistant to a curate, for whom he was to do some part-time teaching. Between 1864 and 1871, following his return from New Zealand, Butler took up painting and had eleven works exhibited at the Royal Academy; most of these are now in the Butler Collection here.

According to Thomas Fuller, Ben Jonson was a Johnian; however, Jonson's statement that he was "taken from school and put to a trade" directly disputes Fuller's account.

Trinity College Trinity College, properly called The College of the Holy and Undivided Trinity, is sometimes confused with Trinity Hall, The Hall of the Holy Trinity of Norwich. History began here in 1324, when Hervey de Staunton, Edward II's Chancellor of the Exchequer, founded The House of the Scholars of St. Michael; it was open only to graduates already in holy orders, six of whom were restricted to the study of theology and one whom was required to take on the mastership without additional remuneration. The building of a library about 1400 and the construction of one of the largest halls in Cambridge did nothing to attract scholars, and the institution languished for some time.

A second establishment from Edward II's time, King's Hall, also had an obscure early history, and apparently no guidelines were set down for the original foundation before it almost faded from sight. Edward III refounded the school in 1337 as the Hall of King's Scholars and set up its statutes. A court-appointed warden was to have complete charge of the thirty-two scholars. A decree of Richard II later established the minimum age for entry as fourteen and set the scholars to the study of logic and grammar. The libidinous nature of the 14-century scholars enters literature when Geoffrey Chaucer uses King's Hall under its early name, Soler Hall, and its scholars as the basis for "The Reeve's Tale" in *The Canterbury Tales*:

Thanne were ther yonge povre scolers two,
That swelten in this halle, of which I seye.
Testif they were, and lusty for to pleye,
And, oonly for hire myrthe and revelrye,
Upon the wardeyn bisily they crye
To yeve hem leve, but a litel stounde,
To goon to mille and seen hir corn ygrounde. . . .

Soler possibly referred to the upper rooms, that is, the sun chambers, of the early hall. New building, which began at the turn of the 15th century, reflected royal benefactions; the stone hall came first and was quickly followed by a small cloistered court and two vaulted gateways on King's Childer Lane and the High Street. In 1546, after Henry VIII had expropriated the land he wanted for Trinity, he amalgamated Michaelhouse and King's Hall to establish a college unequaled in magnificence in Europe. Taking over the structures of the earlier house and hall, he cleared a large site and incorporated the Michaelhouse refectory and King's Hall Chapel.

It was the effort of Dr. Thomas Nevile (Neville), master from 1593 to 1615, that brought about Trinity's position as the "noble and magnificent college" (as the university calendar says). Dr. Nevile moved one of Edward III's original gateways to the west end of the chapel, cleared out some buildings from King's Hall, and developed the Great Court. The chapel includes stonework from the old Franciscan friary, and the antechapel contains an outstanding statuary collection of Trinity's worthies. Henry established only the barest condition for Trinity before his death, and it was Elizabeth who determined the complete statutes of 1560, with a wide-reaching condition that was a noncondition: Trinity was to choose the best people available irrespective of geographical representation. And choose it did, so that The College of the Holy and Undivided Trinity has the most formidable list of men of letters and science of any college of either Oxford or Cambridge.

Two of the earliest scholars at Trinity were George Gascoigne, whose dates of attendance are obscure, and Francis Bacon, who entered in April 1573 at the age of twelve years and three months. He remained in residence for more than three years, except when the university was closed on account of the plague from July 1574 to March 1575; Bacon completed the normal course by December 1575 and was subsequently admitted to the "Society of Ancients" at Gray's Inn. He left Cambridge without a degree, he suggested, because he was aware of the defects within the academic system and because "in the Universities they learn nothing but to believe." In 1614 Bacon was returned to Parliament as the Member for the university There is a memorial statue of Bacon in the Trinity Chapel antechapel. The dramatist George Chapman has been stated to have attended Trinity College around 1574. But Anthony à Wood, one of the sources of information, admits not knowing whether Chapman entered Oxford or Cambridge. Thomas Warton in *The History of English Poetry* first claimed that Chapman was here, but it has not been established how he arrived at this conclusion.

The 17th century has a wealth of literary associations for Trinity. Giles Fletcher the Younger matriculated before 1603 and was elected a scholar on April 12, 1605; he received his B.A. degree in 1606 and became a fellow of Trinity on September 17, 1608. He held a readership in Greek grammar in 1615 and was granted one in Greek literature in 1618. The poet George Herbert had a distinguished academic career here, entering on a scholarship in 1608 and taking up residence on December 18, 1609. His B.A. was granted in 1613, his name being second on a list of seniority; and his M.A. was granted in 1616. Meanwhile, the master, Dr. Nevile, had taken note of Herbert's abilities, and through his offices the poet was elected a minor fellow in 1614 and a major fellow in 1616. In 1617 Herbert was singled out to be a college lecturer, giving the course in Greek grammar; by then he was an accepted classical scholar. The next year the poet became a praelector in rhetoric in the university and decided to enter holy orders; however, he dropped his theology reading when competing for the post of public orator. He was appointed deputy orator on January 18, 1618, and became public orator with a stipend of £30 a year in January 1620. He was now in constant contact with the court and with men of distinction, including Sir Francis Bacon, and subsequently moved into favor in court; indeed, by 1623, when he was to have taken orders, Herbert had decided to enter government instead. He eventually reaffirmed his original decision and was ordained in 1630. On July 3, 1623, Sir John Suckling matriculated as a fellow commoner, at about the age of fourteen if a birth date of 1609 is accurate. Although he gained considerable proficiency in both music and linguistics, it would appear that his learning was more polite than erudite, and he left the university without a degree when he went to Gray's Inn in 1627.

It is believed that Andrew Marvell entered Trinity as a sizar in 1633 on the evidence of Anthony à Wood, who wrote that Marvell was admitted "in matriculam Acad. Cant. Coll. Trinity" on December 14, 1633. The more probable date is 1635, since the established minimum age was fourteen. On April 13, 1638, Marvell was admitted a scholar of Trinity College and received his B.A., most probably, in 1639. College records show that Marvell left about September 24, 1641, when he was expelled because of nonresidence. A possibly aprocryphal story, which

appeared in 1726, states that Marvell early came under the influence of a group of Jesuits who persuaded him to abandon his studies and to go to London, where his father discovered him in a bookseller's shop and forced him to return to the university. Abraham Cowley was chosen a chorister of Trinity College on March 30, 1636; on April 21, his name was entered as "Abraham Coolwy"; and an entry on June 14, 1637, records, "Cowley chosen and admitted Scholar by the King's letter dispensatory." He was granted a B.A. probably in 1639, was admitted a minor fellow in October 1640, and became an M.A. in 1642. It is usually stated that within a year Cowley was forcibly ejected from Cambridge because of Royalist sympathies, but a more reasonable explanation seems to be that he fled before the 1st Earl of Manchester and his commission arrived to administer the Solemn League and Covenant. In February 1661, Cowley was reinstated as a fellow for a period of seven years, preparatory to taking orders. Cowley did a great deal of writing here, including *Naufragium Joculare, The Guardian* (later retitled *Cutter of Coleman Street*), a great part of *Davideis*, and probably at least part of "Vision, Concerning His Late Pretended Highness, Cromwell the Wicked; Containing a Discourse in Vindication of Him by a Pretended Angel and the Confutation Thereof by the Author, Abraham Cowley." At his death in 1667, Cowley bequeathed many of his books to Trinity College.

John Dryden was admitted as a pensioner at Trinity on May 18, 1650, and matriculated in July. He was elected a scholar of the foundation on October 2 and placed under his tutor; he received his B.A. in March 1654 but never took an M.A., probably because, as the holder of a life estate, he would have been assessed approximately seven-eighths of his yearly income. Little is known of Dryden's time at Trinity, but in 1652 he was discommuned and forced to apologize to the vice-master for his rebelliousness.

In the early 18th century the future Poet Laureate Laurence Eusden entered Trinity College; receiving his B.A. in 1708 and his M.A. in 1712, he became a fellow in 1712 and was made Poet Laureate in 1718 after writing some very flattering verses about the 1st Duke of Newcastle's marriage (the laureateship was the duke's to give). The dramatist Richard Cumberland was born in the master's lodge of Trinity College on February 19, 1732, and spent a great deal of his childhood here; following early schooling at Bury St. Edmunds, Suffolk, he entered Trinity in (probably) 1747, took his degree in 1751, and was elected to a fellowship two years later.

The number of 19th-century literary men here is astounding. George Gordon, Lord Byron came up to Trinity from Harrow in 1805 after being unable to attend Christ Church, Oxford. His rooms in the southeast corner of the Great Court he described to his half sister, Augusta, as "superexcellent." Byron's studies were desultory, and most of his time was spent in riding, swimming, boxing, shooting, walking, and reading anything that was not required. Swimming was his undoubted passion, and Byron spent a great deal of time at his favorite pool. After the Christmas vacation he refused to return to Cambridge, simply because he was deeply in debt with no available funds to pay his creditors. He was induced to return in mid-April. His disrespect for the university was highlighted in 1807, when he imported a tame bear, which he walked and lodged in the hexagonal tower above his rooms. His explanation of the bear's residence was that it was going to stand for a fellowship—it reminded him of the dons, but it was better mannered. In 1807 *Poems on Various Occasions* and the aptly titled *Hours of Idleness* appeared. Byron left Cambridge at Christmas 1807 and did not return, except for occasional visits to his cronies, until he took his M.A. in 1808. Trinity's library contains Bertel Thorvaldsen's magnificent statue of Byron, rejected by Westminster Abbey because of the poet's dubious personal reputation.

Thomas Babington Macaulay came up to Trinity College in October 1818 and lodged on Jesus Lane before taking ground-floor rooms in the southeast corner of the Great Court. A brilliant student except in mathematics, he won a prize for a Latin declamation, a Craven scholarship, and the English prizes for his poems "Pompeii" and "Evening." His inability to cope with mathematics almost caused his downfall, for the single tripos, the only path to an honors degree, consisted mostly of mathematics. As a consequence of barely passing in mathematics, he had to face the academic world in 1822 as a poll man (recipient of a pass degree), and after failing twice in his effort, he finally gained a fellowship in October 1824. His one regret throughout his later years was that he had not remained as a resident don. The antechapel of the college chapel contains a memorial statue to Macaulay.

Edward Bulwer-Lytton (Lord Lytton) entered Trinity College as a pensioner in the Easter term of 1822, but disliking the lectures and feeling a slight from his tutor, he moved to Trinity Hall that year. Four years later, Edward FitzGerald took up his place at Trinity; he never stayed in the college but boarded with a Mrs. Perry at 19 King's Parade. The master of Trinity at this period was Christopher Wordsworth, brother of the poet, and FitzGerald's intense dislike of William Wordsworth may have stemmed from his dislike of the master, who, Fitz-Gerald wrote, "used to drawl out the Chapel responses so that we called him the Meeserable Sinner and his brother the Meeserable Poet." In 1827 FitzGerald met Alfred, Lord Tennyson here, but the two did not become intimately associated until later; on the other hand, his friendship with William Makepeace Thackeray was on a firm foundation here in 1829 and 1830 and deepened over the years. FitzGerald left Trinity College after taking his degree in 1830. The college has a FitzGerald-annotated volume of Tennyson's poems, and there is a memorial to the translator of the *Rubáiyát of Omar Khayyám;* George Bernard Shaw was asked to inaugurate the memorial tablet and refused because of his lack of enthusiasm for the poet's work.

One of Trinity's most illustrious members was Alfred, Lord Tennyson, who arrived in February 1828 and, like FitzGerald, never lived in the college. His first rooms were on the top floor at 12 Rose Crescent. Longing for the "hollies and the yews of home," he returned to Somersby, Lincolnshire, for the Easter vacation. Shortly after, he moved to King's Parade, 57 Corpus Buildings; here he purchased a pet snake and would sit in clouds of tobacco smoke, "watching its sinuosities upon the carpet."

In June 1829, Tennyson won the Chancellor's Medal for English Verse on the subject "Timbuctoo." Of the choice of subject much was said, and even the undergraduate body could not contain its derision. Thackeray (who had just entered Trinity) composed a parody of Tennyson:

> The day shall come when Albion's self shall feel
> Stern Afric's wrath and writhe 'neath Afric's steel.
> I see her tribes the hill of glory mount,
> And sell their sugars on their own account,
> While round her throne the prostrate nations come,
> Sue for her rice and barter for her rum.

A significant event in Tennyson's life occurred in June 1828, when Arthur Henry Hallam arrived at Trinity; the two men became intimate friends, and Hallam probably influenced Tennyson's life and genius more than anyone else. Hallam's rooms were on the central staircase on the south side of the New Court, and these are the rooms recalled later in *In Memoriam* when Tennyson saw

> The same gray flats again, and felt
>   The same, but not the same; and last
>   Up that long walk of limes I past
> To see the rooms in which he dwelt.

Both Tennyson and Hallam were elected to the Cambridge Conversazione Society (derisively called the Apostles because the membership was held at twelve), and many of the weekly meetings were held in Hallam's rooms

> Where once we held debate, a band
>   Of youthful friends, on mind and art,
>   And labour, and the changing mart,
> And all the framework of the land;
>
> When one would aim an arrow fair,
>   But send it slackly from the string;
>   And one would pierce an outer ring,
> And one an inner, here and there;
>
> And last the master-bowman, he,
>   Would cleave the mark.

Tennyson worked hard on his poetry here, and in 1830 *Poems, Chiefly Lyrical* appeared; also composed during his undergraduate days were a privately circulated poem, "Sir Launcelot and Queen Guinevere," and "Anacaona," a work of irregular stanzas. From a purely academic point of view Tennyson's time at Trinity was not particularly well spent; while he gained greatly from his intellectual contacts, he was contemptuous of the dons and ultimately of the whole educational institution:

> No!
> Nor yet your solemn organ-pipes that blow
> Melodious thunders thro' your vacant courts
> At noon and eve, because your manner sorts
> Not with this age wherefrom ye stand apart,
> Because the lips of little children preach
> Against you, you that do profess to teach
> And teach us nothing, feeding not the heart.

When Tennyson's father became seriously ill at the beginning of 1831, the son's presence at the Somersby rectory was much desired; Tennyson left Cambridge in February 1831 without taking a degree. A memorial statue to Tennyson is in the antechapel of the Trinity Chapel.

William Makepeace Thackeray, in turn, came up to Trinity in February 1829; while he found the environment here more pleasant than that at Charterhouse, he was still not tempted into any serious academic pursuits. In his first set of examinations (May 1829) he was very nearly at the bottom of the ranking, his position, he said, being where "clever non-reading men were put as in limbo." His other interests took precedence; he formed an essay club, developed a passion for Shelley's poetry, and contributed material to the *Snob*, a nonuniversity paper, which published his parody on Tennyson's "Timbuctoo." Thackeray appears to have fallen into the same kind of habits as Arthur Pendennis in his later novel, and feeling that his studies would be of little ultimate value, he left Cambridge at the end of the 1830 Easter term. Thackeray's rooms during his short stay were on the first floor of E Staircase next to the Great Gateway; these rooms were once occupied by Sir Isaac Newton, and here he wrote his *Principia*. Thackeray was very much aware of his illustrious predecessor and is supposed to have commented to his mother that in future the rooms would be known for his occupancy as well as Newton's. At the end of the century Maurice Baring came up from Eton but did not complete his degree, and the critic Lytton Strachey entered Trinity after spending two years at the University of Liverpool; he gained the Chancellor's Medal in English in 1902 and graduated in history in 1903. It was here during this period that the nucleus of the famous Bloomsbury group was formed.

In 1911 A. E. Housman, the poet and classical scholar, was persuaded to stand for the Latin chair here, vacated in December 1910 by the death of John E. B. Mayor; he was successful and with the appointment was elected a fellow of Trinity College. His inaugural lecture in May was both well attended and well received, and he presented more than thirty different courses during his Kennedy professorship. He soon became acquainted with Thomas Hardy, who sat at the high table when he came to Trinity and maintained a lifelong friendship with Robert Bridges. Housman published *Last Poems* in 1922. He had many favorite country walks on which he conscientiously avoided human contact; he spent the summer holiday of 1935 here with his brother, and even though his health had been failing for three years, they visited the area fully. Housman began lecturing in September, but by November he was in the Nursing Home. Leaving in January 1936 against the wishes of his doctor, he completed the term but had to return to the home; insisting again on taking up his duties, he delivered two lectures in the Easter term before collapsing; he died in the home on April 30 and was buried in Ludlow, Shropshire. There is a memorial tablet in Trinity Chapel. While Housman held his professorship, G.H. Trevelyan was Master of Trinity College (1927–1940).

Trinity Hall   With a situation next to the magnificent Clare College, Trinity Hall (commonly called The Hall but properly titled The Hall of the Holy Trinity of Norwich) has the appearance of the humble cousin of Clare. Frequently confused with Trinity College, or The College of the Holy and Undivided Trinity, The Hall was founded in 1350 by Bishop

William Bateman, who took over a hostel built about 1320 for Benedictine student monks from Ely. The entrance to Trinity Hall is unassuming, almost plain, and contains only a coat-of-arms. Bateman's plan for the college is of modern interest, for his college led the way toward the much narrower professional studies known today.

It is possible that Raphael Holinshed, author of the famous *Chronicles* used by Shakespeare, was a student here, but the evidence is far from conclusive. If he did enter Trinity Hall, he may have been the Holinshed who matriculated in May 1544 and became a scholar in the next academic year. Anthony à Wood's assertion that Holinshed took holy orders has no supportive evidence. In the 17th century, the poet Robert Herrick came here from St. John's; he had entered St. John's as a fellow-commoner (paying double fees because of his family's wealth but gaining only a few perquisites), and living above his means, he was constantly in debt. Thus, his decision to move to Trinity Hall was undoubtedly motivated partly by the saving in costs. Additionally, about 1616 Herrick had determined on a legal career, and The Hall with its emphasis on law was an obvious choice. He received his B.A. in 1617 and his M.A. in 1620; the move here, though, did not solve his financial problems, and the college books show that he was in its debt as late as 1630. The diarist Samuel Pepys spent a short period here in 1650–1651; he had come up from St. Paul's School with a scholarship from the Mercer's Company but left Trinity Hall in 1651 for Magdalene College. Philip Stanhope, 4th Earl of Chesterfield, famous for both his letter writing and his intimacy with Alexander Pope and Jonathan Swift, entered Trinity Hall in 1712; he was in residence little more than a year and later blamed the university for his own "turn for satire and contempt." Of The Hall, though, he had nothing but praise; it was "infinitely the best in the whole University" and "filled with lawyers who have seen the world and know how to live." He left in 1714 without a degree. Later in the century, in 1763, William Hayley came up from Eton, and while he was here began writing poetry; indeed, one of his most popular poems, "Ode on the Birth of the Prince of Wales," appeared in the *Cambridge Collection* at this time. He studied Spanish under Charles Isola, father of Emma Isola, whom Charles Lamb later adopted. Hayley left Cambridge without a degree in 1767.

In 1822 Edward Bulwer-Lytton (Lord Lytton) moved here as a fellow-commoner from Trinity College, where he felt one of his tutors had insulted him. While here he joined the Union Society and achieved some prominence as a speaker. He read English history avidly, published a small volume of poetry, won the Chancellor's Medal for a poem titled "Sculpture" in 1825 and graduated with a B.A. the next year. In the early 20th century J.B. Priestley was an undergraduate here.

CAMELFORD, Cornwall (pop. 1,220)   The stretch of Atlantic coast from Port Isaac north, one of the finest in Cornwall, is inextricably associated with King Arthur and the myriad of legends surrounding his life. The coastal area here is generally characterized as having "formidable cliffs," "savage rocks," and "treacherous water," but Camelford itself is almost 4 miles inland on the Camel River. The village is variously titled in literature: John Leland calls it Kemblen, and William Camden refers to it as Gaffelford. Geoffrey of Monmouth tells of Arthur's last battle at the ancient Slaughter Bridge, which crosses the Camel just a mile north of the village. In pursuit of the treacherous Mordred,

> Arthur was filled with great mental anguish. . . . Without losing a moment, he followed him to that same locality, reaching the River Camblam, where Mordred was awaiting his arrival. Mordred was indeed the boldest of men and always the first to launch an attack. He immediately drew his troops up in battle order. . . .
>   On the other side, Arthur, too, was marshalling his army.

The combat was heavy:

> Arthur continued to advance, inflicting terrible slaughter as he went. It was at this point that the accursed traitor was killed and many thousands of his men with him.

The Camblan River is taken to be the Camel. Layamon, the 12th-century author of *The Brut*, documents the battle too, but he confuses everything a little. The Tamar River forms the border between Devon and Cornwall and is nowhere near Camelford.

> Arthur went to Cornwall   with immeasurable army.
> Mordred heard that,   and held against him
> With countless folk—there were many fated.
> Upon the Tamar   they met together;
> The place called Camelford,   forever will that name endure;
> And at Camelford were assembled   sixty thousand,
> And more thousands besides;   Mordred was their leader.

Michael Drayton retells Geoffrey's story in the first song of *Poly-Olbion:*

> As frantick, ever since her British *Arthurs* blood,
> By *Mordreds* murtherous hand was mingled with her flood.
> For, as that River, best might boast that Conquerours breath,
> So sadlie shee bemoanes his too untimelie death;
> Who, after twelve proud fields against the *Saxon* fought,
> Yet back unto her banks by fate was lastly brought:
> As though no other place on Britaines spacious earth,
> Were worthie of his end, but where he had his birth.

Finally, and perhaps inevitably, Alfred, Lord Tennyson turns Camelford into Camelot, an identification that makes him unique.

Two other literary associations with the village have nothing to do with the West Country legend of King Arthur. Thomas Hardy makes Camelford into Camelton in *A Pair of Blue Eyes.* Stephen Smith and Henry Knight arrive at the Camelton railway station together with "that sombre van which had accompanied them all the way from London. . . ." The second association is entirely different: Camelford became a free borough in 1259 and so remained until the abolition of rotten boroughs under the Reform Act of 1832. James Macpherson, the "Ossian" poet, was one of the members of Parliament from Camelford from 1780 to 1796.

CAMPTON, Bedfordshire (pop. 396)   A small village located at a crossroads and on the Ivel River 6 miles southwest of Biggleswade, Campton shows no signs of 20th-century growth. The village has an exceptionally fine Elizabethan manor house built in 1591 and a 14th-century church with a notable medieval screen. The southwest corner of the churchyard holds the grave of Robert Bloomfield, the Suffolk poet and author of *The Farmer's Boy.* He had retired to nearby Shefford in 1814 after becoming partially blind and suffering from extreme hypochondria and depression and was befriended by Edmund Williamson, the parish priest here. Bloomfield died in Shefford on August 19, 1823, and was buried here. The tombstone notes, "Let his wild native woodnotes tell the rest"; his grave is cared for by the boys of the Robert Bloomfield School in Shefford.

CANONS ASHBY, Northamptonshire (pop. 59)   The name of the hamlet of Canons Ashby, 7½ miles southeast of Daventry, comes down directly from the canons of the Augustinian priory founded here in the mid-12th century, but today the community consists only of a number of small farms, the old manor house, and the parish church (once part of the Augustinian priory church). Very little remains of the old priory except fragments of the gatehouse, a well, and part of the vineyard. The original manor house, built by Sir John Cope with stone quarried from the priory, came into the hands of John Dryden upon his marriage to Cope's daughter in 1551, and the estate eventually passed to the 2d Baronet, the uncle of the poet. Dryden frequently visited here, and his earliest-preserved letter was to his cousin Honor, whom he called his "fairest Valentine" and whom he thanked for the silver inkhorn she sent him at Cambridge. Edward Dryden completed the present manor, a square house with a tower in front and two wings extending to the garden, during the reign of Queen Anne.

Another visitor to Canons Ashby was also related to the owner through marriage. Edmund Spenser, whose wife was a cousin of Sir Erasmus Dryden, was here in 1596 and undoubtedly on many other occasions; a room in the house called by his name commemorates the 1596 visit.

Canons Ashby comes into literature in one specific instance. Lucy Selby uses this as an address in Samuel Richardson's *Sir Charles Grandison.*

CANTERBURY, Kent (pop. 25,950)   A cathedral town and a borough in its own right, Canterbury was inhabited by Belgic tribes long before the Roman invasion and was an important town to the Romans, although it was never fortified. Durovernum Cantiaciorum was established as an administrative and residential center, and baths, a forum, an amphitheater, and large villas were constructed. Life under Roman rule here was peaceful, and the Roman walls that can still be seen were not constructed until the 3d-century menace of Saxon pirates.

By the 6th century Cantwarebyrig had become the capital of the Kentish kingdom ruled by Ethelbert (Aethelbert). The popular belief that St. Augustine, who landed in the shire in 597, began converting the pagans is inaccurate. Conversion had begun under Bishop Liudhard, personal chaplain to Bertha, Ethelbert's wife, almost twenty years before Augustine's arrival, and it was Liudhard's request to Pope Gregory I for missionary assistance that brought Augustine and a contingent of forty monks. When Augustine arrived, Bertha already had a chapel on the site of the present Church of St. Martin, the oldest church still in use in England. Bertha has a firm place in history: the Venerable Bede in his *Historia Ecclesiastica Gentis Anglorum* describes the Queen's worshiping here

> on the east of the city, [in] a church built in ancient times in honour of St. Martin, while the Romans were still in Britain. . . . In this church they first began to to chant the psalms, to pray, to say mass, to preach, and to baptize. . . .

Here Ethelbert was baptized on Whitsunday in 597— an act which assured that Kent and ultimately England would become Christian. It is now thought the font in St. Martin's is the one Augustine used for the King's baptism. Augustine was given the royal palace (probably on the grounds of the Abbey of St. Augustine), an old British church, and the title of Archbishop of Canterbury. The abbey was built outside the walls of the city to seclude the religious community from the bustle of secular life and to allow burial, which was not permitted within the town

Augustine's church gave way to a Saxon cathedral, and soon the entire city became an important religious and educational center. The town and the cathedral suffered from numerous Danish raids, and in 1067 a fire badly damaged Canterbury Cathedral. Archbishop Lanfranc, appointed by William the Conqueror, undertook the rebuilding and set about reconstructing the monastery and cathedral; he based the design of the cathedral on St-Étienne in Caen, his previous post. Of his work, which was finished around 1077, very little remains; most of the Norman parts seen today are the work of Archbishop Anselm, who extended the length of the church and built an enormous choir.

The supremacy of Canterbury and its Archbishop has never been challenged since 1072, when the Accord of Winchester, establishing Canterbury's primacy, was drawn up and attested to by William and Matilda. An event of consequence occurred in 1162, when King Henry II made Thomas à Becket archbishop under the assumption that Becket would be willing to ensure that the "King's Law" included the clergy. Becket, in fact, proved hostile to the King's will, was exiled in 1164, and reconciled in 1170; a second breach occurred, and in France Henry uttered the now-famous words: "Of the caitiffs who eat my bread are there none to free me from this low-born priest?" The challenge was picked up by four knights; William de Tracy, Reginald Fitzurse, Richard le Breton, and Hugh de Morville drew up their plans at Saltwood Castle on December 28 and had an angry interview with the Archbishop in his palace the next day. The knights left to arm themselves, and Becket went through the cloisters to the cathedral and in a door now known as the Martyr's Door. There he was confronted on a staircase (no longer in existence) by the men; he resisted, throwing one man to the ground, and they drew their swords, cutting off the top of his head and splattering blood and brains all over the stones. Alfred, Lord Tennyson uses the murder as the subject for *Becket,* and T. S. Eliot's *Murder in the Cathedral* has the chorus condemn the act:

CANTERBURY
The voice of the Lord will break the cedar-trees,
The Kings and Rulers that have closed their ears
Against the Voice, and at their hour of doom
The voice of the Lord will hush the hounds of Hell
In everlasting silence.

Alfred, Lord Tennyson, *Becket*

Clear the air! clean the sky! wash the wind!
   take stone from stone and wash them.
The land is foul, the water is foul, our beasts
   and ourselves defiled with blood.
A rain of blood has blinded my eyes. Where is England?
   Where is Kent? Where is Canterbury?
. . . .
But this, this is out of life, this is out of time,
An instant eternity of evil and wrong.
We are soiled by a filth that we cannot clean, united to
   supernatural vermin,
It is not we alone, it is not the house, it is not the city that
   is defiled,
But the world that is wholly foul.
Clear the air! clean the sky! wash the wind! take the stone
   from the stone, take the skin from the arm, take the
   muscle from the bone, and wash them. Wash the stone,
   wash the bone, wash the brain, wash the soul! wash
   them wash them!

Miraculous cures attributed to Becket began immediately, and by Easter 1171 Canterbury was a place of pilgrimage. Becket was canonized in 1173; and the next year, the King, penitent and bowing to public pressure, walked barefoot through the city, was scourged in the crypt before the saint's tomb, and kept an all-night vigil. With money raining in, an extensive building program was undertaken, guided by one objective, the placing of the Shrine of St. Thomas. In 1220 the Jubilee of the Martyrdom occurred, and on July 2, the festival day of the translation of St. Thomas, the saint's relics were borne through the stages of the cathedral to the shrine.

Medieval Canterbury, naturally, grew very prosperous, and the town became one of Christendom's major places of pilgrimage. The greatest throng of pilgrims came from London, as do Geoffrey Chaucer's group of twenty-nine in *The Canterbury Tales:*

And specially from every shires ende
Of Engelond to Canterbury they wende,
The hooly blisful martir for to seke,
That hem hath holpen whan that they were seeke.

Chaucer's pilgrims turn from the High Street into Mercery Lane, at which point they pass the Chequers of the Hope, mentioned by Chaucer, with its "Dormitory of the 100 Beds"; this inn has survived but is no longer an inn.

Numerous royal personages visited Canterbury as well; the most spectacular royal association was with Edward the Black Prince, who founded a chantry in the crypt as the price for the papal dispensation to marry his cousin Joan. His last will directed that he be buried in the Chapel of Our Lady in the undercroft, but public demand insisted on his burial on the south side of Becket's tomb in 1376.

The skepticism and inquiry of the 16th century that protested the unreality and formalism of religion throughout Europe had an impact here. Erasmus, the Dutch scholar and humanist, visited Canterbury Cathedral sometime around 1512 in the company of John Colet, Dean of St. Paul's and founder of St. Paul's School. His *Colloquies* comments on the relics for veneration, the haircloth, breeches, blood-marked handkerchief, and a rusted sword point. Both Erasmus and Colet were upset by the commercialism here, but they were even more disgusted when one of St. Thomas's shoes was offered as a relic by the leper hospital at Harbledown. Of the shoe—proffered to all travelers to kiss, for payment, of course—Colet raged, "What would these brutes have? Why doe they not by the same reason offer us their spittle, and the other excrements of the body to be kissed?"

Within twenty years the shrine of St. Thomas and all Becket memorials were destroyed; and the prior and monks were replaced by a dean and twelve canons. Henry VIII's dissolution was complete; even so, the cult of St. Thomas was not broken, as the well-worn stone steps up to the shrine bear witness. A 20th-century pilgrim tried to re-create the medieval scene; leaving from the Old North Gate in Winchester on the most probable date of the first pilgrimage, Hilaire Belloc with two friends (Philip Kershaw and Harold Baker, sometime warden of Winchester College) aimed to reach Canterbury and the shrine of St. Thomas à Becket at the same hour and on the same day as his murder. Arriving, Belloc entered the cathedral:

> It was almost dark. . . I had hoped in such an exact coincidence to see the gigantic figure, huge in its winter swaddling, watching the door from the cloister, and watching it unbarred at his command. I had thought to discover the hard large face in profile . . . the choir beyond at their alternate nasal chaunt; the clamour; the battering of oak; the jangle of arms and of scabbards trailing, as the troops broke in; the footfalls of the monks that fled, the sharp insults, the blows and Gilbert groaning, wounded, and à Becket dead. I listened for Mauclerc's mad boast of violence, scattering the brains on the pavement and swearing that the dead could never rise. . . .
> But there was no such vision.

Near the Infirmary Cloister, leading to the Green Court, is the Dark Entry, a passage immortalized in Richard Harris Barham's *The Ingoldsby Legends.* According to the story, a canon lived without the precinct walls and did not keep the "scant and thin" fare

of the priory: "Ellen Bean ruled his *cuisine.*—He called her 'Nelly Cook.'" Events go well until the canon's "niece" arrives, and Nelly thinks: "They were a little less than 'kin,' and rather more than 'kind.'" After a short period Nelly puts the lady to a test by hiding "the poker and the tongs in that gay Lady's bed!"; six weeks passed, but "the poker and tongs unheeded lay":

> And still at night, by fair moonlight, when all were lock'd in sleep,
> She'd listen at the Canon's door,—she'd through the keyhole peep—
> I know not what she heard or saw, but fury fill'd her eye—
> —She bought some nasty Doctor's-stuff, and she put it in a pie!

After the poisoning Nelly was never seen again, but more than a century later her bones were discovered walled up in the Dark Entry. Now her ghost walks every Friday night:

> And though two hundred years have flown, Nell Cook doth still pursue
> Her weary walk, and they who cross her path the deed may rue;
> Her fatal breath is fell as death! the Simoom's blast is not
> More dire—(a wind in Africa that blows uncommon hot).

Almost nothing exists today of the 11th-century Canterbury Castle; the square-buttressed keep at Wincheap Gate was a prison during the Middle Ages and was attacked by Wat Tyler in 1381. The Royalists held it during the Civil War. Much of Canterbury was destroyed during World War II, and indeed some of the buildings within the cathedral precincts were mutilated by bombs, although the cathedral itself was comparatively fortunate. The postwar impression must have been much like Daniel Defoe's in the 18th century; he writes in *A Tour thro' the Whole Island of Great Britain:*

> The Close or Circumvallation, where the Houses of the Prebendaries, and other Persons belonging to this Cathedral stand, is very spacious and fair. . . . [A]s for the Town, . . . [t]he Houses are truly Antient, and the many Ruins of Churches, Chapels, Oratories, and smaller Cells of Religious People, make the Place look like a general Ruin a little recover'd.

Undoubtedly Canterbury's most famous native son is Christopher Marlowe, who was born early in 1564 in a house (destroyed in World War II) on St. George's Street; he was christened in the parish church of St. George the Martyr on February 26, 1564. Only the tower of the church remains. Marlowe's father was a shoemaker of some importance, and Marlowe's uncle, a draper (or mercer), had a shop on the right side of Mercery Lane going toward the Christ Church Gate of the cathedral. (The lane still retains medieval features such as overhanging upper stories that the dramatist would have known.) Young Marlowe was admitted to King's School at Michaelmas term in 1578 after being awarded a scholarship under the statutes of the school that called for the education of "fifty poor boys." The regulation was not really adhered to: the first places generally went to sons of gentlemen. Most likely Marlowe attended King's before this date as a fee-paying commoner; at age fifteen with only two years to go at school, it was late for a scholarship unless he had had some prior training here.

Marlowe would have walked through the cloisters to get to the school and attended daily mass at the cathedral. He was probably a choirboy at the cathedral since his scholarship to Cambridge specifically mentions his musical ability. Marlowe's known relationship with Canterbury ended with his admission to the university. There is a Marlowe Memorial in the corner of the gardens of the Dane John; Marlowe's statue, blown off its pedestal by World War II bombs, was replaced facing in the wrong direction. A theater dedicated to the playwright is opposite St. Margaret's Church on St. Margaret's Street.

A second native son was Richard Harris Barham, who was born on December 6, 1788, at 61 Burgate Street. He was educated at St. Paul's School but subsequently had little to do with his native town aside from drawing upon it and its lore in *The Ingoldsby Legends*. Thomas Linacre, the scholar and founder of the Royal College of Physicians in London, was born in Canterbury about 1460 and received his earliest education here; little else is known.

Many early literary figures had close ties with the cathedral town; Sir Thomas More, author of *Utopia*, frequently visited Canterbury after his daughter married William Roper. They lived at Roper House, the gateway of which still exists. Following Sir Thomas's execution in London on July 6, 1535, his body was buried in St. Peter in the Tower, London; his severed head, in accordance with custom, was parboiled and impaled on a spike on London Bridge for an indefinitely known period. His daughter was rumored to have obtained the head and to have buried it in a lead casket in the Roper family vault in St. Dunstan's Church in Canterbury. In 1824 an old lead casket containing a head was found in the vault, and the head was assumed to be More's.

A far pleasanter early association exists with Izaak Walton, who married Rachel Floud, a collateral descendant of Archbishop Cranmer, on December 27, 1626, at the Church of St. Mildred with St. Mary de Castro on Stour Street. And Richard Lovelace, Cavalier and poet, is associated with Grey Friars, just off Stour Street. He came into this property, the oldest Franciscan friary in the country, upon the death of his mother in 1633 but was unable to take charge of it until he reached his majority. Lovelace occupied the old building at the water's edge in the garden.

In the early 18th century Daniel Defoe was here investigating a "ghost" story, which resulted in "A True Relation of the Apparition of Mrs. Veal, the Next Day after Her Death to Mrs. Bargrave, at Canterbury, the Eighth of September 1705." He notes: "This relation is matter of fact, and attended with such circumstances as may induce any reasonable man to believe it." Matthew Prior's experiences here in 1711 were none too pleasant; after helping with the peace negotiations preceding the Treaty of Utrecht, he left France and, traveling on a passport issued to Jeremy Matthews, was arrested here (not in Deal, as is usually claimed) on a charge of spying; he was not freed until orders came from London demanding his release. For a time Anne Finch, Countess of Winchilsea, lived on Littlebowne Road at the Moat (now gone).

Nineteenth-century associations are even more extensive than those of previous centuries. John Keats arrived in Canterbury from Margate on May 16, 1817, at a time when "I found my Brain so overwrought that I had neither Rhyme nor reason in it. . . ." He was working on *Endymion* and states in a letter: "I hope the Remembrance of Chaucer will set me forward like a Billiard-Ball. . . ." In early June he went on to the nearby village of "Bo-Peep" (St. Leonards) before returning to London. Later in the century King's School played an important role in the education of Walter Horatio Pater, W. Somerset Maugham, and Hugh Walpole. At the age of fourteen Pater entered the school from a local school in Enfield, Middlesex, and had a very happy time even though he was not particularly interested in the school's sporting activities. Pater went up to Queen's College, Oxford, as a commoner in 1858. He left a clear picture of his life here in "Emerald Uthwart."

The association with W. Somerset Maugham is far-reaching. Living with his uncle in Whitstable, 7 miles away, he entered the school here in 1884 and had a distinctly unhappy time, as he later related in *Of Human Bondage*. In this work Canterbury is thinly disguised as Tercanbury, and King's appears under its own name but is rather superficially described:

> The King's School at Tercanbury . . . prided itself on its antiquity. It traced its origin to an abbey school, founded before the Conquest, where the rudiments of learning were taught by Augustine monks. . . . One or two men of letters, beginning with a poet, than whom only Shakespeare had a more splendid genius, and ending with a writer of prose whose view of life has affected profoundly the generation of which Philip was a member, had gone forth from its gates to achieve fame. . . .
>
> The masters had no patience with modern ideas of education. . . . The dead languages were taught with such thoroughness that an old boy seldom thought of Homer or Virgil in after life without a qualm of boredom. . . . Neither German nor chemistry was taught, and French only by the form-masters; they could keep order better than a foreigner . . . it seemed unimportant that none of them could have got a cup of coffee in the restaurant. . . .

While Philip Carey is tormented on account of his clubfoot, Maugham suffered because of his frailness, his disinclination for games, and his stutter. Like the fictional Philip, Maugham refused to go up to Oxford and persuaded his uncle, the vicar of Whitstable (Blackstable in the novel), to allow him to go to Germany for a year; Philip's sudden inward hesitation at being allowed to go reflects Maugham's own dissatisfaction with his decision:

> He was touched and immensely flattered. It would be pleasant to end up his school-days with glory and then go to Oxford: in a flash there appeared before him the life which he had heard described from boys whom came back in the O.K.S. match or in letters from the University read out in one of the studies. But he was ashamed; he would look such a fool in his own eyes if he gave in now; his uncle would chuckle at the success of the headmaster's ruse.

Maugham's original bitterness eventually disappeared, as he proved conclusively when he gave the original manuscripts of *Liza of Lambeth* and *Catalina* to the school. In 1950 he gave King's the money to build a new boathouse, and in 1958, at the age of eighty-four, he returned to King's to open the new science building, for which he had donated £10,000. At the ceremony, he commented,

> When I was young and travelled a good deal, I found that the English were detested all over the world because they were so class-conscious and sniffy. The public schools were, in my view, largely responsible for creating this class-consciousness. So I suggested to the headmaster that I should provide a certain sum to educate a working-class boy at King's School. But the scheme was a flop; for one thing, working-class parents didn't seem to want their sons contaminated. So after a number of years I said the money should be spent on something else. Hence the Science Building.

His commentary was not exactly meant to please, and he continued in the same way:

> I can't see why England needs public schools. They seem to get on all right without them in France and Italy and the United States.

Maugham died in France on December 16, 1965, following a stroke; his ashes were brought back to Canterbury and on December 22 were interred by the wall of the library which he had helped to build and which he had stocked from his own collection. Permission to bury Maugham in the cathedral had been denied, and only his family were present for the services at King's.

The third literary figure to attend King's, Hugh Walpole, entered the Junior School in the 1896 fall term and spent five terms here. Like Maugham, Walpole was not particularly happy at the school, but the presence of his godfather, Canon A. J. Mason, helped a great deal, for the boy was allowed to spend much time in the canon's house and grounds. When Walpole's father was appointed principal of Bede College in Durham, the boy was removed from King's. Again, like W. Somerset Maugham, Walpole later supported the school generously; he paid for the returfing of the Mint Yard, gave valuable furniture to the establishment, presented his Augustus John portrait to the school, and in February 1938 formally presented it with all his books and manuscripts. The manuscripts are housed in the gate room of Prior Sellingegate over the Dark Entry; one of the boardinghouses is called Walpole House, and there is a Walpole Society as well as endowed Walpole prizes.

Before Maugham's use of Canterbury in *Of Human Bondage*, another novelist made extensive use of the town. A significant part of Charles Dickens's *David Copperfield* occurs here; and specific houses and localities are easily identified. Significantly, no name changes are involved here. David first meets Mr. Wickfield, his aunt's lawyer, in Canterbury:

> At length we stopped before. . . a house with long low lattice-windows bulging out still farther, and beams with carved heads on the ends bulging out too. . . . The old-fashioned brass knocker on the low arched door, ornamented with carved garlands of fruit and flowers, twinkled like a star; the two stone steps descending to the door were as white as if they had been covered with fair linen; and all the angles and corners, and carvings and mouldings, and quaint little panes of glass, and quainter little windows, though as old as the hills, were as pure as any snow that ever fell upon the hills.

The house is assumed to be 71 St. Dunstan's Street, near Westgate. At Miss Trotwood's request for "a

school where he [David] may be thoroughly well taught, and well treated," Mr. Wickfield decides on a local school, unnamed but obviously King's, and David is taken to see the headmaster:

> I went . . . to the scene of my future studies—a grave building in a courtyard, with a learned air about it that seemed very well suited to the stray rooks and jackdaws who came down from the Cathedral towers to walk with a clerkly bearing on the grass-plot . . .
> Doctor Strong looked almost as rusty, to my thinking, as the tall iron rails and gates outside the house; and almost as still and heavy as the great stone urns that flanked them, and were set up, on the top of the red-brick wall. . . .

The house usually associated with Dr. Strong's house is 1 Lady Wootton's Green; however, this identification seems most unlikely in light of Dickens's later description:

> The schoolroom was a pretty large hall, on the quietest side of the house, confronted by the stately stare of some half-dozen of the great urns. . . .

David's early impression of Canterbury is reinforced on a return visit. Dickens writes:

> Coming into Canterbury, I loitered through the old streets with a sober pleasure that calmed my spirits, and eased my heart. There were the old signs, the old names over the shops, the old people serving in them. . . . The venerable cathedral towers, and the old jackdaws and rooks whose airy voices made them more retired than perfect silence would have done; the battered gateways, once stuck full with statues, long thrown down, and crumbled away, like the reverential pilgrims who had gazed upon them; . . . the ancient houses, the pastoral landscape of field, orchard, and garden; everywhere—on everything—I felt the same serener air, the same calm, thoughtful, softening spirit.

When Mr. Micawber arrives in Canterbury, he puts up at "a little inn . . ." where

> he occupied a little room in it, partitioned off from the commercial room, and strongly flavoured with tobacco-smoke. I think it was over the kitchen, because a warm greasy smell appeared to come up through the chinks in the floor, and there was a flabby perspiration on the walls. I know it was near the bar, on account of the smell of spirits and jingling of glasses.

This is probably the 16th-century Sun Hotel, formerly called the Little Inn, on Sun Street. The "county inn" where Mr. Dick stays every alternate Wednesday on his visits to David at school has often been said to be the County Inn (destroyed in World War II); however, another claimant is the Fountain Inn on St. Margaret's Street, where Dickens stayed in 1861 on a public-reading tour. Dickens also once stayed at the Crown Inn, which later became Queen Elizabeth's Guest Chamber. After taking a house at Gadshill in 1856, Dickens was frequently in Canterbury and often brought his guests here.

Another association exists with the novelist Joseph Conrad, who lived in nearby Bishopsbourne from 1919 until his death on August 3, 1924; he was buried in the Roman Catholic portion of Canterbury Cemetery.

CANVEY ISLAND, Essex (pop. 18,110) Set in the Thames Estuary and approached by a bridge, Canvey Island is an extraordinary example of man's refusal to give up land to natural destructive forces. Very little of the island is more than 10 feet above sea level even at low tide; in fact, habitation never really took hold until the 17th century, when some Dutch businessmen and engineers were offered one-third of the island in return for building defenses against the sea. Today, half residential and half resort, Canvey Island has almost won the battle against nature; but any complacency the islanders may have gained was destroyed in the mid-1950s, when a gale accompanied by extremely high tides inundated the island and left 90 percent of the housing uninhabitable. One of the buildings that has stood for more than three centuries, the Lobster Smack Inn in Hole Haven, was unharmed. This is the original of the Thames River inn in Charles Dickens's *Great Expectations* to which Pip takes Magwitch in his attempt to smuggle the convict from the country. Leaving London from Temple Stairs, they journey down the Thames to "below Gravesend, between Kent and Essex, where the river is broad and solitary, where the water-side inhabitants are very few, and where lone public-houses are scattered here and there...." Here they find the inn, "a dirty place enough, and ... not unknown to smuggling adventurers...." However it was then, the pub is now extremely clean and bright and a favorite stop for local yachtsmen.

CAPHEATON, Northumberland (pop. 171) The tiny village of Capheaton, just north of Hadrian's Wall, where the Pennine Chain is often desolate and remote, is splendidly situated between high moorland and greener lowland. It is the seat of Capheaton Hall, built in 1685 by Robert Trollope, the home of the Swinburne family. The family had ruled in Capheaton since the 13th century and took part in the Rising in the North in 1569. Algernon Swinburne spent a great deal of his childhood here, the home of his grandfather, Sir John Swinburne; he also lived in the family home at Bonchurch on the Isle of Wight. One of Swinburne's favorite childhood pastimes was racing his pony across the moors:

The crowning county of England—yes the best! ...
Have you and I, then, raced across its moors
Till horse and boy were well-nigh made with glee
So often, summer and winter, home from school,
And no found that out?

Swinburne did not come to Capheaton only as a child; because of its pleasant associations, he used it as a retreat from disappointment. One such instance occurred in 1862, when his declaration of love to Jane Faulkner, adopted daughter of Sir John Simon, met only with derisive laughter. During this stay he wrote "In Grief and Mortification" and *The Triumph of Time*. One of Swinburne's guests here was Dante Gabriel Rossetti; the undated visit is known to have occurred after Swinburne was sent down from Oxford and before he went to London.

CARDINGTON, Bedfordshire (pop. 377) Just 3 miles southeast of Bedford is the easily recognized village of Cardington. The flat surrounding countryside is populated with giant airsheds, in one of which the famous *R101* was completed in 1930, only to crash in France, killing forty-eight of its fifty-four passengers on its maiden flight. The village contains a fine

old half-timbered barn (Fenlake Barn), an old manor house, and on Warden Road, until recently, an old manor house that once belonged to Sir John Gascoigne. Here the Elizabethan poet and dramatist George Gascoigne was born about 1525. Virtually nothing is known of Gascoigne's life until he went up to Trinity College, Cambridge.

CARISBROOKE, Isle of Wight (pop. 4,767) Situated a little southwest of Newport, the nominal capital of the Isle of Wight, Carisbrooke is now almost completely merged with that town. Two things are noticeable about the village: the impressive 12th-century Norman castle and the crowds of people looking at Carisbrooke Castle. Built on the site of an earlier Roman fort, it is one of the best-preserved and most carefully maintained castles in England, and it is the only major ruin of interest on the Isle of Wight. This was John Keats's view when he stayed here in April 1817; while the island "contained not many Ruins, ...I don't think however I shall ever see one to surpass Carisbrooke castle." Lodging with a Mrs. Cook in the New Village on Castle Road, he had a view of the keep from his rooms, and evidence suggests he had a first-floor bedroom and drawing room in the house now called Canterbury House. Keats writes to John Hamilton Reynolds:

I see Carisbrooke Castle from my window, and have found several delightful wood alleys, and copses, and quick freshes. As for Primroses—the island ought to be called Primrose Island....

He planned to walk over the entire island but abandoned the project after only one week and left for Margate, Kent. When he left, his landlady presented him with a picture of Shakespeare that Keats thought was "nearer to my idea of him than any I have seen." There seems to be no further record of what portrait this was.

CARLISLE, Cumberland (pop. 60,220) Only 9 miles inside the English border and 60 miles west of Newcastle upon Tyne, Carlisle is a border city that suffered much because of its strategic location on the Eden River in the Solway Plain. Daniel Defoe's description of Carlisle in *A Tour thro' the Whole Island of Great Britain* is especially apt; he first terms the Carlisle area "the Frontier Place and Key of *England*" and then goes on:

The City is strong....
King *Henry* VIII fortify'd this City against the Scots, and built an additional Castle to it on the East Side; ... there is indeed another Castle on the West, Part of the Town rounds the Sea, as the Wall rounds the whole, is very firm and strong. But *Carlisle* is strong by Situation, being almost surrounded with Rivers.

The great Hadrian's Wall passed on the north bank of the river, and the Roman settlement of Luguvallium grew up on the southern bank opposite the fortified camp of Petriana. The Romans left the area around 383; in the 9th century, the Danes overran it, only to lose it to the Scots shortly thereafter. It was not until 1092 that William Rufus restored it to England.

Geoffrey of Monmouth in his *Historia Regum Britanniae* places the founding of Carlisle in pre-Roman times:

SOUTHERN ENGLAND

SURREY

SUSSEX

BERKSHIRE

GLOUCESTERSHIRE

SOMERSET

DEVON

ENGLISH CHANNEL

Isle of Wight

The Solent

WILTSHIRE

HAMPSHIRE

DORSET

Eversley

Silchester

○ **Basingstoke**

Holybourne
Alton
Chawton

Selborne

Petersfield
Buriton

North   *Downs*

Bentworth
Steventon
Deane

Alresford

Wey

Andover ●
HAMPSHIRE

Weyhill

Stockbridge
Crawley

Winchester ○

Twyford
Upham

Otterbourne

Bishop's
Waltham
Botley
Wickham

Bedhampton

Portsmouth ●

South Sea

Spithead

Osborne

Newport ●
Carisbrook
Swainston

Shanklin
Bonchurch

Luccombe Chine

Cowes ○

Freshwater
Calbourne

Farringford

The Needles

Netley
Abbey

Titchfield

Itchen

Meon

Southampton

Beaulieu
Beaulieu

Minstead
Lyndhurst
Brockenhurst ●

New Forest

Lymington

Burton

Christchurch

Mudeford

Bournemouth

Avon

Ham

Swindon ○
Chiseldon

*BARBURY
HILL*

Marlborough

Marlborough

*Marlborough
Downs*

Swindon

South Marston

Brokenborough
Charlton

Malmesbury

Kington
St. Michael

Castle Combe
Chippenham
Colerne

Kennet

Bremhill
Calne
Beckhampton

Chittoe
Bromham

South
Wraxall

Trowbridge

Avon

Netheravon

Amesbury
Boscombe
Winterbourne Earls
Winterslow
Dauntsey
Dumford
OLD
SARUM
Wilton
Bemerton

Salisbury
Britford

Combe
Bissett

Alderbury

Romsey

Milston

Devizes
Charlton
St. Peter

All Cannings

Market Lavington

Vale of Pewsey

Salisbury   *Plain*

STONEHENGE

Heytesbury
Longleat

Edington

Chicksgrove
Dinton
Tisbury

Broad
Chalk

Pentridge
Cranborne

Horton

Wimborne
Minster

Charborough

Poole

Corfe
Castle

Swanage

Frome

Wool
West
Lulworth

Mcreton
Owermoigne
Poxwell

Weymouth

*Isle of
Portland*

Hindon
Fonthill
Gifford
Stourton
Mere

Shaftesbury

East Stour

Marnhull

*CRANBORNE
CHASE*

Sturminster Newton

Blandford
Forum

Stour

Bere Regis

Bockhampton
Came
Winterbourne
Sutton Poyntz

Sherborne

Lydlinch

Melbury
Osmund

Evershot

Minterne Magna
Cerne Abbas

Mappowder

Milton
Abbas

Athelhampton
Affpuddle

Godmanstone
Puddletown
Stinsford

Dorchester
Fordington

Winterbourne
Abbas

Maiden Newton

Broadwindsor
Beaminster

Bridport

Charmouth

Lyme Regis

Lewesdon Hill

Blackmoor Vale

DORSET

Longleat

Weyhill

122

Leil, the son of Greenshield, a great lover of peace and justice, succeeded him [Brutus Greenshield]. Leil took advantage of the prosperity of his reign to build a town in the northern part of Britain which he called Kaerleil [Carlisle] after himself.

This was the time when Solomon began to build the Temple of the Lord in Jerusalem and when the Queen of Sheba came to listen to his wisdom.

The town was strongly fortified in the early 12th century, and the red sandstone castle rose on the steep banks of the river, 60 feet above the riverbed. A great moat protects the city side of the castle with its barbican and still-threatening spiked portcullis. The dungeons are terrifying even today with their tongue-smoothed stones where thirsting prisoners licked up the dampness. At the top of the keep is MacIvor's Cell behind a door with four locks and a 3-inch slit for light and air; here Major MacDonald of Tiendrish, the original of Fergus MacIvor in Sir Walter Scott's *Waverley*, was imprisoned:

The place of Fergus's confinement was a gloomy and vaulted apartment in the central part of the Castle; a huge old tower, supposed to be of great antiquity, and surrounded by outworks, seemingly of Henry VIII.'s time, or somewhat later. The grating of the large old-fashioned bars and bolts, withdrawn for the purpose of admitting Edward, was answered by the clash of chains, as the unfortunate Chieftain, strongly and heavily fettered, shuffled along the stone floor of his prison to fling himself into his friend's arms.

Adjacent to the castle is Carlisle Cathedral, begun by the Augustinian canons in 1093. A mixture of gray stone and red sandstone, it is an impressive though imperfect building. The choir is a different matter; one of the finest in an English cathedral, the Decorated east window is superb and contains most of its original 14th-century glass and tracery work. The carved capitals of the choir pillars present a medieval calendar of occupations that can be associated with each month. The cathedral has a close association with Thomas Percy, author of the *Reliques of Ancient English Poetry*, who became dean of Carlisle in 1778, a post he held four years. Another association is with Sir Walter Scott, who married Margaret Charlotte Carpenter (Charpentier) here on December 24, 1797. The daughter of a French refugee, she stayed at 81 Castle Street before the marriage. Some years later Scott admitted that the marriage was not a love match but had been happy nevertheless; he noted:

Mrs. Scott's match and mine was of our own making and proceeded from the most sincere affection on both sides, which has rather increased than diminished during twelve years' marriage. But it was something short of love in all its fervour, which I suspect people only feel *once* in their lives.

John Keats was here on his 1818 walking tour in the company of Charles Armitage Brown; he liked neither the town nor the cathedral and thought "the whole art of yawning might have been learned" here. The two young men had walked 114 miles in five days, and Keats's trouble with a sore throat throughout the trip was an obvious sign of the tuberculosis that was soon to develop. They went from Carlisle to Scotland and Ireland. In the summer of 1853 Dante Gabriel Rossetti came here in the company of William Bell Scott on an unsuccessful painting expedition; the two parted company here, and Rossetti continued on a walking tour of Warwickshire.

Carlisle has often entered into song, and it is featured in the final song of Michael Drayton's *Poly-Olbion*, in which the town and its situation are described:

To *Carlill* being come, cleere *Bruscath* beareth in,
To greet her with the rest, when *Eden* as to win
Her grace in *Carlils* sight, the Court of all her state,
And *Cumberlands* chiefe towne, loe thus shee doth dilate.
What giveth more delight, (brave Citie) to thy Seat,
Then my sweet lovely selfe? . . .

Because this was the land of border disputes, many ballads are set in Carlisle. Perhaps the best known is the true story of "Kinmont Willie." Following a border truce, William Armstrong (Kinmont Willie) leaves the company of a Scottish deputy, is ridden down on the Scottish side of the river, and is captured and delivered to Carlisle Castle:

They led him thro the Liddel-rack,
    And also thro the Carlisle sands;
They brought him to Carlisle castell,
    To be at my Lord Scroope's commands.

Lord Scott of Buccleuch complains of the breach of the truce and, receiving no satisfaction, decides to effect the prisoner's relief as best he can:

We crept on knees, and held our breath,
    Till we placed the ladders against the wa;
And sae ready was Buccleuch himsell
    To mount the first before us a'.

He has taen the watchman by the throat,
    He flung him down upon the lead:
"Had there not been peace between our lands,
    Upon the other side thou hadst gaed."

Buccleuch and his men release Willie from his cell and carry him, still in irons, to a waiting mount before fleeing across the border. Another ballad to include Carlisle is that of William of Cloudsley; outlawed for stealing venison, he returns to town to kiss his wife, is caught, and then is rescued from the market square gallows at the last minute.

CARLTON, Cambridgeshire (pop. 254) Seven miles south of Newmarket near the Suffolk border, Carlton is a small village situated in open country; its 14th- and 15th-century church has ancient glass in the chancel and two bells that have peeled since the Reformation. The church contains the grave of Sir Thomas Elyot, author of *The Boke Named the Governour*, who died here on March 20, 1546. Elyot purchased this estate from Thomas Cromwell in 1540, but Cromwell was attainted before the arrangements were complete, and the estate consequently passed to the crown. It was granted to Sir Thomas, however, in May of that year.

CARTMEL, Lancashire (pop. 313) A cathedral city in miniature, set among the hills of Morecambe Bay and 6 miles east of Ulverston, Cartmel has a magnificent priory church with a square belfry thought to be unique in England. Inside the church is an abundance of 15th- to 17th-century woodwork. The chancel stalls, all 15th-century, are enclosed on three sides by a 17th-century black oak Flemish screen paneled with latticework and beautiful tracery. One of the prize possessions of the church is a first edition of part of Edmund Spenser's *Faerie Queene.*

William Wordsworth spent some time in the churchyard here in 1794 when he was working on *The Prelude* and found the grave of his "honor'd Teacher," William Taylor:

> A plain Stone, inscribed
> With name, date, office, pointed out the spot,
> To which a slip of verses was subjoin'd,
> (By his desire, as afterward I learn'd)
> A fragment from the Elegy of Gray.

The stone is still visible and answers Wordsworth's description perfectly.

CARTMEL FELL, Lancashire On one side of the 1,000-foot fell is Westmorland; on the other the land runs down to Windermere, which is also in Westmorland; Cartmel Fell, in Lancashire, has only a few farm homes and an ancient gem of a chapel. Built in 1504, the chapel was constructed askew as if the builder had followed the rough outlines of the terrain. A deep, tunnellike porch leads to the interior, which still has a great deal of rich woodwork and stained glass and a pre-Reformation Crucifixion that may be unique. The chapel here is the Browhead Chapel of Mrs. Humphry Ward's *Helbeck of Bannisdale.*

CASTLE COMBE, Wiltshire (pop. 363) Castle Combe, 5½ miles northwest of Chippenham, is one of the most frequently photographed villages in England. Set in a deep valley with wooded heights on all sides and By Brook twisting its way through the village, it was once a wealthy weaving center. The Weavers' House, where finished cloth was taken by the villagers, is still by the river; stone cottages cluster about the old market cross; and the bridge over By Brook is a picturesque three-arch stone structure. In 1966 the peacefulness of the village was shattered when Hollywood decided that this was the perfect location for Dr. Dolittle's village of Puddleby-on-the-Marsh. Hollywood put all television aerials underground, built a jetty on By Brook, and hired the local people as extras at 50 shillings a day, with food, drink, and clothes supplied as well.

CASTLETON, Derbyshire (pop. 646) In the heart of the Peak District at the western end of the Hope Valley, Castleton is an old village whose earliest history is contained in the caves where prehistoric people lived and the mines that the Romans worked. Perhaps the best-known cave in England, Peak Cavern (once known as the Devil's Hole) is entered through a 60-foot natural arch in the face of the cliff overlooking the village; even though the mouth of the cave is 114 feet wide, the inside is more awe-inspiring. Here the sound of unseen water permeates every chamber, and the halls of the cave penetrate more than a mile under the hill. Michael Drayton

CASTLE COMBE A picturesque stone-built village in a wooded valley, Castle Combe was selected as Puddleby-on-the-Marsh for the film version of High Lofting's *Dr. Dolittle.*

notes the cave in the twenty-sixth song of *Poly-Olbion:*

> O thou my first and best, of thy blacke Entrance nam'd
> The *Divels-Arse,* in me, O be thou not asham'd,
> Nor thinke thy selfe disgrac'd, or hurt thereby at all,
> Since from thy horror first men us'd thee so to call:
> For as amongst the *Moores,* the Jettiest blacke are deem'd
> The beautifulst of them; so are our kind esteem'd,
> The more ye gloomy are, more fearefull and obscure. . . .

Daniel Defoe visited the Peak District and Castleton when gathering material for *A Tour thro' the Whole Island of Great Britain;* on this cave he comments at length, although he is reluctant to name it:

> [W]e come to the so famed Wonder call'd, saving our good Manners, *The Devil's A——e in the Peak;* Now notwithstanding the grossness of the Name given it, and that there is nothing of similitude or coherence either Form and Figure or any other thing between the thing signified and the thing signifying; yet we must search narrowly for any thing in it to make it a *Wonder.* . . .
>
> On the steep Side of a Mountain there is a large opening very high, broad at bottom, and narrow, but rounding, on the top, almost the Form of the old Gothick Gate or Arches . . . the opening being upwards of thirty Foot perpendicular, and twice as much broad at the bottom at least.
>
> The Arch continues thus wide but a little way. . . . In the middle, (as it were a Street) is a running Stream of Water. . . .
>
> As you go on, the Roof descends gradually, and is so far from admitting Houses to stand in it, that you have not leave to stand upright your self, till stooping for a little way, and passing over another Rill of Water. . . .
>
> This is the whole Wonder. . . .

Before the way was cleared in modern times, visitors had to lie flat in a punt that a guide pushed along through the galleries. In those days George Gordon, Lord Byron visited the cavern in the company of Mary Chaworth:

> I had to cross in a boat a stream which flows under a rock so close upon the water as to admit the boat only to be pushed on by the ferryman, a sort of Charon, who wades at the stern, stooping all the time. The Companion of my transit was M.A.C., with whom I had long been in love and never told it, though she had discovered it without.

The village of Castleton is below the height, and the castle, which is on the high peak over the cavern, is a Norman construction; the land was given to William Peverell after the conquest, and the remaining castle walls are his work. The roofless keep dates from 1176, when it was rebuilt, it is of singularly mammoth construction with walls 8 feet thick and an enclosed area of almost 400 feet. The castle is virtually invulnerable, as Sir Walter Scott describes it in *Peveril of the Peak:*

> William Peveril obtained a liberal grant of property and lordships . . . and became the erector of that Gothic fortress, . . . hanging over the mouth of the Devil's Cavern. . . .
>
> [T]his feudal Baron . . . chose his nest upon the principles on which an eagle selects her eyry, and built it in such a fashion as if he had intended it . . . for the sole purpose of puzzling posterity. . . .

CATFIELD, Norfolk (pop. 485) A village of more than 2,400 acres and a small population, Catfield is 15 miles northwest of Great Yarmouth in the Broads. Its church has a 14th-century tower and a 15th-century font; near the site of the old rectory are a lovely thatched cottage and rectory. William Cowper, the poet, spent some of his school holidays here at the old rectory when his uncle, the Rev. Roger Donne, was vicar of Catfield; he was extremely fond of exploring the area. One of his most memorable holidays took place in July 1752, when with his cousins he drove all over the vicinity in a whiksum snivel, as the old-fashioned gig was called.

CATTHORPE, Leicestershire (pop. 130) At the southernmost tip of Leicestershire, Catthorpe overlooks the Avon River (of Stratford-on-Avon), here a tiny stream. This hamlet is set nicely on a hillside, and its most prized possession is a 13th-century church approached through a modern lych-gate. This parish became the living of the poet John Dyer, author of "Grongar Hill" and *The Fleece,* in 1746. His wife claimed descent (unproved) from William Shakespeare; it was of Dyer that William Wordsworth wrote in 1811:

> Though hasty Fame hath many a chaplet culled
> For worthless brows, while in the pensive shade
> Of cold neglect she leaves thy head ungraced,
> Yet pure and powerful minds, hearts meek and still,
> A grateful few, shall love thy modest Lay. . . .

CERNE ABBAS, Dorset (pop. 511) Seven miles north of Dorchester on the Cerne River, Cerne Abbas is a picture-book village surrounded by rolling downs. There is a particularly impressive specimen of prehistory in the enormous Cerne Giant, a puzzling figure of a man cut into Trendle Hill on the north side of the village. The origin of the ithyphallic figure is unknown, although one legend holds that it was a sheep-devouring giant killed by irritated local people; another, that it was a monument to an ancient fertility god (even in the 19th century women slept on the hillside to cure barrenness); a third, that it was cut into the hillside at the dissolution of the monasteries and depicts a particularly lusty abbot of the local monastery. It is generally believed now that the Cerne Giant dates from the 2d century A.D., during the reign of Commodus, a self-proclaimed reincarnation of Hercules, and thus that the giant is a representation of virility and fertility. The term "giant" is well chosen: the figure is 180 feet high, its shoulders are 45 feet wide, and it holds a club 120 feet long.

William of Malmesbury maintained that the first monastery in Cerne Abbas was founded by St. Augustine, but more likely it dates from the 10th century, when it received an endowment from Ethelmar, Earl of Cornwall. Aelfric, the greatest Anglo-Saxon prose writer, was a monk here before going to Eynsham Abbey in Oxfordshire as abbot in 994. His *Catholic Homilies* and parts of his *Lives of the Saints* were written here. Very little of the abbey buildings remains.

Cerne Abbas becomes Abbot's Cernel in Thomas Hardy's Wessex and is mentioned in *Tess of the D'Urbervilles, The Woodlanders,* "The First Countess of Wessex," and "The History of the Harcomes," and the Cerne Abbas giant on Trendle Hill makes an appearance in *Tess.* The beginning of "The Lost Pyx, a Medieval Legend" deals in detail with Cernel's Abbey. Inside his cell in the ancient abbey the priest first hears the cry:

> Go father, in haste to the cot on the waste.
> And shrive a man waiting to die.

Ignoring the call because of a raging storm, he sees the frowning heaven-set visage and leaves his cell.

In the 20th century Hugh Walpole spent time here in the company of the Anglican monks. Walpole passed his time reading, writing, walking, and talking with the brothers, and the friendship with Father Algy Robertson remained through their lifetimes. Walpole's *Journal* notes:

> I am sure that this is not the *only* life for men to lead, and that it is not *my* life because the starving of sex and creative impulse would turn me silly at my age. I'm equally sure it is the *best* life, and it has got under my skin so that I shall never lose it again.

CHADWELL ST. MARY, Essex Much of the southern portion of Essex is dreary; timeworn, dismal docks stretch for miles along the Thames; industrial buildings either stand on top of one another or rise eerily from undeveloped marshland. But at one time the Southend and Tilbury areas, 2½ miles south of Chadwell St. Mary, were the resorts of fashionable Londoners. West Tilbury, 1 mile east of Chadwell, was the site of a tile works for which Daniel Defoe was secretary from 1694 until 1703, when he was imprisoned in Newgate; he appears to have had a part interest in the works, and the prosperity of the business enabled Defoe to pay off many of the debts still outstanding from his 1692 bankruptcy. During his involvement with the tile factory, Defoe lived here from time to time, across from the church in a thatched daub-and-wattle cottage, the Sleepers, so named because medieval pilgrims slept here before crossing the Thames. (The building is now protected.) Local tradition holds that Defoe was also here in 1718, when he was avoiding arrest on a charge of libel, and that he wrote part of *Robinson Crusoe* here.

CHAGFORD, Devon (pop. 1,715) Made into a stannary (tin-working) town in 1328, Chagford is a lovely little south Devon market town near the Teign River 3 miles northwest of Moretonhampstead. The 13th-century monastery here became a pub and hotel, the Three Crowns Inn, soon after the dissolution in the 16th century; only the outside of the buildings has not been destroyed by renovation. Across the road is the parish church, dedicated to St. Catherine, the patron saint of the tin miners. During the spring and summer of 1944, Chagford was the home of Evelyn Waugh while he was working on *Brideshead Revisited.*

CHALFONT ST. GILES, Buckinghamshire (pop. 2,-074) One of the five Chalfonts in Buckinghamshire, Chalfont St. Giles is 3 miles southeast of Amersham beside the Misbourne River. The village is a lovely old one with well-aged red-brick houses lining a green with a squat 13th-century parish church looming in the background. In the courtyard is the grave of Bertram Mills of circus fame.

CHALFONT ST. GILES This "pretty box" of a cottage where John Milton lived in 1665-1666 when the plague was raging in London is now a Milton museum and contains a rare edition of *Paradise Lost,* which was completed here.

A small hill rises behind the church, and a short distance up the hill is the "pretty box" of a cottage where John Milton lived for about eight months in 1665–1666 while the plague was raging in London. A Quaker friend, Thomas Ellwood, found the cottage for Milton and made all the necessary arrangements. The poet, already blind, had requested Ellwood's help, and the latter's autobiography supplies some interesting information:

> I took a pretty box for him, in Giles Chalfont, a mile from me.... But now being released [from prison] and returned home, I soon made a visit to him, to welcome him into the country. After some common discourses had passed between us, he called for a manuscript of his; which being brought he delivered to me, bidding me take it home with me, and read it at my leisure; and when I had done so, return it to him with my judgement thereupon. When I came home, and had set myself to read it, I found it was that excellent poem which he entitled "Paradise Lost."

Ellwood later comments: "I pleasantly said to him, 'Thou hast said much here of 'Paradise Lost', but what hast thou to say of 'Paradise Found'?" Ellwood cannot really be given credit for the conception of *Paradise Regained,* although he does try to take it. The house, now known as Milton's Cottage and serving as a museum of Milton memorabilia, is open to the public; it is dark with low ceilings, uneven floors, and narrow, twisting staircases. This is the only one of Milton's residences still extant.

CHALK, Kent (pop. 517) Now often considered a part of Gravesend, the boundary port for London, 1½ miles to the northwest, Chalk is on the main road to Dover and has much of the flavor of the Gravesend and Dover ports. After Charles Dickens married Catherine Hogarth, daughter of a colleague on the *Morning Chronicle,* on April 2, 1836, the couple spent their honeymoon in a cottage here; the cottage was on the lane that branched off to Shorne and Cobham. The cottage marked the "one and only" genuine Dickens Honeymoon Cottage is not the cottage where the couple stayed; indeed, that building was on the same lane but has long since disappeared.

Dickens was at work on *Pickwick Papers* then, and no doubt the portion of that work describing Cobham and its park was written here.

Dickens and his wife returned to the cottage for a short time just after the birth of their first son, and the novelist later often walked here from Gadshill. One place that he frequently stopped at was the Church of St. Mary, where the carved figure of a priest grasping a kind of urn by the neck intrigued him. Dickens always nodded at the figure as he passed. For many years the forge here was claimed to be the original of Joe Gargery's in *Great Expectations*, but the one at Cooling has a better claim.

CHAPEL-LE-DALE, Yorkshire (pop. 229) A tiny, isolated village, Chapel-le-Dale is generally known as the best vantage point from which to view one of the county's major landmarks, Ingleborough Hill, but it is also known for its association with Robert Southey. Just above the little chapel with its adjoining manse is the old farmhouse that the poet makes the ancestral home of Dr. Daniel Dove in the miscellany *The Doctor*. Southey's description of the chapel is perfect (although he mentions a nonexistent porch):

> The little chapel called Chapel-le-Dale stands about a bowshot from the family house. . . . A hermit who might wish his grave to be as quiet as his cell could imagine no fitter resting-place. On three sides there was an irregular low stone wall, rather to mark the limits of the sacred ground than to enclose it; on the fourth it was bounded by the brook, whose waters proceed by a subterranean channel from Weathercote Cave. Two or three alders and rowan trees hung over the brook, and shed their leaves and seeds into the stream.

CHARBOROUGH, Dorset (pop. 54) In the rich triangle of farm and dairy land between the North and South Downs, Charborough is 6 miles west of Wimborne Minster in an area of Dorset Thomas Hardy knew well and used under the name Welland in *Two on a Tower*. The observatory in the novel is based on the tower standing in Charborough Park:

> The central feature of the middle distance . . . was a circular isolated hill. . . . The trees were all of one size and age, so that their tips assumed the precise curve of the hill they grew upon. This pine-clad protuberance was yet further marked out from the general landscape by having on its summit a tower in the form of a classical column, which, though partly immersed in the plantation, rose above the tree-tops to a considerable height.

Even though the column was on the "hereditary estate of her husband," Lady Constantine had never visited it. Hardy places folly-cum-observatory, erected in 1790, damaged by lightning in 1838, and rebuilt and enlarged in 1839, on the rise of nearby Weatherbury Castle. The author speculates on the origin of the earthwork at Weatherbury:

> The fir-shrouded hill-top was (according to some antiquaries) an old Roman camp,—if it were not (as others insisted) an old British castle, or (as the rest swore) an old Saxon field of Witenagemote,—with remains of an outer and an inner vallum, a winding path leading up between their overlapping ends by an easy ascent. The spikelets from the trees formed a soft carpet over the route, and occasionally a brake of brambles barred the interspaces of the trunks.

Welland House, the residence of Viviette, Lady Constantine, is based on Charborough House; it is set in a beautifully timbered park with an interesting grotto and, at one time, a herd of Asiatic cattle.

> Leaving his horse at the parsonage he performed the remainder of the journey on foot, crossing the park towards Welland House by a stile and path till he struck into the drive near the north door of the mansion.
> This drive, it may be remarked, was also the common highway to the lower village, and hence Lady Constantine's residence and park . . . possessed none of the exclusiveness found in some aristocratic settlements. . . .
> The long, low front of the Great House, as it was called by the parish, stretching from end to end of the terrace, was in darkness. . . .

The church near the house also forms part of the novel, as does the vicarage occupied by the Reverend Mr. Torkingham.

CHARLBURY, Oxfordshire (pop. 1,231) Located on a hillside overlooking the Evenlode Valley, Charlbury is about 13 miles northwest of Oxford, and one-quarter of its area is the deer park associated with Cornbury House. The house, just across the river from the church, was the home of Robert Dudley, Earl of Leicester, the favorite of Queen Elizabeth I. Rebuilt in the 17th century, it retains much of its earlier flavor and before the construction of Blenheim Place was the largest house in Oxfordshire. It was also the home of Edward Hyde, 1st Earl of Clarendon, who entertained Charles II here. In October 1664 John Evelyn stayed here when on a visit to Oxford and Woodstock. With his entourage he arrived on the evening of October 18 at the house built, as his diary records,

> in the middle of a Sweete dry Park walled with a Dry-wall: The house of excellent free stone. . . . [T]is of ample receite, has goodly Cellars, the paving of the hall admirable, for the close laying of the Pavement. . . . The Lodge is a prety solitude, and the Ponds very convenient; The Parke well stored.

CHARLCOMBE, Somerset (pop. 178) Once a distinct entity 1½ miles north of Bath, Charlcombe is now essentially part of that rapidly expanding city. Henry Fielding, who first came to Bath in 1734, was married that year to Charlotte Cradock at the Church of St. Mary here. When Jane Austen was in Bath from 1801 on, she frequently walked up Beacon Hill and across the fields to Charlcombe, "which," she writes, "is sweetly situated in a little green valley, as a village with such a name ought to be."

CHARLECOTE, Warwickshire (pop. 199) The countryside surrounding Stratford-on-Avon has been virtually untouched by the industrialization of the Midlands; willows line the banks of the Avon, and swans grace the river as it winds through a peaceful valley of pastureland and farms. On the river, 4½ miles east of Stratford, is the village of Charlecote, a place of pleasant cottages, a rebuilt church, and the magnificent Charlecote Park, which has belonged to the Lucy family, William Camden's "renowned ancient family," since the 12th century, when two families who came to England with William the Conqueror intermarried. The Hall, set in open parkland, was begun in 1558 and built in the shape of an E; the house was much altered in the 19th century, but its gatehouse, flanked with polygonal turrets, is purely Elizabethan. The park surrounding the Hall is filled with free-roaming fallow deer.

It is with the deer that the literary association here exists, for this is the site of William Shakespeare's alleged poaching of Sir Thomas Lucy's deer; Nicholas Rowe relates that Shakespeare and some "ill company . . . more than once" robbed

> a park that belonged to Sir Thomas Lucy of Charlecote, near Stratford;—for this he was prosecuted by that gentleman, as he thought, somewhat too severely, and, in order to revenge that ill-usage, he made a ballad upon him . . . so very bitter that it redoubled the prosecution . . . [and] he was obliged to . . . shelter himself in London.

The fact that the story was known and accepted in the 17th century lends some weight to its accuracy, but the truth is that Sir Thomas Lucy did not create the deer park until sometime after the 1585 date of the alleged poaching. It is possible, however, that he had some sort of warren here at the time and was introducing the herd of fallow deer; it is also possible that the poaching occurred on another of Sir Thomas's estates in the neighborhood. Some slight verification of this explanation comes from a visit by Sir Walter Scott in the spring of 1828. After a meal with the owner, Scott was told that the park to which the story refers belonged to another mansion some distance away from where Sir Thomas Lucy lived. Sir Thomas, it has been argued, was the source of Justice Shallow in *Henry IV: Part II* and *The Merry Wives of Windsor;* the latter play, particularly, clearly suggests the accuracy of the identification:

> *Slen.* . . . they may give the dozen white luces in their coat.
> *Shal.* It is an old coat.
> *Eva.* The dozen white louses do become an old coat well; it agrees well, *passant:* it is a familiar beast to man, and signifies—love.
> *Shal.* The luce is the fresh fish; the salt fish is an old coat.

The "dozen white luces" obviously was meant to suggest the three pikes, or luces, in Sir Thomas's coat-of-arms.

A second visitor, Nathaniel Hawthorne, who spent almost seven years in England as United States consul in Liverpool, left an extensive record of his trip.

CHARLES, Devon (pop. 206) This tiny north Devon village on the Bray River is remote and somewhat inaccessible, for it sits on an unmarked, twisting road on the western edge of the Exmoor Forest; but it is a village of character. R. D. Blackmore lived from time to time in the rectory here with his grandfather, John Blackmore, and his uncle Richard. Blackmore's grandfather was the patron of this living, and his uncle was curate and then vicar here. An extremely vivid picture of the rectory emerges in the preface to *Tales from the Telling House:*

> In the hazy folds of lower hills, some four or five miles behind them, may be seen the ancient parsonage, where the lawn is a russet sponge of moss, and a stream trickles under the dining-room floor, and the pious rook, poised on the pulpit of his nest, reads a hoarse sermon to the chimney pots below.

The rookery has disappeared, but opposite the rectory is the nook where Blackmore wrote the first draft of *The Maid of Sker.*

CHARLTON, Wiltshire (pop. 423) On the edge of Charlton Park, 2 miles northeast of Malmesbury, Charlton is a lovely village with many gabled houses, a 13th-century church with fine nave arches and Norman capitals, and an Elizabethan manor (much restored and modernized) in a park of more than 600 acres. This was the country home of the 1st Earl of Berkshire, John Dryden's father-in-law, and it was to this house that the poet came when the plague broke out in London in the summer of 1665; Dryden's eldest son was born here on September 6 of that year. Working conditions, while not perfect because of family problems, were still adequate to enable him to compose *Annus Mirabilis, An Essay of Dramatic Poesy,* and a great deal of *Secret Love, or The Maiden Queen* in his stay of about a year and a half. Dryden returned to London at the end of 1666.

CHARLTON KINGS, Gloucestershire (pop. 5,017) An eastern suburb of Cheltenham looking up to the Cotswolds, Charlton Kings becomes Longfield in Dinah Mulock Craik's *John Halifax, Gentleman;* and across from the Duke of York Inn is Detmore House, where some of the novel was written. From 1930 to 1935, when he was English master at Cheltenham College, C. Day-Lewis lived at Box Cottage; here he wrote *The Magnetic Mountain* and *A Question of Proof.*

CHARLTON ST. PETER, Wiltshire On the south edge of the Vale of Pewsey just north of the Salisbury Plain, Charlton St. Peter, a tiny village with a restored 15th-century church, was the birthplace of Stephen Duck, the "thresher poet," in 1705. The son of extremely poor parents, he was employed as an agricultural laborer at the age of fourteen. With a friend he began to read constantly and to write; with the encouragement and endorsement of various local clergy, he received a royal pension from Queen Caroline, a place at court, and the living in Byfleet, Surrey. Charlton St. Peter holds an annual Duck Festival at the local inn, the Charlton Cat, on June 1. The event is funded by revenues from a land grant given by the 1st Viscount Palmerston.

CHARMOUTH, Dorset (pop. 668) Like all coastal towns in Dorset, Charmouth is in a gap in the coastal hills; situated on the Char River 2 miles northeast of Lyme Regis, the village is a small resort blessed with sand and shingle beaches and cliffs of considerable geological interest. This is where Mary Anning, an amateur geologist and the twelve-year-old daughter of a carpenter, found the skeleton of a 21-foot ichthyosaurus in 1811. She also uncovered an almost-perfect plesiosaurus in 1824 and a pterodactyl in 1828. The area has changed little since Jane Austen wrote in *Persuasion* of

> its high grounds, and extensive sweeps of country, and still more, its sweet, retired bay, backed by dark cliffs, where fragments of low rock among the sands make it the happiest spot for watching the flow of the tide, for sitting in unwearied contemplation, the woody varieties of the cheerful village of Up Lyme . . . a scene so wonderful and

so lovely . . . as may more than equal any of the resembling scenes of the far-famed Isle of Wight: these places must be visited, and visited again. . . .

CHATHAM, Kent (pop. 44,970) Chatham, now merged with Rochester, was a naval base developed by Elizabeth I when the village was unknown. With its strategic position on the Medway, it now has more than 500 acres of royal dockyards and a refitting base for nuclear submarines.

Chatham was one of the boyhood homes of Charles Dickens and is associated with some of his most pleasant memories. In June 1817 the Dickens family moved into 2 (now 11) Ordnance Terrace, on the "boundary" between Chatham and Rochester, where they remained until Lady Day, 1821. Dickens later commented on this boundary confusion in "The Seven Poor Travellers"; "I call it this town, because if anyone present knows to a nicety where Rochester ends and Chatham begins, it is more than I do." Dickens's father was with the Navy Pay Office, and the boy had ample time to explore and store up references for his later writing. He recalls the dockyard and its activities in "One Man in a Dockyard":

It resounded with the noise of hammers beating upon iron. . . . Great chimneys smoking with a quiet—almost a lazy—air, like giants smoking tobacco; and the giant shears moored off it, looking meekly and inoffensively out of proportion, like the giraffe of the machinery creation.

The Ordnance Terrace house was in a row of resolutely plain three-story buildings, and here Dickens's mother began teaching him the rudiments of English and Latin before sending him off to a preparatory day school in Rome Lane (now Railway Street); the school was pulled down in Dickens's lifetime to make way for a new street. By early 1821 John Dickens had pressing financial problems (partly brought on by increasing family demands) and took a less expensive house at 18 St. Mary's Place, sometimes called the Brook. A semidetached house with a plain whitewashed plaster facade, it had a small garden both in front and in back and stood next to Providence Chapel, then a Baptist meeting hall. The now-deteriorated area was relatively rural and uncrowded then, and on the corner of Rhode and Best Streets was the school kept by William Giles, a school that Dickens attended when it was located in Clover Lane. The family attended the 12th-century St. Mary's Church and from an upstairs window in the house the old graveyard is recalled in "A Child's Dream of a Star"; he and his sister, "his constant companion,"

used to say to one another sometimes, Supposing all the children upon earth were to die, would the flowers and the water and the sky be sorry? They believed they would be sorry. For, said they, the buds are the children of the flowers, and the little playful streams that gambol down the hillsides are the children of the water, and the smallest bright specks playing at hide-and-seek in the sky all night must surely be the children of the stars; and they would all be grieved to see their playmates, the children of men, no more.

There was one clear shining star that used to come out in the sky before the rest, near the church spire, above the graves. It was larger and more beautiful, they thought, than all the others, and every night they watched for it, standing hand in hand at a window.

In 1822 John Dickens was recalled to Somerset House in London, and one of the happiest periods of the young Charles's life ended.

Many scenes of Dickens's best-known novels, short stories, and essays are set here or are based on places or people here. *Great Expectations* draws on Dickens's earlier experience of the convicts and the Hulks here. *The Uncommercial Traveller* turns Chatham into Dullborough, where "most of us come from . . . who come from a country town," and describes the town as having "a gravity upon its red brick offices and houses, a staid pretence of having nothing to do, an avoidance of display, which I never saw out of England." David Copperfield, in the novel of that name, fleeing from Murdstone and Grinby's and hoping for a welcome from Betsy Trotwood in Dover, makes his way there via Rochester and Chatham; at night the town seemed "a mere dream of chalk, and drawbridges, and mastless ships in a muddy river, roofed like Noah's arks." David's Sunday-night accommodations here were in the open, "near a cannon . . . happy in the society of the sentry's footsteps. . . ." Dickens's own room in the St. Mary's Place house becomes the room where the old novels stand. In "The Mudfog Papers," he names Chatham "Mudfog."

Pickwick Papers makes the most use of Chatham when Mr. Pickwick's impressions of Chatham, Rochester, Stroud, and Brompton are elaborated: he observes that the towns' principal productions

appear to be soldiers, sailors, Jews, chalk, shrimps, officers, and dockyard men. The commodities chiefly exposed for sale in the public streets are marine stores, hard-baked apples, flat fish, and oysters. The streets present a lively and animated appearance, occasioned chiefly by the conviviality of the military. It is truly delightful to a philanthropic mind, to see these gallant men staggering along under the influence of an overflow, both of animal and ardent spirits. . . .

The famous Chatham Lines, the fortifications of the old town, are the scene of the Pickwick Club's difficulties; and the duel between the offended Dr. Slammer and the innocent and craven Mr. Winkle supposedly occurs in the exercise ground adjacent to Fort Pitt. *The Mystery of Edwin Drood* uses several aspects of the town and disguises them somewhat. The Mitre Inn, for example, where young Dickens often went with his father and where he would sing duets with his sister Fanny, becomes the Crozier and is transplanted to Cloisterham (Rochester). The same inn appears in "The Holly Tree":

There was an inn in the cathedral town where I went to school, which had pleasanter recollections about it than any of these. . . . It was the inn where friends used to put up, and where we used to go and see parents, and to have salmon and fowls, and be tipped. It had an ecclesiastical sign—the Mitre—and a bar that seemed to be the next best thing to a bishopric, it was so snug.

Chatham also furnished many of the names Dickens used in his works; listed in the parish registers for St. Mary's Church are Sowerby (Sowerberry), Tapley, Wren, Jasper, and Weller, and there are Tapley family vaults in the church and gravestones of Wellers in the churchyard.

Chatham is where William Cobbett came in 1784 to enlist in the Marines. Instead, he ended up as a foot soldier and was sent off to Nova Scotia after a year.

CHATSWORTH, Derbyshire (pop. 50) On the Derwent River 9 miles west of Chesterfield, Chatsworth is in the lush ridge land of mid-Derbyshire, which is cut by the beautifully wooded valleys of the Wye, Derwent, and Dove Rivers. In such a setting Chatsworth, seat of the Dukes of Devonshire, was built in the late 17th century. Palladian in style, the house was begun in 1687 for the 4th Earl of Devonshire. Every room here is magnificent, and the decorative touches make Chatsworth one of the truly great English homes; the court artists Louis Laguerre and Antonio Verrio painted walls and ceilings, and Jean Tijou did the ironwork. The outstanding fine arts collection contains works by Reynolds, Van Dyck, Rembrandt, and Canova. The gardens, set in a deer park 10 miles in circumference, virtually defy description. The Emperor Fountain throws up a spout of water 290 feet; a cascade, complete with temple, falls 60 feet over 200 yards of steps; and lovely avenues of trees, including rare conifers, extend throughout the grounds.

Chatsworth is generally conceded to be Pemberley in Jane Austen's *Pride and Prejudice;* this is the place where Elizabeth Bennet is brought by her aunt and uncle, Mr. and Mrs. Gardiner, on their tour of Derbyshire. The group enter Chatsworth from the Beeley side, as Miss Austen's description implies; they come first "to the little town of Lambton [Bakewell, 2½ miles south], the scene of Mrs. Gardiner's former residence," and then to Pemberley:

> The park was very large, and contained great variety of ground. They entered it in one of its lowest points, and drove for some time through a beautiful wood, stretching over a wide extent. . . .
> They gradually ascended for half a mile, and then found themselves at the top of a considerable eminence, where the wood ceased, and the eye was instantly caught by Pemberley House, situated on the opposite side of a valley, into which the road with some abruptness wound. It was a large, handsome, stone building, standing well on rising ground, and backed by a ridge of high woody hills;—and in front, a stream of some natural importance was swelled into greater, but without any artificial appearance. Its banks were neither formal, nor falsely adorned. Elizabeth was delighted. She had never seen a place for which nature had done more, or where natural beauty had been so little counteracted by an awkward taste.

The bend in the road is near Edensor. The grounds are precisely detailed:

> Mr. Gardiner expressed a wish of going round the whole Park, but feared it might be beyond a walk. With a triumphant smile, they were told, that it was ten miles round. It settled the matter; and they pursued the accustomed circuit; which brought them again, after some time, in a descent among hanging woods, to the edge of the water, in one of its narrower parts. They crossed it by a simple bridge, in character with the general air of the scene; it was a spot less adorned than any they had yet visited; and the valley, here contracted into a glen, allowed room only for the stream, and a narrow walk amidst the rough coppice-wood which bordered it. Elizabeth longed to explore its windings; but . . . Mrs. Gardiner, who was not a great walker, could go no farther, and thought only of returning to the carriage as quickly as possible. Her niece was, therefore, obliged to submit, and they took their way towards the house on the opposite side of the river, in the nearest direction. . . .

There are other literary associations with Chatsworth. Thomas Hobbes was tutor and secretary to the

2d and 3d Earls of Devonshire from about 1610 on and spent half his time at an earlier Chatsworth House and half at Hardwick Hall. William Beckford, author of *Vathek,* visited Chatsworth on his English tour of 1779. Finally, William Wordsworth visited Chatsworth on November 6, 1830, on a return journey to Westmorland from Cambridge; he turned aside here to view the famous house. The result of the visit was one of the *Miscellaneous Sonnets,* titled merely "1830":

> CHATSWORTH! thy stately mansion, and the pride
> Of thy domain, strange contrast do present
> To house and home in many a craggy rent
> Of the wild Peak. . . .

CHAWTON, Hampshire (pop. 762) Set near the Wey River, the entire Chawton area is honeycombed with spring-fed streams, all of which flow into the river, and Chawton itself is a delightfully picturesque village with old thatched cottages and a large number of lime trees. The manor house, visible from the Fareham road, dates from the 16th and 17th centuries, while the small house known as Chawton Cottage, originally a posting inn and alehouse, dates from the reign (1689–1702) of William III. The cottage was the home of Jane Austen from July 1809 to May 1817 and is now a Jane Austen Museum. After the death of the Rev. George Austen in Bath in 1805, Mrs. Austen, Jane, Cassandra, and Martha Lloyd, later the wife of Capt. Francis Austen, eventually came here to live. Chawton Manor House was the home of Jane's brother Edward (Austen) Knight, who had adopted the surname Knight in 1812 in accordance with a "names and arms" clause in the will of his cousin Thomas Knight.

The external features of Chawton Cottage are much as they were in the early 19th century, but much of the furniture, all from the correct period, did not belong to the Austens. Indeed, it is fortunate that the interior corresponds at all with the original, for the house was once divided into three tenements. Jane Austen's first three books, *Sense and Sensibility, Pride and Prejudice,* and *Northanger Abbey,* written at the rectory in Steventon, Hampshire, were not published until she settled here; *Mansfield Park,*

CHAWTON   Chawton Cottage, now Jane Austen's House, became the home of that novelist, her mother, her sister, and Martha Lloyd (later Capt. Francis Austen's second wife) in 1805. Writing to her brother Francis less than three weeks after moving in, Jane says:
> Our Chawton Home, how much we find
>   Already in it to our mind:
> And how convinced, that when complete,
>   It will have all other houses beat
> That ever have been made or mended
>   With rooms concise or rooms distended.

Emma, and *Persuasion* were all written here. It was at the desk in the drawing room (whose wood door gave advance warning of intrusion) that she wrote on scraps of paper, which could be easily hidden so that "her occupation should not be suspected by servants, or visitors, or persons beyond her own family party."

By the time *Persuasion* was finished in 1816, Jane Austen was extremely ill. Failing strength made her curtail her activities, and she eventually had to cease gardening, a hobby she enjoyed immensely. She had to rest more and more frequently but would not use the only sofa in the house, as it was usually occupied by Mrs. Austen. Instead, she fashioned a sofa out of chairs and cushions. (A sofa was sufficient luxury to evoke one of William Cowper's best poems.) Seeking a cure in May 1817, she went to Winchester, where she died in July and was buried in the cathedral.

CHEDDAR, Somerset (pop. 2,007)   Much of Cheddar's modern claim to fame goes back to the 18th century, when the little market town, 1¾ miles southeast of Axbridge, produced its own famous cheese; now the name is a generic term, although much cheese is still produced locally. Early, Daniel Defoe writes, "The whole Herd of Cows belonging to the Town, do feed" on the village common; "the whole Village are Cowkeepers," and, he maintains, "it is the best Cheese than *England* affords, if not, that the whole world affords." The area around Cheddar is spectacular; Cheddar Gorge is wild and picturesque with dominant crags, while Cheddar Water forms an impressive lake in the chasm. Hannah More came here to the George Hotel (gone) in the summer of 1789 with William Wilberforce and her sister Martha; appalled by the deterioration in the ecclesiastical ranks (one parish incumbent was drunk as a rule, rowdy, and often unable to preach), the sisters decided to set up Sunday schools which they supplied with their own teaching tracts. They met considerable opposition but took a small house here for 6½ guineas a year and opened a school on Lower North Street (now the Hannah More Cottage, an old people's club).

Samuel Taylor Coleridge and Robert Southey were visitors to the area in 1794, when they stayed at the inn; here they were locked in the attic by the landlord until they could prove they were not highwaymen.

CHELTENHAM, Gloucestershire (pop. 52,809)   Lying at the spot where the Chelt River runs through the western edge of the Severn Plain, Cheltenham, which is shielded by a steep Cotswolds limestone escarpment on the north and east, has a much milder climate than that of the uplands area. The Domesday Book, describing in 1086 what remained essentially true until the 18th century, notes that the settlement had about 200 people and five productive mills on the river, which then ran through the center of the town. While the town was an agricultural center, few merchants and clothiers were located here; as a result, the medieval town was the exception in not having the narrow, twisting streets of the typical Cotswold town.

John Leland describes Cheltenham in his *Itinerary* as a "market town in the vale" and as "a longe towne havynge a market. . . . " And such it might have remained if three springs of mineral water had not been discovered in 1716; the actual discovery of the springs is credited to pigeons, who were seen picking at the formed grains of salt, but it is more likely that the efficacy of the springs had been known locally for years. Nevertheless, the pigeon now has a place of honor in the Cheltenham coat of arms. Cheltenham became a fashionable watering spot after George III's visit in 1788, and the magnificent Royal Crescent was built.

The old Church of St. Mary, in the heart of the town, has a 14th-century tower on a Norman base and a 14th-century rose window. While the arts came with the theatrical and musical productions of Regency times, there have also been more recent developments including the Opera House (now the renovated Everyman Theatre), opened by Lily Langtry in the 1890s. There is also a vigorous educational establishment here dating to Victorian times; a Church of England Training College for male teachers was founded in 1849, a Training College for Women, in 1869; Cheltenham College, one of the earliest Victorian public schools, in 1844; and Cheltenham Ladies' College, in 1853.

Literary associations with Cheltenham really do not begin until the 18th century; the exception is Sir Francis Bacon. Both the rectory and the manor of Cheltenham were confiscated by the crown at the Reformation, and the lands were granted to a series of lessees, one of whom, Sir Francis, obtained the lease in 1598 at an annual rent of £75. He was to keep the chancel of the church in repair and to provide two chaplains, two deacons, the bread and wine for communion services, bells, ropes, and straw. The poet William Shenstone came here in the summer of 1743 and fell in love with the mysterious Miss C, but nothing came of the liaison. The most famous visit of the 18th century was the 1788 royal visit with Fanny Burney in the party as second keeper of the robes to Queen Charlotte; the royal party stayed at the new home of Viscount Fauconberg on Bayhill, where the present Fauconberg House stands. Miss Burney's *Diary and Letters* contains a vivid description of the five weeks' stay, including their attendance at services at the parish church with the Bishop of Gloucester officiating and the choir too overwhelmed to perform. Dr. Samuel Johnson also came to Cheltenham, as Boswell reports.

Cheltenham reached its zenith in the early 19th century. Lord Byron's first visit occurred in 1801, when he was impressed with the view of the Malvern Hills from the top of Bayshill; he probably returned in 1811 and again in 1812, staying at Georgiana Cottage near the corner of what is now Bath Street. In 1812 he was despondent, for Anne Isabella Milbanke had refused his proposal of marriage in the Assembly Rooms, local tradition maintains. But Byron's opinion of the rooms and the entertainment makes that doubtful: "As for your rooms and your assemblies they are not dreamed of in our philosophy." Cheltenham, unlike Bath, was essentially a summer resort, as Jane Austen notes in *Northanger Abbey* when she comments that Mr. King, appointed master of ceremonies here in 1806, retains the identical office in Bath during the winter season. Miss Austen, a visitor here in May 1816 for a period of three weeks, lodged in the High Street and writes of the city and the pumps to her sister Cassandra: "How much is Cheltenham to be preferred in May," and remarks that, according to the newspapers, "the Duchess of Orleans drinks at my Pump." But the pump shared with the duchess is not identifiable. Elizabeth Barrett Browning visited Cheltenham first in January 1819, when she stayed with her aunt Arabella Graham-Clarke on Cambray Street; "Lines Extempore on Taking My Last Farewell of the Statue of Nigeia at Cheltenham" dates from this visit. She returned in 1824.

The Rev. Robert Stephen Hawker was sent to Cheltenham Grammar School in 1821 after an unsuccessful apprenticeship with a solicitor in Plymouth; and his first book of verse, *Tendrils, by Reuben*, was published when he was at the grammar school. Also in 1821 William Cobbett made the first of several trips to Cheltenham, and his *Rural Rides* contains a vitriolic attack on the city. He writes, under the date of November 17:

> *Cheltenham* is a nasty, ill-looking place, half clown and half cockney. The town is one street, there are rows of white tenements, with green balconies, like those inhabited by the tax-eaters round London. Indeed, this place appears to be the residence of an assemblage of tax-eaters. These vermin shift about between London, Cheltenham, Bath, Bognor, Brighton, Tunbridge, Ramsgate, Margate, Worthing, and other spots in England, while some of them get over to France and Italy. . . .
> [He soon left] this resort of the lame and the lazy, the gormandising and guzzling, the bilious and the nervous. . . .

Not satisfied, he returned four years later and found the area even more distasteful; it was 10 P.M., and the town was deserted:

> I did not see more than four or five carriages and, perhaps, twenty people on horseback; and these seemed, by their hook-noses and round eyes, and by the long and sooty necks of the women, to be, for the greater part, *Jews and Jewesses*. The place really appears to be sinking very fast; and I have been told, and believe the fact, that houses, in Cheltenham, will now sell for only just about one-third as much as the same would have sold for only in last October. . . . What a figure this place will cut in another year or two! I should not wonder to see it nearly wholly deserted. It is situated in a nasty, flat, stupid spot, without anything pleasant near it.

So incensed were the townspeople by his scathing comments that when he came here to speak in 1830, he had to be rescued from the mob, and his effigy was burned in the market square.

Edward Bulwer-Lytton (Lord Lytton) and his mother were in Cheltenham numerous times before the publication of *Pelham* in 1828, and he appears to have found the area impressive:

> I was greatly struck with the entrance to the town; it is to these watering places that a foreigner should be taken, in order to give him an adequate idea of the magnificent opulence and universal luxury of England. Our country has in every province what France has only in Paris—a capital consecrated to gaiety, idleness and enjoyment.

This, however, is not quite the view found in Robert Smith Surtees's *Jorrocks' Jaunts and Jollities*. Jorrocks arrives specifically to try the waters even though he has not "astonished his stomach" with such for fifteen years:

> [H]e commenced his visits to the royal spa, and after a few good drenches, picked up so rapidly, that to whatever inn they went to dine, the landlords and waiters were astounded at the consumption of grog, and in a very short

time he was known from the "Royal Hotel" down to Hurlston's Commercial Inn, as the great London Cormorant.

Otherwise, the cockney grocer finds nothing admirable:

> [I]t's nothing but a long street with shops . . . with a few small streets branching off from it, and as to the prom-me-nard, as they calls it, aside the spa, with its trees and garden stuff, why, I'm sure, to my mind, the Clarence Gardens up by the Regent's Park, are quite as fine.

Alfred, Lord Tennyson first arrived in 1843, when he was in a state of deep depression because of having lost all his money in an absurd scheme of machined wood carvings. Tennyson, also physically ill because of irregular eating habits, came here to undergo Dr. James Manby Gully's water cure and at first lodged at 6 Belle Vue Place. Edward FitzGerald noted in an 1844 letter to Frederick Tennyson: "Hydrotherapy has done its worst: he writes the name of his friends in water." That year Tennyson joined his mother and sisters at 10 St. James's Square. Tennyson did not like Cheltenham:

> Cheltenham—a polka, parson-worshipping place of which Francis Close is Pope, besides pumps and pump-rooms, chalybeates, quadrilles, and one of the prettiest counties in England.

He lived in the "tall house" on the square for six years; his room, where parts of *In Memoriam* were written, was the one that overlooked the Great Western Railway station.

George Eliot's visit to Cheltenham precipitated a reference to the church establishment in *Middlemarch*:

> "We will make a journey to Cheltenham in the course of a month or two," Bulstrode said to his wife, Harriet. "There are great spiritual advantages to be had in that town, along with the air and the waters, and six weeks there will be very refreshing for us."

Cheltenham, though, is most strongly associated with James Elroy Flecker, who came here at the age of two in May 1886, when his father took over the headship of the new Dean Close School, half a mile from the city center. At six, Flecker entered the kindergarten department of the Ladies' College; after a time at the grammar school, he entered Dean Close School in 1893. The family lived in the headmaster's house, and the boy's nursery, later his study, overlooked Leckhampton Hall and the rose garden and elms of which the poet later wrote. The elms are described in the posthumously printed poem "November Elms":

> November Evenings! Damp and still
> They used to cloak Leckhampton Hill,
> . . . .
> And send queer winds like Harlequins
> That seized our elms for violins
> And struck a note so sharp and low
> Even a child could feel the woe.

The rose garden appears in "From Grenoble":

> I hate this glittering land where nothing stirs:
> I would go back, for I would see again
> Mountains less vast, a less abundant plain,
> The Northern Cliffs clean-swept with driven foam
> And the rose-garden of my gracious home.

Flecker joined the Consular Service, was posted to the Middle East, where his health broke, and died of tuberculosis in Switzerland on January 3, 1915. His body was returned to England on a British destroyer, and funeral services were held in the Dean Close School chapel, where there is a memorial tablet on the wall just behind the headmaster's stall. Flecker was buried in the cemetery on the outskirts of Cheltenham; a plain gray granite curb surrounds the grave. On the granite cross hangs a wreath of bay, perpetually renewed, and the plot contains an Alexandrian laurel and an *Olearia hastii*, the nearest approximation of the "Oak and Olive" that climate and cemetery rules permit.

There are three final associations with the town. Anthony Trollope lived here for a short time after being transferred back to England from Ireland by the Post Office; Thomas Hardy mentions Cheltenham in *The Woodlanders* and "Incident in the Life of Mr. George Cruickhill"; and C. Day-Lewis was English master at Cheltenham College from 1930 to 1935.

CHERTSEY, Surrey (pop. 22,500) Of the Thames-side villages and towns within a reasonable commuting distance of London, Chertsey is perhaps the only one unaltered by the inevitable urban sprawl. Extraordinarily good planning has allowed this market town, 22½ miles southwest of the metropolis, to retain its rural character. It has heavily wooded areas, commons (including Chertsey Mead), and extensive surrounding green fields. As Matthew Arnold once observed, this "the stillest of country towns leads nowhere but to the heaths and pines of Surrey." A Benedictine abbey was founded here in A.D. 666, and the marshy land was drained by the monks, who banked the Thames for the purpose. The abbey flourished under St. Erkenwald; and from the reign (1216–1272) of Henry III, who granted the Goose and Onion Fair of September 25 (still held), to that (1422–1461; 1470–1471) of Henry VI, who granted the Black Cherry Fair on Eldebury Mount (now St. Anne's Hill), the abbey prospered and figured in history and literature. In 1471 the body of the murdered Henry VI was conveyed by boat to Chertsey Abbey from St. Paul's and Blackfriars, as Raphael Holinshed notes; and the body remained here until Henry VIII had it reinterred at Windsor. William Shakespeare makes use of this in *Richard III* but takes the license of having Lady Anne, Henry's daughter-in-law, accompany the body to the abbey:

> Come, now towards Chertsey with your holy load,
> Taken from Paul's to be interred there;
> And still, as you are weary of the weight,
> Rest you, whiles I lament King Henry's corse.

After the dissolution of the monasteries the abbey, which once covered more than 4 acres, was reduced to a pile of rocks.

Much of the abbey was still extant when Abraham Cowley moved here into a house given him for his services to the crown by Queen Catherine of Braganza in the spring of 1665. Porch House, at the west end of the village on Guildford Street, was a rather extensive timber-and-brick dwelling; so solid was the construction that even though considerably altered it was still in use in 1926, when it was demolished to make way for a row of shops and flats. Cowley wanted to live a retired life, and "The Garden" speaks of this place in that vein:

> I never had any desire so strong, and so like to covetousness as that which I have had always, that I might be master at last of a small house and large garden . . . and there dedicate the remainder of my life only to the culture of them and study of nature.

A summerhouse in the garden where Cowley is said to have worked and his favorite seat under a large sycamore are gone. In July 1667 Cowley caught a chill that resulted in pneumonia and his death on July 28. He is said to have caught the initial cold in the damp evening air working in the fields with his laborers, but Alexander Pope unkindly asserted that the fatal illness resulted from spending the night under a field hedge when returning home after a convivial evening. Cowley's body was taken down the Thames to Whitehall, where it lay in state at Wallingford House before burial on August 3 in Westminster Abbey.

Chertsey also has strong ties with Charles Dickens, who had spent several summers at Elm Cottage (later called Elm Lodge) and uses the town and Pycroft House in *Oliver Twist*. Pycroft House, on Pycroft Street off Guildford Street, is meant to be the Maylies's home, the house burglarized by Oliver Twist, Bill Sikes, and Toby Crackit.

> [T]hey hurried through the main street of the little town, which at that late hour was wholly deserted. . . .
> Quickening their pace, they turned up a road upon the left hand. After walking about a quarter of a mile, they stopped before a detached house surrounded by a wall: to the top of which, Toby Crackit, scarcely pausing to take breath, climbed in a twinkling.

The house is now the junior department of the Sir William Perkins School. The window in the "scullery, or small brewing-place," at the back of the house through which Oliver Twist is eased, feet first, has been removed from the house and is now in the Dickens House on Doughty Street, London.

Thomas Love Peacock, aged three, was brought here by his mother in 1788 to Gogmoor Hall, the home of his maternal grandfather, upon the death of his father. There is no trace of the house. One other rather curious literary association exists with Chertsey; the American ballad "Curfew Must Not Ring Tonight," by Rose Hartwick Thorpe, re-creates an event that occurred here during the Wars of the Roses. Blanche Heriot actually did stop the curfew bell from ringing the time of her lover's execution by climbing the bell tower and clinging to the clapper of the bell until the reprieve came.

CHESHAM, Buckinghamshire (pop. 12,266) Situated on the Hertfordshire border of Buckinghamshire, less than 26 miles from London, Chesham is on the Chess River in an area that once was a center for the boot-and-shoe industry, and some establishments have survived the general migration of the industry to the Midlands. One of the more eccentric men of Chesham is possibly immortalized in literature; Robert Crabbe, who has the dubious distinction of being sentenced to death (a sentence not executed) by Oliver Cromwell for a lack of discipline, lived here for many years, running a hat shop, eating a daily ration of turnip greens and grass, and wearing sackcloth. After being declared insane, he left Chesham for Uxbridge, where he lived the rest of his life as the "English Hermit and Wonder of the Age." This is the man on whom, it is frequently said, Lewis Carroll based the Mad Hatter in *Alice's Adventures in Wonderland;* a second claimant, however, is put forth in Theophilus Carter, a furniture dealer around Oxford, who was noted for his top hat and his eccentricities.

After their marriage in July 1914 D. H. Lawrence and Frieda von Richthofen Weekley came to a cottage, near the windmill, where Gilbert Cannan and his wife lived. Kept from Ireland by the war, the two settled into a very busy existence with Lawrence rewriting *The Rainbow* and beginning his study of Thomas Hardy. Both John Middleton Murry and Katherine Mansfield were among the Lawrences' early visitors. In January 1915 Viola Meynell invited the Lawrences to live in Greatham, Sussex, and they left Chesham.

CHESHUNT, Hertfordshire (pop. 18,000) A town famous for its display of roses, Cheshunt is a suburb of London, a little over 17 miles to the south; the town has a number of outstanding buildings and remains, including one wing of Cheshunt Great House (once the home of Cardinal Wolsey), Cheshunt Park (the home of Richard Cromwell), a 15th-century church, and a manor, Theobalds (pronounced "tib'balds"). Only a few fragments of this manor, built by Lord Burleigh, Queen Elizabeth's Secretary of State, remain. Lord Burleigh was the brother-in-law of Sir Nicholas Bacon, who lived at Gorhambury House in St. Albans and was a frequent visitor here. Burleigh's son Robert Cecil, 1st Earl of Salisbury, exchanged Theobalds with James I for Hatfield.

The earliest literary association with Cheshunt concerns Princess Elizabeth (the future Elizabeth I), who had been staying with John Astley and his family in Chelsea. Around Whitsuntide, 1548, she was sent here to Sir Anthony Denny with her tutor of four months, Roger Ascham, because the familiarity between Astley and the young princess had become alarming. They were here for more than two years before Ascham left (or was dismissed) from his post. A letter of January 28, 1550, notes that he has been "ship-wrecked" by a gale of "recent violence and injury at court"; Ascham left for Cambridge but, returning in the summer, was warmly received by Elizabeth.

It is thought that the dramatist John Lyly almost certainly was here on the occasion of Queen Elizabeth's visit to Burleigh in May 1591, but there is no proof.

CHESTER, Cheshire (pop. 47,863) The cathedral town of Chester is located on a bend in the Dee River, which leads directly to the Irish Sea, 20 miles away; close to Liverpool, 16 miles to the north, the town stands on a rocky escarpment above the riverbed. Chester may well have been occupied and fortified by the ancient Britons, but it became the Romans' foremost western stronghold, Castra Devana. The Britons who reinhabited the town called it Caerleon, and the Anglo-Saxons made the name into Legaceaster, which was later shortened to Chester. Michael Drayton writes of the founding of Chester in the eleventh song of *Poly-Olbion:*

But, in that famous Towne, most happy of the rest
(From which thou tak'st thy name) faire *Chester,* call'd of
  old
ff. Carelegion; whilst proud *Rome* her conquests
  heere did hold
Of those her legions known the faithfull station then,
So stoutly held to tack by those neere *North-wales* men;
Yet by her owne right name had rather called be,
ff. As her the *Britaine* tearm'd, *The Fortresse upon
  Dee,*
Then vainly shee would seeme a Miracle to stand,
Th' imaginary worke of some huge Giants hand:
Which if such ever were, Tradition tells not who.

After the Romans came the Britons and the Anglo-Saxons, and early in the 7th century the Northumbrian King wreaked havoc here. Chester was laid waste, and not until after the Danes had slighted the town and been driven off was it rebuilt by the Mercian king Ethelred. Used as a defensive outpost, it gained importance that culminated in the tenth century. Chester is said to have been the last English town to surrender to William the Conqueror (1070). William, in his turn, fortified the town and made it into a palatine earldom.

Medieval Chester flourished, mainly on trading, until the Dee silted up, and the red sandstone cathedral on St. Werburgh Street, which dates from this period, stands on the site of an earlier Saxon church. The cruciform cathedral was begun by Hugh Lupus as a Benedictine house in 1092. Added to by Anselm, the powerful Archbishop of Canterbury, the abbey quickly gained in stature, and by the end of the 13th century the monks here had fashioned the series of plays now known as the Chester Miracle Plays. The Chester Cycle of plays consisted of twenty-five plays (some attributed to a monk named Randle) and were, at first, no more than semidramatic forms presented in the churches. As their popularity increased, the action was added, and the dialogue became somewhat earthy. Eventually characterizations were developed, and the crowds became too large and too rowdy to be contained in the church. In 1210 the plays were ordered outside by Pope Innocent III, and the guilds quickly became involved both in the building of the mobile pageant wagons (which were drawn by guildsmen from station to station) and in the acting of the plays. Each guild had its own appropriate set play and pageant wagon; the Water Carriers' Guild, for example, produced *The Flood,* and the Carpenters' Guild built the Ark. The abbey's importance remained steady even through the dissolution of the monasteries in the 16th century, and the last abbot of the Benedictine order was chosen to be the first dean of the see of Chester, created in 1541.

Chester Cathedral, with one of the smallest cathedral naves in England and one of the largest chancels, is relatively new, except for the small north transept and 16th-century cloisters. One of the most interesting features of the cathedral is the modern stained-glass gallery depicting more than 125 festivals, angels, and church and political figures, including William Laud, Lancelot Andrewes, Richard Hooker, Thomas à Becket, and St. Anselm.

Chester Castle is thought to stand on an entrenched Saxon earthwork, but most of what is seen today dates from the 19th century and is a series of colonnaded buildings.

In the heart of the city are the Rows, Chester's main

pride. Dating from the Middle Ages, these are galleried streets, two tiers high, with the second level of shops set back with overhanging balustraded walkways. The Rows, possibly a defensive work to ward off Welsh invaders, are now unique in England. The town also contains an outstanding collection of 16th- and 17th-century timbered houses, easily the best in the county and probably the best grouping in England. God's Providence House, which happens to be the only house in Watergate Row to escape the plague, has ornate plasterwork panels (restored in 1862). Bishop Lloyd's House, on the same street, is rich in timbers and plasterwork outside and contains beautiful ceilings and fireplaces inside. Old Leche House, also here, has a carved bargeboard and carved beams. However, Daniel Defoe liked neither the Rows nor the old houses; he writes in *A Tour thro' the Whole Island of Great Britain:*

> It is a very Antient City, and to this Day, the Buildings are very old; nor do the Rows as they call them, add any thing, in my Opinion, to the Beauty of the City; but just the contrary, they serve to make the City look both old and ugly: These Rows are certain long Galleries, up one pair of Stairs, which . . . are to keep the People dry in walking along. . . . [B]ut then they take away all the view of the Houses from the Street[;] . . . besides, they make the Shops themselves dark, and the way in them is dark, dirty, and uneven.

Years earlier John Leland was here. Interestingly enough, while liking the Rows, he comments on them only in comparison with those in Bridgnorth, Shropshire, in his *Itinerary.*

While a fair number of literary figures have some association with Chester, it can claim no important native son. John Donne was in the city in September 1599 for the funeral of Sir Thomas Egerton, son of the Lord Chancellor, who died in Ireland on August 23. The services were held in the cathedral, and Donne was part of the funeral procession: "The sword borne by Mr Jo done." Jonathan Swift was here frequently, for Chester was on the main coaching route between London and Dublin, and many of the old coaching inns still exist: the Pied Bull on Northgate Street, the Falcon Inn (built in 1616 and now a café) on Lower Bridge Street, the Royal Oak (rebuilt in 1919) on Foregate Street, and the Yacht Inn at the corner of Nicholas Street. Swift stayed at the Yacht, and his *Journal to Stella* began there in 1710. Thomas Parnell, who was born in Dublin but whose father was from Cheshire, was also often in Chester on his way back and forth from Ireland. Parnell was on his way from London when he was taken ill and died here in October 1718; he was buried in the churchyard of Holy Trinity Church on October 24. No monument marks the site. Later in the 18th century Samuel Johnson visited the city with the Thrales on the way to Wales. He explored Chester carefully and felt that the cathedral was "not of the first rank." However, he found the city walls impressive and incurred Mrs. Thrale's wrath by detaining young Miss Thrale "beyond her hour of going to bed" to walk the walls at night.

Thomas De Quincey had run away from school when he came here in July 1802 to see his sister Mary, who was living with his mother at the Priory, a house that was in the churchyard of St. John's Church. De Quincey was on his way to Wales to

CHESTER "We got to Chester about midnight on Tuesday: and here again I am in a state of much enjoyment. . . I am daily obtaining an extension of agreeable acquaintance, so that I am kept in animated variety. . . Chester pleases my fancy more than any town I ever saw."

James Boswell to Samuel Johnson, October 22, 1779

wander about, and because of his mother's disapproval he chose to limit his family counsels here to his sister; she, however, was in Ambleside looking for him. Col. Thomas Penson, the young man's uncle, was able to persuade Mrs. De Quincey to allow her son a guinea a week to roam the Welsh countryside. By November De Quincey was in London and had broken completely with his mother. Not until March 1803 did he return to effect a reconciliation, and once again his uncle's intervention was crucial; here he rested from "the dreadful remembrances [of London] in the deep monastic tranquility of St. John's Priory." De Quincey describes the house, said to have belonged to Sir Robert Cotton, the antiquarian, in his *Autobiographic Sketches:*

> It was an exceedingly pretty place: and the kitchen, upon the ground storey, which had a noble groined ceiling of stone, indicated, by its disproportionate scale, the magnitude of the establishment to which once it had ministered. . . . On the upper storey were exactly five rooms— viz., a servants' dormitory . . . shut off into a separate section. . . . But the principal section on this upper storey had been dedicated to the use of Sir Robert, and consisted of a pretty old hall, lighted by an old monastic-painted window in the door of entrance; secondly, a rather elegant dining-room; thirdly, a bedroom. The glory of the house internally lay in the monastic kitchen, and, secondly in what a Frenchman would have called, properly, Sir Robert's own *apartment* of three rooms. . . . Ten rooms there may have been in the Priory, as offered to my mother for less than £500. A drawing-room, bedrooms, dressing-rooms, &c., making about ten more, were added by my mother for a sum under £1000.

One of De Quincey's favorite pastimes here was watching the bore, a curious tidal wave on the Dee. He decided to go up to Oxford, and Worcester was selected because it was the cheapest of the colleges; for some reason De Quincey received only £100 a year from his mother although his full patrimony was £150.

When George Borrow was in the town and praised Chester ale, he commented that if one wanted the famous Cheshire cheese, he should not look for it here. In the autumn of 1828 Arthur Hugh Clough and his brother Charles were sent here to attend King's School, then on Northgate Street but now on Wrexham Road. Clough and his brother were here for only one year before going on to Rugby, where Dr. Thomas Arnold was headmaster. After Charles Kingsley, author of *The Water Babies,* resigned his professorship at Cambridge in 1869, noting that both his head and his pocket needed to be refreshed, he delivered a number of lectures supporting a system of national education before being appointed canon of Chester in August of that year. Installed in November, he did not take up residence until the following year; his time here was pleasant, and a botany class that he began evolved into the Chester Natural History Society. He was appointed canon of Westminster in 1873 and before taking up his new post left Chester for a trip to the United States. Another 19th-century resident of the town was Thomas Hughes, author of *Tom Brown's School Days;* appointed to a judgeship in the county court in July 1882, he moved here with his family to 16 Dee Hills Park. In fact, he built the house called Uffington, which was named after his place of birth. Two other visitors to Chester who should be mentioned are Henry James, who uses Chester in *The Ambassadors,* and Nathaniel Hawthorne, who comments in his *English Note-Books* (1853) that Chester has an ancient smell pervading it. He continues:

> Here and there, about some of the streets through which the Rows do not run, we saw houses of very aged aspect, with steep, peaked gables.... Most of these old houses seemed to be taverns,—the Black Bear, the Green Dragon, and such names. We thought of dining at one of them, but, on inspection, they looked rather too dingy and close, and of questionable neatness. So we went to the Royal Hotel, where we probably fared just as badly at much more expense....

CHESTERFIELD, Derbyshire (pop. 65,200)   In the center of the mining and industrial heartland of Derbyshire's Rother Valley, Chesterfield is an ancient market town noted in the Domesday Book. While one might expect a dull and grimy city, Chesterfield is quite attractive with a number of fine old Tudor (renovated) buildings, lovely parks and recreation areas, and a few architecturally outstanding modern buildings. The principal attraction is the Church of All Saints, whose 228-foot timber-supported spire is so warped that it is 8 feet out of perpendicular.

In 1877 Gerard Manley Hopkins was sent to Mount St. Mary's College here after his ordination at St. Beuno, Wales; his post was that of "assistant to the minister," a euphemistic title for housekeeper and bookkeeper—duties he found most uncongenial. A note to Robert Bridges sums up his feelings:

> Life here is as dank as ditch-water and has some of the other qualities of ditch-water; at least I know that I am reduced to great weakness by diarrhoea, which lasts too, as if I were poisoned.

Hopkins's poem on the foundering and sinking of the *Eurydice* was written here before he left for London in July 1878.

CHESTERFIELD   The extraordinary warped spire on the Church of All Saints in Chesterfield has long drawn the astonished gaze of visitors, including Gerard Manley Hopkins, who served as "assistant to the minister" at Mount St. Mary's College here.

CHEVELEY, Cambridgeshire (pop. 599)   The ducal domain of Cheveley Park, 1 mile west of the village of Cheveley (itself near the Suffolk border 3 miles southeast of Newmarket), is no more, but the estate was once a sumptuous affair with gardens and parklands. The opulence of the house made a lasting impression on George Crabbe, who was shown around it when he delivered medicines to the Duke of Rutland from the doctor to whom he was apprenticed in Wickhambrook from 1768 to 1771. Crabbe later wrote of seeing the house in "Silford Hall":

> Through rooms immense, and galleries wide and tall,
> He walk'd entranced—he breathed in Silford Hall.
>   Now could he look on that delightful place,
> The glorious dwelling of a princely race;
> His vast delight was mixed with equal awe,
> There was such magic in the things he saw.

CHICHELEY, Buckinghamshire (pop. 164)   On the Ouse River 2½ miles northeast of Newport Pagnell, Chicheley has a lovely old church with box pews and some good monuments and a moated manor house, Chicheley Hall, built in 1701 for Sir John Chester. The builder went to some trouble to avoid distractions from the overall graceful qualities of the hall, and such features as the attic, a library where all the books are hidden behind paneled doors, make it especially attractive. In November 1787 William Cowper visited the hall in the company of Mrs. Morley Unwin and Mrs. John Throckmorton and met the Bishop of Norwich.

CHICHESTER, Sussex (pop. 19,944) The site of the modern town of Chichester, 28 miles west of Brighton and 1½ miles northeast of the head of Chichester Harbor, was a settlement of the Regnenses long before the Roman conquest of A.D. 43, as the Roman name for the town, Noviomagus Regnensium, implies. Settled under Cogidubnus when the Romans arrived, the people were anxious to adopt the invaders' ways, and under their client-king they made Chichester one of the earliest and most thoroughly Romanized towns in the land. The present walls of the city follow the line of the Roman walls, and the four major directional streets that meet at the Market Cross are Roman.

When the Roman legions abandoned their colonies here, the Saxon chieftain Aella (Ella) invaded and conquered Sussex in the 5th century and gave the town to his son Cissa, after whom it is named. Saxon Sussex was a bit of a backwater, at least in terms of Christianization; shut off by the densely forested Downs, it was one of the last areas in England to be converted from paganism.

Nine years after the Norman invasion the see was transferred to Chichester, and the building of the cathedral began in 1091, when Ralph de Luffa was consecrated bishop. The building, completed in 1184, was extensively damaged by a fire three years later. Reconstruction began immediately; the Norman clerestory was rebuilt in the Early English style with pointed arches, all capable of supporting far greater weight. Purbeck marble pillars were added, and the vaulted roof was built. Chichester Cathedral is unique among English cathedrals in that the Perpendicular bell tower is completely freestanding. Daniel Defoe comments in *A Tour thro' the Whole Island of Great Britain:*

> The Cathedral here is not the finest in *England,* but is far from being the most ordinary: The Spire is a Piece of excellent Workmanship, but it received such a shock about ——— Years ago, that it was next to Miraculous, that the whole Steeple did not fall down; which in short, if it had, would almost have demolish'd the whole Church.

Medieval Chichester flourished, mostly with the wool trade, and fine buildings—the 13th-century Chantry on Canon Lane, and the 13th-century Guildhall in Priory Park as well as the city walls—can still be seen. The 13th-century chapel of the Bishop's Palace contains a magnificent medieval wall painting called the *Chichester Roundel,* which shows an enthroned Virgin and Child in a quatrefoil border.

Chichester claims two native sons. William Collins was born at 21 East Street, on Christmas Day, 1721, and spent most of his life in this city. His father, a hatter, was twice mayor of Chichester, and his son was educated at the prebendal school here before being sent on to Winchester and Queen's and Magdalen Colleges, Oxford. After a brief period in London, where he was to bring out a volume of poetry with Joseph Warton, Collins returned to Chichester and lived at 11 Westgate Street; he probably spent some time in an insane asylum, perhaps in Chelsea, and at one point this pockmarked poet shocked the citizens

of Chichester by moaning and howling in unison with the choir in the cathedral cloisters. Thomas Warton visited Collins here and noted the young man's failing health in the 1750s. He died here at the Royal Chantry on June 12, 1759, and was buried in St. Andrew's Church. William Hayley, who was born here on October 29, 1749, wrote the inscription for the memorial relief tablet by John Flaxman in the southwest tower of the cathedral.

Early in the 19th century William Blake saw more of Chichester than he could have desired. He had been living in Felpham, "a sweet place for study," since 1800 and in August 1803 in the front garden of that house had an encounter with a great hulk of a drunken soldier. Being soundly turned out, the soldier vowed revenge and secured a comrade's verification to the charge he laid against Blake of seditious language. On January 11, 1804, the Duke of Richmond opened the quarter sessions, and the trial began. The *Sussex Advertiser* reports on January 16, 1804, that Blake had uttered such statements as

> D——n the king, d——n all his subjects, d——n his soldiers, they are all slaves; when Bonaparte comes, it will be cut-throat for cut-throat, and the weakest must go to the wall; I will help him, &c. &c.

Blake's defense was handled by Samuel Rose, but the latter could not keep the poet under control, for every time that the soldier conjured up supportive comments, Blake vehemently and convincingly called out "False!" Character witnesses attested to the accused's "habitual gentleness and peaceableness," and when the jury acquitted the poet, the court erupted in a jubilant uproar.

Another 19th-century visitor to Chichester was

CHICHESTER The octagonal Market Cross, in the center of Chichester where four main roads converge, was built in 1501 by Bishop Edward Story; the cross is crowned with stone pinnacles and ribs which rise to a lantern.

John Keats; he was here on a number of occasions after January 1819 and stayed with the father of Charles Wentworth Dilke at 11 Eastgate Street. His first visit was productive even though he was not especially pleased with his "little Poem call'd 'St Agnes Eve. . . .'" He wrote to his brother and sister-in-law of the stay:

> I was nearly a fortnight at Mr John Snook's and a few days at old Mr Dilke's—Nothing worth speaking of happened at either place—I took down some of the thin paper and wrote on it a little Poem call'd 'St Agnes Eve'—which you shall have as it is when I have finished the blank part of the rest for you. I went out twice at Chichester to old Dowager card parties. I see very little now, and very few Persons—being almost tired of Men and things.

The house is now marked with a plaque.

Later in the century Edward FitzGerald married Lucy Barton, daughter of Bernard Barton, the "Quaker Poet"; they were married at All Saints' Church on November 4, 1856, without one member of the groom's family present. FitzGerald's letters to friends, among them William Makepeace Thackeray, informing them of his marriage, asked that he not be congratulated—a rather ominous start for the disastrous marriage.

W. H. Hudson's visit produced extreme fury over the clergy's indifference to the large number of pubs which sold

> wrecked lives of innumerable men, broken hearts and homes made desolate: famine and every foul disease: feverish dreams and appetites, frantic passions, crimes, ravings of delirium, epilepsy, insanity, and, strewn all over, the ashes of death.

Here, too, he fought in vain to have a white owl removed from its captivity in a kitchen.

In early October 1912, Rupert Brooke came to visit John Middleton Murry, then editor of *Rhythm*, and his wife at nearby Runcton Cottage. Later John Galsworthy stayed in the Anchor Hotel, which he called "excellent," and visited the cathedral.

One of H. G. Wells's novels, *The Wheels of Chance*, has scenes set here. Hoopdriver makes inquiries at the Black Swan; he and Jessie stay at the Red Hotel; and the White Hart is where the "short, thick set, red face" hostler gives Dangle a black eye. An even more modern author has written of the 13th- and 14th-century Arundel tombs in the north aisle of the cathedral. Contemplation of the 14th-century tomb of Richard Fitzalan, Earl of Arundel, and his wife occasioned Philip Larkin's "An Arundel Tomb":

> Side by side, their faces blurred,
> The earl and countess lie in stone,
> Their proper habits vaguely shown
> As jointed armour, stiffened pleat,
> And that faint hint of the absurd—
> The little dogs under their feet.
>
> Such plainness of the pre-baroque
> Hardly involves the eye, until
> It meets his left-hand gauntlet, still
> Clasped empty in the other; and
> One sees, with a sharp tender shock,
> His hand withdrawn, holding her hand.

CHICKSANDS PRIORY, Bedfordshire (pop. 56) In 1150 Rose de Beauchamp of Bedford Castle founded a priory for Gilbertine nuns here on the Ivel River; this was the only English chapter of the order. At the dissolution of the monasteries in the 16th century the estate passed into the hands of the Osbornes, who carefully transformed the priory into a family home; this was the birthplace of Dorothy Osborne in 1627, and here she would

> walk out into a common that lies hard by the house, where a great many young wenches keep sheep and cows, and sit in the shade singing of ballads.

After meeting Sir William Temple in 1648, she corresponded with him, and their letters present an admirable picture of 17th-century life.

CHICKSGROVE, Wiltshire A tiny hamlet 2 miles northeast of Tisbury, Chicksgrove was the birthplace of Sir John Davies in April 1569; the manor house here (rebuilt) was owned by Sir John's father, described by Anthony à Wood as a "wealthy tanner" and by Sir John's admission entry to the Middle Temple as of "New Inn, [a] gentleman." Davies was baptized at the parish church in Tisbury on April 16 and after the death of his father was raised by his mother here.

CHIGWELL, Essex (pop. 62,240) On the edge of the famous Epping Forest 13½ miles northeast of the London conurbation, Chigwell retains a great deal of the feeling of the 19th-century village that was especially attractive to visitors. The Church of St. Mary, originally of Norman construction, had Samuel Harsnett as its vicar from 1597 to 1605. Although he rose to the office of Archbishop of York, Chigwell remained his favorite place, and he showed his affection by founding the grammar school in 1629. His *Declaration of Egregious Popish Impostures*, the source of the names of the fiends mentioned by Edgar in *King Lear,* was written here in 1603. Harsnett was interred in St. Mary's in 1631, and his memorial brass, originally in the chancel floor, is now upright against a pier in the chancel arch. The brass is almost life-size, and Harsnett appears dressed in stole, alb, dalmatic, and cope as Bishop (Norwich and Chester) and not as Archbishop. The Bishop's alb, in quite unusual fashion, is open in the front.

Opposite the church is the King's Head Inn, where Charles Dickens stayed in 1841. Wanting John Forster to join him, he writes, "Chigwell, my dear fellow, is the greatest place in the world. Name your day for going. Such a delicious old inn opposite the churchyard . . . such an out-of-the-way rural place. . . . I say again, name your day." In fact, the old black-and-white coaching inn, becomes the Maypole in *Barnaby Rudge;* the name, though, comes from the old Maypole, not the present one, on Chigwell Row. Dickens's description of the King's Head as "an old building, with more gable ends than a lazy man would care to count on a sunny day" is only slightly exaggerated; the windows are still "old diamond-pane lattices," the floors "sunken and uneven," and the ceilings "blackened by the hand of time, and heavy with massive beams."

A later description of Chigwell by Sir Walter Besant is more hostile but perhaps more relevant to the current town. *All in a Garden Fair* describes the place as so rural as to seem "overdone, an affectation of rurality, a pedantry and pretence, somewhat over-acted, of rusticity." The roadside inns are "picturesque and dirty; their signs—brave old signs, such as the 'Good Intent' and the 'Traveller's Rest' hang creakily over the wooden trough full of water for the horses." Today as then, "Nowhere else so near to London can you hear such singing of birds . . . the nightingale . . . the dove. . . ." The "wild and ghostly" churchyard is on the road between Abridge and Theydon Bois.

CHILTERN HILLS, Bedfordshire Running from southern Oxfordshire across the southern part of Buckinghamshire and thence into Bedfordshire and Hertfordshire, the Chiltern Hills are a range of mainly chalk hills still covered with beech woods, dense and green. The Bedfordshire Chilterns are closely associated with John Bunyan, and most likely it is the area between Ampthill and Barton-le-Clay that becomes the Delectable Mountains in *The Pilgrim's Progress*. Christian sees them first from the house "built by the Lord of the hill . . . for the relief and security of pilgrims":

> [A]nd behold at a great distance [south] he saw a most pleasant mountainous country, beautified with woods, vineyards, fruits of all sorts, flowers also, with springs and fountains, very delectable to behold.

He later "came to the Delectable Mountains":

> [S]o they went up to the mountains to behold the gardens and orchards, the vineyards, and fountains of water, where also they drank and washed themselves and did freely eat of the vineyards. Now there was on the tops of these mountains shepherds feeding their flocks, and they stood by the highway side. The pilgrims therefore went to them, and . . . asked, "Whose Delectable Mountains are these? And whose be the sheep that feed upon them?"

CHILVERS COTON, Warwickshire (pop. 12,770) Just east of Arbury and essentially a part of Nuneaton, Chilvers Coton suffered a great deal of bomb damage

CHILTERN HILLS   An area of outstanding natural beauty which extends roughly from Goring to Hitchin, the Chiltern Hills play an important role in John Bunyan's *The Pilgrim's Progress* as the Delectable Mountains.

during World War II, primarily as a result of its closeness to Birmingham, 17 miles to the west. The 13th-century parish church was bombed on May 17, 1941, and practically destroyed, but in 1946–1947 prisoners of war who were lodged here played a major role in the rebuilding of the church. The College for the Poor, built in 1800 by French prisoners of war at the expense of Sir Roger Newdigate of Arbury Hall, no longer exists in its original capacity, and the old dining room where the chaplain preached to the inmates has been converted into a chapel for the elderly who now are housed at Coton Lodge. At the rear of the building, the college originally had an infirmary, which became an emergency hospital during World War II and which has now evolved into the George Eliot Hospital. Opposite the parish church the free school, erected by Sir Roger Newdigate but founded in 1745 by his mother, originally catered to thirty poor boys and twenty poor girls; however, the numbers rapidly increased because the school was open to all parishioners. The old vicarage in Chilvers Coton was on a 2-acre plot just northwest of the church, and only an old copper beech survived its demolition in 1936.

The vicarage, as well as the other buildings noted here, played an important part in the life and works of George Eliot (Mary Ann Evans). This church is the one she attended while she lived at Griff House; indeed, she was baptized here a week after her birth, but the font used then was destroyed in the air raid in 1941. Chilvers Coton becomes Shepperton in "The Sad Fortunes of the Rev. Amos Barton," and this is the Shepperton Church,

> a very different-looking building five-and-twenty years ago. To be sure, its substantial stone tower looks at you through its intelligent eye, the clock, with the friendly expression of former days; but in everything else what changes! Now there is a wide span of slated roof flanking the old steeple; the windows are tall and symmetrical; the outer doors are resplendent with oak-graining, the inner doors reverentially noiseless with a garment of red baize; and the walls, you are convinced, no lichen will ever again effect a settlement on. . . . Pass through the baize doors and you will see the nave filled with well-shaped benches, understood to be free seats; while in certain eligible corners . . . there are pews reserved for the Shepperton gentility. Ample galleries are supported on iron pillars, and in one of them stands the crowning glory, the very clasp or aigrette of Shepperton church-adornment— namely, an organ. . . .

The figures of the Rev. and Mrs. Amos Barton, who live in the old fashioned vicarage near the church, are based on the Rev. John Gwyther and his wife Emma; Gwyther served as the curate from 1831 to 1838, and the story of their poverty and of the scandal and trouble brought on by the countess was well known when George Eliot was a child. The death of Mrs. Gwyther is accurately presented in Eliot's story, and she was buried opposite the old church tower, where her memorial stone was shaded by a yew tree. The Rev. Amos Barton functions as chaplain of the college and preaches to its collection of inmates:

> At eleven o'clock, Mr. Barton walked forth in cape and boa, with the sleet driving in his face, to read prayers at the workhouse, euphuistically called the "College." The College was a huge square stone building, standing on the best apology for an elevation of ground that could be seen for about ten miles round Shepperton. A flat ugly

district this; depressing enough to look at even on the brightest days.

He makes his way to "the dreary stone-floored room," where he reads "a portion of the morning service to the inmates seated on benches before him."

Chilvers Coton as Shepperton comes into another of the stories in Eliot's *Scenes of Clerical Life*, and again the characters are based on real people. "Mr. Gilfil's Love Story" is set partly here, for the vicar takes two short sermons from his file "every Sunday, . . . and having preached one of those sermons at Shepperton in the morning" goes on to Knebley (Astley) for afternoon services. The Rev. Maynard Gilfil is based on Bernard Gilpin Ebdell, the man who christened Mary Ann Evans; Caterina, his wife, "a little pale woman, with eyes as black as sloes," is drawn from Sarah (Sally) Shilton Ebdell:

> There were not many people in the parish, besides Martha, who had any very distinct remembrance of Mr. Gilfil's wife, or indeed who knew anything of her, beyond the fact that there was a marble tablet, with a Latin inscription in memory of her, over the vicarage pew. The parishioners . . . [said] Mrs. Gilfil looked like a "furriner, wi' such eyes, you can't think, an' a voice as went through you when she sung at church."

The tablet, badly damaged by the bombing, has been repaired and placed in the south side of the nave on the second pillar from the pulpit. Another memorial of interest is the tablet to Signior Dominico Motto, the professor of music brought to Arbury Hall by Sir Roger Newdigate to be Sally Shilton's voice teacher. Also of interest is the tablet tomb of Robert and Christiana Evans (George Eliot's parents) and their twin sons, who died shortly after birth; the graves are near the churchyard cross.

CHIPPENHAM, Wiltshire (pop. 8,439) On the busy road from London to Bath, which lies 13 miles to the southwest, the large market town of Chippenham lies on the left bank of the Avon River. In the 11th century the town was remarkable in having twelve water-powered mills; indeed, up through the industrial revolution the economic base of the town, cloth- and iron-manufacturing industries, depended on the river. This is a dignified town with a number of good Georgian houses interspersed with fine examples of 16th- and 17th-century timber-fronted buildings. Thomas Hardy makes use of Chippenham in *A Pair of Blue Eyes;* here Elfride's funeral carriage is attached to the train carrying Knight and Stephen Smith to Endelstow (St. Juliot).

CHIPPING ONGAR   *See* ONGAR.

CHISLEDON, Wiltshire (pop. 1,688) On the edge of the Marlborough Downs, 3 miles southeast of Swindon, Chisledon has a number of thatched houses and a 13th-century church with medieval bench ends, an old timbered roof, and an intricate Jacobean pulpit. It was one of the favorite spots of the 19th-century nature poet Richard Jefferies of nearby Coate Farm, Swindon. He walked here almost daily and called the small copse of firs "one of his thinking places." The remaining seven of these firs have been scheduled as Trees of Remembrance.

CHISLEHURST, Kent (pop. 8,981) Until the middle of the 18th century Chislehurst was clearly not a part of London, even though the city was less than 12 miles away, but was a relatively rural area on a common with large country weekend homes. Then only London Bridge carried traffic across the Thames; with new bridges and faster means of locomotion, the town became a commuting suburb. Chislehurst contains the remains of Scadbury Hall, the home of Thomas Walsingham and a residence, at several times between 1583 and 1593, of the dramatist Christopher Marlowe. On his first visit Marlowe attended services in the small parish church of St. Nicholas, of which Richard Harvey, Gabriel Harvey's brother and Marlowe's contemporary at Cambridge, was rector. It was this occasion that prompted Marlowe's remark that Harvey was but "an asse, good for nothing but to preach in the Iron Age." The dramatist, here again in May 1593, when London was plague-ridden, was working on *Hero and Leander*. Marlowe returned to London sometime between May 18 and 20, when a court messenger appeared with a warrant for his arrest. Scadbury Hall has been reconstructed at ground level; the lower walls of the hall on which the timbers had rested are gone. An interesting relic in the grounds here has led to a great deal of conjecture; a stone slab, which appears to cover an unmarked grave in an overgrown area, has been hypothesized as the place at which Walsingham may have had Marlowe buried after the brawl in Deptford, London.

The lovely Elizabethan Camden Place, now a golf club, was once the residence of William Camden. He spent his latter years "retired into the country for the recovery of my tender health, where *portum anhelans beatitudenis*, I proposed to sequester myself from worldly business and cogitations." In May 1622, he established a history lectureship at Oxford while still exercising his office of king of arms. In August 1623 he suffered a stroke that left him partially paralyzed, and he died at his home here on November 9, 1623. His body was removed to his house in Westminster and was buried in the south transept of Westminster Abbey on November 19.

John Evelyn was an occasional visitor to Frogpoole (now Frognal) when it belonged to Sir Philip Warwick. And in the 20th century H. G. Wells used Chislehurst in *The Food of the Gods* as the scene of, first, the nursery and, then, the stronghold of Cossar's three Boom-fed sons.

CHISWICK, Middlesex (pop. 40,938) Once a fashionable suburban Thames-side village just west of London, Chiswick is no longer either suburban or villagelike and could hardly be considered fashionable either; since 1965 it has been amalgamated with Brentford, Heston, Isleworth, and Feltham in the Greater London borough of Hounslow. As such, it is now on one of the major approach roads into the West End from Heathrow Airport and the west; and the enormous concrete spider legs of the M4 flyover are a symbol of its modern role. Chiswick was one of England's most fashionable places of residence in the 17th and 18th centuries. Chiswick Mall, easily reached from Hammersmith Mall, affords a glimpse of the past: here lining the bank of the Thames are excellent 18th-century houses; Morton House, Strawberry House, and Walpole House are especially notable. Chiswick House (once known as Chiswick Villa) is one of the finest small aristocratic mansions in the shire. Built in 1729 by the 3d Earl of Burlington as a temple to the arts, the house underwent many changes through the next two centuries but is now in its original state. In time, the house came to the 5th Duke of Devonshire, who added two wings designed by James Wyatt; later it was Edward VII's summer home when he was Prince of Wales, a lunatic asylum, and an emergency fire station in World War II. In 1736 the classic front of Beaufort House was brought here, and chiseled on it is Alexander Pope's memorial:

Inigo Jones put me together
Sir Hans Sloane left me alone
Burlington brought me thither.

Both Pope and John Gay were frequent guests here. The grounds are an excellent example of 18th-century taste in landscape art.

Sir Walter Scott visited Chiswick and saw Chiswick House on May 17, 1828, as his diary records:

I drove out to Chiswick, where I had never been before. A numerous and gay party were assembled to walk and enjoy the beauties of that Palladian dome. The place and highly ornamented gardens belonging to it resemble a picture of Watteau. There is some affectation, but in the *ensemble* the original looked very well.

Literary associations date mostly from Chiswick's fashionable period. Not only was Alexander Pope a guest at Chiswick House; from 1716 to 1719 he lived here with his parents in what is now a small inn, the Fox and Hounds and Mawson Arms just off the Mall, where Pope felt he was "under the wing of my Lord Burlington." He also worked on the *Iliad* here, and his father died here in 1717 and was buried in the Chiswick churchyard. In the 19th century William Makepeace Thackeray was sent to England from India (where he was born) to attend a school on Chiswick Mall run by a Dr. Turner. His experience here was short-lived, and in 1822 he was at Charterhouse. Nevertheless, a strong impression had been made, and the novelist used the area in *Vanity Fair* as the location of Miss Pinkerton's Academy. Boston House on Chiswick Square claims to be the original of Miss Pinkerton's, but a far better case can be put forward for Walpole House on the Mall, since Thackeray clearly locates the school on the Mall. To confuse the issue, the author's illustrations of the school seem to incorporate features of both buildings. Local tradition purports that Horace Walpole lived at Walpole House, but there is absolutely no evidence of this.

In 1876, John Yeats moved his family from London to 8 Woodstock Road, a Norman Shaw house. William Yeats attended the Godolphin School in Hammersmith until 1880, when the family returned to Ireland partly for financial reasons. The Yeats family were again in Chiswick after 1888, at 3 Blenheim Road. "The house," Yeats wrote, "is fine and roomy . . . everything is a little idyllic."

William Ernest Henley and his wife settled for a short time at 1 Merton Road before he became editor of the *Scots Observer* and left for Edinburgh.

CHITTOE, Wiltshire (pop. 158) Sloperton Cottage in Chittoe, a small village 5 miles northwest of Devizes, just outside the Vale of Pewsey, was the home of the Irish poet Thomas Moore from 1817 until his death on February 25, 1852. Moore settled in Chittoe partly to be near the 3d Marquess of Lansdowne, but any idea of working here vanished when his deputy in Bermuda was discovered to have embezzled more than £6,000, for which Moore was held responsible. The poet immediately left for Paris and then went on to Italy, while Lord Lansdowne settled the affair. Moore returned to England in April 1822 and resettled in Chittoe in November of that year. He had met Lord Byron in Venice in 1819 and wrote an invaluable life of the poet here following Byron's death in 1824. Moore died in Chittoe, but because it had no parish church, he was buried in Bromham, about a mile away.

CHRISTCHURCH, Cambridgeshire Situated 4 miles south of Upwell, Christchurch is a small fen village whose fame is recent; the rectory here was the vacation home of Dorothy Sayers beginning in 1917, when her father left Bluntisham and took this living. The area around Christchurch is used in *The Nine Tailors*, and the nearby village of Upwell is undoubtedly Fenchurch St. Paul. The description of the church in that work closely corresponds to the church in Upwell. Lord Peter Wimsey's ancestral home, Denver Ducis, is probably to be located in the Upwell Fen area near Denver, about 9 miles northeast.

CHRISTCHURCH, Hampshire (pop. 16,408) Located 1½ miles from the sea at the confluence of the Avon and Stour Rivers, Christchurch was an important religious center as early as Saxon times, and the modern sprawling town retains some of its early monastic character. Behind Christchurch Quay is the splendid Priory Church with its massive Norman nave, 14th-century reredos, and choir stalls older than those in Westminster Abbey in London. Perhaps the most fascinating aspect of the church is St. Michael's Loft, a large chamber above the Lady Chapel, in which there appears to have been an early altar. Theologians and historians have long been interested in hilltop churches and loft chapels dedicated to St. Michael, which are considered to be possible links to the Coptic Christianity of anchorites in 4th-century Egypt.

The Priory Church seems an appropriate one to contain a monument by Henry Weekes to Percy Bysshe Shelley; the drowned poet's body is represented as having just been washed ashore and is supported on the knees of his second wife, Mary. The monument, originally offered by Mary Shelley to Westminster Abbey but turned down because of Shelley's "doubtful religious views," was given to Christchurch in 1845 by Sir Percy Shelley, the poet's son, who lived in nearby Boscombe.

Two centuries earlier, John Marston, the amoral dramatist who suddenly became conventional, held the living here from 1616 to 1631. Conversion was so complete that he disclaimed the 1633 collected edition of his own plays.

Sir Arthur Conan Doyle makes slight use of Christchurch and the road leading from the town to Beaulieu in *The White Company*. This is the road along which "swaggered Samkin Aylward, true type of the archer who at a hundred and fifty yards' distance could split the wooden peg which fastened the centre of the target." Aylward then encounters John of Hordle, who has been expelled from the abbey, and young Alleyne Edricson, the student.

Frederick William Rolfe, better known as Baron Corvo and author of *Hadrian the Seventh*, spent two periods here, in 1889 and 1891 and is supposed to have decorated "St. Michael's" Roman Catholic Church with a number of frescoes. Two points, though, are in order: St. Michael's is not Catholic, and the Church of the Immaculate Conception and St. Joseph, which is, has a canvas wall mural and not a number of frescoes.

CIRENCESTER, Gloucestershire (pop. 8,200) Frequently referred to as the capital of the Cotswolds, Cirencester (also known as Cicester and pronounced "cis'sester"), on the Churn River about 21 miles southeast of Cheltenham, was one of the largest Roman towns of the 2d century. Although there was a prior Celtic establishment, the Roman Corinium got its start as a small military station at the crossing of the Churn and the juncture of the Fosse Way, Ermine Street, and Akeman Street. It grew rapidly, and because of its situation on open upland country with few if any natural defenses, it was completely walled in; by the end of the 2d century stone-faced walls enclosed the 240-acre city. When Britain was organized by Diocletian into four parts for ease in administration, Corinium became the capital of Britannia Prima; only Londinium (London) was then a larger city.

Following the withdrawal of the Romans, Corinium was harassed by marauders and was simultaneously threatened by Saxon hordes and plagued by the number of refugees seeking sanctuary within the stout city walls. The Saxons massacred the townsmen and, probably, flooded the lower end of the city, turning it into marshland; this event is commemorated in the modern Water Moor Street. By 628 the town's name had become Cirencester, and in 879 Alfred the Great invited the Danes to settle here in order to know where they were and to regroup his forces without harassment.

Norman rule brought peace and prosperity, and Cirencester quickly became an important urban area. Of the 11th-century castle built by William Fitzosbern, nothing remains; it was razed in 1142 by Stephen's forces. The 12th-century abbey has disappeared except for one gateway, called the Spital Gate, on Grove Lane; this was a powerful and wealthy ecclesiastical establishment whose wealth came from the wool trade. The extent of the medieval wool trade is seen in the 15th-century Weavers Hall on Thomas Street, the houses of rich merchants on Coxwell Street, and the restored timber-fronted Fleece Hotel. Daniel Defoe comments briefly in *A Tour thro' the Whole Island of Great Britain*:

> On the *Churne* one of those Rivers stands *Cirencester*, or *Ciciter* for brevity, a very good Town, Populous and Rich, full of Clothiers, and driving a great Trade in Wool. . . . [I]t is sold here in quantities, so great, that it almost exceeds belief: It is generally bought here by the Clothiers of *Wiltshire* and *Gloucestershire*, for the supply of that great Clothing Trade; of which I have spoken already: They talk of 5000 Packs in a Year.

Cecily Hill, a cul-de-sac formerly named Instripp Street, leads to the gates of Cirencester Park, an area of 5,000 acres laid out by the 1st Earl Bathurst, the patron of Alexander Pope, John Gay, Dean Swift, Matthew Prior, Laurence Sterne, and William Congreve. Pope spent at least part of ten summers here from 1715 on; an ornamental summerhouse in the park is known as Pope's Seat, and he is said to have planted many of the trees in the park. The third epistle of Pope's *Moral Essays* was dedicated to Bathurst, and the poet writes to the Misses Blount:

> I am with Lord Bathurst, at my bower; in whose groves we had yesterday a dry walk of three hours. It is the place that of all others I fancy; and I am not yet out of humour with it, though I have had it some months: it does not cease to be agreeable to me so late in the season; the very dying of the leaves adds a variety of colours that is not unpleasant. I look upon it, as upon a beauty I once loved, whom I should preserve a respect for in her decay. . . .

Pope also notes the destruction of part of the village of Sapperton:

> Link towns to towns with avenues of oak,
> Enclose whole downs in walls—'tis all a joke!
> Inexorable Death shall level all
> And trees, and stones, and farms, and farmers fall.

Gay and Swift were here whenever the dean of St. Patrick's was in England, and in the summer of 1726 Gay (undoubtedly with assistance from Pope and Swift) wrote his "Molly Mog; or, The Fair Maid of the Inn" on a return trip from Cirencester. Sterne was also here frequently and sketched a portrait of Bathurst and his home in *Letters from Yorick to Eliza*. The poet Edward Young stood for Parliament here in a contested election in 1721.

CLEOBURY MORTIMER, Shropshire (pop. 1,487) Securely positioned on the Rea River 13 miles south of Bridgnorth, in the Wyre Forest (itself once a royal preserve), Cleobury Mortimer has a partly Norman church with an oaken spire that must be restored every 100 years or so because of the depredations of wind and rain. The spire so curves in the middle as to appear dangerous, which it is not. The church contains a memorial east window to the poet William Langland; the window portrays his childhood. He is seen asleep, the Rea River in front of him, the Malvern Hills in the distance, and masked figures of Truth and Falsehood on either side.

Cleobury Mortimer is traditionally considered the birthplace of Langland sometime around 1330; the assertion comes in John Bale's *Illustrium Majoris Britanniae Scriptorum*:

> [Langland] was born in the county of Shropshire, at a place commonly known as Mortymers Clibery [that is, Cleobury Mortimer], in a poor district eight miles from the Malvern hills. I cannot say with certainty whether he was educated until his maturity in that remote and rural locality, or whether he studied at Oxford or Cambridge. . . .

It is also now thought that Langland received some of his education from the Austin Friars here; part of their original establishment has been incorporated in Woodhouse. The little that is known of the *Piers Plowman* poet derives from internal evidence in the poem and from marginal notations in the Ashburnham manuscript, which contains a Latin note stating that Langland's father was "of gentle birth," one Stacy de Rokayle, who lived at Shipton-under-Wychwood, Oxfordshire. The poet took the name Langland possibly because of his illegitimate birth. The usual argument that such an assumption means that the poet was born in Shipton-under-Wychwood because of a nearby hamlet called Langley is a red herring, since a hamlet by the same name can also be found a few miles from Cleobury Mortimer. A third, more recent claimant as the birthplace is a manor farm called Longlands (next to the parish of Ledbury and near Malvern Priory), where the poet's mother may have lived.

CLEVEDON, Somerset (pop. 8,000) Located where two ranges of hills meet on the Severn Estuary, Clevedon is in a coastal upland area 15½ miles west-southwest of Bristol. Clevedon was a medieval manorial establishment built around Clevedon Court, which dates mostly from the early 14th century. The Great Hall, dated approximately 1320, contains chamfered arches, and the rectangular windows in the chapel are completely filled with reticulated tracery.

The main interest in Clevedon is in the Church of St. Andrew, a Norman to medieval structure which looks out over the Severn to the Welsh mountains and contains the grave of Arthur Henry Hallam, whose death inspired Alfred, Lord Tennyson's *In Memoriam.* Hallam died in Vienna in September 1833 and was buried in the Elton family vault in the manor aisle in January 1834. (The Eltons had owned the hall since the reign of Queen Anne, and Arthur Henry Hallam was the nephew of the 6th Baronet.) Tennyson did not attend Hallam's funeral because it was "too trying an ordeal to face," and it was a number of years before the poet was able to visit the church and the grave. *In Memoriam* is, as Tennyson states, "a poem, *not* an actual biography," and records his thoughts and feelings for fifteen years. He describes the Somerset coast:

The Danube to the Severn gave
    The darken'd heart that beat no more;
    They laid him by the pleasant shore,
And in the hearing of the wave.

There twice a day the Severn fills;
    The salt sea-water passes by,
    And hushes half the babbling Wye,
And makes a silence in the hills.

The Wye is hush'd nor moved along,
    And hush'd my deepest grief of all,
    When fill'd with tears that cannot fall,
I brim with sorrow drowning song.

The large memorial to Hallam in the center of the west wall was erected by Hallam's father, Henry Hallam, the historian, whose own simple epitaph was written by Tennyson. Another poet made a pilgrimage to Hallam's grave after meeting Tennyson in London; in June 1855, Dante Gabriel Rossetti came here with Elizabeth Eleanor Siddal, his model and, later, wife, for a stay of only a few days.

Earlier Samuel Taylor Coleridge, who married Sarah Fricker in the Church of St. Mary Redcliffe in Bristol on October 4, 1795, spent his six-month honeymoon here in a cottage on the banks of the Severn, which Coleridge describes as

                        . . . our cot o'ergrown
With white-flowered Jasmin, and the broad-leaved
    Myrtle,
(Meet emblems they of Innocence and Love!)

A cottage on Old Church Road near the station is claimed to be Coleridge's cottage, but this identification cannot be confirmed, and there are other candidates. Clevedon is often erroneously claimed as the birthplace of Hartley Coleridge, who was in fact born in Bristol.

William Makepeace Thackeray was a frequent guest of Sir Charles, the 6th Baronet, at Clevedon Court. The house becomes the original of Castlewood, the family seat of the Viscounts and Earls of Castlewood, in both *The History of Henry Esmond, Esquire* and *The Virginians:*

The hall of Castlewood was built with two courts, whereof one only, the fountain-court, was now inhabited, the other having been battered down in the Cromwellian wars. In the fountain-court, still in good repair, was the great hall, near to the kitchen and butteries; a dozen of living-rooms looking to the north, and communicating with the little chapel that faced eastwards and the buildings stretching from that to the main gate, and with the hall (which looked to the west) into the court now dismantled.

Also here is the Three Castles Inn of the novels where Davis is the landlord. Although "here" is Clevedon, Thackeray arbitrarily transports Castlewood to Hampshire for his convenience. Finally, Rupert Brooke was a frequent visitor to Clevedon.

CLIFFE-AT-HOO, Kent (pop. 2,581) Located near the Roman Watling Street on Cliffe Creek and the Thames River and immediately across the river from the Saxon kingdom of Essex, Cliffe-at-Hoo (5½ miles east of Gravesend) was the site of a 7th-century synod summoned by Theodore of Tarsus, Archbishop of Canterbury. A century later the Mercian king Offa built a church here and dedicated it to St. Helena, the supposed daughter of Earl Coel ("Old King Cole") of Colchester. Coel did not exist, and St. Helena, who was the mother of the emperor Constantine, had no association with Colchester. The port prospered until a fire devastated the village in the 16th century. The sluice-gate hut that stood on the bank of the canal is thought to be Charles Dickens's model for the sluice house to which Pip is decoyed in *Great Expectations.* The canal once connected a lime quarry with the creek, where the lime was loaded onto Thames barges. Dickens's description tallies with local use and tradition:

It was another half-hour before I drew near to the kiln. The lime was burning with a sluggish stifling smell, but the fires were made up and left, and no workmen were visible. Hard by was a small stone-quarry. . . .
Coming up again to the marsh level out of this excavation—for the rude path lay through it—I saw a light in the old sluice-house. I quickened my pace, and knocked at the door with my hand. Waiting for some reply, I looked about me, noticing how the sluice was abandoned and broken, and how the house—of wood with a tiled roof—would not be proof against the weather much

longer, if it were so even now, and how the mud and ooze were coated with lime, and how the choking vapour of the kiln crept in a ghostly way towards me.

CLIFFORD CHAMBERS, Warwickshire (pop. 347) Clifford Chambers, 2 miles south of Stratford-on-Avon on the Stour River, is a secluded hamlet little changed over the centuries. The Norman doorway of the church is still in use, and the Norman font, although refashioned in medieval times, still serves its original purpose. As might be expected with any location near Stratford-on-Avon, if a Shakespearean association does not actually exist, it will in "legend" or "tradition." Here, for more than three centuries the inhabitants of Clifford Chambers have maintained that this village and not Stratford was the dramatist's birthplace. They argue that since the plague had already reached Stratford in 1564 and John Shakespeare and his wife had lost two children in infancy, they came here to the old rectory, where there were relatives (and no plague).

An irrefutable association exists with Michael Drayton, who was a frequent visitor to the home of Anne Goodere after her 1595 marriage to Henry Rainsford. Indeed, he paid his compliments to the area and his host and hostess in the fourteenth song of *Poly-Olbion*:

Nor of deere *Cliffords* seat (the place of health and sport)
Which many a time hath been the Muses quiet Port.
Yet brags not he of that, nor of himselfe esteemes
The more for his faire site; but richer then he seemes,
Clad in a gowne of Grasse, so soft and wondrous warme,
As him the Sommers heat, nor Winters cold can harme.

Sixteenth-century Clifford Chambers was in Gloucestershire, not Warwickshire.

CLIFTON, Westmorland (pop. 397) Within sight of the Pennines to the north and 2½ miles southeast of Penrith, Clifton has an Early English church, a good manor house, and an important place in English history. The church was built over Saxon foundations by the Normans, and the manor hall has a 15th-century peel tower whose large windows suggest that Clifton Manor was only partially fortified. The historical event that led to Clifton's fame and use in literature occurred in 1745, when the last battle to be fought on English soil took place here. The Scottish army of Prince Charles Edward, retreating northward through the village with the Duke of Cumberland's dragoons in close pursuit, was ambushed by a small force of Highlanders commanded by Lord George Murray; the parish register for December 19 records the burial of the six English dead. The prince's dead were buried, unrecorded, under a large oak known as the Rebel Tree, opposite Town End Farm. This is the battle described by Sir Walter Scott in *Waverley*:

They had passed a large open moor, and were entering into the enclosures which surrounded a small village called Clifton. The winter sun had set, and Edward began to rally Fergus upon the false predictions of the Gray Spirit. . . . Mac-Ivor, with a smile . . . casting his eyes back on the moor, a large body of cavalry was indistinctly seen to hover upon its brown and dark surface. To line the enclosures facing the open ground and the road by which the enemy must move from it upon the village, was the work of a short time.

CLIFTON HAMPDEN, Oxfordshire (pop. 476) The small and isolated Thames-side village of Clifton Hampden with its proper thatched-roof and old-timbered cottages is just 3½ miles southeast of Abingdon and had no claim to literary fame until Jerome K. Jerome found it useful for his *Three Men in a Boat*. From the yew hedge along the banks of the Thames the Barley Mow Inn can be seen on the opposite bank, but the inn is in Berkshire while Clifton Hampden is in Oxfordshire. Jerome and the men tie up at the landing stage at the thatched waterside inn opposite the village:

The "Barley Mow" . . . is, without exception . . . the quaintest, most old-world inn up the river. It stands on the right of the bridge, quite away from the village. Its low-pitched gables and thatched roof and latticed windows give it quite a story-book appearance, while inside it is even still more once-upon-a-timeyfied.

It would not be a good place for the heroine of a modern novel to stay at. The heroine of a modern novel is always "divinely tall," and she is ever "drawing herself up to her full height." At the "Barley Mow" she would bump her head against the ceiling each time she did this.

It would also be a bad house for a drunken man to put up at. There are too many surprises in the way of unexpected steps down into this room and up into that. . . .

CLIFTON REYNES, Buckinghamshire (pop. 120) A small village on the Ouse River a mile east of Olney, Clifton Reynes has a church with a battlemented tower that reminds one of more perilous times. William Cowper, who lived in Olney, was often a guest at the manor house after he met Lady Austen in the summer of 1781 and describes the winter walk past the water mill in *The Task*:

On the flood,
Indurated and fix'd, the snowy weight
Lies undissolved; while silently beneath,
And unperceived, the current steals away.
Not so, where scornful of a check it leaps
The mill-dam, dashes on the restless wheel,
And wantons in the pebbly gulf below:
No frost can bind it there; its utmost force
Can but arrest the light and smoky mist
That in its fall the liquid sheet throws wide.
And see where it has hung the embroider'd banks
With forms so various, that no powers of art,
The pencil or the pen, may trace the scene!
Here glittering turrets rise, upbearing high
(Fantastic misarrangement!) on the roof
Large growth of what may seem the sparkling trees
And shrubs of fairy land. The crystal drops
That trickle down the branches, fast congeal'd,
Shoot into pillars of pellucid length,
And prop the pile they but adorn'd before.

CLIVE, Shropshire (pop. 387) Like many hamlets of medieval origin, Clive is grouped around its old manor house. Clive Hall, the ancient and now-enlarged manor house, was the home of the Wycherley family, which settled in this area as early as 1410, and was the birthplace of the dramatist William Wycherley sometime around 1640. No parish records are available to ascertain a more precise date. All Wycherley's childhood was spent here, and his education was probably managed at home. At the age of fifteen, he was sent from here to France before entering Queen's College, Oxford. Wycherley, as the eldest son, inherited the estate upon the death of his father in 1697 and continued to use and maintain it until after the turn of the 18th century.

CLOPHILL, Bedfordshire (pop. 909) Situated on the Ivel River 3½ miles east of Ampthill, the village of Clophill gives evidence of at least two earlier cultures. One is on the hill on the north side of the village, where the old Perpendicular church stands alone, and the other was probably prehistoric. After the Black Death of 1348 hit the village so severely that when no reliefs (death duties) were paid to the crown "because they are all dead through the pestilence," the old church was abandoned. An even earlier settlement lay southeast of the village at Cainhoe Castle, a massive earthwork mound, probably prehistoric, that was added to in Norman times. Nearby is Wrest Park, and the view of the disused piers at the entrance gateway and the great earthworks of Cainhoe are decidedly similar to Doubting Castle in John Bunyan's *The Pilgrim's Progress*. A sculpted griffin here intimidates anyone who dares scale the mound to Giant Despair's stronghold.

CLOVELLY, Devon (pop. 634) Part of the most spectacular coastal land in north Devon, Clovelly, 10 miles west of Bideford, has a showplace quality because of its setting in a narrow, lush combe between massive crags. The promontory is 300 feet high on its landward side and drops rapidly to the point where a lighthouse stands. Just beyond the lighthouse is a savage reef area which caused more than its share of wrecked ships. The High Street, which, like the rest of the village, admits no cars, drops 400 feet in a series of cobbled steps to the inn by the harbor. All transport is by donkeys, which carry the fish brought into the harbor up the High Street, the coal and provisions for the ships, and even the post. The houses, small, flower-bedecked, and seemingly precariously perched on the side of the hill, have been described as "a waterfall of cottages [which] meets the sea."

Charles Kingsley's father took the living here in 1830, to the dismay of young Charles, who had found the fenland and ghost-ridden Barnack rectory much to his liking. He spent the first summer exploring and studying wild flowers, sea life, and shells. Much later Kingsley described the village in an article for *Fraser's Magazine*. His most vivid memory, described in *Two Years Ago*, was that of a wrecked ship being badly pounded by storm waves. The family's first sight of the ship was in the daylight, and throughout the stormy night they stood on the shore watching the attempted rescue. A more pleasant aspect of the Clovelly area enters *Westward Ho!*, in which Kingsley mentions Freshwater, a cascade on the shore walk. "The Three Fishers" is also set here. Kingsley actually spent very little time here except for the school holidays from Clifton (Bristol), Gloucestershire, and in 1836 the family moved to Chelsea, London. The parish church contains a commemorative plaque.

Both Charles Dickens and Wilkie Collins were in Clovelly in November 1860 on a West Country tour

CLOVELLY   A tiny quay and a pebbled beach (and no vehicular traffic) make this fishing village as attractive now as it was when Charles Kingsley lived here from 1830 to 1836 while his father held this living.

gathering local color for the Christmas story for *Household Words*. Dickens used Clovelly in the 1860 issue of the magazine, only thinly disguising it as Steepways:

> [T]he village was built sheer up the face of a steep and lofty cliff. There was no road in it, there was no wheeled vehicle in it, there was not a level yard in it. From the sea-beach to the cliff top two irregular rows of white houses, placed opposite to one another, and twisting here and there, and there and here, rose, like the sides of a long succession of stages of crooked ladders. . . .

Collins also calls Clovelly Steepways in *A Message from the Sea*. The use of the same name supports the rather positive assertion that Dickens wrote the first chapter of this work.

CLUN, Shropshire (pop. 1,774) This western area of Shropshire, with wild moorland and the Clun Forest, borders on Radnorshire, Wales, and is thereby border country. Clun held an extensive Bronze Age community, one of the oldest settlements in the country. At Pen y Wern, 1½ miles to the southeast, are the ruins of an extensive stone circle with an enormous monolith that crown a 1,258-foot-high hill. And just a little farther southeast are earthwork remains of a 12-acre hill fort said to have been the camp of Caratacus (Caractacus) before his last battle against the Romans at Bucknell. Defeated first at the Medway River, Caratacus rallied the Silures (south Wales and western England) and the Ordovices (north Wales and western England), but the combined forces were defeated. Robert Graves's *Claudius the God* relates a version of the story of the defeat.

The Normans then settled the town and in the 12th century built a castle high on the hill as a defense against the Welsh invaders. Part of the keep, three sides of the old tower, and portions of two round bastions are all that remain. Sir Walter Scott is thought to have used Clun Castle as Garde Douloureuse, from which Eveline Berenger is rescued by Hugo de Lacy, Constable of Chester, in *The Betrothed*. Scott describes the castle as so strongly built and fortified by art that it is totally impregnable:

> The river, whose stream washes on three sides the base of the proud eminence on which the castle is situated, curves away from the fortress and its corresponding village on the west, and the hill sinks downward to an extensive plain, so extremely level as to indicate its alluvial origin.

This is the area so intimately associated with A. E. Housman and, most especially, *A Shropshire Lad*. The opening lines of the fiftieth song immortalize four small villages here, of which Clun is the westernmost:

> Clunton and Clunbury,
>   Clungunford and Clun,
> Are the quietest places
>   Under the sun.

Shropshire natives argue that this stanza is actually a local ditty of much earlier vintage and that *quietest* becomes *prettiest, drunkenest,* and *wickedest* as circumstances require.

CLUNBURY, Shropshire (pop. 713) Located on the Clun River 4½ miles east of the village of Clun, Clunbury is dominated by Clunbury Hill with its prehistoric menhir known as the Fairy Stone, a deposit from the Ice Age glaciers. The valley in which Clunbury lies is rich, fertile land and is covered with extensive orchards. This is part of the area A. E. Housman made use of in *A Shropshire Lad*, and the village is one of four named as "the quietest places/ Under the sun."

COBHAM, Kent (pop. 955) Cobham, a little more than 3 miles west of Rochester, is a pleasant village with a relatively large number of important buildings: Cobham Hall (Tudor) with its park; Owletts, a 17th-century brick mansion with an outstanding ornate plaster ceiling dated 1684 above the stairwell; and the church, which contains possibly the most celebrated collection of medieval brasses in England. The chancel is literally paved with brasses, fifteen in all, the earliest dated 1299, with a Norman-French inscription to Dame Jone de Cobham.

Across from the church is the half-timbered Leather Bottle Inn, immortalized by Charles Dickens in the *Pickwick Papers*. Mr. Pickwick, Mr. Winkle, and Mr. Snodgrass find Mr. Tupman here after his flight from Dingley Dell. This "commodious village ale-house," Mr. Pickwick says, "for a misanthrope's choice . . . is one of the prettiest and most desirable places of residence"; and the three travelers

> entered a long low-roofed room, furnished with a large number of high-backed leather-cushioned chairs of fantastic shapes, and embellished with a great variety of old portraits and roughly-coloured prints of some antiquity. At the upper end of the room was a table, with a white cloth upon it, well covered with a roast fowl, bacon, ale, and et ceteras; and at the table sat Mr. Tupman. . . .

Dickens spent two days here in 1840 with John Forster and Daniel Maclise and later frequently walked with friends from Gadshill for refreshment. The room in which Tracy Tupman drowns his sorrows remains substantially the same except that it has become a veritable Dickens museum; the walls are covered with autograph letters, portraits, and engravings. Fortunately a fire on Good Friday in 1887 only partially destroyed the building, and the rebuilding, which slightly enlarged the structure, was kept basically to the original plan. It is near the inn that Mr. Pickwick discovers the Bill Stumps's stone, and the appropriate stone has since been placed in the proper location.

Dickens, often a guest of Lord Darnley's at the hall, was also a frequent visitor to Cobham Park and had a key that allowed him access at any time. Following Dickens's death at Gadshill, the Swiss chalet in which he did most of his writing was reerected in the grounds of Cobham Park, where it remained until 1961, when it was moved to Rochester.

COBHAM, Surrey (pop. 5,103) Cobham, Surrey, is often confused with Cobham, Kent, with its Dickensian associations, but if the proper designation Church Cobham were used for this Cobham, there would be no confusion. This town, which includes the adjoining hamlet of Street Cobham, is on the Mole River 6½ miles west of Epsom. William Wordsworth attended the partly Norman church here when visiting Francis Wrangham, the curate. Wordsworth felt a great deal of empathy for this man, who had been denied a fellowship at Trinity College, Cambridge, because of his outspoken views.

The church also contains a simple commemorative brass to Matthew Arnold, who lived at nearby Pain's Hill Cottage for fifteen years before his death in 1888 in Liverpool. Arnold's comfortable Victorian cottage was just west of the small 18th-century bridge. Arnold, styling himself "the hermit of the Mole," enjoyed the nearness of Pain's Hill's great cedars, the largest cedars in England; here the canary Mathias

> Saw the cedars of Painshill;
> Here he poured his little soul,
> Heard the murmurs of the Mole.

After four years' companionship Geist, Arnold's dog, was buried

> Between the holly and the beech,
> Where oft we watched thy couchant form,
> Asleep, yet lending half an ear
> To travellers on the Portsmouth Road.

Just above Arnold's cottage is Pain's Hill Mansion, surrounded by magnificent 18th-century gardens, which excited Horace Walpole's praise:

> All is great, and foreign, and rude; the walks seem not designed, but cut through the wood of pines; and the style of the whole is so grand ... that when you look down on this seeming forest, you are amazed to find it contains only a few acres.

COCKAYNE HATLEY, Bedfordshire (pop. 87) A tiny village, Cockayne Hatley is set down a lonely road 5½ miles northeast of Biggleswade. The original Cockayne family manor house long ago disappeared, but the church retains numerous monuments and fine 15th- and 16th-century brasses to the family. W. E. Henley had long been a friend of the Cockayne-Cust family, and he and his wife gained a great deal of strength from them when Margaret, the Henleys' only child, died in 1894. This is the child immortalized in Sir James Matthew Barrie's *Peter Pan* as Wendy; the name developed from her name for Sir James, "Fwendy." When Henley's health broke down after a railway carriage accident in 1903, he made arrangements to be buried here as well, and after he died in Woking, London, on June 11, his ashes were brought to Cockayne Hatley for interment.

COCKERMOUTH, Cumberland (pop. 4,838) One of the oldest Cumberland towns, firmly ensconced in Lakeland, though not itself on a lake, Cockermouth is situated at the confluence of the Cocker and Derwent Rivers 32 miles southwest of Carlisle and has a castle dating from 1134. William Wordsworth was born here on April 7, 1770, at Wordsworth House, an 18th-century building on Main Street. Wordsworth's father was an estate agent to Sir James Lowther, later 1st Earl of Lonsdale, and Wordsworth spent his early years here. The poet later refers to the town and the house many times, especially in *The Prelude:*

> For this, didst thou,
> O Derwent! winding among grassy holms
> Where I was looking on, a babe in arms,
> Make ceaseless music that composed my thoughts
> To more than infant softness, giving me

> Amid the fretful dwellings of mankind
> A foretaste, a dim earnest, of the calm
> That Nature breathes among the hills and groves?
> When he had left the mountains and received
> On his smooth breast the shadow of those towers
> That yet survive, a shattered monument
> Of feudal sway, the bright blue river passed
> Along the margin of our terrace-walk;
> A tempting playmate whom we dearly loved.

The terrace walk, mentioned here, and the garden with its "leafy shade" frequently appear in Wordsworth's poems. *The Prelude,* "The Sparrow's Nest," and "To a Butterfly" all include the garden described in a note to an 1801 poem:

> At the end of the garden of my father's house at Cockermouth was a high terrace that commanded a fine view of the river Derwent and Cockermouth Castle. This was our favourite playground. The terrace wall, a low one, was covered with closely clipt privet and roses, which gave an almost impervious shelter to birds who built their nests there.

It appears that Wordsworth attended the grammar school here for at least a few months, and probably longer, before being sent to school in Penrith and then to Hawkshead after his mother's death in 1778. The school, now gone, was run by the Rev. Joseph Gilbanks and was in the churchyard.

A favorite haunt was the ruined Cockermouth Castle, on a small hill only a few hundred yards up the Derwent from his father's garden; what remains dates mostly from the 13th and 14th centuries. The castle was besieged in the Civil War and partly dismantled; the gatehouse with 7-foot barbican walls, an inner gatehouse, a two-story roofless tower, a

COCKERMOUTH Now in the hands of the National Trust, Wordsworth House was the birthplace of both William and Dorothy Wordsworth; the house, with the Derwent flowing by the foot of the garden, enters into much of his poetry.

kitchen with two fireplaces, and two vaulted dungeons are among the remaining structures. Called by the poet "the shattered monument of feudal sway" in *The Prelude,* it is the subject of "Address from the Spirit of Cockermouth Castle":

"Thou look'st upon me, and dost fondly think,
Poet! that, stricken as both are by years,
We, differing once so much, are now Compeers,
Prepared, when each has stood his time, to sink
Into the dust. Erewhile a sterner link
United us; when thou, in boyish play,
Entering my dungeon, didst become a prey
To soul-appalling darkness. . . ."

Wordsworth left Cockermouth in 1784 after the death of his father; he returned with his sister Dorothy in the spring of 1794 on their way to Whitehaven and found that "all was in ruin, the terrace-walk buried and choked up with the old privet hedge which had formerly been so beautiful. . . ." There is a Wordsworth memorial in the 19th-century All Saints' Church, and a fountain in the park represents Dorothy as a child.

Other associations exist here as well. One of the early scholars at the grammar school was Fletcher Christian, leader of the mutiny on the *Bounty,* who was born at a nearby farmhouse, Moorland Close, in 1764 and spent his early life in this area. In the mid-19th century Ouida (Marie Louise de la Ramée) spent a holiday at Oakhurst on a hill above the Cocker; and Robert Louis Stevenson spent a few days here and at Keswick in 1871 and recorded his impressions in one of his travel essays, "Cockermouth and Keswick." It was here that he met the hatter Smethurst; having left his inn (unspecified), he

turned up a lane and found myself following the course of the bright little river. . . . I came to a dam across the river, and a mill—a great, gaunt promontory of building,—half on dry ground and half arched over the stream. The road here drew in its shoulders, and crept through between the landward extremity of the mill and a little garden enclosure, with a small house and a large signboard with its privet hedge. I was pleased to fancy this an inn, and drew little etchings in fancy of a sanded parlour, and three-cornered spittoons, and a society of parochial gossips seated within over their churchwardens; but as I drew near, the board displayed its superscription, and I could read the name of Smethurst, and the designation of "Canadian Felt Hat Manufacturers."

Sir Hugh Walpole, who lived at Brackenburn in Manesty Park, Keswick, used Cockermouth in his chronicle of the Herries family; the Sunwoods lived here on the edge of town, where "streets were narrow, ill-paved and of a certain odour." The bearbaiting that was a turning point in the life of Reuben Sunwood, the itinerant preacher, also took place here. Finally, the Italian-born Raphael Sabatini was a frequent visitor here and made this his summer home for a number of years before his death in 1950.

COLCHESTER, Essex (pop. 51,900) A location on the tidal part of the Colne River, probably more than anything else, has given Colchester more than 2,000 years of recorded history. The oldest town in England, Colchester faces open heathland to the north and heavy forests and agricultural lands to the east. Some sort of settlement existed here as early as the 7th century B.C.; Camulodonum lay a little west of the current town center on the south bank of the river and was the capital of the ruling Essex tribe, the Trinobantes. The city was ruled by Cunobelin, whose name Geoffrey of Monmouth alters to the now-better-known Cymbeline used by William Shakespeare, and Colchester is the "Royal Town" of the play *Cymbeline.*

The Romans under Claudius invaded the kingdom in A.D. 43. While Robert Graves's *Claudius the God* has Colchester not the initial target of the invasion, it almost certainly was. Graves says that the greatest battles were set in Romford, "along the London to Colchester road—not a road in the Roman sense of course," and that Colchester was given up after a brave stand "by a few old men and a number of women." Historians disagree, claiming that Camulodunum was the prime object of attack, and strong evidence exists of a fierce battle here. By A.D. 50, a *colonia* for retired soldiers had been established on a site adjacent to the original town, and a magnificent Roman temple, built to honor Claudius, stood on the site of the present Castle Museum.

Tradition claims Colchester's name came from the King or Earl Coel mentioned by Geoffrey of Monmouth, who calls the city Kaelcolim. It is this king who is commemorated in the nursery rhyme "Old King Cole" and who is supposed to be the father of St. Helena. The king is mythical, and his name is derived from that of the town; St. Helena, the mother of the emperor Constantine, has no association with Colchester except as its patron saint.

By 1086 the town's population exceeded 1,000, and its Norman castle may have been built by then. By the end of the 11th century the castle existed; today only the keep remains, but it is the largest Norman keep ever built. It is thought that, excluding the Tower of London, Colchester Castle was the first permanently occupied castle in England. By the mid-15th century the castle had become the strongest Essex prison, and in this role it is most famous for a prisoner who was able to escape. Sir Thomas Malory was imprisoned here on October 16, 1454; after committing a series of crimes in Essex, he and John Aleyn broke into a house belonging to John Grene and were caught trying to escape with coffers and chests. Malory escaped on October 30, was apprehended on November 18, and was taken to Marshalsea Prison in London. Colchester tradition maintains that *Le Morte d'Arthur* was begun here, but the conflicting biographical evidence and internal evidence relating to sources suggest a date more closely aligned with Malory's intermittent London imprisonment from 1456 to 1470. After its use as a prison the castle was allowed to fall into partial ruin, and the sale to a 17th-century land speculator and contractor brought about its systematic destruction.

By the 15th century the boundaries of the city expanded, its economic position was enhanced, and it had a thriving religious community. There were a number of important priories, abbeys, and churches: St. Botolph's, an Augustinian foundation, near the south gate; St. John's, on the Mersea Road; St. Leonard's on the Hythe; the Crouched (Crutched) Friars, on Crouch Street; and an enormous scattering of parish churches. Colchester became a clothmaking center by the 13th century, but the dissolution of the monasteries in the 16th century and the simultaneous decline of the cloth trade brought on difficult times; only an influx of Dutch and Flemish clothmakers saved the local industry. This was the environment into which Samuel Harsnett was born, probably in 1561; the son of a pastrycook whose business was located near the Church of St. Botolph, Harsnett was born in that parish, and the parish register for 1561 records his baptism. The church contains a commemorative window that portrays him preaching before Elizabeth I outside St. Paul's Cathedral in London. He probably attended the grammar school in Colchester before going up to Cambridge in 1575, and he returned in March 1587 when he was named headmaster of the grammar school; he remained for eighteen months. He was in the town occasionally after being made archdeacon of Essex in 1603. Harsnett always retained an affection for Colchester and bequeathed his library of mainly theological material to the city in 1631; it is housed in the Harsnett Library Collection in the public library.

Even though the town was strongly Parliamentarian during the Civil War, it had to withstand a two-week siege by Cromwellian forces in 1648 because it had come into the hands of two Royalist commanders in the summer of that year. John Evelyn, who visited the town in July 1656, describes it as "wretchedly demolished by the late Siege." It was this siege that prompted Dr. Samuel Johnson to view the town "with veneration since it had withstood a siege for Charles I." With James Boswell, who was then on his way abroad, he stayed at the town's chief coaching inn, the White Hart Inn, which stood on the south side of the High Street at the present-day Bank Passage.

Daniel Defoe's *Moll Flanders* (1722) sets one of its earliest scenes in this town. Moll states, "It was at Colchester, in Essex, that those people [the Gypsies] left me.... I was now in a way to be provided for...." Only eight years old, she was "put to nurse," and eventually was taken in by the wife of the mayor. Defoe includes no description of the town, but his knowledge of it was intimate from his explorations for *A Tour thro' the Whole Island of Great Britain*. Jane and Ann Taylor, the authors of *Rhymes for the Nursery*, which includes "Twinkle, Twinkle, Little Star," lived at 11 and 12 West Stockwell Street when their father was minister of the Congregational Church in St. Helen's Lane. In more recent times H. G. Wells uses the town in "Mr. Brisher's Treasure"; it is here that Brisher hires a trap.

COLEORTON, Leicestershire (pop. 726)   It is only 3 miles from Ashby-de-la-Zouch to Coleorton, where the lovely 14th-century church contains monuments of the Beaumonts, owners of Coleorton Hall, located on the west side of Charnwood Forest. This was the home of the Leicestershire Beaumont family, one of the few noted English families that predates William the Conqueror and one that has produced prodigious warriors, judges, poets, patrons of poets, and benefactors of the National Gallery. George Howland Beaumont, 7th Baronet, who had known Samuel Johnson and been a close friend of Sir Joshua Reynolds, made his lasting contribution to literature in 1806, when he became a benefactor and friend to William Wordsworth. (The two men became ac-

quainted initially through Beaumont's concern for Samuel Taylor Coleridge, and Beaumont bought property for Wordsworth at the foot of Skiddaw because he believed that Wordsworth's proximity to Coleridge would help both poets.) Wordsworth had discovered that the house in Grasmere, Dove Cottage, was too small for his burgeoning family and accepted Sir George's offer of Hall Farm here for the autumn and winter of 1806–1807.

This was a period of intense activity for Wordsworth; he prepared *Poems in Two Volumes* for publication and worked on "Song at the Feast of Brougham Castle." Coleridge also spent some time here in this period; he parted from his wife Sarah and brought Hartley to Coleorton just before Christmas, 1806. He stayed until April and wrote "An Angel Visitant" for Sara Hutchinson, Mary Wordsworth's sister:

Within these circling hollies woodbine clad—
Beneath this small blue roof of vernal sky—
How warm, how still! Tho' tears should dim mine eye,
Yet will my heart for days continue glad,
For here, my love, thou art, and here am I!

Wordsworth journeyed to London in April for a month's stay and returned with Sir Walter Scott, who visited for a short time. As well as believing Wordsworth to be an exceptional poet, Lady Beaumont was quite confident of his gardening abilities and asked him to lay out her winter garden, which is kept as the poet had it made up. He also wrote a large number of inscriptive verses for the gardens here, including "In the Grounds of Coleorton, the Seat of Sir George Beaumont, Bart., Leicestershire":

The embowering rose, the acacia, and the pine,
Will not unwillingly their place resign;
If but the Cedar thrive that near them stands,
Planted by Beaumont's and by Wordsworth's hands.
One wooed the silent Art with studious pains:
These groves have heard the Other's pensive strains;
Devoted thus, their spirits did unite
By interchange of knowledge and delight.
May Nature's kindliest powers sustain the Tree,
And Love protect it from all injury!
And when its potent branches, wide out-thrown,
Darken the brow of this memorial Stone,
Here may some Painter sit in future days,
Some future Poet meditate his lays....

Wordsworth returned on numerous occasions, in 1818 on his way from London and in the autumn of 1820 after being in Cambridge. On this trip he wrote the King's College sonnets and conceived the idea for the *Ecclesiastical Sonnets* while walking and talking with Beaumont in the grounds. His final trip here in 1841, when he also visited Grace Dieu Priory in Belton, occurred long after Sir George's death when the house had been bought by the Merewethers. Beaumont, whose generosity to the National Gallery resulted in its acquisition of two Rembrandts, also made provision for Wordsworth to receive £100 a year for life for an annual holiday.

Among other visitors to Coleorton Hall and the Beaumonts were Lord Byron, Robert Southey, John Constable, and Sir David Wilkie, whose *Blind Fiddler* Sir George also bequeathed to the nation. There is a memorial to Francis Beaumont in the garden.

COLERNE, Wiltshire (pop. 912) Situated 5 miles northeast of Bath on the Wiltshire-Gloucestershire border, Colerne is quite close to the old Fosse Way. This area was heavily settled by the Romans, for whom Bath was a regional center. The area produced excellent stonemasons and woodcraftsmen over the years, and the parish church holds fine examples of their work. Colerne was the birthplace, around 1446, of the great Renaissance scholar William Grocyn; the date was determined by the rolls of Winchester College, where he was described as *filius teneris de Colerna* in 1463. The college had property here, and his father is thought to have been a copyholder. Euridge Farm, a mile from the town, was one of the Dorset, Wiltshire, and Somerset manors granted to Sir Walter Ralegh before his fall from favor. He lived here only occasionally, preferring his country home in Sherborne, Dorset.

COLESHILL, Buckinghamshire (pop. 560) Although Coleshill is almost a part of Amersham, its larger neighbor 1 mile to the northeast, at one time the village was neither in Buckinghamshire nor on its border. Until 1832 it was a small detached part of Hertfordshire, as Hertfordshire House, 1 mile southwest of the village, recalls. The manor house here was the birthplace of the poet Edmund Waller on March 3, 1606, and he was baptized in the parish church at Amersham. Waller does not appear to have lived here very long before his family's removal to Beaconsfield.

An earlier association exists with Sir Thomas Malory, who was imprisoned here in July 1451 after attacking Humphrey Stafford, 1st Duke of Buckingham at Combe Abbey, Warwickshire. Malory escaped after only two nights in jail.

COLWALL, Herefordshire (pop. 2,043) On the western slopes of the Malvern Hills 4 miles northeast of Ledbury, Colwall is an ideal center for touring and walking the Malverns. Just south of the village on the northern edge of the range of hills was Hope End, the estate bought by Elizabeth Barrett's father late in 1809 or early in 1810; the house was later described by the poet as a "Turkish house . . . crowded with minarets and domes, and crowned with metal spires and crescents." The house was a large one with twenty bedrooms, many of which had elaborately carved marble fireplaces; "Elizabeth's room," as it was known, had a large stained-glass window. Elizabeth Barrett was educated at home and by the age of eight was reading Homer in the original; "The Greeks," she said, "were her demi-gods." Life here was happy until around 1820, when she somehow suffered a spinal injury after trying to saddle her mount alone; the next few years were spent almost wholly in bed. Essentially bankrupt after his wife's death, Barrett sold the estate, and on August 23, 1832, the family left for Sidmouth, Devonshire, before finally settling in London.

"The Deserted Garden" recalls Elizabeth Barrett Browning's childhood pleasure at Hope End and her sanctuary in the woods, while "The Lost Bower" tells of finding a glade of "fresh and dewy glitter" and resolving to return to it daily, but she never found it again:

> Green the land is where my daily
> Steps in jocund childhood played—

> Dimpled close with hill and valley,
> Dappled very close with shade;
> Summer-snow of apple blossoms, running up
> from glade to glade. . . .

> On your left, the sheep are cropping
> The slant grass and daisies pale;
> And five apple-trees stand, dropping
> Separate shadows toward the vale. . . .

"Aurora Lee" also describes Hope End and the scenery.

COMBE ABBEY, Warwickshire The Warwickshire seat of the Earl of Craven, Combe Abbey, 4 miles east of Coventry, is closest to the village of Binley and is often generally located there. The abbey, founded in 1150 by the Cistercians, was one of the three great monastic houses in Warwickshire and was extremely prosperous up to the dissolution of the monasteries, when it was granted to John Dudley, Earl of Warwick and Duke of Northumberland. The abbey reverted to the crown after his execution in 1553 and was purchased by a lawyer, Sir Robert Kelway, whose daughter Anne brought the estate to the 1st Baron Harington by marriage; this was the Lord Harington to whom James I entrusted Princess Elizabeth's care. After both Harington's death and his son's, the abbey passed to his daughter Lucy, whose extravagance so outstripped her means that she was forced to sell the estate. It was then that Elizabeth, Lady Craven became its owner. The estate remained in the family until 1968, when it was auctioned at Sotheby's. The abbey and grounds have been open as a public recreation area since 1966.

Literary associations here go back to the 15th century, when the Cistercians still held the abbey, and place Sir Thomas Malory in an uncertain light. A King's Bench warrant dated January 4, 1450, declares that Malory and twenty-six others waited, fully armed, in the woods of Combe Abbey intending to murder Humphrey Stafford, 1st Duke of Buckingham. The reason for the attack is not at all clear, for the two men had been colleagues, serving together on a royal commission in 1445 and 1446. Malory was not arrested until July 25, 1451, and was taken before the King and his Council and imprisoned at Coleshill, from which he escaped two nights later by swimming the moat. He returned to Newbold Revel, gathered his men, and in a rage "in the manner of an insurrection" forced his way into the abbey on July 28. Malory and his band broke into two chests and two bags, gaining about £46 in gold and silver coins, and took ornaments and jewels valued at more than £40 which belonged to Abbot Richard. Then, the charge states, they carried out "in great destruction and spoliation of the monastery and abbey aforesaid." The next night, they smashed eighteen doors and broke into three iron chests; their two incursions netted them the equivalent of £7,000. Of Combe Abbey today the cloisters and a door leading to the chapter house remain.

COMBE FLOREY, Somerset (pop. 215) The rolling, wooded Quantock Hills, covering 72 square miles, possibly compose the most attractive area in Somerset. There are no towns or large villages to speak of, and the hamlets and scattered farmlands nestle in heather-covered moors, populated with red deer and covered with flowers in season. Appropriately, Combe Florey is a beautiful sandstone village in the heart of the hills. For fifteen years this was the home of the Rev. Sydney Smith, the witty author of *The Letters of Peter Plymley* and the man who Thomas Babington Macaulay claimed was "the greatest master of ridicule since Dean Swift." While Smith's first reaction to his "exile" in Combe Florey was not favorable, immured, he termed it, in "a kind of healthy grave," when he moved into the Old Rectory in 1829, he became attached to his rural parish, although he never quite lost the feeling that "creation would expire before bedtime." He traveled from here to Taunton to speak on the inability of the House of Lords to act on reform and told the story of Mrs. Partington of Sidmouth, who attempted to stem the surges of the Atlantic: "She was excellent at a slop or puddle, but should never have meddled with a tempest." Becoming ill in 1844, Smith left Combe Florey for London, where he died on February 22, 1845. His parishioners erected the commemorative east window in the church.

More recently Combe Florey was the home of Evelyn Waugh, who lived at the manor house from 1956 until his death. Apparently the house and gardens suited the novelist and his quite large family very well, and Waugh enjoyed puttering in the gardens here just as he had done at Piers Court, Stinchcombe, in Gloucestershire. The novelist died here on April 10, 1966.

CONINGSBY, Lincolnshire (pop. 1,031) In the flat fen country in the triangular area appropriately known as Parts of Holland, Coningsby, 9 miles southwest of Horncastle, is noted for the Church of St. Michael and All Angels and its unique 17th-century clock, 16½ feet in diameter and beautifully colored; it has only an hour hand, as was common before the mid-17th century, but the dial is so large that accuracy is possible to five minutes. The Old Rectory is medieval with later additions. Two of the 18th-century incumbents were literary men. Laurence Eusden, often described as the most undistinguished Poet Laureate England ever had, was presented with this living sometime in 1725; he gained the laureateship through the influence of the 1st Duke of Newcastle and wrote insipid verse that was often held up to ridicule. He kept the post here until his death on September 27, 1730. A letter from the poet Thomas Gray describes the Poet Laureate as "a person of great hopes in his youth, though at last he turned out a drunken parson."

John Dyer took the living in 1752 and wrote *The Fleece* here, where he remained until his death in 1758. He was buried in the church, but there is no memorial.

CONISBOROUGH, Yorkshire (pop. 17,190) Conisborough is midway between Doncaster and Rotherham, and its castle dates from about 1180. An earlier structure on the same site was a favorite residence of William the Conqueror (r. 1066–1087). The roofless Norman keep is the oldest surviving round keep in England; the curtain walls dominate the town, and the deep, tree-lined moat is impressive. This whole area next to the Don River figures in Sir Walter Scott's *Ivanhoe*. This is the home of the poor fool Wamba and of the Copmanhurst religious, and Conisborough Castle itself is the home of Athelstane the Unready. Scott writes:

> There are few more beautiful or striking scenes in England than are presented by the vicinity of this ancient Saxon fortress. The soft and gentle river Don sweeps through an amphitheatre, in which cultivation is richly blended with woodland, and on a mount ascending from the river, well defended by walls and ditches, rises this ancient edifice, which, as its Saxon name implies, was, previous to the Conquest, a royal residence. . . .

This wooded hill, about a ten-minute walk from the castle, is the scene of the funeral feast. The tiny hexagonal oratory in the castle is the one from which the revived Athelstane emerges, still in his grave clothes. The threat to hang the fat abbot in cope and stole at the top of the castle can be reconstructed vividly, but the stairs would have proved a tight fit for his portly body.

CONISTON, Lancashire Lying at the northwestern extremity of Coniston Water, Coniston is at the foot of the Old Man and central to the section of Lancashire considered to belong to the Lake District. Coniston Water was the first lake that William Beckford visited on his tour of England from August to October 1779, and the hall, "a ruinated place, as my driver told me, [which] was inhabited by a very ancient man," and its setting intrigued him:

> All down the steeps appeared trunks of decayed trees of the strangest shapes imaginable, whose appearance [in] this misty and showery weather was almost formidable; they seemed to me like spectres frowning upon the pass below.

In 1850, after their June wedding, Alfred Tennyson and his new bride spent part of their honeymoon at Tent Lodge, "the little villa on Coniston Water." He writes:

> We only arrived here last night. Mr. Marshall's park looked as lovely as the Garden of Eden, as we descended the hill to this place. We have a very beautiful view from our drawing-room windows, crag, mountain, woods and lake, which look especially fine as the sun is dropping behind the hills.

Here for the first time Mrs. Tennyson met Thomas Carlyle, who called on the newlyweds at Tent Lodge. A second visitor who stayed for a short time was Coventry Patmore. The Tennysons declined the offer of Tent Lodge as a permanent home but were here again in 1856, when they were visited by Lewis Carroll (Charles Lutwidge Dodgson).

In 1871 John Ruskin bought Brantwood, the house that he said had "the finest view I know in Cumberland or Lancashire," and began to lead a somewhat secluded life. It was a damp country cottage in a state of partial decay, but he spent thousands of pounds in enlarging and repairing it. He added the dining room, studio, tower, and gateway, planted the mile-long grounds beside the lake, and built a harbor. Here he began *Fors Clavigera*, a monthly missive "to the workmen and labourers of Great Britain." From 1870 to 1879 and again in 1883 and 1884 Ruskin commuted from here to Oxford, where he was Slade Professor of Art; around 1878 he adopted a life of seclusion. After the opening of the Grosvenor Gallery, Ruskin attacked James McNeill Whistler's *Nocturnes:* "I never expected to hear a young coxcomb ask two hundred guineas for flinging a pot of paint in the public's face." Whistler brought action for libel, and the jury awarded a settlement of

CONISTON   On the eastern shore of Coniston Water, Brantwood was "a mere shed of rotten timber and loose stone" when John Ruskin purchased the property in 1871. The thousands of pounds and years of work he lavished on the estate turned Brantwood into the magnificent structure it is today.

1 farthing for damages. Ruskin's physical and mental health began to deteriorate seriously in 1887, and he finished his last writing, a chapter in *Praeterita*, in June 1889. On January 18, 1900, he contracted influenza and died two days later. He was buried in the churchyard here on January 25; his grave is marked by a cross carved on all four sides. Ruskin's home is now a museum and is open to the public. Ruskin took a great deal of interest in the Coniston Museum, which now contains such memorabilia as his early drawings and sketches, manuscripts and notebooks, walking stick, box of paints and brushes, and an annotated 14th-century Greek manuscript of the Psalms.

Across the lake from Ruskin's home is a medieval manor that was held by the Countess of Pembroke, "Sidney's sister, Pembroke's mother." Tradition says that Sir Philip Sidney visited the manor.

COOKHAM, Berkshire (pop. 5,848) On the banks of the Thames River 3 miles north of Maidenhead, Cookham is often erroneously believed to be the childhood home of Kenneth Grahame. Indeed, he knew this area well, but he lived in the nearby hamlet of Cookham Dean. However, the village of Cookham was the home of the Young family, of which the most famous member was Sir George, who as a young man fought with Gen. James Wolfe at Quebec. A later Sir George and his family played host to Virginia Stephen (Woolf) at their home, Formosa Place, during the greater part of July 1905.

COOKHAM DEAN, Berkshire (pop. 1,135) Here the Thames River is at its finest with great beechwood forests on gentle hills reaching the banks of the widening river on the east side and level meadows stretching along the west bank. Cookham Dean, a relatively unspoiled village 3 miles north of Maidenhead and east of the parent village of Cookham, was the childhood home of Kenneth Grahame. When his mother died from scarlet fever in 1864, the five-year-old boy was sent here to live with his grandmother, Mrs. John Ingles, at The Mount. Kenneth had also caught scarlet fever, and the disease left him with severe recurring bronchial problems. His father was an alcoholic, and consequently his grandmother, from all accounts a formidable woman of sixty, took on the job of managing the Grahame children. The house, still "beautiful and spacious," was originally a hunting box, and the grounds, which contain a venerable tree marking the edge of Windsor Forest, cover several acres and were ideally suited for childhood wandering. The house contains an area known as the Gallery that was the private domain of the children. Here was their imaginary city, which keeps turning up in the author's work. Grahame's schooling with private tutors and teachers also took place in the Gallery. He left Cookham Dean in the spring of 1866 and spent a short period in Cranbourne before his father summoned him to Edinburgh. The sojourn there lasted only one year.

Almost forty years later, in May 1905 just before retiring from his secretaryship at the Bank of England, Grahame and his wife took a furnished house here called Hillyers, and he began reworking *The Wind in the Willows*. While the Thames-side area obviously provided material for the work, it is not the only locale that influenced the author. The topography of the work is a jumble: Toad Hall is a combination of the manor houses at Harleyford, Mapledurham, and Cliveden; Cookham and Cookham Dean are placed in Cornwall; and the Thames flows into Fowey toward the sea. In August 1907 the Grahames moved into a new house, Mayfield, a sprawling building with a large garden and paddock; the house is now a school. Grahame resigned from the bank in June 1908 and moved to Blewbury in 1910.

COOLING, Kent (pop. 190) In the midst of marshland on the Hoo Peninsula, Cooling has associations with both William Shakespeare and Charles Dickens. The 14th-century Cooling Castle was an early home of the Cobham family, a member of which married the Lollard Sir John Oldcastle, the model for Shakespeare's Falstaff. Oldcastle was considerably more influential than most Lollards, as John Wycliffe's followers were contemptuously called, and his efforts to effect conversions throughout Kent and, in particular, his effort to convert Prince Hal resulted in an accusation of heresy, for which he was tried, convicted, and burned as a heretic—thus he was not the comic character whose name Shakespeare is pressured to change to Falstaff. In fact, in the Epilogue to *Henry IV: Part II* Shakespeare apologizes

> for anything I know, Falstaff shall die of a sweat, unless already he be killed with your hard opinions; for Oldcastle died a martyr, and this is not the man.

The Dickensian association with Cooling is an important one, for this is the village Dickens claimed was Pip's village in *Great Expectations*. Here, in the midst of the dreary marshes, is Pip's home with the Gargerys:

> Ours was the marsh country, down by the river, within, as the river wound, twenty miles of the sea. My first most vivid and broad impression of the identity of things, seems to me to have been gained on a memorable raw afternoon towards evening. At such a time I found out for certain, that this bleak place overgrown with nettles was the churchyard . . . and that the dark flat wilderness beyond the churchyard, intersected with dykes and mounds and gates, with scattered cattle feeding on it, was the marshes; and that the low leaden line beyond was the river; and that the distant savage lair from which the wind was rushing, was the sea; and that the small bundle of shivers growing afraid of it all and beginning to cry, was Pip.

The churchyard at Cooling contains a row of thirteen quite curious gravestones commemorating the Comport family with one large headstone recording the dates. This, of course, was the source of the "five little stone lozenges, each about a foot and a half long, which were arranged in a neat row beside their grave, and were sacred to the memory of five brothers" of Pip. Close to the churchyard is a row of cottages that have been identified as the original of Joe Gargery's forge. The local inn, known as the Horse and Castle, is supposed to have been the prototype of the Three Jolly Bargemen.

COOMBE BISSETT, Wiltshire (pop. 248)   In a remote area on the edge of the downs 3 miles southwest of Salisbury, Coombe Bissett has an old stone arched packhorse bridge across the Ebble River, a 13th-century church, and many old cottages. Coombe Bissett Hill becomes Bissett Hill in Thomas Hardy's Wessex; the hill is the meeting place of Georgy and a "fine-looking young farmer" in "Incident in the Life of Mr. George Crookhill."

CORFE CASTLE, Dorset (pop. 1,402)   The village of Corfe, known by the name of its centuries-old castle, is in the Isle of Purbeck, an isolated peninsula southwest of Bournemouth, and is located on the side of a chalk hill, which is the site of the castle. In Anglo-Saxon and medieval times the entire isle was a royal chase, but by the end of Charles I's reign in 1649 no

large wild game were left, and none have come back. Not until the 10th century was the castle enlarged and fortified when it became King Edgar's (Eadgar's) principal residence.

Corfe has a grim history; Edgar's son Edward was murdered here in 978 by his stepmother, Elfrida, or her attendant, and King John preferred this castle, no doubt because of its inaccessibility, and used it as a prison. In one instance twenty-two knights and barons were starved to death in the dungeons here for espousing the cause of John's nephew Arthur. Later, Edward II was imprisoned here before his execution at Berkeley Castle in Gloucestershire on September 21, 1327. In the Civil War Corfe Castle withstood the initial Roundhead siege under the direction of Lady Bankes, wife of Sir John Bankes (a member of Charles I's Privy Council and also Chief Justice), but the treachery of a Colonel Pitman permitted Parliamentary troops to enter the grounds. The castle was taken, looted, and wrecked. The Bankes family moved to Kingston Lacey, near Wimborne Minster; Dr. Samuel Johnson, who is said to have stopped here on his trip through Devonshire with Sir Joshua Reynolds in 1762, visited the Bankeses at Kingston Lacey and not here, where the castle was a total ruin.

The starkness of the castle and the fickleness of the weather here come into Thomas Hardy's *The Hand of Ethelberta*, in which he calls the castle

CORFE CASTLE   High on a chalk hill on the Isle of Purbeck, Corfe Castle is used by Thomas Hardy as Corvsgate in *The Hand of Ethelberta*.

Corvsgate. Ethelberta starts along "a path on the shore where the tide dragged huskily up and down the shingle without disturbing it and then up the steep crest of land opposite. . . ." On the south side of the castle the day is warm and sunny while to the north the sky is dark and cloudy over the heath as she advances to explore the castle. "Once among the towers above, she became so interested in the windy corridors, mildewed dungeons, and the tribe of daws" that she becomes an imaginary part of history.

CORLEY, Warwickshire (pop. 405) Standing on a high spot with good views over the Warwickshire countryside, Corley is 4½ miles northwest of Coventry close to Corley Rock, an area that still shows traces of its prehistoric walls and terraced hillside. About a mile from the village is a Jacobean hall, now a farmhouse, which is supposed to be the model for Hall Farm in *Adam Bede* by George Eliot (Mary Ann Evans). A brick-enclosed garden stood in front of the house, and the entrance gate is flanked by a griffin *sejant guardant* on each upright. On the northwest side of the estate are a few remaining walnut trees, the last vestiges of "the grand double row" mentioned in the novel.

> Evidently that gate is never opened . . . and if it were opened, it is so rusty, that the force necessary to turn it on its hinges would be likely to pull down the square stone-built pillars, to the detriment of the two stone lionesses which grin with a doubtful carnivorous affability above a coat of arms surmounting each of the pillars. . . . [B]ut by putting our eyes close to the rusty bars of the gate, we can see the house well enough. . . .
> It is a very fine old place, of red brick, softened by a pale powdery lichen, which has dispersed itself with happy irregularity, so as to bring the red brick into terms of friendly companionship with the limestone ornaments surrounding the three gables, the windows, and the door-place. But the windows are patched with wooden panes. . . .

CORNHILL-ON-TWEED,   Northumberland (pop. 585) This border village on the Tweed River is as Scottish as it is English, and, in fact, its railway station is across the border in Coldstream. The river is spanned by an 18th-century bridge on which a 1926 plaque commemorates Robert Burns's first entry into England, on May 7, 1787; the plaque states that "kneeling, [he] prayed for a blessing on his native land in the words:—

> 'O Scotia! my dear, my native soil!
> For whom my warmest wish to heaven is sent!
> Long may thy hardy sons of rustic toil
> Be blest with health, and peace, and sweet content."

CORNWALL, Duchy of (pop. 341,746) A peninsula 75 miles long and, at the Devon border, 45 miles wide, Cornwall is joined to the mainland only by a 5-mile strip of land above the Tamar River, which separates it from Devon. Until the last half of the 19th century it remained isolated from the rest of England; Cornwall was for the Cornish alone, and the name Cornwall itself implied "foreign"; even today the insularity and remoteness of the county remains one of its interesting characteristics. Many of the Cornish still refer to Cornwall as the Duchy and say that they are "going up to England." And this remoteness, com-

bined with Celtic traditionalism, provided sufficient conditions for the Coming of Arthur and other myths. A good deal has been written on the Arthurian legend, much of which is highly speculative. To be sure, an Arthur did exist; further, the legend is generally acknowledged to belong to Celtic tradition, to have originated with the Celtic communities in Wales and Cornwall, and to have been essentially Cornish until the 11th or 12th century. The early references begin with a 7th-century fragment, "Gododin," in which Arthur is mentioned by name but in which his exploits are not enumerated. The next reference is in Nennius's 9th-century *Historia Britonum*, in which Arthur is described as *dux bellorum*, not as a king, and as the leader of twelve specified battles, the last of which is *mons Badonus*, where he received his "mortal wounds." To confuse the issue further, in the 6th century Gildas, a Welsh monk living near Glastonbury, wrote *De excidio Britanniae* (also known as *Liber Querolus*), in which he cites the Mount Badon battle but does not mention Arthur. These battles were fought between the Romanized Celts in Cornwall and the Saxon invaders.

From Nennius's time on the Arthurian legend became widespread. In the 10th-century Welsh *Annales Cambriae*, Arthur appears carrying "the cross of our Lord Jesus Christ on his shoulders" at the Battle of Badon; a full "historical" treatment was undertaken in the 12th century, when Geoffrey of Monmouth devotes two-fifths of *Historia Regum Britanniae* to a romantic treatment of Arthur, and he gives as his source "a certain very ancient book written in the British language" presented to him by Walter, archdeacon of Oxford, but no such work has been discovered. Along the same lines but even more curious is the evidence of the legend, predating Geoffrey, found 1,000 miles away in the Cathedral of Modena, Italy, where a semicircular frieze on the archivolt of the north doorway clearly presents Arthur and his knights.

The story begins on Tintagel Head with the remains of what is known as King Arthur's Castle (also called Tintagel Castle), sitting partly on the cliff and partly on a narrow spit of land where a Celtic monastery existed in what must have been Arthur's time. Here the events surrounding Arthur's birth took place, and a path leads from the castle to a shingle beach and what is alleged to be Merlin's Cave. The graves of Tristan and Iseult are said to be at Arthur's Castle, although much of that Arthurian legend is associated with the mythical land of Lyonnesse. Near the village of Pendoggett is a large encampment consisting of three concentric ramparts and ditches known as Tregeare Rounds or, locally, as Castle Damelioc. Here Gorlois, Duke of Cornwall and husband of Ygerna, was slain by Utherpendragon's men on the night that Uther, magically transformed into the image of Gorlois, seduced Ygerna.

Lyonnesse lies near the Isles of Scilly and supposedly stretched the 26-mile distance between Land's End and the isles and included St. Michael's Mount, near Penzance in Mount's Bay. Lyonnesse is thought to have disappeared into the sea because the land mass is subject to rapid subsidence here (the Isles of Scilly were one island during the Bronze Age, and the remains of walls are visible between the islands). It is possible that the area was a solid mass. Even in the

LAND'S END, CORNWALL   The most westerly point in England is the rocky tip of Cornwall known as
Land's End; 28 miles east of the Isles of Scilly (which can be sighted on a clear day), this area and those
isles are said to have been the solid land mass known as Lyonnesse during the days of King Arthur.

15th century, when Sir Thomas Malory wrote *Le
Morte d'Arthur,* island remains of Lyonnesse possibly
existed. Malory uses the area both as Lyonnesse,
where Tristan is born, and as the country of Surluse,
where "Galahalt, the haute prince," lived.

The end of the Arthur story also occurs in Cornwall. Mordred, who has usurped Arthur's land and
seduced and seized his Queen, is pushed back from
Richborough in Kent to the Camblan (Camel) River
at Camelford in Cornwall, where Mordred is killed
and Arthur mortally wounded: this is the *mons Badonus* mentioned by Nennius and Gildas; the fact
that no Mount Badon exists in the Camel River area
is only mildly disturbing, since battles are known to
have taken place near Bath and the Severn Estuary,
where there are numerous candidates for *mons Badonus* (Badbury, Badbury Hill, Cadbury, and Badbury
Rings). However, both Malory and Geoffrey of Monmouth place the pseudohistorical battle near here,
and the conclusion of the battle is assigned to the
water meadow near Slaughter Bridge just north of
Camelford, where there is also a small entrenchment
known as Arthur's Hall. Mortally wounded, Arthur
directs Sir Bedivere to dispose of Excalibur in a pond
nearby, and only after three attempts does the knight
successfully resolve to throw the sword away. Dozmary Pool, near Bolventor on Bodmin Moor, is the
most popular candidate for this episode. Loe Bar, the
usual second choice, is closer to the scene of the
battle and perhaps the more reasonable alternative.

The West Country supports other legends as well,
many with a more specific religious intent. St. Bur-
yan has a prehistoric ring of nineteen stones with two
menhirs (single upright stones) that tradition says
were pipers and nineteen young girls turned into
stone for dancing on the Sabbath. Saints' wells and
local saints are legion; in Looe, St. Keyne supposedly endowed her well with the medieval quality of
maisterie: whichever of two marriage partners first
drank its water would dominate the other. Drinking
the water of St. Ludgvan's Well near Marazion guaranteed that no child would commit murder, but it
guaranteed no such thing about adults. Water from
the well of St. Cleer on Bodmin Moor cured insanity
but did not prevent it. And, curiously enough, bathing in water from the well of St. Constantine would
bring on rain showers. These superstitions are by no
means extinct. Macabre legends likewise exist, and
among these is the story of Jan Tregeagle, a combination of the Faust legend and classical mythology.
Tregeagle sold his soul to the devil, but the Cornish
saints had mercy on him because he had performed a
single good deed in his lifetime. Consequently, his
spirit was set to such never-ending tasks as emptying
Dozmary Pool with a limpet shell having a hole in it
and weaving ropes of sand. However, the saints did
nothing to stop the pursuit of Tregeagle by demons,
and natives maintain that "Tregeagle moans"—the
wind does not sigh.

COTTERSTOCK, Northamptonshire (pop. 138)   On the
Nen River 2 miles north of Oundle, Cotterstock has
an early-17th-century hall, altered in 1658; E-shaped,
it stands back from the road, and on one side an avenue of elms extends to the river. John Dryden often
stayed here with Elizabeth Steward, his "honoured

cousin and very good friend." An attic room under the western gable was given over to him, and there he wrote many of his fables.

COVENTRY, Warwickshire (pop. 225,000)

In an area of heavy industrial and mining activity, the city of Coventry is a pleasant surprise with its flowered public parks and large, planned green spaces, a pleasing-enough reminder of the massive devastation here in World War II. Indeed, Coventry was battered so badly that the Germans coined the word *coventrated* for "destroyed." The most massive raid occurred on the night of November 14, 1940, when an estimated 400 bombers made their way back and forth over the city, dropping 3,000 incendiaries to illuminate their target, raining down 1,000 high explosive bombs, and parachuting down mines. By daybreak more than 50,000 buildings had been damaged; of the 1,000 or so in the city center, only a few were standing, and the cathedral was burned to the ground. An estimated 500 persons were killed, and twice that number were wounded. This was not the only raid on Coventry, and the end-of-war statistics are horrifying: forty-one raids, 5,566 properties destroyed and 50,479 damaged; and more than 1,200 persons killed, 800 of whom were buried in a mass grave at the London Road Cemetery. From all this arose the new Coventry, a model of civic planning with large green expanses, a new cathedral, and a few salvaged and carefully restored old buildings.

The war aside, the history of Coventry is an interesting one. The Danes ravished the area and the nunnery in the settlement by the Sherbourne River in 1016, but a new Benedictine monastery was founded on the same site by Leofric, Earl of Mercia and his wife Godiva (properly Godgifu) in 1043. It is from this period that the legend of Lady Godiva's ride dates, but the probably apocryphal tale did not emerge in literature until Roger of Wendover, historian to the Abbey of St. Albans between 1188 and 1236 wrote of it:

> The Countess Godiva, a true lover of the Mother of God, longed to free the town of Coventry (Conventrensam) from heavy bondage and servitude, and often . . . begged her husband . . . [to] free the town from that service and from all other heavy burdens.
>
> The Earl constantly refused and . . . forbade her evermore to speak to him again on the matter. Godiva however with womanly pertinacity never ceased to worry her husband on that matter until at last he answered and said, "Mount your horse naked, and ride through the market of the town from the beginning to the end when the people are assembled, and when you return, you shall have what you ask." To which Godiva, replying said, "And if I am willing to do this will you grant me leave?" "I will," he said. Then the Countess, cherished of God, attended by two soldiers, as is said before, mounted her horse naked, letting down her hair and tresses of her head so that her whole body was veiled except for her beautiful legs, and no one saw her as she traversed the market place.

Other accounts exist, but no single version dates the ride, and no contemporary version of it has been found. It is possible that some element of early folklore, especially connected with fertility rites, was the basis of the story or that a verbal misunderstanding occurred; if, for example, Godiva was said to have stripped herself of all her possessions, a 12th-century chronicler could have made the metaphorical statement into a literal one. Undoubtedly she was instrumental in freeing the citizens from a heavy tax, but that is about all that can be said. As far as the legendary Peeping Tom is concerned, he comes into the story far too late to lend it any authenticity; he first appears in the 17th century, when he opened a window "to see the Strange Case" and heard Lady Godiva's horse neigh. He also has been described as "a certain taylour" and "one prying slave."

The monastery in Coventry attracted fine craftsmen, and the town attracted merchants; medieval Coventry flourished, and the guild system had a particularly strong base from 1340 on. From the very inception of the system, the craft guilds gained fame for mystery plays performed on Corpus Christi Day and on other special occasions. There were ten plays in all, each performed in one of the city's ten wards (Gosford Street, Jordan Well, Much Park Street, Bayley Lane, Earl Street, Broadgate, Smithford Street, Spon Street, Cross Cheaping, and Bishop Street). The Coventry Cycle presents the greatest modern problems since the *Ludus Coventriae* was assigned its name in the 17th century; the plays in it have no relationship to the two extant (and authentic) plays in the Coventry Cycle. The *Ludus Coventriae* plays were performed on a Sunday, not the Thursday on which Corpus Christi Day falls; successive plays were given in successve years, and the dialect is that of the northeast Midlands, not of Coventry.

The true Coventry Cycle was performed on mobile carts of two stories (the upper the stage, and the lower the tiring room), which were moved from station to station, accompanied by the liveried craft companies, torchbearers, the mayor, other city dignitaries, and all the trappings of the church. In 1392 the company of smiths put on the trial, condemnation, and Crucifixion of Christ: the "tormentors" had gowns and hoods; God's coat was white leather, and he also had a girdle and a gilt peruke; the devil's mask had a hairy black leather covering; and Pontius Pilate wore a green silk gown, hat, and gloves. The Shearmen and Taylors Guild performed the Nativity, the flight into Egypt, and the murder of the innocents; most important, their repertoire included the song known today as "Lully lulla," the "Coventry Carol." The plays were performed yearly until 1580 and then sporadically until 1591, when they were discontinued. In modern times the two extant plays, the Nativity and the presentation of Jesus in the Temple, have been combined into one, which is performed in the ruins of Coventry Cathedral.

By the 15th century trade had expanded so that Coventry was nationally important, and its extensive walls, begun in 1355, posed a considerable threat to Henry VIII at the time of the dissolution of the monasteries. More than 18 inches thick and almost 3 miles long, they were an impressive defense. Toward the end of the 17th century the manufacture of watches, ribbons, and clocks began to supplant the dwindling cloth trade, and the 18th century saw the beginning of heavy industrialization. The first bicycle manufactured in England was made here, and, appropriately enough, so were the first automobile and the first Dunlop pneumatic tires. Today, many internationally known firms, including Dunlop, Massey Ferguson, Chrysler, Jaguar, Triumph, Courtaulds, and British Celanese, are located here.

Coventry is mostly modern, but a few old structures still exist. St. Mary's Hall, with an entrance on Bayley Lane, was built by the Merchant Guild of St. Mary in 1342 and originally was called the Hall of Our Lady. Next to the 18th-century Church of the Holy Trinity is Priory Lane with a number of black-and-white cottages, including the verger's house, which is said to date from the late 12th century. Of note architecturally is Spon Street, which is being redeveloped; indeed, old shops and dwellings from various parts of the city, which have been dismantled and stored, are being rebuilt here beam by beam alongside existing old buildings *in situ*.

The new cathedral designed by Sir Basil Spence can be called nothing less than a masterpiece; begun in 1954, it was linked to the ruins of the old cathedral. Indeed, a charred cross of burnt timbers which were salvaged from the debris marks the old high altar and has the words "Father Forgive" carved behind it. Inside hangs Graham Sutherland's tapestry, *Christ in Glory in the Tetramorph*, 38 feet wide and 74 feet high. On the wall of the Priory Street entrance is the 25-foot-high bronze *St. Michael and the Devil* by Sir Jacob Epstein.

Literary associations with Coventry are considerable. Sir Thomas Malory appears to have led an exemplary existence until some time around 1445, when he was in Parliament: for some reason, he then embarked on a course of lawlessness, including poaching, assault, extortion, rape, and attempted murder. It is under these circumstances that he became associated with Coventry. In July or August 1450 he was brought here to face a charge of rape, *cum ea carnaliter concubit*, the second time such a charge had been made, and was ordered, it appears, to jail; evidence of the punishment is sketchy. Again, late in July 1451, he was transported here from Newbold Revel after his arrest there on July 25; this time the charge was that of the attempted murder, some twenty months earlier, of Humphrey Stafford, 1st Duke of Buckingham, near Coombe Abbey. Malory was taken to Coleshill, Buckinghamshire, to await an appearance before the King and his Council.

A second early figure here was Michael Drayton, who was probably a page in the service of Sir Henry Goodere either here or at Polesworth; it seems most likely that he was in Coventry with the Gooderes when they lived here in 1572. Also probable is his attendance at the grammar school; indeed, Abraham Holland, son of the headmaster Philemon Holland, refers to Drayton's attendance in a manuscript now in the Bodleian Library. Drayton mentions Coventry in a number of poems and tells of Lady Godiva in *Poly-Olbion*:

Until the *Saxons* raigne, when *Coventry* at length,
From her small, meane regard, recovered state and
 strength,
ff. By *Leofrick* her Lord yet in base bondage held,
The people from her Marts by tollage who expeld:
Whose Dutchesse, which desir'd this tribute to release,
Their freedome often begg'd. The Duke, to make her
 cease,
Told her that if shee would his losse so farre inforce,

His will was, shee would ride starke nak't upon a horse
By day light through the street: which certainly he
 thought,
In her heroïck breast so deeply would have wrought,
That in her former sute she would have left to deale.
But that most princely Dame, as one devour'd with zeale,
Went on, and by that meane the Cittie cleerly freed.

A third Warwickshire native, William Shakespeare, also had associations with Coventry; it is usually asserted that as a boy Shakespeare saw some performance of the Coventry Cycle since his home at Stratford-on-Avon was only 27 miles away. Internal evidence from the plays—"It out-Herod's Herod" (*Hamlet*) and "What a Herod of Jewry is this!" (*The Merry Wives of Windsor*)—is usually cited as proof of this attendance. Of more significance is the use of Coventry in three of the histories. Gosford Green, just east of the 14th-century city, was the venue for the solution of many major political issues, and here the famous "nonduel" between Henry Bolingbroke, Duke of Hereford, and Thomas Mowbray, Duke of Norfolk, recorded in *Richard II* occurred. Here the lists took place, and King's Road, down which Richard walked, is now lined with modern houses and leads to a park. The men prepared for combat, Hereford on a white mount in green velvet and Norfolk on a charger in embroidered crimson velvet; they are ready to begin when Richard stops the duel and with his counselors determines the sentence: Bolingbroke, "we banish you our territories" for ten years; Mowbray, "I with some unwillingness pronounce:/ . . . never to return." Norfolk died in Venice in exile, but Hereford, who went to France for his ten years' exile, returned to England two years after banishment and was crowned Henry IV, successor to the deposed Richard II. The small remains of the once-large Gosford Green has a plaque commemorating the nonduel.

Two other plays make use of the town; in *Henry IV: Part I*, Falstaff and Bardolph are on Tamworth Road when Sir John says:

Bardolph, get thee before to Coventry; fill me a bottle of sack: our soldiers shall march through; we'll to Sutton-Cop-hill to-night.

(Sutton-Cop-hill is Sutton Coldfield.) Part of *Henry VI: Part III* takes place at the city walls; Lancastrians and Yorkists defy each other, and King Edward and Warwick finally resolve the difficulty:

King Edw. What, Warwick, wilt thou leave the town
 and fight?
Or shall we beat the stones about thine ears?
War. Alas, I am not copp'd here for defence!
I will away towards Barnet presently,
And bid thee battle, Edward, if thou dar'st.
King Edw. Yes, Warwick, Edward dares, and leads the
 way.
Lords, to the field: Saint George and victory.

John Evelyn, the first of the itinerant diarists to visit Coventry, in August 1654, was particularly charmed with the town. He records in his diary:

The next place was *Coventry*, where most remarkeable is the Crosse, for *Gotic* worke, & rich gilding. . . . This Citty, has many handsome Churches, a very beautifull Wall, a faire free-Schole & Librarie to it: the streetes full of great Shops, cleane & well pav'd.

In the early 18th century Daniel Defoe came to Coventry on the orders of Robert Harley, 1st Earl of Oxford; here he witnessed the riots accompanying the election and later testified about the rampant corruption and intimidation here. All this he documents in *A Tour thro' the Whole Island of Great Britain:*

> It was a very unhappy Time when I first came to this City . . . the Inhabitants (in short) enraged at one another, met, and fought a pitch'd Battle in the middle of the Street, where they did not take up the Breadth of the Street . . . upon a Shout given, as the Signal on both Sides, they fell on with such Fury with Clubs and Staves, that in an Instant the Kennel was cover'd on both Sides, and, in a Word, they fought with such Obstinacy that 'tis scarce credible.
>
> Nor were these the Scum and Rabble of the Town, but in short the Burghers and chief Inhabitants, nay even Magistrates, Aldermen, and the like.
>
> Nor was this one Skirmish a Decision of the Quarrel, but it held for several Weeks, and they had many such Fights. . . .

Defoe was not impressed with the town: the buildings were "very old and decayed," and the inhabitants were engaged in the "Weaving of Ribbons of the meanest Kind, chiefly Black." About 100 years later, William Cobbett pledged to stand for Coventry in the 1820 parliamentary election; the town had a freemen's franchise and a huge proportion of "out votes" and was, consequently, an expensive seat to contest. Cobbett lost badly, polling only 157 votes; he never mentions the town in *Rural Rides*.

In 1832 George Eliot (Mary Ann Evans) was sent to a school at 48 Little Park Street kept by Rebecca and Mary Franklin, the daughters of a Baptist clergyman. They fostered her musical abilities, but her intense shyness precluded any display of her talents. She left the school in December 1835 because of her mother's illness, but her associations with Coventry remained strong. In March 1841, upon his retirement, Robert Evans brought his daughter to Bird Grove, off Foleshill Road, a semidetached villa then on the outskirts of Coventry; here she met the Brays, who lived at Rosehill, St. Nicholas Street, over the canal and across the fields. They were characterized as freethinkers, and Mary Ann Evans eventually adopted their views to the extent that she refused to attend services with her father. She ultimately agreed to go to church but let it be clearly known that she could embrace neither doctrinal practices nor teaching. In this period at the Brays' home she met Robert Owen, Herbert Spencer, William Makepeace Thackeray, and Ralph Waldo Emerson; she had met Dante Gabriel Rossetti when she was in school. Years later her views of Coventry were used in *Felix Holt, the Radical;* the Rev. Rufus Lyon is a portrayal of the Reverend Franklin she knew in her school days, and Franklin's house in Chapel Yard almost exactly resembled that of the Reverend Mr. Lyon:

> Mr. Lyon lived in a small house, not quite so good as the parish clerk's adjoining the entry which led to the Chapel Yard. . . . He sat this morning, as usual, in a low up-stairs room, called his study, which, by means of a closet capable of holding his bed, served also as a sleeping room. The bookshelves did not suffice for his store of old books, which lay about him in piles so arranged as to leave narrow lanes between them. . . .

The church noted in the novel is the Church of St. Michael; the roads in the Radford area are named from George Eliot's novels (for example, Middlemarch Road and Bede Road), and the road where Bird Grove stands has been renamed George Eliot Road.

In June 1840 Alfred, Lord Tennyson visited Coventry; the fruit of the visit was his poem "Godiva." Tennyson noted in a letter to a friend "that the celebrated Lady Godiva was a reality and no myth":

> She sought her lord, and found him, where he strode
> About the hall, among his dogs, alone,
> His beard a foot before him, and his hair
> A yard behind. She told him of their tears,
> And pray'd him, "If they pay this tax, they starve."
> Whereat he stared, replying, half-amazed,
> "You would not let your little finger ache
> For such as *these?*"—"But I would die," said she.
> He laugh'd, and swore by Peter and by Paul,
> Then fillip'd at the diamond in her ear?
> "Oh ay, ay, ay, you talk!"—"Alas!" she said,
> "But prove me what it is I would not do."
> And from a heart as rough as Esau's hand,
> He answer'd, "Ride you naked thro' the town,
> And I repeal it." . . .

Tennyson even incorporates the aspect of Peeping Tom, though the poet does not remark on his reality:

> . . . one low churl, compact of thankless earth,
> The fatal byword of all years to come,
> Bore a little auger-hole in fear,
> Peep'd—but his eyes, before they had their will,
> Were shrivell'd into darkness in his head,
> And dropt before him. So the Powers, who wait
> On noble deeds, cancell'd a sense misused. . . .

The same story was incorporated into one of the *Imaginary Conversations* by Walter Savage Landor.

Charles Dickens was here in December 1858, as guest of honor at a public dinner at the Castle Hotel; he was presented with a gold repeater watch by the local watchmakers in gratitude for his efforts in raising funds for the Coventry Institute. He had done a reading of *A Christmas Carol* a year previously and commented, in acknowledging the testimonial:

> This watch, with which you have presented me, shall be my companion in my hours of sedentary working at home and in my wanderings abroad. It shall never be absent from my side, and it shall reckon off the labours of my future days. . . . And when I have done with time and its measurement, this watch shall belong to my children. . . . From my heart of hearts I can assure you that the memory of to-night, and of your picturesque and ancient city, will never be absent from my mind. . . .

He bequeathed the watch to John Forster. In *Pickwick Papers* the town is the first stop on the Birmingham-to-London stage, and here Mr. Pickwick, Bob Sawyer, and Sam Weller stop at an unnamed inn, probably the Castle:

> When they stopped to change at Coventry, the steam ascended from the horses in such clouds as wholly to obscure the hostler, whose voice was, however, heard to declare from the mist that he expected the first Gold Medal from the Humane Society on their next distribution of rewards, for taking the post-boy's hat off; the water descending from the brim of which, the invisible gentleman declared, must inevitably have drowned him (the post-boy) but for his great presence of mind in tearing

it promptly from his head and drying the gasping man's countenance with a wisp of straw.

There is a minor literary association with Angela Brazil, the children's writer, who came here to live in 1911; her brother had set up a medical practice, and his two sisters, Angela and Amy, resided with him at 1 The Quadrant. Miss Brazil died here in 1947.

COWES, Isle of Wight (pop. 18,002) There are two distinct towns named Cowes, separated by the Medina River; unfortunately, the distinction between East and West Cowes was seldom made until the 20th century. In most instances, however, it may be assumed that early references are to West Cowes since it is both the landing place for the mainland ferry and the yachting capital of Britain. Virtually every writer who has visited the Isle of Wight has been in Cowes, but two men in particular found the town especially attractive. Leaving the island and Carisbrooke on his way to Winchester in September 1817, John Keats stopped off here and was enchanted by the yachting center. Writing to Fanny Brawne, he comments:

> One of the pleasantest things I have seen lately was at Cowes. The Regent in his Yatch . . . was anchored opposite—a beautiful vessel—and all the Yatchs and boats on the coast, were passing and repassing it; and circuiting and taking about it in every direction—I never beheld anything so silent, light, and graceful.

A more active enthusiast was Edward FitzGerald, who sailed his schooner, the *Scandal*, out of Lowestoft and Aldeburgh in Suffolk. With one or two hands he often sailed down the East Anglia coast and around Dover. In June 1866 he sailed into Cowes and found the marine facilities of an exceptionally high standard. Among the others associated with Cowes is William Davenant, who was imprisoned in the castle in 1650 after being apprehended on his way from France to the Virginia colony. A staunch Royalist, he was held here until he was taken to the Tower of London in 1651.

Charles Lamb was in Cowes on holiday from London with the Burneys in July 1803 and made the town the center for trips to Newport and Carisbrooke Castle. The town can also claim one native son, better known as an educator than as a writer. Dr. Thomas Arnold was born in West Cowes in 1795, and both St. Mary's Church near Norwood House and the Royal Yacht Squadron Club contain memorial brasses. The present St. Mary's was erected in 1867 on the site of the previous church.

COXHOE, County Durham (pop. 3,987) The modern village of Coxhoe in the parish of Kelloe seems bent on its own destruction: the magnesium limestone (dolomite) ridge is being quarried and processed into factory bricks, creating an unusually unpleasant atmospheric pall. But when the 18th-century mansion Coxhoe Hall was built, there were fewer than 100 people in the area, and there was no village. The hall was a castellated stone building with more than twenty-five rooms situated in a 1,000-acre woodland estate. It was in this once-magnificent hall that Elizabeth Barrett (Browning) was born on March 6, 1806. Now nothing remains. The destruction is modern and proceeded in stages: during World War II Italian pris-

oners of war were billeted here, and the interior suffered. Subsequently the National Coal Board took over the property, and with that came the final ruin. Kelloe Church preserves some of the area's identification with Elizabeth Barrett Browning.

COXWOLD, Yorkshire (pop. 251) Coxwold is a picturesque village set at the point where the Vale of York begins to rise to meet the Hambleton Hills. It was the home of Laurence Sterne from 1760 to his death in 1768; offered the quite lucrative living by Lord Fauconberg of Newburgh Priory, he found Coxwold a pleasant change after Sutton-on-the-Forest. Since there was no vicarage when Sterne and his family arrived, they took the cottage near the church at the end of the village. Mrs. Sterne was a late arrival; she was mentally ill, imagining herself to be the Queen of Bohemia, but was apparently thought to have recovered enough to join her husband and daughter. Later, domestic difficulties here led to a final separation.

The house is a long, low Elizabethan building, yellow-washed, with gabled ends and a tiny window in the chimney stack. Sterne's ground-floor study is to the right of the entrance; his bedroom, reached by climbing a compact wooden staircase with a strangely convoluted rail, still contains his powder closet with a remarkable hatch for drawing up a pail of water for his morning ablutions. Sterne named the house Shandy Hall; *shandy* in local Yorkshire dialect means "crackbrained." Here he wrote the last seven books of *The Life and Opinions of Tristram Shandy, Gentlemen, The Sentimental Journey*, and *Journal to Eliza*.

Sterne's incumbency was not without its lighter moments: to celebrate the coronation of George III he had a very large ox roasted at the local inn for his parishioners and served them great quantities of ale to accompany it. Not all members of his flock were happy with the drunken brawl that ensued. After his death in London in 1768, Sterne was first buried there, but in 1969 his body and the original tombstone were brought here and placed outside the south wall of the nave. The house where Sterne lived in Coxwold is now the Laurence Sterne Museum.

CRANBORNE, Dorset (pop. 675) The village of Cranborne, 10 miles northeast of Wimborne Minster, was once the most important settlement in the area known as the Cranborne Chase, a once-forested tract of 700,000 acres with a perimeter of 100 miles. The Stour and Avon Rivers bordered the area, and even in the mid-19th century the chase sheltered an estimated 20,000 deer. After the Norman Conquest, the rights of the chase, a private hunting ground, belonged to the Earls of Gloucester, but the marriage of John, soon to be king, to a Gloucester heiress brought the chase to the crown and made it a forest (that is, a prerogative of kingly right). The rights eventually passed through the Earls of Shaftesbury to the Pitt-Rivers family. In the 18th century the chase was an ungovernable area; smugglers had good cover, and poachers reveled in the abundance of game. Robbery and murder were common, and not until 1830, when Parliament abolished the special rights of the chase, was there any improvement.

The Chase, as this area becomes, and Chaseborough or Chasetown, as Cranborne is called, figure in Thomas Hardy's Wessex, most prominently in *Tess of the D'Urbervilles*. Tess goes to Chaseborough with a group of workers on Saturday night:

> The chief pleasure of these philosophers lay in going every Saturday night, when work was done, to Chaseborough, a decayed market-town two or three miles distant; and, returning in the small hours of the next morning, to spend Sunday in sleeping off the dyspeptic effects of the curious compounds sold to them as beer by the monopolizers of the once independent inns.

The Flower-de-Luce Inn where Alec tells Tess he can "hire a trap, and drive you home with me" had the Fleur-de-lys as its prototype; Hardy's spelling simply reflects period pronunciation. The Chase, "the oldest wood in England," itself is the scene of the first tragedy in Tess's life.

CRANBOURNE, Berkshire (pop. 1,051) In a setting of trees and parkland just southwest of Windsor, Cranbourne was once part of Winkfield but for some years has had its own existence. In the spring of 1866 Kenneth Grahame came to Fernhill Cottage from his grandmother's house in Cookham Dean. He was here only a short time before his father summoned him to Edinburgh; the elder Grahame, an alcoholic, had given up the idea of raising his children after the death of his wife but on this occasion gave it an unsuccessful trial.

CRANBROOK, Kent (pop. 3,829) On a hill high above the Weald on the Crane River 4 miles north of Hawkhurst, Cranbrook is a small town built by industry; the Flemish, attracted by Edward III to break the monopoly of Flanders in the cloth trade, settled here and made this the hub of clothmaking in Kent. The industry prospered, and the rich merchants built a magnificent church which has Father Time and his scythe marking the hours on the tower clock. Nearby on the High Street is the old George Hotel, where Edward I is supposed to have stayed in 1299, where Elizabeth stayed in 1573, and where Edward Gibbon stayed in 1760 when guarding French prisoners of war at Sissinghurst Castle.

The old rectory, which stood on part of the site of Cranbrook School, may have been the birthplace of Phineas Fletcher, son of Giles Fletcher the Elder, in late March or early April 1582; he was baptized by his grandfather at the parish church on April 8. It may well be that his brother Giles was also born and baptized here around 1588, but there is no proof.

CRANFORD, Middlesex (pop. 759) Once a small rural village on the Crane River 3 miles northwest of Hounslow, Cranford is now almost totally inundated by the encroaching housing projects of London, arterial metropolitan roads, and great factories. The ruins of Cranford House stand in a corner of the park with St. Dunstan's Church, whose bells (one of which dates to 1380) have rung, it is said, for every major English victory from Agincourt to Alamein. Thomas Fuller was presented to this church in March 1658; his last three years were spent here and as chaplain to the 1st Earl of Berkeley. Fuller succumbed to typhus (probably) in the summer of 1661

and died in Covent Garden, London, on August 16. He was buried in the church here with 200 London clergy in attendance. There is a memorial tablet on the east wall of the chancel.

CRANHAM, Gloucestershire (pop. 441) Deep in the Cotswolds 5½ miles northeast of Stroud, Cranham lies in a hollow in the hills where much of the atmosphere of the ancient royal beech forest still prevails. James Elroy Flecker was diagnosed as tubercular in Constantinople and was sent back to England for rest and travel; he spent three months in Cotswold Sanatorium here in 1910 and worked on *Don Juan*, his first play, and wrote "Oak and Olive" here:

> When I go down the Gloucester lanes
>   My friends are deaf and blind:
> Fast as they turn their foolish eyes
>   The Maenads leap behind,
> And when I hear the fire-winged feet,
>   They only hear the wind.
>
> Have I not chased the fluting Pan
>   Through Cranham's sober trees?
> Have I not sat on Painswick Hill
>   With a nymph upon my knees,
> And she as rosy as the dawn,
>   And naked as the breeze?

CRAWLEY, Hampshire (pop. 563) Just northwest of Winchester is Crawley, almost entirely of 16th-century construction and a striking example of how the earlier feudal system left its marks on the countryside. Crawley Court, the old manor house, is flanked by a pond, and the village cottages are placed in their proper relationship to the manor house, the 13th-century church, and the pub. This village is traditionally held to be the original of Queen's Crawley in William Makepeace Thackeray's *Vanity Fair*:

> It is related, with regard to the borough of Queen's Crawley, that Queen Elizabeth in one of her progresses, stopping at Crawley to breakfast, was so delighted with some remarkably fine Hampshire beer which was then presented to her by the Crawley of the day ... that she forthwith erected Crawley into a borough to send two members to Parliament; and the place, from the day of that illustrious visit, took the name of Queen's Crawley, which it holds up to the present moment.

CREDENHILL, Herefordshire (pop. 234) This is the land of the cider apple, and 60 percent of the cider consumed in Great Britain is made in Hereford, 4 miles to the southeast; in the spring here the Wye Valley orchards are a riot of color. After taking orders in 1660, Thomas Traherne, the last of the metaphysical poets of the Anglican clergy, took the living in Credenhill in 1661. Traherne held this office until his death in 1674 at Teddington, Middlesex, but from 1669 to 1674 he lived in London and Teddington as chaplain to Sir Orlando Bridgeman. During Traherne's lifetime only *Roman Forgeries* appeared under his name, and, indeed, the manuscript of his poetry was only discovered in a London bookstall in 1897, when it was erroneously ascribed to Henry Vaughan; the 1910 discovery of the Burney manuscript in the British Museum verified Traherne's authorship.

CRICH, Derbyshire (pop. 3,056) A village on a hill, Crich (pronounced "critch") has especially fine views from the top of the ridge out over the lush woodlands of the Derwent Valley and toward Crich Stand and its World War I memorial. With its 12th-century church, Crich is 4 miles west of Alfreton, in an area used in D. H. Lawrence's novels. The village itself appears in *Sons and Lovers.* After Paul Morel, Miriam, and the others visit Alfreton and its church and go on to the manor of South Wingfield, they walk here:

> At last they came into the straggling grey village of Crich, that lies high. Beyond the village was the famous Crich Stand that Paul could see from the garden at home. The party pushed on. Great expanse of country spread around and below. The lads were eager to get to the top of the hill. It was capped by a round knoll, half of which was by now cut away, and on top of which stood an ancient monument, sturdy and squat, for signalling in old days far down into the level lands of Nottinghamshire and Leicestershire.
>
> It was blowing so hard, high up there in the exposed place, that the only way to be safe was to stand nailed by the wind to the wall of the tower. At their feet fell the precipice where the limestone was quarried away. Below was a jumble of hills and tiny villages—Matlock, Ambergate, Stoney Middleton.

CROFT, Yorkshire (pop. 509) Situated 3 miles south of Darlington, the village of Croft, or Croft Spa (named for the baths and mineral waters once in abundance in the area), is cut in half by the winding Tees River. The part of the village north of the Tees in County Durham is known as Hurworth. In 1843 Sir Robert Peel presented the crown living here to the Rev. Charles Dodgson, and for the next twenty-five years the rectory was the family home of Charles Lutwidge Dodgson (Lewis Carroll). The parsonage, located close to St. Peter's Church and still in use, was in the midst of an extremely complicated and exotic garden laid out by the previous incumbent. The house and extensive grounds were a source of delight to the young Lewis Carroll, and the nearby train line stimulated the boy to build his own version, part of which survives. Here also he began two house magazines when on holiday from school at Richmond, Yorkshire, and Rugby. In 1845 he began *Useful and Instructive Poetry,* and in 1849 or 1850 *The Rectory Umbrella.* The latter was full of his caricatures, several of which are now in the Vernon Gallery. Carroll left Croft for Christ Church, Oxford, in May 1850.

The Church of St. Peter, built of local red sandstone quarried from the riverbed, is partly Norman and contains what has been termed "the most fantastic family pew in Yorkshire"; the pew belonged to the Milbanke family of Seaham, County Durham. Standing on oak pillars, the pew is reached by entering the dog gates at the bottom and climbing a winding triple flight of stairs. The canopy above the pew is hung with heavy red curtains to ensure privacy; the result is much like a giant four-poster bed. The church is the spiritual resting place of the Milbanke family, and this is the pew where the bored bridegroom Lord Byron is supposed to have slept a few hours after his marriage to Miss Anne Isabella Milbanke.

CROMER, Norfolk (pop. 4,177) The Cromer area has been fighting the encroaching seas for centuries. At least one previous settlement, Shipden-juxta-Mare, was dumped into the sea around 1400. Cromer is a bustling holiday resort area, but the town's economy is based largely on catching crabs; this is the crab capital of Norfolk, and the fishermen prepare their bait at the eastern end of the beach. The sands here are especially good for bathing, and the eastern end of the shore is protected by 250-foot cliffs. William Camden commented on an early fishing industry in his *Britannia:*

> *Cromer,* where the best lobsters on this coast are taken, was formerly part of *Shipden,* whose church and many houses were swallowed up by the sea. The first attempt for a pier was in the reign of Richard II. It is still a tolerable fishing town, has a fair, and the nave and tower of a handsome church; and a mile to the East is a lighthouse.

The dangers of the coast as well as its lobsters enter Daniel Defoe's *A Tour thro' the Whole Island of Great Britain:*

> *Cromer* is a Market Town close to the shoar of this dangerous Coast, I know nothing it is famous for (besides it's being thus the Terror of the Sailors) except good Lobsters, which are taken on that Coast in great Numbers. . . .

In March 1901, Sir Arthur Conan Doyle stayed at the Royal Links Hotel to recuperate from the effects of enteric fever contracted in the Boer War. It was during his visit that he was told the story of the spectral hound that later was used in *The Hound of the Baskervilles.*

CROMFORD, Derbyshire (pop. 904) In the beautiful Matlock Dale, where the Derwent River meanders about, Cromford is clustered around a great house, an 18th-century church, and the old cotton mills, which were the first water-powered cotton mills in Derbyshire. Sir Richard Arkwright, whose invention the machinery was, began Willersley Castle and the church, both of which were finished by his son Richard. The castle is now a Methodist guesthouse. Mary Ann Evans (George Eliot) and her father were frequent guests of the Arkwright family at the castle, and the scene of the mills so impressed itself that she mentions them in *Adam Bede.*

CROPTHORNE, Worcestershire (pop. 545) Cropthorne, a pleasant little village on the Avon River just over 2 miles west of Evesham, historically belonged to Worcester Cathedral, and the partly Norman church has a reminder of the gift, an early-9th-century cross elaborately carved with lions, intertwined foliage, and a long-necked fabulous creature.

Worcestershire was always Francis Brett Young's first love, and in November 1931 he first saw Craycombe, a derelict Adam house built about 1791. The house was inspected in the early part of 1932 and bought in June; extensive renovation and restoration were completed before the Youngs moved in from Esthwaite Water, Lancashire, in November. The house and the novelist's return to the shire proved a tremendous catalyst, and here he wrote *This Little World, White Ladies, Far Forest, They Seek a Coun-*

try, Portrait of a Village, Dr. Bradley Remembers, The City of Gold, Mr. Lucton's Freedom, and parts of *The Island. Portrait of a Village* contains some excellent commentary on the area, although Monk's Norton, Young claimed, never existed "outside my imagination; [and] . . . the people whom I have devised for its inhabitation are, equally, wholly imaginary. . . ." *This Little World* also concerns the area. The novelist relieved his frustrations in writing to some degree by becoming involved in the work on Craycombe,

> struggling with the beasts at Ephesus (i.e. the builders); cutting off the monstrous tail of red brick in which the Duc d'Aumale housed his train of valets de place, de chambre, and de everything else . . . [and removing] the accretions of brown paint which had incrusted the delicate work of Robert Adam. . . .

With the outbreak of World War II, Young and his wife opened Craycombe House as a guesthouse for broadcasters at Wood Norton and then offered the house and land to the Red Cross for a convalescent hospital because

> we had no right to monopolize that lovely place when it might be enjoyed by so many others. . . . All the daffodils are out in flower, the birds are singing, though sometimes bombs fall near enough to shake us in our beds. But we are not shaken in our belief that nothing can prevent the ultimate triumph of Right in this distracted world.

By this time they had 35 acres under cultivation, and when the Red Cross took over the house, the Youngs moved into the Orangery. They spent only the warm months here anyway and wintered at Talland House near Talland Bay. Craycombe House was sold late in 1944. Young returned to South Africa in July 1945. Among the Youngs' frequent guests here were George Bernard Shaw and G. M. Trevelyan.

CROSTHWAITE, Cumberland (pop. 2,626) Situated in the basin of the Derwent River Valley and virtually a part of Keswick, Crosthwaite holds an enviable position in the Lake District just below the southern slopes of Skiddaw. The Scottish religious St. Kentigern (Cyndern) built a wood-and-wattle church here, and by 1181 a new church had been built here by Cecilia de Romilée, founder of Bolton Abbey. Eight years later the church was given to the Cistercian monks at Fountains Abbey, who added the tower and south aisle. In the present tower are the eight great bells that have sounded for generations, and the ringing chamber has an 1826 admonition to the bell ringers:

> You ringers all, observe these orders well,
> He eightpence pays who overturns a bell,
> He who presumes to ring without consent,
> Shall pay one shilling and it shall be spent,
> And he who rings with either spur or hat,
> Shall pay his eightpence certainly for that.
> He who in ringing interrupts a peal,
> For such offence shall pay a quart of ale.
> In falling bells one penny must be paid,
> By him who stops before the signal's made,
> And he who takes God's Holy name in vain
> Shall pay one shilling and this place refrain.

The churchyard here is where Robert Southey was buried in March 1843; the grave is near the tower on the northwest side of the churchyard. He had died at Greta Hall in Keswick on March 21, and his son says:

> It was a dark and stormy morning when he was borne to his last resting-place, at the western end of the beautiful churchyard of Crosthwaite. . . . But few beside his own family and immediate neighbours followed his remains. His only intimate friend within reach, Mr. Wordsworth, crossed the hills that wild morning to be present.

Wordsworth and his son-in-law had walked the 16 miles from Rydal Mount. Inside the church, opposite the south door, is a memorial figure sculpted in white marble with an inscription by Wordsworth:

> Ye vales and hills whose beauty hither drew
> The poet's steps, and fixed him here, on you
> His eyes have closed! And ye, loved books, no more
> Shall Southey feed upon your precious lore,
> To works that ne'er shall forfeit their renown,
> Adding immortal labours of his own. . . .

Thomas Gray was in Crosthwaite in October 1769 and was impressed with the scenery and the old vicarage, both of which are described in his *Journal.* Sir Hugh Walpole uses Crosthwaite in *The Fortress;* here is the site of the foot-race from "Crosthwaite Church to the Druid's Circle" (Castle Rigg, which is not druidical) that so impressed the young Adam Paris.

CROWBOROUGH, Sussex (pop. 4,894) Crowborough, a fast-growing village spreading itself over Beacon Hill and into the edge of the Ashdown Forest, is midway between Tunbridge Wells and Uckfield. The town is a recent one, even by Sussex standards. Its center is Crowborough Cross, once a hamlet a quarter of a mile distant. Where the crossroads meet is The Downs, the house where Richard Jefferies lived in the winter of 1885–1886; for a three-month period before taking this house, he stayed at Rehoboth Villa, Jarvis Brook. He wrote his last essays, published posthumously as *Field and Hedgerow,* in The Downs, and many of his works, including *The Story of My Heart,* reflect Sussex:

> There, alone, I went down to the sea. I stood where the foam came to my feet, and looked over the sunlit waters. The great earth bearing the richness of the harvest, and its hills golden with corn, was at my back; its strength and firmness under me. The great sun shone above, the wide sea was before me, the wind came sweet and strong from the waves. The life of the earth and the sea, the glow of the sun filled me; I touched the surge with my hand, I lifted my face to the sun, I opened my lips to the wind. I prayed aloud in the roar of the waves. . . .

In 1886 Jefferies left for Goring-on-Sea, near Worthing.

W. E. Henley stayed at the Chummery, South View, in February 1897; he had been ill most of the winter, and his recuperation here was fairly rapid. He commented that this place had "a hideous name, but [was] a pleasant house with a view of the whole Sussex Weald. . . ."

Crowborough's principal writer was Sir Arthur Conan Doyle, who moved into Windlesham after his marriage to Jean Leckie in 1907; the house, a gray-shingled structure, had five gables, two of which contained his study. Doyle wrote a large number of works here, including "Wisteria Lodge" and "The

Bruce Partington Plans," both Sherlock Holmes stories written at his wife's request; he also wrote *The House of Temperley, The Lost World, The Poison Belt, The Valley of Fear,* and "Danger! Being the Log of Capt. John Sirius." He spent a great deal of time traveling, and his great interest in spiritualism began around 1914. The novelist was also very eager to do his part in World War I, and after the first instance of men drowning because of submarine attacks, he suggested the use of rubber life rafts. In the spring of 1930 Doyle was taken ill; he died here on July 7 and was buried in the grounds of the house near a garden hut that he had often used as a study. The headstone, made of British oak, contained his name and age and the inscription, "Steel true, blade straight." After World War II his remains were removed to Minstead, Hampshire. One of Doyle's frequent guests was Rudyard Kipling, who came from his home in nearby Burwash.

CROXALL, Staffordshire (pop. 233)   Situated 7 miles southwest of Burton-upon-Trent on the Mease River, Croxall was inhabited as long ago as Saxon times, as shown by the mound in the churchyard. Nearby are two fine manor houses, Oakley Hall, a 15th-century structure, and Croxall Hall, an Elizabethan structure damaged in 1942 but since rebuilt. Croxall Hall was the seat of the Curzons and later of the Earls of Dorset, and the dramatist and poet John Dryden was a frequent guest of his patron, the 6th Earl. But the fame of the village results from another association, for here lived Lord Byron's cousin Sir Robert Wilmot-Horton and his wife, the Lady Anne, who inspired Byron's "She Walks in Beauty"; the poet first met her at a ball when she was dressed in a glittering black gown, and he wrote the hymn to her beauty the same night:

> She walks in beauty, like the night
>   Of cloudless climes and starry skies;
> And all that's best of dark and bright
>   Meet in her aspect and her eyes. . . .

Of much more significance is Sir Robert's role in the negotiations between Lord Byron and his wife and at the time of Byron's death; Byron had given Thomas Moore the manuscript of his memoirs on the understanding that they would be published after his death. Moore, in turn, sold them to John Murray for £2,000, with the stipulation that they could be redeemed at any time during the poet's lifetime or within three months of his death. Acting on behalf of the poet's half sister, Augusta Leigh, Sir Robert was instrumental in suppressing the memoirs and was, in fact, present in London when the manuscript was burned.

CROXTON KERRIAL, Leicestershire (pop. 414)   High on the Wolds overlooking the Devon Valley, Croxton (pronounced "cros'n") Kerrial, 8 miles northeast of Melton Mowbray, is a small stone village with the remains of a 12th-century abbey whose abbot is said to have brought back a part of the King John's body for interment here. The 13th-century parish church contains forty-two beautifully carved 15th-century bench ends. The living was given to the Rev. George Crabbe in 1813, along with one in Trowbridge, Wilt-

shire, by the Duke of Rutland. There is no evidence that Crabbe ever took up his post here.

CROYDON, Surrey (pop. 243,400)   This was Surrey's largest town before it became an outer borough of Greater London in 1965; nevertheless, historically Croydon belongs to Surrey, and its ties will long be with that shire. Croydon, 10 miles south of London Bridge, has always been on the commuters' route, and its growth in the last fifty years has been considerable: the town center has been moved, the commercial center has been totally shifted out of the old market area around Surrey Street, and high rises soar upward all over the town.

The old center of Croydon lay by the headwaters of the Wandle River at the foot of the chalk hills when the town and its manor were presented to Archbishop Lanfranc by William the Conqueror. Lanfranc founded and built the archepiscopal palace, the summer residence of the archbishops and now part of a girls' school, around a quadrangle, and there is still evidence of Norman work, although much of the palace is considerably newer. By the 18th century the archbishops had determined that Croydon was unhealthy—"on so low and unwholsome a situation"— and moved to nearby Addington Palace.

Croydon prospered throughout the Middle Ages, primarily as a market town, and by the 16th century it was the home of many rich merchants. And by the 18th century Daniel Defoe found it was

> large and full of Citizens from *London*, which makes it so Populous; it is the Antient Palace of the Archbishops of *Canterbury*, and several of them lye buried here; particularly that great Man, Archbishop *Whitgift*, who not only repair'd the Palace, but Built the Famous Hospital and School, which remains there to this Day, to the singular Honour of the Giver.

Literary associations here begin in the 15th century. In 1406 James, Duke of Rothesay, the eleven-year-old heir to the Scottish throne, was sent from Scotland by King Robert III to France to keep him out of the reach of the powerful 1st Duke of Albany; captured at sea, the Duke of Rothesay was brought to Croydon, where he was imprisoned in the palace under Archbishop William Courtenay until 1424, when he was ransomed. During his incarceration, James is said to have written *The Kingis Quair*, the form of which has given rise to the term "rime royal." From his prison tower the King sees Lady Jane Beaufort and describes the experience, his dream, and the promise of success in courtship in the poem:

> Now there was made fast by the tower wall
> A garden fair, and, in the corners set,
> Flourished green herbs, with wattles long and small
> Railed all about; and so the place was set
> With trees, and so with hawthorn hedges knit,
> That nobody, though he were walking nigh,
> Might there within scarce any wight descry.
>
> And on the slender green-leaved branches sate
> The little joyous nightingales, and sang
> So loud and clear the hymns that consecrate
> Are to Love's use; now soft their tune, now strong,
> That all the walls and all the garden rang
> Right of their song. . . .

In the late 19th century William Ernest Henley

came to Ashburton Lodge in Addiscombe, then a completely separate area. He and his family arrived in September 1892; in November their only child became seriously ill, and in December Henley's health broke down. They left Croydon in December.

Even more recently D. H. Lawrence was associated with Croydon for a few years; after qualifying in 1908 from the University of Nottingham, he took up a teaching post at the Davidson Road School. He stayed with the Jones family at 12 and then 16 Colworth Road in Addiscombe, just 3/4 mile from the school. While Lawrence was a success with both teachers and students, he did not find the environment especially inspiring:

> I pick my way over threadbare grass, which is pressed
> Into mud—the space fast shrinks in the builder's hands.

Lawrence was teaching art among other things, but his teaching

> was somewhat suspect. While I [A. W. McLeod] was conferring with a Board of Education Inspector, a boy brought a large pastel drawing, still life, for inspection. After a glance I made an ineffectual attempt to suppress the sketch. The official eye had, however, anticipated my effort. "Is this sent for any particular reason?" I inquired. "Mr. Lawrence thought it was rather good," the boy replied. The artist returned to his class leaving the masterpiece with us.
> "Are you by any chance an artist?" inquired the wary director. "No," I replied. "Neither am I", he commented. "We had better be careful about this man. After the session, without his knowledge, collect a sample of these drawings. I will send them to the Art Department at Kensington for an expert opinion." Later they were returned by the Inspector in person. "Good thing we took the course we did," he reported. "The department highly approves. You'll have a crowd of students down to worry you about them, I expect!"

He continued working on *The White Peacock* and began *The Trespasser*, but he was not temperamentally suited to the teaching position. Indeed, his mother's death in 1910 precipitated what he called his "sick year," and at the end of the 1911 school year he resigned his post upon the advice of his physician. The school is marked with a plaque.

CUCKFIELD, Sussex (pop. 17,334) Along the forest ridge containing the last tracts of Andredsweald, in Roman times a 120-mile-broad swath across southeast England, and just west of Haywards Heath, Cuckfield (pronounced "cookfield") has grown rapidly. The village is usually described as 13th-century, but the manor and attendant lands belonged to William de Warenne, William the Conqueror's cousin, and the King had both a hunting lodge and a chapel here. The town is built on the side of a hill, and the steep High Street is jammed with houses and shops.

A footpath beside the road leads to Cuckfield Park (later called Cuckfield Place), an Elizabethan house with a Tudor gatehouse. Percy Bysshe Shelley was a frequent guest of his uncle, Capt. John Pilfold, here, especially after being sent down from Oxford. Following his marriage to Harriet Westbrook in 1811, he came to get money from his father and grandfather but was unsuccessful. Pilfold, though, was the kindest and most tolerant, and he supplied the young Shelleys with money when they were penniless in Edinburgh. Shelley felt that the house and park of Cuckfield Place were full of "bits of Mrs. Radcliffe."

The novelist William Harrison Ainsworth, who lived at Ovingdean, near Brighton, uses the Sussex countryside in some of his works. He stayed at Cuckfield Park in 1830 and 1831, and Rookwood in the novel of that name is Cuckfield; Ainsworth's reasons for his choice are well defined:

> The supernatural occurrence, forming the groundwork of one of the ballads which I have made the harbinger of doom to the house of Rookwood, is ascribed, by popular superstition, to a family resident in Sussex; upon whose estate the fatal tree (a gigantic lime, with mighty arms and huge girth of trunk, as described in the song) is carefully preserved. Cuckfield Place, to which this singular piece of timber is attached, is, I may state, for the benefit of the curious, the real Rookwood Hall; for I have not drawn upon imagination, but upon memory, in describing the seat and domains of that fated family. The general features of the venerable structure, several of its chambers, the old garden, and, in particular, the noble park, with its spreading prospects, its picturesque views of the Hall . . . its deep glades, through which the deer come lightly tripping down, its uplands, slopes, brooks, brakes, coverts, and groves, are carefully delineated.

Here, writes Ainsworth, Sir Ranulph de Rookwood built "a massive edifice . . . with gate and tower, court and moat complete; substantial enough, one would have thought, to have endured for centuries."
The hall

> . . . was situated near the base of a gently declining hill, terminating a noble avenue of limes, and partially embosomed in an immemorial wood of the same timber. . . . Descending the avenue . . . as you advanced, the eye was first arrested by a singular octagonal turret of brick. . . . This tower rose to a height corresponding with the roof of the mansion; and was embellished on the side facing the house with a flamingly gilt dial, peering, like an impudent observer, at all that passed within doors.

On the gateway, "carved in granite," were "the achievements of the family—the rook and the fatal branch," and on one side was "the hoary summit of a dovecot, indicating the near neighbourhood of an ancient barn," and on the other was the garden, "formal, precise, old-fashioned, artificial, yet exquisite!" It was a "beautiful English garden—*really a garden*—not that mixture of park, meadow, and wilderness, brought up to one's very windows. . . ." Here were "the gayest of parterres and greenest of lawns."

Cuckfield also has an association with a now-little-read 19th-century novelist. Henry Kingsley, younger brother of Charles Kingsley, lived in the 15th-century Kingsley Cottage (then known as At Trees or Attrees) during the last years of his life. He died here on May 24, 1876, of cancer of the tongue, and was buried here; a 9-foot monument stands in commemoration of him.

CULBONE, Somerset The tiny village of Culbone, on the Bristol Channel, is accessible only on foot; the 2-mile footpath from Porlock Weir leads through crowding hills and dense woodlands past a tiny brook to the village: a small house, a smaller cottage, and the smallest church in England. Culbone once supported a leper colony whose members attended services outside this minuscule church. Here, at Ash Farm, a quarter of a mile from the church, Samuel Taylor Coleridge, in the summer of 1797, took the now-famous 2 grains of opium "to check a dysentery." Falling asleep over *Purchas His Pilgrimage* at the lines "In Zandu did Cublai Can build a stately Palace, encompassing sixteen miles of plaine ground with a wall," Coleridge dreamed all of "Kubla Khan, or A Vision in a Dream," which he maintained ran to 200 or 300 lines. Awakening, he began to compose "in a sort of reverie" and managed to write 53 lines before he was "called out by a person on business from Porlock" and detained for more than an hour. Returning to his room, he was no longer able to recall the general scheme of the work and could remember no more than eight or ten scattered images.

R. D. Blackmore and his novel *Lorna Doone* also are associated with Culbone. The original of Plover's Barrows, often claimed to be in Oare, is in fact Broomstreat Farm here.

CULMSTOCK, Devon (pop. 760) Below the Black Down Hills in the Culm Valley 9¾ miles northeast of Tiverton, Culmstock has an interesting parish church with a yew tree growing out of the top of the tower. This village was the longtime home of Richard Doddridge Blackmore, who came here at the age of six in 1831, when his father accepted the curacy and remarried. The "long and rambling" rectory made a lasting impression on Blackmore; it "was not a cheerful place to sit alone in after dark," and "the only access to the kitchen . . . was through a narrow and dark passage, arched with rough flints set in mortar, which ran like a tunnel beneath the first floor rooms. . . ." Here, he says, "even the stoutest heart might flutter a little in the groping process (for the tunnel was pitch-dark at night). . . ." Blackmore, who was educated at Blundell's School in Tiverton, always felt himself a Devonian:

In everything, except the accident of my birth, I am Devonian; my ancestry were all Devonians; my sympathies and feeling are all Devonian, and I now actually possess in Devonshire a nearly perpendicular wood that unfortunately has to pay out more in rates and taxes than it brings in profit to me. . . .

Years later he wrote one of the best fishing stories in any language, "Crocker's Hole," which tells how John Pike, with the young Richard as his companion, caught the large trout which had been desired by all fishermen at Crocker's Hole, a quiet pool in the bend of the Culm.

CUMNOR, Berkshire (pop. 4,197) Perched on the west side of Hurst Hill in the Cumnor Range, the village of Cumnor rises high above Oxford, 3½ miles to the northeast, and looks to the lower reaches of the Cotswolds. The Thames in this part of the country has long inspired poets, but the area most expressly belongs to Matthew Arnold and, in particular, to *The Scholar-Gipsy*. A path from the village drops down into the valley and leads to the ferry where one can cross "the stripling Thames at Bablock-Hithe." This is the area where

In autumn, on the skirts of Bagley Wood—
. . . most the gipsies by the turf-edged way
Pitch their smoked tents. . . .

The village is better known because of a historical event that Sir Walter Scott uses in *Kenilworth* with enough license and imagination to render the history misleading. In 1560 Cumnor Place (the original title of *Kenilworth*) was owned by Anthony Foster, and it was to Cumnor Place that Amy Robsart, accompanied by three other women, came in September while her husband, Robert Dudley, was engaged on a diplomatic mission. On September 6, most of the household attended the Abingdon Fair, and upon their return the servants found Amy's body at the foot of "a paire of staires." Rumors were rampant, and the highly unscrupulous but brilliant Dudley was thought to have engineered her death because of his earlier liaison with Queen Elizabeth and the still-possible marriage with her. Accusations against him were neither investigated nor proved. Scott takes this event and embroiders it, and it is his account that is known today. According to Sir Walter, Leicester secretly established his wife at Cumnor Place, where she is passed off as the wife of his master of the horse, Richard Varney. He describes the estate and village:

The village of Cumnor is pleasantly built on a hill, and in a wooded park closely adjacent was situated the ancient mansion occupied at this time by Anthony Foster, of which the ruins may be still extant. The park was then full of large trees, and in particular, of ancient and mighty oaks, which stretched their giant arms over the high wall surrounding the demesne, thus giving it a melancholy, secluded, and monastic appearance.

Amy's fate is sealed when her admirer Tressilian threatens to charge Varney with seduction; Varney swears to the Queen that Amy is his wife and then insists to Leicester that Tressilian is Amy's lover. Her death is arranged, and only too late does Leicester discover her innocence.

There are a few other literary references to this event. The old play *A Yorkshire Tragedy* alludes to the event when a baker, determined to destroy his family, throws his wife down the stairs and comments:

The only way to charm a woman's tongue
Is, break her neck—a politician did it.

Both John Aubrey and Anthony à Wood refer to Amy's death, and the obscure poet William Julius Mickle wrote a rather long poem on the event in the 18th century; it is thought that the ghost legend began because of the final verses of his work:

And in that Manor now no more
   Is cheerful feast and sprightly ball;
For ever since that dreary hour
   Have spirits haunted Cumnor Hall.
. . . .
Full many a traveller oft hath sigh'd,
   And pensive wept the Countess' fall,
As wand'ring onwards they've espied
   The haunted towers of Cumnor Hall.

Cumnor Hall was demolished by the Earl of Abingdon in the 19th century.

DARESBURY, Cheshire (pop. 104) In a parklike area surrounded by rolling meadows 3 miles southwest of Warrington, Daresbury would have been unremembered by history except that it was at the old parsonage that Charles Lutwidge Dodgson (Lewis Carroll) was born on January 27, 1832, to the Rev. and Mrs. Charles Dodgson. The parsonage was on a glebe farm, 1½ miles from the village itself, and only the gateposts remain. The seclusion of the house where Carroll lived for eleven years could well have influenced the child. There is little doubt of his precocious imagination, and he was on speaking terms with every conceivable form of lower life he could find. One of his more interesting experiments supposedly was encouraging combat among earthworms; he even supplied them with arms (small lengths of pipe) to use.

This is the village referred to in "The Three Sunsets," which in its original form read as follows:

I watch the drowsy night expire
And fancy paints at my desire
Her magic pictures in the fire.

An island farm, 'mid seas of corn,
Swayed by the wandering breath of morn,
The happy spot where I was born.

The local church has been much changed since Carroll's day; the large memorial window, done in red, gold, and blue, shows Carroll in hood and surplice kneeling before the Christ child, while Alice stands beside him. The base panels of the window portray characters from his works: the White Rabbit, the Dodo, the Caterpillar, the Mad Hatter, the Dormouse in a teapot, the March Hare, the Duchess, the Gryphon, the Mock Turtle, the Knave of Hearts, the Cheshire Cat, and the Queen of Hearts. Executed by Geoffrey Webb, the window was paid for from a worldwide subscription.

DARLEY DALE, Derbyshire Pleasantly situated on the Derwent River 3 miles northwest of Matlock, Darley Dale is a tiny hamlet adjacent to the somewhat larger village of Darley. The quarries here are almost as important now as they were in Saxon times, and from this Derwent Valley area stones have been taken for buildings all over England, including the Thames Embankment and Hyde Park Corners.

Nearby Oaker Hill was once planted with two sycamores by two brothers who parted here. When William Wordsworth was on his way from Cambridge to Westmorland in November 1830, he was told of the tradition by his coachman and wrote the sonnet "A Tradition of Oker Hill in Darley Dale, Derbyshire"; they planted their trees, and

. . . like two new-born rivers, they
In opposite directions urged their way
Down from the far-seen mount. No blast might kill
Or blight that fond memorial;—the trees grew,
And now entwine their arms; but ne'er again
Embraced those Brothers upon earth's wide plain;
Nor aught of mutual joy or sorrow knew
Until their spirits mingled in the sea
That to itself takes all, Eternity.

Only one tree remains.

DARTFORD, Kent (pop. 35,680)

. . . the silver Darent, in whose waters clean
Ten thousand fishes play and deck his pleasant
    stream. . . .

So Edmund Spenser viewed the small Darent stream which has nurtured so much industry here in Dartford. About 3 miles from the confluence of the Darent and the Thames and 17 miles east of Charing Cross Station, the town was known to the Romans as Derenti Vadum and to the Saxons as Derentford; the Normans came this way, as did Geoffrey Chaucer's pilgrims on their way to the shrine of St. Thomas à

Becket in Canterbury. The pilgrims stopped here at the chantry high on the hill where the Martyrs' Memorial now stands. Dartford has long been a manufacturing town, and the shire's first paper mill, founded in the 15th century, probably supplied much of the paper for the Shakespeare folio of 1623. Shakespeare uses the fields between Dartford and Blackheath in *Henry VI*, and the King was buried here after his death at the hands of the Duke of Gloucester. Samuel Pepys and Oliver Goldsmith were later visitors to the town, while Jane Austen stayed on two separate occasions at the Bull and George Inn (now the Royal Victoria and Bull) on her way to Godmersham Park, the home of her brother Edward Knight. William Makepeace Thackeray uses Dartford Common in *Denis Duval;* this is the lonely moor where Denis shoots the highwayman.

DARTMOOR, Devon A bleak, desolate, and wild upland granite area of 365 square miles, Dartmoor is famous for its rugged beauty as well as for its prison; within its nationally protected boundaries are lofty tors, moors, combes, dense woodlands, extensive farms, market towns, and a myriad of pitfalls for the traveler. Indeed, sudden fogs and mists can cut visibility to a few inches, while snowfalls capable of toppling heavy oaks are not unknown. More than 1,000 years ago the rugged Dartmoor ponies ran wild here, and today, while still free, the ponies are tame. Evidence of the early civilizations which flourished on Dartmoor is abundant. The prehistoric hill forts, Bronze Age cists, and standing-stone circles and huts scattered about have long stimulated writers, perhaps the best-known work being Sir Arthur Conan Doyle's *The Hound of the Baskervilles:*

> The sun was already sinking when I reached the summit of the hill, and the long slopes beneath me were all golden-green on one side and grey shadow on the other. A haze lay low upon the farthest skyline, out of which jutted the fantastic shapes of Belliver and Vixen Tor. Over the wide expanse there was no sound and no movement. . . . The barren scene, the sense of loneliness, and the mystery and urgency of my task all struck a chill into my heart.

R. D. Blackmore's description in *Christowell: A Dartmoor Tale,* however, probably better captures the moor's full beauty. Finally, Dartmoor really belongs to the regionalist Eden Phillpotts; many of his novels concern rural Devonshire, eighteen of them life on Dartmoor. *The Three Brothers* presents an especially vivid picture of the people and life here.

DARTMOUTH, Devon (pop. 6,700) Beautifully situated on a steep hill on the west side of the estuary of the Dart River facing Kingswear, Dartmouth has much of historical and architectural interest. An important harbor since Roman times, it has sent out many naval expeditions, including one to assist in the 1347 siege of Calais, and is now important both as a fishing port and as a resort. The 15th-century Dartmouth Castle with its Norman keep was the last glimpse of England the passengers of the *Mayflower* had in 1620. Daniel Defoe, who reports his excursion here in *A Tour thro' the Whole Island of Great Britain,* was amazed at the quantity, quality, and price of local fish; on one night, he, his servant, and a friend dined on seventeen pilchards bought "for a

DARTMOOR "A false step yonder means death to man or beast. Only yesterday I saw one of the moor ponies wander into it. He never came out. I saw his head for quite a long time craning out of the bog-hole, but it sucked him down at last. Even in dry seasons it is a danger to cross it, but after these autumn rains it is an awful place."

Sir Arthur Conan Doyle,
The Hound of the Baskervilles

Half-penny" on the quay and dressed "their way . . . with Pepper and Salt" and broiled by the cook at the inn for another farthing. He says: "We really really Din'd for *three Farthings,* and very well too. . . ." The next day his friend " . . . Treated . . . with a Dish of large Lobsters, and I being curious to know the value of such things . . . found that for 6*d.* or 8*d.* they bought as good Lobsters there, as would cost in *London* 3*s.* to 3*s.* 6*d.* each."

The more important literary association here is

DARTMOUTH An ancient seaport now a popular modern resort town with sandy beaches, Dartmouth stands on the west bank of the Dart River. This was the home of the shipman in Geoffrey Chaucer's *Canterbury Tales,* and Chaucer may have modeled his character upon Peter Risshenden, master of the *Magdaleyne.*

with Geoffrey Chaucer, who had been in the town on crown business. Dartmouth is the home of one of the pilgrims in *The Canterbury Tales:*

> A *Shipman* . . . wonynge fer by weste;
> For aught I woot, he was of Dertemouthe.

The shipman, whose "barge ycleped was the Maude-layne," is often identified as John Hawley, a local shipowner to whom St. Sepulchre's Church has a commemorative brass. However, it is most unlikely that Chaucer, who probably knew Hawley, modeled the shipman on him. It is known that a vessel called the *Magdaleyne* from Dartmouth paid customs duties in 1379 and 1391; in the latter year Peter Risshenden was its master and most likely was Chaucer's shipman.

DATCHET, Buckinghamshire (pop. 2,406) Two miles east of Windsor, the Thames-side village of Datchet has a large common surrounded by many pubs and good houses. The High Street leads from the green to the Thames, which has long been of interest to fishermen: Charles II often fished here with, as Alexander Pope said, "the pliant rod now trembling in his hand," and the greatest angler of them all, Izaak Walton, was frequently at Datchet with Sir Henry Wotton, Provost of Eton, "the undervaluer of money . . . a man with whom I have often fished and conversed. . . ."

Datchet is most familiar, though, as the place where Sir John Falstaff is thrown from the buck basket (laundry basket) "among the whitsters in Datchet mead, and . . . [emptied] in the muddy ditch, close by the Thames side" in William Shakespeare's *The Merry Wives of Windsor.* Falstaff reports the incident to Bardolph:

> The rogues slighted me into the river with as little remorse as they would have drowned a bitch's blind puppies, fifteen i' the litter: and you may know by my size that I have a kind of alacrity in sinking; if the bottom were as deep as hell I should down. I had been drowned but that the shore was shelvy and shallow: a death that I abhor; for the water swells a man; and what a thing should I have been when I had been swelled! I should have been a mountain of mummy.

DATCHWORTH, Hertfordshire (pop. 577) A village of yews and ivy-covered elms, Datchworth is 6 miles northwest of Hertford. Its yew trees are associated with Edward Young, who lived in retirement in nearby Welwyn and composed some of *Night Thoughts* under these trees.

DAUNTSEY, Wiltshire (pop. 366) In a particularly scenic part of northern Wiltshire on the Avon River, 6½ miles southeast of Malmesbury the village of Dauntsey was the seat of the Danvers family, into which the 17th-century poet-priest George Herbert married. Herbert first came here in 1627 to the "noble" house, as he called it, to stay with Henry, Lord Danvers, Herbert's stepfather's elder brother. The house was set in a park of oak trees a short distance from the Avon. Here Herbert met Jane Danvers, Henry's kinswoman, whom he later married. The poet composed the epitaph on the tomb of Lord Danvers in the partly 13th-century church.

DAWLISH, Devon (pop. 7,620) Situated between the estuaries of the Teign and Exe Rivers at the mouth of Dawlish Brook, 3 miles northeast of Teignmouth, Dawlish grew from a smuggling port to a fashionable resort late in the 18th century. This part of Devonshire is one of the most favored in England: vegetation is luxurious, palm trees flourish, the sand is golden, and the sea is a dark blue. Many sections of the town, notably the Strand, retain their Regency appearance, and the resort was one of Jane Austen's favorites, as she points out in *Sense and Sensibility* when Robert Ferrars muses how anyone could possibly live in the shire and not be near Dawlish. Another visitor to Dawlish a few years later was John Keats; on a walking tour in 1818, he came here from Teignmouth on March 23 to attend the local fair:

> Over the hill and over the dale,
> And over the bourne to Dawlish—
> Where Gingerbread Wives have a scanty sale
> And gingerbred nuts are smallish.

Charles Dickens explored Dawlish, Teignmouth, Babbicombe, and Torquay in August 1840 when he was visiting his father in Exeter; he worked while here, and "a small farm near Dawlish" later becomes the birthplace of Nicholas Nickleby. Many years after the farm had been sold, "The first act of Nicholas, when he became a rich and prosperous merchant, was to buy his father's old house." He

> altered and enlarged [it]; but none of the old rooms were ever pulled down, no old tree was ever rooted up, nothing . . . was ever removed or changed.

DEAL, Kent (pop. 23,500) Once important as a Cinque Port and the main harbor town in southern England, Deal is now a resort in a well-known fishing area. Julius Caesar and his fleet put in here in 55 B.C. after being beaten back at Dover, but his forces refused to disembark when they saw the local Belgic tribe ready to do battle and awaiting their landing. A standard-bearer of the Tenth Legion shamed the Roman forces by leaping into the water holding the gilded eagle standard aloft; the troops engaged, and victory went to the Romans. By the Middle Ages the town had moved quite a way inland, and then it became subordinate to the Cinque Port of Sandwich.

Among the important survivors of Deal's past is Deal Castle, which Henry VIII had constructed as a defense against possible Catholic invaders from the Continent after he broke with Rome. Severely damaged by a bomb in World War II, it has been restored almost completely, so that it is now as Samuel Pepys saw it when he sailed into the Downs in April 1660 with the fleet. His opinion of the town is rather damaging:

> So we took boat and first went on shore, it being very pleasant in fields; but a very pitiful town Deal is. We went to Fuller's (the famous place for ale), but they have not but what was in the vat.

In a similar fashion two centuries later, William Cobbett damned the town in his *Rural Rides;* it was, he said, "a most villainous place. . . . full of filthy looking people." He continued:

> Great desolation of abomination has been going on here; tremendous barracks, partly pulled down and partly tumbling down, and partly occupied by soldiers. Everything seems upon the perish. I was glad to hurry along through it, and to leave its inns and public-houses to be

occupied by the tarred, and trowsered, and blue-and-buff crew whose very vicinage I always detest.

Deal's literary associations begin with a now-obscure friend of Dr. Samuel Johnson, Mrs. Elizabeth Carter, who was born here and lived at Carter House most of her life; a plaque on the wall of the building (now a hotel) notes: "Royalty and Society were her friends and visited her here." Dr. Johnson especially admired her translating abilities, and this house was bought from the revenues of her translation of Epictetus. In the 19th century Deal was used in literature both by Charles Dickens and by William Makepeace Thackeray. In *Bleak House* Esther Summerson visits the town in the company of Charley. After an all-night coaching trip

we came into the narrow streets of Deal: and very gloomy they were upon a raw misty morning. The long flat beach, with its little irregular houses, wooden and brick, and its litter of capstans, and great boats, and sheds, and bare upright poles with tackle and blocks, and loose gravelly waste places overgrown with grass and weeds, wore as dull an appearance as any place I ever saw. The sea was heaving under a thick white fog; and nothing else was moving but a few early ropemakers, who, with the yarn twisted round their bodies, looked as if, tired of their present state of existence, they were spinning themselves into cordage. . . .
Then the fog began to rise like a curtain; and numbers of ships, that we had no idea were near, appeared. . . . [A]nd when the sun shone through the clouds, making silvery pools in the dark sea, the way in which these ships brightened, and shadowed, and changed, amid a bustle of boats putting off from the shore to them and from them to shore, and a general life and motion in themselves and everything around them, was most beautiful.

In *Denis Duval* Thackeray uses Deal as the location of the Blue Anchor Inn, whose landlady was Mrs. Boniface.

William Ernest Henley spent a recuperative holiday here in May 1895, and Joseph Conrad stayed at the South Eastern Hotel for three weeks in September 1920.

DEAN PRIOR, Devon (pop 243) The small village of Dean Prior, a few miles southwest of Ashburton, is on the southeastern fringe of Dartmoor and is consequently rather bleak and harsh. Following directly upon his chaplaincy to the Duke of Buckingham, Robert Herrick was given this living by King Charles I in September 1629. It was Herrick's first parish appointment and a good one: the parochial district was large and included the villages of Dean Prior, the largest, Dean Combe, and Dean Church, where the church and vicarage were. Herrick was installed officially at the end of October 1630 with an income of £21 a year, and he immediately installed as his housekeeper Prudence Baldwin, the Prue of his poems and a woman younger than he, even though he knew such an impropriety would cause gossip. Area guidebooks assert that he learned "to appreciate his parishioners and take delight in their 'nut brown mirth and russet wit,'" but this was not the case. In many ways Herrick was anything but a good vicar; this is the man who hurled his sermon at the congregation for its inattention, scandalized the local people by keeping a pet pig that he taught to drink cider from a tankard, and was reported for nonresidence in 1640 (probably), when he went to London without

the official approval of the Bishop. It is futile to think of Herrick's hatred of the area as a passing fancy when he writes:

Dean-bourn, farewell; I never look to see
Deane, or thy warty incivility. . . .
Rockie thou art; and rockie we discover
Thy men; and rockie are thy wayes all over.
O men, O manner; there and ever knowne
To be A Rockie Generation!
A people currish; churlish as the seas;
And rude (almost) as rudest Savages. . . .

Such "hate" poems were written throughout Herrick's tenure here; it was, he felt, a bitter exile: he had been "by hard fate sent/ Into a long and irksome banishment." Removed during the Commonwealth, Herrick went to London, but he returned to Dean Prior with the Restoration and continued to minister to the parish, after his own fashion, until his death in October 1674. He was buried in the churchyard in an unmarked grave on October 15, and a commemorative east window and bells were placed in the church in 1929. The old vicarage has been altered, but the cellar where Herrick stored his sack is unchanged.

DEANE, Hampshire (pop. 125) A short distance from the village of Steventon, Deane is one of the two livings held by Jane Austen's father, the Rev. George Austen. He became rector here in 1773, and Jane Austen was a frequent visitor to Deane House, home of the Harwoods. Henry Fielding is supposed to have modeled Squire Western in *Tom Jones* on one of the Harwoods.

DEEPDALE, Yorkshire Just below Barnard Castle and a short distance up the right bank of the Tees River is a deep and narrow valley known as Deepdale. Full of weirdly eroded rock ravines with overhanging cliffs and an abundance of silver fir trees planted in the thick woods, the dale is one of the pleasantest places in north Yorkshire. Sir Walter Scott knew Deepdale well and examined it minutely in the autumn of 1812 when he visited John B. S. Morritt at Rokeby Hall to gather more firsthand material for *Rokeby.*

It was during this visit that Morritt noticed Scott's extraordinary power of observation; Scott noted "down even the peculiar little wild flowers and herbs that accidentally grew round and on the side of a bold crag near his intended cave of Guy Denzil. . . ." The millstone grit cliffs, hung over with heath, harebells, and tufts of grass, are the spot sought by Wilfrid when as a youth he wanted pleasures not "in horse and hawk and hound"

But loved the quiet joys that wake
By lonely stream and silent lake;
In Deepdale's solitude to lie.
Where all is cliff and copse and sky;
To climb Catcastle's dizzy peak,
Or lone Pendragon's mound to seek.

Scott takes a bit of license in suggesting that Pendragon's mound lies in Deepdale; it is actually to the northwest beyond Cotherstone, near the opening of Baldersgill. Catcastle, which Sir Walter refers to as both Cat's Cradle and Cat's Castle, is the small nearby "wild glen where," says Scott, "we had such a clamber on horseback up a stone staircase. . . ."

DENHAM, Buckinghamshire (pop. 1,498) A picture-book village because of its brick-and-timber buildings, pubs around the green, and a small stream, Denham has been photographed more often than any other village in England. Both Pinewood and Rank film studios are here, and more films and television shows have been shot here than can be counted. Denham is fortunate in having two fine houses (both 17th-century), Denham Place and Denham Court, essentially at opposite ends of the village. Denham Court, much altered, was the seat of Sir William Bowyer, whose family was generous to many literary figures including John Dryden and Dr. Samuel Johnson. Dryden was here for a few months beginning in September 1696 when he was at work on Book XII of the *Aeneid;* he returned in August 1697, when he was working on "A Song for St. Cecilia's Day." At this time Dryden was ill with hearing difficulties that had originated in London, and a cold caught in September severely aggravated his deafness.

DENT, Yorkshire (pop. 996) Dent is an inaccessible moorland village of old stone cottages and cobbled streets in one of the smallest Yorkshire dales. The Dee River, fed by many tributary becks, winds through a dale covered with fern and trees, cascades over dark gray rocks, and disappears suddenly underground, only to reappear just as suddenly. High reaches of dark rock loom over a valley where the stone cottages, which once had attached galleries, are situated almost entirely along a narrow, winding, and difficult highway. Hartley Coleridge describes the village, its location, and its road hazards; little but the mode of transportation has changed:

There is a town, of little note or praise;
Narrow and winding are its rattling streets.
Where cart with cart in cumbrous conflict meets;
Hard straining up and backing down the ways
Where, insecure, the crawling infant plays. . . .

Dent was an important wool center, and in the 17th and 18th centuries every man, woman, and child knitted. The first thing a child learned upon entering school was a local knitting song, and by the time one full round of the song was completed, one round of the stocking was supposed to be done. Robert Southey, who relates the story of the "terrible knitters of Dent" in *The Doctor,* describes the industry quite accurately.

DENTON, Kent (pop. 153) One of a number of villages in Kent named Denton, this village is just off the road from Dover to Canterbury, 7½ miles northwest of Dover. With tile-hung houses and timbered cottages, Denton has an Early English church; just outside the village is Tappington Hall, a brick-and-timber Tudor farmhouse. Thomas Gray spent a two-month holiday at the rectory here in May and June 1766 as the guest of "Rev. Billy," the Rev. William Robinson, Mrs. Elizabeth Montagu's brother. Gray visited the coastal area of Kent and was completely entranced by the county; in a letter dated August 26 he writes:

. . . the country is all a garden, gay, rich, & fruitfull, & (from the rainy season) had preserved, till I left it, all that emerald verdure, wᶜʰ commonly one only sees for the first fortnight of the spring.

Tappington Hall was the home of the family of Richard Harris Barham, and the hall was the setting of some of *The Ingoldsby Legends.* He describes the hall and part of its atmosphere in "The Spectre of Tappington":

Tappington (generally called Tapton) Everard is an antiquated but commodious manor-house in the eastern division of the county of Kent. . . . The Glen . . . still frowns darkly as of yore; while an ineradicable blood-stain on the oaken stair yet bids defiance to the united energies of soap and sand.

DERBY, Derbyshire (pop. 142,403) South Derbyshire, an area of soft rolling hills, lazily wandering rivers, extensive arable land which produces abundant crops of wheat and barley, and clay deposits which support a vigorous pottery industry, has its industrial base in Derby (pronounced "dar′be"), the county town and administrative center of the shire. This has always been an important city; at the Norman Conquest, for example, it had more than 2,000 people. Known settlement dates to the extensive Roman colony of Derventio. Under the Anglo-Saxon heptarchy the town became Northwothige; the Danes subdued Northwothige and settled it. After the Treaty of Wedmore (878), the name was changed to Deoraby, from which the present name developed.

The Norman invasion brought almost complete destruction to the town, but it was rebuilt and became a prodigious medieval trading center. The first silk mill in England was introduced here in 1717, and when that industry disappeared, it was supplanted by an artificial-silk industry which also has vanished. Later in the 18th century, in 1773, a more durable industry arose; it was then that the charter for Crown Derby porcelain was granted by George III. The tide of the industrial revolution found Derby extremely flexible, and it now is a major center for the building of locomotives and carriages, produces Rolls-Royce airplane engines, and has a nuclear engineering research plant, chemical factories, engineering concerns, and metal foundries.

Not many old buildings still exist, although there are some around the Market Square. Four of the six medieval churches remain: St. James is of Norman origin but dates mainly from the 14th century, and the parish church of All Saints, elevated to cathedral status in 1927, was greatly rebuilt in 1725 by James Gibbs. Daniel Defoe visited the church when gathering material for *A Tour thro' the Whole Island of Great Britain:*

In the Church of *Allhallows,* or, as the *Spaniards* call it, *De Todos los Santos* All Saints, is the Pantheon, or Burial-Place of the noble, now Ducal family of *Cavendish,* now *Devonshire,* which was first erected by the Countess of *Shrewsbury,* . . . and at this Church is a famous Tower or Steeple, which for the Heighth and Beauty of its Building, is not equalled in this County, or in any of those adjacent.

By an Inscription upon this Church, it was erected, or at least the Steeple, at the Charge of the Maids and Batchelors of the Town, on which Account, whenever a Maid, Native of the Town, was marry'd, the Bells were Rung by Batchelors. . . .

Literary associations with Derby begin in the 17th century. It is generally accepted that Samuel Richardson was a native of Derbyshire, but the specific birthplace is not known. However, a stronger but tenuous link exists between the novelist and Derby, for it is assumed that some of his childhood and youth were spent here because his father has been described as a "joiner of Derby." A more definite relationship is that between Dr. Samuel Johnson and St. Werburgh's Church, located beside Markeaton Brook. The church, one of those counted in the Domesday Survey, was almost totally rebuilt in 1894; the original chancel is now a chapel. Here on July 9, 1735, Samuel Johnson, as the license notes, of St. Mary parish in Lichfield, married Mrs. Elizabeth (Tetty) Porter of the parish of St. Michael in Birmingham. They must have appeared an unusual couple: Johnson, twenty-five and ugly, and Mrs. Porter, forty-five and a widow. But, "Sir," said Dr. Johnson, "it was a love marriage on both sides." More than forty years later, as Boswell reports, he and Dr. Johnson returned here twice, and on neither occasion did Johnson inquire of the church. Also in this century, from 1775 to 1781, Maria Edgeworth attended Mrs. Latuffiere's school, where she studied French and handwriting.

In the mid-19th century Matthew Arnold spent a great deal of time in Derby after being appointed to Her Majesty's Inspectorate for Schools at the behest of the 3d Marquess of Lansdowne. Arnold appears to have lodged at Babington Hall while his tours took him over an eleven-county area. George Eliot (Mary Ann Evans) uses Derby under the name Stoniton in *Adam Bede;* here Hetty is brought to trial for infanticide and found guilty. In the jail here Dinah Morris secures Hetty's confession, and they ride from the jail in a cart to the site of the gallows:

> It was a sight that some people remembered better even than their own sorrows—the sight in that gray clear morning, when the fatal cart with the two young women in it was described by the waiting watching multitude, cleaving its way towards the hideous symbol of a deliberately inflicted sudden death.
> All Stoniton had heard of Dinah Morris, the young Methodist woman who had brought the obstinate criminal to confess, and there was as much eagerness to see her as to see the wretched Hetty.

A later use of Derby occurs in D. H. Lawrence's *Sons and Lovers,* in which it receives passing mention as a market town. A final association is with the Derby ram, and the town has erected an effigy of this famous animal of the ballad in the new shopping mall.

DERBYSHIRE (pop. 757,352) A north Midland county with upland and lowland regions, Derbyshire (pronounced "dar′bi-shire") is in an area of great beauty; roughly rectangular in shape, the county has an area of 650,369 acres. The upland region ends in the High Peak area, most of which lies in the great Peak District National Park. Here high, rock crags rise from heather- and peat-covered moors, and everywhere there are rich pastures and woodlands; this area is also where the Pennines, which run north to the Scottish border and are often called the "backbone of England," begin.

D. H. Lawrence uses the shire extensively, although in many cases the places are not specifically identifiable. *The Virgin and the Gipsy,* for example, is clearly set in a Derbyshire village called Papplewick. This has never been properly located even though some of Lawrence's description seems most vivid:

> Past the gate went the whitish muddy road, crossing the stone bridge almost immediately, and winding in a curve up to the steep, clustering, stony, smoking northern village, that perched over the grim stone mills which Yvette could see ahead down the narrow valley, their tall chimneys long and erect.
> The rectory was on one side of the Papple, in the rather steep valley, the village was beyond and above, further down, on the other side the swift stream. At the back of the rectory the hill went up steep with a grove of dark, bare larches, through which the road disappeared.

Lawrence is never consistent in his use of names; sometimes he uses the real one, sometimes a fictional one, and sometimes both. "Kangaroo" also is placed in the Midlands, probably Derbyshire, but the location is not available; "Wintry Peacock" and "Glad Ghosts" are two other local short stories, both the result of a year's residence at Middleton-by-Wirksworth. Derbyshire also figures importantly in *Lady Chatterley's Lover;* Constance's drive through Derbyshire is certainly based on Lawrence's own Midlands trips in 1925 and 1926 and probably follows those journeys:

> The car ploughed uphill through the long squalid straggle of Tevershall, the blackened brick dwellings, the black slate roofs glistening their sharp edges, the mud black with coal dust, the pavements wet and black. It was as if dismalness had soaked through and through everything. . . .
> A coal cart was coming downhill, clanking in the rain. Field (the driver) started upwards, past the big but weary-looking drapers and clothing shops, the post office, into the little market place of forlorn space, where Sam Black was peering out of the door of the Sun, that called itself an inn, not a pub, and where commercial travellers stayed. . . .
> The church was away to the left among black trees. The car slid downhill, past the Miners' Arms. It had already passed the Wellington, the Nelson, the Three Tuns, and the Sun, now it passed the Miners' Arms, then the Mechanics' Hall, then the new and almost gaudy Miners' Welfare and so, past a few new "villas," out into the blackened road between dark hedges and dark green fields, towards Stacks Gate.
> When Connie saw the great lorries full of steel workers from Sheffield . . . off for an excursion to Matlock, her bowels fainted.

But these locations are virtually impossible to identify, and most critics agree that the journey is a composite of many places known to Lawrence. *Sons and Lovers* is a somewhat different matter; many of the locales are specifically identifiable and mentioned under their own names.

DERWENT RIVER and DERWENT WATER, Cumberland The 34-mile-long Derwent River in Cumberland is one of four northern English rivers of that name. While it is by no means the longest or the most navigable, it is the best known. Rising in the neighborhood of Bow Fell and Scafell, it flows northward to Derwent Water and then northwest to Bassenthwaite Water; a westward turn takes it out to Solway Firth at Workington by way of Cockermouth. John Leland includes the Derwent River in his *Itinerary* and describes it, and a little later Michael Drayton notices the river in Song XXX of *Poly-Olbion:*

> . . . and in her way doth win
> Cleere *Coker* her compeere, which at her comming in,
> Gives Coker-mouth the name, by standing at her fall,

Into faire *Darwents* Banks, when *Darwent* therewithall,
Runnes on her watry Race, and for her greater fame,
Of *Neptune* doth obtaine a Haven of her name. . . .

Another travel writer, Daniel Defoe, notes the Derwent a century later in *A Tour thro' the Whole Island of Great Britain* when he comments that the river "is noted for very good Salmon and for a very great Quantity, and Trout."

More especially, the Derwent is associated with William Wordsworth; it flowed behind his Cockermouth birthplace, as he notes in *The Prelude*, and it recurs frequently in his writing. He calls it the "glory of the vale" in "To the River Derwent" and writes:

Among the mountains were we nursed, loved Stream!
Thou near the eagle's nest—within brief sail,
I, of his bold wing floating on the gale,
Where thy deep voice could lull me! Faint the beam
Of human life when first allowed to gleam
On mortal notice. . . .

Derwent Water was probably the last lake William Beckford visited on his 1779 tour of England. The countryside with its cottages, holly, and oak pleased him; and here he liked the small springs,

conducted from the rock by a trough to supply little natural basins scooped out of the living rock, on the edge of which I noticed several bright jugs of earthenware, that reminded me of Patriarchal times and made me venerate these fountains.

Thomas Edward Brown, the Manx poet, recalls Derwent Water in "Epistola ad Dakyns," written in memory of his friend, and mentions that this is one of the

DERWENT WATER   Seen from Friar's Crag, Derwent Water is probably the best-known lake in the Lake District because of its myriad of associations with William Wordsworth. From this spot on a clear day the cataract of Lodore can be seen in the distance.

places the friend will haunt because of his love for the area.

DEWSBURY MOOR, Yorkshire   A mile to the west of the heavily industrialized town of Dewsbury, Dewsbury Moor was the location to which Miss Wooler removed her school from Roe Head around 1836; this site without the "fine, open, breezy situation of the former" pleased neither Charlotte Brontë, one of the teachers, nor her sister Anne, one of the students. (Emily had already gone to teach in Halifax.) In comparing Roe Head and Dewsbury Moor, Elizabeth Gaskell says this "residence was a much lower site, and the air much less pure and exhilarating to one bred at the wild hill-village of Haworth."

DINTON, Wiltshire (pop. 397)   Built on a hillside 8½ miles west of Salisbury, Dinton is a lovely little village with a fine cruciform church and three houses under the care of the National Trust, two of which have important literary associations. Hyde House, often confused with Little Clarendon, a quarter of a mile to the east, was the birthplace of Edward Hyde, 1st Earl of Clarendon, on Febuary 18, 1609. Besides serving as Charles II's Lord Chancellor and writing *The History of the Great Rebellion,* Hyde began the family that produced two queens; his daughter Anne married the Duke of York, later James II, and was the mother of Mary II (wife of William of Orange) and Queen Anne. The 17th-century building known as Lawes Cottage was the birthplace (1596) and home of Henry Lawes, John Milton's friend, whose invitation brought about the masque of *Comus.* Lawes composed the music for the masque, quite possibly some of it here, and played the Attendant Spirit for the first performance at Ludlow Castle. Milton writes:

Harry, whose tuneful and well measured song
First taught our English music how to span
Words with just note and accent—not to scan
With Midas ears, committing short and long.

DISS, Norfolk   Diss is an attractive old market town on the Waveney River, 20 miles southwest of Norwich; here Tudor, Georgian, and Victorian houses are stacked up along the 6-acre mere, which comes to the edge of the main street; traffic is especially trying on the crooked streets on market days. The restored church has a 13th-century crenellated tower and two superb 15th-century chancel chapels built by local guilds. While the 16th-century poet John Skelton is often claimed as a native (without proof), he was rector here for twenty-five years. He was settled here by April 1504 and signed "Master John Skelton, laureat, parson of Diss in Norfolk" as a witness to a parishioner's will in the same year. Skelton lived an irregular life, and Anthony à Wood's statement that "at Diss and in the diocese Skelton was esteemed more fit for the stage than the pew or pulpit" was undoubtedly correct. Skelton's behavior here was peculiar, and it is now accepted that his actions were questioned by the Bishop of Norwich. One of the accusations was that he lived with a woman and had many children by her; his parishioners had lodged the complaint after a son was born. In keeping with his character, he took to the pulpit on Sunday, held the naked child aloft, queried what fault they found in him, and commented that the child was "as fair as is the best of yours." Many years later he confessed he had been married but could not earlier bring himself to admit the fact openly. Skelton's attacks on Thomas Cardinal Wolsey were made while he held this living, and the poet sought sanctuary in Westminster to avoid imprisonment. The poet retained his post here until his death but spent no time in Diss after 1514. He died at Westminster in 1529. Mere Manor, the Elizabethan rectory, stands on the site of the one Skelton inhabited.

DITCHINGHAM, Norfolk (pop. 997)   The central plateau of Norfolk was once extensive woodland and is now farmland with the scattered villages clustered around commons or greens which were once medieval clearings in the woods. Ditchingham is on the Waveney River 1½ miles north of Bungay. The 15th-century church, which is set away from the village, was restored late in the 19th century. The restoration of the south porch and the addition of the clock tower were undertaken by Sir Henry Rider Haggard in memory of his only son Arthur, who died at the age of nine. The novelist lived at Ditchingham House, his wife's family home. Haggard married Mariana Louisa Margitson in 1880, and nine years later, after he read for the bar and turned to politics, the couple settled here. In Ditchingham Haggard turned to his two loves, writing and agriculture. *Joan Haste, King Solomon's Mines, Allan Quatermain,* and *She* are among the works written here. The novelist died in London in 1925; the 16th-century screen in the church was restored and a window erected in his honor.

DITCHLEY, Oxfordshire   An almost-nonexistent Oxfordshire hamlet 4½ miles northwest of Woodstock, Ditchley was the birthplace of John Wilmot, 2d Earl of Rochester, on April 10, 1647. Much of his childhood was spent here, and he succeeded to the estate upon the death of his father in 1658. Little is known of Wilmot's early life here or of the house itself, although John Evelyn, who visited "Dichley" on October 20, 1664, describes it as "a low antient timber house, with a pretty bowling greene." The present house, built on the site of the original, eventually came into the hands of the family from which the American Confederate general Robert E. Lee was descended. It is now an Anglo-American conference center. Sir Walter Scott, it should be noted, uses Sir Henry Lee and his dog Bevis in *Woodstock.*

DORCHESTER, Dorset (pop. 10,031)   The bustling county town of Dorset, Dorchester sits in the heathland of mid-Dorset, 6 miles north of Weymouth on the Frome (pronounced "frume") River, the longest river wholly in the shire. Dorchester was inhabited long before the Romans arrived, and the nearby Iron Age camp at Poundbury (pronounced "pummery") has yielded extensive remains. The town became the Roman Durnovaria, a settlement of considerable importance. Roman remains are much in evidence: on the grounds of the Dorset County Hall an old building is clearly discernible. One stretch of Roman wall remains on West Walk, and the rest can be traced; a number of Roman cemeteries lie near the Grove; and just to the south a Neolithic henge, Maumbury

Rings (approximately 115 feet in diameter), was turned into an amphitheater by the Romans. The town's street pattern is a typical Roman grid. After the departure of the Romans, little was heard of Dorchester until modern times.

The medieval town thrived and grew, but disastrous fires occurred in the 17th and 18th centuries. In August 1613 a tallow chandler overheated his cauldron, and before the conflagration was brought under control, Holy Trinity and All Saints' Churches and 300 houses were destroyed. Thus Dorchester is architecturally a modern town. The 15th-century Church of St. Peter, at the junction of the High and South Streets, is the only old church remaining. Across from the Shire Hall, where the Tolpuddle Martyrs (early union organizers) were tried, is the timber-framed 17th-century house where Judge George Jeffreys lodged when he held the infamous assizes following the Duke of Monmouth's defeat in 1685. Dorchester still functions as a market town, serving an extensive rural area; this activity is one characteristic Daniel Defoe remarks on in *A Tour thro' the Whole Island of Great Britain:*

> *Dorchester* is indeed a pleasant agreeable Town to live in, and where I thought the People seem'd less Divided into Factions and Parties, than in other Places. . . . The Town is populous, tho' not large, the Streets broad, but the Buildings old, and low; however, there is good Company and a good deal of it; and a Man that coveted a retreat in this World might as agreeably spend his time, and as well in *Dorchester,* as in any Town I know in *England.*

The town has particularly lengthy literary associations with William Barnes and Thomas Hardy. Barnes came here from Sturminster Newton in 1818 to work as a copier of deeds for a Mr. Coombs and made the acquaintance of the Rev. John Henry Richman, rector of St. Peter's, who taught poetic techniques to the young man and lent him as many books as he could read. Barnes also set about learning wood engraving and became so proficient that he was able to submit eight blocks for inclusion in *A Walk round Dorchester.* At the same time he undertook the study of etymology and languages, and here too he became knowledgeable. His first work, *Orra: A Lapland Tale,* was published in 1822, and the following year he secured the mastership of a school in Mere, Wiltshire. His first love was Dorset, though, and in 1835 he returned to Dorchester to take over a very promising school on Durngate Street, where he also lived. The accommodations were much too small as the school grew, and a few years later he took two houses on South Street; Number 40 is marked with a plaque. In 1838 he placed his name on the books at St. John's College, Cambridge, and in 1847 he was ordained by the Bishop of Salisbury. He kept up not only his school while ministering to the parish of Whitcombe (3 miles to the southeast) but also his writing until 1862, when he took the living at Winterbourne Came. Among the volumes produced here are *Poems of Rural Life in the Dorset Dialect, Philological Grammar,* and *Hwomely Rhymes.* Outside St. Peter's Church is a commemorative statue unveiled in 1887 by Christopher Wordsworth, Bishop of Salisbury and brother of William Wordsworth; on the base are lines from "Culver Bell and the Squire."

Thomas Hardy's association with Dorchester dates from 1849, when he began attending a day school conducted by Isaac J. Last, a Nonconformist, and lasted with only intermittent lapses until his death in January 1928. In 1856 he was apprenticed to John Hicks, an architect here, and became acquainted with William Barnes, whose school was next door to Hicks's office. Hardy attended the church at Fordington, where the Rev. Henry Moule preached; Moule's sermons and his eight sons made a lasting impression on the novelist. Indeed, Charles Moule, later a Senior Fellow and President of Corpus Christi College, Cambridge, became the model for Angel Clare in *Tess of the D'Urbervilles.* Hardy left in 1862 for London, where he continued his work in architecture. Partly because of ill health he returned to Dorchester and Hicks's office in 1867 and was by this time determined on a writing career. His first work, *The Poor Man and the Lady,* was rejected by Macmillan and also, in 1869, by Chapman & Hall, whose reader requested an interview. The reader was George Meredith, and it was then that Hardy was advised not to publish the manuscript and to work on "plot." Accordingly, he destroyed the manuscript and wrote *Desperate Remedies,* rejected by Macmillan in 1870 but published under a different imprint in 1871. Hardy's architectural work on restoring old churches was becoming less and less important, and his work at St. Juliot, Cornwall, was among his last. *Under the Greenwood Tree* appeared in 1872 and prompted Leslie (later Sir Leslie) Stephen to invite Hardy to write a serial for the *Cornhill Magazine;* the result was *Far from the Madding Crowd,* which began to run in January 1874 and which the author finished at Bockhampton that summer.

Hardy married in 1874, and after nine years of moving around he rented an unattractive house on Shire Hall Lane and in October began building Max Gate on Wareham Road. The name of the house came from the man who owned a little cottage here which had been a tollgate; the area was known locally as Mack's Gate. Hardy wished to preserve the sound but did not feel he could use the name. (Mack's Gate, however, appears in *The Dynasts.*) He and his wife moved into the house in June 1885; and here he wrote *The Mayor of Casterbridge, The Woodlanders, Tess of the D'Urbervilles, Jude the Obscure,* and other works, including "The Strange House," which concerns Max Gate. In November 1912 Emma Lavinia Hardy died; as Hardy said, it was the end of an unhappy marriage, but some of his best love poetry was written after the bitterness had gone. Hardy remarried in 1914, and the union with Florence Dugdale was a happy one. He died on January 11, 1928, after his wife had finished reading one stanza of the *Rubáiyát of Omar Khayyám:*

Oh Thou, who Man of baser Earth didst make,
And ev'n with Paradise devise the Snake:
For all the Sin wherewith the Face of Man
Is blacken'd—Man's Forgiveness give—and take!

Hardy's many guests here included A. E. Housman, who spent a weekend at Max Gate; John Galsworthy, who found Hardy a "nice, alert old fellow" in 1915; and Hilaire Belloc, with whom Hardy spent an afternoon talking about a legendary storm. The Dorset County Museum contains a reconstruction of Hardy's study at Max Gate and a collection of his manuscripts, and at the Top o' Town is a memorial statue by Eric Kennington.

Dorchester becomes Casterbridge in Hardy's works and appears in at least seven of his novels, eleven short stories, and seven poems; the area is used extensively, and virtually nothing in the contemporary town or its surrounding area is omitted. The more significant places can be picked out from *Far from the Madding Crowd* and, especially, *The Mayor of Casterbridge.* Mrs. Susan Newson and Elizabeth-Jane arrive in Casterbridge in search of Henchard and, approaching the city, rest on the summit of a hill which "commanded a full view of the town and its environs." The hill is Stinsford Hill (Hardy's Mellstock Rise). To the girl the town appears to be "an old-fashioned place . . . huddled all together; and it is shut in by a square wall of trees, like a plot of garden ground by a box-edging." Hardy continues:

> It stood as an indistinct mass behind a dense stockade of limes and chestnuts, set in the midst of miles of rotund down and concave field. The mass became gradually dissected by the vision into towers, gables, chimneys, and casements, the highest glazings shining bleared and bloodshot with the coppery fire they caught from the belt of sunlit cloud in the west.
>
> From the centre of each side of this tree-bound square ran avenues east, west, and south into the wide expanse of cornland and coomb to the distance of a mile or so.

Continuing on their way, Mrs. Newson and Elizabeth-Jane pass down the London road, where "the dense trees of the avenue rendered the road dark as a tunnel." Many of the trees have long since gone. The Newsons wander about the town and

> returned into the High Street, where there were timber houses with overhanging stories. . . . There were houses of brick-nogging, which derived their chief support from those adjoining. There were slate roofs patched with tiles, and tile roofs patched with slate, with occasionally a roof of thatch.

Some of the old buildings remain, but many have disappeared. The "grizzled church, whose massive square tower rose unbroken into the darkening sky," is St. Peter's. The curfew which Mrs. Newson and Elizabeth-Jane hear is still rung. Other clocks strike, one at the jail (which figures more prominently in "The Withered Arm") and one "from the gable of an almshouse" (Napper's Mite). They approach the King's Arms (the proper name) on the High Street. Farfrae enters the town and is directed to the Three Mariners:

> A long, narrow, dimly-lit passage gave access to the inn. . . . The good stabling and the good ale of the Mariners, though somewhat difficult to reach on account of there being but this narrow way to both, were nevertheless perseveringly sought out by the sagacious old heads who knew what was what in Casterbridge.

This is where Elizabeth-Jane and her mother also stay.

On the daughter's trip to see Henchard, she goes up the High Street on a market day (a Wednesday, then, no doubt as now); she passes "the vans of carriers," for then, as now,

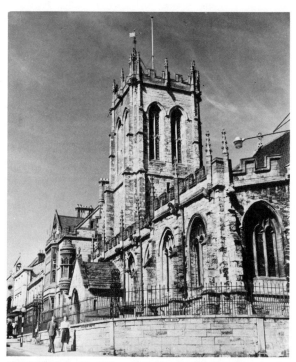

DORCHESTER   The 15th-century Church of St. Peter has associations with both William Barnes and Thomas Hardy; the church,
Hardy writes in *The Mayor of Casterbridge*, showed "how completely the mortar from the joints of the stonework had been nibbled
out by time and weather. . . ."

Casterbridge was in most respects but the pole, focus, or
nerve-knot of the surrounding country life. . . . Casterbridge lived by agriculture at one remove further from the
fountain-head than the adjoining villages—no more. The
townsfolk understood every fluctuation in the rustic's condition, for it affected their receipts as much as
the labourer's. . . .

"Henchard's house was one of the best," Hardy
writes, "faced with dull red-and-grey old brick," and
was located on the High Street. Just before Elizabeth-
Jane's arrival, Henchard and Farfrae talk as they walk

> towards the Bath and Bristol road . . . till they had gone
> down an avenue on the town walls called the Chalk
> Walk, leading to an angle where the North and West
> escarpments met. From this high corner of the square
> earthworks a vast extent of country could be seen.

Chalk Walk is undoubtedly Colliton Walk, which is
placed on the exact top of the Roman wall. Elizabeth-
Jane's request is countered by Henchard's note asking a meeting with Mrs. Newson "at the Ring on the
Budmouth Road." This, Hardy says, is "merely the
local name of one of the finest Roman Amphi-
theatres, if not the very finest, remaining in Britain":
Maumbury Rings.

> The Amphitheatre was a huge circular enclosure, with
> a notch at opposite extremities of its diameter north and
> south. From its sloping internal form it might have been
> called the spittoon of the Jötuns. It was to Casterbridge
> what the ruined Coliseum is to modern Rome, and was
> nearly of the same magnitude. The dusk of evening was
> the proper hour at which a true impression of this
> suggestive place could be received. Standing in the mid-
> dle of the arena at that time there by degrees became

apparent its real vastness, which a cursory view from the
summit at noon-day was apt to obscure.

Henchard recommends that Susan Newson and the
girl take lodgings on the High Street over a china shop

> in the upper or western part of the town, near the Roman
> wall, and the avenue which overshadowed it. The evening
> sun seemed to shine more yellowly there than anywhere
> else this autumn—stretching its rays, as the hours grew
> later, under the lowest sycamore boughs, and steeping
> the ground-floor of the dwelling, with its green shutters,
> in a substratum of radiance which the foliage screened
> from the upper parts.

Henchard and Farfrae both plan entertainments
for "a day of public rejoicing . . . in celebration of a
national event that had recently taken place." Henchard's is held at Poundbury, just northwest of the
town:

> Close to the town was an elevated green spot sur-
> rounded by an ancient square earthwork—earthworks
> square and not square, were as common as blackberries
> hereabout—a spot whereon the Casterbridge people usu-
> ally held any kind of merry-making, meeting, or sheep-
> fair that required more space than the streets would
> afford. On one side it sloped to the river Froom, and from
> any point a view was obtained of the country round for
> many miles. This pleasant upland was to be the scene of
> Henchard's exploit.

Farfrae's fete takes place on West Walk (a name retained today). The Corn Market, which is mentioned
throughout the novel but which has a far more conspicuous role in *Far from the Madding Crowd*, is still
very similar; then, though, the roadway between St.
Peter's Church and the corn exchange was spanned
by an archway. Henchard's walk into the night after
reading his wife's confession takes him to "a bypath
on the river bank, skirting the north-eastern limits of
the town":

> The river—slow, noiseless, and dark—the Schwarz-
> wasser of Casterbridge—ran beneath a low cliff, the two
> together forming a defence which had rendered walls and
> artificial earthworks on this side unnecessary. Here were
> ruins of a Franciscan priory, and a mill attached to the
> same, the water of which roared down a back-hatch like
> the voice of desolation. Above the cliff, and behind the
> river, rose a pile of buildings, and in the front of the pile a
> square mass cut into the sky. It was like a pedestal
> lacking its statue. This missing feature, without which
> the design remained incomplete, was, in truth, the corpse
> of a man; for the square mass formed the base of the
> gallows, the extensive buildings at the back being the
> county gaol.

(This county jail is not the present building, and the
hangman's cottage figures more prominently in
"The Withered Arm.")
Elizabeth-Jane seizes every opportunity to visit her
mother's grave in

> the still-used burial-ground of the old Roman-British
> city, whose curious feature was this, its continuity as a
> place of sepulture. Mrs. Henchard's dust mingled with
> the dust of women who lay ornamented with glass hair-
> pins and amber necklaces, and men who held in their
> mouths coins of Hadrian, Posthumus, and the
> Constantines.

This is allegedly on Fordington Hill (Hardy's Durnover Hill), just outside the town. It is here that

Elizabeth-Jane meets Lucetta, who takes "High-Place Hall—the old stone one looking down the lane to the Market":

> The Hall, with its grey *façade* and parapet, was the only residence of its sort so near the centre of the town. It had, in the first place, the characteristics of a country mansion—birds' nests in its chimneys, damp nooks where fungi grew, and irregularities of surface direct from Nature's trowel. At night the forms of passengers were patterned by the lamps in black shadows upon the pale walls.

Hardy draws on Colliton House for the hall, but he moves it eastward toward North Square. After moving in with Miss Templeham, Elizabeth-Jane is sent on a series of errands which include a trip to the museum; Elizabeth-Jane's statement that she has never seen the museum prompts Miss Templeham to say:

> It is an old house in a back street—I forget where—but you'll find out—and there are crowds of interesting things—skeletons, teeth, old pots and pans, ancient boots and shoes, birds' eggs—all charmingly instructive.

This is not the present Dorset County Museum but was a house on Trinity Street near the Antelope Hotel.

Jopp, "the manager originally displaced by Farfrae's arrival," lives "in Mixen Lane—a back slum of the town, the *Pis Aller* of Casterbridge domiciliation"; the slum of Mill Street is now gone, as most of it was when Hardy wrote. Here the "skimmity ride" is planned at "the Inn called Peter's Finger . . . the church of Mixen Lane";

> Mixen Lane was the Adullam of all the surrounding villages. It was the hiding-place of those who were in distress, and in debt, and trouble of every kind. . . .
> The lane and its surrounding thicket of thatched cottages stretched out like a spit into the moist and misty lowland. Much that was sad, much that was low, some things that were baneful, could be seen in Mixen Lane. Vice ran freely in and out certain of the doors in the neighbourhood; recklessness dwelt under the roof with the crooked chimney; shame in some bow-windows; theft (in times of privation) in the thatched and mud-walled houses by the sallows. Even slaughter had not been altogether unknown here.

Another undesirable part of the town is portrayed after Henchard's bankruptcy:

> Two bridges stood near the lower part of Casterbridge town. The first, of weather-stained brick, was immediately at the end of High Street, where a diverging branch from that thoroughfare ran round to the low-lying Durnover lanes; so that the precincts of the bridge formed the merging point of respectability and indigence. The second bridge, of stone, was further out on the highway—in fact, fairly in the meadows, though still within the town boundary.
> These bridges had speaking countenances. . . .
> For to this pair of bridges gravitated all the failures of the town; those who failed in business, in love, in sobriety, in crime. . . .
> There was a marked difference of quality between the personages who haunted the near bridge of brick and the personages who haunted the far one of stone. Those of lowest character preferred the former, adjoining the town. . . .

The first bridge is at the east end of the High Street,

and the second, Grey's Bridge, figures in a number of other novels and poems, among them *The Trumpet-Major, Far from the Madding Crowd,* and *Life's Little Ironies and a Few Crusted Characters.*

Dorchester appears in many of Hardy's other works. *Far from the Madding Crowd* includes more than twenty specific sites, among them both All Saints' and All Souls' Churches; Troy and Fanny Robin are to be married at the former, but she goes to All Souls' instead and misses the ceremony. The Corn Market, "the low though extensive hall, supported by beams and pillars, and latterly dignified by the name of Corn Exchange," is where Bathsheba takes up her position. "The bridge over the Froom" is Grey's Bridge, over which Fanny Robin passes, and the Swan Bridge is mentioned as well. The White Hart Tavern stood at the lower end of town, and here Troy meets Pennways; also mentioned are the Casterbridge Barracks, the grammar school, and the jail, on a "much-desired spot outside the town":

> Originally it had been a mere case to hold people. The shell had been so thin, so devoid of excrescence, and so closely drawn . . . that the grim character of what was beneath showed through it. . . .
> Then Nature, as if offended, lent a hand. Masses of ivy grew up, completely covering the walls, till the place looked like an abbey; and it was discovered that the view from the front, over the Casterbridge chimneys, was one of the most magnificent in the county. . . .
> This stone edifice consisted of a central mass and two wings, whereon stood as sentinels a few slim chimneys, now gurgling sorrowfully to the slow wind. In the wall was a gate, and by the gate a bell-pull formed of a hanging wire.

Fanny dies at the Casterbridge Union; also mentioned are the King's Arms Inn (North Street), the Post Office, the South Street Almshouses, and the Tailor's Arms.

Dorchester can claim one native author, Llewelyn Powys, who was born here in 1884, when his father was curate of St. Peter's Church. During this time Powys's older brother, Theodore Francis, attended the grammar school.

DORKING, Surrey (pop. 18,115) The ancient town of Dorking is situated at the end of a gap in the North Downs cut by the Mole River; to the northeast is Box Hill, and to the south is Leith Hill. The site attracted settlers from the Iron Age to the Norman period, including Danish invaders on numerous occasions. Dorking, or Darking, as John Aubrey calls it, was Aubrey's home for a brief period in the 17th century.

The White Horse Inn in the center of town dates to the 15th century; although Charles Dickens stayed at the inn, the town is rather more proud of fictional Dickensian associations, some of which are partly conjectural. Sam Weller certainly does journey by coach from Arundel to Dorking "to see his father and pay his duty to his mother-in-law," but the identity of the original of the inn, the Marquis of Granby, kept by Mrs. Weller is uncertain. Dickens's description seems quite exact:

> The Marquis of Granby in Mrs. Weller's time was quite a model of a roadside public-house of the better class— just large enough to be convenient and small enough to be snug. . . .

The bar window displayed a choice collection of geranium plants and a well-dusted row of spirit phials. The open shutters bore a variety of golden inscriptions, eulogistic of good beds and neat wines; and the choice group of countrymen and hostlers lounging about the stable-door and horse-trough afforded presumptive proof of the excellent quality of the ale and spirits which were sold within.

The major claimant, the Old King's Head, is gone, and the field is left to the King's Arms and the White Horse itself, both of which aspire to the honor.

Two other important literary figures are associated with the town. George Gissing lived at 7 Clifton Terrace beginning in April 1898. When Gabrielle Fleury came for a week in October, they decided to live as man and wife. A contemporary of Gissing's, George Meredith, is buried in Dorking Cemetery; he died at his home at Box Hill on May 18, 1909, and his ashes were brought here for interment next to his wife's remains. The simple tombstone contains the following epitaph :

Life is but a little holding, lent
  To do a mighty labour. It is one
With heaven and the stars when it is spent
  To do God's aim. Else die we with the Sun.

At Meredith's death King Edward VII and others wanted to bury him in Westminster Abbey, but the idea was firmly rejected by the family and the executors of his estate.

Just half a mile east of Dorking are the remains of the Deepdene estate, built originally in Palladian style in 1652. John Evelyn, who visited here in 1655, was extremely impressed by its amphitheater garden, and John Aubrey spoke of its "pleasant and delightful solitude" in 1665. In the 19th century, after Thomas Hope had it greatly enlarged, Benjamin Disraeli visited while he was writing *Coningsby.* Indeed, this book is dedicated to Hope's son Henry, since "these volumes were conceived and partly executed amid the glades and galleries of Deepdene."

DORSET HEATHLAND   Although the heathland of Dorset is a diffuse area and its parts bear different names, it is usually thought of as an entity, a brooding wilderness which stretches from Dorchester to Bournemouth with only an occasional break. The natural environment has defied taming: briers and bracken have stubbornly refused to give way to cultivation, and people have now given in to nature. It is, as John Leland comments, "overgrown with heath and moss." Its principal spokesman, Thomas Hardy, makes it into Egdon Heath:

[P]recisely at this transitional point of its nightly roll into darkness the great and particular glory of the Egdon waste began, and nobody could be said to understand the heath who had not been there at such a time. It could best be felt when it could not be clearly seen, its complete effect and explanation lying in this and the succeeding hours before the next dawn: then, and only then, did it tell its true tale. . . . The place became full of a watchful intentness now; for when other things sank brooding to sleep the heath appeared slowly to awake and listen. Every night its Titanic form seemed to await something; but it had waited thus, unmoved, during so many centuries, through the crises of so many things, that it could only be imagined to await one last crisis—the final overthrow.

Egdon Heath (for want of a more accurate name), Hardy contended, could actively influence people, as it often does with the characters in his novels. Moreover, there is sufficient richness in the natural scenery here—ancient barrows; deep, covered pits; stagnant, algae-covered ponds—to assist in creating many effects an author might want.

Practically all of *The Return of the Native* is set upon the heath. Bloom's End, the Yeobrights' cottage, is located on a spur of the heath near Lower Bockhampton. The farmhouse on which Hardy models the cottage is called Bhompston, and even though the house has been greatly altered (it no longer has white palings in front, nor is it "encrusted with heavy thatchings, which dropped between the upper windows"), it is still recognizable as the scene of the mumming. The Devil's Bellows, "a clump of fir trees so highly thrust up into the sky that their foliage from a distance appeared as a black spot in the air above the crown of the hill," is in the eastern part of the heath near Affpuddle. The highway traversing Egdon Heath enters this novel under its real name, Via Iceniana, or the Ikenield Way (also called Icknield Street); in a number of the poems in *Poems of the Past and Present* and in *The Well-Beloved* it become Ickling Way. It is also referred to as the Roman Road in *Time's Laughingstocks and Other Poems.* Mistover Knap, where Captain Vye lives in the hamlet of Mistover, is supposed to be only a short distance from Rainbarrow Hill; all traces of the cottage which once stood there are gone. However, the large pool "bearded all round by heather and rushes" is just north of the barrows under a bank. The Quiet Woman Inn on the old Roman highway was originally known as the Traveller's Rest; later it became the Wild Duck Inn and eventually Duck Farm. Traces of the old inn, including the hatch between the kitchen and the parlor, remain in the present farmhouse. Throop Corner, to which Damon Wildeve escorts Eustacia after the village dancing, is easily identified as the crossroads just south of the tiny hamlet on the heath; Throop Great Pond is in the vicinity. The names of most of the other specific places in *The Return of the Native,* such as Moreford Pond and Bottom Pond, are accurate and are generally located where Hardy places them, although Rainbarrow Hill, placed centrally in the novel (and in *The Trumpet-Major*) to justify an overview of the heath, is transported to its western edge.

Egdon Heath, because it is an integral part of Hardy's Wessex, appears in almost all his works. Donald Farfrae and Elizabeth-Jane, in *The Mayor of Casterbridge,* search the north side of Egdon for Henchard and find him dead at a humble cottage "built of kneaded clay" and now reduced "to a lumpy crumbling surface." The cottage is gone, but "the form of a blasted clump of firs on the summit of a hill" is still distinguishable on Corfe Mullin Heath, near Wimborne Minster. "The Fiddler of the Reels" includes not only a search across Egdon, "a mass of dark heath-land [which] rose sullenly upward to its not easily accessible interior," but also a scene at the Quiet Woman Inn in which Ned discovers Mop Ollamoor has departed with the child. Headless William's Pond is the pool within sight of Norris Hill Farm near Lower Bockhampton. "By the Barrows" concerns Rainbarrow Hill but moves the location toward the middle of the heath. Rushy Pond, on the heath near Casterbridge (Dorchester), appears in "The Withered Arm."

DOVEDALE, Derbyshire Mid-Derbyshire is an area of ridges broken by some of the loveliest river valleys in England; the Derwent, Wye, and Dove all wind through here, and Dovedale, in the southwest part of the mid-county area running through a national park, is a limestone ravine, completely wooded, with an abundance of caves and crags. About 7 miles in length from Thorpe to Beresford Dales, Dovedale is one of the best trout-fishing areas in England.

Michael Drayton speaks of the beauty of the Dove in *Poly-Olbion:*

> This, *Moreland* greatly lik't: yet in that tender love,
> Which shee had ever borne unto her darling *Dove,*
> Shee could have wisht it his: because the daintie grass
> That growes upon his banke, all other doth surpasse.

This was a favorite spot of Izaak Walton and Charles Cotton, and the area comes into *The Compleat Angler.* The first glen at one end of Dovedale is Milldale; here is Viator's Bridge: the discussion between Viator and Piscator of the Dove River and Dovedale explains the area:

> VIAT. Here are the prettiest rivers, and most of them in this country that ever I saw; do you know how many you have in the country?
> PISC. I know them all. . . . [W]e have first the river Dove, . . . which . . . is so called from the swiftness of its current, and that swiftness occasioned by the declivity of

its course, and by being so straitened in that course betwixt the rocks. . . . [It] has as fertile banks as any river in England, none excepted. And this river, from its head for a mile or two, is a black water . . . but is in a few miles' travel so clarified by the addition of several clear and very great springs (bigger than itself) which gush out of the limestone rocks, that before it comes to my house, which is but six or seven miles from its source, you will find it one of the purest crystalline streams you have seen.

At the end of Beresford Dale is the fishing lodge which Cotton built in 1675 and which he and Walton frequently used.

While it is often maintained that Dr. Samuel Johnson bases his Happy Valley of *Rasselas* on Dovedale, there is no real evidence to support this. The Dove Valley, though, becomes the Eagledale of *Adam Bede* by George Eliot (Mary Ann Evans). Arthur Donnithorne, in order to avoid meeting Hetty again, goes off on a fishing excursion to Eagledale, which Adam describes to Hetty as "a wonderful sight—rocks and caves such as you never saw in your life. I never had a right notion of rocks till I went there." One other use of the Dove River merits consideration, although the specific identity of the river is in doubt because other Dove Rivers exist in Yorkshire and Westmorland. Nevertheless, William Wordsworth uses the Dove, generally assumed to be the Derbyshire river, in one of the *Lucy* poems:

> She dwelt among the untrodden ways
> Beside the springs of Dove,
> A Maid whom there were none to praise
> And very few to love.

DOVER, Kent (pop. 40,500) The southeast corner of England and Dover in particular have long been called "the lock and key to the kingdom," and certainly the area has always been attractive to invaders. Centuries before the Roman invasion the northern European Celtic tribesmen used this locality as their access to the country, and attempts continued on into the 20th century. Julius Caesar's initial landing force in 55 B.C. made for Dover, but the hills on both sides of the estuary provided ample opportunity for the natives to defend their land, and so strong a reception did they give Caesar that he altered his plan and sailed north to Deal. The Roman invasion in the 1st century A.D. was far more successful, and Dover became a fully Romanized town; two pharoses were built; the lower half of one still stands in the castle precincts. The Church of St. Mary-in-Castro, also in the castle precincts, was built for the Saxon *burh* (fortified township), which was located where the present 12th-century castle stands. The castle, which John Leland calls "the mayne, strong, and famose castle of Dovar," was essentially finished in the 13th century, and later additions were made simply to accommodate the increased ingenuity of warfare. John Evelyn visited the town on numerous official occasions, stayed at the castle, and attended services at St. Mary's. A later diarist to visit here was William Cobbett, whose favorable opinion of the town and its inhabitants is included in his *Rural Rides:*

> The town of Dover is like other sea-port towns; but really more clean, and with less blackguard people in it than I ever observed in any sea-port before. It is a most picturesque place, to be sure. On one side of it rises, upon the top of a very steep hill, the Old Castle, with all its

DOVEDALE A narrow, wooded river valley, Dovedale is famous for its fishing, its beauty, and its literary associations: Izaak Walton fished here and talked of its beauty, and George Eliot uses the valley in *Adam Bede.*

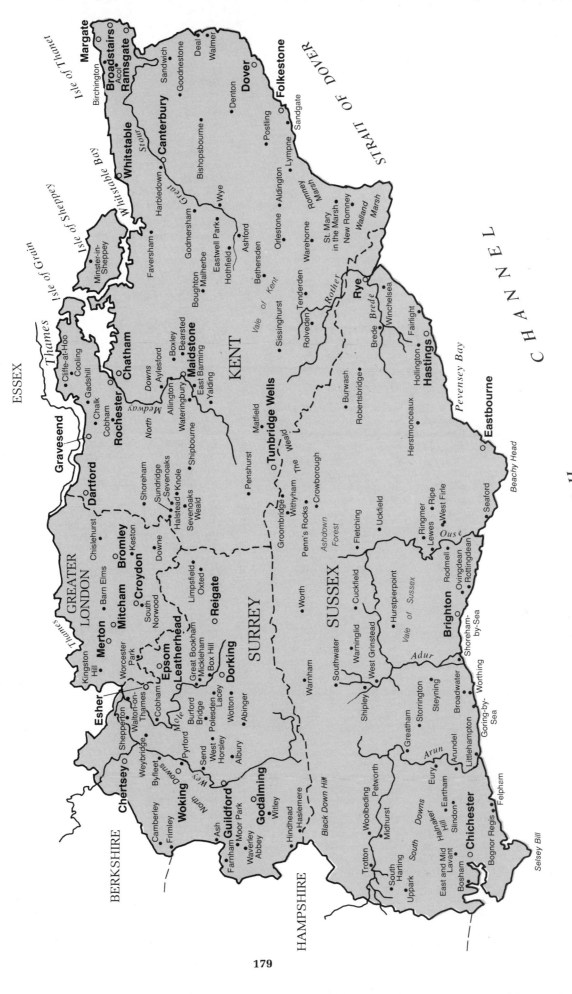

SOUTHEAST ENGLAND

ESSEX

GREATER LONDON

BERKSHIRE

SURREY

HAMPSHIRE

SUSSEX

KENT

Isle of Thanet

Isle of Sheppey

Isle of Grain

Thames

STRAIT OF DOVER

CHANNEL

ENGLISH

Pevensey Bay

Beachy Head

Selsey Bill

Margate
Broadstairs
Acol
Ramsgate
Birchington
Sandwich
Goodnestone
Deal
Walmer
Whitstable
Canterbury
Bishopsbourne
Stour
Dover
Folkestone
Sandgate
Denton
Postling
Lympne
Harbledown
Godmersham
Wye
Eastwell Park
Ashford
Orlestone
Aldington
Romney Marsh
Faversham
Hothfield
Betbersden
St. Mary in the Marsh
New Romney
Walland Marsh
Boughton
Malherbe
Great Stour
Minster-in-Sheppey
Cliffe-at-Hoo
Cooling
Gadshill
Chalk
Cobham
Rochester
Chatham
Medway
North Downs
Aylesford
Allington
Boxley
Bearsted
Maidstone
East Barming
Wateringbury
Shipbourne
Yalding
Vale of Kent
Sissinghurst
Tenderden
Rolveden
Wareborne
Rother
Rye
Brede
Brede
Winchelsea
Fairlight
Hastings
Hollington
Herstmonceaux
Mattfield
Penshurst
Tunbridge Wells
Withyham
The Weald
Groombridge
Penn's Rocks
Crowborough
Ashdown Forest
Burwash
Robertsbridge
Gravesend
Dartford
Chislehurst
Barn Elms
Bromley
Keston
Croydon
Downe
South Norwood
Limpsfield
Oxted
Reigate
Worth
Cuckfield
Warninglid
West Grinstead
Hurstpierpoint
Fletching
Uckfield
Ringmer
Ripe
Lewes
West Firle
Rodmell
Ovingdean
Rottingdean
Brighton
Shoreham-by-Sea
Ouse
Seaford
Eastbourne
Merton
Mitcham
Worcester Park
Epsom
Leatherhead
Great Bookham
Mickleham
Box Hill
Dorking
Kingston Hill
Esher
Walton-on-Thames
Cobham
Burford Bridge
Polesden Lacey
Wotton
Abinger
Shepperton
Weybridge
Byfleet
Pyrford
Send
West Horsley
Albury
Woking
Camberley
Frimley
Ash
Moor Park
Guildford
Farnham
Waverley Abbey
Godalming
Witley
Hindhead
Haslemere
Black Down Hill
Warnham
Southwater
Shipley
Greatham
Petworth
Storrington
Steyning
Broadwater
Worthing
Goring-by-Sea
Adur
Arun
Vale of Sussex
South Downs
Woolbeding
Midhurst
Eartham
Slindon
Arundel
Littlehampton
Felpham
Bognor Regis
Bosham
Chichester
East and Mid Lavant
Hainaker Hill
Eartham
Troton
South Harting
Uppark
Chertsey
North Downs
Wey
Mole
Whitstable Bay

fortifications. On the other side of it there is another chalk hill . . .

The two chalk hills jut out into the sea, and the water that comes up between them forms a harbour for this ancient, most interesting, and beautiful place.

Without doubt the most famous aspect of the town is the chalk cliffs; the most famous of these is known as Shakespeare's Cliff, the place to which the disguised Edgar leads the blind, suicide-bent Gloucester in *King Lear:*

> . . . here's the place:—stand still.—How fearful
> And dizzy 'tis, to cast one's eyes so low!
> The crows and choughs that wing the midway air
> Show scarce so gross as beetles: half way down
> Hangs one that gathers samphire,—dreadful trade!
> Methinks he seems no bigger than his head:
> The fishermen that walk upon the beach,
> Appear like mice. . . .

Samphire, a type of fleshy green plant, still grows there along with brambles and gorse. Edgar accurately estimates the height (approximately 350 feet):

> Ten masts at each make not the altitude
> Which thou hast perpendicularly fell. . . .

The area is also used in *Henry VI: Part II;* "The Sea shore near Dover" is where William de la Poole, Duke of Suffolk, is murdered.

The cliff is also mentioned in one of the Paston letters, dated May 5, 1450, from William Lemner to John Paston. Joseph Addison's visit to Shakespeare's Cliff, before going to the Continent in late August 1699, may have triggered the *Spectator* essay No. 489, which describes his feelings toward the ocean:

> I must confess, it is impossible for me to survey this World of fluid Matter, without thinking on the Hand that first poured it out, and made a proper Channel for its Reception. Such an Object naturally raises in my Thoughts the Idea of an Almighty Being, and convinces me of his Existence, as much as a Metaphysical Demonstration.

Matthew Arnold's "Dover Beach" contains another well-known use of the site, although the situation is reversed; at one point Arnold appears to be beneath the cliffs looking up at the sheer chalk escarpment. Some years before, during the Napoleonic scare, William Wordsworth addressed a sonnet to the Men of Kent, and it is obvious that he was aware of the ancient tradition that eastern Kent had not been conquered by the Normans in 1066; exhorting them, the "Vanguard of Liberty," to "prove your hardiment," he says:

> Left single, in bold parley, ye, of yore,
> Did from the Norman win a gallant wreath;
> Confirmed the charters that were yours before;—
> No parleying now.

Dickensian associations are numerous; in 1852 Charles Dickens spent three months at 10 Camden Crescent, where one of his guests was Wilkie Collins, who arrived after his theatrical tour. Collins was then suffering from an acute attack "of earache and faceache" and during his two-week stay was "cosseted by Mrs. Dickens and cured promptly." Dickens's initial impression of Dover was:

> It is not quite a place to my taste, being too bandy (I mean musical; no reference to its legs), and infinitely too

genteel. But the sea is very fine, and the walks are quite remarkable.

In 1855, at the Lord Warden Hotel, and in 1856, he describes the theater (built in 1790) as "a miserable spectacle—the pit is boarded over, and it is a drinking and smoking place." Parts of *A Tale of Two Cities* take place in Dover; here Lucie Manette is told that her father has been "Recalled to Life." The opening scene of the coach drive to Dover is frequently called some of Dickens's best descriptive writing, and he describes the fortified city as it must have appeared more than 150 years ago:

> The little narrow, rooked town of Dover hid itself away from the beach, and ran its head into the chalk cliffs, like a marine ostrich. The beach was a desert of heaps of sea and stones tumbling wildly about, and the sea did what it liked, and what it liked was destruction. It thundered at the town, and thundered at the cliffs, and brought the coast down, madly. The air among the houses was of so strong a piscatory flavour that one might have supposed sick fish went up to be dipped in it, as sick people went down to be dipped in the sea.

The Uncommercial Traveller also talks of Dover, where "the sea was tumbling in, with deep sounds" and where "the revolving French light at Cape Grisnez was seen regularly bursting out and becoming obscured. . . ."

Dickens's best-known use of the town occurs in *David Copperfield.* David has run away from his Blunderstone (Blundeston) home and made his way to his aunt's home in Dover. His inquiries are met with jocosity but no information, and he sits "on the step of an empty shop at a street corner, near the market place. . . ." This shop was a Mr. Igglesden's bakery shop on Market Square; a modern building on the site bears a commemorative plaque to the fictitious event. David finally receives the necessary directions to find Miss Trotwood from the fly-driver: ". . . 'go right up there,' pointing his whip towards the heights, 'and keep right on till you come to some houses facing the sea. . . .'" The house proves to be "a very neat litte cottage with cheerful bow windows" and a well-tended garden in front, from which Miss Trotwood shoos the donkeys.

Almost every English author has been in Dover at one time or another, usually on the way to the Continent. Oliver Goldsmith returned to England, landing at Dover, from the Continent on February 1, 1756; he had been wandering around France, Switzerland, and Italy after obtaining a medical degree (perhaps at Leiden) and arrived with a cash supply of only a few halfpence. He ultimately went to Southwark, London, to try to support himself by practicing medicine, but possibly he first attempted to set up a surgery in Dover, although no evidence has come to light. In 1784 William Beckford, following homosexual accusations which made numerous court litigations seem inevitable, came to Dover to flee to the Continent. Alone and realizing that fleeing was tantamount to admitting guilt, he determined to return to Fonthill Gifford, Wiltshire:

> I rambled about the Port with heaviness of heart, the weather as gloomy as my spirits; passing along the beach, I came under the perpendicular cliffs crowned by the Castle. Snug under one of these I found to my great surprise a little green spot, enlivened with mignionet and gilly flowers; steps cut out in the rock, leading to strange

dens with something like gothic entrances. . . . Beneath, lie plains of sea; above, nod the Castle walls, and many a crag mottled with samphire.

When Lord Byron spent his last two days in England here in 1816, awaiting favorable winds for the channel crossing, one of the things he did was visit the grave of Charles Churchill, the 18th-century satirist who died on November 4, 1764, in Boulogne. Churchill's body was brought back to Dover, where it was buried in the churchyard of St. Martin's Church on Cannon Street. On the gravestone is a line from *The Candidate:* "Life to the last enjoyed, here Churchill lies." The church also contains a commemorative monument. After his visit to the cemetery, Byron notes the occasion:

I stood beside the grave of him who blazed
The comet of a season. . . .

George Eliot (Mary Ann Evans) and George Henry Lewes stayed at the Lord Warden Hotel in March 1855 on their return from Germany; this was an extremely traumatic period in her life, for she and Lewes were living as husband and wife even though Lewes's wife was alive and presenting the couple with real problems. Another visitor was Henry James, who had lodgings on Marine Parade in 1884 while he was working on *The Bostonians.* Thomas Hardy makes a slight use of Dover (under its own name) in *A Pair of Blue Eyes* and in "A Tradition of 1804"; he also mentions the Strait of Dover in *The Trumpet-Major.*

DOWN HALL, Essex The area known as Epping Forest, once a 60,000-acre royal hunting ground and now only 5,600 public acres protected by an act of Parliament of 1878, is one of the most attractive parts of Essex and has always been especially favored by writers. Down Hall and its parklands, 5½ miles southeast of Bishop's Stortford, between Hatfield Broad Oak and Harlow, on Pincey Brook was the home of Matthew Prior for a little more than a year before his death in Wimpole, Cambridgeshire, in 1721. After a fairly successful political career, including carrying out the negotiations for the Treaty of Utrecht of 1713, which became known as Matt's Peace, he was imprisoned on a charge of treason. Sentenced without trial, he was released after spending two years in prison. With neither money nor prospects, he was persuaded to publish a folio edition of his works for wealthy subscribers; his patron Lord Harley offered an equivalent sum so that Prior could purchase a home and live in relative ease. Harley's only stipulation was that the house revert to him or his heirs upon Prior's death. The sales for the edition of Prior's work produced 4,000 guineas so that the matching amount made the poet quite comfortable. Lord Harley's bringing Prior here to view Down Hall in 1720 occasioned the "Ballad of Down Hall,"

I sing of exploits that have lately been done
By two British heroes, called Matthew and John
And how they rid friendly from fine London town,
Fair Essex to see, and a place they call Down.

Prior says:

There are gardens so stately and arbours so thick,
A portal of stone, and a fabric of brick.

After moving in, in July 1720, Prior built several summerhouses, cut walks in the woods, and dug a small fishpond, but apparently wrote little or no verse.

After Prior's death in 1721, Harley completed here the famous Harleian collection of manuscripts begun by the 1st Earl of Oxford and now in the British Museum. In 1725 Alexander Pope was a guest here of Harley, now the 2d Earl of Oxford, to offer planning advice on the gardens.

DOWNE, Kent (pop. 791) A small village whose name was originally spelled Down, 5½ miles southeast of Bromley, Downe contains both Down Court and Down House, the country house belonging to Charles Darwin, grandfather of Gwen Reverat. The latter wrote the delightful *Period Piece,* in which she states, "Everything at Down was perfect" even though there was "nothing to do but to go for long walks in the steep valleys and great lonely woods, and to get your boots stuck in huge balls of red clay." In front of the veranda the path "was made of large round water-worn pebbles . . . stuck down tight in moss and sand"; outside the window of the white-floored nursery was "a great old mulberry . . . [whose] shadows . . . used to shift about on the white floor." "And on the landing hung a swinging rope with a cross bar, on which we did all kinds of gymnastics." She says, "The flint flavour of the ghost of my grandfather" permeated the entire estate "in a friendly way," but "when I was eleven Grandmamma died and it all came to an end." One of Charles Darwin's guests here before their estrangement was Samuel Butler.

Before the Royal College of Surgeons took over Down House, it had been a private boarding school, to which the Irish-born novelist Elizabeth Bowen was sent after her mother's death in 1911.

DUDDON RIVER, Cumberland Forming a major part of the Cumberland-Lancashire border, the Duddon River rises on Wrynose Fell and then flows for about 21 miles to the Irish Sea near Broughton-in-Furness; there it runs into a 7-mile estuary known as Duddon Sands. William Wordsworth's earliest memories of a day's fishing, when he met with pouring rain and no fish, were negative, but later, when on holiday from Cambridge, he spent many happy hours on the banks of the river.

Through his sonnet sequence *The River Duddon* Wordsworth can be followed accurately in his walk along the Duddon from its Wrynose Fell source until it

. . . expands
. . . over smooth flat sands
Gliding in silence with unfettered sweep!

The fifth sonnet describes Cockley Beck. Emerging from Wrynose Bottom, after 2 miles of stones and somewhat monotonous scenery of "sullen moss and craggy ground," he finds the

. . . Cottage rude and gray;
Whose ruddy children, by the mother's eyes
Carelessly watched, sport through the summer day. . . .

Only the "sheltering pines" are gone. The stepping-stones of Sonnet IX,

> . . . stone matched with stone
> In studied symmetry, . . .

are generally identified as those opposite Dale Head Farm between Cockley Beck and Birks Bridge if Wordsworth is sequentially accurate. Thus, the local tradition which asserts that the stones are those near Seathwaite puts the sonnet in the wrong sequential position, but these stones at Black Hall are far more acceptable once the Faery Chasm of Sonnet XI is identified:

> No fiction was it of the antique age:
> A sky-blue stone, within this sunless cleft,
> Is of the very footmarks unbereft
> Which tiny Elves impressed;—on that smooth stage. . . .

If the chasm is sought above Seathwaite, and not below, it appears to be the rocky gorge crowned by Birks Bridge just after the stepping stones at Black Hall. Here the water, tumbling over a series of falls into a narrow channel, has eroded the rocks into fantastic designs. "The Open Prospect" of fields from which Seathwaite,

> . . . one small hamlet, under a green hill
> Clustering, with barn and byre, and spouting mill[,]

could be seen must be from Pen Crag; the ruins of the mill are on Tarn Beck just below Seathwaite Chapel. The final lines of this sonnet refer to the inn of Newfield, and Dunnerdale is on the east bank of the Duddon:

> . . . then would I
> Turn into port; and, reckless of the gale,
> Reckless of angry Duddon sweeping by,
> While the warm hearth exalts the mantling ale,
> Laugh with the generous household heartily
> At all the merry pranks of Donnerdale!

> [The]. . . deep chasm, where quivering sunbeams play
> Upon its loftiest crags, mine eyes behold
> A gloomy NICHE, capacious, blank, and cold . . .

is located between Pen Crag and Wallabarrow Crag, but the specific niche is unidentifiable. "Return" includes the view from Bootle, and Wordsworth erroneously ascribes the stone circle at Hardknott Pass to the druids. Wordsworth carries on:

> . . . to this hidden pool, whose depths surpass
> In crystal clearness Dian's looking-glass . . .

The bathing pool known as Long Dub is in the Vale of Ulpha. Rising sharply on one side are the crags where the "love-lorn maid" deliberates:

> . . . shall she plunge, or climb
> The humid precipice, and seize the guest
> Of April, smiling high in upper air?
> Desperate alternative! what fiend could dare
> To prompt the thought?

The ramble moves by a house:

> Fallen, and diffused into a shapeless heap,
> Or quietly self-buried in earth's mould,
> Is that embattled House, whose massy Keep
> Flung from yon cliff a shadow large and cold.

Near the head of Holehouse Ghyll is the Old Hall, and nearby is a disused farmhouse which tradition says is Wordsworth's "shapeless heap." Approaching Ulpha Bridge, he comes to an area known as the Sepulchre:

> Yet, to the loyal and the brave, who lie
> In the blank earth, neglected and forlorn,
> The passing Winds memorial tribute pay. . . .

On the east side of the Duddon, near New Close, was a Friends' burial ground without tombstones to mark graves. The poet then arrives at

> The Kirk of Ulpha to the pilgrim's eye
> . . . welcome as a star. . . .

Ulpha is still entered over the ancient stone bridge. Finally, Wordsworth reaches the estuary and sees the river enter the sea:

> Not hurled precipitous from steep to steep;
> Lingering no more 'mid flower-enamelled lands
> And blooming thickets; nor by rocky bands
> Held; but in radiant progress toward the Deep
> Where mightiest rivers into powerless sleep
> Sink, and forget their nature—*now* expands
> Majestic Duddon, over smooth flat sands
> Gliding in silence with unfettered sweep!

DUNMOW, LITTLE, and DUNMOW, GREAT, Essex (pop. 318) Little Dunmow and Great Dunmow, only 2 miles apart near Stansted, are often confused or named as one when ascribing the tradition of the Dunmow flitch; the two villages also are often placed together topographically. The ancient custom of presenting a flitch of bacon to any man "which repents him not of his marriage, either sleeping or waking, in a year and a day" is usually ascribed to Robert Fitzwalter in 1244, but strong evidence indicates that the practice originated with the Augustinian priory founded at Little Dunmow and that the prior examined the husband's claim. The evidence also points out that after the dissolution of the monasteries the tradition passed to the lord of the manor, who then sensibly included the wife in his examination. An early reference to the Dunmow flitch occurs in William Langland's *Piers Plowman*, although here it appears as if both partners are questioned:

> For since the Plague hundreds of couples have married, yet the only fruit they have brought forth are foul words; they live in jealousy, without happiness, and lie in bed quarrelling, so that all the children they get are strife and nagging! If they went to try for the Dunmow flitch, they wouldn't stand a chance without the Devil's help; and unless they were both lying there'd be no bacon for them.

Geoffrey Chaucer's better-known allusion to the flitch occurs in *The Canterbury Tales* when the Wife of Bath speaks of her husbands and her attitude toward them:

> The bacon was not fet for hem, I trowe,
> That som men han in Essex at Dunmowe.

The last time that the lord of the manor presented the flitch was in 1751, but the tradition has not died entirely. In 1855 William Harrison Ainsworth, a bit of a showman himself, revived the old tradition in a somewhat more modern form and added to the original proviso a more easily tested one, that the couple "have not had a brawl in their home." Great Dunmow now hosts this late-Victorian revival, for Little

Dunmow is too tiny to support the modern extravaganza.

Dunmow, as the larger of the two villages is generally called, has a number of strong ties to H. G. Wells, especially with *Mr. Britling Sees It Through.* Wells lived in Little Easton Rectory and in Easton Glebe for more than twenty-five years, and he uses Dunmow as Matching's Easy and the rectory as Mr. Britling's house, the Dower House. The Clavering Arms is the Stag, also known as Plumper's Arms, an old thatched inn opposite the rectory. Claverings, Lady Homartyn's home, is Easton Glebe, a large rambling house on the edge of Lady Warwick's estate here. The barn used for dancing and other activities, adjoining Mr. Britling's house, was transported by Wells from Little Easton. Mertonsome, which Wells designates as a nearby village, cannot be identified.

Dunmow was also the home of Sir George Beaumont, who was host to Samuel Taylor Coleridge during one of the periods when the poet was suffering over his marriage and planning his departure for Malta and Italy (in February 1804 and, most likely, in January as well). William Wordsworth was also a guest of the Beaumonts and more than once spent a few weeks with them here, particularly on those rare trips he took to the east coast to visit his brother Christopher, who was rector at nearby Bocking.

DUNSTABLE, Bedfordshire (pop. 27,200)   The history of Dunstable (pronounced "dun′stabl") goes back to about 3500 B.C., for here in the downs country known as Five Knolls a prehistoric barrow cemetery has been uncovered. The foot of the downs was the site of the ancient British track, the Icknield Way, and later the Romans erected a posting station where their Watling Street crossed the Icknield Way. Around this crossroads, 4½ miles west of Luton, the town of Dunstable grew up, and in the early 12th century Henry I founded a priory here. The town had its own miracle play (or plays) by 1119; produced by the schoolmaster, Geoffrey of Gorham, the play is unknown today, and except for the chance record of an attendant disaster, we would not even know that it existed. For one performance (undoubtedly the last) the copes which Geoffrey borrowed from the Abbey of St. Albans were destroyed in a fire.

In many ways medieval Dunstable was in advance of the times: as early as 1221 there were public health laws, and the prior meted out stiff fines to violators. The town thrived well into the reign of Henry VIII, but with the suppression of the monasteries Dunstable entered a long period of decline, and almost the only substantial sources of income were the town's location on the coaching road and the beginning of a small straw-plaiting industry. The town established a number of good inns in the 17th century, notably the Anchor and the Red Lion; the Sugar Loaf dates from 1717.

Dunstable was the birthplace in 1648 of Elkanah Settle; his father was the landlord of the Red Lion Inn, and the inn was most likely Settle's place of birth. After his education here, he went to Trinity College, Oxford. An early visitor to the town was John Evelyn; as his diary records, he arrived by coach with his son on August 15, 1688, but failed to comment about the inn, the food, or the town. Another figure with associations with an inn in Dunstable, probably the Red Lion, is Jonathan Swift, whose first meeting with Vanessa (Esther Vanhomrigh) probably took place there at the end of December 1707; by 1710 he had become practically an intimate of the house.

There is a more important association with John Bunyan, who places part of *The Pilgrim's Progress* in this vicinity; his Slough of Despond is on Holyhead Road just north of Dunstable on the way to Hockliffe. The narrator first describes the Slough of Despond; Christian and Pliable

> drew near to a very miry slough that was in the midst of the plain, and they, being heedless, did both fall suddenly into the bog. The name of the slough was Despond.

Another part of this general area is included in *The Pilgrim's Progress:* the "tombs" among which the blind are forced to wander were probably the tumuli on the Dunstable Downs; the shepherds speak:

> "From that stile there goes a path that leads directly to Doubting Castle, which is kept by Giant Despair; and these men (pointing to them among the tombs) came once on pilgrimage, as you do now, even till they came to that stile. And because the right way was rough in that place, they chose to go out of it into the meadow, and there were taken by Giant Despair, and cast into Doubting Castle, where, after they had awhile been kept in the dungeon, he at last put out their eyes and led them among those tombs, where he has left them to wander to this very day...."

DUNSTER, Somerset (pop. 705)   Dunster, called "the most beautiful village" in Exmoor because of its timbered medieval houses and its castle, is set at the foot of Conygar Hill, 5 miles west of Watchet. The 11th-century Dunster Castle, built by the De Mohuns probably on the site of a Saxon stronghold, has

DUNSTER   An integral part of Thomas Hardy's Wessex, Dunster has a number of fine old houses along its wide main street. Dunster becomes Hardy's Markton, and the 15th- to 17th-century Luttrell Arms Hotel becomes the Lord Quantock Arms Hotel in *A Laodicean.*

been enlarged over the centuries. In the 13th century Reginald de Mohun was created Earl of Est (Somerset) by the Pope, and less than two centuries later a descendant performed for the feudal serfs an act comparable to that performed in Coventry by Lady Godiva. Here, according to Thomas Fuller, Lady de Mohun obtained common ground for the town "in one day (believe it was a summer one for her ease and advantage) . . . going on her naked feet."

Thomas Hardy uses Dunster and its area as the major setting of *A Laodicean*. Dunster becomes Markton, and the Lord Quantock Arms Hotel, where George Somerset takes rooms, is based on the Luttrell Arms Hotel in Dunster. Somerset notes the commanding view from Stancy Castle (Dunster Castle):

> . . . a terrace to the northwest. . . . was bounded by a parapet breast high, over which a view of the distant country and sea met the eye, stretching from the foot of the slope to a distance of many miles. Somerset went and leaned over, and looked down upon the tops of the bushes beneath. The prospect included the village or townlet close at hand, . . . and amidst the green lights and shades of the meadows he could discern the red brick chapel whose recalcitrant inmate had so engrossed him.

The little adjacent village of Sleeping Green is possibly Carhampton or Withycombe.

DUNWICH, Suffolk (pop. 189) The prosperous medieval port of Dunwich (pronounced "dun'ich") with its six churches now lies at the bottom of the sea, and all that is left is a tiny hamlet, the remains of a 13th-century priory, the chapel of leper-colony hospital, and the still crumbling cliffs, Not much of what is left has changed since Edward FitzGerald, Thomas Carlyle, Jerome K. Jerome, Algernon Swinburne, and Henry James visited here in the 19th century. FitzGerald, who lived in Suffolk almost all his life, frequently visited here from 1855 on, sometimes staying with a Mrs. Scarlet, and on one occasion he brought Carlyle with him. Years later Jerome stayed with the same Mrs. Scarlet.

DURHAM, County Durham (pop. 19,300) Durham is one of the most interesting of the English cathedral and market towns because of its topography: the Wear River has cut deeply into the land, leaving enormous cliffs which contain the old city in a horseshoe shape known as the peninsula, and high rock plateaus on either side of the riverbanks and farmland are within sight from most points in the city. Durham was obviously an important Saxon town; an Anglo-Saxon poem speaks of the "celebrated" city:

> The road to it is steep:
> It is surrounded with rocks,
> And with curious plants:
> The Wear flows round it,
> A river of rapid waves . . .

and of its fame:

> There is in this city
> Also, well known to men
> The venerable St. Cudberth [Cuthbert].

At the end of the 10th century St. Cuthbert's body was brought here from Ripon, Yorkshire, by a devout band of monks in order to escape the pillage and desecration of the Danish invaders. The second canto of Sir Walter Scott's *Marmion* tells the story:

> When the rude Dane burn'd their pile
> The monks fled forth from Holy Isle:
> O'er northern mountain, marsh, and moor,
> From sea to sea, from shore to shore,
> Seven years Saint Cuthbert's corpse they bore.
> . . . .
> Chester-le-Street and Ripon saw
> His holy corpse, ere Wardilaw
>   Hail'd him with joy and fear;
> And after many wanderings past,
> He chose his lordly seat at last,
> Where his Cathedral huge and vast,
>   Looks down upon the Wear;
> There, deep in Durham's Gothic shade,
> His relics are in secret laid.

Part of Durham's uniqueness stems from the fact that from the 10th century until 1836 the bishopric was endowed with political sovereignty. The Bishop, known as Count Palatine or Prince Palatine, made his headquarters here, administered his domain as the representative of the sovereign, minted money, and kept a standing army. Durham is in fact still the "capital" of the county palatine.

Durham Cathedral, which has been called the world's greatest Norman building, stands high above the Wear River on the peninsula. Dr. Samuel Johnson was impressed by the cathedral but not by its beauty: writing to Mrs. Thrale, he comments:

> The Cathedral has a massyness and solidity such as I have seen in no other place. . . . It rather awes than pleases, as it strikes with a kind of gigantick dignity, and aspires to no other praise than that of rocky solidity and indeterminate duration.

But John Ruskin, at the least a far better judge of architecture, called the combination of the river, cathedral, and castle "one of the seven wonders of the world." The cathedral is an imposing structure, and its modern-day inaccessibility serves to remind one of its medieval remoteness. St. Cuthbert's Shrine, originally in the feretory behind the high altar, is now a simple gray stone slab on the original site. It is at this shrine that Scott sets the baptism of Count Witikind in *Harold the Dauntless*. The Venerable Bede's tomb, in the Galilee Porch, does not belong here; a monk named Alfred who was the sacrist at Durham removed Bede's body from his grave in Jarrow about 1022. There is a memorial east window to William Caxton, who has no known association with the cathedral or the town.

Durham's castle (now part of the University of Durham), along with its cathedral, was to be part of a buffer state against Scottish invaders, and its walls once effectively sealed off the peninsula. Some of the original sections of the castle are still being used for their original function: the Great Hall, for example, which leads to one of the "most magnificent dining halls in England," is used by students now just as it was when Sir Walter Scott and the Duke of Wellington dined with Bishop Willam Van Mildert on October 3, 1827. Scott comments in his diary:

> The bright moon streaming in through the old Gothic windows contrasted strangely with the artificial lights within; spears, banners and armour were intermixed with

the pictures of old bishops, and the whole had a singular mixture of baronial pomp with the grave and more chastened dignity of prelacy.

This visit to Durham was by no means Scott's first; earlier he had walked across the Prebends' Bridge on the southwest side of the peninsula, and lines from *Harold the Dauntless* are carved into a stone in the western approach to the bridge:

Grey towers of Durham . . .
Yet well I love thy mixed and massive piles,
Half church of God, half castle 'gainst the Scot,
And long to roam these venerable aisles,
With records stored of deeds long since forgot. . . .

Durham can claim no major literary figure as its own, but two minor 19th-century novelists were born here in the Old Bailey: Jane Porter, author of *Thaddeus of Warsaw*, in 1776, and Anna Maria Porter, author of *The Hungarian Brothers*, in 1780. Other associations with the town are varied. Christopher Smart was sent here as a child in 1732 after the death of his father, and Durham and the area appear frequently in his writings. Most probably he lodged with his uncle, John Smart, or with his schoolmaster from Durham Grammar School. The school, one of two on Palace Green at the time, was on the west side of the green and is now part of the University of Durham. Smart refers to Durham in *Jubilate Agno:* "Let Josiphiah rejoice with Tower Mustard. God be gracious to Durham School." This is a reminder of the 18th-century saying "The City of Durham is famous for seven things—Wood, Water and Pleasant Walks, Law and Gospel, Old Maids and Mustard." Durham mustard is extremely biting. Smart left Durham in 1739 to go up to Cambridge, an opportunity afforded partly because of the Duchess of Cleveland's influence and generosity. The grammar school also was the scene of the very short education in 1819 of Robert Smith Surtees, the creator of John Jorrocks, who remained a year before being apprenticed to a solicitor. The school also has a specific association with literature, for William Makepeace Thackeray based his figure of Dr. Senior in *The Newcomes* on Edward Elder, headmaster here from 1839 to 1853.

Thomas Gray was a frequent visitor to Durham from 1753 to 1765; taking holidays from his academic activities at Cambridge, he often came to stay with Dr. Thomas Wharton and found the environment both beautiful and exciting. Writing in December 1753, he says:

I have one of the most beautiful vales in England to walk in, . . . all rude and romantic, in short, the sweetest spot to break your neck or drown yourself in that ever was beheld.

Hugh Walpole lived in Durham from Easter, 1898, until going up to Emmanuel College, Cambridge, in October 1903. When his father became principal of Bede College of the University of Durham, Walpole became a day boy at Durham School. At Durham, as in many public schools, the day student is made to feel an outcast, and this may partly explain Walpole's early intense dislike of the town and the school. He felt repelled by the environment; he hated what he felt was the snobbishness of the cathedral canons but grudgingly admitted admiration for the cathedral,

DURHAM   Set high on a horseshoe-shaped escarpment cut by the Wear River, Durham Cathedral and Castle, "Half church of God, half castle 'gainst the Scot," is the site of St. Cuthbert's coffin, in the Chapter Library, and of the Venerable Bede's tomb, in the Galilee Porch.

"hanging high in air, perfectly proportioned, pearl-shadowed, and sky defended." The only other aspect of the town to earn his respect was the old subscription library, where he read Scott, Dickens, Trollope, Collins, and Kingsley. Walpole paid only two visits to Durham after he left for Cambridge. The first, in early November 1923, only an overnight stop, awakened memories, he says: "Very few pleasant ones: I walked the streets under the stars and was grateful to God." The second, at the end of June 1929, was an "official" visit to speak at the school on Prize Day. His enjoyment of the affair was greater than he had anticipated: he spent the morning before his speech rediscovering his old haunts, and the next day he attended services at the cathedral. Durham Cathedral is transported to Polchester (Truro, Cornwall) in the *Jeremy* novels because of its physical domination of the town.

Three other figures have had some association with Durham and its educational institutions. Cuthbert Bede (Henry Bradley) was educated at the University of Durham. In 1838 the university decided "by a special grace of convocation" to confer the degree of doctor of civil laws on William Wordsworth. The first honorary graduate and the only one on this occasion, he received the degree in person and went on from the ceremony to a three-week tour of County Durham and Northumberland. Rudyard Kipling also was honored with a Durham degree, in June 1907; it was followed by honorary degrees from Oxford and Cambridge. So popular a recipient was Kipling that the students pulled his carriage up to Palace Green.

DURNFORD, Wiltshire (pop. 394)   Located 2½ miles south of Amesbury, the village of Durnford lies below the Wiltshire Downs on the Avon River. It has a number of flint-and-stone cottages and a church whose 13th-century tower only hints at the age of the structure. Durnford House was the home of John Evelyn's uncle, and Evelyn comments on his visit here in 1654 in his diary:

> We departed [from Salisbury] & dined at a ferme of my *U. Hungerfords* cald *Darneford magna,* situate in a Valley under the Plaine, most sweetly water'd, abounding in Trowts and all things else requisite, provisions exceeding cheape: . . . After dinner continuing our returne we passd over that goodly plaine or rather Sea of Carpet, which I think for evennesse, extent, Verdure, innumerable flocks, to be one of the most delightfull prospects in nature. . . .

DURRINGTON, Sussex (pop. 1,182) In the instance of Durrington population figures are misleading; what appears to be a village of less than 2,000 inhabitants is only 2½ miles northwest of the large seaside resort of Worthing and virtually a part of it. This was the birthplace of John Selden in 1584, and he was baptized here on December 30. The house of brick and flint with a thatched roof, which stood near the John Selden Inn on Selden's Way, was destroyed by fire in the 1950s. The son of a yeoman (says John Aubrey), Selden was educated at Chichester Free School before going up to Hart Hall, Oxford, in 1600.

EAKRING, Nottinghamshire (pop. 326) The red-roofed hamlet of Eakring, 11 miles northwest of Trenton, is often assumed to be the Eakrast of D. H. Lawrence's "Mr. Noon"; he writes,

> The school and the school house were one building. In the front the long schoolroom faced the road: at the back the house premises and garden looked to—the fields and distant forest.

The schoolhouse is attached just as Lawrence describes it, but Eastwood (also in Nottinghamshire) is also a claimant for the setting of this story.

EAMONT BRIDGE, Westmorland and Cumberland (pop. 237) Part of the tiny village of Eamont Bridge, just outside Penrith, is in Cumberland, but the greater part is in Westmorland. Spanning the Eamont River is a fine medieval three-arched bridge. In the immediate vicinity of Eamont Bridge are two Neolithic remains and the 17th-century Yanwath Hall. One of the Neolithic remains is Mayburgh, an earthwork which holds a solitary monolith, and the other relic, the Round Table, roughly circular and originally bound by a ditch, is associated with Arthurian legend. This Round Table has entered into all manner of literature; it first appeared in a ballad collected in Bishop Thomas Percy's *Reliques of Ancient English Poetry,* and describes the combat to free Sir Arthur's men between Sir Launcelot du Lac and the robber chieftain Torquin; this man of more than ample proportions lived on the Cumberland bank of the Eamont in a lair still known as the Giant's Cave. The ballad was known by the end of the 16th century, when William Shakespeare introduced the first line, "When Arthur first in court . . . and was a worthy king," into *Henry IV: Part II.*

Sir Walter Scott mentions this Round Table and Mayburgh in *The Bridal of Triermain:*

> The faithful Page he mounts his steed,
> And soon he cross'd green Irthing's mead,
> Dash'd o'er Kirkoswald's verdant plain,
> And Eden barr'd his course in vain.
> He pass'd red Penrith's Table Round,
> For feats of chivalry renown'd,
> Left Mayburgh's mound and stones of power,
> By Druids raised in magic hour,
> And traced the Eamont's winding way,
> Till Ulfo's lake beneath him lay.

Scott's notes on the Neolithic remains of the table are interesting:

> As the ditch is on the inner side, it could not be intended for the purpose of defence, and it has reasonably been conjectured that the enclosure was designed for the solemn exercise of feats of chivalry, and the embankment around for the convenience of the spectators.

Mayburgh, he says,

> is a prodigious enclosure of great antiquity. . . . In the plain which it encloses there stands erect an unhewn stone of twelve feet in height. Two similar masses are said to have been destroyed during the memory of man. The whole appears to be a monument of Druidical times.

EARL'S CROOME, Worcestershire (pop. 170) Three Worcestershire villages have the name Croome; Earl's Croome, historically the property of the Earls of Warwick, is a peaceful little place near Upton-on-Severn, 9 miles south of Worcester. The nearby 16th-century half-timbered manor house, considerably altered, was the home of Thomas Jeffrey, a justice of the peace for whom Samuel Butler, author of *Hudibras,* acted as a secretary. Just how long Butler served in this capacity or how long he was in residence here is not known.

EARTHAM, Sussex (pop. 158) About the only interest in Eartham, a tiny flintstone village 5½ miles northeast of Chichester, is a small 13th-century church with a Norman chancel. Eartham Hall was the home of William Hayley, a relatively popular poet during the late 18th and early 19th centuries, although Robert Southey commented: "Everything is good about the man except his poetry." Hayley, though, was sufficiently popular to attract various writers to his home, and Edward Gibbon, William Blake, and Robert Southey were often here, as were the artists George Romney and John Flaxman. Because both men were working on editions of Milton, Hayley was able somehow to persuade the anxiety-ridden William Cowper and Mrs. Morley Unwin to join him here. Cowper, although a bit terrified by the height of the Sussex hills here, seemed to enjoy himself:

> This is a delightful place. More beautiful scenery I have never beheld, nor expect to behold. . . . [H]ere I see from every window woods like forests, and hills like mountains—a wilderness in short, that rather increases my natural melancholy, and which, were it not for the agreeables I find within, would soon convince me that mere change of place can avail me little.

Another of Hayley's guests then was the novelist Charlotte Smith.

EASEDALE VALLEY, Westmorland   A lovely mountain valley on the western border of the shire, Easedale descends from White Stones Mountain to Grasmere over a distance of 3½ miles. Grasmere was the longtime home of William Wordsworth, who knew and loved this valley. In the first year he and his sister Dorothy lived in Grasmere, they determined upon the name Black Quarter for the area because it seemed to be the gathering place of dark clouds and storms. Wordsworth later maintained that he had written "thousands of lines" beside Easedale Beck. He often walked from his home past the rocky outcrop known as Buttercup How, over Goody Bridge, along Blentarn Farm, and its gill to Easedale Tarn. "It was an April morning: fresh and clear" describes a walk in the area.

EAST BARMING, Kent   This small village on the Medway River, 2½ miles southwest of Maidstone, has a notable partly Norman church with carved bench ends. Hall Place here was the childhood home of Christopher Smart for almost seven years. Aided by a bequest left to him by Lord Barnard, in 1723, Smart's father bought the 48-acre estate in 1726; indeed, the elder Smart carried a mortgage of £1,300 on the house and land, a considerable sum at the time. Christopher attended school in Maidstone. When Smart's father died in February 1733, the estate was in a precarious financial condition, and the boy and his sister were sent to Durham.

EAST BEDFONT, Middlesex (pop. 2,271)   A peculiar little village 3 miles northeast of Staines and just south of the airport, East Bedfont lies in a triangular area between the Staines and Great South West Roads. It still has its green, a 16th-century manor house, a partly Norman church, and a number of Tudor and Georgian houses. The fame of this village until 1940 was due to the ornamental topiary work in the churchyard; two yew trees were cut into fantastic shapes, representing peacocks. Thomas Hood tells

the story of these trees in one of his early poems, "The Two Peacocks of Bedfont":

> Each Sabbath morning, at the hour of prayer,
>   Behold two maidens, up the quiet green
> Shining, far distant, in the summer air
>   That flaunts their dewy robes and breathes between
> Their downy plumes,—sailing as if they were
>   Two far-off ships,—until they brush between
> The churchyard's humble walls, and watch and wait
> On either side of the wide open'd gate.

There the two maidens "stand—with haughty necks . . . [and]/With pouting lips"; eventually, though, Hood concludes, "Where two haughty maidens used to be,"

> There, gentle stranger, thou may'st only see
>   Two sombre Peacocks.—Age, with sapient nod
> Marking the spot, still tarries to declare
> How they once lived, and wherefore they are there.

Most likely Hood created the legend, for it appears nowhere else, and a note appended to the poem in the *London Magazine* (October 1822) seems to support this. The trees, neglected for some time, were recut from the mid-19th century on.

EAST BUDLEIGH, Devon (pop. 756)   Just north of Budleigh Salterton on the south Devon shore, the village of East Budleigh is a place of striking contrasts. Grazing land here is particularly good, the vivid red seaside cliffs drop precipitously to the water of the bay, and palm trees thrive in an extremely mild climate. This is a lovely village of thatched cottages along a narrow and steep central street; a footbridge spans the Otter River. The local church has a strange collection of carved bench ends including one carved with the family arms of Sir Walter Ralegh. The family pew, dated 1537, was used by Sir Walter and his family for many years; there is also a memorial to the family here. Ralegh was born 1 mile west of here at Hayes Barton, a beautiful Tudor manor house (now a farmhouse), and the room where he was born is at the west end of the house, at the top of a dark, winding staircase. Over the porch is a small room which was his smoking room. At one point the estate was sold by the Ralegh family to a Mr. Duke, and Sir Walter could not persuade Duke to resell the house even with an open-ended offer: "I am most willing to give you whatsoever in your conscience you shall deem it worth." An attempt by an American to remove the entire house to Virginia in 1884 failed because a single 80-foot main beam ran the entire length of the house.

EAST COKER, Somerset (pop. 752)   South Somerset is a region of remote villages and small country towns set deeply in low-lying hills. East Coker, 2 miles southwest of Yeovil, is a lovely stone-built village with a quite good 15th-century manor house. There has been some dispute over the identification of East Coker as Narrobourne in Thomas Hardy's "A Tragedy of Two Ambitions" because the details also fit, slightly less well, the village of West Coker, 1 mile away. Hendford Hill, where Joshua and Cornelius pass a man "unsteady in his gait," lies between Narrobourne and Ivell (Yeovil). Narrobourne Church, of which Joshua Halborough has the living, is the parish church here, and the manor house, the residence of Albert Fellmer, who marries Rosa Halborough, is Coker Court.

A more famous association is with T. S. Eliot, whose ancestors lived in East Coker for several centuries and who commemorates the village in *Four Quartets:*

In my beginning is my end. In succession
Houses rise and fall, crumble, are extended,
Are removed, destroyed, restored, or in their place
Is an open field, or a factory, or a by-pass.
. . . .
Houses live and die: there is a time for building
And a time for living and for generation
And a time for the wind to break the loosened pane
And to shake the wainscot where the field-mouse trots
And to shake the tattered arras woven with a silent motto.

The church contains an Eliot family commemorative window, and after his death in London in 1965 T. S. Eliot's ashes were placed in the church.

EAST DEREHAM, Norfolk (pop. 5,561) This bustling market town (pronounced "der'rum"), on the slope of a hill in rich agricultural land 16 miles west of Norwich, has a history which begins in the early 7th century, when St. Withburga, daughter of the East Anglian king Anna, founded a nunnery here. Her grave site in the church became a place of pilgrimage, and the early town flourished, especially after 798, when the *Anglo-Saxon Chronicle* states, "the body of Wihtburh was found quite sound and free from corruption." St. Nicholas' Church stands on the site of the nunnery.

East Dereham became the home of William Cowper and Mrs. Morley Unwin in 1796. Mrs. Unwin had suffered three paralytic strokes beginning in 1791 when they were living in Olney, Northamptonshire, and Cowper found the job of nursing her extremely disagreeable. In 1796 the pair came to East Dereham, where they could be near Johnny Johnson, Cowper's devoted cousin. Mrs. Unwin died on December 17 and was buried here. Although Cowper's melancholy increased, his physical health seemed to improve somewhat. He was able to work on his translation of Homer and wrote "The Castaway," his last piece, in 1798. He moved to a larger house in town at the end of 1799 and gradually grew weaker; seized with dropsy in early April 1800, he died on April 25. Cowper was buried in the chapel in the north transept of the East Dereham Church. The memorial, by John Flaxman, shows the Bible and a book of Cowper's poems with a palm branch over them; the commemorative window, which depicts the poet, his dog, and his pet hares, is a centenary window. Cowper Congregational Chapel (1874) stands on the site of his house, and the vestry contains woodwork from the bedroom where he died.

The association with George Borrow is actually just outside East Dereham, although Borrow and most of his biographers claim that he was born here; in fact, he was born in Dumpling Green, to the south, on July 5, 1803. The birthplace, a two-story farmhouse, is on a lane off Yaxham Road; Borrow's time here was quite short because of his father's militia duties, but he retained a special warmth for the "beautiful little town in a certain district of East Anglia." Captain Borrow was posted to Colchester in 1803 and then to Winchester before the family returned here for eleven months in June 1809. Borrow recalls the Church of England services in the East Dereham Church in *The Romany Rye* when he with four Gypsy friends attended services in Bushbury, Staffordshire.

EAST LAVANT *See* LAVANT, EAST, AND LAVANT, MID.

EAST STOUR, Dorset (pop. 436) This village in the Blackmoor Vale, an area of rolling hills, thickly wooded copses, and clear rivers, is close enough to Shaftesbury, less than 5 miles to the east, to have some of the advantages of the city as well. An early-19th-century gray stone house just west of the church stands on the site of the original manor house, which belonged to Henry Fielding's maternal grandfather. Fielding lived here with his mother from 1710, when she was left the estate, until 1719 or 1720, when he was sent to Eton. He probably received his earliest education here under the Reverend Mr. Oliver, the curate of nearby Motcombe, an "ignorant and selfish man" who was the prototype of Parson Trulliber in *Joseph Andrews.* Fielding eventually inherited this estate but did not come back to live until after his marriage to Charlotte Cradock in November 1734. When Fielding and his wife did return to East Stour, he managed to run through the remainder of his rather sizable inheritance in the three years in which they occupied the manor. As a consequence of his desperate financial situation he turned to writing and drew in part on his earlier experiences in the area.

EASTBOURNE, Sussex (pop. 62,028) The Eastbourne esplanade, which is 3 miles long, is lined with private homes, good hotels, and flower beds and is uncluttered with shops. Hemmed in by Beachy Head to the west, the town is on Pevensey Bay 23 miles east of Brighton. It was once a Saxon hamlet, but the modern city was laid out in the 1850s as a speculative venture by William Cavendish, later 7th Duke of Devonshire. It came into fashion with the 19th-century trend toward holiday making and is popular today, but Eastbourne is a remarkably unlittered member of the resort genus. The old town center has only a few remaining old houses, and these are clustered on narrow streets around the parish church of St. Mary. Near the church is the Lambe Hotel, said to be 13th-century, and the Old Parsonage, a 16th-century stone-built hall.

Although most literary associations could be expected to date from Eastbourne's modish period, one 17th-century relationship is of interest. John Taylor, the "water poet," arrived in Eastbourne between August 9 and September 3, 1653, and was introduced to a brew called Eastbourne Rug, about which he composed some doggerel:

No cold can ever pierce his flesh or skin
Of him who is well lin'd with Rug within;
Rug is a lord beyond the Rules of Law,
It conquers hunger in a greedy maw,
And, in a word, of all drinks potable,
Rug is most puissant, potent, notable.

Toward the end of the 19th century H. G. Wells took

a cottage "at the end of the town" to recuperate from recurrent hemmorhaging (caused by incipient tuberculosis) in London, where he was teaching at University Tutorial College. Another constant visitor was Lewis Carroll (Charles Lutwidge Dodgson), who frequently stayed at 7 Lushington Road during the Long Vacations from Oxford and regularly attended Christ Church, where some of his last sermons were delivered to a congregation of children. In 1911 Rupert Brooke spent the month of December here with his mother at the Beachy Head Hotel; before he left, he finished his dissertation on John Webster.

Eastbourne's most important literary connection is with Eric Blair (George Orwell), who entered St. Cyprian's School, a public preparatory school run by a Mr. Vaughan Wilkes on the outskirts of the town beyond the promenade and hotels. Blair was intensely unhappy here and escaped at every opportunity to walk on the Downs with Cyril Connolly, who became one of his closest friends. Orwell was under a great deal of strain because of the separation from his family, and bed-wetting was a result of his frustration. Once, ridiculed in front of a stranger at tea and threatened with a caning by the sixth form, Orwell again wet the bed. He was thus caned by the headmaster, and to gain back some self-respect the child reported that the punishment had not hurt. The conclusion and full story he tells in *Such, Such Were the Joys:*

> "How dare you say a thing like that? Do you think that is a proper thing to say? Go in and REPORT YOURSELF AGAIN!"
>
> This time Sim [Mr. Wilkes] laid on in real earnest. He continued for a length of time that frightened and astonished me—about five minutes, it seemed—ending up by breaking the riding crop. The bone handle went flying across the room.

> "Look what you've made me do!" he said furiously, holding up the broken crop.
>
> I had fallen into a chair, weakly snivelling. . . . I was crying partly because of a deeper grief which is peculiar to childhood and not easy to convey: a sense of desolate loneliness and helplessness, of being locked up not only in a hostile world but in a world of good and evil where the rules were such that it was actually not possible for me to keep them.

However, Wilkes's ambition "to train up pupils to win scholarships at public schools, above all Eton," occasionally forced him "to sacrifice financial profit to scholastic prestige"; that is, "he would take at greatly reduced fees some boy who seemed likely to win scholarships and thus bring credit on the school." On these terms Orwell entered St. Cyprian's, and he notes:

> I did not at first understand that I was being taken at reduced fees; it was only when I was about eleven that Bingo and Sim began throwing the fact in my teeth.

Orwell never quite lost the feeling that his treatment was influenced by his status. In the autumn of 1913 he was placed in the scholarship class, and in December, having passed the examination for Wellington College, a school for the sons of military officers near Wokingham, he left Eastbourne.

Cyril Connolly returned to Eastbourne, to 48 St. John's Road, in 1970 and lived there until his death in 1974.

EASTHAMPSTEAD, Berkshire (pop. 1,994)   As late as the 17th century Easthampstead, which is 3 miles east of Wokingham, was a walk of the Royal Forest of Windsor and a favorite hunting area of kings. The manor house (now gone) was the home of Sir William Trumbull, a scholar as well as William III's Secretary of State, who managed to anger Samuel Pepys so much that the diarist left a most unfavorable portrait of him. Upon Sir William's retirement he took up residence here and, at an age close to seventy, made the acquaintance of the sixteen-year-old Alexander Pope. Pope dedicated "Spring" of the *Pastorals* to the old man:

> *You,* that too wise for Pride, too Good for Pow'r,
> Enjoy the Glory to be Great no more,
> And carrying with you all the World can boast
> To all the World Illustriously are lost!

The church here contains a memorial to Elijah Fenton, tutor to Sir William's son; Fenton helped Pope in his translation of the *Odyssey* (an effort Pope belittled in later years), and Pope wrote Fenton's epitaph:

> A poet blest beyond the poet's fate
> Whom heaven kept sacred from the proud and great.

One other possible association of Easthampstead is with Percy Bysshe Shelley and his first wife, Harriet Westbrook, who are thought to have rented Reeds Hill Farm in 1814.

EASTON MAUDIT, Northamptonshire (pop. 125)   A small village 6½ miles south of Wettingborough, Easton Maudit has an especially fine 14th-century church whose tall 15th-century spire can be seen for miles. Quatrefoils top the tower, and flying buttresses support the spire. The interior of the church is renowned

EASTBOURNE   A resort town uncluttered with small shops, Eastbourne was one of Lewis Carroll's favorite vacation sites; in 1965 the Eastbourne Literary Society erected a plaque "to perpetuate his memory" at 7 Lushington Road, where he had stayed.

for its decoration as well as for its monuments. One poignant monument is the simple tiled cross, at the chancel steps, which marks the three small graves of the children of the vicar, Thomas Percy, later Bishop Percy. He was presented to the living here in 1753 and held the post for twenty-nine years. Of great importance was the work he did here, for during this period he collected the ballads eventually published as *Reliques of Ancient English Poetry,* the collection of ballads, sonnets, historical songs, and metrical romances found in a Jacobean manuscript at Shifnal, Shropshire.

Many famous literary men of the period visited Percy here, and a brass tablet on the front pew of the nave notes that Dr. Johnson, Oliver Goldsmith, Edmund Burke, and David Garrick all worshiped here. Dr. Johnson, a frequent guest who made extended stays with Percy, was here in August 1764 and again in September in a state of extreme depression. One of Dr. Johnson's favorite spots in the village was the holly walk, still referred to as Dr. Johnson's Walk.

EASTWELL, Kent (pop. 77) Modern Eastwell, 3 miles north of Ashford, hardly exists, but at one time it was an important country seat with a splendid church (now in ruins) on the Pilgrims' Way. In the 17th and 18th centuries Eastwell Park was a beautiful estate, and it was to this manor that Anne Finch (later Countess of Winchilsea) and her husband came in 1689. Col. Heneage Finch had been in King James II's service, and because he and his wife remained loyal to the Stuart cause, they were forced to seek refuge here with the 4th Earl of Winchilsea, Heneage's nephew. Finch succeeded to the title in 1712, and the environment of Eastwell Manor and Park provided the stimulus for his wife's poetry. Here she listened to the sounds of nature and wrote "The Bird," "To the Nightingale," and the lovely "Nocturnal Reverie" in which the countryside is explored.

Eastwell Park and Manor are used by H. G. Wells in the autobiographical *Tono-Bungay,* even though it is usually noted that the Bladesover of the novel is Uppark, Sussex: it is, in fact, an amalgamation of Uppark, where Wells's mother was housekeeper, and Eastwell Park, which Wells states is "on the Kentish Downs, eight miles from Ashborough." Ashborough is Ashford, but Wells's distance is wrong. He notes accurately enough:

> The park is the second largest in Kent, finely wooded with well-placed beeches, many elms and some sweet chestnuts, abounding in little valleys and hollows of bracken, with springs and a stream and three fine ponds and multitudes of fallow deer. . . . A semi-circular screen of great beeches masks the church and village, which cluster picturesquely about the high road along the skirts of the great park.

EASTWOOD, Nottinghamshire (pop. 8,990) Almost all of northwest Nottinghamshire stretching toward Derbyshire is in the coalfield belt, and mining and colliery towns abound. Eastwood, situated 9 miles northwest of Nottingham and bounded on the west by the Erewash River, is a town of unusual contrasts with pithead machinery strewn about amid the surrounding farmland.

Modern Eastwood is largely a product of the industrial revolution, but it brought forth D. H. Lawrence

EASTWOOD   Typical of the tenemented terrace houses allotted to colliery workers in the industrial South Midlands is 8A Victoria Street, the birthplace of D.H. Lawrence. While he frequently proclaimed his hatred of this colliery area and Eastwood's "ugliness, ugliness, ugliness," Lawrence also believed the area was "the real England—the hard pith of England."

in partial compensation. Lawrence, the fourth of five children, was born at 8A Victoria Street on September 11, 1885, in a house still standing and suitably marked. He describes the local inhabitants in *The Lost Girl:*

> Here we are then; a vast substratum of colliers; a thick sprinkling of tradespeople intermingled with small employers of labour and diversified by elementary school teachers and non-conformist clergy; a higher layer of bank managers, rich millers and well-to-do ironmasters, episcopal clergy and the managers of collieries; then the rich and sticky cherry of the local coal owner glistening over all.

When Lawrence was about two years old, the family moved to the Breach, a hollow below the north end of the town. They lived, as he later wrote, "in the corner house facing the stile . . ."; this house, with its own garden, is now 26 Garden Road and is fully described in *Sons and Lovers:*

> The houses themselves were substantial and very decent. One could walk all round, seeing little front gardens . . . seeing neat front windows, little porches, little privet hedges, and dormer windows for the attics. But that was outside. . . . The dwelling-room, the kitchen, was at the back of the house, facing inward between the blocks, looking at a scrubby back garden, and then at the ash-pits. . . . So, the actual conditions of living in the Bottoms, that was so well built and that looked so nice, were quite unsavoury because people must live in the kitchen, and the kitchens opened on to that nasty alley of ash-pits.

When the boy was six, the family moved to better accommodations at 3 Walker Street, a house Lawrence nicknamed Bleak House because of its exposure to the winds and its view of the miners' tenements. An ash tree near this house appears in *Sons and Lovers* and in an early poem, "Discord in Children." Lawrence spent several years at the local school before going on to Nottingham High School on a scholarship. In 1902 the family moved to 97 Lynn Croft Road, and in the same autumn Lawrence became a pupil-teacher in the local school. He was transferred in 1903 to the Ilkeston Pupil-Teacher Centre in the Wilmot Street Schoolroom, where he remained until 1906.

In much of Lawrence's work Eastwood and the mining area are prominent. The most notable use, perhaps, is in *Sons and Lovers*, in which he calls the town Bestwood, not to be confused with a nearby community of that name. All the houses in which he lived, the places where he played, and the inns (the Sun Inn and the Three Tuns) where his father drank, appear in the novel. The Haggs, in Greasley, a nearby farm where the Chambers family lived, appears as Willey Farm; Felley Mill becomes Strelley Mill; the millpond, Willey Water; and Nethermere, Moorgreen Reservoir. Even the local mines are carefully differentiated: Selston is Selby, Brinsley is Beggarlee, High Park is Spinney Park, and Moorgreen is Minton. Lawrence was in harmony with his environment, rough as it still seems to the visitor; and through Morel he notes:

> I like the pits here and there. I like the rows of trucks, and the headstocks, and the stream in the daytime, and the lights at night. When I was a boy . . . I thought the Lord was always at the pit-top."

The White Peacock takes place in the Eastwood area, and its topography is easily traced on the actual landscape. The Ram Inn on Moorgreen Road is now a private dwelling with the new Ram Inn just opposite; Woodside may be the gamekeeper's lodge near Nethermere but could be the shooting lodge at Beauvale House; and the quarry where Annable dies is probably located at Willey Wood Farm (The Haggs). Highclose is most likely based on Lambclose House (described as Shortlands in *Women in Love*); this is "a long, low, old house, a sort of manor farm that has spread along the top of a slope just beyond the narrow little lake of Willey Water." Here Eastwood masquerades under the name Willey Green. The beginning of *The Lost Girl* is also set in Eastwood, at London House, a draper's shop on the main street, which Lawrence calls Manchester House; the original shop has disappeared. In this instance Eastwood has become Woodhouse, and the Throttle Ha'penny mine stands in Connection Meadow behind the Methodist Chapel. Only a small part of *Aaron's Rod* takes place in Eastwood, but the house described in the early pages is Lawrence's home at Lynn Croft, and Lambclose House becomes Shottle House.

Lawrence's short stories are also frequently set in Eastwood: "Love among the Haystacks" is concerned with haymaking at Hagg Farm:

> The two large fields lay on a hillside facing south. . . . These two fields were four miles from the home farm. But . . . everyone looked forward to the hay harvest at Greasley, it was a kind of picnic. They brought dinner and tea in the milk float which the father drove over in the morn-

ing. The lads and labourers cycled. Off and on, the harvest lasted for a fortnight. . . . [T]he high road from Alfreton to Nottingham ran at the foot of the fields.

"Strike-Pay" refers to Scargill Street, the Methodist Chapel, and the squares of miners' houses. "A Sick Collier" concerns an actual Eastwood mining accident; one of the first scenes of "You Touched Me" takes place in Bromley House, called here Pottery House, now a shopping center. (The same house becomes the Hollies in *The White Peacock* and "The Horse Dealer's Daughter.") "The Christening" takes place on Percy Street. A great number of poems also concern the Eastwood area with the early love poems, such as "Cherry Roberts" and "Dog Tired," set at The Haggs.

Lady Chatterley's Lover, Lawrence's most famous Midlands novel, presents topographical problems. Locally it is argued that the setting is Eastwood and that the ubiquitous Lambclose House has become Wragby Hall. Indeed, the gamekeeper's cottage is claimed to be one of the woodmen's huts on the estate, but there are other claimants, especially Renishaw, just south of Sheffield. Many things keep these identifications from ringing true, not the least of which is the fact that Constance Chatterley's trip begins at a point well north of Nottingham. The points in the trip are well defined from Tevershall to Worsop Castle. It seems best to accept the proposition that the village and manor house of this novel are representative rather than specific.

EATON BRAY, Bedfordshire (pop. 1,509) Eaton Bray, 3½ miles southwest of Dunstable, was one of the last Bedfordshire villages to take to modern farming methods, and its fields were not enclosed until 1860. William Beckford, author of *Vathek*, spent part of his first eleven years here at the castellated residence once owned by John of Gaunt and later by Beckford's father. Virtually no information is available about the boy's stay, but he could not have visited the house after 1770, the year of his father's death and the sale of the estate.

EATON SOCON, Bedfordshire (pop. 3,264) Eaton Socon, once a village of 7,602 acres on the Ouse River 1½ miles southwest of St. Neots, no longer exists but is, according to the bureaucracy, part of St. Neots in Huntingdonshire. The natives refuse to agree to its new geographical placement, and one still finds references to the village as an entity in Bedfordshire. The town was an important coaching stop by the 17th century, and the partly 13th-century White Horse Inn was probably the best-known hostelry. Samuel Pepys stayed here on one of his trips for the Admiralty.

Much later Charles Dickens visited the inn and assured the town's immortality as Eton Slocomb in *Nicholas Nickleby*. It is here that the coach stops on its way to Dotheboys Hall. "The weather was intensely and bitterly cold" as the coach made its way from London with the boys on top:

> At Eton Slocomb there was a good coach dinner, of which the box, the four front outsides, the one inside, Nicholas, the good-tempered man, and Mr. Squeers, partook; while the five little boys were put to thaw by the fire, and regaled with sandwiches.

EBCHESTER, County Durham (pop. 710) This is an undistinguished village set on the east bank of the Derwent River, on the site of a former Roman camp, *Vindomara,* which guarded the river crossing. The parish church of St. Ebba is where Robert Smith Surtees of nearby Hamsterley Hall was christened, and the churchyard contains his grave. A white marble cross with bas-relief lilies marks the grave, which is mossy and weed-covered. Surtees died on March 16, 1864, in Brighton and was brought back here for burial; the church contains a commemorative plaque.

EDGEHILL, Warwickshire A wooded escarpment on Warwickshire's southern border, Edgehill is 3 miles southeast of Kineton. On Stratford Road is the Sunrising Inn, where it is most likely that William Shenstone wrote the lines:

Whoe'er has travell'd life's dull round,
    Where'er his stages may have been,
May sigh to think he still has found
    The warmest welcome at an Inn.

The inscription "Lines Written at an Inn at Henley" was the publisher's and not Shenstone's and no doubt accounts for the erroneous title. Shenstone noted that the lines were written "at an inn on a certain occasion." Had Shenstone been in the Henley-in-Arden area, he would have stayed at Barrels Park in Ullenhall cum Apsley and not in an inn; had he been in Henley-on-Thames, as has also been suggested, he would have stayed at Park Place with the Conways.

EDGWARE, Middlesex (pop. 1,516) On Edgware Road, the old Roman Watling Street, Edgware is just over 11 miles northwest of London and since the 1965 redistricting has been a part of Greater Metropolitan London. At one time it was the site of the Roman station Sulloniacae. The church is mostly 18th-century and heavily restored, but the tower dates from the 15th century. Francis Coventry, a now-obscure poet, was vicar here during the 18th century; the perpetual curacy was granted him by a relative, the 6th Earl of Coventry. The poet's most famous piece, "Pompey the Little, or The Adventures of a Lap Dog," was preferred by Lady Mary Wortley Montagu over *The Adventures of Peregrine Pickle.* Coventry died of smallpox around 1759 and was buried here.

EDIAL, Staffordshire Edial (whose name is pronounced and sometimes spelled "Edjal") is now technically a part of the combined parish of Burntwood, Edial, and Woodhouses, but it is distinct enough in its location just 2½ miles west of Lichfield. Edial was assured lasting fame by an advertisement in the *Gentleman's Magazine* for 1736:

At Edial, near Lichfield, in Staffordshire, young gentlemen are boarded and taught the Latin and Greek Languages, by SAMUEL JOHNSON.

Here Samuel Johnson came, a bridegroom of twenty-six, with his new bride of forty-seven. James Boswell writes:

[H]is appearance was very forbidding: he was then lean and lank, so that his immense structure of bones was hideously striking to the eye, and the scars of the scrophula were deeply visible. He also wore his hair, which was straight and stiff, and separated behind: and he often had, seemingly, convulsive starts and odd gesticulations, which tended to excite at once surprise and ridicule.

The Johnsons made their home in the school, an 18th-century hall. Only three pupils, relates Boswell, showed up for Johnson's tuition: "David Garrick and his brother George, and a Mr. Offely, a young man of good fortune who died early." For almost eighteen months Johnson kept the school going for the three students and was convinced that he had developed a system for the teaching of the classics to overtake all others; he also worked on *Irene* during this period.

Johnson's school was a misadventure and was closed by February 1737; even Mrs. Johnson's £600 was lost. On March 2, with David Garrick, Johnson set out on the 120-mile journey to London. Whether they "rode and tied" their way there, as is claimed, is not certain. Somewhat more acceptable is the story of their financial state reported by Boswell:

Both of them used to talk pleasantly of their first journey to London. Garrick, evidently meaning to embellish a little, said one day in my hearing, "we rode and tied." And the Bishop of Killaloe [Dr. Barnard] informed me, that at another time, when Johnson and Garrick were dining together in a pretty large company, Johnson humorously ascertaining the chronology of something, expressed himself thus: "that was the year when I came to London with two-pence half-penny in my pocket . . . and thou, Davy, with three half-pence in thine."

EDINGTON, Wiltshire (pop. 748) On the northwest edge of the sometimes lonely Salisbury Plain just northeast of Westbury, Edington is a surprise, for there is an enormous cruciform church here which is out of all proportion to the size of the village. The church was built as a priory for the Bonhommes, a foundation similar to the Augustinians. The priory-cum-church has a magnificent exterior, and the interior is outstanding, especially in its series of consecration crosses; all twelve crosses survive inside, and only two are missing outside. This is the church in which George Herbert, the poet-priest of Bemerton, married Jane Danvers on March 5, 1629.

EDMONTON, Middlesex Too close to London (8¾ miles north of the Liverpool Street Station) to be even a dormitory suburb, Edmonton was once part of the vast forested and agricultural area which lay north of the city; but that was centuries ago, and today it is typical of the communities on the edge of London. Even in Daniel Defoe's time the encroachment of London was apparent; in *A Tour thro' the Whole Island of Great Britain* he writes in passing:

Newington, Tottenham, Edmonton, and *Enfield* stand all in a Line N. from the City; the encrease of Buildings is so great in them all, that they seem to a Traveller to be one continu'd Street; especially *Tottenham* and *Edmonton. . . .*

Located in the borough of Enfield since the 1965 redistricting and now a part of Greater London, Edmonton has one large green area in the 50- or 60-acre Pymme's Park and a few noteworthy old buildings, including the 12th-century All Saints' Church, a restored Jacobean house with upper-story pargeting on Bury Street, and Halliwick House.

Edmonton's use in literature dates to 1608, when *The Merry Devil of Edmonton* appeared. Of unknown authorship, although both Shakespeare and Michael Drayton have been suggested as candidates, the play concerns in part Peter Fabell, "a renowned scholar" who was said to have made a Faust-like compact with the devil and cheated him:

> That, for his fame in sleights and magic won,
> Was call'd the merry Fiend of Edmonton.
> If any here make doubt of such a name,
> In Edmonton yet fresh unto this day,
> Fix'd in the wall of that old ancient church,
> His monument remaineth to be seen. . . .

Fabell was supposedly buried in All Saints' Church, but neither the grave nor any record in the register has been discovered.

A second early play dealing with the town has provable historical connections. *The Witch of Edmonton*, by Thomas Dekker and John Ford and (possibly) William Rowley, partly concerns Elizabeth Sawyer, executed in 1621 for witchcraft. Mother Sawyer was the victim of the Stuart witch-hunts. In the play, after extreme persecution by her neighbors, she sells her soul to the devil in return for those powers of which she is accused. Almost all the action of *The Witch of Edmonton* takes place here, and the accounts of bigamy, murder, morris dancing, and the manner of dealing with the devil's familiar are said to be an accurate presentation of 17th-century Edmonton. However, it should be noted that the authors place the town in Hertfordshire and not in Middlesex.

A better-known use of Edmonton occurred in 1782, the year William Cowper's "The Diverting History of John Gilpin" appeared; the story had been told to Cowper by Lady Austen to combat the poet's melancholy. Gilpin's wife and children, his sister-in-law and her child have already journeyed

> Unto the Bell at Edmonton,
> All in a chaise and pair.

There he is to meet them. Mounting his borrowed steed, he races here:

> At Edmonton, his loving wife
> From the balcony spied
> Her tender husband, wondering much
> To see how he did ride.

> "Stop, stop, John Gilpin!—Here's the house!"
> They all at once did cry;
> "The dinner waits, and we are tired:"—
> Said Gilpin—"So am I!"

> But yet his horse was not a whit
> Inclined to tarry there;
> For why?—his owner had a house
> Full ten miles off, at Ware.

At the time of the ride Pymme's Brook was channeled under Fore Street and was "the Wash" of the poem. The Bell Inn, where the anniversary dinner was to be held, is said to be the one on Fore Street at the corner of Gilpin Grove. However, two points, lead to questioning this long-established identification.

First, eight separate "Bell" inns in the town claim this distinction; second, and most damning, is that Cowper, knowing the topography of the area, must have had some inn on the farther, not the near, side of the Wash in mind.

John Keats had very strong ties with Edmonton, for in 1805 he came here to live with his mother and grandmother at a house on Church Street. Keats's time here and at school in nearby Enfield was quite happy. He enjoyed walking along Pymme's Brook to its confluence with the Lea River, and later he wrote some nonsense verse about life here:

> There was a naughty boy
>   And a naughty boy was he,
> He kept little fishes
>   In washing tubs three
>   In spite
>   Of the might
>   Of the Maid
>   Nor afraid
>   Of his Granny-good—
>   He often would
>   Hurly burly
>   Get up early
>   And go
>   By hook or crook
>   To the brook
>   And bring home
>   Miller's thumb,
>   Tittlebat
>   Not over fat,
>   Minnows small
>   As the stall
>   Of a glove. . . .

Keats's mother died in February 1810, and in the following summer young Keats was apprenticed to Thomas Hammond, a surgeon whose office, Wilston, was also on Church Street. The cottage where Keats worked and lived was known as Keats' Cottage; it was demolished in 1931, but a plaque at 7 Church Street commemorates the site. Keats's grandmother died in 1814, but she had provided guardians for her orphaned grandchildren: John Rowland Sandell and a myopic tea dealer, Richard Abbey. Sandell soon relinquished the trust and left Abbey in sole charge. Keats quarreled with Hammond in 1815, left his apprenticeship, and went on to London. In Keats's time here, a footbridge spanned a small brook in the last field entering Edmonton from Enfield; it was this, the poet told Charles Cowden Clarke, that inspired part of "I Stood Tiptoe upon a Little Hill":

> How silent comes the water round that bend;
> Not the minutest whisper does it send
> To the o'erhanging sallows: blades of grass
> Slowly across the chequer'd shadows pass.

> Why, you might read two sonnets, ere they reach
> To where the hurrying freshnesses aye preach
> A natural sermon o'er their pebbly beds;
> Where swarms of minnows show their little heads,
> Staying their wavy bodies 'gainst the streams,
> To taste the luxury of sunny beams
> Temper'd with coolness. How they ever wrestle
> With their own sweet delight, and ever nestle
> Their silver bellies on the pebbly sand.

The bridge is gone, but the public footpath near the church leading to Bury Street and Enfield is thought to have been the poet's route.

Another resident of Edmonton was Charles Lamb; hounded from house to house by the nature of his sister Mary's illness, he found some peace here at Bay Cottage (now called Lamb Cottage and marked with a plaque), the home of a Mr. and Mrs. Walden who had cared for Mary during two of her breakdowns. Lamb joined his sister in May 1833; Bay Cottage is near the railway station, squeezed between two much larger houses. Lamb became increasingly lonely and despondent. In December 1834 he fell while walking on the London road and lacerated his face; within a few days erysipelas set in, and Lamb was unable to fight the acute, febrile disease. He died on December 27 and was buried here in the churchyard of All Saints' Church. The grave is southwest of the church, and on the plain headstone is Henry Francis Cary's epitaph, which says in part:

Yet art thou not all lost; thro' many an age
With sterling sense and humour shall thy page
Win many an English bosom, pleased to see
That old and happier vein revived in thee.

Mary, who survived him by thirteen years, is buried beside her brother. Part of William Wordsworth's intended epitaph is engraved inside the church and includes the final line, "O, he was good, if e'er a good man lived!"

Inside the north door of All Saints' is a double medallion portrait memorial to Lamb and William Cowper; the combination is quite appropriate since Lamb frequented "Johnny Gilpin's," as he called the Bell and often met friends there. Just north of the church is the Lamb Memorial Hall and Institute, a somewhat gray and glum building designed as a literary, social, and recreational center.

EDWINSTOWE, Nottinghamshire (pop. 963) Pleasantly situated on the Maun River in Sherwood Forest, Edwinstowe is the center for Birklands and Bilhagh, two of the most impressive parts of Sherwood Forest, the land of Robin Hood legend. The Church of St. Mary, carefully restored, retains a plain Norman priest's door in the chancel and is the traditionally held site for the marriage of Robin Hood and Maid Marian. A mile north of the church is the magnificent hollow-trunked Major, or Queen, Oak, thought to be 1,400 years old. The tree has a circumference of 30 feet; the massive branches, whose spread exceeds 250 feet, are supported by 2,000 pounds of iron bands and are protected from the weather by more than 1,500 pounds of lead. The tree, naturally, is said to have been a meeting place for Robin and his men.

EDWORTH, Bedfordshire (pop. 82) The tiny village of Edworth, 3½ miles southeast of Biggleswade on the eastern border of Bedfordshire, once held a Roman colony, but what the Romans called the establishment is not known. A few cottages and Manor Farm are about all that remain, but the hamlet attracted a great deal of attention when Agnes Beaumont and her family, dissenters, lived here. She is the woman who caused such inadvertent trouble for John Bunyan that a lynching party almost set out for him. In February 1674 Agnes, who lived with her widower father John, asked John Bunyan to carry her by pillion on his horse to a dissenters' meeting in Gamgay (now Gamlingay), Cambridgeshire. It is

said he remarked, "Your father would be grievously angry if I should." Nevertheless, he acquiesced. Upon their return the father was indeed "grievously angry," had locked Agnes out, and refused her admission to the house unless she promised to give up the dissenters. The old man died the following Tuesday, and by this time gossip had reached such proportions that Bunyan was accused of supplying Agnes with poison to kill her father. An inquest cleared them both. Bunyan alludes to this incident in the second edition of *Grace Abounding to the Chief of Sinners:*

It was reported with the boldest confidence that I had my Misses, my Whores, my Bastards, yea, two Wives at once, and the like. My foes have missed their mark in this their shooting at me. I am not the man.

The Beaumont farmhouse, now forming two brick-and-plaster cottages, is on the east side of Great North Road, off a road opposite the Plough Inn.

EGGLESTONE ABBEY, Yorkshire (pop. 44) The ruins of this Premonstratensian house are beautifully situated in the angle formed by the tiny dell called Thorsgill and the Tees River. The abbey, founded near the end of Henry II's reign, was dedicated to St. Mary and St. John the Baptist. The Premonstratensians were a small order, and they were known as white canons from the color of their habits. While Sir Walter Scott uses the abbey throughout *Rokeby* and describes its "grey ruins" on the bank of the Tees, he transfers all action here at the end; this is the site where the execution of the Knight of Rokeby is prevented, Wilfrid dies from his wounds, and Wilfrid's father is shot and killed by Bertram. Scott explored the abbey in the autumn of 1812, when he was visiting John B. S. Morritt at nearby Rokeby to gather firsthand information for this work:

The reverend pile lay wild and waste,
Profaned, dishonored, and defaced
Through storied lattices no more
In softened light the sunbeams pour,
Gilding the Gothic sculpture rich
Of shrine and monument and niche.
The civil fury of the time
Made sport of sacrilegious crime;
For dark fanaticism rent
Altar and screen and ornament
And peasant hands the tombs o'erthrew
Of Bowes, of Rokeby, and Fitz-Hugh.

John Wycliffe received part of his education here; and contrary to John Leland's statement that Wycliffe was born at Ipreswell, or Hipswell, Yorkshire, he was probably born about 1320 in Wycliffe, about 3 miles downstream from the abbey.

EGHAM, Surrey (pop. 23,563) Half a mile southeast of Runnymede, where, like the stag,

Fair liberty pursu'd, and meant a prey
To lawless power, here turn'd, and stood at bay,

the Magna Carta was sealed in 1215, is Egham, which once belonged to Chertsey Abbey. The principal literary interest here lies with Sir John Denham, whose father built the Place (demolished) near the church and almshouses on the High Street; the poet came into the estate at the death of his father "and was wont to say he would there build a Retiring Place for his

Muses." *Cooper's Hill* describes the prospect here with Windsor on the left and London at a distance on the right; four lines from the poem are inscribed on Denham's mother's memorial tomb in the modern church. Denham lost the estate here in the Civil War.

ELLASTONE, Staffordshire (pop. 243) A small village on the Staffordshire-Derbyshire border, Ellastone is 5 miles southwest of Ashbourne and has the Dove River and its lovely valley just below it; behind the village rise the Weaver Hills, and near the Dove are the remains of the Augustinian Calwick Abbey. Wootton Lodge, one of the finest stately homes in Staffordshire, was bought by Bernard Granville, a peculiar man who grew steadily more difficult with age. Nevertheless, his hospitality was considerable, and among his many visitors were Jean-Jacques Rousseau, who could speak no English and found Granville the only person in the area who could speak French. Rousseau worked on his *Confessions* here during the winter when Granville was absent.

More important, Staffordshire is the Loamshire of George Eliot's novels; Dovedale is Eagledale, and Ellastone is the Hayslope of *Adam Bede*. Robert Evans, the author's father, who, it is maintained, became Adam in the novel, spent his early life here; and the house belonging to Samuel Evans, her uncle, who is said to have become Seth Bede, remains although it is much rebuilt. Her grandfather's house, where Robert had his carpentry workshop, still stands although the workshop is unrecognizable. The description of Hayslope is accurate even today:

> The Green lay at the extremity of the village, and from it the road branched off in two directions, one leading farther up the hill by the church, and the other winding gently down towards the valley. On the side of the Green that led towards the church, the broken line of thatched cottages was continued nearly to the churchyard gate; but on the opposite, northwestern side, there was nothing to obstruct the view of gently-swelling meadow, and wooded valley, and dark masses of distant hill. . . . [A]nd now from his station near the Green he had before him in one view nearly all the other typical features of this pleasant land. . . . the huge conical masses of hill, like giant mounds intended to fortify this region of corn and grass against the keen and hungry winds of the north . . . a more advanced line of hanging woods, divided by bright patches of pasture or furrowed crops. . . . Then . . . the valley, where the woods grew thicker. . . .

Dinah Morris preaches on the Green, as did her prototype, Elizabeth Evans. The Bromley Arms becomes the Donnithorne Arms of the novel; Donnithorne Chase is either Calwick Abbey or Wootton Lodge. The confusion results because both are surrounded by the woodland Eliot writes of:

> [I]t was still scarcely four o'clock when he stood before the tall narrow gate leading into the delicious labyrinthine wood which skirted one side of the Chase. . . . It was a wood of beeches and limes, with here and there a light, silver-stemmed birch. . . . It was not a grove with measured grass or rolled gravel for you to tread upon, but with narrow, hollow-shaped, earthy paths, edged with faint dashes of delicate moss. . . .

The church here

> was [not] remarkable for anything except for the gray age of its oaken pews—great square pews mostly, ranged on each side of a narrow aisle. It was free, indeed, from the

modern blemish of galleries. The choir had two narrow pews to themselves in the middle of the right-hand row. . . . The pulpit and desk, gray and old as the pews, stood on one side of the arch leading into the chancel, which also had its gray square pews for Mr. Donnithorne's family and servants.

ELSFIELD, Oxfordshire (pop. 174) Within sight of Oxford, 3 miles to the southwest, Elsfield is a lovely little village with an especially fine 13th-century church with a Norman font and a 13th-century piscina. Outside, one of the buttresses contains two sundials thought to be 16th-century or earlier.

Dr. Samuel Johnson was a frequent visitor to the village, quite possibly to escape harassment from his London creditors, and undoubtedly knew the sundials in the churchyard. At the time he was holding up production of his *Dictionary* until his M.A. was conferred by Oxford.

Many years later Elsfield was host to another man who was to become an important literary figure. R. D. Blackmore, who was born in Longworth, Berkshire, in June 1825, was brought here as an infant by relatives after the death of his mother four months after his birth. Mary Frances Knight Gordon, wife of the vicar here and the infant's aunt, cared for him at the vicarage, and much later Blackmore used the area in *Cripps the Carrier*, a woodland tale concerning Oxford and Elsfield, in which Master Cripps turns a good number of corners between Beckley and Oxford.

In 1919 Elsfield Manor became the home of John Buchan, who eventually became Lord Tweedsmuir and Governor-General of Canada, and it remained his home until his death in Montreal on February 11, 1940. His ashes were brought home from Canada and interred in the church graveyard.

ELSTOW, Bedfordshire (pop. 412) Almost close enough to Bedford (less than 1½ miles to the north) to be a part of the city, Elstow has been inhabited since before the Norman Conquest and is said to have been a camping site for Offa, King of Mercia. Just south of the Norman Church of SS. Mary and

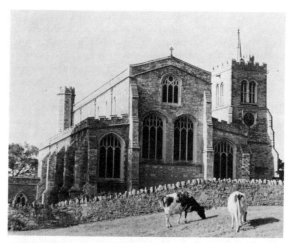

ELSTOW The restored Church of SS. Mary and Helen, a "modernized" structure dating to the founding of Elstow Abbey in 1078, was the site of the christening of John Bunyan; memorial windows in the north and south aisles depict *The Holy War* and *The Pilgrim's Progress*.

Helen are the ruins of a nunnery (part of the cloisters and fishponds) founded by Countess Judith, who was either the sister or the niece of William the Conqueror. The nunnery flourished throughout the Middle Ages and was especially attractive for women of the more aristocratic families. So much wealth was on display here that at various times the sisters were reprimanded by the bishop for their ostentation.

This is the country of John Bunyan. Born in Harrowden, a mile to the east, he was christened here on November 30, 1628, by the Rev. Thomas Kellie. The Norman font with four crouching figures, grotesquely representing the vices cast out by the sacrament of baptism, is still in use. The young boy played on the village green, and later, following his return from the Civil War and his marriage, he settled here and took up his father's trade. The house where Bunyan probably lived was pulled down long ago, but the Bedford Road site is marked with a plaque. Attached to the south end of the house was the forge at which he worked as tinker and brazier. He and his young wife, he said, "came together as poor as poor might be, not having so much household-stuff as a dish and spoon betwixt both." But she did bring two books to the marriage, *The Practice of Piety* and *The Plain Man's Pathway to Heaven.* The couple attended services at the church, where he was a bell ringer. One interesting sidelight, especially since the Bedford dissenting stronghold was so close, is that SS. Mary and Helen was High Church in all respects. Bunyan admitted pleasure in the ritual and display. Bunyan was playing tipcat on the village green, it is said, when he heard a voice saying, "Will thou leave thy sins and go to heaven, or have thy sins and go to hell?"

Elstow's use in *The Pilgrim's Progress* is extensive. At the west end of the church is a double portal whose inner gate is most likely the wicket gate through which Christian flees for refuge after being brought back from the burning mountain by Evangelist. This identification appears to hold up especially well when the nearby detached tower is taken into account. The tower probably is the Castle of Beelzebub, from which the arrows are shot at the passing pilgrims. Also partially identifiable is the "pleasant place, where was built a *stately palace,* beautiful to behold." This house, to which Interpreter takes Christian, is a composite of Houghton House in Houghton Conquest and Elstow Place, a 1619 Tudor mansion (close to the south side of the church), built with stones from the abbey ruins and now in ruins itself. The wall called Salvation, leading to the cross (still standing in part on Elstow Green), can easily be any of a number of the little alleys formed by the houses which run from the road to the green. Vanity Fair, "no new erected business, but a thing of ancient standing," has its basis in the great May abbey fair originating in the 12th century. Bunyan's description of the fair, where "all sorts of vanity" were sold, where "jugglings, cheats, games, plays, fools, apes, knaves, and rogues, and that of all sorts" were to be found, must have been accurate even in his day:

... and at the town [Vanity] there is a fair kept called Vanity Fair. It is kept all the year long; it beareth the name of Vanity Fair, because the town where 'tis kept is lighter than vanity, and also because all that is there sold or that cometh thither is Vanity....

Here are to be seen, too, and that for nothing, thefts, murders, adulteries, false swearers, and that of a blood-red colour.

The Moot Hall contains Bunyan's father's will, in which John Bunyan was left 1 shilling, and the 15th-century pulpit from the church, used when Bunyan attended services there. An upper room at the church holds a lacquer cabinet in which Sir William Temple kept Dorothy Osborne's letters before they were married.

ELY, Cambridgeshire (pop. 8,382) The name of the cathedral town of Ely (pronounced "ēl′ē"), 15 miles northeast of Cambridge, means "eel island," and, indeed, for many years tithes were paid in eels. At one time the Isle of Ely, on the south bank of the Ouse, was an island in the Fens surrounded by willowy marshes; today the marshland is pastureland, orchards, and farmland, and enormous banks have been raised as a barrier against flooding. Michael Drayton calls Ely the queen "of all the *Marshland* Iles" in *Poly-Olbion:*

The Turffe which beares the Hay, is wondrous needful Peat:
My full and batning earth, needs not the Plowmans paines;
The Rils which runne in me, are like the branched vaines
In human Bodies seene; those Ditches cut by hand,
From the surrounding *Meres,* to winne the measured land,
To those choyce waters, I most fitly may compare,
Wherewith nice women use to blanch their Beauties rare.

The magnificent Ely Cathedral, built on the site of a 7th-century monastery, draws thousands of visitors. The Venerable Bede tells the story of the founding in his *Historia Ecclesiastica Gentis Anglorum,* and it seems clear that this was a foundation of both monks and nuns, as was common in those times, and, furthermore, that St. Etheldreda (Aethelthryth) endowed the foundation with the Isle of Ely, which she had obtained as part of her marriage settlement.

The Danes attacked Ely on numerous occasions and were usually repulsed, but in 870 they sacked the house and murdered all the nuns and monks before setting fire to the buildings. The foundation was reestablished by King Edgar with the help of St. Dunstan as a single Benedictine monastery. The first abbot, Brihtnoth, built a new church that was consecrated on Candlemas Day, 970, but after the heroic stand of Hereward the Wake against the Normans a Norman abbot, Simeon, decided that the Anglo-Saxon church was not grand enough for his purposes. Around 1080 the Norman church was begun, and by 1100 the relics of the old church, including the coffin of St. Etheldreda, were transferred to the eastern end of the partially built structure. Work on the church continued for eighty-nine years, and the Norman building still forms the greatest part of the cathedral. The third addition is one of the most exciting; an octagonal area 74 feet across was opened up, and a timber vault, surmounted with another octagonal wooden structure, the Lantern, was built. The Lantern seems to be suspended in midair almost 100 feet above the floor. The sixteen struts bearing the 400-ton weight rest on the octagon pillars, and the eight corner oak pieces for the Lantern itself are 63 feet long and approximately 3 feet thick.

Time, the dissolution of the monasteries, Cromwell, and lack of leadership and money exacted such a severe toll here that by the 18th century writers were beginning to show concern for the cathedral. Daniel Defoe writes in *A Tour thro' the Whole Island of Great Britain* that the cathedral

> ... seen far and wide ... is so ancient, totters so much with every gust of Wind, looks so like a Decay, and seems so near it, that when ever it does fall, all that 'tis likely will be thought strange in it, will be, that it did not fall a hundred Years sooner.

Even by 1830, when William Cobbett came here in conjunction with *Rural Rides,* restoration had not begun:

> [T]his famous building, the cathedral, is in a state of disgraceful irrepair and disfigurement. The great and magnificent windows to the east have been shortened at the bottom, and the space plastered up with brick and mortar, in a very slovenly manner, for the purpose of saving the expense of keeping the glass in repair. Great numbers of the windows in the upper part of the building have been partly closed up in the same manner, and others quite closed up. One door-way, which apparently had stood in need of repair, has been rebuilt in modern style, because it was cheaper; and the churchyard contained a flock of sheep acting as vergers for those who live upon the immense income....

Not until 1839 was the necessary work undertaken, but by the 1870s William Gladstone described Ely as "a pattern for the cathedrals of England." The 16th-century Bishop West's Chapel in the south aisle contains the remains of the giant Essex ealdorman Byrhtnoth, who with his *dryht* (army) was defeated at the Blackwater Estuary in Maldon in 991 by Danish invaders. Byrhtnoth is the warrior commemorated in the 10th-century poem "The Battle of Maldon." A man of great wealth who had given the monastery various manors for its hospitality to him and his men, he promised the abbot even greater wealth if he would make certain that the ealdorman would be buried here if he lost his life in the battle; Byrhtnoth fell on August 10, and the monks recovered his headless body and buried it here in the church. Exhumation of the remains in 1796 showed the man to be of gigantic stature at 6 feet 9 inches. The Danes, it is thought, took away Byrhtnoth's head to use as a drinking vessel, believing they would thereby be imbued with the ealdorman's wisdom and courage.

Ely is best known because of Charles Kingsley's *Hereward the Wake;* the first part of the novel, which concerns Hereward's youth, outlawry, deeds in England and Flanders, and marriage to Torfrida, is the more attractive, but the second part deals in detail with his gallant efforts to defeat the invading Normans. Hereward was not a fictional creation; this

> was Hereward the Wake, Lord of Bourne, and ancestor of the family of Wake, whose arms, of course, are much later than the time of Hereward.

Hereward established himself on the Isle of Ely with a number of Anglo-Saxon refugees, the most important of whom was Morcar, Earl of Northumbria; the Fenland, "a natural fortress," was worth fighting for, Kingsley notes:

> The low rolling uplands were clothed in primeval forest; oak and ash, beech and elm, with here and there perhaps a group of ancient pines, ragged and decayed, and fast dying out in England even then; though lingering still in the forest of the Scotch highlands.
> Between the forests were open woods, dotted with white sheep and golden gorse; rolling plains of rich though ragged turf, whether cleared by the hand of man or by the wild fires which often swept over the hills. And between the wood and the wold stood many a Danish "town," with its clusters of low straggling buildings round the holder's house, of stone or mud below and of wood above; its high dykes round tiny fields....

Historically, in 1069 the band held off William the Conqueror's men, and the fighting continued for two years:

> Then he [William] began to rebuild his causeway, broader and stronger; and commanded all the fishermen of the Ouse to bring their boats to Cotinglade, and ferry over his materials. "Among whom came Hereward in a very narrow canoe, with head and beard shaven lest he should be known, and worked diligently among the rest. But the sun did not set that day without mischief; for before Hereward went off he finished his work by setting the whole on fire, so that it was all burnt, and some of the French killed and drowned."
> And so The Wake went on, with stratagems and ambushes, till "after seven day's continual fighting they had hardly done one day's work...."

The band of Anglo-Saxons set fire to the reeds, as Torfrida had suggested to Hereward:

> A line of flame was leaping above the reed bed, crackling and howling before the evening breeze. The column on the causeway had seen their danger but too soon, and fled—but whither?
> A shower of arrows, quarrels, javelins fell upon the head of the column as it tried to face about and retreat, confusing it more and more....
> On came the flame, leaping and crackling, laughing and shrieking, like a live fiend. The archers and slingers in the boats cowered before it, and fell, scorched corpses, as it swept on. It reached the causeway, surged up, recoiled from the mass of human beings, then sprang over their heads and passed onwards, girding them with flame.
> The reeds were burning around them; the timbers of the bridge caught fire; the peat and fagots smouldered beneath their feet. They sprang from the burning footway, and plunged into the fathomless bog, covering their faces and eyes with scorched hands, and then sank in the black gurgling slime.

The Norman struggle to gain control of the Isle of Ely ended in 1071, when the abbot promised obedience to the Norman invaders in exchange for their sparing the church and the city.

ENFIELD, Middlesex (pop. 102,000) About 12 miles northwest of central London, Enfield is now a large London borough incorporating Enfield, Edmonton, and Southgate but was once a royal hunting ground. Enfield Chase is still an extensive piece of land, although many of its trees and most of the animals are gone. The chase was used heavily by the Tudors. During Cromwell's time the land was confiscated for its timber, but the Restoration saw reforestation and restocking.

Michael Drayton notes the royal hunting ground in *Poly-Olbion:*

> And that he is the Hill, next *Enfield* which hath place,
> A Forrest for her pride, though titled but a Chase.

Her Purlewes, and her Parks, her circuit full as large,
As some (perhaps) whose state requires a greater charge.

Daniel Defoe also mentions the chase and part of its history in *A Tour thro' the Whole Island of Great Britain:*

> This Chase was once a very beautiful Place, . . . but it has suffered several Depredations since that [James I's reign], and particularly in the late Protector's Usurpation, when it was utterly stript, both of Game, and Timber, and let out in Farms to Tenants, for the use of the Publick.
>
> After the Restoration, it was reassumed, and laid open again; Woods and Groves were every where Planted, and the whole Chase stored with Deer: But the young Timber which indeed began to thrive, was so continually Plundered, and the Deer-stealers have so Haras'd the Deer, and both perhaps by those who should have preserved it, as well as by others, that the Place was almost ruined for a Forrest. . . .

Four hunting lodges were at the entrances to the land; East Lodge, used by Charles I, is uninhabited and in rather shabby condition; North Lodge (now called Kilvinton Hall) has been altered a great deal; West Lodge is now a hotel; and South Lodge, virtually unrecognizable, is a hospital. John Evelyn visited West Lodge on June 2, 1676, and records in his diary:

> I went ... to Mr. *Secretary Coventries* Lodge in the Chace, which is a very prety place, the house commodious, the Gardens handsome, & our entertainment very free. . . . To this Lodge are 3 greate ponds, & some few inclosures, the rest a solitarie desert, yet stored with no lesse than 3000 deare &c: These are pretty retreates for Gent: especialy that were studious & a lover of privacy. . . .

It should be noted that South Lodge also claims to be the site of Sir William Coventry's home.

As close to London as it is, Enfield still seems rural, particularly along its Essex and Hertfordshire borders, and there are a number of notable buildings: Enfield Court (built about 1690, and now the lower school of the grammar school); the old vicarage on Silver Street; and Forty Hall (built in 1632), without doubt the most magnificent building in Enfield. Elsynge House, where Elizabeth I stayed as a princess, is nearby, and it is thought that Sir Walter Ralegh was in attendance here.

One of the first mentions of the town in literature occurs in the anonymous play *The Merry Devil of Edmonton* (1608). Many of the courting scenes take place in the chase; Banks, the miller, stops to rest at Enfield Church:

> 'Sfoot, here's a dark night indeed! I think I have been in fifteen ditches between this and the forest. Soft, here's Enfield Church: I am so wet with climbing over into an orchard for to steal some filberts. Well, here I'll sit in the church porch, and wait for the rest of my consort.

Other, more specific relationships begin with John Keats and his brother George, who were sent to school here around 1804. It has been said that the boys were "not yet out of child's dress," but that seems somewhat unlikely. The school, located where the railway station is, was opposite a bend in the New River and was run by a very compassionate and enlightened headmaster, John Clarke, whose son Charles Cowden Clarke became Keats's close friend:

> At the far end of the pond . . . there stood a rustic arbour, where John Keats and I used to sit and read Spenser's "Faery Queene" together, when he left school, and used to come over from Edmonton, where he was apprenticed to Thomas Hammond the surgeon.

Keats remained in school here until the end of 1810, when he entered into his apprenticeship.

The author most strongly associated with Enfield is Charles Lamb, who made this his home from the summer of 1827 until 1833, when he and Mary went to Edmonton. The Lambs had two houses here, both on Gentleman's Row, a group of early-18th-century houses through whose gardens the New River wanders. Lamb describes their first house at Number 17 as "the prettiest compactest house I ever saw" and gives impossible directions for finding it:

> [C]ome down by the Green Lanes. . . . pass the Church; pass the "Rising Sun," turn sharp round the corner, and we are the 6th or 7th house on the Chase; tall elms darken the door.

He omitted a number of turnings and the crossing of the New River before turning right. Both houses are marked with commemorative plaques. Lamb frequented the Crown and Horseshoe Inn and had many guests including William Hazlitt, Thomas Hood, Leigh Hunt, and William Wordsworth. Another visitor, Walter Savage Landor, who was brought to Enfield to meet Lamb by Thomas Worsley (later master of Downing College, Cambridge), and Henry Crabb Robinson, commented on the meeting that Lamb "met me as if I had been a friend of twenty years' standing." In 1833 Lamb moved to Edmonton, where Mary was under the nursing care of a Mrs. Walden.

Down Hadley Road, a little beyond the entrance to Trent Park, is Camlet Moat, an old earthwork which William Camden called the "ruines and rubbish of an ancient house," once belonging to the Mandevilles. Others claimed that it was the site of the chief forester's lodge. No more than a green hump from the road, the site was chosen by Sir Walter Scott as the scene of Lord Dalgarno's murder in *The Fortunes of Nigel:*

> The place at which he stopped was at that time little more than a mound, partly surrounded by a ditch, from which it derived the name of Camlet Moat. A few hewn stones there were, which had escaped the fate of many others that had been used in building different lodges in the forest for the royal keepers. . . . A wild woodland prospect led the eye at various points through broad and seemingly interminable alleys, which, meeting at this point as at a common centre, diverged from each other as they receded, and had, therefore, been selected by Lord Dalgarno as the rendezvous for the combat, which, through the medium of Richie Moniplies, he had offered to his injured friend, Lord Glenvarloch.

There are four other associations with Enfield. Isaac D'Israeli was born in the old schoolhouse in 1766; Frederick Marryat, author of *Mr. Midshipman Easy,* was in a private school here for a time; Walter Pater moved here to Chase Side (demolished) following the death of his father in the 1840s and attended the local school before going on to King's School, Canterbury, in 1853; and Maurice Hewlett attended Palace School as a boarder in 1874–1875 before going on to the International College, Spring Grove, Isleworth.

ENNERDALE BRIDGE, Cumberland The stern mountains Bowness Knott and Great Borne encircle Ennerdale, and its valley, one of the wildest and most attractive in the Lake District, holds Ennerdale Water, 2½ miles long and ½ mile broad, which receives the Liza River at its eastern end and discharges the Ehen at its western end. Where the Ehen joins Crossdale Beck is the village with its 19th-century Norman-style church and its churchyard, the scene of William Wordsworth's "The Brothers." Here is the green field of a churchyard where there

> Is neither epitaph nor monument,
> Tombstone nor name—only the turf we tread
> And a few natural graves.

Leonard talks with the Ennerdale priest in the churchyard and discovers the accident which had claimed his brother James's life:

> Both left the spot in silence;
> And Leonard, when they reached the church-yard gate,
> As the Priest lifted up the latch, turned round,—
> And, looking at the grave, he said, "My Brother!"

EPSOM, Surrey (pop. 18, 804)

> Here lies I and my four daughters
> Died thro. drinking Baryta waters,
> If us 'ad stuck to Epsom salts,
> We wouldn't be lying in these 'ere vaults.

That was an appropriate comment on Epsom salts, and by extension the town of Epsom, until the end of the 18th century, when horse racing became firmly established upon the Downs. On the foot of Banstead Down, less than 18 miles southwest of London, Epsom was little more than a village in a lovely location until the early 17th century, when Henry Wicker tried to enlarge an existing water source for his cattle, only to find they would not drink from the bitter spring. The "bitter purging salt" became famous worldwide within a short time, and people came by the thousands to partake of its medicinal qualities. Indeed, the waters supposedly cured everything from gout to madness.

The spa gained fashion rapidly after the Restoration, when Charles II and his family frequented it and Lord Buckhurst (the future 6th Earl of Dorset) and Nell Gwynn were discreetly lodged in a nearby inn. By the end of the 17th century the well was beginning to dry up, and in 1702 Celia Fiennes, the travel writer, caught the officials replenishing the well from other sources early in the morning. But the greatest damage was probably done by a local apothecary, Dr. Livingstone (Levingstone), who discovered that people would not turn to his newly dug well (whose waters had no medicinal qualities); he bought up the lease on the Old Well and closed it. This and the bathing rage finished Epsom's early popularity; the only reminder in the town is a plaque at the site of the old well.

But Epsom was twice blessed; the era of horse racing brought new prosperity to the town, and the Derby and the Oaks are world-famous. The races did not become permanent until the 18th century, when they were begun by Edward Stanley, 12th Earl of Derby. The major races are named after the earl and his home in Banstead.

One of the earliest figures associated with Epsom was the diarist Samuel Pepys, in June 1663, when he and his company "could hear of no lodging, the town so full; but, which was better, I went towards Ashtead, and there we got a lodging in a little hole we could not stand upright in." He took the waters on June 26 and

> rode through Epsom, the whole town over, seeing the various companies that were there walking; which was very pleasant to see how they are there, without knowing almost what to do, but only in the morning to drink waters.

He stayed at the King's Head in 1667, when Charles II was also in town, and Pepys wrote that he heard "that my Lord Buckhurst and Nelly are lodged at the next house and Sir Charles Sedley with them; and keep a merry house." Pepys returned numerous times to take the waters; walking on the Downs, he came across a shepherd boy reading the Bible to the shepherd.

During the same period John Evelyn had frequent cause to be here because his brother Richard and his wife lived at Woodcote Park. He comments obliquely about the waters upon the death of his brother in March 1670:

> My Bro: being opened, a stone was taken out of his bladder, . . . but his *Livar* so faulty, that in likelyhood [it could not] have lasted much longer, and his kidnis almost quite consum'd: all of this doubtlesse the effects of his intolerable paine proceeding from the stone; & that perhaps by his drinking too excessively of Epsom Waters, when in full health. . . .

John Evelyn's determination to forgo the waters did not last, for he later noted drinking "Epsom water some days." In 1676 Sir George Etherege was involved in a major incident in Epsom, one of the few known events in his life. In 1675 Lord Rochester complained of Etherege's idleness in his "Session of the Poets"; the dramatist responded in his own medium, *The Man of Mode, or Sir Fopling Flutter*, in which Rochester is portrayed as Dorimant. The success of the play increased the rivalry of the men and led to a brawl in Epsom in which a local night watchman was killed, and both men were forced to flee.

In the 18th century Daniel Defoe visited Epsom, as *A Tour thro' the Whole Island of Great Britain* relates, and his sincere pleasure in the town permeates everything he wrote of it:

> About four Miles, over those delicious *Downs*, brings us to *Epsome*, and if you will suppose me to come there in the Month of *July*, or thereabouts, you may think me to come in the middle of the Season, when the Town is full of Company and all disposed to Mirth and Pleasantry. . . .
>
> As, *I say,* this Place seems adapted wholly to Pleasure, so the Town is suited to it; 'tis all Rural, the Houses are Built at large, not many together, with Gardens and Ground about them. . . .
>
> ['T]is the general Language of the Place, *Come let's go see the Town, Folks don't come to* Epsome *to stay within Doors.*

Defoe catalogs all the activities and pleasures: drinking, dancing, listening to music, being serenaded upon arrival, even walking, but unlike Tunbridge

Wells after the morning activities there was "little *stirring*, except Footmen, and Maid Servants, going to and fro of Errands, and Higglers and Butchers, carrying Provisions to People's Lodgings." Even then Epsom was a London suburb at least "in season," as Defoe is quick to point out:

> The greatest part of the Men, I mean of this Grave sort, may be supposed to be Men of Business, who are at *London* upon Business all the Day, and thronging to their Lodgings at Night, make the Families, generally speaking, rather provide Suppers than Dinners; for 'tis very frequent for the Trading part of the Company to place their Families here, and take their Horses every Morning to *London*, . . . and I know one Citizen that practis'd it for several Years together, and scarce ever lay a Night in *London* during the whole Season.

Racing in the mid-19th century attracted George Meredith, and his favorite activity was arriving in time to watch the horses breast the hill; he then ran across the Downs to catch the horses as they passed Tottenham Corner into the straightaway. Later in the century Epsom was the home of George Gissing and his second wife, but this marriage was as unsuccessful as his first. The couple lived here from 1894 to 1897, during which time the novelist worked on *Eve's Ransom, The Whirlpool,* and his critical study of Charles Dickens. The marital situation became intolerable, and Gissing left his wife in 1897.

In January 1908 Hugh Walpole took up a post at Epsom College and taught English and the classics to the lowest form. He soon began work on *Mr. Perrin and Mr. Traill,* whose publication in 1911 was enjoyed by the boys but thoroughly annoyed the staff and college authorities. As they said, while Walpole had carefully placed the school on the coast in Cornwall, the proper identification was obvious to anyone who knew Epsom College and the staff. Because of the resentment of his former colleagues all communcation between Walpole and the college ceased until he apologized in the Preface to the Everyman edition. Years later, in 1937, Sir Hugh Walpole, CBE, gave the main address as the guest of honor at the official Epsom College prizegiving.

Two other minor associations should be mentioned: Hilaire Belloc lectured here on World War I, and H. G. Wells has Benham watch the exercising of the horses here in *The Rsearch Magnificent.*

ESHER, Surrey (pop. 64,186) On rising ground near the Mole River, Esher is 14½ miles southwest of London, but because of its good surrounding open spaces—Esher Common, Arbrook Common, and Oxshott Heath—it does not seem to be an integral part of the metropolitan area. The Saxons were established here, but Esher became important when William the Conqueror granted the land and manor to a monastery in Normandy. It stayed under that jurisdiction until Henry III's Bishop of Winchester bought it back.

The 16th-century Esher church is of interest because the three-story pulpit faces a large chamber pew, much like a box at the opera, built by the Duke of Newcastle to insulate himself and his brother from direct contact with the local inhabitants. Thomas Pelham, Earl of Clare and later Duke of Newcastle, bought the mansion of Claremont in 1715 and immediately began enlarging his estate. Claremont reached its glory when Robert Clive, the famous statesman and soldier, became its owner; he demolished the old house and built the present mansion in 1769 for £100,000. Thomas Babington Macaulay notes that the Surrey natives

> looked with mysterious horror on the stately house which was rising at Claremont, and whispered that the great wicked Lord had ordered the walls to be made so thick in order to keep out the devil, who would one day carry him away bodily.

Claremont came into the hands of the government in 1816, and in 1926 it was bought from the crown and turned into a girls' boarding school.

Shortly after Lord Clare bought Claremont, Richard Steele was a guest; Clare talked to Steele of the election at Boroughbridge, Yorkshire, in which Steele had stood successfully, and the two men plotted parliamentary strategy. In the same period Horace Walpole was a frequent visitor to the old episcopal palace owned by Lord Clare's brother; Walpole delighted in the grounds but strongly disapproved of the sham Gothic additions to Wolsey's Tower. Another of Pelham's guests was James Thomson, who uses Esher in *The Seasons:*

> and Esher's groves,
> Where in the sweetest solitude, embraced
> By the soft windings of the silent Mole,
> From courts and senates Pelham finds repose.
> Enchanting vale!

In 1859 George Meredith had just taken Fairholme (once an old coaching inn, the Bunch of Grapes) for himself and his son Arthur when he encountered an old friend, Janet Duff-Gordon, on whom he modeled Rose Jocelyn in *Evan Harrington.* In 1860 he was induced by the Duff-Gordons to move into Copsham Cottage, then just outside the town on the road to Oxshott, and his work progressed nicely in this location. Both the "Ode to the Spirit of Earth in Autumn" and "Autumn Evensong" were written here and display the influence of the countryside. Meredith's first wife, the daughter of Thomas Love Peacock, died in 1861 after eloping to Italy with a young painter, and in 1864 Meredith remarried and brought his new bride, Marie Vulliamy, here to live. Both Algernon Swinburne and Dante Gabriel Rossetti were frequent visitors before the Merediths moved to Kingston Lodge, Norbiton.

Both Anna Maria Porter and her sister Jane Porter lived their last years here at 85 High Street and are buried in the churchyard.

As a footnote, it could be added that H. G. Wells uses Esher in *The Wheels of Chance.* Hoopdriver stops at the Marquis of Granby Inn, which still exists:

> In the fulness of time, Mr. Hoopdriver drew near the Marquis of Granby at Esher, and as he came under the railway arch and saw the inn in front of him, he mounted his machine [bicycle] again and rode bravely up to the doorway. Burton and biscuits and cheese he had, which, indeed, is Burton in its proper company. . . .

ESTHWAITE WATER, Lancashire Extending 2 miles southeast from near Hawkshead toward Lake Windermere, Esthwaite is relatively small by Lake

District standards. William Wordsworth, who had close associations with Hawkshead, wrote of both this valley and the lake. "The Vale of Esthwaite," probably written in 1786 or 1787, looks to the surrounding scenery, as does a sonnet published in 1807:

> ... when into the Vale I came, no fears
> Distressed me; from mine eyes escaped no tears;
> Deep thought, or dread remembrance, had I none.
> By doubts and thousand petty fancies crost
> I stood, of simple shame the blushing Thrall;
> So narrow seemed the brooks, the fields so small!
> A Juggler's balls old Time about him tossed;
> I looked, I stared, I smiled, I laughed; and all
> The weight of sadness was in wonder lost.

Wordsworth composed "Lines Left upon a Seat in a Yew-Tree Which Stands near the Lake of Esthwaite, on a Desolate Part of the Shore, Commanding a Beautiful Prospect," in 1787, mostly at Hawkshead:

> Nay, Traveller! rest. This lonely Yew tree stands
> Far from all human dwelling, what if here
> No sparkling rivulet spread the verdant herb?
> What if the bee love not these barren boughs?
> Yet, if the wind breathe soft, the curling waves,
> That break against the shore, shall lull thy mind
> By one soft impulse saved from vacancy.

The yew tree was cut down in 1820 for fear of its poisoning local livestock. Book I of *The Prelude* also includes many references to the "Beloved Vale."

Esthwaite Lodge, a Regency house on the west bank of the lake, became the home of Francis Brett Young in June 1929; on a trip to visit Hugh Walpole in Manesty in September 1928, Young found the house and determined to have it. He noted: "There's only a radius of five square miles where I want to live, and that is in the Lake District near Esthwaite Water and Hawkshead." Both *Jim Redlake* and *Mr and Mrs Pennington* were written here. A frequent weekend guest was Hugh Walpole; indeed, the Youngs gave him a room with a view so that he could work on *Judith Paris*. So successful did Walpole find the room that he built a similar one onto his own study. Young eventually found:

> Esthwaite: lovely as it is, is far too remote from London and from my own blue remembered hills; and the Worcestershire rainfall is twenty-three inches against eighty.

He left here for Cropthorne, Worcestershire, in late November 1932.

ETON, Buckinghamshire (pop. 4,505, including school) Seldom does one think of Eton, on the left bank of the Thames, as particularly distinct from Windsor, on the opposite bank; but the two are actually in different counties although they have been connected by a bridge for centuries. The town of Eton can be traced to at least the early 11th century, when it was already a royal manor belonging to Edith, the wife of Edward the Confessor. Following the Norman Conquest and the building of the royal castle across the Thames, Eton (then Eaton) was given to the constable of Windsor Castle. Royal use of Eton was minimal and generally sporting until 1440, when Henry VI founded Eton College as "the first pledge of ... devotion to God." The initial foundation, modeled on Winchester College, was to provide scholarships for seventy highly qualified young men; up to twenty others, all fee-paying and termed "oppidans," could be admitted. Even today there are seventy foundation scholars, and since 1923 the fee has been determined by a means test. Some of the 15th-century buildings and grounds of the college are still in use: the School Yard, a cobbled courtyard, contains the original chapel; and to the left of the yard is the 1443 Lower School. The chapel sustained severe damage from the deathwatch beetle and World War II, but it has been completely restored. For more than three centuries the scholars suffered from the "economies" of keeping the institution, and hardships were grudgingly endured: an 1834 report noted that workhouse inmates were better fed and cared for, and the boys were locked into the Long Chamber (above the Lower School) nightly at 6:30 without lights and allowed one day of visitation each year. But little if any of this dampened the enthusiasm of Etonians.

Michael Drayton comments briefly in *Poly-Olbion:*

> ... *Eaton* is at hand to nurse that learned brood,
> To keepe the Muses still neere to this Princely Flood;
> That nothing there may want, to beawtifie that seate,
> And every pleasure stor'd: And here my Song compleate.

Daniel Defoe's comments in *A Tour thro' the Whole Island of Great Britain* show some early signs of Eton's ultimate prestige, although he places the school in Berkshire:

> [W]e saw *Eaton* College, the finest School for what we call Grammar Learning, for it extends only to the Humanity Class, that is in *Britain,* or, perhaps, in Europe.
> The Building, except the great School Room, is Antient, the Chapel truly *Gothick;* but all has been repaired, at a very great Expence, out of the College Stock, within these few Years. ...
> This College was Founded by King *Henry* VI. ... for the Encouragement of Learning, to Profusion. ...
> This College has a settled Revenue of about Five thousand Pounds *per Annum.* ...

The early association with King's College, Cambridge, still continues, twenty-four places being held for Etonians. William Cobbett's dislike of the public-school concept and what he considered to be the inadequacies of the educational system are revealed in a singular reference to "toad-eating and nonsensical and shoe-licking Eton!" in his *Rural Rides.*

John Evelyn and Samuel Pepys were early visitors here. Evelyn was frequently in Eton, especially after his grandson entered the college, and the comments in his diary are those of a doting grandparent:

> The Scholemaster assured me that there had not ben in 20 years a more pregnant youth in that Place than my Grandson. ...

Pepys, who was here in February 1666, describes the college in his diary:

> ... there find all mighty fine. The school good, and the custom pretty of boys cutting their names in the shuts of the window when they go to Cambridge. ... To the Hall, and there find the boys' verses, "De Peste," it being their custom to make verses at Shrove-tide. I read several, and very good they were; better, I think, than ever I made when I was a boy. ... Thence to the porter's, in the

absence of the butler, and did drink of the College beer, which is very good; and went into the back fields to see the scholars play.

One of the earliest headmasters of Eton was Nicholas Udall, who was appointed to the post in June 1534; among the requirements for assuming the headship were an M.A. degree (Udall received his in July of that year) and bachelorhood; the head was also to "be a man of good character, skilled in grammar and teaching." Before taking the post, Udall prepared *Floures for Latine Spekynge, Selected and Gathered Oute of Terence and the Same Translated into Englysshe* for his pupils. Whether *Ralph Roister Doister* was first prepared for performance here is still a moot question, but Udall was dismissed in 1541 under peculiar circumstances. Early that year he was charged with the crime of buggery and sent to Marshalsea Prison; more likely, the crime was the burglary of church plate from the Eton chapel, and only that; but conviction of the more heinous offense brought about his dismissal.

Another early official of Eton was Sir Henry Wotton, who was given the provostship here in 1624; he was granted a dispensation to allow him to hold the post without taking orders, but he took deacon's orders in 1637 anyway. Izaak Walton, who often visited Sir Henry here, wrote of him:

He was a constant cherisher of all those youths in that school, in whom he found either a constant diligence or a genius that prompted them to learning. . . .

Wotton made an annual trip from here to Boughton Hall, and in the summer of 1639 he went to Winchester, his old school. On his return, seized by a "feverish distemper" from which he never recovered, he died in early December and was buried in the college chapel. In March 1639, John Milton came to Eton to visit friends and met Sir Henry, but there is no record of the meeting. A little later in the 17th century Andrew Marvell was appointed tutor of William Dutton, ward of the Lord Protector, and both Marvell and Dutton took up residence with the family of John Oxenbridge, a fellow of the college. Marvell wrote many poems during his four years here, among them "The First Anniversary of the Government under His Highness the Lord Protector" and various pastorals. He left his post in 1657, probably in September, to take up an appointment as a Latin secretary and colleague of John Milton.

One of the earliest scholars here was Sir John Harington, author of *The Metamorphosis of Ajax* (a delightful work on water closets), who arrived in the 1570s. Both Giles Fletcher the Elder and his son Phineas were students in the 1560s and 1590s respectively. Edmund Waller was admitted shortly after the death of his father on August 26, 1616. Henry Fielding entered Eton in 1719 or 1720 after the death of his mother; young Fielding had had most of his education at home under the tutelage of a Mr. Oliver, a curate. He spent a number of holidays in Salisbury before he left Eton. Both William Pitt the Elder and Henry Fox were his contemporaries here. In 1727 Thomas Gray was sent here "under the auspices of his uncles, and at the expense of his mother"; Gray's father had refused to have anything to do with the boy's education. While Gray was here, Horace Wal-

pole matriculated, and the two became close friends. With Richard West and Thomas Ashton, they formed the Quadruple Alliance, a group with a literary and poetical bent which had considerable influence on both Gray and Walpole. They walked over the playing fields and across the bridge that spans Chalvey Brook, where, says Walpole, they uttered "some pastoral name to the echo of the cascade under the bridge." Tradition now maintains that the "Poet's Walk," an avenue of lime trees, was named for Gray. "Ode on a Distant Prospect of Eton College" was written in 1742, when Gray was in Stoke Poges:

Ye distant spires, ye antique towers,
That crown the watery glade,
Where grateful Science still adores
Her Henry's holy Shade;
And ye, that from the stately brow
Of Windsor's heights th' expanse below
Of grove, of lawn, of mead survey,
Whose turf, whose shade, whose flowers among
Wanders the hoary Thames along
His silver-winding way.

Gray and Walpole both went up to Cambridge in 1734. Another 18th-century student here was the minor poet William Hayley, who entered in 1757 and remained until going up to Trinity Hall, Cambridge, in 1763.

When Percy Bysshe Shelley entered Eton in July 1804, the notorious Dr. John Keate was assistant headmaster, and the discipline in the Lower School was extremely strict. Shelley first lodged with the writing master, Mr. Hexter, and then with the Rev. George Bethell; the young poet was extremely unhappy here and numbered these days as among the most miserable in his life. He did not fit in well, and escaping from school and especially from the games, he would wander all over Eton, Windsor and its park, and the graveyard at Stoke Poges. He was called Mad Shelley and Shelley the Atheist by the boys, and his eccentricities in habits and dress coupled with his dislike of games made him all the more conspicuous. One of his delights, boating on the Thames, is recalled in "The Boat on the Serchio":

. . . "Those bottles of warm tea—
(Give me some straw)—must be stowed tenderly;
Such as we used, in summer after six,
To cram in great coat pockets, and to mix
Hard eggs and radishes and rolls at Eton,
And, couched on stolen hay in those green harbours
Farmers call gaps, and we schoolboys called arbours,
Would feast till eight."

Shelley became interested in the occult and read as widely as possible in the area; on one occasion, somehow securing a skull, he ended up astride a small stream, where he delivered a recommended incantation, drank from the skull three times, and waited. No spirits were aroused because, Thomas Jefferson Hogg says, "probably he had failed to repeat the correct formula of the charm." These early occult experiences are recalled in "Hymn to Intellectual Beauty":

While yet a boy I sought for ghosts, and sped
Through many a listening chamber, cave and ruin,
And starlight wood, with fearful steps pursuing
Hopes of high talk with the departed dead.

I called on poisonous names with which our youth is fed;
I was not heard—I saw them not.. . .

Shelley wrote *Zastrozzi*, a Gothic romance in imitation of Ann Radcliffe, during his last term in Eton; as his reward for finishing at Eton, he went up to Oxford, where his experiences were, if anything, worse. Shelley carved his name in the Upper School, where it can still be seen.

Some forty years later Algernon Charles Swinburne arrived at Easter, 1849, and was described as "a queer little elf, who carried about with him a Bowdlerized Shakespeare, adorned with a blue silk book-marker, with a Tunbridge-ware button at the end of it." Forbidden to read novels as a child, he found his freedom at Eton and read widely, especially the works of Dickens and the unbowdlerized Shakespeare. Swinburne resided at the home of his tutor, Mr. Joynes, and contrary to the usual belief, he was not bullied in the manner of Shelley. He stayed very much to himself, and a great deal of his time was spent in the library sitting cross-legged in the bay window; the window is pointed out to visitors. His slow progress, however, was cause for concern, and by 1853 he was beginning to show signs of rebelliousness. That summer, following some trouble with his tutor, Swinburne was removed from the college to be put under a private tutor. He eventually went up to Oxford. A year after Swinburne left Eton, Robert Bridges entered at the age of nine. His time here was pleasant, and he distinguished himself on the playing fields. Bridges played for the field elevens and in his last year was captain of his house. He left Eton for Corpus Christi College, Oxford, in 1863. In the early 1890's Edward Plunkett (later Lord Dunsany) entered Eton; a not very industrious student who was overly interested in sports, he did poorly and was removed for tutoring before being sent to Sandhurst. Maurice Baring also received his university preparatory work here in the late 19th century.

In the early 20th century Aldous Huxley entered Eton, "where he endured troubling years"; one of the most difficult times occurred toward the end of his stay, when he went blind. Suffering from keratitis, an irritation of the cornea, he was obliged to learn braille and to give up his study of science. He left Eton for Balliol College, Oxford, in 1913 but returned briefly to take a teaching post in 1918. Eric Blair (George Orwell) entered as a King's Scholar in May 1917 and lived in Chamber, a hall in the oldest part of the college. Not confirmed in the Anglican Church before his entrance at Eton, he was confirmed in the chapel by Bishop Charles Gore but remained a total skeptic and cynic. Some of Blair's most memorable times occurred when A. E. Housman came from Oxford to address the Literary Society, of which Blair was a member. Cyril Connolly had also entered from St. Cyprian's in Eastbourne, Sussex, and the two friends often swam in a bend of the Thames River opposite Windsor Castle. This is the spot which becomes Orwell's "Athens" and which he describes as possessing "a subtly delicious exhalation of its own. . . ." Blair left Eton at the end of Michaelmas term in 1921 and spent the next five years in Burma in the Imperial Police. Another 20th-century Etonian was Anthony Powell, author of the *Dance to the Music of Time* novels; he entered in 1919 from a boarding school in Kent

and remained until 1923, when he went up to Balliol College, Oxford.

In addition to the association of scholars and faculty, one or two other connections with Eton should be mentioned. Hilaire Belloc was here on a number of occasions from 1910 to 1915; he first lectured on Marie Antoinette in 1910 and was given, he said, a bad dinner by Edward Lyttelton. He then lectured twice on the war between the outbreak of World War I and December 1915. Finally, H. G. Wells makes use of Eton College in *The Soul of a Bishop;* the Garstein Fellowses' oldest son attends the school.

EUSTON, Suffolk (pop. 248)   This is Breckland, an area of roughly 300 square miles shared by Suffolk and Norfolk, which was once far more heavily populated than it is today. Evidence of extensive early settlement crops up in the tumuli scattered about and in the implements discovered everywhere. Euston, on the Little Ouse River 3 miles southeast of Thetford, is a tiny village of black-and-white timber, thatch and tile, flint, and brick houses on the edge of Breckland. Until the 17th century most of the village stood within the gates of Euston Hall, built during the reign of Charles II and the home of the Dukes of Grafton. Charles was a guest here in 1671, as was the diarist John Evelyn, who had just been appointed to the Council for Foreign Plantations; it was here that Louise de Kéroualle became Charles's acknowledged mistress and that the rumor of a "mock marriage" began. Evelyn denied all knowledge of such a ceremony, but noted in his diary under the date of October 10:

I went that night with Mr. *Tressurer* to *Euston*, a palace of my L: [*Arlingtons*]. . . . It was universaly reported that the faire Lady ——— [Quierovil] was bedded one of these nights, and the stocking flung, after the manner of a married Bride: I acknowledge she was for the most part in her undresse all day, and that there was fondnesse, & toying, with that young wanton; nay 'twas said, I was at the former ceremonie, but tis utterly false, I neither saw, nor heard of any such thing whilst I was there. . . .

Robert Bloomfield later paid tribute to the estate in his first work, *The Farmer's Boy.*

EVERSHOT, Dorset (pop. 291)   The Frome River rises in this small village, 12 miles northeast of Bridport. This is a relatively rural area where travel from east to west is difficult because most roads follow the north-south drainage routes carved into the central chalk downs. Evershot is the Evershead of Thomas Hardy's works and is mentioned in "Interlopers at the Knap," "The First Countess of Wessex," and *Tess of the D'Urbervilles.* Tess, on her way to Clare's home, comes through this village, where she halts for a time:

Three miles farther she cut across the straight and deserted Roman road called Long-Ash Lane; leaving which as soon as she reached it, she dipped down the hill by a transverse lane into the small town or village of Evershead, being now about half-way over the distance.

EVERSLEY, Hampshire (pop. 864)   Formerly a royal hunting ground, the village of Eversley is located exactly on the border of Berkshire. Wild boars were one of the favorite quarries of noble and royal hunts-men and so were allowed to roam freely and mate in woodlands, like those around Eversley, well into the 17th century.

Eversley was the home of Charles Kingsley from 1842, when he was appointed curate, until his death in 1875. He wrote most of his better-known works, *Westward Ho!, The Heroes, The Water Babies,* and *Hereward the Wake,* at the Rectory, a pleasant but undistinguished house near the 18th-century church. He died here on January 23, 1875, and is buried in the church graveyard near an enormous Scotch pine. The grave is marked with a marble cross, on whose base are the words *Amavimus, Amamus, Amabimus.* At the east end of the church there is a bas-relief commemorative portrait.

EWELME, Oxfordshire (pop. 426) The Thames Valley south of Oxford has some of the pleasantest scenery in Oxfordshire. Settled into a beech-wooded niche at the foot of the Chiltern Hills, Ewelme has retained much of the model-village atmosphere it must have had in the 15th century, when Alice, Duchess of Suffolk, planned the village. Besides the church, the ancient almshouses built around a cobblestone courtyard and a school dating from 1437 are the pride of the village; indeed, the village school is claimed to be the oldest in use in the country. The church, built by Dame Alice and her husband William de la Pole, Duke of Suffolk, is an almost-perfect period piece, and here the pair are buried.

Alice, who has frequently been called the greatest lady of her age, was the granddaughter of Geoffrey Chaucer. Chaucer's putative son Thomas had a country seat here, and one of his guests was the poet John Lydgate; both the time and the extent of the visit are uncertain, but it is clear from the "Ballade at the Departyng of Thomas Chaucyr into France" that the date was 1417 or before. The *Troy Book* also refers to the time spent here. When Thomas Chaucer died on November 18, 1434, he was buried in the parish church, and all evidence suggests that Lydgate was present for the funeral service and, indeed, may have taken part in it. The alabaster canopied monument to the Duchess of Suffolk is known throughout the country for its beauty; wooden angels stand on the pinnacles above the canopy. Below is the effigy, with four angels holding the stone pillow for her head and sixteen armored figures standing in the surrounding niches.

The church also contains a wall monument to John Howard, only son of Lord Andover, himself a friend of Edmund Waller. Waller wrote the epitaph for the child, who was so old for his age that

Tis no wonder Death our hopes beguiled.
He's seldom old that will not be a child.

A more recent literary figure is associated with the village. From 1887 on Jerome K. Jerome lived at nearby Gould's Grove, an old farm with a summerhouse called the Nook. Nothing written here ever achieved the success of *Three Men in a Boat,* although *The Passing of the Third Floor Back* was published during this period. Among Jerome's guests were William Wymark Jacobs, Eden Phillpotts, and H. G. Wells. Jerome, who died in Northampton on

June 14, 1927, was cremated there, and his ashes were brought here for burial. The stone marking his grave reads "For we are labourers together with God."

EXETER, Devon (pop. 71,160) Exeter is the meeting place for all the West Country, and it has so functioned since the time of the Dumnonii, a Celtic people of the 2d and 3d centuries B.C. who were the most likely first settlers. Modern excavation has determined that the first settlement was on a plateau near the Exe River, and when the Romans came to Isca Dumnoniorum in A.D. 50, they recognized the strategic nature of the site, especially the red height, now appropriately called Rougemont, north of the town, and set to work to fortify the city. By 670 Exeter had a monastery, the same one in which Wynfrith (later St. Boniface) was educated for nineteen years. Alfred the Great came to the Wessex throne in 871, and in the first year of his reign he fought nine major West Country battles with the Danes before securing any sort of peace. Exter was sacked numerous times until the reign of Edward the Confessor, when the city was rebuilt and the early-7th-century monastery elevated to cathedral status.

With the Norman invasion Exeter's promise of allegiance to William was deemed inadequate, and the town was seized and subdued. Exeter Cathedral, founded in 1112, with twin Norman towers and a west front containing sixty-eight carved figures, has been termed the most original and completely harmonious and symmetrical English cathedral. The cathedral library contains the Codex Exoniensis (the oldest, and as yet untranslated, collection of Anglo-Saxon poetry known) and the manuscript of "The Seafarer." *Eikon Basilike,* an attempt to vindicate the "wisdom, honour, and piety" of Charles I, upon which John Milton based his *Eikonoklastes,* was written by Dr. John Gauden, who later became Bishop of Exeter. Miles Coverdale was also Bishop of Exeter, from 1551 to 1553. Richard Hooker, the 16th-century theologian and author of *Of the Lawes of Ecclesiasticall Politic,* was born in Heavitree, now a suburb of Exeter, and not in Exeter, as is normally claimed. He was educated at the grammar school before going up to Corpus Christi College, Oxford, under the patronage of Bishop John Jewel. There is a commemorative statue to Hooker in the cathedral close. Just opposite the cathedral in the close is an interesting and obscure old building known as Mol's Coffee Shop, which was a meeting place for such Elizabethan sailors as Sir Walter Ralegh and Sir Francis Drake. The three-story building is fronted by an enormous galleon-style double-bay window.

Exeter was fully established during the Middle Ages, when it was considered the westernmost point of "civilization." Trade was good, especially that from cloth, and lavish merchants' houses such as the 15th-century Slepcote Hall were built throughout the city. Rougemont Castle and Exeter both appear in William Shakespeare's *Richard III;* Richard speaks:

Richmond!—When last I was at Exeter,
The mayor in courtesy show'd me the castle,
And call'd it Rouge-mont: at which name I started,
Because a bard of Ireland told me once
I should not live long after I saw Richmond.

Modern writers have been especially fond of Exeter. Thomas Hardy refers to Exeter in a number of his works as Exonbury: it appears in *The Trumpet-Major, Jude the Obscure,* "The Lady Icenway," *The Woodlanders,* "For Conscience' Sake," "The Winters and the Palmleys," *A Pair of Blue Eyes,* and "My Cicely." In most of these works, though, the references to Exonbury, Exonbury Cathedral, and Exonbury Barracks are of passing interest, and Hardy actually sets very few scenes here. On a trip to visit Hardy at his home in September 1885, Robert Louis Stevenson was taken ill and collapsed in the New Lion Inn in Exeter. He stayed in Room 16, where a stained-glass panel in the window and a commemorative inscription have been placed. For five days, from September 9 to 14, the hotel staff ministered to his needs; upon departing, he wrote in the visitors' book, "I cannot leave this house without testifying to the kindness of all in it. If it is ever your ill-fortune to be ill at an inn, be sure it is the New Lion."

Charles Dickens was in Exeter on numerous occasions, the first in 1836 to cover a local election. Three years later he came here searching for a retirement cottage for his parents and found Mile End Cottage, a mile south of the city on the Plymouth Road. Actually it was one house divided into two cottages, one of which was occupied by the landlady. Dickens was enormously pleased with his find:

> I am charmed with the place and the beauty of the country round about.... The situation is charming; meadows in front, an orchard running parallel to the garden hedge, richly-wooded hills closing in the prospect behind, and, away to the left, before a splendid view of the hill on which Exeter is situated, the cathedral towers rising up into the sky in the most picturesque manner possible.

While Dickens makes no specific mention of Exeter in his novels, the opening of *Nicholas Nickleby* refers to the Dibabses' home in "a sequestered part of the county of Devonshire," undoubtedly the cottage occupied by Dickens's parents: "the beautiful little thatched white house one story high, covered all over with ivy and creeping plants, with an exquisite little porch with twining honeysuckle, and all sorts of things." Dickens returned to Exeter twice on his reading tours.

The most extensive use of "the capital of the West," as Exeter is often called, occurs in William Makepeace Thackeray's *Pendennis;* here it becomes Chatteris, a country town near Clavering St. Mary (Ottery St. Mary), with "that quiet little street ... called Prior's Lane, which lies close by Dean's Green and the canons' houses, and is overlooked by the enormous towers of the cathedral; there the captain dwelt modestly in the first floor of a low-gabled house...."

There are numerous minor associations with Exeter: Anthony Trollope lived somewhere in the town for a short time after being transferred from Ireland by the General Post Office. After his second marriage George Gissing lived here, first at 24 Prospect Park and then at 1 St. Leonard's Terrace, in 1891 and 1892, and his sons Walter and Alfred were born in Exeter. The countryside around the town serves as the setting for *The Private Papers of Henry Ryecroft.* Joyce Cary came on holiday to Exeter during part of his 1918 leave from the Nigerian political service. He and his wife were avid hikers and relatively poor at the time, and they spent their holiday hiking, sitting on the banks of the Exe, eating in good country inns, and sleeping in the coastal sea air. Finally, Exeter was the birthplace in 1653 of Thomas D'Urfey. Destined for the church by his French Huguenot parents, he informed them that the astrological disposition of planets at his birth made such plans impossible: "My good stars have ordained me to be a jester and a knight-errant in the fairy-field of poetry, and I shall save more souls with my songs than I ever should have done with my sermons." D'Urfey became a kind of court jester to Charles II, and the two would romp through the palace and sing some of the scurrilous songs written especially for the King.

EYFORD, Gloucestershire (pop. 61) There is little to see at Eyford, 3 miles west of Stow-on-the-Wold, except the natural beauty of the heavily wooded slopes of Eyford Park and a well enclosed by a six-sided wall. Near the well is a carved stone, worn and almost illegible, which says that beside this spring John Milton wrote part of *Paradise Lost.*

EYTON-ON-SEVERN, Shropshire The tiny hamlet of Eyton-upon-Severn is 2 miles south of the Roman colony of Wroxeter and 5½ miles northwest of Much Wenlock, on the Severn River. Edward Herbert, later 1st Baron Herbert of Cherbury, was born at the old hall, the home of his maternal grandmother, Lady Newport, on November 3, 1583, and was christened in the local parish church.

Herbert lived here for most of the first ten years of his life and was schooled privately in this period. Suffering from what now appears to have been epilepsy, he was a slow student at first but extremely inquisitive. At the age of fifteen he was married to Mary Herbert, the daughter of Sir William Herbert, who had made his daughter's marriage to someone bearing the family name the condition of her inheritance. Herbert had been at University College, Oxford, prior to the ceremony and returned there accompanied by both his wife and his mother.

FAIRLIGHT, Sussex (pop. 410) The coastal area stretching east from Hastings is a series of sandstone cliffs, generally tree-covered and overhung with gentle slopes and surprising glens, the most beautiful of which is Fairlight Glen, where a stream cuts through gigantic boulders. The village of Fairlight consists of little more than an attractively placed new church and a series of old coast guard cottages. The churchyard contains the neglected tombstone of Richard D'Oyly Carte, founder of the opera company.

Clive Vale Farm in Fairlight was the destination of Edward Lear, Holman Hunt, and William Rossetti in the summer of 1852. Lear, who was to take painting lessons from Hunt and to give Italian lessons in return, had originally intended to section off the house to ensure privacy and to keep the fact of his epilepsy from Hunt, but the idea of separation was abandoned. Hunt returned to London in the autumn, but Lear stayed, working on *Reggio* and *Thermopylae,* before going on to Hastings to paint a fig tree.

FARINGDON, Berkshire (pop. 3,389) Set in the lovely water meadows surrounding the Thames River in the Vale of the White Horse, Faringdon is built almost wholly of stone; indeed, it exudes an antiquity which is false since almost nothing except the medieval church predates the 17th century. Wadley Hall, a mile from Faringdon on the road to Oxford, was the birthplace on February 20, 1745, of Henry Pye, the man who became probably the most abused and parodied Poet Laureate of all time. Appointed Thomas Warton's successor in 1790, Pye dutifully churned out verses for George III, and one of the birthday pieces, full of feathered choristers and singing groves, prompted the comment:

> And when the *pie* was opened
> The birds began to sing;
> And wasn't that a dainty dish
> To set before a king?

FARNBOROUGH, Hampshire (pop. 21,670) Farnborough, one of two Hampshire service towns, and the whole area are dominated by the Royal Air Force establishment here. Rudyard Kipling was a frequent visitor to Farnborough when his son John attended nearby Wellington College, and Kipling took advantage of the visits to come here. He stayed at the Queen's Hotel on Lynchford Road and often went to nearby Aldershot, which was then the new Royal Air Force establishment. Kipling's interest in planes and the military was a deep and long-lasting one, and he always received preferential treatment at the base.

FARNHAM, Surrey (pop. 22,000) The most westerly town in Surrey, Farnham, on the Wey River 3 miles southwest of Aldershot, has always been an important place because of its location at the end of the Hog's Back at the first gap in the chalk downs east of Hampshire. Travelers have passed this way since the Bronze Age; traders used the route, and this was part of the medieval Pilgrims' Way. Roman ruins have also been excavated here, and the Saxon king Ethelbald is said to have given the land at Farnham to St. Swithun of Winchester. Until the mid-20th century Farnham Castle was the home of the bishops of Winchester.

Standing on a hill with a commanding view of the town and the Wey Valley, the first rudimentary castle was probably built in the 12th century by Bishop Henry of Blois; reconstruction and additional building took place in the late 12th and early 13th centuries. The medieval Farnham Castle was the administrative center of the manor of Farnham, and the Norman keep was added to through the centuries. The structure was certainly magnificent enough to support royal visits at widely separated times from the reign of King John to that of George III. Elizabeth I was here in 1569 as the guest of Bishop Robert Horne when Thomas Howard, 4th Duke of Norfolk and Earl of Surrey, was asked to join her for dinner.

At the end of the meal, referring to the duke's projected marriage to Mary, Queen of Scots, the Queen advised him to take care where he laid his head; two years later he laid it on the block. Many of the Winchester bishops used the castle as a part-time residence. The most important of them was Lancelot Andrewes, author of *Private Devotions*, who served from 1619 to 1626.

During the Civil War, in 1642, the Parliamentarians placed George Wither in charge of the castle, and when he was forced to evacuate Farnham in the following year, he was accused of cowardice. In defense of his honor he published *Se defendendo,* and in 1646, when he felt that Sir Richard Onslow was trying to remove him from the Commission of Peace for Surrey, he brought out the pamphlet *Justitiarius justificatus;* this was judged to be libelous, and Wither was imprisoned. In the interim the castle was held by the Royalists under Sir John Denham, author of *Cooper's Hill;* indeed, Sir John pleaded for Wither's pardon, stating that as long as Wither lived "he should not be the worst poet in England." Twelve years after the Restoration the castle reverted to Winchester.

The town itself is the center of an industry found nowhere else in Surrey, that of hop growing, which was established in England during the Reformation, as a doggerel couplet comments:

> Hops, Reformation, baize and beer,
> Came into England all in a year.

With the rich soil of the neighborhood, the town has always been an important agricultural center, and the old Elizabethan market, with brick-and-timber props, survived until the late 19th century.

Daniel Defoe was much impressed by Farnham's market,

> the greatest Corn-Market in *England, London* excepted; that is to say, particularly for Wheat, of which so vast a quantity is brought every Market-Day to this Market, that a Gentleman told me, he once counted on a Market-Day Eleven Hundred Teams of Horse, ... every Team of which is supposed to bring what they call a Load, that is to say, Forty Bushels of Wheat to Market; which is in the whole, Four and Forty Thousand Bushel....

The old park of about 1,000 acres surrounding the castle was once rich in deer; throughout the centuries poaching caused a steady battle between the diocese and the town, and in Defoe's time the battle still raged:

> The *Farnham* People it seems, or some of the Country Folks, notwithstanding the Liberality and Bounty of the several Bishops, ... have of late been very unkind to the Bishop, in pulling down the Pale of his Park, and plundering it of the Deer, Killing, Wounding, and Disabling, even those they cou'd not carry away.

Defoe was by no means the first literary visitor to Farnham; a very frequent guest at the castle when Bishop George Morley was in residence was Izaak Walton. Walton had suffered under the Protectorate, and after the Restoration, when his old friend Morley was translated to the see of Winchester, Walton spent virtually the rest of his life under the Bishop's roof. Here he wrote his lives of Herbert and Donne. After the marriage of his daughter Anne to William Hawkins, a prebendary of Winchester, in 1676, the old man

spent a few months every year in his son-in-law's home and, indeed, returned there from Farnham in August 1683 to draw his will. Walton died in Winchester on December 15, 1683. Another early association exists with the naturalist Gilbert White, who was sent to school here from Selborne, Hampshire; the experience was pleasant, as he later recalled when visiting his brother here at Mareland and hearing the "sweet peal of bells" from the parish church.

The most famous association with Farnham dates from the 18th century, for The William Cobbett was the birthplace on March 9, 1763, of William Cobbett, the third of four children born to a small farmer and publican. At a very young age Cobbett began working as a field laborer, not only for his father but also in the garden at Waverley Abbey and at Farnham Castle. He could not remember when he had not made his own living:

> When I first trudged afield, with my wooden bottle and my satchel over my shoulder, I was hardly able to climb the gates and stiles.

Cobbett claimed that at the age of eleven (more likely he was fourteen), while clipping box edgings and weeding flower beds at Farnham Castle, he came under the influence of a gardener who inspired him to walk to Richmond to see Kew Gardens. On the trip Cobbett experienced the "birth of intellect" when he stopped under a haystack just outside Richmond to read Jonathan Swift's *A Tale of a Tub;* this experience, he maintained, was the beginning of his awakening. Cobbett left Farnham finally in 1782, when, supposedly off to attend the fair at Guildford, he impulsively boarded a coach for London and eventually went on to the United States. After Cobbett's return from America, he frequently came back to Farnham. He died at Normandy Farm, in Ash, in June 1835 and was buried by the porch of St. Andrew's Church in Farnham; the church contains a commemorative bust and tablet on the south wall.

Farnham comes into William Makepeace Thackeray's *The Virginians;* Harry Warrington, Madame Bernstein, and the Lady Maria, on their way to Tunbridge Wells, stop at "the 'Bush Inn' at Farnham, under which name a famous inn has stood in Farnham town for these three hundred years...." Here Maria is ill and does not join the others for supper; they proceed on their way the next morning:

> Round about Farnham the hops were gloriously green in the sunshine, and the carriages drove through the richest, most beautiful country.

Just to the southeast of Farnham and very near Moorpark, once the seat of Sir William Temple, is small Black Lake Cottage (now Lobs Wood Manor), which Sir James Matthew Barrie gave to his wife in 1900 as a summer house. One eventually rewarding pastime was walking in the wooded areas in the company of the five sons of Arthur Llewelyn Davies and telling them stories. Indeed, here *Peter Pan* was fully developed, and the woods where the pirates and redskins meet in deadly conflict are undoubtedly the ones in which Barrie and the boys roamed; the Mermaids' Lagoon and the Marooners' Rock are nearby:

> The children often spent long summer days on this lagoon, swimming or floating most of the time, playing the mermaid games in the water, and so forth.... When

she stole softly to the edge of the lagoon she might see them by the score, especially on Marooners' Rock, where they loved to bask, combing out their hair in a lazy way that quite irritated her. . . .

They treated all the boys in the same way, except of course Peter, who chatted with them on Marooners' Rock by the hour, and sat on their tails when they got cheeky.

After Sir James's divorce in 1909, he did not return to the cottage here.

Finally, Augustus Montague Toplady, the author of "Rock of Ages," was born on the High Street on November 4, 1740; the house is marked with a plaque, and the church contains a memorial inscription.

FARRINGFORD, Isle of Wight The Freshwater, Freshwater Bay, High Down, and Alum Bay area of the western part of the Isle of Wight is associated mainly with Alfred, Lord Tennyson. Farringford, about 1 mile west of Freshwater Bay, was the Tennyson home from 1853 to 1868. Even after Aldworth at Black Down, Sussex, was built, Tennyson and his family returned here every winter. In the summer of 1853, looking for quiet and seclusion, Tennyson took a lease on Farringford House and had fully settled in by November. It took three years to decide to purchase the house, and in April 1856 it was bought with the revenues from *Maud.* The house was a yellow-brick and stucco building, long and low; the poet's study was at the top. Among the works he composed here are "The Charge of the Light Brigade"; *Maud,* most of which was written in the garden at Swainstown; "Enid," "Vivien," "Elaine," and "Guinevere" in the *Idylls of the King;* and *Enoch Arden,* written in the summerhouse. The Tennysons' home was known for its hospitality, and the lengthy guest list included Prince Albert, the Duke of Argyll, Robert Browning, Lewis Carroll, Arthur Hugh Clough, Charles Darwin, Aubrey de Vere, Edward FitzGerald, Giuseppe Garibaldi, Henry James, Charles Kingsley, Edward Lear, Henry Wadsworth Longfellow, Coventry Patmore, Dean Arthur Stanley, Algernon Swinburne, and William Makepeace Thackeray. In *The Middle Years* Henry James describes Tennyson's after dinner practice of reading aloud, smoking, and drinking port in the drawing room. And Oliver Wendell Holmes comments on Tennyson's

delight in pointing out to me the finest and rarest of his trees, and there were many beauties among them. In this garden of England, where everything grows with such a lavish extravagance of green, I felt as if weary eyes and over-tasted brains might reach their happiest haven of rest.

Tennyson speaks of the place in a short verse:

Where, far from noise and smoke of town,
I watch the twilight falling brown
All round a careless-order'd garden
Close to the ridge of a noble down.

This "noble down" is known now as Tennyson Down, and the poet was often seen striding across it to Alum Bay, where he indulged in his hobby of geologizing. Edward Lear, a frequent guest of the Tennysons (he was a particular favorite of Emily Tennyson), recalls "striding over the downs beside

FARRINGFORD The downland area leading to The Needles, huge chalk stacks on the westernmost tip of the Isle of Wight, has been named Tennyson Down in honor of the poet, whose home for many years was in nearby Farringford. Tennyson and his many guests often made the walk across the town to the Needles.

Alfred with his tousled black beard and flowing cloak, booming out his new "Idylls of the King" in a deep measured voice. . . ." The relationship between Lear and Tennyson deteriorated by the time of Lear's final visit in the autumn of 1869; he found the Poet Laureate's "harshness and egocentricity hard to bear" and simply commented, "I would he were as his poems."

Tennyson's original purpose in coming to Farringford was to find seclusion, but by the mid-1860s he was being inundated by visitors whom he found impossible to escape even on his daily walks to The Needles (Freshwater Peninsula), no matter how early or how late in the day, and after 1868 he spent only the winter, nontourist months here. On a trip across the Solent to Farringford in 1889, Tennyson composed "Crossing the Bar," the poem which by his own request is always placed at the end of every collection of his works. Tennyson had been seriously ill in 1888–1889, and the composition of this poem, according to his son and biographer, "came in a moment":

For tho' from out our bourne of Time and Place
    The flood may bear me far,
I hope to see my Pilot face to face
    When I have crost the bar.

After his death in Ryde on June 28, 1958, Alfred Noyes was buried here in accordance with his request.

FAVERSHAM, Kent (pop. 12,080) Faversham Creek brings the ocean to Faversham, less than 10 miles southeast of Canterbury, and a modest port still operates here. Shipping was of sufficient importance in the Middle Ages to make the town a corporate member of the Cinque Port of Dover, and previously the Romans had used the tidal creek and established a settlement called Durolevum nearby. In 1147 King Stephen founded a Benedictine abbey here, but the only extant part is the guesthouse, now known as Arden's House, at 80 Abbey Street; the street also contains a number of fine old Tudor buildings.

After the dissolution of the abbey in 1538 Thomas Arden (Ardene) secured the lands, the guesthouse, and, eventually, the position of Lord Mayor of Faver sham as well as those of clerk of the courts and controller of customs. On February 15, 1551, after a series of unsuccessful attempts, his wife Alice, her lover Thomas Mosby, and two accomplices, Black Will and Loosebag, finally succeeded in murdering Arden while he was playing draughts with Mosby. Mosby was hanged at Smithfield, Alice was burned at the stake in Canterbury, Black Will was burned at Flushing, and Loosebag was never heard of again. The story, first told by Raphael Holinshed in his *Chronicles,* formed the basis of the 1592 play *The Lamentable and True Tragedie of Master Arden of Feversham in Kent,* a play attributed to Shakespeare, Marlowe, and many others.

Faversham was also on the route taken by Geoffrey Chaucer's Canterbury pilgrims, and Ospringe, a village half a mile away, is a reference point in the tales. A modern pilgrim, Charles Dickens's David Copperfield comes through the town on his way to Dover and Miss Trotwood.

FAWLEY, Berkshire (pop. 192)

Fawley, 4 miles south of Wantage, is near the ancient Ridgeway, which traverses the crest of the Berkshire Downs for a distance of about 20 miles. Although Thomas Hardy rarely leaves central Wessex for the scenes of his works, he uses Fawley extensively in *Jude the Obscure* as the source of Jude's last name and as Marygreen, the scene of his early life. The upper part of the village and its green are as Hardy describes them, with the old well at the edge of the green, the schoolhouse, church, and cottage:

> The cart creaked across the green, and disappeared round the corner by the rectory-house. The boy returned to the draw-well at the edge of the greensward, where he had left his buckets when he went to help his patron and teacher in the loading. . . . The well into which he was looking was as ancient as the village itslf. . . .

The new church whose "tower loomed large and solemn in the fog" is where Phillotson and Sue are remarried after she leaves Jude. The high ridge, Jude's favorite spot because he can catch a glimpse of Christminster (Oxford) from there, is the Ridgeway. The Brown House, with a long stretch of cultivated land sloping up to it, is known locally as the Red House. Jude and Arabella plan to walk here:

> First they clambered to the top of the great down. . . . Then they bore off to the left along the crest into the ridgeway, which they followed till it intersected the highroad at the Brown House aforesaid, the spot of his former fervid desires to behold Christminster. But he forgot them now. . . .
> They reached the Brown House barn—the point at which he had planned to turn back.

The nearby village of Cresscombe is probably Letcombe Bassett.

FELLEY, Nottinghamshire (pop. 17)

Felley, almost too small to be considered an entity, has been put on the map by D. H. Lawrence. Close to his native town of Eastwood, Felley was known intimately by Lawrence, who used it in *The White Peacock* under the name Strelley. (The nearby village actually called Strelley does not figure in the novel.) At the beginning of the novel Lawrence mentions the Austin, or black, canons who once lived here at the 13th-century priory. The establishment was small, not very prosperous, and among the earliest to be dissolved. Felley Mill, the novelist's Strelley Mill, is falling completely into ruin, but just above the mill the pond is visible, as is the spot where the "thin stream" used to fall through the millrace.

FELPHAM, Sussex (pop. 1,619)

On the coast 1 mile northeast of Bognor Regis, Felpham was a quiet rural spot that had changed little when William Blake took possession of a white-walled thatched cottage (known both as Blake's Cottage and as Felpham Cottage) in mid-September 1800. The cottage, on the seaward side of the village, is a long, shallow six-room house with a veranda from which a narrow footpath leads to the sea. On the night before he left London to move here, Blake wrote to Ann Flaxman, the wife of John Flaxman, the sculptor:

> This song to the flower of Flaxman's joy;
> To the blossom of hope, for a sweet decoy;
> Do all that you can and all that you may
> To entice him to Felpham and far away.

His view had not altered by September 21, when he wrote to Flaxman:

> Felpham is a sweet place for study, because it is more spiritual than London. Heaven opens here on all sides her golden gates: her windows are not obstructed by vapours; voices of celestial inhabitants are more distinctly heard, and their forms more distinctly seen; and my cottage is also a shadow of their houses.

It was in the garden here that he saw the "fairy funeral":

> I was walking alone in my garden; there was great stillness among the branches and flowers, and more than common sweetness in the air; I heard a low and pleasant sound, and I knew not whence it came. At last I saw the broad leaf of a flower move, and underneath I saw a procession of creatures, of the size and colour of green and grey grasshoppers, bearing a body laid out on a rose leaf, which they buried with songs, and then disappeared. It was a fairy funeral!

The walks on the shore below the cottage had a great effect upon the poet, and there can be no doubt of the influence in

> To see a World in a grain of sand
> And a Heaven in a wild flower,
> Hold Infinity in the palm of your hand
> And Eternity in an hour.

William Hayley, who lived at the Turret, induced Blake to come to Felpham, but Hayley never understood the visionary poet and became a source of constant irritation. Although he was Blake's patron, he believed Blake's poems were of less consequence than his own and set menial tasks to keep Blake busy: doing the engravings for Hayley's life of Cowper, painting miniatures, teaching local people, and acting as Hayley's amanuensis and reader. An early hint of dissatisfaction, in the form of self-condemnation, comes in a letter to Flaxman:

> I labour incessantly. I accomplish not one half of what I intend, because my abstract folly hurries me often away while I am at work, carrying me over mountains and valleys, which are not real, into a land of abstraction where spectres of the dead wander. This I endeavour to

prevent; I, with my whole might, chain my feet to the world of duty and reality. But in vain! the faster I bind, the better is the ballast; for I, so far from being bound down, take the world with me in my flights, and often it seems lighter than a ball of wool rolled by the wind.

To Thomas Butts Blake complains that "corporeal friends are spiritual enemies" and adds:

Indeed, by my late firmness I have brought down his [Hayley's] affected loftiness, and he begins to think I have some genius. . . .

But this was insufficient, and Blake blurts out, "as if genius and assurance were the same thing." The "late firmness" produced the fifty-page poem *Milton*, in which he represents Hayley's type as Satan. Even if Blake had not been ready to return to London, an incident in August 1803 would have convinced him: a violent and unruly drunken soldier named Scofield broke into Blake's garden and refused to leave. Blake turned on the man and fairly threw him out; the soldier shouted all manner of things, including that he was the King's soldier. Blake's retort, "Damn the King and you too," set the soldier on revenge, and he entered a charge of sedition against Blake, claiming that the poet had uttered all sorts of treasonable statements while running him out of the garden. Blake was forced to trial in Chichester in the next quarter sessions.

Every summer the Quaker poet Amelia Opie stayed with Hayley at the Turret; her record of the day's activities provides a glimpse of what Blake found intolerable. Hayley rose at six o'clock or earlier, at which time he composed devotional verse; at breakfast he read to Mrs. Opie, and after breakfast she read to him. Coffee was served at eleven, and she sang for him as he dressed for dinner, after which he read aloud either his manuscript verse or "modern publications." In the afternoon Mrs. Opie either read to him or sang, and at nine o'clock the servants came in for prayers (Hayley's compositions); just before bed Mrs. Opie sang one of his hymns. Hayley died here in 1820, and Mrs. Opie wrote the epitaph on the church wall.

FENNY BENTLEY, Derbyshire (pop. 156) Watered by tiny Bentley Brook, the village of Fenny Bentley is 2½ miles north of Ashbourne and contains a lovely 15th-century fairy-tale hall, half house, half castle in appearance. Bentley Brook appears in *The Compleat Angler,* when Viator asks, "But what pretty river is this we are going into?"

Why this, sir, is called Bently-brook, and is full of very good trout and grayling; but so encumbered with wood in many places, as is troublesome to an angler.

During the 18th century, after being removed from Rugby, Walter Savage Landor was placed here under William Langley, the rector. Under Langley's tutelage Landor improved his English and Latin versification and worked on his Greek. *Imaginary Conversations* commemorates his time here (Izaak Walton, Charles Cotton, and Oldways discuss Langley and his students), while "The Birth of Poesy," written during the period of twelve to eighteen months when Landor lived here, went through many revisions before its ultimate publication. Landor returned to his home in the autumn of 1792.

FINCHINGFIELD, Essex (pop. 1,236) Finchingfield is probably the most photographed Essex village because of both natural and artificial attractions: a low, squat Norman church on a hill, a duck pond formed by the Pant River, and a large village green. Brent Hall was the birthplace of the metaphysical poet Edward Benlowes, on July 12, 1602, and he retained this home until his financial position was so crippled by the Civil War and various lawsuits that he retired to Oxford. It is said that Francis Quarles wrote his *Emblems, Moral and Divine* at Brent Hall; the friendship between Quarles and Benlowes was deep and long-standing, and Quarles often visited and especially enjoyed his lonely walks along the Pant, where, tradition maintains, much of *Emblems* was composed.

FIRLE *See* WEST FIRLE.

FLETCHING, Sussex (pop. 1,151) Fletching is a small village on the Ouse River, 8 miles north of

FINCHINGFIELD One of the most picturesque villages in Essex, Finchingfield was once the home of Edward Benlowes, an intimate friend of Francis Quarles, whose *Emblems, Moral and Divine* was written here.

Lewes, that was known in the Middle Ages for the manufacture of arrowheads. In the 13th-century church, with its tall broach spire and fragments of 13th-century glass in three lancet windows, Simon de Montfort maintained an all-night vigil before going out to win the Battle of Lewes on May 14, 1264. Another association is of greater significance, for the Sheffield Mausoleum behind the north transept is where Edward Gibbon is buried. The historian was often a guest of the 1st Earl of Sheffield at Sheffield Park, and he came here for a number of months after Lady Sheffield's death in 1793. Gibbon had suffered occasional attacks of severe gout, for which he had secured no treatment in more than thirty years; when the illness reached alarming proportions after his return to London in October 1793, surgery was undertaken. He spent Christmas at Sheffield Park and returned to London in January 1794, expressing the belief that he had yet a "good life for ten, twelve, or perhaps twenty years." He became critically ill on January 15 and died the next afternoon. Lord Sheffield had Gibbon's body brought here for burial in the family tomb. Only the historian's name is engraved in the marble.

FOCKBURY, Worcestershire Located midway between Worcester and Birmingham, just 1 mile northwest of Bromsgrove, Fockbury is in a rich agricultural area which has escaped the urban sprawl associated with the two cities. A. E. Housman was born at Valley House, now known as Housmans, on March 26, 1859, but lived here only a year before his family moved to Bromsgrove, where his father had his law offices. However, Housman's grandparents owned Fockbury House (now Clock House), to which the boy came frequently and to which he moved in 1873 following his father's remarriage.

FOLKESTONE, Kent (pop. 46,170) Folkestone, one of England's prettiest and most popular seaside resorts, took on significance in the Middle Ages as a limb to the Cinque Port of Dover, 7 miles to the northeast, but growth was very slow until the 19th century. As a consequence the Old Town is still a picturesque working-harbor area with attractive old cottages and narrow cobbled streets. Daniel Defoe notes that Folkestone is

eminent chiefly for a multitude of Fishing-Boats belonging to it, which are one part of the Year employ'd in catching Mackarel for the City of *London:* The *Folkestone* Men catch them, and the *London* and *Barking* Mackarel-Smacks, of which I have spoken at large in *Essex,* come down and buy them, with such a cloud of Canvas, and up so high that one would wonder their small Boats cou'd bear it and shout not overset. . . .

William Cobbett also visited Folkestone and on one occasion bemoans the conversion of the military establishment to more domestic purposes, saying, "After having sucked up millions of the nation's money, these loyal Cinque Ports are squeezed again: kept in order, kept down, by the very towers which they rejoiced to see rise to keep down the Jacobins."

One of the best-known attractions in Folkestone is the unique construction known as the Leas, a cliff walk laid out in grass and flowers, pine and broom. On the Leas is a commemorative statue to William Harvey, discoverer of the circulation of the blood, who was born here in 1578.

Much of the town is now the same as when Richard Harris Barham described it in "The Leech of Folkestone" in *The Ingoldsby Legends:*

Rome stood on seven hills; Folkestone seems to have been built upon seventy. Its street, lanes, and alleys—fanciful distinctions without much real difference,—are agreeable enough to persons who do not mind running up and down stairs; and the only inconvenience at all felt by such of its inhabitants as are not asthmatic, is when some heedless urchin tumbles down a chimney, or an impertinent pedestrian peeps into a garret window.

Folkestone was also one of Charles Dickens's favorite holiday spots; he first stayed at the Pavilion Hotel and called the town Pavilionstone whenever it appeared in his works. He describes it, with "crooked street[s] like a crippled ladder," in "Out of Town":

Within a quarter of a century—*circa* 1830, it was a little fishing town, and they do say that the time was when it was a little smuggling town. . . . The old little fishing and smuggling remains. . . . There are breakneck flights of ragged steps, connecting the principal streets by backways, which will cripple the visitor in half an hour. . . . Our situation is delightful, our air delicious, and our breezy hills and downs, carpeted with wild thyme, and decorated with millions of wild flowers, are, in the faith of the pedestrian, perfect.

Dickens noticed the tidal harbor ("At low water we are a heap of mud, with an empty channel in it. . . .") and "the very little wooden lighthouse [which] shrinks in the idle glare of the sun" but

when it is lighted at night—red and green—it looks so like a medical man's, that several distracted husbands have at various times been found, on occasions of premature domestic anxiety, going round it, trying to find the night bell!

In 1855 he took 3 Albion Villas for a family holiday, and the Dickenses were joined in July by Wilkie Collins.

Toward the end of the 19th century Ford Madox Ford was sent to a private school here from his home in Merton, Surrey. A 20th-century visitor was Rupert Brooke, who was here on a walking tour at the end of the Cambridge 1907 term. C. S. Calverley was buried here in February 1884.

Folkestone has an important place in the writings of H. G. Wells; in *The Sea Lady,* his first work in which the town appears, the Sea Lady who becomes Miss Waters retires to Lummidge's Hotel with her maid. In *The Dream* Folkestone is Cliffstone. The most extensive use is in *Kipps,* in which the town figures under its own name. Kipps is apprenticed to Mr. Shallford at the Folkestone Drapery Emporium,

one of the most considerable in Folkestone, and he insisted on every inch of frontage by alternate stripes of green and yellow down the house over the shops. His shops were numbered 3, 5, and 7 on the street, and on his bill-heads 3 to 7.

There is no specific location, however. Later Kipps inherits a stucco house on the Leas; with a balcony painted sea green and gilded, the house has brass-railed windows. The inside is described fully.

FONTHILL GIFFORD, Wiltshire (pop. 309) Near Tisbury and Hindon, this Fonthill is one of two adjacent villages with the same name; Fonthill Bishop is the other, and the two are often called by their common name and are often confused. Fonthill Gifford, an attractive villa just outside the lake-watered Fonthill Park, was the location of the extravaganza in 18th-century building created by the author of *Vathek*, William Beckford, said to be England's wealthiest heir, supposedly inheriting an income of £100,000 per year at the age of ten. This, though, is a fiction, and his actual yearly income was closer to £25,000 or £30,000, still a considerable sum. A great deal of Beckford's childhood was spent in the family home here, and Fonthill Park and House were the scene of one of the biggest coming-of-age parties ever given in southern England. On September 29, 1781, almost 1,000 lamps were hung from the trees in the park and the surrounding grove, lighted skiffs were on the lake, wax torches illuminated the exterior of the house, and an illuminated triumphal arch was placed opposite the portico. And this was not enough: Beckford had three enormous bonfires lit on the downs to remind him of Hector's funeral in Troy; fireworks were displayed throughout the evening, and the greatest *castrato* in Europe, Gasparo Pacchierotti, performed.

It was this mentality which produced Fonthill Abbey. Begun as a tower, the dominant motif, it went on as a great baronial hall and concluded as an abbey. Beckford's plans began as early as 1792, when he directed that the 519 acres of his "Enchanted Gardens and Monastic Demesne" be walled in so that the buildings could appear magically in their complete state. Four years later he began a mock abbey but abandoned in the interim his plans for a tower, which had been started on the other end of the ridge. He commissioned James Wyatt to build "a convent partly in ruins and partly perfect." All the work was said to have been done at night, and during extremely cold weather great bonfires blazed so that the cement and mortar would not freeze. The building proceeded, as Beckford said, "gently, and oh! so slowly, and with all the economy of a Father Guardian of the poorest monasteries." Only one really great day occurred here, at Christmas, 1800, before construction was complete; only the first floor and south and west wings were finished. Beckford entertained Lord Nelson and Sir William and Lady Hamilton in state in the 52-foot dining room, whose table was as long as the room. Following dinner, the guests went upstairs to the St. Michael's Gallery, where the library was screened off from the magnificent setting of Vincenzo de' Rossi's sculpture of St. Anthony. Placed against scarlet draperies, the sculpture was surrounded by jeweled reliquaries, gilt candelabra, hundreds of candles, and music. The *pièce de résistance* came as the guests turned around; here was the great plate-glass oriel window which reproduced the lighted tapers at the shrine of St. Anthony and was Beckford's own reproduction of his experience in the York Cathedral in 1779:

> But what suggested a finer idea of vision and enchantment than anything I ever beheld was—upon my turning round—its reflection on the glazed work of the screen which, as I advanced (all the way communicating my own motion), spread wider and wider and rose every step I took, till the whole in all its varied hues and splendid colouring hung suspended in the air.

Fonthill was finished in 1808, and Beckford packed it with paintings, books, sculpture, and cu-rios. Eventually, deeply in debt, he was forced to sell the sumptuous estate; he kept back his best paintings and other objects but realized £300,000 from the sale, enough to be well out of debt. One of those attending the sale was Thomas Moore, who walked here from his home in nearby Bromham and bought a cup and saucer for his wife. Beckford moved to Bath, where he began another building project. Beckford's magnificent tower crashed down in December 1825 and destroyed some of the abbey as well.

A number of literary figures were at Fonthill Abbey at one time or another. William Hazlitt first visited early in 1822, when he was touring picture galleries, and later saw the contents of the house auctioned off. He called the place "a glittering waste of laborious idleness, a cathedral turned into a shop," and admitted its "heartless desolation and finery." Thomas Hardy makes a passing reference to Fonthill in *Jude the Obscure*, in which it is called by its own name as the possible site for a day's holiday for Jude and Sue.

FORDINGTON, Dorset (pop. 3,705)   Fordington, now a southeast suburb of Dorchester, received a separate entry in the Domesday Book as a manor belonging to the King and later- became part of the Duchy of Cornwall. Overlooking a green is the Fordington church, dedicated to St. George, which underwent extensive restoration in the early 20th century. A Gothic style chapel was built to replace a Georgian chapel, which the vicar thought was not in keeping with the rest of the building. When he decided to restore the church to its proper medieval form, he was urged to leave the structure as it was by his most famous parishioner, Thomas Hardy, but the vicar won out.

Fordington has an extensive place in Hardy's Wessex as Durnover (its Roman name was Durnovania), and in some of the early editions of *The Mayor of Casterbridge* the town is called Drummerford. When Hardy was writing *The Mayor*, Fordington had important agricultural interests:

> Here wheat-ricks overhung the old Roman street, and thrust their eaves against the church tower; green-thatched barns, with doorways as high as the gates of Solomon's temple, opened directly upon the main thoroughfare. Barns indeed were so numerous as to alternate with every half-dozen houses along the way. . . . [A] street ruled by a mayor and corporation, yet echoing with the thump of the flail, the flutter of the winnowing-fan, and the purr of the milk into the pails—a street which had nothing urban in it whatever—this was the Durnover end of Casterbridge.

The granary on Durnover Hill, the place appointed for the meeting of Elizabeth-Jane Newson and Donald Farfrae, "was just within the farm-yard, and stood on stone staddles, high enough for persons to walk under." The barn and the granary, which threw great shadows onto the church, were demolished to make way for the new rectory. Here Farfrae had opened his hay and grain stores. The Church of St. George is the Durnford Church where Mrs. Henchard is buried; the grave is in

> the still-used burial-ground of the old Roman-British city, whose curious feature was this, its continuity as a place of sepulture. Mrs. Henchard's dust mingled with the dust of women who lay ornamented with glass hairpins and amber necklaces, and men who held in their

mouths coins of Hadrian, Posthumus, and the Costantines.

Here Elizabeth-Jane encounters Lucetta.

Hardy's use of Fordington as Durnford is not restricted to *The Mayor of Casterbridge.* In *Under the Greenwood Tree,* after Mr. Maybold learns that Fancy and Dick Dewy are engaged, he

> stood still upon the bridge....
>
> Mr. Maybold leant over the parapet of the bridge and looked into the river. He saw—without heeding—how the water came rapidly from beneath the arches, glided down a little steep, then spread itself over a pool in which dace, trout, and minnows sported at ease among the long green locks of weed, that lay heaving and sinking with their roots towards the current.

Dewy has gone on to Durnford Hill (Fordington Hill), and the bridge where Maybold stands is the one used by Henchard in *The Mayor of Casterbridge.* Durnover Green is used in *The Dynasts,* Durnover Moor is in *The Mayor of Casterbridge* and *Far from the Madding Crowd,* and Durnover Great Field (Durnover Lea) is in "The Alarm," "Winter in Durnover Field," and "Bereft":

> When the summer dawns clearly,
> And the appletree-tops seem alight,
> Who will undraw the curtain and cheerly
> Call out that the morning is bright?

> When I tarry at market
> No form will cross Durnover Lea
> In the gathering darkness, to hark at
> Grey's Bridge for the pit-pat o' me.

FOREST HILL, Oxfordshire Located on the brow of a hill 4 miles east of Oxford, Forest Hill draws literary pilgrims to its 13th-century church, one of the few extant places associated with John Milton. Leaving London at Whitsuntide in 1642, Milton traveled here to see Richard Powell, an improvident and impoverished Royalist, to whom Milton's father had lent £300 in 1627. The yearly interest payment of £24 accrued to the poet. By 1642 Powell's affairs were in a complete muddle, and when he requested more time to find the interest payment, Milton made the trip from London. Here he met Mary Powell, aged seventeen, who became his first wife in the church here in July. The couple went to London immediately after the ceremony, and Milton's *The Doctrine and Discipline of Divorce* is said to have been inspired by the fact that his wife left him to return home after only two months of marriage.

William Julius Mickle, an obscure Scottish poet, came to Forest Hill from London about 1772; settling with a farmer, a Mr. Tomkins, he produced some of his best work in the village. He finished his translation of Luis Vaz de Camões's *Os Lusiadas* and wrote *A History of the Discovery of India, A History of the Portuguese Empire in the East,* and *A Life of Camoens,* among others. Mickle married Tomkins's daughter Mary in 1781 and settled in nearby Wheatley. He died on a visit here on October 28, 1788, and was buried in the parish churchyard.

FORNCETT ST. PETER, Norfolk (pop. 554) Situated in the lovely Tas Valley 10 miles southwest of Norwich, Forncett St. Peter is one of two adjacent parishes with the name Forncett; the second, Forncett St. Mary, is even tinier than its counterpart. The 15th-century church here, with a small Saxon tower and fifty-four richly carved bench ends (some medieval), is one William Wordsworth would have known. His uncle, the Rev. William Cookson, held this living from around 1789 on, and the poet first visited the rector and his new wife in June of that year. Dorothy Wordsworth was already staying in the rectory and, in fact, remained three years. Her brother stayed only a short time before going on to the Yorkshire Dales. He was back for a six-week stay beginning in December 1790 and is thought to have come over occasionally from Cambridge. However, the relationship between uncle and nephew was, at best, strained, and Wordsworth did not care to be here often.

FOSTON, Yorkshire (pop. 93) The tiny North Riding village of Foston, also known as Foston-le-Clay, is located at the edge of the Vale of Pickering about 6 miles southwest of Malton on an unmarked road. Its church, one of the masterpieces of England and possibly the oldest parish church in the country, was served beginning in 1806 by the Rev. Sydney Smith as a nonresident rector (administering the parish from Heslington). He later designed the rectory, 1 mile from the church, which he named The Rector's Head. Smith, a renowned wit, once commented to a local bishop, "You must not think that I am trivial because I am flippant; and I will not think you are serious because you are pompous." His slight eccentricities generally endeared him to his parishioners: he used an old green chariot, christened Immortal, for getting back and forth to the church and dubbed the horse used for his parish rounds Calamity because of its propensity to part company with its rider. Eventually he became not just the rector but a farmer, a very successful breeder of horses, and the village magistrate, chemist, and doctor by virtue of his attendance at medical lectures at the University of Edinburgh. Both nobility and literary personages were among his numerous guests: the Earl of Carlisle and Lord Morpeth were weekly visitors; Sir Humphry Davy and his wife were frequently in Foston; Francis Jeffrey, Smith's cofounder of *The Edinburgh Review,* and Thomas Babington Macaulay were often house guests. Smith was so well liked by his small group of parishioners that when he left the parish to take the living at Combe Florey, Somerset, they erected a plaque inscribed: "He was a faithful friend and counsellor, a seeker of peace, a wit who used his powers to delight and not to wound." *The Letters of Peter Plymley* was written here.

FOUNTAINS ABBEY, Yorkshire This 12th-century Cistercian abbey on the Skell River is England's finest monastic ruin. Set in the beautiful wooded seclusion of Skeldale, it was founded in 1132–1133 by twelve ex-Benedictine monks from St. Mary's Abbey in York and grew to be one of the most powerful and wealthy abbeys in the Cistercian community. In the early years at Fountains the monks were near starvation, and the wild north country forests (now park and farming land) created a stark and forbidding environment. But by the 1300s the abbey had become very prosperous and established a number of daughter houses such as those at Kirkstall and Newminster, and by the early 16th century its prosperity, especially because of the wool trade, made Fountains one of the wealthiest institutions in England.

On one side of the Skell River is an ivy-covered well known as Robin Hood's Well, which may be a memorial of the famous encounter between Robin and "the curtal friar" of Fountains, Friar Tuck. This is the spot traditionally assigned as the one where the celebrated trial of strength takes place and where Robin Hood is thrown into the Skell. "Robin Hood and the Curtal Friar" tells how

> Robin Hood took a solemn oath,
>   It was by Mary free,
> That he would neither eat nor drink
>   Till the frier he did see

until

> . . . coming unto Fountain[s] Dale,
>   No further would he ride;
> There was he aware of a curtal frier,
>   Walking by the water-side.

The two men engage in combat, each resorting to trickery in an attempt to win: Robin Hood summons fifty men, and Friar Tuck an equal number of bandogs. Little John "shot with might and main" until "half a score of the friers dogs/Lay dead upon the plain" and the curtal friar who

> had kept Fountains Dale
> Seven long years or more

calls for a truce. Robin offers him clothing and a fee to forsake Fountains Abbey for the life of an outlaw in the forest, conditions Friar Tuck accepts. A tradition still exists that Robin Hood's bow and arrows, preserved here, disappeared at the dissolution.

FOWEY, Cornwall (pop. 2,255) Fowey (pronounced "foy") clings to the western bank of the Fowey River with a network of tiny streets covering the hills. Neither pavements nor buses exist in the old waterside village, and the streets lined with old houses with cob walls and slate roofs are so narrow as to make passage treacherous. Fowey was one of the many southern river-estuary towns which gained importance in the early Middle Ages, and by the reign (1307–1327) of Edward II, when the Cinque Ports supported a blatant piracy, open warfare existed between those ports and Fowey. Fowey gallants plundered the Normandy coast until Elizabethan times, when the French outfitted an expedition against the town. The great days of Fowey appeared to end in the mid-15th century after the final Lancastrian revolt against Edward IV, but Fowey remained prosperous because of its favorable trade position; it exported chiefly tin, hides, pilchards, herring, and clay and imported salt, woolen cloth, linen, and canvas. Its most valuable import was wine from the south of France and Spain.

Michael Drayton catalogs the river in *Poly-Olbion* along with the Low (Looe):

> Thou *Foy*, before us all,
> By thine owne named Towne made famous in thy fall,
> As *Low*, amongst us heere; a most delicious Brooke,
> With all our sister Nymphes, that to the noone-sted looke,
> Which glyding from the hills, upon the tinny ore,
> Betwixt your high-rear'd banks, resort to this our
>   shore. . . .

John Wolcot, the satirist known as Peter Pindar, came here as a boy in 1751 after his father died and he was left in the care of his uncle. He went to London in 1762 to study to be a surgeon and returned from 1764 to 1767 as his uncle's assistant.

Fowey also has special connections with Kenneth Grahame, whose initial visit in July 1899 was spent convalescing in the Fowey Hotel, from which he proposed to Elspeth Thomson. The marriage, set for July 22, posed a probem in getting the banns read, but Sir Arthur Quiller-Couch solved the problem by finding a "tame curate" in the local billiards room who made the arrangements. The marriage took place in St. Fimbarrus' Church, with Grahame's cousin Anthony Hope Hawkins as best man, and part of the couple's honeymoon was spent here. Grahame was especially fond of "the little grey sea town that clings along one side of the river" (as described in *The Wind in the Willows*) and returned here frequently until 1912.

Fowey is probably more closely associated with Quiller-Couch than with anyone else. While it was his retirement home, Q actually settled at the Haven (which looked out on the harbor) in 1891, when he was still lecturing at Cambridge; there the Divinity School gate often carried the sign "The Professor is not yet in residence" or "The Professor has gone down." In 1913 he helped to have the town's ancient civic status restored, and he served as mayor of Fowey in 1937–1938. He made the town famous as Troy Town in his *Astonishing History of Troy Town*, but he also used other area points of interest in his works, notably Dodman Point on the headland near Gorran Haven. Q died at his home on May 12, 1944,

FOWEY Long famous as a port and sailing center, Fowey was guaranteed a place in literature by Kenneth Grahame, who was inspired by the river setting here and used it (transported) in *The Wind in the Willows*, and by Sir Arthur Quiller-Couch, who transforms it into Troy Town.

and the town erected a commemorative statue on Hall Walk overlooking the harbor.

Alfred, Lord Tennyson was here in June 1848 on his way to Polperro to gather material on the Arthurian legend, but he left no impression of Fowey.

About 2 miles north of the village on the old trade route running to Bodmin is Castle Dore, originally a 2d-century B.C. fortified village and the castle of the Cornish king Mark of Arthurian legend. A partly obliterated stone near here reads " . . . hic iacit Cunomori filius" (" . . . lies here the son of Cunomorus"); the first name is difficult to read but is almost certainly Drustanus (the 6th-century form of Tristran), whom King Mark reportedly buried close to the tomb of Iseult. Adding plausibility to the Arthurian connection is the possibility that the ancient name of the castle may derive from the name of an adjoining building, Carhules, "that belonging to Gourles." The husband of Arthur's mother was Gorlois, and it is entirely possible that Mark succeeded to the kingship.

FRAMLINGHAM, Suffolk (pop. 2,397)   This quiet and attractive market town in the farmlands of eastern Suffolk and its history are dominated by the 12th-century castle, begun by Roger Bigod after Henry I gave him the land about 1100. Bigod's second son, Hugh, was the first of many unsuccessful adventurers who sallied forth from the castle: he supported Henry II in 1154 but then joined Henry's sons in a doomed fight against the crown; his submission to the King brought about the partial destruction of the castle. Subsequent Bigod generations rebuilt the castle and were loyal until Roger, the 5th Earl of Norfolk, aligned himself with the barons against Edward I. For his treason his lands were held forfeit and went to the crown upon his death in 1306. After several transfers, the lands came to the Mowbray family, and John Mowbray, the last Duke of Norfolk in this line, was often in residence here and frequently served as host to John Paston of nearby Paston and Bacton, Norfolk. Paston's letters tell much about life here, and one records the visit of William of Wynflete, then Bishop of Winchester, in 1472 for the christening of the duke's daughter Anne. By 1476 the last of the Mowbray line died, and after a short period of royal control the castle passed to the enormously powerful Howard family. The family held the dukedom of Norfolk, and the poet and unsuccessful courtier Henry Howard, Earl of Surrey, was here frequently as a child and was in attendance at the state funeral of his grandfather, the 2d Duke, who died in 1524. Surrey never succeeded to the estate or the title but was beheaded at the Tower of London in 1547; his father, the 3d Duke, sentenced to a similar fate, was reprieved at the last minute by Henry VIII's death. The church in Framlingham contains all the Howard family tombs, including that of the Earl of Surrey, whose body was brought back from London for the burial.

Framlingham has a slight association with Robert Greene, author of *The Honorable Historie of Friar Bacon and Friar Bungay* (1594), who uses Suffolk and Oxford as the settings of the play. While most of the action in the county takes place in Fressingfield and Harleston, Framlingham is mentioned as a royal hunting area. King Henry III explains where Edward the Prince of Wales has gone:

He posted down, not long since, from the court,
To Suffolk side, to merry Framlingham,
To sport himself amongst my fallow deer. . . .

FRESHWATER PENINSULA, Isle of Wight   The old town of Freshwater, 1 mile from Freshwater Bay in a marshland area at the Yar Estuary, is dominated by the downland walk to The Needles, huge chalk stacks on the westernmost tip of the island. This is Tennyson country; the area from Freshwater to the tip of the island has been named Tennyson Down, and a memorial column has been erected on High Down. The poet made this walk daily from his home in Farringford, and one can visualize him as he walked, black cloak flowing and voice booming out the newest part of, say, *Idylls of the King*, with Edward FitzGerald in the summer of 1859, with Henry Wadsworth Longfellow in 1868, or with any other guest. One of Tennyson's visitors was Arthur Hugh Clough, who came here to try to recover from chronic illness (the Isle of Wight has long had a reputation as a health spa). With a six months' leave of absence from the Education Office, Clough came to Freshwater early in 1861 and stayed until April, during which time he saw a great deal of the Tennysons. Clough died on November 13 in Florence, where he was buried in the Protestant Cemetery. Edward Lear, whose early friendship with Tennyson became quite strained, visited Freshwater in March 1861 and stayed at the Royal Albion Hotel on Freshwater Bay rather than with the Tennysons. The Church of St. Agnes in Freshwater, built in 1908 on a site donated by the poet's son, contains seven Tennyson memorials.

Lewis Carroll spent part of his vacation from Oxford here in 1862 and took great interest in the daily comings and goings of four small children dressed in yellow. He comments in a letter: "They go by in a state of great excitement, brandishing wooden spades, and making strange noises; from that moment they disappear entirely—they are never to be seen *on* the beach. The only theory I can form is that they tumble into a hole somewhere, and continue excavating therein during the day. . . ." On their return they made similar sounds, but he says, "I suppose they are different to them, and contain an account of the day's achievements." At the very end of the century, following the death of her mother, Virginia Stephen (Woolf) spent a summer holiday somewhere on the peninsula with her family.

FRIMLEY, Surrey (pop. 18,390)   Just a few miles southwest of Bagshot, Frimley is on the Blackwater River in an area with extensive military establishments, heath, and fir. The American short-story writer Bret Harte, who spent his last years here and in London, died in Camberley on May 5, 1902, and was buried in the churchyard of St. Peter's Church.

FROLESWORTH, Leicestershire (pop. 220)   Although this little village 5 miles north of Lutterworth officially spells its name Frolesworth, both its post office and its hall spell the name Frowlesworth. The area is especially lovely, with rich farms on nearby hills and a charming group of 18th-century almshouses and chapel around a flowered quadrangle built by Judge

John Smith. The twenty-six houses have been enlarged internally so that now there are only sixteen attached cottages. Alexander Pope commemorated Smith with these lines placed over the porch:

Who built this Alms-House, neat, but void of State
Where Age and Want sit smiling at the Gate?

FYFIELD, Berkshire (pop. 514) Situated 5 miles northwest of Abingdon, the village of Fyfield has a lovely 14th-century manor house with a musicians' gallery, a partly Norman church, and an old elm tree. The elm, an offshoot of the original Fyfield, or Tubney, elm, which measured 36 feet around its hollow trunk, is the tree Matthew Arnold refers to in *The Scholar-Gipsy:*

Maidens, who from the distant hamlets come
  To dance around the Fyfield elm in May,
Oft through the darkening fields have seen thee roam,
  Or cross a stile into the public way.

GADSHILL, Kent Practically enveloped by the sprawling modern cities of Rochester and Stroud, Gadshill still maintains some of the ease of life which has given it its special place in the geography of English literature. This locale is on the Pilgrims' Way, the northern route taken by medieval pilgrims to the Shrine of St. Thomas à Becket at Canterbury, and Geoffrey Chaucer himself passed by on this road as a pilgrim in April 1388. In 1385 he had retired to his property in the area and been appointed justice of the peace for the county; he was also elected knight of the shire in the summer of 1386. In addition, Chaucer lived here while working on *The Canterbury Tales*. Two centuries later William Shakespeare used Gadshill for the encounter between Falstaff and the "two rogues in buckram suits" who grow to eleven in the telling. The choice of the site for the "robbery" in *Henry IV: Part I* was fairly simple: nearby are the ruins of Cooling Castle, once the home of Sir John Oldcastle, from whom Falstaff is probably drawn. The robbery is supposed to have been committed in front of Gadshill Place, a house which later belonged to Charles Dickens.

As a small child Dickens had been impressed by Gadshill Place, most likely, as he said, "because of the old cedar-trees," and in later years he often recalled his father's comment that if he "ever grew up to be a clever man," this house or one like it might be his. The chances of his acquiring the house were fairly remote. Dickens happened to relate this childhood dream to William Henry Wills, an editor of *Household Words;* Wills later happened to have dinner with Mrs. Lynn-Linton, who, having just inherited the place upon her father's death, wanted to dispose of it. In February 1856 the sum of £1,790 was agreed upon, and after an additional outlay of £1,000 for alterations and repairs, Dickens took possession in April, although he had never been in the house prior to the purchase. Gadshill Place was not in-

tended to be a permanent residence, but as he became involved with the house and the area, Dickens was no doubt secretly happy that he could find nothing to his liking in London and ultimately gave up the idea of living in the city. A two-story brick house with a pillared portico, Gadshill Place had fourteen rooms, with Dickens's library and study on the right side of the entrance hall and a billiards room directly behind the study. The grave of Dick, the "best of birds," is beneath the rose tree seen from the dining-room window. Dickens often had a drink "just over the way" at the "rustic alehouse," the Sir John Falstaff, which was a favorite of his and his constant stream of guests. The nearby house which Henry Wadsworth Longfellow and his daughters took on a visit to Dickens is now a school. Charles Eliot Norton, Sir Edward Bulwer-Lytton, and Hans Christian Andersen were among Dickens's other guests. Andersen's stay, beginning on July 7, 1857, proved to be a trial for the whole family. Along with Queen Victoria and Prince Albert, the King of the Belgians, and their respective parties, he was invited to attend the prestigious opening-night benefit (for the widow of Douglas Jerrold) of Wilkie Collins's *The Frozen Deep*. Afterward Andersen was invited to stay a little longer, which he did—for five weeks. After his departure, a card was placed on the dressing table of his bedroom: "Hans Andersen slept in this room for 5 weeks which seemed to the family ages." Collins was a constant house guest, especially during the courtship and subsequent marriage of Dickens's daughter Kate and Charles Collins, Wilkie's brother.

Dickens did not actually do much writing in the house. A Swiss chalet, sent by the French actor Charles-Albert Fechter, was erected on a part of the estate known as the Wilderness, and a tunnel was constructed from the front lawn at Gadshill Place under the highway to the chalet. Here Dickens worked on *A Tale of Two Cities, Great Expectations,*

The Uncommercial Traveller, Our Mutual Friend, and the unfinished *Edwin Drood;* and here Linda, his favorite dog, is buried. As was his usual practice, he spent the day of June 8, 1870, at work in the chalet and was late in leaving it that evening before dinner. The meal had begun before Miss Georgina Hogarth, Dickens's sister-in-law, noticed he was ill; he directed that dinner go on (his last coherent words) and sat at the table attempting to take part in the conversation until he collapsed; he died the next day. Dickens's directions for a simple burial in a small nearby churchyard were being followed when the dean and chapter of Rochester requested his burial in the cathedral there. Family assent was given reluctantly, but before the services were carried out, the dean of Westminster proposed that the abbey was the more fitting place. Dickens, consequently, was buried on June 14, 1870, at Westminster Abbey with only his family, immediate friends, and the abbey clergy in attendance. After Dickens's death his family presented the chalet to the Earl of Darnley, who reerected it at his park in Cobham; finally, in 1961, it went to Eastgate House, the Rochester public museum, where it has been carefully reconstructed.

GAINSBOROUGH, Lincolnshire (pop. 18,689) An old market town 18 miles northwest of Lincoln, Gainsborough looks across the Trent River into Nottinghamshire; the east side of the town is sheltered by a wooded escarpment. It was the site of King Alfred's marriage (868) and the place of King Sweyn's death. The oldest building in Gainsborough, aside from a very small part of the rebuilt church, is Old Hall, a 15th-century baronial hall with an open roof, tie beams, and wind-braced rafters. Gainsborough is the prototype of St. Ogg's in George Eliot's *The Mill on the Floss,* and the descriptive passages are still identifiable.

> It is one of those old, old towns which . . . carries the traces of its long growth and history like a millennial tree. . . . It is a town "familiar with forgotten years." The shadow of the Saxon hero-king still walks there fitfully, reviewing the scenes of his youth and love-time, and is met by the gloomier shadow of the dreadful heathen Dane, who was stabbed in the midst of his warriors by the sword of an invisible avenger, and who rises on autumn evenings, like a white mist from his tumulus on the hill, and hovers in the court of the old hall by the river-side—the spot where he was thus miraculously slain in the days before the old hall was built. It was the Normans who began to build that fine old hall, . . . so old that we look with loving pardon at its inconsistencies. . . .

The Old Hall is the scene of the St. Ogg's bazaar, where Maggie Tulliver has a stall:

> All well-drest St. Ogg's and its neighbourhood were there; and it would have been worth while to come, even from a distance, to see the fine old hall, with its open roof and carved oaken rafters, and great oaken folding-doors, and light shed down from a height on the many-coloured show beneath: a very quaint place, with broad faded stripes painted on the walls, and here and there a show of heraldic animals of a bristly, long-snouted character, the cherished emblems of a noble family once the seigniors of this now civic hall. A grand arch, cut in the upper wall at one end, surmounted an oaken orchestra, with an open room behind it. . . . Near the great arch over the orchestra was the stone oriel with painted glass, which was one of the venerable inconsistencies of the old hall; and it was close by this that Lucy had her stall. . . .

While Gainsborough is inland, it is not so far inland as to be unaffected by tides; indeed, the Bore, or Aegir (eagre), on which Maggie and Tom are caught is a local phenomenon which was once more prevalent than it is now. The rush of tidal water inland from the estuary was greeted with the cry "War the Aigre," and it has caused extraordinary flooding:

> A large company in a boat that was working its way along under the Tofton houses, observed their danger, and shouted, "Get out of the current!"
> But that could not be done at once, and Tom, looking before him, saw death rushing on them. Huge fragments, clinging together in fatal fellowship, made one wide mass across the stream.
> "It is coming, Maggie!" Tom said, in a deep hoarse voice, loosing the oars, and clasping her.
> The next instant the boat was no longer seen upon the water—and the huge mass was hurrying on in hideous triumph.
> But soon the keel of the boat reappeared, a black speck on the golden water.

The Red Deeps, where Maggie and Philip Wakem meet near St. Ogg's, are properly located near Griff Hollows in Warwickshire and have been transplanted here.

GALTRES FOREST, Yorkshire This ancient royal forest (alternatively spelled Gaultres) once covered more than 100,000 acres in the North Riding of Yorkshire and extended from the north wall of York to Boroughbridge, to the north to the village of Crayke and as far east as Bulmer. Galtres is mentioned in Geoffrey of Monmouth's *Historia Regum Britanniae* as the forest of Calaterium in the story of Archgallo and his brother Elidurus the Dutiful. John Leland, librarian and antiquarian to Henry VIII, describes the forest as two parts: the first, nearer York, "moorish and low ground, and having very little wood"; the second, "higher, and reasonably wood," abundant in "wild deer." A few years later William Camden surveyed the forest in greater detail for his *Britannia,* which says it was "shaded in some places with trees, in others . . . wet, flat, full of moist and moorish quaremires."

This is the forest setting in the fourth act of William Shakespeare's *Henry IV: Part II.* The Archbishop of York (Richard Scrope) asks: "What is this forest call'd?" and is answered with "'Tis Gaultree Forest." It is impossible to determine the great plain where the two opposing forces were encamped. Michael Drayton changes the name of the forest to Gautres in *Poly-Olbion* and portrays the forest as a nymph:

> When that great Forrest-Nymph faire *Gautresse* on her way,
> Shee sees to stand prepar'd, with Garlands fresh and gay
> To decke up *Ouze,* before her selfe to *Yorke* she show. . . .

GARSINGTON, Oxfordshire (pop. 930) Snugly placed in the sweeping area between the Chiltern Hills and the Berkshire Downs and only 5 miles southeast of Oxford, Garsington is in one of the loveliest parts of Oxfordshire. The main attraction of the village is the 16th-century Garsington Manor House, which in the 20th century became the home of Philip and Lady Ottoline Morrell, around whom some of the most famous and successful literary personages of their time assembled. One of the earliest and most valued members of the coterie was T. S. Eliot, who made the first of many visits in 1915, although not until 1924 did he meet Virginia and Leonard Woolf here. The Woolfs' first visit, from November 17 to 19, 1917, occurred when both Aldous Huxley and Lytton Strachey were also guests. The group which congregated here had the reputation of being freethinking and free-spoken and became the model of the country life portrayed in Huxley's *Crome Yellow*. Huxley and Woolf never met until a late-June weekend in 1926, when Siegfried Sassoon and Victoria Sackville-West were also here. William Butler Yeats first came to the Morrells in 1919, when he was in Oxford; and Katherine Mansfield came here the first time from Mylor, Cornwall, and thoroughly enjoyed the visits until the intensity of the relationships became such a strain that she felt compelled to break them off. Among the other literary figures who frequented Garsington Manor House were John Masefield, Walter de la Mare, the Sitwells, D. H. Lawrence, and Rupert Brooke.

Earlier the ten-year-old H. Rider Haggard, who was felt to be accomplishing nothing at his school in London, was sent to a school here run by the Rev. H. J. Grahame at the rectory. The influence here, at least in part, was seen later in the name of Quartermain in *King Solomon's Mines*. The source of the name was a farmer here who took a paternal interest in the boy.

GATESHEAD, County Durham (pop. 124,545) Even though Gateshead is typical of many northeastern industrial towns and is especially typical of a sprawling Tyneside town, Dr. Samuel Johnson's comment that it is "a dirty lane leading to Newcastle" is unfair. Daniel Defoe lived somewhere in Gateshead for a few months, and Robert Smith Surtees ventured into political life here. In 1837 Surtees stood for Gateshead's one seat in Parliament in a contest which he felt would be "politically honest" and sensible. The incumbent, Cuthbert Rippon, had a personal life which was thought to be undesirable for a Member of Parliament and was, in addition, a Liberal. However, the race was entered by a third party, an ex-Conservative turned Liberal who wanted to defeat Rippon at all costs, and in the ensuing bitter battle Surtees withdrew his candidacy in disgust. He never offered himself for election again.

GAULTRES FOREST　*See* GALTRES FOREST.

GAWSWORTH, Cheshire (pop. 573) Even though only 3 miles to the old silk-manufacturing town of Macclesfield and quite close to the Jodrell Bank scanning center, Gawsworth has retained its peacefulness and its beauty, notably its fine medieval rectory, with lovely black-and-white walls, an open-roofed hall, and a very old window with diamond panes and a few shields in glass. Other noteworthy buildings are the black-and-white gabled 16th-century hall and the new 18th-century hall built by the 4th Baron Mohun. It was Lord Mohun's duel which William Makepeace Thackeray uses in *Henry Esmond*. Lord Castlewood, embittered by the destruction of his wife's beauty by smallpox and enraged by Mohun's attempted seduction of her, sets out for London to challenge his rival:

[A] cry from the chairmen without, who were smoking their pipes, and leaning over the railings of the field as they watched the dim combat within, announced that some catastrophe had happened, which caused Esmond to drop his sword and look round, at which moment his enemy wounded him in the right hand. But the young man did not heed this hurt much, and ran up to the place where he saw his dear master was down.

Henry Fielding based the character of Maggoty Johnson in *Tom Jones* on Samuel Johnson, a now-obscure 18th-century dramatist who had astounding success in London with an opera, *Hurlothrumbo*. The opera played for more than a month, an extremely long run at the time, but Johnson fell into obscurity almost immediately and retired to Gawsworth as a dance master. He died here in 1773 and is buried in a spinney with his own inscription on a stone:

Here, undisturbed, and hid from vulgar eyes,
A wit, musician, poet, player lies.

The grave is in a wooded area near the church.

One final tenuous association exists with the old hall, once the home of the Fitton family, of whom Mary Fitton is sometimes claimed to be the Dark Lady of Shakespeare's sonnets.

GEDNEY, Lincolnshire (pop. 1,985) Situated in the marshy land around the Wash, Gedney is in the middle of a bulb-growing district 3½ miles east of Holbeach. The Fenland, generally just above sea level, supports lush vegetation and is some of the richest agricultural land in England. Gedney is a scattered village, and it has an excellent partly 13th-century church erected before the Fens were properly drained; as a result, the foundations are anything but firm. The 14th-century south porch has an outstanding old wicket door with four coats of arms and an ivory Crucifixion above it, and the 15th-century nave has old carved beams and bosses on the roof. Richard Hakluyt, author of *Principall Navigations, Voiages, and Discoveries of the English Nation*, came here as vicar in 1612 and retained the post until his death on November 23, 1616. He was buried in Westminster Abbey.

GIGGLESWICK, Yorkshire (pop. 954) Giggleswick is in the western Dales area. Here the broad reaches of the Pennines slope downward to form lovely Dales, which descend from barren stretches of heath and moorland through isolated farms to the busy market towns on the valley floor. Millions of years ago the high rocks in this area split, and land slipped into the gaps known as Craven faults; one of these, known today as Aire Gap, is the only true gap through the Pennines. The village, situated on the Ribble River, is the center of a limestone-quarrying industry, and its most important scenic feature is a "glorious limestone bastion" known as Giggleswick Scar just beyond the village. At the foot of the scar is the ebbing and flowing well to which Michael Drayton refers in *Poly-Olbion*. A spring of extreme irregularity, influenced undoubtedly by environmental factors, the well rises and then flows into a natural stone basin at unpredictable times. Drayton describes the well as a nymph living

Among the mountains high
Of Craven, whose blue heads for caps put on the sky.

The poet tells, too, how the gods rescued the exhausted nymph from a pursuing satyr by changing her into an irregular spring:

Even as the fearful nymph then thick and short did blow,
Now made by them a spring, so doth she ebb and flow.

Giggleswick Scar and the spring were two of the moorland areas explored by Virginia Stephen (Woolf) when she came in the autumn of 1904 to the school to stay with her cousin Will Vaughan, who was then headmaster; she also visited the parsonage at Haworth on this occasion. She was back in Giggleswick from April 12 to 25, 1906, when she lodged with a Mrs. Turner, near the Vaughans' home. On this trip she brought her dog Gurth, with which she took long walks across the moors and delighted in his chasing rabbits and other wildlife.

GILSLAND, Cumberland On the Northumberland border 7 miles northeast of Brampton, Gilsland has a history dating at least to Roman times; near the stony Irthing River are remains of Hadrian's Wall, and part of the old vicarage garden contains fragments of the wall. In the autumn of 1797 Sir Walter Scott, recovering from a disastrous affair with Williamina Belsches (later Lady Forbes), was in the area on holiday with his brother and a friend. Three or four days after their arrival, they were out riding and saw Charlotte Margaret Carpenter (Charpentier), the woman Scott was later to marry. At a ball that evening all three vied for an introduction, and both Capt. John Scott in his regimentals and Adam Ferguson in the uniform of the Edinburgh Volunteers were successful dance partners, but the partially lame Sir Walter escorted her to dinner. Scott courted her here, and tradition holds that he proposed at the Popping Stone, a small rock platform which juts out of the Irthing. She evidently refused his first proposal; Scott went off to the Jedburgh assizes, where his friend Robert Shortreed noted:

Scott was *sair* beside himself about Miss Carpenter;—we toasted her twenty times over—and sat together, he raving about her, until it was one in the morning.

Scott returned to Cumberland after the assizes and pursued his courtship; the couple were married in Carlisle Cathedral on Christmas Eve. In 1805 they returned to Gilsland for a few days after visiting William Wordsworth in Grasmere. Gilsland is used in *Guy Mannering* as the place explored by Vanbeest Brown (Harry Bertram): he had

a desire to view the remains of the celebrated Roman Wall, which are more visible in that direction than in any other part of its extent. . . . "And this then is the Roman Wall," he said, scrambling up to a height which commanded the course of that celebrated work of antiquity. "What a people! whose labours, even at this extremity of their empire, comprehended such space, and were executed upon a scale of such grandeur. . . ."

Hungry, he goes to

the alehouse, . . . situated in the bottom of a little dell, through which trilled a small rivulet. It was shaded by a large ash tree. . . . The outside of the house promised little for the interior. . . .

The inn, Scott's notes indicate, was

called Mumps's Hall, that is, being interpreted, Beggar's Hotel. . . . It was a hedge alehouse, where the Border farmers of either country often stopped to refresh themselves and their nags. . . . [The area was] a barren and lonely district, without either road or pathway, emphatically called the Waste of Bewcastle.

Another of Scott's works, *St. Ronan's Well*, is based on observations made at Gilsland in 1797.

GLASTONBURY, Somerset (pop. 4,325) Mid-Somerset, mostly lowland and generally known as the Plain of Sedgmoor, or the Levels, was covered with water until a network of rhines (drainage ditches) was built. Internal "islands" dot the area, although none of these is "an island in the sea, . . . inaccessible on account of bogs and inundation of lakes" and approached only by boat, as William of Malmesbury wrote. Glastonbury, on the Brue River 5 miles southwest of Wells, is near an Iron Age settlement uncovered at the end of the 19th century. Much of the history of Glastonbury cannot be verified. The Venerable Bede in his *Historia Ecclesiastica Gentis Anglorum* began part of Glastonbury's legend when he related the story of the Christianization of King Lucius in the 2d century in Glastonbury; no historical Lucius has ever been discovered. William of Malmesbury, from whom most of the early history of Glastonbury comes, repeated Bede's account of Lucius and added details of missionaries and of the establishment of the Old Church of St. Mary, possibly, he says, by the actual disciples of Christ. William was not responsible for another legend about the founding of Glastonbury, which says that Joseph of Arimathea came to England to convert the heathen and leaned on his staff here, where it took root. A thorn on Wirrall Hill, supposed to be the survivor of this event, was destroyed in the Civil War; there is what is said to be an offshoot in the abbey grounds. William of Malmesbury disbelieved these accounts and credited the founding of the community here to the Celtic saints, especially St. Patrick, in the first half of the 5th century.

Modern discoveries have enabled a rough history of the abbey to be drawn. As is now known, the site of the Chapel of St. Michael on Glastonbury Tor was the location of both a previous chapel, destroyed in 1275 by an earthquake, and a pagan shrine. With the advent of missionaries in the 5th century, the old summit shrine was sanctified and moved to the more sheltered area where the abbey was built. The first abbey, founded in A.D. 688, was basically a series of clay-and-wattle oratories, some of which survived in a rebuilt form until after the Reformation. The 7th-century monastery was richly endowed by King Ine of Wessex, and a stone church was built to become the principal church at Glastonbury (the remains of this church were discovered under the west end of the medieval nave). By the Norman Conquest in 1066, Glastonbury was an extraordinarily wealthy monastic community, and the new church was barely completed when the 1184 fire devastated the site. The medieval Benedictine monastery was begun immediately with generous crown support. The edifice was not completed until just before the dissolution of

GLASTONBURY The ruins of Glastonbury Abbey are what is left, legend says, from an establishment begun by Joseph of Arimathea. St. Patrick supposedly retired here and was elected abbot, and this is, so it is said, the Fairy Isle of Avalon, where King Arthur and Guinevere lived and were buried.

the monasteries, when the buildings were taken apart fairly thoroughly. It is amazing that as much of the abbey remains today as it does. Many of the small buildings external to the abbey church itself—the Abbot's Kitchen, the Tribunal, the Abbot's House, the Tithe Barn, and the Fish House—were left alone and are in almost perfect condition today.

Glastonbury has long been identified with the Arthurian legends. In one variation Arthur and the armies of Cornwall and Devon lay siege to the abbey after Melwas, King of Aestiva Regio (modern Somerset), carries away Guinevere and is accused of *violatam et raptam;* the abbot restores Guinevere to Arthur. In the same account nearby Glastonbury Tor becomes Chrétien de Troyes's Isle de Voirre, where life is perfect and there are no temperature extremes, no tempests, and "no noxious beasts." The most famous association comes through the identification of Glastonbury as the Fairy Isle of Avalon and through a story which, at least in part, concerns Henry II and Abbot Henry of Blois. Michael Drayton's *Poly-Olbion* is perhaps the best starting point:

> O three times famous Ile, where is that place that might
> Be with thy selfe compar'd for glorie and delight,
> Whilst *Glastenbury* stood? exalted to that pride,
> Whose Monasterie seem'd all other to deride?
> . . . .
> When not great *Arthurs* Tombe, nor holy *Josephs* Grave,
> From sacriledge had power their sacred bones to save;
> He who that God in man to his sepulchre brought
> Or he which for the faith twelve famous battels fought.

John Selden of the Inner Temple, who annotated the poem, relates the story of the discovery of King Arthur's grave in 1191 (the facts are confused, since Henry II died in 1189 and Henry of Blois in 1171):

Henry the *second* . . . heard it affirmed that in *Glastenbury* . . . *Arthur* was buried twixt two pillars, gaue commandement to *Henry of Blois* then Abbot, to make search for the corps: which was found in a wooden coffin (*Girald* saith Oken, *Leland* thinks Alder) some sixteene foote deepe; but after they had digged nine foot, they found a stone on whose lower side was fixt a leaden crosse . . . with his name inscribed, and the letter side of it turn'd to the stone. He was then honored with a sumptuous monument, and afterward the sculs of him and his wife *Guineuer* were taken out (to remaine as separat reliques and spectacles) by *Edward Longshanks* and *Elianor.*

In April 1278 the supposed bodies of King Arthur and Queen Guinevere were reinterred in a shrine in the center of the choir, where they are said to have remained until the dissolution in 1539. In 1934 the base of this shrine was discovered, and the site is now marked. Geoffrey of Monmouth notes that Arthur "was mortally wounded [in the battle with Mordred] and was carried off to the Isle of Avalon, so that his wounds might be attended to," but he does not locate Avalon. Sir Thomas Malory also writes of the isle without identification, and Alfred, Lord Tennyson in "The Passing of Arthur" follows suit:

> " . . . I am going a long way
> With these thou seest—if indeed I go—
> For all my mind is clouded with a doubt—
> To the island-valley of Avilion;
> Where falls not hail, or rain, or any snow,
> Nor ever wind blows loudly; but it lies
> Deep-meadow'd, happy, fair with orchard lawns
> And bowery hollows crown'd with summer sea,
> Where I will heal me of my grievous wound."

(Tennyson, by the way, spent part of his honeymoon here.) John Leland asserted that Arthur was a frequent visitor here but cited no source for his information.

There are two recent associations: John Masefield's *Badon Parchments* deals with the legend, and John Cowper Powys's *A Glastonbury Romance* is set in modern times. One association outside the Arthurian canon should be mentioned: Thomas Hardy makes Glastonbury into Glaston Twelve Hides, the place were Mother Lee dies in "A Trampwoman's Tragedy."

GLINTON, Northamptonshire (pop. 356) Located on the edge of fenland 3 miles southeast of Market Deeping, Glinton is a model village of neatly kept houses with roofs of thatch or Collyweston slate and a 12th- to 15th-century church near the heart of the village. John Clare attended school here for almost five years; under the mastership of a man named Seaton, young Clare learned to read and write and to understand the rudiments of mathematics. The school itself was located in the vestry of the church, and the graveyard served as the playground. Clare attended the church from his home in Helpston, a mile to the west.

GLOSSOP, Derbyshire (pop. 20,531) Near the Cheshire border 13 miles east of Manchester, Glossop has an outstanding location at the northern end of the area leading to Kinder Scout, 2,088 feet in height, and to parklands of waterfalls, heath, moor, and gorges. Hilaire Belloc, who stopped here during a lecture tour of the north of England and Scotland, disliked it intensely:

Do you know the filthy village of Glossop? It is inhabited entirely by savages. I tried every inn in the place and found each inn worse than the last. It stinks for miles. Rather than sleep in such a den I started walking back to Manchester with a huge bag.

GLOUCESTER, Gloucestershire (pop. 90,134) Histories of Gloucester (pronounced "glos'ter"), situated on the east bank of the Severn River 37 miles north-northeast of Bristol, usually start with the Roman settlement of Glevum. However, there were prior settlements here. Geoffrey of Monmouth explains the founding of "Kaerglou" in his *Historia Regum Britanniae*. Genvissa, Claudius's daughter and an extremely beautiful girl, was married to Arvirargus, who

> made up his mind to give some special mark of distinction to the place where he had married her. He suggested to Claudius that the two of them should found there a city which should perpetuate in times to come the memory of so happy a marriage. Claudius agreed and ordered a town to be built which should be called Kaerglou or Gloucester. Down to our own day it retains its site on the bank of the Severn, between Wales and Loegria. Some, however, say that it took its name from Duke Gloius, whom Claudius fathered in that city. . . .

The facts are somewhat different. Caer Glow, which became the Roman Glevum, was the site of a court held by Aulus Plautius. For some time Glevum was the headquarters of the Augustan Legion (Second Legion), and ultimately the 50-acre site became one of four *colonia* (areas of land grants for demobilized troops), along with Colchester, York, and Lincoln.

The Saxons lived here immediately after the Roman withdrawal, and Gloucester achieved prominence as the capital of the kingdom of Mercia. The Normans refashioned the 7th-century monastery and began the great cathedral in 1089. Dedicated in 1100, the cruciform cathedral is 425 feet long and is battlemented; the tower, which many feel is its outstanding architectural feature, was not begun until the mid-15th century. A fire in 1122 destroyed much of the Norman church, and fire marks can be seen on some of the round pillars in the nave.

Gloucester came into its own following the refusal of the abbots at Bristol and Malmesbury to accept the remains of Edward II, murdered on September 21, 1327, at Berkeley Castle. In December the abbot here demanded the body so that the King could be afforded a proper Christian burial. Edward's tomb, in the north aisle of the choir, is a masterpiece of medieval art. Crowned, he lies in his robes with angels supporting his head. The cathedral and this monument quickly became a shrine to the martyred King, and the thousands of pilgrims who came to pray at the shrine made money offerings sufficient to enable later abbots to carry on an extensive rebuilding program.

The early travel writers had a great deal to say about the town, its location, and the cathedral. John Leland, Henry VIII's antiquarian and librarian, left one of the earliest descriptions of the town:

> The towne of Gloucestar is auncient, well buildyd of tymbar, and large, and strongly defendyd with waulls, wher it is not fortified with a depe streame of Severne watar. In the waull be 4. gates by este, west, northe and southe, and soe bere the names, but that the est-gate is commonly caullyd Aillesgate. . . .

> The beautie of the towne lyeth in too crossing stretes, as the gates of the towne ly; and at the place of the midle metynge, or quaterfors of these stretes, is aquaduklyd incastellid.

Michael Drayton includes Roman vineyards in *Poly-Olbion* but notes:

> . . . now th' All-cheering Sun the colder soyle deceaves,
> *ff* And us (heere tow'rds the Pole) still falling Southward leaves:
> So that the sullen earth th' effect thereof doth prove;
> According to their Books, who hold that he doth move
> From his first Zeniths poynt; the cause we feele his want.
> But of her Vines depriv'd, now *Gloster* learens to plant
> The Peare-tree every where: whose fruit shee straines for juce.

Daniel Defoe mentions neither grapes nor pears in *A Tour thro' the Whole Island of Great Britain* and calls Gloucester "an antient middling City, tolerably built, but not fine"; he adds that "the Cathedral is all I see worth Recording of this Place":

> The Cathedral is an old venerable Pile, with very little Ornament within or without, yet 'tis well built; and tho' plain, it makes together, especially the Tower, a very handsome Appearance. . . .
> The Whispering Place in this Cathedral, has for many Years pass'd for a kind of Wonder; but since, experience has taught us the easily comprehended Reason of the Thing: And since there is now the like in the Church of St. *Pauls*, the Wonder is much abated.

About a century later William Cobbett stopped off in Gloucester on one of many visits, but he was unable to get along with either the town or its inhabitants. Railing at an event in the town and at the inhabitants for allowing it, he writes in *Rural Rides*:

> [W]hen I came to Gloucester, I found that I should run a risk of having no bed if I did not bow very low and pay very high; for what should there be here, but one of those scandalous and beastly fruits of the system, called a "music-meeting!" Those who founded the cathedrals never dreamed, I dare say, that they would have been put to such uses as this! They are, upon these occasions, made use of as *Opera-Houses;* and, I am told, that the money which is collected goes, in some shape or another, to the clergy of the church, or their widows, or children, or something. . . . From this scene of prostitution and of pocket-picking I moved off with all convenient speed, but not before the ostler made me pay 9*d.* for merely letting my horse stand about ten minutes. . . .

Gloucester has only a few literary associations, but it does have two native sons. John Taylor, known as the water poet, was born here of humble parents on August 24, 1580; little is known of his early life except that he was educated at the local grammar school for a time. He subsequently left for London, where he apprenticed himself to a waterman. The second native son, William Ernest Henley, was born on August 23, 1849, at 1 Eastgate Street to a struggling bookseller and his wife, who was a descendant of Joseph Warton. The Henleys moved all around Gloucester, and an early visitor to one of their homes was William Makepeace Thackeray. Henley attended the Crypt Grammar School in 1861 when the headmaster was Thomas Edward Brown, the poet. Even though Brown disliked Gloucester and teaching, he made a favorable and lasting impression on Henley, who later commented that Brown's presence was "a call from the world outside, the great, quick, living world. . . . What he did for me, practically, was to suggest such possibilities in life and character as I had never dreamed." Henley's schooling was often interrupted, partly because of his father's precarious finances but mainly because of his own physical state. By 1861 he was suffering from tuberculosis of the bone, which jeopardized his life, and from this date one foot was always tightly bound while the second was swollen and bandaged. In 1865 one leg was amputated below the knee, and when he was later told that to save his life he would have to lose the second leg, he went to Edinburgh and placed himself in the care of Prof. Joseph Lister (later Lord Lister). His leg was saved. Henley left Gloucester for London shortly after his father died in 1867.

In the 17th century William Davenant, often called William Shakespeare's natural son, was knighted here (1643) for his part in securing French arms for the Royalist forces, and a 19th-century visitor to Gloucester was Elizabeth Barrett (Browning), who lived here from July 1821 to the spring or summer of 1822; not much is known of her stay except that she became seriously ill and was taken to the Spa Hotel for medical treatment. Hilaire Belloc lectured at Gloucester on World War I and stayed at the New Inn (early 15th century), an establishment on Northgate Street built to accommodate visitors to Edward's shrine.

One of the most delightful of Beatrix Potter's children's stories, *The Tailor of Gloucester*, is set here, and, indeed, the model for the tailor's house and shop is on College Street.

GODALMING, Surrey (pop. 18,643)   The twin town of Guildford, 4 miles to the north, Godalming (pronounced "god'alming") shares the same heritage and the same river, the Wey; like Guildford this town was bequeathed to Ethelwald by his uncle, Alfred the Great. Since the town occupies the bed of the river valley, it is so hemmed in by the hills that expansion is inhibited and access is difficult. Godalming's medieval importance can be described in one word: wool. Around the 12th century large numbers of Flemish weavers and dyers settled in this area, and the industry prospered greatly. By the 16th century emphasis was on kerseys and blue kerseys. The town was able to keep the wool trade going long after Farnham and Guildford lost theirs, mostly because, as John Aubrey said, "their colours are not equalled by any in England." The industrial revolution brought the introduction of a knitting framework to the town, and the wool industry survives to the present.

Many older buildings have survived here, among them the White Hart Inn, opposite the town hall (itself known as either the Pepper Pot or the Pill Box), a lovely half-timbered Tudor building; the 17th-century red-brick King's Arms Inn, near the bridge; and a number on Church Street and the High Street.

Probably the most famous local person is the 18th-century Mary Tofts, "the rabbit woman." She had been weeding a field when she was startled by a rabbit; she then discovered an unaccountable passion for rabbits and promptly was delivered of eighteen of her own, according to her local doctor and George I's official physician. Needless to say, no fe-

male in Godalming would thereafter eat a rabbit for fear of following Mary Tofts's course. After a German physician announced his skepticism and she was imprisoned a few weeks, she confessed that it was all a hoax. The episode inspired William Hogarth's *Cunicularii, or The Wise Men of Godlyman* and *Credulity, Superstition and Fanaticism.*

An important literary association is with Aldous Huxley, who was born here on July 26, 1894, the youngest of three sons of Leonard and Julia Arnold Huxley. With his brothers Julian (the biologist) and Trev (who committed suicide in 1914), he spent his childhood here, where his father was a master at Charterhouse. Overcoming near blindness, Aldous was sent at the age of nine to nearby Hillside School, a preparatory school and probably the source of Bulstrode in *Eyeless in Gaza:*

> "To-morrow," Anthony was thinking, "there'll be algebra with old Jimbug." The prospect was disagreeable; he wasn't good at maths, and, even at the best of times, even when he was only joking, Mr. Jameson was a formidable teacher. "If Jimbug gets baity with me, like that time last week. . . ." Remembering the scene, Anthony frowned; the blood came up to his cheeks. Jimbug made sarcastic remarks at him and pulled his hair. He had begun to blub. (Who wouldn't have blubbed?) A tear had fallen on to the equation he was trying to work out and made a huge round blot.

Family holidays were spent in the Lake District and in Switzerland, and in 1908 Huxley was sent to Eton.

Charles Dickens also knew this area well and used it in *Nicholas Nickleby;* on their way to Portsmouth, Nicholas and Smike pass through Godalming, where "they bargained for two humble beds" before continuing their journey, "a harder day's journey than yesterday's, for there were long and weary hills to climb. . . ."

Finally, in 1872 the Charterhouse School was moved out of London to a location 1 mile north of Godalming. It has a number of literary mementos in its museum from its former days including the manuscript of William Makepeace Thackeray's *The Newcomes* and items concerning Joseph Addison and Richard Steele.

GODMANSTONE, Dorset (pop. 111)   On the Cerne River 2½ miles south of Cerne Abbas, the tiny village of Godmanstone has one claim to fame: the thatched Smith's Arms is probably the smallest pub in England. The church here, which dates partly from the 12th century, may have been attended by Matthew Prior from time to time. The story that Prior frequently visited his grandfather here is apocryphal; Prior's grandfather died many years before the poet's birth. His grandmother, though, was still alive, and Prior may well have visited her. She is probably the "Widdow Pryor" who was buried in 1674 according to the church register. Prior's "The Old Gentry" exhibits his knowledge of the agricultural life of the area.

GODMERSHAM, Kent (pop. 233)   Set in the floor of the Stour Valley 6 miles northeast of Ashford, the village of Godmersham is little more than a Georgian brick mansion and the grounds of Godmersham Park. The area, which is full of water meadows and gigantic oak trees, was a pleasant setting for Jane

Austen. Her brother Edward Knight, his name changed as a condition of his inheriting the estate from a relative, took possession of the park in 1797, and Miss Austen was here frequently between 1798 and 1809; her last-known visit occurred in 1813. Even though *Mansfield Park* is set specifically in Northamptonshire, much of the story was drawn from the house in Godmersham, where "the grandeur of the house astonished" her and "the rooms were too large for her to move in with ease." With her brother's family she attended services at the parish church just outside the brick walls of the park. The church is noted for its naïve medieval relief of a mitered bishop, undoubtedly Thomas à Becket, the earliest-known image of the saint.

GODSTOW, Oxfordshire   A 3-mile walk to the northwest of Oxford is Godstow, the site of a 12th-century nunnery of which only scant ruins survived the Civil War. Godstow is a romantic place, for the village is associated with Fair Rosamond, Rosamond Clifford, the daughter of Walter de Clifford and the acknowledged mistress of Henry II. The convent was richly endowed by Henry, and here he is supposed to have met the daughter of the great house of Clifford. The legend which has grown up around the King and his mistress first emerged from the chronicler John Stow, who told the stories of the possibility of the poisoning of Rosamond by Queen Eleanor and of the silk thread. He writes:

[She] dyed at Woodstocke where King Henry had made for her a house of wonderful working, so that no man or woman might come to her but he that was instructed by the King. . . . [B]ut when she was dead, she was buried at Godstow in an house of nunnes, beside Oxford, with these verses upon her tombe:

Hic jacet in tumba Rosa mundi, non rosa munda:
Non redolet, sed olet, quae redolere solet.

The pun on Rosamond's name was first mentioned by Giraldus Cambrensis. In 1191, a few years after Rosamond's death here in 1176, the grave was the richest monument in the church, complete with silken hangings, lamps, and candles; it had obviously been made into a place of personal pilgrimage (Henry was still alive). Bishop Hugh of Lincoln ordered the removal of the monument from the church to the chapel; church, chapel, and convent are now gone; only the boundary walls, a 15th-century doorway, and the shell of the chapel remain.

Thomas Deloney is one of the first to have used the story in a ballad, published in 1607. Found by Queen Eleanor, Rosamond pleads for her life:

But nothing could this furious Queene therewith appeased be:
The cup of deadly poyson fil'd, as she sat on her knee.

She gaue this comely Dame to drinke, who tooke it from her hand:
And from her bended knee arose, and on her feet did stand;
And casting vp her eyes to Heauen, she did for mercy call:
And drinking vp the poyson then, her life she lost with all.

And when that death through euery limbe, had done his greatest spight:

Her chiefest foes did plaine confesse she was a glorious wight.
Her body then they did intomb, when life was fled away:
At Godstow, neere to Oxford Towne as may be seene this day

Some years later Michael Drayton composed "The Complaint of Rosamund"; he also included "The Epistle of Rosamond to King Henry the Second" and "Henry to Rosamond" in *Englands Heroicall Epistles*. Another 16th-century version, Samuel Daniel's *The Complaint of Rosamond*, is related by Rosamond's ghost, and the erotic narrative has a moral emphasis which was echoed by later writers. Rosamond's ghost tells how the "wronged Queene . . ./ forc'd me to take the poyson she had brought" and concludes;

Then were my funerals not long deferred,
But doone with all the rites pompe could deuise:
At *Godstow,* where my body was interred,
And richly tomb'd in honorable wise.
Where yet as now scarce any note descries
    Vnto these times, the memory of me,
    Marble and Brasse so little lasting be.

Raphael Holinshed recounted the story in his *Chronicles,* and in the 18th century Joseph Addison used the story in an opera simply entitled *Rosamond.*

In early March 1879 Gerard Manley Hopkins took a few hours off from his studies at Oxford to come to Godstow, where he discovered that on both sides of the Cherwell the aspens had been cut down:

My aspens dear, whose airy cages quelled,
Quelled or quenched in leaves the leaping sun,
All felled, felled, are all felled. . . .

Godstow was the destination of the rowing party consisting of the Rev. Robinson Duckworth, Lorraine, Alice, and Edith Liddell, and Lewis Carroll (Charles Lutwidge Dodgson) on Friday, July 4, 1862; it was on this excursion that *Alice's Adventures in*

GODSTOW   A lovely Thames-side village, Godstow, writes Lewis Carroll, was where "We had tea on the bank there and did not reach Christ Church again till quarter past eight," He later added the note, "On which occasion I told them the fairy-tale of Alice's adventures underground."

Wonderland was first told to the girls. Later Carroll wrote:

> I distinctly remember, now as I write, how, in a desperate attempt to strike out some new line of fairy-lore, I had sent my heroine straight down a rabbit-hole, to begin with, without the least idea what was to happen afterwards. And so, to please a child I loved (I don't remember any other motive), I printed in manuscript, and illustrated with my own crude designs—designs that rebelled against every law of Anatomy or Art (for I had never had a lesson in drawing)—the book which I have just had published in facsimile.

GOLDERS GREEN, Middlesex With no pretension toward suburbia, Golders Green is less than 2 miles from Hampstead and part of the Greater Metropolitan London borough of Hendon; it is a bustling urban community with only a very few vestiges of its early rural environment. Golders Hill House was the home of Jeremiah ("Mungo") Dyson, the very generous friend of Mark Akenside, the physician and poet born in Newcastle upon Tyne; indeed, Akenside was often here, sometimes in residence, and once, "recovering from a fit of sickness," he wrote:

> Thy verdant scenes, O Goulder's hill,
>   Once more I seek, a languid guest:
> With throbbing temples and with burden'd breast
> Once more I climb thy steep aerial way.
> O faithful cure of oft-returning ill,
>   Now call thy sprightly breezes round,
>   Dissolve this rigid cough profound,
> And bid the springs of life with gentler movement play. . . .

He recovered, as the "ode" continues, "Goulder's hill, by thee restored. . . ." It was Dyson's generosity that made the physician and destroyed the poet. Dyson allowed Akenside £300 a year, a house, and a chariot so that he could live like a gentleman until his medicine could support him properly. Many years after Akenside had been here, William Wordsworth wrote:

> I am not infrequently a visitor on Hampstead Heath, and seldom pass the entrance of Mr. Dyson's Villa on Golder's Hill, without thinking of the pleasures which Akenside often had there.

Later residents of Golders Green were Alec and Evelyn Waugh, whose family built the house at 145 North End Road when the postal address was Hampstead. Soon afterward the Post Office changed its designation; Evelyn Waugh writes:

> My father deplored the change, and, as far as was possible, ignored it, because Hampstead had historic associations, with Keats and Blake and Constable, while Golders Green meant, to him, merely a tube station. I, at that self-conscious age, minded more, for I knew, as he did not, that the district had somehow acquired a slightly comic connotation. . . .

The nucleus of the village, he says,

> comprised an old bow-fronted inn, the Bull and Bush, famous in Cockney song, standing back from the road in a beer-garden in which the tables stood in bowers of creeper and climbing rose; a building called "the Rooms" which served as an infant school, a village hall and on Sundays as a place of worship; a post office and village shop kept by an irascible man named Mr Borely. He was surly with all his customers and positively savage with children until he got into some trouble with the postal

authorities. . . . There was also a dairy named Tooley's. . . . Round these institutions clustered the cottages, their gardens full of flowers and washing and gossip. . . . Of all this no trace survives except in the name of the Bull and Bush, now quite rebuilt with an asphalt car park covering its lawns and arbours.

Alec Waugh's reaction was not the same, as *The Early Years of Alec Waugh* illustrates:

> It all looks very different there today. In the spring of that year North End was a village, Golders Green did not exist and buses stopped at Child's Hill, but in July the Hampstead and Highgate tube was opened and very soon villas were running out to Hendon and shops were clustering at the crossroads. . . .
>
> No one passing Underhill today would be able to guess at the kind of family life that we enjoyed there. A subsequent owner has installed a petrol station in the garden; there is a perpetual roar of traffic; there is no sense of privacy. It was a very different place in 1910 with its lawns and greenhouses and rose-beds behind the shelter of high hedges.

GOLDINGTON, Bedfordshire (pop. 1,097) Now part of a rapidly growing Bedford, Goldington has not been fortunate enough to preserve reminders of unique days. Just west of the old village was Newnham Priory, of which there is no visible evidence; Warden Abbey is now covered over with a housing estate. The village center, though, still has its green, and nearby is the 17th-century hall, now a hotel. The hall was the 19th-century home of William Kenworthy Browne, a close friend of Edward FitzGerald. FitzGerald was especially fond of staying here "in the land of old Bunyan," where there were "such poplars as only the Ouse knows how to rear."

GOODNESTONE, Kent (pop. 438) Sometimes called Goodnestone-by-Adisham to distinguish it from a second village in Kent of the same name, this village, whose name is pronounced "goonston," is 5 miles southwest of Sandwich. Here are a lovely 13th-century church, Dutch-style houses with curved and molded end gables, and Goodnestone Park, once the home of Sir Brook Bridges. This is a village Jane Austen knew well, for she was often here at Rowling House, 1 mile to the east, after the marriage of her brother Edward to Sir Brook's daughter in 1791; from here she wrote of village social life (the dances at the park) and on one occasion, "in great distress" when leaving, bemoaned her inability to decide whether to give a servant half a guinea or a crown. She attended services at the parish church on her visits.

Montague Rhodes James, the writer of ghost stories, was born here at the old rectory in 1862; he was baptized in the parish church and received his first education in the village.

GOODRICH, Herefordshire (pop. 441) Tucked under the shadow of a semicircle of mountains 4 miles southwest of Ross, Goodrich lies in one of the most picturesque stretches of the Wye River Valley; on a wooded hill overlooking the valley are the moated remains of the 12th- to 14th-century Goodrich Castle, built as part of the defense system against Welsh raiders. Goodrich Court, pulled down in 1950, was a sham Gothic castle whose wood paneling was rescued and placed in the church. The living of Goodrich church was held by the Royalist grandfather of

Jonathan Swift, the Rev. Thomas Swift, whose 1636 house is now a farm. Dean Swift came here in April or May 1727 and presented the church with a chalice which had belonged to his grandfather and arranged for a commemorative tablet to him. This area is renowned for its cider apples (Herefordshire makes 60 percent of the cider consumed in Great Britain), and Swift ordered some of the local cider for friends in London and for himself in Ireland.

In 1793, on a tour of the West Country, William Wordsworth came here from Bristol and visited the castle, where he met the little girl who became the heroine of "We Are Seven":

> "Sisters and brothers, little Maid,
> How many may you be?"
> "How many? Seven in all," she said,
> And wondering looked at me.
>
> "And where are they? I pray you tell."
> She answered, "Seven are we;
> And two of us at Conway dwell,
> And two are gone to sea.
>
> "Two of us in the church-yard lie,
> My sister and my brother;
> And, in the church-yard cottage, I
> Dwell near them with my mother."

Wordsworth returned some fifty years later and could find neither her nor anyone else who interested him.

GORING-BY-SEA, Sussex (pop. 653) Generally called Goring, this village is 1 mile west of Worthing in a secure position near Highdown Hill, which has the prototype of all chalk gardens; the plants seem to grow directly from a chalk-and-flint rubble bed without the use of an earth foundation. The village is proud of its Norman church and of Goring Castle (built in 1790 by Sir Bysshe Shelley, the poet's grandfather), but it would prefer to forget John Taylor's doggerel narrative "A New Discovery by Sea with a Wherry from London to Salisbury," which recounts a night in Goring with fleas,

> Who in their fury nip'd and skip'd so hotly,
> That all our skins were almost turned to motley.

The poet and naturalist Richard Jefferies spent the last nine months of his life at Sea View (now known as Jefferies House) and died here on August 14, 1887. He was buried in the cemetery at Broadwater, 2 miles to the northeast.

GORLESTON-ON-SEA, Norfolk (pop. 20,391) A triangular area bounded by Norwich on the west, Sea Palling on the north, and Lowestoft on the south defines the district known as the Norfolk Broads, an expanse of water with large navigable approach channels, all linked together to afford almost 200 miles of inland sailing and boating. Gorleston is part of this network and overlooks the Yare River and the sea in a prominent position at the mouth of Yarmouth Harbor. Edward FitzGerald, whose marriage to Lucy Barton, daughter of Bernard Barton, the "Quaker poet," was extremely unsatisfactory, followed his wife here in 1847 after marital problems in London. They lived here for almost nine months, during which time they were visited by George Borrow, who was living in nearby Oulton Broad. The separation of the FitzGeralds effected here was permanent.

GOSFORTH, Cumberland Seven miles southeast of Egremont in the foothills of the west Cumberland fells, Gosforth contains one of the country's greatest treasures, the ancient Gosforth Cross, more than 14 feet high; its importance lies in its probable date and its carving; the cross is thought to date from the early Scandinavian settlement here in the 9th or 10th century. The crosshead of the tapering shaft is unique: it is carved with the triquetra, an emblem of the Trinity, and not a cross. The carving on the shaft is of great interest; the round part is thought to represent Yggdrasill, the Scandinavian world-supportive sacred ash tree; the square part is thought to depict the *Völuspa*. One of the sides of the cross shows a stag, a wolf, and a horseman (probably Odin); another shows an upside-down horseman and dragons attacking the gods (probably the last great battle) and two figures (probably Loki and his wife, who is catching drops of poison meant to kill Loki); on the third side are two embattled horsemen and a dragon.

When Hugh Walpole's family lived in Durham, he spent a number of school holidays here at Sower Myre Farm, owned by a family named Armstrong. Walpole later described the farm in "The Lake District," published in *English Country*. He did a lot of climbing, including ascents of Scafell Pike and Great Gable, and a good deal of walking, particularly over Sty Head into Borrowdale and on to Keswick, when he explored the Wast Water and Derwent Water areas; of Lodore Falls, he said that they were not much but that "in the winter they must be lovely."

GRANTCHESTER, Cambridgeshire (pop. 489) A tranquil village replete with thatch and timber-and-plaster buildings, Grantchester has been adopted by Cambridge undergraduates and tutors so that it is now almost part of the university town, 2½ miles to the northeast. There are remains of an old Roman camp, and the partly Saxon and Norman church has a beautiful 14th-century chancel, some medieval glass, and a carved medieval tomb. Facing the church was a riverside cottage known as the Orchard, the house where Rupert Brooke first had rooms in Grantchester; the building now houses tearooms. His sitting room in front looked toward the church, and his bedroom was immediately above it. The owner of the house, a Mrs. Stevenson, let him use the river garden, and Brooke's full room and board came to 30 shillings a week. Shortly after moving here in June 1909, he received his Tripos results, a second, and immediately began work on an essay concerning John Webster for the Shakespeare scholarship. Brooke described the place as "golden and melancholy and sleepy and enchanted. I sit neck-deep in dead red leaves." Among his frequent guests were James Elroy Flecker, then a student at Gonville and Caius College, Jacques Raverat, and Gwen Darwin (later Raverat), the author of the delightful *Period Piece*.

By Christmas, 1909, Brooke leased half of the Old Vicarage, a ramshackle red-brick house with three stories, dormer windows, and an attic; Brooke had three rooms, and his bedroom had once been the

GRANTCHESTER   Beloved by Cambridge undergraduates and tutors as well as by literary pilgrims, Grantchester is on a cutting of the Granta, as the Cam River is called south of Cambridge. Literary associations here include Geoffrey Chaucer, Lord Byron, and Rupert Brooke.

nursery. The living room, below the bedroom, had a glass door with yellow panes of Art Nouveau design, which the poet claimed was like sunshine on a wet day. At the back of the house was a large overgrown garden, marked off by ancient chestnut trees, leading down to the riverbank. D. H. Lawrence, in one of his letters, notes that Brooke, dressed in pajamas, would read poetry "at Grantchester upon the lawns where the river goes." "The Old Vicarage, Grantchester," written in May 1912 at the Café des Westens in Berlin, where Brooke was recuperating from a breakdown ("Here am I, sweating, sick, and hot"), immortalizes the vicarage and the village:

But Grantchester! ah, Grantchester!
There's peace and holy quiet there,
Great clouds along pacific skies,
And men and women with straight eyes,
Lithe children lovelier than a dream,
A bosky wood, a slumbrous stream,
And little kindly winds that creep
Round twilight corners, half asleep.

He continues:

Say, do the elm-clumps greatly stand
Still guardians of that holy land?
The chestnuts shade, in reverend dream,
The yet unacademic stream?
Is dawn a secret shy and cold
Anadyomene, silver-gold?
And sunset still a golden sea
From Haslingfield to Madingley?
And after, ere the night is born,
Do hares come out about the corn?
Oh, is the water sweet and cool,
Gentle and brown, above the pool?

The pool is Byron's Pool, just outside the village on the Trumpington Road; named for the poet, it has been a famous swimming hole for centuries and

holds associations with numerous writers besides Brooke. Geoffrey Chaucer, John Dryden, Edmund Spenser, John Milton, and Lord Byron are all said to have sat by the muddy cut or to have swum in it, though the pool itself is far less attractive than the paths leading to it. Brooke refers again to the pool in this poem:

In Grantchester, in Grantchester. . . .
Still in the dawnlit waters cool
His ghostly Lordship swims his pool,
And tries the strokes, essays the tricks,
Long learnt on Hellespont, or Styx.
Dan Chaucer hears his river still
Chatter beneath a phantom mill.
Tennyson notes, with studious eye,
How Cambridge waters hurry by . . .

Brooke often swam here, and on one occasion at least, in August 1911, when she was staying at the vicarage with the Neeveses, so did Virginia Stephen (Woolf).

After an extensive tour of the United States, Canada, Hawaii, Samoa, Fiji, New Zealand, and Tahiti, Brooke had almost no time back here before going into active war service in 1914; he died of acute blood poisoning following a sunstroke on April 23, 1915, on the island of Scyros. One of his last poems reflects on England, and no doubt Grantchester, and speaks for all who died in World War I:

If I should die, think only this of me:
That there's some corner of a foreign field
That is for ever England. There shall be
In that rich earth a richer dust concealed;
A dust whom England bore, shaped, made aware,
Gave, once, her flowers to love, her ways to roam,
A body of England's, breathing English air,
Washed by the rivers, blest by suns of home.

GRANTHAM, Lincolnshire (pop. 26,030) At the southern edge of the narrow limestone edge known as the Lincoln Edge 25 miles south of Lincoln, Grantham, an ancient town built astride the Great North Road, once had a castle and may even have been walled. The antiquity of this modern industrial town is hard to capture, but some feeling of earlier times exists near the church; otherwise there is not even a hint of John Evelyn's description of "a pretty Towne,"

situated on the side of a botome; which is large, & at distance inviron'd with ascending grounds, that for pleasure I think it comparable to most [inland] places of *England*: famous is the Steeple for the exceeding height of the Shaft, which is of stone. . . .

The town was a royal manor at the time of the Domesday Survey (1086), and royalty has had a great deal to do with Grantham. King John once held court at the Angel Inn; this was the final stop when Queen Eleanor's body was being transported from Harby, Nottinghamshire, to London in 1290; and Edward IV endowed the grammar school and incorporated the town in the second year of his reign.

St. Wulfram's Church, located on the site of a 7th-century Saxon church and a later Norman church, is the pride of Grantham: its 281-foot spire is a landmark for miles around. An interesting aspect of the church is the priest's residence over the south porch; a spiral staircase leads to the room with its fireplace and recessed sink. The room now contains a chained library; eighty-three of the original volumes are still fastened with their chains.

Near the church is King's School, the old grammar school, built by Richard Fox, bishop and statesman; the building is still in use as a hall and chapel even though the school itself has newer quarters in the area. Isaac Newton attended the school from 1654 to 1658, and a few years later the young Colley Cibber entered King's. He remained until 1687 and later commented in *An Apology for the Life of Colley Cibber, Comedian:*

> And such learning as that school could give me, is the most I pretend to (which though I have not utterly forgot, I cannot say I have much improv'd by study), but even there I remember I was the same inconsistent creature I have been ever since! always in full spirits, in some small capacity to do right, but in a more frequent alacrity to do wrong; and consequently often under a worse character than I wholly deserv'd. A giddy negligence always possess'd me, and so much, that I remember I was once whipp'd for my *theme,* tho' my master told me, at the same time, what was good of it was better than any boy's in the form.

Another pupil here, William Cecil, was destined to political fame as Elizabeth I's Lord Treasurer, Lord Burghley.

Daniel Defoe visited Grantham while gathering material for *A Tour thro' the Whole Island of Great Britain:*

> From hence we came to *Grantham,* famous for a very fine Church and a Spire Steeple, so finely built, and so very high, that I do not know many higher and finer built in *Britain....*
> This is a neat, pleasant, well-built and populous Town, has a good Market, and the Inhabitants are said to have a very good Trade, and are generally rich. There is also a very good Free-School here.

Another passing visitor to the town was the poet John Clare, who stayed at the Crown and Anchor after running away from Burghley House, 21 miles south. Finding no work here, he went on to Newark-upon-Trent, Nottinghamshire. A far later visitor not only stayed in Grantham but used it in one of his works. With Phiz (Hablot Knight Browne), Charles Dickens stopped at the George on January 30, 1838, on their way north to look at Yorkshire schools. He said the George was "the very best inn I have ever put up at" and later appears to have intended this to be the George Inn of *Nicholas Nickleby:*

> Twenty miles further on, two of the front outside passengers wisely availing themselves of their arrival at one of the best inns in England, turned in, for the night, at the George at Grantham.

The George and New Inn at Greta Bridge is often confused with the George here in Grantham.

GRAPPENHALL, Cheshire (pop. 1,945) Situated on the Bridgewater Canal, Grappenhall is just off the main road 2½ miles southeast of Warrington. The cottages are still thatched, and the church, remodeled in 1539, contains an old carved chest and some old glass. The curiosity of the church is above the west window of the tower; here is the figure of a grinning cat, quite possibly the original of the Cheshire Cat, for Charles Lutwidge Dodgson (Lewis Carroll) lived a few miles away in Daresbury until the age of eleven.

GRASBY, Lincolnshire (pop. 338) Situated on the western edge of the Lincolnshire Wolds, an area of rolling hills, deep valleys, and small streams, the village of Grasby, 3 miles northwest of Caistor, commands an extensive view of the patchwork of woods, fields, and farms of the area. The 13th-century church, the village school, and the old rectory were all rebuilt in the 19th century. Grasby is closely linked with Alfred, Lord Tennyson, whose brother Charles took the living here in 1835. Charles Tennyson Turner (he took his great-uncle's surname when he succeeded to the Turner estate) brought his young wife here in 1837. She was the sister of Emily Sellwood, who 13 years later became the wife of Alfred Tennyson. Tennyson frequently visited his brother at the vicarage, and, indeed, Tennyson's family often spent part of the summer in Grasby. Tennyson presented the church with its lovely east window, and when Charles Tennyson Turner and his wife died in 1879, Lord Tennyson set up a white marble memorial tablet which reads, in part:

> True poet, surely to be found
> When Truth is found again.

These lines are from "Midnight, June 30, 1879," the prefatory poem to the *Collected Sonnets* (1880) of Charles Tennyson Turner; it is a lament of his brother's death.

GRASMERE, Westmorland (pop. 1,173) Central Westmorland contains almost every feature of mountain scenery known to man, and it is probably the most satisfying section for the visitor. The landscape has been virtually unchanged by human habitation, and Grasmere is beautifully central, being 3½ miles northwest of Ambleside on its own lake with the Langdale Pikes and Helvellyn in sight. Grasmere is intimately associated with the Lake poets, especially William Wordsworth, almost to the detriment of its fantastic surroundings.

Wordsworth and his sister Dorothy arrived in Grasmere on December 20, 1799, to settle at Dove Cottage (originally an inn called the Dove and Olive Branch, or the Dove and Olive Bough, as Wordsworth called it), in the area of the village known as Town End. Dove Cottage, whose name is of fairly recent date and not Wordsworth's, is at the foot of the hill where the old Ambleside road drops to the lakeshore; the Wordsworth Museum here was once a barn. After his marriage in 1802 to Mary Hutchinson in Brompton, Yorkshire, the couple settled here, where three of their children were born (John, 1803; Dora, 1804; and Thomas, 1806). The house is best described in Thomas De Quincey's *Recollections of the Lakes and the Lake Poets;* he first saw the "white cottage with two yew trees breaking the glare of its white walls" in the summer of 1807:

> A little semi-vestibule between two doors prefaced the entrance into what might be considered the principal room of the cottage. It was an oblong square, not above eight and a half feet high, sixteen feet long, and twelve broad; very prettily wainscoted from the floor to the ceiling with dark polished oak, slightly embellished with carving. One window there was—a perfect and unpretending cottage window, with little diamond panes, embowered, at almost every season of the year, with roses; and, in the summer and autumn, with a profusion of jessamine and other fragrant shrubs.

GRASMERE

      . . . for thus I live remote
From evil-speaking; rancour, never sought,
Comes to me not; malignant truth, or lie.
Hence have I genial seasons, hence have I
Smooth passions, smooth discourse, and joyous thought:
And thus from day to day my little boat
Rocks in its harbour, lodging peaceably.
      William Wordsworth, "Personal Talk"

Much of Wordsworth's best work was written or begun at Dove Cottage, and from here he set out on his walks over the fells and to the lakes. "A Farewell" was written just before his departure for Gallow Hill, Yorkshire, in 1802:

> FAREWELL, thou little Nook of mountain-ground,
> Thou rocky corner in the lowest stair
> Of that magnificent temple which doth bound
> One side of our whole vale with grandeur rare;
> Sweet garden-orchard, eminently fair,
> The loveliest spot that man hath ever found,
> Farewell!—we leave thee to Heaven's peaceful care,
> Thee, and the Cottage which thou dost surround.

The four sonnets entitled "Personal Talk," written in the house, describe the cottage and its atmosphere. Wordsworth was quite interested in his garden and orchard, which rose steeply from the rear of the house, and while the last stanza of "A Farewell" deals especially with these, "The Green Linnet" is perhaps a better description of his land:

> Beneath these fruit-tree boughs that shed
> Their snow-white blossoms on my head,
> With brightest sunshine round me spread
>   Of spring's unclouded weather
> In this sequestered nook how sweet
> To sit upon my orchard-seat!
> And birds and flowers once more to greet,
>   My last year's friends together.

Other poems specifically associated with the orchard and garden include "To a Butterfly," "The Redbreast Chasing a Butterfly," and "The Kitten and the Falling Leaves."

Many other Wordsworth poems deal with tales, legends, or events in the Grasmere area. Part of "The Recluse" tells of the extremely severe 1800 winter and the March mildness thereafter; "The Brothers" re-lates a story told by an Ennerdale shepherd; and "Rural Architecture" describes "three rosy-cheeked school-boys" who

> To the top of GREAT HOW did it please them to climb:
> And there they built up, without mortar or lime,
> A Man on the peak of the crag.

> They built him of stones gathered up as they lay:
> They built him and christened him all in one day,
> An urchin both vigorous and hale;
> And so without scruple they called him Ralph Jones.
> Now Ralph is renowned for the length of his bones;
> The Magog of Legberthwaite dale.

Both "The Oak and the Broom" and "The Waterfall and the Eglantine" are drawn from Wordsworth's walks on the mountain path by Nab Scar. "The Waggoner" was suggested by an employee of the owner of Greta Hall; Benjamin, the name of the hero as well as the original name of the poem, was factually accurate, Wordsworth maintained. The young man's expedition during the evening, night, and morning catalogs Grasmere Vale:

> Sky, hill, and dale, one dismal room,
> Hung round and overhung with gloom;
> Save that above a single height
> Is to be seen a lurid light,
> Above Helm-crag—a streak half dead,
> A burning of portentous red;
> And near that lurid light, full well
> The ASTROLOGER, sage Sidrophel,
> Where at his desk and book he sits,
> Puzzling aloft his curious wits;
> He whose domain is held in common
> With no one but the ANCIENT WOMAN,
> Cowering beside her rifted cell,
> As if intent on magic spell;—
> Dread pair that, spite of wind and weather,
> Still sit upon Helm-crag together!

He continues over Dunmail Raise, through Thirlmere, and to St. John's Vale.

Wordsworth and his expanding family were at Coleorton, Leicestershire, in 1807; soon after their return in July they took Allan Bank, a house at the south end of the village at the foot of Easedale. The house had been built by a Liverpool lawyer named Crump, who allowed Wordsworth to lay out the parkland below the house. *The White Doe of Rylstone* dates from this period, as does the ballad of the Green orphans of Blen Tarn Ghyll; the parents of the orphans, the oldest of whom was eleven, were lost in a snowstorm. The Wordsworths took in one of the children, Sally, and provided for her, and other villagers did the same for the other children. The Greens' double grave is in the Grasmere churchyard:

> Who weeps for strangers? Many wept
>   For George and Sarah Green;
> Wept for that pair's unhappy fate,
>   Whose grave may here be seen.

> By night, upon these stormy fells,
>   Did wife and husband roam;
> Six little ones at home had left,
>   And could not find that home.

In 1811 the Wordsworths once again moved, this time to the old Grasmere vicarage by the bridge opposite the church. It was a much easier house to manage, but because of its location it was extremely damp. Within a year and a half the two youngest children, Catherine and Thomas, died, and the family moved to Rydal Mount, 2 miles from here, in May 1813.

Wordsworth is not the only Lake poet to be associated with Grasmere and was, in fact, the magnet for two important visitors who also lived here. Samuel Taylor Coleridge first stayed with the Wordsworths at Dove Cottage in the spring of 1800 and was back again on his way to Malta in 1803, when he was ill and impoverished. At that time Mary Wordsworth nursed him for more than a month, and Wordsworth forced him to accept a loan of £100. Indeed, in November 1808, after the Wordsworths' move to Allan Bank, Coleridge, whose two boys were in school in Ambleside, arrived in Grasmere and remained until February 1809; his study was the room immediately to the left of the front door.

The other visitor was Thomas De Quincey; he had tried unsuccessfully three or four times to meet Wordsworth but never had the courage to complete the arrangements. Finally, in November 1807, he accompanied Sarah Coleridge and her children to Grasmere from Bristol and was then to meet the older poet. De Quincey was overcome with fright at the prospect, and it was Mrs. Wordsworth who put him at his ease; he realized that his anxieties had been so extreme that he had taken no account of the great man at all. Soon after the party's arrival, the entire group and Coleridge made a tour to Ambleside, over Kirkstone Pass, along Brothers Water to Patterdale, and then to Elsmere. De Quincey and Wordsworth left the group here and walked to Penrith, Wordsworth reading *The White Doe of Rylstone* aloud that evening. De Quincey went on to Keswick, Cumberland. He too shared Allan Bank with the Wordsworths and Coleridge until February 1809.

In March 1809 De Quincey took possession of Dove Cottage and began a program of walking 14 or more miles a day. Dorothy Wordsworth was to superintend alterations and additions to the cottage and, most particularly, to get bookcases built for his library of more than 5,000 volumes. De Quincey's study was the room at the top of the stairs, which had been the parlor during Wordsworth's occupancy, a room with an especially good view of the countryside. He retained the house for an extended period even though he was frequently in London, Westhay (Wrington), and Edinburgh. His addiction increased, and he admitted that at one stage he took enough opium "to kill some half-dozen dragoons, together with their horses." Sometime before 1816 he met Margaret Simpson, whose father, a local farmer, lived in Nab Cottage, where De Quincey often stayed. Wanting to marry her, he attempted to conquer his addiction and was, for a short time, successful. A son, christened William, was born in November 1816, and he and Margaret were married in the Grasmere church the following February. In 1817–1818 De Quincey had an especially difficult time in which he was haunted by human figures, huge moving architectural figures, and silvery lakes of human faces; his daughter Margaret was born in this period. Coleridge was a frequent visitor and guest here. The De Quinceys moved to Rydal in 1821, but they returned to Dove Cottage in the autumn of 1825 and remained until leaving permanently for Edinburgh in 1830.

Other associations in Grasmere are with the stream of literary visitors, especially but not exclusively to the Wordsworths. Charles and Mary Lamb visited Grasmere in 1802 when they were staying in Keswick with Coleridge; they did not meet Wordsworth, but they stayed at Dove Cottage for a few days. Sir Walter Scott was here in 1805; his fame secured by the success of *The Lay of the Last Minstrel*, Scott and his wife made a long trip to see the Cumberland and Westmorland lakes and to visit Wordsworth. Later Scott talked of the enthusiastic reception they received from Wordsworth. On at least one of the days Wordsworth showed them the lakes, and with Humphry Davy, the chemist, the two men climbed Helvellyn. William Hazlitt's first visit to the Lake District and to Grasmere probably was in 1807, when he painted portraits of Coleridge and the eleven-year-old Hartley Coleridge in Keswick before coming here to do Wordsworth's portrait. Hazlitt was involved in some sort of amatory escapade at which the local population appears to have been so highly incensed that he was forced to flee in order to escape jail. Wordsworth apparently extricated Hazlitt and gave him money and clothes to facilitate an escape. Some years later, in 1818, John Keats came through Grasmere from Ambleside on his way to visit Wordsworth at Rydal Mount; he later claimed to have recognized Wordsworth's "ancient woman," Helm Crag, from the poem.

Both the partly 13th-century Church of St. Oswald and the churchyard in Grasmere are intimately connected with Wordsworth. The church, near Dove Cottage, is massive and dark with the unusual interior feature of a two-story continuous north arcade (16th and 17th centuries). The font is medieval, and a carved stone, thought to be part of an ancient cross, is 800 years old. The interior is described in *The Excursion:*

Not raised in nice proportions was the pile,
But large and massy; for duration built;
With pillars crowded, and the roof upheld
By naked rafters intricately crossed,
Like leafless underboughs, in some thick wood,
All withered by the depth of shade above.
Admonitory texts inscribed the walls,
Each, in its ornamental scroll, enclosed;
Each also crowned with wingèd heads—a pair
Of rudely-painted Cherubim. The floor
Of nave and aisle, in unpretending guise,
Was occupied by oaken benches ranged
In seemly rows; the chancel only showed
Some vain distinctions, marks of earthly state
By immemorial privilege allowed;
Though with the Encincture's special sanctity
But ill according. An heraldic shield,
Varying its tincture with the changeful light,
Imbued the altar-window; fixed aloft
A faded hatchment hung, and one by time
Yet undiscoloured. A capacious pew
Of sculptured oak stood here, with drapery lined. . . .

The "oaken benches" were removed in 1841, much to the poet's disgust, but the ends of the benches have been placed near the tower door. The "capacious pew" near the sanctuary was provided by Sir Daniel le Fleming in 1633. On the wall opposite the pew is a memorial to Wordsworth with an inscription from John Keble's "Oxford Lectures on Poetry." It should be noted that the church in Bowness-on-Windermere also claims to be Wordsworth's model.

The churchyard, "almost wholly free/From interruption of sepulchral stones," is not like that now, but Wordsworth's general description is still applicable; the graves of the Sympson family, for example, can be identified:

> Whence comes it, then, that yonder we behold
> Five graves, and only five, that rise together
> Unsociably sequestered, and encroaching
> On the smooth play-ground of the village-school?

Wordsworth planted eight of the yew trees (seven remain), and near one of them is the poet's grave; he died at Rydal on April 23, 1850, and was buried here near the Rothay River. Here also are the graves of Mary Hutchinson Wordsworth (died 1859), his sister Dorothy (died 1855), his children Catherine and Thomas, and his daughter Dora Wordsworth Quillinan. Just northwest of these graves is the grave of Hartley Coleridge, who died here on January 6, 1849; the site of the grave was chosen by Wordsworth. One additional memorial is of interest; just a few feet beyond these graves is the grave of Anne Clough, mother of Arthur Hugh Clough, and the stone above her grave has a memorial inscription to him and his sister Anne Jemima Clough, the first principal of Newnham College, Cambridge.

GRAVESEND, Kent (pop. 39,460)   The boundary port for London, lying 24 miles southwest of the city on the south bank of the Thames, Gravesend has always been important as a port and is the modern home of more than 200 river pilots. Its old town has become derelict in spite of its fine old buildings and excellent location. The fame of Gravesend in many ways is not associated with the port. The parish church of St. George attracts an annual flood of American tourists who come to see the grave of the American Indian princess Pocahontas, who was buried in the chancel of the old church in 1617. However, there now appears to be some doubt about the specific place of burial (even though the parish register contains the entry "Rebecca Wrothe, Wyff of Thomas Wrothe, gent, a Virginian born Lady, here was buried in the Chauncell") because a skeleton unearthed in 1907 during building operations in the churchyard proved to be that of a female Indian.

Because Gravesend is a port, its best literary associations are those of transients. Sir Philip Sidney spent his last days on English soil here before embarking on the his expedition of November 1585 to the Netherlands, where he was fatally wounded at Zutphen in September 1586. Not very fond of the town, Charles Dickens uses Gravesend only for landings and embarkations in his works and notes that the place was too low for a family holiday, as suggested by Joseph Tuggs in *Sketches by Boz.* In *David Copperfield,* Mr. Peggotty and Ham land here from Great Yarmouth on their way to visit David at Salem House, Blackheath, and Peggotty and Micawber sail from here. There is another far more definite Dickensian association with Gravesend: a cottage on the canal bank made from an inverted fishing boat on low brickwork walls. The 30-foot-long boat formed the upper room, and windows were cut into the area where the rudder had been. The whole thing was much like Phiz's original drawings of the Peggottys' house, which Dickens placed at Great Yarmouth. An 1844 Gravesend guide called the boat-cottage old at that time, and it is likely that if Dickens derived the idea of Peggotty's house from an actual place, this was it. It is also often claimed that Gravesend is the town referred to as Muggleton in *Pickwick Papers,* but all things considered, Town Malling appears to be a far better choice. Dickens stayed at Waite's Hotel in Gravesend in April 1857, when he was overseeing alterations to Gadshill.

There are other transient literary associations. William Cowper spent part of an August 1758 holiday in the town; and John Evelyn, who frequently called the city Grays-in-Kent, was present for a variety of official purposes. Evelyn sailed from Gravesend to the Continent on court-appointed duties, attended the royal yacht races here, and made the necessary arrangements for the treatment of the sick and wounded from the wars with the Dutch. Samuel Pepys was also often here on official business and frequented the Ship and the Swan; he appears to have especially enjoyed eating venison, drinking, and talking to the landlord (who "undeceives" him about the Dutch fleet) at the Ship. Joseph Conrad uses this area in "Heart of Darkness"; he locates the ship where the story is told off Gravesend. Finally, H. G. Wells uses Gravesend in *Tono-Bungay.* George Ponderevo stays at the Good Intent Inn (unidentified) before sailing on the *Maud Mary.*

GRAZELEY, Berkshire (pop. 32)   Four miles south of Reading and quite close to the Hampshire border, Grazeley, little more than a hamlet, was once the home of Mary Mitford. Her father, Dr. George Mitford, was a spendthrift and lost enormous sums of money in various speculations and in whist. When his daughter won a £20,000 lottery in 1797, he built a house in Grazeley on the site of a fine old place which he had torn down. Just as the family fortunes diappeared, so has their house.

GREASLEY, Nottinghamshire (pop. 6,279)   The village of Greasley, 7 miles northwest of Nottingham, centrally placed in the rich coal belt of the North Midlands, is not primarily a colliery town but a part of the agricultural area which exists alongside the mining communities. Only a short distance from Eastwood, the early home of D. H. Lawrence, Greasley is a community which he knew well and used in his works. The young Lawrence was frequently found here at Hagg Farm, the home of the Chambers family. *The White Peacock* describes the countryside in a wet May:

> [T]he light of the dandelions was quite extinguished, and it seemed that only a long time back had we made merry before the broad glare of these flowers. The bluebells lingered and lingered; they fringed the fields for weeks like purple fringe of morning. The pink campions came out only to hang heavy with rain; hawthorn buds remained tight and hard as pearls.

In *Sons and Lovers* Hagg Farm appears as Willey Farm with its house, gardens, and fields, Nethermere (Moorgreen Reservoir), and Willey Water all in their proper places. "Love among the Haystacks" describes haymaking in the Greasley fields, and the farm or events in which Lawrence had a part appear in "A Modern Lover," "Second Best," and "The Shades of Spring," all landscaped with "large farms . . . and far off coal mines" and farms situated "less than a hundred yards from the wood's edge." These are the fields where "barley stood in rows, the blond tresses of corn streaming on to the ground."

GREAT BOLAS *See* BOLAS MAGNA.

GREAT BOOKHAM, Surrey (pop. 1,566) Great Bookham, 2 miles southwest of Leatherhead, once belonged to the great abbey at Chertsey; indeed, the chancel of the parish church was built by John de Rutherwyk, builder of the abbey. Lying back from the main road, the village has little changed over the years and today is much as it was when Fanny Burney settled here at the Hermitage on the corner of East Street in 1793 after her marriage to Gen. Alexandre d'Arblay. They spent four pleasant years here, enjoying "the beautiful country around us in long and romantic strolls," and D'Arblay imposed his own methods and standards of gardening upon the cottage grounds. Madame d'Arblay tells of his clearing a "considerable compartment of weeds" and showing his work to the gardener, who declared "he had demolished an asparagus bed! M. d'A protested, however, nothing could look more like *des mauvaises herbes*." She also says, "His greatest passion is for transplanting. Everything we possess he moves from one end of the garden to another, to produce better effects." *Camilla*, written here, was so successful (earning more than 3,000 guineas) that they were able to build Camilla Cottage (later Camilla Lacey). The writing of this book was interrupted, Miss Burney said, by only one episode, the birth of a child.

A second novelist is also associated with Great Bookham, for the Rev. Samuel Cooke, a friend of the D'Arblays, was Jane Austen's godfather; she frequently visited the old rectory (gone). Here she heard much of her predecessor firsthand and in 1813 wrote: "Perhaps I may marry young Mr. D'Arblay." On her 1814 visit she was working on *Emma* and visited Box Hill, where one of the scenes of that novel is set.

GREAT CASTERTON, Rutland (pop. 259) Situated on the Wash (Gwash) River 8½ miles to the east of Oakham, Great Casterton has a history going back to a recently discovered Stone Age settlement, in which the skeleton of a Stone Age man with his weapons and tools placed nearby was found. Excavations reveal that this site epitomizes the history of Roman building in England: a 1st-century fort, complete with a defensive ditch and bank; the remains of a town occupied continuously from the 1st to the 5th century; the site of a villa occupied from the late 4th century on; and part of the great Roman road Ermine Street.

In 1817 John Clare came to Great Casterton from Helpston, Northamptonshire, in search of work and met a young woman, Martha Turner, who became "Sweet Patty of the Vale":

And I would go to Patty's cot,
And Patty came to me.

Each knew the other's every thought
Under the hawthorn tree.
And I'll be true for Patty's sake
And she'll be true for mine,
And I this little ballad make
To be her valentine.

She was only eighteen years old, and her parents, who were cottage farmers, objected strenuously to her marrying Clare because of his poverty. Their objections were overcome, and the couple finally married in 1820 after a small annuity had been settled on the poet. The Clares stayed here only a short time before going to the cottage in Helpston where his parents lived.

GREAT DUNMOW *See* DUNMOW, LITTLE, AND DUNMOW, GREAT.

GREAT GONERBY, Lincolnshire (pop. 1,279) Two miles northwest of Grantham overlooking the Vale of Belvoir, Great Gonerby sits on what was once the steepest hill on the Lincoln Edge on the former Great North Road between Edinburgh and London. Sir Walter Scott uses the hill in *The Heart of Midlothian* as the site where Jeanie Deans is ordered to "Stand and deliver":

Taking leave of her Lincolnshire Gaius, Jeanie resumed her solitary walk, and was somewhat alarmed when evening and twilight overtook her in the open ground which extends to the foot of Gunnerby Hill, and is intersected with patches of copse and with swampy spots. The extensive commons on the north road, most of which are now enclosed, and in general a relaxed state of police, exposed the traveler to a highway robbery in a degree which is now unknown, except in the immediate vicinity of the metropolis. Aware of this circumstance, Jeanie mended her pace when she heard the trampling of a horse behind. . . .

The hill has now been cut down quite a bit, and the new A1 bypasses the village.

GREAT GRIMSBY *See* GRIMSBY.

GREAT HASELEY, Oxfordshire (pop. 550) Located 4 miles southwest of Thame, Great Haseley, while a lovely little village, is often bypassed by the traveler because of its lack of known literary or historical associations. Christopher Wren was once the rector here, and near the church stand an ancient tithe barn with a vast tiled roof and the old manor house behind a stone wall.

John Leland completed the appointed rounds for Henry VIII and was presented to the living here in April 1542. He preached in the church, described "the fair chauncelle of Haseley," and commented on the surrounding area in his *Itinerary*. Leland held the living until his death in 1552, although in the early years he was frequently at his house in the parish of St. Michael le Querne in London. From 1550 on, after an incapacitating mental collapse, his Great Haseley income was received by his brother, who used it for the Lelands' support.

GREAT LANGDALE *See* LANGDALE, GREAT, AND LANGDALE, LITTLE.

GREAT MALVERN, Worcestershire (pop. 9,092) Beautifully situated on the slopes of the Malvern Hills

GREAT MALVERN   Seen from the Malvern Hills, the Priory Church of SS. Mary and Michael, all that remains of the 11th-century Benedictine monastery, dominates the town of Great Malvern. Here at the priory William Langland is believed to have been educated.

and sheltered by them from the west wind, Malvern, or Great Malvern, is one of the most underrated resort areas and beauty spots in England. The Malverns, offering unparalleled views into Herefordshire and Wales to the west and across the patchwork countryside of Worcestershire to the east, are crossed by footpaths on the lower slopes and untrammeled land with free access on the upper reaches. Great Malvern, 9 miles southwest of Worcester, is one of six Malverns in the vicinity; it was the site of an endowed hermitage (1085) from which a Benedictine monastery was founded.

The Priory Church of SS. Mary and Michael is the pride of Malvern; set among cedar, ilex, pine, and yew trees, the church has a 14th-century bell which still peals four times a day and two bells dating from 1611. The interior of the church holds the greatest attraction for visitors because of the great East Window in which thousands of fragments of original glass have been painstakingly put back in their proper places. Much of the restoration work on the glass was initiated by the ghost-story writer Montague Rhodes James in 1910. Half of the elaborately carved stalls in the church are 15th-century; the grotesques forming the armrests are unequaled in Worcestershire and perhaps in England. The priory church became the parish church at the dissolution of the monasteries in the 16th century, when the townspeople bought it from the crown for £20.

One of the earliest writers of medieval alliterative verse, William Langland, is assumed to have had some association with the priory; he knew this area, according to *Piers Plowman:*

In a summer season   when soft was the sun,
I clothed myself in a cloak   as I shepherd were,
Habit like a hermit's   unholy in works,
And went wide in the world   wonders to hear.
But on a May morning   on Malvern hills,
A marvel befell me   of fairy, methought.
I was weary with wandering   and went me to rest
Under a broad bank   by a brook's side,

And as I lay and leaned over   and looked into the waters
I fell into a sleep   for it sounded so merry.

It also seems certain that the view inspiring the opening lines is the one over the Severn Valley. If Langland is identified as the dreamer of the poem, it may well be that he was educated here at the priory.

Malvern College for Boys, established in 1865, is housed in an impressive set of buildings, and here C. S. Lewis attended school for one year.

George Bernard Shaw's plays were regularly presented at the drama festivals here, and Malvern virtually became a second home for him during festival time; he was often seen striding over the hills. Hugh Walpole and Francis Brett Young frequently attended the festivals, and it is partly due to Young that the natural beauty of these hills is unchanged. He was asked to give evidence before the Ministry of Health in 1939 about the quarrying of this land, "sacred soil in the history of English Literature." Mentioning Langland, "the father of English Poetry . . . Elizabeth Barrett Browning . . . Masefield and Housman," he concluded that Malvern's revitalization came

through the establishment by Sir Barry Jackson, of our Annual Dramatic Festival which had attracted a large number of visitors from the Continent and the United States. . . . It is no use trying to establish an English Bayreuth or Salzburg if there is a prospect of its surroundings being blasted to bits. . . .

GREAT MARLOW, Buckinghamshire (pop. 5,355) Marlow, called Great Marlow to distinguish it from the village of Little Marlow 2 miles to the northeast, is a busy Thames-side town with a wide and attractive High Street. Within easy commuting distance of London, 32½ miles to the east, the town has a long and rich history. The old manor belonged to the Saxon Algar before William the Conqueror expropriated it for Queen Matilda. The old parsonage on St. Peter's Street is the oldest building in the town, some of the stone window frames and the roof dating from the 14th century.

Just across the river on the Berkshire side of the Thames is the delightful Compleat Angler Hotel, named in honor of Izaak Walton, who often fished here; the windows of the hotel are particularly interesting, with paintings of the fish Walton describes in his work. The area around Marlow, an especial favorite of Jerome K. Jerome, is described in detail in *Three Men in a Boat:*

> Marlow is one of the pleasantest river centres I know of. It is a bustling, lively little town; not very picturesque on the whole, it is true, but there are many quaint nooks and corners to be found in it, nevertheless—standing arches in the shattered bridge of Time, over which our fancy travels back to the days when Marlow Manor owned Saxon Algar for its lord, ere conquering William seized it to give it to Queen Matilda, ere it passed to the Earls of Warwick or to worldly-wise Lord Paget, the councillor of four successive sovereigns.
>
> There is lovely country round about it, too, if, after boating, you are fond of a walk, while the river itself is at its best here.

Jerome spent a great deal of time here toward the end of his life before he moved to Belsize Park.

Marlow's most famous literary episode began on February 14, 1817, the date Percy Bysshe Shelley leased Albion House on West Street for a period of twenty-one years to commence on December 21. Shelley committed himself to the three adjoining houses and a 4-acre meadow next to the house as well. He and Mary Godwin and their first child, William, took up residence after a stay in Bath. Almost immediately after they arrived, Fanny Godwin, Mary's half sister, died very tragically, and the body of Harriet Shelley was found in the Serpentine, where she had drowned herself. During the early part of his stay here Shelley produced "A Proposal for Putting Reform to the Vote throughout the Kingdom. By the Hermit of Marlow" and "An Address to the People on the Death of Princess Charlotte" under a similar pseudonym. Mary also was productive, and the manuscript of *Frankenstein,* begun on the Continent, was finished and the page proofs corrected here. Shelley and Mary Godwin married a few weeks after Harriet's death, and in September 1817, when Clara Evelina was born, the poet was working on *Laon and Cythna* (later *The Revolt of Islam*). Shelley's health was bad in 1817, and he was advised to winter abroad in Italy; after arranging a rental for the house, he left Marlow in early February 1818, and Mary followed in a few days.

Perhaps the main reason Shelley settled here in 1817 was that Thomas Love Peacock, who had moved to Great Marlow in 1815, secured Albion House for the Shelleys. The two saw much of each other, and Shelley sought Peacock's advice on *The Revolt of Islam.* In the 1815–1819 period, Peacock discovered that his forte probably lay in the satiric novel; *Headlong Hall, Melincourt,* and *Nightmare Abbey* were all completed here; and *Calidore* was begun. Peacock and Shelley roamed the countryside within a radius, they claimed, of 16 miles and undoubtedly tested every pub and inn in that circle. Peacock said that the quality of an inn could be determined by the state of its mustard pot and would

GREAT MARLOW   Called "a bustling, lively little town" by Jerome K. Jerome, The Thames-side village of Great Marlow was the home of Percy Bysshe Shelley and Mary Godwin in 1817.

enter an establishment, call for a mustard pot, and stay or leave without an explanation of his behavior.

In 1894 Hugh Walpole was sent to school here after being in school in Truro for a year. His experiences here were most unpleasant, and *The Crystal Box* recalls some of the physical and emotional tortures inflicted on the young boys by boys in the upper classes. Walpole's time was cut short when his parents discovered in 1896 how things were, and he was then sent to the junior school of the King's School in Canterbury.

GREAT MILTON, Oxfordshire (pop. 403)   An engaging small village less than 10 miles southeast of Oxford, Great Milton is one of three Oxfordshire Miltons often confused with each other. It contains a fine old gabled house alleged to have been the home of the ancestors of John Milton; indeed, the traditional assumption, that Milton spent holidays here as a boy, is based partly on the fact that his father was the ranger of a forest in this area.

GREAT SAXHAM, Suffolk (pop. 184)   The tiny village of Great Saxham, 5 miles west of Bury St. Edmunds and 8½ miles east of Newmarket, was once dotted with moated farmhouses, a few remnants of which remain. Thomas Carew, who stayed at the seat of the Crofts family here and was extraordinarily pleased with their hospitality, had a tendency to antagonize those who employed or befriended him, but his relationship with Sir John Crofts apparently never suffered on this account. Carew wrote "To Saxham" in praise of his handsome treatment and Sir John:

> The strangers welcome, each man there
> Stamp'd on his chearfull brow, doth weare;
> Nor doth this welcome, or his cheere
> Grow lesse, 'cause he staies longer here.
> There's none observes (much lesse repines)
> How often this man sups or dines.
> Thou hast no Porter at the doore
> T'examine, or keep back the poore;
> Nor locks, nor bolts; thy gates have bin
> Made onely to let strangers in. . . .

GREAT TEW　Because the village of Great Tew is a prize example of early planning and careful maintenance, much is just as it was when Thomas Hobbes, Edward Hyde, and Abraham Cowley visited the Falklands at the manor house. The house has been rebuilt, but the gardens remain.

GREAT TEW, Oxfordshire (pop. 354)　This village, 9 miles southwest of Banbury, is unusually attractive and, because of early planning, has the appearance of a park lined with 17th-century honey-colored cottages complete with scallop-thatched roofs, mullioned windows, and gables. One of the prizes of the village is the partly Norman parish church by the gates of the park.

In the 17th century the manor house was inhabited by Lucius Cary, 2d Viscount Falkland, who died at Newbury in 1643. His house was an intellectual center for some of the most important men of London and Oxford; indeed, both Thomas Hobbes and Edward Hyde, 1st Earl of Clarendon, are known to have visited here. Probably in 1639, Abraham Cowley met Lord Falkland here and soon after wrote "To the Lord Falkland, for His Safe Return from the Northern Expedition against the Scots." Cowley, knowing that the house was always open to loyal Royalists, was frequently here from 1643 on to avoid the local fighting.

GREAT WYRLEY, Staffordshire (pop. 2,701)　On the edge of the Black Country, Great Wyrley has the advantage of being only a few miles from the southern portion of Cannock Chase. For centuries this village, 2 miles south of Cannock, was virtually unknown, but in the early 20th century it was marked by a series of events. Between February and August 1903, eight cases of horrible animal mutilation occurred, and on August 8 George Edalji, an Indian who was the son of the local vicar, was arrested although he staunchly proclaimed his innocence. He was found guilty of the crime even though another maiming took place while he was in custody, and a second mutilation occurred in November, while he was in the Lewes Prison engaged, ironically, in making feed bags for horses. Three years later Edalji was mysteriously released from prison, and he appealed to Sir Arthur Conan Doyle for help. Doyle, convinced of the young man's innocence, investigated the case from December 1906 to the following August and met Edalji at the Grand Hotel in London in January 1907, when he discovered that the young man suffered from eight diopters of myopia; that is, he was half blind in daylight. Sir Arthur sent a dossier to the Home Office in late April or May concerning the case and, in true Holmesian fashion, identified the real perpetrator of the crimes as Peter Hudson, who had been expelled from Walsall Grammar School, knew animals, and had been apprenticed to a butcher. In May 1907 Edalji was proclaimed "not guilty," but even with the proof which had emerged nothing was done about Hudson.

GREAT YARMOUTH, Norfolk (pop. 56,771)　Norwich, Lowestoft, and Sea Palling form the triangular boundaries of the Norfolk Broads, a series of open and navigable expanses of water linked by streams, rivers, and artificial channels. Great Yarmouth, a fishing town, coast guard station, and resort area 19 miles east of Norwich, has a coastal location on the eastern side of the Broads at the mouth of the Yare River and the influx of the Bure River. It was a fishing village shortly after the Romans left England and became the center of the herring trade by the 11th century. Indeed, the free fair held in September and October, the peak of the fishing season, began at this time, and the influx of traders and visitors from all over England and the Continent was enormous and often turbulent. William Camden notes the longstanding battles between the Cinque Ports and Great Yarmouth in his *Britannia:*

> The walls were built about A.D. 1340, and in a little time the inhabitants became so rich and powerful as frequently to attack their neighbours of Leostoffe and the Cinque ports at sea, with great loss on both sides. They had probably a pique against them because they themselves were not allowed the privilege of the Cinque ports, which old *Garianonum* and their ancestors enjoyed under the Count of the Saxon shore. . . . Their spirit being lowered, and their wealth declining, they were forced to apply themselves to trade and the herring fishery, . . . large shoals are found on this coast. It is incredible what a great fair is held here at Michaelmas, and what quantities of herrings and other fish are sold.

During the Middle Ages, when the wool trade was of great importance in East Anglia, Yarmouth shipped wool and woven cloth to the Low Countries and dealt heavily in herring and other fish. Michael Drayton's *Poly-Olbion* refers to the fishing industry; the Yare comes

> To *Yarmouth* . . . her onely christned Towne,
> Whose fishing through the Realme, doth her so much renowne,
> Where those that with their nets still haunt the boundless lake,
> Her such a sumptuous feast of salted Herrings make,
> As they had rob'd the Sea of all his former store,
> And past that very howre, it could produce no more.

Henry III granted permission for the town's defense system, and Camden notes that the town is

> fortified both by nature and art. Though almost surrounded with water, to the West by the river, over which is a draw-bridge, and on the other sides by the sea, except the North, where it joins to the land, yet it has very stout walls, which, with the river, form a long square; in which, besides the towers on the East, is a mount or fort. . . .

EASTERN
ENGLAND

NORTH

SEA

The Wash

LINCOLNSHIRE

Langham •   Holt •   Cromer •
Barningham Winter •   • Mundesley
  Paston •   • Bacton
• Houghton Hall   Heydon •   Happisburgh
  Buxton • • Lamas   • Catfield

○ **King's Lynn**   Bawdeswell •   *Norforlk Broads*
    East Dereham •   North   • Mautby
  • Tuddenham   Caister
  West Bradenham •   **Norwich** ○   next Yarmouth
        Great Yarmouth

HUNTINGDON-
SHIRE
Water
• Newton
• Leverington
• Wisbech

CAMBRIDGE-
SHIRE
AND
ISLE OF ELY

NORTHAMPTON-
SHIRE

AND

PETERBOROUGH

Keyston
• Little Gidding
• Alconbury
Leighton Bromswold
• Brampton
Kimbolton • Buckden
St. Neot's

Ely ○   Bluntisham
Huntingdon   • St. Ives
• Hemingford Grey
• Impington

Cambridge
Grantchester •
Trumpington •
Wimpole   *Gog-Magog Hills*

• Hilgay   Merton •
  Breckland   Forncett St. Peter •
Weeting •   • Thetford
Brandon •   *Ouse*
  Euston •   Kenninghall •
Honington •   • Sapiston   Diss •
      Waveney

NORFOLK

Ditchingham •   Roos Hall
  Bungay   Beccles •
  Blundeston
  Oulton
  Lowestoft ○
  • Kessingland

SUFFOLK
  Southwold •
• Wetheringsett   Dunwich •
  Framlingham •   Rendham •
Bury St. Edmunds   • Great Saxham
Newmarket   Hawstead •
Cheveley •   **Stowmarket** ○   Parham •   • Great Glemham
Carlton •   Lidgate •   Bredfield •   *The Sandlings*   • Aldeburgh
• Wickhambrook   Boulge •   *Orford Ness*
  • Lavenham   Woodbridge •   Sutton Hoo
Long Melford •   **Ipswich** ○   • Hollesley
Sudbury •

Little
Ouse

Great
Cam

HERTFORDSHIRE

Audley End •
Finchingfield •
Dunmow •
Hatfield Broad Oak •
Down Hall •

Stour
Brantham •
Colne
Blackwater
Braintree •
• Witham

Colchester
Thorpe-le-Soken •
  Harwich
  Landguard Point
  Walton •
  The Naze

Chelmer
Maldon •

Epping Forest
• Ongar
Waltham Holy Cross
High Beech •
Loughton •   Navestock •
Chigwell •

ESSEX

GREATER LONDON
• Stratford
Chadwell St. Mary •

Southend-on-Sea
Stanford-le-Hope •
Canvey Isle
Thames
Foulness Point

Thames

KENT

In fact, for almost six centuries the inhabitants of Yarmouth were crowded into this area, and the Rows were created to house the population. These were 145 incredibly narrow roads (Row 95 was only 27 inches wide at one point) sloping down to the river. Yarmouth doggedly maintained its compressed nature until the end of the 18th century, when sea bathing became fashionable. The 19th century saw the addition of some quite fashionable Regency-style buildings and the construction of the Wellington and Britannia Piers. Today gardens abound, the seafront has been fully developed, and the area where nets were spread to dry is now overspread with caravans.

Daniel Defoe was much interested in Yarmouth and its development. He comments in *A Tour thro' the Whole Island of Great Britain:*

> YARMOUTH is an antient Town, much older than *Norwich;* and at present, tho' not standing on so much Ground, yet better Built; much more Compleat; for number of Inhabitants, not much inferior; and for Wealth, Trade, and advantage of its Situation, infinitely superior to *Norwich.*

He goes on to note the buildings:

> The Key reaching from the Draw-Bridge almost to the *South-Gate,* is so spacious and wide, that in some Places 'tis near One hundred Yards from the Houses to the Wharf. In this pleasant and agreeable range of Houses are some very magnificent Buildings, and among the rest, the Custom-House and Town-Hall, and some Merchants Houses, which look like little Palaces, rather than the Dwelling-Houses of Private Men.
> The greatest Defect of this beautiful Town, seems to be, that tho' it is very Rich and encreasing in Wealth and Trade, and consequently in People, there is not Room to enlarge the Town by Building. . . .

Yarmouth can claim one native literary figure; Anna Sewell, author of *Black Beauty,* was born on March 30, 1820, in a gabled and timbered house (1641) on Church Plain next to Fisherman's Hospital; the house, now known as Sewell House, is marked with a plaque. In 1867 she moved from here to Old Catton, where she died eleven years later and was buried in the Friends' burying ground at Lamas. Another writer lived here for almost seven years. George Borrow came here with his wife on the advice of Thomas Gordon Hake, a physician in Bury St. Edmunds. Mrs. Borrow's health had not been good, and Borrow was himself in an agitated state after the 1851 appearance of *Lavengro* when he referred to the critics, whose reviews had been unfavorable, as foaming vipers, sycophants, and lackeys. The Borrows made their home at 24 Trafalgar Place after short periods of residence at 169 King Street and 37–39 Camperdown Place. From here Borrow ranged all over Norfolk on his Gypsy ramblings until 1860, when he and his wife went to London.

Sometime after November 10, 1655 (the date of the official charge), the Royalist poet John Cleveland was apprehended in Norwich, where he had been living with Edward Cooke. Considered to be a "person of great abilities and so able to do the greater disservice" to the government, Cleveland was imprisoned here, possibly on Middlegate Street, for three months.

Yarmouth has also entered literature; one of the earliest works to include the town was Thomas Nashe's *Lenten Stuffe: The Praise of Red Herring.*

Nashe had long been involved in controversy with Gabriel Harvey and claimed in 1597 that he had to flee to Yarmouth. In return for the people's warmth and hospitality, he said, "I pay them again praise of their own town and the red herring." Nashe probably died here about 1601.

The best-known use of Yarmouth occurs in Charles Dickens's *David Copperfield.* The author came to Norfolk and Suffolk first in 1848 to obtain local color for the novel and stayed in Somerleyton Hall in Somerleyton with Sir Samuel Morton Peto. In 1849 Dickens was back and stayed at the Royal Hotel, Marine Parade, and his fascination with the Rows gave him the idea of describing Yarmouth as the "Norfolk gridiron." He thought this "the strangest place in the wide world, one hundred and forty-six miles of hill-less marsh between it and London," and, impressed by the landscape near the port, decided to "try his hand" with it. He places the home of the Peggotty family and Little Em'ly on the open Denes; David is brought here from Blunderstone (Blundeston, Suffolk) to stay for two weeks when his mother remarries:

> Yarmouth . . . looked rather spongy and soppy, I thought, as I carried my eye over the great dull waste that lay across the river. . . .
> As we drew a little nearer, and saw the whole adjacent prospect lying a straight low line under the sky, I hinted to Peggotty that a mound or so might have improved it; and also that if the land had been a little more separated from the sea, and the town and tide had not been quite so much mixed up, like toast and water, it would have been nicer. . . .
> When we got into the street (which was strange enough to me), and smelt the fish, and pitch, and oakum, and tar, and saw the sailors walking about, and the carts jingling up and down over the stones, I felt I had done so busy a place an injustice. . . .

David is carried on Ham's back from the cart to the boathouse and notes the dreariness of the Denes:

> [W]e turned down lanes bestrewn with bits of chips and little hillocks of sand, and went past gas-works, rope-walks, boat-builders' yards, ship-wrights' yards, ship-breakers' yards, caulkers' yards, riggers' lofts, smiths' forges, and a great litter of such places, until we came out upon the dull waste I had already seen at a distance; when Ham said:
> "Yon's our house, Mas'r Davy!"
> I looked in all directions, as far as I could stare over the wilderness, and away at the sea, and away at the river, but no house could *I* make out. There was a black barge, or some other kind of superannuated boat, not far off, high and dry on the ground, with an iron funnel sticking out of it for a chimney and smoking very cosily; but nothing else in the way of a habitation that was visible to *me.*
> "That's not it?" said I. "That ship-looking thing?"
> "That's it, Mas'r Davy," returned Ham.

David passes through Yarmouth on his way to school near London, and it is at the Duke's Head Inn that he meets William, the "friendly and companionable waiter." A second inn, the Buck Inn on the Market Square, is where David later meets Ham Peggotty. David returns home from school when his mother dies and is fitted for a suit of mourning by Mr. Omer; it is now thought that Dickens had 74 Middlegate Street in mind. Steerforth and David, who come to Yarmouth from Steerforth's home, are thought to be at the Star Hotel when they meet the "ain't I volatile?"

Miss Mowcher. Finally, it would seem apparent from the descriptions toward the end of the novel that Dickens himself must have experienced one of the gales which periodically attack Yarmouth:

> The tremendous sea itself, when I could find sufficient pause to look at it, in the agitation of the blinding wind, the flying stones and sand, and the awful noise, confounded me. As the high watery walls came rolling in, and, at their highest, tumbled into surf, they looked as if the least would engulf the town. As the receding wave swept back with a hoarse roar, it seemed to scoop out deep caves in the beach, as if its purpose were to undermine the earth. When some white-headed billows thundered on, and dashed themselves to pieces before they reached the land, every fragment of the late whole seemed possessed by the full might of its wrath, rushing to be gathered to the composition of another monster. . . . [M]asses of water shivered and shook the beach with a booming sound; . . . the ideal shore on the horizon, with its towers and buildings, rose and fell; the clouds flew fast and thick; I seemed to see a rending and upheaving of all nature.

During the storm the ship breaks up, and Ham tries to rescue "the solitary man upon the mast." With ropes around his body and held by men on shore

> he made for the wreck, rising with the hills, falling with the valleys, lost beneath the rugged foam, borne in towards the shore, borne on towards ship, striving hard and valiantly. . . . At length he neared the wreck. He was so near, that with one more of his vigorous strokes he would be clinging to it—when, a high, green, vast hill-side of water, moving on shoreward, from beyond the ship, he seemed to leap up into it with a mighty bound, and the ship was gone!
> Some eddying fragments I saw in the sea, as if a mere cask had been broken, in running to the spot where they were hauling in. Consternation was in every face. They drew him to my very feet—insensible—dead.

And, shortly after, Copperfield is led to the shore by an old fisherman who knew him and Em'ly as children to identify yet another body, Steerforth's:

> And on that part of it where she and I had looked for shells . . . —among the ruins of the home he had wronged—I saw him lying with his head upon his arm, as I had often seen him lie at school.

GREATHAM, Sussex (pop. 60) A tiny village on the Arun River 6 miles northeast of Arundel, Greatham (pronounced "gret'tam") has a fine 16th-century manor house, a 13th-century slate-steepled church, and modern literary associations with Padraic Colum and D. H. Lawrence. Near the village on the Rackham road is Shed Hall, a house constructed from cowsheds, which was loaned to Colum in 1912 for his honeymoon; the property belonged to Viola Meynell, who loaned it to D. H. Lawrence three years later when he was finishing *The Rainbow*. Lawrence makes the hall the setting for the title story in the collection *England, My England* even though he transplants it to Hampshire as Crockham Cottage:

> The timbered cottage with its sloping, cloak-like roof was old and forgotten. . . . Lost all alone on the edge of the common, at the end of a wide, grassy, briar-entangled lane shaded with oak, it had never known the world of today. . . .
> The house was ancient and very uncomfortable. But he did not want to alter it.

GREENHEAD GHYLL, Cumberland The Vale of Grasmere contains an extraordinary number of locations used in Wordsworth's works, and Greenhead Ghyll (Greenhead Gill), one of these on the eastern border of west Cumberland, 9 miles south of Keswick, is the scene of "Michael." Wordsworth notes that he was writing of real places:

> The sheepfold remains, or rather the ruins of it. The character and circumstances of Luke were taken from a family to whom had belonged, many years before, the house we lived in at Town End. The name of the Evening Star was not given to this house, but to another on the same side of the valley, more to the north.

The finished sheepfold on the lower slope of the hill is not the one referred to; Michael's was much higher up:

> If from the public way you turn your steps
> Up the tumultuous brook of Green-head Ghyll,
> You will suppose that with an upright path
> Your feet must struggle; in such bold ascent
> The pastoral mountains front you, face to face.
> But, courage! for around that boisterous brook
> The mountains have all opened out themselves,
> And made a hidden valley of their own.
> No habitation can be seen. . . .

Michael's home:

> . . . on a plot of rising ground
> Stood single, with large prospect, north and south,
> High into Easedale, up to Dunmail-Raise,
> And westward to the village near the lake;
> And from this constant light, so regular,
> And so far seen, the House itself, by all
> Who dwelt within the limits of the vale,
> Both old and young, was named *The Evening Star*.

The house was gone even when Wordsworth was writing.

GRENDON UNDERWOOD, Buckinghamshire (pop. 283) A straggling village just off the road from Aylesbury to Bicester, 10 miles south of Buckingham, Grendon Underwood was at one time in Bernwode Forest. An old rhyme tells of an early reputation which has no validity today even though the village is close to the industrial county town of Buckingham:

> Grendon Underwode
> The dirtiest town that ever stode.

Just off the highway at the junction of the Aylesbury road is a farmhouse known now as Shakespeare House, but in the 16th and 17th centuries it was the Old Shipe Inn. The association with Shakespeare is recounted in John Aubrey's *Brief Lives* (and has been adopted in local lore):

> The Humour of the Constable in Midsomernight's Dreame, he happened to take at Grendon, in Bucks (I thinke it was Midsomer night that he happened to lye there) which is the roade from London to Stratford, and there was living that Constable about 1642, when I first came to Oxon.

Some of the names Shakespeare uses in *A Midsummer Night's Dream* are those of people he is supposed to have met during his stay. There is no evidence except Aubrey's and the casual similarities of names to support the assertion.

GRIMSBY, Lincolnshire (pop. 110,510) The Lincolnshire coast is a vast expanse of sand dunes and buckthorn and, as a flat area, is subject to considerable flooding. Grimsby (also called Great Grimsby), set near the mouth of the Humber River 15 miles southeast of Hull, is the largest town on the Lincolnshire coast. It was originally a Danish settlement, and by medieval times it had become one of the foremost ports in the world; it then steadily declined because of the silting up of the harbor. Not until the 19th century, when the Freshney River was diverted to form a new dock, did Grimsby begin its period of phenomenal growth, and today it handles more than half a billion tons of fish annually. There are a great number of ancillary products as well: nets (which must be braided by hand), chemicals, cattle foodstuffs, and cod-liver oil are among the most valuable.

Daniel Defoe notices the town in *A Tour thro' the Whole Island of Great Britain:*

> *Grimsby* is a good Town, but I think 'tis but an indifferent Road for Shipping; and in the great Storm, (*Ann.* 1703.) it was proved to be so, for almost all the Ships that lay in *Grimsby* Road were driven from their Anchors, and many of them lost.

The literary fame of Grimsby is due to its use in the early-14th-century verse romance "The Lay of Havelok the Dane." Partly historical in character, the tale relates that the English king Athelwold, at his death, commands Godrich, Earl of Cornwall, to arrange the marriage of Goldborough, the King's daughter, to the strongest and fairest man who can be found. At the same time the Danish Regent orders the drowning of Prince Havelok, who is saved through the good offices of Grim, the fisherman ordered to drown him. Grim with his family and Havelok flee Denmark and land in England:

> In Humber Grim bigan to lende,
> In Lindeseye, riht at the north ende.
> Ther sat his ship up-on the sond,
> But Grim it drou up to the lond;
> And there he made a litel cote
> To him and to hise flote.
> Bigan he there for to erde,
> A litel hus to maken of erthe. . . .

Havelok becomes the husband of Goldborough, whose guardian sees Havelok only as the kitchen knave he has become; Havelok's identity is revealed to his wife by an angel, and he eventually returns to Denmark and regains the throne. Moreover, he raises an army and later adds England to his kingdom. The name Havelok (Abloye) is said to be the Welsh counterpart of Anlaf; Havelok uses the name Cuaran in the scullery, and the historical Anlaf Curan, son of the Viking king Sihtric, later king of Northumbria, was driven into exile in Scotland and married the daughter of Constantine III.

GRISEDALE TARN, Westmorland In the northwest section of Westmorland, the Grisedale glen descends from Fairfield northeast to Ullswater; the glen is traversed by Grisedale Beck, which has as its source Grisedale Tarn at the head of the glen. Perhaps no tarn of the Lake District seems lonelier, more secluded, or more impressive than this one. William and Dorothy Wordsworth and their brother John, a sailor, were here in 1800 before parting for the last time, and a return trip in June 1805 awakened memories of that trip in the poet. Here he wrote "Elegaic Verses in Memory of My Brother, John Wordsworth, Commander of the E. I. Company's Ship the Earl of Abergavenny, in Which He Perished by Calamitous Shipwreck, Feb. 6th, 1805":

> Here did we stop; and here looked round
> While each into himself descends,
> For that last thought of parting Friends
> That is not to be found.
> Hidden was Grasmere Vale from sight,
> Our home and his, his heart's delight,
> His quiet heart's selected home.

Continuing, he asks:

> —Brother and friend, if verse of mine
> Hath power to make thy virtues known,
> Here let a monumental Stone
> Stand—sacred as a Shrine. . . .

About 100 yards down from the tarn, a plaque has been placed on a rock with an inscription from the "Elegaic Verses."

GROOMBRIDGE, Sussex Situated 3½ miles southwest of Tunbridge Wells, Groombridge was historically half in Kent and half in Sussex; the old Sussex part did not appear until the railroad arrived here, but the Kent side of the village, which was a Saxon settlement, has a superb 17th-century manor house standing on the site of a Norman castle. From the 15th century on Groombridge Place belonged to the family of the 17th-century poet Edmund Waller, but in 1618 John Packer bought the estate and built the house which stands today. It was Packer's son Philip who was the friend of both Samuel Pepys and John Evelyn. Evelyn's diary calls this "a pretty Melancholy seate, well wooded & watred" and notes attending services at the "Chapell . . . built by his Father, in remembrance of K: Charles the 1. his safe return out of *Spaine.*" Evelyn may have had a hand in laying out the grounds here.

More recently, from 1903 to 1913, the Cottage was the home of Mark Rutherford (William Hale White); he had retired from the Admiralty in 1891 and after settling here produced *More Pages from a Journal* and *Last Pages from a Journal* (posthumously) as Rutherford and *John Bunyan* as White. His second marriage, to Dorothy Vernon Smith, took place in the parish church here in 1911; he died at his home on March 14, 1913, and was buried in the parish churchyard.

GUILDFORD, Surrey (pop. 40,000) Guildford, pleasantly situated in the Wey Valley, is a large county town within easy commuting distance of London, about 30 miles to the northeast. It sits on a chalk gap between Guildown and Pewley and has long been a part of the major route to the south, but there seems to be no evidence of Roman settlement here. A remarkable discovery in 1928 confirmed a gory event in British history. When King Cnut (Canute) died in 1035, his illegitimate son Harold Harefoot seized the throne. Traveling over what was later known as the Pilgrims' Way, Alfred, Cnut's stepson, was journeying to Winchester to press his own claim to the throne when he was greeted by Earl Godwin, who lavishly entertained him and his 200 men. During the night Alfred and his troop were seized and murdered (some were badly tortured), and the bodies were hastily thrown into a common shallow grave on Guildown. On one of his journeys through Guildford in the 18th century Daniel Defoe noted that the local gallows stood in plain sight of the town on what has proved to be the spot on Guildown which yielded up Alfred and his men. Defoe's suggestion was that the placement enabled the townspeople to see the writhings of the condemned.

By the time of the medieval pilgrimages to the shrine of St. Thomas à Becket in Canterbury, Guildford's prosperity was ensured. The Pilgrims' Way passed through the town, and many pilgrims stopped at the partly Saxon and Norman St. Mary's, or Middle, Church on the High Street. The early affluence of Guildford came from the cloth trade, especially wool; in fact, Guildford cloth, often called Hampshire Kersey, was well known in Italy by the 15th century. In addition, a particular kind of blue cloth was manufactured here; in 1619, when the prosperity of the industry was declining, the inhabitants of Abbott's Hospital determined to support the industry by wearing garments only of this particular cloth, as they still do.

Guildford is linked with King Arthur; in the 14th-century *Le Morte Arthur*, Launcelot is brought by the lord of the manor to Astolat (Guildford), following the jousts at Winchester in which he is wounded by Sir Ector de Maris. Sir Thomas Malory's *Le Morte d'Arthur* actually has two places which could be Guildford: one is the same Astolat as in the earlier work, and the second is Castel Galafort in the Grant St. Graal. One of the earliest-known references to Guildford in literature occurs in *The Owl and the Nightingale* (ca. 12th century), and the poet may well have been a native. The verse debate is written in southwestern dialect, but the rhymes themselves appear to suggest a Surrey or Sussex derivation. The way in which Master Nicholas of Guildford is mentioned, as the possible arbiter of the debate, suggests that he may well have been the author of this poem. This Nicholas lived in Patisham, Dorset, as the poem states. John of Guildford, a known versifier, is also often mentioned as the poet, partly on the appended evidence of a 17th-century owner of one of the two manuscripts.

The High Street and its famous inn, the Red Lion (now White, the Chemist's), have probably received greater attention from literary personages than any other part of the town; the High Street, as Dickens once said, is "the most beautiful High Street in England." It is a marvelous hodgepodge of slowly evolved buildings that seem to fit together particularly well, and it is unadorned with neon signs. But Dickens does not really use Guildford in his novels; his characters merely pass through the town. In *Nicholas Nickleby* Mr. Crummles and company pass down the High Street en route to Portsmouth, and in *David Copperfield* Dora and David spent that one extraordinary day somewhere near here, but, then, they really did not know where they were. John Evelyn was here on August 22, 1653, "to rejoice at the famous Inn the Red Lion, & went to see the Hospital, & Monument of *Geo: Abbot*, late A:Bish: of Canterbury. . . ." John

Aubrey noted that accommodations in Guildford were perhaps the best in England: "the Red Lion particularly can make 50 beds, the White Hart [where Saintsbury's stands] is not quite so good, but has more noble rooms." Samuel Pepys often visited Guildford on his way back and forth between London and Portsmouth on Admiralty business, and he describes the Red Lion in his diary (May 4, 1661) as "the best Inn" in the town. In 1662 he notes cutting asparagus from the garden of the Red Lion for his supper, "the best that ever I eat in my life." In 1668, on a return trip from Portsmouth, he and his companions found the inn "so full of people, and a wedding" that they were forced to take lodgings in a "private house . . . mighty neat and fine." Jane Austen frequently passed through Guildford from Alton and once bought gloves on the High Street, not because the shop looked like a glover's but "rather because it was near. . . ." In 1813 she visited the town in leisure, had a long and comfortable breakfast, perhaps at the Red Lion, and explored the castle, the bowling greens, and the shops. Even William Cobbett, who does not tend to be lavish with praise, on one of his *Rural Rides* wrote that Guildford was "the prettiest, and, taken all together, the most agreeable and most happy-looking town that I ever saw in my life." The novelist Charlotte Smith was buried in St. John's Church here in 1806, following her death in Tilford on October 28.

There are a number of more recent associations of this sort. Lewis Carroll was a frequent guest at the Chestnuts on Castle Hill; the house belonged to his sisters and is marked with a plaque. On his visits he attended the old Church of St. Mary's and, indeed, preached at the church on January 3, 1898. He came here for the Christmas holidays from Oxford, continued work on Part II of his *Symbolic Logic,* and began a series of lectures in logic at Abbott's Hospital on January 5. The following day he was ill with influenza, and within a week bronchial symptoms set in. He died at the Chestnuts on January 14, 1898, and was buried in the Guildford Cemetery at the top of a steep hill called the Mount. The grave is marked with a relatively simple marble cross, and underneath "Rev. Charles Lutwidge Dodgson" has been chiseled out "Lewis Carroll," as he directed, so that children could remember "their friend." On July 18, 1874, while walking on a hillside near Guildford, Lewis Carroll was struck with a line of nonsense on which he built *The Hunting of the Snark:* "For the Snark was a Boojum, you see."

Rudyard Kipling and his wife often spent weekends here in the late 19th and early 20th centuries with John St. Loe Strachey, editor of the *Spectator.* Kipling particularly enjoyed walking in this area and in June 1900 composed a light verse about Guildford and the Pilgrims' Way:

There runs a road by Merton Down—
  A grassy track to-day it is—
An hour out of Guildford town,
  Above the river Wey it is.

Guildford is part of the setting in H. G. Wells's *The Wheels of Chance:* Hoopdriver lodges one night at the Yellow Hammer Coffee Tavern (unidentified), and the Beaumonts lodge at the Earl of Kent (also unidentified), whose sign Hoopdriver sketches. Hilaire Belloc comments on Guildford:

> They sell good Beer at Haslemere
> And under Guildford Hill

Undoubtedly he tasted the Guildford Hill brew when he passed along the Pilgrims' Way on his re-creation of the medieval pilgrimages in December 1902. On July 12, 1953, at his home in Shipley, Sussex, Belloc, aged eighty-two, was found lying on the floor near the burning fireplace in his sitting room, which was engulfed in smoke. Belloc, in a state of severe shock and badly burned, was brought here to the Mount Alvernia Nursing Home of the Franciscan missionaries (Belloc had adopted Catholicism many years before). He received the last sacraments on July 13 and died in the nursing home three days later. His body was taken to West Grinstead, Sussex, for burial.

HADLEY WOOD, Middlesex Once a tiny village in Middlesex where nightingales sang and now a part of the Greater London metropolitan area, Hadley Wood is only 10½ miles north of King's Cross Station, London; here C. Day-Lewis died on May 22, 1972.

HADLOW, Kent (pop. 2,264) Hadlow lies in the flat Medway plain 4 miles northeast of Tonbridge. Its exact location can be spotted from miles away because of a fantastic folly tower built in the 1840s by Walter Barton May. Hadlow has been conjectured to be the birthplace of William Caxton, whose only comment on his place of birth was that he was born "in Kent in the Weeld." No specific evidence supports Hadlow's claim, and a far better case can be made for Tenterden.

HAGLEY, Worcestershire (pop. 1,728) At the foot of the Clent Hills, an area of woodlands, shrubs, pools, and walking country, 3 miles south of Stourbridge, the village of Hagley is modern except for the graceful Palladian Hagley Hall and its Ionic temple in a splendidly landscaped park. The home of the Lytteltons since the 16th century, the Hall became the property of the 1st Baron Lyttelton, who was Chancellor of the Exchequer and a friend of Alexander Pope and patron of James Thomson, author of *The Seasons*. Pope and Joseph Addison both visited Lyttelton and Thomson here when the original timbered hall was standing. Thomson spent every autumn here from 1739 on and made numerous visits in spring and summer as well. In August 1743 he wrote of the park:

> The park, where we pass a great part of our time, is thoroughly delightful, quite enchanting. It consists of several little hills, finely tufted with wood, and rising softly one above another; from which one sees a great variety of at once beautiful and grand, extensive prospects: but I am most charmed with its sweet, embowered retirements, and particularly with a winding dale that runs through the middle of it.

He worked on a revision of *The Seasons* here, and "Spring" contains a fine description of the Park:

> There along the dale
> With woods o'erhung, and shagged with mossy rocks
> Whence on each hand the gushing waters play,
> And down the rough cascade white-dashing fall
> Or gleam in lengthened vista through the trees,
> You silent steal; or sit beneath the shade
> Of solemn oaks, that tuft the swelling mounts
> Thrown graceful round by Nature's careless hand,
> And pensive listen to the various voice
> Of rural peace....

Horace Walpole was another early visitor to Hagley Hall and its gardens and noted that here was such beauty in the "woods, rills, cascades, and . . . thickness of verdure . . . that I quite forgot my favourite Thames!"

William Shenstone was frequently at Harborough Hall, the timber-built Elizabethan hall belonging to his maternal grandparents; "Elegy XV" ("In Memory of a Private Family in Worcestershire") relates his impression of his mother's home. On one occasion Shenstone visited Hagley from nearby Halesowen, and he became such a good friend of Thomson that the latter returned the visit on numerous occasions.

The 1st Baron Lyttelton was a minor poet himself and is included in Dr. Samuel Johnson's *Lives of the Poets*. Johnson had been Lyttelton's guest in 1774 but had little regard for him as a poet.

HALESOWEN, Worcestershire (pop. 28,212) With the Clent Hills to the south and the Black Country to the north, Halesowen, though it is only 7 miles southwest of Birmingham, has a country feeling due perhaps to its location on the Stour River. It is industrial, to be sure, but no factory obtrudes, although all manner of goods, from anchors and buttons to nails and rivets, are produced here. About 1 mile out of town are the ruins of the 13th-century Premonstratensian Halesowen Abbey; one wall of the 200-foot abbey church is now the wall of a barn, and many parts of the abbey were incorporated in the 19th-century farm buildings. William Shenstone's "The Ruined Abbey, or The Effects of Superstition" refers to Halesowen Abbey:

> . . . through the land the musing pilgrim sees
> A tract of brighter green, and in the midst
> Appears a mouldering wall, with ivy crown'd,
> Or Gothic turret, pride of ancient days!
> Now but of use to grace a rural scene,
> To bound our vistas. . . .

About 1 mile north of the church is the Leasowes (known locally as "Lezzers"), the birthplace of William Shenstone on November 18, 1714; that is, Shenstone claimed that he was born here, but the matriculation entry at Pembroke College records his birthplace as Wickstone. The poet's father owned the Leasowes and was churchwarden of the Halesowen parish church, where William was baptized on December 6. The boy obtained his earliest schooling at a dame school run by Sarah Lloyd, whom he commemorates in "The Schoolmistress":

> A russet stole was o'er her shoulders thrown;
> A russet kirtle fenced the nipping air;
> 'Twas simple russet, but it was her own;
> 'Twas her own country bred the flock so fair;
> 'Twas her own labor did the fleece prepare;
> And, sooth to say, her pupils ranged around,
>   Through pious awe, did term it passing rare;
>   For they in gaping wonderment abound,
> And think, no doubt, she been the greatest wight on ground.

His education continued at the grammar school here and then at Solihull before his admission to Oxford. He lived here on the family estate with a guardian until 1745 and at the age of thirty-one, after his guardian's death, took over the estate himself. Sharing the home with his brother Thomas, a nonpracticing attorney, Shenstone began what he considered his life's work: the extensive landscaping of the grounds. He kept himself practically penniless with his lawns, valleys, "natural" beds of water, and priory; but in Dr. Samuel Johnson's words, it did become "a place to be visited by travellers, and copied by designers." Shenstone, though, was frequently depressed and commented in 1749: "I lead the unhappy life of seeing nothing in the creation so idle as myself." In the same vein Horace Walpole commented:

> Poor man! he wanted to have all the world talk of him for the pretty place he had made, and which he seems to have made only that it might be talked of.

Thomas Gray also noted that Shenstone's

> whole philosophy consisted in living against his will in retirement, and in a place which his taste had adorned, but which he only enjoyed when people of note came to see and comment it.

James Thomson came on a number of visits from Hagley, where the two had met, and Shenstone commemorated the autumn 1747 trip by placing a memorial inscription on one of the seats in the grounds.

Returning from a trip in an attempt to secure a pension, Shenstone caught a "putrid fever" and died here in 1763; he was buried on February 15 next to his brother just outside the parish church, where a plain upright stone and a recumbent slab mark the grave. Only his name and "Ob. 11 Feb. 1763, AEt 49" are on the marker. In the west end of the church is a marble tablet surmounted by an urn whose commemorative lines conclude:

>   Reader! if genius, taste refined
> A native elegance of mind;
> If virtue, science, manly sense,
> If wit that never gave offence;
> The clearest head, the tenderest heart
> In thy esteem e'er claim'd a part—
> Ah! smite thy breast, and drop a tear,
> For, know, thy Shenstone's dust lies here.

Ten years after Shenstone's death, Oliver Goldsmith made a pilgrimage here and found the ruined grounds and overgrown walks a reflection of his own *The Deserted Village.*

Francis Brett Young was born on June 29, 1884, at the Laurels, a substantial red-brick Victorian house just outside Halesowen. Like Shenstone, he was christened in the parish church, which he later described as

> a structure of great beauty. The grace and ingenuity of successive ages of priestly architects had embellished its original design with many beautiful features, and the slender beauty of its spire had imposed an atmosphere of dignity and rest upon the rather squalid surroundings of this last of the black-country towns.

The son of a doctor, Young spent his holidays here from school at Sutton Coldfield, Warwickshire, and from Epsom College, London. He discovered Shenstone's poetry quite early and made him a kind of hero because his was the only great name associated with the town. Young read and memorized line after line of the poet's work, and when the rector teased him about his adoration and asked if he remembered anything Shenstone wrote, the boy quoted these lines from "The Ruined Abbey":

>   Each angry friar
> Crawl'd from his bedded strumpet, muttering low
> An ineffectual curse.

When his mother later asked if he had any idea what a "bedded strumpet" was, he replied, "No, but I always thought they were such lovely-sounding words." While he was Epsom College, his mother became ill, and the circumstances of his homecoming are told in *The Young Physician;* Epsom becomes St. Luke's. Arriving home from St. Luke's, Edwin Inglesby is met by his aunt Laura and not allowed to see his mother; the next morning, all the shades are drawn:

> "She's gone," he said, "in the night?"
> "Yes, in the night. She passed away quite quietly. . . ."
> "She was alive when I came yesterday. And you wouldn't let me see her. *You,* of all people. . . . She hated you. She told me so, and she'd hate you for this more than anything." His father took him to the room.

At a dance in Edgbaston, near Birmingham, Young met Jessica Hankinson, a student at the Anstey Physical Training College, then housed at the Leasowes here, who became his wife in 1908 after he had served as ship's doctor on the Holt Lines' *S.S. Kin-*

tuck. He became homesick for England during the year abroad and, returning to the Laurels in May 1907, wrote:

> I have just emerged from a dream . . . walking amid the greenest of hedgerows that told me a thousand times over that I was in my own England. It was Spring, for there were violets, and the poignant sweet cowslips. . . .

After taking a locumship in Bloxwich, Staffordshire, for a short time, he never again spent much time in Halesowen, but his love of Worcestershire was lifelong. The church contains a commemorative plaque.

HALLIFORD, Middlesex   Halliford consists of the hamlets of Upper and Lower Halliford, one old and one new, standing side by side half a mile east of Shepperton. In the early 1820s Thomas Love Peacock acquired a country residence here, Vine Cottage, where he lived until his death. The house, consisting of two old cottages, was close enough to the Thames that the author was able to indulge his love of the river. The decline in his production of literary works began in the mid-1820s, and after the death of his mother in 1833, he commented that he was unable to write anything of interest. As an examiner for the East India Company, he advanced the cause of steam navigation, an act which eventually almost doubled the company's trading volume, and defended the company brilliantly from various attacks and encroachments, especially when the Liverpool and Cheshire combine tried to destroy the company's monopoly of the Indian salt trade. Peacock rose to the post of chief examiner in 1836 and held it until 1856, when he resigned in deference to advanced age and John Stuart Mill. Peacock died here on January 23, 1866, and was buried in the churchyard at Shepperton.

A second resident of Halliford was George Meredith, Peacock's son-in-law. In 1849 Meredith married Mary Ellen Peacock Nicholls, a widow some seven years his senior with a young daughter; the marriage was not a particularly good one even at the start, and the couple struggled for years against overwhelming poverty. In 1853 Peacock took them into his own house and then secured another cottage for them shortly after the birth of their only child in June; the detailed course of the estrangement between the Merediths later appeared in *Modern Love,* and Meredith's own unhappiness was expressed succinctly in "No Sun warmed my roof-tree . . . the marriage was a blunder." Meredith's wife went off with Henry Wallis, the artist, in 1858, and Meredith laid claim to his son and left for London.

HALNAKER, Sussex   Pronounced "hannaker," this minuscule hamlet, 3½ miles northeast of Chichester, has an 18th-century tower mill which was in ruins in 1913 when Hilaire Belloc visited Halnaker and wrote about the mill:

> Sally is gone that was so kindly
>   Sally is gone from Ha'nacker Hill.
> And the Briar grows ever since then so blindly
>   And ever since then the clapper is still,
>   And the sweeps have fallen from Ha'nacker Mill.
>
> H'anacker Hill is in Desolation:
>   Ruin a-top and a field unploughed.
> And Spirits that call on a fallen nation

> Spirits that loved her calling aloud:
> Spirits abroad in a windy cloud.

He set the poem to a high-pitched, plaintive melody, and there is a phonograph record of his singing the words.

HALSTEAD, Kent (pop. 565)   A tiny village 4½ miles northwest of Sevenoaks, Halstead has been bypassed by the dormitory suburbs of London and has kept the charm it had when Edith Nesbit lived with her family at the Hall from 1871 to 1877. The "long low red-brick house" she later described as commonplace except for the covering of roses, ivy, and jasmine; the family lived here in days of prosperity, and much of the country life in Halstead provided a background for her later works.

HALTON HOLEGATE, Lincolnshire (pop. 341)   On the southern edge of the Lincolnshire Wolds 1 mile southeast of Spilsby, Halton Holegate looks out across the Fens. Its 15th-century church, built almost entirely of local sandstone, has stepped buttresses, a 14th-century font, and a number of fine old monuments. Of special interest is the stone effigy of a 14th-century cross-legged crusader with one lion on his shield and a second at his feet, described by Alfred, Lord Tennyson in "Locksley Hall Sixty Years After":

> Yonder in that chapel, slowly sinking now into the ground,
> Lies the warrior, my forefather, with his feet upon the hound.
>
> Cross'd! for once he sail'd the sea to crush the Moslem in his pride;
> Dead the warrior, dead his glory, dead the cause in which he died.

At one time Drummond Rawnsley, father of H. D. Rawnsley (later Canon Rawnsley), was rector here. A local farmer, Gilbey Robinson, is the one who gave the young H. D. the advice that Tennyson preserves in "The Churchwarden and the Curate":

> An' thou'll be 'is Curate 'ere, but, if iver tha meäns to git 'igher,
> Tha mun tackle the sins o' the Wo'ld, an' not the faults o' the Squire.
> An' I reckons tha'll light of a livin' somewheers i' the Wowd or the Fen,
> If tha cottons down to thy betters, an' keeäps thysen to thysen.
> But niver not speäk plaain out, if tha wants to git forrards a bit,
> But creeä along the hedge-bottoms, an' thou'll be a Bishop yit.
>
> Naäy, but tha *mun* speäk hout to the Baptises here i' the town,
> Fur moäst on 'em talks ageän tithe, an' I'd like tha to preäch 'em down,
> Fur *they*'ve bin a-preächin' *mea* down, they heve, an' I haätes 'em now,
> Fur they leäved their nasty sins i' *my* pond, an' it poisoned the cow.

HAM, Wiltshire (pop. 160)   On the Berkshire border 4 miles southwest of Hungerford, Ham is set amid rolling chalk hills and lovely woodland; from 1924 to

1932 Ham Spray House here was the home of the biographer and critic Lytton Strachey. The Georgian house with views to the downs was a pleasant change from the damp house in Tidmarsh, Berkshire, where he had lived almost seven years; here he worked on *Elizabeth and Essex, Portraits in Miniature,* and *Characters and Commentaries.* Strachey died in Ham on January 21, 1932; his ashes were scattered, and a bronze commemorative plaque was placed in the Strachey Chapel at the Chew Magna church, Somerset.

HAMPOLE, Yorkshire (pop. 118) About 6 miles northwest of Doncaster, the tiny village of Hampole was once the location of an important Cistercian priory, founded in 1170 by William de Clarefai for the White Ladies. Among the few scattered known facts is that Richard Rolle, the mystic known as the Hermit of Hampole, spent the last years of his life here. One of the most popular divines of the 14th century, he wrote his works mostly in rhyme for the "unlered and lewed" and presents an extremely good example of early Northumbrian dialect. From the Vienna manuscript and the *English Martyrology* he is known to have lived *in solitudine campii* and "led a solitary life in a wood near to the monastery of *Hampole,* to which place he was wont often to repaire and sing songs." Indeed, the Cistercian nuns looked upon him with veneration and considered him a saint; there are references to Rolle miracles in the Douai manuscript written at Shene.

Rolle neither took orders nor became a doctor of divinity; in fact, he left Oxford at the age of nineteen and styled himself a hermit and irregular teacher. He died at Hampole on September 30, 1349, in the midst of an outbreak of the plague and most likely was buried within the precincts of the nunnery. There is no direct evidence that he contracted the plague, however likely it may seem. In 1393 his body was reinterred in the priory, and by 1508 it was removed to its own chapel. With the dissolution and eventual destruction of the buildings and grounds, his remains were lost.

HAMPTON AND HAMPTON COURT, Middlesex Situated on the north bank of the Thames River in the borough of Twickenham and within 15 miles of Waterloo Station in London, Hampton has the remains of an 18th-century village (on Thames, Church, and the High Streets) and has preserved numerous 17th-century houses, including the Old Grange and Orme House. The center of the village is St. Mary's Church, a rather disappointing example of the church architecture of the 1830s. Near the church is Hampton House, now known as Garrick's Villa and the residence of David Garrick from 1757 until his death in 1779. Garrick was then at the height of his fame, and the entertaining here was lavish. Horace Walpole, known to be particular in such matters, was a guest at at least one of these parties and remarked, "*Sur assez bon ton* for a player." Dr. Samuel Johnson was a guest on many occasions and once visited the Bell, which he found "neat and clean within." There are numerous stories connected with Johnson's visits: when Garrick protested at his pulling down finely bound books, he retorted, "Lookee David, you do understand plays, but know nothing of books!" He also suggested that Garrick connect the two sides of the grounds, which are split by a public road. On the lawn Garrick built a classical temple to house Louis-François Roubillac's statue of Shakespeare, for which Garrick sat. The original of the work is now in the British Museum.

Not all the other literary associations here are fully documented. As a very young child Robert Herrick came to his aunt's home shortly after the death of his father in November 1592. The circumstances surrounding the elder Herrick's death were strange (he fell from an upper-story window of their London home just after having drawn his will), and the family may well have come here to escape gossip. Where his aunt, Anne Campion, lived is not known. Thomas Gray spent a short time here in June 1758 with Lady Cobham before going on to Strawberry Hill. Charles Dickens made some use of Hampton in *Oliver Twist, Nicholas Nickleby,* and *Our Mutual Friend.* In *Oliver Twist* Bill Sikes and Oliver

> reached a town. Here against the wall of a house, Oliver saw written up in pretty large letters, "Hampton." They lingered about, in the fields, for some hours. At length they came back into the town; and, turning into an old public-house with a defaced sign-board, ordered some dinner by the kitchen fire.
>
> The kitchen was an old low-roofed room; with a great beam across the middle of the ceiling, and benches, with high backs to them, by the fire; on which were seated several rough men in smock-frocks, drinking and smoking.

The inn is thought to have been the Red Lion (later rebuilt) or the White Hart. *Nicholas Nickleby* talks of Hampton on race days:

> The little race-course at Hampton was in the full tide and height of its gaiety.... Every gaudy colour that fluttered in the air from carriage seat and garish tent top, shone out in its gaudiest hues. Old dingy flags grew new again, faded gilding was re-burnished, stained rotten canvas looked a snowy white, the very beggars' rags were freshened up, and sentiment quite forgot its charity in its fervent admiration of poverty so picturesque.

The fatal duel takes place on the riverbank near Twickenham. *Our Mutual Friend* contains many references to this general vicinity, and Betty Higden flees from the White Lion (the Red Lion) from the questioners:

> "For the Lord's love don't meddle with me!" cried old Betty, all her fears crowding on her. "I am quite well now, and I must go this minute."
>
> She caught up her basket as she spoke.... Nor did she feel safe until she had set a mile or two of by-road between herself and the market-place, and had crept into a copse, like a hunted animal, to hide and recover breath. Not until then for the first time did she venture to recall how she had looked over her shoulder before turning out of the town, and had seen the sign of the White Lion hanging across the road, and the fluttering market booths, and the old grey church, and the little crowd gazing after her but not attempting to follow her.

Anthony Trollope's *The Three Clerks* also uses Hampton for its setting; Jessamine House here becomes Surbiton Cottage:

> There are still, however, some few nooks within the reach of the metropolis which have not been be-villaed and be-terraced out of all look of rural charm, and the

little village of Hampton, with its old-fashioned country inn, and its bright, quiet, grassy river, is one of them. . . .

It was here that the Woodwards lived. Just on the outskirts of the village, on the side of it furthest from town, they inhabited not a villa, but a small old-fashioned brick house, abutting on to the road, but looking from its front windows on to a lawn and garden, which stretched down to the river.

The grounds were not extensive, . . . but the most had been made of it; it sloped prettily to the river, and was absolutely secluded from the road.

Finally, Jerome K. Jerome brings the protagonists of *Three Men in a Boat* to Hampton, where

the sunny river, from the Palace up to Hampton Church, is dotted and decked with yellow, and blue, and orange, and white, and red, and pink.

Harris, he says,

wanted to get out at Hampton Church, to go and see Mrs. Thomas's tomb.

"Who is Mrs. Thomas?" I asked.

"How should I know?" replied Harris. "She's a lady that's got a funny tomb, and I want to see it."

But Harris did not see the "funny tomb" and would have been disappointed if he had; the tomb is a simple life-size effigy.

The village of Hampton traditionally claims that Claire Clairmont, the woman whose place in the lives of Shelley and Byron is well known, was buried in an unmarked grave in the churchyard here. However, this seems most unlikely since she died in Florence.

Divorcing the village of Hampton from the magnificent Hampton Court Palace less than 1 mile to the east is impossible because in many ways the village grew up adjacent to the old manor house. Situated in magnificent parkland on the Thames, Hampton Court dates from before the Norman Conquest, when the small Saxon manor belonged to Earl Algar. By 1240 the estate had been sold to the prior of the Hospital of St. John of Jerusalem for 1,000 marks (roughly £556) so that the already-established preceptory near Hampton Court could be moved here. The estate was extensive, covering more than 2,000 acres, and had on it a house, a dovecote, and a chapel. The Knights Hospitallers added to the buildings, and Henry VII, after his victory at Bosworth Field in 1485, spent time here with the religious community. Five years after Henry's death, Thomas Wolsey secured the lease of Hampton from the Knights Hospitallers and embarked on an ambitious building program. The old house was razed, and elaborate drainage systems and walled-in gardens were begun; the drainage and water systems alone are said to have cost almost £50,000.

The palace, covering about 8 acres, was a series of two-story structures clustered around the two main courtyards and numerous smaller ones with cloisters. In all there were 1,000 rooms, including a chapel, multiple kitchens and sculleries, the Great Hall, a banqueting hall, a suite for the King, and 280 bedrooms for guests. The richness of the surroundings cannot even be imagined: eighteen chambers were hung with Arras tapestry, Wolsey's own rooms were hung with cloth of gold, Venetian carpeting covered sixty rooms, and Italian Renaissance tapestry was bought by the case lot. In addition, the Cardinal had 500 retainers, sixteen priests, eighty kitchen

servitors and a master chef, and 100 washerwomen here along with scores of others. The opulence and ostentation caused John Skelton, who was not on the friendliest terms with Wolsey, to turn to satiric verse; the Cardinal, he writes,

. . . ruleth all the roast
With bragging and with boast,
Borne up on every side
With pomp and with pride.

And he says:

The Kynge's Courte
Shoulde have the excellence;
But Hampton Court
Hath the preemynence.
And Yorkes Place,
With my lord's grace,
To whose magnifycence
To all the conflewence,
Sutys and supplycacons,
Embassades of all nacyons.

What really seems to have made the prelate unbearable was the arrival of the Cardinal's hat, which William Tyndale reported "was set on a cupboard and tapers about, so that the greatest Duke in the land must make curtesie thereto." Wolsey's attitude irritated even Sir Thomas More, who made more than one comment about the hat and the Cardinal's mistress, "the daughter of one Lark," and their children.

Wolsey was forced to turn the palace over to Henry VIII in the summer of 1525, after being asked why Hampton Court had been built on such a magnificent scale and replying, "To show how noble a palace a subject may offer his sovereign." Henry took the offer seriously. He got rid of some of the trappings of the disgraced and dead Archbishop, enlarged the house and the Great Hall, and redecorated completely. Henry's natural son by Elizabeth Blount, Henry Fitzroy, Duke of Richmond, spent a great deal of time here in the company of the young Henry Howard, Earl of Surrey. Here in 1537 the earl struck a courtier who insinuated that he sympathized with the "Yorkist insurgents," and he was imprisoned at Windsor on that account. Perhaps in the same year (although 1544 also is possible, since the chapter of the Garter was held here then) Surrey penned the "Description and Praise of His Loue Geraldine," his first love:

Honsdon did first present her to mine iyen:
Bright is her hewe, and Geraldine she hight.
Hampton me taught to wishe her first for mine:
And Windsor, alas, dothe chase me from her sight.
Her beauty of kinde her vertues from aboue.
Happy is he, that can obtaine her loue.

Geraldine was Elizabeth Fitzgerald, daughter of the 9th Earl of Kildare, and she was about nine years of age in 1537.

Queen Elizabeth made few changes at Hampton when she came to the throne, and Sir Francis Bacon conveys an excellent impression of the gardens in his essay on them. Some of the plants set out here had been brought back from foreign countries for her by Sir Walter Ralegh, Sir John and Sir Richard Hawkins, and Sir Francis Drake.

Hampton Court gained in popularity during the reign of James I and his wife Anne, who spent their first Christmas here in 1603 amid much splendor. Samuel Daniel, made Master of the Queen's Revels during the last months of Elizabeth's reign, wrote a new masque for the Queen and selected other pieces for the performance. The newly formed King's Company of Comedians performed the plays, and since William Shakespeare's name appears on the list, it is reasonable to assume that he was in attendance. Tradition says that Ben Jonson was ejected from the performance of Daniel's *The Vision of the Twelve Goddesses* for his outspoken criticism and unruly behavior, although the account may be exaggerated. John Taylor, the "water poet," also visited Hampton Court about this time and wrote of the Paradise Room, where some needlework done by Queen Mary hung:

> In Windsor Castle and in Hampton Court
>   In that most pompous room called Paradise,
> Whoever pleases thither to resort
>   May see some works of hers of wondrous price.
> Her greatness held it no disreputation
>   To hold the needle in her royal hand;
> Which was a good example to our nation,
>   To banish idleness throughout the land.

With the accession of Charles I, Hampton was almost the sole residence of the royal family, and Charles added much to the wealth and splendor of the palace. Ironically, in view of his love of Hampton Court, Charles was imprisoned here by the Parliamentarians in 1648 but was treated much like a privileged (but restricted) guest and was allowed to receive visitors. John Evelyn came on September 10, just about six weeks after the start of the King's imprisonment:

> I went to *Hampton Court,* where I had the honour to kisse his Majesties Hand, and give him an Account of severall things I had in charge, he being now in the power of those execrable Villains who not long after mu[r]der'd him. . . .

Evelyn was to return to Hampton Court.

The palace was a favorite of Oliver Cromwell's, and, indeed, from here in 1657 Mary Cromwell, the Protector's "Little Mall," married Thomas Belayse, 2d Viscount Fauconberg. Andrew Marvell wrote "Two Songs" in honor of the nuptials and read the poem here. The following year, knowing that Cromwell was ill and that his daughter Elizabeth, whose infant son had just died, was dying of cancer, Marvell described how the two tried to keep their sufferings from each other:

> She, lest he grieve, hides what she can her pains,
> And he, to lessen hers, his sorrow feigns. . . .

Charles II brought his new bride Catherine of Braganza here for their honeymoon. Evelyn, back again, noted in his diary that she

> arived, with a traine of Portugueze Ladys in their mo[n]strous fardingals or *Guard-Infantas:* Their complexions *olivaster,* & sufficiently unagreable: *Her majestie* in the same habit, her foretop long & turned aside very strangely: She was yet of the handsomest Countenance of all the rest, & tho low of stature pretily shaped, languishing & excellent Eyes, her teeth wronging her mouth by stiking a little too far out: for the rest sweete & lovely enough. . . .

Evelyn's commentary was more generous than that of Edward Hyde, 1st Earl of Clarendon, who was Charles's Lord Chancellor. He described the retinue as "old, ugly and proud, and incapable of any conversation with persons of quality and a liberal education." The Guarda Infanta, the most virtuous of the virtuous, were horrified when Charles's mistress, Barbara Villiers, Lady Castlemaine, gave birth to their son during the royal couple's honeymoon. However, as Samuel Pepys notes in his diary under the date of Sunday, June 22, 1662:

> This day I am told of a Portugal Lady, at Hampton Court, that hath dropped a child already since the Queen's coming, but the King would not have them searched whose it is; and so it is not commonly known yet.

Pepys was frequently at Hampton Court and usually journeyed, as was the custom, up the Thames. With Charles, who was often at Hampton, the grounds and palace underwent extensive changes; Evelyn describes them admirably:

> *Hampton Court* is as noble & uniforme a Pile & as Capacious as any *Gotique* Architecture can have made it: There is incomparable furniture in it . . . [and] many rare Pictures. . . . The Gallery of Hornes is very particular for the vast beames of staggs. . . . The *Queenes* bed was an Embordery of silver on Crimson Velvet, & cost 8000 pounds, being a present made by the states of *Holland* . . . . The great looking-Glasse & Toilet of beaten & massive Gold was given by the Q: Mother &c. . . . The Greate hall is a most magnificent roome: The Chapel roofe incomparably fretted & gild. . . . The *Park* formerly a flat, naked piece of Ground, now planted with sweete rows of *lime-trees,* and the Canale for water now neere perfected. . . . The Cradle Walk of horne-beame in the Garden, is for the perplexed twining of the Trees, very observable &c: Another *Parterr* there is which they call *Paradise* in which a pretty banqueting house, set over a Cave or Cellar. . . .

The bower described as "horne-beame" is, in fact, wych elm.

When William of Orange and Mary gained the throne in 1689, they were thoroughly entranced by Hampton's seclusion and beauty. Queen Mary examined every room herself, and together the couple decided to have Sir Christopher Wren redesign the State Rooms. These are the massive rectangular structures whose mathematical precision stands in poor contrast to the old Tudor expanses. In *A Tour thro' the Whole Island of Great Britain* Daniel Defoe comments on the building program:

> Whoever knew *Hampton-Court* before it was begun to be rebuilt, or alter'd, by the late King *William,* must acknowledge it was a very compleat Palace before, and fit for a King; and tho' it might not, according to the modern Method of Building, or of Gardening, pass for a Thing exquisitely fine; yet it had this remaining to itself, and perhaps peculiar; namely, that it shewed a Situation exceedingly capable of Improvement. . . .
>
> This Her Majesty Queen *Mary* was so sensible of, that while the King had order'd the pulling down the old Apartments, . . . [she then] fix'd upon a Building formerly made use of chiefly for landing from the River, and therefore call'd the *Water Gallery.* . . .
>
> The Queen had here her Gallery of Beauties, being the Pictures, at full Length, of the principal Ladies attending upon her Majesty, or who were frequently in her Reti-

nue. . . . Her Majesty had here a fine Apartment, with a Sett of Lodgings, for her private Retreat only, but most exquisitely furnish'd; particularly a fine Chints Bed, then a great Curiosity. . . .

Defoe goes on at great length, noting the "Fountain and *Jette d'Eau's*" planned for the King and the cartoons William had imported. William, indeed, wanted another Versailles, and the work was nowhere near completion when he died in 1702.

Queen Anne, faced with her brother-in-law's heavy debts, stopped the building program; she came to Hampton fairly frequently in the early years of her reign and entertained numerous literary figures here. Not in good health when she ascended the throne, she suffered increasingly from gout and dropsy; it was said that her fondness for food was matched only by her husband's fondness for drink. Jonathan Swift encountered the Queen at this time:

> We made our bows and stood, about twenty of us, round the room while the Queen looked at us with her fan in her mouth, and once in a minute said about three words to some that were nearest to her; and then she was told that dinner was ready and went out. . . . I dined at Her Majesty's board of green cloth. It is much the best table in England and costs the Queen £1,000 a month while she is at Windsor or Hampton Court, and is the only mark of magnificence or royal hospitality that I can see in the Royal household.

Swift disliked having dinner here or anywhere because of the size of the tips required.

An incident at Hampton Court during Anne's reign brought about one of the most famous 18th-century poems. Arabella Fermor, the 7th Baron Petre, and Sir George Brown were invited for an evening of cards at the lodging residence of a Hampton Court official. Here, Lord Petre cut off a lock of Miss Fermor's hair, and a distinct estrangement occurred between the two families. Alexander Pope, attempting to force a reconciliation, wrote *The Rape of the Lock*, whose whole setting is here. Early in the poem Pope conveys a fairly representative portrait of the palace:

> Close by those meads, forever crowned with flowers,
> Where Thames with pride surveys his rising towers,
> There stands a structure of majestic frame,
> Which from the neighboring Hampton takes its name.
> Here Britain's statesmen oft the fall foredoom
> Of foreign tyrants and of nymphs at home;
> Here thou, great Anna! whom three realms obey,
> Dost sometimes counsel take—and sometimes tea.
>   Hither the heroes and the nymphs resort,
> To taste awhile the pleasures of a court. . . .

Pope, though, thought the whole court routine dull.

Another event in the same year found its way into literature. A party of eighteen, including one Member of Parliament, were at the Toye, an inn in Hampton, for an evening of drinking and jesting. Sir Cholmondley Deering, the Member of Parliament for Kent, quarreled with Richard Thornhill, knocked him down, and broke seven of his teeth. In the duel which followed, no seconds were used, and no distance was paced off. Sir Cholmondley was killed, and Thornhill, ultimately tried for murder, escaped with a conviction of manslaughter and was sentenced to be "burned in the hand." Three months later, Thornhill was murdered by two men on horseback, who chased him from Hampton Court nearly to Chiswick. An essay in *The Spectator* by Richard Steele deals with dueling and this event and makes Thornhill into Spinamont:

> But alas! in the Dominions of *Pharamond,* by the Force of a Tyrant Custom, which is misnamed a Point of Honour, the Duellist kills his Friend whom he loves; and the Judge condemns the Duellist, while he approves his Behaviour.

After Anne's death in 1714, George I, who had little English, arrived in England with his two mistresses, later known in court circles as the Maypole (Madame Schulemburg, who was tall and thin) and the Elephant and Castle (Madame Kielmannsegge, who was enormously fat). Horace Walpole met the Maypole when he was a child and was terrified because of her

> two fierce black eyes, large and rolling beneath two lofty arched eyebrows; two acres of cheek spread with crimson, an ocean of neck that overflowed and was not distinguished from the lower part of her body, and no part restrained by stays.

He also related the incident of her being carried through the streets and popping her head from the window of the sedan chair in response to the crowd's noise. Asking, "Good people, why do you abuse us? We come for all your goods," she was met with the response, "Yes, damn ye! and for our chattels too." With King George in residence life was tedious and dull; Alexander Pope had the misfortune of being at the palace during one of the King's visits:

> I can easily believe that no lone house in Wales, with a mountain and a rookery, is more contemplative than this Court. . . . In short, I heard of no ball, assembly, basset table, or any place where two or three were gathered together except Madame Kielmannsegge's, to which I had the honour to be invited and the grace to stay away.

One of George's few planned events here was scheduled for the summer of 1718, when the King's Company of Actors was to put on two plays a week; the first, *Hamlet,* was eventually presented on September 23, and the second, *Henry VIII,* was chosen by the King. Colley Cibber, then Poet Laureate, played Cardinal Wolsey and proceeded directly to the royal box to deliver the whispered speech to Thomas Cromwell:

> A word with you.
>   [*To the* Secretary.
> Let there be letters writ to every shire,
> Of the king's grace and pardon. The griev'd commons
> Hardly conceive of me; let it be nois'd
> That through our intercession this revokement
> And pardon comes. . . .

The reason for Cibber's action was obvious: George often accused the ministers of taking credit for duties they had been told to perform.

James Thomson wrote of Hampton Court during this time:

> Here languid Beauty kept her pale-faced courts:
> Bevies of dainty dames of high degree
> From every quarter hither made resort:
> Where from gross mortal care and business free,
> They lay poured out in ease and luxury.

George never came to Hampton Court during the last seven years of his reign, and the palace was overrun with squatters who did not respond to royal edict.

George III, at the start of his long reign, set out to regularize the places of the now-traditional squatters and established the first Grace-and-Favour residents; two centuries later the privilege still exists. Hannah More, who often visited David Garrick's villa, lived at the palace for a short time and wrote to Horace Walpole:

> The private apartments are almost all full; they are occupied by people of fashion, mostly of quality; and it is astonishing to me that people of large fortune will solicit for them. Mr. Lowndes has apartments next to these, notwithstanding he has an estate of £4,000 a year.

Not only the wealthy were granted apartments; the rule was that those who had performed a service to the country were eligible, and the families of these men were occasionally impoverished. In 1776 Samuel Johnson asked for lodgings here:

> My lord.... Some of the apartments at Hampton Court are now vacant, in which I am encouraged to hope that, by application to your lordship, I may obtain a residence. Such a grant would be considered by me a great favour; and I hope, to a man who has had the honour of vindicating His Majesty's government, a retreat in one of his houses may not improperly or unworthily be allowed.

Johnson did not get the accommodations. Horace Walpole, son of Sir Robert Walpole, George II's Prime Minister, often visited family members in these apartments and on one occasion had a nasty mishap:

> It was dusk; there was a very low step at the door, I did not see it; it tripped me up. I fell headlong on the stones, and against the frame of a table at the door, and battered myself so much that my whole hip is as black as my shoe, besides bruising one hand, both knees, and my left elbow, into which it brought the gout next day.

Hampton Court and its grounds had been opened to the public by George II, and in the 18th and 19th centuries many persons visited the vast estate. Fanny Burney, author of *Evelina*, visited it in the company of David Garrick, and in May 1828 Sir Walter Scott made one of his three or four trips here. He records:

> *May 25.*—After a morning of letter-writing, leave-taking, papers-destroying, and God knows what trumpery, Sophia and I set out for Hampton Court, carrying with us the following lions and lionesses—Samuel Rogers, Tom Moore, Wordsworth, with wife and daughter. We were very kindly and properly received by Walter and his wife, and had a very pleasant day.

Thomas Moore, noting this trip in his *Journal*, comments that the public "were all *eyes* after Scott, the other scribblers not coming in for a glance." Another visitor was Mary Mitford. Finally, Jerome K. Jerome included Hampton Court in *Three Men in a Boat*, but in contrast to his approach elsewhere, he made no attempt to describe the vast and much-written-about palace. Rather, he wrote of the famous maze, for which Harris has a map guaranteeing an easy exit. Harris picks up many lost souls: the group walk and walk and finally become mired in the center:

> Whatever way they turned brought them back to the middle. It became so regular at length, that some of the people stopped there, and waited for the others to take a walk round, and come back to them. Harris drew out his map again, after a while, but the sight of it only infuriated the mob, and they told him to go and curl his hair with it. Harris said that he couldn't help feeling that, to a certain extent, he had become unpopular.

They "sang out for the keeper" who turns out to be "new to the business; and when he got in, he couldn't get to them, and then *he* got lost."

> They had to wait until one of the old keepers came back from his dinner before they got out.
> Harris said he thought it was a very fine maze, so far as he was a judge. . . .

Victoria encouraged applications for the Grace-and-Favour apartments, and until recently fifty of these were available at the sole discretion of the sovereign. Today the highest, most luxurious, and largest rooms on the top floor are unoccupied, the problem of hauling up milk and bread and groceries through an open window proving to be too much of a strain for the elderly tenants. Still, more than twenty-five apartments in the palace are occupied by the families of men who have been distinguished in the arts and sciences or the services, and other houses in the parks and gardens or on the green outside the gates are Grace-and-Favour apartments.

HAMPTON-IN-ARDEN, Warwickshire (pop. 1,157) In the 16th century, the thickly wooded Forest of Arden covered an area of 200 or so square miles north and west of the Avon River, but today the great forest is little more than an occasional clump of freestanding trees. The name Hampton-in-Arden is at least a reminder of those days, but the village is now more of a dormitory, lying as it does midway between Coventry and Birmingham. With a 17th-century packhorse bridge crossing the Blithe River and some fine 17th-century cottages, Hampton-in-Arden has long been accepted as the scene of William Shakespeare's *As You Like It*.

HAMPTON WICK, Middlesex Now in the borough of Twickenham and part of the Greater London area, Hampton Wick is about 12 miles southwest of the Waterloo Station on the north bank of the Thames River opposite Kingston-on-Thames. Hampton Court Park is the combined size of Kensington Gardens and Hyde Park, and the contiguous Bushy Park is renowned for its flowering chestnuts and lime trees planted in a triple avenue. The lodge (now part of the National Physical Laboratory) was once the residence of the park ranger, and when the 1st Earl of Halifax held the post in the early 18th century, Richard Steele was a frequent guest; he dedicated the fourth volume of *The Tatler* to Halifax and wrote of Bushy Park in one of the essays. Steele took a house and garden here in the summer of 1708; already deeply in debt, he borrowed £1,000 from Joseph Addison to set his "country box" like a villa in miniature and then gave it the whimsical name of the Hovel, perhaps out of excessive pride. The Hovel and its occupants come into William Makepeace Thackeray's *Henry Esmond*; the protagonist spends a night at the Hovel as a guest of the Steeles:

> Indeed Harry had ridden away from Hampton that very morning, leaving . . . [Captain and Mrs. Steele] by the ears; for from the chamber where he lay, in a bed that was

none of the cleanest, and kept awake by the company which he had in his own bed, and the quarrel which was going on in the next room, he could hear both night and morning the curtain lecture which Mrs. Steele was in the habit of administering to poor Dick.

At night it did not matter so much for the culprit; Dick was fuddled, and when in that way no scolding could interrupt his benevolence. Mr. Esmond could hear him coaxing and speaking in that maudlin manner, which punch and claret produce, to his beloved Prue, and beseeching her to remember that there was a *distiwisht officer ithe rex roob,* who overhear her. She went on, nevertheless, calling him a drunken wretch, and was only interrupted in her harangues by the Captain's snoring.

In the morning, the unhappy victim awoke to a headache and consciousness, and the dialogue of the night was resumed.... But Dick was charming, though his wife was odious....

In the mid-19th century R. D. Blackmore and his wife had a "comfortable villa" in Hampton Wick when the novelist was teaching in Twickenham. They remained from 1854 until late 1859.

HAMSTERLEY, County Durham There are several instances of duplicate villages in County Durham, and the Hamsterleys are a case in point. This Hamsterley is near the sprawling industrial complex of Consett, which is responsible for a good deal of visible pollution. The British Steel Works, frequently called "Britain's worst-sited steelworks," provides an eerie dominance to an area which would otherwise belong to sheep.

Hamsterley Hall, in well-wooded grounds east of the village, was the birthplace of Robert Smith Surtees in 1803, more than a quarter of a century before the first small mill was erected. The Hall, a mixture of 18th- and 19th-century construction, was famous for its lovely grounds and large pack of hounds. From 1825 to 1838 Surtees lived in London, where he wrote *Jorrocks' Jaunts and Jollities,* but returned when he succeeded to the estate upon his father's death. A suggestion from John Gibson Lockhart, Sir Walter Scott's son-in-law and biographer, induced Surtees to write two of the later novels, *Handley Cross* and *Hillingdon Hall,* in which Hamsterley Hall is undoubtedly depicted and in which Jorrocks reappears.

Surtees was appointed justice of the peace and deputy lieutenant for County Durham in 1842 and painstakingly fulfilled his duties. He had a bit of the sporting Jorrocks in him, and for two years he kept a large pack of hounds here.

HANLEY, Staffordshire (pop. 67,891) A largely industrial area now called Stoke-on-Trent and formed from the amalgamation of Burslem, Hanley, Longton, Tunstall, Stoke, and Fenton, Hanley has been one of the foremost towns involved in pottery making since at least the 16th century. Ideally located above the Trent River and close to the Grand Trunk Canal, Hanley was a logical place for the pottery industry to develop because of adequate supplies of clay, water, and coal. Archaeological evidence points to pottery making here as early as Neolithic times; the Romans and Saxons also are known to have potted in the area. By the 18th century, when the master potters Josiah Wedgwood, Aaron Wood, John Flaxman, Josiah Spode, Thomas Minton, and others appeared, the industry was not only highly developed but ready for

new processes. All the pottery towns grew haphazardly but rapidly throughout the 17th, 18th, and 19th centuries, and they seem much the same, all on the same main road. In the 20th century this lack of distinction affected J. B. Priestley, as he notes in his *English Journey:*

There is no city. There are still these six little towns. After federation into one city had been first suggested, the inhabitants of these towns argued and quarrelled most bitterly for years.... But when you go there, you still see the six towns, looking like six separate towns. Unless you are wiser than I was, you will never be quite sure which of the six you are in at any given time; but at least you will be ready to swear that you are nowhere near a city that contains three hundred thousand people.... For what distinguishes this district, to my eye and mind, is its universal littleness. Everything there is diminutive. Even the landscape fits in.... And unless I am sadly wrong, unless I was so dominated by this idea of littleness that I could not use my eyes, the very people are small; sturdy enough, of course, and ready to give a good account of themselves; but nearly all stunted in height.

On May 27, 1867, Arnold Bennett, the man who made the "Five Towns" famous in literature, was born at 90 Hope Street; the house, at the corner of Hope and Hanover Streets, was demolished in 1961, but a plaque has been placed on the new structure. Bennett's father was a potter, schoolmaster, and pawnbroker and then became a solicitor; at times the family fortunes were quite low. The Bennetts moved to Burslem when Arnold was still a child. The Potteries play an important role in his works, and the towns are always disguised with the same names: Tunstall becomes Turnhill, Burslem is Bursley, Hanley is Hambridge, Stoke becomes Knype, and Longton is Longshaw. *Anna of the Five Towns, Clayhanger, Hilda Lessways, The Old Wives' Tale,* and *These Twain* are all set in this area.

A second author to use the Potteries and Hanley as a setting for a novel was H. G. Wells, who places *In the Days of the Comet* here. This is the district in which Leadford lives, and the towns of Clayton, Leer, Overcastle, and Swathinglea mentioned by Wells are identical with Bennett's towns.

HAPPISBURGH, Norfolk (pop. 574) The Norfolk coast from Happisburgh (also spelled Hasbro' but always pronounced "haze'bro") northwest to Blakeney is subject to constant assault from the sea. As a consequence, this village, snugly settled in sand dunes 5 miles east of North Walsham, has had to erect defenses to protect its land. The treacherous Hasbro' Sands offshore are signaled by both the red-and-white striped lighthouse and the tall tower of the Perpendicular St. Mary's Church, but the beach area is pleasant and quite safe.

On a motoring visit here Sir Arthur Conan Doyle got the idea for "The Adventure of the Dancing Men" from the small son of Mr. Cubbitt, the owner of Hill House Hotel, where he stayed; it was Cubbitt's son who wrote his signature in dancing men. Doyle worked on the story in the Green Room.

HARBLEDOWN, Kent (pop. 896) Only 1 mile west of Canterbury, Harbledown was the last village on the medieval Pilgrims' Way. There was then a leper hospital, St. Nicholas' Hospital, which was of interest to the pilgrims since it preserved one of St. Thomas à Becket's shoes as a relic. Indeed, the shoe was still around in the 16th century, when it was presented to Erasmus and John Colet to kiss ceremoniously. Erasmus was not openly hostile to the offer, but Colet's reaction was extreme and not a little vulgar, ending with "[w]hy doe they not by the same reason offer us their spittle, and other excrements of the body to be kissed?"

Harbledown is the "Bobbe-up-and-doun" of Geoffrey Chaucer's *Canterbury Tales:*

> Woot ye nat where ther stant a litel toun
> Which that ycleped is Bobbe-up-and-doun,
> Under the Blee, in Caunterbury Weye?

"Bobbe-up-and-doun" is still an apt description of the Harbledown switchback.

HARDWICK, Oxfordshire (pop. 41) So small now as to be less than a hamlet, Hardwick is a lonely place about 5 miles north of Bicester with little remaining to show its early history and importance. The old gray church hides behind a farm which is all that remains of the ancient manor house of the Earls of Effingham. Equally bereft of its history is the adjacent community of Tusmore, where there was once a magnificent manor house. There are only scant remains now: a medieval oak granary set on piles of stones with a dovecote over it.

The lake, more than 8 acres in extent, tradition says was excavated in Elizabeth's reign by a renegade Catholic priest who was undetected during the 12 years he labored here. One arm of the lake is crossed by a balustraded bridge, and nearby is a Temple of Peace built as a memorial to Alexander Pope about 1770. The Tudor mansion at Tusmore belonged to the Fermors, a staunch Catholic family, who literally had moved their house here from Somerton in the 16th century. Pope was a frequent guest, and *The Rape of the Lock* was occasioned by an incident involving Arabella Fermor and Lord Petre, who cut off a lock of Miss Fermor's hair. The incident led to a definite coolness between two families that had once been on good terms, and John Caryll, a relative of Lord Petre, persuaded Pope to write the poem to heal the breach. In the memorial temple is a stone inscribed with a verse from Pope's work.

HAREFIELD, Middlesex (pop. 2,812) A rural English village in the Greater London area seems unlikely, but Harefield, 4 miles north of Uxbridge, is just that. With an area of more than 4,600 acres, agriculture is still the main employment here, as it has been since the 12th century. Originally the northern stretches of outer London were the hunting grounds and playgrounds of the wealthy as well as rich farming land, and at one time there were more than twenty-five farms in this village alone. Both Cripps Farm and Colney Farm date to the 14th century. The Church of St. Mary the Virgin here is not impressive outside, but inside it is overwhelming with its ornately carved altar rails and its monuments to the Ashbys, Newdigates, and Tarletons. Most impressive is the Jacobean monument to Alice, Dowager Countess of Derby and the Lady of Harefield Manor, to whom Edmund Spenser dedicated "The Teares of the

Muses"; she was also the "sweet Amaryllis" of his "Colin Clout's Come Home Again."

John Marston wrote an entertainment for Lady Alice, and she acted the part of Zenobia in Ben Jonson's *The Masque of Queens,* but it is John Milton's association with the dowager countess that is the most famous. Probably in 1633, he wrote *Arcades* for her, and it was performed on the grounds of Harefield Manor "by some Noble persons of her Family...." Milton's presence here is debated, but in 1632 he retired to Horton, only 12 miles away, and the work displays such specialized knowledge of the grounds and setting that at least one preproduction visit is indicated. He notes the hill in the background:

> When Ev'ning gray doth rise, I fetch my round
> Over the mount, and all this hallow'd ground,
> And early ere the odorous breath of morn
> Awakes the slumb'ring leaves, or tassell'd horn
> Shakes the high thicket, haste I all about....

And he accurately describes both

> ... the smooth enamell'd green
> Where no print of step hath been....

and the long avenue of elms leading to the house where the Countess was to sit:

> Under the shady roof
> Of branching Elm Star-proof,
>   Follow me;
> I will bring you where she sits....

It is also possible that Milton visited Henry Lawes here when the latter was attached to the 1st Earl's household as a musical tutor; Lawes is known to have been here for the performance of *Arcades.*

The original Harefield Manor, which stood very near the church, burned to the ground in 1660, when Sir Charles Sedley held the estate. The accident is said to have resulted from his carelessness in adopting the then-dangerous practice of reading in bed.

Probably apocryphal is the tradition that William Shakespeare and his players performed *Othello* here for Queen Elizabeth I at the end of July 1602. With an accepted date now of 1604 for the earliest recorded production, the story loses its credibility. However, it is known that Sir John Davies's *A Lotterie* was specifically written and performed for Elizabeth's visit.

HARLINGTON, Bedfordshire (pop. 862) The small village of Harlington, 12 miles south of Bedford, retains much of its 17th-century charm because of a number of pleasant old half-timbered houses and inns and the manor house associated with John Bunyan. The house stands behind a brick wall so high that only the upper part is visible from the road, but inside, in the long, low paneled Great Parlour, everything is much as it was when Bunyan appeared before the owner, Francis Wingate, in November 1660. Bunyan had been preaching at nearby Samsell when he was arrested and brought here to appear before Wingate, a justice of the peace; also in residence then were Wingate's father-in-law, Dr. Lindall, vicar of Harlington, and his brother-in-law, Dr. William Foster, a noted ecclesiastical lawyer from Bedford. Bunyan refused Wingate's offer (as Bunyan recorded it), "If you will promise to call the people no more together, you shall have your liberty to go home," and the justice of the peace had no choice under the Act of Uniformity in Public Worship but to arrest Bunyan. He was kept in the attic overnight and transferred to Bedford Gaol the next day. Just beyond the church is a great old oak tree known as Bunyan's Oak. Its hollow trunk has been filled with earth to construct a kind of pulpit or platform. Bunyan is supposed to have preached from this oak.

HARPENDEN, Hertfordshire (pop. 13,750) Harpenden, 5 miles south of Luton and about 24 miles northwest of London, is an unspoiled country town which has been affected neither by the industrial revolution nor by the urban sprawl characteristic of this area, and the wide streets are comfortably tree-lined. It has a few noteworthy houses, including the former Bull Inn, Bower House, and The Hall. Mackery End, a brick house with curvilinear gables dating from 1666 that stands at a slight distance northeast of the town, has usually been identified as the house described by Charles Lamb in his essay "Mackery End, in Hertfordshire." Despite the use of the name, the house he describes, which belonged to relatives named Gladman, was the adjacent farmhouse, now refaced. Lamb lived here as a child but wrote from a distance of forty years:

The oldest thing I remember is Mackery End; or Mackarel End, as it is spelt, perhaps more properly, in some old maps of Hertfordshire; a farm-house,—delightfully situated within a gentle walk from Wheathampstead. . . . The house was at that time in the occupation of a substantial yeoman, who had married my grandmother's sister. His name was Gladman.

He continues:

At first, indeed, she [Bridget] was ready to disbelieve for joy; but the scene soon reconfirmed itself in her affections—and she traversed every outpost of the old mansion, to the wood-house, the orchard, the place where the pigeon-house had stood (house and birds were alike flown)—with a breathless impatience of recognition. . . .

HARRINGTON, Lincolnshire (pop. 94) Situated 4 miles northwest of Spilsby in an area dominated by the Lincolnshire Wolds, Harrington, which is surrounded by rolling hills, has a 15th-century and extensively renovated church and the partly Elizabethan Harrington Hall, the home of the Amcotts from the mid-17th century on. A later generation of this family knew the Rev. George Clayton Tennyson quite well, and the young Alfred Tennyson frequently came to the Hall from the rectory in Somersby, 1 mile to the northeast. He later remembered the paneled walls with their quaint carvings, the walled-in garden, and the rooks; he had these last in mind when he wrote *Maud:*

Birds in the high Hall-garden
    When twilight was fading,
Maud, Maud, Maud, Maud,
    They were crying and calling.

HARROGATE, Yorkshire (pop. 56,330) A spa town and conference center 18 miles north of Leeds and 19 miles west of York, Harrogate reached its zenith between the 16th and 19th century; in particular, the

more than eighty mineral springs which flow here made it a fashionable resort by the 18th century. Even today a 200-acre grassland called the Stray reaches into its very heart and reminds one of the town's past. Oliver Goldsmith mentions "the wells . . . where there was a great deal of company" in *The Vicar of Wakefield,* but greater use is made of Harrogate in Tobias Smollett's *The Expedition of Humphrey Clinker.* Matthew Bramble arrives "to satisfy my curiosity, rather than with any view of advantage to my health. . . ." "Harrigate," he writes to Dr. Lewis,

is a wild common, bare and bleak, without tree or shrub, or the last signs of cultivation; and the people who come to drink the water, are crowded together in paltry inns, where the few tolerable rooms are monopolized by the friends and favourites of the house, and all the rest of the lodgers are obliged to put up with dirty holes, where there is neither space, air, nor convenience.

The first taste of the water, he reports, "has cured me of all desire to repeat the medicine.—Some people say it smells of rotten eggs, and others compare it to the scourings of a foul gun. . . . As for the smell, if I may be allowed to judge from my own organs, it is exactly that of bilge water. . . ." Bramble says its only effects "were sickness, griping, and unsurmountable disgust.—I can hardly mention it without puking." The custom of bathing in tubs, immortalized by Bramble, continued until 1852.

HARROW-ON-THE-HILL, Middlesex Although everyone knows and refers to this town, 10 miles northwest of London, as Harrow, its proper name is Harrow-on-the-Hill, and the borough of which it is part (now in Greater London) is known as Harrow. In the Domesday Book (1086), Harrow was Herges, a manor belonging to the Archbishop of Canterbury and consisting of 15,000 acres, but the town had existed for centuries earlier. Michael Drayton notes the town's hill location in *Poly-Olbion:*

As *Colne* come on along, and chanc't to cast her eye
Upon that neighbouring Hill where *Harrow* stands so hie,
She *Peryvale* perceiv'd prankt up with wreaths of wheat,
And with exulting tearmes thus glorying in her seat;
Why should not I be coy, and of my Beauties nice,
Since this my goodly graine is held of greatest price?

Harrow has a wealth of 18th-century buildings as well as earlier ones, one of the best of which is the King's Head, dating partly from 1533. St. Mary's Church, on the 408-foot slope of the hill near the old school buildings, was called "the visible church" by Charles II because of its location. The church was founded by Lanfranc, Archbishop of Canterbury, and was consecrated by St. Anselm; Thomas à Becket was here twelve days before his murder in 1170; and Thomas Cranmer surrendered the church and manor to Henry VIII in 1544. Charles Lamb's comment to William Wordsworth in a letter thanking him for a copy of *The Excursion* sums up the atmosphere of the church:

One feeling I was particularly struck with as what I recognized so very lately at Harrow Church on entering it after a hot and secular day's pleasure—the instantaneous coolness and calming, almost transforming, properties of a country church just entered—a certain fragrance which it has—either from its holiness, or being shut all the week, or the air that is let in being pure country—exactly what you have reduced to words, but I am feeling I cannot. . . .

"Summer" in James Thomson's *The Seasons* notes:

> Say, shall we wind
> Along the streams? or walk the smiling mead?
> Or court the forest glades? or wander wild
> Among the waving harvests? or ascend,
> While radiant summer opens all its pride,
> Thy hill, delightful Shene? Here let us sweep
> The boundless landscape: now the raptured Eye,
> Exulting swift, to huge *Augusta* send,
> Now to the Sister Hills that skirt her plain,
> To lofty Harrow now. . . .

The fame of the town comes from its school (Eton's main rival), founded by John Lyon in 1572, originally for the poor of Harrow; today there are fifty-six buildings and playing fields belonging to Harrow School, and most are clustered together in a half-mile-square area around West Street and the High Street. Of greatest interest are the Old Schools (1611 and still in use) and the fourth-form room, where the black oak paneling is the unofficial work of centuries; here the young scholars carved their names or initials, and from these alone the school's roll can be called. One of these scholars, Richard Brinsley Sheridan, entered Harrow School from a school in Dublin in 1762 and was said to be "remarkable only in his degree of idleness and carelessness"; he remained until 1768, two years after the death of his mother, when he left for London to live with his father and brother. He returned to the town for a short time in 1780, when he and his wife lived in a grand style which they could ill afford at the Grove.

George Gordon, Lord Byron is perhaps Harrow's best-known student; entering in April 1801, he became known as a rebel, an idler, and a mischief-maker in quick order. The first half of his stay here was unhappy, but becoming a school leader gave him a firm attachment to Harrow. He drove himself to the extreme to achieve some measure of physical or athletic success in spite of his lameness and played cricket against Eton with a runner taking his place. Byron was one of the prime movers in the rebellion caused by the appointment of Dr. George Butler as headmaster upon the death of Dr. Joseph Drury; he and others favored Drury's brother Mark, and in open defiance of Butler's appointment tore down gratings in a room, stating these made the room too dark, and refused a dinner invitation from the new head. Byron satirized Butler as Pomposus in "On a Change of Masters at a Great Public School":

> So you, degenerate, . . .
> . . . seat Pomposus where your Probus sate.
> Of narrow brain, yet of a narrower soul
> Pomposus holds you in his harsh control;
> Pomposus, by no social virtue sway'd,
> With florid jargon, and with vain parade;
> With noisy nonsense, and new-fangled rules,
> Such as were ne'er before enforced in schools.
> Mistaking pedantry for learning's laws,
> He governs, sanction'd but by self-applause. . . .

Byron later regretted his rudeness and apologized to Butler for this vitriol, and he also claimed to have

kept the rebel group from burning down the fourth-form room by pointing out the initials carved by their predecessors. He frequented Mother Barnard's, the local inn, and is said to have overcome his acute self-consciousness by bellowing, "This bottle's the sun of our table." He recalled the school in the 1806 poem "On a Distant View of the Village and School of Harrow on the Hill":

> Again I revisit the hills where we sported,
>   The streams where we swam, and the fields where we fought;
> The school where, loud warn'd by the bell, we resorted,
>   To pore o'er the precepts by pedagogues taught.
>
> Again I behold where for hours I have ponder'd,
>   As reclining, at eve, on yon tombstone I lay;
> Or round the steep brow of the churchyard I wander'd,
>   To catch the last gleam of the sun's setting ray.

The Peachey Stone, a favorite spot, is at the edge of the churchyard, and it was here in 1822, after her death at a convent in Bagna Cavallo, that Allegra, Byron's daughter by Claire Clairmont, was buried. Byron chose the spot under the church porch and also directed that the tablet be erected.

The poet carved his initials in the fourth-form room twice, once in nondescript lower-case letters next to the name Stedman and once in elegant capitals under the name R. B. Sheridan. Byron went up to Trinity College, Cambridge, in 1805. Harrow suffers from Byron mania, and once even the telephone exchange was Byron.

Another 19th-century literary figure here was the novelist Anthony Trollope; he had been at Winchester College in 1826, but his father's move to Harrow Weald in 1827 brought Trollope's removal from that school. As a day pupil and a town boy, he suffered a measure of ridicule and persecution. Indeed, Dr. Butler stopped him in the street once and asked "whether it was possible that Harrow School was disgraced by so disreputably dirty a little boy." When Trollope left Harrow in 1834, he commented: "[N]o attempt had been made to teach me anything but Latin or Greek, and very little attempt to teach me those languages."

Charles Stuart Calverley came to Harrow in September 1846 after spending three months at Marlborough. He showed little academic interest and a great deal of athletic ability. His intermittent work, however, occasionally reached a high level, and in 1850 he secured a Balliol scholarship with some Latin verses.

J. A. Symonds entered Harrow in May 1854 and took little interst in anything except reading; avoiding sports and contact with fellow students, he was extremely shy by the time he left for Balliol College, Oxford.

John Galsworthy entered the school in the summer term of 1881. He was first a member of a Mr. Colbeck's house, one of the Small Houses; but at the end of a year he moved to Moreton's, where he was head of the house for two years. Galsworthy's time here was pleasant, and he captained the football team and won the mile and a half before going up to New College, Oxford, in 1886. Edward Robert Bulwer Lytton, the 1st Earl of Lytton (Owen Meredith), was educated here briefly before he was removed for private tutoring on the Continent, and so were Sir Robert Peel, the historian G. M. Trevelyan, Sir Winston Churchill, and Sir Terence Rattigan. Hilaire Belloc lectured here in 1910–1911.

In the spring of 1868 Matthew Arnold took Byron House because he liked its "old countrified look," and in 1871 he had as his guest the Duke of Genoa, son of King Victor Emmanuel II. Arnold left Harrow in 1873 for Cobham, Kent, where he lived until his death in Liverpool in 1888. In the year that Arnold left Byron House, Charles Kingsley took a large house (now Kingsley House) on the London Road; he remained only a short time.

Henry Pye, the Poet Laureate appointed by George III but much ridiculed by his contemporaries, is commemorated with an urn in the Church of St. John the Baptist. He died in nearby Pinner on August 11, 1813.

HARROW WEALD, Middlesex A very small village 2½ miles north of the larger Harrow-on-the-Hill, Harrow Weald (now a part of Greater London in the new borough of Harrow) retains a sense of space and a feeling of country. Anthony Trollope lived on a farm, Julians, here after he had been taken from Winchester College in 1827; the farmhouse was built by his father, but when his father's business failed, the house was let, and the family moved to another farmhouse, Julians Hill, on the same road. This farmhouse later became the subject of *Orley Farm*. The young boy, a day pupil at Harrow School, walked the 3 miles to school daily. In 1831, when his mother returned from the United States after having written *The Domestic Manners of the Americans* (published 1832), the family was again solvent and moved back to its own home. Trollope's misery was acute throughout this period: "I had not only no friends, but was despised by all my companions." The Orley Farm in South Harrow has no connection with Trollope.

Another resident of Harrow Weald was Sir William Schwenck Gilbert, who purchased the Norman Shaw mansion of Grimsdyke House in Grimsdyke Park. Buying the house in 1890, Gilbert spent many pleasant years here and wrote the libretti for *Utopia Limited* and *The Grand Duke* during this period. His passionate fondness for wildlife made him issue orders to his gamekeeper and staff that nothing was to be caught or trapped; indeed, even birds and deer entered the library without fear. Sir William and Lady Gilbert held annual Christmas parties for the village children, a practice kept up long after his death. Gilbert had often said that he wanted to die on a summer's day in his garden, and indeed he did on May 29, 1911. After rescuing a young woman from drowning in a lake on the estate, he had a fatal heart attack; his ashes were interred at the church in Great Stanmore.

Nearby is Bentley Priory, now taken over by the Royal Air Force, which has placed an antiquated Spitfire on one of the priory lawns and Nissen huts on the others. The original priory was taken over at the dissolution of the monasteries in the 16th century and later demolished; the present building dates from the 18th century. William Wordsworth, Thomas Moore, and Sir Walter Scott all visited here when the property belonged to the 1st Marquess of Abercorn. In fact, all through the early spring of 1807, when Scott was in London doing research on

John Dryden, he reserved at least one day in the weekend to be here. Cantos I and II of *Marmion* were composed here and sent to James Ballantyne, the publisher, from Bentley Priory.

In the 20th century, from his days at the university on, Joyce Cary was a frequent guest at the Glade, the large home of the Ogilvie family. Cary had known both William Heneage and Frederick Ogilvie at Clifton College in Bristol, and on one of his early visits he was attracted to Gertrude, one of the three Ogilvie sisters. Cary was here in April 1916 recuperating from asthma, insomnia, and unhealed wounds, the result of the Cameroon campaign. His interest in Gertrude increased; they were engaged in May, married in June, and here for six weeks after their honeymoon before he left for Nigeria in August. Cary was back on leave in February 1918 and remained until July; when he left the Nigerian service in 1920, he and his family settled in Oxford.

HARROWDEN, Bedfordshire Harrowden is often not distinguished from Elstow, of which it is an adjunct, but the hamlet does have its own style. It was the birthplace of John Bunyan in November 1628; the house where he was born has long been pulled down, but a footpath from Elstow leads to a plaque marking the site. The son of a tinker and brazier, Bunyan is thought to have had no formal schooling except for a short period in Bedford; he claimed to have had his education from a copybook and a primer. Most of Bunyan's life was spent in this general area and especially in Elstow.

HARTFORD, Huntingdonshire (pop. 460) Hartford was once a small, pleasant riverside village; but now with Huntingdon, a little more than 1 mile to the southwest, it is part of the county seat. In less crowded times (1765), William Cowper found the village very attractive and became especially fond of it, noting that the 12th-century church "is very prettily situated upon a rising ground, so close to the river that it washes the wall of the church yard."

HARTINGTON, Derbyshire (pop. 879) Just east of Beresford Dale, through which the Dove River meanders, and 8 miles southwest of Bakewell, Hartington is surrounded by limestone hills. The river here separates Derbyshire and Staffordshire, and less than 1 mile from the village is the secluded Pike Pool; hidden in the luxuriant growth of trees is the almost-inaccessible one-room Fishing House which Izaak Walton and Charles Cotton used. Built in 1674 by Cotton, whose home was the nearby Beresford Hall, this is the Fishing House described in *The Compleat Angler*. Piscator takes Viator to this spot to fish:

> PISC. . . . But look you, sir, now you are at the brink of the hill, how do you like my river, the vale it winds through like a snake, and the situation of my little fishing-house?
>
> VIAT. Trust me, 'tis all very fine, and the house seems at this distance a neat building.
>
> PISC. Good enough for that purpose. . . .
>
> VIAT. Stay, what's here over the door? PISCATORIBUS SACRUM. Why then, I perceive I have some title here; for I am one of them, though one of the worst; and here below it is the cypher too you speak of, and 'tis

prettily contrived. Has my master Walton ever been here to see it, for it seems new built?

PISC. Yes, he saw it cut in the stone before it was set up; but never in the posture it now stands; for the house was but building when he was last here, and not raised so high as the arch of the door.

HARTSHILL, Warwickshire (pop. 2,560) The view from the ridge on which the mining village of Hartshill rests extends to Derbyshire on clear days, and no fewer than forty churches can be counted in the panorama. Located 3 miles south of Atherstone, Hartshill is thought to have held a Roman camp, and there is evidence of a prehistoric settlement at nearby Oldbury Camp. Sometime between March 26, 1563, and March 25, 1564 (most likely 1563), the village was the birthplace of Michael Drayton. John Aubrey wrote that Drayton's father was a butcher (he said the same of Shakespeare's father), but of this there is no evidence. Indeed, Drayton maintained he was "nobly bred." Tradition describes two sites as the birthplace, one (now gone) near the chapel and the other on the north side of the green at the corner of the Atherstone Road. In his works Drayton called Hartshill "Rowland of the Rock" because of the quarrying.

HARWICH, Essex (pop. 13,046) Harwich has always been important because of its position on a peninsula between the Stour and Orwell Rivers, naturally protected from the extreme force of the sea. For ten centuries Harwich has served as a berth for every conceivable type of ship, from those of the invading Danes to those of the French during the Hundred Years' War. The present town with its many narrow cobbled streets is in a transitional stage, and much is unlovely, particularly the decayed remnants of its long past.

Whether or not John Skelton visited Harwich is not known, but he was familiar enough with it to use the town in the introductory lines of "The Bowge of Court":

At Harwich port slumbering as I lay
In mine hostes house called Powers Key.

Daniel Defoe was in Harwich in 1668 and went up the Orwell River to Ipswich, and a century later, in 1763, Dr. Samuel Johnson was here to see James Boswell off to Holland. In 1703, during the War of the Spanish Succession, Richard Steele was posted to Languard Fort, Suffolk, to command the garrison there and early in 1704 took rooms at the Queen's Arms on the High Street here. Local residents, the Elliotts, who were staunch Whig supporters, became his friends, and he often was a guest in their home on St. James's Street; the house was the next-to-last one on the southeast corner. In 1704 and 1705 the Elliotts entertained many of Steele's friends including Joseph Addison and Jonathan Swift.

Finally, Christopher Marlowe sets part of *Edward II* in Harwich. It is here that Queen Isabella, Prince Edward, and Sir John of Hainault land from France to encounter the King.

HASLEMERE, Surrey (pop. 10,100) Lying in the hollow between Hindhead and Black Down, about 13 miles southwest of Guildford, Haslemere is often erroneously referred to as the home of Alfred, Lord Tennyson, whereas his home Aldworth is 2 miles to the east and in Sussex. This market town is a lovely place with old gabled houses and cottages on the High Street. An alley off the High Street leads away from the town toward the church, in which the Poet Laureate is remembered. It was here that he attended services when at Aldworth, and a commemorative window by Sir Edward Burne-Jones depicts Sir Galahad's vision of the Holy Grail.

It was the Wealden beauty and remoteness which drew literary figures to this area in the late 19th and early 20th centuries. In May 1862, on his walk over the Downland region, George Meredith came to Haslemere from Milford, where he had spent the night, and lunched here, "drinking," as he said, "copious ale." Mary Ann Evans (George Eliot) came to Brookbank, a house in the Shottermill area, in 1871 for a few months, and here she wrote part of *Middlemarch*. Gerard Manley Hopkins was a frequent visitor to Court's Hill Lodge, his parents' home from 1885 on, and a window in the north aisle of the church commemorates him. Sir Arthur Wing Pinero spent a holiday in the Grayswood area just to the northeast in July 1890. He was working on *The Second Mrs. Tanqueray,* and it is thought that the second and third acts were written here. Finally, Virginia Stephen (Woolf) spent part of the spring of 1902 with her family at Hindhead Copse, the home of Sir Frederick Pollock.

HASTINGS, Sussex (pop. 72,410)

Then duke William sailed from Normandy into Pevensey, on the eve of Michaelmas [28 September]. As soon as his men were fit for service, they constructed a castle at Hastings. When king Harold was informed of this, he gathered together a great host, and came to oppose him at the grey apple-tree, and William came upon him unexpectedly before his army was set in order. Nevertheless the king fought against him most resolutely with those men who wished to stand by him, and there was great slaughter on both sides. King Harold was slain, and Leofwine, his brother, and earl Gurth, his brother, and many good men. The French had possession of the place of slaughter, as God granted them because of the nation's sins.

Thus the *Laud Chronicle* of the *Anglo-Saxon Chronicle* tells of the Battle of Hastings, which, in fact, occurred 6 miles inland at Battle; even today Hastings is still accorded the site of the battle that was a significant turning point in English history. Hastings, however, preceded William the Conqueror and was an important and accessible Saxon port often harried by the Danes. The small river which led to the sea was gradually blocked up here, and after the great storm of 1287, which wreaked havoc along the entire coast, the port was abandoned.

The Old Town of Hastings is a warren of narrow streets spreading down from the Norman castle to the fishing harbor, and here the old timbered cottages are neatly tucked away. Originally two main streets ran through the Old Town, All Saints and High Streets, but the 1960s saw what Sir Nikolaus Pevsner claimed was "the Rape of Hastings indeed"; then, a third, the Bourne, was built, and everything in its path was demolished. Among the survivors are two of the seven medieval churches: St. Clement's and All Saints'. The modern resort town, which lies west of the Old Town, came into its own in Victorian times, when the community of St. Leonard's-on-Sea was incorporated into Hastings.

HASTINGS Once strategically perched on the cliff overlooking the harbor, the Norman castle here is now but the ruin of man and weather. Hastings, though, prospers and has hosted a number of literary figures from Samuel Pepys to Henry James.

There are few literary associations with Hastings before its inception as a resort. In the 17th century Samuel Pepys in his post at the Admiralty would have known its role as a Cinque Port although he makes only passing reference to it in his diary, and in the next century Daniel Defoe in *A Tour thro' the Whole Island of Great Britain* caustically comments that Hastings, Rye, and Winchelsea have "little in them to deserve more than a mere mention." Thomas Chatterton, who created the 15th-century monk of Bristol, Thomas Rowley, "discovered" one of the monk's poems on the Battle of Hastings.

One of the earliest literary visitors was Leigh Hunt who came here with his family for a holiday in 1812, the year before he was imprisoned for his attack on the Prince Regent; during his stay here he began *The Story of Rimini*, a long poem which he finished in the Horsemonger Lane Gaol. John Keats was first in Hastings in 1815 and returned in 1817, at which time he visited the painter Benjamin Haydon, who had lodgings at New England Bank in the nearby hamlet of Bo-Peep (now part of Hastings). George Gordon, Lord Byron spent a three weeks' holiday here in July 1814 with his half sister, Augusta Leigh, who had given birth to their child Medora in April. In 1823 Charles and Mary Lamb stayed at 4 York Cottages on a holiday in which they felt they were "doing dreary penance." Lamb disliked the "detestable Cinque port," as he calls Hastings in his essay "The Old Margate Hoy," noting:

> I love town, or country; but this . . . is neither. I hate these scrubbed shoots, thrusting out their starved foliage from between the horrid fissures of dusty innutritious rocks; which the amateur calls "verdure to the edge of the sea."

He continues:

> There is no home for me here. There is no sense of home at Hastings. It is a place of fugitive resort, an heterogeneous assemblage of seamews and stockbrokers, Amphitrites of the town, and misses that coquet with the Ocean. If it were what it was in its primitive shape, and what it ought to have remained, a fair honest fishing-town, and no more, it were something—with a few straggling fishermen's huts scattered about, artless as its cliffs, and with their materials filched from them, it were something.

Lamb half apologized for his lack of being good-natured by placing the blame on "the salt foam [which] seems to nourish a spleen."

He had, however, written to John Bates Dibdin about the little church at nearby Hollington, and Lamb's description of it—"Seven people would crowd it like a Caledonian Chapel"—persuaded Thomas Hood to spend his honeymoon here. Another visitor to Hastings at this time was the poet George Crabbe; already an old man of seventy-six, he had for some time led a retired life, punctuated only by a few visits to his son and some of his closest friends such as Samuel Hoare. Hoare and his family were here at 34 Wellington Square in 1830, when Crabbe, on a visit to see them, was struck by a coach just as he emerged from his own. Injured only slightly, he did not have to alter any of his holiday plans.

Almost twenty-five years later Edward Lear came to the home of Frederick North, Member of Parliament for Hastings, after having spent a number of weeks at Fairlight with Holman Hunt and William Rossetti; his visit was planned: he had come to paint a fig tree which North's gardener had been raising. Lear brought with him a stuffed jackdaw which he wired into every conceivable position for his work; he had not, however, told Hunt and Rossetti of his plans, perhaps because he knew that he would be met with derision. Lear had planned to return to London in January 1853 but remained here until the end of the winter because the ceiling in his London flat had fallen in. Dante Gabriel Rossetti is also associated with the town; after the death of his father he came to join Elizabeth Siddall, who was here for reasons of health. The poet stayed at 12 East Parade (now part of the Cutter Hotel) near her lodgings, and even though he remained in the town for two months, after a week he had found Hastings, like Newcastle, "rather slow." He was here again in the spring of 1860 with Elizabeth Siddall on account of her "extreme illness," and believing that she was dying and that no marriage to her could last very long, he married her at St. Clement's Church on May 23 with only the clergy and a stranger and his wife (probably caretakers) in attendance. "The Song of the Bower" shows his attitude to the marriage:

Nay, but my heart when it flies to thy bower,
　What does it find there that knows it again?
There it must droop like a shower-beaten flower,
　Red at the rent core and dark with rain.
Ah, yet what shelter is still shed above it,—
　What waters still image its leaves torn apart?
Thy soul is the shade that clings round it to love it,
　And tears are its mirror deep down in thy heart.

John Addington Symonds married a local girl, Catherine North, at St. Clement's on November 10, 1864, and the young couple lived for a short time in her parents' home on Old London Road. The same year Thomas Carlyle had lodgings at 117 Marina (marked with a plaque).

Coventry Patmore first saw Hastings as a child when the town was almost as fashionable a watering place as Brighton; at that time he saw the Mansion House and decided to live there, so his brother declared later. The Queen Anne house, now known as Old Hastings House and hidden behind a magnolia tree, came into his hands in 1875. The choice of Hastings for a home may well have been prompted by the fact that his daughter Emily was at this time a novice, Sister Mary Christina, at the St. Leonard's-on-the-Sea Convent of the Holy Child Jesus. When Patmore's wife died in April 1880, Hastings became the recipient of a marvelous memorial: he began the construction of the Church of St. Mary Star of the Sea on All Saints Street almost immediately, and the Gothic building was completed by 1883. In the meantime, on June 13, 1861, Patmore's daughter, who was tubercular, died at the convent and was buried there. Patmore left for Lymington in 1891, when the owner of the Mansion House died and the new owner refused to honor the poet's lease. Among Patmore's many guests here were Gerard Manley Hopkins, who visited for a few days after the summer of 1883 when they first met and again in August 1885; Robert Bridges; and Charles Lutwidge Dodgson (Lewis Carroll), who visited the seventy-year-old man on October 4, 1890. Dodgson noted that he "called on Mr. Coventry Patmore (at Hastings) and was very kindly received by him, and stayed for afternoon tea and dinner." Carroll knew the town rather well, for he often spent a few days here with his mother's sisters, the Misses Lutwidge, during his early college years.

The novelist Mark Rutherford (William Hale White) lived first at 9 High Wickham (1892) and then at 5 High Wickham (1895). Retiring from the Civil Service, in which he had been assistant director of contracts in the Admiralty, he worked on *Catharine Furze* and began *Clara Hopgood* here. Henry James was a frequent visitor to Hastings and recorded his attitude toward the resort in *Portraits of Places*.

In April 1902 Rupert Brooke spent a holiday here with his mother and brother; he passed his time reading Carlyle and walking on the sea front, at one point noting how the breakers

look very ghostly under the white glare of the powerful incandescent (or electric?) lamps. Vast swollen greynesses heaving tumultuously and flashing out suddenly into a sheet of spray . . .

at which point he broke off. He was back with his mother in April 1905, when they stayed at the Palace Hotel.

Another early-20th-century association exists with H. G. Wells, who makes the town the location of Cavendish Academy, the school attended by the young Arthur Kipps; the days were a "grey routine," but other remembrances which came through

included countless pictures of sitting on creaking forms, bored and idle; of blot licking and the taste of ink; of torn books with covers that set one's teeth on edge; of the slimy surface of the laboured slates; of furtive marble-playing, whispered story-telling, and of pinches, blows, and a thousand such petty annoyances being perpetually "passed on" according to the custom of the place; of standing up in class and being hit suddenly and unreasonably for imaginary misbehaviour; of Mr. Woodrow's raving days, when a scarcely sane injustice prevailed; of the cold vacuity of the hour of preparation before the bread-and-butter breakfast; and of horrible headaches and queer, unprecedented internal feelings, resulting from Mrs. Woodrow's motherly rather than intelligent cookery.

After World War I Sir Henry Rider Haggard bought North Lodge here. He was frequently away from the Maze Hill house because of his work as a member of the Empire Settlement Committee, but his study was in an archway room over the road.

HATFIELD, Hertfordshire (pop. 5,695) Hatfield was once Bishop's Hatfield; it is on the Lea River 6 miles southwest of Hertford and stands near the Great North Road, the modern roadway over the route of one of the old Roman roads out of London. Hatfield was an important Saxon town soon after Edward the Elder fortified Hertford; and in the 15th century John Morton, Bishop of Ely, built Hatfield Palace. The structure was made of brick, and parts of it still exist, some having been incorporated into a newer structure.

When James I succeeded to the throne in 1603, his desire to have Theobalds in Cheshunt was so great that Sir Robert Cecil, Lord Burleigh's son and owner of the estate, was given Hatfield and created Earl of Salisbury in exchange for Theobalds. Cecil embarked on an extensive renovation program and built what is now one of the most important Jacobean mansions in England. The new mansion, in the shape of an E in honor of the late Queen, cost close to £40,000, a fantastic sum. The east and west walls of the two-story Great Hall are intricately paneled and screened, and the other two are richly tapestried. The main staircase has no equal; the newel posts are individually carved with fantasy figures and children. Two galleries, the Cloisters, or Armoury, and the Long Gallery, extend from end to end in the main gallery. The Long Gallery with its antechambers is 150 feet long, and the floor-to-ceiling paneling is an outstanding example of contemporary craftsmanship. The grounds are as magnificent as the house, and here as well Sir Robert spared no expense. The Lea River was used to supply water for the gardens, and an extensive vineyard (since destroyed) was planted. John Evelyn comments briefly on the house and vineyard as "rarely well water'd and planted" in his diary, and Samuel Pepys, who visited Hatfield in July 1661, notes:

> I . . . walked all alone to the Vineyard, which is now a very beautiful place again; and coming back I met with Mr. Looker, my Lord's gardener (a friend of Mr. Eglin's), who showed me the house, the chapel with brave pictures, and, above all, the gardens, such as I never saw in all my life; nor so good flowers, nor so great gooseberries, as big as nutmegs.

Probably the earliest literary association at Hatfield is with Princess Elizabeth and her tutor, Roger Ascham, who were in residence here in the late autumn and early winter of 1548. Far more recently Lewis Carroll (Charles Lutwidge Dodgson) was a guest of Roger Arthur Talbot Gascoyne-Cecil, the 3d Marquess of Salisbury and the Cecil who restored the family to its former position of political power as Prime Minister in 1885–1886, 1886–1892, and 1895–1902. Carroll was first at Hatfield at the New Year in 1870, when he was surrounded by a large number of children and invented part of the story of *Sylvie and Bruno* (not published until 1889) for their amusement. A number of the scenes in the work were inspired by the surroundings of Hatfield. On a subsequent visit in 1874 Carroll told the story of Prince Uggug, which he later incorporated in the same work.

Hatfield has two inns of note, the 1794 Red Lion (recently enlarged) and the 18th-century Eight Bells, located on Fore Street. It was the latter inn to which Charles Dickens most likely came in 1835 when he was a reporter covering a fire at Hatfield House, and it appears that in October 1838 he and Phiz (Hablot Knight Browne) stayed at the Salisbury Arms (no longer an inn) when they made their "bachelor excursion" to the West Country. Dickens's knowledge of Hatfield comes into *Oliver Twist;* Sykes, in flight after the murder of Nancy, finally reaches the village and enters the Eight Bells:

> At last he got away, and shaped his course for Hatfield.
> It was nine o'clock at night, when the man, quite tired out, and the dog, limping and lame from the unaccustomed exercise, turned down the hill by the church of the quiet village, and plodding along the little street, crept into a small public-house, whose scanty light had guided them to the spot. There was a fire in the tap-room, and some country-labourers were drinking before it. They made room for the stranger, but he sat down in the furthest corner, and ate and drank alone, or rather with his dog: to whom he cast a morsel of food from time to time.

After the episode over the hat, Sykes leaves the inn and

> turned back up the town, and getting out of the glare of the lamps of a stagecoach that was standing in the street, was walking past, when he recognised the mail from London, and saw that it was standing at the little post-office. He almost knew what was to come; but he crossed over, and listened.

The "little post-office" then adjoined the Salisbury Arms. Sykes finds refuge nearby:

> There was a shed in a field he passed, that offered shelter for the night. Before the door were three tall poplar trees, which made it very dark within; and the wind moaned through them with a dismal wail.

Poplar trees are not common in this area, but there are poplars near Great Nast Hyde.

Dickens also uses Hatfield in "Mrs. Lirriper's Lodgings"; the churchyard here contains the grave of Mr. Lirriper, not because he was a native of Hatfield but because

> he had a liking for the Salisbury Arms, where we went upon our wedding-day, and passed as happy a fortnight as ever happy was.

Lirriper's younger brother also makes an appearance in Hatfield; a bit of a scapegrace, he stays at the Salisbury Arms for two weeks and leaves without paying his bill.

HATFIELD BROAD OAK, Essex (pop. 1,564) The county of Essex contains not only the 5,600-acre Epping Forest, the remainder of what was once a royal forest, but a second and much smaller portion as well—Hatfield Forest. Less than 1 mile from the southern edge of Hatfield Forest is the village of Hatfield Regis or Hatfield Broad Oak, as it is now known. The Broad Oak of the name, it has been conjectured, may have arisen from one of the legendary oaks mentioned in the Domesday Book; some were extremely large: the Doodle Oak, for example, was almost 60 feet in circumference at its base. By 1135 there was a substantial Benedictine priory here, and the priory was important by June 1423, when John Lydgate was appointed to the priorate. His term of office probably lasted until April 8, 1434, when he received permission to return to the monastery at Bury St. Edmunds, Suffolk; however, he apparently was in residence at Hatfield only from 1423 to 1426, for he seems to have spent the other eight years in Paris, London, and Windsor. It seems unlikely that he worked on *The Fall of Princes* here, although local tradition suggests that he did.

HATHERSAGE, Derbyshire (pop. 1,694) A Peak District village on the Derwent River 10 miles north of Bakewell, Hathersage and the surrounding area are known to have been inhabited long before the Romans reached England; indeed, Carl Wark is an Iron Age hill fort just outside the village. The church, dating mainly from the 14th and 15th centuries but partly incorporating an earlier structure, has crenelations carved with human and animal faces; notable are a tiger's head and the head of a muzzled bear. The churchyard is of great importance to those interested in balladry and legend, for here near a large yew tree is the grave of Little John, friend to Robin Hood. Legend states that after burying Robin at Kirklees, Little John came here in sorrow, preparing to die; the church is said to have held his cap and bow for many years. The grave is now in the care of the Ancient Order of Foresters.

Close to the church is the old vicarage in which Charlotte Brontë was a guest in 1845 of her friend Ellen Nussey, who was here with her brother, the vicar. Miss Brontë's pearl-inlay writing desk, one of her shawls, and a pair of her slippers are in the vicarage. The village, its houses and church, and the

HATHERSAGE "At this thought I turned my face aside from the lovely sky of eve and lonely vale of Morton--I say lonely, for in that bend of it visible to me, there was there was no building apparent save the church and the parsonage, half hid in trees. . ."
Charlotte Brontë, *Jane Eyre*.

surrounding countryside play an extensive part in *Jane Eyre*. Even the surname is local; the Eyre family's coat of arms is over the church porch, and its brass portraits are in the church itself. Hathersage is, of course, Morton in the novel; after the interrupted wedding, Jane flees from Thornfield Hall and is left at Whitcross because her funds will take her no farther:

> Whitcross is no town, nor even a hamlet; it is but a stone pillar set up where four roads meet: white-washed, I suppose to be more obvious at a distance and in darkness. Four arms spring from its summit: the nearest town to which these point is, according to the inscription, distant ten miles; the farthest, above twenty. From the well-known names of these towns I learn in what county I have lighted; a north-midland shire, dusk with moorland, ridged with mountain: this I see. There are great moors behind and on each hand of me; there are waves of mountains far beyond that deep valley at my feet. . . .
> I struck straight into the heath; I held on to a hollow I saw deeply furrowing the brown moorside; I waded knee-deep in its dark growth; I turned with its turnings, and finding a moss-blackened granite crag in a hidden angle, I sat down under it. High banks of moor were about me; the crag protected my head: the sky was over that.

Because of a later reference to the hour's journey from Hathersage, Whitcross has been determined to be the crossroads at the Fox House Inn above Grindleford Bridge. Morton is first described from a distance:

> I heard a bell chime—a church bell.
> I turned in the direction of the sound, and there, amongst the romantic hills, whose changes and aspect I had ceased to note an hour ago, I saw a hamlet and a spire. All the valley at my right hand was full of pasture-fields, and cornfields, and wood; and a glittering stream ran zigzag through the varied shades of green, the mellowing grain, the sombre woodland, the clear and sunny lea.

Jane searches for shelter and finds the vicarage, since enlarged but still situated as Miss Brontë describes it:

> In crossing a field, I saw the church spire before me: I hastened towards it. Near the churchyard, and in the middle of a garden, stood a well-built though small house, which I had no doubt was the parsonage. I remembered that strangers who arrive at a place where they have no friends, and who want employment, sometimes apply to the clergyman for introduction and aid.

Moorseats, the home of St. John Eyre Rivers, was one of the homes of the Eyre family and is the obvious source of Moor House, even though there is another Eyre claimant at Stanage Edge. Located near the edge of the moor about three-quarters of a mile from the village, Moor House has been enlarged since Miss Brontë's description of the "black, low, and rather long house," but the environment is unchanged:

> They loved their sequestered home. I, too, in the grey, small, antique structure, with its low roof, its latticed casements, its mouldering walls, its avenue of aged firs— all grown aslant under the stress of mountain winds; its garden, dark with yew and holly—and where no flowers but the hardiest species would bloom—found a charm both potent and permanent. They clung to the purple moors behind and around their dwelling—to the hollow vale into which the pebbly bridle-path leading from their gate descended; and which wound between fern-banks first, and then amongst a few of the wildest little pasture-fields that ever bordered a wilderness or heath, or gave sustenance to a flock of grey moorland sheep, with their little mossy-faced lambs. . . . [M]y eye feasted on the outline of swell and sweep—on the wild colouring communicated to ridge and dell, by moss, by heath-bell, by flower-sprinkled turf, by brilliant bracken, and mellow granite crag.

The "pebbly bridle-path" is still there. A little later St. John instructs Jane to go out the kitchen door and "take the road towards the head of Marsh Glen . . ." where he will meet her for a walk. They soon are "treading the wild track of the glen":

> The stream descending the ravine, swelled with past spring rains, poured along plentiful and clear, catching golden gleams from the sun, and sapphire tints from the firmament. As we advanced and left the track, we trod a soft turf, mossy fine and emerald green, minutely enamelled with a tiny white flower, and spangled with a star-like yellow blossom: the hills, meantime, shut us quite in; for the glen, towards its head, wound to their very core.

HAVERTHWAITE, Lancashire (pop. 853) Haverthwaite has a beautiful location in Cumbria in the River Leven Valley, 5 miles northeast of Ulverston. Well-kept gardens with yew trees, a 19th-century church, and an inn dominate the village. Arthur Ransome, the author of many delightful children's stories, made his home at Hill Top, a house overlooking Furness Fells, just northwest of the village, from 1949 until his death in June 1967.

HAWKSHEAD, Lancashire (pop. 575) Near the head of Esthwaite Water in the midst of tree-covered hills, Hawkshead is one of the loveliest villages in the Lake District. An old market town 5 miles southwest of Ambleside, it is of interest primarily because of William Wordsworth, who was sent to school here from Cockermouth in 1778. The Free Grammar School, founded by Edwin Sandys (later Archbishop of York), is a two-story building with a sundial over the porch; the upper story holds the library. The schoolroom contains many old benches and desks, undoubtedly the most valuable of which is the one in which the young Wordsworth cut his name; the carved area is protected by glass. He spent eight years here in the company of approximately 100 boys, and of the four masters who taught him, Wordsworth referred to the Rev. William Taylor (who died while Wordsworth was in school) in "Address to the Scholars of the Village School of ———":

> Here did he sit confined for hours;
> But he could see the woods and plains,
> Could hear the wind and mark the showers
> Come streaming down the streaming panes.
> Now stretched beneath his grass-green mound
> He rests a prisoner of the ground.
> He loved the breathing air,
> He loved the sun, but if it rise
> Or set, to him where now he lies,
> Brings not a moment's care. . . .

In other works Taylor is given the name Matthew.

Wordsworth lodged with Dame Ann Tyson in a joiner's cottage here; the cottage which he calls "a Sanctity, a safeguard, and a love!" is said to be located in a secluded corner just off the main street near the village center. He writes in *The Prelude* that in bed he watched

> The moon in splendour couched among the leaves
> Of a tall ash, that near our cottage stood;
> Had watched her with fixed eyes while to and fro
> In the dark summit of the waving tree
> She rocked with every impulse of the breeze.

However, even though this cottage has been accepted as correct for more than 100 years, its authenticity seems to be in doubt. Much of Wordsworth's description does not fit well: he states that the brook was

> boxed
> Within our garden. . . .

But the brook in Hawkshead runs (or ran) through no garden. The only stream runs under one of the streets. He says that "fronting our cottage" stood

> A smooth rock wet with constant springs
> Sparkling from out a copse-clad bank. . . .

In an earlier text the location is even more precise:

> An upright bank of wood and woody rock
> That opposite our rural dwelling stood. . . .

Not one cottage in Hawkshead can boast this sight, and "our rural dwelling" may be significant. In another place he remarks on Ann Tyson's walking with him:

> She guided me;
> I willing, nay—nay wishing to be led. . . .

This was a natural statement if they were outside the village. Finally, he notes that he would catch hold of a wall or a tree walking to school; a tiny wall was possible, but not the tree.

A more logical identification of the house is Green End Cottage in the tiny hamlet of Colthouse, half a mile to the east. The cottage lies under the wooded side of Claife Height from which a small beck, an "unruly child of mountain birth," ran down through the garden before entering Black Beck. The rock and wood referred to above are most likely Spring Wood at Colthouse, and from here Wordsworth's comments about walking make sense. One other piece of evidence seems relevant: according to Wordsworth's son William, the poet once pointed out "a spot on the eastern side of the valley and out of the village" as the place where he had lived.

While in school here, Wordsworth usually attended services in the mostly 16-century church, which sits on a mound above the village. He

> Saw the snow-white church upon her hill
> Sit like a throned lady sending out
> A gracious look all over her domain.

However, if the day were either very warm or very wet, he and Ann Tyson would attend services at the Quaker meetinghouse halfway up the hill above the hamlet of Colthouse.

A modern but minor literary association exists with Francis Brett Young, who spent part of the summer in 1908 here with his fiancée and a chaperon; they walked in the hills and rowed on Esthwaite Water during their holiday.

HAWORTH, Yorkshire (pop. 3,923) It is virtually impossible to disassociate this moorland town from the Brontë family; indeed, any description of the area— bleak, windswept, raucous with the cry of rooks, and gruff—brings images from the novels to mind. The village is not attractive even in the roughest of Yorkshire ways, and yet the pure rudeness of the place establishes its character very well. The Rev. Patrick Brontë brought his family here from Thornton, Yorkshire, shortly after the birth of Anne at the end of March 1820. In fact, he came here about a month before Anne's birth to assume his duties, and his family joined him in April. Of the church where Anne, Emily, and Charlotte heard their father preach only the old tower remains, although some of the pews are in the parsonage and the pulpit has been placed in the village church at nearby Stanbury. The "new" church (1881), built long before the village was engulfed by the Brontë cult, contains a Brontë memorial chapel dating from 1964. The town has a Heathcliff Café, a series of Brontë shops, and a stable of Brontë buses, although to its credit the plain vicarage is now the Brontë Parsonage Museum. The museum committee has done its best to keep the house as it was in the Brontës' time. The same door admits visitors to the museum as admitted the family and parishioners, and all the downstairs rooms have been arranged as Charlotte's biographer Elizabeth Celghorn Gaskell describes them. To the right of the entrance is the Reverend Mr. Brontë's study, the dining room is just opposite, and the stone staircase is much as it was when it contained the large family clock. The parlor, left of the main entrance, is where the three curates, later described in *Shirley*, took tea with Mr. Brontë and where Charlotte upbraided them for their intolerance. This is also the room where Anne, Charlotte, and Emily, under the pseudonyms Acton, Currer, and Ellis Bell, worked on their poetry and read their manuscripts to one another. Here Emily wrote *Wuthering Heights*, derived from local legend and, to be sure, truth, although she occasionally altered the local names: Grimshaw, an old Wesleyan, becomes Earnshaw, and Sutcliffe becomes Heathcliff. The apostles' cupboard described in *Jane Eyre* as "a great Cabinet—whose front, divided into twelve panels, bore in grim design the heads of the twelve Apostles," is in the museum.

Shortly after the completion of *Wuthering Heights* the Brontë family suffered what has been popularized as the "trilogy of death." Branwell, who for quite some time had led a dissolute life, involving excesses of opium and drink, is supposed to have received a rather nasty message of renunciation from his mistress, had a fit of some sort, and died at the parsonage in September 1848. The day of the funeral in St. Michael's Church was a very wet one, and Emily caught cold. She died ten weeks later, on December 19, and was buried in the same cemetery. The couch on which she died has been kept *in situ* in the dining room of the parsonage. Anne, who had exhibited the family tubercular traits for some time, died the following May in Scarborough, where she had gone to take the air and was buried there with only Charlotte and a friend in attendance.

Charlotte returned to Haworth and her father. At the end of 1852 Arthur Nicholls, Mr. Brontë's young curate of eight years' standing, finally proposed to her in her sitting room, from which, Charlotte says, "I half led, half put him out. . . ." Mr. Brontë's strong opposition to marriage produced a delay and Nicholls's departure, but eventually the father relented, and Charlotte and Nicholls were married in the local church on June 29, 1854, with only two friends in the congregation. Indeed, Mr. Brontë did not attend, and Miss Wooler, Charlotte's old schoolmistress, gave the bride away; the villagers stood in attendance outside the church. After an Irish honeymoon to meet the Nicholls family, the couple returned to the parsonage,

and within nine months Charlotte was dead. In November, after their return, Charlotte and her new husband walked over a part of the moors to a favorite spot of hers, a waterfall now known as the Brontë Waterfall, 2 miles west beyond the church along Enfield Side. Rain began while they were out, and the severe cold Charlotte caught aggrevated her already-unstable tubercular condition. She died on March 31, 1855, and was buried at St. Michael's, in a grave next to Emily's. Matthew Arnold's "Haworth Churchyard" commemorates a December 1850 meeting between Charlotte Brontë and Harriet Martineau before describing the churchyard here:

There on its slope is built
The moorland town. But the church
Stands on the crest of the hill,
Lonely and bleak; at its side
The parsonage-house and the graves.

Strew with laurel the grave
Of the early-dying!

Much of Haworth and the surrounding area is unchanged from the mid-19th century; the Black Bull Inn, which Branwell frequented, is still there and is the pub from which Emily rescued her dog, later using the event in *Shirley*. The snow-covered mountains beyond the parsonage which Emily characterized as

A distant, dreamy, dim blue chain
Of mountains circling every side

are not really mountains; they are the Pennine moors, so well delineated in the early scenes of *Wuthering Heights*. Across these moors, about 3 miles to the west, is the bleak weather-beaten ruin of High Withins, or Top Withins, often thought to be the model for Heathcliff's Wuthering Heights. It is far more likely that his residence is a combination of High Withins and Ponden Hall, just across the Brontë Bridge in the Sladen Valley. Ponden Hall was also the prototype for Thrushcross Grange in the same novel. The hall was well known to the Brontë sisters when the Heaton family owned it; the family had a magnificent library, including a Shakespeare first folio and an especially extensive collection of travel books, and it is hardly surprising that this was the original of Edgar Linton's library in *Wuthering Heights*.

Among Charlotte's guests at the parsonage were Harriet Martineau and William Makepeace Thackeray, both of whom attended church services with her. Mrs. Gaskell was frequently here, especially after she was asked by the Reverend Mr. Brontë to write Charlotte's biography. Virginia Stephen (Woolf) visited the parsonage in the autumn of 1904 when she was staying in Giggleswick with a cousin; the visit proved to be an important one, for it provided the material for her first accepted piece of writing, an article which appeared in the December 21, 1904, issue of *The Guardian*.

HAWORTH   Ponden Hall, 2 miles over the Yorkshire moors from Haworth, is the source of Thrushcross Grange, the home of the Lintons in Emily Brontë's *Wuthering Heights*.

HEADINGTON, Oxfordshire (pop. 5,328) With modern urban expansion Headington has been almost swallowed up by its large neighbor, Oxford, 2½ miles to the southwest. There is a superficial similarity between the two places because much of the crumbling stone used in the Oxford colleges came from

HAWORTH MOOR While the bleak and windswept Haworth Moor generally evokes the memory of the Brontë sisters, Top Withens, now in ruins, was the model for the Earnshaws' home in *Wuthering Heights.*

the quarries here. The village has a literary association which it prefers not to acknowledge but which reflects no discredit upon the community. On May 1, 1878, dressed as Prince Rupert, Oscar Wilde attended a fancy-dress ball here given by Mrs. Morrell; this was his first real attempt at masquerading. All the social chronicles of the time carried some sort of commentary (usually long and vitriolic) about his appearance here, and this episode and its aftermath have sometimes been thought to be the catalyst for his later behavior.

HELL KETTLES, County Durham Legends abound in the rural areas of County Durham, and here at the confluence of the Skerne and Tees Rivers a little northeast of Croft, are three harmless pools of water which have been associated with numerous stories. The ponds are said to be bottomless: they are, in fact, from 14 to 19 feet deep. They are said to contain huge fighting pike; the fish are generally innocuous stickleback. They are said to be boiling sulfurous springs; they are alkaline springs with very little sulfur in them. The ponds are explained as the creation of an earthquake or, equally implausibly, by Daniel Defoe as waterlogged coal pits. Michael Drayton, coming down the Tees from Barnard Castle, gives voice to the Skerne and Hell Kettles in *Poly-Olbion;* the Skerne

> . . . spieth near her banke
> (That from their loathsome brimms do breathe a sulphurous sweat)
> Hell-Kettles rightly cald, that with the very sight,
> This Water-nymph, my Skerne, is put in such affright,
> That with unusual speed, she on her course doth haste,
> And rashly runnes herselfe into my widened waste.

HELM CRAG, Westmorland From one angle Helm Crag, the prominent hill overlooking Grasmere from

1½ miles to the northwest, resembles an old woman, the "ancient Woman" John Keats claimed to have recognized from William Wordsworth's poetry on his 1818 tour. Wordsworth had alluded to the woman and noticed the echo effect:

> —When I had gazed perhaps two minutes' space,
> Joanna, looking in my eyes, beheld
> That ravishment of mine, and laughed aloud.
> The Rock, like something starting from a sleep,
> Took up the Lady's voice, and laughed again;
> That ancient Woman, seated on Helm-Crag
> Was ready with her cavern; Hammar-Scar,
> And the tall Steep of Silver-how, sent forth
> A noise of laughter; southern Loughrigg heard,
> And Fairfield answered with a mountain tone;
> Helvellyn far into the clear blue sky
> Carried the Lady's voice,—old Skiddaw blew
> His speaking-trumpet;—back out of the clouds
> Of Glaramara southward came the voice;
> And Kirkstone toss'd it from his misty head.

HELPSTON, Northamptonshire Helpston, a typical west Fen village situated 7 miles north of Peterborough, on reclaimed land, is clustered around a crossroads with the finest surviving medieval cross in the county at one corner; the partly 13th-century church, dedicated to St. Botolph, was rebuilt in 1865 on its original Saxon foundations. The surrounding fenland has for centuries supported the local population with wheat, sugar-beet, and potato crops; the wetter part of the Fens yields the warped remains of bog oak from what was once great forest land.

Helpston was the birthplace on July 13, 1793, of John Clare, styled "the Northamptonshire peasant poet." Clare's birthplace, a gray stone, thatched cottage on the west side of the main road, was a tenement house which his parents inhabited all their married lives. Clare, a twin whose sister was thought to be the stronger at birth but who died shortly afterward, attended a dame school in the village, where he learned to spell a little "and to read from the Bible," and was employed in watching sheep and goats by the age of seven. His literary ambitions were kindled by a chance outing to nearby Stamford, where he bought a shilling copy of James Thomson's *Seasons*. Clare describes this area as:

Acres of little yellow weeds,
The wheat-fields' constant bloom
That ripen into prickly seeds
For fairy curry-combs,
To comb and clean the little things
That draw their nightly wain,
And so they scrub the bettle's wings
Till he can fly again.

In 1809 the proprietor of the local Blue Bell hired Clare to tend horses, plow 6 or 8 acres, and weed, but his employment here and in other menial jobs was generally unsuccessful because of his greater interest in writing. After a trip to Newark in 1812, Clare joined the militia and was sworn in at Peterborough; the relationship was not a successful one, and he returned to Helpston in May 1813. He lived with his parents, who were themselves extremely poor, until his marriage in 1819, when he moved into a white-washed cottage (marked with a plaque) next door. Here his family grew rapidly; there were four children in four years and more than eight in all. In November 1819, Clare met John Taylor, the publisher who first put Clare in print.

Clare's *Poems Descriptive of Rural Life and Scenery* and *The Village Minstrel* describe life in the village and were published and fairly well received before the first clear signs of mental illness appeared in late 1823. Clare's problems, not alleviated by his ever-increasing family, were in the first instance financial, and after 1824 the necessity to consult good physicians often took him on expensive trips away from Helpston, trips which did little more than lighten his purse. After eventual hospitalization at High Beech in 1837, he was finally certified and removed to Northampton in 1841. Both *The Shepherd's Calendar* and *The Rural Muse* were products of the transitional period prior to his lasting confinement, although many of the poems in the later volume had been composed far earlier. "On Seeing a Skull on Cowper Green" (Copy Green), for example, was composed in May 1813 when bones were found on the nearby green.

Wert thou a Poet, who in fancy's dream
Saw Immortality throw by her veil,
And all thy labours in Fame's temple gleam
In the proud glory of an after-tale?

Clare essentially spent the last twenty-seven years of his life in mental institutions. Death came on May 20, 1864, in Northampton, ten days after he suffered a particularly bad seizure. In earlier moments of lucidity Clare had dictated unusually precise arrangements for his burial:

I wish to lye on the North side of the churchyard, about the middle of the ground, where the Morning and Evening sun can linger the longest on my Grave. I wish to have a rough unhewn stone, something in the form of a mile stone, so that the playing boys may not break it in their heedless pastimes, with nothing more on it than this Inscription: "Here rest the hopes and ashes of John

Clare." I desire that no date be inserted thereon, as I wish it to live or dye with my poems and other writings, which if they have merit with posterity, it will, and if they have not it is not worth preserving.

Most of his instructions were carried out; the inscription, however, reads: "A Poet is born not made." There is a commemorative monument to Clare on the village green.

HELVELLYN, Cumberland and Westmorland The third highest mountain in the Lake District, Helvellyn rises on the Cumberland-Westmorland border 10 miles north of Ambleside. It is an extremely popular challenge to the climber; indeed, one of the most frequently used ascents is the arête of Striding Edge, whose crest, a mass of shattered pinnacles, Thomas De Quincey called that "awful curtain of rock."

An incident on the mountain more than 150 years ago, the death of Charles Gough, has been recorded in literature; Gough fell in a lonely spot here and died, and for three months his terrier Foxey never left the body. The whole matter was investigated, and while some points remain in doubt, what De Quincey called "the sublime and mysterious fidelity of the dog" has been established. Both William Wordsworth and Sir Walter Scott climbed the peak after this incident, and both wrote of the event. Wordsworth's "Fidelity" tells the story and comments:

The Dog, which still was hovering nigh,
Repeating the same timid cry,
This Dog, had been through three months' space
A dweller in that savage place.

Yes, proof was plain that, since the day
When this ill-fated Traveller died,
The Dog had watched about the spot,
Or by his master's side. . . .

Scott's "Hellvellyn" is far more descriptive of the scenery and captures the solitude of the area:

I climb'd the dark brow of the mighty Hellvellyn,
    Lakes and mountains beneath me gleam'd misty and wide;
All was still, save by fits, when the eagle was yelling,
    And starting around me the echoes replied.
On the right, Striden-edge round the Red-tarn was bending,
And Catchedicam its left verge was defending,
One huge nameless rock in the front was ascending,
    When I mark'd the sad spot where the wanderer had died.

References to Helvellyn are found in numerous other poems by Wordsworth, including "To ———, on Her First Ascent to the Summit of Helvellyn," "To the Same," "To Joanna," and "Musings near Aquapendente," which recalls climbing Helvellyn with Scott:

Where once together, in his day of strength,
We stood rejoicing, as if earth were free
From sorrow, like the sky above our heads.

HEMINGFORD GREY, Huntingdonshire (pop. 749) There are two parts to the Ouse River village of Hemingford Grey: the old part, which contains the oldest inhabited house in England; and the new part, which is rapidly expanding along the road to St. Ives, 1½ miles to the east. The village, on the south side of the Ouse, has a two-story manor house built about 1160 of Northamptonshire stone and still inhabited. Izaak Walton used to fish here because of the local Pomeranian bream, a fish not found in many English rivers.

HENLEY-ON-THAMES, Oxfordshire (pop. 9,490) Within commuting distance of London, 35½ miles to the east, and near the borders of Buckinghamshire and Berkshire, Henley-on-Thames is often called "one of the most enchanting towns in Oxfordshire." Located on the Thames River where it begins to be noticeably wider, Henley looks to the river and great rolling elm and beech woods on softly undulating hills. Summer sees the Thames populated with a variety of rivercraft—punts, skiffs, canoes, and launches—and the autumn colors are practically unequaled in the country. In 1839 Henley was the site of the first modern river regatta, and the event now occurs annually in July. The main street is lined with elegant Georgian houses; there are also a number of timbered houses and an outstanding example of 14th-century architecture in Chantry House. About 1420 this house came into the hands of the church, and a school was begun; in 1604 a grammar school was started on its upper floor, and some part of the school came under the patronage of Lady Elizabeth Periam. On the floor below the open timber-roofed grammar school she maintained twenty boys; Lady Elizabeth was the sister of Francis Bacon, who is known to have visited here. By 1778 all the boys were being schooled together, and by the mid-19th century the school was defunct; Chantry House was then sold to the Red Lion Inn.

The inn, still in business, has distinct associations with three literary figures: William Shenstone, Samuel Johnson, and Charles Dickens. It was here about 1750 that Shenstone is said to have written on a window of the inn what has become his most famous verse:

Whoe'er has travell'd life's dull round,
  Where'er his stages may have been,
May sigh to think he still has found
  The warmest welcome at an inn.

However, it is more likely that the lines apply to the Sunrising Inn in Edgehill, Warwickshire. Dr. Johnson stayed at the Red Lion with James Boswell in 1776.

Charles Dickens's *Our Mutual Friend* uses the Henley area quite extensively: it is to Henley that Lizzie Hexham comes to escape the attentions of Bradley Headstone and her thoughts of Eugene Wrayburn, and in this general Thames-side area she finds Betty Higden:

In those pleasant little towns on Thames, you may hear the fall of the water over the weirs, or even, in still weather, the rustle of the rushes; and from the bridge you may see the young river, dimpled like a young child, playfully gliding away among the trees, unpolluted by the defilements that lie in wait for it on its course, and as yet out of hearing of the deep summons of the sea.

Lizzie finds work at a mill, based on Marsh Mill, about half a mile away from Henley. The most dramatic parts of the novel are set on the towpath and at Plashwater Weir; the weir, in fact, was placed about 32 miles above London and located between Henley and Hurley:

Plashwater Weir Mill Lock looked tranquil and pretty on an evening in the summer time. A soft air stirred the leaves of the fresh green trees, and passed like a smooth shadow over the river, and like a smoother shadow over the yielding grass. The voice of the falling water, like the voices of the sea and the wind, was an outer memory to a contemplative listener. . . .
The creaking lock-gates opened slowly, and the light boat passed in as close as there was room enough, and the creaking lock-gates closed upon it, and it floated low down in the dock between the two sets of gates, until the water should rise and the second gates should open and let it out. . . .
The water rose and rose as the sluice poured in, dispersing the scum which had formed behind the lumbering gates, and sending the boat up. . . .

After Lizzie rescues Eugene from the water following his beating by Bradley Headstone, she takes him to the Angler's Inn (the Red Lion). Sometime later, in a "darkened and hushed room" in the inn "with the river outside the windows flowing on to the vast ocean," she and Eugene, "a figure on the bed, swathed and bandaged and bound, lying helpless on its back, with its two useless arms in splints at its sides," are married by the Rev. Frank Milvey:

As the bridegroom could not move his hand, they touched his fingers with the ring, and so put it on the bride. When the two plighted their troth, she laid her hand on his, and kept it there. When the ceremony was done, and all the rest departed from the room, she drew her arm under his head, and laid her own head down upon the pillow by his side.

The 20th century brought the very young Eric Blair (George Orwell) here; his father returned to England on leave with his family in July 1907, and they took Nutshell, a small house on Western Road. The father returned to India, leaving his growing family here and joined them upon retirement from the Foreign Service four years later. At the age of five Orwell was sent to Sunnylands, a nearby day school, where he remained until the family moved to Shiplake-on-Thames in 1912. Three years later the family returned to Henley and took a semidetached house at 36 St. Mark's Road, where they remained until leaving for London in 1917.

HEREFORD, Herefordshire (pop. 46,503) Hereford, the county town of the old county of Herefordshire (amalgamated with Worcestershire in 1974), was founded originally as a settlement near the Welsh Marches to protect the more inland areas of England after the West Saxons crossed the Severn River early in the 7th century. Hereford, on the north bank of the Wye River in a very attractive setting, was the Saxon capital of West Mercia. Mercian influence and rule were extensive; only recently has it come to light that Mercian scholarship has been underrated.

The Cathedral Church of the Blessed Virgin Mary (now properly the Cathedral Church of the Blessed Virgin Mary and St. Ethelbert) dates from the early 10th century, but the first church was replaced by a much grander structure between 1012 and 1052. The new church was destroyed within three years of its completion by the insurgent Welsh; reconstruction began in 1079. Although the cathedral is mainly

Norman, changes over the centuries have added styles from every period. It is most noted for its chained library and an internationally famous *mappa mundi,* drawn about 1300 and one of the oldest maps of the world. The chained library of nearly 1,500 volumes is one of the largest in the world; the chains of each volume are securely fastened to rods on the 17th-century oak bookcases. The Church of All Saints, on the High Street, also has an outstanding chained library.

Hereford's economy has always been based on the nearby countryside; orchards of cider apples surround the town, and 60 percent of the cider consumed in Great Britain is made here. More important, the rich pastureland grazes large herds of the famous red-and-white Hereford cattle, which supply some of the best beef in the world; the Hereford stock markets are known worldwide.

Hereford was visited by the early travel writers but has few literary associations other than those. Daniel Defoe was here when compiling material for *A Tour thro' the Whole Island of Great Britain* and was not much impressed by anything other than the cathedral:

> It is truly an old, mean built, and very dirty City, lying low, and on the Bank of *Wye,* which sometimes incommodes them very much, by the violent Freshes that come down from the Mountains of *Wales;* for all the Rivers of this County, except the *Diffrin-Doe,* come out of *Wales.*
> The chief Thing remarkable next to the Cathedral, is the College, which still retains its Foundation Laws. . . .
> The great Church is a magnificent Building, however Antient, the Spire is not high, but handsome, and there is a fine Tower at the West End, over the great Door or Entrance. The Choir is very fine, tho' plain, and there is a very good Organ. . . .

Even Michael Drayton finds little to sing of in *Poly-Olbion:*

> Whose reason whil'st he seekes industriously to knowe,
> A great way he hath gon, and *Hereford* doth showe
> Her rising Spires aloft; when as the Princely *Wye,*
> Him from his Muse to wake, arrests him by and by.

Virtually the only other literary association is with the last metaphysical poet of the Anglican Church, Thomas Traherne, who was born here in 1637. Traherne was the son of a Hereford shoemaker of Welsh descent, and despite poverty he was educated here before entering Brasenose College, Oxford in 1653. It is possible that he was raised by one Philip Traherne, a well-to-do innkeeper and later Lord Mayor of Hereford. The poet's works were unknown until 1910, when the Burney manuscript discovered in the British Museum verified that a manuscript book of poetry found in a London street bookstall was indeed Traherne's and not Henry Vaughan's.

One other minor literary relationship exists; Elizabeth Barrett (Browning) frequently visited the Elizabethan Kinnersley Castle, the home of her uncle John Altham Graham-Clarke and his wife, when she was living at nearby Colwall. David Garrick was born here at the Raven Inn on February 19, 1717, and Nell Gwyn (Gwynne) is supposed to have been born on Gwynne Street on February 2, 1650; a tablet marks the house. London, however, also claims her birth.

HERMITAGE, Berkshire (pop. 502) Situated in the south downlands of Berkshire 4 miles northeast of Newbury, Hermitage has a nearby prehistoric earthworks known as Grimsbury Castle and itself contains the site of a Roman villa. In January 1918 D. H. and Frieda Lawrence moved into Chapel Farm Cottage, where they remained until the owners, the Radford family, needed the house again in May. The Lawrences went to Middleton-by-Wirksworth in Derbyshire and then returned to Hermitage in May 1919. So poor that they could not even afford to buy fuel, they picked up wood chips after trees had been felled. They applied for passports, which appeared in mid-autumn, and Lawrence then left for Florence by way of Paris, where he met Frieda, who had first gone to Baden-Baden to see her mother.

HERSTMONCEUX *See* HURSTMONCEUX.

HEXHAM, Northumberland (pop. 8,843) In times past Hexham, which is 15 miles west of Newcastle upon Tyne, was known as Halgutstad, Hangustald, Hexildesham, and Hextoldesham. It was once the seat of a county palatine, an entity under no political jurisdiction except its own. The history of this market town is known back to the 7th century, when Wilfrid, Archbishop of York, founded an abbey here; all that is left of the original Anglo-Saxon church, completed in 678, is a fine crypt. The crypt and most likely at least part of the original structure were built of stones taken from the nearby Roman town of Corstopitum at Corbridge, and some of the dedicatory inscriptions to pagan Roman gods are still visible. The Venerable Bede in his *Historia Ecclesiastica Gentis Anglorum* describes the building of the abbey, which is said to be the finest monastic structure "north of the Alps." The abbey church now in use was begun in the 12th century and contains two relics of quite exceptional interest: the first is the cross of St. Acca, Bishop of Hexham from 709 to 732; the other is the original frithstool, or sanctuary chair, known as St. Wilfrid's Chair. Because of its location, Hexham played a part in border warfare and in the Jacobite rebellion of 1715. Sir Walter Scott uses

HEREFORD The half-timbered Old House in Hereford dates to 1621 and is one of the few remaining structures in the town which the metaphysical poet Thomas Traherne would have known.

Hexham Abbey in *Rokeby* when he has Bertram comment:

Edmund, thy years were scarcely mine
When, challenging the Clans of the Tyne
To bring their best my brand to prove.
O'er Hexham's altar hung my glove;
But Tynedale, not in tower nor town,
Held champion meet to take it down.

There is no factual basis for the belief that the hanging of a glove in the chancel of the abbey was the ultimate challenge.

In the summer of 1853 Dante Gabriel Rossetti was here at the White Horse Inn and "contemplated the quiet beauty of the old town." He later recalled that he and William Scott Bell "sat and looked at the market-place from the deep window of an inn some centuries old and talked of friends for one pleasant hour, while sun and air seemed whispering together, and the 'hovering pigeons' touched the street." Rossetti does not mention the abbey or the splendid Tynedale scenery.

In more recent times a Georgian house with bow windows on Battle Hill was the birthplace of Wilfrid Wilson Gibson on October 2, 1878; only a portion of the house next to the General Post Office remains. Gibson, educated privately, achieved some of his greatest success with *Whin,* an anthology of Northambrian poetry.

HEYDON, Norfolk (pop. 213) A small village 5 miles west of Aylsham, Heydon consists of little more than an old manor hall, a church, and a few cottages. The manor house was built between 1581 and 1584 by an auditor of Elizabeth I's Exchequer, and it became the home of William Earle Bulwer in the 18th century and remained in the family for a considerable period. Edward Bulwer-Lytton (Lord Lytton) was not born in Heydon, but he was frequently at the manor house throughout his youth and early adulthood and worked on many of his novels here.

HEYTESBURY, Wiltshire (pop. 496) Somewhat dominated by its position on the edge of the Salisbury Plain, Heytesbury (pronounced "hāt′is-bry"), 4 miles southeast of Warminster on the Wylye River, actually possesses excellent views of the rolling hills of Wiltshire. The village has a 13th-century church with a medieval bell, a grouping of 15th-century (rebuilt) almshouses, and a lovely parkland containing Heytesbury House, the home for many years of Siegfried Sassoon. Many of Sassoon's poems deal with the area, among them "Eulogy of My House," "Awareness of Alucin," "In Heytesbury Wood," "On Edington Hill," and "Outlived by Trees":

A beech, a cedar, and a lime
Grow on my lawn, embodying time.
A lime, a cedar, and a beech
The transcience of this lifetime teach.

Beech, cedar, lime, when I'm dead Me
You'll stand, lawn-shadowing, tree by tree;
And in your greenery, while you last,
I shall survive who shared your past.

One of Sassoon's guests here was T. E. Lawrence, who was stationed at nearby Bovington Camp. Sassoon died here on September 1, 1967, and was buried near Bath at Downside Abbey.

HIGH BEECH, Essex (pop. 504) Perched somewhat precariously on the verge of Epping Forest less than 15 miles from central London, High Beech is a village protected by stringent building codes and common land, which forestall total immersion. This was the "home" of John Clare from 1837 to 1841, for High Beech was the location of Dr. Allen's private mental asylum. Clare was fortunate in being placed in Dr. Allen's care, for the doctor's treatment was unusually enlightened: he stated that here "together with domestic comfort, diversity of occupations and amusements suited to their various states, the retirement, pure air and sweet scenery around, afford ample scope for walks without annoyance, and apparently without restraint, which, with judicious moral and medical management combine with acknowledged requisites to assist the disturbed and diseased mind to regain its tranquillity." The asylum was a complex of three houses, Lippitt's Hill Lodge and Springfield House, both of which are extant, and Fairmead House, demolished in the late 19th century. Clare was encouraged to walk through the forest and to write; and, most important, he was temporarily relieved of his pressing financial problems. Clare's happiness here is apparent:

I love the Forest and its airy bounds,
Where friendly Campbell takes his daily rounds:
I love the breakneck hills, that headlong go,
And leave me high, and half the world below;
I love to see the Beech Hill mounting high,
The brook without a bridge and nearly dry,
There's Bucket's Hill, a place of furze and clouds,
Which evening in a golden blaze enshrouds. . . .

"The brook without a bridge" still runs across Fairmead, and Bucket's Hill was the local name for nearby Buckhurst Hill. Clare could be found sitting, thinking, and writing at Fern Hill behind the chapel; Fern Hill is there and basically unchanged, but the chapel was demolished in 1872 to make room for the present church. Clare could sit here knowing that

. . . giant London, known to all the world,
Was nothing but a guess among the trees,
Though only half a day from where we stood.

Wanting to go home to his first love, Clare left the asylum in 1841 by simply walking off and reached Northborough, Northamptonshire, three days later. Anything but cured, he failed to recognize his wife Patty and could not believe that Mary, his first love, was dead: he insisted that he had seen her only twelve months before when, in fact, she had been dead for six years.

It is possible that Clare may have met Alfred, Lord Tennyson, who lived here from 1837 to 1840, since Tennyson is known to have been acquainted with Dr. Allen. Tennyson came here from Somersby in Lincolnshire and lived, quite unhappily, at Beech Hill House (now rebuilt). In particular, he disliked the area, complaining that it was devoid of nature and had "a want of men and birds." There were two aspects of life here that he did like: skating on the pond in winter and being able to see Waltham Abbey from his house. Tennyson left High Beech in 1840 for Tunbridge Wells, Kent.

HIGH WYCOMBE, Buckinghamshire (pop. 40,384) A heavily industrialized city and a large market town, High Wycombe has an especially good location for a dormitory suburb on the Wye River 10 miles east of Maidenhead and 34 miles northwest of London. Only a few old buildings are left here, but they are all clustered together at the west end of the High Street, a fact which must have helped preserve them.

An early visitor here was Dr. Samuel Johnson, who stayed at Wycombe Abbey in 1783; this structure was never an abbey and is now one of the best-known girls' schools in the country. A somewhat later traveler in the same area was Robert Louis Stevenson, who recorded his impressions in an 1875 essay, "An Autumn Effect." "[W]ith a sufficiency of money and a knapsack," he roamed the countryside here and

> had this first enthusiasm to encourage me up the long hill above High Wycombe. . . . A pall of grey cloud covered the sky, and its colour reacted on the colour of the landscape. Near at hand, indeed, the hedgerow trees were still fairly green, shot through with bright autumnal yellows, bright as sunshine. But a little way off, the solid bricks of woodland that lay squarely on slope and hill-top were not green, but russet and grey. . . . The whole scene had an indefinable look of being painted, the colour was so abstract and correct, and there was something so sketchy and merely impressional about these distant single trees on the horizon that one was forced to think of it all as of a clever French landscape. . . .
>
> Overhead there was a wonderful carolling of larks which seemed to follow me as I went. Indeed, during all the time I was in that country the larks did not desert me. The air was alive with them from High Wycombe to Tring; and . . . they began to take such a prominence over other conditions, and form so integral a part of my conception of the country, that I could have baptized it "The Country of Larks."

T. S. Eliot spent a relatively short time at High Wycombe after he married Vivienne Haigh Haigh-Wood in 1915; he took up a post at the grammar school and taught French, mathematics, history, geography, art, and swimming. At the time he made frequent trips to London, where he met Wyndham Lewis, James Joyce, and Ezra Pound. It was Pound who encouraged Eliot's adoption of a writing career and persuaded him to settle permanently in England. After less than a year's teaching, Eliot left High Wycombe for London.

HIGHAM-ON-THE-HILL, Leicestershire (pop. 553) Higham-on-the-Hill, on the Leicestershire-Warwickshire border 3 miles from Hinckley, is a modern village, and just a mile away is Lindley Hall, the birthplace of Robert Burton on February 8, 1577. The Burtons were a well-established family (a Burton had carried Henry VI's banner in France), and this had long been the family home. Burton spent his childhood here and was schooled at Sutton Coldfield and Nuneaton before going up to Oxford.

HIGHGATE, Middlesex For years Highgate was always thought of as a part of London, and since the redistricting of 1965 it has actually been placed in Greater London; but at one time this community, just northeast of Hampstead, was partly in Middlesex. Highgate has cared for its buildings, and the 18th-century village of old Highgate, on the top of the hill, centers in The Grove, mostly 18th-century, which leads from the High Street to the Old Hall (1691). Without doubt the oldest and finest house in the town is Cromwell House; Waterlow Park, secluded on the

slopes of the hill, has several small lakes which attract a wide variety of wildlife; and Lauderdale House, located in the park and now its teahouse, was the home of Nell Gwyn.

As might be expected of a town so close to Hampstead and London, Highgate is overflowing with literary associations, and early travelers noted its situation and beauty. Michael Drayton writes of Highgate in *Poly-Olbion:*

> Then *Hie-gate* boasts his Way; which men do most frequent;
> His long-continued fame; his hie and great descent;
> Appointed for a gate of London to have been,
> When first the mighty *Brute,* that City did begin.

And Daniel Defoe comments on its social structure in *A Tour thro' the Whole Island of Great Britain:*

> The *Jews* have particularly fixt upon this Town for their Country Retreats, and some of them are very Wealthy; they live there in good Figure, and have several Trades particularly depending upon them, and especially, Butchers of their own to supply then with Provisions kill'd their own way; also, I am told, they have a private Synagogue here.

Many figures of importance lived in Highgate: Sir Francis Bacon had lodgings here when he was keeping his terms at Gray's Inn, and Andrew Marvell lived in a cottage near Waterlow Park, where he had a garden

> So with roses overgrown
> And, lillies, that you would it guess
> To be a little wilderness. . . .

There is a commemorative plaque on the long, low brick wall which forms the park boundary.

Highgate's most prominent literary resident was Samuel Taylor Coleridge, who, defeated by his addiction to opium, put himself in the hands of Dr. James Gillman on April 9, 1816. The house was at 3 The Grove, and Coleridge spent the rest of his life here. His room

> looked upon a delicious prospect of wood and meadow, with a gay garden full of colour under the window. . . . There he cultivated his flowers, and had a set of birds for his pensioners, who came to breakfast. . . . He might be seen taking his daily stroll up and down near Highgate, with his black coat and white locks and a book in his hand, and was a great acquaintance of the little children.

He found the Gillmans' hospitality expansive and generous, and for eighteen years he could frequently be seen in his favorite spot at the top of Highgate Hill, where he has been described as looking "like a sage escaped from the inanity of life's battle." Millfield Lane, just beyond the curve on West Hill, is where Coleridge and John Keats met in 1819; Keats describes the meeting in a letter to George and Georgiana Keats:

> Last Sunday I took a Walk towards Highgate and in the lane that winds by the side of Lord Mansfield's park I met Mʳ Green our Demonstrator at Guy's in conversation with Coleridge—I joined them, after enquiring by a look whether it would be agreeable—I walked with him a[t] his alderman-after-dinner pace for near two miles I suppose[.] In those two Miles he broached a thousand things—let me see if I can give you a list—Nightingales, Poetry—on Poetical Sensation—Metaphysica—Differ-

ent genera and species of Dreams—Nightmare—a dream accompanied by a sense of touch—single and double touch—A dream related—First and second consciousness—the difference explained between will and Volition—so m[an]y metaphysicians from a want of smoking the second consciousness—Monsters—the Kraken—Mermaids—Southey believes in them—Southey's belief too much diluted—A Ghost story—Good morning—I heard his voice as he came towards me—I heard it as he moved away—I heard it all the interval—if it may be called so. He was civil enough to ask me to call on him at Highgate Good Night!

Ralph Waldo Emerson also visited the poet here, in 1833. Coleridge died on July 25, 1834, and a postmortem determined that there was no apparent physical cause for his suffering and addiction. He was buried originally in the graveyard of Highgate School, and in 1866 the tomb was transferred to the crypt of the school chapel. In 1961 the body was again moved, this time to St. Michael's Church on South Grove Street, where the tomb now rests in the center aisle of the church; on this occasion John Masefield delivered the funeral oration.

Gerard Manley Hopkins was at the Highgate Grammar School on Hampstead Lane from 1854 to 1863 while his family was living in neighboring Hampstead. His nine years here must not have been pleasant ("I had no love for my schooldays"), although he won a number of prizes; two of them were won with "The Escorial" and "A Vision of Mermaids." He left for Balliol College, Oxford, in April 1863. From 1886 to 1905 A. E. Housman resided here; he was still working in the Patent Office as a Civil Service clerk, a period he referred to as purgatory, when he took Byron Cottage, 17 North Hill Road. He wrote *A Shropshire Lad* here. Housman was one of the first to become interested in preserving the old aspects and attitudes of Highgate. When brushwood was cleared from the center of the wood so that, in his opinion, too much of the Archway could be seen, he caustically wrote to the *Standard:*

> Now when we stand in the center, we can divide our attention between Juggins' porter and our neighbours' washing. Scarlet flannel petticoats are much worn in Archway Road, and if anyone desires to feast his eyes on these picturesque objects . . . let him repair to the centre of Highgate Wood!

George Eliot (Mary Ann Evans), who lived at 4 Cheyne Walk, Chelsea, after her May 1880 marriage to the New York banker John W. Cross, died there the following December. She was buried in the Highgate Cemetery next to her earlier common-law husband, George Henry Lewes. Christina Rossetti, who died in London on December 29, 1894, is also buried here. Coventry Patmore lived at Bowden Lodge for a short time after his second marriage in 1864.

In the 20th century both T. S. Eliot and John Betjeman were associated with Highgate; Betjeman was born here on August 28, 1906, and was educated at the grammar school where Eliot taught English for a time. Indeed, Betjeman once handed his English master a tiny notebook entitled *The Best of Betjeman;* his later poem "Summoned by Bells" portrays Edwardian Highgate through the eyes of a small boy.

Finally, Hans Christian Andersen, who visited the old Archway on Hornsey Lane to get a good view of London, saw "the great world metropolis mapped out in fire" before him. The old stone archway designed by John Nash was replaced with a steel structure in 1897, and the view extends to the Essex marshes, St. Paul's, and the City.

HILGAY, Norfolk (pop. 1,491)   With the Wissey River below it, the hillside village of Hilgay, 3 miles south of Downham Market, is just west of Breckland, an area once cultivated but now allowed to revert to its wilderness state. An avenue of lime trees leads to the 18th-century church, a rather abbreviated affair with a squat tower. In 1621 Phineas Fletcher, author of *The Purple Island, or The Isle of Man,* was presented with this living, and he remained here until his death at the end of 1650; his place of burial is not known. One of Fletcher's guests here may have been Francis Quarles, author of *Emblems,* since one of the globes in that work is inscribed with the name Hilgay.

HINCKLEY, Leicestershire (pop. 34,100)   An old market town whose longtime industry has been the manufacturing of gloves, Hinckley is now reaching out to become a part of the sprawling metropolis of Leicester, 15 miles to the northeast. Hinckley gained early fame for its fair, and it is to this that William Shakespeare refers in *Henry IV: Part II* when Davy asks Judge Shallow,

> . . . and, sir, do you mean to stop any of William's wages about the sack he lost the other day at Hinckley fair?

John Cleveland (whose name is properly spelled Cleiveland) came to Hinckley from Loughborough in 1621, when his father was presented with this living. The boy's education was undertaken by the Rev. Richard Vines (Vynes), and Cleveland proved an apt and industrious pupil; he left Hinckley in 1627, when he matriculated at Christ's College, Cambridge.

HINDHEAD, Surrey (pop. 1,536)

> From north to south it [the heath] extends from Binfield (which cannot be far from the borders of Buckinghamshire) to the South Downs of Hampshire, and terminates somewhere between Liphook and Petersfield, after stretching over Hindhead, which is certainly the most villainous spot that God ever made. Our ancestors do, indeed, seem to have ascribed its formation to another power; for the most celebrated part of it is called "*the Devil's Punch Bowl.*"

The land around Hindhead, 9 miles southeast of Farnham, is indeed the "villainous" heathland that William Cobbett describes; the escarpment here faces north, but the land is peculiarly rough for the South Downs. Here is the Devil's Punch Bowl, a deep valley carved from the same sandstone ridge on which Hindhead is situated; Daniel Defoe likens the environment to Arabia Deserta in *A Tour thro' the Whole Island of Great Britain:*

> Here is a vast Tract of Land . . . which is not only Poor, but even quite steril, given up to Barrenness, horrid and frightful to look on, not only good for little, but good for nothing; much of it is a Sandy Desert, and one may frequently be put in Mind here of *Arabia Deserta.* . . . This Sand indeed is check'd by the *Heath,* or *Heather,* which grows in it, and which is the common product of Barren Land, even in the very *Highlands* of *Scotland;* but the Ground is otherwise so Poor and Barren, that the

Product of it feeds no Creatures, but some very small Sheep, who feed chiefly on the said *Heather*, and but very few of these, nor are there any Villages, worth mentioning, and but few Houses, or People for many Miles far and wide. . . .

The desolation of the country here partly accounts for the onetime high incidence of robbery, violence, and murder; the most famous crime occurred on September 24, 1786, when a nameless sailor stopped at the Red Lion on his way to his ship at Portsmouth. He was well off (a curiosity considering that he was on his way to his ship) and bought three tramps at the inn a number of rounds before leaving the Red Lion in their company. At the edge of the Punch Bowl the three murdered and robbed him, stripped off his clothes, and threw the body into the hollow, where two laborers found it shortly afterward. The murderers were caught that night in Steep, were tried and convicted at Kingston Assizes, and hung in chains at the scene of the crime. The unknown sailor lies in a grave behind the church.

Nobody liked a good story—and a murder—as much as Charles Dickens, and he uses this event in *Nicholas Nickleby*. Nicholas and Smike pass the Punch Bowl on their way to Portsmouth; they spend the night at Godalming before continuing the journey over "long and weary hills":

> They walked upon the rim of the Devil's Punch Bowl; and Smike listened with greedy interest as Nicholas read the inscription upon the stone which, reared upon that wild spot, tells of a murder committed there by night. The grass on which they stood, had once been dyed with gore; and the blood of the murdered man had run down, drop by drop, into the hollow which gives the place its name. "The Devil's Bowl," thought Nicholas, as he looked into the void, "never held fitter liquor than that!"

Hindhead was a popular but not populous area when Sir Arthur Conan Doyle arrived in January 1897 and rented a part of Moorlands, a guest establishment, so that he could oversee the building of his new home, then seriously behind schedule; by October the family was able to move into Undershaw, named from the grove of trees overhanging the gables and house frontage. Doyle wrote prolifically here, probably because of his inextricable marital situation; his wife was terminally ill, and he was deeply in love with Jean Leckie, an affair that his "Ma'am," as he called his mother, not only accepted but fostered. By the spring of 1898 he had finished *Round the Fire Stories* for *The Strand*, and in the autumn he began *A Duet, with an Occasional Chorus*. Sherlock Holmes, though, was dead, and Doyle so intended him to stay, but the offer of $5,000 for American rights to resuscitate the master detective in 1903 brought about a spate of new books beginning with *The Adventure of the Empty House*.

Doyle had been undergoing a deep personality shift, said to be another result of his personal situation, and his harsh, domineering side became more and more visible. However, he was still capable of extreme generosity: on one occasion in 1906 he hosted a considerable number of men from the French Fleet who had expressed a desire to meet the King, Sir John Fisher (the "*grand amiral anglais*"), and Doyle. "*Bienvenue*" was posted at the entrance gate, a huge marquee tent was raised, four brass bands were in attendance, and girls distributed flowers. This was Doyle's way of giving "them a real rousing welcome." On July 4, 1906, at the age of forty-nine, his wife Louise died of the tuberculosis that she had fought for thirteen years and was buried here with a marble cross marking her grave. Doyle gave up the house in 1907.

In early November 1894 William Ernest Henley took a fortnight's holiday here at the Log House, and in 1896 Virginia Stephen (Woolf) was here on holiday with her family in a house at the top of the Downs.

HINDON, Wiltshire (pop. 415) The tiny hamlet of Hindon, 9 miles south of Warminster, was entirely rebuilt after a fire destroyed it in 1765. Historically, Hindon was an early pocket borough which returned "John Lyly, gent." as its Member of Parliament in February 1589. A second political aspirant was not so fortunate; Benjamin Disraeli unsuccessfully contested the seat here.

Just above the town on the downs is a fine stand of trees known as Great Ridge Wood to which W. H. Hudson frequently came; he records seeing deer bound through the forest in *A Shepherd's Life* and comments on the area "where ravens bred down to about thirty-five or forty years ago." In the spring and summer of 1909 he lived

> at the Lamb Inn, a famous posting-house of the great old days, and we had three pairs of birds—throstle, pied wagtail, and flycatcher—breeding in the ivy covering the wall facing the village street, just over my window. I watched them when building, incubating, feeding their young, and bringing their young off. . . . It was on the morning of the day I left, and one of the little things flitted into the room where I was having my breakfast. I succeeded in capturing it before the cats found out, and put it back on the ivy.

HITCHIN, Hertfordshire (pop. 17,300) Located on the Hiz, one of England's smallest rivers, Hitchen is 8

HINDHEAD Called "villainous" by William Cobbett and "frightful" by Daniel Defoe, the heathland around Hindhead is characterized by its wildness and desolation. This is the Devil's Punch Bowl, one of the most remote parts of the heath, which found its way into literature after a particularly brutal 18th-century murder.

miles northeast of Luton and about 32 miles north of London. Hitchin contained a monastery in the 8th century, in Offa's time, and it still has several attractive streets with old houses. The medieval Church of St. Mary, set in a spacious churchyard and partly surrounded by period houses, is battlemented, and its tower stands on Norman foundations which incorporate Roman bricks. The inside is even more impressive, with a wall painting, *The Adoration of the Magi*, thought to be the work of Rubens, and a good collection of medieval to 18th-century brasses, including one commemorating Robert Hinde (Hind), who died in 1786 and is said to be the original of Uncle Toby in Laurence Sterne's *Tristram Shandy*. Hinde, indeed, had a house with a drawbridge in Preston, where he fired off the celebration salvos mentioned in the novel and maintained an army of farmhands and children.

Sometime around 1559 George Chapman was born at Mount Pleasant, a house on the higher ground of the town. Very little is known of his life even after his career as a dramatist began, although it is often assumed that a great deal of his writing was done here. A plaque on 35 Tilehouse Street records his residence:

> The learned shepherd of fair Hitchin Hill, as his young contemporary William Browne describes him in his Britannia's Pastorals, himself records in The Teares of Peace that it was while he was "on the Hill next Hitchin's hand" the shade of Homer filled his bosom with a "floode of soule."

Much more is known of John Bunyan's Agnes Beaumont, the girl whose father died shortly after barring her from his home in Edworth when she had gone off with Bunyan to a dissenters' meeting. The old man's death brought a charge of murder by poison on Bunyan and Miss Beaumont, but they were cleared by the inquest. The grave of Agnes Beaumont Story is in the graveyard behind the Baptist Chapel on Tilehouse Street, and in the Salem Chapel is a chair which Bunyan presented to the incumbent minister.

Part of Edward Bulwer-Lytton's *Eugene Aram* concerns Hitchin.

HOCKLIFFE, Bedfordshire (pop. 497) Situated on the Roman Watling Street and later settled by the Saxons, Hockliffe has long depended on road traffic for its support. In Tudor days carriages and other traffic often overran the road into the adjoining fields; numerous inns sprang up to service the travelers, and several remain, among them the fine Old White Horse. Hockliffe is the supposed birthplace of Thomas Hoccleve (Occleve), the author of *De regimine principum*, sometime about 1370, but nothing more is known.

At the turn of the twentieth century Arnold Bennett took Trinity Hall Farm, a rather nondescript house (except for its name), for three years. The garden, orchard, and meadows surrounding the house were the main attraction for Bennett. He brought his parents and sister here from Burslem when his father was ill with softening of the brain. The illness is fully described in *Clayhanger*. His father died in January 1902 and was buried in Chalgrove Cemetery. Among Bennett's frequent guests here was H. G. Wells, who became the target of one of his host's favorite games.

Bennett would "sail" china dinner plates from the table for his guests to catch. Wells, in a pique about the recurring missiles, once threw a cushion at Bennett, causing extensive damage. In 1903 Bennett moved to Fountainebleau.

HODDESDON, Hertfordshire (pop. 12,500) The ancient village of Hoddesdon, 4 miles southeast of Hertford and near the Lea River, was once rich in old inns. The Bull, the Maidenhead, and the Thatched House have been demolished, but the Salisbury Arms, formerly the Black Lion, is mid-16th century, and the Bell is mid-17th century. This part of Hertfordshire has been a favorite fishing area for centuries and was of especial interest to Izaak Walton; indeed, the old Thatched House was the place where he "was wont to repair for my morning cup of ale." *The Compleat Angler* mentions the inn:

> . . . [F]or my purpose is to drink my morning's draught at the Thatched House in Hoddesdon, and I think not to rest till I come thither, where I have appointed a friend or two to meet me. . . .

Around 1720, on his way to Down Hall, Essex, for the first time, Matthew Prior stopped at the Bull,

> Near a nymph with an urn, that divides the highway,
> And into a puddle throws mother of tea. . . .

The nymph was a conduit head for the High Street. Just 1 mile away are the remains of the old moated Rye House; more was extant when Dante Gabriel Rossetti arrived here with George P. Boyce in a hansom cab they had hired in London for the trip. They arrived a little after 5 o'clock and, after waiting some time for their meal, Rossetti became drunk and quarrelsome. He is said to have fallen down in the unlighted passageway leading to the dungeons here and to have lost his overcoat (which in its torn state was retrieved by Boyce).

HOGHTON, Lancashire (pop. 910) About equidistant from Preston and Blackburn, Hoghton (pronounced "haw'ton") has views to the Welsh mountains, the Yorkshire moors, and the Lakeland mountains; here the Ribble and the Darwen flow below the battlemented walls of Hoghton Tower, built in 1565 by Sir Thomas Hoghton. James I visited here when Sir Richard Hoghton held the manor, and it is said that on this occasion in jest the King knighted the loin of beef and made it Sir Loin forever more. The tower was badly damaged in the Civil War and was abandoned in the 18th century; it has since been restored and is presently occupied by a De Hoghton once again. However, it was in a ruinous state when William Harrison Ainsworth used it for the final scenes of *The Lancashire Witches*. Charles Dickens also described it in its decayed state in his story "George Silverman's Explanation."

HOLFORD, Somerset (pop. 160) Located in the rolling, wooded Quantock Hills, where red deer are still common, Holford is in a particularly attractive setting. A lane beside the small church here leads to Alfoxton House (old spelling, Alfoxden), the home of William Wordsworth and his sister Dorothy in 1797. Samuel Taylor Coleridge was less than 3 miles away at the Lime Street Cottage in Nether Stowey, and the poets, by this time firm friends, found walking in the

Quantocks and conversing with each other pleasant and profitable. Indeed, a number of the more productive walking sessions involved an extensive exploration of poetic theories which led to collaboration on the *Lyrical Ballads*. Wordsworth's favorite walk can still be re-created: a path on the right side of Alfoxton House leads to Holford Combe and a small stream and continues through the woods to the summit of the Quantocks; this is the scene of "Upon smooth Quantock's airy ridge we roved." Wordsworth is supposed to have done most of his work in a small cottage on the Manor House grounds.

More recently, Virginia Woolf and her husband stayed at the Plough Inn in August 1912 before leaving on August 18 for a honeymoon on the Continent. A year later, after showing signs of recovery at Miss Thomas's Nursing Home in Twickenham, Virginia Woolf was sent back to Holford on her doctor's advice in the hope that the Quantocks and Holford with their pleasant memories would help even more. However, her stay here was marked by intense depression and increased resistance to food, and on September 8, sixteen days after her arrival, she returned to London.

HOLLESLEY, Suffolk (pop. 575)   A tiny east Suffolk village 6 miles southeast of Woodbridge, Hollesley (pronounced "hōz'li") is known throughout England as the site of an open borstal. In 1936 Brendan Behan was involved in an Irish Republican Army bombing campaign and three years later was sentenced to serve three years at this reform school. Part of his *Borstal Boy* tells of his experiences here:

> The buildings were big, rambling and timbered like the headquarters of the Horse Show or the Phoenix Park Racecourse buildings in Dublin. They were built about 1880 or 1890, I'd have said, to imitate a Tudor great house. . . .
> I liked these buildings because they were more unlike a jail than any place could be.

HOLLINGTON, Sussex   Hollington has become an arm of Hastings, 2½ miles to the south; yet its 13th-century red-roofed church has an especially fine setting in a wood. This village and its old church were the ones which Charles Lamb loved so much; on his trip to Hastings in 1823 with his sister Mary, he walked here and later described the church in great detail to John Bates Dibdin:

> Let me hear that you have clamber'd up to Lover's Seat. . . . And go to the little church, which is a very protestant Loretto, and seems dropt by some good angel for the use of a hermit, who was at once parishioner and a whole parish. It is not too big. Go in the night, bring it away in your portmanteau, and I will plant it in my garden. It must have been erected in the very infancy of British Christianity, for the two or three first converts; yet hath it all the appertances of a church of the first magnitude, its pulpit, its pews, its baptismal font; a cathedral in a nutshell. Seven people would crowd it like a Caledonian Chapel. . . . It reminds me of the grain of mustard seed.

The Lover's Seat Lamb mentions is at Fairlight.

Because of Lamb's description, Thomas Hood was persuaded to spend his honeymoon in nearby Hastings and to visit the church in 1825.

HOLME PIERREPONT, Nottinghamshire (pop. 184)   This rather secluded village on the Trent River about 4½ miles southeast of Nottingham has an old manor house in the park which was the home of the grandparents of Francis Beaumont. Since the distance between Holme Pierrepont and his birthplace and childhood home at Grace Dieu is less than 20 miles, it is assumed that he was often here.

Another association with this village exists with John Oldham, sometimes called the English Juvenal, who lived here with his patron, the Earl of Kingston, until his death in 1683 at the age of thirty. He is buried here in the 13th-century church, and in the nave arcade, facing the entrance, is an ornate tablet, said to be the work of Grinling Gibbons, to the "Young Oldham," a "poet of merit." At a much later date Holme Pierrepont was often visited by Lord Byron.

HOLMER GREEN, Buckinghamshire   Situated 4 miles northeast of High Wycombe on the heath side of the road, Holmer Green is now very much a part of the creeping suburbs of London. The so-called heath once supported acres of the famous Bucks Black Cherry orchards, and a spattering of blossoms is still visible in spring; but a heath it no longer is.

The old village was set around a large green where cricket and football were played, and near the Valiant Trooper was a large Victorian cottage belonging to the Polidori family, relatives of Dante Gabriel and Christina Rossetti (there is a modern house on the site). Both poets spent a great deal of time here, Christina living with Uncle Polidori for many years and Dante spending his summers here until 1839, when the Polidoris returned to London. Nothing remains to link the two to the village, but Christina's "Song" recalls the area:

> When I am dead, my dearest,
>   Sing no sad songs for me;
> Plant thou no roses at my head,
>   Nor shady cypress tree;
> Be the green grass above me
>   With showers and dewdrops wet;
> And if thou wilt, remember,
>   And if thou wilt, forget.

HOLNE, Devon (pop. 285)   The Dartmoor Chase, on whose southeast border Holne is located, is noted for its rugged beauty and its impression of desolation. The small village of Holne, 4 miles west of Ashburton, was the birthplace of Charles Kingsley on June 12, 1819. The old parsonage where the family lived was a thatched affair and has been described as "a cosily sheltered house overlooking Dartmoor Chase." Kingsley was baptized in the local church, which has a very fine painted screen, a pulpit with an hourglass, and a Kingsley memorial window. The family lived in Holne for only a short time before moving to Burton-upon-Trent, Staffordshire.

HOLT, Norfolk (pop. 2,249)   A market town 10 miles southwest of Cromer, Holt is almost wholly Georgian because of a fire which almost completely destroyed the town in 1708. Sir John Gresham, Lord Mayor of London, gave Holt its grammar school in 1555 for the free education of thirty scholars; the old market-square manor (rebuilt) housed the students until

1900, when new buildings were erected on Cromer Road and the school was renamed Gresham's School. From 1920 to 1925 W. H. Auden attended the school, but he was not a particularly good student and was, by his own admission, "a difficult child." He recalled his Holt days in "The Old School."

HOLY ISLAND *See* LINDISFARNE.

HOLYBOURNE, Hampshire (pop. 565) Located on the busy main road from Winchester to Guildford and practically forming a part of bustling Alton, Holybourne is not the quiet village it was in the mid-19th century, when Elizabeth Gaskell decided to settle here. As a surprise present for her husband she bought The Lawns from an advance of £2,600 on *Wives and Daughters* from her publishers and came to inspect her purchase on November 12, 1865. After attending church that morning, she had a fatal heart attack and was buried in the Unitarian Chapel Cemetery in Knutsford, Cheshire.

HOLYWELL, Oxfordshire (pop. 846) Once a completely separate entity, Holywell has become a small appendage to Oxford. Kenneth Grahame, who died in 1932, was first buried in Pangbourne, Berkshire, but his body was later transferred to the St. Cross churchyard, a much more fitting place, considering his lifelong love of and admiration for Oxford and the shire. The epitaph on the tombstone reads:

> To the beautiful memory of Kenneth Grahame, husband of Elspeth and father of Alastair, who passed the River on the 6th of July 1932, leaving childhood and literature through him the more blest for all time.

HONINGTON, Suffolk (pop. 225) Honington is situated on the southeastern edge of Breckland, a 300-square-mile area shared by Suffolk and Norfolk which was under heavy cultivation in ancient times but has been allowed to revert to its natural state. This is a region permeated by small streams and meres, and its character has been maintained by the planting of large groups of conifers. Honington, on a tributary of the Little Ouse River 7 miles southeast of Thetford, was the birthplace of Robert Bloomfield on December 3, 1766. After his father's death in 1767, Bloomfield's mother kept a dame school in their wattle-and-daub cottage, and from her the child first learned to read and write. He also received some education at Ixworth from a schoolmaster named Rowell. On the whole, Bloomfield's education was in his own hands, and his mother's remarriage around 1775 made self-sufficiency even more necessary. He worked for a time on a farm on the Euston estate and then went to live with his uncle, William Austin, in nearby Sapiston. Although his diminutive size precluded farmwork of any sort, he did gain a great deal of information and inspiration for *The Farmer's Boy* at this time. He left Honington for London in 1781.

HONITON, Devon (pop. 3,008) Situated on the Otter River, Honiton has a long history, although a series of fires from the early 18th century on have destroyed all vestiges of its antiquity. The village has long been famous for its lacemaking; originally a cottage industry introduced by the Flemish, this is one of the few which can still compete from the cottage because

mechanical expertise has not found a way to duplicate the intricate patterns, some using more than 400 bobbins for a single pattern. William Shakespeare knew the fame of Honiton lace and its makers and alludes to it in *Twelfth Night:*

> The spinsters and the knitters in the sun,
> And the free maids that weave their thread with bones,
> Do use to chant it.

Daniel Defoe was quite favorably impressed with Honiton and comments in *A Tour thro' the Whole Island of Great Britain* that it

> may pass not only for a pleasant good Town,...but stands in the best and pleasantest Part of the whole County; and I cannot but recommend it to any Gentlemen that Travel this Road, that if they please to observe the prospect for half a Mile, till their coming down the Hill and to the Entrance into *Honiton*, the view of the Country is the most beautiful Landskip in the World—a meer Picture; and I do not remember the like in any one Place in *England*.

HORNCASTLE, Lincolnshire (pop. 3,459) Situated 21 miles east of Lincoln on the Bain River at its juncture with the Waring River, Horncastle is so named because of its location on a hornlike section of land formed by the meeting of the two rivers. The medieval St. Mary's Church, restored and partially rebuilt, has a number of chained books and a chest dating to 1690. Near the church in the marketplace is a house with a noticeable number of windows that was the home of Emily and Louisa Sellwood. Louisa married Charles Tennyson Turner, Alfred Tennyson's brother, at St. Mary's in 1836. Emily, who was a bridesmaid, had met the future Lord Tennyson first in 1830 but had hardly seen him since. Now the poet, who escorted her to the church, fell in love with her:

> "O happy bridesmaid, make a happy bride!"
> And all at once a pleasant truth I learn'd,
> For, while the tender service made thee weep,
> I loved thee for the tear thou couldst not hide,
> And prest thy hand, and knew the press return'd.

It was not until 1850 that they were married in Shiplake.

Horncastle has long been known for its annual horse fair, which ran for ten days in August until the turn of the 20th century. The fair, once the biggest in England, and the town are included in George Borrow's *The Romany Rye:*

> Leaving the house of the old man who knew Chinese but could not tell what was o'clock, I wended my way to Horncastle....
> The town was a small one, seemingly ancient, and was crowded with people and horses. I proceeded, without delay, to the inn to which my friend the surgeon had directed me. "It is of no use coming here," said two or three ostlers, as I entered the yard—"all full—no room whatever"....

Borrow devotes a number of chapters to the fair and describes in detail the stories told by the Suffolk jockey and the Hungarian.

HORTON, Buckinghamshire (pop. 1,027) On the Colne River 3½ miles southeast of Eton, Horton is now being dragged into the suburban complex of London, although it still retains its triangular village green. Its squat, ancient church is a visible reminder of its long association with John Milton. Milton's father moved here from Hammersmith, and after being awarded his M.A. degree at Cambridge in July 1632, the poet settled here with his family. Tradition maintains that the house, pulled down in 1795, was near the church where a manor house now stands. Milton's "Horton Period" was especially productive; among the works he wrote here were "How Soon Hath Time," "At a Solemn Musick," *Arcades, Comus, Lycidas,* various shorter works, and, probably, *L'Allegro* and *Il Penseroso.* From Horton Milton traveled to nearby Langley, where he had access to the library in St. Mary's Church. In April 1637 Milton's mother was buried in the chancel of the Horton church, and in late April or early May Milton left the village for a trip to the Continent.

HORTON, Dorset (pop. 351)   The part of Dorset southwest of Cranborne is rich agricultural land with grain fields and pasturelands containing hints of the once-extensive Cranborne Chase; villages here such as Horton, 4½ miles southwest of Cranborne, tend to be small. This is the Lornton of Thomas Hardy's Wessex and enters "Barbara of the House of Grebe" in *A Group of Noble Dames.* On the brow of a barren hill is the old wayside inn called the Lornton Inn, where "The chaise which had been seen waiting . . . was, no doubt, the one they had escaped in. . . ." The inn stands a little distance from the village at the intersection of the Wimborne–Cranborne and Shaftesbury–Ringwood roads.

HOTHFIELD, Kent (pop. 315)   The great house was pulled down after World War II, but Hothfield, 3 miles northwest of Ashford, is beautiful in summer, when gorse and bracken flourish on the higher ground and bog asphodel (a protected species) grows in abundance in the area called "the bogs." A curiosity here is the cone-shaped mound encircled by great elms just outside the park. This is an old icehouse; few have survived in England. Swinsford Old Manor, a Tudor house just south of the village, was the home of Alfred Austin from 1867 to 1913; made Poet Laureate in 1896, he loved his garden here, and his walk between the elms with an espaliered beech walk has been preserved. The beauty of the spot has been described in *The Garden That I Love.* Austin died in Ashford on June 2, 1913.

HOUGHTON, Norfolk (pop. 175)   The coastal area of northwest Norfolk is a series of contrasts and surprises: Houghton, about equidistant from King's Lynn and Hunstanton, is fenlike in appearance and consists of little more than Houghton Hall, a few cottages, and a church inside the estate parkland. The hall, the third one on the site, is an enormous mansion 450 feet long built for Sir Robert Walpole, Prime Minister and Chancellor of the Exchequer and father of Horace Walpole. Sir Robert, who had been born in Houghton, had the hall designed in part to contain his magnificent collection of paintings, statuary, books, and furniture.

Horace Walpole spent a great deal of time at this house in his youth, and after Sir Robert's resignation as Prime Minister in 1742, both father and son were here frequently. The author disliked the fenlike nature of the area almost as much as he disliked the

county and its inhabitants, but the house itself with all its grand compensations was another matter. Indeed, the collection here prompted his "Sermon on Painting." Houghton Hall eventually passed to Sir Robert's reckless and dissolute grandson, and much of the art collection was sold to Catherine the Great of Russia. Horace Walpole's feelings about the events appear in a 1761 letter:

> I love Houghton; Houghton, I know not what to call it, a monument of grandeur or ruin! . . . For what has he built Houghton? for his grandson to annihilate, or his son to mourn over.

The sale itself was

> the most signal mortification to my idolatry of my father's memory it could receive. It is stripping the temple of his glory and his affection.

Sir Robert was buried in the churchyard, and after Horace Walpole died in London on March 2, 1797, he was buried here as well; there is no monument to either man.

HOUGHTON CONQUEST, Bedfordshire (pop. 560)   There are two villages in Bedfordshire with the name Houghton, and they are often difficult to keep straight: Houghton Regis (Dunstable Houghton), with important earthworks, is near Dunstable in the southern part of the county, while Houghton Conquest (Bedford Houghton) is 2½ miles north of Ampthill and closer to Bedford. On the hill near the village is Houghton House, built for Mary Herbert, Countess of Pembroke, sister of Sir Philip Sidney. Tradition states that Sidney wrote *Arcadia* under one of the trees in the park adjoining the house. This is wrong because the countess did not receive this land grant from James I until 1615 and Sidney was mortally wounded at Zutphen in 1586.

This area has a far more specific association with John Bunyan, for his House Beautiful in *The Pilgrim's Progress* is a composite of Houghton House and Elstow Place. This was

> a very stately palace before him, the name whereof was Beautiful, and it stood just by the highway side.

Houghton House was a combination of red brick, stone, and terra cotta and was of enormous size. The Hill Difficulty which Christian climbs following his refreshment at the spring is also located here:

> There was also in the same place two other ways beside that which came straight from the gate; . . . the narrow way lay right up the hill (and the name of the going up the side of the hill is called Difficulty). Christian now went to the spring and drank thereof to refresh himself, and then began to go up the hill. . . .

This is the northern slope of Houghton Park. At the time Bunyan was writing, the slope was terraced, and each arbor had its own settle:

> Now about the midway to the top of the hill was a pleasant arbour, made by the Lord of the hill, for the refreshing of weary travellers. Thither therefore Christian got, where also he sat down to rest him.

HOUNSLOW, Middlesex   Hounslow, 2½ miles southwest of Brentford and 13½ miles west of London, is an intensely built-up area in a Greater London borough which includes Feltham, Heston, Isleworth, Brentford, and Chiswick; in Elizabethan times, however, this was one of the greatest wheat-growing areas in the country. The terrain is quite flat, and William Cobbett, speaking in the 19th century of the general area as well as of Hounslow Heath, notes in *Rural Rides:*

> With the exception of the land just round Crookham and the other villages, nothing can well be poorer or more villainously ugly. It is all first cousin to Hounslow Heath, of which it is, in fact, a continuation to the westward. There is a clay at the bottom of the gravel; so that you have here nasty stagnant pools without fertility of soil.

Even today the heath has the same appearance, although it is considerably diminished in size. John Leland also notes the area in his *Itinerary:*

> There rennith a lande water thorough the hethe of Hundeslaw as a drene to the hole hethe, that is of a great cumpace, and I passid by a bridge of tymbre over it.

For hundreds of years the heath had a reputation for highway robbery and murder, and for many of these years gibbets, to dispense instant justice, were arrayed all about. Jonathan Swift, in a bitter satire on those "excellent and moral men" initially chosen for Irish bishoprics, says:

> It unfotunately has uniformly happened that as these worthy divines crossed Hounslow Heath, on their road to Ireland, to take possession of their bishopricks, they have been regularly robbed and murdered by the highwaymen frequenting that common, who seize upon their robes and patents, come over to Ireland, and are consecreted in their stead.

Tobias Smollett uses the notoriety of the heath in *The Adventures of Roderick Random:* there was excitement when

> Strap road up to the coach door, and told us in a great fright, that two men on horseback were crossing the Heath (for by this time we had passed Hounslow), and made directly towards us.

In William Harrison Ainsworth's *Old St. Paul's,* King Charles II is robbed on his journey across the heath:

> Charles was laughing heartily, and desired his attendants, who were neither numerous nor well-armed, to take care they were not robbed again between this place and Oxford; "though," added the monarch, "it is now of little consequence, since we have nothing to lose."
> "Is it possible your Majesty can have been robbed?" asked the landlord, who stood cap in hand at the door of the carriage.
> "I' faith, man, it *is* possible," rejoined the King. "We were stopped on Hounslow Heath by a band of highwaymen, who carried off two large coffers filled with gold, and would have eased us of our swords and snuff-boxes, but for the interposition of their captain. . . .

HUCKNALL, Nottinghamshire (pop. 19,980) Until recently this mining town midway between Nottingham and Sutton-in-Ashfield was known as Hucknall Torkard from the medieval landowners in the area. Saxon workings dating to the 8th century have been uncovered in the Church of St. Mary Magdalen, located on the busy Market Square, and it is with this church that George Gordon, Lord Byron is intimately associated. Byron died in Greece on April 19, 1824, and his body was sent back to London, where it lay in state from June 30 until July 12, when it was determined that he was not destined to lie in the Poets' Corner of Westminster Abbey. He was then brought here for interment in the family vault. The King of Greece presented the slab of blue marble, marked simply "BYRON," for the tomb, and a perpetual lamp burns in his memory. The chancel also contains a memorial bust. The family vault contains the coffins of the wicked 5th Baron Byron, of the poet's mother, Catherine Byron, of his great-grandmother, Lady Frances, and of his daughter Augusta Ada. In 1938 the Byron family vault was opened, and it was found that Lord Byron's coffin was not fastened, that the body of the poet was in a perfect state of preservation, and that he was, indeed, lame in the right foot.

There have been many visitors to the shrine of Lord Byron; among them was D. H. Lawrence, whose frequently quoted letter (to Rolf Gardiner in 1926) comments on his excursions from Eastwood:

> How well I can see Hucknall Torkard and the miners! Didn't you go into the church to see the tablet, where Byron's heart is buried? My father used to sing in the Newstead Abbey choir, as a boy.

American authors visiting Hucknall have included Washington Irving, Nathaniel Hawthorne, and Joaquin Miller.

HUGHENDEN, Buckinghamshire (pop. 2,523) Situated 1 mile north of High Wycombe, with which it is usually associated, the village of Hughenden lies in the Hughenden Valley along a pleasant stream and rolling parklands, 35 miles northwest of London. The old flint church is surrounded by trees in a parklike setting, and just beyond the church is Hughenden Manor, the home of Benjamin Disraeli, Earl of Beaconsfield, from 1847 to 1881. Brought up in nearby Bradenham, Disraeli purchased the manor here after learning that his childhood home could not be obtained permanently. He married the widow of Wyndham Lewis in 1839 and with her money was able to buy and maintain this estate. He modernized the house in 1862 in a mixture of Flamboyant Gothic and aggressively romantic styles; one room in the house, his study, remains just as it was when he died. On the desk are his pens and writing paper, the correspondence with Queen Victoria survives, and the manuscripts of his novels are here along with his complete library.

With the death of his "perfect wife" in 1872 Disraeli concerned himself with the renovation (not for the better) of the 13th- and 14th-century Hughenden Church of St. Michael and All Angels. After his death in London on April 19, 1881, his body was brought here for burial in the churchyard. The memorial tablet on the north wall of the chancel above his stall was erected by Queen Victoria:

> To the dear and honoured memory of
> Benjamin, Earl of Beaconsfield, this
> memorial is placed by his grateful
> Sovereign and friend, Victoria R.I.
> *Kings love him that speaketh right.*

The Queen also commanded that his banner, sword, and helmet as a Knight of the Garter be brought here from Windsor and placed over the chancel arch. Victoria did not attend the funeral but made a trip to Hughenden a few days after the services and placed a wreath of primroses (Disraeli's favorite flower) on the grave; she declared April 19 Primrose Day, and members of the Primrose Society place a wreath on the grave annually.

HUGHLEY, Shropshire (pop. 67) The village of Hughley, in a rich agricultural region dominated by the limestone ridge of Wenlock Edge, is country dotted with lovely small wooded areas, narrow winding lanes, and glistening small streams. The church in Hughley is the village's most notable attraction aside from the landscape, and it has a rather rare 13th-century altar stone complete with five consecration crosses. Hughley is one of the villages A. E. Housman uses in *A Shropshire Lad*, but as the poet later admitted to his brother, his use is purely "romantic":

> The vane on Hughley steeple
> Veers bright, a far-known sign,
> And there lie Hughley people,
> And there lie friends of mine.
> Tall in their midst the tower
> Divides the shade and sun,
> And the clock strikes the hour
> And tells the time to none.
>
> To south the headstones cluster,
> The sunny mounds lie thick;
> The dead are more in muster
> At Hughley than the quick.
> North, for a soon-told number,
> Chill graves the sexton delves,
> And steeple-shadowed slumber
> The slayers of themselves.

Housman's "far-known sign" was, in fact, buried away in a valley, and the suicides simply did not occur; the "slayers of themselves" were basically church wardens, vicars, and vicars' wives, all quite respectable people, in neatly tended graves in consecrated ground. But Housman, who changed the name of the actual village, erred: "I did not apprehend that the faithful would be making pilgrimages to these holy places."

HULL, Yorkshire (pop. 317,800) Officially named Kingston-upon-Hull, this city is now the third largest port in England, and its open docks expand annually to receive Scandinavian timber, Australian and New Zealand wool, and Danish dairy products. On a low plain at the entrance of the Hull River into the estuary of the Humber River, Hull has also long drawn its support from the sea: enormous fishing fleets are based here, and traditions of the sea abound. Geoffrey Chaucer notes the fame of Hull seamen in an offhand way in the Prologue to *The Canterbury Tales* when he compliments the Shipman:

> But of his craft to rekene wel his tydes,
> His stremes and daungers him bi sydes,
> His herberwe and his mone, his lode-menage,
> There nas noon swich from Hulle to Cartage.

In *Historia Regum Britanniae* Geoffrey of Monmouth explains that the river was named for Humber, King of the Huns, who was put to flight by Leocrinus, the local King. "Humber retreated as far

as the river and was then drowned beneath its waters, giving his name to the stream."

John Evelyn was impressed enough in the 17th century to comment on the rich fenny land surrounding Hull in his diary. Andrew Marvell had lifelong associations with the city; he was brought here from Winestead at the age of three in 1624, when his father was appointed headmaster of the local grammar school. No evidence shows where the family lived, and information about Marvell's early life is scanty. He is known to have attended the grammar school before going up to Trinity College, Cambridge, in 1633, and he then spent a fairly long period abroad. Returning to Hull in late December 1658 or early January 1659, he stood for Parliament and was returned overwhelmingly on January 10. He remained the Member for Hull until his death in 1678 and was noted for the special interest he took in his constituents; there is a memorial statue at the corner of Saville and George Streets. The Guildhall has a very good collection of Marvell's political letters, and the City Library has a special collection of his works.

Hull contains a very curiously named old street, Land of Green Ginger, which gave its name to Winifred Holtby's novel. The street, off Whitefriargate, was apparently named after the tradeswoman who tempted customers with a sweet called green ginger. The town also appears in *South Riding*, under the name Kingsport.

HUMBER RIVER, Yorkshire The Humber River is actually the estuary of the Ouse and Trent Rivers on the east coast of England. Varying in breadth from 1 to 7¼ miles, it runs for 38 miles before flowing into the North Sea at Spurn Head and is best known for the higre (eagre), or bore, a tidal wave which rushes up the river. Long-standing tradition says that the name of the river commemorates Humber, King of the Huns. Geoffrey of Monmouth in *Historia Regum Britanniae* relates that Humber and his forces met Leocrinus in the general vicinity of Hull and there did battle: "When the two forces made contact, Leocrinus forced Humber to flee. Humber retreated as far as the river and was then drowned beneath its waters, giving his name to the stream."

Michael Drayton traveled all over the country between 1613 and 1622 collecting material on the natural beauty of England, especially about rivers and streams, for his *Poly-Olbion*. He describes the sound of the river:

> . . . What flood comes to the deep
> Than Humber that is heard more horribly to roar?
> For when my Higre comes, I make my either shore
> Even tremble with the sound that I afar do send.

In "At a Vacation Exercise in the College," John Milton catalogs the English rivers and alludes to the King of the Huns and the vocal characteristic of this river: "Humber loud, that keeps the Scythian's name." Andrew Marvell, a man who had grown up and lived on the Humber River and knew it well, uses it in "To His Coy Mistress"; banteringly suggesting how he would celebrate his mistress's charms and complain of her reservedness—if "Had we but World enough, and time"—he comments, "I by the Tide/Of Humber would complain," before going on to plead to "let us sport us while we may." Finally, in Winifred

Holtby's *South Riding* the Humber becomes the Leame.

HUNSDON, Hertfordshire (pop. 538) The village of Hunsdon, 4 miles east of Ware, was a royal hunting area and seat in the time of Henry VIII, and his children were frequently here. It is possible that Hunsdon was the birthplace of Henry Howard, Earl of Surrey, in the winter or early spring of 1517. There are no records of his birth anywhere, and the claim of this village is based on landholdings of his grandfather, the 2d Duke of Norfolk, in one of whose houses Howard is known to have been born. (The other houses are in Framlingham, Suffolk, and Kenninghall, Norfolk, and the claim made by the former is more generally accepted.) Howard did, however, meet Lady Elizabeth Fitzgerald here for the first time sometime around 1537. The daughter of the 9th Earl of Kildare, she is the "fair Geraldine" of Surrey's sonnets. Howard notes the meeting in "Description and Praise of His Loue Geraldine":

From tender yeres, in Britain did she rest,
With a kinges childe, who tasteth ghostly food.
Honsdon did first present her to mine iyen:
Bright is her hewe, and Geraldine she hight.

In 1537 Geraldine was about nine years of age.

HUNTINGDON, Huntingdonshire (pop. 8,812) Technically both the town and the county of Huntingdon do not exist; the former has been Huntingdon and Godmanchester since 1961, and the latter, which was part of Huntingdon and Peterborough, has since 1974 been amalgamated with Cambridgeshire. Godmanchester, which cannot be separated from Huntingdon, was an important Roman establishment and is the oldest town in the county; recent excavations show Roman occupation on the northern, or Huntingdon, side of the Ouse as well. Huntingdon was a large Saxon town from the 7th century on; it was controlled by the Danes until Edward the Elder drove their army from the area. Edward, then, is the nominal founder of the modern *burh* and began its ditch fortification, which can be observed descending from Mill Common to Alconbury Brook. William the Conqueror saw the importance of the river crossing and ordered the construction of a wooden castle; only the earthworks remain.

The town gained in stature, received its first charer from King John in 1205, and by the end of the 13th century contained three hospitals, sixteen churches, and three monasteries. The advent of the Black Death in the mid-14th century caused a decline and even in the 18th and 19th centuries Huntingdon was not especially prosperous. Only now are planned government expansion and industrialization beginning to alleviate chronic unemployment here.

Early visitors to Huntingdon would be unable to recognize it now in its expanded state. On August 31, 1654, John Evelyn writes that it

is a faire antient Towne, a sweete river running by it, and the Country about it so abounding in Wheate, that when any King of England passe thro it, they have a costome to meete his Majestie with an hundred plows....

Daniel Defoe notes some of the same qualities but also (in keeping with his personality) comments:

It is full of very good Inns....
Here are the most beautiful Meadows on the banks of the River *Ouse*, that I think are to be seen in any Part of *England;* and to see them in the Summer Season, cover'd with such innumerable Stocks of Cattle and Sheep, is one of the most agreeable Sights of its Kind in the World.
This Town has nothing remarkable in it....

The admired fields now bear council houses. William Cobbett rode here some years later and found Huntingdon "one of those pretty, clean, unstenched, unconfined places that tend to lengthen life and make it happy." Never one to praise anything unnecessarily, he seemed unable to contain his effusiveness for the county town and the shire. Undoubtedly part of his reason for liking Huntingdon was that expansion into the first quarter of the 19th century had bypassed the town and left it, to his mind, unspoiled:

Huntingdon is a very clean and nice place, contains many elegant houses, and the environs are beautiful. Above and below the bridge, under which the Ouse passes, are the most beautiful meadows that I ever saw in my life.... Here are no reeds, here is no sedge, no unevenness of any sort. Here are *bowling-greens* of hundreds of acres in extent, with a river winding through them, full to the brink. *One* of these meadows is the *race-course;* and so pretty a spot, so level, so smooth, so green, and of such an extent I never saw, and never expected to see.... I think it would be very difficult to find a more delightful spot than this in the world.

Huntingdon Grammar School, once a medieval hospital on the market square, was where Samuel Pepys (and earlier Oliver Cromwell) received part of his education. Pepys came here at the age of nine and remained for almost four years; after the Parliamentarian victory here, he returned to London and became a scholar of St. Paul's. The two-story grammar school, whose original Norman front is intact, is now the Cromwell Museum. In 1765 William Cowper came to the town after leaving the care of Dr. Nathaniel Cotton at St. Albans and went into lodgings which had been secured for him. He had responded so well to treatment that his family did not hesitate to allow him this freedom; within a few months of his arrival he became quite attached to the town of fewer than 2,000 inhabitants. By September he met the Unwins, and two months later he took lodgings in their home on the High Street. Cowper's original rate as a paying guest (80 guineas a year) was halved because of his financial straits; he frequently attended services at the Norman Church of St. Mary, just south of the Market Place. Following the Rev. Morley Unwin's death in July 1767 (he fell from a horse), Cowper and Mrs. Unwin went to Olney, the place most closely associated with the poet.

HURSTMONCEUX, Sussex (pop. 1,495) For a small village, Hurstmonceux (spelled Herstmonceux by the Post Office), 4 miles northeast of Hailsham, has an extraordinary number of fine houses as well as a castle with a strange history. The 15th-century castle was once one of the great brick masterpieces in southern England and in 1777 was the property of Robert Hare, a canon of Winchester. His second wife wanted him to build Hurstmonceux Place from the castle materials so that the Hare family estates could pass to her children and not to Francis Hare-Naylor, her stepson.

Her schemes did not work out, and Francis Hare-Naylor retained Hurstmonceux until the death of his wife. The second of their four sons was the rector here; his curate, John Sterling, was Thomas Carlyle's friend. Hurstmonceux Castle fell further into ruin and remained in that state until 1929, when it was restored by Col. Claude Lowther.

In the middle of the 18th century Horace Walpole visited Hurstmonceux and described it before it was ruined:

> The chapel is small, and mean; the Virgin and seven long lean saints, ill done, remain in the windows. There have been four more, but they seem to have been removed for light; and we actually found St. Catherine and another gentlewoman with a church in her hand, exiled into the buttery. . . . The draw-bridges are romantic to a degree; and there is a dungeon, that gives one a delightful idea of living in the days of soccage and under such goodly tenures. They showed us a dismal chamber which they called *Drummer's*-hall, and suppose that Mr. Addison's comedy is descended from it.

Walter Savage Landor usually spent at least one week here every summer with Julius Charles Hare and his family.

HURSTPIERPOINT, Sussex (pop. 3,099) With exceedingly fine views to the Devil's Dyke and Ditchling Beacon, Hurstpierpoint, 8 miles north of Brighton, entered the tempestuous life of Percy Bysshe Shelley in 1811; at that time, on a visit to his uncle in Cuckfield, he met Elizabeth Hitchener, a schoolmistress, here. She became everything to Shelley; indeed, he saw her as a paragon of wisdom, virtue, and genius. It was to Elizabeth that Shelley wrote the one account that exists of his unhappy marriage, and he later induced her to join the Shelley "extended household." But this grouping lasted only five months; Shelley was disillusioned by his paragon, and she was promised £100 a year to compensate for the loss of her school.

Much later in the 19th century, Little Rockley became the home of William Harrison Ainsworth. From 1869 to 1878 he lived in the house here with his unmarried daughter and wrote *Boscobel* and *The Manchester Rebels* (original title, *The Good Old Times*).

HURSTWOOD, Lancashire Hurstwood is usually considered part of the slightly larger village of Worsthorne, half a mile away, and the combination, referred to as Worsthorne with Hurstwood, with a combined population of 1,358, is located just east of Burnley. Hurstwood Hall is a low 16th-century stone house with gables and small windows. Of more interest is a village house dating from 1579 and originally called the Hall, which belonged to Edmund Spenser's family; it is thought that the poet spent some of his youth here. Spenser was a Lancashire man except by the accident of his London birth, and this branch of the family traces itself to the 13th century in the shire. After receiving his M.A. degree at Cambridge in 1576, Spenser came here for a stay of perhaps two years. It is now fairly certain that at this time he met Rose Dyneley, the Rosalind of his poetry, who lived in the nearby village of Cliteroe with her widowed mother, but the circumstances under which they met are not known. Spenser fell in love with her, but she married his rival, the Menalcas of *The Shepheardes Calender*. In that work the advice of Hobbinoll (Gabriel Harvey) to Colin Clout clearly points to the North Country and, most obviously, to Lancashire:

> Then, if by me thou list advised be,
> Forsake the soyle that so doth thee bewitch:
> Leave me those hilles where harbrough nis to see,
> Nor holy-bush, nor brere, nor winding witche:
> And to the dales resort, where shepheards ritch,
> And fruictfull flocks, bene every where to see:
> Here no night-ravenes lodge, more black then pitche,
> Nor elvish ghosts, nor gastly owles doe flee.

In all probability the *Calender* was begun at this time, but the rejected suit and the need to earn a living forced Spenser back to London.

ILAM, Staffordshire (pop. 200) The Manifold Valley is one of the loveliest in the north Midlands, and Ilam (once called Islam) has a prize location 5 miles northwest of Ashbourne with the valley laid out in front and the 1,000-foot Bunster Hill just behind, shielding the entrance to the Dove Valley. Three miles north of the village are Thor's Caves, with a 40-foot entrance, into which the Manifold River, joined by the Hamps, disappears. The river reappears near cliffs in the church grounds at Ilam and then pushes its way to meet the Dove a mile or so farther southwest. This is an area so beautiful that it is called Paradise. The rebuilt (but probably 13th-century) church contains two old paper wreaths, properly known as maiden's garlands, which traditionally were left in the church after the funeral of a betrothed girl; this type of wreath is employed by William Shakespeare in *Hamlet* when Laertes denounces the parish priest.

The hall and park in Ilam once belonged to the Congreve family, and in 1687 the dramatist William Congreve came here to convalesce after an illness. In a grotto in the estate grounds he wrote the very successful *The Old Bachelor;* Dryden like the play, but Jeremy Collier did not and became rather vicious about the dramatist in his *Short View of the Immorality and Profaneness of the Stage.* Congreve's reply that the play was written to "amuse himself in a slow recovery from a fit of sickness" prompted the retort "What his disease was I am not to enquire, but it must have been a very ill one to be worse than the remedy."

Years later Samuel Johnson made his way here and visited the grounds of the estate and the place where Congreve had penned the play. This was not Johnson's first visit, for he had grown up in Lichfield and knew the Staffordshire area well. In 1777 he and James Boswell were in nearby Ashbourne, Derby-shire, when Dr. Johnson decided on this visit. Boswell records:

> Dr. Johnson obligingly proposed to carry me to Islam, a romantick scene, now belonging to a family of the name of Port, but formerly the seat of the Congreves. I suppose it is well described in some of the Tours. . . .
> I recollect a very fine ampitheatre, surrounded with hills covered with woods, and walks neatly formed along the side of a rocky steep, on the quarter next the house, with recesses under projections of rock, overshadowed with trees; in one of which recesses, we were told, Congreve wrote his "Old Bachelor."

From this visit has emerged the apocryphal story of Dr. Johnson's experimenting with corks in the underground river. What in fact occurred Boswell says:

> We viewed a remarkable natural curiosity at Islam; two rivers bursting near each other from the rock, not from immediate springs, but after having run for many miles under ground. . . . [T]he gardener . . . said . . . he had put in corks, where the river *Manyfold* sinks into the ground, and had catched them in a net, placed before one of the openings where the water bursts out. Indeed, such subterraneous courses of water are found in various parts of our globe.

The Dovedale area, mentioned above as Paradise, is claimed to be the inspiration for the Happy Valley in *Rasselas,* the piece written to pay for the funeral of Johnson's mother. The description of the valley does not exactly fit this area, especially in Johnson's lushness of detail, but the similarities are marked:

> The sides of the mountains were covered with trees, the banks of the brooks were diversified with flowers; every blast shook spices from the rocks, and every month dropped fruits upon the ground. All animals that bite the grass, or brouse the shrub, whether wild or tame, wandered in this extensive circuit, secured from beasts of prey by the mountains which confined them. . . .
> The valley, wide and fruitful, supplied its inhabitants

with the necessaries of life, and all delights and superfluities were added at the annual visit which the emperor paid his children. . . .

ILCHESTER, Somerset (pop. 449) On the Yeo River, in a green and spacious valley with well-wooded hills and a variety of small streams, the pre-Roman village of Ilchester became a heavily fortified Roman station on the Fosse Way before becoming a Saxon stronghold. It was a medieval town of some importance, and a black friary, founded during the reign (1272–1307) of Edward I, became the educational center of south Somerset. Around 1214 Ilchester was the birthplace of the scholar Roger Bacon; little is known of his early life or parentage, but his father was evidently in good circumstances since Bacon received some or all of his education at the friary. He was admitted to orders at Oxford by 1233 and appears to have had no further association with Ilchester after this date. It was Bacon who predicted the invention of submarines, microscopes, and telescopes and who served as the model for the Friar Bacon of Robert Greene's play *The Honorable Historie of Friar Bacon and Friar Bungay.*

Thomas Hardy uses the town because of its site as the county's main prison for seven centuries. The function arose naturally from its royal manor, churches, and southerly position. In "A Trampwoman's Tragedy," the Ilchester jail, built in 1188, becomes the Ivelchester jail where the trampwoman's fancy man is hanged.

ILKESTON, Derbyshire (pop. 31,990) A market town 8 miles northeast of Derby, Ilkeston overlooks the Erewash Valley in an area which was once almost wholly given over to collieries; it is now heavily engaged in textile manufacturing, and the last coalfield was abandoned in 1966. D. H. Lawrence became a pupil-teacher here in 1903, when he was transferred from Eastwood to the Pupil-Teacher Centre in the Wilmot Street Schoolroom. (Wilmot Street is off Bath Street, the main thoroughfare running from the railway station to the market square.) Lawrence remained at this post for two years and later used the town in *Sons and Lovers.* Paul Morel and some friends make an expedition to the Hemlock Stone through Ilkeston, Stanton Gate, and Trowell.

ILMINGTON, Warwickshire (pop. 536) In an area where the Warwickshire plains begin to rise to the Cotswolds, Ilmington lies 3½ miles northwest of Shipston-on-Stour. A village full of mellow stone cottages and winding streets, it has a battlemented Norman church and a nearby manor, Compton Scorpion, which was the birthplace of the poet, author of vignettes, and courtier Sir Thomas Overbury in 1581. He was baptized in the parish church at Barton-on-the-Heath on June 18. The manor here belonged to his maternal grandfather, and Overbury was probably here often as a child.

ILSINGTON, Devon (pop. 1,134) The secluded village of Ilsington is located on the eastern fringe of Dartmoor about 3½ miles southwest of Bovey Tracey. John Ford, the dramatist, was born in an ancient manor house, Bagtor, close to the churchyard. The old house with massive stone walls and elaborate stonework was pulled down in the mid-1800s, but a house there now, also called Bagtor, stands on the approximate site of the original. The actual date of Ford's birth is not known, but he was baptized in the local church on April 17, 1586.

IMPINGTON, Cambridgeshire (pop. 876) Just north of Cambridge, Impington is set in a broad expanse of orchard land and contains one of the relatively new Cambridgeshire experimental village colleges. Its small church, mostly 14th- and 15th-century, stands against a band of trees, and the red-brick Impington Hall, set in a park, dates from the mid-16th century. Although there have been numerous additions to the hall, Samuel Pepys would still be able to recognize it as the old family mansion, and the Pepys and Talbot family arms are carved into the garden entrance. Here lived Pepys's uncle, Talbot Pepys, whom the diarist visited from Cambridge on numerous occasions. Once, after his uncle's death, he

[w]alked in the orchard with my cozen Roger, and there discoursed about my uncle's will, in which he did give me good satisfaction, but tells me I shall meet with a great deal of trouble in it. However, in all things he told me what I am to expect and what to do. To church, and had a good plain sermon. At our coming in the country-people all rose with so much reverence; and when the parson begins, he begins "Right Worshipfull and dearly beloved" to us.

INGLEWOOD FOREST, Cumberland At one time Inglewood Forest extended from Penrith to Carlisle, had a circuit of 60 miles, and was heavily populated with wild deer and other game; it no longer exists. The forest was the scene of the exploits of Adam Bell, Clim of the Clough, and William of Cloudesley, who were outlawed for breaking the game laws. The story of the rescue of William of Cloudesley, under sentence of death in Carlisle, and the King's subsequent pardon of the men is told in the 16th-century ballad "Adam Bell, Clim of the Clough, and William of Cloudesley." William Wordsworth uses both the ancient forest and its legend of Adam Bell in "Suggested by a View from an Eminence in Inglewood Forest":

The forest huge of ancient Caledon
Is but a name, no more is Inglewood,
That swept from hill to hill, from flood to flood:
On her last thorn the nightly moon has shone;
Yet still, though unappropriate Wild be none,
Fair parks spread wide where Adam Bell might deign
With Clym o' the Clough, were they alive again,
To kill for merry feast their venison.

INGS, Westmorland A small hamlet 2 miles east of Windermere, Ings has fragments of an early British settlement and a 1743 church. The church, with a few stones from an earlier structure, was built by Richard Bateman, who brought the Italian marble floor from Leghorn. Bateman, born here to a very poor family, became quite wealthy in London, and it is his story that William Wordsworth alludes to in "Michael." At the church, set in brass, are the poet's words:

There's Richard Bateman, thought she to herself,
He was a parish-boy—at the church door
They made a gathering for him, shillings, pence,

And halfpennies, wherewith the neighbours bought
A basket, which they filled with pedlar's wares;
And, with this basket on his arm, the lad
Went up to London, found a master there,
Who, out of many, chose the trusty boy
To go and overlook his merchandise
Beyond the seas; where he grew wondrous rich
And left estates and monies to the poor,
And, at his birthplace, built a chapel floored
With marble, which he sent from foreign lands.

Wordsworth does not tell the whole story, for less than a year after the rebuilding was begun, Bateman was poisoned by the captain of one of his own cargo ships. The rest of "Michael" is set at nearby Greenhead Ghyll.

IPSDEN, Oxfordshire (pop. 708)   On Icknield Way 4 miles south of Wallingford, Ipsden is a village with a mainly 13th-century church and Ipsden Manor House, the birthplace of Charles Reade on June 8, 1814. Reade was the youngest of eleven children and the seventh boy; his early life here was congenial and happy. He was sent off to school in Iffley in 1822, but from 1829 to 1831 he spent his time here, pursuing a strenuous course of logic preparatory to matriculating at Oxford.

IPSLEY, Worcestershire (pop. 934)   There are two Ipsleys in Worcestershire, and this one, Upper Ipsley, is on the eastern outskirts of Redditch, athwart the Roman Rycknield Street. Just beyond the church is Ipsley Court, where Walter Savage Landor spent much of his boyhood. In 1786 the estate, which had belonged to his mother's second cousin, came to the family, who frequently stayed here after that time. Landor never forgot his pleasure here and later wrote:

In youth twas here I used to scare
A whirring bird or scampering hare,
And leave my book within a nook
Where alders lean above the brook.

IPSWICH, Suffolk (pop. 96,500)   Informally the county seat of East Suffolk, Ipswich is situated on the north bank of the Gipping River, which at this point enters the estuary of the Orwell, and has long been an important port and a means of access to all of East Anglia. Throughout the Middle Ages it flourished as a port; the guilds played an important role in town government, and the prosperity of medieval Ipswich is acknowledged in the documents of the Merchant Gild of Corpus Christi, which instituted the 14th-century Corpus Christi feast, designed the Church of St. Mary-le-Tower (rebuilt in the 19th century), and helped create a large body of mystery plays (all lost) for the town. This was the nature of the city when Thomas Wolsey, who became Archbishop of York and later a cardinal, was born about 1473 on Silent Street, next to 3 The College Gateway bookshop. A grazier's son, after his phenomenal rise to power he wanted to build a great college here; it was begun, and Wolsey's Gate on College Street, red-brick with the royal coat of arms, is the only relic, for when Wolsey fell, his college project did so as well.

Early prosperity in Ipswich was based on cloth as well as on shipping, and the economic decline here following the Middle Ages meant a dearth of old buildings; an exception is the Georgian Great White Horse on Tavern Street, which since 1799 has been one of the particularly characteristic coaching inns of England. In October 1835 Charles Dickens, a reporter covering the parliamentary election here for the *Morning Chronicle,* is said to have stayed at the inn for two or three weeks. He later immortalized it in *Pickwick Papers.* Mr. Pickwick stays in Room 32, where he has the adventure with the woman in yellow curlpapers. Dickens's description of the inn is so unkind that the landlord threatened a libel action. The inn is

rendered the more conspicuous by a stone statue of some rampacious animal with flowing mane and tail, distantly resembling an insane cart-horse, which is elevated above the principal door. The Great White Horse is famous in the neighbourhood, in the same degree as a prize ox, or county paper-chronicled turnip, or unwieldy pig—for its enormous size. Never were such labyrinths of uncarpeted passages, such clusters of mouldy, ill-lighted rooms, such huge numbers of small dens for eating or sleeping in, beneath any one roof, as are collected together between the four walls of the Great White Horse at Ipswich.

Dickens probably did not actually dislike the town or the inn, for he stayed at the Great White Horse on three other occasions, twice on reading tours (1859 and 1861) and once on a trip to the north. The "insane cart-horse" still rampages over the main entrance, but whatever remains of the inn's formerly moldy or ill-lit nature now seems in keeping with its long tradition.

Dickens claimed that the original of Westgate House in *Pickwick* was not in Bury St. Edmunds, as he states in the book, but in Ipswich, supposedly in the parish of St. Nicholas; the house, however, has escaped detection. The famous green gate which Job Trotter opens and closes behind him, where Sam Weller is embraced by Alfred Jingle's body servant, is pointed out as the gate adjoining the churchyard just a few yards from Church Street. The "kind of courtyard of venerable appearance" where Sam quite unexpectedly meets Job is near St. Clement's Church.

The Dickensian "paper-chronicled turnip" analogy was neither new nor unfounded. The surrounding area had long been known for the cultivation of turnips, and five years before Dickens's visit William Cobbett comments favorably on Ipswich and its turnip growing in his *Rural Rides:*

Ipswich is in a dell, meadows running up above it, and a beautiful arm of the sea below it. The town itself is substantially built, well paved, everything good and solid, and no wretched dwellings to be seen on its outskirts. . . . [T]hen the country round about it [is] so well cultivated; the land in such a beautiful state, the farmhouses all white, and all so much alike; the barns, and everything about the homesteads so snug; the stocks of turnips so abundant everywhere; the ploughman so expert; the furrows, if a quarter of a mile long, as straight as a line, and laid as truly as if with a level: in short, here is everything to delight the eye. . . .

Today Ipswich itself seems much less like a rural center than a modern city, and Cobbett's words strike a chord only at some distance from it.

Christchurch Mansion, a 16th-century building in Christchurch Park, is now a museum and art gallery and has on display a number of the personal relics of

Edward FitzGerald, who spent almost all his life in Suffolk. He lived in Wherstead Lodge (now gone) near here from 1825 to 1835. George Meredith wrote a weekly column for *The Ipswich Journal* from 1860 on; when in town, he often rode out into the nearby countryside, where he held forth on national political issues to the local people. In the same decade H. Rider Haggard attended Ipswich School. In the twentieth century G. K. Chesterton spent part of his honeymoon here and later wrote what has been called "an interminable ballad" on the White Horse Inn.

IREBY, Cumberland (pop. 369) Once a market town, Ireby, now a tiny village, played host to John Keats in the summer of 1818, when he walked here from Bassenthwaite, just a few miles south, and stopped at the inn, which he termed "a dull beggarly looking place." The inn did, though, offer an attraction; hearing a great deal of thumping and thudding above him, Keats discovered a dancing class in session and was thoroughly delighted to watch the young dancers. Nearby is High Ireby, the location of Sir Hugh Walpole's monstrous house in *Fortress*, a castle of a home built on spite, which knew fine days but which, like its owner, deteriorated:

> The building was dark, naked and repellent. The stone seemed to have blackened under rain as though it had been smoked. The wood behind the house moaned and wailed. A pile of earth stood near the flagged path in the garden as though in preparation for a grave, and all the plants were beaten down with the wind. A tree somewhere rocked and screamed.

ISLEWORTH, Middlesex On the Thames River 12 miles west of London and now part of the Greater London borough which includes Hounslow, Feltham, Heston, Brentford, and Chiswick, Isleworth (pronounced "iz′el-worth") is an old town which has retained the nucleus of its old village. Indeed, there are a number of old houses, the remains of the 15th-century Church of All Saints, the 18th-century London Apprentice Inn, and the magnificent Syon House, in its great park along the river. Originally a Brigittine abbey, the nunnery was dissolved in the 16th century, and buildings and parkland were granted to Edward Seymour, Duke of Somerset, who built the core of the present building. The present house was the joint project of Robert Adam and Sir Hugh Smithson, 1st Duke of Northumberland, and the facade is crowned with the lead Percy lion brought from the Northumberland London home. The house contains a considerable art collection, and the Long Gallery, 136 by 14 feet, is an unusual room.

William Camden's *Britannia*, enlarged by Richard Gough, describes Syon House:

> The entrance into this magnificent villa from the great Western road is through a beautiful gateway, adorned on each side with an open colonnade. . . . Here, amid large clumps of stately trees, and over a continuation of the serpentine river mentioned before in the garden, the visitor is conducted to this princely mansion, and by a large flight of steps ascends into the great hall, which is a noble oblong room, ornamented with antique marble colossal statues. . . . This is a square apartment, finished in a very uncommon style; the floor is of scaglioli, and

the walls in fine relief, with gilt trophies, &c. But what particularly distinguishes this room are twelve large columns and sixteen pilasters of verde antique, . . . [O]n the columns are twelve gilt statues. This leads to the dining-room, which is finished with a very chaste simplicity, and is ornamented with beautiful marble statues and paintings in chiaro obscuro, after the antique.

Both the original and the new Syon House have literary associations, and one in particular exposes the corrupt practices of the 16th-century church. Elizabeth Barton, the Holy Maid of Kent, was frequently a guest of the monks and sisters here, especially when she was offering prophecies about Henry VIII's intention of divorcing Queen Catherine. She categorically stated that, "in the name and by the authority of God," she forbade the divorce and that if Henry pursued his planned course, he "should no longer be king of this realm . . . and should die a villain's death." Sir Thomas More visited here on at least two occasions and treated her with "suspicious reverence." When Thomas Cranmer was elevated to the see of Canterbury, he was directed to determine the maid's prophetic powers, and after two months of exhaustive questioning he forced a confession from her which implicated at least six known clerics in the fraud. Sir Thomas was named as an abettor of the treasonable conspiracy in the bill of attainder drawn up by Parliament in January 1534 but met the charges successfully, partly because of the existence of a letter from him warning Elizabeth Barton to avoid politics.

John Evelyn visited Thistleworth, the Isleworth home of Sir Clepesby Crew, in February 1648, and returned to the town and Syon House during the plague of 1666, when Charles II held his Council here. He was not impressed with the house, as his diary shows:

> I viewed that seate, belonging to the E. of *Northumberland* built out of an old *Nunnerie*, of stone, & faire enough, but more celebrated for the Garden than it deserves; yet there is excellent Walle fruit, & a pretty fountaine, nothing else extraordinarie. . . .

Horace Walpole's opinion certainly did not match Evelyn's; Walpole felt that Syon House was a "palace of palaces." His attitude toward Osterley Park here and its great house (now owned by the National Trust) was somewhat different; its classical facade and a large courtyard appeared ostentatious, and Walpole thought the Etruscan Room (an Adams experiment) "a profound tumble into bathos." The drawing room, he says, was "worthy of Eve before the Fall," and while the ornamental lake in the park was admirable, the park was "the ugliest spot of ground in the universe"—a considerable complaint.

A number of other literary figures are associated with Isleworth. Around 1790 or 1791, in the midst of the impeachment trial of Warren Hastings, in which he played a major role, Richard Brinsley Sheridan lived at Lacy House (long gone) by the riverside. In 1802, Percy Bysshe Shelley attended Syon House Academy, a boarding school run by a Reverend Dr. Greenlaw; the academy is not to be confused with Syon House. The school, now called Syon Park House, is on the London Road almost opposite the lane leading to Syon Park and is enclosed by high walls. The schoolrooms have vanished, and there is no trace of the playground. During his two-year stay here Shelley was most unhappy, and he was acutely aware of being oppressed by his schoolmates. Indeed, stanzas forming part of the Dedication to *The Revolt of Islam* most probably refer to his time at Syon House Academy and not to Eton, where he went in 1804:

> Thoughts of great deeds were mine, dear Friends, when first
>   The clouds which wrap this world from youth did pass.
> I do remember well the hour which burst
>   My Spirit's sleep: a fresh May-dawn it was,
>   When I walked forth upon the glittering grass,
> And wept, I knew not why; until there rose
>   From the near schoolhouse, voices, that, alas!
> Were but one echo from a world of woes—
> The harsh and grating strife of tyrants and of foes.
>
> And then I clasped my hands and looked around—
>   —But none was near to mock my streaming eyes,
> Which poured their warm drops on the sunny ground—
>   So, without shame, I spake:—"I will be wise,
>   And just, and free, and mild, if in me lies
> Such power, for I grow weary to behold
>   The selfish and the strong still tyrannise
> Without reproach or check." I then controlled
> My tears, my heart grew calm, and I was meek and bold.

The local association with Robert Louis Stevenson was short-lived. For a few months in the autumn of 1863 he was a boarder at the Burlington Lodge School run by a Mr. Wyatt in the Spring Grove area; the house was later named St. Vincents. Stevenson came here from Edinburgh Academy before going on to another private school in Edinburgh. Maurice Hewlett attended the International College, now the Teachers' Training School, on Borough Road in 1875. The musician Frederick Delius was also a student at the college, and the artist Vincent van Gogh lived in Twickenham Road in 1876 when he was teaching Sunday school and residing with a Mr. Jones.

IVINGHOE, Buckinghamshire (pop. 810) A small market village on the eastern border of Buckinghamshire, Ivinghoe is set on the lower slopes of the Chiltern Hills. Ivinghoe Beacon, rising 904 feet above the village to the northeast, presents some fine views. This village is the source of the name of Sir Walter Scott's novel *Ivanhoe*. Scott acknowledged that "an old rhyme" suggested the name and quotes the circumstances and the rhyme in the Introduction to the novel. He transcribes the first two village names correctly but uses his own spelling for the third:

> [T]he Author chanced to call to memory a rhyme recording three names of the manors forfeited by the ancestor of the celebrated Hampden, for striking the Black Prince a blow with his racket, when they quarreled at tennis:
>
> > Tring, Wing, and Ivanhoe,
> > For striking of a blow,
> > Hampden did forego,
> > And glad he could escape so.

JARROW, County Durham (pop. 30,840) The history of Jarrow is an eventful one. It is unfortunate that Jarrow is now more often recalled as the "town that was murdered," its sufferings brought to light by the horrible hunger march (Jarrow Crusade March) of 1936, when 200 unemployed marched on London, rather than with its glorious past. But Jarrow is also the place where English literature and learning began.

St. Paul's Church and Monastery stands near an estuary known as the Jarrow Slake, close to the confluence of the small Don River and the Tyne. The monastery, founded in 681, and sister to the Monkwearmouth, is where the Venerable Bede (born about 673) lived and died (735). He entered the order at the age of seven, as he states at the end of his *Historia Ecclesiastica Gentis Anglorum,* received deacon's orders at nineteen, and was ordained a priest at thirty. His education at the hands of Abbot Benedict and Ceolfrith was fortunate, for the libraries at Jarrow and Monkwearmouth had been endowed by Benedict Biscop with one of the finest European collections of patristic literature. Here Bede produced more than seventy-five major works, including his treatise *De natura rerum,* which is remarkable in assigning natural causes to phenomena. Most important, he finished, four years before his death, *Historia Ecclesiastica Gentis Anglorum,* which provides the earliest collected information about the civilizing of England. Bede's task was to present historical truth, and the fact that most of the nonhistorical work is hagiographic detracts little from his history. At Bede's death he was buried in the monastic graveyard, but a little less than three centuries later his remains were transported to Durham, where he was buried in the Galilee Porch of the cathedral.

Very little of the original monastic buildings remains, but the Church of St. Paul contains a number of interesting associations with Bede. The Saxon chancel, with its original stone walls, is as he knew it and is still in use. On the outer part of the east wall are two upright marked monoliths which are thought to be the ones referred to by Bede as the site chosen by King Ecgfrith (Ecgfrid) of Northumbria for the placement of the altar. A chair that was reputedly Bede's is against the north wall of the sanctuary; its disrepair has been accelerated by centuries of marauding visitors. The east window, which depicts Bede, blue-robed and holding a book, on the left side of Christ, is modern.

JERVAULX ABBEY, Yorkshire The Cistercian Jervaulx (pronounced "jar'vis") Abbey was a refounded abbey—a somewhat unusual situation produced because the original abbey, near the head of Wensleydale, proved too harsh even for the abstemious Cistercians, and the present site on the Ure River, in a conveniently lush setting about 6 miles southeast of Middleham, was chosen for the new abbey. Today the area is famous for the lovely Wensleydale cheese made by the Jervaulx monks. At the dissolution of the monasteries in the 16th century the recipe was passed on to a few local farmers, who were pledged to keep the exact formula secret; years of experimentation by outsiders eventually suggested that the special flavor was, in part, the result of using ewe's milk.

Richard Rolle, the Hermit of Hampole, is traditionally associated with Jervaulx Abbey. Here he is said to have frequently received the usual alms, bread and white and red herrings, given to those the abbey termed *pauperibus hermitis et pueris.* Sir Walter Scott uses Jervaulx Abbey and its prior in *Ivanhoe.* He describes Prior Aymer as "well known for many miles around as a lover of the chase, of the banquet, and, if fame did him not wrong, of other worldly pleasures still more inconsistent with his monastic vows." What is curious is that Scott uses the Cistercian establishment here as the prior's community when the author undoubtedly knew of its deserved reputation for austerity rather than for the license required by Prior Aymer.

KEDLESTON, Derbyshire (pop. 79) Known primarily because of the Hall, undoubtedly the finest Georgian house in England, Kedleston is so close to Derby, 4 miles to the southeast, that it will probably be incorporated into the county town. When the Hall was first built by James Paine and Robert Adam for the 1st Baron Scarsdale, the whole village, except the church, was moved so that the land could be made into parkland. One of the early visitors to the Hall was Samuel Johnson, whose opinion is recorded in Boswell's *Life:*

> Dr. Johnson thought better of it to-day, than when he saw it before; for he had lately attacked it violently, saying, "It would do excellently for a town-hall. The large room with the pillars (said he) would do for the Judges to sit in at the assizes; the circular room for a jury-chamber; and the room above for prisoners." Still he thought the large room ill lighted, and of no use but for dancing in; and the bed-chambers but indifferent rooms; and that the immense sum which it cost was injudiciously laid out.

A few years later, William Beckford visited the Hall on his English tour of August–October 1779.

KEGWORTH, Leicestershire (pop. 2,139) Situated in the northwestern tip of Leicestershire 7 miles from Loughborough on the Soar River, Kegworth is now heavily industrialized, much to the detriment of its early charm. Before factories came to Kegworth, Thomas Moore lived here with his wife shortly after their marriage. Their house, The Cedars, which still stands on the Loughborough Road, has a bay window and a red porch. It was here that Moore wrote some of the *Irish Melodies* while his wife gardened nearby. Their daughter, Anastasia, was born here before Moore and his family left in 1813.

KELLOE, County Durham (pop. 1,003) Kelloe is a remote Durham village, of interest only because of its slight association with Elizabeth Barrett (Browning). While the area is badly scarred by coal mining and quarrying, it contains small areas of surprising natural beauty, and this is true of the tiny Kelloe parish church dedicated to St. Helen, which is situated in a lovely tiny valley on a private dirt road maintained by the National Coal Board. Medieval pilgrims came to see the famous Kelloe Cross, a work quite possibly of Anglo-Saxon date. St. Helen, to whom the church is dedicated, dreamed that an angel revealed to her the position of the True Cross, and the Kelloe Cross portrays this dream with the figures of her son, the emperor Constantine, St. Helen, and Judas, the latter being commanded by her to dig for the Cross.

Modern pilgrims come to see the small church in which Elizabeth Barrett and her older brother were christened on February 10, 1808. The 18th-century font is still in the church, and the parish register records the baptism. A marble tablet set into the south wall of the church commemorates the poet:

To
commemorate the birth
in this parish, of
ELIZABETH BARRETT BROWNING
who was born at Coxhoe Hall
March 6th 1800,
and died at Florence, July 29th 1861

———

A Great Poetess, A Noble Woman,
A Devoted Wife

———

KELMSCOTT, Oxfordshire (pop. 152) Kelmscott has retained its charm over the centuries, and even the 20th century seems to have made no distinct impression upon the village. This locale in Oxfordshire is often and easily confused with Kelmscott House on the Thames near Hammersmith, but this Kelmscott is in the upper Thames Valley, 15 miles west of Oxford. The main attraction of the village is Kelmscott Manor House, an Elizabethan structure once belonging to William Morris; the house, of light gray stone behind walls so high that only the gabled roof can be seen from the road, is now owned by the Society of Antiquaries and is open to the public. The stone courtyard was an especial favorite of Morris's, and he would often stand here beneath the mullioned windows, whose formality he greatly admired. He had the yew hedge here cut into the shape of a dragon.

Morris and Dante Gabriel Rossetti together took Kelmscott Manor in July 1871, and a business agreement was made with seven members of the Pre-Raphaelite Brotherhood whereby each member invested £20 in the joint venture. That Morris and Rossetti were involved together here is curious because the two were already somewhat alienated, and their association was to cease entirely in 1874. The greatest problem arose when Rossetti and two others demanded their legal share of the firm's considerable assets, which without question were all due to Morris's energy, ideas, and business acumen, and the dissolution of the partnership left bitter feelings all around. Morris, whose property Kelmscott Manor really was, did everything to make the house fulfill his expectations of beauty, and he fully carried out the exhortation in "The Beauty of Life":

> Have nothing in your houses that you do not know to be useful or believe to be beautiful.

Morris delighted in the work of the craftsman—indeed, he was disparaged by many as "the poetic upholsterer"—and made and designed almost everything used in this house, including the wallpaper, carpets, fabrics, and stained glass. Perhaps his greatest venture was the establishment in 1890 of the Kelmscott Press because of his determination to see books set in beautiful and legible type (he designed the type fonts), on good-quality paper, and in the finest leather bindings possible. Another of his efforts was the formation of the Society for the Protection of Ancient Buildings. Morris did some of his best writing here, including *Notes from Nowhere*, *Love Is Enough*, a great deal of *Sigurd the Volsung*, and *Three Northern Love Stories*. He left here by 1878 for Hammersmith, where he died on October 3, 1896, after finishing the famous *Kelmscott Chaucer*; his body was brought back to Kelmscott for burial in the churchyard. Much in keeping with Morris's life and attitudes, his coffin was carried to the church on an old farm cart, and both cart and coffin were decorated with willow bows, vine leaves, flowers, and moss. The grave is marked with a simple coped stone on which are carved some vine leaves and an oak branch.

Rossetti spent a great deal of time here from 1871 to 1874; one of his longest stays occurred after his first breakdown, when he was here from September 1872 until January 1874. Upon his return in March or April there were new signs of a breakdown. He was suffering from auditory hallucinations and from the "persecution mania of paranoia," and by the end of July he left Kelmscott for good.

KELSTON, Somerset (pop. 175)   A tiny village on the Avon River 3½ miles northwest of Bath, Kelston has held a manor at least since the 14th century and became the seat of Sir John Harington's family when his father married Etheldreda, natural daughter of Henry VIII, who granted her the monastic forfeitures of three places including Kelston. Sir John, the Queen's godson, inherited the estate upon his father's death and spent a great deal of time here, especially when he was out of favor in court; and indeed Elizabeth, infuriated by his translating the story of Giocondo in Lodovico Ariosto's *Orlando Furioso*, banished him to Kelston until he translated the complete work. In 1592, on her visit to Bath, Elizabeth stayed here with Sir John, who was then high sheriff of Somerset; he was in and out of favor over the next few years and in 1602 wrote a complete account (published posthumously) of Elizabeth's last illness. Harington died here on November 20, 1612. Kelston remained in family hands until 1776.

KEMPSFORD, Gloucestershire (pop. 664)   The village of Kempsford, 3 miles south of Fairford on the Thames-Severn Canal, has possible associations with Geoffrey Chaucer. A walk by the river, in what is now the vicarage garden, is named after Lady Maud, sister of John of Gaunt's wife, Lady Blanche; the scanty remains of the manor are at the end of the walk. Tradition states that the tower of the parish church was built by John of Gaunt as a memorial to Blanche after her death in the plague of 1369 and that Chaucer, whose patron was Lady Blanche, wrote at least part of *The Book of the Duchess* here.

KENDAL, Westmorland (pop. 20,760)   A city of beautiful gray limestone buildings, Kendal is located in the lovely valley of the Kent River 9 miles southeast of Windermere and 20 miles north of Lancaster. A Roman fortification, Alauna, flourished on the south side of the city, where the remnants of the Norman castle now stand. The 12th-century castle, which stands on a green hill with an overgrown moat and weathered battlements, was the birthplace of Catherine Parr, the lucky sixth of Henry VIII's wives. In the 14th century the Flemish established a woolen industry here; the river provided pure water for washing the wool and for powering the mills, and within a short time both Kendal Green and its "milk white cloth" (no longer made) became famous.

Kendal's woolen industry is the source of the first literary allusions to the town; references to Kendal Green occur frequently in medieval ballads, and Michael Drayton notes it in *Poly-Olbion*, the

> . . . *Can* first creeping forth, her feet hath scarcely found,
> . . . gives that Dale her name, where *Kendale* towne doth stand,
> For making of our Cloth scarce match'd in all the land.

William Shakespeare refers to the industry in *Henry IV: Part I;* in the Boar's Head Tavern, following the Gadshill episode, Falstaff embroiders his side of the story and enlarges the number of "rogues in buckram" to eleven:

> But, as the devil would have it, three misbegotten knaves in Kendal green came at my back and let drive at me.

The green color was obtained by first dyeing the material with the yellow of the plant known as dyer's greenweed and then redyeing it with a blue dye extracted from woad. The milk-white cloth was also produced in pieces with hand-colored red, blue, or green dots; called "ermine" or "spotted cotton," this fabric is referred to in one of the ballads of Flodden Field:

> The left-hand wing with all his rout
> The lusty Lord Dacre did lead
> With him the bows of Kendal stout
> With milke-white coats and crosses red;
> There are the bows of Kendal bold
> Who fierce will fight, and never flee.

Thomas Gray was in Kendal on his trip to the North Country in 1770 and describes the castle and the general area in a letter to Richard West, who amended Gray's description and included it in his own *Guide to the Lakes*. Gray writes:

> [T]he dusk of evening coming on I enter'd *Kendal* almost in the dark, & could distinguish only a shadow of the Castle on a hill.
> . . . [I] went up the Castle-hill. the Town consists chiefly of three nearly parallel streets almost a mile long. except these all the other houses seem as if they had been dancing a country-dance & were out: there they stand back to back, corner to corner, some up a hill, some down without intent or meaning. along by their side runs a fine brisk stream, over which are 3 stone-bridges. the buildings (a few comfortable houses excepted) are mean, of stone & cover'd with a bad rough-cast. near the end of the Town stands . . . the Church . . . [with] 4 chappels, . . . one of the *Pars*, another of the *Sticklands*, . . . the 4th of ye *Bellingcams*, a family now extinct.

Hanging near the Billingham Chapel are a sword and helmet, said to commemorate Sir Roger Billingham. However, tradition also holds they commemorate an unrelated event involving Colonel Briggs, a Kendal magistrate and Cromwellian officer, and Maj. Robert Philipson, a Cavalier who lived on Belle Island in Lake Windermere. Briggs besieged Philipson on the island, but Philipson's brother caused the siege to be lifted after only a few days; the following Sunday, determined on revenge, Philipson and his troops rode into Kendal, and the major rode into the church during services. From this point on accounts vary, but evidently his helmet and sword were knocked off and hung in the church as a memorial to his insolence. The story, told in a ballad entitled "Robin the Devil," is the basis of Scott's story of Bertram Risingham's killing Oswald in the church at Rokeby and being killed himself in the nave:

> A horseman arm'd, at headlong speed—
> Sable his cloak, his plume, his steed.
> Fire from the flinty floor was spurn'd,
> The vaults unwonted clang return'd!—
> One instant's glance around he threw,
> From saddlebow his pistol drew.
> Grimly determined was his look!
> His charger with the spurs he strook—
> All scatter'd backward as he came,
> For all knew Bertram Risingham!
> Three bounds that noble courser gave;
> The first has reach'd the central nave,
> The second clear'd the chancel wide,
> The third—he was at Wycliffe's side.
> Full levell'd at the Baron's head,
> Rung the report—the bullet sped—
> And to his long account, and last,
> Without a groan dark Oswald past!

> All was so quick, that it might seem
> A flash of lightning, or a dream.

Scott's notes refer to the incident here.

William Wordsworth commemorates John Gough, a Kendal native, in *The Excursion*. Blinded by smallpox before the age of three and known as The Blind Philosopher, Gough became an outstanding teacher of mathematics and botany:

> No floweret blooms
> Throughout the lofty range of these rough hills,
> Nor in the woods, that could from him conceal
> Its birthplace; none whose figure did not live
> Upon his touch. The bowels of the earth
> Enriched with knowledge his industrious mind;
> The ocean paid him tribute from the stores
> Lodged in her bosom; and, by science led,
> His genius mounted to the plains of heaven.

When Wordsworth composed this poem and placed Gough in the churchyard, the blind man was still alive. A second Kendalian appears in *The Prelude*; James Patrick, source of "The Wanderer," is buried near the Presbyterian meetinghouse which Wordsworth occasionally attended. Samuel Taylor Coleridge also wrote of John Gough in *Omniana*, under the title "The Soul and Its Organs of Sense":

> The every way amiable and estimable John Gough of Kendal is not only an excellent mathematician, but an infallible botanist and zoologist. He has frequently at the first feel corrected the mistakes of the most experienced sportsmen with regard to the birds or vermin which they had killed. . . . As to plants and flowers, the rapidity of his touch appears fully equal to that of sight; and the accuracy greater.

Of all the Lake District authors Thomas De Quincey had the strongest association with Kendal; he was on the staff of the *Westmorland Gazette* from its inception and served as its editor in 1819 and 1820; he once commented that in this town he noted "more interesting conversations, as much information and more natural eloquence in conveying it" than he had found "usually in literary cities or in places professedly learned."

Alfred, Lord Tennyson used another Kendalian, George Romney, the portrait painter, in "Romney's Remorse." The story of Romney's life is a strange one; leaving his wife and two children here with half his savings, he went to London, where he became famous and rich, but he never sent for his wife and only occasionally visited Kendal, although he supported his family generously. At sixty-five, mentally and physically broken, he returned to his wife of thirty-seven years, who nursed him for the rest of his life. Tennyson tells of these last years; delirious and speaking to his wife, the artist queries:

> Nurse, were you hired? or came of your own will
> To wait on one so broken, so forlorn?
> Have I not met you somewhere long ago?
> I am all but sure I have—in Kendal church—
> O yes! I hired you for a season there,
> And then we parted; but you look so kind
> That you will not deny my sultry throat
> One draught of icy water. There—you spill
> The drops upon my forehead. Your hand shakes.
> I am ashamed. I am a trouble to you,
> Could kneel for your forgiveness. Are they tears?

For me—they do me too much grace—for me?
O Mary, Mary!

Kendal's one literary son, whose work is not much read today, is Richard Brathwaite (Braithwaite), author of *Barnabae Itinerarium (Drunken Barnaby's Four Journeys)*. Born in 1588 on his father's estate, called Burneshead or Burneside, he was educated here before matriculating at Oriel College, Oxford, in 1604 as a commoner. He appears to have taken over the family estate here after the death of his father in 1610 and eventually became deputy lieutenant of Westmorland and a justice of the peace. *Barnabae Itinerarium* was written here and published in 1638.

KENILWORTH, Warwickshire (pop. 16,419) Almost equidistant from Warwick and Coventry, Kenilworth has little history predating the 12th century, when Geoffrey de Clinton, Henry I's Chamberlain and Treasurer, was given the estate. The first structure here was probably an earth-and-timber fortress of the motte-and-bailey type and possibly stood on the site presently occupied by the inner court of Kenilworth Castle. The history of the castle is long and complex. Virtually impregnable because small streams to the west and south were dammed to form an enormous mere, Kenilworth Castle was made a royal establishment by King John, who strengthened its defenses. In 1248 Henry III presented the royal stronghold to his sister Eleanor, wife of Simon de Montfort, Earl of Leicester, and thereby made one of his worst errors, for Montfort became his greatest enemy. Building his military strength here, the Earl of Leicester met the King in battle at Lewes on May 14, 1264, captured Henry, imprisoned his son Edward, and for all practical purposes became England's ruler. After more than a year Prince Edward escaped and prepared to do battle at Evesham, Worcestershire; on August 4, 1265, Montfort was killed, and the rebellion quelled. Only Kenilworth remained to be subdued, and its siege lasted from the spring of 1266 until nearly Christmas. Nothing would break the defenses; even the Archbishop of Canterbury, induced to appear at the walls and excommunicate those within, met with derision; but disease and dysentery brought a surrender.

Kenilworth was presented to Henry's second son, Edmund Crouchback, founder of the Lancastrian branch of the house of Plantagenet. During the reign of Edward II the castle became his prison and the site of the signing of his abdication in 1327. This event, of course, is used by Christopher Marlowe in *Edward II;* the Earl of Leicester states:

Be patient, good my lord, cease to lament.
Imagine Killingworth Castle were your court,
And that you lay for pleasure here a space,
Not of compulsion or necessity.

And here, accurate to history, Marlowe has Edward abdicate:

Leices. My lord, the king is willing to resign.
Bishop. If he be not, let him choose.
K. Edw. O would I might, but heavens and earth conspire
To make me miserable! Here receive my crown.
Receive it? No, these innocent hands of mine
Shall not be guilty of so foul a crime.

He of you all that most desires my blood,
And will be call'd the murtherer of a king,
Take it. What, are you mov'd? Pity you me?

When Blanche, daughter of the 1st Duke of Lancaster, married John of Gaunt, the castle began to take on even greater proportions under his building program. John built the Great Hall and the adjoining State Apartments and turned Kenilworth into a palace. It has been suggested that Geoffrey Chaucer visited Kenilworth while John of Gaunt was in possession. Kenilworth again became a royal property in 1399 when John's son usurped the throne, but Henry IV added nothing to the buildings. Meanwhile, royal use of Kenilworth continued, and William Shakespeare places Henry VI on the castle terrace when he hears the news of Jack Cade's defeat:

Clif. He [Cade] is fled, my lord, and all his powers do yield;
And humbly thus, with halters on their necks,
Expect your highness' doom of life or death.
K. Hen. Then, heaven, set ope thy everlasting gates,
To entertain my vows of thanks and praise!
Soldiers, this day have you redeem'd your lives,
And show'd how well you love your prince and country:
Continue still in this so good a mind,
And Henry, though he be unfortunate,
Assure yourselves, will never be unkind:
And so, with thanks and pardon to you all,
I dismiss you to your several countries.

Not until Henry VIII came to the throne did a renewed building program begin; he had the Lodgings constructed (on the site of the present Leicester's Building), but they were probably insubstantial, and nothing of them remains.

Elizabeth I gave the castle to Robert Dudley, Earl of Leicester, and probably assisted his great building program. The story of Elizabeth's attentions to Leicester is well known, and she frequently visited him here. The most famous visit occurred in July 1575, some fifteen years after the death of Amy Robsart, the earl's first wife, who was killed when she fell, supposedly by accident, down the stairs at Cumnor Place in Berkshire. The Queen was Leicester's guest for nineteen days, and the expenses were enormous: more than £100,000 was spent on the festivities, and 320 hogshead of beer were consumed. Leicester commissioned George Gascoigne to create the entertainment for Her Majesty, and he did well; *The Princelye Pleasures of the Courte of Kenelwoorth* eulogizes his cleverness. Arriving from the lakeside, Elizabeth was greeted by the Lady of the Lake surrounded by nymphs, all on a floating island. The next day, Sunday, after church, Gascoigne writes:

There was nothing done until the evening at which time there were fireworks shewed upon the water, the which were both strange and well executed: as sometimes, passing under the water a long space, when all men had thought they had been quenched, they would rise and mount out of the water againe, and burn very furiously untill they were consumed.

The days were all filled, and great numbers of people came from all over to see the festivities. It has been suggested that the young William Shakespeare, then a boy of eleven, was brought to see the *Hocks Tuesday* play put on by the Coventry players, and while there is no external supportive evidence, Oberon's recollections in *A Midsummer Night's Dream* are said to be Shakespeare's own recollection of the affairs at Kenilworth:

> My gentle Puck, come hither: thou remember'st
> Since once I sat upon a promontory,
> And heard a mermaid, on a dolphin's back,
> Uttering such dulcet and harmonious breath,
> That the rude sea grew civil at her song,
> And certain stars shot madly from their spheres
> To hear the sea-maid's music.

Leicester was the brother-in-law of Sir Henry Sidney, the father of Sir Philip, and the nephew was frequently here, including the time of the Queen's 1575 visit. It was here that Philip Sidney met Penelope Devereux, who became the Stella of his poems.

This period of Kenilworth's history is richly presented in Sir Walter Scott's *Kenilworth;* the approach to the castle is described when the countess nears it for the first time:

> The outer wall of this splendid and gigantic structure enclosed seven acres, a part of which was occupied by extensive stables, and a pleasure-garden, with its trim arbours and parterres, and the rest formed the large base-court, or outer yard, of the noble Castle. The lordly structure itself, which rose near the centre of this spacious enclosure, was composed of a huge pile of magnificent castellated buildings, apparently of different ages, surrounding an inner court, and bearing, in the names attached to each portion of the magnificent mass, and in the armorial bearings which were there blazoned, the emblems of mighty chiefs who had long passed away. . . . A large and massive Keep, which formed the citadel of the Castle, was of uncertain though great antiquity. . . . The external wall of this royal Castle, was, on the south and west sides, adorned and defended by a lake partly artificial, across which Leicester had constructed a stately bridge. . . .

The interior is described as well, and so is the July 1575 visit of Queen Elizabeth. Scott places Sir Walter Ralegh at Kenilworth for the occasion of the Queen's arrival:

> The word was passed along the line, "The Queen! The Queen! Silence, and stand fast!" Onward came the cavalcade, illuminated by two hundred thick waxen torches, in the hands of as many horsemen, which cast a light like that of broad day all around the procession, but especially on the principal group, of which the Queen herself, arrayed in the most splendid manner, and blazing with jewels, formed the central figure.

The ladies of the court were carefully dressed so as not to detract from Her Majesty, but the courtiers were magnificent, according to Scott, since they were "free from such restraints as prudence imposed on the ladies. . . ."

> Leicester, who glittered like a golden image with jewels and cloth of gold, rode on her Majesty's right hand, as well in quality of her host, as of her Master of the Horse. The black steed which he mounted had not a single white hair on his body, and was one of the most renowned chargers in Europe, having been purchased by the Earl at large expense for the royal occasion. . . . The rider well became the high place which he held. . . .

Scott describes the hunt and implies a proposal of marriage from Leicester to the Queen; the attendants wait for the chase, "[b]ut Leicester had another chase in view":

> "No, Leicester, not so!" answered the Queen, hastily; "but it is madness, and must not be repeated. Go—but go not far from hence—and meantime let no one intrude on my privacy."
> While she spoke thus, Dudley bowed deeply, and retired with a slow and melancholy air. The Queen stood gazing after him, and murmured to herself—"Were it possible—were it *but* possible?—but no—no—Elizabeth must be the wife and mother of England alone."

The marriage between Amy Robsart and Leicester, according to Scott, was a secret; and indeed, Scott avers that it was generally believed that she was the wife of Richard Varney, Leicester's master of the horse. Scott has Amy die at Cumnor Place shortly after the Queen's visit and has Varney contrive her death. In fact, the novelist has taken great license here: the marriage between Amy Robsart and Robert Dudley, Earl of Leicester, was never a secret, and most important, the Countess of Leicester was killed fifteen years before Elizabeth's visit to Kenilworth. Scott, of course, paid many visits to Kenilworth and in 1828, after the publication of his novel (1821) on one of his many trips to London was gratified to find that the ruins were being protected both from the elements and from vandals.

Kenilworth's importance decreased steadily after the Earl of Leicester's death in 1588, and almost two years later the castle was sold to James I for the grand sum of £14,000. The castle fell into ruin until 1937, when Sir John Siddeley (later 1st Baron Kenilworth) bought the estate. It was given to the people of Kenilworth in 1958 and is now in the hands of the Ministry of Public Buildings and Works.

One other literary association with Kenilworth should be mentioned: Charles Dickens, accompanied by Phiz (Hablot Knight Browne), stopped here on a Midlands tour after being in Leamington Spa. The writer was captivated by the newly restored ruins and wrote to his wife that they drove in a post chaise to Kenilworth,

> where I really think we *must* have lodgings next summer, please God that we are in good health and all goes well. You cannot conceive how delightful it is. To read among the ruins in fine weather would be perfect luxury.

The area is remembered briefly in *Dombey and Son;* the group come here from Warwick for

> A stroll among the haunted ruins of Kenilworth, and more rides to more points of view: most of which, Mrs. Skewton reminded Mr. Dombey, Edith had already sketched, as he had seen in looking over her drawings. . . .

KENNINGHALL, Norfolk (pop. 3,669) About equidistant from Diss to the southeast and Attleborough to the north, Kenninghall contains a well-preserved mixture of Tudor and Georgian houses and a mostly 15th-century church. Kenninghall Place, the Tudor house just east of the village, was built of red and blue brick by Thomas Howard, 2d Duke of Norfolk, and grandfather of the poet and courtier Henry Howard, Earl of Surrey, and it may be that the house was the poet's birthplace. He is known to have been a frequent childhood visitor here until his grandfather's death in 1524, and when his father succeeded to the title, this became the family's principal residence from 1524 to 1529.

One of the early guests here was John Leland, who left a brief commentary about Kenninghall in his *Itin-*

erary; William Camden had little to say about Kenninghall in his *Britannia.*

In 1532 Surrey's marriage to Francis de Vere, daughter of John de Vere, 15th Earl of Oxford, was arranged, but because the couple were so young (Surrey was only fourteen) they were not permitted to live together until 1535, when they took up residence here. Their first son, Thomas, was born in March 1536, and Surrey and his wife were again in residence in 1538 and in 1539 when their second son, Henry, was born. Surrey was doing a great deal of writing at this time and had probably begun his blank-verse translation of the *Aeneid.* The estate of Kenninghall appears to have been confiscated in 1546 and given to the Seymours after Surrey and his father had been arraigned on the charge of treason that cost Surrey his life (his father was eventually released).

John Skelton was a frequent guest and first met Jane Scrope, Lady Wyndham's daughter, here. Jane, three sisters, and Lady Wyndham were all at the Benedictine nunnery at Carrow; it was Jane Scrope for whom *Phyllyp Sparowe* was written. Thomas Churchyard, the poet, was taken into the household, probably as a ten-year-old page, sometime around 1544.

KESSINGLAND, Suffolk (pop. 2,056)   A fishing village 4½ miles southwest of Lowestoft, Kessingland has suffered the depredations of the sea for centuries but has been more fortunate than other nearby coastal villages; it is now a favorite holiday area with caravans and tiny summer bungalows in abundance. The thatch-roofed village church with a lofty tower has served as a sighting point for sailors for more than 300 years. Around 1900 H. Rider Haggard bought Cliff Grange (now the Grange), a large house which stands on the cliffs; it was formerly a coast guard station, and all its rooms were named after seamen. Here he wrote *Rural England, The Poor and the Land,* the result of a Colonial Office commission, and *Ayesha* and had Rudyard Kipling as a frequent guest. Indeed, Kipling and his family took over Cliff Grange for the summer of 1914 and were here when war was declared; they left in mid-August for London.

KESTON, Kent (pop. 1,029)   A small village with an old windmill on its common, Keston is 3½ miles southeast of Bromley on the edge of London. Dinah Mulock Craik, who lived at Shortlands, near Bromley, after her marriage, was buried in Keston following her death at her home on October 12, 1887.

KESWICK, Cumberland (pop. 4,437)   Keswick (pronounced "kes′ick") may well be the most delightfully situated town in the Lake District because of its location at the north end of Derwent Water, the widest of the lakes, with 3,053-foot Skiddaw bulking large above it. Keswick is located on the Greta River 13 miles southeast of Cockermouth. The houses of gray slate are typical of the North Country, and the Moot Hall, rebuilt in 1813, on the market square, is an island.

Thomas Gray, an early visitor to the Lake District and Keswick, left some remarkable descriptions of the scenery, descriptions interlaced with a measure of fear of the looming mountains and their precipices. In 1769 he wrote:

> . . . by the side of this hill, wch almost blocks up the way, the valley turns to the left & contracts its dimensions, till there is hardly any road but the rocky bed of the river. the wood of the mountains increases & their summits grow loftier to the eye, & of more fantastic forms: among them appear *Eagle's-cliff, Dove's-nest, Whitedale-pike,* &c: celebrated names in the annals of Keswick.

William Wordsworth spent some time here at Windy Brow, a farmhouse owned by William and Raisley Calvert on Latrigg; he probably stayed here all of January 1794 before going on to Armathwaite to visit John Spedding, an old schoolfellow. In April he borrowed the house for six weeks and then left for Whitehaven in mid-May. The more important Keswick associations at this time, however, were with Samuel Taylor Coleridge and Robert Southey. At the end of July 1800, Coleridge moved into Greta Hall, which stands on a low hill facing the tentlike encampment of mountains; to the right are the vale and lake of Bassenthwaite, and to the left Derwent Water, Lodore Falls, and the Borrowdale Mountains. Most of Coleridge's best writing had already been done, and his marital problems were worsening. Nevertheless, the second part of "Christabel" and "Ode to Dejection" were written at this time. By August, 1802, when Charles and Mary Lamb arrived for a visit, Coleridge's rheumatic and neuralgic conditions had worsened, and his addiction to laudanum and opium had greatly increased. The habit was fixed by 1803. The Lambs stayed for three weeks, and on one occasion the three climbed Skiddaw and Scafell. Of the scenery Lamb writes:

> . . . such an impression I never received from objects of sight before. . . . We have seen Keswick, Grasmere, Ambleside . . . we have clambered up to the top of Skiddaw. . . .

Coleridge's "Hymn before Sunrise, in the Vale of Chamouni" came about on this excursion, and the description is unmistakably that of this area. Upon a medical suggestion of the value of a change in climate, Coleridge went to Malta in 1803, leaving his family at Greta Hall. Before Christmas, 1806, his marital problems had reached a crisis; his patience with Sarah, he claimed, was gone, but Coleridge himself had the more difficult personality. Sarah refused a formal separation, and Coleridge left with their eldest son Hartley for Coleorton, Leicestershire, to join William and Dorothy Wordsworth. He returned to Keswick only occasionally as a visitor.

In September 1803 Robert Southey brought his family to Greta Hall, then a two-family dwelling. Southey's family responsibilities were already enormous, and they were to become greater still. The old pantisocratic scheme formulated by Coleridge and Southey at Oxford had brought a third party into the plan, Robert Lovell of Bristol, and the three men had married three sisters. By 1803 Lovell was dead, and his widow and child had been taken into the Southey household. When Coleridge abandoned his family, Southey took on the responsibility of the third sister and maintained them all for the rest of his life. He is known once to have exclaimed, "To think how many mouths I must feed out of one inkstand!" When he came to Greta Hall, he brought a library of 4,000 volumes, and by his death it had grown to more than 14,000.

By 1807, when it became clear that the hall was to be his home for life, Southey entered into a vigorous plan of renovation and restoration, and in 1809 he bought the whole house. He then turned as vigorously to his work; he solved some of his financial troubles by becoming a steady contributor to the *Quarterly Review*, from which he eventually received £100 an article. In 1813 he was offered the Poet Laureateship because of Sir Walter Scott's generosity. The post had been offered to Scott, who declined it, suggested it be offered to Southey, and visited here to persuade the poet; Southey accepted the honor and its stipend on condition that the traditional birthday ode not be written. Southey had many other visitors as well. William Hazlitt came for the first time in 1803, when he was painting Wordsworth's and Coleridge's portraits; De Quincey and Percy and Harriet Shelley were also guests. Shelley arrived from York in November 1811 on the way to Ireland; he first took lodgings at Townhead and within two weeks moved to Chestnut Cottage, just outside the town. He describes the cottage in an early letter and comments on Greta Hall:

> . . . awfully beautiful. Our window commands a fine view of two lakes, and the giant mountains which confine them. But the object most interesting to my feelings is Southey's inhabitation.

The Shelleys frequently accepted Southey's hospitality but left for Ireland on February 3, 1812, without even a farewell. Another visitor some years later was Walter Savage Landor, who came here from Wast Water; he stayed two days at the hall.

A letter to Grosvenor Bedford dated October 2, 1834, tells of the tragedy that befell Southey; he was parted from his wife

> by something worse than death. Forty years she has been the life of my life; and I have left her this day in a lunatic asylum.

A few years after her death in 1837, he married Caroline Bowles; his own state of health was deteriorating, and the last year of his life was spent in a trancelike state. He died here on March 21, 1843, and was buried in the Crosthwaite churchyard.

When John Keats was on a walking tour of the Lake District in the summer of 1818, he stayed in Keswick and wrote to his brother Thomas that he thought the entrance into the Keswick Valley "surpassed Winandermere—it is richly wooded and shut in with rich-toned Mountains." Following dinner here on June 29, he and Charles Armitage Brown

> set forth about a mile and a half on the Penrith road, to see the Druid temple. We had a fag up hill, rather too near dinner time, which was rendered void by the gratification of seeing those aged stones, on a gentle rise in the midst of Mountains, which at that time darkened all round, except at the fresh opening of the vale of St. John.

His druid circle is the Neolithic stone circle at Castlerigg, about 2 miles from the town; thirty-eight stones form a circle 100 feet across, and ten stones stand inside the ring. Keats later draws on Castlerigg in *Hyperion*:

> . . . like a dismal cirque
> Of Druid stones, upon a forlorn moor,

> When the chill rain begins at shut of eve,
> In dull November, and their chancel vault,
> The Heaven itself, is blinded throughout night.

Sir Hugh Walpole uses the stone circle as the end point of a footrace in *The Fortress*. Thomas Edward Brown spent a part of every summer vacation here from 1873 to 1892; he first stayed at St. John's Terrace and later at Lake View. John Galsworthy spent the 1887 Long Vacation from New College, Oxford, here with three companions; they formed a reading party and found Keswick ideally suited to their needs. Galsworthy climbed Scafell on this trip and had absolutely no fear of the height; he became acrophobic at a later date.

A significant 20th-century association with Keswick is that of Sir Hugh Walpole, who lived nearby at Brackenburn, Manesty Park, from 1923 until his death in 1941. He regularly attended church services either here at St. John's or in the village of Grange; emerging from St. John's one February morning, he noted:

> The view from the churchyard was superb, the hills ranged like battlements. All is so quiet then. In front, the hills, just touched with roses; behind, the little gray street, quite silent, thin spirals of smoke coming from the chimneys. The churchyard scattered with snowdrops.

He decided that he would be buried in this churchyard and made the necessary arrangements. Many of the scenes in the "Herries" novels take place in Keswick; the town is the site of Pomfret Herries's home, Westaways, one of the most beautiful in Keswick "because he wished to have a better house than any of his neighbours." It had been expensive,

> but it was a beautiful house. . . .
> In fine proportion, its roof covered with red tiles, the wrought ironwork across its front showing like lace against the stone, the house was oblong without gables. The windows were for their period most modern. They were sash windows, a great rarity, and they were beautifully spaced. The doorway had fluted columns and over it there was a charming and delicate fanlight.
> The house was outside the town near to Crosthwaite Church, and the gardens ran down to the weeds and rushes of the lake-end. The garden held lime trees and the lawn was bordered with tubs of orange and bay trees.

A memorable chapter in *Judith Paris* describes a visit to the Southeys. The poet seemed scholarly, and there were books everywhere, but Judith was most deeply impressed with the young Hartley Coleridge,

> a very extraordinary being. This was a boy of some fifteen or sixteen years of age; he had a small restless body dressed in clothes too young for it, the short blue cloth jacket, the white trousers and open frilled shirt of boys junior to him. Dark hair strayed untidily over his forehead, but his eyes were the strangest part of him, burning with intelligence and yet at the same time lost, as he gazed about the room, in a kind of abstract wonder.

The Keswick Museum has a number of relics of Walpole and Southey.

KEYSTON, Huntingdonshire (pop. 182)   The name of this small Huntingdonshire village, just off the Thrapston Road 4 miles southeast of Huntingdon, is properly Keystone and was most likely a boundary marker for the western edge of the shire. On January 16, 1616, John Donne was given the benefice here on the understanding that the parish would be served by a curate paid from Donne's revenues. There is no evidence that Donne was ever here, and he resigned the post on October 20, 1621.

KIDDERMINSTER, Worcestershire (pop. 45,510) Set on the Stour River 15 miles north of Worcester and 19 miles southwest of Birmingham, Kidderminster was anciently called Sour-in-Usmere and was in royal hands until the 12th century. Long famed for its carpet manufacturing, an industry established in the mid-18th century, the town has been engaged in the cloth trade since at least the 14th century and was the source of "*Kidderminster* Stuffs call'd Lindsey Woolseys ... very rarely made any where else," as Daniel Defoe claims in *A Tour thro' the Whole Island of Great Britain*. One of the outstanding buildings in Kidderminster is the partly 14th-century St. Mary's Church, which stands on a hill overlooking the Stour; elsewhere modernization has destroyed much of the town's antiquity. Close to the town center, in the Bull Ring, is a commemorative statue of Richard Baxter, the Presbyterian divine and reformer who was assistant preacher in the town on two occasions, the first in 1641–1642. The outbreak of the Civil War presented him with a major problem: almost all Worcestershire supported Charles I, and Baxter, a believer in limited monarchy, sided with Parliament. He ultimately retired to Coventry, and after the Parliamentarian victory and his own serious illness he returned to his work in Kidderminster in 1647. The *Saints Everlasting Rest* was written here in 1650, and his pulpit is preserved in the Unitarian Chapel.

Kidderminster was the birthplace of Edward Bradley (Cuthbert Bede) on March 25, 1827; he was educated at the grammar school here before going up to University College, Durham, in 1845. Following his graduation there and a subsequent year at Oxford because he was too young to take orders, he returned to Kidderminster, where he worked in the clergy schools for a little more than a year. Ordained in 1850, he took the curacy of Glatton-with-Holme, Huntingdonshire.

KIDDINGTON, Oxfordshire (pop. 181) The tiny Glyme Valley villages of Nether Kiddington and Over Kiddington share everything but a single name and are usually referred to as one; 4½ miles northwest of Woodstock, Kiddington has something left from the Britons, Romans, and Saxons, and the Normans built the church hidden behind trees in Kiddington Park. The church was modernized in the 14th century, when the chancel was shortened, but the beautiful grotesque heads were left intact. In October 1771 the Rev. Thomas Warton was appointed to this living and took up his post immediately; he had already begun his history of English poetry and while here finished the volumes up to the end of Elizabeth's reign. The fourth volume, which would have moved up to Pope, was never written, but he did produce "a specimen of history" in the model history of Kiddington. After 1785 Warton combined his parish duties with those of the Camden Professorship of History at Oxford, and that year, upon the death of William Whitehead, he became Poet Laureate. Shortly after a trip to Bath to take the waters for his gout, Warton suffered a paralytic stroke in the Sen-

ior Common Room at Trinity College on May 20, 1790, and died the next day.

KIMBOLTON, Huntingdonshire (pop. 920) In a deep, wooded valley along the Kym River 10 miles southwest of Huntingdon, Kimbolton is an unspoiled village with a number of attractive houses fronting on the High Street. The person who built Kimbolton Castle is not known with certainty, but in 1522 Henry VIII gave the castle to Sir Richard Winfield and made an additional grant of building materials. Most likely Winfield moved the site of the castle to its present location, although the present building is largely 18th-century and the work of Sir John Vanbrugh. In his *Itinerary* John Leland notes:

> The castelle is dowble dikid, and the building of it meately strong. . . .
> Syr Richard Winfield buildid new fair lodgyns and galeries apon the old foundations of the castelle.

Later, when Daniel Defoe came to know it, the castle, in the hands of the Duke of Manchester's family, was

> that most nobly situated and pleasant Seat of the Duke of *Manchester,* called *Kimbolton,* or *Kimbolton Castle,* where no Pains or Cost has been spar'd to make the most beautiful Situation still more beautiful, and to help Nature with Art.

These quotations might as well refer to two different castles. The earlier castle is important in William Shakespeare's plays, for it is in this castle that Queen Katharine dies after banishment from the court in *King Henry VIII*. In actual fact Catherine of Aragon was imprisoned in the castle in 1534 and spent the last two years of her life in rooms which, though greatly altered, are still pointed out. The building now houses the scholars of Kimbolton Grammar School and is open to the public only in summer.

KING'S LANGLEY, Hertfordshire (pop. 2,504) On the Gate River just south of Hemel Hempstead and less than 25 miles from London, King's Langley once belonged to Eleanor, wife of Edward I, and at that time the village name was changed from Chiltern Langley to Queen's Langley. It later became King's Langley. Queen Eleanor began a building program here, and by 1236 the accomodations were sufficient to house the royal family and its retinue, and the young Prince of Wales not only had his own accommodations and servants here but a camel and a lion cub in the park. After becoming King in 1307, Edward II continued to spend a great deal of time here, especially in the company of Piers Gaveston, one of the main figures in Christopher Marlowe's *Edward II*. Edward brought back the sycophant's remains after his execution and buried Gaveston in the 14th-century Dominican priory adjacent to the palace; his grave has not been located.

Edward III's fifth son, Edmund of Langley, later 1st Duke of York, was born here in 1341. Edmund was three times Regent when Richard II was abroad and upon the death of his brother John of Gaunt in 1399 was made Steward of England "until Henry, Earl of Derby, shall sue for the same." At this point the exiled Henry invaded England and forced Richard to surrender. The story is related in William Shakespeare's *Richard II;* the scene in "Langley, the

Duke of York's garden," is where the Queen learns of Richard's fate from the gardener:

> King Richard, he is in the mighty hold
> Of Bolingbroke: their fortunes both are weigh'd:
> In your lord's scale is nothing but himself,
> And some few vanities that make him light;
> But in the balance of great Bolingbroke,
> Besides himself, are all the English peers,
> And with that odds he weighs King Richard down.

After Richard's murder at Pontefract, Bolingbroke returned the King's body to the priory here for burial; Edmund was buried here as well, in 1402. The buildings are now used as a school.

KING'S LYNN, Norfolk (pop. 24,110)   The northwest coastal region of Norfolk, which sweeps down to the Wash, is an area of sand, low cliffs, saltings, tidal inlets, and here, around King's Lynn (also known as Lynn Regis), marshland. The ancient market town, which flourished as a medieval port, is on the Ouse River near the confluence of the Nare; once called Bishop's Lynn (Lynn Episcopi), when the town belonged to the Bishop of Norwich, it became King's Lynn at the dissolution of the monasteries.

Modern times have not brought more than light industry here, and as a consequence the town has a wealth of old buildings, medieval to Georgian, in good repair and now well protected by the joint operations of the Town Council and the Preservation Society. The Guildhall (now the Town Hall) dates to 1423; the quayside wooden warehouse of the Hanseatic League dates from 1428; the Greenland Fisheries, on All Saints' Street, is a 1605 timbered house; and Clifton House has an Elizabethan watchtower. St. Margaret's Church has the unusual feature of twin towers and a central lantern.

William Camden includes the town in his survey in *Britannia:*

> This is a large town almost surrounded by a deep ditch and walls, and divided by two little rivulets, over which are about 15 bridges. And though it is more modern, and not long ago called *Bishop's Linne,* having belonged to the bishops of Norwich to the time of Henry VIII (for it rose out of the ruins of an older town opposite to it, in Marshland, now called *Old Lynne* and *Lynne Regis*), yet for the safe entrance of its harbour, the resort of merchants, the beauty of the buildings, and the wealth of the inhabitants, it may claim the chief rank after Norwich among the Iceni.

Years later Daniel Defoe visited "*Lyn,* another Rich and Populous Thriving Port-Town," as he calls it in *A Tour thro' the Whole Island of Great Britain.* His opinion of it was very high; he says in part:

> It is a beautiful well built, and well situated Town, at the Mouth of the River *Ouse,* and has this particular attending it, which gives it a vast Advantage in Trade; Namely, that there is the greatest Extent of Inland Navigation here, of any Port in England, London excepted. . . .
> Here are more Gentry, and consequently is more Gayety in this Town than in *Yarmouth,* or even in *Norwich* itself; the Place abounding in very good Company.

King's Lynn claims both Margery Kempe and Fanny Burney as natives. Margery Kempe, whose *Book of Margery Kempe* was not discovered until 1934 (until then only an eight-page fragment was known to exist), was born here about 1373. The daughter of a prosperous merchant who served five times as mayor of Lynn, she married John Kempe, also of Lynn, around 1393 and bore him fourteen children before they agreed to a future life of abstinence. Margery Kempe's religious fervor increased after the birth of her first child. She was then mad for six months before she had a vision of Christ which restored her sanity. Her frequent "cryings" and weepings "full boisterously," as she described them, are noted in her book, which she dictated in 1436 after travel to the Holy Land, Danzig, and Rome. She also enumerates her conversations with Christ, the Virgin Mary, St. Peter, St. Paul, St. Catherine, "or whatever saint in heaven she had devotion to."

The second native author, Fanny Burney, was born on June 13, 1752, either at St. Augustine's House on Chapel Street (on the site of an Austin friary) or at 84 High Street. Her father was the organist of St. Margaret's, and, in fact, the Snetzler organ built to his specifications in 1743 to increase the dulciana stop, which he introduced to England, is on display in the church. Fanny Burney was, by her own account, a backward child and had no knowledge of her letters until 1760, the year in which the family moved to London.

One other literary association exists with King's Lynn, for Eugene Aram was an usher at the grammar school when the body of an unknown man was discovered in Knaresborough, Yorkshire. Even though it was not the body of Daniel Clarke, a friend of Aram's who had disappeared under strange circumstances, Aram was later tried and convicted for complicity in Clarke's murder and was executed by hanging. Thomas Hood's poem *The Dream of Eugene Aram, the Murderer* recounts the schoolmaster's days here prior to his arrest:

> Like sportive deer they cours'd about,
>   And shouted as they ran,—
> Turning to mirth all things of earth,
>   As only boyhood can;
> But the Usher sat remote from all,
>   A melancholy man!
>
> His hat was off, his vest apart,
>   To catch heaven's blessed breeze;
> For a burning thought was in his brow,
>   And his bosom ill at ease:
> So he lean'd his head on his hands, and read
>   The book between his knees!

Edward Bulwer-Lytton (Lord Lytton) uses the same story in his novel *Eugene Aram.*

KINGSBRIDGE, Devon (pop. 2,946)   In the richest agricultural district of Devon, called by John Leland "the frutefullest part of all Devonshire," Kingsbridge, frequently named the capital of South Hams, stands at the head of the Kingsbridge Estuary 11 miles southwest of Totnes. The grammar school dates to 1670, and the Shambles, a 16th-century market arcade (rebuilt in 1796), is noteworthy. Pindar Lodge in Dodbrooke (now a parish within Kingsbridge) was the birthplace of John Wolcot, better known as Peter Pindar, in 1738; he was baptized at the 16th-century Dodbrook Church on May 9. His birthplace, now a hotel, originally faced Ebrington Street. Wolcot's education, begun at the grammar school before his father's death in 1751, was taken over by an uncle, John Wolcot of Fowey, and the satirist went on to school in Liskeard and Bodmin.

KINGSBURY, Middlesex Kingsbury once was a refreshingly rural spot on the Brent River 7 miles northwest of St. Paul's Cathedral in London, but now it is a dormitory suburb of the city and retains only its ancient church. Sometime in 1771 Oliver Goldsmith took a room in a farmer's house here near the 6-mile stone in the Kingsbury Green area known as the Hyde. He used Hyde Farm as a summer residence and spent much of his time here in the last years of his life. Here he wrote *She Stoops to Conquer* and most of *The Grecian History* and compiled the greater part of *An History of the Earth and Animated Nature.* His lodgings here were only temporary, and he retained his London flat during the entire period. He came to the house (on Edgware Road) in March 1774 but, feeling ill, returned to London, where he died on April 4. Two of Goldsmith's visitors here were William Julius Mickle and James Boswell; Goldsmith was not at home, and Boswell's inquisitiveness got the better of him:

> . . . having a curiosity to see his apartment, [I] went in and found curious scraps of descriptions of animals, scrawled upon the wall with a black lead pencil.

KINGSTON HILL, Surrey (pop. 6,749) Once considered the capital of the county of Surrey, being the seat of the County Council and having usurped the assizes from Guildford in 1930, Kingston-upon-Thames, of which Kingston Hill is a distinct area, was amalgamated with Malden, Coombe, and Surbiton in 1965 and thus became the Royal Metropolitan Borough of Kingston-upon-Thames. The Kingston area owes its very long history to its location: it was the first place above London Bridge where the Thames was fordable. Kingston Hill, which lies in the northern section of the Royal Borough, and Kingston are almost purely residential, the only important commercial diversion being the Saturday market.

In *Britannia* William Camden claims that three kings, Athelstan, Edwy, and Ethelred, were crowned here and that the town was anciently called Moreford; to this list, in the additions by Richard Gough, are appended:

> Edward the elder A.D. 900, Edmund A.D. 940, Edward the martyr A.D. 975, and another Etheldred or Edred A.D. 978. . . .

And, he continues:

> It was called Kyningestun, *formosus ille locus*, in Egbert's council A.D. 838. Leland supposes the new town was built in the Saxon times. The bridge is the oldest over the Thames, except London bridge.

Samuel Pepys was often in Kingston on his way to Windsor and frequently stopped off at an inn for a meal or overnight accommodations; but the "neat inn" where he ate in 1665 has not been identified. Daniel Defoe was singularly unimpressed with the town; he comments in *A Tour thro' the Whole Island of Great Britain:*

> *I say,* satisfy'd with this [what I had seen], I came back directly to *Kingstone*, a good Market-Town, but remarkable for little, only that they say, the Antient *British* and

Saxon Kings were usually Crown'd here in former Times, which I still neither assert or deny.

The major literary association in Kingston Hill is with John Galsworthy, who was born at Parkfield on August 14, 1867; then, for the next nineteen years, he lived all about the area. Shortly after his birth, the Galsworthy family moved into Coombe Warren, (later called Coombe Court and demolished in 1931), where they remained until 1875, when the house became much too small for them; they then took Coombe Leigh (now called Coombe Ridge) until 1878. That year the family took Coombe Croft, which is still as it was then, but returned in 1881 to Coombe Leigh, where they remained until moving into London in 1886. Galsworthy was educated at home by a series of governesses and tutors until the age of nine, when he was sent to school in Bournemouth, and he spent all his school holidays here. The Coombe Hill and Kingston Hill area made a deep impression on him, and it later played an important role in *The Forsyte Saga.* Robin Hill, the Forsyte house, is placed at Coombe Warren, and the description of the grounds and coppice is actual:

> Almost from their feet stretched ripe corn, dipping to a small dark copse beyond. A plain of fields and hedges spread to the distant grey-blue downs. In a silver streak to the right could be seen the line of the river. . . .
> Thistledown floated round them, enraptured by the serenity of the ether. The heat danced over the corn, and pervading all, was a soft, insensible hum, like the murmur of bright minutes holding revel between earth and heaven.

Galsworthy also portrays the rurality of the period:

> From where he sat he could see a cluster of apple-trees in blossom. Nothing in Nature moved him so much as fruit-trees in blossom; and his heart ached suddenly because he might never see them flower again. . . . Blackbirds sang recklessly in the shubbery, swallows were flying high, the leaves above him glistened; and over the fields was every imaginable tint of early foliage, burnished by the level sunlight, away to where the distant 'smoke-bush' blue was trailed along the horizon.

The house, however, Galsworthy says, "I built with my imagination."

Charles Dickens mentions Kingston in *Nicholas Nickleby* as the first stop on the trip from London taken by Nicholas and Smike.

KINGSTON LISLE, Berkshire (pop. 220) Kingston Lisle is located on the southern edge of the Vale of the White Horse 4½ miles west of Wantage. As the first part of the name signifies, the village was once a royal demesne. The 14th-century chancel of the church has extraordinarily clear medieval wall paintings; one is an extremely good portrayal of Herod and Herodias, in the dress of a Norman king and queen, watching Salome dance. The most famous aspect of the village is the Blowing Stone, linked in legend with King Alfred (r. 871–899), who is said to have used it as a trumpet to assemble his men. A 3-foot-high block of red sandstone which is supposed to have stood on White Horse Hill, it is now in a cottage garden near the main road turning to the village. Thomas Hughes, whose paternal grandmother, Mary Anne Hughes, made her home here (probably Kingston Lisle House) from 1833 on, uses the stone with "petrified antediluvian rat-holes" in *Tom Brown's School Days:*

> "What is the name of your hill, landlord?"
> "Blawing Stwun Hill, sir, to be sure."
> [READER. "*Sturm?*"
> AUTHOR. "*Stone*, stupid—the Blowing *Stone*."]
> "And of your house? I can't make out the sign."
> "Blawing Stwun, sir," says the landlord. . . .
> "What queer names! say we, sighing at the end of our draught, and holding out the glass to be replenished.
> "Bean't queer at all, as I can see, sir," says mine host . . . "seeing as this here is the Blawing Stwun, his self," putting his hand on a square lump of stone, some three feet and a half high, perforated with two or three queer holes, like petrified antediluvian rat-holes, which lies there close under the oak. . . . "Like to hear un, sir?" says mine host, . . . and he, without waiting for a reply, applies his mouth to one of the rat-holes. Something must come of it, if he doesn't burst. Good heavens! I hope he has no apoplectic tendencies. Yes, here it comes, sure enough, a gruesome sound between a moan and a roar, and spreads itself away over the valley, and up the hillside, and into the woods at the back of the house, a ghost-like awful voice.

The village of Kingston Lisle, just below the Blowing Stone Inn, was the home of "Squire Brown, J.P for the county of Berks . . . where he dealt out justice and mercy in a rough way, and begat sons and daughters, and hunted the fox, and grumbled at the badness of the roads and the times."

Hughes's grandmother, who had lived in London, had a wide range of literary friends, including William Harrison Ainsworth, to whom she told local legends and folklore. Ainsworth was a frequent guest here and, indeed, was promised every comfort and facility, including his meals at any hour. He worked on both *Guy Fawkes*, dedicated to Mrs. Hughes, and *Jack Sheppard* here and used his hostess as the model for Mrs. Compton, "the good old lady" of whom it was said "no one living . . . does more good" in *Old St. Paul's.*

KINGSTON-UPON-HULL   *See* HULL.

KINGTON ST. MICHAEL, Wiltshire (pop. 437)   Lying 3 miles north of Chippenham off the road to Malmesbury, Kington St. Michael, an attractive village, has lovely 16th-century gabled stone almshouses on the main street and a 13th-century, partially reconstructed church with a Norman font. On March 12, 1626, John Aubrey, the antiquarian, was born at a house called Easton Piers (now Easton Piercy or Percy) in this parish; the house no longer exists but another Cotswold-stone house stands on the site. Aubrey was first educated privately by the rector of Leigh Delamere and then at the Blandford Grammar School. No great lover of his hometown, he later described the surrounding area as "a dirty claye country" and the natives as "phlegmatique . . . slow and dull, and heavy of spirit." He goes on:

> [H]ereabout is but little tillage or hard labour. They only milk cowes and make cheese; they feed chiefly on milke meates, which cooles their braines too much and hurts their inventions.

The natives, he says, are

> melancholy, contemplative and malicious, their persons plump and feggy by consequence whereof come more law-

suits out of North Wilts—at least double to the southern parts.

The parish church contains a commemorative window.

KIRBY WISKE, Yorkshire (pop. 190)   This tiny village on the Wiske River in northeastern Yorkshire was the birthplace of Roger Ascham in 1515. There is no village record of his birth or baptism, for such records were not kept until a century later, and not much is known about Acham's early life here except that the family was not well off. It is known that Ascham's father once had a farm at Newsham, just across the river from Kirby Wiske, and that the farm failed. The elder Ascham, however, had an enthusiasm for the benefits of education and managed to place his son in the local grammar school. Roger Ascham was later taken into the family of Sir Anthony Wingfield and educated with Wingfield's son; Wingfield, in fact, sent Ascham to St. John's College, Cambridge.

KIRKBY LONSDALE, Westmorland (pop. 1,393)   One of the most beautiful villages in the Lake District, Kirkby Lonsdale sits on a hill above the Lune River 12 miles southeast of Kendal. The area has been inhabited since prehistoric times, as the circle of twenty upright stones 1½ miles to the northeast bears witness; and the Romans had a camp here. An early-15th-century bridge, the oldest in Westmorland and called the Devil's Bridge, spans the Lune here. John Ruskin praised the village when he said that the English river, moorland, and forest were at their best here and that the view from the Brow overlooking the Lune Valley was "one of the loveliest scenes in England."

Kirkby Lonsdale's literary fame comes from the village of Casterton, 1 mile to the northeast, the location of Casterton Girls' School. The institution was originally at Cowan Bridge, 2 miles to the southeast in Lancashire. In the earlier location the Brontë sisters attended the Clergy Daughters' School; Maria and Elizabeth entered first, and Charlotte and Emily followed in a few months (September 1824). Maria and Elizabeth both died within a short period of entering school, and by the autumn of 1825 Charlotte and Emily had returned to their Haworth, Yorkshire, home. Elizabeth Gaskell's *Life of Charlotte Brontë* describes the school:

> It is a long, low bow-windowed cottage, now divided into two dwellings. It stands facing the Leck, between which and it intervenes a space, about seventy yards deep, that was once the school garden. Running from this building, at right angles with what now remains of the school-house, there was formerly a bobbin-mill. . . . Mr. Wilson adapted this mill to his purpose; there were schoolrooms on the lower floor, and dormitories on the upper. The present cottage was occupied by the teachers' rooms, the dining-room and kitchens, and some smaller bed-rooms. . . . The other end forms a cottage, with the low ceilings and stone floors of a hundred years ago; the windows do not open freely and widely; and the passage up-stairs, leading to the bed-rooms, is narrow and tortuous; altogether, smells would linger about the house, and damp cling to it. But sanitary matters were little understood thirty years ago.

The area plays a major role in Charlotte Brontë's

Jane Eyre. The school becomes Lowood School, and Kirkby Lonsdale becomes Lowton, the nearest town to the school. From Jane's windows she sees

> two wings of the building; there was the garden; there were the skirts of Lowood; there was the hilly horizon. My eye passed all other objects to rest on those most remote, the blue peaks. It was those I longed to surmount; all within their boundary of rock and heath seemed prison-ground, exile limits. I traced the white road winding round the base of one mountain and vanishing in a gorge between the two. How I longed to follow it further!

Casterton Hall in the novel is probably the manor here. Miss Brontë later said she never would have written what she did of Lowood School had she known it would be so easily recognized.

KIRKLEES, Yorkshire This tiny village on the Calder River in the West Riding of Yorkshire, 2 miles from Brighouse, contains the remains of a Cistercian nunnery founded in 1155. The prioress's lodging is the traditional scene of the death of Robin Hood, and a small closet is pointed out as the exact place of his death. The tradition is of an extremely early date and clearly predates William Camden, to whom the information was given by Sir John Savile. At least three major ballads—"A Gest of Robyn Hode," "Robin Hoode His Death," and "Robin Hood's Death and Burial"—deal with his death. Ill and convinced that only by being bled will he recover, he comes to Kirklees Priory, where his near kinswoman is the prioress.

> And when he came to fair Kirkly-hall
>   He knockd all at the ring,
> But none was so ready as his cousin herself
>   For to let bold Robin in.

The bleeding begins in a "private room" locked by the prioress, where "did he bleed all the live-long day,/Until the next day at noon" when he realizes that he has been betrayed. Unable to escape, he summons Little John with the traditional three blasts upon his horn. Forbidding Little John to destroy the nunnery by fire, Robin Hood directs his own burial:

> . . . a broad arrow I'll let flee;
> And where this arrow is taken up,
>   There shall my grave digged be.

The grave site, on a high, flat piece of land in the midst of a very thick stand of trees, is enclosed by an iron railing, and at the back of the site is a broken block of stone which contains the very much debated inscription:

> Hear Underneath dis laitle Stean
> Las Robert earl of Huntington
> Naer arcir ver az hie sa geud
> An pipl kaul him Robin Heud
> Sick utlauz az he an iz men
> Vil england nivr si agen.
>   Obit 24 Dekembris, 1247

The inscription, spelling, and rhymes do, it is true, point to a 19th-century date for the raising of the stone, but the epitaph, plus two other lines (Full thirteen years and something more/These no[r]thern parts he vexed sore), appear in a far older ballad and are reputed to have been put on the original gravestone by the prioress of Kirklees. Michael Drayton in *Poly-Olbion* refers to the Calder River and Robin Hood:

> She [the Calder] in her course on Kirkley cast her eye,
> Where merry Robin Hood, that honest thief, doth lie.

The nearby inn, the Three Nuns, originally a guesthouse provided by the priory for visitors, has stained-glass windows portraying figures from the legend: Robin Hood, the guilty prioress, Little John, and Friar Tuck.

Charlotte Brontë knew this area quite well: she began attending Miss Wooler's School in nearby Birstall in 1832 and many times walked to Kirklees. Kirklees Hall (of Jacobean origin) becomes the Nunnely of *Shirley*, and various other episodes take place in this general vicinity.

KIRKSTALL, Yorkshire (pop. 5,526) On the banks of the Aire River, in the West Riding of Yorkshire, the village of Kirkstall, which is a part of the borough of Leeds, is fast becoming a satellite of that city. The most distinctive feature of the village is the ruined Cistercian Kirkstall Abbey, second in state of preservation and extent only to Fountains Abbey, Yorkshire. The white monks, as members of the community were known because of the color of their habits, most often founded their houses in undeveloped valleys, and the monks here, besides farming, began the coal-mining operations for which the Leeds area is now famous. They employed a simple method of divination: they found that the clay superstructure over the coal beds, for some reason, grew clover with unusually large leaves.

The abbey suffered badly at the dissolution of the monasteries and was surrendered in 1539 by Joseph Ripley, the last abbot, who continued to live in the inner gatehouse, a Norman building, which was kept in good repair. The gatehouse now forms part of the Abbey House Museum, and the original narrow spiral Norman staircase is still in use.

Thomas Gray visited the abbey on his northern trip in 1762 and wrote to Dr. Thomas Wharton that the "lofty towers . . . were the truest objects for my glass I have yet met with anywhere." The glass, a small telescope which he frequently used on this tour, he described as "a plane-convex mirror of about four inches in diameter, on a black foil." William and Dorothy Wordsworth were here on their return from Coleorton, Leicestershire, in 1807. They stayed at New Grange with Mrs. Jane Pollard Marshall, with whom they explored Kirkstall Abbey, Wharfedale, and Bolton Abbey before going on to Grasmere. Robert Southey's "Mary the Maid of the Inn" is based on a historical event here involving Mary Clarkson, niece of Joe Sutcliffe, landlord of the Star and Garter Inn. Miss Clarkson, who fell in love with one William Bradford and promised to marry him secretly, stumbled onto his complicity in the murder of a Leeds merchant when she discovered the attempt to bury the body in Kirkstall Abbey, and she subsequently helped both to apprehend and to convict Bradford. This is the story on which Southey bases the poem, but the poet tells it differently.

KIRKSTONE PASS, Westmorland The highest mountain pass open to the motorist in this region of the Lake District, Kirkstone Pass links Windermere to Patterdale and reaches a height of 1,489 feet at its summit. At the peak between Caudale Moor and Red Screes is the Kirkstone Pass Inn, formerly known as the Travellers' Rest. William Wordsworth and his sister Dorothy often walked up the pass, and he wrote "The Pass of Kirkstone" in June 1817:

> List to those shriller notes!—*that* march
> Perchance was on the blast,
> When, through this Height's inverted arch,
> Rome's earliest legion passed!
> —They saw, adventurously impelled,
> And older eyes than theirs beheld,
> This block—and yon, whose church-like frame
> Gives to this savage Pass its name.
> Aspiring Road! that lov'st to hide
> Thy daring in a vapoury bourn,
> Not seldom may the hour return
> When thou shalt be my guide. . . .

KNEBWORTH, Hertfordshire (pop. 1,629) Knebworth lies on the Great North Road about 25 miles north of London and 8 miles northwest of Hertford, but the old village is about 1 mile west and has a 260-acre park containing a partly 12th-century church. A great deal of work has been done on the church, and it is now a hodgepodge of styles and periods; the tower dates from 1420, the Lytton Chapel from the 16th century, the porch from the 17th, and the chancel from the 19th. The Tudor manor house was begun in 1492 by Sir Robert Lytton on the site of an earlier castle and is still in family hands.

Edward Bulwer, later 1st Baron Lytton, came here in 1811 when his mother inherited the estate, and it was she who took the name Bulwer-Lytton. The eight-year-old Edward was sent in rapid succession to a number of schools in Fulham, Salisbury, Brighton, and then Rottingdean, Sussex, and school holidays were usually spent here even after he went up to Trinity College, Cambridge. The curious "affair" with Lady Caroline Lamb occurred at her home in nearby Brocket Park, where Lytton spent a great deal of his time; his ultimate appraisal was simple: "On both sides I think it had little to do with the heart but a great deal with the imagination." By 1825 he was an infrequent guest at Knebworth, and a period of estrangement followed his marriage in 1827 to Rosina Doyle Wheeler.

Lytton gained a parliamentary seat for St. Ives before he inherited Knebworth in 1843, and it is his renovated house which remains. His mother had torn down three wings of the house, and Lord Lytton medievalized the remainder in true Victorian fashion, installing sham Gothic windows, cementing the brickwork to imitate stone, and adding roof battlements and plaster gargoyles. Inside, the house is much the same mixture of real and sham, and according to one account the staircase is papier-mâché. *The Caxtons, My Novel,* and *What Will He Do with It?* all were written here, and the house contains first editions of Lytton's works, the manuscripts of *The Last Days of Pompeii, The Caxtons,* and *My Novel,* a plaster cast of his hand, and a series of letters written to him by Charles Dickens, who was a frequent guest here. According to Dickens, Lytton was "talkative, anecdotal and droll, looked young and well, laughed

KIRKSTONE PASS
> —Who comes not hither ne'er shall know
> How beautiful the world below;
> Nor can he guess how lightly leaps
> The brook adown the rocky steeps.
> Farewell, thou desolate Domain!
> William Wordsworth, "The Pass of Kirkstone"

heartily and enjoyed some games we played with great zeal."

Lytton was a good host and an interested patron of the arts, and over the years his literary guests included Benjamin Disraeli, Matthew Arnold, and Wilkie Collins. The library collection contains the manuscript of *Lucile,* the now-obscure verse novel written by Owen Meredith, the pseudonym of Lord Lytton's son, the 1st Earl of Lytton.

KNIGHTON, Leicestershire So close to Leicester, 2 miles to the northwest, as to be essentially a part of the city (indeed, the official residence of the vice-chancellor of the University of Leicester is here), the village of Knighton once caused William Cobbett anguish. Visiting Leicester in April 1830, he walked to Hailstone and Knighton and was disturbed by the economic disparity in these communities:

> Standing on the hill at Knighton, you see the three ancient and lofty and beautiful spires rising up at Leicester; you see the river winding down through a broad bed of the most beautiful meadows that man ever set his eyes on; you see the bright verdure covering all the land, even to the tops of the hills, with here and there a little wood, as if made by God to give variety to the beauty of the scene. . . . But go down into the villages; . . . and then look at the miserable sheds in which the labourers reside! Look at these hovels, made of mud and of straw; bits of glass, or of old off-cast windows, without frames or hinges frequently, but merely stuck in the mud wall. Enter them, and look at the bits of chairs or stools; the wretched boards tacked together to serve for a table; the floor of pebble, broken brick, or of the bare ground; look at the thing called a bed; and survey the rags on the backs of the wretched inhabitants. . . .

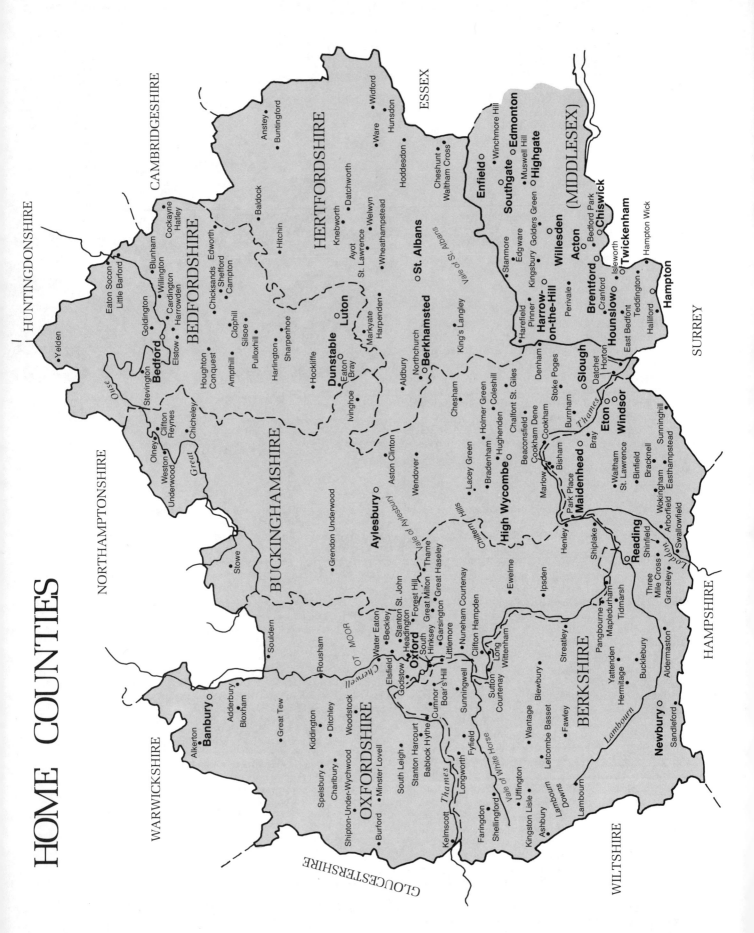

HOME COUNTIES

KNOLE, Kent   A mile east of Sevenoaks, but not part of that town, is Knole (now owned by the National Trust), whose parklands are roughly 6 miles in circumference; it is a simple matter for visitors to imagine themselves displaced five centuries in time. Thomas Bourchier, Archbishop of Canterbury, created the present fabric of the manor, in appearance a travesty of Oxford. Thomas Cranmer lived here for seven years, until Henry VIII expressed a desire to have the manor for a residence (" . . . as for Knole, it standeth on a sound, perfect and wholesome ground; and if I should make abode here, as I surely mind to do now and then, I will live at Knole"); Cranmer complied. The manor remained crown property until 1566, when Queen Elizabeth I gave it to a cousin, Thomas Sackville, the courtier, poet, and dramatist. Sackville purchased the estate freehold in 1603, and since that time Knole has belonged to the Sackville family.

Thomas Sackville, author of *A Mirror for Magistrates*, coauthor with Thomas Norton of *Gorboduc*, and Lord Treasurer under Elizabeth, spent thousands of pounds on the interior of the house, including importing Italian craftsmen for the plasterwork and carvings. A large part of the present interior fabric is thus his doing. Whether by accident or by design, Knole is linked to the passage of time: there are 7 courtyards (days per week), 52 staircases (weeks per year), 365 rooms (days per year), and, it is said, 1440 individual stairsteps (minutes per day).

It was from Thomas Sackville that the remainder of the Sackville family descended, a family which according to its most famous modern member, Victoria Sackville-West (born here on March 9, 1892), was "a race too prodigal, too amorous, too weak, too indolent, and too melancholy." Undoubtedly one of the best descriptions of the house and the family is her work *Knole and the Sackvilles*. There have been many illustrious visitors over the centuries. An early guest of the 2d Earl of Dorset was John Donne, who received the benefice at Sevenoaks in July 1616; he made an annual summer trip to Sevenoaks and usually stayed here at Knole with the earl. In the late 17th and early 18th centuries the 6th Earl, the patron of John Dryden, entertained numerous literary figures, including Dryden, William Wycherley, Alexander Pope, and Matthew Prior. It was this Sackville who paid Dryden's pension after William III dismissed him as Poet Laureate. The dining room where Sackville entertained is known as the Poets' Parlour, but it is not open to the public. Dante Gabriel Rossetti and Holman Hunt attempted to paint in the park of the estate when Rossetti was working on *The Meeting of Dante and Beatrice in the Garden of Eden*, but he found painting in the rain unpleasant. A much later frequent guest of Victoria Sackville-West's was Virginia Woolf, who was often here in the 1920s when the relationship between the two women flourished. Knole is the setting for *Orlando*, and the manuscript is preserved here.

KNOWLE, Warwickshire (pop. 2,535)   The distance between Knowle and Birmingham is generally stated to be 9½ miles, but in fact the village is only 4 miles from the southeast boundary of the growing urban mass. The village, though, has kept a measure of its former isolation and is especially proud of its timbered guild house and Grimshaw Hall, dating to the 16th and 17th centuries. Walter Savage Landor was sent to a school here in 1780, at the age of five, and remained until 1785, when he was sent to Rugby. Of his years here and of the school at the time very little is known.

KNOWSLEY, Lancashire (pop. 1,175)   Only a few miles southwest of Liverpool, Knowsley has become part of its urban area because of the infiltration of housing estates. The Hall, home of the Stanley family, the Earls of Derby, is now a 360-acre safari park with elephants, lions, hippopotamuses, and giraffes kept under "natural" conditions. It would be wrong, however, to think of this venture as solely a modern idea since a 19th-century Lord Stanley kept an extensive personal menagerie here. The Stanleys, who have occupied the estate since the 14th century, in fact ruled as kings of the Isle of Man from the 15th to the 18th century and have had a great deal of influence on English history as statemen and, especially, as warriors. One Stanley was a hero of Flodden Field and was immortalized by Sir Walter Scott in *Marmion:*

"Charge, Chester, charge! On, Stanley, on!"
Were the last words of Marmion.

The 5th Earl, Ferdinando, was a patron of the arts, owner of a company of actors, and the Amyntas of Edmund Spenser's "Colin Clout's Come Home Again."

In 1832 Edward Lear was invited by Lord Stanley (later 14th Earl of Derby) to come to Knowsley to live and to make drawings of his collection of animals. Lear kept diaries here but destroyed them, and, indeed, little is known of his time at the Hall. He did, though, comment:

The uniform apathetic tone assumed by lofty society irks me *dreadfully* . . . nothing I long for half so much as to giggle heartily and to hop on one leg down the great gallery—but I dare not.

He amused Lord Stanley's grandchildren and great-grandchildren (and probably himself) with drawings and nonsense verse. He worked here intermittently until 1837, and more than 100 of his drawings are in the library. Lear returned on other occasions, in 1841 working on *Views in Rome and Its Environs,* in 1845 working on a book on Abruzzi, and in 1849 and 1855 visiting. Another frequent 19th-century guest at Knowsley was Matthew Arnold.

In the 20th century Hilaire Belloc was here after telling his constituents in Salford that he would not stand a second time for Parliament; he was given the run of the library on this trip and on all subsequent visits. He noted it was "one of the most glorious libraries in Europe, and what is especially remarkable, really and properly kept up to date." And, he continued, it was "the most domestic, the most enwrapping library in Britain."

KNUTSFORD, Cheshire (pop. 6,500)   A market town near the Birken River 15 miles southwest of Manchester, Knutsford is a pleasant community with some old black-and-white houses and inns in its narrow streets. Inextricably linked with Elizabeth Gaskell, Knutsford was the place to which she was brought in 1811 as a thirteen-month-old child after her mother died. Elizabeth Cleghorn Stevenson was raised by her Aunt Lumb at Heathside (now Heathwaite House); marked by a plaque, the house of many windows stands at the top of the town overlooking the heath. The story of the journey in which two grandfathers take a motherless grandchild to Manchester from London appears in *Mary Barton*. The girl spent her childhood here, except for three years in school in Stratford-on-Avon, Warwickshire. On August 30, 1832, she married William Gaskell here at the Unitarian Chapel, a 17th-century brick structure with lattice-paned windows. Following a honeymoon in Wales, the couple settled in Manchester, but Mrs. Gaskell frequently returned to Knutsford. After her death at Holybourne, Hampshire, in 1865, she was buried in the Unitarian churchyard; the grave is marked by a simple cross, lilies of the valley, and rose trees. The King's Coffee House, a 20th-century building, contains a medallion portrait of Mrs. Gaskell and the titles of her works carved in stone.

Much of Mrs. Gaskell's writing, begun to counteract her grief at the death of her only son, concerns Knutsford which itself masquerades under various names. Knutsford, obviously, is Cranford in the novel of the same name, a village of lavender and lace, with "rules and regulations for visiting and calls" not to exceed a quarter of an hour and to be returned within three days. It was, as well,

> in possession of the Amazons; all the holders of houses above a certain rent are women. If a married couple come to settle in the town, somehow the gentleman disappears; he is either fairly frightened to death by being the only man in the Cranford evening parties, or he is accounted for by being with his regiment, his ship, or closely engaged in business all the week in the great neighbouring commercial town of Drumble, distant only twenty miles on a railroad. In short, whatever does become of the gentlemen, they are not at Cranford.

Mrs. Gaskell specifically uses a number of locations in the town, including Shire Lane, the George Inn, Darkness Lane, and the Assembly Rooms, and in this work Brook House stands near the chapel:

> That lady lived in a large house just outside the town.

A road, which had known what it was to be a street, ran right before the house, which opened out upon it without any intervening garden or court. Whatever the sun was about, he never shone on the front of that house.

The old shop in which Miss Matty sells tea is identified as a house at the top of the George Yard; from the window a "shower of comfits and lozenges . . . came from time to time down upon their [the children's] faces as they stood up-gazing at Miss Matty's drawing-room windows" after her long-lost brother Peter returns from India.

In *Ruth* the Brook Street Unitarian Chapel becomes Mr. Benson's Dissenting Chapel in Eccleston, and in *Wives and Daughters* Knutsford is Hollingsford. The old school described here is probably the one in Knutsford, which had indeed been a girls' school near the entrance to Cumnor Towers:

> The countess and the ladies, her daughters, had set up a school, not a school after the manner of schools nowadays . . . but a school of the kind we should call "industrial," where girls are taught to sew beautifully, to be capital housemaids, and pretty fair cooks, and, above all, to dress neatly in a kind of charity uniform devised by the ladies of Cumnor Towers. . . .

Cumnor Towers is based on Tatton Park, $3\frac{1}{2}$ miles to the north. The Royal George Hotel is where guests were charmed by

> the shining oak staircase and panelled wainscot, the old oak settles and cupboards, Chippendale cabinets, and old bits of china. . . .

Knutsford appears as Duncombe in "Mr. Harrison's Confession," as Eltham in "Cousin Phyllis," as Hamley in "A Dark Night's Work," and as Barford in "The Squire's Story." In the last-named short story about Edward Higgins, the highwayman, Mrs. Gaskell uses the old office of weights and measures on the heath. Thomas De Quincey also writes of Higgins in "Highwaymen."

A minor 20th-century association exists with Knutsford as well. In April 1911 John Galsworthy stayed here and frequented The King's Coffee House when commuting daily to Manchester for rehearsals of *The Little Dream*.

LACEY GREEN, Buckinghamshire (pop. 905) Alternatively spelled Lacy Green, this village lies along the ridge extending from Whiteleaf in southern Buckinghamshire. Here is the pub with the delightful name of the Pink and Lily Inn which was a favorite spot of Rupert Brooke and his friends before World War I. The pub displays photographs of Brooke and a few lines of doggerel written here.

LAKE DISTRICT, Cumberland, Westmorland, and part of Lancashire William Wordsworth describes the Lake District thus in *A Description of the Scenery of the Lakes in the North of England:*

> Days of unsettled weather, with partial showers, are very frequent; but the showers, darkening, or brightening, as they fly from hill to hill, are not less grateful to the eye than finely interwoven passages of gay and sad music are touching to the ear. Vapours exhaling from the lakes and meadows after sunrise, in a hot season, or, in moist weather, brooding upon the heights, or descending towards the valleys with inaudible motion, give a visionary character to everything around them.

The district itself is a compact area, about 25 miles wide and some 30 miles long, with a total area of about 900 square miles. In an incomparable setting in the Cumbrian Mountains, it contains more than sixty lakes and tarns and some of the highest mountains in England. The geology of the district is one of its most fascinating aspects, as innumerable visitors and residents have attested. Large Ice Age glaciers carved out the valleys, most of which are U-shaped, and the rubble from the glaciers, dammed up at the ends of the valleys, caused the formation of the characteristic district finger lake, long and narrow. The slopes into the valleys are smooth-surfaced because of the planing effect of the glaciers' movement, and each valley is separated from the next by high fells covered with short grass and a variety of shrubs. The valleys, in their turn, open out into low pasture and farm lands. From a central dome formed during the Miocene epoch, all the Lake District rivers radiate; the Ennerdale, Wasdale, Eskdale, Langdale, Easedale, Matterdale, and Borrowdale Rivers, for example, each rise near Scafell Peak. The rivers are unpolluted and generally unnavigable.

Habitation of the Lake District dates from Neolithic times, and evidence of religious edifices can be found in Castlerigg, near Keswick, and Long Meg and Her Daughters, in Little Salkeld. In the Bronze Age the area was on the major trading route between the Pennines and Ireland. Both the Eden and the Lune Valleys were British routes, and later Roman inhabitants found these valleys of special strategic importance. The Norse invaders found the Lake District particularly attractive because of the similarity to their Scandinavian homeland. After the Normans arrived, various parts of the district were fortified to hold back the Scots—indeed, border warfare had been endemic for centuries.

The main occupations in Cumbria (as the area has been known officially since the 1974 amalgamation act), besides a very extensive tourist business, are sheep raising in the uplands and agriculture in the more fertile lower valleys. Wildlife flourishes, although the introduction of pesticides and mechanization have taken a considerable toll, and includes daffodils, bracken, primroses, brier roses, ermine, foxes, and red deer. Trout and salmon are found in the waters, but their take is rigidly controlled.

The most notable of the literary figures, and the only indigenous poet, was William Wordsworth, who was born at Cockermouth, educated at Penrith and Hawkshead, lived at Grasmere and Rydal, where he died, and was buried in Grasmere churchyard. Wordsworth was in every corner of the district, and his works reflect this. Most important, possibly, is *The Prelude,* and the country concerned in Books I and II of that work is the area around Esthwaite

Water, Windermere, Coniston, the Old Man, and the Langdales. The eastern margin of Esthwaite Water on the road from Hawkshead to Sawtry is described thus:

> . . . I fixed my view
> Upon the summit of a craggy ridge,
> The horizon's utmost boundary; far above
> Was nothing but the stars and the grey sky.
> She was an elfin pinnace; lustily
> I dipped my oars into the silent lake,
> And, as I rose upon the stroke, my boat
> Went heaving through the water like a swan;
> When, from behind that craggy steep till then
> The horizon's bound, a huge peak, black and huge,
> As if with voluntary power instinct
> Upreared its head. . . .

Ironkeld Ridge is the "craggy ridge, / The horizon's utmost boundary," and the "huge peak, black and huge, / As if with voluntary power instinct" is the summit of Wetherlam.

The Wordsworthian references are clearly too numerous to list, but some seem especially apt. The stream in "The Fountain" is Hawkshead Beck; Windermere is described in *The Prelude* (Book II) and in "There Was a Boy"; Yewdale also comes into *The Prelude,* and the place where the boy hangs

> Above the raven's nest, by knots of grass
> And half-inch fissures in the slippery rock

is Holme Fells. Dove Cottage in Grasmere is specifically alluded to in many poems and is now a museum. Its orchard is even more frequently referred to: "Personal Talk" is probably the most intimately associated with it, but "A Farewell," "The Green Linnet," "To a Butterfly," "The Kitten and the Falling Leaves," and "The Redbreast Chasing the Butterfly" are also important. Grasmere Church and the attendant churchyard are carefully described in *The Excursion.* "Two heath-clad rocks" which Wordsworth describes

> . . . ascend
> In fellowship, the loftiest of the pair
> Rising to no ambitious height . . .

rise about 50 feet above the lower road from Grasmere to Rydal very near the third mile marker to Ambleside. "The Primrose of the Rock" is on the right-hand side of the vale from Rydal to Grasmere, closer to Rydal, and is also called the Glow Worm Rock because of the number of glowworms that Wordsworth and his sister Dorothy saw there. "The Waggoner" also refers to this now-roseless rock; close by the rock is the "pool base to the eye of heaven," where Wordsworth sees the leech gatherer ("Resolution and Independence"). Greenhead Ghyll, the scene of "Michael," is near Grasmere, and Loughrigg Tarn, on the south face of the fell, is the scene of the "Epistle to Sir George Beaumont." Many more sites have been located this precisely.

The Lake poets are, of course, the group most intimately associated with the area. Samuel Taylor Coleridge lived for a time at Greta Hall in Keswick, where he left his wife and family, and spent time with Wordsworth and his family on various occasions for periods ranging from a few days to a few months. Robert Southey, who ended up supporting a myriad of relatives under the roof of Greta Hall, first moved there in 1803 with his own family and his widowed sister-in-law and her child. Southey and his families lived there for the rest of their lives, and Southey was buried in the churchyard at Crosthwaite. Thomas De Quincey came to Grasmere first in 1808, at which time he met Wordsworth; he shared Allan Bank with the Wordsworths and Coleridge for a few months before taking possession of Dove Cottage. For a brief period he and his family lived at Rydal, but they returned to Grasmere and Dove Cottage, where they remained until 1830, when they moved permanently to Edinburgh.

Harriet Martineau, the author of a quite early and good *Complete Guide to the English Lakes,* came to Ambleside in 1845 and built The Knoll, her home until her death on June 27, 1876. She was buried in Birmingham. In 1871 John Ruskin bought Brantwood, overlooking Coniston Water and the mountain called Coniston Old Man, where he eventually adopted a life of seclusion; here Ruskin lived for

LAKE DISTRICT Tarn Hows, Lancashire, near Coniston, typifies the great beauty and variety of the Lake District. Near here John Ruskin lived from 1872 until his death in 1900.

twenty years and died on January 20, 1900; he was buried in the Coniston churchyard close to the school. Manesty, near Keswick, was the home of Sir Hugh Walpole from 1924 until his death on June 1, 1941; his "Herries" series, the chronicle of a district family, was begun there in 1927. Much to Walpole's consternation, he was never fully accepted as one of the natives because he lacked their blood, a point reiterated frequently in the Herries novels. He often attended services in Keswick at St. John's Church, where he was buried. He includes Keswick, Watendlath, Borrowdale, and Skiddaw in his works.

The resident 19th-century authors, of course, drew a host of visitors, but the area figures in earlier literature as well. The North Country's claim to King Arthur as a Strathclyde hero brings Arthurian legend to Cumbria, but the associations are not nearly so clear-cut here as they are in Cornwall. Penrith is the assumed location of the grave of the giant Torquin slain by Sir Launcelot at Eamont Bridge. The latter site is also the location of Arthur's Round Table, a natural feature of the landscape thought by Sir Walter Scott to have been a tournament field of sorts. Birdoswald, Cumberland, the Roman camp of Camboglanna, is held by the proponents of the northern Arthur school to be the site of Camblan, Arthur's last battle.

The early "travel" writers Camden, Leland, Drayton, and Defoe were all in the Lake District at one time or another and left their impressions of the landscape, weather, and people. Daniel Defoe writes:

Here, among the Mountains, our Curiosity was frequently moved to enquire what high Hill this was, or that; and we soon were saluted with that old Verse which I remembered to have seen in Mr. *Cambden*, viz.

Inglebrough, Pendle-hill *and* Penigent,
Are the highest Hills between Scotland *and* Trent.

Indeed, they were, in my Thoughts, monstrous high; but in a Country all mountainous and full of innumerable high Hills, it was not easy for a Traveller to judge which was highest.
Nor were these Hills high and formidable only, but they had a kind of unhospitable Terror in them.

He continues:

[W]e entred *Westmoreland,* a Country eminent only for being the wildest, most barren and frightful of any that I have passed over in *England,* or even in *Wales* it self; the West Side, which borders on *Cumberland,* is indeed bounded by a Chain of almost unpassable Mountains, which, in the Language of the Country, are called *Fells. . . .*

Thomas Gray began a fairly extensive tour of the Cumbrian lakes in July 1769 from York; his *Journal of a Tour in the Lakes* minutely describes his journey and feelings. Approaching Ulleswater, as he spells it, Gray comes to the area used in William Wordsworth's "I Wandered Lonely as a Cloud":

Walked over a spongy meadow or two, and began to mount this hill through a broad and straight green alley among the trees, and with some toil gained the summit. From hence saw the lake opening directly at my feet, majestic in its calmness, clear and smooth as a blue mirror, with winding shores and low points of land covered with green enclosures, white farmhouses looking out among the trees, and cattle feeding. The water is

almost everywhere bordered with cultivated lands gently sloping upwards till they reach the feet of the mountains, which rise very rude and awful with their broken tops on either hand.

Ten years later William Beckford toured the lakes from August to October. One of the most memorable sights, he claimed, was that at Morecambe Bay:

There was nothing wanting to complete noble landscape scenery. The land bordering upon the sands consisted of corn fields, green enclosures and woods, while churches, villages and romantic old castles were well dispersed over the picture. Sometimes we saw fine woods of oak and beech descending almost to the sands and sloping upwards to the mountains. Here a group of rocks frowned over some pretty bay, within which green islands shot up, continually varying their forms as we proceeded. We passed close to reefs and shoals—dark, jagged and fully exposed by the recession of the tide.

The late 18th and 19th centuries found virtually every important author attracted to the district. Sir Walter Scott was first here in 1797, taking a holiday in Gilsland; from this time on his trips to the area (Helvellyn and Bowness-on-Windermere) were frequent, and many local events, traditions, and scenes occur in his writings. Charles and Mary Lamb visited the lakes in 1802 and stayed with Coleridge in Keswick; they also tried to visit Wordsworth in Grasmere. The following year William Hazlitt first came to the lakes to paint portraits of Coleridge and his son Hartley in Keswick and of Wordsworth in Grasmere; this was the beginning of a fairly long association with the poets. Percy and Harriet Shelley were residents of Keswick for a few months in 1811 before they went to Ireland; in 1818 John Keats made an extensive tour of the Lake District, and in 1824 Charlotte Brontë attended school near Kirkby Lonsdale and later used the area as Lowton in *Jane Eyre*. Among other literary figures associated to some degree with Cumbria are Alfred, Lord Tennyson, Edward FitzGerald, Matthew Arnold, Edward Lear, Thomas Carlyle, and Beatrix Potter.

LALEHAM, Middlesex (pop. 775) The frequent references to Laleham as a Victorian backwater are unfair, for although this Thames-side village retains a great deal of its Victorian flavor, it is certainly not a backwater. The village has been the same for centuries because there is no room for expansion, located as it is in a crook of the Thames just south of Staines. Laleham is best known for the association with Matthew Arnold and his father, Dr. Thomas Arnold, who began his first private school here in 1819. Matthew was born here on December 24, 1822, in a house whose location has been marked by a cedar tree on Ashford Road. Dr. Arnold loved the area here and was reluctant to move to Rugby in 1828. There is little information about Matthew's early days here, but he did return to Laleham in the 1830s as a pupil in the school then managed by his uncle, the Rev. John Buckland. He made many later visits to Laleham, and his affection for the village dictated this as his burial place. Arnold died in Liverpool on April 15, 1888, and was buried here in the churchyard of All Saints; the grave, which is shared with his son Thomas (1852–1868) and his grandson, is tree-shaded and lies southeast of the church. The marble-margined site has a plain headstone with the inscription, "There is sprung up a light for the righteous and joyful gladness for such as are true-hearted."

LAMAS, Norfolk (pop. 216) Situated in the triangular Norfolk area between Norwich, Lowestoft, and Sea Palling known as the Broads, Lamas is 9 miles north of Norwich on the Bure River, which with its tributaries connects almost all the lakes. The proper name of the village is actually Lammas with Little Hautbois; the post office insists on the spelling Lamas. The village has a Quaker burial ground as well as the churchyard adjacent to the parish church, and in the former Anna Sewell was buried in 1878. The author of *Black Beauty,* published only one year before her death, Miss Sewell was crippled in early childhood by what has been described as a severe spraining of both ankles.

LAMBOURN, Berkshire (pop. 2,193) Close to the Wiltshire border and 8 miles north of Hungerford, Lambourn is situated on the Lambourn River in a hollow of the Berkshire Downs. It is a particularly attractive village with a 12th-century church and Victorian almshouses clustered around a flowered courtyard. The village appears in Charles Kingsley's *Two Years Ago* under the name Whitbury.

> "Is this Whitbury?" asked Stangrave.
> It was Whitbury, indeed. Pleasant old town, which slopes down the hill-side to the old church,—just "restored," ... to its ancient beauty of gray flint and white clunch checker-work, and quaint wooden spire. Pleasant churchyard round it, where the dead lie looking up to the bright southern sun, among huge black yews, upon their knoll of white chalk above the ancient stream. Pleasant white wooden bridge, with its row of urchins dropping flints upon the noses of elephantine trout, or fishing over the rail with crooked pins.... Pleasant new National School at the bridge end ... [It is] an ugly pile enough of bright red brick.... Pleasant, too, though still more ugly, those long red arms of new houses which Whitbury is stretching out along its fine turnpikes....

LANCASTER, Lancashire (pop. 47,720) In the 1086 Domesday survey, Lancaster was identified as a small hamlet near the great manor of Halton; now Halton virtually does not exist, and Lancaster is well known. Lancaster dates at least to Roman times, and some traces of the Romans' station and wall still exist. There is also evidence of extensive 7th- and 8th-century Anglo-Saxon settlement here. The medieval town, granted its charter in 1193, flourished until the Scots destroyed it, including the castle, in 1322 and again in 1389; John of Gaunt restored the castle, and his Gateway Tower is one of the finest in England. The town grew as a market town and in the 18th century had a brief period as a port before the Lune Estuary silted up.

When John Leland visited Lancaster in the 16th century, he noted in his *Itinerary:*

> Lancastre Castel on a hille strongly buildid and wel repaired. Ruines of an old place (as I remembre of the Catfelds) by the castel hille. The new toune (as thei ther say) buildid hard by yn the descent from the castel....

Only a short time later William Camden commented in his *Britannia:*

> Though it be at present but thinly peopled, and all the inhabitants farmers (the country about it being culti-

vated, open, flourishing and not bare of wood,) in proof of its Roman antiquity they sometimes find coins of emperors, especially at the friery. For that is said to be the site of the antient city, which the Scots burnt....

Even in the 18th century little was altered: Daniel Defoe writes in *A Tour thro' the Whole Island of Great Britain:*

> *Lancaster* is the next, the County Town, and situate near the Mouth of the River *Lone* or *Lune.* The Town is antient; it lies, as it were, in its own Ruins, and has little to recommend it but a decayed Castle, and a more decayed Port ... but, as before, here is little or no Trade, and few People.

For all its history, few important authors have had anything to do with Lancaster. John Keats was here in May 1818, when he and Charles Armitage Brown were beginning their walking tour of the lakes. The town was in the midst of preparing for a parliamentary election, and Keats was annoyed by the rowdiness and the ruffians and by the two-hour wait for dinner. He and Brown left the next morning at 7:00 A.M. for Bolton-le-Sands, where they breakfasted. A later visitor, John Ruskin, stayed at the King's Arms.

LANDGUARD POINT, Suffolk The East Anglia coastline from Felixstowe in the south to Kessingland in the north is a crumbling mass of stone and beach, buffeted by high winds, flooded by the sea, and invaded repeatedly. Whole towns, such as Dunwich and Slaughden, have been swept out to sea, and large parts of others have been destroyed. Just southeast of Harwich is the appropriately named Landguard Point, a headland forming the most southerly part of Suffolk and guarding the mouth of the Orwell River. This is a desolate, moorlike area with cold easterly gale-force winds sweeping across it, and a less appropriate place for Sir Richard Steele cannot be imagined. With the rank of captain in the 2d Baron Lucas's newly formed regiment, he was stationed here shortly after the death of William III. Steele endured the isolated existence for only a few months and then, pulling rank, took lodgings in the nearby village of Walton, which is essentially part of Felixstowe.

LANGAR CUM BARNSTON, Nottinghamshire Langar cum Barnston, an ecclesiastical amalgamation of two parishes, lies 9 miles southeast of Nottingham and possesses the notable 13th-century Church of St. Andrew, often referred to as the Cathedral in the Vale. The vale is the Vale of Belvoir (pronounced "beaver"), and the church overlooks the area from an open field. The Langar rectory, a Georgian house of ivy-covered brick, was the birthplace of Samuel Butler on December 4, 1835; the house, situated on a slight rise, is now called Langar House. *The Way of All Flesh,* Butler's posthumously published autobiographical novel, refers to Langar as Battersby-on-the-Hill, the place to which the Rev. Theobald Pontifex (Canon Butler) and his new bride come:

> Battersby-on-the-Hill was the name of the village of which Theobald was now rector. It contained 400 or 500 inhabitants, scattered over a rather large area, and consisting entirely of farmers and agricultural labourers. The rectory was commodious, and placed on the brow of a hill which gave it a delightful prospect.

The church, as the Butler family first knew it,

was then an interesting specimen of late Norman, with some early English additions. It was what in these days would be called in a very bad state of repair, but forty or fifty years ago few churches were in good repair.

The misery of the childhood Butler spent here made him determine never to raise any children of his own and, indeed, never to marry. Young Butler suffered extremely at the hands of his parents, especially his father, who strongly believed that education must involve harsh physical discipline:

> When Ernest was in his second year, Theobald, as I have already said, began to teach him to read. He began to whip him two days after he had begun to teach him.
>
> "It was painful," as he said to Christina, but it was the only thing to do and it was done. The child was puny, white and sickly, so they sent continually for the doctor, who dosed him with calomel and James's powder. All was done in love, anxiety, timidity, stupidity, and impatience. They were stupid in little things; and he that is stupid in little will be stupid also in much.

After leaving Cambridge, having been destined to take orders, Butler fought bitterly with his father and emigrated to New Zealand.

LANGDALE, GREAT, and LANGDALE, LITTLE, Westmorland

Two valleys are separated by Lingmoor Fell and overlooked by the impressive Langdale Pikes. Great and Little Langdale have a background of lofty fells, including Bow Fell, 2,960 feet, and Crinkle Crags, 2,818 feet. Extending 3½ miles east to Elterwater, where it joins Great Langdale, Little Langdale descends from Wrynose Pass, the meeting point of Westmorland, Cumberland, and Lancashire, to the head of Windermere. This is the lower of the two dales, and its natural scenery is in proportion, for the lakes, waterfalls, and woodlands are smaller. Here is Loughrigg Tarn on the southern face of Loughrigg Fell, which William Wordsworth describes minutely in "Epistle to Sir George Beaumont":

> Ah, Beaumont! when an opening in the road
> Stopped me at once by charm of what it showed,
> The encircling region vividly exprest
> Within the mirror's depth, a world at rest—
> Sky streaked with purple, grove and craggy *bield*,
> And the smooth green of many a pendent field
> And, quieted and soothed, a torrent small,
> A little daring, would-be waterfall.
> One chimney smoking and its azure wreath,
> Associate all in the calm Pool beneath,
> With here and there a faint imperfect gleam
> Of water-lilies veiled in misty steam. . . .

A second poem associated with the tarn is a fragment begun in July or August 1844 after a visit during which Wordsworth discovered what appeared to be a dark-shaped and sharply defined fossil on the smooth stone; the fossil, in fact, was the shadow of a daisy, said a member of the party, "projected upon it with extraordinary precision by the intense light of an almost vertical sun":

> So fair, so sweet, withal so sensitive,
> Would that the little Flowers were born to live,
> Conscious of half the pleasure that they give;
>
> That to this mountain-daisy's self was known
> The beauty of its star-shaped shadow, thrown
> On the smooth surface of this naked stone!

The Excursion also deals with Little Langdale; "The Solitary" makes his home here near Blea Tarn, and the narrator and the Pedlar make their way across Little Langdale.

Great Langdale extends 5 miles southeast from Three Shire Stone on the Cumberland border to Elterwater and follows the highest mountain ridges which surround the vale. Here, where the villages are few and small, is one of the best-known localities associated with Wordsworth: Dungeon Ghyll is the scene of "The Idle Shepherd Boys; or, Dungeon-Ghyll Force":

> It was a spot which you may see
> If ever you to Langdale go;
> Into a chasm a mighty block
> Hath fallen, and made a bridge of rock:
> The gulf is deep below:
> And, in a basin black and small,
> Receives a lofty waterfall.

The fall itself is about 90 feet high. Samuel Taylor Coleridge mentions Dungeon Ghyll and Langdale Pike in "Christabel."

LANGHAM, Norfolk (pop. 283)

Just a few miles inland from the sea and with salt marshes only a few miles away, Langham is 5 miles northwest of Holt; it is also known as Langham Bishops. From 1843 on Langham Manor Cottage (razed in 1883) was the home of Capt. Frederick Marryat, author of *Mr. Midshipman Easy* and numerous other works; he had bought the property in 1830 before his extensive travels in Belgium, Canada, and the United States following his early retirement from the Royal Navy. When he decided to settle here, he devoted a great deal of time to writing and introduced scientific farming methods to turn a profit. His books prospered, but his farm did not. His heavy writing program took its toll of his never very healthy constitution, and the Admiralty's refusal to reinstate him in the Navy precipitated his death. In a raging fury over its decision, he burst a blood vessel in his lungs and almost killed himself. The death of his eldest son, Frederick, some six months later broke him completely, and he died here on August 9, 1848. Captain Marryat was buried in the churchyard, and the Burne-Jones window is a memorial.

LANGLEY MILL, Derbyshire (pop. 4,536)

Near the Derbyshire-Nottinghamshire border but definitely in Derbyshire, Langley Mill is considered to belong to Eastwood, Nottinghamshire, of which it is essentially a part. The village, on the Erewash River 3 miles north of Ilkeston, is deep in the colliery district. The Eastwood area is associated with D. H. Lawrence and his novels, in which Langley Mill appears in several guises. It is Lumley in *The Lost Girl;* the story begins here and at Woodhouse (Eastwood). Lawrence's description of Lumley is anything but flattering:

> It was a long straggle of a dusty road down in the valley, with a pale grey dust and spatter from the pottery, and big chimneys bellying forth black smoke right by the road. Then there was a short cross-way, up which one saw the iron foundry, a black and rusty place. A little further on was the railway junction and beyond that more houses stretching to Hathersedge, where the stocking factories were busy. Compared with Lumley, Wood-

house, whose church could be seen sticking up proudly and vulgarly as an eminence, above trees and meadow-slopes, was an idyllic heaven.

The village is also where James Haughton makes his final attempt at gaining a fortune by beginning a cinematograph. In *Sons and Lovers*, Langley Mill appears under its own name when Paul Morel and his friends take an excursion to the manor house at Wingfield (South Wingfield) and also appears as Sethley Bridge, where the group catch "a train . . . amid all the bustle of the Bank Holiday crowd."

LARTINGTON, Yorkshire (pop. 179) This tiny village in the North Riding of Yorkshire, 2 miles north-west of Barnard Castle, County Durham, is interesting primarily because of the claim that the original "Master Humphrey's Clock" which intrigued Charles Dickens at Barnard Castle is now in the railway station here.

LAUNCESTON, Cornwall (pop. 3,979) On the Kensey River near its confluence with the Ottery and Tamar Rivers, Launceston (pronounced "lawn' ston") became a military stronghold under the Normans because its location between the tidal Tamar River and the north coast made it the key to the duchy of Cornwall. The first structure here, probably wooden at least in part, was replaced with a completely stone building in the 13th century by Richard, Earl of Cornwall. From the reign of Edward the Black Prince until the present day, the castle (whose keep is well preserved) has remained in the hands of the Dukes of Cornwall.

In 1538 John Leland, Henry VIII's librarian and antiquarian, visited Launceston. Crossing the Tamar at New Bridge, he passed the Augustinian priory "by a fair wood side" and entered the town through one of the medieval gates. He records his impression of the castle:

> The large and auncient castelle of Launstun stondith on the knappe of the hille by south litle from the paroche chirch. Much of this castel yet stondith: and the moles that the kepe stonde [*th on*] is large and of a terrible highth.

In the market square is the White Hart Hotel, once one of the most famous coaching inns in the West Country with a reputation for exceptionally good food. This hotel, now a Trust House, accommodated Robert Southey on his West Country trip in 1802. The open courtyard into which Southey's coach pulled is now the glass-roofed main lounge, and around the lounge playbills dated 1772 once were posted. Southey had left Falmouth in the morning and, with one stop to change horses and two for food, reached Launceston by six o'clock that evening: "What a country for travelling is this! Such rapidity on the roads! Such accommodation at the resting places! We advanced fourteen leagues to-day without fatigue or exertion."

Thomas Hardy was first in Launceston on his way to St. Juliot in March 1870; he left the train here and hired a horse-drawn four-wheeler to take him on. The town becomes St. Launce's in his works and is most prominently used in *A Pair of Blue Eyes*. Stephen Smith first leaves the train here, just as did Hardy, on his way to Endelstow (St. Juliot). Elfride Swancourt, on her way to meet Stephen in Plymouth, rides here on Pansy to catch the train: "Presently the quaint gables and jumbled roofs of St. Launce's were spread beneath her, and going down the hill she entered the courtyard of the Falcon." The Falcon Hotel, kept by Mrs. Buckle, is drawn from the White Hart. Among the other places in Launceston which Hardy mentions are a bank, where Stephen's £200 deposit is placed, the castle ruins, the town hall, and Hill Street. A poem written after his Cornish pilgrimage in 1913, "St. Launce's Revisited," recalls Hardy's first excursion in the area; the inn is probably the White Hart:

> At the inn
> Smiling high, why is it
> Not as on my visit
>   When hope and I were twin?
> . . . .
> Here I hired
> Horse and man for bearing
> Me on my wayfaring
>   To the door desired.

The "desired" door was that of the rectory in St. Juliot, where Emma Lavinia Gifford lived; this was the woman who was to become Hardy's first wife.

LAVANT, EAST, and LAVANT, MID, Sussex (pop. 697) Both these hamlets, on the Lavant River 2½ miles north of Chichester, belong to the same parish, but each has its own church. Mid Lavant, which is largely sprawled along the roadway, lacks some of the charm of East Lavant, but its literary association more than makes up for any defects. Here, at a cottage owned by a Mrs. Poole, William Blake was a frequent visitor from Felpham, and it was to Mid Lavant that he and his party came after his acquittal on charges of treason in Chichester in 1804.

LAVENHAM, Suffolk (pop. 1,305) In the heart of what is still an important agricultural area, Lavenham, one of the loveliest preserved towns in England, represents the high point of the wool trade. Its early wealth is apparent in the large number of richly decorated homes and in the fine medieval timbered houses, especially the Guild Hall (which has served both as a prison and as an almshouse) and the Wool Hall (a covered market now effectively incorporated into the Swan Hotel). Henry VIII, to support his war against France, imposed heavy taxes upon the woolen industry and, not incidentally, on the workers; extensive rioting took place here in 1525. This is the case which Thomas Howard, 3d Duke of Norfolk, who lived in nearby Framlingham, pleads to the King in William Shakespeare's *Henry VIII*:

> The clothiers all, not able to maintain
> The many to them longing, have put off
> The spinsters, carders, fullers, weavers, who
> Unfit for other life, compell'd by hunger
> And lack of other means, are all in uproar
> And danger serves among them.

But trade declined, and even with Queen Elizabeth's attempts to restore the industry (it was decreed that every deceased Englishman was to be wrapped in a woolen shroud), Lavenham, like the other wool towns, slipped quietly out of sight. Today it supports itself with the tourist trade, and antique shops abound.

Shilling Old Grange on Shilling Street was the home of the Taylor Family, whose main contribution to literature will never be forgotten even though the name of the author is seldom remembered. Here in 1806 Jane and Ann Taylor composed *Rhymes for the Nursery*, which includes the verse (composed by Jane) which every child knows, "Twinkle, Twinkle, Little Star." A second house in the village erroneously claims this distinction; Jane Taylor did, in fact, live in this house after some years in London, but the verses were written before her stay there.

LAVINGTON   *See* LENTON.

LAW HILL, Yorkshire   Law Hill is not a location in the usual sense of the word; rather, it is a seat on Southowarm Bank, 1½ miles east of Halifax. It was to the hall that Emily Brontë came in 1837 as a teacher in Miss Patchett's school, then located here; how long she remained at the post is debatable. It may have been as short a time as six months or as long as eighteen; nevertheless, she missed Haworth intensely, as the poems written here reflect:

What language can utter the feeling
  Which rose, when in exile afar,
On the brow of a lonely hill kneeling,
  I saw the brown heath growing there?

It was scattered and stunted, and told me
  That soon even that would be gone:
It whispered, "The grim walls enfold me,
  I have bloomed in my last summer's sun."

The influence of this period upon her literary life is striking: most of the background material for *Wuthering Heights* came from this experience. Earnshaw was the name of a fellow teacher, the history of the owners of Law Hill provided the story, and Wuthering Heights was modeled on nearby High Sutherland and its situation. The house sat on a "bleak hill-top [of] . . . earth [that] was hard with black frost." Because of its exposed hilltop location, "the architect had foresight to build it strong: the narrow windows are deeply set in the wall, and the corners defended with large jutting stones. . . . [G]rotesque carving [was] lavished over the front, and especially about the principal door. . . ."

LEAMINGTON, Warwickshire (pop. 44,989)   Situated 2 miles east of Warwick on the Leam River, Leamington (pronounced "lem'ington") or, to give it its proper title, Royal Leamington Spa is almost a new town in that it had virtually no history or population until the end of the 18th century. Its history begins in 1786, when one hot and one cold bath were opened for a few invalid visitors; at that time Leamington was so obscure that mail coaches came no closer than Warwick. Two centuries earlier, however, William Camden, whose family had property here, noted a saline spring in his *Britannia*:

. . . also *Leamington,* so called from the little river *Leam,* which waters this part of the county, where is a salt spring.

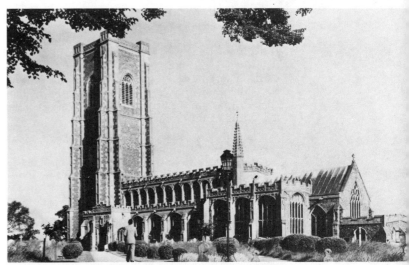

LAVENHAM   This clerestoried church built with profits from the wool trade (as was much of the village of Lavenham) was attended by Jane and Ann Taylor during their childhood.

Shortly after the first spring was opened, a more spacious system of baths was developed from a new well, and Leamington quickly became well known (although not greatly frequented) as a spa. Even in 1800 no more than 300 people lived in the town, but the springs continued to well up, and a rapid building program ensued. The Parade was built between 1810 and 1830, and the Pump Room came into being in 1814. The visit of the Prince Regent in 1819 helped publicize the town, and sometime before 1830 the Regent Hotel became fashionable, for in that year the Duchess of Kent and her eleven-year-old daughter, Princess Victoria, stayed there. It was probably this visit that eventually permitted the affixing of Royal to the town's name.

Two miles east of Leamington is the renowned Midland Oak; said to be 900 years old, the tree is traditionally held to mark the center of England. This is "that Crosse" in Michael Drayton's *Poly-Olbion:*

Hence, Muse, divert thy course to *Dunsmore,* by that Crosse
Where those two mightie waies, the *Watling* and the *Fosse,*
Our Center seeme to cut.

Literary associations with Royal Leamington Spa do not begin until it gained its 19th century reputation. Charles Lamb was one of the first visitors, in August 1819; coming here from Cambridge, he visited the circulating library, where he first met the subject of his essay "Ellistoniana":

My first introduction to E., which afterwards ripened into an acquaintance a little on this side of intimacy, was over a counter of the Leamington Spa Library, then newly entered upon by a branch of his family. . . . With what an air did he reach down the volume, dispassionately giving his opinion upon the worth of the work in question, and launching out into a dissertation on its comparative merits with those of certain publications of a similar stamp, its rivals! his enchanted customers fairly hanging on his lips, subdued to their authoritative sentence. So have I seen a gentleman in comedy *acting* the shopman.

Robert Smith Surtees often stayed in Leamington when he hunted with Mr. Thornhill's Warwickshire Hounds; he and Thornhill first stayed in the Royal Hotel (one of the three main hotels), but discovering that the port decanters held only three-quarters of a bottle of port, he decided to try the Bedford, then run by a Mr. Gumm. Surtees's opinion of the Bedford appeared in print in the *New Sporting Magazine* in the spring of 1824:

> As to the Bedford, BY GUMM, no one should think of going there who has not a hardy constitution and a long purse: and the large hotels are too numerous and too empty to spare many guests for the small ones. Still we can hardly say that we are sorry for the inn-keepers, for there certainly never were a more rapacious set gathered together, as every person that has ever had any dealings with them can testify. Their delinquencies have led to the formation of a club.

All the hotels ignored the attack except one, and Gumm, in accordance with the law, entered a suit against the printer, Rudolph Ackermann, first asking damages of £500 and later raising the sum to £1,000. Counsel for the magazine did a superbly witty job in the defense, but the Lord Chief Justice summed up for the plaintiff, and the jury obediently found for Gumm and assessed damages at 1 farthing. Leamington probably became part of the setting of Surtees's *Handley Cross*.

John Ruskin paid several visits during 1840–1841 and 1847; under the care of Dr. Henry Jephson, the most fashionable physician of the period, Ruskin had long been in ill health and was sent here to take the cure. He stayed at the Bedford Hotel before taking lodgings at 53 Russell Terrace. In 1838 Charles Dickens and Phiz (Hablot Knight Browne) arrived in Leamington from London and stayed at Copp's Royal Hotel, where after a very cold journey they found "a roaring fire, an elegant dinner, a snug room, and capital beds" awaiting them. They stayed only one night before going on to Warwick and Kenilworth, but Dickens's impressions were such that he later used the hotel in *Dombey and Son*:

> [I]n this flow of spirits and conversation, the Major continued all day: so that when evening came on, and found them trotting through the green and leafy road near Leamington, the Major's voice, what with talking and eating and chuckling and choking, appeared to be in the box under the rumble, or in some neighbouring haystack. Nor did the Major improve it at the Royal Hotel. . . .

Copp's Royal Hotel was demolished in 1847 to make way for the railway line to Rugby.

Another author to use Leamington and Copp's Royal Hotel was William Makepeace Thackeray, who set "Dennis Haggarty's Wife" in *Men's Wives* here; Jemima Amelia Wilhelmina Molloy Gam, a rather selfish, heartless, and ill-bred woman, does her husband hunting here:

> There was an odious Irishwoman and her daughter who used to frequent the Royal Hotel at Leamington some years ago, and who went by the name of Mrs. Major Gam. Gam had been a distinguished officer in his Majesty's service, whom nothing but death and his own amiable wife could overcome. The widow mourned her husband in the most becoming bombasine she could muster, and had at least half an inch of lamp-black round the immense visiting tickets which she left at the houses of the nobility and gentry her friends.

Nathaniel Hawthorne, American Consul in Liverpool from 1853 to 1858, was frequently in Leamington and when here usually lived at 10 Lansdowne Crescent, near the town hall. *Our Old Home* contains an extensive section on "Leamington Spa," for it was one of Hawthorne's favorite places.

One of the most famous modern associations of the spa is with John Betjeman's poem "Death in Leamington":

> She died in the upstairs bedroom
>   By the light of the ev'ning star
> That shone through the plate glass window
>   From over Leamington Spa.
>
> Beside her the lonely crochet
>   Lay patiently and unstirred,
> But the fingers that would have work'd it
>   Were dead as the spoken word.
>
> And Nurse came in with the tea-things
>   Breast high 'mid the stands and chairs—
> But Nurse was alone with her own little soul,
>   And the things were alone with theirs.

LEATHERHEAD, Surrey (pop. 27,269) Situated on the historic route from London to the south coast, Leatherhead is an attractive old country town on the Mole River 4 miles southwest of Epsom and 18 miles southwest of London. It has narrow streets, gabled Tudor houses, and the Running Horse Inn (ca. 1520), which stands near the bridge over the Mole and has served ale for more than 400 years. Some badly chosen restoration, including an unattractive modern refacing, has changed the inn considerably, but it is still the Tudor alehouse that the poet John Skelton knew when he came here from the court at Nonsuch to fish. This is the inn that prompted "The Tunnyng [Brewing] of Elynour Rummyng"; in August 1525 the local ale taster certified that Alinora Romyng, common tippler of ale, was selling "at excessive price by small measures," and she was fined accordingly. Alinora's face, Skelton wrote,

> . . . would aswage
> A mannes courage.
>
>   Her lothely lere
> Is nothynge clere,
> But vgly of chere,
> Droupy and drowsy,
> Scuruy and lowsy;
> Her face all bowsy,
> Comely crynklyd,
> Wounderslly wrynkled,
> Lyke a rost pygges eare,
> Brystled wyth here.

Richard Brinsley Sheridan lived at Randell's Farm, across from the cemetery entrance, for fifteen months in 1808 and 1809 and delighted in fishing in the nearby Mole. After his death on July 8, 1933, at Heath Farm, Walton-on-the-Hill, Surrey, Anthony Hope, as Sir Anthony Hope Hawkins was known, was buried in the parish churchyard here.

LECHLADE, Gloucestershire (pop. 1,034) The Thames River flows nearby and the Leach and Coln flow into this village, 24 miles west of Oxford; Lechlade was once involved in heavy barge traffic between

LECHLADE   Rowing up the Thames from Windsor in 1815, Percy Bysshe Shelley, Thomas Love Peacock, and Mary Godwin stopped here at the Trout Inn (probably), where Peacock insisted that Shelly eat well-peppered mutton chops to restore his vitality.

the Thames and the Severn, but much of this activity is gone. The 15th-century church was built partly of stone quarried from an ancient priory, and some of the clerestory windows contain fragments of the original glass. In 1815 Percy Bysshe Shelley, Mary Godwin, and Thomas Love Peacock rowed up the Thames from Windsor and stayed at the inn here for a couple of days. Shelley's "A Summer Evening Churchyard" was inspired by the Lechlade Church and its pathway to the river:

> The dead are sleeping in their sepulchres:
> And, mouldering as they sleep, a thrilling sound,
> Half sense, half thought, among the darkness stirs,
> Breathed from their wormy beds all living things around,
> And mingling with the still night and mute sky
> Its awful hush is felt inaudibly.

LEDBURY, Herefordshire (pop. 3,154) An old market town almost equidistant from Hereford (13 miles northwest), Worcester (16 miles northeast), and Gloucester (17 miles southeast), Ledbury is set among pastures and streams in a broad plain east of the Wye River, an area that is picturesque rather than beautiful. Located as it is on the west side of outliers of the Malvern Hills, the town is an excellent base from which to explore the surrounding countryside. Ledbury has changed little over the years: the 17th-century timbered Market House is still supported by its original oak posts, and crowding both sides of Church Lane are the black-and-white timbered houses which lead to the partly Norman church with its "golden vane surveying half the shire."

The earliest literary association here is only a claim: Ledbury often asserts that it was the birthplace of William Langland around 1330. However, a more likely birthplace is Cleobury Mortimer, Shropshire. The association with William Wordsworth is far more tenable; he visited here numerous times on his stays at Brinsop Court (5½ miles southeast), where his brother-in-law Thomas Hutchinson and his wife lived. On one of these occasions he learned

of the legend of St. Katherine of Ledbury and wrote his sonnet on the subject:

> When human touch (as monkist books attest)
> Nor was applied nor could be, Ledbury bells
> Broke forth in concert flung adown the dells,
> And upward, high as Malvern's cloudy crest;
> Sweet tones, and caught by a noble Lady blest
> To rapture! Mabel listened at the side
> Of her loved mistress: soon the music died,
> And Catherine said, Here I set up my rest.
> Warned in a dream, the Wanderer long had sought
> A home that by such miracle of sound
> Must be revealed:—she heard it now, or felt
> The deep, deep joy of a confiding thought;
> And there, a saintly Anchoress, she dwelt
> Till she exchanged for heaven that happy ground.

Elizabeth Barrett Browning and Robert Browning were also visitors; as a child, Elizabeth Barrett lived at Hope End, near Colwall, and both her parents are buried here.

Ledbury's most famous native is the Poet Laureate John Masefield, who was born on June 1, 1878, at The Knapps. He obtained some education locally before going to King's School, Warwick, from which he was apprenticed at the age of fourteen aboard a windjammer sailing around Cape Horn. He never lost his love for this town, "pleasant to the sight, / Fair and half-timbered houses black and white," or for his native shire; and many of his later poems recall the surrounding countryside, where he never heard "the west wind but tears are in my eyes." The wind

> . . . comes from the west lands, the old brown hills,
> And April's in the west wind, and daffodils.

> It's a fine land, the west land, for hearts as tired as mine,
> Apple orchards blossom there, and the air's like wine.
> There is cool green grass there, where men may lie at rest,
> And the thrushes are in song there, fluting from the nest.

Perhaps even more revealing of his love is "London Town"; even though "London Town's a fine town"

LEDBURY The black-and-white timbered houses which line both sides of Church Lane are those which John Masefield, a native of Ledbury, called "pleasant to the sight."

and "London ale is right," it is the one town he is "glad to leave behind"; his strongest desire is

> . . . for the road, the west road, by mill and forge and fold,
> Scent of the fern and song of the lark by brook, and field and wold,
> To the comely folk at the hearth-stone and the talk beside the fire,
> In the hearty land, where I was bred, my land of heart's desire.

LEEDS, Yorkshire (pop. 457,081) A city, a county borough, and a parliamentary borough returning six Members of Parliament, Leeds is an excellent example of what the industrial revolution could do in typical Yorkshire sheep country. Sheep have always grazed high on the Yorkshire moors, and farming families have always sheared, spun, and woven wool. When machinery was introduced, cottage-industry work declined, and the manufacture of worsteds and woolens moved to the mills on the banks of the Aire, Colne, and Calder Rivers. When steam power was introduced and the use of coal and water became necessary for efficient production, Leeds found itself ideally located. No matter where in the city one is, there is extensive evidence of industrial affluence, from the rather flamboyant architecture of the Infirmary and the Corn Exchange to the little-known but decidedly fantastic Temple Mill with its east facade done up like an Egyptian temple.

Leeds is probably the model for the town of Millcote in Charlotte Brontë's *Jane Eyre.* Her description makes the identification seem inevitable: "Millcote was a large manufacturing town on the banks of the

A—[Aire]: a busy place enough, doubtless; so much the better; it would be a complete change at least." Mary Ann Evans (George Eliot) also may have found the town a change, but she did not have any pleasant memories of it following her visit in 1868. She comments in a letter: "We do not often see a place which is a good foil for London, but certainly Leeds is in a lower circle of the great town—Inferno." She refers to the city in her works only in passing: Dinah Morris in *Adam Bede* comes to Leeds "to visit a holy woman that preaches there."

Leeds was the birthplace of the now-little-read Alfred Austin; born on May 30, 1835, into a strong Roman Catholic family, he became Poet Laureate upon the death of Alfred, Lord Tennyson in 1892. The post was undoubtedly gained through his flattery of Lord Salisbury, and his official verse has been termed "memorably bad."

In 1916 John Galsworthy spent some time here when he was interested in the case of George Sauter, who was imprisoned as an enemy alien in Lofthouse Park internment camp at Wakefield. While preparing the case he was eventually to plead before the Home Office Advisory Committee, Galsworthy stayed at the Queens Hotel on City Square.

LEICESTER, Leicestershire (pop. 263,000) The county seat, a university center, a cathedral city, and a heavily industrial district, Leicester (pronounced "les'ter") stands on the navigable Soar River in an area of access routes in all directions. While its known history dates from about A.D. 52, Geoffrey of Monmouth tells of a pre-Roman foundation here by the son of Bladud:

> After Bladud had met his fate in this way [trying to fly], his son Leir was raised to the kingship. Leir ruled the country for sixty years. It was he who built the city on the River Soar which is called Kaerleir after him in the British tongue, its Saxon name being Leicester. He had no male issue, but three daughters were born to him. Their names were Goneril, Regan and Cordelia.

Geoffrey concludes the story with Leir's death in Gaul and Cordelia's bringing Leir's body home for burial. This is, of course, the story used by William Shakespeare in *King Lear,* and it may even be true that the dramatist meant Leicester for the opening scene of the play, "A Room of State in King Lear's Palace." History differs somewhat from this account, and there is no evidence of any large pre-Roman settlement here.

The city has seen its share of English history, from the meeting in 1201 of the outraged barons, a meeting which eventually resulted in the Magna Carta, to the place where Thomas Cardinal Wolsey, stripped of power, died. The 12th-century Abbey of St. Mary de Pratis is in ruins now, but the site of the Lady Chapel is traditionally pointed out as containing Wolsey's grave. Shakespeare has Griffith describe Wolsey's death to Queen Katharine in *Henry VIII:*

> At last, with easy roads, he came to Leicester,
> Lodg'd in the abbey; where the reverend abbot,
> With all his covent, honourably receiv'd him;
> To whom he gave these words,—*O, father abbot,*
> *An old man, broken with the storms of state,*
> *Is come to lay his weary bones among ye;*
> *Give him a little earth for charity!*

So went to bed; where eagerly his sickness
Pursu'd him still: and three nights after this,
About the hour of eight,—which he himself
Foretold should be his last,—full of repentance,
Continual meditations, tears, and sorrows,
He gave his honours to the world again,
His blessed part to heaven, and slept in peace.

On May 28, 1645, during the Civil War, Prince Rupert and Sir Marmaduke Langdale attacked the town, and by May 31 it had fallen. The young John Bunyan took part in the three-day siege, and tradition maintains that the death of a young man who had taken his place on guard duty brought about Bunyan's conversion. There is no proof of which side he fought on, and a fruitless debate has raged for years as to which side would have been more acceptable. Indeed, the account linking Bunyan and the siege of Leicester has been proved incorrect in its description of the battle. One certain connection of Bunyan with Leicester does exist: soon after his license to preach was approved on May 9, 1672, he was here to hold services.

William Cobbett was in Leicester on the Midland tour included in his *Rural Rides*. He arrived on April 25, 1830, and noted:

Leicester is a very fine town; spacious streets, fine inns, fine shops, and containing, they say, thirty or forty thousand people. It is well stocked with gaols, of which a new one, in addition to the rest, has just been built, covering three acres of ground! And, as if *proud* of it, the grand portal has little turrets in the castle style, with *embrasures* in miniature on the caps of the turrets. . . . Our forefathers built abbeys and priories and churches, and they made such use of them that gaols were nearly unnecessary.

This was not Daniel Defoe's impression; he is not nearly so socially conscious as Cobbett:

Leicester is an ancient large and populous Town. . . . They have a considerable Manufacture carry'd on here, and in several of the Market Towns round here for Weaving of Stockings by Frames; and one would scarce think it possible so small an Article of Trade could employ such Multitudes of People as it does; for the whole County seems to be employ'd in it. . . .

Another earlier association is with Jonathan Swift, whose mother was a native of this area. She was a Leicestershire Herrick and a relation of the poet Robert Herrick, whose father lived here. After the death of his uncle Godwin Swift in 1688 and the receipt of his degree at Trinity College, Dublin, young Swift was frequently here as a visitor, although he strongly disliked what he termed the "meddlesome gossip" in this very provincial city. A 1692 letter to the Rev. John Kendall expresses his feelings:

The people is a lying sort of beast (and I think in Leicester above all parts that ever I was in).

In spite of his dislike of Leicester, he visited his mother here until her death in 1710. With other members of the Herrick family she is buried in St. Martin's Church.

LEIGHTON, Shropshire (pop. 234) A tranquil village on the Severn River 3½ miles north of Much Wenlock, Leighton has a Georgian house and church and clipped yews everywhere. Leighton Lodge was the birthplace of Mary Webb on March 25, 1881; the daughter of a Welsh schoolmaster, she was first educated privately at home before being sent to a Southport school for two years. Miss Webb spent almost her entire life in Shropshire, and *Precious Bane* and *Gone to Earth* both deal with the shire. Bonmere Pool, 3 miles south of Shrewsbury, is the Sarn Mere of *Precious Bane.*

LEIGHTON BROMSWOLD, Huntingdonshire (pop. 242) An exposed village high on the Huntingdonshire wolds, Leighton Bromswold is 7 miles northwest of Huntingdon and overlooks the Spaldwick Valley; its exact location is easily signaled to the traveler by the old tower on the church. George Herbert was presented with the living here on July 25, 1625, in conjunction with the prebendaryship of Layton Ecclesia. The church was then in a dilapidated state; because of Herbert's efforts the building is now one of the most interesting in the county. About 1626 he had the aisled nave replaced and the 13th-century doorways incorporated in the outer arches of the newly built porches. All the Jacobean furnishings are due to him: a font, the seating, the chancel screen, and the twin pulpits, one for preaching and the other for praying. Interestingly enough, Herbert quite possibly was never in Leighton Bromswold or in the church; he had attempted to sign over the post to Nicholas Ferrar, who lived at nearby Little Gidding. Declining his friend's generosity, Ferrar urged Herbert to undertake the necesary restoration and agreed to oversee all the work.

LENTON, Lincolnshire (pop. 117) A small village 7½ miles southeast of Grantham, Lenton actually has two names (the other, not much used, is Lavington); the church here is mainly 13th-century with a 15th-century chancel. In 1883 Edward Bradley, better known as Cuthbert Bede, author of *The Adventures of Mr. Verdant Green*, was presented the living here by the 1st Baron Aveland. Coming from Stretton, Rutland, where he had been an indefatigable worker (for example, he fully restored the church), he again undertook extensive public work. He established a free library and local-improvement societies in the six years before his death. Bradley died in the vicarage on December 12, 1889, and was buried in Stretton.

LETCOMBE BASSETT, Berkshire (pop. 161) The prehistoric Ridgeway crosses the downs high above the village of Letcombe Bassett, and the Saxons had a hill fort, Segsbury Camp, close to the present village. The church, high on a hill overlooking the village and its stream, is basically Norman and has unusually fine Norman carving in the capitals of the filled-in doorway and on the chancel arch. Following the 1st Earl of Oxford's fall from power in the early 18th century, Jonathan Swift left London and came to the vicarage here. The Rev. John Geree was an old acquaintance of Swift's, and the priest made the necessary arrangements for Swift to live at Letcombe Bassett with room and board fixed at 1 guinea a week. Swift arrived on June 3, 1714, and remained until August 16.

This village is most likely the model for Cresscombe in Thomas Hardy's *Jude the Obscure*. On the small river just a short distance from the village is a small thatched cottage standing in the midst of extensive beds of watercress; this is the location of the cottage belonging to Arabella's parents. Hardy's description seems particularly apt:

> In three minutes he [Jude] was out of the house and descending by the path across the wide vacant hollow of corn-ground which lay between the village and the isolated house of Arabella in the dip beyond the upland. . . .
> . . . .
> Passing the few unhealthy fir-trees and cottage where the path joined the highway, he hastened along, and struck away to the left, descending the steep side of the country to the west of the Brown House. Here at the base of the chalk formation he neared the brook that oozed from it, and followed the stream till he reached her dwelling. A smell of piggeries came from the back, and the grunting of the originators of that smell.

LEVERINGTON, Cambridgeshire (pop. 2,484) On the Isle of Ely, once an island separated from the rest of the shire by fenland and waterways, Leverington is 2 miles northwest of Wisbech, set in lovely orchards cultivated on reclaimed land. A wall memorial in the medieval Leverington church commemorates Capt. Anthony Lumpkin, a name familiar to every reader of Oliver Goldsmith's *She Stoops to Conquer;* the captain died in 1780, seven years after Goldsmith's play was produced. It is traditionally held that Goldsmith was a guest of the Lumpkin family here and that he took the captain's name for his play. It is also thought that he wrote at least part of the play under the village mulberry tree, but no evidence of this exists.

LEWES, Sussex (pop. 11,960) Very near here the South Downs rise to more than 700 feet, and Lewes itself lies partly in a hollow and partly on a hill. Situated on the Ouse River 8 miles northeast of Brighton, the town is a compact one which once overlooked a broad estuary. Indeed, the area now known as The Brooks was once a sea lake. The Saxons settled the town, and Alfred the Great recognized its importance when he ordered it to be fortified. But it was Norman influence which increased Lewes's importance. The unique stone castle with its twin keeps was then undertaken. Construction must have posed problems since the castle is built on two mounds instead of the usual one. In 1620 much of the structure was pulled down for building materials and sold for 4 pence a load.

By the 15th century Lewes was a prosperous town, especially as the Sussex wool trade flourished, and many great houses were built. Anne of Cleves House, so named because Anne was given Lewes Priory as part of her divorce alimony and not because she ever lived here, is a timber-framed house with magnificent beaming; and Barbican House, a medieval to 18th-century building, is now the Sussex Archaeological Society's general museum and has an excellent collection of Saxon jewelry.

Daniel Defoe liked Lewes on his visit, as he writes in *A Tour thro' the Whole Island of Great Britain:*

> *Lewis* is a fine pleasant Town, well built, agreeably scituated in the middle of an open Champaign Country, and on the Edge of the *South Downs,* the pleasantest, and most delightful of their kind in the Nation; it lies on the Bank of a little wholesome fresh River, within Twelve Miles of the Sea; but that which adds to the Character of this Town, is, that both the Town and the Country adjacent, is full of Gentlemen of good Families and Fortunes. . . .

A second traveler, William Cobbett, was also here, and he, too, was pleased with what he saw:

> The town itself is a model of solidity and neatness. The buildings all substantial to the very outskirts; the pavements good and complete; the shops nice and clean; the people well-dressed; and, though last not least, the girls remarkably pretty, as, indeed, they are in most parts of Sussex; round faces, features small, little hands and wrists, plump arms, and bright eyes. The Sussex men, too, are remarkable for their good looks. . . . The inns are good at Lewes, the people civil and not servile, and the charges really (considering the taxes) far below what one could reasonably expect.

Another traveler, John Evelyn, actually spent a great deal of his childhood in Lewes at the home of his maternal grandparents, the Stansfields (variously Standsfield); they lived at the Cliffe, then on the outskirts of Lewes. Here Evelyn passed a number of years with an overindulgent grandmother; he later wrote in his diary:

> I was soone after sent for into Surrey, and my Father would very willingly have weaned me from my fondnesse of my too indulgent Grand-mother, intending to have me sent to Eaton; but being neither so provident for my owne benefit, unreasonably terrified with the report of the severe discipline there; I was sent back againe to Lewes, which perversenesse of mine, I have since a thousand times deplor'd.

His grandfather died in 1627, and after the remarriage of Eleanor Stansfield to William Newton in 1630, the family moved to the Grange, Southover, then on the other side of Lewes. Evelyn attended the Free School for seven years but was an undistinguished student by his own account:

> The 3d. of Apr: 1637 I was sent for from Schoole; where till about the last Yeare I had been extreamely remisse in my studies; so as I went to the Universitie, rather out of shame of abiding longer at Schoole, than for any fitnesse, as by sad experience I found, which put me to relearne all that I had neglected, or but perfunctorily gaind.

With his grandparents Evelyn attended services at All Saints Church, where both the Stansfields are buried; after going up to Balliol College, Oxford, he returned to Lewes many times to administer his property here.

Another early resident was Sir Thomas Browne, author of *Religio Medici,* who lived here for a short time after the death of his father. Browne's mother, Anna Garraway Browne, was a native of Lewes.

Probably the most famous resident of this town was Thomas Paine, who settled here as an exciseman and tobacconist in 1768; he lived at Bull House, a half-timbered building dating from 1450, just off the High Street and opposite St. Michael's Church. He married Elizabeth Ollive, the daughter of his Quaker landlord, on March 26, 1771, at St. Michael's Church, but the marriage proved unsuccessful, and a deed of separation was signed on June 4, 1774. Paine spent his evenings at the White Hart Inn, a Georgian coaching inn, where he would engage in heated political debates and, it is said, received regularly the copy of Homer (known as the "Headstrong Book") presented to the most obstinate debater the next morning. Becoming embroiled in the excisemen's agitation for increased salaries, he drew up a list of grievances which he presented to the Members of Parliament. Paine was unsuccessful and shortly thereafter, on April 8, 1774, was dismissed from his post and left for London. Thomas "Clio" Rickman and the "Citizen of the World," Paine's biographer, was born here in 1761.

Samuel Johnson once stayed at a house on the High Street now known as Shelleys Hotel; it appears to be a Georgian building, but the facade hides an old Elizabethan inn called the Vines. Johnson's visit left an indelible mark on the Shelley family when he reacted to a child who had become a nuisance by picking her up, putting her into a cherry tree, and walking off. Only hours later at dinner, when the child was missed, did he remember leaving her there. The tree for a long time was known as Dr. Johnson's cherry tree.

William Harrison Ainsworth, who lived in nearby Brighton, uses the Grange in Southover as the Mock Beggars' Hall in *Ovingdean Grange* (1860):

> Though ancient, the house was in excellent preservation; the hard grey Caen stone of which it was constructed looking as fresh as if it had only just left the mason's chisel, and promising to resist the destructive action of the weather for centuries to come. On either side of the porch—to approach which a couple of steps leading into a small court had to be descended—was a far-projecting wing, furnished with bay mullioned windows. The wings had gable roofs, and on the northerly side of the habitation there was a massive stone chimney of very ornamental construction. A tolerably extensive garden was attached to the house; laid out in the old-fashioned style, planted with yew-trees and evergreens, possessing good walls for fruit, and watered by the brook that flowed through the valley.

At the end of the 19th century, beginning on May 1, 1899, George Gissing stayed at the White Hart Inn while awaiting the arrival of Gabrielle Fleury from Rouen.

Lewes has a 20th-century association with Virginia and Leonard Woolf, who leased Asham House from 1912 to 1919; this house is said to be the setting for "A Haunted House." On June 3, 1919, they bought the Round House, which had once been a windmill; standing on Lewes Hill near the castle, the house turned out to be totally unsuitable, and they soon left for Rodmell.

LEWESDON HILL, Dorset There are no villages here, just a hill and a few scattered houses, but the location offers an unparalleled view of Marshwood Vale, a huge bowl of gorse-strewn land. About halfway along the road from Crewkerne to Lyme Regis are the twin hills of Lewesdon and Pilsdon Pen, themselves so intertwined that from a distance few can tell them apart. At the western end of Pilsdon Pen on the northwest slope of Lewesdon is Racedown Lodge, at one time the home of William Wordsworth and his sister Dorothy. Located in a fold of the Dorset hills, the lodge was rebuilt and refurnished by John Pinney, whose son was a close friend of the Wordsworths. The house, which was offered to Wordsworth essentially rent-free, is a square brick structure presently visible from the road just north of Birdsmoorgate. Some changes were made in the house in the 20th century, but the original is outwardly unaltered, and the bedroom and attic floors are as they were in 1795, when the Wordsworths lived there. To the west and south of the house were a flower garden, an extensive kitchen garden, and an orchard. The Wordsworths arrived on September 26 for a stay of two years and had brought with them from London the three-year-old son of Basil Montagu, whom they had taken in following his mother's death.

Wordsworth had written virtually nothing in the two years preceding his stay in Lewesdon, but things were different here, as *The Prelude* relates:

> . . . Nature's self, by human love
> Assisted, through the weary labyrinth
> Conducted me again to open day,
> Revived the feelings of my earlier life,
> Gave me that strength and knowledge full of peace,
> Enlarged, and never more to be disturbed.

Their stay here was, according to Dorothy's letters, a very happy one. Wordsworth began "The Old Cumberland Beggar" in 1795, if the watermark on the paper is a correct indication of the date, and by the spring of 1797 had completed "The Ruined Cottage," which later became Book I of *The Excursion;* he also wrote *The Borderers,* which Covent Garden rejected. "Goody Blake and Harry Gill," while written later at Alfoxden in Holford, Somerset, describes the abject poverty of many of the Dorsetshire people. "If Lucy Should Be Dead," even though written in Germany in 1799, is set here; the recorded approach to the house from the east as the moon sets corresponds in every detail to the approach to Racedown Lodge. Mary Hutchinson, later Wordsworth's wife, and her brother Henry arrived for a long visit in the early spring of 1797. They departed on June 5, the same day that Samuel Taylor Coleridge arrived; Wordsworth noted more than forty years later "a distinct remembrance of his arrival. He did not keep to the high road, but leaped over a gate and bounded down a pathless field by which he cut off at an angle." Coleridge and the Wordsworths took long walks over the downs while they read or recited poetry to each other.

LICHFIELD, Staffordshire (pop. 22,672) Now rapidly modernizing, Lichfield still has a great deal of its ancient charm; situated 17 miles southeast of Stafford, the town is located almost in the middle of England. Its name, meaning "the field of corpses," refers to an unsupported tradition that thousands of Christians were martyred here by the Roman emperor Diocletian in 286. The Venerable Bede first referred to this legend in his writings, and many later writers followed suit.

After the Norman Conquest, the Normans built a church on the site of the present cathedral. The cathedral, one of the smallest in England, was built between 1195 and 1293; the Lady Chapel was added in the 14th century. The three graceful sandstone spires which dominate the city are known as "the Ladies of the Vale." The west front of the building is rich in sandstone statuary, but all but 5 of the 113 statues in the arcades and panels are 19th-century. Over the doorway to the chapter house are the figures of famous churchmen, including George Herbert, Bishop Thomas Ken, Archbishop William Laud,

Izaak Walton, and Richard Hooker, and the stalls and the bishop's throne are the 19th-century work of Samuel Evans, the uncle of George Eliot (Mary Ann Evans) and the Seth Bede of her novel *Adam Bede*. The panels are richly carved biblical scenes, and the ends of the stalls show the figures of the Apostles. Over the 13th-century chapter house is the cathedral library, which contains about 8,000 volumes. Its most prized possession by far is St. Chad's Gospel, an illuminated manuscript of 110 vellum leaves written in about 700; and it also has Chaucer's *Canterbury Tales*, written and illuminated in about 1435, a 13th-century illuminated copy of the laws of Justinian, and a 13th-century manuscript of the decretals of Gregory IX. Also there, but not in the same class as these volumes, is Samuel Johnson's marked copy of Dr. Robert South's *Sermons*, the book quoted in Johnson's *Dictionary*.

William Camden wrote of the early history of Lichfield in his *Britannia*:

> The city stands low, but is tolerably large and neat, divided into two parts by a pool of clear water of no great depth; but these two parts are united by two banks, with vents under them.... The farther part is ... remarkable for a most noble church, surrounded by a fair wall, like a castle, encircled with very handsome houses of prebends and the bishop's palace. It has three beautiful and lofty stone spires, and was for many ages past the seat of a bishop.

John Leland surveyed the city for his *Itinerary* but was unimpressed since

> all the substaunce of it stondithe apon a low and equall ground, only the close and the cathedrale churche, withe a longe streate, that lyethe northe on the bridge of the towne is somewhat apon a highe ground. There is no token that evar the towne was waullyd.

Somewhat later Daniel Defoe found Lichfield an "indifferent" city even though he was impressed by the cathedral,

> one of the finest and most beautiful in *England*, especially for the Outside, the Form and Figure of the Building, the carv'd work'd, Imagery, and the three beautiful Spires; the like of which are not to be seen in one Church, no not in *Europe*.

The houses in the cathedral close, he says, were "well-built . . . and well inhabited."

The town's most illustrious association is with Samuel Johnson, who was born here on September 18, 1709; the house on Bread Street in Market Square, near the corner of Sadler Street, which was his father's bookstore, is now a Johnson Museum. The baby was christened immediately after birth in the bedroom of the house, probably by the Rev. William Baker of St. Mary's Church. The baptism is recorded in the parish register. Johnson was put out to a wet nurse on George Lane, and when he was returned to his mother in November, he was almost blind and was riddled with disease. As a child he suffered from scrofula, the king's evil, a tubercular infection of the lymphatic glands in the neck; an operation left enormous scars as well as some facial disfigurement. Johnson also suffered from smallpox as an infant; again the scars were disfiguring. In 1712 he was taken to London by his mother, who believed that the royal touch of Queen Anne would cure the scrofula; Johnson remembered the occasion in later years. The young

LICHFIELD Standing at the corner of Bread Street in Market Square, Samuel Johnson's birthplace has changed little since Michael Johnson built it in 1707-1708; the house is now a Johnson Museum.

Samuel attended a dame school run by Dame Oliver on Dam Street, within 400 feet of his home, where he learned to read; the building is marked with a plaque. After leaving Dame Oliver's in 1716, he was tutored for a year before entering the Lichfield Grammar School on St. John Street, opposite the old Hospital of St. John; the brick grammar school had four gables and a single oak-paneled room. The grammar school is now at Borrowcop Hill, but the old building on St. John Street is still there. Promotion to the Upper School brought Johnson under a stern disciplinarian who believed strongly in indiscriminate flogging; Johnson later remembered that Mr. Hunter

> "was very severe, and wrong-headedly severe. He used (said he) to beat us unmercifully; and he did not distinguish between ignorance and negligence; for he would beat a boy equally for not knowing a thing, as for neglecting to know it. He would ask a boy a question, and if he did not answer it, he would beat him, without considering whether he had an opportunity of knowing how to answer it. For instance, he would call up a boy and ask him Latin for a candlestick, which the boy could not expect to be asked. Now, Sir, if a boy could answer every question, there would be no need of a master to teach him."

At another time, reflecting on the extreme discipline, he observed, "Sir, I am afraid that what they gain at one end, they will lose at the other."

Johnson was a precocious child, and his family sent him to school in Stourbridge for a short period before he was apprenticed in his father's bookstore. The family's financial situation was such that university work was impossible, and Johnson spent his working hours reading in the shop:

> ". . . not voyages and travels, but all literature, Sir, all ancient writers, all manly: though but little Greek, only

some of Anacreon and Hesiod: but in this irregular manner (added he) I had looked into a great many books, which were not commonly known at the Universities, where they seldom read any books but what are put into their hands by their tutors; so that when I came to Oxford, Dr. Adams, now master of Pembroke College, told me, I was the best qualified for the University that he had ever known come there."

How Johnson managed to get to Oxford is not wholly clear, but he had to leave after a little more than one year's residence and returned home. After the elder Johnson died early in December 1731 and was buried at St. Michael's Church, east of the city, Johnson found it necessary to support himself and secured a post in Market Bosworth. He returned to Lichfield frequently, especially later when he was in nearby Edial. Johnson's mother and brother Nathaniel are buried at St. Michael's Church, and the inscription on Mrs. Johnson's tombstone was composed by Samuel.

Two old inns here are associated with Dr. Johnson: the Three Crowns (marked with a plaque) and the Swan. In early July 1774 Johnson and the Thrales stayed at the Swan on Bird Street for four days on their way to Wales. At this time Johnson so strongly disapproved of Mrs. Thrale's "morning nightgown and close cap" that he refused to take the family out until she had changed her clothes. In March 1776 he took James Boswell to the Three Crowns (an office building now stands on the site), where Boswell

saw here, for the first time, *oat ale;* and oat cakes, not hard as in Scotland, but soft like a Yorkshire cake, were served at breakfast. It was pleasant to me to find, that "*Oats*," the "*food of horses*," were so much used as the *food of the people* in Dr. Johnson's own town. He expatiated in praise of Lichfield and its inhabitants, who, he said, were "the most sober, decent people in England, the genteelest in proportion to their wealth, and spoke the purest English." I doubted as to the last article of this eulogy. . . .

On Sunday, March 24, they visited a friend, Mrs. Cobb, and her niece at their home, the Friary, and Dr. Johnson and Mrs. Cobb attended services at St. Mary's.

There are numerous other memorials and traditions associated with Dr. Johnson: the Bishop's Palace in the cathedral close was the residence of Gilbert Walmesley, a close friend; the Dean's Walk in the close was one of Johnson's favorite spots, and he frequently extolled its virtues. Another favorite walk was to Stowe Pool, and midway along the pool is Johnson's Willow, a descendant grown from cuttings of the original tree; adjacent to the pool is the Parchments, where a venture of Johnson's father into the parchment trade met with disaster. Both Stowe Hill and Stowe House were open to Johnson at any time; indeed, part of his *Lives of the Poets* was written here. A memorial bust of Dr. Johnson is in the south-transept chapel of the cathedral, and in Market Square is the famous sculpture of him; on the plinth is a relief sculpture, one piece of which depicts his penance in the Uttoxeter market. The town commemorates Johnson's birth date; in the morning there is a wreath-laying ceremony, and in the evening a candlelight supper in the Guildhall with liveried footmen in attendance. David Garrick was also a native of Lichfield and attended the grammar school here.

In the deanery on the north side of the cathedral lived the young Joseph Addison, whose father was appointed dean of Lichfield in 1683. The pleasant life here was marred in June 1684, when Addison's mother died; services were held in the cathedral, and she was buried in the choir. Addison attended the Lichfield Grammar School for a time before entering Charterhouse in London in 1686 as a gentleman commoner. There he met Richard Steele, and from 1686 through their university days Steele spent many of his holidays in the Addison home.

The George, on Bird Street, has an interesting literary association with George Farquhar, who stayed here in 1705 when he was probably in the military as a recruiting officer. The inn becomes the setting of *The Beaux' Strategem*, and it has been claimed that it was noted especially for its ale:

Aim. I have heard your town of Lichfield much famed for ale; I think I'll taste that.
Bon. Sir, I have now in my cellar ten tun of the best ale in Staffordshire; 'tis smooth as oil, sweet as milk, clear as amber, and strong as brandy; and will be just fourteen year old the fifth day of next March, old style.
Aim. You're very exact, I find, in the age of your ale.
Bon. As punctual, sir, as I am in the age of my children. I'll show you such ale!—Here, tapster, broach number 1706, as the saying is.—Sir, you shall taste my *Anno Domini.* . . .

Sir Walter Scott, who was well acquainted with "the bluest of the bluestockings," Anna Seward, known as the Swan of Lichfield and the daughter of the canon residentiary of the cathedral, was often here. Miss Seward, little read today, was a poet and a prolific letter writer who attached herself to Sir Walter and barraged him with letters, which he regularly answered; Scott, feeling it his duty to do so, visited her and, indeed, wrote the epitaph for her tombstone in Lichfield Cathedral. He had to pay for his attentions, however, for when she died in March 1809, she bequeathed her poetry to him with the injunction to publish it immediately together with a short biography which he was to write. Scott was also to take control of publishing her vast correspondence (of which she kept copies), but he declined this task. He later comments:

The despair which I used to feel on receiving poor Miss Seward's letters, whom I really liked, gave me a most unsentimental horror for sentimental letters. I am now doing penance for my ill-breeding, by submitting to edit her posthumous poetry, most of which is absolutely execrable. This, however, is the least of my evils, for when she proposed this bequest to me, which I could not in decency refuse, she combined it with a request that I would publish her whole literary correspondence. This I declined on principle, having a particular aversion at perpetuating that sort of gossip; but what availed it? Lo! to ensure the publication, she left it to an Edinburgh bookseller. . . .

Scott uses Lichfield and some of its history in *Marmion:*

Short is my tale: Fitz-Eustace' care
A pierc'd and mangled body bare
To moated Lichfield's lofty pile;
And there, beneath the southern aisle
A tomb, with Gothic sculpture fair,
Did long Lord Marmion's image bear.
(Now vainly for its sight you look;

'Twas levell'd when fanatic Brook
The fair cathedral storm'd and took;
But, thanks to Heaven and good Saint Chad,
A guerdon meet the spoiler had!)

The storming of the cathedral, which had been garrisoned by Royalist forces in the Civil War, was directed by Sir John Gill and Lord Brook; Brook was killed when a musket shot went through the visor of his helmet, and, it was claimed, he was shot in the eye from St. Chad's Church on St. Chad's Day. This eye, he said, would see the destruction of all such English cathedrals.

LIDGATE, Suffolk (pop. 268)   About 6½ miles southeast of Newmarket and just south of the Kennet River is the tiny village of Lidgate (old spelling, Lydgate), which was the birthplace of John Lydgate, the poet-monk, in, most likely, 1370. He leaves his readers in no doubt about his birthplace, noting it in *Aesop's Prologues* as an apology: "Haue me excusyd, I was born in Lydgate." Further, twice in *The Fall of Princes* he describes the village in terms no longer relevant, it seems:

Born in a vyllage which is called Lydgate,
Be olde tyme a famous castel toun

and

I was born in Lidgate,
Wher Bachus licour doth full scarsli fleete.

Nothing more is known of his life until he entered the monastery at Bury St. Edmunds, Suffolk, about 1385.

LILLEY, Hertfordshire (pop. 381)   Just south of the old Icknield Way (a prehistoric track used by Neolithic and Bronze Age people), Lilley, 4 miles northeast of Luton, was the 17th-century birthplace of James Janeway, author of *A Token for Children, Being an Account of the Conversion, Holy and Exemplary Lives, and Joyful Deaths of Several Young Children*, a book the author felt responsible parents should give their children because a "child is never too little to go to hell." One Janeway heroine is seen looking in a mirror and saying,

What a pity such a pretty maid
As I should go to hell.

Another association exists with Rupert Brooke, who often walked here from Cambridge and later incorporated the village into one of his poems:

The Roman road to Wendover,
By Tring and Lilley Hoo.

LIMPSFIELD CHART, Surrey   Lying about 1 mile east of Oxted in the Holmesdale Valley, Limpsfield Chart is overshadowed by the larger village of Limpsfield, which H. G. Wells uses as Dr. Fremisson's home in *Jane and Peter* and in which the composer Frederick Delius was buried in 1934 after his death in France. Richard Church was married in the parish church in 1916 and lodged on the High Street near the present Bull Inn; he moved to the 14th-century Comfort's Cottage in Staffhurst Wood in 1927 before leaving for London.

In the little hamlet literary associations are legion,

for here Edward Garnett and his wife Constance built The Cearne in 1896. A reader for T. Fisher Unwin, Garnet chose a wooded area overlooking the valley for his home, and here his guest list reads like a who's who in literature: W. H. Hudson, Joseph Conrad, John Galsworthy, Edward Thomas, W. H. Davies, D. H. Lawrence, Hilaire Belloc, Ford Madox Ford, Rupert Brooke, Henry James, Stephen Crane, and George Bernard Shaw.

LINCOLN, Lincolnshire (pop. 62,403)   A cathedral city and the county town, Lincoln is on the west bank of the Witham River 33 miles northeast of Nottingham. Situated at the center of the limestone ridge known as the Lincoln Edge, the town lies at a gap forged by the river, which established its strategic importance. Here the Romans built their town named Lindum Colonia, a chartered town and fortress for the Ninth Legion; by A.D. 71 it had become a settlement for retired soldiers. Of the Roman gates in the walled town, the north gate, called Newport Arch, is still standing and in use. There are excellent remains of the Roman walls, one of which contains a stone interval tower. The ruins of what is now thought to have been a basilica and temple have been found in Bailgate.

Lincoln became a Saxon city under Mercian rule, and the Danes made it the chief borough of the five of their Danelagh; Danish influence can still be felt in such street names as Danesgate and Hunsgate.

The Normans had the most substantial effect upon the city, and under them Lincoln became one of the most important cities in the realm. William the Conqueror ordered the building of the castle in 1068, and the site chosen was the crest of the 210-foot hill in the southwestern quarter of the Roman *colonia* above the river. Under the Normans the focus of religious life changed; the church was given vastly more power, and the bishops were expected to be not only men of prayer and scholarship but competent administrators. William transferred the see of Dorchester to Lincoln and placed Remigius, the first Norman to be given a bishopric, in charge. Remigius began the new cathedral around 1072, and on Ascension Day twenty years later it was consecrated. Probably the most outstanding feature of the cathedral is the windows: the rose window, known as the Bishop's Eye because it looks in from the old episcopal seat, and the Dean's Eye, which looks in from the deanery gardens, both contain beautiful fragments of medieval glass and flowing decorated tracery, a feature rarely found in English churches.

The cathedral library contains first editions of *Paradise Lost, Don Quixote,* and part of the *Faerie Queene;* the Thornton manuscript of Richard Rolle, known as the Hermit of Hampole; and one of the four extant copies of the Magna Carta. Robert Southey's comment on the cathedral rather sums up its location and aspect:

Never was an edifice more happily placed, overtopping a city built on the acclivity of a steep hill. To see it in full perfection it should be in the sunshine of an autumnal evening, when the red roofs and red-brick houses would harmonise with the sky and the fading foliage.

Lincoln retains a few Norman houses in the area of the High Street, now known as Steep Hill. Dernstall Lock, its original name, was the scene of a legendary event that found its way into literature. Dernstall Lock was supposed to be a barrier, locked at sunset, to keep in the Jews who lived on the hill; it was the home of the child Little St. Hugh, who was said to have been murdered by the Jews in 1255. The story, which is contained in many contemporary records, including the *Annals of Waverley*, the work of Matthew Paris, and the *Annals of Burton*, relates that the boy Hugh was crucified in contempt of Christ, after much torture and suffering, by the Jews of Lincoln. Numerous old ballads refer to Hugh of Lincoln, and in most

> Yesterday was brave Hallowday,
>   And, above all days of the year,
> The schoolboys all got leave to play,
>   And little Sir Hugh was there.
>
> He kicked the ball with his foot,
>   And keeped it with his knee,
> And even in at the Jew's window
>   He gar the bonnie ba flee.

"Dear Hugh" is induced by "an apple reid and white" to "get the ba"; he is then led to the Jewess's "ain chamber" where

> She's laid him on a dressin-board
>   Whare she did often dine;
> She stack a penknife to his heart,
>   And dressed him like a swine.

The story varies somewhat from version to version but was the source of the Prioress's story in Geoffrey Chaucer's *The Canterbury Tales*:

> O yonge Hugh of Lyncoln, slayn also
> With cursed Jewes, as it is notable,
> For it is but a litel while ago. . . .

Lincoln entered Arthurian legend as well, and indeed some of the manuscripts from which Sir Thomas Malory drew his material are in the cathedral library. Here, according to Geoffrey of Monmouth in his *Historia Regum Britanniae*, Arthur defeated the Saxon horde:

> They let a few days pass and then they marched to the town of Kaerluideoit, . . . situated upon a hill between two rivers, in the province of Lindsey: it is also called by another name, Lincoln. As soon as they had arrived there with their entire force, keen as they were to fight with the Saxons, they inflicted unheard-of slaughter upon them; for on one day six thousand of the Saxons were killed, some being drowned in the rivers and the others being hit by weapons. As result, the remainder were demoralized. The Saxons abandoned the siege and took to flight.

John Leland includes a long section on Lincoln in his *Itinerary*:

> It is easy to be perceivid that the toune of Lincoln hath be notably buildid at 3. tymes. The first building was yn the very toppe of the hille, the oldest part wherof inhabited in the Britans tyme, was the northethest part of the hille, directely withoute Newport gate . . . After the destruction of this old Lincoln men began to fortifie the souther parte of the hille, new diching, waulling and gating it, and so was new Lincoln made out of a pece of old Lincoln. . . .
> The third building of later tymes was in Wikerford, for commodite of water: this parte is enwallid wher it is not defendid with the ryver and marisch ground.

LINCOLN This "old confusd towne, very long, uneven & confragose, steep & raged" according to John Evelyn, still has this character in part as the timbered houses on the western side of the celebrated High Bridge spanning the Witham River attest.

Not long after, Michael Drayton refers to Lincoln and its river in *Poly-Olbion*:

> By this to *Lincolne* com'n, upon whose loftie Scite,
> Whilst wistly *Wytham* looks with wonderfull delight,
> Enamoured of the state, and beautie of the place,
> That her of all the rest especially doth grace,
> Leaving her former Course, in which she first set forth,
> Which seemed to have been directly to the North. . . .

John Evelyn visited the town in August 1654 and found it "an old confusd towne,"

> very long, uneven & confragose, steepe & raged, but has formerly ben full of good houses, especialy Churches & *Abbies*, especialy the Minster, comparable to that of York it selfe, abounding with marble pillars, a faire front. . . . [T]he Souldiers had lately knocked off all or most of the Brasses which were on the Gravestones, so as few Inscriptions were left: They told us they went in with axes & hammers, & shut themselves in, till they had rent & torne of some barges full of Mettal; not sparing the monuments of the dead, so helish an avarice possess'd them.

Evelyn's "old confusd towne" had changed little by the time Daniel Defoe visited here when gathering material for *A Tour thro' the Whole Island of Great Britain*. Defoe found it "an antient, ragged, decay'd, and still decaying City" in which even the "Hog-Styes, were built Church-Fashion . . . with Stone Walls and arch'd Windows and Doors." He thought a little better of the cathedral, which he describes as a "noble Structure" but not equal to Lichfield even though its situation is "infinitely more to Advantage." His conclusion, though, still damns the town:

> [I]t is an old dying, decay'd, dirty City; and except that Part, which, as above, lies between the Castle and the Church, on the Top of the Hill, it is scarce tolerable to call it a City.
> Yet it stands in a most rich, pleasant, and agreeable Country. . . .

Years later William Cobbett "came to this famous ancient Roman station, and afterwards grand scene of Saxon and Gothic splendour...." He arrived in the middle of the fair, and while amazed at the numbers of sheep and cattle and the prices they commanded, he was bitterly distressed by the prices of tradesmen's horses, for

> those who live on the taxes have money to throw away; but those who *pay* them are ruined, and have, of course, no money to lay out on horses.

However, in general, he was pleased by the town, its

> ancient castle and the magnificent cathedral on the *brow* of a sort of ridge which ends here; for you look all of a sudden down into a deep valley, where the greater part of the remaining city lies.... The cathedral is, I believe, the *finest building in the whole world*. All the other that I have seen (and I have seen all in England except Chester, York, Carlisle, and Durham) are little things compared with this. To the task of describing a thousandth part of its striking beauties I am inadequate....

There are only a few other specific literary associations with Lincoln. Samuel Daniel was attached to Sir Edward Dymoke's household here. Although the dates are uncertain, Daniel appears to have been in Sir Edward's service from about 1585 to 1592. Letters substantiate these dates, and the usually accepted date of 1585 for Daniel's entering the Pembroke household must probably be postponed to 1592. George Herbert, who took holy orders late in life, was made a prebendary of Lincoln Cathedral in the summer of 1626 by Bishop John Williams. The poet's only duty here was to preach once a year, and even that could be done by proxy. Herbert did not even attend his institution in the cathedral on July 5; that, too, was done by proxy. But in 1629, shortly after his marriage to Jane Danvers, he preached a Pentecost sermon at the cathedral. A later association exists with Edward Bulwer-Lytton (Lord Lytton), whose parliamentary seat for St. Ives was swept away with the Reform Bill of 1832; he sat for Lincoln from November 1832 until his retirement from parliamentary life in 1841. One other person should be noted: Alfred, Lord Tennyson, who is closely associated with the shire but not with Lincoln, is commemorated in a large bronze statue standing on the Minster Green. The Tennyson Research Centre is in Lincoln.

LINDISFARNE, Northumberland (pop. 586)

The ancient kingdom of Northumbria has long been known as the cradle of English Christianity, and this small island (also known as Holy Island), less than 2 miles long and about 2 miles wide, was first settled by missionaries from Iona. The term "island" is not quite accurate because Lindisfarne is connected to Beal on the mainland by a 3-mile causeway which is covered only at high tide. It was for this reason that the Venerable Bede termed Lindisfarne a "semi-isle." The monastery founded here was within sight of the royal city of Bamburgh, and in the tradition of the Irish model on which it was based, the monastic community was in close contact with the King. The monastery was Celtic in both origin and practice, although with the decision of the Whitby Synod (664) to accept the Roman Easter instead of the Celtic one the Ionian missionaries returned home.

Cuthbert, probably the favorite Northumbrian saint and actually a Scotsman, served his novitiate and received formal training at Melrose and Ripon Abbeys before coming to Lindisfarne. He spent three years in a hermit's retreat on the Inner Farne, was made bishop in 685, and built an oratory on Farne Island, where the small church now stands and where he died in 687. While neither the early church nor the monastery has left any traces, two manuscripts of the period are of considerable interest: the Lindisfarne Gospels and the *Liber Vitae*, both now in the British Museum. The 7th-century Gospels, written in honor of the canonization of St. Cuthbert in 698, are masterpieces of early monastic art. These four Gospels in the Vulgate text are decorated with illuminated capitals and written in Anglo-Saxon majuscule script; an Anglo-Saxon gloss was added in the 10th century. The *Liber Vitae*, a list of names in alternating gold and silver letters, was for centuries kept at the high altar of Durham Cathedral. What is remarkable is that these manuscripts escaped a savage Danish assault in 793; fearing a second attack, the monks left Lindisfarne in 875 carrying with them a stone sarcophagus containing Cuthbert's body and undoubtedly the Gospels and *Liber Vitae*.

Not until the 11th century was the monastery refounded under the jurisdiction of the Benedictine rule of Durham; at this time the name Holy Island first appeared. Neglect rather than explicit destruction seems to account for the ruin of the buildings; the last straw was the giving of the lands to Theophilus Howard, Baron Howard deWalden, who with the help of hereditary regalian rights brought about the final ruination of the monastic buildings when he removed the lead from the roofs.

The second canto of Sir Walter Scott's *Marmion* is set in a convent at Lindisfarne. Scott admitted that the convent was entirely fictitious, for there has never been a nunnery on Holy Island. This is the scene of the live interment of Constance of Beverley in the "vault of Penitance,/Excluding light and air," for breaking her vow. Scott based this event on fact, for more than once the religious who broke the vow of chastity was placed in a niche just large enough to contain the body, given a token portion of food, and walled up with the words *vade in pacem*.

> For there were seen in that dark wall,
> Two niches, narrow, deep, and tall:
> Who enters at such grisly door
> Shall ne'er, I ween, find exit more.
> In each a slender meal was laid,
> Of roots, of water, and of bread....

It should be noted that Scott's referring to the building here as Saxon ("In Saxon strength that Abbey frown'd") is a common misusage of the period. The buildings were Norman.

LISKEARD, Cornwall (pop. 4,377)

A small market town and an ex-stannary town, Liskeard (pronounced "lis'card") is built on a hill almost exactly equidistant from Plymouth and Launceston. The Liskeard Grammar School, which closed in 1849, numbered two men of letters among its pupils. The Rev. Robert Stephen Hawker, later vicar of Morwenstow, was sent from Plymouth to the school for a short time, and John Wolcot (Peter Pindar) also received part of his education here. Wolcot was the churchman-cum-doctor who later said that a physician's role was that of observing nature and giving "her a shove on the back if he sees her inclined to do right." There is also an Arthurian association in the neighborhood. Just a short distance north on the main road are several tors, one group of which is called Arthur's Bed. It has been put forth that the word *bed* is a possible corruption of the Anglo-Saxon *beth*, "grave," but there is no evidence at all to suggest that this argument applies to this case.

LITTLE BARFORD, Bedfordshire (pop. 121) The Ouse River, just west of the main road in Little Barford, has been flooding and claiming lives since the 13th century, when the first recorded fatalities took place. Situated 2 miles south of St. Neots, Little Barford has never been large; indeed, today it consists of a row of cottages and a Victorian manor house dominated by a large power station. The village was the birthplace of Nicholas Rowe, the dramatist and Poet Laureate, in June 1674. He was born in the home of his maternal grandfather, Jasper Edward, and baptized in the local church on June 30. The Edward cottage, with a projecting upper story, stands on the east side of the road which enters Little Barford and is appropriately marked.

LITTLE DUNMOW *See* DUNMOW, LITTLE, AND DUNMOW, GREAT.

LITTLE GIDDING, Huntingdonshire (pop. 42) This tiny village, 10 miles northwest of Huntingdon, is probably one of the best known in England because of the establishment by Nicholas Ferrar in 1626 of a small but self-supporting religious community known as the "Protestant Nunnery." Daily life was strictly regulated, and the twenty-four hours of the day saw constant religious services. Ferrar built a large house (only its platform remains) overlooking the valley and is traditionally held to have restored the local church; it is far more likely that he rebuilt it on a new site as a private chapel and not as a parish church. Many of the items in the church are of Ferrar's taste and time, including a brass baptismal font dangerously surrounded by brass spikes.

Joseph Henry Shorthouse, a minor novelist of the late 19th century, describes the community in *John Inglesant*. Among Ferrar's guests here were George Herbert and Richard Crashaw; Crashaw's intimacy with Ferrar is often thought to have had much to do with the development of the poet's religious views. Perhaps, though, Little Gidding and its early associations are most widely known today because of the influence of Ferrar's beliefs and practices upon T. S. Eliot. The poet knew of Charles I's visit in 1633, when the King was received with due respect, and early in "Little Gidding" in the *Four Quartets* the figure of Charles, "a broken king," appears. He came to "kneel/Where prayer has been valid" in the private chapel-cum-church:

If I think, again, of this place,
And of people, not wholly commendable,
Of no immediate kin or kindness,
But some of peculiar genius,
All touched by a common genius,
United in the strife which divided them;

If I think of a king at nightfall,
Of three men, and more, on the scaffold
And a few who died forgotten
In other places, here and abroad,
And of one who died blind and quiet,
Why should we celebrate
These dead men more than the dying?

LITTLE LANGDALE *See* LANGDALE, GREAT, AND LANGDALE, LITTLE.

LITTLE OUSEBURN, Yorkshire (pop. 210) A tiny village 7 miles northeast of Knaresborough, Little Ouseburn contains Thorp Green Hall, the home of the Rev. Edmund Robinson and his family in the mid-19th century. It was to the hall that Anne Brontë came in March 1841 as governess to the Robinsons' three daughters; she was joined by her brother Branwell in 1843, when he was engaged as a tutor to the younger Edmund Robinson. Branwell's time here was most unsatisfactory; while his sister's presence and influence no doubt kept his drinking and opium addiction under partial control, it had no effect upon his relationship with Mrs. Robinson. Miss Brontë left her position in June 1845, and within a few weeks Branwell was dismissed. While here, Miss Brontë attended Holy Trinity Church with the Robinsons — the Reverend Mr. Robinson was not, it should be noted, the incumbent, nor is it likely that he ever took up a living. *Agnes Grey* deals with the life of a governess, and the portrayal of the Murray family is based on the Robinsons:

I did not see her [Mrs. Murray] till eleven o'clock on the morning after my arrival; when she honoured me with a visit, just as my mother might step into the kitchen to see a new servant-girl; yet not so, either, for my mother would have seen her immediately after her arrival, and not waited till the next day; and, moreover, she would have addressed her in a more kind and friendly manner, and given her some words of comfort as well as a plain exposition of her duties; but Mrs. Murray did neither. . . .

LITTLE SALKELD, Cumberland (pop. 87) Five miles northeast of Penrith is the tiny village of Little Salkeld, and high above the village is Long Meg and Her Daughters, a Bronze Age stone circle second in size only to Stonehenge. Of the sixty-seven stones making up the circle, Long Meg is a tapering stone, 18 feet high and 15 feet around, which weighs more than 15 tons. Facing her and forming a sort of doorway are her four daughters.

Some of the stones have disappeared since William Wordsworth first came upon them and tallied their number at seventy-two. He notes:

When I first saw this monument, as I came upon it by surprise, I might over-rate its importance as an object; but, though it will not bear a comparison with Stonehenge, I must say I have not seen any other relique of those dark ages which can pretend to rival it in singularity and dignity of appearance.

He later composed "The Monument Commonly Called Long Meg and Her Daughters near the River Eden," a sonnet meditating on their past.

Years earlier Michael Drayton had seen the stones and included them in *Poly-Olbion*:

Stones seventie seven stand, in manner of a Ring,
Each full ten foot in height, but yet the strangest thing,

Their equall distance is, the circle that compose,
Within which other stones lye flat, which doe inclose
The bones of men long dead, (as there the people
say). . . .

LITTLEHAMPTON, Sussex (pop. 12,597) The Arun
River Valley is one of impressive natural beauty.
Rising near Pulborough, the river cuts its meander-
ing way across the South Downs toward the sea at
Littlehampton. The valley constituted one of the
rapes of Sussex after the Norman Conquest, with its
defensive castle at Arundel, 3½ miles to the north,
and its port here. At the time of the conquest, Littlehampton was a functioning Saxon port, which the
invaders were quick to put to their use, ferrying
passengers back and forth to Normandy and later
receiving great quantities of the Caen stone used in
building churches all over Sussex. The 18th century
and the fashion of sea bathing brought some attention, but this fad did not leave the town much altered.
It has become a family resort area, especially appeal-
ing because of wide, sandy beaches and the Mediterranean-like harbor full of small pleasure craft.

George Gordon, Lord Byron came here to visit
Edward Noel Long in the summer of 1806 and established himself, his dog, and his horses at the Dolphin
Inn. One of his first activities was to walk down to
the pier, where he amused himself by firing at oyster
shells. Samuel Taylor Coleridge spent September
1817 here and met the Rev. Henry Francis Cary, the
translator of Dante, on the beach; Cary was reciting
Homer to his son when Coleridge approached saying,
"Sir, yours is a face I should know; I am Samuel Taylor Coleridge." A final visitor during the century was
Mary Ann Evans (George Eliot), who spent the summer of 1862 here working on *Romola*, which was
being serialized in *Cornhill Magazine*.

From the winter of 1906–1907 until February
1918 John Galsworthy spent great periods of time
here because working conditions were quite good. In
March 1907 he came to work on *Strife*, and in December 1910 he finished all the revisions of *The
Patrician*. The period from January to March 1911,
split between here and London, he spent on *The
Man of the World* (later called *The Fugitive*) and
began *The Pigeon*. At Christmas of that year he
worked on revisions for *The Patriot* (later titled *The
Mob*), two studies ("The Grand Jury" and "Gone"),
and two poems ("Persia—Mortiura" and "Hetaira").
April 1914, October and December 1917, and January and February 1918 were all spent at the Beach
Hotel; on these trips he spent a great deal of time in
searching for a country home. A final association
exists with Hilaire Belloc, who had his weekly barrel
of ale sent from the brewery here to his home in
Slindon.

LITTLEMORE, Oxfordshire (pop. 1,640) So close to
Oxford, 2½ miles to the northwest, as to be virtually a
part of the city, Littlemore was the location of a 12th-
century nunnery; the chapel has vanished, but the
16th-century Minchery Farm once formed part of the
nunnery and incorporated part of an older religious
building (a 15th-century door, a lovely oak staircase,
and many old windows) in its construction. Littlemore was a place of great consequence in the 19th-
century religious movement, for John Henry Cardinal Newman was the vicar here from 1841 until
1845, when he was received into the Roman Catholic
Church. Neither church nor parsonage was here
then; indeed, one irony is that Newman's mother laid
the foundation stone of the new church, a good example of Gothic Revival. A farmhouse was converted
into a set of rooms for the followers of Newman and
Dr. Edward Pusey, and it was from here that the
famous *Tracts for the Times* originated. Newman
first lived in a cottage, now the George Inn, and
when the church was under construction, in a house
now known as St. George's. He later moved into the
new parsonage.

Newman's conversion to Catholicism was the one
blow from which the Oxford movement could not
recover, but in retrospect it seems strange that no one
associated closely with either Newman or the movement saw the impending signs of conversion. He
retired from Oxford to Littlemore in 1842 as his
religious doubts increased, and in October 1845 Father Dominic the Passionist received him into the
Roman Church at the Anglican rectory.

Some years later Littlemore became the home of
Hilaire Belloc and his family. They lived in rooms
here before settling in the upper part of 36 Holywell,
from the back of which there was a view of Wadham
College. Belloc was then lecturing in Lancaster and
other parts of northern England for the University
Extension Program. In November 1896 *The Bad
Child's Book of Beasts* was published, and after a trip
to the United States in late 1896 and early 1897, Belloc began work on *Danton* and *A Moral Alphabet*.
Belloc and his family remained in the house on
Holywell until the winter of 1899–1900, when they
moved to London.

LIVERPOOL, Lancashire (pop. 747,490) The leading
port for the transatlantic trade in England, Liverpool,
on the east bank of the Mersey River, was settled at
least as early as the 1st century A.D. but grew slowly
before and during the Middle Ages because of its
remoteness in this northwest corner of Lancashire,
31 miles west of Manchester. What really made a
town of fewer than 2,000 inhabitants in 1650 become
a boom town by the 1730s was the Liverpool triangle
trade, whereby English manufactured goods were exported for West African slaves, who were then traded
in the New World for sugar and rum. Immigrants to
the Americas left from Liverpool in the nineteenth
century, the most notable group being the Irish after
the potato famine.

Daniel Defoe visited here at least three times and
comments on its growth in *A Tour thro' the Whole
Island of Great Britain:*

Liverpoole is one of the Wonders of *Britain* [;] . . . the
Town was, at my first visiting it, about the Year 1680, a
large, handsome, well built, and encreasing or thriving
Town; at my second Visit, *Anno* 1690, it was much
bigger than at my first seeing it, and, by the report of the
Inhabitants, more than twice as big as it was twenty
Years before that; but, I think, I may safely say at this my
third seeing it, for I was surpriz'd at the View, it was
more than double what it was at the second; and, I am
told, that it still visibly encreases both in Wealth, People,
Business and Buildings: What it may grow to in time, I
know not.

He continues:

In a word, there is no Town in *England, London* excepted, that can equal *Liverpoole* for the fineness of the Streets, and beauty of the Buildings; many of the Houses are all of Free Stone, and compleatly finished; and all the rest (of the new part I mean) of Brick, as handsomely built as *London* itself.

But the city grew too rapidly; in 1801 the population stood at 78,000; by 1850 it exceeded 310,000, and today the metropolitan area contains more than 1 million people. The result of such rapid growth was overcrowding and squalor; and at one point, it is said, an estimated 40,000 people were packed like rats into 4,000 cellars. Victorian Liverpool was a curious mixture of extraordinary affluence, underscored by some of the remaining opulent Victorian buildings, and extreme poverty.

Changes were forced on the city by population expansion, the trade pattern, and World War II. Indeed, as one would expect of an important port, bomb damage here was extensive, and large parts of the city were blown up beyond any possible reconstruction.

Liverpool is a city with two modern cathedrals. The foundation stone for the Anglican cathedral was laid in 1904, and while the building was consecrated in 1924, it is still not complete. The Roman Catholic cathedral dates to 1847, when a small amount of building took place in Everton. This structure was abandoned, and in the 1930s a new set of plans for a building larger than St. Paul's was drawn up, but the program was abandoned during the war. In 1953 new plans incorporating the crypt were drawn up, and the cathedral was consecrated in 1967. Giving the appearance of a space-age edifice, the building is capped by an immense baldachino. Inside, 2,000 people can be seated within 8 feet of the celebrant of the mass.

The earliest literary association with Liverpool is said to be with Geoffrey Chaucer, who might have been here in the party of Elizabeth, Countess of Ulster, in 1357. There are two native-born Liverpudlians: Felicia Browne (Hemans) and Arthur Hugh Clough. Felicia Hemans was born at 118 Duke Street (marked with a plaque) on September 25, 1793; the daughter of a merchant, she lived here for seven years before financial reverses forced her father to move to Wales; there he injudiciously had her first volume of poetry published when she was fourteen. She returned in 1827 for her sons' education and lived in a house (gone) on Wavertree High Street until 1831. Clough was born at 9 Rodney Street (marked with a plaque) on January 1, 1819, and lived here for only four years before his family emigrated to Charleston, South Carolina. The family returned briefly in 1828 to put Arthur and his elder brother in school in Chester and then, in 1829, in Rugby, where he formed a lifelong friendship with Dr. Thomas Arnold and his son Matthew (Matthew was to commemorate Clough in *Thyrsis*). Clough accepted the headship of University Hall, London, in 1849, and after returning from Paris divided his time between Liverpool and London. His sister Anne, who became the first principal of Newnham College, Cambridge, recalled that he wrote "The Bothie of Tober-na-Voulick" in one of the upper-story rooms at 59 Vine Street. One other important native of Liverpool who must be mentioned was the statesman William Ewart Gladstone, who was born at 62 Rodney Street in 1809.

At the age of thirteen William Hazlitt came to Liverpool from Wem, Shropshire, to stay with Unitarian friends of his father. The visit with the Tracey family involved a number of firsts for the young Hazlitt. He began to read Fe'nelon's *Télémaque*, went to the theater for the first time, and was introduced to the established church, of which he apparently thought little. John Keats was at the Crown Inn for one night in May 1818; he came to bid good-bye to his brother George and his wife, who were sailing to the United States, and he went on to Lancaster for the beginning of his walking tour of the Lake District. Matthew Arnold gave a lecture called "The Methods of Science" at University College in 1882. Back again in April 1888 to meet his daughter Lucy, who was returning from the United States, he stayed at his sister's home in Dingle Bank and suffered a fatal heart attack on April 15. He was buried in the churchyard at Laleham, Middlesex.

Charles Dickens was first here in 1847, when he and his company of amateur actors performed Ben Jonson's *Every Man in His Humour* for the benefit of Leigh Hunt. In the 1850s and 1860s he was here on various reading tours, and he usually performed in St. George's Hall. On these occasions he generally stayed at the Adelphi Hotel, although in 1844 he stayed at Radley's. He mentions Liverpool in many of his works but normally only as a port. It becomes "that rich and beautiful port" in *Martin Chuzzlewit* when the younger Chuzzlewit and Tapley return to England after their experiences in the United States:

> Bright as the scene was . . . it was nothing to the life and exultation in the breasts of the two travellers, at the sight of the old churches, roofs, and darkened chimney stacks of Home. The distant roar, that swelled up hoarsely from the busy streets, was music in their ears; the lines of people gazing from the wharves, were friends held dear; the canopy of smoke that overhung the town was brighter and more beautiful to them than if the richest silks of Persia had been waving in the air.

The "cheap tavern, where they regaled upon a smoking steak," cannot be identified. In "Poor Mercantile Jack," Dickens sketches the slums of Liverpool:

> . . . a labyrinth of dismal courts and blind alleys, called "entries," kept in wonderful order by the police, and in much better order than by the Corporation, the want of gaslight in the most dangerous and infamous of these places being quite unworthy of so spirited a town. . . . Many of these sailors' resorts we attained by noisome passages so profoundly dark that we felt our way with our hands. Not one of the whole number we visited was without its show of prints and ornamental crockery, the quantity of the latter, set forth on little shelves and in little cases in otherwise wretched rooms, indicating that Mercantile Jack must have an extraordinary fondness for crockery to necessitate so much of that bait in his traps. . . .

Later in the 19th century Gerard Manley Hopkins was sent here from Bedford Leigh to the Church of St. Francis Xavier to do parish work among the Irish. The death of a blacksmith, one of his charges, prompted "Felix Randall the Farrier" in April 1880:

> "O he is dead then? my duty all ended,
> Who have watched his mould of man, big-boned and hardy-handsome
> Pining, pining, till time when reason rambled in it and some
> Fatal four disorders, fleshed there, all contended."

Thomas Hardy attended the dramatization of *Far from the Madding Crowd* on February 27, 1882; he mentioned Liverpool in that work, in *A Pair of Blue Eyes*, and in *Desperate Remedies*. In the last of these, Mr. and Mrs. Manston live at 133 Turngate Street.

On September 1, 1906, Hugh Walpole arrived in Liverpool as lay minister at the Mersey Mission for Seamen and lodged at 32 Peel Street, which was operated by a Miss Hales. In a characteristic manner, before going to the mission he visited the public reading room and the circulating library. Walpole held the post only six months before leaving for London, but in the interim he convinced his family that his ordination was impossible. H. G. Wells includes Liverpool in "A Dream of Armageddon" in *Twelve Stories and a Dream;* Cooper the solicitor works here.

Nathaniel Hawthorne was United States Consul here from 1853 to 1857, when he lived on Duke Street and then in Rock Park. Hawthorne's experiences in Liverpool and England are described in *Our Old Home;* the consulate

> was located in Washington Buildings (a shabby and smoke-stained edifice of four stories high, thus illustriously named in honor of our national establishment), at the lower corner of Brunswick Street, contiguous to the Goree Arcade, and in the neighborhood of some of the oldest docks. This was by no means a polite or elegant portion of England's great commercial city, nor were the apartments of the American official so splendid as to indicate the assumption of much consular pomp on his part. A narrow and ill-lighted staircase gave access to an equally narrow and ill-lighted passageway on the first floor, at the extremity of which, surmounting a door-frame, appeared an exceedingly stiff pictorial representation of the Goose and Gridiron, according to the English idea of those ever-to-be-honored symbols.

LOLHAM BRIDGES, Rutland An area near Great Casterton, Lolham Bridges is associated with the Northamptonshire poet John Clare, who came here in 1817 shortly after arriving at Great Casterton from Helpston. He visited a friend here, "where King Street crosses the flood-meadows and marshes of the Welland." This area is the scene of his poem "The Last of March."

LONDON (pop. 7,379,041) Spread along both banks of the Thames River, 40 miles from the estuary to the North Sea, London covers an area of about 1,000 square miles; today it is properly known as Greater London, since it has become a conurbation of thirty-two London boroughs and since the old City is now only a financial and commercial area in its center. Roughly the shape of a squashed oval, London supports an extremely dense population in an environment which still includes a great number of green spaces: parks, playing fields, and old village commons abound, while skyscrapers have been kept to a bare minimum, at least by comparison with other large cities around the world. Indeed, single-family dwellings are the dominant form of housing in the Greater London area. Furthermore, even though London is the sixth largest city in the world, with a good deal of 20th-century expansion behind it, it has maintained a healthy respect for its past and has preserved perhaps more ancient buildings than any other metropolis in the world.

From Pre-Roman Times to the 16th Century The area of ancient London was marshy on both sides of the serpentine Thames, but the land was higher on the north side, where in two places hills rose abruptly 25 or 30 feet above the river. This is the only area where an early city could have existed, and it is generally assumed that the ancient Britons had a hill fortress on the westernmost of the two hills. On the other hill the Romans later began their settlement. Of the ancient Britons here nothing is known, although Geoffrey of Monmouth in his *Historia Regum Britanniae* accounts for the city in this way:

> Heli had three sons: Lud, Cassivelaunus and Nennius. Lud, the eldest of these, accepted the kingship after his father's death. He was famous for his town-planning activities. He re-built the walls of the town of Trinovantum and girded it round with innumerable towers. He ordered the citizens to construct their homes and buildings there in such a style that no other city in the most far-flung of kingdoms could boast of palaces more fair. . . . However many other cities he might possess, this one he loved above all and in it he passed the greater part of each year. As a result it was afterwards called Kaerlud and then, as the name became corrupted, Kaerlundein. In a later age, as languages evolved, it took the name London. . . .

Around 1200 Layamon added his bit to the tale and possibly originated the myth of Brutus in this connection; Brutus

> . . . found a pleasant place   upon a water stream;
> There he did raise up   a very rich borough,
> With bowers and with halls,   and with high stone walls.
> When that city was made,   it was most glorious.
> The city was very well built,   and he set a name on her
> He gave her a glorious name,   Troy the new,
> To remind his kindred   when they were come.
> Since then the people,   a long time after,
> Gave up that name,   and Trinovant named it.
> Within a few winters   it befell after,
> There arose from Brutus' kin   one who was a high king,
> Lud was he called;   he loved that city greatly;
> He had it named Lud   throughout his folk,
> Had it called Kaerlud,   after that king.

Quite naturally, the town has its place in Arthurian legend; here Utherpendragon first sees Ygerna, wife of Gorlois:

> The next Eastertide Uther told the nobles of his kingdom to assemble in that same town of London, so that he could wear his crown and celebrate so important a feast-day with proper ceremony. They all obeyed. . . .
> Among the others there was present Gorlois, Duke of Cornwall, with his wife Ygerna, who was the most beautiful woman in Britain. When the King saw her there among the other women, he was immediately filled with desire for her, with the result that he took no notice of anything else, but devoted all his attention to her. . . . When Ygerna's husband saw what was happening, he was so annoyed that he withdrew from the court without taking leave.

Arthur, too, retreated here and "convened the bishops and clergy of the entire realm" to plan "the best and safest [action] for him to do, in the face of this invasion by the pagans."

The Romans arrived in A.D. 43 and subsequently placed their settlement on the twin hills which are today crowned by St. Paul's Cathedral and the Smithfield Market; the Thames was bridged at this point, and the modern Gracechurch Street led from the Romans' bridge to their basilica in the heart of Londinium. Within a short time of its establishment, Londinium had become a thriving port, and the trading town was soon linked to the north, south, east, and west of the island by a vast road network. The Romans had little trouble in subduing the early Britons in this region, and Londinium prospered; this prosperity, in turn, attracted the attention of Boadicea, Queen of the Iceni, who led her people against the city in A.D. 61. Londinium was sacked and burned, but a new basilica was then erected (roughly on the site of the modern Leadenhall Market) and, said Tacitus, the city was soon restocked with merchants. So large and important did London become that it superseded the Roman capital of Camulodunum (Colchester) in importance; its commercial success and its relatively less isolated position vis-à-vis the provincial tribes led to its assumption of the role of capital city. A system of roads radiated from London, with Ermine Street running north to Lincoln, Watling Street northwest to St. Albans, the Colchester Road east to Colchester, and the Silchester Road west to Silchester. As Roman peace settled over the city and its administrative bodies, farms and villages grew up in the surrounding countryside; indeed, settlement outside the city was encouraged, and each area had a well-defined personality, some of which survives to the present and suggests a plurality in Roman London's administration which has only recently been confirmed.

Saxon London flourished but not without conflicts. One such conflict centered in an attempt by Mellitus, St. Augustine's companion priest, to convert the Londoners, and various accounts of the episode point to already well-established religious cults, probably drawn directly from the Roman versions. Augustine wrote that the people were "hostile to Christianity," and the Venerable Bede in his *Historia Ecclesiastica Gentis Anglorum* comments, "But the people of London refused to receive Mellitus, preferring to serve idolatrous high priests." Mellitus, in fact, was unable to perform his duties here and was forced to flee to Canterbury, where Augustine was safely established. Through all this London was a populous urban center with an international market (according, for example, to Bede). The city fell to the Danes; in 886 it was recaptured by Alfred the Great, who had its walls rebuilt. Later the Danes regained the city and became part of its heterogeneous population.

Saxon London was peaceful, prosperous, and populous and enjoyed a favored status up to the Norman invasion. Edward the Confessor began both Westminster Abbey and Westminster Palace on Westminster Eyot in the Thames River; the abbey, built to house a Benedictine monastery, was consecrated on December 28, 1065, only a few days before Edward's death. His decision to build both abbey and palace on this site was prompted by a desire to create a court center completely removed from the commercial city; further, because of the proximity of the two buildings, church and state were effectively linked. Edward was buried in his new abbey in January 1066, and Harold II may have been crowned here. Nevertheless, from the time of Harold's death (October 14, 1066) to the reign of Elizabeth II, all monarchs except Edward V (who was murdered before he was crowned) and Edward VIII (who abdicated before his coronation) have been crowned in the abbey. The cruciform abbey with its low roof stood for more than 200 years, during which time Edward was canonized, before Henry III (r. 1216–1272) decided to build the magnificent abbey we see today.

The Norman Conquest was the turning point in London's development, and extensive building took place during the late 11th century after William I had shown special favor to the city. This monarch took care not to destroy London needlessly, and in return for its surrender he allowed the citizens to retain their rights; he built his palace and stronghold on the eastern boundary of the City, beyond Chancery Lane and Holborn. Indeed, William's central keep, known as the White Tower (because of its whitewashing in 1241), with the rest of the more recent complex, is what is today known as the Tower of London; the concentric moated castle did not appear for another two centuries. Early Norman London flourished until 1135, when a fire swept through it from end to end; rebuilding began almost immediately, this time in stone; the streets were paved; and a primitive sewage system of open sewers and conduits was put into operation. Along the Strand the great houses of medieval London, usually ecclesiastical palaces, were constructed, and by 1400 two archbishops, sixteen bishops, twenty abbots, and six priors owned dwellings in London.

Self-government in the City of London began at the end of the 12th century, and self-determination grew in proportion to the growth of the guilds, which provided, among other things, the funds needed to finance ambitious building programs and expeditions abroad. The trades flourished in several distinct areas, especially north and south of Cheapside along streets called Wood, Milk, Honey, Iron, and Poultry on the north and Bread, Candles, Soap, and Fish on the south. Medieval London was also known for its prejudices and superstitions, and the expulsion of the Jews in 1290 is notable; the medieval anti-Jewish legends which grew up, as for example in "The Prioress's Tale" in Geoffrey Chaucer's *The Canterbury Tales,* were generally accepted as fact.

It is London's great buildings that are the principal means whereby the past survives here, and one of the most famous is the Tower of London. Actually, the Tower, whose gardens cover 18 acres, is a conglomerate of every flourishing English architectural style from the Norman on and has served as prison, palace, and fortress and as home of the Royal Mint, the Public Records Office, and the Royal Observatory. But it is as a jail that the Tower is best known, and it is with the Bloody Tower and the Traitor's Gate that most literary figures are associated; indeed, through the gate on their way to prison or execution passed such figures as Sir Thomas More, Queen Anne Boleyn, Lady Jane Grey, and James, Duke of Monmouth. The Bloody Tower took its present name by the 16th century; it is the assumed site of the murders of Edward V and his brother the Duke of York and gained the epithet "bloody" following, as Sir Thomas More wrote, "the dolorous end of those babes." The Tower held early political prisoners as well, most frequently those found guilty of treason. Later, depending on their influence, political prisoners such as Sir Walter Ralegh were permitted comfortably furnished rooms, servants, and visits from their families, but here, as well, sufferings such as those recounted in John Foxe's *The Book of Martyrs* were commonplace. Since the inception of the tower, because of its security it has held the crown jewels and regalia, and since 1870, excepting a period during the war years when they were hidden outside London, they have been on display in Wakefield Tower.

Westminster Abbey has been a royal foundation (called a "Royal Peculiar" and responsible only to the reigning monarch) since its inception; indeed, the collegiate body, consisting of a dean and four canons, is still appointed by the crown, although the abbey is financed wholly through subscriptions and endowments. Originally a Benedictine monastery, it met the usual fate at the dissolution of the monasteries in the 16th century. After briefly regaining its monastic status under Mary, it was fully reconstituted under Elizabeth I as the Collegiate Church of St. Peter in Westminster. The Shrine of Edward the Confessor once drew many pilgrims, and near the shrine or in the Henry VII Chapel many English monarchs have been buried. Richard II and his Queen, Anne of Bohemia, Eleanor of Castile, Mary, Queen of Scots, Elizabeth I, and Mary I are but a few of the monarchs in the abbey. Here as well are the Unknown Warrior's grave (World War I), the magnificent Battle of Britain commemorative window in the Royal Air Force Memorial Chapel, the Statesmen's Aisle (where such men as Sir Robert Peel, William Gladstone, Benjamin Disraeli, and William Pitt are buried), and the Poets' Corner (where the tombs and memorials of many of the great men of letters, beginning with Geoffrey Chaucer, are to be found).

Another important, basically medieval building is St. Paul's Cathedral. The first, wooden church was destroyed by fire in the 7th century; the second, built of stone by St. Erkenwald (Earconwald), was destroyed by the Danes in the 9th century; and the third burned in 1087. The last-named church, rebuilt by Maurice, Bishop of London, and supported by the new king, William Rufus, was on a grand scale. This was Old St. Paul's, which endured until the Great Fire in 1666; it stood within the precincts bounded by Paternoster Row on the north, Old Change on the east, Carter Lane on the south, and Creed Lane and Ave Maria Lane on the west and was enclosed by walls. Cloisters, residences, and a chapter house were constructed in the precincts, and some of the remains of the chapter house are still visible in the gardens south of the present nave. Without doubt, the most famous aspect of the cathedral was Paul's Cross, an open-air pulpit which was the scene of many extraordinary and, often, inciting sermons. Old St. Paul's was the scene in 1377 of the heresy trial of John Wycliffe, on whose behalf John of Gaunt appeared. In many ways this trial portended what was to come, since Old St. Paul's became one of the major locations for trials concerning witchcraft and sorcery, the convicted being taken from here to be burned at the stake at Smithfield. The church, which had been enormously wealthy from the 14th century on, was despoiled in the Reformation; the high altar was taken down and replaced with a plain table, the reredos was totally destroyed, and all the monuments, except that to John of Gaunt, were damaged. In 1628 James I

undertook a major restoration, which continued until the outbreak of the Civil War, when the destruction proceeded in an orderly fashion. Carved woodwork became firewood, windows were smashed, and lead was melted down for bullets. The existing tombs were savaged, and a contemporary description of the building as "a loathsome Golgotha" was undoubtedly apt.

There were many other important churches in medieval London, but of the thirteen major ones only the Church and Hospital of St. Bartholomew the Great has had a continuous existence on the same site. Rahere, who appears to have been a *jongleur* in various wealthy households, fell ill on a pilgrimage and vowed the founding of a hospital dedicated to St. Bartholomew in exchange for his recovery. Upon his return to London, he founded the hospital on a site indicated as appropriate by the saint, who then appeared and demanded a church as well. Rahere became the first prior and was buried here in 1144 in a magnificent canopied tomb. Another of these magnificent churches was that of St. Martin le Grand, which stood until 1538 at the junction of the roads at Cheapside where the General Post Office buildings now stand. This church was of great importance on two counts: first, the bell in the tower gave the nightly signal for curfew to be rung throughout the City; second, and more significantly, it had the right of sanctuary. The Church of St. Mary Overy, on the south bank of the Thames, was founded originally, says John Stow, as a "house of sisters" by Mary Awdrey upon the death of her lover. The convent later was made a college of priests by Swithen, a noblewoman, and in the 12th century two Norman knights founded here a great priory, of which the present Church of St. Saviour was the chapel. The original chancel, two transepts, and the Lady Chapel have now been incorporated into the present Southwark Cathedral.

John Gower (1325?–1408) John Gower, Geoffrey Chaucer's "moral Gower," presumably a member of the Inner Temple (this affiliation is totally unsubstantiated and probably erroneous), resided in the Priory of St. Mary Overy beginning possibly in 1377; his quarters are thought to have been on Montague Close, between the church and the river. In 1398 he and Agnes Groundolf, "both parishioners of St. Mary Magdalene, Southwark," were married by special license granted by William of Wykeham, Bishop of Winchester, in his own chapel with the chaplain of St. Mary Magdalene officiating. Gower was instrumental in restoring St. Mary Overy and, says John Leland, contributed lavishly himself and secured aid from his "powerful friends." Even though Gower went blind around the turn of the 15th century, his residence here continued, and it is assumed that he spent the rest of his life at the priory. In August 1408 he made his will (preserved at Lambeth) and left instructions for his burial in the Chapel of St. John the Baptist at St. Mary Overy. Gower died between August 15 and October 24, and John Stow writes that he was

> buried on the north side of the said church, in the chapel of St. John, where he founded a chantry: he lieth under a tomb of stone, with his image, also of stone, over him: the hair of his head, auburn, long to his shoulders, but curling up, and a small forked beard; on his head a

chaplet, like a coronet of four roses; a habit of purple, damasked down to his feet; a collar of esses gold about his neck; under his head the likeness of three books, which he compiled. The first, named *Speculum Meditantis*, written in French; the second, *Vox Clamantis*, penned in Latin; the third, *Confessio Amantis*, written in English. . . .

William Langland (1330?–?1400) The long literary history of London begins in the Middle Ages with William Langland, assumed author of *Piers Plowman*. Because of an autobiographical passage in the C text, he is thought to have lived in London at some time:

> Thus I awoke, and found myself on Cornhill, where I lived with Kit in a cottage, dressed like a beggar— though not, believe me, in high favour with the idle hermits and beggars who hang around London, for I put them into my verses and spoke as Reason taught me.

Langland probably was a minor cleric (educated at the Priory of Great Malvern) who took only minor orders because of the death of his patron or patrons and was therefore unable to advance in the church. As a result, he belonged to the class of medieval clerics known as unbeneficed clergy, as he reports in *Piers* (that is, if the reading can be taken as autobiographical):

> And though the friends who helped me then have since died, I have never found any life that suited me, except in these long, clerical robes. If I'm to earn a living, I must earn it by doing the job that I've learned best. . . .
>
> So I live in London, and also on London, and the tools that I work with are my Paternoster and Prayer Book, and sometimes my Book of Offices for the Dead, and my Psalter and Seven Penitential Psalms. And with these I sing for the souls of those who help me; and I expect the folk who provide me with food, to make me welcome when I visit them once or twice a month.

Geoffrey Chaucer (1345?–1400) Without doubt the best-known early figure associated with the greater London area was Geoffrey Chaucer; with him, legend, tradition, and fact are so interwoven that they are often difficult to separate. The year of Chaucer's birth is unknown, but the usually accepted date of about 1340 seems to be three or four years in error if the poet's testimony in 1386 at the Scrope-Grosvenor trial—that he was then "forty years old and more"— and the evidence of military service in France in 1359 are accurate. The son of John Chaucer, a vintner, and his wife (probably Agnes), the poet was born in a tenement in the parish of "St. Martin at Vintry, between the tenement of William le Gauger on the east and that which belonged to John le Mazclyner on the west" (thought to have been near Whittington Gardens on Upper Thames Street). This was not a particularly attractive location, as Guildhall documents reveal: Walbrook was periodically "stopped up by divers filth and dung thrown therein by persons who have houses along the said course, to the great nuisance and damage of all the city." Chaucer and his family are assumed to have attended services at St. Martin at Vintry (long since destroyed), and it is also assumed that he had some education at the Inner Temple.

By May 1357 he was in the service of Elizabeth, Countess of Ulster, the wife of Prince Lionel, but how long he was in this household is not known; he was, though, ransomed from France after being taken prisoner at Reims in 1359, and he received payment from the prince until 1360. Of the next seven years nothing is known. Possibly as early as 1366 Chaucer married Philippa Roet; the marriage is traditionally assigned to the Savoy Palace on the Embankment (the present Savoy Chapel stands on the approximate site). Tradition also records that the Savoy Madonna over the altar was a gift from Chaucer. In 1374 Chaucer took lodgings at Aldgate; a Latin lease dated "48 Edward III. A.D. 1374" granted "the whole of the dwelling house above the Gate of Aldgate, with the rooms built over, and a certain cellar beneath, the same gate, on the South side of that gate, and the appurtenances thereof; to have and to hold the whole of the house aforesaid, with the rooms so built over, and the said cellar. . . ." In exchange for the life grant, Chaucer had to maintain the property. On Aldgate about 25 feet from the corner of Jewry Street, the foundations for the medieval gate with its apartments in the city wall were discovered (where the street runs today), and the Aldgate Post Office holds a plaque noting Chaucer's nearby residence. In 1369 Blanche of Lancaster, wife of John of Gaunt, died of the plague and was buried at Old St. Paul's; it is assumed that Chaucer was present at the September 12, 1374, memorial service which John of Gaunt attended, especially if *The Book of the Duchess* was read then.

In 1386 Chaucer sat as a Member of Parliament (which probably met in the Great Chapter House of Westminster), and his employment as Controller of the Customs and Subsidy of Wools, Skins, and Hides in the Port of London, a post he had held since 1374, was terminated; in the same year he gave up the lodgings over Aldgate, but in the twelve-year period here he had translated Boethius's *De consolatione philosophiae* and written *Troilus and Criseyde, Parlement of Foules, Hous of Fame,* and the *Legend of Good Women*. Chaucer, it is thought, had already retired to Kent, where he was elected Knight of the Shire in 1386. He seems to have had severe financial problems in the next few years, but Richard II's reaching his majority in May 1389 changed Chaucer's prospects; John of Gaunt was reinstated in the court's favor, and Chaucer, in his turn, became "clerk of our Works at our Palace of Westminster, our Tower of London, our Castle at Birkhamstead, our Manors of Kennington, Eltham, Clarendon, Shene [Richmond], Byfleet, Chiltern Langley, and Feckenham, our Lodges at Hatherburgh in our New Forest, and in our other parks and our Mews for falcons at Charing Cross." He probably lived in Greenwich in 1390, but he did not give up his Kent residence until December 4, 1399, when he took a fifty-three-year lease of a house in the gardens of Westminster Abbey. It was "a tenement, with its appurtenances, situate in the garden of St. Mary's Chapel"; the house, somewhere on the site of the present Henry VII Chapel, was sheltered by the southeast walls of the abbey church, "nigh to the White Rose Tavern." The poet's last-recorded pension payment was made on June 5, 1400, and if the inscription on his tomb is correct, he died on October 25 of that year. Chaucer was the first literary figure to be buried at Westminster Abbey, and the choice of his site dictated the location of what today is known as the Poets' Corner.

There are many more Chaucerian associations with

the City and what is now Greater London; he loved "[t]he citye of London that is to me so dere and sweete, in which I was forth growen; and more kindly love have I to that place than to any other in yerth." *The Canterbury Tales* begins here:

> Bifil that in that seson on a day,
> In Southwerk at the Tabard as I lay
> Redy to wenden on my pilgrymage
> To Caunterbury with ful devout corage,
> At nyght was come into that hostelrye
> Wel nyne and twenty in a compaignye,
> Of sondry folk, by aventure yfalle
> In felaweshipe, and pilgrimes were they alle,
> That toward Caunterbury wolden ryde.

On the east side of Borough High Street in Southwark is an alley called Talbot Yard, and here at the alley entrance is the Old Tabard Inn. This is not, of course, Chaucer's Tabard, but the original inn from which the pilgrims set out stood very near this spot until its demolition in 1629. The medieval pilgrims, of whom Chaucer may have been one, made their way out of London down Tabard Street (Kent Street then) to modern Kent Street and Watling Street. Among the other Greater London areas mentioned in Chaucer's works are Deptford, Dartford, Chepe (Cheapside), Dartmouth, Greenwich, Eltham, and Hatcham. Hatcham is especially significant, for the poet himself was robbed here twice at the Foul Oak in 1390, and "The Reeve's Prologue" refers to this:

> Lo Depeford! and it is half-wey pryme
> Lo Grenewych, ther many a shrewe is inne!

(Historically, Greenwich included Hatcham.) Chaucer's "gentil Pardoner" came from the Hospital of St. Mary Rounceval, founded by 1236 by Gilbert, the Marshal of England, Earl of Pembroke; the hospital stood on what is today Northumberland Avenue and was part of the site occupied by Northumberland House and Gardens.

Thomas Occleve (1370?–1426) Thomas Occleve (Hoccleve), author of *De regimine principum*, lived for some time at Chester's Inn, Strand, before being granted sustenance by the King at Southwick Priory in Hampshire.

John Lydgate (1370?–?1451) Another early figure associated with the city is John Lydgate, who between 1390 and 1400 made the acquaintance of Chaucer and his son Thomas; an introduction to the court brought him into direct contact with the Prince of Wales, later Henry V, whose subsequent victory at Agincourt and return to London Lydgate celebrated in verse. When in London during this time, Lydgate stayed at the town house belonging to the monastery at Bury St. Edmunds; John Stow describes the house, known as Buries Markes in St. Mary Axe (Aldgate), as

> one great house, large of rooms, fair courts, and garden-plots....

With the accession of Henry VI, Lydgate acted as court poet, although it is not thought that an official title was conferred. Various state and other events were held in Westminster Hall, on the south side of New Palace Yard, and shops and stalls were set up along the walls of the hall:

> Within this Hall, neither riche nor yet poore,
> Wolde do for aught, althogh I sholde dye:

> Which seeing I gat me out of the doore,
> Where Flemynge on me began for to cry.
> Master, what will you require or by?
> Fyne felt hatts or spectacles to rede,
> Lay down you sylver and here you may spede.

"London Lickpenny" is especially topographical.

Sir John Paston (1421–1466) Sir John Paston, whose correspondence (and his wife's) gives a remarkable insight into 15th-century England, had chambers in the Temple, and the letters often reflect life in the city in an interesting way, as the following illustrates:

> [M]ine aunt Mundeford ... dare not adventure her money to be brought up to London for fear of robbing. For it is said here that there goeth many thieves betwixt this and London. . . .

William Caxton (1422?–1491) One of the most important men of the mid-15th century was William Caxton, who, though born in the Weald of Kent at Tenterden, was a Londoner in all but birth. Apprenticed to the mercer Robert Large in 1438, Caxton probably resided in Large's house at the northeast corner of Old Jewry. This house, a substantial building, was originally a synagogue and had been presented to the Mendicant Friars by Henry III in 1271. Caxton's apprenticeship lasted until 1446, when he established himself in Bruges, and he undertook various royal commissions over the next twenty-five years. Having learned the art of printing on the Continent, Caxton returned to England and London in 1476; under the auspices of Bishop Islip, he set up his presses at the walls of Westminster Abbey. Caxton's house is believed to have been on the site of the old Almonry on Little Dean Street; it was just to the left after the turning into Tothill Street from Storey's Gate. Here from 1477 to 1491 he printed more than 18,000 pages and translated more than twenty-five French, Dutch, and Latin works. Caxton died in 1491 and was buried either in St. Margaret's Church, Westminster, or in the adjoining churchyard near the abbey. There is no record of his death, and the church registers for the period include only one notation recording 6 shillings 8 pence "atte bureying of William Caxton" and a second for 6 pence "for the belle atte same bureying." A memorial tablet was erected by the Roxburghe Club in 1820, and in 1833 the London printers and publishers raised a stained-glass window, inscribed by Alfred, Lord Tennyson in Caxton's honor. The window was destroyed during World War II.

Thomas Malory (d. 1471) Sir Thomas Malory's relationship with London is more a relationship between Malory and London's jails. About two years after the 1450 episode at Combe Abbey, Warwickshire, when Sir Thomas and his men carried out "great destruction and spoilation of the monastery and abbey," Malory was imprisoned in Marshalsea Prison in Southwark (off Borough High Street, roughly between present-day Mermaid Court and Talbot Yard). When charged, Malory pleaded not guilty and "put himself on the country"; that is, he asked for trial by a jury of Warwickshire men. The April 28 trial date came, but the jurors did not, and Malory was remanded in custody for about a year. It is thought that his release came when he bribed a jailer. Orders for his rearrest were issued; Malory was brought before the King and Council at Westminster, and a second jury was ordered; again, in January 1454, the jury failed to appear, and Malory was sent to Marshalsea, where no bail was granted. Indeed, so exasperated were the King and Council that the prison marshal was threatened with a £1,000 fine if the prisoner escaped. Somehow in May Malory arranged bail and swore to return on October 29 for recommittal with a guarantee of £400 (£200 from Sir Thomas and £20 each from ten others); he failed to turn up, but the explanation—that John Hampton, the governor of the Colchester Castle, where Malory was being held on suspicion of a felony, would not allow it—was accepted. In November he was back in Marshalsea, where he remained until being removed to the Tower of London in May 1455. He presented letters patent from the King and six guarantors when asking for a pardon in February 1456, but the courts dismissed not only the guarantors but also the pardon. In January 1457 he was transferred to the more secure Newgate Prison, on Newgate Street at the corner of Old Bailey where the Central Criminal Court now stands. From here he was moved again to the nearby Ludgate Prison; as was often the case in the Middle Ages, the apartments over Ludgate (which then spanned the street and was part of the City's walls) were being used as a prison.

In October 1457 Malory was released on a personal penalty of £400 (plus £60 from three other guarantors) and ordered to appear on December 28, at which time he was recommitted to Marshalsea. He was freed by Easter of the next year. By 1471 he was back in London (perhaps in prison), where he died on March 12; he was buried two days later in the Chapel of St. Francis in the Grey Friars Monastery. His grave was on the south side of the chapel under the fourth window. The church stood on part of the site occupied by the General Post Office on Newgate Street near the Central Criminal Court building. If, as is generally assumed, Sir Thomas had easy access to a library when he was composing *Le Morte d'Arthur*, he probably used the library of the Grey Friars Monastery.

16th and Early 17th Centuries The 16th century, from the Reformation on, is in many ways the beginning of modern times, especially with respect to England's literature. While the Reformation itself was directed at the relation between church and state and was largely inspired by Henry VIII's complicated matrimonial and fiscal affairs, it is obvious that the ending of the old order brought new possibilities in all aspects of English life, not just the literary. In many ways the church was anachronistic and far from popular, and in the final analysis Henry's attack was carried off rather easily. It began when Henry's cardinal, Thomas Wolsey, failed to secure the King's divorce from Catherine of Aragon. Wolsey was dismissed as Lord Chancellor in October 1529, and Henry sought to establish that the state had the authority to grant the divorce; to that end the Reformation Parliament was convened in November 1529.

Henry continued through five more wives and was succeeded in 1547 by Edward VI, his son by Jane Seymour (who died a few days after his birth). Edward's death would bring the Catholic Mary to the throne, but the Earl of Warwick coerced Edward into declaring Mary illegitimate and thereby set the line of succession to Lady Jane Grey, Warwick's daughter-in-law and the grandniece of Henry VIII. Warwick, now Duke of Northumberland, and Lady Jane were imprisoned in the Tower and executed for their pains, and Mary came to the throne. Marrying Philip II of Spain and determined to return England to the Catholic fold, she had a violent reign; when "Bloody" Mary died on November 17, 1558, there was much jubilation.

Elizabeth I clearly was eminently suited for the crown (she had a solid Renaissance education as well as a good grasp of the religious problems of her country), and the benefits of the Reformation became associated with her name. Elizabethan England was a dynamic society, and London, in particular, reaped the rewards as it became the artistic and cultural capital. The population increased rapidly (75,000 in the City alone and 150,000 outside the gates), and Southwark became a part of London proper early in the 17th century. Elizabeth's reign, however, was not without incident, the greatest problems being those of Mary, Queen of Scots, the war with Spain, the rapid growth of the more democratic House of Commons as an independent voice in the government (in opposition to the House of Lords), and the question of Elizabeth's successor. The last-named problem was solved by designating James VI of Scotland, son of Mary, Queen of Scots, as heir apparent, and his reign provided the necessary unification of Scotland and England.

Walter Besant has described the London of Edward III as "a city of palaces" and that of Elizabeth as "a city of ruins," and his meaning was not restricted to buildings. Henry had managed to shatter the monasteries and religious foundations as well as many of England's beliefs and traditions. However, Elizabethan London had much green space; the area south of Chepe was probably the most populous, with the population just outside the City walls growing rapidly, especially around St. Giles Cripplegate. London still had no docks, and the loading and unloading of cargo took place in the Pool below London Bridge. As the volume of trade increased, London took on the aspect of a prosperous city and, as such, led the way in the founding of grammar schools and theaters. St. Paul's, the Blue Coat School, the School of St. Thomas (previously founded by the Mercers' Company), the Merchant Taylors' School (now at Charterhouse), St. Saviour's School, and St. Olave's School came at this time, and Charterhouse was founded a few years later. Between 1570 and 1600 seven theaters were built (four were public: the Globe at Bankside, the Curtain in Shoreditch, the Red Bull on St. John's Street, and the Fortune on Whitecross Street; and three were private: the Blackfriars, the Whitefriars, and the Cockpit, or Phoenix), and numerous companies of actors emerged.

The twenty-two years of James I's reign were difficult ones, as James had a somewhat anachronistic view of the monarchy, believing, as he did, in the divine right of kings. Confrontations took place between the King and Parliament and the King and the judiciary, and James also got himself and England embroiled in the Thirty Years' War, which brought about extremely depressed conditions in England: trade, especially the cloth trade, fell off drastically, and devaluations of the pound reflected the country's weakness in international markets. Great Britain and

Spain were at war in 1624, a fact which added to Charles I's problems when he came to the throne in 1625.

John Skelton (1460?–1529)   An important cleric of this period with strong ties with London was John Skelton, whose first appearance seems to have been in 1491, when he became tutor to the King Henry VII's second son, Prince Henry (later Henry VIII). Toward the end of the century the affair of Perkin Warbeck, whose supporters were camped on nearby Blackheath, caused the Queen to remove her children—and most probably the staff, including Skelton—from Eltham to Coldharbour and then to Windsor for greater safety. Back at the Great Hall, Skelton met Desiderius Erasmus through Sir Thomas More, and the great humanist later described Skelton as *Britannicarum literarum lumen et decus*. Between March and June 1498, Skelton entered holy orders with a title from the Abbey of St. Mary of the Graces (long gone but then located near the Tower), and by 1504 he had assumed the living of Diss, Norfolk.

Skelton appears to have been back in Westminster by 1512, when he was appointed *orator regius*, and by 1516 he was established in one of the abbey houses near the Sanctuary Tower (these houses were a little northwest of St. Margaret's Church, approximately where the Middlesex Guildhall now stands). Skelton's reputation as a satirical wit increased, and he attacked both the lax clergy and Cardinal Wolsey with equal effectiveness. Wolsey, who had been Skelton's patron for many years, becomes "Son of the Wolf," and when he dissolved a convocation called by Archbishop William Warham at St. Paul's in 1522 and ordered it to meet at Westminster, Skelton responded:

> Gentle Paul, laie doune thy sweard,
> For Peter of Westminster hath shauen thy beard.

"Why Come Ye Nat to Courte?" followed immediately, and Wolsey's style and character are further described:

> Twit, Andrew, twit, Scot,
> Ge hame, ge scour the pot:
> For we have spent our shot.
> We shall have a *tot quot*
> From the Pope of Rome,
> To weave all in one loom
> A web of linsey-woolsey,
> *Opus male dulce:*
> The devil kiss his cule!
> For, whiles he doth rule
> All is warse and warse,
> The devil kiss his arse!

With the circulation of this poem almost immediately after "Speke Parrot," Wolsey's patience was at an end, and the "poet laureate" was forced to seek refuge in the abbey at Westminster, where he remained for the rest of his life; no reconciliation was ever effected with Wolsey. Skelton died in the abbey precincts on June 21, 1529, a scant four months before Wolsey's downfall, and was buried before the high altar of St. Margaret's Church, just across from Westminster Hall. An alabaster stone with the words *Ionnes Skeltonvs, vates Pierivs, hic sitvs est* marks the grave; both stone and inscription are gone.

Sir Thomas More (1478–1535)   Sir Thomas More, Lord Chancellor of England, was born in the early morning of February 7, 1478 (New Style), at the family home on Milk Street, Cheapside; nothing remains of the house. More's earliest education took place at St. Anthony's Free School on Threadneedle Street (possibly about where the Bank of England now stands), but about 1490 More was placed in the household of John Morton, Archbishop of Canterbury and Lord Chancellor; after a period at Canterbury Hall, Oxford, he was called back to London by his father, who was concerned about the impact of the new learning upon his son's religious orthodoxy. Thus, in 1494 he came to New Inn, preparatory to entering one of the Inns of Court; in less than two years he completed his preliminary study and entered Lincoln's Inn, where he became an outer (junior) barrister in the shortest possible time and, as a reward for his extensive legal knowledge and ability in disputation, was appointed reader of law at Furnival's Inn (this inn was located off Holborn between Brooke Street and Leather Lane). Through William Grocyn, rector of the Church of St. Lawrence Jewry (just off Aldermanbury opposite the Guildhall), he was invited to preach there, and More accordingly delivered a series of lectures on St. Augustine's *De civitate Dei*. The church contains a commemorative window.

When his early religious questioning came to an end, More's energies were thrown into secular life, and he even sat in Parliament in 1504. After becoming an undersheriff of the City in 1510, a post he kept until 1519, he was appointed a reader at Lincoln's Inn in 1511. Even this early More sometimes attended the Old Church in Chelsea (restored after a 1941 direct bomb hit) and occasionally acted as a server and crucifer as well as a chorister.

After his 1505 marriage to Jane Colt, the couple lived in Bucklersbury in the parish of St. Stephen, Walbrook, but nothing remains of this house. Four children were born here; within a month of his wife's death More, remarried to a widow with one child, took Crosby Place on Crosby Square (off Bishopsgate) for a short time; *Utopia* and *The History of King Richard III* were both written here. In 1524 More bought land in Chelsea, then essentially a country village, to build a home; Erasmus, who had met Sir Thomas in 1499 but who never visited him here, writes:

> More hath built near London upon the Thames side a commodious house, neither mean nor subject to envy, yet magnificent enough; there he converseth with his family, his wife, his son and daughter-in-law, his three daughters and their husbands, with eleven grandchildren....

While the new house was being built west of the Old Church, More and his family rented a nearby farmhouse, now known as Lindsey House (rebuilt). Sir Thomas's home is gone, but its location and that of its outbuildings have been discovered. Just where Battersea Bridge meets the Embankment was More's private landing stage; the house itself, a two-story brick structure with an inner court, stood about halfway up present Beaufort Street and was actually astride the street just about where the modern Covent Chapel stands. In its time, More's estate was quite elaborate; a kitchen garden lay on the west, enclosed formal gardens were on the north and east, orchards were all around, and a small zoo was constructed.

More succeeded Wolsey as Lord Chancellor in October 1529, just as the problems in connection with Henry's divorce of Catherine were beginning to dominate English politics; he was able to keep both the Court of Chancery and the Star Chamber current in their cases, and thus the rhyme:

When More some time had Chancellor been
No more suits did remain,—
The like will never more be seen,
Til More be there again.

More's resignation as Lord Chancellor on May 16, 1532, was inevitable; while he never actually entered into open opposition toward Henry's divorce, he felt it appropriate to retire to his Chelsea home. More's act, though, compromised Henry, who could never forgive his ex-Lord Chancellor. Sir Thomas's refusal to attend Anne's coronation on June 1, 1533, as well as his involvement in the case concerning the "holy maid of Kent," Elizabeth Barton, who prophesied the King's damnation and death, brought More before the Council. The Act of Succession, which made Elizabeth heir apparent and Mary illegitimate and which abjured "any foreign potentate" while demanding full renunciation of the Pope, called for an oath of adherence from all English subjects. More was summoned to Lambeth to appear before the commissioner but was in an unyielding mood and refused to take the oath. He was committed on April 17, 1534 to the Beauchamp Tower in the Tower of London, where he remained for just over fourteen months; during this time he wrote *A Dialoge of Comfort against Tribulacion, A Treatice to Receave the Blessed Body of Our Lorde,* and *A Treatice upon the Passion of Chryste.*

More's family was severely affected by his imprisonment; his estates were confiscated, and his health was undermined. His wife sent pleas for leniency to Henry, but both King and More remained obdurate. Three times Thomas Cromwell confronted More with the conditions of the 1534 act conferring the title Supreme Head of the Church upon Henry, and each time More replied only that he was a faithful subject. Finally, on July 1, 1535, the physically broken Sir Thomas was brought before a special commission at Westminster Hall, where without counsel he was charged with high treason. The end was inevitable; More was found guilty and sentenced to be hanged, drawn, and quartered at Tyburn. On July 5 the King changed the execution order to beheading, and on the following day, carrying a red crucifix in his hand, he left the Tower for execution. Meeting a woman from a neighboring inn who offered him a glass of wine for strength to face the ordeal, he replied in characteristic fashion, "Marry, good woman, my Master, Christ, had vinegar and gall and not wine given him to drink." More stumbled on the steps to the block, but his humor remained: "I pray you Master Lieutenant, see me safe up, and for my coming down, let me shift for myself." He told the executioner:

"Pluck up thy spirits, man, and be not afraid to do thy office; my neck is very short; take heed therefore thou strike not awry for the saving of thine honesty."

He asked him to wait until his beard was moved aside for "it had never committed treason."

Some confusion exists regarding More's burial; his head was impaled on London Bridge (in a standard procedure) and later was retrieved by his favorite daughter, Margaret Roper, who preserved it until her death in 1544. At that time the head is thought to have been placed in a leaden box and interred in the Roper family vault at St. Dunstan's Church, Canterbury. The headless body was interred in the Chapel of the Tower and was later moved to the Church of St. Peter ad Vincula. Modern London contains many memorials to Sir Thomas More, the most impressive being the modern sculpture by L. Cubitt Bevis. Here, sitting in front of the More Chapel which he restored in 1528, Sir Thomas overlooks the Thames; he wears the chain and Tudor rose presented by Henry across his knees and the red crucifix he carried to his execution around his neck.

Miles Coverdale (1488–1568) It was at Sir Thomas More's home in London that Miles Coverdale first met Thomas Cromwell, a man who became his most influential and powerful friend, but Coverdale's Catholicism (he had taken priest's orders in 1514 and entered the Austin friary at Cambridge) was not a problem during these troubled times, for as he told Cromwell, his desire was for nothing but his books and his conduct in all other matters would be guided by Henry VIII's adviser. In 1548 Coverdale became chaplain to King Edward VI and almoner to Queen Catherine Parr and was thus often in the royal residences in London and elsewhere. Coverdale preached occasionally at Old St. Paul's and at Westminster Abbey and as a prelate sat in the House of Lords in 1552 and 1553. On March 3, 1563, he was collated to the living of St. Magnus the Martyr on Lower Thames Street, where he remained until 1566, when the government tried to enforce a stricter observance of the liturgy than Coverdale would accept. Resigning the living, he preached as an itinerant and without sanction throughout London, including in his visits the Churches of St. Bartholomew the Less and Holy Trinity in the Minories. Coverdale was living somewhere in the parish of St. Bartholomew when he died in February 1568; he was buried on February 19 in the Church of St. Bartholomew by the Exchange (gone). Coverdale's remains were carefully disinterred in 1840 and taken to the Church of St. Magnus the Martyr on Lower Thames Street, where he was buried in a vault in the south aisle.

Sir Thomas Wyatt (1503?–1542) The poet Sir Thomas Wyatt, a court favorite from about 1518 on, seems, like so many of his contemporaries, to have had special experience of London's dungeons. In May 1534 he was involved in a fight with "the serjeants of London, in which one of the serjeants was slain. For this Mr. Wyatt is committed to the Fleet" (the Fleet stood mostly on the site of the present Congregational Memorial Hall on Farringdon Street, just north of Ludgate Circus). This imprisonment lasted only a short time, and it made little difference to Wyatt's position in court. Sir Thomas, though, again found himself in trouble in 1536, when Henry was ridding himself of Anne Boleyn, who was then in prison on five charges of adultery and one of incest. Wyatt, suspected of being one of her lovers or believed to have important information regarding the Queen's behavior, was probably confined in the crypts at this time, and it has been maintained that an inscription in his hand existed into the 19th century. He was released in June, with no charges laid, several weeks after the Queen's execution and was still not out of favor with Henry.

Over the years Wyatt undertook numerous diplomatic missions for the King before retiring to his home in Allington, Kent; the retirement was short-lived and in 1541 he was imprisoned in the Tower on the capital charge of treason. One account of the affair maintains that Wyatt insisted on his innocence, while another contends that he "confessed upon his examination, all the thinges, objected upon him" and admitted the seriousness of his actions which had "proceeded from him in his rage and folishe vaynglorios fantazie," yielding "himself only to his majesties mercy." Whatever his approach, it worked, and he was pardoned "*pour estre personnage de bon esprit.*" Indeed, Henry not only forgave him but added to his landholdings; the only condition was that Wyatt was compelled to take back his wife, from whom he had been separated for fifteen years because she had committed adultery (so had he, for that matter). Sir Thomas was still undertaking commissions for the crown at the time of his sudden death in Sherborne, Dorset, in 1542.

Nicholas Udall (1505–1556) The dramatist and scholar Nicholas Udall was first known to have been in London in the company of John Leland in 1533, when the two men undertook the writing of Latin and English verses for pageants celebrating the entry of Anne Boleyn to the City after her marriage to Henry VIII. Some five years later Udall was "outlawed" in the City for the nonpayment of a £20 tailor bill; and in March 1541, when he was headmaster at Eton, he was brought before the Privy Council on two charges: complicity in stealing silver from the college and buggery. In front of the Council he confessed to the second and more heinous crime and was committed to Old Marshalsea Prison in Southwark, off the Borough High Street, between the present Mermaid Court and Talbot Yard. Udall was dismissed from his post as headmaster, but his imprisonment lasted only a short time, and neither his scholastic reputation nor his chances for preferment were ruined. He found favor under Mary and in December 1555 was appointed to the headship of St. Peter's Grammar School, which was later annexed to Westminster (the school was behind the abbey, with its buildings ranged around Little Dean's Yard). Udall died a month after receiving the post and was buried in St. Margaret's Church, across from Westminster Hall, on December 23. The parish register there recorded his name as Nicholas Yevedale. It is possible that Udall's *Ralph Roister Doister,* considered by most to be the earliest English comedy, was written for performance by the boys at St. Peter's, but a similar and earlier claim is made by Eton.

John Leland (1506?–1552) The antiquarian John Leland was born in London around 1506 and received his early education at St. Paul's School, in St. Paul's Churchyard, the largest and most important school in the City in the early 16th century. The school, founded by John Colet, was for the children of citizens who could read and write Latin and English before admission. Leland proceeded from here to Christ's College, Cambridge; finding court favor under Henry VIII, he became King's librarian by 1530

and spent much of his time at the royal residences. Leland and Nicholas Udall composed elaborate verses in English and Latin for the pageants attending Anne Boleyn's first entry into London, and Leland reaped his reward that year when he was made the King's antiquarian, an office with neither predecessor nor successor. From this commission came the invaluable *Itinerary;* in a probable nine-year period (the author claimed six years) Leland not only carried out Henry's order to search out English antiquities in the libraries of abbeys, cathedrals, colleges, priories, and all administrative units but also sought out Roman, Saxon, and Danish remains to include in his catalog. Leland claimed, in presenting the manuscript to Henry, "as a Newe Yeares Gyfte," that he was "totally inflammed with a love to see thoroughly al those partes of this your opulente and ample reaulme." Even though Leland held a number of livings outside London (for example, Great Haseley, Oxfordshire), he kept a house in the City in the parish of St. Michael-le-Querne, at the west end of Cheapside. Here he spent time arranging his voluminous notes and became insane, it is said, by overtaxing his brain with his antiquarian studies. Even so he retained at least two of his benefices and was never in need; he died on April 18, 1552, and was buried in St. Michael's Church, approximately on the site of the St. Paul's Underground Station; both the church and the monument were destroyed in the Great Fire.

Roger Ascham (1515–1568) The educator and scholar Roger Ascham was first associated with London in 1545, when he presented a copy of *Toxophilus* to Henry VIII at Greenwich; he eventually gained royal favor, was appointed tutor to Princess Elizabeth in 1548, and took up residence at Cheshunt, Hertfordshire. While this post gave him the opportunity to use the teaching system later recommended in *The Scholemaster,* he found his court duties distasteful and resigned his post in 1550 to return to Cambridge. In late 1553 or early 1554, after an extended period on the Continent, Ascham was appointed Latin Secretary to Queen Mary and possibly lodged in the Middle Temple, just off Fleet Street.

In January 1554 Ascham married Margaret Howe, probably here in London, and later he and his family lived in the parish of St. Sepulchre, where he worked on *The Scholemaster.* In November 1568 Ascham taxed his always-precarious health by staying up for many nights in succession working on a Latin poem celebrating the anniversary of Queen Elizabeth's accession on November 17. He became very ill on December 23 and survived another week in severe pain before dying on December 30, 1568. He was buried on January 4 in St. Stephen's Chapel of St. Sepulchre's Church; there is no memorial to be seen.

John Foxe (1516–1587) Enduring a life of persecution and poverty during the 16th-century religious conflicts, John Foxe was in and out of London frequently from 1559 on, the time when he returned from the Continent. He preached one of his most powerful sermons at St. Paul's Cross on Good Friday, 1570, and renewed vigorously his attacks upon Catholicism. He died here in London on April 18, 1587, and was buried in St. Giles Cripplegate.

Henry Howard (1517?–1547) Henry Howard, Earl of Surrey (a courtesy title), had a long connection with the royal family, especially as a companion to Henry

VIII's natural son Henry Fitzroy, Duke of Richmond, and consequently with London. His major associations with London began in June 1533, when he carried the fourth sword before the King at the coronation of Anne Boleyn. In 1536 he presided as Earl Marshal, in the Duke of Norfolk's stead, at the trial of Anne Boleyn; he also took part in the Westminster jousts which celebrated the marriage of the King to Anne of Cleves, and on April 23, 1541, he was elected Knight of the Garter with investiture at Westminster Abbey.

Surrey's temperamental and ungovernable nature frequently got him into difficulties: in July 1542 the Privy Council imprisoned him in the Fleet (on the site of the present Congregational Memorial Hall on Farringdon Street) for having issued a challenge to John à Leigh. Freed in early August on a 10,000-mark bond, he promptly traveled to Newcastle upon Tyne to join his father, who was gathering troops for an expedition into Scotland. Within a year Surrey was in trouble in London again, this time accused of "a lewde and unsemely manner of walking in the night abowght the stretes and breaking with stone-bowes off certeyne wyndowes." A second charge was brought that he had eaten flesh in Lent; to this charge he pleaded a dispensation, and to the first he pleaded guilty but later argued a case of special circumstances. In his satire on London he presents himself, a gay young aristocrat roistering about the London streets, as a crusader against the moral ills of London:

London, hast thou accused me
Of breach of laws, the root of strife?
Within whose breast did boil to see,
So fervent hot, thy dissolute life,
That even the hate of sins that grow
Within thy wicked walls so rife,
For to break forth did convert so
That terror could it not repress.

. . . .

In secret silence of the night
This made me, with a reckless breast,
To wake thy sluggards with my bow—
A figure of the Lord's behest,
Whose scourge for sin the Scriptures show.

Surrey was imprisoned again in the Fleet for a little over one month but was fully restored in the King's favor by October, when he traveled abroad in aid of Emperor Charles V. During the next few years he served in Montreuil and Boulogne, whence he was recalled in 1546, though not in disgrace, as is popularly believed. He was not imprisoned and, in fact, received a grant (including Wymondham, Norfolk) from the King in April of that year.

A long-standing feud with the 1st Earl of Hertford arose when the dying Henry was nearing his decision on the post of regent for Edward VI's minority rule. Surrey's rashness in demanding his father's cause overstepped the bounds of propriety, and his insistence on a new coat of arms which included the arms of Edward the Confessor (a quartering forbidden by the Royal College of Arms) precipitated his fall. Hertford construed the new quartering as treasonous, and Surrey was arrested on December 12, 1546, to answer charges before the Privy Council. In the meantime, other unfounded allegations were made— affecting foreign dress and employing a foreign jester—which the Council, for some reason, took

seriously, and Surrey was ordered to the Tower of London. Unlike most prisoners of high rank, Surrey was led through the streets of London to the Tower instead of being conveyed there secretly; but the Council had greatly misjudged the public's sympathy for Surrey, and the walk was something of a triumph. Assuming that Surrey wanted to usurp the throne from Edward, King Henry had a charge drawn to that effect. Tried in the Great Hall of the Guildhall, just off Aldermanbury, on January 13, 1547, on a charge of treason, Surrey was found guilty by the panel of jurors, who debated his fate for only eight hours. He was to be taken from the Tower to Tyburn, where he was to be hanged, drawn, and quartered. In the final event the sentence was changed to the more humane beheading on Tower Hill; the scaffold stood on Tower Hill above and across from the walls, just a few steps from the Seamen's Memorial; a plaque marks the spot. Execution was carried out quickly on January 19, mostly because the King was near death, and the Privy Council wanted no part of the blame. Howard was buried in the 7th-century Church of All Hallows (Allhallows), Barking, near the Tower, but in 1614 his body was removed to the family church in Framlingham, Suffolk, where a large monument was erected. During Surrey's final seven weeks in the Tower, he wrote extensively, including making poetical paraphrases from the penitential Psalms and from the first five chapters of Ecclesiastes.

Thomas Churchyard (1520?–1604)   Never succeeding in gaining the preferment and patronage he desired, Thomas Churchyard died here in 1604 and was buried at St. Margaret's Church, Westminster, on April 4.

George Gascoigne (1525?–1577)   The poet George Gascoigne probably entered the Middle Temple, off Fleet Street, around 1548 after leaving Trinity College, Cambridge, without a degree. Well known for his extravagance, for which he was disinherited, Gascoigne is said to have been imprisoned in 1548 for dicing, but the circumstantial evidence now points to a lawyer named Gastone and not to George Gascoigne. His activities until 1548 are unknown, but that year he entered the Middle Temple, and in 1555 he went over to Gray's Inn, on Gray's Inn Road; in and out of residence for a number of years, he produced *Supposes* here in 1566 and followed it with the five-act tragedy *Jocasta*. Around this time, undoubtedly in financial trouble, he "determined to abandon all vain delights and to return to Gray's Inn, there to undertake again the study of common laws," but a better means of regaining his fortunes appeared in the person of Elizabeth Breton, mother of the poet Nicholas Breton and a well-to-do widow, whom he married before October 1568, when the Lord Mayor of London set a commission to look into the couple's possible misuse of Breton's property. His extravagance was still not under control, and he was unable to take his seat as Member of Parliament for Midhurst, because a petition, without doubt from his creditors, charged him with insolvency, atheism, and manslaughter as well as with being "a common rhymer and a deviser of slanderous passages against divers persones of great calling."

Thomas Norton (1532–1584)   Thomas Norton may have been born in the City in 1532, but he is known to have been admitted to the Inner Temple in 1555.

About the time he was called to the Bar, *Gorbuduc* was produced at the Inner Temple. Norton followed an extremely successful legal and political career until his religious zeal brought him to the Tower of London in 1583.

Thomas Sackville (1536–1608)   The 1st Earl of Dorset and Baron Buckhurst, Thomas Sackville had a long association with London, its theater, and the court; he settled here at the age of seventeen in 1553, when he was mentioned in the pardon roll for some unknown reason. Subsequently, he was admitted to the Inner Temple, where his father was governor, and ultimately was called to the bar. The Induction to *A Mirror for Magistrates* was begun around 1557, and after writing the Induction and the "Complaynt of Henrye Duke of Buckingham," he handed over the manuscript to William Baldwin and George Ferrers for completion. More important is his contribution in the first English dramatic tragedy, *Gorboduc*, written with Thomas Norton, a fellow student, and produced at the Inner Temple on January 6, 1562; Sackville was wholly responsible for the final two acts. The play was printed by Wynkyn de Worde, Caxton's successor, at the Falcon in Falcon Court, off Fleet Street. Sackville turned to politics seriously by 1557, when he was returned to Parliament for Westmorland; he lived for a time on the site of 19–20 Bow Street and frequented the nearby Cock Tavern. Sackville died suddenly at the Council table at Whitehall on April 19, 1608, and lay in state at Dorset House on Fleet Street until his funeral at Westminster Abbey on May 26. He was buried in the Sackville Chapel in Withyham, Sussex.

Sir Edward Dyer (1543–1607)   Sir Edward Dyer, author of "My mind to me a kingdom is," was in London and present in court circles by 1566, but he somehow fell out of favor, although neither the cause nor the date of the royal displeasure is known. By November 1572, when he was living at Leicester House (demolished 1680) on the Strand with his patron the Earl of Leicester, Dyer became consumptive, and he regained Elizabeth's favor when it was suggested to her that the cause of his illness was her disfavor. Within a year Dyer returned to court and, if still not a resident at Leicester House in 1575, was at least a frequent guest there. Here he met Sir Philip Sidney, eleven years his junior, and the two became "the two very diamonds of her maiesties courte for many speciall and rare qualities." Here, as well, around 1579 he met Edmund Spenser. In 1596, after some time abroad on diplomatic missions, Dyer was appointed chancellor of the Order of the Garter, which required the holder to have at least the rank of knight. Accordingly, Dyer was knighted in April 1596. He lived in retirement soon after at Winchester House (between Bankside and the south end of London Bridge and recalled today with the name Winchester Street), where he died early in May 1607. He was buried on May 11 in the chancel of Southwark Cathedral.

William Camden (1551–1623)   The antiquarian and historian William Camden was born on May 2, 1551, in a house on Old Bailey Street, which runs parallel to part of the old city wall connecting Lud Gate and New Gate. His father, a printer, appears to have undertaken Camden's earliest education, but the boy is known to have entered Christ's Hospital, a blue-coat school (originally intended to serve the poor boys of London), on the site of the earlier Grey Friars Monastery (on Newgate Street and now covered by the General Post Office). Camden remained here until approximately 1563, when he suffered from the plague at Islington. Upon recovery he was sent to St. Paul's School (in the shadow of Old St. Paul's, roughly in the present churchyard), where he remained until going up to Magdalen College, Oxford, in 1566. Returning to London in 1571 without employment, he felt free to pursue his antiquarian studies and gathered the materials which formed the basis of his *Britannia*.

In 1575 he secured a mastership at the 14th-century Westminster School, whose buildings surround Little Dean's Yard, adjacent to Westminster Abbey and Dean's Yard. During his tenure here Camden worked on *Britannia*, which appeared in 1586 and passed through three London editions in four years. With the resignation of the headmaster of Westminster School in February 1593, Camden succeeded him in March; the new master lodged, said John Aubrey later, in the "gatehouse by the Queen's scholars' chambers in Dean's Yard." From here, when the students were at play he would wander forth to copy inscriptions from the ancient tombs of the abbey. In October 1597 Camden was made Clarenceux king-of-arms, an appointment which freed him from his teaching responsibilities. Camden's later years were spent in retirement in Chislehurst, Kent, where the first signs of his fatal illness appeared at the end of August 1621, when the antiquarian began vomiting blood. Two years of irksome illness followed, and on August 18, 1623, he suffered a paralytic stroke. He died on November 9 and was buried in Westminster Abbey on November 19. The grave, in the southern transept in the Poets' Corner, is marked by a white marble monument showing him with his left hand on his *Britannia* and inscribed with an incorrect age, seventy-four.

Edmund Spenser (1552–1599)   The poet Edmund Spenser was probably born in the East Smithfield area of London around 1552. He was educated at the newly founded Merchant Taylors' School (1561), then off Upper Thames Street on Suffolk Lane, and may have been one of its first pupils. Entering as a "poor boy," he received two gowns in 1569, one early in the year and the other in April; a second account-book entry reads "To Emond Spensore, scholler of the Mrchante Tayler scholles, at his gowinge to Pembrocke Hall in Chambridge." By 1577 or 1578 Spenser was a member of the 1st Earl of Leicester's household at Leicester House on the Strand (where Essex Street is now), and here he met Sir Philip Sidney, nephew of the earl, and Sir Edward Dyer; the three, along with Fulke Greville, formed the Aeropagus Club, which held its meetings at the House and debated and experimented in a variety of English metrical styles. *The Shepheardes Calender*, entered in the Stationers' Register on December 5, 1579, was completed here, and *The Faerie Queene* was begun here in the same year. In July 1580, probably because of the influence of Leicester and his nephew, Spenser was appointed secretary to 14th Baron Grey de Wilton, newly appointed Lord Deputy for Ireland. He left for Ireland in August and returned to England only twice until the end of 1598.

His first trip back, in October 1589, with Sir Walter Ralegh, was for the dual purpose of publishing the finished first three books of *The Faerie Queene* and of seeking favor from the Queen. Spenser had long realized the desolation of his Irish life, but no other employment was offered, although Elizabeth did sweeten the Irish position a little by granting an annual pension of £50. At the end of 1595 he returned to London to get Books 4, 5, and 6 of *The Faerie Queene* into print. Still in London in September, he was at court at Greenwich in his search for preferment and there wrote the dedication to the *Fowre Hymnes*. Preferment did not come, and in November Spenser was at the home of the 1st Earl of Essex (formerly Leicester House). His treatise *A View of the Present State of Ireland*, written at this time, was not published until after his death. Early in 1597 Spenser returned to Ireland, where political problems (sparked by Hugh O'Neill, 2d Earl of Tyrone) were coming to a head, and the poet was dispatched to London with a report of the rebellion.

Shortly after his arrival, broken physically and mentally, he fell ill at his lodgings on King Street (once a thoroughfare running from Charing Cross to Westminster Hall beside Whitehall Palace), where he died on January 13, 1599; Spenser was buried in the Poets' Corner of Westminster Abbey near the grave of Chaucer. "His hearse," said Camden, was "attended by poets, and mournful elegies and poems, with the pens that wrote them, were thrown into his tomb." The Earl of Essex bore the funeral expenses, and Anne Clifford, Countess of Dorset, raised the freestone monument in Spenser's memory in 1620; it was fully restored in more durable marble in 1778. The stories surrounding Spenser's poverty, including Ben Jonson's assertion that he starved to death, are undoubtedly without base, for it is unlikely that a pensioner of the crown and the bearer of an official governmental dispatch from Ireland would starve to death in a city where he had so many friends and admirers. Perhaps the most singular expression of Spenser's love for London occurs in "Prothalamion":

> At length they all to mery *London* came,
> To mery London, my most kyndly Nurse,
> That to me gaue this Lifes first natiue sourse:
> Though from another place I take my name,
> An house of ancient fame.
> . . . .
> . . . there standes a stately place,
> Where oft I gayned giftes and goodly grace
> Of that great Lord, which therein wont to dwell,
> Whose want too well now feeles my freendles case. . . .

Sir Walter Ralegh (1552?–1618) Sir Walter Ralegh was first in London in the spring of 1576, when he was described as "of the Middle Temple." There is no reason to believe that Ralegh was a student of law, and there was never any stipulation that legal study was required for residence in the Temple. As a resident he had certain privileges: he was entitled to use the Temple Library, could claim a seat in the Round Church, and could enter his name for chambers—all appropriate steps for an aspiring young politician. Located just off Fleet Street, the Middle and Inner Temples, while distinct institutions, really make up one precinct with harmonious buildings dating from the 12th through the 20th century. The church which Ralegh attended belonged originally to the Order of the Knights Templars, and a chancel, added to the east side of the church between 1220 and 1240, effec-

tively forms a separate church, used today for services. Ralegh spent almost a year here before moving to Islington, then a relatively unspoiled area north of the City. Exactly where Sir Walter resided has escaped detection, but the Old Queen's Head on Queens Head Road (demolished in 1829) was strongly associated with him. He is said also to have lived at the Old Pied Bull, which stood very near the site of the present public house at the corner of Theobarton and Upper Streets. Both these inns also claimed that Ralegh smoked his first pipe there—an unlikely event since the Virginia expedition did not occur until some years later.

Shortly after Ralegh left Islington, his hot temper involved him in trouble with Sir Thomas Perrot, and the two men, arraigned before the lords of the Council on February 7, 1580, were committed to the Fleet, where they remained for six days until sureties were found for their keeping the peace. Ralegh was free a little more than a month before he was confined to Old Marshalsea (between Mermaid Court and the next street north off the Borough High Street, Southwark); this time he and a man named Wingfield were committed for a "fray beside the tennis court at Westminster." After serving in Ireland, Ralegh was granted Durham House on the Strand by Elizabeth, although her right to do so was not entirely clear. Sir Walter took possession in the summer of 1583 and retained the house until 1603. Among Ralegh's guests were Sir Philip Sidney, George Chapman, Michael Drayton, George Peele, Thomas Lodge, Thomas Campion, John Marston, and John Aubrey, who commented:

> I well remember his study, which was a little turret which looked over and into the Thames, and had the prospect which is pleasant perhaps as any in the world, and which not only refreshes eiesight but cheers the spirits and (to speake my mind) I believe enlarges an ingeniose man's thoughts.

Here Ralegh wrote some of his poetry, *A Report of the Fight about the Iles of the Açores,* and *The Discoverie of the Large, Rich and Beautiful Empyre of Guiana* and cultivated tobacco in the garden.

Ralegh's favor in court kept increasing, and he was perhaps at the height of his ascendancy when his secret marriage (after seduction) to Elizabeth Throckmorton, one of the Queen's maids of honor, was discovered. Enraged by Sir Walter's actions, Elizabeth imprisoned both the courtier and his wife in the Tower of London; eventually Ralegh, through flattery and, incidentally, some useful service to the Queen at Dartmouth, was restored. The couple settled in Sherborne, Dorset, but Ralegh was back in London in 1593 as a Member of Parliament. At this time his dedication to literature and science led to his membership in the Society of Antiquaries, the nucleus of the group which began to meet at the Mermaid Tavern on Bread Street (on the east side just a few doors down from Cheapside); indeed, Ralegh has been credited with suggesting the meeting place. Among the many men who joined in the discussions from time to time were Edmund Spenser, Christopher Marlowe, Thomas Kyd, Thomas Dekker, John Donne, Francis Beaumont, John Fletcher, William Shakespeare, Ben Jonson, and Sir Francis Bacon. By the early spring of 1593 the "School of

Night" or "Sir Walter Rawley's School of Atheisme" was flourishing and meeting at Durham House; a pamphleteer noted

> much diligence was said to be used to get young gentle-men to this school, wherein both Moyses and our Sauiour, the old and new Testaments are iested at and the schollars taught among other things to spell God backwards.

Warrants were issued in May for those involved, but Marlowe died within a month, and Sir Walter undoubtedly had left for Sherborne after Parliament was dissolved in April.

After the Guiana and Cadiz expeditions Ralegh was in constant attendance at court, but the trouble which then arose between Ralegh and the Earl of Essex and continued over the years was to play a large role in Ralegh's ultimate downfall. Moreover, the allegation that Sir Walter actively opposed James's claim to the throne predisposed the new monarch against Ralegh, and in a very short time he moved against the courtier. Ralegh was stripped of his post of captain of the guard, forced to resign the governorship of Jersey and the wardenship of the stannaries, removed from holding the patent of wine licenses, and compelled to leave Durham House. In July Ralegh was summoned before the Council to answer charges of knowledge of plots "to surprise the king's person" concocted between the 8th Baron Cobham and Count Aremberg or by William Watson. Ralegh first denied all knowledge of the plots but then admitted to knowledge of pertinent correspondence and was committed to the Tower on July 17, 1603; he was brought to trial in Winchester in November. Charged on what today would be considered inadequate evidence and prejudged guilty by virtue of the examination of the Council on a charge of treason, he was unable to offer absolute proof of innocence, and a guilty verdict was inevitable. Ordered to be executed on December 11, he was reprieved on December 10 and sent to the Tower on December 16.

Ralegh had apartments in the upper story of the Bloody Tower, and his entire family and personal servants lived here with him at a cost of £200 a year. Prince Henry became attracted to his cause, and his encouragement brought about Ralegh's *History of the World*. Ralegh's laboratory in the Tower Garden for experiments and the compounding of drugs, a lath-and-plaster hut, became the daily meeting place of many men of consequence, including Ben Jonson. Around 1610 Ralegh sought permission to lead another expedition to Guiana, and on March 19, 1616, the King ordered his release. The expedition set sail on June 12, 1617, and was disastrous from the start; when Sir Walter returned to Plymouth in the middle of June 1618, he left directly for London to meet his fate. He was arrested, not in Plymouth, as is usually stated, but in Ashburton, Devon, by Sir Lewis Stucley (Stukeley), his cousin, and then returned to Plymouth, where Ralegh considered fleeing to France. Before he could implement his plan, he was transported to London, where he was again detained unguarded; attempting to flee from England, he was apprehended at Gravesend and put in the Tower.

This time Ralegh's examination by the commissioners, headed by the Lord Chancellor Francis Bacon, was undoubtedly fair, and Sir Walter might have saved himself had he not become enmeshed in the tangle of lies he presented. Bacon and the Commission of Inquiry brought Ralegh before them on October 22, at which time he was told that he was guilty of abusing James's confidence and that the 1603 execution was now to be carried out. Neither Ralegh's appeal before the King's Bench nor his plea for the King's mercy met with success; sentenced for immediate execution, he was taken to the Gate House in Old Palace Yard, where he wrote:

> Euen such is tyme which takes in trust
> Our youth, our Ioyes, and all we haue,
> And payes vs butt with age and dust:
> Who in the darke and silent graue
> When we haue wandred all our wayes
> Shutts up the storye of our dayes.
> And from which earth and graue and dust
> The Lord shall rayse me up I trust.

(The Gatehouse Prison lay on the west side of Storey's Gate just before it meets Tothill Street). On Friday, October 29, Sir Walter mounted the scaffold in Palace Yard; when the placement of his head on the executioner's block was objected to, he made the now-famous reply, "What matter how the head lie, so long the heart be right?" Sir Walter's remains were given to his wife, and the headless body was buried in the chancel of the 16th-century St. Margaret's Church, which contains a memorial window inscribed by James Russell Lowell. Lady Ralegh had the head embalmed and kept it in a red leather bag until her death, when it passed to her son Carew; what ultimately happened to it is not known.

Richard Hakluyt (1552?–1616) The geographer and historian Richard Hakluyt received his early education at Westminster School, where his interest in geography and travel literature first appeared. After going up to Christ Church, Oxford, in 1570 and taking orders, he had little more to do with London until May 1602, when he was appointed prebendary of Westminster. Made archdeacon in 1603, he held this post until his death on November 23, 1616, and was buried in Westminster Abbey on November 26; there is a commemorative monument.

Sir Philip Sidney (1554–1586) One of the most brilliant figures of the early Elizabethan period was the soldier, statesman, courtier, and poet Sir Philip Sidney, whose association with London began almost at birth, for his grandfather possessed a house near St. Anthony's School on Threadneedle Street; for a short time, too, Sir Philip's father had the lease of Durham House. This house and its grounds, which stood in the area now enclosed by Robert Street, Adam Street, the Strand, and Adelphi Terrace, later came into the hands of the 1st Earl of Essex, who tried to secure a marriage agreement between his daughter Penelope Devereux, later Lady Rich, and Sir Philip. Sir Philip had lodgings at Gray's Inn early in his career, and when in London he took part, as did Sir Walter Ralegh, in tournaments held in the Tilt Yard (just opposite the Banqueting Hall toward St. James's Park) of Whitehall Palace. Sidney is also associated with Crosby Place, the magnificent mansion once belonging to Sir Thomas More which stood on the site now occupied by Crosby Square. This mansion was slated for demolition in the 19th century, when a public subscription saved it; it was then appropriately moved stone by stone to Danvers Street, Chelsea, where Sir Thomas More had once had his country residence, and is now in use by the Federation of University Woman.

Essex Street was the site of Essex House, so named when the Earl of Essex held the house and called Leicester House when Robert Dudley, Sidney's uncle, held it. Here in 1578–1579 Sir Philip first met Edmund Spenser, who was in Leicester's employ, and Sir Edward Dyer; these three, along with Fulke Greville, formed the Aeropagus Club. In September 1583 Sidney married Frances Walsingham, daughter of Sir Francis Walsingham; the couple divided their time between Walsingham House here and Barn Elms, Surrey. When their first child, Elizabeth, was born in 1585 (after Sidney had incurred the Queen's wrath by trying to join Sir Francis Drake's expeditionary force to the Spanish coast without royal consent), the Queen stood as godmother and attended the christening service at the 15th-century St. Olave's Church on Hart Street.

In November 1585 the Queen, all forgiving, granted Sidney the governorship of Flushing. He left London in November and traveled to the Low Countries to assume his duties; in September 1586, taking part in the battle at Zutphen, he rashly discarded his leg armor, and on the third charge he took a bullet in the left thigh. He managed a return to the camp, but the wound became infected, and he lingered until October 17. On November 1, a troop of 1,200 English soldiers escorted the body to Sidney's ship *The Black Pinnace*, which with black sails set out for England; arriving at Tower Hill under escort on November 5, the coffin was taken to the Minories at Aldgate. Here the body lay in state for more than three months until financial problems were resolved. Finally, on February 16, 1587, the funeral procession with thirty-two aged gownsmen at its head, one for each year of Sidney's life, made its way to Old St. Paul's with Sir Fulke Greville, Sir Edward Dyer, Edward Wotton, and Thomas Dudley bearing the coffin. Sidney was buried in the choir aisle, and a simple wooden tablet with eight indifferent lines of verse was raised in commemoration.

John Lyly (1554?–1606)   Of John Lyly's long association with London, unfortunately only scattered pieces of information are known for certain. Gabriel Harvey said he knew Lyly "in the Savoy" when *Euphues: The Anatomy of Wit* was being written; the great Palace of the Savoy, owned in the 14th century by John of Gaunt, was restored by Henry VII, who made it into "a charitable foundation, to harbour an Hundred poor People, Sick or Lame, or Travellers." Obviously, Lyly did not fit into any of these categories, but the management was especially lax about the directions. His literary fame was secure by 1579, and within four years he had begun dramatic efforts for the children's acting companies of the Chapel Royal and St. Paul's Cathedral. Most probably, he was made vice-master of the boys of the St. Paul's and Savoy acting companies in April 1585, but the assumption of his holding such a post is inferred only from further statements by Harvey.

Lyly had sought court favor as early as 1585 and, indeed, seems to have been made some vague prom-

ise that he would be given the mastership of the revels, but in 1595 he wrote:

> I was entertained your Majesty's servant by your own gracious favour, strengthened with conditions that I should aim all my course at the Revels (I dare not say with a promise but a hopeful item to the reversion).

In 1589 he probably was the "John Lyly, gent," who became Member of Parliament for Hendon, and he continued to serve in Parliament for Aylesbury until the early 1600s. Lyly was married at the Church of St. Clement Danes in 1583, and the register of St. Bartholomew the Less records that on September 10, 1596, "John the sonne of John Lillye gent was christened." Subsequently, three or perhaps four children were christened there; the child in doubt is Elizabeth, who was buried there on May 14, 1605. From 1596 or so on, Lyly lived in the Hospital of St. Bartholomew, which was served by the Church of St. Bartholomew the Less; he remained there until his death in November 1606, but no monument or tombstone with his name has survived the extensive restoration of the church. Of London Lyly wrote in *Euphues and His England*:

> It [England] hath in it twentie and six Cities, of the which the chiefest is named *London*, a place both for the beautie of buyldinge, infinite riches, varietie of all things, that excelleth all the Cities of the world: insomuch that it maye be called the Store-house and Marte of all *Europe*. Close by this Citie runneth the famous Ryuer called the Theames, which from the head wher it ryseth named *Isis*, vnto the fall Middway it is thought to be an hundred and forescore myles. That can there be in anye place vnder the heauens, that is not in this noble Citie either to be bought or borrowed?

Lancelot Andrewes (1555–1626)   One of the most notable early figures in the Anglican Church, Lancelot Andrewes was born in the parish of All Hallows (Allhallows), Barking, in 1555, and was educated at the Coopers' Free Grammar School before going to the Merchant Taylors' School, on the west side of Suffolk Lane, just off Upper Thames Street. Within a few years of taking orders in 1580 he was presented with the living of St. Giles Cripplegate on Fore Street and was appointed a prebendary of St. Paul's; he also lectured three times a week at St. Paul's. Made chaplain in ordinary to Queen Elizabeth, Andrewes refused two bishoprics but finally accepted the deanship of Westminster shortly before the Queen's death and in this post took part in the coronation of James I. He became bishop of Winchester in 1619 and was, in fact, the last bishop to use Winchester House in London as the episcopal residence. It was located in Southwark, west of the Church of St. Mary Overy and east of the Clink Prison, and was described by Stow in *A Survey of London* as

> a very fair house, well repaired, [with] a large wharf and landing-place, called the bishop of Winchester's stairs.

Andrewes died here on September 26, 1626, and was buried in Our Lady's Chapel in the Church of St. Mary Overy, Southwark.

George Peele (1556–?1596)   Another native Londoner, the dramatist George Peele, was born in July 1556, possibly on July 25, the son of James Peele, who probably lived in the parish of St. James Garlickhithe, since the child was baptized in the Church of St. James, which stood on Upper Thames Street near Garlick Hill (destroyed in the 1666 fire; the present building was designed by Sir Christopher Wren). The family lived for a time on Seething Lane in the parish of St. Olave Jewry before the elder Peele became clerk of Christ's Hospital and the family took the Clerk's House at Christ's Hospital. This famous blue-coat school stood on Newgate Street where the General Post Office now stands, originally the site of the Grey Friars Monastery. Peele entered Christ's, probably as a free scholar, by 1562, for he is known to have been in the grammar school in 1565. He was more frivolous than scholarly, and he must have been back in London from Oxford in 1579, for in September Christ's board of governors ordered the elder Peele to "discharge his house . . . of his son George Peele, and all other of his household which had been chargeable to him," suggesting that he was living a riotous life.

It is probable that from 1581 to 1592, or at least during part of the period, Peele was living on Bankside, the area south of the Thames roughly between Blackfriars Bridge and London Bridge; his *Merrie Conceited Jests of George Peele, Sometime a Student in Oxford* notes that when his daughter was aged ten they were living on Bankside. Though a district of brothels, bull- and bear-baiting gardens, and disreputable taverns from the Middle Ages until the 18th century, this area was frequented by the theatrical set in the 16th and 17th centuries. Peele resided somewhere on Clink Street (named after the famous Clink Prison for debtors, "indiscreet" prostitutes, and rowdies, and the source of the modern slang "in the clink"). The register at Southwark Cathedral contains an April 25, 1587, entry for the burial of "Annys Pyll," who is thought to have been the dramatist's first wife, and an entry in St. Olave's parish register, Southwark, relates that "George Peele and marye Yates" were married "p[er] license" on December 26, 1591; this is by no means conclusive evidence of a second marriage, although it corresponds to Peele's residence. When and where Peele died is not known, but in 1598 Francis Meres asserted in *Palladis Tamia* that the dramatist was syphilitic: "As Anacreon died by the pot: so George Peele by the pox." A burial entry for November 9, 1596, at St. James's Church, Clerkenwell, recording "George Peele, householder," may refer to the dramatist.

The *Merrie Conceited Jests* mentions various localities and taverns in and near London; the tavern on Sea Coal (Seacoal) Lane is supposedly the one he frequented; Anthony the barber is directed to "George's common abode,"

> which was at a blind alehouse in Sea-coal Lane. There he found George in a green jerkin, a Spanish platter-fashioned hat, all alone at a peck of oysters.

Peele also "supped" at the White Horse on Friday Street; one night

> he met with an old friend of his, who was so ill at the stomach, hearing George tell him of the good cheer he went to, himself being unprovided both of meat and money, that he swore he had rather have gone a mile about than have met him that instant.

Thomas Kyd (1558–1594)   Thomas Kyd was born in London, probably in late October or early November 1558, and was baptized on November 6 at the Church of St. Mary Woolnoth (the present church dates to the 18th century). The parish entry for that day notes, "Thomas, son of Francis Kyd, *Citizen and Writer of the Court Letter of London*." Where the Kyd family lived is not known, but this was a quite well-to-do parish in a lively commercial district (now the banking district); by the end of 1594 the family had moved to the neighboring parish of St. Mary Colchurch. At the age of seven, Kyd was enrolled at the Merchant Taylors' School, on Suffolk Lane; the school, founded in 1561, was moved to Charterhouse in 1875. The dramatist remained here possibly until 1573 or 1575.

There was a close relationship between Christopher Marlowe and Kyd, and shortly before Marlowe's death on June 1, 1593, in a tavern in Deptford, Kyd was arrested on a charge of libeling foreigners. London at this time was particularly troubled: unemployment was rampant, the plague was at hand, and what could be called libelous graffiti had sprouted up all over the metropolis. The Privy Council had ordered that the source or sources be found and those arrested who refused to tell the "truth" be tortured at Bridewell (located between what are today Bridewell Place, New Bridge Street, and Tudor Street), which was then a prison for brief imprisonment and flogging and was used as a refuge and training place for homeless apprentices. The original charge of libel laid against Kyd was changed to one of heresy, when as the document relating to his arrest relates:

> 12 May 1593
> vile hereticall Conceiptes
> denyinge the deity of Jhesus
> Christe o^r Savio^r fownd
> amongst the papr^s of Thos
> Kydd prisoner

Then, added in a different hand, and probably at a later date, were the words

> wch he affirmethe that he
> had from Marlowe.

Probably tortured at Bridewell, Kyd is said to have implicated Marlowe, and the allegation has also been made that Marlowe's subsequent murder suggests political ramifications rather than mere atheism. Kyd died in December 1594 (on December 30 his mother repudiated his estate—Kyd was undoubtedly in debt), and he is thought ot have been buried at St. Mary Colchurch.

Thomas Lodge (1558?–1625)   The dramatist Thomas Lodge, whose father, Sir Thomas Lodge, was Lord Mayor of London, may well have been born in the City, but no records are available. He entered the Merchant Taylors' School, on Suffolk Lane, on March 23, 1571, and left for Oxford in 1573. After receiving his B.A., he entered Lincoln's Inn in 1578 but early abandoned any pretenses for law. Far more interested in literature, he fell into disgrace with his family, undoubtedly forfeited his mother's legacy, and was cut from his father's will. He was in and out of London, sailing to the Canaries in 1588 and to South America in 1591, before he left the city for Low Leyton in 1596.

Having abandoned law earlier, he now abandoned literature and took a medical degree before returning to London to practice. He lived first on Warwick Lane, then on Lambert Hill (gone), and finally on Old Fish Street, where he died in 1625.

George Chapman (1559?–1634)   The poet, translator, and dramatist George Chapman is first noted in Philip Henslowe's diary under the date of February 12, 1596, when *The Blind Beggar of Alexandria* was first produced. More likely, Chapman had been in town for a few years, especially since *The Shadow of Night* appeared in quarto in 1594. Indeed, while it is assumed that he was associated with Gray's Inn and had lodgings in the inn, it is not known when this was. Chapman's collaboration with Ben Jonson and John Marston on *Eastward Hoe* brought about the imprisonment of all three men (who were to have their ears cut and noses split) for their references to the rapaciousness of James's Scottish following. Jonson and Chapman were obviously together at Marshalsea, as a letter from Jonson to the 1st Earl of Salisbury discloses:

> I am here, my most honoured lord, unexamined and unheard, committed to a vile prison, and with me a gentleman (whose name may perhaps have come to your lordship), one Mr. George Chapman, a learned and honest man.

Nothing is known of Chapman's residences; he died on May 12, 1634, in the parish of St. Giles-in-the-Fields, and a monument in the form of a Roman altar, designed by Inigo Jones, was erected; the present inscription is a second cutting.

Eastward Hoe is set in various parts of London and contains many references to the city. The play opens on Goldsmith's Row in Cheapside, an area where the goldsmiths were set up, and says John Stow:

> the most beautiful frame of fair houses and shops that be within the walls of London, or elsewhere in England.... It containeth in number ten fair dwelling-houses and fourteen shops, all in one frame, uniformly built four stories high, beautified towards the street with the Goldsmiths' arms and the likeness of woodmen, in memory of his name, riding on monstrous beasts, all which is cast in lead, richly painted over and gilt....

In the play Golding tells Quicksilver:

> Methinks I see thee already walking in Moorfields without a cloak, with half a hat, without a band, a doublet with three buttons, without a girdle, a hose with one point and no garter, with a cudgel under thine arm, borrowing and begging threepence.

The disreputable Moorfields was once empty marshland just beyond the City's north wall where women dried their wash, archery was practiced, and apprentices tied bones to their shoes to skate on the frozen area. The Cock Tavern, mentioned by Security in answer to Golding's question, may well have been on the east side of Bow Street, just south of Broad Court:

> But, Dad, hast thou seen my running gelding dressed today?
> *Sec.* That I have, Frank. The ostler o' th' Cock dressed him for a breakfast.

The Isle of Dogs, which is mentioned, is a peninsula formed where the Thames makes a sharp loop between, roughly, Limehouse and Blackwell Tunnel. The reference to the Counter, where Quicksilver, Sir Petronel Flash, and Security are held, could be any one of a number of London's prisons.

Robert Greene (1560–1592)   The dramatist, pamphleteer, and profligate Robert Greene appeared in London about 1587, some time after he married Dorothy, "a gentleman's daughter of good account," by whom he had a child before deserting her. According to Greene, his life in town was extremely vicious, but contemporary commentary relates that while his habits were irregular, he was innocent of "any notorious crime." He did father an illegitimate son, Fortunatus, by the sister of Cutting Ball, the leader of a band of thieves who was hanged at Tyburn. Greene's death in London occurred after a dinner party at which herrings and Rhenish wine were served. According to Gabriel Harvey, not an unbiased observer, Greene, deserted by all of his former friends, was in extreme poverty and during his illness was ministered to by the people with whom he had lodgings, a poor shoemaker and his wife. He died on September 3, 1592, and the following day was buried in the New Churchyard near Bethlehem Hospital (Bedlam, the site of the present Liverpool Street Station of British Rail).

Francis Bacon (1561–1626)   One of the most influential men of his time—lawyer, courtier, statesman, philosopher, and essayist—was Francis Bacon, son of Lord Keeper Sir Nicholas Bacon, who was born in London on January 22, 1561, at York House on the Strand; the house, once the lodging of the archbishops of York, stood just southeast of the intersection of Villiers Street and the Strand and adjoined York Place, a residence of the Queen; between the two ran common gardens, fields, and lanes. When Nicholas Bacon became Keeper of the Great Seal, he promptly moved into York House, as did successive Lord Keepers. Francis Bacon was baptized three days after his birth at the old Church of St. Martin-in-the-Fields; the birth register entry can still be seen. William Rawley's statement that Bacon was "born in York House or York Place in the Strand" has stirred up controversy, just as has the church register, since it reads *Mr.* Francis Bacon; the Lord Keeper's other children were not so designated, and the *Mr.* is inserted above the line and in paler ink. On the line below is inserted "Filius Dm Nich Bacon Magni Anglie Signilli Custodis," also in paler ink.

Bacon was admitted as an "ancient" to Gray's Inn on June 27, 1576, but before he took up residence, he left for France at the Queen's command with Sir Amias Paulet. Recalled at his father's death in February 1579 and discovering that his patrimony was far smaller than anticipated (indeed, he received the smallest portion of any of the children), Bacon took up residence in 1 Coney Court (now Gray's Inn Square). His chambers, which he retained nearly fifty years, overlooked the gardens to Highgate Hill; the gardens, entered from a narrow opening on Gray's Inn Square, are as lovely and peaceful today as when they inspired Bacon's "Of Gardens." Sir Walter Ralegh and Bacon conversed here frequently, and even in the 1960s two old catalpa trees, planted by Bacon's instructions from slips brought by Ralegh from the New World, survived in a propped-up state. After a three years' term Bacon was called to the bar on June 27, 1582, and began his parliamentary career sitting as the Member for Melcombe Regis in 1584; he subsequently was the Member for Taunton, Somerset, in 1586, for Liverpool in 1588, for Southampton in 1597, and for Cambridge in 1614.

With Elizabeth's death in 1603, Bacon was forced to secure James's favor, no easy task because of prior conflicts with Sir Edward Coke and with Sir Robert Cecil, who were now especially influential. James knighted Bacon in July 1603 and made him learned counsel in 1604, but Bacon was still unable to gain preferment. On May 10, 1606, he married Alice Barnham at the medieval Marylebone parish church (destroyed by World War II bombs); it was located on the western side of Marylebone High Street, just opposite Beaumont Street, where a small church garden now stands. Not until the death of Cecil, Earl of Salisbury, in 1612 was Bacon able to gain a place of privilege in court; Bacon's proposal to James that Coke be removed as Chief Justice and placed instead on the King's Bench and that he himself be made Attorney General was accepted. Then the early animosity between Bacon and Coke reached extreme proportions as the two argued the cause of royal prerogative and judicial independence. Bacon was appointed Lord Keeper in March 1617 and became Lord Chancellor and Baron Verulam in 1618. In succeeding Lord Ellesmere as Lord Chancellor, Bacon took possession of York House; when the 2d Duke of Lennox attempted to persuade Bacon to part with York House, he was met with, "For this you will pardon me. York House is the house where my father died, and where I first breathed; and there will I yield my last breath, if so please God and the King." January 1621 saw an expansive sixtieth-birthday celebration in York House, and Ben Jonson paid his homage to one

> Whose even thred the Fates spinne round, and full,
> Out of their Choysest, and their whitest wool.

And the same month James created Bacon Viscount St. Albans. During this period, busy as he was, Bacon wrote at least twelve drafts of *Novum Organum*.

Bacon's power and stature continued to increase, but he was not without enemies, and even though James had called him "most laborious, affectionate, [and] . . . faithful," he was charged on two counts of bribery in 1621. Bribery was neither uncommon nor necessarily illegal, and Bacon felt certain of acquittal, as he wrote to the Marquis of Buckingham "I know I have clean hands and a clean heart, and I hope a clean house for friends or servants." He hoped only to be denied office; on May 1 the Great Seal was delivered to the Committee of Peers at York House. Bacon was too ill to attend sentencing on May 3, when he was fined £40,000, imprisoned at the King's pleasure, excluded from Parliament, disabled from holding any state office, and prevented from coming within the verge of the court (the jurisdictional area of Marshalsea Court). His imprisonment in the Lieutenant's House in the Tower of London lasted only a few days, but the conditions thoroughly alarmed him, and he implored Buckingham to secure his release since "to die before the time of His Majesty's grace, and in this disgraceful place, is even the worst that could be."

On September 20, 1621, the King issued a pardon protecting Bacon from all legal demands other than those from the parliamentary sentence, but the prohibition from being within 12 miles of the court was not relaxed until the spring of 1622. From that time on, Bacon kept to his house in St. Albans, Hertfordshire, and although a full pardon never came, he was admitted to the King's presence in January 1623. Finally, in March 1626, he took ill; John Aubrey's *Brief Lives* recounts how

> it came into my Lord's thoughts why flesh might not be preserved in snow, as in salt. They were resolved they would try the experiment presently. . . . The snow so chilled him that he immediately fell so extremely ill that he could not return to his lodgings (I suppose then at Gray's Inn), but went to the Earl of Arundel's house at Highgate, where they put him into a good bed warmed with a pan, but it was a damp bed that had not been lain in about a year before. . . .

Bacon died on April 9 at Arundel House, where the Church of St. Michael, South Grove Street, now stands and was buried in St. Michael's Church, St. Albans.

Samuel Daniel (1562–1619) Sometime after leaving his post as tutor to Anne Clifford, daughter of the Countess of Cumberland, Samuel Daniel appeared in London, and it has been suggested that the arrival correlates with the death of the Poet Laureate Edmund Spenser in 1599 and that he became the new Poet Laureate. Daniel, who was well received in court after James's accession in 1603, lived on Old Street in the parish of St. Luke's near Bunhill Fields; here he wrote most of his dramatic pieces. Many of his masques, such as *Tethys Festival, or The Queenes Wake*, were performed at Whitehall, and in February 1614 *Hymens Triumph* was played at Somerset House on the Strand. (On the site of the present Somerset House, a coldly menacing 18th-century classical building, was a palace for the Queens of England.) From a statement in *The Tragedie of Philotas* (1607), which notes that Daniel had been "liuing in the country about four yeares since," it is assumed that he left London around 1603 and returned to the city only occasionally.

Michael Drayton (1563–1631) While much of Michael Drayton's life in London is known, there are also the usual conjectures and traditions to deal with. That Drayton was at an Inn of Court cannot be proved; the belief rests solely on a reference in William Cavell's *Polimanteia . . . : A Letter from England to her Three Daughters, Cambridge, Oxford, Innes of Court*. A second unsupported assertion is certainly possible: Drayton is said to have drunk at the Devil Tavern (on the site of 1 Fleet Street) with Ben Jonson. Drayton appeared in London, by 1597, at which time Philip Henslowe's diary notes that he was writing for the stage; his lodgings when he was with the Lord Admiral's Company are thought to have been in the area of the Church of St. Dunstan in the West. The favor Drayton found under Elizabeth was not as readily available under James, but the fault was the poet's, and his 1604 "A Paean Trimphall for the Societie of Goldsmiths Congratulating His Highnes Entring the Citie" met only contempt. Drayton was working on the monumental compilation of *Poly-Olbion* during this period, and he wrote extravagantly of London:

> Built on a rising Bank, within a Vale to stand,

And for thy healthfull soyle, chose gravell mixt with sand
And where faire *Tames* his course into a Crescent casts
(That, forced by his Tydes, as still by her he hasts,
He might his surging waves into her bosome send)
Because too farre in length, his Towne should not
extend.

Drayton's satirical "The Moon Calf" refers to the fashionable piccadill (an expansive collar), from which the present-day Piccadilly has taken its name:

In euery thing she must be monstrous: Her Picadell aboue her crowne vp-beares: Her Fardingale is set aboue her eares.

Drayton's last residence was on Fleet Street, according to John Aubrey, "at the bay-window house next the east end of St. Dunstan's Church"; here he died in December 1631. He was buried near Chaucer and Spenser in the Poets' Corner of Westminster Abbey, and in January 1632 the Countess of Dorset raised a commemorative monument.

Christopher Marlowe (1564–1593) Mid-16th century London held many attractions for the ambitious, and the playwright Christopher Marlowe probably came directly here after receiving his M.A. at Cambridge in 1587. He may well have been in the City between 1584 and 1587 in connection (quite possibly) with Elizabeth I's secret service, since the Privy Council assured the Cambridge authorities that Marlowe's absences in term resulted from his being employed "in matters touching the benefitt of his Countrie." Nonetheless, shortly after the M.A. was conferred, Marlowe came to London, and his dramatic fame was assured with the acting of both parts of *Tamburlaine the Great* by the Lord Admiral's Company in 1587. By September 1598 Marlowe had lodgings with Thomas Watson in the library of Norton Folgate near the Curtain Theatre, but the thirteen years Marlowe spent in London are as elusive as were his earliest years in Canterbury.

As well as writing constantly, Marlowe appears to have spent some time violating the Queen's peace; on September 9, 1589, he and Thomas Watson were arrested on suspicion of murder and imprisoned at Newgate Prison (the site was at the corner of Newgate Street and Old Bailey). Marlowe and William Bradley, an innkeeper's son who had sought legal protection against three men (including Watson), were fighting on Hog Lane (part of the present-day Worship Street between Curtain Road and Norton Folgate); Watson appeared, and Bradley was killed. Marlowe and Watson entered a plea of self-defense, and on September 19 the jury found in their favor. Again in 1592 he was in trouble in Shoreditch and was bound over to Sir Owen Hopton. Marlowe, a frequent visitor to Sir Walter Ralegh at Durham House on the Strand, where he undoubtedly met Edmund Spenser, was also part of the group of independent thinkers who have been dubbed the "School of Night" which met at Ralegh's house. Marlowe was a close friend of George Peele, George Chapman, John Marston, Thomas Nashe (Nash), and Thomas Kyd, all of whom undoubtedly visited Marlowe in his lodgings.

In 1591 Marlowe and Kyd began sharing lodgings; then on May 12, 1593, Thomas Kyd was arrested after a raid on his rooms turned up papers denying the divinity of Jesus. It is assumed that under torture

Kyd implicated Marlowe, for the document relating to Kyd's arrest had appended (probably) in a different hand:

wᶜʰ he affirmethe that he
had from Marlowe.

Kyd maintained that the papers were Marlowe's and self-righteously denounced the dramatist's treasonable and atheistic opinions. Kyd reported Marlowe's

custom when I knewe him first & as I heare saie he contynewd it in table talk or otherwise to iest at the devine scriptures gybe at praiers, & stryve in argument to frustrate & confute what hath byn spoke or wrytt by prophets & such holie menn....

On May 18 the Privy Council called for Marlowe's apprehension; he was found in Chislehurst, Kent, at the home of Sir Francis Walsingham, Elizabeth's "chief of security," but was required only daily attendance at the Council "until he be licensed to the contrary"—a remarkably lenient approach considering the seriousness of the charge.

On May 30, Marlowe and three other men, Ingram Frizer (Frisar), Nicholas Skeres, and William Pooley, were at a tavern in Deptford and, according to the record at the inquest:

After supper the said Ingram & Christopher Morley were in speech & uttered one to the other divers malicious words for the reason that they could not be at one nor agree about the payment of the sum of pence, that is, le recknynge, there.

A fight occurred, and Marlowe was killed. He was buried on June 1 at the Church of St. Nicholas in Deptford, and Frizer was pardoned by the Queen on June 28. What the brawl was really about has not been ascertained; Pooley, though, was a known double agent, and he and Frizer had been associated with Sir Francis Walsingham; Skeres himself appears to have been involved in the Babington plot. In all, they were an unsavory bunch, and the result of the fracas was described at the inquest: Christopher Marlowe "then and there instantly died" of "a mortal wound over his right eye to the depth of two inches & of the width of one inch." Many were not saddened by his death, including Robert Greene, who was so malicious in his *Groats-worth of Witte, Bought with a Million of Repentance* that the publisher felt obliged to censor some of the material; others paid posthumous tribute, notably Michael Drayton:

Next *Marlow* bathed in the *Thespian* springs
Had in him those braue translunary things,
That the first Poets had, his raptures were,
All ayre, and fire, which made his verses cleere,
For that fine madnes still did he retaine,
Which rightly should possesse a Poets braine.

Marlowe probably frequented the Mermaid Tavern on Bread Street, a house or two down on the northwest corner nearest Cheapside. Much of *Edward II* is set in London; the palace is located in Westminster, and there are various specific references to Fleet Prison, the Tower of London, the New Temple, and Lambeth.

William Shakespeare (1564–1616) When William Shakespeare arrived, London had a population of around 300,000, and the gates were still closed and guarded at night. The actual date of his appearance is unknown, and there is no record of him from 1585 until 1592, when Robert Greene wrote in his *Groatsworth of Witte, Bought with a Million of Repentance:*

> There is an upstart crow, beautified with our feathers, that with his *Tygers heart wrapt in a Players hide* supposes he is as well able to bombast out a blank verse as the best of you; and, being an absolute *Johannes Factotum,* is in his own conceit the only Shake-scene in a country.

It is not clear exactly how Shakespeare entered the theater, but from about 1594 on he was a member of the Lord Chamberlain's Company and possibly had belonged to this company or another earlier. After 1597 the Lord Chamberlain's Company, with Richard Burbage as its chief actor, worked out of the most famous of Elizabethan theaters, the Globe, on Bankside in Southwark; the theater was approximately 450 feet east of the steps leading down from Southwark Bridge and about 50 feet south of the road. Bankside (between Blackfriars and Southwark Bridges), then given over primarily to various public amusements (gardens and theaters, brothels, taverns of varying repute, and bull- and bear-baiting gardens), is now dominated by warehouses. It is thought that Shakespeare lived in the vicinity of the Globe, and the assumption is reasonably well founded since the actor and owner of the Rose, Edward Alleyn, Philip Henslowe, George Peele, John Fletcher, Francis Beaumont, and Philip Massinger all resided here. Shakespeare is also said to have lived on Worship Street, "six doors from Norton Folgate." Another residence which may be associated with Shakespeare in 1598 was on Great St. Helen's; one William Shakespeare lived here that year, as assessment records show. The dramatist did lodge with the French Huguenot Mountjoy family at the corner of Silver (gone) and Monkwell Streets at the City Wall, possibly, from 1598 until 1604. When Shakespeare finally left London for Stratford-on-Avon cannot be determined, but his move is generally placed around September 1611. There is a memorial in the Poets' Corner of Westminster Abbey.

There are places other than theaters definitely associated with the dramatist; he was among the leading literary figures including Edmund Spenser, Ben Jonson, Francis Beaumont, John Fletcher, Philip Massinger, Christopher Marlowe, John Donne, and Sir Walter Ralegh who frequented the Mermaid Tavern (destroyed in the Great Fire), on the northwest corner of Bread Street at Cheapside. St. Saviour's Church (Southwark Cathedral), on the Borough High Street, claims to be the "Cathedral Church of the Theatre," and Shakespeare as well as other theatrical figures (Jonson, Beaumont, Fletcher, Henslowe, and Alleyn) attended services here; many were buried here too, including Edmund Shakespeare, the dramatist's younger brother. William Shakespeare was no doubt in attendance on December 31, 1607, when the church register states, "Edmund Shakespeare, a player, [was] buried in ye church with a forenoon knell of the great bell." In 1912 an alabaster memorial to the dramatist was placed in the cathedral. Shakespeare also knew St. Giles Cripplegate, which he attended for the christening of his nephew, and St. Paul's Cathedral and St. Paul's Courtyard, which was once the location of innumerable booksellers (publishers); here many of the dramatist's works were first published: *Venus and Adonis* and *The Rape of Lucrece* at the sign of the White Greyhound, *The Merry Wives of Windsor* at the Flower de Luce and the Crown, *The Merchant of Venice* at the Green Dragon, *Richard III* at the Angel, *Troilus and Cressida* at the Spread Eagle, *Titus Andronicus* at the Gun, and *King Lear* at the Bull. *Othello* was published in the New Exchange on the Strand, a huge shopping complex under one roof, much like a modern shopping center, just north of Durham House.

When Shakespeare arrived in London, only two theaters existed, the Theatre and the Curtain, both on the north side of the Thames in Shoreditch; the location of the Theatre, built and owned by James Burbage, is marked by a plaque on 90 Curtain Road at the corner of New Inn Yard. The Curtain, which did not take its name from the theatrical curtain but from the curtain wall of Holywell Priory, stood on present-day Hewett Street. In 1596 Burbage converted a house in the City into a theater, Blackfriars; the site, originally part of a Dominican monastery, is now covered by Playhouse Yard, just off Printing House Square. Burbage was not the first to try to establish a theater in the City; although meeting with heavy opposition from nearby residents, he was successful. He died in 1597 before the rebuilding was complete, and his son Richard took over the project; it soon became the only professional theater in London with a roof on it. The theater was rebuilt on Bankside as the Globe. Shakespeare bought an interest in it, and the site is commemorated by a plaque on a brewery in Park Street. In March 1613 Shakespeare bought property in the precinct; the building is said to have been the gatehouse of the monastery, and it was bequeathed to his daughter Susanna Hall. The conveyance describes the property as "abutting upon a streete leading down to Puddle Wharffe on the east part, right against the King's maiestie's Wardrobe" and "now or late . . . in the tenure or occupacon of one William Ireland." Shakespeare's will describes the house as "situat lying and being in the Blackfriers in London, near the Wardrobe." Today Ireland Yard, on the west side of St. Andrew's Hill, recalls this; Wardrobe Place points toward the site of the Wardrobe.

London references in Shakespeare's plays are abundant, and the following are merely representative of the more important ones. The histories are the plays with the most obviously specific locations. *Henry VI: Part I* begins in Westminster Abbey with the funeral of Henry V, and the third scene of Act I takes place "before the gates of the tower," when the Lord Protector has

> . . . come to survey the Tower this day:
> Since Henry's death, I fear, there is conveyance.—
> Where be these warders, that they wait not here?
> Open the gates: Gloucester it is that calls.

"The Temple Garden," where the Duke of Somerset, the Earls of Suffolk and Warwick, and Richard Plantagenet meet, for, as Suffolk states,

> Within the Temple-hall we were too loud;
> The garden here is more convenient[,]

was possibly the area south of Crown Office Row known as the Inner Temple Gardens or more likely, and so held traditionally, the gardens adjacent to Garden Court, just behind Fountain Court on the east side. Here Lancastrians and Yorkists first identify themselves by plucking red and white roses. Warwick, who "love[s] no colours . . . pluck[s] this white rose with Plantagenet"; Suffolk, "this red rose with young Somerset"; and Vernon, "this pale and maiden blossom here . . . my verdict on the white rose side." Their discussion finished, the four go to dine in the Middle Temple, where dinner is eaten in "messes" (that is, in groups of four); like many of the nobility, the Duke of York was probably a member of the Temple. Edmund Mortimer is "brought in a chair by two Keepers" to a room in the tower, and his nephew Richard Plantagenet is sent for and told that the title rests in the Mortimer line. Shakespeare takes some license with the meeting of Parliament which opens Act III; historically, this Parliament of Bats met in Leicester, not in London, but the brawling actually did occur. The word *bat* refers to the clubs used, but Shakespeare changed the method of combat:

> The bishop and the Duke of Gloucester's men,
> Forbidden late to carry any weapon,
> Have fill'd their pockets full of pebble stones,
> And, banding themselves in contrary parts,
> Do pelt so fast at one another's pate,
> That many have their giddy brains knock'd out. . . .

Scenes i and v of Act V occur in the palace in London.

Henry VI: Part II introduces many other glimpses of London; "the Duke of Gloucester's house" undoubtedly refers to the house which stood on Old Gloucester Street, Holborn. Here the spirit of Margery Jourdain, a witch burned at Smithfield, foretells the fates of the King and the Dukes of Suffolk and Somerset. The "hall of justice" where Henry sentences Dame Eleanor Cobham, Margery Jourdain, Southwell, Hume, and Bolingbroke, the first to banishment on the Isle of Man, the second to "Smithfield . . . burn'd to ashes," and the other three "strangled on the gallows," is possibly Westminster Hall itself; trials, especially of this importance, were common there. Cardinal Beaufort dies "so bad a death," one which "argues a monstrous life," in his bedchamber in the Bishop of Winchester's Palace on Bankside near the Clink. The early scenes with the rebel Jack Cade and his followers are set on Blackheath, about 5 miles to the southeast; from here, following the skirmish in which Sir Humphrey Stafford and his brother are killed, Cade and his rebellious band march into London itself. They are first reported in Southwark; and then since they "hath gotten London Bridge;/The citizens fly and forsake their houses." Cade leads his forces to Cannon Street, where he sits "upon London stone" and commands that "the pissing-conduit run nothing but claret wine this first year of our reign." The stone (supposedly a Roman *milliarium*) no longer exists, but a fragment of it was built into St. Swithin's Church opposite Cannon Street Station. Cade's men then march to Smithfield to encounter the King's forces. Capturing and executing Lord Say and his son-in-law, Cade leads his rabble band to Southwark, where Shakespeare makes a curious mistake; Cade directs the rebels

> Up Fish Street! down Saint Magnus' corner! kill and knock down! throw them into Thames!

Both these places are on the City side of the Thames, not Southwark, as the scene location directs. The battle took place in the area of Lower Thames Street, and a monument commemorating the event stands on Fish Street Hill (then Fish Street). The Church of St. Magnus the Martyr (the present church dates from after the Great Fire) stood on the south side of Lower Thames Street.

Henry VI: Part III has only eight scenes set in London, with the opening scene occurring in the Houses of Parliament; here York's demand that he and his heirs ascend the throne after Henry's death is acceded to. It is in the Tower of London that Henry resigns the government to the Earl of Warwick and later is murdered by Gloucester.

Most of *Richard III* takes place in London; the second scene, merely "London: another street," depicting the solemn and lonely funeral procession for Henry VI, contains many locational details. The body of the murdered King is first taken to St. Paul's Cathedral and then borne toward the monastery in Chertsey. The procession with the Lady Anne as the solitary mourner was to stop for one day at the Blackfriars Monastery (off Queen Victoria Street) before going on; Gloucester's directions to the bearers of the corpse are thought to be a slip on Shakespeare's part:

> *Glo.* Sirs, take up the corse.
> *Gent.* Towards Chertsey, noble lord?
> *Glo.* No, to White Friars; there attend my coming.

Directing the body to Whitefriars Monastery, off Fleet Street and to the west of St. Paul's, not only would delay the trip but also would be in the wrong direction. In the same scene Gloucester attempts to woo the Lady Anne and, giving her a ring, urges her

> . . . presently [to] repair to Crosby House;
> Where, . . .
> . . . .
> I will with all expedient duty see you. . . .

Crosby House, then in Bishopsgate, roughly on the site of the present Crosby Square, was dismantled and the banqueting hall reerected in 1910 on the Embankment in Chelsea, near the corner where Danvers Street enters Cheyne Walk. Clarence's ghastly murder takes place in the Tower of London, and the body is hidden

> . . . in some hole,
> Till that the duke give order for his burial. . . .

When Queen Elizabeth, the young Duke of York, the Archbishop of York, and the Duchess of York receive the news that Lord Rivers, Lord Grey, and Sir Thomas Vaughan are being imprisoned at Pomfret (Pontefract, Yorkshire), they seek safety:

> *Q. Eliz.* Come, come, my boy; we will to sanctuary.—

The Sanctuary, a place of refuge for criminals probably from the time of Edward the Confessor on, was on the approximate site of the Guildhall in Westminster. It is at Baynard's Castle that Richard is proclaimed King after Gloucester sets the stage:

> If you thrive well, bring them to Baynard's Castle;
> Where you shall find me well accompanied
> With reverend fathers and well learned bishops.

This was a considerable building on the riverbank in Blackfriars at the point of Blackfriars Bridge when

Henry VI ascended the throne in 1422; the building eventually came into the hands of Richard, Duke of York, father of Gloucester, and became Gloucester's chief London residence.

Richard II is set in both England and Wales. While the opening scene in some editions is placed at "Windsor: a room in the palace," it is more likely—since Windsor has always been designated as a castle—that Shakespeare meant the Old Palace of Westminster. Originally the residence of Edward the Confessor, the buildings surrounded the Old Yard; the New Palace Yard dates from William II's building of Westminster Hall, and the hall known today dates from the time of Richard II. The Duke of Lancaster's Palace, the location of the second scene, in Shakespeare's time was known as the Hospital of the Savoy, a hospital endowed by Henry VII. The great Palace of the Savoy, with its stone towers and stone water gates, stood northwest of the present Cleopatra's Needle between the Strand and the Embankment (approximately from Adam Street to just beyond Savoy Street); it is here that Gaunt and the Duchess of Gloucester discuss the coming combat between Bolingbroke and Thomas Mowbray, and from here Gaunt travels to Gosford Green, near Coventry, to watch the trial by combat. Gaunt is then an old man, and the banishment of his son "till twice five summers have enrich'd our fields" weighs heavily. When Gaunt becomes "grievous sick," Richard recognizes a chance to refill his "coffers . . . grown somewhat light"; praying that Gaunt's physician help the patient "to his grave immediately," the King comes to Ely House (Ely Place), once the episcopal palace of the bishops of Ely; consisting of about 20 acres when John of Gaunt held the residence, it was on the north side of Holborn Hill, where Ely Place runs north off Charterhouse today. It should also be noted that Ely House enters *Richard III;* Gloucester refers to it and its gardens:

> My lord of Ely, when I was last in Holborn
> I saw good strawberries in your garden there:
> I do beseech you send for some of them.

Shakespeare takes a bit of historical license in placing Act IV of *Richard II* in Westminster Hall so that the deposition will have greater dramatic effect; in fact, the deposition most likely occurred in the Tower of London, in the King's chief chamber, to which Richard was escorted after being lodged in Westminster. The "street leading to the tower" down which the deposed Richard is conveyed on his way to imprisonment in Pomfret Castle is probably the corner of the Minories.

London locations are scattered about in *Henry IV: Part I.* The opening scene, "a room in the palace," occurs in the old palace of Westminster, and the next London locale is "Eastcheap: a room in the Boar's Head Tavern." The inn, a well-known meeting place for men of letters, stood near London Bridge in Eastcheap, just at the open space at the lower end of Gracechurch Street, where Cannon, King William, and Gracechurch Streets, Eastcheap, and the access road to the bridge converge. The building which the dramatist knew as the Boar's Head was destroyed in the Great Fire. One point which should be made here is that the Boar's Head is a prochronism; the tavern existed in the early 16th century but not in the 15th, when Prince Hal and Falstaff lived. One of the exchanges at the Boar's Head between Prince Hal and Falstaff produced the following reference:

> *Fal.* . . . 'Sblood, I am as melancholy as a gib-cat or a lugged bear.
> *P. Hen.* Or an old lion, or a lover's lute.
> *Fal.* Yea, or the drone of a Lincolnshire bagpipe.
> *P. Hen.* What sayest thou to a hare, or the melancholy of Moor-ditch?
> *Fal.* Thou hast the most unsavoury similes. . . .

Today a lane, running from approximately 87 Fore Street to Chiswell Street, is the site of Moorfields, Shakespeare's Moor-ditch; a fenlike waste area then, it was an extremely offensive place crossed with stinking ditches and common sewers. In 1527 Moorfields was first drained, and in 1606 walks were laid out. In a room at the Boar's Head Falstaff's "two rogues in buckram suits" become eleven. A few centuries later Oliver Goldsmith described a visit to Shakespeare's Boar's Head, "still kept at Eastcheap," and noted how he used Hal's chair and sat before the fire in the room where Falstaff told his story.

Henry IV: Part II also leads to widely scattered parts of the metropolis. The London street where Sir John and his page walk undoubtedly lay not far from the Boar's Head and was probably within view of St. Michael's Church; in the course of their conversation a number of specific localities are mentioned. Bardolph, says the page to Falstaff, has "gone to Smithfield to buy your worship a horse"; Smithfield, a corruption of "smooth field," was used as a cattle market for more than seven centuries but was also the site of a Friday horse fair notorious for its swindling. The markets were bounded roughly by Farringdon Road, Cowcross, Aldersgate Street, and Long Lane and Smithfield Street. Sir John's comment on Bardolph, "I bought him in Paul's, and he'll buy me a horse in Smithfield," refers to Paul's Walk, the name applied to the middle aisle of the nave of the Old St. Paul's Cathedral; it was the meeting place of rogues and idlers, and much commerce was conducted there. In Act III, scene ii, Falstaff comments that he met Justice Shallow at Clement's Inn, an Inn of Chancery located on the north side of the Strand just opposite the Church of St. Clement Danes; the present little street known as Clement's Inn marks the location. The same scene contains an oblique reference to London when Falstaff says to Justice Shallow, "We have heard the chimes at midnight, Master Shallow." The chimes are those of St. Clement Danes on the Strand, made famous in the nursery rhyme "Oranges and lemons say the bells of St. Clement's." (The Church of St. Clement's, on Clement's Lane off King William Street, makes the same claim.) The impending death of Henry IV is set in "a room in the palace" at Westminster; however, more detailed information is available. The King directs;

> . . . bear me hence
> Into some other chamber: softly, pray.

Asking Warwick the name of "the lodging where I first did swoon," he is told, "Tis call'd Jerusalem, my noble Lord," and directs his removal there:

> Laud be to God!—even there my life must end.
> It hath been prophesied to me many years,
> I should not die but in Jerusalem;
> Which vainly I suppos'd the Holy Land:—

But bear me to that chamber; there I'll lie;
In that Jerusalem shall Harry die.

The chamber, which no longer exists because of the extensive repairs and rebuilding of the abbey, was attached to the southwest tower of the abbey close to the cloisters. Finally, the coronation of Henry V takes place in Westminster Abbey; in a street near the abbey, presumably on the way to the old palace, the newly crowned King is greeted by "that vain man," Falstaff, and banishes him, "on pain of death . . ./Not to come near our person by ten mile." Falstaff and his companions (Shallow, Pistol, and Bardolph) are taken into custody and carried to the Fleet, approximately on the site of the present Congregational Memorial Hall on Fleet Lane off Farringdon Street, just north of Ludgate Circus.

Henry VIII, whose sole or multiple authorship has long been debated, must be included here if for no other reason than that this play was the reason for the disastrous fire which destroyed the Globe on St. Peter's Day, June 29, 1613. A number of contemporary accounts describe the conflagration, and one John Chamberlain who recounts the burning claims it "fell out by a peale of chambers," that is, was caused by the firing of small cannon; the original stage directions called for the discharging of chambers in Act IV, scene i. The "antechamber in the palace" of the opening scene of the play was probably at Greenwich Palace, Henry's favorite, rather than Westminster; the last act, it should be noted, specifically puts Greenwich in London. After the arrest of the Duke of Buckingham and Lord Abergavenny on a charge of high treason, Brandon refers to Nicholas Hopkins as "a monk o' the Chartreux"; this is an allusion to a member of the ancient establishment of Charterhouse, which is a corruption of Chartreux. The second scene of the same act presents another aspect of London; Buckingham's surveyor, wishing to impeach his master, tells the King:

> Not long before your highness sped to France,
> The Duke being at the Rose, within the parish
> Saint Lawrence Poultney, did of me demand
> What was the speech among the Londoners
> Concerning the French journey. . . .

Sir John Poultney (Pountney) owned The Row, a great crenelated mansion with a massive stone tower which stood southwest of the old Church of St. Laurence in St. Laurence Lane (now Laurence Pountney Lane), and the present Duck's Foot Lane (from about 151 Upper Thames Street to Laurence Pountney Hill) is a corruption of Duke's Foot Lane—that is, the narrow lane to and from the duke's mansion, the Rose. "The presence chamber in York Place" was Cardinal Wolsey's London palace, built on land north of Westminster Abbey. When Wolsey became Archbishop of York in 1514, he undertook a massive building and beautification program and added a hall, chapel, and multiple kitchens; it was Wolsey, as well, who added the land known as Scotland Yard (because it was the usual visiting residence of the Scottish kings) to the estate. Indeed, tradition holds that Henry first met Anne Boleyn here, and the effect on Henry led to the downfall of Catherine of Aragon, Wolsey, and the English Roman Catholic Church as well as, ultimately, Anne Boleyn.

> *K. Hen.* My lord chamberlain,
> Pr'ythee, come hither: what fair lady's that?

> *Cham.* An't please your grace, Sir Thomas Bullen's
> daughter,—
> The Viscount Rochford,—one of her highness' women.
> *K. Hen.* By heaven, she is a dainty one,—Sweetheart,
> I were unmannerly to take you out,
> And not to kiss you.

When the Cardinal falls (Act III, scene ii), he is told:

> . . . to confine yourself
> To Asher House, my Lord of Winchester's,
> Till you hear further from his highness.

Wolsey makes over all his worldly possessions to the King; historically these included sufficient gold and gilt plate to cover two trestle tables, vast quantities of silk, satin, velvet, sarcenet, and "a thousand pieces of fine Holland cloth"; the palace, belonging to the see of York, was not his to deed over. Nevertheless, Henry wanted it (just as he had wanted Hampton Court) and moved quickly to take the palace before legal formalities could entangle the property. He renamed it:

> Sir,
> You must no more call it York Place, that's past:
> For since the cardinal fell, that title's lost:
> 'Tis now the king's, and call'd Whitehall.

The only important scene with Anne Boleyn in the play takes place in "an antechamber in the Queen's apartments" and would properly have been set in the anterooms of Bridewell Palace, between Fleet Street and the Thames and bounded roughly by New Bridge Street and by Bouverie Street and Temple Avenue. The medieval Bridewell took its name from a holy well dedicated to St. Bride, or St. Bridget (recalled today in the Church of St. Bride just west of Bride Lane off Fleet Street). This is also the setting of the later scene in which Catherine is visited by Cardinals Wolsey and Campeius. Catherine's trial is set in "a hall in Blackfriars," the Dominican monastery, established in 1278, built of stones from the City Wall and from William de Montfichet's castle. It was an especially well-favored foundation and usually supplied the royal confessors and entertained visiting foreign dignitaries. Shakespeare places Queen Catherine's trial in the hall in 1532 (the tribunal actually sat from May 31 to July 23, 1533), and she did not plead her own cause. At present Act V is usually set in "London: a gallery in the palace"; Shakespeare, however, undoubtedly knew that Princess Elizabeth had been born at the palace in Greenwich and would not have changed the birthplace. The christening of the princess, with Archbishop Thomas Cranmer of Canterbury as the godfather and "the old Duchess of Norfolk/And Lady Marquis Dorset" as the godmothers, takes place in "the palace yard" of Greenwich. The porter's comment "Do you take the court for parish garden?" is often edited to read "Paris garden" because that garden, situated on Bankside in Southwark (between the Swan Theatre and the Thames just west of the Falcon Inn), was familiar enough to be distinguished on contemporary maps and was exactly opposite the Palace of Bridewell.

The Merry Wives of Windsor, while set in Windsor and the adjacent forest, contains two interesting references to London. The bear-baiting garden in Paris Garden and Sackerson are alluded to by Slender:

> *Slen.* . . . Why do your dogs bark so? be there bears i' the
> town?

Anne. I think there are, sir; I heard them talked of.

Slen. I love the sport well; but I shall as soon quarrel at it as any man in England.—You are afraid if you see the bear loose, are you not?

Anne. Ay, indeed, sir.

Slen. That's meat and drink to me now. I have seen Sackerson loose twenty times; and have taken him by the chain: but, I warrant you, the women have so cried and shrieked at it that it passed:—but women, indeed, cannot abide 'em; they are very ill-favoured rough things.

Another reference is contained in a speech by Sir John Falstaff to Mrs. Ford:

Come, I cannot cog, and say thou art this and that, like a many of these lisping hawthorn buds that come like women in men's apparel, and smell like Bucker's-bury in simple-time. . . .

The Bucklersbury area, well known from a very early time, was inhabited mostly by druggists and purveyors of herbs and simples; this, of course, is the reference by Sir John.

Other Shakespearean plays are associated with London in a variety of capacities. *The Comedy of Errors* was first performed in Gray's Inn Hall, built between 1556 and 1560; it sustained much damage during World War II but has been rebuilt. *Twelfth Night* had its first performance in Whitehall in 1601 and its second with the lawyers of the Middle Temple in 1602, with Queen Elizabeth and Shakespeare present; the Middle Temple also suffered extensive bomb damage but has been restored completely. *Othello* was probably first performed in 1604 at the old Banqueting Hall (burned 1619), of Westminster, which stood on the site of today's magnificent hall. The Great Bed of Ware, 10 feet wide and 11 feet long, to which Shakespeare refers in *Twelfth Night,* is at the Victoria and Albert Museum; with a richly carved 16th-century headboard, columns, and a canopy, the bed is said to be able to sleep six people comfortably. A few other associations should be mentioned. The great Northumberland House, once the home of Shakespeare's Hotspur, stood approximately on part of the site now occupied by the General Post Office on St. Martin's-le-Grand. The only known correspondence to which Shakespeare was a partner is a letter from Richard Quiney (Quyney) which asks for financial assistance and was posted "ffrom the Bell in Carter Lane, the 25 October, 1598." The Bell Inn was south off the present-day Carter Lane, in the vicinity of Playhouse Yard. Finally, of all the pubs near the Elizabethan Globe which Shakespeare may have used, only one survived into the 20th century: the George Inn, its old beams intact, is tucked neatly inside a courtyard in Southwark.

Thomas Campion (1567–1620) The poet, musician, and physician Thomas Campion may have been born in London on February 12, 1567, and was baptized on February 13 at St. Andrew's Church, at the southwest corner of Holborn Viaduct where it runs into Holborn Circus. Little is known of Campion's early life, although he is known to have lived in a house "built with divers fair lodgings for gentlemen, all of brick and timber," near the corner of Chancery Lane and Cursitor Street. Campion lived there until 1576, when his father, a cursitor (court officer), died. His mother's remarriage in 1577 brought about a move to an unknown destination, and her death in 1580 and his stepfather's remarriage left Campion with two foster parents. After attending Peterhouse College, Cambridge, he was admitted in April 1586 to Gray's Inn, described then as "a sort of academy or gymnasium fit for persons of their station, where they learn all kinds of music, dancing, and other such accomplishments and diversions which are suitable for their quality and such as are practiced at court." He did not leave Gray's Inn before 1594 except, possibly, in 1591, when he may have joined the 2d Earl of Essex's forces helping Henry IV of France against the Spanish invaders of Brittany; he was never called to the bar.

Although Campion contributed verses to Sir Philip Sidney's 1591 edition of *Astrophel and Stella* and published *Poemata* and *A Booke of Ayres,* little more is known until 1605, when he took a degree in medicine at the University of Caen; however, he was soon back in London and in 1607 produced a masque in honor of the marriage of Lord Hay, which was presented before James I at Whitehall. In 1613 his *Masque on St. Stephen's Night* was performed in the Banqueting Hall at Whitehall for the marriage of Robert Carr, Earl of Somerset, to Lady Frances Howard, the divorced and notorious wife of the 3d Earl of Essex; the Banqueting Hall, on Whitehall and Horse Guards Avenue, is all that remains of Whitehall Palace. It was at this time that Campion visited the Tower of London to minister to his patron, Sir Thomas Monson, who was imprisoned for complicity in the murder of Sir Thomas Overbury. Campion died on March 1, 1620, and was buried the same day in the old Church of St. Dunstan-in-the-West, on the north side of Fleet Street just west of Fetter Lane.

Sir John Davies (1569–1626) In 1587 Sir John Davies (Davys), a minor poet and politician, entered the Middle Temple (between the Victoria Embankment and Fleet Street) and in 1595 was called to the bar; he was debarred for breaking a cudgel over the head of a fellow barrister and readmitted following an open apology to his victim. He died at his house on the Strand during the night of December 7–8, 1626, the night his appointment as Lord Chief Justice was announced; Davys was buried at St. Martin-in-the-Fields. He mentions the Paris Garden, as did Shakespeare, in his *Epigrammes:*

Publias, student at the common law,
Oft leaves his books, and for his recreation,
To Paris Garden doth himself withdraw. . . .

Thomas Middleton (1570–1627) The dramatist Thomas Middleton was possibly a native of London and was baptized at the old Church of St. Lawrence Jewry, in front of the Guildhall. Nothing specific is known of Middleton until he entered Gray's Inn, off Gray's Inn Road, probably in 1596, since a 1580 birthdate has been newly established. His first writing for the stage was probably in 1599, when *The Old Law* was composed, and by 1601–1602 he was one of the regular contributors to the Lord Admiral's Company. In September 1620, in recognition of his services to London, he was appointed city chronologer. Nothing of these official writings remains. His political drama *A Game at Chess* met with unparalled success, playing for nine consecutive days and producing revenues of £1,500, before James I was forced by the Spanish Ambassador to stop the performances and reprimand the company and the author. Middleton, who had long lived at Newington Butts, Surrey, died there in late June 1627.

He based Moll Cutpurse in *The Roaring Girle* on Mary Firth, who lodged in the Drury Lane area and who, tradition says, was the first Englishwoman to smoke a pipe in the streets of London. *The Blacke Booke* refers to

passing through Birchin Lane, amidst a camp-royal of hose and doublets. . . .

Birchin Lane, almost opposite Clement's Lane, off the north side of Lombard Street, was inhabited mostly by drapers.

Thomas Dekker (1570?–1632) Somewhere in London around 1570, the dramatist Thomas Dekker was born, but the first definite record is dated January 1598, when he is noted in Philip Henslowe's diary: "Lent unto Thomas Dowton, the 8 of Jeneway 1597, twenty shillings, to by a books of Mr. Dickers, xxx." Henslowe also bailed Dekker out of the Counter, where he had been put for a debt of 40 shillings in February 1598, the same year he began writing for Henslowe. It is believed that Dekker was, for a time, in the Fleet Prison (near Fleet Lane off Farringdon Street, where the Congregational Memorial Hall now stands), and for some reason from 1613 to 1619 he was imprisoned in the original King's Bench Prison, on the Borough High Street near Angel Place in Southwark. Dekker continued writing and collaborating after his release from prison, and it is thought that he died in 1632.

Dekker wrote some remarkably graphic accounts of the people who frequented Paul's Walk (the middle aisle of the nave of Old St. Paul's Cathedral):

At one time, in one and the same rank, yea, foot by foot, and elbow by elbow, shall you see walking the knight, the gull, the gallant, the upstart, the gentleman, the clown, the captain, the appel-squire, the lawyer, the usurer, the citizen, the rankrout, the scholar, the beggar, the doctor, the idiot, the ruffian, the cheater, the puritan, the cut-throat, the high-man, the low-man, the true-man, and the thief. Of all trades and professions some; of all countries some. Thus, whilst Devotion kneels at her prayers, doth Profanation walk under her nose in contempt of religion.

Many of Dekker's works contain references to specific places in London. *The Gulls Horne-Book* asks: "Did many think you come wrangling into the world about no better manners, than all his lifetime to make privy searches in Birchin Lane for whalebone doublets?" Birchin Lane, north off Lombard Street, was noted as a place for trade in men's ready-made clothes.

Without doubt, *The Shoemaker's Holiday, or A Pleasant Comedy of the Gentle Craft* provides as effective a set of descriptions of contemporary life and locations in London as can now be found. Rowland Lacy, nephew of the Earl of Lincoln, remarks on the preparations for the French wars of Henry V:

The men of Hertfordshire lie at Mile-end;
Suffolk and Essex train in Tothill-fields;
The Londoners and those of Middlesex,
All gallantly prepar'd in Finsbury,
With frolic spirits long for their parting hour.

The Guildhall, seat of government for the City of London, where "Lacy . . . shall receive his pay," is just off Aldermanbury Street; this site has held a gov-ernment establishment since Saxon times, and it was here that Henry Howard, Earl of Surrey, was tried on a charge of treason. Simon Eyre, the shoemaker, bids farewell to Rafe:

[H]ere's five sixpences for thee; fight for the honour of the gentle craft, for the gentlemen shoemakers, the courageous cordwainers, the flower of St. Martin's, the mad knaves of Bedlam, Fleet Street, Tower Street and Whitechapel; crack me the crowns of the French knaves; a pox on them; crack them; fight by the Lord of Ludgate; fight, my fine boy!

St. Martin's appears to refer to the old Church of St. Martin's (on Ludgate Hill west of St. Paul's Cathedral), which was destroyed in the Great Fire and rebuilt by Sir Christopher Wren. Bedlam, of course, is the old Bethlehem Hospital where the mentally ill were kept in relatively primitive conditions; it was located where the Liverpool Street Station of British Rail stands today.

The "Lord Mayor's garden, Old Ford," where Act II begins, was then outside of London in a relatively secluded area. Simon Eyre's shop, at "the sign of the last," was in Tower Street, just off Shaftesbury Avenue, north of Cambridge Circus, and it is to this place "of the gentle craft" that the disguised Lacy comes in search of employment. Hodge's comment (Act III, scene i) refers to the Church of St. Mary Overy, which stood on the south bank of the Thames east of the Bishop of Winchester's London residence:

Portagues, thou wouldst say; here they be, Firk; hark, they jingle in my pocket like St. Mary Overy's bells.

Act IV begins in "The Old Change," more properly, the Old Exchange, located near the old cathedral church of St. Paul's just south of Carter Lane; it held all manner of shops including the seamster's shop in which Jane works. The Church of St. Faith, where Hammon and Rose are to be married, was commonly called St. Faith under Paul's and, notes Stow, "served for the stationers and others dwelling in Paul's churchyard, Paternoster row, and the places adjoining." The London Stone, an irregular block of stone to which Firk refers (Act IV, scene v), used to stand on the south side of Cannon Street; in 1798 it was put into a wall niche in St. Swithin's Church, but after this structure was severely damaged in World War II, the stone was removed and is now secure in one wall of the Bank of China, which stands on the site of the church. Simon Eyre, now Lord Mayor of London, relating the marriage plans of Lacy and Rose, tells Lady Madgy:

[T]rip and go, my brown queen of periwigs, with my delicate Rose and my jolly Rowland to the Savoy; see them link'd, countenance the marriage; and when it is done, cling, cling together, you Hamborow turtle-doves.

The area of the Savoy is roughly bounded today by the Strand and Savoy Place on the north and south, and Savoy Street and, say, Adam Street on the east and west. The feast is to occur in the "great new hall in Gracious Street corner, which our master [Simon Eyre], the new lord mayor, hath built"; Gracious Street is Gracechurch Street, and the specific area here is between Fenchurch and Leadenhall Street, north of the Leadenhall Market. In 1445 Lord Mayor Sir Simon Eyre, a draper, not a shoemaker, gave a large mansion to the city, and the name of Leadenhall Street derives from this hall, which had a lead roof. In contradiction to Dekker, Eyre did not name the building for the reason set forth by the King:

> . . . we'll have it call'd
> The Leadenhall, because in digging it
> You found the lead that covereth the same.

Neither did Eyre build the structure. In the same scene Dekker also explains (equally erroneously, for Dick Whittington acquired the rights) the beginning of the Leadenhall Market:

> *Eyre.* . . . They are all beggars, my liege; all for themselves, and I for them all on both my knees do entreat, that for the honour of poor Simon Eyre and the good of his brethren, these mad knaves, your grace would vouchsafe some privilege to my new Leadenhall, that it may be lawful for us to buy and sell leather there two days a week.
> *King.* Mad Sim, I grant your suit, you shall have patent To hold two market-days in Leadenhall.
> Mondays and Fridays. . . .

Dekker's *The Seven Deadly Sinnes of London* and *The Belman of London* also deal with the city.

John Donne (1572–1631)   One of the most important literary figures of this period was the poet and divine John Donne, who was born between January 24 and June 19, 1572, on Bread Street; his was a Roman Catholic family, and Donne later claimed that no other English Catholic family had suffered as much as his. Indeed, his mother, the daughter of the playwright John Heywood, was a collateral descendant of Sir Thomas More, who lost his head rather than betray his faith. Donne's father, a successful ironmonger, was looking to a prosperous career in January 1576, when he died leaving six children, of whom John Donne was the eldest; his mother's remarriage brought the children a most suitable stepfather in Dr. John Syminges. Sometime after the marriage, the family moved to a house on Bartholomew Close, where John Donne and his brother Henry were educated privately by a Catholic tutor. Under this strong family influence, Donne left London in October 1584 to matriculate at Hart Hall (Hertford College), Oxford, in full knowledge that he would never take a degree since that meant subscribing to the Act of Supremacy and accepting the Thirty-Nine Articles. Donne's stepfather died in July 1588 and was buried on July 15 at the partly 15th-century Church of St. Bartholomew the Less, now incorporated into St. Bartholomew's Hospital; Donne was undoubtedly in attendance. Donne's mother again remarried and moved to St. Saviour's parish, Southwark; it can be assumed that Donne knew Southwark well.

Donne was back in London, more or less permanently, by May 1591, when he became a student at Thavies Inn (gone but on Fetter Lane between Holborn and the Records Office adjoining the Church of St. Andrew on the west). On May 6, 1592, he moved to Lincoln's Inn, the 14th-century foundation on the west side of Chancery Lane, Holborn. Donne's name disappears from the records here in 1594; presumably the requirements for proceeding to final legal training were then complete. Through military service with Ralegh and Essex, he met Thomas Egerton, the son of the Lord Keeper, and secured a post as secretary to Sir Thomas, probably late in 1597; it seems most likely that Donne had abandoned formal

Catholicism by the time he entered Egerton's service. He quickly became part of the establishment at York House, traditional home of the Lord Keeper, and was often in attendance at court (Whitehall, Greenwich, Nonsuch, and Richmond). Donne became Sir Thomas's parliamentary observer in 1600, the same session to which Sir George More brought his daughter to London from Loseley Park, Surrey.

Ann (Anne) More, Lady Egerton's niece, had first met Donne at York House before this sitting of Parliament. Unable to win Sir George's consent, they married secretly in December before she had to return with her father to Loseley for Christmas. This elopement was what Izaak Walton called "the great error of his [Donne's] life," for not only was it a breach of civil and canon law but it also assured the wrath of the Lord Keeper. Donne took lodgings in the house of a Mr. Haines beside the Savoy, from which he wrote to Sir George in February 1601 breaking the news of the marriage. Sir George's reaction was to be expected; he first had Donne committed to the Fleet Prison (where the present Congregational Memorial Hall stands on Fleet Lane and Farringdon Street) and then had him dismissed as Egerton's secretary. Sir Thomas, though, was not antipathetic to Donne's situation, and on February 12 secured the poet's release from the Fleet. Donne returned to his lodgings, though still nominally under restraint, and there he received the news that the Court of High Commission had upheld the validity of his marriage.

Donne and his wife went to Pyrford, Surrey, and then to Mitcham, Surrey; although he was having difficulty in getting employment, Donne kept an apartment on the Strand at the house of a Mr. Tincomb (not in Whitehall, as is often claimed). Around 1606 he became a frequent visitor to the Strand house belonging to Magdalen Herbert, mother of George Herbert, and became a close friend of Edward Herbert, later Lord Herbert of Cherbury. Donne frequented the Mitre Tavern on Fleet Street, on the western corner of Old Mitre Court, which was also patronized by the *bon vivant* and poet Thomas Coryate. Finding another patron in Sir Robert Drury, Donne took a house on Drury Lane after a period abroad. Walton claims that Donne paid no rent here, but that seems unlikely. In any event the Donnes resided here until 1621. During this period a son, Nicholas, who died in infancy, was baptized in the Church of St. Clement Danes on August 3, 1613, and a three-year-old daughter, Mary, was buried in the same church on May 18, 1614.

Donne felt certain of court preferment after his epithalamion in honor of the marriage of Robert Carr, Earl of Somerset, and Frances Howard, the notorious Countess of Essex and by 1614 was optimistic, but his hopes were crushed when the King let it be known again that Donne's only preferment would come through holy orders. By the end of November 1614, Donne acquiesced to James's wishes and entered the church; he was ordained deacon and priest on January 23, 1615, in the large chapel in the bishop's palace on the north side of St. Paul's Cathedral. Almost immediately preferment arrived in the form of an appointment as Chaplain-in-Ordinary, and in June Donne preached at the Inns of Court and the Camberwell Church on Camberwell Church Street.

What was quite possibly Donne's first court duty occurred on April 21, 1616, when he preached at the Palace of Whitehall; his court preachings then followed a regular pattern, one sermon every April with the exception of the years 1618, 1620, 1621, 1625, and 1626, when he appeared twice in the month. Employment was now the least of his problems; already holding the livings of Keyston, Huntingdonshire, and Sevenoaks, Kent (both from 1616), he was chosen divinity reader at Lincoln's Inn on October 24, 1616.

Donne's first sermon at St. Paul's occurred on March 24, 1617, when he preached at Paul's Cross, the open-air pulpit northeast of the cathedral. His fortunes were rapidly improving, but on August 15 Ann Donne died after giving birth to a stillborn child. She and the child were buried in a common grave on August 16 at the Church of St. Clement Danes, east of Aldwych on the Strand. Donne vowed, says Walton, "never to bring . . . [his surviving seven children] under the subjection of a step-mother," and he kept his promise. Donne preached his first sermon after his wife's death here—the incumbent rector had died and no successor had been found—and took as "his text . . . a part of the Prophet Jeremy's lamentation, 'Lo, I am the man that hath seen affliction.'" He erected a monument to his wife on the north side of the chancel; a tombstone carved by Nicholas Stone did not survive the 1681 rebuilding by Sir Christopher Wren. A trip abroad as chaplain to the 1st Viscount Doncaster prompted the "Sermon of Valediction at My Going into Germany" at Lincoln's Inn on April 18, 1619. Donne was disappointed in his failure to secure the deanship of Salisbury, but on September 12, 1621, as Walton relates,

> the king sent to Dr. Donne and appointed him to attend him at dinner the next day. When his Majesty was sate down, before he had eat any meat, he said after his pleasant manner, "Dr. Donne, I have invited you to dinner; and, though you sit not down with me, yet I will carve to you of a dish that I know you love well; for knowing you love London, I do therefore make you Dean of Paul's; and when I have dined, then do you take your beloved dish home to your study, say grace there to yourself, and much good may it do you.

Elected dean on November 22, he was installed the same day; he also became prebendary of Chiswick, as his predecessor had been. Late in the year, he moved into the deanery, on the southwest side of the cathedral, and preached at St. Paul's on Christmas Day. The deanery, Stow's "fair old house," had a long tradition of hospitality.

St. Paul's was in very poor condition, because of past calamities, the most important of which occurred on June 4, 1561, when the already shaky spire was again struck by lightning and burned down to the roof. A temporary roof of boards and lead was raised, but repairs lagged, and what with the damage of the fire and the exposure to the elements, extensive deterioration took place. Donne set out to repair the chapel and worked assiduously on the cathedral for the remainder of his life. With the business of St. Paul's pressing him, Donne preached his last sermon at Lincoln's Inn in 1622 (either February 2 or May 30) and presented the memorial window, inscribed "Io: Donne/Dec:S:Pauli," in the chapel (second window on the north side). Donne resigned his chambers at the end of 1624.

In November 1623 Donne became seriously ill with "spotted fever" or "relapsing fever" (probably typhoid), and recovery was not expected; throughout the illness he kept extensive journals of his thoughts and prayers, which resulted in *Devotions upon Emergent Occasions, and Several Steps in My Sickness:*

> No man is an island entire of itself; every man is a piece of the continent, a part of the main. If a clod be washed away by the sea, Europe is the less, as well as if a promontory were, as well as if a manor of thy friend's or of thine own were. Any man's death diminishes me, because I am involved in mankind, and therefore never send to know for whom the bell tolls; it tolls for thee.

In the spring of 1624 Donne received the benefice of the medieval Church of St. Dunstan-in-the-West, on the north side of Fleet Street just west of Fetter Lane; it was rebuilt in the 19th century and restored after bomb damage. In 1625, when the plague was ravaging London, Donne sought refuge in the Chelsea country house of Sir John Danvers, the husband of Magdalen Herbert, to whom Donne had earlier sent his *Divine Poems.* The house stood on the northwest corner of Danvers Street opposite Paulton's Square. Donne's "Elegy ix: The Autumnal" was written of her.

> No spring nor summer beauty hath such grace
>   As I have seen in one autumnal face.
> Young beauties force our love, and that's a rape;
>   This doth but counsel, yet you cannot 'scape.
> If 'twere a shame to love, here 'twere no shame;
>   Affection here takes reverence's name.
> Were her first years the golden age? That's true;
>   But now they are gold oft tried and ever new.
> That was her torrid and inflaming time,
>   This is her tolerable tropic clime.

Lady Danvers died in 1627 after nursing many of the Chelsea victims of the plague, and Donne preached her funeral service in Chelsea Old Church.

Although Donne's health was now failing, as the dean of St. Paul's he refused to give up preaching as long as he could mount the steps to the pulpit; in December 1630 he made out a holograph will. The rumor that he was dead (probably a confusion raised by the death of his mother the same year) had the lie put to it when he appeared in Whitehall to preach on Ash Wednesday, February 23. Taking his text from Psalm 68 and titling the sermon "Death's Duell," he was virtually preaching his own funeral service. Donne continued to conduct cathedral business until mid-March 1631 and died on March 31; he was buried in St. Paul's Cathedral on April 3. His request for a simple and private funeral could not be met, for, as Walton notes:

> [B]eside an unnumbered number of others, many persons of nobility and of eminency for learning, who did love and honor him in his life, did show it at his death by a voluntary and sad attendance of his body to the grave, where nothing was so remarkable as a public sorrow.

Walton also claimed that Donne was persuaded in his last illness that "a monument [should be] made for him" and that with this resolution Donne had, first, a wooden urn carved to his specific dimensions and a board of the height of his body delivered to the deanery. This done, he secured a painter, and

> Several charcoal fires being first made in his large study, he brought with him into that place his winding-sheet in his hand and, having put off all his clothes, had

this sheet put on him and so tied with knots at his head and feet and his hands so placed as dead bodies are usually fitted to be shrouded and put into their coffin or grave. Upon this urn he thus stood with his eyes shut. . . . In this posture he was drawn at his just height; and when the picture was fully finished, he caused it to be set by his bed-side, where it continued . . . till his death . . . [when it was] thus carved in one entire piece of white marble as it now stands in that church. . . .

The epitaph is Donne's own composition. When the fire of 1666 destroyed Old St. Paul's, only Donne's monument survived. In the modern St. Paul's it has been placed on the eastern side of the south choir aisle, almost exactly where it stood before the destruction of the older cathedral. Donne, it should be noted, was a member of Sir Walter Ralegh's group, which included William Shakespeare, Ben Jonson, Christopher Marlowe, Francis Beaumont, and John Fletcher, who met at the celebrated Mermaid Tavern on Bread Street, one or two doors in from the corner of Cheapside on the west side.

Ben Jonson (1572–1637) Ben Jonson, who shares with William Shakespeare preeminent literary importance during the reigns of Elizabeth I and James I, is similarly difficult to trace through London. He was probably born on Northumberland Street (formerly Hartshorne Lane, between the Strand and Craven Place) around June 11, 1572, a month or two after the death of his father. It is known that after his mother's remarriage the family lived on Hartshorne Lane. Although Jonson's stepfather was a bricklayer, the child obtained a first-rate education, beginning at an establishment in the Church of St. Martin-in-the-Fields and then, by a singular stroke of good fortune, at Westminster School. The antiquarian William Camden is said to have paid the boy's expenses:

Camden, most reverend head, to whom I owe
  All that I am in arts, all that I know
(How nothing's that!); to whom my country owes
  The great renown and name wherewith she goes;
Than thee the age sees not that thing more grave,
  More high, more holy, that she more would crave.

Camden was then one of the masters in the 14th-century school, whose buildings surround Little Dean's Yard, and Jonson later dedicated two plays to his "most reverend head." Jonson's formal education undoubtedly ended early, and most plausibly he followed his stepfather's masonry trade; he is believed to have worked on the wall on the west side of Chancery Lane and on the entrance gate to the Lincoln's Inn precincts.

Between 1592 and 1596 (more likely 1592), Jonson married at the 14th-century Church of St. Giles Cripplegate on Fore and Wood Streets (restored in the 1540s and the 1950s); of Jonson's wife nothing is really known aside from his comment that she was "a shrew, yet honest," and that they lived apart for five years. The parish record at St. Martin-in-the-Fields notes a burial on November 17, 1593, as "Seplta fuit Maria Jonson peste"; the name is a common one, but the register entry suggests this was Jonson's daughter:

Here lies, to each her parents' ruth,
Mary, the daughter of their youth;
Yet all heaven's gifts being heaven's due,
It makes the father less to rue.
At six months' end she parted hence
With safety of her innocence. . . .

Jonson's first son, Nicholas (born 1596), died of the plague in 1603 and was buried in the Church of St. Botolph without Bishopsgate; Jonson, who was away when the child died, claimed a vision of the child "of manly shape" and of the growth "he shall be at the resurrection"; to the "child of my right hand" he says:

Rest in soft peace, and asked, say, "Here doth lie
  Ben Jonson his best piece of poetry;
For whose sake henceforth all his vows be such
  As what he loves may never like too much."

By July 1597 Jonson was both a player and playwright of Philip Henslowe's company and possibly acted the role of Hieronimo in Thomas Kyd's *The Spanish Tragedy*. He is also probably the "Benjamin Iohnson" imprisoned in the Old Marshalsea Prison (in the Borough High Street, Southwark, between Mermaid Court and Talbot Yard) in mid-July 1597 for his part in writing "a lewd plaie . . . contanynge very seditious and sclandrous matter"; the play was *The Isle of Dogs*, begun by Thomas Nash and finished by Jonson; he was released on October 8. Within a year Jonson was imprisoned at Newgate (on part of the site occupied by the Central Criminal Court on Old Bailey and Newgate Streets) for the murder of Gabriel Spencer, one of Henslowe's men; the duel took place in Hoxton Fields beyond Shoreditch. Tried in October at the Old Bailey, he pleaded guilty and escaped the gallows by claiming the "benefit of clergy," that is, the ability to read the Latin Bible. He did not escape the punishment of branding, but was freed after being "branded" with a cold iron, a penalty which suggests he had influence somewhere. In mid-September, *Every Man in His Humour* was produced by the Lord Chamberlain's Company at the Curtain (on the east side of Curtain Road just south of Hewett Street); tradition holds that William Shakespeare recommended the play and acted in it.

Jonson was one of many who frequented the Mermaid Tavern, on the west side of Bread Street one or two doors down from the corner of Cheapside; "Inviting a Friend to Supper" celebrates the tavern and its delicious wine:

But that which most doth take my muse and me,
Is a pure cup of rich Canary wine,
Which is the *Mermaid's* now, but shall be mine.

Jonson had attracted notice in court by this time, and after the *Entertainment of the Queen and Prince at Althrope* Jonson prepared *The Masque of Blackness*, which was produced at the old Palace of Whitehall on Twelfth Night, 1605. The dramatist also visited Sir Walter Ralegh in the Tower of London and was made tutor to Ralegh's son for a visit to the Continent. Returning to London on June 29, 1613, he witnessed the burning of the Globe Theatre, and ten years later his personal library was destroyed in a fire. Jonson recalls the experience in "An Execration upon Vulcan":

And why to me this, thou lame Lord of fire,
  What had I done that might call on thine ire?
Or urge thy Greedie flame, thus to devoure
  So many my Yeares-labours in an houre?
I ne're attempted, *Vulcan*, 'gainst thy life;
  Nor made least line of love to thy loose Wife. . . .

In a legal document dated the same year, he claims to

be domiciled at Gresham College, formerly the town house of Sir Thomas Gresham, located between Bishopsgate and Old Broad Street, where Palmerston House now stands. It is probable that Jonson had only temporary refuge here. James granted the dramatist a pension of 100 marks in 1621, and in October of that year he was granted the reversion of the office of the master of the revels. In 1621, as well, Jonson helped to celebrate Sir Francis Bacon's sixtieth birthday at York House and wrote of the occasion in *"Lord BACONS Birth-day"*:

> . . . This is the sixtieth yeare
> Since *Bacon,* and thy Lord was borne, and here;
> Sonne to the grave wise Keeper of the Seale,
> Fame, and foundation of the English Weale.
> What then his Father was, that since is hee,
> Now with a Title more to the Degree;
> *Englands* high Chancellor: the destin'd heire
> In his soft Cradle to his Fathers Chaire,
> Whose even Thred the Fates spinne round, and full,
> Out of their Choysest, and their whitest wooll.

Early in 1626 Jonson became ill with palsy and then dropsy, and his health began to deteriorate seriously; he had just returned to his dramatic work in 1625 with the *Staple of News,* and it is generally assumed that he was forced into this because of poverty. In 1628 he appears to have suffered a stroke and was confined at first to his chambers and eventually to his bed; according to John Aubrey, he was living "in the house under which you passe as you goe out of the Churchyard into the old Palace"; the little cottage stood between St. Margaret's Church and Westminster Abbey. Jonson's health declined quite slowly, and he died on August 6, 1637; he was buried in Westminster Abbey under a square flag of blue marble which was incised "O rare Ben Jonson." (One suggestion has been that the first two words should have been combined to form *orare* and that the epitaph thus reads "Pray for Ben Jonson," because of his recusant Catholicism.) One point of a rather macabre interest is that Ben Jonson's head is possibly not in his tomb; the skull, it is said, was examined and then placed in the coffin of the famous surgeon John Hunter; a second point of interest is that Jonson was buried upright either because of a joke by Bishop John Williams, dean of the abbey, that Jonson could never hope to attain more than two square feet of abbey space or because the dramatist wanted to be ready for the Resurrection. In 1728 a commemorative bust was placed on the south wall of the Poets' Corner by the 2d Earl of Oxford.

Other places in London are closely associated with Jonson's life: he frequented the Dog and the Triple Tun, both of which have disappeared, and the Devil Tavern (on the south side of Fleet Street at the present Number 1), where he helped establish the famous Apollo Club, one of the City's first literary clubs and the place where the famous "Tribe of Ben" congregated. Well into the late 18th century, Jonson's inscription hung over the door to the Apollo, the apartment where the celebrated club met; it read in part:

> Welcome all, who lead or follow,
> To the Oracle of Apollo.
> Here he speaks out of his Pottle,
> Or the Tripos, his Tower Bottle:
> All his Answers are Divine,
> Truth itself doth flow in Wine.
> Hang up all the poor Hop-Drinkers,

> Cries Old Sym, the King of Skinkers;
> He the half of Life abuses,
> That sits watering with the Muses.

"Old Sym, the King of Skinkers" was the landlord.

A complete survey of the allusions to London in Jonson's plays is beyond the realm of possibility here, but some of the highlights can be taken up. *Every Man in His Humour* is set wholly in London; Captain Bobadill is described as a "Paul's Man," a ne'er-do-well who frequented the main aisle of St. Paul's Cathedral. Master Stephen reports that because he dwells in Hogsden (Hoxton, then a northeast suburb)

> I shall keep company with none but the archers of Finsbury, or the citizens that come a ducking to Islington ponds!

In the 16th and 17th centuries, because of rioting and the plague, places of entertainment had to lie outside the City. The second act, set in the "garden of Kitely's house" in Old Jewry, was the area bounded on the north by the Guildhall and on the south by Cheapside; the synagogue was on Lothbury Street near the intersection of Old Jewry. Kitely directs Cash to tell Master Lucar

> He shall ha' the grograns at the rate I told him,
> And I will meet him on the Exchange anon.

The present Royal Exchange, between Threadneedle Street and Cornhill, opposite the Bank of England, is the third on this site. Kitely, then, describes Cash to Downright as

> . . . a jewel, brother.
> I took him of a child up at my door,
> And christ'ned him, gave him mine own name, Thomas;
> Since bred him at the Hospital. . . .

The hospital is Christ's Hospital, originally the Grey Friars (Franciscan) Monastery (on Newgate Street); the school was moved to Sussex in 1902. Moorfields, where part of the second act takes place, is just north of the London Wall and was a deserted marshland where archery was practiced, where women dried their washing, and where apprentices skated on bones tied to their shoes in winter. Finally, Coleman Street, where Justice Clements resides, is essentially an extension of Old Jewry Street, running northeast from Lothbury to the London Wall.

Epicoene, or The Silent Woman, also set in London, adds references to those in *Every Man in His Humour.* Truewit, while discoursing on women, alludes to the 1609 rebuilding of Aldgate:

> How long did the canvas hang afore Aldgate? Were the people suffer'd to see the city's Love and Charity, while they were rude stone, before they were painted and burnish'd? No.

Aldgate, one of the four original gates to the City, was located on the present Aldgate Street about 25 feet east of the corner of Jewry Street; the foundations of the wall and the easternmost gate have been discovered. The rebuilt gate was pulled down in 1761. Sir Amarous La-Foole is "a precious mannikin," who "has a lodging in the Strand," a very fashionable lodging place in the late 16th and early 17th centuries; parallel with the bank of the Thames, it runs from Temple Bar to Charing Cross. The enormous medieval houses and palaces of ecclesiastics and nobility which lined the Strand were taken over at the Reformation by the wealthy, and the long process of conversion (and, inevitably, deterioration) was started. In Act II, when Truewit encounters Morose, he comments,

> Marry, your friends do wonder, sir, the Thames being so near, wherein you may drown so handsomely; or London-bridge, at a low fall, with a fine leap, to hurry you down the stream; or, such a delicate steeple i' the town, as Bow, to vault from; or a braver height, as Paul's.

The Bow is the Church of St. Mary-le-Bow, on Bow Lane on the south side of Cheapside. This church determines a true Cockney, for to have that distinction one must be born within the sound of its bells. "Paul's" of course, refers to the cathedral. Mrs. Otter refers twice to the Paris Garden:

> 'Fore me, I will *na-ture* 'em over to Paris-garden, and *na-ture* you thither too, if you pronounce 'em again.

and

> By my integrity, I'll send you over to the Bank-side; I'll commit you to the master of the Garden, if I hear but a syllable more.

The garden, on Bankside in Southwark, west of the Falcoln Inn between the Swan Theatre and the Thames, was a popular bear-baiting garden. Truewit's St. Pulchre, "You would think he meant to murder all St. Pulchre's parish," is the original 12th-century Church of St. Sepulchre, rebuilt in the 15th century and again after the Great Fire, on Holborn Viaduct just east of the intersection of Snow Hill. Finally, Jonson mentions the Great Bed of Ware, which is now in the Victoria and Albert Museum.

The Prologue to *The Alchemist* sets the scene of the play in London for specific reasons:

> Our scene is London, 'cause we would make known,
>   No country's mirth is better than our own.
> No clime breeds better matter for your whore,
>   Bawd, squire, imposter, many persons more. . . .

However, the play is more specifically set in the area of Blackfriars. Face declares he first met Subtle

>   . . . at Pie-Corner,
> Taking your meal of steam in, from cooks' stalls. . . .

Located directly in front of the Smithfield Central Market in West Smithfield, Pie-corner was noted for its cookery shops. The Renaissance speculator Sir Epicure Mammon, awaiting the appearance of Subtle at Lovewit's house, states:

>   This night I'll change
> All that is metal in my house to gold:
> And, early in the morning, will I send
> To all the plumbers and the pewterers,
> And buy their tin and lead up; and to Lothbury
> For all the copper.

Lothbury, an extension of Throgmorton Street between Bartholomew Lane and Princes Street, says Stow,

> is possessed for the most part by founders, that cast candlesticks, chafing-dishes, spice mortars, and such like copper or laton works, and do afterward turn them with the foot, . . . making a loathsome noise to the by-passers . . . and therefore by them disdainfully called Lothberie.

Reference is made to the Temple Church; Face states:

> Here's one from Captain Face, sir,
> Desires you meet him i' the Temple-church,
> Some half-hour hence, and upon earnest business.

He calls it "the round"; the church, round in form like others belonging to the Knights Templars, was modeled on the Church of the Holy Sepulchre in Jerusalem. Although heavily bombed during World War II, it has retained much of its 12th-century architecture.

Bartholomew Fair concerns the great cloth fair held in the churchyard of the Priory of St. Bartholomew, Smithfield, from at least the time of Henry II until 1855; Cloth Fair, approximately parallel to Long Lane, commemorates this. Jonson's play presents a good general picture of the 17th-century goings-on at Bartholomew tide. Of the many locales mentioned, one is noteworthy here; John Littlewit comments:

> A poxe o' these pretenders to wit! your *Three Cranes, Miter,* and *Mermaid* men! Not a corne of true salt, nor a graine of right mustard amongst them all.

The Three Cranes, just east of the Vintners' Hall at Southwark Bridge, took its name from the three-story cranes of timber which were placed on Vintry Wharf to unload wines. The sign of the three birds was a popular pun on the commercial aspect of the area.

Thomas Heywood (1574?–1641)   As is often the case with important early literary figures, facts concerning the relationship between London and Thomas Heywood are scarce. A native of Lincolnshire by his own account, he became a member of Philip Henslowe's company, the Lord Admiral's, and probably served his apprenticeship with this group. He later became a "*switzers* to players (I mean the hired men)" who "make but a hard and hungry life of it by strowting vp and down after the Waggon" from town to town. It seems fairly certain that he lived on Bankside near the Rose, an area favored by actors and writers, until the Queen's Men moved to the Curtain in Shoreditch around 1603. Most likely Heywood married an "Aenn Butler servt. to Mr. Venn," probably on June 13, 1603, and an Ann Hayward, probably his daughter, was buried on January 12, 1622. He married again on January 18, 1633, when the parish register at the Church of St. James, Central Street, Clerkenwell, records the marriage of "Thomas Hayward & Jane Span: lic. from the Facul"; the marriage took place in the church of the suppressed Benedictine nunnery of St. Mary, whose church served as the parish church. Soon after the marriage, the couple moved to Clerkenwell, a now densely populated, light-industrial area; in Heywood's time it was separated from the City by Moorfields and was more rural than urban. Heywood died in August 1641 and was buried on August 16 in the Church of St. James, Clerkenwell.

John Marston (1575?–1634)   John Marston, who was presented with the living of Christchurch, Hampshire, in 1616, was living in the London parish of Aldermanbury at the time of his death, but he had earlier been imprisoned at Marshalsea (near Mermaid Court) for his collaboration in *Eastward Hoe*. He died on June 25, 1634, and was buried the next day near the altar of Temple Church. The gravestone (gone) read "Oblivioni Sacrum."

Thomas Coryate (1577?–1617)   Thomas Coryate, author of *Coryats Crudities Hastily Gobled Up in Five Moneths Travells in France, Savoy, Italy, Rhoetia Comonly Called the Grisons Country, Helvetia Alias Switzerland, &c, &c*, obviously lived in London, probably at St. James's Palace, when he was a hanger-on in court, and frequented the Mermaid Tavern, on the east side of Bread Street. After a trip abroad, which he estimated covered 1,975 miles, and the publication of his journal, he had a "chamber in Bowelane," from which he wrote to Sir Michael Hicks on November 15, 1610.

John Fletcher (1579–1625)   Of John Fletcher's life in London, only scattered bits are known. He came here from Rye, Sussex, when his father was made Bishop of London, and the family lived in Chelsea, on the south side of Cheyne Walk just east of Chelsea Old Church. Fletcher's mother was buried in the original Chelsea church, and it is reasonable to assume that the dramatist was present for the service. He returned to the City after being at Bene't (Corpus Christi) College, Cambridge, if he is the "John Fletcher of London" on the university's records; this is highly likely since Bishop Fletcher had been president of the college. Around 1607 Fletcher's relationship with Francis Beaumont developed, and they took a house on Bankside, perhaps on Clink Street, where other theatrical persons lived. Here, according to John Aubrey:

> They lived together on the Banke side, not far from the playhouse, both bachelors, lay together, had one wench in the house between them, which they did so admire, the same cloaths and cloake, &c, between them.

They frequented the Mermaid Tavern, one or two doors down on the northwest side of Bread Street from the corner of Cheapside, along with Shakespeare, Ben Jonson, Christopher Marlowe, John Donne, and Sir Walter Ralegh. In 1625 the plague was raging in London, and, says Aubrey, accepting an invitation to escape to the country,

> [h]e stayed but to make himsele a suite of cloathes, and while it was makeing fell sick of the plague and died.

Fletcher died on August 29, 1625, and was buried the same day, as was the invariable practice with plague victims; no memorial was erected.

John Webster (1580?–?1625)   Most of the details of John Webster's life have been obscured by time, but he is usually assumed to have been born in London around 1580. He was probably apprenticed to his father's trade, that of a tailor, and was a freeman of the Merchant Taylors' Company in 1604, when he was assessed charges for James I's coronation. Sometime after this time he began collaborating with Thomas Dekker, and one of the fruits of that collaboration, *Westward Hoe*, was acted by the Children of Paul's in December 1604. Webster is believed to have lived on the west side of Shoreditch High Street, just north of Holywell Lane, an area of rooming houses, where Richard Burbage also lodged. Webster may have resided in the Middle Temple and was possibly admitted to study law on August 1, 1598. The dramatist is often identified as being the John Webster who married Isabell Sutton at the Church of St. Leonard, on the east side of Shoreditch High Street. Neither the date of Webster's death nor his place of burial is known, but St. Andrew's Church, Holborn, often claims his grave and sometimes claims he was its parish clerk.

John Taylor (1580–1653)   John Taylor, the "water poet," was apprenticed to a London waterman before serving Elizabeth "seven times at sea"; retiring from the service with a "lame leg," he returned to his earlier trade. He was a "collector of the perquisite of wine enacted by the lieutenant of the Tower" for about fourteen years and was commissioned to arrange the Thames water pageants in honor of Princess Elizabeth in 1613 and in welcome of Charles I's return from Scotland in 1641. Taylor's lodgings in London cannot be verified until June 1653, when he took the license of the Crown Inn on Long Acre, near Covent Garden, in what is today Hanover Square. When Charles was executed, Taylor changed the inn sign to that of the Mourning Crown; this, though, was a dangerous sentiment, and upon reflection he hung his portrait in its stead. Taylor died at the Poet's Head in December 1653 and was buried on December 5 at the Church of St. Martin-in-the-Fields. One of Taylor's best-known pieces refers to Tyburn (the modern Connaught Place), upon which the gallows stood:

> I have heard sundry men oftimes dispute,
> Of trees that in one yeare, will twice beare fruit.
> But if a man note Tyburn 'twill appeare,
> That that's a tree that bears twelve times a yeare.

Sir Thomas Overbury (1581–1613)   One of the more tragic figures of this period was the poet and courtier Sir Thomas Overbury, member of a distinguished political family; he came to London in 1598, when he entered the Middle Temple and resided in the Inns of Court. On a pleasure trip in 1601 to Scotland, he was introduced to Robert Carr, the man who was to be his nemesis. Overbury was well received in court after 1603, when Carr arrived to attend James I; indeed, Overbury was looked on as Carr's tutor. In 1606 the relationship was more or less formalized as he became Carr's secretary and adviser, and it was reported that "Overbury governed Carr and Carr governed the King." When Carr, now Viscount Rochester, became involved with the notorious Countess of Essex, Frances Howard, Overbury encouraged the affair early by writing many of the letters and poems with which Carr pursued his suit. However, Overbury's opinion of the suitability of the countess as Carr's mistress was not the same as his opinion of her as Carr's wife, and, indeed, Sir Thomas voiced his disapproval of any marriage. Rochester, not wishing to break with Overbury, hesitated, but under sharp prodding from his mistress he effected Overbury's imprisonment at the critical moment. Thus, with Sir Thomas out of the way, the marriage took place.

Whether Carr, now Earl of Somerset, expected Overbury's imprisonment to be anything but short-lived has never come to light; however, it appears that the countess was determined to put him out of the way. She arranged the dismissal of the unimpeachable lieutenant of the Tower of London and had him replaced by Sir Gervase Helwys, who would do as he was bid. Thus a personal appointee from the countess, Richard Weston, became Overbury's jailer, and a systematic, slow poisoning (by means of arsenic and mercury) was undertaken. Overbury, of course, complained; no concern was shown, and he was denied visitors. So confident was the countess of her scheme that she allowed Overbury access to two eminent physicians, who found nothing unnatural in his condition. Within months Overbury's condition was critical, and he was diagnosed as consumptive. Losing patience, the countess ordered "a clyster of corrosive sublimate" administered. On September 15, around 5 A.M., Sir Thomas died in the Bloody Tower (some say he was suffocated at the end) and was buried on the same day at St. Peter's ad Vincula within the tower walls; the body was wrapped only in a sheet and was not placed in a coffin. About a year later a commission formed to look into his death found all parties guilty, and only the earl and his countess escaped the gallows. *Sir Thomas Overburie His Wife . . . New Newes and Divers More Characters* was not published until after the author's death.

Philip Massinger (1583–1640) Like many of the dramatists of the period, Philip Massinger is difficult to trace. In 1613 he was certainly in prison, undoubtedly the famous Clink Prison (on Clink Street, Bankside), and was also an established writer for Philip Henslowe. For some reason in 1623 he switched his allegiance to the Queen's Company, but three years later he returned to the King's Company. He married and had a house on Bankside, Southwark, when he died suddenly in mid-March 1640. According to Anthony à Wood,

> He went to bed well, and was dead before morning; whereupon his body, being accompanied by comedians, was buried about the middle of that ch. yard belonging to St. Saviour's Church there, commonly called the Bullhead ch. yard. . . .

There are a few irregularities here. First is the payment of a £2 burial fee, which indicates Massinger was a "stranger" in the parish, that is, a nonparishioner; if, indeed, he were living in Bankside, this is puzzling unless, perhaps, he did convert to Catholicism, as is sometimes suggested. Second is the register note stating that Massinger was buried inside and not outside the church; the tradition, possibly false, that Massinger was buried in the same grave as John Fletcher was begun by Sir Aston Cokayne's elegy:

> In the same Grave *Fletcher* was buried here
> Lies the Stage-Poet Phillip Massinger:
> Playes they did write together, were great friends:
> And now one Grave includes them at their ends. . . .

The church contains a memorial window.

Most of Massinger's plays or those in which he had a hand are set outside London or outside England; *The City Madam*, a comedy licensed on May 25, 1632, is a notable exception. Moorfields, where

> . . . some chandlers daughters
> [Were] Bleaching linen. . . .

was the marshy area just beyond the City's north wall, and the Exchange, the Royal Exchange built by Sir Thomas Gresham, was originally called the Bourse, the name which the courtesan Shave'em uses:

> I am starv'd,
> Starv'd in my pleasures; I know not what a coach is,
> To hurry me to the Burse, or Old Exchange:
> The neathouse for musk-melons, and the gardens,

> Where we traffic for asparagus, are, to me,
> In the other world.

The neathouse was a well-known garden and nursery near Chelsea. Goldwire's allusion to St. Martin's

> Thou shalt have thy proper and bald-headed coachman;
> Thy tailor and embroiderer shall kneel
> To thee, their idol: Cheapside and the Exchange
> Shall court thy custom, and thou shalt forget
> There e'er was a St. Martin's. . . .

is not really clear since the parish of St. Martin's has been distinguished historically as a sanctuary, a bridewell, a spittle, and an almshouse, but Shave'em's entry in the last scene "in a blue gown" presents her in the livery of Bridewell Prison.

Edward Herbert (1583–1648) Edward, 1st Baron Herbert of Cherbury, elder brother of the poet and divine George Herbert, was first in the City in 1600, when he presented himself to the court and gained the attention of the aging Queen Elizabeth. His next confirmed appearance was not until 1611, when his dueling and quarrelsome nature were as well known as his attractiveness (so he claimed) to women. A flirtation with Lady Ayres had an abrupt end when the irate Sir John attacked Herbert in Scotland Yard (an area north of Whitehall and not the present building) and left him badly beaten, stabbed, and unrepentant. Dismissed as British Ambassador in Paris in 1624 after offending King James, he was in London often thereafter and in 1629 became Lord Herbert of Cherbury. Herbert was committed to the Tower of London for a short time in the spring of 1642 for an indiscretion committed in the parliamentary debate on Charles I's struggle with Parliament; in this case an apology secured his release. From September 1643 on he made his home on the south side of Great Queen Street near the corner of Wild Street, where he died on August 20, 1648, without benefit of clergy. By his own request he was buried in the Church of St. Giles-in-the-Fields at midnight "without pomp or other ceremonies as is usual"; a flat marble stone (now gone) with a Latin inscription was placed over the grave.

Francis Beaumont (1584–1616) Francis Beaumont, who may have been born in his father's London residence (but more likely Grace Dieu), undoubtedly knew the metropolis as a child, but his first confirmed association with London occurred in 1600, two years after his father's death, when he entered the Inner Temple under the sponsorship of his two brothers. He matriculated "Specialiter, Gratis, Comitive" because his father had been a bencher, and he had external lodgings somewhere. Sometime early, Beaumont (and his elder brother Sir John) made the acquaintance of Michael Drayton and Ben Jonson, and by 1607 he was on such good terms with Jonson as to address him as "dear friend" in an encomium. The aspiring dramatist frequented the Mermaid Tavern (a house or two below the northwest corner of Bread Street just off Cheapside), where Ben Jonson held forth, and described the "combat of wits" here in an epistle to Jonson:

> What things have we seen
> Done at the "*Mermaid*." Heard words that have been
> So nimble, and so full of subtle flame,
> As if that every one from whence they came
> Had meant to put his whole wit in a jest,
> And had resolved to live a fool the rest
> Of his dull life. . . .

It may have been at the Mermaid that Beaumont and Fletcher first met, but the suggestion that Jonson introduced the two is unsupported. Beaumont also frequented the Mitre Inn, at the top of Mitre Court a few feet off Fleet Street. Probably by 1608 Beaumont and Fletcher lived

> together on the Banke side, not far from the playhouse, both bachelors, lay together, had one wench in the house between them, which they did so admire, the same cloaths and cloake, &c, between them.

Their lodgings were probably on Clink Street. Beaumont died on March 6, 1616, at Sundridge, Kent, and was buried on March 9 in Westminster Abbey, just in front of St. Benedict's Chapel. The grave, to the right of Chaucer's, has no monument and neither name nor date to distinguish it. It was Beaumont who wrote the often-quoted lines on the abbey:

> Mortality, behold and fear
> What a change of flesh is here!
> Think how many Royal bones
> Sleep within these heaps of stones.
> Here they lie, had realms and lands,
> Who now want strength to stir their hands. . . .

Many of the plays by Beaumont and those by Beaumont and Fletcher have to do with London. *The Knight of the Burning Pestle,* undoubtedly performed in Blackfriars, is set partly in the city, although specific locations are hard to come by. Mile End, of which Mistress Merrythought and her son Michael speak, was then a suburban area about 1 mile northeast of Aldgate where troops were often mustered:

> *Mist. Mer.* Where be we now, child?
> *Mich.* Indeed, forsooth, mother I cannot tell, unless we be at Mile-End. Is not all the world Mile-End, mother?
> *Mist. Mer.* No, Michael, not all the world, boy; but I can assure thee, Michael, Mile-End is a goodly matter. . . .

Humphrey, whose "bride is gone" and who has "been beaten twice," says he

> . . . will wear out my shoe-soles
> In passion in St. Faith's church under Paul's.

The original St. Faith's was a parish church just outside the walls of Old St. Paul's Cathedral; as the cathedral grew, St. Faith's had to be demolished (ca. 1260), and the parishioners were then granted the right to worship in the crypt of the new cathedral. In effect, St. Faith's church carried on its offices under the choir of St. Paul's. In the final scene of the play Ralph enters "with a forked arrow through his head" and commends his soul "to Grocers' Hall," not the building standing today but on the same site on the north side of Poultry, just after it changes from Cheapside, facing Princes Street. The new hall, built in 1970 to replace a late-19th-century building destroyed by fire in 1965, belongs to a corporation which dates to the medieval guilds.

Giles Fletcher the Younger (1588–1623) Giles Fletcher the Younger may have been born in London about 1588 and may have been educated at the Westminster School, but there is no corroboration for Thomas Fuller's statement.

George Wither (1588–1667) The poet and pamphleteer George Wither (Withers) appears to have settled in London around 1610 and ended up in Lincoln's Inn in 1615 after spending some time in one of the minor Inns of Court. From the beginning Wither seems to have adopted his aggressive writing style; and his abusive works often landed him in jail. In 1613, when *Abuses Stript and Whipt* appeared, the pointed verses on revenge, ambition, lust, and weakness, among others, offended the authorities and Wither was promptly placed in the Old Marshalsea Prison (on the east side of the Borough High Street in Southwark, between Mermaid Court and Talbot Yard), where he "wasted in despair"; he noted he had fallen

> into the displeasure of the state: and all my apparent good intentions were so mistaken by the aggrauations of some yll affected towards my indeavors, that I was shutt up from the society of mankind.

He wrote prolifically in prison, but none of this material was found offensive. *Wither's Motto: Nec habeo, nec careo, nec curo* (printed 1621) was looked on favorably by many for the vision of morality it conveyed, but even so the authorities felt that it was negative about the current political situation and committed him a second time to Marshalsea. On this occasion he never came to trial, possibly because of his claim that Michael Drayton had approved the work.

A staunch Puritan, Wither was involved in the political upheavals of the Civil War, and when sentenced to die for treason felt extremely bitter that he owed his survival to Sir John Denham's plea that "so long as Wither lived he [Denham] would not be accounted the worst poet in England." He continued to write prolifically and stayed out of major trouble until 1660, when he returned to a house in the Savoy and was arrested for an unpublished manuscript on the reactionary nature of the House of Commons. The verse paper brought about his imprisonment in Newgate (on Newgate Street, on the site of the present General Post Office). Wither appeared before the House of Commons on March 24, 1662, and was committed to the Tower of London to await impeachment but was released on bond for good behavior. Wither died at his home in the precincts of the Savoy (roughly bounded by the Strand, Savoy Place, Adam Street, and Savoy Street) on May 2, 1667, and was buried "within the east door" of the Queen's Chapel of the Savoy.

Robert Herrick (1591–1674) The poet and preacher Robert Herrick, a native of London, was baptized at the old parish church of St. Vedast, on the east side of Foster Lane, on August 24, 1591. The church, mostly destroyed in the Great Fire, was rebuilt by Sir Christopher Wren from 1670 to 1673, sustained heavy bomb damage in World War II, and has been much restored. Herrick's father was a goldsmith, and the family lived on Goldsmith's Row, a series of ten 15th-century houses so magnificent in their decoration that they were a tourist attraction; Stow calls them

> the most beautiful frame of fair houses and shops that be within the walls of London, or elsewhere in England, . . . beautified towards the street with the Goldsmiths' arms and the likeness of woodmen, in memory of his name, riding on monstrous beasts, all which is cast in lead, richly painted over and gilt. . . .

Herrick's father, Nicholas, died on November 9,

1592, in peculiar circumstances; having made out a will on November 7, he died from injuries received in a fall (or jump) from an upper-story window of his house. Giles Fletcher the Elder became one of the three administrators of the estate after an investigation brought about a verdict of accidental death. Herrick possibly was educated at Westminster School in Little Dean's Yard in the abbey precincts before he was apprenticed for ten years to his uncle, Sir William Herrick, on August 25, 1607; Sir William's shop was on Wood Street, probably at the corner of Goldsmith Street.

Herrick pursued his apprenticeship until 1613, when he entered St. John's College, Cambridge, as a fellow commoner, and after taking orders and the living at Dean Prior, Devonshire, was back in London only occasionally until the autumn and winter of 1640. At that time he came hoping to get his first volume of poems published and took lodgings on Little Almonry Street near Westminster Abbey. When Herrick, a devoted royalist, was ejected from Dean Prior in 1647, he is thought to have returned to London. Anthony à Wood claimed he lived "in St. Anne's parish in Westminster," but no such parish existed then. In all likelihood Herrick was living on St. Anne's Lane (now St. Ann's Street) in St. Margaret's parish near the Almonry, where he had lived before. He frequented the Mermaid Tavern, on Bread Street a door or two from the corner of Cheapside. Herrick's "His Teares to Thamasis" sums up his feelings toward London:

I send, I send here my supremest kiss
To thee, my silver-footed Thamasis.
No more shall I reiterate thy Strand,
Whereon so many stately structures stand:
Nor in the summer's sweeter evenings go,
To bathe in thee, as thousand others doe:
No more shall I along thy christall glide,
In barge with boughes and rushes beautifi'd,
With soft-smooth virgins for our chaste disport,
To Richmond, Kingstone, and to Hampton-Court:
Never againe shall I with finnie ore
Put from or draw unto the faithfull shore,
And landing here, or safely landing there,
Make way to my beloved Westminster,
Or to the golden Cheap-side, where the earth
Of Julia Herrick gave to me my birth.

Francis Quarles (1592–1644)   The popular poet Francis Quarles, of whom Horace Walpole once said, "Milton had to wait till the world had done admiring Quarles," entered Lincoln's Inn in 1608; he never seriously intended to follow the legal profession but was, according to his wife, desirous of settling differences between friends and neighbors. He had lodgings at Lincoln's Inn, on the west side of Chancery Lane, and on one occasion, it is said, because of his fondness of music he sold his "Inn-of-court gowne" to buy a lute case. On May 28, 1618, at St. Andrew's Church, Holborn, he married Ursula Woodgate, by whom he had eighteen children. Quarles was occasionally in London after leaving Lincoln's Inn, and in 1626 he prosecuted the case of a woman pickpocket in the old Sessions House (rebuilt and now converted to offices) in Clerkenwell opposite the Church of St. James. Quarles was appointed chronologer to the City of London, a post he held from

1639 until his death on September 8, 1644; he was buried in the Church of St. Olave, on Seething Lane.

Izaak Walton (1593–1683)   Izaak Walton, fisherman and chronicler of the lives of John Donne and George Herbert, came to London from his birthplace of Stafford to apprentice himself, probably as a seamster, or tailor, to a relative. In 1625 he was admitted to the Company of Ironmongers, whose hall is located on the east side of Aldersgate Street, but it seems likely that Walton made his living as a draper rather than as an ironmonger. His London residences are well documented; of the first Sir John Hawkins writes:

He dwelt on the north side of Fleet Street in a house two doors west of the end of Chancery Lane, and abutting on a messuage known by the sign of the Harrow.

Here Walton had both his shop and his house. In 1632 he moved to the next-to-last house on the west side of Chancery Lane before it reaches the Strand but probably did not retain the former residence as a shop. At one time he attended the Church of St. Bride at the foot of Fleet Street (rebuilt by Wren between 1671 and 1703 and again after World War II), and he also attended St. Dunstan-in-the-West on Fleet Street, probably because his friend John Donne was vicar there; indeed, Walton himself was a vestryman in the church until 1644. Walton's first wife was buried there on August 25, 1640. Because of Dr. Donne, Walton is also associated with Chelsea Old Church, on the southeast corner of Old Church Street and Cheyne Walk; almost totally destroyed by the Germans in 1941, the church was fully rebuilt on its original plan; even the fragments of the old monuments were carefully collected and pieced together. Here Walton came in 1627 for the funeral service for Magdalen, Lady Danvers, mother of the poet George Herbert; Walton recalls that he

saw and heard this Mr. John Donne (who was then Dean of St. Paul's) weep and preach her funeral sermon in the parish church of Chelsea, near London, where she now rests in her quiet grave, and where we must now leave her. . . .

For many years after leaving London in 1644, Walton lived in Winchester, Hampshire, and his visits to London were generally unrecorded. However, he was back in 1658, when he scratched his initials on the commemorative tablet in Westminster Abbey to Isaac Casaubon, "that man of rare learning and ingenuity." Between 1658 and 1662 Walton moved to the Clerkenwell area, which he did not like; thus, when his friend George Morley became bishop of Winchester, Walton found a second home in the bishop's palace.

George Herbert (1593–1633)   George Herbert had a long association with London, beginning in 1600, when his mother, Magdalen, took a house on Charing Cross where Edward Herbert and his wife lived. Herbert's early schooling took place at home, but in 1605, at the age of twelve, he was sent to Westminster School, whose buildings surround Little Dean's Yard, a short walk southward from his home. He was at first a day scholar and later, after winning a scholarship, became a boarder before going up to Trinity College, Cambridge, in 1609. He was not really back in London until he sat for Montgomeryshire in Parliament in the winter of 1624; then he was in Westminster for the sittings of the House of Commons and met daily with his fellow members in St. Stephen's Chapel, which stood at right angles to Westminster Hall.

By 1622 Magdalen Herbert had married Sir John Danvers, a man nearly half her age and about the age of his stepson George, and the two lived in Chelsea at Danvers House (roughly the area bounded today by Danvers Street, Old Church Street, Cheyne Walk, and Paulton's Square). Herbert himself was staying here in December 1625, when John Donne was a frequent guest. Herbert's mother died in 1627 after nursing Chelsea's early victims of the plague and was buried in Chelsea Old Church, where Dr. Donne preached the memorial service, which undoubtedly was attended by George Herbert.

Thomas Carew (1595?–1640)   Thomas Carew, the poet, was brought by his parents to London at an early age from West Wickham, Kent, and while the family lived on Chancery Lane between Fleet and Carey Streets, the exact location of the house is unknown. After becoming a B.A. at Oxford in 1611, he entered the Middle Temple, where, according to his father, he did "little at law"; dissatisfied with his son's progress, Sir Matthew sought employment for the young man and sent him to Florence as Sir Dudley Carleton's secretary. Dismissed on account of "slanderous insinuations" against Sir Dudley and his wife in 1616, Carew could secure no new position and returned to his father's house. He became a court favorite and attended the November 3, 1616, investiture of Charles as Prince of Wales at Whitehall; the poet became one of Charles I's favorites and a gentleman of the King's Privy Chamber in 1628. Probably at this time (or in 1630, when he became a server at the King's table) Carew took lodgings on King Street (gone, but it once ran beside Whitehall Palace from Charing Cross to Westminster Hall). Among Carew's frequent guests were Ben Jonson (then Poet Laureate), Sir William Davenant, and Sir John Suckling. Carew was one of the *beaux esprits* at the Mermaid Tavern on Bread Street, a house or two down on the northwest corner off Cheapside. He died in London, probably in the house on King Street, on March 22, 1640, and was buried at St. Dunstan-in-the-West.

James Shirley (1596–1666)   Very few facts have been confirmed about the life of James Shirley, but he was born on September 18, 1596, and according to Anthony à Wood (who is frequently in error) the birthplace was in or near the parish of St. Mary Woolchurch (since incorporated into St. Mary Woolnoth). On October 8, 1608, he was admitted to the Merchant Taylors' School, on the west side of Suffolk Lane, where he remained until going up to St. John's College, Oxford, in 1612. After taking orders and subsequently being converted to Catholicism, he returned to London no later than 1625; according to Anthony à Wood, he took up residence in Gray's Inn, between Holborn and Theobalds Road. It is possible that the "Matthias Shirley, son of John Shirley," baptized in 1624 at St. Giles Cripplegate was his son. Probably the peak of his career occurred in 1634, when *The Triumph of Peace*, for which he wrote the text, was performed by the members of the four Inns of Court in the Banqueting Hall at Whitehall Palace, all that remains of the palace.

Shirley left London around 1636 for Ireland and returned only occasionally until (probably) 1640; with the 1642 suppression of plays, he was, said Anthony à Wood,

> hereupon forced to leave London, and so, consequently his wife and children who were afterwards put to their shifts.

It is not exactly clear what Shirley did at this juncture, and he may have joined the Earl of Newcastle's forces; however, as the King's cause deteriorated, Shirley "retired obscurely to London" and took up residence in Whitefriars, where he returned to schoolmastering and continued to write for the stage. At the time of the Great Fire, in September 1666, Shirley and his wife were still in Whitefriars, supposedly near the Inner Temple Gate, and were driven from their home by the holocaust; they found lodgings in the parish of St. Giles-in-the-Fields, where, according to Anthony à Wood, "being in a manner overcome with affrightments, disconsolations, and other miseries, occasion'd by that fire and their losses," they died within twenty-four hours of each other and were buried in the same grave on October 29 in the churchyard of St. Giles-in-the-Fields. *The Constant Maid, The Lady of Pleasure, The Wedding,* and *The Witty Fair One* are all set in London.

From Charles I until George I   With the death of James in 1625, Charles I assumed the throne; his reign was fraught with political mismanagement from the start. Charles had inherited the belief that kings were intended by God to reign, and the imposition of his authoritarian rule at a time of growing unrest because of religious and political suppression precipitated the Civil War. Trouble began immediately when Parliament met in June 1625 and the King refused either to explain his foreign policy or to account for the expected costs of this policy. The 1626 Parliament proved even more difficult; Charles, unable to justify the failure of the expedition against Cádiz, dissolved Parliament. Matters worsened as the arrogant Duke of Buckingham involved England in a war with France and Charles arranged a heavy loan (declared illegal by the Chief Justice) to finance the operation. When Parliament met in 1628, it drafted the Petition of Right, which forced the monarch to recognize four important principles: no taxation without consent, no imprisonment without cause, no martial law without war, and no forced quartering of troops. Between the third and fourth sittings of Parliament, the Duke of Buckingham was assassinated; and the fourth Parliament brought forward three resolutions condemning the King's behavior.

No other Parliaments met until 1640; England seemed to enjoy a measure of peace and prosperity for nearly ten years, but the issues continued to pile up. The Bishops' War broke out. Charles convened Parliament in April 1640 to raise money for the Scottish war, and when the members insisted upon debating their complaints, Charles dissolved the so-called Short Parliament. The new Long Parliament, meeting in November, had one of Charles's most trusted advisers beheaded and condemned his rule.

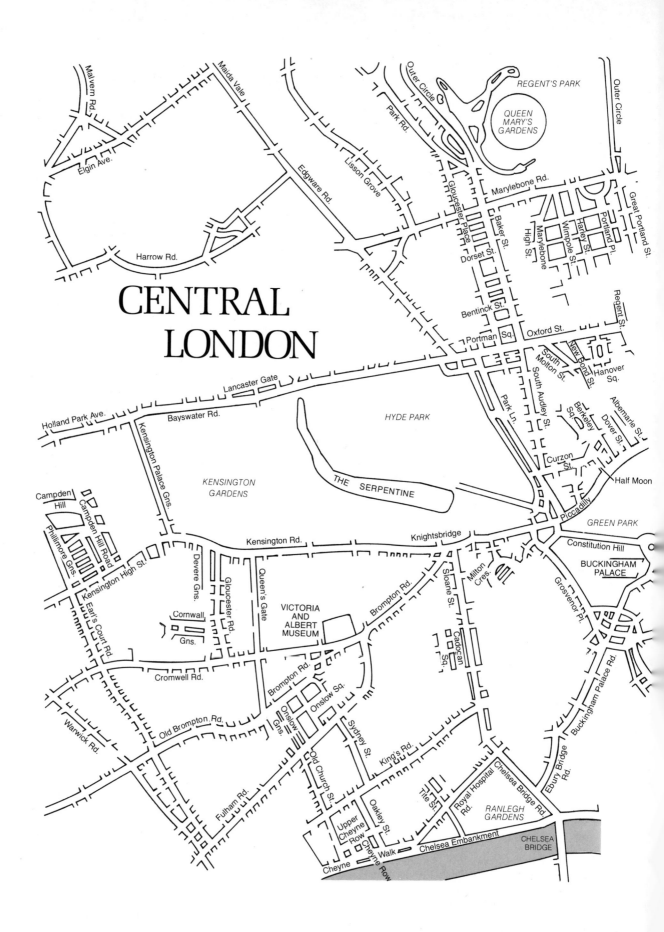

CENTRAL LONDON

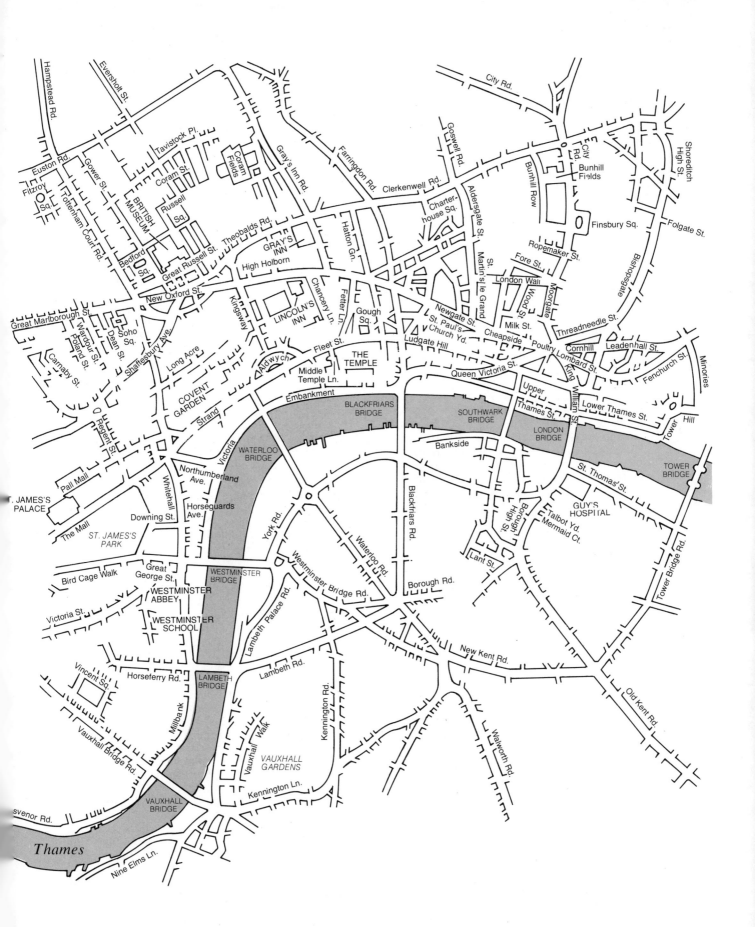

By 1641 both the Royalists and the Parliamentarians were building armies; and when Charles could not accept the Nineteen Propositions and flew the royal banner at Nottingham, military activity intensified. Early fighting went well for the King, but after Oliver Cromwell became second-in-command of the New Model Army in 1645 and soundly defeated the Royalists at the Battle of Naseby, the tide turned. In the spring of 1646 Charles escaped to the camp of the Scots; they, though, had reached an agreement with the Parliamentarians and upon their departure in 1647 handed the King over. Held in Northamptonshire, Newmarket, and Hampton Court, from which he escaped in November, Charles then fell into the hands of the Governor of the Isle of Wight, a staunch Parliamentarian, and was brought to trial on a charge of high treason on January 20, 1649. Sentenced on January 27, he was executed on January 30 outside the Banqueting Hall at Whitehall. To John Milton, then Latin Secretary for the Council, fell the task of explaining the regicide to the rest of the world.

With Charles's death, the "Commonwealth and Free State" was created by the Rump Parliament, which, however, was dissolved by troops when it delayed in making many of the changes the Parliamentarians wanted. A group of 140 handpicked Puritans made Cromwell Lord Protector and created a single-chamber Parliament. Before his death in September 1658, Cromwell agreed to a version of the Humble Petition and Advice, a Protectorate arrangement restoring the upper parliamentary house and making the Protectorate hereditary. His son Richard, England's second Lord Protector of the Realm, struggled to maintain the government, but gave up in May 1659 when he was unable to reconcile the conflicting interests. The Long Parliament, restored by Gen. George Monck, dissolved itself after summoning a Convention Parliament, which called Charles II to the throne.

In April 1660, Charles drafted his Declaration of Breda, which included provisions for amnesty, and was proclaimed King in May. Even though Charles sought tolerance, a new Act of Uniformity required the clergy to subscribe to the Thirty-Nine Articles, to use a new book of prayer, and to take a new oath of supremacy. Almost 2,000 clerics were removed from their benefices, and the 1664 Conventicle Act severely limited the right of assembly of Nonconformists, whose clergy were restricted by the Five-Mile Act from coming within that distance of places where they had previously preached. Finally, the 1673 Test Act, Lord Macaulay said,

> provided that all persons holding any office, civil or military, should take the oath of supremacy, should subscribe a declaration against transubstantiation, and should publicly receive the sacrament according to the rites of the Church of England.

Charles had little control over Parliament, and the subsequent passage of the Corn Laws and the Navigation Acts had far-reaching consequences.

Charles died a Roman Catholic in 1685, having been converted on his deathbed; more important, he did not leave an heir, although he had fathered at least fourteen illegitimate offspring. From the time of Charles through to the house of Hanover, religious questions were of the utmost importance; preferments were difficult to obtain and equally difficult to keep; as "The Vicar of Bray" points out, "In good King Charles's golden days" one became "a zealous high-churchman." "When royal James possess'd the crown," the "church of Rome" one "found would fit"; with "royal Anne" one "became a tory"; and with "George in pudding-time," why, "one became a whig, sir."

> And this is law that I'll maintain
> Until my dying day, Sir,
> That whatsoever King shall reign,
> Still I'll be the Vicar of Bray, Sir.

Charles's brother, the Duke of York, came to the throne as James II, pledging to preserve church and state "as it is now by law established" while intending to reestablish the Church of Rome. This brought about the quickly quelled rebellion of the Duke of Monmouth; Monmouth was executed, and Judge George Jeffreys's Bloody Assizes wiped out a considerable number of Monmouth's Protestant followers. Macaulay writes:

> The court was hung, by order of the Chief Justice, with scarlet; and this innovation seemed to the multitude to indicate a bloody purpose....
> More than three hundred prisoners were to be tried. The work seemed heavy; but Jeffreys had a contrivance for making it light. He let it be understood that the only chance of obtaining pardon or respite was to plead guilty. ... Two hundred and ninety-two received sentence of death.

James's Declaration of Indulgence firmly stated his position: "We cannot but heartily wish, as it will be easily believed, that all the people of our dominions were members of the Catholic Church." He proceeded to appoint Catholics as fellows and president of Magdalen College, Oxford (which under the statutes he could not do), and clearly overreached his authority; in a second Declaration of Indulgence on April 27, 1688, the King repeated that "his purpose was immutably fixed" and that he would "employ those only who were prepared to concur in his design." He ordered the declaration "to be read, on two successive Sundays at the time of divine service, by the officiating ministers of all the churches and chapels of the kingdom." This finally provoked the clergy, and the Archbishop of Canterbury and six other prelates drafted a petition which claimed the declaration was illegal because the King "was not constitutionally competent" to deal with matters ecclesiastic and which affirmed their intention to ignore both James's directive and his declaration. The seven were brought before the King in Council on a charge of seditious libel, and their trial at the King's Bench was long and emotional before the jury, which met all night closely guarded by men from both groups, brought in a verdict of not guilty. The birth of James's son assured a Catholic succession. On the day of the bishops' acquittal seven peers of the realm invited William of Orange to take the English throne. William landed at Torbay (modern Tor Bay) on November 5, 1688, with his forces, and James was forced to flee to France. In January 1689, the Convention Parliament declared that James had abdicated and formally offered the dual crown to William III, Charles I's grandson, and Mary II, daughter of James II.

The reign of William and Mary was marked internally by widespread reforms and externally by a shift to a pro-Dutch and anti-French foreign policy. By 1701 William was eager to do battle with France over various matters of European succession, but his death in 1702 forestalled his designs. Princess Anne, James II's younger daughter and a Protestant, who took the throne at William's death, had borne five children by 1700 (in eighteen pregnancies), but the only child to survive infancy died in 1700. Thus Anne agreed to the Act of Settlement of 1701, which designated the Hanoverian succession to the Stuart line. Scotland disputed the Hanoverian right of succession, but the problem was formally resolved with the adoption of the Act of Union in 1707.

London during this ninety-year period was overcrowded, and its water supplies were polluted. James I's attempt to control the city's growth by prohibiting new building resulted only in further crowding and the construction of inferior dwellings (so that if they were pulled down, as the code provided, the loss would not be great). By 1637, contrary to the law, 1,360 houses in an area from Westminster through St. Martin-in-the-Fields to Bloomsbury, Holborn, and Clerkenwell had been built outside the City wall. The 2d Earl of Leicester, attempting to develop part of his Leicester Fields estate, was required to plant the open area with trees and to provide walkways; some of this survives today in Leicester Square. Francis Russell, 4th Earl of Bedford, also held land here, in the form of a newly inherited Covent Garden estate; while permitted to build as many houses "fit for the habitacions of *Gentlemen* and men of ability" as he liked, he was to be overseen by one of the King's four newly appointed commissioners, including the Surveyor General of Works, Inigo Jones. Jones designed the new square, planning the Covent Garden Church, as Bedford demanded, as the focal point of the development with rows of stucco terraced houses whose front doors opened onto vaulted arcades facing the church. When the building was finished, Bedford obtained a license to establish a fruit and vegetable market, which as it expanded, eventually pushed the more affluent residents out.

During the Civil War those who could left the city, and many buildings were abandoned. In 1642 weeds were rampant in the courts of Whitehall Palace, and it was, said one pamphleteer, "a Palace without a Presence":

> You may walk into the Halls. . . . You may walk into the Presence Chamber with your hat, spurs and sword on. And if you will presume to be so unmannerly, you may sit down in the Chair of State.

During the Protectorate only stone and brick structures could be built on existing foundations. The Restoration changed some of the rules, but great areas of the city were still covered with vastly overcrowded, ramshackle hovels and deteriorated tenements in which people and rats fought each other for space. It was in these overcrowded areas that the bubonic plague of 1664–1665 took most of its 70,000 victims in a population then estimated at around 460,000. Harrison Ainsworth describes the beginning of the plague in *Old St. Paul's:*

> The whole city was panic-stricken: nothing was talked of but the plague—nothing planned but means of arresting its progress—one grim and ghastly idea possessed the minds of all. Like a hideous phantom stalking the streets at noonday, and scaring all in its path, Death took his course through London, and selected his prey at pleasure. . . . [G]risly shapes appeared at night—strange clamours and groans were heard in the air,—hearses, coffins, and heaps of unburied dead were discovered in the sky, and great cakes and clots of blood were found in the Tower moat. . . .
>
> From Drury Lane it spread along Holborn, eastward as far as Great Turnstile, and westward to St. Giles's Pound, and so along the Tyburn Road. Saint Andrew's Holborn was next infected, and as this was a much more populous parish than the former, the deaths were more numerous within it. For awhile the disease was checked by Fleet Ditch; it then leaped this narrow boundary, and ascending the opposite hill, carried fearful devastation into St. James's, Clerkenwell. At the same time, it attacked Saint Bride's: thinned the ranks of the thievish horde haunting Whitefriars, and proceeding in a westerly course, decimated Saint Clement Danes.
>
> Hitherto, the city had escaped.

The plague was followed by London's most spectacular visitation, the Great Fire of 1666. On Sunday, September 2, 1666, a fire broke out in a baker's house on Pudding Lane, between Lower Thames and Eastcheap Streets near London Bridge; there appeared to be no cause for alarm, and the Lord Mayor, awakened in the early hours, showed nothing but contempt for the small blaze, noting, "Pish! a woman might pisse it out." Even Samuel Pepys, also roused from his bed, saw no need to worry. August, though, had been very dry, and occasional gusts of wind soon spread the fire and sparks up and down Pudding Lane and Fish Street Hill into Lower Thames Street and down to the riverside wharves, which were loaded with coal and wood. Bucket brigades were totally ineffective, as were the rudimentary fire engines, which were unable to get through streets packed with personal belongings. Pepys again viewed the fire and reported to King Charles

> that, unless His Majesty did command houses to be pulled down, nothing could stop the fire. . . . [T]he King commanded me to go to my Lord Mayor from him, and command him . . . to pull down before the fire every way.

Pepys went down Watling Street "as well as I could" because of the fleeing hordes of people:

> At last met my Lord Mayor in Cannon Street, like a man spent, with a hankercher about his neck. To the King's message, he cried, like a fainting woman, "Lord! what can I do? I am spent: people will not obey me. I have been pulling down houses, but the fire overtakes us faster than we can do it."

By the evening of September 2 the fire had spread as far north as Cornhill and almost as far west as Cheapside; then, on September 3 St. Paul's and the Guildhall were engulfed in flame. Ainsworth's novel, drawn from contemporary sources, describes the end of Old St. Paul's:

> It now became evident also, from the strange roaring noise proceeding from the tower, that the flames were descending the spiral staircase, and forcing their way through some secret doors or passages to the roof. . . . [T]he fierce glare of the flames lighted up the painted windows at the head of the choir with unwonted splendour. Overhead was heard a hollow rumbling noise like that of distant thunder, . . . while fluid streams of smoke

crept through the mighty rafters of the roof, and gradually filled the whole interior of the fabric with vapour. Suddenly a tremendous cracking was heard, as if the whole pile were tumbling in pieces. . . .

[T]he flames, which had long been burning in secret, burst through the roof at the other end of the choir, and instantaneously spread over its whole expanse. . . . At this juncture, a strange hissing sound was heard, as if a heavy shower of rain was descending upon the roof, and through the yawning gap over the choir there poured a stream of molten lead of silvery brightness. Nothing can be conceived more beautiful than this shining yet terrible cascade, which descended with momentarily increasing fury, sparkling, flashing, hissing, and consuming all before it. All the elaborately carved woodwork and stalls upon which it fell were presently in flames. . . . [A]nother fiery cascade burst through the roof near the great western entrance . . . flooding the aisles and plashing against the massive columns. At the same moment, too, a third stream began to fall over the northern transept. . . .

The flames continued. "Nothing," John Evelyn noted, "but the almighty power of God was able to stop them, for vaine was the help of man: on the fift it crossed towards *White-hall,* but ô the Confusion was then at that Court." Finally, an earlier proposal was adopted:

[N]othing was like to put a stop, but the blowing up of som many houses, as might make a ⟨wider⟩ gap, than any had yet ben made by the ordinary method of pulling them downe with Engines; This some stout Seamen proposed early enought to have saved the whole Citty; but some tenacious & avaritious Men, Aldermen &c. would not permitt, because their houses must have ben ⟨of⟩ the first: It was therefore now commanded to be practised. . . .

Mercifully the wind died down at the same time, and the fire was brought under control; 395 acres in the City were destroyed, including St. Paul's, the Guildhall, the Royal Exchange, and the Customs House, eighty-seven parish churches, forty-four City company halls, and more than 13,000 homes. Almost 250,000 people were left homeless. As long after the fire as March 1667, the debris was still smoldering, and it was no longer possible to tell where streets had been.

Charles was concerned with laying out a commodious new City, with wider streets and brick and stone buildings only. There were, though, conflicting claims to sites, and many of the multiple rebuilding schemes were untenable. John Evelyn wanted to erect all public buildings on a wide embankment along the Thames and rid the city of the "horrid smoke," which as he earlier had complained, "obscures our Churches, and makes our Palaces look old, which fouls our Clothes, and corrupts the Waters."

Sir Thomas Browne (1605–1682) Sir Thomas Browne, physician and author of *Religio Medici,* was born in the parish of St. Martin-le-Grand on October 19, 1605; a plaque at the entrance to the church notes that he was born somewhere in the immediate vicinity. Browne was baptized at St. Michael-le-Querne (at the approximate site of St. Paul's Underground Station), which burned in the Great Fire. After his father's death and his mother's remarriage, Browne was under the care of guardians who sent him to Winchester College, but he probably had some early education in London. After settling in Norwich, Norfolk, in 1637, Browne rarely traveled from home, except possibly to visit his eldest son, Dr. Edward

Browne, at his home here in Crane Court; the house, which stood at the far end of the court, was later owned by the Royal Society and then by the Philosophical Society.

Sir William Davenant (1606–1668) Sir William Davenant (often D'Avenant), frequently said to be the natural son of William Shakespeare by the wife of an Oxford innkeeper, came to London in 1622 as a page to Frances, Duchess of Richmond, and later served Fulke Greville, 1st Baron Brooke. With Greville's murder in 1628, Davenant became a hanger-on at court and began to pursue a writing career; *The Cruel Brother* (1627) and *The Just Italian* (1629) were both produced at the theater in Blackfriars. Davenant attracted the attention of Queen Henrietta Maria and by 1630 was signing himself "Servant to Her Majesty." Many of Davenant's masques, including *The Temple of Love,* were acted at the Banqueting Hall at Whitehall, and more than half a dozen plays were written under the express patronage of King Charles. Sixteen months after Ben Jonson's death in August 1637, the Poet-Laureateship became Davenant's at the Queen's request. About this time Davenant lost his nose; illness is often cited in explanation, but more dramatic causes have been advanced. Sir John Suckling, in *A Session of the Poets,* notes:

Surely the company would have been content,
If they could have found any precedent;
But in all their records, in verse or in prose,
There was not one *laureate without a nose.*

He goes on to explain the matter of the missing nose:

　　　　　　. . . a foolish mischance,
That he had got lately travelling in France.

Anthony à Wood states:

The said mischance, which Sir John [Suckling] mentions, happened to Davenant through a dalliance with a handsome black girl in Axe Yard in Westminster, . . . which cost him his nose. . . .

Axe Yard stood on the southwest side of Parliament Street where King Charles Street enters from the west.

In 1639 Davenant was appointed "governor of the King and Queen's Company, acting in the Cockpit in Drury Lane" and was granted a patent to erect a playhouse "behind the Three King's Ordinary in Fleet Street." A confirmed Royalist, Davenant was knighted in 1643 and imprisoned in the Tower of London from 1650 to 1652. The first edition of *Gondibert* was published while he was a prisoner, and the fact that he was not executed is thought to have been the result of the intervention of John Milton, then Latin Secretary to the Commonwealth. After his release Davenant had lodgings on Charterhouse Yard, just north of Carthusian Street, in 1655. *The Siege of Rhodes,* produced in 1656 at Rutland House (the modern Rutland Place on Charterhouse Square), was essentially the first opera ever produced in England, and in it were introduced painted stage sets and the first English woman, Mrs. Edward Coleman, to appear upon the stage.

At the Restoration Davenant and Thomas Killigrew received licenses to form two new companies of players; Davenant's company, the Duke's (named for the Duke of York, later James II), opened first in Salisbury Court (now John Carpenter Street) and then moved to Portugal Street in Lincoln's Inn Fields. Davenant renovated the old Dorset Garden Theatre, which had been suppressed by the Puritans, and used it until the new theater was ready in June. A covered tennis court on Portugal Row was converted into the Duke's Theatre, which had the first full-scale movable scenery in any English theater; Davenant had lodgings behind the theater. He died on April 7, 1668, and two days later was buried in the Poets' Corner of Westminster Abbey; Samuel Pepys reports in his diary:

> 9th. I up and down to the Duke of York's playhouse, there to see, which I did, Sir W. Davenant's corpse carried out towards Westminster, there to be buried. Here were many coaches and six horses, and many hackneys, that made it look, methought, as if it were the burial of a poor poet. He seemed to have many children, by five or six in the first mourning-coach, all boys.

At one time Davenant also had lodgings in the Middle Temple and on Tothill Street.

Edmund Waller (1606–1687) Edmund Waller, admitted a member of Lincoln's Inn in July 1622, claimed to have sat in Parliament that year as the Member from Amersham; however, he could not have been a voting member since the borough's disenfranchisement was not lifted until 1624. Later, he represented the constituencies of Ilchester, Chipping Wycombe, Amersham, and St. Ives. On July 5, 1631, he married Anne Banks, the wealthy daughter of John Banks and a ward of the court, at the 15th-century St. Margaret's Church across from Westminster Hall, but difficulties arose because Waller had not secured permission for the marriage from her guardians. Waller's involvement with Lady Dorothy Sidney, the Sacharissa of his poems, dates from around 1635, about a year after the death of his wife in childbirth; and later (1660–1665), when Lady Dorothy lived on the site now occupied by the Royal College of Surgeons, Waller was probably a visitor there.

He generally supported the majority position when Charles and the Commons were at odds, but, a courtier by nature, he eventually fully supported the King. He became involved in what is now known as Waller's plot; this scheme, to secure London for the King, was laid in part in Waller's house in Holborn in Hatton Garden, but secrecy was not achieved, and on May 31, 1643, Waller and others were arrested. Waller disclosed all he knew, no doubt in the hope of saving his life, and after a trial at the Guildhall was thrown into the tower, where he remained until November 1644. Both Houses of Parliament agreed to accept a £10,000 fine in lieu of execution, and Waller was banished from the realm. In 1651, when his banishment was lifted, he returned to London and bought property on the west side of St. James's Street (about where Number 64 now stands) in 1653 and lived here until his death. His *A Panegyrick to My Lord Protector* appeared in 1654, and at the Restoration he resumed his political career as the Member of Parliament for Hastings. Shortly after Charles II took the throne, Waller wrote *To the King, upon His Majesties Happy Return*. Charles read the poem and commented that he thought it much inferior to the panegyric; Waller replied, "Sir, we poets never succeed as well in writing truth as in writing fiction."

Waller attended the old St. Bride's Church (restored after the Great Fire and after World War II), at the foot of Fleet Street. He was a temperate man, drinking, it is said, nothing stronger than water; as a consequence, John Aubrey's account that "——made him damnably drunk at Somerset House, where at the waterstairs he fell down, and had a cruel fall" might well be exaggerated, if not false. Concerned with the rebuilding of parts of London, Waller wrote "Upon His Majesty's Repairing of Paul's" in 1640 and about St. James's Park in 1661; he noted that the man who could throw a ball as from a "smoking Culverin" must have his park to match:

> Of the first Paradise there's nothing found,
> Plants set by heav'n are vanisht, & the ground;
> Yet the description lasts, who knows the fate
> Of lines that shall this Paradise relate?

The completion of Somerset House occasioned the 1665 poem *Upon Her Majesty's New Buildings at Somerset House.*

Thomas Fuller (1608–1661) Thomas Fuller probably first came to London in June 1642, when he preached at the Inns of Court; he was soon appointed minister of the Queen's Chapel of the Savoy. The accusation that he took the Solemn League and Covenant twice in the Savoy Chapel (in late August and September 1643) and that he invited others to do so is false since Fuller left London probably in late July and certainly no later than early August to join the Royalist forces in Oxford. Returning in 1646, he stayed at the Crown, the shop belonging to his publisher, John Williams, in St. Paul's Courtyard and about this time became intimate with Sir John Danvers, the stepfather of George Herbert and Lord Herbert of Cherbury, whose home in Chelsea he frequently visited. Fuller was working on *The History of the Worthies of England* all during this period. In March 1647 he preached at the medieval Church of St. Clement (rebuilt), on King William Street, in 1655–1656 at St. Clement's and St. Bride's, and occasionally at St. Luke's (Sidney Street, Chelsea), Westminster Abbey, St. Martin's, St. Dunstan-in-the-West, St. Bride's, St. Paul's, and St. Botolph's Church without Bishopsgate.

Fuller was appointed to the living of Cranford (now part of the Greater London metropolitan area) in 1658, but he returned to the city frequently. Especially favored by the King, he was created D.D. in August 1660 and resumed his post at the Savoy and his prebendary post at Salisbury. More preferment was on its way when Dr. Fuller returned to London from Wiltshire and contracted a fever, probably typhus; preaching at the Savoy in August 1661, he finished his sermon after commenting to his congregation, "I find myself very ill, but I am resolved by the grace of God to preach this sermon to you though it be my last." He was helped from the pulpit and taken to lodgings in Covent Garden, where the doctor ordered a phlebotomy; 20 ounces of blood were taken. He died on August 16 and was taken to Cranford for burial.

John Milton (1608–1674) One of the outstanding men of his age, John Milton was born in London on December 9, 1608, almost certainly in a second-floor bedroom of the Spread Eagle, a tenement in a larger house called the White Bear on Bread Street. The house appears to have been just a little south of Cheapside on the east side of the street, where a small court opened up just beyond the present third doorway. Milton was baptized on December 20 at All Hallows (gone), on Bread Street. In 1877 this parish was united with St. Mary-le-Bow, where a commemorative plaque hangs on the west wall facing the churchyard. Milton had some of his education at home and entered St. Paul's around 1620; if that date is correct, he was then in the fourth form. His walk to school would have taken him down Watling Street to the east end of St. Paul's Churchyard. Around 1632 his father gave up the Bread Street residence for one in Hammersmith, where Milton possibly wrote "Ad Patrum."

Sometime after 1639 Milton took lodgings in St. Bride's Churchyard near Fleet Street, where he undertook the tutoring of his two nephews, Edward and John Phillips. "Epitaphium Damonis" was written at this time, and the work on an epic concerning Arthur was begun. These lodgings proved too small, and probably in the autumn of 1640 he leased a house, "a pretty garden-house," probably at the end of Golden Lion Court on Aldersgate Street; *Of Reformation Touching Church Discipline in England, Animadversions upon the Remonstrant's Defence, against Smectymnuus,* and *The Reason of Church-Government Urg'd against Prelaty* were among the works written before he went off in May 1641 to Forest Hill, Oxfordshire, and returned with a Royalist wife, Mary Powell. Less than two months later she returned to her father's home; whatever the specific cause of the separation, it appears that *The Doctrine and Discipline of Divorce,* was written essentially on their honeymoon, if the date inscribed on the pamphlet in the British Museum, "Aug. 1st," is correct. From 1643 to 1645 Milton resided in a house about halfway down Maidenhead Court on the north side.

In the summer of 1645 Milton moved to a larger house in the Barbican off Aldersgate, where he was able to take in more students. As the Royalist cause became more and more precarious, Mary Powell Milton's family found more and more reason to effect a reconciliation with the poet and placed her in the home of William and Hester Blackborough (Milton's relatives) on St. Martin's-le-Grand Lane so that she could plead her cause; Milton finally relented and placed his wife in lodgings in St. Clement's Churchyard until the Barbican house was ready for occupancy in October. Their first child, Anne (lame and probably mentally retarded), was born on July 29, 1646; by this time Milton's in-laws were residing with him, and after Powell's death in December 1646 difficulties arose during which Mrs. Powell called her son-in-law a "harsh choleric man" and accused him of turning out his wife. Around August 1647 Milton moved his family to High Holborn into a smaller house on the northwest side of the square, which "opened backwards into Lincoln's Inn Fields." Here a second daughter, Mary, baptized at the Church of St. Giles-in-the-Fields on November 7, 1648, was born, and Milton wrote *The Tenure of Kings and Magistrates.*

In March 1649 Milton was invited to take up the post of Secretary for the Foreign Tongues (Latin Secretary) at a salary of approximately £730 a year; later that spring Milton took lodgings in Charing Cross to be nearer Whitehall. The house, "next door to the Bull Head Tavern at Charing Cross, opening in Spring Gardens," was abandoned in mid-November, when the Council of State ordered that Milton have lodgings in Whitehall, and he was given an apartment in Scotland Yard. Milton had been warned that he was endangering his already-weakened eyesight, but he chose to ignore the warning, noting his eyes were incidental to "outward view." Milton was almost totally blind by March 1651, and by the end of the year he had taken another "pretty garden house" in Petty France, the area between Tothill Street and Buckingham Gate. Near the northeast corner of the street with a garden reaching back to St. James's Park, the house later belonged to Jeremy Bentham and was occupied by William Hazlitt (it was demolished in 1877). The birth of a daughter, Deborah, on May 2, 1652, and the death of Milton's wife three days later left the now totally blind poet with four children under six years of age. On November 12, 1656, Milton married Katherine Woodcock at the Church of St. Mary Aldermanbury, and a daughter was born in October 1657. In the following February Milton's wife died and was buried in St. Margaret's Church, Westminster, where there is a memorial window.

In May 1660, foreseeing the dangers resulting from the failure of the Protectorate, Milton fled from his home and went into hiding in Bartholomew Close, just off Smithfield. He was here when his *Pro Populo Anglicano Defensio* was ordered to be burned publicly in the yard of Newgate Prison, and here he remained until late August. In September he reappeared and rented a house in Holborn near Red Lion Fields, the modern Red Lion Square. In November Milton was arrested, but on December 15 the Commons decided he should have full benefit of the Indemnity Bill: a full pardon was accordingly granted. Shortly afterward, he took a house at the far end of Jewin Street off Aldersgate. One of Milton's most frequent guests here was Andrew Marvell, who had helped plead the case before the Commons. Milton was now working on *Paradise Lost: A Poem in Twelve Books* and rose every morning, it is said, at 4 A.M., preparatory to beginning dictation at seven; the story is related how Milton, if kept waiting by his amanuensis, would roar out, "I want to be milked."

The need for a wife to take over a badly mismanaged household led to Milton's marriage on February 24, 1663, to Elizabeth Minshull at the medieval Church of St. Mary Aldermary. Following the marriage, Milton took a substantial house on the present Bunhill Row (leading to Bunhill Fields) at the approximate site of the college. Here he finished *Paradise Lost, The History of Britain, Paradise Regained,* and *Samson Agonistes,* and here he remained for the rest of his life except for an eight-month period in Chalfont St. Giles, Buckinghamshire, when the plague was ravaging London. In February 1674 John Dryden, then Poet Laureate, and Edmund Waller called on Milton; during this visit or another, Dryden requested permission to turn *Paradise Lost* into a heroic opera in rhyming couplets. Milton is reported to have answered,

"Well, Mr. Dryden, it seems you have a mind to tag my points, and you have my leave to tag them. But some of them are so awkward and old-fashioned that I think you had as good leave them as you found them."

Dryden's *The State of Innocence and Fall of Man* was never acted.

Milton's health was now declining, and he was suffering from gout; he died here in November 1674, probably on November 8, and was buried on November 12 in the Church of St. Giles Cripplegate. A plaque marks the grave near the pulpit, and in 1793 the brewer Samuel Whitbread erected a memorial executed by John Bacon. Among the many other London places associated with Milton are the Church of St. Anne and St. Agnes, where he attended Mrs. Blackborough's funeral service; the Mitre Bookstore and the Blue Anchor on Falcon Court, where *Samson Agonistes, Paradise Regained,* and other poems were first offered for sale; the Coffee Club of the Rota at New Palace Yard, Westminster, of which he was probably a member; Mark Lane, where Cyriack Skinner lived; and the Inner Temple, where Milton's brother Christopher lived after being called to the bench in 1660. There is a memorial to Milton in the Poets' Corner of Westminster Abbey.

Sir John Suckling (1609–1642) Most of Sir John Suckling's early life is wrapped in obscurity; he is often held to have been educated at Westminster School simply because John Aubrey made a note to question the headmaster on the matter. He was, however, admitted to Gray's Inn on February 23, 1627, and became a popular figure at court. Returning to England from abroad in 1632, he devoted himself primarily to the pleasures of court life: cards and dice were almost an addiction, as he reports in *A Session of the Poets:*

> . . . [Suckling] loved not the Muses so well as his sport;
> And
> Prized black eyes, or a lucky hit
> At bowls, above all the Trophies of wit;
> But *Apollo* was angry, and publiquely said
> 'Twere fit that a fine were set on his head.

He frequented Piccadilly Hall, a gaming house with gardens, bowling greens, and walks which stood at the northeast corner of Haymarket just about where Coventry Street enters; John Aubrey relates that Suckling constantly made so many reckless wagers in the gaming rooms that his sisters followed him one day to the "Piccadill bowling-green crying for the fear he should lose all their portions." At this time he was living somewhere on St. Martin's Lane and also frequented the Bear Tavern at the Bridge Foot. Sir John's first play, *Aglaura: A Tragedy,* was produced at Blackfriars and at court, and probably at the King's request he changed it into a tragicomedy. He was a frequent guest at Thomas Carew's house on King Street along with Ben Jonson and William Davenant. "A Ballade: Upon a Wedding" celebrating the marriage of Roger Boyle, Baron Broghill, to Lady Margaret Howard, daughter of the 2d Earl of Suffolk, refers to Suffolk House (first known as Northampton House and then as Northumberland House), near Charing Cross on the site of the present Northumberland Avenue. A Royalist, Suckling fled from the country and apparently committed suicide by poison in Paris in 1642.

Edward Hyde, 1st Earl of Clarendon (1609–1674) Upon the deaths of his two elder brothers, Edward Hyde became heir to the paternal estate and was forced away from the church, which had been his father's intent for him; consequently, Hyde became a member of the Inner Temple (1625). His interests lay elsewhere, however, and he was not called to the bar until 1633. He remained in London, sitting in Parliament and wielding enormous power throughout the difficult years preceding the Commonwealth; after the Restoration, Hyde returned to London from abroad and was raised to the peerage. Lord Clarendon died in Rouen on December 9, 1674, and was buried in Westminster Abbey on January 4, 1675.

Richard Crashaw (1612?–1649) Richard Crashaw was born somewhere in London, probably in 1612 or 1613, to the Rev. William Crashaw, a scholarly Puritan minister, and received his early education at the 17th-century Charterhouse, established for "forty poor boys" of London, which stood on Charterhouse Square. He spent only a short time in London in late 1643 while on his way to Paris and died in Loreto, Italy, after embracing Roman Catholicism and being appointed a canon of the Cathedral of Santa Casa.

Samuel Butler (1612–1680) When the author of *Hudibras* actually came to London is not really known, but Samuel Butler is believed to have been a student at Gray's Inn and to have resided there. He frequented Will's Coffee House (1 Bow Street) when he lived on Rose Street, where he died of tuberculosis in complete poverty on September 25, 1680. He was buried in St. Paul's Church, Covent Garden, at the expense of William Longueville, a bencher of the Inner Temple. According to John Aubrey, who attended the funeral, his grave is

> in the north part next the church at the east end. His feet touch the wall. His grave, two yards distant from the pilaster of the dore (by his desire), six foot deepe.

Anthony à Wood, however, claims Butler is buried "at the west end of the said yard, on the north side, and under the wall, of the church; and under that wall which parts the yard from the common highway." A monument has been erected in the Poets' Corner at Westminster Abbey.

Butler's *Hudibras* makes much use of London. Near Hyde Park Corner during the Civil War a fort was built, and near the present Marble Arch a checkpoint was set up for travelers entering or departing from London. Everyone helped with the defenses; the women,

> From ladies down to oyster wenches
> Labour'd like pioneers in trenches;
> Fell to their pick-axes and tools
> And help'd the men to dig like moles. . . .

Of the squire "whose name was Ralph," Butler said:

> The Chaos, too, he had decried,
> And seen quite through, or else he lied;
> Not that of pasteboard, which men shew
> For groats, at fair of Barthol'mew. . . .

The medieval Bartholomew's Fair in West Smithfield went on with many changes, mostly for the worse, until 1855; but during the 17th century the puppet shows which portrayed such biblical concepts as the chaos and the creation were extremely popular. At the north end of Abingdon Street (then known as Lindsay Lane) was a tavern called Heaven (now occupied by the committee rooms of the House of Commons). In the 17th century two subterranean passages called Hell and Purgatory tunneled under the old Exchequer Chamber; in *Hudibras* the tavern is False Heaven and placed at the end of Hell:

Tossed in a furrious hurricane,
Did Oliver give up his reign,
And was believed, as well by saints
As moral men and miscreants,
To founder in the Stygian ferry,
Until he was retrieved by Sterry,
Who in a false erroneous dream,
Mistook the New Jerusalem,
Profanely for th' apocryphal
False Heaven at the end o' th' Hall;
Whither it was decreed by fate,
His precious reliques to translate.

John Cleveland (1613–1658) John Cleveland (properly spelled Cleiveland) came to London after Oliver Cromwell released him from imprisonment in Great Yarmouth, Norfolk. He resided in Gray's Inn (where he probably met Samuel Butler) only a short time before "an intermittent fever seized him, whereof he died [April 29, 1658], a disease at that time epidemical"; he was buried in the medieval Church of St. Michael, Paternoster Royal (destroyed in the Great Fire).

Jeremy Taylor (1613–1667) Jeremy Taylor, remembered best for *The Rule and Exercises of Holy Living* and *The Rule and Exercises of Holy Dying*, spent short periods in London after taking holy orders in 1633 at Cambridge and served as a substitute preacher at St. Paul's Cathedral. Living in Wales from about 1645 on, he frequented London to oversee the publication of his works and preached in numerous churches and chapels, including St. Gregory's under St. Paul's, then located (says Stow) "near unto the cathedral church of St. Paul," St. Mary Magdalen on Milk Street, and the Earl of Rutland's Chapel. With the help of John Evelyn, to whom he became "my Ghostly Father," Taylor settled in London from 1650 until 1658, when he left for Ireland.

Sir John Denham (1615–1669) While Sir John Denham reputedly had his early education in London, he cannot really be verified here until the 1630s, when he entered Lincoln's Inn, Holborn, to study law; called to the bar in 1639, he had married Ann Cotton at St. Bride's Church, Fleet Street, on June 25, 1634, and the couple had settled with his father in Egham, Surrey. Denham had already begun gambling, and as his habit increased, so did his family's fears. By the time he inherited the Surrey estate in 1638, he was deep in debt. Shortly after the beginning of the Civil War, Denham, a strong Royalist, was captured at Farnham Castle and imprisoned briefly in London before being sent on to Oxford; he was later barred from being within a 20-mile radius of London. At the Restoration he received his rewards: multiple land grants and the post of Surveyor General of Works; in this capacity he superintended the erection of many official London buildings and is almost certainly the architect of Burlington House (rebuilt and enlarged in 1715), just beyond the Burlington Arcade. Denham was by now a widower, and he married again on May 25, 1665, at Westminster Abbey. The couple lived in Great Scotland Yard, then a wide yard surrounded by buildings, one of which held the residence and offices of the Royal Architect. Lady Denham, many years her husband's junior, carried on openly as the Duke of York's mistress, and he frequently visited her here. In 1666 Denham suffered a period of madness, first attributed to his disgrace and by Andrew Marvell to a blow on the head; nevertheless, while he was convalescing, Lady Denham died, supposedly by a cup of poisoned chocolate. Samuel Pepys credited Sir John with the murder, while John Aubrey accused the Countess of Rochester; and the general population demanded a lavish funeral at St. Margaret's Church, Westminster. Interestingly enough, the post mortem showed no signs of poison. Sir John suffered dislike at court over the next few years and was ridiculed by most of his contemporaries. He died in Great Scotland Yard in mid-March 1669 and was buried in the Poets' Corner of Westminster Abbey. There is no monument.

Richard Lovelace (1618–1658) Poet and Cavalier, Richard Lovelace was born in 1618 in his father's manor house in Woolwich and after his father's death in 1628 was sent to Charterhouse (on the north side of Charterhouse Square), a 17th-century school established for "forty poor boys" of London. Belonging to a wealthy Kentish family, he inherited the family estate at Bethersden in 1633 and went up to Oxford. Lovelace was a great favorite at court before becoming actively involved in the Kentish petition framed by Royalists on the Kings's behalf. Indeed, Lovelace had the temerity to present the petition to the House of Commons and was accordingly committed to the Gatehouse on April 30, 1642. The prison (in the gatehouse of the wall which stood just slightly north of Westminster Abbey almost opposite the present Tothill Street) is probably where he wrote:

Stone walls do not a prison make,
  Nor iron bars a cage:
Minds innocent and quiet take
  That for an hermitage:
If I have freedom in my love,
  And in my soul am free,
Angels alone, that soar above,
  Enjoy such liberty.

Lovelace was released after seven weeks on "good security," that is, £20,000 bail; the charges were dropped, but he was confined to London. "The Vintage to the Dungeon" dates to this period; he became intimate with a group of poets and wits, including Thomas Rawlins, Sir John Suckling, and Charles Cotton the elder, who met regularly at the Fleece Tavern off Covent Garden. Late in 1645 or early in 1646 he joined the Royalist forces (hence forgoing his bail) in Oxford and eventually fled abroad. He returned in 1648 and was committed to Petre House (Peterhouse) Prison for his part in the Kent uprising on June 9; the prison stood on the west side of Aldersgate Street, opposite the new Ironmongers' Hall. "Mock Song" from this period shows his belief that the King's cause had vanished, and "To Lucasta, from Prison: An Epode" shows the despair and disillusionment of the Cavaliers. Virtually nothing is known about his life after his release on April 9, but he is said to have lived in a cellar in Long Acre in the vicinity of Rose Street. Anthony à Wood states that having consumed his patrimony for a lost cause,

he . . . became very poor in body and purse, was the object of charity, went in ragged cloaths . . . and mostly lodged in obscure and dirty places, more befitting the worst beggars and poorest of servants.

Lovelace died in 1658 on Gunpowder Alley (now

Shoe Lane) and was buried at the west end of St. Bride's Church, (rebuilt after the Great Fire and the 1940 bombing).

Abraham Cowley (1618–1667) Abraham Cowley's 1618 birthplace is claimed by two parts of London: the parish of St. Michael-le-Querne, Cheapside, and (more acceptably) Serjeant's Inn, on the south side of Fleet Street almost opposite Red Lion Court. The seventh and posthumous child of a stationer, Cowley entered the 14th-century Westminster School (the buildings surround Little Dean's Yard) around 1628 and became a King's Scholar in short order. His precocity was soon evident, and his first collection of poems, *Poeticall Blossomes,* appeared in 1633, four years before he went up to Cambridge. Cowley was not back in London until his return from France in 1654, probably as a Royalist agent; arrested and imprisoned on April 12, 1655, he recanted officially the next year and was released, but this act of submission to Oliver Cromwell did much to cloud Cowley's later prospects. Cowley may have been living in King's Head Yard (probably near the southeast corner of Chancery Lane on Fleet Street) and frequented the King's Head Tavern. He was one of the first members of the newly formed Royal Society but was unsuccessful in gaining the mastership of the Savoy:

> Savoy missing Cowley came into the court,
>   Making apologies for his bad play;
> Every one gave him so good a report,
>   That Apollo gave heed to all he could say.

Cowley was eventually restored to favor and granted land in Chertsey, Surrey, where he died on July 28, 1667. John Evelyn attended the funeral:

> Went to Mr. *Cowleys* funerall, whose Corps Lay at Wallingford house [part of the Admiralty building stands on the site], & was thence conducted to Westminster Abbey in an *Hearse* with 6 horses, & all funebrual decency, neere an hundred Coaches of noble men & persons of qualitie following, among these all the Witts of the Towne, Divers Bishops & Cleargy men: &c. He was interred next *Jeofry Chaucer* & neere *Spencer* &c: [a goodly Monument since erected.] I returned home. . . .

John Evelyn (1620–1706) The associations of John Evelyn, one of the two great diarists of this period, with London and its inhabitants are extensive; he was admitted to the Middle Temple in February 1637 and to Balliol College, Oxford, in May; he did not finish there and returned to the chambers his father had secured. The

> new Lodgings (that were formerly in Essex-Court) being a very handsome appartment just over against the Hall-Court; but 4 payre of stayres high; which gave us the advantage of the fairer prospect. . . .

His father's death and a trip abroad disrupted Evelyn's course of study, and by the end of January 1642 he describes himself as "studying a little; but dauncing and fooling more." A loyal supporter of King Charles I, Evelyn was present "just at the retreate" at the Battle of Brentford but did not join the Royalist forces because the area all around the family estate at Wotton, Surrey, was held by the Parliamentarians, and he feared he and his brothers would be "expos'd to ruine, without any advantage to his Majestie." Refusing to subscribe to the Solemn League and Covenant, Evelyn went abroad in 1643 and did not return permanently until 1652, when he and his wife settled at Sayes Court, Deptford, on the banks of the Thames, where a small memorial park marks the site of the original gardens. Seven of Evelyn's children were born here, and Jeremy Taylor, a frequent guest, christened Evelyn's fourth son George "in the withdrawing-roome at *Says Court*" on June 7, 1657. Evelyn was a member of the vestry of the Church of St. Nicholas, whose medieval tower still stands near the bridge on Deptford Green. Evelyn regularly spent many months in town especially in winter, and often attended St. Clements Eastcheap, St. Gregory's under St. Paul's (long gone), or Exeter Chapel, particularly when Taylor was preaching at the latter two. In May 1658 he stayed with his brother in Covent Garden and attended Covent Garden Chapel; he also took "the aire in *Hide-park*," saw a coach race there, and then "collationd with my Bro: ⟨in⟩ Spring Garden." The winter of 1659–1660 Evelyn "tooke Lodgings at the 3 feathers in Russel-streete Covent Garden"; the building was on the site of the present Number 17.

Evelyn was on the Strand on May 29, 1660, for the triumphal return of Charles II:

> This day came in his Majestie *Charles* the 2nd to London after a sad, & long Exile, and Calamitous Suffering both of the King & Church: being 17 yeares: This was also his Birthday, and with a Triumph of above 20000 horse & foote, brandishing their swords and shouting with unexpressable joy: The wayes straw'd with flowers, the bells ringing, the streets hung with Tapissry, fountaines running with wine. . . . I stood in the strand, & beheld it, & blessed God. . . .

Evelyn raced in the royal yacht with the new monarch on the Thames in October 1661 and was more frequently in the City than in Sayes Court until 1662, when he gave up his lodgings in Westminster. One of the most delightful events in his diary is recorded on December 1, 1662, when he saw

> the strange, and wonderfull dexterity of the sliders on the new Canall in St. *James's* park, perform'd by divers Gent: & others with *Scheets*, after the manner of the *Hollanders*, with what pernicitie & swiftnesse they passe, how sudainly they stop in full carriere upon the Ice, before their *Majesties*. . . .

He vividly recounts the Great Fire in the diary and tells how "with my Wife & Sonn" he went by coach "to the bank side in Southwark," where he saw "the miserable & calamitous spectacle . . . like the top of a burning Oven. . . . *London* was, but is no more." Evelyn, like Samuel Pepys, reacted strongly to the threat of a Dutch invasion in June 1667, when he heard "the Enemie might adventure up the Thames even to Lond"; thus, "The alarme cause me . . ." he relates, "to send away my best goods, plate, &c: from my house to another place." Pepys was a very good friend and frequently dined with Evelyn at Sayes Court; indeed, when Pepys was committed to the Tower of London from the late spring of 1679 until February 1680, Evelyn visited him and on one occasion (July 3) sent "a piece of *Venison*" and went along to help him eat it.

Charles knew the diarist's capabilities well and entrusted him with various commissions; he was concerned with London street improvement, the Royal Mint, the repair of Old St. Paul's, and the founding of "a Royal Hospital for Emerited Souldiers." The Wren-built hospital is on Royal Hospital Road, north of the Chelsea Embankment. In November 1683, pressed by City business and concerned about his daughters' educations, Evelyn and his "whole Family (except my little Grandson, & his Nurse" took "the house of one Mr. Dive's, in Villars streete in Yorke-buildings in the Strand." From 1696 to 1700 he met weekly with Richard Bentley, the Royal Librarian, Sir Christopher Wren, John Locke, and Isaac Newton at St. James's Palace. On one of his winter sojourns in the City, Evelyn lived on Surrey Street, and he often dined at Pontack's Tavern, one of London's most fashionable eating places from 1688 to 1780, which stood at the east corner of Abchurch Lane and Lombard Street. In July 1699 Evelyn, again "finding my Occasions calling ⟨me⟩ so often to Lond:," took a house, "nine doors up, on the east side" of Dover Street and used it almost exclusively until his death in 1706. From late 1705 on Evelyn was in failing health; his infirmities increased, and his last diary entry is dated February 3, 1706. He died at his home here on February 27 and was buried at Wooton on March 4.

Of the hundreds of London associations with Evelyn, the following few may be of interest. He frequently dined on Saturday night with fellow members of the Royal Society at Samuel Pepys's home on Villiers Street. The area covered today approximately by Surrey, Howard, and Norfolk Streets, just south of the Strand, was once covered by the inn belonging to the Bishop of Bath and later to the 14th Earl of Arundel. Under his grandson, Henry Howard, 6th Duke of Norfolk, the house became the life center of the arts in London, and it was this man whom Evelyn persuaded to donate the famous Arundel marbles to Oxford in September 1667. Evelyn visited Edward Hyde, 1st Earl of Clarendon, whose house, on the north side of Piccadilly roughly between Old Bond and Berkeley Streets, Evelyn said was "the best contrived, most useful, graceful and magnificent house in England"; the 10th Earl of Northumberland, whose "new front towards the Gardens, is tollerable, were it not drown'd by a too massie, & clowdy pair of stayers of stone, without any neate Invention"; and the 2d Duke of Buckingham, whose Chelsea house had belonged to Sir Thomas More. Virtually every part of 17th-century London is mentioned in Evelyn's diary, and at one time or another he attended services at the Churches of St. Albans (Wood Street), St. Andrew (Holborn, where his son was married), St. Andrew's Undershaft, St. Bartholomew, St. Bride, St. Clement Danes, St. Clement, St. Dunstan-in-the-West, St. Giles-in-the-Fields, St. James (Piccadilly), St. Lawrence Jewry, St. Margaret, St. Martin's-in-the-Fields, St. Martin's (Ludgate), St. Mary-le-Bow, St. Mary Magdalen (Milk Street), St. Mary Magdalen (Old Fish Street), St. Michael (Cornhill), and St. Thomas (Regent Street) and the Chapel of the Savoy.

Andrew Marvell (1621–1678)   Eventually an ardent republican, Andrew Marvell had practically nothing to do with the political strife between Charles and Parliament or with London until John Milton, Latin Secretary for the Commonwealth, proposed Marvell as his assistant as early as 1653; the post was not granted until 1657 (probably September). Tradition holds that Marvell had a cottage (demolished) north of Lauderdale House on Highgate Hill. He retained his post under Richard Cromwell and the Long Parliament and was voted lodgings in Whitehall. He

then successfully stood for Parliament as the Member from Hull in 1659, and retained the seat until his death. Although Marvell was abroad during much of the period between 1662 and 1665, he was instrumental in helping John Milton survive the Restoration.

Before his fall from power in 1667, Edward Hyde, 1st Earl of Clarendon, built a huge mansion on the north side of Piccadilly, partly from the stones from St. Paul's, and furnished it lavishly with (alleged) gifts from foreign ambassadors. Nicknamed Dunkirk House (the populace believed he had sold Dunkirk to the French), Holland House, and Tangiers House, the house was the beginning of Clarendon's downfall; Marvell wrote "Upon His House" after Parliament discussed Hyde's impeachment:

> Here lie the sacred bones
> Of Paul beguiled of his stones:
> Here lie golden briberies,
> The price of ruined families;
> The cavalier's debenture wall,
> Fixed on an eccentric basis:
> Here's Dunkirk-Town and Tangier-Hall,
> The Queen's marriage and all,
> The Dutchman's *templum pacis*.

The reference to the Queen undoubtedly concerned the inscription tacked on a gibbet near the estate walls:

> Three sights to be seen,
> Dunkirk, Tangier, and a barren Queen.

Marvell had lodgings on Maiden Lane (the present Number 9) in his last years; here the Lord Treasurer, the 1st Earl of Danby, came with an offer of the King's patronage, which Marvell refused rather than compromise his Parliamentary convictions. He died on August 16, 1678, of purely natural causes (contrary to rumor) and was buried on August 18, according to John Aubrey, "under the pews in the south side of St. Giles' Church in the Fields, under the windows wherein is painted on glass a red lion." There is no evidence of the grave; a black marble slab and epitaph on the north wall erected in 1764 by Marvell's nephew record that "near to this place lyeth the body of Andrew Marvell, Esquire."

Henry Vaughan (1622–1695)   Welsh-born Henry Vaughan had only a passing association with London, where he arrived in the summer or fall of (probably) 1640 to pursue the study of law in accordance with his father's wishes. There is no record of Vaughan at any of the Inns of Court, and he was never called to the bar. The Civil War interrupted his studies, but "A Rhapsodis, Occasionally Written upon a Meeting with Some of His Friends at the Globe Tavern" refers to his London days and alludes to the Strand and Fleet Street, site of the tavern.

John Aubrey (1626–1697)   John Aubrey had relatively little to do with London until 1646, when he came to study law at the Middle Temple; he was never called to the bar. At the Restoration, though, he returned and with James Harrington was part of the Rota Club, which met at Miles's Coffee House in Old Palace Yard:

> Here we had a balloting box, and balloted how things should be carried by way of Tentamens. The room was every evening full as it could be crammed. Mr. Cyriack

Skinner, an ingeniose young gentleman, scholar to John Milton, was chairman.

Where he stayed at this time is not known, but in 1673 he was lodging on Gray's Inn Lane. He frequented the Bagneo on Newgate Street (opened December 1679 and later called Royal Bagnio Coffee House), which he claimed was "built by Turkish Merchants"; its services were advertised as "sweating, rubbing, shaving, hot bathing, and cupping, after the Turkish model."

John Bunyan (1628–1688) John Bunyan, one of the most important and active dissenters of this difficult period, has a number of associations with London; indeed, records exist of his addresses to congregations exceeding 1,500 in Southwark, probably at the Zoar Chapel (between Summer and Great Guildford Streets). He also preached at Pinner's Hall, a place now recalled only in the narrow lane of that name leading off Old Broad Street. He made his last trip to London from Reading, Berkshire, in August 1688 in order to effect the reconciliation of a neighbor and his father; Bunyan had suffered an attack of "sweating sickness" in the spring, and the trip was cold and rainy. He reached the house of a friend, John Strudwick, a grocer doing business at the sign of the Star on Snow Hill; the house stood on the southeast side of the intersection of Cock Lane. He had what appeared to be a mild cold but preached at Whitechapel on August 19; he became extremely feverish two days later and died at Strudwick's house on August 31. Bunyan was buried at Bunhill Fields, called by Robert Southey "the Campo Santo of the Dissenters" and by Anthony à Wood "the fanatical burying-place called by some 'Tyndal's burying place.' " The recumbent effigy (which has been renewed because of damage from the weather) was added to the tomb in 1882. There is a memorial statue on Eagle Street, and a stained-glass window in the north transept of Westminster Abbey portrays Bunyan and four episodes from *The Pilgrim's Progress*.

John Dryden (1631–1700) John Dryden is first found in London around 1648, when he entered the 14th-century Westminster School (in Little Dean's Yard), but there are no records of his time here before he went up to Cambridge. He may have settled in London in 1654 after receiving his B.A., but between 1659 and 1663 he had a residence on the south side of the Strand just opposite Bedford Street. Within a year of the Restoration he may have been residing near or in Lincoln's Inn Fields with Sir Robert Howard, and in 1663 he lived on the north side of Lincoln's Inn Fields where the Soane Museum is now. Dryden met Howard through Herringman, a bookseller in the New Exchange on the Strand; the friendship led to an introduction to Sir Robert's sister, and in December 1663 Dryden married Lady Elizabeth Howard, a twenty-five-year-old of doubtful reputation whose intellectual abilities and temper left much to be desired. On November 30 they received a license for marriage (the consent of the parents is noted on the license even though she was of age) at St. Swithin's Church (destroyed in World War II), where they were married on December 1. With the outbreak of the plague in July and August 1665, they left for Charlton, Wiltshire, the small estate settled on them by her father.

The Wild Gallant was produced unsuccessfully in 1663, and *The Rival Ladies* appeared successfully in 1664. Early in 1664 Dryden was frequenting Will's Coffee House, at 21 Bow Street (sometimes referred to as Number 1) in Covent Garden. Here Samuel Pepys found Dryden on February 3, 1664,

> where I never was before: where Dryden, the poet, I knew at Cambridge, and all the wits of the town, and Harris the player, and Mr. Hoole of our College. And had I had time then, or could at other times, it will be good coming thither, for there, I perceive, is very witty and pleasant discourse.

Dryden held forth as the acknowledged head of the group and occupied the place of honor in the winter beside the fireplace and in the summer in the corner of the first-floor balcony overlooking the street. *The Indian Emperor* appeared in 1665, and after the plague and the Great Fire had closed the theaters by the end of 1666, Dryden dedicated nearly 100 quatrains of *Annus Mirabilis* to the fire:

> Already laboring with a mighty fate,
> She shakes the rubbish from her mounting brow,
> And seems to have renewed her charter's date,
> Which Heav'n will to the death of time allow.

> More great than human now, and more August,
> New deified she from her fire does rise;
> Her widening streets on new foundations trust,
> And, opening, into larger parts she flies.

Within four days of William Davenant's funeral in April 1667, Dryden was appointed Poet Laureate with a stipend of £200 a year; it was later increased to £300. From 1673 to 1682 Dryden and his family lived on the Strand in Salisbury Court (then just slightly west of what is today called Dorset Rise). Dryden's house was almost at the end of the court. It is often maintained that during this period the Poet Laureate was living on Fetter Lane (about Number 16), but this is probably in error since the parish rate books list him as in Salisbury Court, "on the water side of the street."

While living on the Strand and frequenting Will's Coffee House, Dryden was severely beaten on his return from Will's on December 18, 1679. The band of ruffians who set upon him may have been in the employ of the Earl of Rochester (and possibly the Duchess of Portsmouth), who had been satirized in the 3d Earl of Mulgrave's *Essay on Satire*, which Dryden was said to have written or at least corrected. The incident took place on Rose Alley where the Lamb and Flag is today. The event is commemorated with a plaque on Rose Alley.

Much of Dryden's literary productivity after *Annus Mirabilis* was for the theater; he became a shareholder in the King's Company after the enormous successes of *Secret Love, or The Maiden Queen, Sir Martin Mar-All* (which opened the newly built Duke's Theatre in 1671), and *The Tempest*. The Duke's Theatre had been the Dorset Garden Theatre (approximately where John Carpenter Street is today), originally named for its position in the gardens of Dorset House. The King's Company also took over the premises of the original Duke's Theatre, on Portugal Street nearly opposite the entrance of Carey Street; some confusion inevitably arises because of the same names, but the theaters were usually designated by location, that is Lincoln's Inn Fields Theatre for the latter and Dorset Garden Theatre for the former. Dryden's contract with Thomas Killigrew called for three new plays yearly in return for 1¼ shares of the 12¾ shares held by the company. From 1668 until 1682 Dryden produced some fourteen plays, most of which gave offense to those satirized and many of which contributed, John Evelyn said, to the degeneration and pollution of the stage.

Dryden produced more than dramatic pieces during his later years, and *Absalom and Achitophel* (which dealt with the 1st Earl of Shaftesbury's attempt to exclude the Duke of York from the succession and set the Duke of Monmouth on the throne) came out in November 1681, just before Shaftesbury was to be indicted. *The Medall*, possibly written at the suggestion of Charles II, and *MacFlecknoe* appeared in 1682. Charles's death meant that Dryden was now reliant on the patronage of James II, who continued all his predecessor's offices, except the butt of malmsey accompanying the laureateship. Within a few months of James's accession, Evelyn notes:

> *Dryden* the famous play-poet & his two sonns, & Mrs. *Nelle* (Misse to the late . . .) were said to go to Masse; & such purchases were no greate losse to the Church.

Dryden was converted toward the end of 1685, and *The Hind and the Panther* is an elaborate argument of the case for his new church.

After the 1688 uprising and James's flight, Dryden was stripped of the laureateship (which was given to Thomas Shadwell), and about this time he took a house on Gerrard Street in Soho; Dryden described the house, now Number 43, as "the fifth door, on the left hand [i.e., south], coming from Newport Street." He remained here, still in attendance nightly at Will's Coffee House and still writing, until his death on May 1, 1700. He suffered from gout in his later years, and when in (probably) April 1700 gangrene took hold of one toe, he refused the advice of his physician to amputate. The body lay in state at the Royal College of Physicians until the funeral on May 13. Fifty carriages of friends followed the hearse to Westminster Abbey, and fifty more carriages of the curious followed. For almost a quarter of a century the grave was unmarked; then, in 1720, perhaps because of Alexander Pope's allusion to the "rude and nameless stone," a simple monument, later replaced by an effigy, was erected in the Poets' Corner between Chaucer and Cowley.

Other Dryden associations include the site of the present Buckingham Palace and its gardens, where the Mulberry Garden existed during the reigns of Charles I and Charles II; a fashionable place of entertainment and rendezvous, it was a favorite resort of Dryden and Mrs. Anne Reeve, the woman said to be his mistress and referred to in Thomas Mathias's *The Pursuits of Literature:*

> Nor he, whose essence, wit, and taste, approved,
> Forget the *Mulberry-tarts* which Dryden loved.

The Nursery, a seminary for the education of children for the stage, located on Golden Lane, is mentioned in *MacFlecknoe:*

> Near these a Nursery erects its head,
> Where queens are form'd, and future heroes bred;
> Where unfledg'd actors learn to laugh and cry,
> Where infant punks their tender voices try,
> And little Maximins the gods defy.

One of Dryden's publishers, Jacob Tonson, had his first shop at the Judge's Head (some say the King's Head) on Chancery Lane, possibly on the southeast corner; Tonson was late with his payments, and under a print of the publisher Dryden wrote:

> With leering looks, bull-faced, and freckled fair,
> With two left legs and Judas-coloured hair,
> And frowzy pores, that taint the ambient air. . . .

He sent it with the message, "Tell the dog that he who wrote these lines can write more." Payment, one assumes, followed. Finally, at 1 Fleet Street was Child's Bank, England's oldest private bank, dating to the late 16th century. Dryden was one of the bank's early clients, as were Charles I's widow, Charles II, James II, and William and Mary.

Samuel Pepys (1633–1703) The diarist Samuel Pepys, the son of a tailor, was born on February 23, 1633, in Salisbury Court, St. Bride's parish, and was baptized in the Church of St. Bride (rebuilt after the Great Fire and gutted in the 1940 blitz), which still contains the font in which he was baptized. Pepys's family sent him from the City to Huntingdon because of the Civil War, but he returned around 1646 and was enrolled in the 16th-century St. Paul's School in the churchyard of St. Paul's Cathedral. Here he studied Greek, Latin, Hebrew, and geography before going up to Cambridge in 1650. After graduation he probably entered the service of his cousin, Sir Edward Montagu of Hinchingbrooke (later 1st Earl of Sandwich), who had lodgings at Whitehall Palace in Westminster, and most likely Pepys had a chamber there.

Pepys married Elizabeth Marchant de Saint-Michel, the fifteen-year-old daughter of a French Huguenot refugee, on October 10, 1655, "according to the rites of the Protestant church"; they had their wedding dinner at a tavern somewhere on Fish Hill Street. However, with respect to the laws of "republican England," they were not legally married, and on December 1 a city magistrate performed the civil ceremony at St. Margaret's Church. This, of course, explains why Pepys maintained October 10 was their anniversary while records are available only for the December date. He and his new wife lived with Lord Sandwich, and Pepys recalled the time in his diary in 1667:

> Lay long in bed, talking with pleasure with my poor wife, how she used to make coal fires, and wash my foul clothes with her own hand for me, poor wretch! in our little room at my Lord Sandwich's. . . .

Before beginning his diary in 1660 (the date August 1658 also has been suggested), Pepys moved to a small house in Axe Yard (approximately where King Charles Street enters Parliament Street). He frequented the local pubs and coffeehouses and was at the Star in Cheapside when Gen. George Monck enlarged the Rump Parliament:

> In Cheapside there was a great many bonfires, and Bow-bells and all the bells in all the churches as we went home were a-ringing. . . . The number of bonfires, there being fourteen between St. Dunstan's and Temple Bar, and at Strand Bridge I could at one time tell thirty-four fires. In King Street seven or eight; and all along, burning, and roasting and drinking for rumps. There being rumps tied upon sticks and carried up and down. The butchers at the May Pole in the Strand rang a peal with their knives when they were going to sacrifice their rump.

He often noted being at Will's, "where Hawley ... brought a piece of his Cheshire Cheese and we were merry with it" and "where [on another occasion] like a fool I stayed and lost 6d. at cards." There is, though, some confusion over the identification of Will's. It is usually thought that Pepys meant Will's Coffee House under Scotland Yard Gate because of the proximity to Westminster, but this identification must be erroneous since the first recorded mention of the coffeehouse does not occur until 1702. More likely Pepys meant (as did many others who also called it Will's) Wells Coffee House in Scotland Yard, which belonged to a Mrs. Wells and is first mentioned in 1696.

In July 1660 Pepys took the clerkship of the acts (that is, he was a member of the Navy Board, whose office was on Seething Lane facing Crutched Friars). He left his home in Axe Yard when he was given lodgings on the east side of Seething Lane just north of the entrance of Pepys Street. He attended the 15th-century Church of St. Olave ("our own church"), on Hart Street, and was present for the return to the old ceremonials of the Church of England:

> Mr. Mills did begin to nibble at the Common Prayer, by saying "Glory be to the Father," &c., after he had read the two psalms; but the people had been so little used to it, that they could not tell what to answer.

An even more delightful observation is entered on October 26, 1662:

> Put on my new scallop, which is very fine. To church, and there saw the first time Mr. Mills in a surplice; but it seemed absurd for him to pull it over his eares in the reading pew, after he had done, before all the church, to go up to the pulpitt, to preach without it.

Throughout 1660 and 1661 Pepys seemed willing to allow his bacchanalian colleagues, Admirals Sir William Batten and Sir William Penn, to run the Navy Office, but by 1662 he was working hard at putting it in order. Indeed, when the plague broke out in 1665, he refused, unlike many Londoners, to leave his post, although in early July he sent his wife and her two maids to Woolwich. Pepys remained on Seething Lane and made two or three trips a week to Hampton Court on business before joining his wife at the end of August:

> 31st. Up: and, after putting several things in order to my removal, to Woolwich; the plague having a great increase this week, beyond all expectation, of almost 2,000, making the general Bill 7,000, odd 100; and the plague above 6,000. Thus this month ends with great sadness upon the public, through the greatness of the plague everywhere through the kingdom almost. Every day sadder and sadder news of its increase. In the City died this week 7,496, and of them 6,102 of the plague. But it is feared that the true number of the dead this week is near 10,000. . . .

Also in 1665, Pepys first met John Evelyn, who lived at Sayes Court, and the two men formed a lasting friendship.

On December 31, 1665, Pepys returned to his London house on Seething Lane, where on September 2, 1666, he was awakened because "of a great fire . . . in the City," which he viewed from an upper-story window; "being unused to such fires as followed, I thought it far enough off, and so went to bed again, and to sleep." By September 5, with the fire raging out of control, Pepys sent his money and plate to Sir

William Rider at Bethnal Green and buried his wine and his Parmesan cheese in the garden; he climbed to the top of the 7th-century Church of All Hallows, on Byward Street, and saw

> everywhere great fires, oil-cellars, and brimstone, and other things burning. . . . [T]he fire being spread as far as I could see it. . . .

He and Sir William Penn decided on the course of action which saved the Navy Office: they pulled down all surrounding buildings, using Navy Office personnel drawn from Woolwich and Deptford.

Trouble with Pepys's eyesight had begun earlier, and in May 1669 he was forced to abandon his diary:

> And thus ends all that I doubt I shall ever be able to do with my own eyes in the keeping of my journal, I being not able to do it any longer, having done now so long as to undo my eyes almost every time that I take a pen in my hand; and, therefore, whatever comes of it, I must forbear. . . .

Following a trip to France and Holland, Elizabeth Pepys contracted a fever and died on November 10, 1669; she was buried in the crypt of St. Olave's Church. Her husband erected the memorial marble bust beyond the altar and the pulpit, a spot which Pepys chose so that he could look upon her likeness during services. Pepys's professional advancement was rapid, and when the Duke of York refused to accept the Test Act and resigned from the Admiralty, Pepys was appointed "Secy. for the affairs of the Navy." As administrative head of the Navy, in whom all powers except those reserved to the monarch were vested, he felt the necessity of representing the Navy Office in Parliament and successfully stood as the Member for Castle Rising and then for Harwich.

In 1679, however, Pepys came extremely close to execution on Tower Hill for treason; accused of being a papist and of being implicated in the murder of Sir Edmund Berry Godfrey, a London magistrate, the diarist was committed to the Tower of London on May 22. This was the time that John Evelyn visited Pepys and sent venison to him. With an unshakable alibi and the support of Charles II (who effectively saved him by dissolving Parliament for eighteen months), Pepys was released on bail in August 1679; the proceedings, however, were not dropped until June 1680. He lost his Admiralty post and moved temporarily into York Buildings; somewhat later he moved to 12 Buckingham Street, where he stayed until 1687. John Evelyn was a frequent guest in both houses and called the Saturday evenings spent together "our Saturday academics."

Reinstated as a public servant in 1683 and restored to his post in the Admiralty in 1684, Pepys moved in 1687 to 14 Buckingham Street, from which he conducted Admiralty business. His fortunes, though, were tied to the Stuarts, and when James II fled, Pepys retired from the Admiralty and, somewhat later, left London for Clapham. Not particularly happy there, he was visited by Evelyn, who said it was

> a very noble, & wonderfully well furnished house, especialy with all the Indys & Chineze Curiositys, almost any where to be mett with, the Offices & Gardens exceedingly well accomodated for ⟨pleasure⟩ & retirement:

Pepys died in Clapham on May 26, 1703, and was buried in the crypt of St. Olave's Church on Hart Street.

The Pepys memorial, designed by Sir Arthur Blom-field, was erected in 1884.

Other Pepysian associations afford a look at various parts of 17th-century London. St. James's Park, from its inception under Charles II until it became an established lounging place, was one of the diarist's favorite spots:

> December 1st. [1662] To . . . the Parke, where I first in my life, it being a great frost, did see people sliding with their skeates. . . .
>
> nd. [March 1661] To St. James's Park, where I saw the Duke of York playing at Pelemele [*paille maille*], the first time that ever I saw the sport.

The latter, of course, is the source of the words Pall Mall. Pepys also frequented the gardens at Gray's Inn, a resort of the fashionable; here he would walk "all alone, and with great pleasure, seeing the fine ladies walk there. Myself humming to myself. . . ." He took Elizabeth Pepys "to observe fashions of the ladies, because of my wife's making some clothes." One of Pepys's favorite early drinking spots was the Rhenish Wine House owned by Matthew Prior's uncle on Cannon Row; here the Admiralty officer conducted business, drank, and flirted. He spent time in many taverns and coffeehouses: the Rose in Covent Garden, at the corner of Catherine and Russell Streets but torn down in 1776; the Cock, on Fleet Street just opposite the gate of Middle Temple Lane (where he "drank, and ate a lobster, and sang, and mightily merry. So, almost night, I carried Mrs. Pierce home"); the Bear, on the Thames at the foot of the bridge leading to the Exchange; and the Bell, on King Street, a thoroughfare which once ran from Charing Cross to Westminster Hall beside White-hall Palace, where he was once invited to dinner but had to pay his own bill. He visited the Coffee Club, or the Coffee Club of the Rota (in New Palace Yard, Westminster), founded by James Harrington. Pepys came here first with Muddiman, "a good scholar, [and] an arch rogue" and "gave 18*d.* to be entered at the Club." He knew the Common Garden Coffee House, near the New Exchange; the Crowne Tavern, on Threadneedle Street ("behind the Exchange," Pepys says), where, being admitted a member of the Royal Society on February 15, 1665, he and other members came for a meal; the Floating Coffee House, moored in the center of the Thames; and the Marybone (Mary-le-Bone) Gardens Coffee House, covering most of Beaumont Street, Devonshire Street, and Devonshire Place, a fashionable public pleasure garden with graveled walks, a bowling green, an eating establishment, and space for entertainment and exhibitions.

Sir Charles Sedley (1639–1701) Sir Charles Sedley knew London as a child, for he was baptized in the Church of St. Clement Danes, and may have been born somewhere in the City in March 1639. However, the first definite association does not occur until after the Restoration, when he entered Parliament as the Member from New Romney and became a leading member of the court wits, the group which so flagrantly and repeatedly broke the peace. The stories of Sir Charles' debaucheries, many of which are contained in Samuel Pepys's diary, are legion; on July 1, 1663, Pepys relates that Sedley, Sir Thomas Ogle, and Charles Sackville (later 6th Earl of Dorset) became superbly drunk at Oxford Kate's in Bow Street, Covent Garden:

> Mr. Batten telling us of a late triall of Sir Charles Sydly the other day, . . . for his debauchery a little while since at Oxford Kates; coming in open day into the Balcone and showed his nakedness—acting all the postures of lust and buggery that could be imagined, and abusing of scripture. . . .

The tavern stood across the street from the present columned theater. The Lord Chief Justice "did . . . give him a most high reproofe," and for his part in the escapade Sedley was bound "to his good behavior" and fined £5,000. On February 23, 1657, he had married Catherine Savage at St. Giles-in-the-Fields; their daughter Catherine may have been baptized in the Church of St. Clement Danes. Still a member of the court, Sedley was involved in another serious escapade in 1668, as Pepys records:

> Pierce do tell me, among other news, the late frolic and debauchery of Sir Charles Sedley and Buckhurst, running up and down all the night, almost naked, through the streets; and at last fighting, and being beat by the watch and clapped up all night. And how the King takes their parts. . . .

Sedley also frequented the Cock Tavern near the Magistrate's House, Bow Street, Covent Garden.

Sedley's first comedy, *The Mulberry Garden,* was produced at Drury Lane, "the house infinitely full" on May 18, 1668, with "the King and Queen[,] . . . all the Court," and Pepys in attendance; everyone "do expect great matters" from the pen of the renowned court wit, "but," says Pepys,

> the play, when it come, though there was here and there a pretty saying, and that not very many neither, yet the whole of the play had nothing extraordinary in it at all, neither of language nor design; . . . insomuch that I have not been less pleased at a new play in my life, I think. And which made it the worse was, that there never was worse music played—that is, worse things composed. . . .

In February 1669 Sedley again broke the peace, or more properly, had it broken for him; on January 31 in St. James's Park the actor Edward Kynaston, who bore a startling resemblance to Sir Charles and who affected his dress and manners, was "exceedingly beaten by sticks by two or three that saluted him [as the baronet], so that he is mightily bruised and forced to keep his bed." *Bellamira, or The Mistress*, Sedley's second comedy and his best play, was produced in Drury Lane in 1687. For some time Sedley lived in a house on Great Queen Street. Even though a man of less than perfect morals himself, he was estranged from his daughter, who became James II's mistress and Countess of Dorchester for her services; Sir Charles did, however, occasionally visit her at 24 St. James's Square. He "conceived a hatred to James" and became part of the group ready "to dispossess him of his throne and dominions":

> Being asked one day, why he appeared so warm against the King, who had created his daughter a Countess, "It is from a principle of gratitude I am so warm," returns Sir Charles; "for since his Majesty has made my daughter a Countess, it is fit I should do all I can to make his daughter a Queen."

He died in his Haverstock Hill cottage, Hampstead, on August 20, 1701, and was buried in Southfleet, Kent, where many of his ancestors were also buried.

William Wycherley (1640?–1716) William Wycherley probably made his first appearance in London in November 1659, when he was admitted to the Inner Temple after leaving Oxford without a degree and resided somewhere in the Temple. He seems to have been more fit for pleasure than for law; his first play *Love in a Wood, or St. James's Park,* possibly drafted at this time, but presented in 1671, brought the author immediate fame and the interest of Barbara Villiers, Duchess of Cleveland. Encountering Wycherley on Pall Mall, she called to him from her carriage, "You, Wycherley, you are a son of a whore!" The remark alluded to a song in the play:

> When parents are slaves
> Their brats cannot be any other,
> Great wits and great braves
> Have always a punk for their mother.

Charles II's mistress drove on; Wycherley gave chase to ask: "Madam, you have been pleased to bestow a title on me which generally belongs to the fortunate. Will your ladyship be at the play tonight?" To his statement that he would await her even though he would "disappoint a very fine woman who has made me an assignation," she replied, "So you are sure to disappoint a woman who has favoured you for one who has not." "Yes," said Wycherley, "if she who has not favoured me is the finer woman of the two. But he who will be constant to your ladyship till he can find a finer woman is sure to die your captive." She appeared that night in the King's box; Wycherley entertained her appropriately and began his entry into the circle of wits at court. He led a fashionably dissolute life and at some point took up residence on the west side of Bow Street "over against the Cock." *The Country Wife* was presented successfully in 1675 by the King's Company at the Portugal Street theatre in Lincoln's Inn Fields, and *The Plain Dealer* followed in 1676, though undoubtedly written earlier.

Wycherley's excesses caught up with him in 1678, when he became ill, and King Charles is said to have given him sufficient funds for a recuperative holiday in Montpelier. He returned in the late spring of 1679, but before coming to London he met the rich widowed Countess of Drogheda, whom he married secretly in 1680. The couple settled in a Bow Street house on the site of the present colonnaded theater. The countess was an extremely jealous woman, and their brief marriage was uncomfortable for Wycherley, who was not allowed to venture farther than across the street to the Cock Tavern. Even then, it was said, he sat at an open window facing the street so that his wife could be certain no women were present. At her death she left her entire estate to him, but the contested will produced legal complexities which ruined Wycherley; in fact, he was thrown into the old Fleet Prison (near the junction of Fleet Lane and Farringdon Street) for debt. Here "the plain dealer" remained for seven years, unable to get support from his father or the publisher of his most successful play; James II, though, ordered payment of the dramatist's debts and the granting of a £ 200 pension. Wycherley, however, would not give a full accounting of his finances and so remained in prison a few more months until his father cleared up the remaining debts.

Wycherley's friendship with Alexander Pope allegedly began in 1704, and their published correspondence, shows many alterations in Pope's letters and greatly misrepresents the relationship. Determined to prevent his nephew from inheriting his estate, Wycherley (at the age of seventy-five) married Elizabeth Jackson on December 20, 1715, by special license at his Bow Street house; he died on January 1, 1716. Wycherley received the last rites of the Roman Catholic Church (to which he had evidently reverted after his rescue from prison by James) and was buried in the vaults of the Covent Garden Church of St. Paul, rebuilt after a fire in 1795. Wycherley frequented Will's Coffee House at 21 Bow Street (sometimes called 1 Bow Street), one of the most famous coffeehouses; indeed, here, it is said, "out of pure compassion for his exotick Figour, narrow circumstances, and humble appearance," Wycherley admitted Pope "into his society."

Wycherley's four plays, all set in London, contain numerous references to specific places and events. The widowed Lady Flippant, in *Love in a Wood,* relates that she has

> constantly kept *Covent-Garden*-Church, St. *Martins,* the Play-Houses, *Hide-Park, Mulbery-Garden,* and all other the publick Marts where Widows and Mayds are expos'd[.]

Martha meets Dapperwit "in the Piazzo," an open arcade on two sides of Covent Garden and a favorite place of rendezvous. Dapperwit's statement, "If I had met you in *Wheatstones*-Park with a drunken Foot-Soldier, I should not have been jealous of you," alludes to an area known for its prostitutes and its toughness; indeed, a letter to Wycherley from Thomas Shadwell asks,

> If they break Windows when they're Drunk,
> And at late hours, wake *Whetstone's* Punk,
> That has all day been hard at Service,
> With Clerk and Prentice, *Tim* and *Gervas.*

Among the other places referred to in the play are Pepper Alley (an undesirable area led to by Pepper Stairs at the Thames), the New Spring Garden at Vauxhall, and Bridewell Prison.

Hippolita and Prue in *The Gentleman Dancing-Master* complain that they have not been permitted "to see a play in twelve-month," "to go to *Ponchinello* . . . [or] Paradise," "to take a Ramble to the Park . . . [or] Mulberry-gar'n," or "to eat a Sillybub in new Spring-gar'n." The Punchinello booth at Charing Cross was run by Anthony Devolto (di Voto); Samuel Pepys went there on numerous occasions and found it "prettier and prettier" (March 20, 1667). Paradise, according to John Evelyn, was a room in Hatton Garden which was

> furnished with the representations of all sorts of animals, handsomely painted on boards or cloth, & so cut out & made to stand & move, fly, crawll, roare & make their severall cries, as was not unpretty: though in it self a meere bauble. . . .

Don Diego's statement that "the Graves of my Ancestors [lie] in Great Saint *Ellens* Church" refers to the medieval Great St. Helen's Church in Bishopsgate, where Sir Thomas Gresham, founder of the Royal Exchange, is buried.

Mrs. Aphra Behn (1640–1689) Although most of the life of Mrs. Aphra Behn is clouded in obscurity, it is known that she died in London on April 16, 1689, and was buried in Westminster Abbey.

Thomas Shadwell (1642?–1692) The Poet Laureate Thomas Shadwell first appeared as a student in London at the Middle Temple, just west of the intersection of Chancery Lane with Fleet Street, after leaving Cambridge around 1658. Few specifics are available about his private life here, and what is available is fragmentary. He resided in Salisbury Court (which ran parallel to and east of the present Dorset Rise, just south of Fleet Street) at the same time as John Dryden, when they were still on friendly terms. Shadwell's first play, *The Sullen Lovers*, was produced at Lincoln's Inn Fields in 1668; *The Miser* (1672) was dedicated to the 6th Earl of Dorset, at whose home Shadwell sat and drank ale "all day long," according to Nell Gwyn. At least eight more plays appeared before the feud with Dryden broke out in the open in 1682, the year in which Dryden's *The Medall* and *MacFlecknoe or A Satyr on the True-Blew-Protestant Poet, T. S.* and Shadwell's *The Medal of John Bayes: A Satyr against Folly and Knavery* appeared. The satires, motivated partly by political reasons and partly by a matter of literary taste (in particular, Shadwell's reverence of Ben Jonson) were vitriolic and libelous. Shadwell won when Dryden was removed as Poet Laureate and Historiographer Royal after James fled and the posts were given to Shadwell. About this time he moved to Chelsea, where he lived at 60 Cheyne Walk; there he died suddenly on November 19, 1692, but not by his own hand, as is sometimes claimed. Shadwell was buried in Chelsea Old Church, just west of his house, and there is a memorial in the Poets' Corner of Westminster Abbey.

Shadwell frequented the Devil Tavern, favored by Ben Jonson, at 1 Fleet Street; and the Rose, adjoining the Drury Lane Theatre at the corner of Catherine and Russell Streets, figures in his plays. The famous Pie Corner, on Giltspur Street at the end of Cock Lane, comes into *The Woman-Captain*, and *The Squire of Alsatia* is placed in Whitefriars; from the time of James I through that of William III this was a place of sanctuary and, as such, attracted all sorts of abandoned and shady characters. They gave the area the cant title Alsatia, and Shadwell used the cant of the inhabitants in his play.

Elkanah Settle (1648–1724) Dryden's rival during Charles II's reign and much supported artistically by the university communities, Elkanah Settle had his early schooling at the 14th-century Westminster School, whose buildings surround Little Dean's Yard, before going up to Oxford. He returned to London without a degree and possibly went through a very large fortune in 1666, the same year that *Cambyses King of Persia: A Tragedy* was performed at Lincoln's Inn Fields. The play's success determined Settle's continued activity with bombastic drama and assured his rivalry with Dryden. The two engaged in vicious attacks, and Dryden's prediction that Settle would be reduced to Bartholomew Fair audiences eventually came true. On February 28, 1674, he married Mary Warner at St. Andrew's Church, Holborn, and in 1691 he was made London Laureate and turned out pageant after pageant for the city. His resources steadily decreased, however, and around 1718 he was forced to take his place as a poor brother at the 14th-century

Carthusian priory on Charterhouse Square. He died on February 12, 1724, and may be buried in Charterhouse Square, but the registers covering the period 1710–1740 are missing.

Thomas Otway (1652–1685) One of the most unfortunate literary people in this period was the dramatist Thomas Otway, who came to London to take a small role in Aphra Behn's *The Forc'd Marriage* and was thus introduced to the theater, which was to play an important role in his short life. All of Otway's plays except *The Atheist, or The Second Part of the Soldier's Fortune* were presented at the Dorset Garden Theatre, south of Fleet Street on the east side of John Carpenter Street. In financial difficulty because of his excesses, especially in drink, Otway enlisted in the Army in 1678 and was sent to Holland; he returned to London late in 1679 and again began writing for the stage, with *The Orphan* appearing in 1680. How destitute he was over the next five years is a matter of debate, and various stories have arisen concerning his death. He is said to have drunk cold water in an overheated condition after pursuing the murderer of a friend and to have died of a fever caused by his condition; Dr. Johnson added another factor when he stated that Otway, almost naked and "in a rage of hunger," begged a shilling from a gentleman in a coffeehouse. Given a guinea, Otway "bought a roll, and was choked with the first mouthful." What is known is that Otway had lodgings in the Bull on Tower Hill and that he died there on April 14, 1685. He was buried in the churchyard of St. Clement Danes on the Strand. Otway is thought to have lived on Fetter Lane at one time. *The Atheist* presents a good rendering of the cries of the tradesmen on the Upper Walk of the New Exchange on the Strand.

Nahum Tate (1652–1715) One of the least well-known Poet Laureates, Nahum Tate, who is probably best remembered for his revision of William Shakespeare's *King Lear* in which Cordelia marries Edgar and lives happily forever after, had a long but untraceable association with London. He was, though, buried in the churchyard of St. George the Martyr, Borough High Street, Southwark, in 1715.

Thomas D'Urfey (1653–1723) The dramatist, poet, and wit Thomas D'Urfey, generally known as Tom Durfey, was in London by 1676, when his first play, *The Siege of Memphis, or The Ambitious Queen*, was performed at the King's Theatre. During his years here he wrote thirty-two plays and some 500 poems under the patronage of Charles II (who liked to have him liven up the court), James II (who was a bit more cautious in his relationship), William and Mary (for whom he changed his politics and his religion), and Queen Anne (who was delighted at his lampoon of the heir apparent, Electress Sophia: "The Crown's too weighty for the shoulders of 'Eighty'! "). Toward the end of his long life, he fell upon bad times, and a number of benefits staged for his relief were supported by such men as Joseph Addison and Richard Steele. D'Urfey died somewhere in London on February 26, 1723, and was buried in St. James's Church, Piccadilly (restored after being bombed in World War II), where a slab of Yorkshire stone reading "Tom D'Urfey, dyed Feb.ry ye 26th, 1732" [sic] was placed on the south outside wall. One of D'Urfey's favorite resorts was the Queen's Arms Tavern on Newgate Street, where the General Post Office now stands.

Thomas Southerne (1659–1746) Coming to London from Ireland to study law, Thomas Southerne entered the Middle Temple in 1678, but there is no record of his being called to the bar. His first play, *The Loyal Brother*, complimentary to the Duke of York, opened in 1682 at the then newly built Drury Lane Theatre and was most successful. Southerne determined on a dramatist's career in 1688 when the Glorious Revolution brought William and Mary to the throne, and many of his subsequent plays were produced at Drury Lane. For a number of years he lived on Tothill Street (approximately where Number 4 is now), where John Dryden is thought to have visited him. While there, he attended services at Westminster Abbey; at some other time he lived in the vicinity of Covent Garden and attended services at St. Paul's, Covent Garden. He was living on Great Smith Street in 1746, when he died on May 26.

Daniel Defoe (1660?–1731) When Daniel Defoe reached London, that "great Center of England," with "such a Prodigy of Buildings, that nothing in the World does, or ever did, equal it, except old *Rome*, in *Trajan's* Time," he admits that the scope of his native city was too "difficult to be described . . . in the narrow Compass of a letter." He goes on:

> It is the Disaster of *London*, as to the Beauty of its Figure, that it is thus stretched out in Buildings[;] . . . this has spread the Face of it in a most straggling, confus'd Manner, out of all Shape, uncompact, and unequal. . . .

Sometime in 1660 (probably between July and October) Defoe was born in the parish of St. Giles Cripplegate; his father, James Foe, was a prosperous tallow chandler and a Nonconformist. (Defoe added the prefixed *De-* to his name around 1703.) His first religious education came from his father, and the family attended dissenting services on Bishopsgate Street. Since the usual educational channels were not open to Defoe because of his religion, in 1672 he was sent to a dissenters' school, the Rev. Charles Morton's academy at Newington Green, a rural area northeast of the City with fewer than 150 houses (now part of the London borough of Hackney). It is interesting to note that one of Defoe's schoolfellows, Timothy Cruso, gave his name to what is probably the author's most famous novel.

In 1676 Defoe was apprenticed to Charles Lodwick, a Cornhill merchant; and in 1683 he opened up a business as an agent, not a hosier, on Freeman's Court, just opposite Change Alley on the north side of Cornhill. On New Year's Day, 1684, Defoe married Mary Tuffley at the original medieval St. Botolph's Church, at the junction of Aldgate and Houndsditch; the marriage, a happy one, produced eight children. Even so, Defoe was an inveterate traveler; indeed, between 1684 and 1688, traveling over most of England, he made copious notes for *A Tour thro' the Whole Island of Great Britain*. His business prospered until 1692, when he went bankrupt; Defoe was one of nineteen "merchant insurers" who, insuring ships in the war with France, failed that year. Defoe fled to the asylum offered by the Mint (where he was legally safe for one month) and then escaped to Bristol, where he remained until a (rare) arrangement in which he repaid £12,000 within ten years was concluded. By 1697 Defoe was living somewhere in

London and when here took almost all of his meals at Pontack's (on the east side of Abchurch Lane); this was the "celebrated French eating-house" where a delicious meal was served for 4 to 5 shillings and a bottle of wine (the owner's father was described by John Evelyn as "the . . . President of Bordeaux") sold for 7 shillings.

Defoe, as a dissenter, felt extreme pressure under James II and openly welcomed and supported William (and Mary), calling him "William, the Glorious, Great, and Good, and Kind." Already branded a dangerous Whig, Defoe encountered real trouble with the December 1702 publication of *The Shortest Way with the Dissenters*. In this paper Defoe, posing as a "high flyer" (a High Church Tory), attempted to discredit the Tories by reducing their arguments to absurdities. The sale of the anonymous pamphlet was enormous, but it was not seen as satire. The dissenters threatened to hang the anonymous author, while a young Tory clergyman praised the work from his pulpit. Indignant at the lack of public comprehension, he issued *A Brief Explanation of a Late Pamphlet, Entitled . . . Dissenters*, which forced the government to order his arrest and to offer a reward for his apprehension. Arrested on May 20, 1703, he was imprisoned at Newgate (the medieval gatehouse on the south side of Newgate Street near the entrance of Giltspur Lane); the prison information for *The Fortunes and Misfortunes of the Famous Moll Flanders* came from this experience. He admitted to his pamphlet, and his penalty was severe: to pay a fine of 200 marks, to stand in a public pillory on three separate occasions at the end of July, and to remain in Newgate until the Queen saw fit to release him. Furthermore, he was bound to guarantee seven years' good conduct. Before the public pillorying, though, he composed "Hymn to the Pillory," a work which swung public sympathy and support to his side. On August 1, the final day of his disgrace, Defoe was led into the Strand, where the pillory had been set up just within Temple Bar; the crowd accompanying him from Newgate was exultant, and the pillory was garlanded with flowers. Instead of the traditional rotten eggs and garbage, Defoe was pelted with flowers during his two hours, and his poem was sung out by the crowd, with emphasis no doubt on

> Tell them the men that placed him here
>   Are scandals to the times;
> Are at a loss to find his guilt,
>   And can't commit his crimes.

Three months more were spent in jail before he was finally released.

One of Defoe's most remarkable accomplishments during Anne's reign was the production of *The Review*, which greatly influenced other periodical writers. Around 1708 he and his family settled first in a house on the north side of Stoke Newington Church Street and then at Number 95; Defoe enlarged the latter place, which is marked with a plaque. Here he occasionally frequented the Three Crowns, the village pub. Imprisonment in 1713 on a charge of libel was of short duration, and Defoe was granted a pardon under the great seal. *The Life and Strange Surprizing Adventures of Robinson Crusoe*, written in Stoke Newington, appeared in 1719, and *Moll Flanders, A Journal of the Plague Year*, and *The History and Remarkable Life of Colonel Jacque, Commonly Call'd Col Jack* came out in 1722. His last major fictional work, *The Fortunate Mistress*, was published in 1724.

From 1724 until 1730 Defoe lived in relative peace and comfort at his home, but in that summer he claimed that he was struck a blow by a "wicked, perjur'd and contemptible enemy" and went into hiding in the maze of streets around Newgate. Early in 1731, still not feeling safe enough to rejoin his family, Defoe took lodgings on Ropemaker Alley (the present Ropemaker Street), where he died on April 26, 1731, from a "lethargy," according to the parish register. As a dissenter he was buried in Bunhill Fields, the Nonconformists' graveyard (between City Road and Bunhill Row), where the gravedigger identified him as "Mr. Dubow"; the grave was first marked by a small white marble slab, which was replaced with a granite obelisk on September 16, 1870. A stained-glass window in the Butchers' Hall portrays him in elegant court attire with a tricornered velvet hat under his arm.

Along with many of his contemporaries, the novelist visited a long list of coffeehouses: the Amsterdam, on Bartholomew Lane; the British, described as opposite Suffolk Street at 27 Cockspur Lane, where "the Scots generally go"; Jonathan's, 20 Exchange Alley; Jones's, Finch Lane; Robin's, Exchange Alley; and Waits, Bell Yard, Gracechurch Street. One other, Elford's Coffee House, deserves more than passing mention for its literary importance; located on George Street, Elford's had an entrance from Birchin Lane through White Lyon Yard and was usually described as being on Birchin Lane. It had on display,

> to be seen and read Gratis, ... also an Account of a Man living alone 4 Years and 4 Months in the Island of John Fernando, which they brought with them.

The man was obviously Alexander Selkirk, and Defoe probably first read here the account which some years later was molded into *Robinson Crusoe*.

Defoe's familiarity with London is seen clearly in *Moll Flanders*, for Moll is born in Newgate, has lodgings in Hammersmith, and attends Bartholomew Fair, where she meets "a gentleman extremely well dressed and very rich," who begs her to "trust myself in a coach with him." They drive "to the Spring Gardens, at Knightsbridge," and eventually back to the city:

> [H]e stopped the coach at a house where, it seems, he was acquainted, and where they made no scruple to show us upstairs into a room with a bed in it. At first I seemed to be unwilling to go up, but after a few words I yielded to that too. ...

The house was on the Strand; returning to the coach three hours and much drink later, he falls asleep, and Moll robs him and

> opening the coach door, stood ready to jump out while the coach was going on; but the coach stopping in the narrow street beyond Temple Bar to let another coach pass, I got softly out, fastened the door again, and gave my gentleman and the coach the slip both together. ...

At another point Moll, holding a package while a maid returns to get her mistress for the Barnet coach, flees:

> I walked away and turning into Charterhouse Lane, made off through Charterhouse Yard, into Long Lane, then crossed into Bartholomew Close, so into Little Britain, and through the Bluecoat Hospital, into Newgate Street.

She walks in "St. James's Park, where I saw abundance of fine ladies in the Park, walking in the Mall"; here she lifts Lady Betty's gold watch as

> the crowd ran to see the king go by to the Parliament House.
> The ladies ran all to the side of the Mall, and I helped my lady to stand upon the edge of the boards on the side of the Mall, that she might be high enough to see. ...

Moll is eventually carried back to Newgate, where a woman under sentence who "pleaded my belly" sings "the following piece of Newgate wit":

> "If I swing by the string,
> I shall hear the bell ring,
> And then there's an end of poor Jenny."

The bell is that of St. Sepulchre's on Holborn Viaduct, which was tolled on execution days.

Matthew Prior (1664–1721) The early life of the poet and diplomat Matthew Prior becomes somewhat more precise when his father brought the family to London; the Priors lived on Stephen's Alley, near King Street, Westminster, where the elder Prior went into the wine trade, an occupation in which two of his brothers, Arthur and Samuel, were already well established. Prior was sent to the 14th-century Westminster School (the buildings surround Little Dean's Yard), where he had reached the middle of the third form (around 1677) when his father died. Unable to continue at school, he was taken into his uncle's establishment, the Rhenish Wine House, to help keep the accounts; the house was in Cannon Row, east of and parallel to Parliament Street. It was at here that Prior is said to have met the 6th Earl of Dorset, for whom he translated some of Horace's odes and Ovid's verses and for whom he composed an ode in Latin. Ultimately Dorset sought Prior's permission and his uncle's to return the boy to school (at the earl's cost); there he became a King's Scholar in 1681. Following graduation from St. John's College, Cambridge, an appointment as the tutor to the 5th Earl of Exeter's sons, and the ambassadorship to The Hague, Prior was in and out of London over the years. From 1700 on his commitments here increased; in June 1700 he was given a seat on the Board of Trade and Plantations, and he sat in the House of Commons for East Grinstead in 1701.

Sometime before 1706 Prior bought a house in Westminster just off Great George Street, approximately where Horse Gardens Road is today. Prior's house, near the entrance of King Charles Street, became a popular location for the intrigues of the Tories. After the Tories regained power in 1710, Prior was promised a new commission in customs, which he took up on January 28, 1712. Back and forth to France on various missions, he was recalled a few months after Anne's death in 1714, when he and a number of others were ordered arrested by Sir Robert Walpole; Prior first appeared before the Secret Committee on June 16, 1715. He was imprisoned until the end of 1716 and kept himself occupied by writing the *Answer to the Secret Committee, Alma, or The Progress of the Mind*, and shorter poems. After his release he retired to Down Hall, Essex; he died on September 18, 1721, at the 1st Earl of Oxford's estate in Wimpole, Cambridgeshire, and was buried according to the directions of his will in the Poets' Corner of Westminster Abbey at the feet of Spenser. He also wanted a monument erected to hold the bust executed by Antoine Coysevox, and the epitaph was to be composed by Dr. Robert Freind; for these vanities he left £500.

Prior mentions the Rhenish Wine House in *The Hind and the Panther Transvers'd to the Story of the Country Mouse and the City Mouse:*

> What wretch would nibble on a hanging shelf,
> When at Pontack's he may regale himself?
> Or to the house of cleanly Rhenish go,
> Or that at Charing Cross, or that in Channel Row?

Pontack's, at the corner of Abchurch Lane and Lombard Street, was long one of London's most fashionable eating places. Another coffeehouse which Prior frequented, often in the company of Jonathan Swift, was the Smyrna (Smirna), at 58 and 59 Pall Mall, which "stood on the north side . . . at the corner of Crown Court on the east side." Prior was a regular visitor to 35 St. Martin's Street, the home of Sir Isaac Newton, who had an observatory atop his house. At least one of Prior's mistresses lived on Long Acre; the wife of a soldier, she was the Chloe to whom many of the poet's poems are addressed. It is also believed that Betty Cox, another mistress whom he addresses as Emma, lived in Long Acre. Prior also at one time lived on Leicester Square, in the tenth house up from the bottom on the east side.

Jonathan Swift (1667–1745) To document fully the comings and goings of Jonathan Swift in London is impossible. To begin with, he was undoubtedly in the City while employed by Sir William Temple at Moor Park, Surrey, but the specific associations are unavailable. Serving as chaplain and secretary to the Earl of Berkeley in Dublin, Swift returned to England in 1701, 1702, and 1703; by 1708 he was a frequent guest at the house of Sir Andrew Fountaine in Leicester Fields, and Richard Steele's publication of "Morning in Town" brought him to the attention of London writers and society in general. "A Description of a City Shower" (1710) is a vivid account of the City:

> Now from all parts the swelling kennels flow,
> And bear their trophies with them as they go:
> Filth of all hues and odours seem to tell
> What street they sailed from, by their sight and smell.
> They, as each torrent drives with rapid force,
> From Smithfield or St. Pulchre's shape their course,
> And in huge confluent join at Snow Hill ridge,
> Fall from the conduit prone to Holborn Bridge.
> Sweeping from butchers' stalls, dung, guts, and blood,
> Drowned puppies, stinking sprats, all drenched in mud,
> Dead cats and turnip-tops come tumbling down the
> flood.

On his 1710 visit to London, Swift first lodged on Pall Mall, but he writes to Stella (Esther Johnson) on September 20, "Tomorrow I change my lodgings in Pall Mall for one in Bury Street, where I suppose I shall continue while in London." These lodgings (where he also stayed in 1713 and 1722) were on the west side of the street, about halfway down from Jermyn Street; Swift says:

> I have the first floor, a dining-room and bed-chamber, *at eight shillings a week, plaguy dear*, but I spend nothing for eating, never go to a tavern, and very seldom in a coach; yet after all it will be expensive.

He visited Elliott's Coffee House and White's Coffee House on St. James's Street and Robin's Coffee House in the Exchange; at Elliott's on November 19, he

> christened our Coffeeman Elliot's child; where the rogue had a most noble supper, and Steele and I sat among some scurvy company over a bowl of punch. . . .

White's, originally on the east side of the street, had moved to the west side, to Number 69, when Swift came to know it; here he claimed Robert Harley

> never passed by White's Chocolate-House (the common Rendezvous of infamous Sharpers and noble Cullies) without bestowing a curse upon that famous academy, as the bane of half the English nobility.

The Devil Tavern at 1 Fleet Street was another of his resorts, and here on October 12, "I dined to-day with Dr. Garth and Mr. Addison . . . and Garth treated."

In 1711 Swift had a succession of lodgings in London; he lived on Leicester Square for a short time, but on April 26 he moved to Church Street (now Old Church Street) in Chelsea "for the air." He was suffering from pains in the head and felt the walk into London would be an adequate substitute for the exercise he had gotten in Dublin. "It is two good miles," he writes, "and just five thousand and seven hundred and forty-eight steps."

> I got here with Patrick and my portmanteau, for sixpence, and pay six shillings a week for one silly room, with confounded coarse sheets. I lodge just over against Dr. Atterbury's house; and yet, perhaps, I shall not like the place better for that.

And he did dislike Chelsea. The summer was hot, and Swift complained:

> It was bloody hot walking today; and I was so lazy, I dined where my new gown was, at Mrs. Van Homrigh's, and came back like a fool, and the Dean of Carlisle has sitten with me till eleven.

He swam in the Thames at the foot of Old Church Street and visited the famous Chelsea Bun House (on Pimlico Road, just west of the More Street intersection), where he bought a bun which was stale. On July 4 he "left Chelsea for good," and he returned only twice to visit the dean of Carlisle.

Swift went from Chelsea to a house on Suffolk Street, only a few doors away from that of Esther Vanhomrigh (pronounced "vanummery"), the Vanessa of his poetry. He frequented Pontack's, the "famous dining place" at 16–17 Lombard Street, where he recounts, "Pontack told us, although his wine was so good, he sold it cheaper than others; he took but seven shillings a flask. . . ." He also often stopped at the Smyrna (Smirna) Coffee House, 58–59

Pall Mall, in the company of Matthew Prior after the two had walked around Hyde Park. The Thatched House Tavern, 74–76 St. James's Street, was another favorite spot, where the Brothers' Club, a group formed to secure patronage for appropriate men of letters and to engage in literary warfare against the Whigs, met.

From the end of September to December 1712 Swift lodged on Ryder Street between Duke and Bury Streets, and here on the same street (probably near the northeast corner of Bury Street) Vanessa lived from 1712 to 1714. Swift frequently went to Truby's (Trubey's) Coffee House in St. Paul's Churchyard and writes:

> At Childs or Trubys never once had been,
> Where town and country vicars flock in tribes
> Secured by numbers from the layman's gibes
> And deal with vices of the graver sort,
> Tobacco, censure, coffee, pride and port.

Child's was also located in the churchyard. Swift had become the Tories' leading political writer, and he fully anticipated a reward for his services, a deanery in England, but the reward was slow in coming. In April 1713 the Queen appointed Swift Dean of St. Patrick's Cathedral in Dublin, but not until the accession of George I and the downfall of the Tory party did Swift return to his native Ireland and his preferment. He made only two trips back to England, in 1726 and 1727; on the latter trip he lodged chiefly on New Bond Street "over against the Crown and Cushion" before leaving England forever.

Other important Swiftian associations in London are scattered over his years here. Button's Coffee House, on Russell Street, Covent Garden, was where Joseph Addison presided over literary meetings which included Pope, Swift, Gay, Steele, and Cibber. The Bell Coffee House, on King Street, Westminster, originally a tavern, was where the October Club, whose members were mostly Tories, met:

> [W]e are plagued with an October Club, that is, a set of above a hundred Parliament men of the country, who drink October beer at home, and meet every evening . . . to consult affairs and drive things on to extreme against the Whigs.

Swift also visited the Fountain Tavern, a social headquarters for many Tories, located in Fountain Court (now Numbers 103 and 104 on the Strand). He was often the guest of Robert Harley, 1st Earl of Oxford, at 14 Buckingham Street in the Adelphi, where Pepys had also lived; and he visited Isaac Newton's home at 35 St. Martin's Street, Soho. The 3d Earl of Burlington's house (a superb Palladian house on the north side of Piccadilly now housing the Royal Academy of Arts), was another residence where Swift could be found; here he enjoyed teasing the good-tempered duchess. On Swift's last two trips to England, he frequented the Cocoa Tree Chocolate House, which stood on Pall Mall, on the site of the Royal Automobile Club.

Two other associations should be mentioned: the home of the astrologer and almanac maker John Partridge, whom Swift ridicules in *Predictions for the Year 1708 . . . by Isaac Bickerstaff Esq.*, was on Henrietta Street, and Lemuel Gulliver of *Travels into Several Remote Nations of the World* lived on Fetter Lane off Fleet Street.

William Congreve (1670–1729)   The dramatist William Congreve entered the Middle Temple in 1691, but he was never a serious or enthusiastic reader of law, although he pursued his study here for three years. Between March 1691 and August 1692 he was well received as a poet and became a friend of John Dryden, and in March 1693 *The Old Bachelor* was produced at the Theatre Royal on Drury Lane; Dryden had seen the manuscript the preceding summer and along with Thomas Southerne and Everard Maynwaring had helped to polish it. The play ran for fourteen nights, a fantastic run in those days, and Congreve was granted the "privilege of the house" for an unprecedented six months. The dramatist at this time was probably living somewhere on Southampton Street. The success of this first play was undoubtedly instrumental in his placing *The Double Dealer* on the same stage in November; however, it was not really a success, though a better play.

Because of problems at the Theatre Royal, the Lord Chamberlain granted a new license for plays at the new Lincoln's Inn Fields Theatre, on the north side of Portugal Street almost opposite the entrance of Carey Street, and Congreve became one of its managers. The theater opened on April 30, 1695, with his *Love for Love,* which ran with only a few breaks until the end of the year. Congreve guaranteed the company one new play each year but was unable to fulfill his promise. His most financially successful play, *The Mourning Bride,* saved the foundering company in 1697 and swelled the dramatist's already-large reputation, but it was three years before he had another play ready to produce. The Lincoln's Inn Fields Theatre produced Congreve's masterpiece and last play, *The Way of the World,* in 1700. He did not, though, desert the theater: he wrote a masque and the libretto for an opera and in 1705 became the first manager of Her Majesty's Theatre, Haymarket.

Private means, civil service commissions (which involved no toil), and the financial success of his plays allowed Congreve to lead a quiet and private life from 1705 on. Leaving a house somewhere on Arundel Street, from 1706 on he lived on Surrey Street with his friends Mr. and Mrs. Porter; Mrs. Porter's sister, Anne Bracegirdle, whom the dramatist visited, lived on nearby Howard Street. Voltaire visited him at the Porters' house:

> Mr. Congreve had one defect, which was his entertaining too mean an idea of his own first profession, that of a writer, though it was to this he owed his fame and fortune. He spoke of his works as trifles that were beneath him, and hinted to me in our first conversation that I should visit him upon no other foot than that of a gentleman who led a life of plainness and simplicity. I answered that had he been so unfortunate as to be a mere gentleman, I should never have come to see him; and I was very much disgusted at so unseasonable a piece of vanity.

By 1714 Congreve's intimacy with Anne Bracegirdle seems to have been displaced by that with the 2d Duchess of Marlborough, whose second daughter, Lady Mary Godolphin was almost certainly his child. Indeed, that hypothesis goes a long way toward explaining Congreve's bequest of £10,000 to the duchess. Congreve suffered internal injuries from a coach accident in the autumn of 1728; he grew steadily weaker and died on Sunday morning, January 19,

1729. The following Sunday his body lay in state at Westminster Abbey, and the funeral service was conducted in the King Henry VII's Chapel. He was buried in the abbey, and Henrietta, Duchess of Marlborough erected the memorial tablet in the gallery next to the chapel.

Congreve was a member of the Kit-Cat Club, which met in the Upper Flask Inn, on the southeast corner of Heath Street at the intersection of East Heath Road; he was considered one of the "three most honest-hearted and good men" of the group, which included Joseph Addison and Sir Richard Steele. Congreve frequented Will's Coffee House, at 21 Russell Street (sometimes called 1 Bow Street) and the Fountain Tavern, at the Strand end of Fountain Court (gone but between Numbers 103 and 104), and often ate at Pontack's, one of the period's most famous eating places, at the corner of Abchurch Lane and Lombard Street. He was also a frequent guest at Isaac Newton's home, 35 St. Martin's Street.

The Way of the World, set in London, mentions a number of specific locations, although "a chocolate-house," where the play opens, cannot be identified. Mirabell asks, "Well, is the grand affair over? You have been something tedious," and receives the reply:

> Sir, there's such coupling at Pancras, that they stand behind one another, as 'twere in a country dance. Ours was the last couple to lead up; . . . so we drove round to Duke's Place; and there they were rivetted in a trice.

At the Church of St. Pancras (destroyed by fire), on Pancras Lane, as at the Church of St. James, Duke Place, marriages could be performed without the proclamation of banns and without a special license. Mirabell bids the servant to tell "Dame Partlet . . . [to] meet me at one o'clock by Rosamond's Pond . . . " The pond is in St. James's Park. Mirabell and Fainall "take a turn before dinner" in the Mall (St. James's Park), a very fashionable area; the second act is set there. Lady Wishfort, threatening to "send for Robin from Locket's," probably refers to Locket's Coffee House in Spring Gardens, Charing Cross, but a second coffeehouse of the same name existed on Gerrard Street, Soho. Foible engages in the same sort of raillery as Lady Wishfort:

> He! I hope to see him lodge in Ludgate first, and angle into Blackfriars for brass farthings, with an old mitten.

The prisoners at Ludgate let down containers on a rope to beg alms from passersby.

Colley Cibber (1671–1757)   Without doubt the most maligned poet of this period was the Poet Laureate Colley Cibber, the hero of Alexander Pope's vicious satire *The Dunciad.* The son of the Danish sculptor Caius Gabriel Cibber, the dramatist was born on November 6, 1671, on Southampton Place, in a house on the northwest corner next to Bloomsbury Square, and was baptized at the Church of St. Giles-in-the-Fields. About 1690 he joined Thomas Betterton's company at the Theatre Royal, and here he muffed his first line on stage, to be delivered to Betterton. Betterton demanded Cibber be fined:

> "Why, sir," said the prompter, "he has no salary."— "No?" said the old man; "why then, put him down ten shillings a week, and forfeit him five shillings."

After Cibber married in 1693 and his acting career provided inadequate revenues, he turned to writing:

> It may be observable too that my muse and my spouse were equally prolific; that the one was seldom the mother of a child, but in the same year the other made me the father of a play. I think we had a dozen of each sort between us, of both which kinds some died in their infancy, and near an equal number of each were alive when I quitted the theatre.

Even so, he was plagued with financial problems and spent part of 1697 in the Gatehouse Prison (in the wall almost directly in front of the entrance to Westminster Abbey) for debt. From 1711 to 1714 he resided in Spring Gardens, then a fashionable district.

Through a series of intrigues Cibber gained a one-third management of the Drury Lane Theatre, which subsequently reached a prosperity hitherto unknown. He entered into political writing at the death of Queen Anne but did not give up the management of the theater, near which he moved in 1721, taking a house on the west side of Wellington Street, three doors north of Tavistock Street; he became Poet Laureate in December 1730. He wrote *An Apology for the Life of Mr. Collery Cibber, Comedian* after retirement from the theater in 1730. Cibber claimed that the laureateship resulted from his Whig connections, and it must be admitted that his literary work alone gives him a poor claim to the honor. This certainly provoked *The Dunciad,* in which the Goddess of Dullness creates Cibber King of the Dunces:

> Thou, Cibber! thou, his [Eusden's] laurel shalt support;
> Folly, my son, has still a friend at court.
> Lift up your gates, ye princes, see him come!
> Sound, sound, ye viols; be the cat-call dumb!

Cibber moved to the site of 19 Berkeley Square, where he died on December 11, 1757. He was buried in the Danish Church which his father had built on Wellclose Square, Whitechapel (the new London borough of Tower Hamlets); the church stood on the site of St. Paul's School. Cibber frequented Button's Coffee House, on the south side of Russell Street two doors from the corner of Covent Garden, Tom's Coffee House, 17 Russell Street, and White's Coffee House, 68–69 St. James's Street, after it became a private club in 1736.

Joseph Addison (1672–1719)   With the essayist, poet, and statesman Joseph Addison London associations are especially numerous; in 1686 he was sent by his father, the dean of Lichfield, to Charterhouse, the 17th-century school founded for "forty poor boys" on the north side of Charterhouse Square (the school remained here until 1872). Addison entered as a gentleman commoner and met Richard Steele, with whom he formed a lifelong friendship. After going up to Queen's College, Oxford, in May 1687, he made frequent trips to London to further his developing literary career and probably stayed on College Street. Following an extended European tour (1699–1704), financed by a Treasury grant when Charles Montagu (subsequently 1st Earl of Halifax) realized what an asset Addison would be to the Whigs, he returned to London permanently and took up a seat in the Kit-Cat Club, which regularly met in the Upper Flask Inn on the southeast corner of Heath Street and East Heath Road; Addison also frequented

St. James's Coffee House, near St. James's Palace, where he would meet Steele.

As the Whigs gained power, Addison was asked to write occasional pieces, such as *The Campaign* (December 14, 1704), on the Duke of Marlborough's victory at Blenheim. Before the poem was finished, he was appointed Commissioner of Appeal in Excise, and in July 1705, after the Whig success and the return of Lord Somers and Halifax to the Privy Council, he was appointed Undersecretary of State; in 1706 he accompanied Halifax to the Hanoverian court to discuss the Act of Settlement. When Richard Steele's first wife died in December 1706, Addison joined him at 9 Bennet Street and remained until October 29, a short time after Steele's remarriage. For a brief period before his appointment as secretary to the Lord Lieutenant of Ireland in 1708 (effectively Secretary of State), he sat in Parliament as the Member for Lostwithiel, Cornwall, and had a house in Sandy End, Fulham (now part of the London borough of Hammersmith). He stood as godfather to Elizabeth Steele at St. James's Church, Piccadilly, before leaving for Ireland in April 1709; upon his permanent return in 1710 he took lodgings on St. James's Place (two blocks south of Steele's house on Bennet Street) with his secretary and cousin Eustace Budgell; even though he sat in Parliament for Malmesbury, Wiltshire, he was able to devote time to his literary activities and contributed to the final issues of Steele's *Tatler*.

At this time Steele and Addison decided to launch *The Spectator;* the first issue appeared on March 1, 1711. In October Addison took a house on Kensington Square, where Edward Wortley Montagu would also live. Attached to the arrangement was a proviso that Addison "be nice in the choice of a cook," deemed necessary because the essayist's taste for plain cooking was not shared by his friends. From 1710 on Addison frequented Will's Coffee House (1 Bow Street), Child's Coffee House (Warwick Lane, near St. Paul's), St. James's Coffee House (near St. James's Palace), the Grecian Coffee House (Devereux Court on the Strand), and the Cocoa Tree Chocolate House (south side of Pall Mall); the first issue of *The Spectator* noted:

> There is no place of general Resort, wherein I do not often make my Appearance; sometimes I am seen thrusting my Head into a Round of Politicians at *Will's.* . . . Sometimes I smoak a Pipe at *Child's.* . . . I appear on *day* nights at St. *James's* Coffee-House. . . . My Face is likewise very well known at the *Grecian,* the *Cocoa-Tree,* and in the Theatres both of *Drury-Lane* and the *Hay-Market.* I have been taken for a Merchant upon the *Exchange,* . . . and sometimes pass for a *Jew* in the Assembly of Stock-Jobbers at *Jonathan's.*

At Will's, Addison first met Alexander Pope in the autumn of 1711, probably in the company of William Wycherley, but Pope was not here often because neither the diet nor the hours suited him. The political wilderness into which Addison had been thrust by the rise of the Tories ended with Queen Anne's death; the government, vested in a regency, appointed Addison secretary in August. To be closer to the government, he took lodgings on Cecil Street in the Strand; the street stood between Adam Street and Savoy Court, about twelve doors beyond Adam. Addison was once again disappointed; he was not made Secretary of State, as he hoped, but given another undersecretaryship.

In December 1715 Addison was appointed one of the commissioners of trades and plantations, and in the summer of 1716 both the *Whitehall Courant* and the *General Post* carried the note, "Joseph Addison, Esq, is to be married to the Countess of Warwick." There is no evidence of any sort of courtship, and the two were married on August 9 in the Church of St. Edmund the King and Martyr on Lombard Street. Addison then took up residence at Holland House, the duchess's home, although he also maintained a house on Albemarle Street. Holland House, a large E-shaped Jacobean house north of Kensington High Street on the west side of Holland Walk, was almost totally destroyed during World War II, but the beautiful front courtyard remains and has been fully restored by the London County Council; the grounds are as they were originally laid out with avenues of lime trees. The fulfillment of Addison's political ambition came in April 1717, when he was appointed Secretary of State; illness, however, kept him from taking a very active part in the government, and he vacated the post in mid-March 1718. He first became ill in June 1717, and there were more severe recurrences in August, September, November, and December; it now appears that he suffered a slight stroke in the December illness. A daughter, Charlotte, was born on January 30, 1719, and was christened at St. Martin-in-the-Fields. Addison's health continued to fail, and he died at Holland House on June 17, 1719. His body lay in state in the Jerusalem Chamber of Westminster Abbey and was buried on the night of June 26 in the Albemarle Vault in the King Henry VII's Chapel. Addison had reflected:

> When I look upon the tombs of the great, every emotion of envy dies within me: when I read the epitaphs of the beautiful, every inordinate desire goes out; . . . when I see kings lying by those who deposed them, when I consider rival wits placed side by side, or the holy men that divided the world with their contests and disputes, I reflect with sorrow and astonishment on the little competitions, factions, and debates of mankind. When I read the several dates of the tombs, of some that died yesterday, and some six hundred years ago, I consider that great day when we shall all of us be contemporaries, and make our appearance together.

Places here associated with Addison are legion, and *The Spectator* alone catalogs London during the period. Addison frequented the George, a fashionable chocolate house on Pall Mall, and on February 29, 1708, invited Jonathan Swift to dine at two o'clock that afternoon with Steele in the party. Addison attended services at St. James Garlickhythe, on Garlick Hill north of Upper Thames Street, where he discovered "the excellency of Common Prayer":

> When being at *St. James's Garlick-hill* Church, I heard the Service read so distinctly, so emphatically, and so fervently, that it was next to an Impossibility to be unattentive.

He delighted in the Royal Exchange:

> It gives me a secret Satisfaction, and, in some measure, gratifies my Vanity, as I am an *Englishman,* to see so rich an Assembly of Country-men and Foreigners consulting together upon the private Business of Mankind, and making this Metropolis a kind of *Emporium* for the Whole Earth.

Vauxhall also pleased him; the name, it should be noted, was originally Fulke's Hall, named after Falkes (Fulke) de Breauté, a Norman warrior during the reign of King John. It was ultimately corrupted to Vauxhall; the site was also known as Spring Gardens. The approximately 12-acre site, bounded roughly by Leopold Street, Upper Kennington Lane, St. Oswald's Place, and Goding Street, became the resort of all the wit, fashion, and rank of London; Addison (and Sir Roger de Coverley) visit the gardens, which had become the haunt of the Cyprians:

> When I considered the Fragrancy of the Walks and Bowers with the Choirs of Birds that sung upon the Trees, and the loose Tribe of People that walked under their Shades, I could not but look upon the place as a kind of *Mahometan* Paradise.

Just as John Dryden made Will's Coffee House the resort of wits, so Addison made Button's on the south side of Russell Street, about two doors from Covent Garden. The proprietor, Daniel Button, had at one time been in the service of the Countess of Warwick, but contrary to popular belief Addison did not set Button up in business after his marriage since the coffeehouse had been established in 1712 or 1713, three or four years before Addison married Lady Warwick. Tradition maintains that when Addison had suffered any vexation from his wife, he would repair here before going on to a tavern where he would stay too long and drink too much. It was at Button's that Addison presided over his "literary club" (Steele, Cibber, Swift, Gay, and Dr. John Arbuthnot) and "gave his little senate laws," as the envious Alexander Pope sniped.

Addison also frequented Giles's Coffee House, although there is some confusion as to which one he used: the more likely was located on St. Martin's Lane and was described officially "as the resort of Frenchmen" as early as 1715; the second was on Pall Mall. Speculating on coffeehouse politicians on the death of the French King,

> I afterwards called in at *Giles's*, where I saw a Board of *French* Gentlemen sitting upon the Life and Death of their *Grand Monarque*. Those among them who had espoused the Whig Interest, very positively affirm'd, that he departed this Life about a Week since, and therefore proceeded without any further delay to the Release of their Friends on the Gallies, and to their own Re-establishment. . . .

He went on to Jenny Man's Coffee House, Charing Cross:

> I saw an *alerte* young Fellow that cocked his Hat upon a Friend of his, who entered just at the same time with my self. . . . Well *Jack*, the old Prig is dead at last. Sharp's the Word. Now or never Boy. Up to the Walls of *Paris* directly.

The Smyrna (Smirna) Coffee House, 59 Pall Mall, Garraway's Coffee House, 4 Exchange Alley, and Will's Coffee House are mentioned in *The Spectator*:

> I have known Peter publishing the whisper of the day by eight o'clock in the morning at Garraway's, by twelve at Will's, and before two at the Smyrna. . . .

The Devil Tavern, 1 Fleet Street, famous as the resort of Ben Jonson and his circle, kept up its reputation in the 18th century, when Addison, Swift, and Sir Samuel Garth took the place of "glorious Ben."

The Hum-Drum Club held its silent meetings at the King's Head, 22 Ivy Lane:

> The *Hum-Drum* Club, of which I was formerly an unworthy Member, was made up of very honest Gentlemen, of peaceable Dispositions, that used to sit together, smoak their Pipes, and say nothing 'till Mid-night.

Sir Richard Steele (1672–1729) Soon after the death of his father in 1677, Dublin-born Richard Steele was placed under the care of an uncle, Henry Gascoigne, a governor of Charterhouse, to which the twelve-year-old Steele was nominated in November 1684. (The 17th-century school, founded for "forty poor boys," was on the north side of Charterhouse Square until 1872.) Two years after Steele's entrance, Addison entered Charterhouse, and the two became lifelong friends. After Steele went up to Christ Church, Oxford, he was not heard of in London until 1700, when he had lodgings in the parish of St. Martin-in-the-Fields and was involved in a duel with a young Coldstream Irish officer named Kelly whom Steele had talked out of a previous duel with a fellow soldier. Kelly, convinced that Steele was shielding the offender, demanded satisfaction from Steele, and the two met just before nightfall on June 16, 1700, in Hyde Park; Steele, determined to disarm or disable Kelly, actually ran him through but did not kill him. This experience and, no doubt, an incompatability between the style of military life and his own forms of dissipation seem to have drawn Steele to writing, and he put out *The Christian Hero,* which his men felt was hypocritical.

The Funeral was presented at the Drury Lane Theatre in 1701, and in September Steele moved to Wandsworth, Surrey (now in the London borough of Wandsworth); here he had rooms in a house which was a school for girls (he stayed only a month). Steele was now in debt, and when he became involved with an alchemist in Bethnal Green (Steele supplied the funds), he became so insolvent that he considered selling his captaincy in Lord Lucas's regiment. His second play, *The Lying Lover,* was a dismal failure, "damned," as Steele said, "for its piety." Then, in May 1705 he married a wealthy widow, Margaret Ford Stretch; of the marriage little is known, but it is reasonable to assume that Steele's motives were at least partly mercenary. When his wife conveniently died in late 1706, Steele was left with a substantial income, but even so, during her short married life Steele appeared in common pleas court for a debt of £600. The pair lodged over Keen's Apothecary Shop at 9 Bennet Street, and Steele began frequenting St. James's Coffee House. He secured a number of small appointments, for example, as gentleman waiter to Prince George, the Danish husband of Queen Anne.

At his wife's funeral, Steele supposedly met Mary Scurlock, his "Dear Prue" (again a woman of means), whom he married on September 9, 1707. It was long believed that they were married at St. Margaret's Church, Westminster, but they were actually married at the Church of St. Mary Somerset (demolished 1867), on Lower Thames Street near the corner of Fish Street Hill. They first lived in her old place on Swallow Street and then took a house on Bury Street, "third door, right hand, turning out of Jermyn Street," Steele states, where Number 21 or Number 22 stands today. Steele began reappearing at the Fountain Tavern (at the head of Fountain Court on the Strand where Numbers 103 and 104 stand) but was still having problems with his creditors. He spent May 1708 sleeping at "Leg the Barber's, opposite the Devil Tavern in Charing Cross," that is, across from 1 Fleet Street. Steele's first daughter, named Elizabeth (just as was his natural daughter born in 1700), was born on March 26, 1709, and was christened at St. James's Church, Piccadilly, with Joseph Addison standing as one of the godfathers.

Steele's literary career took a sharp turn for the better; he was appointed writer of *The Gazette,* the official government journal, in May 1707, but the desire of the ministries to keep the publication out of trouble gave no scope to the essayist's talents. *The Tatler,* undoubtedly conceived because of government restraints, was launched in March 1709 under the name of Isaac Bickerstaff, a man who frequented White's Chocolate House on St. James's Street and Will's Coffee House at 1 Bow Street; the latter, Steele writes,

> is very much altered since Mr. *Dryden* frequented it; where you used to see *Songs, Epigrams,* and *Satyrs,* . . . the Learned now dispute only about the Truth of the Game.

Steele set up *The Tatler* so that all accounts of poetry came from Will's, "all accounts of gallantry, pleasure, and entertainment" from White's, all accounts of learning from the Grecian Coffee House at 19 Devereux Court, and all accounts of "FOREIGN and DOMESTICK NEWS" from St. James's Coffee House, 87 St. James's Street. Still having periodic financial difficulties, Steele was locked up in the Bull-Head (a sponging house for debtors being held pending a court decision), on Vere Street (then located near the corner of Sheffield and Portugal Streets, perpendicular to Sheffield Street). Perhaps the best illustration of Steele's money problems and attitudes is the story later related by Dr. Johnson in *Lives of the English Poets:*

> Sir Richard Steele having one day invited to his house a great number of persons of the first quality, they were surprised at the number of liveries which surrounded the table; . . . one of them inquired of Sir Richard how such an expensive train of domestics could be consistent with his fortune. Sir Richard very frankly confessed . . . that they were bailiffs who had introduced themselves with an execution, and whom, since he could not send them away, he had thought it convenient to embellish with liveries that they might do him credit while they stayed.

The last issue of *The Tatler* appeared on January 2, 1711, its demise precipitated by political reasons: the Whigs were out of power, and many of Steele's more obvious barbs at Robert Harley, the Tory leader, were unappreciated by the government.

The Tatler was not long without a successor: on March 1, 1711, the first issue of the joint venture of Addison and Steele, *The Spectator,* came out. Steele moved his family to Bloomsbury Square (the fifth house in a row of ten on the east side of the street up from Southampton Place), and he was elected to the House of Commons as the Member for Stockbridge, Hampshire, in 1713. Becoming embroiled in a vicious battle with the Tories, he issued *The Importance of Dunkirk Consider'd* and *The Crisis,* which actually brought about his expulsion from the House on

March 18, 1714, for "uttering seditious libels." In July the Bloomsbury Square house was let, and the Steeles took 26 St. James's Street, a big brick house opposite Park Place. Steele's political fortunes again rose with the accession of George I; he was then appointed deputy lieutenant for Middlesex and governor of the Drury Lane Theatre. He was returned to Parliament as the Member for Boroughbridge, Yorkshire, and was knighted in 1715. In the autumn Steele leased a "country" cottage on Paradise Row, Chelsea; this was a line of attractive 17th-century houses running from Flood Street to Burton's Court along what is now Royal Hospital Road. In the same period he also established a residence in York Buildings just south of the Strand.

On December 26, 1718, Steele's "dear and honoured" Prue died and was buried in Westminster Abbey. Steele continued his duties at the theater and in Parliament, but his health was failing, and in 1724 he retired to his late wife's estate in Carmarthen, Wales, where he died on September 1, 1729.

While the associations in London with Sir Richard Steele are overwhelming, they are not exclusively those of *The Tatler* and *The Spectator.* Steele had many residences in town: in 1707 he had lodgings on Great Smith Street, Westminster, and in 1712 and 1722 he had houses on Villiers Street in the Strand. The first house (1712), directly across from Number 43, had a concert room that could hold 200 people; the second (1722) was located closer to the Strand on the east side of the street. Steele also lived on Kensington Square. He was a member of the famous Kit-Cat Club, whose meetings were held regularly at the Upper Flask Inn on the east side of Heath Street, Hampstead (just south of the intersection of East Heath Road). He frequented the Devil Tavern, 1 Fleet Street, with Addison and Swift, and he could also be found at the Thatched House Tavern on St. James's Street, where Numbers 74–76 are today. In the ill-fated *The Lying Lover,* Steele explicitly refers to Pontack's, the "celebrated French eating house" on the eastern corner, where Abchurch Lane intersects Lombard Street; Latine states, "Your great supper lies on my stomach still. I defy Pontack to have prepared a better o' the sudden." Steele could also be found with Addison at Button's Coffee House, on the south side of Russell Street about two doors from Covent Garden, and at Shanley's Coffee House in Covent Garden; the fifth number of *The Lover* mentions these two and offers advice to new arrivals in the city:

> I think it necessary to assign particular places of resort to my young gentlemen as they come to town, who cannot expect to pop in at Button's on the first day. . . . I recommend it, therefore, to young men to frequent Shanley's some days before they take upon them to appear at Button's.

Many of the letters written to Prue were dated from London coffeehouses: George's Chocolate House, Pall Mall; Rolls Coffee House, Chancery Lane; and Tennis Court Coffee House, in the Cockpit, Whitehall, near Treasury Passage. Steele stayed at the Devil Tavern in Devil Tavern Yard, Charing Cross, not the tavern at Temple Bar which Ben Jonson and Samuel Pepys patronized. Finally, the Triumphant Chariot, in the space between Hamilton Place and the Pillars of Hercules (an inn at the western end of Piccadilly), was almost certainly the "petty tavern" where Steele and Richard Savage wrote a hurried pamphlet to sell for 2 guineas so they could have a meal.

The Tatler and *The Spectator,* of course, mention many places in London. Drury Lane, Steele writes:

is the only part of Great Britain where the tenure of vassalage is still in being. All that long course of buildings is under particular districts, or ladyships, after the manner of lordships in other parts, over which matrons of known abilities preside. . . . This seraglio of Great Britain is disposed into convenient alleys and apartments, and every house from the cellar to the garret is inhabited by nymphs of different orders, that persons of every rank may be accommodated.

Steele led his band of "Twaddlers" from Shire Lane to Dick's Coffee House (Richard's Coffee House), at the rear of 8 Fleet Street overlooking Hare Court, in the October 27, 1709, number:

[W]e marched down Sheer-lane, at the upper end of which I lodge. When we came to Temple-bar, sir Harry and sir Giles got over; but a run of the coaches kept the rest of us on this side of the street; however, we all at last landed, and drew up in very good order before Ben Tooke's shop, who favoured our rallying with great humanity; from whence we proceeded again, until we came to Dick's coffee-house. . . .

Steele also delighted in walking in Lincoln's Inn Gardens, which lay in front of the chapel in the inn precincts, and devoted space to them in *The Tatler* and later in *The Theatre.* The Trumpet, on Sheer Lane (Shire Lane), Temple Bar, is also included in *The Tatler:*

After having applied my Mind with more than ordinary Attention to my Studies, it is my usual Custom to relax and unbend it in the Conversation of such as are rather easy than shining Companions. . . . This is the particular Use I make of a Set of heavy honest Men . . . [whose] Conversation is a kind of Preparation for Sleep. . . . This I look upon as taking my first Nap before I got to Bed. The Truth of it is, I should think my self unjust to Posterity, as well as to the Society at the *Trumpet,* of which I am a Member, did not I in some Part of my Writings give an Account of the Persons among whom I have passed almost a Sixth Part of my Time for these last Forty Years.

The Royal Exchange, an enclosed shopping center under one roof on the Strand, was still a fashionable and tempting lounging place when Number 454 of *The Spectator* appeared:

[W]e came into the Centre of the City, and Centre of the World of Trade. the *Exchange* of *London.* As other Men in the Crowds about me were pleased with their Hopes and Bargains, I found my Account in observing them, in Attention to their several Interests. I, indeed, look'd upon my self as the richest Man that walk'd the *Exchange* that Day. . . . It was not the least of the Satisfactions in my Survey, to go up Stairs, and pass the Shops of agreeable Females; to observe so many pretty Hands busy in the Foldings of Ribbands, and the utmost Eagerness of agreeable Faces in the Sale of Patches, Pins, and Wires, on each Side the Counters. . . .

Nicholas Rowe (1674–1718)   The dramatist and Poet Laureate Nicholas Rowe first came to Highgate to the Free Grammar School, opposite the present Gatehouse Tavern; then, in 1688, he was elected a King's Scholar at the 14th-century Westminster School, in Little Dean's Yard. He entered the Middle Temple, off Fleet Street, and was called to the bar in 1696, but his father's death in 1692 provided him with sufficient income to leave a profession in which he had no interest and to begin a writing career. He continued to live in the Temple precincts, on Inner Temple Lane; the extremely political *Tamerlane* was produced in 1702 and was resurrected annually at the Drury Lane Theatre on November 5 (the date of William III's landing in England and of the Gunpowder Plot) until 1815. Other plays followed, but perhaps Rowe's chief accomplishment was his six-volume edition of Shakespeare's plays, *"revis'd and corrected,"* arrived at, he claimed, through a careful comparison of the various extant versions. Although his text contains many obvious errors, he did restore several scenes in *Hamlet, Romeo and Juliet, Henry V,* and *King Lear.* An ardent Whig, he frequented the Cocoa Tree Chocolate House on the south side of Pall Mall. Rowe held a number of government posts and finally achieved recognition when he was appointed Poet Laureate on August 1, 1715. The only identified residence of Rowe was on King Street, Covent Garden, where he died on December 6, 1718; he was buried in the Poets' Corner of Westminster Abbey, where there is an elaborate monument with an inscription by Alexander Pope.

George Farquhar (1678–1707)   The Irish dramatist George Farquhar has few associations with London, although his works were performed here. He appears to have come to the city from Dublin in (probably) 1697, and his first play, *Love and a Bottle,* was produced in December 1698 at Drury Lane; but where he lived and how he supported himself are unknown. Early in the next year Farquhar visited the Mitre Tavern (on the west corner of Old Mitre Court and Fleet Street), where he discovered Anne Oldfield, who was reading passages from Beaumont and Fletcher's *The Scornful Lady;* she ultimately "created" two of Farquhar's heroines, Silvia in *The Recruiting Officer* and Mrs. Sullen in *The Beaux' Stratagem.* Probably in 1703 he entered into an unfortunate marriage with a Yorkshire woman, who, it is said, "knowing that he was much too dissipated to think of matrimony unless advantage was annexed to it," let it be known that she had an income of £700 a year. In fact, she had nothing, but to Farquhar's

honour be it spoken, though he found himself deceived, and his circumstances embarrassed, yet he never once upbraided her for the cheat, but behaved to her with all the delicacy and tenderness of an indulgent husband.

The story is somewhat doubtful because of the irony involved, but the comments on divorce in *The Beaux' Stratagem* imply that Farquhar's experience with marriage was not altgether fortunate.

For two years nothing of Farquhar's appeared on the stage, but *The Recruiting Officer* opened in 1706 at Drury Lane, and its immediate success made it a stock piece of the company. Strained financially, Farquhar was promised a new commission if he sold his old one to pay his debts; the 2d Duke of Ormonde unfortunately was dilatory, and the dramatist's poverty became acute. Farquhar and his family were forced to give up their lodgings in York Buildings (a two-block area at the southeast angle of Villiers

Street and the Strand) when the commission did not arrive. They moved to the most miserable sort of back garret on St. Martin's Lane (between Long Acre and St. Martin's Place), where Robert Wilks, a fellow Irishman, found Farquhar in a state of considerable agitation. Wilks gave the family 20 guineas and exhorted Farquhar to write a new play: *The Beaux' Stratagem* was the result, but Farquhar fell ill while writing it and composed most of the play in bed. On April 29, 1707, supposedly the night of a benefit performance, Farquhar died and was buried, at the expense of Wilks, in the Church of St. Martin-in-the-Fields. Among Farquhar's papers was found a pitiful letter to Wilks:

> DEAR BOB,—I have not anything to leave thee to perpetuate my memory, but two helpless girls; look upon them sometimes, and think on him that was to the last moment of his life thine,
>
> G. Farquhar

The Constant Couple and *The Twin-Rivals* are full of references to London, and, indeed, the same places often occur in both plays. The Prologue to *The Constant Couple* mourns the loss of the Duke's Theatre in Dorset Garden:

> Ah, friends! Poor Dorset-Garden house is gone;
> Our merry meetings there are all undone....

This theater, at the southeast corner of John Carpenter Street, with its rather checkered existence, was patronized by the City rather than by the Court, as had been intended; by 1697 theatrical performances were only occasional, and on June 1, 1709, *The Daily Courant* carried a notice that "The Play House at Dorset Stairs is now pulling down" and that firewood was to be had cheap. Much of the play is set in "the Park," St. James's, and Standard invites Vizard to join him after the walk:

> [I]f your're my friend, meet me this evening at the Rummer; I'll pay my way....

The Rummer Tavern, at 45 Charing Cross, "two doors from Locket's, between Whitehall and Charing Cross," was kept by Samuel Prior, Matthew Prior's uncle. Sir Harry Wildair's question, "What lord has lately broke his fortune at the Groom-porter's?" refers to the groom porter, a court official, whose offices were in St. James's Palace; the chambers were a legalized resort for high-stake gambling, encouraged especially between Christmas and Epiphany. Both John Evelyn and Samuel Pepys came here to see the gambling. Part of Act IV of this play takes place in Covent Garden, and part of Act V is set in Newgate Prison, on the site of the Central Criminal Court building on Newgate Street. The Epilogue mentions the Rose Tavern, and Hippolito's and Locket's as places of resort after the theater:

> Now all depart, each his respective way,
> To spend an evening's chat upon the play;
> Some to Hippolito's; one homeward goes,
> And one with loving she retires to th' Rose,
> . . . .
> To coffee some retreat to save their pockets,
> Others, more generous, damn the play at Locket's;
> But there, I hope, the author's fears are vain,
> Malice ne'er spoke in generous champagne.

The Rose was on Russell Street, Covent Garden,

next to the Drury Lane Theatre; Locket's (Lockitt's) was on Charing Cross, two doors from the Rummer Tavern; and Hippolito's Coffee House was in Covent Garden.

In *The Twin-Rivals* Rosamond's Pond, where the Footman finds one of the ladies "paring her nails," was in the southwest corner of St. James's Park until it was filled up in 1770. The St. Alban's Tavern, on St. Alban's Street, Pall Mall, was "celebrated for political and fashionable dinners and meetings" throughout the 18th century.

Thomas Parnell (1679–1718) Irish-born Thomas Parnell, one of the earliest proponents of the night school, spent only brief periods in England. On one visit, in 1710, he lived on St. James's Place, where he was visited by Alexander Pope. Parnell was a member of the Scriblerus Club, which Jonathan Swift had formed. He came back to London in 1718 and met many of his old friends, including John Gay, before embarking on his return trip; however, he took ill in Chester, where he died.

Edward Young (1683–1765) Edward Young, author of *The Complaint, or Night-Thoughts on Life, Death and Immortality,* had little to do with London; and it is doubtful that he even attended the theater in Drury Lane when either *Busiris* or *Revenge* appeared. The first, a failure, was ridiculed rather harshly by Henry Fielding; the second had only a modest popularity. Appointed chaplain to George II in April 1728, he preached before the House of Commons on the martyrdom of Charles I in February 1729. Young at this time was living on his Oxford fellowship and a pension from Philip Wharton, Duke of Wharton. On May 27, 1731, he married Lady Elizabeth Lee at St. Mary-at-Hill Church; the Reverend Mr. Young was in London only occasionally after this date. He was, it should be noted, a frequent guest at Voltaire's lodgings at the White Perruke on the south side of Maiden Lane in 1727.

John Gay (1685–1732) Tracing John Gay's early life in London is extremely difficult; he came here from Barnstaple, Devonshire, around 1702 as an apprentice to a silk mercer on the Strand and remained until 1706, when he was released, probably on account of ill health. He was in London again in 1707 as Aaron Hill's amanuensis; becoming a part of the elite group formed by Jonathan Swift and the Scriblerus Club, he took to journalism and contributed to *The British Apollo,* a question-and-answer newspaper. In 1712 Gay became secretary to the elderly Duchess of Monmouth, who took over Monmouth House in Chelsea shortly before Gay left her employ in 1714. The house, where Gay lived for a short time, stood at the north end of Lawrence Street (where Number 16 now stands); *Rural Sports* appeared early in 1713, and *The Shepherd's Week* and "The Fan" in 1714. Gay was in Devonshire for part, if not all, of 1715, and *Trivia, or The Art of Walking the Streets of London* appeared in 1716.

Gay's first four plays, *The Wife of Bath, The What D'ye Call It, Three Hours after Marriage,* and *The Mohocks,* were not successful, and he was away from London until probably 1720. He must have been back when he gathered in £1,000 from the publication of two volumes of poetry and speculated (and lost) in South Sea stock. (He would sometimes stay with the 3rd Earl of Burlington in Piccadilly if he was not with the

Duchess of Queensberry at Douglas House off Peter-sham Road.) The volumes of poetry led Princess Caroline to invite Gay to Leicester House to read to her *The Captives*, a tragedy produced in 1724 at Drury Lane. Gay did little further literary work until January 29, 1728, when *The Beggar's Opera* opened at Lincoln's Inn Fields Theatre, on Portugal Street just about opposite Carey Street; the first four nights produced £693/13/6 for the author, and John Rich, the manager of the theater, received more than £4,000 for the first thirty-six performances. A note in Alexander Pope's *The Dunciad* summarized the success of the play:

> It was acted in London sixty-three days. . . . It spread into all the great towns of England. . . . It made its progress into Wales, Scotland, and Ireland, where it was performed twenty-four days together. It was lastly acted in Minores. The fame of it was not confin'd to the Author only. . . . The person who acted Polly, till then obscure, became all at once the favourite of the town; her Pictures were engraved and sold in great numbers; her Life written; books of Letters and Verses to her publish'd; and pamphlets made even of her Sayings and Jests.

Encouraged by such success, Gay prepared the sequel *Polly*, but the Lord Chamberlain forbade its production, probably because of the earlier caricature of Sir Robert Walpole and his Whig administration. Between January 1728 and the restriction of *Polly* late in the year Gay had lodgings in Whitehall, where he became seriously ill. The Duchess of Queensberry, who had been banished from court for soliciting subscriptions for *Polly* within the precincts of St. James, and the duke, who had resigned his court appointments in her support, undertook Gay's care here and at their seat in Amesbury, Wiltshire. Returning from Wiltshire in November 1732 to the Queensberrys' house on the southeast corner of Old Burlington Street, Gay "was attacked by an inflammatory fever" and died on December 4. He lay in state at Exeter Change (on the north side of the Strand between Burleigh and Southampton Streets) and was buried in the Poets' Corner of Westminster Abbey. The hearse bearing the body was trimmed in black and white feathers and was attended by three mourning coaches. Alexander Pope was one of the pallbearers. The Queensberrys erected a monument with an epitaph by Pope; at Gay's request the duke and duchess added the flippant,

> Life is a jest; and all things show it.
> I thought so once; but now I know it.

Gay frequented the Rose Tavern "by the playhouse" at the corner of Catherine and Russell Streets, Covent Garden, and it is often maintained that "Molly Mog, or The Fair Maid of the Inn" was intended as a compliment to a waitress here:

> Says my Uncle, I pray you discover
>   What hath been the cause of your woes,
> That you pine and you whine like a lover?
>   —I have seen *Molly Mog* of the *Rose*.

Mrs. Mary Mogg, a waitress here, is also associated with the Rose (still standing) in Wokingham, Berkshire, and that tavern often claims the distinction. Gay was often to be seen at Button's Coffee House, on the south side of Russell Street two doors from Covent Garden, and at White's Coffee House, at 69 St. James's Street. Finally, like so many other literary figures of the time, Gay was a regular visitor to Sir Isaac Newton's home and observatory at 35 St. Martin's Street.

Trivia is a walking catalog of early-18th-century London; Gay calls to William Fortescue "to leave the Temple's silent walls." They walk "through the long Strand," where the great town houses stood:

> Behold that narrow street which steep descends,
> Whose building to the slimy shore extends;
> Here Arundel's famed structure reared its frame;
> The street alone retains an empty name:
> . . . .
> Where statues breathed, the work of Phidias' hands,
> A wooden pump or lonely watch-house stands.
> There Essex' stately pile adorned the shore,
> There Cecil's, Bedford's, Villiers', now no more.

Villiers's residence was York House. In Piccadilly, Gay knew well Burlington House (now the Royal Academy, with additions to house the Royal Society, the Society of Antiquaries, the Linnean Society, the Chemical Society, the Geological Society, and the Astronomical Society):

> Yet Burlington's fair palace still remains;
> Beauty within, without porportion reigns.
> Beneath his eye declining art revives,
> The wall with animated picture lives;
> There Handel strikes the strings, the melting strain
> Transports the soul, and thrills through every vein;
> There oft I enter (but with cleaner shoes)
> For Burlington's beloved by every Muse.

Handel lived at Burlington House for three years. Some of the less desirable parts of London also are mentioned:

> Or who that rugged street would traverse o'er,
> That stretches, O Fleet Ditch, from thy black shore
> To the Tower's moated walls? Here steams ascend
> That in mixed fumes the wrinkled nose offend.
> Where chandlers' cauldrons boil, where fishy prey
> Hide the wet stall, long absent from the sea.
> And where the cleaver chops the heifer's spoil
> And where huge hogsheads sweat with trainy oil,
> Thy breathing nostril hold. . . .

The Seven Dials, seven streets radiating from a middle column set with seven sundials, was laid out in 1693 and became one of the worst criminal areas in London (Hogarth summed up its horror in *Gin Lane*); here, warns Gay:

> . . . do not thou, like that bold chief, confide
> Thy venturous footsteps to a female guide;
> She'll lead thee with delusive smiles along,
> Dive in thy fob, and drop thee in the throng.

A second disreputable area was Watling Street, behind St. Paul's, where no one would

> . . . the dangers share,
> When the broad pavement of Cheapside is near?

Another place to be avoided, he claims, is the Mews, on the site of Trafalgar Square and a well-known gamesters' district: "Pass by the Mews, nor try the thimble's cheats." More fashionable and reputable locations come into *Trivia*:

> O bear me to the paths of fair Pell Mell;
> Safe are thy pavements, grateful is thy smell!
> At distance rolls along the gilded coach,

Nor sturdy carmen on thy walks encroach;
No lets would bar thy ways were chairs denied,
The soft supports of laziness and pride....

And in winter with its "nitry wind" and "snow descend[ing] in flaky sheets"

At White's the harnessed chairman idly stands,
And swings around his waist his tingling hands:
The sempstress speeds to 'Change with red-tipped nose;
The Belgian stove beneath her footstool glows....

The 'Change, the covered shopping plaza on the Strand, was on a definite downward trend with space taken up by quack doctors and other charlatans and prostitutes plying their trade. In Covent Garden stands the "famous temple," St. Paul's Church

That boasts the work of Jones' immortal hands;
Columns with plain magnificence appear,
And graceful porches lead along the square....

A shoppers' directory is included:

Shall the large mutton smoke upon your boards?
Such Newgate's copious market best affords.
Wouldst thou with mighty beef augment thy meal?
Seek Leadenhall; St. James's sends thee veal.
Thames Street gives cheeses; Covent Garden fruits;
Moorfields old books; and Monmouth Street old suits.
Hence mayst thou well supply the wants of life,
Support thy family, and clothe thy wife.

Gay's publisher (and Alexander Pope's until a quarrel), Bernard Lintot, occupied 7 Fleet Street (now absorbed by Number 10), two doors beyond the gate to Middle Temple Lane, where Gay asks

...let my labours obvious lie,
Ranged on thy stall....

The Beggar's Opera is set entirely in London, many of the scenes being located in Newgate Prison, at the corner of Old Bailey and Newgate Streets and partly occupied today by the Central Criminal Court building. Macheath is lodged in Newgate, where Lockit directs him to "Hand me down those fetters there" because Macheath knows "the custom." Tyburn, the public hanging site, near Marble Arch on the southside of Bayswater Road (marked by a tablet), is where Macheath is to be executed:

Since laws were made, for every degree,
To curb vice in others, as well as me.
I wonder we han't better company
    Upon Tyburn tree.
But gold from law can take out the sting;
And if rich men, like us, were to swing,
'Twould thin the land, such numbers to string
    Upon Tyburn tree.

Actually, modern research has revealed that the gallows (removed in 1783 when the official execution site was changed to Newgate) stood exactly at the northwest curb of Bayswater and Edgeware Roads. Hockley-in-the-Hole, a notorious bull- and bear-baiting garden and Marybone (Marylebone) are mentioned as places where Fitch should go "to learn valour." The flowers in Covent Garden were already well known:

But when once plucked 'tis no longer alluring,
To Covent Garden 'tis sent (as yet sweet),
There fades, and shrinks, and grows past all enduring,
Rots, stinks, and dies, and is trod under feet.

Alexander Pope (1688–1744)   Another of London's many native writers was Alexander Pope, who was born on May 21, 1688, in a house at the bottom of Plough Court facing Lombard Street. Pope's father, a linen draper, retired from business the year his son was born and soon moved his family to Binfield, Berkshire. After private tutoring at home and a disagreeable but short time at school in Twyford, Hampshire, Pope was placed in a school here run by Thomas Deane; the school was first located in Marylebone and then near Hyde Park Corner. In this latter location, thought to be what later became Down Street, Pope claimed to have composed the juvenile play based on John Ogilby's translation of the *Iliad*. Pope maintained that at the age of twelve he first visited Will's Coffee House in Covent Garden and met John Dryden, but this seems unlikely and is possibly just another of the exaggerations in which he indulged in his later years. He left school in 1700 for Binfield, where he studied on his own; he returned to London in 1703 to study French and Italian. Pope contended that his physical condition, including a curvature of the spine, was caused by excessive study rather than by (probably) Pott's Disease; his full-grown height was 4 feet 6 inches, and his deformity left him extremely sensitive to pain.

By 1706, when *Pastorals* was in print, Pope was introduced to town life by William Wycherley, forty-eight years his senior. Pope blamed the 1710 breach between the two on Wycherley's taking offense at the young poet's frank criticism of the old man's work and, in fact, altered letters to prove his point; the genuine letters have since proved Pope's inversion of the truth. Around 1712 the painter Charles Jervas put Bridgewater House (at the western end of Cleveland Row where Cleveland Square is now located) at Pope's disposal, and for more than five years Pope wrote here and studied painting. By the end of 1712 he knew Addison, Congreve, Gay, Swift, Arbuthnot, and Thomas Parnell and probably had met all of them at Will's Coffee House, 1 Bow Street. On other visits to the City, Pope stayed with the 3d Earl of Peterborough on Bolton Street and with the 1st Earl Bathurst on St. James's Square; at one time he owned a house on Berkeley Square (where Number 9 now stands) to be near the 3d Earl of Burlington, and he was a constant visitor to Burlington House (now the Royal Academy of Arts) in Piccadilly. Pope visited Martha and Teresa Blount, who lived on Bolton Street, just west of Pope's Berkeley Square residence, and on Wellbeck Street and, indeed, left his Berkeley Square house to Martha, who died there in 1762. Pope also once had lodgings "at Mr. Digby's, next door to the Golden Bull," on the west side of St. James's Street.

In the company of Matthew Prior and John Gay, he visited John Sheffield, Duke of Buckingham, at Buckingham House (superseded by Buckingham Palace); upon the duchess's death the house passed to John, Lord Hervey, whom Pope makes into Sporus, "this bug with gilded wings," in *An Epistle to Dr. Arbuthnot*. Dr. John Arbuthnot's house, where Pope often could be found, was at 11 Cork Street; court physician and creator of John Bull, Arbuthnot is probably best remembered as the addressee in Pope's *Epistle*:

P. Shut, shut the door, good John! fatigued, I said;
Tie up the knocker, say I'm sick, I'm dead.

The Dog Star rages! nay 'tis past a doubt,
All Bedlam, or Parnassus, is let out. . . .

Pope frequented the Fountain Coffee House on the Strand (probably Number 101), and from Howel's Coffee House on Wild Street he writes, "In the town it is ten to one, but a young fellow may find his strayed heart again, with some Wild Street or Drury Lane damsel." He also went to Button's Coffee House, on the south side of Russell Street about two doors from Covent Garden, and Tom's Coffee House, on Devereux Court near Temple Bar; the latter was run by Thomas Twining, founder of the house of Twining, which still is trading at 216 the Strand. White's Chocolate House, at 69 St. James's Street, comes into *The Dunciad:*

　　　　　　　. . . Still, still remain
Cibberian forehead, and Cibberian brain.
. . . .
This mess, tossed up of Hockley Hole and White's;
Where dukes and butchers join to wreathe my crown,
At once the bear and fiddle of the town.

Hockley Hole, not far from Clerkenwell Green, was an amphitheater for bear- and bull-baiting. In the same poem Pope mentions the Fleet Ditch; immediately west of Blackfriars Bridge, the Fleet, which ran into the Thames, was a broad and limpid stream rising in the high ground of Hampstead and was fed by numerous wells (for example, Clerken-well):

　　　　　　　. . . By Bridewell all descend,
(As morning prayer and flagellation end),
To where Fleet Ditch, with disemboguing streams,
Rolls the large tribute of dead dogs to Thames. . . .

The Ring in Hyde Park (much smaller than the present Ring Road) was once the fashionable place to be seen; Pope mentions it in *On the Characters of Women: An Epistle to a Lady* and writes to Martha Blount:

She glares in balls, front-boxes, and *the Ring*,
A vain, unquiet, glittering, wretched thing.

The Devil Tavern, at 1 Fleet Street, (frequented by Ben Jonson and by Pepys, Addison, Steele, and Swift), comes into *The Dunciad* and in *The First Epistle of the Second Book of Horace: To Augustus* with regard to Jonson, who "swears the Muses met him at the Devil." In a much lighter vein Pope writes of John Moore, the inventor of worm powder:

Oh learned friend of Abchurch Lane
Who sett'st our entrails free!
Vain is thy art, thy powder vain,
Since worms shall e'en eat thee.

Indeed, virtually no place in London escapes inclusion in Pope's works (Duck Lane, the Church of St. Mary-le-Bow, the Royal Mint, Bedlam, Soho, Smithfield, and Tyburn are but a few), and "A Farewell to London" reflects the generosity of Burlington:

Luxurious lobster-nights, farewell,
　For sober studious days,
And Burlington's delicious meal,
　For salads, tarts, and peas.

Finally, Henry St. John, 1st Viscount Bolingbroke, to whom Pope dedicated *An Essay on Man*—

Awake; my St. John! leave all meaner things
To low ambition, and the pride of kings.

—had a house on Golden Square where Pope and Swift both dined.

From George I to Victoria　Hanoverian London was probably the largest city in the world; it was a congested and bewildering place although parts had been carefully planned after the Great Fire. Political strife was not over even though the Act of Settlement had assured the succession of the house of Hanover, and within a year of George I's succession, both Henry St. John, 1st Viscount Bolingbroke, and James Butler, 2d Duke of Ormonde, fled to France, where the Old Pretender's court was planning an invasion of Britain. The Septennial Act (1716) allowed the Whigs to gather strength, but the leadership of Robert Walpole was short-lived because of dissension in Whig ranks. James, 1st Earl Stanhope, brought about both an effective party reconciliation and one between the King and the Prince of Wales, whose interests were felt to be reversionary.

Walpole resumed office in the summer of 1721 after the bursting of the South Sea Bubble. The South Sea Company had been granted extensive trading privileges in return for a payment of £7 million and the assumption of three-fifths of the national debt. While the scheme was not entirely witless, the speculation was, and the whole thing came down in September 1720. Another crisis arose in the mid-1720s, when William Wood, an ironmaster from Wolverhampton, Staffordshire, was granted a patent for debased coinage for Ireland. The furor continued for two years, with Jonathan Swift attacking the plan vigorously before Walpole revoked the patent. After the accession in 1727 of George II (for the first time since Anne's death, the sovereign spoke English), Walpole continued with a remarkably effective government; he lowered import duties to stimulate British manufacturing and proved that prosperity was viable even with a national debt. However, relations with continental Europe deteriorated, and the episode of Jenkins's Ear forced Walpole into a war against Spain. Indeed, Walpole's time was running out, and his resignation in 1742 left England in rather poor shape militarily.

During the immediately following years, one government succeeded another, only to founder; dissension again broke out in the Whig party, with William Pitt doing obeisance to the Prince of Wales and the all-too-common 18th-century concern of reversionary interest reemerging. The conflict was eliminated when Prince Frederick predeceased George II, and Pitt, ever mindful of his political situation, returned to the King's fold. England became peaceful and prosperous, the War of the Austrian Succession concluded with the Treaty of Aix-la-Chapelle, the annual budget was down to about £2,500,000, and the Gregorian calendar was adopted; one major blot on the Whig leadership was sustained in 1753, when the government denied Jews the right of naturalization.

By 1753, though, Anglo-French conflict had begun in North America, and the new government, which rushed to conclude a set of pro-Austrian treaties, actually precipitated the Seven Years' War. Naval supremacy became an urgent concern, and by 1763 Great Britain had become a major sea power. In the interim George II died, and to the throne came his twenty-two-year-old grandson George III, who wanted to end the "bloody and expensive war." The usual postwar problems—a large national debt and heavy taxation—were among Britain's most pressing concerns; the King surrounded himself with younger and less astute men, and within five years two governments went down; the second had the honor of putting through both the 1764 Sugar Act and the 1765 Stamp Act.

American independence soon followed, and the ensuing war involved France and Spain. There were also problems in India, and, indeed, it was partly a trade concession to the East India Company that helped bring about the Boston Tea Party. The pressure of increased taxation and higher government spending and the Gordon Riots combined to topple the government in 1782; moreover, a movement for reform was on its way as England moved into its industrial revolution. A coalition government faltered, and the younger William Pitt was called on to form a minority government. His time was not an easy one, but he held on tenaciously. When his government passed a bill adding 100 Irish seats to the Commons and creating twenty-eight peers, the King rejected it because of opposition to Catholicism. Pitt formed another government three years later, and the Battle of Trafalgar ensured that England could not be invaded.

With Pitt's death in 1806, George III was forced to accept another coalition government, which led Parliament through the abolition of the slave trade the next year. A new government foundered over the appropriate military stance, and when Napoleon resorted to economic sanctions against Britain (all but stopping the Continental trade) and the Americans boycotted British goods, unemployment in England reached a peak. However, 1813 saw an improvement militarily, and the Battle of Waterloo brought a successful conclusion to this period in June 1815.

Possibly the most significant events at this time concern the effect of the industrial revolution; the upheavals, while not particularly dramatic, altered every facet of English life. As the revolution took root in the north and the Midlands, the face of London changed drastically, mostly because long-established trades moved out of the metropolis to seek cheaper labor and to be closer to raw materials. While London's eminence as a manufacturing center declined, its position as an international port and trade center was enhanced. At the beginning of the 19th century perhaps one-quarter of its population was connected in some way with the port and its activities; by the end of the century, the country was exporting more than £7 million of goods and importing almost £6 million. Even earlier Daniel Defoe had commented on the volume of shipping in *A Tour thro' the Whole Island of Great Britain*:

> That Part of the River *Thames* which is properly the Harbour, and where the Ships usually deliver or unload their Cargoes, is called the *Pool*.... In this Compass I have had the Curiosity to count the Ships as well as I could, *en passant*, and have found above Two thousand Sail of all Sorts, not reckoning Barges, Lighters or Pleasure-Boats, and Yatchs; but of Vessels that really go to Sea.
>
> It is true, the River or Pool, seem'd, at that time, to be pretty full of Ships; it is true also, that I included the Ships which lay in *Deptford* and *Black-Wall* Reaches, and in the Wet Docks....

Later, London lost ground to Liverpool (built to take care of the burgeoning textile industry in the Midlands) and Newcastle upon Tyne. Brokerage firms set up their headquarters here, and trading companies often had their central offices in the metropolis. Even more significant, at least in the long run, was the advent of firms dealing in marine insurance, which by mid-century made London the insurance capital of Europe. Lloyd's first list of ships appeared in 1734; its famous register appeared in 1765, and its specialist underwriting (the first in England) began in the 1780s. Banks branched out into the Midlands as the industrial revolution took hold, and this plus the establishment of a clearinghouse in 1775 made the City the world's leading financial center.

The end of the Napoleonic Wars, though, produced an all-too-common condition: a postwar debt, inflation, and unemployment. Parliament in 1815 was controlled by agricultural interests, which jammed through the protectionist Corn Law; industrial and general discontent was inevitable. The reign of George IV saw the reduction of import duties, a new sliding scale for the fixed Corn Law, and the beginning of law reform under Sir Robert Peel. Serious dissension in Ireland since 1801 on the question of Catholic emancipation forced the government to try to pass an act of emancipation. The passage of the bill in 1829 and the death of George in 1830 combined with an ill-conceived stance against constitutional reform to bring down the government. It was time for reform, and the result was the Whig Reform Bill, which was introduced in 1831. But passage was difficult, and the bill enacted in 1832 did not offer complete reform: representation still did not reflect the population. The Whigs, however, carried on, ending slavery in British colonies, passing the New Poor Law, which provided for a national board in London, granting governmental powers to large but previously unincorporated industrial areas, and turning to problems of health and education.

Samuel Richardson (1689–1761) Much of Samuel Richardson's early life is bathed in obscurity, but he was in London with his family by 1698, when they lived in the area of Tower Hill, either in St. Botolph's parish, Aldgate, within the limits of the City, or in the Liberty of Smithfield. By 1700 the Richardson family was living on Mouse Alley, which ran south from East Smithfield to what is now St. Katherine's Docks. Traditionally Richardson has been thought to have been uneducated, but it is now believed that he had some education at either Christ's Hospital or the Merchant Taylors' School on Suffolk Lane. At the latter there is a record of a Samuel Richardson entering the second form in 1701 and advancing to the third before leaving in 1702, and this well could have been the novelist since his father's financial difficulties would account for the boy's removal. In 1703 the family moved to Rosemary Lane (gone), inside the City near the Minories and immediately north of the Tower of London, and in 1706 the seventeen-year-old apprenticed himself to a printer, John Wilde, for a period of seven years. The term expired on July 2, 1713, and by July 13, 1715, he had become a freeman of the company and a citizen of London.

Not until 1721, the year in which he joined James Leake in the printing business and rented a house the printer had previously leased in Salisbury

Square, is Richardson heard of here again. That year he married Martha Wilde, the daughter of his former master; of the six children born to the couple between 1722 and 1730, not one survived infancy. Richardson's wife died on January 23, 1731, and was buried in a family vault at St. Bride's Church. In February 1733 Richardson married Elizabeth Leake, by whom he had six children, four daughters surviving him. He remained in the Salisbury Square area the rest of his life, taking a house across from the first in 1728, another farther down the square in 1734, and in 1736 a larger house on the northwest corner of the square, where he lived almost twenty years. Suffering from some sort of nervous disorder which plagued him for the rest of his life, he found a country house a necessity, and in 1738 he leased 40 North End Crescent, North End Road, in Fulham. Here in the three-story brown-brick house Richardson's writing career began; on his weekend trips most of *Pamela, or Virtue Rewarded, Clarissa, or The History of a Young Lady*, and *The History of Sir Charles Grandison* were composed, often in the garden. Richardson entertained many literary figures, especially at the Fulham house; Edward Young stayed with the publisher-novelist on his trips from Welwyn, Hertfordshire, and Dr. Johnson and Boswell were frequently here. Boswell relates:

> One day at his country house at Northend, where a large company was assembled at dinner, a gentleman who was just returned from Paris, willing to please Mr. Richardson, mentioned to him a very flattering circumstance,—that he had seen his Clarissa lying on the King's brother's table. Richardson observing that part of the company were engaged in talking to each other, affected then not to attend to it; but by and by when there was a general silence, and he thought that the flattery might be fully heard, he addressed himself to the gentleman, "I think, Sir, you were saying something about,"— pausing in a high flutter of expectation. The gentleman provoked at his inordinate vanity, resolved not to indulge it, and with an exquisitely sly air of indifference answered, "A mere trifle, Sir, not worth repeating."

In 1754 the landlord of the Fulham house raised the rent from £25 a year to £40, and Richardson moved to 247 King's Road, in nearby Parson's Green. Facing the green, the house, which tradition maintained was once the dower house of Catherine of Aragon, was in sore need of repair, and the garden was badly neglected. Richardson, curiously, spent more than £300 in repairs almost immediately. His printing establishment prospered over these years, but in 1752 an apprentice accidentally set fire to the building, and instead of rebuilding the severely damaged premises Richardson built new facilities on the north side of White Lion Court, which ran north into Fleet Street. Richardson suffered a stroke on June 28, 1761, and died at his Parson's Green home on July 4; he was buried in the center aisle of St. Bride's Church. St. Bride's, gutted during the 1940 bombing, has been restored to Sir Christopher Wren's original plans; the Richardson monument actually survived the bombing, and an unusual story is associated with it. It is said that an American scholar specializing in Richardson was in London right after the war and visited St. Bride's; finding the coffins and corpses all stacked on one side, ready for reinterment when the rebuilding was complete, he searched for the novelist's body and touched him on the nose.

Richard Savage (1697?–1743)   At best the life and circumstances of Richard Savage are tangled; by his own account he was the natural son of Richard Savage, 4th Earl Rivers, by Anne, Countess of Macclesfield. What is known from parish records at St. Andrew's Church, Holborn Viaduct, is that a child was baptized as Richard Smith on January 18, 1697, with Newdigate and Dorothea Ousley as godparents and Lord Rivers in attendance. This child was placed in the care of a baker and his wife in Covent Garden. Dr. Johnson's *An Account of the Life of Mr Richard Savage* says that Lady Macclesfield held her son in contempt, even though she had openly proclaimed her adultery to secure a divorce, and that she used every means available to keep the child in abject poverty:

> [H]is father, the Earl Rivers, was seized with a distemper which in a short time put an end to his life. He had frequently inquired after his son, and . . . on his deathbed . . . demanded a positive account of him, with an importunity not to be diverted or denied. His mother, who could no longer refuse an answer, determined at least to give such as should cut him off for ever from that happiness which competence affords, and therefore declared that he was dead. . . .
>
> The Earl did not imagine there could exist in a human form a mother that would ruin her son without enriching herself, and therefore bestowed upon some other person 6000*l.* which he had in his will bequeathed to Savage.

It was the death of his nurse, a Mrs. Lloyd, whose effects Savage examined, which precipitated the discovery of his true mother. Not until November 1715, when he was taken into custody for writing treasonous (Jacobite) doggerel, is there any real information about Savage. He was probably placed in the Fleet Prison, roughly the site of the Congregational Memorial Hall on Fleet Lane. His release came quickly, and other verses, such as *The Convocation*, and plays, such as *Love in a Veil*, followed; Savage, though, was impecunious, and his choice of companions was open to question, although such literary figures as Alexander Pope and Sir Richard Steele frequently came to his rescue.

For some part of this period Savage lodged in Richmond; and on November 20, 1727, he and two drinking companions, Merchant and Gregory, "went . . . to a neighbouring coffee-house, and sat drinking till it was late, it being in no time of Mr. Savage's life any part of his character to be the first of the company that desired to separate." At Robinson's Coffee House in Charing Cross, "Merchant with some rudeness demanded a room," only to be told a good fire was blazing in the next partition, "which the company were about to leave." For some reason the answer was unsatisfactory; Johnson continues:

> Merchant . . . rushed into the room, and . . . soon after kicked down the table. This produced a quarrel, swords were drawn on both sides, and one Mr. James Sinclair was killed. Savage, having likewise wounded a maid that held him, forced his way with Merchant out of the house[;] . . . they were taken in a back court. . . .
>
> Being secured and guarded that night, they were in the morning carried before three justices, who committed them to the Gatehouse [at Westminster], from whence, upon the death of Mr. Sinclair, which happened the same day, they were removed in the night to Newgate. . . .

The question was whether Savage's act was one of

self-defense, and the evidence was contradictory. Sinclair had so sworn on his deathbed, and Savage never denied running his sword through Sinclair but claimed self-defense; on the other hand, one prosecution witness claimed Sinclair was unarmed, while another claimed that the point of Sinclair's sword was "towards the ground" when Savage struck. The trial concluded with "Mr. Page's. . .eloquent harangue":

> "Gentlemen of the jury, you are to consider that Mr. Savage is a very great man, a much greater man than you or I, gentlemen of the jury; that he wears very fine clothes, much finer clothes than you or I, gentlemen of the jury; that he has abundance of money in his pocket, much more money than you or I, gentlemen of the jury; but, gentlemen of the jury, is it not a very hard case, gentlemen of the jury, that Mr. Savage should therefore kill you or me, gentlemen of the jury?"

Sentenced to death by the notorious hanging judge, Savage had only the hope of a royal pardon, and this his mother, it is said, did everything possible to prevent. He was imprisoned at Newgate Prison, on the east side of Old Bailey, facing Newgate Street, and the intercession of Frances Thynne, Countess of Hertford, brought about his pardon on March 9, 1728. It is noteworthy that Sir Francis Page later "confessed that he had treated him [Savage] with uncommon rigour."

Following his release, Savage was given living accommodations on Arlington Street, by Lord Tyrconnel. Tyrconnel, nephew of Savage's mother, was possibly attempting to rectify some of the wrongs done to the poet and, indeed, received him "into his family, treated him as his equal, and engaged to allow him a pension of 200*l.* a year." For a time it looked as if all would go well for the "unfortunate Savage," but eventually he and Tyrconnel became estranged, and Savage's fortunes fell; he left London with sufficient money raised through subscription to live for a year in Wales but apparently squandered all but a few pence in a week in Bristol, where he died in the debtors' prison in 1743. *London and Bristol Compar'd* was written in prison there:

> Now silver *Isis* bright'ning flows along,
> Echoing from *Oxford's* Shore each classic Song;
> Then weds with *Tame*; and these, O *London*, see
> Swelling with naval Pride, the Pride of Thee!
> Wide deep unsullied *Thames* meand'ring glides
> And bears thy Wealth on mild majestic Tides.

John Dyer (1699–1758)   The author of "Grongar Hill," John Dyer was educated here at the Westminster School before being placed in his father's law office.

James Thomson (1700–1748)   Though a Scot by birth, James Thomson, author of *The Seasons,* spent most of the last twenty-three years of his life in the London and Richmond areas. Educated in Scotland and destined for the church, Thomson refused to enter the ministry and decided on a literary career. Armed with letters of reference, supposedly tied in a handkerchief, he arrived in London in late February 1725 and promptly had his pocket picked as he wandered around; the letters, however, were not much missed, and he stayed for a time at Montrose House on Hanover Square. Thomson's means were inadequate for such a life, and he became tutor to Charles, Lord Binning's son Thomas Hamilton, in East Barnet,

Hertfordshire. The post was of short duration, and Thomson returned, perhaps to 30 Charing Cross, the home of the bookseller John Millan. He was already working on "Winter," and three coffeehouses claim the distinction of being the place of composition. The Dane Coffee House, between the Upper and Lower Malls in Hammersmith, is one such claimant, as is the Dover Coffee House, whose only location is Hammersmith. The third is the Doves Coffee House, described in 1740 as "just over the High Bridge and at the commencement of the Upper Mall" in Hammersmith. The Doves (Dove) Inn still exists between Sussex House and the river. It seems well within reason to assume these inns are the same and only the name has changed over the years.

"Winter" appeared in March 1726, probably the same year in which Thomson acted as a tutor at "Mr. Watt's Academy in Little Tower Street" (now Tower Street). He moved almost directly across from the Admiralty when he was working on "Summer," which was probably almost completed in this house, seven or eight doors down from the corner. Thomson later took a house in Lancaster Court (no longer extant, but it led from the Strand pretty much where Lancaster Place and Wellington Street now lie) and for a period received his mail "at the Lancaster Coffee House, Lancaster Court in the Strand, London." "Spring" was issued in 1728, and "Autumn" first appeared in the completed work *The Seasons* in 1730.

In the autumn of 1730 Thomson decided to quit London, although he retained his Lancaster Court apartment until 1736, when he moved to a cottage in Richmond, Surrey. He died there on August 27, 1748, and was buried in the Richmond parish church; there is a memorial to Thomson in the Poets' Corner of Westminster Abbey. At least three other London coffeehouses are associated with the poet: Long's, on Queen Square, Westminster; Man's, near Charing Cross, where on September 13, 1736, he and one other "were admitted Free Masons at Old Man's Coffee House, Charing Cross"; and the Smyrna (Smirna) Coffee House, 59 the Strand, where subscriptions for *The Seasons* were accepted.

David Mallett (1705–1765)   The Scottish-born David Mallett (changed from Malloch in 1724 because "there is not one Englishman that can pronounce it") first arrived in London in August 1723 on his way to taking a post as tutor to the Duke of Montrose's sons in Hampshire. He was here frequently after *Eurydice* was performed at Drury Lane in 1730–1731, and although he continued to write steadily for the theater, he did not achieve any notable success until the revised version of *Alfred* (a masque written with James Thomson). A man of dubious reputation, who Dr. Johnson said "had talents enough to keep his literary reputation alive so long as he himself lived," Mallett lived somewhere on Arlington Street in 1746–1747 and from 1758 until his death on April 21, 1765, at 7 St. George Street. He was buried in St. George's Cemetery, South Audley Street, but there is no monument.

Henry Fielding (1707–1754)   Henry Fielding had a long association with London in various capacities; he seems first to have been in the City around 1728, when his *Love in Several Masques* was played at the Drury Lane Theatre before he went off to study classics at the University of Leiden, where he stayed only a short time because of financial problems. He returned to London by February 1730, "having no choice," he said, "but to be a hackney-writer or a hackney coachman." Fielding had married Charlotte Cradock in Charlcombe, Somerset, in November 1734, and the two lived rather extravagantly for some time in East Stour, Dorset. When they returned to London in 1736, they probably lived on Buckingham Street in the Strand with some of her relatives, while Fielding took to playwriting again and managed the Haymarket Theatre. He opened his tenure with the highly successful *Pasquin: A Dramatick Satire on the Times,* which attacked current political corruption. The attack, of course, fueled the government's opposition to freedom in the theater, and in 1737, when Fielding followed *Pasquin* with *The Historical Register for the Year 1736,* in which Sir Robert Walpole, undisguised, is mercilessly attacked, Walpole retaliated by pushing through Parliament the new Licensing Act. The legislation put an end to Fielding's work; he entered the Middle Temple and was called to the bar on June 20, 1740. The same day the benchers of the Inn assigned him chambers at 4 Pump Court, east of Middle Temple Lane. Up three flights of stairs, the chambers, which Fielding retained for life, were low-ceilinged with paneled walls, and the windows of the sitting room and bedroom looked out on the buildings of Brick Court.

During this period Fielding published *The History of the Adventures of Joseph Andrews and of His Friend Mr. Abraham Adams;* and in 1743 he produced *The Life of Mr. Jonathan Wild the Great,* a notorious criminal who was finally hanged; Wild lived at 68 Old Bailey. This was not an especially happy period in the novelist's life: not only was he in financial difficulties and badly crippled with gout, but his daughter Charlotte was dying from some unspecified ailment, and his wife, he said, was "in a condition very little better." Charlotte, "one of the very loveliest creatures ever seen," died in February 1742 and was buried at St. Martin-in-the-Fields. Concerned with his wife's health, Fielding took her to Bath in the autumn of 1744 to take the waters; there she died shortly after their arrival and was buried in London in the chancel vault of St. Martin-in-the-Fields. Fielding then took up residence in Beaufort Buildings with his daughter, his sister Sarah, and Mary Daniel, his wife's maid. (The 17th-century Beaufort Buildings, just about opposite Exeter Street, surrounded a courtyard and communicated with the Strand by a long, narrow passage.) In November 1747, amid much derision, Fielding married his first wife's maid at the Church of St. Benet on Paul's Wharf, a small passageway between Queen Victoria Street and Upper Thames Street. He told friends he could find no better mother for his children or nurse for himself, and the marriage was extremely successful; she fulfilled, he said,

> excellently well her own, and all the tender offices becoming the female character . . . besides being a faithful friend, an amiable companion, and a tender nurse.

Their first child was christened in February 1748 but died within ten months and was buried at St. Paul's Church, Covent Garden; two other children (both girls) were later baptized in the same church.

Fielding, in the meantime, had thrown himself into the fray against the Stuart pretender to the throne and edited two separate weeklies from 1745 to 1747 in defense of the house of Hanover. His reward came quickly, for in December 1748 he was made justice of the peace for Westminster and took up a new residence at Magistrate's House, 19–20 Bow Street; later he became magistrate for Middlesex as well. It is said that Fielding was one of the two best justices in the 18th century; the other was his half brother, Sir John Fielding. The office was unpaid, and previous magistrates had supported themselves through fees and bribes. Fielding worked hard against corruption and successfully reduced the "income" of the office, he said,

> by composing, instead of inflaming, the quarrels of porters and beggars . . . and by refusing to take a shilling from a man . . . I had reduced an income of about £500 a year of the dirtiest money upon earth, to little more than £300. . . .

He was instrumental in ending what were termed "common" riots and prison break-ins (to effect the release of prisoners) and spent his entire Bow Street life as a social reformer; he began the "Bow Street Runners" (men who aided the meager police force as thief takers and did much to improve police and magistrate relations with the public), which eventually evolved into the Metropolitan Police.

The History of Tom Jones, a Foundling appeared in 1749; *Amelia* followed in 1751. Fielding was suffering from deteriorating health; so bad was his gout that he was frequently unable to walk, even though his legs were wrapped in bandages, and had to take to a wheelchair. He was ordered to Bath just when the 1st Duke of Newcastle prevailed upon him to draft a proposal to suppress "those murders and robberies which were every day committed in the streets"; Fielding thus remained in London over the winter, and asthma and dropsy were added to his gout. In May 1754 he and his family moved to Fordhook Avenue in then-suburban Acton, which was known for its mineral spa, but in June Fielding was finally persuaded to seek a warmer climate and left for Portugal. For a short time he seemed to benefit from the change, but he died in Lisbon on October 8 and was buried in the British Cemetery. Fielding frequented the Shakespeare Head Tavern (gone) in Covent Garden and Tom's Coffee House (gone) at 8 Russell Street, Covent Garden, and mentioned Garraway's Coffee House (gone), 3 Exchange Alley, off Cornhill, in *Amelia.* Fielding lived for a short time on Essex Street and is commemorated by a plaque on Essex Hall.

Specific London locations are extensive in Fielding's three major works, and there are many references to well-known contemporaries. Tom Jones's arrival in the metropolis is described:

> But Jones . . . was an entire stranger in London; and as he happened to arrive first in a quarter of the town the inhabitants of which have very little intercourse with the householders of Hanover or Grosvenor Square (for he entered through Gray's Inn Lane), so he rambled about some time before he could even find his way to those happy mansions where fortune segregates from the vulgar . . . but the peer unluckily quitted his former house when he went for Ireland . . . so that, after a successless inquiry till the clock had struck eleven, Jones at last yielded to the advice of Partridge, and retreated to the Bull and Gate in Holborn, that being the inn where he had first alighted. . . .

Tom's entrance into London via Gray's Inn Lane was in the region of King's Cross; once called Portpool Lane, it was a squalid area running from Holborn to King's Road (now Theobalds Road) and Liquorpond Street (now Clerkenwell Road). The Bull and Gate Inn was on the west side of Lincoln's Inn Fields, just east of Little Turnstile Street. Most of the rest of this part of the novel takes place in London, more specifically in Westminster. Tom begs off an invitation "to dinner at the tavern" from Mr. Nightingale on the ground that "his clothes . . . were not yet come to town":

> To confess the truth, Mr. Jones . . . had not one penny in his pocket; a situation in much greater credit among the ancient philosophers than among the modern wise men who live in Lombard Street, or those who frequent White's chocolate-house.

With Mr. Nightingale, Tom attends the masquerade in search of Sophia; they

> arrived at that temple where Heydegger, the great Arbiter Deliciarum, the great high-priest of pleasure, presides. . . .

The masquerades put on by George II's master of the revels were held at the Haymarket Opera House (Her Majesty's Theatre on Haymarket). Nightingale escapes from old Mr. Nightingale and marries Nancy:

> [T]he mother, Mr. Jones, Mr. Nightingale, and his love stepped into a hackney-coach which conveyed them to Doctors' Common; where Miss Nancy was, in vulgar language, soon made an honest woman, and the poor mother became, in the purest sense of the word, one of the happiest of all human beings.

The Doctors' Common was an area near St. Paul's Church where marriage licenses could be secured for a civil ceremony, and there was a chapel here as well. Jones resides on Bond Street, "in a very reputable house, and in a very good part of town." Squire Western, searching for Sophia, lodges

> in Piccadilly, where he was placed by the recommendation of the landlord at the Hercules Pillars at Hyde Park Corner; for at the inn, which was the first he saw on his arrival in town, he placed his horses, and in those lodgings, which were the first he heard of, he deposited himself.

This famous coaching inn, standing just next to Apsley House at the western end of Piccadilly, is where Sophia is brought and locked in her room "with no other company than what attend the closest state prisoner, namely, fire and candle." Other places mentioned in the novel are Bridewell, Exchange Alley, Tyburn, Billingsgate ("that gate, which seems to derive its name from a duplicity of tongues"), Grub Street, Will's Coffee House (1 Bow Street in Covent Garden), Button's Coffee House (Russell Street, "on the south side about two doors from Covent Garden"), and Newgate Prison.

Joseph Andrews also uses London and the immediate environs; Joseph is brought to the city with Lady Booby before the death of Sir Thomas and promptly becomes involved with fashionable things: "His hair was cut after the newest fashion"; "he applied most of his leisure hours to music"; "he behaved with less seeming devotion" when "he attended his lady at church (which was but seldom)"; "but his morals remained entirely uncorrupted":

> She would now walk out with him into Hyde Park in a morning, and when tired, which happened almost every minute, would lean on his arm, and converse with him in great familiarity. Whenever she stept out of her coach, she would take him by the hand, and sometimes, for fear of stumbling, press it very hard; she admitted him to deliver messages at her bedside in a morning. . . .

Many specific references to parts of London are scattered throughout the novel; having saved the young woman "in danger of . . . [a] ravisher," Adams and the girl encounter the "set of young fellows. . . in pursuit of a diversion which they call 'bird-baiting'":

> This, if thou art ignorant of it (as perhaps if thou hast never travelled beyond Kensington, Islington, Hackney, or the Borough, thou mayst be), . . . is performed by holding a large clap-net before a lantern, and at the same time beating the bushes: for the birds . . . immediately make to the light, and so are enticed within the net.

Kensington, west of the City, held popular pleasure gardens; Islington, to the north, had a spa and tea gardens where the fashionable gathered on Sundays; Hackney, to the northeast, was an acceptable suburban living area; and the Borough (Southwark) held a mixture of prisons, brothels, and a famous fair. At various times Fielding introduces the Bear Garden in Clerkenwell (at Hockley-in-the-Hole), which was the scene of rough and violent sports such as bull and bear baiting and wrestling; Mother Haywood's in Covent Garden, a notorious house of prostitution; St. James's Coffee House, a Whig meeting place at 87 St. James's Street; the Inner and Middle Temple; and the Park (The Mall in St. James's Park).

Samuel Johnson (1709–1784)

Tho' grief and fondness in my breast rebel,
When injur'd Thales bids the town farewell,
Yet still my calmer thoughts his choice commend,
I praise the hermit, but regret the friend,
Resolved at length, from vice and London far,
To breathe in distant fields a purer air,
And, fix'd on Cambria's solitary shore,
Give to St. David one true Briton more.

Probably more than any other 18th-century figure, Dr. Samuel Johnson is particularly associated with London. Johnson was first brought to London at the age of two and one-half, suffering from scrofula (the "King's evil"), when, records Boswell,

> His mother, yielding to the superstitious notion, . . . carried him to London, where he was actually touched by Queen Anne.

They stayed with John Nicholson, a bookseller whose shop, the King's Arms, was on Little Britain Street; on March 30, 1712, Mrs. Johnson took the child to St. James's for the expected cure. Much later, Johnson

> "had (he said) a confused, but somehow a sort of solemn recollection of a lady in diamonds, and a long black hood." This touch, however, was without any effect.

Johnson, then, had no other association with London until early March 1737, when he gave up his school in Edial, Staffordshire, and came here with David Garrick, one of his pupils; tradition established by Garrick says that they "rode and tied" their way, and Johnson claimed:

> ". . . I came to London with two-pence half-penny in

my pocket." Garrick overhearing him, exclaimed, "eh? what do you say? with two-pence half-penny in your pocket?"—JOHNSON. "Why, yes; when I came with two-pence half-penny in *my* pocket, and thou, Davy, with three half-pence in thine."

How he supported himself is not known, but "his first lodgings were at the house of Mr. Norris, a staymaker, in Exeter-street, adjoining Catherine-street, in the Strand" (the present intersection with Wellington Street covers the site). Undoubtedly, part if not all of *London* was composed here; Johnson frequented "the Pine-Apple in New-street, just by"; there

> "I dined (said he) very well for eight-pence. . . . I had a cut of meat for six-pence, and bread for a penny, and gave the waiter a penny; so that I was quite well served. . . ."

Johnson's New Street is New Row, off St. Martin's Lane opposite St. Martin's Court. *Irene* was begun in the five months in the Exeter Street lodgings, and in July Johnson moved to the Golden Heart, Church Street, Greenwich, where he planned to work on the final two acts of the play. He was also contributing verse and prose to the *Gentleman's Magazine*.

Johnson returned to Edial in the late summer of 1737 to wind up his affairs and to bring Tetty to London. Their first lodgings were on Woodstock Street, but they soon moved to a house at 6 Great Castle Street, parallel to Oxford Street and east of Regent Street. Here Johnson finished *London* and *Irene*, which he thought was "fit for the stage." Boswell notes:

> Mr. Peter Garrick [David's brother] told me, that Johnson and he went together to the Fountain Tavern, and read it over, and that he afterwards solicited Mr. Fleetwood, the patentee of Drury-lane theatre, to have it acted at his house; but . . . it was not acted till 1749, when his friend David Garrick was manager of that theatre.

The Fountain Tavern stood in Fountain Court, which entered the Strand between Numbers 103 and 104. Johnson was employed by Edward Cave, publisher of the *Gentleman's Magazine,* and "as an adventurer in literature" he became one of those writers who haunted St. John's Gate, Clerkenwell:

> He told me [Boswell], that when he first saw St. John's Gate, the place where that deservedly popular miscellany was originally printed, he "beheld it with reverence."

The old gatehouse, the nave of the church, and the crypt are still standing. *London* appeared in May 1738, and in the same year he and Tetty took new lodgings in Boswell Court (gone) on Carey Street, north of the Strand, where the law buildings now stand. Johnson remained here for three years, still working for Cave, but in the next few years of this rather hand-to-mouth period he had at least three other residences, on Bow Street, on Fetter Lane, and in Holborn.

Johnson began his editorial and critical work on *Macbeth* after publishing *An Account of the Life of Mr Richard Savage* in 1744. Just when Johnson made the acquaintance of Savage is uncertain, but the two men became friends:

> [A]s Savage's misfortunes and misconduct had reduced him to the lowest state of wretchedness as a writer for bread, his visits to St. John's Gate naturally brought Johnson and him together.

Boswell says the two

> were sometimes in such extreme indigence, that they could not pay for a lodging; so that they have wandered together whole nights in the streets. Yet in these almost incredible scenes of distress, we may suppose that Savage mentioned many of the anecdotes with which Johnson afterwards enriched the life of his unhappy companion, and those of other Poets.

The contract for *A Dictionary of English Language* was signed on June 18, 1746, and *The Plan of a Dictionary of the English Language* appeared in the following year. About this time Johnson moved to 17 Gough Square, north of Fleet Street; here

> he had an upper room fitted up like a counting-house for the purpose, in which he gave to the copyists their several task. The words, partly taken from other dictionaries, and partly supplied by himself, having been first written down with spaces left between them, he delivered in writing their etymologies, definitions, and various significations. The authorities were copied from the books themselves, in which he had marked the passages with a black-lead pencil, the traces of which could easily be effaced.

Johnson's extreme aggressiveness has often been ascribed to an underlying sense of inadequacy and insecurity, and the front door of the Gough Square house (marked with a plaque) still has a massive chain for protection. The three-story house had the dining and family sitting rooms on the ground floor, a bedroom and paneled withdrawing room on the first, and two more bedrooms on the second; the kitchen, as was frequently the case, was in the basement and contained a stone sink and two alcoves for

LONDON   Less than a minute's walk from the famous Ye Olde Cheshire Cheese, 17 Gough Square was Dr. Samuel Johnson's home from 1749 to 1759. The only one of his many London addresses to survive, the house, now the property of Dr. Johnson's House Trust, is a Johnsonian museum and contains a first edition of the *Dictionary*, which may be examined.

fireplaces. The work on the *Dictionary* was proceeding well but was insufficient to keep Johnson active:

> He therefore not only exerted his talents in occasional composition, very different from Lexicography, but formed a club in Ivy Lane, Paternoster Row, with a view to enjoy literary discussion, and amuse his evening hours.

The Vanity of Human Wishes appeared in January 1749, and "in 1750 in the character for which he was eminently qualified, a majestic teacher of moral and religious wisdom," he began *The Rambler,* which appeared twice weekly for two years.

During this period Tetty was almost constantly ill; she had, by most accounts, taken to excessive drink and was also using opiates heavily. As well, she was now celibate and living at Priory House, just opposite Frognal Lane in Hampstead, where Johnson frequently joined her. Tetty's death came on March 17, 1752, and she was buried in the church in Bromley, Kent. Johnson retained the Gough Square house, where Joshua Reynolds became a frequent guest, until February or March 1759. In the meantime the *Dictionary* was finished, and Johnson's fame was secure even though his financial condition was not. Indeed, in March 1756 he was under arrest for the sum of £5/18/0 and had to apply to Samuel Richardson for funds. Johnson moved from Gough Square to lodgings first in Staple Inn, at Number 2 in the first court south of Holborn, and then in Gray's Inn, north of Holborn. In 1759 and 1760 Johnson also lived at 2 Holborn, up under the roof, and wrote *The Prince of Abissinia* so

> that with the profits he might defray the expence of his mother's funeral, and pay some little debts which she had left. He told Sir Joshua Reynolds, that he composed it in the evenings of one week, sent it to the press in portions as it was written, and had never since read it over.

Shortly thereafter he moved to 1 Inner Temple Lane, south off Fleet Street, opposite Chancery Lane, and remained here until 1765. About this time he made the acquaintance of the Cock Lane ghost, which purportedly gave messages to an eleven-year-old girl named Parsons who lived at 33 Cock Lane off Giltspur Street; this was a slum area in Johnson's day, and in Chaucer's time it was the only street on this side of the City where prostitutes were legally permitted to reside. The ghost delivered its messages in the form of scratching sounds when the child was in bed:

> Churchill in his poem entitled "The Ghost" availed himself of the absurd credulity imputed to Johnson, and drew a caricature of him under the name of "POMPOSO," representing him as one of the believers of the story of a Ghost in Cock-lane.... Johnson was one of those by whom the imposture was detected. The story had become so popular, that he thought it should be investigated; and in this research he was assisted by the Reverend Dr. Douglas, now Bishop of Salisbury, the great detecter of impostures; who informs me, that after the gentlemen who went and examined into the evidence were satisfied of its falsity, Johnson wrote in their presence an account of it, which was published in the newspapers and Gentleman's Magazine....

The child, whose father was the clerk of St. Sepulchre's Church, was discovered scratching a piece of wood under the blanket.

The accession of George III in 1760 signaled the end of Johnson's financial problems:

> [E]arly this year Johnson having been represented to him as a very learned and good man, without any certain provision, his Majesty was pleased to grant him a pension of three hundred pounds a year....
> Sir Joshua Reynolds told me, that Johnson ... said he wished to consult his friends as to the propriety of his accepting this mark of the royal favour, after the definitions which he had given in his Dictionary of *pension* and *pensioners*.... Sir Joshua answered that...certainly the definitions in his Dictionary were not applicable to him. Johnson, it should seem, was satisfied, for he did not call again till he had accepted the pension....

In May 1763 James Boswell, "after having been enlivened by the witty sallies of Messieurs Thornton, Wilkes, Churchill, and Lloyd ... boldly repaired to Johnson," whose "Chambers were on the first floor of No. 1, Inner-Temple-lane":

> He received me very courteously: but, it must be confessed, that his apartment, and furniture, and morning dress, were sufficiently uncouth. His brown suit of cloaths looked very rusty: he had on a little old shrivelled unpowdered wig, which was too small for his head; his shirt-neck and knees of his breeches were loose; his black worsted stockings ill drawn up; and he had a pair of unbuckled shoes by way of slippers. But all these slovenly particularities were forgotten the moment that he began to talk.

Sometime during the 1763–1764 winter (Boswell claims February) the Literary Club was formed with Sir Joshua Reynolds having "the merit of being the first proposer of it"; the other original members included Edmund Burke, Oliver Goldsmith, Dr. Christopher Nugent (Burke's father-in-law), Sir John Hawkins, Topham Beauclerk, Bennet Langton, and Anthony Chamier:

> They met at the Turk's Head, in Gerrard-street, Soho, one evening in every week, at seven, and generally continued their conversation till a pretty late hour.... Their original tavern having been converted into a private house, they moved first to Prince's in Sackville-street [Number 23], then to Le Telier's in Dover-street, and now meet at Parsloe's, St. James's-street [Number 85].

The tavern was at 9 Gerrard Street; of the other locations mentioned by Boswell, the club met at Prince's only while Dr. Johnson was alive. This was also the period in which he visited the Thrales at their Park Street home in Southwark; he became almost one of the family with apartments allocated to him in their house here and at Streatham. At the end of 1765 or early in 1766 Johnson took "a good house in Johnson's Court, Fleet Street, in which he had accommodated Miss Williams with an apartment on the ground floor, while Mr. Levitt occupied his post in the garret; his faithful Francis was still attending upon him." He remained at Number 7 for ten years working on *A Journey to the Western Islands of Scotland* and his edition of Shakespeare. Johnson had long been in the habit of frequenting "the library at the Queen's House," as Boswell records, and in February 1767,

> as soon as he [Johnson] was fairly engaged with a book, on which, while he sat by the fire, he seemed quite intent, Mr. Barnard [the librarian] stole round to the apartment where the King was, and, in obedience to his Majesty's

commands, mentioned that Dr. Johnson was then in the library. His Majesty said he was at leisure, and would go to him. . . . Being entered, Mr. Barnard stepped forward hastily to Dr. Johnson, who was still in a profound study, and whispered him, "Sir, here is the King." Johnson started up, and stood still. His Majesty approached him, and at once was courteously easy.

The King "enquired if he was then writing anything"; Johnson's answer that he had "pretty well told the world what he knew" and that he "thought he had already done his part as a writer" was met by, "'I should have thought so too, (said the King,) if you had not written so well.'" Queen's House was, in fact, Buckingham House (now Palace), which George III bought in 1762 and where he established the King's Library.

Dr. Johnson's health had begun to decline in the early 1770s, and on numerous occasions he practically lived with the Thrales, where Mrs. Thrale's ministrations were especially desired. Johnson moved again in 1776 to 8 Bolt Court, just off Gough Square and was still making frequent excursions from the City. Strained relations with Mrs. Thrale and increasing despondency made Johnson attempt to re-create some of his old pleasures; Boswell notes:

> On Friday, April 6, he carried me to dine at a club, which, at his desire, had been lately formed at the Queen's Arms, in St. Paul's Church-yard.

The Queen's Arms was at the western end of St. Paul's Churchyard. Johnson suffered a stroke in mid-June 1783 which left him with partial dysphasia; recovery was slow. Even so, he formed another club, the Evening Club, which met "at the Essex Head, now kept by an old servant of Thrale's. . . . We meet twice a week." The Tavern (rebuilt) was at 40 Essex Street and fairly close to Dr. Johnson's home. His health was deteriorating rapidly, and asthma, dropsy, and gout (as well as, possibly, testicle cancer) compounded his earlier problems with the stroke; he died at his Bolt Court house on December 13, 1784, and was buried on December 20 in Westminster Abbey near the monument to William Shakespeare. A monument planned for the abbey was placed in St. Paul's Cathedral; it depicts Dr. Johnson somewhat incongruously in flowing robes.

Virtually nothing in London escaped Dr. Johnson's notice, and he is associated with almost everything. He regularly attended services at St. Clement Danes Church, on the Strand, which was so badly damaged in May 1940 by bombs that the bells sounding "oranges and lemons" were thrown to the ground and broken. They have been recast from the original metal and replaced in the steeple; a particularly unfortunate statue of Johnson stands outside at the eastern end of the church. He frequented many of the 18th-century inns and coffeehouses, although James Boswell never mentions Ye Olde Cheshire Cheese in Wine Office Court, north off Fleet Street; the tavern is normally associated with Johnson and advertises that he, Goldsmith, Boswell, and others were often there. Dr. Johnson's seat is pointed out, and it is in many ways reasonable to assume his patronage when he lived on nearby Gough Street. At the Crown and Anchor Inn (gone), 37 Arundel Street in the Strand, Johnson quarreled with Dr. Thomas Percy, collector of the *Reliques*, over the merits of Alnwick Castle,

hereditary home of the Percys. The Devil Tavern at 1 Fleet Street was the scene of an all-night party in 1751 in honor of Charlotte Lennox's first novel, and the Mitre Tavern (gone) at the west corner of Old Mitre Court and Fleet Street was a favorite haunt. Johnson also frequented Hummums's Hotel (the corner of Russell Street, facing Covent Garden), Tom's Coffee House (17 Russell Street, Covent Garden), St. James's Coffee House (87, later 88, St. James's Street), the Old Baptist Head (St. John's Lane, Clerkenwell; the signboard showed John the Baptist's head on a charger), Old Slaughter's Coffee House (74–75 St. Martin's Lane), the Anchor Inn, Bankside; Don Saltero's Coffee House (18 Cheyne Walk, Chelsea), and Jack's Coffee House (Dean Street, Soho). Dr. Johnson visited Thomas Sheridan, father of the dramatist, at his home at the northeast corner of Bedford Court; the location affords a view of the length of Henrietta Street, across which Johnson had to walk. On one occasion a fellow guest at Sheridan's recorded Johnson's approach:

> I perceived him at a good distance, walking along with a peculiar solemnity of deportment, and an awkward sort of measured step. At that time . . . stone posts were in fashion, to prevent the annoyance of carriages. Upon every post, as he passed along, I could observe he deliberately laid his hand; but missing one of them, when he had got some distance, he seemed suddenly to recollect himself, and immediately returning back, carefully performed the accustomed ceremony, and resumed his former course. . . .

Johnson also visited Samuel Richardson on Salisbury Square and the 4th Earl of Chesterfield on Grosvenor Square (where Johnson "was kept [so] long in waiting in his Lordship's antechamber" when Chesterfield was with Colley Cibber "that he went away in a passion"). He also visited David Garrick at the Adelphi and Boswell in his many lodgings—22 Gerrard Street, Downing Street (opposite Number 10), 22 Poultry, Great Queen Street (on the site of the Freemasons' Hall), Half Moon Street, Old Bond Street, and across from the Albany off Piccadilly. Finally, from Dr. Johnson, a view of London: "Why, Sir, you find no man, at all intellectual, who is willing to leave London. No, Sir, when a man is tired of London, he is tired of life; for there is in London all that life can afford."

John Cleland (1709–1789)   Where John Cleland was born is unknown, although it was probably London, but in 1722 he entered the 14th-century Westminster School, whose buildings surround Little Dean's Yard. Not until 1748 is he recorded again in London; he was at that time imprisoned for debt in the old Fleet Prison, on Farringdon Street near the entrance of Fleet Lane, and here he wrote *Fanny Hill: Memoirs of a Woman of Pleasure* before his release in 1752. Because of the licentiousness of the work he was summoned before the Privy Council, to which he pleaded poverty as the cause. At one time Cleland lived in an old house facing the Thames on the Strand, between Savoy Court and Savoy Street; he spent his last years at a house (gone) in Petty France and died there on January 23, 1789.

Laurence Sterne (1713–1768)   The novelist-clergyman Laurence Sterne's early trips to London were often in connection with his literary work. On one occasion, Stephen Croft provided an expense-paid trip if the novelist would act as his companion; they arrived in early March 1760 and lodged with Nathaniel Cholmley, Croft's son-in-law, on Chapel Street, Mayfair. While Sterne was here, he arranged the publication of the first part of a second edition of *The Life and Opinions of Tristram Shandy*, two additional volumes of *Tristram*, and two volumes of sermons; he then took lodgings on St. Alban's Street, where he stayed for more than two months before returning home; when he did, it was in style, for he was now a rich man with his own carriage and two horses, and he had been feted for his entire stay in London. He returned just before Christmas that year to see two new volumes of *Tristram* through the press and preached his first and only London sermon at the Foundling Hospital on Guildford Street on the first Sunday in May. Most probably he had lodgings on Waterloo Place, just off Pall Mall, until June. On a third visit, in November 1761, again for seeing *Tristram Shandy* through its printing, he met Dr. Samuel Johnson at Sir Joshua Reynolds's home at 47 Leicester Square. Here Sterne read the dedication from the new volume of *Tristram* to the 1st Viscount Spencer (though "nobody desired him to"), and after he had finished six or so lines, Dr. Johnson commented, "I told him it was not English, Sir." Sterne fell ill on this trip and left for the south of France in January; he returned to England in 1764 and stayed here for a time with friends on John Street, near Berkeley Square.

Sterne was back in January 1767, when he took lodgings at 41 Old Bond Street and complained heartily that no one was frequenting St. James's Coffee House, 87 St. James's Street. He met Elizabeth Draper, the wife of an East India Company official, with whom he carried on an open flirtation until she was ordered back to India by her husband. The rather mournful *Letters from Yorick to Eliza*, begun at this time, was never intended for publication. Many of Sterne's "love letters" to Eliza were dated from Mount's Coffee House (Mount Coffee House; The Mount; Mount Street Coffee House), on Grosvenor Street. Suffering from tuberculosis since 1762, when the disease injured his voice, Sterne contracted influenza in February 1768, and within a few weeks pleurisy set in. He died in his lodgings on March 18, and it is said that just at his death he raised his arm and murmured, "Now it is come." A private ceremony was conducted in St. George's Church, Hanover Square, and Sterne was buried in St. George's Burial Ground, on Hyde Park Place, Bayswater; the site is now the playground of the Hyde Park Nursery School. The story that Sterne's body was stolen by grave robbers a few weeks later and taken to Cambridge is apparently true; it was used for an anatomy lecture and was quietly returned to the grave after (it is said) the Rev. Thomas Greene, Dean of Salisbury, recognized the skull. In 1969 Sterne's remains were reinterred in Coxwold, Yorkshire.

Sterne visited Tobias Smollett's apartment at 16 Lawrence Street, Chelsea, and frequented Don Saltero's Coffee House, 18 Cheyne Walk.

William Shenstone (1714–1763)   William Shenstone spent his entire life in Halesowen, Worcestershire, and visited London only briefly. On a 1739 trip he found "George's to be economical"; George's Coffee House, without Temple Bar on the Strand, stood between the entrance to Devereux Court and Essex Street. It was almost opposite St. Clement's Church and was probably 213 the Strand, three houses west of Devereux Court. In January 1741 Shenstone writes from "Mr. Wintle's Perfumer, at the King's Arms, by Temple Bar, Fleet Street" and attended the theater. Shenstone never strayed far from this area and in February 1743 was at Nando's (Nandoe's or Nondoe's) Coffee House, 15 Fleet Street. He lodged nearby, "between the two coffee-houses, George's and Nando's, so that I partake of the expensiveness of both, as heretofore." He shows concern about the safety of London streets:

> London is really dangerous ... the pickpockets formerly content with mere filching, make no scruple to knock people down with bludgeons in Fleet Street and the Strand, and that at no later hour than 8 o'clock at night; but in the Piazzas, Covent Garden, they come in large bodies, armed with couteaus, and attack whole parties. ...

In March 1745 he dates his letters from "Mr. Shuckburgh's, Bookseller in Fleet Street your Brother's Lodgings" and may well have had lodgings on Jermyn Street.

William Whitehead (1715–1785)   Not often do Poets Laureate fall into almost total oblivion, but William Whitehead (Poet Laureate from 1757 on) is an exception. He came to London in 1745, when he became tutor to the ten-year-old Viscount Villiers, and lived in the 3d Earl of Jersey's London home. He spent a few years traveling abroad with his charge and was back in London when the laureateship, which Thomas Gray refused, fell to him. He continued to live with Lord Jersey in winter until 1769, when his former pupil succeeded to the title. At that time he moved to 3 St. James's Place and prepared *A Trip to Scotland* for performance at the Drury Lane Theatre on January 6, 1770; he remained here until 1772. Then or perhaps later, he moved to Charles Street, off Berkeley Square, where he died on April 14, 1785. He was buried in the Grosvenor Chapel on South Audley Street.

Thomas Gray (1716–1771)   A native Londoner, Thomas Gray was born at 39 Cornhill (rebuilt) on December 26, 1716; he was the only one of the twelve Gray children born to survive infancy. Gray's father both neglected his son and treated him harshly, while Mrs. Gray's milliner's business clothed and educated him. Gray was taken to Burnham, Buckinghamshire, by an uncle and spent very little time in London until 1738, when he left Cambridge and returned to his father's house for six months, uncertain over what career to follow. His friendship with Horace Walpole, begun at Eton, brought at least a temporary answer when the Prime Minister's son suggested a joint grand tour, financed by Walpole, beginning in March 1739. In the autumn of 1741, after his return, Gray studied law, but his father's death (he had been ill all year) left him in an unexpectedly precarious financial condition, and he redirected his studies toward a degree in civil law at Peterhouse College, Cambridge, where he remained for the rest of his life with only occasional forays into the city.

In the 1750s, after the Cornhill house had burned down (May 1748), Gray had several different lodgings on Jermyn Street, and when the British Museum opened on January 15, 1759, the poet was one of the first to visit it. He lodged on Southampton Row, and his bedroom window looked out over a southwest garden wall of flowers. Gray spent most of the next thirty months in London working in the Reading Room of the museum and at some point changed to rooms on Russell Square (where the Imperial Hotel now stands). Gray also stayed with Lady Cobham on Hanover Square in October and November 1759 and frequented Ranelagh Gardens (part of the Royal Hospital grounds). After this, his visits were curtailed by failing health. He was buried in Stoke Poges, Buckinghamshire, but a monument commemorates him in the Poets' Corner of Westminster Abbey.

Horace Walpole (1717–1797) The writer and collector Horace Walpole, later 4th Earl of Orford, and the son of Sir Robert Walpole, Prime Minister under George II, was born at 5 Arlington Street (now replaced by Number 22) on September 24, 1717, and spent his early childhood here and at his father's summer home in Chelsea, on the east side of Tite Street, where the Royal Hospital stands today. The property had an L-shaped orangery, and Lady Walpole's grotto in the lower part of the garden was built of shells from the Channel Islands. The *Gentleman's Magazine* noted:

Whilst patriots murmur at the weight
  Of taxes that support the State;
See how the isles obeisance pay
  To W-l-p-le's most auspicious sway!
Each little isle with generous zeal
  Sends grateful every precious shell;
Shells in which Venus and her train
  Of nymphs ride stately o'er the main . . .
To make the W-l-p-le grotto fine
  And rival grotto Caroline.

("Grotto Caroline" belonged to George II's Queen.) Walpole's father, of course, had possession of 10 Downing Street (crown property) from 1732 on, and during his tenure as Prime Minister the house was enlarged and extensively altered for official use. Following his education at Eton and King's College, Cambridge, and a grand tour of the Continent with Thomas Gray, Walpole returned to London and his father's Downing Street address and then resided on Arlington Street (across from Number 5) after Sir Robert's resignation in 1742. This house continued to be Horace Walpole's main address long after Sir Robert's death in 1745, although he spent time in Houghton, Norfolk, at the family estate.

In 1747 Walpole took Strawberry Hill, in Twickenham, Middlesex, where he spent most of his time and considerable money, and which he made over in the Gothic style, although he retained his London house. Walpole frequented Ranelagh Gardens, which opened in 1742 as public pleasure gardens; today the Chelsea Royal Hospital occupies the entire site. He attended opening night, where there was, he said, "much nobility and much mob"; although his early preference was for Vauxhall Gardens, his taste changed, and by 1744 this slender man, dressed usually in gray or lavender with a silver-embroidered waistcoat and gold-buckled shoes, was in constant attendance. He attended a masquerade here in the Venetian manner in 1749 and says there was

nothing Venetian in it but was by far the best understood and prettiest spectacle I ever saw: nothing in a fairy tale ever surpassed it.

In November 1749 Walpole was robbed by the "gentleman highwayman" James Maclaine (M'Clean) and barely escaped serious injury when Maclaine's pistol accidentally discharged and the bullet grazed Walpole's cheek before going through the roof of the carriage.

Walpole served as the parliamentary member for Castle Rising, Norfolk, from 1754 to 1757 and for King's Lynn from then until 1768. In October 1779 he took 40 (now 11) Berkeley Square (not actually square); his house on the east side of the square has long been gone, and the site contains a large modern building. Here Walpole died on March 2, 1797, and was buried in Houghton, Norfolk.

Walpole frequented coffeehouses and private members' clubs, including the Bedford Coffee House, "in the north-east corner [of Covent Garden], near the entrance to Covent Garden Theatre"; St. George's Coffee House, "without Temple Bar, Strand" (at 123 the Strand, between the entrance to Devereux Court and Essex Street); Wildman's Coffee House, on Bedford Street in the Strand; White's Club (White's Chocolate House, which became a private members' establishment in 1736), at 68 and 69 St. James's Street; and Brooks's Club at 60 St. James's Street. The latter two were notorious gaming houses. The novelist often visited Mrs. Elizabeth Montagu, "queen of the bluestockings," at her home on Upper Berkeley Street (on the northeast corner of Gloucester Place) and Mrs. Mary Granville Delany, another bluestocking, at 33 St. James's Place. Walpole knew intimately Sir Hans Sloane, the physician and collector, and in February 1753 writes:

Sir Hans Sloane is dead, and has made me one of the trustees to his museum. . . . He valued it at four score thousand: and so would anybody who loves hippopotamuses, sharks with one ear, and spiders as big as geese! It is a rent charge to keep the foetuses in spirits!

Chelsea Manor House, bequeathed to the nation, was not retained by the government, but the invaluable "productions of nature and art" formed part of the original British Museum collection. Three years later Theodore (Theodor von Neuhof), the German adventurer and self-styled King of Corsica, died in poverty in Soho. Walpole paid for his tombstone at St. Anne's Church and wrote the poetic inscription:

The grave, great teacher, to a level brings
Heroes and beggars, galley-slaves and kings;
But Theodore this moral learned ere dead;
Fate poured its lessons on his living head,
Bestowed a kingdom, and denied him bread.

Elizabeth Carter (1717–1806) The woman who Dr. Johnson said "could make a pudding as well as translate Epictetus from the Greek and work a handkerchief as well as compose a poem," Elizabeth Carter died in her lodgings on Clarges Street on February 19,1806, and was buried in the grounds of the Grosvenor Chapel on South Audley Street.

Mark Akenside (1721–1770) Mark Akenside, known chiefly for *The Pleasures of Imagination*, first came to London in 1743, and then, after a time abroad, attempted to establish a medical practice at North End,

Hampstead. His practice languished while his literary productivity rose; after 1747, when Jeremiah Dyson banished the struggling physician's financial concerns by fitting up a house on Bloomsbury Square for him, allowing him an allowance of £300 a year, supplying a chariot, and procuring patients, Akenside wrote little more. He rose steadily in the medical profession and was living at 33 Craven Street when he was appointed physician to Queen Charlotte. Akenside moved to 12 Old Burlington Street, where he lived for the rest of his life; he died on June 23, 1770, supposedly in the same bed in which Milton died, and was buried at the Church of St. James, Piccadilly.

Like other 18th-century figures, Akenside was a frequenter of coffeehouses including Serle's (Searle's or Searl's), at the "corner of Lincoln Inn's Square" (probably at the corner of Serle and Portugal Streets), and Tom's, on Devereux Court near Temple Bar. The latter, which belonged to Thomas Twining (of the house of Twining) from 1706 on, was a resort of men of learning in the 1760s, and Akenside spent many winter evenings there.

Tobias Smollett (1721–1771) Eighteenth-century London was a magnet for aspiring writers including the Dumbartonshire physician Tobias Smollett, who came to the city in 1739 to seek his literary fortune. He served as surgeon's second mate in the Royal Navy, and in Jamaica he met (and may have married) Anne Lassells, but he returned alone to London, where he established a home and surgery somewhere on Downing Street. (His wife joined him in 1747.) Early in 1746 Smollett was living on Chapel Street (now 11 Aldford Street), where he stayed two years and frequented the British Coffee House, opposite Suffolk Street. Indeed, this was where he heard the news of the Battle of Culloden in April 1746, which inspired "The Tears of Scotland." In 1748, when the Smollett family moved to Beaufort Buildings on the Strand, approximately opposite Exeter Street, *The Adventures of Roderick Random* appeared.

Because Smollett's daughter was tubercular, he took a country home at 16 Lawrence Street, Chelsea, in 1750; Monmouth House consisted of four houses, and he held the central unit on the western side. The house was a "plain, yet decent habitation, which opened backwards into a very pleasant garden, kept in excellent order"; Chelsea Public Library has a watercolor of the house. Smollett was active in the literary life of London, and according to his own account in *The Expedition of Humphry Clinker,*

[E]very Sunday his house is opened to all unfortunate brothers of the quill, whom he treats with beef, pudding, and potatoes, port, punch, and Calvert's entire butt beer.

Indeed, Smollett's house was visited by many leading literary figures including Oliver Goldsmith, David Garrick, and Dr. Samuel Johnson. Smollett patronized a number of the local taverns and coffeehouses, including the White Swan Tavern, on the Thames east of the Botanical Gardens, and Don Saltero's Coffee House, 18 Cheyne Walk; it was Smollett's presence in the latter that prompted George Canning's "On the Tragedy of Elvira." In the meantime, Smollett was writing steadily, and with *The Adventures of Peregrine Pickle* and *The Adventures of Ferdinand Count Fathom* the author gave up his medical practice.

From 1756 to 1759 Smollett was editor of *The Critical Review*, a Tory and church paper with offices on Paternoster Row; it was in the last year that Smollett met with difficulty. On November 24, 1759, he was convicted of libeling Adm. Sir Charles Knowles, fined £100, and sentenced to three months' imprisonment at King's Bench Prison, on the north side of Scovill Road off the Borough High Street in Southwark. His time in prison was pleasant enough, and his visitors, including David Garrick and Oliver Goldsmith, came frequently. Released by February 25, 1760, with a promise of keeping the peace for seven years and the security of £500 from himself and £250 each from two others, Smollett returned to Chelsea, where the bells of Chelsea Old Church rang out for his return. *The Life and Adventures of Sir Launcelot Greaves* is based on his experiences in prison, which

appears like a neat, little regular town, consisting of one street, surrounded by a very high wall, including an open piece of ground, which may be termed a garden, where the prisoners take the air, and amuse themselves. . . . Tradesmen of all kinds here exercise their different professions. Hawkers of all sorts are admitted to call and vend their wares as in any open street of London. Here are butchers'-stands, chandlers'-shops, a surgery, a taphouse well frequented, and a public kitchen, in which provisions are dressed for all the prisoners gratis, at the expense of the publican.

Smollett had been tubercular for some time, and asthma became a problem in 1761. His daughter's death in 1763 was a severe blow and filled him "with unutterable sorrow"; she was buried in Chelsea Old Church in the center aisle next to her maternal grandmother, Elizabeth Leaver. Smollett then abandoned all literary activity, and within two months of Elizabeth's death he and his wife left England and settled in Nice. He returned to England twice (1766 and 1768) before his death on September 17, 1771, in Italy.

References to London in Smollett's works, especially *Humphry Clinker*, are plentiful. Tom King's Coffee House, on the south side of Covent Garden opposite Southampton Street, comes into *The Adventures of Roderick Random:*

It being now near two o'clock in the morning, . . . Billy Chaten being unable to speak or stand, was sent to a bagnio and Banter and I accompanied Bragwell to Moll King's Coffee House, where, after he had kicked half a dozen hungry whores, we left him to sleep on a bench and directed our course towards Charing Cross. . . .

The original of Hugh Strap in the same novel was Hugh Newson, who lived "in the lodge of the terrace at the foot of Buckingham Street. . . ." In *Humphry Clinker* Matthew Bramble describes the metropolis to Dr. Lewis on various occasions:

London is literally new to me. . . . What I left open fields, producing hay and corn, I now find covered with streets, and squares, and palaces, and churches. I am credibly informed, that in the space of seven years, eleven thousand new houses have been built in one quarter of Westminster. . . . Pimlico and Knightsbridge are now almost joined to Chelsea and Kensington. . . .

London and Westminster are much better paved and lighted than they were formerly. The new streets are spacious, regular, and airy; and the houses generally convenient. . . . But, notwithstanding these improvements, the capital is become an overgrown monster; which, like a dropsical head, will in time leave the body and extremities without nourishment and support.

Bramble is annoyed at many aspects of this "overgrown monster"; his lodgings are so small "there is not room enough to swing a cat," and he breathes "the steams of endless putrification," which would "produce a pestilence, if they were not qualified by the gross acid of sea-coal."

> I start every hour from my sleep, at the horrid noise of the watchmen bawling the hour through every street. . . . If I could drink water, I must quaff the maukish contents of an open aqueduct, exposed to all manner of defilement; or swallow that which comes from the river Thames, impregnated with all the filth of London and Westminster—Human excrement is the least offensive part of the concrete, which is composed of all the drugs, minerals, and poisons, used in mechanics and manufacture, enriched with the putrefying carcasses of beasts and men; and mixed with the scourings of all the wash-tubs, kennels, and common sewers, within the bills of mortality.
> This is the agreable potation, extolled by the Londoners, as the finest water in the universe. . . .

Bramble and his entourage lodge "in Golden-square, at the house of one Mrs. Norton" (east of Regent Street and south of Beak Street) and visit Ranelagh Gardens, the public pleasure gardens which adjoined the Chelsea Royal Hospital grounds (the hospital occupies the entire site today). Two more divergent views of those frequenting the amusement place could not be found; to Matthew Bramble:

> One half of the company are following at the other's tails, in an eternal circle; like so many blind asses in an olive-mill, where they can neither discourse, distinguish, nor be distinguished; while the other half are drinking hot water, under the denomination of tea, till nine or ten o'clock at night, to keep them awake for the rest of the evening. As for the orchestra, the vocal music especially, it is well for the performers that they cannot be heard distinctly.

To Lydia Mitford, however:

> Ranelagh looks like the inchanted palace of a genie, adorned with the most exquisite performances of painting, carving, and gilding, enlightened with a thousand golden lamps, that emulate the noon-day sun. . . . While these exulting sons and daughters of felicity tread this round of pleasure, or regale in different parties, and separate lodges, with fine imperial tea and other delicious refreshments, their ears are entertained with the most ravishing delights of music, both instrumental and vocal. There I heard the famous Tenducci, . . . and it warbled so divinely, that, while I listened, I really thought myself in paradise.

Bramble visits the British Museum,

> which is a noble collection, and even stupendous, . . . but great as the collection is, it would appear more striking if it was arranged in one spacious saloon, instead of being divided into different apartments, which it does not entirely fill. . . .

This view could not even be conceived of today. Of the library, Bramble observes:

> It would likewise be a great improvement, with respect to the library, if the deficiencies were made up, by purchasing all the books of character that are not to be found already in the collection—They might be classed in centuries, . . . and catalogues printed of them and the manuscripts. . . .

Win Jenkins visits the Tower of London with her mistress "to see the crowns and wild beastis; and there was a monstracious lion, with teeth half a quarter long" which the keeper warns her to avoid "if I wasn't a maid; being as how he would roar, and tear, and play the dickens. . . . " Vauxhall Gardens, Covent Garden, and Clerkenwell also enter the novel.

Christopher Smart (1722–1771) When Christopher Smart came to London from Cambridge around 1750 or 1751 and had lodgings somewhere in the vicinity of St. James's Park, he became ill and was confined for a short period in Bethlehem Hospital (Bedlam, on the site of the present Liverpool Street Station). On this trip he probably met the bookseller John Newbery and his stepdaughter Anna Maria Carnan, whom he married in 1752 without the consent or knowledge of the authorities at Cambridge, where he was a fellow. The marriage most likely took place at St. Bride's Church, Fleet Street, although no records exist. Smart returned to the university, and the marriage was discovered, but he seems not to have left until 1755; the couple, however, resided more or less permanently with Newbery at Canonbury Tower in Islington. Here at least one of Smart's children was born. During this period Smart was often ill, and on May 6, 1757, he was admitted to St. Luke's Hospital, Old Street, an insane asylum from the 18th century until 1916, when the Bank of England took over the premises. He was listed in the "Curable Patients Book" but was discharged as uncured on May 11, 1758.

Smart's whereabouts are unknown from his discharge from St. Luke's until February 3, 1759, when he was again hospitalized, probably in a private clinic run by a Mrs. Potter in Bethnal Green. Of his *Jubilate Agno*, which was begun in 1759, only about one-third survives. Following his release in 1763, he roomed with a Mrs. Barwell on Park Street and was especially delighted with the terrace, which overlooked St. James's Park. Dr. Samuel Johnson visited Smart on various occasions throughout his hospitalizations; Boswell reports a conversation with Dr. Charles Burney:

> "How does poor Smart do, Sir; is he likely to recover?" JOHNSON. "It seems as if his mind had ceased to struggle with the disease; for he grows fat upon it." BURNEY. "Perhaps, Sir, that may be from want of exercise." JOHNSON. "No, Sir, he has partly as much exercise as he used to have, for he digs in the garden. Indeed, before his confinement, he used for exercise to walk to the alehouse; but he was *carried* back again. I did not think he ought to be shut up. His infirmities were not noxious to society. He insisted on people praying with him; and I'd as lief pray with Kit Smart as any one else. Another charge was, that he did not love clean linen; and I have no passion for it."

It was during this commitment, it is believed, that Smart wrote *A Song to David*. He visited Dr. Burney and his daughter at 50 Poland Street, when he was noted as

> one of the most unfortunate of men—he has been twice confined in a madhouse, and, but last year, sent a most affecting letter to papa to entreat him to lend him half a guinea. He is extremely grave, and has still great wildness in his manners, looks, and voice.

His financial problems led to his commitment to King's Bench Prison, on Scovill Road, Southwark, on April 26, 1770; with the consensus that Smart was best off here, a subscription was raised, and the privilege of the rules was secured for him. In this way he was allowed a measure of freedom and permitted to walk in St. George's Fields. Smart died in prison on May 21, 1771, and was buried, not in the churchyard at St. Paul's, as is usually stated, but in the Church of St. Gregory by St. Paul's (long destroyed).

Oliver Goldsmith (1730–1774) Irish-born Oliver Goldsmith arrived in London in 1756 after being on the Continent for a few years; destitute, he found employment as a chemist's assistant on Fish Street Hill and through the help of friends, especially Dr. J. F. Sleigh, whom he had known in Ireland, was able to set up a medical practice on Bankside in Southwark. *The Bee* makes it apparent that he knew London well:

> You then, O ye beggars of my acquaintance, whether in rags or lace; whether in Kent-street or the Mall; whether at the Smyrna or St. Giles's, might I be permitted to advise as a friend, never seem to want the favour which you solicit.

Kent Street (now Tabard Street and Old Kent Street) was "sacred" to broom men and beggars. Goldsmith's medical practice was unsuccessful, and he drifted into a quasi-literary position as a corrector for Samuel Richardson, whose shop was in Salisbury Court. Both this post and his next, as usher at the Peckham school kept by the Reverend Mr. Milner, were short-lived. In April 1757 he entered the employ of Ralph Griffiths, publisher of *The Monthly Review*, and lodged above the shop "at the sign of the Dunciad," on Paternoster Row, Cheapside; later that year he may have lodged in a squalid garret near Salisbury Square. He returned to Peckham for a short period, but, determined to secure a post as a "hospital mate" on the coast off Coromandel, he presented himself for examination at the Surgeons' Hall, where he was found "not qualified."

Goldsmith moved to lodgings in Green Arbour Court by the end of 1758; the court no longer exists, but Goldsmith's rooms were on the northeast corner of the present Seacoal and Green Arbour Lanes. Washington Irving, who visited the lodgings before their demolition, called it "a region of washerwomen," and said it was made up of

> tall and miserable houses, the very intestines of which seemed turned inside out, to judge from the old garments and frippery that fluttered from every window.

Goldsmith's poverty was still extreme, but he frequented the Temple Exchange Coffee House on Fleet Street, near Temple Bar, when he could afford it. Many of his 1757–1758 letters are dated from here; others are addressed to him at "the Temple Exchange Coffee-house . . . where the waiter George . . . took charge of them" and where he met the Rev. Thomas Percy, not yet bishop of Dromore but already a collector of material for the *Reliques*. Percy visited Goldsmith in his Green Arbour Court lodging, as did Tobias Smollett, who recruited him to write for *The British Magazine*. Goldsmith's literary reputation was building, and by the end of 1760 he had moved to 6 Wine Office Court (rebuilt), off Fleet Street; Ye Olde Cheshire Cheese, which claims the patronage of Dr. Samuel Johnson, James Boswell, and Goldsmith, is at the entrance to the court on the east side. *The Citizen of the World*, which had been

LONDON   Possibly the best-known London pub, Ye Olde Cheshire Cheese, which was rebuilt in 1667 after the Great Fire, stands on the location of the guesthouse of a 13th-century Carmelite monastery. Among the pub's many patrons were Samuel Johnson, Oliver Goldsmith, and William Butler Yeats.

begun in January 1760, was completed here, and Dr. Johnson paid his first call on May 31, 1761.

Goldsmith moved again at the end of 1762, to Islington, then a rural suburb; still short of money and no doubt wishing to avoid his creditors, he may have had rooms in Canonbury Tower before lodging with Mrs. Elizabeth Fleming at a cost of £50 a year for room and board. For a brief period from December 1763 to March 1764 Goldsmith resided in Gray's Inn, although he kept up his rent at Mrs. Fleming's. It must have been during this period that Dr. Johnson came to his friend's rescue:

> "I received one morning a message from poor Goldsmith that he was in great distress, and as it was not in his power to come to me, begging that I would come to him as soon as possible. I sent him a guinea, and promised to come to him directly. I accordingly went as soon as I was drest, and found that his landlady had arrested him for his rent, at which he was in a violent passion. . . . He then told me that he had a novel ready for the press, which he produced to me. I looked into it, and saw its merit; told the landlady I should soon return, and having gone to a bookseller, sold it for sixty pounds. . . ."

The Vicar of Wakefield appeared in 1766, and by the middle of 1767 Goldsmith had taken up residence in Islington again, this time in Canonbury House (the tower of Queen Elizabeth's hunting lodge). In Islington he took his "shoemaker's holidays," dining across the fields at Highbury Barn on two courses and a pasty for 10 pence (including the waiter's penny) and taking tea at White Conduit House, where the public house of the same name stands on Barnsbury Road. On one occasion Goldsmith encountered the three daughters of a merchant to whom he owed money. Washington Irving relates the incident:

> With his prompt disposition to oblige, he conducted them about the garden, treated them to a tea, and ran up a bill in the most open-hearted manner imaginable; it was only when he came to pay that he found himself in one of his old dilemmas—he had not the wherewithal in his pocket.

Goldsmith also attended the group of lettered and quasi-literary men who met at the Crown Tavern on Islington Lower Road.

By 1768 Goldsmith was well known as an author, and he returned to the City, where he took quarters in the Middle Temple at 2 Garden Court; his apartments opened on the library staircase. A little later Goldsmith moved to better quarters at 3 King's Bench Walk in the Middle Temple, where Dr. Johnson visited him. With the success of *The Good-natur'd Man,* which earned around £500 for him at Covent Garden, he moved to 2 Brick Court in the Middle Temple, where he had two old-fashioned and reasonably sized rooms and a smaller sleeping closet; Goldsmith spent £400 on the lease and another £100 on the furnishings. The sitting room, which overlooked Essex Court, was furnished with Wilton carpets, blue moreen-covered sofas and chairs, blue moreen curtains, chimney glasses, and bookshelves. His second-floor rooms were just above those of the jurist Sir William Blackstone, who complained of the noise from his "revelling neighbour."

In December 1769 Goldsmith was appointed Professor of Ancient History of the Royal Academy, and he published *The Deserted Village* in May 1770. For the next four years until his death, he spent his summers in Kingsbury, Middlesex. *The Mistakes of Night* (later titled *She Stoops to Conquer*) was finished in 1772, but Goldsmith had some difficulty in securing a producer. George Colman at Covent Garden rejected it but was finally persuaded of its potential by Dr. Johnson, who led a large group on opening night. Goldsmith was in Kingsbury when he became ill in mid-March 1774 and returned to London for medical advice. On March 25, when his fever increased, he sent for William Hawes, an apothecary surgeon, but in the end attempted a self-cure with Dr. James's Fever Tablets. Goldsmith grew steadily weaker, and he died in strong convulsions on April 4. He was buried privately in the churchyard of Temple Church; the inscribed stone slab marks only the approximate site. Two years later the Literary Club erected a memorial in Westminster Abbey; this is a medallion portrait by Joseph Nollekens with an epitaph by Johnson.

Many other locations in London are associated both with Goldsmith and with his works. He was an inveterate frequenter of coffeehouses including the Globe Tavern and Coffee House, 133 Fleet Street, and the Grecian Coffee House, Devereux Court on the Strand, where he often ate; the Turk's Head Coffee House, 9 Gerrard Street, Soho (gone), where the Literary Club met; and Old Slaughter's Coffee House, 77 St. Martin's Lane, of which Goldsmith wrote: "If a man be passionate he may vent his rage among the old orators at Slaughter's Coffee-house and damn the nation because it keeps him from starving." On one occasion when Goldsmith was, as usual, late for a Literary Club dinner at St. James's Coffee House (87 St. James's Street), the other members of the group composed humorous verses about him; in response he penned "Retaliation":

> If our landlord supplies us with beef, and with fish,
> Let each guest bring himself, and he brings the best dish:
> Our Dean shall be venison, just fresh from the plains;
> Our Burke shall be tongue, with a garnish of brains;
> Our Will shall be wild-fowl, of excellent flavour,
> And Dick with his pepper shall heighten their savour:
> Our Cumberland's sweet-bread its place shall obtain,
> And Douglas is pudding, substantial and plain:
> Our Garrick's a salad; for in him we see
> Oil, vinegar, sugar, and saltness agree:
> To make out the dinner, full certain I am,
> That Ridge is an anchovy, and Reynolds is lamb;
> That Hickey's a capon, and by the same rule,
> Magnanimous Goldsmith a gooseberry fool.

Goldsmith often visited Northumberland House, on the west side of Northumberland Street (formerly Hartshorne Lane), when the Rev. Thomas Percy lived there in the 1770s as chaplain to the 1st Duke of Northumberland; it was here, the story goes, that calling by appointment, Goldsmith mistook the liveried footman for the duke. In the 18th century the Islington area became a popular spa; advertisements called it the new Tunbridge Wells, and hundreds flocked here. Goldsmith writes in *The Citizen of the World:*

> Here the inhabitants of London often assemble to celebrate a feast of hot rolls and butter; seeing such numbers, each with their little tables before them, employed on this occasion, must no doubt be a very amusing sight to the looker-on but still more so to those who perform the solemnity.

In the same work he describes Vauxhall Gardens:

> [U]pon entering the gardens, I found every sense overpaid with more than expected pleasure: the lights everywhere glimmering through the scarcely-moving trees, the full-bodied concert bursting on the stillness of the night, the natural concert of the birds in the more retired part of the grove, vying with that which was formed by art; the company gaily dressed looking satisfaction, and the tables spread with various delicacies, all conspired to fill my imagination with the visionary happiness of the Arabian lawgiver, and lifted me into an ecstasy of admiration.

Finally, St. Dunstan's clock, mentioned in *The Vicar of Wakefield,* was, in fact, in the Earl of Hertford's Regent's Park home (called St. Dunstan's), where it was taken from the old Church of St. Dunstan.

Charles Churchill (1731–1764) The now-little-read satiric poet Charles Churchill was born in February 1731 on Vine Street, Westminster (gone), when his father was curate of the nearby Church of St. John the Evangelist. At the age of eight Churchill was sent to the 14th-century Westminster School, whose buildings surround Little Dean's Yard, and after a rather young marriage in 1748 he and his wife lived with the Rev. Charles Churchill. The poet's life is obscure for some time, but he is thought to have returned to the metropolis to take charge of some property belonging to his wife before he was ordained. With his father's death in 1758, he was made curate of St. John's, but the income (£100 a year) was insufficient to support his family, and he opened a school somewhere in Westminster. He also taught in a ladies' boarding school run by a Mrs. Dennis at 24 Queen Square, where the Homeopathic Hospital now stands. Churchill was noted for his disreputable behavior, although not at the "ladies' Eton"; his preaching was such that "sleep, at his bidding, crept from pew to pew," and his marriage lasted only until February 1761. *The Rosciad*, a satire on leading actors and actresses, appeared in 1761, and Churchill's contemporary fame was secure. He frequented the Bedford Coffee House in Covent Garden and eventually had a house at Richmond and at Acton Common. He died abroad in November 1764 and was buried in Dover.

William Cowper (1731–1800)   William Cowper, one of the most widely read poets of his day, had a long but sporadic relationship with London; following the death of his mother in 1737 and a few years in a boarding school in Hertford, he was sent to Westminster School, the buildings of which surround Little Dean's Yard, between the abbey and Dean's Yard. The entire school then was taught in the Great Hall (the old monks' dormitory), and behind the rod table (from which two birch rods protruded from a drawer) were the masters' chairs (dating to the reign of Henry VIII). Much later Cowper noted that he became "adept in the infernal art of lying" to the masters; "Table Talk" refers specifically to his time at Westminster, and "Tirocinum, or A Review of Schools" conveys his attitude:

Ye once were justly famed for bringing forth
Undoubted scholarship and genuine worth,
And in the firmament of fame still shines
A glory bright as that of all the signs,
Of poets raised by you, and statesmen, and divines,
Peace to them all! those brilliant times are fled,
And no such lights are kindling in their stead.
Our striplings shine indeed, but with such rays
As set the midnight riot in a blaze,
And seem, if judged by their expressive looks,
Deeper in none than in their surgeons' books.

At school he enjoyed the usual holiday pastimes such as visiting the Tower of London or the great hospital at Bedlam; at the latter he was both much upset by the misery and suffering and somewhat entertained by the whimsy of the inmates. In a 1748 letter, though, he wrote, "I was angry at myself for being so [amused]."

Cowper left Westminster School in 1749 and was articled to a solicitor named Chapman whose offices were on Ely Place, Holborn; Cowper's uncle, Ashley Cowper, lived on Southampton Row (the ninth house on the east side after Cosmo Place), where the poet was a regular visitor, partly in the courtship of his cousin Theodora. All the Cowpers attended St. George's Church on Queen Square. Some accounts of Cowper's life relate that while articled to Chapman, the poet lived at 62 Russell Square, but Cowper himself writes that he lived for "three years with Mr. Chapman, the Solicitor, that is to say, I slept three years in his house; but I lived, that is to say, I spent my days, in Southampton Row." Nevertheless, in 1748 he entered the Middle Temple and in 1752 took chambers on Inner Temple Lane, where he remained, unhappily as it turns out, for close to a year.

He attended services at St. George-the-Martyr on Queen Square at this time. Cowper was called to the bar in 1754 and took lodgings in Pump Court, where, he said, "there are lime trees, and where the sound of water passing into pails and pitchers, is rather agreeable." The courtship of his cousin Theodora was brought to an end in 1756, when Ashley Cowper forbade the two to marry on grounds of consanguinity. Cowper was turning more and more to literature, but in 1759 he received the sinecure appointment of commissioner of bankrupts with an annual salary of £60.

Signs of mental instability were appearing, and the offer of the office of clerk of the journals called for an examination at the bar in the House of Lords in 1763. Cowper at this point was on the brink of suicide, and, in fact, "the merciful depths of insanity" occurred the week of the examination. On the appointed day, breakfasting at Richard's Coffee House (also Dick's Coffee House), 8 Fleet Street, he read a newspaper item which he felt was a personal affront. Deciding on immediate suicide, he rushed to Tower Wharf on the Custom House Quay to drown himself, but the water was too low. He had already attempted suicide with laudanum and found that he could not drink it; the third attempt came the next day, when he tried to hang himself in his rooms in Fig Tree Court. Cowper wrote later:

By the eternal Providence of God, the garter which had held me till the bitterness of temporal death was past, broke before eternal death had taken place upon me.

His cousin, Maj. William Cowper, saw that pursuing the clerkship was impossible, and after care in London for a short time, Cowper was removed to an asylum in St. Albans, Hertfordshire. Here he was visited by numerous relatives including Martin Madan, a strong Calvinistic preacher, whose visit increased the poet's horror and despair and produced:

Man disavows, and Deity disowns me,
Hell might afford my miseries a shelter;
Therefore, Hell keeps her ever-hungry mouths all
            Bolted against me.

There are two other Cowper associations of note. One concerns John Beyer, a linendraper at 3 Cheapside, who was the model for John Gilpin in "The History of John Gilpin":

John Gilpin was a citizen
    Of credit and renown,
A trainband captain eke was he
    Of famous London town.

"Table Talk" also contains many references to London, including a passage on the Gordon Riots and one on the historic giants from St. Dunstan's Church which were removed by the Earl of Hertford to St. Dunstan's, his Regent's Park home. These figures, badly mutilated and damaged in the Great Fire, formed an effective simile for mediocre poets:

When labor and when dulness, club in hand,
Like the two figures at St. Dunstan's stand,
Beating alternately, in measured time,
The clockwork tintinnabulum of rhyme,
Exact and regular the sounds will be;
But such mere quarter-strokes are not for me.

Richard Cumberland (1732–1811)   Poet, emissary to Spain, friend of Lord Byron, Sir Walter Scott, and

Thomas Moore, and author of forty plays and two novels, yet largely forgotten today, Irish-born Richard Cumberland came to Westminster School, whose buildings surround Little Dean's Yard, from a school in Bury St. Edmunds, Suffolk, in 1744; his first lodgings at the school were with William Cowper. After Cambridge, he did not return to London until sometime after the mid-1750s, when he had begun writing for the stage. At that time he was living in the Abingdon Buildings (where the gardens now are), near Westminster Abbey; *The Brothers*, which was produced at Covent Garden in 1769, was his first considerable success, and David Garrick produced *The West Indian*, probably Cumberland's best play, in 1771. By this time he was living in one of the corner houses on Queen Anne Street at Wimpole Street and frequenting the British Coffee House, opposite Suffolk Street, Charing Cross, with Garrick, Oliver Goldsmith, and Sir Joshua Reynolds. Cumberland retired to Tunbridge Wells but died in London at the home of Henry Fry, 30 Bedford Place, on May 7, 1811, and was buried in Westminster Abbey.

James Macpherson (1736–1796) Only once during the Ossian controversy did James Macpherson come to London; in 1761, at the express invitation of the 3d Earl of Bute, Macpherson arrived and in December had issued by public subscription *Fingal*, which was soon denounced as spurious. He did not return to the city until 1766, after serving as secretary to the Governor of West Florida for two years. Then he settled in Manchester Buildings (gone) and Norfolk Street before moving in 1792 to Fludyer Street, which stood west off Parliament Street, just below King Charles Street, where the Treasury now is. In 1780 Macpherson became the Member of Parliament for Camelford, Cornwall, and retained this seat after the 1790 election although he never addressed the House. Macpherson died in Badenoch, Inverness-shire, on February 17, 1796, and his body was returned to London, where it was buried in the south transept of Westminster Abbey, near the Poets' Corner, on March 15.

Edward Gibbon (1737–1794) The historian Edward Gibbon was born on April 27, 1737, at his maternal grandfather's home (gone) in Putney and is remembered today by Gibbon Walk. The only one of seven children to survive infancy, Gibbon suffered from various physical ills in childhood and was frequently cared for by an aunt, Catherine Porten, because of his mother's "delicate" condition. He attended a day school here before being sent to a public school at Kingston-on-Thames, where his experiences were most unpleasant. The death of his mother in December 1747 and his father's retirement to Buriton, Hampshire, left the child here in the care of his aunt and grandfather, and he was soon absorbed in *The Arabian Nights*, Pope, and Dryden. With the bankruptcy of the elder Porten, Gibbon's aunt set up a boardinghouse in Dean Yard for the Westminster School, probably mostly to benefit her nephew. Gibbon entered the school in 1748 or 1749, but serious illness forced his withdrawal in 1750. Not until he became independent, following his father's death late in 1770, was Gibbon able to settle in London again; in 1772 he took the lease of 7 Bentinck Street, where he remained for eleven years. He very seldom left

London and became a habitué of London clubs and coffeehouses (Brooks at 60 St. James's Street, the Cocoa Tree Coffee House at 28 Pall Mall, and Almack's Tavern at 49–50 Pall Mall); during the early part of his residence, he began *The History of the Decline and Fall of the Roman Empire*, which had been conceived on a visit to Rome in 1764. From September 1783 until May 1793 Gibbon lived in Lausanne, but he returned to England permanently following the death of Lady Sheffield, the wife of his intimate friend John Baker Holroyd, Baron Sheffield (later Earl of Sheffield). Gibbon settled with a friend at 74 St. James's Street in November and was now suffering from serious and frequent attacks of gout; he had received medical attention for the problem in 1761 but had ignored any treatment for the condition in the interim. He underwent three operations and spent Christmas at Sheffield Park, Lord Sheffield's home in Fletching, Sussex; returning to London, he appeared to be much improved in health and said on January 15 that he felt he would still have a "good life for ten, twelve, or perhaps twenty years." He became critically ill that night and died the following afternoon; Gibbon was buried in the Sheffield family vault in the Fletching Church.

Other London locales associated with Gibbon include St. James's Church, Piccadilly (where he tripped over a gravestone and sprained an ankle); the Rose Tavern (gone), at the corner of Catherine and Russell Streets (where he dined with his father and David Mallett, or Malloch, in 1763); and 14 John Adam Street, the Adelphi Hotel, or Osborne's (where he stayed upon his return from Lausanne in 1788 to superintend the publication of the last volumes of *The Decline and Fall*).

John Wolcot (1738–1819) John Wolcot, better known as Peter Pindar, came to London in 1762 to pursue the study of medicine and lodged with his uncle; he returned to the West Country two years later as a medical assistant in Fowey, Cornwall, until becoming the physician to Sir William Trelawny, who was appointed to the governorship of Jamaica in 1767. Returning to London in 1769 for the sole purpose of taking orders and securing the lucrative living of St. Anne, Jamaica, which was Sir William's to bestow, Wolcot was ordained deacon (June 24) and priest (June 25) by the Bishop of London and returned to Jamaica immediately. With Sir William's death in 1772, he dropped the clerical calling and practiced medicine in the West Country until the success of some songs and poems prompted his removal to London in 1781.

To Wolcot's wealth of London addresses specific years can be assigned only occasionally. In 1793 he lived on Southampton Street (not Southampton Row, as is usually stated), and the next year he moved to Tavistock Row, which in the 18th century was a row of houses facing into Covent Garden just beyond Southampton Street (it should not be confused with the present-day Tavistock Street). He also resided at 7 Great Newport Street, 1 Aldford Street, and 1 Gildea Street. In 1800 he was at 1 Chapel Place, and in 1810, after two other moves to Camden Town and 94 Tottenham Court Road, he was on Howland Street, when his house was very nearly destroyed by fire and a servant girl was killed. Wolcot died on January 14, 1819, at Montgomery Cottage,

Somers Town, and was buried, as he directed, in the churchyard of St. Paul's Church, Covent Garden, next to Samuel Butler.

Henry Pye (1745–1813) In some ways the 18th-century Poets Laureate, Nahum Tate, Nicholas Rowe, Laurence Eusden, Colley Cibber, William Whitehead, Thomas Warton, and Henry James Pye, were ill-chosen men; none except Warton compares well with later figures. Indeed, Henry James Pye was relegated to a footnote, "H. J. Pye (1745–1813), author of *Alfred*, an epic (1801) and many other volumes of worthless verse; poet laureate, 1790–1813," in Alfred C. Baugh's *A Literary History of England*. Pye was born somewhere in London on February 20, 1745, and was educated privately at home. Pye spent most of his time from 1766 on at the family estate in Faringdon, Berkshire, although he sat in the Commons as the Member for Berkshire from 1784 on. At some point he settled at 2 Buckingham Gate, where it enters Birdcage Walk; he was appointed a police magistrate for Westminster in 1792. There is a memorial in the parish church in Pinner. Pye was the man whom Sir Walter Scott termed "eminently respectable in every thing but his poetry."

Hannah More (1745–1833) Hannah More came to London from Bristol in 1773 or 1774, at which time she was introduced to David Garrick and soon became an intimate of both Garrick and his wife. In 1777 she had a house on Henrietta Street, Covent Garden, and in 1778 she took up residence on Gerrard Street. The intimacy with the Garricks grew, and after David Garrick's death in 1779, Miss More was invited to take up companionship residence at 5 Adelphi Terrace; she remained for twenty years.

Mrs. Charlotte Smith (1749–1806) The woman who has been called "probably the most popular novelist in the English-speaking world in the 1790s," Mrs. Charlotte Smith (née Turner) was born on King Street (the number is not known) on May 4, 1749, and lived here until her mother's death in 1752. After an arranged marriage at the age of fifteen, she lived with her in-laws in the city and fled to Lys Farm, Hampshire, after her invalid mother-in-law's death. When her husband Benjamin's flair for extravagance and backing of wild schemes led to his imprisonment at the King's Bench Prison on Scovell Road, Southwark, around 1784, Mrs. Smith and their children remained with him throughout the seven months' confinement. Separation eventually occurred (ca. 1787), and Mrs. Smith, now the sole support of the family, turned to writing in earnest. The extremely successful *Emmeline, or The Orphan of the Castle*, which Sir Walter Scott praised highly, appeared in 1788, and others followed regularly until 1799; toward the end of her life, Mrs. Smith lived on Baker Street, four or five doors up from Marylebone Road.

Richard Brinsley Sheridan (1751–1816) Although his father and family had come to London from Dublin, Ireland, before 1757, Richard Brinsley Sheridan did not join them until late 1758 or early 1759; Thomas Sheridan, a successful teacher of elocution, had a house on Frith Street, where the boy spent all his holidays from Harrow (1762–1768). Two years after his mother's death in 1766, the boy was brought home from Harrow and educated privately in Latin and mathematics by Lewis Ker, a retired physician. Sheridan's father moved the family to Bath in 1770,

and there they became acquainted with the Linley family, whose daughter Elizabeth the dramatist was later to marry. Miss Linley had been persecuted by the attentions of Maj. Thomas Mathews, and after helping her to escape the Welshman by fleeing to Lille, France, in March 1772, Sheridan returned to London, where he dueled with Mathews. In early May, after Mathews called the dramatist "a liar and a treacherous scoundrel," they fought in three different locations, starting at the Ring at Hyde Park (considerably smaller and farther inside Hyde Park than today's Ring). After drawing a crowd, they moved to a tavern at Hyde Park Corner, where a crowd also gathered; finally they moved to the Castle, at the northeast corner of Bedford and Henrietta Streets, where Mathews was disarmed. Both fathers opposed marriage between Sheridan and Elizabeth Linley.

Sheridan entered the Middle Temple on April 6, 1773, at just about the time Linley ceased opposing his daughter's marriage; as a consequence, Sheridan broke with his father, gave up his career in law, and married Elizabeth. The ceremony, arranged by special license, took place on April 13 at Marylebone Church, which stood on the Marylebone High Street opposite the entrance to Beaumont Street; the church was gutted in World War II, and the site is now a garden. The marriage was announced in the *Gentleman's Magazine*: "Mr. Sheridan of the Temple to the celebrated Miss Linley of Bath." The couple eventually took a house at 22 Orchard Street, Portman Square, and Sheridan turned to the theater. Both *The Rivals* and *The Duenna* were written here; these works were produced at Covent Garden, and the second was unrivaled as an opera, with seventy-five performances during the season (*The Beggar's Opera* had sixty-three). Sheridan became an extremely popular dramatist, and in June 1776 he took over the patent for the Drury Lane Theatre (officially, the Theatre Royal) from the aging David Garrick. With his father-in-law and Dr. James Ford, he bought Garrick's share in the theater for £35,000; and two years later they bought the other shares from Garrick's partner, Willoughby Lacy, for the same amount. Sheridan remained manager until 1788 and part owner until 1809. In 1777 he moved to Great Queen Street, near the theater, on the site of the present Freemasons' Hall, and was working on *The School for Scandal*, the play which brought the title "the modern Congreve" to Sheridan.

In March 1777 Sheridan became a member of Dr. Johnson's Literary Club, which met at the Turk's Head, 9 Gerrard Street, Soho. Through his association with Charles James Fox, Sheridan became interested in politics, and in 1780 he was returned as the Member of Parliament for Stafford; he was a persuasive orator during his thirty-two-year parliamentary career. In 1783 and 1784 Sheridan and his family lived somewhere on Albemarle Street, Piccadilly, and in 1784 and 1785 on Bruton Street, just off Berkeley Square. Sheridan was possibly already in financial difficulties, and, it is said, the Bruton Street house was so often beset by bailiffs that food had to be introduced to the house over the railings. Sheridan was heavily involved in the impeachment proceedings against Warren Hastings, and his speech at Westminster Hall on the matter of the Begums of Oudh has become one of the most memorable in the records of Parliament;

the entire body including the gallery applauded, an unprecedented occurrence. In 1792 he took a house on Jermyn Street, but in that year both Sheridan's wife and daughter died. From 1795, the year in which he married Esther Jane Ogle, daughter of the dean of Winchester, until 1802, Sheridan lived at 10 Hertford Street (originally, Garrick Street), Berkeley Square; Gen. John Burgoyne, who lost the Battle of Saratoga to Benedict Arnold, also lived here. Sheridan's interest in government and the Drury Lane Theatre continued, and in 1802 he moved to 37 St. James's Place.

The House of Commons was meeting on the night of February 24, 1809, on the question of the conduct of the war in Spain when it suddenly was lit up by extraordinary light:

> [I]t was ascertained that the Theatre of Drury Lane was on fire. A motion was made to adjourn; but Mr. Sheridan said, with much calmness, that "whatsoever might be the extent of the private calamity, he hoped it would not interfere with the public business of the country." He then left the House; and . . . witnessed, with . . . fortitude . . . the entire destruction of his property. It is said that, as he sat at the Piazza Coffee-house during the fire, taking some refreshment, a friend of his having remarked on the philosophic calmness with which he bore his misfortune, Sheridan answered, "A man may surely be allowed to take a glass of wine by his own fireside."

The Piazza Coffee House (Great Piazza Coffee House) stood at the northeast angle of Covent Garden Piazza. The fire brought chaos to Sheridan's financial affairs; he had already underwritten the extra costs (£75,000) of rebuilding the theater, and by 1811 he had to sell his books to pay bills, many of which were brought about by an excessively extravagant life. In the spring of 1813 he was arrested and taken to Took's Court (north off Cursitor Street), a sponging house, where he spent a short period (a sponging house was a kind of halfway house where debtors were placed until they paid their debts or were placed in debtors' prison). Sheridan became ill late in 1815, and, living then at 17 Savile Row, he became bedridden the following spring. (It is now believed the correct house number was 14, not 17; this was a house given to Sheridan for his use by the Duke of Wellington.) He was still debt-ridden at this time, and at least one report stated that an order which had been issued for his arrest was forestalled by his physician. Sheridan died here on July 7, 1816, and the reports that he died unattended and in abject poverty were untrue; Charles Brinsley Sheridan, the dramatist's son, wrote to his half brother:

> You will be soothed by learning that our father's death was unaccompanied by suffering, that he almost slumbered into death, and that the reports which you may have seen in the newspapers of the privations and the want of comforts which he endured are unfounded. . . .

Sheridan's body was taken to the home of Peter Moore, (Member of Parliament for Coventry) on Great George Street, where it lay in state until July 14. Sheridan was buried in the Poets' Corner at Westminster Abbey on an exceptionally grand scale; he had wanted to be buried near Fox, but, at least in modern terms, the more appropriate place was chosen. *The Times* spoke of Sheridan as a man

> whom it has been the fashion for many years to quote as a bold reprover of the selfish spirit of party; and throughout

a period fruitful of able men and trying circumstances, as the most popular specimen in the British Senate of political consistency, intrepidity, and honour.

Many other locations in London are associated with the dramatist. He was frequently at Burlington House, now the home of the Royal Academy of Arts, but then the unofficial headquarters of the Whig party. Sheridan also was a member of White's Chocolate House (a private members' club from 1736 on and famous as a gaming house) and of the Cocoa Tree Chocolate House (a private club from 1745 on), at 46 Pall Mall from 1757 to 1787, at 64 Pall Mall until 1799, and then at 64 St. James's Street. He also frequented Brooks's Club at 60 St. James's Place; the headquarters of the Whigs and Liberals for many years, it has been called "the most famous political club that will ever have existed in England," for its members included Edmund Burke, David Hume, Charles Fox, Edward Gibbon, Horace Walpole, and Sheridan.

Thomas Chatterton (1752–1770)   "The marvelous boy," as William Wordsworth later called him, Thomas Chatterton came to London from Bristol in late April 1770; he first lived somewhere in Shoreditch and frequented the Chapter Coffee House, on Paternoster Row at the corner of Paul's Alley. A letter to his mother notes that he was "quite familiar" there. In June Chatterton moved to 39 Brooke Street, the first house from the corner of Holborn on the west side; a dreary place, it was pulled down in 1880, but a commemorative plaque was placed on the current building in 1928. Chatterton did not fare well in the metropolis, and his poems of Thomas Rowley, passed off as those of a 15th-century Bristol monk, were greeted with suspicion and hostility. He was literally starving but refused the aid of friends, and in the greatest despair, on the night of Friday, August 24, 1770, at the age of eighteen, he took arsenic. (It has been said that he was driven to suicide when a baker refused him a loaf of bread.) On August 29 he was buried in the grounds of Shoe Lane Workhouse (also known as St. Andrew's Workhouse, approximately where 41–43 Shoe Lane stands); the register at St. Andrew's Church contains the erroneous entry "William Chatterton Brooke's Street 28," but added later in a different hand is "the poet T. . . ." In 1828 a number of bodies were removed from the graveyard, and it is thought that Chatterton's was one of those taken to St. Andrew's Garden on the west side of Gray's Inn Road; however, in 1892 other remains from the original burial ground were taken to the City of London Cemetery at Little Ilford, and it is possible that Chatterton's remains are there.

Fanny Burney (1752–1840)   Mme. Alexandre d'Arblay, who is far better known under her maiden name, Fanny Burney, came to London in 1760, when her father moved his family here from King's Lynn, Norfolk; they lived in a house in the grounds of the Royal Hospital, Chelsea, where Dr. Charles Burney was the organist for twenty-three years. As a child she lived for a time at 50 Poland Street, Soho. In 1771 Dr. Burney, his second wife, and the rest of the family moved to a house on the east side of Queen Square, where they stayed until 1774. Fanny Burney was entirely self-educated and is said not even to have known the alphabet when she was eight years old, but by the time she was living on Queen Square she had begun

Evelina, or The History of a Young Lady's Entrance into the World. She claimed not to have committed it to paper until it was completely worked out mentally. In 1774 the Burneys moved to 35 St. Martin's Street (the home of Sir Isaac Newton); here *Evelina* was written and presented for publication. Appearing anonymously, it was well received and eventually brought Miss Burney to Dr. Samuel Johnson's attention. A second novel, *Cecilia, or Memoirs of an Heiress,* appeared in 1782, but it was not the equal of *Evelina.* In 1786 she took the post of second keeper of the robes under Madame Schwellenberg with many misgivings, which were borne out in her five unhappy years of service.

Fanny Burney met General d'Arblay, formerly adjutant general to the Marquis de Lafayette, and they were married on July 31, 1793, in Mickleham, Surrey, and repeated their vows on August 1 at the Sardinian Embassy's Catholic Chapel on Sardinia Street. Following a very difficult period in France, Madame d'Arblay and her son returned to London; when she was nursing her ill father, she lived at 23 Chenies Street, where her sister Charlotte (Mrs. Clement Francis) lived, and then she moved to 63 Lower Sloane Street, Chelsea, close to the Old Burial Ground, where her father was buried. From this point on she devoted herself to her son (ordained deacon in 1818 and priest in 1819 and appointed minister of Ely Chapel in 1836) and to the preparation of her father's memoirs. From 1818 to 1828 she lived at 11 Bolton Street and in 1828 moved to 1 Half Moon Street, where she remained until 1836. She spent 1838 and probably at least part of 1839 at 22 Mount Street before moving, shortly before her death, to 29 Grosvenor Street; here she died on January 6, 1840.

Evelina is full of references to London; Evelina stays on Queen Anne Street and attends the Drury Lane and Haymarket Theatres and visits St. James's Park,

> a long straight walk of dirty gravel, very uneasy to the feet; and at each end instead of an open prospect, nothing is to be seen but houses built of brick.

Ranelagh Gardens, adjacent to the Royal Hospital in Chelsea, was

> a charming place; and the brilliancy of the lights, on my first entrance, made me almost think I was in some enchanted castle or fairy palace. . . .

But Evelina's first visit to Vauxhall Gardens, a 12-acre site also known as Spring Gardens, bounded roughly by Leopold Street, Upper Kennington Lane, St. Oswald's Place, and Goding Street, was most disagreeable because of the company; however,

> The garden is very pretty, but too formal; I should have been better pleased, had it consisted less of straight walks, where
>
> > Grove nods at grove, each alley has its brother.
>
> The trees, the numerous lights, and the company in the circle round the orchestra make a most brilliant and gay appearance; and had I been with a party less disagreeable to me, I should have thought it a place formed for animation and pleasure.

George Crabbe (1754–1832)   Aldeburgh, Suffolk, is the place most frequently associated with George Crabbe, but his start in the literary world must be

placed in London. Abandoning an unsuccessful medical practice (for which he had practically no training) and borrowing a few pounds, he came to the metropolis in April 1780 and found lodgings with a Mr. Vickery, a hairdresser, somewhere close to the Exchange. When Vickery moved his family to 119 Bishopsgate (seven doors from Cornhill), Crabbe went too. He spent evenings in a small coffeehouse near the Exchange and tried in vain to gain patronage from Lord North, the Earl of Shelburne, and Edward, Baron Thurlow; finally, at the beginning of 1781, he wrote to Edmund Burke about his desperate state. In March Crabbe, in total despair, paced back and forth over the old Westminster Bridge contemplating suicide before Burke came to his rescue. Burke persuaded Robert E. James Dodsley to publish *The Library* and took Crabbe into his own home in Beaconsfield, Buckinghamshire. Years later, Crabbe returned to London; in 1813, with his wife, who, although ill, wanted to be in the metropolis, he stayed at Osborne's Hotel (the Adelphi), which stood at 1–4 John Adams Street. In 1817, on another trip, Crabbe had lodgings at 37 Bury Street while he arranged for the publication of *Tales of the Hall;* on other occasions he stayed at Hummums's Hotel, which stood where Russell Street enters Covent Garden.

William Blake (1757–1827)

> 'Twas on a Holy Thursday, their innocent faces clean,
> The children walking two and two, in red and blue and green,
> Grey-headed beadles walked before with wands as white as snow,
> Till into the high dome of Paul's they like Thames' water flow.
>
> O what a multitude they seemed, these flowers of London Town!
> Seated in companies they sit with radiance all their own.

Without question one of the most significant figures of this period was the poet, painter, engraver, and visionary William Blake, born on November 28, 1757, at 28 Broad Street (now Broadwick Street). In the 1960s a large building was put up on this site, and nothing now remains from Blake's time. His was a comfortably off family, and Blake was christened on December 11 at St. James's Church, Piccadilly; the ornate marble font by Grinling Gibbons used for Blake's christening has survived. When he was ten, Blake was sent to Henry Pars's drawing school on the Strand, then the best school in the City; it was on the north side of the Strand, approximately where Agar Street enters. By 1769 he was writing verse, and his wanderings through the nearby fields and villages made a strong impression on him:

> How sweet I roamed from field to field,
> And tasted all the summer's pride,
> Till I the prince of love beheld
> Who in the sunny beams did glide!

In 1771 Blake was apprenticed to the engraver William Ryland, whom Blake did not like because of his face, which Blake is supposed to have said "looks as if he will live to be hanged," and he was, twelve years later, for forgery. From Ryland, Blake went to James Basire, an engraver whose works were at 31 Great

Queen Street (the building, then Number 30, was just opposite the Freemasons' Hall); here Blake remained until 1778, and the training in fundamentals served him well in later years. In the summers Blake was set to recording many of the monuments in the old churches of London, especially those in Westminster Abbey, and in the winter to engraving the work. After the apprenticeship ended, he became a student at the Antique School (on St. Martin's Lane) of the Royal Academy under George Michael Moser, its first keeper; Blake was still living at home and was making his living by engraving and painting watercolors, but he soon left the academy because he disliked the influence of Sir Joshua Reynolds and found the academic method of studying stifling.

On August 18, 1782, Blake married Catherine Sophia Boucher in the Battersea Church, and the couple set up house at 23 Green Street (gone) on Leicester Square. After the death of Blake's father in 1784, they moved to 27 Broad Street, next to Blake's mother and his brother James. Blake set up as a printer and engraver with James Parker and brought his younger brother Robert to live with him; this was the year that Blake exhibited *War Unchained by an Angel, Fire, Pestilence, and Famine Following* and *Breach in a City: The Morning after a Battle* at the Royal Academy. Robert, however, was ill, and Blake attended him until his death in February 1787. Some sort of disagreement with Parker, coupled with Robert's death, precipitated Blake's move to 28 Poland Street; here *Songs of Innocence* was written. Lacking the money to hire a compositor, he claimed that the vision of his dead brother inspired him to send out his wife with (supposedly) their only half crown to purchase materials; he then engraved both the words and designs and hand-painted the pages after printing. *The Book of Thel* appeared in 1789, and *The Marriage of Heaven and Hell* was finished in 1790. The next year Blake, at the request of the bookseller Joseph Johnson, undertook the illustrations for Mary Wollstonecraft's *Original Stories from Real Life;* Johnson's shop, at 72 St. Paul's Churchyard, was also the scene of weekly dinners to which Blake, William Godwin, Thomas Paine, and Mary Wollstonecraft were intermittently invited.

In 1793 Blake and his wife moved to 13 Hercules Buildings in Lambeth, a one-story structure on the west side immediately after Westminster Bridge Street; it is now rebuilt as a series of tenements. In the garden house at the end of the gardens the Adam and Eve episode is said to have occurred. Thomas Butts, who kept the Blakes alive by buying on the average one drawing a week, arrived and found them in the summerhouse. Blake supposedly called out, "Come in! it's only Adam and Eve, you know!" whereupon Butts discovered they had been reading aloud passages from *Paradise Lost* while unclothed. Blake was prolific during these years but quite poor; however, the appearance of *Songs of Experience, Europe: A Prophecy,* and *The First Book of Urizen* in 1794 and *The Song of Los* and *The Book of Ahania* in 1795 helped a little. Blake also had aid from John Flaxman, the sculptor, who initiated a scheme whereby the poet-engraver went to Felpham, Sussex, where William Hayley was undertaking *The Life of Cowper.*

When he returned to London in January 1804,

following the sedition trial in Chichester, Sussex, Blake settled on the first floor at 17 South Moulton Street; here he began both *Jerusalem* and *Milton.* He exhibited at the Royal Academy for the last time in 1808 with *Christ in the Sepulchre Guarded by Angels* and *Jacob's Dream,* and his last attempt to display his work publicly came in May 1809 at his brother's house on Broad Street; the exhibit was not well attended, but one of those who did view the work was Charles Lamb. In 1821 Blake, who was now unable to get much work, moved to 3 Fountain Court on the Strand; the court stood where Numbers 103 and 104 on the Strand are today. He often visited the home of Charles Aders, a wealthy merchant from an old German family, at 11 Euston Square, and here met both Samuel Taylor Coleridge and Henry Crabb Robinson.

In 1821 Blake was commissioned by John Linnell to engrave the *Illustrations of the Book of Job,* perhaps his most beautiful work; Linnell, himself a struggling artist, was virtually supporting Blake at this time. Sundays were often spent with Linnell and his family, who lived at Old Wyldes, Hampstead Way, Hampstead; the farm was north of Hampstead Heath between North End and the Spaniards Inn. Blake's health was declining at this time, and, indeed, he was working in bed. He died at Fountain Court on August 12, 1827, and was buried with a Church of England service in Bunhill Fields (the Nonconformists' cemetery west off City Road) on August 17. Neither stone nor marker was placed on the "common grave" (19 shillings), and the record at Somerset House reveals that the grave is numbered "77, east and west; 32, north and south." There is now no means of identifying the grave, but a small blackened stone near the obelisk marking the grave of Daniel Defoe is in the general area. There is a commemorative monument to Blake in St. Paul's Cathedral, and an entire room in the Tate Gallery is devoted to his works.

Three final associations might be noted. The village of Paddington, once an area of green fields with an estate known as Tyburnia, was laid out for extensive building in the early 1800s; and building began almost immediately, as the poet noted:

What are those Golden builders doing? Where was the
   burying-place
Of soft Ethinthus? near Tyburn's fatal Tree? Is that
Mild Zion's hill's most ancient promontory, near
   mournful
Ever-weeping Paddington?

At one time he had relatives living in the general area of Hampstead, and Blake knew "the lovely hills of Camberwell" and "the fields of corn at Peckham Rye"; later he writes:

The fields from Islington to Marylebone,
To Primrose Hill and Saint John's Wood,
Were builded over with pillars of gold,
And there Jerusalem's pillars stood.

Her little ones ran in the fields,
The Lamb of God among them seen
And fair Jerusalem his bride
Among the little meadows green.

Pancras and Kentish town repose

Among her golden pillars high,
Among her golden arches which
Shine upon the starry sky.

In *Jerusalem* he notes how the Spitalfields silk throwers, crowded together in their houses behind sealed windows, could hear

The shuttles of death sing in the sky to Islington and Pancras,
Round Marylebone to Tyburn's river, weaving black melancholy as a net. . . .

William Beckford (1759–1844)   The eccentric author of the Gothic novel *Vathek*, William Beckford, was not born in Fonthill Gifford, Wiltshire, as is usually stated, but at 22 Soho Square, where his father, Lord Mayor of London, had lived since 1752. To say the least, Beckford had a good life as a child; at the age of five he took piano lessons from the eight-year-old Wolfgang Amadeus Mozart, and at the age of eleven he inherited a fortune estimated to earn around £100,000 a year on a capital of £1,000,000. After his father's death, he spent little time in London until after Fonthill Abbey was completed; then he lived at 16 Dover Street, at 22 Grosvenor Square (where Sir William and Lady Hamilton, as well as Horatio Nelson, were guests), and at 4 Devonshire Place. From about 1822 on he frequently rode his white Persian mare Deborah in Hyde Park.

William Cobbett (1763–1835)   The essayist and political activist William Cobbett had a long and sporadic association with London; in 1782 he came to the City from Farnham, Surrey, on his way to the Guildford Fair. Actually, he arrived on a whim, for he met the London stagecoach on the road and simply jumped in. From a man he met on the journey, he secured employment as a "quill-driver" (copy clerk) to a Mr. Holland, an obscure attorney with chambers in Gray's Inn. Cobbett remained with Holland for eight or nine months and spent Sundays walking in St. James's Park. Unhappy in his employment but resisting his father's order to return home, he was quite possibly desperate when he enlisted in the armed services the next year. He served eight years in the Army, most of which time was spent in Canada. On one return trip to London, Cobbett married Ann Reid on February 5, 1792, in the church at Woolwich.

In early July 1800, after a period in the United States, Cobbett came directly to lodgings in St. James's Street. He began *Porcupine's Gazette* (October 30, 1800). It failed by the end of November 1801, partly, claimed Cobbett, because of the General Post Office and difficulties over shipment to the United States. He moved to 11 Pall Mall, where he set up a bookseller's shop in partnership with John Morgan at the Crown and Mitre. *The Political Register* was begun through private subscription in January 1802 and was published weekly until his death in 1835. In March 1803 Cobbett sold the book business and moved to lodgings somewhere in Westminster before moving to Botley, Hampshire. His first real trouble with the government occurred with his June 1810 sedition trial for an article on military flogging; he insisted on pleading his own case, but after only five minutes' deliberation the jury found him guilty. Cobbett was fined £1,000 and spent two years in Newgate Prison, on the southeast corner of Newgate Street and Old Bailey. His imprisonment was com-

fortable enough: he hired a considerable part of the head jailer's lodging for the period, was allowed visitors from 12 noon until 10 P.M., and was even able to continue *The Register*. His release on July 9, 1812 (on bail of £3,000 and two sureties of £1,000), was celebrated with a dinner for 600 at the Crown and Anchor Tavern, at 37 the Strand, a gathering place of Radicals.

Cobbett continued to live in Hampshire, although his business was in London. In 1821 he moved *The Register's* publishing office to 1 Clement's Inn, but the offices were subsequently moved three more times, to Johnson's Court (on Fleet Street between Red Lion Court and Bold Court), to 183 Fleet Street, and then to 11 Bolt Court. In 1832, at the age of sixty-nine, when he was elected to Parliament as the Member from Oldham, Lancashire, Cobbett took up residence at 21 Crown Street, Westminster, a house with

a door opening on the park . . . looking across the parade and over the Mall, and having in the background of the view the lofty column standing in Waterloo Place. . . .

Early in 1834 he gave up these lodgings and moved into Bolt Court. But evening parliamentary hours and the routine of the House of Commons disturbed him, and, indeed, his political career was a failure. Attending meetings of the House in May 1835, he became ill and retreated to Normandy Farm in Ash, Surrey, where he died on June 18.

Ann Radcliffe (1764–1823)   Called "the 1st poetess of romantic fiction" by Sir Walter Scott, Ann Ward Radcliffe, who is best known today for *The Mysteries of Udolpho,* was born at 19 Holborn (demolished) on July 9, 1764, and baptized at the nearby St. Andrew's Church. Little is known of her London life, but after marriage in 1787 to William Radcliffe, a law student who was later proprietor of the *English Chronicle,* she traveled extensively. She spent the last eight years of her life at 5 Stafford Row (gone, but it once stood approximately where Bressenden Place leads into Buckingham Palace Road); here she died on February 7, 1823. Mrs. Radcliffe was buried in the old burying ground belonging to the parish of St. George, Hanover Square, on Hyde Park Place.

Robert Bloomfield (1766–1823)   The rustic poet Robert Bloomfield came to London from Sapiston, Suffolk, in 1781, when he was apprenticed to his brother Nathaniel, a shoemaker, and lived in a garret in his brother's house at what is now 14 Telegraph Street, east off Moorgate. They later moved to Blue Hart Court (gone) on Bell Alley (now Great Bell Alley). Bloomfield was married in 1790, and the couple lived somewhere in London in extreme poverty: it took a number of years even to acquire their own bed. By the time he became undersealer in the Seal Office, his health was failing, and he left London around 1814. One of the London places Bloomfield visited was Ranelagh Gardens in Chelsea:

A thousand feet restled on mats—
    A carpet that once had been green;
Men bowed with their outlandish hats,
    With corners so fearfully keen.
Fair maids, who at home in their haste
    Had left all clothing else but a train,
Swept the floor clean as slowly they paced,
    Then—walked round and swept it again.

William Wordsworth (1770–1850) The association between London and William Wordsworth reads more like a long list of dinner invitations than anything else, although he did take many trips here from his homes in the Lake District, particularly after he had achieved fame. His first trip followed his Cambridge degree in January 1791, when he stayed at Wyke House in Islington with John Robinson, Member of Parliament for Harwich. Of more importance was his probably seven-month stay in London beginning in December 1792, when he resided with his brother Richard in his chambers in Staple Inn, a group of half-timbered buildings originally dating to the 16th century, rebuilt in the 18th, and restored in the mid-1950s. Wordsworth spent February to August 1795 here with Basil Montagu at 7 New Square in Lincoln's Inn in an attempt to prove that "cataracts and mountains will not do for constant companions." It was during this period that Wordsworth made frequent calls in Somers Town on William Godwin, who was then at the height of his fame as the author of *An Enquiry Concerning the Principles of Political Justice* and *Things as They Are, or The Adventures of Caleb Williams.* Wordsworth also stayed with Montagu in 1796.

Not until 1802 did Wordsworth pay another visit here of any significance; following a trip to France to see Annette Vallon and their daughter Caroline, he stayed in London for almost three weeks. Coming from Dover by coach, he crossed the old stone Westminster Bridge (the present one dates to 1852):

Earth has not anything to show more fair:
Dull would he be of soul who could pass by
A sight so touching in its majesty:
This City now doth, like a garment, wear
The beauty of the morning; silent, bare,
Ships, towers, domes, theatres, and temples lie
Open unto the fields, and to the sky. . . .

On this visit Basil Montagu was again his host in Paper Buildings, King's Bench Walk, where he had rooms during law terms. Wordsworth visited the Lambs at 16 Mitre Court Buildings, also King's Bench Walk, and Charles Lamb took both Dorothy and William to "Bartelmy Fair," thus supplying some of the material for *The Prelude:*

            . . . the Fair,
Holden where martyrs suffered in past time,
And named of St. Bartholomew. . . .

Now, though, it is

            . . . a phantasma,
Monstrous in colour, motion, shape, sight, sound!

Here he sees "A Parliament of Monsters":

     Albinos, painted Indians, Dwarfs,
The Horse of knowledge, and the learned Pig,
The Stone-eater, the man that swallows fire,
Giants, Ventriloquists, the Invisible Girl,
The Bust that speaks and moves its goggling eyes,
The Wax-work, Clock-work, all the marvellous craft
Of modern Merlins, Wild Beasts, Puppet-shows,
All out-o'-the-way, far-fetched, perverted things,
All freaks of nature. . . .

Until 1855 St. Bartholomew's Fair was held at Bartholomew tide (August 24) in Smithfield, the site of the execution of many Protestants during the reign of Queen Mary.

In 1806 Wordsworth stayed with Sir George and Lady Beaumont at 29 Grosvenor Square, with Basil Montagu on Thornaugh Street, Russell Square, and with his brother Christopher in Lambeth, "near the work house." Neither "Stray Pleasures" nor "Star-Gazers" was written in London, but both recapture his mood while he roamed the streets:

What crowd is this? what have we here! we must not pass
   it by;
A Telescope upon its frame, and pointed to the sky:
Long is it as a barber's pole, or mast of little boat,
Some little pleasure-skiff, that doth of Thames's waters
   float.

Wordsworth returned the next year for a month with an entourage—Mary Wordsworth, Sara Hutchinson (her sister), Samuel Taylor Coleridge (who went on to Bristol), and Hartley Coleridge—from Grasmere; they stayed with Montagu and with Christopher Wordsworth. Sir Walter Scott was also in London, working on his edition of Dryden in the British Museum, and Wordsworth and Sir Walter took the ten-year-old Hartley to the Tower of London; Wordsworth's frugality, however, would not allow him to purchase tickets for the Jewel House, and they went to the Armouries instead. There were many other short trips to London, in 1808 to see *The White Doe of Rylstone* through the press, in 1812, when he stayed with the Beaumonts on South Audley Street, in 1815, when Benjamin Haydon took a life mask of Wordsworth before breakfast at 41 Great Marlborough Street, and in 1817–1818, when he was attempting to wind up the tangled estate of his brother Richard. This last trip became protracted, and Wordsworth was forced to take lodgings on Mortimer Street, where John Keats, whom Wordsworth had met at Haydon's, came to dinner on January 5.

Following the 1820 Continental trip, Wordsworth, Mary, and Dorothy stopped in London for a fortnight, and Wordsworth was invited to dine at Holland House, a rather unexpected invitation since the poet was a staunch enemy of the Whigs. Wordsworth made numerous visits to Samuel Rogers at 22 St. James's Place and to Charles Aders at 11 Euston Square. On one occasion Aders had as his dinner guests Charles Lamb, Samuel Rogers, Samuel Taylor Coleridge, John Flaxman, and William Wordsworth (who fell asleep). "The Reverie of Poor Susan," it should be noted, probably refers to the treed plot of ground that stood just where Wood Street enters Cheapside; Wordsworth transformed the rooks to a thrush:

At the corner of Wood Street, where daylight appears,
Hangs a Thrush that sings loud, it has sung for three
   years:
Poor Susan has passed by the spot, and has heard
In the silence of morning the song of the Bird.

Wordsworth's attitude toward London is best summarized in *The Prelude:*

But though the picture weary out the eye,
By nature an unmanageable sight,
It is not wholly so to him who looks
In steadiness, who hath among least things
An under-sense of greatest; sees the parts
As parts, but with a feeling of the whole.

There is a commemorative statue of Wordsworth in Westminster Abbey.

Sir Walter Scott (1771–1832)   Sir Walter Scott's trips to London from Scotland were relatively infrequent, but the frequency increased after his daughter Sophia and son-in-law John Lockhart were residing here. Scott was in London as a four-year-old child when it was thought the waters at Bath "might be of some advantage to my lameness." He and an aunt traveled "to London by sea," and

> we made a short stay, and saw some of the common shows exhibited to strangers. When, twenty-five years afterwards, I visited the Tower of London and Westminster Abbey, I was astonished to find how accurate my recollections of these celebrated places of visitation proved to be. . . .

Actually Scott's return trip with his wife was in the spring of 1799 before he was called back to Edinburgh by his father's death; besides being introduced "to some literary and fashionable society with which he was much amused," he spent time examining "the antiquities of the Tower and Westminster Abbey and . . . [making] some researches among the MSS. of the British Museum." Scott was becoming established as a literary figure when he came to London in 1803 "as soon as the Court rose, in hopes of seeing [Dr. John] Leydon once more before he left England; but he came too late." Staying at "No. 15 Piccadilly West" (the home of M. Charles Dumerque, a French surgeon-dentist), he visited the firm of Longman and Rees, who "are delighted with the printing [of the *Minstrelsy*]."

By the time of his visit early in 1806, Sir Walter's reputation was set:

> I have been very much fêted and caressed here, almost indeed to suffocation, but have been made amends by meeting some old friends. . . . If you are celebrated for writing verses or for slicing cucumbers, for being two feet taller or two feet less than any other biped, for acting plays when you should be whipped at school, or for attending schools and institutions when you should be preparing for your grave,—your notoriety becomes a talisman—an "Open Sesame" before which everything gives way—till you are voted a bore, and discarded for a new plaything. . . . [T]his is a consummation of notoriety which I am by no means ambitious of experiencing. . . .

He was invited to dine at Holland House, on the west side of Holland Walk, a kind of social headquarters and informal place of rendezvous for the Whigs; and on the same trip Caroline, Princess of Wales (a resolute Tory separated from her Whig husband), invited Sir Walter to Montagu House, Blackheath,

> to recite some verses of his own, . . . but [he] introduced a short account of the Ettrick Shepherd [James Hogg], and repeated one of the ballads of the *Mountain Bard*, for which he was then endeavouring to procure subscribers. The Princess appears to have been interested by the story, and . . . she desired that her name might be placed on the Shepherd's list. . . .

The next year Scott worked energetically in the British Museum gathering material for his edition of Dryden; on this occasion he met William Wordsworth. Scott, it should be noted, loved the theater, attended it on every possible occasion, and was acquainted with many of the leading actresses and actors.

Sir Walter's literary activities kept him away from London for a number of years, but in 1815 in the publisher John Murray's drawing room at 50 Albemarle Street, Scott met the man who "hits the mark where I don't even pretend to fledge my arrow," Lord Byron. Scott was concerned about their disparate personalities, being led to expect "a man of peculiar habits and a quick temper," but he "was most agreeably disappointed in this respect." They met almost daily for two months and were enormously drawn to each other even though they were opposites in many respects: Scott believed Napoleon was not a gentleman, but Byron believed he was not a democrat; Byron felt a "spot of adultery" would do Scott some good, but Scott believed a "dash of chastity" would work wonders for Byron. The two, Scott writes,

> Like the old heroes in Homer . . . exchanged gifts. . . . [F]or Byron sent me . . . a large sepulchral vase of silver. It was full of dead men's bones, and had inscriptions on two sides of the base. One ran thus:—"The bones contained in this urn were found in certain ancient sepulchres within the long walls of Athens, in the month of February 1811." The other face bears the lines of Juvenal—"*Expende—quot libras in duce summo invenies?—Mors sola fatetur quantula sint hominum corpuscula.*"

Their final meeting took place in Long's Hotel, on the southeast corner where Clifford Street joins New Bond Street; just across was Stevens' Hotel, where Sir Walter and the Irish poet Thomas Moore dined frequently in the early years of their friendship. In the spring of the same year Scott was invited twice to "a snug little dinner that will suit him" at Carlton House by the Prince Regent. "Before he returned to Edinburgh . . . the Regent sent him a gold snuff-box, set in brilliants, with a medallion of his Royal Highness's head on the lid. . . ."

In London on Court of Sessions business in 1821 and frequently afterward, Scott stayed at the Waterloo Hotel, 85–86 Jermyn Street; in 1821 he attended the coronation of George IV. When Sir Walter was here in 1826, he stayed with the Lockharts at 25 Pall Mall, and in April 1828, when he received the last proof sheets for *St. Valentine's Day, or The Fair Maid of Perth*, he stayed at 24 Sussex Place, Regent's Park, to which the Lockharts had moved. On this trip Sir Walter sat for Benjamin Haydon at his house at 22 Lisson Grove:

> *May 5.*—Breakfasted with Haydon, and sat for my head. I hope this artist is on his legs again. The King has given him a lift, by buying his clever picture of the Mock Election in the King's Bench prison. . . . He is certainly a clever fellow, but too enthusiastic, which, however, distress seems to have cured in some degree. . . . Yet it was very little I could do to help [the Haydons].

Scott's health was failing, and he suffered three strokes between February 15, 1830, and April 1831. He left Abbotsford for Italy in September 1831 but first stayed with his daughter in London, where Washington Irving and Thomas Moore were often dinner companions; near Nijmegen, Netherlands, on June 9, 1832, he suffered a fourth and paralytic stroke but insisted on returning to Scotland; he arrived in London on June 13:

> Owing to the unexpected rapidity of the journey, . . . Charles Scott drove to the St. James's Hotel in Jermyn Street [Number 76], and established his quarters there before he set out in quest of his sister and myself [J. G. Lockhart]. When we reached the hotel, he recognised us

with many marks of tenderness, but signified that he was totally exhausted. . . .

The newspapers issued daily reports until July 7, when he was carried from the hotel on a litter to travel home; there he died on September 21. There is a memorial in Westminster Abbey.

Sydney Smith (1771–1845)   The man to whom the label "peripatetic" applies so aptly, at least in London, Sydney Smith, is impossible to follow here with any great certainty until 1839; however, he has left a myriad of addresses scattered throughout the metropolitan area. His father's refusal to support his study of law compelled him to take orders in 1794, and his first-known London residence followed his marriage (1800) and resignation as tutor to Michael Hicks Beech in Edinburgh, where he had begun the *Edinburgh Review*. In 1803 he lodged at 8 Cavendish Street and at 77 Guildford Street for short periods before settling at 8 (now 14) Doughty Street, Holborn (marked with a plaque). Smith's wit and honesty were already known when he was seeking a clerical post, and a few random sermons left the congregations convinced of his madness. Sir Thomas Bernard, though, was favorably impressed and secured Smith's appointment as preacher to the Foundling Hospital; he also preached in the Berkeley and Fitzroy Chapels. Income from lecturing on moral philosophy at the Royal Institution allowed him to move to 18 Orchard Street, Marylebone, in 1806, and his wry sense of humor together with his Whig politics gave him entree to Holland House, Holland Walk, social headquarters of the Whigs from 1716 on. When the Whigs came to power in 1806, Smith was given the living at Foston-le-Clay but was able to avoid residence there until 1808; in the interim the anonymous *The Letters of Peter Plymley* on Catholic emancipation appeared. On an 1811 visit Smith lodged at Miller's Hotel, 74 (then 81) Jermyn Street, and from 1818 through 1835, when he was frequently in London, he stayed at his brother's home, 20 Savile Row (until 1833) or at 47 Hertford Street (1834). Smith had already determined that he was unfit for a bishopric but was enormously disappointed that he never had the chance to refuse one; instead he became canon residentiary of St. Paul's Cathedral in September 1831 and then spent three months a year in London attending to his duties. In 1831 he spent some time in the Amen Corner area; in 1834 he was at both 25 Brook Street and 18 Stratford Place before taking 26 Cartwright Gardens, off Tavistock Place; and from 1836 to 1839 he had the lease of 34 Cartwright Gardens. Smith became a familiar figure at the Athenaeum Club in Pall Mall at Waterloo Place. With his brother Courtenay's death in 1839, Smith inherited £50,000 and bought 56 Green Street, Mayfair. His interest in theological dogma and reform increased until his final illness in 1844; he was brought to London from Combe Florey and died on Green Street on February 22, 1845. Smith was buried in Kensal Green Cemetery.

Samuel Taylor Coleridge (1772–1834)   The myriad of London associations with Samuel Taylor Coleridge extend over his lifetime; following his father's death in 1781, the nine-year-old obtained a place at Christ's Hospital, the blue-coat school, through the influence of the judge Sir Francis Buller, one of the Rev. John Coleridge's former pupils. The school stood on Newgate Street and was part of the Grey Friars Monastery. The friendship between Charles Lamb and Coleridge, who lodged at the school and spent all his holidays here alone, began here, and Lamb's later essay "Christ's Hospital Five-and-Thirty Years Ago" drew directly from the pain and suffering of his friend:

> I was a poor friendless boy. My parents, and those who should care for me, were far away. Those few acquaintances of theirs, which they could reckon upon being kind to me in the great city, after a little forced notice, which they had the grace to take of me on my first arrival in town, soon grew tired of my holiday visits. . . . [A]nd, one after another, they all failed me, and I felt myself alone among six hundred playmates.

It was supposedly in his last year that the incident in which the boy's hand made contact with a gentleman's pocket occurred on the Strand. In anger, the man responded, "What! so young and so wicked?" and accused Coleridge of trying to pick his pocket. Sobbing, the boy explained he had been pretending to be Leander swimming the Hellespont; the stranger, completely mollified by the answer, gave Coleridge a free subscription to the circulating library on King Street. At Christ's he began writing verse, most of which was published later in *Juvenile Poems*.

Coleridge returned in December 1793 after the "furnishings" episode at Cambridge and on Chancery Lane saw a sign, "Wanted a few smart lads for the 15th Elliot's Dragoons"; at the place of enlistment the sergeant twice tried to dissuade him, but the third time Coleridge prevailed and was enlisted as Silas Tomkyn Comberbacke. Even though totally unfit for this life, he remained until he was discovered and his brothers bought him out. By December 1794 he was residing at the Angel Inn (possibly the Angel Inn, Coffee House, Tavern, and Hotel behind St. Clement's Church on the Strand) and with Charles Lamb was frequenting the Salutation and Cat at 17 Newgate Street, where they ate Welsh rabbit, drank "egg-hot," and smoked "oronooko." Later he lodged on the Strand at Number 21. In 1801 and 1802, as his dependence on opium was increasing, he was at 10 King Street in Covent Garden, and in January 1804, before going to Malta, he stayed at 7 Barnard's Inn (gone,) on the south side of Holborn between Numbers 22 and 23.

Back in London in 1806, Coleridge took lodgings in the Strand for a time and then went to the Lambs, "ill, penniless, and worse than homeless" and afraid "even to cowardice, to ask for any person, or of any person." After separating from his wife, he stayed with the Basil Montagus at 55 Frith Street, just off Soho Square, until an argument four days after his arrival again sent him off in anger. He is thought to have lived at Brown's Coffee House, 7 Mitre Court, Fleet Street, for a time, and for another period in 1807 he stayed with Charles and Mary Lamb at 54 Southampton Buildings. Basically, though, these "residences" were periods of escape due, he said, to "bitter consciousness of my own infirmities and increasing irregularity of temper" from John Morgan's household on Portland Place (now 7 Addison Bridge Place) and then at 71 Berners Street, north off Oxford Street. Both these houses are marked with plaques. An increased interest in the arts led directly to the 1811–1812 lecture series on Shakespeare and other poets, delivered at the meetings of the Philosophical Society in its hall (gone) at the far end of Crane Court (a tiny opening north off Fleet Street between Fetter Lane and Red Lion Court). *Osorio*, retitled *Remorse* (written years earlier), was produced successfully at the Drury Lane Theatre early in 1813. After the appearance of *Remorse*, Coleridge was sitting in the coffee room of a hotel when he

> heard his name coupled with a coroner's inquest, by a gentleman who was reading a newspaper to a friend. He asked to see the paper, which was handed to him with the remark that "It was very extraordinary that Coleridge the poet should have hanged himself just after the success of his play; but he was always a strange mad fellow."— "Indeed, sir," said Coleridge, "it is a *most extraordinary* thing that he should have hanged himself, be the subject of an inquest, and yet that he should at this moment be speaking to you." ... The newspaper related that a gentleman in black had been cut down from a tree in Hyde Park, without money or papers in his pockets, his shirt being marked "S. T. Coleridge"; and Coleridge was at no loss to understand how this might have happened, since he seldom travelled without losing a shirt or two.

Coleridge was, though, using opium more and more heavily in this period and in mid-April, after leaving his lodgings at 42 Norfolk Street, put himself in the hands of James Gillman, a surgeon living at 3 The Grove in Highgate, Middlesex (now a part of London); here he spent the last eighteen years of his life. Under Gillman's roof, it appears as if there might have been some progress in the control of Coleridge's addiction, and he was able to turn more vigorously to his writing. *Sibylline Leaves* appeared in 1816, and *Biographia Literaria*, as well as considerable philosophical writings, in 1817. From about 1822 on, although he was often confined to bed, Coleridge managed to see friends and even to travel up the Rhine with the Wordsworths (1828) and to visit Cambridge (1833). He began a steady decline thereafter, though, and died in Highgate on July 25, 1834. He was buried in St. Michael's Church, South Grove Street, Highgate, where the Gillmans raised the memorial tablet with a long inscription. Coleridge had composed his own epitaph, which was deemed "inapplicable to the place in which he was buried":

> Stop, Christian passer-by: Stop, Child of God,
> And read, with gentle breast. Beneath this sod
> A poet lies, or that which once seemed he—
> O, lift a thought in prayer for S. T. C.—
> That he who many a year with toil of breath
> Found death in life, may here find life in death:
> Mercy for praise—to be forgiven for fame—
> He asked, and hoped through Christ. Do thou the same.

There is a memorial in Westminster Abbey.

Robert Southey (1774–1843) Robert Southey, the man in whose behalf Sir Walter Scott declined the Poet-Laureateship in 1813 because he was "already provided for," entered the 14th-century Westminster School, whose buildings surround Little Dean's Yard, on April 1, 1788, and is said to have made little academic progress, preferring to read books of his own choosing. In 1792 he was expelled for writing an article in the school magazine protesting flogging, which he claimed was the invention of the devil. He did not return to the metropolis until February 1797;

his views on pantisocracy and his revolutionary ideas had changed, and he entered Gray's Inn, off Holborn, to study law. This, though, was unsuccessful (he found the study a "laborious indulgence"), and he left in the same spring. The bond between Southey and Coleridge, if such it can be called, brought Southey to the Salutation and Cat, 17 Newgate Street, where he accused his brother-in-law of "culpable supineness" in abandoning his family in Keswick; out of necessity Southey took over the responsibility of supporting both families. Southey accepted the laureateship in 1813 on the condition that he need not write the dreary birthday odes, and in the autumn at St. James's Palace the oath of office was "administered by a fat old gentleman-usher in full buckle." Southey died in Keswick and was buried at the church in Crosthwaite, but there is a commemorative monument in Westminster Abbey.

Jane Austen (1775–1817) While it was mostly the publication of her novels that brought Jane Austen to London, she also visited her brother Henry here. After *Sense and Sensibility* appeared anonymously in 1811 (she guaranteed it against loss), she spent great parts of every year at her brother's home at 23 Hans Place, a narrow opening just off Pont Street, and, indeed, spent all the autumn of 1815 nursing him through a severe fever and slow convalescence. It was at this time that the Prince Regent (later George IV) requested James Stanier Clarke, the librarian, to take Jane Austen to Carlton House to "show her its glories." (Carlton House stood between Pall Mall and the Mall where Carlton House Terrace now stands.) Clarke told her that the Prince Regent greatly admired her works and that she could dedicate her next work to him. The "discreet royal command" was followed, and *Emma* was "most respectfully dedicated" to him. In this novel the Knightly family resides on Brunswick Square, north of Guildford Street:

> "Ah! my poor dear child, the truth is, that in London it is always a sickly season. . . ."
> "No, indeed, *we* are not at all in a bad air. Our part of London is so very superior to most others!—You must not confound us with London in general, my dear sir. The neighbourhood of Brunswick Square is very different from almost all the rest. . . . Mr. Wingfield thinks the vicinity of Brunswick Square decidedly the most favourable as to air."

Miss Austen visited the equestrian showplace, the (Royal) Astley Amphitheatre (gone, but at 225 Westminster Bridge Road), in 1796 and uses it in *Emma*; here, without the influence of Emma, Robert Martin and Harriet Smith reach an understanding.

Charles Lamb (1775–1834) Quite possibly the literary figure of this period most closely associated with London is Charles Lamb, who was born on February 10, 1775, at 2 Crown Office Row, east of Middle Temple Lane. Rebuilt between 1863 and 1864, his birthplace is marked by a plaque; "I was born," Lamb writes,

> and passed the first seven years of my life in the Temple. Its church, its halls, its gardens, its fountain, its river, I had almost said ... these are of my oldest recollections. . . .
> Indeed, it is the most elegant spot in the metropolis. . . . What a cheerful, liberal look hath that portion of

it, which, from three sides, overlooks the greater garden: that goodly pile

> "Of building strong, albeit of Paper hight,"

confronting, with massy contrast, the lighter, older, more fantastically shrouded one, named of Harcourt, with the cheerful Crown-office Row (place of my kindly engendure), right opposite the stately stream, which washes the garden-foot with her yet scarcely trade-polluted waters . . . a man would give something to have been born in such places.

Lamb's father, a scrivener who served as the assistant to Samuel Salt, a bencher of the Inner Temple, is Lovel in "The Old Benchers of the Inner Temple." Lamb was baptized on March 10 at the Temple Church, as the registers there indicate. His earliest schooling was at home, and about 1781 he joined his sister Mary at the coeducational academy run by William Bird in Bond Stables (destroyed), off Fetter Lane. Lamb later recalled: "O how I remember our legs wedged in to those uncomfortable sloping desks, where we sat elbowing each other." He obtained a nomination to the blue-coat school Christ's Hospital (the old Grey Friars Monastery on Newgate Street, where the General Post Office now stands) through Samuel Salt in 1782, and two later essays, "On Christ's Hospital, and the Character of the Christ's Hospital Boys" and "Christ's Hospital Five-and-Thirty Years Ago," describe the foundation thoroughly:

> I was a hypochondriac lad; and a sight of a boy in fetters, upon the day of my first putting on the blue clothes, was not exactly fitted to assuage the natural terrors of initiation. . . . I was told he had *run away*. This was the punishment for the first offence. As a novice I was soon after taken to see the dungeons. These were little, square, Bedlam cells, where a boy could just lie at his length upon straw and a blanket—a mattress, I think, was afterwards substituted—with a peep of light, let in askance, from a prison-orifice at top, barely enough to read by. Here the poor boy was locked in by himself all day, . . . and here he was shut up by himself of *nights*, out of reach of any sound, to suffer whatever horrors the weak nerves, and superstitition incident to his time of life, might subject him to.

On the whole, though, Lamb seems to have been happy here and to have acquired some considerable skills.

Lamb left Christ's in November 1789, and what he did until September 1791, when he took a clerkship at the South Sea Company, 19 Old Broad Street, is mostly unknown, although he did work for Joseph Paice, a merchant at 27 Bread Street Hill, for a short time. "The South-Sea House," which first appeared in the *London Magazine* in August 1820, recalls his days there:

> Reader, in thy passage from the Bank . . . didst thou never observe a melancholy-looking, handsome, brick and stone edifice to the left—where Threadneedle Street abuts upon Bishopsgate? . . .
> This was once a house of trade,—a centre of busy interests. The throng of merchants was here—the quick pulse of gain—and here some forms of business are still kept up, though the soul be long since fled. Here are still to be seen stately porticoes; imposing staircases; offices roomy as the state apartments in palaces—. . . the still more sacred interiors of court and committee-rooms, . . . the oaken wainscots hung with pictures of deceased gov-

ernors and sub-governors, of Queen Anne, and the two first monarchs of the Brunswick dynasty. . . .

In April Lamb entered the employ of East India House, on Lime Street at the northwest corner of Leadenhall, where he remained for thirty-three years. Salt, who had secured the post for Lamb, died this year, and the family had to move from the Temple, but there is no record of their new location. The terms of Lamb's appointment were the usual: sureties were posted, and he served three years without a salary. In 1794 the Lamb family moved to 7 Little Queen Street (now merged into Kingsway); Holy Trinity Church covers the site of the house. By December Lamb was frequenting the Salutation and Cat, 17 Newgate Street, where he would sit and listen to Samuel Taylor Coleridge.

It was on September 22, 1796, in the Little Queen Street house, that Mary Lamb, in a temper with a young apprentice girl, attacked her with a knife and fatally stabbed Mrs. Lamb as she tried to intervene. The insanity was to be recurrent, and Charles Lamb (then just of age) took on the responsibility of her care as her legal guardian. At the end of 1796 or early in 1797 the family moved to 45 Chapel Street (now Chapel Market), Pentonville, to be near Mary during her initial confinement. Aunt Hetty's death in February 1797 and funeral at St. James's Church, Clerkenwell, prompted Lamb to write, "Thou too art dead. . . ." Mary was back with the family from April to December 1797 but relapsed that month, as "Written on Christmas Day, 1797" indicates. After the death of John Lamb Sr., in April 1799, Charles took lodgings at 36 Chapel Street and had Mary with him; during this time whenever some sign that madness was returning occurred, Lamb, carrying a straitjacket, would walk Mary to the Hoxton Asylum. Later, as Lamb's finances improved, she was cared for privately.

Feeling marked in the Chapel Street area, the two took John Gutch's offer of rooms at 27 Southampton Buildings, off Holborn, but stayed only until April 1801, when they moved to 16 Mitre Court Buildings, where they remained for eight years. Lamb was writing for various newspapers to add to his income and published *John Woodvil* in 1802. The next year he produced his verse on the Quaker Hester Savory who died three months after her marriage:

> When maidens such as Hester die
> Their place ye may not well supply,
> Though ye among a thousand try
>   With vain endeavour.

William Hazlitt appeared at East India House, either late in 1804 or early in 1805, with a letter of introduction, and the two men became immediate friends, with Hazlitt frequently at the Lambs's home. Through Hazlitt, Lamb met William Godwin, who induced Charles and Mary to write the *Tales from Shakespear,* which appeared in January 1807. A far more interesting commission followed in 1808, when Longmans asked him to edit selections from Elizabethan dramatists; Lamb's position as a critic was then established. On May 1, 1808, the Lambs stood as best man and bridesmaid at St. Andrew's Church, Holborn, for the marriage of William Hazlitt and Sarah Stoddart.

Late in March 1809 they made a temporary move

to 34 Southampton Buildings before taking the lease of 4 Inner Temple Row, "where," Charles Lamb stated, "I mean to live and die." The accommodation, he says,

> looks out upon a gloomy churchyard-like court, called Hare Court, with three trees and a pump in it. . . . I was born near it, and used to drink at that pump when I was a Rechabite of six years old.

For an annual rent of £30 they had two third-floor rooms and five fourth-floor rooms with an inner private staircase. Henry Crabb Robinson and Hazlitt both visited here, and Samuel Taylor Coleridge was here and at all of their London addresses. Lamb produced essays steadily throughout this period, and in October 1817 they moved to 20 Great Russell Street, Covent Garden; their rooms were on the first floor over an ironmonger's; the houses have been rebuilt and altered so that Number 20 is now two places. Of the area Lamb wrote:

> We are in the individual spot I like best in all this great city. The theatres with all [their noises; Covent Garden] dearer to me than any gardens of Alcinous, where we are morally sure of the earliest peas and 'spargus; Bow Street, where the thieves are examined within a few yards of us.

It was during his residence here (until 1823) that Lamb wrote the early essays of *Elia*.

The first set of essays was published separately in 1823, the year in which the Lambs moved to Colebrook Row (now 64 Duncan Terrace and marked by a plaque) in Islington; it was a detached cottage then, and New River ran in front of the house. Lamb writes:

> George Dyer, instead of keeping the slip that leads to the gate, had, deliberately, staff in hand, in broad open daylight, marched into the New River. . . . Who helped him out they can hardly tell . . . but between 'em they got him drenched thro' and thro'. . . .

Lamb then dubbed the New River "Stream Dyerian"; he described the house in a letter to Bernard Barton, the Quaker poet and future father-in-law of Edward FitzGerald:

> I have a cottage in Colebrook (properly Colnbrook) Row, Islington; a good cottage, for it is detached; a white house with six good rooms; the New River (rather elderly by this time) runs (if a modest walking pace can be so termed) close to the foot of the house, and behind is a spacious garden with vines (I assure you) pears, strawberries, parsnips, leeks, carrots, cabbages, to delight the heart of old Alcinous.

One of Lamb's guests, Thomas Hood, felt the house was "a cottage of ungentility, for it had neither double coach house nor wings. Like its tenant it stood alone." Other guests included Mary Russell Mitford, Mary Shelley, Bryan Procter, and Harrison Ainsworth. Lamb's health began to weaken, and he was considering retirement from East India House when he became seriously ill in the 1824–1825 winter. Charles and Mary Lamb left London for Enfield in 1827, but he returned to London on various occasions and was at 6 Frith Street when William Hazlitt died.

Of the many other London associations, only a few will be noted. Lamb was asked by Adm. James Burney to give away his daughter at her wedding at the Church of St. Mildred, at the angle formed by Cannon and Queen Victoria Streets; only the tower of the church survived World War II, and the churchyard has been laid out in a garden. Here, though, because of the solemnity of the occasion, Lamb was moved to mirth:

> I could not resist the importunities of the young lady's father, whose gout unhappily confined him at home, to act as parent on this occasion, and *give away the bride*. Something ludicrous occurred to me at this most serious of all moments—a sense of my unfitness to have the disposal, even in imagination, of the sweet young creature beside me. I fear I was betrayed to some lightness, for the awful eye of the parson—and the rector's eye of Saint Mildred's in the Poultry is no trifle of a rebuke—was upon me in an instant, souring my incipient jest to the tristful severities of a funeral.

In October 1823 he wrote an indignant essay about Westminster Abbey for *London Magazine* because

> after attending the choral anthems of last Wednesday at Westminster, and being desirous of renewing my acquaintance, after lapsed years, with the tombs and antiquities there, I found myself excluded; turned out like a dog, or some profane person, into the common street, with feelings not very congenial to the place, or to the solemn service which I had been listening to. It was a jar after that music.

Lamb was frequently at the brilliant and witty breakfasts given by Samuel Rogers at his home at 22 St. James's Place, as were Sir Walter Scott, Thomas Moore, Lord Byron, William Wordsworth, Madame de Staël, Sydney Smith, Washington Irving, and many others.

Walter Savage Landor (1775–1864) At Christmas 1794 Walter Savage Landor took up residence at 38 Beaumont Street after being rusticated from Trinity College, Oxford, for firing a pistol at the window of an "obnoxious tory" having a party for "servitors and other raff" and for refusing to offer an explanation. His mission here was to perfect himself "by means of masters, in French & Italian [and to improve my knowledge of Greek]." He eventually went off to Wales. Most of the period between 1798 and 1802 was spent here, although only his 1801 address of New Court (then entered from Carey Street at the intersection of Serle Street) is known. Landor traveled extensively in the next years and did not return to London until 1832, when he stayed on Upper Brook Street; on this visit he was a guest at the Countess of Blessington's home at the end of Seamore Place (now Curzon Street). With Henry Crabb Robinson he went to Highgate to call on Samuel Taylor Coleridge, who was, Landor said, "infirm in his limbs . . . but retained all his energy of mind, and all his sweetness, variety, and flexibility of language." Landor returned in May 1836 to spend an evening at Lady Blessington's new home, Gore House, on Kensington High Street (on the site of the Royal Albert Hall), but stayed a month and met Charles Dickens here. Indeed, Landor was later godfather to Walter Landor Dickens and visited with the novelist's family on Devonshire Terrace for the christening.

William Hazlitt (1778–1830) William Hazlitt lived with his family, after their return from the United States in August 1787, in lodgings near the Montpelier Tea Gardens and on Percy Street, before they moved to Wem. He was sent to the New College for Protestant Dissenters at Hackney, a "seminary of unorthodox religion" (between Tresham Avenue and Urswick Road) in 1793 by his father, a Unitarian preacher; here Hazlitt experienced "repeated disappointments" and "long dejection," and he went so far as to write his own papers (for example, "On the Political State of Man") rather than to use the set pieces. Deciding he was not cut out for the ministry, he returned home. He came back frequently to London, where he met the Godwins and, through them, Charles Lamb. After periods abroad studying art, Hazlitt spent more and more time here; in 1799 he took lodgings at 12 Rathbone Place, near William Godwin's bookshop on Hanway Street, and up to 1805 he seldom missed a Wednesday evening at-home in Mitre Court with Charles and Mary Lamb. He later recalled the evenings:

> When a set of adepts, of *illuminati*, get about a question, it is worth while to hear them talk. They may snarl and quarrel over it, like dogs; but they pick it bare to the bone, they masticate it thoroughly.
>
> This was the case formerly at L[amb]'s—where we used to have many lively skirmishes at their Thursday [Wednesday] evening parties. . . . There was L[amb] himself, the most delightful, the most provoking, the most witty and sensible of men. He always made the best pun, and the best remark in the course of the evening. . . . How often did we cut into the haunch of letters, while we discussed the haunch of mutton on the table! How we skimmed the cream of criticism! How we got into the heart of controversy!

For about three years Hazlitt lived with his brother at 109 Great Russell Street (probably not at today's Number 109) and made the acquaintance of Sarah Stoddart, whom he married on May 1, 1808, at St. Andrew's Church, at Holborn Circus. Charles Lamb stood as best man, and Mary Lamb as bridesmaid. The Hazlitts went to Winterslow, where Mrs. Hazlitt had some property, but they returned to London in 1812 shortly after the birth of their second child in 1811 and took 19 Petty France, off Buckingham Gate. The house, once owned by Jeremy Bentham, is where John Milton lived from 1652 to 1660. Hazlitt was practically penniless at the time, and the move to London was designed to gain literary employment. He gave a series of philosophical lectures at the Russell Institution, Great Coram Street, which Henry Crabb Robinson called "hardly tolerable" since Hazlitt "seems to have no conception of the difference between a lecture and a book." He read the lecture in a monotone, "not once daring to look on his audience" and "read . . . so rapidly that no one could possibly follow him." He did, however, complete the series.

Hazlitt's marriage was not particularly successful; indeed, both parties were at fault, but they were kept together by the common bond of their child until the autumn of 1819. Hazlitt lost his lease on the Petty France house at the end of 1819 and took lodgings in 9 Southampton Buildings; here he met Sarah Walker, one of his landlord's two daughters, and almost immediately fell in love with her ("When I sometimes think of the time I first saw the sweet apparition, August 16, 1820") and in 1821 proposed getting rid of that "ill-advised connection in marriage" by divorcing his wife in order to marry her.

The artist Benjamin Haydon describes the situation to Mary Russell Mitford:

> He has fallen in love with a lodging-house hussy, who will be his death. He has been to Scotland and divorced his wife although he has a fine little boy by her; and after doing this to marry this girl, he comes back and finds she has been making a fool of him in order to get presents, and in reality has been admitting a lover more favoured. Hazlitt's torture is beyond expression. . . .

The latter was not quite true; Hazlitt produced *Liber Amoris, or The New Pygmalion.* Quite naturally he took new lodgings, at 10 Down Street, off Piccadilly, but this must have been after he wrote to Thomas Noon Talfourd on February 12:

> My Dear Sir,—I have been arrested this morning, and am at a loss what to do. Would you give me a call to talk the matter over, and see if your influence could procure me any terms of accommodation?

Hazlitt was married again, in April 1824, to a widow named Bridgewater, worth about £300 a year, and the couple left for the Continent. Hazlitt returned to England in October 1825, leaving his wife behind, and when "at the end of a fortnight he wrote her, asking her when he should come to fetch her . . . the answer that he got was that she had proceeded on to Switzerland with her sister, and that they had parted for ever!" The new Mrs. Hazlitt was bitterly resented by her stepson, whom Hazlitt adored; Hazlitt's grandson, years later, wrote:

> It appears that my father was excessively hurt and indignant at the whole affair from the first outset, . . . and when he joined his father and step-mother abroad, he, mere child as he was, seems to have been very pointed and severe in his remarks upon the matter. This probably gave Mrs. Hazlitt a foretaste of what she might have to expect on her return to England. . . .

Hazlitt's life became very solitary; he had rooms for a while at 40 Half Moon Street, at 34 Southampton Buildings, and then at 3 Bowerie Street. His final move in London was to 6 Frith Street, where he died of stomach cancer on September 18, 1830. He was neither destitute nor alone at his death. Charles Lamb and three others were with him, and a few months before his death he had received considerable sums for his *Conversations of James Northcote.* Hazlitt was buried on September 23 in the churchyard of St. Anne's Church on Wardour Street. A large memorial with a long epitaph was erected, but in 1870 it was removed, and the present memorial substituted. Many of Hazlitt's essays deal at least in part with London: "The Indian Jugglers," for example, describes an act which played at the Olympic New Theatre on Newcastle Street, Strand, in the winter of 1815. "The Fight," which recounts the battle between Bill Neat and Tom Hickman on December 11, 1821, at Hungerford, and which reads like a roll call of period boxers, includes London and Chancery Lane when Hazlitt tries to learn the locale of the fight.

Thomas Moore (1779–1852) While Thomas Moore, the Irish-born poet and friend of Lord Byron, is seldom read in modern times, his major poetic work, *Irish Melodies,* contains such still-familiar pieces as "Believe Me If All Those Endearing Young Charms," "The Harp That Once through Tara's

Halls," and "The Last Rose of Summer." Schooled in Dublin, he arrived in London in 1799 to enter the Middle Temple; it should be noted that he had many London addresses, some of which undoubtedly were unrecorded. One of his earliest lodgings was at 44 George Street, where he had a front room up two flights of stairs; he then took quarters at 46 Wigmore Street. From August 1803 until November 1804 Moore was in Bermuda (via Norfolk, Virginia) as the Admiralty registrar, a post which he felt was not worth his time to keep, and settled at 28 Bury Street upon his return (some sources give the number as 27).

When *Epistles, Odes and Other Poems,* containing a rather severe attack on the United States, appeared in 1806, the *Edinburgh Review,* under the editorship of Francis Jeffrey, gave it a savage review. Jeffrey, of course, is the man who also attacked William Wordsworth, Lord Byron, Leigh Hunt, and John Keats. Moore, though, reacted:

> Though, on the first perusal of the article, the contemptuous language applied to me by the reviewer a good deal roused my Irish blood, the idea of seriously noticing the attack did not occur to me, I think, till some time after.

He discovered Jeffrey was in London to see friends in July and sent a challenge to him. The duel was set for Chalk Farm, around the northern and western end of Regent's Park Road; waiting for the pistols to be readied, Moore told a joke to Jeffrey, who

> had scarcely time to smile at this story, when our two friends, issuing from behind the trees, placed us at our respective posts ... and put the pistols into our hands. They then retired to a little distance; the pistols were on both sides raised; and we waited but the signal to fire, when some police officers, whose approach none of us had noticed, and who were within a second of being too late, rushed out from a hedge behind Jeffrey; and one of them, striking at Jeffrey's pistol with his staff, knocked it to some distance into the field, while another running over to me, took possession also of mine. We were then replaced in our respective carriages, and conveyed, crestfallen, to Bow Street.

No bullet was found in Jeffrey's pistol. Some years later Byron ridiculed the affair in *English Bards and Scotch Reviewers;* after Moore demanded an explanation and an apology, the two men met and became very close friends. Moore and Jeffrey also became friendly, and Moore thereafter made frequent contributions to the *Review.*

On March 25, 1811, Moore married Bessie Dyke, an actress, at St. Martin-in-the-Fields, on Trafalgar Square, and the two determined on life in the country, although Moore was frequently back in the metropolis. Between 1812 and 1814 he visited Leigh Hunt, who was imprisoned at Horsemonger Lane Gaol, on Harper Street (once called Horsemonger Lane), Southwark, for libeling the Prince Regent (later George IV), and frequently dined with Hunt. In 1814 Moore had lodgings at 38 Duke Street, and in 1816 he was at 19 Bury Street (the next street west). For a while in 1817 he had lodgings at 11 Duke Street, and in the same year he was also at 44 Davies Street, when his oldest daughter, Barbara, died of consumption. The defalcation of his deputy in Bermuda in 1819 made Moore liable for £6,500, and he fled to the Continent until 1822, when the Admiralty reduced the

debt to £1,000 and the 2d Marquess of Lansdowne helped to pay it off.

Moore's town lodgings from 1824 to 1833 were many; in 1824 he was at 24 Bury Street, in 1825 at 58 Jermyn Street, in 1829 at 15 Duke Street, in 1829 and 1830 at 19 Bury Street and in 1833 back at 15 Duke Street. Moore regularly dined with Lord Byron at Stevens' Hotel, on the northeast corner of Clifford Street at New Bond Street; was often at the 17th-century Holland House, on Holland Walk in Kensington (the informal headquarters of Whig politicians well into the 19th century); and was frequently invited to the famous breakfasts at Samuel Rogers's house at 22 St. James's Place. *Lalla Rookh* was published from Paternoster Row, at the sign of the Ship and Black Swan; without a single word having been written, Longmans paid £3,000 for the manuscript, the highest advance given for a poem to that time.

Leigh Hunt (1784–1859) Thomas Moore's good friend and the close friend of many other literary figures, Leigh Hunt, entered Christ's Hospital (the Grey Friars Monastery on Newgate Street, where the General Post Office partly stands now) on November 24, 1791, and remained for eight years. The boys lived in twelve wards, each in the charge of a "nurse," usually the widow of a liveryman. Hunt was placed in the Grammar School (with "insolent Greek and haughty Rome") rather than in the Writing School or the Mathematical School. His *Juvenilia* appeared in 1801, and seven years later he launched the weekly *The Examiner* with his brother John.

In 1812, the year in which Hunt was imprisoned for libel, he was living at 35 Great Portland Street; at a political dinner, the usual toast to the Prince Regent was omitted, and the *Morning Post* brought the fact to light and published a poem describing the prince as the "Protector of the Arts," the "Maecenas of the Age," and the "Adonis of Loveliness." This was too much for Hunt, and *The Examiner* replied:

> This Adonis in loveliness was a corpulent man of fifty and short, this delightful, blissful, wise, honourable, virtuous, true and immortal prince was a violator of his word, a libertine over head and ears in disgrace, a despiser of domestic ties, a companion of gamblers and demireps, a man who has just closed half a century without one single claim on the gratitude of his country or the respect of posterity.

Tried for libel, both John and Leigh Hunt were found guilty and sentenced to two years in jail and fined £500; guaranteed freedom and the cancellation of their fines for abstaining from all attacks on the regent, both men chose jail. Hunt was imprisoned at the Horsemonger Lane Gaol, the present recreational grounds on Harper Road (formerly Horsemonger Lane), off the Borough High Street, Southwark. Continuing to edit *The Examiner,* Hunt made his prison room into a bower with wallpaper of trellised roses, a skyscape on the ceiling, and a constant supply of fresh flowers; here he had many visitors including Charles Lamb, Thomas Moore (who brought Lord Byron on one occasion), Percy Bysshe Shelley, and John Keats. Upon his release he took a house (long gone) at 13 Lisson Grove, where he was visited by William Wordsworth and Lord Byron, who delighted in riding the rocking horse belonging to Hunt's small son.

After a period abroad until 1825, Hunt settled his family in Highgate Hill, where they remained until a move to Epsom in 1828. Between 1830 and 1832 he was back in the Lisson Grove area but moved to 22 Upper Cheyne Row (then Number 4):

> From the noise and dirt of the New Road, my family removed to a corner in Chelsea, where the air of the neighbouring river was so refreshing, and the quiet of the "no thoroughfare" so full of repose, that although my fortunes were at their worst, and my health almost at a piece with them, I felt for some weeks as if I could sit still forever, embalmed in the silence.

The rear of the house looked out on a small garden, and lime trees lined the very noisy Upper Cheyne Row; Hunt, though, was undisturbed and was actually interested in the cries of the hawkers:

> I fancied they were unlike the cries in other quarters of the suburbs. . . .
>
> There was an old seller of fish, in particular, whose cry of "Shrimps as large as prawns" was such a regular, long-drawn and truly pleasing melody, that in spite of its hoarse and, I am afraid, drunken voice, I used to wish for it of an evening, and hail it when it came. It lasted for some years; then faded and went out; I suppose, with the poor old weather-beaten fellow's existence.

Hunt's life here was becoming more and more intolerable, though, and from Thomas and Jane Carlyle, who took 5 Cheyne Row (now Number 24), a picture of the Hunts emerges. Hunt, Carlyle said, "talks forever about happiness and seems to me the very miserablest man I ever sat and talked with," but it was Marianne Hunt who was really impossible. "She torments my life out with borrowing," Jane Carlyle wrote; everything is

> begged of me because "Missus has got company and happens to be out of the article"; in plain unadorned English, because "missus" is the most wretched of managers, and is often at the point of not having a copper in her purse.

Hunt left Chelsea for 32 Edwardes Square, Kensington, in 1840, his financial situation still desperate. Two royal grants of £200 came his way, and Sir Percy Shelley settled a yearly pension of £120 on him in 1844. From 1851 to 1853 Hunt lived at 2 Phillimore Terrace (now Phillimore Gardens); he spent his last years at 27 (now 16) Cornwall Road (now Rowan Road), Hammersmith. Hunt's health declined from about 1857 on, and he died in Putney at the home of Charles Reynell on August 28, 1859; he was buried in the Kensal Green Cemetery, where a bust by Joseph Durham was placed on the grave in 1869. The memorial is inscribed with a line from "Abou Ben Adhem":

> Write me as one who loves his fellow-men.

(Kensal Green Cemetery was one of seven "hygienic" cemeteries brought into existence between 1832 and 1841 in an attempt to suppress the kind of graveyard horrors described in *Bleak House*.)

Thomas De Quincey (1785–1859)   Thomas De Quincey, essayist and author of *Confessions of an English Opium Eater*, came to London in November 1802 from Wales; planning to borrow £200 from his inheritance in order to live, he approached a Mr. Brunell, a moneylender or a lender's agent, at 61 Greek Street. He got no money, but Brunell "allowed me to sleep in a large unoccupied house, of which he was tenant. Unoccupied, I call it, for there was no household or establishment in it." At this time 61 Greek Street was in a row of tumbledown lodgings. Here De Quincey met a deserted waif (perhaps Brunell's illegitimate daughter), "a poor, friendless child, apparently ten years old":

> [A]nd, amidst the real fleshly ills of cold, and, I fear, hunger, the forsaken child had found leisure to suffer still more (it appeared) from the self-created one of ghosts. I promised her protection against all ghosts whatsoever: but, alas! I could offer her no other assistance. We lay upon the floor, with a bundle of cursed law papers for a pillow. . . .

De Quincey was quite ill and experiencing much difficulty sleeping; he walked the streets by day and made friends with London's outcasts, especially a prostitute named Ann:

> One night, when we were pacing slowly along Oxford-street, . . . I requested her to turn off with me into Soho-square: thither we went: and we sat down on the steps of a house, which to this hour, I never pass without a pang of grief, and an inner act of homage to the spirit of that unhappy girl, in memory of the noble act which she there performed. Suddenly, as we sat, I grew much worse: . . . all at once I sank from her arms and fell backward on the steps.

She "ran off into Oxford-street, and . . . returned to me with a glass of port-wine and spices." Soon after De Quincey received £10 from a family friend and left London in March 1803. He made arrangements with Ann that when he returned, in approximately one week,

> she should wait for me, at six o'clock, near the bottom of Great Titchfield-street, which had been our customary haven, as it were, of rendezvous. . . .

There was no sign of her when he returned:

> [A]ccording to our agreement, I sought her daily, and waited for her every night, so long as I stayed in London, at the corner of Titchfield-street.

De Quincey returned from Oxford in 1804 to search for Ann and to meet Charles Lamb, who was then living at 16 Mitre Court Buildings. The same year he awoke one morning "with excruciating rheumatic pains of the head and face, from which I had hardly any respite for about twenty days." A college acquaintance whom he chanced upon recommended opium:

> My road homewards lay through Oxford-street; and near "the *stately* Pantheon," (as Mr. Wordsworth has obligingly called it) I saw a druggist's shop. The druggist, unconscious minister of celestial pleasures!—as if in sympathy with the rainy Sunday, looked dull and stupid, just as any mortal druggist might be expected to look on a Sunday: and when I asked for the tincture of opium, he gave it to me as any other man might do: and furthermore, out of my shilling returned to me what seemed to be a real copper half-penny, taken out of a real wooden drawer.

The chemist's shop was at 173 Oxford Street, just at the corner of Poland Street. When De Quincey left Oxford in 1808, he intended to study law at the Middle Temple and probably did for a few terms. He lived first at 82 Great Titchfield Street, the scene of the abortive rendezvous with Ann, and then at 5

Northumberland Street (now Luxborough Street) with a friend, Richard Smith. By the summer of 1809 he was dividing his time among Grasmere, Wrington, and London, and by 1812 he abandoned his halfhearted pursuit of law. On a return trip in 1814, he had lodgings on the south side of Waterloo Bridge, somewhere near the Surrey Theatre.

De Quincey's opium eating had increased to 320 grains of laudanum a day, and he was attempting to stabilize or even give up the habit during this period. In 1821, in another attempt to break the addiction, he came to London in search of literary work; settling at 4 York Street (Tavistock Street), Covent Garden, he visited Charles and Mary Lamb frequently and began the *Confessions* in the autumn. By this time he no longer had pleasure from opium, but an attempt at detoxification in the summer of 1822 was only partially successful. A burst of literary energy occurred as the effect of the opiate decreased, but both morbidity and depression increased proportionately. By 1825 De Quincey was moving from place to place to avoid creditors and at one time was at 4 Eccleston Street and at another with the publisher Charles Knight in his house on Pall Mall East before returning to Grasmere.

George Gordon, Lord Byron (1788–1824)   George Gordon, Lord Byron was a London native almost by accident; the poet's father, John Byron ("mad Jack"), after the death of his first wife left him penniless, married Catherine Gordon of Gight, Scotland, and took her to the Continent, where he squandered almost all her property before bringing her to London. Here, on January 22, 1788, at 16 Holles Street, an inexpensive lodging house off Cavendish Square, George Gordon was born; his clubbed right foot was noticed at birth, but not until eleven years later was proper treatment begun. Byron was christened on February 29 at the Marylebone parish church (gone) on Marylebone High Street, and within six months mother and son left for Aberdeen, Scotland. When Byron succeeded to the title in 1798, his mother returned him to England (to Nottingham), and in July of the next year John Hanson, Mrs. Byron's attorney, rescued the child and brought him to the Hansons' home in Earl's Court. He arranged for medical attention for the boy and placed him in a school run by Dr. Glennie in Dulwich. Early in 1800 Mrs. Byron settled on Sloane Terrace and systematically undid the work of Hanson and Glennie by keeping the child home from school and undermining all the school's discipline. Hanson, in turn, got Byron into Harrow in the spring of 1801, and part of the summer holiday was spent at Earl's Court and part at 16 Piccadilly, where his mother had rooms.

Byron was frequently in London after going up to Trinity College, Cambridge, in 1805. In January 1807 he was at Dorant's Hotel, 1 Albemarle Street, when he distributed copies of *Poems on Various Occasions* and tried to raise funds for his enormous and growing debt at the university. At the beginning of 1808, back at Dorant's Hotel, he fell into "an abyss of sensuality" which almost ruined both his health and his finances. He was at Cox's Hotel, 55 Jermyn Street, when he read the vicious criticism of *Hours of Idleness* in the *Edinburgh Review* and, it is assumed, worked here on his reply, *English Bards and Scotch Reviewers;* on March 13, 1809, he took his seat in the House of Lords, Thomas Moore says, in

a state more lone and unfriended, perhaps, than any youth of his high station had ever been reduced to on such an occasion. . . .

After 1811 Byron was a frequent dinner guest of the 3d Baron Holland and Lady Holland at Holland House, on Holland Walk, which had become an informal meeting place for Whig politicians and writers; here he met both Samuel Rogers and Thomas Moore. At Melbourne House (now the Scottish Office in Whitehall), the home of the 1st Viscount Melbourne and Lady Melbourne (the mother-in-law of Lady Caroline Lamb), he met Anne Isabella (Annabella) Milbanke, Lady Melbourne's niece, in March 1812.

Byron was living at 8 St. James's Street (rebuilt, now Byron House) in 1812, when the first two cantos of *Childe Harold's Pilgrimage* appeared and he "awoke one morning and found myself famous." The publisher was John Murray at 50 Albemarle Street; the offices, now at Number 5A, have many relics and manuscripts of the poet. The same year, on Saturday, October 12, the fourth and present Drury Lane Theatre on Catherine Street, officially the Theatre Royal, opened with Shakespeare's *Hamlet* and an address written by Byron; it notes the 1809 catastrophe:

> In one dread night our city saw, and sigh'd,
> Bow'd to the dust, the Drama's tower of pride:
> In one short hour behold the blazing fane,
> Apollo sink, and Shakespeare cease to reign.

Byron was a frequent visitor to Leigh Hunt, imprisoned at the Horsemonger Lane Gaol on a charge of libel from 1812 to 1814, and, indeed, was later often at Hunt's Lisson Grove house. In January 1813 Byron took lodgings at 4 Bennet Street, just off St. James's Street, and retained them for more than a year. Here he wrote the Oriental tales, *The Giaour, The Bride of Abydos,* and *The Corsair,* and changed the name of the street to Benedictine Street on his letters.

In what is now believed to be an attempt to extricate himself from the incestuous affair with his half sister Augusta Leigh and to rid himself of the incautious Lady Caroline Lamb, Byron courted Anne Isabella Milbanke at Melbourne House and at 63 Portland Place, Sir Ralph Milbanke's London home. His first proposal in 1812, made through Lady Holland, was refused, but after rather extensive correspondence Miss Milbanke accepted his second proposal. After their marriage in Seaham, County Durham, in 1815 and a honeymoon of more cloud than sunshine, they settled at 139 Piccadilly Terrace, a house belonging to the Duchess of Devonshire. Lady Byron, who was pregnant, invited Augusta Leigh for a visit; then, in a state of exasperation brought on by his wife's "humourless sensitivity" and by mounting debts and drink, Byron evidently hinted boldly about his relationship with Augusta (and perhaps Lady Caroline, as well). Augusta Ada (a strange name for Lady Byron to choose in the circumstances) was born on December 10, 1815, and on January 15 Lady Byron and the baby left to visit her parents. Convinced that Byron was mentally deranged, she had Sir Ralph notify her husband that she would never return; since Lady Byron offered no concrete reasons for her departure, rumors centering on Byron's relations with his half sister soon began. Lord Byron signed the separation agreement and left England, never to return, on April 24, 1816.

Byron suffered from malaria while abroad, and his death in Greece on April 19, 1824, was hastened by the bleeding doctors insisted on for his fever. His embalmed body was returned and arrived in the Thames Estuary on June 29; he lay in state at the home of Sir Edward Knatchbull at 20 Great George Street while a controversy raged over his burial in Westminster Abbey. Byron was buried in the family vault at Hucknall (Hucknall Torkard); 145 years later a memorial was placed in the abbey.

There are a multitude of other London associations with Lord Byron. He frequently stayed at Long's Hotel, on the east corner of Clifford Street where New Bond Street enters; and this, in fact, was the scene of the last meeting with Sir Walter Scott in 1815. Another haunt was Stevens' Coffee House and Hotel on the northeast corner of Clifford and New Bond Streets; Thomas Moore writes:

> [D]uring the first months of our acquaintanceship we dined together alone, and as we had no club in common to resort to . . . our dinners used to be at the St. Alban's [St. Alban's Street, Pall Mall], or at his old haunt, Stevens'.

Byron did belong to the Cocoa Tree Chocolate House at 64 St. James's Street, a private members' club established in 1745 from the original 1689 coffeehouse; he writes to Moore on April 9, 1814:

> I am but just returned to town[;] . . . I have been boxing, for exercise, with Jackson for this last month daily. I have also been drinking, and on one occasion, with three other friends at the Cocoa-Tree from six till four, yea, until five in the matin. We clareted and champagned till two, then supped, and finished with a kind of regency punch composed of Madeira, brandy, and *green* tea, no *real* water admitted therein.

Jackson was John Jackson, the noted black pugilist known as Gentleman Jackson who was instrumental in making boxing a legitimate sport in England; from his home at 4 Lower Grosvenor Place, he gave Byron boxing lessons. At one time Byron also lived in the Albany, off Piccadilly, as did Jackson. Byron's illegitimate child Allegra, by Claire Clairmont, William Godwin's stepdaughter, was baptized at St. Giles in the Fields Church.

Richard Harris Barham (1788–1845)   The wit, author of *The Ingoldsby Legends*, and priest Richard Harris Barham was educated at St. Paul's School, which was located in the churchyard of the cathedral until 1884. Indeed, he became a minor canon of St. Paul's Cathedral in 1821, and three years later he was made priest in ordinary of the Chapel Royal. From 1821 to 1824 Barham lived at 51 Great Queen Street, Holborn; his literary work was generally on the fringe of his other activities and often resulted from chance events. Thus, he composed one piece while recovering from a confining accident, and a second came about after a friend pirated and printed the first chapters so that Barham had to go on. Indeed, *The Ingoldsby Legends* arose from helping to get *Bentley's Miscellany* started. Barham lived at 1 Paul's Churchyard until 1839, when he moved to 1 Amen Corner (gone), where Sydney Smith had lived; Barham died here on June 17, 1845, and was buried at St. Mary Magdalene, Old Fish Street, where he had been priest. The church burned in 1885, and the commemorative plaque was moved to St. Martin within

Ludgate. St. Paul's also holds a commemorative monument. The Salopian Coffee House at 41 Charing Cross was one of the places Barham frequented.

Percy Bysshe Shelley (1792–1822) and Mary Wollstonecraft Godwin Shelley (1797–1851)

> London; that great sea whose ebb and flow
> At once is deaf and loud, and on the shore
> Vomits its wrecks, and still howls on for more.
> Yet in its depths what treasures!

One of the most unusual men of this period was Percy Bysshe Shelley, of whom is told a very revealing story concerning his outlook on life: an early question by his mother about the best school for her son prompted the answer, "Oh, send him somewhere where they will teach him to think for himself." To this she replied, "Teach him to think for himself? Oh, my God, teach him rather to think like other people!" He spent the summer of 1810 before going up to Oxford at the home of his cousin, John Grove, in Lincoln's Inn Fields, and returned to his house on a number of occasions. Expelled from Oxford on March 25, 1811, for "contumaciously refusing" to answer university officials on the pamphlet *The Necessity of Atheism* and already on difficult terms with his father, Shelley came to London and took lodgings with Thomas Jefferson Hogg (also expelled) at 15 Poland Street. He took long walks in the gardens at the Inns of Temple, in Kensington Gardens, and in Hyde Park; he also walked in his sleep and was once discovered in Leicester Square, almost half a mile from his lodgings.

Sometime after mid-April Shelley began to visit the family of John Westbrook, whose daughter was at school in Fulham with Shelley's sisters. Westbrook was the retired landlord of Mount's Coffee House (variously, the Mount and Mount Street Coffee House), Grosvenor Square, and now had a house at 23 Chapel Street (now Aldford Street). Shelley found Harriet Westbrook feeling persecuted and in agreement with his radical views; as a consequence, he decided to elope with but not marry her in order to effect her escape. It was Hogg who convinced Shelley of the desirability of marriage. The couple left London from the Bull and Mouth Tavern, and were married in Edinburgh, Scotland, on August 28, 1811.

Shelley was generally away from London until 1813, although on an autumn trip in 1812 he was frequently at William Godwin's house on Skinner Street, where he met Mary Wollstonecraft Godwin in October. Shelley and his wife returned in April 1813 and stayed on Chapel Street and in an Albemarle Street hotel before going to lodgings on Half Moon Street. They eventually took a house somewhere in Pimlico, where their daughter Ianthe Elizabeth was born in June. They then renewed their wedding vows (March 24, 1814) at St. George's Church, on St. George's Street, Hanover Square, in order to regularize their Scottish marriage (the laws differed) and to ensure Ianthe's legitimacy. Shelley met Mary Godwin at her father's house again in early May, and Harriet's absence in Bath (she and Shelley were already estranged) provoked a separation. On July 28, 1814, after meeting at Hatton Gardens, Shelley and Mary eloped to Calais; the elopement, of course, could not have the benefit of matrimony. Returning to London because of lack of funds, they spent 1814 in many different lodgings evading bailiffs. Together and separately they lived at 26 Nelson Square in Southwark, 15 Old Bond Street, and Southampton Buildings, where Shelley stayed with Thomas Love Peacock while trying to sort out his life. Shelley was so deeply in debt by October that he was forced to meet Mary secretly in Gray's Inn Gardens on Sundays, on Sundays because people could not be arrested for debt on that day and secretly because Mary's father William Godwin, a freethinker, had become a very conventional father when his daughter ran off with a married man. They also met at Staple Inn, St. Paul's Cathedral, and Bartlett's Buildings, a cul-de-sac at the end of Skinner Street, off Snow Hill. For a short time Shelley and Mary Godwin lived at 41 Hans Place, and either at this house or another unidentified one, Mary gave birth to a son, Charles Bysshe, on November 30.

Early in 1815, Shelley's financial situation brightened enormously. The death of his grandfather, Sir Bysshe Shelley, changed Sir Timothy's outlook when he realized his son could now legally entail the estate; to avoid such a possibility, Shelley's father decided to come to terms. In return for giving up all interest in the family estate, Shelley received a lump sum of £7,400 (which paid most of his debts) and a yearly income of £1,000 (£200 of which he settled on Harriet). They left London in July, eventually going to France, and returned to England (to Bath) in September. Sometime in November 1816 Harriet Shelley disappeared from her father's London house and left no trace; on December 10 her body was recovered from the part of the Serpentine known as the Long Water in Kensington Gardens, where she had drowned herself. The inquest revealed she was in an advanced state of pregnancy. She was probably buried in the churchyard in Paddington, in the northern portion of the churchyard on the east side in the second grave north of a person named Holloway; there is no marker. The Lord Chancellor denied Shelley custody of his two children.

On December 30, 1816, at St. Mildred's Church, at Cannon and Queen Victoria Streets (only the tower remains), Shelley and Mary Wollstonecraft Godwin were married by license in the presence of William Godwin, with whom they had been reconciled. Throughout 1815 and 1816, Shelley and Mary, together and separately, had lived at 13 Lower Grosvenor Place (then called Arabella Road), right after the birth of a stillborn child, at 26 Marchmont Street, and at 13 and 32 Norfolk Street. For a short time the Shelleys lived with Leigh Hunt at 13 Lisson Grove, where Hunt proved to be very supportive; they then took lodgings at 19 Marbledown Place before moving to Great Marlow, Buckinghamshire.

In February 1818 the Shelleys returned to lodgings at 119 Great Russell Street, and on March 9 their children William and Clara, as well as Allegra Byron, Lord Byron's daughter by Claire Clairmont, were christened at St. Giles-in-the-Fields. Two days later, taking Allegra with them, they left for Italy, where Shelley drowned on July 8, 1822. There is a commemorative tablet in Westminster Abbey.

Mary Shelley and her son Percy Florence, born in 1819 and the only Shelley child to survive childhood, returned to London in 1823; she probably stayed with her father for a short time before moving to 5 Bartholomew Road, where she stayed from 1824 to 1827. That year she joined her father at 49 Gower Place off Gordon Square, where they lived until 1833, and then moved to New Palace Yard. In 1836 she lived for a while at 36 North Bank (off Lodge Road) and from 1837 to 1839 was at 41D Park Street, where she edited and annotated Shelley's poetry; she also had lodgings at 51 George Street. Around 1846 she moved to 24 Chester Square, where she died on February 1, 1851; she was buried in Bournemouth, where her son was living.

Two other London associations should be mentioned: Whitestone Pond, at the complex intersection of East Heath Road and Heath Street in Hampstead, is where Shelley sailed paper boats for the children while visiting Leigh Hunt in the Vale of Health; and the Horsemonger Lane Gaol, on Horsemonger Lane (now Harper Street), Southwark, is where Shelley visited the imprisoned Hunt from 1812 to 1814.

Frederick Marryat (1792–1848) Capt. Frederick Marryat was born on Great George Street, the western extension of Bridge Street, where the Treasury now stands, on July 10, 1792, and was educated privately. He ran away from different schools—Great Ealing School and Holmwood, on Baker Street, Enfield—several times in trying to escape to the sea, and in 1806 he was able to persuade his father to secure him a position on the *Impérieuse* under the command of Thomas, Lord Cochrane. He rose to the rank of captain before retiring in 1830; when he returned to England in 1832, he lodged at 38 St. James's Place and applied himself to editing the *Metropolitan Magazine* from 1832 to 1835. From 1837 to 1839 or so, he had possession of 8 Duke Street, and in 1841 and 1844 he stayed at 120 Pall Mall. When Marryat was not in a London house, he lived at Gothic Lodge, Woodhayes Road, Wimbledon, from 1839 to 1843. The London house most closely associated with him is 3 Spanish Place (marked with a plaque); here he wrote *Masterman Ready, or The Wreck of the Pacific*. There must have been times that Marryat's publishers, or at least the compositors, wished he had never taken to writing, for

his handwriting was so minute that the compositor having given up the task of deciphering it in despair, the copyist had to stick a pin in at the place where he had left off to ensure his finding it again when he resumed his task.

In 1843 Marryat left London for Langham, Norfolk.

John Clare (1793–1864) The "Northamptonshire peasant poet," as John Clare is often styled, had a few associations with London, beginning in March 1820, when he enjoyed celebrity status in literary circles. He stayed with the publishers Taylor & Hessey at 96 Fleet Street; his *Poems Descriptive of Rural Life and Scenery* had already appeared, and other works had been published in the *London Magazine*. On a second trip in May he attended one of the monthly dinners held at Waterloo Place for contributors. Here he was introduced to Charles and Mary Lamb, John Hamilton Reynolds, Thomas Hood, and William Hazlitt. Clare made other trips for the same reason and usually visited George Reynolds at 19 Lamb's Conduit Street. John Hamilton Reynolds, the son, was also the friend of John Keats and a minor poet in his own right. John Clare's mental condition was unstable by 1824; and poverty, an ever-increasing family, and drink took their steady toll. On the 1824 trip he stayed with a Mrs. Emmerson, with whom he had corresponded for some time; she had moved to Stratford Place in 1822 and promised he should have "the most elevated spot in the house"—this was his "sky chamber." In July he stood at the bottom of Oxford Street, as did George Borrow, to watch Byron's funeral cortege cross London. From 1825 on Clare had numerous breakdowns and made frequent trips here from Northampton to see Dr. George Darling, the physician in charge of his case.

John Keats (1795–1821) The last of the great triad of poets of this period, John Keats was born on October 31, 1795, at the Swan and Hoop Livery Stables, which his maternal grandfather, John Jennings, leased and where his father was head ostler; a plaque at 85 Moorgate commemorates the site. Keats was baptized on December 18 at St. Botolph's Church without Bishopsgate, and sometime before 1801 the family moved to Craven Street; his father by then had taken over the livery business. In 1804 Keats's father died after a fall from a horse, and his mother remarried in less than three months. This marriage was most unhappy, and the Keats children were sent to their grandmother, Mrs. Jennings, at Ponders End, Edmonton; Keats's mother died in 1810, and the poet remained with Mrs. Jennings until 1814, when he returned to London. He entered Guy's Hospital, on St. Thomas's Street, on October 1, 1815, to train in the joint medical school of Guy's and St. Thomas's (the latter demolished when the London Bridge Station was built); living at 8 Dean Street (now Stainer Street) in Southwark, he directed Charles Cowden Clarke to the address, stating it was easy to find,

if you would run the Gauntlet over London Bridge, take the first turning to the left and then the first to the right. . . .

Keats was lodging alone and was unhappy when he wrote:

O Solitude! if I must with thee dwell,
    Let it not be among the jumbled heap
    Of murky buildings; climb with me the steep,—
Nature's observatory—whence the dell,
Its flowery slopes, its river's crystal swell,
May seem a span. . . .

Keats's poetic career took a turn for the better when Leigh Hunt, whom Keats had visited in the Horsemonger Lane Gaol, published "O Solitude" in *The Examiner* in May 1816. At the same time, Dr. Astley Cooper, one of the greatest surgeons at St. Thomas's, took an interest in Keats and arranged for him to live on St. Thomas's Street, over a tallow chandler's shop. Keats passed his apothecary's examination in July and became one of the first licensees under the Apothecaries Act for Examining and Licensing; the partly 17th-century Apothecaries Hall is on Blackfriars Lane. With his interest in poetry increasing, he did not complete his medical studies. He was now living with his brothers at 76–78 Cheapside; the house stretched over the passage leading to Bird-in-Hand Court and the Queen's Arms Tavern (later Simpson's). Here most of the work which appeared in *Poems,* including "On First Looking into Chapman's Homer," was written. In October or November Keats

met the artist Benjamin Haydon, whose studio was at 41 Great Marlborough Street, and the two became close friends; indeed, Haydon took Keats to see the Elgin marbles, which the 7th Earl of Elgin first displayed at 137 and 138 Piccadilly and thus inspired "On Seeing the Elgin Marbles" and influenced Keats's "Ode on a Grecian Urn." Keats was spending a lot of time visiting Leigh Hunt in the Vale of Health:

For what there may be worthy in these rhymes
I partly owe to him. . . .

In fact, Keats probably first met Percy Bysshe Shelley there in December 1816.

In March or April 1817, Keats moved to 19 Well Walk, Hampstead Heath, with his brothers. Hampstead Heath was then a wild, natural countryside with expanses of open fields and bog and marsh; the land teemed with flora, and in spring the blossoms of the wild cherry, bullace plum, pear, and crab-apple trees made the area especially attractive. Their tall, narrow house, next to the Green Man (later the Wells Hotel), was pulled down when the public house was enlarged. Keats was on holiday off and on until October 1817, at which time he was working on *Endymion.* In mid-December he replaced John Hamilton Reynolds as drama critic for *The Champion* for a few weeks over the Christmas holidays, and on December 28 at Benjamin Haydon's house, 22 Lisson Grove, the "immortal dinner" occurred; here he met William Wordsworth for the first time. Also at the dinner were Charles Lamb, William Cosmo Monkhouse, and Edwin Henry Landseer. Keats, who saw Wordsworth on other occasions when the older poet was in town, found him a didactic egoist and reacted badly; on one occasion when Wordsworth was holding court, Keats in agreement opened his mouth to speak, and Mrs. Wordsworth touched Keats's arm, saying "Mr. Wordsworth is never interrupted." Finally, Keats could stand no more and simply wrote to Reynolds in exasperation, "I will have no more of Wordsworth or Hunt in particular."

The year 1818 was a tumultuous one for Keats. His brother Tom, whom Keats nursed throughout his final illness, died of tuberculosis and was buried in the family grave in the Church of St. Stephen (gone), Coleman Street; he met Fanny Brawne and moved to Wentworth Place (now Keats House), in Keats Grove. The house, which was Charles Armitage Brown's, was surrounded by open heath and was actually two cottages (combined in 1838); the garden still follows much the same design that Keats knew, but the plum tree under which he is said to have written "Ode to a Nightingale" is now an ivy-covered stump. In January 1819 "The Eve of St. Agnes" was written, and in February the fragment "The Eve of St. Mark"; the period of greatest activity came in April and May, when "La Belle Dame sans Merci," "On a Dream," and the great odes "To Psyche," "On a Grecian Urn," "To a Nightingale," and "On Melancholy" were written. Fanny Brawne and her mother took over the half of Wentworth Place which Charles Wentworth Dilke had occupied, and in early October 1819, having finished "To Autumn," Keats resolved to live through journalism and moved to lodgings at 25 Great College Street, off Dean's Yard, where Church House now is. Keats determined to live away from Fanny, but a trip to Hampstead broke his intention, and by October 19 he returned to Wentworth House. He and Fanny became officially engaged, and under the pressures of failing health and a foreseeably long engagement he took to laudanum. Brown, though, discovered the activity and exacted a pledge of abstinence, which was actually kept. On February 3, as Brown reported, Keats became chilled but

> [h]e mildly and instantly yielded—a property in his nature towards any friend—to my request that he should go to bed. I followed with the best immediate remedy in my power. I entered the chamber as he leapt into bed. On entering the cold sheets, before his head was on the pillow, he slightly coughed, and I heard him say, "That is blood from my mouth." I went towards him; he was examining a single drop of blood upon the sheet. "Bring me the candle, Brown, and let me see this blood." After regarding it steadfastly, he looked up in my face, with a calmness of countenance that I can never forget, and said: "I know the colour of that blood;—it is arterial blood;—I cannot be deceived in that colour; that drop of blood is my death-warrant—I must die."

Keats was well enough in March 1819 to attend the unveiling of Haydon's *Christ Entering Jerusalem*, done in the style of the old masters, in which he included Voltaire, Wordsworth (head bowed devoutly), William Hazlitt (the detached observer), and Keats (the bright, animated viewer). A trip to Scotland, prescribed by the doctor, was aborted in Gravesend, and Keats took lodgings in Kentish Town to be near Leigh Hunt's family on Mortimer Terrace. He became desperately ill at Hunt's home and was moved in there; even so, he saw *Lamia, Isabella, The Eve of St. Agnes and Other Poems* through publication before returning to Wentworth Place, where Mrs. Brawne and Fanny nursed him. In July Percy Bysshe and Mary Shelley invited Keats to Pisa to live with them; he left on the *Maria Crowther* with Joseph Severn on September 17, 1820, and he died in Rome on February 23, 1821; Keats was buried in the Protestant Cemetery there, his tombstone engraved:

> Here lies one whose name was writ in water.

Both Hampstead parish church and Westminster Abbey contain memorials. Wentworth Place is now a Keats Museum and has, among other things, Keats's leather-covered book of lecture notes from Guy's and St. Thomas's, which contains delightful drawings decorating the borders and the comment, "In disease medical men guess, if they cannot ascertain a disease they call it nervous."

There are additional London associations with Keats. He spent a great deal of time at 96 Fleet Street, the offices of Taylor & Hessey, Publishers, and the home of John Hessey. "Keats' dearest friend," John Hamilton Reynolds, lived at 19 Lamb's Conduit, and the poet was often here. Finally, Charles Cowden Clarke lived at 9 Craven Hill, a home Keats frequently visited. Keats's poetry was remarkably unspecific locationally, but one poem in particular is of interest:

> Souls of Poets dead and gone,
> What Elysium have ye known,
> Happy field or mossy cavern,
> Choicer than the Mermaid Tavern?
> Have ye tippled drink more fine
> Than mine host's Canary wine?

> Or are fruits of Paradise
> Sweeter than those dainty pies
> Of venison? O generous food!

The Mermaid, frequented by William Shakespeare, Ben Johnson, Christopher Marlowe, Sir Walter Ralegh, John Donne, Francis Beaumont, and John Fletcher, stood on the west side of Bread Street a house or two beyond the corner of Cheapside.

Thomas Carlyle (1795–1881)   The author most deeply associated with Chelsea is probably Thomas Carlyle; he found 5 (now 24) Cheyne Row, in May 1834 after lodging for a short time at 33 Ampton Street, where he and his wife had stayed for a few months in 1831–1832 when he was seeking a publisher for *Sartor Resartus*. The Cheyne Row rent was £35 a year, and Carlyle's enthusiasm is displayed in a letter to his wife; there was

> a broad highway with huge shady trees, boats lying moored and a smell of shipping and tar. Battersea Bridge is a few yards off; the broad river with white-trousered, white-shirted Cockneys dashing about like arrows in their long canoes of boats and beyond the green beautiful knolls of Surrey with their villages.

Here in a rooftop room he soundproofed to deaden local noises, Carlyle wrote *The French Revolution*; after many months of painstaking work, he gave the first volume to John Stuart Mill to read, but Mill returned only its charred remains: a servant had used it to light an upstairs fire. Carlyle had no other draft of the text and had destroyed his notes; Mill, Carlyle told his wife, was terribly disturbed, and "we must endeavour to hide from him how serious this business is to us." Five months later he completed the new volume. Carlyle and his wife spent the rest of their lives here and entertained all the literary and intellectual figures of the day: Leigh Hunt, Charles Dickens, William Makepeace Thackeray, and Lord Tennyson were only a few. Jane Carlyle died peacefully in her carriage on April 24, 1866, and Carlyle remained here until his death on February 4, 1881, and was buried in his native Scotland. Today the house is Carlyle Museum, owned by the National Trust.

Thomas Hood (1799–1845)   Thomas Hood, a social-reform poet whose works served as the models for an entire school of social-protest poetry and a notable writer of humorous verse, was born on May 23, 1799, at 31 Poultry (now the Midland Bank); his father, a prosperous bookseller, had his son educated in public schools in London, including one located at 45 Lothbury. Entering a now-unknown merchants' trading house about 1812, Hood suffered from ill health (now thought to have been rheumatic heart disease) and was sent to relatives in Dundee, Scotland. In the 1820s he lived here at 1–3 Robert Street (a plaque marks the house) and became involved with the publishing firm of Taylor & Hessey, 96 Fleet Street, as assistant editor of their *London Magazine*, as well as a constant contributor, and became acquainted with such figures as Charles Lamb, William Hazlitt, Thomas De Quincey, and John Hamilton Reynolds, whose sister Jane he married in May 1825 at St. Botolph's Church. Lamb's "On an Infant Dying as Soon as Born" was occasioned by the death of Hood's first child. In 1829 he moved to Rose Cottage on Vicars Moor Lane, Winchmore, and from

1832 to 1835 he lived in Lake House, Wanstead. At the end of 1834, when some sort of publisher's failure (it is thought) bankrupted him, Hood fled to the Continent until 1840, when he began writing for the *New Monthly Magazine,* of which he became editor in 1841. He wrote "The Song of the Shirt" at 17 Elm Tree Road, St. John's Wood, where he spent his last years. In 1844 he began *Hood's Magazine,* but the undertaking proved too great for his fragile health. He became bedridden at Christmas 1844 and died at Devonshire Lodge, 28 Finchley Street (marked with a plaque), on May 3, 1845. Hood was buried in the Kensal Green Cemetery, where a monument was erected in 1854.

Victorian and Later Periods   From a population of 1,225,694 in 1821, London reached 6,586,269 at the turn of the 20th century. An estimated 90,000 persons crossed London Bridge daily in 1837, the year of Queen Victoria's accession; indeed, congestion in the city was extremely serious. Metropolitan living conditions then were generally ghastly, and the provisions for sanitation—if that is what open cesspools, stagnant gullies, rotting privies, and gas-filled sewers can be called—were disgraceful. The Thames, the source of the water supply, was so heavily polluted by the sewers, stable dung, and rubbish and offal from slaughterhouses that its color was green black and its consistency that of runny glue. This, along with the horrid state of 218 acres of shallow, low-lying burial grounds and the smoke-laden and foggy atmosphere, produced a cholera outbreak in 1849 which carried off 400 persons a day at its peak. Typhus was common, and hordes of rats came up through the open sewers in search of food, often attacking humans, particularly children.

Not surprisingly, social reform became a major concern. Educational grants established primary schools, and school inspectors were appointed; the first national Public Health Act was passed in 1848. Factory inspectors were appointed in 1833, and in 1844 children under ten and women were denied employment in mines.

In politics, Sir Robert Peel was still very much in control of his party, and by the election of 1841 he had built such a loyal following among the Tories that his subsequent moves for reform were readily accepted. While he simplified and reduced tariff restrictions, brought back the income tax within his ministry's first year, set forth principles for banking and currency in the Bank Charter Act, and established a solid banking and credit system with residual powers vested in the Bank of England, his greatest impact came in 1846, when he secured the repeal of the Corn Laws.

After the repeal of the Corn Laws, Peel was unable to retain control of the Conservatives, and the young Benjamin Disraeli, despite prejudice because of his family's religious background, his literary abilities, and his manner, eventually gained control of the Conservatives. Disraeli led in the passage of the Reform Act of 1867, which almost doubled the electorate and created forty-six new borough and county seats. In 1868 the Liberals with William Gladstone won the elections; he and his Cabinet, perhaps the best in the 19th century, accomplished much: the Irish Land Act of 1870 afforded some safeguards to

Irish tenant farmers, the Trade Union Act of 1871 legalized unions, and the Ballot Act of 1872 provided for the secret ballot. The Education Act of 1870, though, alienated the dissenters, and the Licensing Acts of 1871 and 1872 alienated the brewers, who came over to the Conservative party and carried Disraeli to power "in a torrent of gin and beer" in 1874.

Disraeli embarked on a program of social legislation, geared to the interests of the masses. Effective slum clearance came about with the Artisans' and Labourers' Dwellings Improvement Act; the 1875 Public Health Act created a public health authority in every area of Britain; the 1878 Factory Act legislated a fifty-six-hour workweek; and additional legislation set up the machinery for some health and old-age insurance. The general election of March 1880 returned the Liberals and Gladstone to power, with Joseph Chamberlain, who openly proclaimed a radical program of "municipal socialism," the dissident element. Gladstone's most pressing problems were abroad: in the Transvaal, where the Boers defeated the British; in Egypt, where he ordered the bombardment of Alexandria to counter a national revolt; in the Sudan, where Charles Gordon and his troops were massacred in Khartoum; and in Ireland, where there was great support for Irish home rule. Victoria's evident dislike of Gladstone grew over the years (she referred to him in 1892 as an "old, wily, and incomprehensible man of 82½"), and when his resignation was forced, the Queen was pleased.

In many ways Victoria's successor, Edward VII, was totally unprepared for his role. Until the age of fifty, he had been forbidden by the Queen to read any of the Prime Minister's reports of Cabinet meetings, and he had generally been excluded from both family and court affairs. By this time the labor movement had become politically motivated. New social legislation was adopted; national secondary education was established; free school meals for needy children and a school medical service were provided; an Old Age Pensions Act for persons seventy years of age and over was drafted; and a trades board was created to establish wages in industries lacking union strength. Edward died in May 1910 (while considering abdication), and his politically inexperienced son George V came to the throne.

Ford Madox Ford called London of the 19th century "the world town"; it was then the greatest urban center in the world, and between 1821 and 1901 its population increased by 5,360,575. The city had a rising crime rate until Peel's Metropolitan Police Force (established in 1828) slowed it down. Executions, though fewer, were still carried out in public despite the protests of many influential people such as Charles Dickens; indeed, not until 1868 were executions made private. Prostitution was rampant; in the 1860s an estimated 80,000 women were professional prostitutes, and that number did not include the dolly-mops (amateurs) or the vast number of mistresses of men wealthy enough to possess apartments. There were about 3,000 brothels, ranging from the very smartest of houses, such as Kate Hamilton's or the Argyll Rooms on Shaftesbury Avenue, to filthy courts off Bluegate Fields, where all the rooms in each house were used for prostitution.

Transportation in London came in for special attention during this period. Omnibuses revolutionized London in 1829, Joseph Aloysius Hansom introduced the "patent safety cab" in 1834, and by 1838 numerous railway lines had been laid down. The effects were considerable; thousands of Londoners were displaced as entire areas were demolished for the rail lines, hotels, and terminals, and many of them moved into already-overpopulated areas. Furthermore, the metamorphosis of suburban areas brought an uncountable number of pedestrians, vehicles of all sorts, horses, and market animals to jam the streets of London. The underground, proposed to cut congestion, opened in 1863 and carried 30,000 passengers in open carts between Paddington and the City on its inaugural day.

The problem of public health was urgent: communicable diseases were common, and a major outbreak of cholera killed 4,000 persons in 1866. While the 1870 Education Act established universal elementary education, this did not alter the fact that children as young as five were often put to work; even their small income (usually less than 6 pence a day) was often essential for a family's survival. If the child did get to school, the mother often took his place at work and left younger children at home drugged with a healthy dose of Godfrey's Cordial or other preparations of opium and treacle.

One of the most striking aspects of Victorian London was the rapidity and opulence of building programs; streets are barely identifiable from one decade to another because of construction. Trafalgar Square and the Embankment are particularly impressive, but the list included the Post Office (1873), the Wool Exchange (1874), the Knightsbridge Barracks (1879), the City of London School (1882), St. Paul's School and the Brompton Oratory (1884), the Stock Exchange (1885), and the Guildhall School of Music and the Guildhall Art Gallery (1886). Between 1855 and 1866 the Royal Victoria, Millwall, South-West India, Royal Albert, and Tilbury Docks were built; and in 1897 the Blackwell Tunnel was opened.

Probably nothing could rival the period between 1840 and 1860 when the Houses of Parliament and the Crystal Palace were built. The old Palace of Westminster (the conglomerate of buildings around Westminster Hall) burned to the ground in 1834, when workmen overstuffed a stove with wooden tallies from the office of the clerk of works. Work on the houses began in 1840, and the House of Lords was finished in 1847. There was, according to Nathaniel Hawthorne, American consul in Liverpool, "nothing . . . more magnificent and gravely gorgeous." In 1849 Prince Albert proposed the Great Exhibition to the Society of Arts, but the scheme met considerable opposition, especially when the lowest estimated cost was £120,000. Fresh plans created the Crystal Palace, a monumental structure almost 2,000 feet long and 400 feet wide, containing 30 miles of guttering, 200 miles of wooden sash bars, and 900,000 square feet of glass; its purpose was to display, William Makepeace Thackeray stated, "England's arms of conquest . . . the trophies of her bloodless war," that is, 19,000 exhibits of the industrial revolution. The profits from its success bought a long stretch of land between Kensington Gardens and Cromwell Road, where eventually schools, museums, concert halls, and homes of learned societies rose in Prince Albert's name, a long-overdue tribute. The Exhibition Hall, renamed the Crystal Palace and moved to Sydenham, was destroyed by fire in 1936.

Thomas Babington Macaulay (1800–1859) While Thomas Babington Macaulay is now most often considered a historian, he was also an important man of letters. He was brought to London from Rothley Temple shortly after his birth, and the family lived on Birchin Lane for two years before moving to 5 The Pavement (marked with a plaque) in Clapham, where he attended Mr. Greaves's Day School. Finishing at Trinity College, Cambridge, he rejoined his family at their Great Ormond Street address (on the site of the present Homeopathic Hospital) in 1823 after keeping separate lodgings on Frith Street for a short time. He entered Lincoln's Inn while retaining his fellowship at Trinity College and was called to the bar in 1826. Three years later he took chambers at 8 South Square, off Gray's Inn Road.

By 1828 Macaulay had essentially given up the law, and as an ardent Whig he took a seat in Parliament in 1830 as the Member from Calne, Wiltshire; he became an intimate of Holland House in Kensington, which was then, he said, the resort of "wits and beauties, of painters and poets, of scholars, philosophers, and statesmen." After spending four years in India setting up a national education system and reforming the penal system, he returned to London in 1838 and was elected Member of Parliament for Edinburgh; he settled at 3 Clarges Street, but he went to his sister and brother-in-law's home at 12 Great George Street in 1839, when he became Secretary for War in the 2d Viscount Melbourne's Cabinet. Macaulay had begun *The History of England* in 1839 but suspended all work on it while in the Cabinet. He moved late in 1840 to the Albany where he led

> a sort of life peculiarly suited to my taste, college life in the West-end of London. I have an entrance hall, two sittingrooms, a bedroom, a kitchen, cellars, and two rooms for servants,—all this for ninety guineas a year. . . .

When Melbourne's government fell and the secretaryship vanished in 1841, Macaulay was able to publish his *Lays of Ancient Rome* and *Critical and Historical Essays*. He reentered Parliament in 1846 but soon lost his seat and, in fact, his interest in politics. The leisure was now at hand for his *History*, and the first two volumes appeared in 1849; he continued his literary and historical work, reading constantly in the British Museum, of which he was a trustee, and visiting the scenes of historical events. He bought Holly Lodge (where Queen Elizabeth College now stands), on Campden Hill in Kensington, in 1856 to be near Lord and Lady Holland; here Macaulay took great delight in his extensive gardens except for the dandelions, which were anathemas to him:

> I thought I was rid of the villains; but the day before yesterday, when I got up and looked out of my window, I could see five or six of their great, impudent, flaring yellow faces turned up at me. . . . How I enjoyed their destruction! Is it Christianlike to hate a dandelion so savagely?

Created Baron Macaulay of Rothley in 1857, he never spoke in the Lords and, indeed, was well aware he could not finish his *History*; Lord Macaulay died on December 28, 1859, and was buried in the Poets' Corner of Westminster Abbey.

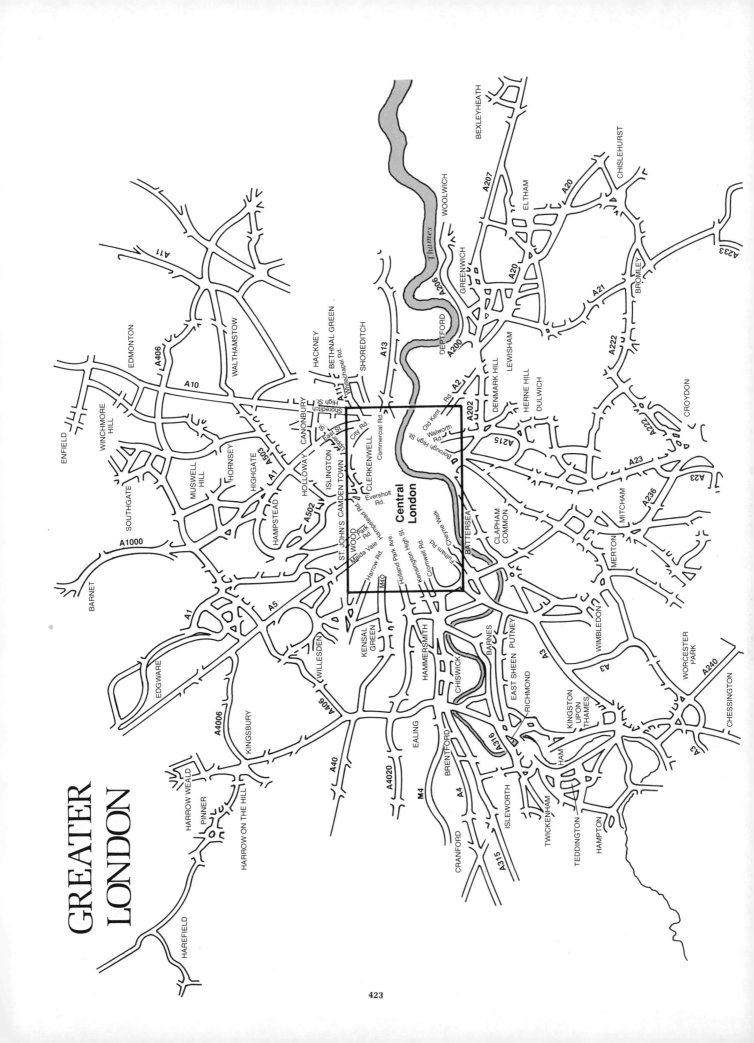

GREATER LONDON

Central London

HAREFIELD

HARROW WEALD

PINNER

HARROW ON THE HILL

EDGWARE

A4006

KINGSBURY

A40

A4020

M4

A4

CRANFORD

A315

ISLEWORTH

BRENTFORD

EALING

A406

WILLESDEN

KENSAL GREEN

HAMMERSMITH

CHISWICK

A316

RICHMOND

TEDDINGTON

HAMPTON

TWICKENHAM

HAM

KINGSTON UPON THAMES

BARNES

EAST SHEEN

PUTNEY

A3

WIMBLEDON

WORCESTER PARK

A240

CHESSINGTON

A3

MERTON

MITCHAM

A236

A23

CROYDON

A222

A222

A215

CLAPHAM COMMON

BATTERSEA

DULWICH

HERNE HILL

DENMARK HILL

LEWISHAM

A202

A2

A200

A205

DEPTFORD

GREENWICH

WOOLWICH

A207

ELTHAM

A20

A20

A21

BROMLEY

CHISLEHURST

A233

BEXLEYHEATH

Thames

Old Kent Rd.

Walworth Rd.

Borough High St.

Fulham Rd.

Cheyne Walk

Cromwell Rd.

Kensington High St.

Holland Park Ave.

Harrow Rd.

Maida Vale

Hampstead Rd.

Park Rd.

St. JOHN'S WOOD

CAMDEN TOWN

Eversholt Rd.

CLERKENWELL

City Rd.

Commercial Rd.

ISLINGTON

HOLLOWAY

CANONBURY

Essex Rd.

East St.

Liverpool St.

Shoreditch High St.

Whitechapel Rd.

A111

A13

SHOREDITCH

BETHNAL GREEN

HACKNEY

A10

A502

A1

A503

HIGHGATE

HORNSEY

MUSWELL HILL

HAMPSTEAD

A406

WALTHAMSTOW

EDMONTON

WINCHMORE HILL

A11

SOUTHGATE

ENFIELD

A1000

BARNET

A1

A5

423

Harriet Martineau (1802–1876)   Harriet Martineau made a short trip to London from Dublin in September 1831 to talk with various publishers about her stories and finally persuaded Charles Fox to publish them with half the profits returning to the author; however, not until 1832 did she move to London. Then she took rooms at 6 Conduit Street but joined her mother and her aunt at 17 Fludyer Street, Westminster (Fludyer Street stood west off Parliament Street, just below King Charles Street where the Treasury now is). Miss Martineau remained here until leaving London in 1834: in the meantime she was extraordinarily successful and claimed to have dined out six days a week, to have advised Cabinet ministers, and to have supported poor-law reforms with information drawn from Lord Brougham's private papers. She returned to London in 1849 and stayed at 17 Westbourne Street, Bayswater; *Deerbrook* had been published in 1839, and from Charlotte Brontë (writing as Currer Bell), Miss Martineau now received a note acknowledging "a new and keen pleasure" that "*he* had derived" from the work and enclosing a copy of *Shirley*. The author of *Deerbrook* invited "Currer Bell, Esq." (but wrote "Dear Madam" in the note) to tea on December 10. Miss Brontë's normal unease was overcome, and the tea passed pleasantly.

Thomas Lovell Beddoes (1803–1849)   On June 5, 1817, Thomas Lovell Beddoes entered the 17th-century Charterhouse, originally founded for "forty poor boys" of London, on the north side of Charterhouse Square. Here Beddoes distinguished himself by outrageous behavior and a passion for Elizabethan dramatists. Here, as well, he began writing, and *The Bride's Tragedy* was, at least in part, written before he left for Pembroke College, Oxford. His education was interrupted in the summer of 1824 when his mother died in Florence, and that same year he resided for a time at 2 Devereux Court. After receiving his bachelor's degree in 1825, he lodged at 6 Devereux Court before going to Göttingen to study medicine. Subsequently Beddoes was in England briefly two or three times before he committed suicide in Basel, Switzerland, on January 26, 1849.

Edward Bulwer-Lytton, Lord Lytton (1803–1873)   One of the early popular Victorian novelists, Edward Bulwer-Lytton was born on May 25, 1803, at 31 Baker Street, a house which the family kept until the fall of 1807, after Gen. William Bulwer died. Mrs. Lytton took her family to Knebworth when she inherited the estate in 1811 and added Lytton to her surname; Lytton had some early schooling in Ealing and Fulham before that move. Before March 1821 he was living at 10 Seymour Street. After Cambridge and an extensive stay in Paris, Lytton returned here and met Rosina Doyle Wheeler, who was living in the city with her uncle. A woman of remarkable beauty, she encouraged his attentions while his mother, who strongly disapproved of the match, stopped his generous allowance immediately upon their marriage in 1827. Soon after *Pelham* was published in 1828, Lytton bought a house at 36 Hertford Street, but the couple lived in Fulham until January 1830, when they took occupancy here. Lytton was reconciled with his mother about this time, and his £1,000 allowance was restored.

The marriage proved ill-advised, and Lytton's election to Parliament as the Liberal Member for St. Ives in 1831 (and subsequently for Lincoln) and his literary activities (he was finishing *Eugene Aram*) provided grounds for the estrangement. Rosina and the children, Emily and Robert, went to Berrymead Priory, Acton, in 1834, and Lytton let the Hertford Street house when he took lodgings in the Albany. Interestingly enough, in the year of greatest marital conflict *The Last Days of Pompeii* was published.

Lytton's friendship with Benjamin Disraeli grew, and Disraeli converted him to Toryism; in 1852 Lytton was returned to the House of Commons as the Member from Hertfordshire. From 1836 on he was energetically writing and contributed, in addition to his novels, several successful plays, a host of essays, and two volumes of *Athens: Its Rise and Fall*. In 1866 he took the lease of 12 Grosvenor Square and lived his last five years here. Lord Lytton died in Torquay on January 18, 1873, and was buried in the Poets' Corner of Westminster Abbey. There is also a memorial in St. Paul's Cathedral. It should be noted that Robert Bulwer-Lytton, 1st Earl of Lytton, better known as Owen Meredith, was born in his father's Hertford Street house on November 8, 1831.

George Borrow (1803–1881)   The intriguing author of *Lavengro* and *The Romany Rye*, George Borrow, was articled unsuccessfully to a solicitor in Norwich before he came to London in April 1824 to try his luck. He had rooms at 16 Millman Street when he did some indifferent reviewing for Sir Richard Phillips's *Monthly Magazine*. During this period Borrow spent some time in the company of the artist Benjamin Haydon, as *Lavengro* relates; he first visited Haydon with his brother:

> At length we were shown into the studio, where we found the painter, with an easel and brush, standing before a huge piece of canvas, on which he had lately commenced painting a heroic picture. The painter might be about thirty-five years old; he had a clever intelligent countenance, with a sharp gray eye—his hair was dark brown, and cut à-la-Rafael, as I was subsequently told, that is, there was little before and much behind— . . . he had a broad muscular breast, and I make no doubt that he would have been a very fine figure, but unfortunately his legs and thighs were somewhat short.

At Holy Lands, a hostelry on the Strand, Borrow met Francis Arden, an "Irish gallant" who introduced him to the bear pits, pubs, dogfights, and theaters; Arden becomes Francis Ardry in *Lavengro*. The first night Francis

> proposed that we should go to the play to see Kean; so we went to the play, and saw—not Kean, who at that time was ashamed to show himself, but—a man who was not ashamed to show himself, and who people said was a much better man than Kean—as I have no doubt he was—though whether he was a better actor I cannot say, for I never saw Kean.

The second time they went to

> shall I say?—why not?—a gaming house, where I saw Francis Ardry play and lose five guineas, and where I lost nothing, because I did not play, though I felt somewhat inclined; for a man with a white hat and sparkling eye held up a box which contained something which rattled, and asked me to fling the bones. "There is nothing like flinging the bones!" said he, and then I thought I should like to know what kind of thing flinging the bones was; I, however, restrained myself.

"Some of the places" where they went, Borrow states, "were very strange places indeed ... and, among other strange places to which Francis Ardry conducted me was a place not far from the abbey church of Westminster." Here they "saw a dog destroy a great many rats in a very small period"; this was the old Westminster Pit, where the celebrated terrier Billy is said to have killed 500 rats in 5½ minutes.

Borrow was in the City when Lord Byron's body was being taken from Great George Street to Hucknall Torkard (now Hucknall), Nottinghamshire:

> I found myself about noon at the bottom of Oxford Street, where it forms a right angle with the road which leads or did lead to Tottenham Court. . . . Just then I hear various voices cry "There it comes!" and all heads were turned up Oxford Street, down which a hearse was slowly coming: nearer and nearer it drew; presently it was just opposite the place where I was standing, when, turning to the left, it proceeded slowly along Tottenham Road; immediately behind the hearse were three or four mourning coaches[;] . . . behind these came a very long train of splendid carriages, all of which, without one exception were empty.
> "Whose body is in that hearse?" said I to a dapper-looking individual ... who stood beside me on the pavement. . . .
> "The mortal relics of Lord Byron." . . .

Borrow was unable to get anything published, and around May 12, 1825, in a typical state of despondency, "almost mechanically my feet conducted me to London Bridge," and "found myself in a street or road, with terraces on either side, and . . . leading . . . to the south-east." He was in a crowd, which he decided to follow, because he "had a desire to know whither all this crowd was going, and for what purpose," and eventually reached "a kind of low dingy town [Southwark], in the neighbourhood of the river," where the annual Blackheath Fair was being held. He met Jasper Petulengro, who offered him money, but Borrow refused the generosity and returned to the City, where he lived on bread and water until leaving London on a walking tour later in the month.

About two years later, when Borrow returned to sit for Haydon and took rooms at 26 Bryanston Street, his *Romantic Ballads*, translated from the Danish, appeared. In early December 1829, when he stayed at 17 Great Russell Street, he was attempting to get his translation of Johannes Ewald's *The Death of Balder* published. Before his next major stay in the city, he had met Mrs. Mary Clarke, and when Borrow, with his sombrero, servant, and horse, arrived in London before his marriage to her on April 23, 1840, at St. Peter's Church, Cornhill, he stayed at the Spread Eagle Inn on Gracechurch Street. In November of the same year, staying at 58 Jermyn Street, he took the manuscript of *The Zincali* to John Murray, 50 (now 50A) Albemarle Street. Following a trip to Cornwall, while engaged in research at the British Museum, he stayed at 53A Pall Mall (he had also stayed here in 1848).

Having by 1860 become an established, although not necessarily a reputable, figure, he and his family moved to London; after staying briefly at 21 Montagu Street, they took posession of 22 Hertford Square, where he remained until 1874. Borrow's wife, who

died on January 30, 1869, is buried in the Brompton Cemetery; the tombstone contains a peculiar inscription, "To the Blessed Memory of My Mother, Mary Borrow, who fell asleep in Jesus." In 1874 Borrow returned to Oulton Broad, where he died in 1881; he was buried here in Brompton. *Lavengro* contains numerous references to London.

Benjamin Disraeli (1804–1881) A man of enormous Victorian importance, Benjamin Disraeli was born on December 21, 1804, at 22 Theobalds Road (then 6 King's Road); the house, called Disraeli House, was marked by a plaque in 1904. He was not, as he claimed, born in a library in the Adelphi. Probably the most significant event in his life occurred when his father, Isaac D'Israeli, quarreled seriously with the Sephardic Synagogue of Bevis Marks in 1813 and had his children baptized on July 31, 1817, at St. Andrew's Church, Holborn; but for this event, Disraeli's political career could never have taken place since Jews, by law, were then excluded from Parliament. In 1817 or 1818 the D'Israeli family moved to 6 Bloomsbury Square, and the family attended services at St. George's Church. Disraeli was privately educated at a dame school on Colebrook Row, Islington, and then in Walthamstow. At the age of seventeen, he was articled to a solicitors' firm in the Old Jewry and in 1824 entered Lincoln's Inn, where he remained for nine terms before he removed his name.

Disraeli was interested in making his mark on the world in ways other than law and turned to literature; the first volume of *Vivian Grey* was an enormous success. He entered Parliament in 1837, when the stench from the Thames, which he once described as "a Stygian pool reeking with ineffable and intolerable horrors," still reached the Houses. (As late as the summer of 1858, £1,500 worth of lime was used weekly to cut the odor, and in 1859 the sum of £17,733 was spent on chalk, lime, chloride of lime, and carbolic acid in order to help.) In August 1839 Disraeli married Mrs. Wyndham Lewis, the widow of a former colleague, at St. George's Church, Hanover Square; and the couple resided at her home at 93 Upper Grosvenor Street for thirty-three years (with time out at 10 Downing Street when he was Prime Minister). By 1872 six major novels, including *Coningsby, or The New Generation, Sybil, or The Two Nations*, and *Lothair*, had been produced.

The death of Mrs. Disraeli, now Viscountess Beaconsfield, of cancer in November 1872 was keenly felt by Disraeli, and he retired to Hughenden but kept a residence at 2 Whitehall Gardens, opposite Whitehall Court where it enters Horse Guards Avenue, until the Conservatives suffered a heavy defeat in the 1880 elections. Created Earl of Beaconsfield in 1876 and working hard on *Endymion* even though his health was failing, he took 19 Curzon Street (marked with a plaque) upon his retirement from active politics; the house, secured by the £10,000 advance on the novel, had "a look of spick and span newness, with no pictures, and no busts or engravings, only a few pieces of Dresden China." He finished *Endymion* before he died here on April 19, 1881. He was buried in Hughenden, next to his wife. There is a commemorative statue of Disraeli in Parliament Square as well as one in the Statesmen's Aisle of Westminster Abbey. One of the few London places frequented by Beaconsfield was the Cider Cellar Tavern in the basement of 21 Maiden Lane.

Harrison Ainsworth (1805–1882)   A Manchester-born author of popular historical romances, William Harrison Ainsworth came to London in 1824 to finish his legal training with Jacob Phillips of the Inner Temple but found himself more deeply involved with the literary world than with his legal studies. He lodged at 6 Devereux Court, off the Strand. Ainsworth became acquainted with John Ebers, manager of the Opera House and a book publisher, and through him met Anne Frances Ebers, whom he married in 1826; the couple first lived at 4 Sussex Place, off the Outer Circle in Regent's Park. Deciding to abandon the law, he went into business as a publisher and had his office and a bookstore at 27 Old Bond Street, but this, too, he abandoned after only eighteen months. He had moved to the Elms in Kilburn, then a small village north of London; here he wrote *Rookwood*. From 1835 to 1841 Ainsworth lived at Kensal Lodge, Harrow Road; the house overlooked the fields and woods, and here he wrote *Jack Sheppard* and some of *The Tower of London*. Shortly after becoming editor of *Bentley's Miscellany* in 1840, he moved to the larger Kensal Manor, where he was visited by many of the leading literary figures of the time, among them Charles Dickens, Richard Harris Barham, and William Makepeace Thackeray; after his death in Reigate, Ainsworth was buried in the Kensal Green Cemetery.

Many of his works deal at least in part with London, and *Old St. Paul's* is a standard reference work for the Great Fire of 1666 and the plague. *The Tower of London*, mostly written at the Sussex Hotel on Bouverie Street, is virtually a history of the great fortress; Ainsworth desired in part

> to exhibit the Tower in its triple light of a palace, a prison, and a fortress.

He describes the building of the tower: "In 1078 . . . the Tower of London was founded by William the Conqueror, who appointed Gundulph, Bishop of Rochester, principal overseer of the work." "Fourteen years later," he continues, ". . . the White Tower was greatly damaged by a violent storm." Repairs began immediately, and Ainsworth follows the history to the time of his chronicle, the mid-16th century:

> [T]he Tower of London comprehended within its walls a superficies of rather more than twelve acres. . . . Consisting of a citadel or keep, surrounded by an inner and outer ward, it was approached on the west by an entrance called the Bulwark Gate, which has long since disappeared. The second entrance was formed by an embattled tower, called the Lion's Gate, conducting to a strong tower flanked with bastions, and defended by a double portcullis, denominated the Middle Tower. The outworks adjoining these towers, in which was kept the menagerie, were surrounded by a smaller moat, communicating with the main ditch. A large drawbridge then led to another portal, . . . forming the principal entrance to the outer ward, and called the By-ward or Gate Tower. The outer ward was defended by a strong line of fortifications; and at the north-east corner stood a large circular bastion, called the Mount.

The Duke of Northumberland's trial for high treason takes place in Westminster Hall. "Closely confined within the Beauchamp Tower" before being escorted to the hall, he and his sons

> descended a short spiral stone staircase, and, passing under an arched doorway, . . . entered upon the Green. The whole of this spacious area, from Saint Peter's Chapel to the Lieutenant's lodgings—from the walls of the tower they had quitted, to those of the White Tower, was filled with spectators.

Disorder occurs when Gunnora Braose breaks "through the ranks of the guards":

> Order being restored, the procession set forth. . . . Taking its course across the Green, and passing beneath the gloomy portal of the Bloody Tower, the train entered an archway at the left of the By-ward Tower, and crossing the drawbridge, drew up at the head of the stairs leading to the river.

There are, of course, many other references and accurate descriptions of London and its buildings here.

Elizabeth Barrett Browning (1806–1861) and Robert Browning (1812–1889)   A popular but relatively minor poet of the Victorian period is Elizabeth Barrett Browning, who was brought to London by her father from Sidmouth in 1836; the Barretts first lived at 74 (now 99) Gloucester Place, a brick house built about 1805. Elizabeth Barrett, not wanting to leave Devonshire, wondered how she would survive "walled up like a transgressing nun, and out of hearing of that sea": she was depressed at first by the "want of horizon" and so sat, seeing

> Fog only, the great tawney weltering fog,
> Involve the passive city, strangle it
> Alive, and draw it off into the void
> Spires, bridges, streets and squares, as if a sponge
> Had wiped out London.

Eventually, though, London became "a wonderful place—the living heart and center of an immense circle of humanity—the fountain of intellect—of Art in all its forms—of the highest memories consecrated by genius: it is your Fletcher's London, our Shakespeare's London, my Chaucer's London." In April 1838 the Barretts moved to 50 Wimpole Street, the residence most often associated with the poet (a plaque on the present building marks the site); the same year her first volume of poetry, *The Seraphim and Other Poems*, appeared. However, her health, already precarious because of a spinal injury received when trying to mount her pony at Hope End around 1820, forced her to spend the next three years in Torquay. Returning in September 1841, a year after her brother's drowning death, she took to her rooms and developed a terror of meeting anyone new; she was still ill and was taking fairly large doses of morphine, which she was never able to do without, even later in Italy. In 1843 "The Cry of the Children," "A Vision of Poets," "The Last Bower," and "To Flush, My Dog" appeared, as well as a volume of poetry. In an 1844 volume she included a few lines in praise of Robert Browning, a then still relatively obscure poet.

Browning had been born on May 7, 1812, at Hanover Cottage, Southampton Street (gone), Camberwell, where his family lived for twenty-five years. Since his Nonconformity barred him from Oxford and Cambridge, he enrolled in the newly founded University of London for its first term and took digs on nearby Gower Street. However, within a very short period he gave up both the rooms and the university and went home. He continued to live with his parents until 1846; *Paracelsus* appeared in 1835, *Sordello* in 1840, and between 1841 and 1846, seven plays in verse, including *Pippa Passes*. In 1836 Mary Russell Mitford invited him to her home at 56 Russell Square; as she noted:

> Mr Wordsworth, Mr Landor, and Mr White dined here. I like Mr Wordsworth. . . . Mr Landor is a very striking-looking person, and exceedingly clever. Also we had a Mr Browning, a young poet, and Mr Proctor, . . . and quantities more of poets.

Following Elizabeth Barrett's praise in her 1844 *Poems*, Robert Browning wrote to her in January 1845; "I love your verses with all my heart, dear Miss Barrett," followed by "I do, as I say, love these books with all my heart—and I love you too." Her reply was immediate, and although the two corresponded constantly, they did not meet until May. Elizabeth Barrett's father was tyrannical and selfish, and he even forbade her going to Italy when the doctors recommended it. Browning, convinced that getting her out of the Wimpole Street house offered the only possible hope, persuaded her to marry him secretly on September 12, 1846, at St. Marylebone Parish Church, on Marylebone Road. As she later wrote, "There was no elopement in the case, but simply a private marriage." The windows in the north aisle of the church commemorate the marriage. This was the first and only time before they left for Italy that they had met outside her father's home; Elizabeth Barrett Browning returned to Wimpole Street for the next week. On September 19 she, her dog Flush, and her maid Wilson met Browning at Vauxhall Station, and they left for Italy. Barrett never forgave his daughter and was never reconciled to her.

The Brownings returned to England in 1851 and took up residence at 26 Devonshire Street (now Boswell Street), where they stayed until September; here they received Thomas Carlyle, Samuel Rogers, and Barry Cornwall. On a second trip in June 1852 they resided at 58 Welbeck Street (now a hotel), and Browning probably met Dante Gabriel Rossetti at this time. He is known to have visited Rossetti frequently at 16 Cheyne Walk from 1862 on and may well have been at The Hermitage, Rossetti's cottage on West Hill in Highgate. Elizabeth Barrett Browning's last trip to England occurred in 1855, when they came to 13 Dorset Street (rebuilt); most of *Aurora Leigh* was finished, and many of their friends, including Alfred, Lord Tennyson and Rossetti, visited them. Indeed, in this house Rossetti made his famous sketch of Tennyson reading *Maud* aloud.

After Elizabeth Barrett Browning's death on June 29, 1861, in Florence, Browning decided immediately to "go away, break up everything, go to England, and live and work and write." After taking temporary lodgings, he settled at 19 Warwick Crescent and became quite withdrawn. *Dramatis Personae*, which included "Abt Vogler" and "Rabbi Ben Ezra," appeared in 1864, and with this volume came recognition. As did Lord Lytton, Oscar Wilde, and J. E. Millais, he began to take part in the literary evenings that Ouida (Marie Louise de la Ramée) held at her apartment in the Langham Hotel (across from All Souls' Church,

Langham Place), and in 1866 his sister Sarianna came from Paris to live with him. Browning by then was much sought after, and observers often wondered how he could ever reconcile his creative life and his active social life. In 1868–1869 *The Ring and the Book* appeared, and beginning in 1871 a series of dramatic or narrative poems followed. He moved to 22 De Vere Gardens, his last home, in 1888; from 1886 on he was frequently at 87 Oakley Street, the home of "Speranza," the pseudonym of Lady Wilde, the poet, Irish patriot, and mother of Oscar Wilde.

Browning habitually spent at least part of each year abroad and died in Venice on December 12, 1889; he was buried in the Poets' Corner of Westminster Abbey on December 31. It should be noted that Browning wrote the inscription for the memorial window to Queen Victoria in St. Margaret's Church, across from Westminster Hall.

Edward FitzGerald (1809–1883) Edward FitzGerald had at least ten different addresses in London from 1830 on, but he was in most of them for only short periods until after his disastrous marriage to Lucy Barton in 1856. Lodgings in the 1830s were at 27 Southampton Row; in the 1840s he became fascinated with Charlotte Street (Rathbone Place turns into Charlotte at Percy Street); in 1840, 1844–1845, and 1848 he was at Number 19, in 1843 at Number 18, and in 1846–1847 at Number 60. In 1843 he also lived for a time with William Makepeace Thackeray at 13 Coram Street. He worked on the *Rubáiyát of Omar Khayyám* at 24 Greenberry Street in St. John's Wood. He had, at one time, bachelor lodgings at 31 Great Portland Street, and after his separation from his wife he returned to his old quarters in March 1858. FitzGerald also lodged at 39 Bolsover Street from 1848 to 1850, at 17 Old Gloucester Street in 1854, and at 60 Lincoln's Inn Fields in June 1854 after a trip to Alfred, Lord Tennyson's home in Farringford.

Alfred, Lord Tennyson (1809–1892) Easily the most celebrated Victorian poet as well as Poet Laureate from 1850 on, Alfred Tennyson often visited Arthur Henry Hallam's home at 67 Wimpole Street from 1832 until Hallam's death in September 1833; this "dark house . . . in the long unlovely street" is recalled in *In Memoriam*:

> . . . I see
> Betwixt the black fronts long-withdrawn
> A light-blue lane of early dawn,
> And think of early days and thee. . . .

On an 1833 visit with his sister Mary and with Hallam, he viewed the Elgin marbles, the Tower of London, and the Zoological Gardens, where through microscopes they looked at "moths' wings, gnats' heads, and at all the lions and tigers which lie perdus in a drop of spring water." On trips to London following Hallam's death, Tennyson frequented Bertolini's and the Cock Tavern, on Fleet Street opposite the gate of Middle Temple Lane:

> O plump head-waiter at The Cock,
>   To which I most resort,
> How goes the time? 'Tis five o'clock.
>   Go fetch a pint of port:
> But let it not be such as that
>   You set before chance-comers,
> But such whose father-grape grew fat
>   On Lusitanian summers.

He often stayed with James Spedding at 60 Lincoln's Inn Fields or with Edmund Lushington at 1 Mitre Court when he did not have his own lodgings,

> the last house, Norfolk Street, Strand, at the bottom of the street on the left; the name is Edwards which you will see projecting from the door on a brass plate.

Tennyson met Thomas Carlyle at least as early as 1840, and he was frequently at Carlyle's home at 5 (now 24) Cheyne Walk, in Chelsea. Carlyle's detailed description of the poet, Tennyson's son said, was the most accurate:

> Alfred is one of the few British and foreign figures (a not increasing number I think) who are and remain beautiful to me, a true human soul, or some authentic approximation thereto. . . . One of the finest looking men in the world. A great shock of rough dusky hair; bright, laughing, hazel eyes; massive aquiline face, most massive yet most delicate; of sallow brown complexion, almost Indian looking, clothes cynically loose, free-and-easy, smokes infinite tobacco. His voice is musical, metallic, fit for loud laughter and piercing wail[;] . . . I do not meet in these late decades such company over a pipe! we shall see what he will grow to.

On an 1842 visit to St. Paul's Cathedral with Edward FitzGerald, Tennyson commented when they were in the middle of the "central roar" that "This is the mind; that is a mood of it." On one trip in 1844 he stayed at the old Hummums's Hotel, on the south corner of Russell Street where it enters Covent Garden. Probably the most important of Tennyson's early associations was his membership in the Sterling Club (founded in 1838 as the Anonymous Club); here he would meet Carlyle, William Makepeace Thackeray, Charles Dickens, Walter Savage Landor, Daniel Maclise, Leigh Hunt, Barry Cornwall, and Samuel Rogers. He even attended some of the historic literary breakfasts at Rogers's home at 22 St. James's Place.

After his marriage in 1850 to Emily Sellwood, the poet much preferred his Haslemere (Aldworth) and Farringford homes to London but was here in February 1850 staying at 25 Mornington Place, off Hampstead Road. Tennyson had with him the manuscript of *In Memoriam*, but on his return to Farringford he discovered his "book of Elegies" was missing. He wrote immediately to Coventry Patmore and asked, "Will you go to my old chambers and institute a vigorous inquiry?" Patmore, after great difficulty with the landlady, found the manuscript at the back of a closet. On a trip in 1858 with his wife and two children, he stayed at Little Holland House (gone), 6 Melbury Road, Kensington, and there Tennyson began "Lancelot and Elaine." After the Rev. George Granville Bradley, a friend of long standing, became Dean of Westminster, Tennyson was a frequent guest at the Deanery; while he was staying there in April 1883, Archdeacon Frederic William Farrar asked him to compose an epitaph on Caxton for the painted window subscribed by the London printers at St. Margaret's Church, across from Westminster Hall. Tennyson complied and felt the epitaph was one of his best:

> Thy prayer was "Light—more Light—while Time shall last,"
> Thou sawest a glory growing on the night,

> But not the shadows which that light would cast,
> Till shadows vanish in the Light of Light.

On this trip he and his son Hallam wandered around the abbey and climbed the chantry; listening to the combined sounds of choristers and organ, Tennyson commented, "It is beautiful, but what empty and awful mockery if there were no God!"

After Lord Tennyson's death at Aldworth on October 6, 1892, his body was taken to the Chapel of St. Faith, Westminster Abbey, and he was buried in the Poets' Corner next to Robert Browning.

Elizabeth Cleghorn Gaskell (1810–1865) Elizabeth Cleghorn Stevenson, better known as Mrs. Gaskell, was born at 23 (now 93) Cheyne Walk, Chelsea, on September 29, 1810; with her mother's death shortly after her birth, she was sent to her aunt in Knutsford. The story of the trip is told in *Mary Barton* when the "babby" is taken from London. In 1827 she was back in the city, staying with her father and stepmother at 3 Beaufort Street, and she returned here frequently. Indeed, she nursed her father through his last illness here in 1829 and then stayed alternately with two of her uncles, one living at 25 Brook Street and one on Park Lane. For a time in the late 1850s Mrs. Gaskell stayed at 17 Cumberland Terrace, Regent's Park. *North and South* begins and ends in a fashionable house in London, but the picture of Harley Street is an artificial one.

William Makepeace Thackeray (1811–1863) Born in India on July 18, 1811, William Makepeace Thackeray was sent to relatives in Chiswick, then a London suburb, in 1817, two years after his father died, and attended a school in Southampton before being sent to a school run by a Dr. Turner in Chiswick; the school was in Walpole House on Chiswick Mall. In 1822 Thackeray was sent to the 17th-century Charterhouse, a school founded originally for "forty poor boys" of London, and first boarded in a Mr. Penny's house, Wilderness Row on Clerkenwell Road. In 1824 he moved to the home of a Mrs. Boyes, probably on Charterhouse Square (the buildings of Charterhouse stand on the north side of the square). He entered the Middle Temple in 1831 and took rooms at 1 Hare Court; his chambers, on the ground floor, had oak wainscoting and set-in bookcases. He read with the special pleader, a Mr. Taprell, and quickly came to believe that the preparatory study was "one of the most cold-blooded, prejudiced pieces of invention that ever a man was slave to." Thackeray, it should be noted, knew he would come into a quite large patrimony in 1832 and consequently was desultory in most of his studies.

In May 1833 Thackeray bought *The National Standard*, a weekly literary periodical which failed in February 1834, and this, coupled with his general improvidence, left him penniless. Following a period in Paris studying art and his marriage to Isabella Shawe, he returned to London and lived for a short time in 1837 at 18 Albion Street, off Bayswater Road, where his mother and stepfather lived and where his eldest daughter, Anne, was born. In relative poverty, the family moved to 13 Coram Street (then Great Coram Street), Brunswick Square, where Thackeray engaged in journalism in an effort to support his family; indeed, he did some reviewing for *The Times* and was often in Paris on business. Both Alfred, Lord Tennyson and Edward FitzGerald were frequent visitors here and elsewhere, and here he wrote *The Paris Sketch Book.* Returning from Belgium, where he had gone on business in 1840, he found his wife suffering from a mental breakdown; various remedies were tried, with Thackeray always at her side, but by 1843 she was hopelessly insane and in 1844 had to be placed in care in the country. The children were sent to their grandmother in Paris, and Thackeray moved to 27 Jermyn Street; he had begun *Vanity Fair* in 1841 and worked on it and *The Luck of Barry Lyndon* here.

Thackeray moved in 1845 to 88 St. James's Street, next to St. James's Coffee House. *The Snobs of England,* serialized in *Punch* in 1846–1847, made Thackeray famous; and in 1846, reunited with his children, he moved to 13 (now 16) Young Street. Here, in the first-floor bedroom, he dictated *The History of Henry Esmond Esq.* and finished *Vanity Fair.* He was called to the bar at the Middle Temple in 1848, and between that year and 1850 or 1851 he had chambers at either 10 (gone) or 2 Crown Office Row. One of Thackeray's greatest admirers (indeed, the second edition of *Jane Eyre* was enthusiastically dedicated to the "Satirist of *Vanity Fair*") was Charlotte Brontë, and in June 1850, when she and her sister Anne were in London, the two met Thackeray at her publisher's offices at 32 Cornhill. (There is a commemorative plaque on the door of the present building.) The series of lectures titled *The English Humourists of the Eighteenth Century,* delivered at the Assembly Rooms, 26 Pall Mall, put the seal on his fame and led directly to his highly successful lecture tours in the United States in 1852 and 1855. *The History of Pendennis* appeared between 1848 and

1850, and *The History of Henry Esmond Esq.,* the only one of his works to appear without being serialized, was published in 1852. The Queen Anne period of the latter work was thoroughly researched at the British Museum and in the library of the Athenaeum Club (on the corner where Pall Mall enters Waterloo Place), to which he was elected in February 1851.

Thackeray moved to 36 Onslow Square, where he completed *The Newcomes,* wrote *The Virginians* and *Lovel the Widower,* and worked on the *Roundabout Papers* in his first-floor study. In 1860 his life became dominated by *The Cornhill Magazine,* of which he was the first editor; in 1861 he built a red-brick Queen Anne–style house at 2 Palace Green (marked with a plaque) in Kensington and moved into the house in February 1862. He died here quite suddenly during the night of December 23–24, 1863, from an "effusion of the brain," and was buried in Kensal Green Cemetery; there is a commemorative bust in Westminster Abbey. Thackeray frequently attended St. Mary Abbots Church on the Kensington High Street; and he especially enjoyed the Cider Cellar Tavern in the basement of 21 Maiden Lane and Rules Restaurant on Southampton Street, Covent Garden.

London associations with Thackeray's novels are so abundant that only a sample can be given here. The best starting place, perhaps, is *Vanity Fair;* "Miss Pinkerton's academy for young ladies, on Chiswick Mall," is Walpole House, where Thackeray had himself attended school. The Sedley family's home was at 62 Russell Square, while the Osborne's was at Number 96. The group, composed of "Jos and Miss Sharp . . . on the front seat" and "Mr. Osborne sitting bodkin opposite, between Captain Dobbin and Amelia," take a coach to Vauxhall Gardens:

LONDON   On seeing 16 Young Street, Kensington, for the first time, William Makepeace Thackeray commented: "It has the air of a feudal castle. I'll have a flagstaff put over the coping of the wall and hoist a standard when I'm home!" Here Thackeray lived from 1846 to 1853 and wrote *Vanity Fair, Pendennis,* and *Henry Esmond.*

> [T]he hundred thousand *extra* lamps . . . were always lighted; the fiddlers, in cocked-hats . . . played ravishing melodies under the gilded cockle-shell in the midst of the Gardens; the singers, both of comic and sentimental ballads . . . charmed the ears there; the country dances, formed by bouncing cockneys and cockneyesses, and executed amidst jumping, thumping, and laughter; the signal . . . announced that Madame Saqui was about to mount skyward on a slack-rope ascending to the stars; the hermit . . . always sat in the illuminated hermitage. . . .

Raggles's house, in which Becky and Rawdon stay in London, is 22 Curzon Street:

> When you came to 201 there was a hearty welcome, a kind smile, a good dinner, and a jolly shake of the hand from the host and hostess there, just for all the world, as if they had been undisputed masters of three or four thousand a-year—and so they were, not in money, but in produce and labour—if they did not pay for the mutton, they had it; if they did not give bullion in exchange for their wine, how should we know? Never was better claret at any man's table than at honest Rawdon's; dinners more gay and neatly served. His drawing-rooms were the prettiest, little, modest salons conceivable: they were decorated with the greatest taste, and a thousand knick-knacks from Paris. . . .

"Lord Steyne's town palace stands in Gaunt Square, out of which Great Gaunt Street leads," so Thackeray writes:

> Gaunt House occupies nearly a side of the Square. The remaining three sides are composed of mansions that have passed away into Dowagerism—tall, dark houses,

with window-frames of stone, or picked out of a lighter red.... Brass plates have penetrated into the Square— Doctors, the Diddlesex Bank Western Branch—the English and European Reunion, &c.—it has a dreary look—nor is my Lord Steyne's palace less dreary. All I have ever seen of it is the vast wall in front, with the rustic columns at the great gate, through which an old porter peers sometimes with a fat and gloomy red face— and over the wall the garret and bedroom windows, and the chimneys, out of which there seldom comes any smoke now.

Most probably this is Lansdowne House on Berkeley Square, although a good case can be made for Harcourt House (demolished) on Cavendish Square. The sponging house where Rawdon Crawley is taken is in Took's Court, off Cursitor Street. This is not Crawley's first time here ("You'll find your old bed, Colonel, and everything comfortable"); this house is where Richard Brinsley Sheridan was held.

Any number of taverns and coffeehouses as well as private clubs are mentioned in *Vanity Fair*. "The Piazzi Coffee-House," also known as Great Piazzi Coffee House, where Jos Sedley dines alone, is most likely the one which stood in the northeast angle of the Covent Garden Piazza although some claim has been made for Evans's Coffee House, at 43 King Street, Covent Garden. The Cocoa Tree, where Rawdon Crawley "won two hundred of him [Osborne]," was actually the Cocoa Tree Chocolate House, which Thackeray would have known at 64 St. James's Street; and Slaughter's Coffee House ("Someone inquired ... regarding ... [George Osborne], where it was said he and his friend Captain Dobbin had left town") was actually Old Slaughter's Coffee House at 74 and 75 St. Martin's Lane and not the Slaughter's Coffee House close to Newport Street on St. Martin's Lane, which had ceased to exist by this time. Here Dobbin lodges on his return from India:

> Long years had passed since he saw it last.... There, however, stood the old waiter at the door in the same greasy black suit, with the same double chin and flaccid face, with the same huge bunch of seals at his fob, rattling his money in his pockets as before, and receiving the Major as if he had gone away only a week ago.

It was also here that

> Jos ... could enjoy his hookah ... with such perfect ease, and could swagger down to the theatres, when minded, so agreeably, that, perhaps, he would have remained altogether at the Slaughters' had not his friend, the Major, been at his elbow.

The Swan with Two Necks, an ancient house on Lad Lane, is the place from which Sir Pitt Crawley and Becky leave London for Queen's Crawley (Crawley, Hampshire):

> [T]he worthy Baronet whom he drove to the City did not give him one single penny more than his fare. It was in vain that Jehu appealed and stormed; that he flung down Miss Sharp's bandboxes in the gutter at the 'Necks, and swore he would take the law of his fare.

The coaching inn was originally called the "Two Necked Swan in Lad Lane," supposedly a corruption of "two nicks," the cuts made by the Dyers' Company and the Vintners' Company on the upper mandible of swans; Lad Lane was absorbed by Gresham Street in 1848. Other locations mentioned or alluded to include Greek Street (where Becky lives), St.

James's Street, Park Lane (where Miss Crawley has a house), Coventry Street (where Becky hires her diamonds), and Charterhouse, which becomes Whitefriars, the school young Rawdon Crawley attends through Lord Steyne's interest.

The History of Pendennis in some ways offers even more locational information: Pen attends Gray Friars (Charterhouse), and he comes down from St. Boniface, Oxbridge (Trinity College, Cambridge), "with his friend Mr Bloundell. They put up at a hotel in Covent Garden, where Bloundell had a tick, as he called it, and took the pleasures of the town very freely...." This was probably Old Slaughter's, although Thackeray is not specific. Pen returns after being "plucked" at the university and "hastened to the inn at Covent Garden" before walking "off to his uncle's lodgings in Bury Street"; here he tells Major Pendennis that he has failed his examination and is deeply in debt. In the depths of despair, Pen

> paced the streets. He remembers, he says, the prints which he saw hanging up at Ackermann's window in the rain, and a book which he read at a stall near the Temple....

Rudolph Ackermann's print shops were located at 96 the Strand and 191 Regent Street. Leaving London for Chatteris (Exeter) two days later, Pen "took his place at the Bull and Mouth, Piccadilly, by the Chatteris coach for that evening"; the Bull and Mouth Inn at 12 St. Martin's le Grand had begun to function as a coaching post in 1819. Once again in London:

> The very first acquaintance of his own whom Arthur met, as the coach pulled up at the Gloster Coffee House, was his old friend Harry Foker, who came prancing down Arlington Street behind an enormous cab-horse.

The Gloster Coffee House was probably the White Horse Cellar, a well-known coaching station in Piccadilly. The "pretty little theatre" to which Thackeray refers in terms of Lord Colchicum, who "received dramatic professors of all nations at his banquets—English from the Covent Garden and Strand houses, Italians from the Haymarket, French from their own pretty little theatre, or the boards from the Opera where they danced," was St. James's Theatre on King Street.

Pen "was entered as a member of the Upper Temple, and was reading hard for the bar"; he is then at Lamb Court, where Major Pendennis visits him:

> The feeble and filthy oil-lamps, with which the staircases of the Upper Temple are lighted of nights, were of course not illuminating the stairs by day, and Major Pendennis, having read with difficulty his nephew's name under Mr Warrington's on the wall of No. 6, found still greater difficulty in climbing the abominable black stairs....

Crown Office, just off Middle Temple Lane, was the model for Lamb Court. The club called the Back Kitchen met "at the Fielding's Head in Covent Garden":

> The Fielding's Head had been a house of entertainment, almost since the time when the famous author of "Tom Jones" presided as magistrate in the neighbouring Bow Street; his place was pointed out, and the chair said to have been his, still occupied by the president of the night's entertainment.

The Fielding's Head was the Cider Cellar Tavern,

located in the basement of 21 Maiden Lane, just next to the Adelphi Theatre. Pen and Warrington go to see Captain Shandon "[i]n the Fleet Prison. . . . [where] [h]e is the king of the place":

> They went through the anteroom, where the officers and janitors of the place were seated, and passing in at the wicket, entered the prison. The noise and the crowd, the life and the shouting, the shabby bustle of the place, struck and excited Pen. People moved about ceaselessly and restless, like caged animals in a menagerie. . . .
> They went through a court up a stone staircase, and through passages full of people, and noise, and cross lights, and black doors clapping and banging;—Pen feeling as one does in a feverish morning dream.

The Fleet, a debtors' prison on Fleet Lane, was torn down in 1846; the site is now occupied mostly by the Congregational Memorial Hall. The Claverings take a house (unidentified) on Grosvenor Square, where Pen and his uncle visit. Clement's Inn, opening off the Strand, once held an Inn of Chancery which masquerades here as Shepherd's Inn, the place where Captain Costigan lives:

> Bred up, like a bailiff or a shabby attorney, about the purlieus of the Inns of Court, Shepherd's Inn is always to be found in the close neighbourhood of Lincoln's Inn Fields, and the Temple. Somewhere behind the black gables and smutty chimney-stacks of Wych Street, Holywell Street, Chancery Lane, the quadrangle lies, hidden from the outer world; and it is approached by curious passages and ambiguous smoke alleys, on which the sun has forgotten to shine. . . . In a mangy little grass-plat in the centre rises up the statue of Shepherd, defended by iron railings from the assaults of boys. The Hall of the Inn, on which the founder's arms are painted, occupies one side of the square, the tall and ancient chambers are carried round other two sides, and over the central archway, which leads into Oldcastle Street, and so into the great London thoroughfare.

Pen walks in the vicinity of the Temple Garden on many occasions:

> Fashion has long deserted the green and pretty Temple Garden, in which Shakespeare makes York and Lancaster to pluck the innocent white and red roses which became the badges of their bloody wars. . . . Only antiquarians and literary amateurs care to look at the gardens with much interest, and fancy good Sir Roger de Coverley and Mr Spectator with his short face pacing up and down the road; or dear Oliver Goldsmith in the summerhouse, perhaps meditating about the next "Citizen of the World." . . . The poetical figures live in our memory just as much as the real personages,—and . . . the young gentleman chose the Temple Gardens as a place for exercise and meditation.

Other locations in and around London in this novel include the Vauxhall Gardens, Fleet Street, Paternoster Row, Dobree's (a pawnbroker's) on Charlotte Street and Gilbert Street, the Theatre Royal on the Strand, John Tilbury's at 48 Mount Street, and Brook's (a private club) at 60 St. James's Street.

In *The History of Henry Esmond Esq.*, Henry Esmond visits General Webb at his home at 22 Golden Square, and the Dowager Viscountess Castlewood comes "from Lincoln's Inn-Fields to Chelsey" to Castlewood Hall,

> to a pretty new house. . . . The walls were still open in the old house as they had been left by the shot of the Commonwealthmen. A part of the mansion was restored

and furbished up with the plate, hangings, and furniture brought from the house in London.

Lady Castlewood's house is perhaps modeled on Queen's House, 16 Cheyne Row; for years tradition maintained that Catherine of Braganza lived here, but the house was built in 1717, twenty-four years after she returned to Portugal. The house at 7 Kensington Square is where "the Right Honourable Henry St. John, Esquire," Lord Ashburnham, and Captain and Mrs. Richard Steele, among others, congregate on that memorable evening when "all the satiric compliments which Mr. St. John" pays Mrs. Steele are received as genuine, and

> As for poor Dick, we were obliged to leave him alone at the dining-table, where he was hiccupping out the lines from the "Campaign," in which the greatest poet had celebrated the greatest general in the world; and Harry Esmond found him, half an hour afterwards, in a more advanced stage of liquor, and weeping about the treachery of Tom Boxer.

The Newcomes also contains a number of specific references to London. The marriage between Lady Clara Pulleyn and Barnes Newcome takes place in St. George's Church, Hanover Square:

> Finer flounces, finer bonnets, more lovely wreaths, more beautiful lace, smarter carriages, bigger white bows, larger footmen, were not seen, during all the season of 18—, than appeared round St. George's, Hanover Square, in the beautiful month of June succeeding that September when so many of our friends, the Newcomes, were assembled at Baden.

Here "[b]efore the service . . . a woman of vulgar appearance and disorderly aspect, accompanied by two scared children" enters the church and, although "requested to retire by a beadle," must be "induced to quit the sacred precincts of the building by the very strongest persuasion of a couple of policemen." The Cave of Harmony, which some of the Newcomes frequent, was most likely Evans's Coffee House, at 43 King Street in Covent Garden, famous for its food and music. Colonel Newcome has a residence at 37 Fitzroy Square (once the home of the Pre-Raphaelite painter Ford Madox Brown), and after the colonel is bankrupt, Clive, his family, and the colonel lodge on nearby Howland Street. The colonel, Clive, and Pen all attended Grey Friars (Charterhouse), and Colonel Newcome, destitute and unable to bear the Campaigner (Mrs. Mackenzie), becomes a pensioner of the Hospital of Grey Friars:

> He wore the black gown of the pensioners of the Hospital of Grey Friars. His order of the Bath was on his breast. He stood there among the poor brethren, uttering the responses to the psalm. The steps of this good man had been ordered hither by Heaven's decree: to this almshouse!

The Virginians offers yet further London locations. The Lamberts live on Dean Street, and when in London Harry Warrington "would go to the 'Star and Garter' in Pall Mall, or to an inn in Covent Garden." Both places existed, and the unnamed inn was the Bedford Coffee House "under the Piazza Covent Garden" in the northeast corner; from here on one occasion Warrington "sought out proper lodgings at the Court end of town, and fixed on some apartments in Bond Street. . . ." Charterhouse masquerades as Chartreux School in this work. Finally, many of the fashionable clubs on St. James's Street and on Pall Mall enter this work; there are others, either under their own or other names: Brook's, at 60 St. James's Street, which becomes the Regent (*Vanity Fair, Pendennis, Men's Wives,* "Ravenswing"); Black's, on St. James's (*The Adventures of Philip*); Blight's, on St. James's (*The Snobs of England*); Boodle's, at 28 St. James's, which is Foodle's (*The Snobs of England*); and White's (originally White's Chocolate House and, after 1755, Arthur's), at 68–69 and then 37–38 St. James's Street (*The Luck of Barry Lyndon, The Snobs of England, The Virginians,* and *The Adventures of Philip*). The *Roundabout Papers*, of course, also includes a wealth of factual detail about Victorian London.

Charles Dickens (1812–1870) London locations associated with Charles Dickens and his works are as numerous as those of William Shakespeare and Dr. Samuel Johnson, and volumes have been written on the subject. Born in Portsmouth in 1812, Dickens spent much of the period from 1822 until 1860, when he moved to Gadshill, in London; for a brief time the family lived at 10 Norfolk Street (now 22 Cleveland Street), by the side of the Middlesex Hospital. (Indeed, when applying for book privileges at the British Museum in 1830, Dickens used this as his address even though he had not lived here since 1823.) In 1823 John Dickens, whose finances were generally in an untidy state, felt the need of additional retrenchment and moved his family to 16 Bayham Street (gone), Camden Town, "about the poorest part of the London suburbs, then," as John Forster states; "the house was a mean small tenement, with a wretched little back-garden abutting on a squalid court." In fact, the property was not as bad as Forster makes it out to be; the cottages were new (built in 1821), and in the meadow behind the main row of houses haymaking went on in season; furthermore, people of some importance, including one Bow Street magistrate and the engravers Francis Engleheart and Francis Holt, lived here. The family's affairs worsened yet further in 1823, and the Dickenses moved to 4 (now 147) Gower Street (demolished around 1895), where Mrs. Dickens, like Mrs. Micawber and with the same results, attempted to retrieve the family fortunes by opening a school for young girls. A brass plaque reading "MRS. DICKENS'S ESTABLISHMENT" was put up; flyers were distributed, but no one even inquired.

By this time John Dickens could no longer hold off his creditors, and he was arrested and placed in Marshalsea Prison, on the Borough High Street, Southwark. Extensive knowledge of debtors' prisons is displayed in Dickens's works, and special mention can be made of the Fleet in *The Pickwick Papers* and Marshalsea in *David Copperfield* and *Little Dorrit*. To survive, the remaining members of the family pawned or sold virtually every object in the house; then a relative, James Lamert, came to the rescue by obtaining a job for the child at Warren's Blacking Manufactory, where the Charing Cross Station now stands. Dickens recalls:

The blacking warehouse was the last house on the left-hand side of the way, at old Hungerford Stairs. It was a crazy, tumble-down old house, abutting of course on the river, and literally overrun with rats. . . . My work was to cover the pots of paste-blacking: first with a piece of oil-paper, and then with a piece of blue paper; to tie them round with a string; and then to clip the paper close and neat all round, until it looked as smart as a pot of ointment from an apothecary's shop.

Here he earned 6 or 7 shillings a week (he could not remember which) and gathered the material to create Murdstone and Grinby's warehouse "down in Blackfriars" in *David Copperfield.*

The household on Gower Street was broken up in 1824, with Mrs. Dickens and the family (except Charles and Fanny) joining John Dickens at the prison. Fanny was at the Royal Academy of Music, and Charles lodged with Mrs. Elizabeth Roylance, whom the family had long known at her house on Little College Street (now College Place), probably Number 37 (demolished); he supported himself here and joined his family at the prison on Sundays. Almost completely cut off from his parents and extremely lonesome, he was found lodgings in a "back attic . . . at the house of an insolvent court agent, who lived in Lant Street in the Borough, where Bob Sawyer [*The Pickwick Papers*] lodged many years afterwards." The landlord and his family, who were very kind to the child, are the Garland family in *The Old Curiosity Shop.* The elder Dickens was released from prison when a legacy was paid into court, and the family, after a short period with Mrs. Roylance, moved to a small tenement in Somers Town. The blacking firm had moved to the southwest corner of Chandos Place and Bedford Street in Covent Garden, where the boy worked until a quarrel occurred between his father and Lamert.

At this time (1824) Charles Dickens entered Wellington House Academy, a "classical and commercial" establishment (on the north side of Granby Road where it enters Hampstead Road), which was revived as Salem House in *David Copperfield;* here Dickens said the boys trained white mice better than the master trained the boys. For the early part of Dickens's schooling the family lived near the school. Leaving here after two years without having particularly distinguished himself, Dickens became a clerk to Charles Molloy, a solicitor with offices at 8 New Court, Lincoln's Inn; he was soon transferred by his father to the service of Edward Blackmore, whose offices were at 1 South Square (then Holborn Buildings), Gray's Inn. The family moved to 17 Polygon Road, Somers Town, a far more respectable area than their other Somers Town home; it is here that Harold Skimpole (*Bleak House*) settles in an area "where there were at that time a number of poor Spanish refugees walking about in cloaks, smoking little paper cigars." John Dickens with commendable perseverance learned shorthand to become a parliamentary reporter and appears to have had lodgings where his son joined him at 25 Fitzroy Square, somewhere in Highgate, and probably in Fulham in 1832 and 1833. Charles, too, took up shorthand and went through a probationary period of almost two years during which he reported for the proctors in Doctors' Commons, St. Paul's Churchyard; he relates the frustrations of learning the system in *David Copperfield* and describes the courts (destroyed 1867) where he worked in *Sketches by Boz:*

Crossing a quiet and shady courtyard paved with stone, . . . we paused before a small, green-baized, brass-headed nailed door, which, yielding to our gentle push, at once admitted us into an old quaint-looking apartment, with sunken windows and black carved wainscotting, at the upper end of which, seated on a raised platform of semicircular shape, were about a dozen solemn-looking gentlemen in crimson gowns and wigs.

In 1833 Dickens tried bachelor lodgings on Cecil Street (a lost street between Adam Street and Carting Lane in the Strand), but, he wrote, "The people at Cecil Street put too much water in the hashes, lost the nutmeg-grater, attended on me most miserably . . . and so I gave them warning, and have not yet fixed on a local habitation." Without much doubt he went from here to 15 Buckingham Street and most likely had rooms on the top floor on the east side; here Betsy Trotwood finds rooms for David Copperfield. In the meantime, in 1830, Dickens had met Maria Beadnell, the daughter of a banker, and when her family discovered that he was courting their daughter and that she was empty-headed enough to encourage an impecunious shorthand reporter, they sent her off to Paris "to complete her education." The time abroad produced the correct effect from the parents' point of view, but desiring to show her man-hunting abilities (as her letters illustrate), she never broke with Dickens. During the time that Dickens worked as a parliamentary reporter (in the Old House of Commons) and was living at 18 Bentinck Street (rebuilt), he was working on his *Sketches*, forty-five of which appeared in two years. In late December 1834 he took rooms at 13 Furnival's Inn (which stood off Holborn between Brooke Street and Leather Lane where the Prudential Building is), once an Inn of Chancery but lodging houses by the 18th century; by early 1836 he had moved to Number 15, where the rooms were much better. These are probably the rooms which become John Westlock's Furnival's Inn apartment in *Martin Chuzzlewit*:

> There are snug chambers in those Inns where the bachelors live, and, for the dissolute fellows they pretend to be, it is quite surprising how well they get on. . . . His rooms were the perfection of neatness and convenience. . . . There is little enough to see in Furnival's Inn. It is a shady, quiet place, echoing to the foot-steps of the stragglers who have business there, and rather monotonous and gloomy on Sunday evenings.

And in *The Mystery of Edwin Drood*, Mr. Grewgious, whose own chambers are "over the way" at Staple Inn, comments, "Furnival's is fireproof and specially watched and lighted."

On April 2, 1836, Dickens married Catherine Thomson Hogarth, daughter of a colleague on the *Morning Chronicle;* the ceremony took place at St. Luke's Church, Sydney Street, Chelsea, and was performed by the Rev. Charles Kingsley, father of the novelist. For a few weeks before the marriage Dickens lived at 18 Selwood Place in order to be permitted to marry at St. Luke's. The marriage ultimately produced nine children who survived and much unhappiness. Dickens and his wife stayed at Furnival's Inn, where the novelist worked on *The Pickwick Papers* and *Oliver Twist*. *Pickwick* was then being serialized, and when Robert Seymour, the illustrator, committed suicide after the first number, William Makepeace Thackeray called on Dickens with two or three drawings in hand and proposed that he be taken on in that capacity. In 1837 Dickens removed his wife, son, and sister-in-law Mary to 48 Doughty Street (off Theo-

LONDON   Charles Dickens's residence at 48 Doughty Street, now called The Dickens House, is the headquarters of the worldwide Dickens Fellowship and a museum of Dickens memorabilia, including manuscript pages of his early books and the velvet-topped portable desk which Dickens himself designed.

balds Road), a three-story, twelve-room house on the east side of the street. *The Pickwick Papers* and *Oliver Twist* were completed here, and *Nicholas Nickleby* was begun. The house is now a Dickens museum. The completion of *Pickwick* was celebrated at the Prince of Wales Coffee House, 10 Leicester Place, where Dickens presided; Harrison Ainsworth was one of those in attendance. During his days here Dickens enjoyed walking into the country, and one of his favorite places was Jack Straw's Castle in Hampstead, as he wrote to Forster:

> You don't feel disposed, do you, to muffle yourself up, and start off with me for a good brisk walk, over Hampstead Heath? I knows a good 'ous there where we can have a red-hot chop for dinner, and a glass of good wine. . . .

Indeed, tradition asserts that on occasion Dickens used a small front bedroom there.

In 1839 Dickens moved an ever-increasing household to 1 Devonshire Terrace, at York Gate; it was, he said, "a house of great promise (and great premium), undeniable situation, and excessive splendour" at the northern end of New Road (now Marylebone Road). The site is now covered by Ferguson House, a somewhat ugly yellow building with a porch which has a bas-relief of Dickens and some characters from the novels finished or written here: *Barnaby Rudge, The Old Curiosity Shop, Martin Chuzzlewit, A Christmas Carol, The Cricket on the Hearth, Dombey and Son*, and *David Copperfield*. Henry Wadsworth Longfellow was a visitor here in 1842 and commented on the ravens which had inspired Grip in *Barnaby Rudge:*

> I write this from Dickens's study, the focus from which so many luminous things have radiated. The raven [kept in a stable on the south side of the garden] croaks in the garden, and the ceaseless roar of London fills my ears.

The first raven died in 1841, probably from eating a meal of white paint; its successor, "comparatively of weak intellect," died in 1845, probably on account of "the same illicit taste for putty and paint...." Dickens commented:

> Voracity killed him, as it did Scott's; he died unexpectedly by the kitchen fire. He kept his eye to the last upon the meat as it roasted, and suddenly turned over on his back with a sepulchral cry of "Cuckoo."

Dickens and his family remained here, except for periods away from London, until 1851; in 1844, though, he had temporary lodgings at 9 Osnaburgh Terrace, off Albany Street, when he rented out Devonshire Terrace because the family was going to the Continent.

The Dickens family made many trips to Italy and Switzerland, but in 1847 they were called back on account of their eldest son's illness with scarlet fever. The child was being cared for by his maternal grandmother on Albany Street, Regent's Park, and since the Devonshire Terrace home had been let, Dickens took accommodations at nearby 1 Chester Row from the end of February until June. Dickens's fifth son was born here. By 1851, when the novelist's family of six sons and two daughters had outgrown Devonshire Terrace, he bought the lease of Tavistock House (rebuilt), Tavistock Square. Hans Christian Andersen, who visited him here in 1857, described the house:

> A large garden, with a grass plot and high trees, stretches behind the house, and gives it a countrified look in the midst of this coal and gas-steaming London. In the passage from street to garden hung pictures and engravings.... On the first floor was a rich library, with a fireplace and a writing-table, looking out on the garden.... The kitchen was underground, and at the top of the house were bedrooms. I had a snug room looking out on the garden, and over the tree-tops I saw the London towers and spires appear and disappear as the weather cleared or thickened.

Here Dickens wrote, either wholly or partially, *Bleak House, Hard Times, Little Dorrit, A Tale of Two Cities,* and *Great Expectations.*

Always interested in the theater, Dickens arranged a whole series of juvenile theatricals for production in Tavistock House, including Henry Fielding's *Tom Thumb* on January 6, 1854. Thackeray was in the audience, and frequently so was Wilkie Collins. The latter, in fact, wrote at least two of the presentations, including *The Frozen Deep,* a play of great personal significance for Dickens. As early as 1854 the novelist expressed unhappiness over his marital situation, and in another two years he wrote, "I find the skeleton in my domestic closet is becoming a pretty big one." Ellen Ternan played in Collins's *The Frozen Deep* with Dickens in a production in Manchester in August 1857; and it was his attraction to her that precipitated the separation from his wife in May 1858. He wrote to a friend:

> The domestic unhappiness remains so strong upon me that I can't write, and (waking) can't rest, one minute. I have never known a moment's peace or content, since the last night of The Frozen Deep.

There was a scandal, but everyone, including John Forster in his biography, avoided any mention of the situation. Indeed, not until 1939 was anything known factually; and even today evidence is, at best, scanty. In any event Dickens kept Tavistock House and, probably, at least some of the children and set up Ellen Ternan, by now his mistress, in her own house.

Dickens had by then determined to leave London, and after Gadshill, the house which he had desired from childhood, came onto the market, he went there in 1860. Dickens, though, could not be totally content away from London society (and Ellen Ternan), nor could his daughters be kept from the important London season; as a consequence, he took furnished quarters in town for a few months almost every year. In 1861 these were at 3 Hanover Terrace in Regent's Park; in 1862, at 16 Hyde Park Gate (on the site of the modern apartment building); in 1864, at 57 Gloucester Place; in 1865, at 16 Somers Place; in 1866, at 66 Southwick Street; and in 1870, at 5 Hyde Park Place. When Dickens died at Gadshill on June 9, 1870, of "an effusion on the brain," there was no question as to his burial place; the service at Westminster Abbey was a simple one, and he was buried in the Poets' Corner, where there is a monument as well.

Among the other places in London associated with Dickens rather than with his works are Ye Olde Cocke Tavern, 22 Fleet Street; Ye Olde Cheshire Cheese Tavern, which still flourishes in Wine Office Court; the Great Piazzi Hotel, Covent Garden, where he stayed in 1844 and 1846; and Rules Restaurant, which was established in its present location on Maiden Lane in 1798. Dickens was also a visitor at Thomas Carlyle's home at 24 Cheyne Row and at Daniel Maclise's home at 4 Cheyne Walk; indeed, Maclise's *Nickleby* portrait of Dickens not only is probably the artist's finest work but is an extremely good likeness of the author. "Here we have," exclaimed Thackeray, "the real identical man, Dickens!"

No description of literary London can omit extensive reference to *The Pickwick Papers* and *David Copperfield,* and the major concentration here will be on these two works. It is notable that Mr. Pickwick knew London as a topographer, an archaeologist, and a naturalist, for how else could he have produced the "Speculations of the Source of the Hampstead Ponds, with Some Observations on the Theory of Tittlebats"? These researches alone must have carried him to every pond in Hampstead, especially Whitestone Pond. However, it is on Goswell Street (today Goswell Road, but then a street which ran from Aldersgate to just north of Old Street) that

> Mr. Samuel Pickwick burst like another sun from his slumbers, threw open his chamber window, and looked out upon the world beneath. Goswell Street was at his feet, Goswell Street was on his right hand—as far as the eye could reach, Goswell Street extended on his left; and the opposite side of Goswell Street was over the way.

Traveling to the coach stand at St. Martin's le Grand (down Aldersgate) "with his portmanteau in hand," he directs the driver to Golden Cross, Charing Cross (approximately where Nelson's statue stands), but the driver obviously misjudged the distance when he said, "Only a bob's vorth, Tommy," because the fare was 1 shilling up to 1 mile and 1 shilling 6 pence for 1½ miles. After the fracas with the driver, the group of Pickwick, Winkle, Tupman, and Snodgrass depart in *The Commodore* for Rochester. Pickwick and Wardle return in pursuit of Jingle and Miss Wardle and arrive at the White Hart (gone) in the Borough:

> The reader would look in vain for any of these ancient hostelries among the Golden Crosses and Bull and Mouths, which rear their stately fronts in the improved streets of London. If he would light upon any of these old places, he must direct his steps to the obscurer quarters of the town. . . .
> In the borough, especially, there still remain some half-dozen old inns, which have preserved their external features unchanged. . . . Great, rambling, queer, old places they are, with galleries and passages and staircases wide enough and antiquated enough to furnish materials for a hundred ghost stories. . . .

Sam Weller, the boot, is asked by Jingle if he knows "'what's-a-name—Doctors' Commons'" and where it is:

> "Paul's Churchyard, sir; low archway on the carriage-side, bookseller's at one corner, hot-el on the other, and two porters in the middle as touts for licences."

The bookseller, F. Hurst, and the hotel, St. Paul's Coffee House, both occupied 5 St. Paul's Churchyard (although the coffeehouse moved to Number 6 in 1838). Wardle's "lawyer, Mr. Perker, of Gray's Inn," accompanies the group in its confrontation of Jingle and Miss Wardle.

In Bury St. Edmunds Pickwick receives the communication dated August 28, 1830, from Messrs. Dodson and Fogg of Freeman's Court, Cornhill, telling Pickwick that they had "been instructed by Mrs. Martha Bardell to commence an action against you for a breach of promise of marriage," with damages of £1,500, and that "a writ has been issued against you in this suit in the Court of Common Pleas. . . ." On his immediate return to London Pickwick goes to the offices of Dodson and Fogg "[i]n the ground-floor front of a dingy house, at the very furthest end of Freeman's Court. . . ."

> The clerks' office . . . was a dark, mouldy, earthy-smelling room, with a high wainscotted partition to screen the clerks from the vulgar gaze, a couple of old wooden chairs, a very loud-ticking clock, an almanac, an umbrella-stand, a row of hat-pegs, and a few shelves, on which were deposited several ticketed bundles of dirty papers. . . .

It is generally believed that Dickens meant Freeman's Court in Cheapside, since one existed there relatively recently, but in fact until the building of the new Royal Exchange in 1844 a Freeman's Court existed in Cornhill between the old Royal Exchange and Finch Lane; the new Exchange destroyed the court. It is clear that Dickens intended Cornhill, since Weller "safely deposited him [Pickwick] in Cornhill. . . . [Then] Mr. Pickwick walked on abstractedly, crossed opposite the Mansion House, and bent his steps up Cheapside." The stop for Pickwick's "glass of brandy and warm water" at the "[s]econd court on the right-hand side—last house but vun on the same side the vay" could have been Grocer's Hall Court if they had not gone beyond the Poultry, but Honey

Court (Lane), just east of Milk Street in Cheapside, seems the better choice.

Refreshed, Pickwick and Sam resume their walk to Gray's Inn only to find that since it is "eight o'clock . . . the majority of the offices had closed for that day." Perker was out of town, but his clerk Lowten could be found at the Magpie and Stump:

> [T]he hostelry in question was situated in a court, . . . approximating to the back of New Inn. . . .
> This favoured tavern, sacred to the evening orgies of Mr. Lowten and his companions, was what ordinary people would designate a public-house. . . . [A] large black board, announcing in white letters to an enlightened public that there were 500,000 barrels of double stout in the cellars of the establishment, left the mind in a state of not unpleasing doubt and uncertainty as to the precise direction in the bowels of the earth in which this mighty cavern might be supposed to extend.

The Magpie and Stump stood on the corner of Portugal Street in Lincoln's Inn Fields, where the Black Jack Tavern (later known as the Jump since Jack Shepherd is supposed to have bolted out one of the windows there) stood until 1897. Pickwick's introduction of the old inns produces the series of recollections on inns from Jack Bamber; "'strange old places,'" he calls them and first tells of the "'very dusty skeleton, in a blue coat, black knee-shorts, and silks'" which "'fell forward in the arms of the porter,'" eighteen months after the man's death. Next he relates the episode of Clifford's Inn, whose "'[t]enant . . . took a dose of arsenic.'" Clifford's Inn stood just behind St. Dunstan's Church, Fleet Street, until 1935, when it was demolished; one finely paneled room was saved and reconstructed at the Victoria and Albert Museum. Bamber concludes his storytelling with "The Old Man's Tale about the Queer Client," which begins "'In the Borough High Street, near Saint George's Church and . . . the smallest of our debtors' prisons, the Marshalsea.'" This, of course, was where Dickens's father had been imprisoned. Dickens has Bamber note: "'[T]his part of London I cannot bear.'" The story ends in a miserably furnished lodging to which the hackney coach is directed:

> [I]t was quite dark; and proceeding by the dead wall in front of the Veterinary Hospital, they entered a small by-street which is, or was at that time, called Little College Street, and which, whatever it may be now, was in those days a desolate place enough, surrounded by little else than fields and ditches.

The association here is with College Place (then Little College Street), a not very attractive area east of the Royal Veterinary Hospital.

Mr. Pickwick and Sam set off the next day from the Bull Inn, Whitechapel (the center for coaches to and from the northeast), on the site of the present Aldgate Avenue. Sam's "'Not a wery nice neighbourhood, this, sir'" brings on the observation "'that poverty and oysters always seems to go together.'" since there seems to be "'a oyster-stall to every half-dozen houses.'" Preparing for the legal proceedings, Pickwick lodges "in very good, old-fashioned, and comfortable quarters, to wit, the George and Vulture Tavern, and Hotel, George Yard, Lombard Street"; the George then adjoined the east side of the Church of St. Edmund the King and is now at 3 Castle Court; Mr. Pickwick's stay here is short-lived, as he and his three companions and Sam travel back to Dingley Dell for Christmas.

Not until the Pickwickians come back and the discourse on lawyer's clerks and their habits takes place does the work return to London:

> There are several grades of Lawyers' Clerks. There is the Articled Clerk; who has paid a premium and is an attorney in perspective.... There is the salaried clerk—out-of-door or indoor, as the case may be—who devotes the major part of his thirty shillings a week to his personal pleasure and adornment.... There is the middle-aged copying clerk, with a large family, who is always shabby, and often drunk. And there are the office lads in their first surtouts, who feel a befitting contempt for boys at day-schools, club as they go home at night for saveloys and porter, and think there's nothing like "life."...

Pickwick, back at the George and Vulture, sees his attorney, Mr. Perker, before breaking all precedents in going to the offices of Serjeant Snubbin on Old Square, Lincoln's Inn. The junior counsel, Mr. Phunky, is sent for from his chambers in nearby Holborn Court, Gray's Inn, but, Dickens adds, it "is South Square now." Bob Sawyer and Ben Allen direct Pickwick to Lant Street, "'near Guy's ... little distance after you've passed St. George's Church—turns out of the High Street on the right-hand side of the way.'" The Borough Market office, where Allen sleeps "under the firm impression that he lived there and had forgotten the key" after accompanying Pickwick and company to London Bridge, was a fruit and vegetable market just south of St. Saviour's, Southwark. Sam is called to the "Blue Boar, Leaden'all Markit" by his father as the trial draws near:

> Looking round him, he there beheld a sign-board on which the painter's art had delineated something remotely resembling a cerulean elephant with an aquiline nose in lieu of trunk. Rightly conjecturing that this was the Blue Boar himself, he stepped into the house and inquired concerning his parent.

The tavern is not fully identifiable, but perhaps the most likely claimant was the Spread Eagle on Gracechurch Street (then between Numbers 83 and 84).

The case of Bardell versus Pickwick takes place in the Guildhall (rebuilt); a note written from Garraway's ordering "[c]hops and Tomata sauca" is introduced in evidence. Garraway's, known to Jonathan Swift, Joseph Addison, and Daniel Defoe and mentioned in *Martin Chuzzlewit, Little Dorrit,* and *The Uncommercial Traveller,* was located at 4 Exchange Alley until 1832, when it moved to Number 3. Found guilty of breach of promise and vowing to pay "'not one farthing of costs or damages,'" Pickwick has two months' freedom before the opposite party "'can issue execution ... for the amount of the damages and taxed costs.'" The Pickwickians "'dispatched [Sam] to the White Horse Cellar to take five places by the half-past-seven o'clock coach next morning'" for Bath. The White Horse Cellar stood at the corner of Arlington Street, Piccadilly, on the site later occupied by the Ritz:

> The travellers' room at the White Horse Cellar is of course uncomfortable.... It is the right-hand parlour, into which an aspiring kitchen fire-place appears to have walked, accompanied by a rebellious poker, tongs, and shovel. It is divided into boxes for the solitary confinement of travellers, and is furnished with a clock, a looking-glass, and a live waiter....

Returning from Bath, Pickwick again is at the George and Vulture, but three days later, "just as all the clocks in the city were striking nine individually, and somewhere about nine hundred and ninety-nine collectively," Pickwick is presented with an execution order by "'Namby, Bell Alley, Coleman Street.'" (Bell Alley, greatly rebuilt, connected Coleman Street to Moorgate Street.) "The coach, having turned into a very narrow and dark street, stopped before a house with iron bars to all the windows...." Here Pickwick is shown into a "coffee-room ... a front parlour," before being taken "off to Chancery Lane," where "[t]here were two judges in attendance at Serjeant's Inn" (the second small court opening into Fleet Street beyond Old Mitre Court). Here the "'have-his-carcass'" was readied, and "Pickwick was ... to be ... taken to the warden of the Fleet Prison and there detained until the amount of the damages and costs ... was fully paid and satisfied." (The Fleet Prison stood on Farringdon Street, approximately where the Congregational Memorial Hall stands today.) Pickwick "sat for his portrait" before being led "through the inner gate and ... descending a short flight of steps. The key was turned after them; and Mr. Pickwick found himself, for the first time in his life, within the walls of a debtor's prison."

In order to attend his master, Sam Weller, his father, and Mr. Solomon Pell concoct a plan "In a lofty room, ill-lighted and worse ventilated," in "Portugal Street, Lincoln's Inn Fields." After Pell prepares the "writ ... for the sum of twenty-five pounds and costs of process," Sam and his father, "the plaintiff and defendant walking arm-in-arm, the officer in front, and eight stout coachmen bringing up the rear," go off to the Fleet. On the way they stop at Serjeants' Inn Coffee House, which stood close to the entrance of the inn until 1838. Mrs. Bardell and Tommy, Mrs. Cluppins, and the Raddles take a Hampstead stage to Spaniards Tea Gardens; the Spaniards, which was a favorite spot of the author, is still on the heath. Here Mr. Jackson of Dodson and Fogg finds Mrs. Bardell and under the pretense of carrying her back to the city on urgent business with her lawyers carries her off to the Fleet "'in execution for them costs....'" Convinced by Perker (who comes to the prison from his home on Montague Place, Russell Square) that he should pay the greatly reduced costs, Pickwick leaves the prison and takes up quarters again at the George and Vulture.

In many ways *David Copperfield* is even more representative of Dickens's London than *Pickwick.* London does not enter the novel until David is sent to school here:

> What an amazing place London was to me when I saw it in the distance.... We approached it by degrees, and go, in due time, to the inn in the Whitechapel district, for which we were bound. I forget whether it was the "Blue Bull", or the "Blue Boar"; but I know it was the Blue Something....

The inn was the Blue Boar, between Numbers 29 and 31 on Whitechapel Road, and was the center for East Country coaches (Mr. Pickwick also uses it). The almshouses David visits with Mr. Mell in Southwark are unidentifiable but may have been those erected by Edward Alleyn in Soap Yard. Salem House is, of course, Wellington House Academy, which Dickens attended. After the death of his mother, the ten-year-old David is given a position "in the service of Murdstone and Grinby":

> Murdstone and Grinby's warehouse was at the water side. It was down in Blackfriars. Modern improvements have altered the place; but it was the last house at the bottom of a narrow street, curving down hill to the river, with some stairs at the end, where people took boat. It was a crazy old house with a wharf of its own, abutting on the water when the tide was in, and on the mud when the tide was out, and literally overrun with rats.

Even though Dickens places the factory in Blackfriars, it is identical to Warren's Blacking Factory at Hungerford Stairs, off the Strand. David remains with the firm even after it moves to 3 Chandos Street and frequents the same places that Dickens did, the bystreets of the Adelphi, Covent Garden, Fleet Street, and "a little public-house close to the river, with an open space before it. . . ." This was the Fox under the Hill, at the foot of Ivy Lane (Ivy Bridge Lane), just about where Carting Lane is today; the Embankment swept Ivy Lane out of existence.

During this time David lodges with Mr. Micawber on "Windsor Terrace, City Road," the John Dickens home at 16 Bayham Street. The Micawbers' financial situation has always been precarious, and at length "Mr. Micawber's difficulties came to a crisis, and he was arrested early one morning, and carried over to the King's Bench Prison in the Borough." When David visits him, he is given the same advice Dickens claimed his father delivered from Marshalsea Prison:

> [T]o take warning by his fate; and to observe that if a man had twenty pounds a year for his income, and spent nineteen pounds nineteen shillings and sixpence, he would be happy, but that if he spent twenty pounds one he would be miserable. After which he borrowed a shilling off me for porter. . . .

When Mrs. Micawber joins her husband, David finds "a little room . . . outside the walls in the neighbourhood of that Institution"; it is

> a quiet back-garret with a sloping roof, commanding a pleasant prospect of a timber-yard, and when I took possession of it . . . I thought it quite a paradise.

This is obviously Dickens's Lant Street room. David "walked to and fro daily between Southwark and Blackfriars, and lounged about at meal-times in obscure streets"; the Micawbers, eventually freed from prison, join David in the same lodging house.

David's flight to Dover to his aunt, Betsy Trotwood, begins "near the Obelisk, in the Blackfriars Road"; the obelisk was erected in 1771 in honor of Brass Crosby, Lord Mayor of London, but by 1773 was badly cracked. After a long period in Dover and Canterbury, David returns to London on his way to visit the Peggottys at Yarmouth:

> We went to the "Golden Cross," at Charing Cross, then a mouldy sort of establishment in a close neighbourhood. A waiter showed me into the coffee-room: and a chambermaid introduced me to my small bedchamber, which smelt like a hackney-coach, and was shut up like a family vault.

The Golden Cross, just about where Nelson's statue is, was the major coaching inn of the West End. David attends a performance of *Julius Caesar* and the new Pantomime at the Covent Garden Theatre, returns to

the Golden Cross for "some porter and oysters," and runs into Steerforth, who is instrumental in getting David's room, Number 44, "'a little loft over the stable'" changed to Number 72, "a great improvement—not being at all musty, and having an immense four-post bedstead." David accepts Steerforth's invitation to spend a few days at his mother's home in Highgate:

> It was a genteel old-fashioned house, very quiet and orderly. From the windows of my room I saw all London lying in the distance like a great vapour, with here and there some lights twinkling through it.

This was probably Church House in South Grove, off Highgate High Street.

After a time in Suffolk, David "drove to Lincoln's Inn Fields, where I found my aunt up," and the next day they proceed to "the office of Messrs Spenlow and Jorkins, in Doctors' Commons"; on the way, however, they

> made a pause at the toy-shop in Fleet Street, to see the giants of Saint Dunstan's strike upon the bells—we had timed our going, so as to catch them at it—at twelve o'clock—and then went on towards Ludgate Hill and St. Paul's Churchyard.

The toy shop was Harrison's at 31 Fleet Street, and the famous clock, removed to Regent's Park when the new church was built in 1833, has since been returned to the church. They go on:

> Doctors' Commons was approached by a little low archway. Before we had taken many paces down the street beyond it, the noise of the city seemed to melt, as if by magic, into a softened distance. A few dull courts and narrow ways brought us to the sky-lighted offices of Spenlow and Jorkins. . . .

Doctors' Commons, in St. Bennet's Hall, St. Paul's Churchyard, was dissolved in 1861 when the law courts were demolished. When David undertakes his apprenticeship, his aunt has already determined on his lodgings:

> [S]he produced from her pocket an advertisement, carefully cut out of a newspaper, setting forth that in Buckingham Street in the Adelphi there was to be let furnished, with a view of the river, a singularly desirable and compact set of chambers, forming a genteel residence for a young gentleman. . . .

This, of course, is Dickens's chambers at Number 15; the rooms

> were on the top of the house . . . and consisted of a little half-blind entry where you could see hardly anything, a little stone-blind pantry where you could see nothing at all, a sitting-room, and a bedroom. . . . [A]nd, sure enough, the river was outside the windows.

Ely Place, just off Charterhouse Street, Holborn, is where David goes to meet Agnes the morning after the dissipation of his first dinner party.

Spenlow's house is on Norwood Road, and here David falls so distractedly in love with Dora that he haunts the area; needing a confidant, he searches out Traddles, who had mentioned that

> he lived in a little street near the Veterinary College at Camden Town, which was principally tenemented . . . by gentlemen students, who bought live donkeys and made experiments on those quadrupeds in their private apartments. . . .
> I found the street was not as desirable a one as I could

have wished it to be, for the sake of Traddles. The inhabitants appeared to have a propensity to throw any little trifles they were not in want of, into the road: which not only made it rank and sloppy, but untidy too, on account of cabbage-leaves.

This is, of course, Dickens's house on College Place. David's trip to Yarmouth brings the news that "little Em'ly" has run off with Steerforth, and David and Peggotty return to the metropolis in search of the girl. Peggotty's lodgings, "of a very clean and cheap description, over a chandler's shop, only two streets removed from me," were, in fact, on Market Street in Hungerford Market, then two streets west of Buckingham Street, between Craven and Villiers Streets. Having proved Barkis's will, David takes his old nurse

> to see some perspiring Waxworks, in Fleet Street (melted, I should hope, these twenty years); and by visiting Miss Linwood's Exhibition, which I remember as a Mausoleum of needlework, favourable to self-examination and repentance; and by inspecting the Tower of London; and going to the top of St. Paul's.

The "perspiring Waxworks" was not Madame Tussaud's but Mrs. Salmon's, at Water Lane and Great Tower Street; Miss Linwood's exhibition of old masters executed in needlepoint was either in the Hanover Square Rooms or in Savile House, Leicester Square, depending on whether the date is from the author's life or David's.

After David's engagement to Dora, Miss Trotwood appears "ruined" and installs herself with her nephew on Buckingham Street. Mr. Dick is taken to Peggotty's old rooms:

> [T]here was a low wooden colonnade before the door (not very unlike that before the house where the little man and woman used to live, in the old weather-glass), which pleased Mr. Dick mightily.

David's attempt to "freshen . . . [his] wits a little" leads him east past Somerset House:

> There was an old Roman bath in those days at the bottom of one of the streets out of the Strand—it may be there still—in which I have had many a cold plunge. . . . I tumbled head foremost into it, and then went for a walk to Hampstead.

Fed by a natural spring, the Roman Bath, which probably is not Roman since its brickwork dates to the 17th century, is on Strand Lane, a narrow pedestrian alley just off Surrey Street. Tommy Traddles is "now lodging up behind the parapet of a house in Castle Street, Holborn"; the actual name then was Castle Yard and is today Furnival Street. Here David determines to master shorthand for "reporting the debates in Parliament." Micawber also has changed his lodgings, to "near the top of Gray's Inn Road," and his name. The terrifying interview with Mr. Spenlow and Miss Murdstone, who greets David with "her chilly fingernails," takes place in "a certain coffee-house, which, in those days, had a door opening into the Commons, just within the little archway in St. Paul's Churchyard"; this was undoubtedly St. Paul's Coffee House (also known as St. Paul's & Doctors' Commons Coffee House), at 5 St. Paul's Churchyard and, from 1838 on, at Number 6.

Returning home from Dr. Strong's house in High-

gate "one snowy night," David "naturally took the shortest way . . . through St. Martin's Lane."

> Now, the church which gives its name to the lane, stood in a less free situation at that time; there being no open space before it, and the lane winding down to the Strand.

There "on the steps of the church . . . was the stooping figure" of Mr. Peggotty, and the two go into the Golden Cross (the entire area was wiped out by the creation of Trafalgar Square, but this courtyard stood between 140 and 141 St. Martin's Lane). As David's marriage approaches, he "removed from Buckingham Street, to a pleasant little cottage" on the Highgate Road, but the church where Dora and David are married is unknown. Eventually David and Peggotty search for Martha, hopeful that she has news of Little Em'ly:

> We had come, through Temple Bar, into the city. . . . We were not far from Blackfriars Bridge, when he turned his head and pointed to a solitary female figure. . . .
> We crossed the road, and were pressing on towards her. . . . [W]e followed at a distance: never losing sight of her, but never caring to come very near. . . .
> She went on a long way. Still we went on. . . . At length she turned into a dull, dark street, where the noise and crowd were lost. . . .

They "were now down in Westminster," and "in the narrow water-side street by Millbank . . . we came up with her." Millbank probably takes its name from the smock mill which was here; Dickens's description of the area is frightening:

> There were neither wharves nor houses on the melancholy waste of road near the great blank Prison. A sluggish ditch deposited its mud at the prison walls. Coarse grass and rank weeds straggled over all the marshy land in the vicinity. In one part, carcasses of houses, inauspiciously begun and never finished, rotted away. In another, the ground was cumbered with rusty iron monsters of steam-boilers, wheels, cranks, pipes, furnaces, paddles, anchors, diving-bells, windmill-sails, and I know not what strange objects. . . . Slimy gaps and causeways, winding among old wooden piles, with a sickly substance clinging to the latter, like green hair, and the rags of last year's handbills offering rewards for drowned men fluttering above high-water mark, led down through the ooze and slush to the ebb tide. There was a story that one of the pits dug for the dead in the time of the Great Plague was hereabout; and a blighting influence seemed to have proceeded from it over the whole place.

Today the Tate Gallery sits on the site of the penitentiary, and the Embankment is replete with massive buildings; nothing remains of this horror. Here Martha is saved from the Thames and leads David and Peggotty to Em'ly. Following the death of Dora and the emigration of Peggotty and Em'ly and the Micawbers, David goes abroad; on his return to "London on a wintery autumn evening," he goes to Gray's Inn Coffee House, where he discovers that Traddles now has chambers in Gray's Inn, 2 Holborn Court; the coffeehouse in 1838 was at 19 and 20 Gray's Inn and was "the next house on the east from the Holborn Gate."

Dickens's first attempt at novel writing, as opposed to the loosely joined sketches in *Pickwick,* was *Oliver Twist;* during the later years of William IV's reign Oliver, escaping from the workhouse, trudges the 75 or so miles to the metropolis. Meeting the Artful Dodger in Barnet, he enters London by way of the Islington Turnpike:

> They crossed from the Angel into St. John's Road; struck down the small street which terminates at Sadler's Wells Theatre; through Exmouth Street and Coppice Row; down the little court by the side of the workhouse; across the classic ground which once born the name of Hockley-in-the-Hole; thence into Little Saffron Hill; and so into Saffron Hill the Great. . . .

"The street," Dickens relates, "was very narrow and muddy, and the air was impregnated with filthy odours"; indeed, Oliver has never seen "[a] dirtier or more wretched place." In these surroundings he is introduced to Fagin and his crew; Dickens does not exaggerate conditions:

> Covered ways and yards, which here and there diverged from the main street, disclosed little knots of houses, where drunken men and women were positively wallowing in filth; and from several of the door-ways, great ill-looking fellows were cautiously emerging. . . .

Even the parish priests making their rounds were accompanied by plainclothes policemen. A time of "picking the marks out of the pocket-handkerchiefs" precedes Oliver's first expedition with Dawkins and Charlie Bates. Caught after his comrade lifts Mr. Brownlow's handkerchief, Oliver is taken to the magistrate:

> The crowd had only the satisfaction of accompanying Oliver through two or three streets, and down a place called Mutton Hill, when he was led beneath a low archway, and up a dirty court, into this dispensary of summary justice, by the back way. It was a small paved yard into which they turned; and here they encountered a stout man with a bunch of keys in his hand.

The police office where Oliver is taken was 54 Hatton Garden, and the archway led to Hatton Yard; Mutton Hill, by the way, got its name from the days when prostitutes, "laced muttons," worked the area.

Oliver is pitied and rescued by Mr. Brownlow, who takes him by coach

> over nearly the same ground as that which Oliver had traversed when he first entered London in company with the Dodger; and, turning a different way when it reached the Angel at Islington, stopped at length before a neat house, in a quiet shady street near Pentonville.

Pentonville was then an outlying suburb; the great prison did not get built until around 1840. Recaptured by Nancy, Oliver is carried back to Fagin's lair, which has been changed to Whitechapel:

> At length they turned into a very filthy narrow street, nearly full of old-clothes shops [and] . . . stopped before the door of a shop that was closed and apparently untenanted; the house was in a ruinous condition, and on the door was nailed a board, intimating that it was to let: which looked as if it had hung there for many years.

Fagin's journey to Bethnal Green via Spitalfields sets the stage for Oliver's trip to Chertsey; Sikes and Oliver

> made their way through Hosier Lane into Holborn.
> "Now, young 'un!" said Sikes, looking up at the clock of St. Andrew's Church, "hard upon seven!" . . . They held their course at this rate, until they had passed Hyde Park corner, and were on their way to Kensington. . . .

After the failure of the robbery, Fagin goes to the Three Cripples (fictitious) on Saffron Hill.

Much later the story returns to an undisclosed West End hotel where Nancy relates Monks's conspiracy to Rose Maylie, and almost simultaneously Oliver discovers Mr. Brownlow's new address on Craven Street (probably Number 39). Noah Claypole and Charlotte Sowerberry, now his wife, arrive in London after rifling "the money from . . . [old Sowerberry's] till," and Noah

> crossed into St. John's Road, and was soon deep in the obscurity of the intricate and dirty ways, which, lying between Gray's Inn Lane and Smithfield, render that part of the town one of the lowest and worst that improvement has left in the midst of London.

Here they come into contact with Fagin, and Claypole (or Morris Botter), because he is unknown in London, is sent to Bow Street to find out about the Artful Dodger; this Bow Street Police Court was a four-story house on the west side of the street. On her second attempt to meet Rose Maylie on London Bridge, Nancy is followed by Claypole:

> A mist hung over the river, deepening the red glare of the fires that burnt upon the small craft moored off the different wharfs, and rendering darker and more indistinct the mirky buildings on the banks. The old smoke-stained storehouses on either side, rose heavy and dull from the dense mass of roofs and gables, and frowned sternly upon water too black to reflect even their lumbering shapes. The tower of old Saint Saviour's Church, and the spire of Saint Magnus, so long the giant-warders of the ancient bridge, were visible in the gloom. . . .

Because she is afraid of the bridge, Nancy directs Rose and Mr. Brownlow to steps leading to the water:

> The steps to which the girl had pointed, were those which, on the Surrey bank, and on the same side of the bridge as Saint Saviour's Church, form a landing-stairs from the river. To this spot, the man bearing the appearance of a countryman hastened unobserved. . . .
> These stairs are a part of the bridge; they consist of three flights. Just below the end of the second, going down, the stone wall on the left terminates in an ornamental pilaster facing towards the Thames. At this point the lower steps widen. . . .

Nancy's murder in Whitechapel forces Sikes to run:

> He went through Islington; strode up the hill at Highgate on which stands the stone in honour of Whittington; turned down to Highgate Hill, unsteady of purpose, and uncertain where to go; struck off to the right again, almost as soon as he began to descend it; and taking the foot-path across the fields, skirted Caen Wood, and so came out on Hampstead Heath. Traversing the hollow by the Vale of Health, he mounted the opposite bank, and crossing the road which joins the villages of Hampstead and Highgate, made along the remaining portion of the Heath to the fields at North End, in one of which he laid himself down under a hedge, and slept.

But Sikes returns to London in desperation and arrives at Jacob's Island:

> Near to that part of the Thames on which the church at Rotherhithe abuts, . . . there exists the filthiest, the strangest, the most extraordinary of the many localities that are hidden in London. . . .
> To reach this place, the visitor has to penetrate

through a maze of close, narrow, and muddy streets, thronged by the roughest and poorest of waterside people, and devoted to the traffic they may be supposed to occasion. . . .

In such a neighbourhood, beyond Dockhead in the Borough of Southwark, stands Jacob's Island, surrounded by a muddy ditch, six or eight feet deep and fifteen or twenty wide when the tide is in, once called Mill Pond, but known in the days of this story as Folly Ditch.

The actual house to which Sikes goes was 18 Eckell Street in Metcalf Yard (all are gone); Jacob's Island itself lay east of St. Saviour's Dock. Finally, Fagin, tried, found guilty, and sentenced to "die on Monday," is placed in the condemned cell at Newgate, within "[t]hose dreadful walls . . . which had hidden so much misery and such unspeakable anguish."

The Old Curiosity Shop is unique in the Dickensian canon in that it has the name of a specific London place for its title but has very little material on London for topographical annotation. Most important, the Old Curiosity Shop on Portsmouth Street, just off Lincoln's Inn Fields, is spurious; the description from the novel does not tally with the actual building, and the name was applied to the store in 1868 when a Mr. Tesseyman took over the premises. There have been many attempts to locate this shop (Dickens writes "a fine broad road was in its place"), but 10 Green Street (now Orange Street), often identified with the shop, will not work since the "fine broad road" (Charing Cross Road) was not built until 1887. A second possibility, 24 Fetter Lane, almost opposite the Records Office, was once the kind of shop Dickens meant and had been one of the author's early haunts. The description fits here far better; Dickens's knowledge of the place helps in the search, but there is no further proof. Quilp is described as living on Tower Hill, possibly Number 2 (long gone), or 6 Tower Dock, which faced the entrance to the tower; and Quilp's Wharf, on the Surrey side of the Thames, was later known as Butler's Wharf. Simon Brass's house has been identified as 10

LONDON   The Old Curiosity Shop on Portsmouth Street boasts that it is the shop "immortalised by Charles Dickens," but, indeed, it is not. The shop's location does not tally with Dickens's description, and the name was first applied to the building seventeen years after the novel appeared.

Bevis Marks, located between St. Mary Axe and Creechurch Lane (Bevis Marks is a corruption of Buries Marks—Buries, limits—and was the boundary of the property of the Bury St. Edmunds abbots). When Little Nell and her grandfather leave London, they probably go by way of Tottenham Court Road to Parliament Hill.

With *Barnaby Rudge* there are many complications because the novel is set in the London of the early part of George III's reign and many major topographical changes had taken place by the time Dickens was writing. Gabriel Varden has his shop and home in Clerkenwell, "the venerable suburb—it was a suburb once . . . towards that part of its confines which is nearest to the Charter House, and in one of those cool, shady streets of which a few . . . yet remain. . . ." Varden's house is unidentifiable, but Carlisle House, where the masquerade is held, was the famous assembly rooms kept by the notorious Mrs. Cornleys; it was pulled down in 1803, and St. Patrick's Roman Catholic Chapel was erected on the site of the ballroom. The Paper Buildings (Number 3) in the Temple, where Mr. Chester has his rooms, burned down in 1838, but the present building Dickens would have known. Coming into London, the trio of Lord George Gordon, Gashford, and Grueby "rode the whole length of Whitechapel, Leadenhall Street, and Cheapside, and into St Paul's Churchyard. Arriving close to the cathedral, Lord George halted," looked at the dome of St. Paul's, and

shook his head, as though he said "The Church in Danger!" . . . So along the Strand, up Swallow Street, into the Oxford Road, and thence to his house in Welbeck Street, near Cavendish Square. . . .

After Haredale's accusation against Gashford to Lord George on the steps of Westminster Hall, Gashford, following Hugh and Dennis, the hangman, proceeds up Parliament Street (then narrow), past St. Martin's Church, to Tottenham Court Road, "at the back of which, upon the western side, was then a place called Green Lanes."

This was a retired spot, not of the choicest kind, leading into the fields. Great heaps of ashes; stagnant pools, overgrown with rank grass and duckweed; broken turnstiles; and the upright posts of palings long since carried off for fire-wood, which menaced all heedless walkers with their jagged and rusty nails, were the leading features of the landscape. . . . [V]ery poor the people were who lived in the crazy huts adjacent. . . .

Green Lanes ran almost exactly where Cleveland Street is today. Some of the Roman Catholic chapels which were destroyed were rebuilt on the same site. Of these, the most important was the Duke Street Chapel, dedicated to Saints Anselm and Cecilia, which was rebuilt and, with the change of the name Duke Street to Sardinia Street, became the Sardinia Street Chapel. The Boot Tavern, where Hugh suspects Barnaby is being held, was at 116 Cromer Street, off Gray's Inn Road. It is to Sir John Fielding's house, 4 Bow Street, that Haredale goes to get the elder Rudge committed to Newgate, which is subsequently under attack. The authorities finally decide on a show of strength:

At the Lord President's in Piccadilly, at Lambeth Palace, at the Lord Chancellor's in Great Ormond Street, in the Royal Exchange, the Bank, the Guildhall, the Inns of

Court, the Courts of Law, and every chamber fronting the streets near Westminster Hall and the Houses of Parliament, parties of soldiers were posted before daylight. A body of Horse Guards paraded Palace Yard; an encampment was formed in the Park, where fifteen hundred men and five battalions of militia were under arms; the Tower was fortified. . . .

The Lord President, the 2d Earl Bathurst, lives in Aspley House (now the Wellington Museum); the 1st Baron Thurlow, the Lord Chancellor, lives at 145 Great Ormond Street. Even so, the mob rampages:

> In two hours, six-and-thirty fires were raging—six-and-thirty great conflagrations; among them the Borough Clink in Tooley Street, the King's Bench, the Fleet, and the New Bridewell. . . . The firing began in the Poultry, where the chain was drawn across the road, where nearly a score of people were killed on the first discharge. Their bodies . . . [were] hastily carried into St Mildred's Church. . . .
> At Holborn Bridge, and on Holborn Hill, the confusion was greater than in any other part; for the crowd that poured out of the City in two great streams, one by Ludgate Hill, and one by Newgate Street, united at that spot, and formed a mass so dense, that at every volley the people seemed to fall in heaps. At this place a large detachment of soldiery were posted, who fired, now up Fleet Market, now up Holborn, now up Snow Hill—constantly raking the streets in each direction.

The riot is broken: Gordon goes to the Tower of London, and Hugh is hanged before Newgate.

About a third of the action of *Martin Chuzzlewit* occurs in London, but Dickens tends to be fairly vague in his references in this work. Mrs. Todgers's boardinghouse cannot be located; neither can the Chuzzlewits' offices, although they stand "in a very narrow street somewhere behind the Post Office. . . ." The immortal Mrs. Gamp, though, lodges on Kingsgate Street, High Holborn,

> at a bird-fancier's, next door but one to the celebrated mutton-pie shop, and directly opposite to the original cat's-meat warehouse; the renown of which establishments was duly heralded on their respective fronts.

Kingsgate Street is no more, but it and its houses (accurately portrayed) stood at the corner of Southampton Row and Theobalds' Road where the School of Arts and Crafts was erected. Tom seeks lodgings at 3 Terrett's Place, off Upper Street in Islington, and Tom and Fips arrange to meet on Fleet Street at the Temple Gate, which gives access to Middle Temple Lane. Fips then

> led the way through sundry lanes and courts, into one more quiet and more gloomy than the rest, and, singling out a certain house, ascended a common staircase: taking from his pocket, as he went, a bunch of rusty keys.

These chambers were in Pump Court, and Dickens later describes the special atmosphere of the Temple. Tom and Ruth have arranged to meet in Fountain Court before going home, and on one occasion, "Either she was a little too soon, or Tom was a little too late," and she meets John Westlock instead. The dinner invitation follows, and they go to his lodgings in Furnival's Inn.

The London topography of *Dombey and Son* is also somewhat elusive; only approximately can Mr. Dombey's house or offices, the residence of the Toodles, Gills's shop, or Cousin Feenix's residence be located. The Dombeys' house, with its "circular back" and "two gaunt trees in the gravelled yard," is "in the region between Portland Place and Bryanston Square"; about the offices Dickens writes:

> [T]he offices of Dombey and Son were within the liberties of the City of London, and within hearing of Bow Bells. . . . Gog and Magog held their state within ten minutes' walk; the Royal Exchange was close at hand; the Bank of England with its vaults of gold and silver "down among the dead men" underground, was their magnificent neighbour. Just round the corner stood the rich East India House. . . .

Since the East India Company, which stood on the west side of Lime Street where it enters Leadenhall Street, was "just round the corner" from Dombey's offices, it is generally assumed that his premises were in a court off Gracechurch Street. Sol Gills's shop can be located on the north side of Leadenhall Street at Number 157, and this helps to establish Dombey's location since Walter, Sol's nephew, who works for Dombey, has to cross the road to enter his uncle's shop and home. Dombey and Edith Skewton are married at All Souls' Church, Langham Place, the same church where little Paul is christened and where Mrs. Dombey and the child are buried. Before the ceremony Cousin Feenix is shaved at Long's Hotel, which stood on the southeast corner of Clifford Street and New Bond Street, and his house is on Brook Street, Grosvenor Square.

The London of *Bleak House* is interesting largely for its conveyance of atmosphere, but a number of points are of specific interest as well. It is arranged "for . . . [Esther] being forded, carriage free . . . [to arrive at] White Horse Cellar, Piccadilly," the same location used in *Pickwick*. And Esther duly arrives in "a London particular," that is, a fog. Mr. Guppy, who lives at 87 Penton Place, meets her, and they

> drove slowly through the dirtiest and darkest streets that ever were seen in the world (I thought) . . . until we passed into sudden quietude under an old gateway, and drove on through a silent square until we came to an odd nook in a corner, where there was an entrance up a steep, broad flight of stairs, like an entrance to a church.

The offices of Kenge and Carboy are at 13 Old Square, and the gateway was that which formed the entrance into Lincoln's Inn from Chancery Lane. On the morning expedition Esther, Ada, Richard, and Caddy Jellyby meet up again with Miss Flite and are taken to her lodgings at the top of the building which houses Krook's shop; this is generally thought to have been in Chichester Rents, between Star Yard and Chancery Lane. Mr. Snagby's offices are "[o]n the eastern borders of Chancery Lane, that is to say, more particularly in Cook's Court, Cursitor Street. . . ." These, in fact, were in Took's Court and were probably at Number 22; Tulkinghorn's own house is of great interest since it was 58 Lincoln's Inn Fields, the residence of John Forster and the place where "The Chimes" (supposedly about St. Dunstan-in-the-West) was read to a select group on December 2, 1844. It was

> a large house, formerly a house of state. . . . let off in sets of chambers now; and in those shrunken fragments of its greatness, lawyers lie like maggots in nuts. But its roomy staircases, passages, and antechambers still remain; and even its painted ceilings, where Allegory, in Roman helmet and celestial linen, sprawls. . . .

The inquest into the death of the mysterious "Nemo" is held at the Sol's Arms, the Old Ship Tavern at the corner of Chichester Rents and Star Yard. Nemo is buried in the graveyard of St. Mary-le-Strand in Russell Court (where York Street, Covent Garden, now is),

> a hemmed-in churchyard, pestiferous and obscene. . . .
>
> With houses looking on, on every side, save where a reeking little tunnel of a court gives access to the iron gate. . . .

(The graveyard of St. Clement Danes is also identified as the site, but the description does not seem to fit as well.) Mr. Turveytop's dancing academy is at 26 Newman Street, and even at the beginning of the 20th century the dancing room extended from the building. Bell Yard needs no identification, but Tom-all-Alone's needs both identification and explanation for the 20th-century reader. This was one of the most wretched, unsanitary, and criminal of the 18th-century rookeries:

> It is a black, dilapidated street, avoided by all decent people; where the crazy houses were seized upon, when their decay was far advanced, by some bold vagrants, who, after establishing their own possession, took to letting them out in lodgings. Now, these tumbling tenements contain, by night, a swarm of misery. As, on the ruined human wretch, vermin parasites appear, so, these ruined shelters have bred a crowd of foul existence that crawls in and out of gaps in walls and boards; and coils itself to sleep, in maggot numbers, where the rain drips in; and comes and goes, fetching and carrying fever. . . .

Jo shuffles through the maze of courts and tenements between Great Russell Street and St. Giles High Street. The sponging house called Coavinseo by Mr. Skimpole was Sloman's Sponging House at 2 Cursitor Street.

Nicholas Nickleby opens in London; Ralph Nickleby's house was probably 6 James Street (Golden Square), and Mr. Squeers lodges at the Saracen's Head on the north side of Snow Hill:

> The inn itself garnished with another Saracen's Head, frowns upon you from the top of the yard; while from the door of the hind boot of all the red coaches that are standing therein, there glares a small Saracen's Head, with a twin expression to the large Saracens' Heads below. . . .
>
> When you walk up this yard, you will see the booking-office on your left, and the tower of St. Sepulchre's church, darting abruptly up into the sky, on your right, and a gallery of bedrooms on both sides.

The construction of the Holborn Viaduct blotted the inn out of existence, but a second was built in its place. Most of the other places mentioned in this novel are unspecified in the sense that only street names (which are easily found) are given and the exact houses and other buildings are not.

In *Little Dorrit* Dickens uses the London Coffee House (24 Ludgate Hill), Marshalsea Prison, the Jerusalem Coffee House (a subscription house for East India and China merchants on Fleece Passage, later known as Cowper's Court, between 32 and 33 Cornhill), and the Church of St. George the Martyr in Southwark (where Little Dorrit is christened, later spends a night in the vestry, and then, still later, is married). The church has a stained-glass window depicting Little Dorrit. Dickens, it should be noted, was accused of basing the collapse of Mrs. Clennam's abode upon the collapse of quarters on Tottenham Court Road in the summer of 1857; *Little Dorrit*, as the author established, was in proof when this happened.

The London in *A Tale of Two Cities* is that of the earlier half of George III's reign: Tellson's Bank on Fleet Street is the original Child's Bank at 1 Fleet Street, and the odd-job man for Tellson's, Jerry Cruncher, lives on Hanging Sword Alley, an almost-imperceptible turning off Whitefriars Street. (The alley was once known as Blood Bowl Alley from the notorious Blood-Bowl House immortalized in the ninth plate of Hogarth's *Industry and Idleness* series.) After Charles Darnay's trial at the Old Bailey, Sydney Carton takes Darnay

> down Ludgate Hill to Fleet Street, and so, up a covered way, into a tavern.

This is said, almost without doubt, to be the Cheshire Cheese in Wine Office Court, and, indeed, a tablet there professes to show where they sat. (The Cock, just opposite until 1887, made the same claim.) Dr. Manette's house is generally accepted as 10 Dean Street, Soho. Lucie Manette's marriage to Charles Darnay most likely takes place in St. Anne's Church in Soho.

Localities in "Lunnon town" used in *Great Expectations* include Barnard's Inn (where Pip stays with Mr. Pocket and which Biddy once calls Barnard's Hotel, thinking it was a place kept by one Barnard), Hummums's Hotel in Covent Garden, and (probably) St. George's Church in Camberwell (where Wemmick and Miss Skiffins are married). *Our Mutual Friend* mentions the Six Jolly Fellowship Porters Inn, that place with "not a straight floor, and hardly a straight line," a "narrow lopsided jumble of corpulent windows heaped one upon another. . . ." Until very recently it was accepted that this was the Grapes in Limehouse, but the Prospect of Whitby now makes the same claim (somewhat less realistically, it would seem). The Grapes, destroyed in World War II, has been rebuilt on Narrow Street overlooking the river. The Lammles' wedding takes place in St. James's Church, Piccadilly; and in the paved square churchyard of St. Peter's Church, Cornhill, Bradley Headstone makes his vehement declaration of love to Lizzie Hexham. Finally, even though most of *The Mystery of Edwin Drood* is set in Rochester, there are some London sites: Mr. Grewgious has offices at 10 Staple Inn, and the inscription

$$J \quad {}^{P} \quad T$$
$$1747$$

on which Dickens facetiously comments, stands for Principal John Thomson, president of the inn for two terms in 1747. Grewgious eats dinner at Wood's Hotel, actually within the archway of Furnival's Inn, where Rosa Bud eventually has lodgings.

Edward Lear (1812–1888) Edward Lear was born on May 12, 1812, in Bowman's Lodge (gone), an "elegant Georgian house" on the corner of Holloway and Seven Sisters Roads where an Elizabethan archery range had stood. The youngest of twenty-one children (seven of whom died in childhood), he was cared for by his eldest sister, Ann, twenty-two years his senior. Lear was an epileptic, suffering from his first seizure, which he called "the demon," at the age of five or six, and from the age of fifteen and one-half, the time of his father's retirement, had to earn his own living. At this time he and his sister took rooms at 28 Upper North Place, and Lear supported them both through his drawing. In 1830 his *Illustrations of the Family of Psittacidae, or Parrots,* with hand-colored plates, appeared under the aegis of the Zoological Society, and in 1831 he and his sister moved to 124 Albany Street.

For some years after 1837 Lear spent most of his time abroad, but returning to London in the winter of 1845, he stayed at 27 Duke Street, where he finished his book on Abruzzi and worked on his first nonsense volume, *A Book of Nonsense,* by Derry down Derry; in the same period he was engaged as drawing master to Queen Victoria, and some lessons were given at Buckingham Palace, where he liked to stand with his back to the huge blazing fireplace. However, every time he took up this position, the attendant lord-in-waiting called him to view something on the other side of the room. Only later did Lear discover that "a subject must not stand with his back to the fire in the presence of his monarch." Leaving England again in December 1846, Lear did not return until 1849, when he wanted to gain entrance to the Royal Academy and took lodgings at 17 Stratford Place, a cul-de-sac running north off Oxford Street; he gained membership in the academy in January 1850. Three years later, enjoying some prosperity as a painter, he stayed at 65 Oxford Terrace, but ill health forced his move to Alexandria in December. Again in London in the winter of 1854–1855, he was ill, and between January and May he went out only once: "I now imitate the conduct of marmots, dormice, truffles, tortoises, & other hybernating things with the utmost strictness until summer comes." He lived in Corfu until May 1857, when he took "a redboom at Hamsens 16 Upper Seymour Street, Squortman Pare, and also a rorkwoom or Stew-jew at 15 Stratford Place"; Lear went back and forth from 1857 on, sometimes staying with Holman Hunt in Chelsea. He died on January 29, 1888, in San Remo, Italy, where he was buried.

Charles Reade (1814–1884)   A novelist whose works often exposed Victorian social injustices, Charles Reade spent almost all his life in London after taking his degree at Oxford; indeed, even when he was fellow, bursar, dean of arts, and vice president of Magdalen College, he kept rooms here and was in town more than was generally acceptable. In 1836, just a year after his election as a fellow, he entered his name at Lincoln's Inn Fields as a law student, but his studying appears to have been little more than dining the requisite number of times in the hall. He was called to the bar at Lincoln's Inn on January 16, 1843, although he never really practiced law. In 1837 he entered into correspondence with Mrs. Laura Seymour, the actress, when she was living at 13 Jermyn Street, and she soon became his mistress. He had permanent lodgings on Leicester Square until (probably) 1855; the following year he took 6 Bolton Row (gone), where he wrote *It Is Never Too Late to Mend,* an attack on prison conditions, the historical romance *The Cloister and the Hearth, Hard Cash,* an attack on mental institutions, and many plays. Laura Seymour was also his landlady, and the two were together until her death in 1879.

Between 1866 and 1879 Reade lived at 19 and 12 Albert Gate, opposite Sloane Street; the first residence, described in *A Terrible Temptation,* was "an old-fashioned, mean-looking house, in one of the briskest thoroughfares of the metropolis; a cabstand opposite to the door, and a tide of omnibuses passing it." Lady Bassett is taken to Mr. Rolfe by the maid:

> She opened the glass folding-doors, and took them into a small conservatory, walled like a grotto, with ferns sprouting out of rocky fissures, and spars sparkling, water dripping. Then she opened two more glass folding-doors, and ushered them into an empty room, the like of which Lady Bassett had never seen; it was large in itself, and multiplied tenfold by great mirrors from floor to ceiling, with no frames but a narrow oak beading; opposite her, on entering, was a bay-window all plate-glass, the central panes of which opened, like doors, upon a pretty little garden that glowed with color, and was backed by fine trees belonging to the nation; for this garden ran up to the wall of Hyde Park.

With the death of Laura Seymour on September 27, 1879, Reade gave up the Albert Gate house and moved to 3 Blomfield Villas, Uxbridge Road, where he died on April 11, 1884; he was buried next to Laura Seymour in the churchyard at Willesden, then a northern suburb. There is a monument to Reade in St. Paul's Cathedral.

Anthony Trollope (1815–1882)   The novelist Anthony Trollope was also a native Londoner; he was born on April 24, 1815, at 6 (probably) Keppel Street, one block northwest of the British Museum. His father was a sometime scholar, barrister, and (later) failed gentleman farmer who during this period had chambers in Lincoln's Inn; indeed, the midsummer holiday from Winchester College, to which Anthony had been selected a scholar in 1826, was spent here wandering around the old and sometimes deserted buildings of the Inns of Court. The elder Trollope decided around 1827 to move to Harrow, and Trollope did not return to London until 1834, when he came to take the clerkship's examination for the General Post Office, which was then in St. Martin's le Grand, opposite the present General Post Office. The story of the examination for his fitness is told in the opening chapters of *The Three Clerks.* Trollope was a junior clerk from 1834 to 1841, but the years were ones of profit for neither the postal service nor him; he was living "by the Marylebone Workhouse, on to the back door of which establishment my room looked out." It was here, in anger because Dr. Samuel Johnson wrote sneeringly of "Lycidas," that he threw his *Lives of the Poets* out the window.

In 1859 the General Post Office transferred him to England from Ireland to take charge of the eastern postal district: by then *The Warden, Barchester Towers,* and *Doctor Thorne* had appeared. Resigning from the General Post Office in 1867 (eight years before becoming eligible for a pension), he now devoted full energies to writing. In 1872 he lived at 3 Holles Street and then at 39 Montagu Square, where he remained for seven years. The Plantagenet Palliser (later Duke of Omnium) novels, begun in 1868–1869, were finished here. He moved to Harting in his last years but returned frequently to London. In November 1882 Trollope was at Garland's Hotel, 15 Suffolk Street, when he suffered a paralytic stroke; from here he was taken to a Marylebone nursing home, 34 Welbeck Street (rebuilt and part of Welbeck Mansions), where he died on December 6. Trollope was buried in the Kensal Green Cemetery. He had been a member of the famous Garrick Club, on Garrick Street, as were Charles Dickens and William Makepeace Thackeray.

Trollope's *The Small House at Allington* uses the Pimlico area; the newly betrothed Lady Alexandrina refuses her future husband's request to live in the area:

> If, indeed, they could have achieved Eaton Square, or a street leading out of Eaton Square—if they could have crept on to the hem of the skirt of Belgravia—the bride would have been delighted. And at first she was very nearly taken in with the idea that such a proposal was made to her. Her geographical knowledge of Pimlico had not been perfect, and she had very nearly fallen into a fatal error.

The series of novels involving Plantagenet Palliser contain many references to London. One of the most striking specific uses of London occurs in *Phineas Redux*: the murder of the odious Bonteen on Lansdowne Passage, one of the two entrances to Berkeley Square at the eastern end of Curzon Street; at that time the passage was separated from the street by a flight of steps (now there is an easy gradient):

> There is a dark, uncanny-looking passage running from the end of Bolton Row, in May Fair, between the gardens of two great noblemen, coming out among the mews in Berkeley Street, at the corner of Berkeley Square, just opposite to the bottom of Hay Hill. It was on the steps leading up from the passage to the level of the ground above that the body was found. The passage was almost as near a way as any from the club to Mr. Bonteen's house in St. James's Place. . . .

Charlotte Brontë (1816–1855), **Emily Brontë** (1818–1848), **and Anne Brontë** (1820–1849)   Charlotte Brontë had only sporadic and slight contact with London beginning in 1842, when she and Emily were on their way to Brussels to study French and German with Constantin Héger, preparatory to opening their own school in Haworth. Accompanied by the Rev. Patrick Brontë, they stayed, says Elizabeth Gaskell, "at the Chapter Coffee House, Paternoster Row—a strange, old-fashioned tavern. . . ." The coffeehouse stood at 50 Paternoster Row, adjoining Paul's Alley; closed in 1854, it reopened in 1856 as a tavern, the Chapter Wine House, and was later almost totally rebuilt. Mrs. Gaskell writes:

> Paternoster Row . . . is a narrow flagged street, lying under the shadow of St. Paul's. . . . Half-way up, on the left-hand side, is the Chapter Coffee-house. . . . It had the appearance of a dwelling-house, two hundred years old or so, such as one sometimes sees in ancient country towns; the ceilings of the small rooms were low, and had heavy beams running across them; the walls were wainscotted breast high; the staircase was shallow, broad, and dark, taking up much space in the centre of the house.

Charlotte and Emily returned to England when Miss Elizabeth Branwell was dying, and only Charlotte resumed her studies in Belgium. Accordingly, in January 1843, she made her way to London:

> She had intended to seek out the Chapter Coffee-house . . . but she seems to have been frightened by the idea of arriving at an hour which, to Yorkshire notions, was so late and unseemly; and taking a cab, therefore, at the sta-

tion, she drove straight to the London Bridge Wharf, and desired a waterman to row her to the Ostend packet: . . . at first [she was] refused leave to ascend to the deck. "No passengers might sleep on board," they said, with some appearance of disrespect. She looked back to the lights and subdued noises of London—that "Mighty Heart" in which she had no place—and, standing up in the rocking boat, she asked to speak to some one in authority on board the packet.

In 1848 a letter from Messrs. Smith and Elder, the publishers who had issued Currer Bell's (Charlotte's) *Jane Eyre*, brought Charlotte and Anne to London. (Acton Bell's, or Anne's, *The Tenant of Wildfell Hall* and *Agnes Grey* and Ellis Bell's, or Emily's, *Wuthering Heights* had been published by T. C. Newby.) Confusion had arisen, and because Newby believed that Acton, Ellis, and Currer were one author, he had guaranteed that author's next work to an American publisher. Smith and Elder had promised the sheets to a different company:

> With rapid decision, they resolved that Charlotte and Anne should start for London that very day, in order to prove their separate identity to Messrs. Smith and Elder. . . .

Mrs. Gaskell continues:

> [I]n the quiet of Haworth Parsonage . . . they had resolved to take a cab, if they should find it desirable, from their inn to Cornhill; but that, amidst the bustle and "queer state of inward excitement" in which they found themselves, . . . they quite forgot even the possibility of hiring a conveyance; and when they set forth, they became so dismayed by the crowded streets, and the impeded crossings, that they . . . were nearly an hour in walking the half-mile they had to go.

Identifying themselves to Mr. Smith at 65 (now 32) Cornhill, they declined to stay at his home but did allow him to plan some activities for them; Charlotte Brontë writes that after the day's events she was "in grievous bodily case" upon returning to the Chapter Coffee House but prepared to expect "the ladies of Mr. Smith's family," only to discover that "they were to go to the opera":

> The performance was Rossini's "Barber of Seville,"—very brilliant, though I fancy there are things I should like better. We got home after one o'clock. We had never been in bed the night before; had been in constant excitement for twenty-four hours; you may imagine we were tired. The next day, Sunday, Mr. Williams came early to take us to church; and in the afternoon Mr. Smith and his mother fetched us in a carriage, and took us to his house to dine.

On Monday they went to "the Royal Academy, the National Gallery, dined again at Mrs. Smith's, and then went home to tea with Mr. Williams at his house." Desiring to hear Dr. George Croly preach, they were taken to the little St. Stephen's Church, just behind Mansion House, and afterward they were driven through Kensington Gardens, where Miss Brontë was "struck with the beauty of the scene, the fresh verdure of the turf, and the soft rich masses of foliage."

After Anne's death in 1849, Charlotte made only three more trips to London; she met William Makepeace Thackeray at the publishers' offices, where a plaque commemorates the meeting:

> I can only just notify what I deem three of its chief incidents:—a sight of the Duke of Wellington at the

Chapel Royal (he is a real grand old man), a visit to the House of Commons (which I hope to describe to you some day when I see you), and last, not least, an interview with Mr. Thackeray. . . . The giant sate before me; I was moved to speak to him of some of his short-comings (literary of course); one by one the faults came into my head, and one by one I brought them out, and sought some explanation or defence. He did defend himself, like a great Turk and heathen; that is to say, the excuses were often worse than the crime itself. The matter ended in decent amity; if all be well, I am to dine at his house this evening.

She also attended his lectures on the English humorists. On one occasion Thackeray hosted a party for her at the Greyhound on Kensington Square, but her uncommunicative shyness was so forbidding that he escaped to his club. *Villette,* published in 1853, reflects, at least in part, some of Miss Brontë's reaction to the city:

> Finding myself before St. Paul's, I went in. I mounted to the dome. I saw thence London, with its river, and its bridges, and its churches; I saw antique Westminster, and the green Temple Gardens, with sun upon them, and a glad, blue sky of early spring above; and, between them and it, not too dense a cloud of haze.
>
> Descending, I went wandering whither chance might lead. . . . I got into the Strand; I went up Cornhill; I mixed with the life passing along; I dared the perils of crossings. . . . Since those days I have seen the West End, the parks, the fine squares; but I love the city far better.

Westminster Abbey contains memorials to Emily, Anne, and Charlotte Brontë.

Arthur Hugh Clough (1819–1861)   Not until the autumn of 1849, when he took over the headship of University Hall (an institution which furnished tuition and living accommodations to students attending University College) did Arthur Hugh Clough have any great association with London. University Hall, just off Gordon Square in Bloomsbury, was Clough's home, and "Dipsychus" was written at the end of his first year; he was lonely and dissatisfied: "Nothing is very good anywhere, I am afraid. I could have gone cracked last year with one thing or another, I think, but the wheel comes round." One of his greatest pleasures was visiting the Thomas Carlyle home on Cheyne Walk, Chelsea. After Clough's marriage in the summer of 1854, he lived near Regent's Park and then, in 1859, in the Camden Hill area. He left England for a trip abroad in 1861 on doctor's orders and died in Florence, after an attack of malaria and a paralysis, on November 13.

Charles Kingsley (1819–1875)   Charles Kingsley was brought to Chelsea in 1836, when his clergyman father took the living there; the family lived at the Rectory, a spacious Georgian house with a large garden, on the east side of Old Church Street, just south of King's Road. Kingsley entered King's College (now part of the University of London), which is housed in the easternmost wing of Somerset House, but he found London dismal and his father's parishioners boring, ugly, and splay-footed, and he eagerly awaited going up to Magdalene College, Cambridge. After his ordination in 1842 and serving as his father's curate at St. Luke's Church, he took the living of Eversley, and was only a visitor to London until 1851, when he preached a sermon entitled "The Message of the Church to the Labouring Man" in an unspecified London church. The incumbent, who knew the sermon was to present the views of Christian Socialists, rose in protest at the end of the sermon; the press took up the battle, and the Bishop forbade Kingsley to preach in the London diocese. The prohibition was lifted shortly thereafter. In 1873 Kingsley was appointed canon of Westminster, but ill health prevented his taking up the post immediately, and his first sermon at Westminster was preached in November 1874. However, pleurisy contracted in the United States further weakened him, and he died in Eversley on January 23, 1875. A commemorative service was held at Westminster Abbey, and a memorial bust was placed in the "chapel of minor poets."

Mary Ann Evans (1819–1880)   George Eliot (Mary Ann Evans) settled in London in 1851, when she decided to support herself as a free-lance writer; having already reviewed R. W. Mackay's *The Progress of the Intellect* in *The Westminster Review* and having become acquainted with the publisher John Chapman, she boarded at the Chapmans' residence on the Strand (Number 142). Problems arose because Mrs. Chapman and the children's governess (Chapman's mistress) became extremely jealous of Marian (as she now signed herself), and the novelist fled to Coventry. There is no evidence that she had also become Chapman's mistress, although she did return to the Chapman household within a few months and remained there until 1853. In that autumn she took her own lodgings at 21 Cambridge Street and shortly after met George Henry Lewes, whose 1841 marriage had dissolved after his wife gave birth to two children fathered by Thornton Leigh Hunt. Lewes, who had had the first child registered as Edmund Lewes and remained on friendly terms with his wife and Hunt, was unable to sue for divorce since he had condoned the adultery; as a consequence, Lewes and Eliot were unable to marry. Eliot, however, regarded their relationship, beginning in 1854, as essentially a marriage. They had lodgings in East Sheen and Richmond before moving to Holly Lodge, (now) 31 Wimbledon Park Road, in February 1859; she writes that the house (marked with a plaque)

> is very comfortable, with far more of vulgar indulgences in it that I ever expected to have again; but you must not imagine it a snug place, just peeping above the holly bushes. Imagine it rather, as a tall cake, with a low garnish of holly and laurel.

However, she quickly tired of the area, and by June she wanted "to get rid of this house, cut cables and drift about." *The Mill on the Floss* was written here. At Michaelmas, 1860, they moved to 10 Harewood Square, where they stayed six months before moving to 16 Blandford Square on December 17; *Silas Marner* was published in 1861 while she was working on *Romola.* In 1863 the couple went to The Priory, 21 North Bank (gone), just off Lodge Road in Regent's Park; here she held her famous Sunday receptions and wrote *Felix Holt, Middlemarch,* and *Daniel Deronda.* Lewes died here on November 28, 1878, and for some time following his death George Eliot not only was unable to write but went into seclusion before undertaking the completion of Lewes's *Problems of Life and Mind.*

Years before Lewes's death, Eliot had met John Walter Cross, an American banker who handled most of her financial affairs. She began to depend on him in the very ways she had depended upon Lewes, and on May 6, 1880, they were married at St. George's Church, Hanover Square. (Cross was forty; she was sixty-one.) Following a trip abroad and a short time in Witley, they moved to 4 Cheyne Walk, Chelsea (marked with a plaque); in early December they attended a concert at St. James's Hall (where the Piccadilly Hotel stands), and there she caught the cold which brought about her death on December 22. She was buried in Highgate Cemetery.

John Ruskin (1819–1900) One of the most influential Victorian writers, John Ruskin, was born in London, at 54 Hunter Street (gone), off Brunswick Square, on February 8, 1819; the present house is marked with a plaque. Ruskin's father was a successful wine merchant, specializing in sherry, and his mother was an especially dour woman who believed in neither toys nor playmates. When he was four, the family moved to 26 Herne Hill, then on the southern outskirts of London, where they remained until 1844; the house is marked with a plaque. Ruskin writes of the house in *Praeterita*:

> [T]he house itself, three storeyed, with garrets above, commanded, in those comparatively smokeless days, a very notable view. . . . The front was richly set with old evergreen, and well grown lilac and laburnum. The rear garden was renowned for its pears, as well as having a mulberry tree, a black Kentish one, and gooseberry and blackcurrant bushes. . . .

Ruskin's education was managed at home by his mother, with whom he constantly read the Bible, and his father, with whom he read the 18th-century classics; his father also encouraged his writing and artistic skills. At the age of fifteen he was sent to a school run by the Rev. Thomas Dale at Peckham, and three days a week he attended lectures in logic, English literature, and translation at King's College (the easternmost wing of Somerset House on the Strand). When he entered Christ Church, Oxford, as a gentleman commoner in 1836, his mother took lodgings to be near her son and oversee his education; the same year he fell in love with Adèle Domecq, the daughter of his father's partner, but parental intervention stopped the affair.

After graduation from Oxford in 1842 and a trip to the Continent, Ruskin moved back in with his parents; he was hard at work on what turned out to be the first volume of *Modern Painters*. The book appeared in May 1843 and had considerable success; at this point the family moved to 163 Denmark Hill, a large house with 7 acres of grounds. Soon after *Modern Painters* was published, J. M. W. Turner became a frequent visitor to the house. In Perth, in April 1848, Ruskin married Euphemia (Effie) Chalmers Gray, the daughter of Scottish family friends; after their honeymoon they set up house at 31 Park Street. The house was unsuitable to Ruskin, who complained of a dead brick wall opposite his window, and they moved to 36 Herne Hill, in an area he had known earlier. In 1851 he met Dante Gabriel Rossetti, whom he befriended, Edward Burne-Jones, and John Everett Millais, whom Ruskin wanted to accompany him to Switzerland. Ruskin's wife fell in love with Millais, and as soon as he was elected to the Royal Academy, she left Ruskin. She was granted an uncontested annulment, justified since the five-year-old marriage had never been consummated.

Ruskin, following the collapse of his marriage, returned to his parents' home on Denmark Hill, escaping only infrequently to lecture at the Working Men's College at 31 Red Lion Square (founded by Frederick Denison Maurice, the Christian Socialist, in 1854). Ruskin had earlier met Thomas Carlyle and was often to be found at Carlyle's home at 24 Cheyne Row. By 1858, when he was in Italy again for a short time working on the fifth volume of *Modern Painters,* it was obvious that Ruskin was gradually going mad; he was able to function well until a few years after his mother's death in 1871 and, indeed, held onto his Slade professorship at Oxford. Following Mrs. Ruskin's death, he sold the Denmark Hill house and moved to Coniston in the Lake District, where he died on January 20, 1900. There is a commemorative bronze medallion in the Poets' Corner of Westminster Abbey.

Matthew Arnold (1822–1888) When Matthew Arnold took up residence in London in 1847 as the private secretary to the 3d Marquess of Lansdowne, President of the Council in Lord John Russell's Liberal ministry, he probably lodged first at 101 Mount Street. *The Strayed Reveller and Other Poems, by A* was published in 1849. By 1851 Arnold proposed marriage to Frances Lucy Wightman, daughter of Sir William Wightman, a judge of the Court of Queen's Bench, who opposed the match because Arnold had neither sufficient nor secure income. Lansdowne then secured his appointment as an inspector for the Committee of the Council on Education, and objections to the marriage were overcome. The couple stayed at Justice Wightman's residence at 38 Eaton Place, off Ebury Street, until February 1855, when they moved to 11 Belgrave Square but still dined nightly at Eaton Place. In 1852 *Empedocles on Etna and Other Poems* appeared under the initial A, and Arnold's poetic reputation seemed secure. By December 1856 Arnold and his wife had given up their own home and were back at Eaton Place; in 1857 he was elected to the Oxford Chair of Poetry. In February 1858 he and his wife took up residence at 2 Chester Square, just east of his father-in-law's home; here they remained until 1866, just before *New Poems* was published, when they moved to West Humble, near Dorking, and then to Harrow-on-the-Hill. Arnold, it should be noted, was a member of the Athenaeum Club, whose premises are at the intersection of Waterloo Place and Pall Mall.

Thomas Hughes (1822–1896) After finishing at Oxford in 1845, Thomas Hughes came to Lincoln's Inn (where he had been admitted on January 1) to read for the bar, but moved over to the Inner Temple on January 1, 1848, and was called to the bar ten days later. He became a Queen's counsel in 1869 and a bencher in 1870. Hughes was never an outstanding lawyer, perhaps because of his extreme involvement in the Christian Socialist movement led by Frederick Denison Maurice and in political matters. In 1848 Hughes had married Frances Ford, and for a time the couple lived on Upper Berkeley Street while he shared chambers with John M. Ludlow at 3 Old Buildings, Lincoln's Inn. In 1853 Hughes and Ludlow decided upon their own "communistic experiment" and jointly built and occupied a house in Wimbledon where Hughes wrote *Tom Brown's School Days;* the extremely successful experiment lasted four years before Hughes returned to the city.

Hughes and his wife then resided at 113, 33, and 80 Park Street, Grosvenor Square, during which time he became involved with the Working Man's College on Great Ormond Street. Increasingly concerned with social reform, Hughes sat in the House of Commons as the Member for Lambeth (1865–1868) and for Frome (1868–1874). In 1882, after three trips to the United States and being appointed county-court judge, Hughes and his family left for Chester.

Coventry Patmore (1823–1896)   Coventry Patmore's childhood was divided between his parents' London residence at 12 Greek Street and a "country" house at Highwood Hill in Hendon (now the London borough of Barnet); he was educated at home and as a child met William Hazlitt at Basil Montagu's home on Bedford Square. His subsequent education (six months at a branch of the Collège de France in Saint-Germain) was brought to an end when his father could no longer support him, and, indeed, in 1845, his father went bankrupt over some bad railway speculations and fled from England, leaving Patmore to support himself. He first turned to translating and to writing for periodicals, but in November 1846 Richard Monckton Milnes secured him a post in the British Museum as a supernumerary assistant in the Department of Printed Books. By then he had taken lodgings at 12 Arundel Street in the Strand. *Amelia* was written about Emily Augusta Andrews, to whom he proposed on Hampstead Heath on May 17, 1847; they were married at St. John's Church, Church Row, Hampstead, in September. The Patmores first lived in a small house (burned down) in The Grove, Highgate Rise, where Alfred Tennyson, John Ruskin, Thomas Carlyle, and Robert Browning were frequent guests. Patmore was one of the Pre-Raphaelite Brotherhood, and meetings often took place in his home, which, it should be noted, frequently changed. He moved from Highgate to Kentish Town, then to Elm Cottage, Hampstead, next to 14 Percy Street (marked with a plaque), near Bedford Square, and then to "a charming early Victorian cottage" at 3 Mount Vernon, Hampstead.

The first part of Patmore's *The Angel in the House*, "The Betrothal," appeared anonymously in 1854, "The Espousals" in 1858, and "Faithful Forever" in 1860; the final portion, "The Victories of Love," a poem of bereavement, appeared in 1862, the year his wife died of tuberculosis. After her death Patmore went to Rome, where he joined the Roman Catholic Church and met Marianne Caroline Byles, whom he married on July 18, 1864, at the Church of St. Mary of the Angels in Bayswater; the family settled at Bowden Lodge in Highgate. The new Mrs. Patmore was quite well off, and Patmore resigned his post at the British Museum at the end of 1865; they then moved to Heron's Ghyll, near Uckfield. Patmore frequently returned to London, sometimes visiting with Thomas Carlyle at 24 Cheyne Row, Chelsea; for a short period in 1874 Patmore had a furnished house in Campden Hill. His second wife died in 1880, and he married for a third time on September 13, 1881, at the procathedral in Kensington. On later trips to London Patmore stayed at the Grosvenor Hotel and was a frequent guest at the home of Wilfrid and Alice Meynell at 47 Bayswater Road.

William Wilkie Collins (1824–1889)   The first English novelist to write mystery stories and the author of *The Moonstone*, Wilkie Collins was born at 11 New Cavendish Street (not Tavistock Square) on January 8, 1824; his father, William Collins, the landscape painter, moved his family to Pond Street in Hampstead in 1826, to Hampstead Square in 1829, to a house in the Bayswater area in 1830, and to Regent's Park in 1838. Collins was sent to Maida Hill Academy and then to a boarding school in Highbury run by a Mr. Cole. Here he was often punished for petty misdemeanors and left school toward the end of 1840; he took an apprenticeship with Antrobus and Company, tea importers, on the Strand. Here, too, he did not distinguish himself and spent most of his time working on a novel, later published as *Antonina, or The Fall of Rome*. Collins repeatedly asked for or took long summer leaves of absence from the firm, and it is just as well that his father's pleasure with the novel was such that he persuaded his son to enter Lincoln's Inn as a law student. After the death of the elder Collins in February 1847, Mrs. Collins and her two sons moved to 38 Blandford Square, an area Collins was to stay in almost all the rest of his life. He was called to the bar on November 21, 1851, but had no more aptitude for law than he had for trade. He was versatile, though, and exhibited at the Royal Academy in 1849 and had *Antonina* published in 1850.

In March 1851 Collins met Charles Dickens at Ivy Cottage, the Bayswater home of Augustus Egg, and their subsequent friendship was particularly close. In fact, on May 16 of that year, he and Dickens appeared in the major roles in Edward Bulwer-Lytton's *Not So Bad as We Seem*, produced at Devonshire House, which stood on the east side of Stratton Street at Piccadilly, by the Guild of Literature and Art to raise funds for indigent artists and authors. By August 1850, Collins and his mother and brother had moved to 17 Hanover Terrace, where Holman Hunt frequently visited; the house also became a favorite meeting spot of the Pre-Raphaelite Brotherhood. *Basil: A Story of Modern Life* appeared in 1852, and Collins became a contributor to *Household Words*. Collins and Dickens took numerous holidays together in the 1850s, and in June 1855 Dickens produced Collins's *The Lighthouse* at Tavistock House and then at Campden House, Church Street, Kensington. A regular guest at the Hanover Terrace house was Edward Lear, who so closely resembled Collins that the two were frequently confused. In April 1856, returning from Paris with Dickens, Collins took rooms in Howland Street, off Tottenham Court Road, in a house run by a rather unpleasant landlady, a Mrs. Glutch; he lasted here three weeks but used the experience for an article for *Household Words*. In 1857 the Collins family was at 2 Harley Place, although Mrs. Collins was in the country.

Early in 1859 (probably), Collins met Caroline Elizabeth Graves (whom he never married) and began an almost nomadic London existence. They lived for seven months at 2 New Cavendish Street before moving to 12 Harley Street, where they remained for five years. In 1860 *The Woman in White* appeared, and in 1862 *No Name;* at the end of 1864 they moved to 9 Melcombe Place, and three years later they moved to 90 (now 65) Gloucester Place (marked with a plaque). *Armadale* had been published in 1866, and in 1868, the year *The Moonstone* was published, there is a bit of mystery about Collins's life, for in October Caroline Graves married;

indeed, what had happened between her and Collins is not known, but her daughter remained with Collins throughout the mother's marriage. At this time he formed a liason with Martha Rudd, known as Mrs. Dawson, and in the next five years fathered three illegitimate children. Marian was born at 33 Belsover Street (exactly nine months after Caroline Graves's marriage); Harriet was born in the same house in 1871; and a son was born at 10 Taunton Place on Christmas Day, 1874. All the children were given the surname Dawson and were recognized in Collins's will, but only the son's birth was registered with the name William Charles Collins Dawson. In the 1870s Caroline returned to Collins at 65 Gloucester Place and remained with him as Mrs. Graves until his death. The Gloucester Place house is in a row of pleasant Georgian houses, and Dickens was here for dinner "to warm the house."

Collins was deeply upset by Dickens's death in 1870 and attended the Westminster Abbey funeral even though he had been advised against it. By March 1874 he was suffering from "extensive gout attacks," and both Collins and his doctor claimed it attacked him in the eyes, a medical impossibility. He took laudanum to relieve the pain, and his dependence upon the drug became extreme. Eventually he consumed a wine glass full nightly in order to sleep; what is amazing is that the drug never impaired his faculties so seriously that he was unable to work, although admittedly the caliber of his work declined steadily. During his last ten years he withdrew from society but not to the extent of becoming a hermit; he was, in fact, almost an invalid by 1880. At the end of 1887 the lease expired on the Gloucester Place house; he and Caroline Graves moved to 82 Wimpole Street (rebuilt), where he suffered a paralytic stroke on June 30, 1889. He was not expected to recover, but in August he was able to leave his third-floor sickroom. Collins developed bronchitis and died here on September 23; he was buried in the Kensal Green Cemetery on September 27 with Holman Hunt, Arthur Wing Pinero, and Oscar Wilde among those in attendance. Collins's will directed that a simple stone cross not exceeding £25 in cost be placed on the grave. When Caroline died in June 1895, she, too, was buried in Kensal Green, in the same grave, but her name is not on the gravestone.

R. D. Blackmore (1825–1900) Richard Doddridge Blackmore had only passing contact with London except for the years 1849 to 1854; he entered the Middle Temple as a law student on January 27, 1849, under the tutelage of John Warner of the Inner Temple and was called to the bar on June 7, 1852. (From 1853 to 1857 he is listed as residing at 3 Essex Court, in the Temple, but these were probably only his professional chambers.) On November 8, 1853, he married Lucy Maguire at Trinity Church in the parish of St. Andrew, Holborn; the church records list his residence as Rochester Square. He and his wife may have lived there after the marriage; their marriage was kept secret for some time, not because his father-in-law was Anglican while his wife was Roman Catholic but rather because her family was Roman Catholic and they were married in the Anglican Church. Advised to give up law and engage in some sort of outdoor activity because of severe epileptic seizures, Blackmore determined on a teaching career and went to Welles-

ley House School in Twickenham. Later, after he had bought land in Teddington and embarked on market gardening, he was frequently at Covent Garden to sell his fruit; *Alice Lorraine* tells of produce being sent here by Martin Lovejoy. In October 1881, Blackmore was at the Arts Club, along with Thomas Hardy, for a dinner in honor of "Tourgeneff."

Dante Gabriel Rossetti (1828–1882) and Christina Rossetti (1830–1894) The Anglo-Italian family of Gabriele Rossetti was a remarkable Victorian group with two scholars (the father and daughter Maria), two outstandingly creative literary personalities (Dante Gabriel and Christina), and an important member of the Pre-Raphaelite Brotherhood (William). Dante Gabriel Rossetti (christened Gabriel Charles Dante at All Souls Church on Langham Place) was born on May 12, 1828, at 38 Charlotte Street (later 106–110 Hallam Street); the house, with others, was demolished in 1928 for an apartment block called Rossetti House, and the original memorial plaque was placed over the main entrance of the new building. William Michael was born here in 1829, and Christina Georgina in 1830. Both boys were educated first at home and then at "Mr. Paul's," a neighboring preparatory school, in 1837. A Church of England day school (with some boarders) and staffed mostly by clergy, it was "an education experience of average stupidity" for the Rossettis.

About the time the boys entered King's College (in the easternmost wing of Somerset House on the Strand), Gabriele Rossetti moved his family to a larger house at 50 Charlotte Street. In 1841, after leaving King's, Dante Gabriel enrolled at Henry Sass's, a Bloomsbury drawing school heavily favored by the academicians, which brought out the worst in Rossetti. He was a bad student, boisterous, idle, sarcastic, and temperamental; his habit of mimicry also led to difficulty. He abandoned Sass's in 1845 for the Antique School of the Royal Academy, where he spent two years in the same manner; in 1848 he persuaded Ford Madox Brown, then a widower of twenty-six and not really well known, to accept him as a student. Rossetti worked daily in Brown's Clipstone Street studio but rebelled at having to begin from scratch; consequently, he left Brown's tutelage and went to Holman Hunt at 7 Cleveland Street, where once again he was forced back to the beginning. Rossetti had his own studio in the autumn of 1849 at 72 Newman Street and was now painting in earnest, but forced to leave after some difficulties over the Pre-Raphaelite Brotherhood, he took 74 Newman Street, a gloomy place where the rain pelted dismally on the dirty skylight. "The Blessed Damozel" appeared in the first issue of *The Germ* in 1850.

When financial problems forced the family to move to 38 Arlington Road in Camden Town, Rossetti first shared 17 Red Lion Square with Walter Deverell, but then was persuaded by Brown to share the Newman Street studio. The arrangement was almost unworkable: Rossetti kept Brown from working, often painted all night, and translated sonnets for breakfast; he was "working hard and doing nothing." In the spring of 1852 he was sharing The Hermitage on West Hill, Highgate, with Edward Bateman, and about this time he became secretly engaged to Elizabeth (Lizzie) Siddal. Rossetti is said to have discovered Lizzie in a milliner's shop on Cranbourn Alley, which was at the very end of Cranbourn Street, on the northeast side of Leicester Square. For some reason, possibly Lizzie, Rossetti was driven from his parents' home, and in November 1852 he found second-floor rooms (a large studio, a pleasant sitting room, and a small bedroom) at 14 Chatham Place. *Ecce Ancilla Domini* was exhibited in 1850, but severe criticism made Rossetti give up oils for watercolors and determine never to exhibit again. However, he did exhibit in the 1852 Winter Exhibition of Watercolors on Pall Mall; one of those at the showing was John Ruskin, who admired Rossetti's work. Ruskin first came to the Chatham Place studio in April 1854 and became a powerful and influential patron.

From the autumn of 1854 on Rossetti was teaching figure drawing and watercolor at the Working Men's College, 31 Red Lion Square, and by the summer of 1855 was an occasional guest of Robert and Elizabeth Barrett Browning. Robert Browning also was frequently in Rossetti's studio; Rossetti's meeting Alfred, Lord Tennyson at the Brownings just before their departure for Italy led to the 1857 illustrations for Edward Moxon's edition of Tennyson's *Poems*. During this period he had some difficulties with Lizzie, who had a series of illnesses, real or imaginary; he also took as a mistress a model, Fanny Cornforth (Sarah Cox), who was "a strapping blonde from Wapping." He set her up on Tennyson Street, Battersea, and the flat became "a favourite resort." After marrying Lizzie in the spring of 1860, they settled in Spring Cottage, Downshire Hill, in Hampstead.

In 1861 Rossetti, William Morris, Edward Burne-Jones, and others formed the firm of "fine art workmen" known as Morris, Marshall, Faulkner and Company. Some of their most successful early works were the stained-glass windows designed by Rossetti. In May 1861 Lizzie gave birth to a stillborn child, and after this she entered a mentally unbalanced state from which she never fully recovered. On February 10, 1862, Dante Gabriel Rossetti, Lizzie, and Algernon Swinburne ate at the Sablonière Restaurant on Leicester Square; Lizzie, taking laudanum to stifle the pain from acute neuralgia, did not want to miss the occasion but became unnaturally animated during the meal. Rossetti took her home, went off to teach at the college, and, returning home about midnight, found her unconscious beside an empty laudanum bottle; she died the following morning and was buried in the Rossetti family plot in Highgate. At the funeral Rossetti could not be stopped from putting a Bible and a red-edged manuscript book of original verses in the coffin (perhaps as a peace offering), but seven years later he had the coffin opened and the verses retrieved.

Rossetti left the Chatham Place house first for 77 Newman Street, then for 59 Lincoln's Inn Fields, where George Meredith and Swinburne were frequent guests, and finally went to 16 Cheyne Walk, Chelsea, a house which was known as Tudor House and the Queen's House and supposedly was the residence of Sir Thomas More and Queen Catherine. In fact, the house dates from 1717. Rossetti planned to find a joint tenant: Swinburne was the first applicant, and Ruskin was gently dissuaded from joining them. Meredith became a second inmate, and William Ros-

setti the third. Meredith did not last long; it was rumored that his sensibilities were affronted by the sight of Rossetti devouring a plate of ham surrounded by six bleeding eggs for breakfast, but more likely he departed after Rossetti threw a cup of tea in his face at breakfast. Some of Swinburne's more exotic behavior, such as sliding naked down the handrail of the staircase, could also have been contributory. Although the house was badly run, with rats and mice everywhere, Rossetti lavished a great deal of time, energy, and money on it.

Without doubt, the greatest peculiarity of the house after Swinburne left were its other inmates. A wombat was an early acquisition, and when it was discovered having eaten the straw hat of a patron as she sat for a portrait, Rossetti cried out, "Oh, poor wombat! it is so indigestible!" There were peacocks in the garden and armadillos and kangaroos, squirrels, dormice, a raccoon, and Jessie and Bobby, two owls. The actress Ellen Terry wrote:

> He bought a white bull because it had "eyes like Janey Morris", and tethered it on the lawn. . . . Soon there was no lawn left—only the bull. He invited people to meet it, and heaped favours on it, until it kicked everything to pieces, when he reluctantly got rid of it.

Rossetti bought a white peacock, which immediately hid under the sofa in the drawing room and stayed there until it died. He compensated by buying white dormice, which he sat "on tiny bamboo chairs." After their winter's hibernation he gave a spring party for their awakening:

> "They are awake now," he said, "but how quiet they are! How full of repose!"
> One of the guests went to inspect the dormice more closely, and a peculiar expression came over his face. It might almost have been thought he was holding his nose.
> "Wake up, little dormice," said Rossetti, prodding them gently with a quill pen.
> "They'll never do that," said the guest. "They're dead. I believe they have been dead some days."

Because of the cacophonous shrieks of the peacock calling to its mate after a fallow deer had trampled on its tail until all the feathers were out, all leases to this day on Cheyne Walk have a clause forbidding the keeping of peacocks.

In 1866 Rossetti began to suffer from hydrocele and in 1867 from chronic insomnia; he was, though, still able to go out, frequenting, for example, Rules Oyster Bar (still flourishing in Covent Garden), and to receive guests, among them Henry James, in the spring of 1869. Within two years, however, his health was in a serious decline: he suffered from insomnia, depression, hypersensitivity, failing sight, and a loss of self-control. Chloral and spirits were of no help, and in 1872, becoming temporarily irrational and suffering auditory delusions, he was taken to Roehampton, where he attempted suicide with laudanum, and upon his survival he was left a hemiplegic. He was in Bognor off and on over the next eight years, and only on rare occasions did he visit his mother and sister at 30 Torrington Square. On December 11, 1881, his left side was paralyzed from his use of chloral, and he died at Birchington-on-Sea on April 9, 1882. In June 1887 Holman Hunt unveiled a bronze medallion of Rossetti designed by Ford Madox Brown; it surmounts a drinking fountain designed by John Seddon opposite 16 Cheyne Walk on the Chelsea Embankment. In January 1970 thieves ripped the bronze portrait from the fountain, presumably to sell it for scrap, but a new cast was made, and in 1971 "Rossetti with a tap in his tummy," as J. M. Whistler called it, was back in its proper place.

Christina Rossetti suffered from ill health throughout her life and in the 1870s especially from Graves' Disease; she remained within the confines of the family, living at 56 Euston Square from 1869 to around 1876 and then at 30 Torrington Square, where she died of cancer on December 29, 1894. She was buried in the Highgate Cemetery; Christ Church, Woburn Square, has an altarpiece with paintings by Sir Edward Burne-Jones in her memory.

George Meredith (1828–1909) George Meredith came to London in 1844 from the Moravian School at Neuwied, Germany, and lived with his father in the St. James area. In February 1846 he was articled to Richard Stephen Charnock, a solicitor with an office at 44 Paul's Alley, but later abandoned the law. By 1848 he had met Edward Peacock, Thomas Love Peacock's son, through whom he met Mary Ellen Peacock Nicholls, a widow with a young child; in 1849 Meredith was lodging at 153 Ebury Street. On August 9, 1849, shortly after he came of age and received the remainder of his inheritance, Meredith and Mrs. Nicholls were married at St. George's Church, Hanover Square, and went to live in Weybridge. The marriage was a difficult one, and Meredith disclaimed the paternity of his wife's child in 1858; she subsequently went off with Henry Wallis, the artist. Immediately following the separation, Meredith came to London and lodged at 8 Hobury Street, Chelsea; here he wrote *The Ordeal of Richard Feverel.* In later years whenever he came to London from Esher and Box Hill on business with his publisher, he frequently stayed with Dante Gabriel Rossetti on Cheyne Walk. The original Diana of *Diana of the Crossways,* Mrs. Caroline Norton, lived at 2 Storey's Gate, just beyond the end of Great George Street, where Meredith visited her. Meredith was elected to membership in the Garrick Club, 15 Garrick Street, in 1864 and retained his membership until 1899. After his death on May 18, 1909, at Box Hill, simultaneous services were held in Dorking and Westminster Abbey.

Henry Kingsley (1830–1876) As a child, Henry Kingsley, the novelist and brother of Charles Kingsley, lived in the Rectory on Old Church Street after 1836, when his father was given the Chelsea living; he was educated at King's College in the easternmost wing of Somerset House on the Strand before going up to Worcester College, Oxford. From 1871 to 1873 he was at 24 Bernard Street, where he wrote *Oakshott Castle* and *Reginald Hetherege.* He also lived at 88 Forbes Road in Kentish Town before retiring to Cuckfield, where he died.

William Hale White (1831–1913) Better known as Mark Rutherford, William Hale White had an early but sporadic relationship with London in the capacity of a Unitarian preacher; in the 1850s he was hired by John Chapman of Chapman and Hall, whose offices were at 11 Henrietta Street, Covent Garden, and then at 193 Piccadilly. Chapman gave White lodgings in his own home at 142 the Strand, and here White met Mary Ann Evans (George Eliot) for the first time.

White, however, was still unble to support himself through literature and in 1854 became a clerk in the Registrar General's office in Somerset House on the Strand. In the next year he was transferred to the Admiralty, where he remained until his retirement in 1891. For some time he lived at 69 Marylebone Road and was for a short period registrar of births, deaths, and marriages for Marylebone.

William Morris (1834–1896) Willim Morris, poet, designer, craftsman, and social reformer, came to London from Oxford in 1856, when the architectural firm of George Edmund Street, to which he was articled, moved its offices here; Morris lived at 1 Gordon Street with Edward Burne-Jones, who had left Oxford without a degree. Dante Gabriel Rossetti, who had met Morris some years before, convinced him that he too ought to paint, and Morris consequently quit his post and took a studio with Burne-Jones at 17 Red Lion Square. In the same year *The Defence of Guenevere and Other Poems* was written. In 1859, after his marriage to Jane Burden, he moved to 41 Great Ormond Street until The Red House in Bexleyheath was ready for their occupancy. The marriage was unhappy, and in 1865 Morris and his family moved from The Red House to 26 Queen Square; here the greater part of the house was given over to Morris's workshop; marital discord increased even further, fueled, as it turned out, by Rossetti's transparent infatuation with Jane. Morris also began to write again, and the scheme for *The Earthly Paradise* was completed by 1866. In 1871 he settled at Kelmscott Manor in Kelmscott, Oxfordshire, but returned to London and Kelmscott House (marked with a plaque) in Hammersmith in 1878; facing the Thames, the house also became his workshop. Needing more space to set up the Kelmscott Press in 1891, he and the engraver-printer Walker Emery used part of nearby Sussex House and within seven years produced fifty-three titles, including the famous *The Works of Geoffrey Chaucer.* By 1883 Morris was involved in the Democratic (later Social Democratic) Federation, and with George Bernard Shaw at his side helped to lead the November 13, 1887, "Bloody Sunday" demonstration to Trafalgar Square. Following a voyage to Norway Morris died at Kelmscott House on October 3, 1896, and was buried in Kelmscott, Oxfordshire.

Samuel Butler (1835–1902) In the face of stern opposition from his parents about earning his living as a painter, Samuel Butler fled to New Zealand in 1859 to make his way as a sheep breeder; selling his holdings at just the right time, he doubled his original stake before returning in 1864. He took chambers at 15 Clifford's Inn, Fetter Lane; the 14th-century Inn of Court, then a complex of shops, gardens, residences, and passageways, gave way to progress in the form of modern apartments and offices in 1935. (One finely paneled room was saved and reerected in the Victoria and Albert Museum.) Butler's second-floor apartment of three rooms and a pantry was to be his home for the rest of his life. At first, still intent on becoming a painter—and, indeed, he did exhibit at the Royal Academy—he studied at Francis Stephen Cary's and then at Heatherley's school. His daily life was scrupulously planned—he spent seven hours a day painting, practicing the piano, and writing—and he would tolerate no deviation from his plan. *Family Prayers* was painted this year, and *The Evidence for* *the Resurrection of Jesus Christ . . . Critically Examined* was printed at his own expense the same year.

In 1869 continuous overwork and emotional problems began to exact their toll on Butler; in addition, a tumorlike growth appeared at the back of his neck, and he heard loud noises in his head before going to sleep. He attracted little literary notice until 1872, when *Erewhon* appeared anonymously. The book was too "impious" for his family, and at their request all relations ceased. A series of books on evolution, *Life and Habit, Evolution, Unconscious Memory,* and *Luck or Cunning,* appeared in the late 1870s and the 1880s. In May 1902, in a state of indifferent health, Butler left alone for a trip to Sicily and collapsed in Rome; he was brought back to London by Alfred, his faithful servant, and died on June 18, 1902, in a London nursing home. His body was cremated in Woking, as he had directed, and his ashes were dispersed. The largely autobiographical *The Way of all Flesh* was published posthumously in 1903; the original of Alathea Pontifex, Butler's longtime friend Eliza Mary Ann Savage, lived at 22 Beaumont Street, off the Marylebone High Street. It was she whom Butler called "the best, kindest, wittiest, most lovable, and, to my mind, handsomest woman I had ever seen."

Sir Walter Besant (1836–1901) Besant first came to London to attend Stockwell Grammar School, an affiliate of King's College, before going on to King's itself. After a 6-year period (1861–1867) at the Royal College, Mauritius, he returned to England and settled somewhere in London; from 1896 until his death here on June 9, 1901, Sir Walter lived at Frognal End (marked with a plaque), 18 Frognal Gardens, in Hampstead. He was buried on Church Row, just north of the Hampstead Parish Church.

Sir William Schwenck Gilbert (1836–1911) Sir William Schwenck Gilbert was born at 17 Southampton Street, the home of his maternal grandfather, on November 18, 1836, and was baptized at St. Paul's Church, Covent Garden. Traveling with his parents in 1838, he was kidnapped on the Via Posilippo in Naples by a band of brigands and ransomed for £25; years later he claimed to recognize the site of the kidnapping. At the age of ten Gilbert was sent to the Western Grammar School in Brompton, where he remained until going to Great Ealing School, Ealing, in 1849; here his literary and artistic talents were soon visible. In 1855 he began his studies at King's College (in the easternmost wing of Somerset House on the Strand) and planned on going up to Oxford. He finally took his B.A. at London University in 1857 but had entered the Inner Temple as a student on October 11, 1855. Of the £300 Gilbert inherited in 1861, £100 was used to pay his call to the bar in 1863; a second third of the legacy was used to furnish his rooms in Clement's Inn; and the final third was used to gain access to (Sir) Charles James Watkin Williams's chambers. His income from the law was less than £100 a year, and he took to supplementing it through writing. He contributed to *Cornhill, London Society, Tinsley's Magazine,* and *Temple Bar* and became the drama critic for the *Illustrated Times,* all while he continued military duties in the 3d Battalion, Gordon Highlanders. He reached the rank of major before his retirement in 1883.

Gilbert's theatrical career began in 1866 with *Dul-camara, or The Little Duck and the Great Quack,* and the next year he married Lucy Agnes Blois Turner, settling at 21 Eldon Road, South Kensington; they attended the nearby St. Mary Abbots Church. Gilbert and his wife moved to 8 Essex Villas, where they remained until 1876. The collaboration between Gilbert and (Sir) Arthur Sullivan was set in motion when the German Reeds introduced the two men in 1870, but their first major joint effort, *Trial by Jury,* did not open at the Royalty Theatre on Dean Street (opposite Bateman Street, where Number 73 now stands) until 1875. The long partnership (interrupted between 1890 and 1893, apparently by an argument over carpeting for the Savoy Theatre) was so successful that Richard D'Oyly Carte built the Savoy Theatre for their works; the theater opened in 1881 with *Patience,* which satirized generally the aesthetic movement and particularly Oscar Wilde and his daily trip to see Lillie Langtry with a single lily.

In 1878 Gilbert and his wife moved to The Boltons, essentially an extension of Gilston Road, in Chelsea West, where they remained for three years. After the enormous successes of the early operettas, Gilbert was a very wealthy man, and in 1883 he moved into 39 Harrington Gardens, South Kensington. The house, marked by a plaque, was built to Gilbert's specifications and is an elaborate combination of medieval Dutch and Victorian English styles. Gilbert put his wealth to use in other ways; he built and owned the Garrick Theatre on St. Martin's Place, which opened in 1889 with Sir Arthur Wing Pinero's *The Profligate.* In 1890 he purchased the Norman Shaw house, Grimsdyke, in Harrow Weald; he also had other addresses in London, including 36 Prince's Gardens, from 1894 to 1898, and a town house, from 1907 to 1911, at 90 Eaton Square. Gilbert's writing for the theater during these years met with no success, and not even renewed collaboration with Sullivan achieved the previous brilliance. Sir William Schwenck Gilbert died of heart failure at his Harrow Weald home on May 29, 1911; a commemorative medallion on the Embankment opposite Charing Cross Station notes:

His foe was Folly
And his weapon wit.

Algernon Charles Swinburne (1837–1909) Algernon Charles Swinburne, born on April 5, 1837, on Chester Street (probably Number 7), was not expected to survive more than an hour or so after birth, and most of his childhood was spent in the open air at Bonchurch on the Isle of Wight and at Capheaton in Northumberland. He returned to London from Oxford in 1860 and remained here, in general, for the rest of his life. He first lodged near Edward Burne-Jones's residence at 62 Great Russell Street; in 1861 and 1862 he was at 12 Grafton Way, off Fitzroy Square, and in the same decade he resided at 124 Mount Street, off Berkeley Square, and 18 Grosvenor Place, off Knightsbridge.

Swinburne had met Dante Gabriel Rossetti at Oxford, and from 1862 to 1872, he wrote, they "lived on terms of affectionate intimacy; shaped and coloured on his side, by cordial kindness and exuberant generosity, on mine by gratitude as loyal and admiration as fervent as ever strove and ever failed to express all the sweet and sudden passion of youth towards greatness in its elder." Indeed, Swinburne had dined with Rossetti and Lizzie on the night she died and gave evidence at the inquest. After Lizzie's death Swinburne took the lease on Rossetti's house (17 Newman Street), but not for long. Rossetti had already taken 16 Cheyne Walk, at an expensive rent of £110 a year with the view to sharing with two others; impulsively, Swinburne became the first tenant but proved to be erratic, in that he was often away and had some sort of a drinking problem. Rossetti also became increasingly concerned about Swinburne's abnormal sex life. When Swinburne was in residence, he worked in his sitting room to the right of the front door. Here he completed *Chastelard* and worked on his *Poems and Ballads;* Rossetti's suggestion in 1863 that he begin a study of Blake led to a formulation of the principles of the aesthetic movement. Swinburne perpetually flitted back and forth, to Paris, to the country, to the sea, and neither he nor the rent was available on a regular basis. Rossetti consequently broke the tenancy in an "affectionate and cordial" letter, and the two remained the best of friends.

It is now thought that Swinburne suffered from epilepsy, and after an especially severe seizure he left London for the Isle of Wight and the Continent. In 1865 he took 36 Wilton Crescent, Belgravia, where he corrected the proofs of *Atalanta in Calydon*, which brought literary success. When the earlier-written *Chastelard* was published, questioning of the author's literary morals began. From 1865 to 1870 he lived at 22 Dorset Street, and in 1866 the storm began to rage when *Poems and Ballads* appeared. Attacked for its "feverish carnality," the book was withdrawn by the publisher within three months; a second publisher was found, but the literary scandal was enormous. An attempt to prosecute fell through; *Punch* called him "Mr. Swineborn," and the newspapers carried daily legendary stories about his eccentricities. A period of frenzied literary activity, whirlwind trips to the country, and excesses in living style (drinking and masochistic encounters) added to his health problems; and he suffered a particularly bad seizure in the Reading Room of the British Museum in July 1868. After an enforced holiday, he lodged at 12 North Crescent and then took rooms at 3 Great James Street, off Theobalds Road, where he resided, except for a short time in 1879, until he left London for good. By September of that year his physical state had deteriorated so rapidly that Theodore Watts (later Watts-Dunton) rescued him and, with the consent of Lady Jane Swinburne, took the poet into his own home, The Pines, 2 (now 11) Putney Hill, Putney. Here for thirty years Swinburne's regimen was strictly controlled, and, encouraged to write, he wrote twenty-three volumes of prose, poetry, and plays. Swinburne died in Putney on April 10, 1909, and was buried in Bonchurch. Watts-Dunton survived him by five years.

Marie Louise de la Ramée (1839–1908)   Best known for the children's classic *A Dog of Flanders* and by her pseudonym Ouida (a childhood corruption of her Christian name), Marie Louise Ramé (self-styled to de la Ramée) visited London in 1851 with her parents to see the Great Exhibition. In 1859, at the age of twenty, she came to live at 11 Ravenscourt Square (marked with a plaque) and gained an introduction to Harrison Ainsworth; her literary career began with his inclusion of a short piece, "Dashwood's Drag, or

The Derby and What Came of It" in *Bentley's Miscellany* in 1859. Sixteen more undistinguished tales (none was ever reprinted) appeared by 1860. From that year on she lived almost exclusively in Italy, but on trips to England stayed either at her mother's home at 51 Welbeck Street or in apartments in the Langham Hotel (an ugly building now part of the British Broadcasting Corporation properties), on Langham Place, and presided over a kind of literary salon there. Those in attendance included Robert Browning, Oscar Wilde, and Lord Lytton.

Wilfrid Scawen Blunt (1840–1922)   About the turn of the twentieth century Wilfrid Scawen Blunt, already seriously affected by illness, lived at 100 Mount Street, off Berkeley Square.

John Addington Symonds (1840–1893)   John Addington Symonds, essayist, poet, and biographer, spent a little time in London at 7 Half Moon Street in 1854, but not until after his health had broken at Oxford did he settle here. Shortly after his marriage in November 1864, he and his wife came to 13 Albion Street, where they remained for a short time before moving to 47 Norfolk Square. Since his health would not permit holding a fellowship at Oxford, Symonds determined on a career in law but found that this, too, was unsuitable; 1867 was the last year that Symonds spent any considerable time in London, and he died in Rome on April 19, 1893.

Thomas Hardy (1840–1928)   In 1862, when his father determined that he earn his own living, Thomas Hardy ventured to London with a prudently purchased return ticket in his pocket; he had had some architectural experience in Dorchester and upon arrival here in May secured a post with the firm headed by Arthur Blomfield, whose offices were located at 8 St. Martin's Place. Hardy lodged at 16 Westbourne Park Villas for the five years of his employment. Blomfield moved his offices to 8 Adelphi Terrace in 1863, and here Hardy

> sat . . . drawing, inside the eastern-most window of the front room on the first floor above the ground floor. . . . I saw from there the Embankment and Charing Cross Bridge built, and, of course, used to think of Garrick and Johnson.

The room where he worked, he continues, "contained at that date a fine Adams mantel-piece in white marble, on which we used to sketch caricatures in pencil." Hardy first appeared in print in *Chambers's Journal* (March 18, 1865), with "How I Built Myself a House" (he never did). His work for Blomfield was that of a "Gothic" draftsman, the same work he had done for the firm of John Hicks in Dorchester. He took classes in French at King's College (the easternmost wing of Somerset House on the Strand), began to write poetry, and spent time in the National Gallery and at Exeter Hall (372 the Strand), where Jenny Lind performed.

Ill health forced Hardy's return to Dorchester; he submitted *The Poor Man and the Lady* to Chapman and Hall after it had been turned down by Alexander Macmillan and came to London in March 1867 to meet with their reviewer, who had also refused it. The reader was George Meredith, who suggested that Hardy begin a novel, "one with a more complicated plot. . . ." Hardy was back in London off and on through the early 1870s and in 1870 worked at Clement's Inn for a brief period; in 1874 he settled in Westbourne Park to establish residency for his marriage to Emma Lavinia Gifford on September 17, 1874, at St. Peter's Church, Elgin Avenue, Paddington; they settled for almost two years at St. David's, Hood Road, Surbiton, where he wrote *The Hand of Ethelberta* and worked on *The Return of the Native*. After a time in Sturminster Newton, they moved to The Larches, 1 Arundel Terrace, Trinity Road, in March 1878; here he became critically ill after a lung hemorrhage and returned to his native Dorset in 1881.

Hardy did, though, come to London frequently; in June 1878 he was elected to the Saville Club, where he met Edmund Gosse and James Russell Lowell, then the American Minister in London; in April 1891 he was elected to the Athenaeum Club, at the corner of Pall Mall and Waterloo Place, and would frequently stay here when in town. By 1896 Hardy was making frequent trips to the Royal Hospital for old and disabled soldiers (Royal Hospital Road in Chelsea) and its attendant military museum to authenticate the details of the Napoleonic Wars for *The Dynasts*. Hardy died at his home in Dorchester on January 11, 1928; three simultaneous church services were held, one at St. Peter's Church, Dorchester, another at Stinsford (near his birthplace), and one at Westminster Abbey. His ashes were buried in the Poets' Corner; serving as pallbearers were Sir James Matthew Barrie, John Galsworthy, Edmund Gosse, A. E. Housman, Rudyard Kipling, and George Bernard Shaw. His heart, as he directed, is interred in the grave of his first wife in Stinsford.

London is not really a part of Thomas Hardy's Wessex, but various sections of the city play a minor role in his works. He mentions Bloomsbury, Bond Street, Boswell Court, Buckingham Palace, Charing Cross, 41 Charles Square (Hoxton), Chelsea, Gower Street, Green Park, the (old) Houses of Parliament, 20 John Street, Lancaster Place, Lincoln's Inn Fields, the Strand, Warwick Street, Waterloo Station, and Spring Gardens in *Desperate Remedies;* Baker Street, Berkeley Square, the British Museum, the Grosvenor Hotel in Pimlico, Hyde Park, the Mint, Nightingale Lane, and Paddington Station, Piccadilly, in *A Pair of Blue Eyes;* the Barbican, Burlington House, Cheapside, St. Giles Cripplegate Church, Doctors' Commons, Kew, the Poets' Corner of Westminster Abbey, and Westminster Bridge in *The Hand of Ethelberta;* St. Paul's Cathedral in *The Trumpet-Major* and *The Mayor of Casterbridge;* the Royal Observatory at Greenwich in *Two on a Tower;* the law courts, the London docks, and Long Acre in *Jude the Obscure;* and Covent Garden in *The Well-Beloved*. Many of his short stories and poems also contain references to London.

William Henry Hudson (1841–1922) The earliest years in England (and probably London) of the Argentinian-born William Henry Hudson are almost a complete mystery. Poverty in England and, perhaps, health problems, which had begun in Buenos Aires in 1856, may have induced his 1876 marriage to Emily Wingrave, a woman fifteen years his senior. Hudson's wife ran a boarding house at 11 Leinster Square, Bayswater, and the couple lived there until the enterprise failed in 1884. A second boarding house failed in 1886. Hudson's first novel, *The Purple Land That England Lost*, attracted little attention,

and they settled in lodgings in Ravenscourt Park for a short time before moving to 40 St. Luke's Road, Kensington, when Emily Hudson inherited that house (marked with a plaque). They kept up the mortgage payments only by renting out the lower floors. Here all Hudson's ornithological works were written; *The Naturalist in La Plata* brought him a measure of prominence but little financial reward.

Hudson was granted a civil list pension of £150 a year in 1901 and was thus enabled to travel around the country and write the books on the English countryside which finally brought him fame (*Afoot in England* and *A Shepherd's Life*) and *Green Mansions*, his best-known work. The outbreak of World War I did not affect Hudson as it did many of his contemporaries, probably because the character of his work and his interest in nature kept him remote from politics. His wife died in 1921, and his health, too, was deteriorating; he died in London on August 18, 1922. In the same year a not very attractive public monument which depicts Rima of *Green Mansions* (by Jacob Epstein) was erected in Hyde Park, where the bird sanctuary was also established in his memory. One other London association with Hudson is at 16 Gerrard Street, a tavern before World War I which attracted many writers including Hudson, Hilaire Belloc, G. K. Chesterton, John Masefield, Norman Douglas, John Galsworthy, Joseph Conrad, and William H. Davies.

Henry James (1843–1916) The American-born writer and naturalized British citizen Henry James knew England as a child but did not settle here, in London, until late in 1876, when he took a set of small rooms at 3 Bolton Street, off Piccadilly, where he remained for ten years. (He did, however, have rooms for a short time in 1878 at 7 Half Moon Street.) Here in Bolton Street he produced *The American, Watch and Ward, The Europeans, Daisy Miller, Washington Square, The Portrait of a Lady, The Bostonians,* and *The Princess Casamassima,* but it was *Daisy Miller* in 1878 which first brought him international acclaim. James was lionized and, supposedly, dined out 140 times during 1878 and 1879; one of the many homes to which he was invited was that of the literary critic Edmund Gosse, at 29 Delamere Terrace, where Robert Browning, George Moore, and Algernon Swinburne often met. In 1884 James's sister joined him, and in 1886 he moved to 34 De Vere Gardens:

> My small house seems most pleasant and peculiar (in the sense of being my own), and my servants are as punctual as they are prim—which is saying much.

The house was marked with a plaque in 1949. Here James wrote *The Tragic Muse, The Spoils of Poynton,* and *What Maisie Knew*.

In 1898 James left London for Rye, where he remained until the end of 1912; working on his autobiography and staying at the Reform Club (where he always kept a room), he was persuaded by his secretary, Theodora Bosanquet (who was sharing a flat at 10 Lawrence Street), to take two rooms at the back of that flat; she noted:

> Chelsea began to make its appeal to him before long. He walked about and made little purchases in the shops. He liked talking to the people; he liked the kind of village atmosphere that he found there. . . . And then he found a delightful flat round the corner at Carlyle Mansions. . . .

He moved into 21 Carlyle Mansions, Cheyne Walk, on January 5, 1913, and had two front rooms overlooking the river; "just at hand, straight across the River," he wrote, "by the ample and also very quiet Albert Bridge, lies the very convenient and in its way also very beguiling Battersea Park." It was an excellent choice by his own admission. On his seventieth birthday a group of friends presented him with his portrait, to be painted by John Singer Sargent, a fellow American living at 31 Tite Street; Sargent finished the portrait in ten sittings. It was, said James,

> Sargent at his very best and poor old H. J. not at his worst; in short, a living breathing likeness and a masterpiece of painting. I am really quite ashamed to admire it so much and so loudly—it's so much as if I were calling attention to my own fine points. I don't alas, exhibit a "point" in it, but am all large and luscious rotundity—by which you may see how true a thing it is.

A confirmed Anglophile, James was much dismayed by the outbreak of World War I and became a naturalized citizen in 1915. "The odd thing is," he wrote, "that nothing seems to have happened and that I don't feel a bit different.... The process has only shown me virtually what I *was*." At the beginning of 1916, when he was already ill, he was awarded the Order of Merit; the news was brought to him by Edmund Gosse, who looked at the seemingly unconscious man and leaned over the bed to whisper, "Henry, they've given you the O.M." There was no reply, and Kidd, the maid, commented softly that James was too far gone to hear. Gosse left, and the author, opening his eyes, said, "Kidd, turn off the light to spare my blushes." When James died on February 28, 1916, his ashes were taken to the James family plot in the Cambridge, Massachusetts, cemetery, but Chelsea Old Church has a commemorative plaque to "a resident of this Parish who renounced a cherished citizenship to give allegiance to England in the first year of the Great War." There is also a commemorative tablet in Westminster Abbey.

Robert Bridges (1844–1930)

> Then boys I heard, as they went to school, calling;
> They gathered up the crystal manna to freeze
> Their tongues with tasting, their hands with snowballing;
>   Or rioted in a drift, plunging up to the knees;
> Or peering up from under the white-mossed wonder,
> "O look at the trees!" they cried, "O look at the trees!"
>   With lessened load a few carts creak and blunder,
> Following alone the white deserted way,
> A country company long dispersed asunder;
>   When now already the sun, in pale display
> Standing by Paul's high dome, spread forth below
> His sparkling beams, and awoke the stir of the day.

Poet Laureate from 1913 on, Robert Bridges was never comfortable in London; in November 1869 he entered St. Bartholomew's Hospital on Little Britain as a student and graduated with an M.B. in 1874. His intention was to retire from medicine at the age of forty, for then he would have gained the knowledge of men necessary for his work as a poet. He was house physician at Bart's and lived at 50 Maddox Street; in 1877, as the hospital's casualty physician, he recorded seeing 30,940 patients, averaging 1.28 minutes on each patient, and prescribing 200,000 medicines containing iron. In 1877 he moved to 52 Bedford Square with his mother, and he kept this residence, where Gerard Manley Hopkins was a visitor, until he left London. In 1878 he was appointed assistant physician of the Hospital for Sick Children on Great Ormond Street; later he went to the Great Northern Hospital in Holloway. In 1876 *The Growth of Love: A Poem in Twenty-four Sonnets* appeared, and two volumes of *Poems, by the Author of the Growth of Love* followed in 1879 and 1880. In June 1881 Bridges suffered an attack of pneumonia and empyema and in November left for Italy to recuperate. He never returned to medicine or to London.

Bram Stoker (1847–1912)   The Irish-born novelist and Sir Henry Irving's personal manager for twenty-seven years, Bram Stoker, whose only claim to literary fame is the Gothic horror romance *Dracula*, had one known London address: 4 Durham Place, Chelsea.

William Ernest Henley (1849–1903)   William Ernest Henley came to London in 1867 and lodged in 11 Bateman Buildings, a small passageway off the south side of Soho Square; at that time he was trying to earn his living by writing, but by 1873 the tubercular condition of his right foot was so serious that he had to leave. He eventually went to Edinburgh, where he put himself in the care of Prof. Joseph Lister and where he wrote "Invictus." Lister's radical new approach eventually saved Henley's leg, and he returned to London late in 1876. Taking rooms at 1 The Parade in Shepherd's Bush, he became editor of *London*, a weekly paper which had its editorial offices at 281 the Strand:

> Down through the Ancient Strand
> The spirit of October, mild and boon
> And sauntering, takes his way
> This golden end of afternoon....

By June 1978 he was at 11 Adelaide Grove, Shepherd's Bush, and turned to critical work for the *Athenaeum, St. James's Gazette, Vanity Fair,* and *Saturday Review* when *London* ceased publication. After marrying in Edinburgh that April, he and his wife were at 4 Earl's Terrace, Devonshire Road, in December but moved to 36 Loftus Road at Easter, 1879; for a brief period in 1880 Henley was editor of *Pan* at 22 Tavistock Street. Another move occurred in 1881, when the Henleys took a small house at 51 Richmond Gardens.

As editor of the *Magazine of Art* in 1882, he championed the causes of Auguste Rodin and James McNeill Whistler, and his friendship with Rodin was lifelong. After an 1886 trip to Paris, Henley and his wife settled at 1 Merton Road, Chiswick, where a daughter was born in 1888. Henley and his family returned to Edinburgh that year. When the *Scots Observer*, of which Henley was editor, moved its offices to London and became the *National Observer* in 1892, Henley took the lease of 1 Great College Street, Westminster, and found a house in Addiscombe as well. The death of his only child (the "Reddy" of Sir James Matthew Barrie's *Sentimental Tommy*) in 1894 dealt Henley a blow from which he never recovered, and he gave up both the Westminster and Addiscombe houses. He returned to London frequently and in 1896 was at 9 Barnes Terrace; in 1901 he had a flat at 19 Albert Mansions in Battersea, although he was most often in Woking then. After his death in 1903 a memorial bust sculpted by Rodin was placed in the crypt of St. Paul's Cathedral. Many of Henley's poems, especially *London Voluntaries,* deal with aspects of London, and when Christ's Hospital was moved from the old Grey Friars Monastery on Newgate Street in 1902, Henley composed an affectionate sonnet on the occasion:

So went our boys when Edward Sixth, the King,
Chartered Christ's Hospital, and died. And so
Full fifteen generations in a string
Of heirs to his bequest have had to go.
Thus Camden showed, and Barnes, and Stillingfleet,
And Richardson, that bade our Lovelace be;
The little Elia thus in Newgate Street;
Thus to his Genevieve young S. T. C.
With thousands else that, wandering up and down,
Quaint, privileged, liked and reputed well,
Made the great School a part of London Town
Patent as Paul's and vital as Bow Bell:
    The old School nearing exile, day by day,
    To certain clay-lands somewhere Horsham way.

Mrs. Humphry Ward (1851–1920)   Although little read today, Mrs. Humphry Ward had an enormous following until her death here on March 24, 1920, and, indeed, was considered so persuasive a writer that President Theodore Roosevelt, encouraged by the British government, requested a series of articles from her on the efforts of the Allies in World War I. She was granted access to anything she wanted, toured the battlefields, and wrote *Letters to an American Friend, Towards the Goal,* and *Fields of Victory.* She first settled in London with her husband in 1881, at 61 Russell Square, when she joined the staff of *The Times;* in 1891 she and her husband moved to 25 Grosvenor Place, where she remained until her death.

George Moore (1852–1933)   Once heralded as an innovator in fiction, George Moore appeared in London early in the 1880s after an abortive attempt to paint in France; from 1881 to 1883 he lived at 17 Cecil Street (it ran south off the Strand approximately twelve doors east of Adam Street), where he worked on *A Modern Lover.* Before he returned to Ireland in 1901 to help plan the Abbey Theatre, he lived at 8 King's Bench Walk (1888–1896), where he wrote *Esther Waters,* and in the late 1890s at 92 Victoria Street, off Buckingham Palace Road. Here William Butler Yeats persuaded Moore to return to Dublin and help initiate what became the Irish literary renaissance. Disillusioned by the political situation and with what he considered the narrowness of the Irish mentality, Moore returned to London in 1911 and settled at 121 Ebury Street (marked with a plaque); here he was visited by Yeats, H. G. Wells, Arnold Bennett, George Bernard Shaw, and possibly Thomas Wolfe, who lived at Number 75 in 1930–1931 when he was working on *Of Time and the River.* Moore died here on January 21, 1933. The principal figure of *Esther Waters* was drawn from the wet nurse of the minor novelist and dramatist Gilbert Frankau, who passed his childhood at 32A Weymouth Street.

Oscar Wilde (1854–1900)   Possibly the major spokesman for the late-19th-century aesthetic movement in England was Oscar Wilde, whose first-known association with London occurred a year or two after he came down from Oxford, when he joined the St. Stephens Club on the Victoria Embankment at the outrageous membership cost of £42 a year. In 1876 he

took rooms at 13 Salisbury Street with Frank Miles; calling it Thames House, Wilde found it "untidy and unromantic" but stayed two years and held a daily 5:30 At-Home to which such people as the actresses Lillie Langtry and Ellen Terry frequently came. Wilde often visited with his mother at 1 Ovington Square. In 1878, forced into finding cheaper lodgings, Wilde ventured into Chelsea, to 1 Tite Street, a house known as Skeats House (because a Miss Elizabeth Skeats had lived there); Wilde immediately changed the name to Keats House. By this time he was well established in artistic and literary circles, was known for his extravagant dress and his wit, and had published *Poems* in 1881. He left Miles in the Tite Street house in December 1881 for an American lecture tour. Returning in April 1883, he took rooms at 9 Charles Street (now Carlos Place), Grosvenor Square, where a Mr. and Mrs. Davis kept lodgings "for single men of distinction"; his rooms on the top floor consisted of an oak-paneled sitting room with an adjacent small bedroom.

After a second trip to the United States and a provincial English lecture tour, Wilde married Constance Lloyd on May 29, 1884, at St. James's Church, Paddington. The marriage was one of opposites: she was as morally conventional as he was unconventional; Wilde, though, was quite lyrical about his

grave, slight, violet-eyed little Artemis, with great coils of heavy brown hair which make her flower-like head droop like a blossom, and wonderful ivory hands which drew music from the piano so sweet that the birds stop singing to listen to her.

They settled at 16 (now 34 and marked with a plaque) Tite Street, Chelsea; and even though they were by no means well off, they had the interior of the house redone by the artist Edward Godwin, with some help from James McNeill Whistler. Long before the craze for whiteness, Godwin painted the front door white, painted the hall with a high-gloss white, and covered the stairs in a white matting. "I have," wrote Wilde, "a dining room done in different shades of white, with white curtains embroidered in yellow silk: the effect is absolutely delightful, and the room is beautiful." The walls of his study were yellow, the woodwork was enameled in red, and he worked on a table which had belonged to Thomas Carlyle. It was the upstairs drawing room in which Whistler had a hand; he and Wilde had been the closest of friends, although there were frictions. Invited to Wilde's wedding, Whistler sent the telegram, "Am detained. Don't wait"; on another occasion, when Wilde, who was known to polish up Whistler's quips, said to him, "Ah, I wish I'd said that!" he retorted, "You will, Oscar, you will." But Whistler put aside the estrangement and painted dragons on the blue drawing-room ceiling and two peacock feathers set in the plaster; he also placed two of his etchings on the buttercup-yellow walls.

Wilde became editor of *The Lady's World* in 1887 and changed the name to *The Woman's World;* in 1888 he published *The Happy Prince and Other Tales.* He frequented the Crown in Charing Cross, the Albemarle Club at 13 Albemarle Street off Piccadilly, the Café Royal at 68 Regent Street, and Kettner's at 29 Romilly Street. *The Picture of Dorian*

Gray appeared in 1890, and both *Lord Arthur Savile's Crime and Other Stories* and *A House of Pomegranates* were published in 1891. For years Wilde had been enamored of the famous Lillie Langtry, and at one time he walked down Piccadilly daily to her Belgravia home carrying a single lily, which he said symbolized both the aesthetic movement and the woman. It was this that William Schwenck Gilbert satirizes through Reginald Bunthorne in *Patience:*

Though Philistines may jostle,
You will rank as an apostle
    In the high aesthetic band
If you walk down Piccadilly
With a poppy or a lily
    In your medieval hand.

It was inevitable that Wilde should turn to the theater, but he never wrote a play for the actress to whom he was so greatly attracted. *Lady Windermere's Fan* premiered in 1892 at St. James's Theatre, which stood at 23–24 King Street, and *Salomé* (written for Sarah Bernhardt and in French) was held back by the censor until 1893 for publication and was not produced until 1896 in Paris. *A Woman of No Importance* was produced in 1893; and in October of this year, ostensibly to get work done, Wilde took a ground-floor bedroom and communicating sitting room at 10 St. James's Place, a private hotel. After the production of *Lady Windermere's Fan,* Wilde was earning huge sums of money, and his life was being increasingly dominated by Lord Alfred Douglas, whom he had first met in 1891; the relationship between the two infuriated the 8th Marquess of Queensberry, Douglas's father and the originator of the rules of modern boxing, and to bring it to a close Queensberry left an inflammatory note for Wilde at the Albemarle Club. In the note he accused Wilde of sodomy; urged on by Lord Douglas, Wilde sued the "Screaming Scarlet Marquis" for criminal libel. Wilde's case collapsed on April 3, 1895, and he was then liable for prosecution for the offenses of which he had been made to appear guilty.

During the trial Wilde had rooms at the Cadogan Hotel, 75 Sloane Street; and on the day Queensberry was found not guilty, Wilde was arrested at the hotel, denied bail, and taken to Holloway Prison. Tried at the Sessions House, better known as the Old Bailey (on the site of the present Central Criminal Court), Wilde testified brilliantly, and the jury was unable to reach a verdict; he was released on bail of £2,500 pending a second hearing, which began on May 20. Unable to secure lodgings, he stayed at his mother's home at 146 Oakley Street, Chelsea, but life here was unbearable, and Wilde was invited to stay at the home of his friend Ada Leverson and her husband in Cornfield Gardens (so infamous was Wilde at this time that the Leversons had to obtain the consent of their servants before inviting him). The Tite Street house and its contents were sold for a pittance before the trial; production of Wilde's plays ceased; and his books were withdrawn from circulation. Friends implored him to flee to France, but he refused; as his brother said, "Oscar is an Irish gentleman; he will stay and face the music." Wilde's wife remained firmly in the background and, indeed, seemed to have no clear understanding of the charges against her hus-

band. The second trial began, and on May 25 Wilde was found guilty on six counts (only one of which he said had any foundation) and sentenced to "be imprisoned and kept to hard labour for two years." Transferred to the Reading Gaol from Pentonville on November 13, 1895, he stood at the Clapham Junction in a sharp autumnal rain, jeered at by a crowd. Wilde never returned to London.

A few other associations here with Wilde deserve mention. He frequently attended the Rhymers' Club, which met in a second-floor room of the Ye Olde Cheshire Cheese in Wine Office Court; he was often at Lillie Langtry's home at 18 Pont Street and wrote "The New Helen" for her. Finally, Marie Louise de la Ramée, better known as Ouida, had apartments in the Langham Hotel (now British Broadcasting Corporation property in Langham Place) where she presided over a kind of literary salon in the mid-1880's; Wilde was one of many in attendance.

Marie Corelli (1855–1924) Born Mary Mackay on Gloucester Terrace, Bayswater, in 1855, Marie Corelli (as she is better known) moved to Box Hill, Surrey, at a very young age. However, her father, after a stroke, returned with his family to 47 Longridge Road, Kensington, in 1883; she had been planning a musical career and began a series of concert appearances in 1884 but abandoned them suddenly to write. *A Romance of Two Worlds* and *Vendetta* appeared in 1886; *Thelma* (1887) attracted a wide audience. Following the successes of *Barabbas* in 1893 and *The Sorrows of Satan* in 1895, she left for Stratford-on-Avon in 1899.

Sir Arthur Wing Pinero (1855–1934) Arthur (later Sir Arthur) Wing Pinero was born on May 24, 1855, at 21 Dalby Terrace, Islington, not on Old Kent Road or the Seven Dials, as is often claimed; today this is a drab market and industrial area, but then, as Pinero recalls, "it was a pleasant enough locality." As a boy Pinero was sent to a school on Exmouth Street (Exmouth Market) in Clerkenwell, although he was removed at the age of ten when the family's financial situation deteriorated. He was then taken into his father's offices on South Square, off Gray's Inn Road, and on Prince Street (now Bedford Row), and when his father retired in 1870, he took a job as a clerk in a circulating library on Wigmore Street. However, following the family tradition, Pinero began law studies at Lincoln's Inn Fields; he also attended night classes at the Birkbeck Institute, where he became interested in elocution.

When his father died in 1874, Pinero gave up the law and became involved in the theater in Edinburgh. Two years later he acted in *Armadale* at the Globe Theatre and, in fact, gained considerable stature playing character roles. His first play, *£200 a Year,* was performed at the Globe for the benefit of Francis Henry Macklin in 1877, and in the next fifty-five years he wrote fifty-four plays of one sort or another. In 1883, after marrying the actress Myra Holme (Myra Emily Wood), Pinero lived at 66 St. John's Wood Road; here he would begin writing at teatime and was not to be disturbed until after breakfast the next morning. At one time he lived at 63 Hamilton Terrace, and *The Second Mrs. Tanqueray,* which established Pinero's eminence, premiered at St. James's Theatre (at 23–24 King Street until

1957) in 1893. In 1910 he moved to 115A Harley Street, a rose-colored brick Georgian house which was actually on Devonshire Street, and he remained here until sometime in the 1920s. Pinero died in the Marylebone Nursing Home after emergency surgery on November 23, 1934, and funeral services were held in the Marylebone parish church.

Sir Henry Rider Haggard (1856–1925)   After finishing school and spending more than five years in South Africa, Henry (later Sir Henry) Rider Haggard brought his family to London, where he read for the bar; he was called to the bar at Lincoln's Inn in 1884, but like many other literary figures he discovered that law was not for him. *Cetwayo and His White Neighbours* had been published in 1882, and *King Solomon's Mines* appeared three years later. Haggard lived at 69 Gunterstone Road in Hammersmith in 1885, and about the time *She* was published he moved to 13 King's Bench Walk. From the turn of the twentieth century on Haggard was involved in government commissions and traveled extensively on behalf of the Royal Colonial Institute, the Dominions Royal Commission, and the Empire Settlement Committee. He settled on 24 Redcliffe Square as a London address, and here he died on May 14, 1925.

Thomas Anstey Guthrie (1856–1934)   The humorist, dramatist, and satirical novelist F. Anstey was born Thomas Anstey Guthrie on August 8, 1856, at 7 St. George's Court, South Kensington, and his family moved when he was a child to 6 Phillimore Gardens. Educated at a private school in Surbiton and at King's College School before going up to Cambridge, he was called to the bar by the Middle Temple in 1880, but like many of the literary figures of the time he never practiced. In 1921 he took up residence at 24 Holland Park, where he lived until his death on March 10, 1934.

George Bernard Shaw (1856–1950)   In 1876, a year after his mother had left his father and come to London, George Bernard Shaw came to his mother's home at 13 Victoria Grove (now Netherton Grove), but life here was hardly more satisfactory than it had been in Ireland. He frequented art galleries, the British Museum (especially the Reading Room), and concert halls, and spent his first two years in rather desultory jobs. He began his first novel, *Immaturity* (not published until 1921 in the United States and 1930 in Great Britain), in 1879, the same year he began working for the Edison Telephone Company. In 1881 he moved (with his mother) to 37 Fitzroy Street, contracted smallpox, and completed an unsalable novel. After he had recuperated from smallpox, they moved to 36 Osnaburgh Street, where they lived until the spring of 1887; here he wrote *Cashel Byron's Profession* and became a member of the Fellowship of the New Life, which met at 17 Osnaburgh Street. A schism in this group resulted in the Fabian Society. Shaw became a polished orator and debater and with William Morris and Mrs. Annie Besant tried to lead the "Bloody Sunday" march (November 13, 1887) to Trafalgar Square; he had still not turned to the theater when he and his mother moved to 29 Fitzroy Square. The house is marked by a commemorative plaque ("From the coffers of his genius he enriched the world"), which also notes his service as a vestryman and borough councillor of St. Pancras

parish. It was here, so the story goes, that he turned Fitzroy Square into a ballet practice arena. Shaw wrote in *The Star* for February 21, 1890:

> I found Fitzroy Square, in which I live, deserted. It was a clear, dry cold night; and the carriage-way round the circular railing presented such a magnificent hippodrome that I could not resist trying to go just once round in Vincenti's fashion. It proved frightfully difficult. After my fourteenth fall I was picked up by a policeman. "What are you doing here?" he said, keeping fast hold of me. "I'bin watching you for the last five minutes." I explained, eloquently and enthusiastically. He hesitated a moment, and then said, "Would you mind holding my helmet while I have a try? It don't look so hard." Next moment his nose was buried in the macadam and his right knee was out through its torn garment. He got up bruised and bleeding, but resolute. "I never was beaten yet," he said, "and I won't be beaten now. It was my coat that tripped me." We both hung our coats on the railings, and went at it again. . . . [B]y four o'clock the policeman had just succeeded in getting round twice without a rest or a fall. . . . We were subsequently joined by an early postman and by a milkman, who unfortunately broke his leg. . . .

Shaw's first play, *Widowers' Houses*, was soundly denounced; *Mrs. Warren's Profession* was denied a license by the Lord Chamberlain, ostensibly because of a hint of incest; and the successful *Arms and the Man* opened at the Avenue Theatre on April 21, 1894, and ran until July. In September 1896 Shaw met Charlotte Frances Payne-Townshend at the home of Beatrice and Sidney Webb; a wealthy Irish woman who lived at 10 Adelphi Terrace, she undertook to do his secretarial work, and they were married on June 1, 1898, in the registry office on the Strand. At that time Shaw was ill from overwork, and Miss Payne-Townshend came to the Fitzroy Square home to nurse him; upset by the discomfort in which he was living, she proposed to move him to the country. Shaw, it is said, insisted on the marriage (unconsummated) so that she would not suffer from any scandal; after Shaw's recovery in the country, they returned to 10 Adelphi Terrace, where, among other things, he wrote *Man and Superman, Major Barbara, Androcles and the Lion,* and *Pygmalion*.

In 1906, after spending many years looking for a country home, he found the New Rectory in Ayot St. Lawrence but did not live in it permanently for many years. In October 1927 he and his wife moved from Adelphi Terrace to 4 Whitehall Court (where the Shell Mex Building is now), and here he wrote *The Adventures of the Black Girl in Her Search for God*. Shaw's wife had for years suffered from Paget's disease of bone, and her mind was affected before she died in September 1943. Shaw, during World War II, retired to his Ayot St. Lawrence home, where he died on November 2, 1950, at the age of ninety-four. It should be noted that Shaw places Eliza Doolittle under the portico of St. Paul's, Covent Garden, in the first act of *Pygmalion*.

George Gissing (1857–1903)   After being expelled from Owens College, Manchester, for stealing college funds to support a prostitute (Marianne Helen Harrison) and spending a short time in prison and a long time in the United States, George Gissing made his way back to England and lived with Marianne in dismal lodgings at 22 Colville Place, behind the Tottenham Court Road police station. They had but one room here; Gissing describes the residence in *The Private Papers of Henry Ryecroft*. In January 1879 Gissing married Marianne, and the couple moved to 70 Huntley Street. Gissing frequented the Reading Room of the British Museum, where he read classical literature, as Ryecroft does. He wrote for *The Cornhill Magazine* to support himself, while his wife "degenerated into a drunken virago"; they lived apart for a year or so before her death in a Lambert slum although the novelist sent her a regular allowance. In 1884 he moved to 7K Cornwall Terrace, Marylebone, where he lived until 1890. The Reardons' house in *New Grub Street* faithfully copies this house:

> It was undeniable that on a fine day one enjoyed extensive views. The green ridge from Hampstead to Highgate, with Primrose Hill and the foliage of Regent's Park in the foreground; the suburban spaces of St John's Wood, Maida Vale, Kilburn; Westminster Abbey and the Houses of Parliament, lying low by the side of the hidden river. . . .
>
> A sitting-room, a bedroom, a kitchen. But the kitchen was called dining-room, or even parlour at need; for the cooking range lent itself to concealment behind an ornamental screen, and the walls displayed pictures and bookcases, and a tiny scullery which lay apart sufficed for the coarser domestic operations. . . . Of necessity, Edwin Reardon used the front room as his study.

In 1891, soon after Marianne's death, Gissing entered into a second disastrous marriage with a serving girl, and in the same year *New Grub Street* appeared. He left London and returned only infrequently to visit Clara Elizabeth Collet, the Labor correspondent of the Board of Trade, at 36 Berkeley Road, Crouch End; much later, he entrusted the education of his two sons from this marriage to her if anything happened to him. He was also a member of the Omar Khayyám Club, which often gathered for meals at Pagani's Restaurant on Great Portland Street. Gissing died in Saint-Jean-de-Luz, France, on December 28, 1903. At one time he lived at 33 Oakley Gardens, Chelsea (marked with a plaque). Both *The Nether World* and *New Grub Street* contain extensive references to London.

Joseph Conrad (1857–1924) Józef Theodor Konrad Korzeniowski, born in Poland on December 3, 1857, became the naturalized British subject Joseph Conrad in 1886, but he had been in London briefly on and off beginning in 1878. On August 21, 1880, he boarded the 1,200-ton *Loch Etive*, bound for Sidney, as third mate; he was the youngest officer on board, and he describes the event in *Chance*. The next year, he sailed as second mate on the *Palestine*, a London barque of 425 tons: the ship was too small, the captain too old for his first command, and the pay too little. Again, the experience was used, the *Palestine* becoming the barque *Judea* in *Youth*:

> "The ship also was old. Her name was the *Judea*. Queer name, isn't it? . . . She had been laid up in Shadwell basin for ever so long. You may imagine her state. She was all rust, dust, grime—soot aloft, dirt on deck. To me it was like coming out of a palace into a ruined cottage. She was about 400 tons, had a primitive windlass, wooden latches to the doors, not a bit of brass about her, and a big square stern. . . .
>
> "We left London in ballast—sand ballast—to load a cargo of coal in a northern port [Newcastle] for Bangkok. . . ."

Conrad was probably back in London at the end of May 1889, awaiting his new command; he had lodgings in Bessborough Gardens, near Vauxhall Bridge, and began *Almayer's Folly* at this time. After a trip to the Congo, Conrad was very ill and spent almost two months in the German Hospital here, suffering from such severe gout that he was bedridden for six weeks before he recovered sufficiently to be sent to a Swiss hydropathic establishment. He took his second command on the *Torrens* and on its second voyage in 1893 met John Galsworthy.

Back in January 1894, Conrad settled at 17 Gillingham Street, off Vauxhall Bridge Road, where he had stayed from 1891 on; by this time his sea life was over. In June of that year he submitted *Almayer's Folly* to T. Fisher Unwin (26 Paternoster Square, but bombed out in World War II), who accepted it in August, and began *An Outcast of the Islands* in November. In March 1896 he married Jessie George. While the critical reception of his novels was extremely good, the reading public did not take to his works for another fifteen years. During this period one of Conrad's earliest friends, Galsworthy, often had Conrad and his family at his home at 14 Addison Road, just west of Holland Park, and the Conrads sometimes took over the house when Galsworthy was away. Indeed, Conrad's second son, John Alexander, was born here on August 2, 1906. In 1904 Conrad lived at 17 Gordon Place to be near his collaborator, Ford Madox Ford, and in November 1905 he and his family were at 32 St. Agnes Place when his eldest son, Borys, contracted scarlet fever and had to be put into a nursing home in Kensington Park Road.

Success came to Conrad in 1910 after *Lord Jim*, *Nostromo*, and *Under Western Eyes* appeared, and he eventually settled at Bishopsbourne. A favorite London restaurant of Conrad's was Overton's, at 5 St. James's Street; here, having ordered everything in advance, he told his future mother-in-law of his plans to marry her daughter, and here he and his bride dined on their wedding day. Conrad was also a member of the Athenaeum Club at Pall Mall and Waterloo Place.

Edith Nesbit (1858–1924) The author of *The Railway Children*, Edith Nesbit was born at 38 Lower Kennington Lane on August 19, 1958, but had little to do with London for some time following her father's death in 1862 until 1899, when Well Hall (gone) on Well Road became her home. Here she not only raised her own four children by Herbert Bland, and a number of his illegitimate children, but entertained such guests as H. G. Wells, G. K. Chesterton, and Frederick Rolfe as well as writing voluminously. Her fictional family, the Bastables, lived at Moat House, drawn from the moated Tudor house which belonged to William Roper and his wife, Margaret, Sir Thomas More's daughter. Three years after Bland's death in 1914, Edith Nesbit remarried, and although she and her new husband, Thomas Tucker, tried to maintain Well Hall as a guesthouse, they were forced to give it up in 1922.

Francis Thompson (1859–1907) Because of the nature of his life, specifying London associations with the poet Francis Thompson is a little like sweeping in all

London without bringing forth exact details. Schooled at Ushaw College, Ushaw, and then dropping out at Owens College, Manchester, after failing his examinations three times, Thompson resolved to make his living in London by writing. Almost immediately upon his arrival in November 1885, with little means of subsistence, he was attacked by neuralgia and other ills and resorted to opium for relief. Thompson went successively through every phase of poverty; he was forbidden entrance to the Guildhall Library because his clothes were ragged and filthy; he sold matches to theatergoers in Covent Garden and held their horses; and he slept in alleys and doorways, the theater porch, boxes and crates, and the church entrance in the garden. It was a churchwarden of St. Martin-in-the-Fields who tried to help Thompson, and surely this church is meant when he writes of

> . . . Jacob's ladder
> Pitched between Heaven and Charing Cross.

When he had the funds, he frequented the Pillars of Hercules, in Soho Square, built over an archway which leads to Manette Street.

In 1888 his first two poems were published by Wilfrid Meynell in his *Merry England*, but opium and privation had exacted a heavy toll. The Meynells convinced Thompson that hospitalization was the only hope of recovering and breaking his opium habit; afterward he stayed with the Premonstratensian monks at Storrington, Sussex, before returning to London. Thompson never had a home of his own here; rather he was such a frequent guest at the Meynells that he was more like a resident when they were living at 47 Palace Court, off Bayswater Road. Thompson babysat with the children and took them into the neighboring Kensington Gardens. He also stayed with the Meynells at 2A Granville Place, near Portman Square. He had never really been in good health, and by the summer of 1907, after his tuberculosis had become serious, he was persuaded to enter the Hospital of St. John and St. Elizabeth on Circus Road, St. John's Wood, where he died on November 13. He was buried in the Catholic cemetery at Kensal Green.

Jerome Klapka Jerome (1859–1927) When the colliery business in Walsall proved unsuccessful, Jerome Clapp Jerome brought his family to London, where he set up as an ironmonger in the East End; his son, Jerome Klapka Jerome, was sent to the Marylebone Grammar School until 1873, when he began to fend for himself. Not until 1889 is he specifically located in London; at that time, working on *The Idle Thoughts of an Idle Fellow* and *Three Men in a Boat*, he had lodgings in a block of flats at Chelsea Bridge and Ebury Bridge Roads, Chelsea Gardens. Here his top-floor drawing room overlooked the river and Battersea Park. Within a year he had moved into 33 Tavistock Place (gone) with George Wingrave (the George of *Three Men*) and finished both works. During his last years he lived somewhere in Belsize Park.

Sir Arthur Conan Doyle (1859–1930) Although Sir Arthur Conan Doyle came from a staunch Irish Catholic family living in Edinburgh, he had early contact with London, for his grandfather, John, the portrait painter and caricaturist, lived at 17 Cambridge Terrace in Hyde Park, and his uncle Richard, the illustrator for *Punch* and designer of its cover, had his studio on Finborough Road. Conan Doyle was probably first at his uncle's at Christmas 1874, when he spent three weeks sightseeing (the Crystal Palace, Madame Tussaud's, the Tower of London, St. Paul's Cathedral, and Westminster Abbey) and attending the theater, but the real London association did not begin until Doyle set up a medical practice in Southsea in 1882 and wrote his first Sherlock Holmes adventure, *A Study in Scarlet*. The author came up to discuss another Holmes adventure with Stoddart of *Lippincott's Magazine* and at dinner met Oscar Wilde for the first time; the outcome was *The Sign of Four*. Doyle was not an enthusiastic medical practitioner, and after a trip to Vienna to study he set up as an oculist in March 1890 at 2 Devonshire Place, just west of Harley Street; this was a fashionable location for physicians, but Doyle never had a patient. Living at 23 Montagu Place, he decided in June to abandon medicine.

From later in 1890 until 1903 Doyle lived at 12 Tennison Road, South Norwood, and by 1891 the Holmes stories were appearing regularly in *The Strand*. Doyle tired of Holmes and devised his death in 1893 in a life-and-death struggle with Professor Moriarty; the public, though, was not pleased, and Doyle was forced to bring Holmes back in another adventure. Doyle served as an unpaid senior physician in the field hospital at Bloemfontein, South Africa, during the Boer War, and on his return he stayed at Morley's Hotel, Trafalgar Square. His 1885 marriage to Louise Hawkins had been on difficult ground for some time, but divorce was out of the question not only because of religion but because of Louise's tuberculosis. "Ma'am" (Doyle's name for his mother) not only knew of the situation and approved of Doyle's relationship with Jean Leckie but was a driving force in his life until her death. From about 1900 on Doyle had a flat at 15 Buckingham Mansions, Victoria Street, where he usually stayed when in town. On August 9, 1902, at Buckingham Palace, Prince Edward knighted Doyle and "made me Deputy-Lieutenant of Surrey, whatever that means," as he wrote to his brother Innes.

At the Grand Hotel, Charing Cross, Doyle met George Edalji, a vicar's son who had spent three years in Lewes Prison for eight horrible mutilations of animals in Great Wyrley. Edalji had proclaimed his innocence, and when he was mysteriously released from prison (he was neither pardoned nor paroled, and his sentence was not up), he appealed to Doyle for help. They met at the hotel in January 1907, and when Sir Arthur discovered that Edalji suffered eight diopters of myopia (that is, he was able to see forms only in bright light), he was able to prove conclusively that, since the mutilations were nocturnal, Edalji was innocent. Louise Doyle died in 1906, and on September 18, 1907, Doyle married Jean Leckie at St. Margaret's Church, Westminster, with only relatives and one or two friends in attendance. The reception, in the Whitehall Rooms of the Hotel Métropole, included Sir James Matthew Barrie, Jerome K. Jerome, Bram Stoker, and George Edalji among the 250 guests.

It is the Sherlock Holmes stories that so concern London; it was in July 1877 or 1878 that Holmes came down from Oxford and "took rooms in Montague Street, just round the corner from the British Museum." This was Number 24, a four-story Georgian house later incorporated into the Lonsdale Hotel. He used the facilities of the Pharmaceutical Society on Great Russell Street to gain his knowledge of toxicology; Dr. Watson's office was at 6 Southampton Place (then Southampton Street). The *Post Office London Directory*, in fact, records a Dr. John Watson at this address. Watson had taken his medical degree at the University of London Medical School on Gower Street. Watson contemplates the economizing he must do (*A Study in Scarlet*) in one of London's then most expensive bars, the American Bar of the Criterion Hotel, on Piccadilly Circus. A plaque (stolen; only four holes in the stone remain) on the facade of the building noted that here Watson and young Stamford met and Stamford told the doctor of

> a fellow who is working at the chemical laboratory up at the hospital. He was bemoaning himself this morning because he could not get someone to go halves with him in some nice rooms which he had found, and which were too much for his purse. "By Jove!" I cried; "if he really wants someone to share the rooms and the expense, I am the very man for him. I should prefer having a partner to being alone."

After eating at the Holborn Restaurant (demolished) just across the street, Watson meets Holmes at St. Bartholomew's Hospital; a plaque recalls the meeting. The day after Holmes and Watson meet, they see "a suite in Baker Street which would suit us down to the ground." The accomodation, at 221B Baker Street,

> consisted of a couple of comfortable bedrooms and a single large airy sitting-room, cheerfully furnished, and illuminated by two broad windows. So desirable in every way were the apartments [that] we at once entered into possession.

LONDON A caped and helmeted bobby, wet pavements, and a London "particular" bring to life the atmosphere of Sir Arthur Conan Doyle's Sherlock Holmes and Dr. Watson.

(The Abbey National Building Society occupies the same site, but Number 109 still has its original facade, similar to the Holmes-Watson residence.)

Paddington Station is the departure point for many of their famous cases, such as *The Hound of the Baskervilles* and "Silver Blaze," and a number of concert halls, theaters, and music halls and Covent Garden come into the canon. Holmes recovers the Countess of Morcar's £20,000 blue carbuncle from the crop of a leftover Christmas goose at Covent Garden Market; halfway through *A Study in Scarlet* Holmes proposes a break:

> "And now for lunch, and then for Norman-Neruda. Her attack and her bowing are splendid, what's that little thing of Chopin's she plays so magnificently: Tra-la-la-lira-lira-lay."

Wilma Norman-Neruda (afterward, Lady Hallé) performed at St. James's Hall (demolished in 1904 for the Piccadilly Hotel), and in the midst of "The Redheaded League," Holmes proposes another "visit to St. James' Hall to hear the Spanish violinist Pablo Sarasate." Holmes visits the Haymarket Theatre (properly the Theatre Royal), the Albert Hall ("The Adventures of the Retired Colourman"), and Hengler's Circus ("The Case of the Veiled Lodger"), where the Palladium now stands.

Like many other Victorian figures, Holmes enjoys dining at the Café Royal (rebuilt 1923 and severely bombed in World War II), knows Claridge's Hotel, and enjoys the Grosvenor Hotel, the Charing Cross Hotel, the Midland Hotel, and the Northumberland Hotel (actually the Northumberland Arms and now called The Sherlock Holmes, at the corner of Northumberland Street, Strand, and Craven Passage). He also makes considerable use of the Thames, especially in the river chase of Jonathan Small:

> It was a little past seven before we reached Westminster Wharf, and found our launch awaiting us. Holmes eyed it critically.
> "Is there anything to mark it as a police boat?"
> "Yes; the green lamp at the side."
> "Then take it off."
> The small change was made, we stepped on board, and the ropes were cast off.

They "passed the City [as] the last rays of the sun were gilding the cross upon the summit of St. Paul's. It was twilight before . . . [they] reached the Tower." On finishing "The Case of the Dying Detective," Holmes comments: "When we have finished at the police station, I think that something nutritious at Simpson's would not be out of place." Simpson's Strand location is unchanged. One final note: the Whitbread-tied pub The Sherlock Holmes has been converted in part into a museum of Sherlockiana and has the reconstructed Baker Street sitting room (from the 1951 Festival of Britain Exhibition) on display.

A. E. Housman (1859–1936) Although he had been a brilliant student at Oxford, A. E. Housman failed his examinations, apparently as a by-product of unfulfilled homosexual love for a fellow student, and returned to Bromsgrove to study for the Civil Service examination. From 1882 to 1892 he worked as a higher-division clerk in the Patent Office in London and lodged with Moses John Jackson at 82 Talbot Road, Bayswater; during this time he worked on

Latin studies in the Reading Room of the British Museum at night and wrote a number of articles which eventually caught the eye of the academic community. About the time that Jackson went to India in 1887, Housman moved to 17 North Road, Highgate, and remained there until 1905, when he moved to 1 Yarborough Villas, Pinner, Middlesex; here he wrote most of *A Shropshire Lad*. He had already attracted considerable academic notice and in 1892 applied for the vacant chair of Latin and Greek at University College. The chair was to be divided at this time, and while Housman preferred the Latin chair, he stated his desire to be considered for the other if his preference went to someone else. It did not, and he retained the post until 1911, when he was successful in obtaining the Latin chair at Cambridge.

Kenneth Grahame (1859–1932) Orphaned at a young age and schooled by his grandmother in Oxford, Kenneth Grahame spent many holidays with his uncle John Grahame in Sussex Gardens, and when university training was financially impossible, he worked for his uncle Robert, a parliamentary agent with offices in Westminster. At this time he lived with his uncle at Draycott Lodge (gone), between King's Road and Fulham Road. One of Grahame's earliest discoveries was his love for Soho, and from 1876 on he made it a practice to eat there at least once a week; at dinner one night toward the end of his first year he met Frederick James Furnivall, founder of the Early English Text Society, and Grahame joined Furnivall's New Shakespeare Society in June 1877.

On January 1, 1879, Grahame began work as a clerk in the Bank of England, where he remained until ill health forced his retirement in 1908. For convenience he moved to a Threadneedle Street flat and enjoyed the National Gallery and Trafalgar Square, where as "Pastels" relates, he watched pigeons, people, and sidewalk artists. Around 1882 he moved to a top-floor flat at 65 Chelsea Gardens, with a superb view over the Thames and Battersea Park; he rode the ferry steamer, which ran between Chelsea Embankment and London Bridge, to and from work. On May 7, 1886, Grahame took part at the Grand Theatre in Islington in an unlicensed production by Furnivall of Percy Bysshe Shelley's *The Cenci*, in which he played Giacomo; in the audience were Robert Browning, George Bernard Shaw, James Russell Lowell, George Meredith, and Sir Percy and Lady Shelley. An interview with William Ernest Henley led to Grahame's contributing to the *National Observer*, of which Henley was editor, and the two men became close friends; Grahame was often at Henley's home and at the regularly scheduled Friday dinners at Verrey's Restaurant, 233 Regent Street, held for *Observer* contributors. Grahame, though, would not leave his position at the bank and rose to become secretary of the bank in 1898, at the age of thirty-nine. In the autumn of 1894 he and Thomas Greg, a barrister, took a joint lease on 5 Kensington Crescent, where he remained until his marriage.

Critically ill in 1899 from pneumonia and empyema, Grahame was nursed at home by his sister and spent hours writing "baby-talk" *billets-doux* to Elspeth Moulton, whom he had met in 1897. They were married in 1899 and took a long lease on 16 Phillimore Place (marked with a plaque) in Campden Hill. Their only child, Alastair, born prematurely in 1900, was "a sickly, physically handicapped, sensitive but not over-bright child," badly spoiled by his parents. *The Wind in the Willows* was first told to him as a series of bedtime stories. In 1903 Grahame was again critically ill, this time after being shot by a lunatic at the bank. Grahame and his family left London for Cookham Dean, Berkshire, in 1905.

Frederick Rolfe (1860–1913) A man guided by eccentricity and fantasy, Frederick Rolfe ("Baron Corvo") was born in the City at 42 Cheapside (rebuilt), on July 22, 1860; educated here, he left school at fourteen and became a pupil-teacher and an unattached Oxford student. Between 1900 and 1903, while working on *Hadrian the Seventh*, he lived at 69 Broadhurst Gardens, Hampstead, and about 1904 moved to 15 Cheniston Gardens. He left England for a holiday in Venice in 1908 and remained there until his death in 1913.

Sir James Matthew Barrie (1860–1937)

> I wrote and asked the editor if I should come to London, and he said no, so I went, laden with charges from my mother to walk in the middle of the street (they jump out at you as you are turning a corner), never to venture forth after sunset, and always to lock up everything (I who could never lock up anything, except my heart in company).

Against the advice of Frederick Greenwood, editor of *St. James's Gazette*, Scottish-born James (later Sir James) Matthew Barrie appeared in London in March 1885 and took his first lodgings somewhere on Great Windmill Street; Jerome K. Jerome, who knew Barrie at this time, said the lodgings were "in a turning out of Cavendish Square...." He moved from here to Guildford Street, and in 1887 and 1888 *When a Man's Single: A Tale of Literary Life* appeared serially in the *British Weekly*. In June 1888 he joined the Savage, a club with headquarters in Lancaster House (which stood on Savoy Street) before moving its premises to Adelphi Terrace in the 1890s; this is the Wigwam in *When a Man's Single*. Barrie had rooms in Furnival's Inn, which stood between Brooke Street and Leather Lane, on the north side of Holborn, when his first book, *Better Dead*, was published in November 1887 and was at 14 Old Quebec Street in 1889. *Auld Licht Idylls*, *A Window in Thrums*, and *My Lady Nicotine* were published in 1889 and 1890, and Barrie was beginning to think of the theater; in 1890 he moved to 15 Cavendish Street, where he remained while working on *The Little Minister*, his first long novel, and *Richard Savage*, his first full-length play.

Barrie moved again in 1893, to 14 Bryanston Street, and the next year was married in Kirriemuir, Scotland, to Mary Ansell, a young actress. They settled at 133 Gloucester Road, South Kensington, and he finished *Margaret Ogilvy*, a tribute to his mother. After completing the autobiographical *Sentimental Tommy* and *Tommy and Grizel*, Barrie never returned to the novel form except for the three variations on the Peter Pan theme. In 1897 he met Mrs. Sylvia Llewelyn Davies, the mother of five boys, who lived at 23 Campden Hill Square, and he adopted the children in all but name. It was one of these children who provided the dramatist with some copy for *Peter Pan*:

> "You'll be sick tomorrow, Jack, if you eat any more chocolates," Sylvia remarked severely to her small son

during a picnic at which the dramatist was one of the guests.

"I shall be sick tonight," replied the child laconically, helping himself to another sweetmeat.

So delighted was Barrie at this epigram that he offered the child a royalty of a halfpenny a performance for the copyright.

Indeed, it was for these children that Barrie's Peter Pan stories were created. In 1902, when *The Little White Bird* appeared, he and his wife moved to an old Georgian brick house, Leinster Corner, on Bayswater Road, off Lancaster Gate and facing Kensington Gardens; here he would walk his dog (variously described as Porthos, a St. Bernard, and Luath, a Newfoundland) in the gardens and would buy toys for the dog in a nearby toy store (carefully stating they were for a child).

The Admirable Crichton ran for 328 performances at the Duke of York's Theatre on St. Martin's Lane before being replaced by *Little Mary* in September 1903. The same year Barrie and his wife moved to 100 Bayswater Road (marked by a plaque), where he wrote the immortal *Peter Pan;* produced at the Duke of York's Theatre on December 27, 1904, the play was not believed ready for production by Charles Frohman and Sir Herbert Beerbohm Tree. Barrie, however, was confident; attendance was sparse at first, but then children of all ages came in droves until the play closed in April, only to be revived every Christmas thereafter. Also written in the Bayswater Road house were *Alice-Sit-by-the-Fire* and *What Every Woman Knows*. Barrie's marriage, which had never been solid, fell apart, and in 1908 he lived at 17 Stratton Street, off Piccadilly, before moving to 1–3 Robert Street (marked by a plaque) after his October 1909 divorce. His rooms here were on the top floor, with windows to the river.

In May 1912 a bronze of Peter Pan, sculpted by Sir George Frampton and commissioned by Barrie, appeared in Kensington Gardens; Barrie put it there specifically for children to play around, and the base was ordered to be a "carven tree trunk." In 1929 he made out his will so that the Hospital for Sick Children on Great Ormond Street would receive all the proceeds of *Peter Pan*, and the benefit to the hospital has been great: both a Barrie Wing and a Peter Pan Ward have been constructed from the funds. Sir James died on June 19, 1937, and was buried in Kirriemuir, Scotland.

Eden Phillpotts (1862–1960)   Noted especially for his novels of the Devonshire countryside, the novelist and poet Eden Phillpotts had only a short association with London around 1900, when he lived for a time at 4 Portugal Street.

William Wymark Jacobs (1863–1943) William Wymark Jacobs is rarely remembered today by name, but his short stories, especially "The Monkey's Paw," are still read. He was born in Wapping on September 8, 1863, into a poor family and remembered the nagging financial problems that beset his family. The elder Jacobs was a wharfinger, and the family's early home was on a Thames wharf; educated in a private school in the City, he imbibed a great deal of the dockside atmosphere which later appeared in his works. He attended Birkbeck College before joining the Civil Service in 1879; he remained in the service for twenty years while he built up a literary reputa-

tion. In the 1930s he lived at 15A Gloucester Gate, in Regent's Park West, and from 1937 until his death on September 1, 1943, he lived at Elm Tree Road Mansions, on Elm Tree Road in St. John's Wood.

Sir Anthony Hope Hawkins (1863–1933)   Sir Anthony Hope Hawkins, far better known as Anthony Hope, author of *The Prisoner of Zenda*, was born on February 9, 1863, in Clapton, where his father, the Rev. Edwards Comerford Hawkins, was headmaster of St. John's Foundation School for the Sons of Poor Clergy. In the 1880s he was at 1 Brick Court, just off Middle Temple Lane, and after being called to the bar by the Middle Temple in 1887, he again resided with his father, who then held the living of St. Bride's Church, Fleet Street. His law career was most successful, but his literary interests came to dominate his life when he worked out the plot of *The Prisoner of Zenda*. Published in April 1894, it was instantly acclaimed, and Hope left the legal profession. There followed many novels, none quite as successful as *The Prisoner*, which was dramatized and produced at St. James's Theatre on King Street (where Numbers 23–24 now stand) in January 1896. Following his 1903 marriage to Elizabeth Sheldon, Hope resided at 41 Russell Square, where the couple remained until around 1917; ill health forced him to move to Walton-on-the-Hill and to exchange his large town residence for a smaller one. Later he took a lease on 14 Gower Street.

Rudyard Kipling (1865–1936)   Even though Rudyard Kipling knew the Fulham area of London from 1872 to 1882 as a schoolboy, it was not until after he had published *Departmental Ditties, Plain Tales from the Hills*, and six volumes of short stories in India that he returned to England and London in 1889. He stayed at first with the family of his uncle by marriage, Sir Edward Burne-Jones, at the Grange (gone), North End Road, where as a child he had listened to William Morris ("Uncle Topsy") tell stories about the Vikings and had met Robert Browning. Soon, however, he took "an eyrie from which to survey London," rooms on the fifth floor of Embankment Chambers, at the foot of Villiers Street (Number 43). The building is now called Kipling House and is marked with a plaque. *Something of Myself* relates:

> My rooms were above an establishment of Harris the Sausage King, who, for tuppence, gave as much sausage and mash as would carry one from breakfast to dinner when one dined with nice people who did not eat sausage for a living.

In *The Light That Failed* Dick Heldar takes rooms "overlooking the Thames" near Charing Cross. Lunches were often spent with Sidney Row, editor of *St. James's Gazette*, at Sweeting's Restaurant on Fleet Street, and from March 1890 on Kipling and William Ernest Henley dined at Sherry's on Regent Street. Kipling's parents arrived back in England from Lahore (where John Lockwood Kipling had been curator of the museum) and lived at 29 Wynnstay Gardens before settling nearby at 101 Earl's Court Road.

Kipling, in the meantime, met Charles Wolcott Balestier, with whom he wrote *The Naulahka* in 1892 after he married Balestier's sister Caroline by special license on January 18 at All Souls Church on Langham Place; there were only five in the congregation, including Henry James, who gave the bride away. Immediately following the ceremony the new bride rushed off to nurse her mother, who was one of many stricken at the time with influenza. Kipling and his wife were reunited two days later at Brown's Hotel on Dover Street (which has a Kipling Room to commemorate his many visits) and sailed for the United States on the *Teutonic*. They settled in Brattleboro, Vermont, but it was not a pleasant experience, and they returned to England in September 1896. Settling in Rottingdean, Kipling was back in London frequently, especially after war had been declared and his son John (killed in action in 1915) had enlisted; he lunched regularly at the Athenaeum, at the corner of Pall Mall and Waterloo Place. For twenty years Kipling had suffered with acute pain and hemorrhaging from an undiagnosed duodenal ulcer. He became seriously ill on January 12, 1936, and was taken to the Middlesex Hospital, where emergency surgery was performed. He died on January 18, and his ashes were buried in the Poets' Corner of Westminster Abbey on January 23.

William Butler Yeats (1865–1939)   Acclaimed by T. S. Eliot as "the greatest poet of our time—certainly the greatest in this language, and so far as I am able to judge, in any language," William Butler Yeats was brought to London two years after his birth when his barrister father came to study art and paint portraits. The family's first home was at 23 Fitzroy Road (marked with a plaque), and here he spent the next seven years, although they were interspersed with frequent trips to his mother's home in Sligo. In 1874 John Butler Yeats moved his family to 14 Edith Villas (Edith Road), where the poet recalled later that he used to sail a model boat, *The Rose*, in the Round Pond in Kensington Gardens; two years later the family moved to Chiswick, to 8 Woodstock Road, a Norman Shaw house. Yeats attended the Godolphin School in Hammersmith until 1880, when the family returned to Ireland partly for financial reasons. The Yeats family were again in Chiswick after 1888, at 3 Blenheim Road; "The house," Yeats wrote, "is fine and roomy . . . everything is a little idyllic." The elder Yeats and his wife again came to London in 1887, and their son joined them at 58 Eardley Crescent after *Mosada* had been published. It was here at the end of the summer that Yeats's mother had two strokes, the first of which seriously affected her mind. Yeats was constantly back and forth to Ireland, and his numerous residences read like a map of London.

Yeats met William Ernest Henley, then editor of the *Scots Observer* (later the *National Observer*), at his home in Chiswick and spent many Sunday evenings there and at 1 Great College Street, Westminster, when Henley moved there; at Henley's homes he met Kenneth Grahame, Oscar Wilde, and George Wyndham. Yeats was one who did not reject Wilde after his arrest and, indeed, visited him at his mother's Oakley Street house before the trial. In 1895 Yeats, a founding member of the Rhymers' Club, which met in an upper room of Ye Olde Cheshire Cheese in Wine Office Court, moved away from his family to Fountain Court (in the Temple) and then to 18 (now 5) Woburn Walk, where he had "two rooms in one of the little old houses in Woburn Buildings, a stone-flagged alley . . . running eastward from . . . Woburn Place." Here he lived with his mistress, Olivia Shakespear ("Diana

Vernon") until 1917. Yeats was often at Augusta, Lady Gregory's apartment in Queen Anne's Mansions, Queen Anne's Gate, talking of plays and the theater. He continued to spend at least half his time in London, even during the founding of the Irish Literary Theatre; John Masefield was one of Yeats's Monday-evening visitors and met John Millington Synge here on one of those occasions. Masefield called the apartment "the most interesting room in London at that time" and said:

> After 1904–05, [Yeats] added to the room a big dark-blue lectern, on which his Kelmscott Chaucer stood, between enormous candles in big blue wooden sconces. These candles, when new, stood four feet high, and were as thick as a skip's oar.

After Yeats left for his 1903–1904 American lecture tour, he was not to return to London for any long period until the winter of 1912–1913. Ezra Pound, whom he had met many years earlier at the home of Olivia Shakespear (12 Brunswick Gardens), made life tolerable for Yeats in 1912–1913, when he was suffering from eye problems, frequent severe headaches, and a digestive disorder which reduced him to a milk diet. Pound read to him and taught him to fence. Yeats married Georgie Hyde-Lees at the Harrow Road registry office on October 20, 1917, and Pound was their best man; Yeats wrote to Lady Gregory:

> I wish you could see Woburn Buildings now—nothing changed in plan but little touches here and there, and my own bedroom (the old bathroom), with furniture of unpainted unpolished wood such as for years I have wished for. Then there is a dinner service of great purple plates for meat, and various earthenware bowls for other purposes. Then too all is very clean.

The Yeatses gave up the house here, preparatory to going to Ireland, but spent a few months at Oxford first. For a short time after the 1919 United States tour, they stayed at Ezra Pound's flat at 10 Kensington Church Walk, but Yeats was then not in London for any length of time until the summer of 1935, when he stayed at 17 Lancaster Gardens. Yeats died in Roquebrune, France, on January 28, 1939, but the outbreak of World War II postponed his burial in Ireland until 1948. Memorial services were held at St. Martin-in-the-Fields in 1939.

Beatrix Potter (1866–1943)   The author of delightful children's stories, Beatrix Potter was born at 2 Bolton Gardens, Kensington, on July 28, 1866; her father, a barrister who never practiced, was a North Country man of considerable property, and her mother had inherited money from Lancashire cotton fortunes. The house where Miss Potter spent the first thirty-nine years of her life is gone; the Bousefield Primary School stands on the site. She did not attend any school and was rigidly controlled by her parents; only occasional summer trips broke the regularity of her otherwise dull and conventional environment. After she became interested in the countryside on a Lake District holiday, she and her governess smuggled pet rabbits and all manner of creatures into the London nursery, where Miss Potter spent hours drawing and studying them. *The Tale of Peter Rabbit* was written here to amuse the sick child of a former governess. Finding a publisher for the tale was no easy task (Miss Potter first had the book printed privately), but eventually she came to Frederick Warne

& Co., 15 Bedford Street, Covent Garden. The association was personal, as well, and against her parents' wishes she became engaged to Norman Warne, the publisher's son, in 1905; he died a few months after their engagement, and Miss Potter took the opportunity to break from her parents and moved to Near Sawrey, Lancashire, where she had bought a farm.

H. G. Wells (1866–1946) After struggling to free himself from two inappropriate apprenticeships and gaining a measure of academic respectability as a pupil-teacher in Midhurst, H. G. Wells in 1884 received a studentship and maintenance grant to attend the Normal School of Science (later Royal College), in South Kensington, where during his first year he studied under Thomas Henry Huxley. He took rooms in Westbourne Grove in a house without a bathroom; a cousin who visited him was so appalled by his living conditions that he took Wells off to his two aunts, who let rooms in their house at 181 Euston Road. Wells's early feelings toward London are described in *Tono-Bungay:*

> I find myself with a certain comprehensive perception of London, complex indeed, incurably indistinct in places and yet in some way a whole that began with my first visit and is still being mellowed and enriched.

He remained here throughout his student days. His first year under Huxley was enormously successful (he was one of three in Huxley's class to obtain a first-class pass at the end of the year), but his second and third years were a catastrophe. Spending more time in the library than in the laboratory, he failed his third-year examination. Again, *Tono-Bungay* relates the event:

> So one day I found myself sitting in a mood of considerable astonishment in Kensington Gardens, reflecting on a recent heated interview with the school Registrar in which I had displayed more spirit than sense. I was astonished chiefly at my stupendous falling away from all the militant ideals of unflinching study I had brought up from Wimblehurst. I had displayed myself, as the Registrar put it, "an unmitigated rotter."

As a result, the best Wells could do was take up "an ill-paid assistantship in some provincial organized Science School or grammar school," and this he did at the Holt Academy in Wrexham, Denbighshire, Wales.

After a disastrous attempt at teaching and a serious illness, he returned to London virtually penniless in June 1888, determined to "make his way"; he first took part of an attic room on Theobalds Road but soon moved in again with his aunts, who had moved to 12 Fitzroy Road. In May 1889 the household moved to a larger house, Number 46 on the same road, where Wells remained until his marriage. By 1890 he had secured his bachelor of science degree with a first class in zoology and a second in geology and in 1891 became a full-time tutor at University Tutorial College; leasing 28 Maldon Road, Wandsworth, "a solid eight-roomed corner house," in October, he married his cousin Isabel Mary Wells on October 31, 1891, at the Wandsworth parish church. The marriage was a failure, and Wells was unfaithful within a few months. Prompted by rather severe hemorrhaging in May 1893, Wells gave up his tutorial post and his marriage when he ran off with Amy Catherine Robbins (the original of the protagonist of *Ann Veronica*), one of his students at the college. When they returned to London in 1894, they came to 7 Mornington Place, but because the landlady was intrusive, they moved around the corner in March to 12 Mornington Terrace. The divorce from Isabel came through in January 1895, and Wells and Jane (as she eventually was called) were married in October. Wells had been successful with a number of short stories by this time, and *The Time Machine* was published in 1895.

Wells and his wife left London in 1896; he was, however, frequently in the city and met George Gissing, for example, at a dinner meeting of the Omar Khayyám Club at Frascati's that year. In 1901 he received an invitation to join the Fabians and to be available for dinners and meetings took accommodations at 6 Clement's Inn, just north of St. Clement Danes Church on the Strand. A group of Fabians calling themselves the "Co-efficients" (including Bertrand Russell, Beatrice and Sidney Webb, Wells, and Richard Burdon Haldane) met at the Ship Tavern in Whitehall and at St. Ermin's Hotel on Caxton Street. In May 1909 Wells took 17 Church Row in Hampstead for Jane and their two sons, and he stayed here as well when he was not in Woldingham, Surrey, with Amber Reeves when she was having their child. (Wells also had a second illegitimate son, Anthony, by Rebecca West.) It was here that he worked on *The History of Mr Polly, The New Machiavelli,* and *Marriage.*

In May 1913 Wells took quarters at 52 St. James's Court, Westminster, and in the late 1920s he gave up his house in Dunmow and afterward had a string of London addresses (often more than one at the same time). One of these was a flat, Number 120, at 4 Whitehall Court; in 1928 and 1929 he lived in St. Ermin's Hotel. In the autumn of 1928 Wells took a modern flat (Number 47) in Chiltern Court, an ornate building on Marylebone Road, just east of Baker Street; here Charlie Chaplin visited him when the actor was working on *City Lights* in 1930. He had broken with Odette Kuen by this time and now wanted "Moura" (Marie von Benckendorf, then Baroness Budberg) to marry him; she, though, refused to give up her title and independence for his "sexual annuity," and they maintained separate homes. Wells wrote, "She will stay with me, eat with me, sleep with me. . . . But she will not marry me"; Wells had to make do with a "symbolic wedding" at the Quo Vadis in Soho.

In 1936 Wells took 13 Hanover Terrace, a Regency house (marked with a plaque) overlooking Regent's Park which had been the home of Alfred Noyes in the 1920s and 1930s; Wells descended on Noyes on the Isle of Wight by plane to discuss the lease. He stayed here throughout World War II, stubbornly refusing to leave London even when the blitz raged around him and the door to the house was blown in. Next door in the garden of an empty house was "that bloody sycamore . . . a complete repudiation of any belief in any intelligent god." For *The Countryman* he wrote:

> Like most of my erstwhile neighbours . . . next-door has gone away, but he retains his lease . . . [and] this hoggish arboreal monster. . . . Every day when I go out to look at my garden I shake my fist at it and wish for the gift of the evil eye; every day it grows visibly larger,

ignoring my hatred. . . . This tree of mud, this dirty, ugly witless, self protecting tree. . . .

Wells had himself photographed shaking his fist at the tree. In the spring of 1941, he had George Orwell (Eric Blair) here for their first meeting, and in this house he wrote his last work, *Mind at the End of Its Tether.* Wells died here on August 13, 1946; J. B. Priestley gave the address at the services in Golders Green, and his sons Gip Wells and Anthony West took the ashes to the Isle of Wight and scattered them over the sea.

There are a myriad of London associations with Wells's novels, although they are generally not as specific as one might wish; furthermore, Wells makes up names as he goes (for example, Jules Restaurant on Jermyn Street in *Joan and Peter* may be Rules Restaurant, 35 Maiden Lane, on the Strand). *The Invisible Man* makes use of Great Portland Street where Griffin lodges; Bedford Street, where the invisible man knocks down a passerby; Oxford Street, where the invisible man makes contact with, among others, the man with the basket of soda-water siphons, a Salvation Army band, and two street urchins (who pursue his footsteps); and Drury Lane, where Griffin enters a theatrical costume establishment.

Lionel Johnson (1867–1902) Lionel Johnson came directly to London from Oxford in 1890 and took lodgings at 20 Fitzroy Square; in October 1895 he moved to 7 Gray's Inn Square, and a few years later to New Square, Lincoln's Inn. His health, never especially good, was further undermined by his intemperance and late-night work; in late September 1902 he fell on Fleet Street, fractured his skull, and died on Octobeer 4 in St. Bartholomew's Hospital. Johnson was buried in Kensal Green Cemetery.

Enoch Arnold Bennett (1867–1931) (Enoch) Arnold Bennett came to London in March 1889, when he took up a junior post as a solicitor's clerk with the firm of Le Brasseur & Oakley, in New Court, Lincoln's Inn Fields, a red-brick structure just behind the Royal Courts of Justice on the Strand. The early experiences of Edward Larch in *A Man from the North* are Bennett's, and New Court and Lincoln's Inn Fields become New Sergeant's Inn:

> New Serjeant's Court was a large modern building of very red brick with terra-cotta facings, eight storeys high. . . . In the centre of the court was an oval patch of brown earth, with a few trees . . . struggling towards sunlight. . . . Round this plantation ran an immaculate roadway of wooden blocks, flanked by an equally immaculate asphalt footpath.

Bennett first lived at 46 Alexandra Road in Hornsey and then on Raphael Street, Knightsbridge, before becoming a paying guest at the home of Frederick Marriott's family at 6 Victoria Grove (now Netherton Grove) in the spring of 1891. Bennett abandoned the clerkship and its attendant tedium and on January 1, 1894, became assistant editor of the weekly journal *Woman* (90 Shaftesbury Avenue) by contributing £300 toward the firm's capital. He worked a little more than half time at this task and became editor of the journal in 1896; in 1897 *Woman* moved its offices to 11 Fetter Lane. At the end of October 1897, he took a three-year lease on 9 Fulham Park Gardens. Here he kept the clock set exactly one quarter hour

fast as "a mark of . . . scorn for most people's casual attitude to time-keeping"; another quirk was that he ate rice pudding at almost every meal. He began on *Anna of the Five Towns* and *The Grand Babylon Hotel* here.

Resigning from *Woman* in 1900, Bennett joined his parents in Hockliffe until his father's death. He then moved to 7 Halsey House, Red Lion Square, for a short time before going on to France in 1903; there in 1907 he married Marie Marguerite Soulié, a French actress. In 1912, when he was well established financially, they returned and stayed at 14 St. Simon's Road, Putney. With the outbreak of World War I, Bennett involved himself in the war effort, and he and his wife took 12B St. George Street, Hanover Square, in 1919; during the last months of the war Marguerite Bennett lived at 53 Oxford Street, and her husband stayed at the Royal Yacht Club, 80 Piccadilly; marital trouble had begun years earlier. They returned briefly to the St. George Street house before Bennett left his wife and his home in 1921; he moved to 75 Cadogan Square, just west of Sloane Street, where he remained until 1930.

The year after separating from his wife, Bennett fell in love with an English actress, Dorothy Cheston, by whom he had a daughter, Cheston Bennett, in 1926. In November 1930 he took a modern apartment (Number 97) in Chiltern Court, on Marylebone Road, and went abroad at the end of the year. He was ill with what was diagnosed as influenza when he returned in January 1931 but, in fact, was found in February to be suffering from typhoid fever, and he died on March 27. The borough council, for the last time, spread straw on the road to deaden noises for an ill person; on this occasion because it rained and everything became slippery, after midnight a milk dray skidded and overturned, crashing milk churns all over. *Imperial Palace,* written in 1930, pictures the Savoy Hotel:

> The great front-hall was well lighted; but the lamps were islands in the vast dusky spaces. . . . Behind the long counters to the right of the double revolving doors at the main entrance shone the two illuminated signs, "Reception" and "Enquiries," always at the same strength day and night. . . . The grill-room, which gave on a broad corridor opposite the counters, had several lights; in theory it opened for breakfasts at 6 A.M., but in fact it was never closed, nor its kitchen closed.

John Galsworthy (1867–1933) The Nobel Prize winner John Galsworthy was born into a solicitor's family which had made its wealth in 19th-century land speculation; they led a comfortable life in Kingston Hill before moving to Kensington in 1886, the year he went up to Oxford. In partnership with two other men, his father bought land in Regent's Park and built a row of ten houses (now called Cambridge Gate) in which the Galsworthy family settled (at Number 8) in 1887, and Galsworthy continued to use the family house until his marriage in 1905. After obtaining a second class in jurisprudence at Oxford in 1889, Galsworthy was called to the bar by Lincoln's Inn in 1890 and for the next four years had chambers at 5 Stone Buildings, Chancery Lane. In 1894 Galsworthy moved his chambers to 3 Paper Buildings, King's Bench Walk, and for some time shared rooms with G. H. Harris at 3 Palace Street; he also maintained a small flat in St. Margaret's Mansions, Victoria Street.

By this time Galsworthy had formed a distaste for the law and had begun to write; he took 2 Cedar Studios, Glebe Place, off King's Road, in 1894 to this end. He actually gave up his law offices around 1896, although he was officially their tenant until 1900; he also had three more residences (besides his family's home) between this date and his marriage: 4 Lawrence Mansions, on the Chelsea Embankment, 10 Tor Gardens, off Campden Hill Road, and 16A Aubrey Walk, in Campden Hill. *From the Four Winds* appeared in 1897 under the name of John Sinjohn, and the publication of *Jocelyn* was settled with Gerald Duckworth over dinner at the Junior Carlton Club, the setting of most of that story.

On September 23, 1905, Galsworthy married Ada Cooper Galsworthy, the divorced wife of his first cousin, at St. George's Church on St. George Street, Hanover Square. They took a lease on 14 Addison Road, where Galsworthy wrote his first play, *The Silver Box* (originally titled *The Cigarette Box*), and saw *The Man of Property* through the press. Both were highly successful, and Galsworthy's position was secure. *Fraternity, Strife, Justice,* and *The Patrician* at least in part, were also written here. He traveled extensively in these years and in 1912 took a flat at 1 Adelphi Terrace, where Arnold Bennett and his wife were dinner guests; the acquisition of a house in Manaton kept Galsworthy out of London for longer periods of time, but when back he would always find time to eat at Simpson's and Romano's, two of his favorite restaurants.

Returning from work in a French hospital in the spring of 1917, Galsworthy and his wife began to look for a new town house and stayed at 1–3 Robert Street. The telegram offering Galsworthy a knighthood was sent here in December 1917, when the Galsworthys were away; as soon as possible, Galsworthy sent a wire declining the honor and, though concerned because the wire was sent late, was confident that the silence would not be perceived as consent. However, it was, and the knighthood was announced; Galsworthy insisted on a cancellation of the honor and got it. On September 27, 1918, Galsworthy took possession of Grove Lodge (marked with a plaque), on Admiral's Walk off Hampstead Grove. Among Galsworthy's many visitors here were John Masefield, Sir James Matthew Barrie, Hugh Walpole, and Arnold Bennett. In May 1922 *The Forsyte Saga,* written largely in the ground-floor study here, appeared as an entity, and ten years later his "distinguished art of narration which takes its highest form in *The Forsyte Saga*" brought him the Nobel Prize for Literature. Galsworthy died here on January 31, 1933, and memorial services were held in Westminster Abbey on February 9; the Dean of Westminster refused to place Galsworthy's ashes here, and thus Galsworthy's own wish was complied with:

Scatter my ashes!
  Let them be free to the air,
  Soaked in the sunlight and rain,
  Scatter, with never a care
  Whether you find them again.
  Let them be grey in the dawn,
  Bright if the noontime be bright,
  And when night's curtain is drawn
  Starry and dark with the night.
  Let the birds find them and take
  Lime for their nests, and the beast,
  Nibbling the grizzled grass, make
  Merry with salt to his feast.
Scatter my ashes!
  Hereby I make it a trust;
  I in no grave be confined,
  Mingle my dust with the dust,
  Give me in fee to the wind!
              Scatter my ashes!

Galsworthy's ashes were scattered from the top of Bury Hill on March 28.

George William Russell (1867–1935) George William Russell, the Irish poet, painter, and mystic who wrote as Æ, spent almost his entire life in Ireland although he spoke at Albert Hall in London on November 1, 1913, to protest the arrest of James Larkin for sedition and to berate the position of employers in the Dublin labor disputes. After his wife's death in 1932 Russell came to London and lived at 41 Sussex Gardens in 1933 and 1934; suffering from cancer, he moved that year to 1 Brunswick Square, off Coram Street. Æ died in Bournemouth on July 17, 1935.

Hilaire Belloc (1870–1953) In September 1870, two months after his birth, the part-French Hilaire Belloc was brought to the home of his maternal grandmother at 17 Wimpole Street. He and his mother were here only a short time before returning to France, but in August 1871 the Belloc family inherited 11 Great College Street from Josiah Parkes, and Belloc's mother received the sum of £20,000. Belloc, his mother, and his sister moved into the house in December, while his father, a French barrister, remained in France, where he died in 1872. As a child Belloc attended the Church of Notre Dame de France just off Leicester Square and had his first

LONDON The 17th-century Grove Lodge on Admiral's Walk in Hampstead, which was once inhabited by John Constable, was the home of John Galsworthy from 1918 until his death in 1933; his ground-floor study, which looked out on the garden, can be seen from Windmill Hill at the back of the house.

schooling with a Mrs. Shiel on Great College Street. Belloc's mother lost almost her entire inheritance when she gave large sums to a lodger who worked on the London Stock Exchange; as a consequence, she had to let the London house in November 1878. Meanwhile, she took her family to Slindon, where her aged mother lived. From 1879 to 1889 the family resettled in London, but only vague addresses are known: somewhere in Hampstead where Belloc attended a school on Heath Brow, somewhere in Bloomsbury in 1888 and 1889, and on Brompton Square after June 1889.

After marrying Elodie Hogan, Belloc took a lease on 104 Cheyne Walk (marked with a plaque) in the winter of 1900. Only a short distance from the Battersea Bridge, the three-story house of brick washed with plaster had a sitting room with windows looking to the great warehouses on the south bank or up the Thames to Putney; here Belloc had the first telephone (1724 Kensington) installed on the street. He frequented the Mont Blanc Restaurant (which stood at 16 Gerrard Street) and met G. K. Chesterton in the winter of 1900—a memorable evening, Belloc declared, for their conversation was held over bottles of Moulin à Vent. Belloc had already published *Verses and Sonnets* and *The Bad Child's Book of Beasts* and was hard at work on other pieces: *Robespierre, The Path to Rome,* and *Emmanuel Burden, Merchant* stand out. Granted a certificate of naturalization in April 1902, he decided to read for the bar and began to take his evening meals at Gray's Inn. When examination time came, Belloc presented himself, took one look at the examination papers, and left. He was so seriously ill in January 1905 with a pleuropneumonia that the Last Sacrament was given.

Belloc decided to seek adoption as a parliamentary candidate and stood for Salford in 1905; he was returned as the Liberal Member in the 1906 landslide. After the election he gave up the Chelsea house and took his family to Shipley but retained a tiny flat on Victoria Street where he could stay when Parliament was in session. He later shared a flat at 6 Lord North Street in Westminster with Maurice Baring to be closer to Parliament. Belloc was returned in the 1910 election, but he resigned his seat later that year and retired to Sussex. In 1913 he frequently came to London, staying in lodgings on Wellington Square and dining at the Café Monico (if he wanted Barsac and oysters), Prince's Grill (if he wanted good marrow bone), or Rules, the Café Royal, Overton's, Gow's, and Romano's.

It was some years after his wife's death in 1914 before Belloc was interested in society again, and he had also thrown himself into the war effort. He was, however, elected to the very exclusive Sussex Club, the Literary Society, and the Reform Club and was an original member of the Saintsbury Club, and these obligations brought him to London frequently. The first dinner of the Saintsbury Club was held on Prof. George Saintsbury's eighty-sixth birthday (October 23, 1931) at Vintners' Hall on Vintners Place, and Belloc gave the first oration. (The hall dates from 1671 and contains the heavily paneled Court Room, "the oldest inhabited apartment in the City.") They had an 1878 Latour to which Belloc reacted characteristically: "Healey [Maurice Healy]! Healey!" he shouted, "this is wine!" His oratory was unforgetta-

ble: "Hilaire rose, swayed, and there were but three words he uttered: 'I am drunk.' And he was." He then pulled himself together and gave a magnificent talk on the slight differences between good and bad writing and good and bad wine, between a misplaced comma and a slightly loose cork. But his talk was not recorded, and Belloc could not remember a word of it the next day.

On a January 1942 trip to London, Belloc suffered a slight stroke at the Reform Club and was taken back to Shipley; his memory was impaired, and sustained work was impossible. He died in Guildford on July 17, 1953, and a few days after the funeral service in West Grinstead a Solemn Requiem Mass was sung in Westminster Cathedral.

William Henry Davies (1871–1940)   The "hobo poet," Welsh-born William Henry Davies, described himself as having "picked up knowledge among tramps in America, on cattle boats, and in the common lodging-houses in England." He went back and forth between Wales and the United States, where he tramped thousands of miles, jumped freight trains, and occasionally worked. On a trip to the Klondike exploring for gold, he fell while trying to hop a freight and severed his right foot at the ankle; he then returned to England, where he became a peddler of pins, laces, and needles and an itinerant street singer. By 1905, unable to find a publisher for *The Soul's Destroyer and Other Poems,* he was living in an old building that served as a refuge for down-and-outers on Marshalsea Road. He persuaded C. A. Watts & Co., in Johnson's Court off Fleet Street, to publish the volume on condition that Davies would do his utmost to dispose of the copies. He sent one copy to George Bernard Shaw, asking the dramatist to remit half a crown or to return the volume; Shaw, seeing the merit of the work, helped greatly by suggesting several critics to whom copies should be sent. Indeed, one of those, Edward Thomas, set Davies up in "a small cottage in the Weald of Kent [at Sevenoaks]. . . ."

In 1914 Davies was living at 18 Whitcomb Street, Soho, and in 1915 he moved to 11 Aldwych, where he remained for two years, working on *Forty New Poems.* Sometime before 1914 he lived at 29 Clarence Gardens, east of Regent's Park. He was one of the group of writers that included Walter de la Mare, Rupert Brooke, Robert Frost, John Masefield, W. H. Hudson, Hilaire Belloc, John Galsworthy, and Joseph Conrad who met at St. George's Restaurant, St. Martin's Lane, or at the Mont Blanc Restaurant, 16 Gerrard Street. From 1916 to 1922 Davies resided at 14 Great Russell Street; after his marriage in 1923, he and his wife settled eventually in Nailsworth, where he died in 1940.

Sir Max Beerbohm (1872–1956)   The youngest child of a prosperous grain merchant *émigré,* Henry Maximilian Beerbohm was born at 57 Palace Gardens Terrace (marked with a plaque) on August 24, 1872; his earliest education took place at a preparatory school on Orme Square and then at Charterhouse, the 14th-century Carthusian Priory reestablished as a school for boys in 1611 and moved to Godalming by Beerbohm's time. He lived with his family at 48 Upper Berkeley Street from the 1890's until his marriage in 1910 and wrote *Zuleika Dobson,* the fantasy about Oxford, here. Forced out of Rapallo, Italy, in 1915 and again in 1939, Beerbohm returned to England to broadcast for the BBC at the old Langham Hotel on Langham Place. After his death in Italy in 1956, his ashes were placed in the crypt of St. Paul's Cathedral.

Ford Madox Ford (1873–1939) He was born Ford Hermann Hueffer and had his name changed by deed poll in 1919 to Ford Madox Ford; he was the son of the music critic Francis Hueffer, the nephew of William Rossetti, and the grandson of the Pre-Raphaelite painter Ford Madox Brown. As a child, Ford lived with his parents for a time at 90 Brook Green and was frequently at his grandfather's home at 1 St. Edmund's Terrace, St. John's Wood; indeed, Ford and his mother lived for a period in Brown's house. Educated privately, he wrote his first novel, *The Shifting of the Fire,* at eighteen and married Elsie Martindale in 1894. By 1897 he had met Joseph Conrad, with whom he collaborated on *The Inheritors* and *Romance,* and around this time moved to 10 Airlie Gardens, off Campden Hill Road. His marriage was now breaking up, and the situation was not helped by the fact that Viola Hunt, Ford's mistress, lived at 80 Campden Hill Road. Through this period he produced his trilogy on Catherine Howard, *The Fifth Queen and How She Came to Court, Privy Seal,* and *The Fifth Queen Crowned.*

In 1908, living at 84 Holland Park Avenue, Ford began the *English Review* but financial problems forced its sale within one year. Around 1912 he moved into the Campden Hill house known as South Lodge (marked with a plaque), where he remained until 1918, and was visited by Henry James, H. G. Wells, Joseph Conrad, and Arnold Bennett. In 1910 his wife brought suit for the restitution of conjugal rights, and twenty-one years later she sued the *Throne* newspaper for calling Miss Hunt Mrs. Ford Madox Hueffer and won. *The Good Soldier,* thought by many to be Ford's best work, appeared in 1915. Ford held a commission in the Welsh Regiment during World War I and after 1922 spent his remaining years in Paris, Provence, and the United States. Before the war he was part of the literary group that frequented the Mont Blanc Restaurant, 16 Gerrard Street, Soho.

Walter de la Mare (1873–1956) Walter de la Mare, born in Charlton, Kent was educated at the 16th-century St. Paul's School, originally in St. Paul's Courtyard but moved to the Hammersmith Road in 1884 (the school moved again in 1968 to Barnes). In 1890 he entered the employ of the Anglo-American Oil Company in London and lived from 1899 to 1908 at 195 Mackenzie Road, where he wrote *Songs of Childhood* (under the name Walter Ramal) and *Henry Brocken.* In 1908 he moved to Worbeck Road, and from 1912 to 1925 de la Mare and his family were at 14 Thornsett Road. Before World War I he was part of the group of literary figures including W. H. Davies, Rupert Brooke, and Robert Frost that frequented St. George's Restaurant St. Martin's Lane, and the Mont Blanc Restaurant, 16 Gerrard Street. After his death in Twickenham on June 22, 1956, his ashes were placed in the crypt of St. Paul's Cathedral.

G. K. Chesterton (1874–1936) One of the most popular figures of this late Victorian period was Gilbert Keith Chesterton, critic, illustrator, short-story writer, and novelist; born on May 29, 1874, at 11 Sheffield Terrace off Campden Hill Road (a house no longer standing), he was baptized at St. George's Church, Kensington, a church just oppposite the dominating waterworks tower. "I indignantly deny,' Chesterton later wrote, "that the church was chosen because it needed the whole water power of West London to turn me into a Christian." When he was still very young, the family moved to 11 Warwick Gardens, just south of Kensington High Street, where Chesterton was to live until the turn of the century; he attended St. Paul's School, which had been moved to Hammersmith from the City in 1884, and it was decided that he should attend the Slade School of Art rather than the university since his talents seem to lie in that direction. Chesterton began working for a publisher on Paternoster Row (totally rebuilt since World War II) and even in later years referred to himself as a journalist rather than as a writer. He had already met Hilaire Belloc at the Mont Blanc Restaurant and later illustrated at least two books for Belloc; his first book of poems, *The Wild Knight*, financed by his father, appeared in 1900. Chesterton married Frances Blogg at St. Mary Abbots Church, Kensington, in 1901, and the marriage brought about the beginnings of Chesterton's religious questionings. For the first five months of their married life, the couple lived on the north side of Edwardes Square; moving to 60 Overstead Mansions in Battersea Park, he finished *The Napoleon of Notting Hill* and *Orthodoxy* before leaving London for Beaconsfield in 1908.

Maurice Baring (1874–1945) Maurice Baring was born in Mayfair on April 27, 1874; after leaving Cambridge without a degree, he entered diplomatic service in 1898, spent a year in London with the Foreign Office, and later was attaché in Paris, Copenhagen, and Rome. He kept a residence at 3 Gray's Inn Place from 1899 to 1930 even though he was frequently out of the country acting as a war correspondent for the *Morning Post* during the Russo-Japanese War from 1904 on, covering the civil conflict in Constantinople in 1909, and representing *The Times* in the Balkans in 1912. In 1930 he moved to 18 Cheyne Row, where he remained through most of the 1930s.

W. Somerset Maugham (1874–1965) Parisian-born W. Somerset Maugham, orphaned at ten and reared by an uncle in Whitstable, entered St. Thomas's Hospital, on the south side of the Thames between Westminster Bridge and Lambeth Bridge, in 1892 as a "perpetual student"; that is, he could stay on permanently without qualifying, but he actually did qualify in 1897. The medical school, of 13th-century monastic origin, has always been involved in charity work, and this was particularly the case in the 1890s when the borough of Lambeth (which the hospital adjoins) was a slum area. In fact, when Maugham was here, St. Thomas's handled 25,000 outpatients every year. Maugham took lodgings at 11 Vincent Square, Westminster, with a Mrs. Foresman, whose portrait, somewhat modified, appears in *Cakes and Ale:*

> Mrs. Hudson's name had been given to me by the secretary of the medical school at St. Luke's. . . . She had a house in Vincent Square. I lived there for five years, in two rooms on the ground floor. . . . Mrs. Hudson was a little, active, bustling woman, with a sallow face, a large aquiline nose, and the brightest, the most vivacious, black eyes that I ever saw. . . . She had a heart of gold. . . .

The house, still there, belongs to the Church Commission. St. Thomas's, of course, is the St. Luke's Hospital of *Cakes and Ale* and *Of Human Bondage;* Philip Carey "chose St. Luke's because his father had been a student there. . . .." All the experiences at St. Luke's Hospital are based on Maugham's at St. Thomas's. At the end of Maugham's second year, he became a clerk in the Out Patients Department and later, as an obstetrical clerk, delivered sixty-three children; *Liza of Lambeth*, his first novel, published in his last year of medical school, deals with the period he spent as an *accoucheur* in the slums.

Maugham regretted never practicing after qualifying, but the success of *Liza* persuaded him that he could earn his living as a writer. Even though he wandered abroad, he almost always retained accommodations somewhere in London. Around 1910 he had lodgings at 23 Mount Street, in 1911 at 6 Chesterfield Street (marked with a plaque), between 1923 and 1926 at 43 Bryanston Square, and in the late 1920s at 213 King's Road, Chelsea. Maugham's brother, Frederic Herbert Maugham, 1st Viscount Maugham, who was Lord Chancellor, lived at 73 Cadogan Square, and although the brothers detested each other, Maugham often visited because he was especially fond of his sister-in-law and her children. When Maugham was put on Joseph Goebbels's black list during World War II, the novelist was ordered back to England with other nationals. After Maugham died in Nice on December 16, 1965, his ashes were buried in Canterbury.

Edgar Wallace (1875–1932)   Edgar Wallace was born at 7 Ashburnham Grove, Greenwich, on April 1, 1875; the illegitimate son of Mary Jane (Polly) Richards, an actress, by Richard Horatio Edgar Marriott, an actor, he was raised by George Freeman, a Billingsgate fish porter, and his wife. The Freemans lived at 6 Tressilian Crescent, Deptford (marked with a plaque). Wallace attended St. Peter's Infant School on Thames Street, but school was not exactly his forte, and by the age of eleven he was playing truant to sell newspapers at Ludgate Circus; a plaque there commemorates his earliest newspaper work. Wallace left Reddin's Road School in Peckham at the age of twelve and worked as both a printer's boy and a newsboy before taking successive employment in a shoe shop, in a mackintosh factory, on a Grimsby trawler, as a milk roundsman, as a roadmaker, and as a builder's laborer. He eventually served with the Royal West Kent Regiment in South Africa, and after the Boer War he became a Reuters correspondent and a correspondent for the *Daily Mail*. *The Four Just Men*, his first success, was produced upon his return. Around 1930 he and his wife and daughter were living at 31 Portland Place; Wallace died in Hollywood, California, on February 10, 1932, while writing the script for *King Kong*.

John Buchan, 1st Baron Tweedsmuir (1875–1940)   The prolific novelist and statesman John Buchan, Lord Tweedsmuir came to London and the Middle Temple following his failure to gain a fellowship at Oxford; in 1900 he was living at 4 Brick Court, and in the following year he was called to the bar. Somewhat later he took the lease of 3 Plowden Buildings on Middle Temple Lane. After his 1907 marriage to Susan Grosvenor, he lived at 40 Hyde Park Square until 1910; Buchan subsequently had two other London addresses, 13 Bryanston Street (1910–1912) and 76

Portland Place (1912–1919) before deciding that the need of a more private life necessitated a move from the metropolis to Elsfield, Oxfordshire.

Rafael Sabatini (1875–1950)   A novelist about whom little is known, Rafael Sabatini lived at 25 Fitzjohns Avenue in 1925 and at 22 Pont Street in the 1930's.

Edward Thomas (1878–1917)   Born somewhere in Lambeth on March 3, 1878, Edward Thomas was educated at St. Paul's School before going up to Oxford in 1897. Before World War I, in which he died, Thomas lived for some time at 61 Shelgate Road, Battersea, and was one of that large group of poets including W. H. Davies, Rupert Brooke, Walter de la Mare, and Robert Frost who frequented St. George's Restaurant, St. Martin's Lane, Covent Garden, and the Mont Blanc Restaurant at 16 Gerrard Street.

Wilfrid Wilson Gibson (1878–1962)   W. W. Gibson's first real association with London began about 1912, when he was part of a group of artists and writers, including John Middleton Murry, Henri Gaudier-Brzeska, Ezra Pound, and Rupert Brooke, who met at a café at 67 Frith Street, Soho; with Brooke, John Drinkwater, and others he helped found *New Numbers,* a short-lived poetry magazine. Gibson was a frequent guest at Edward Marsh's home, 5 Raymond Buildings, off Gray's Inn Place, along with Brooke, Walter de la Mare, W. H. Davies, Edmund Blunden, Siegfried Sassoon, and John Drinkwater. Marsh, who was editor of *Georgian Poetry,* published much of Gibson's early work. From 1934 to 1939 Gibson lived at 26 Nassington Road, Hampstead, and wrote of Hampstead Heath:

> Against the green flame of the hawthorn-tree
> His scarlet tunic burns;
> And livelier than the green sap's mantling glee
> The spring fire tingles through him headily
> As quivering he turns
>
> And stammers out the old amazing tale
> Of youth and April weather;
> While she, with half-breathed jests that, sobbing, fail,
> Sits, tight-lipped, quaking, eager-eyed and pale
> Beneath her purple feather.

Edward John Moreton Drax Plunkett, 18th Baron Dunsany (1878–1957)   Edward John Moreton Drax Plunkett, Lord Dunsany, author of tales of the supernatural and fantasy, was born at 15 Park Square, Regent's Park, on July 24, 1878; from around 1925 until 1940, when he left England, he lived at 66 Cadogan Square and here wrote *The Curse of the Wise Woman* and *My Talks with Dean Spanley.*

John Masefield (1878–1967)   John Masefield's first-known address in London dates to 1911, but he lived in the city earlier since he attended the Monday Evenings which William Butler Yeats held in 18 Woburn Buildings and met John Millington Synge there. They would walk home together, as Masefield later recorded:

> Often at night I tread those streets again,
> . . . .
> And now I miss that friend who used to walk
> Home to my lodgings with me, deep in talk,
> Wearing the last of night out in still streets
>   . . . Now I miss
> That lively mind and guttural laugh of his. . . .

In 1911, when he was working on *The Everlasting*

Mercy, Masefield lived at 30 Maida Avenue, and in 1912 and 1913 he was at 14 Well Walk, Hampstead, and worked on *Dauber* and *The Widow in the Bye Street*. He was part of the large group of writers and critics (including Ford Madox Ford, W. H. Hudson, Hilaire Belloc, G. K. Chesterton, Joseph Conrad, and John Galsworthy) who met in the Mont Blanc Restaurant, 16 Gerrard Street, before World War I. Named Poet Laureate in 1930, he lived at 18 Mecklenburgh Square from 1932 to 1935, the year he was awarded the Order of Merit. After his death on May 12, 1967, he was buried in the Poets' Corner of Westminster Abbey; there is a commemorative monument in the abbey as well. Masefield's attitude toward London is summed up as

London Town's a fine town, and London sights are rare,
And London ale is right ale, and brisk's the London air,
And busily goes the world there, but crafty grows the mind,
And London Town of all towns I'm glad to leave behind.

Harold Monro (1879–1932)   Harold Monro had an extremely checkered background before he eventually settled in London and became successful. After founding the Samurai Press and trying to live abroad (he bought a mill in Switzerland which was flooded out), he came to London and founded the *Poetry Review* at 93 Chancery Lane in 1911. Two years later he established the Poetry Bookshop at 35 Boswell Street (formerly Devonshire Street); the bookshop remained at this location until 1926, when it was moved to 38 Great Russell Street. In the Boswell Street location most of the significant poets of the time held readings, and in 1913 Robert Frost and his wife, "by pure accident," the poet claimed, took rooms above the bookshop. (It was Francis Stewart Flint, by the way, who met Frost here, knew he was an American because of his shoes, and suggested he look up a compatriot, Ezra Pound.) From about 1930 on Monro was in increasingly poor health, and he died in Broadstairs on March 16, 1932.

Alfred Noyes (1880–1958)   Information on Alfred Noyes is scanty at best, and only three London associations are known. In the 1920s he resided at 85 Cadogan Gardens, and in 1927 he married his second wife at the Brompton Oratory on Brompton Road; the couple lived from then through the early 1930s at 13 Hanover Terrace, Regent's Park. Finally, his popular poem "The Highwayman" recalls the Spaniards Inn, an old tollhouse on the edge of Hampstead Heath.

Dame Rose Macaulay (1881–1958)   After living with her parents for many years in Wales and near Cambridge, Dame Rose Macaulay eventually made her way to London and settled at 63 Edgware Road in the 1920's, when her fame as a poet, literary critic, and novelist was beginning. *Told by an Idiot* and *Orphan Island* were both finished here before she moved to St. Andrew's Mansions, a large apartment complex on Dorset Street. Throughout most of the 1930s she had a flat at 7–8 Luxborough Street. Rose Macaulay died in London on October 30, 1958, shortly after she had been made DBE.

John Drinkwater (1882–1937)   In the 1930s John Drinkwater lived at 14 Ashburn Gardens, South Kensington, and at North Hall, Mortimer Crescent, off Greville Road. He maintained his residence at 9 The Grove, Hampstead, from 1935 until his death on March 25, 1937.

Virginia Stephen Woolf (1882–1941)   After his marriage to Julia Prinsep Duckworth (widow of Herbert Duckworth), Leslie (later Sir Leslie) Stephen took the five-story brick house at 22 Hyde Park Gate, where his daughter Virginia Stephen (Woolf) was born on January 25, 1882. (The house is marked by a plaque commemorating Sir Leslie.) Even though she was never christened, her godfather was James Russell Lowell, who was a frequent visitor when he was United States Minister to Great Britain; later, after he was replaced by President Grover Cleveland's own nominee, Lowell returned every summer. The children's nursery was at the very top of the gloomy, dismal house, far removed from Sir Leslie's study, where from 1882 on he edited *The Dictionary of National Biography;* The four children by this marriage were educated at home, and the training was excellent. The success of the *Dictionary*, the publication of Virginia's own paper *The Hyde Park Gate News*, and summer holidays in Cornwall should have been the seeds of security and unity within the house, but the reverse was true. Her half sister Laura was already showing signs of mental illness, and her half brother Gerald Duckworth was making advances: "I still shiver with shame," Virginia Woolf wrote many years later, "at the memory of my half-brother, standing me on a ledge, aged about six or so, exploring my private parts." With her mother's death in 1895 and her sister Julia's death in 1897, the situation became even more desperate, and she suffered the first of her recurrent breakdowns.

Sir Leslie's death in 1904 freed the family from this house, and most of them moved to 46 Gordon Square in Bloomsbury. Virginia was sufficiently recovered from her breakdown to join them in January 1905. The house was the antithesis of her father's home and was a considerable distance away; here a brilliant group of people whom her elder brother Thoby had met at Cambridge assembled: Lytton Strachey, John Maynard Keynes, Roger Fry, Clive Bell, and Leonard Woolf. Thoby's death in 1906 and her sister Vanessa's marriage to Clive Bell prompted a move, and with her brother Adrian she leased 29 Fitzroy Square, a house once occupied by George Bernard Shaw and now marked by a plaque commemorating her stay. She was working on *Helymbrosia* (eventually *The Voyage Out*) and reinstituted the Thursday-evening gatherings begun by Thoby. In February 1909 she accepted Lytton Strachey's proposal, but when he eventually called off the engagement because of his homosexuality, she "let him go gently" says Quentin Bell. She, Adrian, John Maynard Keynes, Duncan Grant, and Leonard Woolf shared 38 Brunswick Square (gone) in Bloomsbury in late 1911 and 1912, and on August 12 in the latter year she married Woolf in the St. Pancras registry office.

After their honeymoon, the Woolfs took lodgings at 13 Clifford's Inn and began to divide their time between here and Asham House, near Lewes. Virginia came to London in September 1913 to see her doctors and on the afternoon of September 9 attempted suicide with 100 grains of veronal. She was then in and out of nursing homes, and not for another two or three years did she return to some semblance of normal life. The Hogarth Press, on Victoria Street, which published her books, was established by Virginia and Leonard Woolf in 1917. The couple bought the lease of 52 Tavistock Square (where the Tavistock Hotel now stands) in Bloomsbury in January 1924, and here, as well as in Rodmell, she worked on *Mrs. Dalloway* and *To the Lighthouse*. A diary entry for May 26 of that year shows her London:

> London is enchanting. I step out upon a tawny coloured magic carpet, it seems, and get carried into beauty without raising a finger. The nights are amazing, with all the white porticos and broad silent avenues.

The couple moved the Hogarth Press to 39 Mecklenburgh Square (gone) in mid-August 1939 and at the end of the month moved in their personal possessions. As World War II intensified, they spent more and more time in Rodmell, and in September 1939 the square was bombed and the press severely damaged. They first moved the press to Letchworth, Hertfordshire, and eventually to Rodmell.

While London permeates Virginia Woolf's novels, the references often are not very specific. Mr. and Mrs. Ambrose in *The Voyage Out* are met on the Embankment, pausing to look on the Thames; indeed, the Embankment wall has a curious fascination for the author:

> The embankment juts out in angles here and there, like pulpits; instead of preachers, however, small boys occupy them, dangling string, dropping pebbles, or launching wads of paper for a cruise. . . .
>
> Some one is always looking into the river near Waterloo Bridge. . . . Sometimes the flats and churches and hotels of Westminster are like the outlines of Constantinople in a mist; sometimes the river is an opulent purple, sometimes mud-colored, sometimes sparkling blue like the sea. It is always worth while to look down and see what is happening.

In her sadness Mrs. Ambrose, noting "how little London had done to make her love it, although thirty of her forty years had been spent in a street," becomes even further depressed on the drive to the East End and the docks:

> Observing that they passed no other hansom cab, but only vans and waggons, and that not one of the thousand men and women she saw was either a gentleman or a lady, Mrs. Ambrose understood that after all it is the ordinary thing to be poor, and that London is the city of innumerable poor people. . . .
>
> "Lord, how gloomy it is!" her husband groaned. "Poor creatures!"

In *Night and Day* the Hilbery home, with its "sophisticated drawing-room" and traditional values, is on Cheyne Walk, Chelsea, while the Denham home is in Highgate, and Ralph's office is in Lincoln's Inn Fields. The story takes place in the streets and parks: the Strand, the Embankment, Charing Cross Road, Kingsway, Southampton Row, Regent's Park, and Kew Gardens. Ralph Denham on one occasion walks from his rooms in the Temple to Chelsea:

> The streets were empty enough on Sunday night. . . . The gusts, sweeping along the Strand, seemed at the same time to blow a clear space across the sky in which stars appeared. . . . He walked in the direction of Chelsea.
>
> But physical fatigue, for he had not dined and had tramped both far and fast, made him sit for a moment

upon a seat on the Embankment. . . . [He] pressed on, with the wind against him. The image of the lighthouse and the storm full of birds persisted, taking the place of more definite thoughts, as he walked past the Houses of Parliament and down Grosvenor Road, by the side of the river.

Jacob's Room mentions "Mudie's corner in Oxford Street," where "all the red and blue beads had run together on the string"; St. Paul's, with its dim interior "haunted by ghosts of white marble"; Parliament Hill, where "at this hour they were burning Guy Fawkes"; and the British Museum, which

> stood in one solid immense mound, very pale, very sleek in the rain, not a quarter of a mile from him. The vast mind was sheeted with stone; and each compartment in the depths of it was safe and dry. . . .
>
> Stone lies solid over the British Museum, as bone lies cool over the visions and heat of the brain. Only here the brain is Plato's brain and Shakespeare's; the brain has made pots and statues, great bulls and little jewels, and crossed the river of death this way and that incessantly. . . .

Wyndham Lewis (1882–1957) Wyndham Lewis, born on a yacht near Amherst, Nova Scotia, on November 18, 1882, was not brought to England until 1893, when his parents separated and he and his mother settled somewhere in London. He entered the Slade School of Fine Art in 1898 but left in 1901 before finishing his course. In 1914, the year that *Blast* first appeared, Lewis established his Rebel Art Center at 38 Great Ormond Street and was living at 4 Percy Street. He served as an artillery officer in World War I, and after being demobilized, he settled at 20A Campden Hill Gardens in 1919, the year after *Tarr* was published. In the 1920s, fighting for the seclusion he needed for his work, he first lived at 37 Redcliffe Road and then at 33 Ossington Street; this last address he kept into the early 1930s. At that time he had two other residences, 31 Percy Street and 121 Gloucester Terrace. In 1935 and 1936 Lewis lived at 21 Chilworth Street. Lewis and his wife left for the United States in 1939 for a lecture tour and, caught up in World War II, remained on the North American continent, in poverty, until the end of the war. They then returned to London, where Lewis worked for the British Broadcasting Corporation as the art critic for *The Listener*.

Sir Hugh Walpole (1884–1941) Sir Hugh Walpole was the son of an Anglican clergyman who had been the incumbent at St. Mary's Cathedral, Auckland, New Zealand, when his son was born and who brought his family back to England before the turn of the twentieth century. After living in Canterbury and Durham, the Rev. George Henry Somerset Walpole took the living in Lambeth in January 1904. Hugh Walpole had already entered Emmanuel College, Cambridge, and over the next years spent only his vacations from school or work at the rectory. Finally obtaining his father's consent not to be ordained and spending a year abroad, Walpole settled at 20 Glebe Place, Chelsea, in February 1909 to devote himself to writing; he also had a job with the London Literary Agency and Curtis Brown. His first novel, *The Wooden Horse*, was accepted by Smith and Elder early in February of the same year, and in the same month he dined with Henry James at the Reform Club; the friendship formed here was lasting. *Mar-*

adick at Forty and *Mr Perrin and Mr Traill* were both written before he moved to 16 Hallam Street in May 1911; in Hallam Street *The Duchess of Wrexe* was written, but by 1913 Walpole had given up London for a time.

Walpole served with the Russian Red Cross in Galicia and then headed the Anglo-Russian propaganda office in Petrograd; his observations of the first revolution later gave rise to *The Dark Forest* and *The Secret City*. He did not return permanently from Russia until November 1917, when he took rooms somewhere on Bury Street, St. James's, and then on Ryder Street. Even so, he did not really settle until after his return from the United States in 1920, when he bought the lease (paying a £2,500 premium as well) of 24 York Terrace, a corner house which he described as

> overlooking Regents Park at both ends. It has a little garden in front of it, it is old Georgian and very solid, and has wonderful big rooms—one high room with a big view of the park will make a wonderful library.

Here the "young" writers of the Society of Writers (including Siegfried Sassoon, Edmund Blunden, Edith Sitwell, and Evelyn Waugh) met to plan a suitable memorial for Thomas Hardy's eighty-first birthday. Walpole gave up York Terrace before a second trip to the United States and on his return took a service flat on Berkeley Street before moving to 90 Piccadilly, at the corner of Half Moon Street. He kept this bachelor flat even though he had Brackenburn in Manesty and was frequently out of the country. In 1940 he was involved in the war effort in broadcasting for the British Broadcasting Corporation.

Because Walpole was unable to stay in his flat, he took rooms at the Dorchester Hotel on Park Lane, where he was during the blitz attack on November 15, 1940, when all the ceilings and all but one wall at 90 Piccadilly were blown in. He left London immediately (indeed, the war exacted a great toll on him) and retired to Brackenburn, but just four months before his death in 1941 he returned to inspect Number 90 and found it was "like Lazarus raised from the dead."

Dame Ivy Compton-Burnett (1884–1969)   The London associations with Ivy Compton-Burnett, author of *Brothers and Sisters*, began in 1902, when she entered Royal Holloway College of the University of London; graduating in classics in 1906, she published her first novel, *Dolores,* five years later. From 1916 to 1929 she lived at 59 Leinster Square and from 1934 on shared a London flat, 5 Braemar Mansions, Cornwall Gardens, Kensington, with Margaret Jourdain. Dame Ivy retained the flat after Miss Jourdain's death in 1951 and wrote *Mother and Son,* the James Tait Black novel, here; she died here on August 27, 1969, and her ashes were buried in the Putney Vale Cemetery.

D. H. Lawrence (1885–1930)

London
Original, wolf-wrapped
In pelts of wolves, all her luminous
Garments gone.

London, with hair
Like a forest darkness, like a marsh
Of rushes, ere the Romans
Broke in her lair.

Such was D. H. Lawrence's view of London. Raised in the heavily industrial and coal-mining area of Nottinghamshire, he first came to London in October 1908 to take up a teaching post at the Davidson Road School (later the Davidson Road Secondary Modern School) in Croydon, where he remained until 1920. Contrary to the usual statement that he resigned his teaching post, he contracted pneumonia in November 1911, and even though his doctor forbade returning to work, he would not resign; indeed, he asked for and received an immediate leave. However, he was forced into a resignation on March 19, 1912.

When Lawrence left his post in November 1911, he was not to return to London until 1914, at which time he stayed with a friend (Gordon Campbell, later 1st Baron Glenavy) at 9 Selwood Terrace, Kensington; he had already met Frieda von Richthofen Weekley in Nottingham, and by this time her divorce from Prof. Ernest Weekley was final. Lawrence and she were married in the registry office of the district of Kensington with John Middleton Murry as one of the witnesses. For five months after August 1915 they lived in the ground-floor flat of 1 Byron Villas (marked with a plaque) in the Vale of Health, Hampstead, before moving to Cornwall. Lawrence's war years were not easy ones because of an aristocratic German wife, and, indeed, they were expelled from Zennor in the hysteria over spying and returned to London. They stayed at 138 Earl's Court Square before they were lent a flat at 44 Mecklenburgh Square by Hilda Doolittle, the American poet known as H. D. They remained here until January 1918, during which time he worked on *Women in Love* while they were being "occasionally pestered by agents of the Criminal Investigation Department." Lawrence and his wife left London for Derbyshire in 1918 and then left England permanently at the end of 1919, making only very brief and occasional visits back. On one such visit, in 1923, they stayed at 110 Heath Street.

London is the setting for a number of Lawrence's short stories; "The Last Laugh," in which Lorenzo (Lawrence's nickname) bids his guests farewell at midnight in Hampstead, is based on an event at the house of Ernest Rhys. Ezra Pound, Ford Madox Ford, and William Butler Yeats were also there, and after the others had read some of their poetry, Lawrence was asked to oblige; he took a book from his pocket, turned his back on the audience, and read, in a barely audible voice, for the better part of an hour. With murmuring filling the background, Rhys suggested "[W]hy not stop for a while now and begin again at midnight?"

Marguerite Radclyffe Hall (1886–1943)   The Bournemouth-born Radclyffe Hall, whose 1928 novel *The Well of Loneliness* was banned in Britain because of its treatment of lesbianism, had a number of different London addresses, but the specific dates in some cases are unavailable. She lived for a time at Talbot House, St. Martin's Lane, and at 1 Swan Walk, on the Chelsea Embankment, where her cousin resided, and for some years before 1915 she lived with a friend at 59 Cadogan Square. She also bought a house at 37 Holland Street, where she lived for four years. Miss Hall died in London on October 7, 1943, and was buried in Highgate Cemetery.

Rupert Brooke (1887–1915)   Rupert Brooke's association with London was both short and generally casual since his stays were most frequently visits. He was, for example, an avid theatergoer, beginning in 1901, when he saw *Richard II*, and he was enchanted by Sir James Matthew Barrie's *Peter Pan,* which "[i]n reality no doubt," he told Lytton Strachey, "is very ridiculous." In 1911 in order to work on his essay on Webster, which gained him a fellowship at King's College, he came to London to work in the British Museum and stayed in John Maynard Keynes's rooms at 21 Fitzroy Square until he secured his own rooms at 76 Charlotte Street. Over the next few years he was in and out of town, staying with a friend in Raymond Buildings, Gray's Inn, and meeting various literary figures. In January 1913, he visited Katherine Mansfield at her Chancery Lane address, spent an evening with Hugh Walpole at Gray's Inn, lunched with Walter de la Mare and William Davies at the Moulin d'Or, and had coffee with William Butler Yeats and Ezra Pound in Woburn Buildings. On other trips he often ate at Ye Olde Cheshire Cheese in Wine Office Court with John Middleton Murry, and on April 15, 1912, attended a "birthday dinner at 10 Downing Street," where the guests included George Bernard Shaw and his wife, Edmund Gosse, Sir James Matthew Barrie, John Masefield, and Prime Minister Henry Herbert Asquith and his family. For a short time in 1913 he lodged at 5 Thurloe Street.

After returning from a United States trip in June 1914, Brooke made another round of London: meeting the sculptor Henri Gaudier-Brzeska at the Moulin d'Or; eating with Barrie, Shaw, Yeats, G. K. Chesterton, Harley Granville-Barker, Gerald du Maurier, and Mrs. Patrick Campbell at the Savoy; breakfasting at Gray's Inn with Siegfried Sassoon and W. H. Davies; lunching with Henry James and Marie Belloc-Lowndes; and the next day having lunch with D. H. Lawrence at the Ship Restaurant. It was on that night at dinner at 10 Downing Street that he sat opposite Winston Churchill, First Lord of the Admiralty, whom he had not met before. Churchill offered to help him obtain a commission if war should come; Brooke received his commission in the Royal Navy in September 1914 and died on the island of Scyros on April 23, 1915, from blood poisoning.

Katherine Mansfield (Murry) (1888–1923) and John Middleton Murry (1889–1957)   New Zealand–born Katherine Beauchamp, better known as Katherine Mansfield, arrived in London with her two sisters in April 1903 to enter Queen's College on Harley Street. The school, with the atmosphere of a university, had about forty boarders, or "compounders," as they called themselves, who lived at 41 Harley Street or on the top floor of Number 45, the college itself. The two residences were joined by a boot passage, and the Beauchamp girls were at Number 45 in a room overlooking Mansfield Mews. (Katherine Mansfield's nom de plume did not come from these mews; Mansfield was her grandmother's surname and Katherine Beauchamp's middle name.) She took cello lessons at the London Academy of Music to escape Queen's, which was oppressive. In 1906 she returned to New Zealand, determined not only to be a writer but to be so objectionable at home that she would be sent away. Not until 1908, however, did her father agree to her return; he made her a small allowance and fixed her accommodations in Beauchamp Lodge, a tall, gaunt building which stood behind Paddington Station next to the canal. The lodge was a hostel for music students.

> Westbourne Grove looked as she had always imagined Venice to look at night, mysterious, dark.... She was more than glad to reach Richmond Road, but from the corner of the street until she came to No. 26 she thought of those four flights of stairs. Oh, why four flights! It was really criminal to expect people to live so high up. Every house ought to have a lift, something simple and inexpensive, or else, an electric staircase like the one at Earl's Court—but four flights!

On March 2, 1909, in the Paddington registry office Katherine Mansfield married a singing teacher named George Bowden, whom she left the next day for reasons unknown. Pregnant, she was sent to the Continent by her mother, who did not realize that Bowden was not the father. Returning to London in January 1910, she lived at the Strand Palace Hotel before moving in the summer to 133 Cheyne Walk. Early in the next year she took a three-room flat on the top floor of Clovelley Mansions, Gray's Inn Road. "The Last Romantic" describes the sitting room. In the meantime Katherine Mansfield had met John Middleton Murry, (a native of London), and in April 1912 he moved into the same building; both were impoverished and had joined together in an attempt to save *Rhythm*. In November 1912 they moved into a dingy room on Chancery Lane and then into Number 57, an office flat from which the periodical was published. But *Rhythm* failed almost immediately, and the two went abroad. On their return in March 1914 they took two very drab rooms at 102 Edith Grove and in July took the top floor of a house on Arthur Street. They were constantly forced to seek new accommodations because of their financial and marital situations.

Murry and Mansfield had been well acquainted with D. H. Lawrence and Frieda von Richthofen Weekley and stood as witnesses for their July 1914 marriage. For a time in 1915 Katherine Mansfield and Murry lived on Elgin Crescent, Nottinghill Gate, before they moved into 5 Acacia Road, St. John's Wood, and often picnicked on Hampstead Heath with Lawrence and his wife. Returning from France and Mylor, Cornwall, in the autumn of 1916, they took separate lodgings. Katherine Mansfield took 141A Old Church Street, Chelsea, but facing the information that she was tubercular, she and Murry left for France. Upon their return, they went to Murry's lodgings at 47 Redcliffe Road. By this time Mansfield had secured a divorce, and the two were married in early May 1918. They settled at 2 Portland Villas, East Heath Road (marked with a plaque), in a house which they christened the Elephant because of its size and grayness, but by this time Katherine Mansfield was seriously tubercular. From May 1919 on she was back and forth to France in an effort to fight the disease, and in August 1922 she was at 6 Pond Street (gone), Hampstead, the home of Dorothy Brett, the artist, while Murry lived in a room in the house next door. Refusing sanatorium care, she left for the Gurdjieff Institute in Fontainebleau, whose methods of cure stressed such things as religious reincarnation and organic harmony; Miss Mansfield died on January 9, 1923, less than three months after her arrival.

Greatly disturbed by his wife's death, John Middleton Murry worked strenuously over the next few years and produced his books on Keats, D. H. Lawrence, Blake, and Shakespeare; in 1925 he was living at 18 York Buildings, off John Adam Street, and following his second marriage he and his wife settled at 149 Whitehead's Grove.

Joyce Cary (1888–1957) Shortly after his birth on December 7, 1888, in Londonderry, Ireland, Arthur Joyce Cary was brought to London by his father, an English-trained engineer of Irish birth; the family first settled somewhere in Nunhead and then on Kitto Road, in the same area. However, "the real heart of the family" was the Gunnersbury, Middlesex, home of Dr. Tristram Cary and his wife. Most of Joyce Cary's holidays were spent in Ireland, especially after his mother's death in 1898. After poor examination results at Oxford in the spring of 1912 (he discovered in July that he had managed to get a fourth-class degree), he settled at 10 Store Street, where he began a novel on the Paris he knew in 1906–1907 and 1911. Completely broke, he left England in October 1912 to serve with the British Red Cross in the Montenegrin Army during the Balkan Wars (1912–1913) and to gather material for writing; in 1913 he joined the Colonial Service and was posted to Nigeria. Cary was in England on occasional leaves, mostly in Harrow Weald, but was often in London on day trips after he settled in Oxford in 1920.

The Horse's Mouth makes vivid use of London, and Gully Jimson is certainly a Londoner:

> I was walking by the Thames. Half-past morning on an autumn day. Sun in a mist. Like an orange in a fried fish shop. All bright below. Low tide, dusty water and a crooked bar of straw, chicken-boxes, dirt and oil from mud to mud. Like a viper swimming in skim milk. . . .
> Such as Thames mud turned into a bank of nine carat rough from the fire.

Thomas Stearns Eliot (1888–1965)

> Sweet Thames, run softly, till I end my song.
> The river bears no empty bottles, sandwich papers,
> Silk handkerchiefs, cardboard boxes, cigarette ends
> Or other testimony of summer nights. The nymphs are
>   departed.
> And their friends, the loitering heirs of City directors;
> Departed, have left no addresses.
> By the waters of Leman I sat down and wept . . .
> Sweet Thames, run softly till I end my song,
> Sweet Thames, run softly, for I speak not loud or long.

Thomas Stearns Eliot was an Englishman and a Londoner by choice; in Europe to finish his doctoral dissertation, "Knowledge and Experience in the Philosophy of F. H. Bradley," when World War I broke out, he did not return to the United States and Harvard University, where he had been teaching. Rather he came to London and secured a job teaching French and Latin at the Highgate School. In 1915 he married Vivienne Haigh-Wood, and before World War I and for some time after they lived in Carlyle Mansions, Cheyne Walk, Chelsea. Eliot began working as a clerk in Lloyds Bank, Ltd., Lombard Street, where he remained for eight years. In the early 1920s the Eliots lived at 5 Chester Row, where Herbert Read often visited them; Read relates:

> After the *Criterion* dinners, which generally lasted too long for me to catch my last train home, I would sometimes spend the night at Chester Terrace. I remember

how on one such occasion I woke early and presently became conscious that the door of my room which was on the ground floor, was slowly and silently being opened. I lay still and saw first a hand and then an arm reach round the door and lift from a hook the bowler hat that was hanging there. It was a little before seven o'clock and Mr. Eliot was on his way to an early communion service.

Coming home from the bank,

> At the violet hour, when the eyes and back
> Turn upward from the desk, when the human
>   engine waits
> Like a taxi throbbing waiting,

Eliot would take the underground at Moorgate (also mentioned in the poem). *The Waste Land* was not his first publication, but it ensured his international reputation.

Sometime in the 1920s Eliot moved to 68 Glentworth Street (then Clarence Gate Gardens) and around 1929 moved to Number 98. Before Eliot resigned from the bank, I. A. Richards called on him at work and was shown to a "big table [which] almost entirely filled a little room under the street." Richards tells that shortly after being in the bank, he met one of the branch officials in the Alps, with whom the following interchange took place:

> *Mr. W.:* You know him, I suppose, as a literary man, as a writer and . . . er . . . and . . . er . . . as a poet?
> *I.A.R.:* Yes, he's very well known, you know, as a critic and as a poet.
> *Mr. W.:* Tell me, if you will—you won't mind my asking, will you? Tell me, is he, in your judgement, would you say, would you call him a good poet?
> *I.A.R.:* Well, in my judgement—not everyone would agree, of course, far from it—he *is* a good poet.
> *Mr. W.:* You know, I myself am really very glad indeed to hear you say that. Many of my colleagues wouldn't agree at all. They think a Banker has no business whatever to be a poet. They don't think the two things can combine. But I believe that anything a man does, whatever his *hobby* may be, it's all the better if he is really keen on it and does it well. I think it helps him with his work. If you see our young friend, you might tell him that we think he's doing quite well at the Bank. In fact, if he goes on as he has been doing, I don't see why—in time, of course, in time—he mightn't even become a Branch Manager.

In 1927, the year he became a British subject, Eliot joined Fabr & Gwyer (now Faber & Faber), becoming a director in 1929, and would go to their offices at 24 Russell Square three times a week; indeed, for many years this was his London address. It was at the Church of St. Stephen at the corner of Gloucester Road and Southwell Gardens that Eliot served as churchwarden for twenty-five years and was on the church council until his death. Eliot died in London on January 4, 1965, and his ashes were buried in East Coker; there is a memorial in Westminster Abbey.

The Waste Land and *Four Quartets* especially are full of references to the city; in the former the crowd

> Flowed up the hill and down King William Street,
> To where Saint Mary Woolnoth kept the hours
> With a dead sound on the final stroke of nine.

"Mr. Eugenides, the Smyrna merchant"

> Asked me in demotic French
> To luncheon at the Cannon Street Hotel
> Followed by a weekend at the Metropole.

"And," continues Eliot,

> ... along the Strand, up Queen Victoria Street.
> O City city, I can sometimes hear
> Beside a public bar in Lower Thames Street,
> The pleasant whining of a mandoline
> And a clatter and a chatter from within
> Where fishermen lounge at noon. ...

The interior of the Church of St. Magnus the Martyr on Lower Thames Street, he felt, was "one of the finest among Wren's interiors."

> ... the walls
> Of Magnus Martyr hold
> Inexplicable splendour of Ionian white and gold.

In *Four Quartets*, set

> In the uncertain hour before the morning
> Near the ending of interminable night

he "met one walking," the master, "half forgotten, half recalled," who concludes:

> From wrong to wrong the exasperated spirit
> Proceeds, unless restored by that refining fire
> Where you must move in measure, like a dancer.
> The day was breaking. In the disfigured street
> He left me, with a kind of valediction,
> And faded on the blowing of the horn.

Ivor Brown (1891–1974)   In the 1940s and 1950s, Ivor Brown, critic and novelist, lived at 20 Christchurch Hill in Hampstead.

Agatha Christie (1891–1976)   The author of *The Mousetrap* and a plethora of mystery stories, Agatha Christie lived at 58 Sheffield Terrace, off Campden Hill Road, for a time.

Victoria Sackville-West (1892–1962)   Born into a wealthy and titled family (her father was the 3d Baron Sackville) on March 9, 1892, Victoria Sackville-West lived mostly in London after her 1913 marriage to Sir Harold Nicholson. In the 1920s the couple were at 182 Ebury Street (gone), where she worked on *The Land*, the poem which brought her the Hawthornden Prize in 1927. In 1930 they moved to 4 King's Bench Walk, which they retained until 1945; at this juncture both Victoria Sackville-West and Sir Harold became involved with the Fascist magazine *Action*, edited by Sir Oswald Mosley, whose offices were at 5 Gordon Square, Bloomsbury. Nicholson withdrew from the Fascist activity as soon as he understood its purpose and direction. In the King's Bench Walk house Victoria Sackville-West finished one of her best-known works, *All Passion Spent* (1931). For a time in the 1950s they lived at 10 Neville Terrace.

Dorothy Sayers (1893–1957)   One of the first women graduates of Oxford, Dorothy Sayers, who with Agatha Christie helped make mystery writing a respectable genre in the 20th century, had an intimate knowledge of London, which she displayed primarily through the adventures of Lord Peter Wimsey. For many years Miss Sayers made her home at 24 Great James Street, Bloomsbury; she later retired to Witham, where she died on December 17, 1957.

Richard Church (1893–1972)   Richard Church was born in Battersea on March 16, 1893; he lived at 19 Holland Park in the mid-1930s and at 13 Old Square from 1935 to 1940. Here he worked on the Femina–Vie Heureuse prizewinning novel *The Porch*. As a

boy and youth he had worked at the quay at the customhouse on Lower Thames Street, near St. Mary-at-Hill.

Aldous Huxley (1894–1963)   Before he settled in the United States in 1937, Aldous Huxley had a few associations with London; he was one of the many literary people who have lived in the Albany, off Piccadilly, at one time or another. In 1917, serving as a clerk on the Air Board, he lived with his father and stepmother at 16 Bracknell Gardens, Hampstead, and from June 1919 to December 1920 he had his own flat at 18 Hampstead Hill Gardens. In 1921 he lived at 36 Regent Street, and later in the 1920s he resided at 44 Prince's Gardens, behind the Victoria and Albert Museum.

John Boynton Priestley (1894–   )   The London associations of J. B. Priestley, while obviously spanning a great deal of time, are traceable only through the 1940s and 1950s; he had completed *The English Comic Characters*, *The English Novel*, *The Good Companions*, and *Laburnum Grove* before he took up residence at 3 The Grove in 1935. Here he finished *When We are Married*, in which he played the lead in 1938, before moving to 5 Crown Office Road in 1939; during World War II Priestley did a great deal of broadcasting for the British Broadcasting Corporation, and in the 1940s he lived at 27–28 Well Walk in Hampstead. He lived at the Albany, off Piccadilly just west of Sackville Street, and visited Edward Knoblock (Priestley's collaborator on the dramatization of *The Good Companions*) at 21 Ashley Place and at 11 Montagu Place.

A. J. Cronin (1896–   )   Scottish-born Archibald Joseph Cronin, author of *The Keys of the Kingdom* and *The Citadel*, abandoned medical practice in London in 1926 on account of illness and spent his time writing; *Hatter's Castle* appeared in 1931. He lived at 3 Eldon Road in the 1930s before he emigrated to the United States.

Alec (1898—   ) and Evelyn (1903–1966) Waugh   Both Alec (July 8, 1898) and Evelyn (October 28, 1903) Waugh were born at 11 Hillfield Road, Hampstead, and spent their childhoods here; neither was educated here except for early periods preceding entrance to Sherborne School and Lancing College. Much later, after separating from his wife, Alec Waugh lived at 24 Earl's Terrace.

Elizabeth Bowen (1899–1973)   Elizabeth Bowen, novelist and short-story writer, lived at 2 Clarence Terrace, off the Outer Circle west of Regent's Park, from 1935 until the death of her husband in 1952.

Sir Noël Coward (1899–1973)   Playwright, actor, wit, composer, director, and virtual jack-of-all-trades, Noël Coward had five plays on the boards in London in 1925, and after *Bitter-Sweet*, his most popular musical, was produced in 1929 and any fear of poverty was banished, he took 111 Ebury Street, Belgravia, in the early 1930s. From about 1935 to 1955 he lived at 17 Gerald Road, just a block southwest. He was knighted in 1970 and lived his last years (for health and tax reasons) in Switzerland and Jamaica, where he died on March 26, 1973.

George Orwell (1903–1950)   Although he never abandoned his original name of Eric Blair, in later years he was so closely identified with the name George Orwell, and indeed answered to it, that only a few intimates knew his real name. In accordance with Orwell's will, no biography of the writer exists, and the usual biographical details are consequently difficult to verify. Born in Bengal in 1903, he moved to London with his family at the end of 1917, when his sixty-year-old father enlisted in the armed forces. The family was living at 23 Cromwell Crescent, Earl's Court, and from here Orwell entered Eton. His mother moved the family in the following spring to 23 Mall Chambers, Notting Hill Gate, where they stayed for three years. Deciding not to go to a university in 1921, Orwell followed the family tradition and went off to Burma to serve in the Imperial Police. At the end of 1927, already perceiving that the Burmese no longer wanted alien control and feeling some guilt for his role, he tried to assuage his feelings by living the life of an outcast in London and Paris. He took a room here at 10 Portobello Road in a house run by a Mrs. Craig; it was a "cheap, small, and austere" accommodation, and he stayed in it until leaving for Paris in 1928. Upon his return in 1930, he went to Southwold, where he worked on *Down and Out in Paris and London.* In 1934–1935 he worked in a bookshop at South End Green, Hampstead (where a coffee bar now stands) in return for lodging; here he worked on *Keep the Aspidistra Flying.* The building is marked with a plaque. In 1943–1944 he lived at 101A Mortimer Crescent, Hampstead, and had just finished the manuscript of *Animal Farm* when bombs struck his lodgings. On one occasion he went to one of his favorite pubs, the Fitzroy Tavern, Charlotte Street, where he became too noisy and bothersome and was asked to leave; he then went on to the Wheatsheaf on Rathbone Place, which sold "delicious Scotch ale."

Cyril Connolly (1903–1974)   Cyril Connolly, founder and editor of *Horizon,* lived at 25 Sussex Place, off the Outer Circle on Regent's Park West, at one time.

Cecil Day-Lewis (1904–1972)   The Poet Laureate Cecil Day-Lewis lived somewhere in London during World War II when he was working for the Ministry of Information, but his one known London address dates only to 1954, when he lived at Crooms Hill in Greenwich. He retained the house until his death on May 22, 1972, at Hadley Wood.

Christopher Isherwood (1904–   )   For a time before his emigration to the United States in 1939, Christopher Isherwood, author of *Goodbye to Berlin,* lived at 19 Pembroke Gardens, south of Kensington High Street.

Louis MacNeice (1907–1963)   The Irish-born poet and dramatist Louis MacNeice was in London as a lecturer in Greek at the Bedford College for Women from 1936 to 1940; and from the late 1930s through the early 1940s he settled at 16A Primrose Hill, off Regent's Park Road. Turned down by the Royal Navy, he served as a London fire watcher during World War II:

> When our brother Fire was having his dog's day
> Jumping the London streets with millions of tin cans
> Clanking at his tail, we heard some shadow say
> "Give the dog a bone"—and so we gave him ours;
> Night after night we watched him slaver and crunch away
> The beams of human life, the tops of topless towers.

Here he worked on *Autumn Journal* and *The Poetry of W. B. Yeats* and began writing and producing for the British Broadcasting Corporation. In the mid-1940s MacNeice moved to 10 Wellington Place, St. John's Wood, and here his most successful radio verse play, *The Dark Tower* (with music by Sir Benjamin Britten), and *Collected Poems 1925–1948* were finished. In 1950 and 1951 he was with the British Council as director of the British Institute in Athens, and he moved again in the 1950s to 52 Canonbury Park South, but from 1955 until 1960 he was at 2 Clarence Terrace, Regent's Park. In 1962 MacNeice moved to Aldbury, where he spent the rest of his life; he died of pneumonia on September 3, 1963, in St. Leonard's Hospital, Shoreditch, and memorial services were held at All Souls Church on Langham Place on October 17.

Christopher Fry (1907–   )   Author of *The Lady's Not for Burning,* Christopher Fry for a period in the 1950s and 1960s lived on Blomfield Road, first at Number 27 and then at Number 37. Much acclaimed as a bright new star when he first appeared, Fry saw his reputation somewhat diminish over the years.

Stephen Spender (1909–   )   Stephen Spender entered University College School in London before going to Oxford; in the mid-1930s he lived at 25 Randolph Crescent and was working on the materials later incorporated into *Trial of a Judge* and *The Still Centre.* During World War II Spender was with the National Fire Service; "Thoughts during an Air Raid" was the result of his experiences then:

> Of course, the entire effort is to put myself
> Outside the ordinary range
> Of what are called statistics. A hundred are killed
> In the outer suburbs. Well, well, I carry on.
> So long as the great "I" is propped upon
> This girdered bed which seems more like a hearse,
> In the hotel bedroom with flowering wallpaper
> Which rings in wreaths above, I can ignore
> The pressure of those names under my fingers
> Heavy and black as I rustle the paper,
> The wireless wail in the lounge margin.
> Yet supposing that a bomb should dive
> Its nose right through this bed, with me upon it?
> The thought is obscene.

In 1970 Spender was appointed professor of English at University College, London.

Sir Terence Rattigan (1911–1977)   Sir Terence Rattigan, among England's most successful modern playwrights, was a native of London. His first play, *French without Tears,* was performed in 1936, and for a time Rattigan resided at the Albany (a small street north off Piccadilly, just east of the Burlington Arcade).

Pamela Hansford Johnson (1912–   ) and C. P. Snow (1905–   )   Pamela Hansford Johnson, born in London on May 29, 1912, grew up in the Clapham area; the product of a middle-class family, she was educated locally. Her first novel, *This Bed Thy Centre,* appeared in 1935 and was immediately successful. At one time she lived at 6 Cheyne Walk, Chelsea, and immediately preceding her marriage in 1950 to C. P. Snow, the scientist and novelist best known for his sequence of novels involving Lewis Eliot, she was living at 6 Cheyne Row, Chelsea. During the 1950s and 1960s Miss Johnson and Snow had their home at 199 Cromwell Road, Kensington West; here she wrote *Cork Street, Next to the Hatter's,* and Snow worked on *The Two Cultures and the Scientific Revolution.*

Dylan Thomas (1914–1953) The generally accepted date for Dylan Thomas's first appearance in London is 1932, but now it does not look as if he could have been here before August 1933, when he came for two reasons. The first and most important was to see about publishing in the *New English Weekly,* and the second was to visit his recently married sister and her husband (Nancy and Hayden Taylor), who were living on a houseboat on the Thames. It was at this time that Thomas, after a long drinking session in a local pub, fell into the Thames on his way home; he could not swim, and his brother-in-law fished him out with a boathook. He was in town frequently after that date, and in 1934 he lodged on Parton Street (between Southampton Row and Red Lion Square), an area of decayed three-story Georgian structures. His *18 Poems* was published that year, and in August and part of September he stayed in Battersea with Pamela Hansford Johnson, later the wife of C. P. Snow. During these early years he frequented the Café Royal on Regent Street because in the part of the structure equipped with bare marble-topped tables, he could order a cheap ham sandwich and drink legally no matter what the time was, in defiance of the licensing laws. The Café Royal, though, has a strict policy with respect to drunkenness, and Thomas was often evicted; in fact, in 1935 he was barred for a time on account of his behavior.

In the autumn of 1942 Thomas and his wife Caitlin moved into 9 Wentworth Studios (gone), on the east side of Manressa Road. It was in a row of single-story houses with a glass roof, and they had one large room, "an archaic bathroom, and a kitchen behind a curtain." The roof leaked, and water came in under the door. They lived here until the German raids began again in 1944. Thomas wrote a great number of poems in the nearby Godfrey Street home of Constantine Fitzgibbon, later his biographer, whom Thomas had first met in 1944. The local pubs he drank in are legion: the Australian, the Crossed Keys, the Red House, the Markham, the Pier Hotel, the Angelsea, and the Princess. His favorite was the King's Head and Eight Bells (now modernized), beside the river on Cheyne Walk. He did not, contrary to popular local belief, patronize the Six Bells, as it had been bombed out very early in the war. He wrote for the British Broadcasting Corporation and was a reader for its Third Programme during the war; his superiors (who were, as well, his friends) had to keep him sober until after the show. As Roy Campbell recalled, "Dylan had only one weakness—he could not read correct poets like Pope or Dryden." Campbell continued:

> I used to keep him on beer all day till he had done his night's work. . . . It was with Blake and Manley Hopkins that Dylan became almost Superman; but we had bad luck with Dryden. Dylan had got at the whisky first and he started behaving like a prima donna. . . . There were only two minutes to go and I rushed back to the studio and found Dylan snoring in front of the mike with only twenty seconds left. He was slumped back in his chair, with an almost seraphic expression of blissful peace. I shook him awake, . . . and [he] was almost sober when he got the green light, though he did bungle the title as "Ode on Shaint Sheshilia's Day"; but after that his voice cleared up and I began to breathe again.
>
> When he had finished reading the "Ode" I got another

fright: he began to beckon me wildly with his arms and point to the page before him. I got the engineer to switch off the mike and slipped into the studio again. Dylan had forgotten how to pronounce "Religio Laici". I told him and slipped out. He had about three shots at it, bungled it, gave it up; and then went on reading.

On a trip to London in March 1946, Thomas was rushed off to St. Stephen's Hospital on Fulham Road after he had collapsed with acute alcoholic gastritis and nervous hypertension. Thomas, by the way, never suffered from either the cirrhosis of the liver or the tuberculosis that he claimed. At this time he and Caitlin had been staying in a basement flat on Markham Square. They returned to London in 1951 just prior to his American tour and took a basement flat at 54 Delancey Street; the housing, belonging to Margaret Taylor, was inadequate, and an old caravan was placed in the rear garden for Thomas's study. Almost nightly until they left for the United States, he drank at the nearby Mother Redcap or Finches. Three other places in London favored by Thomas were Ye Olde Cheshire Cheese, in Wine Office Court, the Fitzroy Tavern, on Charlotte Street, and the Marquis of Granby, where Charlotte Street meets Rathbone Place and Percy Street.

Doris Lessing (1919–   ) Doris Lessing, born in Kermanshah, Iran, and raised in Rhodesia, where she remained until 1949, wrote of her early months here in *In Pursuit of the English:*

> It was a nightmare city I lived in for a year; endless miles of heavy, damp, dead building on a dead, sour earth, inhabited by pale, misshapen, sunless creatures under a low sky of grey vapour. Then, one evening, walking across the park, the light welded buildings, trees and scarlet buses into something familiar and beautiful, and I knew myself to be at home. Now London is to me the pleasantest of cities, full of the most friendly and companionable people. . . . It is the variegated light of London which creates it; at night, the mauvish wet illumination of the city sky; or the pattern of black shadow-leaves on a wall; or, when the sun emerges, the instant gaiety of a pavement.

For a time in the 1960s she lived at 60 Carrington Street, and in the 1960s and 1970s she lived at 58 Warwick Road; here she worked on *Briefing for a Descent into Hell* and *The Story of a Non-marrying Man.*

Kingsley Amis (1922–   ) Best known, perhaps, for *Lucky Jim,* Kingsley Amis is a native Londoner. Born on April 16, 1922, he received his first education at the City of London School before going up to St. John's College, Oxford. From 1965 to 1968 he resided at 108 Maida Vale.

John Osborne (1929–   ) The original "angry young man," John Osborne is a native of London; born on December 12, 1929, he is the son of a commercial artist and a barmaid. At one point Osborne lived at 15 Woodfall Street, Chelsea. *Look Back in Anger* appeared in 1956, and in 1957 *The Entertainer* was produced. During the 1960s Osborne lived at 11A Curzon Street.

LONG MELFORD, Suffolk (pop. 2,635) Possibly the most impressive single thoroughfare in Suffolk, Long Melford's main street is flanked by houses and shops of dignity and charm and of disparate architectural styles. The village is an old one (evidence of Roman settlement has been unearthed), and its medieval prosperity was based on the wool trade; Long Melford held one of the elaborate manor homes of the abbot of Bury St. Edmunds (14 miles to the north), and both Melford Hall and Kentwell Hall are Elizabethan. The Church of the Holy Trinity, a Suffolk wool church with excellent flush work, dates to the 14th century, although the Clopton Chantry Chapel is ascribed to 1496 or so. Around the walls of the chapel is a carved scroll inscribed with fragmentary verses generally attributed to John Lydgate, the monk of Bury, although he died some forty-five years before the chapel was completed. However, he was a familiar figure to the Clopton family, and there is, therefore, some validity to the claim. The final lines of one of the poems were taken by John Masefield for the motto of "The Everlasting Mercy."

More recently, in 1965, Hall Mill became the home of Edmund Blunden; he attended Holy Trinity and wrote the church guidebook, which is still being sold. Blunden lived here until his death in 1974 and was buried in the churchyard.

Long Melford comes into George Borrow's *Lavengro;* Belle (Isopel Berners), whom Borrow meets with the Flaming Tinman, cites her background:

> "None of your Rommany chies, young fellow . . . you had better be civil. . . . I would have you to know that I come of Christian blood and parents, and was born in the great house of Long Melford."

She later explains that "the great house" was the workhouse in Long Melford.

LONG WITTENHAM, Berkshire (pop. 694) Nestled between the Sinodun Hills and Wittenham Clump, a wooded adjoining hill, Long Wittenham is an attractive village on the banks of the Thames River 10 miles due south of Oxford. The village's main road, next to the double curves of the river, is absolutely straight, and from the top of the hill both the Vale of the White Horse to the west and vast plains backed by the Chiltern escarpment can be seen. The village road leads to a six-arch bridge spanning the Thames into Oxfordshire, and nearby is the Barley Mow Inn, which is associated with Jerome K. Jerome's *Three Men in a Boat.* Here the men camp; the narrator describes the scene:

> It is without exception, I should say, the quaintest, most old world inn up the river. It stands on the right of the bridge, quite away from the village. Its low-pitched gables and thatched roof and latticed windows give it quite a story book appearance, while inside it is even more once-upon-a-timeyfied.

LONGLEAT, Wiltshire The seat of the Marquess of Bath and called the most magnificent house in England by Thomas Babington Macaulay, Longleat (2½ miles west of Warminster) is an outstanding survival of 16th-century architecture; built by Sir John Thynne, it is crowned with a myriad of domes, sculpted figures, and cupolas and contains not only one of the finest private art collections in England but a library of more than 30,000 volumes, including a Caxton printing of Raoul Lefèvre's *The Recuyell of the Historyes of Troye* (ca. 1475), the first book printed in English, and an autograph letter written by Samuel Daniel. A number of the books in the collection belonged to Bishop Thomas Ken, who was offered hospitality here by the 1st Viscount Weymouth after he refused to give allegiance to William III. One of the earliest mentions of this seat occurs in "To the Honourable Lady Worsley at Longleate." In 1824 George Crabbe and Thomas Moore were here as the guests of the 2d Marquess of Bath.

LONGTON, Staffordshire (pop. 37,812) At the southern end of the now-amalgamated area of the Potteries, Longton is now part of the 36-square-mile complex of Stoke-on-Trent, formed from the pottery towns of Tunstall, Burslem, Longton, Hanley, and Stoke, with Fenton added in. Indeed, even the great old pottery firms have been merged into a megalith called Allied Potteries. Longton is the Longshaw of Arnold Bennett's "Five Towns" novels.

LONGTOWN, Cumberland On the highroad 9 miles north of Carlisle, Longtown is the last English town on the main western road to Scotland; here a five-arch stone bridge spans the Esk River. The 17th-century church at Arthuret contains monuments to the Graham family of nearby Netherby Hall, the home of "fair Ellen," the Graham heiress who eloped with "young Lochinvar." Sir Walter Scott tells the story in the fifth canto of *Marmion:*

> He staid not for brake, and he stopp'd not for stone,
> He swam the Eske river where ford there was none;
> But ere he alighted at Netherby gate,
> The bride had consented, the gallant came late:
> For a laggard in love, and a dastard in war,
> Was to wed the fair Ellen of brave Lochinvar.

LONGWORTH, Berkshire (pop. 773) Situated in the northwest section of the shire with a fine view across the Thames into the Cotswolds, Longworth is noted for its parish church and its native son Richard Doddridge Blackmore, whose father was curate in charge here. The church is an excellent example of the transition from the massive Norman building (the 13th-century north arcade) to the slender and delicate Early English building (the 14th-century south arcade). The 13th-century font is the one in which Blackmore was christened shortly after his birth on June 7, 1825. Three months after his birth, an epidemic of scarlet fever wiped out almost half the population of the village, including the author's mother. The elder Blackmore, because of his grief unable to remain in the village, soon took the living at Culmstock. Longworth was also the birthplace of Dr. John Fell, Dean of Christ Church, Oxford.

LOOE, Cornwall (pop. 3,750) East Looe and West Looe, connected by a Victorian bridge just above the estuary of the united Looe Rivers, are two distinct little towns in the Looe Urban District. East Looe, as a prosperous fishing village, dominates. It is a jumble of narrow cobbled streets overhung with lovely medieval houses; West Looe is clustered around the very interesting Church of St. Nicholas, which for almost 300 years functioned as the guildhall. Looe has always been a dissenting community, and when the town was exporting large quantities of pilchards to the Catholic Mediterranean countries, the inhabitants expressed their feelings in a rhyme which is still common in the village:

Long life to the Pope! May he live to repent
And add just six months to the term of his Lent,
And tell all his vassals from Rome to the Poles
There's nothing like pilchards for saving their souls!

Looe Island, off the coast, was mistaken by the Germans in World War II for a royal aircraft carrier; it was virtually bombed out of the bay, and over the German radio Lord Haw-Haw announced the complete destruction of the *Ark Royal*.

Wilkie Collins, here on his West Country tour in the summer of 1850, declared that Looe was "one of the most primitive places in England." From childhood on Eric Blair (George Orwell) was a frequent visitor to Looe, and many years later, in September 1927, he waited until his family was again in convivial surroundings here to inform them that he had resigned his commission in Burma and was planning to write. Katherine Mansfield, already ill with tuberculosis, arrived here in May 1918 to attempt one of many cures. She stayed at the Headland Hotel and, as she wrote in a letter, had "a really vast room with three windows all south . . . . clean as a pin, gay, with a deep armchair, [and] a bed with two mattresses. . . ." She remained only a short time on this occasion but returned at the end of June for a five weeks' stay.

LORTON, Westmorland (pop. 326) Situated in the Lorton Vale, which extends from Crummock Water to Cockermouth, Lorton is on the Cocker River 4 miles southeast of Cockermouth. The village is known because William Wordsworth's "Yew-Trees" talks of the old village yew, "of vast circumference and gloom profound":

There is a Yew-tree, pride of Lorton Vale,
Which to this day stands single, in the midst
Of its own darkness, as it stood of yore:
Not loth to furnish weapons for the bands
Of Umfraville or Percy ere they marched
To Scotland's heaths: or those that crossed the sea
And drew their sounding bows at Azincour,
Perhaps at earlier Crecy, or Poictiers.

Some 150 years before, George Fox preached to such a crowd of Quakers here that many climbed into the tree. Fox noted in his *Journal* that the tree "was so full of people that I feared they would break it down."

LOTHERSDALE, Yorkshire (pop. 454) A small North Riding village 5 miles southwest of Skipton, Lothersdale was the village to which Charlotte Brontë came in June 1839 as governess to the youngest child in the family of a wealthy industrialist named Sidgwick; the time was far from pleasant, for as she writes to Emily,

The children are constantly with me. As for correcting them, I quickly found that was out of the question; for they are to do as they like. A complaint to the mother only brings black looks on myself, and unjust, partial, excuses to screen the children. . . . [Mrs. ———] cares nothing about me, except to contrive how the greatest possible quantity of labour may be got out of me; and to that end she overwhelms me with oceans of needlework; yards of cambric to hem, muslin nightcaps to make, and, above all things, dolls to dress.

Mrs. Sidgwick was a constant scold, and the children were "pampered, spoilt, [and] turbulent." The Sidgwick home, Stonegappe Hall, which can be seen from above the village, becomes Gateshead Hall; this is Jane Eyre's early "home," and the "red-room . . . a spare chamber" where Mr. Reed dies is where Jane is locked in after the incident with John Reed.

LOUGHBOROUGH, Leicestershire (pop. 30, 370) Loughborough (pronounced "luff'boro"), the second largest town in the county, situated 11 miles north of Leicester, is England's "Town of the Bells." Bells have been cast here for more than 100 years; the chief of these is the great Paul of St. Paul's Cathedral in London, which stands more than 9 feet high and weighs more than 16½ tons. There are bells in Loughborough as well, and the Grand Carillon in Queen's Park is one of the finest in England. Much of the early prosperity of the city came from the hosiery trade, and Loughborough was the scene of Luddite rioting in the early 19th century.

Two centuries earlier, in June 1613, John Cleveland (properly spelled Cleiveland) was born here and was baptized at the Church of SS. Peter and Paul (now All Saints'). His early years were spent in Loughborough, and his first education took place in All Saints' Church, where his father was schoolmaster; the family then moved to Hinckley, Leicestershire.

LOUGHTON, Essex (pop. 5,749) One of the numerous towns and villages on the southeastern edge of the Epping Forest, once the hunting ground of monarchs, Loughton (pronounced "low'ton") has merged its identity with that of London. Loughton Hall (rebuilt) once belonged to Sir Robert and Lady Mary Wroth, daughter of Robert Sidney, Earl of Leicester, and niece of Sir Philip Sidney, who is said to have been a frequent visitor when the house belonged to Lady Mary's father. Later Ben Jonson was often here and dedicated *The Alchemist* to Lady Mary; indeed, the hall was a fashionable meeting place for literary figures of the late 16th and early 17th centuries. Loughton Hall itself comes into literature much later, when Charles Dickens undoubtedly used an event here as the basis for the fire at the great house and the fortunate tolling of the bell in *Barnaby Rudge*. In December 1836 a fire destroyed fifty rooms; the occupants and part of the mansion were saved by the butler, who was awakened by the clamor of the bell in the library; the bell was set to ringing by bits of falling masonry. Most likely Dickens heard this story when staying in nearby Chigwell.

For some months Rudyard Kipling lived with a farmer and his family in a farmhouse, now replaced by two cottages, directly opposite Golding's Hill Pond. Kipling had been sent from India to school in Southsea, Hampshire, where the headmaster, a retired naval captain, was a pleasant-enough sort, but his wife, a religious fanatic, was an extremely cruel woman, applying discipline mainly through physical abuse and fear. When Kipling's mother returned to England in March 1877, he was found to be almost blind and was brought here on holiday. An incident soon after their arrival (his mother went up to his room to say goodnight, and he threw up his arm to ward off the supposed blow) terminated his education at Southsea. He stayed on here until the autumn, when he went to the United Services College at Westward Ho!, Devon. Sarah Martin, author of "Old Mother Hubbard," was buried here in 1826, and W. W. Jacobs, author of "The Monkey's Paw," lived at The Outlook, Park Hill, in the early 20th century.

One rather well-known work was composed here by someone whose name is never recognized in connection with it: Sarah Flower, the actress, was living at Woodbury Hall when she wrote "Nearer, My God, to Thee," the hymn sung as the *Titanic* sank. Her sister Elizabeth composed the music.

LOUTH, Lincolnshire (pop. 9,536) One of the best-preserved Georgian towns in England, Louth is on the eastern edge of the 40-mile upland area of Lincolnshire known as the Wolds. In this area of rolling hills and deep valleys, the village lies in a valley where the Wolds come down to the marsh. Louth's importance began in 1139, when Bishop Alexander of Lincoln gave land here to a colony of Cistercian monks from Fountains Abbey. The abbey built here was one of the largest in the country and flourished until it was devastated by the plague; built just east of the town proper, it was almost totally destroyed at the dissolution of the monasteries in the 16th century. The townspeople and the monks were goaded into open rebellion at the suppression when Henry VIII called the men of Lincolnshire, "the rude commons of one of the most brute and beastly shires of the whole realm." The King had a number of the rebels as well as the vicar summarily executed.

In 1816 Alfred, Lord Tennyson and his brothers were sent to the grammar school here, which was then located on Schoolhouse Lane; the school, refounded by Edward VI and bearing his name, is now part of a school for girls. Tennyson had a miserable time and was bullied by both the headmaster, the Rev. T. Waite, and his schoolfellows; so unhappy was he that years later he was unable to walk down the lane where the school was:

> How I did hate that school! The only good I ever got from it was the memory of the words, "sonus desilientis aquae," and of an old wall covered with wild weeds opposite the school windows. I wrote an English poem there, for one of the Jacksons; the only line I recollect is "While bleeding heroes lie along the shore."

He left the school in 1820 to study at home in Somersby with his father.

Another scholar of the school was Capt. John Smith, one of the founders of Virginia.

LOWESTOFT, Suffolk (pop. 41,768) The triangular limits of the Norfolk Broads are defined by Sea Palling, Norwich, and Lowestoft (pronounced "lo'stoft"), the southern limit and the easternmost point in England. Situated 10 miles south of Yarmouth, Lowestoft has suffered through many invasions and privations, but the worst undoubtedly was the savage attack of the Luftwaffe beginning in 1939. Much has been lost here, but quite possibly the tradition of defiance of the equally merciless sea has helped the town to survive. Originally settled by the Danes at Lowestoft Ness, the town was well populated by 1308, when it received its market charter, and it became an extremely important medieval fishing center (fishing

is still important in the 20th century). Herring, sole, plaice, and cod were the main catches, and by the time of Henry VIII fourteen ships were engaged in fishing as far away as the Icelandic waters. Today much of the rebuilt town caters to the holiday trade.

The literary history of Lowestoft begins in 1567, when Thomas Nashe (Nash) was born here; his father, sometimes described as a preacher and a minister, was probably no more than a curate. Nashe was baptized in November of that year (the record is preserved in the church) and was educated here. In *Lenten Stuffe: The Praise of Red Herring*, he mentions the early discord between Lowestoft and Great Yarmouth in which Richard II had to intervene. Two centuries later George Crabbe frequently rode here to Normanston Park to visit Sarah Elmy, his fiancée, who was residing with the Misses Blackwell and Waldron. In the 19th century Lowestoft became one of Edward FitzGerald's favorite spots. From 1865 on he was here at least once a year, usually for an extended period, and he stayed at 11 and 12 Marine Terrace and at the Suffolk Hotel. He spent long hours walking the shore "longing for some fellow to accost me who might give some promise of filling up a very vacant place in my heart." Eventually he met Joseph Fletcher, the redheaded Posh, on whom FitzGerald grew so dependent that he commissioned the building of a herring lugger, *Meum and Deum*. FitzGerald planned to operate the lugger with his friend, but in the end he turned it over to Posh. He and his boatman sailed frequently until the latter's death in 1877, when FitzGerald lost all interest in sailing. On a trip to Lowestoft in 1857, the year *The Romany Rye* was published, FitzGerald met its author, George Borrow, who lived in Oulton Broad.

As a port Lowestoft has attracted many people but perhaps none who became as famous as the Polish immigrant Joseph Conrad, who in May 1878 stepped off the *Mavis* knowing only one or two words of English, acquainted with no one, and having little money. Within two months he had signed on a coaster, *The Skimmer of the Seas*, which plied its way between here and Newcastle upon Tyne; he began learning English on board the ship, and his experiences were later called on in his writing. Lowestoft, Conrad said, was his "spiritual birthplace." Finally, Hilaire Belloc was sent here to convalesce after collapsing from overwork following his United States lecture tour in 1898.

LOWICK, Lancashire (pop. 14) On the Crake River 5 miles north of Ulverston, the hamlet of Lowick is dominated by Lowick Hall, which dates in part to Norman times. During the short period that Arthur Ransome lived at the manor (1947–1949), he undertook extensive repairs and restoration work.

LOWTHER, Westmorland (pop. 407) The great house of Lowther was once the pride of the county, but all that remains are a shell and a 3,000-acre parkland estate containing deer, wallabies, and native cattle and sheep. Set on the bank of the Lowther River 4 miles south of Penrith, the house was the one-time home of the Earls of Lonsdale, and to it came Mary, Queen of Scots when Sir Richard Lowther was one of her supporters. The 2d Earl of Lonsdale was a

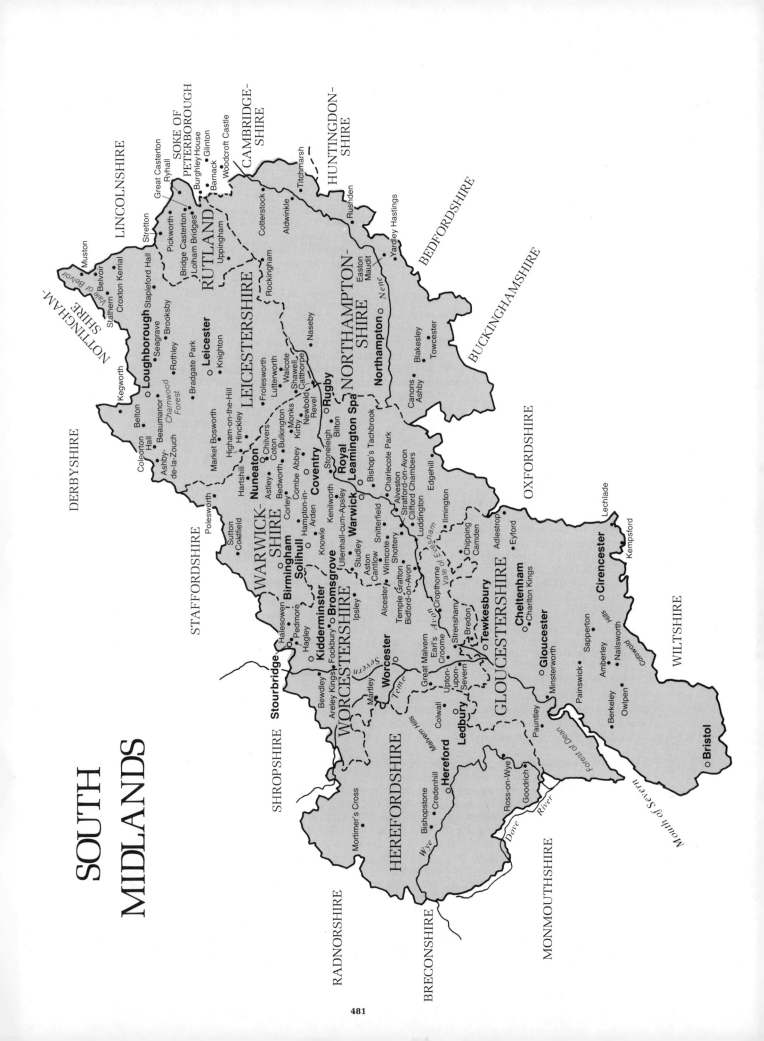

SOUTH MIDLANDS

481

patron of literature and the arts and a friend of William Wordsworth, who probably met Lord Lonsdale in the company of his wife and Sir George and Lady Beaumont in August 1807. After this meeting Wordsworth usually spent a few days each autumn at the earl's home here or at his other residence, Castle Whitehaven. It was to Lord Lonsdale that Wordsworth dedicated *The Excursion:*

> OFT, through thy fair domains, illustrious Peer!
> In youth I roamed, on youthful pleasures bent;
> And mused in rocky cell or sylvan tent,
> Beside swift-flowing Lowther's current clear.
> —Now, by thy care befriended, I appear
> Before thee, LONSDALE, and this Work present,
> A token (may it prove a monument!)
> Of high respect and gratitude sincere.

LUCCOMBE CHINE, Isle of Wight   Between Shanklin and Ventnor, Luccombe Chine is one of the most picturesque areas on the Isle of Wight, with high limestone cliffs and a winding, wooded glen. John Keats came here from Carisbrooke and Shanklin on August 17 or 18, 1817, and undoubtedly his visit to the great cave prompted his sonnet "On the Sea":

> It keeps eternal whisperings around
>   Desolate shores, and with its mighty swell
>   Gluts twice ten thousand Caverns, till the spell
> Of Hecate leaves them their old shadowy sound.

LUDDINGTON, Warwickshire (pop. 105)   Just 3 miles southwest of Stratford-on-Avon and itself on the Avon River, Luddington has very little to offer today's visitor; its old church and its records have unfortunately vanished, for here, tradition maintains, William Shakespeare and Anne Hathaway were married. The claim rests solely on a statement made about Anne Hathaway's native village and the vicar who held this living. Around 1750 the Rev. Joseph Greene, then headmaster of the Stratford grammar school, wrote:

> His [Shakespeare's] wife was the daughter of one Hathaway, a substantial yeoman in the neighbourhood of Stratford, probably *of a* place about a mile from thence call'd *Luddington,* where a *substantial* family of *that name and occupation still reside....*

The second bit of evidence is that Thomas Hunt, allegedly one of Shakespeare's masters at the grammar school (it is assumed that the poet attended the school) was vicar of this parish.

LUDLOW, Shropshire (pop. 5,674)   A market town about 27 miles south of Shrewsbury, Ludlow is undoubtedly one of the finest towns in England; its appeal is literary, historical, and aesthetic. It has rich and well-preserved half-timbered buildings and a mellowness created by the extensive use of red sandstone. Ludlow Castle, built by Roger de Montgomery, Earl of Shrewsbury, in 1085, has been enlarged and its fortifications strengthened over the centuries. One of many castles erected as border defenses against the Welsh, the castle was the point from which Wales and the border were governed. Its history until the time of Henry VII was stormy, but when Henry Tudor, himself a Welshman, assumed the throne after killing Richard III on Bosworth

Field, the area became one of peace through his royal influence.

Henry directed that the castle become the seat of jurisdictional power over the western border counties, and in 1559 Queen Elizabeth appointed Sir Henry Sidney Lord President of the Marches, a post he kept for twenty-seven years. Sidney brought his family here, and his young son Philip would have known the area very well. In 1631 the official post of Lord President came to the 1st Earl of Bridgewater, and he assumed the official residence two years later. In September 1634, on Michaelmas Night, John Milton's masque *Comus,* with music by Henry Lawes, was presented here in the Great Hall (60 feet long and 30 feet wide) with the earl's family taking part in the performance; tradition holds that Milton was in attendance.

Another 17th-century writer, but one whose political views were diametrically opposed to Milton's, also has a link with Ludlow Castle. In 1660 the 2d Earl of Carbery was appointed Lord President, and he named Samuel Butler to the secretaryship. Butler's rooms were above the 14th-century gateway, and here he worked on part of *Hudibras.* Butler held the position for about a year, resigning when he appeared to have made an advantageous marriage.

Daniel Defoe was in Ludlow some years later and commented on the beauty of the countryside, the decay of the castle, and the state of the town in *A Tour thro' the Whole Island of Great Britain:*

> The Situation of this Castle is most Beautiful indeed; there is a most spacious Plain or Lawn in its Front, which formerly continu'd near two Miles; but much of it is now enclosed. The Country round it is exceeding pleasant, fertile, populous, and the Soil rich. . . .
> The Castle itself is in the very Perfection of Decay, all the fine Courts, the Royal Apartments, Halls, and Rooms of State, lye open, abandoned and some of them falling down; . . . Time, the great Devourer of the Works of Men, begins to eat into the very Stone Walls, and to spread the Face of Royal Ruins upon the whole Fabrick.
> The Town of *Ludlow* is a tolerable Place, but it decays *to be sure* with the rest. . . .

Ludlow has a second outstanding architectural monument, the cathedral-like Church of St. Lawrence. While the 135-foot Perpendicular spire of the sandstone church dominates the town, the interior of the edifice is even more impressive with exquisitely carved chancel stalls. The stalls are 15th-century, and the humor of the carvings is matched by the variety. Among them are a fox dressed in bishop's clothes, the devil making off with an alewife for giving short measure, a peddler complete with pack struggling to pull off his boots, a man warming himself by the fire with two slabs of bacon behind him, and various chained animals.

Ludlow and St. Lawrence's Church come into four parts of A. E. Housman's *A Shropshire Lad;* his celebration and love of the Shropshire countryside are well known, and it seems most appropriate that after his death in a Cambridge nursing home on April 30, 1936, and subsequent cremation in London, his ashes were brought here and placed under the north wall of the church. The commemorative tablet, which faces Wenlock Edge and Long Wynd, mentions him only as

Author of "A Shropshire Lad"
Born 26 March, 1859   Died 30 April, 1936
Good Night.   Ensured Release,
Imperishable Peace
Have These For Yours.

Housman wrote his own funeral verses, which conclude:

> We now to peace and darkness
>   And earth and thee restore
> Thy creature that thou madest
>   And wilt cast forth no more.

Ludlow was the birthplace of Stanley Weyman on August 7, 1855; the son of a solicitor, he was educated at the grammar school here before being sent on to the Shrewsbury School. After finishing at Oxford and being called to the bar, he remained at 54 Broad Street with his family until his marriage in 1895. He used Ludlow as the setting of *The New Rector*.

LUTON, Bedfordshire (pop. 136,390) The planners and builders of the late 19th and the 20th centuries must take the responsibility for this modern industrial complex, which is spreading its suburbs over all available space. It is even possible that Dunstable, 4½ miles to the west, may eventually be taken over. Part of Luton, though, predates modern times: Walud's Bank, northwest of the city, was a Neolithic camp, and Dray's Ditches, to the northeast, was an extensive Iron Age stockade. Medieval Luton was an important market town dealing with the wares of tanners, dyers, turners, coopers, and farmers, and a few notable medieval buildings still survive (Moat House at Biscot and the gatehouse of Someries).

Literary associations with Luton are solely of the 20th century. George Bernard Shaw was brought to a hospital here from Ayot St. Lawrence, Hertfordshire, where he had broken his leg in September 1950 while pruning trees in his garden. He was making a good recovery here when kidney trouble developed. Shaw was operated on and remained in the hospital until October 4, when his request to return home was granted. He died in Ayot in November. Joseph Conrad moved to Someries on September 10, 1907, and remained more than a year; he took a farmhouse on the Luton Hoo estate of Sir Julius Wernher. Conrad was in a period of depression over his problems with *Chance* and turned to two other pieces: "Il Conde" was completed during this period, and *Razumov* (later called *Under Western Eyes*) was begun in January 1908. At the beginning of 1909 Conrad and his wife moved to Aldington, Kent.

LUTTERWORTH, Leicestershire (pop. 2,092) Lutterworth's High Street rises steeply from the bridge over the River Swift and leads to the 12th-century parish church, which contains two remarkable medieval wall paintings; here, almost 7½ miles northeast of Rugby, John Wycliffe made his home from 1374, when he took this living, for ten years until his death. He spend much of his time working on the first English translation of the Bible while also attending to his responsibilities at Oxford. Suffering a paralytic stroke here in 1382 or 1383, he was able to resume his duties; but on December 28, 1384, he became ill during services and was carried through what is now called Wycliffe's Door to the rectory, where he died on December 31. Wycliffe was buried in the churchyard, but in 1415 the Council of Constance ordered that the body be disinterred, burned, and thrown into the Swift (this was done in 1428). There is a commemorative mural, but many of the display items in the church claimed as Wycliffe's, such as a chair, a table, and an embroidered vestment, have been proved to be of a later date.

LYDLINCH, Dorset (pop. 294) The tiny River Lydden runs through the village of Lydlinch, in the Vale of Blackmoor 3 miles west of Sturminster Newton. The gentle hills here are covered with thickly wooded patches, but to the Dorset poet William Barnes the character of the village was gained from its bells:

> When vrozen grass, so white's a sheet,
> Did scrunchy sharp below our veet,
> An' water, that did sparkle red
> At zunzet, wer a-vrozen dead;
> The ringers then did spend an hour
> A-ringen changes up in tow'r;
> Vor Lydlinch bells be good vor sound,
> An' like by all the naïghbours round.

LYME REGIS, Dorset (pop. 3,000) The tiny Lym River gushes through the center of the town of Lyme Regis, which is set at the mouth of the river where it flows into Lyme Bay, and for centuries the town was one of the most important ports on the south coast. The Domesday Book (1086) records the manor here, and its royal title was bestowed when Edward I (r. 1272–1307) used the harbor during his wars with the French. The original Cobb, a curved breakwater needed because of the lack of a natural harbor, was built by Edward, and in following centuries Lyme Regis prospered as a port. In 1685, when the Duke of Monmouth landed at the Cobb, Lyme Regis became the touch point of a revolution, since the Duke proclaimed his own right of succession and accused James II of having murdered Charles II. Lyme Regis became the rallying point for thousands of volunteers including Daniel Defoe; the ill-equipped army then marched off to Axminster and total defeat. Lyme Regis then went into a decline and did not become fashionable as a resort until the late 18th century.

When Henry Fielding was here in the early 18th century, he fell in love with Sarah Andrew, an heiress and possibly Fielding's cousin, who lived with her uncle Andrew Tucker, a local official. Tucker's disapproval of the match—he may have wanted his own son to wed her—made Fielding take matters into his own hands. He tried to carry off Miss Andrew and in the process seems to have uttered threats against her uncle; indeed, Tucker had to get a restraining order to keep Fielding away. It is Sarah Andrew who becomes Sophia in *Tom Jones*.

The resort was a particular favorite of Jane Austen; she spent her summer holidays here in 1803 and 1804 and wrote: "A very strange stranger it must be who does not see charms in the immediate environs of Lyme to make him wish to know it better." The house where she stayed in the old port still stands. Not only was *Persuasion* written here, but one of its most famous scenes was enacted in the town. The steps from the upper to the lower Cobb where Louisa Musgrove fell are still in place, and Bay Cottage (now a café) on Marine Road is where Captain Harville has rooms and Louisa recuperates. The impact of the novel on Lyme Regis is well illustrated by an event which occurred more than sixty years later. Alfred, Lord Tennyson visited here in 1867 with friends who wanted to take him to the Cobb to see the landing place of the Duke of Monmouth. Tennyson, his irritation showing, said, "Don't talk to me of the Duke of Monmouth; show me the exact spot where Louisa Musgrove fell."

In the 20th century Virgina Stephen (Woolf) holidayed here at Little Park with her family for a fortnight in April 1900; and John Galsworthy spent a few weeks here in February and March 1907, when he began work on *Strife*. Neither his lodging nor Kenneth Grahame's is known; Grahame spent most of the spring and summer of 1911 here before going on to Fowey, Cornwall.

LYMINGTON, Hampshire (pop. 18,000) On a tidal river of the same name in southern Hampshire, Lymington is the largest and possibly the most attractive town in the New Forest, although it offers a number of incongruous contrasts such as the stable Georgian facades on Quay Hill facing the bustling modern yacht basin. With the dual attraction of the New Forest and the water, Lymington became the home of Coventry Patmore in 1891. The Lodge, "a bluish building, standing coyly askew among trees, very retired and dowdy-looking," is on a small promontory looking out to the Isle of Wight. Much of the once relatively extensive grounds (more than 3 acres) surrounding the house have dropped into the mud of the estuary. Two of Patmore's more frequent guests, Francis Thompson and Alice Meynell, were especially fond of the house and of the solitude here. Patmore died in the Lodge on November 26, 1896, and was buried in the Catholic portion of the Lymington parish cemetery. At his request he was shrouded in the habit of the Franciscan order; his grave is marked with an obelisk.

Edward Gibbon became the Member of Parliament for the borough in 1774. After a relatively undistinguished parliamentary career, he retired in 1783 to Lausanne to finish *The History of the Decline and Fall of the Roman Empire*. Although he never lived in the borough, he had an extensive knowledge of Hampshire, having served in the Hampshire Militia (1759–1763) and having spent his early adulthood at the manor house in Buriton.

In one of his numerous excursions in search of inspiration and enforced activity, Dante Gabriel Rossetti came to the home of William Allingham, a minor 19th-century poet, in September 1867. He remained nine days, took no active interest in the area, saying he found nothing of interest, and refused to go to the Isle of Wight to meet Alfred, Lord Tennyson because of a fear of seasickness.

LYMPNE, Kent (pop. 592) Situated 2½ miles west of Hythe, Lympne (pronounced "lim") was once the Roman Portus Limenus, a fort built in this verdant area around the 3d century to help keep off Saxon invaders; at that time a branch of the Rother (usually then called the Limen or Limene) flowed here before entering the sea at Hythe. The settlement was on the Roman Stane (Stone) Street, which led due north to Canterbury, and the fortress (in a field near the castle) covered some 10 acres. The present Lympne Castle (restored), built around 1360 on the site of a house belonging to the Archbishops of Canterbury, looks across Romney Marsh to Dungeness and served as a lookout from Roman times through World War II.

H. G. Wells uses Lympne in both *The First Men in the Moon* and *Kipps*. He describes the general area in the first of these works:

> Certainly if any one wants solitude, the place is Lympne. It is in the clay part of Kent, and my bungalow stood on the edge of an old sea cliff and stared across the flats of Romney Marsh at the sea. In very wet weather the place is almost inaccessible.... I doubt if the place would be there at all, if it were not a fading memory of things gone for ever. It was the big port of England in Roman times, Portus Lemanus, and now the sea is four miles away. All down the steep hill are boulders and masses of Roman brickwork, and from it old Watling Street, still paved in places, starts like an arrow to the north.... And where the port had been were the levels of the marsh, sweeping round in a broad curve to distant Dungeness....
>
> That outlook on the marsh was. indeed, one of the finest views I have ever seen.

Lympne, of course, is where Cavor lives, works, and experiments and where a great deal of the action of the novel occurs. In *Kipps* the castle is the object of the excursion with Helen, Mrs. Walshingham, Coote, and young Walshingham. It is the day on which "Kipps had clambered to the battlements of Heart's Desire." The group goes past "Portus Lemanus, up the steep slopes towards the castle on the crest":

> The Castle became a farm-house, and the farm-house, itself now ripe and venerable, wears the walls of the castle as a little man wears a big man's coat.... One climbs the Keep, up a tortuous spiral of stone, worn to the pitch of perforation, and there one is lifted to the centre of far more than a hemisphere of view. Away below one's feet, almost at the bottom of the hill, the Marsh begins and spreads and spreads in a mighty crescent that sweeps about the sea, the Marsh dotted with the church towers of forgotten mediaeval towns, ... and round the north, bounding the wide perspective of farms and houses and woods, the Downs, with their hangers and chalk-pits, sustain the passing shadows of the sailing clouds.

LYNDHURST, Hampshire (pop. 2,931) Located in part of the most beautiful area of the New Forest, Lyndhurst is approached on roads that give a false impression that this is a private park. Here are wide grass shoulders, adjacent woodland, and large numbers of the wild New Forest animals: cows, donkeys, pigs, and ponies. All the animals are actually owned and tallied by the Court of Verders, which is the absolute legal body in the New Forest, and Lyndhurst is, in fact, the administrative center of the New Forest with the Verders' Court sitting in the 17th-century Queen's House.

It seems appropriate that this somewhat fantastic setting was the home of Mrs. Reginald Hargreaves, neé Alice Liddell, the original of Lewis Carroll's Alice in *Alice in Wonderland,* for whom the story was composed at Oxford when Alice's father was dean of Christ Church. Her grave is in the parish churchyard. The large parish church, situated on a bank at the end of the town, has stained-glass windows which are all the work of the Pre-Raphaelite school; included are works by William Morris and Dante Gabriel Rossetti.

From 1900 on Virginia Stephen (Woolf) often spent part of her summer holidays here at Fritham House with her family. The New Forest held many attractions for her, especially riding, and these periods were among her happiest.

LYNMOUTH, Devon Because this tiny village and harbor on the north coast of Devon is situated between steep wooded hills on the west and the sea on the east, its growth has been held in check, but its position at the mouth of the Lyn River also brought its worst disaster, in 1952. The Lyn violently overflowed its banks following an unusual storm over Exmoor. Lynmouth was deluged by a flood so severe that more than 100 homes were wiped out, twenty-eight bridges were damaged or destroyed, and thirty-one people were killed. Fortunately the rather pictur-

esque thatched houses on the harbor and promenade were unharmed. This district of the town is much as it was when Robert Southey visited here in the early 19th century and declared that Lynmouth was "the finest spot, except Cintra and the Arrabida" that he had ever seen.

Initially Percy Bysshe Shelley was of the same enthusiastic opinion as Southey; Shelley and his first wife came here from Wales in June 1812. Shelley, then engaged in writing rather outspoken pamphlets, tried to get his *Letter to Lord Ellenborough, Occasioned by the Sentence Which He Passed on Mr. D. J. Eaton, as Publisher of the Third Part of Paine's Age of Reason* published, but the Barnstaple publisher destroyed seventy-four of the seventy-five printed copies when he discovered the nature of the work. From here Shelley and Harriet sent out, in bottles and boxes, the *Dedication of Rights,* a piece which so upset the provincial authorities that they notified the Home Office about Shelley's activities. Shortly after this incident, in August, the couple left for Tremadoc, Wales. The "myrtle twined cottage" where Shelly stayed is now Shelley's Cottage Hotel and as a historic building is under a preservation order.

MABLETHORPE, Lincolnshire (pop. 2,852) A holiday center on the sand-dune coast of Lincolnshire 13 miles east of Louth, Mablethorpe has been flooded over the centuries, and the extremely heavy floods of 1953 prompted the construction of concrete defenses to stave off future inroads from the sea. But the sea has taken its toll, for St. Peter's Church as well as numerous old houses have been swept away. In the 19th century the Tennyson family spent their summer holidays in a cottage close to "the long low line of tussocked dunes"; Alfred, Lord Tennyson later recalled, "I used to stand on this sand-built ridge and think that it was the spine-bone of the world." He remembered the wide expanse of marshland to the west:

> Whether the high field on the bushless Pike,
> Or even a sand-built ridge
> Of heapèd hills that mound the sea,
> Overblown with murmurs harsh,
> Or even a lowly cottage whence we see
> Stretched wide and wild the waste enormous marsh,
> Where from the frequent bridge,
> Like emblems of infinity,
> The trenchèd waters run from sky to sky. . . .

Here Alfred and his brother Charles celebrated the publication of *Poems by Two Brothers*, and around 1837 Alfred Tennyson wrote a fragment (later given to the *Manchester Athenaeum Album*) about the village:

> Here often when a child I lay reclined:
>   I took delight in this fair strand and free;
> Here stood the infant Ilion of the mind,
>   And here the Grecian ships all seem'd to be.
> And here again I come, and only find
>   The drain-cut level of the marshy lea,
> Gray sand-banks, and pale sunsets, dreary wind,
>   Dim shores, dense rains, and heavy-clouded sea.

The beach was firmly imprinted on Tennyson's memory, and years later he recalled the flat Lincolnshire coast accurately in "The Last Tournament":

> Arthur deigned not use of word or sword,
> But let the drunkard, as he stretched from horse
> To strike him, overbalancing his bulk,
> Down from the causeway heavily to the swamp
> Fall, as the crest of some slow-arching wave,
> Heard in dead night along that table-shore,
> Drops flat. . . .

But the area has changed a great deal as an English resort.

Mablethorpe comes into two separate literary pieces. Jean Ingelow of Boston wrote of the terrible 1571 storm and flooding in "High Tide on the Coast of Lincolnshire":

> "For evil news from Mablethorpe,
>   Of pyrate galleys warping down;
> For shippes ashore beyond the scorpe,
>   They have not spared to wake the towne:
> But while the west bin red to see,
> And storms be none, and pyrates flee,
> Why ring 'The Brides of Enderby'?"

Later D. H. Lawrence has Paul Morel's family, preparing for a Mablethorpe holiday, come across the Ingelow poem. Paul has read it aloud:

> "But," interrupted Mrs. Morel, "what *is* the 'Bride of Enderby' that the bells are supposed to ring?"
> "It's an old tune they used to play on the bells for a warning against water. I suppose the Bride of Enderby was drowned in a flood," he replied. He had not the faintest knowledge what it really was. . . .

(There was, of course, no "Brides of Enderby," but a tune by that name was later composed.) The Morels arrived here at their vacation cottage,

> a house that stood alone over the dyke by the highroad. There was wild excitement because they had to cross a little bridge to get into the front garden. But they loved

486

the house that lay so solitary, with a sea-meadow on one side, and immense expanses of land patched in white barley, yellow oats, and green root-crops, flat and stretching level to the sky.

Miriam and Paul walk the sands

towards Theddlethorpe. The long breakers plunged and ran in a hiss of foam along the coast. It was a warm evening. There was not a figure but themselves on the far reaches of sand, no noise but the sound of the sea. . . . It was quite dark when they turned again. The way home was through a gap in the sandhills, and then along a raised grass road between two dykes. The country was black and still. From behind the sandhills came the whisper of the sea.

MACKWORTH, Derbyshire (pop. 223) A small village 3 miles northwest of Derby, Mackworth contains the remnants of Mackworth Castle and a rebuilt 14th-century church. The chancel is at least half a century older than the rest of the church and is rich in pinnacles, buttresses, and a priest's doorway, but its interior is modern and somewhat overwhelming in its display of alabaster. One of the few known early facts about Samuel Richardson is connected with this church. Richardson's family was from somewhere in Derbyshire, undoubtedly around this area, for he was baptized here on August 19, 1689; an obscure reference in a much later letter written by his daughter Ann dates his birth as July 31. By 1698 the Richardson family was in London, but absolutely nothing is known of the nine years Samuel probably spent here.

MADELEY, Staffordshire (pop. 2,883) Close to the heavily industrialized Stoke-on-Trent complex and the sprawling colliery area of Newcastle-under-Lyme, 5 miles to the east, Madeley nevertheless has a country setting. The church, mainly Perpendicular, has a 14th-century tower and a 13th-century arcade and chancel arch, and nearby Madeley Manor, recently become a College of Education, stands on the site of an old castle. The older structure, of which only a few walls remain, belonged to Sir John Offley in the 17th century; Izaak Walton held Sir John as his "most honoured friend" and was frequently here; indeed, he is said to have been here when the Parliamentarians did their damage. Walton's great admiration of Offley and his many good deeds led to the author's dedication of *The Compleat Angler* to Sir John. Walton attended the church on his visits, and Sir John paid a fitting tribute to Walton in the north aisle with a memorial window portraying the miracle of the fishes.

MAIDEN NEWTON, Dorset (pop. 597) Where the little Hooke River flows into the Frome, in a lovely setting, lies the village of Maiden Newton, 8 miles northwest of Dorchester. This village becomes Chalk Newton in Thomas Hardy's Wessex and is used in "Interlopers at the Knap" (*Wessex Tales*), *Tess of the D'Urbervilles,* and *Under the Greenwood Tree.* The White Horse Inn, where Helena's boy is placed in the custody of the bailiff ("Interlopers"), was an Elizabethan building demolished at the end of the 19th century. In *Tess* Hardy brings Tess through Chalk Newton on her way to Flintcombe Ash (Dole's Ash); here she "breakfasted at an inn," and because "several young men were troublesomely complimentary to her good looks"

. . . Tess resolved to run no further risks from her appearance. As soon as she got out of the village she . . . took a handkerchief from her bundle and tied it round her face under her bonnet, covering her chin and half her cheeks and her temples, as if she were suffering from toothache. Then with her little scissors, by the aid of a pocket looking-glass, she mercilessly snipped her eyebrows off, and thus insured against aggressive admiration she went on her uneven way.

MAIDENCOMBE, Devon Maidencombe is a small village on the south Devon coast, 3 miles south of Teignmouth in the very heart of the so-called Devon Riviera. The beaches here are sandy, and the vegetation is luxurious, including even palm trees. Following his return from the United States in September 1896, Rudyard Kipling and his wife came to Rock House, Rock House Lane. They always remembered with distaste the time spent in the village until the spring of 1897, mostly since the house, booked in advance, was one in which they were never comfortable because of its *fêng shui,* which produced a spirit of despondency. Kipling worked on *Stalky and Co.* here before leaving for London in the spring while he searched for a more suitable house in Kent and Sussex.

MAIDENHEAD, Berkshire (pop. 37,280) Close enough to London, 25 miles to the east, to be considered a bedroom suburb, Maidenhead is actually a busy resort and pleasure-boating center on the Thames River. Spanning the river here are two of the finest bridges over the Thames; one is a balustraded road bridge built in 1772 by Robert Taylor, a stonemason's son, and the other is the railway bridge with flat brickwork spans designed by Isambard Brunel.

Daniel Defoe was not impressed by the town when he was here in the 18th century and gives it only the slightest mention in *A Tour thro' the Whole Island of Great Britain:*

There are Two other Towns on the *Thames,* which I have already mentioned, *viz. Henly* and *Maidenhead,* which have little or nothing remarkable in them; but that they have great Business also, by the Trade for Malt and Meal and Timber for *London.* . . .

H. G. Wells uses Maidenhead briefly in at least three of his works: in *The Secret Places of the Heart* a group of diners come here, "at night, in the neighbourhood of Hardy and Martineau"; in *The Food of the Gods,* the first giant wasp is killed at the estate of Lieut. Col. Rupert Hick here; and in *Joan and Peter* Maidenhead is where the gardener mows a lawn and the swans on the Thames are fed.

Maidenhead can claim one and possibly two native sons. Sir George Etherege, the creator of the Restoration comedy of manners, may have been born here about 1635. More recently, Hugh Lofting was born here on January 14, 1886. *The Story of Dr. Dolittle* and other books about Dr. Dolittle emerged from letters Lofting wrote to his children from the western front during World War I. Lofting left England permanently in 1912 for the United States and eventually settled in New York.

MAIDSTONE, Kent (pop. 47,630) Maidstone, as Michael Drayton states in *Poly-Olbion,* is the "only christned Towne" of the Medway River, and it is the river, which cuts the town in half, that has helped Maidstone to play its role in history. In the ancient past there were iguanodons on the shores of the great Wealden Lake, and when a new coat of arms was granted to the town in 1949, one of the creatures reappeared as a heraldic supporter, "iguanodon proper collared gules." From the Middle Ages on, Maidstone was actively involved in the milling of flour from the rich agricultural lands nearby, in eel fishing, and in crystallizing salt in primitive iron pans. Later its economic interest was mainly in the agricultural products of the Weald, and when hops were introduced into Kent in the 1500s, Maidstone became the center of the Kentish brewing industry. Indeed, the town fathers have given the iguanodon the company of a horse's head "gorged with a chaplet of hops fructed proper" in the town crest.

The beautiful 14th-century All Saints Church and the remains of the old college were the home of William Grocyn from 1506 when he became the warden of All Saints; numbered among his guests were Erasmus and Sir Thomas More, once his pupil. Grocyn apparently suffered a stroke in 1518 and died here before October 1519; he was buried in the church he served for thirteen years.

In 1648 Richard Lovelace was one of 900 Royalists captured by Gen. Thomas Fairfax in or near the 14th-century Perpendicular parish church. He was sentenced on June 8 and committed to Peterhouse in London the next day. John Evelyn, as his diary notes, was in Maidstone on official business on various occasions and, indeed, records this particular insurrection under the date of May 23:

> There was a rising now in *Kent*, my Lord of *Norwich* being in the head of them and their first rendezvous in *Broome-fild*, next my house at *Says-Court* whence they went to *Maidstone,* & so to *Colchester* where there was that memorable siege:

Earlier, in 1542, Sir Thomas Wyatt of nearby Allington was made chief steward of the manor of Maidstone shortly before his death. Samuel Pepys was in Maidstone in March 1669 and notes more than once that he "had a mighty mind to see" the town, and he was not disappointed. He

> walked all up and down the town, and up to the top of the steeple, and had a noble view, and then down again: and in the town did see an old man beating of flax.... [I]n the street also I did buy and send to our inne, the Bell, a dish of fresh fish. And so, having walked all round the town, and found it very pretty, as most towns I ever saw, though not very big, and people of good fashion in it, we to our inne to dinner, and had a good dinner....

Sometime later, between 1726 and 1732, Christopher Smart attended the Maidstone Free School after his father had bought a large estate in East Barming. Even in his darkest and most desperate times, Smart retained a great deal of affection for both the town and its inhabitants.

In a house (gone) in Mitre Lane (now Bullock Street) off the High Street, William Hazlitt was born on April 10, 1778. His father, an Irishman, was minister of the Unitarian Chapel on Earle Street where Hazlitt was baptized on June 21. Within two years the Reverend Mr. Hazlitt quarreled bitterly with his dissenting congregation, removed his family to Ireland, and later sailed to the United States. These first few years appear to be William Hazlitt's only contact with Maidstone. The Maidstone Museum and Art Gallery, actually Chillington Manor, a red-brick Elizabethan mansion on St. Faith's Street, contains relics concerning the essayist.

Despite Charles Dickens's fondness for the town, he mentions Maidstone only in "The Seven Poor Travellers" and *David Copperfield*. It is possible that he planned to give the town a large role in *The Mystery of Edwin Drood* by making the county jail the scene of Jasper's imprisonment. It has been conjectured (like Gravesend and Town Malling) that Maidstone is the Muggleton of the *Pickwick Papers* because of its description as

> a corporate town, with a mayor, burgesses, and freeman.... Muggleton is an ancient and loyal borough, mingling a zealous advocacy of Christian principles with a devoted attachment to commercial rights....

Mr. Pickwick, then, observes "with an air of curiosity":

> There was an open square for the market-place, and in the centre of it, a large inn with a sign-post in front, displaying an object very common in art, but rarely met with in nature—to wit, a blue lion, with three bow-legs in the air, balancing himself on the extreme point of the centre claw of his fourth foot. There were, within sight, an auctioneer's and fire-agency office, a cornfactor's, a linen-draper's, a saddler's, a distiller's, a grocer's, and a shoe-shop.... There was a red brick house with a small paved court-yard in front, which anybody might have

MAIDSTONE Just behind the beautiful 14th-century All Saints Church a gateway leads to the remains of the old collegiate college, the home of a master and twenty-four chaplains. When William Grocyn was Master, he had Thomas More as a pupil and Erasmus living in his house.

known belonged to the attorney; and there was, moreover, another red brick house, with Venetian blinds and a large brass door-plate, with a very legible announcement that it belonged to the surgeon.

Both descriptions fit Maidstone and its marketplace quite well.

One other use of the town occurs in William Makepeace Thackeray's *Denis Duval*. Dr. Barnard and Denis stop at the Bell here on their journey to London.

MALDON, Essex (pop. 13,840) The center of the town of Maldon stands on the summit of a hill overlooking the location of the Anglo-Saxon defeat by the Danish invaders commemorated in "The Battle of Maldon." This poem, one of several recorded in the *Anglo-Saxon Chronicle,* was entered for the year 991, when the giant Essex ealdorman Byrhtnoth and his *dryht* (retainers) defended the Blackwater Estuary against a band of Norsemen most probably led by Anlaf Tryggvason. The Viking invaders, encamped on Northey Island (joined to the mainland by a causeway at low tide), were delayed in their attack by the incoming tides. In an instance of folly Byrhtnoth withdrew his men holding the causeway and allowed the Norsemen to cross. Battle lines were drawn up on the shore of the Blackwater, and in the ensuing three-day battle Byrhtnoth was slain. Ely Cathedral contains what are alleged to be Byrhtnoth's remains, except for the head. Legend holds that his skull was used as a drinking vessel by the Danes in the hope that the ealdorman's courage and intelligence would pass to them; his skeleton, exhumed in 1796, showed him to be of gigantic stature at 6 feet 9 inches. All Saints' Church in Maldon contains a commemorative statue.

MALHAM, Yorkshire (pop. 142) A tiny and remote upper Airedale village, Malham (pronounced "mawm") is set against a great amphitheater of limestone cliffs 285 feet high, from which the Aire River issues by a subterranean passage. About 4 miles north of the village are the lonely Malham Tarn and Tarn House. In 1769 Thomas Gray, after visiting nearby Gordale Scar, came to this village, which he noted was "in the bosom of the mountains, seated in a wild and dreary valley . . . on the cliffs above hung a few goats; one of them danced and scratched an ear with its hind foot in a place where I would not have stood stockstill for all beneath the moon."

Almost 100 years later Malham Tarn became part of the inspiration for Charles Kingsley's *The Water Babies,* written primarily to amuse Kingsley's son. Kingsley was staying at Malham Tarn House, then owned by Walter Morrison, an eccentric Yorkshire millionaire; it was through Morrison's good offices that Kingsley got a firsthand picture of the complicated countryside. The "great patches of flat limestone rock, just like ill-made pavement," over which Tom flees correspond perfectly to the gigantic limestone overhang of Malham Cove. The "beautiful caves of tufa" are also here; tufa (essentially travertine) is abundant in the area. Malham has a water elf of its own named Janet, and behind a curtain of moss and travertine is a well-concealed cave, "Janet's water home." Among other 19th-century visitors to Walter Morrison's home were John Ruskin and Charles Darwin, neither of whom left records of their stay.

MALLERSTANG, Westmorland (pop. 221) In the Vale of Eden, a narrow, steep-sided valley between Wild Boar Fell and High Seat (each of which is more than 2,300 feet high), is Mallerstang. Located on the Yorkshire border 5 miles south of Kirkby Stephen, the area can hardly be described as a village. The ruined Pendragon Castle, reputedly the home of Utherpendragon, father of King Arthur, stands on a knoll away from the Eden River (the course of the river was different in earlier times), and a local rhyme alludes to the Arthurian connection:

Let Uther Pendragon do what he can,
Eden shall run as Eden ran.

In actual fact, the first structure here dates from Norman times; it later came into the hands of the Cliffords and was attacked and burned during numerous border raids. Lady Anne Clifford had it repaired in the 17th century, and these are the ruins seen today.

MALMESBURY, Wiltshire (pop. 2,700) Although the general area around Malmesbury, 15 miles west of Swindon, has been flattened by the Avon River and its tributary, the Inglebourne, this is actually a hill town. Malmesbury (pronounced "mawmz'bury") dates to 640, when an Ionian monk or hermit, Maildulf, and a few followers arrived and chose the rocky site above the forest and rivers as the location of a small British monastery which eventually became a Benedictine order. From its early days the order had a school, and one of the pupils was Aldhelm, an extraordinary scholar, a writer of songs, and an inventor; he is said to have built England's first organ, "a mighty instrument with innumerable tones, blown with bellows and enclosed in a gilded case." Upon his death Aldhelm was brought here and buried in the church.

By the time King Athelstan came to the throne in 924, Malmesbury and its abbey were powerful and prestigious. Athelstan added to its wealth, and the town, too, received its benefactions. The old abbey was once a place of pilgrimage, but in the mid-12th century the great Norman abbey was built; the only part of this abbey now functioning is the section of the nave which was converted into a parish church. At the dissolution of the monasteries in the 16th century Malmesbury Abbey was sold (for £1,516/15) to a wealthy cloth merchant, who set up looms in the building. The church is still beautiful today, and the tower window contains portraits of Maildulf, Aldhelm, Egelmer (a monk who tried to fly), and William of Malmesbury. The monk fashioned a flying machine of wings attached to his hands and feet and took off from the abbey tower; he broke both legs in the fall. William of Malmesbury, born around 1090 in south or west England, was brought up at this abbey and eventually wrote *Gesta Regum Anglorum* and *Gesta Pontificum Anglorum* here. He served as the monastic librarian and probably died here around 1143.

Malmesbury—or rather Westport, a community now integrated into the city—was the birthplace of

Thomas Hobbes on April 5, 1588. Hobbes's father was the vicar of Charlton and Westport, and the boy first was a pupil in the Westport School, removing at eight to the Malmesbury school. Another literary association is with Joseph Addison, who was first returned to Parliament for Malmesbury on October 9, 1711, in an uncontested election; he stood for Parliament here a number of times and was in the town frequently. William Cobbett visited Malmesbury two or three times; he had a number of comments on the town in his *Rural Rides*:

> This town, though it has nothing particularly engaging in itself, stands upon one of the prettiest spots that can be imagined.... [T]his is a very pleasant place. There remains more of the abbey than, I believe, of any of our monastic buildings, except that of Westminster, and those that have become cathedrals.... [T]he abbey is used as the church, though the church-tower is at a considerable distance from it. It was once a most magnificent building; and there is now a *doorway* which is the most beautiful thing I ever saw, and which was, nevertheless, built in Saxon times, in "the *dark* ages," and was built by men who were not begotten by Pitt nor by Jubilee George.

In 1869 W. H. Hudson came from South America to live in Malmesbury before going on to London, where he settled. He returned in 1908 and climbed the abbey up to the roof.

MALVERN   *See* GREAT MALVERN.

MANATON, Devon (pop. 387) A village picturesquely set on the eastern slopes of Dartmoor 3½ miles south of Moreton Hampstead, Manaton looks south to Hound Tor and southwestward to Bowerman's Nose, a curious outcropping of rock. Wingstone, a farmhouse just north of the village, is where John Galsworthy and Ada Galsworthy (his cousin's wife) spent some time after his father's death and before divorce papers were served on her in 1904; they then spent their honeymoon here and retained the house for almost fifteen years. The Galsworthys had an unusual arrangement, for while they were technically summer lodgers, they had access to the guest portion of the house all year round. *Buttercup Night* records how Galsworthy discovered Wingstone on a walking tour in 1904; the meadow by which he originally reached the house, Cross Park, figures in *The Patrician*, "The Apple Tree," and *The Skin Game*. He enjoyed extensive walks in the area to moor grave, Hound Tor Gate, and Hayne Down and mentions all of them in his diary. Galsworthy wrote most of *Fraternity* and parts of *The Eldest Son, The Mob,* and *The Freelands* here; *The Second Flowering* was begun after he tried to enlist for war service in 1918 and was rejected because of vision problems. In the summer and autumn of 1914 George Bernard Shaw and Harley Granville-Barker visited Galsworthy here.

Another writer who spent some time here was Rupert Brooke, who came to stay with Lytton Strachey at the end of term in 1909; Brooke was mulling over the possibility of giving up classics and concentrating on English literature in his fourth year at Cambridge but came to no resolution here.

MANCHESTER, Lancashire (pop. 732,900) Situated 31 miles east of Liverpool on the Irk, Irwell, and Medlock Rivers, Manchester seems to have originated in Roman times, in A.D. 79, when an earth-and-timber fort was placed on a plateau of 250,000 acres near the Irwell by Agricola's legions. Under Hadrian the fortification was partially rebuilt in stone, but Roman occupation was intermittent, and the town was finally abandoned in the 4th century. At some date before 1086 the center of Manchester was moved 1 mile farther north. Probably by the 9th century a church stood on the site of the present cathedral, and in the 11th century a Norman manor was built nearby. Within two centuries Manchester developed a flourishing market and grew in population, but it was not until the 14th century, with the importation of Flemish weavers, that growth became rapid. Within a short time the town's prosperity enabled Thomas de la Warr to turn St. Mary's into a collegiate church, part of which survives in Chetham's Hospital.

The accession of Elizabeth in 1558 eventually brought increased trade to Manchester, and by the early 17th century the manufacture of fustian, a combination of linen and cotton, began. Daniel Defoe was in Manchester before the industrial revolution and saw the town before its period of greatest growth; he recorded his admiration in the following passage:

> [W]e came on to *Manchester,* one of the greatest, if not really the greatest meer Village in *England.* It is neither a wall'd Town, City, or Corporation; they send no Members to Parliament; and the highest Magistrate they have is a Constable or Headborough; and yet it has a Collegiate Church. . . .

Later in his discussion he notes: "I cannot doubt but this encreasing Town will, some time or other, obtain some better Face of Government, and be incorporated, as it well deserves to be." However, not until 1838 did Manchester receive its charter of incorporation. Manchester was in an especially good position for the industrial revolution. The Bridgewater Canal, which transports coal from Worsley, was built; ultimately it was extended to Liverpool so that the cotton industry, headquartered here, could export directly. The first cotton mills were built in the 1780s, and when industry shifted westward in the 19th century, the city built the Manchester Ship Canal to keep the port alive. Indeed, the canal is still in operation today, and Manchester is now the fourth largest port in the country.

The present-day conurbation centered in Manchester includes most of southeast Lancashire and northeast Cheshire, and the industrial estate at Trafford Park is the largest in England. Many changes have occurred in relatively recent times; much of Manchester was flattened by bombs in World War II, and exciting redevelopment schemes have been evolved and implemented. Most of the old Market Square, with its black-and-white houses and cellared shops, was destroyed in December 1940, and the redesigned area, retaining two 18th-century buildings missed by the bombs, is extremely attractive. The cathedral suffered badly: its windows were blown out, and the Lady Chapel and Regimental Chapel were destroyed. Fortunately, the thirty Tudor canopied choir stalls with elaborately crafted misere-ere seats (two men playing backgammon, pigs dancing to bagpipes, a fox riding a hound, and two men fighting, one seated on a camel, the other on a unicorn) came through unscathed. Manchester is also noted for its patronage of the arts: the rebuilt Palladian Free Trade Hall is the home of the Hallé Orchestra; the City Art Gallery on Mosley Street has an outstanding collection of English works dating from the 16th century, and the Whitworth Gallery has a superb collection of English watercolors and drawings and an unrivaled provincial display of the work of contemporary artists. The John Rylands Library has a collection of more than 250,000 books, including a number printed before 1501 and the oldest example of European printing with an unchallenged date (1423) in the world.

Manchester claims three native-born authors, the best known of whom, Thomas De Quincey, was born at a house (gone) at the corner of Tasle and Red Cross Streets (now Cross and John Dalton Streets) on August 15, 1785, not at the Farm, Moss Side, where he was taken within a few weeks, or at Greenhay Hall (erroneously Greenheys, for that is the name of the district). On September 23 he was baptized at the 18th-century St. Ann's Church. In 1791 his family moved to Greenhay Hall, later described in his *Autobiographic Sketches:*

> Greenhay, a country-house, newly built by my father, at that time was a clear mile from the outskirts of Manchester; but in after years, Manchester, throwing out the *tentacula* of its vast expansions, absolutely envelopéd Greenhay; and, for anything I know, the grounds and gardens which then insulated the house may have long disappeared. Being a modest mansion, which (including hot walls, offices, and gardener's house) had cost only six thousand pounds, I do not know how it should have risen to the distinction of giving name to a region of that great town; however, it *has* done so. . . .

De Quincey's father died in 1793, and the boy was sent to Salford for lessons from a guardian, the Rev. Samuel Hall, for a few years. With a brother, who as De Quincey wrote, "first laid open to me the gates of war," he made daily trips, except for Sunday, to the Reverend Hall; and they passed a mill where a number of child laborers initiated a feud which was to be carried on twice daily:

> [A]nd the result was pretty uniform—viz., that my brother and I terminated the battle by insisting upon our undoubted right to run away. *Magna Charta,* I should fancy, secures that great right to every man; else, surely, it is sadly defective. But out of this catastrophe to most of our skirmishes, and to all our pitched battles except one, grew a standing schism between my brother and myself. . . . Twice, at least, in every week, but sometimes every night, my brother insisted on singing "Te Deum" for supposed victories he had won; and he insisted also on my bearing a part in these "Te Deums."

When their mother sold Greenhay and left for Bath in 1797, Thomas and one brother, probably Richard, boarded here for one month with a young married couple named Kelsall; it was, De Quincey said, one of the happiest months of his life. He then attended school in Bath and Winkfield, Wiltshire, before being returned to Manchester in 1801 to attend the grammar school. The move here was highly favored by his guardians because of the headmaster, Charles Lawson, no mean scholar but unfortunately a man growing old, pedantic, and inefficient; of him De Quincey comments:

> The head-master was substantially superannuated for the duties of his place. Not that intellectually he showed any symptoms of decay; but in the spirits and physical energies requisite for his duties he *did;* not so much age, as disease, it was that incapacitated him. In the course of a long day, beginning at seven A.M. and stretching down to five P.M., he succeeded in reaching the farther end of his duties. But how? Simply by consolidating pretty nearly into one continuous scene of labour the entire ten hours.

The school was then on Long Millgate, in the city center. De Quincey was in poor health that winter, and apparently his only solace was the presence of Lady Carbery, whom he had met in Bath; they studied Hebrew together. Unable to gain his guardians' permission to leave Manchester Grammar School, he borrowed £10 from Lady Carbery, paid his school servants' tips, and escaped in the early hours of a July 1802 morning. De Quincey had packed his trunk and secured the help of the head groom to carry it downstairs at 3:30 A.M.; just at the head's door the trunk slipped and crashed down, but Lawson never woke. The trunk was sent on, and De Quincey with a backpack began his walk via Altrincham to Chester, where his mother was living.

The second Mancunian is the novelist William Harrison Ainsworth, and the third is Frances Eliza Hodgson Burnett. Ainsworth was born at 21 King Street (gone) on February 4, 1805; there is a plaque on the National Westminster Bank. The only son of a solicitor, he was educated, like De Quincey, at the grammar school and later wrote of it in *Life and Adventures of Mervyn Clitheroe.* After finishing at the school, Ainsworth was articled to a solicitor here for three years before going to London to complete his legal training. Frances Burnett, author of *Little Lord Fauntleroy,* was born at 141 York Street (now Cheetham Hill Road) on November 24, 1849, and her childhood years were spent at 19 Islington Square (gone), Salford. Her family emigrated to the United States in 1856, and the novel was written there.

Numerous other literary associations exist with Manchester: William Beckford visited Manchester during his tour of England from August to October 1779 and explored a subterranean section of the 3d Duke of Bridgewater's canal, which had been finished in 1772. Elizabeth Cleghorn Gaskell settled here after her marriage in 1832 to the Rev. William Gaskell, minister of the Cross Street Unitarian Chapel. They lived first at 14 Dover Street, then on Oxford Road, and in 1842 moved to 121 Upper Rumford Street (the houses are gone). Again they moved, this time to 84 Plymouth Grove. *Mary Barton,* begun in 1844 after the death of their only son, presents a vivid picture of the area, factory life, and living conditions here in the 1840s:

> Berry Street . . . was unpaved; and down the middle a gutter forced its way, every now and then forming pools in the holes with which the street abounded. Never was the Old Edinburgh cry of "Gardez l'eau," more necessary than in this street. As they passed, women from their doors

tossed household slops of *every* description into the gutter; they ran into the next pool, which overflowed and stagnated.... Our friends ... picked their way till they got to some steps leading down into a small area, where a person standing would have his head about one foot below the level of the street, and might at the same time, without the least motion of his body, touch the window of the cellar and the damp muddy wall right opposite. You went down one step even from the foul area into the cellar in which a family of human beings lived. It was very dark inside. The window-panes were many of them broken and stuffed with rags, which was reason enough for the dusky light that pervaded the place even at midday. After the account I have given of the state of the street, no one can be surprised that on going into the cellar inhabited by Davenport, the smell was so foetid as almost to knock the two men down. Quickly recovering themselves, as those inured to such things do, they began to penetrate the thick darkness of the place, and to see three or four little children rolling on the damp, nay wet, brick floor, through which the stagnant, filthy moisture of the street oozed up; the fire-place was empty and black; the wife sat on her husband's chair, and cried in the dank loneliness.

After 1851 one of Mrs. Gaskell's frequent visitors at Plymouth Grove was Charlotte Brontë, whose first trip to Manchester in July 1846 was made with her father, who came here for cataract surgery. During his month-long recuperative period at 83 Mount Pleasant (gone, but a plaque marks the site), Boundary Street, she began *Jane Eyre*. Among Mrs. Gaskell's other guests were Thomas Carlyle, Harriet Beecher Stowe, and Charles Dickens. The Cross Street Chapel contains a memorial to Mrs. Gaskell, who died on November 12, 1865, in Holybourne, Hampshire; she was buried in Knutsford, Cheshire.

In 1872 George Gissing entered Owens College, now the University of Manchester, as an exhibitioner; Gissing was a brilliant student and won almost every prize and scholarship available, including the Shakespeare Scholarship. However, his propensity to engage in amorous adventures became not only his misfortune but, in this instance, his disgrace. He met Marianne Helen Harrison, a prostitute, and devoted all of his resources to reforming her; eventually, unable to support her, he stole from the college and was caught. He was, of course, dismissed summarily from Owens and, indeed, spent a period in prison. Upon his release, with assistance from friends, he left for the United States. In 1877 Francis Thompson came from Ushaw College in Ushaw, County Durham, to study medicine (the choice was his father's, not his), and after six years of study, during which he failed his examinations three times, he left the college and began a life of aimless wandering which culminated in disaster in London, where he became addicted to opium.

The most extensive use of Manchester in literature occurs in the works of Charles Dickens, who made one of his first trips here in 1843, when he presided at a meeting in the Free Trade Hall to raise money for the *Athenaeum*. In 1847 and 1848 he returned again for charitable reasons, the first time to raise funds for needy men of letters and the second to raise money to purchase William Shakespeare's birthplace in Stratford-on-Avon. Another trip, in 1852, was for the inauguration of the Manchester Free Libraries; the meeting, held at Campfield (originally called the Hall of Science), was also attended by Edward Bulwer-Lytton (Lord Lytton) and William Makepeace Thackeray. Both Dickens and Thackeray were to speak, but Thackeray delivered only one sentence of his carefully worked-out talk before sitting down, unable to continue. Dickens spoke on the use of literature in society. Dickens was also here in 1857, for a free reading of *A Christmas Carol* in the Free Trade Hall; in 1858, when he stayed at the Adelphi Hotel and presided over the annual meeting of the Institutional Association of Lancashire and Cheshire and distributed prizes; in the 1860s; and in 1869, for his final visit. There is also a personal connection between Dickens and Manchester, for around 1841 his elder sister Fanny married Harry Burnett, a retired operatic performer, and settled here on Upper Brook Street. It was their crippled son who became the prototype of Paul Dombey.

Manchester is Coketown, in a fairly thin disguise, in *Hard Times:*

It was a town of red brick, or of brick that would have been red if the smoke and ashes had allowed it; but as matters stood it was a town of unnatural red and black like the painted face of a savage. It was a town of machinery and tall chimneys, out of which interminable serpents of smoke trailed themselves for ever and ever, and never got uncoiled. It had a black canal in it, and a river that ran purple with ill-smelling dye, and vast piles of building full of windows where there was a rattling and a trembling all day long, and where the piston of the steam-engine worked monotonously up and down like the head of an elephant in a state of melancholy madness. It contained several large streets all very like one another, and many small streets still more like one another, inhabited by people equally like one another.

Dickens writes of Coketown on "a sunny midsummer day," for "there was such a thing sometimes," even here under the industrial pall:

Seen from a distance in such weather, Coketown lay shrouded in a haze of its own, which appeared impervious to the sun's rays. You only knew the town was there, because you knew there could have been no such sulky blotch upon the prospect without a town. A blur of soot and smoke, now confusedly tending this way, now that way, now aspiring to the vault of Heaven, now murkily creeping along the earth, as the wind rose and fell, or changed its quarter: a dense formless jumble, with sheets of cross light in it, that showed nothing but masses of darkness:—Coketown in the distance was suggestive of itself, though not a brick of it could be seen.

And, he continues:

The streets were hot and dusty on the summer day, and the sun was so bright that it even shone through the heavy vapour drooping over Coketown, and could not be looked at steadily.... There was a stifling smell of hot oil everywhere. The steam-engines shone with it, the dresses of the Hands were soiled with it, the mills throughout their many stories oozed and trickled it.... [T]he mills, and the courts and alleys, baked at a fierce heat. Down upon the river that was black and thick with dye, some Coketown boys who were at large ... rowed a crazy boat, which made a spumous track upon the water as it jogged along, while every dip of an oar stirred up vile smells.

It should be noted that Preston, Rochdale, and Oldham have also laid claim to Coketown, but the description seems to fit Manchester best. Dickens again uses Manchester in *Nicholas Nickleby,* for this was the home of the originals of the Cheeryble brothers; in the Preface Dickens states:

> [T]here *are* two characters in this book which are drawn from life. . . . But those who take an interest in this tale, will be glad to learn that the BROTHERS CHEERYBLE, live; that their liberal charity, their singleness of heart, their noble nature, and their unbounded benevolence, are no creations of the Author's brain; but are prompting every day (and oftenest by stealth) some munificent and generous deed in that town of which they are the pride and honour.

These were the brothers William and Daniel Grant, with whom Dickens claimed that he "never interchanged any communication" in his life; however, that statement is known to be in error. In 1838, one year before *Nicholas Nickleby* was published, he and John Forster, with a letter of introduction from Harrison Ainsworth, were the guests of Gilbert Winter of Stock House (gone), Cheetham Hill Road; here they met the Grants, who owned a town residence, although they preferred the one in Ramsbottom, where their factory was located. Their warehouse, a large, roomy building, was at 15 Cannon Street and was marked by a later owner as Cheeryble House.

Four other associations with Manchester can be noted: Sir Walter Ralegh is traditionally held to have visited the mathematician John Dee in the Audit Room of The Hall, a 14th-century building. Charles Swain, now a little-read poet, was born on Every Street on January 4, 1801; his was basically a business career, but he wrote a great deal of verse, some of which was set to music and was once very popular. He died at his home, Prestwich Park, and is buried in Prestwich churchyard. Another minor native poet, Isabella V. Banks, was born on Oldham Street on March 25, 1821; she attended the long-established school for young ladies at Cheetham and married George Linnaeus Banks at the Collegiate Church here on December 27, 1846. Finally, John Galsworthy was first here early in 1908 for the rehearsals of *The Silver Box* and *Strife*, which were produced at the Duke of York's Theatre in March. In 1911, returning for the rehearsals of *The Little Dream*, he stayed at the Midland Hotel. On May 18, 1927, he was again in Manchester, when the university made him an honorary doctor of letters.

MANESTY, Cumberland   Four miles south of Keswick in the Borrowdale Valley, Manesty is a locality rather than a village. Situated on Derwent Water, this parklike area has the Derwent Fells behind it and is a few miles north of the Jaws of Borrowdale. For almost twenty years this was the home of Sir Hugh Walpole; Brackenburn, on a plateau cut into the steep slopes of Cat Bells about 250 feet above the level of the lake, is made of Cumberland stone, which Walpole once described as "one of the loveliest stones in the world, having a shade of green like a tulip leaf, a purple depth like a bishop's ring, and a dove-shadowed grey over all." He came to the area in October 1923 and found Brackenburn at the beginning of November.

> Day with a star indeed, because on it I bought what I hope will be the abode of my old age—Brackenburn, Manesty Park, Derwentwater. Came on it quite by chance—a stray remark from the owner of our Keswick hotel. Above Grange in Borrowdale. A little paradise on Cat Bells. Running stream, garden, lawn, daffodils, squirrels, music-room, garage, four bedrooms, bath— All!

The house, bought without a survey and against advice, became Walpole's refuge for the rest of his life. He enlarged the upper floor and made the old music room on top of the garage into his study; he later added a third story to the house. Walpole began the "Rogue Herries" novels here in mid-1927, and the manuscript of *Rogue Herries* was completed in January 1929. The completion of *Judith Paris* followed in 1930; *The Fortress*, in 1931; and *Vanessa*, in 1932.

Walpole spent many periods abroad before World War II and lived in London for a short time after hostilities began, but he came back to Brackenburn after the October 1940 bombing of the capital, an event which seems to have affected his health. Soon after his return, all the symptoms of delayed shock appeared; nevertheless, he insisted on returning to London for two BBC talks and stayed for some time, during which a heart condition was diagnosed. Walpole, always a bit eccentric about medical care, refused to have an electrocardiogram made and was back permanently at Brackenburn in May 1941. On May 26 he suffered a diabetic coma (he had initially refused to treat this condition, and not until 1928 was it controlled with insulin), and on May 28 the attending physician diagnosed a severe coronary thrombosis. Walpole died here on June 1, 1941, and was buried at St. John's in Keswick.

While Walpole lived here, there were many invited guests and a number of curiosity seekers, "who," he said, "peer into my windows, invade my garage, discuss my books loudly, and so on." J. B. Priestley, then editor of *These Diversions*, was extended an offer to visit after he had invited Walpole to contribute to the series. Priestley first arrived in September 1925, and the two men spent long hours walking on the fells; they became intimate friends, and Priestley came on frequent visits. Sinclair Lewis was a guest in July 1928 shortly after he married Dorothy Thompson, and Francis Brett Young, who had been in Liverpool for the opening of the dramatized version of *The Iron Age*, called *The Furnace*, visited Walpole in September of that year. The two men walked over Cat Bells and talked of books. W. H. Auden, "the young poet," as Walpole described him, visited Brackenburn in 1934.

The area around Brackenburn is used extensively in the latter part of *The Fortress;* Adam Paris's cottage is placed on Cat Bells, and much of the scenery in the novel could be seen from Walpole's study:

> Adam, turning on his side, caught the light from the window. The morning clouds, fiery with gold, were piling up above Walla Crag. *His* field—the field of all his life with its five little trees and its arch of sloping green—rolled into the glow; then, as though with a sigh of satisfaction, held the light; the little trees stood up and stretched their morning limbs.

Behind the house the ground rises sharply through bracken to the isolated and barren tops of the fells, the area Adam climbs to embrace the world:

> As he mounted, . . . [t]he Lake rose and he saw that the

sun had veined it with patterns of light, here there were pools of grey and ashen pallor and there deep shadows of saffron—all confined by the hills, Skiddaw, Saddleback, Walla Crag.

Adam ran and then "lay on the turf":

He stood up. Below him was Derwentwater to the east, Newlands to the west veiled now in the shadow of the lengthening day. He saw Catchedicam to the left of Helvellyn top, and southwards was Langdale Pike o' Stickle. Why should he ever return? He started to run again on a surface so buoyant that it seemed to run with him. Up the easy slope of Maiden Moor, Scafell and Gable coming up to meet him between Eel Crag and Dale Head. Why should he ever return? Borrowdale and Grange were below and now the Pillar was in view between Dale Head and Hindscarth. He might race on for ever—Hindscarth and Robinson, then down to Bettermere across to Ennerdale, over to Waswater, to Eskdale and the sea!

MAPLEDURHAM, Oxfordshire (pop. 2,042) Below Oxford the Thames River becomes the idealized English river of song and verse; numerous waterside inns have their own moorings, and houses have flower-strewn gardens that reach the river's edge. Just 3½ miles northwest of Reading is one of the most delightful villages on the Thames, Mapledurham. This is a secluded village, almost completely hidden by rolling hills and rich woodland, and the old mill on the river is perhaps the best on the Thames. The 17th-century rose-red brick almshouses are decked with cobbles and flowers and cluster near the prize of the village, Mapledurham House, often called the "finest Tudor home in England." The house was built by Sir Michael Blount, and its lofty chimneys rise high above the high-pitched roof. The name Blount recalls Alexander Pope, whose portrait by Charles Jervas hangs here. Pope was closely associated with both Martha and Teresa Blount and was a frequent guest here. Martha was his constant correspondent and his "scornful beauty"; it was from London to Mapledurham where

She went to plain-work, and to purling brooks,
Old fashion'd halls, dull aunts, and croaking rooks,
She went from Op'ra, park, assembly, play,
To morning walks, and pray'rs three times a day.

The house is partially hidden by a church of many centuries, which is itself unique in that there is a Roman Catholic chapel in the south aisle. The 14th-century chapel was built by Sir Robert and Lady Amice Bardolph and now belongs to the Blount heirs. One wonders if Pope ever attended services in the chapel.

More recently John Galsworthy made this secluded hamlet the location of the Shelter, Soames Forsyte's home in *The Forsyte Saga:*

It was full late for the river, but the weather was lovely, and summer lingered below the yellowing leaves. Soames took many looks at the day from his riverside garden near Mapledurham that Sunday morning. With his own hands he put flowers about his little house-boat, and equipped the punt, in which, after lunch, he proposed to take them on the river.

MAPPOWDER, Dorset (pop. 157) On the north side of the North Dorset Downs, 6 miles northeast of Cerne Abbas, Mappowder has a delightful church with distinctive gargoyles and a pinnacled tower. Standing near the church at the entrance to Newleaze House (the Old Rectory) is the cottage to which Theodore Francis Powys moved in 1940. He had become a recluse after his marriage in 1905, and he moved here from Chaldon Herring for greater seclusion. Powys died here on November 27, 1953, and is buried in the churchyard.

MARGATE, Kent (pop. 42,500) Often referred to as the Blackpool of Kent, Margate has an unusual location; 4 miles north of Ramsgate, it is situated on the Isle of Thanet (no longer an island). Thanet was inhabited by the Belgae before the Roman invasion. Once antiquarians attempted to derive Thanet from the Greek *thanatos*, "death," and supported the derivation by noting that "there be no snakes in Tanet and the earth that is brought from thence will kill them." In Roman and early Saxon times, Thanet was separated from the mainland by the Stour and Wantsum Rivers, and the two gave direct access to the Thames Estuary at high tide.

Margate is an extensive modern resort area; it has a long promenade, gardens, a lido, and the Dreamland Amusement Park, and many old buildings have been destroyed to make way for the holiday maker. Indeed, Margate was a placid fishing village when the first bathing machine was introduced in 1753. The geological material on which Margate is built is chalk, and at the bottom of Grotto Hill is The Grotto, an extensive underground folly of rooms and passageways covered, in set patterns, with thousands of seashells. Since its discovery in 1837 all sorts of speculations have arisen over its origin; especially untenable, but popular, is the argument that Phoenician traders built The Grotto. Marie Corelli, author of *The Mighty Atom*, describes The Grotto as "one of the most beautiful, fantastic, and interesting relics of the ancient days that exist in England or anywhere else."

One of the earliest visitors to Margate was the poet William Cowper, who came here on leave from his government duties in August 1763; already showing signs of mental illness, he found only temporary relief and returned to London still brooding about his financial state. Thomas Gray visited "Bartholomew Fair by the seaside" in 1766. Richard Brinsley Sheridan was summoned to Margate in the summer of 1788, when his father died here while on his way from Dublin to Lisbon on doctor's orders. Sheridan arranged for the funeral here, and his father was buried in the north aisle of St. Peter's Church. Early in the 19th century John Keats made several trips here; he first came for a short time in July 1816 and returned on at least two occasions. Writing to his brother George in August, he penned the lines:

E'en now, I'm pillow'd on a bed of Flowers,
That crown a lofty Cliff, which proudly towers
Above the Ocean Waves. The Stalks, and Blades
Checquer my Tablet with their quivering shades.
On one side, is a field of drooping Oats;
Through which the Poppies show their scarlet Coats;
So pert, and useless, that they bring to Mind
The scarlet Coats, that pester human kind.
And on the other side, outspread, is seen
Ocean's blue mantle, streak'd with purple & green.
Now 'tis I see a Canvassed Ship, and now

Mark the bright silver curling round her prow.
I see the Lark down dropping to her Nest,
And the broad winged Sea Gull, never at rest. . . .

A second trip in April 1817 is of more significance. Keats had been at Carisbrooke, on the Isle of Wight, where he began *Endymion*. He continued work on the poem here, and many of its passages which give glimpses of the sea are certainly derived from the seascapes at Margate.

As a young child Edward Lear was sent to the town around 1819 for treatment of his epilepsy. He was put on a course of exercises and spa waters to improve his condition. In 1821 Charles and Mary Lamb spent a week's holiday here, a vacation which years later resulted in "The Old Margate Hoy." Lamb noted that this was their first seaside experience, during which "many circumstances combined to make it the most agreeable holiday of my life":

> We have been dull at Worthing one summer, duller at Brighton another, dullest at Eastbourne a third, and are this moment doing dreary penance at—Hastings!—and all because we were happy many years ago for a brief week at—Margate.

Finally, William Cobbett reacts characteristically to Margate in his *Rural Rides:*

> I left Ramsgate to my right about three miles, and went right across the island to Margate; but that place is so thickly settled with stock-jobbing cuckolds, at this time of the year, that having no fancy to get their horns stuck into me, I turned away to my left when I got within about half a mile of the town.

William Makepeace Thackeray introduced the seaside town into *A Shabby Genteel Story.* Mr. Gann frequents the Bag of Nails, and Lord Cinqbars and Mrs. Carrickfergus and her retinue stay at Wright's Hotel. Later, William Ernest Henley entered the Royal Sea-Bathing Infirmary to secure treatment for the tubercular condition of his right leg. He first stayed in lodgings next to the concert hall and in a few months (February 1873) was admitted to the infirmary. Through the spring and early summer he underwent treatment, and in August, when the doctor decided to amputate, Henley left for Edinburgh, where he put himself under the care of Joseph Lister, whose revolutionary methods at that time had gained little acceptance.

MARKET BOSWORTH, Leicestershire (pop. 886) This town, 10 miles west of Leicester, has had licensed markets since 1285, and the present owners of the manor retain a royal charter allowing the operation of a private market. (There are only seven such markets in England.) The most famous association of the town is with the Battle of Bosworth Field (1485), in which Richard III was slain. This, of course, is the setting of the last few scenes of William Shakespeare's *The Tragedy of King Richard III* and the site of the utterance of Richard's famous line, "A horse! a horse! my kingdom for a horse!"

The literary fame of the village dates from a somewhat later period, when Dr. Samuel Johnson took up a position as an usher at the grammar school on the marketplace. Johnson's salary was £20 per year with living accommodations provided. The statutes of the school stated that the accepted appointee must have a B.A. degree and "be free from infectious and contagious diseases and be honest, virtuous, and learned." The patron of the school was Sir Wolstan Dixie, owner of Bosworth House, where Johnson lodged. Johnson was, as well, to act as a kind of lay chaplain to Sir Wolstan. The owner of Bosworth Hall was a bit of an autocrat and treated Johnson with a great deal of harshness. A disagreement with his employer finally resulted in his leaving the post and going to Birmingham to live temporarily with an old school friend. Some of the more pleasant moments in Market Bosworth were the evenings at the rectory with the Rev. Beaumont Dixie and his wife, the sister of Andrew Corbet, an old friend.

MARKET LAVINGTON, Wiltshire (pop. 904) On the north edge of the Salisbury Plain and 5½ miles south of Devizes, Market Lavington has a 14th-century church, an irrigation method dating to Anglo-Saxon times, and the Green Dragon Inn. The irrigation method, consisting of dew ponds built high on the downs, is one of those working traditions handed down from generation to generation. A large hollow is dug and then packed with puddled clay, slaked lime, and straw; this is covered with stone and firmly tamped down. The pond was started by the first rainfall, and nightly condensation (which always exceeds daily evaporation) supplies the pond with cool water.

In April 1908 Rupert Brooke came to the Green Dragon, where John Maynard Keynes had arranged a meeting of the Society (a Cambridge club); in fact, Brooke was really having his first encounter with the nucleus of the Bloomsbury group. Among those present were G. E. Moore, R. G. Hawtry, Robert Calverley Trevelyan, and Lytton Strachey. Strachey wrote to Virginia Stephen (Woolf): "Of course it finally destroyed me, the coldest winds you can imagine sweeping over the plain, and inferior food, and not enough comfortable chairs. But on the whole I was amused."

MARKYATE, Hertfordshire (pop. 1,340) Situated 4½ miles southeast of Dunstable, Markyate is on the Roman Watling Street, and Markyate Cell is a restored mansion built on the site of a former nunnery. Soon after his mother's death in 1737, William Cowper was sent to a school here on the High Street run by a Dr. Pitman; the two-year stay was not a happy one, and Cowper suffered at the hands of older boys, one of whom was expelled for his abuses. The onset of eye trouble in 1739 prompted Cowper's removal from the school and placement in the home of an eminent surgeon and oculist, a Dr. Disney. Cowper's early treatment at this school was not forgotten, and "Tyrocinium" is a long tirade against such establishments:

> Lascivious, headstrong, or all these at once;
> That in good time the stripling's finished taste
> For loose expense and fashionable waste
> Should prove your ruin, and his own at last;
> Train him in public with a mob of boys,
> Childish in mischief only and in noise.

MARLBOROUGH, Wiltshire (pop. 4,976) An ancient city in the Kennet River Valley on the boundary of Savernake Forest and on the busy road from London to Bath, Marlborough (pronounced "mawl'bro") is noted for its very wide main street, its famous public school, and its attractive inns and coaching stops. This area of Wiltshire is downland, and there are, as well, an enormous number of tumuli, mounds, and other relics of prehistoric existence. Indeed, traces of Neolithic and Roman occupation have been found near Castle Mound, and traditionally the great mound Maerl's Barrow on the grounds of Marlborough College is associated with Arthurian legend and is fondly hoped to be the burial place of the magician Merlin. However, the mound was actually an important part of the town's defenses, and a wooden Saxon structure was built on it; later this was replaced by a flint-and-stone building.

The town was always attractive to the English monarchs, especially because Savernake Forest was a royal hunting ground: Henry II spent Christmas here with Thomas à Becket in attendance, and King John seemed especially partial to the town; he was married in the castle chapel in 1189 and granted the town's royal charter in 1204. Fires devastated the town in 1653, 1679, and 1690; fortunately, some fine quaint medieval half-timbered buildings escaped the fires and are to be found in the narrow back alleys behind the Georgian-lined High Street. St. Mary's Church was rebuilt after the 17th-century fires, and the salvageable parts of the old church were incorporated in the new; the old Norman pillar is still marked by its brush with the fires. St. Peter's Church, on the other side of the street, was the scene of the ordination of Thomas Wolsey.

One of the earliest visitors here was John Evelyn, who came to Marlborough from Windsor on May 9, 1654, and noted the fire damage:

> Din'd at *Marlborow*, which having lately ben fired, was now new built: At one end of this Towne we saw my Lord *Seamors* house, but nothing observable save the Mount. . . .

Samuel Pepys's concern was with his accommodations even though he noted the prodigious stones on the Downs and wrote that they reminded him of Stonehenge; he also was interested in house construction:

> Before night come to Marlborough, and lay at the Hart; a good house, and a pretty fair town for a street or two; and what is most singular is, their houses on one side having their pent-houses supported with pillars, which makes it a good walk.

Daniel Defoe was extremely interested in the stones Pepys had noticed:

> I am come now to *Marlborough:* On the Downs, about Two or Three Miles from the Town, are abundance of loose Stones, lying scattered about the Plain; some whereof are very large, and appear to be of the same kind with those at *Stonehenge,* and some larger. They are called by the Country People, not for want of Ignorance, *The Gray Weathers.*

Both Evelyn and Pepys were entertained in the Duke of Somerset's home. Somewhat later the house was in the hands of Frances, Countess of Hertford (later Duchess of Somerset), a patron of many poets. By this time the grounds had been styled to the times with sham ruins, a grotto, and artificial cascades. One of the countess's guests was the poet James Thomson, who probably wrote parts of "Spring" here. Indeed, this section of *The Seasons* is dedicated to the countess, and some of the descriptions reflect the Marlborough area.

The house continued its curious history and became a famous coaching inn a few years later; an announcement of the conversion appeared in the August 17, 1752, issue of the *Salisbury Journal and Devizes Mercury:*

> I beg leave to inform the Publick that I have fitted up the Castle at Marlborough in the most genteel and commodious manner, and opened it as an Inn, where the Nobility, Gentry, etc., may depend on the best accommodation and treatment; the favour of whose company will always be gratefully acknowledged by their most obedient Servant, George Smith, late of the Artillery Ground, London. Neat Post Chaises.

MARLBOROUGH Downland tracks, tumuli, sarsen stones known as Grey Wethers, and other evidence of prehistoric existence dot the landscape surrounding the ancient town of Marlborough and have been commented on by many writers including Samuel Pepys and Daniel Defoe, who compared the stones here with those at Stonehenge.

The inn and grounds were taken over by Marlborough College, and the inn was the first building in which the school was housed. Charles Stuart Calverley was here for three months in 1846 before being admitted at Harrow, and William Morris was educated at the school from 1848 to 1851 before going up to Exeter College, Oxford. Hallam Tennyson, son of Lord Tennyson, came to the Marlborough school in 1866 because the headmaster, Granville Bradley, was a man whom Tennyson knew and respected as a scholar. Lord Tennyson was here on several occasions, and on the first he wrote "The Victim," which as Hallam later said, his father began "in view of the old cut yews (opposite his window). . . . And he expressed great delight at the choir of birds in the trees here." Tennyson's room, in Lady Hertford's old home, was the green dressing room which overlooked the clipped yews and the lime circle of the old garden. Sir Anthony Hope Hawkins, who excelled in athletics, Siegfried Sassoon, John Betjeman, and Louis MacNeice also were educated here.

MARLOW *See* GREAT MARLOW.

MARNHULL, Dorset (pop. 1,213) The name Marnhull is a corruption of the ancient name of this village of northern Dorset, situated about 5 miles southwest of Shaftesbury. Once more appropriately called Marlhill on account of the common white clay which hardens into freestone on exposure to air, the village was formerly widely noted for its drunkenness and debauchery and was called "the booziest place in Dorset." Marnhull is Thomas Hardy's Marlott and Tess's birthplace: "The village of Marlott lay amid the northeastern undulations of the beautiful Vale of Blackmore . . . [in an area] in which the fields are never brown and the springs never dry. . . ." This is the home of the Durbeyfield family, and the Pure Drop Inn, where "there's a very pretty brew in the tap" and where John Durbeyfield drinks to celebrate Tess's marriage, may well have been the Crown. (The name, however, was probably picked up from inns of the same name at Wootton Glanville and Wareham.) Hardy also mentions Rolliver's, most likely the Blackmoor Vale Inn on the west side of the village. Marlott is used mainly in *Tess of the D'Urbervilles*, but it is mentioned in "Squire Petrick's Lady" (*A Group of Noble Dames*).

MARTINDALE, Westmorland (pop. 195) On the east side of the wooded shore of Ullswater, 10 miles southwest of Penrith, is the valley community of Martindale. The forested area here is the only area in the country where a herd of wild red deer roams freely. The much-restored and very remote old Norman Church of St. Martin, on Howe Grain, about a 1,000 feet above sea level, has been rebuilt many times, beginning in 1633. William Wordsworth and his sister Dorothy found their way here; Dorothy left a description of the church in her *Journals*, and William used it in *The Excursion*. St. Martin's is the roofless chapel where the old peat gatherer takes shelter from the storm:

. . . long and hopelessly we sought in vain:
Till, chancing on that lofty ridge to pass
A heap of ruin—almost without walls
And wholly without roof (the bleached remains

Of a small chapel, where, in ancient time,
The peasants of these lonely valleys used
To meet for worship on that central height)—
We there espied the object of our search,
Lying full three parts buried among tufts
Of heath-plant, under and above him strewn,
To baffle, as he might, the watery storm:
And there we found him breathing peaceably. . . .

MARTLEY, Worcestershire (pop. 739) A tidy old village 7 miles northwest of Worcester, Martley has a number of good 18th-century buildings, a fine 17th-century rectory, and an outstanding gray and red sandstone church. Located down a pleasant side lane with low-lying meadows below it, the basically Norman and medieval church has an interior perhaps unequaled in England. Original Norman tiles form part of the altar step, and the chancel walls are covered with 13th- and 15th-century wall paintings in an excellent state of preservation.

Martley was the birthplace of Charles Stuart Calverley on December 22, 1831; the son of the Rev. Henry Blayds (this name, which had been assumed at the beginning of the 19th century, was replaced by the original name Calverley in 1852), he spent most of his early life here and had his first education from private tutors at home before entering Marlborough and then Harrow in 1846.

MATFIELD, Kent (pop. 669) The Weald of western Kent is an area containing rich farmland, great houses, and Royal Tunbridge Wells, 5 miles northwest of the village of Matfield, the home for many years of Siegfried Sassoon; he lived at Weirleigh, a tall red-brick house, before World War I. Here Sassoon worked on the first poems he published, and here in his studio in a pique burned all his copies of *Verses* "with the exception of the 'black buckrams.'" *The Weald of Youth*, "an attempt to compose an outline of my mental history," describes far more than that and shows much of his life at Weirleigh:

To be aware of a glimmer of light at my open window; to hear a cock crowing from the farm beyond the wood . . . to listen for the first thrush or blackbird out in the dewy dimness of the garden: and then to slip on some clothes and creep downstairs. . . . The house, with its stair-creaking silences, its drowsing stuffiness, and the queerness of its reflection in mirrors and the glass of dark pictures—this was only a vacated residue of the night before.

MAUTBY, Norfolk (pop. 92) Five miles northwest of Great Yarmouth, Mautby is in the Norfolk Broads, a triangular area (bounded by Norwich, Sea Palling, and Lowestoft) of open expanses of navigable water with approach channels linking more than thirty of the Broads. The small, partly Norman church has a thatched roof and some very good 14th-century glass. The village was probably the birthplace of Margaret Mautby (Mauteby), the wife of John Paston, who is known for the correspondence which reveals much of the history and social practices of the 15th century. Indeed, some of the letters were written here. Margaret Paston returned to Mautby after her husband's death and died here in 1484; she was buried in the south aisle (destroyed) of the church.

MAYFIELD, Staffordshire (pop. 1,232) Mayfield is actually two villages, Upper Mayfield, perched on a hill overlooking the Dove Valley, and Lower Mayfield, nestled against the river in the valley. Situated on the Derbyshire-Staffordshire border 2 miles southwest of Ashbourne, it has a lovely location surrounded by woods and fields. The higher village is full of old stone houses, while the lower one has a Norman and Perpendicular church and an old textile mill.

Between the two villages is the gray stone Mayfield Cottage (now Standcliffe Farm), where Thomas Moore lived from 1811 to 1817. Just married in March 1811, Moore and his wife Bessie came to Mayfield after a short time in Kegworth, Leicestershire, and their choice appears to have been excellent: "I could not possibly have a more rural or secluded corner to court the Muses in," Moore related. From the cottage Moore could hear the bells of the Ashbourne Church, "the Cathedral of the Peak":

> Those evening bells! Those evening bells.
> How many a tale their music tells.
> Of youth, and home, and that sweet time
> When last I heard their soothing chime.
>
> Those joyous hours are passed away
> And many a heart that then was gay
> Within the tomb now darkly dwells
> And hears no more those evening bells.

As Moore's family increased, the necessity of adding to his income became urgent, and Longmans was induced to pay £3,000 for a yet unproduced or unconceived poem. Many ideas and false starts occurred before Moore hit upon *Lalla Rookh,* most of which was written in his study here. By 1815 he was sufficiently pleased to offer the publishers a look at the incomplete manuscript, which they declined, stating that they would wait for the finished piece. The following year was financially disastrous for Longmans, and Moore offered them back their advance and suggested rescinding the contract. Moore's daughter Olivia Byron (after Lord Byron) died a few months after her birth in 1815 and was buried in the churchyard here.

MEDWAY RIVER, Kent   For centuries the Medway River has played an important role in Kentish history. The river rises in two headstreams in Sussex and one in Surrey and courses 70 miles northeast past Maidstone and Rochester, where it effectively forms part of the Thames Estuary. It is, in fact, the Medway that traditionally has created the division between the Men of Kent, on the eastern bank, and the Kentish Men, to the west. The wild flowers of the Medway Valley are said to be the richest in England, and the river itself, although now barren of trout, is well stocked with the less particular carp, some of which have been known to exceed 20 pounds. John Milton refers to the "Medway smooth" in "At a Vacation Exercise in the College," and only a few years earlier Michael Drayton sang the praises of the river and its "Martiall and Heroique spirits" in *Poly-Olbion:*

> This *Medway* still had nurst those navies in her Road,
> Our Armies that had oft to conquest born abroad;
> And not a man of ours, for Armes hath famous been,
> Whom she not going out, or comming in hath seen:
> Or by some passing Ship, hath newes to her been brought,
> What brave exploits they did; as where, and how, they fought.

And, of course, as Drayton notes, Edmund Spenser writes of the marriage of the Medway and the Thames in the *Faerie Queene.*

One of the most amusing stories concerning the Medway is associated with Samuel Pepys, who had visited the river fortifications numerous times in his official capacity at the Admiralty. He apparently had no confidence in arrangements which included "a chain at the stakes" to stop the Dutch; and when the Dutch forces actually penetrated the river defenses, he panicked and sent his wife to Brampton, Huntingdonshire, to bury his gold for safekeeping. Just about a year earlier John Evelyn had been in the area "in order to the march of 500 Prisoners to *Leeds-Castle*" and thought the area "by the *Medway* river . . . very agreeable, the downes & prospect." Christopher Smart, who was sent to school in Maidstone on the Medway, refers to the river as the "sweetest daughter of the ocean" and as the "silver Medway" whose surface "views the reflected landscape." The riverbank was lined with oak trees, the "bent oaks" of "The Hop Garden," and here as a child he fished and as a man mourned the death of his friend Theophilus Wheeler while the Medway

> shall flow
> In sullen silence silvery along
> The weeping shores. . . .

MELBURY OSMUND, Dorset (pop. 278)   Off the main road from Yeovil to Dorchester, 1½ miles northwest of Melbury Bubb, this little village, with stone-and-thatch houses scattered among the trees, is called Little Hintock in Thomas Hardy's Wessex. Melbury Sampford, 1½ miles to the south, becomes King's Hintock, and Minterne Magna, 7 miles to the southeast, is Great Hintock. The Hintocks are mentioned in *Tess of the D'Urbervilles* and *The Mayor of Casterbridge,* and most of the action of *The Woodlanders* occurs in this general neighborhood. Mentioned are Tutcombe Bottom and Delborough, said to be a nearby hamlet, where Giles Winterborne goes to live. The Horse, an inn on Hintock Green, appears in "A Trampwoman's Tragedy."

MELLS, Somerset (pop. 830)   Mells, an unpretentious village 3 miles northwest of Frome and south of Bath, was once closely associated with the great Benedictine establishment at Glastonbury and was one of the easternmost of the abbey's holdings. The plan to design the village in the shape of a cross with its four streets intersecting at the 16th-century church was completed only on the north side of the village when John Horner, the last local steward to the abbot of Glastonbury, bought the property at the dissolution of the monasteries. The Tudor manor house, with gables and mullioned windows, became the Horner family seat, and this house and this family inspired the children's rhyme "Little Jack Horner." The poem, which first appeared in a 1770 pamphlet, "The Pleasant History of Jack Horner," was based on a fictitious story of the transportation of the title deeds to the manor. The deeds (that is, the plum) were said to have been sent to Henry VIII in a pie but were stolen on the way.

More recently Mells was associated with Thomas Hardy and his Wessex. "The First Countess of Wessex" (*A Group of Noble Dames*) begins at King's-Hintock Court (Melbury Sampford, Dorset) and then moves to Falls Park, which is Mells. Hardy puts an almost accurate distance of 20 miles between the two places, and the description of Falls Park and its mansion leaves little doubt of the identification:

> Falls-Park . . . was altogether a more modest centre-piece to a more modest possession than [King's-Hintock Court]. . . . Its Palladian front, of the period of the first Charles, derived from its regular features a dignity which the great, many gabled heterogeneous mansion of his wife could not eclipse.

The Three Man Gibbet mentioned in the story is on the road from Wells to Bristol.

MEOLE BRACE, Shropshire (pop. 2,259)   A secluded village less than 2 miles from the town of Shrewsbury, Meole Brace has more than a normal share of visitors because of its outstanding church. Built where a Norman church once stood, the 19th-century building has some of the most beautiful modern windows in England. Most of these were executed by William Morris from designs by Sir Edward Burne-Jones, and the chancel work contains more than 150 figures.

A frequent mid-19th-century visitor was Samuel Butler; in school in Shrewsbury from 1847 to 1854, he came to Meole Brace to see his aunt, Mrs. Edward Bather. She was a kindly woman, the wife of an archdeacon, and a fairly accomplished pianist. Butler later recalled, "My great delight was to get her to play the overtures of *Rodolinda* and *Atalanta*, which were her stock pieces. . . ." An early-20th-century regional author lived here from 1902 until her marriage in the village church in 1912; Mary Webb, whose novels are set mostly in Shropshire, moved to Lyth Hill, 3 miles to the south.

MERE, Wiltshire (pop. 1,847)   Situated on the eastern edge of the Vale of Blackmoor and set below downland slopes which may have been Roman vineyards, Mere is the meeting point of Wiltshire, Dorset, and Somerset. There are two famous old coaching inns here: the Old Ship and the modernized Talbot, where Charles II is said to have stayed in disguise after the Battle of Worcester. The pinnacled Perpendicular church retains some of its 13th-century features, but the tower for which many Wiltshire churches are justly famous is its most impressive attribute. Just southwest of the church is a long, low Tudor house known as the Chantry; its gardens slope down to a stream which escapes from the garden wall. Here William Barnes, the Dorset poet, kept his school after coming from Dorchester. When he arrived in 1823, the school was in a different location, but after his marriage in 1827, he took the Chantry and accepted boarders. He trimmed the lawn with a scythe and turned the old coach house into a workshop. Barnes took great delight in his trees and flowers, and when he left in 1835 for a better school in Dorchester, he wrote of the garden:

> No more at breezy eve or dewy morn
>   My gliding scythe shall shear thy mossy green;
> My busy hands shall never more adorn,
>   My eyes no more may see this peaceful scene.
> But still, sweet spot, wherever I may be,
>   My love-led soul shall wander back to thee.

MERTON, Norfolk (pop. 164)   A village consisting of a manor house, a basically 14th-century church inside the manor parklands, and a few scattered houses bordering Breckland (an expanse of uncultivated heath), Merton is 10 miles north of Thetford. The old manor house, badly damaged and partially destroyed by a fire in 1956, was mostly Jacobean, dating to 1610, and had two wings added in 1830 and 1843 respectively; it was hodgepodge of gables and buttresses. Inside the park is the church with a Norman tower and fragments of 14th-century glass.

The son of one of Edward FitzGerald's closest friends was the Rev. George Crabbe, the poet's grandson, who was the vicar here for many years; FitzGerald was in the habit of visiting Merton quite frequently, especially in summer. He suffered from a heart condition for years and died here at the Old Rectory (now called Silverdale) in his sleep on the night of June 13–14, 1883, and was buried at Boulge, Suffolk.

MERTON, Surrey   Merton, Surrey, no longer officially exists except for its inhabitants; in 1965 it was amalgamated with the boroughs of Mitcham, Wimbledon, and Morden (all formerly in Surrey) into one of the outer boroughs of Greater London. Jointly the population exceeds 175,000 and about 75,000 of the inhabitants live in Merton. Before the Norman Conquest, Merton belonged to Harold, and under William the Conqueror a great Austin priory was founded here in 1115 by the sheriff of Surrey, Gilbert le Norman. In 1130 its site was moved to the banks of the Wandle River, and its prosperity and importance increased immeasurably. It became a royal favorite, and the priory school became well known in a relatively short time; indeed, both Thomas à Becket and Walter de Merton, later founder of Merton College, Oxford, and Bishop of Rochester, were educated here.

Throughout the next two centuries Merton continued to gain wealth and favors, so much so that when Henry VIII dissolved the religious foundations, he kept Merton and its £1,000 yearly revenue for himself. The buildings were then quarried for Nonsuch, and virtually nothing was left. William Camden describes Merton in his *Britannia*:

> The clear little river *Wandle*, full of excellent trouts, rises not far from hence at *Cashalton*, and passing by *Morden* leaves on its West bank *Merton*, situate in a most fruitful spot. . . . At present this place shews only the ruins of a monastery, founded by Henry I. at the instigation of Gilbert sheriff of Surrey, and famous for the parliament held at it under Henry III.

Richard Gough later added:

> All that remains of *Merton* abbey are the outer walls of flint, inclosing 65 acres, the river Wandle running through them: a chapel and two gates. . . . [A]nd the site is occupied by two calicoe printing manufacturers, and a copper mill, employing altogether near 1000 persons.

The "two calicoe printing manufacturers" and the copper mill are of importance because of their literary association. In 1881 William Morris bought a print factory here at the abbey, where with William De Morgan he produced wallpaper, household decorations, and pottery. (Morris's establishment had been moved from Queens Square, London, because of a lack of space.)

Ford Hermann Hueffer (later changed by deed poll to Ford Madox Ford) was born in Merton on December 17, 1873. Grandson of the artist Ford Madox Brown, nephew by marriage of William Rossetti, and son of a noted music critic, he had a creatively oriented youth. His childhood was spent here, and he attended a private school in Folkestone. Also associated with Merton are William Ernest Henley, who frequently visited a friend, George Wyndham, here from July 1879 on, and Richard Brinsley Sheridan, who rented Church House for a short time.

MICKLEHAM, Surrey (pop. 795) Midway between Leatherhead and Dorking in the Mole Valley, Mickleham is one of the most attractive spots in Surrey; here the Mole has cut through the chalk walls of the Mickleham Downs, and every summer the river goes underground, swallowed up by the chalk bed. The phenomenon of "swallows," as this disappearance of the river is called, was fully investigated in the mid-20th century; it seems that the swallow holes are, in reality, chalk-bed fissures which absorb a constant amount of water, and thus in summer, when the flow of water is reduced, the river "dries up," only to reappear near Leatherhead.

The Mole has frequently been written of; Michael Drayton talks of its strange underground passage (trees have disappeared into enormous potholes in modern times) in *Poly-Olbion*:

ff. *Mole* digs her selfe a Path, by working day and night
(According to her name, to shew her nature right)
And underneath the Earth, for three miles space doth creep....

Edmund Spenser writes in the *Faerie Queene*:

Mole, that like a nousling mole doth make
His way still underground, till Thames he overtake.

And John Milton refers to it as the "sullen *Mole*, that runneth underneath" in the catalog of rivers in "At a Vacation Exercise in the College." Even Alexander Pope notes the river in his *Windsor Forest* as the "sullen Mole, that hides his diving flood." Earlier John Evelyn visited the area and on August 26, 1655, wrote:

... went to view the *Swallow* famous for the diving of the river *Darking* there, & passing under ground at the foote of a huge white Cliffe or precipice, looking West-ward, the Channell where the water sinks in, being full of holes; It not rising til some miles distance about *Letherhead*....

Daniel Defoe was quite interested in the phenomenon of the swallows, but he was highly indignant that "Men of Learning" dealing with "a Case so easily discover'd and so near" could be so unenlightened as to suggest the river swirled up again at Leatherhead. He quotes William Camden's "erroneous" explanation in *Britannia* and rages on for some time before stating "[I]t is thus, and no more":

But the true State of the Case is this, the Current of the River being much obstructed by the Interposition of those Hills, called *Box-Hill*, which tho' descending in a kind of Vale, as if parted to admit the River to pass, and making that Descent so low as to have the appearance of a level, near a Village call'd *Mickleham*: I say, these Hills yet interrupting the free Course of the River, it forces the Waters *as it were* to find their way thro' as well as they

can; and in order to this ... the Waters sink insensibly away, and in some Places are to be seen, (*and I have seen them*) little Chanels which go out on the sides of the River, where the Water in a Stream not so big as would fill a Pipe of a quarter of an Inch Diameter, trills away out of the River, and sinks insensibly into the Ground.

The village itself holds a great deal of interest: near the church with its Norman tower is the red-brick Old House, dated 1663, the home of George Meredith's second wife, Marie Vulliamy, a woman of Swiss Huguenot descent whom he had first met in Norfolk; the couple were married here in September 1864 and took Flint Cottage in Box Hill in 1867. Meredith was also in Mickleham earlier on his walk across the Downs, and he stayed at an inn here on his way from Copsham to Burford Bridge. He delighted in the nightingales by the banks of the Mole. Across from the church is the entrance to Norbury Park, one of the finest parks in the shire and the home of the Stidulphs, friends of John Evelyn; the diarist visited the estate on his 1655 trip and felt the "*yew & Box, as render the place extremely agreable, it seeming to be summer all the winter for many miles prospect.*"

Mickleham's most important literary association is with Frances Burney, later Madame d'Arblay; after leaving her royal post as second keeper of the robes in July 1791, she eventually made her way here to her sister Susanna's home near Norbury Park. Fanny Burney stayed with the Phillipses for some time and was a frequent visitor to Norbury Park, then owned by an old family friend. At this time Louis-Marie-Jacques-Amalric Narbonne, the French Minister of War, and a number of other French refugees had established themselves at Juniper Hall, where Fanny Burney met Gen. Alexandre d'Arblay, Tallyrand, and Madame de Staël. A February 1793 letter from Fanny Burney to her father contains early hints of her feelings toward D'Arblay:

M. D'Arblay is now indisposed. This latter is one of the most delightful Characters I have ever met, for openness, probity, intellectual knowledge, & unhackneyed manners.

Within two weeks she adds:

M. D'Arblay is one of the most singularly interesting Characters that can ever have been formed. He has a sincerity, a frankness, an ingenuous openness of nature that I had been injust enough to think could not belong to a French Man. With all this, which is his *Military portion,* he is passionately fond of literature, a most delicate critic in his own language, well versed in both Italian & German, & a very elegant Poet.... [H]e has been writing an English address *a Mr Burney,* (i.e., M. le Docteur) joining in M^e De Stahl's request. I cannot send it you, because it is a precious morsel of elegant broken English, & I must keep it amongst my treasures: but I will produce it when I return, for your entertainment.

The admiration quickened, and they were married at the Mickleham Church on July 31, 1793. The d'Arblays settled in nearby Bookham.

From 1865 to 1883 Marie Corelli lived at Fern Dell.

MID LAVANT *See* LAVANT, EAST, AND LAVANT, MID.

MIDDLEHAM, Yorkshire (pop. 652) The open and wooded upland moor area in which Middleham lies is perhaps one of the most beautiful of the Yorkshire dales; the surrounding limestone hills are covered with heather, bilberries, and cotton grass. The village is often called the Windsor of the North in deference to its prominent position when the once-magnificent castle was in the hands of the Nevilles. Richard III, who married Anne Neville, lived in the castle for a substantial period, and when he was here, the court musicians were always in attendance. The castle was taken over by the crown following the Battle of Barnet in 1471, and by the mid-17th century it had become a local source of building materials. Fortunately, the keep and the castle walls have been essentially untouched, and the ruins are impressive. Around the market square are some extremely fine Georgian houses, and the old church, dedicated to St. Alkelda, contains a good collection of old glass.

Charles Kingsley, who visited the village from Malham when he was gathering material for *The Water Babies*, found that it was full "of so much bustle, and robing and unrobing" that he could find no time to think. Kingsley was one of the last canons of the Collegiate Church of St. Alkelda and generally enjoyed his visits here, no matter what his complaints were. William Shakespeare was stirred by the castle and its history and used "a park near Middleham Castle in Yorkshire" (*Henry VI: Part III*) as the residence of the Archbishop of York, the Earl of Warwick's brother. It is to this castle that Edward IV is sent as a prisoner when the Kingmaker manages to restore the throne to Henry VI.

Edward Bulwer-Lytton uses much of the same situation and environment in *The Last of the Barons*, in which he describes the last exciting days of Richard Neville and the feelings of Edward, who was brought here as half guest, half captive.

MIDDLETON-BY-WIRKSWORTH, Derbyshire (pop. 911) One of the oldest industries in England, tin mining, was begun here by the Romans, and the originally worked caves can still be seen. Limestone quarrying replaced the mining, and local limestone is still shipped all over England. Middleton-by-Wirksworth, 1½ miles northwest of the parent town, has a lovely location in the Derwent Vale, in an area abundantly blessed with wild flowers. For one year D. H. Lawrence lived in Mountain Cottage here. His sister Ada rented the place for him, and Lawrence moved in at the beginning of May 1918; he describes the location of the cottage:

It is in the darkish Midlands, on the rim of a steep valley, looking over darkish, folded hills—exactly the navel of England, and feels exactly that.

It seems that "Wintry Peacock" was inspired by a dream Lawrence had here and by his acute appreciation of the Derbyshire winter landscape. A letter to Katherine Mansfield (February 1919) describes his feelings:

I climbed with my niece to the bare tops of the hills. Wonderful it is to see the footmarks on the snow—beautiful ropes of rabbit prints, trailing away over the brows; heavy hare marks; a fox, so sharp and dainty, going over the wall; birds with two feet that hop; very splendid straight advance of a pheasant; wood pigeons that are clumsy and move in flocks; splendid little leaping marks of weasels, coming along like a necklace chain of berries; odd little filigree of the field mice; the trail of a mole—it is astonishing what a world of wild creatures

one feels round one, on the hills in the snow. From the height it is very beautiful. The upland is naked, white like silver and moving far into the distance, strange and muscular, with gleams like skin.

"Glad Ghosts" deals specifically with the area and describes Lord Lathkill's place as

an old Derbyshire stone house at the end of the village of Middleton: a house with three sharp gables, set back not very far from the high road, with a gloomy moor for a park behind.

MIDHURST, Sussex (pop. 1,890) Midhurst is the center of one of the most beautiful areas in Sussex; overlooking the Rother River, 12 miles north of Chichester, it is an old market town full of attractive houses and fine old inns. There is an air of spaciousness and gentility here, partly because of the huge expanse of marshy land on the north side of town and partly because of the wide 18th-century layout of North Street. The original town center is around the market square and the church, mainly 15th-century but considerably restored in 1881, while the most attractive and mellowed areas are on North, Red Lion, and South Streets. South Street has the huge and beautiful Spread Eagle Inn, which dates to 1430 and was well known in coaching days; its only known literary connection is with Hilaire Belloc, who often cycled here with John Phillimore from Shipley.

Just north of the town and across the river are the ruins of the magnificent Tudor house of Cowdray. The first house built here was that of the Norman Bohuns, around 1300, and by marriage the house passed to Sir David Owen, natural son of Owen Glendower. In 1529 Sir William Fitzwilliam, Lord Keeper of the Privy Seal, Lord High Admiral, and later Earl of Southampton, bought and completed the house except for a few touches added by his half

MIDHURST   Midhurst's South Street contains the lovely 14th-century Spread Eagle, one of the best-known coaching inns of its day. Its locally brewed beer was later a favorite of Hilaire Belloc's, and he often cycled here from his home in Shipley.

brother Sir Anthony Browne. It was Sir Anthony, it is said, who caused the ultimate extinction of his line. He had been given Battle Abbey in 1538 and converted the abbot's house to his own use; while feasting there on one occasion, he was cursed by a monk, who prophesied that the line would end "by fire and water." In 1793 the 8th and last Viscount Montague (Sir Anthony's son was the 1st) drowned while trying to shoot the Laufenburg Falls in the Rhine, and Cowdray caught fire, leaving the remains seen to this day.

There are a number of important literary associations with Midhurst and Cowdray. Although it is only conjectured that John Lyly was here in August 1591 as a guest at Cowdray, it is known that Dr. Samuel Johnson and Philip Metcalfe visited the house in 1782. Johnson, as usual, was not easily impressed, but this house and its contents, including the Roll of Battle Abbey and many excellent paintings, brought about the comment:

> Sir . . . I should like to stay here four-and-twenty hours. We see here how our ancestors lived.

The most famous association is with H. G. Wells, who came here as a chemist's apprentice under Samuel Cowap after the school fiasco in Wookey, Somerset, and attended the newly reopened grammar school to study Latin. Wells's apprenticeship lasted only for the trial month and was far too costly for his mother to maintain; thus, at the end of the month the young man persuaded the headmaster of the school, Horace Byatt, to allow him to stay on and to live in the headmaster's house. Wells became a full-time pupil here on February 23, 1881. Six weeks later, however, his mother secured another apprenticeship for him at a draper's in Southsea, Hampshire, and he left Midhurst. The experience in Southsea was distasteful, and with two full years to run on the apprenticeship Wells left. He returned to Midhurst, became an undermaster in the grammar school (which was located across from the gates to Cowdray Park), and shared rooms with the other assistant master over a High Street sweetshop run by a Mrs. Walton. Wells studied, took the examinations offered by the Education Department in 1884, and gained a studentship to the Normal School of Science, South Kensington, London, a bursary of a guinea a week, and the possibility of taking a B.S. degree.

Midhurst appears often in Wells's writings. The town becomes Wimblehurst in *Tono-Bungay;* George Ponderevo's story of being brought to Wimblehurst from Bladesover parallels Wells's experiences after leaving Uppark:

> I took up my new world in Wimblehurst with the chemist's shop as its hub, set to work at Latin and materia medica, and concentrated upon the present with all my heart. Wimblehurst is an exceptionally quiet and grey Sussex town, rare among south of England towns in being largely built of stone. I found something very agreeable and picturesque in its clean cobbled streets, its odd turnings and abrupt corners, and in the pleasant park that crowds up one side of the town. The whole place is under the Eastry dominion, and it was the Eastry influence and dignity that kept its railway station a mile and three-quarters away. Eastry House is so close that it dominates the whole; one goes across the market-place (with its old lock-up and stocks), past the great pre-reformation church, a fine grey shell, like some empty skull from which the life has fled, and there at once are the huge wrought-iron gates. . . .

Here George "speedily mastered the modicum of Latin necessary for my qualifying examinations, and—a little assisted by the Government Science and Art Department classes that were held in the Grammar School—went on with my mathematics." He "made no friends among the young men of the place at all"; he had "no love-affair to tell of"; and his "adolescent years at Wimblehurst were on the whole laborious, uneventful years that began in short jackets and left me in many ways nearly a man. . . ." *The Wheels of Chance* also uses Midhurst, for there Wells includes his sweetshop room, which had a slanted ceiling:

> He [Hoopdriver] came into Midhurst by the bridge at the water-mill, and came up the North Street; and a small shop flourishing cheerfully the cheerful sign of a teapot, and exhibiting a brilliant array of tobaccos, sweets, and children's toys in the window, struck his fancy. A neat bright-eyed little old lady made him welcome, and he was presently supping sumptuously on sausages and tea. . . . The room had a curtained recess and a chest of drawers, for presently it was to be his bedroom . . . very comfortable it was indeed. The window was lead framed and diamond paned, and through it one saw the corner of the vicarage and a pleasant hill crest in dusky silhouette against the twilight sky.

Also among the visitors to Midhurst are the Beaumonts, who put up at the Angel Hotel:

> You must not think that a strain is put on coincidence when I tell you that next door to Mrs. Wardor's—that was the name of the bright-eyed, little old lady with whom Mr. Hoopdriver had stopped—is the Angel Hotel, and in the Angel Hotel on the night that Mr. Hoopdriver reached Midhurst, were "Mr." and "Miss" Beaumont, our Bechamel and Jessie Milton.

MILSTON, Wiltshire (pop. 162)   A small village on the Avon River 3 miles north of Amesbury, Milston has a 13th-century church with 15th-century windows; this area is the center of Salisbury Plain, and the landscape is gently rolling. Milston was the birthplace of Joseph Addison on May 1, 1672; his father, Lancelot Addison, was the newly installed rector, and the family lived in the substantial thatched rectory about 50 yards from the church. The rectory burned down in 1681 and was rebuilt; the second rectory was later demolished, but a stone in the garden of the present rectory marks the site. Addison was christened the day he was born, perhaps because of a delicate constitution, and the font with its leaf-carved base and dormer cover is still in use. The family left Milston in 1683, when the Reverend Mr. Addison became the dean of Lichfield.

MILTON ABBAS, Dorset (pop. 579)   Milton Abbas, 6 miles southwest of Blandford Forum, is one of the loveliest and most historically interesting villages in Dorset; it is a model 18th-century village of unsurpassed beauty (officially rated the prettiest in England). The old abbey here was established by Athelstan as a community of secular clergy around 840, but in 964 Cyneward established the Benedictine order which controlled the foundation until the

MILTON ABBAS This model 18th-century village was created here by the 1st Earl of Dorchester between 1782 and 1787, and becomes an important part of Thomas Hardy's Wessex as Middleton Abbey in *Tess of the D'Urbervilles*.

dissolution of the monasteries in the 16th century. Then John Tregonwell bought the abbey buildings and presented the church to the town. In the 18th century Joseph Damer bought the estate, and that is when all the changes came about. This is the man Horace Walpole described as

> the most arrogant and proud of men, with no foundation but great wealth and a match with the Duke of Dorset's daughter. His birth and parts were equally mean and contemptible.

When Damer bought the property, the village of between 500 and 600 inhabitants was prosperous and lay south of the church on both sides of the stream; it had a market, a fair, a brewery, a school, and almshouses. But to Damer, later Lord Milton and 1st Earl of Dorchester, these were a blight, and he tackled the problem by buying up or condemning village properties until he had the whole area. Then the old village was replaced by a model village of his own design.

The village is an integral part of Thomas Hardy's Wessex and may well be the "Abbey south" of Blackmoor Vale in "The Last Pyx" (*Poems of the Past and Present*). It is certainly Middleton Abbey in *Tess of the D'Urbervilles* and *The Woodlanders*. In the latter Mrs. Charmond makes Middleton Abbey her temporary residence. The surrounding area is described as Marshcombe Bottom, and on the road from Middleton to Little Hintock (Melbury Osmund) Dr. Fitzpiers is thrown into the road. Middleton Gate in the same novel is a toll station on the turnpike between Little Hintock and Middleton. In "The Revisitation" (*Time's Laughingstocks and Other Poems*) Milton Abbey Woods become Milton Woods.

MINSTEAD, Hampshire (pop. 804) A New Forest village set in a maze of lanes, Minstead, 2½ miles northwest of Lyndhurst, has a curious 13th-century church overlooking the village and a small green.

With rubble-and-daub walls, dormers, and gabled windows, the church would be mistaken for a farmhouse except for its brick tower (1774); it was the 17th- and 18th-century local builders, familiar with domestic but not ecclesiastic architecture, who transformed the church. The churchyard contains the grave of Sir Arthur Conan Doyle, who died in Crowborough, Sussex, on July 7, 1930; Doyle was first buried in the garden of his home there, but after World War II his remains and the British-oak headstone inscribed "Steel true, blade straight" were brought here to an area he knew and loved. Just a few years before his death he and his second wife, Jean Leckie, who also is buried here, bought Bignell Wood, a half-timbered cottage, and lived in it intermittently until 1930.

MINSTER-IN-SHEPPEY, Kent (pop. 3,059) Situated on the northwest coast of Sheppey (the Isle of Sheep), an island connected to the mainland by the Kingsferry Bridge over the Swale Channel, Minster-in-Sheppey dates to the 7th century, when Sexburga, the widow of the Kentish king Ercombert, founded a nunnery here. The establishment, which was sacked by the Danes in 855 and by Earl Godwin two centuries later, gave the village its name. The nunnery was reestablished after each destruction, and the abbey church was rebuilt in the early 12th century. One of the many medieval monuments is to Sir Robert de Shurland, Baron of Sheppey and Lord Warden of the Cinque Ports, of whom Richard Harris Barham writes in "Grey Dolphin" in *The Ingoldsby Legends*. Barham makes Sir Robert into Ralph. The knight is banished from court after killing Father Fothergill, "a friar of the Augustine persuasion." Edward I (Longshanks), then King, is anchored in the mouth of the Thames, and Sir Ralph swims to the royal barge and begs the King's pardon. Returning to the shore, he meets a witch who prophesies his death by means of his horse; "'He has saved your life Ralph Shurland, for the nonce; but he shall yet be the means of your losing it for all that!'" Barham continues:

> He dropped the rein, drew forth Tickletoby, and, as the enfranchised Dolphin, good easy horse, stretched out his ewe-neck to the herbage, struck off his head at a single blow. "There, you lying old beldame!" said the Baron; "now take him away to the knacker's."

Three years later, walking on the beach and again seeing the witch, Sir Ralph comes upon Grey Dolphin's skull; he throws it across the beach, feels "an odd sort of sensation in his right foot," and discovers "a horse's tooth was sticking in his great toe!" Gangrene sets in, and he dies:

> In the abbey-church at Minster may yet be seen the tomb of a recumbent warrior, clad in the chain-mail of the 13th century. His hands are clasped in prayer; his legs, crossed in that position so prized by Templars in ancient, and tailors in modern days, bespeak him a soldier of the faith in Palestine. Close to his great toe lies sculptured in bold relief a horse's head....

MINSTER LOVELL, Oxfordshire (pop. 708) The Windrush River, which slowly winds its way around Oxfordshire and Gloucestershire, makes its way through gently rolling hills and at Minster Lovell is spanned by a 15th-century stone bridge. The village, with many old stone houses, contains the 15th-century Old Swan Inn; a ruined manor house, Minster Lovell Hall; and a Perpendicular church by the river. The manor house figures in two tragic legends, the medieval "Mistletoe Bough Legend" and that of "Lovell the dog." The former tells of a young girl who, while playing hide-and-seek on Christmas Eve, hid in a heavy wooden chest and was trapped. The second concerns the all-powerful Lovell family; Francis Lovell, a known supporter of the pretender Lambert Simnel, hid in a secret room following the defeat of Simnel at Stoke in 1487; only one other person, a trusted manservant, knew the room. The servant died suddenly, and Lovell, unable to escape, starved to death. This Francis Lovell, devious and sinister, is referred to in

> The Cat, the Rat, and Lovell the dog
> Rule all England under our hog.

He also appears, along with Catesby and Ratcliff, in William Shakespeare's *Richard III*.

MINSTERWORTH, Gloucestershire (pop. 319) Dating from Saxon times, Minsterworth, 3½ miles southwest of Gloucester on the banks of the Severn, became the property of the abbey (minster) of Gloucester soon after the Norman Conquest. The church here has been flooded by the Severn, and a 15th-century font in the "new" church bears water marks. Salmon fishing is especially good here, and there is a carving of three salmon in a net above an arcade capital in the church.

Minsterworth was the birthplace of the now-obscure World War I poet Frederick William Harvey. H. G. Wells spent a number of holidays here at the Elms, a farm kept by his uncle Charles; Wells came here first in 1886.

MINTERNE MAGNA, Dorset (pop. 203) On the Dorset Downs just 2 miles north of Cerne Abbas, Minterne Magna sits beneath High Stoy (860 feet), one of the hills forming the southern boundary of Blackmoor Vale, Thomas Hardy's Valley of the Little Dairies, which was used extensively in *Tess of the D'Urbervilles* and *The Woodlanders* and was mentioned in "The Lost Pyx" (*Poems of the Past and the Present*). Minterne Magna becomes Great Hintock, one of the group of villages composing the Hintocks in *The Woodlanders* (Melbury Osmund becomes Little Hintock, and Melbury Sampford, King's Hintock). The villages are also mentioned in *Tess of the D'Urbervilles* and *The Mayor of Casterbridge*. Giles Winterborne of *The Woodlanders* is buried in the churchyard of Great Hintock Church; and Great Hintock House, the residence of Mrs. Charmond, is based either on Turnford House, near Blandford Forum, or Upcerne House, just a mile farther south on the road to Cerne Abbas.

MITCHAM, Surrey Mitcham, Surrey, no longer exists, having in 1965 been amalgamated with Wimbledon, Merton, and Morden to form one of the thirty-two outer boroughs of Greater London. The full borough population is more than 175,000, and about 70,000 of the inhabitants reside in Mitcham. The town, on the Wandle River 2¼ miles southeast of Wimbledon and 3¾ miles northwest of Croydon, was once an area noted for fields and meadows, and lavender and wild herbs grew on the same rich black mold which now supports suburban detached cottages. The commons here, though, is a throwback to the past with inns surrounding the oldest cricket green in the world.

An early inhabitant of the village was John Donne, who came here with his family in 1606 after having effected a reconciliation with Sir George More, his father-in-law. Donne had experienced a number of difficult years following his secret marriage, but after the reconciliation he took a house on Whitford Lane, where modern housing now stands. The house, destroyed in 1840, was two-storied with projecting gables in front and a wing to the left. Here four more children were born to the Donnes, all of them baptized in the parish church of St. Peter and St. Paul. While Donne lived here, he was frequently at court and attracted the notice of the King; indeed, it was during this period that King James determined that if Donne were to get any preferment, it would have to be in the church. The family remained in Mitcham until November 1611, when John Donne accompanied Sir Robert Drury to the Continent and his wife and children went to the Isle of Wight to be with Sir John Oglander, Ann's brother-in-law.

Sir Walter Ralegh also had an association, however slight, with Mitcham. His wife bought him a house here, which he sold to raise funds for the second expedition to Guiana; it is doubtful that the Raleghs were ever in residence. The house is not the same one that John Donne inhabited, as is sometimes claimed; the dates do not fit.

MONKS KIRBY, Warwickshire (pop. 559) The Roman Fosse Way lies less than 1 mile away, and an ancient camp and an early monastery were both in Monks Kirby, although neither remains now; the town lies 7 miles northeast of Coventry. All that remains of early times is the church dedicated to St.

Edith, the Saxon abbess of Polesworth and daughter of King Egbert. The church is full of monuments to the Feildings of nearby Newnham Paddox; these were ancestors of the novelist Henry Fielding, who altered the spelling of the name.

In July 1450 Sir Thomas Malory and three others were accused of breaking into the house of one Hugh Smyth and of raping Mistress Joan Smyth. The intent of the charge is unclear, since the word *rape* carried meanings both of forced sexual intercourse and of abducting (perhaps by force). Malory also seized goods and chattels worth £40. Not apprehended, he raped another woman in Coventry eight weeks later.

The patron of John Donne and others, Sir Henry Goodere was born in Monks Kirby and spent most of his boyhood here with Michael Drayton, who was probably attached to the family as a page.

MONTACUTE, Somerset (pop. 739) This Somerset village 4 miles west of Yeovil held a Norman castle at one time, and in the first decade of the 12th century the manor and the entire village (an area still called The Borough) were made over to the Burgundian abbey at Cluny, and a priory was founded. Following the execution of Catherine Howard and her paramour Thomas Culpepper in 1542, these lands came into the possession of Sir Thomas Wyatt, who probably was here shortly after receiving them. John Leland, Henry VIII's librarian, comments:

> The ancient town we now call Montacute
> Chose Wyatt as its lord and patron.

The lands reverted to the crown after Wyatt's death later in the same year.

MOOR PARK, Surrey The most westerly parts of Surrey are unspoiled reaches of sandy heathland, green commons, and woodlands; here the Downs have narrowed into an area known as the Hog's Back, an essentially rural thin strip of chalkland between Guildford and Farnham commanding beautiful views at an altitude of a little over 500 feet. Just 1½ miles southeast of Farnham is Moor Park, originally Compton Hall; a 17th-century mansion now called Moor Park Cottage and serving as a center for adult Christian education, it became Moor Park when it was bought by Sir William Temple, diplomat, statesman, scholar, and husband of Dorothy Osborne. (Remembered for her letters to Sir William before they were married, she died here in February 1695 and was buried in Westminster Abbey.) Sir William laid out the gardens, it has been said, in both French and Dutch styles, "but his fine taste enabled him to retain the sweetness of the old English garden...." When he came here (probably from Sheen, the modern Richmond), at the close of 1689, Jonathan Swift accompanied him temporarily as his secretary and companion before returning to Ireland in May. Swift was back by Christmas, 1691, when he was reemployed by Temple, who had promised to secure employment for him in Ireland. The employment there had not been forthcoming, and Swift spent the next few years here, at one time entertaining King William III in the gardens when Sir William was ill. The young King, it is said, taught the poet how to cut asparagus in the Dutch way and eat both tip and stalk. Swift remained until May 1694, when Sir William's offer of prefer-

ment seems to have removed any scruples Swift may have had about entering the church merely for support. There was some estrangement after 1694, but fresh promises from Temple induced a return in April 1696. Swift retained his Irish prebendary until January 1698, when he relinquished it to a neighboring cleric.

During his last stay at Moor Park, Swift wrote *A Tale of a Tub* and *The Battle of the Books* and worked on Temple's manuscripts. Here, also, he met the (probably) ten-year-old "Stella," to whom he wrote his *Journal;* she was Esther Johnson, whose mother, the companion to Temple's sister and an intimate of the family, lived in one of the two cottages (now gone) at the driveway entrance to the estate. (The claim, by the way, that Esther was Sir William's natural child is without foundation.) Following Temple's death in 1699, Swift returned to Ireland as chaplain secretary to Lord Berkeley.

Near the estate is Mother Ludlam's Cave (90 by 140 feet), where, it is said, once dwelt a witch who was the reputed owner of the cauldron in Frensham Church; here, too, was the spring of Ludwell which supplied Waverley Abbey until it suddenly dried up in 1216. Swift puts the names together in "A Description of Mother Ludwell's Cave" but makes no reference to the witch:

> I that of Ludwell sing, to Ludwell run,
> Herself my Muse, her spring my Helicon.
> The neighbouring park its friendly aid allows,
> Perfum'd with thyme, o'erspread with shady boughs.
> Its leafy canopies new thoughts instil,
> And Crooksbury supplies the cloven-hill;
> Pomona does Minerva's stores dispense,
> And Flora sheds her balmy influence.

William Cobbett brought his son here in October 1825, as his *Rural Rides* relates, and pointed out the cave, the hill where Swift ran for exercise, and the spot where Sir William's heart was buried:

> From Waverley we went to Moore Park.... Here I showed Richard Mother Ludlum's Hole; but, alas! it is not the enchanting place that I knew it, nor that which Grose describes in his Antiquities! The semicircular paling is gone; the basins, to catch the never-ceasing little stream, are gone; the iron cups, fastened by chains, for people to drink out of, are gone; the pavement all broken to pieces; the seats for people to sit on, on both sides of the cave, torn up and gone; the stream that ran down a clean paved channel now making a dirty gutter.... Near the mansion, I showed Richard the hill upon which Dean Swift tells us he used to run for exercise, while he was pursuing his studies here; and I would have showed him the garden-seat under which Sir William Temple's heart was buried, agreeably to his will; but the seat was gone, also the wall at the back of it....

A sundial marks the burial place.

MORECAMBE BAY, Lancashire and Westmorland Technically considered part of the Lake District, Morecambe Bay, 10 miles wide and 18 miles long, is a sea inlet which has spawned a popular resort area rivaling Blackpool with an arrangement of promenades, a marineland, and illuminated piers in both Heysham and Morecambe. The bay and its village are renowned for shrimps, the view, and the sands. The tiny Morecambe Bay shrimps, which are potted and sent all over the world, are caught from horse-drawn carts fitted with nets, and the daytime panorama here includes views northward of Coniston Old Man, Helvellyn, Saddleback, the Langdale Pikes, and the peaks of Skiddaw and Scafell. The sands are treacherous, but for centuries the route from Lancaster to Ulverston led across them; many lost their lives here, and once an entire party of wedding guests was swept out to sea. Today walkers are permitted to cross only with an official guide. William Beckford crossed the sands on his English tour from August to October 1779, as did Ann Radcliffe around 1790; traveling in the early morning, she recalls:

> We took the early part of the tide, and entered these vast and desolate plains before the sea had entirely left them, or the morning mists were sufficiently dissipated to allow a view of distant objects; but the grand sweep of the coast could be faintly traced. . . . The tide was ebbing fast from our wheels, and its low murmur was interrupted, first, only by the shrill small cry of seagulls. . . . [I]t was sublimely interesting to watch the heavy vapours beginning to move, then rolling in lengthening volumes over the scene, and as they gradually dissipated, discovering through their veil the various objects they had concealed—fishermen with carts and nets stealing along the margin of the tide, little boats pulling off from the shore, and the view still enlarging as the vapours expanded. . . .

MORESBY, Cumberland (pop. 1,102)   A coastal mining village 2½ miles northeast of the harbor town of Whitehaven, Moresby is a cliffside town fortified by the Romans. The old rectory was the home of William Wordsworth's son the Rev. John Wordsworth, who married Isabella Curwen in Workington in June 1830 and took the living here. Wordsworth, accompanied by his daughter Dora, came for a visit in 1832, undoubtedly to see his new grandchild Jane. In mid-June Walter Savage Landor arrived from Whitehaven (following his exile of almost eighteen years) in search of Wordsworth. The two men went on to Wasdale.

MORETON, Dorset (pop. 365)   This hamlet on the Frome River (also spelled Froom and pronounced "frume") becomes Moreford in Thomas Hardy's "The Fiddler of the Reels" (*Life's Little Ironies*). He locates it 2 miles past Stickleford (Tincleton), an accurate measurement of the distance between the real villages. The hill near the village is called Moreford Rise in "The Slow Nature" (*Wessex Poems*), in which a poor husbandman is gored to death by an escaped bull.

About 2 miles northeast of Moreton is Clouds Hill, originally a gamekeeper's cottage and later the home of T. E. Lawrence. The house, taken over by the National Trust and open to the public, is hidden from the road by an immense hedge of rhododendrons. Lawrence first rented the house in 1923, when he was stationed at Bovington, and then bought it in 1925 for use as a holiday home. He began to use the house permanently after he left the Royal Air Force in 1935 but lived here only two months before being killed in a motorcycle accident. The house has been left with his furnishings, and no electricity has been put in. Lawrence was buried in the churchyard at Moreton.

MORPETH, Northumberland (pop. 96,004)   The town of Morpeth, 16½ miles north of Newcastle upon Tyne, in many ways has not changed in the four centuries since John Leland was here and described it as "a market town. . . . Wansbeke, a praty ryver, rynnithe threge the syde of the towne. . . . [T]he fayre castle standing upon a hill. . . . The towne is long and metely well buylded with low housys, the streets pavyed." By 1664 little of "the fayre castle" remained, but the ruins still stand impressively high above the river. Near the castle is the partly 14th-century Church of St. Mary, which still maintains the old North Country custom of tying the church gates when a newly married couple emerges from the church; the couple cannot pass until the groom pays a toll. Morpeth is included in William Cobbett's "Progress in the North" (*Rural Rides*) and receives one of his frequent castigations, for this "great market town. . . . a solid town . . . has the disgrace of seeing an enormous new gaol rising up in it. From cathedrals and monasteries we are come to be proud of our gaols, which are built in the grandest style, and seemingly as if to imitate the Gothic architecture."

Morpeth comes into the writings of two authors. Mark Akenside, a Northumberland native, was inspired on a visit in 1738 to begin *The Pleasures of Imagination*:

> O ye Northumbrian shades, overlook
> The rocky pavement and the mossy falls
> Of solid Wensbeck's limpid stream;
> How gladly I recall your well-known seats,
> Beloved of old, and that delightful time
> When, all alone, for many a summer's day,
> I wandered through your calm recesses, led
> In silence by some powerful hand unseen.
>   Nor will I e'er forget you. . . .

Morpeth also occurs in George Borrow's *Lavengro*.

MORTIMER'S CROSS, Herefordshire   A hamlet on the Lugg River 5½ miles northwest of Leominster, Mortimer's Cross has primarily a historical claim to fame; here on February 2, 1460, the Yorkists under Edward de Mortimer, Earl of March (later Edward IV), defeated the Lancastrians led by the Earl of Pembroke. The commemorative obelisk was erected in 1799. William Shakespeare sets part of the action of *Henry VI: Part III* on "a Plain near Mortimer's Cross in Herefordshire"; here the incident of the three suns occurs:

> *Edw.* Dazzle mine eyes, or do I see three suns?
> *Rich.* Three glorious suns, each one a perfect sun;
> Not separated with the racking clouds,
> But sever'd in a pale clear-shining sky.
> See, see! they join, embrace, and seem to kiss,
> As if they vow'd some league inviolable:
> Now are they but one lamp, one light, one sun.
> In this the heaven figures some event.

And thus, the opening lines of *The Tragedy of King Richard III* are set:

> Now is the winter of our discontent
> Made glorious summer by this sun of York;
> And all the clouds that lour'd upon our house
> In the deep bosom of the ocean buried.

MORWENSTOW, Cornwall (pop. 597)   The northernmost parish in Cornwall, bordering the gale-swept Atlantic coast, Morwenstow is 6 miles north of Bude above a deep wooded combe (valley). The village is named after Morwenna, the Welsh Mwynen, daughter of Brynach Wyddel by Corth, not Modwenna, as John Leland proclaimed. The two were often confused or identified as one. Morwenna migrated to Cornwall from Wales, established a cell at Marham Church, and came to this area. Leland noted *"in villa, quae Modwenstow dicitur, S. Modwenna quiescit,"* but, in fact, Modwenna, who postdates Morwenna by two centuries, is buried at Burton-on-Trent; St. Morwenna is buried here.

Even the Rev. Robert Stephen Hawker, whose parish this was for more then forty years, believed the Modwenna story and wrote of it. Hawker was here first at Coombe Cottage in November 1824 for his honeymoon. Like almost everything else in his life, his marriage was unusual. He came down from Oxford at the age of nineteen, his degree not completed, and proposed to Charlotte I'Ans, a woman more than twice his age. After finishing the requirements for a B.A. degree and graduating in 1828, he came here to read for orders. His affection for the area had already been illustrated with these lines:

Welcome, wild rock and lonely shore!
Where round my days dark seas shall roar,
And thy gray fane, Morwenna, stand
The beacon of the Eternal Land.

When he was presented with this living by Bishop Henry Phillpotts of Exeter, there had been no resident vicar for more than 100 years, and the vicarage was in such a ruinous state as to be uninhabitable. Hawker and his wife proceeded to build a new vicarage near the church on a plot of land chosen because the sheep sheltered there from storms. The house contains five chimneys, in complete disregard of orthodox building style, four of which are replicas of the towers of churches with which Hawker had been in some way associated: Stratton (where his father had been curate), Whitstone (where he had married Charlotte I'Ans), North Tamerton (where he had been curate), and Magdalen Hall, Oxford. The fifth chimney posed a problem; Hawker explained: "The kitchen chimney perplexed me very much, till I bethought me of my mother's tomb; and there it is, in its exact shape and dimensions." Over the doorway of the house he had this verse carved:

A House, a Glebe, a Pound a Day;
A Pleasant Place to Watch and Pray.
Be true to Church—Be kind to Poor,
O Minister! for evermore.

Hawker's parishioners were a varied lot, and he "had to soothe the wrecker, to persuade the smuggler, and 'to handle serpents' in my intercourse with adversaries of many a kind." One of his initial acts was to offer a reward for the recovery of bodies from shipwrecks; he was upset at the usual practice of searching the body and then hiding it; and he made certain that every dead seaman received a Christian burial. In 1849 he began restoring the church, and the 1849 window portraying St. Morwenna teaching Aethelwulf's daughter Editha is one of Hawker's errors. One of his undertakings was introducing a pagan harvest tradition into the church: within fifty years the Harvest Festival became a standard celebration in England and the United States. Hawker also built and maintained St. Mark's School.

A path near the church leads to the edge of Vicarage Cliff, where Hawker built a wooden hut which he used as a study; this was where he wrote most of his works including the celebrated *Footprints of Former Men in Far Cornwall,* "The Quest of the Sangreal," "And Shall Trelawney Die," and "Legend of St. Cecily." It should be noted that many of the Cornish legends Hawker included in *Footprints* appear for the first time there. In 1848 Hawker was visited by Alfred, Lord Tennyson when he was gathering information on Arthurian legends. Hawker and Tennyson talked of Cornish and Arthurian legends on their walks, and Tennyson left Morwenstow with a large number of Hawker's books and manuscripts concerning Arthurian lore. It is all the same difficult to credit Hawker's assertion that he introduced the Arthurian cycle to Tennyson. Hawker's first wife died in Morwenstow in February 1863 and was buried outside the chancel of the church. Within two years Hawker married Pauline Anne Kuczynski, a governess at nearby Chapel Farm. His death in Plymouth, Devon, nine years and three children later, was equally unusual in that he embraced the Roman Catholic faith the day before he died.

Less than half a mile south of Morwenstow is an almost perfect example of a 16th-century manor house, Tonacombe. The hall, only 30 feet long, contains a minstrels' gallery, a large open fireplace, and open timbers; and the glass panes in some of the latticed parlor windows are the originals. This hall is said to be the model for the chapel in Charles Kingsley's *Westward Ho!*

MUCH WENLOCK, Shropshire (pop. 14,149) Much Wenlock, 14 miles southeast of Shrewsbury, sits at the northern tip of the narrow limestone ridge known as Wenlock Edge, which runs from here southwest to Wistanstow. Wenlock Edge is of outstanding natural beauty and dominates the rich agricultural land of southeast Shropshire. The town of Much Wenlock, situated in the hills with extensive copses, vales, streams, and meadows all around it, was a settled location before the Danish invasions. In the 7th century a priory was founded here by St. Milburga, granddaughter of the Mercian king Penda, and it flourished until the time of the Danish invasions. The invaders razed the buildings, which remained in a derelict state until Lady Godiva restored them and helped reestablish the foundation. Reestablished after the Norman invasion, the priory became the center of Cluniac activity in England and flourished until the dissolution of the monasteries in the 16th century.

The early Shropshire building style, generally called box-frame, is well preserved here; the buildings have three distinctive features: a local red-sandstone base, intricately and extravagantly patterned external woodwork, and a Welsh slate roof. The old Guildhall's timbered facade is a marvel, especially if one appreciates that the final timbering was done in two days; the entire pattern had been precut and numbered, like modern prefabrications, and the carpenters had only to peg it together.

This area around Wenlock Edge and the Wrekin is a part of Shropshire having many associations with A. E. Housman, and Much Wenlock is probably the area written of in Part XXXI of *A Shropshire Lad:*

On Wenlock Edge the wood's in trouble;
His forest fleece the Wrekin heaves;

The gale, it plies the saplings double,
    And thick on Severn snow the leaves.

'Twould blow like this through holt and hanger
    When Uricon the city stood:
'Tis the old wind in the old anger,
    But then it threshed another wood.

Mary Webb lived in Much Wenlock in the early twentieth century.

MUDEFORD, Hampshire Lying on a bay in Christchurch Harbour 1½ miles southeast of Christchurch, of which it is a ward, Mudeford has excellent sands for bathing and is a pleasant holiday spot. Sir Walter Scott arrived here on holiday in 1807, when he was working on *Marmion;* he stayed with William Stewart Rose at Gundimore, and the two explored the south coast thoroughly, rode in the New Forest, and sailed to the Isle of Wight. It is quite likely that this trip gave rise to the allusion to Bevis of Hampton in *Marmion:*

    Well has thy fair achievement shown,
    A worthy meed may thus be won;
    Ytene's oaks—beneath whose shade
    Their theme the merry minstrels made,
    Of Ascapart, and Bevis bold,
    And that Red King, who, while of old,
    Through Boldrewood the chase he led,
    By his loved huntsman's arrow bled—
    Ytene's oaks have heard again
    Renew'd such legendary strain. . . .

MUNDESLEY-ON-SEA, Norfolk (pop. 1,161) Situated 5 miles northeast of North Walsham on the section of the Norfolk coast which is severely pounded by the sea, Mundesley has suffered numerous depredations even though it is on a small cliff structure. Indeed, the action of the sea has eroded the cliff structure, fields, houses, and even the breakwater in the past century alone. The sands, though, are wide and safe, and the water is shallow. There are associations here with the poet William Cowper, who visited the village numerous times between 1752 and 1796. On his first excursion in July 1752, he came from Catfield, where he was having a holiday with his uncle, the Rev. Roger Donne. Three of the *Delia* poems, including the one begging a lock of hair "merely to defraud/Thy spoiler of his prey," were written at Mundesley on this first visit. Cowper came again on numerous occasions, once in August 1793 from North Tuddenham and off and on from 1795 to 1800, when he stayed with his cousin in the High Street; the house is now called Cowper's House.

MUSBURY, Devon (pop. 370) Situated 3 miles southwest of Axminster in some of the most fertile grassland in east Devon, Musbury is just east of the Axe River, and its restored church contains a particularly fine 1611 memorial to the Drake family. In 1938 Cecil Day Lewis made Musbury his home; moving from Cheltenham, he took Brimclose here and stayed until after World War II began. His delight with the rich Devon countryside appears in *The Buried Day:*

    Over the hill-top it was wild country. Thistle-clocks
    came ghosting down to us in swarms as the summer

deepened. The sky issued an unearthly mewing, and looking up I saw three buzzards circling there in the blue, gliding like skaters round a frozen pond. . . .
    But throughout that first spring and summer all was exuberance. The low, bramble hedge and the deep ditch between our garden and the fields seemed a flimsy defence against the thrusts of wild nature, which teemed and tossed against us.

As hostilities in Europe increased, Day Lewis gave up Brimclose for London, where he went to work for the Ministry of Information.

MUSTON, Leicestershire (pop. 261) Situated in the far northern tip of the country on the Devon River and a little over 5 miles northwest of Grantham, Lincolnshire, Muston is easily overlooked because of its location. The village green has an ancient market cross, and the chiefly 14th-century church contains remarkable old benches carved with poppyheads. Muston's literary importance is related to the fact that the living here, together with that at Allington, was presented to the Rev. George Crabbe after the Duchess of Rutland persuaded Lord Thurlow to exchange Crabbe's two Dorsetshire parishes for these more lucrative ones. He and his wife settled at the Muston parsonage on February 25, 1789, and remained until 1792, when Crabbe moved to Parnham and took the livings at Sweffling and Great Glemham; he left a curate in charge at Muston.

Until his return in October 1805, his life was unfortunate; following the deaths of five of their seven children, Mrs. Crabbe became melancholic and ultimately lost her reason. The years in Muston were productive ones for Crabbe despite the gravity of his wife's illness. In 1807 *The Parish Register* appeared; in 1810, *The Borough;* and in 1812, *Tales in Verse.* In October 1813 Sarah Crabbe died, and growing ill himself Crabbe became convinced he was about to die and asked that his wife's grave be kept open for him. He did recover his health, and in June 1814 he was presented with the living at Trowbridge, Wiltshire, a post he gladly took.

MUSWELL HILL, Middlesex (pop. 9,508) Now the steepest hill in London, Muswell Hill formerly belonged to the borough of Clerkenwell and until 1900 was known as "Clerkenwell detached." Situated 5½ miles north of King's Cross Station, the village once had a holy well which was a medieval place of pilgrimage. William Ernest Henley lived in Stanley Lodge here from April 1896 until October 1898; the house was originally designed as a pub but was never used as such. The author moved from here to Worthing.

MYLOR, Cornwall (pop. 2,039) Located in an area of lush vegetation and sparkling sands in southern Cornwall known as the Riviera, the village of Mylor, 2 miles northeast of Falmouth on Mylor Creek off Falmouth Harbour, overlooks Carrick Roads, a superb waterway between Falmouth and St. Mawes. Among the yews in the churchyard of the partly Norman Mylor church is a medieval wheel-headed cross 17 feet tall, the largest cross in the county. In 1916

Katherine Mansfield and John Middleton Murry came to a cottage here from Zennor, where they had tried to live with D. H. Lawrence and his wife. The grounds of the cottage ran down to the water's edge, and they found the environment pleasant and peaceful: syringa and magnolia grew in the front, and a herb garden took up the back. Miss Mansfield's restlessness, which was apparent in frequent trips to Garsington and London, became acute, and when Murry took a job in the War Office in London, she also returned.

NAILSWORTH, Gloucestershire (pop. 3,500) Nailsworth is an attractive Cotswold village situated in a valley just 4 miles south of Stroud. While this is the bacon-curing center of Gloucestershire with more than 1,500 pigs being killed and cured here weekly, the village is best known for the Nailsworth Ladder, a chalky hill with an average gradient of 1 in 3. Nailsworth was the home of William Henry Davies, the Welsh-born "tramp poet," author of *Autobiography of a Super Tramp.* Davies roamed thousands of miles in the United States and Canada and did itinerant work; he traveled by a variety of methods, one of which, hopping freight trains, led to an accident in Renfrew, Ontario, when he fell and the wheels of a train severed his foot above the ankle. He did not settle down until after the publication of various volumes of poetry and his marriage in 1923; he came to Nailsworth in 1931 and eventually settled in Glendover, where he died on September 26, 1940.

NASEBY, Northamptonshire (pop. 416) Near the source of the Avon, Welland, and Nene Rivers, this small village, 7 miles southwest of Market Harborough, has a long history which includes a strange link with Anglo-Saxon literature. The original Old English name of the village, Hnaefes burh, "the fortress of Hnaef," is of great interest. It was not a name in ordinary use and, indeed, was reserved for the hero Hnaef, the Half Dane, Lord of the Hocingas, who is referred to in *Beowulf* and *Widsith.* Nowhere outside heroic poetry is the name recorded, and its use here is unparalleled as well as unexplained.

Naseby, of course, has another niche in English history, for here was fought the decisive battle in the Civil War; just to the north of the village is a column, erected in 1936, commemorating the event:

Battle of Naseby 14 June 1645
From near this site Oliver Cromwell led the cavalry

charge which decided the issue of the battle and ultimately that of the Great Civil War.

This column and plaque were put in place to rectify an 1823 error which placed the spot on the opposite side of the road and had an inscription stating that the Battle of Naseby

led to the subversion of the Throne, the Altar, and the Constitution, and plunged this nation into anarchy and civil war, leaving a useful lesson to British kings and British subjects.

For many years Thomas Carlyle fought unsuccessfully to have the correction made. The battle was Charles's last chance to maintain his rule, and he and Prince Rupert came to the field leading 7,000 men; events might have been different if Cromwell, having ridden all night from Ely, had not arrived just in time to spur on his men. Thomas Babington Macaulay calls on this moment of tension in *The Battle of Naseby:*

Stout Skippon hath a wound; the centre hath given
  ground:
  Hark! hark!—What means the trampling of horsemen
  on our rear?
Whose banner do I see, boys? 'Tis he, thank God, 'tis he,
  boys.
  Bear up another minute: brave Oliver is here.

Their heads all stooping low, their points all in a row,
  Like a whirlwind on the trees, like a deluge on the
  dykes,
Our cuirassiers have burst on the ranks of the Accurst,
  And at a shock have scattered the forest of his pikes.

Edward FitzGerald often spent time here at his parents' estate and attended services at the parish church; he considered himself a cut above the local people and wore a loud blue surtout to church. The lyric "The Meadows of Spring" was written here:

Then the clouds part,
  Swallows soaring between;

The spring is alive,
  And the meadows are green!

I jump up, like mad,
  Break the old pipe in twain,
And away to the meadows,
  The meadows again!

NAVESTOCK, Essex (pop. 720)   A dormitory town 6 miles north of Romford, Navestock is understandably proud of its medieval church dedicated to St. Thomas the Apostle and the nearby rose garden set in a deep depression in the churchyard. There a sundial captures the story with its inscription: "An enemy landmine fell here on 21st September 1940." The crater was caused by the mine, which exploded in the tree where it was caught, and the destruction was great; the church was so badly damaged that many parishes would not have repaired it. But it was fully restored, and its pagoda tower, which had been only slightly damaged, attests to 13th-century building skills.

An early vicar of the church was the Rev. William Stubbs, a distinguished historian and later Bishop of Oxford, to whom Algernon Swinburne came for tutoring after leaving Balliol College in the summer of 1859. Swinburne stayed in the vicarage (now called Marleys) on the green with Stubbs and remained here until the summer of 1860, just before his return to Balliol in October.

NEAR SAWREY, Lancashire (pop. 417)   Situated between Hawkshead and the Windermere ferry (to Bowness-on-Windermere), Near Sawrey and its small companion, Far Sawrey, are actually one village, Sawrey, divided into two hamlets. On the Lancashire (west) side of Lake Windermere, the village has many lovely old cottages set among trees and gardens. One of these, Hill Top Farm, behind the Town Bank Arms, became the home of Beatrix Potter, author of *The Tale of Peter Rabbit* and other children's stories. She had been in Near Sawrey in 1896 with her parents and stayed at Lakeland (now Ees Wyke); in 1905 she bought the farm, ostensibly to get over the sudden death of her fiancé, and lived here for the rest of her life. In 1913 she married William Heelis, a Westmorland solicitor, and they moved to Castle Cottage across the meadow and turned to raising sheep. She dedicated *The Tale of Benjamin Bunny* to "The Chilren of Sawrey" and used the village as the setting for *Ginger and Pickles* and *The Pie and the Patty Pan* as well as for many other stories. The kitchen at Hill Top Farm was used for the illustration in *The Tale of Tom Kitten*. Miss Potter died here on December 22, 1943; she bequeathed her house and much of the surrounding land to the National Trust, and the house is open to the public.

NETHER STOWEY, Somerset (pop. 578)   Located on the eastern slope of the Quantocks, Nether Stowey is a small village nestled in rolling woodlands typical of the northern reaches of the area. The Quantock Hills are in a small protected area, 12 miles long and 6 miles wide, which is designated officially as an area of outstanding natural beauty, something that Samuel Taylor Coleridge and William Wordsworth discovered at the end of the 18th century. On Coleridge's first

NEAR SAWREY Springtime in the Lake District must be accounted one of its wonders and was especially attractive to Beatrix Potter, who made her home here from 1905 to 1943.

visit to the village with Robert Southey in August 1794, he met Thomas Poole, the man whom Coleridge later called "My brother by gift of God"; and the two poets unfolded their pantisocratic scheme to Poole, who was known for his outspoken egalitarian principles, before they returned to Bristol.

Coleridge married Sarah Fricker in 1795, and after six months in Clevedon, followed by an attempt to live with his mother-in-law in Bristol, he was invited to Nether Stowey by Poole. The Coleridges arrived with their infant son David Hartley in December 1796. Their small, drab, and dark Lime Street cottage had been obtained by Poole and opened onto his land. In the spring of 1797 Coleridge said he was already an expert gardener, but perhaps on account of his "equalitarian principles" his garden was weed-ridden; he felt it "unfair to prejudice the soil towards roses and strawberries." The cottage (enlarged) where he lived is now called Coleridge Cottage Museum and is under the care of the National Trust. In July 1797 Wordsworth and his sister Dorothy joined the Coleridges for a two-week stay and found Alfoxton House at Holford, 3 miles away, which they rented that year. Once again Thomas Poole made the arrangements and stood as security for the rent. In the meantime everyone lived in the small three-bedroom Lime Street cottage. Within a few days Charles and Mary Lamb arrived and met Wordsworth for the first time; their stay lasted only a week, during which time long walks were taken, usually with both Wordsworth and Coleridge, in the Quantock Hills. On one occasion Coleridge was forced to remain at home; he had been scalded when a skillet of boiling milk was upset upon him, and the incident produced the poem "This Lime-Tree Bower My Prison."

On November 13, 1797, Coleridge and the Wordsworths began their walk to Watchet, Linton, and the Valley of Stones, the trip on which *The Rime of the*

NETHER STOWEY   The Lime Street cottage where Samuel Taylor Coleridge brought his wife and infant son in December 1796 is now a Coleridge museum; the kindness and generosity of Tom Poole, Coleridge's "brother by gift of God" who secured the house for the poet, perhaps changed the course of English poetry, for here Coleridge wrote all his major poetry except "Kubla Khan."

Ancient Mariner was begun. Almost without exception Coleridge's best-known works derive from this period: only "Kubla Khan" was not written in the Lime Street cottage. The summer of 1798 brought another well-known visitor, William Hazlitt, who arrived for a few weeks' stay and met Wordsworth at this time; with Coleridge they made an enjoyable excursion to Cheddar, the home of the famous cheese. Shortly after Hazlitt's departure, Coleridge went to Germany with the Wordsworths, leaving Sarah and their two sons behind. He returned only briefly in July 1799 and then, dissatisfied with his surroundings, left with his family for Ottery St. Mary.

Besides Coleridge Cottage Museum, there is one other place of interest in the village, the house on Castle Street which served as Poole's home and bookstore. The bookstore was always open to Coleridge and the Wordsworths; indeed, Coleridge often helped himself to the collection, sometimes returning the books years later with full marginal notations. Coleridge, in fact, firmly believed that the right of ownership was directly proportional to the degree of understanding and had nothing to do with the purchase of a book.

NETHERAVON, Wiltshire (pop. 728)   On the Salisbury Plain 5 miles north of Amesbury, Netheravon is the center of a large military district; indeed, William Cobbett's famous "acre of hares" is now an acre of the Royal Air Force. The village contains a lovely 13th-century church with (quite possibly) a late Saxon tower, which is of interest since it contains a small

Saxon doorway 17 feet above the ground. It is now thought that this was either the private chapel of one of the village residents or the sacristan's residence. The Rev. Sydney Smith was the curate here from 1794 to 1797. The squire of the parish was Michael Hicks-Beach, and with his encouragement the young curate set about to provide a Sunday school for the villagers. Hicks-Beach also helped Smith to aid the parish poor. Smith became the tutor of Hicks-Beach's eldest son; they planned to visit Weimar, but hostilities there forced a diversion to Edinburgh.

William Cobbett visited Netheravon often, and in 1826 he reported of frequently having heard "this valley described as one of the finest pieces of land in all England. . . .'' He goes on to describe Hicks-Beach property:

> I had been at Netheravon about eighteen years ago, where I had seen a great quantity of hares. It is a place belonging to Mr. Hicks Beach, or Beech, who was once a member of parliament. I found the place altered a good deal; out of repair; the gates rather rotten; and (a very bad sign!) the roof of the dog-kennel falling in!

NETLEY ABBEY, Hampshire (pop. 1,396)   Originally open to the coast, the Cistercian Netley Abbey, perhaps the finest monastic ruin in England, was begun in 1239. The community for some reason was not especially prosperous at the dissolution of the monasteries in the 16th century, when the site and lands were granted to Sir William Paulet, later Marquess of Winchester, who converted the church and cloister buildings into a residence. In the 18th century the building materials were sold by the owner, Sir Berkeley Luce, and demolition was begun; again the remains were saved when the tracery of the great west window collapsed on the purchaser.

Alexander Pope spent early August 1734 at Mount Bevis, the home of the 3d Earl of Peterborough, and a letter to Martha Blount on August 5 describes a stop at Netley Abbey on a sailing trip around the Isle of Wight. Here they explored the ruins, "lunched in the woods," and sketched the abbey.

In a letter dated October 1764, Thomas Gray describes Netley Abbey as standing

> in a little quiet valley which gradually rises behind the ruins into a half-circle crowned with thick wood. Before it, on a descent, is a thicket of oaks, that serves to veil it from the broad day, and from profane eyes, only leaving a peep on both sides, where the sea appears glittering through the shade, and vessels, with their white sails, glide across and are lost again. . . . I should tell you that the ferryman who rowed me, a lusty young fellow, told me that he would not, for all the world, pass a night at the Abbey, there were such things seen near it.

Gray's superstitious ferryman was possibly referring to the ghost of the building contractor. (Gray had also been here in 1755.) A few years earlier, in 1752, William Cowper and his cousin Harriet walked here from Southampton, where he was staying on holiday, and a visit by William Lisle Bowles prompted "Sonnet to Netley Abbey."

NEW ROMNEY, Kent (pop. 2,072)   The Romney Marsh area is a vast flatland that is just above sea level and is even below it at times; winter on the marshes is cold, wet, and foggy, and summer brings its share of fog as well. The marshes have been an ideal entry point for smugglers over the centuries; and, it is said, only a man born and bred here could find his way through the marshy channels. Even today reports of immigrant smuggling are fairly frequent. Often referred to as the capital of the Marsh, New Romney, 9 miles southwest of Hythe, was originally a Cinque Port, but by the early 13th century the sea had retreated, and New Romney was established 2 miles east of the first town, now called Old Romney. Toward the end of the 13th century great storms battered the Kentish coast, and the Rother River, which ran into St. Mary's Bay here, dramatically altered its course and ran westward to Rye.

In 1897 George Gissing came to stay with an old friend, Dr. Henry Hicks, and here he learned he had tuberculosis. Hicks sent the novelist to a specialist, Philip Pye-Smith, who in turn sent Gissing to Budleigh Salterton, Devon. There is a second literary association with Dr. Hicks in the following year; H. G. Wells came from Seaford, Sussex, to see the physician in August. Wells was dangerously ill with an abscess on a previously damaged kidney and was kept in New Romney for the prescribed treatment; during his recuperation he had a number of visitors, including Henry James, Edmund Gosse, and Sir James Matthew Barrie. Wells later used the area extensively in *Kipps;* here Arthur wonders why "he had come into the care of an aunt and uncle instead of having a father and mother like other little boys." Kipps later returns "to break the news of his engagement":

> He was now a finished cyclist, but as yet an unseasoned one; the south-west wind, even in its summer guise, as one meets it in the Marsh, is the equivalent of a reasonable hill, and ever and again he got off and refreshed himself by a spell of walking.

In *The First Men in the Moon,* the two clerks who take charge of Bedford's gold represent a bank in New Romney.

In the summer of 1906, after a short stay at Brockenhurst, Rupert Brooke came to the Rugby Home Mission Camp here; the camp was intended to serve as a place where impoverished Notting Hill area boys were taught to observe the rules of cricket and to read "above their station." Brooke had, at the time, finished at Rugby and come here to help. Finally, many of Sheila Kaye-Smith's works have the Romney Marsh area as their background.

NEWARK-UPON-TRENT, Nottinghamshire (pop. 25,-030) No town in the shire has greater historical significance than Newark, the ancient borough often called The Key to the North. Near the eastern boundary of Nottinghamshire and almost equidistant from Nottingham and Lincoln, Newark was inhabited in Roman and Saxon times; indeed, evidence of a Saxon church has been unearthed. The 12th-century castle was enlarged and made more nearly impregnable by Gilbert de Gaunt, and in 1216 King John was carried here on a litter from Swineshead and died on October 18. From the reign (1216–1272) of Henry III until the mid-17th century the history of the castle is one of turbulence and bloodshed. It changed hands many times before being destroyed after its surrender in the Civil War. Newark was staunchly Royalist, and one of its defenders was John Cleveland, an extremely

popular poet whose works were mainly political satires; indeed, he wrote some verse at this time. He is believed to have lived in a house at the entrance to Stodman Street, but this seems unlikely, for it was the residence of the Governors of the Castle.

It is Newark's inns which have the firmest literary associations. Near the marketplace is the Saracen's Head Inn (now a bank), one of the innumerable places where Charles I is supposed to have slept and which Sir Walter Scott uses in *The Heart of Midlothian.* This is the inn at which Jeanie Deans stops. Next to the Saracen's Head was the Clinton Arms, originally called the Kingston Arms, where Lord Byron stayed when he was seeing a volume of poems through the press of a Newark printer. Alfred, Lord Tennyson stayed at the old Spread Eagle Inn in February 1828 on his way to Cambridge from Somersby, and years later George Eliot (Mary Ann Evans) stayed at the Ram Inn near the castle.

Finally, there are associations in Newark with John Clare, who worked for a nurseryman named Withers for a few months. Clare came here in 1821 from his home in Helpston after an unsuccessful apprenticeship. He tried to join the militia in Newark but was rejected because of his height.

NEWBOLD REVEL, Warwickshire The ancient Britons had a camp on the top of nearby Edge Hill; the Romans constructed Fosse Way in the vicinity; and the Mowbrays built a castle in Brinklow, the nearest village (4 miles east of Coventry), but very little of this exists today. Newbold Revel is a seat made new in the early 18th century, but it was built on the site of a previous manor which belonged to the family of Sir Thomas Malory. For centuries the identity of the author of *Le Morte d'Arthur* was only guessed at, and although George Lyman Kittredge believed the Malory family of Newbold Revel was the one to which the author belonged, not until a manuscript of *Le Morte d'Arthur* was found at Winchester College in 1934 was a more positive identification assured. This manuscript, more complete than William Caxton's version, is not believed to be a holograph; nevertheless, it contains a valuable statement at the end of what Caxton designated as Book IV:

> And this booke endyth where as Sir Launcelot and Sir Tristrams com to courte. Who that woll make any more lette him seke other bookis of Kyng Arthure or of Sir Launcelot or Sir Tristrams. For this was drawyn by a knight presoner Sir Thomas Malleore that God sende hym good recover. Amen.

This, coupled with the previously printed note at the end of Book VII, makes the identification clear.

Still, little is known of Malory's early life: he was born here about 1410 and inherited the family estates at the age of twenty-three. Sometime around 1440 Malory married, and one son was born who died, it would appear, before 1450, the beginning of Sir Thomas's "orgy of lawlessness." Then, between June 1450 and July 1451, he committed a dozen serious crimes, including attempted murder, theft, robbery, rape, and extortion, and was arrested here on July 25, 1451, after breaking into the park at Caludon, where he did damage amounting to £500 and carried off six of the Archbishop of Canterbury's deer. Malory was back within a few years, and, borrowing money, he sat for Parliament in March 1456; his failure to repay the debt landed him in prison in London. He was back here in 1459, having escaped from prison, but was recaptured at Lent, 1460. He died (perhaps in prison) in 1471 and was buried in the Grey Friars Monastery, London.

NEWBURY, Berkshire (pop. 14,710)   Newbury, a large, prosperous, and cheerful old town, now a racing center, has a prized place on the road from London to Bath. It is known to have been settled long before the Romans saw its strategic importance in the Kennet Valley below the steep slopes of the Berkshire Downs and garrisoned the area. After the Norman Conquest the town was again fortified with the building of Donnington Castle, which, says John Evelyn in his diary, was "famous for the Battail, siege, & that this last [the Castle] had ben the possession of old *Geofrie Chaucer.* . . ." There is no evidence to support or refute Evelyn's assertion.

Since Tudor times Newbury has depended upon the cloth industry, especially woolens. The town's reputation in this respect is due to the almost-legendary figure of Jack of Newbury, one John Smalwode (John Winchombe). The son of a London draper, Smalwode came here as an enterprising young apprentice, married the master's daughter, and became the master clothier of Newbury; he entertained Henry VIII and Catherine of Aragon, Henry's first wife, and covered the floor of the royal seating area with pieces of wool valued at £100 per cloth. Northbrook Street contains the remains of the house in which Smalwode entertained Henry and his Queen, and just across the small bridge is the magnificent Cloth Hall. The overhanging upper story of the hall is supported on oak pillars, and the columns on either side of the doorway are oak.

Daniel Defoe writes of Newbury in *A Tour thro' the Whole Island of Great Britain,* commenting first on the battles of the Civil War; then he notes:

> This Town of *Newbury* is an antient cloathing Town, though, now, little of that Part remains to it; but it retains still a manufacturing Genius, and the People are generally imployed in making *Shalloons,* a kind of Stuff, which, though it be used only for the Lineing and Insides of Mens Cloaths, . . . yet it becomes so generally worn, both at Home and Abroad, that it is increased to a Manufacture by itself, and is more considerable, than any single Manufacture of Stuffs in the Nation.

A later traveler to Newbury was William Cobbett, who mentions the town frequently in his *Rural Rides;* it was then a major market town and close to his Hampshire home in Botley. He does not discuss the cloth industry but comments on the political structure of the town and on the natural elements of the landscape:

> In going along we saw a piece of wheat with cabbage-leaves laid all over it at the distance, perhaps, of eight or ten feet from each other. It was to catch the *slugs.* The slugs, which commit their depredations in the *night,* creep under the leaves in the morning, and by turning up the leaves you come at the slugs, and crush them, or carry them away.

In more recent times Newbury becomes Kennetbridge in Thomas Hardy's *Jude the Obscure;* the au-

thor first makes the town the residence of the composer of the hymn that haunts Jude. Jude travels here, and his sense of disappointment with the man forms a decisive episode in his life. Later, for a short period, he and Sue reside in "Kennetbridge, a thriving town not more than a dozen miles south of Marygreen [Fawley]. . . ." When Arabella appears in Kennetbridge, the Chequers Inn, Jack Inn, and Temperance Hotel are mentioned specifically.

NEWBY BRIDGE, Lancashire   Lying in attractive surroundings on the Leven River at the foot of Lake Windermere, 5 miles northwest of Cartmel, Newby Bridge is a perfect center for exploring the Lake District, but its own beauty tends to attract visitors. Here the Leven surges swiftly beneath the old bridge before crashing down into the wooded gorge below, and the village lies in the shelter of the mountains to the west. The Newby Bridge Hotel was where Arthur Ransome stayed in 1930 when he was writing *Swallows and Amazons;* Ransome frequently used the Lakeland area, especially Windermere, for the setting of his children's books.

NEWCASTLE-UNDER-LYME, Staffordshire (pop. 64,-580)   An old industrial town full of collieries, ironworks, and potteries, Newcastle-under-Lyme is set in a rural environment 16 miles north of Stafford; it was once strongly fortified with a castle set near the great Forest of Lyme, but both are only distant memories. Newcastle was a famous educational center by the end of the 16th century, and in May 1882 Arnold Bennett was sent to the middle school here from his home in Burslem. (The school has since been transferred to Wolstanton and is known as the Wolstanton County Grammar School.) Bennett rose to be head boy before leaving in 1885 to take up an apprenticeship in his father's law office, preparatory to reading law in London. Earlier, in 1831, Dinah Mulock (Craik) was brought to a house in Lower Street when her father took a church post here; the family later moved to 2 (now 7) Mount Pleasant.

NEWCASTLE UPON TYNE, Northumberland (pop. 291,300)   Novocastrians, as Newcastle upon Tyne natives are called, are immensely proud of their city, and modern civic planners, while temporarily creating a jumbled mess as they rip out the Victorian and Edwardian city center, are trying to preserve as much of the old city as possible. Originally a station called Pons Aelii on the great Roman wall which stretched across the North Country from Wallsend to Carlisle, Newcastle was later dominated by a massive Norman castle built in 1172. Like other major fortified northern cities, the town was constantly involved in border warfare, especially because of its proximity to the major political and religious center of Durham; it was once fully walled in, but only part of the walls to the west remains. Two Norman churches, St. Andrew's and St. John's, are still in use, and the medieval Church of St. Nicholas, which gained cathedral status in the late 19th century, contains an imperfect manuscript of Richard Rolle's *Paraphrase of Psalms and Canticles.* John Leland, who was not prone to exaggeration, comments in his *Itinerary:* "The strength and magnificence of the walling of this town surpasseth all the walls of the cities of England and most of the towns of Europe." Another well-traveled writer spent a few days here beginning on September 30, 1706. Traveling to Scotland as Alexander Goldsmith, Daniel Defoe (a secret agent for Robert Harley) stayed here and got in touch with John Bell, the postmaster, who supplied him with money and fresh horses; Defoe may well have stopped over with Bell unless the risks were thought to be too great. He comments on the town in *A Tour thro' the Whole Island of Great Britain*.

Newcastle is the native town of Mark Akenside, best known as a physician in the 18th century and as the author of *The Pleasures of Imagination* in the 20th. He was born on November 9, 1721, at 33 Butcher Bank, now Akenside Hill, in an area as poverty-stricken then as it is now. At the age of seven he was playing in his father's butcher shop when a meat cleaver fell on his foot and lamed him for life. He attended a local private academy, where he showed poetic gifts, and was strongly encouraged in academic pursuits by his parents. Members of the dissenting community, his parents raised the money to send him to the University of Edinburgh to train for the ministry in 1739. There he changed his mind, decided to take up medicine, returned the money to his family, and ultimately took his medical degree in Leiden.

It was this town and not Gateshead which held bad memories for the young Oliver Goldsmith. He left for Bordeaux from Edinburgh on the *St. Andrews*, which was forced into port at Newcastle because of a severe storm. A letter to his uncle Thomas Contarine posted from Leiden takes up the story:

> We all went a-shore to refresh us after the fatigue of our voyage. Seven men and I were one day on shore, and on the following evening as we were all very merry, the room door bursts open: enters a serjeant and twelve grenadiers with their bayonets screwed: and puts us under the King's arrest. It seems my company were Scotsmen in the French service, and had been in Scotland to enlist soldiers in the French army. I endeavoured all I could to prove my innocence; however, I remained in prison with the rest a fortnight, and with difficulty got off even then. Dear Sir, keep all this a secret, or at least say it was for a debt; for if it were once known at the university, I should hardly get a degree.

This is the basis of the story that Goldsmith was imprisoned in Gateshead for a bad debt. In January 1795 William Wordsworth was in Newcastle; he came here from Greystoke, Penrith, Lancashire, to be with his sister Dorothy, who was visiting relatives, the Griffiths.

The town has often been an occasional host to other literary figures. Elizabeth Barrett (Browning), with whom the entire area has casual but specific associations, spent July through September 1815 with her maternal grandparents, the Graham-Clarkes, who owned a very large and dignified North Country home called Fenham Hall. Robert Smith Surtees of nearby Hamsterley Hall in County Durham was articled to a Mr. Purvis here from 1822 to 1825; the offices were probably on Grainger Street. Dante Gabriel Rossetti, complaining of "continually returning illness" to one of his more sympathetic London aunts, obtained £12 from her and came here to the home of William Bell Scott but stayed for only two days before going off to paint. Finally, William

Makepeace Thackeray locates the Elephant and Cucumber Hotel in *Jeames's Diary* in Newcastle.

NEWINGTON BUTTS, Surrey   Now a part of London and called Newington, Newington Butts was a semirural district when the dramatist Thomas Middleton lived here (site unknown) from 1609 until his death in late June 1627. He was buried in the parish church (demolished in the 18th century) on July 4.

NEWMARKET, Suffolk (pop. 9,767)   Newmarket, the racing town, while actually in Suffolk, is almost entirely surrounded by Cambridgeshire. There is nothing new about the market, and the town's known history dates back to the 1st century A.D., when the Icenian settlement of Queen Boadicea at nearby Exning was struck by the plague and moved here. There is a survival of this early period and its troubles in the 7th-century earthworks on Newmarket Heath called the Devil's Dyke, a fortification raised to stall the Mercian raids in East Anglia. The ditch, its history, and its legend are described by Michael Drayton in *Poly-Olbion*:

> I, by th' *East Angles* first, who from this Heath arose,
> The long'st and largest Ditch, to check their *Mercian* foes;
> Because my depth, and breadth, so strangely doth exceed,
> Mens low and wretched thoughts, they constantly decreed,
> That by the Devils helpe, I needs must raised be,
> Wherefore the *Devils-Ditch* they basely named me.

Before Newmarket became the racing capital of England, the heath was well known for its curative and restorative powers. Indeed, George Herbert, whose health always seemed to be in a perilous state, occasionally came here from Oxford to partake of the "good air and pleasure," which, however, had no beneficial effects.

Interestingly enough in light of the later development of Newmarket into the headquarters of British horse racing, the Icenian coins bore the image of a horse, and the Iceni were noted for their horses and chariots. It was not until 1619, under James I's encouragement, that the first horse race was run here. James was so enamored of the sport that decisions of state were made more often in Newmarket than in London or Windsor. In fact, John Donne had to journey here in November 1614 to inform the King of his decision to enter the church and to receive assurances of preferment from the crown. The audience took place in the small palace which James had constructed in what is now Palace Street. Donne had to make the same trip a second time from London in late January or early February 1615 to present himself as a priest to the King. Samuel Pepys was here with King Charles II later in the 17th century.

Enthusiasm for Newmarket and the races was not limited to monarchs and a special few. It seems natural for Daniel Defoe, with his known penchant for "investments," to have come here yearly for the races; he would not miss them, as he commented, "for anything in the world." Another visitor to the races, but probably only once, was William Congreve, who was here for the Autumn Race in 1707. Finally, George Crabbe, at the age of eleven or twelve, was sent here from his home in Aldeburgh to attend the school kept by Richard Haddon, a mathematician, but remained only a short time.

NEWPORT, Shropshire (pop. 3,456) An old market town about 18 miles east-northeast of Shrewsbury, Newport has a medieval cross in its wide main street, a partly 14th-century church with a collection of more than fifty brasses, and a grammar school founded in 1656. One of the early students in the school was the satirist Thomas Brown, who is best known for his lines beginning "I do not love thee, Doctor Fell." Brown remained here until going up to Christ Church, Oxford, in 1678.

NEWSTEAD, Nottinghamshire (pop. 928) Newstead is now a sought-after residential district in wooded countryside about 9 miles north of Nottingham. Its main historical attraction is Newstead Priory (not Newstead Abbey, as it is usually written), founded by Henry II in 1170 as an atonement for the murder of Thomas à Becket. The priory, properly termed Prioratus Sancte Marie de Novo Loco in Foresta Nostra de Scirwurda, was never wealthy; and indeed in 1536 it was on the list of religious establishments with incomes of less than £200 which were the first to be suppressed by Henry VIII. After the priory was formally deeded to the crown in 1539, Sir John Byron took possession of the house, lands, church, priory, and the rest in May. This was the Byron known as "Little Sir John with the Big Beard," who was descended from the Byrons who fought at Crécy and Bosworth Field. It was from this family that George Gordon, 6th Baron Byron, descended.

Byron's two immediate predecessors seriously embarrassed the estate, which was in financial straits when the poet succeeded to the title in the summer of 1798 at the age of ten. While Byron did not take up residence at Newstead until 1808, he was here before that date. Indeed, he was brought to the family seat during the summer of his succession. He, his mother, and his nurse attempted to live here for some time, and a tutor was actually engaged for the boy. Byron returned on visits in 1799 and in 1800. After "escaping" from his mother in Southwell, he spent

part of the summer of 1803 in the caretaker's lodge on the estate; refusing to return to Harrow, he was offered the hospitality of the manor by Lord Grey, to whom it had been rented. Byron's return to school in January 1804 was precipitated by an unpleasant incident (sometimes alleged to have been homosexual) involving Lord Grey. When Byron left Cambridge in July 1808, he was determined to settle here and, even though practically destitute, began renovations to make the priory habitable. The property had been severely damaged by the "Wicked Byron," the poet's great-uncle, who killed the master of Annesley; this Byron lived out his life in the scullery and kept cattle in the abbot's dormitory. It might have been said of the priory then that

> Through thy battlements, Newstead, the hollow winds whistle,
> Thou, the hall of my fathers, art gone to decay:
> In thy once smiling garden the hemlock and thistle
> Have choked up the rose which late bloomed in the way.

The poet had his odd moments as well. His dog, the Newfoundland Boatswain, died mad and was buried in the garden here. Byron's somewhat misanthropic commentary on the dog's death concludes:

> To mark a friend's remains these stones arise;
> I never knew but one, and here he lies.

When the gardener was excavating the dog's grave, he uncovered a skull which Byron in one of his moods sent to Nottingham to have made into a drinking cup; it was returned "with a very high polish and a mottled colour like a tortoise shell" and set in heavy silver; this was the goblet passed around to Byron's Cambridge friends on the occasion of the housewarming and many times thereafter.

Byron's determination to keep the estate is presented quite strongly in a letter of 1809 in which he wrote:

> Newstead and I stand or fall together. I have now lived on the spot, I have fixed my heart upon it, and no pressure, present or future shall induce me to barter the last vestige of our inheritance.

However, in 1817 Byron sold the priory to Col. Thomas Wildman, who had been in his form at Harrow and who subsequently undertook a great deal of restoration. Restoration was completed after the priory was purchased in 1860 by W. F. Webb, a noted explorer and an intimate friend of Dr. David Livingstone. Webb turned Newstead into a memorial to both Byron and Livingstone, who wrote *The Zambesi and Its Tributaries* here.

Most of the modern interest in the priory derives from Lord Byron; his chambers (originally the abbot's) have been kept undisturbed; here are his bedstead with its gilded coronets and the oriel window, his writing table, and his inkstand. Indeed, this is the prototype of the Gothic chamber in a Norman abbey where Don Juan slept and dreamed of Aurora Raby. *Don Juan*, in fact, graphically describes the natural charms of Newstead, and in front of the priory is the lake of the poem. The circular desk on which Byron wrote a portion of *Childe Harold's Pilgrimage* has been preserved, as have the poet's papers, which indicate that this poem was initially to be entitled *Childe Byron* and was designed for private circulation

NEWSTEAD There is no sense of the hall "gone to decay," nor is there evidence of the "once smiling garden" being choked by "hemlock and thistle"; the Corporation of Nottingham has taken over the care of Lord Byron's family home and the gardens, and the priory is now a memorial to Byron and David Livingstone.

only. Here also are Byron's crockery, boxing gloves, singlesticks, carved oak chairs set with embroidery done by Augusta Leigh (Byron's half sister), and the rapier with which the 5th Baron killed William Chaworth. The entire estate has been kept in perfect order, realizing Lord Byron's wish:

Haply thy sun, emerging, yet may shine,
 Thee to irradiate with meridian ray;
Hours splendid as the past may still be thine,
 And bless thy future as thy former day.

One popular misstatement made to visitors is that Byron's chambers have not been occupied since the poet's death; this is untrue. Indeed, two writers well known in their own right have slept there and noted the fact. Washington Irving, who visited Newstead when Colonel Wildman owned the priory and who the colonel thought was "a very fine man for an American," used the bedroom for some time and wrote about it in letters to his brother. The second person who used the room was Joaquin Miller, who observed that the moonbeams reflected from the mirror onto his face were the obvious source of the ghostly apparitions which Byron saw here. Wildman also entertained Thomas Moore, Byron's biographer, on numerous occasions.

NEWTON ABBOT, Devon (pop. 14,640) The "new town" dates back seven centuries; part of the town belonged to Torre Abbey, whence the second part of its name. Lying at the head of the Teign Estuary with cider orchards stretching southward, Newton Abbot has almost joined up with Torquay, a few miles to the south. Sir Arthur Quiller-Couch was sent to Newton Abbot College from his home in Bodmin before he went on to Clifton College in Bristol.

NORBURY, Derbyshire (pop. 365) On the Staffordshire-Derbyshire border 5 miles southwest of Ashbourne, Norbury is on the Dove River; here are a fine church and a manor house reached by a deep-cut country lane. The manor house, belonging to the Fitzherberts, has been greatly altered, but its grounds still encircle the old church. The church is noted for fragments of 10th-century Saxon crosses, one containing a figure with a staff, and a collection of Fitzherbert monuments.

Derbyshire and Norbury, as Stonyshire and Norbourne, occupy a prominent place in George Eliot (Mary Ann Evans) country; further, just across the Dove is Ellastone, the Hayslope of *Adam Bede*. In fact, Roston, 1 mile to the southeast, was the birthplace of Eliot's father, Robert Evans, and of his brother, who become Adam and Seth Bede of the novel.

NORBURY, Shropshire (pop. 148) The tiny village of Norbury, 15 miles southeast of Shrewsbury, has a new church with a 14th-century tower and font; this village was the birthplace of Richard Barnfield in 1574, and he was baptized at the old font (in the old church) on June 18. His early education probably took place in nearby Bishop's Castle, although there is no evidence of this.

NORHAM, Northumberland (pop. 697) A Tweed-side village of lovely proportions, Norham (originally called Ubban Ford), like many other border towns, was long an important part of the battleground between England and Scotland. The Norman church and the remains of the great Norman castle testify to the village's early importance; indeed, both the church and the castle were part of the County Palatine of Durham until 1882. Norham Castle, begun in 1121 by Bishop Rannulf Flambard, was maintained by the Durham bishops, not the crown, as a northern defense against both the Scots and the English until 1583. Situated on a steep south bank overhanging the Tweed, the castle was repeatedly taken and retaken during the wars and border skirmishes between the two countries and played an important role in the Battle of Flodden Field. Sir Walter Scott uses Norham Castle and the surrounding area as the setting of the opening of *Marmion:*

Day set on Norham's castled steep,
And Tweed's fair river, broad and deep,
 And Cheviot's mountains lone;
The battled towers, the donjon keep,
The loophole grates, where captives weep,
The flanking walls that round it sweep,
 In yellow lustre shone.

NORTH TAMERTON, Cornwall (pop. 344) Eight miles north of Launceston on the Tamar River, North Tamerton is a small village whose only literary association is with the Rev. Robert Stephen Hawker, the rather eccentric poet-priest more likely to be associated with nearby Morwenstow. Hawker, who was ordained deacon in 1829, was appointed to the curacy here in the same year. With essentially no living accommodations available, Hawker and his wife created a house, Trebarrow, from two small cottages by knocking out walls and adding a veranda and rooms. Hawker left here in 1834, when he was presented with the living at Morwenstow.

NORTH TUDDENHAM, Norfolk (pop. 301) With the small Tud River running through the surrounding meadows, the scattered village of North Tuddenham is a small and secluded place 3 miles east of East Dereham. The church, Decorated and Perpendicular, with fine examples of 15th-century glass, is much as William Cowper would have known it in July 1795, when he came to live in the untenanted parsonage with Mrs. Morley Unwin; under the guardianship of Johnny Johnson, his devoted cousin, they moved in October to Dunham Lodge in Dunham, where they passed the winter.

NORTHAM, Devon (pop. 5,420) Located 1½ miles north of Bideford and almost 1 mile east of Westward Ho!, Northam has a grass mound called Bone Hill which is said to contain the remains of the Danes slain by King Alfred's men in a 9th-century engagement. The village becomes the imaginary home of Amyas Leigh and the burial place of Salvation Yeo in Charles Kingsley's *Westward Ho!* St. Margaret's Church, which Kingsley mentions, contains a memorial to Thomas Berry, who at one time owned Burrough House, just south of the village; the present building dates from 1868. Kingsley used the older house (which belonged to the Thomas Leigh family in his time) as the home of Mrs. Leigh and her two sons. The description of the locality the young Amyas sees on his return from hearing John Oxenham speak in Bideford is credible even today:

> So he goes up between the rich lane-banks, heavy with drooping ferns and honeysuckle; out upon the windy down toward the old Court, nestled amid its ring of wind-clipt oaks; through the gray gateway into the homeclose; and then he pauses a moment to look around; first at the wide bay to the westward, with its southern wall of purple cliffs; then at the dim Isle of Lundy far away at sea; then at the cliffs and downs of Morte and Braunton, right in front of him; then at the vast yellow sheet of rolling sandhill, and green alluvial plain dotted with red cattle, at his feet, through which the silver estuary winds onward toward the sea. Beneath him, on his right, the Torridge, like a land-locked lake, sleeps broad and bright between the old park of Tapeley and the charmed rock of the Hubbastone, where, seven hundred years ago, the Norse rovers landed to lay siege to Kenwith Castle, a mile away on his left hand. . . .

NORTHAMPTON, Northamptonshire (pop. 12,608) Situated in the Nene River Valley 21½ miles northwest of Bedford, the county town of Northampton was an ancient British settlement, a Saxon town, and a Norman stronghold; its great castle was begun in the early 12th century. The city was walled in then, and one mark of its early importance was the granting of its first market charter in 1189. Not much of the old town has survived; a few years after Charles II ordered the demolition of the castle in retaliation for the town's strong support of the Parliamentarian forces, a great fire gutted almost the entire town. Daniel Defoe visited Northampton sufficiently long after the fire that extensive rebuilding was taking place and called it

> the handsomest and best built Town in all this part of *England;* but here, as at *Warwick,* the Beauty of it is owing to its own Disasters, for it was so effectually and suddenly burnt down, that very few Houses were left standing, and this, tho' the Fire began in the Day-time, the Flame also spread itself with such Fury, and run on with such terrible Speed, that they tell us a Townsman being at Queen's Cross upon a Hill, on the *South* Side of the Town, about two Miles off, saw the Fire at one End of the Town then newly begun, and that before he could get to the Town it was burning at the remotest End, opposite to that where he first saw it; 'tis now finely rebuilt with Brick and Stone, and the Streets made spacious and wide.

Three notable churches were spared by the flames; the most significant is the Crusaders' Church of the Holy Sepulchre. A round church and one of five English churches built after the Crusades and modeled on the Holy Sepulchre in Jerusalem, it is said to be most like the original; it dates from about 1100 and is thought to have been built by Simon de Senlis, 1st Earl of Northampton. St. Peter's Church, which dates from the mid-12th century, stands on the site of a previous Saxon foundation and has incorporated some Saxon carvings into the present fabric. The last is St. Giles's Church, which has been rebuilt over the centuries, and now little of its Norman heritage remains; the chancel, which has some blocked Norman arches, dates from the 13th century, and the transepts and chapels from the 14th.

The name Northampton, according to the gloss in Michael Drayton's *Poly-Olbion,* derives from "*North-avonton,* the towne upon the North of *Avon*," since the Nene River was once called the Avon. Indeed,

William Camden reaches virtually the same conclusion in his *Britannia:*

> The Avon advances with a gentle stream a little way below this, and soon after receives an increase from a little river from the North, where at their conflux stands a town, called from the river *Northafandon,* by contraction *Northamton,* surrounded on the West by one river, on the North by the other.

These explanations, though, are erroneous for at least two reasons; first, the name, even in the *Anglo-Saxon Chronicle,* never had any similarity to the Avon, as these authors want to suggest; second, *hampton* means "at the high farm," and the locational element *north* was added later.

The principal literary association in Northampton is with John Clare, the "Northamptonshire peasant poet." Suffering from long periods of depression and unable to cope with his environment, Clare was removed from his home in Northborough in June 1837 and placed in an asylum in High Beech, Essex, for treatment. In 1841 Clare was reexamined by a physician from Peterborough, Fenwick Skrimshaw, and certified insane; arrangements were then made to transfer Clare to the Northampton General Lunatic Asylum. The 3d Earl Fitzwilliam, whose father had supplied the Northborough cottage and grounds, paid all the poet's expenses here for the twenty-two years that he was in the asylum. The institution (now St. Andrew's Hospital for Mental Diseases), which had opened in August 1838, had facilities to care for thirty private patients and fifty-two pauper patients; while its location was pleasant enough, it was then by no means the pleasant and almost lavish place it is today.

During the first thirteen years of his confinement, Clare was permitted to wander freely, and he would often sit for hours under the portico of All Saints' Church watching the children play or scribbling down idle thoughts in his small notebook. Clare was writing at this time, and two poems from 1844, "The Sleep of Spring" and "Graves of Infants," both show a degree of sanity and acceptance of his situation. What may be Clare's best poem, "I am, who knows, who cares?" was written here in January 1848. In 1854 the headship of the institution changed, and with the new administration Clare's freedom was restricted; he was, in fact, confined to the grounds. His last lines were written here in 1861:

> 'Tis Spring, warm glows the south,
> Chaffinch carries the moss in his mouth
> To filbert hedges all day long,
> And charms the poet with his beautiful song;
> The wind blows bleak o'er the sedgy fen,
> But warm the sun shines by the little wood,
> While the old cow at her leisure chews her cud.

In May 1864, at the age of seventy, he suffered a paralytic seizure; he lingered for ten days before dying in the afternoon of May 20. In an earlier moment of lucidity, in 1844, he had laid down specific instructions for his burial, and these were carried out in Helpston, although not to the letter. One person who came to see Clare and left an account of a friend's visit was Mary Russell Mitford, who wrote in *Recollections of a Literary Life:*

> His delusions were at that time very singular in their character. Whatever he read, whatever recurred to him from his former reading, or happened to be mentioned in

conversation, became impressed on his mind as a thing that he had witnessed and acted in. My friend was struck with a narrative of the execution of Charles the First, recounted by Clare, as a transaction that occurred yesterday and of which he was an eye-witness—a narrative the most graphic and minute, with an accuracy as to costume and manners far exceeding what would probably have been at his command if sane. . . .

Several other literary associations are of interest. Northampton was probably the birthplace in 1612 of Anne Dudley (Bradstreet), who has been called America's first woman poet. Little is known of her life here, and even her place of birth has been questioned; however, her father, Thomas Dudley, resided in Northampton, and it is likely that she grew up in this town. Two years after her marriage in 1628 to Simon Bradstreet, a Nonconformist minister, the couple emigrated to America. For seven years William Cowper wrote verses for the parish clerk at All Saints' to accompany his Bill of Mortality registering local deaths. Cowper commented at one point, "A fig for poets who write epitaphs on individuals; I have one that serves 200 people." In this century Jerome K. Jerome was taken ill on a motor tour of England and was brought to Northampton General Hospital, where he died on June 14, 1927. His body was cremated here, and his ashes were interred at Ewelme, Oxfordshire.

Finally, there are two commemorative statues in front of the public library on Abington Street, to Thomas Fuller and John Dryden, both natives of the shire. The library has an excellent collection of John Clare memorabilia, including his death mask, a bust by Henry Behnes, and a portrait by Atkinson Grimshaw.

One use of Northampton in literature should be mentioned. William Shakespeare uses the old castle in *King John;* here the court decides that Robert has won his suit, and the King knights Philip, bastard son of Richard Coeur de Lion.

NORTHBOROUGH, Huntingdonshire (pop. 207) Originally, the village of Northborough, while within the bounds of Northamptonshire, was under the political jurisdiction of the soke of Peterborough; the powers descended to the bishopric at the Reformation, and in 1576 Bishop Scambler was forced to sell the "lordship," as it was called, to Elizabeth, who immediately bestowed it on her Lord Treasurer Burghley and his descendants. With the Local Government Act of 1888 the soke became an administrative county in its own right, although it was still included at least historically in Huntingdonshire; then, in 1965, it was united with that county and lost its independence. One more change took place in 1974, when major redistricting occurred, and Northborough was absorbed into Cambridgeshire.

The village, 2 miles southeast of Market Deeping, is a pleasant, straggling affair of stone-built cottages with thatched and tiled roofs and a 14th-century manor house. In 1832 John Clare, "the Northamptonshire peasant poet," moved to a cottage on the estate, then belonging to the 2d Earl Fitzwilliam. Already suffering from mental illness and without the money to stock or secure the place, he was totally dependent upon his friends. The six-room house had a doorway built to Clare's specifications; facing away from the road, it gave him a quick way out if he saw guests approaching. He planted the flower gardens and most of the orchard (much as they are today); gooseberries and currants were planted beneath the pear and apple trees so that he could

> Walk round the orchard on sweet summer eves,
> And rub the perfume from the black currant leaves.

Clare felt exiled here, although his home was less than 3 miles away at Helpston, and describes his feelings in "The Flitting":

> I've left my own old home of homes,
>   Green fields and every pleasant place;
> The summer like a stranger comes,
>   I pause and hardly know her face.
> I miss the hazel's happy green,
>   The blue bell's quiet hanging blooms,
> Where envy's sneer was never seen,
>   Where staring malice never comes.

Written as a companion poem, "Remembrance" catalogs the country of his youth and includes Langley Bush, Eastwell Spring, Lea Close Oak, Crossberry Way, Swordy Well, and Hilly Snow.

By 1837 it was apparent that Clare could not function in society, and arrangements were made by John Taylor, his publisher, to have the poet taken to High Beech, Essex, for treatment.

NORTHCHURCH, Hertfordshire (pop. 1,378) Actually part of Berkhampsted, 1½ miles to the southeast, but a parish in its own right, Northchurch has a Saxon church and some fragments of Grim's Dyke to attest to its long history. The church and its churchyard contain a memorial brass and gravestone to a feral child, "Peter the Wild Boy," who was found in a forest near Hannover, Germany, walking on all fours, climbing trees with squirrellike agility, and eating grass. Brought to England in 1726 by George I, the boy was first exhibited in court as a curiosity, but the church plaque states: "[A]fter ablest masters had failed to make him speak he was sent to a farm, where he ended his inoffensive life in 1785, aged about 72 years." Jonathan Swift was taken up in the craze over Peter and wrote that the child was a Christian and had been taken to court dressed all in green; Swift and Dr. John Arbuthnot then coauthored a pamphlet, *The Most Wonderful Wonder That Ever Appeared to Be the Wonder of the British Nation,* about Peter.

From 1776 to 1780 Maria Edgeworth spent her school holidays here at Edgeworth House with her father and stepmother, who had returned from Ireland because of Mrs. Edgeworth's health. Shortly after her stepmother's death in 1780 and her father's remarriage (to his sister-in-law), Miss Edgeworth went to London.

NORTON MALREWARD, Somerset (pop. 140) Just northeast of the Mendip Hills and 5 miles southeast of Bristol is the tiny parish of Norton Malreward. The village was said to be the birthplace of Thomas Rowley, the 15th-century monk whom the poet Thomas Chatterton invented as the author of his antique poems and *The Ryse of Peyncteynge in England.*

NORTON ST. PHILIP, Somerset (pop. 448) Six miles south of Bath is Norton St. Philip ("North Town with a church dedicated to St. Philip"), which contains the 13th-century George Inn, believed to be the oldest inn in use in England and at one time the guesthouse for the Carthusian priory in nearby Hinton Charterhouse. The inn, with a stone-built ground floor and two upper stories of timber and plaster, is known to have functioned as an alehouse in 1397. Across a meadow from the George is a church with a stone monument which Samuel Pepys and his wife visited. Pepys writes (of "Philips Norton") in his journal:

> I walked to the Church . . . and here saw the tombstone where on there were only two heads cut, which, the story goes, and credibly, were two sisters, called the Fair Maids of Foscott, that had two bodies upward and one belly, and there lie buried.

The monument has been mutilated through the years. The local tradition is that one of these Siamese twins died a rather long time before the other and that the surviving sister had to carry her dead sister about. A tomb of a Knight Templar noted by Pepys disappeared by the 18th century. The church bells, "a very fine ring of six bells, and they mighty tunable," are still in use. Pepys and his entourage "dined very well" for 10 shillings at the George before proceeding to Bath.

Norton St. Philip is one of the two places generally believed to be the birthplace in 1562 or 1563 of Samuel Daniel. Thomas Fuller's assertion that the birthplace was Taunton seems to have no credibility, and Anthony à Wood's statement that Daniel was born in the vicinity of "Philips Norton" or the nearby village of Beckington seems more reasonable. The site of Beckington may be the more plausible of the two villages because Daniel is known to have retired there.

NORWICH, Norfolk (pop. 126,236) Norwich (pronounced "nor'ich" or "nor'ij") is a cathedral and university town 18½ miles west of Great Yarmouth

NORWICH Daniel Defoe's 18th-century commentary about Norwich includes the statement "The publick Edifices are chiefly the Castle, antient and decayed, and now for many Years past made use of for a Jayl." Today the castle is in total ruin and serves only as a tourist attraction.

on the navigable Wensum River just north of its confluence with the Yare. Prehistoric people were active throughout the area, but for some inexplicable reason they avoided this general locality; so did the Romans. The Saxon settlements have been only roughly placed: one was along King Street, another in the vicinity of St. Martins'-at-Palace and along Palace Street, and a third along St. Benedict Street and across the river. A market area also seems to have flourished in Tombland, an open expanse central to the three. When the Normans subjugated the inhabitants, they also built a large bailey surrounded by a moat on an old Saxon-raised mound; here the first wooden fortification was built. Later a stone keep and wall, towers, and a gatehouse were constructed.

Not long after the Normans arrived, Norwich Cathedral was begun; it was the Norman practice to place bishops' sees in important cities where the bishops could act in both spiritual and secular affairs, and so the pre-Norman see at Thetford was moved here, as were fragments from that cathedral. The original plan called for the founding of a cathedral and palace and a Benedictine monastery of sixty monks. The bishop was granted the central area of Tombland, which he did not enclose but over which he claimed that the citizens had no rights, and the foundation stone of the cathedral was laid in 1096. Building went rapidly, and the cathedral was consecrated in September 1101.

The priory became an exceptional institution in the Middle Ages and left records of the details of monastic life running over four centuries; indeed, detailed rolls exist from 1272 (older ones were destroyed by fire that year) until the dissolution of the monasteries in the 16th century. On the average, there were sixty monks here until the Black Death drastically reduced the figures, and there were also numerous clerks and servants. The fire in 1272 originated in a dispute over the jurisdiction of the town going back to the bishops' claim to the central area. The feud erupted at the Tombland Fair between the priory and the town's citizenry. The prior ordered the priory to put up its defenses and brought in armed mercenaries from Yarmouth, who razed the town. The citizens replied by attacking the priory, burning goodly portions of it. The citizens were heavily fined as a consequence of the riots, and thirty citizens were sentenced to death by dragging, one was burned, and numerous others were hanged.

Medieval Norwich became an extremely prosperous town; the early 13th century saw it well established in the cloth and leather trades, and its worsteds were renowned. Medieval prosperity is reflected in the more than thirty extant churches dating from this time. The 14th century saw the town almost wiped out by the Black Death and the serious economic and social consequences fomented the Peasants' Revolt of 1381. By the 15th century four more monastic institutions—the Black Friars, the Grey Friars, the White Friars, and the Augustinians— were flourishing in the city, and the great Benedictine nunnery of Carrow lay just outside the town. In addition, a college of priests was established at St. Mary-in-the-Field, and two hospitals, that of St. Paul and the Great Hospital, had been founded. Nevertheless, the century was one of unquiet; the worsted trade declined, and general lawlessness prevailed. The letters written by John and Margaret Paston bring much of this into vivid relief and show a great deal of concern with the problems of the time; living in nearby Paston, they had town houses here: the 12th-century Music House (now Wensum Lodge), on King Street, and Crown Court, off Elm Hill. The Norman Maid's Head (18th-century facade) is mentioned in their letters.

While the reign of Henry VII restored some of the needed law and order, Norwich's economic fortunes fluctuated considerably until modern times, and there were many unsuccessful attempts to make the cloth industry profitable. One of these schemes was to import Dutch weavers, as mentioned by Michael Drayton in *Poly-Olbion:*

> That hospitable place to the Industrious *Dutch,*
> Whose skill in making Stuffes, and workmanship is such,
> (For refuge hither come) as they our ayd deserve,
> By labour sore that live, whilst oft the *English* starve;
> On Roots, and Pulse that feed, on Beefe and Mutton spare,
> So frugally they live, not gluttons as we are.

But the Dutch, who had fled from persecution, found fresh persecution here, as Norwich clergy tried to drive the "Outlandishe" into the Laudian church, and many of the *émigrés* returned to Holland or fled to America.

Early writers were impressed by the large size of Norwich. William Camden devoted a great deal of space (with Richard Gough's later additions) to discussing the town's history and buildings in his *Britannia.* One interesting question that Camden raised, not taken seriously by later writers, was the extent of Roman influence:

> Without going back into fabulous antiquity, or to the ideas of Polydore Vergil and those who fancy they find the name of *Norvicus* in that of the *Ordovices,* who never existed here, one may fairly trace the Romans hereabouts by their many marks, though the city probably had not a being till they left the island.

Daniel Defoe, who often used Camden and Leland's *Itinerary* as sources, ignored the Romans in *A Tour thro' the Whole Island of Great Britain* and was especially taken with the people and the known past. He saw the walls of the city as "taking in more Ground than the City of *London,*" but he notes,

> much of that Ground lying open in Pasture-Fields and Gardens; nor does it seem to be, like some antient Places, a decayed declining Town, and that the Walls mark out its antient Dimensions; for we do not see Room to suppose that it was ever larger or more populous than it is now: But the Walls seem to be placed, as if they expected that the City would in time encrease sufficiently to fill them up with Buildings.
>
> The Cathedral of this City is a fine Fabrick, and the Spire-Steeple very high and beautiful; it is not antient . . . yet the Church has so many Antiquities in it, that our late great Scholar and Physician, Sir *Tho. Brown,* thought it worth his while to write a whole Book to collect the Monuments and Inscriptions in this Church. . . .

Norwich can lay claim to being the birthplace of two writers and the home of many others. All available evidence points to Robert Greene's being born here in 1558; he probably attended the local grammar school, founded before 1240 and refounded by Edward VI in 1547. What could have been an important event in Greene's life occurred on a trip home in 1584 or 1585 when he attended services at St. Andrew's and heard the parish priest, a man whom he greatly admired, call on the congregation to give up its sinful and immoral ways. Greene's somewhat debauched life in London is well known, and the dramatist then vowed to give up his old ways. He returned to London and his old friends, and his weak will immediately took over. Little else is known of Greene's existence here except that his parents, he said, were "respected for their gravity and honest life."

The second native, Harriet Martineau, was born on June 12, 1802, in a distinguished house, Gurney Court, on Magdalen Street. Gurney Court has pedimented and canopied doorways and is entered from 31 Magdalen Street. Soon the Martineaus moved to a large Georgian house at 24 Magdalen Street, where the author was privately tutored until 1813, when she and a sister attended a school directed by the Rev. Isaac Perry. Her formal education came to an end when Perry left Norwich in 1815. Miss Martineau's deafness began during childhood, and by the time she was sixteen her hearing problem was extremely serious. She also suffered from anosmia. Miss Martineau continued to live here except for brief periods in Bristol, Newcastle upon Tyne, and Dublin until she left for London in 1834.

The earliest literary figure to be associated with the town was Juliana of Norwich, the anchorite who wrote *XVI Revelations of Divine Love;* she is thought to have been a Benedictine nun at Carrow Abbey just outside the city walls and to have lived the greater part of her life in St. Julian's churchyard here. She died in Norwich in 1443, but her burial place is not known. Margery Kempe visited her here. John Skelton came to Carrow sometime around 1506, when he visited Jane Scrope and her mother, Lady Wyndham. The visit occasioned *The Boke of Phyllyp Sparowe,* a delightful medieval bird mass lamenting the death of Jane's pet sparrow:

> That vengeaunce I aske and crye,
> By way of exclamacion,
> On al the whole nacion
> Of Cattes wilde and tame:
> God send them sorrow and shame!
> That Cat specially
> That slew so cruelly
> My litle pretty sparow
> That I brought vp at Carow.
>   O cat of churlyshe kynde,
> The feend was in thy minde
> Whan thou my byrd vntwynde.
> I wolde thou haddest ben blynd!

Jane Scrope had asked Skelton to compose an epitaph for the sparrow after Gib, the convent cat, had done his misdeed. Dame Margery of the poem was Margery Carrow, the senior nun who would conduct the service.

Another early literary association exists with the balladeer and pamphleteer Thomas Deloney, who worked as a silk weaver in Norwich around 1585 and may have been born here about 1563. Nothing more is known.

In 1637 Sir Thomas Browne arrived here from Shibden Hall, Yorkshire; in 1641 he married Dorothy Mileham, and between 1643 and 1662 twelve children were born to the couple. Browne lived here quietly for forty-five years, during which time he wrote *Pseudodoxia Epidemica,* "Hydriotaphia," and *The Garden of Cyrus;* it is unlikely, contrary to the usual claim, that he wrote *Religio Medici* here since at least a surreptitious copy existed in 1642. The house where Browne lived is gone, but it was near the present Lamb Inn. John Evelyn visited Sir Thomas, "that famous Scholar & Physition . . . now lately knighted" (by Charles II at St. Andrew's Hall), on October 18, 1671, and left an interesting account in his diary:

> Next morning, I went to see Sir *Tho: Browne* (with whom I had sometime corresponded by Letters tho never saw before) whose whole house & Garden being a Paradise & Cabinet of rarities, & that of the best collection, especialy Medails, books, Plants, natural things, did exceedingly refresh me after last nights confusion: . . . He likewise led me to see all the remarkeable places of this antient Citty, being one of the largest, & certainly (after *London*) one of the noblest of England, for its venerable Cathedrall, number of Stately Churches, Cleanesse of the streetes; & buildings of flint, so exquisitely headed & Squared, as I was much astonish'd at; Sir Tho: told me they had lost the art, of squaring the flint, which once they [were] so excellent in: & of which the Churches, best houses & Walls are built. . . .

Browne died here at seventy-seven on October 19, 1682, the day of his birth, and was buried at St. Peter Mancroft; there is a commemorative statue outside the church. Workmen digging in the chancel of the church in 1840 accidentally broke open his coffin lid; the skull was removed and given to the Norfolk and Norwich Hospital, where it remained until 1922, when it was returned to the coffin.

George Crabbe was ordained a priest at the cathedral in August 1782 by the Bishop of Norwich. At the time Crabbe was licensed as a curate to the Reverend Mr. Bennet, rector of Aldeburgh, Suffolk.

One of the most renowned persons ever to live in and write about Norwich was George Borrow, author of *Lavengro* and *The Romany Rye;* his father, a captain in the West Norfolk Militia, retired to Norwich in 1816, when his son was thirteen. Their small house on Willow Lane was reached through a passageway now known as Borrow's Court, and young George received this part of his education at the grammar school under Dr. Edward Valpey. The youth was already interested in languages and spoke Gaelic, much to his father's dislike:

> "God help the child! I bear him no ill-will, on the contrary, all love and affection; but I cannot shut my eyes; there is something so strange about him! How he behaved in Ireland! I sent him to school to learn Greek, and he picked up Irish!"
> "And Greek as well." said my mother. "I heard him say the other day that he could read St. John in the original tongue."

But the father's main concern was "[t]hat ever son of mine should have been intimate with the Papist Irish, and have learnt their language."

By the time Borrow left school, he knew Latin, Greek, French, Italian, Spanish, and Romany, as well as Gaelic. In March 1819 Borrow was articled to a firm of Norwich solicitors, Messrs. Simpson and Rockham of Tuck's Court, St. Giles':

> [T]he scene of my labours was a strange old house, occupying one side of a long and narrow court, into which,

however, the greater number of the windows looked not, but into an extensive garden, filled with fruit trees, in the rear of a large, handsome house. . . .

During the lunch period when he, as the most junior member of the firm, was left behind "to take care of the premises, to answer the bell, and so forth," he took from his desk the poems of Dafydd ap Gwilym. With the death of his father in 1824, Borrow gave up the solicitors' office and went to London, where he had a Grub Street garret. He returned frequently to Norwich to visit his mother in the Willow Lane house; after his marriage, when he lived in Oulton, he would stay in lodgings on Lady Lane.

In *Lavengro* Borrow expresses his feelings toward Norwich and Norfolk:

> A fine old city, truly, is that, view it from whatever side you will; but it shows best from the east, where the ground, bold and elevated, overlooks the fair and fertile valley in which it stands. Gazing from those heights, the eye beholds a scene which cannot fail to awaken, even in the least sensitive bosom, feelings of pleasure and admiration. At the foot of the heights flows a narrow and deep river, with an antique bridge communicating with a long and narrow suburb, flanked on either side by rich meadows of the brightest green, beyond which spreads the city; the fine old city, perhaps the most curious specimen at present extant of the genuine old English town. Yes, there it spreads from north to south, with its venerable houses. . . . Now, who can wonder that the children of that fine old city are proud of her, and offer up prayers for her prosperity? I, myself, who was not born within her walls, offer up prayers for her prosperity, that want may never visit her cottages, vice her palaces, and that the abomination of idolatry may never pollute her temples.

In this work he also writes extensively about the Danish influence here and comments on the former annual horse fair:

> I was standing on the castle hill in the midst of a fair of horses.
> I have already had occasion to mention this castle. It is the remains of what was once a Norman stronghold, and is perched upon a round mound or monticle, in the midst of the old city. Steep is this mound and scarped, evidently by the hand of man; a deep gorge, over which is flung a bridge, separates it, on the south, from a broad swell of open ground called "the hill;" of old the scene of many a tournament and feat of Norman chivalry, but now much used as a show-place for cattle, where those who buy and sell beeves and other beasts resort at stated periods.

Here Borrow renewed his acquaintanceship with Jasper Petulengro, the Gypsy whom he had first met in Yaxley, Huntingdonshire; Jasper took Borrow back to the Gypsy camp on Mousehold Heath northeast of the city:

> We descended the hill in the direction of the north, and passing along the suburb reached the old Norman bridge, which we crossed; the chalk precipice, with the ruin on its top, was now before us; but turning to the left we walked swiftly along, and presently came to some rising ground, which ascending, we found ourselves upon a wild moor or heath.

Lav-engro, the Romany term for "Word-Master," was the name applied to Borrow in his youth by Ambrose Smith.

Three other associations should be noted. Charles Dickens stayed at the now-demolished Royal Hotel on the Market Place on a reading tour in 1861; he read at St. Andrew's Hall and observed that his audience was

> a very lumpish audience indeed . . . an intent and staring audience. They laughed, though, very well, and the storm made them shake themselves again. But they were not magnetic, and the great big place (St. Andrew's Hall) was out of sorts somehow.

This was not his first excursion to Norwich; in 1848 he wrote to John Forster about the need of mental stimulation and queried, "What do you say to Norwich and Stanfield Hall?" This moated Tudor house had just been the scene of the murders of Isaac Jeremy, the Recorder of Norwich, and his son by James Bloomfield Rush. After the party arrived, Dickens confessed that the house was unattractive and has "a murderous look that seemed to invite such crime." (It is, perhaps, worth noting that this had been the home of Sir John Robsart, the father of Amy Robsart.)

George Meredith stayed at the home of the headmaster of the Norwich Grammar School, a Mr. Jessop, who took Meredith to Cambridge, where they dined at the High Table at St. John's College. Shortly thereafter, in September 1862, Meredith placed his son Arthur in Jessop's care at the grammar school.

Finally, from 1867 to 1884 Anna Sewell lived at 125 Spixworth Road, where she wrote *Black Beauty*.

NOTTINGHAM, Nottinghamshire (pop. 278,800) The county town of the shire, Nottingham dominates the area with its history, legend, and industry. Located on the north bank of the Trent River 15 miles east of Derby, this large market town is thought to have had a Roman settlement, but no trace of it has been found. It was left to the Saxons to colonize Snotingaham; the initial *S* was lost in the 12th century under Norman influence. The *Winchester Chronicle* records the invasion of the Danes and the subsequent siege by Alfred and Ethelred in 869, but no battle occurred, and a temporary peace was effected. A second invasion in the spring of 874 brought all Mercia, including the modern boroughs of Nottingham, Lincoln, Derby, Leicester, and Stamford, under Danish control, and Nottingham became the chief Danish burgh and so remained until the reconquest of Danish-held territory in 919 by Edward the Elder and his sister Ethelfleda (Athelflaed).

With the Norman invasion the history of Nottingham becomes inextricably linked with the castle William ordered William Peverell to build in 1068 on the high rock cliff of Castleton. This brought about the epithet Peverell of the Peak, which Sir Walter Scott uses in his Derbyshire novel *Peveril of the Peak*. During the Norman period the town grew peacefully in two distinct districts, the Normans settling in the French borough near the castle and the Saxons on St. Mary's Hill. Each borough had its own set of laws and customs, town hall, and mint. The town became important and, because of its proximity to the hunting district of Sherwood Forest, retained its close ties with the monarchy. Indeed, Edward IV proclaimed himself King here and denounced as a traitor the Earl of Warwick, "the Kingmaker" (killed at nearby Barnet), whom Edward Bulwer-Lytton graphically portrays in *The Last of the Barons*.

Michael Drayton sings the praises of the town and its river in *Poly-Olbion*, and in the same song he tells the story of Robin Hood, whose statue stands just outside the castle walls. Drayton's account of Robin Hood's band is one of the pleasantest in the rich Robin Hood literature. Robin Hood is associated with Nottingham mostly because of his enemies, particularly the sheriff, and the principal sources of the association are the ballads. The third fit (section) of "A Gest of Robin Hode" relates how Little John enters the service of the sheriff to betray him to Robin; and the fifth and sixth fits recount the circumstances leading to the slaying of Robin's prime enemy. "Robin Hood and the Monk" tells of the outlaw journeying from his forest hideout to the city to hear mass; traveling with Little John, Robin loses his temper over a lost shooting wager, strikes his companion, and

> When Robyn came to Notyngham,
>   Sertenly withouten layn,
> He prayed to God and myld Mary
>   To bryng hym out saue agayn.
>
> He gos in to Seynt Mary chirch,
>   And kneled down before the rode;
> All that euer were the church within
>   Beheld wel Robyn Hode.

The monk sitting next to Robin discovers his identity and rouses the sheriff, who takes the outlaw captive in the Church of St. Mary, the Perpendicular church in the original Saxon borough. Nottingham is also featured in "Robin Hood's Death," "Robin Hood and the Potter," "Robin Hood and the Butcher," "Robin Hood and the Tinker," "Robin Hood and the Beggar, I," "Robin Hood's Delight," and "Robin Hood's Progress to Nottingham." This is by no means a complete list of the ballads in which the town is mentioned.

There are more exact literary associations with the town as well. Philip Massinger's *A New Way to Pay Old Debts* is set in "the country near Nottingham," and the Unitarian Chapel on High Pavement was one of the many chapels where Samuel Taylor Coleridge preached in 1796. A few years later George Gordon, Lord Byron attended the same chapel. In 1798, when Byron succeeded to the family estates at Newstead and the family financial situation was too precarious to maintain the priory, Byron and his mother rented Newstead to Lord Grey and took lodgings here, first for a short time on Pelham Street and then on St. James Street. The Nottingham Corporation has recently acquired the latter home. After the poet took his seat in the House of Lords, he gave his maiden speech on behalf of the Luddite rioters of Nottingham. William Wordsworth and his wife had an enforced visit in the town in 1831, when Mary Wordsworth became ill on a trip; she was taken to the home of a chemist and minor poet, William Howitt, in the marketplace across from Long Row. The Wordsworths remained overnight. The children's poet Ann Taylor, who is most frequently associated with Lavenham, Suffolk, married the Rev. Joseph Gilbert and came to Nottingham to live. She died in 1866 and is buried here. Sir James Matthew Barrie took a job with *The Nottingham Journal* on Pelham Street in January 1884 and had lodgings in "one of the pleasant little groves of dwellings between Sherwood Street and Addison Street." He was particularly fond of walking around the castle in the dark, "an uncouth stranger," as he termed himself, "a book in each pocket, and . . . thoughts three hundred miles due north. . . ." He occasionally frequented the Kettle Club, a meeting place of reporters, but his intense dislike of the club and its low atmosphere kept him from going there often. "When a Man's Single" uses his experiences here, with Nottingham as Silchester and the *Journal* as the *Mirror:*

> The Mirror's offices are nearly crushed out of sight in a block of buildings left in the middle of a street for town councils to pull down gradually. This island of houses, against which a sea of humanity beats daily, is cut in two by a narrow passage, off which several doors open. One of these leads up a dirty staircase to the editorial and composing rooms of The Daily Mirror, and down a dirty stair to its printing rooms.

Barrie remained in the town and with the newspaper until October 1884, when he went to London.

Nottingham was the birthplace and residence of William Thompson, the pugilist turned preacher, better known as Bendigo; this is the man familiar to Sir Arthur Conan Doyle's readers as "The Pride of Nottingham." Many broadsides concern Thompson and his unique method of dealing with the local rowdies in his congregation:

> But the roughs they kept on chaffin' and the uproar it was such
> That the preacher in the pulpit might be talking double Dutch,
> Till a working man he shouted out, a-jumpin' to his feet,
> "Give us a lead, your reverence, and heave 'em in the street."
>
> Then Bendy said, "Good Lord, since I first left my sinful ways,
> Thou knowest that to Thee alone I've given up my days,
> But now, dear Lord" (and here he laid his Bible upon the shelf)
> "I'll take with your permission just five minutes for myself."

The writer most intimately connected with Nottingham is D. H. Lawrence, who entered Nottingham High School on a scholarship in September 1898; too frail to work in the coal mines in the Eastwood area, young Lawrence attended the high school until July 1901, when he became a general clerk at Haywood's, a surgical-goods manufacturer on Castle Gate, at a salary of 13 shillings a week. He remained only a few months before taking a post as a pupil-teacher at Ilkeston and Eastwood and decided to take a teacher's training course at Nottingham University College. He entered the college (it became the University of Nottingham in 1948) in September 1906 and qualified in June 1908. "Nottingham's New University" refers to "that dismal town/where I went to school and college" and goes on to comment on the new buildings erected by Lord Trent (Sir Jesse Boot), with whom Lawrence's grandfather had quarreled:

> Little I thought, when I was a lad
> and turned my modest penny
> over on Boot's Cash Chemists counter
> That Jesse, by turning many
>
> millions of similar honest pence
> over, would make a pile

that would rise at last and blossom out
in grand and cakey style

into a university. . . .

In 1912 Lawrence met Frieda von Richthofen Weekley, the wife of Prof. Ernest Weekley, at their home on Victoria Crescent, and the two eloped in May.

Nottingham is used extensively in Lawrence's works. George Saxton's trip to the city in *The White Peacock* describes the area of Nottingham High School; *The Rainbow* describes the old University College where Ursula becomes a student:

> She liked the hall with its big stone chimney piece and its Gothic arches supporting the balcony above. To be sure the arches were ugly, the chimney-piece of cardboard-like carved stone with its armorial decoration looked silly just opposite the bicycle stand and the radiator, whilst the great notice board with the fluttering papers seemed to slam away all sense of retreat and mystery from the far wall. Nevertheless, amorphous as it might be, there was in it a reminiscence of the wondrous, cloistral origin of education.

In *Sons and Lovers*, Haywood's becomes Jordan's:

> a big warehouse, with creamy paper parcels everywhere, and clerks, with their shirt sleeves rolled back—going about in an at-home sort of way. The light was subdued, the glossy cream parcels seemed luminous, the counters were of dark brown wood.

One of Lawrence's short stories, "Goose Fair," describes the riots in 1831, when Lord Grey's second reform bill was rejected. "The White Stocking" is also set in Nottingham.

NOTTINGHAMSHIRE (pop. 712,681) One of the North Midlands counties, Nottinghamshire is steeped in the legend of Robin Hood, England's most popular and elusive folk hero. At least two major areas claim him and his band of merry men, and over the years he has been authoritatively identified as a forest elf, a sun god, a god of witches, and a Scandinavian deity. He has also been identified as the last Saxon warrior to hold out against the Normans (to be compared with Hereward the Wake), a leader of peasant revolts, and a roughneck yeoman; in addition, he has been assigned reality and a peerage as Robert Fitz-Ooth, Earl of Huntingdon. However uncertain some of the facts behind the legend are, there are a few known historical facts which may have a bearing on his identification. The portion of the 1230 Pipe Roll pertaining to Yorkshire mentions one "Robertus Hood *fugitivus*," and he appears first in William Langland's *Piers Plowman:*

> He [Sloth] began *Benedicite* with a belch   and knocked on his breast
> And stretched and snored   and slumbered at last.
> "Awake, wretch!" quoth Repentance   "and run thee to shrift."
> "Should I die on this day   I'd not trouble to look.
> I know not *Paternoster*   as the priest it singeth,
> But I know rhymes of Robin Hood   and Earl Randolph of Chester,
> But of our Lord or our Lady   not the least ever made."

Robin had become a historical figure by the time of Andrew of Wyntoun's *Chronicle of Scotland* under the date 1283:

Lytill Ihon and Robyne Hude
Waythmen were commendyd gude;
In Yngilwode and Barnysdale
Thai oysyd all this tyme thare trawale.

The Middle Ages saw Robin Hood at the peak of his popularity; balladeers and minstrels made him God-fearing, just, chivalrous, dignified, cheerful, and gracious while fighting the local agent of central government (the sheriff of Nottingham), ecclesiastical landowners, and other wealthy landholders. He has been said to have been born at Locksley about 1160, but of this there is no proof, and most critics believe he is the creation of the balladeer. His characteristics evolved from the ballad makers: his sanctuary was the forest, and he would not eat until either a guest or an adventure turned up:

Robin Hood took a solemn oath,
   It was by Mary free,
That he would neither eat nor drink
   Till the frier he did see.

Neither would he recruit a man until he had been tested in friendly combat: in "Robin Hood and the Scotchman," Robin states simply:

"But eer I employ you . . .
   "With you I must have a bout. . . ."

Friar Tuck almost brought this practice to an end when he dumped Robin Hood into a stream:

And coming to the middle stream,
   There he threw Robin in:
"And chuse thee, chuse thee, fine fellow,
   Whether thow wilt sink or swim."

Robin Hood swam to a bush of broom,
   The frier to a wicker wand;
Bold Robin is gone to shore,
   And took his bow in his hand.

Robin and Friar Tuck reached an agreement:

"If thou wilt forsake fair Fountains Dale,
   And Fountains Abbey free,
Every Sunday throughout the year,
   A noble shall be thy fee.

"And every holy day throughout the year,
   Changed shall thy garment be,
If thou wilt go to fair Nottingham,
   And there remain with me."

One of the pleasantest accounts of Robin Hood is contained in the twenty-sixth song of Michael Drayton's *Poly-Olbion:*

The merry pranks he playd, would aske an age to tell,
And the adventures strange that *Robin Hood* befell,
When *Mansfield* many a time for *Robin* hath bin layd,
How he hath cosned them, that him would have betrayd;
How often he hath come to *Nottingham* disguised,
And cunningly escapt, being set to be surprizd.
In this our spacious Isle, I thinke there is not one,
But he hath heard some talke of him and little *John;*
And to the end of time, the Tales shall ne'r be done,
Of *Scarlock, George a Greene,* and *Much* the Millers sonne,
Of *Tuck* the merry Frier, which many a Sermon made,
In praise of *Robin Hood,* his Out-lawes, and their Trade.

He goes on to list all Robin's virtues.

NOTTINGHAMSHIRE Major Oak near Edwinstowe in Sherwood Forest is said to be 1,400 years old; this site, tradition says, Robin Hood used as a meeting place for his men.

While Yorkshire's Barnesdale Forest also claims Robin Hood (and the court rolls at the manor of Wakefield associate him with Thomas, Earl of Lancaster), Nottinghamshire's Sherwood Forest is certainly not going to renounce its favorite folk hero; he is held to have married Maid Marian at Edwinstowe and to have used the Major, or Queen, Oak near there as a meeting site for his men. Maid Marian is said to have lived in Blidworth, as did Will Scarlet, who is supposedly buried in the churchyard there; and Friar Tuck lived in the same general area. No matter how many Nottinghamshire places have claimed associations with Robin Hood and his men, historians have had as much difficulty in tracing Robin as the sheriff of Nottingham had. It should perhaps be noted that the earliest ballads reflect the hard times that were an integral part of medieval social conditions.

NUN APPLETON HALL, Yorkshire About 2 miles from Bolton Percy in a bend in the Wharfe River is the private mansion of Nun Appleton Hall, once the home of Gen. Lord Fairfax, a leading figure in the Restoration. Indeed, Nun Appleton Hall, whose grounds contain the scanty ruins of a Cistercian priory, was the place where the scheme for restoring the monarchy was hatched, and it was from here that the word was carried by a Fairfax to Gen. George Monck at Coldstream, touching off the uprising.

From 1650 to 1652 Andrew Marvell was tutor to Lord Fairfax's daughter and only child, Mary, in a house which has been described as a "picturesque brick mansion with stone copings" set in "a noble park with splended oak trees." A herd of some 300 deer was kept, and the extensive flower gardens Marvell said were laid out in the figure of a fort:

The sight does from their bastions ply
The invisible artillery;
And at proud Cawood Castle seems
To point the battery of its beams,
As if it quarrelled in the seat
The ambition of its prelate great.

During his time here Marvell wrote *Upon Appleton House, to My Lord Fairfax*, which relates the history of the house and the family, "Before the Hill and Grove at Bilborough," which also concerns the house, and "Hortus." The old north front of Nun Appleton Hall is still standing, but the rest of the house has been severely altered.

NUNEATON, Warwickshire (pop. 66,979) A northern Warwickshire industrial and market town on the Coventry Canal 9 miles north of Coventry, Nuneaton is in the heart of the area's coalfields and displays all the characteristics of places tainted by the industrial revolution. Robert Burton, author of *The Anatomy of Melancholy*, was educated for some time at the grammar school here, but the fact that he was here is known only from a reference in his will. Nuneaton's major literary association is with the novelist George Eliot (Mary Ann Evans), for this is the heart of Eliot country. Born at South Farm, Arbury, just a few miles away, she moved with her family to Griff House when she was four months old. The house, which was her home for twenty-one years, is now a hotel on the main Nuneaton-Coventry road about 1 mile from the church in Chilvers Coton and is secluded by elm and chestnut trees. Her first schooling took place at a nearby dame school kept by a Mrs. Moore; at the age of eight she was sent to a much larger school kept by a Miss Wallington. The first school no longer exists but was a double-fronted cottage opposite the entrance gate to Griff House. Christiana Evans, the novelist's mother, became seriously ill late in 1835 while Mary Ann was in school in Coventry, and the girl returned to Griff House before the end of that year. Following her mother's death in February 1836, Mary Ann took over all housekeeping duties but was able, with private tutors and visiting masters, to keep up her study of modern and ancient languages and music. She remained here with her father until his partial retirement and move to Coventry in 1841.

Most of Eliot's novels and poems are at least partly set in or drawn on places and people here; these include *The Mill on the Floss, Adam Bede, Middlemarch, Felix Holt, the Radical, Scenes of Clerical Life*, and *Brother and Sister*. Much of the material in the largely autobiographical *The Mill on the Floss* is taken from here; the childhood of Maggie and Tom Tulliver parallels that of the novelist and Isaac Pearson Evans in the "trimly-kept, comfortable dwelling house as old as the elms and chestnuts that shelter it"; its "great attic . . . ran under the old high-pitched roof":

> This attic was Maggie's favourite retreat on a wet day, when the weather was not too cold; here she fretted out all her ill-humours, and talked aloud to the worm-eaten floors and the worm-eaten shelves, and the dark rafters festooned with cobwebs. . . .

Behind Griff House was a large fruit, vegetable, and flower garden, which evidently served as the original of Hall Farm garden in *Adam Bede:*

> Adam walked round by the rick-yard, at present empty of ricks, to the little wooden gate leading into the garden—once the well-tended kitchen-garden of a manor-house; now, but for the handsome brick wall with stone coping that ran along one side of it, a true farmhouse garden, with hardy perennial flowers, unpruned fruit-trees, and kitchen vegetables growing together in careless, half-neglected abundance. In that leafy, flowery, bushy time, to look for any one in this garden was like playing at "hide-and-seek."

A third aspect of Griff House enters yet another novel, for the garden walk leading to the summer-house is transplanted to Lowick Manor in *Middlemarch*.

Just to the right of Griff House and barely visible in the field is Griff Pond; now suffering from many attempts to fill it in, the pond is not nearly as impressive as Eliot makes Round Pond in *The Mill on the Floss*, where Maggie and Tom fish:

> They were on their way to the Round Pool—that wonderful pool, which the floods had made a long while ago: no one knew how deep it was; and it was mysterious, too, that it should be almost a perfect round, framed in with willows and tall reeds, so that the water was only to be seen when you got close to the brink.

Other local spots are used later in the novel when Maggie runs away to the Gypsies after pushing Lucy into the mud of a pond in a garden near Garum Firs; the lane down which Maggie runs is Gypsy Lane, a trackway along which Gypsies actually did camp. The lane runs past Griff House toward Bulkington, a few miles southeast. Maggie

presently passed through the gate into the lane, not knowing where it would lead her. . . . She turned through the first gate that was not locked, and felt a delightful sense of privacy in creeping along by the hedgerows. . . . Sometimes she had to climb over high gates, but that was a small evil; she was getting out of reach very fast, and she should probably soon come within sight of Dunlow Common, or at least some other common. . . . At last, however, the green fields came to an end, and Maggie found herself looking through the bars of a gate into a lane with a wide margin of grass on each side of it.

Going on,

[s]he crept through the bars of the gate and walked on with new spirit. . . . [A]t the next bend in the lane Maggie actually saw the little semi-circular black tent with the blue smoke rising before it, which was to be her refuge from all the blighting obloquy that had pursued her in civilized life. She even saw a tall female figure by the column of

NUNEATON Griff House, George Eliot's home for twenty-one years, is now a hotel but has changed outwardly only a little; it is still a "trimly-kept, comfortable dwelling as old as the elms and chestnuts that shelter it. . . ."

smoke—doubtless the gypsy mother, who provided the tea and other groceries. . . .

About a mile west of Griff House is Arbury Mill, which is Darlcote Mill in *The Mill on the Floss;* exterior and interior are much changed, but the description of the area around the stream as seen from the bridge still rings true:

> Just by the red-roofed town the tributary Ripple flows with a lively current into the Floss. How lovely the little river is, with its dark, changing wavelets! . . . I remember those large dipping willows. I remember the stone bridge.
> And this is Darlcote Mill. . . . Even in this leafless time of departing February it is pleasant to look at—perhaps the chill damp season adds a charm to the trimly-kept comfortable dwelling house, as old as the elms and chestnuts that shelter it from the northern blast. The stream is brimful now, and lies high in this little withy plantation, and half drowns the grassy fringe of the croft in front of the house.

Eliot, though, transports the mill from the Ribble to the Idle River near where it enters the Trent (the Floss) in the vicinity of Gainsborough (St. Ogg's), so that it becomes a tidal river for the flood sequence.

The nearly exhausted shale quarries where Maggie meets Philip Wakem lie between Coventry Road and the Griff arm of the Coventry Canal; this was once a beautiful spot, but some of its naturalness has been spoiled. So closely associated has the area become with the novel that it is now known by Eliot's name, the Red Deeps:

> Insignificant I call it, because in height it was hardly more than a bank; . . . imagine this high bank crowned with trees, making an uneven wall for some quarter of a mile along the left side of Darlcote Mill and the pleasant fields behind it, bounded by the murmuring Ripple. Just where this line of bank sloped down again to the level, a by-road turned off and led to the other side of the rise, where it was broken into very capricious hollows and mounds by the working of an exhausted stone-quarry—so long exhausted that both mounds and hollows were now clothed with brambles and trees. . . .

The canal area enters a number of George Eliot's works; the *Brother and Sister* sonnets refer to the "brown canal," that part of the structure between Griff Hollows and Marston Bridge:

> Slowly the barges floated into view,
> Rounding a grassy hill to me sublime
> With some Unknown beyond it, whither flew
> The parting cuckoo toward a fresh spring-time.
>
> The wide-arched bridge, the scented elder-flowers,
> The wondrous water rings that died too soon,
> The echoes of the quarry, the still hours
> With white robe sweeping on the shadeless noon,
>
> Were but my growing self, are part of me,
> My present Past, my root of piety.

The quarry referred to was one of the Gypsy Lane quarries which were being worked during George Eliot's early childhood and not the Griff Hollows Quarry, which was opened later.

The three stories in *Scenes of Clerical Life* are set in this area and drawn from real events and people. "The Sad Fortunes of the Reverend Amos Barton" is set mostly in Chilvers Coton, itself virtually a part of Nuneaton, while parts of "Mr. Gilfil's Love Story"

and almost all of "Janet's Repentance" are set here. In the first, Mrs. Jennings lives at the Wharf, most probably the Wharf Inn on the Coventry Canal; also mentioned in this story is the Oldinport Arms, based on the Old Newdegate Arms Hotel on Newdegate Street, roughly where the present Newdegate Arms Hotel is situated. Here Mr. Hackel (a portrayal of Robert Evans) presides

> at the annual dinner of the Association for the Prosecution of Felons, held at the Oldinport Arms, [where] he contributed an additional zest to the conviviality on that occasion by informing the company that "the parson had given the Squire a lick with the rough side of his tongue."

Nuneaton becomes Milby in "Janet's Repentance," and the Nuneaton parish church, which Mary Ann Evans attended, is Milby Church. The town

> was a dingy-looking town, with a strong smell of tanning up one street and a great shaking of hand-looms up another; and even in that focus of aristocracy, Friar's Gate, the houses would not have seemed very imposing to the hasty and superficial glance of a passenger. . . .

From this it is apparent that the chief residential area was near the church on, say, Orchard Street (Church Street) and Friar's Gate (Bond Gate), and the nearby middle class attended services here:

> The well-dressed parishioners generally were very regular church-goers, and to the younger ladies and gentlemen I am inclined to think that the Sunday morning service was the most exciting event of the week; for few places could present a more brilliant show of out-door toilets than might be seen issuing from Milby church at one o'clock.

The home of J. W. Buchanan and his wife Nancy, the prototypes of the Dempsters,

> lay in Orchard Street, which opened on the prettiest outskirt of the town—the church, the parsonage, and a long stretch of green fields. It was an old-fashioned house, with an overhanging upper storey; outside, it had a face of rough stucco, and casement windows with green frames and shutters; inside, it was full of long passages, and rooms with low ceilings.

The house was destroyed in World War II, and the once-beautiful garden now forms part of the George Eliot Memorial Garden. Living on Orchard Street, three doors from the Dempsters on the Bridge Street side, was Mrs. John Robinson, the Mrs. Pettifer of "Janet's Repentance." In the story and in reality the incumbent was a nonresident; the Hon. and Rev. R. Bruce Stapleton becomes "the Hon. and Rev. Mr. Prendergast," who on special occasions "read the prayers—a high intellectual treat." The Reverend Stapleton's curate, the Rev. Hugh Hughes, served the parish for fifty-two years, during forty of which he was also headmaster of the grammar school, and officiated at most christenings, weddings, and funerals. The old grammar school where

> old Mr. Crewe, the curate, in a brown Brutus wig . . . on a week-day imparted the education of a gentleman—that is to say, an arduous inacquaintance with Latin through the medium of the Eton Grammar—to three pupils in the upper grammar-school

was badly damaged in the 1941 bombing; the tower, though, is the original. Sarah Hughes becomes "our good Mrs. Crewe. . . . Dear tiny woman!" who had the onerous task of preparing the Bishop's collation. George Eliot's Rev. Edgar Tryan and his persecutions are also real; Tryan is based on the Rev. J. E. Jones, Evangelical curate of the Stockingford Chapel (the chapel on "Paddiford Common"), and Jones did secure the Bishop's approval of and permission to deliver the Sunday-evening lectures in this parish church. The persecutions by the lawyer Robert Dempster and his cronies took place in 1829, and it was at the Bull Hotel, which becomes the Red Lion, on the Market Place, that Dempster and his anti-Tryanites meet over their brandy and water. The attorney, at what was thought to be the culmination of the effort to get rid of Tryan, appears "at the large upper window" where he addresses the anti-Evangelical mob. The Rev. J. E. Jones died of consumption, as does Mr. Tryan, but unlike Tryan he was not buried here but in the Withington, Gloucestershire, church. The Reverend Mr. Tryan, writes George Eliot,

> was buried as he had desired: there was no hearse, no mourning-coach; his coffin was borne by twelve of his humble hearers, who relieved each other by turns. But he was followed by a long procession of mourning friends, women as well as men.
>   Slowly, amid deep silence, the dark stream passed along Orchard Street. . . .
>   It was a cloudy morning, and had been raining when they left Holly Mount; but as they walked, the sun broke out, and the clouds were rolling off in large masses when they entered the churchyard. . . .

It should be noted that while Eliot generally portrays people realistically, Janet Dempster is not an accurate presentation of Nancy Buchanan.

The church gravestones and memorial tablets here tell much of George Eliot's people: the Buchanan (Dempster) family tablet is on the King Edward Road side of the churchyard, and nearby are the graves of Nancy's mother, Mrs. Wallington (Mrs. Raynor), and J. W. Buchanan's mother (Mamsey Dempster). Mrs. John Robinson (Mrs. Pettifer) is buried only a short distance from the Buchanan tomb. John Evarad, who was made into Mr. Jerome, William Cradock, who became Mr. Landor, and the William Bull family, who became the Phipps banking family, are also here.

Associated to some extent with Nuneaton, and specifically with the Old Newdegate Arms Hotel, is *Felix Holt, the Radical;* in 1832 serious rioting occurred in front of the hotel during the local elections. From the upper windows the magistrates read the Riot Act to the mob below, and in putting down the disturbance, during which the Scots Greys were called in, many persons, including the two magistrates, were injured. This, of course, is the source of the riot scene in *Felix Holt.*

NUNEHAM COURTENAY, Oxfordshire (pop. 277)
Nuneham Courtenay, 6 miles southeast of Oxford, is an 18th-century planned village; the houses on both sides of the main street were brought here from Stanton Harcourt in 1764 by the 1st Earl Harcourt. Then the medieval village lay around the old manor, but Harcourt rearranged the buildings here and added a magnificent park and a grand manor house that still exists today. The village is just over 2,100 acres in size, and Nuneham Courtenay Park alone consists of 1,200 acres; the enclosures (for deer, emu, and kangaroo) are well designed, and the park slopes down to the Thames.

One of the earliest literary associations of Nuneham Courtenay was with the Poet Laureate William Whitehead, the son of a Cambridge baker and a friend of Earl Harcourt, who wrote many of the inscriptions on the statues, tablets, and urns scattered through the park. Whitehead was unconcerned by the earl's mass displacement of the villagers and, indeed, suggested that their lot was improved since they were

> Well pleased to house their little train
> In happier mansions warm and dry.

Alexander Pope was an earlier 18th-century visitor to the Harcourt family's home; the 1st Viscount Harcourt was a close friend of Pope's, and the poet was a frequent guest after the family moved here in 1718. In fact, until recently there was a pane of red glass here on which Pope recorded the completion of the fifth volume of the *Iliad* (brought from Stanton Harcourt).

Among the 1st Earl Harcourt's guests were Horace Walpole and Fanny Burney, who left a detailed account of her August 1786 visit in her diary. With the King and Queen, who were already in the garden, she is annoyed at not being met in the "straggling, half-new, half-old, half-comfortable, half-forlorn" mansion and reacts:

> To arrive at a house where no mistress or master of it cared about receiving me; to wander about, a guest uninvited, a visitor unthought of; without even a room to go to, a person to inquire for, or even a servant to speak to!

In the 19th century the Harcourts again were involved with a literary figure, Edward Lear. George Granville Harcourt and his wife, Frances, Lady Waldegrave, invited Lear to Nuneham Courtenay first in August 1855, at which time Lady Waldegrave commissioned two paintings in Palestine if Lear went there as planned in the spring. Lear was again invited to the manor house in August 1860, this time to do two paintings of the grounds.

OARE, Somerset (pop. 85)   Situated on the East Lyn River at the Devon border, Oare is an extremely small parish and hamlet whose name has become enmeshed with that of R. D. Blackmore's *Lorna Doone.* Here in the Doone Valley (named after the book) is the little church where the elder Ridd is buried, where the younger Ridd pilfers the gutter lead to make bullets, and where the wedding of Lorna Doone and John Ridd is disturbed by a shotgun blast. A window on the south side of the nave is pointed out as the one through which Carver Doone shoots Lorna as she stands at the altar; from this window his markmanship would have been remarkable, if not technically impossible. The Snowe family mentioned in the novel is real, and Nicholas Snowe, whose death in 1691 is commemorated on a tablet in the church, is the Farmer Snowe of the novel. The church also contains a commemorative medallion portrait of Blackmore, who wrote part of the novel at Parsonage Farm; the farm is the scene of one raid. Locally, Snowe's house, next to the church, is thought to be the original of Plover's Barrows Farm. This is not the case, and the real house of John Ridd, Broomstreat Farm, is 2 miles east of Oare in Culbone.

ODCOMBE, Somerset (pop. 523)   Three miles west of Yeovil, in a countryside dotted with remote villages and farmhouses, are the hamlets of Upper and Lower Odcombe, known jointly as Odcombe. Odcombe was the birthplace of Thomas Coryate around 1577. His father was the rector of Odcombe, and Thomas was born in the old parsonage. Virtually nothing is known about Coryate's life until he went up to Oxford in 1596. He appears to have lived aimlessly for a number of years and returned to Odcombe from London in early March 1606, when his father died. According to a traditional story, because of Coryate's ability to keep the body from decomposing the Rev. George Coryate was not buried until mid-April.

Sometime in May 1608 Coryate left England on the first of his extensive travels and produced *Coryats Crudities.* Before his second trip, in 1612, he returned to Odcombe, gave a valedictory address at the market cross, and, possibly as a pagan gesture, hung his shoes in the Odcombe Church, where they remained for more than a century. The church contains a memorial window.

OARE R.D.   Blackmore places the shooting of Lorna Doone here at the altar of the 14th-century Oare Church in the Exmoor Valley: "the sound of a shot rang through the church.... Lorna fell across my knees, when I was going to kiss her ... a flood of blood came out upon the yellow wood of the altar steps; and at my feet lay Lorna...."

OLD BOLINGBROKE, Lincolnshire Situated 3½ miles west of Spilsby on the southern edge of the Lincolnshire Wolds, the rambling hamlet of Old Bolingbroke appears a place of little consequence, but it is the most historic and probably the finest village in the Wolds. The first Norman Earl of Lincoln built the castle here in the 12th century, and two centuries later John of Gaunt, just married to Blanche, the 1st Duke of Lancaster's heir, came here to live. In the castle on (perhaps) April 3, 1367, Henry of Bolingbroke, later Henry IV, was born. Local tradition holds that Geoffrey Chaucer was a frequent visitor to the castle and is thought to have been here shortly after Blanche's death in December 1369 because of the meeting with John of Gaunt depicted in *The Book of the Duchess:*

> . . . so at the laste
> I was war of a man in blak,
> That sat and had yturned his bak
> To an ook, an huge tree.
> "Lord," thoght I, "who may that be?
> What ayleth hym to sitten her?"

OLD PARK, County Durham (pop. 820) Three miles northeast of Bishop Auckland, Old Park is in an area of County Durham which can be extremely wild and desolate. Old Park Farm was the 18th-century home of Dr. Thomas Wharton, Thomas Gray's friend; the poet was frequently here in the 1760s and advised Wharton on his gardens and experimental farm.

OLD SARUM, Wiltshire At the eastern end of the old Roman Portway, which linked it with Silchester, Old Sarum has a special place in English history. Little remains but vast earthworks and foundations, but the view down to Salisbury, a little more than 1 mile to the south, is impressive. Salisbury, indeed, is the successor to Old Sarum, and its name was originally New Sarum. Old Sarum was the general site of the Roman fortress Sorbiodunum, but the earthworks strongly suggest the possibility of an Iron Age occupation, and some scattered remains of that period have been found. The huge mound of multiple earthworks, covering 56 acres, was in use by the Saxons, who called it Searobyrg, "the dry town."

In 1070 William the Conqueror assembled his victorious forces here before disbanding them; he later fortified Old Sarum and created a new bishopric here. Bishop Osmund built the great Norman cathedral (the foundations are in outline), but the hill location was so exposed that the tower suffered considerably from the weather. When the castle was seized from the Bishop by the King's forces in 1139, the difficulties also became personal. The cathedral and its clergy were directly in conflict with the castle and its forces and directly in line with any fighting to the northwest. Petitions to move to the lower meadows were made to the Pope, and the reasons were clearly set forth: the military interfered with the free movement of the clergy; the site was exposed and uncomfortable, water was lacking, and sanitary conditions were appalling. The clergy even added, pathetically, that the white glare from the chalk escarpment was impairing their sight. Papal permission was forthcoming, and on April 28, 1220, the cornerstone for the new cathedral was laid in Salisbury. Seven years later Old Sarum Cathedral was abandoned, and within a short period the town was a desolate quarry for builders.

Even so, when John Leland visited the site in 1535 and wrote of it in the *Itinerary,* part of the cathedral and the Chapel of Our Lady were still standing. Samuel Pepys visited the site on his way to Salisbury in June of 1668 and notes:

> [B]efore I came to the town [Salisbury] I saw a great fortification, and there 'light, and to it and in it; and find it prodigious, so as to fright me to be in it all alone at that time of night, it being dark. I understand, since, it to be that that is called Old Sarum.

Daniel Defoe came here when gathering material for *A Tour thro' the Whole Island of Great Britain;* he was especially interested in the number of good old remains in this area of England:

> Old *Sarum* is as remarkable as any of these, where there is a double Entrenchment, with a deep Grasse, or Ditch, to either of them; the Area about 100 Yards in Diameter, taking in the whole Crown of the Hill, and thereby rendering the Ascent very difficult: Near this, there is one Farm House, which is all the Remains I could see of any Town in or near the Place, for the Encampment has no Resemblance of a Town; and yet this is call'd the Borough of old *Sarum,* and sends two Members to Parliament, *who,* those Members can justly say, *they represent,* would be hard for them to answer.

Defoe was one of the first to comment on Old Sarum as a rotten borough. Indeed, until the Reform Act of 1832 the borough returned two members, and a stone in a nearby field, known as Election Acre, marks the site where local elections were held. William Cobbett also commented on local politics in his *Rural Rides.*

There is surprisingly little use of Old Sarum in literature; the best-known use, perhaps, occurs in Thomas Hardy's "On the Western Circuit" (*Life's Little Ironies and a Few Crusted Characters*). It is "to the earthworks of Old Melchester [Salisbury]" that Charles Bradford Raye and Anna walk from Melchester.

OLNEY, Buckinghamshire (pop. 2,651) The northern part of Buckinghamshire is noted for its flat and gentle countryside, many little rivers, and marshes. Olney, happily situated in this setting along the Ouse River (often called the Great Ouse to distinguish the river from others of that name), retains its 18th-century character. Its early economy was based partly on the lacemaking cottage industry; and indeed, until the 1950s handmade lace was still a visible industry here. An early tanning industry also survives. Olney is perhaps best known as the original site of the Shrove Tuesday pancake race, a tradition which began here in the 15th century.

For almost twenty years Olney was the home of the poet William Cowper; he came here from Huntingdon in September 1767 with Mrs. Morley Unwin to convalesce after a serious illness. The two lived in the rectory with John Newton, the curate, until their own residence was available in early December. Their house, Orchard Side (now the Cowper and Newton Museum), on the High Street, is of red brick and has a "prison like appearance"; the poet and Mrs. Unwin lived in the western half of the house for sixteen years. It was a small place (the parlor was only 13 feet square), close to the most squalid part of Olney. A number of Cowper's letters and works refer to the depressed economic conditions and to the lace industry here. He also comments on the dull life: "Occurrences here," he writes, " . . . are rare as cucumbers at Christmas." In 1771 he began working on the hymns he contributed to the *Olney Hymns* and by 1773 finished most of the sixty-eight. Early in January of that year Cowper again became mentally deranged, and even Mrs. Unwin was unable to do much to help him; Cowper, in fact, accused her of poisoning his food. He moved back into the vicarage in April, attempted suicide in October, and remained with Newton for thirteen months. Upon his return home, he began again to keep animals, including three leverets, Puss, Tiney, and Bess, all males despite their names, and took up gardening in earnest. Part of *The Task*, written during this period, is devoted to "The Garden":

> The morning finds the self-sequestered man
> Fresh for his task, intend what task he may;
> . . . if the garden with its many cares,
> All well repaid, demand him, he attends
> The welcome call, conscious how much the hand
> Of lubbard Labour needs his watchful eye,
> Oft loitering lazily, if not o'erseen,
> Or misapplying his unskilful strength.
> Nor does he govern only or direct,
> But much performs himself. . . .

A 1783 letter to Newton describes the love for his Olney garden:

> The very stones in the garden-walls are my intimate acquaintance. I should miss almost the minutest object, and be disaggreeably affected by its removal, and am persuaded that were it possible I could leave this incommodious nook for a twelvemonth, I should return to it again with rapture, and be transported with the sight of objects which to all the world beside would be at least indifferent.

The Task was the result of Lady Austen's request for a blank-verse poem on the subject of a sofa; one subject led to another, and Cowper "brought forth," as his advertisement to the first edition states, " . . . instead of the trifle which he at first intended, a serious affair—a Volume!" Cowper first met Lady Austen here in the summer of 1781, and visits between the two were frequent. In October 1782 she told the poet a story remembered from her childhood; this tale became "The Diverting History of John Gilpin."

At the back of Orchard Side is a summerhouse where the poet often worked; a Cowper Memorial Chapel in the church has a window showing Cowper, Newton, and the leverets. Cowper and Mrs. Unwin left Olney for Weston Underwood, 1½ miles away, in 1786.

ONGAR, Essex (pop. 1,142) The more proper but seldom-used name of this village, about 23 miles northeast of London, is Chipping Ongar, but even the post office uses the shortened form. The lane to the church was the center of the medieval community, and behind the church is a castle mound which may have been strengthened before the Norman Conquest. In 1811 Isaac Taylor, an engraver and dissenting minister who served as pastor here for eighteen years, moved his family from Colchester to Castle House, just under the shadow of the motte. Jane and Ann Taylor already had published *Original Poems for Infant Minds by Several Young Persons, Rhymes for the Nursery* (which contains Jane Taylor's "Twinkle, Twinkle, Little Star"), and a volume of children's hymns; here they concentrated on more hymn writing. In 1814, when Ann married, the Taylors moved to Peaked Farm; Jane left for Ilfracombe, Devon, and Marazion, Cornwall, with her brother, but after August 1816, she was rarely away from Ongar. In 1823, after a short trip to Olney, Buckinghamshire, she became ill and died on April 13, 1824; she was buried in the churchyard of the chapel, where a simple monument marks her grave.

ORLESTONE, Kent (pop. 383) Situated on the edge of the Romney Marshes 5 miles southwest of Ashford, Orlestone and the immediately surrounding area are barely above sea level and are cut by numerous deep dikes. Smuggling occurred here as late as the 19th century, but now much of the country is used for the grazing of sheep and the raising of tulips. Capel House in Orlestone was the home of Joseph Conrad from the end of June 1910 until early 1919, when he went to Wye before going on to Bishopsbourne. He finished *Victory* here in June 1914, immediately prior to a trip to his homeland, Poland, in July, the last peaceful month in Europe for some time. Conrad worked on *Chance* and "Within the Tides" while living in Orlestone.

OSBORNE, Isle of Wight The 1,000-acre Osborne Park, in the north of the island, was purchased in 1845 by Queen Victoria as a quiet retreat for the royal family, and the existing 18th-century Osborne House was enlarged by Thomas Cubitt under the direction of Prince Albert. The south wing of the house is now a convalescent home for officers of the Army, Navy, and Air Force.

The former royal residence is almost always associated with the royal family and with Alfred, Lord Tennyson, who from 1862 on was often here with his family when the Queen was in residence. Tennyson's warm personal relationship with the soverign lasted until his death. A far different relationship, a working one, existed between the Queen and Edward Lear. An April 1846 publication, by Lear, *Illustrated Excursions in Italy,* caught the Queen's attention, and she requested his services as a drawing master. He began a series of twelve lessons here on July 15, 1846, but found life more difficult than he had imagined since Osborne House was in the process of being rebuilt. The lessons begun here were finished later in London.

OSWESTRY, Shropshire (pop. 12,300) Tucked between pastureland and the isolated hill country of the Welsh border 17 miles northwest of Shrewsbury, Oswestry has had a turbulent history which has left deep scars. Its name is based on the legend of St. Oswald, for here in 641, as the *Anglo-Saxon Chronicle* relates:

> Oswald, king of Northumbria, was slain by Penda the Mercian at *Maserfeld* [*Oswestry, Sa*] on 5 August, and his body was buried at Bardney. His holiness and miracles were afterwards abundantly made manifest through-

out this island, and his hands are at Bamburgh uncorrupted.

The field in question is said to be the one across from the grammar school. After the battle St. Oswald's body was nailed to a tree, and somehow it fell to the ground, where it was retrieved by an eagle. St. Oswald's Well, in a nearby dingle, is said to be the spot where waters gushed forth as the body was raised from the ground. One other feature of the town is notable: the Croeswylan (Weeping Stone) on Morda Street is the base of a cross erected in 1559 during a visitation of the plague that carried off 1 in every 7 persons in Oswestry.

A native Shropshire poet, Thomas Churchyard, who was born in Shrewsbury around 1520, wrote of the town:

> As Ozwestry, a pretie towne full fine,
> Which may be lov'd, be likte and praysed both.
> It stands so trim, and is maintayned so cleane,
> And peopled is with folk that well doe meane:
> That it deserves to be enrolled and shryned
> In each good breast, and every manly mynde.

Another native Shropshire poet was born just outside the town; Plas Wilmot was the birthplace of the World War I poet Wilfred Owen on March 18, 1893. After receiving his early education here, he entered Birkenhead Institute. Owen was killed in France a week before the armistice in November 1918.

OTTER RIVER, Devon Flowing 24 miles southwest past Honiton and Ottery St. Mary to enter the English Channel at Otterton, the Otter River is one of many in England of the same name, most of which were named for the animals which inhabited them. Michael Drayton in the first song of his *Poly-Olbion* correctly comments on this reason for the naming of the stream:

> . . . *Otrey* (that her name doth of the Otters take,
> Abounding in her banks). . . .

Drayton also provides a place in history for the Otter and Axe Rivers:

> For where
> Great *Brute* first disembarqu't his wandring Trojans, there
> ∫ His offspring (after long expulst the Inner land,
> When they the *Saxon* power no longer could withstand)
> Found refuge in their flight; where *Ax* and *Otrey* first
> Gave these poor soules to drinke, opprest with grievous thirst.

Samuel Taylor Coleridge, a native of Ottery St. Mary, once referred to the Otter River as that "wild streamlet of the West" along which as a child he "skimmed the smooth thin stone"; here he noted the banks of "willows grey" and sand which

> veined with various dyes,
> Gleam'd through thy bright transparence. . . .

While his later recollection is clearly pleasant, Coleridge did have an extremely unpleasant experience with the river. In the autumn of 1780, he ran away from home after being tormented by his brother Frank. He rested on a small hill that sloped down to the banks of the Otter, where, after reflecting on the misery others must be feeling for him, he fell asleep.

The night was stormy, and, feeling cold, Coleridge dreamed that he was pulling a blanket over him; in so doing, he rolled down the hillside to within only a few feet of the river's edge but did not waken, it is claimed, until about 4 A.M. He was discovered by a search party after he cried out for help; he was so cold, wet, and stiff that he was unable to walk.

William Makepeace Thackeray, who uses the Exeter and Ottery St. Mary areas under the names Chatteris and Clavering St. Mary in *Pendennis,* changes the Otter River into the Brawl. He describes it as "the rapid and shining Brawl winding down from the town and skirting the woods of Clavering Park" and as a stream which had been spoiled "as a trout-stream" by the factory owners. He also mentions the river in *The Newcomes.*

OTTERBOURNE, Hampshire (pop. 809) This fairly large south Hampshire village, on the main road from Winchester to Southampton, is located on the Itchen River. It is renowned for its support of the 19th-century Oxford movement, principally by Charlotte Mary Yonge, who was born here in 1823. Elderfield, where she was born, is on the east side of the village's main street, and she lived here for the greater part of her life. Educated at home by her father, who designed and built the local church, she came under the influence of John Keble, vicar of the neighboring village of Hursley and of Otterbourne from 1836 to 1866. With Keble's instruction and encouragement, Charlotte Yonge wrote novels in support of the Oxford movement, among them *The Heir of Redclyffe* and *The Daisy Chain,* and devoted all the profits from her writings to religious causes. She died on March 24, 1901, and was buried in the Otterbourne churchyard. A simple granite molding marks her grave, which is located at the foot of the commemorative cross to Keble.

OTTERBURN, Northumberland (pop. 350) Northumberland has often been described as a battlefield, not a county, and this village has certainly made its contribution to the history of the area. Today Otterburn is a pleasant and peaceful village. At Lammastide, 1388 (one ballad sets the date as Wednesday, August 19, under the light of a full moon), the battle between Hotspur (Henry Percy) and the 2d Earl of Douglas took place near here. Sent from Alnwick by his father, the 1st Earl of Northumberland, Hotspur encountered the Douglas in Newcastle upon Tyne, where, during a two-day skirmish, the Scotsman relieved Hotspur of his horse and his pennon and threatened to raise the pennon from the highest point of Dalkeith Castle. Douglas taunted Percy to attack that night, a challenge that was let pass, and the Scots band moved north, pillaging and burning everything in its path. Reaching Otterburn, about 30 miles from Newcastle, the Scots wanted to make for Carlisle to join up with the rest of their forces, but the Douglas would hear none of this; he wanted to remain and goad Hotspur into battle. The Northumbrians, except for Hotspur and the other Percys, were convinced erroneously that all Scotland stood behind the earl. Hotspur, in a rash moment, with 600 knights and 8,000 infantrymen, who were weary after a 32-mile march, attacked the Scots troops. The battle was a disaster for both sides: the Earl of Douglas was killed; the English were totally defeated; Hotspur was taken prisoner; and the burn ran red with blood for days. Numerous ballads celebrate the battle and, incidentally, the location:

The Otterbourne's a bonnie burn,
  'T is pleasant there to be. . . .

The same ballad describes the meeting between the Douglas and Hotspur:

When Percy wi the Douglas met,
  I wat he was fu fain;
They swakked their swords, till sair they swat,
And the blood ran down like rain.

But Percy with his good broad sword,
  That could so sharply wound.
Has wounded Douglas on the brow,
  Till he fell to the ground.

Bishop Thomas Percy's *Reliques of Ancient English Poetry* includes "The Battle of Otterbourne," and Francis J. Child's *English and Scottish Popular Ballads* contains numerous versions of the ballad including at least one that must be spurious. Sir Walter Scott's "Battle of Otterburn" includes what has traditionally been ascribed to the Douglas, a premonition of his own death:

But I hae dreamed a dreary dream,
Beyond the Isle of Skye,
I saw a dead man win a fight
And I think that man was I.

The ballad "The Battle of Chevy Chase" is often thought to be an accurate description of this battle but is, in fact, a combination of the Battles of Otterburn, Homildon Hill, and Piperden.

OTTERY ST. MARY, Devon (pop. 4,005) Ottery St. Mary, a market town on the Otter River 12 miles northeast of Exeter, is one of numerous small English towns with an obscure history. Only 6 miles southwest of Honiton, it has been involved in the making of Honiton lace since Elizabethan times; this is one of the few true cottage industries still being carried on in England, primarily because technology has not yet found a way to duplicate the extremely intricate process which may include 400 or more separate bobbins just to plait one pattern. The town still keeps its 17th-century tradition of rolling a blazing tar barrel through the street on November 5 to celebrate Guy Fawkes Day, and no doubt as a child Samuel Taylor Coleridge watched the annual event. The vicarage (gone) of Ottery St. Mary was the poet's birthplace on October 21, 1772; his father, the Rev. John Coleridge, was both the parish priest and the headmaster of the Free Grammar School, sometimes known as Old King's School. Coleridge had a relatively uneventful childhood except for an attempt at running away in the autumn of 1780, after he was rather badly tormented by an older brother, Frank. His father died quite suddenly in October 1781, and young Samuel was sent to Christ's Hospital in London. He returned to Ottery St. Mary seldom after that; when he did return at a much later date to see his brother Frank, he was informed that because of his known unorthodox views he was unwelcome. Coleridge was far more closely attached to the town than it was to him. The only item commemorating

the poet here is a small, badly tarnished plaque which merely notes the town as his place of birth.

William Makepeace Thackeray's mother and stepfather, Maj. Carmichael Smyth, settled in Larkbeare, a spacious Georgian residence about 1½ miles from Ottery St. Mary in the Tale Water Valley, when Thackeray was a student at Charterhouse, London, and he frequently spent his school holidays here. In *Pendennis* Ottery St. Mary becomes Clavering St. Mary, the "little town" near which Pendennis's home, Fairoaks, is situated. Fairoaks is modeled on Larkbeare, although Thackeray takes some slight license with geography. Thackeray describes the town from the prospect of Fairoaks:

Looking at the little old town of Clavering St. Mary from the London road as it runs by the lodge at Fairoaks, and seeing the rapid and shining Brawl winding down from the town and skirting the woods of Clavering Park, and the ancient church tower and peaked roofs of the houses rising up amongst the trees and old walls, . . . the place appears to be so cheery and comfortable that many a traveller's heart must have yearned towards it from the coach-top. . . . Clavering is rather prettier at a distance than it is on a closer acquaintance. The town, so cheerful of aspect a few furlongs off, looks very blank and dreary. Except on market days there is nobody in the streets. The clack of a pair of pattens echoes through half the place, and you may hear the creaking of the rusty old ensign at the "Clavering Arms," without being disturbed by any other noise.

The implication is that Fairoaks is virtually in the town; Larkbeare is not. And, indeed, the "Fairoaks lawn [which] comes down to the little river Brawl" has been transported to the adjacent valley just as has Clavering Park on the other side of the house. The original of the Abbey Church of Clavering St. Mary is undeniably the Collegiate Church of Ottery St. Mary:

On the south side of the market rises up the church, with its great grey towers, of which the sun illuminates the delicate carving; deepening the shadows of the huge buttresses, and gilding the glittering windows and flaming vanes. The image of the patroness of the church was wrenched out of the porch many centuries ago.

The Queen Anne rectory, "a stout broad-shouldered brick house," was the one in which Coleridge was born.

OULTON BROAD, Suffolk (pop. 4,644) Located in the triangular expanse of land known as the Norfolk Broads, Oulton Broad is one of the more than thirty areas which contain open expanses of water with navigable channels. Despite centuries of belief that these lakes were glacially formed, they are, in a sense, artificial, in that they resulted from repeated diggings for peat. Oulton Hall and its summerhouse (both gone), which overlooked the Broad, became George Borrow's home in 1840, when he married Mary Skepper Clarke, a persistent widow, who, it is said, persevered "in her intention of capturing him." Borrow had spent a substantial part of the summer of 1832 here with the Skepper family; he then met the young widow.

Most of Borrow's remaining years, with the exception of the five following his wife's death in 1869, were spent here, where he worked on *Lavengro, The Bible in Spain*, and *The Romany Rye* in the summerhouse, which had been converted into a library-cum-study. His affinity with and love of the East Anglian Gypsies created numerous problems locally, as Borrow encouraged their local encampments. Sir Samuel Morton Peto of nearby Somerleyton Hall objected strenuously to Borrow's permission for the Romanies to camp anywhere on his estate near St. Michael's Church, and Borrow ridiculed Peto in *The Romany Rye* in the person of Mr. Flamson Flaming. It is possible that Borrow's portrait is not merely a reaction to Peto's objections to the Gypsies, since Peto managed (possibly unscrupulously) to buy from Borrow the right to run a railway from Lowestoft to Reedham over Borrow's property at an enormous profit. Borrow returned in 1874 to Oulton Hall, where he could often be seen walking across the Broads, cape streaming out behind and an extremely large and unfashionable hat perched on his head. He lived here until his death on July 26, 1881; he was buried in the churchyard at Brompton, London, but there is a memorial window in the church at Oulton.

The Elizabethan Oulton High House, which is often erroneously located in nearby Oulton rather than Oulton Broad, belonged to the Fastolf family, whose member Sir John is said to have been made into the unforgettable Sir John Falstaff by William Shakespeare. The church at one time contained brasses to both Sir John, who died in 1459, and his wife Catherine, but only the matrices in the chancel floor exist to show their position.

OVINGDEAN, Sussex (pop. 476) Tucked into a deep valley of the South Downs 3 miles southeast of Brighton, Ovingdean is comfortably settled in a pastoral area. It has an impressive Saxon and Norman church with Roman tiles worked into a blocked-up north-wall door. The village and its history come into William Harrison Ainsworth's *Ovingdean Grange*. Noting that "fairer spot than this cannot be found amidst the whole range of the South Downs—nor one commanding more delightful views," Ainsworth describes the village:

> [I]mmediately beneath us ... is a pretty little village, nestling amid a grove of trees, above whose tops you may discern the tower of a small, grey old church. With this village we trust to make you more intimately acquainted by-and-by. It is Ovingdean. On the left, and nearer the sea, you may discern another, and considerably larger village than Ovingdean....
> Behind and around on every side, save towards the sea, are downs—downs with patches of purple heather or grey gorse clothing their sides—downs with small holts wthin their coombs, partially cultivated, or perfectly bare—everywhere downs.

The grange itself, he declares, "as it now appears, is a fair-proportioned, cheerful-looking domicile, and with its white walls and pleasant garden, full of arbutuses, laurestines, holms, and roses, offers a very favourable specimen of a Sussex farmhouse," but in 1651, the time of Charles II's supposed escape over the South Downs, Ovingdean Grange was already old,

> having been built in the reign of Henry the Eighth. Constructed of red brick, chequered with diamonds formed of other bricks, glazed, and of darker hue, mingled with flints, it seemed destined to endure for ages,

and presented a very striking frontage, owing to the bold projections of its bay-windows with their stone posts and lintels, its deep arched portal with a stone escutcheon above it, emblazoned with the arms of the Maunsels, at that time its possessors, its stone quoins and cornices, its carved gables, its high roof, covered with tiles encrusted with orange-tawny mosses and lichens, and its triple clusters of tall and ornamented chimney-shafts.

Local legend holds that Charles lodged here during his escape to France; however, license has been taken—Charles was never east of Brighton.

OVINGHAM, Northumberland (pop. 562) In the 19th century the village of Ovingham situated on the Tyne River, contained a public school, Ovingham School, to which Robert Smith Surtees was sent at some time, but he left for the grammar school in Durham in 1818. Although the dates of his attendance are not known, he chronicled the everyday events of school life here in detail and forty years later used the information in *Mr. Sponge's Sporting Tour* and, probably, in *Hillingdon Hall*. The school was kept by the Rev. James Birkett, who probably survives as Mr. Slooman, the schoolmaster of Hillingdon Hall:

> Slooman being on best of terms with himself, coughed and hemmed and stroked his chin, and looked complacently around, as much as to say, "I am Sir Oracle, and when I ope my lips let no dog bark." He was a little, bristly-headed, badger-eyed, pedantic, radical schoolmaster, who formed his own glebe. . . .

No doubt also the Reverend Mr. Birkett, who had "the most ludicrous propensity for making and hoarding up walking sticks" and who "could not see or hear of a promising sapling but that he would be at it and, having converted it into a walking stick, would add it to his already redundant collection," is Mr. Jogglebury Crowdey of *Mr. Sponge's Sporting Tour*. In this novel Crowdey always sneaks out at night to steal his neighbor's saplings, carve them into "gibbey-sticks," and put them aside as knobbly investments for his descendants.

OWERMOIGNE, Dorset (pop. 298) The little village of Owermoigne, 6 miles southeast of Dorchester, lies just north of the road from Weymouth to Wareham and 3 miles from a portion of the Dorset coast which consists of high cliffs and unpopulated downland. This seclusion enabled the village to engage in a great deal of 19th-century smuggling. The Gothic church was rebuilt in 1883, and many of its early features have disappeared.

Owermoigne becomes Nether Moynton in Thomas Hardy's Wessex and is the background for "The Distracted Preacher" (*Wessex Tales*). The church is no longer as Hardy describes it:

> The light showed them to be close to the singing-gallery stairs, under which lay a heap of lumber of all sorts, but consisting mostly of decayed framework, pews, panels, and pieces of flooring, that from time to time had been removed from their original fixings in the body of the edifice and replaced by new.

Here are the "little barrels bound with wood hoops" which Lizzie calls "tubs of spirit that have accidentally floated over in the dark from France." Hardy describes the standard method of tapping the keg and drawing off the contents; the preacher asks, "How do you wish me to get it out—with a gimlet, I suppose?"

> "No, I'll show you," said his interesting companion; and she held up with her other hand a shoemaker's awl and a hammer. "You must never do these things with a gimlet, because the wood-dust gets in; and when the buyers pour out the brandy that would tell them that the tub had been broached. An awl makes no dust, and the hole nearly closes up again. Now tap one of the hoops forward."

The liquid was replaced by taking mouthfuls of water and "putting . . . lips to the hole, where it was sucked in . . . from pressure." The house where Lizzie Newbury lives is drawn from the house opposite the rectory:

> It stood within a garden-hedge, and seemed to be roomy and comfortable. . . .
> As he now lived there, Stockdale felt it unnecessary to knock at the door. . . . He advanced to the parlour, as the front room was called, though its stone floor was scarcely disguised by the carpet, which only overlaid the trodden areas, leaving sandy deserts under the furniture. But the room looked snug and cheerful.

However, the orchard does not adjoin her garden. The excisemen make their raid here, and the place where an exciseman is tied to a tree is Warmwell Cross, the point at which the Dorchester and Weymouth roads (A352 and A353) split.

OWLPEN, Gloucestershire (pop. 79) A tiny Cotswold village with a lovely manor house dating in part to Elizabethan times and placed in a setting of yew trees, Owlpen is 2½ miles east of Dursley and midway to Nailsworth and sits in a hollow of the hills. It has a curious old church (redesigned in 1828), whose prize possession is the cross on the altar; made of alabaster, it is set with twenty-nine amethysts. Robert Bloomfield, the Suffolk poet, visited here and recorded his impressions in his journal:

> The village of Owlpen stands under the hanging woods at the top of Uley Vale; it is very small, and near its curious and obscure church runs the little rill, with several natural cascades.. . .The country immediately round this valley on the high ground, is every where intersected by stone walls; for stone, a brick thickness, more or less, is the invariable consequence of digging ten inches into the ground; they are merely piled, without mortar, easily made, and as easily mended; a strange desolate appearance!

OXFORD, Oxfordshire and Berkshire (pop. 94,900, including 1,260 in university colleges and halls) Among the most famous university towns in the world, Oxford appears to be carefully tucked in between the Cherwell (pronounced "char'well") and Thames Rivers. One of the little-known and surprising facts about the city is its location: it is situated in two counties, Oxfordshire and Berkshire. Within easy commuting distance of London, 63 miles to the southeast, the town has a recorded history spanning more than 1,000 years, and its attendant influence has led to cloth, sheep, cars, shoes, a religious movement, and even a marmalade being named after it. The town's early history is somewhat obscure, and

most of the early beliefs concerning its founding must be regarded as legend. The lively old innovator Geoffrey of Monmouth (who may have studied here about 1129) in one of his more amusing fictions has Oxford and the university system founded more than 1,000 years before the birth of Christ by Memphric, a great-grandson of Brutus and a direct descendant of Aeneas. A little more accurately, Oxford was the site of a nunnery founded in the early 8th century by Frideswide, a king's daughter who was betrothed to King Algar of Leicester, a man whom she disliked intensely and from whom she was forced to flee. In terms of actual recorded history, there is no explicit record before a 910 entry in the *Anglo-Saxon Chronicle*, but from then on Oxford's history is well documented.

Alfred the Great is often credited with founding an academic institution here, but this is unlikely since his death in 899 occurred more than two centuries before the first scholar can be identified. What is true is that Alfred played an important role in the building of the first real town here when he realized the tactical importance of militarizing the Oxenforde vicinity if the Wessex kingdom was to remain free of Danish intrusion. Oxford thus became a buffer between the Danelaw of the north and the Wessex of the south. It appears that the early town was constructed all at once and was completely walled, with walks laid out symmetrically. Indeed, this basic plan is still preserved in the main streets: at the central crossing of Carfax (that is, Quatre Foix, "four ways," or Carrefours) four roads radiate at right angles to each other. The long-anticipated problems with the Danes materialized in 1009, when the town was beseiged; for the next six years or so, it changed hands fairly often, but in 1015 the two forces, after protracted negotiations, reached a peace agreement. The town was by all accounts quite prosperous and by the middle of the 11th century had a population in excess of 3,000.

By 1071 the construction of the castle had begun, and the donjon's early completion may have acted as a deterrent to uprisings against the Normans. What happened to Oxford between 1071 and the Domesday survey (1086) is an enigma, but clearly some kind of disaster occurred. The population dropped by more than two-thirds, and more than half of the houses were recorded as "waste" and unoccupied. A visitation of the plague would probably not have escaped record, so the most reasonable explanation may be that the Normans engaged in a short reign of terror to subdue a very independent Oxford population.

By the 12th century numerous religious houses, Franciscan, Dominican, Carmelite, and Augustinian, had been established, and their scholastic inclinations were well known. However, what actually brought about early academia is not known. At first, a few scholars arrived from Paris; the English, though, continued to seek their educations abroad, but soon they joined the small bands of scholars here or at Cambridge. The critical influence was brought to bear on Oxbridge when Louis VII expelled all English scholars and visitors because of an academic-royal dispute and Henry II retaliated by forbidding the English to go abroad for study. Thus, in only a few weeks more than 2,000 students and masters, suddenly finding themselves in England without a real academic center, ended up in Oxford and Cambridge.

Attitudes developed which later were solidified into those called "the town" and "the gown." The town made certain that the gown population paid for the inconveniences it created and looked upon the academic community as a plague of thieves, lechers, and drunkards. The gown, in its turn, believed itself beyond town corporation power and gradually usurped the powers of the civic body, beginning what turned out to be a 700-year struggle over rights. While the early fault is not easy to determine, it is clear that the town was guilty of charging exorbitant rents, prices, and interest rates and that the gown's initial arrogance and freedom from secular control helped keep the warfare going. Royal favor descended on the university and royal disfavor on the town, and the church generally proved indulgent to the gown. It is no wonder there was extensive town-gown fighting; Hastings Rashdall, the Oxford historian, comments that there is probably not a yard of ground between St. Martin's and St. Mary's where blood was not spilled in these disputes.

The first recorded major killing and riot occurred in 1209, when two innocent clerks were hanged by the townspeople for the murder of a local woman; the last-known killing occurred in 1857, when a townsman stabbed a gownsman to death with a butcher knife. The riot in 1209 caused the gownsmen to leave en masse, and the "balance" was not restored until five years later, when a papal legate set the conditions of penance on the town: reduction of rents, an annual feast for 100 poor scholars, an annual fine of 52 shillings for the relief of poor scholars, public penance of the involved townsmen, and the church's right to mete out all punishments for scholars.

The most horrific bloodletting came in February 1355 when students (who had probably already had a good deal to drink) complained that a local vintner's wine was sour and unfit for human consumption before throwing a tankard and its contents in his face. The ensuing town-gown riot continued for the better part of three days with unusually barbaric fighting. Anthony à Wood relates: "[T]he townsmen subtilly and secretly sent about four-score armed men into the parish of St. Giles in the north suburb," where they attacked "certain scholars walking after dinner in Beaumont Fields." The students barricaded the gates; 2,000 townsmen and country folk fought the gownsmen "till after vesper-tide" and then broke through the West Gate. The university scholars fled to their quarters, only to be dragged out, beaten, and killed. The fighting continued two more days, and at the end sixty-three scholars and an untold number of townsmen had died, nineteen halls were destroyed at least in part, and numerous shops and houses were burned. A year later the commission of inquiry appointed by the crown handed down its verdict, and the settlement found for the university. The town was stripped of most of its remaining power, fined in perpetuity, and made to perform a yearly penance of celebrating a mass for the dead scholars, in front of the university community, at St. Mary's. Only in 1825 was the Lord Mayor able to demand this humiliating penance be revoked.

Even though both the crown and the church re-

garded the university with extreme favor, teaching was generally indifferent, if it existed at all, until 1221, when the Dominican friars established their primary seat of learning here. Three years later the Franciscans emulated them, and perhaps modern Oxford began to exist at this point. A hall, established from a grant by William of Durham at the end of the 13th century for four M.A.'s to live and pursue the study of theology, became University College, the first-established college at Oxford. Meanwhile John de Balliol, also of County Durham, maintained a number of scholars here as a penance; his wife Dervorguilla (Devorguila) carried out the penance after his death, and Balliol College came into existence. The Bishop of Rochester, Walter de Merton, turned over his extensive landholdings here and an endowment to the university; the statutes he devised for Merton College became the model for all other collegiate units and, as amended, are in use today. The 14th-century building of the first lecture room, near the present-day Old Schools Quadrangle, pretty well established the university.

The student body continued to live scattered throughout the town, although students usually became members of halls or hospitia; these were always headed by principals (usually graduates) but had no endowments, property, or corporate existence. The important point is that the university appeared first; the halls and colleges developed to answer a specific need, that of establishing "study communities" and, in the case of the colleges, that of furnishing financial aid for the pursuit of the M.A. and other higher degrees. Each college was totally self-contained, and most of the governing bodies of the colleges were established with the foundations; these are identical save in name for all of the colleges except Christ Church, whose dean is appointed for life by the crown; the head of each of other bodies is elected until retirement by the fellows of the college. New fellows are appointed by the head and fellows of a given institution, and every holder of a chair is a fellow of one of the colleges, not necessarily the college at which he professes. Every one of the old colleges except All Souls has undergraduates and some graduate research students. At All Souls, in a truly medieval tradition, every member is a graduate and no tutoring is done. As a consequence, the College of All Souls of the Faithful Departed neither is considered a part of the university nor is entitled "to present candidates . . . for matriculation."

The old examination system, a public oral disputation between opponents and respondents, was overhauled in the early 19th century after it had so decayed that a degree in history was supposedly granted for the response of "Alfred the Great" to the question "Who founded University College?" The new system allowed for honors and pass degrees, but the principal subjects were still classics and mathematics. As with other modern British universities, the written examinations now occur in June and consist of about a dozen three-hour papers followed by a viva voce examination; the usual course for the B.A. extends over three years with the exception of classics, which requires four years. The M.A. is awarded automatically upon payment of a fee seven years after matriculation. At present there are twenty-four men's colleges; three mixed societies, mostly for graduates;

five women's colleges; and five permanent private halls.

The High Street, called by Nathaniel Hawthorne "the noblest old street in England," intersects Carfax, a street of much nonuniversity interest. The old tower standing here is the only remaining part of the medieval Church of St. Martin, the officially designated town church, as opposed to St. Mary the Virgin, the official university church. The old tower and original church have one of the few confirmed and plausible associations with William Shakespeare outside Stratford-upon-Avon. He frequently stopped in Oxford on his way to London, but where he lodged on the early trips is not known. Most likely, it was not the Crown Inn, now 3 Cornmarket Street, since as the best inn in Oxford, it was likely to have been much too expensive for the unemployed and newly married playwright. However, in time Shakespeare became the intimate friend of the innkeeper, John D'Avenant, and the dramatist frequently stayed at the Crown as his fortunes improved. After William Davenant was born in late February 1606, Shakespeare stood as the child's godfather and as such was present when the christening took place in March at St. Martin's; the font at which the service was held is now in All Saints' Church. The story that Shakespeare was Davenant's father was produced by William Oldys, who cited Alexander Pope and Thomas Betterton as his sources. The house at 3 Cornmarket (now owned by the Oxford Corporation and open to the public) was altered in 1927, and when the 16th-century walls were stripped, a painted design of fruit and flowers with inscriptions in black Tudor lettering was found. William Davenant obtained his early education at the Free School, and later he was a member of Lincoln College. Another native, Anthony Wood, self-styled Anthony à Wood, was born on December 17, 1632, in a house (gone) opposite the gate of Merton College. Before he began his *Athenae Oxonienses*, he inherited two garrets in the family house and converted one into a hermit's retreat by the addition of a large chimney. Here he devoted his life to writing the *Athenae;* never sociable, he became increasingly disagreeable and misanthropic as he exaggerated the importance of his work and grew increasingly deaf. His final illness began on November 1, 1695; he died seven days later and was buried in the outer chapel of Merton College, where a monument was erected.

Just west of Oxford is the parish of St. Thomas, the living presented to Robert Burton on November 29, 1616, by the dean and chapter of Christ Church. He is said to have built the south porch of the church. Burton had been at the university (Brasenose and Christ Church) beginning in 1593 and had proceeded B.D. in 1614. He held this and a living in Selgrave, Leicestershire, until his death. *The Anatomy of Melancholy* was written here, and the Apologetical Appendix is explicitly dated "From my Studie in Christ-Church, Oxon, December 5, 1620." Burton's death occurred at Christ Church on January 25, 1640, a date he is said to have foretold from a calculation of his nativity. He was buried in the north aisle next to the choir of Christ Church, and the monument, on the upper-right pillar of the aisle, was erected by Burton's brother William; the inscription below the bust is one he wrote himself.

There are many medieval associations with the early church, the university, or the town (as distinguished from the specific colleges), although often only scattered bits of evidence bear on the connection. One of the most eminent thinkers of medieval Europe, Roger Bacon, is traditionally said to have begun his university studies at Oxford, but while no matriculation record exists, there is no reason to doubt that Bacon studied here. Furthermore, tradition asserts that he belonged to the order of Franciscans, whose house and grounds stood both within and without the city walls (joined by a gateway). Bacon spent an indefinite period of time in Paris but probably returned to Oxford around 1250; his superiors sent him away in 1257, and he spent many of the succeeding years in confinement on the Continent. He is said to have died here after 1294 and to have been buried at the abbey, now somewhere west of St. Ebbe's Church.

Another medieval scholar, John Duns Scotus, was associated with this Franciscan order. Richard Rolle received part of his education here, but the dates are difficult to verify. At an early age his abilities were noticed by Thomas de Neville, Archdeacon of Durham, who maintained Rolle at Oxford, possibly as early as 1314. John Lydgate was most likely sent here from the monastery at Bury St. Edmunds after 1386 to finish his education, but this assertion rests purely on a statement by John Bale. If Lydgate was here, he was most likely associated with Gloucester Hall, to which the Benedictines generally sent their young scholars. Oxford comes into Geoffrey Chaucer's *Canterbury Tales*, for in the train of pilgrims is "[a] clerk ... of Oxenford" who "looked holwe" and wore a short coat "ful thred bare." It is in "The Miller's Tale" that Chaucer displays some knowledge of the town and nearby Oseneye (Osney).

Another untraceable association is with John Skelton; he came here after leaving Cambridge without a degree, but the date is not known. By 1490, in his preface to *Eneydos*, Caxton describes Skelton as the "late created poet laureate in the university of Oxford," a title which loosely designated someone distinguished in rhetoric and letters rather than a poet.

Michael Drayton had some uncertain association with Oxford and mentions Oxford in *Poly-Olbion*:

These preparations great when *Charwell* comes to see,
To *Oxford* got before, to entertaine the Flood,
Apollo's ayde he begs, with all his sacred brood,
To that most learned place to welcome her repaire.

The impression is of secondhand knowledge, and Drayton displays none of the special affection which might be expected had he matriculated at any one of the colleges; his name does not appear on any university list.

The English Protestant who advanced the cause of the Reformation in England, Hugh Latimer, met his death here with Nicholas Ridley on October 16, 1555; in an untenable position when the Catholic Mary Tudor came to the throne in 1553, Latimer refused to bow to Catholicism and was arrested in September. Tried in Oxford, he was sentenced to be burned at the stake in the ditch outside the city wall with Ridley, whom he exhorted, "We shall this day light such a candle, by God's grace, in England, as I trust shall never be put out." In the next year Thomas Cranmer was burned at the stake. The site of the executions on Broad Street is marked with a concrete cross, and the Gothic Martyrs Memorial in St. Giles commemorates them.

Thomas Sackville, 1st Earl of Dorset and coauthor of *The Tragedy of Gorboduc,* is thought to have been a member of Hart Hall here, but he did have a decidedly important association with the university later. A politically astute man, Sackville held favor under Mary, Elizabeth I, and James I; and through Elizabeth's influence he secured the chancellorship of Oxford on December 17, 1591. In 1600 Sackville displayed his admiration and affection for Oxford by giving an extensive part of his personal book collection to the Bodleian Library and in donating a bust (still extant) of Thomas (later Sir Thomas) Bodley, who more than anyone else was responsible for the outstanding university library. After books and manuscripts donated by Humphrey, Duke of Gloucester, were removed from the Divinity School in 1550, Oxford had been without a structured library facility until 1598, when Bodley pledged a vast sum for reconstruction of the facilities and purchase of scholarly materials. By 1602 the library reopened, but in a short period it was unable to house the rapidly expanding collection; this was partly Sir Thomas's fault, for he arranged with Her Majesty's Stationers' Company that one copy of every book published in England be presented to the Bodleian.

In the same period George Chapman is said to have studied here; Anthony à Wood observes:

> Sure I am that he spent some time in Oxon, where he was observed to be most excellent in the Latin and Greek tongues, but not in logic or philosophy, and therefore I presume that was the reason why he took no degree there.

Somewhat later Thomas Warton, in *The History of English Poetry* (1774–1781), echoes Wood and adds on unknown authority that Chapman spent two years at Trinity. In keeping with this, Chapman refers to "Academickes" who

> ever rate
> A man for learning, with that estimate
> They made of him, when in the schooles he liv'd;
> And how so ere he scatter'd since, or thriv'd,
> Still they esteeme him as they held him then. . . .

The university's association with Abraham Cowley is also difficult to establish, although there is some fragmentary evidence. Cowley went up to Trinity College, Cambridge (not Oxford, as is often stated), in June 1637, and received the degrees of B.A. in 1639 and M.A. in 1642. In 1643, with the Roundhead successes, Cowley was ejected from the university and retired here to St. John's College, a Royalist stronghold, where he remained two years; Oxford, "the British Muse's second fame," he writes:

> . . . that to loved Charles's sight
> In these sad times giv'st safety and delight. . . .
> Amidst all the joys which heaven allows thee here,
> Think on thy sister, and then shed a tear.

He was created M.D. here on December 2, 1657, by governmental decree, an act said to suggest a reward for espionage.

In the autumn of 1665, when the plague was ravaging London, Parliament decided to meet in Oxford, where there was less chance of contagion; and with

this parliamentary group came Andrew Marvell, the Member for Hull; he took the time to visit the Bodleian on September 30.

Samuel Pepys was here three years later for a day of sightseeing, and he would have put the modern tourist to shame with the whirlwind nature of his short stay. In less than a full day Pepys "did" the university and found Oxford "a very sweet place . . . a mighty fine place and well seated"; he took time to have a shave and his hair done for half a crown, overtipped the staff that served him, ate strawberries, and finally visited the butteries because of his curiosity about the Child of Hales. The Child of Hales, whose real name was John Middleton, was a court giant whose hand (17 inches long) was preserved in the cellar of Brasenose College. The now-obscure metaphysical poet Edward Benlowes spent his final years here after he gave up Brent Hall in Finchingfield, Essex; he passed most of his time reading in the Bodleian before his death here on December 18, 1676. A few years later Jonathan Swift, who stopped off on his way to Moor Park from Ireland, found Oxford society so congenial that he decided to take his M.A. here and made arrangements to pick up the few weeks of needed residence early in 1692. In June, on the strength of testimonials from Dublin, he was admitted B.A., and the M.A. was conferred on July 5.

In the 18th century a large number of visitors came to what was then an academic shrine. Alexander Pope's first trip was in the summer of 1714, when he abandoned his books and other serious work for a brief stay; he found the dons "all very honest fellows" and felt well entertained. So greatly impressed was he by this reception and the scenery that he returned in 1717. To Teresa and Martha Blount he writes:

> [T]he moon rose in the clearest sky I ever saw, by whose solemn light I paced on slowly, without company, or any interruption to the range of my thoughts. About a mile before I reached Oxford, all the bells tolled, in different tones; the clocks of every college answered one another; and told me, some in a deeper, some in a softer voice, that it was eleven o'clock.

Dr. Johnson, whose experience with Pembroke College had been bad, made frequent trips back to Oxford from 1754 on. On the first he lodged at Kettel Hall near Trinity College and met the Rev. Thomas Warton, who was a fellow at Trinity. The two enjoyed walking together and frequently made the trip to Elsfield, about 3 miles away. Johnson undertook a trip in 1759 at Warton's urging, and on this occasion he was made M.A.

Sometime around 1782 Jane Austen and her sister Cassandra arrived in Oxford to attend a school run by a Mrs. Cawley, the widow of a principal of Brasenose. They remained only for a year or two before being sent to Reading, but Oxonian associations remained strong, and in both *Northanger Abbey* and *Mansfield Park* university undergraduates are portrayed.

In June 1794 Oxford became the planning place for the pantisocratic scheme evolved by Samuel Taylor Coleridge. Through the offices of an undergraduate at University College Coleridge met Robert Southey, and during this short initial acquaintanceship Southey was converted to both Unitarianism and pantisocracy. Another Lake poet, William Wordsworth, was in Oxford at a much later date and was inspired to compose two sonnets on Oxford, including one which expresses his admiration for the community:

> Ye sacred Nurseries of blooming Youth!
> In whose collegiate shelter England's Flowers
> Expand, enjoying through their vernal hours
> The air of liberty, the light of truth;
> Much have ye suffered from Time's gnawing tooth:
> Yet, O ye spires of Oxford! domes and towers!
> Gardens and groves! your presence overpowers
> The soberness of reason. . . .

Charles Lamb also wrote of Oxford, but "Oxford in the Vacation," curiously enough, was written during a visit to Cambridge. In one of his descriptions of Oxford, "the heart of learning under the shadow of the mighty Bodley," he writes:

> Here I can take my walks unmolested, and fancy myself of what degree and standing I please. I seem admitted *ad eundum*. . . . I can rise at the chapel-bell, and dream that it rings for *me*. In moods of humility I can be a Sizar, or a Servitor. When the peacock vein arises, I strut a Gentleman Commoner. In graver moments, I proceed Master of Arts. . . .

Lamb visited in 1800 and again several years later with William Hazlitt, who commented that Lamb and "the old college were hail-fellow well met." On a July 1810 excursion, Hazlitt records in "Character of the County People," the local tailor

> was ordered to make a pair of brown or snuff-coloured breeches for my friend Charles Lamb;—instead of which the pragmatical old gentleman (having an opinion of his own) brought him home a pair of "lively Lincoln-green," in which he rode in triumph in Johnny Tremain's cross-country caravan through Newberry, and entered Oxford, "fearing no colours." . . .

Hazlitt's essay "On Going on a Journey" also records a trip to Oxford.

Richard Brinsley Sheridan was invited to attend Lord Greville's investiture as chancellor in July 1809 and had himself been proposed as a recipient of an honorary degree. The degree, however, was held up by two men on the board, one of whom was opposed to Sheridan because of nonpayment of tithes. The story was known all over the universty, and when Sheridan entered the hall for the ceremony, he was greeted by cries of "Mr. Sheridan among the Doctors." To his great delight and that of the audience, Sheridan was given a seat with those receiving the honorary degrees.

John Keats spent some time here with Benjamin Bailey in September 1817 while Bailey was studying for examinations, and according to *Rural Rides,* William Cobbett was here in November 1821, when he made a few acid observations about university life:

> Upon beholding the masses of building, at Oxford, devoted to what they call "*learning,*" I could not help reflecting on the drones that they contain and the wasps they send forth! However, malignant as some are, the great and prevalent characteristic is *folly:* emptiness of head; want of talent; and one half of the fellows who are what they call *educated* here, are unfit to be clerks in a grocer's or mercer's shop.

A more accurate picture of mid-19th century life at Oxford is presented in *The Adventures of Mr. Verdant Green, an Oxford Freshman* by Cuthbert Bede (Edward Bradley). Bradley himself was not an Oxonian but may have studied here in 1849.

The experiences of Dante Gabriel Rossetti at Oxford are almost beyond belief. In the spring of 1855, under the influence (and with the money) of John Ruskin, Rossetti brought Lizzie Siddal to Dr. Henry Acland, Reader in Anatomy, fellow of Christ Church and All Souls, for diagnosis and treatment. Both Ruskin and Rossetti were convinced that Lizzie was near death, and they were surprised to discover that her ailment was not physical but caused by "mental power long pent up and lately over-taxed." By July or August 1857 Rossetti was living at 87 High Street opposite The Queen's College with Edward Burne-Jones and William Morris, and the three were busily engaged in painting medieval themes from Sir Thomas Malory's *Le Morte d'Arthur* on the Union Debating Hall. In October they moved to 13 George Street and brought Algernon Swinburne, who was at Balliol, into the group. The young men ignored the technical problems of painting the walls and used the tempera process on unprepared, newly built, and unwhitewashed walls; because of this technical incompetence, the work was unlikely to survive, but, in fact, the walls were admirably restored in 1936. Rossetti left immediately upon completion of the work for Matlock, Derbyshire, to see Lizzie, who was again acting out her acute "illness."

For some reason Oxford seems to have had a great deal to do with two men who have perhaps the most illustrious names in children's literature. Lewis Carroll (Charles Lutwidge Dodgson) spent almost all his adult life here at Christ Church, and Kenneth Grahame had his early education here. Grahame, who came of a solid middle-class Scots family, was placed in St. Edward's School, a newly founded but still anarchic establishment, on Michaelmas Day, 1868. (The buildings were on New Inn Hall Street but were moved to Summertown in 1873.) Grahame spent the next seven years here, where apparently to his family's surprise he not only survived but did extremely well. Finishing the upper sixth and already interested in literature and writing, Grahame was not permitted to go on to the university; his uncle put the family attitude nicely: nature had played a rather dirty trick on the family by putting a literary cuckoo into a respectable Scots' nest. After Grahame's death in Pangbourne on July 6, 1932, and his interment there, his remains were later brought to St. Cross (Holywell) and placed in the same grave as his son.

Another late-19th-century Scotsman wrote of Oxford and his time at Balliol; Andrew Lang looked back affectionately at the ten years (1865–1875) spent here:

> A land of waters green and clear
>   Of willows and of poplars tall,
> And in the Spring-time of the year,
>   The white may breaking over all,
> And Pleasure quick to come at call;
>   And summer rides by marsh and wold,
>   About the towers of Magdalen roll'd:
> And strange enchantments from the past,
>   And memories of the friends of old,
> And strong Tradition binding fast
>   The flying terms with bands of gold,—
> All these hath Oxford. . . .

From her marriage in 1872 until 1881 Mrs. Humphry Ward lived at 5 (now 17) Bradmore Road. After the publication of *Robert Elsmere* she defended her work to William Gladstone, who felt the novel attacked Christianity, at the warden's lodge of Keble College.

The association of William Butler Yeats with Oxford was both extensive and sporadic. His first contact occurred in 1888, when he was sent here by Alfred Nutt, the publisher, to transcribe a rare Caxton volume of Aesop in the Bodleian. In a letter to Katherine Tynan he writes:

> I walked about sixteen miles on Sunday, going to the places in Matthew Arnold's poems—the ford in the *Scholar Gipsy* being the most interesting. How very unlike Ireland the whole place is—like a foreign land (as it is).

After finishing his work on the Caxton manuscript, Yeats was not back until November 1917, when he was here for a little over two months after his marriage to Georgie Hyde-Lees. They lodged at 45 Broad Street (gone), and Yeats then met Robert Bridges for the first time. The Yeatses left in January 1918 but returned in October 1919, when they took 4 Broad Street (gone), opposite Balliol near the Cornmarket. Their tenancy was interrupted by a trip to the United States, but upon their return both Bridges and John Masefield (living at Boar's Hill) were frequent guests. About this time Yeats made an appearance at the Oxford Union to denounce the British government's use of the Black and Tans to track down the militant members of the Irish Republican Army. During this period Yeats became a close friend of Sir Maurice Bowra, President of Wadham College. After Yeats's return to Ireland in 1922, he came to Oxford only twice more, in November 1930 for a short English holiday, when he stayed with John Masefield at Boar's Hill, and in May 1931 to receive an honorary doctor of letters degree.

Toward the end of the 19th century Hilaire Belloc took a house on Holywell Street and made his living by taking pupils and giving extension lectures. In 1894 he began speaking at the Oxford Union and in 1898 defended popular education against Andrew Lang. When he was over eighty, Belloc refused an honorary fellowship offered by Balliol College. His love of Balliol did not carry over to the university as a whole, and in his "Moral Alphabet" of 1899, he treats it thus:

> O stands for Oxford, salubrious seat
> Of learning! Academical Retreat!
> Home of my Middle Age! Malarial Spot
> Which people call Medeeval (though it's not)
> The marshes in the neighbourhood can vie
> With Cambridge, but the town itself is dry
> And serves to make a kind of Fold or Pen
> Wherein to herd A Lot of Learned Men. . . .

He could, though, speak of Balliol and allow "Dons admirable," "Dons of might," and

> regal Dons!
> With hearts of gold and lungs of bronze,
> Who shout and bang and roar and brawl
> The Absolute across the hall. . . .

Thomas Hardy came to Oxford in June 1893 to do research on *Jude the Obscure* and took a hotel room near Carfax, "a spot . . . called The Fourways [Quatre Voies] in the middle of the city." He was here through Commemoration and walked in the quadrangles, watched the boat races, and familiarized himself with the city. Oxford, of course, is Christminster, the city of Jude's dreams. Jude's first view of the town is still much the same:

> Grey stoned and dun-roofed, it stood within hail of the Wessex border, and almost with the tip of one small toe within it, at the northernmost point of the crinkled line along which the leisurely Thames strokes the fields of that ancient kingdom. The buildings now lay quiet in the sunset, a vane here and there on their many spires and domes giving sparkle to a picture of sober secondary and tertiary hues.

There are many specific allusions in this novel: the High Street becomes Chief Street; Merton Street with its cobblestone pavings is Old Time Street, the location of Crozier College. Carfax is Four Ways, and the colleges take on new identities: Christ Church is probably Hardy's Cardinal College; Balliol is Biblioll; and either Corpus Christi or New College is Sarcophagus. The Church of St. Mary-the-Virgin masquerades as the church with the Italian porch; the Martyrs' Cross is little changed as "the cross in the pavement which marked the spot of the Martyrdoms." Jude courts Sue in the Turf Tavern in St. Helen's Passage, and the description of the Cathedral of Cardinal College leaves no doubt of its identity:

> From his window he could perceive the spire of the Cathedral, and the ogee dome under which resounded the great bell of the city. The tall tower, tall belfry windows, and tall pinnacles of the college by the bridge he could also get a glimpse of by going to the staircase.

And "the circular theatre with that well-known lantern above it" must be the Sheldonian. On their later return to Christminster, Jude and Sue lodge on Mildew Lane (unidentified), where the gruesome murder of the children takes place. As Sue's outlook changes, she frequents St. Silas's Church, which Hardy locates in Beersheba, the most populous area in the city. Beersheba is probably a pseudonym for Jericho, and St. Silas's is undoubtedly the Church of St. Barnabas. With Jude's final return to Christminster after he and Sue separate, he is met at the station by Arabella, and fantasies crowd in on him as they walk home:

> "Fancy! The Poet of Liberty used to walk here, and the great Dissector of Melancholy there!"
> "I don't want to hear about 'em! They bore me."
> "Walter Raleigh is beckoning to me from that lane—Wycliffe—Harvey—Hooker—Arnold—and a whole crowd of Tractarian Shades—"
> "I *don't want* to know their names. . . ."
> "I must rest a moment," he said; and as he paused, holding to the railings, he measured with his eye the height of a college front. "This is old Rubric. And that Sarcophagus; and up that lane Crozier and Tudor: and all down there is Cardinal with its long front, and its windows with lifted eyebrows, representing the polite surprise of the University at the efforts of such as I."

One may walk down St. Aldate's Street to reconstruct Jude's walk. Hardy mentions many other places, some of which cannot be identified. Unfortunately, one of these is the house in which Jude dies; it is, we are told, in "a yet more central part of the town" and, we know, relatively close to the Sheldonian Theatre. While *Jude* is the main Hardy work involving Oxford, the town appears under its own name in *A Pair of Blue Eyes* and "The Son's Veto," and under the name Christminster it comes into "Squire Petrick's Lady." Here the Marquis of Christminster is alleged to be the father of Anna Petrick's son Rupert.

Henry James lodged for a short time in 1894 at 15 Beaumont Street while he worked on "The Altar of the Dead"; Oxford, says James, "lends sweetness to labour and dignity to leisure." He includes the town in *Portraits of Places* and sets part of "The Passionate Pilgrim" here:

> [Oxford] seems to embody with undreamed completeness a kind of dim and sacred ideal of the Western intellect,—a scholastic city, an appointed home of contemplation. No other spot in Europe, I imagine, extorts from our barbarous hearts so passionate an admiration. . . . Over all, through all, the great corporate fact of the University prevails and penetrates. . . .

In the 20th century probably no more intimate association exists than with Joyce Cary. After giving up a possible art career, Cary took cram courses in Edinburgh and persuaded his father of the value of an Oxford education. He planned to read for a law degree so that if a literary career proved impossible, he could obtain a more conventional job. Barely passing his first entrance examinations, he entered Trinity College in October 1909. With this, a lifelong love of Oxford and all it represented began. By 1920, after some restless years with the British Red Cross, the Irish Agricultural Organization Society, and the Nigerian political service, Cary and his family took a ninety-nine-year lease on 12 Parks Road, a large semidetached Victorian house about 20 yards north of Keble College. Not well off, Cary hit the very bottom of his finances in January 1922 and, reluctant to move his family from their home, rented out the ground floor. With the birth of a third child, Cary found working conditions impossible at home and rented a top-floor room of a house on Rawlinson Road so that he could write. In 1935, after he secured a new publisher (Victor Gollancz) for his third novel, the financial picture began to brighten. Neither of his first two novels made any money, but *The African Witch* was made a Book Society choice and sold more than 15,000 copies. From 1940 on, with *Charley Is My Darling*, the books began to flow: *A House of Children* and *Herself Surprised* (James Tait Black Memorial Prize) in 1941, *To Be A Pilgrim* in 1942, and *The Moonlight* in 1946. Late in 1946 or early in 1947, Cary's wife, Trudy, was found to have cancer, and from that point on his productivity was halted. Her death in December 1949 affected him greatly. From the early 1950s on Cary's Sunday-evening "at-homes" attracted such guests as Enid Starkey, W. H. Auden, Lord David Cecil, and Helen Gardner. In 1955 it was discovered that he was suffering from disseminated neuritis, and he died in Oxford on March 29, 1957, and was buried at St. Giles.

Numerous other 20th-century literary figures have had some sort of Oxford association. In 1906 Rupert Brooke stopped in Oxford to see his friend Arthur Eckersley and to explore Oxford for the first time; he was especially delighted with writing letters in the Oxford Union Debating Society clubroom. Rudyard Kipling was one of three (with Mark Twain, or Samuel Langhorne Clemens, and Gen. William Booth) who received honorary doctorates from the university in June 1907. Kipling was frequently here after World War I on business for the Rhodes Trust and in 1919 was often found in the company of T. E. Lawrence; he resigned his post with the trust in 1925. H. G. Wells uses Oxford in a number of his works: Marjorie Pope, the second of Pope's daughters in *Marriage*, studies at Oxbridge, and Sir Roderick Dover, Trafford's friend, is "Late Professor of Physics" here. *The Passionate Friends* mentions Oxford, and the Mediated Universities Club is here. Finally, in *Joan and Peter* Oswald dines with Bleep at St. Osyth's (not identified), and the students at Ruskin College are described as oldish young men with rough North Country accents. A. E. Housman, who had been a student at St. John's College, toured Oxford with Robert Bridges, Poet Laureate, in 1924 and found the old man (then seventy-nine) active and "correctly opinioned." In June 1931 John Galsworthy received a D.Litt. degree at the Encaenia after delivering a very well-attended Romanes lecture in the previous month; and in 1952 W. Somerset Maugham received an honorary degree along with Dean Acheson, the United States Secretary of State. There is more recent and slightly longer association with Dylan Thomas; in mid-March 1946, after hospitalization in London, he and his family moved into Holywell Ford Cottage on the river, just outside the college walls. The cottage belonged to a Derbyshire friend, Alan Taylor, and was at best rudimentary. It was really no more than a very large summerhouse or studio of one fully furnished room with cooking facilities. But it had no plumbing other than an outdoor earth closet, a feature not at all pleasing to the family. The cottage was the Thomas home for a year.

Both C. S. Lewis, a fellow at Magdalen College, and J. R. R. Tolkien, a fellow at Pembroke and then Merton, frequented the back bar at the Eagle and Child on St. Giles's Street, and Dorothy Sayers sets the marriage of Lord Peter Wimsey and Harriet Vane at St. Cross Church. Helen Denver, Lord Peter's irksome sister-in-law, writes that they "found the place—an obscure little church in a side-street, very gloomy and damp looking." The bride, she continues, had a "most incredible assortment of bridesmaids—all female dons!—and an odd dark woman to give her away, who was supposed to be the Head of the College." Lord Peter and his man Bunter stay at the Mitre on the night before the wedding. Finally, after her 1923 marriage to Alan Cameron, Elizabeth Bowen made Old Headlington her home until she inherited the family Irish estate in 1928. She received an honorary D.Litt. degree from Oxford in 1957 and returned to the town for a short time in 1960.

While one can sum up Oxford by the well-known "Johnson endured the University; Gibbon rejected it; it rejected Shelley," perhaps it is just as well to remember that Matthew Arnold could call it

> That sweet city with her dreaming spires
> She needs not June for beauty's heightening,
> Lovely all times she lies, lovely tonight!

All Souls College   For 500 years The College of All Souls of the Faithful Departed stood unique among Oxford and Cambridge colleges in maintaining the medieval tradition of admitting only graduates; only with the founding of Nuffield College in 1937 and St. Anthony's College in 1948 did any other Oxford colleges reinstate the medieval graduate tradition. Founded in 1438 by Henry Chichele, Archbishop of Canterbury, All Souls was dedicated to Henry V and "the English captains and other subjects who drank the cup of bitter death" during the Hundred Years' War. Called "the greatest of all war memorials," it was established both as a chantry and as an academic institution.

The gatehouse and library date from 1438 and 1442 respectively, but the basic construction, an overwhelming hodgepodge of Renaissance and Gothic motifs, is the later work of Nicholas Hawksmoor, who, Horace Walpole maintained, had "blundered into a picturesque scenery not void of grandeur...." The chapel is an especially interesting specimen of 15th-century Perpendicular Gothic; in 1664 the ruins of the first reredos were covered over, and the Last Judgment was painted on the covering boards. John Evelyn, who came to Oxford on numerous occasions—as a student at Balliol College, as a concerned parent when his son was here, and as a visitor when Viscount Cornbury was vice-chancellor—was taken to see the new painting on October 25, 1664, and describes it in his diary as

> the largest piece of Fresco painting (or rather in Imitation of it, for tis in oyle [of *Terpentine*]) in England, & not ill design'd ... yet I feare it will not hold long, & seemes too full of nakeds for a Chapell....

Whether or not the "nakeds" were the reason, the fresco was removed by the fellows in 1714, but in 1870 the canopies of the original reredos were discovered and an effective restoration took place; indeed, some of the medieval coloring can still be seen.

The roll at All Souls seems to contain a preponderance of churchmen—Gilbert Sheldon and Cosmo Gordon Lang, both Archbishops of Canterbury, and Herbert Hensley Henson, Bishop of Durham—as well as men of science: Christopher Wren and Thomas Linacre, classicist and eventually physician to Henry VIII. Jeremy Taylor is one of the best known of the college's minor literary figures; he was recommended to the fellowship by Archbishop William Laud in 1635; Sheldon objected to his candidacy. The fellows eventually acquiesced, and Taylor was admitted as a probationary fellow on November 5, 1635, and as a perpetual fellow in January 1636. Taylor's reputation as a preacher here at St. Mary's was extremely good, and he probably worked on *The Rule and Exercises of Holy Living* and *Holy Dying*. He left Oxford in 1658, when he was preferred to the living at Uppingham, Rutland. In 1708 Edward Young became a law fellow and had the reputation of having more genius than common sense (so said Alexander Pope). He eventually received degrees of bachelor of civil law on April 23, 1714, and doctor of civil law in June 1719. Edward Hyde, 1st Earl of Clarendon, as one of the King's advisers, lived at All Souls while Charles I had his headquarters here during the Civil War. Finally, T. E. Lawrence was a fellow of All Souls.

Balliol College   Balliol College is one of three Oxford institutions claiming the distinction of being the oldest college; Merton was founded in 1264, just around the time Balliol came into existence, and University College dates from 1280 or 1249, depending on whose view one chooses. Balliol College was founded by John de Balliol, a man who, fortunately for Oxford, seems to have had his share of both temper and fight; in serious trouble with the church in Durham and Northumberland for having "unjustly vexed and enormously damnified the Churches of Tynemouth and Durham," he was scourged and ordered to do penance by providing for sixteen poor scholars who were to receive 8 pence a week for sustenance. Living accommodations were found for them on the site of the present master's house. The endowment was made by 1265, and 1263 is generally accepted as the founding date. With Balliol's death in 1269, his wife showed concern for the state of her husband's soul by raising the student stipend; in 1282 she issued a charter of incorporation in which the scholars (students in the arts) were to be basically self-governing, electing a principal among themselves, but to be subject to two external masters, one clerical and one lay.

The college flourished, and John Wycliffe was first a fellow and later master of Balliol; the dates are uncertain, but the period of the mastership is generally assumed to be 1356 to 1361. By the middle of the 15th century Balliol had become one of the outstanding resorts of Renaissance leaders. The college itself was little affected by the Reformation, but the Civil War found its membership much reduced and its debts increased. The penury was long-lived though not continuous, and by the 18th century the buildings were terribly run down. As buildings were replaced, not always in the best of taste (for example, the 1860 rebuilding program of Alfred Waterhouse), Balliol began its long tradition of firsts in the schools (final examinations). One of the few remaining old buildings here, the library (formerly the Hall) in the little front quadrangle off Broad Street, contains a small but valuable collection of Browning memorabilia including a portrait painted by his son and a copy of the old yellow book which the poet found in a Florentine bookstall in the Piazza of San Lorenzo in June 1860 and turned into *The Ring and the Book*.

The earliest literary association in a long list is often claimed but never proved. According to Anthony à Wood, who had something to say about everyone, Sir Edward Dyer "received some of his academical education in Oxon, particularly, as I conceive it in Ball. College or Broadgate's Hall." It appears most likely that Dyer, the author of "My mind to me a kingdom is," came here in 1558, around the age of sixteen; Wood, in *Athenae Oxonienses*, claims that Dyer's "natural inclination to poetry and other polite learning as also his excellence in bewailing and bemoaning the perplexities of love, were observed by his contemporaries." The date of Dyer's departure is thought to be 1561; he left without a degree and undoubtedly went abroad.

Not quite a century later, in May 1637, Balliol saw the arrival of John Evelyn:

> I was sent from Schole to the University, rather out of shame of abiding longer *sub ferula,* than, for that fitnesse to have ben expected from one had well employed his time....

Evelyn's experiences at Balliol differed only a little from his Southover days, and with an unfortunate choice of tutor he profited less from his studies than from his attendant activities and friendships. In February 1640, he left for the Middle Temple in London to study law. His diary notes the move under the date of April 11 and comments, "I was sent to London . . . so as my being at the University, in regard of these avocations was of very small benefit to me." An interesting sidelight to Evelyn's years here concerns Nathaniel Conopios, a Greek who Evelyn observed was "the first I ever saw drink Coffe, which custome came not into England til 30 years after." Twenty-nine years later Evelyn returned to Oxford for an honorary D.C.L. conferred for his role in obtaining the Arundelian marbles for the university. He attended the opening of the New Theatre (the Sheldonian), and the honorary degrees were conferred six days later, July 15, at "the Convocation house . . .":

> Here being all of us rob'd in Scarlet, with Caps & hoods &c: in the Porch, we were led in by the Professor of Laws, & presented respectively by name & a short elogie &c: to the *Vice-Chancelor* who sate in the Chaire, with all the Doctors & heads of houses & Masters about the roome, which was exceeding full: Then began the Publique Orator, his speech, directed chiefly to the *Chancelore,* the *Duke of Ormond,* in which I had also my Compliment in Course: This ended, we were called up, and Created Doctors according to the forme. . . .

Adam Smith was a Snell exhibitioner here from 1740 to 1746 and received a B.A. degree in 1744. He showed no later interest in Oxford (and complained of ill-treatment when here); indeed, the university never accorded him an honorary degree, as was customary with such illustrious graduates.

At the end of the 18th century Balliol became the college of Robert Southey, but this was not the poet's first choice. He had been expelled from Westminster School in London for protesting against excessive flogging in an impromptu school magazine, *The Flagellant,* and was rejected by Christ Church because of the incident. Balliol, though, accepted him at Michaelmas, 1792, and he matriculated on November 2. Although Southey and the college were not mutually beneficial (his tutor said to him, "Mr. Southey, you won't learn anything by my lectures; so, if you have any studies of your own, you had better pursue them"), there was no feeling of enmity. About the time of his father's death in 1793 Southey was introduced to Samuel Taylor Coleridge by a University College undergraduate; within a short period, Southey, converted to Unitarianism and pantisocracy (a scheme he and Coleridge later pursued), left Balliol without a degree. He later wrote of his years here:

> All I learnt was a little swimming and a little boating . . . and with respect to its superiors, Oxford only exhibits waste of wigs and want of wisdom; with respect to the undergraduates, every species of abandoned excess.

Arthur Hugh Clough entered Balliol from Rugby on a scholarship in 1837 and took second-class honors four years later. His first lodgings were in small garret rooms in the quadrangle. Moving to the ground floor of the quadrangle, he spent at least one winter without a fire and without any company. His desire for solitude was extremely strong, and an enormous personal religious struggle was beginning.

Clough failed to secure a Balliol fellowship in the fall of 1841 but gained an Oriel fellowship in the spring. Matthew Arnold came up to Balliol with a classical scholarship in November 1840 and gained the coveted Newdigate Prize in 1843 for his poem on Oliver Cromwell. Arnold's friendship with Clough was strengthened here; there were Sunday breakfasts in Clough's rooms, occasional boating on the Cherwell, and walks in the Cumnor Hills. Arnold's examinations in 1844 resulted in second-class honors in *litterae humaniores;* however, the following spring he was able to redeem himself with his election to a fellowship at Oriel College. He returned to the university in 1857 as professor of poetry, and many of his lectures from his ten-year tenure have become classics in criticism. His Preface to *Essays in Criticism* eulogizes the "beautiful City" of Oxford, which he sees "whispering . . . the last enchantments of the middle ages"; but he also characterizes the university as the "home of lost causes, and forsaken beliefs, and unpopular names, and impossible loyalties."

When Charles Stuart Calverley came up from Harrow in 1850, he was already known for his Latin versification, his extraordinary powers of verbal memory, and his high spirits. His Latin won both a scholarship and the Chancellor's prize in 1851, while his high spirits (really breaches of discipline and pranks) won his expulsion from Balliol in 1852; he went over to Cambridge. Just a few years later, Balliol had on its hands yet another political radical and nonconformist, Algernon Swinburne. He matriculated on January 24, 1856, and kept term regularly during his first three years here. In the autumn of 1857 Swinburne met three men who were to have a great impact on his life: Dante Gabriel Rossetti, Edward Burne-Jones, and William Morris, who were decorating the Debating Hall of the Oxford Union. Toward the end of his tenure, Swinburne took rooms on Broad Street; his landlady, upset by his late hours, republican views, and ungentlemanly activities, complained to the authorities, who eventually came to believe Swinburne dangerous. Prof. Benjamin Jowett felt the necessity to act after Swinburne read a paper supporting Mazzini and Orsini against Napoleon III at the Union in May. Jowett was concerned that Swinburne would be sent down, an act which the tutor felt would "make Balliol as ridiculous as University had made itself about Shelley," and consequently convinced the poet to withdraw in the summer of 1859. Returning briefly in October, Swinburne left for good in November and seldom came back. He never lost his bitterness over the episode, and it is said that he left Oxford with neither a degree nor a regret.

John Addington Symonds came up to Balliol from Harrow in 1858, and he eventually achieved distinction with a double first in classics and the Newdigate Prize for "The Escorial." He took an open fellowship at Magdalen College in October 1862 after failing to secure one at The Queen's College.

Gerard Manley Hopkins matriculated in April 1863, and after getting through Smalls (the first examination for the B.A. degree), he wrote, "proceeded to booze at the Mitre. . . ." Hopkins was converted to Catholicism as an undergraduate and left the university with a double first in *litterae humaniores* in June 1867. He met Robert Bridges, a commoner at Corpus

Christi, and the two became close friends. Bridges, in fact, prepared the first collected edition of Hopkins's poems. Joining the Jesuit order, he was named assistant to Father Parkinson, priest of the mission here, in December 1878. After he left in October 1879, he never returned. Bridges often visited him in 1879, and the two were frequently seen walking up the Cowley Road. Hopkins later recalls the

> Towery city....
>   and branchy between towers
> Cuckoo-echoing, bell-swarmed, lark-charmed, rook-
>   racked, river rounded. ...

Anthony Hope Hawkins was an undergraduate from 1881 to 1884 and was president of the Oxford Union.

One of the most brilliant academic careers any literary figure had at Balliol was Hilaire Belloc's. Having wandered from one activity to another and one country to another, Belloc finally decided on a university career and was accepted by Balliol for Hilary term, 1893. In December he was awarded one of two Brackenbury scholarships and in 1895 gained a first in history. His early life of loneliness and poverty apparently caused him to strive for acceptance here; he had an extraordinarily wide circle of friends and became a brilliant speaker as well as one of the most outstanding presidents the Oxford Union has ever known. Belloc's first rooms were on the left-hand side of the ground floor, Staircase No. 3, in the main quadrangle, but in 1894 he was at 6 St. Aldates Street with three other Oxonians. Following his marriage in 1896 Belloc settled for a short time at 5 Bath Place before moving to Littlemore. His attitude is best summed up by "To the Balliol Men Still in Africa": "Balliol made me, Balliol fed me."

In 1913 Aldous Huxley came up to Balliol College from Eton; he took an honors degree in English literature and went back to Eton to teach in 1918. Another Etonian was Anthony Powell, whose Oxford reminiscences are contained in the early volumes of his "Dance to the Music of Time" novels. Cyril Connolly came up from Eton in the 1920s, and Graham Greene came up from school in Berkhamsted, Hertfordshire, and took a second in modern history in 1925.

Brasenose College Usually called B.N.C., Brasenose (founded in 1509 and once considered a new college) is properly The King's Hall and College of Brasenose; its name is taken from the brazen-nose door knocker on a 15th-century bronze mask. The brazen nose is now above the High Table in the 16th-century Hall, but the nose on the gate has been there since the old hall was built. The original Brasenose Hall has long since disappeared, but its kitchen remains in a quadrangle with the chapel and library. The old gate tower, a superb example of early-16th-century architecture, was orginally the principal's lodging.

The college has always had a preeminent reputation on the games field and the Cherwell, and its scholarly reputation has suffered accordingly. Indeed, literary associations, except for some modern ones, are unusually difficult to establish. John Foxe is said to have entered Brasenose in 1532 and to have attended Magdalen College simultaneously. Some circumstantial and biographical evidence supports this claim, but there is no record of his matriculation. Foxe, however, does mention Brasenose a number of times in *Actes and Monuments,* although there is no evidence of personal association. Finally, Foxe's chamber mate here supposedly was Alexander Nowell, later dean of St. Paul's, a lifelong friend, and a member of Brasenose. The most likely explanation is that Foxe was here for a brief period as a private pupil of John Harwenden before transferring to Magdalen.

Another early scholar here was Richard Barnfield, author of *The Affectionate Shepherd,* who entered on November 27, 1589; before taking his degree in 1592, he had been suspended for an unknown offence and formed a lasting friendship with Michael Drayton. "John Marston, aged 16, a gentleman's son, of co. Warwick," matriculated here on February 4, 1592; contrary to Anthony à Wood's assertion that Marston was a member of Corpus Christi, this entry and one adjoining the confirmation of the B.A. degree in 1594 clearly indicate that this was the dramatist. In the same period Robert Burton was a commoner; he was sent to Brasenose, probably from the free school of Sutton Coldfield, Warwickshire, in the 1593 Long Vacation. In 1599 he was elected a student (fellow) of Christ Church, where for the sake of form and not for lack of scholarship he was assigned a tutor.

The 17th century saw the late-discovered metaphysical poet Thomas Traherne appear at Brasenose; of an impoverished Hereford family, Traherne managed to enter the college in 1653 and took his B.A. in 1656. In 1657 he took the living of Credwell, Herefordshire, and by 1669 had taken two additional degrees and holy orders.

Early in the 19th century Richard Harris Barham was a Brasenose scholar who was originally intended for the bar. But Barham took orders in 1813 and left no record of his undergraduate life here. After two unsuccessful efforts to secure fellowships at Brasenose and Trinity, Walter Pater succeeded in 1864; he came into residence immediately and took his M.A. degree in 1865. He eventually rented 2 Bradmore Road, where he was joined by his two sisters. However, even though Pater had an "external" residence, his real home was his set of rooms at the college. His life here, which is often termed "monotonous," afforded him a great deal of time to work, and *Marius the Epicurean* and *Imaginary Portraits* both date to this period. Pater moved away from Oxford in 1886 but returned to 64 St. Giles's in 1893; he contracted rheumatic fever in June 1894 and, although thought to be recovering, died suddenly on July 30. He was buried in the cemetery of St. Giles's Church. In 1897 John Buchan, later 1st Baron Tweedsmuir and Governor-General of Canada, entered on a scholarship. The same year he won the Stanhope Historical Prize for his essay on Sir Walter Ralegh and in 1898 captured the Newdigate Prize for his poem on the Pilgrim Fathers. As an undergraduate he was commissioned to write a history of the college for the Robinson series and was president of the Union in 1899; he managed to cap a brilliant career here with a first in *litterae humaniores* that year but was unable to secure a fellowship. A more recent student at Brasenose was John Middleton Murry, who took a first in honor moderations in 1910 and a second in *litterae humaniores* in 1912. William Golding came here in 1932 and received his B.A. in 1935.

One of the few literary references to Brasenose occurs in Robert Greene's *The Honourable History of*

Friar Bacon and Friar Bungay. This is the location of the cell where Friar Bacon (Roger Bacon) has "contrived and framed a head of brass. . . ." Edward Bradley makes Brasenose Verdant Green's College.

Christ Church College Christ Church, often called the House from its Latin title, Aedes Christi, is one of the two Oxford colleges considered socially prestigious and traditionally aristocratic in membership (Magdalen is the other). The college, founded in 1525 by Thomas Cardinal Wolsey, was built on the site of the early priory of St. Frideswide. In four years Wolsey spent money like a drunken prince: the buildings were planned on a grander scale than ever before conceived. In his attempt to make the church here worthy of the college, Wolsey did away with the three west bays of the old monastic church, and consequently Christ Church is the smallest cathedral in England. With Wolsey's disgrace in 1529, Henry VIII took the project over, completing most of what Wolsey had planned and finally endowing the establishment. "Great Tom" in Tom Tower rings 101 times nightly at 9:05 P.M. (9 o'clock Oxford meridian time); the number of peels are the number of members "on the foundation" in 1680. Until the early 20th century this was also curfew hour, and any man returning after the gates were shut paid "gate money."

The hall, on the southeast side of the quadrangle, is the largest medieval hall in Oxford and is extremely impressive with its carved and gilded hammer-beam roof and its display of portraits, probably the finest collection of any of the colleges. The full-length portraits by Lely, Gainsborough, Reynolds, and Lawrence are of many of the more famous Christ Church men, but those who became poets are generally missing unless they had an academic or political claim as well. Sir Thomas More is in a blue fur-lined gown; John Lily is in a relatively simple blue gown; Robert Burton, holding *The Anatomy of Melancholy,* appears in a black gown and skullcap; and Charles Lutwidge Dodgson (Lewis Carroll) is represented as much for his mathematical and general academic accomplishments as for his writings. Bishop John Fell, whose portrait presents him resplendent in miter and cope, was among the greatest of the Christ Church men and one of its greatest benefactors; he is probably best known today because of the Thomas Brown incident. Brown was threatened with expulsion because of some sort of exuberant activity; when he sent Dr. Fell a letter of apology, he was offered a pardon on condition that he translate, on the spot, Martial's epigram, "I do not love thee, Sabidius, nor can I say why: I can only say this, I do not love"; Brown's reply has become a classic:

> I do not love thee, Dr. Fell,
> The reason why I cannot tell;
> But this I know, and know full well,
> I do not love thee, Dr. Fell.

The list of literary men associated with Christ Church is especially rich. Sir Thomas More entered Canterbury Hall (later absorbed into Christ Church) around 1492 at the age of fourteen; he learned Greek from Thomas Linacre, and William Grocyn was another of his tutors. More was here for just under two years and left without a degree to enter New Inn in London, the usual step preparatory to entering one of the four Inns of Court. Sir Thomas was later elected

high steward of Oxford and with Henry VIII's support helped the forces of the Reformation, that is, the Greek scholars who favored the new learning.

About seventy-five years later, in January of 1568, Sir Philip Sidney came up from Shrewsbury at the age of thirteen. The boy was in frail health, and his uncle, the Earl of Leicester, chancellor of the university, solicited a papal dispensation for the eating of meat in Lent for "my boy Philip Sidney, who is somewhat subject to sickness." The plague broke out in Oxford in 1571, and the colleges were accordingly closed; Sidney left and never returned to take his degree. His classmate, William Camden, entered Magdalen College in 1566 under the patronage of Dr. Thomas Cooper; then, under Dr. Thomas Thornton's protective wing, Camden was admitted to Broadgates Hall and transferred to Christ Church when Thornton was promoted to a canonry here. He was later an unsuccessful candidate for a fellowship at All Souls. Camden first supplicated for his B.A. in June 1570, without result, and he then reapplied three years later but failed to complete the degree requirements. He later described himself as B.A. of Christ Church, but it is not known if he ever received the degree. Richard Hakluyt was elected to a studentship in 1570 and graduated with a B.A. on February 19, 1574, and an M.A. on January 27, 1577. He pursued an early interest in geography and read "whatever printed or written discoveries and voyages I found extant, either in Greek, Latin, Italian, Spanish, Portugal, French, or English languages." It is also possible that he lectured here after taking his degree. About the same time George Peele arrived from Christ's Hospital, London; he first entered Broadgates Hall (Pembroke) on March 29, 1571, but by December 20, 1574, he had settled at Christ Church. He was admitted to the B.A. degree in June 1577 and determined during the following Lent term (determining is the disputation to prove fitness). While here, Peele gained a reputation as a poet, possibly began his "Tale of Troy," and enjoyed a rather frantic social life. His M.A. was granted in the autumn of 1579, and sometime between March 1 and October 18, 1580, he married Ann Cooke of nearby St. Aldate's parish; the parish register has disappeared, but the ceremony most probably took place here. Christ Church is also often stated to be John Marston's college, but this is Anthony à Wood's error; Marston was a member of Brasenose.

Robert Burton has associations with both Brasenose and Christ Church; he came to Christ Church as a student (called fellow in other colleges) from Brasenose in 1599 and was placed under the tutelage of Dr. John Bancroft. Receiving his B.D. in 1614, he took the living of St. Thomas the Martyr in 1616; within five years there appeared *The Anatomy of Melancholy,* which Burton said was undertaken to suppress his own melancholy. Bishop Kennet says Burton's despondency was so great that his only relief was going to the bridge over the Cherwell and listening to the bargemen swear at each other, "at which he would set his hands to his sides and laught most profusely." Burton died here on January 25, 1640, and was buried in the north aisle of the cathedral; the epitaph is his own composition.

Ben Jonson is one of the men who had a Christ Church degree but not a Christ Church education. He came in the summer of 1619 as the guest of

Richard Corbet, a poet and senior student of the college, for the formal confirmation of his M.A. degree on July 19; the degree, Jonson told William Drummond of Hawthornden, was "by their favour, not his studie." Thomas Otway is another dramatist associated with the college; he entered from Winchester College as a commoner on May 27, 1669. He was more interested in the theater than in his studies and left Oxford in 1672 without a degree.

Sir Richard Steele came up from Charterhouse, London, in 1689 and in November was "elected to the university"; he is entered on the Dean's Entry Book on December 21 as "Richardus Steele, commoner." He was unable to secure a studentship here, and an application made to Merton College secured him a post as a *portionista*, or postmaster (poor scholar); Steele transferred to Merton in August 1691. In 1746 Thomas Percy entered Christ Church; he graduated with a B.A. degree in 1750 but without an especially distinguished record.

Probably the most renowned of Christ Church's literary graduates is John Ruskin, who matriculated in October 1836 and took up residence as a gentleman commoner in January. A number of aspects in Ruskin's life were unique here: he had a valet with him in Peckwater Quadrangle, and his mother took rooms at 90 High Street. From London, Ruskin's father joined his family on weekends, and Ruskin himself took tea with his mother daily. He competed for the Newdigate Prize on three separate occasions and was finally successful with "Salsette and Elephanta." The year 1840 was an eventful one on two counts. Ruskin met J. M. W. Turner, the watercolorist, whose works had impressed him a few years before; he was eventually to defend Turner's art in his *Modern Painters*. The same year Ruskin was forced to leave the university because of a complete breakdown in his health, and he moved to the Continent with his family in September. He remained away from Christ Church for a year and a half but took a B.A. degree in 1842 with an almost-unheard-of honorary fourth in classics and mathematics. Ruskin's M.A. degree was conferred in 1843. Almost a quarter of a century later Felix Slade endowed a professorship of fine arts here, and John Ruskin filled the chair as the first Slade Professor. Between 1870 and 1884 he gave numerous lectures and courses, a number of which were published; while Ruskin's courses were not well attended by the undergraduates, his inaugural lecture on February 8, 1870, which had been announced for the museum, had to be adjourned to the larger Sheldonian Theatre. The intensity of his work and his devotion to academic affairs undermined his health, and illness forced him to resign in 1879. Reelected to the professorship to succeed Sir William Richmond in 1883, Ruskin delivered a very well-received series of lectures, "The Art of England," but the pressures of his overextended public lecturing, combined with the university's refusal to support an extension of his drawing school (while voting funds for a laboratory for performing vivisection), brought about his final resignation in 1884. During his tenure here Ruskin had also been made an honorary fellow of Corpus Christi College.

The Manx poet T. E. Brown matriculated as a servitor in 1849 and took a double first in classics and law and history in 1853. He became a fellow at Oriel in 1854.

Charles Lutwidge Dodgson (Lewis Carroll) spent almost forty-seven years here but never succeeded to a chair. He matriculated at The House on May 23, 1850, took up residence on January 24, 1851, and virtually never left Oxford again. His first set of rooms was in Peckwater Quadrangle. Carroll's studentship was exemplary; as a first-year student he won a Boulter scholarship; in his second year he took first-class honors in mathematics and second-class honors in classics; and in October 1854 he obtained a first in the Final Mathematical School. In October 1855 he began lecturing on mathematics and at the same time he was made a master of the House (that is, he was a B.A. enjoying M.A. privileges within the walls of Christ Church but not having enough terms to be an M.A.). His M.A. was conferred in 1857. He became a full-fledged lecturer in 1856, and in October he met Ruskin, who later advised him on artistic matters. He also met William Makepeace Thackeray, who was here to deliver a paper on George III; they breakfasted together the morning after the lecture. Carroll underwent many periods of doubt before deciding to take orders, and he was not ordained a deacon until December 1861. He did not proceed to take priest's orders, perhaps partly because of his shyness and a congenital stammer and possibly, as well, because of a lack of desire to undertake regular parochial work. Carroll's love of boating was well known, and his literary career was under way in July of 1862; his diary records: "I made an expedition *up* the river to Godstow with the three Liddells; we had tea on the bank there, and did not reach Christ Church till half-past eight." Added later on the opposite page is the entry: "On which occasion I told them the fairy-tale of "Alice's Adventures Underground," which I undertook to write out for Alice." This Alice was Alice Liddell, the young daughter of the dean of Christ Church, and the book became known as *Alice's Adventures in Wonderland*. The day of the excursion was always remembered as "that golden afternoon," and Carroll later recalled

the cloudless blue above, the watery mirror below, the boat drifting idly on its way, the tinkle of the drops that fell from the oars as they waved so sleepily to and fro. . . .

Alice also recalled the blazing sun and a very hot afternoon; actually, meteorological records show that the day was rather cool and quite wet.

Carroll moved in November 1868 to a suite of ten rooms on the first floor near the present entrance of the junior common room, in the northwest corner of Tom Quadrangle; this was his final Oxford residence. He created a photographic studio on the roof and entertained frequently in his rooms. In 1869 *Behind the Looking-Glass* (published as *Through the Looking-Glass*) was finished, and in 1876 *The Hunting of the Snark* appeared, and in 1881 he resigned his lectureship and delivered his final lecture on November 30. Carroll left Oxford for Guildford on December 23, 1897, to spend Christmas there with his sisters and died there on January 14, 1898.

Stanley Weyman took a second in modern history here in 1877, and more recently W. H. Auden matriculated in 1925, began experimenting with poetic forms as an undergraduate, and attracted considerable notice as a poet before graduating in 1928. After becoming an American citizen, he held the professorship of poetry from 1956 to 1960 and lived on the col-

OXFORD: "THE SHEEP SHOP" "She looked at the Queen, who seemed to have suddenly wrapped herself up in wool. Alice rubbed her eyes, and looked again. She couldn't make out what had happened at all. Was she in a shop? And was that really—was it really a *sheep* that was sitting on the other side of the counter?"
Lewis Carroll, *Through the Looking-Glass and What Alice Found There.*

lege grounds from 1972 until his death in Vienna in 1974.

Corpus Christi College Founded in 1516 or 1517, Corpus Christi has always been a small but distinguished college. By the time Richard Fox (Foxe) founded Corpus Christi, monastic influence was on the wane; Fox thus established a college for the training of secular clergy, with emphasis on the teaching of Latin, Greek, and theology. The original plan accommodated twenty fellows, twenty *discipuli* (between the ages of twelve and seventeen at admission), and four to six sons of wealthy noblemen or lawyers; today there are almost 300 faculty and students. Within a few years of opening its doors, Corpus Christi became the college of Nicholas Udall, who was admitted as a scholar on June 18, 1520, and graduated with a B.A. degree in May 1524; he became a *scholaris* (probationary fellow) in September of that year and was admitted a *socius* (full fellow) two years later. In the next few years he lectured on Greek and logic and may have written *Thersites*, although his authorship of this work is uncertain. Udall left Oxford in 1529 and was kept from receiving the M.A. until July 1534, probably because of religious nonconformity. Another early scholar at Corpus Christi was Richard Hooker, whose place as a "humble student" in 1568 was secured by Bishop John Jewel. Upon Jewel's death in 1571, Hooker found a patron

in Edwin Sandys, and in 1573 he was elected a scholar of the foundation (the statutes of the college stated an upper age limit of nineteen for the election of scholars except in the case of unusual attainment, which this was judged to be). Hooker was graduated with a B.A. degree in January 1574 and received an M.A. degree in 1577, the year in which he also obtained a fellowship. For some reason, probably an offense to the Puritan vice-president of the college, John Barfoot, Hooker was among a small group of scholars expelled for a month in October 1579. He returned in November and continued his studies until he took holy orders around 1581; he relinquished his fellowship upon the occasion of his marriage later that year.

Thomas Carew is often mentioned as a member of Corpus Christi, following Anthony à Wood, but Carew matriculated at Merton College in 1608. A century later, in 1702, Edward Young came up as an independent member from Winchester College; he had been on the election roll for New College but was over the age limit before a place fell vacant. He resided at the warden's lodge here while at New College and then entered Corpus Christi as a gentleman commoner in 1702. In 1708 he was appointed to a law fellowship at All Souls.

In the 19th century Dr. Thomas Arnold became a student here, and John Ruskin was admitted as an honorary fellow when he was Slade Professor of Fine Art. Ruskin's rooms were on the first floor of Staircase No. 2 in the Fellows' Building, and many of the choicest items in his art collection were displayed there. A later Victorian was Corpus Christi's most distinguished literary student. In October 1863 Robert Bridges came up as a commoner from Eton and soon met Gerard Manley Hopkins, who was at Balliol. The friendship was to be of great importance to both men, and Bridges later edited Hopkins's poems. Bridges distinguished himself as an oarsman and in 1867 stroked the college boat to a second. He took a second in *litterae humaniores* in 1867 and for some time following graduation had only occasional contacts with the university. In 1895, his poetic reputation secure, he was urged to compete for the chair of poetry but declined; that year he was made an honorary fellow of the college.

Exeter College In 1314 Exeter College was founded by Walter de Stapleton, Bishop of Exeter, to provide instruction for the men of Cornwall and Devon. The dean and chapter of Exeter were to nominate thirteen scholars, eight from Devon, four from Cornwall, and one other as chaplain. But the formal establishment lacked permanence and discipline, and in 1566 the statutes were changed, and new fellowships were endowed. The college then entered a period of flourishing academic activity and stability which was undermined only by the Civil War. The connection with the West Country is maintained in the 20th century by fifteen or more Stapleton scholars, all born or educated there. Exeter's 19th-century chapel contains a magnificent tapestry by William Morris of the Burne-Jones painting *The Star of Bethlehem.*

Literary associations with Exeter go back to the early 17th century and John Ford. He is probably the John Ford, "Devon gen f.," who matriculated on March 26, 1601, since this John Ford left the university in 1602 and was admitted to the Middle Temple (as was the dramatist) in November of that year. There is slightly more information about the college career of William of Tavistock (William Browne). He entered about 1603—or as Anthony à Wood states, "about the beginning of the reign of James I"—and went down without a degree to study law at Clifford's Inn and later at the Inner Temple in London. He returned to Exeter at the beginning of 1624 and became a tutor. An entry on the college rolls dated April 30, 1624, records the matriculation of "William Browne, son of Thomas Browne, gentleman of Tavistock, matriculated, age 33." It is possible, but highly unlikely, that Browne had not matriculated in 1603; nevertheless, on August 25, 1624, he was admitted to the degree of M.A., which was officially conferred in 1625.

In 1842 James Anthony Froude, the historian, became a fellow of Exeter; he took deacon's orders in 1844 and resigned his fellowship five years later when a tutor seized a student's copy of Froude's *Nemesis of Faith,* tore it up, and consigned it to the fire. Froude returned later as Regius Professor of Modern History and lived at Cherwell Edge (now Linacre College).

After a very "crooked start in life," he said, Richard Doddridge Blackmore matriculated at his father's college on scholarship from Blundell's School in Tiverton, Devon, on December 7, 1843. A sound classical scholar, an enthusiastic fisherman, and a keen observer of nature, he took a second in classics in 1847 and was admitted to an M.A. degree in 1852.

Probably the most famous Exeter literary man is William Morris, who matriculated in June 1852 and took up residence the following January. He came up from early private education with an extraordinary amount of knowledge, a fantastic (but not photographic) memory, and a habit of incessant reading. His close friendship with Edward Burne-Jones, a friendship that lasted until Morris's death in 1896, began here. With Burne-Jones and William Fulford, another undergraduate at Exeter, he formed the Brotherhood, a group concerned with an ascetic life, and determined not to take orders as planned. Two years after obtaining his final Schools, he returned with Burne-Jones, Dante Gabriel Rossetti, and others to work on the decoration of the Debating Hall of the Oxford Union Society. Morris worked on one of the bays of a wall and on the roof; the plaster was improperly prepared, and the pre-Raphaelite frescoes did not survive intact (they have been restored).

In more recent times both Alfred Noyes and J. R. R. Tolkien were Exeter undergraduates. Noyes published his first poetry, *The Loom of Years,* while he was here, and Tolkien was later made an honorary fellow.

Hertford College Hertford College (pronounced "hart'ford") has a deceptively modern appearance, and indeed its founding date is generally listed as 1874; but the history of this establishment is mixed with that of Hart Hall, which was founded on this site in 1283 or 1284 by Elias de Hertford; the fortunes of the college then became a bit confused. In the 14th century the Bishop of Exeter, Walter de Stapleton, and his successors leased the hall to anyone who had need of it (including, for example, William of Wykeham, who rented Hart Hall until New College was completed). In fact, the college was in desperate straits until well into the 18th century,

and it did not become a college in its own right until the principalship of Dr. Richard Newton in that century; even as late as 1818 a new vice-principal could not be found. In 1820, when nearby Magdalen Hall burned to the ground, its members moved to the Hertford site; and by the time the Baring banking family became interested in the plight of the college, Hart Hall was virtually nonexistent. The Baring benefactions thus created the modern college around 1874, and the name Hertford was resumed.

One of the early college worthies is William Tyndale, the translator of the Bible, who entered Magdalen Hall at the beginning of Easter term, 1510, under the name William Hychyns (the Tyndale family, possibly on migrating to the north during the Wars of the Roses, assumed the surname Hychyns). John Foxe says that Tyndale not only improved "himself in knowledge of tongues and other Liberal arts" but read extensively in theology and did some private tutoring. Tyndale was awarded a B.A. degree in July 1512 and received his M.A. in July 1515; from here he went on to Cambridge. Samuel Daniel entered Magdalen Hall as a commoner in 1579 and stayed at Oxford about three years, during which time, according to Anthony à Wood, he "improved himself much in academical learning" because of an excellent tutor. However, Wood continues, "His glory being more prone to easier and smoother studies than in pecking and hewing at logic, he left the university without the honour of a degree."

Within two years of Daniel's leaving Oxford, eleven-year-old John Donne was admitted to Hart Hall with his younger brother Henry in October 1584. It was not usual for boys so young to be entered in the university, although there were precedents for the practice. The main reason for Donne's early arrival was the Oath of Supremacy; because of the drift in the country toward Rome, all Oxonians except students younger than sixteen had to swear to the oath; quite naturally, having taken care to raise her family in the old creed, Donne's mother sent the children to the university at an age when the oath was not required. Donne had relatives living in Oxford; his uncle Robert Dawson and his wife kept the Blue Boar Inn (where the public library now stands) at the corner of St. Aldate's Street and Blue Boar Lane. Henry (later Sir Henry) Wotton, who entered Hart Hall at the same time, shared rooms with Donne. Donne's time here had to be less than the full three years (twelve terms), since he would then have to matriculate and take the oath. Izaak Walton's assertion that Donne moved to Cambridge in 1588 is possible but unprovable. Many years later, on October 16, 1610, the M.A. degree was conferred on Donne by decree of convocation.

In January or February 1602, Thomas Hobbes entered Magdalen Hall and might easily have had a distinguished university career but for the effect of lax discipline and ecclesiastic disputation on his character; as John Aubrey states, he spent most of his time snaring jackdaws and reading travel books. Despite this lack of application Hobbes was granted the B.A. degree in February 1608. In the Lent term of 1622 Edward Hyde, later 1st Earl of Clarendon, entered Magdalen Hall; he was granted a B.A. degree in February 1626. He had failed to obtain a demyship at Magdalen College despite a royal mandate. At the end of the 17th century Jonathan Swift appeared at

Hart Hall; with the help of Sir William Temple, he gained two degrees from Oxford in a short time. He was admitted to the B.A. degree on June 14, 1692, on the strength of testimonials from Trinity College, Dublin, and to an M.A. on July 5.

A little more than 100 years later Robert Stephen Hawker entered Magdalen Hall from Pembroke College; he had married Charlotte I'Ans, aged forty-one, before transferring to Magdalen Hall, where he received his B.A. degree in 1828 and his M.A. in 1836. The year before he completed his degree, Hawker won the Newdigate Prize with a poem on Pompeii.

A far more modern association is that of Evelyn Waugh, who matriculated on a scholarship from Lancing, Shoreham-by-Sea, Sussex, in 1922. Waugh comments in *A Little Learning:*

> Hertford was a respectable but dreary little college. When Mr. Bowlby announced my scholarship to the school, he described it in a phrase which, by reason of its combination of patronage with grammatical infelicity, amused my father intensely, as "a very rising college". If I can believe my children, it has not yet risen to a higher position than it enjoyed in my time. In my time there was no scholar of importance among the dons. . . .
> The advantages were a good kitchen and a unique system by which term was kept merely by residence; there were neither roll-calls nor chapels as there were at other colleges, to take one early from bed on cold mornings.

His first rooms were, by his own account, modest:

> [A]rriving late, I found the only set available were in the oldest building, that looked out on New College Lane. They were over the J.C.R. buttery in which teas were prepared and my chief memory of the staircase is of the rattle of dish-covers on foggy afternoons and the smell of anchovy-toast and honey buns as the scouts filled their trays.

As an undergraduate Waugh knew Graham Greene, who was at Balliol, slightly and "stood on friendly terms though barely in friendship" with Anthony Powell, also at Balliol. Waugh scraped a third in 1926 and noted:

> The only serious regret of my Oxford life is the amount of time which I wasted on my books in my last term. Had I known I was to get a third, I would readily have settled for a fourth.

Waugh presents a fair picture of his undergraduate life in *Brideshead Revisited.*

Jesus College The first Oxford college founded after the Reformation, Jesus College required more than 100 years to become stabilized and realize sufficient endowments to gain importance. Founded in 1571 by Hugh Price, the college was designed to cater mainly to the Welsh. Until the early 20th century Jesus was at least half Welsh, but now the number of Welsh students has dropped to about one-fifth.

Lancelot Andrewes, later Bishop of Winchester, was nominated to a fellowship by the founder of Jesus in 1576; Andrewes was also elected to a fellowship at Pembroke the same year. He seems to have resigned in 1580 or 1581. Henry Vaughan entered Jesus College in 1638; there is no evidence of his matriculation, although his twin brother Thomas matriculated at Jesus on December 14, 1638. Vaughan, says John Aubrey, "stayed not att Oxford to take any degree." The external evidence supplied by "On Sir *Thomas Bodley's* Library, the Author

Being Then in Oxford" seems to establish that Vaughan was an Oxonian but not necessarily a member of Jesus College. He left without a degree in the autumn or summer of 1640 and went to London, where he spent some time studying law. T. E. Lawrence entered from Oxford High School in 1906 and took a first in history in 1910; his thesis, required for the degree, was later published as *Crusader Castles.* In 1906–1907 Frederick Rolfe was here as secretary to Dr. Hardy.

Lincoln College Probably no college in Oxford or Cambridge has had a wider influence on religious matters than Lincoln. Founded in 1427 and properly called The College of the Blessed Mary and All Saints, Lincoln, in the University of Oxford, it was designed as a theological training ground for refuting Wycliffite heretical dogma. It is often assumed that in 1620 Sir William Davenant entered Lincoln College, where he studied under Daniel Hough; his tenure is traditionally said to have been short, but there is no evidence for this assumption. During the Civil War Thomas Fuller resided at Lincoln College for seventeen weeks; he joined the Royalist forces here in August 1643 after preaching a heated sermon in London showing his discontent with Puritanism and then refusing to take the oath. John Wesley was here for nine years beginning in 1726, and his rooms over the passage between the two quadrangles have been carefully restored and can be seen by the public. More recently, Edward Thomas came up to Oxford from St. Paul's School as a noncollegiate student in 1897 but gained a scholarship in history here in 1898. He was graduated with a second two years later.

There is one female association with this college. Mark Pattison, the 19th-century rector, had much to do with the education of women and was also largely responsible for Lincoln's discarding many of its medieval trappings and becoming a modern and progressive institution. One of his houseguests was Mary Ann Evans (George Eliot); she, unkindly, probably portrays Pattison in *Middlemarch* as that deadly-dry, humorless pedant Mr. Casaubon.

Magdalen College Dominating the scene at Magdalen (pronounced "maud'lin") is the extraordinarily graceful bell tower, described by James I as "the most absolute building in Oxford" and by Thomas Babington Macaulay as that "singularly venerable tower." The tower, begun in 1492 and completed seventeen years later, rises 150 feet and is crowned with open parapets and pinnacles. The college, founded by William of Waynflete, became the wealthiest foundation in the university, and it is still one of the three richest. The oldest part of the college, the 13th-century wall in High Street, was part of the Hospital of St. John the Baptist, but the original pilgrim's door is now partly covered by the roadway. Waynflete's statutes provided for a president, forty fellows (there are now fifty-nine fellows and seven lecturers), and thirty scholars called demies (there are now two senior demies and twenty-five demies). (A demy receives half the allowance of a fellow and, therefore, half the name.) The medieval cloister around the Great Quadrangle is itself impressive, but even more impressive are twenty-five stone figures more than 400 years old which crown the buttresses on three sides of the quadrangle.

Around 1532 John Foxe entered Magdalen, and he

may also have attended Magdalen College School. His university career may have begun at Brasenose, but his degrees were all granted here, the B.A. in July 1537 and the M.A. in July 1543. He became a probationary fellow in July 1538, advanced to full fellow status the next year, and held a joint lectureship in logic in 1539–1540. Although Foxe always identifies himself with Magdalen in his works, he disliked compulsory chapel, was annoyed that within seven years he had to take orders or lose his fellowship, and rebelled against enforced celibacy. As a consequence, he and five others resigned their posts in July 1545.

Miles Coverdale visited Magdalen in 1551. In 1566 William Camden also appeared; apparently his patron, Dr. Thomas Cooper, a fellow here, secured Camden's position. Most likely Camden was a servitor (so Anthony à Wood claims); in any event, he remained only a short time. Failing to gain a demyship, he migrated to Broadgates Hall (Pembroke College). One of the first-known facts about John Lyly places him at Magdalen in the spring of 1569; he entered, probably as a commoner, at the age of sixteen and matriculated on October 8, 1571, when he was described as *plebi filius*. He evidently neglected his academic studies and by the time he was admitted to a B.A. degree in April 1573 was known as a poet and wit "averse to the crabbed studies of logic and philosophy." Unable to obtain a fellowship, he was, he says in *Euphues*, "sent into the country" by the university authorities. His M.A. was granted in June 1575.

George Wither was at Magdalen from 1604 to 1606 but took no degree. In 1689 Joseph Addison, who originally entered his father's college, Queen's, gained a demyship at Magdalen after numerous resignations protesting James II's order to elect a Roman Catholic president in 1687; the college refused the command. Addison took his M.A. degree in 1693 and became a fellow in 1698; he was renowned as a classical scholar and noted for his extreme shyness and late-night study. He was also noted for his frequent walks around the grounds; Addison's Walk (then Water Walk) lies east of the New Building and the Grove. Addison resigned his fellowship in 1711 because of his frequent absences but had given up actual residence in 1699.

William Collins also secured a demyship at Magdalen; coming up to Queen's in 1740 from Winchester, he transferred here in 1741 upon his election. During his time at the university he became acquainted with Gilbert White, who was at Oriel, and published *Persian Eclogues* before taking his B.A. degree on November 18, 1743. A few years later, on April 3, 1752, Edward Gibbon entered as a gentleman commoner. His previous schooling at a day school in Putney, at Kingston-on-Thames, at Putney Bridge, and at Westminster School, London, was haphazard, and he entered, he said, "with a stock of erudition which might have puzzled a doctor, and a degree of ignorance of which a schoolboy might be ashamed." Later he acknowledged that the time spent here was a waste:

> To the university of Oxford I acknowledge no obligation; and she will as cheerfully renounce me for a son as I am willing to disclaim her for a mother. I spent fourteen months at Magdalen College; they proved the fourteen months the most idle and unprofitable of my whole life.

Gibbon's interest in Roman Catholicism culminated when he was received into the church; this step, in fact, signaled the end of his university career; his father removed him and placed him with a friend in Putney to overcome the Catholic influence. Gibbon was not, as is often stated, expelled from Magdalen. Henry James Pye, later a much-ridiculed Poet Laureate, entered as a gentleman commoner in 1762; he received an M.A. in 1766 and a D.C.L. in 1772.

In May 1803 John Wilson (Christopher North) entered, also as a gentleman commoner, from Glasgow College; he won the Newdigate Prize with "The Study of Greek and Roman Architecture." His B.A. degree in 1807 followed "the most illustrious examination within the memory of man," and he proceeded to the M.A. degree in 1810. John Addington Symonds, after a double first in classics at Balliol, was elected a fellow in 1826; the following spring he won the chancellor's prize for an essay, "The Renaissance." Never having been very strong and having a tendency toward tuberculosis, Symonds had to leave Magdalen because of a complete physical breakdown six months later. Charles Reade entered in 1831 on a demyship and read privately with Robert Lowe as an undergraduate. Taking a third, he received his B.A. in June 1835, was elected a fellow the following month, and later was elected Vinerian scholar; he proceeded to an M.A. degree in 1838. Reade became bursar of the college in 1844; he was also elected dean of arts and proceeded to shock the more austere faculty by parading around in a green coat with brass buttons. He received a D.C.L. degree in 1847 and assumed the vice-presidency of Magdalen four years later. His rooms were at 2 New Building. From this point on Reade took less interest in the college and its activities (in fact, he acquired permanent lodgings in London); however, he retained his fellowship until his death in April 1884.

Oscar Wilde came to Magdalen from Trinity College, Dublin, on a demyship on October 17, 1875; he was a good student and took a first in the honor finals in Trinity term, 1878. In *De Profundis* Wilde later wrote that there were "two great turning points in my life . . . when my father sent me to Oxford, and when society sent me to prison." He came under the influence of John Ruskin, Slade Professor of Fine Art, and in June 1878 won the Newdigate Prize for his poem *Ravenna*. Wilde's three rooms overlooking the Cherwell on what is called the kitchen staircase were fully paneled and noted for their exotic qualities.

T. E. Lawrence was a senior demy here from 1910 to 1914. Compton Mackenzie, an undergraduate here in the early 1900s, describes university life in *Sinister Street*. In 1925 C. S. Lewis was elected a fellow and held the post until 1954, when he left to become Professor of Medieval and Renaissance English at Cambridge; he had earlier been at University College as an undergraduate.

The Poet Laureate John Betjeman, who entered Magdalen from Marlborough College, recalls his time here and his rooms in the final chapter of *Summoned by Bells*:

> My walls were painted Bursar's apple-green;
> My wide-sashed windows looked across the grass
> To tower and hall and lines of pinnacles.
> The wind among the elms, the echoing stairs,
> The quarters, chimed across the quiet quad

From Magdalen tower and neighbouring turret-clocks,
Gave eighteenth-century splendour to my state.
Privacy after years of public school;
Dignity after years of none at all. . . .

He admits he "cut tutorials with wild excuse" and spent too much time at the George Restaurant, but he was always kept in line by an "insistent inner voice of guilt." On Sundays, he passed by "college chapels with their organ-groan" and stacked bicycles "[t]o worship at High Mass at Pusey House," and he writes fondly of "[d]inner with Maurice Bowra," the man whose "company/Taught me far more than all my tutors did."

Merton College   Merton College, the oldest residential college, has one of the longest and most notable histories of the Oxford colleges and was the first educational institution in England to depart from the student monastic model. In 1262 Walter de Merton, "sometime Chancellor of the illustrious Lord, Henry, King of England," allotted revenues from two Surrey manors for the support of clerks studying at a university, and by 1264, when Henry III granted his approval of Merton's plan, it was decided to house the students in their own buildings. As a result, Merton was better able to provide for and influence its students. Much of the original structure is still here, and walking through a stone-vaulted chamber into the Mob Quadrangle is a step back to the Middle Ages; on all sides are 14th-century buildings complete with mullioned windows. The library is exceptional; the paneled roof has Tudor heraldic bosses, and the paneling, screens, and bookcases are Elizabethan. There are medieval tiles in the floor, some fragments and panels of old glass in the windows, a number of chained volumes, and a display of Max Beerbohm cartoons.

Traditionally, both John Wycliffe and Geoffrey Chaucer are connected with Merton, but it is now fairly well established that the John Wyclif here was not John Wycliffe the reformer and theologian. Chaucer's connection is difficult to prove; a close friend toward the end of his life was one Strode, "one of the most illustrious ornaments of Merton College." It would seem fair, then, to assume that Chaucer at least visited Oxford. Finally, there is no historical basis for the assertion that John Gower was educated here.

On May 14, 1602, Philip Massinger, styling himself the son of a gentleman from Salisbury (*Sarisburiensis, generosi filius*), entered St. Alban's Hall (incorporated into Merton in 1882). The gossipy Anthony à Wood comments that Massinger did not apply himself to the study of logic and philosophy and was far more deeply involved with poetry and romances. Either on this account or because of his father's death in 1606, Massinger left without a degree. Thomas Carew, who Anthony à Wood claimed was at Corpus Christi College, apparently matriculated at Merton on June 10, 1608; he proceeded to a B.A. degree on January 31, 1611, and went on to the Middle Temple in London to read law. Anthony à Wood was also a Merton man. The family home was just outside the college grounds; Wood matriculated in May 1647 and within a few months was made a postmaster. His undergraduate career was undistinguished, and, indeed, he took five years to obtain his degree. His M.A. was granted in December 1655.

Richard Steele transferred from Christ Church to Merton in August 1691, when he was elected a postmaster here. He had been unable to secure a senior scholarship at Christ Church, and his transfer from his "loved and ever-honoured tutor" must have been difficult. Steele secured a slight reputation as a scholar, but there was some trouble, notably with old Anthony à Wood, who had become deaf, misanthropic, tyrannical, and detested. Steele left without a degree on March 3, 1692, and volunteered for the Life Guards. George Saintsbury, critic, historian, and author of *Notes on a Cellar Book*, matriculated here in 1863 as a classical postmaster and received a first in classical moderations in 1865 and a second in *litterae humaniores* in 1866. He failed to secure a fellowship and left Oxford in 1868; much later, in 1909, he was elected an honorary fellow of Merton.

More recently Merton housed Sir Max Beerbohm, who felt that his character was influenced for the worse by Oxford. Beerbohm came up from Charterhouse, London, took no degree, and left in 1892. In 1939 he received an honorary D.Litt. from the university, and in 1942 he was made an honorary fellow of Merton College. T. S. Eliot came here in 1914 following time spent at Harvard and the Sorbonne; he had already finished his doctoral dissertation at Harvard and spent his time here absorbed in the study of Greek philosophers, especially Aristotle. Eliot was made an honorary fellow in 1949.

Louis MacNeice, an undergraduate from 1926 to 1930, describes his time here in *The Strings Are False;* he also sets part of *Autumn Sequel* in Oxford and asks

Where are Saucer Hall
And Peckwater Inn and Bocardo? Where are the grey
Friars and the black friars? Gone to the wall;

And the wall has gone—or is going with little delay.
Duns Scotus, William of Ockham and Roger Bacon,
Wycliffe and even Wolsey, have had their day;

The trivium and quadrivium are forsaken. . . .

Finally, Edmund Blunden, a fellow here from 1931 to 1944, became Professor of Poetry in 1967, and J. R. R. Tolkien, a fellow of Merton and Professor of English Language and Literature from 1945 to 1959, completed *The Lord of the Rings* here in 1955.

New College   This college is properly titled St. Mary College of Winchester in Oxford, and New College is a nickname, although it is the only name the foundation has ever known. Established in 1379 by William of Wykeham, founder of Winchester College, the college originally admitted only Winchester boys but opened its doors to all students in the 19th century. The Winchester tie, though, is still strong. The college is essentially as it was in the 14th century, and the chapel, on the north side of the Great Quadrangle, retains its original 14th-century glass in all except the great west window. The now-fading "new" west window is from cartoons of Sir Joshua Reynolds, and below the window are the figures of the Seven Virtues; Charity is a portrait of Elizabeth Linley, wife of Richard Sheridan. Unlike other early colleges at Oxford, New College was founded specifically for undergraduates and, in fact, may have been the first college to employ the tutorial approach systematically.

In the mid-15th century William Grocyn was here as a scholar; admitted from Winchester College in 1465, he became a full fellow in 1467. This was the beginning of an outstanding academic career which reached its zenith when he became one of the first, if not the first, to teach Greek publicly in the university. Sir Henry Wotton matriculated in New College as a commoner from Winchester College on June 5, 1594. He remained only two years before transferring to The Queen's College. For the next century there were no outstanding literary figures at New College; then, in 1702, Edward Young entered from Winchester College as a commoner. For a short time he lived in the warden's lodge, but with the death of the warden he transferred as a gentleman commoner to Corpus Christi College in anticipation of lower expenses. In 1789 Sydney Smith came up from Winchester, where he had been a prefect. He became a scholar of New College on February 5. After two years of residence he succeeded to a fellowship and took orders a few years later.

Lionel Johnson won the Winchester scholarship in December 1885; seven months later he won the Goddard scholarship for his ability in the classics. Johnson came up in October of the same year and had a distinguished but not outstanding career. He took a second in classical moderations in 1888 and a first in *litterae humaniores* in 1889 and was well known in local literary circles. A contemporary of Johnson's was John Galsworthy, but the two do not appear to have known each other. Coming from Harrow, Galsworthy matriculated on October 15, 1886; he read law and took a second in jurisprudence in 1889; the second may have been the result of too much time spent in the Mitre Inn playing bar billiards. There is a commemorative plaque in the cloisters.

One of the more recent wardens of New College has left an indelible mark on the literary world. The Rev. William Archibald Spooner, whose name has given us the term "spoonerism," was an absent-minded Victorian clergyman who supposedly told a first-year man that to get around Oxford well he needed "a well-boiled icicle." Many of his other slips have become famous, although some are no doubt apocryphal.

Oriel College   The House of the Blessed Mary the Virgin in Oxford, commonly called Oriel College, of the Foundation of Edward II of famous memory, sometime King of England is one of Oxford's oldest colleges, founded in 1326, and erroneously claims as its founder King Edward II. The real founder was Adam de Brome, the King's almoner, who was given a license to found a college for a provost and ten scholars. After establishing the college, then called Mary's College, in 1324, he turned it over to the King. Today nothing exists of the medieval college, and the oldest current building was erected in Tudor times.

It is said, without foundation, that William Langland was a student here, but it is known that Sir Walter Ralegh was about 1568. The date cannot be established, but Ralegh entered Oriel at the age of fifteen or sixteen, which age would suggest 1568, if his correct birth date is 1552. Anthony à Wood notes

that Ralegh was in residence for three years, and the college books contain his name in 1572. In 1604 Richard Brathwaite (Braithwaite), author of *Barnabae Itinerarium (Drunken Barnaby's Four Journeys)*, entered as a commoner and spent several years here before his father determined on a law career for him and sent him to Cambridge.

The celebrated naturalist Gilbert White was admitted as a commoner in December 1739 but did not enter into residence until November 1740. On June 17, 1743, he received his testamur (certificate that he passed his examinations) and a few days later his B.A. The following March he was elected a fellow of Oriel College, proceeded to an M.A. degree in October 1746, and received deacon's orders the following April. He unsuccessfully stood for the provostship following the death of Dr. Hodges in 1757 and shortly thereafter claimed, by right of fellowship seniority, the vacant living of Moreton-in-Pickney, Northamptonshire, which he planned to serve in a nonresidential capacity, as had been customary for years. The new provost did not accept this situation with pleasure and was even more deeply incensed when White continued his residence in Selborne, Hampshire, while retaining his fellowship.

John Henry Newman was elected a fellow of Oriel College on April 12, 1822, and when he was ordained a deacon in 1824, he was appointed to the curacy of St. Clement's Church. Two years later he gained a tutorship at Oriel, and when the living of St. Mary's Church (the university church) fell vacant, it was granted to Newman. The Oxford movement had already begun although it had not yet taken on its final form. In 1832 Newman was forced to resign his tutorship, and by 1839 Newman's reservations about the Anglican Church were many and well known. In 1843 he resigned the living of St. Mary's and left Oxford, and in 1845 he was received into the Catholic Church.

Both Dr. Thomas Arnold and his son, Matthew Arnold, were elected to fellowships at Oriel; the elder Arnold gained his in 1815 and resided here until his ordination and preferment to the Laleham church. Matthew was elected in 1845 and held the fellowship only two years. One of his colleagues was Thomas Hughes, author of *Tom Brown's School Days*, who came up from Rugby in the spring of 1842. Hughes already had a reputation as a fairly decent cricketer and, indeed, played in the 1843 Oxford-Cambridge match at Lord's. After graduating with a B.A. degree in 1845, he went to London, where he read for the bar. His novel *Tom Brown at Oxford* presents a fairly accurate picture of contemporary Oxford, and, in fact, St. Ambrose's is Oriel.

Arthur Hugh Clough, after obtaining a second at Balliol in 1841, was elected to an Oriel fellowship; within a year he was appointed a tutor and discovered the pleasures of teaching. He began writing seriously at this time, and "The New Sinai," "Qui Laborat, Orat," "Qua Cursum Ventus," and "The Questioning Spirit" date from this period. By the time that Ralph Waldo Emerson visited him at the end of the winter term in 1847, Clough was already considering leaving Oxford. Unable to sign the Thirty-nine Articles and unwilling to enter the church, Clough gave up his tutorship in April 1848 and his fellowship the following October. He returned to Oxford for several weeks in the autumn of 1849 and stayed in cheap lodgings in Holywell near the Parson's Pleasure.

Pembroke College Originally Broadgates Hall, an early medieval institution, Pembroke College came into existence in 1624, nominally founded by James I, and took its name from William Herbert, 3d Earl of Pembroke, then chancellor of the university. Originally the college was intended to cater to young men from Abingdon School, and there is still a close association with the school. The college occupies the original medieval site, and the refectory of Broadgates is now the college library.

The first literary association with Pembroke is only probable; John Heywood is traditionally said to have been a member of Pembroke, and it has been suggested that Heywood was sent here after being a choirboy, at royal expense; indeed, one of his later epigrams refers to Broadgates:

> Alas poor verdigales must lie in the streete:
> To house them, no doore in the citee made meete.
> Syns at our narow doores they in can not win,
> Send them to Oxforde, at Brodegates to get in.

One of the earliest scholars here was William Camden, who was admitted in the 1560s after failing to secure a demyship at Magdalen. His interest in antiquarian research began during this period; Camden transferred to Christ Church when his patron, Dr. Thomas Thornton, was elevated to a canonry there. In March 1571 George Peele entered Broadgates from Christ's Hospital, London, and probably remained here until 1574, when he transferred to Christ Church. Francis Beaumont matriculated at Broadgates Hall, and, in fact, his birth date (1584) is calculated from the entry in the university register: "Broadgates, 1596, Feb. 4, Francisc. Beaumont Baron. fil. aetat 12." Beaumont's father died during the young man's second year here, and both Francis and his brothers Henry and John probably left without taking degrees. Sir Thomas Browne entered Broadgates as a fellow commoner at the beginning of 1623; his B.A. degree was confirmed on June 30, 1626, and his M.A. on June 11, 1629. He then turned to medicine and practiced first somewhere in Oxfordshire.

The most famous Pembroke man of letters had only a short association with the college; Samuel Johnson entered as a commoner on October 31, 1728. His family's poverty had precluded his attending a university, and Johnson was able to enter Pembroke only when Andrew Corbet offered to undertake the young man's expenses so that Johnson could read with Corbet's son. Johnson's tutor, William Jorden, was a kind and worthy man but not a scholar; the outset of Johnson's university career is best related in the story told to James Boswell:

> The first day after I came to college I waited upon him [Jorden] and then stayed away four. On the sixth, Mr. Jorden asked me why I had not attended. I answered I had been sliding upon the ice in Christ Church meadow. And this I said with as much *nonchalance* as I am now talking to you. I had no notion that I was wrong or irreverent to my tutors. *Boswell:* "That, Sir, was great fortitude of mind." *Johnson:* "No, Sir, stark insensibility."

Another of the numerous Johnsonian anecdotes concerns a fine of 2 pence which Jorden imposed on Johnson for nonattendance at lectures. Paying the fine, Johnson commented, "Sir, you have sconced me twopence for non-attendance at a lecture not worth a penny." Johnson had impressed the college authorities with his wide reading; and, contrary to his claim that he disregarded all power and authority and Bishop Thomas Percy's claim that Johnson tried to incite the students to rebel against college discipline, Johnson is said to have attended lectures regularly and to have been well behaved.

By 1729 Johnson's money was running out, and some sort of disagreement with Corbet affected the early promise of tuition. Thus, while poverty finally brought an end to Johnson's university career, it is also clear that he often exaggerated his own poor state and could not accept help from other quarters because of his vanity. Contrary to Boswell's assertion that Johnson was here three years, the college books show that he was in continual residence only until December 12, 1729; he was here only briefly after that date, and in October 1731 his name was removed from the rolls.

Johnson did revisit Oxford later and always retained a great deal of affection for Pembroke and Oxford. On his first return in 1754, when he came to do research on his dictionary, he resided at Kettel Hall for five weeks and became intimate with Thomas Warton at Trinity, with whom he reexplored Oxford. On this visit Johnson was coldly received by the master of Pembroke; trying to secure a subscription to the dictionary and being turned down, Johnson remarked, "There lives a man who lives by the revenues of literature, and will not move a finger to support it." Johnson's rooms were over the gateway in what was then the top of the tower. The college owns a number of memorabilia and is proudest of Sir Joshua Reynolds's portrait of Dr. Johnson, which hangs in the senior common room. There is a bust of Johnson in the library, which also houses a collection of his early letters and essays and the manuscript of his *Prayers and Meditations*. One other item of interest is the old gossip's great china teapot; Johnson was a tea drinker *extraordinaire* and was often known to consume twenty cups in an evening.

William Shenstone is often said to have been one of Dr. Johnson's contemporaries, but this cannot have been the case unless most of the information known about Johnson is in error. Shenstone matriculated here as a servitor in May 1732, almost nine months after Johnson left. Even though Shenstone's name remained on the books until 1742, he took no degree.

In 1820 Thomas Lovell Beddoes became a commoner of Pembroke College and a well-known eccentric and rebel about campus. In 1821 he published *The Improvisatore*, a small pamphlet of which he was soon ashamed and which he suppressed. The following year *The Bridge's Tragedy*, a play which he had written in 1819 while at Charterhouse in London, was published. He commenced with a B.A. degree in 1825, the year in which he wrote *The Second Brother* and *Torrismond*, two dramatic fragments; within a few months of receiving his degree, he went to Göttingen to study medicine and returned in April 1828 to receive his M.A.

The Rev. Robert Stephen Hawker matriculated at

Pembroke on April 28, 1823, and during the 1824 vacation his father informed him that there were no finances to maintain him at Oxford. In true Hawker fashion, he solved the problem. At the age of nineteen, he proposed to Charlotte I'Ans, a woman of forty-one, and married her in November; the means of staying on at the university had been found. However, upon his return after Christmas, he was unable to stay at Pembroke and transferred to Magdalen Hall (Hertford College).

From 1926 to 1945 J. R. R. Tolkien was a fellow of Pembroke and Professor of Anglo-Saxon. *The Hobbit* was written here.

The Queen's College The Queen's College was founded in 1340 or 1341; the later date is that listed in the charter, which sets out an elaborate scheme for the provision of a provost and twelve scholars representing Christ and the Twelve Apostles. Founded by Robert of Eglesfield, a native of Cumberland and chaplain to Queen Philippa, for whom the college was named, Queen's was originally under her patronage. The scholars, mainly from the Lake District, were to be students of theology and were to wear blood-red robes in hall to commemorate the Passion and be supported by seventy-two "poor boys," or disciples; the fellows are still summoned to dinner by a trumpet in term time. Another tradition, established because the distance between Oxford and the Lake District was too great to allow the scholars to travel home over Christmas vacation, is still maintained: the Boar's Head Procession and Dinner on Christmas Day and the Needle and Thread Feast on New Year's Day. On the latter occasion the bursar presents each guest with a needle and thread and comments, "Take this and be thrifty."

The foundation here was impoverished in the 15th and 16th centuries, and Queen's admitted *commensales* (paying guests). In 1535 there were fourteen such commoners, and by 1612 the number had increased to 194. Among the early *commensales* were John Wycliffe, Henry Cardinal Beaufort, and Henry V. The library, built between 1692 and 1695 to house Bishop Thomas Barlow's bequest, is one of the most splendid buildings here and has four Shakespeare folios and a first edition of *Paradise Lost*.

Thomas Middleton, the dramatist, is usually assumed to have been educated here before going to Gray's Inn in London in 1593 to study law; however, with a now-established birth date of 1580 (not 1570), the 1593 Gray's Inn Thomas Middleton is certainly not the dramatist. There is, though, a Thomas Middleton of London, noted in the university registers as *pleb. fil.*, who matriculated here in April 1598 at the age of eighteen. Age, residence, and social rank compare well and point to this being the dramatist. Sir John Davies matriculated at Queen's on October 15, 1585; he was admitted to the Middle Temple in London two years later and was graduated with a B.A. degree in 1590. Sir Henry Wotton, another diplomat, entered Queen's from New College in 1586; during his undergraduate days he wrote *Tancredo*, based on Tasso's *Gerusalemme liberata*, and became acquainted with John Donne. In 1588 Wotton received a B.A. degree and immediately upon graduation left for a Continental tour. A third early literary and political figure, Sir Thomas Overbury, became a

gentleman commoner in the Michaelmas term, 1595, and matriculated on February 27, 1596. His reading of logic and philosophy seems to have been extraordinarily good, and he graduated with a B.A. degree at the end of 1598 before entering the Middle Temple.

William Wycherley entered as a gentleman commoner, probably in 1659, after being in the south of France, where he abandoned his Protestant faith (about 1655); he lived in private lodgings. Part of the reason for Wycherley's attendance at Queen's (a school noted for its strong theological bent) was his family's desire to have him reconciled to Protestantism; Wycherley neither formally matriculated nor had his name entered on the college books. In May 1687 Joseph Addison came up from Charterhouse in London; already a good classical scholar and Latin versifier, he attracted the notice of Dr. Lancaster, one of the fellows and later college provost, who procured a demyship at Magdalen for him. William Collins came to Queen's from Winchester College on March 24, 1740, as a commoner after having failed to secure a place at New College; after his election to a demyship at Magdalen, he transferred there in July 1741. Walter Pater came up to Queen's as a commoner from Canterbury in 1858 and took a second in greats in 1862.

More recently, Edmund Blunden came up to Brasenose in 1914 from Christ's Hospital but had his studies interrupted by World War I. Returning to Queen's in 1919, he published three volumes of verse, including the Hawthornden Prize-winning "The Shepherd," before graduating in 1923.

St. John's College Based on a foundation by Archbishop Henry Chichele for Cistercian monks in 1437, the present College of St. John the Baptist was founded after the suppression by Henry VIII of St. Bernard's College. The establishment has been presented to Christ Church by Henry VII; and in 1555 Sir Thomas White, a wealthy London merchant, former Lord Mayor, and devout Roman Catholic, endowed two scholarships for boys from Reading, one of which was later granted to William Laud. Among the other reserved fellowships, the Merchant Taylors' School received an extremely high proportion of the total of forty-three, and even today fifteen are granted to Merchant Taylors', or more than New College grants to Winchester or Christ Church to Westminster. The library built by Archbishop Laud contains John Wycliffe's Old Testament and Apocrypha (said to be an autograph copy), a Little Gidding book by Nicholas Ferrar, a number of Caxton volumes including a Chaucer, and a good collection of Laudiania including the Archbishop's red-morroco–bound diary, his ebony-and-ivory walking stick (used on his walk to the block), and the skullcap worn on his execution day in 1645.

James Shirley came up to St. John's from the Merchant Taylors' School in 1612; he was destined to take holy orders, but Anthony à Wood relates that Laud, then president of St. John's, held the common view that physical perfection was absolutely necessary for any cleric; Wood goes on to report that though impressed with the young Shirley's abilities, Laud advised the young man against taking orders because of the facial disfigurement caused by a mole on the left cheek. Whether this had anything to do with Shirley's ultimate decision is not known, but he left Oxford as an undergraduate for St. Catherine's Hall, Cambridge. During the Civil War, Oxford was a hotbed of Royalist activity, and partly on this account Abraham Cowley ended up here in 1644 after being ejected from Trinity College, Cambridge. He became the intimate friend of many of the Royalist leaders, including members of the Jermyn family, who were responsible for much of Cowley's later political activities. After numerous political missions abroad and a long period of imprisonment because of mistaken identity, Cowley took up the study of medicine (possibly as a cover for his real activities), and was granted an M.D. on December 2, 1657, by government order, an act which, says Anthony à Wood, infuriated Cowley's friends. Cowley retired to Kent and appears to have had nothing further to do with Oxford.

A more modern association with St. John's was that of A. E. Housman, who entered from Bromsgrove School on an open scholarship in the autumn of 1877. He gained a first in moderations in 1879, but two years later he failed to obtain honors in greats because of emotional problems brought on by an unsuccessful homosexual affair. Housman went home to study for the civil service examination and returned for one term to read for a pass degree in classics. He did not bother to pay for or take up his degree until 1892, when he was appointed Professor of Latin at University College, London.

More recently Kingsley Amis came up from the City of London School in 1940; his education was interrupted by World War II, and he did not receive his degree until 1949.

Somerville College   One of the modern colleges, Somerville Hall was founded in 1879 and takes its name from the distinguished 19th-century mathematician Mary Somerville, one of the founders. Originally designed for twelve students, the college has long since expanded its student body and outgrown Walton Manor, a Queen Anne mansion with extensive additions. When the school took over new facilities in 1886, it assumed the name Somerville College. Even with its short history, Somerville can claim to be the institution of four modern novelists. Supported by her uncle and grandfather, Rose Macaulay entered here from Oxford High School in 1900 and three years later was awarded an *aegrotat* (degree without examination). Dorothy Sayers, who was born in Oxford on June 13, 1893, entered Somerville on a scholarship in 1912 and later used an imaginary women's college and this university town in *Gaudy Night* and *Busman's Honeymoon*. After leaving Somerville, she remained in Oxford as a reader for Blackwell's until 1919. Vera Brittain, whose time in Oxford overlapped Dorothy Sayers's, recalls her university days in both *Testament of Youth* and *A Testament of Friendship*, the latter remembering her relationship to another Somerville student, Winifred Holtby.

Trinity College   Founded in 1555 by Sir Thomas Pope, a successful civil servant, Trinity College actually has antecedents dating to the 13th century, when Durham College was founded by the prior and convent of Durham as a residence for their Benedic-

tine brothers studying at Oxford. Within a year of the founding of Trinity College, Sir Thomas installed a president, twelve fellows, and eight scholars; from the outset Trinity admitted commoners and included in that group a liberal sprinkling of students from good county families. The college prospered under its first presidents, and many of its early scholars became important figures in church and state. At first the buildings lay quite far back from Broad Street, and parts of the medieval structure are still incorporated in a number of buildings in the quadrangle.

Around 1573 Thomas Lodge came to Trinity from the Merchant Taylors' School in London as a servitor to Edward Hoby. He graduated with a B.A. degree on July 8, 1577, supplicated for his M.A. in February 1581, and was incorporated M.D. in 1602. Other than Anthony à Wood's assertion that Lodge had begun writing verse as an undergraduate here, virtually nothing is known of Lodge's years at Oxford. Whether George Chapman ever was at Trinity (or at Oxford, for that matter) around 1574 is not known, for the assertions rest upon Anthony à Wood's statement:

> [S]ure I am that he spent some time in Oxon, where he was observed to be most excellent in the Latin and Greek tongues, but not in logic or philosophy, and therefore I presume that that was the reason why he took no degree there.

Sir John Denham matriculated on November 18, 1631; he was examined for the B.A. degree, but there is no record of one being granted. Indeed, if Anthony à Wood's comment on Denham is accurate, the reason was simple; Denham was

> a slow and dreamy young man, given more to cards and dice than to study; his seniors and contemporaries could never in the least imagine, at that time, that he would be able to enrich the world with his fancy, or by the issue of his brain, which he afterwards did.

One of the most famous early students, John Aubrey, entered as a gentleman commoner in May 1642. His antiquarian tastes were apparent early, and one of his contributions was a plate of Osney Abbey to Sir William Dugdale's *Monasticon*. Aubrey left Oxford in 1643, driven out by both the Civil War and smallpox; he entered the Middle Temple in London in 1646 but frequently returned to Oxford even though he never resumed his studies. In June 1697, on his way from London to Draycott, he became ill and died here; he was buried in the Church of St. Mary Magdalene. Elkanah Settle, later Poet Laureate of the City of London, matriculated in July 1666 but left without taking a degree.

Thomas Warton's association with Trinity began with his matriculation in March 1743 and lasted until his death in 1790. After graduating with a B.A. degree in 1747, he went on to take orders and to do tutorial work at Trinity. His M.A. was granted in 1750, he was elected a fellow in 1751, and his B.D. degree was granted in 1767. He was not known for strict attention to his academic duties and did not even regard them seriously enough to meet his tutorials regularly. By Warton's time coffeehouses had become the acknowledged centers of learning, gossip, serious discussion, and wit; indeed, many of them contained large libraries. In 1780 Warton noted "the many libraries founded in our coffee houses for the benefit of such as have neglected or lost their Latin and Greek." He went on to say that with the laced coffee and other drinks "in these libraries, instruction and pleasure go hand in hand, and we may pronounce . . . that learning no longer remains a dry subject." Warton suffered a stroke in the college common room on May 20, 1790, and died the next day; he was buried in Trinity College Chapel. William Lisle Bowles was also a student here and received his B.A. in 1792.

At the same time a less amiable student appeared at Trinity College. On November 13, 1792, Walter Savage Landor matriculated here and took up residence in January 1793. His university career was difficult; he refused, for example, to enter any competitions with his Latin verses, even though he maintained they were the best in the university. He became noted for his eccentricities, declared himself a republican, and wrote an ode to George Washington. He was known as the "mad Jacobin" and in this role managed to get himself rusticated for two terms (not for a year, as is usually stated) for a volley fired at the shuttered windows of an outspoken Tory. Landor refused to explain his conduct; the authorities were willing to reinstate the young scholar, but the incident caused a violent dispute with Landor's father, who refused to allow his son to return. Landor recalled pleasantly strolling along Addison's Walk at Magdalen and sculling on the Isis; the latter pleasure, he confessed, was partly perverse, as his excitement was increased because he could not swim.

John Henry Newman entered Trinity College from a private school in Ealing in December 1816 and came into residence in June 1817. He gained a Trinity scholarship in 1818 and a reputation as an extremely hardworking student. Disaster struck when he was called for his viva voce a day earlier than expected; Newman broke down completely and was unable to stand for the examination. After seven different attempts, he had to retire and barely managed to obtain his degree, his name finally appearing "below the line" of the second division of the second class.

Sir Arthur Quiller-Couch entered as a classical scholar in 1882; writing for the *Oxford Magazine*, he adopted the pseudonym Q. In 1884 he took a first in classical moderations, and in 1886 a second in *litterae humaniores;* he stayed an additional year as a lecturer in classics before going to London. Quiller-Couch's feelings toward the university were summed up with the publication of *The Oxford Book of English Verse* (1900), dedicated to his old college, "a house of learning, ancient, liberal, humane, and my most kindly nurse."

Herman James Elroy Flecker was here from 1902 to 1906 and was constantly seeking accommodations. His first room was on Broad Street overlooking a blank wall which was to be covered with creeper his mother had sent. Not patient enough to wait for the growth, he was allotted Dr. Johnson's rooms at Pembroke but soon left those because they were sunless; the third set of rooms he repapered because the original paper reminded him of the blue carnations of the sanatorium where he once had recovered from scarlet fever. As soon as the new paper was hung, again Flecker moved; and this was not the last time. He took his B.A. degree in 1906.

A little later, in October 1909, after barely passing the entrance examination, Joyce Cary entered Trinity to take a law degree; the law was to be something to fall back on if he could not make writing a successful career. In his second year he took lodgings on Broad Street with John Middleton Murry, but their friendship disintegrated within a few months. Cary was a joiner: among his clubs were the Hilton, the Gryphon (a very serious literary group founded by Quiller-Couch), the Elizabethan (founded by Cary and friends), and the Petronius, but Cary's time with any organization was usually quite brief. When examination time came in 1912, Cary, who had spent his time reading widely, writing, and, of course, socializing, was totally unprepared; he received a fourth and shortly thereafter went to London. After leaving the Nigerian political service in 1920, he and his wife settled in Oxford at 12 Parks Road, near Keble College and opposite the University Parks.

Much more recently Sir Terence Rattigan spent his undergraduate days here in the late 1920s and early 1930s.

University College For many years University College, originally The Great Hall of the University of Oxford, supported its claim of being the oldest Oxford College by maintaining that Alfred the Great was its founder, and a 1727 decision by the Court of King's Bench confirmed this origin as "fact." However, University's actual history as a college dates from 1249, when William of Durham bequeathed 310 marks for the support of between ten and twelve masters of arts to study theology; even this fact is not accepted by Merton and Balliol Colleges as establishing University as the oldest institution, since its statutes date from 1280. The original site of the college was near Brasenose, and the present location was acquired with two purchases in 1332 and 1336.

An early literary association with University College is that of Edward Herbert, later Lord Herbert of Cherbury, who entered as a gentleman commoner in May 1596. Soon after his arrival his father died, and under the guardianship of Sir George More a marriage to Mary Herbert (a relation whose inheritance depended on marrying someone with the same family name) was arranged. They were married in February 1598, and both returned to Oxford accompanied by his mother. He appears to have applied himself diligently and to have done well, but there is no record either of his receiving a degree or of his leaving the college. In the 18th century Richard Jago entered as a servitor in October 1723 and took his B.A. degree in 1736 and the M.A. in 1739. This century probably was the period during which University College was most blessed with its fellows: Sir Robert Chambers, William Scott, John Scott, and Sir William Jones, all friends of Dr. Samuel Johnson, who frequently visited here. Most likely it was a 1776 trip with Boswell, when the men dined in the hall, that Johnson refers to when he later recalled having "drunk three Bottles of port without being the worse for it. University College has witnessed this!"

The most famous person associated with University College is Percy Bysshe Shelley. He came up from Eton, matriculated in April 1810, and entered residence in October. His rooms were next to the hall on the first floor in the corner of the quadrangle and are now in use as the junior common room. The Oxford countryside became a favorite of Shelley's, and he and Thomas Jefferson Hogg (who later wrote *Shelley at Oxford*) often took long walks, especially to a pool in the quarry at the foot of Shotover Hill; a favorite pastime on these walks was shooting with dueling pistols at anything except human beings. Shelley's refusal to follow the university curriculum, coupled with the publication in February 1811 of *The Necessity of Atheism,* brought about the end of his career here. Called before the authorities on Lady Day after sending copies to the heads of all colleges, Shelley refused to answer any of their questions and denied the authorship. Hogg's attempt to intervene in a legislative way resulted in both receiving a summary expulsion, and they left on the following morning, March 26. The poet is commemorated by the Shelley Memorial in the main quadrangle; the sculpture by Edward Onslow Ford represents the drowned Shelley. The Sophocles volume Shelley was carrying when he drowned is in the Bodleian.

C. S. Lewis matriculated at University College in 1918 and had an outstanding record as a classical scholar. He later returned as a fellow and tutor of Magdalen College. Another modern author who received his undergraduate training here was Stephen Spender, who met both W. H. Auden of Christ Church and Cecil Day-Lewis of Wadham College at this time.

Wadham College   Often called "the youngest old foundation" at Oxford, Wadham College was founded in 1610 by Nicholas Wadham of Merifield, Somerset, and his wife Dorothy, "to the praise, glory, and honour of Almighty God, for the increase of sound letters and the common utility of this Kingdom." The college, whose statutes appear to be years ahead of their time in terms of liberality and freedom from bigotry, was built on the site of an older Augustinian friary, and stone and wood craftsmen were imported from Somerset. There has been essentially no alteration to the fabric of the college, and Wadham now stands as an extremely fine example of Renaissance architecture. Historically, the college has been Whig and Low Church, and after resisting a crown attempt in 1618 to install an ineligible Scotsman in a fellowship, it admitted Carew Ralegh, Sir Walter's son, as a fellow the next year.

Sir Charles Sedley entered Wadham College as a fellow commoner on March 22, 1656; he is known to have taken a degree, but there is no evidence as to when he left. John Wilmot, 2d Earl of Rochester, matriculated as a fellow commoner in 1660 at the age of thirteen and showed an early penchant for writing verse and for displaying his lifelong cynicism. He was created an M.A. in September 1661, and in 1662 presented to the college four silver pint mugs, which have been preserved.

In far more modern times Cecil Day-Lewis, created Poet Laureate in 1968, received his university training here. After graduating in 1927, he taught school for a short time; he returned to Oxford in 1951 as Professor of Poetry, a chair he held until 1956. Day-Lewis describes his rooms in *The Buried Day:*

> That summer term, my last in college, was made all the more enchanting by the situation of the rooms into which I had moved after my first year: they overlooked the main quadrangle in front . . . while from my bedroom window at the back I had the famous garden spread

below me—its herbaceous borders and flowering shrubs, the lawns with the gloss of centuries on them, the fabulous copper beech, and to my left, beyond the grey-black wall which enclosed the Warden's garden, the tops of the tulip tree and judas tree that grew there.

During World War I Wadham College was turned into a rest and recuperation center for officers who were awaiting reassignment on the western front. Robert Graves was billeted here and had fond memories of the college and of Oxford; he returned numerous times, especially from his Boar's Hill residence.

Worcester College   Worcester College is one of the Oxford University colleges which, although it has an 18th-century founding date, is based on an older institution. In the 13th century Sir John Gifford founded Gloucester Hall, by way of penance, for students from Gloucester Abbey, and the Hall was later opened to many other Benedictine monks; as a result, a number of buildings were erected "in common." The Hall declined seriously until Sir Thomas Cookes declared his intention of granting £10,000 to fund a college with a provost, six fellows, and eight scholars, but this did not actually take place until 1714, thirteen years after his death. The oldest of the buildings here, the original monks' houses, are medieval; the best are on the south side of the quadrangle, although there are others north of the chapel.

When Worcester was still Gloucester Hall, Thomas Coryate entered (1596) but left without a degree and cannot be traced until he is associated with Prince Henry's household. Richard Lovelace matriculated on June 27, 1634, from Charterhouse and was, said Anthony à Wood, "the most amiable and beautiful person that ever eye beheld"; indeed, the cap-and-gown portrait of Lovelace in the dean's house easily confirms this. Lovelace's extraordinary looks certainly played a large part in his academic attainments; when Charles I and the court were here in 1636, one of the Queen's retinue was so taken by the poet's appearance, "innate modesty, virtue, and courtly deportment" that she persuaded the university chancellor, Archbishop William Laud, to incorporate Lovelace as an M.A. two years early. Lovelace left for the court this year and returned to Oxford probably late in 1645, when it was a Royalist stronghold; he remained until the town surrendered in 1646 and then left England to fight abroad in the service of the French King.

Nearly two centuries later, in December 1803, Thomas De Quincey matriculated after failing to get into Christ Church. He remained off and on for 3½ years even though his name remained on the college books until 1810; his rooms were on Staircase No. 10. He formed early opinions of his undergraduate colleagues and thought them "so ill-read in English literature as not to be worth cultivating." He later commented: "[F]or the first two years of my residence in Oxford, I compute that I did not utter one hundred words." He found the lectures unsatisfactory and by 1804 was making frequent trips to London. De Quincey's last days here, during his examinations, are still shrouded in confusion, but the most reasonable explanation appears to be the following. His first-day paper in Latin was so good that one of the examiners, Dr. Edmund Goodenough of Christ Church, called De Quincey the cleverest man he had ever met and implied that if the next day's viva voce were as brilliant, the young scholar would probably have been the best man the university had seen. De Quincey, though, disappeared the night before the viva voce, not because he was nervous but because he thought the system unfair and erratic. At the last moment the examination format was changed; instead of being conducted in Greek, which would have illustrated De Quincey's proficiency, it was decided to examine in Latin. His leaving merely illustrated contempt for a system which he felt offered no real evidence of intellectual attainment. Much later, in his *Autobiographic Sketches*, he publicized his attitude toward the university and his college:

> Oxford, ancient Mother! I owe thee nothing . . . [but] at this moment when I see thee called to thy audit by unjust and malicious accusers—even with the ears of inquisitors and the purposes of robbers—I feel towards thee something of filial reverence and duty.

Henry Kingsley matriculated from King's College, London, in 1850 but left in 1853 without a degree to explore the Australian gold fields with fellow students. Part of *Ravenshoe* is set here; after being rusticated, Charles Ravenshoe takes a "Last Glimpse of Oxford":

> The front of Magdalen Hall. . . . All Souls . . . St. John's. . . . Exeter, and all Brasenose. In front, the Radcliffe, the third dome in England, and beyond, the straight façade of St. Mary's, gathering its lines upward ever, till tired of crocket, finial, gargoyle, and all the rest of it, it leaps up aloft in one glorious crystal, and carries up one's heart with it into the heaven above.

OXTED, Surrey (pop. 3,284) Beneath the Surrey Downs, 11 miles southeast of Croydon, Oxted belonged to Earl Godwin's wife at the Norman Conquest, when it was given to Eustace II, Count of Boulogne. The village High Street is lined with a number of fine 18th-century cottages, and the half-timbered Bell Inn is extremely picturesque. Just north of the town Ravensbrook House (now apartments), at the base of Snats Hill, was the home of the American novelist Stephen Crane and Lady Cora Stewart in 1897; here he worked on the short stories for *The Open Boat, and Other Tales of Adventure*.

PADSTOW, Cornwall (pop. 2,779) Padstow is a quaint Cornish port on the south side of the estuary of the Camel River, 11 miles northwest of Bodmin. The first name of the community here was the Cornish Lodenek, but the place was also known as Petrockstow after St. Petroc, and from this its modern name derives. The saint came here after spending some years in an Irish monastery, established an oratory, and performed numerous miracles. The Bodmin Gospels, the only early Cornish monastic book to survive, is designed specifically for liturgical use and is of especial interest because of the marginal notations recording local manumissions at the altar of the monastery. Padstow, indeed, was the ecclesiastical capital of Cornwall until the Norman Conquest.

John Leland, who passed through here on his 1538 expedition to Cornwall, commented that Padstow was "a good quick Fischar Town, but unclenly kept." There are two quays here. The North Quay, which is approached by the narrow and twisting High Street, contains the 15th-century Abbey House, which is connected to the monastery by a subterranean passage. The South Quay holds the 16th-century Court House, often called either Ralegh's Court House or Ralegh Court, which is the place where Sir Walter Ralegh held court as warden of Cornwall; here he collected the dues to which he was entitled. In the 20th century J. D. Beresford played host to D. H. Lawrence at Porthcothan from December 1915 until March 1916.

PAINSWICK, Gloucestershire (pop. 2,639) The old Cotswold wool town of Painswick, which dates to the 14th century, is set on a hillside 3½ miles northeast of Stroud and 6 miles southeast of Gloucester; the gray stone houses of characteristic Cotswold construction look down on a lovely valley. The 15th-century church still retains burn marks from the Civil War, when the building was fired to force the Parliamentarians to surrender. The churchyard contains 100 yews, some of which date to 1714; for many years, tradition holds, there were only 99 trees here because the devil uprooted the hundredth every time it was planted.

In the summer of 1897 Virginia Stephen (Woolf) escaped to the vicarage here from Hyde Park Gate in London; the depression caused by her half sister Stella's death, she claimed, was alleviated by the beautiful churchyard and peacefulness of the area. James Elroy Flecker delighted in the Painswick area and Painswick Beacon with its view to the Severn Bridge when confined to the Cotswold Sanatorium in nearby Cranham. He found this a perfect spot in which to picnic, even in January, when coal had to be brought along to make tea. "Oak and Olive" refers to this spot:

> Have I not chased the fluting Pan
>   Through Cranham's sober trees?
> Have I not sat on Painswick Hill
>   With a nymph upon my knees,
> And she as rosy as the dawn,
>   And naked as the breeze?

PANGBOURNE, Berkshire (pop. 1,936) The village of Pangbourne, located at the junction of the Thames and Pang Rivers, is a popular boating area, but because it is on the main road from Oxford to Reading, the village center is often flooded with cars. The architecture here is largely Edwardian, but Bere Court (rebuilt) was the summer residence of the abbots of Reading Abbey in the 13th century. At the dissolution of the monasteries in the 16th century it came into the hands of John Dudley, Duke of Northumberland, who supported Lady Jane Grey's bid for the throne and was beheaded for this part in the affair.

The riverside Swan Hotel is one of the inns noted

in Jerome K. Jerome's *Three Men in a Boat;* the location is described thus:

> The reaches down to Pangbourne woo one for a sunny sail or for a moonlight row, and the country round about is full of beauty. We had intended to push on to Wallingford that day, but the sweet smiling face of the river here lured us to linger for a while....

Far more important is Church Cottage, located at the top of Pangbourne Hill, for this was the home of Kenneth Grahame from 1924 to 1932. Church Cottage had an old village lockup for a tool shed and a ship's bell at the front door. The illustrations for *The Wind in the Willows* (originally written as a series of letters to be read as a bedtime story for Grahame's son) were done here even though this was not the actual location of the book. By the beginning of 1932 Grahame was suffering from high blood pressure, advanced arteriosclerosis, and what has been termed "fatty degeneration of the heart." On the night of July 5, 1932, he suffered a cerebral hemorrhage and died the following morning. The funeral took place on July 9 at St. James the Less Church in Pangbourne, and he was buried in the churchyard here. His body was later transferred to Holywell churchyard, Oxford.

PARHAM, Suffolk (pop. 337) A small village on the Ore River 2 miles southeast of Framlingham, Parham has long been known for its romantic moated grange; in an area where the average rainfall is only 20 to 30 inches a year, the moats, created by the removal of building clay and often not intended for defense, served a valuable storage purpose. In 1772 George Crabbe, who was apprenticed to a Woodbridge surgeon, met John Tovell's niece Sarah Elmy, who was residing here with her uncle at Ducking Hall; she became the Mira of his early poems. Crabbe and Miss Elmy were soon engaged, but prudently she refused to set a date for the marriage because of his circumstances; he continued to call on her here over the next ten years, but as his circumstances declined, her family became more firmly set against the marriage. Not until after he had achieved success with *The Library* and *The Village* in 1783 and had taken orders were they married. Upon the death of Tovell in 1792, Crabbe, who was executor, inherited this estate and brought his family to Parham; however, his wife's relatives, who had never accepted the marriage, contributed to Crabbe's unhappiness here, and in 1796 he took the living of Great Glemham.

PARK PLACE, Berkshire Situated on the northern Berkshire-Oxfordshire border, Park Place is a seat 1 mile southeast of Henley-on-Thames. In June 1760 Thomas Gray, Lady Carlisle, and Harriet Speed were here as the guests of Gen. Henry Seymour Conway. Miss Speed had inherited £30,000 from Lady Cobham, and at this time everyone, including Gray, expected the poet and Miss Speed to marry. What specifically happened during the visit is not known, but the two did not marry. Mention has been made that Gray's spirits were beaten "by a pack of women," and Miss Speed married Baron de la Peyrière in January 1761. Gray's visit ended in August 1760, when he returned to Cambridge.

PARKGATE, Cheshire (pop. 5,195 with Neston) A shrimping village on the Dee Estuary with views toward the Welsh mountains, Parkgate has been officially amalgamated with Neston to form the Neston cum Parkgate Urban District. It was a fashionable sailing center well into the 19th century; now although the estuary is silted up, the area is gaining popularity as a tourist spot.

As the favored port for Ireland, with frequent ship service, Parkgate attracted many literary travelers including Jonathan Swift, who regularly landed and departed here. The *Journal to Stella* notes: "[W]e made our Voyage in 15 hours just.... I got a Fall off my Horse, riding here from Parkgate, but no Hurt...." Years later from Ireland Thomas De Quincey noted that the "passage is very dangerous ... in general not more than three days ... but sometimes much longer"; his concern was well founded, for here on August 10, 1637, John Milton's college friend Edward King drowned a mile or so off the coast when his ship mysteriously foundered on a calm day. The tragedy evoked "Lycidas":

> Bitter constraint, and sad occasion dear,
> Compels me to disturb your season due;
> For *Lycidas* is dead, dead ere his prime,
> Young *Lycidas*, and hath not left his peer:
> Who would not sing for *Lycidas?* he knew
> Himself to sing, and build the lofty rhyme.
> He must not float upon his wat'ry bier
> Unwept....

Another drowning here is used by Charles Kingsley in "The Sands of Dee"; a young girl perishes driving her father's cattle home:

> The western tide crept up along the sand,
>   And o'er and o'er the sand,
>   And round and round the sand
> As far as eye could see.
> The rolling mist came down and hid the land:
>   And never home came she.

PASTON, Norfolk (pop. 281) Paston, 4 miles northeast of North Walsham, is a coastal village which has fought the depredations of the sea for centuries; the assault of the sea is never-ending, and the entire coast is lined with defenses to safeguard the land. The village was the home of Sir William Paston, "the Good Judge" and the founder of the Paston family. His son John and John's wife Margaret (Mautby), whose letters reveal the social, economic, and political turmoil and structure of the 15th century, lived at the old manor house here, of which nothing remains except the great flint barn built in 1581. The 14th-century church with medieval wall paintings, where the Pastons worshiped, is little changed; at the east end are a number of Paston family monuments, some of which cannot be identified with accuracy. However, it is thought that the center tomb is John Paston's and that it was brought here from Bromholm Priory in Bacton.

PATTERDALE, Westmorland (pop. 916) Patterdale is situated on alluvial land between Grisedale and Goldrill Becks at the southern end of Ullswater. An attractive tourist village surrounded by mountains, 8½ miles north of Ambleside, it is an excellent walking center and base for climbing the 3,118-foot Helvellyn. The old inn at Patterdale played host at one time or another to every Lake poet; when Sir Walter Scott and William Wordsworth (with Humphry Davy) came here in August 1805, the inn was so crowded because of the Charles Gough story of Helvellyn that the only available accommodation was the sitting room. The three men climbed Helvellyn the following day and in their climb passed the great hollow of Red Tarn, whose isolation caused Wordsworth to write:

There sometimes doth a leaping fish
Send through the tarn a lonely cheer;
The crags repeat the raven's croak,
In symphony austere;
Thither the rainbow comes—the cloud—
And mists that spread the flying shroud;
And sunbeams; and the sounding blast,
That if it could, would hurry past;
But that enormous barrier holds it fast.

PAUNTLEY, Gloucestershire (pop. 161)   Pauntley, on the Leadon River 7 miles west of Gloucester, was Dick Whittington's birthplace about 1358, but here, at least, the legend first mentioned in the play *The History of Richard Whittington* is told in a different way. Indeed, the only fact in the play which is accurate is that Whittington married Alice Fitzwaryn. Whittington's father was Sir William Whittington, and his mother was the widow of Sir Thomas Berkley of Cubberley, who was closely related to the powerful and wealthy lords of Berkeley. The family home was the moated Pauntley Court, which has been resurrected through the efforts of the Poet Laureate John Masefield; he raised £500 to convert the house into a Home for Young Wayfarers and offered to keep the fund at full strength by giving free poetry readings within a 40-mile radius of the village.

PEAK FOREST, Derbyshire (pop. 420)   A small Peak District stone village in what was once a royal forest, Peak Forest is at an altitude of 980 feet, 5 miles northeast of Buxton. Between here and Castleton is Eldon Hole, one of the Wonders of the Peak; known as the Bottomless Pit until 1770, when its bottom was located, the hole is on the side of Eldon Hill; connected to Eldon Hole is a fine stalactite cave. Michael Drayton includes this feature of the landscape in *Poly-Olbion:*

For *Elden* thou my third, a Wonder I preferre
Before the other two, which perpendicular
Dive'st downe into the ground, as if an entrance were
Through earth to lead to hell, ye well might judge it here,
Whose depth is so immense, and wondrously profound,
As that long line which serves the deepest Sea to sound,
Her bottome never wrought, as though the vast descent,
Through this Terrestriall Globe directly poynting went
Our *Antipods* to see, and with her gloomy eyes,
To glote upon those Starres, to us that never rise. . . .

Some years later Daniel Defoe was in the area gathering material for *A Tour thro' the Whole Island of Great Britain;* he was generally unimpressed by the wonders of the Peak District, and he had been especially put out by the Devil's Hole near Castleton because of its other, generally earlier name, the Devil's Arse. However, Eldon Hole did impress him:

The remaining Article, and which, I grant, we may justly call a WONDER, is *Elden Hole. . . .* [T]his opening goes directly down perpendicular into the Earth, and perhaps to the Center; it may be about twenty Foot over one way, and fifty or sixty the other; it has no Bottom, that is to say, none that can yet be heard of. . . .

This I allow to be a Wonder, and what the like of is not to be found in the World, that I have heard of, or believe. . . .

What Nature meant in leaving this Window open into the Infernal World, *if the Place lies that way,* we cannot tell: But it must be said, there is something of Horror upon the very Imagination, when one does but look into it. . . .

Thomas Hobbes, author of *Leviathan,* relates that he rolled stones into the hole, which plunged "to the depths of Hell."

PEDMORE, Worcestershire (pop. 494)   To the southeast of Stourbridge are the Clent Hills, an extremely pleasant area of woodlands, shrubs, and pools, and tucked under Wychbury Hill, one of the foothills, is Pedmore, 1½ miles south of Stourbridge and now almost connected to that larger town. In the 18th century Pedmore was the home of Cornelius Ford, a cousin of Samuel Johnson and fifteen years his senior; indeed, the young Samuel came for a few days' visit at the end of 1725 and stayed six months. Here, under the guidance of his cousin, Johnson was completely immersed in the writings of Congreve, Addison, and Prior. After his stay, he returned home to Lichfield, but in 1726, when he was at nearby Stourbridge in school, he frequently visited Pedmore.

PENN'S ROCKS or Penns in the Rocks, Sussex   Just 2½ miles north of Crowborough in the general area of Ashdown Forest is Penn's Rocks, a seat once belonging to Lord Gerald and Lady Wellesley. After a sojourn in Majorca in 1933, William Butler Yeats came here to hide from photographers and journalists. He returned frequently until August 1938, a year before his death.

PENRITH, Cumberland (pop. 10,923)   Because Penrith has been bypassed by the M6 motorway, it has not suffered much from the depredations of modern town planning. The town, which lies at the foot of Penrith Beacon (937 feet) on the Eamont River, almost 18 miles southeast of Carlisle, consists today largely of red-sandstone buildings. The 14th-century castle, now in ruins, was an important stronghold during all the border warfare. The Church of St. Andrew has a memorial to the 2,260 Penrith citizens who succumbed to the plague during Elizabeth I's reign and three noteworthy glass portraits: one is of a crowned king; the other two are of Richard, Duke of York, and his wife Cecily Neville, who were the ancestors of every British monarch. She was the twenty-third child of Ralph Neville, Shakespeare's Earl of Westmorland; two of their children became kings, and a granddaughter married Henry VII. A curiosity on Bridge Lane in Penrith is a rare plague stone, where the plague-ridden townspeople washed their money in vinegar when paying for goods brought in from the countryside.

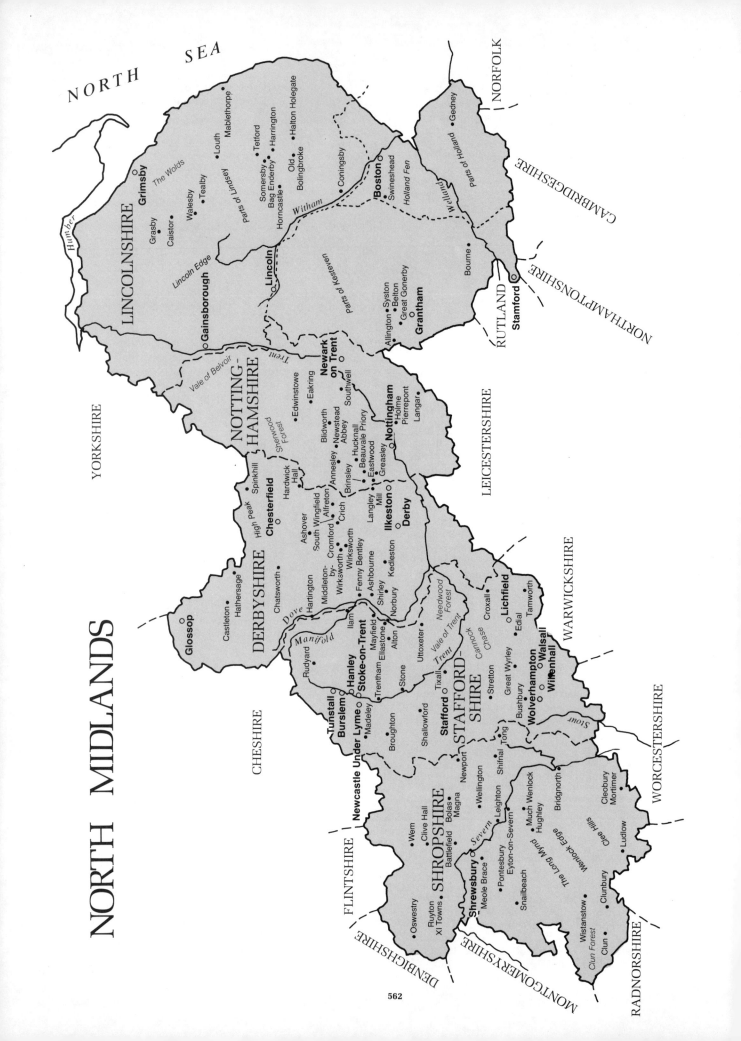

NORTH MIDLANDS

NORTH SEA

YORKSHIRE

Humber

LINCOLNSHIRE

Grimsby
The Wolds
Louth • Mablethorpe
Walesby • Tealby
Somersby • Tetford
Grasby • Bag Enderby • Harrington
Caistor • Horncastle • Halton Holegate
parts of Lindsey • Old • Bolingbroke
Coningsby
Witham
Lincoln Edge
Boston
Swineshead
Holland Fen
parts of Holland
Welland
Lincoln
Gainsborough
parts of Kesteven
Allington • Syston
Belton
Great Gonerby
Grantham
Bourne

NORFOLK

CAMBRIDGESHIRE

RUTLAND
Stamford
NORTHAMPTONSHIRE

Trent
Vale of Belvoir
NOTTING-HAMSHIRE
Newark on Trent
Edwinstowe
Eakring
Southwell
Sherwood Forest
Blidworth • Newstead Abbey
Annesley • Hucknall • Beauvale Priory
Nottingham
Holme Pierrepont
Langar

LEICESTERSHIRE

Spinkhill
Hardwick Hall
Chesterfield
High Peak
Ashover
South Wingfield • Alfreton
Crich
Brinsley • Eastwood • Greasley
Langley Mill
Ilkeston
Derby

DERBYSHIRE
Castleton • Hathersage
Dove
Chatsworth
Hartington
Middleton-by-Wirksworth • Cromford • Wirksworth
Fenny Bentley
Ashbourne
Shirley • Norbury
Kedleston

WARWICKSHIRE

Glossop

Manifold
Rudyard
Hanley
Stoke-on-Trent
Ilam
Mayfield
Trentham • Ellastone
Alton
Stone
Uttoxeter
Tixall
Trent
Vale of Trent
Needwood Forest
Cannock Chase
Croxall
Lichfield
Edial • Tamworth
Great Wyrley
Bushbury
Wolverhampton • **Walsall**
Willenhall

Tunstall
Burslem
Newcastle Under Lyme
Madeley
Broughton
Shallowford
Stafford
STAFFORD-SHIRE
Tong
Stour

CHESHIRE

FLINTSHIRE

Wem • Clive Hall
Battlefield • Bolas Magna
Wellington
Newport
Shifnal
Leighton
Eyton-on-Severn
Much Wenlock • Hughley
Bridgnorth
Cleobury Mortimer

SHROPSHIRE
Oswestry
Ruyton XI Towns
Shrewsbury
Meole Brace
Severn
Pontesbury
Snailbeach
The Long Mynd
Wenlock Edge
Clee Hills
Ludlow
Wistanstow
Clun Forest
Clun
Clunbury

WORCESTERSHIRE

DENBIGHSHIRE

MONTGOMERYSHIRE

RADNORSHIRE

562

John Leland said little about Pereth, as he called the town, but Daniel Defoe, a couple of centuries later, obviously liked it:

> *Perith*, or *Penrith*, is a handsome Market Town, populous, well built, and, for an Inland Town, has a very good share of Trade. It was unhappily possessed by the late Party of *Scots* Highland Rebels, when they made that desperate Push into England. . . . However, to do Justice even to the Rebels, they offered no Injury to the Town, only quartered in it one Night, took what Arms and Ammunition they could find, and advanced towards *Kendal*.

Thomas Gray first explored Penrith in September 1769, when he "dined," he said, "with Mrs Bucken on trout and partridges." He went on to Ullswater and Watermillock, where he saw the mountains "rude and awful with their broken tops." Within twenty-five years Ann Radcliffe visited Penrith and noticed the old houses straggling along the north road; her thoughts are recorded in *Observations during a Tour in the Lakes:*

> Penrith, despite its many symptoms of antiquity, is not deficient in neatness. The houses are chiefly white, with door and window cases of the red stones found in the neighbourhood. Some of the smaller have over their doors dates of the latter end of the sixteenth century. The town lies . . . spreading prettily along the skirts of the mountain, with its many roofs of blue slate, among which the church rises near a dark grove.

Penrith has a close and, in some ways, unhappy association with William Wordsworth. His mother was born here, and Burrowgate, a house now rebuilt, was where she died and where he and the other Wordsworth children lived after the death of their father in 1783. This was the house in which his grandfather and Uncle Kit lived, and the environment was disagreeable to the young children. For a year Wordsworth attended a dame school kept by Mrs. Ann Birkett, who, Wordsworth later said, was "no bad teacher but indifferent to method"; she read *The Spectator* to the children and had them learn extensive passages from the Bible. The students were required to keep the country festivals; on Easter, for example, they rolled pace eggs on the top of Penrith Beacon, no doubt a pleasant undertaking. From the dame school here Wordsworth was sent to Hawkshead to continue his education. Another Wordsworthian association comes through his wife, Mary Hutchinson; although her aunt's home in Penrith cannot be found, her mother's grave is near the northeast corner of the church tower. Incidentally, the well-kept parish registers provide sufficient details to prove the Hutchinsons were Penrith people and to disprove Thomas De Quincey's assertion that the Wordsworths and the Hutchinsons were cousins.

Sir Walter Scott had a lifelong attraction to Penrith, its surrounding area, and Eamont Bridge, and the town held a double fascination because of his interest in Arthurian legend. Sir Launcelot supposedly killed the giant Torquin at Eamont Bridge, and tradition says the Giant's Grave, in the churchyard, is the burial site of Torquin. Other claims make this the grave of Owen Caesarius, a knight of gigantic stature, who is variously called a pagan, a Christian, the slayer of Torquin, and the hero of Inglewood Forest who rid that place of vicious wild boars. Scott

was fascinated by the problem and by the stones and never passed through Penrith without stopping to see them.

PENSHURST, Kent (pop. 1,531) The village of Penshurst, 4 miles southwest of Tonbridge, is situated at the confluence of the Eden and Medway Rivers and is largely unspoiled by the passage of time. It is rich in timbered houses; and perhaps its most attractive spot, opposite the Leicester Arms Hotel, is Penshurst, a group of half-timbered houses set in the form of a hollow E which creates an inhabited gateway to the churchyard. Penshurst Place is why the village is known; the magnificent medieval hall, central to the estate, was built in 1340 and has had many additions, including work as late as the 19th century. The Elizabethan work, especially Buckingham Building, was done after Edward VI granted the estate on April 6, 1552, to his Chamberlain and Chief Steward, Sir William Sidney, grandfather of the poet, soldier, and courtier Sir Philip Sidney.

Penshurst was Sir Philip's birthplace on November 30, 1554, and the family's position was such that the boy had as godparents "the grete King, Phillipe of Spain," after whom he was named (as Sir William's diary records), the 1st Earl of Bedford, and the Duchess of Northumberland. Much of Sidney's early life was spent here, and it was to Penshurst that he retreated on the occasion of being banished from Elizabeth's court for speaking his mind. It was partly the surrounding countryside (as well as that at Wilton, Wiltshire) which inspired *Arcadia*. The nature images in the *Astrophel and Stella* sonnet sequence are also drawn from Penshurst. Sir Philip left England from Gravesend, Kent, on November 10, 1585, as part of the expeditionary force sent to the Netherlands; at Zutphen in late September 1586, his thigh was shattered by a musket. Fulke Greville, one of Sidney's closest friends, wrote:

> [B]eing thirsty with excess of bleeding, he called for drink, which was presently brought to him; but as he was putting the bottle to his mouth he saw a poor soldier carried along, who had eaten his last at the same feast, ghastly casting his eyes at the bottle, which Sir Philip perceiving, took it from his mouth before he drank and delivered it to the poor man with these words, "Thy necessity is greater than mine."

Sidney underwent a crude form of surgery; gangrene set in and he died in Arnhem on October 17. The helmet surmounted with a porcupine (the family crest) that was carried at Sir Philip's funeral at St. Paul's Cathedral, London, is in the Great Hall.

Penshurst was frequently the center of a literary coterie, and one of the earliest to receive patronage, encouragement, and employment from the Sidneys was Edmund Spenser, who first met Sir Philip in 1577 or 1578; indeed, *The Shepheardes Calender* is dedicated to Sidney and was partly written here. Spenser seems to have divided most of his time during this period between the Sidney homes here and in London. Ben Jonson enjoyed Sir Robert Sidney's hospitality, which he said imposed none of the indignities to which men of letters were usually subjected. Jonson's attitude is neatly summed up in "To Penshurst"; he describes the estate, the fertility of the land and its subsequent bounty, and then the rapport of the Sidneys with the local people and with their guests:

> Here no man tells my cups, nor, standing by
> A waiter doth my gluttony envy,
> But gives me what I call, and lets me eat;
> He knows below he shall find plenty of meat.
> Thy tables hoard not up for the next day,
> Nor when I take my lodging need I pray
> For fire or lights or livery; all is there
> As if thou then wert mine, or I reigned here;
> There's nothing I can wish, for which I stay.

The beneficence of the Sidneys extended into the 17th century; Sir Robert's rather remarkable grandchild Dorothy is the Sacharissa of Edmund Waller's poetry, and it was she whom he courted unsuccessfully after the death of his first wife. "To Penshurst," one of the amatory verses written to Dorothy, comments on the estate:

> Ye lofty beeches, tell this matchless dame
> That if together ye fed all one flame,
> It could not equalize the hundredth part
> Of what her eyes have kindled in my heart!
> Go, boy, and carve this passion on the bark
> Of yonder tree, which stands the sacred mark
> Of noble Sidney's birth. . . .

The park now contains Sacharissa's Walk, commemorating the place where Waller courted Lady Dorothy. John Evelyn also visited Penshurst on a few occasions and under the date of July 9, 1652, comments in his diary:

> [W]e went to see *Penshurst* being the E. of *Licesters*, famous onc⟨e⟩ for its Gardens & excellent fruit: and for the noble Conversation which was wont to meete there. . . . It stands also in a park, is finely water'd: & was now full of Company, upon the marriage of my old fellow-Collegiate, Mr. Robert Smith, who married my L: Dorothy Sidney, widdow of the Earle of *Sunderland.*

Later, Robert Southey visited here and wrote about Penshurst and its occupants:

> Sidney here was born,
> Sidney, than whom no gentler, braver man
> His own delightful genius ever feign'd
> Illustrating the vales of Arcady
> With courteous courage and with loyal loves.
> Upon his natal day the acorn here
> Was planted. It grew up a stately oak,
> And in the beauty of its strength it stood
> And flourish'd, when his perishable part
> Had moulder'd dust to dust. That stately oak
> Itself hath moulder'd now, but Sidney's fame
> Lives and shall live, immortalized in song.

PENTRIDGE, Dorset (pop. 150) Lying just north of the 600-foot Pentridge Hill, the village of Pentridge is central to the Dorset area known as Cranborne Chase, once a great royal hunting ground. It is a cul-de-sac village with easy access to the prehistoric Dorset Cursus. Pentridge was the home of the aunt and uncle of the poet William Barnes, who made frequent trips here. His poem "Pentridge by the River" describes a town on the Stour River (which is nowhere near here), but Pentridge has no river:

> PENTRIDGE!—oh! my heart's a-zwellèn
> Vull o' jaÿ wi' vo'k a-tellèn
> Any new o' thik wold pleäce
> An' the boughy hedges round it,

> An' the river that do bound it
> Wi' his dark but glis'nèn feäce.
> Vor there's noo land, on either hand,
> To me lik' Pentridge by the river.

The village figures in Thomas Hardy's Wessex as Trantridge; in *Tess of the D'Urbervilles*, Tess journeys here to visit her reputed relative and to gain assistance for her family. The Slopes, where Mrs. D'Urberville lives, was

> a country house, built for enjoyment pure and simple, with not an acre of troublesome land attached to it beyond what was required for residential purposes, and a little fancy farm kept in hand by the owner, and tended by a bailiff.
> The warm red-brick lodge came first in sight, up to its eaves in dense evergreens. . . . [T]he house proper . . . was of recent erection—indeed almost new—and of the same rich crimson color that formed such a contrast with the evergreens of the lodge. Far behind the bright-hued corner of the house, which rose like a red geranium against the subdued colors around, stretched the soft azure landscape of the Chase, a truly venerable tract of forestland, one of the few remaining woodlands in England, of almost primeval date, wherein Druidical mistletoe was still found on aged oaks, and where enormous yew-trees, not planted by the hand of man, grew as they had grown when they were pollarded for bows.

No house in Pentridge answers this description.

PENZANCE, Cornwall (pop. 19,964) Like almost every town in Cornwall, Penzance was founded by a saint, in this case, St. Anthony, whose small chapel overlooked Mount's Bay. The Domesday Book records the name of the district from Penzance to Mousehole as Alwareton, but by the reign (1327–1377) of Edward III the name was changed, and the annual Penzance Fair existed. Because Penzance was exposed to the sea, it suffered an unusual number of attacks. The list of attackers includes the Spaniards, who landed in 1549; Parliamentarian forces under the command of Gen. Thomas Fairfax, from 1646 on; and French, Algerians, and Turks, until the 1750s. Penzance has an extremely famous native son: the founder of the Jewish colony here was Abraham Hart, whose grandson, the spirit merchant Lemon Hart, secured a rum-trade monopoly and supplied the Royal Navy. His name is still on the label of a popular rum.

Edmund Spenser landed in Penzance with Sir Walter Ralegh in 1589 on their way from Ireland, where Spenser was private secretary to the Lord Deputy, Lord Grey de Wilton. Their landing here was undoubtedly occasioned by Sir Walter's interests: he was warden of the stannaries and lieutenant of the county. Spenser had already completed the first three books of the *Faerie Queene* to present to Queen Elizabeth, and he describes their approach to Mount's Bay in "Colin Clout's Come Home Again," dedicated to Ralegh. The Scottish schoolmaster John Davidson, a quite popular late-19th-century poet, came here from London in the early 20th century. Depressed and in ill health, he drowned himself on March 23, 1909, and was buried at sea.

From 1905 on Penzance was the special favorite of W. H. Hudson, and in 1915, when he was more than eighty years old, he began wintering here. He stayed at 22 North Parade and frequented Bridger's Book Store. He returned yearly for six years and was often visited by John Galsworthy, who made the easy journey from St. Ives. The Penzance Registry Office was the scene of the marriage of Caitlin Macnamara and Dylan Thomas on July 11, 1937. They had gone to Mousehole in late spring and made the short trip here for the ceremony.

One obvious modern association occurs with W. S. Gilbert and Arthur Sullivan's *The Pirates of Penzance.* The entire first act is set on "[a] rocky sea-shore on the coast of Cornwall," and the basic material is derived from stories and traditions of local piracy.

PERIVALE, Middlesex Somehow Perivale, now part of Greater London, maintains a semirural atmosphere even though it is only 1½ miles north of Ealing; it straddles the Brent River here. On one side of the river is a modern housing estate, while on the other are traces of the old village. At one time Perivale was wheatland, as Michael Drayton points out in *Poly-Olbion*:

> . . . [A]nd chanc't to cast her eye
> Upon that neighbouring Hill where *Harrow* stands so hie,
> She *Peryvale* perceiv'd prankt up with wreaths of wheat,
> And with exulting terms thus glorying in her seat;
> Why should not I be coy, and of my Beauties nice,
> Since this my doogly grain is held of greatest price?
> No manchet can so well the courtly palat please,
> As that made of the meale fetcht from my fertile *Leaze*,
> Their finest of that kind, compared with my wheate,
> For whitenesse of the Bread, doth look like common Cheate.

The grain has been gone for more than 100 years.

PERRANPORTH, Cornwall Five miles southwest of Newquay on the Atlantic coast, Perranporth is noted for its fine sand beach and its excellent surfing. Three churches, all dedicated to St. Piran (for whom the village is named) have been built here. After floating here on a millstone St. Piran built an oratory on Penhale Sands which was buried from the 11th century until its rediscovery in 1835. A second church was begun in 1150 a quarter of a mile to the east; in the 15th century it too was buried in the dunes. The current parish church, built in 1804, was placed 1½ miles farther inland at Perranzabuloe.

Almost equidistant between these villages is St. Piran's Round, an undated ancient amphitheater 130 feet wide. The round was used centuries ago for the performance of mystery plays, which have lately been revived. The *Ordinalia*, the Cornish cycle, consists of three long plays, *The Origin of the World, The Passion of Our Lord,* and *The Resurrection;* it is comparable to the English cycles of Wakefield, York, Coventry, and Chester. Because of the multitude of local references, most of the *Ordinalia* is believed to have been written by one or more members of Glasney College at Penryn. The cycle was so long that performances lasted more than three days, and the plays were generally given on major religious holidays and at Whitsuntide. Unlike the English cycles, the Cornish cycle took place in "rounds," circular earth banks around the *plen-an-gwary* (playing place). Traditionally, the east side of the arena held the main stage and was the location of heaven and God's throne, the north side was hell, and the central area contained the paraphernalia for the major action.

Another medieval Cornish play, unique in English literature, was performed here. In the Middle Ages the Cornish clergy wrote plays about the lives of the numerous local saints. The only extant play is the 15th-century *Bewans Meriasek (Life of Meriasek),* which begins with a delightful scene of a Cornish priest who likes his drink teaching Latin and the alphabet to a group of small boys.

PETWORTH, Sussex (pop. 2,435) Located 14 miles northeast of Chichester, Petworth has a remarkable feudal air with its 14th-century Church of Our Lady of Pity (a most unusual dedication), its old village buildings, a network of narrow cobbled streets, and its great manor house. At the center of the village is the tiny marketplace with an arcaded 18th-century town hall; and throughout Petworth are fine half-timbered Tudor houses and Georgian buildings. It is the manor house here which is most outstanding. Set in a park measuring 10 miles around, the mansion once belonged to the Northumberland Percys. Joscelyn (Josceline), brother of Henry I's Queen Adeliza, married the Percy heiress Lady Agnes and was given the home by the Queen. Charles Seymour, 6th Duke of Somerset, set about building the present structure after his marriage in 1682 to Elizabeth Percy, the orphaned daughter of the 11th Earl of Northumberland. The grandest room is the State Room, which Grinling Gibbons was given a free hand to decorate; and while the room contains a fair treasury of art works, all is drenched in the lavishness of Gibbons's carvings. Petworth contains an overwhelming art collection, which includes works by Lely, Gainsborough, Turner, Reynolds, Hoppner, Van Dyck, Holbein, Hals, Rembrandt, Hogarth, and Claude Lorraine. William Hazlitt viewed the galleries, and while they did not command a separate entry in *Sketches of the Principal Picture-Galleries in England,* he did compare the Claude Lorraines favorably with those now in the National Gallery. One of the other items displayed is the sword Henry Percy, William Shakespeare's Hotspur, used in the Battle of Shrewsbury.

Daniel Defoe visited Petworth while preparing *A Tour thro' the Whole Island of Great Britain* and thought it "one of the finest Piles of Buildings, and the best model'd Houses then in Britain." He was distressed by the Duchess of Somerset's death in 1722, "while these Sheets were writing," but composed himself to write:

> [I]t cannot be said, that the Situation of the House is equally design'd, or with equal Judgment as the rest; the Avenues to the Front want space, the House stands as it were with its Elbow to the Town, its Front has no *Visto* answerable, and the West Front look'd not to the Parks or fine Gardens, but to the old Stables.
> To rectify this . . . the Duke was oblig'd to pull down those Noble Buildings; I mean the Mews, or Stables, the finest of their kind in all the South of England. . . .

Defoe's complaint about the situation of the house was a frequent one in the 18th and 19th centuries; and one handbook even compared the house to "a strip of indifferent London terrace." William Cobbett also comments on Petworth and its manor in *Rural Rides:*

> Petworth is a nice market town, but solid and clean. . . . Lord Egremont's house is close to the town, and with its out-buildings, garden walls, and other erec-

tions, is, perhaps, nearly as big as the town; though the town is not a very small one. The park is very fine, and consists of a parcel of those hills and dells which Nature formed here when she was in one of her most sportive modes. . . . It is, upon the whole, a most magnificent seat, and the Jews will not be able to get it from the *present* owner; though, if he live many years, they will give even him a *twist*.

About the only literary personage to visit Petworth as a guest was Edward Lear, who met the 3d Earl of Egremont in the 1820s.

Petworth House was the birthplace of the poet Wilfrid Scawen Blunt on August 17, 1840; the second son of wealthy Roman Catholic parents, he was educated at two of the finest Catholic schools in England, Stonyhurst and St. Mary's, Oshott. He inherited the family estates in 1872 and spent the rest of his life traveling and residing at Crabbet Park when in England.

PICKERING, Yorkshire (pop. 3,503)   The site of this lovely North Riding market town in the Vale of Pickering has been continuously inhabited since prehistoric times. The vale, a broad trough of clay, once drained to the east, but glacial activity obstructed the original outlet, and the new lake which was formed ultimately forced its outlet westward. Consequently, from their source near the sea the Derwent and its branches flow for many tortuous miles essentially in the wrong direction before joining the Ouse and Humber Rivers to empty into the North Sea. The town's Norman church contains some of the most beautiful medieval frescoes in England; two of the scenes depict St. Christopher, larger than life-size, carrying the Christ Child through waters reminiscent of the ancient neighboring lake and the 9th-century martyr King Edmund being put to death with bows and arrows. A more appropriate place for Richard Rolle, the hermit and mystic of Hampole, cannot be imagined. Most likely he preached his first sermon as a hermit here; Rolle settled here under his patron, John de Dalton, as his *Office of St. Richard Hermit* states.

PICKWORTH, Rutland (pop. 116)   The village of Pickworth, 5 miles northwest of Stamford, is one of the few country villages which suffered damages in the Wars of the Roses. On a hilltop stands a 14th-century arch with carved capitals, all that remains of the local church, which is said to have been destroyed by soldiers along with the village after the Battle of Losecoat Field in 1470.

In the autumn of 1817 John Clare came here for occasional work as a limeburner. When the men dug a kiln just west of the church, they found human bones (probably from the Battle of Losecoat Field) and the foundations of earlier habitation. This was the background which inspired "Elegy on the Ruins of Pickworth." "On a Sunday Morning" was inspired by the old church.

PIEL ISLAND, Lancashire   A tiny island guarding the channel to Barrow Harbour, Piel Island is 4 miles southeast of Barrow-in-Furness and is connected to the mainland by a causeway; it is essentially unpopulated, with only an inn and the magnificent ruins of Piel Castle, properly the Pile or Peel of Fouldrey, which was built by the abbot of Furness in the early

14th century as a defense against raiding Scots. This is where Lambert Simnel and his men landed in June 1487 and where he was proclaimed Edward VI and held his court, but the rebels were crushed by Henry VII's forces at Stoke-on-Trent.

William Wordsworth commemorates the castle in "Elegiac Stanzas Suggested by a Picture of Peile Castle, in a Storm, Painted by Sir Geo. Beaumont." He was vacationing in nearby Rampside in 1794 when he saw the castle:

> I was thy neighbour once, thou rugged Pile!
> Four summer weeks I dwelt in sight of thee:
> I saw thee every day; and all the while
> Thy Form was sleeping on a glassy sea.

Beaumont painted two pictures of Piel Castle and gave one to Wordsworth; however, after Sir George's death Lady Beaumont took back the work and presented it to Sir Uvedale Price of Foxley.

PILGRIMS' WAY, THE   The term "Pilgrims' Way," designating the route followed by medieval pilgrims to the shrine of St. Thomas à Becket in Canterbury, wrongly implies a single set route into the town. In fact, two major and distinct routes existed. The southern route, for Continental pilgrims landing at Southampton, led directly north to Winchester and the popular shrine of St. Swithun. From there, perhaps after staying at the Pilgrims' Hall in the close, the pilgrims went on to Farnham, across the southern edge of the Hog's Back to Guildford, Shere, Dorking, and Reigate, and then along the high ridge of the North Downs through Titsey Hill, Otford, Wrotham, Snodland, Kit's Coty House, and Charing. The final stop, where they joined the northern pilgrims at Harbledown, occurred just outside Canterbury after the southern travelers had almost completed the part of their trip known as the "Route of the Five C's": Charing, Challock, Chilham, Chartham, and Canterbury. The southern route, anciently used by Bronze Age traders, involved a difficult, perilous, and long trip. In some places it followed quite good roads (as from Southampton to Guildford), but in others, mere tracks, particularly along the southern slope of the North Downs, a route taken to avoid the hazardous marshes. In contrast, the northern route was easier to follow, since the Roman road ran directly from London to Canterbury through a populous and relatively flat region where accommodation was easy to come by. Even from as far north as Northumbria the road and its branches were fairly safe and unusually direct. Unfortunately, there is little specific information about the route farther north; distance and sparsely populated areas did not encourage the journey. It is known, though, that the small Church of St. Helen in Kelloe, County Durham, was a stopping place because of its tradition of the holy Cross and that nearby Quarringdon Hill was known as the "signing bank," where the pilgrims made the sign of the Cross as they caught sight of Durham Cathedral.

The northern route is used by Geoffrey Chaucer's pilgrims in *The Canterbury Tales*. Leaving the Tabard Inn in Southwark, London, on April 17, they journeyed the 20 miles to Dartford by way of Depeford (Deptford) and Grenewych (Greenwich), where Harry Bailley admonishes the Reeve to begin his tale.

"Sey forth thy tale, and tarie nat the tyme

Lo Depeford! and it is half-way pryme.
Lo Grenewych, there many a shrewe is inne!
It were all tyme thy tale to bigynne."

On April 18 the company proceeds the 12 miles or so
to Rouchestre (Rochester):

"My lord, the Monk . . . by myrie of cheere,
For ye shul telle a tale trewely.
Loo, Rouchestre stant heer faste by!
Ryde forth, myn owene lord, brek nat oure game."

The third day's trip takes them 18 miles through
Sidyngborne (Sittingbourne) to Ospringe, before
which time the Summoner threatens, in anger, to

telle tales two or thre
Of freres, er I come to Sidyngborne.

Then, after a relatively short journey on April 20,
they meet the southern pilgrims at Harbledown and
proceed to the martyr's shrine; in the Prologue to
"The Manciple's Tale," "Bobbe-up-and-doun" is a
play on the name Harbledown and the mode of
transportation:

Woot ye nat where ther stant a litel toun
Which that ycleped is Bobbe-up-and-doun
Under the Blee, in Canterbury Weye?

"Blee," or Blean Woods (now a national nature re-
serve), is where the pilgrims are joined by "[a] man
that clothed was in clothese blake."

In the 20th century Hilaire Belloc traced the 120-
mile southern route of the pilgrims; with two others
he left from the Old North Gate in Winchester in
December 1902 on what they calculated as the most
probable date of the first pilgrimage. They arrived in
Canterbury at the cathedral on the same date and at
the same time as Becket's murder, December 29. The
weather Belloc also held to be the same: clear, cold,
and windless.

PILTON, Devon (pop. 2,406) Well located in some of
the most spectacular coastal scenery in north Devon,
where cliffs can sheer off straight down to the water's
edge, Pilton consists of two villages half a mile north
of Barnstaple. East Pilton, almost 20 times larger than
West Pilton, is actually in the borough of Barnstaple.
It was to Broadgate Villa (now two cottages, Fairmead
and Fairview), on the corner of Bellaire and Bellaire
Drive, that Saki (H. H. Munro) was brought as a two-
year-old child after his mother's death in Burma. His
father, of the Bengal Staff Corps and inspector general
of the police, brought his three children here to live
with their grandmother and two aunts. The stern and
unsympathetic discipline of Aunts Augusta and Tom
had a strong effect upon Saki, the most sensitive of
the children, but as his sister later wrote, "We had
only to be ill and everything was changed at Broadgate, scolding was a thing of the past." Munro was
educated privately at Pencarwick in Exmouth and at
the Bedford School in Bedford before his father's return from Burma in 1888.

PINDAR'S GREEN, Yorkshire Essentially part of
Wakefield, only 2 miles away, Pindar's Green has an
obvious connection with the Robin Hood legend.
Giving his name to this area, George-à-Greene, the
pinner (poundkeeper) of Wakefield, was long known
as a man who could exact a penalty from trespassers

THE PILGRIMS' WAY   The southern route for Continental pilgrims to the shrine of St. Thomas à Becket in Canterbury was a much
more difficult track than the northern route; particularly hazardous
was the southern slope of the North Downs, as here in Newlands
Corner, Surrey.

regardless of rank. Into this trap, as the ballad "The
Jolly Pinder of Wakefield" relates, came Robin Hood,
Scarlet, and John, who

have forsaken the king's highway
And made a path over the corn.

In one version of the fight George-à-Greene takes
on all three men at once and fights until the three
Yorkshire men have had their swords "broke fast into
their hands." In his usual persuasive manner Robin
asks:

. . . wilt thou forsake thy craft,
And live in green wood with me?

The pinner agrees to join the band after his term of
service expires on Michaelmas Day. The same event
and locality are introduced into *George a Greene, the
Pinner of Wakefield* (1599), attributed to Robert
Greene, and a prose history of the same name (1706).

PINNER, Middlesex Near the Hertfordshire border,
2½ miles northwest of Harrow-on-the-Hill, Pinner
has a proper village High Street lined with some fine
old buildings; many of the shops and houses are
Georgian, and the Queen's Head dates from 1705,
even though it bears the date 1580. The village
church, neatly tucked away on a lane leading off the
High Street, dates from 1321 but stands on an earlier
earthworks site. The church contains the grave of the
Poet Laureate Henry James Pye, a man often described as "eminently respectable in everything but

his poetry"; indeed, his dramatic efforts were no better. While staying at Pinner Wood House, Albury Drive, in 1831–1832, Edward Bulwer-Lytton (Lord Lytton) wrote parts of *Eugene Aram*. A. E. Housman lived at 1 Yarborough Villas (gone), Devonshire Road, for a short time before taking up his post as Kennedy Professor of Latin at Cambridge.

PLACE FELL, Westmorland A mountain 2,154 feet high just 1 mile northeast of Patterdale, Place Fell is opposite the dominant Helvellyn and its sides slope down to the edge of Ullswater. With the help of Lord Lonsdale, William Wordsworth acquired Broadhow, a 17th-century cottage, but he never lived in it. Probably on a short tour along Ullswater in November 1805, Wordsworth decided not to live in the cottage.

PLYMOUTH, Devon (pop. 221,229) Situated on Plymouth Sound between the estuaries of the Plym and Tamar Rivers, on the edge of the lush agricultural region known as the South Hams, Plymouth is the only industrial center in the area and the largest city in the West Country. The modern city, whose predecessor received only passing mention as a hamlet named Sutton in the Domesday Book, was formed by the amalgamation of three old towns, Plymouth, Devonport, and Stonehouse. Plymouth supported an extensive Stone Age colony, and unearthed coins from the period immediately preceding the Roman invasion point to a strong 1st-century culture, but there is no evidence at all of Roman occupation. Medieval Plymouth grew from the original fishing port on the banks of Sutton Pool, and in the late 14th century the Valletorts, who acquired the manor, were influential enough to induce the prior of Plympton to develop the harbor area; thus by the Hundred Years' War the fishing village had taken on naval importance. Plymouth's location made it vulnerable to invasion, and the last French invasion, in 1403, saw

more than 600 houses burned and most of the inhabitants killed or taken prisoner. Plymouth grew enormously and became the major port of embarkation for the great Elizabethan sailors: Hawkins, who sailed into the Gulf of Mexico; Drake, who sailed around the world and returned with a ship laden with gold and silver; and Ralegh, who left to settle the New World. However, Plymouth's prosperity was checked when more than one-third of the population was killed off by the plague during the reign of Charles I.

Plymouth has a special place in history as a seaport: five times Sir Walter Ralegh sent out ships and men from Plymouth to settle Virginia, and each time he and they met with failure. Then, on September 6, 1620, the Pilgrim Fathers set out on the *Mayflower* in their second attempt at sailing (their first departure in August was aborted when the *Speedwell* sprang a leak).

Because Plymouth has been an important naval base, dockyard, and civilian port for three centuries, the center of the city and most of its dock area were completely obliterated during World War II. About all that is left of old Plymouth is the area around Sutton Pool. One of the earliest references to Plymouth and the Hoe is the description of the match between Corineus and Gogmagog in Michael Drayton's *Poly-Olbion*:

> All, doubtful to which part the victorie would goe,
> Upon that loftie place at *Plimmouth* call'd the *Hoe*,
> These mightie Wrastlers met; with many an irefull looke
> Who threatened, as the one hold of the other tooke:
> But, grapled, glowing fire shines in their sparkling eyes.

The dock area and sailing accessibility were two of the reasons that Samuel Johnson came here on holiday in 1762. He had just been granted a state civil-list pension, and upon his arrival the commissioner of the dockyard provided a yacht for Johnson and his companion, Sir Joshua Reynolds. The two men became especially fond of the trip out to the Eddystone Rocks. William Beckford arrived in August 1779 just when the Franco-Spanish Fleet was lying off the coast, and the town was filled with troops anticipating imminent bombardment and land attack. He noted in his diary on August 15 that the Plymouth "inhabitants are all in confusion, filled with alarms and suspicions, staring about with rusty guns in one hand and telescopes in the other." Beckford and his former tutor, Dr. Lettice, were arrested as spies as they took out notebooks to record their observations of the events. The Rev. Robert Stephen Hawker in his youth lived for a time with his grandfather, the Rev. Robert Hawker, vicar of Charles Church. Hawker received his earliest education from his grandfather, whom he alienated by sending carriages and protestations of love to older spinsters of the Charles Church congregation and other pranks. Hawker spent his school holidays here and was articled for a few months to a local lawyer. In June 1875 he returned to Plymouth and took lodgings at 9 Lockyer Street, attending St. James's Church on occasion. Severe illness, coupled with reservations about the Protestant faith which he had preached for more than forty years, brought him into the Catholic Church immediately before his death on August 15, 1875. A solemn requiem mass was celebrated on August 18 at

PLYMOUTH Overlooking Drake's Island in Plymouth Sound, the Hoe is of both historical and literary interest. Sir Francis Drake is said to have been playing bowls here while waiting for the correct tide for sailing to engage the Armada, the *Mayflower's* second and successful attempt to sail for the New World was from the Hoe, and Corineus and Gogmagog met in combat here.

Plymouth Catholic Cathedral, and he was buried in Plymouth Cemetery; the brass cross on his coffin simply states: "Robert Stephen Hawker . . . who Died in the Catholic Faith. . . ."

Charles Dickens first visited here on a reading tour in 1855 and stayed at the West Hoe Hotel. On this occasion his public readings took place in Stonehouse, which was, he writes, "on top of a windy and muddy hill, leading (literally) to nowhere; and it looks (except that it is new and mortary) as if the subsidence of the waters after the Deluge might have left it where it was." Dickens was here again in 1861 on a second tour. There are references to the town in *Bleak House* and *David Copperfield;* Plymouth is where Mrs. Micawber's relatives are influential.

This area in Devon is too far west for Thomas Hardy's Wessex novels, but he does use it occasionally under its own name. He mentions the Plymouth Barbican in "The Duchess of Hamptonshire" and refers briefly to the town in *Desperate Remedies.* Plymouth is used in *A Pair of Blue Eyes;* Stephen Smith walks on the Hoe, from which he can see "the wide Sound, the breakwater, the lighthouse on far-off Eddystone." Elfride Swancourt comes to Plymouth from her father's Endelstow (St. Juliot, Cornwall) vicarage when she is planning to marry Stephen. A few of Hardy's later poems, those which followed his first wife's death, deal with Plymouth, at least in part; he recalls the trip never made to her birthplace and states that now a

> phantom draws me by the hand
> To the place—Plymouth Hoe—
> Where side by side in life, as planned,
> We never were to go!

"Places" and "The Marble Sheeted Town" also concern Plymouth.

Hilaire Belloc was in Plymouth in July 1914, when he observed the British Fleet on maneuvers during that waiting period. The ships were steaming eastward, "like ghosts, like things made themselves out of mist," as he writes in *The Cruise of the "Nona."* The *Nona,* indeed, is itself sent here from St. Ives in that work. Finally, H. G. Wells uses the naval town in *Marriage:* Marjorie Pope is sent to the home of her cousin, Susan Pendexter, when it is suspected that Marjorie intends to elope.

POLESDEN LACEY, Surrey   The Mole River has cut a large gap in the North Downs near Dorking, 2½ miles southeast of the seat of Polesden Lacey, and Ranmore (Ranmer) Common, in the care of the National Trust, has magnificent views over Holmesdale and the Tillingbourne Valley. In this environment is Polesden Lacey, a 19th-century house with lovely rose gardens, which stands on the site of a much earlier house bought by the dramatist Richard Brinsley Sheridan at the end of the 18th century after his marriage to Esther Jane Ogle, daughter of the dean of Winchester. He sold off some of his shares in Drury Lane to purchase the estate and, indeed, created some of his financial difficulties in the process. Sheridan and his wife spent relatively little time here, preferring to be at Dean Ogle's in Southampton.

POLESWORTH, Warwickshire (pop. 6,277)   The early role of Polesworth, a village on the Anker River 4 miles east of Tamworth, is part of the tangle of Anglo-Saxon history. The 9th-century nunnery here was built for Modwena, who was joined by Edith (Editha), King Egbert's daughter; it is to her that the church is dedicated. After the Norman Conquest, when Marmion, Lord of Tamworth, seized the abbey, a second St. Edith appeared to him in a dream and stabbed him with her crozier. He promptly returned the estate. The vicarage near the church now covers the site of the house built on the nunnery ruins by Sir Henry Goodere, in whose service Michael Drayton was a page in his early years. Because of the dedications to "Queen Isabel and Richard II" and "Mary the French Queen and Charles Brandon," it is assumed that Drayton most probably attended school in the Abbey Gatehouse (still there); he wrote "To Henry Goodere I confess myself to be beholding, for the most part of my education." Drayton attended Thomas Goodere's funeral here in 1585 and was often back between 1603 and 1612. He watched or perhaps learned the sport of hawking then and showed his appreciation to his host in later works. Drayton may have met John Donne here, although the recorded visits do not overlap. Donne's first visit probably occurred in February 1614, soon after the marriage of Princess Elizabeth to the Elector Palatine, Frederick V; he remained until April. Another literary figure whom Goodere supported was Ben Jonson, who also wrote of the hawking he observed here and of the library.

POLGIGGA, Cornwall   About 2 miles southeast of Land's End, the westernmost point of the English mainland, Polgigga is little known. Its association with Dylan Thomas stretches belief because of Polgigga's remoteness and lack of habitation and Thomas's general preference for urban life and its amenities. Thomas spent a little over two months in 1936 at a cottage owned by Wyn Henderson. He was brought here to get some work done, and, in fact, "lots and lots of work," he writes, is "saving me . . . not from any melodramatic issues but just from sheer unhappiness. . . ." On the other hand, Polgigga was not his sort of place:

> I'm not a country man; I stand for, if anything, the aspidistra, the provincial drive, the morning café, the evening pub; I'd like to believe in the wide open spaces as the wrapping around walls, the windy boredom between house and house, hotel and cinema, bookshop and tube-station; man made his house to keep the wind and the weather out, making his own weathery world inside; that's the trouble with the country: there's too much public world between private ones.

POLPERRO, Cornwall   Located 5½ miles east of Fowey on the south coast, Polperro was once a den of pirates, and its pilchard fleet has made its runs since the Middle Ages. It is strung out along a narrow and steep valley, with its lime-washed cottages clinging to the hillsides and built directly into a small harbor sheltered by two seawalls. One of the earliest visitors to Polperro was Alfred, Lord Tennyson, who came in a boat from Fowey on June 20, 1848, in search of local traditions about King Arthur. Tennyson called on the Dr. Jonathan Couch and read some of his current verses about King Arthur to the doctor. Couch later commented that he thought the verses were "prolix and modern" and that he certainly could not approve of the poet's slouch or slovenly dress. This Dr. Couch was the grandfather of Sir Arthur Quiller-Couch, who often visited him here in his youth. Couch's home, for some time a smugglers' museum, is now in private hands. Sir Hugh Walpole, who made Polperro a private retreat from 1912 to 1921, was first in the village in September 1911, when he discovered that it was "beyond any kind of question absolutely my dream place." Returning in 1912, he found the Cobbles, a whitewashed cottage at the beginning of the cliff path, and he moved in on March 13, 1913. The Cobbles, a small place with a sitting room and two bedrooms, was accessible only on foot. Henry James, who visited him here, sent "a convenient and solid oak Desk" and a mirror as housewarming gifts. Each time Walpole came to Cornwall he experienced the same elation; on November 5, 1915, he writes:

> The most wonderful coming into Cornwall I've ever had. Most perfect November day. Almost dizzy with happiness. Eggs and bacon at Liskeard, a shave at Looe, then walked over. Sea mists and dazzle, trees golden and *such* quiet. Just walked down the road into my cottage.

Walpole gave up the Cobbles in September 1921 but returned to Polperro occasionally until 1931; on these trips he stayed with John Curtis, a local fisherman, whose wife Annie had looked after Sir Hugh when he lived in his own cottage. Among other things he had worked on *The Dark Forest*, *The Green Mirror*, and *The Cathedral* during these years.

PONTEFRACT, Yorkshire (pop. 21,560) Also spelled and pronounced "Pomfret," this bustling city near the confluence of the Aire and Calder Rivers is an important rail center and is on the direct road route to the north. Besides being known for an 11th-century castle, the town has long been famous for its Pomfret cakes, liquorice lozenges stamped with the outline of the castle. It is believed that 13th-century Benedictine monks originated the cakes, but the extensive early liquorice "plantations" no longer exist, and the raw materials are imported from Turkey. One might assume that John Evelyn, with his strong horticultural bent, would have commented on the cakes in his diary, but no mention is made of the sweets or the raising of liquorice. It is the Plantagenet castle, dating from 1080, which ensures Pontefract's place in history, for this was the scene of the murder of Richard II in 1400. William Shakespeare's statement in *Richard II*,

> . . .the mind of Bolingbroke is chang'd;
> You must to Pomfret, not unto the Tower,

was undoubtedly an exigency of dramatic structure. In fact, Richard came here by a circuitous route: first the King was incarcerated at Leeds, then at Pickering Castle, then at Knaresborough, and finally at Pomfret Castle. The death scene in the play, in which Sir Pierce stabs Richard after he had set upon the keeper for refusing the first taste of the prepared meal, is also dramatic license. Archbishop Scrope, close at hand and most likely in a good position to ascertain the facts, declared that at the end of January 1400 Richard died a very mean death after full starvation for fifteen days.

Shakespeare also mentions Pontefract Castle in *Richard III*. As Ratcliff conducts Rivers, Grey, and Vaughan to execution, the group passes the castle, and Rivers is prompted to comment on Richard's grisly death:

> O Pomfret, Pomfret! O thou bloody prison
> Fatal and ominous to noble peers!
> Within the guilty closure of thy walls
> Richard the Second here was hack'd to death. . . .

Jonathan Swift's later comment sums up the general attitude toward the town: "I love Pomfret," he wrote. "Why? It is in all our histories."

PONTESBURY, Shropshire (pop. 2,815) With evidence of prehistoric settlement here on Pontesford Hill and Pontesbury Hill, Pontesbury has had only one brush with history when a Mercian and a West Saxon king clashed here in the 7th century. The town lies 8 miles southwest of Shrewsbury and overlooks the Rea Valley. Roseville was the home of Mary Webb for a few years after her marriage in 1912 to Henry B. L. Webb, a minor writer who used the name John Clayton. Here they ran a truck garden, and she wrote *The Golden Arrow*, perhaps her best-known work. The couple left for Lyth Hill, where they built a cottage.

POOLE, Dorset (pop. 77,936)

> If Poole was a fish poole, and the men of Poole fish,
> There'd be a poole for the devil and fish for his dish.

This 18th-century couplet was a popular estimation of the early corruption of Poole, for pirates, smugglers, rebels, and lawbreakers in general abounded here over the centuries; the long, deep chines which led down to the gaps in the cliffs around Poole Harbour were excellent cover for smuggling well into the 19th century. Five miles west of Bournemouth, Poole is on a tongue of land on the north side of the second largest natural harbor in the world; formed by the projection of the Isle of Purbeck, the harbor is 7 miles wide and 4½ miles long.

By the mid-16th century Poole had been constituted a county in its own right, and piracy and smuggling were the order of the day; flagrant violations of the judicial system occurred because the town had its own court of admiralty, and many times the mayor stood in open defiance of the crown. Poole was isolated during the Civil War because it supported Oliver Cromwell while the rest of Dorset supported Charles I, and a battle inside the town walls, entry having been gained by the bribing of a captain in the Parliamentarian forces, left most of Cromwell's men dead. Today Poole's role as a port is a minor one, and its prosperity is based on light industry and tourism. One interesting sidelight is the phenomenon that the harbor has four tides a day, just as has the entire coastal area from Weymouth to Southampton.

The harbor and coastline attracted Michael Drayton, who tells the story of Poole in *Poly-Olbion*:

> When *Poole* (quoth shee) was young, a lustie Sea-borne Lass,
> Great *Albyon* to this Nymph an earnest suter was;
> And bare himselfe so well, and so in favour came,
> That he in little time, upon his lovelie Dame
> *ff*. Begot three mayden Iles, his darlings and delight:

The eldest, *Brunksey* call'd; the second, *Fursey* hight;
The youngest and the last, and less then the other,
Saint *Hellens* name doth beare, the dilling of her Mother.
And, for the goodlie *Poole* was one of *Thetis* traine,
Who scorn'd a Nymph of hers, her Virgin-band should staine,
Great *Albyon* (that fore-thought, the angrie Goddesse would
Both on the Dam and brats take what revenge shee could)
I'th bosome of the *Poole* his little children plac't:
First, *Brunksey; Fursey* next; and little *Hellen* last;
Then, with his mightie armes doth clip the *Poole* about,
To keep the angrie Queene, fierce *Amphitrite* out.

In *A Tour thro' the Whole Island of Great Britain* Daniel Defoe calls Poole "a considerable Sea-port, and indeed the most considerable in all this Part of *England,*" but he was more deeply impressed by one aspect of its trade:

> This Place is famous for the best, and biggest Oysters in all this Part of *England,* which the People of *Pool* pretend to be famous for Pickling. . . . 'Tis observ'd more Pearl are found in the *Pool* Oysters, and larger than in any other Oysters about *England.*

Poole has few literary associations, and it is best known in Thomas Hardy's works; nevertheless, a number of literary figures were here. In June 1866 Edward FitzGerald visited Poole, "a place I had long a very slight Desire to see; and which was not worth the seeing." Robert Louis Stevenson took Bonallie Towers in the Bransome Park area as a temporary home in November 1884 before he purchased Skerryvore in Bournemouth, early in 1885. W. E. Henley and his wife spent part of November with the Stevensons.

As Hardy's Havenpool, Poole takes on its main literary importance; it appears under that name in *The Mayor of Casterbridge, The Hand of Ethelberta,* "Barbara of the House of Grebe," and "To Please His Wife." The town provides the backdrop for the last-mentioned story; Jolliffe enters St. James's Church to give thanks for escaping a shipwreck:

> The interior of St. James's Church, in Havenpool Town, was slowly darkening under the close clouds of a winter afternoon. It was Sunday: service had just ended. . . .
> For the moment the stillness was so complete that the surging of the sea could be heard outside the harbour-bar. Then it was broken by the footsteps of the clerk going towards the west door. . . .

The Georgian building on the High Street which was turned into a hospital was most likely the model for the merchant's house:

> The worthy merchant's home, one of those large, substantial brick mansions frequently jammed up in old fashioned towns, faced directly on the High Street, nearly opposite to the grocery shop of the Jolliffes. . . .

The High Street is where the Pippards live, and Sloop Lane is where Emily Hanning lives before her marriage.

PORLOCK, Somerset (pop. 965) The village of Porlock lies at the bottom of a broad wooded valley known as the Vale of Porlock, on the northern edge of Exmoor on Porlock Bay. Robert Southey was especially fond of Porlock and stayed at the ancient Ship Inn; indeed, Southey's corner is pointed out to credulous visitors:

> Porlock, thy verdant vale so fair to sight,
> Thy lofty hills which fern and furze embrown,
> The waters that roll musically down
> Thy woody glens, the traveller with delight
> Recalls to memory.

William Wordsworth visited Porlock in 1797, and Samuel Taylor Coleridge frequented the Ship, especially in Southey's company. This village was also the home of the now-infamous man whose interruption of Coleridge's reverie at Ash Farm in Culbone brought an end to "Kubla Khan." R. D. Blackmore, both before and during the time he was writing *Lorna Doone,* was on various occasions in Devon and Somerset and frequented the bookstore in Porlock.

PORTLAND, ISLE OF, Dorset (pop. 12,431) Situated 4 miles south of Weymouth, the Isle of Portland, 4½ miles long and 2 miles wide, is not really an island since it is connected to the mainland by Chesil Bank, a long, narrow ridge of shingle. On the north side of the island is Portland Castle, built by Henry VIII in 1520; and near the village of Easton is a second castle, Pennsylvania Castle, built in 1800 for John Penn. The high, rocky peninsula sinks gradually as it reaches Portland Bill, its furthermost tip, and here, where there was once a bird sanctuary, is a clutter of buildings (kiosks, restaurant, toilets) which detract somewhat from its splendor. Portland was inhabited slightly by the Romans and the Saxons, but the area has always been rather isolated. Many of the traditional ways were kept for centuries: all the sons of a man who died intestate shared equally, and a man never married "till his intended wife is pregnant, and it was hardly ever broken in the memory of man but when the woman falsely assures the man that she was breeding."

In medieval times the inhabitants of the Isle of Portland were noted for their prowess with the sling, and this is the simple explanation of the name Isle of Slingers, which Thomas Hardy often uses for the area in his Wessex. It is mentioned in *The Trumpet-Major,* "The Melancholy Hussar," "A Tradition of 1840," and "The Souls of the Slain," and it is the principal scene of action in *The Well-Beloved.* In the last-named novel Isaac Pierston walks through the Street of Wells, actually Fortune's Well, a village at the entrance to the island which derived its name from a spring arising behind the inn:

> A person who differed from the local wayfarers was climbing the steep road which leads through the sea-skirted townlet definable as the Street of Wells, and forms a pass into that Gilbraltar of Wessex, the singular peninsula once an island, and still called such, that stretches out like the head of a bird into the English Channel. It is connected with the mainland by a long thin neck of pebbles, "cast up by rages of the sea," and unparalleled in its kind in Europe.

He climbs the steep hill and walks toward Eastern Village (Easton), where he stops in front of the Caros' cottage. The house stood close to Pennsylvania Castle; just before the gates which form the northern entrance to the castle is a small lane, with the cottage at the corner. Avice Caro and Pierston walk all over the island and to the Beal, or Portland Bill, where they pass Cave Hole, "the treacherous cavern . . . into which the sea roared"; its roof has been eroded by the action of the ocean. After Avice's recitation at the village hall, she and Pierston "climbed homeward slowly by the Old Road":

> At the top they turned and stood still. To the left of them the sky was streaked like a fan with the lighthouse rays, and under their front, at periods of a quarter of a minute, there arose a deep, hollow stroke like the single beat of a drum, the intervals being filled with a long-drawn rattling, as of bones between huge canine jaws. It came from the vast concave of Deadman's Bay, rising and falling against the pebble dyke.
> . . . They [the winds] brought it up from that sinister Bay to the west, whose movement she and he were hearing now.

The old church at Church Hope is in ruins, but the headstones are still in place:

> [T]he old Hope Churchyard . . . lay in a ravine formed by a landslip ages ago. The church had slipped down with the rest of the cliff, and had long been a ruin. It seemed to say that in this last local stronghold of the Pagan divinities, where Pagan customs lingered yet, Christianity had established itself precariously at best.

Just below the cliff is Rufus Castle, or Bow-and-Arrow Castle, Hardy's Red King's Castle; Pennsylvania Castle becomes Sylvania Castle, the temporary residence of Marcia Bencomb. Twenty years later Pierston returns to Portland as the tenant of the castle,

> a dignified manor-house in a nook by the cliffs, with modern castellations and battlements; and he had walked through the rooms, about the lawn, and into the surrounding plantation of elms, which on this island of treeless rock lent a unique character to the enclosure. In name, nature, and accessories the property within the girdling wall formed a complete antithesis to everything in its precincts.

After another time lapse, Pierston meets the third Avice at Sandsfoot Castle, called Henry VIII's Castle, "on the verge of the rag-stone cliff"; nearby Hope Cove is where Avice and Leverre have their near escape from drowning, for they had moved dangerously close to the Race:

> [T]he tide ran round to the north, but at a special moment in every flood there set in along the shore a narrow redux contrary to the general outer flow, called "The Southern" by local sailors. It was produced by the peculiar curves of coast lying east and west of the Beal; these bent southward in two back streams . . . [and] united outside the Beal, and there met the direct tidal flow, the confluence of the three currents making the surface of the sea at this point to boil like a pot, even in the calmest weather. The disturbed area, as is well known, is called the Race.

The Race is caused by the extreme velocity of the tide between the land and the Shambles; it is dangerous for large vessels in rough weather and disastrous for small ones at any time.

The Shambles, 4 miles off the tip of the island, is a sandbank which has taken thousands of lives including that of Richard Wordsworth, the poet's brother, who went down with 300 of his men in the 1805 wreck of the *Avergavenny*.

PORTSMOUTH, Hampshire (pop. 258,400) Referred to as Pompey by the Royal Navy, Portsmouth has always been the naval capital of England because of its good harbor, and during World War II the city was a prime bombing target because of its naval importance. Today Portsmouth is bursting at its seams and incorporating surrounding areas into its expanding metropolitan area. Southampton is approaching from the west, and no doubt some day a new megalopolis, to be dubbed Solent City and to include Winchester to the north, will exist here in fact, if not in name. Before World War II the High Street had many lovely 17th- to 19th-century houses; the destruction, though leveling these, spared the 12th-century and later cathedral and much of literary interest.

Charles Dickens was born on the north side of the city at 387 Commercial Road, Mile End, on February 7, 1812. The house, renumbered 393 and now the Dickens Birthplace Museum, is an unpretentious two-story building with a dormer window and a small fenced-in front garden. The now densely populated Mile End area was then known as Landport and was comparatively rural. Dickens was baptized in the Church of St. Mary, Kingston (gone); St. Mary's par-

PORTSMOUTH The house where Charles Dickens was born is now the Dickens Birthplace Museum. On an 1838 visit to Portsmouth with John Forster, Dickens recalled being "watched by a nurse through a low kitchen window almost level with the gravel walk" and being "carried from the garden one day to see the soldiers exercise. . . ."

ish register is in the Portsea parish church, where a stained-glass window commemorates his baptism. When Dickens was four months old, his family moved to 16 Hawke Street, a larger house with a much better location. The three-story house, with a proper basement (an unusual feature in English houses of that period), was destroyed in the war. The family lived here from Midsummer Day in 1812 to Midsummer Day in 1814, when they moved to London. Dickens renewed his acquaintance with Portsmouth in 1838 to obtain local color for *Nicholas Nickleby*. Vincent Crummles lodges in St. Thomas's Street with Bulph, the pilot; this is assumed to be No. 78. Miss Snevellicci has rooms at a tailor's on Lombard Street, and Nicholas Nickleby has lodgings over a tobacconist's shop on the Common Hard, "a dirty street leading down to the dockyard." The old Portsmouth Theatre where Nicholas has his theatrical success was on the High Street on the site of the present Cambridge Barracks. The local tradition which maintains that Dickens asked for a small part in a production here in order to have a better understanding of the theater must be apocryphal. Portsmouth seldom appears in his works; it is merely mentioned in *The Uncommercial Traveller*, and in *Great Expectations* it becomes Provis, the town where Magwitch lands. When Dickens ended his first reading tour in Portsmouth in 1866, he stopped to see his birthplace and was upset to find he remembered nothing of it at all.

A second native of Portsmouth was George Meredith, who was born in his grandfather's house at 73 High Street (gone) on February 12, 1828; Meredith's father, like his grandfather, was a tailor and naval outfitter here. The house contained the family's living quarters upstairs, and the ground floor of the house was divided into two parts, with the shop in the front and the workshop behind. Here young Meredith lived ten years, attending St. Paul's Day School in Southsea, where he learned a little Latin and history and made observations which ultimately appear in *Evan Harrington*. Melchisedec Harrington, the glorified tailor known as "the great Mel" or "the Marquis," is Melchizedek Meredith, the author's grandfather; and Lymport-on-the-Sea is obviously Portsmouth. The circumstances of the novel are drawn directly from the Meredith family background: the original Melchizedek was laid out in yeomanry uniform, sword and helmet at his side; one daughter, the real Louisa, married, not a Portuguese, but a man in the Consular Service who eventually settled well in Portugal; another, Harriet, married a brewer; the third married a professional soldier, not unlike Major Strike; the one surviving son, Augustus, who planned to become a doctor, was forced to take on both an apprenticeship and the family debts. The High Street creditors are certainly real.

Jane Austen was a frequent visitor to Portsmouth from Southampton when her brother Capt. Francis Austen was based here. She especially enjoyed the beauty of the seaside in spring; describing a visit, she writes:

> [T]hough it was really March, it was April with its mild air, brisk, soft wind, and bright sun occasionally clouded for a minute, when everything looked beautiful under the influence of such a sky, with the shadows pursuing each other on the ships at Spithead and the islands beyond. . . .

She disliked the social life of the officers and their wives, and *Mansfield Park* may well include a comment on this experience by Fanny Price. Fanny finds that society here offers her nothing: "The men appeared to her all coarse, the women all perty, everybody underbred. . . ."

William Wordsworth was here in 1793, and watching the fleet in preparation for the French wars, he was depressed by what he felt would be a long and misery-ridden war. Sir Walter Scott was in Portsmouth in early 1807 and was quite disturbed by seeing convict work gangs; he wrote to his wife, "One thing displeases me, which was the sight of convicts in their irons going up and down some part of the yards. There is something very degrading in the idea of a free born Briton in chains." On his second visit in 1831, preparatory to sailing to Malta on October 29, he stayed at the Fountain Inn, where he received many visitors including the Literary and Philosophical Society of Portsmouth. Thomas Hardy was similarly interested in the French problem, and *The Trumpet-Major* concerns the south coast's anticipation of the landing of Napoleonic forces. Bob Lovejoy, the trumpet-major's brother, visits Captain Hardy (a collateral branch of the Thomas Hardy family) in Pos'ham (Portesham, Dorset) before coming to Portsmouth to join Nelson's flagship *Victory*. Hardy also briefly mentions the town in "Geographical Knowledge."

Kenneth Grahame, when he was at St. Edward's School in Oxford, spent pleasant school holidays here with his uncle, Jack Ingles, a commander aboard H.M.S. *Hercules*. Finally, Portsmouth can claim as a native son Sir Walter Besant, who was born at 3 St. George's Square (gone) on August 14, 1836; his father, a local merchant, decided to educate him at home, and not until the age of twelve was he sent to St. Paul's Day School in Southsea; he stayed only until the end of the first term. He returned home for eighteen months before continuing his education at Stockwell Grammar School in London.

POSTLING, Kent (pop. 111) On the southern edge of the North Downs 3 miles north of Hythe, Postling is too tiny even to support a pub. Just outside the village is Pent Farm, rented by Joseph Conrad from Ford Madox Ford between 1898 and 1909; a number of Conrad's best-known works, *Lord Jim*, *Typhoon*, and *Nostromo* among them, were written here. Numerous writers, including H. G. Wells, who lunched on dry bread and Guinness, and George Bernard Shaw, who had cocoa and a biscuit, visited Conrad. Conrad and his wife moved from here to Aldington, Kent, in January 1909.

POWDERHAM, Devon (pop. 153) Only 6½ miles from Exeter on the road to Dawlish, this village has grown up around Powderham Castle, from which its name is taken. On the west side of the estuary of the Exe River, the castle for centuries was the principal seat of the Courtenays, Earls of Devon, and is a mixture of architectural styles and periods from the 14th through 19th century. The Courtenays and Powderham Castle have often been blamed for the social ruin of William Beckford, the author of *Vathek*, but this accusation seems a little strong. Beckford visited the Courtenays in August 1779 on an English tour; having already displayed homosexual inclinations some two years previously, he formed an extremely sentimental attachment to William Courtenay, Viscount Courtenay's young son. It is this William Courtenay who is said ultimately to have caused the novelist's disgrace. Beckford and his wife visited the castle again in September and October 1784, just about the time the estrangement between the two was beginning.

POXWELL, Dorset (pop. 77) A remote hamlet about 1½ miles inland and 5 miles southeast of Dorchester, Poxwell is in the heart of Thomas Hardy's Wessex; this is lonely hill country with the remains of a druidical circle nearby. Poxwell's manor house, dating to the 17th century, was the prototype of Oxwell Hall, the residence of Squire Benjamin Derriman in *The Trumpet-Major:*

> The hall was as interesting as mansions in a state of declension usually are. . . .
> The rambling and neglected dwelling had all the romantic excellencies and practical drawbacks which such mildewed places share in common with caves, mountains, wildernesses, glens, and other homes of poesy that people of taste wish to live and die in. Mustard and cress could have been raised on the inner plaster of the dewy walls at any height not exceeding three feet from the floor; and mushrooms of the most refined and thin-stemmed kinds grew up through the chinks of the larder paving. . . . The keenness was gone from the mouldings of the doorways. . . . The iron stanchions inside the window-panes were eaten away to the size of wires at the bottom where they entered the stone.

PRESTON, Lancashire (pop. 112,800) One of the oldest boroughs in Lancashire, the early town of Preston was located near the site of the Roman fortress of Walton-le-Dale, which overlooked the Ribble River. Preston's medieval importance was assured because of its position on a major north-south route and its central location in the county, 28 miles northeast of Liverpool and 31 miles northwest of Manchester. Sixteenth-century Preston, a stronghold of Roman Catholicism, held out, even violently, against the Reformation; in the 17th century Preston was severely hit by the plague, more than one-third of its population being carried off; and 18th-century Preston was a leader in enfranchisement, extending the vote to "all inhabitants" (twenty-one and male) in 1768.

Eighteenth-century industrial growth here was based on an earlier cottage industry of cotton and woolen weaving; the water frame for cotton spinning was invented here by Richard Arkwright, and the first spinning mill was built in 1770 by Samuel Horrocks. By 1835 there were more than forty mills, and over 280,000 pounds of cotton yarn were produced monthly. The cotton famine during the American Civil War threatened to destroy Preston economically, and only in the 20th century did other industries emerge to broaden the economic base.

The first literary association with the town dates to 1563, when Roger Ascham sat in Parliament for Preston; it was a short-lived tenure, for the seat was reassigned to the town mayor's son before the session was dissolved. Daniel Defoe visited Preston to gather material for *A Tour thro' the Whole Island of Great Britain* and decided:

> *Preston* is a fine Town, and tolerably full of People, but not like *Liverpoole* or *Manchester*. . . . Here's no Manufacture; the Town is full of Attorneys, Proctors, and Notaries, the Process of Law here being of a different Nature than they are in other Places, it being a Dutchy and County Palatine, and having particular Privileges of its own. The People are gay here, though not perhaps the richer for that; but it has by that obtained the Name of *Proud Preston.*

Francis Thompson was born at 7 Winckley Street (marked with a plaque) on December 18, 1859. His childhood, about which little is known, was spent here, and he was strictly raised in the Roman Catholic Church. He was sent to Ushaw College, Ushaw, County Durham, at the age of eleven to get a classical education and to prepare for the priesthood. His family moved to Ashton-under-Lyne in 1864. "The Hound of Heaven" derives from his childhood here. Years later, Thompson commented,

> I was born in 1858 or 1859 (I never could remember and don't care which) at Preston in Lancashire. Residing there, my mother more than once pointed out to me, as we passed it, the house wherein I was born; and it seemed to me disappointingly like any other house.

The strength of this Roman Catholic community drew another poet to it in 1882; his confinement at Manresa House, Roehampton, suspended, Gerard Manley Hopkins took charge of St. Wilfred's parish here for a short time before going on to the Cumberland coast, where he took part in his first mission.

One final association with Preston is debated, at least in part. Charles Dickens, who stayed at the Bull in 1845 when he was working on *Hard Times*, visited the town expressly to see the effects of a strike on a manufacturing town, but as he wrote:

> Except the crowds at the street-corners reading the placards *pro* and *con*, and the cold absence of smoke from the mill-chimneys, there is very little in the streets to make the town remarkable.

He thought Preston a "nasty place" instead of the town he expected, and he called the Bull an "old, grubby, smoky, mean, intensely formal red-brick house, with a narrow gateway and a dingy yard." He returned in April 1869, when his reading tour was brought to an abrupt end; he had been taken ill the previous week, and this reading, which had been scheduled for April 22, was canceled by Dickens's doctor. Preston figures under its own name in "George Silverman's Explanation," one of the novelist's lesser-known works. The debated point concerning Dickens and Preston has to do with *Hard Times* and the claim that this is the original of Coketown. However, Rochdale, Oldham, and Manchester also claim the distinction, and the case for Manchester appears the strongest.

PRINCETOWN, Devon (pop. 2,061, excluding prisoners) Modern guidebooks often exhort their readers: "Do not waste your time visiting Princetown. It is known only for its prison." A more unfortunate view of this town, about 22 miles northeast of Plymouth, cannot be imagined. This is the highest town on Dartmoor and the bleakest, with gale-force winds, fog, and snow and a very heavy annual rainfall (often in excess of 100 inches). Indeed, the moor is one place not to be caught unawares; more frightening than anything else is the sheer intensity of natural forces here: in this century, for example, oak trees were uprooted by the weight of a winter snowfall.

What is interesting, in light of the tremendously difficult survival conditions, is that the immediate vicinity contains evidence of extensive Bronze Age life. The prison was intended originally for French and American prisoners in the Napoleonic Wars and was not used for criminals until late in the 19th century. These morbid influences undoubtedly were at work in April 1901, when Sir Arthur Conan Doyle was here with Fletcher Robinson, a Dartmoor native; they stayed at Rowe's Duchy Hotel, where, as Doyle wrote:

> I am in the highest town in England. Robinson and I are exploring the Moor over our Sherlock Holmes Book. I think it will work out splendidly, indeed. I have already done nearly half of it. Holmes is at his very best, and it is a highly dramatic idea—which I owe to Robinson.

The book is *The Hound of the Baskervilles*. Robinson knew all the folktales, devil legends, and water-bogle stories connected with the area and supplied the details of the devil hounds for this story from local legend. Watson, Sir Henry Baskerville, and Dr. Mortimer arrive at Baskerville Hall shortly after Selden's escape from prison; Watson's musings comment on the scenery and the murderer:

> Our wagonette had topped a rise and in front of us rose the huge expanse of the moor, mottled with gnarled and craggy cairns and tors. A cold wind swept down from it and set us shivering. Somewhere there, on that desolate plain, was lurking this fiendish man, hiding in a burrow like a wild beast, his heart full of malignancy against the whole race which had cast him out. It needed but this to complete the grim suggestiveness of the barren waste, the chilling wind, and the darkling sky....
> We had left the fertile country behind and beneath us.... The road in front of us grew bleaker and wilder over huge russet and olive slopes, sprinkled with giant boulders.

PUDDLETOWN, Dorset (pop. 761)   Puddletown is 5 miles northeast of Dorchester on the main road to Blandford Forum; on both east and west sides of the village are marvelous manor houses, and the Piddle River runs through the center. Between Puddletown and Wareham is a great expanse of open heath, the Egdon Heath (Dorset heathland) of Thomas Hardy's novels; this is a wild heathland full of bracken and rare wild flowers and of relatively remote villages. The church here, with its 15th-century timbered roof, box pews, pre-Norman font, and handsome Jacobean pulpit, is one Thomas Hardy knew well, for his grandfather played the bass viol in the minstrels' gallery. The south side of the church contains the Athelhampton Chantry, where the 13th- to 15th-century altar tombs, effigies, and brasses to the Martyn family are found. The Martyns owned Athelhampton Hall, a 15th-century manor 1 mile to the east.

Athelhampton Hall becomes Hardy's Athelhall in "The Dame of Athelhall." More important is Waterston Manor, 2 miles to the west, also a Martyn home, which becomes Weatherbury Farm in *Far from the Madding Crowd*. Hardy moves the manor closer to the village and renames the village itself Weatherbury; indeed, the house has suffered fire damage and subsequent alterations since the novel was completed. To Gabriel Oak it is

> a hoary building, of the early stage of Classic Renaissance as regards its architecture....
> Fluted pilasters, worked from the solid stone, deco-

rated its front, and above the roof the chimneys were panelled or columnar, some coped gables with finials, and like features still retaining traces of their Gothic extraction. Soft brown mosses, like faded velveteen, formed cushions upon the stone tiling, and tufts of the houseleek or sengreen sprouted from the eaves of the low surrounding buildings. A gravel walk leading from the door to the road in front was encrusted at the sides with more moss—here it was a silver-green variety, the nut-brown of the gravel being visible to the width of only a foot or two in the centre.

Little Weatherbury Farm, the home of Boldwood, most likely is modeled on nearby Druce Farm; the "house stood recessed from the road, and the stables, which are to a farm what a fireplace is to a room, were behind, their lower portions being lost amid bushes of laurel." Warren's Malthouse has long been demolished and is now a small park. The church also enters the novel:

> The tower of Weatherbury Church was a square erection of fourteenth-century date, having two stone gurgoyles on each of the four faces of its parapet....
> Weatherbury tower was a somewhat early instance of the use of an ornamental parapet in parish as distinct from cathedral churches, and the gurgoyles, which are the necessary correlatives of a parapet, were exceptionally prominent.... All the eight were different from each other ... [but] only that at the south-eastern corner concerns the story.... This horrible stone entity was fashioned as if covered with a wrinkled hide; it had short, erect ears, eyes starting from their sockets, and its fingers and hands were seizing the corners of its mouth, which they thus seemed to pull open to give free passage to the water it vomited.

Here Fanny Robin and her child are buried, and eight months later so is Francis Troy; later still, Gabriel Oak and Bathsheba are married here. The Weatherbury Great Barn at Bathsheba's farm is probably based on an old tithe barn at Abbotsbury.

PULLOXHILL, Bedfordshire (pop. 648)   A quiet hilltop village, Pulloxhill has been a backwater until recently, when it has been threatened by the growth of Ampthill, only 3 miles to the northwest. There is an early Saxon settlement at nearby Kitchen End, and there are also the remains of a gold mine worked in the 18th century and earlier, marked on recent ordnance survey maps. This location is used by John Bunyan in *The Pilgrim's Progress* as the "little hill called Lucre, and in that hill a silver mine"; and the nearby meadow is called "Gold Close." The gold was shining yellow talc mixed with yellow, claylike earth; the mine, though, was worked in Bunyan's day.

PYRFORD, Surrey (pop. 1,179)   Pyrford is on the Wey River 6 miles northeast of Guildford, in an area somewhat saturated with water. The Wey Valley is very wide at this point, and the river divides into no fewer than seven streams; the valley floor is also extremely flat here. Pyrford became an "asylum" for John Donne around 1601; he had secretly married the sixteen-year-old Ann (Anne) More, daughter of Sir George More, and Sir George's discovery of the marriage led directly to Donne's imprisonment and the loss of his position as secretary to the Lord Keeper, Sir Thomas Egerton (Sir George's brother-in-law). Following Donne's release, the young couple were offered sanctuary (and support probably) here by Francis Wolley, Ann's cousin through Sir Thomas's first wife. Here the couple lived for almost four years; their first two children were born and christened here. Donne left for Peckham in 1605, but Wolley's hospitality and help were not forgotten; the Donnes christened their fourth child in his honor in 1607.

Another 17th-century association is with John Evelyn, who visited Denzil Onslow at his seat here in 1681 when there

was much company, & such an extraordinary feast, as I had hardly ever seene at any Country Gent: table in my whole life.... The seate stands on a flat, the ground pastures, rarely watred, & exceedingly improved; since Mr. Onslow bought it of Sir *Rob: Parkhurst,* who spent a faire Estate &c: The house is Timber, but commodious, & with one ample dining roome, & the hale adorned with paintings of this kind from the life. . . .

In the 20th century H. G. Wells mentions Pyrford in *The War of the Worlds;* the narrator passes through here on his return from Leatherhead.

QUORN, Leicestershire (pop. 2,417) The proper name of this village is Quorndon, but few insist on it; topographers, cartographers, and gazetteer writers have used Quorn for decades. The village is world-renowned for both the Quorn Hunt and the Quorn Kennels. The granite church has two unusual medieval stone screens and a very fine Norman doorway with a double row of chevrons. In D. H. Lawrence's *The Rainbow,* Quorn becomes Beldover, the town to which the Brangwens move:

It was an old, quiet village on the edge of the thronged colliery-district. So that it served, in its quaintness of odd old cottages lingering in their sunny gardens, as a sort of bower or pleasaunce to the sprawling colliery-townlet of Beldover, a pleasant walk-round for the colliers on Sunday morning, before the public-houses opened.

The Brangwens' house "stood in a quiet little side-street near the large church."

RAMPSIDE, Lancashire (pop. 481) On the Furness coast in northern Lancashire near Piel Island, Rampside is a well-known bathing place and in the 18th century was a health resort as well. In June 1794 Dorothy Wordsworth came here from White-haven, Cumberland, to stay with cousins, the Barkers, and William joined her in August from Keswick. The Barkers' house was close to the seashore, and Wordsworth had a fine view of Piel Castle, about which he later wrote. The house was sold after the death of Francis Barker in 1797 and eventually became an inn; it has been completely rebuilt.

RAMSGATE, Kent (pop. 19,861) Ramsgate, 4 miles southeast of Margate and one of a trio of Isle of Thanet holiday resorts, has an unusual symmetry observable from its eastern pier: on the right, the colonnaded Wellington Crescent, and on the left, the Georgian Nelson Crescent; both stand on low cliffs which run down to the harbor. With its Norman Church of St. Lawrence, Ramsgate still seems an old-world seafaring town, much unlike the other resort areas; here cargo boats unload, fishing boats ply the outer harbor, and seagoing pleasure yachts moor at the yacht marina. Princess Victoria played here on the wide expanses of sand, had her lessons at home (probably), now St. Winifred's School, and rode a favorite white donkey in the grounds.

Daniel Defoe was an early visitor to this "small port, [whose] Inhabitants are mighty fond of having us call it *Roman's-Gate;* pretending that the *Romans* under *Julius Caesar* made their first attempt to land here." William Cobbett cites Ramsgate as one of the places inhabited by "an assemblage of tax-eaters." "These vermin," he says, "shift about between London, Cheltenham, Bath, Bognor, Brighton, Tunbridge, Ramsgate, Margate, Worthing, and other spots in England...."

Jane Austen came to Ramsgate, most likely, in 1803, when her brother Frank was stationed here; the only evidence is Sir Samuel Egerton Brydges's statement in his *Autobiography:* "The last time I think that I saw her was at Ramsgate in 1803." She undoubtedly combined this visit with one to God-mersham. Miss Austen later used her knowledge of the area in *Pride and Prejudice* and *Mansfield Park;* in the first, Georgiana Darcy "last summer . . . went . . . to Ramsgate; and thither also went Mr. Wickham, undoubtedly by design . . . she was persuaded to believe herself in love, and to consent to an elopement." In the second novel it is here that Tom Bertram discovers the problem of determining whether or not young ladies are "out":

> "I went down to Ramsgate for a week. . . . I made my bow in form [to Mrs. Sneyd and her two daughters]. . . . They looked just the same; both well dressed, with veils and parasols like other girls; but I afterwards found that I had been giving all my attention to the youngest, who was not *out,* and had most excessively offended the eldest."

Another visitor was Samuel Taylor Coleridge, who from 1816 on came here each October with the Gillmans.

RAVENSPUR, Yorkshire Ravenspur is the usual spelling of this once-thriving seaport at the mouth of the Humber River near Spurn Head, but it was also called Ravenspurn, Ravenser, Ravensrode, and Ravenspurgh. In the mid-14th century it was a wealthy but small port, and by 1500 it was gone, swept away by the sea along with a number of other fishing villages. The single surviving trace of the port, a cross erected to commemorate the landing of Henry Bolingbroke in 1399, was later moved to the grounds at Holyrood House, Hendon. William Shakespeare refers both to Bolingbroke's landing and the port in *Richard II* when Green comments to the Queen, "I hope the king is not yet shipp'd for Ireland" and states:

> The banish'd Bolingbroke repeals himself,
> And with uplifted arms is safe arriv'd
> At Ravenspurgh.

READING, Berkshire (pop. 100,400) Reading (pronounced "red'ing") is the largest town in Berkshire as well as its county town. It stands on the Kennet River near the confluence with the Thames, 36 miles west of London. There is nothing surprising about the amoebalike spread of the town, and it has now almost encompassed all of Caversham, Tilehurst, Earley, and Calcot. Because of its position, Reading has always been inhabited, and there is extensive evidence of an Iron Age settlement around Southcote House. The area became important to the Romans and was on the direct route from the Hampshire colony of Silchester (Calleya Atrebatum), itself a model city of almost 100 acres.

By the time of the Domesday Survey in 1086, Radynges had developed into a settlement of thirty or so houses, and it prospered throughout the Middle Ages. Henry I founded the abbey in 1121 as a memorial to his son, who died when the *White Ship* sank; the abbey suffered horribly at the dissolution of the monasteries under Thomas Cromwell, Henry VIII's "hammer of the monks," who celebrated closing the abbey by publicly hanging and quartering the abbot and a few of his monks. In better days the abbey made a tremendous contribution to medieval literature and music, for this was where "Sumer is icumen in" was written sometime around 1240. There is a lively debate over the dating of this piece of music because of its notation, but the generally accepted view now ascribes it to the 13th century. A stone tablet in the Chapter House walls is inscribed with the work, which was written to be sung in a sort of round by six people, two singing a two-part ground base for "Sing cuckoo" and the others the verse to the turn. Sizable parts of the abbey ruins are extant. The central tower with its pillar is certainly the most memorable, for here Thomas à Becket consecrated the church, and the marriage of John of Gaunt to Blanche of Lancaster occurred. The old stone seats of the Chapter House are still in place, and on these William of Malmesbury must have sat when he came here and found the monks "a noble pattern of holiness and an example of delightful and unwearied hospitality."

A number of early travelers and diarists visited Reading and left comments on the city. John Leland, who included extensive notes on Reading in his *Itinerary*, was favorably impressed by the area:

> Yet it is a very auncient toun, and at this tyme the best toun of al Barkshire. There was a castelle in the Saxons tyme in this towne: and the name of Castelle-Streat yet remaynithe. . . .

John Evelyn, who was here in May 1654 and who usually had something to say about every place he visited, mentions only that he and his wife stayed over. About half a century later Daniel Defoe inspected Reading, and in *A Tour thro' the Whole Island of Great Britain* he focuses on the economy:

> *Reading,* a very large and wealthy Town, handsomly built, the Inhabitants rich, and driving a very great Trade. The Town lies on the River *Kennet,* but so near

the *Thames,* that the largest Barges which they use, may come up to the Town Bridge, and there they have Wharfs to load, and unload them. Their chief Trade is by this Water-Navigation to and from *London,* though they have necessarily a great Trade into the Country, for the Consumption of the Goods which they bring by their Barges from *London,* and particularly Coals, Salt, Grocery Wares, Tobacco, Oyls, and all heavy Goods.

William Cobbett, whose *Rural Rides* often treats the economic problems of the areas he visited, was more deeply concerned with the Reading population and his own reception; he writes:

> I have seldom seen a number of persons assembled together, whose approbation I valued more than that of the company of this day. . . . This has been a fine meeting at Reading! I feel very proud of it. . . .
> I came on horseback 40 miles, slept on the road, and finished my harangue at the end of *twenty-two hours* from leaving Kensington; and I cannot help saying that is pretty well for "*Old* Cobbett."

Other writers had some sort of association with Reading, but many of these were unhappy. John Bunyan came here in an attempt to reconcile a father and son, but riding from Reading to London he caught the cold from which he died. Stephen Duck, frequently referred to as the "phenomenon of Wiltshire," had been quite successful in court and had aroused the envy of many of the 18th century's more able writers. When the rumor of his being nominated Poet Laureate to succeed Laurence Eusden began, Jonathan Swift wrote a thoroughly contemptuous epigram:

> Thrice happy Duck! Employed in threashing stubble,
> Thy toil is lessened, and thy profits double.

In 1755 Duck's mind began to give way, and he was subject to increasing periods of depression and melancholy. On March 21, 1756, he drowned himself in the trout stream behind the Black Lion Hotel.

The relationship between Reading and Samuel Taylor Coleridge was hardly one of the more pleasant ones in his life. On December 4, 1793, Coleridge enlisted in the 15th Dragoons under the name Silas Tomkyn Comberbacke; while his enlistment can easily be understood in the light of his problems at the university and his debts, his choice of the Dragoons leaves much to be explained, since he was a totally inept horseman. His training, if such it could be called, took place here; he nursed his fellow soldiers, wrote their letters, and was discharged on April 10. Jane Austen came to Reading and spent some time at the Abbey School (over the abbey gateway) while her family lived in Steventon.

By the gardens on the riverbank not too far from the site of the abbey is the old Reading Gaol, described in Charles Reade's *It Is Never Too Late to Mend:*

> Therefore our story drags us . . . to a massive castellated building, glaring red brick with white stone corners. . . .
> Two round towers flank the principal entrance. . . . The castle is massive and grand. . . .
> Between the central towers is a sharp arch, filled by a huge oak door of the same shape and size, which, for further security or ornament, is closely studded with large diamond-headed nails. . . . You slip under a porch into an enclosed yard, the great door shuts almost of itself. . . .

Passing into the interior of the vast building, you find yourself in an extensive aisle traversed at right angles by another of similar dimensions, the whole in form of a cross. In the centre of each aisle is an iron staircase, so narrow that two people cannot pass. . . .

The novel, subtitled *A Matter of Fact Romance,* was motivated by accounts of the extreme cruelty in the Birmingham Gaol and by a desire to bring about social reform.

The most famous association with the jail in Forbury Road is with Oscar Wilde, who was imprisoned here from November 1895 until his release on May 19, 1897. Wilde was transferred here from Pentonville Prison on the instigation of Richard Burdon Haldane, later Viscount Haldane. This was a period of total misery for Wilde; he was unable even to clean his shoes and went so far as to comment, "If I could but feel clean, I should not feel so utterly miserable." He wrote "De Profundis," a long letter to Lord Alfred Douglas which contained the very moving explanation of his conduct; the work was posthumously published in 1905. He wrote in the evenings, when he knew he would be undisturbed. He put his plank bed across the two wooden trestles in his cell to make a table, and as he commented, "It was a very good table, too." Wilde's cell was marked C.3.3. *The Ballad of Reading Gaol* was probably written after his release, although the occasional claim is made that Wilde composed the poem under his prison number and completed it in 1896. It was published in 1898 after Wilde had gone abroad to Berneval, France. Parts V and VI of the ballad are especially moving:

But this I know, that every Law
  That men have made for Man,
Since first Man took his brother's life,
  And the sad world began,
But straws the wheat and saves the chaff
  With a most evil fan.

This too I know—and wise it were
  If each could know the same—
That every prison that men build
  Is built with bricks of shame,
And bound with bars lest Christ should see
  How man their brothers maim.

Reading is used extensively in the works of Thomas Hardy. While he merely includes the town in *The Hand of Ethelberta,* "The Son's Veto," and *Desperate Remedies,* he relies on it heavily in *Jude the Obscure* as Aldbrickham. Unfortunately the changes in Reading have been so great that some of the specific places are unidentifiable. The house on Spring Street where Jude and Sue live and where Jude works as a monumental mason is well specified but impossible to locate; the house is relatively close to the Prince Inn, where Arabella stays when she comes from London to see Jude. The hall where Jude attends a public lecture was "not far off"; and when Little Father Time arrives by train in Aldbrickham searching for his father, he has a long walk to the area before finding "the way to the little lane" where the house is. Other places mentioned include the George Inn, where Jude and Arabella and later Jude and Sue stay; the Temperance Hotel; and the Office of the Superintendent Register. The unnamed church in which Jude and Sue work as ornamentors is placed close to the village of Gaymead, about 2 miles from Aldbrickham. This has frequently been identified as Theale, but a far more likely identification (and now generally accepted) is the village of Shinfield, a few miles to the south. Gaymead is used more specifically in "The Son's Veto" as the location of the Reverend Mr. Twycott's parsonage and church and his wife's native village.

The men in Jerome K. Jerome's *Three Men in a Boat,* coming upstream, finally catch sight of the city:

The river is dirty and dismal here. One does not linger in the neighbourhood of Reading. The town itself is a famous old place, dating from the dim days of King Ethelred. . . .

In later years, Reading seems to have been regarded as a handy place to run down to, when matters were becoming unpleasant in London. Parliament generally rushed off to Reading whenever there was a plague on at Westminster; and, in 1625, the Law followed suit, and all the courts were held at Reading. It must have been worth while having a mere ordinary plague now and then in London to get rid of both the lawyers and the Parliament.

REDRUTH, Cornwall (pop. 36,240) In the southernmost section of Cornwall, 9 miles southwest of Truro, is Redruth, now part of the Camborne-Redruth Urban District, the largest industrial area in western Cornwall; the amalgamation forms the largest nucleus of population in the duchy. Like many Cornish towns, Redruth has extremely narrow streets; it is built on two hills, and between it and Camborne is Carn Brea, whose granite heights rise to 738 feet. The crown of Carn Brea is covered with all the paraphernalia necessary to druid worship: a cave, standing stones, remains of cromlechs, circles, rock basins, and a grove of trees. Indeed, 18th-century scholars argued that some of the vermicular grooves in some of the rock basins were used for the blood of sacrifices, possibly human. George Borrow refers to this determination. He came to Cornwall in December 1853 to meet his local relations, and in January 1854 he set out on a walking tour of the county. He climbed Carn Brea, which reminded him of "huge rhinoceroses piled upon one another," and then examined the stone basins:

On top of the Carn there are two little basins about seven feet from each other; three mysterious little holes about the diameter of a penny seemed to have connected them. . . . In the principal basin—the horrid place of sacrifice—there are outlets for the blood to stream down.

REIGATE, Surrey (pop. 56,088 including Redhill) An old market town at the foot of the North Downs, Reigate is on the southwest perimeter of London and is now a community of commuters. The town once belonged to William de Warenne, who was created Earl of Surrey by William Rufus and to whom the land was granted; the main De Warenne holding was at Lewes, but the family also built the castle here.

When the De Warenne line died out, the castle passed to the Howards, Dukes of Norfolk, but they made little use of the castle, and by the time of James I it was in a state of decay. Today nothing remains of the structure, and the scarped site, some 50 feet high, has been turned into a public flower garden.

In 1216 the De Warennes founded a small house for the Austin friars just south of the High Street, where there are still remains of some of the old priory walls. At the dissolution of the monasteries in the 16th century it came into the hands of Lord Howard of Effingham, who built the present house; it later became the property of John Somers. The 3d Earl bequeathed it to his daughter, Lady Henry Somerset. William Butler Yeats was a frequent guest at the Somerset house.

The exact location of an early literary association cannot be established authoritatively; however, John Foxe, the martyrologist and author of *Actes and Monuments*, was engaged for five years as a tutor to the orphaned children of Henry Howard, Earl of Surrey, after his execution in January 1547. The children were placed in the care of their aunt, the Duchess of Richmond, who chose Foxe as their tutor. It is not known absolutely whether the duchess lived at the priory or at the castle. Reigate was visited by Daniel Defoe, and although he mentioned other rotten boroughs in *A Tour thro' the Whole Island of Great Britain*, he ignored that aspect of this town.

In more modern times the novelist William Harrison Ainsworth moved to Belvedere, St. Mary's Road, from Tunbridge Wells in 1878; earlier he had often stayed with his brother at Hill View Lodge on Glovers Road. Now an old man well past the crest of his literary and social fame, Ainsworth had already sold off most of his family property and settled into a solitary life here with his second wife. He died here on January 3, 1882, and was buried at Kensal Green Cemetery, London.

RENDHAM, Suffolk (pop. 287) The tiny village of Rendham, almost equidistant between Great Glemham and Saxmundham, was the home of George Crabbe from 1801 to 1805; leaving the living at Muston, Leicestershire, to a curate in 1792 to take over the executor's duties of his wife's uncle's estate, he and his family first lived in Parham, but family dissension drove him away. Then in 1796, when he became curate of both Great Glemham and Sweffling, he took Great Glemham Hall, where he led a very retired life; about 1801, after he had obtained a stay of the Bishop of Lincoln's order of his return to Muston, Crabbe moved to Lady Whincups, opposite the parsonage, when Dudley North sold the hall. He reestablished residence at Muston in 1805.

REY CROSS CAMP, Yorkshire High on the summit of Stainmore, just off the main road 6 miles west of Bowes, is the Roman camp of Rey Cross, topped by a fragment of an old cross with its pediment. The cross, probably antedating the Romans and surrounded by an entrenchment, is thought perhaps to have marked the frontier between Scotland and the early kingdom of Northumbria. The lovely song "Allen-a-Dale" in Sir Walter Scott's *Rokeby* describes the cross as a meeting place:

Allen-a-Dale has ne'er belted a knight
Though his spur be as sharp and his blade be as bright;
Allen-a-Dale is no baron or lord,
Yet twenty tall yeomen will draw at his word;
And the best of our nobles his bonnet will vail,
Who at Rere-cross on Stanmore meets Allen-a-Dale.

RICHMOND, Surrey (pop. 39,276) On the sloping south bank of the Thames River just under 10 miles southwest of Waterloo Station, London, Richmond is more London than Surrey, although it was not always urban. Indeed, the town was known as Sheen until Henry VII renamed it Richmond after his own Yorkshire title, Earl of Richmond. By the early 14th century the manor was permanently in the hands of the crown and became a favorite residence of the monarchs from Edward III through George II. The original structure was partially destroyed by Richard II after the death here of his wife, Anne of Bohemia, and a fire in 1497 completed the destruction. Henry VII rebuilt it, but Cromwellian forces dismantled most of the estate, and only a Tudor gateway and some minor outbuildings have been preserved. The old Star and Garter, now a home for disabled war veterans, commands an especially good view of the town, although the "unrivalled landscape" emphasized in Sir Walter Scott's *The Heart of Midlothian* is no longer dominant:

A huge sea of verdure with crossing and intersecting promontories of massive and tufted groves, was tenanted by numberless flocks and herds, which seemed to wander unrestrained and unbounded through the rich pastures. The Thames, here turreted with villas, and there garlanded with forests, moved on slowly and placidly, like the mighty monarch of the scene, to whom all its other beauties were but accessories, and bore on its bosom an hundred barks and skiffs, whose white sails and gaily fluttering pennons gave life to the whole.

Scott's description, though the most famous, was not the first; James Thomson describes the view in "Summer" in his *Seasons:*

Say, shall we wind
Along the streams? or walk the smiling mead?
Or court the forest glades? or wander wild
Among the waving harvests? or ascend,
While radiant Summer opens all its pride,
Thy hill, delightful Shene? Here let us sweep
The boundless landscape. . . .

Thomson had a small cottage on Kew Foot Lane before taking Rosedale House in 1736 (part of the house is now incorporated in the Royal Richmond Hospital). It was probably here that he wrote "Rule Britannia."

Thomson's earlier friendship with Alexander Pope, who was living in Twickenham, only a mile away, quickly deepened, and many visits were made back and forth until Pope's death in 1744. William Collins was another frequent guest. Thomson is said to have become overheated walking the short distance from Richmond to Hammersmith; he contracted a high fever and began treatment which probably would have been effective if he had not succumbed to the temptation of the extremely fine weather to venture out again. The fever reappeared, and he died on August 27, 1748; burial was in the churchyard of St. Mary Magdalene here. The parish churchyard also contains the grave of Mary Elizabeth Braddon, author of *Lady Audley's Secret*, who lived the last forty years of her life at Lichfield House (now Lichfield Court), Sheen Road, and died in her home on February 4, 1915.

John Evelyn visited the home of Henry Brounckers in Sheen in late August 1678; Brouncker's home was formerly the Carthusian priory in West Sheen, where, Evelyn notes, "there yet remaining one of their solitary Cells with a Crosse. . . ." Evelyn particularly enjoyed the "severall pretty Villas, and fine Gardens of the most excellent fruites" within the priory grounds and was especially impressed with that belonging to Sir William Temple; in 1688 he visited Temple's estate, of which he wrote: "The most remarkable thing is his Orangerie & Gardens; where the wall Fruite trees are most exquisitely nailed & applied, far better than in my life I had ever noted...." Toward the end of June 1689 Jonathan Swift was also at Temple's estate as his secretary. It is thought that both Swift and Sir William left for Moor Park toward the end of the following year.

Charles Dickens was a frequent visitor to Richmond. In 1836 he rented Elm Cottage (now Elm Lodge) on Petersham Road, and for twenty years he kept his wedding anniversary at the Star and Garter Inn, reserving a table which "commanded a view of the river from the Crest of Richmond Hill." The same inn, almost certainly, was the scene of the party which celebrated the completion of *David Copperfield;* among Dickens's guests at the celebration were both William Makepeace Thackeray and Alfred, Lord Tennyson. When Dickens wrote *Pickwick Papers,* he used Richmond and its surroundings for the pleasant retreat owned by Tracy Tupman where he walked on the terrace in the summer months. From 1855 to 1859 George Eliot (Mary Ann Evans) and George Henry Lewes lived at 7 Clarence Row and then at 8 Parkshot; here she wrote *Scenes of Clerical Life* and *Adam Bede.* Charles Lamb took a month's holiday here in late August and early September 1804 and enjoyed wandering along the banks of the Thames. In 1914 Virginia and Leonard Woolf lived at 17 The Green and in 1915 moved to Hogarth House, Paradise Road. Finally, H. G. Wells uses the town in *The History of Mr. Polly,* as the location of the Roebuck Inn to which Mr. Polly goes with his fellow shop assistants to stand for drinks after coming into the legacy left by his father.

RICHMOND, Yorkshire (pop. 6,750)   In the midst of Swaledale, Richmond has somehow maintained the atmosphere of a storybook medieval town, and the British Council acknowledged Richmond's special character by calling it "typically English." The town is on the Swale River and is dominated by a magnificent 11th-century castle, which occupies the summit of a cliff overlooking the river. Indeed, protected on three sides by the formidable cliff structure and on the fourth by the massive keep, the castle itself was never under siege. An early comment by John Leland in his *Itinerary* that "Richemont is pavid" (that is, "cobbled") is true even in the 20th century. Many of the wynds (ancient alleys) are still cobbled, and the town is unwilling to pave the cobbles over.

Richmond is one of many localities that figure in both Arthurian and Robin Hood legends, although here the claims are not well substantiated. Local tradition holds that King Arthur and his knights met on the hilltop in front of the castle, and this is one of numerous places where Arthur and his entourage are supposed to be sleeping, waiting for the garter to be cut and the magic horn to be sounded. Their underground chamber is said to be hidden beneath the castle, somewhere off Castle Walk; local legend has it that one Potter Thompson stumbled on their sleeping place but neglected to perform the ritual. The castle also has a connection with Robin Hood, for it contains Robin Hood's tower. In contrast, the 18th-century ballad "The Sweet Lass of Richmond Hill" belongs to Richmond, Yorkshire, and not to Richmond, Surrey, as is usually claimed. The song was written by Leonard MacNally, an Irish barrister, for the purpose of courting a local girl, Frances I'Anson, whom he later married.

Lewis Carroll (Charles Lutwidge Dodgson) was sent to Richmond School in 1844, at the age of twelve,

RICHMOND, YORKSHIRE   The ruins of the magnificent 11th-century castle dominate the town from their hilltop position, and in an underground chamber beneath the castle King Arthur and his entourage are said to be sleeping and awaiting the ritual of the garter and horn to awaken them.

from his home in Croft, Yorkshire. The school had an excellent scholastic reputation under James Tate, Sr. and Jr., and it was the headmaster, James Tate, Jr., who recognized the young Lewis Carroll's talent; note his rather interesting advice to the Reverend Mr. Dodgson:

> You must not entrust your son with a full knowledge of his superiority over other boys. Let him discover this as he proceeds. The love of excellence is far beyond the love of excelling. . . .

Carroll remained here until 1846, when he was sent on to Rugby.

RIDGEWAY, THE, Berkshire and Wiltshire The Ridgeway is a prehistoric trackway which extends some 20 miles along the crest of the Berkshire Downs overlooking the Kennet Valley. Used as a main trading route during the Bronze Age, although of earlier origin, it was especially important as an access route from the Thames River settlements to the major religious center at Avebury in Wiltshire. The name Ridgeway (sometimes spelled as two words) was normally applied to an unpaved track following the ridges across country; such ways provided dry routes above the lowland marshes and sloughs and were passable even in winter, when the valley routes were treacherous. The ways once connected settlements but now do not generally link communities. Kenneth Grahame, who lived in Blewbury and Cookham Dean, loved to walk the Ridgeway and wrote of its isolation:

> At once it strikes you out and away from the habitable world in a splendid, purposeful manner, running along the highest of the Downs, a broad green ribbon of turf, with but a shade of difference from the neighbouring grass, yet distinct for all that. No villages nor homesteads tempt it aside or modify its course for a yard. . . .

Yet this isolation is not dehumanized:

> Out on that almost trackless expanse of billowy Downs such a track is in some sort humanly companionable: it really seems to lead you by the hand.

An earlier writer used the Berkshire Downs, the Vale of the White Horse, and the Ridgeway quite extensively in one of his works. Thomas Hughes places the Brown family home in Kingston Lisle in *Tom Brown's School Days*, and the Ridgeway, which passes very near the village, is described as

> a place that you won't forget, a place to open a man's soul, and make his prophesy, as he looks down on that great Vale spread out as the garden of the Lord before him, and wave on wave of the mysterious downs behind, and to the right and left the chalk hills running away into the distance, along which he can trace for miles the old Roman road, "the Ridgeway" ("the Rudge," as the country folk call it), keeping straight along the highest back of the hills. . . .

RINGMER, Sussex (pop. 1,359) Ringmer is only 2½ miles northeast of Lewes. Visitors to the music festival at nearby Glyndebourne who pass through Ringmer to avoid Lewes must be astonished by the large, richly painted signpost of a turtle, the village's patron. This is Timothy the Tortoise, whose carapace is in the Natural History Museum in London and who crawled to fame through the naturalist Gilbert White and his book *The Natural History and Antiquities of Selborne*. Timothy belonged to Mrs. Rebecca Snooke, White's aunt, who lived at Delves House, where the author was a frequent visitor. White was fascinated by the tortoise, and when his aunt died, he took the reptile back to his home in Selbourne, where he observed it closely:

> On the first of November I remarked that the old tortoise, formerly mentioned, began first to dig the ground in order to the forming its hybernaculum, which it had fixed on just beside a great tuft of hepaticas. It scrapes out the ground with its fore-feet, and throws it up over its back with its hind; but the motion of its legs is ridiculously slow, little exceeding the hour-hand of a clock; and suitable to the composure of an animal said to be a whole month in performing one feat of copulation. Nothing can be more assiduous than this creature night and day in scooping the earth, and forcing its great body into the cavity. . . .

A rookery which White observed is also here.

For centuries before White and Timothy the village was famous for its bad roads and mud, and Daniel Defoe notes the problem in *A Tour thro' the Whole Island of Great Britain*:

> Sometimes a whole Summer is not dry enough to make the Roads passable: Here I had a sight, which indeed I never saw in any other Part of *England*: Namely, that going to Church at a Country Village, not far from *Lewis*, I saw an Ancient Lady, *and a Lady of very good Quality, I assure you*, drawn to Church in her Coach with *Six Oxen*; nor was it done in Frolick or Humour, but meer Necessity, the Way being so stiff and deep, that no Horses could go in it.

The 14th-century Ringmer Church is said to be the one to which Defoe refers.

RIPE, Sussex (pop. 277) A peaceful village 7 miles east of Lewes, Ripe became the home of Malcolm Lowry in January 1956; White Cottage, near the Lamb, was where, on doctor's orders to find a secluded place to help his manic-depressiveness and alcoholism, Lowry was once again able to write. He finished the short-story volume *Hear Us O Lord from Heaven Thy Dwelling Place* before he died here on June 27, 1957; Lowry is buried in the churchyard.

RISINGHOE, Bedfordshire Risinghoe is an uninhabited location about 4 miles from Bedford on the Ouse River just beyond Goldington, itself part of Bedford. Here by the site of an old mill is a mound named Risinghoe by 10th-century Danish invaders, and nearby is a small bridge known as Bloody Battle Bridge. Risinghoe is part of the Bedfordshire landscape used in John Bunyan's *The Pilgrim's Progress*: this is the hill to which Worldly Wiseman directs Christian:

> But behold, when he was got now hard by the hill, it seemed so high . . . that Christian was afraid to venture further, lest the hill should fall on his head. Wherefore there he stood still, and wooted not what to do. . . . There came also flashes of fire out of the hill that made Christian afraid. . . .

John Leland erroneously describes the artificial mound in his *Itinerary* as the one-time castle keep of the Espec family. The most likely explanation is that this was some sort of Danish signal station, a point more in keeping with Bunyan's "flashes of fire."

ROBERTSBRIDGE, Sussex   The Rother River, winding its way across the broad east Sussex plain, forms a lovely setting for the small hamlet of Robertsbridge (Rotherbridge), 4¾ miles north of Battle; but because of its position on the main road to Hastings the village suffers from excessive traffic. Of the 12th-century Cistercian abbey founded here, there are only the scantiest remains at Abbey Farm at the end of Fair Lane; at the top of the village is the George Inn, an old coaching inn where in recent times Hilaire Belloc stayed when he began the tramp through Sussex described in *The Four Men*. An earlier visitor to the village was Horace Walpole whose experiences were distressing; he writes:

> The roads grew bad beyond all badness, the night dark beyond all darkness, our guide frightened beyond all frightfulness. However, without being at all killed, we got up, or down—I forget which, it was so dark,—a famous precipice called Silver Hill and about ten at night arrived at a wretched village called Rotherbridge. . . . But alas! there was only one bed to be had: all the rest were inhabited by smugglers, whom the people of the house called mountebanks; and with one of whom the lady of the den told Mr. Chute he might lie. We did not at all take to this society, but, armed with links and lanthorns, set out again upon this impracticable journey.

Dante Gabriel Rossetti came to nearby Scalands in March 1870; being ordered by his physician to leave London and rest, he accepted Madame Bodichon's offer of this house. He had previously, in 1854, stayed here with Elizabeth Siddall. During his recuperation he completed "The Stream's Secret," "Barren Spring," and "He and I" before beginning to take chloral. "Youth's Spring Tribute," "The Love Letter," "Love Sweetness," and "The Monochord" were all written here before *Poems by D. G. Rossetti* appeared at the end of April.

ROBIN HOOD'S BAY, Yorkshire   This picturesque and remote old fishing village with its little houses and shops tightly crowded together probably once was named Fyling (Fylingdales Moor is nearby) but later was named after Robin Hood, who, it is said, frequently came here when he was forced out of his usual Nottinghamshire retreats. The village, set on the edge of the sea with its narrow main street careening sharply down to the ever-encroaching water, was once the haunt of smugglers.

ROBIN HOOD'S BAY   Once the haunt of smugglers because of its numerous caves and hiding places, Robin Hood's Bay has suffered much from the encroaching sea, and many of the early fishing cottages have been swept out to sea.

ROCHDALE, Lancashire (pop. 91,290)   Sitting astride the Roch River 10½ miles north of Manchester, with the Rossendale Fells rising to the north, Rochdale has become so industrialized, especially with the cloth trade, that its natural beauties have been obliterated. A total of 122 steps lead high above the town hall to the medieval St. Chad's Church and the churchyard where John Collier, the 18th-century Lancashire dialect poet who wrote as Tim Bobbin, is buried. Born the son of a poor blind parson, he came here as a schoolmaster in 1739 and held the post until his death in 1786.

Another literary association began here in 1855 when Robert Bridges's mother married the Rev. John Edward Nassau Molesworth, and Rochdale Vicarage became their new home. Bridges had been sent to Eton from Walmer and continued at the school until going up to Corpus Christi College, Oxford, in 1863. In August 1866 Gerard Manley Hopkins, who had met Bridges at Oxford, came here on his way to Birmingham, "where I have some business"—that of seeing John Henry Cardinal Newman at the Oratory in Birmingham. Hopkins had planned to stop in Rochdale after going to Birmingham but came here first because Newman was abroad.

Rochdale also claims to have been used as the model for Charles Dickens's Coketown, the "town of red brick" in *Hard Times*. However, Preston, Oldham, and Manchester have also been identified as Coketown, and the case for Manchester seems the strongest.

ROCHESTER, Kent (pop. 55,460)   Its present significance confirmed by its status as a cathedral city as well as a river port, a market town, and a borough in its own right, Rochester dates its importance from its location as a crossing point on the Medway River when the area was inhabited by the Belgic tribes. Under the Romans Durobrivae thrived from its location on Watling Street, the road from the channel ports to London, and it received Roman walls at an early date. The Danes periodically invaded and destroyed the town until Alfred the Great defeated them decisively in the late 9th century.

The aftermath of the Norman Conquest brought major changes to Rochester; the Normans fortified the town, and a Norman monk, Gundulf, consecrated as bishop, immediately began building Rochester Cathedral, Rochester Castle, and a monastery. Most of Gundulf's cathedral has been superseded, but the unadorned south-aisle arcade and the crypt are two noteworthy exceptions; the medieval graffiti scratched on the piers in the crypt are also worth searching out. The cathedral library is outstanding and contains, among other things, the *Textus Roffensis* (1115–1124), Coverdale's 1535 Bible, and the 1539 Great Bible.

Early writers made extensive use of Rochester or commented on it. Geoffrey Chaucer uses Rouchestre in *The Canterbury Tales* as one of the marking points of the journey; the band of pilgrims arrive here on April 18, and Harry Bailly requests the monk not to break the game of the tales:

> "My lord, the Monk," quod he, "be myrie of cheere,
> For ye shul telle a tale trewely.
> Loo, Rouchestre stant heer faste by!
> Ryde forth, myn owene lord, brek nat oure game. . . ."

John Lyly uses the contemporary city as the scene of *Mother Bombie.* A far less pleasant view of Rochester occurs in William Shakespeare's *Henry IV: Part I;* here nothing of the castle or cathedral is mentioned: there is only malicious gossip directed at its inn:

> *2 Car.* Peas and beans are as dank here as a dog, and that is the next way to give poor jades the bots: this house is turned upside down since Robin ostler died.
> *1 Car.* Poor fellow! never joyed since the price of oats rose; it was the death of him.
> *2 Car.* I think this be the most villanous house in all London road for fleas: I am stung like a tench.

Today, of course, neither the King's Head nor the Bull (called the Royal Victoria and Bull since Queen Victoria stayed there) claims any association with either the poet or the play.

The diarists also included Rochester in their itineraries. Samuel Pepys was in Rochester on numerous occasions for Admiralty business and recorded some of his impressions of the cathedral and the city in April 1661:

> Then to Rochester, and there saw the Cathedral.... Then away thence, observing the great doors of the church which, they say, was covered with the skins of the Danes. So to the Salutation tavern, where Mr. Alcock and many of the town came and entertained us with wine and oysters and other things.... Here much mirth, but I was a little troubled to stay too long, because of going to Hempson's, which afterwards we did.... Here we had, for my sake, two fiddles, the one a bass viol, on which he that played played well some lyra lessons, but both together made the worst music that ever I heard.

John Evelyn's first trip to Rochester was probably in July 1640, and he, too, returned frequently on business. In August 1663 he records a trip to Scots Hall and comments on the parish church:

> Whence...to *Scots hall,* a right noble seate, uniformely built, handsome Gallery, it stands in a Park well stored, fat & good land: we were exceedingly feasted by the young knight & in his pretty Chapell heard an excellent sermon....
> In the Church-yard of the Parish-Church I measured an over-grown Yew-tree that was 18 of my paces in compasse out of some branches of which, torne off by the Winds, were divers goodly planks sawed....

Daniel Defoe, too, was in Rochester, and while he was less strongly impressed by the town than by the Royal Navy's complex, he certainly is not malicious in his commentary in *A Tour thro' the Whole Island of Great Britain:*

> There's little remarkable in *Rochester,* except the Ruins of a very old Castle, and an antient but not extraordinary Cathedral; but the River and its Appendices are the most considerable of the kind in the World. This being the Chief Arsenal of the Royal Navy of *Great-Britain.* The Buildings here are indeed like the Ships themselves, surprisingly large, and in their several kinds Beautiful....

Another of the early travelers who commented on Rochester was William Cobbett in his *Rural Rides;* under date of December 4, 1821, he notes:

> Rochester . . . is a small but crowded place, lying on the south bank of the beautiful Medway, with a rising ground on the other side of the city.... *Rochester* itself, and *Chatham,* form, in fact, one main street of about two miles and a half in length.—Here I was got into the scenes of my cap-and-feather days! Here, at between sixteen and seventeen, I enlisted for a soldier.

ROCHESTER   More closely associated with Charles Dickens than anyone else, Rochester, its cathedral, and its gateway play important roles in *Pickwick Papers, Great Expectations,* and *The Mystery of Edwin Drood.* Dicken's own desire "to lie in the little graveyard belonging to the Cathedral at the foot of the Castle wall" was denied when the Dean and Chapter at Westminster Abby requested his burial there.

By far the most obvious association with Rochester occurs with Charles Dickens and his works. As a child, when the Dickens family lived in Chatham, the elder Dickens and his son frequently walked in the Medway area around Chatham and Rochester; the novelist later recalled to John Forster:

> How he thought the Rochester High Street must be at least as wide as Regent Street, which he afterwards discovered to be little better than a lane; . . . and how, in its town hall, which had appeared to him once so glorious a structure that he had set it up in his mind as the model on which the genie of the lamp built the palace for Aladdin, he had painfully to recognise a mere mean little heap of bricks, like a chapel gone demented.

Dickens first describes Rochester in "The Great Winglebury Duel," but it is *Pickwick Papers,* which emphasizes the town. Mr. Pickwick, with Mr. Tupman, Mr. Winkle, and Mr. Snodgrass, comes by coach from London:

> "Magnificent ruin!" said Mr. Augustus Snodgrass, with all the poetic fervour that distinguished him, when they came in sight of the fine old castle.
> "What a study for an antiquarian!" were the very words which fell from Mr. Pickwick's mouth as he applied his telescope to his eye.
> "Ah! Fine place," said the stranger, "glorious pile—frowning walls—tottering arches—dark nooks—crumbling staircases—old cathedral too—earthy smell—pilgrims' feet worn away the old steps—little Saxon doors—confessionals like money-takers' boxes at theatres— . . . fine place—old legends too—strange stories: capital"; and the stranger continued to soliloquize until they reached the Bull Inn, in the High Street, where the coach stopped.

The Bull Inn (now the Royal Victoria and Bull), on

the High Street, a "good house—nice beds" and superior to "Wright's next house,...[where they] charge you more if you dine at a friend's than they would if you dined in the coffee-room" was also where Dickens stayed on his visit in 1845. The yard is now smaller, the stables are gone, and the ballroom or assembly room upstairs, where Tracy Tupman and the stranger encounter Dr. Slammer, was later made into the dining room. The bar where Tupman buys the tickets was opposite the coffee room. Dickens stayed in Mr. Pickwick's room, No. 17, and Mr. Tupman and Mr. Winkle had rooms 13 and 19, which were intercommunicating.

> Behind it rose the ancient castle, its towers roofless and its massive walls crumbling away, but telling us proudly of its own might and strength, as when, seven hundred years ago, it rang with the clash of arms or resounded with the noise of feasting and revelry. On either side, the banks of the Medway, covered with corn-fields and pastures, with here and there a windmill or a distant church stretched away as far as the eye could see, presenting a rich and varied landscape, rendered more beautiful by the changing shadows which passed swiftly across it as the thin and half-formed clouds skimmed away in the light of the morning sun. The river, reflecting the clear blue of the sky, glistened and sparkled as it flowed noiselessly on....

The Rochester which Mr. Pickwick knew and which Dickens so graphically describes has changed: Pickwick's bridge has been replaced, but some of the original supporting balustrades were retained as coping for the esplanade embankment. The view is gone from both sides of the bridge.

Rochester also figures in *David Copperfield*, for the runaway makes his way through Rochester on his route from London to Dover; he crosses over

> the bridge at Rochester.... One or two little houses, with the notice, 'Lodgings for Travellers', hanging out, had tempted me; but I was afraid of spending the few pence I had, and was even more afraid of the vicious looks of the trampers I had met or overtaken. I sought no shelter, therefore, but the sky....

In *Great Expectations*, Rochester assumes a more important role as the market town. Miss Havisham's house, Satis House, is not to be confused with the actual house of that name in the city; Dickens took the name and applied it to Restoration House, a red-brick E-shaped building dating from 1857. The exterior of Satis House

> was of old brick, and dismal, and had a great many iron bars to it. Some of the windows had been walled up; of those that remained, all the lower were rustily barred. There was a court-yard in front, and that was barred.... [A]t the side of the house there was a large brewery. No brewing was going on in it, and none seemed to have gone on for a long time.

The interior of the present house (occasionally open in summer) contains a wealth of dark paneling taken from the church in nearby Frindsbury, and Miss Havisham's room, a dignified and paneled drawing room, offers a decided contrast to the room Pip saw full of vanished dreams:

> It was spacious, and I dare say had once been handsome, but every discernible thing in it was covered with dust and mould, and dropping to pieces. The most prominent object was a long table with a tablecloth spread on it, as if a feast had been in preparation when the house

and the clocks all stopped together. An épergne or centre-piece of some kind was in the middle of this cloth; it was so heavily overhung with cobwebs that its form was quite undistinguishable; and, as I looked along the yellow expanse out of which I remember its seeming to grow, like a black fungus, I saw speckled-legged spiders with blotchy bodies running home to it....

> I heard the mice, too, rattling behind the panels.... But the blackbeetles took no notice of the agitation, and groped about the hearth....

The Bull also enters the novel as the Blue Boar (the Blue Boar Inn here does not fit Dickens's description). It is at the Bull that the celebration concerning Pip's apprenticeship takes place. Pip remembers only

> that they wouldn't let me go to sleep, but whenever they saw me dropping off, woke me up and told me to enjoy myself. That, rather late in the evening Mr. Wopsle gave us Collins's ode, and threw his blood-stain'd sword in thunder down, with such effect that a waiter came in and said, "The Commercials underneath sent up their compliments, and it wasn't the Tumblers' Arms."

Across from Eastgate House on the High Street is a half-timbered building with three gables and projecting bay windows; this is the site of Mr. Pumblechook's premises. They

> were of a peppercorny and farinaceous character, as the premises of a corn-chandler and seedsman should be. It appeared to me that he must be a very happy man indeed, to have so many little drawers in his shop: and I wondered when I peeped into one or two on the lower tiers, and saw the tied-up brown paper packets inside, whether the flower-seeds and bulbs ever wanted of a fine day to break out of those jails, and bloom.

In fact, in Dickens's time this was the building used by a William Fairbairn, a seed merchant, and the small rows of seed drawers described in the novel were in his shop.

The most detailed use of Rochester occurs in the unfinished *The Mystery of Edwin Drood;* here, only thinly disguised, it is Cloisterham, where "[t]he low sun is fiery and yet cold behind the monastery ruin, and the Virginia creeper on the Cathedral wall has showered half its deep-red leaves down on the pavement." In the center of the "drowsy city" where the streets are silent and narrow is the Nuns' House, Miss Twinkleton's Seminary, "a venerable brick edifice whose present appellation is doubtless derived from the legend of its conventual uses." This is Eastgate House, an Elizabethan mansion, which for many years in the 19th century actually served as a school; it is now a city museum with an excellent collection of Dickens's books and manuscripts. Nearly opposite Eastgate House is a half-timbered building which was Mr. Sapsea's premises:

> Over the doorway is a wooden effigy, about half-life-size, representing Mr. Sapsea's father, in a curly wig and toga, in the act of selling. The chastity of the idea, and the natural appearance of the little finger, hammer, and pulpit, have been much admired.

The carved figure which Dickens describes was actually from another auctioneer's premises at St. Margaret's Banks. The "old stone gatehouse crossing the Close, with an arched thoroughfare passing beneath it," where the verger Tope and Jasper live, faces Pump Lane; indeed, College or Chertsey's

Gatehouse is now usually referred to as Jasper's. It should be noted that Dickens's description involves characteristics from the Prior's and the Deanery Gatehouse as well. The crypt of the cathedral is the scene of Jasper's night excursion under Durdle's guidance, and later he crosses "what was once the vineyard, belonging to what was once the monastery. . . ."; this is now an open space of lawn and giant plane trees known as the Vines. The Travellers' Twopenny, which Durdles and Jasper pass after wandering in the crypt, was a lodging place, originally called the Duck, at the junction of Frog Alley and Crow Lane. In Rochester the inn was also known as Kit's Lodging House and was locally designated as the Travellers' Threepenny; indeed, in manuscript Dickens used Threepenny but changed it in the proof sheets. Minor Canon Corner, "a quiet place in the shadow of the Cathedral" where the Rev. Septimus Crisparkle and his mother live, is just beyond Jasper's Gatehouse and the west door of the cathedral. The Crozier, the orthodox hotel at which Datchery puts up, has had two claimants; one is the Mitre in Chatham, an inn which Charles Dickens knew as a child. However, Dickens rather clearly places the Crozier in Rochester, and the case for the Crown Hotel here is thereby far stronger. (The Crown also was Wright's, which is considered "very dear" in *Pickwick Papers*.)

One or two of Dickens's minor works also include Rochester: "The Seven Poor Travellers" has as its setting the High Street House for Poor Travellers endowed by Richard Watts, an early Member of Parliament:

> a clean white house of a staid and venerable air, with a quaint old door (an arched door), choice, little, long, low lattice windows, and a roof of three gables.

Rochester is also Dullborough Town in *Sketches by Boz*.

Dickens's last visit to Rochester from Gadshill, only a few days before his death, was to gather information for *The Mystery of Edwin Drood*. On June 6 he looked at Restoration House and then walked about the Vines; it was the latter which he used for the final interview between Datchery and Princess Puffer, the chapter finished on June 8, the day before he died. There is a commemorative plaque to Dickens in the cathedral.

ROCKINGHAM, Northamptonshire (pop. 163) On the site of ancient Rockingham Forest, 10 miles northeast of Market Harborough, the stone-built village of Rockingham is nestled at the foot of the castle hill with the Welland River running along the base of the hill. At one end of the village's steep main street is the Butter Cross, which supposedly marked the center of the forest, and on both sides of the street are thatched-roof ironstone houses with small gardens.

Rockingham Castle, whose keep was built by William the Conqueror for use as a royal hunting box, is the oldest "house" in the shire to be continuously inhabited. By the end of the 15th century the castle had fallen into decay, and after Elizabeth I granted it to Sir Edward Watson (son-in-law of Lord Chief Justice Sir Edward Montagu), he built the long gallery from stone quarried from the Norman keep, restored the Great Hall, and added the kitchen wing. More resto-

ROCKINGHAM Snugly placed at the bottom of the castle hill with the Welland River running through the town, Rockingham is securely placed in literature because of the mainly Elizabethan Rockingham Castle, which was the model for Chesney Wold in Charles Dickens's *Bleak House*.

ration was undertaken by his son and grandson, and the house is still in the hands of the Watson family.

In the mid-19th century the Hon. Richard and Mrs. Watson, friends of Charles Dickens, held the house, and it is small wonder that the novelist seized every opportunity to visit them here. Writing of his November 1849 visit to John Forster, he describes the environment:

> Picture to yourself, my dear F., a large old castle, approached by an ancient keep, portcullis, etc., filled with company, waited on by six-and-twenty servants; the slops (and wine-glasses) continually being emptied; and my clothes (with myself in them) always being carried off to all sorts of places; and you will have a faint idea of the mansion in which I am at present staying. . . . Of all the country-houses and estates I have yet seen in England, I think this is by far the best. Everything undertaken eventuates in a most magnificent hospitality. . . .

Dickens returned the next winter, when he and a country carpenter built "a very elegant little theatre"; the novelist acted as the manager and presented his first play here in January. The playbills for these plays are preserved in the library. Dickens wrote substantial parts of *Bleak House* here, and Rockingham Castle and its grounds become Chesney Wold, transplanted to the watery landscape of Lincolnshire. At the end of the terrace is the Yew Walk which becomes the Ghost's Walk of the novel. The house is seen from a distance:

> It was a picturesque old house, in a fine park richly wooded. Among the trees, and not far from the residence, he pointed out the spire of the little church of which he had spoken. . . . The house, with gable and chimney, and tower, and turret, and dark doorway, and broad terrace-

walk, twining among the balustrades of which, and lying heaped upon the bases, there was one great flush of roses, seemed scarcely real in its light solidity, and in the serene and peaceful hush that rested all around it. To Ada and to me, that, above all, appeared the pervading influence.

The "shady, ancient, solemn little church" with the carved oak pulpit is much closer to the house than Dickens places it. The Sondes Arms, an old inn on the road to the castle, is the prototype of the Dedlock Arms. The long drawingroom of Chesney Wold, as Dickens describes it, is the one here, except that the family portraits are actually in the hall and the fireplace is surmounted by an overmantel and not by a portrait.

RODMELL, Sussex (pop. 205)   On the chalk downs of Sussex, the Ouse and Cuckmere Rivers cut their wide valleys to the sea, and in such a valley is the hamlet of Rodmell, a village of flint houses and walls. The original manor house was presented to Anne Boleyn by Henry VIII, and the young princess Elizabeth used to walk on the Downs, where one gap is still known as the Princess Gap. Monk's House, a two-story brick-and-flint house, weatherboarded on the street side, became the home of Virginia and Leonard Woolf in July 1919. The ground floor was paved with brick, and the house had no bath, hot water, or toilet. The years here were ones of intense activity with *Jacob's Room, Freshwater and the Hours* (later *Mrs. Dalloway*), *To the Lighthouse, Orlando,* and *The Waves* published during this period. Virginia Woolf's mental instabilities increased from about 1914 on, and the advent of World War II contributed greatly to her problems. Leonard Woolf removed his wife to Mecklenburgh Square, London, in 1939, but the 1940 bombing raids necessitated bringing her back to the relative calm of Sussex. Nonetheless, in a manic-depressive state, she drowned herself in the Ouse River here on March 28, 1941; her ashes were buried in the garden.

Among the Woolfs' many guests were T. S. Eliot, in September 1920, Victoria Sackville-West, in the autumn of 1924, and Stephen Spender, in September 1939.

ROKEBY, Yorkshire (pop. 131)   Sir Walter Scott's attachment to Rokeby and its history probably began shortly after his first visit in June 1809, when Rokeby Hall was owned by John B. S. Morritt, to whom Scott ultimately dedicated his poem. The hall stands on the site of the original Mortham Tower, burned to the ground by the marauding Scots in the 14th century but rebuilt early in the 15th century. The tower fell into disrepair and was still in ruins when Scott knew it (it has since been completely restored). The present Rokeby Hall is set on the right bank of the Tees River, below the "right fair bridge" near Egglestone Abbey, in a heavy stand of trees. John Leland describes the bridge in his *Itinerary* as having three arches; now there are only two.

Scott began work on *Rokeby* in December 1811 and plied Morritt for details of the environment and for historical information. By March 1812, after destroying the first canto partly because of his inability to get the details right, Scott decided upon a visit and arrived *en famille* for a week in the autumn. The mound,

"[r]aised by that legion long renowned," is a small Roman camp behind the Morritt Arms; in spite of numerous agricultural passes over it, its outline remains relatively clear. Mortham Tower itself, sitting high on the right bank of the Greta, appeared directly in front of Wilfrid "when he issued from the wood":

'Twas a fair scene! The sunbeam lay
On battled tower and portal grey;
And from the grassy slope he sees
The Greta flow to meet the Tees. . . .

The "lone dwelling of the dead" over which the elm trees intertwined their branches to form a canopy, this

massive monument,
Carved o'er in ancient Gothic wise
With many a scutcheon and device

was brought to the riverbank from Egglestone Abbey about the turn of the century.

Rokeby is also used in one of Charles Dickens's novels. He stayed at the George and New Inn here with Phiz (Hablot Knight Browne) in January 1838, when he was collecting material about northern schools for *Nicholas Nickleby*. Rokeby is the place where Squeers, Nicholas, and the small boys depart from the coach to be taken the rest of the way to "the delightful village of Dotheboys [Bowes, Yorkshire]" by pony cart. And this is also the place where Nicholas is given some money and a blessing by John Browdie. The George and New Inn was made into a lodging house in the early 1900s.

An old ballad, "The Hunting of the Felon Sow," tells the tale of a fierce old sow that terrorized the local woods. Ralph of Rokeby gave the creature to the friars of Richmond, and three monks were sent to fetch her. She put up such a fight that

they fled all three
They fledd away by Watling Street
They had no succor but their feet
It was more the pity.

ROLVENDEN, Kent (pop. 1,194)   Rolvenden is almost a small version of Tenterden, 3 miles to the northeast, with brick and weatherboarded houses and green verges lining its main thoroughfare. The 13th- to 15th-century church has an unusual squire's pew over the south chapel; it is carpeted and, with its Chippendale chairs and table, is furnished more like a sitting room than a church pew. Great Maytham Hall on the Rolvenden Layne Road was the home of Frances Hodgson Burnett from 1888 until 1900; *The Secret Garden* may well have been based on the high-walled garden here:

It was the sweetest, most mysterious-looking place any one could imagine. The high walls which shut it in were covered with the leafless stems of climbing roses which were so thick that they were matted together. . . . All the ground was covered with grass of a wintry brown and out of it grew clumps of bushes which were surely rose-bushes if they were alive. . . . There were other trees in the garden, and one of the things which made the place look strangest and loveliest was that climbing roses had run all over them and swung down long tendrils. . . .

ROMFORD, Essex (pop. 115,960)   As is often the case with towns located on the edge of London, Romford has become part of the sprawling metropolis, but in the 16th century it was an area of fashionable country residences. Francis Quarles was born of a very prosperous family at Stewards in 1592. Their estate of more than 320 acres covered the area of the present Western, Eastern, and Victoria Roads. When the later Romford Hall was built on the site of Stewards, the name Stewards was transferred to a farmhouse with which the Quarles family had no association. Quarles's father died in 1599, and at his mother's death in 1605 he inherited the estate. Following his education at Christ's College, Cambridge, and Lincoln's Inn in London and a period of almost seven years in Germany in the retinue of Princess Elizabeth, he settled here and quickly gained the reputation of a quiet, studious man because he rose at 3:00 A.M. to get to his books. That may well be true, but a more likely explanation is simply that this is the only time that the father of eighteen children could find solitude.

ROMSEY, Hampshire (pop. 5,779)   Located in the valley of the Test River, one of the greatest trout fishing streams in England, Romsey has long been a center for sportsmen and pilgrims. The old market town contains one of England's best Norman buildings in Romsey Abbey and one of the finest examples of 18th-century architecture in Broadlands. The 10th-century abbey looks as if it were designed for military purposes because of its low tower and solid walls, but the interior is remarkably beautiful, with a pair of semicircular chapels and a fine rood in the west-facing wall of the transept. Set in a large park, Broadlands, whose house and gardens were remodeled by Lancelot Brown (Capability Brown), was once the home of Lord Palmerston, and after his death in 1865 it became the property of his stepson and his wife, Mr. and Mrs. William Francis Cowper-Temple. Dante Gabriel Rossetti visited the Cowper-Temples through the month of August 1876; while he would have liked to be inactive, he found that private rooms had been so set up that work was almost inescapable. He drew a great deal and worked extensively on "The Blessed Damozel."

Broadlands itself becomes Deansleigh Park in Thomas Hardy's "Dame the Fourth: Lady Mottisfont" (*A Group of Noble Dames*). Hardy, though, creates locational problems for his readers by making Deansleigh Park the seat of Sir Ashley Mottisfont. Mottisfont Abbey, 4 miles northwest of Romsey, was obviously Hardy's source of the name but cannot be Deansleigh since it is not visible from a bridge crossing the river. Embley Park (2 miles west of Romsey), which becomes Fernell Hall in the same story, was the childhood home of Florence Nightingale.

ROOKHOPE, County Durham (pop. 582)   Rookhope, a valley about 5 miles long through which Rookhope Burn runs before emptying into the Wear River, is northwest of Stanhope in the most beautiful part of the Weardale. "Rookhope stands in a pleasant place/ If the false thieves wad let it be" is the way the ballad "Rookhope Ryde [Raid]" puts it. Sir Walter Scott's *Harold the Dauntless* uses the entire Weardale and Tyneside areas, but most extensively Rookhope. This is the setting of the second canto and the location of the home of Jutta and Wulfstane and their daughter Metelill, whose hand Harold demands in marriage.

ROOS HALL, Suffolk   A seat half a mile from Beccles, Roos Hall is a glowing brick Tudor manor with many old turrets and chimneys; at one time the manor belonged to Sir John Suckling's father, who purchased it about 1600 at the insistence of his second wife. The elder Suckling had planned to have his son purchase the reversion of the manor from his stepmother, but Sir John failed to do this, and the manor came into the family of Sir Edwyn Rich when Suckling's widow married him.

ROSS-ON-WYE, Herefordshire (pop. 4,607)   A spectacular position on a curve of the Wye River is only one of Ross's outstanding features; 12 miles southeast of Hereford and 16 miles west of Gloucester, looking toward the Welsh hills, it is a delightful market town of steep streets lined with Georgian houses. The 17th-century arcaded market hall is the

ROSS-ON-WYE   Lying in a bend of the Wye River, the market town of Ross-on-Wye is somewhat of a memorial to John Kyrle, the "Man of Ross" celebrated by Alexander Pope in his *Moral Essays*. The pinnacles on the church spire in the background are only one of the many public benefactions of Kyrle.

center of Ross; there are two sets of 17th-century almshouses, Webb's Hospital and Rudhall's, and on the High Street are two shops created from the home of John Kyrle, Alexander Pope's "Man of Ross" in "Of the Use of Riches" in *Moral Essays:*

Behold the market-place with poor o'erspread!
The Man of Ross divides the weekly bread:
He feeds yon almshouse, neat, but void of state,
Where age and want sit smiling at the gate:
Him portion'd maids, apprenticed orphans blest,
The young who labour, and the old who rest.
Is any sick? the Man of Ross relieves,
Prescribes, attends, the medicine makes and gives:
Is there a variance? enter but his door,
Balk'd are the courts, and contest is no more. . . .

Kyrle spent most of his eighty-seven years here and devoted all his considerable spare income to works of charity: he gave the town its first public water supply, constructed the causeway to the Wilton Bridge, built the pinnacles on the church spire, and laid out The Prospect, a public garden near the church. His house, turned into the King's Arms Inn before becoming shops in 1804, is marked with a plaque; the garden behind his home has a curious mosaic of a swan made of horses' teeth.

Samuel Taylor Coleridge was here in 1794 during his tour of Wales; he stayed at the King's Arms Inn and is said to have written on the shutters of the inn:

Richer than misers o'er their countless hoards,
Nobler than kings, or king-polluted lords,
Here dwelt the man of Ross! O trav'ller, hear,
Departed merit claims a reverent tear.
If 'neath this roof thy wine-cheered moments pass,
Fill to the good man's name one grateful glass. . . .

Daniel Defoe's experience here, as related in *A Tour thro' the Whole Island of Great Britain,* is worthy of inclusion:

We came to Ross, a good old Town, famous for good Cyder, a great Manufacture of Iron Ware, and a good Trade on the River *Wye;* and nothing else as I remember, except it was a monstrous fat Woman, who they would have had me gone to see. But I had enough of the Relation, and so I suppose will the Reader, for they told me she was more than three Yards about her Wast; that when she sat down, she was oblig'd to have a small Stool plac'd before her, to rest her Belly on, and the like.

In 1807 Robert Bloomfield stayed at the Swan when touring the Wye, and at the Royal Hotel, which has a commemorative plaque, Charles Dickens and John Forster met in 1867 with Dickens's manager, a native of Ross, to discuss the projected American reading tour. Forster knew "of some degeneration of some function of the heart" and had been concerned when Dickens complained from Birmingham of "so severe a pain in the ball of my left eye that it makes it hard for me to do anything." Forster was unalterably opposed to the tour; the manager was strongly in favor, and Dickens decided to go.

ROTHLEY, Leicestershire (pop. 2,264)   Situated beyond the eastern edge of the Charnwood Forest, 6 miles north of Leicester, Rothley has a Norman church whose churchyard holds an impressive Saxon cross almost 12 feet high. Hidden away from the village is Rothley Temple, founded as a preceptory during the reign of Henry III by the Knights Tem-

plars and later the family home of the Babingtons, as well as the birthplace of Thomas Babington Macaulay on October 25, 1800. The youngster later spent at least a few summer and autumn months here yearly and retained a great deal of affection and enthusiasm for the place; indeed, when he was elevated to a peerage in 1857, he decided to be titled Baron Macaulay of Rothley. Rothley Temple (now Rothley Court Hotel) is set among stately old trees in a somewhat untamed park. The house itself is of that English variety which, though added to by every generation, remains harmonious. On the side of the house, seemingly guarding the entrance to the 13th-century chapel, is a well-worn stone cross-legged knight.

ROTTINGDEAN, Sussex (pop. 2,769)   On the coast about 4 miles southeast of Brighton is the village of Rottingdean, once a superior watering place and now projecting an aspect of the way Brighton must have been two or three centuries ago. A peaceful place in the only gap in the hills between Brighton and Newhaven, it was at one time a smugglers' haven, and, indeed, an early story of a haunted house on this coast has now been explained by the noises coming up through a smuggler's cave in a tunnel. The Sussex attitude toward smuggling is well characterized by Rudyard Kipling's "Smugglers' Song" in *Puck of Pook's Hill:*

If you wake at midnight, and hear a horse's feet,
Don't go drawing back the blind, or looking in the street,
Them that asks no questions isn't told a lie.
Watch the wall, my darling, while the Gentlemen go by!

Five and twenty ponies
Trotting through the dark;
Brandy for the Parson,
'Baccy for the Clerk
Laces for a lady, letters for a spy,

And watch the wall, my darling, while the Gentlemen go by!

People often turned to the wall; a story, for example, is related of a Sussex parson who feigned illness to keep the church closed when contraband had been hastily stored in the pews to evade the revenue men. Pebble-walled houses line the High Street, and larger Georgian houses line the village green. The flint-and-stone Church of St. Margaret (Saxon and Norman) has many windows designed by Sir Edward Burne-Jones, who lived in a house on the green for twenty years. The three lancets of the east window given in honor of the marriage of Burne-Jones's daughter were executed by William Morris. Burne-Jones died here in 1898 and is buried in the churchyard.

Partly on account of Sir Edward and his wife, Rudyard Kipling settled in Rottingdean for a time. Kipling, the nephew of Lady Burne-Jones, first spent part of a summer holiday here in 1882 and moved to North End House (which belonged to the Burne-Joneses) in June 1897. He wrote "Recessional" here, and in September, a month after his son John was born, Kipling moved to the Elms, a house with an islandlike setting on the village green. He began telling the *Just So Stories* to family groups late in the summer of 1898 and worked on *Kim.* In 1899 Kipling was very ill in New York City (where his eldest daughter died), and from that time on he did not spend winters in England. But summers here became increasingly unpleasant because of the number of literary pilgrims who came to Rottingdean to get a glimpse of him; he moved to Bateman's, near Burwash, in 1902. "The Sea and the Hills" in *The Five Nations* was inspired by the surroundings here, and "Sussex" well summarizes his attitude toward the Downland:

No tender-hearted garden crowns,
  No bosomed woods adorn
Our blunt, bow-headed, whale-backed Downs,
  But gnarled and writhen thorn—
Bare slopes where chasing shadows skim,
  And through the gaps revealed
Belt upon belt, the wooded, dim
  Blue goodness of the Weald.

While Kipling's association here is the major one, there are others of consequence. In the early 19th century, in a vicarage on the village green, Dr. Redman Hooker kept a very fashionable school to which Edward Bulwer-Lytton was sent in 1814; this was the boy's fourth school, and he seems to have adjusted better here than elsewhere. The fragment *Lionel Hastings* deals with life here. In 1818 Dr. Hooker suggested to Lady Lytton that a public school where discipline would become important was the next appropriate step, but Bulwer-Lytton, told by his mother that she had selected Eton, revolted, said he had had enough of scholastic restrictiveness, and demanded and got a tutor.

In 1909 D. H. Lawrence lodged for a short time on the High Street, and in February or March 1910 Katherine Mansfield came here to recuperate from an operation for peritonitis and in May suffered from an attack of rheumatic fever. She worked steadily throughout the period and wrote most of her sea poems before she returned to London in the summer. Virginia and Leonard Woolf visited Maurice Baring when he lived here, and Alfred Noyes, who lived in Rottingdean for a number of years, derived much of his sea and Downland imagery from his experiences on the Sussex coast. "Mist in the Valley" captures the very essence of Rottingdean:

Mist in the valley, weeping mist
  Beset my homeward way.
No gleam of rose or amethyst
  Hallowed the parting day;
A shroud, a shroud of awful gray
  Wrapped every woodland brow,
And drooped in crumbling disarray
  Around each wintry bough.

ROUSHAM, Oxfordshire (pop. 103)   The small village of Rousham (pronounced "row'sham"), on the Cherwell River 5 miles north-northeast of Woodstock, has a partly Norman church and the Jacobean Rousham House, silhouetted on a ridge overlooking the river. Built for Sir Robert Dormer and landscaped by William Kent, the house was a meeting place in the 18th century for Alexander Pope, John Gay, and Horace Walpole, all friends of the Dormer family. All three stayed here at one time or another, and all were impressed by the gardens; Walpole writes:

It has reinstated Kent with me; he has nowhere shown so much taste. The house is old and was bad. He has improved it, stuck as close as *he* could to Gothic, has

made a delightful library and the whole is comfortable—the garden is Daphne in little; the sweetest little groves, streams, glades, porticos, cascades and river, imaginable; all the scenes are perfectly classic. . . .

ROYAL LEAMINGTON SPA   *See* LEAMINGTON.

RUDSTON, Yorkshire (pop. 492)   Briton, Dane, Roman, and Anglo-Saxon have all inhabited Rudston, 5 miles west of Bridlington, and the Rud Stone, a megalith in the churchyard, attests to the village's ancient heritage. The western side of the village, backed by the Wolds, holds Rudston House, Long Street, the birthplace of Winifred Holtby on June 23, 1898; here she spent most of her life until going up to Somerville College, Oxford. In the garden of the house is a small dell with a bubbling spring known locally as part of the Woe Waters (the Gypsy Race and its tributaries), since they burst forth, supposedly, when some national disaster is about to occur. The waters rise in *South Riding* and *The Land of Green Ginger* when calamity is imminent. Many local places enter Miss Holtby's works: Hull is Kingsport, Beverley becomes Flintonbridge, Bridlington is Hardrascliffe, and Rudston is Anderby. The tessellated Roman pavement at Breeze Farm, uncovered by Henry Robson (a friend of the Holtbys) in 1933, is the basis for the story "Pavements at Anderby," in which Robson becomes Ted Burroughs:

Within three days, the pattern lay revealed, the conventional border round the edges broken, but the sagging centre, where the hypocaust flues had subsided, almost perfect, displaying a girl in a grey limestone tunic, her black hair bound with a terra-cotta fillet, regarding with consternation a broken mirror. The background was white, the design very fresh and delicate.

Miss Holtby died in 1935 and was buried in the churchyard; the grave is marked by a marble book, half-open, and the inscription,

God give me work till my life shall end
And life till my work is done.

RUDYARD, Staffordshire (pop. 78)   In an area in the Staffordshire "lake district," Rudyard, 2 miles northwest of Leek, is at the southern end of Rudyard Lake, a reservoir nearly 2 miles in length with glorious woods coming down to its banks. The tiny village and the lake were the source of Rudyard Kipling's first name; Lockwood Kipling and Alice Macdonald became engaged here in the 1860s, and so fondly did they remember the area that when their son was born in India, they named him after this place.

RUGBY, Warwickshire (pop. 59,396)   The rural atmosphere for which Rugby, 15 miles northeast of Warwick on the Avon River, was long known has disappeared, and the railway junction seems to dominate the town. Nothing is as important to the town as its famous public school; Rugby School came into being in 1567 with the death of Lawrence Sheriff, who, married but childless, left all the rents of property here and in Brownsover and one-third of his Middlesex property to provide a school for boys. Two of the most striking features of Rugby have been family continuities and the return of former students to teaching and administrative posts here. The Rugby Chapel, perhaps the heart of the school, was rebuilt after the tercentenary and has served as a memorial to thousands of former students. The War Memorial Chapel alone contains the names of more than 600 who died in World War I and all those who died in World War II.

The number of literary figures who have attended Rugby is impressive in its quality. When Walter Savage Landor entered in 1785, he already had a reputation for irascibility, and his difficultness increased over the years. He was under the tutelage of Dr. Thomas James, basically the classics master, whom he irritated. Finally, there was open conflict over some of Landor's Latin verses: feeling that Dr. James had chosen the worst of his works, Landor wrote highly insulting remarks on the fair copy. When a second incident of the same sort followed, Landor's father was consulted. Told that his son's rebelliousness was intolerable and that he was inciting the other boys to rebellion, the senior Landor was given the choice of removing his son or having him expelled. The boy was then put under a private tutor in Ashbourne, Derbyshire.

One of the most important decisions ever made at Rugby took place in 1827, when Dr. Thomas Arnold was encouraged to apply for the mastership. Given every assurance by the board of governors that his educational reforms would be accepted, he submitted his name and was selected on the strength of one referee's comment that Arnold "would change the face of education all through the public schools of England." Arnold was appointed regius professor of history at Oxford in 1841 but remained at Rugby until his death on June 12, 1842; he was buried at the entrance to the chancel in Rugby Chapel; the grave is marked by a plain marble slab. Dr. Arnold's presence here determined the presence of one of the most illustrious Rugbeians, his son Matthew, whose education had begun at Laleham, Middlesex, under the guidance of his uncle, the Rev. John Buckland. After spending the 1836–1837 academic year at Winchester, he entered Rugby and in 1840 won the poetry prize for "Alaric at Rome," his first-recorded poetic attempt; the same year he was elected to an open classical scholarship at Balliol College, Oxford. In 1847 Arnold returned briefly to Rugby as a master. In 1857 he wrote "Rugby Chapel" to commemorate his father; he felt impelled to write the poem after a reviewer of Thomas Hughes's *Tom Brown's School Days* charged Dr. Arnold with narrowness and humorlessness:

> There thou dost lie, in the gloom
> Of the autumn evening. But ah!
> That word, *gloom*, to my mind
> Brings thee back, in the light
> Of thy radiant vigor, again;
> In the gloom of November we pass'd
> Days not dark at thy side;
> Seasons impaired not the ray
> Of thy bouyant cheerfulness clear.
> Such thou wast! and I stand
> In the autumn evening, and think
> Of bygone autumns with thee.

Matthew Arnold is commemorated in the Poets' Corner of Rugby Chapel.

Arthur Hugh Clough entered Rugby a year after Dr. Arnold took the headship; the Arnolds took a keen interest in Clough and frequently invited him

into the private part of the house. Clough, whose parents were in the United States, excelled in games, swimming, and running and was said to be "the best goal-keeper of his day." His academic attainments also were of the first order; he became ready for the sixth form so rapidly that he had to be delayed a year. In 1836 Clough gained the Balliol scholarship and went up to Oxford in October 1837; he has also been commemorated in the Poets' Corner of the chapel. During Clough's eight years here, Thomas Hughes, author of *Tom Brown's School Days*, entered from a private school near Twyford, Hampshire; like Clough, Hughes was something of an athlete and played for the Rugby eleven against Marylebone at Lord's in his last year. His academic attainments were not great, and he went up to Oriel College, Oxford, in the spring of 1842.

The Rugby of these times was later described in what has become the prototype of school stories, *Tom Brown's School Days;* Hughes claimed not to have been the Tom Brown of the book, but the attitudes and doings of the protagonist were much akin to Hughes's. He describes the school and the town:

> The coachman shook up his horses, and carried them along the side of the school close, round Dead-man's corner, past the school-gates, and down the High Street to the Spread Eagle....
> Tom's heart beat quick as he passed the great school-field or close, with its noble elms, in which several games at football were going on, and tried to take in at once the long line of gray buildings, beginning with the chapel, and ending with the School-house, the residence of the head-master, where the great flag was lazily waving from the highest round tower.

There is a commemorative statue of Judge Hughes on the lawn of the Temple Reading Room.

In February 1846 Lewis Carroll (Charles Lutwidge Dodgson) entered Rugby from school in Richmond, Yorkshire; he exhibited few of the normal schoolboy enthusiasms, but he was academically gifted and took a number of prizes in his five years here. A letter to the Rev. Charles Dodgson from Archibald Campbell Tait, the headmaster, noted that "[h]is mathematical knowledge is great for his age" and prophesied that he "will do himself credit in classics." Carroll went up to Christ Church, Oxford, in January 1851. He, too, is commemorated in the chapel; the memorial in the south transept features the company from *Alice's Adventures in Wonderland*.

Dame Rose Macaulay was born here on August 1, 1881, while her father was assistant master at Rugby; her family left four years later when her father took up a post in Varazze, Italy. Another native of Rugby, Rupert Chawner Brooke was born at 5 Hillmorton Road on August 3, 1887. His father was a tutor at the school, and the boy spent all his early life here; in 1891 William Parker Brooke became housemaster of School Field, into which the family moved that year. In the summer of 1897 he entered school at Hillbarrow and became friends with Duncan Grant and James Strachey, the younger brother of Lytton. Then, in 1901, he entered "as a new boy" at School Field, a massively late-Victorian house of alternating red and blue bricks with substantial mullions. Brooke's entire training was "on the classical side," that is, in Latin, Greek, French, Scripture, history, English, geography, and mathematics, and he spent eleven hours a day at his work. In June 1906 his poem "The Bastille" won a school prize, and that year he entered King's College, Cambridge. On January 24, 1910, Brooke's father died, and Brooke felt impelled to attend the funeral even though he fiercely resented the ceremony. "There are things," he wrote to a friend, "pieces of folly, or bad taste, or wanton cruelty—in the Christian, middle-class way of burying the dead that make me ill. . . ." Another letter explained his newfound circumstances:

> I cannot find continuity between that time and this. . . . Now, and lately, though, I am well and bursting with activity. I work like a Professor, and feel the Spring in my bones. I am acting Housemaster in my father's place till the end of the term. Then we are to be turned from this place by cold strangers, into a little house with a patch of grass in front, on a road, stiff and ugly. . . .

The house to which Mrs. Brooke moved was a three-story detached house on Bilton Road, and its gray-stucco facade was, indeed, "stiff and ugly" and depressing. Brooke returned to Rugby at frequent intervals until his last visit in August 1914; the war only vaguely disturbed him at first; he admitted:

> I'm so uneasy—subconsciously. All the vague perils of the time—the world seems so dark—and I'm vaguely frightened. I feel hurt to think that Germany may be harmed by Russia. And I'm anxious that England may act rightly. I can't *bear* it if she does wrong.

But his decision to enlist came quickly enough; early in December he accepted a commission in the Royal Navy, and he sailed with the Anson Battalion, 2d Naval Brigade, for Antwerp on October 4. Brooke died on the island of Scyros, where he was buried in an olive grove, on April 23, 1915. A monument to Brooke in the Poets' Corner of the chapel is fittingly inscribed with one of his last poems:

> If I should die, think only this of me:
>   That there's some corner of a foreign field
> That is for ever England. There shall be
>   In that rich earth a richer dust concealed;
> A dust whom England bore, shaped, made aware,
>   Gave, once, her flower to love, her ways to roam,
> A body of England's, breathing English air,
>   Washed by the rivers, blest by suns of home.

Kenneth Grahame visited Rugby on at least two occasions, once when his son Alastair entered the school and again when the child left six weeks later after a very unhappy time. Hilaire Belloc lectured here on World War I a number of times. Finally, Charles Dickens uses the railway junction here as Mugby Junction in a special Christmas-issue story in *All the Year Round*.

RUSHDEN, Northamptonshire (pop. 15,000) A footwear-manufacturing town to the south of the Nene Valley and 12 miles southeast of Kettering, Rushden has a 15th-century church which draws visitors because of its magnificence. Outside is a wealth of gargoyles, grotesques, and clowns, and above the fan-vaulted north porch is a room with a fireplace; inside, beautiful medieval screens enclose the chancel, transept, and chancel chapels, and a remarkable arch across the middle of the nave recalls Wells Cathedral. The best monuments in the church are those to the Pembertons, owners of the 16th- and 17th-cen-

tury Rushden Hall (restored) in a public park southwest of the church. Robert Herrick was a guest of Sir Lewis Pemberton here in 1623 and recalls his visit in "A Panegyrick to Sir Lewis Pemberton":

> . . . but all things even
>   Make for thy peace, and pace to heaven.
> Go on directly so, as just men may
>   A thousand times, more sweare, then say,
> This is that *Princely Pemberton*, who can
>   Teach man to keepe a God in man:
> And when wise poets shall search out to see
>   Good men, *They find them all in Thee*.

RUYTON-OF-THE-ELEVEN-TOWNS,   **Shropshire**
Also known as Ruyton-XI-Towns, this village, which is 8½ miles northwest of Shrewsbury, was originally a group of eleven townships surrounding the local manor house. The amalgamation of this complex in 1301 created not only one of the longest village names but one of the longest village streets in England. The village is located in the rich arable farmland just north of the Severn River and its many tributaries, and its church has the ruins of a 14th-century castle in the churchyard. The north wall of the church contains a small opening which may well be a rare example of an anchorite's cell.

In 1881 Arthur Conan Doyle came here as an apprentice to the local physician, Dr. Elliot. Elliot was known for his short temper, and Doyle was often annoyed by the daily display of irritability. He commented that the doctor, "though outwardly a gentleman," had not one single idea in his head; he left his apprenticeship in October.

RYDAL, Westmorland (pop. 503) The village of Rydal, on the smallest of the lakes, Rydal Water (½ mile broad and ½ mile long), and its park follow the Rothay River on its course from Grasmere to Ambleside. Nab Scar sits toward the north, and Loughrigg Fell to the south. Rydal Mount, for four centuries the early home of the Flemings, was the home of William Wordsworth from May 1813 until his death; "the beauty of the situation," writes Wordsworth, is

> being backed and flanked by lofty fells, which bring the heavenly bodies to touch, as it were, the earth upon the mountain tops, while the prospect in front lies open to a length of lovely valley, the extended lake, and a terminating ridge of low hills.

When the poet took possession, he had never been in the house. Within two years he began to suffer regularly from what now appears to be trachoma, which was to afflict him for the rest of his life.

The number of works he wrote here was enormous, and many local allusions occur in them. "November 1," written in December 1815, celebrates the sight from his house of snow on the mountain.

In 1826 the poet bought the field known as Rashfield (now Dora's Field) just below his garden; there was some doubt that he could keep his lease for the mount, and "Composed When a Probability Existed of Our Being Obliged to Quit Rydal Mount as a Residence" was written at this time:

> The doubt to which a wavering hope had clung
> Is fled; we must depart, willing or not;
> Sky-piercing Hills! must bid farewell to you
> And all that ye look down upon with pride,

With tenderness imbosom; to your paths,
And pleasant Dwellings, to familiar trees
And wild-flowers known as well as if our hands
Had tended them....

Wordsworth seems to have solved the problem of the lease by threatening to build on the lower ground so that the new house would be visible from the mount. The field, planted in daffodils by the poet and then given to his daughter, is now in the care of the National Trust and is not the one referred to in "I Wandered Lonely as a Cloud" because the poem predates the purchase and planting by more than twenty years. Near the gate to the field was the pollard oak with primroses which sheltered the wren's nest:

This, one of those small builders proved
   In a green covert, where, from out
The forehead of a pollard oak,
   The leafy antlers sprout;

RYDAL   The field just below the garden at Rydal Mount, the home of William Wordsworth from 1813 until his death in 1850, is known as Dora's Field and is in the care of the National Trust. Wordsworth set out the daffodils here after he won a guarantee from the de Flemings that his tenancy would be permanent.

For She who planned the mossy lodge,
   Mistrusting her evasive skill,
Had to a Primrose looked for aid
   Her wishes to fulfil.

Under another oak is the pool where the goldfish from the library were placed:

Removed in kindness from their glassy cell
To the pure waters of a living well;
An elfin pool, so sheltered that its rest
No winds disturb.

The grounds at Rydal Mount are inseparably associated with many poems; a winding terrace led to the arbor; the path here led to what Wordsworth called the Far Terrace, which in turn led to a well of clear water known as Nab's Well. A great deal of the preliminary work for his poetry took place while he paced back and forth here, and part of his affection for the Far Terrace, beyond the summerhouse, was that he had constructed it:

                    Yet on the mountain's side
A POET'S hand first shaped it; and the step
Of that same Bard—repeated to and fro
At morn, at noon, and under moonlight skies
Through the vicissitudes of many a year—
Forbade the weeds to creep o'er its grey line.

The summerhouse is associated especially with "Contrast: the Parrot and the Wren":

This moss-lined shed, green, soft, and dry,
Harbours a self-contented Wren,
Not shunning man's abode, though shy,
Almost as thought itself, of human ken.

Rydal Water also enters Wordsworth's poetry on various occasions, and he even composed by the side of the lake. The view from the southeastern end of the lake included the island in which was found "The Wild Duck's Nest," Nab Cottage where Hartley Coleridge lived, and the path to Grasmere which passed the Leech Gatherer's Pool. Of the works written here, two of the *Evening Voluntaries* are of note, especially

Soft as a cloud is yon blue Ridge—the Mere
Seems firm as solid crystal, breathless, clear,
And motionless; and, to the gazer's eye,
Deeper than ocean, in the immensity
Of its vague mountains and unreal sky!

On the whole, Wordsworth's life was very happy at Rydal Mount; in October 1842 he received a civil-list pension, and upon the death of Robert Southey in 1843 he was offered the Poet-Laureateship, which he declined on account of age. Sir Robert Peel, who secured the poet's pension, tried to persuade him to accept the honor, and feeling under obligation to Sir Robert, Wordsworth accepted but wrote virtually nothing after this date. By 1845 the poet estimated that more than 500 visitors appeared here yearly, and the strain occasionally showed on the old man. He became ill with pleurisy in March 1850 and died here on April 23; he was buried in the churchyard at Grasmere.

Many of Wordsworth's guests were literary figures. They included Sir Walter Scott in 1825 and Dr. and Mrs. Thomas Arnold in the summer of 1831 and many times thereafter. On these occasions Dr. Arnold preached in the small Rydal Chapel, where

Wordsworth had been a chapel warden in 1833. Other guests were Matthew Arnold, Thomas De Quincey, George Eliot (Mary Ann Evans), Harriet Martineau, John Keats (who found no one home), Hartley Coleridge, Edward FitzGerald, Nathaniel Hawthorne, Thomas Carlyle, and Ralph Waldo Emerson. The last two were not great admirers of Wordsworth, Emerson thinking his mind narrow and too English and Carlyle regarding his speech as prolix and thin. A year before Wordsworth's death, Lady Jane Swinburne brought her young son to Rydal Mount to see Wordsworth, and the old poet was told that Algernon was already acquainted with his poetry; Wordsworth's comment was merely that there was nothing in his poetry that could do any harm and some things that could do some good.

Another of the writers associated with the Lake District lived here for a few years. Thomas De Quincey lived in Fox Ghyll, a cottage owned by his father-in-law, from 1821 to 1824. At the time his opium addiction was steadily increasing, and his financial position was becoming increasingly precarious; he and his family left when the cottage was sold in early 1825 and eventually returned to Dove Cottage, Grasmere.

RYE, Sussex (pop. 4,150) "Winchelsea," wrote Coventry Patmore, "is a town in a trance, a sunny dream of centuries ago; but Rye is a bit of the old world living pleasantly on, in ignorance of the new." Standing high above the sea with its old and now-useless seaport below, Rye was once a hill fort with formidable ramparts to ward off invaders. Situated on the Rother River 11 miles northeast of Hastings, Rye was of relative significance in the mid-13th century but became especially important around 1350, when it was incorporated as a full member of the Cinque Ports. Long before that, the Romans had established themselves here, and even before that an important ridgeway from the estuary through Rye to Uckfield eventually linked up with the way from Lewes to London.

In Saxon times this was an isolated area with Saxons and Jutes to the east and west and the great Forest of Anderida and the English Channel to the north and south, and growth and development were relatively slow. There was little interest in the area in the century after the Norman Conquest, and Rye's importance as a port probably dates to 1287, when a great storm wracked the coast, swept Old Winchelsea, on a hill opposite Rye, out to sea, and changed the course of the Rother so that it flowed past Rye.

The sea began to recede in the 15th century, and the estuary silted up. Nothing much came of an attempted recovery, and in the 18th century Daniel Defoe notes in *A Tour thro' the Whole Island of Great Britain:*

> Rye would flourish again, if her Harbour, which was once able to receive the Royal Navy, cou'd be restor'd; but as it is, the Bar is so loaded with Sand cast up by the Sea, that Ships of 200 Tun chuse to ride it out under *Dengey* or *Beachy,* tho' with the greatest danger, rather than to run the hazard of going into *Rye* for shelter. . . .

On the marshes below Rye is the moss-covered ruin of Camber Castle, a reminder of early fortifications here; some of the 14th-century town walls on

RYE   While little is known of the early life of the dramatist John Fletcher, it is known that he was baptized by his father in the Norman Church of St. Mary on December 20, 1579. A window portraying the kings of Bethlehem was the last one designed by Edward Burne-Jones.

the north side of the town remain. The other walls have been eaten away by the sea. The Church of St. Mary, built about 1180, has a locally made (ca. 1560) clock which has seen service for 400 years with its great pendulum swinging back and forth in front of the parishioners. The present quarter boys date from 1969, but the originals (one of which was discovered to be a quarter girl during a cleaning and regilding in 1902) are in the north chapel. Rye is also noted for its inns, and excluding clubs with bars, there are said to be seventeen here, including one of the most famous in England. A long, steep cobbled street leads to the 15th-century Mermaid Inn, which is still reminiscent of early days when smugglers sat with their pistols on view. The George Hotel, an old coaching inn, looks Georgian, but 15th-century timbers, fireplaces, and beaming are behind the facade.

Rye has had a number of important literary associations from the 16th century on. It was the birthplace of the dramatist John Fletcher, in December 1579. He was born probably at the Old Vicarage House (demolished ca. 1703) and, as the parish church registers indicate, was baptized on December 20. His father, the Rev. Richard Fletcher, later Bishop of London, held the living here. A second building, the half-timbered Fletcher's House (tearooms beside the church), claims the possible distinction of being the dramatist's birthplace.

The town received no literary notice for a little more than two centuries; then William Makepeace Thackeray based the unfinished *Denis Duval* on the notorious 17th-century smugglers the Weston brothers. Living with his Alsatian mother and his grandfather (a barber and a smuggler), Denis is sent to

Pocock's Grammar School, Thackeray's name for the old grammar school on the High Street,

> where I learned to speak English like a Briton born as I am, and not as we did at home, where we used a queer Alsatian jargon of French and German. At Pocock's I got a little smattering of Latin, too, and plenty of fighting for the first month or two. . . .

The major association with Rye is with Henry James, who first rented Point Hill in nearby Playdon and then the Old Rectory before settling at Lamb House in 1898; the house, a Georgian building on West Street, is now in the care of the National Trust. What has been called the house's "comfortable opulence" must have appealed greatly to James when he acquired it. A room just to the right of the entrance hall is a memorial; here are his desk, portraits from all ages, and books by his contemporaries. One item of interest is a page proof from *The American* in which James inserted six words for one, a departure from customary compression. James usually worked in the small garden house, (totally destroyed by a bomb in 1940), and there he wrote, or rather dictated, all his later books including *The Wings of the Dove*, *The Ambassadors*, and *The Golden Bowl*.

James's earliest years here were pleasant ones, and he had many guests. Joseph Conrad first visited Lamb House in 1901 and came here frequently from that time on. Conrad had befriended the young and ill Stephen Crane, who was living at Brede, 5 miles to the west, and introduced him to James, whose reaction was characteristic; he disliked Crane's Bohemian ménage and refused to be of much help. The relationship between James and H. G. Wells, seriously strained in the early 20th century, was reestablished on the occasion of William James's visit in the summer of 1908, and when Wells arrived, he discovered that G. K. Chesterton was in Rye on holiday and introduced him to Henry James. One of the most frequent guests here was Hugh Walpole, who was first invited for the weekend of April 26, 1909; his diary entry for that date predicted pretty well what their relationship was to become:

> Spent a wonderful week-end with Henry James. Much more wonderful than I had expected. I am very lucky in my friends. The house and garden are exactly suited to him. He is beyond words. I cannot speak about him.

Walpole drove down from Manesty fairly frequently after this stay, and in 1909, just after he had finished *Maradick at Forty*, Walpole recalled, James tried to persuade him to stay "more or less indefinitely." James left Lamb House and Rye at the end of 1912 for London, where he died in 1916.

There are other associations as well: Charles Kingsley commemorated the 1850 sinking of the *Mary Sandford* in "The Three Fishers":

> Three corpses lay out on the shining sands
>   In the morning gleam as the tide went down,
> And the women are weeping and wringing their hands
>   For those who will never come home to the town;

> For men must work, and women must weep,
> And the sooner it's over, the sooner to sleep;
>   And good-bye to the bar and its moaning.

Rudyard Kipling uses the early smuggling of the Rye port in "Simple Simon" in *Rewards and Fairies*: Dan and Una go down to Rabbit Shaw to see Cattiwow and his men unearth "a middlin' big log sticked in the dirt at Rabbit Shaw. . . ."

Three more minor associations with Rye include (Marguerite) Radclyffe Hall, author of the lesbian novel *The Well of Loneliness*, who lived in Rye for a time, and Sheila Kaye-Smith, who was born in St. Leonards-on-Sea and included the area in her works. Indeed, many of her novels depict the influence of the Sussex landscape on its inhabitants, and numerous scenes in *Sussex Gorse* are set in Rye. Finally, Ford Madox Ford's *The Half Moon* concerns Rye, as does part of *Some Do Not*, and Malcolm Lowry spent his Cambridge vacations here at Jeake's House when Conrad Aiken lived there.

RYHALL, Rutland (pop. 666)   Ryhall is a small Rutland village beside the Wash (Gwash) River just north of Stamford. John Clare sometimes came here from Pickworth, 3 miles away, and sat by the hedgerow to find inspiration for his poetry. He once went to the local post office to post a packet of his poems to the printer but could not pay the extra penny required because he came after the normal posting time.

RYLSTONE, Yorkshire (pop. 118)   An attractive West Riding village 7½ miles north of Skipton, Rylstone (Rilstone) once held the "old sequestered hall" of the Nortons, a family that lost the whole of its Yorkshire estates for its part in the Rising in the North in 1569. Led by the 7th Earl of Northumberland and the 6th Earl of Westmorland, the rising, in support of the "old religion" and Mary, Queen of Scots, was doomed from the start; William Wordsworth takes a local story and adds it to the known facts in *The White Doe of Rylstone*. The poet has the Norton banner raised here (although it was raised at Ripon) and mentions the church and its bells:

> "When the bells of Rylstone played
> Their Sabbath music—"God us aydc,"
>   That was the sound they seem'd to speak."

The bells disappeared with the old tower in the 19th century. A square tower, probably a hunting and watch tower, at the end of the ridge, is thought to have been built by Richard Norton:

> High on a point of rugged ground
>   Among the wastes of Rylstone Fell,
> Above the loftiest ridge or mound
>   Where foresters or shepherds dwell,
> An edifice of warlike frame
> Stands single (Norton Tower its name);
>   It fronts all quarters, and looks round
> O'er path and road, and plain and dell,
> Dark moor, and gleam of pool and stream,
>   Upon a prospect without bound.

ST. ALBANS, Hertfordshire (pop. 35,840) Few towns in England can rival St. Albans in its wealth of history or its convenient location; situated some 20 miles northwest of London on the Ver River, the town was named after Alban, the first Christian martyr in England, who was executed in the 3d or 4th century just outside the Roman town of Verulamium. St. Albans claims descent from that Roman town, but there was a prehistoric settlement here at Prae Wood, a richly wooded plateau very near the later Roman settlement. Verulamium was first directed by the military forces, but then (in a procedure unique for Roman cities in Britain) it was turned over to the citizens, who were given all the rights of Roman citizenship. The city prospered until A.D. 61, when Boadicea, Queen of the Iceni, enraged by British submission to Roman rule, destroyed the town when the Governor was absent. A second Roman city rose early in the 2d century, and it incorporated part of the original site in an enlarged ovoid form. The city declined with Roman withdrawal, but evidence exists of a highly sophisticated Roman-based culture here until around A.D. 450.

The story of modern St. Albans begins when the heathen Alban, who hid a fugitive priest from his pursuers and was gratefully baptized by the priest, was martyred. The Venerable Bede relates the story in his *Historia Ecclesiastica Gentis Anglorum*. It would appear that a church and a shrine dedicated to the saint existed here by the early 5th century, and the great Benedictine abbey, which is usually said to have been founded by the Mercian king Offa in 793, was more probably given official status by him. The newer town grew up around the monastery, and after the Norman invasion the present church structure was begun.

Like most other English cathedrals, St. Albans is a mixture of styles and periods, although much is Norman. The first Norman abbot, Paul of Caen, made numerous procedural reforms and began the building program. His contempt for his Saxon predecessors (he called them *Rudes et Idiotas*) led to much innovation, and within eleven years of assuming the abbacy he had rebuilt the entire church and all attendant buildings except the buttery and the bakehouse. The material for the building was quarried from the old Roman Verulamium, and even to the present day materials are supplied from the same source. The abbey possesses the finest group of medieval wall paintings in England (covered over in the 16th century); they were painted freehand on damp plaster in earth colors and bound with lime or skimmed milk.

The medieval town flourished along with the abbey, and a famous school of history, under the direction of Roger of Wendover, author of *Flores Historiarum (Flowers of History)*, began here; a later historian at the abbey was the celebrated Matthew Paris. One very famous English cleric owes his fame to the medieval abbey; the family of Nicholas Breakspear, later Pope Adrian IV and the only Englishman ever to ascend the papal throne, owned abbey lands here, and the boy was most likely educated in the abbey school. The Shrine of St. Alban brought a large number of medieval pilgrims, and the townspeople built a sizable stock of inns and hostels, some of which (for example, the Peahen) have been rebuilt. On Fishpool Street old building fronts cover even older buildings, possibly medieval hostels.

The town has had a checkered political existence, beginning in 1213 with a great assembly of barons and clergy here to air their grievances against King John; at that time a draft of the document which later became the Magna Carta was read. The Wars of the Roses touched the town with two important battles fought in the streets; Lancastrian forces occupied the town in 1455, when they were attacked after the Yorkist forces broke through their defenses. Henry VI was in St. Albans at the time and was captured, it is said, after taking refuge in a baker's shop. The

ST ALBANS   Important remains of the Roman city of Verulam-ium–walls, an amphitheater, and a hypocaust–exist in the public park at modern-day St. Albans. Here on a hill opposite the Roman walled city, Alban was beaten and beheaded for aiding a Christian priest in flight from Roman persecution, thus becoming the first Christian martyr in England.

second skirmish occurred in 1461, when the Yorkist forces were routed by Queen Margaret's troops, who were given the right to loot as their reward. It is the first of these battles of which William Shakespeare writes in *Henry VI: Part II;* here are laid three scenes, the first of which concerns the town and its environs. The King, his followers, and Queen Margaret are described hawking for waterfowl (undoubtedly on the Ver River) when the interrupting episode of the miracle at the Shrine of St. Alban occurs; Gloucester uncovers the truth:

> Then, Saunder, sit there, the lyingest knave in Christendom. If you hadst been born blind, thou mightst as well have known all our names as thus to name the several colours we do wear. Sight may distinguish of colours; but suddenly to nominate them all, it is impossible.

The story of the beggar's faking his restored sight is documented, although Shakespeare adds the crippling. The other two scenes concern the fighting on St. Peter's Street after the eastern defenses on Chequer Street have been broken. Early in the play Margery Jourdain (Jordan) prophesies the place of the Duke of Somerset's death:

> Let him shun castles;
> Safer shall he be upon the sandy plains
> Than where castles mounted stand.—

The Duke of Somerset does indeed meet death at a castle in St. Albans. Richard Plantagenet and Somerset fight, and Somerset is killed:

> *Rich.* So, lie thou there;—
> For underneath an alehouse' paltry sign,
> The Castle in Saint Albans, Somerset
> Hath made the wizard famous in his death.—

The building was, of course, the Castle Inn, an alehouse with the sign of a castle; a plaque on the modern site marks the scene. It should be noted that Shakespeare has used dramatic license here; Richard Plantagenet was only three years of age in 1455.

The ancient town of St. Albans established an abbey school; by the 10th century the school had an international reputation, and a few centuries later Thomas Walsingham was able to comment in his *Gesta Abbatum* that

> no better or more fruitful school, none more useful to scholars or offering greater opportunity could be found in that day in England.

Because the school was associated with the abbey, it suffered in the monastic suppressions of the 16th century; however, in 1553 Edward VI granted the mayor and the burgesses "full power, authority and right" to establish a grammar school in the Lady Chapel of the cathedral. In 1871 the school was moved to Gate House, which it still occupies. One important literary association exists with the school; the dramatist James Shirley arrived in the St. Albans area about 1620 after having taken orders, probably at Cambridge. Shirley's time in the church was short, and in 1623 he took up the mastership of the grammar school; he held it until 1625 and in the two-year period became a fervent Roman Catholic. Sometime later, Shirley is known to have written a tragedy entitled *St. Albans,* which was entered in the Stationers' Register but never was printed.

Literary traditions and associations in St. Albans reach back to the time of Arthur, and Geoffrey of Monmouth's *Historia Regum Britanniae* records one of the first Arthurian tales of the town. According to Geoffrey, German forces led by Octa and Eosa ravaged parts of England but were not repulsed by Loth of Lodonesia, who had been given charge of the kingdom during Utherpendragon's illness. Uther orders a litter:

> They put the King in his litter and set out for St Albans. . . . When Octa and Eosa were informed of the Britons' arrival and of the fact that their King had been brought along in a litter, they were too proud to fight him, on the grounds that he had had to be carried there. According to them Uther was already half-dead and it was not decent for such great men as themselves to fight with a person in that state. They thereupon retired into the town, leaving the gates wide open to show that they were not afraid of him.

Uther besieged the city and "breached the walls" before the Saxons resisted; eventually Octa and Eosa were slain, but the King's illness took "an even more serious turn," and the enemy plotted his death:

> While Uther lay ill in the town of St Albans, they sent spies disguised as beggars, who were to discover how things stood at court. When the spies had obtained all the information that they wanted, they discovered one additional fact which they chose to use as a means of betraying Uther. Near the royal residence there was a spring of very limpid water which the King used to drink when he could not keep down any other liquids because of his illness. These evil traitors went to the spring and polluted it completely with poison, so that all the water which welled up was infected. When the King drank some of it, he died immediately.

Sir Thomas Malory also uses St. Albans in *Le Morte d'Arthur;* Merlin prophesies victory:

> It was done as Merlin had devised, and they carried the king forth in an horse-litter with a great host toward his enemies. And at St Albans there met with the king a great host of the north. And that day Sir Ulfius and Sir Brastias did great deeds of arms, and King Uther's men overcame the northern battle and slew many people, and put the remnant to flight. And then the king returned unto London, and made great joy of his victory.
>
> And then he fell passing sore sick. . . .

In Malory's version, Utherpendragon dies in London, and there is no mention of poison.

Edmund Spenser writes of the old Roman city in "The Ruines of Time"; wandering beside the Ver, he comes upon "[a] Woman sitting, sorrowfully wailing" and "askt what vexed her so":

> I was that Citie, which the garland wore
> Of *Britaines* pride, deliuered vnto me
> By *Romane* Victors, which it wonne of yore;
> Though nought at all but reuines now I bee,
> And lye in mine owne ashes, as ye see:
> *Verlame* I was; what bootes it that I was
> Sith now I am but weedes and wastfull gras?

Verlame catalogs her virtues of "[h]igh towers, faire temples, goodly theatres," which were then in ruins and notes her defenders and attackers:

> That stout *Pendragon* to his perill felt,
> Who in a siege seauen yeres about me dwelt.
> But long ere this *Bunduca* Britonnesse
> Her mightie hoast against my bulwarkes brought,
> *Bunduca,* that victorious conqueresse,
> That lifting vp her braue heroick thought
> Boue womens weaknes, with the *Romanes* fought,
> Fought, and in field against them thrice preuailed:
> Yet was she foyld, when as she mee assailed
> And though at last by force I conquered were
> Of hardie *Saxons,* and became their thrall. . . .

Michael Drayton notes the derelict state of the old Roman town in *Poly-Olbion,* but is more deeply interested in the modern St. Albans and its history:

> Behold that goodly Fane, which ruind now doth stand,
> To holy *Albon* built, first Martyr of the Land;
> Who in the faith of Christ from *Rome* to *Britanne* came,
> And dying in this place, resign'd his glorious Name.
> In memory of whom, (as more than halfe Divine)
> Our English *Offa* rear'd a rich and sumptuous shrine
> And Monastary heere: which our succeeding kings,
> From time to time endow'd with many goodly things.
> And many a Christian Knight was buried heere, before
> The Norman set his foote vpon this conquered shore. . . .

A later topographical writer, Daniel Defoe, devotes very little space to this important area in his *Tour thro' the Whole Island of Great Britain,* noting only:

> [I]t has a great Corn Market, and is famous for its antient Church, built on the Ruins, or part of the Ruins of the most famous Abbey of *Verulam;* the Greatness of which, is to be judg'd by the old Walls, which one sees for a Mile before we come to Town.
>
> In this Church as some Workmen were digging for the Repairs of the Church, they found . . . the Corps of a Man, the Flesh not consum'd, but discolour'd; by the Arms and other Painting on the Wall, it appear'd that this must be the Body of *Humphry* Duke of *Gloucester* . . . [and] must have lain Buried there 277 Years.

The most famous literary personage associated with St. Albans is Sir Francis Bacon, whose father, Sir Nicholas, Lord Keeper to Elizabeth I, held Gorhambury House, a short distance from the town. Sir Nicholas built the house from the ruins of the original St. Albans Abbey, and Elizabeth visited frequently around 1560. Sir Francis, who came into the estate upon his brother's death in 1601, enlarged the house (the existing porch is his work) and greatly modernized the interior. (Bacon's Gorhambury survives as a fragment and ruin in the park, and the present Gorhambury House, which contains numerous portraits, books, and other memorabilia of the time, dates to 1784.) So extensive and lavish were Bacon's rebuilding and life-style that John Aubrey commented that Bacon's existence was "as if the court were there, so nobly did he live." Bacon began Freemasonry here, and the house and grounds are said to have been set out symbolically. After his disgrace in 1621 over charges of corruption and his short imprisonment in the Tower of London, Bacon retired to Gorhambury, where he engaged in full-time scientific research and writing; *The Advancement of Learning* dates from this period. An experiment of preservation through chilling is said to have brought on the severe bronchitis which caused his death in London in 1626; his body was returned to St. Albans for burial at the 10th-century St. Michael's Church. Bacon's grave is thought to be somewhere in the Saxon chancel; there is also an impressive marble sculpture erected by Bacon's cousin and heir, Sir Thomas Meautys. Unlike most 17th-century memorials, Bacon's effigy is characteristic and depicts him sitting with his eyes closed; the inscription reads *Sic Sedebat.*

Other important literary figures associated with St. Albans include William Cowper, author of *The Task,* and Charles Dickens. Cowper was in St. Albans for an eighteen-month period beginning in December 1763. After several "attempts" at suicide in London, followed by increasing signs of madness, Cowper was placed under the care of Dr. Nathaniel Cotton at the Collegium Insanorum, an E-shaped Tudor building, and Cotton's sympathetic care and skill were such that within five months Cowper showed signs of improvement. However, he remained an additional twelve months before leaving with no money and in debt to Dr. Cotton in June 1765. Cotton himself was a minor poet and friend of Edward Young.

Charles Dickens was in St. Albans on numerous occasions and uses the locale in *Bleak House.* He stayed at the Queen's Hotel on Chequer Street when searching for local color, and he stayed at the Salisbury Arms in 1835, when he saw and reported on the great fire at Hatfield House. Dickens specifically places Bleak House near St. Albans, not actually in the town, and describes the house in great detail:

> [W]e came to St. Albans[,] near to which town Bleak House was. . . . When we turned out of the town, round a corner, . . . [t]here was a light sparkling on the top of a hill before us, and the driver, pointing to it with his whip, and crying, "That's Bleak House!" put his horses into a canter, and took us forward at such a rate, up-hill though it was, that the wheels sent the road-drift flying about our heads like spray from a water-mill. Presently we . . . turned into an avenue of trees, and cantered up towards . . . an

old-fashioned house, with three peaks in the roof in front, and a circular sweep leading to the porch.

Three buildings claim the distinction of being Bleak House. Gombards, an early Georgian house at the top of Gombards Road, is often credited as the correct place; the objection that it is in St. Albans is invalid since it was on the northern outskirts of the town 150 years ago. The position of the house, christened Bleak House, relative to the abbey church is correct, and so are the characteristics of the surrounding area. The second claimant, Great Nast Hyde, a late-17th-century house on the St. Albans–Hatfield road, not only fits the general description but has an avenue of trees leading to it and the correct number of gables. The third claimant, the three-gabled Bleak Hall in Kensworth, has a brickfield nearby and appears to fit the description except for one thing. When *Bleak House* was written, this place consisted of three cottages and had no gables and no name; "Bleak Hall" came into existence in the summer of 1852 after the earliest parts of the novel appeared.

Three other associations should be noted. Sir John Mandeville, the 14th-century author of *The Voyage and Travels of Sir John Mandeville, Knight,* states in the Prologue of that work that he "Johan Maundeville, chevaler" was born and educated in St. Albans; indeed, nothing is known of Mandeville's life except that which can be gleaned from his *Travels.* Dr. Samuel Johnson stopped in St. Albans with the Thrales on their Welsh tour, and H. G. Wells uses the area in *In the Days of the Comet.*

ST. COLUMB MAJOR, Cornwall (pop. 2,880) Lying 6 miles east of Newquay on the Melanhyl River, St. Columb Major (also called St. Columb) is a market town noted for a 14th-century church with a four-tiered tower, possibly the finest in Cornwall. This market town is noted for its ancient custom, still kept, of hurling on Shrove Tuesday and the following Saturday; the game is played here with an applewood ball covered with silver. About 3 miles east of the town is Castle-an-Dinas, an Iron Age fort with ramparts. A slightly later alteration of the earth fort enclosed 6 acres in an elliptical doubly entrenched camp. This is the traditional site, according to legend, of King Arthur's hunting seat. Once, no doubt, the area was heavily forested and abundant in game, especially deer, which Arthur is said to have chased on the Tregan Moors. As proof of the legend, a stone here is pointed out as bearing a hoofprint of the King's horse.

ST. IVES, Cornwall (pop. 8,267) Set on a peninsula with the sea to the north and south, St. Ives grew up around an oratory established in the late 5th century by St. Ia (Eia), from whom the town has taken its name. The present 15th-century church, dedicated to St. Ia, was built on the site of an earlier Norman building, which in turn had been erected on the site of the original oratory. The town is a jumble of narrow streets, clustered stone cottages, and a fishing harbor which was once the center of pilchard fishing in the south and is now used primarily by vacationers.

By the end of the 14th century, St. Ives was a flourishing little fishing town, but by the time John Leland, antiquarian and librarian to Henry VIII, was in Cornwall in 1538, this port, like others in the area, was having difficulty with sand piling up in the harbor; the front had been "sore oppressid and overcoverid with Sandes that the stormy Windes and Rages castith up there." Sand is still a problem.

With its bracing climate and attractive intellectual atmosphere, St. Ives has long been a favorite of writers as well as of painters, sculptors, and potters. By the 19th century the town had become an art center second only to London; then James McNeill Whistler and Walter Sickert were the best-known painters here. In the 20th century Ben Nicholson, Dame

ST. IVES, CORNWALL   Especially attractive because of its climate, St. Ives has long been a favorite of artists and writers; Virginia Stephen Woolf was first brought here on family vacations as a child and later returned on her own. She draws heavily on the area in *To the Lighthouse.*

Barbara Hepworth, and Bernard Leach have worked in St. Ives. Edward Bulwer-Lytton, later Lord Lytton, was a Member of Parliament for St. Ives in 1830, Kenneth Grahame spent a part of his honeymoon here in 1899 before returning to Fowey, and John Galsworthy spent more than a fortnight here in March and April 1916. During this time Galsworthy made numerous trips to Penzance to visit W. H. Hudson; Hudson came to St. Ives in return. Sir Hugh Walpole was another frequent visitor to St. Ives before he acquired the Cobbles in Polperro in 1913. Coming from Epsom in 1908, he spent April here with the Charles Marriott family and met Havelock Ellis, who was living here. Walpole returned again in May 1912 and began *Fortitude;* he also visited relatives in Truro, where he had lived as a child.

The most notable literary figure connected with St. Ives is Virginia Stephen (Woolf); her first-known visit here was in 1882, when her parents took Talland House (now flats), which became their summer home for more than twelve years. Life here, as she recalled, was "shabby" in a casual and untidy way, and Cornwall became a childhood Eden. Among the frequent visitors to the household were George Meredith, James Russell Lowell, and Henry James; Meredith, in fact, took great delight in sitting under a tree in the garden and reading his poetry aloud to anyone who would listen. One of Virginia Stephen's earliest playmates here was Rupert Brooke, whose family holidayed here in April 1889; both authors later recalled romping together over the sand beach. Sir Leslie gave up Talland House in 1895 following his wife's death, but he probably would have given up the house in any event because the building of a hotel in 1894 obstructed its view. These were not the only years Virginia Stephen spent in St. Ives; in April and early May 1908 she was at Trevose House, and in April 1914, when she was ill, she spent a short time somewhere in the town. A number of Virginia Woolf's works reflect the St. Ives area in particular and the Cornish coast in general. The early setting of *Jacob's Room* of a Cornish coastal town is often assumed to be St. Ives, and all the sea imagery can be credited to her experiences here. The most important work in this respect is *To the Lighthouse*, where the local allusions are clear. The lighthouse is modeled on that on Godrevy Island on the east side of the bay:

> James looked at the Lighthouse. He could see the white-washed rocks; the tower, stark and straight; he could see that it was barred with black and white; he could see the windows in it; he could even see washing spread on the rocks to dry.

Later she describes the environment when the boat is docked:

> On the left a row of rocks showed brown through the water which thinned and became greener and on one, a higher rock, a wave incessantly broke and spurted a little column of drops which fell down in a shower. One could hear the slap of the water and the patter of falling drops and a kind of hushing and hissing sound from the waves rolling and gambolling and slapping the rocks as if they were wild creatures who were perfectly free and tossed and tumbled and sported like this for ever.

Another author to use St. Ives and its harbor was Hilaire Belloc, an avid sailor who put into port here on various occasions. In *The Cruise of the "Nona"*

ST. IVES, HUNTINGDONSHIRE   For centuries travelers to and from St. Ives have crossed the old bridge, which dates to 1425; on the bridge stands one of three remaining bridge chapels in England. This chapel is unique in that it is two-storied, with the chapel at road level and the priest-custodian's residence below.

he "confesses to a complete ignorance of going round the land, that is, of turning the point of Cornwall and of passing from the northern to the southern coast." And he goes on, "Three times have I set out from St. Ives with the firm intention of passing the Longships, and putting her round up-Channel. Never have I done so." It was St. Ives he put into after getting caught in the force of a storm so violent that the three-day trip from Bideford was shortened to less than twelve hours.

ST. IVES, Huntingdonshire (pop. 3,092)   Historically in Huntingdonshire, 5¼ miles east of Huntingdon, St. Ives has recently been redistricted into Cambridgeshire. This market town on the Ouse River is one of the prettiest towns in the country; the river, which is bordered by extensive meadowlands, splits into two by the church dedicated to St. Ivo and reunites at the Waits. The Red House on Market Hill was the birthplace and childhood home of Theodore Watts (later Watts-Dunton) on October 12, 1832; the son of a solicitor, he joined the family firm, in which he remained until setting up his own practice in London. The elder Watts kept his law office in the Market Hill house.

ST. JULIOT, Cornwall (pop. 229)   The tiny Valency Valley village of St. Juliot, 5½ miles north of Camelford on the west coast of Cornwall, is on an early trade route from Ireland to the Continent, and gold lunulae, complete with the geometric patterns of known Irish workmanship of the period, have been found here.

Thomas Hardy first came to St. Juliot in March 1870 from nearby Launceston to finish the architectural renovation of the church for the Dorchester firm of John Hicks. His trip from Launceston was over virtually the same road traveled by John Leland three centuries previously; even in the 16th century it must have been much as Hardy later described it:

> Scarcely a solitary house or man had been visible along the whole dreary distance of open country they were traversing. . . .The only lights apparent on earth were some spots of dull red, glowing here and there upon the distant hills . . . smouldering fires for the consumption of peat and gorse-roots where the common was being broken up for agricultural reasons.

Hardy was received at the Old Rectory (now a private home) by Emma Lavinia Gifford, the incumbent's sister-in-law and, eventually, Hardy's first wife. An inspection of the church, locally known as St. Jilt and dedicated to the martyr St. Julietta, about whom very little is known, revealed that the tower was cracked. The bells lay on the transept floor; the roof timbers were cracked, rotting, and the nesting place of numerous sparrows; bats hung from the ivy covering the timbers; and the bench ends were rotten. For the restoration Hardy made painstaking notes and drawings, one of which is preserved in the church. Local excursions with Miss Gifford are often recalled in Hardy's poetry, usually of a much later date. "Green Slates" is of a trip they made on March 9, 1870, to the nearby quarries at Penpethy, and "Beeny Cliff" and "Places" contain details of a trip on March 10. Two earlier poems recall events connected with Hardy's first departure: "At the Word 'Farewell'" describes their first parting, and "The Frozen Greenhouse" relates the extreme damage of an overnight frost:

> . . . the stove was forgot
> When we went to bed,
> And the greenhouse plants
> Are frozen dead!

"When I Set Out for Lyonnesse," which Hardy began on his first outward trip, describes his feelings toward Miss Gifford; "Under the Waterfall" recalls an early picnic; "Why Did I Sketch" records a drawing session in the rain; and many other poems contain local allusions. The marriage, of which her family never approved, was "wrought [with] division," as Hardy recalls after Emma's death in "After a Journey," but in 1913 he placed a tablet in her memory in the church in St. Juliot.

The village is important in *A Pair of Blue Eyes*, which was partially written here. The setting of the novel is Cornwall with the exception of a few events in London. St. Juliot becomes Endelstow, and the rectory becomes the Endelstow rectory where Elfride and her father, Parson Swancourt, reside. The West Endelstow Church of St. Agnes is modeled on St. Jilt's, although Hardy has transported it to the other side of the rectory, nearer to the sea and the summit of the hill where "[n]ot a tree could exist . . . nothing but the monotonous grey-green grass." Actually, Hardy seems to have adopted some of the characteristics of the site of the church at Forrabury (Boscastle) for the West Endelstow Church. Most likely Endelstow House, the home of Lord Luxellian, never existed here, but a house of a matching description was once about 20 miles south of St. Juliot. The Crags, the ancient manor house occupied by Mrs. Troyton,

which stood close to the vicarage, was probably based on Tregrylls, a house on the opposite side of the Valency Valley. The Welcome Home Inn kept by Martin Cannister and his wife Unity may be based partly on the Ship at Boscastle.

In September 1938 Siegfried Sassoon made a pilgrimage to "the scene of [Hardy's] long lost romance." He found such poems as "Beeny Cliff" still enjoyable, and others rose significantly in his estimation as a result of the greater familiarity.

ST. JUST-IN-PENWITH, Cornwall (pop. 5,030) Often called St. Just, St. Just-in-Penwith (so named to distinguish it from St. Just-in-Roseland) is the westernmost town in England. Standing 1½ miles inland from Cape Cornwall, the town and its surrounding area are unusually rich in antiquities. The locality was a tin-mining center in the Bronze Age, and the large medieval church contains a 5th- or 6th-century stone inscribed with the Chi-Rho monogram formed by the first two letters (XP) of the Greek Christos. On Bank Square is Plen-an-gwary, an amphitheater 126 feet in diameter, where medieval Cornish mystery plays were performed.

Charles Dickens spent part of a three-week Cornish holiday here in 1842; he had hoped to use the duchy as part of the setting in *Martin Chuzzlewit* but found he could not do so easily. Indeed, the only bit of this remote area of Cornwall which does appear in his work occurs in *A Christmas Carol*, in which the second spirit takes Scrooge across the Cornish moors to Land's End and then out to Longships Lighthouse, 1½ miles out to sea:

> To Scrooge's horror, looking back, he saw the last of the land, a frightful range of rocks, behind them and his ears were deafened by the thundering of water, as it rolled, and roared, and raged among the dreadful caverns it had worn, and fiercely tried to undermine the earth.
> Built upon a dismal reef of sunken rocks, some leagues or so from shore, on which the waters chafed and dashed, the wild year through, there stood a solitary lighthouse. Great heaps of seaweed clung to its base, and storm-birds—born of the wind, one might suppose as seaweed of the water—rose and fell above it, like the waves they skimmed.

ST. LEONARD'S-ON-SEA, Sussex While it is incorrect to regard St. Leonard's-on-Sea by itself, since it has been considered a part of Hastings since 1850 and has been under the control of Hastings Corporation since 1872, this west side of Hastings does have a distinctive history as well as unique architectural features. Moreover, any literary figure through the early 20th century knew it as a separate place. St. Leonard's was the first seaside residential area developed on this part of the Sussex coast, and when the piles for the piers were being driven, an extensive submerged forest (an extension of today's St. Leonard's Forest) was discovered 800 or 900 feet from shore; indeed, the forest is thought once to have reached as far as Pevensey. Sounding like a 20th-century conservationist, Michael Drayton writes in *Poly-Olbion* of the destruction of this forest to keep iron foundries supplied:

> These Forrests as I say, the daughters of the *Weald*
> (That in their heavie breasts, had long their greefs conceal'd)

Foreseeing, their decay each howre so fast came on,
Under the axes stroak, fetch many a grievous grone,
When as the anviles weight, and hammers dreadfull
    sound,
Even rent the hollow Woods, and shook the queachy
    ground.

. . . .

These yron times breed none, that minde posteritie.
Tis but in vaine to tell, what we before have been,
Or changes of the world, that we in time have seen;
When, not devising how to spend our wealth with waste,
We to the savage swine, let fall our larding mast.
But now, alas, our selves we have not to sustaine,
Nor can our tops suffice to shield our Roots from raine.

St. Leonard's has had numerous visitors including George Eliot (Mary Ann Evans) in 1853 and Edward Lear in July 1859 and August 1860. Before the first visit Lear felt disheartened by his life in London and came here to rest and work. He imposed a strict order on his day, which, while conducive to work, could not have provided the needed rest. Rising at 5½ (as he wrote), he began work at six and broke for breakfast at nine; he continued working until five, when he allowed dinner to take "to 5¾ at most." Then, "to 7½ paint again"; after cleaning his brushes, he walked and wrote "to 9½," at which point he read Sophocles for "½" before bed. He kept up this routine until November, when he returned to the city. A more important St. Leonard's association is with Sheila Kaye-Smith, who was born here on February 4, 1887. Her novels show a great deal of regional influence, especially *Sussex Gorse*, with many of its scenes set in Rye, *Joanna Godden*, set mainly in the Romney Marsh region, and *Tamarisk Town*. Finally, Mary Webb, author of *Precious Bane*, died here on October 8, 1927, after a short illness.

ST. MARY IN THE MARSH, Kent (pop. 278)   A remote village 2 miles north of New Romney, St. Mary in the Marsh has a Norman church typical of the central marsh area; a lichen-covered roof and pale gray walls create a pleasant impression, and one of the bells dates to the 14th century. Just by the door is a memorial plaque to Edith Nesbit (Mrs. Bland-Tucker), who died at The Long Boat in nearby Jesson St. Mary in 1924; she had made her last home in the seaside resort beginning in 1921. She is buried in the churchyard near a bush of rosemary, and the simple wooden nameplate on the grave was carved by her second husband.

ST. MICHAEL'S MOUNT, Cornwall (pop. 59)   St. Michael's Mount, a large granite rock about 1 mile in circumference, sits in Mount's Bay 3 miles east of Penzance and at low tide is connected to Marazion on the mainland by a causeway. As in the case of numerous other Cornish localities, the history of St. Michael's Mount is an inextricable mixture of legend and fact. St. Michael the Archangel is supposed to have appeared to a hermit living here. The mount was a sanctuary and place of pilgrimage by the mid-5th century, and by 1044 the shrine was granted by Edward the Confessor to the Abbey of Mont-St-Michel, which it resembles. It was during this period that the Benedictine priory was built, and by 1190 a royal castle was added to the complex; also at this time the abbot was granted the right to hold a market or fair on the mainland at what is now Marazion (old

name, Market Jew). Neither the monastery nor its adjacent buildings were demolished during the 16th-century suppressions because of the strategic location in the bay; they were actually kept in repair and garrisoned by the crown.

Mount St. Michael is closely associated with one of the more fantastic exploits of King Arthur, the battle with the cannibal giant (Mont-St.-Michel claims the same battle). Geoffrey of Monmouth relates how the giant takes Helena (Duke Hoel's niece) and flees here, how Helena dies of fright, and how Arthur incapacitates the giant by giving "him such a blow that, although it was not mortal, all the same the blood ran down his face and into his eyes and prevented him from seeing." Ultimately Arthur killed the giant with "a lethal blow by driving the whole length of the blade into his head just where his brain was protected by the skull." The difficulty with placing the encounter here is that Duke Hoel and his niece are natives of Normandy, more than a giant step away.

Charles Dickens visited here in 1842, and George Borrow visited in January 1854, when he came to the duchy to meet his Cornish relatives. He walked the causeway at low tide and visited the castle,

> a castellated high house seated upon a lofty hill rising from the sea on the North East side of Penzance Bay, accessible also by a narrow causeway overflowed at flood-tide, opposite to Marazion or Market Jew. Ascended by a flight of steps to a small town or village; then mounted a hill by a rugged path, till we came to a sort of bastion. . . . Ascended the hill to the principal entrance. . . . Candles brought to show the vault. There is in this Castle a stone vault below the Chapel about six and a half feet high in which a skeleton was found. . . .

The skeleton was probably that of the Yorkist leader Sir John Arundell, who was killed in 1471 in an attempt to wrest the mount from Lancastrian forces under the Earl of Oxford.

ST. NEOTS, Huntingdonshire (pop. 6,680)   Situated on the Ouse River 8 miles southwest of Huntingdon, St. Neots (pronounced "nēts") came into existence when a monastery was established early in the 12th century; there are now only scattered remains of its foundations. The monastery was given to the manor in 1117 and soon was granted the right to hold a market. The present Market Place was set out at that time, and today's market is one of the best in the area.

George Gissing, who was in St. Neots in April 1900, uses the little town in *Will Warburton*, published posthumously in June 1905. He was quickly attracted to the town and writes to Gabrielle Fleury on April 20:

> Ah! if you had been with me at St Neots! The delicious silence of the fields! No sound but the larks singing! And the sense that no hateful city was anywhere near! If you had been there with me, to walk or sit hand in hand, silently, and to gather the spring flowers.

SALCOMBE, Devon (pop. 2,384)   The most southerly resort in Devon, Salcombe has scenic splendors unsurpassed in England, especially in the area 2 miles southwest around Bolt Head and Bolt Tail. About 3 miles south of Kingsbridge, the village is replete with lemon and orange trees, palm trees, shimmering sands, and glistening white houses. For many years the historian and friend of Alfred, Lord Tennyson,

SALCOMBE The Mediterranean-like resort area of Salcombe and its parish church can claim to be the inspiration for one of the most frequently quoted poems in English literature. Here the peals of church bells summoning parishioners to evensong as the yacht on which Alfred, Lord Tennyson was a guest left the harbor brought about "Crossing the Bar."

James Anthony Froude, made his summer home here at the Moult and then at Woodville (now Woodcot), both between North and South Sands. Tennyson was a frequent guest at Froude's homes and was here following an especially severe attack of rheumatic gout in May 1889; he was convalescing on board the *Sunbeam*, belonging to Earl Brassey, and they put into harbor here to allow Tennyson's visit. He left on Sunday evening just as the bells rang for evensong, and as the yacht reached a sandbar, Tennyson perceived the ringing sound as "a surfy, slow, deep, mellow voice" which became "a hollow moan [as it] crossed the bar. . . ." In October he composed "Crossing the Bar"; he directed his son, "Mind you put 'Crossing the Bar' at the end of all editions of my poems."

SALFORD, Lancashire (pop. 199,400) Older than Manchester and situated on the west bank of the Irwell River, Salford is central to the group of closely linked industrial cities in the area known as SouthEast Lancashire. Indeed, this area was once called Salfordshire, and Manchester was part of Salford Manor at the time of the Domesday survey (1086). Thomas De Quincey, who was born and raised in Manchester, was sent to school here with his elder brother William in 1793. The school, which was kept by the Rev. Samuel Hall, was 2 miles from the De Quincey home, Greenhay Hall. William has been characterized as an unruly bully, and he initiated Thomas into the "gates of war." De Quincey's *Autobiographic Sketches* comments:

> We fought every day; and, generally speaking, *twice* every day; and the result was pretty uniform—viz., that my brother and I terminated the battle by insisting upon

our undoubted right to run away. *Magna Charta,* I should fancy, secures that great right to every man; else, surely, it is sadly defective.

Thomas was saved by the factory girls. He left school in Salford in 1797, when Greenhay was sold.

Frances Hodgson Burnett, author of *Little Lord Fauntleroy,* spent her childhood at 19 Islington Square. The Hodgson family emigrated to Knoxville, Tennessee, in 1865.

William Harrison Ainsworth, includes Ordsall Hall, a partly 15th-century manor, in *Guy Fawkes.* Hilaire Belloc stood for Parliament as the Liberal candidate in 1905 and was warned by the party that since the Catholic-Anglican issue was explosive, his religious affiliation should not be mentioned. He began his first address:

> Gentlemen, I am a Catholic. As far as possible, I go to Mass every day. This [taking a rosary out of his pocket] is a rosary. As far as possible, I kneel down and tell these beads every day. If you reject me on account of my religion, I shall thank God that he spared me the indignity of being your representative.

These opening remarks were met with astonished silence and then with thunderous applause; on polling day, January 13, 1906, Belloc won easily. When Parliament was dissolved in December 1909, Belloc decided not to stand because not only did he detest "the vulgar futility of the whole business," but he had no desire "to see myself placarded on the walls in twenty ridiculous attitudes, and with any number of false statements or suggestions attached to my name." However, he was persuaded to stand and again was returned by a substantial margin. Belloc stayed with the 4th Baron Stanley of Alderley during most of his campaigning.

SALISBURY, Wiltshire (pop. 28,260) At the confluence of the Avon, Bourne, and Wylye Rivers and the meeting point of four river valleys in the sheltered area below the downs, Salisbury is in one of the most enviable positions in the shire and in England. The town is among the most pleasant in the county, and some of its attractiveness can be attributed to the fact that it was a "planned" town of the 13th century. Salisbury is unique among English cathedral towns in that its exact founding date is known; there was simply no town here before 1220. Salisbury, known also as New Sarum, grew up around the magnificent Salisbury Cathedral after papal permission was granted to reestablish the Old Sarum Cathedral here. Many of the stones from Old Sarum were placed in the gateway and long wall of the new close as the old cathedral was quickly dismantled. Under the direction of Bishop Richard Poore, Elias de Dereham (a canon who was involved in other building projects, notably Winchester Castle) began the planning and building. The Chapel of the Holy Trinity and All Saints (wrongly called the Lady Chapel) was completed and dedicated in 1224, and the original project was complete by the end of the century, when the enormous spire, 404 feet high, was erected; Salisbury Cathedral thus exists as the only older English cathedral, excepting St. Paul's, built generally to one man's design, of one period, and of one construction.

The cathedral virtually defies description with its great spire dominating the countryside and with its magnificent close, which still seems a miniature medieval town even though some Georgian houses are intermingled with the older ones. Hemyngsby contains a medieval hall and chapel, and Walton Canonry, named after Isaac Walton, Izaak Walton's son, and often visited by the famous father, is here as well. The capstone of the lofty cathedral spire holds a small lead box which was placed there in 1375 and which contains a small fragment of cloth then believed to be a relic of the Virgin. The relic was placed in the spire to protect it from lightning and other disasters. The spire is the highest in England and the third highest in Europe.

Michael Drayton's *Poly-Olbion* makes little reference to Salisbury, but the illustration and the gloss for the illustration demonstrate the interest he had in the town. Salisbury is portrayed as a buxom wench standing at the Avon with a castlelike cathedral balanced rather precariously on her head. The gloss comments on the town, but more specifically on the cathedral, and quotes one of Drayton's sources, Robert of Gloucester.

There are a number of unusual and interesting features in the cathedral, and its attachments are fabulous. The cathedral was built with 12 doors, 365 windows, and 8,760 columns, to correspond to the months, days, and hours of the year. Several monuments are of particular note because of their literary connections. One is an old plaque recently discovered in the choir and reinstalled by the 16th Earl of Pembroke; this was the memorial to one of the family's most illustrious members, and the plaque now includes the lines ascribed to William Browne (William of Tavistock):

Underneath this sable hearse
Lies the subject of all verse:

Sidney's sister, Pembroke's mother.
Death, ere thou hast slain another
Fair and learned and good as she,
Time shall throw a dart at thee.

Two other memorials are also notable: the north transept contains a bust of Richard Jefferies, the Wiltshire poet, and a new window at the eastern end of the north choir aisle commemorates George Herbert, poet and rector of nearby Bemerton. Designed by George Webb, the window is based on two of Herbert's poems, "The God of Love My Shepherd Is" and "Love-Joy," and shows the poet's kneeling figure at the bottom left of the window.

The cloisters, which suffered severe neglect and abuse in the 17th and 18th centuries, are the earliest and largest in any English cathedral; they were originally intended to provide passage from the cathedral to the octagonal chapter house, which is believed by many to be the outstanding part of Salisbury Cathedral and the best-designed chapter house in England.

The cathedral library (built in 1445) is a treasury of early manuscripts, including a 10th-century Gallican Psalter with an interlinear Anglo-Saxon gloss; a second 10th-century Gallican Psalter with a list of old Breton saints; the only extant copy of *Fons Jacobi*, a 15th-century devotional book; and a 15th-century copy of William Caxton's *Golden Legend*, printed by Wynkyn de Worde. The most famous document is one of the four existing copies of the Magna Carta; one other is in Lincoln, and two are in London. This copy is the most nearly perfect of the four, even though the seal is missing.

As with many English cathedral cities, one tends to ignore the town and emphasize the cathedral; in the case of Salisbury this is inordinately unfair. St. Martin's Church has four outstanding modern painted glass windows in its old walls and a 15th-century corbel of a nun's head wearing glasses, an extremely rare depiction. St. Thomas's Church contains outstanding Doom paintings, especially the one above the chancel arch. A great deal of the original 13th-century planning of the town is still in evidence; the first streets, built to the north and east of the close, crossed at right angles to each other, and the squares are still known as "checquers"; many of these still exist, some with their medieval houses still intact. Later street design here was often in the gridiron pattern.

Salisbury has generally had more than its share of prosperity. While its medieval economy was based on sheep, other trades were important, and many Londoners still flock to Salisbury's makers of boots and shoes, the survivors of a large leather industry. Nevertheless, the judgment that Salisbury was founded on woolpacks is basically fair. Salisbury Plain supported the sheep well, but with the industrial revolution Salisbury lost most of its cloth industry to areas better able to supply power, and now the great plain supports armored vehicles and immense wheat crops.

Salisbury first enters the *Anglo-Saxon Chronicle* in 1004, prior to its actual founding, but tradition ascribes a much earlier founding date: Geoffrey of Monmouth in his *Historia Regum Britanniae* places the treacherous mass slaughter wreaked on Vortigern and his men by Hengist and his forces near here and relates that the name of the city was then Kaercaradduc. Geoffrey, though, seems muddled about Salisbury and this general area in Wiltshire, for he goes on to tell how Aurelius rebuilt York, London, and Winchester after the Saxons destroyed them and then

> visited the monastery near Kaercaradduc, which is now called Salisbury. It was there that were buried the leaders and princes whom the infamous Hengist had betrayed. A monastery of three hundred brethern stood there, on Mount Ambrius, for it was Ambrius, so they say, who had founded the monastery years before. As Aurelius inspected the place in which the dead lay, he was moved to compassion and burst into tears.

Mount Ambrius could possibly be Avebury, but Geoffrey seems to have confused it with Amesbury and ultimately with Stonehenge, where Merlin finally erects the Giants' Ring.

Returning to the history that actually happened, one finds literary travelers impressed both with the town and, curiously, with the running water in the streets. John Leland was here between 1535 and 1543. Before going on to discuss the town, he comments:

> Al the streates in a maner of New Saresbyri hath litle streamelettes and armes derivyd out of Avon that rennith thorough them.
> The site of the very toun of Saresbyri and much ground therabout is playne and low, and as a pan or receyver of most part of the water of Wyleshire.

The running water comes up again in John Evelyn's diary (July 20, 1654), but things had obviously changed somewhat:

> [T]he Merket place, ... together with most of the streetes are Watred by a quick current & pure streame, running through the middle of them, but are negligently kept, when with small charge they might be purged, & rendred infinitely agreable, & that one of the sweetest Townes in *Europe;* but as 'tis now, the common buildings are despicable, & the streetes dirty.

However, Evelyn was impressed with the cathedral, which he calls "the compleatest piece of *Gotic-Worke in Europe*...." It would appear that by the time Daniel Defoe arrived here to gather material for *A Tour thro' the Whole Island of Great Britain* the water in the streets was even worse then his predecessors had noted:

> [T]ho' I do not think it at all the pleasanter for that which they boast so much of; namely, the Water running thro' the middle of every Street, or that it adds any thing to the Beauty of the Place, but just the contrary; it keeps the Streets always dirty, full of Wet and Filth, and Weeds, even in the middle of Summer.

The condition was not unusual for an English meadow town, and it persisted well into the 18th century. One should note that Salisbury Cathedral sits on the water, which can be viewed there if one is persistent.

Salisbury has an enormous number of literary associations in its history but can claim only one native son, Philip Massinger, who was christened in the Church of St. Thomas on November 24, 1583. Massinger's father was a member of the Earl of Pembroke's household, and while the facts concerning the dramatist's life are scanty, it is normally assumed that his early education was at the grammar school here. John Foxe became a Canon of Salisbury in 1563, the year *The Book of Martyrs* appeared. From 1630 until his death in 1633, George Herbert twice a week left the parish services in Bemerton in the hands of a curate and walked to the cathedral to hear the music, for which it was renowned from the Middle Ages on. A visitor somewhat later in the 17th century was Samuel Pepys; in June 1668 he and his wife stayed at the George Inn (now gone), where they "lay in a silk bed; and very good diet." He toured the city the next day and found it "a very brave place." His diary continues:

> The river goes through every street; and a most capacious market-place. The city great, I think greater than Oxford. But the Minster most admirable; as big, I think, and handsomer than Westminster: and a most large Close about it, and houses for the officers thereof, and a fine palace for the Bishop.

Pepys's admiration for the city was not carried over to his "reckoning, which was so exorbitant, and in particular in rate of my horses, and *7s. 6d.* for bread and beer" that he left in anger. Sometime prior to 1683, when his family moved to Lichfield, Joseph Addison had a bit of schooling here and at Amesbury, but records of this are not specific. A final 17th-century association is with Edward Young, who came to live in the close when his father was given a prebendal stall and later made dean of the Cathedral; indeed, the inscription on the memorial to the dean, who died in 1705, was written by the poet.

In the 18th century young Henry Fielding was a frequent visitor to his maternal grandmother, Lady Gould, at Number 14 in the close; by 1722, after Lady Gould had won court custody of her grandchildren, he spent all school holidays from Eton here. Oliver Goldsmith visited Salisbury in the autumn of 1762, and *The Vicar of Wakefield* was first published here in 1766.

In the 19th-century William Lisle Bowles was closely associated with the cathedral (prebendary of Stratford in 1804, prebendary of Major Par Altaris in 1805, and canon residentiary in 1828); he died here in the close on April 7, 1850. Among the century's visitors to the town were William Cobbett, William Barnes, and W. H. Hudson. Cobbett's view of the town is contained in his *Rural Rides*, and William Barnes was ordained here on March 14, 1848. Hudson, here on a market day around the turn of the twentieth century, comments in *A Shepherd's Life:*

> Business is business and must be attended to, in fair or foul weather, but for business with pleasure we prefer it fine on market-day.... The numbers—the people and the animals! The carriers' carts drawn up in rows on rows ... each brings its little contingent. Hundred and hundreds more coming by train; you see them pouring down Fisherton Street in a continuous procession, all hurrying market-wards. And what a lively scene the market presents now, full of cattle and sheep and pigs and crowds of people standing round the shouting auctioneers!... And what a profusion of fruit and vegetables, fish and meat, and all kinds of provisions on the stalls.... The Corn Exchange is like a huge beehive, humming with the noise of talk, full of brown-faced farmers.... You would think that all the farmers from all the Plain were congregated there.

One of the earliest 20th-century authors to visit Salisbury was Hilaire Belloc, who came here from the *Nona* (moored at Picket Post) for mass on June 29, 1914, and heard of the assassination of Archduke Francis Ferdinand at Sarajevo on June 28. He returned shortly after the outbreak of World War I and spoke on the war at the Godolphin School for Girls.

Salisbury and its environs have been used quite extensively in literature. Anthony Trollope was inspired to write the "Barchester" novels, especially *The Warden*, here. He writes in his autobiography:

> In the course of the job [surveyor for the General Post Office] I visited Salisbury, and whilst wandering there one mid-summer evening round the purlieus of the cathedral I conceived the story of *The Warden*,—from whence came that series of novels of which Barchester . . . was the central site.

Trollope, though, clearly tried to prevent any future attempt to establish a specific association for his novels; nevertheless, his basic description has most often led to the claim that Barchester was Salisbury (the claim is also made for Winchester):

> [L]et us call it Barchester. Were we to name Wells or Salisbury, Exeter, Hereford, or Gloucester, it might be presumed that something personal was intended. . . . Let us presume that Barchester is a quiet town in the West of England, more remarkable for the beauty of its cathedral and the antiquity of its monuments, than for any commercial prosperity; that the west end of Barchester is the cathedral close, and that the aristocracy of Barchester are the bishop, dean, and canons, with their respective wives and daughters.

Often cited as evidence in this argument is *Framley Parsonage*, the third novel in the series, which is more firmly located as near Salisbury.

Charles Dickens uses Salisbury extensively in *Martin Chuzzlewit;* he had been all over the south and west of England in 1842 searching for local color and, indeed, changed the location of the projected novel from Cornwall to Wiltshire after the trip. "The fair old town of Salisbury" figures prominently in the novel, and his early reference to the cathedral must be based on personal observation:

> [F]inally, the service being just over, Tom took the organ himself. It was then turning dark, and the yellow light that streamed in through the ancient windows in the choir was mingled with a murky red. As the grand tones resounded through the church, they seemed, to Tom, to find an echo in the depth of every ancient tomb, no less than in the deep mystery of his own heart.

However, the author makes a curious mistake a few chapters later when he writes:

> And, lo! the towers of the Old Cathedral rise before them, even now! and by-and-bye they come into the sheltered streets, made strangely silent by their white carpet; and so to the Inn for which they are bound. . . .

Calling the majestic spire "towers" could simply be an oversight, and errors are not unknown in Dickens's works. The description of the great bustle at Salisbury market is still accurate:

> [A]nd the thoroughfares about the Market Place [were] filled with carts, horses, donkeys, baskets, waggons, garden-stuff, meat, tripe, pies, poultry, and huckster's wares of every opposite description and possible variety of character. Then there were young farmers and old farmers, with smock-frocks, brown great-coats, drab great-coats, red worsted comforters, leather-leggings, wonderful

shaped hats, hunting-whips, and rough sticks, standing about in groups, or talking noisily together on the tavern steps, or paying and receiving huge amounts of greasy wealth. . . . Also there were farmers' wives in beaver bonnets and red cloaks, riding shaggy horses. . . .

Tom Pinch probably stayed at the Ox, which stood in Ox Row facing the Market Place until its license was revoked in 1924; the claim that Dickens actually intended to portray the George Inn cannot be considered because that inn had been changed by the time of Dickens's first visit to Salisbury. The White Hart Inn on St. John Street is supposedly where John Westlock entertains Martin Chuzzlewit and Tom Pinch at dinner; this is

> the hall a very grove of dead game, and dangling joints of mutton. . . . And behold, on the first floor, at the court-end of the house, in a room with all the window-curtains drawn, a fire piled half-way up the chimney, plates warming before it, wax candles gleaming everywhere, and a table spread for three, with silver and glass enough for thirty. . . .

Finally, William Makepeace Thackeray uses the historical personages of Bishops Gilbert and Hadley in *The Virginians*.

Salisbury is central to Thomas Hardy's Wessex and is given the name Melchester. The town is brought into a dozen works, including its most extensive use in *Jude the Obscure*. It is to Melchester that Sue comes when she enters Melchester Normal School; the building which suggested the school is still a teachers training college and fronts the beautiful west face of the cathedral from just outside the close:

> It was an ancient edifice of the fifteenth century, once a palace, now a training school, with mullioned and transomed windows, and a courtyard in front shut in from the road by a wall.

Only incidental changes have occurred since that writing. Jude's "lodgings . . . near the Close Gate would not have disgraced a curate . . . ," and he looks for employment:

> His first work was some carving at the cemetery on the hill; and ultimately he became engaged on the labour he most desired—the Cathedral repairs, which were very extensive, the whole interior stonework having been overhauled, to be largely replaced by new.

Indeed, around 1870 Sir George Gilbert Scott worked on the cathedral; a great deal of work was carried out on the tower and spire and on the interior of the building. Following Sue's expulsion from the school, she and Phillotson are married here in a church which figures under its own name. Jude, who has been asked to give Sue away, takes her there:

> [O]n turning the corner they found themselves close to a grey Perpendicular church with a low-pitched roof—the church of St. Thomas.
> "That's the church," said Jude.
> "Where I am going to be married?"
> "Yes."

Besides the cathedral, the close and its gate, and the Church of St. Thomas, the novel mentions the Market House and the Red Lion Inn. The final part of *Tess of the D'Urbervilles* is played out in this general area at Stonehenge, but before Tess and Angel reach there from Bramhurst Manor House (Moyle's Court), they must pass through "the steepled city of Melchester":

> It was about midnight when they went along the deserted street, lighted fitfully by their few lamps, keeping off the pavement that it might not echo their footsteps. The graceful pile of cathedral architecture rose on their right hand, but it was lost upon them now. Once out of the town they followed the turnpike road, which plunged across an open plain.

Two on a Tower mentions the palace and the close; and *The Hand of Ethelberta* includes the cathedral, the close, the White Hart Hotel (where Lord Mountclere stays), the Red Lion (where Ethelberta stays), the town hall, and the High Street. "The First Countess of Wessex," "Barbara of the House of Grebe," and "The Marchioness of Stonehenge" all make some use of Melchester, as do "On the Western Circuit" and "Incident in the Life of Mr. George Crookhill." A small part of *The Trumpet-Major* also takes place here. Hardy's poems which mention Salisbury under its own name include "In a Cathedral City" and "The Impercipient," and "My Cicely" presents the cathedral disguised as "Poore's olden Episcopal See." The schoolhouse residence of Fancy Day in *Under the Greenwood Tree* can still be seen, and both the Red Lion and the White Hart Inns are still in business.

In the early 20th century both H. G. Wells and Coventry Patmore introduced Salisbury into their works; in Wells's *The Secret Places of the Heart*, Dr. Martineau leaves Hardy at the station here, and both of them, as well as V. V. and Miss Seyffert, stay at the Old George Hotel. The opening section of Patmore's *The Espousals* is entitled "The Cathedral Close":

> Once more I came to Sarum Close,
> With joy half memory, half desire,
> And breathed the sunny wind that rose
> And blew the shadows o'er the Spire,
> And toss'd the lilac's scented plumes,
> And sway'd the chestnut's thousand cones,
> And fill'd my nostrils with perfumes,
> And shaped the clouds in waifs and zones,
> And wafted down the strain
> Of Sarum Bells, when, true to time,
> I reached the Dean's, with heart and brain
> That trembled to the trembling chime.
> 'Twas half my home, six years ago.
> The six years had not alter'd it:
> Red-brick and ashlar, long and low,
> With dormers and with oriels lit.

Also in modern times, William Golding, who taught at Bishop Wordsworth's School from 1935 to 1940, when he joined the Royal Navy, is thought to have used the original building program at the cathedral as the basis for *The Spire*. The model of the cathedral is described early in the book:

> The model was like a man lying on his back. The nave was his legs placed together, the transepts on either side were his arms outspread. The choir was his body, and the Lady Chapel where now the services would be held, was his head. And now also, springing, projecting, bursting, erupting from the heart of the building, there was its crown and majesty, the new spire. They don't know, he thought, they can't know until I tell them of my vision! And laughing again for joy, he went out of the chapter house to where the sun piled into the open square of the cloisters. And I must remember that the spire isn't every-

thing! I must do, as far as possible, exactly what I have always done.

SALISBURY PLAIN, Wiltshire Salisbury Plain is a great undulating chalkland which extends from the eastern border of Wiltshire at Westbury to Warminster on the west and, from north to south, between the Vale of Pewsey and Salisbury. About 280 square miles in size, it is now largely under cultivation except for a substantial area under the control of the War Department. Five rivers cut through the plain, and the Avon, Bourne, and Wylye River Valleys fringe the area; the plain attains an average height of 400 to 500 feet and reaches 775 feet on Westbury Down. It contains many ancient British and Roman camps and remains including Yarnbury Castle (an ancient earthworks), Woodhenge (a Neolithic earthworks discovered in 1925 and probably a forerunner of Stonehenge), Vespasian's Camp (a Roman earthworks constructed over an earlier site), and Stonehenge (late Stone or early Bronze Age).

For centuries authors have recorded their reactions to this vast area with few villages and even fewer streams, and many have found it awe-inspiring. Michael Drayton devotes part of *Poly-Olbion* to Salisbury Plain and, indeed, claims it is "renowned everie where"; he continues, speaking in defense of all plains but using Salisbury specifically:

> The Larke to leave her Bowre, and on her trembling wing
> In climing up tow'rds heaven, her high-pitcht Hymnes to sing
> Unto the springing Day; when gainst the Sunnes arise
> The earlie Dawning strewes the goodly Easterne skies
> With Roses every where: who scarcelie lifts his head
> To view this upper world, but hee his beames doth spred
> Upon the goodlie *Plaines;* yet at his Noonesteds hight,
> Doth scarcelie pierce the Brake with his farre-shooting sight.

John Evelyn often compared other parts of England to Salisbury Plain, and his comment in his diary (July 22, 1654) is illustrative of his view. He had been to a small plain village, Durnford Magna:

> After dinner continuing our returne we passed over that goodly plaine or rather Sea of Carpet, which I think for evennesse, extent, Verdure, innumerable flocks, to be one of the most delightfull prospects in nature and put me in mind of the pleasand lives of the Shepherds we reade of in *Romances* & truer stories. . . .

Daniel Defoe appeared to be overwhelmed by the number of remains and barrows upon the plain and even tried to catalog them in *A Tour thro' the Whole Island of Great Britain* after writing:

> The Downs and Plains in this Part of *England* being so open, and the Surface so little Subject to Alteration, there are more Remains of Antiquity to be seen upon them, than in other Places, *for Example,* I think they tell us there are three and fifty antient Encampments, or Fortifications to be seen in this one County. . . .

There are "hundreds" of barrows, he says, "especially in the North part of this County," and they have "suffr'd very little Decay."

The plain enters literature as well. William Shakespeare sets one scene of *Richard III* here; Buckingham, being led to his execution, crosses the plain.

Thomas Chatterton's "The Battle of Hastings" includes a description of the plain:

> The hungrie traveller upon his waie
> Sees a huge desarte alle arounde hym spreadde,
> The distaunte citie scantlie to be speede,
> The curlynge force of smoke he sees in vayne,
> Tis to far distaunte, and his onlie bedde
> Iwimpled in hys cloke ys on the playne,
> Whylst rattlynge thonder forrey oer his hedde,
> And raines come down to wette hys harde uncouthlie
> bedde.

In 1793 William Wordsworth made a trip to the West Country and walked across the plain; he had been on the Isle of Wight, staying with William Calvert, and the two men came on foot to this area. Calvert left Wordsworth here; *The Prelude* refers to the initial part of Wordsworth's downland trek:

> There on the pastoral Downs without a track
> To guide me, or along the bare white roads
> Lengthening in solitude their dreary line,
> While through those vestiges of ancient times
> I ranged, and by the solitude overcome,
> I had a reverie and saw the past.

Wordsworth spent three days wandering here and

> Saw multitudes of men, and here and there
> A single Briton in his wolf-skin vest
> With shield and stone-axe, stride across the Wold;
> The voice of spears was heard, the rattling spear
> Shaken by arms of mighty bone, in strength,
> Long mouldered, of barbaric majesty.

The poet also completed "Guilt and Sorrow; or Incidents upon Salisbury Plain" after this journey.

Between 1880 and 1882 Salisbury Plain became the special love of W. H. Hudson, who stayed in an unidentified downland cottage loaned to him by Sir Edward Grey (later Viscount Grey). *A Shepherd's Life*, with its predominant figure Caleb Bawcombe, the shepherd, has been called "a fugue of Salisbury Plain." Hudson writes:

> It may be fancy, or the effect of contrast, but it has always seemed to me that just as the air is purer and fresher on these chalk heights than on the earth below, and as the water is of a more crystal purity, and the sky perhaps bluer, so do all colours and all sounds have a purity and vividness and intensity beyond that of other places. I see it in the yellows of hawkweed, rock-rose, and bird's foot trefoil, in the innumerable specks of brilliant colour—blue and white and rose—of milk-wort and squinancy-wort, and in the large flowers of the dwarf thistle, glowing purple in its green setting; and I hear it in every bird-sound, in the trivial songs of yellowhammer and cornbunting, and of dunnock and wren and whitethroat.

In this work Hudson first named his favorite village Winterbourne Bishop and stated that it was close to Bustard Down and contained a Bustard House.

Salisbury Plain is part of Thomas Hardy's Wessex, and in one case he refers to it as the Great Mid-Wessex Plain. In *Tess of the D'Urbervilles* it is given no name; Tess and Angel Clare leave Melchester (Salisbury) in their flight:

> [T]he moon had now sunk, the clouds seemed to settle almost on their heads, and the night grew as dark as a cave. However, they found their way along, keeping as much on the turf as possible, that their tread might not resound, which it was easy to do, there being no hedge or fence of any kind. All around was open loneliness and black solitude, over which a stiff breeze blew.

"On the Western Circuit" uses the Great Mid-Wessex Plain, and Anna is raised in an unidentified village, probably near Stonehenge.

SANDGATE, Kent Almost a part of Folkestone, 1½ miles to the east, and just beyond the Leas (a cliff-top expanse of lawns and gardens) lies Sandgate with its 16th-century beach-front castle being slowly washed into the sea. For a little more than ten years Sandgate was the home of H. G. Wells; in September 1908 he rented two Beach Cottages, right on the shore, a house he describes as having "a back door slap upon the sea. . . . The shrimps will come in and wack about on the dining-room oil-cloth." A later letter calls Sandgate and Folkestone "the most habitable place I've ever been in," and he observes, "For an elderly invalid (as I practically am) it is incomparable." Within a few months Beach Cottages proved to be insufficient for his needs, and he and his family moved to Arnold House (now 20 Castle Road). This semidetached house with a garden running down to the beach is situated in a sheltered area known as the Sandgate Riviera, where palmettos flourish and where the cliff rising up to the Leas cuts off the winds. Wells, though, was interested in a house of his own design and rather promptly embarked on the building of Spade House, the dwelling most often associated with him. Spade House, just above Arnold House, was not ready for habitation until late 1900. From the first Wells took up with Joseph Conrad of nearby Pent Farm, and Conrad was a frequent visitor here; as he noted, the trip between Sandgate and Pent Farm took only half an hour by bicycle. Another was Stephen Crane, who stayed with the Wellses in September 1899 on his way to catch the channel ferry.

The Wells family moved into Spade House on December 8, 1900, and the new house was a great deal different from their other residences here; it was of a rough finish with buttresses, iron casements, leaded lights, and a low-eaved roof of Westmorland tile. It was here mostly that Wells lived with his second wife Jane in a basically polygamous relation with Amber Reeves. George Gissing, of whom Jane Wells was especially fond, was here on many occasions, and it was to Sandgate that he came in June 1901 before entering a sanatorium in Nayland, Suffolk. Wells's wife tried to fatten him up during his stay here, and, in fact, it was she who helped break the news to Gabrielle Fleury that Gissing's remaining in England for treatment was, in Dr. Hicks's opinion, a matter of life or death. George Bernard Shaw was a visitor to Spade House in 1902 and was taken to see Conrad at Pent Farm. The affair came off rather badly when Conrad was unable to perceive Shaw's teasing manner and when Conrad's wife was unable to deal successfully with both Shaw's and Wells's diets. Arnold Bennett also stayed with Wells; Bennett had returned from the Continent in late 1906 and stopped on his way to Edinburgh, where he was going for speech therapy. The ostensible reason for visiting Wells was to get advice on the wisdom of publishing some of his more sensational serials in book form, but his real reason was to establish a legal residence here for his marriage to Eleanor Green—a sensible maneuver except that she knew nothing of the impending marriage and, in the final event, did not cooperate. After running off to Touquet, France, in April 1909 with Amber Reeves, Wells decided to give up Spade House; suffering a sizable financial loss in the process, he took a house in Hampstead, London, for his wife and children.

SANDLEFORD, Berkshire (pop. 35) Sandleford is usually lumped with Newbury, 2 miles to the north, but the hamlet exists in its own right and is the location of the 18th-century Sandleford Priory (incorporating 13th-century ruins) built by Mrs. Elizabeth Montagu. Here were entertained many of the leading figures of the 18th century: Samuel Johnson, Oliver Goldsmith, William Cowper, Edmund Burke, and Sir Joshua Reynolds. Cowper writes of the feathered trappings in the drawing room:

> The birds put off their feathery hue
> To dress a room for Montagu.

Dr. Johnson, as ever candid, relates that while admiring Mrs. Montagu's generous nature and placing a high value on her company, he thought she possessed no critical ability. Boswell records an incident reflecting Johnson's estimation:

> One day at Sir Joshua's table, when it was related that Mrs. Montagu, in an excess of compliment to the author of a modern tragedy, had exclaimed, "I tremble for Shakespeare"; Johnson said, "When Shakespeare has got Jephson for his rival, and Mrs. Montagu for his defender, he is a poor state indeed."

The term "bluestocking," which arose in this period, was derived not from the color of a woman's stockings but from those worn by Benjamin Stillingfleet, whose company was much valued on the literary evenings. The group itself coined the expression by refusing to begin "without our blue stockings."

SANDWICH, Kent (pop. 3,913) Sandwich, 5 miles southwest of Ramsgate on the Stour River, is an ancient Cinque Port which retains much of its old character even though it is now 2½ miles away from the sea at Pegwell Bay. However, it has refused to lose its seafaring past, and the queer winding streets, ancient houses, and quayside are charming reminders of the town's one-time importance. It was from here that Gnaeus Julius Agricola set sail to round Caledonia and return to establish that Britain was an island and here that Hengist and Horsa landed to begin English history. In April 1759 Thomas Paine arrived from Dover to set up in business as a stay maker, and on September 17 he married Mary Lambert at St. Peter's Church, which still rings a daily 8 P.M. curfew. The couple lived at 20 New Street until Paine's business failed and they left for Margate.

This town is included in many of William Wymark Jacobs's short stories about longshoremen.

SAPISTON, Suffolk (pop. 174) Set in a Suffolk countryside of sand and scrub, the village of Sapiston, 10 miles northeast of the cathedral town of Bury St. Edmunds, once held a farm belonging to William Austin, an uncle by marriage of Robert Bloomfield, the "Suffolk poet." As a child of eleven, after his mother's remarriage and the beginning of a new family, Bloomfield was sent here from Honington to be under his uncle's care and to find a vocation. Austin's house stands on the green near the church. Bloomfield was employed in farm labor for four years, before it was determined that his small size precluded such work, and he left to take up an apprenticeship in London. It was Sapiston which provided the bucolic inspiration of his later poetry.

SAPPERTON, Gloucestershire (pop. 494) Situated 5 miles west of Cirencester, Sapperton overlooks the lovely Golden Valley, while the Frome River winds its way past the village. The stately grey stone Daneway House and sections of the church date in part to the 14th century, and the church contains marvelously carved Elizabethan bench ends and altar table. The gabled Penbury Park was the home of John Masefield throughout World War II and after, and here he worked on and published *Land Workers* and *Collected Poems*.

SCARBOROUGH, Yorkshire (pop. 40,520) A fishing village, spa, and coastal town rolled into one, Scarborough sits on the east coast of the North Riding, 42 miles northeast of York. The huge cliffs which form the headland have been important throughout the centuries, first as the Romans built a signal station and later as the Normans raised their castle. The harbor was developed in the crook of the south bay, and today cobles and mules, drifters and trawlers vie with each other for harbor space. The oldest part of the town, excepting the castle, lies south of the headland, and Church Steps is a cobbled way leading to the Church of St. Mary with its Fisherman's Aisle. Here in the churchyard is the grave of Anne Brontë, who died at 2 The Cliff (where the Grand Hotel stands) on May 28, 1849. Mortally ill in Haworth, she was determined to make the unbelievable trip from Haworth to see the scenes of her own *Agnes Grey;* she and Charlotte, accompanied by Ellen Nussey, arrived on May 25, and she drove on the sands the next day. These are the sands where Weston and Agnes Grey meet:

> [W]hen my foot was on the sands and my face towards the broad, bright bay, no language can describe the effect of the deep, clear azure of the sky and ocean, the bright morning sunshine on the semicircular barrier of craggy cliffs surmounted by green swelling hills, and on the smooth, wide sands, and the low rocks out at sea. . . . And then, the unspeakable purity and freshness of the air.

Anne Brontë had been to Scarborough earlier as governess of the children of the Robinson family of Thorp Green Hall; in 1841 their lodgings on St. Nicholas Cliff, built on a terrace high up on the cliffside, commanded the finest view of the sea in Scarborough.

There are many other literary associations here, beginning with the realm of fancy, for all Yorkshire is Robin Hood land. In "The Noble Fisherman, or Robin Hood's Preferment," Robin decides

> I will to Scarborough goe,
> That I a fisherman brave may be

for fishermen have more money "[t]hen any mer-

SCOTLAND

NORTHEAST ENGLAND

Berwick-upon-Tweed

Norham
Tillmouth
Cornhill-on-Tweed
Branxton
Tweed

Lindisfarne
Farne Islands

Bamburgh

CUMBERLAND

Cheviot Hills
Redesdale
Aln

Alnwick
Warkworth

NORTHUMBERLAND

NORTH SEA

Otterburn
Wallington House
Wansbeck

Morpeth

Capheaton

Seaton Sluice

Newcastle
Upon Tyne

Hadrian's Wall

Ovingham

Jarrow

Hexham
Tyne

Gateshead
Whitburn

PENNINES

Derwent

Ebchester

Sunderland

Seaham

Rookhope

Ushaw
Brancepeth

Durham

Weardale

Wear

Coxhoe

Old Park

Hartlepool

DURHAM

Seaton Carew
Tees Bay

WESTMORLAND

Staindrop

Barnard
Castle

Hell Kettles

Lartington
Woden Croft

Rey Cross Camp
Bowes
Egglestone
Abbey

Rokeby

Tees

Sockburn

Croft-on-Tees

Cleveland Hills

Whitby
Robin Hood's Bay

(Barnesdale Forest)

Swaledale

Richmond

NORTH YORK MOORS

Scarborough

Wensleydale

Ure

Yafforth

Vale of Pickering
Pickering
Brompton-by-Sawdon

Dent

Middleham
Jervaulx Abbey

Kirby Wiske

West Tanfield

Chapel-le-Dale

Nidderdale

Coxwold

Flamborough Head

YORKSHIRE

Ripon

Sheriff Hutton
Sittenham
Foston-le-Clay

Rudston

Bridlington

LANCASHIRE

*Malham
Tarn*

Fountains Abbey

Stillington

Boroughbridge

Sutton-on-the-Forest

Vale of York

Giggleswick

Bolton Abbey

Knaresborough

Ouse

Lothersdale

Skipton

Harrogate

York

Airedale

Bishopthorpe

Derwent

The Wolds

KEIGHLEY MOOR

Calverley

Nunappleton

Holderness

CHESHIRE

Haworth

Kirkstall

Kingston upon Hull

HAWORTH MOOR
Thornton

Leeds

Aire

Winestead

Shibden Hall

Law Hill
Kirklees

Birstall

Pontefract

Humber

Dewsbury

Wakefield

Spurn
Head

LINCOLNSHIRE

Silkstone

Hampole

Don

Conisbrough

Wharncliffe
Side

DERBYSHIRE

Sheffield

NOTTINGHAMSHIRE

SCARBOROUGH   The popular resort area of Scarborough is dominated by the ruined Norman castle on the cliff headland north of the town; here Anne Brontë came shortly before her death to visit the scenes of her own *Agnes Grey*.

chant, two or three." The widow who runs his rooming house and owns a boat employs Robin under the name Simon, and he ultimately saves the boat and crew from a French cruiser bearing down on them by having the crew tie him with his bow to the mast and "vowing never a Frenchman will I spare." When Simon and the crew board the ship, they find £12,000, of which Robin says:

> . . . with this gold, for the opprest
> In habitation I will build,
> Where they shall live in peace and rest.

After Scarborough became a popular spa in the 18th century, Richard Brinsley Sheridan used the town as the setting for *A Trip to Scarborough,* produced at Drury Lane in 1777. A little earlier Tobias Smollett used the resort in *The Expedition of Humphry Clinker;* Matthew Bramble and his entourage arrive on June 24, but, he says, "Scarborough seems to be falling off, in point of reputation." Bramble does not stay long, not because of dislike but because of a humiliating (in his eyes) episode; Melford writes:

> One morning, while he was bathing in the sea, his man Clinker took it in his head that his master was in danger of drowning; and, in this conceit, plunging into the water, he lugged him out naked on the beach, and almost pulled off his ear in the operation. You may guess how this achievement was relished by Mr. Bramble, who . . . has the most extravagant ideas of decency and decorum in the oeconomy of his own person. . . .

Two final associations are with Wilkie Collins, who visited the spa at the end of September 1857 for a short time, and John Galsworthy, who stayed for a week in August 1909 and finished the third act of *Justice.*

SCILLY, ISLES OF (pop. 1,940)

> We'll rant and we'll roar like true British sailors
> We'll rage and we'll roam o'er the salt seas,
> Until we strike soundings in the channel of old England
> From Ushant to Scilly is thirty-five leagues.

So goes the chorus of an Elizabethan sea chantey still sung today in the pubs of St. Mary's. At the entrance to the English Channel, 25 miles southwest of Land's End, the Isles of Scilly (never the Scilly Isles) consist of approximately 145 small islands set at a latitude of 49°55′N and a longitude of 6°19′W, in an area about 30 miles in circumference. The climate here is so mild that "spring" flowers are often picked as early as November. There are really only two seasons here, spring and summer, and the Scillonian economy is based primarily on flower growing and a bit of tourism. Access to the archipelago from Penzance on the mainland is by helicopter or boat. Owned mostly by the Duchy of Cornwall, six of the islands (St. Mary's, St. Agnes, Gugh, Bryher, Tresco, and St. Martin's) are inhabited; often the others support a tuft or two of grass and a few shags at best. St. Mary's, the largest island (1,611 acres and 1,534 people), holds Hugh Town, the ostensible capital of Scilly; St. Martin's, 2 miles north of St. Mary's, is all of 552 acres, three "towns" (Higher, Middle, and Lower Town), and 100 people; and Gugh, joined to St. Agnes (Agnes, commonly) by a low-water bar, is kept from deserted status by its population of 2.

Tradition says that the Isles of Scilly are the high ground of a land once joined to Cornwall and then inundated by a great flood. Some support for this conjecture is raised by the phenomenal number (50 in 4,042 acres) of granite burial chambers dating to the Bronze Age (England and Wales contain a total of 250, one-fifth of which are here). This was not the Isles of the Dead; bodies were not brought from the mainland. Indeed, extensive evidence of very early habitation at the water's edge proves that most if not all of the islands were once joined in a solid land-mass; submerged walls between the islands are visible proof that they were united. However, the question of whether the island mass ever was joined to the mainland is still debated. Many stories of submerged villages, churches, and other ruins are brought out as proof that these isles were joined to Cornwall and are used to prove that these are the remnants of Arthurian Lyonnesse, a country of incomparable fertility and beauty holding many villages, 140 churches, bountiful orchards, and contented people.

Depending on the particular account of Arthur, Lyonnesse is the country of Tristram's birth, the place of Mordred's death, or the country of Surluse, ruled by Galahalt. Geoffrey of Monmouth, who wrote of Arthur in about 1136, mentions nothing of this country, but subsequent authors enlarged upon the story and the locations. Sir Thomas Malory writes that Meliodas, "lord and king of the country of Liones," was the father of Tristram. More extensive use of the isles occurs in Alfred, Lord Tennyson's "Morte D'Arthur" and "The Passing of Arthur"; to establish an authentic mood and setting for the pieces, Tennyson visited St. Mary's in 1860 and stayed at Captain Tregarthen's hotel for a few days. "These islands," he writes on September 9, "are very peculiar and in some respects very fine. I never saw anything quite like them." The reason for the "peculiarity" was simple: "West Indian aloes here [are] 30 feet high, in blossom, and out all winter, yet the peaches won't ripen; vast hedges of splendid geraniums, [are] a delight to the eye, yet the mulberry won't ripen." When Tennyson sketched out in prose some of his ideas, he described Lyonnesse and Camelot:

On the latest limit of the West in the land of Lyonnesse, where, save the ricky Isles of Scilly, all is now wild sea, rose the sacred Mount of Camelot. . . . [A]t the top of the Mount was King Arthur's hall, and the holy Minster with the Cross of gold. . . .

The Mount was the most beautiful in the world, sometimes green and fresh in the beam of morning, sometimes all one splendour, folded in the golden mists of the West. But all underneath it was hollow, and the mountain trembled, when the seas rushed bellowing through the porphyry caves. . . .

The Isles of Scilly appear elsewhere in early literature; Snorri Sturluson's 13th-century *Saga of Olaf Tryggvesson* records:

While he lay in the isles he heard of a seer, or soothsayer on the islands who could tell beforehand things not yet done, and what he foretold many believed were really fulfilled. . . . He therefore sent one of his men . . . and bade him say he was the king; for Olaf was known in all countries. . . .

Now when the messenger came to the soothsayer and gave himself out for the king he got the answer "Thou are not the king, but I would advise thee to be faithful to thy king."

Olaf's meeting with the hermit brings about his conversion and baptism; traditionally St. Helen's is the scene of the baptism by the Welsh hermit St. Elidius. (It is known that at the time of King Olaf's wander-

ings hermits were cloistered at both St. Helen's and Tresco.) When Olaf returned to Norway, he forced his subjects to give up their pagan ways, but probably not as Henry Wadsworth Longfellow writes,

King Olaf from the doorway spoke
"Choose ye between two things my folk
To be baptized or given up to slaughter!"

Another tradition, quite separate from these legends, places a vast submerged forest here. The 15th-century *Itinerarium* of William Worcester describes such a land, which extended from St. Michael's Mount to the Isles of Scilly. William Camden later calls this land Lyonnesse in his *Britannia*.

There are other than legendary associations here. John Leland, who visited the isles probably shortly after the dissolution of the monasteries, writes of the problems here, especially those of St. Mary's: "The houses of St. Mary's were sore defacid and woren," he states and continues, "[F]ew men were glad to inhabit these islettes for all the plenty for robbers by sea that take their cattle by force. The robbers be Frenchmen or Spaniards." Edward Hyde, later 1st Earl of Clarendon, came to the isles with Prince Charles and his Council on March 4, 1646; attempting to keep the prince in English territory as long as possible, Hyde was forced to take Charles to Jersey in mid-April when the Parliamentary fleet threatened their safety. Algernon Swinburne's visit moved him to write of "[a] small sweet world of wave encompassed wonder," and George Eliot (Mary Ann Evans) and George Henry Lewes came to St. Mary's in April 1857. Here she finished "Janet's Repentance" (*Scenes of Clerical Life*) on April 18; within the next month she finished "Mr. Gilfil's Love Story (*Scenes*) and, in fact, wrote the Epilogue on Fortification Hill. Hugh Walpole spent a fortnight on St. Mary's in July 1931, when he wrote the entire 15,000-word preface to his 1932 centenary anthology of Sir Walter Scott's novels, *The Waverley Pageant*. More recently Sir Arthur Quiller-Couch used the isles in *Major Vigoureux*, and Thomas Hardy mentions Scilly in both *A Laodician* and *The Trumpet-Major*.

SEAFORD, Sussex (pop. 9,800) Northwest of Seaford the South Downs rise to a height of over 700 feet, and just east of the town are long views toward the Seven Sisters. Situated 2¾ miles southeast of Newhaven, Seaford was at one time a Cinque Port. A prehistoric camp on Seaford Head presents evidence that the area was inhabited 2,000 years ago, and Roman graves found there point to some degree of Romanization. At that time the Ouse River turned parallel to the sea at Meeching and did not enter the sea until it reached Splash Point in Seaford; indeed, herrings and porpoises swam upstream to Liford, almost 7 miles away, as late as the 11th century. In time Seaford became an important and prosperous Cinque Port for Lewes and contributed five ships and eighty men to the English armament in 1347. While the town encountered the normal medieval problem from French raids, the biggest disaster here was the Great Storm of 1579; the Ouse flooded rapidly, burst its banks, and cut a new path to the sea at the point where Newhaven now stands. Seaford thus lost its access to Lewes and, of course, its livelihood. The town's subsequent popularity as a resort did not begin until the 19th century, and Seaford is now characterized by red-brick houses.

It has long been maintained that the newly appointed Poet Laureate, Alfred, Lord Tennyson, wrote his "Ode on the Death of the Duke of Wellington" at Seaford; in fact, the ode was written in the Green Room at Chapel House in Twickenham. Appearing on November 18, 1852, the morning of the funeral, it was Tennyson's first completed work since he became Poet Laureate, and he and his wife had not been in Seaford long enough for it to have been written here. The house the Tennysons took, Seaford House, is long gone, but the hilltop garden, capped with cedars, remains. Of little doubt is the fact that the Downs influenced Tennyson immensely, and most likely he revised and polished the ode here.

George Meredith was in Seaford numerous times. He and his wife, the daughter of Thomas Love Peacock, frequently came to Seaford before their total estrangement; they stayed with the FitzGeralds (nephews of the poet Edward FitzGerald); later, Meredith spent Christmas of 1857 here alone on Marine Parade. He returned periodically over the next ten or fifteen years, and "The House on the Beach," descriptive of the Sussex coast, was written here:

> The house on the beach had been posted where it stood, one supposes, for the sake of the sea-view. . . . Sea delighted it not, nor land either. Marine Parade fronting it to the left, shaded sickly eyes, under a worn green verandah, from a sun that rarely appeared. . . . Belle Vue Terrace stared out of lank glass panes without reserve, unashamed of its yellow complexion. A gaping public-house, calling itself newly Hotel, fell backward a step. Villas with the titles of royalty and bloody battles claimed five feet of garden, and swelled in bow-windows beside other villas which drew up firmly, commending to the attention a decent straightness and unintrusive decorum in preference. On an elevated meadow to the right was the Crouch. The Hall of Elba nestled among weather-beaten dwarf woods further toward the cliff.

The description of the great flood which caused so much devastation (and inconvenience) he drew from his own experiences: the wind roared, the rain beat down, and the waves crashed on the shore: "Sleep was impossible," he wrote, "black nights favoured the tearing fiends of shipwreck."

In September 1898 William Ernest Henley came to Steine Villa to recuperate from surgery performed in June. The house, while attractive, was thought to be unhealthy, and he moved in October to 5 West View.

SEAGRAVE, Leicestershire (pop. 286)   Located in a valley in the Wolds 10 miles north of Leicester, Seagrave took its name from the family that held the manor in feudal days, made a significant contribution to history, and then vanished. The Segraves' church still stands, with a silver fish for a weathervane, a lovely old gnarled 14th-century chest, and a musical instrument, called a serpent from its shape, that dates from the 16th century. For the last ten years of his life Robert Burton, author of *The Anatomy of Melancholy*, was rector here; he was presented with this living by George, Lord Berkeley, about 1630. There is little evidence that this preferment made any difference to the solitary life Burton was

living in Oxford, and he paid little attention to his duties here, visiting Seagrave only occasionally.

SEAHAM, County Durham (pop. 23,410)   Originally called Seaham Harbour, Seaham has been a port in the shadow of Newcastle upon Tyne since the 18th century. Heavy industrialization has affected the community, and little of its preindustrial beauty remains. For three years Lord Byron courted Anne Isabella Milbanke, daughter of Sir Ralph Milbanke, owner of Seaham Hall, on the northern outskirts of the town. The match seemed a good one: Miss Milbanke, whom Byron called Princess of the Parallelograms, had shown an avid interest in poetry, theology, and mathematics; and the marriage, by special license, took place in the drawing room here on January 2, 1815.

Sometime later Byron recalled the scene and wrote: "I shall never forget the 2nd of January 1815! Lady Byron was the only unconcerned person present; Lady Noel, her mother, cried; I trembled like a leaf, made the wrong responses, and after the ceremony called her Miss Milbanke." Byron and his new wife resided here for a very short time after their honeymoon; but Byron loathed the place, and before leaving for London in March 1815 wrote: "Upon this dreary coast, we have nothing but county meetings and shipwrecks; and I have this day dined upon fish, which probably dined upon the crews of several colliers lost in the late gales. . . ." Seaham Hall was given to the county council for use as a hospital in 1927, and any former elegance has been eradicated by clinical linoleum floors, waiting rooms, and aspidistras. All that remains of its association with Byron is the fireplace in the drawing room.

SEATHWAITE, Lancashire (pop. 120)   Set centrally in the Vale of Seathwaite, along which the Duddon River flows, Seathwaite has an unparalleled view of Lakeland with Greyfriars Mountain, the Old Man of Coniston, and Dow Crag to the northeast. The Duddon Valley here is, as William Wordsworth describes it, a

> deep chasm, where quivering sunbeams play
> Upon its loftiest crags. . . .

The few village houses are tucked in among the slopes and rocks, and a modern church stands on the site of an old chapel which John Ruskin tried to save. The vicar was Robert Walker, Wordsworth's "wonderful Walker," and the chapel itself is included in the Duddon River sonnet sequence. Wordsworth notes the "Gospel Teacher"

> knew
> Whose good works formed an endless retinue:
> A Pastor such as Chaucer's verse portrays;
> Such as the heaven-taught skill of Herbert drew;
> And tender Goldsmith crowned with deathless praise!

Walker, born at Under-Crag in Seathwaite in 1709, was one of twelve children; sickly as a child, he was allowed to attend the local dale school held in the old church and became curate here in 1735. He and his wife raised eight children on an income that eventually only slightly exceeded £50 a year; they raised their own food, sheared sheep, spun and wove wool, tanned leather, and made their own shoes; extra wool was sold at the market. His grave is in the churchyard under an immense yew where he frequently distributed food and clothes to the parish needy; Book VII of Wordsworth's *The Excursion* describes Walker's character.

SEATON CAREW, County Durham (pop. 2,170)   In the industrial north, Seaton Carew, just south of Hartlepool on the east coast, could be a resort with its long sand beaches and bracing sea breezes but is as yet unused excepted by Teeside natives. H. G. Wells chose this location for Melville's home in *The Sea Lady,* and here Melville, the authority for the story of the sea lady, would have had the opportunity to learn sea lore and legend.

SEATON SLUICE, Northumberland   A once-thriving port for the shipment of local coal, Seaton Sluice is now, with its red-tiled roofs, a haven for artists, and architecture enthusiasts swarm to the area to see the nearby magnificent 17th-century hall, Seaton Delaval, thought by many to be Sir John Vanbrugh's finest work. Fire destroyed part of the hall in 1752 and 1882, but the hall was completely restored. The house obviously impressed Sir Walter Scott, who comments on it in *Marmion.* Here the abbess of St. Hilda notes various aspects of the Northumbrian coast as she and the "five fair nuns" sail to Lindisfarne, Monkwearmouth, and Tynemouth Priory, and then

> They marked amid her trees the hall
> Of lofty Seaton-Delaval.

SELBORNE, Hampshire (pop. 2,004)   Most descriptions of Selborne emphasize its seclusion. Lying where the tiny Oakhanger Stream has cut so deep a valley in the hills that the beech-covered Selborne Hanger appears to isolate the village, it does have a peaceful air about it. Gilbert White was born in the vicarage on January 18, 1720, and not, as is often stated, at the family home, the Wakes, now a joint museum and library dedicated to White and Capt. Lawrence Oates, the Antarctic explorer. White spent little time away from this area and even after his ordination preferred a curacy here to a living anywhere else. As curate he lived first at the parsonage but moved to the Wakes when it came into his possession in 1763. One of White's favorite walks can be traced today because of the path he constructed; a narrow lane at the side of the Queen's Head Inn leads down into a steep ravine known as the Lythe and eventually through the beech wood. Another favorite path is familiar to readers of *The Natural History and Antiquities of Selborne;* this route, called the Zigzag, is just to the right of the Selborne Arms and leads to Selborne common at the top of the Hanger. White died in Selborne on June 26, 1793, and was buried in the church graveyard; a simple marker indicates his grave: "G. W. 1793." The church contains a memorial tablet and a memorial window depicting St. Francis Assisi and the birds; in the garden of the library and museum is the sundial which White constructed. The most effective memorial is the fact that the National Trust took over the entire area to preserve its beauty.

SELBORNE   The Wakes, where Gilbert White wrote *The Natural History and Antiquities of Selborne*, is now the Gilbert White Museum and the Oates Memorial Library, the latter in honor of the Antarctic explorer Capt. Lawrence Oates.

SEND, Surrey (pop. 1,290)   Modern Send is fast on its way to becoming an outpost of nearby Woking, but the old part, on the Wey River, has kept its charm; here are the remains of the 12th-century Augustinian Newark Priory, founded (more probably, refounded) by Ruald de Calva and his wife. The site was known as Aldebury, and the priory was also known as Newstead and De Novo Loco juxta Guildford. In 1807 Thomas Love Peacock, who was living in nearby Chertsey, often met Fanny Faulkner here; the two were engaged, but "through underhand interference of a third person" some sort of misunderstanding occurred, and the engagement was broken. She married another man and died within a year. Peacock's sincerity in the affair was demonstrated as late as 1842, when he wrote "Newark Abbey, August, 1842, with a Reminiscence of August, 1807":

> For all too well my spirit feels
> The only change this scene reveals:
> The sunbeams play, the breezes stir,
> Unseen, unfelt, unheard by her,
> Who, on that long-past August day,
> First saw with me these ruins gray.

SENNEN, Cornwall (pop. 663)   The westernmost village on the mainland of England, only 1 mile east of Land's End, Sennen is of special interest to tourists speculating on the kingdom of Lyonnesse and to walkers traversing the length of the United Kingdom or some part of it for the benefit of charity. Near the hillside Church of St. Senana are the Iron Age remains of Maen Castle (a promontory fort), Chapel Carn Brea (a late Stone Age or early Bronze Age grave), and Table Men (a rock associated with King Arthur). Sennen is reputedly the site of the Battle of Vellan-Drucher, in which Arthur, leading the forces of seven Cornish chieftains, annihilated the Danish invaders and put an end to Danish incursions here.

Following the battle, a victory banquet was held on the large rock now known as Table Men.

SEVENOAKS, Kent (pop. 12,780) Sevenoaks is a modern commuters' town, 5 miles northwest of Tonbridge and a little more than 22 miles southeast of London. Often included in Sevenoaks is the great house of Knole, whose long entrance road begins in the town. The church has an especially good west tower; part of the building dates to the 13th century. In 1616 John Donne received the benefice here from Thomas Egerton, Lord Ellesmere; the living, which had no duties attached to it, was an endowed parish. Donne first stopped here in the summer of 1617 on his way to Knole, seat of the Earl of Dorset and preached here for the first time. He then returned yearly to take the pulpit and stayed at Knole.

In the 19th century Dante Gabriel Rossetti, on a painting holiday, took a room on the High Street before joining Holman Hunt in the Knole park; Rossetti remained three weeks before returning suddenly to London. In July 1894 H. G. Wells took 23 Eardley Road, Tusculum Villas, near the station. Wells's wife Jane was tubercular, and the doctors felt that the climate here, together with enforced rest, would help her condition; the couple left for London in mid-autumn. In the summer of 1920 Virginia Stephen Woolf and her husband stayed at Long Barn, and Victoria Sackville-West and her husband, Sir Harold Nicolson, visited here. The lesbian relationship was known to both Leonard Woolf and Sir Harold, and from this Virginia Woolf drew the idea for *Orlando*.

SEVENOAKS WEALD, Kent (pop. 912) Situated 2½ miles south of Sevenoaks, this village is often called simply Weald; here at Siddolph's Cottage, on Eggpie Lane, W. H. Davies lived when he wrote *The Autobiography of a Super-Tramp*. The cottage was supplied by Edward Thomas, and Davies notes, "[M]y rent, coal and light . . . [were] paid mysteriously by Thomas and his friends." At one point in his sojourn here Davies broke his wooden leg, and the local carpenter fashioned a replacement.

SEWINGSHIELDS, Northumberland The great wall of Hadrian, built by Roman mercenaries between A.D. 122 and 163, ran 73 miles from Wallsend on the Tyne River (the Roman Sedgedunum) across Northumberland and through Cumberland to end at Solway Firth. Supplanting an ineffective earthwork mound, Hadrian's Wall (as it is popularly known), with camps, fortifications, and mile castles at strategic points, was occupied by the Romans for almost three centuries.

The area around Sewingshields, where the wall was built on rather impressive heights, is associated with Arthurian legend, and North Country tradition has Arthur, his court, Queen Guinevere, and thirty pairs of hounds immured in a cavern below the castle (gone) in an enchanted sleep. A horn and garter lie at the cave entrance awaiting the time of discovery; when the finder blows the bugle and cuts the garter with the "sword of stone," Arthur and his entourage will awaken. A local story tells of a 19th-century shepherd who sat on the crags knitting when not seeing (tending) his sheep; one day his clud (wool) rolled off, and in pursuing it he found the cave in which Arthur and the others sleep. He followed an eerie light shining in the distance and discovered the sword, garter, bugle, and assembled sleepers; instinct seems to have prompted the old man to cut the garter, and true to legend the sleepers all sat up. But he neglected to blow the bugle, perhaps because of his alarm, and the occupants fell back into their sleep. Arthur, in the few moments he was awake, managed to address the shepherd:

> O woe betide that evil day
> On which this witless wight was born,
> Who drew the sword, the garter cut,
> But never blew the bugle horn.—

This was rather well put for someone just coming out of a deep sleep. Numerous other area stories about Arthur have no convincing connection with the accepted Arthurian traditions; indeed, many are out of keeping with the chivalric code. For example, one tale relates a heated argument between the King and Guinevere during which he throws a 20-ton rock at her and she wards off the blow with a comb.

Sir Walter Scott uses this location as Seven Shields in *Harold the Dauntless*. Scott makes the castle the site of Harold's "probation": he is "within a lone castle to press a lone bed" and here is converted mystically from his barbaric and demonic ways.

SHAFTESBURY, Dorset (pop. 3,093) Shaftesbury, a market town in the far north of Dorset, is on a 700-foot chalk plateau overlooking the Blackmoor Vale, and many of its old cobbled streets run precipitously down sharp embankments. That the town is ancient is indisputable, but Geoffrey of Monmouth's claim that the city was founded by Rud Hud Hudibras, the ninth king of the Britons in direct descent from Brutus, and that it was once called Paladur cannot be substantiated. This is the town about which Geoffrey says, "There the Eagle spoke, while the wall was being built. If I believed its Sayings to be true, I would not hesitate to hand them down to history with my other material." What is known is that Alfred the Great endowed a Benedictine nunnery here in 880 and that the abbey was well established and prosperous by 981, when Edward the Martyr was buried here.

The town was once known as Shaston, and it is under this name that it appears in the works of Thomas Hardy. It is mentioned in *Tess of the D'Urbervilles* but is most important in *Jude the Obscure*. Hardy comments on the ancient history of Shaston when he introduces the town and incorporates an observation made by Michael Drayton in *Poly-Olbion*:

> SHASTON, the ancient British Palladour,
>
> "From whose foundation first such strange reports arise,"
>
> . . . was, and is, in itself the city of a dream. Vague imaginings of its castle, its three mints, its magnificent aspidal Abbey, the chief glory of South Wessex, its twelve churches, its shrines, chantries, hospitals, its gabled freestone mansions . . . throw the visitor, even against his will, into a pensive melancoly. . . .

Many of the specific locations used by Hardy in *Jude* are traceable: Old Groves Place, the home of Phillotson and Sue after their marriage, is an old house with a projecting porch and mullioned windows just beyond Bimport Street close to the place where the roads branch off to Motcombe and East Stour. Hardy also mentions the abbey and Abbey Walk and locates Castle Green here. The Duke's Arms is modeled on the Grosvenor Arms, an 18th-century hotel on the Commons (the market square). Shaftesbury appears under the name Shastonb'ry in "The Vampirine Fair."

SHALLOWFORD, Staffordshire A hamlet on Meece Brook 3 miles east of Eccleshall, Shallowford consists of little more than a farm and its outbuildings, and it is this farm, once known as Halfhead Farm, to which literary pilgrims flock. From about 1644 until almost the end of his life, Izaak Walton lived or visited here frequently; indeed, he appears to have sought refuge here at the outbreak of the Civil War. The brick-and-timber outbuildings are much as he knew them, but the farmhouse, now the Izaak Walton Cottage and Museum (rebuilt), has twice burned down since it opened in 1924. Walton left this farm to the town of Stafford, his birthplace, with the stipulation that its rent be used to provide the apprenticeship of two boys, coal for the needy, and a marriage portion for one servant girl. Walton wrote of his feelings for this corner of Staffordshire:

Here give my weary spirits rest,
And raise my low-pitched thoughts above
Earth, or what poor mortals love:
Thus, free from lawsuits and the noise
Of Princes' courts, I would rejoice;
Or with my Bryan and a book,
Loiter long days near Shawford brook....

SHANKLIN, Isle of Wight (pop. 11,615 with Sandown) Located in the southeastern part of the Isle of Wight, Shanklin is fortunate in being both protected from heavy Atlantic gales in winter and situated so as to receive every possible benefit from the Gulf Stream. The Gulf Stream encourages the growth of luxurious tropical vegetation, and the East Chine (Cleft) shelters its good sand beaches. Shanklin sits high on the cliff, and lifts take bathers and vacationers down to the sands. The Old Village area of Shanklin has thatched cottages and the Crab Inn, where Henry Wadsworth Longfellow stayed when he visited the island in 1868. A fountain near the Crab carries lines that he wrote in the inn.

O traveller, stay thy weary feet;
Drink of this fountain pure and sweet;
It flows for rich and poor the same.
Then go thy way, remembering still
The wayside well beneath the hill,
The cup of water in His name.

John Keats had been here in 1819, hoping to help his delicate health with fresh sea breezes. He arrived almost penniless at the end of June; local tradition maintains that he was at Eglantine Cottage, 76 High Street, and a plaque commemorating his visit is on the cottage wall. Keat's description of the rooms he shared with James Rice is a little vague (unlike his letters from Winchester, which do impart some information), and there is no specific clue to the location of the house. To his sister he wrote, "Our window looks over house tops and cliffs onto the sea, so that

when ships sail past the cottage chimneys you may take them for Weathercocks," but this is not helpful. While here, he worked on *Otho the Great*, which he considered a potboiler, *Lamia*, possibly *Hyperion*, and undoubtedly the "Bright Star" sonnet. Keats did not find the health he sought even though he took a daily walk across the cliff top, a walk today known as Keats' Green. However, by early August he was disturbed by his environment: he was clearly not getting any better; the voice of the landlady across the way, probably a Mrs. Warder, was annoying; and he had clear need of a library. Hoping to solve at least the latter two problems, he and Charles Armitage Brown, who had joined him in August, went to Winchester.

In 1863 Gerard Manley Hopkins spent the summer vacation from Balliol College, Oxford, here with his parents and the rest of his family. Although this was three years before his actual conversion to Roman Catholicism, the period was one of inner controversy, and he found himself walking a great deal to gain time to reflect.

SHAP, Westmorland (pop. 1,005) A lofty moorland village with superb views of the fells, Shap, situated 10 miles from Penrith, is the only Westmorland location to have had an abbey, but the 12th-century Shap Abbey was never successful and fell into ruin and disuse after only a short time. Little remains today. Stone Age circles at nearby Addendale and Gunnerkeld are evidence of an earlier history, and Shap itself was near the Roman routeway.

Anthony Trollope mentions Shap in *Can You Forgive Her?* The coach passengers stop here just long enough "to thank Heaven they had not been Shappites":

There is a station at Shap, by which the railway company no doubt conceives that it has conferred on that somewhat rough and remote locality all the advantages of a refined civilization; but I doubt whether the Shappites have been thankful for the favour.... Shap ... lay high and bleak among the fells, and was a cold, windy, thinly-populated place....

SHARPENHOE, Bedfordshire At the southern edge of the flat north country of Bedfordshire, the hamlet of Sharpenhoe and the Sharpenhoe Clappers with their tree-covered lower slopes present a striking combination. The Clappers are in the care of the National Trust as an area of natural beauty. Christened in the parish church, Thomas Norton may have been born here and not in London in 1532; called to the bar, about 1561, he maintained a successful law practice in addition to his writing and came into political prominence when sitting as the Member of Parliament for Gatton (1558), Berwick (1562), and London (1572, 1580). With age came sternness, and in later life he described himself as "a mortar-bearer in the work of God"; to others, though, he was a "rackmaster-general" in his ferreting out of Roman Catholics in those days of elevated intolerance. Norton died at Sharpenhoe Manor (Bury Farm contains the original moat) on March 10, 1584.

SHARPHAM, Somerset (pop. 79) Sharpham is 2 miles southwest of Glastonbury in the low-lying Sedgemoor plain, which once was covered with water and is now a maze of rhines (drainage ditches) interspersed with dairy farms in an unusually peaceful countryside. Sir Edward Dyer is often erroneously said to have been born at Sharpham Park in October 1543; while little is known of the author of "My mind to me a kingdom is" until he went up to Oxford, it is known that he was born and raised in Weston Zoyland. Henry Fielding is a real native son, born at Sharpham Park on April 22, 1707, in the room known as the Harlequin Chamber. The 16th-century manor, now a farmhouse, was owned by Fielding's maternal grandfather, and Fielding's parents, who married without consent, used this as their home for three years until moving to East Stour, Dorset. Many years later, in *The History of Tom Jones*, Fielding used this manor house and its setting as the model for Squire Allworthy's "Gothick style of building ... that ... rival'd the beauties of the best Grecian architecture...." Fielding continues:

> It stood on the south-east side of a hill, but nearer the bottom than the top of it, so as to be sheltered from the north-east by a grove of old oaks....
>
> In the midst of the grove was a fine lawn, sloping down towards the house, near the summit of which rose a plentiful spring, gushing out of a rock covered with firs, and forming a constant cascade of about thirty foot, ... that with many lesser falls winded along, till it fell into a lake at the foot of the hill, about a quarter of a mile below the house on the south side, and which was seen from every room in the front.

SHAWELL, Leicestershire (pop. 181)   The small brook flowing through the back gardens of this Leicestershire village, 3 miles south of Lutterworth, eventually empties into the Avon River. For almost fifty years Alfred, Lord Tennyson was a visitor at the rectory (now Old Rectory) here; the rector's wife, Sophy Elmhirst, had been a ward of Tennyson's father. Tennyson did a great deal of writing in the garden summerhouse, to which he was driven because he was not permitted to smoke his pipe in the house itself. The local claim that part of *In Memoriam* was composed here could well be true because Tennyson worked on the poem for seventeen years.

SHEFFIELD, Yorkshire (pop. 522,000)   Set in a depression in the south Pennine slopes, Sheffield is on the Don River almost equidistant from Manchester and York; it is a city of one-way streets and few notable early buildings. Sheffield has been the focal point of the uncharted kingdom of Hallamshire for centuries and as such has been known as a center for cutlery. Indeed, the chapter house at Sheffield Cathedral has a modern window commemorating Geoffrey Chaucer's *The Canterbury Tales* simply because the Miller of Trumpington "A Sheffeld thwitel [small knife] baar ... in his hose." Daniel Defoe notes Chaucer's use in *A Tour thro' the Whole Island of Great Britain* and the antiquity of the town's reputation for cutlery; the town, he says, "is very populous and large, the Streets narrow, and the Houses dark and black, occasioned by the continued Smoke of the Forges which are always at work...." He was, though, impressed with the scope of manufacturing here: "They talked of 30000 Men employed in the whole; but I leave it upon the Credit of Report." Little had changed by 1760, when Horace Walpole

visited Sheffield, "one of the foulest towns in England in the most charming situation." However, his opinion was not entirely negative, as he tells George Montagu in a letter, because "One man there has discovered the art of plating copper with silver—I bought a pair of candlesticks for two guineas, that are quite pretty." The man, Thomas Bolsover, discovered the process in 1742, and Sheffield is still noted for its silver-plating. William Cobbett was similarly impressed seventy years later with "black Sheffield";

> It was dark before we reached Sheffield; so that we saw the iron furnaces in all the horrible splendour of their everlasting blaze. Nothing can be conceived more grand or more terrific than the yellow waves of fire that incessantly issue from the top of these furnaces, some of which are close by the way-side.

In the same century John Ruskin began planning "a Utopia in England"; placing £7,000 in trust for the Guild of St. George, he embarked on an ambitious scheme of establishing self-supporting settlements where "the highest wisdom and the highest treasure need not be costly or exclusive." In May 1871 he called for support from landlords and workers to take part in experiments in agriculture, industry, and art and set up numerous communities accordingly. St. George's Farms proved a failure with the exception of one at Barmouth; a few of the industrial experiments were successful, especially in Langdale, where handmade linen was revived, and in Laxey, Isle of Man, where a similar industry prospered; the artistic branch of St. George's Guild was established here in the form of a museum in 1875. Originally established in a cottage in Walkley, the museum was taken over by the Sheffield Corporation in 1890 and moved to Meersbrook Park; here were displayed the many drawings of medieval buildings in France and Italy that Ruskin had commissioned, as well as his own collection of minerals and gems, drawings, and some manuscripts. Most of this material is now on loan to Reading University. At Abbeydale, 3½ miles southwest of Sheffield, he bought 13 acres of land, where life was to be lived "with no steam engines ... and no railroads"; his plan here did not work, and the land was turned into a market garden. This is now the Abbeydale Industrial Hamlet, which displays early machinery.

Sir Arthur Conan Doyle came to Sheffield in the summer of 1878 as a medical apprentice to a Dr. Richardson in one of the poorer sections of town; Doyle's assistantship lasted three weeks, and he left in anger, writing hotly, "These Sheffielders would rather be poisoned by a man with a beard than be saved by a man without one." Charlotte Brontë includes Sheffield in *Jane Eyre;* here is the ball at which the officers of the garrison "put all our young knife grinders and scissor merchants to shame." Finally, John Galsworthy was made an honorary doctor of letters at Sheffield University on July 5, 1930.

SHEFFORD, Bedfordshire (pop. 2,216)   Although Shefford's known history goes back to Roman times and some earlier finds have been made, its recent history dates from 1225, when a market was established here. The market specialized in hides, and a number of fellmongers and tanners made their homes in Shefford. Because the village stands on the road to London, it has long been an important post stop, and Dorothy Osborne of nearby Chicksands Priory received her letters from Sir William Temple from here. The post came early, leaving Shefford at 4 A.M., and when Miss Osborne did not receive the expected missive, she "chid the carrier for coming so soon."

Shefford was the last home of Robert Bloomfield, who retired to North Bridge Street in 1812; he spent short periods in London, Dover, and Canterbury, but in midsummer of 1814, suffering from semiblindness, marked hypochondria, and acute poverty, he returned permanently to Shefford. Almost mad by 1823, he died on August 19 and was buried in Campton, about 1 mile southwest of this village. He had been befriended by the rector there, the Rev. Edmund Williamson, who provided what comfort he could to Bloomfield.

SHELLINGFORD, Berkshire (pop. 221) A confusing village at best, Shellingford is also known (but less properly) as Shillingford and until recent redistricting was located in Berkshire 2½ miles southeast of Farringdon; now it is in Oxfordshire. It is a village sheltered by woodlands and has a basically 13th-century church. For three months (April to June) in 1921 Minchen's Cottage was the home of William Butler Yeats and his family. They had let their Oxford home and waited here for the "storm," the violence following the 1919 Dáil meeting and subsequent suppression, to break. Yeats's wife, Georgie, was pining for Ballylee, he said, and during the interim he began "Meditations in Time of Civil War." They went on to Thame in June before setting out for Ireland.

SHEPPERTON, Middlesex (pop. 2,858) The Middlesex area including Shepperton was once in the hands of St. Dunstan, and some sort of church has stood on the same site for more than 1,000 years. Shepperton is on the Thames River 2 miles east of Chertsey, in an area where boating is popular in summer. One of the early rectors was William Grocyn, who held this living in addition to All Hallows in Maidstone, St. Lawrence Jewry, and East Peckham from 1504 to 1513. How much time, if any, he spent here is not known, and the tradition that Erasmus visited him here is most likely wishful thinking; even so, Erasmus's ghost is said to haunt the rectory.

More recent associations do exist with Thomas Love Peacock and his son-in-law George Meredith, both of whom lived in Halliford, half a mile to the east. Peacock's daughter Margaret, who died at the age of three, is buried near the church porch, and Peacock wrote the epitaph on the tombstone, which includes the lines:

> The half-formed words of liveliest thought
>   That spoke a mind beyond thy years,
> The song, the dance, by nature taught,
>   The sunny smiles, the transient tears.

Peacock died in his Halliford home on January 23, 1866, and is buried in the churchyard here.

There is no foundation for the story that George Eliot (Mary Ann Evans) stayed at the rectory when writing *Scenes of Clerical Life* and that this is the Shepperton of her work.

SHERBORNE, Dorset (pop. 7,094) Sherborne, a market town on the Yeo River in northwest Dorset, is situated in the midst of rolling chalk downs. Some houses here date from the 15th century, but recorded history goes back much further. There is evidence of an earlier religious community, but a bishopric was established here in 705 and became one of the leading centers of learning in England. The first bishop, Aldhelm, a great scholar and the leader of an advanced intellectual movement, was the first Anglo-Saxon known to have written in Latin, and his works reveal an extensive knowledge of both Christian and classical authors. The episcopacy's last bishop before a Benedictine monastery was established in its place was Asser, known for his biography of King Alfred and a chronicle of English history. An unsupported tradition maintains that Alfred was educated under the monks here. The original Norman structure was razed in the 12th century, and the present golden-stone abbey dates primarily from that century. Many of the monastic buildings are incorporated into the Sherborne School, just beyond the south porch of the abbey; the school, used for the setting of the second filming of James Hilton's *Goodbye, Mr. Chips*, had among its pupils John Cowper Powys, C. Day-Lewis, and Alec Waugh.

Medieval Sherborne was a flourishing community, heavily involved in the wool trade, but the monastic and the lay were in conflict, especially over the building of a separate parish church in the abbey, Allhalowes. The Wykeham Chapel contains an effigy to Sir John Horsey, a friend of Sir Thomas Wyatt, who died here on October 6, 1542. Wyatt was riding from London to Falmouth on a diplomatic mission when he contracted a violent fever and stopped here, undoubtedly at Horsey's home. The fever turned into pneumonia, against which there was no hope. Following his death, he was buried in the abbey. Just where Wyatt was buried is not known, although it is popularly believed to be in the Horsey family tomb in the Wykeham Chapel.

SHANKLIN
O traveller, stay thy weary feet;
Drink of this fountain pure and sweet. . . .
Henry Wadsworth Longfellow

The first Sherborne Castle, just east of the market town, belonged to the abbey and eventually was acquired by the see of Salisbury through St. Osmund, who is said to have been instrumental in the later downfall of Sir Walter Ralegh, that is, if prayer could accomplish it. The Bishop laid a curse on the castle, that "whosoever should take these lands from the bishopric or diminish them in great or in small, should be accursed not only in this world but also in the world to come unless in his lifetime he made restitution thereof." Ralegh, who had seen the castle on a trip from Plymouth to London via Sherborne, pleaded his cause to Queen Elizabeth, adding to his supplications an expensive jewel; she ultimately induced the Bishop to part with the building, and Ralegh undertook a ninety-nine year lease. Initially planning to alter the medieval edifice, Ralegh and his wife eventually began to build a new structure; the 16th-century central portion of the mansion is his. Before his fall from favor in 1603, Ralegh attempted to convey Sherborne Castle to his son Wat, but because of a technical flaw in the deed James I took the estate and gave it to Robert Carr, a court favorite. A stone seat by the old bridge is where Ralegh was supposedly doused with water when smoking a pipe. Another seat across the stream is associated with Alexander Pope, who visited here occasionally on his yearly trips to the south from London.

As Sherton Abbas, this town is an integral part of many of the works of Thomas Hardy, who uses many specific locations in and around the town. It is mentioned in *Tess of the D'Urbervilles*, *The Mayor of Casterbridge*, "Squire Petrick's Lady" (*A Group of Noble Dames*), "Interlopers at the Knap" (*Wessex Tales*), and *Jude the Obscure*. In the last-named novel the Sherton Turnpike is where Oak and Coggan overtake Bathsheba, whom they have mistaken for a horse thief, on her escape to Bath to meet Troy. The turnpike gate still stands at the top of the hill on the road from Weatherbury (Puddletown) to Sherborne. The town takes on a far more important role in "Anna, Lady Baxby" (*A Group of Noble Dames*) and in *The Woodlanders*. Almost all the action of "Anna" takes place at Sherton Castle (Sherborne Castle) at the time of the Great Rebellion, and Hardy has based his story on actual events. In 1642 the Marquess of Hertford fortified the castle for King Charles and garrisoned men there against the coming attack by the 5th Earl of Bedford; the owner, Lord Digby, was married to Bedford's sister, who was in residence at the time. Not only was Lord Bedford's message to his sister telling her to leave unheeded, but Lady Digby rode to the Parliamentarian camp and warned her brother that "he should find his sister's bones in the ruins" if he attacked. Hardy follows historical fact fairly closely, changing the name Digby to Baxby, and has Lord Baxby arrive with sufficient reinforcements to justify Bedford's decision to spare the castle.

Other specific locations are used in *The Woodlanders*: Grace Fitzpiers comes to Sherton from Little Hintock (Hermitage), ostensibly to go to the market but really to catch a glimpse of Giles Winterborne. On this trip, traveling down Sheep Street, she remembers first seeing him "standing under his apple-tree" close to the 16th-century conduit and then "making cider in the courtyard of the Earl of Essex Hotel." This hotel is probably modeled on the New Inn (gone). After meeting, she and Giles proceeded to the abbey, where "they walked about the Abbey aisles and presently sat down" and talked of her marital plight. The Three Tuns Inn, to which Giles takes her for refreshment and to which Lord Melbury takes his men for

the same purpose, is unidentifiable. Sherborne Abbey may be the place described as the "abbey north of Blackmore Vale" in "The Lost Pyx" (*Poems of the Past and Present*).

SHERIFF HUTTON, Yorkshire (pop. 615) Within 10 miles of York in the Vale of York, Sheriff Hutton is a tiny village which once held a superb castle belonging to the Nevilles. The 14th-century castle ruins, joined to a farmhouse, in prouder times guarded the Gaultres Forest. The castle had many historic visitors, among them the Earl of Warwick, Richard III, and the Countess of Surrey. It was at the countess's invitation that John Skelton spent the Christmas season of 1522 here shortly after she became his patroness. This was the time of Skelton's conflict with Thomas Cardinal Wolsey, whom he called a "son of a wolf" in 1515; the cardinal's power and position had forced Skelton to seek sanctuary within the precincts of Westminster Abbey, and this was his first excursion from sanctuary. During his stay in Sheriff Hutton, he began *A Goodly Garland or Chapelet of Laurell*.

SHIBDEN HALL, Yorkshire Although Shibden Hall (now a museum), located in the tiny Shibden Valley, is close enough to the populous wool center of Halifax to be a part of it, the 1-mile distance to the town includes a strategically placed ridge, and the 15th-century hall is remarkably secluded. Between 1634 and 1636, after his return from Leiden, Dr. Thomas Browne practiced medicine here and wrote *Religio Medici*. His move to Norwich, Norfolk, in 1637 was instigated by Sir Thomas Lushington, his former tutor, who was then rector of Burnham Westgate, a small village in northwest Norfolk.

SHIFNAL, Shropshire (pop. 3,303) About 17 miles east of Shrewsbury, Shifnal has lovely narrow old streets lined with half-timbered and Georgian houses and an inn, the Nag's Head, which dates from the 14th century and still retains much of its original appearance. This may have been the birthplace of the satirist Thomas Brown in 1663, but there is no specific information; however, here at Priors Lee Hall, outside the town, the old folio manuscript which formed the basis for Bishop Thomas Percy's *Reliques of Ancient English Poetry* was discovered. About 1760 Percy was here visiting Humphrey Pitt when he discovered an old manuscript which a maid was using to light fires; two pages were missing, and fifty-four folio leaves had been torn in half; however, 195 ballads, sonnets, metrical romances, and historical songs remained, and these became the basis of the rest of the collection.

Another possible literary association is with Charles Dickens, who may have used the town in *The Old Curiosity Shop*; his description of its narrow streets and half-timbered houses is such that one can easily visualize Shifnal. It should be noted that Shrewsbury claims the same distinction.

SHILLINGFORD See SHELLINGFORD.

SHINFIELD, Berkshire (pop. 2,143) Only 3½ miles south of Reading, Shinfield is now merely a suburb of that county town and is rapidly being transformed into a large and modern residential district. The old Church of St. Mary, on a hillock, has a Norman doorway and some medieval windows. Shinfield is usually identified as Gaymead in Thomas Hardy's *Jude the Obscure* and "The Son's Veto" (*Life's Little Ironies and a Few Crusted Characters*). The unnamed church on which Jude and Sue work as decorators, however, may actually be the one in the adjacent parish. Gaymead's role in "The Son's Veto" is more important, for this is the location of the Reverend Mr. Twycott's parsonage and church and his wife's native village:

> In a remote nook in North Wessex, forty miles from London, near the thriving county-town of Aldbrickham, there stood a pretty village with its church and parsonage, which she knew well enough, but her son had never seen. It was her native village, Gaymead, and the first event bearing upon her present situation had occurred at that place when she was only a girl of nineteen.

The Church of St. Mary is the scene of the wedding between Sophy and the rector, and here Mr. Twycott is buried; the vicarage Hardy describes is comparatively new. A small brass plaque recently discovered in the floor has proved to be a memorial to George Mitford, father of Mary Mitford.

SHIPBOURNE, Kent (pop. 498)   Four miles north of Tonbridge, Shipbourne (pronounced "shib'bon") has a 19th-century village center, a church with enormous protruding gargoyles, and Fairlawne (Fairlawn), the birthplace of Christopher Smart in April 1722. His birth date may be April 11, but he was christened at the parish church on May 11. Smart's father was steward to William, Viscount Vane, the younger son of Lord Barnard, owner of Raby Castle, with which Smart was later associated. Christopher's first four years were spent here, and he returned frequently even after Lord Barnard had arranged for his education at Maidstone. *Jubilate Agno* contains at least two specific references to Shipbourne:

> For I bless God in SHIPBOURNE FAIRLAWN the
> meadows·the brooks the hills

and

> Let Mary rejoice with the Carp—the ponds of Fairlawn
> and the garden bless the master.

Much of the nature imagery in *A Song to David* also is derived from the wooded countryside here.

SHIPLAKE, Oxfordshire (pop. 1,554)   Rising high above the winding Thames 4 miles northeast of the populous metropolitan area of Reading, Shiplake is situated in a lovely part of the Oxfordshire countryside. The parish church is especially beautiful and is worth visiting for its windows of medieval glass. Shiplake was one of the favorite spots of Alfred, Lord Tennyson, for it was here on June 13, 1850, that he married Emily Sarah Sellwood after a ten-year separation caused by Tennyson's inability to support a family. Tennyson and Miss Sellwood had met again in the spring of 1850 at the home of her cousins, the Rawnsleys. The poet had been promised a yearly royalty if *In Memoriam* was published, and upon this condition the engagement was renewed. It was a quiet wedding (the cake and the dresses arrived late), but Tennyson remarked, "The peace of God came into my life before the altar when I wedded her."

After the ceremony the couple drove toward Pangbourne; Tennyson composed a poem for Rawnsley, who performed the ceremony:

> Vicar of this pleasant spot
>   Where it was my chance to marry,
> Happy, happy be your lot
>   In the Vicarage by the quarry.
> You were he that knit the knot!
>
> Sweetly, smoothly flow your life.
>   Never tithe unpaid perplex you,
> Parish feud, or party strife,
>   All things please you, nothing vex you,
> You have given me such a wife!

One of the wedding guests, Mary Russell Mitford, left a description of the village and the church:

> A large and beautiful pile it is. The tower, half clothed with ivy, stands with its charming vicarage and its pretty vicarage garden on a high eminence, overhanging one of the finest bends of the great river.... This is Shiplake church, famed far and near for its magnificent oak carving, and the rich painted glass of its windows, collected, long before such adornments were fashionable, by the fine taste of the late vicar, and therefore filled with the very choicest specimens of mediaeval art....

Between 1865 and 1879 Algernon Swinburne made many trips here to his parents' home, Holmwood, and the arrangements for him to live with Theodore Watts-Dunton were made here in 1879.

Shiplake became the home of the family of George Orwell (Eric Blair) at the beginning of term in 1912. They took Roselawn on Station Road and enjoyed the country feeling here; young Eric especially liked exploring on Binfield Heath, just above the village, and fishing in the abandoned quarry in the woods beyond their house. At the end of 1915 the Blairs moved back to Henley-on-Thames.

SHIPLEY, Sussex (pop. 1,011)   The Adur River running past Shipley, itself 6 miles south of Horsham, has cut a deep gap in the South Downs south of the village, but here great farms and orderly woodlands have existed for hundreds of years. Numerous old hammer ponds (a hammer pond is one in which water was stored for driving a hammer mill) are hidden by the trees, and the 12th-century Shipley church is a beautiful building reached by a stone causeway supposedly built at the same time as the church. The composer John Ireland is buried in the church graveyard, as is the actress Anny Ahlers.

Shipley became Hilaire Belloc's home in March 1906, when he bought King's Land, a 5-acre estate which included an eleven-gabled house whose oldest parts date to the 14th century. The house had a walled-in garden, about 1 acre in extent. King's Land had originally been a shop, and when Belloc took occupancy, the walls were lined with little drawers and the shelves were leather-fringed to keep out the dust. The flagstoned dining room was next door, and off it was the poet's study. A very devout Catholic, Belloc had one upstairs room furnished as a chapel. In 1913 he built the Trolls, a hut at the end of the garden, as a study and covered one wall with an ordnance survey map measuring 14 by 22 feet. Belloc began bottling his own wines at this time and also had a weekly barrel of ale brought in from Littlehampton. Life here was pleasant and happy until the death of his wife, Elodie, on February 2, 1914; Belloc shut off her room and never entered it again. His boat, the *Nona*, which comes into his writing, finally became irreparable, and many of his old friends banded together and presented him with the *Jersey*, then the oldest ship in Lloyd's Register (launched in 1846). Belloc contracted pneumonia after a stroke in 1950 but was well enough to play an extensive role in his eightieth-birthday celebrations in Sparta Field opposite the house in July, but from then on his health deteriorated. On July 12, 1953, he was found lying near the fireplace in his home, the room filled with smoke. Suffering from severe shock and burns, Belloc was taken to the Mount Alvernia Nursing Home of the Franciscan missionaries in Guildford, where he died on July 16. He was buried at West Grinstead by his wife's side. Belloc, it should be noted, composed the epitaph for Anny Ahlers. Since Belloc's death Shipley Windmill, the only existing smock mill in West Sussex, has been restored in his memory. (A smock mill has its top floor of wood, while a tower mill has its top floor of brick.)

SHIPTON-UNDER-WYCHWOOD, Oxfordshire (pop. 667)

Six miles southwest of Chipping Norton on the Evenlode River, Shipton has a number of extremely good old homes built when the village was a major sheep and wool market. The Elizabethan Shipton Court stands in beautiful grounds with an ornamental lake, and nearby is the Shaven Crown Inn with a 15th-century gateway. It is possible that one of the earliest English poets, William Langland, was born here but complete proof is lacking. The possibility is based on a Latin note (apparently of the 15th century) appended to the Ashburnham manuscript of *Piers Plowman*, now in Dublin, which states that the poet's father was of gentle birth, was known as Stacy de Rokayle, and lived at Shipton-under-Wychwood. It goes on to note that De Rokayle was a tenant of Lord "le Spenser in comitatu Oxon." But John Bale later named Cleobury Mortimer in Shropshire as Langland's birthplace. The argument that Cleobury Mortimer is the better choice because of the nearby village of Langley, from which the poet's name can be derived, is spurious; there is a hamlet called Langley here as well. Other arguments, though, favor the Shropshire village.

SHIRLEY, Derbyshire (pop. 233)

A tiny village in the especially lovely Dovedale area of Derbyshire, 4 miles southeast of Ashbourne, Shirley has a partly 14th-century church closely associated with the ancient Shirley family and with the Powys family. The church contains memorials to the Shirleys, one of whom died in the Battle of Shrewsbury and whose valor Shakespeare praises in *Henry IV: Part I*. The Old Vicarage, just north of the village, was the birthplace of John Cowper Powys on October 8, 1872, and of Theodore Francis Powys on December 20, 1875; their father, the Rev. Charles Francis Powys, was vicar here from 1872 until 1879, when he took his family to Dorchester.

SHOREHAM, Kent (pop. 1,509)

A Downs village on the Darent River, Shoreham remains incredibly remote and peaceful even though it is less than 5 miles north of Sevenoaks and thus is under the influence of London. Water House, just a short distance from the bridge over the Darent, was the home of Samuel Palmer, the visionary and painter who was strongly influenced by William Blake. Palmer lived here for almost five years, and it is known that Blake visited here at least once before his death in 1827. A more recent association exists with Edward John Moreton Drax Plunkett, 18th Baron Dunsany. Lord Dunsany inherited Dunstall Priory at the death of his mother in 1916 and frequently spent time here. He died in Dublin in 1957, and his body was brought to the churchyard at Shoreham for burial.

SHOREHAM-BY-SEA, Sussex (pop. 11,500)

In ancient times a wide estuary ran inland here for 5 miles through the South Downs; the Romans recognized its importance, for they built not only a harbor but an east-west access road. Shoreham-by-Sea, at the mouth of the Adur River 6 miles west of Brighton, consists actually of two Shorehams, with Old Shoreham slightly to the north. In medieval times this was an important port, and in the 14th century it was actually the most important port on the south coast. The manor of Shoreham was part of the landholdings of William de Braose, lord of the Rape of Bramber, and successive members of the family probably built the magnificent Church of St. Mary de Haura. Subsequently the manor and the church with its parish were formed into New Shoreham; at that time the old village became untenable as a port because the river silted up.

Daniel Defoe was impressed by the occupations attendant to the port when he was here and notes in *A Tour thro' the Whole Island of Great Britain* that the "Sea-faring Town" is

> chiefly inhabited by Ship-Carpenters, Ship-Chandlers, and all the several Trades depending upon the Building and Fitting up of Ships, which is their chief Business; and they are fam'd for neat Building, and for Building good Sea-Boats; that is to say, Ships that are wholesome in the Sea, and good Sailors....
>
> The Builders of Ships seemed to plant here, chiefly because of the exceeding Quantity and Cheapness of Timber in the Country behind them...

From 1880 to 1892 W. H. Hudson took occasional holidays in Shoreham with Morley Roberts; Hudson was especially fond of the sea and indulged in a kind of ritual whenever he was here. Walking into the edge of the surf, he would scoop up a handful of salt water and drink it as some sort of reunification with nature. He loved the mud flats of the Adur at ebb tide, when the sandpipers were out, but mostly when the stream was turned into a great river by flooding; then he would view it from the Downs, "his Downs," above the town:

> I myself prefer to approach the downs on the north side.... The climb up the steep smooth escarpment is a good preparation, an intensifier of the pleasure to follow. Those who know the downs are all agreed that it *is* a rare pleasure to be on them. And when we have had our upward toil on a hot day, and ... have experienced that sense of freedom and elation which is the result of rising from a low level into a rarefied atmosphere, these purely physical sensations are succeeded by a higher, more enduring pleasure, which the mind receives from the pros-

pect disclosed . . . the vast round green hills extending away on either hand to the horizon.

Two of Hudson's favorite activities were frequenting the shipbuilder's yard here and taking long walks to the Devil's Dyke, Bramber, Chactonbury Ring, and Cissbury.

After the publication of Alec Waugh's *The Loom of Youth* made it impossible for Evelyn Waugh to attend Sherborne, he was hurriedly placed at Lancing College here on May 9, 1917; he describes his first view of the college in *A Little Learning:*

> Lancing was monastic; indeed, and medieval in the full sense of the English Gothic revival; solitary all of a piece, spread over a series of terraces sliced out of a spur of the downs.

Waugh remained here until he went to Oxford in 1921.

Another writer associated with Shoreham is Algernon Swinburne; his "On the South Coast" obviously concerns Shoreham, the Adur, and (almost without doubt) the New Shoreham Church:

> Eastward, round by the high green bound of hills that fold
> the remote fields in,
> Strive and shine on the low sea-line fleet waves and beams
> when the days begin;
> Westward glow, when the days burn low, the sun that
> yields and the stars that win.
>
> Rose-red eve on the seas that heave sinks fair as dawn
> when the first ray peers;
> Winds are glancing from sunbright Lancing to Shore-
> ham, crowned with the grace of years;
> Shoreham, clad with sunset, glad and grave with glory
> that death reveres.

Finally, part of George Moore's *Esther Waters* is set here; Woodview is modeled on Buckingham House (gone), and Esther visits Swiss Gardens.

SHOTTERY, Warwickshire Shottery, once a village in its own right about 1 mile west of Stratford-on-Avon, is now basically a part of that literary mecca. Here is the cottage, a house of twelve rooms, where the family of Anne Hathaway, William Shakespeare's wife, is supposed to have lived; Richard Hathaway, a yeoman farmer, inherited the property; and, indeed, Hathaways lived in the house from 1470 until 1911. The cottage was purchased by the trustees of the Shakespeare Birthplace Trust in 1892, and the timbered and thatched house and gardens have been carefully restored to their original state. It should be emphasized that there is no clear proof that the cottage was ever Anne Hathaway's home; the assumption is made because about 1750 the Rev. Joseph Greene, then headmaster of the Stratford Grammar School, first wrote:

> His [Shakespeare's] wife was the daughter of one Hathaway, a substantial yeoman in the neighbourhood of Stratford, probably *of a* place about a mile from thence call'd *Luddington*...

He later revised the statement:

> ... probably *at that* place about *half* a mile from thence call'd *Shotteriche,* where a *creditable* family of *the name aforemention'd 'till within these few years resided.*

SHOTTERY   A short distance from the heart of Shakespeare country, Shottery contains what is purported to be the home of Anne Hathaway, who became William Shakespeare's wife in 1582. The timbered building, now smaller than in the 16th century, is called Anne Hathaway's Cottage and is owned by the Shakespeare Birthplace Trust.

The first reference to this cottage as Anne Hathaway's occurs in *Picturesque Views on the Warwickshire Avon* (1795): .

> The cottage in which she is said to have lived with her parents is yet standing, and although I have doubts as to the truth of the relation, I have yet given a faithful representation of it in the annexed view;—it is still occupied by the descendants of her family, who are poor and numerous;—to this same humble cottage I was referred, when pursuing the same inquiry, by the late Mr. Harte of Stratford. . . .

Mr. Harte was a descendant of Shakespeare's sister.

After the 1582 marriage in an unidentified place, it is possible that Shakespeare and his bride (eight years older than he) lived with her parents here before the dramatist went off to London; this suggestion has been made because Shakespeare had no visible means of support and his own father's fortunes were declining and his family increasing, thus precluding his support of the new family. But there is a lot of conjecture about this.

SHREWSBURY, Shropshire (pop. 56,188) Shrewsbury (pronounced "shroz'bry"), 42 miles northwest of Birmingham, in the center of Shropshire, is attractively situated in a loop of the Severn River; two bridges (one English and one Welsh) provide access to the town; and the pink sandstone castle, dating from the 13th century, protects its landward side. Quite possibly the most striking aspect of Shrewsbury is its wealth of black-and-white half-timbered buildings, most of which have been adapted to modern use without any serious loss of antiquity. The houses are generally located on "shuts," very narrow passages

SHREWSBURY Featuring a wealth of black-and-white half-timbered buildings, Shrewsbury is one of the most attractive towns in the heavily industrial North Midlands. The narrow passages, known as shuts, on which many of these houses are located were known to Sir Philip Sidney and Samuel Butler, who attended the Free Grammar School of Edward VI.

whose names are distinctive, even as English street names: Grope Lane, Pride Hill, Butcher Row, Shoplatch, and Dogpole are representative. At the spot where the High Cross once stood, the body of Hotspur was displayed to put an end to the rumors that he was still alive.

Shrewsbury is associated historically with the battle fought in 1403 at Battlefield, 3 miles north of the town. William Shakespeare describes the event in *Henry IV: Part I,* but he has the forces camp "near Shrewsbury," when, in fact, Hotspur actually came here from Chester on his way to meet Owen Glendower and was greeted with the royal banner flying from the castle. Shrewsbury had a significant early history as well, and at one time the Austin, Black, and Gray Friars had flourishing foundations here. Even earlier, Shrewsbury, because of its position astride the main Midland routes leading into Wales, was the seat (then called Pengwern) of the early Welsh princes. Indeed, it was not until after the late-8th-century conquest by the Mercians that Scrobesbyrig became English.

Michael Drayton was impressed by the river and Shrewsbury's location and praises "that faire towne" in *Poly-Olbion;* the Severn

> . . . oft taking leave, oft turnes, it to imbrace;
> As though she onely were enamored of that place,
> Her fore-intended course determined to leave,
> And to that most lov'd Towne eternally to cleave:
> With much ado at length, yet bidding it adue,
> Her journey towards the Sea doth seriously pursue.

Another early traveler, Daniel Defoe, who was here to gather material for *A Tour thro' the Whole Island of Great Britain,* was impressed by the "beautiful, large, pleasant, populous, and rich Town; full of Gentry, and yet full of Trade too":

> This is really a Town of Mirth and Gallantry. . . .
> Over the Market-house is kept a Kind of Hall for the Manufactures . . . they speak all *English* in the Town, but on a Market-Day you would think you were in *Wales.*
> Here is the greatest Market, the greatest Plenty of good Provisions, and the cheapest that is to be met with in all the *Western* Part of *England.* . . .
> Mr. *Cambden* calls it a City: 'Tis at this Day, says he, a fine City well-inhabited: But we do not now call it a City, yet 'tis equal to many good Cities in *England,* and superior to some.

Even William Cobbett, when he was here in 1830 on his tour of the Midlands, found Shrewsbury a pleasant place; he writes in *Rural Rides:*

> Shrewsbury is one of the most interesting spots that ever man beheld. . . . It is curiously enclosed by the river Severn which is here large and fine, and which, in the form of a *horse-shoe,* completely surrounds it, leaving of the whole of the two miles round only one little place whereon to pass in and out on land. . . . The environs of this town, especially on the Welsh side, are the most beautiful that can be conceived. The town lies in the midst of a fine agricultural country, of which it is the great and almost only mart.

Cobbett goes on to discuss economic disparity, the tommy system of paying wages, and immigration. Finally, lamenting that no one takes the *Political Register* or has bought his *Advice to Young Men,* he is still able to conclude, "I cannot quit Shrewsbury without expressing the great satisfaction that I derived from my visit to that place."

Just opposite the castle is the school (now a library, art gallery, and museum), whose operations have been transferred across the river to Kingsland. The schoolrooms have been left intact and are still lined with lockers and woodwork into which the initials of generations of schoolboys have been cut. Part of the original school is often stated to have been a timbered "gable" on School Lane, which both Sir Philip Sidney and Fulke Greville attended. Known as the Free Grammar School of Edward VI, the school was not located on School Lane but in a house on Ratonyslone (Rotten Lane), near the Castle Gate and town prison; the school moved in 1595. Both Sidney and Greville entered it on October 17, 1564, and remained until spring, 1568, or slightly earlier, when they went up to Christ Church and Broadgates Hall, Oxford. Sidney brought a servant, Marshall, and his own famulus, Randall Calcote, with him. A far later literary figure was also a student here; in 1847 Samuel Butler was sent to the school, where his grandfather had been headmaster for almost forty years. Butler's time at school was not a happy one, although it was far superior to the schooling experience at home under his father, who was a strict taskmaster. The Shrewsbury school, according to Butler, was cramped, old, grimy, and dark; and there was no area, except "the low and squalid feeding chambers," for sitting rooms for the younger forms. Dr. Benjamin Kennedy, the headmaster, becomes Dr. Skinner in *The Way of All Flesh;* while the portrait is not a sympathetic one, Butler considered it faithful. The novelist remained here until 1854, when he went up to St. John's College, Cambridge. A little later Stanley Weyman entered the school from the Ludlow Grammar School. Shrewsbury School had a tuck shop as early as the 16th century, and even at that time the students could buy the famous Shrewsbury cakes there; the shop front now quotes from Richard Harris Barham's *The Ingoldsby Legends;*

On, Pailin, Prince of Cake Compounders,
The mouth liquifies at the very sound of thy name.

Barham's legend is a little changed from the original, which appeared in "A Legend of Shropshire."

The most famous native son of Shrewsbury is Charles Darwin, who was born at the Mount on February 12, 1809, and spent seven years at Shrewsbury School. Numerous literary figures also have distinct associations with the town. Shrewsbury was the birthplace, around 1520, of Thomas Churchyard, often described as a "miscellaneous writer," who was a contributor to *A Mirror for Magistrates.* Little is known about his childhood except that at an early age he was attached to the Earl of Surrey's household. In 1705 George Farquhar, the Irish-born dramatist, was in Shrewsbury and stayed at the Raven Inn (demolished 1954) on Castle Street. Here he wrote *The Recruiting Officer,* which he dedicated "To All Friends round the Wrekin," for

The kingdom cannot show better bodies of men, better inclinations for the service, more generosity, more good understanding, nor more politeness, than is to be found at the foot of the Wrekin.

This play, which depicts local life, is an accurate representation of the early-18th-century town and some of its inhabitants.

At the end of the 18th century Samuel Taylor Coleridge was in Shrewsbury as a prospective candidate for the vacant ministerial post and was invited to preach at the Unitarian Chapel in January 1798. However, he had already decided that he could not accept the post when he heard of the pledge of a £150 annuity from the Wedgwood brothers, whose generosity was intended, as Coleridge stated, "to prevent . . . his going into the ministry," a calling for which they thought he was unsuited. Coleridge eventually returned their money. William Hazlitt, then aged twenty, was living with his father, also a dissenting minister, in Wem. He walked to Shrewsbury to hear Coleridge preach and recalls the experience in "My First Acquaintance with Poets":

It was in January, 1798, that I rose one morning before daylight, to walk ten miles in the mud, and went to hear this celebrated person preach. Never, the longest day I have to live, shall I have another walk as this cold, raw, comfortless one, in the winter of the year 1798. . . . When I got there, the organ was playing the 100th psalm, and, when it was done, Mr Coleridge rose and gave out his text, "And he went up into the mountain to pray, HIMSELF ALONE." As he gave out his text, his voice "rose like a steam of rich distilled perfumes," and when he came to the last two words, which he pronounced loud, deep, and distinct, it seemed to me, who was then young, as if the sounds had echoed from the bottom of the human heart, and as if that prayer might have floated in solemn silence through the universe.

A few years later, in November 1802, Thomas De Quincey arrived in Shrewsbury on his way to London from Wales; without money and friends he spent the night at an unremembered inn where he received

the exceptional treatment of being given sleeping accommodations in the unused ballroom.

In 1838 Charles Dickens and Phiz (Hablot Knight Browne) were in Shrewsbury; this was the first time Dickens stopped here. Their accommodations in the old coaching inn, the Lion Hotel, are described in a letter to Dickens's elder daughter:

We have the strangest little rooms (sitting-room and two bedrooms altogether), the ceilings of which I can touch with my hand. The windows bulge out over the street, as if they were little stern windows in a ship. And a door opens out of the sitting-room on to a little open gallery with plants in it, where one leans over a queer old rail, and looks all downhill and slant-wise at the crookedest black and yellow old houses, all manner of shapes. To get into this room we come through a china closet. . . .

Most of the old inn has been rebuilt, and inevitably only some of the atmosphere of Dickens's time survives. The town of Shrewsbury may be described in *The Old Curiosity Shop;* the same claim is made by Shifnal:

In the streets were a number of old houses, built of a kind of earth or plaster, crossed and recrossed in a great many directions with black beams, which gave them a remarkable and very ancient look. The doors, too, were arched and low, some with oaken portals and quaint benches, where the former inhabitants had sat on summer evenings. The windows were latticed in little diamond panes, that seemed to wink and blink upon the passengers as if they were dim of sight.

Dickens and Browne attended a bespeak (benefit) at the theater on their first night in town and thoroughly enjoyed themselves; so funny did Phiz find the actors that the "indecent heartiness" of his laughter, according to Dickens, made the man in the next box suffer "the most violent indigestion." Dickens stayed a second time at the Lion Hotel in 1858, while on a provincial reading tour.

A. E. Housman, as would be expected, includes Shrewsbury in *A Shropshire Lad;* the section entitled "The Welsh Marches" refers to this area in a historical context:

High the vanes of Shrewsbury gleam
Islanded in Severn stream;
The bridges from the steepled crest
Cross the water east and west.

The flag of morn in conqueror's state
Enters at the English gate:
The vanquished eve, as night prevails,
Bleeds upon the road to Wales.

During World War I Hilaire Belloc lectured here. Finally, Mary Webb, a Shropshire novelist, was buried here in 1927. Her novels, by and large, are romantic pictures of Shropshire life, set in the northern part of the county, and Shrewsbury is Silverton.

SIDMOUTH, Devon (pop. 8,448) Sidmouth, lying where the Sid River cuts through the high cliffs into Sidmouth Bay, was an extremely fashionable resort area in the 19th century. It still is an attractive seaside resort with subtropical vegetation, but more than 35 percent of its present residents are old-age pensioners. The consequence is that the economic base of the community revolves around the vacationer and the pensioner. The town contains many

Regency and Victorian buildings, although a few old cottages are still inhabited by the remaining local fishermen.

On Jane Austen's summer holiday here with her family in 1801, she is supposed to have met the man whom she might have married if he had not died quite suddenly soon after they reached an understanding. In September 1814, as the result of a fairly long correspondence with Charlotte Ridout, George Crabbe came here to meet her and to propose; Crabbe's first wife had died in 1813, and he frequently expressed a strong desire to remarry. An entry in cipher in his diary for September 26 relates his declaration and her acceptance. But this affair came to nothing; at some time after December 12 that year one of the parties broke the engagement.

In 1833 Sidmouth was a fashionable watering place, and Elizabeth Barrett (Browning) and her family came here for a stay of just over two years. They leased 7–8 Fortfield Terrace, the house, Elizabeth Barrett writes, "which the Grand Duchess Helena had, not at all *grand*, but extremely comfortable and cheerful." (The house is now apartments.) In the late spring of 1833 they moved into a "ruinous house" (unidentified, but 7–8 Fortfield Terrace may have been two houses) before taking a rather spacious Georgian house called Belle Vue, about five minutes' walk to the beach. The house (now the Cedar Shade Hotel) looked out over the cricket green and the Esplanade. The Barretts remained at Belle Vue until the summer of 1835, when they moved to what the poet called their "ancient house upon the beach," where they remained until leaving for London. "The Sea-Mew" and "The Little Friend," both written for the Rev. George Hunter's daughter Mary, date from this period.

Sidmouth becomes the seaside town of Baymouth in William Makepeace Thackeray's *Pendennis*. One major scene, the ball, is set here, but Baymouth is where, early in the novel, Pendennis comes to see Mr. Foker. Not finding Foker at his lodgings, Pen

went down to the rock, and walked about on the sand, biting his nails by the shore of the much-sounding sea. It stretched before him bright and immeasurable. The blue waters came rolling into the bay, foaming and roaring hoarsely....

The town also merits mention in *Pendennis* as the spa where the Countess Dowager of Rockminster has a house on the Marine Parade and where the Earl of Trehawke, Lord Lieutenant of Devon, visits. H. G. Wells places his story "The Sea Raiders" in Sidmouth; here the curate, the seaman, and the two schoolboys see the school of giant and intelligent octopuses making one of their south-coast raids.

Two 20-century figures who have been to Sidmouth are Rupert Brooke, who spent part of his April 1909 vacation from King's College, Cambridge, with his family at a house on the Esplanade, and George Bernard Shaw, who spent several weeks in April 1919 at the Victoria Hotel on the Esplanade in an attempt to recover from pernicious anemia.

SILCHESTER, Hampshire (pop. 390) Located on the northern edge of Hampshire only a few miles from Reading, Silchester has had a strange history. Once a Roman town called Calleva Atrebatum and a rival of Winchester as one of the two most important towns in the area, it unaccountably ceased to exist and, indeed, has proved impossible to dig up. Founded on the site of an earlier Celtic community, the Roman town had streets laid out in typical Roman fashion leading to the Forum, three temples, and an amphitheater outside the walls. Silchester was the usual prosperous Roman colony, but for some reason it was abandoned, and now the only survivals are the high city walls, more than a mile in circumference. Only after the Middle Ages was the area resettled.

Geoffrey of Monmouth, in his *Historia Regum Britanniae*, notes: "After the death of Uther Pendragon, the leaders of the Britons assembled from their various provinces in the town of Silchester," where Dubricius was the Archbishop of the City of Legions. Here the fifteen-year-old Arthur was crowned King of Britain by Dubricius under circumstances of extreme urgency, for the Saxons, hearing of Uther's death, had already overrun large areas.

SILKSTONE, Yorkshire (pop. 1,652) On the edge of the moors 4 miles west of Barnsley in the West Riding of Yorkshire is Silkstone, a small village with an interesting association with the Robin Hood legend. Canon Hall, which sits in a woodland about a mile from the village, contains a bow known as Little John's and traditionally associated with that most powerful of archers. The bow, which requires 160 pounds of force to draw it fully, has been at Canon Hall since the 18th century, when the owners of Hathersage Hall succeeded to this estate (Little John is said to be buried in Hathersage). There is no explanation of how the bow came to be retained at Hathersage Hall or why it was constructed to need so much force.

SILSOE, Bedfordshire (pop. 585) This is a pleasant little village of many thatched or tile-roofed cottages with projecting upper stories, 3½ miles southwest of Ampthill. The pride of the village is Wrest House and Park, longtime home of the Grey family. The Greys held the estate for nearly seven centuries, from about 1280 until after World War I, when the family line died out. Today's pavilion was the original banqueting house, where important banquets were held, but the present manor house (holding the National Institute of Agricultural Engineers) dates from the 19th century, when Earl de Grey destroyed all the old structure and built the French-style house. This is not the house John Selden knew when he was steward to Henry Grey, 9th Earl of Kent, or when he visited later. Another household member was Samuel Butler, who was employed by Elizabeth, Countess of Kent, around 1628; Butler spent several years here and painted in his leisure. Thomas Carew was a frequent visitor to the seat and wrote in general of his visits in "To My Friend G. N., from Wrest":

I breathe, sweet Ghib, the temperate air of Wrest,
Where I, no more with raging storms oppress'd,
Wear the cold nights out by the banks of Tweed,
On the bleak mountains, where fierce tempests breed,
And everlasting winter dwells; where mild
Favonius and the vernal winds exiled,
Did never spread their wings; but the wild north
Brings sterile fern, thistles and brambles forth....

SILVERDALE, Lancashire (pop. 895) On the northeast edge of Morecambe Bay, Silverdale has a good view toward Piel Island, Walney Island, and, on clear days, the Isle of Man as well as the northernmost mountains of Wales. To the east, from Castlebarrow Head, one can see to Black Combe, Cumberland, and the fells of Westmorland. Silverdale was a refuge from Manchester for Elizabeth Gaskell, who frequently stayed here at Lindeth (Gilbraltar) Tower and planned and wrote many of her novels here. Her study was at the top of the tower. Silverdale is the most likely candidate for Abermouth in *Ruth*. Charlotte Brontë is said to have stayed in the village as a girl, but nothing more is known.

SISSINGHURST, Kent (pop. 1,004) The beautiful and calm appearance of Sissinghurst Castle, 1½ miles northeast of Cranbrook, gives no indication of its bloody and horrendous history. It was built by Sir John Baker (known posthumously as Bloody Baker for his sadistic torture of Protestants during Mary Tudor's reign) and probably finished by his son, Sir Richard. Family fortunes declined steadily, however, and so did the house. Even so, in 1752 Horace Walpole was able to comment:

> You go through an arch of the stables to the house, the court of which is perfect and very beautiful. This has a good apartment, and to a fine gallery a hundred and twenty feet by eighteen, which takes up one side: the wainscot is pretty and entire; the ceiling vaulted and painted in a light genteel grotesque. The whole is built for show; for the back of the house is nothing but lath and plaster.

The billeting of French prisoners here during the Napoleonic Wars brought complete decay. One of the officers on guard duty during the Seven Years' War was the historian Edward Gibbon, who commented that "the duty was hard, the dirt oppressive." The woodwork was stripped off for firewood, and about 1800 the main mansion was demolished; what was left, however, was turned into one of the beauty spots of Kent by Victoria Sackville-West and her husband Sir Harold Nicolson when they bought the structure in 1930. She writes of finding the place:

> I fell in love; love at first sight. I saw what might be made of it. It was Sleeping Beauty's Castle: but a castle running away into sordidness and squalor; a garden crying out for rescue.

Over the next ten years they restored the house and gardens; the first floor of the tower contained Victoria Sackville-West's study, and here she wrote *All Passion Spent* and *The Eagle and the Dove*. The gardens which the Nicolsons created are virtually open-air rooms, especially the White Garden with its gray or white plants only, the basically medieval herb garden with fennel, woad, tansy, and carraway, and the formal rose gardens. Victoria Sackville-West died in the Priest's House (16th-century) by the White Garden in 1962. One of the most frequent guests here was Virginia Stephen Woolf; she and her husband were first here in September 1930 and returned often.

Richard Church also made his home at the Priest's House, where he died in 1972.

SITTENHAM, Yorkshire In the Vale of Pickering 4 miles southwest of Malton, Sittenham was the birthplace of the poet John Gower about 1320. Gower's family also possessed considerable estates in Nottinghamshire and Suffolk, and information at Sitten-

ham is extremely scanty. However, it is known that Gower was reported back in the village on a visit from London in 1346, when he witnessed a local deed and signed the document. A century or so later a note of identification reading "Sir John Gower the Poet" was added to the document.

SKIPTON, Yorkshire (pop. 12,840) Down from the eastern heights of the Pennines in one of the dales on the Aire River is Skipton, a busy market town on the once-active Liverpool–Leeds Canal. The canal, still open, is used generally for pleasure craft, and summer tourists often arrive by water to see the great castle of the Cliffords. The 14th- to 17th-century castle and the partly 14th-century Church of the Holy Trinity are at the top of the High Street commanding an imposing view of the town. One gateway of the original Norman castle is still standing, and another gateway contains the famous shell room, built of sea shells and fossils collected on the 3d Earl of Cumberland's voyages. The tiny interior courtyard has many carved armorial bearings; on one of them the wyvern supporters unmistakably belong to William Shakespeare's "boist'rous Clifford," who died at Ferrybridge. In the courtyard is a yew tree planted by Lady Anne Clifford, whose tutor Samuel Daniel became in the 1590s. Lady Anne experienced two unsuccessful marriages and finally devoted herself to books and the contemplative life, in which Daniel figured.

Both Edward Bulwer-Lytton, with *Eugene Aram*, and Thomas Hood, with *The Dream of Eugene Aram*, have associations with Skipton. The real Eugene Aram, a schoolmaster from Knaresborough, Yorkshire, who was tried and convicted in York of the murder of Daniel Clarke, lived here for a short time before his marriage to Annie Spence (Madeline Lester in the novel) and after their marriage before moving to Lofthouse, Yorkshire.

SKIPTON Holy Trinity Church, which is partly 14th-century, is still much as it was when Samuel Daniel, tutor to Lady Anne Clifford, lived with the Cliffords in the castle. The church was also the scene of the marriage of the real Eugene Aram to Annie Spence.

Skipton was the home of Rudyard Kipling's paternal grandmother, with whom he spent the long summer holiday of 1882 after his last term at the United Services College in Westward Ho! in Devon. Kipling wrote only one Yorkshire-based story, "On Greenhow Hill," in which Private Learoyd (who appears in a number of Kipling's stories) describes his childhood and youth in Skipton.

SLINDON, Sussex (pop. 546)   The edge of the Arun Valley, where Slindon is located 3½ miles west of Arundel, is an area of impressive natural beauty. The flint-and-stone village has a dramatic location on the slope of the Downs with a view southward to the sea, and the main street rises steeply to a miniature village square which caps the hill. Slindon Cottage (actually the dower house of the Slindon estate, an area of 3,500 protected woodland acres) became the home of Hilaire Belloc in July 1878. The house lies in the southern end of the Fairmile Bottom, about half a mile from the main road. When here, Belloc occasionally attended mass at St. Philip Neri in Arundel. After spending the summer of 1879 in France, Belloc left Slindon, but he returned in 1905 when he leased Courthill Farm, a Georgian house on the northern slope of the hill behind the town.

Belloc's love of Sussex, the Weald, and its people is clearly defined in "The South Country":

> I will gather and carefully make my friends
>   Of the men of the Sussex Weald,
> They watch the stars from silent folds,
>   They stiffly plough the field.
> By them and the God of the South Country
>   My poor soul shall be healed.
>
> If I ever become a rich man,
>   Or if ever I grow to be old,
> I will build a house with deep thatch
>   To shelter me from the cold,
> And there shall the Sussex songs be sung
>   And the story of Sussex told.

Belloc's mother died here at the age of ninety-five on March 29, 1925, and is buried here.

SLOUGH, Buckinghamshire (pop. 84,210)   Slough (pronounced "slow" to rhyme with "cow") has long been an industrial center and was at one time the source of a famous panacea, Elliman's Embrocation, a liniment whose qualities made its originator a millionaire. The formula is still prepared in the town, but now it is done under the auspices of the Horlicks complex. Three other famous products were the results of local ingenuity: both the crimson rambler rose and Cox's Orange Pippins were developed here, and the well-known Mrs. Simkins Pink was the result of the work of a matron at the Slough Workhouse.

Only one literary association of consequence exists here, and that is with the side of Charles Dickens's life that was generally kept under Victorian wraps. Around 1866 or 1867 he lived at Elizabeth Cottage on the south side of the High Street; the cottage burned down in 1889, and a shop now stands at Numbers 162 and 164 on the site. Dickens came here with Ellen Ternan when he was attempting to evade Victorian convention. *Our Mutual Friend* documents his impressions of the area between High Wycombe and Slough.

SNAILBEACH, Shropshire   A tiny hamlet in the Hope Valley 2 miles south of Minsterley, Snailbeach has a small chapel which comes into literature as the chapel used by the mining community in Mary Webb's *Gone to Earth:*

> The chapel and minister's house at God's Little Mountain were all in one—a long, low building of grey stone surrounded by the graveyard, where stones, flat, erect, and askew, took the place of a flower-garden. Away to the left, just over a rise, the hill was gashed by the grey steeps of the quarries.

SNITTERFIELD, Warwickshire (pop. 691)   Overshadowed by Stratford-on-Avon, 3½ miles to the south, Snitterfield has a special place in Shakespeare country, for this was the birthplace of his father John as well as the home of his grandfather Richard and his uncle Henry until their deaths. The village is high-lying, and its 13th-century church, which was once in the Worcester diocese, is ringed with elms, while the churchyard is approached by an avenue of firs. One of the outstanding features of the church is the woodwork in the chancel, especially the altar rails and the stall fronts; another is the 14th-century font with eight carved heads.

In addition to the Shakespearean associations here, which are actually based on conjecture (even though it is reasonable to assume the dramatist knew the area well), the poet Richard Jago was appointed curate here in 1737. Born in Beaudesert and educated at Solihull and at University College, Oxford, he gained the living here in 1754 through the support of Viscount Clare (later Earl Nugent). With a family of seven children to support, he also held the livings of Harbury, Warwickshire, and Chesterton, Warwickshire; these benefices, though, were given up in 1771, when he gained the living of Kimcote, Leicestershire. Jago's permanent residence throughout was in the rectory at Snitterfield; here he undertook many improvements to the vicarage and grounds, and his daughters planted the group of three silver birch trees, known as "the three ladies," on the lawn. Jago died here on May 8, 1781, and was buried in a family vault under the middle aisle of the church. A memorial slab which had been set in the floor of the nave has since been moved to the vestry.

SOAR RIVER   The 40-mile-long Soar River rises on the east border of Warwickshire and flows northeast and northwest to the Trent; along its way it flows through Charnwood Forest, one of the most beautiful sections of Leicestershire. Its beauty and location so greatly impressed Michael Drayton that he devotes an unusually large passage in *Poly-Olbion* to his memories of days when he and others were guests of the Beaumont family at Grace Dieu Priory in Belton. The point from which Drayton views the river, "On Sharpley . . . and Cadmans aged rocks," was only a few minutes' walk from the Beaumont estate:

> O Charnwood, be thou cald the choycest of thy kind,
> The like in any place, what flood hath hapt to find?
> No tract in all this isle, the proudest let her be,
> Can shew a sylvan nymph, for beautie like to thee. . . .

Geoffrey of Monmouth involves the Soar River in his story of King Leir and his three daughters:

Three years later Leir died; and Aganippus, King of the Franks, died too. As a result Leir's daughter Cordelia inherited the government of the kingdom of Britain. She buried her father in a certain under-ground chamber which she had ordered to be dug beneath the River Soar, some way downstream from Leicester.

SOCKBURN, County Durham (pop. 37) Difficult of access because it is hemmed in by the Tees River on three sides and lacks a bridge to cross the river, Sockburn is a small community at the southernmost tip of the county and can only be reached from the north, through Yorkshire. Sockburn Farm, almost centrally located in the peninsula, is where William and Dorothy Wordsworth came in the spring of 1799 on their return from Germany. The 18th-century brick house with tall chimneys (still as it was then, except for a late Victorian door) belonged to Thomas Hutchinson, the great-uncle of Wordsworth's future wife. Here during the winter of 1799 William Wordsworth fell in love with Mary Hutchinson and worked on parts of *The Prelude* and "The Poet's Epitaph." In October 1799, Wordsworth and his sister were joined by Samuel Taylor Coleridge, whose experiences here did not have the happy consequences of Wordsworth's. In the space of two days, the length of his visit, Coleridge, already a married man with a family, fell in love with Sara Hutchinson, Mary's sister. Part of the inspiration for "Love," which he wrote here, was prompted by his visit to the little Sockburn Church, now in ruins, only a short distance from the house. In the church was the effigy of the worm-conqueror Conyers; Sara

> . . . lean'd against the armed man
> The statue of the armed Knight;
> She stood and listen'd to my lay,
>   Amid the lingering light.

The legend of the Worm of Sockburn to which this poem refers is one of the many northern legends concerning a dragon or "fiery flying serpent." In this case the legend is a bit sketchy: Sir John Conyers, lord of the manor, slew the "worm" in the field just outside the farmhouse, but that is basically the extent of traditional knowledge. The worm's crime, traditionally is that of devouring man, woman, and child, but according to a late verse fragment, probably written in the 19th century by the historian Robert Surtees, it is that of eating the Bishop of Durham. From the time of Richard I (r. 1189–1199) until the dissolution of the county palatine in 1836, every bishop upon first entering his diocese, either on the ancient Croft Bridge or in the middle of the Tees River, was met by the lord of Sockburn manor. The bishop was presented with the falchion (now in Durham Cathedral Museum) with which "the champion Conyers slew the worm, dragon, or fiery flying serpent." After taking the falchion, the bishop returned it to the lord of Sockburn and wished him health and enjoyment of the manor. Wordsworth, when cutting across the field from the Northallerton Road, passed the large limestone marker showing the worm's grave; the marker is still in the field.

SOLIHULL, Warwickshire (pop. 52,243) Today the sprawl of Birmingham, 6 miles to the northwest, reaches Solihull, and it is probably only a matter of time before the pleasant mixture of old and new here

disappears. Timber-frame houses and shops line the High Street; and the partly 13th-century church is dedicated to Alphege (Aelfheah), the Archbishop of Canterbury martyred by the Danes in 1012. The well-known Solihull School (rebuilt 1882) dates from about 1560 (it was one of a number founded by Edward VI) and not from 1381, a date often suggested as its beginning. Among the scholars at the school were William Shenstone, who came here from Sarah Lloyd's school in Halesowen, and Richard Jago, another minor poet, who was a classmate and lifelong friend. There is a near association with Samuel Johnson, who applied for a schoolmaster's post here and was rejected by the trustees on the grounds that

> he has the caracter of being a very haughty ill-natured gent: and y^t he has such a way of distorting his fface (w^h though he cannot help) ye gent(lemen) think it may affect some young lads.

SOMERSBY, Lincolnshire (pop. 44) At the southern end of the Wolds, 5½ miles northeast of Horncastle, Somersby is the heart of the Tennyson country; the village looks south to the Fens and has fine views toward the sea and down the Lymm Valley. Dr. George Clayton Tennyson took the living here in 1808, and on August 6, 1809, Alfred Tennyson was born in the two-story rectory. The fourth of twelve children, he was baptized in the partly 18th-century church two days after his birth. The old rectory, with a pantiled roof, an oriel window, and a second-story iron balcony, has an unusual feature of a hall, or refectory, which Dr. Tennyson and a servant built to feed and educate the large family; it has tall windows and gables. This, of course, is the hall which figures in *In Memoriam:*

> At our old pastimes in the hall
>   We gambolled, making vain pretence
>   Of gladness, with an awful sense
> Of one mute Shadow watching all.

The pleasant drawing room, lined with books, overlooked the trim and tidy lawn, one side bordered with elms and the other with larches and sycamores; just beyond a lily and rose border lay

> A garden bower'd close
> With plaited alleys of the trailing rose,
> Long alleys falling down to twilight grots,
> Or opening upon level plots
> Of crowned lilies, standing near
> Purple-spiked lavender. . . .

This sloped down to the parson's field, where the swift brook of "Ode to Memory" ran; it

>   loves
> To purl o'er matted cress and ribbed sand,
> Or dimple in the dark of rushy coves,
> Drawing into his narrow earthen urn,
>   In every elbow and turn,
> The filtered tribute of the rough woodland. . . .

The brook is more fully delineated in "A Farewell" and is also described in *In Memoriam*. This stream, it should be noted, is not the one described in "The Brook."

At the age of eight Alfred was sent to the grammar school at Louth, where he spent a miserable four years before being allowed to return to Somersby to tutelage by his father. The Reverend Dr. Tennyson, although a stern taskmaster, was an excellent (but self-taught) scholar, and the boys had regular instruction in Latin and Greek, the fine arts, mathematics, and natural science; indeed, after Louth, this was their only education until they took their places at Trinity College, Cambridge, in 1828. Dr. Tennyson died in 1831 and was buried in a plain tomb west of the tower of the church, and on a Christmas Eve, years later, the poet reflected:

> Tonight ungathered let us leave
> This laurel, let this holly stand:
>   We live within the stranger's land,
> And strangely falls our Christmas-eve.
>
> Our father's dust is left alone
>   And silent under other snows:
>   There in due time the woodbine blows,
> The violet comes, but we are gone.

"The Two Voices," published in 1842 and dated 1833, refers to services at the Somersby church:

> Like softened airs that blowing steal,
> When meres begin to uncongeal,
> The sweet church bells began to peal.
>
> On to God's house the people prest:
> Passing the place where each must rest,
> Each entered like a welcome guest.

The new incumbent at Somersby allowed the Tennyson family to remain at the old rectory, and they did so for six years. Here Tennyson wrote in his attic study, which was approached by a dark and difficult private staircase:

> O darling room, my heart's delight,
> Dear room, the apple of my sight,
> With thy two couches soft and white,
> There is no room so exquisite,
> No little room so warm and bright,
> Wherein to read, wherein to write.

From their meeting at Cambridge until his death, Arthur Henry Hallam was a frequent guest of the Tennyson family, and a great bond grew up between Hallam and, especially, the poet's mother. In *In Memoriam* Tennyson later recalls these visits:

> O bliss, when all in circle drawn
>   About him, heart and ear were fed
>   To hear him, as he lay and read
> The Tuscan poets on the lawn:
>
> Or in the all-golden afternoon
>   A guest, or happy sister, sung,
>   Or here she brought the harp and flung
> A ballad to the brightening moon. . . .

One of the poet's favorite walks from the garden rivulet went north beyond the stream toward Tetford. He describes the deeply chaneled brook in "Geraint and Enid":

> But at the flash and motion of the man
> They vanished panic-stricken, like a shoal
> Of darting fish, that on a summer morn
> Adown the crystal dykes at Camelot
> Come slipping o'er their shadows on the sand,
> But if a man who stands upon the brink
> But lift a shining hand against the sun,
> There is not left the twinkle of a fin
> Betwixt the cressy islets white in flower. . . .

In the two-year period before Tennyson and his mother moved to High Beech, Essex, Edward FitzGerald was a frequent guest at Somersby and, like Hallam, was especially fond of Mrs. Tennyson. He referred to her as "[o]ne of the most innocent and tender-hearted ladies I ever saw."

SOULDERN, Oxfordshire (pop. 402)   Deep in a woodland hollow 7 miles southeast of Banbury, Souldern has been inhabited at least since Saxon times, for here is a pagan Saxon cemetery which has yielded pottery fragments known to have been made before A.D. 500. The rebuilt Norman church has an avenue of may trees leading to it, and the small Norman north doorway is still in place. Much of Souldern is as William Wordsworth knew it when he frequently came to visit his college friend Robert Jones, who was rector here. Wordsworth describes the church and its environs in notes to his *Ecclesiastical Sonnets*, No. XVIII, "Pastoral Character," and delineates the holy and unholy ground, now marked by the distinguishing line of a wall, after a visit in the summer of 1820:

> Where holy ground begins, unhallowed ends,
> Is marked by no distinguishable line:
> The turf unites, the pathways intertwine;
> And, whereso'er the stealing footsteps tends,
> Garden, and that Domain where kindred, friends,
> And neighbours rest together, here confound
> Their several features, mingled like the sound
> Of many waters, or as evening blends
> With shady night.

SOUTH CADBURY, Somerset (pop. 135)   Southern Somerset villages are often especially pleasing, quite frequently secluded, and occasionally interesting; and South Cadbury, 8½ miles northeast of Yeovil, has all these attractions. On a nearby hill is Cadbury Castle, an earthwork fort known to have been a town and fortress for more than 4,000 years. Archaeological excavations in 1967 established that the hill fort was refortified around A.D. 500, at about the time the Saxons arrived, for here a new leader arose to oppose the invading Saxons. Tradition has for centuries maintained that Cadbury Castle is King Arthur's Camelot, and part of the reason for the 1967 excavations was to find some sort of historical evidence to support the legend. Although the evidence did not establish that this was Camelot, the 6th-century refurbishment was found to be on a large scale, and the discovery of extensive pottery fragments pointed to a relatively wealthy community. Michael Drayton describes "*Arthurs* ancient seat" in *Poly-Olbion* and places it here. The gloss explains:

> By South *Cadbury* is that *Camelot;* a hill of a mile compasse at the top, foure trenches circling it, and twixt every of them an earthen wall; the content of it, within, about xx. acres. . . . Antique report makes this one of *Arthurs* places of his Round Table, as the Muse here sings.

Drayton, though, simply adds his own view to the well-known traditions which, assuming a Camelot, seek to locate it. Sir Thomas Malory sets Arthur's residence at Camelot but identifies it no further, and although glossaries appended to *Le Morte d'Arthur* have suggested, rather without basis, that Camelot is to be identified with Winchester, Malory specifically uses Winchester under its own name, and it would seem that Camelot must have another identity.

From 1754 to 1756 Charles Churchill was curate in South Cadbury.

SOUTH HARTING, Sussex Set securely at the foot of the hills near the Hampshire border, the Hartings are a group of small hamlets noted for their church, often referred to as the Cathedral of the Downs, and for their marvelous downland walks. The village main street is lined with red-brick Georgian houses; Ladyhold Park (gone), outside the village, was visited by Alexander Pope when John Caryll owned it. The Grange (now Northend House) was the home of Anthony Trollope during the last years of his life; he moved here in 1880 and maintained his astonishing writing schedule until he suffered a stroke in 1882. Believing himself to be an uninspired journeyman, he insisted on writing 2,500 words every day, not in itself an immense number, at the rate of 250 words every fifteen minutes between 5:30 A.M. and breakfast. Trollope died in London, after a stroke, on December 6, 1882, and was buried here; at the time of his death he was at work on *The Land-Leaguers*. A case in the partly 13th-century church contains Trollope's paperknife, pen, and letter scales.

Both H. G. Wells and Hilaire Belloc used South Harting in their works. Wells states, "Both the Ship and the Coach and Horses were excellent inns" in *The Research Magnificent:*

> From Haslemere he [Benham] . . . had wandered into a pretty district beset with Hartings. He had found himself upon a sandy ridge looking very beautifully into a sudden steep valley that he learned was Harting Coombe; he had been through a West Harting and a South Harting and read finger-posts pointing to others of the clan. . . .

Here also Belloc leaves his traveling companions to return home in *The Four Men:*

> "Come back with me," I said, "along the crest of the Downs; we will overlook together the groves at Lavington and the steep at Bury Combe, and then we will turn south and reach a house I know of upon the shingle . . . and to-night once more, and if you will for the last time, by another fire we will sing yet louder songs, and mix them with the noise of the sea."
> But Grizzlebeard would not even linger.

SOUTH HINKSEY, Berkshire (pop. 312) Two separate hamlets named North and South Hinksey exist side by side a little more than 1 mile south of Oxford. South Hinksey is on the Thames River; while there was an Anglo-Saxon settlement here, little else is known of its ancient history. The closeness of the village to Oxford is part of the reason that Matthew Arnold includes it in the landscape of *The Scholar-Gipsy:*

> And once, in winter, on the causeway chill
> Where home through flooded fields foot-travellers go,
> Have I not pass'd thee on the wooden bridge,
> Wrapt in thy cloak and battling with the snow,
> Thy face toward Hinksey and its wintry ridge?

The path the gipsy used has pretty much lost its view, but Oxford's towers and spires can still be seen from the road. Here, too, is Bagley Wood, where

> In autumn, on the skirts of Bagley Wood—
> . . . most the gipsies by the turf-edged way
> Pitch their smoked tents. . . .

SOUTH LEIGH, Oxfordshire (pop. 327) South Leigh, 7 miles northwest of Oxford, is set in attractive meadowland. The village church contains an exceptional gallery of 14th- and 15th-century sacred wall paintings which survived under layers of Puritan whitewash. The paintings were in such fine shape that when the whitewash was stripped off, they could be restored line by line. John Wesley preached his first sermon in this church in 1725.

Not until the 20th century did South Leigh have any sort of literary association, and then it was as if a dervish had appeared upon the scene. In 1947 Margaret Taylor bought the Manor House, a whitewashed cottage without any modern conveniences, to house Dylan Thomas and his family. It was a very large cottage in a field at the far end of the straggling village, and after the Thomases arrived, village life was never the same. Everyone, for example, knew what happened after Thomas had a caravan (ostensibly his studio) brought to the back garden of the house; Caitlin Thomas, who knew her husband's drinking habits, in a fit of pique tried to tip the caravan over, with Thomas inside. He promptly had his studio moved to the other side of the village next to the pub. Shortly before the Thomases left in early 1949, an incident occurred which South Leigh still recalls each Christmas. Just before the holiday, Thomas bicycled to nearby Whitney to do some Christmas shopping and, of course, had the requisite number of beers to put him in the proper spirit; cycling home with a basket full of nuts, he collided with a lorry. An old woman going by commented, "You've spilt your nuts, sonny!" and did not stop. Thomas was taken to Radcliffe Infirmary with a broken tooth and a broken arm. As the ambulance took him home, he was able to persuade the men of the brigade to stop at every pub on the way.

SOUTH MOLTON, Devon (pop. 2,832) Central Devon is squeezed between the heights of Dartmoor and Exmoor, and its northernmost point is the hilly market town of South Molton. On the Mole River 10½ miles southeast of Barnstaple, South Molton is an ancient town known to have been settled before the Norman Conquest. It is known especially because Charles II was first proclaimed King here in 1660. The grammar school, endowed originally in 1686, was apparently attended by R. D. Blackmore as a weekly boarder in 1833; he would ride down the Charles Hill in a pony carriage on Monday mornings and return to the rectory in Charles on Friday or Saturday night. Blackmore uses the town in *Lorna Doone* and attempts to characterize it when he writes, "Southmolton is a busy place for talking." Doubtless he meant to brand the town, but gossiping is anything but unusual in small towns and villages anywhere. The George Hotel on Broad Street also enters the novel as the place where Master Stickles fills the brandy bottle which saves his life:

> ". . . I happened to have a little flat bottle of the best stoneware slung beneath my saddle-cloak, and filled with the very best *eau de vie*, from the George Hotel, at Southmolton. The brand of it now is upon my back. Oh, the murderous scoundrels, what a brave spirit they have spilled!"

SOUTH NORWOOD, Surrey (pop. 15,391) South Norwood, 10 miles south of London Bridge, was originally an ecclesiastical district in the larger parish of Croyden; however, since Croyden is now one of the outer boroughs of Greater London, South Norwood is technically in London. When Sir Arthur Conan Doyle found a house here at 12 Tennison Road in June 1890, there was still a great deal of the country about South Norwood, and the Surrey hills could be seen in the distance. The house, a red-brick building with white windows, had a balcony over the front door and a rather large walled-in garden. Doyle was on a strict writing schedule when he was here, working from 8 A.M. until noon and from 5 until 8 P.M., and in fairly rapid succession he produced "The Adventure of the Blue Carbuncle," "The Adventure of the Speckled Band," "The Adventure of the Noble Bachelor," "The Adventure of the Engineer's Thumb," and "The Adventure of the Beryl Coroneto." At this point, as he wrote to "Ma'am," as he called his mother, he was considering "slaying Holmes in the last and winding him up for good and all. He takes my mind from better things." Ma'am, though, was horrified at the thought and refused to countenance the idea. "The Adventure of the Copper Beeches" followed, and *The Refugees* was finished in early 1892 at about the time that *The Strand* magazine asked Doyle for more Sherlock. In a fit of exasperation, he responded to the request, as he wrote to Ma'am, "Under pressure I offered to do a dozen for a thousand pounds, but I sincerely hope that they won't accept it now." They did, and Doyle wrote. In 1893, when Doyle's wife was diagnosed as tubercular, they left for Switzerland, living there off and on until Doyle's trip to the United States in September 1894.

SOUTH WINGFIELD, Derbyshire (pop. 1,605) Astride the old Roman road running 2 miles west of Alfreton, South Wingfield is often referred to simply as Wingfield and is known chiefly for the ruined Wingfield Manor House. The manor was constructed along grand lines; indeed, the ruins are 416 feet long and more than 250 feet wide. The banqueting hall still has an original bay window with extremely good tracery work. Wingfield Manor is often called D. H. Lawrence's favorite ruin, and in fact it plays a part in *Sons and Lovers*, for Paul Morel and his friends make an excursion here:

> The manor is of hard, pale grey stone, and the outer walls are blank and calm.... In the first courtyard, within the high broken walls, were farm-carts, with their shafts lying idle on the ground, the tires of the wheels brilliant with gold-red rust. It was very still.
> All eagerly paid their sixpences, and went timidly through the fine clean arch of the inner courtyard. They were shy. Here on the pavement, where the hall had been, an old thorn-tree was budding. All kinds of strange openings and broken rooms were set in the shadow around them....
> There was one tall tower in a corner, rather tottering, where they say Mary Queen of Scots was imprisoned.

SOUTH WRAXALL, Wiltshire (pop. 301) About 5 miles east of Bath, South Wraxall is located in one of the wooded dell areas for which western Wiltshire is well known. Near the 15th-century church is Wraxall Manor (15th- to 16th-century), which is approached through a 15th-century gatehouse; the manor, which belonged to Sir Walter Long, is now known for its

Ralegh Room. Here, it is said, the first pipes of tobacco were smoked in England.

SOUTHAMPTON, Hampshire (pop. 180,100) The burgeoning city of Southampton, on the south coast of Hampshire, together with Portsmouth eventually will envelop the entire southern part of the county. If present proposals become a reality, Solent City (as it is derisively called) will swallow up the Itchen Valley and Winchester and extend as far north as the hamlet of Stoke Charity. Southampton's recorded past, like that of most of this area, begins with the Roman invasion in the 1st century A.D., when the town had its first major use as a port; as a port it has always flourished, and it now claims to be the gateway to England. Southampton's importance, especially as a port, increased throughout the Middle Ages, particularly because the town was the disembarkation point for Continental pilgrims on their way to the shrine of St. Thomas à Becket at Canterbury, Kent. The only major medieval structure in the town is the Bar Gate, which formed the original north entrance; while parts of the original walls are extant in other sections of the city, notably by the Royal Pier, the gate seems out of place in this ultramodern city. Southampton unfortunately was badly blitzed during World War II, and massive reconstruction took place thereafter; consequently, while literary associations exist from the early 14th century on, there are few physical reminders. However, Southampton is an attractive modern city.

The metrical romance *Bevis of Hampton* (ca. 1300) concerns the murder of Sir Guy, the Earl of Southampton, by his wife and is set in this town; Michael Drayton also relates the story in *Poly-Olbion*. Southampton is traditionally accepted as the birthplace of Nicholas Udall during the Christmas season about 1505, and it is also thought that he received some of

SOUTHAMPTON   While much of Southampton was badly bombed during World War II and the city has an ultramodern appearance, some parts of the medieval wall around the city still exist. It was here (probably) that Nicholas Udall was born about 1505.

his education here. Nothing, though, is really known of his life until he entered Winchester College in 1517; it is from this matriculation date that his birth date is assumed. John Leland visited the town in 1538, made his way down the High Street from Bar Gate, and commented in his *Itinerary* that this major street is "[o]ne of the fairest streates that ys yn any town of al England, and it is wele buildid for timbre building." Sir Fulke Greville, Lord Brooke, took advantage of the English political tradition of standing for a safe parliamentary seat in an area not necessarily the same as one's residence and won a by-election here in early 1581. The constituency honored him on January 27, 1581, by enfranchising him as a burgess of Southampton. The city has a specific association with William Shakespeare, and it is conceivable that he knew the town well. It is frequently assumed that Shakespeare was a guest of Henry Wriothesley, 3d Earl of Southampton, either at Beaulieu or at Titchfield; if these conjectures are true, it is highly likely that the dramatist also was in Southampton. The second act of *Henry V*, set here in "a council chamber," shows Henry's departure for France and the conspiracy against the King by Richard, Earl of Cambridge, Henry, Lord Scroop (Scrope) of Masham, and Sir Thomas Grey of Northumberland.

A royal visit in 1750 enhanced the popularity of the town; although there was no chance of its becoming as fashionable a spa as, say, Bath or Royal Tunbridge Wells, Southampton did gain a great deal from the visit. Horace Walpole, who visited the town in 1755, remarked that sea bathing was well established. Alexander Pope, Jonathan Swift, Voltaire, and Thomas Gray all subsequently took short holidays here. Soon after taking chambers in the Middle Temple in 1752, William Cowper came here on holiday with his cousin Harriet. They stayed for a couple of months, enjoying long walks from Southampton to Netley Abbey, Freemantle, and Redbridge. The recreational facilities of Southampton have also been attractive to yachting enthusiasts including Richard Brinsley Sheridan. Following his marriage to Jane Ogle, daughter of the dean of Winchester, in 1795, he and his wife spent a great deal of time at his father-in-law's home near here. Sheridan thoroughly enjoyed sailing on Southampton Water in a small cutter named *Phaedria* after the magic boat in Spenser's *Fairie Queene*.

The town was still a fashionable watering place and spa when Jane Austen resided here from 1806 to 1809. She first lived with her brother Francis and later moved into her own house at 3 Castle Square (neither residence has survived). The Dolphin on the High Street, with its large Georgian bow windows, was the town's social center, and balls which Jane Austen is known to have attended were held here fortnightly during the winter months. There is little information on John Keats's visit here; all that is known is that he stayed overnight at an inn on his way to the Isle of Wight in April 1817. William Makepeace Thackeray, who uses the Royal George Hotel in Chapter LVIII of *Vanity Fair* as the place where Dobbin and Joseph Sedley stop after landing from the *Ramchunder,* attended school here for a short time after his arrival from India; from here he was sent to school in Chiswick, London. George Meredith stayed at the Pear Tree Green belonging to

a Mr. Price on a two-week honeymoon in September 1864 with his second wife, Marie Vulliamy; he was working on *Vittoria* at the time. A friendship with Frederick Augustus Maxse, begun in 1858, brought Meredith back to Southampton for two months in the autumn of 1867. Maxse had retired that year as a rear admiral and decided to stand as the Radical candidate here. The two campaigned hard during these months but were badly beaten; Meredith rather primly suggested that the defeat occurred because "bribery was done there. We on our side were not guilty of it, I know." He felt that Southampton was "a very corrupt place" and was quite convinced that "bourgeoise corruption had eaten into the workers." Meredith makes Southampton into Bevishampton in *Beauchamp's Career*. W. H. Hudson landed at Southampton from Buenos Aires in May 1869 and took a room here for a few days. He left no information about his time here and professed much later in London not even to remember the town.

Southampton is an integral part of Thomas Hardy's Wessex but rarely if ever appears under a name other than its own, probably because its locational use is generally casual. Southampton is mentioned in *Tess of the D'Urbervilles, The Hand of Ethelberta, The Trumpet-Major, Two on a Tower, A Laodicean, A Pair of Blue Eyes,* and "Barbara of the House of Grebe" and "The Lady Icenway" (*A Group of Noble Dames*). The Southampton docks appear in "Embarkation," "Departure," and "The Colonel's Soliloquy" (*Poems of the Past and Present*), and Southampton Water appears in *A Pair of Blue Eyes. Desperate Remedies* uses three relatively specific but unidentifiable places: a railway station, a hotel to which Manston takes Cytherea, and the White Unicorn Hotel, where Owen and Cytherea Graye stay.

Two final notes about Southampton should be made. George Saintsbury, known mostly as a critic and a professor of rhetoric and English Literature at Edinburgh University, was born at a house (gone) at the corner of Briton Street and Orchard Place on October 23, 1845. Even though his family left Southampton when he was fairly young, he retained a deep affection for the city and returned for a short time after his retirement in 1915. He was buried here in 1933 in the Old Cemetery. Charles Browne, better known as the American humorist Artemus Ward, died in Radley's Hotel (now the Royal Mail House) on March 6, 1867, after becoming ill on a boat trip from Jersey.

SOUTHEND-ON-SEA, Essex (pop. 140,000) One of the largest seaside resorts in England, Southend-on-Sea sits on the estuary of the Thames opposite Sheerness; its nearness to London, only 42 miles to the west, attracts droves of weekenders and day-trippers, and the town is overrun with fun fairs, winkle and cockle stands, pubs, and mud. Jane Austen uses the resort town in *Emma* as the place where the Knightley family holidays; Mr. Woodhouse and Mrs. Knightley talk of the vacation:

> "And, moreover, if you must go to the sea, it had better not have been to South End. South End is an unhealthy place. Perry was surprized to hear you had fixed upon South End."
> "I know there is such an idea with many people, but

indeed it is quite a mistake, sir.—We all had our health perfectly well there, never found the least inconvenience from the mud; and Mr. Wingfield says it is entirely a mistake to suppose the place unhealthy. . . . "

SOUTHGATE, Middlesex (pop. 39,112) Now not only in the Greater London borough of Enfield but also amalgamated with that town, Southgate has essentially lost its identity; it has, though, retained its village green and a few fine houses. The High Street has a rather stark conglomerate forming a technical college, and it is almost impossible to visualize William Camden's description of Southgate in his *Britannia* as "a hamlet of Edmonton." James Henry Leigh Hunt was born in Southgate on October 19, 1784, when his father, an extremely impractical man of sanguine temperament, was tutor to the nephew of the 3d Duke of Chandos; it was from the duke's nephew, James Henry Leigh, that Hunt got his full complement of Christian names. Hunt was especially fond of this area of the shire and later writes in his *Autobiography:*

> [I]t is a pleasure to me to know that I was even born in so sweet a village as Southgate. I first saw the light there on the 19th of October 1784. It found me cradled, not only in the lap of the nature which I love, but in the midst of the truly English scenery which I love beyond all other. Middlesex in general, like my noble friends' county of Warwickshire, is a scene of trees and meadows, of "greenery" and nestling cottages; and Southgate is a prime specimen of Middlesex. It is a place lying out of the way of innovation, therefore it has the pure, sweet air of antiquity about it; and as I am fond of local researches in any quarter, it may be pardoned me if in this instance I would fain know even the meaning of its name. There is no Northgate, Eastgate, or Westgate in Middlesex: what, then, is Southgate? No topographer tells us. . . .

SOUTHPORT, Lancashire (pop. 78,925) A garden city by the sea, Southport, 18½ miles north of Liverpool, has turned its greatest handicap into its greatest asset. For more than 100 years the retreating sea has exposed mile upon mile of sandy beach. What was once a desert has been transformed into outstanding parks, gardens, and the artificially constructed 86-acre Marine Lake for boating and bathing. Southport is where Mary Webb received part of her education; from 1897 to 1899 she attended Longsight at 1 Albert Road.

SOUTHSEA, Hampshire Originally considered the twin town of Portsmouth, Southsea has become the city's residential area, and its population is included in the Portsmouth figures. The town, with its 19th-century terraced stucco houses facing the sea, is a resort area with good sand and shingle beaches, typical resort amusements, and innumerable lodging houses. George Meredith, who lived in Portsmouth, was sent to St. Paul's Day School here when he was eight or nine by his two Portsmouth aunts, who had taken over his education after the death of his mother in 1833. He was remembered as a solitary figure, and in 1838, after his father's bankruptcy, he escaped to London before being sent to a private school in Petersfield, Hampshire. Also a pupil at St. Paul's was Sir Walter Besant, who attended this school before leaving for Stockwell Grammar School in London.

Southsea was the first English soil that Rudyard Kipling remembered; he arrived here from Bombay with his parents and his sister Trix in December 1871. The usual practice of civil servants abroad was to return the children to England for their education, and the Kiplings followed this practice. Kipling and his sister were boarded with Capt. Henry Holloway, R.N., and his wife Rosa at 4 Campbell Road; the Kiplings selected the name from the newspaper and knew little, if anything, about the Holloways. Aunty Rosa was a religious fanatic who through a series of distorted and peculiar circumstances convinced the young Kipling that God lived behind the cooker in the kitchen because it was hot there. To escape her cruelty and the aggressiveness and incidental cruelty of the Holloways' son, Kipling began to tell lies as the autobiographical "Baa, Baa, Black Sheep" relates:

> Consequently, when he failed at school he reported that all was well, and conceived a large contempt for Aunty Rosa as he saw how easy it was to deceive her. "She says I'm a little liar when I don't tell lies, and now I do, she doesn't know," thought Black Sheep. Aunty Rosa had credited him in the past with petty cunning and stratagem that had never entered his head. By the light of the sordid knowledge that she had revealed to him he paid her back full tale.

The partial blindness which developed in these years went unnoticed by the Holloways; only three weeks before the arrival of Kipling's mother and his consequent removal from the house did a friend of his parents discover the child's plight. *Something of Myself,* Kipling's autobiographical fragment, relates some events of this period; and the opening chapter of *The Light That Failed* draws heavily upon his experiences here.

In April 1881 H. G. Wells began serving a second apprenticeship here at Hyde's Drapery Emporium on King's Road; he lasted two years in what he termed a "soul-destroying occupation" before leaving. His leaving, in fact, was acceptable to his mother only because his threat of drowning himself was taken seriously; *The History of Mr. Polly* specifically relates his experiences, while *Kipps,* in which young Kipps is apprenticed to a draper in Folkestone, Kent, is clearly a transposition of the locations of this period.

Sir Arthur Conan Doyle's experiences in Southsea were far more pleasant than those of Kipling or Wells, and he retained many good memories of the area long after leaving it. He set up a medical practice at 1 Bush Villas, Elm Grove, in September 1882; here he both received his first payment, the sum of 29 guineas, for "Habakuk Jephson's Statement," published in *Cornhill Magazine* in July 1883, and wrote his first four novels, including *A Study in Scarlet,* which introduced Sherlock Holmes to the public. Doyle became restless, and his desire to change his life-style took him to Berlin in October 1890. The ostensible reason for his visit was to learn about Dr. Robert Koch's discoveries concerning tuberculosis (the disease which killed his wife some years later), but Doyle was already toying with the idea of giving up the medical profession. The couple came back for a short time in November and returned from Vienna in March 1891 only long enough to arrange for their household effects to be moved to London.

Thomas Hardy, who uses some Hampshire locations, particularly Winchester, in his works, calls Southsea Solentsea in *The Hand of Ethelberta* and

"An Imaginative Woman" (*Wessex Tales*). In the latter story Coburgh House, 13 New Parade, is the location of Robert Trewe's lodgings before they are temporarily relinquished to the Marchmills at his landlady's request. The local cemetary is the site of the terrifying experience Mr. Marchmill has when he finds his wife lying across the grave of Robert Trewe.

SOUTHWATER, Sussex (pop. 932) Southwater, a small village 3 miles south of Horsham, holds Newbuildings Place, which came into the hands of Wilfrid Scawen Blunt's family in the mid-18th century. Blunt inherited Newbuildings Place, along with other family holdings, with the death of his elder brother in 1872 but did not make this his home until 1895, when he left Crabbet Park. Here Blunt entertained William Butler Yeats, Hilaire Belloc, Francis Thompson, and Padraic Colum. Blunt died here on September 10, 1922, and was buried, according to his wishes, in the woods behind the house. The stone tomb is engraved with lines from his poetry.

SOUTHWELL, Nottinghamshire (pop. 3,085) Southwell, pronounced "suth''l" by outsiders and "south-well" by natives of the town, is hidden in a hollow in the midst of the rolling downs which border the Vale of Trent, some 7 miles west of Newark. There is some evidence of a Roman establishment here, but an early reference to Southwell in the Venerable Bede's *Historia Ecclesiastica Gentis Anglorum* cannot be taken for fact: Paulinus, he says, is the implied founder of the church here and baptized "in the presence of King Edwin . . . a great number of people, in the river Trent, near the city, which in the English tongue is called Tiovulfingacestir. . . ." Tiovulfingacestir is always glossed as Southwell. William Camden takes this up in his *Britannia* and expands the information to include Paulinus as the founder of the church here, but on what authority Camden bases his statement has not been discovered.

Southwell Minster, properly the Church of St. Mary, is a superb edifice of mostly Norman origin and contains what has been described as the richest stone screen (dated 1330) in the country and which John Ruskin called the gem of English architecture. The Madonna sits enthroned high up on the screen; along the top is a row of carved heads, some with plants growing out of their mouths and some grotesquely ugly; over the three stone stalls are elaborately carved foliage and flowers, each sufficiently detailed that every leaf or flower has a stem. There are in all 289 intricately carved figures.

In 1803, having leased Newstead to Lord Grey, Lord Byron's mother rented Burgage Manor on Burgage Green here; it was a three-story wooden house with a garden and trees; Byron spent holidays from Harrow and Cambridge here until 1807 or 1808, and on one occasion carved his name on the roof of the tower of St. Mary's; the carving was removed years ago. He made a number of friends in Southwell and was encouraged to write the verses later published as *Hours of Idleness*. Later Byron frequented the Saracen's Head, the oldest inn in the town, originally known as the King's Arms. It was a coaching inn on the route to Lincoln, and the Champion Stagecoach stopped here to change horses and collect passengers and mail. The carrier, John Adams, was well known

to Byron; and when he died "of drunkenness," the poet penned an epitaph:

John Adam lies here, of the Parish of Southwell,
A carrier who carried his can to his mouth well,
He carried so much, and he carried so fast,
He could carry no more so was carried at last.
For the liquor he drank, being too much for one,
He could not carry off, so it is now carry on.

Across from Lady Byron's house was the Burbage, the home of Byron's cousin Mary Chaworth, who is the Eliza of his early poems.

In 1828, when he was preparing his life of Byron, Thomas Moore stayed at the Saracen's Head.

SOUTHWOLD, Suffolk (pop. 2,753) The village of Southwold, 11 miles south of Lowestoft at the mouth of the Blyth River, with its expansive greens is especially attractive. Southwold had a particularly bad fire in 1659, and the open greens were the result of that experience; subsequent construction took place around the greens, and each one differs. One important survivor was St. Edmund's Church, which is noted for its flush work (a typical Suffolk blending of flint and freestone into an intricate and structurally sound design), its richly carved chancel stalls, and the medieval pulpit, which is a blaze of paint.

For centuries the town was involved in fishing, with herring and sprats being two of the main catches, and while Daniel Defoe notes this in *A Tour thro' the Whole Island of Great Britain*, he seems more deeply interested in the yearly gathering of swallows:

[A]nd lodging in a House that looked into the Churchyard, I observ'd in the Evening an unusual multitude of Birds sitting on the Leads of the Church; Curiosity led me to go nearer to see what they were, and I found they were all *Swallows;* that there was such an infinite Number that they cover'd the whole Roof of the Church, and of several Houses near, and perhaps might, of more Houses which I did not see; this led me to Enquire of a grave Gentleman whom I saw near me, what the meaning was of such a prodigious Multitude of Swallows sitting there. . . . *I perceive, Sir,* says he, *you are a Stranger to it;* you must then understand first, that this is the Season of the Year when the Swallows, *their Food here failing,* begin to leave us, and return to the Country, *where-ever it be,* from whence I suppose they came; and this being the nearest to the Coast of Holland, they come here to Embark. . . .

This was more evident to me, when in the Morning I found the Wind had come about to the North-west in the Night, and there was not one Swallow to be seen. . . .

Defoe includes a long account of the Battle of Solebay with the Dutch, and he states, contrary to the modern view, that "the *English* fleet was worsted"; Samuel Pepys's account of the battle agrees with Defoe's.

By far the most important literary association of Southwold is with Eric Blair (George Orwell), whose family moved into 40 Stradbrook Road in 1921; Southwold was then, as Orwell later noted, a typical smaller "lower-upper-middle to middle-middle" class resort area. He loved to fish and did so at every opportunity. After Eton in 1921, he decided on a Civil Service career and enrolled at Mr. Hope's "tutorial establishment" in Southwold to prepare for the July 1922 examinations. Placing seventh in the examinations, he then had to learn to ride before he could take up a post in Burma, where he was stationed for five years. Upon his return in August 1927, he spent some time with his parents at their new address, 3 Queen Street. In 1930, after returning from Paris, Orwell lived in Southwold off and on for a few years, during which time he wrote reviews for *Adelphi;* he also acted as tutor to an Anglo-Indian family with three boys, whom he frequently took on long walks across the estuary to Walberswick. He and his parents moved into Montague House on the High Street; Orwell took possession of this property when his parents left for Bramley. Here he worked on *Days in London and Paris,* which Victor Gollancz published as *Down and Out in Paris and London.* It is worth noting that Blair included the name of a Suffolk River, the Orwell, in his pseudonym.

Two other writers associated with Southwold are R. D. Blackmore, who spent a holiday here in May 1894, and Agnes Strickland, the biographer, who died here and was buried in the churchyard in 1874.

SPELSBURY, Oxfordshire (pop. 410) In the lovely Evenlode Valley just north of Charlbury, Spelsbury is an old-fashioned village of thatch and stone and contains a fine row of 17th-century gabled almshouses. The parish church is an odd affair with a totally rebuilt Norman tower, 13th-century nave arches, a 20th-century chancel arch, and a score of sumptuous monuments. John Wilmot, 2d Earl of Rochester, who died in Woodstock on July 26, 1680, was buried in the north aisle of the church; there is neither an inscription nor a monument to mark the grave.

SPITHEAD, Isle of Wight The name Spithead is ambiguous: it applies to the roadstead at the entrance of Portsmouth Harbour in Hampshire, to the whole area of the English Channel which separates the Isle of Wight from the Hampshire mainland, and, in the 18th century, to the coastal area on the Isle of Wight within a few miles of Ryde. In June 1793 William Wordsworth spent a month on the Isle of Wight, somewhere, as he said, "near Spithead." His enjoyment of the stay with William Calvert is illustrated in a poem written a year or so later:

> How sweet to walk along the woody steep
> When all the summer seas are charmed to sleep
> While on the distant sands the tide retires.

Wordsworth's biographer Mary Moorman suggests that "the woody steep" represents the Ryde area, and this is quite possible.

STAFFORD, Staffordshire (pop. 32,190) The county town of the shire, Stafford is on the Sow River 27 miles north of Birmingham; it lies in the broad green belt separating the northern and southern industrial areas of the county. The town's history dates to Saxon times, when St. Bertram, or Bertelin, prince of the powerful Mercian kingdom, renounced his royal position and established a hermitage here. The town is often assumed to be the one meant in the prophecies ascribed to Merlin in Geoffrey of Monmouth's *Historia Regum Britanniae:*

> The source of the River Amne shall turn into blood; and two kings will fight each other at the Ford of the Staff [Stafford] for the sake of a Lioness.

William Camden surveyed Stafford for inclusion in his *Britannia:*

> Edward the Elder built a castle on the North bank of the river, A.D. 914. . . . Then as well as now it was the head of the whole county, but derives its greatest glory from the adjoining castle of Stafford, which the barons Stafford built for their residence.

Stafford Castle, to which Camden refers, was 1½ miles southwest of the town. Demolished by Parliamentary forces during the Civil War, when the town stood firmly Royalist, it was replaced by another castle on the same site in the 19th century; this castle too is now in ruins.

Stafford has retained many of its old buildings, and two of its churches are of particular note. The tiny Church of St. Chad contains some of the finest Norman work in England. The cruciform St. Mary's Church has an extremely rare 14th-century octagonal tower and a 12th-century font described as one of the strangest in England. In the shape of an irregular quatrefoil, the font has weird figures with slightly human faces on grotesquely formed bodies: beneath these figures on the bowl are four enormous lions and below these on the base are four grotesque animals.

Stafford abounds in old houses, some Tudor and many Elizabethan and newer. A timbered and thatched cottage on Mill Street, now a shop, is dated 1610, and close by is a group of almshouses from the same century. High House on Greengate Street is undoubtedly the gem of the town; a timbered dwelling built in 1550, it is four stories high with quite fine gables. Chetwynd House, now the post office, is an impressive brick-and-stone structure dating from 1745. Daniel Defoe in *A Tour thro' the Whole Island of Great Britain* comments that Stafford is

> an old and indeed antient Town, and gives Name to the County; but we thought to have found something more worth going so much out of the Way in it. The Town is however neat and well built, and is lately much encreas'd; nay, as some say, grown rich by the Cloathing Trade. . . .

The town's most famous literary association is with its native son Izaak Walton, who was born in a house (gone) on Eastgate Street on August 9, 1593. (A plaque on No. 62–62A marks the site.) He was baptized in the Norman font at St. Mary's and appears to have had some schooling here before being apprenticed in London. Walton never lost his love of the town or the shire and left his smallholding in Shallowford to the corporation here with the proviso that the rent be used to furnish the apprenticeship of two poor boys, the marriage portion for a servant girl, and coal for the needy. St. Mary's has a commemorative bust of Walton.

The dramatist Richard Brinsley Sheridan also had strong ties with the town as its Member of Parliament from 1780 to 1806; six years after he gave up his seat here, he tried to regain it but was unsuccessful. When in town he frequently stayed at Chetwynd House. One of the town's chief industries, then as now, was the manufacture of boots and shoes, and the dramatist's toast to the town, "May the trade of Stafford be trod underfoot by all the world," is well known.

Some years later, if the evidence in *The Romany Rye* is accurate, George Borrow served as a hostler at the Swan Hotel, an old inn complete with a plaster front and bow windows. Having parted from Isopel Berners in nearby Mumpers Dingle, he took the post here:

> The inn, of which I had become an inhabitant, was a place of infinite life and bustle. Travellers of all descriptions, from all the cardinal points, were continually stopping at it; and to attend to their wants, and minister to their convenience, an army of servants, of one description or another, was kept. . . . Truly a very great place for life and bustle was this inn. And often in after life, when lonely and melancholy, I have called up the time I spent there, and never failed to become cheerful from the recollection.

The publican, in Borrow's estimation, was "a very kind and civil person" who

> knew his customers, and had a calm clear eye, which would look through a man without seeming to do so. The accommodation of his house was of the very best description; his wines were good, his viands equally so, and his charges not immoderate; though he very properly took care of himself. He was no vulgar innkeeper, had a host of friends, and deserved them all.

Borrow left the inn after a few months and went on to Horncastle.

A second association with the Swan is ascribed to Charles Dickens, who is thought to have referred to it as "the extinct town inn, the Dodo" when he stayed for one night. He later wrote of the inn in *Reprinted Pieces.*

STAINDROP, County Durham (pop. 1,347) The line from Christopher Smart's *Jubilate Agno* "For my grounds in New Canaan shall infinitely compensate for the flats and mains of Staindrop Moor" illustrates the feeling many have for this rather barren area. Almost 24 miles southwest of Durham, this single-streeted town on the moors can be bleak and forlorn, and the weather is not good: heavy summer rains and driving winter snowstorms come sweeping in from the nearby Pennine Chain, and there can be snow on the moors here when crocuses are blooming only 6 miles away.

Raby Castle, standing in a park almost adjacent to the small town of Staindrop, is an impressive sight with its ancient deer park still containing a herd of deer. Sir Walter Scott's *Rokeby* refers to the setting of the village and its castle:

> Staindrop who from her silver bowers,
> Salutes proud Raby's battled towers.

The "license to embattle and crenellate" all the towers, houses, and walls was granted to John de Neville in 1398, and he and his successors made the castle into such a superb example of a feudal stronghold that John Leland described it as "the largest castel of lodgings in all the north country." In the enormous Barons' Hall on the north side of the courtyard, where the Rising in the North was plotted in 1569, a large band of warriors assembled, according to William Wordsworth's *The White Doe of Rylstone*, to pledge their allegiance to the lords of Raby:

> Seven hundred knights, retainers all
> Of Neville, at their master's call,
> Had sate together in Raby's Hall.

The most famous association of the castle is with Christopher Smart. Placed in school in Durham in 1733, he spent his school holidays here at the invitation of the Duchess of Cleveland. Fascinated by his brilliance, she allowed him £40 per year and induced him to use Raby Castle as his holiday home. Smart spent a great deal of time here for six years and later gratefully acknowledged his debt to the household in an ode he wrote when Henry Vane became Lord Barnard in 1754.

> Was it not he, whose pious cares
> Upheld me in my earliest years,
>   An chear'd me from his ample store,
> Who animated my designs,
> In *Roman* and *Athenian* mines,
>   To search for learning ore?
> . . . .
> Can I forget fair *Raby's* tow'rs,
>   How awfull and how great!
> Can I forget such blissful bow'rs,
>   Such splendour in retreat!
> Where me, ev'n me, an infant bard,
> Cleveland and Hope indulgent heard.

However, for much of the time that Smart was here, all was not unmixed bliss. He fell in love with Lady Anne Vane, daughter of Lord Barnard, but marriage was impossible.

> For I saw a blush in Staindrop Church, which was of God's own colouring,
> For it was the benevolence of a virgin shewn to me before the whole congregation.

At one time the two tried to elope, only to be caught by her family; no doubt the torments of Smart's ambiguous position, possibly coupled with other observations, led Lord Barnard and Lady Anne later to claim to have foreseen the poet's ultimate madness.

STAMFORD, Lincolnshire (pop. 10,100) Probably no finer town than Stamford, the southern gateway to Lincolnshire, exists in the county. On the Welland River 16½ miles northwest of Peterborough, it held a Roman camp, a Danish settlement (the Danes' capital of Fenland), and a Norman stronghold. The ancient town of locally quarried and now-mellow stone had a 7th-century priory, St. Leonard's, whose chapel (now in ruins) is just off the Spalding road. In the 12th century Stamford was a prosperous wool center, and by the 16th century Stamford cloth was known throughout Europe; the attendant wealth is evident in the richness of 16th-century architecture still to be seen. An old stone bridge crosses the Welland, and the view to St. Mary's Hill supports Sir Walter Scott's comment that this is "the finest scene between London and Edinburgh." At one time Stamford was a center of learning, attested to by one of Stamford School's prize possessions: one wall contains a pointed archway known as Brasenose Gateway, which was part of Brasenose Hall in the 14th century, when students who seceded from Oxford came here. The brazen-nose knocker was on the gateway until it was returned to the college in 1890.

It is as an educational seat that Stamford enters Michael Drayton's *Poly-Olbion:*

> . . . *Stamford,* which so much forgotten seemes to bee;
> Renown'd for Liberall Arts, as highly honoured there,
> As they in *Cambridge* are, or *Oxford* ever were. . . .

Daniel Defoe, too, mentions Brasenose and adds that tradition maintains "the Schools were first erected by *Bladud,* King of the *Britains;* the same whose Figure stands up at the King's Bath in the City of *Bath,* and who liv'd 300 Years before our Saviour's Time." Defoe liked the town, and many years later William Cobbett "harangued" here at "a very fine and excellent inn, called Standwell's Hotel, which is, with few exceptions, the nicest inn that I have ever been in."

George Gascoigne died here at the home of his biographer George Whetstone on October 7, 1577, and later John Clare frequently walked to Stamford from nearby Helpston. Clare was befriended by Octavius Gilchrist, a grocer whose shop was (possibly) on the High Street opposite the public library; it was Gilchrist who took Clare to London for the first time.

STANFORD-LE-HOPE, Essex (pop. 3,379) A small Thames-side village 5 miles southwest of Pitsea, Stanford-le-Hope became the home of Joseph Conrad in 1896; he and his wife took a small house which Conrad described as a "damned jerry-built rabbit hutch." Here he settled down to writing and finished *The Nigger of the "Narcissus"* in January 1897. The Conrads found the house intolerable and the intellectual climate unbearable and moved to the Elizabethan (rebuilt) Ivy Walls, a farmhouse on the edge of the village, where they were visited by Stephen Crane and John Galsworthy, who had met Conrad aboard the *Torrens* in Adelaide Harbour. Conrad gave up on Stanford in 1898 and moved to Postling, Kent.

STANMORE, Middlesex Formerly a northern dormitory suburb 2 miles northeast of London and now a part of Greater London by the 1965 redistricting act, Stanmore, on a hill slope, was once heavily engaged in agriculture; but about the only free ground today is the wooded common at an altitude of 505 feet. St. John's Church, on Church Road, is the most picturesque part of the old village; here a barn has been converted into a set of cottages. The dramatist Sir William Schwenck Gilbert is buried here; he died after a heart attack at his home Grimsdyke House in Harrow Weald on May 29, 1911, and his ashes were brought here from Golders Green. The tombstone is surmounted by a white angel, and the inscription is on a horizontal slab.

STANTON HARCOURT, Oxfordshire (pop. 699) Between the Windrush and Thames Rivers 6 miles west of Oxford, Stanton Harcourt lies at the north end of the Vale of the White Horse. Numerous thatched farmhouses line the winding roads near the Thames; and at one end of the village, surrounded by high embattled walls, are two towers, one belonging to the church and one belonging to the historic, and now restored, seat of the Harcourts. The Harcourts were here from the 10th century on; their house began to fall into ruin in the 18th century, when the family moved to Nuneham Courtenay. The remaining tower, once part of the family chapel, is now known as Pope's Tower after Alexander Pope, who divided his time between here and Cirencester, Gloucestershire, in the summer of 1718. He had been given the full use of the tower when the Harcourts abandoned Stanton Harcourt for Nuneham Courtenay; here he

found a measure of isolation, interrupted by visits from John Gay, and finished his work on the *Iliad.* Indeed, one pane of glass in the tower was inscribed "In the year 1718, Alexander Pope finished here the Fifth Volume of Homer"; the pane was removed to Nuneham Courtenay.

Pope's refuge in the tower, on the fourth floor up steep and winding narrow stairs, was a wood-paneled room with leaded windows and a view of the old manor, the parish church, and the lovely manorhouse courtyard. Pope never mentioned the grisly associations of his tower and may not have known of them. Two stories involve the punishment of a female member of the Harcourt family and the nailing up of a room in the tower. In one, Lady Frances was guilty of adultery with a neighboring prior and was duly punished; the nailed-up room, called the Adultery Chamber, is where her ghost ostensibly walks. In the other, Lady Alice was murdered by her lover, the Harcourts' domestic chaplain, and is said to haunt the Lady Pool and to moan uncontrollably if the water level falls too low. This version seems to have been taken more seriously, and in 1865 the Bishop of Oxford was called upon to exorcise the pool. Pope was pleased with his place here, and an undated letter to Lady Mary Wortley Montagu contains an elaborate description of Stanton Harcourt:

> [I]n a poetical fit you'd imagine it had been a village in Amphion's time, where twenty cottages had taken a dance together, were all out, and stood still in amazement ever since. . . . One would expect, after entering through the porch, to be let into the hall. Alas nothing less—you find yourself in a brewhouse. From the Parlour you think to step into the drawingroom, but opening the iron-nailed door, you are convinced by a flight of birds about your ears and a cloud of dust in your eyes, that 'tis the pigeonhouse.

The church contains the remains of the 1st Viscount Harcourt's son Simon, whose epitaph Pope wrote.

An occurrence on one of John Gay's visits has become a part of the English literary heritage. Pope and Gay saw two lovers near the house struck by lightning and killed. Both poets wrote accounts of the episode to their friends, and Oliver Goldsmith was sufficiently impressed by the story to incorporate it in *The Vicar of Wakefield:*

> "I never sit thus," says Sophia, "but I think of the two lovers, so sweetly described by Mr. Gay, who were struck dead in each other's arms under a barley mow. There is something so pathetic in the description that I have read it an hundred times with new rapture."—"In my opinion," cried my son, "the finest strokes in that description are much below those in the Acis and Galatea of Ovid. . . ."

A memorial stone to the two was set up outside the church by Lord Harcourt, and the epitaph was written by Pope.

STANTON ST. JOHN, Oxfordshire (pop. 397) This stone village of the St. Johns of Surrey, only 4 miles northeast of Oxford, has an important place in literature, for Stanton St. John was the home of John Milton's father and grandparents, and the young Milton traditionally is said to have spent some of his childhood here. Milton's father was for some time estranged from his parents and, indeed, was disinherited because of his conversion to Protestantism.

STAPLEFORD HALL, Rutland Lying 4½ miles southeast of Melton Mowbray on the Leicestershire-Rutland border, Stapleford Hall is a seat with no population except the inhabitants of the house itself. The hall dates to 1500, but so many additions have been made that the architecture is a patchwork. Stapleford and its park are frequently identified as the Stapleford of Thomas Hardy's "Squire Petrick's Dame" in *A Group of Noble Dames*, but a far better case is made for Stalbridge, Dorset, especially since the author rarely sets his scenes this far north and since he specifically states that "the splendid old mansion [is] now pulled down."

STAPLETON, Gloucestershire Formerly a separate urban district but now included in the city of Bristol, Stapleton lies on the northeast side of that city; the one-time isolation of the village is gone, but green spaces remain in Stoke Park, Pur Down, and Eastville Park. Facing the park and near the church is the house (marked with a plaque) where Hannah More was born on February 2, 1745; the daughter of the master of the free school here, she was educated at home by her father.

STATHERN, Leicestershire (pop. 531) In the lovely Vale of Belvoir (pronounced "beaver"), Stathern is an old village of red-and-white cottages and a very attractive medieval church with a 13th-century doorway and an arcaded 14th-century font. This living was presented to the Rev. George Crabbe in 1785, and he and his young wife and infant moved into the village parsonage, where they lived until after the death of the Duke of Rutland, whose preferment this was. Then, in 1789, with the widowed duchess's help, Crabbe received the joint livings of Muston and Allington and settled in the Muston parsonage in February.

STEVENTON, BEDFORDSHIRE *See* STEVINGTON, BEDFORDSHIRE.

STEVENTON, Hampshire (pop. 195) At the beginning of the rise of the chalk hills which traditionally are held responsible for the clarity and purity of water in the Test Valley is the tiny village and parish of Steventon, where Jane Austen was born on December 16, 1775, the youngest of seven children. In the 18th and early 19th centuries, the scattered cottages of the village were gathered around the church, the rectory, where Jane Austen was born and lived 23 years, and the manor house, now deserted and in a bad state of repair. The Rev. George Austen was rector here for more than forty years and from 1773 on held a joint living with nearby Deane. Although Jane Austen's birthplace was demolished more than a century ago, its location is easily determined, since the field where the house stood has in it a modern pump on the same spot as the Austen family pump. Jane Austen wrote *Pride and Prejudice, Sense and Sensibility,* and *Northanger Abbey* here, but they were not published until after she moved to Chawton in 1809. The 13th-century church contains a memorial brass to the author, erected in 1936, and it also preserves the old manorial and family pews. There is also a memorial to Anne Austen, the first wife of Jane's brother James, as well as one to James himself.

STEVINGTON or STEVENTON, Bedfordshire (pop. 467) Stevington, situated on the Ouse River 4½ miles northwest of Bedford, at one time consisted of mainly stone buildings; the church is partly Saxon, and below its wall is an ancient holy well. Still standing in the village is an old cross which figures in John Bunyan's *The Pilgrim's Progress;* the walk from the holy well (Bunyan's Sepulchre) between the village walls to the cross, is Christian's:

> Now I saw in my dream that the highway up which Christian was to go was fenced on either side with a wall, and that wall is called Salvation. Up this way therefore did burdened Christian run, but not without great difficulty, because of the load on his back.
> He ran thus till he came at a place somewhat ascending, and upon that place stood a cross, and a little below in the bottom, a sepulchre.

STEYNING, Sussex (pop. 1,875) A market town at the foot of a hill 1 mile west of the Adur River and 5 miles northwest of Shoreham, Steyning (pronounced "stain'ing") has what has been called "a fragment of a Norman church," but there is probably no finer Norman work in the country on such a scale. Church Street, one of the shire's best streets, is lined with 15th-century buildings, gabled houses, and Chantry House, the home of Miss Shackleton Heald, where William Butler Yeats often stayed in the 1930s. Yeats began *Purgatory* here.

STILLINGTON, Yorkshire (pop. 510) This small village, 10 miles north of York and just north of Sutton-on-the-Forest, is typical of the villages scattered throughout the Vale of York. In the 18th century the hamlet could not support its own vicar and shared one with the parish of Sutton—a not very happy arrangement for either the parishioners or the vicar from the 1740s to 1760s, Laurence Sterne. Sterne acquired this living through the influence of his wife, and although it almost doubled his income, he could not hide his dislike of the parish. Sterne preached on Sunday morning at Sutton and then traveled the short distance here to preach in the afternoon. Stillington Hall, belonging to Stephen Croft, was a frequent stop for the disgruntled vicar, and it is fortunate that Croft knew how to handle Sterne's violent outbursts of temper, for otherwise *Tristram Shandy* probably would never have seen the light of day. Sterne supposedly pitched the manuscript of the novel into the blazing fireplace in a pique, and Croft rescued the manuscript and calmed the author.

STINSFORD, Dorset (pop. 374) Just 1½ miles east of Dorchester, the village of Stinsford has kept its early remoteness and integrity; it is of interest to literary pilgrims as possibly the central site in Thomas Hardy's country, for it is important in both his life and his works. Growing up in nearby Bockhampton, he attended the parish church here, where his father was one of the musicians, and taught in the Sunday school from 1855 on. The churchyard is full of Hardy's ancestors; his first wife, Emily Lavinia, who died in 1912, is buried here, and the inscription (after thirty-eight years of unhappy marriage) reads simply "This for Remembrance"; the poem "I Need Not Go" refers to Hardy's wife and this churchyard. Hardy's second wife, Florence Dugdale, also is bur-

STINSFORD The Mellstock of Thomas Hardy's Wessex, Stinsford and its church played a major role in the novelist's life. Next to the grave of his first wife, Emma Lavinia Gifford, Hardy's heart was interred after his death in 1928.

ied here. Hardy died at his home in Dorchester on January 11, 1928, and while his ashes were interred in Westminster Abbey, London, his heart was buried here beside his first wife's grave. The 13th- to 15th-century church has a commemorative window to him.

Stinsford is the Mellstock of Hardy's Wessex, and the village enters many of his works: it is Jude's birthplace in *Jude the Obscure*, the home of "Mop" Ollamoor in "The Fiddler of the Reels" (*Life's Little Ironies and a Few Crusted Characters*), the site of the marriages of Cynthia Graye to Manston and Edward Springrove in *Desperate Remedies* (it is thought), and the place where Wildeve and Thomasin were to be married in *The Return of the Native*. It also appears in *Tess of the D'Urbervilles*, *The Mayor of Caster-bridge*, *Far from the Madding Crowd*, and numerous poems, including "A Church Romance," "The Dead Quire," and "The Noble Lady's Tale." The use of Mellstock is most central in *Under the Greenwood Tree*, although, to be sure, Hardy amalgamates several of the area villages and houses under this general name. Mellstock Lane, where the novel opens, is the road leading north from Mellstock Cross, the intersection of two rural roads on the Tincleton road, about 2 miles east of Dorchester. Dick Dewey's house is a mixture of two houses, one of which has vanished and the other had been so altered as to lose its relevance. The last call of the evening is at the vicarage, modeled on the house standing next to the church. Christmas services take place in the Mell-

stock Church, which had long been noted for its musicians' gallery (gone):

> The gallery of Mellstock Church had a status and sentiment of its own. . . . The gallery, too, looked down and knew the habits of the nave to its remotest peculiarity and had an extensive stock of exclusive information about it; while the nave knew nothing of the gallery people, as gallery people, beyond their loud-sounding minims and chest notes. Such topics as that the clerk was always chewing tobacco except at the moment of crying Amen; that he had a dust-hole in his pew; that during the sermon certain daughters of the village had left off caring to read anything so mild as the marriage-service for some years, and now regularly studied the one which chronologically follows it . . . were stale subjects here.

It is also thought that Stinsford is the Carriford of *Desperate Remedies;* Mr. Raunham resides at the vicarage. Knapwater House, the residence of Miss Aldclyffe, is modeled on the 18th-century Kingston Maurward House, which stands in a wooded park:

> The house was regularly and substantially built of clean grey freestone throughout. . . . The main block approximated to a square on the ground plan, having a projection in the centre of each side, surmounted by a pediment. From each angle of the inferior side ran a line of buildings lower than the rest, turning inwards again at their further end, and forming within them a spacious open court, within which resounded an echo of astonishing clearness. These erections were in their turn backed by ivy-covered ice-houses, laundries, and stables, the whole mass of subsidiary buildings being half buried beneath close-set shrubs and trees.

Finally, it should be noted that a more modern literary figure is associated with Stinsford; in 1972 Cecil Day-Lewis, Poet Laureate, novelist, and Hardy devotee, was buried in the churchyard here.

STOCKBRIDGE, Hampshire (pop. 862) Situated on the Test River and noted for trout fishing, Stockbridge consists of a short and wide single street with generally nondescript 19th- and 20th-century buildings. On June 18, 1631, Bishop John Davenant appointed his nephew Thomas Fuller to the prebend of Netherbury-in-Ecclesia in Salisbury; it was called "one of the best prebends in England," and Fuller stopped in Stockbridge on the way to assume his duties. Here, as he mentions in *The History of the Worthies of England,* he looked "over an ingenious plow, which could be drawn by dogs and managed by one man."

In the 18th century Stockbridge was one of the infamous rotten boroughs, whose existence enabled men such as Richard Steele to serve their country. Steele, who was in financial difficulties at the time, stood for Parliament here in 1713 and secured fifty of the seventy-one burgesses' votes. Not the least of his considerations in deciding to stand was the fact that as a Member of Parliament he secured parliamentary immunity from the bailiffs who were hounding him.

STOKE DAMEREL, Devon (pop. 10,441) Now basically a part of the municipal borough of Devonport and retaining its autonomy only as an ecclesiastical district, Stoke Damerel was the birthplace of the Rev. Robert Stephen Hawker on December 3, 1803. He was born in the old rectory, 6 Morley Street, and baptized in the parish church. The boy lived here only a short time before moving to nearby Stratton when his father took the living there.

STOKE-ON-TRENT, Staffordshire (pop. 240, 428)

Spode, Wedgwood, Minton, Copeland, and Coalport are known worldwide as the names of incomparable pottery and porcelain, and all of them are manufactured here at Stoke-on-Trent, 16 miles north of Stafford on the Trent River. The town was originally called Stoke-upon-Trent or just Stoke, but in 1910 the five towns of the Potteries, Burslem, Tunstall, Hanley, Longton, and Stoke, were amalgamated with Fenton to form Stoke-on-Trent, a city and county borough whose extended area exceeds 21,000 acres; indeed, even the potteries have been made into the large conglomerate called Allied Potteries. Then in 1974, with the bill reforming local government, changes were made, and the county-borough status was lifted.

Stoke-upon-Trent was the birthplace of Dinah Maria Mulock, afterward Mrs. Craik, on April 20, 1826; her father, a minister, had a small congregation and was not financially secure in his post. The author's early education was mostly private, and she remained here until about 1846, when she went to London. The writer most intimately associated with the Potteries is Arnold Bennett, many of whose novels deal with the area in detail; Stoke becomes Knype in his works. It is here that Janet Orgreave and Edwin Clayhanger meet the train carrying George Edwin Cannon, the child of Hilda Lessways. In April 1888 H. G. Wells stayed in the town with William Burton, a fellow student at the Normal School (later Royal College) of Science in South Kensington, London. By this time Burton was a prosperous chemist and was aware of Wells's recurrent health problems. Indeed, almost as soon as the author arrived, he had an attack, and the fresh hemorrhage caused a relapse. Wells stayed until June, when he had recovered enough to return to London. A final note should be made of J. B. Priestley's view of the Potteries, as put forth in his *English Journey;* he writes:

This district, Bennett's famous Five Towns, consists of six towns, Burslem, Fenton, Hanley, Longton, Stoke and Tunstall, which have now been merged into one city, called Stoke-on-Trent. This city has a population of nearly three hundred thousand, but it has no real existence as a city of that size. There is no city. There are still these six little towns. After federation into one city had been first suggested, the inhabitants of these towns argued and quarrelled most bitterly for years. Finally, the obvious advantages of federation carried the day, and there appeared, on paper, the mythical city of Stoke-on-Trent.

STOKE POGES, Buckinghamshire (pop. 1,714)

From the northern edge of Slough (2 miles away) a lane leads to Stoke Poges, a village with two manor houses, a Norman church, and all the ambiance of a remote, leafy Buckinghamshire community. Stoke Poges once held Stoke Park (gone), an Elizabethan manor house belonging to Sir Edward Coke, Lord Chief Justice of England, and Stoke Court (originally West End House), the house intimately associated with Thomas Gray and his "country churchyard." The poet's first association with the ancient manor appears to have been in early June 1742, when he

came here to live with his aunt and uncle, the Rogerses, who owned the estate. The house was in the northern part of the parish and was reached by a meadow path from the church which went by the 16th-century hospital. Within a few days of his arrival Gray wrote his "Ode to Spring," and in August the "Ode on a Distant Prospect of Eton College." Windsor and Eton are only a few miles south, and from the garden of the house, it is said, he could see (visualize, perhaps)

> Ye distant spires, ye antique towers,
> That crown the watery glade,
> Where grateful Science still adores
> Her Henry's holy Shade;
> And ye, that from the stately brow
> Of Windsor's heights th' expanse below
> Of grove, of lawn, of mead survey....

In the autumn, probably, Gray began the "Elegy Written in a Country Churchyard." His uncle's death in October of that year left just sufficient funds for his widow to bring her two sisters to live here with her, and Gray's mother and another sister arrived later that autumn. Gray spent his Cambridge holidays here studying and working on the "Elegy" for the next eight years, and when his mother died on March 11, 1753, she was buried in the family tomb on the south side of the churchyard. This is, as well, the grave of Anna Rogers. Gray composed their epitaph. The poet ceased to live here after 1759. Tradition erroneously maintains that some of the "Elegy" was composed as Gray sat on the tomb, but it was finished three years before Mrs. Gray's death. The path to the church is lined with rose trees, and it was up this path that the body of Thomas Gray was borne in August 1771 after his death in Cambridge on July 30. Gray was buried in the same tomb as his mother, although the plaque

STOKE POGES Rose trees line the walk from the lych gate to the Norman church immortalized in Thomas Gray's "Elegy Written in a Country Churchyard." Gray was buried here, in the same tomb as his mother, in 1771, but the inscription on the grave makes no mention of the poet.

on the grave makes no mention of the poet. There is, however, a memorial plaque on the church wall. An additional monument is the cenotaph erected by John Penn in the adjacent field, now called Gray's Field. Twenty feet high and designed by James Wyatt, the monument is most generously described as an overgrown tea caddy; it has a number of stanzas from the "Elegy" chipped into its sides. A debate exists over whether the Stoke Poges Church is the church described in the poem; churches in Upton and Harefield are said to be closer to the poetic description, but Gray has no specific association with either of these claimants.

A 19th-century author has a slight association with Stoke Poges and was also attracted to the churchyard. Percy Bysshe Shelley, when a student at Eton from 1804 to 1810, often escaped to this village and spent some time in the vicinity of the church.

STONE, Staffordshire (pop. 6,500)   Stone is a pleasant old town, 7 miles north of Stafford, with the Trent River and the Trent and Mersey Canal running parallel just to the south. Bury Bank, which dates to the 7th century, is the alleged site of the fortified palace of the Mercian king Wulfhere, a convert to Christianity and the father of St. Werburga (Werburh); plagued by constant strife and warfare, he reverted to paganism and murdered his Christian sons because they clung to their new faith. At the foot of Abbey Street are the remains of a priory founded by Ermenhilda, Wulfhere's wife, in memory of her murdered sons; a few walls and the vaulted cellar of the Priory House are all that remain.

Without doubt the most famous native of Stone is Peter de Wint, one of England's great watercolorists, who was born here in 1784, but another figure, the poet Richard Barnfield, is of more interest here. He came to the tiny village of Darlaston, 1½ miles northwest of Stone, after a short time in London. Barnfield is remarkable in being remembered, since only five copies of his three books of verses are known, and his two now most famous poems were stolen by a pirate publisher and put out under William Shakespeare's name. For centuries (and occasionally even today) these poems were included in Shakespeare's *The Passionate Pilgrim;* "An Ode" is one of the frequently quoted poems:

> Fie, fie, fie; now would the cry
> *Teru Teru*, by and by:
> That to heare her so complaine,
> Scarce I could from Teares refraine:
> For her griefes so liuely showne,
> Made me thinke vpon mine owne.

These last lines are the ones which prompted Algernon Swinburne to call Barnfield "the first adequate English laureate of the nightingale." Barnfield died at his home (gone) in 1627 and was buried either in the Church of St. Michael or in its churchyard on March 6; his grave is unknown.

STONEHENGE, Wiltshire   Situated about 10 miles north of Salisbury against the vastness of the Salisbury Plain, whose average elevation is 450 feet, the immense stone monoliths of Stonehenge are somewhat diminished, but a closer view proves Stonehenge to be as impressive as anticipated. Some main-

tain that the stone circles are druidical, but they are not; others have conjectured that the circular setting of stones, uprights and lintels, which is surrounded by earthworks, was once an ancient British work, a Saxon labor, a Danish construction, and even an early Egyptian work. While modern inquiry has established a date of erection about 3,500 years ago, during the late Neolithic period and the early Bronze Age, it has not completely established the purpose of the circle. Excavations in 1919 began the laborious process which determined that three specific building periods occurred and that each Stonehenge marked a drastic change. Stonehenge I consisted of the bank, the ditch, the Aubrey Holes, the Heelstone (a 15-ton block of sarsen sandstone), and an unspecified but clearly central feature. The cremations, bone pins, and mace-head found in the Aubrey Holes have dated this part of the structure. Stonehenge II is the Double Bluestone Circle (a series of radically arranged stone holes below ground level), the Avenue, and the Causeway and dates to about the 17th century B.C. The final building stage is usually broken into three parts, but briefly this period (around 1500 B.C.) was one of remodeling: more than eighty enormous blocks of sarsen were brought here from the Marlborough Downs, and the trilithons, the Sarsen Circle, the Four Stations, and the Slaughter Stone were put in place. The stones range from 8 to 22 feet high, are 6 feet broad, and about 3 feet thick; the largest is estimated to weigh 50 tons. An outer circle, about 99 feet in diameter, contains fifteen pairs of stones with lintels; the smaller inside circle has forty unlinked stones. Yet more central is a series of lintel-linked uprights in the form of a horseshoe, and inside this is a smaller horseshoe of unlinked stones. What is known is that the Heelstone, 256 feet from the center of Stonehenge, is the place over which the sun (*hele*) rises almost perfectly on the summer solstice; the name Heelstone, however, came about in another way. Around 1660 John Aubrey, the antiquarian who discovered the holes since named after him, mentioned:

> One of the great stones that lies down on the west side ... hath a cavity something resembling the print of a man's foot.

His reference was to another stone, but the name was later transferred to the present Heelstone. Indeed, it seems unlikely that primitive people would go to this extent to create a calendar; of course, rites of some sort were once performed here, but speculation is futile since their purpose is not known.

Stonehenge has been visited by an enormous number of literary people, many of whom left their impression of the place. "*Stonendge* the greatest Wonder of *England*," as Michael Drayton refers to it, was too good not to be rhapsodized over in the third song of *Poly-Olbion:*

> Dull heape, that thus thy head above the rest doost
>   reare,
> Precisely yet not know'st who first did place thee there;
> But Traytor basely turn'd to *Merlins* skill doost flie,
> And with his Magiques doost thy Makers truth belie:
> Conspirator with Time, now growen so meane and
>   poore,
> Comparing these his spirits with those that went before;
> Yet rather art content thy Builders praise to lose,
> Then passed greatnes should thy present wants disclose.

The assumption that Stonehenge was the work of Merlin was not original with Drayton; if anyone can be accused of starting this hare, it is Geoffrey of Monmouth. In his *Historia Regum Britanniae,* Geoffrey relates that Merlin tells Aurelius to build a lasting monument for his battle dead:

> "[S]end for the Giants' Ring which is on Mount Killaraus in Ireland. In that place there is a stone construction which no man of this period could ever erect, unless he combined great skill and artistry. The stones are enormous and there is no one alive strong enough to move them. If they are placed in position round this site, in the way in which they are erected over there, they will stand forever."
>
> At these words of Merlin's Aurelius burst out laughing. "How can such large stones be moved from so far-distant a country?" he asked. "It is hardly as if Britain itself is lacking in stones big enough for the job!"

Merlin, naturally, worked all manner of magic to dismantle the Irish stones, sail them here, and re-erect them; ultimately Utherpendragon, says Geoffrey, was buried within the Giants' Ring.

Some years later William Camden collected all the conjectures concerning the possible builders of the site in his *Britannia.* John Evelyn visited Stonehenge on July 22, 1654, and was most impressed with

> a stupendious Monument, how so many, & huge pillars of stone should have ben brought together, erected som, other Transverse on the tops of them, in a Circular *area* as rudly representing a Cloyster, or heathen & more natural Temple: & so exceeding hard, that all my strength with an hammer, could not breake a fragment: which duritie I impute to their so long exposure.... About the same hills are divers mounts raisd, conceiv'd to be antient intrenchments, or places of burial after bloudy fights: We now went by the *Devizes* ... *Stonhenge* app(e)ares like a Castle at a distance.

Evelyn's last remark is accurate even today.

In the 18th century also Stonehenge had its share of literary visitors. Daniel Defoe includes a lengthy description of it in *A Tour thro' the Whole Island of Great Britain* and decides on its early purpose:

> I shall suppose it, as the Majority of all Writers do, to be a Monument for the Dead, and the rather, because Men's Bones have been frequently dug up in the Ground near them. The common Opinion that no Man could ever Count them, that a Baker carry'd a Basket of Bread, and laid a Loaf upon every Stone, and yet could never make out the same Number twice; *This,* I take, *as a meer Country Fiction,* and a Ridiculous one too; ... and I have seen them told four Times after one another, beginning every Time at a different Place, and every Time they amounted to 72 in all....

Thomas Chatterton wrote of the megaliths in "The Battle of Hastings":

> A wondrous pyle of rugged mountaynes standes,
> Placd on eche other in a dreare arraie,
> It ne could be the worke of human handes,
> It ne was reared up bie menne of claie.
> Here did the Brutons adoration paye
> To the false god whom they did Tauran name,
> Dightynge hys altarre with greete fyres in Maie,
> Roastynge theyr vyctualle round about the flame,
> 'Twas here that Hengyst did the Brytons slee,
> As they were meete in council for to bee.

Thomas Warton the Younger penned a sonnet in praise of the ancient monument, in which he consid-ers the early theories concerning the builders; he asks whether Merlin

> Or Druid priests, sprinkled with human gore,
> Taught mid thy massy maze their mystic lore:
> Or Danish chiefs, enriched with savage spoil,
> To Victory's idol vast, an unhewn shrine,
> Reared the rude heap: or in thy hallowed round
> Repose the kings of Brutus' genuine line;
> Or here those kings in solemn state were crowned:
> Studious to trace thy wondrous origin,
> We muse on many an ancient tale renowned.

William Wordsworth, in a deeply depressed state about the impending French wars, crossed Salisbury Plain from Portsmouth, Hampshire, in 1793. He spent a few days wandering leisurely among the multitude of barrows and the stones here; after considering the disasters of war, he wrote of Stonehenge and the plain in "Guilt and Sorrow; or Incidents upon Salisbury Plain." His forlorn traveler, crossing the plain at dusk, comes upon no evidence of human habitation:

> Once did the lightning's faint disastrous gleam
> Disclose a naked guide-post's double head,
> Sight which, tho' lost at once, a gleam of pleasure shed.
>
> No swinging sign-board creaked from cottage elm
> To stay his steps with faintness overcome;
> 'Twas dark and void as ocean's watery realm
> Roaring with storms beneath night's starless gloom;
> No gipsy cower'd o'er fire of furze or broom;
> No labourer watched his red kiln glaring bright,
> Nor taper glimmered dim from sick man's room;
> Along the waste no line of mournful light
> From lamp of lonely toll-gate streamed athwart the night.

Among other visitors were Henry James, who commented on "the pathless vaults beneath the house of history," and W. H. Hudson, who queried, when he first saw the structure, "Was this *Stonehenge?* this cluster of poor little gray stones, looking in the distance like a small flock of sheep or goats grazing on that immense down?" Another disappointed viewer, Ralph Waldo Emerson, referred to Stonehenge as "a group of brown dwarfs on a wide expanse."

The most famous use of Stonehenge in literature is Thomas Hardy's penultimate scene of *Tess of the D'Urbervilles.* From Melchester (Salisbury), after Tess kills Alec D'Urberville and is reunited with Angel Clare, they walk across the "open loneliness and black solitude" of the plain:

> "What monstrous place is this?" said Angel.
> "It hums," said she. "Hearken!"
> He listened. The wind, playing upon the edifice, produced a booming tune, like the note of some gigantic one-stringed harp. No other sound came from it, and lifting his hand and advancing a step or two, Clare felt the vertical surface of the wall. It seemed to be of solid stone, without joint or moulding. Carrying his fingers onward, he found that what he had come in contact with was a colossal rectangular pillar; by stretching out his left hand he could feel a similar one adjoining.... Angel, perplexed, said, "What can it be?"
> Feeling sideways, they encountered another tower-like pillar, square and uncompromising as the first; beyond it another and another. The place was all doors and pillars, some connected above by continuous architraves.
> "A very Temple of the Winds," he said.
> The next pillar was isolated; others composed a trilithon; others were prostrate, their flanks forming a cause-

way wide enough for a carriage; and it was soon obvious that they made up a forest of monoliths grouped upon the grassy expanse of the plain. . . .

"It is Stonehenge!" said Clare.

"The heathen temple, you mean?"

Here Tess sleeps on an oblong slab until the pursuers from Wintoncester (Winchester) appear at dawn and take her into custody. Another use of Stonehenge occurs in H. G. Wells's *The Secret Places of the Heart:* Sir Richmond Hardy, traveling in the West Country with Dr. Martineau in search of the "mysteries in man's soul," meets Miss Grammont here.

STONELEIGH, Warwickshire (pop. 1,893) The trees from the old Forest of Arden still shelter Stoneleigh on the Leamington side, and the village itself contains a number of fine black-and-white–timbered cottages across from a row of tall chimneyed almshouses built by Alice Leigh, Duchess of Dudley, one of the few women in England ever to be created a duchess in her own right. A little more than 2 miles east of Kenilworth, Stoneleigh Abbey and its grounds have been in the hands of the Leighs since the reign of Elizabeth I. The village church is the town's pride, and although some of the exterior Norman carving is crumbling because of the elements, the beautiful interior is in excellent condition. The present estate has preserved the old monastic buildings, and the Abbot's House is in very good condition. The house itself is rich in finely carved wood, and the Cipriani work in the saloon is unequaled. Recently the entire west wing of the house was taken over for a museum by the county council.

In the early 19th century James Henry Leigh inherited the house, and soon after the death of the Rev. George Austen, his widow (nee Leigh) and daughter Jane came to Stoneleigh before settling in Southampton. Mrs. Austen, Leigh's cousin, was both impressed and disturbed by the vastness of Stoneleigh:

We cannot find our way about it. I mean the best part; as to the offices, which were the Abbey, Mr Leigh almost despairs of ever finding his way about them. I have proposed setting up direction posts at the angles.

The view to the river from the Queen's Bedroom, (named for Queen Victoria's 1858 stay) is called Jane Austen's View.

A second Stoneleigh association is with George Gordon, Lord Byron, a good friend of James Henry Leigh's son, who had been Byron's fag at Harrow. The two dined here together on the evening before Byron left England for the last time.

STONYHURST, Lancashire Situated 4 miles southwest of Clitheroe, the renowned Jesuit college Stonyhurst did not begin here until 1794, and the estate was originally the home of the Shireburnes, a Catholic family. Sir Richard began Stonyhurst in 1590, and upon his death his son, another Sir Richard, kept on with the building program; by 1615 Stonyhurst was half complete. Distrustful of the new Anglican Church but unwilling to jeopardize his estate and wealth, the first Sir Richard attended Anglican services, his ears stuffed with cotton wool so that his soul would not be in peril from the heresies. His son followed the same course, but both his grandson and

his great-grandson refused such a halfway commitment and suffered the consequences; one was that the building program was never completed. Eventually the estate came into the hands of the Welds, who had married into the Shireburne family, and Thomas Weld gave the estate to the Jesuit colony which had been driven out of Saint-Omer. The French refugees found the estate in ruins and rebuilt it in the 19th century. The library has a number of outstanding authenticated items, including *The Golden Legend* published by Caxton, Froissart's *Chronicles,* and, most important, the 7th-century Gospel of St. John which St. Cuthbert held on his deathbed and which was put into the stone coffin with the saint's body.

Alfred Austin, later Poet Laureate, was educated here, and Wilfrid Scawen Blunt entered Stonyhurst in 1853; he believed at one point that he might join the priesthood but later wrote, "The Jesuit novitiate is the most mentally crushing process ever invented." Blunt left in 1858 to join the diplomatic service.

Arthur Conan Doyle, who came from a strict Roman Catholic family in Edinburgh, was sent here on account of the religious orientation and the iron discipline. Because of the distance from home, Doyle spent some Christmases here, and he writes that on one occasion he and two friends ate:

Two turkeys, one *very* large goose, two chickens, one large ham and two pieces of ham, two large sausages, seven boxes of sardines, one lobster, a plate full of tarts and seven pots of jam. In the way of drink we had five bottles of sherry, five of port, one of claret and two of raspberry vinegar; we had also two bottles of pickles.

A later literary figure with a long association with Stonyhurst was Gerard Manley Hopkins, who entered on September 9, 1870, and remained until entering St. Beuno's, North Wales, in 1874. He spent the summer holiday in 1872 with the Stonyhurst Jesuit community, which made an excursion to the Isle of Man. In July and August Hopkins was examined *De universa philosophia,* taught classics for a short time at the college, and made another retreat to the Isle of Man. Returning from Douglas, he was sent to Manresa House in Roehampton to teach rhetoric but returned to Stonyhurst in 1883 and 1884; he met Coventry Patmore, a convert to Catholicism, on Speech Day in 1883. Hopkins was sent in 1884 to Dublin, where he held the interdependent posts of the chair in classics at University College and a fellowship in the Department of Classics, Royal University of Ireland.

STORRINGTON, Sussex (pop. 1,388) Storrington is a jumble of Sussex stone, Edwardian-facaded, and concrete modern houses, and even the monastery's Abbey House is basically new. Situated 8 miles by road northeast of Arundel, Storrington has the full natural scenic advantages of both the South Downs and the Arun Valley. Storrington Priory was the Premonstratensian establishment to which Francis Thompson was induced to come around 1889. Thompson had failed in his attempt to join the priesthood in Ushaw, in his attempt to qualify in medicine in Manchester, and in his attempt to earn his own livelihood in London. Addicted to opium after reading De Quincey's *Confessions of an English Opium Eater* and suffering severe bouts of neuralgia, Thompson was eventually rescued by Wilfrid Meynell and was sent here to recuperate after hospitalization. Much of Thompson's poetry was written here, as was the "Essay on Shelley." An incident here was the force behind "Daisy"; out walking one day, Thompson encountered a child, one of nine in a family, the last four of whom were named for flowers (Rose, Daisy, Lily, and Violet):

Oh, there were flowers in Storrington
On the turf and on the spray;
But the sweetest flower on Sussex hills
Was the Daisy-flower that day!

A second literary association of the priory is with Hilaire Belloc, who sometimes attended midnight mass here at Christmas when he was living in Slindon or Shipley. After mass the older members of the party would join the monks to drink Arquebus.

STOURBRIDGE, Worcestershire (pop. 35,130) An industrial town on the Stour River at the gateway to the Black Country, Stourbridge is 5 miles southwest of Dudley and 11½ miles west of Birmingham. With proximity to coalfields and a good quantity and quality of local clay, the town inevitably became industrialized; indeed, as early as Elizabethan times its glass industry was important. Now there are ironworks as well.

The Bluecoat School, founded in 1667, stands on the main road, but King Edward's Grammar School on the High Street is even older. Originally a long, low brick building set back off the street between the Vine Inn and the Old Horse Inn, this was the school to which Samuel Johnson was sent in 1726 upon the advice of a cousin, Cornelius Ford, of nearby Pedmore. Johnson's specific status here is not known, but it may be that he acted as assistant to Mr. Wentworth for the younger boys; he was engaged in academic and creative pursuits himself and, besides translating Horace, composed a poem on St. Simon and St. Jude and "Festina Lente." Much later in life, as Boswell reports, Johnson made the following discrimination over his education at the grammar school in Lichfield and the one here:

"At one, I learned much in the school, but little from the master; in the other [here], I learnt much from the master, but little in the school."

During the six months (not a year, as is usually thought) Johnson often visited Green Close, the home of Cornelius Ford's half brother, Gregory Hickman, just next to the Old Horse Inn. In 1731 Johnson competed unsuccessfully for the usher's post here; the present grammar school is not the one Johnson attended but has been rebuilt on the same site.

STOURTON, Wiltshire (pop. 302) The village of Stourton, 3 miles northwest of Mere on the downs which separate Wiltshire and Somerset, is actually a part of the great house and estate of Stourhead on its southeastern edge and is often so identified. The Stourhead estate with its magnificent grounds, on the southern edge of the old Forest of Selwood, predates the Norman Conquest and belonged to the Stourton family until after the 8th Baron was publicly hanged in the Salisbury marketplace in the 16th century for a double murder. In 1720 Henry Hoare, Sir Richard Hoare's younger brother, bought the estate from the trustees, tore down the old manor house, built a new Palladian-style house, and renamed it Stourhead. The house is filled with art treasures collected through the years, and the pleasure gardens, laid out by Henry Hoare's son about 1744, are unparalleled in the shire. The son was also responsible for Alfred's Tower, a landmark said to designate the spot where Alfred the Great defeated the Danes in 878. The gardens are about 2 miles in circumference, and contain caves, grottoes, temples, and a wealth of statuary including some brought here from Rome and Herculaneum. In a grotto on the northwest side of the small lake are two pieces of John Michael Rysbrack's work, *Neptune* and the *Sleeping Nymph;* the latter is the one celebrated by Alexander Pope, and his lines are carved on the basin beneath the statue:

Nymph of the grot, these sacred springs I keep
And to the murmur of these waters sleep;
Ah! spare my slumbers, gently tread the cave
And drink in silence or in silence lave.

STOWE, Buckinghamshire (pop. 189) Situated 3 miles northwest of Buckingham, Stowe is both a hamlet and a former ducal seat but is now a well-known public school; the original builder of Stowe was Sir Richard Temple, whose house was somewhat smaller than today's central block. Temple's son Richard, Viscount Cobham, came into the estate and engaged Charles Bridgeman to develop the gardens; Bridgeman embarked on a revolutionary form of landscaping: the ha-ha, a sunken and invisible fence which allowed parts of the garden to merge into the wilder, natural countryside. Later Bridgeman worked with William Kent to lay out the lakes, follies, and vistas that quickly became the talk of the age. Kent then added the Temple of Worthies, which held busts of Shakespeare, Bacon, Milton, Locke, and others, and the Temple of Ancient Virtue. Cobham added to the house, as did his nephew, the 2d Earl Temple. One of Cobham's early and frequent visitors was Alexander Pope, who dedicated the first of his *Moral Essays* to him and who describes the intent of the landscape designers in *An Epistle to the Right Honourable Richard Earl of Burlington.* Most likely Jonathan Swift also visited here; William Congreve was often at Stowe, and Cobham remembered his visits with a commemorative statue by Kent. In 1922 Stowe was sold, and it opened in 1923 as a public school with ninety-seven scholars.

STOWMARKET, Suffolk (pop. 6,508) Located on the Gipping River in the central Suffolk farming plain, Stowmarket is presently favored with a busy market and with light industry; at one time it was important as a port along the river from Ipswich, 12½ miles to the southeast. The church contains an extremely old and still-functioning organ, a very rare wig stand, and a number of good monuments and portraits including one of Dr. Thomas Young, tutor to the young John Milton in London. After Dr. Young was preferred to the living here, he frequently had the poet as his guest at the Old Vicarage on Milton Road. The mulberry tree in the garden of the vicarage which Milton is supposed to have planted blew down in the mid-20th century; in any event, there is little evidence to support the claims once made on its behalf. In 1766 and 1767 George Crabbe attended Richard Haddon's school here; he suffered from the school bully, who, Crabbe later relates, would make "the trembling youngsters flee." But the bully's stupidity matched his cruelty; the master asked him the product of 6 times 5; the bully closes his eyes and heaves a sigh:

"Come, six times count your fingers—how he stands! Your fingers, idiot!"—"What of both my hands?"

STRATFORD, Essex Virtually a part of London now, Stratford is a mere 3½ miles northeast of the Liverpool Street Station and within the municipal and parliamentary limits of the West Ham area of London. Gerard Manley Hopkins was born here at the Grove on July 28, 1844, and was christened in the local Anglican church. The family moved at an early but unspecified date to Hampstead, London, where he spent his boyhood.

STRATFORD-ON-AVON, Warwickshire (pop. 11,-616) This old market town, 8 miles southwest of Warwick, stands where a Roman road once crossed the Avon River. The old estate was granted to the Bishop of Winchester by the Mercian king Offa, and the southern bank of the Avon was heavily settled by Anglo-Saxons; a Saxon burial ground has been discovered there. The monks from Worcester built on the site of the present manor house; the town grew in medieval times, especially as a market, and gained its charter from Edward VI in 1553. However, all Stratford's early history has been eclipsed by its prominence as the birthplace of William Shakespeare, which virtually every aspect of the town reflects.

What must be established first is that most of the information about Shakespeare and Stratford is conjectural; only a very few specific bits of evidence exist. His usual birth date, April 23, 1564, is only a guess; he was christened in the parish church, Holy

Trinity, on April 26, and the date of birth is assumed from this date. The entry in the register, which is open to the appropriate spot, reads "Gulielmus filius Johannes Shakspere." The house which is said to be his birthplace and is under the care of the Shakespeare Birthplace Trust is a half-timbered building on Henley Street. In 1552 John Shakespeare, the dramatist's father, rented a house somewhere on Henley Street, and in October 1556 he purchased a structure on Henley Street, next to the birthplace, as a shop for the sale of wool and other commodities. The two buildings undoubtedly had interior doorways. In 1575, eleven years after William's birth, John Shakespeare bought the building known as the birthplace from Edmund Hall, and it seems plausible to assume that this was the house in which he was earlier just a tenant and in which William was born. The house remained in family hands until 1806, when John Hart's widow sold the encumbered estate, and in September 1847, a committee of trustees bought the property for the nation. The interior of the birthplace has none of the original furniture but has been furnished authentically with similar period pieces. An upper room has been assigned, by a very old tradition, to be the birth room, and the wool shop and store have been made into a museum of relics associated with Shakespeare or the period. In the latter half of 1564 Stratford was visited by the plague, and in six months 238 people, or one-sixth of the town's population, died; not one member of the poet's family was counted in that toll, a point which is often said to attest to the high sanitation standard of the Shakespeare family. That may be so, but in April 1552 John Shakespeare was fined by the corporation "for garnering an unsavory harvest under his own window" and again in 1558, with four others, "for not kepying ther gutters cleane."

The records of the Stratford Free School, the grammar school for this period, no longer exist, but it is assumed that Shakespeare began his education here around 1571 and remained only until 1577, when his father's fortunes began to decline. The only requirement for admission to the school in addition to age was that a boy be able to read; Shakespeare was undoubtedly taught this skill at home with a hornbook, such as he later refers to in *Love's Labour's Lost*:

Cost. O, they have lived long on the alms-basket of words! I marvel thy master hath not eaten thee for a word; for thou art not so long by the head as *honorificabilitudinitatibus*: thou are easier swallowed than a flapdragon.
Moth. Peace; the peal begins.
Arm. Monsieur [*to Hol.*], are you not lettered?
Moth. Yes, yes; he teaches boys the hornbook;—What is a, b, spelt backward with the horn on his head.

Or he may have been taught through an A B C book, to which he alludes in *King John*:

. . . My dear sir,—
Thus, leaning on mine elbow, I begin,—
I shall beseech you—that is question now;
And then comes answer like an ABC-book. . . .

The grammar school had been begun by the old guild in the first half of the 15th century, and Edward VI re-created the school as the King's New School of Stratford-upon-Avon. The training would have been

STRATFORD-ON-AVON The half-timbered house on Henley Street where William Shakespeare probably was born is now in the hands of the Shakespeare Birthplace Trust; while it is furnished appropriately, none of the original furniture has survived.

mostly in Latin, but Greek was possibly included, for the schoolmaster during most of this time was the scholar Thomas Hunt, later vicar at Luddington. The Latin grammar was William Lily's, the standard 16th-century text, which Shakespeare quotes in a number of plays including *The Taming of the Shrew:*

> Master, it is no time to chide you now;
> Affection is not rated from the heart;
> If love have touch'd you, nought remains but so,—
> *Redime te captum quam queas minimo.*

What Shakespeare did after he left school is not known. John Aubrey, who cannot be considered totally reliable, claimed that Shakespeare was apprenticed to a butcher, but of this there is no proof. Another tradition claims he acted as a pupil-teacher at the Stratford school, and a third has him apprenticed in a law firm.

The next actual information concerning Shakespeare is in 1582, the year of his marriage to Anne (Agnes) Hathaway, and of this, too, little evidence exists. The marriage bond authorizing the marriage in the episcopal archives at Worcester is dated November 28, 1582; the surety for the bond was put up by two residents of Shottery, Anne Hathaway's village, and the bond itself was unusual in that although Shakespeare was three years under age, there is no evidence of parental consent. The wedding probably took place in early December, but no church records have come to light to establish the place. It is thought, though, that the most likely place would have been Luddington, where Hunt was vicar. Since Anne Hathaway was obviously pregnant at the time of the marriage, much has been made of the two Shottery husbandmen who acted as surety, but neither William nor his father could have raised the £40. Additionally, if a precontract, that is, a formalized betrothal, had existed for some months, the situation can be explained; the precontract was frequently recognized as equivalent to marriage with all its attendant rights and privileges. It is often stated that the newly married couple lived with the dramatist's family here; however, John Shakespeare's declining resources and his need to provide for his wife and his four remaining young children make this seem unlikely. More realistically, the couple lived with her widowed mother in the big Shottery cottage, although Susanna was christened here at Holy Trinity on May 26, 1583. The twins Hamnet and Judith were born less than two years later and were baptized on February 2, 1585. Shortly after this, Shakespeare left for London; it has also been suggested that Shakespeare went abroad at this point for some unknown reason, and foreign colloquialisms in the plays are cited as proof. Tradition ascribes the reason for the departure to a poaching incident at Sir Thomas Lucy's estate at Charlecote, although the reason could have been connected with the religious issues of the times, since Sir Thomas has been characterized as an ardent and bigoted Protestant and the Ardens (Shakespeare's maternal family) were Romanists who had been involved in a conspiracy against the Queen's life.

Little has been discovered about the life Shakespeare's family led during these years. His son Hamnet died in 1596 and was buried on August 11 at Stratford, and it is usually assumed that the dramatist was here for some part of that summer. Shakespeare appears to have had a direct interest in establishing a home in Stratford, and in the spring of 1597 he bought New Place, a house with nearly an acre of land in the center of the town. He paid £60 for the property, an astonishingly low figure, but New Place was "in great ruyne and decay and unrepayred," and the need for extensive restoration must have influenced the sale price. While Shakespeare did a great deal of work on New Place to make it habitable, the only description of the estate dates from almost fifty years before the dramatist bought it, when John Leland described it as standing

> ... by the north syde of this chapell a praty howse of brike and tymbar. ...

Only the foundations of New Place are left, and the area, under the care of the Shakespeare Birthplace Trust, has been planted beautifully with flowers and herbs appropriate to the plays. It should be noted that New Place was wantonly destroyed in 1759 by its owner, the Rev. Francis Gastrell, who wanted the house as a summer place; in 1756, annoyed by the influx of pilgrims to see the mulberry tree which Shakespeare was said to have planted and sat under, the splenetic clergyman cut the tree down, much to the annoyance of the townspeople. Indeed, they threw rocks through the windows at New Place in retaliation. Three years later, feeling his privacy to be increasingly invaded during his summer residence here and having no kind feelings for the association, he decided the corporation had overstepped its municipal authority in demanding the usual poor rate due on any structure valued at over 40 shillings and gave orders for the demolition of New Place. The townspeople could do nothing, but they vowed "never to suffer a man of the same name to reside in Stratford."

On June 5, 1607, Shakespeare's daughter Susanna married Dr. John Hall at Holy Trinity Church, and it seems fairly obvious that Shakespeare was at the ceremony. Dr. Hall and his wife lived at Hall's Croft (then Old Town), a house and surgery, which the dramatist would have known intimately. A many-gabled house with an overhanging upper floor and a walled garden (owned by the Birthplace Trust), it has the internal atmosphere of a middle-class Tudor home, and Dr. Hall's dispensary is stocked with the appropriate apothecary equipment. Shakespeare appears to have been back and forth from London frequently during these years, but he probably returned to take up permanent residence in 1611, perhaps as early as September. The next years were quiet and uneventful, and on February 10, 1616, his younger daughter Judith was married to Thomas Quiney, a Stratford man nearly four years her junior; the marriage took place without a license, for the lack of which the couple was fined and threatened with excommunication. Since there is no known reason for such a hurried wedding, it has been supposed that the dramatist's failing health was the cause; Shakespeare had prepared his will in January under the direction of a Warwick solicitor.

Shakespeare's death occurred on Tuesday, April 23, 1616, and according to the Rev. John Ward, who became the vicar in 1662 and recorded many local comments concerning the dramatist from those who knew him, Shakespeare was visited by Michael Drayton and Ben Jonson in the latter part of March, on which occasion the three men had a "merry meeting" in a local pub. Ward noted they "drank to hard, for Shakespeare died of a feavour there contracted." The funeral of "Will. Shakespere, gent.," as the parish register states, occurred on April 25; he was buried in the chancel of Holy Trinity, as was appropriate for the owners of the tithes. The grave, near the northern wall of the chancel, is covered with a slab bearing the well-known inscription:

GOOD FREND, FOR IESVS SAKE FORBEARE
TO DIGG THE DVST ENCLOASED HEARE;
BLESTE BE THE MAN THAT SPARES THES STONES,
AND CVRST BE HE YT MOVES MY BONES.

Whether the poet chose these words is debatable, but the relevance of the inscription is important, for an ancient charnel house containing a vast collection of bones stood almost next to his grave. The monument to the poet was erected sometime previous to the 1623 folio edition of the plays, as the Leonard Digges verses prefacing the volume show:

Shake-speare, at length thy pious fellows give
The world thy Workes: thy Workes, by which, out-live
Thy Tombe, thy name must: when that stone is rent,
And Time dissolves thy Stratford Moniment,
Here we alive shall view thee still.

The monument on the north wall of the chancel consists of a life-size bust in an ornamental arch; tradition says that the sculptor, Ghurart Janssen (often Anglicized to Gerard Johnson), worked from a posthumous cast of Shakespeare's face, and many sculptors are in agreement. The bust was originally painted, in the fashion of the day, with Shakespeare's eyes light hazel, his hair and beard auburn, the doub-

let scarlet, the gown black, and the collar and wristbands white; but at the instigation of the critic Edmund Malone in 1793, the bust was covered with a coat of white paint. Malone deserved the anonymous castigation placed in the visitors' book in 1810:

Stranger, to whom this monument is shown,
Invoke the poet's curses on Malone,
Whose meddling zeal his barbarous taste betrays,
And daubs his tombstone as he marr'd his plays.

The white paint was removed in 1861, and sufficient color remained to restore the original shades.

Next to Shakespeare's grave is that of his wife, to whom he left his "second best bed." On the other side of the poet's grave is that of Thomas Nash, first husband of Elizabeth Hall (Shakespeare's granddaughter), and then the grave of Dr. John Hall. Last is the grave of Susanna Hall, whose inscription has had its problems:

Witty above her sexe, but that's not all,
Wise to Salvation was good Mistris Hall,
Something of Shakespere was in that, but this
Wholy of him with whom she's now in blisse.
Then, Passenger, ha'st ne're a teare,
   To weepe with her that wept with all?
That wept, yet set hereselfe to chere
   Them up with comforts cordiall.
Her love shall live, her mercy spread,
When thou hast ne're a teare to shed.

In 1707 the memorial slab was taken up and the verses removed to make way for a new inscription to Richard Watts; but in 1836, the stone was removed from Watts's grave, and the original lines were restored.

There are a number of other interesting monuments, epitaphs, and associations here, including one that may have been the germ of the idea for Ophelia's

STRATFORD-ON-AVON Holy Trinity Church, reflected in the Avon, contains the graves of William Shakespeare, his wife, his daughter Susanna Hall, and her husband Dr. John Hall. The graves of the twins, Hammet and Judith, are in the churchyard near the riverbank.

drowning. On a December day in 1569, one Katherine Hamlett, spinster (the nominal echo is interesting), died by drowning in the Avon near Tiddington; the inquest decided that her death was not suicide but that "going with a milk-pail to draw water at the river, standing on the bank [she] slipped and fell in, and was drowned:" Another early death here may also have influenced the dramatist; in 1564, when the plague ravished Stratford, a daughter, Margaret, was born to Charlotte Clopton, of an influential family. Soon thereafter the mother was striken by the plague. The urgency of the situation demanded quick burial, and the body was rushed to the family vault in Holy Trinity. For some reason the vault was opened several days later, and Charlotte was discovered standing at the doorway dead. Perhaps this was the background for the scene of Juliet's awakening in the tomb to find the bodies of Romeo and Paris beside her. Margaret Clopton may also have been the source of Ophelia's drowning, for she drowned herself in the fishpond at Clopton House, "sick for love." Another of the monuments of interest is that of John Combe, Shakespeare's friend, about whom a tradition concerning usury exists. A few years before Combe's death, Shakespeare is supposed to have composed a satirical epitaph:

> Ten in the hundred lies here engrav'd,
> 'Tis a hundred to ten his soul is not sav'd,
> If any man ask, who lies in this tomb,
> Ho! ho! quoth the Devil, 'tis my John-a-Combe.

Stratford abounds in monuments and dedications to the dramatist; in the Bancroft Gardens is the Lord Ronald Sutherland Gower monument of Shakespeare atop a pedestal with the figures of Prince Hal, Falstaff, Lady Macbeth, and Hamlet in characteristic poses around him. The greatest modern memorial is the magnificent Royal Shakespeare Theatre, the second construction on the site. The first theater, excepting the library and gallery, was completed in April 1879 and was called everything from "a paltry and impertinent business" which was "an insult to the memory of Shakespeare" to a "striped sugar stick." The architect had evidently been thinking of the old Globe, and what arose here on the riverbank was a brick building with some half timbering and a motley assortment of sham-Gothic decorative pieces. The structure lasted until March 6, 1926, when it was totally destroyed by fire; fortunately all the paintings, books, and statuary were saved by a human chain. The present theater was rebuilt as directed, a building "simple, beautiful, convenient," to a design by Elisabeth Scott, grandniece of Sir Gilbert Scott. The new theater, much maligned at first (called both a factory and a tomb), opened on April 23, 1932, with a production of *Henry IV: Part I.*

It is inevitable that virtually every writer has been in Stratford at some time and has commented on the town, its dramatist, or the plays. To catalog the writers here is unnecessary, but a sample makes interesting reading. Staying at the White Lion Inn (later a house) on Henley Street, Horace Walpole had hoped to find the town "smug, and pretty, and *antique*, not *old*," but was disappointed in what he found. The Shakespeare bust in Holy Trinity had just been repaired (the coloring and gilt were restored, and the broken-off bits renewed); and Walpole's disgust is captured in his remark, "Lady Caroline Petersham is not more vermil-

STRATFORD-ON-AVON   The Royal Shakespeare Theatre, overlooking the Avon, presents William Shakespeare's plays yearly from April to October.

lion." Stratford was still a wheat and malt market town, and little was made of the Shakespearean association until some years later, when David Garrick, at the height of his dramatic career, was made a freeman of the town and invited to help raise funds to replace the crumbling town hall. The corporation wrote to him that it was "ever desirous of Expressing Gratitude to all who do Honour and Justice to the memory of Shakespeare, & highly sensible that no person in any Age hath Excelled you" and asked him for a bust, portrait, or sculpture of the dramatist to start its fund raising. From this was born the Shakespeare Jubilee, and preparations began for a September 1769 extravaganza. Dr. Samuel Johnson was conspicuously absent; although a close friend of Garrick and an editor of Shakespeare, he refused to participate in the jamboree, and his decision influenced many in his coterie. Oliver Goldsmith and Edmund Burke did not turn up either, but an assorted number of minor dramatists appeared, among them Hugh Kelly, William Kenrick, Nathaniel Lee, and Love, names which today are never recognized. James Boswell not only attended the jubilee but wrote:

> Upon this occasion I particularly lamented that ... [Johnson] had not that warmth of friendship for his brilliant pupil, which we may suppose would have had a benignant effect on both. When almost every man of eminence in the literary world was happy to partake in this festival of genius, the absence of Johnson could not but be wondered at and regretted.

William Cowper, who is not known to have attended the celebration, did write of it and of Garrick in *The Task:*

> For Garrick was a worshipper himself;
> He drew the liturgy, and framed the rites
> And solemn ceremonial of the day,
> And call'd the world to worship on the banks
> Of Avon famed in song. Ah, pleasant proof

That piety has still in human hearts
Some place, a spark or two not yet extinct.
The mulberry-tree was hung with blooming wreaths. . . .

The 19th century saw a steady procession of visitors. One of the first, John Keats, came in October 1817 with Benjamin Bailey and was repelled by the commercialization of Shakespeare's birthplace. On at least two occasions Sir Walter Scott stopped in Stratford. On the first, in July 1821 on his trip home following George IV's coronation, he wrote his name on the wall of the room in which Shakespeare is said to have been born. Scott's second visit occurred on a spring trip to London in 1828, when he

visited the tomb of the mighty wizard. It is in the bad taste of James I's reign; but what a magic does the locality possess! There are stately monuments of forgotten families; but when you have seen Shakespeare's, what care we for the rest. All around is Shakespeare's exclusive property.

On this visit he also went to nearby Charlecote, the scene of the alleged deer stealing. Elizabeth Cleghorn Gaskell was sent to Miss Byerly's School at Avonbank here in 1821 from Knutsford, Cheshire, where she was living with an aunt. A visit to Clopton House during her three years here provided the material for her first published work, a contribution to William Howitt's *Visits to Remarkable Places*. In 1840 Alfred, Lord Tennyson and Edward FitzGerald stopped in Stratford after an accidental meeting in Warwick; Tennyson writes that they

saw Shakespeare's monument. I should not think it can be a good likeness. That foolish fellow painted it white all over, and served poor Johnny Combe, who lies on a monument near, in the same way. . . . By which fancy of Malone we have in all probability lost the colour of Shakespeare's hair and eyes, which perhaps would do the world very little good to know, but would have been a little satisfaction to poor physiognomists like myself. We went also into the room where they say he was born. Every part of it is scribbled over with names. I was seized with a sort of enthusiasm, and wrote mine, tho' I was a little ashamed of it afterwards: yet the feeling was genuine at the time, and I did homage with the rest.

Charles Dickens, who stayed first at the Red Horse when he arrived in Stratford, came to meet with the committee formed to purchase Shakespeare's birthplace. Dickens's entry in his diary reads much like the staccato style associated with Alfred Jingle:

Stratford—Shakespeare—the birthplace, visitors, scribblers, old women—Qy. whether she knows what Shakespeare did, etc.

His signature and that of Phiz (Hablot Knight Browne) are said to have been scribbled on one of the plaster panels in the birth room, but the panel has since been destroyed. Dickens did, though, visit the church. The guest book (May 1821 to September 1848) which he signed at the birthplace was auctioned at Sotheby's in 1898 and fetched £56; other signatories included Scott and Washington Irving, who had stayed at the Red Horse Hotel on Bridge Street in 1815. For a short time in recent years the hotel was known under Irving's name, and the room where he wrote his essay on Stratford preserves his

chair and poker. Irving is a bit acid about the birthplace, accepts the deer-stealing tradition, and writes of the bust and tombstone:

A flat stone marks the spot where the bard is buried. There are four lines inscribed on it, said to have been written by himself, and which have in them something extremely awful. . . .

Just over the grave, in a niche of the wall, is a bust of Shakespeare, put up shortly after his death, and considered as a resemblance. The aspect is pleasant and serene, with a finely arched forehead; and I thought I could read in it clear indications of that cheerful, social disposition, by which he was as much characterized among his contemporaries as by the vastness of his genius.

In the summer of 1853 Dante Gabriel Rossetti was on a walking tour in the area; extremely depressed about personal matters, he had more than once contemplated suicide before arriving here. He stayed at the Red Horse Inn and composed a rather damning sonnet about the Reverend Gastrell:

This tree, here fall'n, no common birth or death
    Shared with its kind. The world's enfranchised son,
    Who found the trees of Life and Knowledge one,
Here set it, frailer than his laurel-wreath.
Shall not the wretch whose hand it fell beneath
    Rank also singly—the supreme unhung?
    Lo! Sheppard, Turpin, pleading with black tongue
This viler thief's unsuffocated breath!

Rossetti's moral justification of free love, "On Plucking a Honeysuckle," was begun en route and worked on at the inn.

Nathaniel Hawthorne, who spent many years as United States consul in Liverpool, visited Stratford and was especially interested in the Avon. Another American author joined in the doings at Stratford during Queen Victoria's Jubilee in 1887 when the memorial fountain here was unveiled with a great deal of fanfare; Henry Irving, the actor, unveiled the work, whose finials represent Puck, Mustardseed, Peaseblossom, and Cobweb; Oliver Wendell Holmes wrote a poem for the occasion which Irving read, a poem which could by no means be called good:

Here lark and thrush and nightingale shall sip,
    And skimming swallows dip,
And strange shy wanderers fold their lustrous plumes
Fragrant from bowers that lent their sweet perfumes
Where Paestum's rose or Persia's lilac blooms;
Here from his cloud the eagle stoops to drink
    At the full basin's brink,
And whet his beak against its rounded lip,
His glossy feathers glistening as they drip.

Toward the close of the century the poet and dramatist Oscar Wilde was asked to take part in another civic function here, the unveiling of the 65-ton Gower bronze of Shakespeare. Wilde spoke rapturously about the Shakespeare Memorial Theatre as "one of the loveliest buildings erected in Britain for many years" and read a sonnet by a local poet (whose name is lost). Among other 19th-century visitors were Matthew Arnold, who said of the bust in Holy Trinity, "Thou smilest, and art still, Out-topping knowledge"; Thomas Carlyle, who scratched his name on the window of the room in which Shakespeare is said to have been born; and Robert Browning, who placed his signature on a wall panel in the same room and later wrote of Stratford and Shakespeare in "Bishop Blougram's Apology":

> He leaves his towers and gorgeous palaces
> To build the trimmest house in Stratford town;
> Saves money, spends it, owns the worth of things,
> Guilio Romano's pictures, Dowland's lute;
> Enjoys a show, respects the puppets, too,
> And none more, had he seen its entry once,
> Than "Pandulph, of fair Milan cardinal."
> Why then should I who play that personage,
> The very Pandulph Shakespeare's fancy made,
> Be told that had the poet chanced to start
> From where I stand now (some degree like mine
> Being just the goal he ran his race to reach)
> He would have run the whole race back, forsooth,
> And left being Pandulph, to begin write plays?
> Ah, the earth's best can be but the earth's best!

Mary Mackay, better known under her pseudonym Marie Corelli, first arrived in the town in the summer of 1899; she rented Dower House and Hall's Croft before settling into Mason Croft on Church Street in 1901. Here she lived the rest of her life with Bertha Vyver, her friend and companion. Miss Corelli rather looked upon herself as Shakespeare's executrix, and while her efforts deserve some praise, she was very aggressive and self-conscious in her dealings and earned considerable dislike. She often meddled in municipal, theatrical, and ecclesiastical affairs; indeed, she kept Sir Theodore Martin from erecting a memorial to his wife Helen Faucit, the actress, in Holy Trinity Church, and the resulting court proceedings were unpleasant. She had her own gondola, *The Dream*, which she used on the Avon (and fired her first Venetian gondolier for drunkenness); she drove through Stratford in a chaise drawn by two Shetland ponies; and she refused to set the clocks at her house to "summer time," preferring "God's time." But much to her credit, she saved a number of old houses and fought to have the memorial theater give up its use of bowdlerized texts.

When Marie Corelli took Mason Croft, it was in a dilapidated state, and she did extensive renovation, but the good done to the house seemed futile when the terms of her will became known. She died here on April 21, 1924, and was buried in the Stratford Cemetery; her grave is marked by an angel of Carrara marble. Under the terms of the will, Miss Vyver was to keep Mason Croft for the remainder of her life (she died in 1941). Then Mason Croft was to function as a meeting place "for the annual or provincial meeting of scientists connected with the Royal Institution of Great Britain" and as a base for "distinguished persons visiting Stratford-upon-Avon from far countries, who should be selected and recommended to the trustees by the Council of the Society of Authors and who would otherwise seek their quarters in a hotel." The accommodations however, were "absolutely . . . [to exclude] actors, actresses, and all persons connected with the stage." Mason Croft was to be maintained by royalties, and never in her most lucid moments did Marie Corelli foresee that the income would not last forever; her books were to be immortal. The house and its contents were eventually sold, after the provision of the will was declared void, and today the house is the Shakespeare Institute of the University of Birmingham. A recent reaction to Marie Cor-

elli and Mason Croft comes from Hugh Walpole, who visited Stratford with his brother at the end of July 1940:

> An old servant . . . showed us round. Small, white-haired, bespectacled, in a black silk dress and apron. "I hope you were a friend of Miss Corelli's and never spoke or wrote harm of her," she said, her eyes flashing. . . . "She was a sweet little lady." . . .
> She took us over everything—all as it had been in M. C.'s lifetime. All dead or dying. The harp, the faded photographs, paper roses, cracked looking-glasses, a spinning-wheel from which a moth flew out, faded books. . . . Above all the famous gondola, and the Christmas card her gondolier had sent her just before he was killed in France. The ink she had used corroded in the ink-bottles. Rows of hideous china ornaments in her bedroom. The paddock thick with grass, and her old pony over forty! The garden with no flowers, only weeds. . . . Death and decay over everything.

Three other 20th-century visitors of note were William Butler Yeats, Mark Twain (Samuel Clemens), and John Galsworthy. Yeats, who was here in April 1901, spent his days reading in the library of the Shakespeare Institute and his evenings at the theater, where the history plays were being performed. Twain was shown the restored Harvard House by Marie Corelli in 1907, and Galsworthy paid his first visit to Stratford, so says his diary, in August 1916, a rather astonishingly late date. He stayed at the Shakespeare Hotel, where he had "*The Winter's Tale* bedroom." On August 5, the second day of his visit, he read a paper, "The Islands of the Blessed," to an audience of about 250 people.

STREATLEY, Berkshire (pop. 793) An unspoiled village of lovely Georgian houses on the Thames River, Streatley is located opposite Goring, between Reading and Wallingford. From the summit of Streatley Hill the splendid view upstream takes in the Thames as it nears Goring Gap Gorge between the Berkshire Downs and the Chiltern Hills. After the death of Thomas Norton on March 10, 1584, at his home in Sharpenhoe, his body was brought to the church here for burial. Much later the village became the home of Kenneth Grahame for a short time; after forging a close friendship with Sidney Ward, Grahame borrowed his 14th-century cottage on the main street of the village. From here Grahame made his excursions along the prehistoric Ridgeway and on one occasion, after a 20-mile trek across the track, returned for an enormous meal, "pipes, bed, and heavenly sleep."

STRENSHAM, Worcestershire (pop. 194) Situated 4½ miles southwest of Pershore and very near the Gloucestershire border, Strensham is really two hamlets, Upper and Lower Strensham, both of which seem partly of another time even though the motorway pulsates nearby. Close to the Avon River and down a long lane stands a historic church, its 14th-century tower dominating the landscape and looking to the Malvern Hills to the west and to Bredon Hill to the east. Strensham was the birthplace of Samuel Butler in 1612; his father, a farmer, leased land here which for centuries was known as Butler's tenement. Butler was baptized in the parish church on February 8 and spent all his childhood in Strensham; Anthony à Wood's assertion that the author of *Hudibras* was born in Bartonbridge, near Worcester, is unsubstantiated. Butler's earliest-known education was at the grammar school in Worcester.

STRETTON, Rutland (pop. 141) So small a village that one does not expect a church and a vicar, Stretton is located 8 miles northwest of Stamford on the Great North Road. The old church here has coffin fragments more than 800 years old, and it is thought that a lid from a Saxon coffin was fashioned into a tympanum for the Norman doorway. This was the church to which Cuthbert Bede (Edward Bradley) came as rector in the mid-19th century. During his twelve-year tenure at Stretton he wrote *The Adventures of Mr. Verdant Green, an Oxford Freshman*, a fantasy story of university life which secured his place in literature. Bede was also an adept artist, and a number of his pen-and-ink sketches are preserved here; of special interest is one showing the chancel before the extreme restorations which he sponsored. After his death in Lenton, Lincolnshire, on December 12, 1889, Bradley was buried here. Another literary association is with the old manor, the home of Humphrey, Duke of Gloucester, whom William Shakespeare uses in *Henry IV: Part II, Henry V,* and *Henry VI: Parts I and II*. The title Good Duke Humphrey by which he was known had nothing to do with his moral probity but referred to his position as "the most lettered prince in the world" and his patronage of scholarship.

STRETTON, Staffordshire The hamlet and seat of Stretton Hall, 3 miles southwest of Penkridge, has traditionally been associated with William Congreve and *The Old Bachelor*. Congreve visited the estate here, and it has been claimed that the idea for the play and the work on it originated here in Stretton. However, a similar claim is made for the manor house and the village of Aldermaston.

STUDLEY, Warwickshire (pop. 3,147) On the Worcestershire border 3½ miles southeast of Redditch, Studley has been known for the manufacture of needles since the late 17th century; the village is on the Arrow River and has a fine prospect over the wooded countryside. The slight remains of a priory have been incorporated into a farmhouse, and the church has a fine Norman doorway, a 14th-century stone coffin lid carved with a beautiful cross, and the grave of Dorothy Lyttelton, Walter Savage Landor's cousin. It was she who managed to reconcile Landor with his father and whose grave the poet visited. At the age of eighty, Landor confessed to having wanted to marry her in his youth but had felt he could not approach her at that time because of his unknown future. "On the Dead" recalls their being in the chancel for services.

STURMINSTER NEWTON, Dorset (pop. 1,958) Set in the midst of Blackmoor Vale, Sturminster Newton is the primary market town for the Stour farm and dairy lands. The old mill on the Stour River dates from the 17th century and has much of the original brickwork; the roof is partly tiled in stone, and the mill is still operative. Just outside the town, on the opposite bank of the Stour, are Castle Hill and the ruins of what is often referred to erroneously as Sturminster Newton

Castle. This is not a castle but the ruins of a stone house of, most likely, medieval origin; indeed, the site is traditionally held to have been a royal hunting lodge belonging to King Alfred the Great during the later part of his reign (871–899). In the 19th century the ruins were always referred to as the castle ruins: William Barnes, the Dorset poet, describes the remains in "The Castle Ruins":

> There, down the rufless walls did glow
> The zun upon the grassy vloor,
> An' weakly-wandren winds did blow
> Unhinder'd by a door;
> An' smokeless now avore the zun
> Did stran' the ivy-girded tun.

Barnes was born at nearby Pentridge Farm on March 20, 1801, and received his education here. He left school at the age of sixteen and was articled to a solicitor in Dorchester. The lectern in the local church is a memorial to Barnes.

A gray stone mansion called Riverside Villa on the outskirts of the town was the home of Thomas Hardy and his first wife from July 1876 to 1878. Hardy called this period "our happiest time"; "A Two Year Idyll," "Overlooking the River Stour," and "The Music Box" all refer to this time. While living at Riverside he wrote *The Return of the Native*, but the primitive landscape depicted in *The Native* is totally alien to the soft, undulating countryside of the Stour Valley. Sturminster Newton becomes Stourcastle in *Tess of the D'Urbervilles*, but the town has only passing use in the novel: in the opening chapters John Durbeyfield sees a doctor here who tells him he has fat around his heart; Tess and Abraham have just passed through the town on their way to deliver bees in Casterbridge (Dorchester) when Prince is run through by the shaft on the noiseless mail cart.

SUDBURY, Suffolk (pop. 7,045) The comment of Daniel Defoe that he knew "nothing for which this town is remarkable, except for being very populous and very poor," while accurate to a point (Sudbury is relatively populous), is incorrect in that the town was usually prosperous. Located on the Stour River 16 miles south of Bury St. Edmunds, Sudbury has for centuries been a regional center of the cloth trade and the local market town. Its earlier prosperity was based on the wool trade in the 14th and 15th centuries, and when the wool trade declined, Sudbury became a market town and silk-weaving center. The town is best known as the birthplace of Thomas Gainsborough, who is commemorated with a birthplace museum on Gainsborough Street.

Defoe is not the only writer who formed a poor impression of Sudbury; Charles Dickens made it the Eatanswill of the *Pickwick Papers*. Dickens had been here as a reporter for the 1834 and 1835 elections, and his earlier comment about the town does more to explain its pseudonym and his attitude than the book:

> Open house is kept at all the inns in the town; the voters are seen reeling about the streets in a beastly state of intoxication. Cooping and other manoeuvres have been resorted to to procure voters.

Sudbury thus seems an obvious choice for Mr. Fulcher's election, which Mr. Pickwick wants to observe. While the inns of the various factions can be identified, they no longer exist: the Town Arms, headquarters of the Blues, was modeled on the Rose and Crown, which burned to the ground on New Year's Day, 1922. The Rose and Crown was on King Street, close to the marketplace. The Peacock, headquarters of the Buffs and the place where both Tupman and Snodgrass lodge and where "The Bagman's Story" is told, was the Swan Inn, which adjoined the Corn Exchange.

SUNDERLAND, County Durham (pop. 190,510) Known as Wearmouth in Saxon times, when it had a small, almost totally monastic population, Sunderland has become the largest town, the commercial capital, and the chief port of County Durham. In 674 Benedict Biscop founded the Monastery of St. Paul's at Monkwearmouth, the portion of the modern town north of the Wear, and by the 12th century the name "Sunderland" refers to an area "sundered from the monastic lands" by the Wear River; only at the end of the 19th century did Monkwearmouth become part of the larger Sunderland. Monkwearmouth, the sister monastery to the one in Jarrow, was the occasional "home" of the Venerable Bede, who came here to study at the monastic library and to receive help and inspiration from Abbot Benedict. The libraries here and at Jarrow contained one of the best collections of patristic literature outside Rome. The Church of St. Peter's in Monkwearmouth is partly Saxon (the tower and adjoining wall on the west end) and has an extremely good collection of Saxon carved stonework preserved under glass. Unfortunately the church is generally kept locked because of vandalism.

Sunderland has an "association" with Oliver Goldsmith resulting from a misreading of history; he is supposed to have been arrested and possibly imprisoned for a bad debt here. This story should be associated with Newcastle upon Tyne, Northumberland, and the imprisonment had nothing to do with a bad debt. However, there is evidence of an association with Robert Smith Surtees, for he married Elizabeth Fenwick of Bishopwearmouth here on May 29, 1841.

Just north of Monkwearmouth, the beach and resort area known as Roker (pronounced "ro'ka") holds a monument to the Venerable Bede. The 24-foot-tall gray cross on one side depicts scenes from Bede's life (arriving at Jarrow as a child, writing his *Historia Ecclesiastica Gentis Anglorum,* and translating the Gospel of St. John) and on the other portrays associated contemporaries (King Ceolwulf of Northumbria, to whom the history was dedicated, Archbishop John, who taught Bede to sing, Trumbert of Lastingham, who taught him Latin and divinity, and Benedict Biscop, the founder of the monasteries).

SUNDRIDGE, Kent (pop. 1,814) Situated 3 miles west of Sevenoaks, Sundridge has an extremely fine 13th-century church and Sundridge Old Hall, a 15th-century timber-framed building with a great hall illuminated by a twelve-light window. Tradition asserts that around 1613 the old church here was the scene of the marriage of Francis Beaumont and Ursula Isley, daughter of Henry Isley, of an old Sundridge family. Beaumont and his wife lived here following their marriage (the house is gone), and their two

children were born here, one after Beaumont's death here on March 6, 1616. He was buried on March 9 in Westminster Abbey, London.

SUNNINGHILL, Berkshire (pop. 5,839) In the southeast section of Berkshire near the Surrey border and only 5 miles southwest of Windsor, Sunninghill is an area of estates and large parks, much in favor because the road here leads to Ascot. It has often been asserted that the old manor of Sunninghill once belonged to Thomas Carew, but in fact it belonged to Thomas Carey, who was granted the lands by Charles I in 1630. The vicarage garden contains two old trees, one planted by Edmund Burke and the other by the 4th Earl of Chesterfield. One of the large houses here once belonged to George Ellis, a very good friend of Sir Walter Scott, who often visited here. Scott described his friend as the best talker he had ever known. Ellis was obviously a good listener as well, for under a tree on the estate Scott once recited the first three cantos of *The Lay of the Last Minstrel* (at the time unpublished).

SUNNINGWELL, Berkshire (pop. 518) Below Foxcombe Hill in the northern part of the county and close to the Thames, Sunningwell has a partly 13th-century battlemented church with medieval woodwork in a transept screen and a unique heptagonal porch. Sometime after 1250, when Roger Bacon was in nearby Oxford, tradition says that he used this church tower to pursue his study of astronomy and to test the telescopes he was building. Around the end of 1551, about when he took orders, John Jewel secured this living, which he held until religious problems under Queen Mary forced him to flee. While he was here, he built the seven-sided porch, now known as Jewel's Porch, and gave the church a beautifully carved altar table. A model of the 13th-century church in the porch shows Bacon dressed as a Franciscan friar and holding an astrolabe.

SUTTON, Cheshire (pop. 4,563) Situated in the Macclesfield parish, Sutton (once called Sutton Downes) has a lovely old hall with an adjacent ancient chapel (restored) and a modern church. Sutton is usually designated as the birthplace of Raphael Holinshed, whose *Chronicles* William Shakespeare used for a large number of his plays. Holinshed is thought to have been the son of Ralph Holinshed (or Hollingshed) of Cophurst in this township. No definite information is available about the chronicler until he appeared in London in 1548 working in the printing office of Reginald Wolfe.

SUTTON COLDFIELD, Warwickshire (pop. 40,000) Sutton Coldfield, once a medieval market town, is now a suburb of Birmingham, 7 miles to the southwest, and the residents of this royal borough have protested vehemently about a proposal to merge the two towns. Sutton Park, an area of 2,400 acres filled with woodlands, lakes, moorland, meadow, and streams, was given to the people of Sutton Coldfield in the 16th century by Bishop John Veysey. Sutton then became an important weaving town, again because of Bishop Veysey, who introduced the weaving of kersey, built fifty-one houses for the weavers, paved the streets, built Moor Hall, founded Bishop Veysey's Grammar

School when he was in his seventies, and spent another thirty years overseeing his various benefactions.

William Shakespeare, who was without doubt familiar with this area, mentions Sutton Coldfield in *Henry IV: Part I* when he brings Sir John Falstaff's "army" here:

> Bardolph, get thee before to Coventry; fill me a bottle of sack: our soldiers shall march through; we'll to Sutton-Cop-hill to-night.

In the late 16th century Robert Burton spent some time as a scholar at the free school here, as he mentions in "Digression of the Aire." Finally, in 1891 Francis Brett Young entered Iona, a mixed school kept by the two Misses Cull. Only seven years old, he was extremely homesick, and his suffering from migraine did not help his adjustment. A letter written in 1927 to Miss Susie Cull recalls these early years:

> But my private sanctuary, of which no other soul knew was the banks of a little ditch of a little stream at the end of the Tamworth Road. Here, unknown to anybody, I indulged my passion for running water, constructing in sand and mud, enormous works of hydraulic engineering, staging naval battles, wrecks and tempest, absorbed and utterly happy.

SUTTON COURTENAY, Berkshire (pop. 863) On the Thames just 2 miles south of Abingdon, Sutton Courtenay has been a village since Saxon times; its church dates in part to the 12th century, and its churchyard contains the grave of Prime Minister Herbert Henry Asquith, 1st Earl of Oxford and Asquith. The churchyard also contains the grave of Eric Blair (George Orwell), who died in London on January 21, 1950, after a long struggle against tuberculosis.

SUTTON HOO, Suffolk On the north bank of the Deben River, almost directly across from Woodbridge on the south bank, is Sutton Hoo, a private farm estate which was launched into literary importance in July 1939. This is the site of the now-famous barrows, whose partial excavation has revealed a 90-foot-long clinker-built ship and a royal burial chamber, presently dated between A.D. 640 and 660. The yield from the first three of the eleven barrows was meager, but the fourth tumulus, excavated first in July 1939, yielded a series of ship's nails in their proper positions, and the diggers were able to effect a complete reconstruction of the ship. Even more startling was the finding of the unmolested burial chamber of an early, unidentified East Anglian king. The treasure, under the assumption that it was buried with the intent that it should never be found, became the property of the owner of the land, who promptly gave it to the British Museum and to the Ipswich Museum. The former received the bulk of the find, which was only properly examined, evaluated, and displayed in 1945, at the end of World War II.

An examination of the standard, helmet, shield, and musical instrument have shown them to be extremely relevant to the Old English epic *Beowulf;* indeed, some scholars have hopefully suggested a more than coincidental relationship to the poem. But even before the detailed examination took place, the historic and geographic similarities of the Sutton Hoo burial site with those described in the epic were noted:

> Then the people of the Weather-Geats made a place of shelter on a promontory, which was high and broad, widely visible by seafarers, and in ten days they built the monument for the man bold in battle. They built a wall around the leavings of the flames, as wise men might nobly devise. Into the barrow they put the rings and jewels, all such adornments such as men hostile in mind had taken from the hoard earlier. They left the wealth of nobles to the earth to hold, gold in the earth, where it still exists as useless to men as it was before.

The helmet "bound in wire" which Hrothgar gives Beowulf is extraordinarily like the Sutton Hoo helmet, which shows traces of silver wire; the shield is of some significance in that it was placed with a number of other items in the center of the ship, just as were the funereal offerings in the poem. There is no chemical evidence of a body in the cenotaph; it may be that this represented the public (and possibly pagan) burial of a Christian East Anglian king who was buried in consecrated ground elsewhere. The frame of the standard probably contained gold-embroidered cloth because of the surviving evidence of an inlaid gold purse frame (with the cloth gone); the standard is described in *Beowulf* as *segen gyldenne* or *segn eall-gylden.* Other barrows remain to be excavated.

SUTTON-ON-THE-FOREST, Yorkshire (pop. 502) This village in the Vale of York, like many of the Vale villages, is self-contained, quiet, and largely free from the confusion and bustle of York, only 8 miles to the south. Sutton Hall, a mid-18th-century manor house, dominates the village now just as it did when Laurence Sterne was vicar. Sterne's choice of vocation, while clearly an expedient one since he had no family resources to fall back on, was unwise in that he did not seem to have a vocation for the priesthood. He was, however, maintaining a family tradition, for his uncle Jacques had taken the same course and was influential enough to secure this living for his nephew. Sterne ultimately also held the living at nearby Stillington, preaching here in the morning and at Stillington in the afternoon.

Initially, Sterne lived in York, and his duties here were performed by a curate; but in 1741 he married Elizabeth Lumley, of a minor country gentry family, and her dowry money enabled them to make the parsonage habitable. The couple and their one child, Lydia (born in 1747 and christened by her father in the parish church), then lived in the vicarage for twenty years. The marriage was not successful: Sterne was quick-tempered and given to philandering, and his wife was mentally ill and subject to strange delusions. In one well-documented case she is said to have believed herself to be the Queen of Bohemia and required transport through the nearby fields in a one-horse chaise with as much accompanying noise as possible.

Under these conditions Sterne wrote *A Political Romance,* an anonymous pamphlet satirizing the major ecclesiastical problems at York under the guise of a petty village squabble, and began the writing of *The Life and Opinions of Tristram Shandy, Gentleman.* No doubt *Shandy,* which in local Yorkshire dialect means "crackbrained," was drawn from personal experience. The first two volumes were finished here, but Sterne was unable to secure a publisher and published them in York at his own expense in 1759. In 1760 Sterne moved to Coxwold after receiving the lucrative living from Lord Fauconberg.

SUTTON POYNTZ, Dorset

SUTTON POYNTZ, Dorset   The wild heathland of south Dorset contains a number of small villages that would have remained virtually unknown had it not been for Thomas Hardy and his Wessex poems and novels. Rarely does Hardy use a village as tiny as this one for the major locale of a novel, but without doubt Sutton Poyntz, just north of Weymouth, is Overcombe in *The Trumpet-Major*. There is more to Overcombe than to Sutton Poyntz, and the fictitious name is clearly formed from those of two nearby villages, Upwey and Bincombe, from which Hardy also borrows characteristics. Hardy bases his story and the characters' attitudes on verifiable historical information: the natives of this part of southern England were extremely concerned about the landing of Napoleonic forces, which they thought inevitable. With their superstitious natures prodding them on, the people trained a local militia, stockpiled weapons and ammunition in churches, and arranged a beacon warning system. Hardy takes some license with Overcombe Mill, the joint residence of Miller Loveday and the Garlands, since he bases its description on the mill at Upwey and not on the mill which stood here originally. The Duke of York Inn, from which Simon Burden is routed by the influx of military personnel, is on the main road of the village; and the Old Ship was in the adjoining village of Preston. The Overcombe Cross, described as an open cross "[o]n the other side of the mill pond," is in an open area used as a rendezvous point and arena for the local villages. Overcombe Down, where the soldiers camp and pass in review in front of the King, is Bincombe Down; from the top of this hill the soldiers make "a zigzag path down the incline from the camp to the riverhead at the back of the [miller's] house." Dammer's Wood is nearby Came Wood.

Sutton Poyntz is also mentioned briefly as Overcombe, one of the villages which markets its wares in Casterbridge (Dorchester), in *The Mayor of Casterbridge*. In "The Burghers" (*Wessex Poems*) Hardy sets the meeting time of the friends when the "sun had wheeled from Grey's to Dammer's Crest." Grey's is either Grey's Bridge in Dorchester or the adjacent Grey's Wood, while Dammer's Crest is in Came Wood at Sutton Poyntz.

SWAINSTON HOUSE, Isle of Wight

SWAINSTON HOUSE, Isle of Wight   Called Swainston Hall since part of it (the 13th-century oratory) has become a tutorial college, Swainston House (burned in World War II) was the home of Sir John Simeon, the intimate friend of Alfred, Lord Tennyson. The two men were frequently together, walking on the downs as Tennyson recited his newest work or talked out ideas for another poem; in fact, *Maud* resulted, says Aubrey Thomas de Vere, from "a suggestion made by Sir John Simeon, that, to render the poem [an earlier one beginning "O that 'twere possible"] fully intelligible, a preceding one was necessary." The poem was written, but that "too required a predecessor; and thus the whole work was written, as it were, backwards." Sir John is one of three referred to in "In the Garden at Swainston," written after Sir John's death in 1870.

Nightingales warbled without,
  Within was weeping for thee;
Shadows of three dead men
  Walk'd in the walks with me,
  Shadows of three dead men, and thou wast one of the three.

SWALLOWFIELD, Berkshire (pop. 1,587)

SWALLOWFIELD, Berkshire (pop. 1,587)   Almost on the Hampshire border on the Blackwater River, Swallowfield is 6 miles south of Reading. In 1851 Mary Mitford moved to a small cottage at the green near the gates to the park; three roads join here where the group of brick cottages stands. She had, for some time, tried to live on a very small income (a public subscription finally relieved her of her father's debts) and was just able to manage in Swallowfield. When Miss Mitford arrived, her health was already broken, and a carriage accident hastened her death. She died on January 10, 1855, and she was buried among the trees in the churchyard on the banks of the Blackwater River. A stone cross marked her grave.

Sometime later Wilkie Collins was a frequent guest of Sir George Russell, and on one of these occasions he undoubtedly heard of the family heirloom, the Pitt Diamond, which probably inspired Collins's novel *The Moonstone*.

SWANAGE, Dorset (pop. 7,500)

SWANAGE, Dorset (pop. 7,500)   The only town on the Isle of Purbeck, Swanage lies 10 miles southeast of Wareham; to the south is Peveril Point, with its distorted limestone cliffs, and to the north is Ballard Cliff, a confusion of crumbling limestone to which plant life clings precariously. Swanage was a port as early as 877, for the *Parker* and *Laud Chronicles* of the *Anglo-Saxon Chronicle* state:

In this year came the host into Exeter from Wareham, and the pirate host sailed west about, and they were caught in a great storm at sea, and there off Swanage one hundred and twenty ships were lost. And Alfred the king rode after the mounted host with his levies as far as Exeter. . . .

The ships probably met their destruction by Peveril Point, where jagged rock proliferates just below the surface. A granite commemorative column to Alfred on the seafront is rather incongruously capped with cannon balls taken in the Crimea.

Swanage becomes Knollsea in Thomas Hardy's Wessex and is mentioned in "The Distracted Preacher" (*Wessex Tales*), in "On the Western Circuit" (*Life's Little Ironies and A Few Crusted Characters*), and, most important, in *The Hand of Ethelberta*. Hardy describes the town as

a seaside village lying snug within two headlands as between a finger and thumb. Everybody in the parish who was not a boatman was a quarrier, unless he were the gentleman who owned half the property and had been a quarryman, or the other gentleman who owned the other half, and had been to sea.

Knollsea Church is the scene of the secret marriage between Lord Mountclere and Ethelberta. Hardy, it should be noted, had lodgings here for a short time in 1875.

SWANAGE   The Knollsea of Thomas Hardy's Wessex, Swanage is the scene of the marriage of Ethelberta and Lord Mountclere.

SWINBROOK, Oxfordshire (pop. 167)   A small brook meets the Windrush in the meadows outside Swinbrook (2 miles east of Burford), and the village consists of lovely stone houses, an inn, and a partly 13th-century gray stone church. In the churchyard is the grave of Nancy Mitford, author of *The Pursuit of Love*, who died in Versailles on June 30, 1973. That novel is set in the Elizabethan manor at Asthall, 1 mile to the southeast.

SWINDON, Wiltshire (pop. 60,390)   Swindon, the largest industrial town in Wiltshire, is really two towns, Old Swindon, with its market and lovely Georgian inns and houses, and the New Town; the two are separated by an expanse of wooded land. About 10 miles north of Marlborough and almost 78 miles west of London, Swindon was once a hilltop village, and in the early 1800s fewer than 500 families lived here. However, in the 19th century the Great Western Railway placed its works here, and the town grew quickly. A mile and a half to the southeast are Coate Farm and Coate Water, a reservoir which is now partly a bird sanctuary. Coate Farm was the birthplace of Richard Jefferies on November 6, 1848, and the old farmhouse now belongs to the town corporation. Jefferies wandered over the entire area as a child, and he later recalled:

> There was a hill to which I used to resort ... the labour of walking three miles to it, all the while gradually ascending, seemed to clear my blood of heaviness accumulated at home.... I began to breathe a new air and to have a fresher aspiration ... at every step my heart seemed to obtain a wider horizon of feeling.... I was utterly alone with the sun and the earth.

The attic rooms where Jefferies worked are now appropriately given over to a museum:

> I chose the highest room, bare and gaunt, because as I sat at work I could look out and see more of the wide earth, more of the dome of the sky.

Part of the space in the museum is devoted to the local "hammerman poet," Alfred Williams, who died in 1930. The area which Jefferies saw from his work-room and described in *Meadow Thoughts* is changed greatly; then, as he wrote, the

> old house by the silent country road, [was] secluded by many a long, long mile and yet again secluded within the great walls of a garden ... lime tree branches overhung the corner....

Today the roadway has encroached on the land, and even the wall has been pushed back. Coate Water, which now belongs to the town corporation and over which Jefferies sailed boats as a child, inspired *Bevis: The Story of a Boy*. A house on Victoria Road in Swindon was also inhabited by Jefferies.

SWINESHEAD, Lincolnshire (pop. 1,895)   Just 1 mile northeast of the village of Swineshead, itself 6 miles southwest of Boston, are the remains of the Cistercian Swineshead Abbey, founded in 1148, and the remains of Manwarings, a Danish camp 180 feet in diameter with a double fosse. The abbey comes into William Shakespeare's *King John* as Swinstead Abbey, but it is not to be confused with the Lincolnshire village of that name. Shakespeare uses the tradition that the King came here from battle and died; Hubert carries the news:

> *Hub.* The king, I fear, is poison'd by a monk:
> I left him almost speechless and broke out
> To acquaint you with this evil, that you might
> The better arm you to the sudden time,
> Than if you had at leisure known of this.
>   *Bast.* How did he take it; who did taste to him?
>   *Hub.* A monk, I tell you; a resolved villain,
> Whose bowels suddenly burst out: the king
> Yet speaks, and peradventure may recover.

And, indeed, King John, carried into "the orchard in Swinstead Abbey" when "[t]he tackle of my heart is crack'd and burn'd," dies. Historically, this account is totally unfounded; about all that is true is that King John rested here on October 12, 1216, on his way from King's Lynn. Undoubtedly, he was ill when he arrived, but he stopped at Sleaford and Hough-on-the-

Hill before reaching Newark Castle, where he died on October 19.

SYSTON, Lincolnshire (pop. 172) Set between the Witham River and a 500-acre hillside park 3 miles north of Grantham, Syston has a restored Norman church and the 16th-century Old Hall (rebuilt 1830). Syston is one of the villages which claim to be the Willingham of Sir Walter Scott's *The Heart of Midlothian;* in the company of Madge Wildfire, Jeanie Deans approaches the village on a Sunday:

They were now close by the village, one of those beautiful scenes which are so often found in merry England, where the cottages, instead of being built in two direct lines on each side of a dusty high-road, stand in detached groups, interspersed not only with large oaks and elms but with fruit-trees, so many of which were at this time in flourish, that the grove seemed enameled with their crimson and white blossoms. In the centre of the hamlet stood the parish church, and its little Gothic tower, from which at present was heard the Sunday chime of bells.

TAMWORTH, Staffordshire (pop. 11,171) At the confluence of the Tame and Anker Rivers 6½ miles southeast of Lichfield, Tamworth is on the Warwickshire border and was once claimed by both shires. In 1319 Edward II granted the Warwickshire side to the burgesses, and town charters were granted in 1560 and 1663; in 1889 the town was amalgamated and formally placed in Staffordshire. William Camden includes the market town separately in each county in his *Britannia;* under the Staffordshire heading he relates the history, and of the Warwickshire part he writes:

> At the confluence of Anker and Tame stands ·*Tamworth* ... a market-town, where Robert Marmion, to whom the Conqueror gave it, built a castle.... The church is in Staffordshire. Here was a hospital founded by Philip Marmion, 15 Edward I. The town was the seat of the Mercian kings till destroyed by the Danes. It lay in ruins till 914, when Ethelfleda restored it, and built its castle. See more of it in Staffordshire.

The Mercian king Offa built a great palace where the market stalls are now, and around the town he dug a deep entrenchment, of which there are a few remains. Every succeeding Mercian king lived here until the Danes destroyed the town in the 8th century. Ethelfleda (Aethelflaed), King Alfred's daughter, rebuilt the defense system as a timbered palisade, and then erected a castle. The curtain wall is 20 feet high and 10 feet thick and contains Saxon herringbone work of the finest quality; the inside mount, 100 feet in diameter at the top, was raised to 130 feet.

Some of the Saxon castle survived, and the Normans added to it, but the round keep and the tower are the work of the Marmions. "Robert de Marmion, Lord of Fontenay," says Sir Walter Scott, "a distinguished follower of the Conqueror, obtained a grant of the castle and town of Tamworth, and also the manor of Scri-

velby, in Lincolnshire." Four Marmion barons held the demesne until Philip de Marmion died without an heir during the reign of Edward I. Scott uses Tamworth in *Marmion* when Lord Marmion makes his way to Norham, Northumberland:

> They hail'd Lord Marmion:
> They hail'd him Lord of Fontenaye,
> Of Lutterward, and Scrivelbaye,
>   Of Tamworth tower and town;
> And he, their courtesy to requite,
> Gave them a chain of twelve marks' weight,
>   All as he lighted down.
> 'Now, largesse, largesse, Lord Marmion,
>   Knight of the crest of gold!
> A blazon'd shield, in battle won,
>   Ne'er guarded heart so bold.'

The castle was greatly added to and changed during the Tudor and Jacobean periods.

The town has a Decorated and Perpendicular collegiate church, the Church of St. Editha, which stands on the site of an 8th-century church; the 15th-century church tower has a unique double-spiral staircase. In a space just over 6 feet wide two sets of steps corkscrew upward, so fashioned that the floor of one is the ceiling of the second; one entrance is inside the church, while the other is in the churchyard. Two windows in St. George's Chapel and three clerestory windows were designed by Ford Madox Brown and executed by William Morris; one portrays William the Conqueror giving Tamworth to Marmion, and the other shows events in the life of St. Editha, including her striking one of the Marmions with her crozier for his acts against her convent.

The most impressive literary use of Tamworth occurs in William Shakespeare's *Richard III*. Historically the Earl of Richmond camped on the plain here before the Battle of Bosworth Field, and here, according to the dramatist, delivered the following speech to his comrades:

> Fellows in arms, and my most loving friends,
> Bruis'd underneath the yoke of tyranny,
> Thus far into the bowels of the land
> Have we march'd on without impediment;
> And here receive we from our father Stanley
> Lines of fair comfort and encouragement.
> The wretched, bloody, and usurping boar,
> That spoil'd your summer fields and fruitful vines,
> Swills your warm blood like wash, and makes his trough
> In your embowell'd bosoms,—this foul swine
> Lies now even in the centre of this isle,
> Near to the town of Leicester, as we learn:
> From Tamworth thither is but one day's march.
> In God's name, cheerly on, courageous friends,
> To reap the harvest of perpetual peace
> By this one bloody trial of sharp war.

TAUNTON, Somerset (pop. 31,300) Taunton, the county town of Somerset, is almost 45 miles southwest of Bristol, on the Tone River, in the lovely Vale of Taunton Deane. Michael Drayton's inclusion of Taunton, the Vale of Taunton Deane, and the Tone River in *Poly-Olbion* seems apt:

> What eare so empty is, that hath not heard the sound
> Of *Tauntons* fruitfull *Deane?* not matcht by any ground;
> By *Athelney* ador'd, a neighbourer to her Land:
> Whereas those higher hills to view fair *Tone* that stand,
> Her coadjuting Springs with much content behold. . . .

Taunton's history dates at least to King Ine of Wessex, who founded the town in 710 and built an earthwork fort to serve as a military outpost. The fortification built by Ine consisted of a large external ditch, mound, and palisade around a second, far deeper ditch, which protected the citadel. This citadel area was later incorporated in a Norman castle. King Alfred (r.871–899) conferred various royal privileges on the town, and by the 10th century it was given to the abbot and monks of Winchester Cathedral. The Norman castle, partly 12th-century and restored, was tended for its owners by stewards and constables of the castle, one of whom was Thomas Chaucer (1417), the son of Geoffrey Chaucer.

Sir Francis Bacon sat as the Member of Parliament for Taunton when Parliament convened on October 29, 1586, and a number of years later John Donne was the Member for Taunton in the Addled Parliament (April 5–June 7, 1614), in which he served on four select committees. Neither of these representatives lived in Taunton. Samuel Daniel was born in or near Taunton in 1562, according to Thomas Fuller, who admits that he acquired his information through "some of his [Daniel's] late surviving acquaintances. . . ." This information may not be accurate, particularly since some of Fuller's other conjectures about Daniel are known to be in error. Indeed, there seems to be a better case for Beckington than for Taunton. A known native son is Alexander William Kinglake, a relatively minor 19th-century historian who was born in Wilton House, Upper High Street, on August 5, 1809. In 1846, on a trip to the Quantocks, Walter Savage Landor noted that he "met Mr. Kinglake the author of 'Eothen,' and dined at his mother's. Never was a day spent more to my satisfaction." Samuel Taylor Coleridge, who lived in nearby Nether Stowey, preached here at the Mary Street Chapel first in May 1798 and frequently thereafter.

In 1831 Taunton was the site of an important speech by the Rev. Sydney Smith of nearby Combe Florey about the stubborn resistance in the House of Lords to reform. Smith emphasized his point by the story of Mrs. Partington, a native of Sidmouth, who tried to hold back the great swells from the Atlantic. "[S]he was," Smith stated, "excellent at a slop or puddle, but should never have meddled with a tempest." Taunton becomes Thomas Hardy's "Toneborough, in Outer Wessex"; in "For Conscience' Sake" (*Life's Little Ironies*), it is here that the ill-fated meeting between Leonora and Milborne is to take place. In "The Honourable Laura" (*A Group of Noble Dames*) Laura is secretly married to Capt. James Northbrook in the Church of St. Mary Magdalen. In *A Laodician* Toneborough becomes a barracks town, but Hardy moves it northwest some 12 miles or so nearer Stancy Castle (Dunster). Charles Dickens makes passing use of an unspecified locality in the Vale of Taunton in *Nicholas Nickleby;* it is in Taunton Vale that Mrs. Nickleby, as a girl, visits the Hawkins family twice a year.

TAVISTOCK, Devon (pop. 6,056) Much of Dartmoor and many of its towns have legends and superstitions unique to the area. For example, Tavistock, on the western edge of Dartmoor on the Tavy River, was supposedly founded by Ordulf, the giant Saxon whose enormous thigh bones are on exhibition at the church. Ordulf was the sort of hero who engaged in prodigious physical feats: he was able to kill an ox with a single blow or cross the Tavy River in a single stride; he was Christian as well, in that he is designated the founder of the original Saxon abbey on whose foundation the later Benedictine abbey was built. Ordulf's sister Elfryth is part of Tavistock's legendary history. The Wessex king Edgar (Eadgar) heard of her beauty and deputized Aeoelwold to discover if she was worthy of being his consort; the deputy, who had fallen in love with her, emphasized her plainness, and the two were granted permission to marry. Some years later, when Edgar discovered the duplicity, Aeoelwold conveniently met with a fatal hunting accident, and the King married his not-too-bereaved widow; it was Elfryth's son who became the monastery's first real patron.

William Browne, also known as William of Tavistock, was born here in 1591. The author of *Britannia's Pastorals*, containing many allusions to the area, he was educated at the local grammar school, which was then still under the jurisdiction of the monks. Browne is best known as the disputed author of the epitaph of the Countess of Pembroke, "Sidney's sister, Pembroke's mother." He may have died here in 1643, but no absolute evidence exists.

TEALBY, Lincolnshire (pop. 507) Nestled under a steep slope of the Lincolnshire Wolds on land lush with vegetation, Tealby, just east of Market Rasen, has an attractive position beside the Rase River. Many of the old houses here have been expensively restored, and the church dates partly from Norman times. Just south of the village was Bayons Manor, whose name derives from the original owner of the estate, William the Conqueror's half brother Odo, Bishop of Bayeux. The original fortified structure was succeeded by a Tudor house and by Bayons Manor, the seat of Alfred, Lord Tennyson's grandfather; both Alfred and his brother Charles spent a great deal of time here as children. Their uncle, Charles Tennyson D'Eyncourt, built the stately manor house with its towers in 1840; it was not long after that Edward Bulwer-Lytton (Lord Lytton) stayed at Bayons Manor and wrote *The Last of the Barons* in the tapestry room of the tower. The estrangement between the poet's family and the D'Eyncourts increased after Bulwer-Lytton called Tennyson a "school miss" and Tennyson retaliated. The house gradually fell into ruin in the 20th century, and only the towers and some of the walls survived. In 1964 the remains were blown up so that the parkland area where it was located could be put under cultivation.

TEDDINGTON, Middlesex   A Thames-side residential village which grew into an enormous middle-class suburb after World War I, Teddington is now part of the Greater London area. Remains of the old village can still be found near the river, especially in the lock area, which marks the boundary of the tidal and nontidal Thames. The High Street retains its pleasant old sleepiness, and here standing opposite each other are the two parish churches of the village, St. Alban's and St. Mary's. The Chapel of St. Mary, the smaller of the two and once the parish church, dates from the 16th to the 19th century but is now in a state of some neglect; nevertheless, it is this church with which there are literary associations. The earliest, with Thomas Traherne, cleric and author of *Centuries of Meditations*, has insufficient evidence to establish specific dates, but he was undoubtedly the curate here for some time before his death. Most certainly he was in Teddington when Sir Orlando Bridgman, Lord Keeper and the man to whom Traherne was chaplain, was removed from office and retired to his house here. Traherne died here in October 1674 and was buried at St. Mary's on October 10; his grave site is not known.

A more recent association is with R. D. Blackmore. The death of his uncle, the Rev. Henry Hey Knight, in 1857 enabled Blackmore to give up his teaching career, much disliked, and turn to horticulture, something of which he had no practical knowledge. When Blackmore selected Teddington, it was a country village within easy distance of London and well beyond the pall of the smoky metropolis; indeed, it was "as rural as anything between Hyde Park and Bristol," and *Lorna Doone* (written but not set here) explains the author's feeling for the area:

> And I for my part can never conceive, how people who live in towns and cities, where neither lambs nor birds are (except in some shop-windows), nor growing corn nor meadow-grass, nor even so much as a stick to cut or a stile to climb and sit down upon—how these poor folk get through their lives without being utterly weary of them, and dying from pure indolence, is a thing God only knows, if His mercy allows Him to think of it.

Blackmore completed Gomer House (named after his favorite dog) in 1860; he spent the rest of his life here and wrote fifteen of his novels during these years. In 1887 his left arm was partially paralyzed,

but his energies were undiminished, and he continued writing and experimenting in his garden. He died here at his home after a lengthy illness on January 20, 1900, and was buried on January 25 in the churchyard of St. Mary's, where he attended services. Gomer House (gone) was in Doone Close opposite the station.

Sir Noël Coward was born in Teddington on December 16, 1899; his father, a musical-instruments salesman, encouraged his son's professional ambitions and allowed the boy to appear in his first play at the age of twelve. Coward's early education took place here.

TEIGNMOUTH, Devon (pop. 10,017)   One of Devon's oldest seaside resorts, situated at the mouth of the Teign River, Teignmouth (pronounced "tin'muth") faces a problem involving the redevelopment of its harbor. For centuries the district has been a resort as well as a port and shipbuilding area; to continue this traffic, there is a pressing need to deepen the harbor channel, but the construction of a breakwater is opposed vehemently because of a fear that the natural supply of sand for the Riviera-like southern beach will be cut off. If the beaches vanish—and opponents to the channel-deepening scheme are certain they will—a very important part of the town's economy, the tourist, will also presumably vanish. Since more than 50 percent of the working force in town is employed by some industry associated with the harbor, a protracted discussion is likely.

John Keats lived here with his brother Tom for a few months in 1818; a house at 20 The Strand has a plaque which maintains it was his residence. This claim is based purely on the 1901 evidence of an old Teignmouth native who claimed that Keats, who had dined in his father's home, lived at either 20 or 21. Eventually, the site was narrowed to Number 20; however, Keats said there was a "bonnet shop" across the way where he talked to the young salesclerks, and there is no evidence of such an establishment. Keats at first had a poor opinion of Devon and its people: the men were "gutless," and the shire was

> a splashy, rainy, misty, snowy, foggy, haily, a muddy, slip-shod country. The hills are very beautiful—when you get a sight of 'em. The primroses are out, but then you, perforce, are in: the cliffs are of a fine deep colour, but then the clouds are constantly vieing with them.

But as he explored the countryside in the good March weather, he altered his opinion; and by the end of March he writes:

> For there's Bishop's teign
> And King's teign
> And Coomb at the clear teign head
> Where close by the stream
> You may have your cream
> All spread upon barley bread.

"Close by the stream" is the refreshment house, Coombe Cellars, where cockles are brought up from the mud flats below and served with rich Devonshire cream; Keats's barley bread is no longer served, but the barley fields are still there. Keats attended the famous nearby Dawlish Fair on March 23, and by the beginning of April he was working on "Isabella, or the Pot of Basil"; the poem, contrary to some local belief, was not completed until after Keats left

Teignmouth at the beginning of May. Another visitor to the town was Gerard Manley Hopkins, who came here in August 1874 with the Beaumont community on its country holiday; he left no impression of the area at all.

TEMPLE GRAFTON, Warwickshire (pop. 314)

Piping Pebworth, dancing Marston,
Haunted Hillborough, hungry Grafton,
Dodging Exhall, Papist Wixford,
Beggarly Broom and drunken Bidford.

"Hungry Grafton," hungry because its poor, stony soil will not support much, lies 5 miles west of Stratford-on-Avon on fairly high ground with fine views toward the Cotswold Hills as far as Cheltenham. The church here, dedicated to St. Andrew, was rebuilt in 1875; its tower has a fine timbered belfry, and the brooch spire is shingled. Hillborough Manor is 16th-century, and its 14th-century dovecote may have been built by the monks of Evesham Abbey. It is the predecessor of the 19th-century church, which is of possible interest here; the earlier church is believed to be the one in which William Shakespeare married Anne Hathaway (Luddington is another claimant). In the episcopal registers at Worcester, under the date of November 27, 1582, there exists a license for the marriage of "William Shakespeare and Anna Whatley" of Temple Grafton. To confuse the issue, there is evidence of a marriage bond for which Fulk Sandells and John Richardson (both named in Richard Hathaway's will) of Shottery bound themselves in surety of £40 so that "William Shagspere" and "Anne Hathwey" may "lawfully solemnize matrimony together, and in the same afterwardes remain and continew like man and wiffe"; it is dated November 28. The discrepancies have given rise to a number of hypotheses. One is that clerical error has crept in and that the extreme variations in spelling may account for the error. A second explanation is that Anne Hathaway was a widow when Shakespeare married her, but the obvious point is that the bond held much greater authority than the license. Another explanation, well within the realm of possibility, is that the license refers to another William Shakespeare who lived in the Worcester diocese, and a fourth possibility is that Shakespeare traveled alone to Worcester to get the license, thus necessitating a special license, and that he listed Anne Hathaway at a temporary residence in Temple Grafton. This last explanation even can account for the listings of Temple Grafton in the license and Shottery in the bond, since in the latter she would be described as domiciled with her father and in the former she would be described in the place where she was living and where she planned to marry. In any event, it is because of the Worcester license that Temple Grafton claims to be the site of the marriage.

TENTERDEN, Kent (pop. 3,438)
On the edge of the Weald and surrounded by hop plantations, Tenterden is situated 10 miles north of Rye; there is still a great deal of evidence of its early prosperity, which derived partly from its Cinque Port privileges. Although well inland, as a "limb" of Rye it was a corporate member of the Cinque Ports and had its dock at Smallhythe, 2 miles to the south, in the days when the sea still came up this far at high tide. At one end of the wide, grass-lined High Street, with its Georgian and half-timbered houses, is the William Caxton pub, a perpetuation of the now-suspect theory that Tenterden was the printer's birthplace sometime around 1422. Caxton himself stated that he was born "in Kent in the Weald" but gave no more information; Hadlow, near Tonbridge, is another claimant.

TETFORD, Lincolnshire (pop. 367)
Tetford lies 6 miles northeast of Horncastle among the lovely wooded uplands of the Wolds with a fine 14th-century church and Nab Hill rising to the west. Samuel Johnson came here in January 1764 from nearby Langton, where he was staying with Bennet Langton; Boswell says Johnson "had the advantage of a good library" at the Langton seat. Johnson came here to address the Tetford Club at the White Hart Inn, which is still much as it was in the 18th century.

TEWKESBURY, Gloucestershire (pop. 4,704)
Tewkesbury lies 11 miles north of Gloucester on the Warwickshire Avon River at its confluence with the Severn. An old town of timbered black-and-white houses, it is surrounded by flat river meadows with the Cotswolds visible to the south and east and the Malvern Hills to the west. The entire area is steeped in history, and just outside the town, near the junction of the Severn and Swilgate Brook, is a now-peaceful meadow tract known as Bloody Meadow; here, on May 4, 1471, the famous Battle of Tewkesbury was fought. William Shakespeare's *Henry VI: Part III* recalls the battle. Margaret and her Lancastrian forces, exhausted from their march on May 3 from Bristol, were met and slaughtered by the Yorkist army of Edward IV; the Wars of the Roses temporarily ended. As Edward's brother later says in *Richard III:*

Now is the winter of our discontent
Made glorious summer by this sun of York;
And all the clouds that lour'd upon our house
In the deep bosom of the ocean buried.

King Edward, Gloucester, and Clarence murder Edward, Prince of Wales, Margaret's son, after the battle; according to Shakespeare, this caused Clarence's horrific nightmare. *Richard III* relates the episode:

The first that there did greet my stranger soul
Was my great father-in-law, renowned Warwick;
Who cried aloud, *What scourge for perjury*
Can this dark monarchy afford false Clarence?
And so he vanish'd: then came wandering by
A shadow like an Angel, with bright hair
Dabbled in blood; and he shriek'd out aloud,
Clarence is come,—false, fleeting perjur'd Clarence,—
That stabb'd me in the field by Tewkesbury;—
Seize on him, Furies, take him to your torments!
With that, methought, a legion of foul fiends
Environ'd me, and howled in mine ears
Such hideous cries that, with the very noise,
I trembling wak'd, and for a season after,
Could not believe but that I was in hell,—
Such terrible impression made my dream.

Edward, Prince of Wales, was buried in the Norman abbey here; the abbey dates mainly from the 12th century, but one tradition holds that it is built on the site of an abbey erected in the 7th century by St. Theoc. Robert Fitzhamon, one of William Rufus's relatives, began the present structure in 1102, and Henry I's natural son Robert, Earl of Gloucester, finished it in 1123 and gave it to sixty Benedictine monks. The abbey church had always been shared by the Benedictines and the townspeople, and this circumstance saved it from Thomas Cromwell's henchmen at the dissolution of the monasteries in the 16th century. Given the option to buy the abbey, the citizens banded together and raised the necessary £483. A number of abbey buildings survive, and the abbey tower is without comparison in the country. The high altar, made of marble and consecrated 700 years ago, is the longest in England.

Daniel Defoe includes a number of brief comments on Tewkesbury in *A Tour thro' the Whole Island of Great Britain* and is especially impressed by the church, which

> may indeed be call'd the largest private Parish Church in *England;* I mean, that is not a Collegiate or Cathedral Church. This Town is famous for the Great, and as may be said, the last Battle, fought between the two Houses of *Lancaster* and *York,* in which *Edward* IV. was Conqueror. . . .

In the early 19th century William Cobbett was here and commented that Tewkesbury is "a good substantial town" where

> there are the finest meadows that ever were seen. In looking over them, and beholding the endless flocks and herds, one wonders what can become of all the meat!

TEWKESBURY "At the Hop Pole in Tewkesbury, they stopped to dine, upon which occasion there was more bottled ale, with some more Madeira and some port besides; and here the case-bottle was replenished for the fourth time."

Charles Dickens, *Pickwick Papers.*

There are two literary associations of importance in Tewkesbury: Charles Dickens uses the Hop Pole in *Pickwick Papers.* Mr. Pickwick's journey brings him here:

> At the Hop Pole at Tewkesbury, they stopped to dine, upon which occasion there was more bottled ale, with some more Madeira and some port besides; and here the case-bottle was replenished for the fourth time.

A second Victorian novel deals with Tewkesbury in far greater depth. This town becomes Norton Bury in Dinah Mulock Craik's *John Halifax, Gentleman.* Miss Mulock arrived in Gloucestershire in 1852 for a vacation at Charlton Kings and visited here; caught in a sudden rainstorm and taking cover, she watched the vignette that was to become the opening scene of the novel:

> And there stood the little girl, with a loaf in one hand and a carving-knife in the other. She succeeded in cutting off a large slice, and holding it out.
> "Take it, poor boy!—you look so hungry. Do take it."
> But the servant forced her in, and the door was shut upon a sharp cry.
> It made John Halifax start, and look up at the nursery window, which was likewise closed. We heard nothing more. After a minute he crossed the street, and picked up the slice of bread. Now in those days bread was precious, exceedingly. The poor folk rarely got it; they lived on rye or meal. John Halifax had probably not tasted wheaten bread like this for months: it appeared not, he eyed it so ravenously. . . .

When the rain ended, Miss Mulock lunched at the Bell, a half-timbered inn (rebuilt in 1696) on Church Street across from the abbey. While lunching, she discovered that a wealthy tanner had once owned the building, and that established her protagonist's trade. The name Halifax on a tombstone in the churchyard then provided his surname. The bowling green with its thick yew hedge lies behind the Bell, and the Bell is transformed into the house of Abel Fletcher:

> "Please to take me to that clematis arbour; it looks over the Avon. Now, how do you like our garden?"
> "It's a nice place."
> He did not go into ecstasies, as I had half expected. . . .
> "It's a *very* nice place."
> Certainly it was. A large square, chiefly grass, level as a bowling green, with borders round. Beyond, divided by a low hedge, was the kitchen and fruit garden—my father's pride, as this old-fashioned pleasaunce was mine.

The view is extremely pleasant:

> [C]lose below, flowed the Avon—Shakespeare's Avon—here a narrow, sluggish stream, but capable, as we at Norton Bury sometimes knew to our cost, of being roused into fierceness and foam. Now it slipped on quietly enough, contenting itself with turning a flour-mill hard by, the lazy whirr of which made a sleepy, incessant monotone which I was fond of hearing.
> From the opposite bank stretched a wide green level, called the Ham—dotted with pasturing cattle of all sorts. Beyond it was a second river, forming an arch of a circle round the verdant flat. But the stream itself lay so low as to be invisible from where we sat; you could only trace the line of its course by the small white sails that glided in and out, oddly enough, from behind clumps of trees, and across meadow-lands.

Abel Fletcher's mill in an alley "which lay between the High Street and the Avon" is the Abbey Mill (now a restaurant). The "Old Tudor House," a black-and-white building dating to 1540, is on the High Street and has had a variety of uses; in the novel this is "the Mayor's house of fourteen windows" where Ursula Marsh lives.

Tewkesbury, by the way, was noted for one other quality in Shakespeare's days. In *Henry IV: Part II* Falstaff comments of Poins: "His wit's as thick as Tewkesbury mustard."

THAME, Oxfordshire (pop. 4,790) Thame (pronounced "tame"), which is 16 miles east of Oxford, was an old market town even at the time of the Domesday Book (1086), and the 300-acre park was enclosed as long ago as Saxon times. The 18th-century house in the park was built on the site of a 12th-century abbey, of which there are some rather good remains, particularly the south front and the abbot's lodge (ca. 1520); the lodge is beautifully paneled. The main street (so wide that a whole group of buildings, including the municipal halls, were placed on a central island) contains an Elizabethan gabled stone schoolhouse (built in 1569) with mullioned windows, which has been taken over by various commercial enterprises and no longer functions as a school. Here Anthony à Wood received part of his education, and the immortal Dr. Fell ("I do not love thee, Dr. Fell"), Dean of Christ Church, was also a student. More recently Thame was for a short time the home of William Butler Yeats after his marriage to Georgie Lees. The couple came here to Cuttlebrook House (now The Red House Children's Book Shop), 42 High Street, in the summer of 1921, and their son William Michael was born here in August. Shortly after, they returned to Ireland.

The old Spread Eagle Inn in Thame is immortalized in *An Innkeeper's Diary* by John Fothergill, the innkeeper here between World Wars I and II. Fothergill remarked of the town that "even its vices and faults are miserable," but he probably knew Thame and its people too well.

THETFORD, Norfolk (pop. 3,990) One of the few English towns to have extensive Saxon remains, Thetford is in the Breckland area of Norfolk at the confluence of the Thet River and the Little Ouse, 14 miles north of Bury St. Edmunds; indeed, a small part of Thetford is in Suffolk. Breckland (heathland tracts once spasmodically cultivated and now relapsed into wilderness) covers about 300 square miles in Norfolk and Suffolk; today it is an area of sparse population, but the early inhabitants found the land and climate suited to simple farming. There are many remains of their life here: tumuli, domestic implements, and arrowheads are in abundance.

Saxon Thetford was the seat of the King of East Anglia, and the castle, part of the Saxon defense works, commanded the Icknield Way and was surrounded by ramparts. The Normans saw the defensive possibilities of the Saxon castle and constructed their own structure (probably wooden since there are no remains) on the site. As an important ecclesiastical center and the location of the see of East Anglia (from 1075 until around 1094), Thetford had at least five major religious foundations, all of which have left remains.

Thetford contains a goodly number of fine old buildings in addition to its churches: the Ancient House is a 15th-century black-and-white building with an overhanging story, and the Bell Hotel is mostly Elizabethan with an open gallery. William Camden visited Thetford and wrote of it extensively in his *Britannia:*

> It is at present but thinly inhabited, though a large town, was formerly very populous and, besides other monuments of antiquity, shews an immense artificial hill, fortified with a double rampart, and formerly, as is reported, with walls. This is supposed by some a Roman work, by others the work of the Saxon kings under whom it long flourished.

Michael Drayton was more deeply interested in Thetford's situation than in its history; as he records in *Poly-Olbion:*

> This *Waveney* sung before, and *Ouse the lesse,* whose spring
> Towards *Ouse the greater* poynts, and downe by *Thetford* glides,
> Where shee cleere Thet receives, her glory that divides,
> With her new-named Towne, as wondrous glad that shee,
> For frequency of late, so much esteemd should be:
> Where since these confluent Floods, so fit for Hauking lye,
> And store of Fowle intice skil'd Falconers there to flye.

Henry Howard, Earl of Surrey, was here in 1536; Henry VIII's favored but illegitimate son, Henry Fitzroy, Duke of Richmond, who was the husband of Mary Howard, died in London on July 22, and it was decided to bury him here with the Howards.

The most important literary association of Thetford is with Thomas Paine, who was born here on January 29, 1737, on White Hart Street. Paine attended the grammar school (founded 1566), where he had no Latin because of his Quaker father's objections to the books and where he showed decided mathematical abilities. He left school at thirteen to join his father's stay-making business, in which he remained for three years. He then joined a privateer, the *Terrible.* Paine spent little time after this in Thetford until 1761, when he was appointed a supernumerary officer for the Excise Department.

THORNTON, Yorkshire (pop. 5,400) There are several Yorkshire towns and villages of this name, and they are often confused. This particular village is in the county borough of Bradford, of which it is almost a part. Thornton was the birthplace of Richard Rolle, the Hermit of Hampole, about 1300, but more importantly this is the heart of Brontë country, and the area calls to mind *Jane Eyre, Shirley, Wuthering Heights,* and a myriad of details from the novels. From 1815 to 1820 the Rev. Patrick Brontë and his wife Maria lived in the parsonage on Market Street; the simple terraced house is marked by a plaque. Here were born Charlotte (April 21, 1816), Patrick Branwell (July 23, 1817), Emily Jane (August 20, 1818), and Anne (March 25, 1820). Shortly after Anne's birth the family moved to the parsonage at Haworth, which has monopolized the memory of the Brontës.

THORPE-LE-SOKEN, Essex (pop. 1,130) Thorpe-le-Soken, 12 miles east of Colchester, is associated historically with the 17th-century Huguenot refugees, and their influence can still be felt in the village. In 1912 Arnold Bennett returned from France, having achieved fame with *The Old Wives' Tale* and *Clayhanger;* the next year he bought Comarques, a Queen Anne house, badly in need of repair, across from the vicarage. He completely restored the house and furnished it in the manner of the Second Empire. With the outbreak of World War I Bennett really ceased living here, but he retained possession of the house until after he and his wife separated in 1921.

THREE MILE CROSS, Berkshire   Both the name of this village and its general location are obvious; Three Mile Cross lies 3 miles south of Reading at the junction of three roads. The village is small; its hall, its library, and a small workman's cottage are all memorials to Mary Russell Mitford. Her family moved here from Reading after her father, Dr. George Mitford, had managed to squander an enormous fortune; on her tenth birthday, Mary was permitted to buy a lottery ticket and to choose the number. Dr. Mitford hoped that winning the lottery would satisfy his London creditors; he was an inveterate gambler who was said to have "an unhappy love of speculation and an equally unfortunate skill at whist." The ticket was the winning number, and the Mitfords received £20,000, a sum which allowed the debts to be paid off, a house to be bought, and the good doctor to gamble in earnest. By 1820 all the money was gone, and the family moved to the small cottage here.

Miss Mitford began writing to provide an income for the family and to pay off some of her father's extensive debts. Three Mile Cross was the source of the sketches of village life which were ultimately published as *Our Village.* She describes the village:

> A long, straggling, winding street at the bottom of a fine eminence. We will begin at the lower end. The tidy, square, red cottage on the right hand, with the well-stocked garden by the side of the road, belongs to a retired publican from a neighbouring town.
> Next, though parted from it by another long garden with a yew arbour at the end, is the pretty dwelling of the shoemaker. He has one pretty daughter, the champion, protectress, and playfellow of every brat under three years old.

In 1837 Miss Mitford was granted a civil-list pension, but even this, combined with her writing income, did not allow her to meet Dr. Mitford's debts. After he died in 1842, a public subscription was raised to free Miss Mitford from the burden. A few years later she moved to nearby Swallowfield, where she lived until her death.

THRELKELD, Cumberland (pop. 559)   Situated at the head of St. John's Vale, 3½ miles northeast of Keswick, Threlkeld is towered over by the irregular ridge of the 2,847-foot Blencathra (now called Saddleback); St. John's Beck is the local stream. There is abundant evidence of prehistoric habitation here, and the shaft of an old lead mine is still visible. The village, once known for its wrestlers and huntsmen, is now known for its annual sheep-dog trials.

Sir Walter Scott uses the area in *The Bridal of Triermain,* in which he mentions the tradition that the sun never shines on the tarn here and that at midday stars are reflected in the water:

> Above his [Arthur's] solitary track
> Rose Glaramara's ridgy back,
> Amid whose yawning gulfs the sun
> Cast umber'd radiance red and dun
> Though never sunbeam could discern
> The surface of that sable tarn,
> In whose black mirror you may spy
> The stars, while noontide lights the sky.

According to Scott, Arthur

> . . . his way pursued
> By lonely Threlkeld's waste and wood,
> Till on his course obliquely shone
> The narrow valley of SAINT JOHN,
> Down sloping to the western sky,
> Where lingering sunbeams love to lie.

Scott refers to the mountain in early editions of this poem as Glaramara and altered the name later to "stern Blencathra."

A more recent use of Blencathra occurs in Hugh Walpole's *A Prayer for My Son,* which has as its background a house on the slopes of the mountain:

> As they reached the bend of the climbing hill and saw St. John's in the Vale below them it was all that Rose could do to keep back a cry, for the little narrow valley was bursting with life. Every tree seemed to be swelling with importance, the purple-veined tranquil smoke from the farm chimney moved upward with an exultant promise, sheep and cows raised their heads to gaze as though they expected some skyward manifestation. The light was so clear that detail, the green glitter of a leaf, the bubbling pause of the stream before a black stone, the dark lustre of a heap of manure, these things shone like sharp jewelled fragments.

TILLMOUTH, Northumberland   Tillmouth is the name of the area at the mouth of the Till River, which joins the Tweed River here, and this is the area that with Norham and Wark was laid to waste through the centuries by the military adventures of the English and the Scots. A great part of Sir Walter Scott's *Marmion* takes place in this general vicinity, and Tillmouth is the location of "the chapel fair/Of Tillmouth upon Tweed" to which the monk leads Clare following Marmion's death at the Battle of Flodden Field. The chapel, which has been, as one architect stated, "hopelessly restored," no longer retains any visible association with the 16th century.

TINTAGEL, Cornwall (pop. 1,307)   The coastal area north of Port Isaac is some of the most beautiful and wild country in Cornwall, and it is little wonder that it plays such an important role in legend. Strictly speaking, Tintagel is the name of a parish, and Trevena is the name of the village, but even British cartographers and guidebooks forgo accuracy for the better-known description. Trevena itself contains the Old Post Office, a 14th-century manor house which once housed a branch post office; King Arthur's Hall, a modern granite building that serves as headquarters of the Fellowship of the Roundtable and has probably the largest collection of Arthurian manuscripts and literature in the world; and a variety of "Merlins" and "Launcelots" engaged in the flourishing tourist business. Just west of Trevena the legends begin. About

A.D. 500 a Celtic monastery was established on the headland here by St. Juliot; little is known of Celtic missionary life, and all that remains is the remnant of a *leachta* (high grave) in the form of a 3-foot-high stack of masonry blocks surmounted with a cross. The headland remained in ecclesiastical control after the monastery disappeared until 1145, when following complicated and doubtful legal maneuvers the land came to Reginald, Earl of Cornwall, one of Henry I's illegitimate sons. When the castle was first built and even when it was added to in 1235 by Richard, Earl of Cornwall, the brother of Henry III, the headland was far more securely joined to the mainland; the drawbridge, for example, was supported on cliffs now crumbled into the sea. John Leland visited Tintagel in 1538 in his antiquarian search and noted that sheep were grazing in the donjon of Tintagel. However, the drawbridge was still in its original position, linking the outer wards with a "high terrible cragge environid with the Se." Leland observed: "[I]t hath beene a large thing."

Mostly, however, Tintagel is the heart of Arthurian legend, thanks to the combination of bits of history and the fertile imagination of Geoffrey of Monmouth. In literature Arthurian references predate the 12th-century *Historia Regum Britanniae* of Geoffrey by at least five centuries, but Arthur's full glory emerges in the two-fifths of the *Historia* devoted to him. Geoffrey claimed to have as his source "a certain very ancient book written in the British language" which was given him by Walter, Archdeacon of Oxford, but no such book has been found. Arthur, says Geoffrey, was born in Tintagel, a child illegitimately conceived but born in wedlock to Ygerna, wife of Gorlois, Duke of Cornwall, who was defeated by the forces of Utherpendragon at Castle Damelioc (Tregeare Rounds). Utherpendragon, disguised to appear as Gorlois by Merlin's magic, had "spent that night [of the battle] with Ygerna and satisfied his desire by making love with her." Geoffrey continues:

> He [Utherpendragon] returned to Tintagel castle, captured it and seized Ygerna at the same time, she being what he really wanted. From that day on they lived together as equals, united by their great love for each other. . . .

Alfred, Lord Tennyson renders the birth somewhat differently, although he still identifies Tintagel as the birthplace:

> Then Uther in his wrath and heat besieged
> Ygerne within Tintagil, where her men,
> Seeing the mighty swarm about their walls,
> Left her and fled, and Uther enter'd in,
> And there was none to call to but himself.
> So, compass'd by the power of the King,
> Enforced she was to wed him in her tears,
> And with a shamefull swiftness: afterward,
> Not many moons, King Uther died himself,
> Moaning and wailing for an heir to rule
> After him, lest the realm should go to wrack.
> And the same night, the night of the new year,
> By reason of the bitterness and grief
> That vext his mother, all before his time
> Was Arthur born, and all as soon as born
> Deliver'd at a secret postern-gate
> To Merlin, to be holden far apart
> Until his hour should come. . . .

TINTAGEL Both time and the elements have exacted their toll on the Cornish coast, and many once-secure structures have slipped into the sea. Now precariously perched on a rocky headland called Tintagel Head and stretching out over a narrow causeway to the "island" are the remains of Tintagel Castle, the legendary birthplace of King Arthur.

Tennyson visited Tintagel on at least two occasions: in 1848, when he was gathering Arthurian material; and in 1887, following publication of the *Idylls*. On this occasion he examined "Merlin's Cave." It is perhaps Merlin's Cave, underneath the castle, where Arthur was first taken before being placed in the care of old Sir Anton and his wife. Sir Thomas Malory's *Le Morte d'Arthur* basically follows Geoffrey's account of Arthur's beginnings, and, as in the other accounts, he does not have Arthur return to Tintagel except possibly when Arthur leads the Cornish chieftains to victory over the Danes at Sennen. Of course, Tintagel is mentioned in most of the substantial body of Arthurian literature. It is impossible to document all this literature, but óne thing which should be emphasized is that the extant castle cannot be Arthur's birthplace, as it is of a later date.

Algernon Swinburne spent a number of weeks in Tintagel during the summer of 1865 in the company of John William Inchbold, the painter. They did a great deal of swimming and riding on their holiday, and Swinburne began *Atalanta in Calydon* at this time.

TISBURY, Wiltshire (pop. 1,420) Tisbury lies between Salisbury and Shaftesbury, a few miles north of the A30; included in the parish of Tisbury, but practically a village in its own right, is the Wardour estate with its two castles. Tisbury is one of the shire's oldest towns and contains an ancient barn 200 feet long complete with two thatched porches and gigantic timbers. The Norman and later church is a good example of a cruciform structure with a central tower; the nave, transepts, and crossing all date from the 12th century.

In early April 1569, the poet Sir John Davies was born in nearby Chicksgrove, and church records here show that he was christened on April 16. Virtually nothing is known of his life here except that his father, variously described as a wealthy tanner and a gentleman, died when the child was quite young. There is also a 20th-century literary association: when Rudyard Kipling's parents returned permanently from India in the late 1880s, they settled here, and Rudyard, then living in London, visited frequently. In the summer of 1894 Kipling and his wife lived at Arundell House for three months. Kipling's mother died here in November 1910 and was buried in the churchyard; his father, who died the following January, also is buried here.

The ruined Wardour Castle was built in the 14th century, but habitation of the area predates it by a number of centuries; in the 11th century, the property belonged to Sir Walter Walleram. Eventually the castle came into the hands of Lord Arundell, a Royalist, who blew it up during the Civil War when he could not dislodge the occupying Parliamentarian forces under Edmund Ludlow. The estate stayed in the Arundell family, and the 8th Baron Arundell built the new Wardour Castle (now a girls' school) in the 18th century. In *Jude the Obscure* Thomas Hardy has Jude and Sue visit here from Melchester (Salisbury) and the training college:

They reached the Park and Castle and wandered through the picture-galleries, Jude stopping by preference in front of the devotional pictures by Del Sarto, Guido Reni, Spagnoletto, Sassoferrato, Carlo Dolci, and others. Sue paused patiently beside him, and stole critical looks into his face as, regarding the Virgins, Holy Families, and Saints, it grew reverent and abstracted. When she had thoroughly estimated him at this, she would move on and wait for him before a Lely or Reynolds.

TITCHFIELD, Hampshire (pop. 1,915)   The village of Titchfield is 2 miles from the mouth of the Meon River, and just to the north is the site of a beautiful Premonstratensian abbey (now gone). Founded soon after 1214, the abbey of white canons played host to a number of royal visitors including Richard II and Anne of Bohemia and Henry V. It managed to survive about a year following the Suppression Act of 1536 and was turned over to the crown in mid-December 1537. The manor, abbey, and lands at Titchfield were then granted to Thomas Wriothesley, later Lord Chancellor and Earl of Southampton, as was also the monastic establishment at Beaulieu. Wriothesley quickly got to work, converting some of the buildings for domestic uses, tearing down those in need of extreme repair, and building a tall and turreted gatehouse into the long nave of the church. Place House, as the new house was known, was finished no later than 1542, when Wriothesley had to secure a pardon from the crown for fortifying the house without the necessary royal license. John Leland visited New Place after its completion and comments in his *Itinerary*, "Mr. Wriothesley hath builded a right stately house embateled and having a goodely gate and conducte (conduit) casteled in the middle of it. . . ."

Nicholas Udall visited Titchfield in 1541, but whom he visited and why he came here have escaped detection. It is possible that the village contained some Udall relatives (or Uvedale, as the name was usually spelled in Hampshire), since relatives were known to exist in this part of the county. Samuel Daniel visited his brother-in-law, John Florio, here when he was tutor to the 3d Earl of Southampton.

Place House remained in the Wriothesley family's hands for several generations, a circumstance that gave rise to a local tradition concerning William Shakespeare. Since the 3d Earl was the playwright's patron, it is often assumed that Shakespeare visited the earl's houses at Titchfield and Beaulieu. No biographical evidence supports this contention.

TITCHMARSH, Northamptonshire (pop. 620)   Maintaining its seclusion by being set well away from the main road to Peterborough, Titchmarsh, situated 2 miles northeast of Thrapston, has a notable church dating in part to the 13th century with a richly carved 15th-century tower. A set of 18th-century almshouses with dormer windows and an important old elm tree are nearby. The tree marks the site of the long-vanished manor house where John Dryden spend his childhood. When the family moved here and the length of their stay are not known. It does, though, appear that the Drydens remained in Titchmarsh for some time, especially since both of the poet's parents are buried in the church. Most likely the family home broke up with the death of his mother on June 14, 1676, and Dryden then returned only in the summers to visit his other relatives.

The village was also the home of Mrs. Elizabeth Pickering Creed, Dryden's cousin and a cousin to Samuel Pepys, who often refers to her in his diary. It was Mrs. Creed who executed the paintings in the chancel and chapel of the church; the chapel work is especially interesting. These are monuments executed on wood; one is to her brother, the Rev. Theophilus Pickering, and the second to her cousin and his parents. On top of this memorial is a bust of Dryden, complete with a sixty-four-line inscription which reads in part:

[W]e boast he was bred and had his first learning here, where he has often made us happy by his kind visits and most delightful conversation.

TIVERTON, Devon (pop. 9,712)   Situated 12 miles north of Exeter, Tiverton is an old market town with a partly 12th-century castle, but modern industry is slowly engulfing it. Beginning in the Middle Ages, when the town fell under the patronage of the Courtenays, the Earls of Devonshire, its prosperity was based first on the wool trade and then on lacemaking; indeed, the richness of the wool trade led to a number of municipal endowments, among them Waldron Almshouses, Greenway's Almshouses, and Peter Blundell's School. The Perpendicular St. Peter's Church contains some of the Courtenay family tombs and the rather finely carved Greenway Chapel.

At the age of twelve, R. D. Blackmore was sent to Blundell's School from Culmstock. His name is entered on the school register for August 26, 1837, just as his father's was on August 13, 1809, and his uncle Richard's on February 19, 1816. It is also believed that his grandfather attended the school. The fame of Blundell's School rests mostly on the way Blackmore describes it in *Lorna Doone;* this is John Ridd's school:

> The school-house stands beside a stream, not very large, called "Lowman," which flows into the broad river of Exe, about a mile below. This Lowman stream, although it be not fond of brawl and violence (in the manner of our Lynn), yet is wont to flood into a mighty head of waters when the storms of rain provoke it. . . . And in the very front of the gate, just without the archway, where the ground is paved most handsomely, you may see in copy-letters done a great P. B. of white pebbles.

Blackmore not only describes the school accurately but places it correctly in the town:

> At the top of the hill rose the fine old church, and next to it facing the road itself, without any kind of fence before it, stood the grammar-school of many generations. This was a long low building, ridged with mossy slabs, and ribbed with green where the drip oozed down the buttresses. But the long reach of the front was divided by a gable-projecting a little into the broad high road. And here was the way beneath a low stone arch into a porch with oak beams bulging and a bell-rope dangling and thence without any door into the dark arcade of learning.

When Blackmore attended Blundell's, the school was in the old building, from which it was transferred in 1882 to a site about 1 mile away. The original buildings were purchased by a group of former students and given to the board of governors in 1946. A number of the features of the school described in the novel still exist: the Ironing Box (the triangle of turf where John Ridd and Robin Snell fight) is identifiable, as are the lime trees, the porches, and the causeways. The first two years of his time here Blackmore spent in lodgings with Mrs. George Folland on Barrington Street, and in 1839 he became a resident student.

There is one other literary connection with Tiverton: Henry Fielding is said to have lived here when he was working on *Tom Jones.* The house, which had a spread eagle over the door, is now named Fielding's Lodge and is marked with a plaque. Fielding is said to have gone to nearby Prior Park every day to dine with Ralph Allen.

TIXALL, Staffordshire (pop. 282) A small mid-Staffordshire village 3½ miles east of the county town, Tixall is set in some of the most attractive area of the shire. Cannock Chase, 26 square miles of protected forest and moorland and once the hunting ground of Plantagenet kings, lies just to the south; the Trent and Sow Rivers flow nearby; and broad pasturelands surround the village. The old hall here was demolished long ago, and its Georgian successor met the same fate in 1927; however, the Tudor gatehouse with domed turrets has been preserved and is now scheduled as a national monument. The house belonged to the Astons, but even William Camden did not see the original building, as he notes in his 1607 edition of *Britannia:*

> It was a handsome building, the first story of stone, the rest of timber and plaster, and is engraved in Plot, Pl. XXIX. It is taken down, and another mansion built near it, still remaining.

Camden goes on to say that Sir Walter Aston was the patron of Michael Drayton, who praises his patron lavishly in *Poly-Olbion:*

> The noble Owners now of which beloved place,
> Good fortunes them and theirs with honor'd titles grace:
> May heaven still blesse that House, till happy Floods you see
> Your selves more grac't by it, then it by you can bee.
> Whose bounty, still my Muse so freely shall confesse,
> As when she shall want words, her signes shall it expresse.

Drayton was here frequently as Aston's guest, as was John Fletcher; indeed, as early as 1609 or 1610 Fletcher appealed to "that noble and true lover of learning" to come to his aid and dedicated *The Faithful Shepherdess* in part to Aston:

> Dear sir, then,
> Among the better souls, be you the best,
> In whom, as in a centre, I take rest
> And proper being; from whose equal eye
> And judgment nothing grows but purity.
> Nor do I flatter, for, by all those dead,
> Great in the Muses, by Apollo's head,
> He that adds anything to you, 'tis done
> Like his that lights a candle to the sun:
> Then be, as you were ever, yourself still,
> Moved by your judgment, not by love or will. . . .

A third literary figure associated with the Aston family but at a later date is Izaak Walton; he occasionally stopped by on his fishing expeditions with Charles Cotton, and after his *Lives* was published, he presented a copy to the family.

TONG, Shropshire (pop. 421) Many consider Tong the showplace of Shropshire. Set in a beautiful undulating countryside 3 miles east of Shifnal, it has a number of lovely half-timbered houses, thatched cottages, an 18th-century castle, and an ancient church. The "new" castle is on the site of a much earlier fortification built originally by the Vernons, one of whom, Sir Richard Vernon, was Speaker of the Commons in 1426. His son George (later Sir George) is supposedly Sir Walter Scott's "King of the Peak" in *Peveril of the Peak.* It is the church which excites the most interest. Frequently reminding commentators of Westminster Abbey, the early-15th-century Church of St. Bartholomew was built on the site of an earlier collegiate church, and on the slope below it are the remains of the medieval college. St. Bartholomew's, complete with a small crenellated spire, contains a rich collection of monuments, many of delicately carved alabaster. The font is 15th-century, as is the west window, and three screens are medieval. The prize possession of the church, a gem-encrusted silver ciborium said to have been designed by Hans Holbein, is kept behind a locked door which opens with the insertion of the appropriate coin.

Both the village and the church have been immortalized by Charles Dickens in *The Old Curiosity Shop;* the church, indeed, is the scene of Little Nell's death. Dickens and Phiz (Hablot Knight Browne) were in Shrewsbury in 1838, and there is good reason to suppose that they made the trip here at that time. Dickens later assured Archdeacon Lloyd that Tong Church was the one described:

> It was a very aged, ghostly place; the church had been

built many hundreds of years ago, and had once had a convent or monastery attached; for arches in ruins, remains of oriel windows, and fragments of blackened walls, were yet standing; while other portions of the old building, which had crumbled away and fallen down, were mingled with the churchyard earth and overgrown with grass, as if they too claimed a burying-place and sought to mix their ashes with the dust of men.

The Vernon Chantry (Golden Chapel) is Dickens's "baronial chapel":

[A]nd here were effigies of warriors stretched upon their beds of stone with folded hands—cross-legged, those who had fought in the Holy Wars—girded with their swords, and cased in armour as they had lived. Some of these knights had their own weapons, helmets, coats of mail, hanging upon the walls hard by, and dangling from rusty hooks. Broken and dilapidated as they were, they yet retained their ancient form, and something of their ancient aspect.

All the local color of the latter part of the novel is derived from Tong and its surrounding area.

TORQUAY, Devon (pop. 51,970) In 1968 a new town was created amalgamating Torquay, the largest and most famous seaside resort in Devonshire; Brixham, the most active fishing port on the south Devon coast; and Paignton, one of the largest caravan and camping sites on the south shore. The new town is called Torbay, but because it is still the sum of its parts, the original distinctions, boundaries, and names are more useful than the new. The panoramic setting of the town and bay of Torquay is superb: the hills are high and heavily wooded; the bay is wide and of a deep blue known only on this coast; and subtropical trees and vivid flowers add color and contrast.

Torquay can claim one native: Agatha Christie was born here in 1891 and was educated privately at home by her mother.

TORQUAY The lush subtropical vegetation and picturesque walks on the cliffs above Tor Bay are two of the attractions of Torquay. Charles Kingsley and his wife wintered here at Livermead Cottage (replaced by Livermead Cliff) in 1853–1854 because of her health. Kingsley, a devoted naturalist, especially enjoyed his daytime wanderings over the rocks and cliffs and his nighttime examinations of his findings under the microscope.

Walter Savage Landor came here from Clifton, Gloucestershire, in June 1837; his original plan was for a six weeks' holiday, but he stayed almost six months. He had been here forty years earlier when he thought that Torquay was "the most beautiful and retired bay in England, covered with woods all round, and containing but six or seven thatched cottages." Upon his return, although he found Torquay "filled with smart, ugly houses, and rich hot-looking people," he was still able to call it "the most beautiful watering place in the British dominions, [though] deprived of its ancient refinement." He visited the town again in August 1840, when he attended the Regatta Ball before going on to Exmouth.

Elizabeth Barrett (Browning) was sent here for reasons of health by her London physician, Dr. Chambers, in September 1838. Accompanied by her favorite brother Edward, she first stayed with her aunt and uncle, Mr. and Mrs. John Hedley, who lived on the Braddons, a hill on the northern edge of the town. Soon she and Edward, known affectionately as "Bro," moved to 3 Beacon Terrace, considered the warmest area in the town because it is sheltered by Beacon Hill. At the end of September they moved to 1 Beacon Terrace, the Bath House, where they lived for the next two years; this has since become the Hotel Regina and looks much as it did when Elizabeth Barrett lived there. During this period, as she slowly regained her health, she wrote "The Crowned and Wedded Queen," which appeared in the February 1840 *Athenaeum*. Another piece, "A Night Watch by the Sea," appeared two months later in the *Monthly Chronicle* but was never reprinted because of its painful associations. On July 11, 1840, Bro went out sailing with Charles Vanneck and Capt. Carlyle Clarke, both experienced sailors, in *La Belle Sauvage*, and the ship sank off Teignmouth, probably after having been caught in a sudden and violent storm. The bodies of Vanneck and Clarke were washed ashore immediately, but Edward Barrett's body was not recovered until August 4; he was buried in Tor Churchyard two days later. Any gain in Elizabeth's health was lost by the experience, and not until 1841 was she able to begin a slow, eleven-day trip in a private carriage back to London and Wimpole Street, even though her local doctor had pronounced her unfit for travel. Alfred, Lord Tennyson paid a very short visit to Torquay in 1838 on his way to visit Bernard Barton, the Quaker poet, and Benjamin Disraeli was also a visitor. Edward Bulwer-Lytton (Lord Lytton), who frequently wintered at the Union Hotel, eventually bought Argyll Hall, Warren Road; he died here on a visit on January 18, 1873, and was buried in the Chapel of St. Edmund in Westminster Abbey in London.

Kenneth Grahame had private lodgings for about two weeks in June 1899 when he was convalescing but moved on to Fowey, Cornwall, because of his discomfort here. George Bernard Shaw stayed at the Hydro Hotel (gone) when he was writing *Common Sense about the War*. He visited nearby Buckfast Abbey at Buckfastleigh, where he is supposed to have debated the respective merits of the Authorized and Douai Versions of the Bible with his guide. Oscar Wilde, on an excursion with Lord Alfred Douglas, visited Torquay, and the two were photographed together by a local photographer. Wilde later commented that this had been a "thoroughly enjoyable excursion." From about 1901 until 1929 Eden Phill-potts made his home at Eltham, Oak Hill Road, and wrote here many of the Dartmoor novels for which he is known. In April 1908 Rupert Brooke took seaside lodgings on Beacon Terrace, where he worked on the sonnet "Seaside" for ten days before going to Market Lavington, Wiltshire. John Galsworthy was a frequent visitor in 1914 and 1915, when his mother was in Torquay during her final illness. Living in nearby Manaton, he found the journey an easy one, and when he came, he stayed at the Torbay Hotel on Torbay Road. He was in attendance at Hazelmere, where his mother was staying, when she died in early May 1915. Thomas Hardy makes a passing mention of Torquay under its real name in *A Pair of Blue Eyes*. Finally, Sean O'Casey made a flat in Villa Rosa, 40 Trumlands Road, his home from 1955 on. He published *The Drums of Father Ned* and *Behind the Green Curtains* before his death here on September 18, 1964.

TOTNES, Devon (pop. 4,525)   Set on a steep hill above the Dart River, Totnes has an especially favorable location in the rich Devonshire agricultural area known as the South Hams. This area has the mildest climate in England. Flowers bloom until mid-December, and farming is the most important activity; the famous Devon, or clotted, cream is produced from a particular breed of Devon cow raised here. The South Hams was described by John Leland, Henry VIII's antiquarian and librarian, as "the frutefullest part of all Devonshire." Totnes Castle, a Norman structure built on a mound of igneous rock, took the site of a previous Saxon fortification, but if certain traditions are allowed, this site belonged to Brutus, the legendary founder of Britain. In his *Historia Regum Britanniae*, Geoffrey of Monmouth has Brutus seek "the promised island" and come "ashore at Totnes." The island, then known as Albion, "was uninhabited except for a few giants," whom Brutus and his men forced into mountain caves after finding the island "most attractive." Later, celebrating a festival at the port where he landed, Brutus and his men are set upon by Gogmagog and twenty other giants; Geoffrey relates the battle between Corineus, one of the Romans, and Gogmagog, the 12-foot giant. Geoffrey then has Gogmagog heaved off the "nearby" coast; the actual distance Corineus carries the giant is more than 9 miles. Michael Drayton uses Geoffrey's story about the founding of Britain in *Poly-Olbion*:

> For *Albion* sayling then, th' arrived quicklie heere . . .
> And in this verie place where Totnesse now doth stand,
> First set their Gods of *Troy*, kissing the blessed shore. . . .

In the pavement near the East Gate is a granite block known as the Brutus Stone, and to this day the mayor of Totnes stands on the stone to proclaim a new sovereign.

Totnes has an Arthurian association as well. According to Geoffrey of Monmouth, following the battles of Lincoln and Caledon Wood Arthur drove a hard bargain with the invading Saxons and allowed them to leave the island for Germany "if they left behind all their gold and silver. . . ." The Saxons also promised tribute, and Arthur, in keeping with the

times, retained hostages to guarantee payment. Then, says Geoffrey:

> As the Saxons sailed away across the sea on their way home, they repented of the bargain they had made. They reversed their sails, turned back to Britain and landed on the coast near Totnes. They took possession of the land, and depopulated the countryside as far as the Severn Sea.

From 1938 to 1955 Tingrith, a Victorian house on Ashburton Road, was the home of Sean O'Casey and his family; coming here from London, he finished his six-volume autobiography and wrote such plays as *Red Roses for Me*, *Cock-a-Doodle-Dandy*, and *The Bishop's Bonfire* before leaving for Torquay.

TOWCESTER, Northamptonshire (pop. 2,383)   Claiming to be the oldest town in the county and lying on the Roman Watling Street, Towcester (pronounced "toaster") lies on the Tove River 8½ miles southeast of Northampton; the Romans built the walled town of Lactodorum here, and from it there was also a lesser road linking Alchester to Dorchester-on-Thames. After the Roman settlement was abandoned, the Saxons took over the area and built the first church, of which nothing remains.

The arrival of the Normans a little over a century later signaled new life for the town; they built a new church, parts of which have been incorporated into the present 13th- to 15th-century church. The church organ is of more than passing interest; highly ornamented and continental in origin, it was given to the church in 1817 by the 3d Earl of Pomfret. What makes the instrument especially notable is that it was the organ installed in Fonthill Abbey at Fonthill Gifford, Wiltshire, by William Beckford, the eccentric author of *Vathek*. The old Talbot Inn, built in 1707 and now a bank, was one of the major stagecoach stops between London and Holyhead, and Dean Swift was frequently here on his travels back and forth from Ireland.

Towcester's most important literary association is claimed to be with Charles Dickens and his *Pickwick Papers:* the town is reputed to be the Eatanswill of that novel. The Saracen's Head Inn is said to be the inn in the novel, but despite the town's vociferous claims, the case does not appear to be very good, especially in light of the author's early comments about this stage stop:

> We have traced every name in schedules A and B without meeting that of Eatanswill; we have minutely examined every corner of the Pocket County Maps issued for the benefit of society by our distinguished publishers, and the same result has attended our investigation. We are therefore led to believe that Mr. Pickwick . . . purposely substituted a fictitious designation for the real name of the place in which his observations were made. . . . In Mr. Pickwick's note-book, we can just trace an entry of the fact that the places of himself and followers were booked by the Norwich coach; but this entry was afterwards lined through, as if for the purpose of concealing even the direction in which the borough is situated.

TREGEARE ROUNDS, Cornwall   Approximately 5 miles south of Tintagel and 1 mile north of the hamlet of Pendoggett is Tregeare Rounds, an ancient earthwork fort consisting of three concentric ramparts and ditches with an overall diameter of 1,344 feet. The encampment, known locally as Damelioc or Castle Damelioc, is connected with Arthurian legend. After Utherpendragon offends Gorlois, Duke of Cornwall, during an important feast-day celebration in London by paying excessive attention to Ygerna, Gorlois refuses to return to the court celebration he had left without leave. Utherpendragon "swore an oath that he would ravage Gorlois' lands, unless the latter gave him immediate satisfaction," records Geoffrey of Monmouth in *Historia Regum Britanniae*. When satisfaction was not forthcoming, the King harried Cornwall, setting fire to its towns and castles. Gorlois secured Ygerna at Tintagel, since she was obviously the attraction, and took himself to Damelioc to await Irish reinforcements. On the night that Utherpendragon appeared at Tintagel in the guise of Gorlois, the battle was joined at Tregeare Rounds, and "Gorlois was among the first to be killed."

TRENTHAM, Staffordshire (pop. 3,141)   Tucked into the most beautiful part of the Potteries area on the Trent River, Trentham has none of the industrial qualities of its neighbors Stoke-on-Trent, 3 miles northeast, and Newcastle-under-Lyme, 3½ miles north. Its church (rebuilt) stands on the site of a 7th-century nunnery founded by St. Weburga (Werburh) and a subsequent 12th-century priory; in fact, the Norman pillars were part of the priory. The village was for centuries famous as the location of Trentham Hall, built in 1633 and rebuilt in 1838 by the architect who designed the Houses of Parliament; in the 17th century this was the home of Sir William Leveson Gower, a friend of John Dryden. Dryden is thought to have been here in the summer or autumn of 1680 or 1681; while no specific evidence of such a visit to Sir William exists, the dedication of *Amphitryon* recalls such an event:

> I must confess withal, that I have had a former encouragement from you for this address; and the warm remembrance of your noble hospitality to me, at Trentham, when some years ago I visited my friends and relations in your country, has ever given me a violent temptation to this boldness.

In the 19th century Trentham played host on numerous occasions to Benjamin Disraeli, who calls it Brentham in *Lothair:*

> The breakfast-room at Brentham was very bright. It opened on a garden of its own, which, at this season, was so glowing, and cultured into patterns so fanciful and finished, that it had the resemblance of a vast mosaic. The walls of the chamber were covered with bright drawings and sketches of our modern masters, and frames of interesting miniatures. . . .

The house was demolished, but the grounds (now public gardens) still retains some of the qualities Disraeli knew:

> It was an Italian palace of freestone; vast, ornate, and in scrupulous condition; its spacious and graceful chambers filled with treasures of art, and rising itself from statued and stately terraces. At their foot spread a gardened domain of considerable extent, bright with flowers, dim with coverts of rare shrubs, and musical with fountains. Its limit reached a park, with timber such as the midland counties only can produce. The fallow deer trooped among its ferny solitudes and gigantic oaks; but beyond the waters of the broad and winding lake the scene became more savage, and the eye caught the dark form of the red deer on some jutting mount, shrinking with scorn from communion with his gentler brethern.

TROTTON, Sussex (pop. 421)   Trotton is a village in West Sussex which consists essentially of a few notable cottages, a 14th-century church, Trotton Place, and a medieval bridge over the Little Rother River. The church has one of the most impressive interiors in the county, including well-preserved 14th-century wall paintings showing the Seven Deadly Sins and the Seven Acts of Mercy. The best of the church's interior features is one of the most magnificent brasses in England, which lies on a tomb in the chancel in front of the altar; the tomb, which dominates the church, is that of Thomas, 5th Baron Camoys, who commanded part of Henry V's army at Agincourt. One would like to think that the prophetic words Shakespeare put into Henry's speech to Montjoy in *Henry V* have relevance here:

> And many of our bodies shall no doubt
> Find native graves; upon the which, I trust,
> Shall witness live in brass of this day's work:
> And those that leave their valiant bones in France,
> Dying like men, though buried in your dung-hills,
> They shall be fam'd; for there the sun shall greet them,
> And draw their honours reeking up to heaven,
> Leaving their earthly parts to choke your clime.

The brass is about 9 feet long with Lord Camoys wearing the Order of the Garter; his second wife, Hotspur's widow, Elizabeth (called "Gentle Kate" in William Shakespeare's *Henry IV: Part I*), is at his left.

Near the old bridge over the Little Rother is the rectory (rebuilt) where Thomas Otway was born on March 3, 1652. The son of Humphrey Otway, the curate here, he lived in Trotton for only three years before his father became the rector at Woolbeding, 5 miles to the southeast. The church contains a commemorative brass plaque on the south wall of the chancel.

TROUTBECK, Westmorland (pop. 486)   Delightfully settled in a valley 3 miles southeast of Ambleside, with Lake Windermere to the south and Kirkstone Pass to the north, Troutbeck is a village of old stone houses, many of which are gabled and round-chimneyed, and a much-restored church with a magnificent Burne-Jones east window on which, local tradition says, both William Morris and Ford Madox Brown, who were fishing nearby, helped. Briery House, the 19th-century home of Sir James Kay-Shuttleworth, was the scene of the first meeting between Charlotte Brontë and Elizabeth Gaskell in August 1850. Miss Brontë's visit was her first to Westmorland, and she spent a great deal of the time in Sir James's carriage seeing the area. She refers to the visit in her letters:

> The scenery is, of course, grand; could I have wandered about amongst those hills *alone*, I could have drank in all their beauty; even in a carriage with company, it was very well. Sir James was all the while as kind and friendly as he could be: he is in much better health. . . .
> If I could only have dropped unseen out of the carriage, and gone away by myself in amongst those grand hills and sweet dales, I should have drank in the full power of this glorious scenery. In company this can hardly be.

TROWBRIDGE, Wiltshire (pop. 14,388) Trowbridge, just inside Wiltshire's western boundary, on the Biss River 12 miles southwest of Chippenham, is now the administrative center of the county. The town was once the site of a major settlement of Flemish weavers, whose skills brought wealth to the area; indeed, the fabric known as West of England broadcloth is still manufactured here. The Parade contains a number of 18th-century cream-colored stone houses belonging to wealthy wool merchants, and the homes of weavers are easily distinguishable because their upper-story windows are always large to admit extra light. One of the newer industries here is brewing, and Ushers (part of the Watney Mann Group) has its main brewery here.

The church in Trowbridge has been much altered over its history; the original medieval timbered nave roof has been restored and placed on new walls. John Leland describes the church in his *Itinerary* as "lightsum and fair." Trowbridge and this church were the concern of the Rev. George Crabbe for almost twenty years; he arrived here in early June 1814, shortly after the death of his wife. The rectory, across the road from the church, was a pleasant gray stone building with gables and mullioned windows; Crabbe's study was on the southeast side. On one occasion, having left the study in its normal disarrayed state, he went to Bath; upon his return, the rector found that his granddaughter had put his books into perfect order. Crabbe thanked her, replaced the books where they had been, commenting, "My dear, grandpapa understands his own confusion better than your order and neatness." Crabbe's early tenure here was difficult because the parishioners had preferred another candidate, and, indeed, they even demonstrated against him. However, they were quickly won over, although Crabbe did scandalize his congregation by his outspoken attacks on the monarchy. In fact, upon the King's death, the text of Crabbe's sermon was "The sting of death is sin." He wrote *Tales of the Hall* and the manuscript of what was later to be called *Posthumous Tales* was found at his death. Crabbe died here on February 3, 1832, and was buried in the chancel of the church; the memorial statue is by E. H. Bailey, and the epitaph says in part that though "he broke through the obscurity of his birth he never ceased to feel for the less fortunate."

TRUMPINGTON, Cambridgeshire (pop. 820) An old village, settled near the Cam River on the busy A10, Trumpington is only 2 miles south of Cambridge and has long been a favorite of undergraduates and dons. The 14th-century Church of SS. Mary and Michael (restored) has a fine display of medieval glass in the east window and a brass to Sir Roger de Trumpington dated 1289. On the road to Trumpington from Cambridge is the oldest native milestone in the country, and, in fact, this English milestone was taken from an earlier Roman mile marker. Placed in position by Trinity College in 1729, it was originally painted with the arms of Trinity Hall.

Trumpington Street, which begins at King's College and Peterhouse in Cambridge, makes its way to the church here and passes the spot where the Cam separates Grantchester from Trumpington, and that is the location of Chaucer's Mill, as it was known.

This was the mill designated by Geoffrey Chaucer in "The Reeve's Tale" of *The Canterbury Tales:*

> At Trumpyngtoun, nat fer fro Cantebrigge,
> Ther gooth a brook, and over that a brigge,
> Upon the whiche brook ther stant a melle;
> And this is verray sooth that I yow telle:
> A millere was their dwellynge many a day.
> As any pecok he was proud and gay. . . .

The poet's topographical details are quite accurate; the old bridge was about a quarter of a mile downstream, and the fenny area to which he later refers in the same tale was probably the area between the river and the road.

Chaucer's use of the area virtually assured that other writers would at least visit it and, more probably, use it. William Wordsworth, while an undergraduate at St. John's College, was fond of walking here and later recalled the scene in *The Prelude:*

> Beside the pleasant Mill of Trompington
> I laughed with Chaucer in the hawthorn shade;
> Heard him, while birds were warbling, tell his tales
> Of amorous passion. And that gentle Bard,
> Chosen by the Muses for their Page of State—
> Sweet Spenser, moving through his clouded heaven
> With the moon's beauty and the moon's soft pace,
> I called him Brother, Englishman, and Friend!
> Yea, our blind Poet, who, in his later day,
> Stood almost single; uttering odious truth—
> Darkness before, and danger's voice behind,
> Soul awful—if the earth has ever lodged
> An awful soul—I seemed to see him here
> Familiarly. . . .

Associations with Chaucer's Mill are also often ascribed to Alfred, Lord Tennyson; that he knew the mill when an undergraduate at Trinity College, Cambridge, is undeniable. It is even considered possible that it is the mill described in "The Miller's Daughter":

> I loved the brimming wave that swam
>   Thro' quiet meadows round the mill,
> The sleepy pool above the dam,
>   The pool beneath it never still,
> The meal-sacks on the whiten'd floor,
>   The dark round of the dripping wheel,
> The very air about the door
>   Made misty with the floating meal.

Tennyson, though, commented, "The mill was no particular mill; if I thought at all of any mill it was that of Trumpington near Cambridge." In fact, references to "the wolds" and "the white chalk-quarry" are far more reminiscent of the area around his boyhood home in Somersby, Lincolnshire. A more recent use of the mill is that in Rupert Brooke's "The Old Vicarage, Grantchester":

> In Grantchester. in Grantchester. . . .
> Still in the dawnlit waters cool
> His ghostly Lordship swims his pool,
> And tries the strokes, essays the tricks,
> Long learnt on Hellespont, or Styx.
> Dan Chaucer hears his river still
> Chatter beneath a phantom mill.
> Tennyson notes, with studious eye,
> How Cambridge waters hurry by . . .

It should be noted that the successor to Chaucer's Mill was destroyed by fire in 1928.

TRURO, Cornwall (pop. 12,640) Although Bodmin is the officially designated county town, Truro is the location of the administrative offices of the Duchy of Cornwall and is its cathedral town as well. Truro grew up at the confluence of the Kenwyn and Allen (St. Allen) Rivers at the head of Falmouth Harbor, 11¾ miles north of Falmouth; it is still an important tin-smelting center. The independence of the Cornishmen was recognized by Richard de Lucy, who, upon receiving the estate from King Stephen in the 12th century, converted some of the holdings into free burgage areas. As a consequence, the town had an early court of its own and the right of independent management. In the 13th century the Dominicans settled on the west side of the town, and in 1259 both their monastery and the Chapel of St. Mary on the east side of town were consecrated. From Saxon times until the 19th century the diocese of Cornwall was in a rather parlous state. One Cornish vicar is known to have ordered white wine for communion, and another refused to enter his church, although he would gladly talk to his parishioners outside while dressed in a flowered gown and smoking a hookah. In 1876, after the see of Cornwall was reestablished, the 16th-century St. Mary's was designated Truro Cathedral. Four years later the building of the new cathedral commenced; part of the older church was integrated into the structure, and the final work, on the two west towers, was completed in 1909.

In many ways it was through the good offices of Sir Hugh Walpole that Truro became a place of literary pilgrimage. His first visit occurred in the late summer of 1889, when as a child he was on his way to New York from New Zealand. During a six-month stay with his maternal grandparents on Strangeways Terrace, he was enrolled in the nearby High School for Girls, where he learned to read and write. After three years in the United States he returned to England for the rest of his schooling; his parents expressed a desire to Anglicize him, and he first attended Newham House in Truro, a small, select school for the sons of clergymen run by a Mr. and Mrs. Haddrell. The boy was, in fact, one of only six pupils. Walpole returned many times to visit Truro, and as late as 1922 he found the town "as moving as ever. Town looking exactly the same, but I mix it up in my mind now with Polchester until I scarcely know which is which." Truro is, of course, the Polchester of *Jeremy*, *Jeremy and Hamlet*, and *The Cathedral*. Walpole had watched the building of the cathedral here and knew it well. His view might have been that of Archdeacon Brandon, who enters the cathedral from his house in the precincts after crossing the green:

> The Cathedral hung over him, as he stood, feeling in his pocket for his key, a huge black shadow, vast indeed to-day, as it mingled with the grey sky and seemed to be taking part in the directing of the wildness of the storm. Two little gargoyles, perched on the porch of Saint Margaret's door leered down upon the Archdeacon. The rain trickled down over their naked bodies, running in rivulets behind their outstanding ears, lodging for a moment on the projection of their hideous nether lips. . . . Once inside, he was at the corner of the St. Margaret Chapel and could see, in the faint half-light, the rosy colours of the beautiful Saint Margaret window that glimmered ever so dimly upon the rows of cane-bottomed chairs, the dingy red hassocks, and the brass tablets upon the grey stone walls.

Harmer John, begun in 1922 at the home of Lauritz Melchior in Copenhagen and not finished until years later, concerns the arrival of a Scandinavian gymnast in Polchester and the ultimate rejection of him by the townspeople. Finally, *The Old Ladies,* begun in 1923, deals with three old ladies in a Polchester lodging house.

John Wolcot, the satirist and poet Peter Pindar, came here from Jamaica in 1773. He had taken holy orders but had left the church and decided to settle and practice medicine in Truro. However, he remained only six years before moving to Helston after many disagreements with the town corporation. A tablet in the cathedral commemorates Sir Arthur Quiller-Couch.

TUNBRIDGE WELLS, Kent (pop. 33,691) Without doubt one of the most elegant towns in England and just 35 miles southeast of London, Tunbridge Wells (or Royal Tunbridge Wells, as it is properly but rarely called) has had an illustrious career as a spa. In Regency days it rivaled Bath. The discovery of the efficacious waters occurred in 1606, and within ten years Tunbridge had become a popular health spa. The town's reputation was secured in 1630, when Queen Henrietta Maria, recuperating after the birth of the future Charles II, and her retinue stayed in tents pitched on the common. The Pantiles, an 18th-century addition, is a traffic-free precinct of shops, some of which are 17th-century and are shaded by lime trees; the name of the area comes from the large roofing tiles laid as a walk after Queen Anne had complained about the unpaved paths. Beau Nash came from Bath as master of ceremonies in 1735 and remained for twenty-five years. But in the second half of the 18th century, as the popularity of inland resort areas declined, an attractive city was left behind.

Many literary figures have visited Tunbridge over the years. John Evelyn came here in June 1652 and stayed for a number of days. In Rye he met his wife and mother-in-law, who had been in Paris; Evelyn's wife, pregnant and ill after the trip,

> had a greate desire to drink Tunbridge Waters; I carried them thither, where I staied in a very sweete place, private & refreshing, and also tooke the Waters my self a few daies, 'til the 23rd when buisinesse calling me homewards. . . .

On this occasion their lodgings were at Rusthall; Evelyn returned in September 1661, when his wife was again here, and this time he said: "Walking about the solitudes (not) far from our Lodging, I greately admired at the extravagant turnings, insinuations, & growth of sertaine birch trees among the rocks."

A second 17th-century visitor was William Congreve, who came "to drink steel for an attack of the spleen" shortly after being made a commissioner (one of three) of the hackney coaches in May 1695; he was still here in August. The 17th-century Tunbridge was often characterized as a place of scandal, gambling, and sexual license; indeed, the wells were frequently referred to as *les eaux de scandale*. John Wilmot, Earl of Rochester, not exactly known for his pure living, described the madness of the season here:

> Here Lords, Knights, Squires, Ladies and Countesses,
> Changlers, and barren women, Semptresses,

Were mixed together; nor did they agree
More in their Humours than their Quality.
Here, waiting for Gallant, young Damsel stood,
Leaning on Cane, and muffled up in Hood:
The would-be Wit, whose business was to woo,
With Hat removed, and solemn scrape of Shoe,
Advances bowing, then genteelly shrugs,
And ruffled Foretop into Order tugs.

In the 18th century, Tunbridge became a bit less frivolous, and, coincidentally, only a few figures of literary note appeared: Joseph Addison was probably here with the 3d Earl of Sunderland in July 1712 after Parliament rose, and John Gay was here in the entourage of the 3d Earl of Burlington in July and August 1725.

Daniel Defoe included Tunbridge in *A Tour thro' the Whole Island of Great Britain;* after noting the presence of the Prince of Wales, Defoe comments:

> The Ladies that appear here, are indeed the glory of the Place; the coming to the Wells to drink the Water is a meer matter of custom; some drink, more do not, and few drink Physically: But Company and Diversion is in short the main business of the Place; and those People who have nothing to do any where else, seem to be the only People who have any thing to do at Tunbridge.

However, he then notes a more negative aspect before commenting on the general environment:

> As for Gaming, Sharping, Intrieguing; as also Fops, Fools, Beaus, and the like, *Tunbridge* is as full of these, as can be desired, and it takes off much of the Diversion of those Persons of Honour and Virtue, who go there to be innocently recreated: However a Man of Character, and good behaviour cannot be there any time, but he may single out such Company as may be suitable to him, and with whom he may be as merry as Heart can with.
>
> The Air here is excellent good, the Country Healthful, and the Provisions of all sorts very reasonable.

A century later a long association between the town and William Makepeace Thackeray began. An 18th-century house called Rock Villa (now Thackeray House) on the common is where he stayed in August–September 1860, but he had, in fact, been in Tunbridge Wells frequently from about 1823 on. In 1825 he lived at Bellevue, and later he stayed in Mount Ephraim, where the house is marked with a plaque. One result of the 1840 visit was "Tunbridge Toys" in the *Roundabout Papers,* but the more extensive use of the town is in the better-known *The Virginians.* Thackeray's description of the town, its inhabitants, and their habits is quite specific: the White Horse is "the most modish place for dining at the Wells" and the place where Harry Warrington meets the adventurer Captain Batts. Thackeray captures the atmosphere of the town when he discusses Warrington's activities:

> Though our Virginian lived amongst the revellers, and swam and sported in the same waters with the loose fish, the boy had a natural shrewdness and honesty which kept him clear of the snares and baits which are commonly set for the unwary. He made very few foolish bets with the jolly idle fellows round about him, and the oldest hands found it difficult to take him in. He engaged in games out-of-doors and in, because he had a natural skill and aptitude for them, and was good to hold almost any match with any fair competitor. He was scrupulous to play only with those gentlemen whom he knew, and always to settle his own debts on the spot.

TUNBRIDGE WELLS The heart of Tunbridge Wells, the Pantiles is a pedestrian walkway, and the actual spring is below ground level in a recess. Fifteen of the original pantiles are at the foot of the steps which lead to the upper level.

Alfred, Lord Tennyson moved to Tunbridge Wells in 1839 after a doctor had advised his mother to leave Essex, but he quickly disliked the town:

> My people are located at a place which is my abomination, viz. Tunbridge Wells in this county; ... are half killed by the tenuity of the atmosphere and the presence of steel more or less in earth, air and water. I have sometimes tried to persuade them to live abroad but without effect, and I dare say you in your exile agree with them that there is no place like an English home.

Tennyson's antipathy was shared, and in 1841 the family moved to Boxley, near Maidstone.

At the turn of the 20th century Joyce Cary and his brother Jack were sent to the Hurstleigh School here after their father remarried. There is not much information about the novelist's three years here, and he left for Clifton College in Bristol in the autumn of 1903. John Galsworthy and his wife Ada first came here in October 1915 for the therapeutic baths and returned in August 1918, when they stayed at the Spa Hotel. Tunbridge Wells also enters modern literature, for H. G. Wells includes the resort town in *The Food of the Gods;* here the circus proprietor captures the two gigantic chicks which have been fed on Keraklesphorbia, the food also known as Boom Food. And Mr. Bensington, the "[li]ttle man who started the whole thing," comes here for care.

TUNSTALL, Lancashire (pop. 96) A minuscule village 3 miles south of the Westmorland village of Kirkby Lonsdale, Tunstall is located near the confluence of the Lune and Greta Rivers. The church has a 13th-century chest, an elaborately carved gravestone of the same period, a fine 15th-century Belgian-glass east window, and a Roman altar stone dedicated to Hygeia and Aesculapius. The church has changed a little since Charlotte Brontë and her sisters attended services here; they had been sent to the Clergy Daughter's School in nearby Cowan Bridge. The cottages which formed the original Lowood School in *Jane Eyre* can still be seen; Jane arrives at the school:

> Led by her [Miss Miller] I passed from compartment to compartment, from passage to passage, of a large and irregular building; till, emerging from the total and somewhat dreary silence pervading that portion of the house we had traversed, we came upon the hum of many voices, and presently entered a wide, long room, with great deal tables, two at each end, on each of which burnt a pair of candles, and seated all round on benches, a congregation of girls of every age, from nine or ten to twenty.

The food was "Abominable stuff!" Miss Brontë declared, and the sanitation system was virtually nonexistent; a fever which broke out in the school claimed the lives of at least forty girls:

> That forest dell, where Lowood lay, was the cradle of fog and fog-bred pestilence; which, quickening with the quickening spring, crept into the Orphan Asylum, breathed typhus through its crowded schoolroom and dormitory and, ere May arrived, transformed the seminary into a hospital.
>
> Semi-starvation and neglected colds had predisposed most of the pupils to receive infection; forty-five out of the eighty girls lay ill at one time.... Many, already smitten, went home only to die; some died at the school, and were buried quietly and quickly, the nature of the malady forbidding delay.

Tunstall church appears as Brocklebridge Church, where "[w]hen we set out cold, we arrived at the church colder; during the morning service we became almost paralyzed." Then they took their "same penurious portion observed in . . . [their] ordinary meals . . . between services" in a room above the porch.

Elizabeth Gaskell describes the trek to Tunstall in *The Life of Charlotte Brontë:*

> The path from Cowan Bridge to Tunstall Church . . . is more than two miles in length, and goes sweeping along the rise and fall of the unsheltered country, in a way to make it a fresh and exhilarating walk in summer, but a bitter cold one in winter, especially to children whose thin blood flowed languidly in consequence of their half-starved condition. The church was not warmed, there being no means for this purpose. It stands in the midst of fields, and the damp mists must have gathered round the walls, and crept in at the windows.

Maria (who becomes Helen Burns in the novel) and Elizabeth came to the school first from the parsonage in Haworth, Yorkshire, and Charlotte and Emily came in September 1824, only a few months later. Maria died in the spring of 1825 of tuberculosis, and Elizabeth died of the same disease in the summer. The other two girls returned for the autumn term but were removed before the winter.

TUNSTALL, Staffordshire (pop. 22,740) Now a part of the conurbation known as Stoke-on-Trent, formed in 1910 from Burslem, Hanley, Longton, Tunstall, and Stoke (the five Pottery Towns) and Fenton, Tunstall, the northernmost pottery town, still has no more open green space than any of the others. The Wedgwood, Minton, Spode, Copeland, and Coalport pot-

tery firms have been swept into one enormous firm, Allied Potteries, but the individual company names and methods have been retained. The amalgamation has undoubtedly provided a measure of economic security, but, as J. B. Priestley notes in his *English Journey:*

> [T]he general impression is of an exceptionally mean, dingy provinciality, of Victorian industrialism in its dirtiest and most cynical aspect. The look of these places bears no proper relation to the work that goes on in them. It seems to me monstrous that good craftsmen, whose families have been working for generations perhaps with Wedgwoods or Adams or Spode, should be condemned to live in such miserable holes as these.

Tunstall is, of course, the Turnhill of Arnold Bennett's novels of the Potteries and is described in *Clayhanger:*

> They passed through the market-place of the town of Turnhill, where they lived. Turnhill lies a couple of miles north of Bursley [Burslem]. One side of the market-place was barricaded with stacks of coal, and the other with loaves of a species of rye and straw bread. This coal and these loaves were being served out by meticulous and haughty officials, all invisibly braided with red-tape, to a crowd of shivering, moaning, and weeping wretches, men, women and children—the basis of the population of Turnhill. Although they were all endeavouring to make a noise, they made scarcely any noise, from mere lack of strength. Nothing could be heard, under the implacable bright sky, but faint ghosts of sound....

Most of Chapters 4 and 5 were inspired by a Tunstall potter turned Methodist minister who wrote *When I Was a Child,* and the Bastille of the novel, the Workhouse, is where Darius witnesses a flogging on his first day:

> The Bastille was on the top of a hill about a couple of miles long, and the journey thither was much lengthened by the desire of the family to avoid the main road....
>
> In the low room where the boys were assembled there fell a silence, and Darius heard some one whisper that the celebrated boy who had run away and been caught would be flogged before supper. Down the long room ran a long table. Some one brought in three candles.... Then somebody else brought in a pickled birch-rod, dripping with the salt water from which it had been taken, and also a small square table. Then came some officials, and a clergyman, and then . . . the governor of the Bastille, a terrible man.... [T]hen a captured tiger, dressed like a boy, with darting fierce eyes, was dragged in by two men, and laid face down on the square table, and four boys were commanded to step forward and hold tightly the four members of this tiger. And, his clothes having previously been removed as far as his waist, his breeches were next pulled down his legs. Then the rod was raised and it descended swishing, and blood began to flow; but far more startling than the blood were the shrill screams of the tiger.... The boys in charge of the victim had to cling hard and grind their teeth in effort to keep him prone.... The screaming grew feebler, then ceased; then the blows ceased; and the unconscious infant (cured of being a tiger) was carried away leaving a trail of red drops along the floor.

TWICKENHAM, Middlesex (pop. 102,110) One of Twickenham's boundaries consists of almost 10 miles of the Thames River, and even in early times the large houses of the gentry and nobility were strung along the riverbank here. Today, while part of the massive Greater London borough of Richmond-upon-Thames, Twickenham has preserved some of its former grandeur. There is little industry in this primarily residential area, and Twickenham probably has a greater number of literary ghosts than any other town or village in Middlesex. Even so, it did not attract the attention of the early topographers, and the comment in William Camden's *Britannia* is obviously an addition by Richard Gough since the houses mentioned do not date from the 16th century.

One of the earliest and most important residents here was Sir Francis Bacon, who appears to have been given Twickenham Park by the young Earl of Essex. Bacon's parliamentary conduct in 1594 had offended Queen Elizabeth, and the logic and morality in his explanatory letter to Lord Burghley, his uncle, did nothing to reconcile the differences; Essex had tried all manner of things in presenting Bacon's suit and keenly felt the Queen's rejection, to which end he commented (according to Bacon):

Master Bacon, the queen hath denied me yon place for you, and hath placed another; I know you are the least part of your own matter, but you fare ill because you have chosen me for your mean and dependence; you have spent your time and thoughts in my matters. I die if I do not somewhat towards your fortune; you shall not deny to accept a piece of land which I will bestow upon you.

The land covered most of the area known today as St. Margaret's; Bacon eventually entertained the Queen here, but his major concern was in finding "a place much convenient for the trial of my philosophical conclusions." Some of his *Essays* were written here, and he lived here until about 1605.

Sir John Suckling was born at his father's house (where Kneller House stands) in Whitton (now part of Twickenham) in late January or early February 1609 and was baptized at the parish church on February 10. Nothing more of Suckling's early life is known, and even the belief that he was educated at Westminster in London is based on conjecture. Around 1605 Lucy Harington, Countess of Bedford, secured the lease to Twickenham Park, and the country house became a "court of literature." John Donne, whose patroness she was, was frequently here in the summer and autumn of 1608 and dedicated a number of his poems to her. "Twickenham Garden" alludes to the gardens of this house but contains no local reference. Ben Jonson, George Chapman, Samuel Daniel, and Michael Drayton were all here often until 1612, when the countess gave up the estate.

In 1660 Edward Hyde, 1st Earl of Clarendon, bought York House (now Council Offices) and maintained it until his impeachment trial and subsequent escape to the Continent in 1667. The house, it should be noted, has a 20th-century association, for it was used in the film of Henry Fielding's *Tom Jones*.

Twickenham reached its literary zenith in the 18th century, and one of that century's most important residents here was Alexander Pope, who secured the lease on a villa and 5 adjacent acres in 1718, about a year after his father's death. Pope's Villa was located in Crossdeep, and the house there still bears that name; however, the present Victorian mansion, which has been turned into St. Catherine's Convent for Girls, is the third on the site (Pope's house was pulled down early in the 19th century by Lady Howe,

who was annoyed by the number of pilgrims). From the time when he took the villa, Pope worked on both the gardens and the house, a two-story structure facing the Thames on a bend of the river. The expanse of land which allowed him to indulge his passion of landscape gardening was not without problems, but it is said that he planted the first weeping willow in England on the frequently flooded lawn stretching down to the Thames. The principal garden was across the main road from Hampton Court to London and it was under this road that Pope constructed his underground grotto:

Lo! the AEgerian Grot,
Where nobly pensive St. John sat and thought,
Where British sights from dying Wyndham stole,
And the bright flame was shot through Marchmont's soul:
Let such, such only tread this sacred floor,
Who dare to love their country, and be poor.

The grotto, which survives on the convent estate (permission can be gained to see it), is a cold and gloomy place about 9 feet high and lined with great slabs of gray rock. Parts of the ceiling contain rock crystals, flints, and shells, and some fragments of the old mirrors used for light refraction from a central lamp are still in evidence. Here, almost unbelievably, the "Wasp of Twickenham" wrote his satires, *An Essay on Man, The Dunciad, Moral Essays,* and his epistles. Here, too, he entertained his numerous visitors, so many that sometimes he bemoaned his hospitality: John Gay, Dean Swift, Lady Mary Wortley Montagu, and William Congreve were frequent guests, and Voltaire might have become one if he had not dropped a singularly gross remark at dinner in front of Pope's mother and if he had not shaken the staunchly Roman Catholic woman with his avowal of atheism.

By 1743 Pope's health was declining, and he set about a final revision of his works. He died on May 30, 1744, at his home and was buried in the Twickenham churchyard beside his parents; there is a commemorative monument on the north wall of the church.

Pope was a frequent visitor to Marble Hall, built by George II for Henrietta Howard, later Countess of Suffolk. The King's mistress took up residence and made the hall a center of society and wit. Dean Swift, noting the lavishness of the building and furnishings, penned

Now she will not have a shilling
To raise the stairs or build a ceiling.

Marble Hall, now under the care of the Greater London Council, subsequently housed a second royal mistress, Mrs. Fitzherbert, whose questioned private marriage to the Prince of Wales, later George IV, is supposed to have taken place here. It has often been assumed, because of the location of the house, that Mrs. Fitzherbert was the original "Lass of Richmond Hill" tactfully referred to in the line "I'd crowns resign to call thee mine."

Twickenham's second major resident in the mid-18th century was Horace Walpole, who owned Strawberry Hill; the house and grounds are now part of a larger complex belonging to the Roman Catholic St. Mary's Training College. The house was originally a houseman's cottage and had also been inhabited by Poet Laureate Colley Cibber. Walpole engaged four architects to carry out his renovation plans and changed the name from Strawberry Hill to Chopped Straw Hill; later the original name was restored. He added to the building, making it a castellated Gothic mansion which William Beckford once called "a species of Gothic mousetraps." Walpole describes the house in an early letter to Gen. Henry Seymour Conway, father of Anne Seymour Damer, to whom Walpole later bequeathed the property, contents, and a preservation annuity of £2,000 a year.

> It is a little-plaything-house that I got out of Mrs. Chenevix's shop and is the prettiest bawble you ever saw. It is set in enamelled meadows, with philigree hedges. . . . Two delightful roads that you would call dusty, supply me continually with coaches and chaises; barges as solemn as barons of the exchequer move under my window; Richmond Hill and Ham-Walks bound my prospect: but thank God, the Thames is between me and the Duchess of Queensberry. Dowagers as plenty of flounders inhabit all around, and Pope's ghost is just now skimming under my window by a most poetical moonlight. I have about land enough to keep such a farm as Noah's, when he set up in the ark with a pair of each kind, but my cottage is rather cleaner than I believe his was after they had been cooped up together forty days.

Walpole spared no expense on his project: the library bookcases were copied from a screen design in St. Paul's; the gallery has a fan-vaulted ceiling copied from the Henry VII Chapel in Westminster Abbey; and many windows contained painted glass collected all over Europe. Indeed, Walpole had few scruples about his collecting, and whatever money could buy, he obtained. Here he wrote *The Castle of Otranto* and his historical memoirs, and here he established the Strawberry Hill Press, whose first production was a volume of Thomas Gray's Pindaric odes. Walpole was a frequent visitor to Marble Hall after Mrs. Howard became its resident. He also visited Pope's estate and said of the grounds:

> [I]t was a singular effort of art and taste to impress so much variety and scenery on a spot of five acres. The passing through the gloom from the grotto to the opening day, the retiring and then again assembling shades, the dusky groves, the larger lawn, and the solemnity of the termination of the cypresses that led up to his mother's tomb, are managed with exquisite judgment. . . .

One of Walpole's annual guests was the poet Thomas Gray, who spent a part of every long vacation from Cambridge here; he first visited in May 1747, just after Walpole secured the place and most probably met William Hogarth here then. One of the strangest acquisitions Walpole made was that of the "lofty vase" in which Gray's cat died.

Walpole's love of this Thames-side area is captured in:

> Where silver Thames round Twit'nam meads
> His winding current sweetly leads;
> Twit'nam the Muse's fav'rite seat,
> Twit'nam the Graces' loved retreat.

Walpole died in London on March 2, 1797, and the contents of the house were sold in 1842.

In the same period Henry Fielding was living in Twickenham, it is thought, on Back Lane (now Holly Lane); he married his second wife on November 27, 1747, and their first child, William, was christened in the parish church in February. The house where they lived is traditionally held to have been "a quaint, old fashioned wooden structure," now a row of cottages. Fielding is assumed to have worked on *Tom Jones* when living here. He and his family probably lived here for only a short time before moving to Bow Street, London, when Fielding was appointed a justice of the peace for Westminster.

About this time Daniel Defoe visited James Johnstone, Secretary of State for Scotland, who owned Orleans House (restored) in a small park just beyond the road leading to the ferry. Defoe comments that Johnstone's orchard had "the best collection of fruit of all sorts of most gentlemen in England," and "[h]is slopes are for his vines, of which he makes some hogsheads a year, are very particular."

In 1775 Samuel Johnson, James Boswell, and Sir Joshua Reynolds visited Richard Owen Cambridge at his "beautiful villa on the banks of the Thames, near Twickenham"; Reynolds went on ahead alone because Johnson was late. When Johnson and Boswell arrived, the doctor in his usual manner allowed social grace to take second place to his interest in Cambridge's library:

> Johnson ran eagerly to one side of the room intent on poring over the backs of the books. Sir Joshua observed, (aside,) "He runs to the books as I do to the pictures: but I have the advantage. I can see much more of the pictures than he can of the books." Mr. Cambridge, upon this, politely said, "Dr. Johnson, I am going with your pardon, to accuse myself, for I have the same custom which I perceive you have. But it seems odd that one should have such a desire to look at the backs of books."

The visit was a pleasant one, though, and "Johnson was here solaced with an elegant entertainment, a very accomplished family and much good company. . . ."

Twickenham retained its charm through the 19th century, and the stream of literary residents did not lessen. Charles Dickens's first country home, in the summer of 1838, was at 4 Ailsa Park Villas opposite St. Margaret's railway station. The cottage, shut in by a wealth of large trees, was ideally placed for rest and writing. Dickens uses Twickenham in *Nicholas Nickleby*: Morleena Kenwigs receives an invitation to picnic at Twickenham Ait, more popularly called Eel Island. The Twickenham area also occurs in *Little Dorrit* as the location of the Meagles' cottage:

> It was a charming place (none the worse for being a little eccentric) on the road by the river, and just what the residence of the Meagles family ought to be. It stood in a garden, . . . and . . . was defended by a goodly show of handsome trees and spreading evergreens. . . . It was made out of an old brick house of which a part had been altogether pulled down, and another part had been changed into the present cottage. . . . Within view was the peaceful river and the ferry-boat, to moralize to all the inmates, saying: Young or old, passionate or tranquil, chafin or content, you, thus runs the current always.

During his summer stay Dickens worked on *Nicholas Nickleby*, and, indeed, a great deal of local color shows through in that work. Among the novelist's visitors that summer were William Makepeace Thackeray, John Forster, and Douglas Jerrold.

Alfred, Lord Tennyson made Twickenham his home from 1850 through 1852; he left Warninglid, Sussex, and moved into Chapel House, Montpelier Row, which had a terrace between the Thames and the road to Richmond. Tennyson had become Poet Laureate in 1850, and the number of visitors here was considerable; many were welcome, among them Thackeray, Harrison Ainsworth, Coventry Patmore, and Edward FitzGerald, but the unasked, eager for a glimpse of the great man, made him decide to leave. Tennyson's study was known as the Green Room, and the "Ode on the Death of the Duke of Wellington" was written here. The Tennysons' second child was born at Chapel House on August 11, 1852, and christened in September with many in attendance. Robert and Elizabeth Barrett Browning were planning their return trip to Italy when a letter from Emily Tennyson inviting them to Twickenham for the event intercepted them in London; Mrs. Browning replied:

> We had resolved on leaving England on the fifth, but you offer us an irresistible motive for staying, in spite of fogs and cold. So you will see us on Tuesday, and we shall come in time for the ceremony: we would not miss the christening for the world.
>
> And I must tell you, a baby has screamed in this house ever since we have been in England, much to my sympathy . . . only, as the child grows fatter and fatter I have come to consider the screaming to be a sign of prosperity. Still, it is very painful to hear a young child: when he cried I was always near crying myself. Only the fact is that these little creatures *will* make much ado about nothing sometimes, and we are wrong in reading their ills too large through our imagination.

In the autumn the Twickenham meadows flooded badly, and the Tennysons resolved to move.

The novelist R. D. Blackmore, author of *Lorna Doone,* was associated with Twickenham from 1854 to 1858; after abandoning the profession of law, Blackmore took a post at the Wellesley House Grammar School as a classics master. The school, on Hampton Road, is still standing and is the Fortesque House School. While teaching here, Blackmore published *Poems by Melanter, Epullia,* and *The Bugle of the Black Sea, or The British in the East.* The death of Blackmore's uncle, the Rev. Henry Hey Knight, in 1857 enabled the novelist to give up this detested career and to turn to horticulture at nearby Teddington.

Edward Lear visited Strawberry Hill in December 1863. He wrote in his diary of the dinner:

> The people I sate next to bored me to death . . . the large

drawing room was *horribly* cold: & all things horribly dull. Society at Strawberry Hill—unless a great fete—is a misery.

As if this was not enough, his room faced the stables. It took him nine years to make a return visit, and this time was more "ghastly" than the first. He had a minuscule room with a view to a wall, and he left at 7 A.M., vowing never to return.

At the end of June 1910 Virginia Woolf entered Miss Thomas' Nursing Home, Burley Park, for a rest cure. The home, which has been described as "a kind of polite madhouse for female lunatics," may not have been the best choice. Reading, writing, and visiting were all suppressed, and Virginia Woolf was kept mostly in a darkened room while good food was constantly pressed upon her. She remained until mid-June, when she left in the company of Miss Thomas, the proprietress, on a walking tour of Cornwall. Miss Woolf was under care again at the home in February 1912 and in July 1913 and was back in her own lodgings at 65 St. Margaret's Road on October 9, 1914; she left for 17 The Green, Richmond, Surrey, a week later.

A later resident of Twickenham was the poet and novelist Walter de la Mare, who lived at 4 South End House, Montpelier Row, until his death here on June 22, 1956. His ashes were buried in the crypt of St. Paul's Cathedral.

TWYFORD, Hampshire (pop. 2,214) Due south of Winchester on the Itchen River is the fairly undistinguished village of Twyford, which is associated with two literary figures, one English and one American. Alexander Pope was sent to school here in 1696, at the age of eight. The school in the then-remote village was excellent, but Pope's time here was apparently unhappy. There are two versions of his leaving, one that he was expelled and the other that he was removed, but the same cause is attributed in both. Pope's sister says he satirized some of his headmaster's faults (an intolerable act in a school then), for which he was "whipped and ill-used"; she goes on to say that he was "taken from thence on that account." The school was located in a house known as Segar's Buildings (demolished in the 1960s for a housing estate). The other author with whom the village is associated is Benjamin Franklin, who wrote a fair portion of his *Autobiography* at Twyford House, the home in 1771 of the Bishop of St. Asaph. Franklin, in fact, heads the first entry in his *Autobiography*, "Twyford, at the Bishop of St Asaph's, 1771."

UCKFIELD, Sussex (pop. 3,385) Uckfield, 9 miles northeast of Lewes, is probably most sensibly described as two villages, the old village, whose center lies at the T junction at the top of the High Street, and the new village, which is a series of housing estates and undistinguished modern shops creeping out from the town center. Fanny Burney came to Uckfield in 1779 and found of interest only an epitaph in the old churchyard:

> A wife and eight little children had I,
> And two at a birth who never did cry.

The epitaph is gone.

In 1865 Coventry Patmore bought a dilapidated house with about 400 acres of land just outside the village. Renaming the house Heron's Ghyll, he had it rebuilt in the Gothic style, although he omitted the usual overelaborate Victorian detailing except for the dining room's medallioned bay windows, where the seven "heroines of poetry"—Eve, Helen, Dido, Kriemhild, Guinevere, Laura, and Beatrice—were installed. The hermitage built in the woods for Patmore's study was off-limits even to his family. His poem "Winter" describes this area:

> Though not a whisper of her voice he hear,
> The buried bulb does know
> The signals of the year,
> And hails far Summer with his lifted spear.
> The gorse-field dark, by sudden, gold caprice,
> Turns, here and there, into a Jason's fleece;
> Lilies, that soon in Autumn slipp'd their gown of green,
> And vanish'd into earth,
> And came again, ere Autumn died, to birth,
> Stand full-array'd, amidst the wavering shower,
> And perfect for the Summer, less the flower. . . .

Patmore sold the estate in 1874 to the 15th Duke of Norfolk; the house had become, he said, too expen-

sive to maintain, and his family was grown and leaving home. He left for London and then Hastings.

UFFINGTON, Berkshire (pop. 480) The village of Uffington, 4 miles south of Faringdon, is placed squarely in the middle of the Vale of the White Horse, a valley running in a southwesterly direction a few miles from Oxford. The vale takes its name from the enormous galloping horse (374 feet from nose to tail) cut into the highly visible White Horse Hill (856 feet high), and the name appears to have been first used in the early 12th century. Various claims as to its age and origin have been made; one dates it to the 1st century A.D.; another places it in the Iron Age. One claim is that the horse was hewn out of the chalk in honor of Epona, a Celtic protector of horses; another is that the horse was done to celebrate the victory of Alfred the Great and his brother over the Danes in 870, but the *Anglo-Saxon Chronicle* makes no mention of the figure. A third and, in some ways, a more plausible explanation is that it may have been the totem animal of the Celtic tribe that inhabited Uffington Castle, a double-ditched camp just above the horse.

Michael Drayton visited the vale and comments in *Poly-Olbion*:

> And but that *Evsham* is so opulent and great,
> That thereby shee her selfe holds in the soveraigne seat,
> This *White-horse* all the Vales of *Britaine* would or'ebeare,
> And absolutely sit in the imperiall Chaire. . . .

Daniel Defoe visited the vale when he was amassing material for *A Tour thro' the Whole Island of Great Britain*:

> [T]he whole of the Story is this; Looking *South* from the Vale, we see a Trench cut on the Side of a high green

Hill, this Trench is cut in the Shape of a Horse, and not ill-shap'd I assure you. The Trench is about Two Yards wide on the Top, about a Yard deep, and filled almost up with Chalk, so that at a Distance, for it is seen many Miles off, you see the exact Shape of a *White Horse;* but so large, as to take up near an Acre of Ground, some say, almost Two Acres. From this Figure the Hill is called, in our Maps, *White Horse Hill,* and the low, or flat Country under it, the *Vale of White Horse.*

The village has chalk-and-thatch cottages and a fine 12th-century church which contains eleven of the original twelve Stations of the Cross carved into panels. Uffington was the birthplace of Thomas Hughes on October 22, 1822, and most of his early life was spent here. The opening chapters of *Tom Brown's School Days* describe both the vale and the village. White Horse Hill fascinated Hughes:

And then what a hill is the White Horse Hill! There it stands right up above all the rest, nine hundred feet above the sea, and the boldest, bravest shape for a chalk hill that you ever saw. Let us go up to the top of him, and see what is to be found there. . . . Yes, it's a magnificent Roman camp, and no mistake. . . .
"And in this place [Ashdown] one of the two kings of the heathen and five of his earls fell down and died, and many thousands of the heathen side in the same place." After which crowning mercy, the pious king [Alfred], that there might never be wanting a sign and a memorial to the country-side, carved out on the northern side of the chalk hill, under the camp, where it is almost precipitous, the great Saxon White Horse. . . .

He also wrote of the village custom of scouring the White Horse in his book of that name; it takes four men more than three weeks to clean the weeds from the figure, and at one time an annual festival accompanied the ritual; every seventh year there were additional rituals:

The owld Whit Horse wants zettin to rights,
And the squire hev promised good cheer,
Zo we'll gee un a scrape to kip un in zhape,
And a'll last for many a year.

Hughes left Uffington for schooling in Twyford, Hampshire, in 1830 and then went on to Rugby. There is a memorial plaque in the church, and the new village hall (1975) is called the Thomas Hughes Memorial Hall.

ULDALE, Cumberland (pop. 228) Just a little over a mile south of Ireby, Uldale is in an isolated section of Cumberland on fairly high moorland. Hugh Walpole makes this the home of David Herries in the novel *Judith Paris,* part of his "Herries" chronicle:

Uldale is on the farther side of Skiddaw and looks over the moor to the Solway Firth. The sprawling flanks of Skiddaw spread between Uldale and the town of Keswick.

It is to Fell House here that the newborn infant Judith is taken by Squire Gantry after the death of her parents, and it is at Fell House that she is raised by her much older half brother David and his family:

Fell House was a pleasant building, square-shaped, its brick rose-coloured, a walled-in garden, many fruit trees, the farm buildings with all the animals and the odours, a Gothic temple beyond the lawn, pigeons in the loft, swelling downs stretching almost to the sea, Skiddaw

against the windows, and the road where the coaches ran not so far away that you could not hear the horses.

The house cannot be identified.

ULLENHALL CUM APSLEY, Warwickshire (pop. 499) From a hill above the village of Ullenhall, 2½ miles northeast of Henley-in-Arden, the Cotswolds and the Malvern Hills can be seen. Immediately below is the 18th-century Barrels Hall and Park, the home of Robert Knight, Baron Luxborough, and his wife Henrietta; Lady Luxborough was separated from her husband because of her conduct, which she described as "more than prudence or decency allows," with a minor poet, John Dalton. She was, in effect, banished to Barrels, forbidden to leave England, and not permitted to travel within 20 miles of London or on the Bath Road at Colnbrook. Such restrictions did little to dampen her enthusiasm for minor literary figures, and both Richard Jago and William Shenstone were frequently here.

ULLSWATER, Cumberland Second in size of the English lakes, Ullswater is often considered the first in beauty; beginning 5 miles southwest of Penrith, it extends for 7½ miles from Pooley Bridge to Patterdale and averages about ½ mile in width. The lake area has three well-defined reaches: the lower, at the north, is pastoral; the middle is overhung by steep fells on the southern shore and is wooded with park-like fells on the northern; and the higher is the grandest, with St. Sunday Crag at 2,756 feet. In 1802 William Wordsworth and his sister Dorothy were in the woods beyond Gowbarrow Park on a return trip to Grasmere from Eusmere; here he was inspired to write "I Wandered Lonely as a Cloud":

That floats on high o'er vales and hills,
When all at once I saw a crowd,
A host, of golden daffodils;
Beside the lake, beneath the trees,
Fluttering and dancing in the breeze.

Dorothy's *Journal* comments:

We saw a few daffodils close to the water-side. We fancied that the lake had floated the seeds ashore, and that the little colony had so sprung up. But as we went along there were more and yet more; and at last, under the boughs of the trees, we saw that there was a long belt of them along the shore, about the breadth of a country turnpike road. I never saw daffodils so beautiful.

About halfway down the western shore of the lake is a secluded glen where the Aira flows. The force (waterfall) cascades down more than 60 feet, just a short distance above Lyulph's Tower; Wordsworth writes of the area in "Airey-Force Valley":

—Not a breath of air
Ruffles the bosom of this leafy glen.
From the brook's margin, wide around, the trees
Are steadfast as the rocks; the brook itself,
Old as the hills that feed it from afar,
Doth rather deepen than disturb the calm
Where all things else are still and motionless.

Lyulph's Tower, built by the Duke of Norfolk, has an important role in "The Somnambulist." The "Pleasure-house" was occupied by an artist in Wordsworth's day, and from him the poet heard of the young sleepwalker awakened either by the cold-

NORTHWEST
ENGLAND

SCOTLAND

NORTHUMBERLAND

• Longtown

Birdoswald • • Gilsland

Brampton •

Solway Firth

○ **Carlisle**

Eden

DURHAM

CUMBRIAN MTS.

CUMBERLAND

• Uldale

• Little Salkeld

Cockermouth •

Bassenthwaite
SKIDDAW
Bassenthwaite

Eamont
Bridge • **Penrith**

Moresby •

• Lorton

Keswick •

○ Brougham
• Clifton
• Lowther

Derwent Water
Buttermere

Watendlath •

Ullswater

Ennerdale Bridge •

Ennerdale
Water

• Manesty

• Place Fell

Martindale •

• Shap

St. Bee's Head •

Borrowdale •
Wasdale • *HELM CRAG*

Wythburn •

Patterdale •

WESTMORLAND

GREAT GABLE

Gosforth • ▲ *SCAFELL*
PIKE

Grasmere •

Kirkstone Pass

Esthwaite Water

Rydal •

Ambleside •
Troutbeck •
Windermere •
• Ings

Mallerstang •

Seathwaite •

Coniston •

Bowness-on-Windermere •

Esthwaite Lodge •

Near
Sawrey •

Windermere

○ **Kendal**

Bootle •

Coniston
Water

Lowick •
Haverth-
waite •

Newby
Bridge
Cartmel •

• Crosthwaite

Duddon

Leven

Burton-in-
Kendal •

• Kirkby Lonsdale

• Ireby

Silverdale •

• Tunstall

Irish

Isle of
Walney

Morecambe
Bay

Rampside •

Lune

○ **Lancaster**

YORKSHIRE

Sea

Wyre

Flyde

Stonyhurst •

PENNINE

Wycoller •

• Whalley

MTS.

Preston ○

Ribble

• Hurstwood

• Hoghton

LANCASHIRE

○ **Southport**

○ **Wigan**

Rochdale ○

Liverpool
Bay

• Knowsley

Manchester
○ ○
Salford

○ **Liverpool**

• Grappenhall

• Parkgate

Mersey

Knutsford •

• Daresbury

• Alderley Edge

DERBYSHIRE

CHESHIRE

Macclesfield ○

• Sutton

Gawsworth •

FLINTSHIRE

○ **Chester**

• Bosley

Brereton-cum-Smethwick •

STAFFORDSHIRE

DENBIGHSHIRE

SHROPSHIRE

ness of the stone floor on her bare feet or by difficulty in opening the door:

> While 'mid the fern-brake sleeps the doe,
>   And owls alone are waking,
> In white arrayed, glides on the Maid
>   The downward pathway taking,
> That leads her to the torrent's side
>   And to a holly bower;
> By whom on this still night descried?
> By whom in that lone place espied?
>   By thee, Sir Eglamore!

Lyulph's Tower and Ullswater both enter into part of Sir Walter Scott's *The Bridal of Triermain*. The vision seen by Sir Roland de Vaux, whose family held Cumbrian land before the Norman Conquest, forces him to seek help from Lyulph, "that sage of power," who is "sprung from Druid sires":

> The faithful Page he mounts his steed,
> And soon he cross'd green Irthing's mead,
> Dash'd o'er Kirkoswald's verdant plain,
> And Eden barr'd his course in vain.
> He pass'd red Penrith's Table Round,
> For feats of chivalry renown'd,
> Left Mayburgh's mound and stones of power,
> By Druids raised in magic hour,
> And traced the Eamont's winding way,
> Till Ulfo's lake beneath him lay.

Ulfo's Lake is Ullswater.

UPHAM, Hampshire (pop. 576) The village of Upham, on an unnumbered road 2½ miles northwest of Bishop's Waltham, is noted for the discovery, in 1849, of an extensive Roman villa which has not yet been entirely excavated and as the birthplace of Edward Young, in June 1683. Young spent only a very short time here, for his family moved to Salisbury when his father, rector of Upham, was "collated to a prebendal stall" at Salisbury Cathedral.

UPPARK, Sussex At the top of a hill, on the crest of the Downs 1 mile south of the Harting hamlets and 4 miles southeast of Petersfield, is the magnificent seat of Uppark (often spelled Up Park), built in the late 1680s, for the 3d Baron Grey of Werk, later Earl of Tankerville. The great house could be situated here only because Lord Tankerville's grandfather had invented a pump which brought water up from a low-lying spring. A later owner, Sir Matthew Featherstonhaugh, brought carpets, furniture, paintings, and *objets d'art* from the Continent by the boatload; in 1780 his twenty-seven-year-old son, Sir Harry, brought the beautiful fifteen-year-old Emma Hart here as his mistress, but this relationship lasted little more than a year; she subsequently carved her place in history by becoming Sir William Hamilton's wife and Lord Nelson's mistress. Sir Harry kept close company with the Prince of Wales for more than twenty-five years, and after a serious breach in their relationship he retired to Uppark. Here, well over the age of seventy, Sir Harry scandalized the West Sussex gentry by marrying his head dairymaid, Mary Ann Bullock. When he died in 1846, the house passed to his wife and then to her sister Frances, who carefully kept Uppark as it had been during Sir Harry's lifetime.

It was in Uppark's preserved state that H. G. Wells came to know the house and its mistress; in need of employment, Wells's mother became Miss Featherstonhaugh's housekeeper when her son was fourteen years old. Wells lived here off and on throughout his apprenticeship years and drew on his intimate knowledge of the house in *Tono-Bungay*, in which Bladesover becomes a combination of Eastwell, Kent, and Uppark. He locates the house "up on the Kentish Downs":

> The house was built in the eighteenth century, it is of pale red brick in the style of a French château, and save for one pass among the crests which opens to blue distances, to minute, remote, oast-set farmhouses and copses and wheat fields and the occasional gleam of water, its hundred and seventeen windows look on nothing but its own wide and handsome territories.

Wells, like George Ponderevo, had full use of the library and read "Tom Paine's 'Rights of Men,' and his 'Common Sense,' excellent books, once praised by bishops," "a translation of Voltaire's 'Candide' and 'Rasselas,'" and an unexpurgated *Gulliver's Travels*. "[T]he big saloon" (the double-cube saloon)

> was a huge long room with many windows opening upon the park, and each window—there were a dozen or more reaching from the floor up—had its elaborate silk or satin curtains, heavily fringed, a canopy (is it?) above, its complex white shutters folding into the deep thicknesses of the wall. At either end of that great still place was an immense marble chimney-piece. . . . Down the centre of the elaborate ceiling were three chandeliers, each bearing some hundreds of dangling glass lustres, and over the interminable carpet—it impressed me as about as big as Sarmatia in the store-room Atlas—were islands and archipelagoes of chintz-covered chairs and couches, tables, great Sevres vases on pedestals, a bronze man and horse. Somewhere in this wilderness one came, I remember, upon a big harp beside a lyre-shaped music-stand, and a grand piano. . . .

George is sent from here for his first apprenticeship to Wimblehurst, just as Wells went to Midhurst for his.

As Wells severed his various apprenticeships, he returned from time to time and was extremely grateful for Miss Featherstonhaugh's generosity when he came back from a teaching experience on the Welsh border. Refereeing a football match, Wells was kicked in the back by a student and had his kidney ruptured; a lung hemorrhage which occurred while he was recovering put him back in bed. Wells was given an attic room, a coal fire, good food, and extraordinarily generous hospitality for three months. *The Research Magnificent* mentions Up Park by name as the county seat near Harting where the Morrises live:

> The house was a little long house with a veranda and a garden in front of it with flint-edged paths; the room in which they sat and ate was long and low and equipped with pieces of misfitting good furniture, an accidental-looking gilt tarnished mirror, and a sprinkling of old and middle-aged books. Some one had lit a fire, which cracked and spurted about cheerfully in a motherly fireplace, and a lamp and some candles got lit.

UPPINGHAM, Rutland (pop. 2,453) A pleasant little town 6 miles south of Oakham with green fields all around it, Uppingham is the shire's second largest town and perhaps its most famous. The earthworks of an ancient castle rise on a hill, and one of the original school buildings stands near the church. The Norman church (restored) retains an ancient font and the pulpit from which Jeremy Taylor preached when he held this living from 1638 to 1642. As soon as he received the post on March 23, 1638, he came here to reside, in marked contrast to the previous nonresident rector. Taylor served the parish well until (probably) the summer of 1642, and here he was married, and his small son died.

Taylor ministered not only to his small congregation but to the boys of the now-famed Uppingham School. Founded in 1584 by Robert Johnson, the school carried on in the one-room building in the church grounds until Dr. Edward Thring became headmaster in 1853. He made the school what it is by emphasizing not only the classics and English but the arts and modern languages; he built stately castlelike buildings and found time to champion higher education for women. Two of the outstanding students at the school were Norman Douglas and James Elroy Flecker.

UPTON-ON-SEVERN, Worcestershire (pop. 2,004) On the right bank of the Severn River 11 miles south of Worcester, Upton-on-Severn is a charming old market town with a picturesque quayside. Its most famous building is the White Lion Inn on the High Street, which enters Henry Fielding's *Tom Jones* ("our hero . . . brought his companion, or rather follower, safe into the famous town of Upton"):

> Mr. Jones and his fair companion no sooner entered the town, than they went directly to that inn which in their eyes presented the fairest appearance to the street.

URE RIVER, Yorkshire Rising in the North Riding on the western border of the county about 7 miles west of Muker, the Ure River flows east and then southeast for some 50 miles before being fed by the Swale River and eventually forming the Ouse. It has been traditionally held that Sir Walter Ralegh introduced the abundant crayfish into this river. This is one of the myriad erroneous stories about Ralegh, for as William Camden notes in his *Britannia,* " . . . hence runneth Ure downe a maine, full of Creifishes, ever since Sir Christopher Medcalfe in our remembrance brought that kinde of fish hither out of the South part of England."

USHAW, County Durham (pop. 2,987) On an unnumbered minor road about 5 miles west of Durham is a town which is the home of Ushaw College, the Roman Catholic College of St. Cuthbert. This college, succeeding one founded at Douai by William Cardinal Allen in 1568 and destroyed during the French Revolution, has been the English training ground for priests since 1808. The college has an extensive theological library containing more than 130 books dated before 1500 and a large collection of relics of saints, including a 13th-century gold ring set with a big sapphire, said to have come from St. Cuthbert's

coffin when it was opened in 1540. There is no explanation of how a 13th-century ring appeared in the coffin of a man who died in the 7th century. Francis Thompson, author of "The Hound of Heaven," received a large part of his education here before going to Owens College, now the University of Manchester. Ushaw College has preserved a number of Thompson's original manuscripts.

UTTOXETER, Staffordshire (pop. 5,363) Uttoxeter (pronounced "ū-tox′eter") is a relatively pleasant and unspoiled market town which still derives much of its prosperity from its Wednesday cattle market; it is located 14 miles northeast of Stafford and 18 miles north of Lichfield in an area of rich pastureland and looks down on the Dove River and the Derbyshire border. Uttoxeter Church was badly rebuilt in fake Gothic in 1828, but the 14th-century tower retains much of its original beauty.

One of the best-known stories associated with a literary figure originated here around 1780, when Dr. Samuel Johnson came to do penance for an earlier sin of pride. James Boswell relates the incident in *The Life of Samuel Johnson:*

> To Mr. Henry White . . . he mentioned that he could not in general accuse himself of having been an undutiful son. "Once, indeed, (said he,) I was disobedient; I refused to attend my father to Uttoxeter-market. Pride was the source of that refusal, and the remembrance of it was painful. A few years ago I desired to atone for this fault. I went to Uttoxeter in very bad weather, and stood for a considerable time bareheaded in the rain, on the spot where my father's stall used to stand. In contrition I stood, and I hope the penance was expiatory."

Sometime in 1731 the young Johnson had refused to tend his father's stall here; the elder Johnson was ill at the time and, indeed, died about six weeks later of an inflammatory fever. Michael Johnson's room at the Red Lion Inn, just opposite his stall on the market square, was known as Mr. Johnson's room and was fitted with bookshelves for storage; the boy often stayed here with his father. In commemoration of the penance, a bas-relief has been placed on the conduit of the marketplace.

Years later Nathaniel Hawthorne made the same pilgrimage, which he described in *The English Notebooks:*

> It had been my previous impression that the marketplace of Uttoxeter lay immediately round-about the church; . . . a walk of a minute or two brings a person from the centre of the market-place to the church-door; and Michael Johnson might very conveniently have located his stall and laid out his literary ware in the corner at the tower's base. . . . But the picturesque arrangement and full impressiveness of the story absolutely require that Johnson shall not have done his penance in a corner . . . but shall have been the very nucleus of the crowd. . . . I am resolved, therefore, that the true site of Dr. Johnson's penance was in the middle of the market-place.

WAKEFIELD, Yorkshire (pop. 60,430) Wakefield, located some 9 miles southwest of Leeds, is still a thriving center of the woolen industry, which it attracted originally in the 15th century because of a low tax rate. Coal is also mined extensively in the area, which is in the industrial heart of Yorkshire. Almost certainly, the 15th-century Wakefield Cycle of thirty-two plays, also known as the Towneley Mysteries, belongs to this particular Wakefield because of the large number of local allusions. This medieval mystery cycle differs from other cycles in that the craft guilds presented it on fixed stages at specific places on the procession route. The audience moved from play to play, while the evidence is that in York and Chester the play itself moved from station to station. A few years ago, the town successfully revived *The Second Shepherd's Play* at St. Mary's on the Bridge, the 14th-century cathedral chantry on Calder Bridge.

The Robin Hood legend is based in Wakefield, for the popular hero is traditionally supposed to have been born somewhere in the city, and both "A Gest of Robyn Hode" and "The Jolly Pinder of Wakefield" concern Wakefield. In the latter ballad Robin Hood with Little John and Scarlet leaves the main highway, makes a path through the grain, and incurs the pinner's (pinder's) anger. The pinner of Wakefield seems to have been specially able at extracting the appropriate fine from trespassers, and a combat begins when Robin refuses to heed him. In a similar vein, the play *George-a'-Greene, the Pinner of Wakefield,* attributed to Robert Greene, deals with Robin Hood and another of the well-known local heroes: George-a'-Greene, the local poundkeeper, who defeats all contestants at quarterstaff. He defies the prince's demand for tribute, elopes with the judge's daughter, and defeats Robin Hood, who is forced into the challenge match with George by Maid Marian. The legend is also related in William Hazlitt's *Tales and Legends.*

Mirefields, 30 Westgate, was the birthplace of George Gissing on November 22, 1857. Gissing's father, a pharmaceutical chemist, was a man of "strong impulses towards culture" and a student of literature, the classics, politics, and economics, much like Nicholas Peak in *Born in Exile.* With a firm belief in the value of a first-rate education, he initiated an early study in classics for his son; this, along with a natural predilection for study, made George Gissing (and his father) "an intellectual placed in uncongenial circumstances"; so, too, are the heroes of his novels. Gissing was an indifferent pupil at Harrison's Back Lane School until his father's death in 1870, when he and his brothers were sent to board at Lindow Grove School in Alderley Edge, Cheshire. After leaving Owens College in Manchester, he visited Wakefield, infrequently at first but more often later (after his first two unfortunate marriages), when his mother was caring for his eldest son Walter at 9 Wentworth Terrace.

Oliver Goldsmith is not known to have been personally acquainted with Wakefield, but no doubt on one of his northern trips prior to writing *The Vicar of Wakefield* he passed through the town. The first two chapters of the novel are set here in "an elegant house" before the suddenly impoverished vicar and his family leave for the "small cure" (identified as Kirby Moorside, Yorkshire) 70 miles away. John Galsworthy visited Lofthouse Park Internment Camp here in 1916, when he was working on the case concerning George Sauter that he was to plead before the Home Office Advisory Committee; he did not stay in Wakefield but in Leeds.

Sandal Castle, 3 miles south of Wakefield in the parish of Sandal Magna, was an important York stronghold in the Wars of the Roses and was used by William Shakespeare in *Henry VI: Part III.* The interior of the castle is the scene of the development of Richard's persuasive and cunning personality.

The "plains near Sandal" are the location of the historic Battle of Wakefield (1460), which resulted in the defeat of the York faction and the death of the Duke of York.

WALCOTE, Leicestershire So small as to have no population listed in current gazetteers, Walcote, 2 miles east of Lutterworth, has an assured place in literary history because of H. G. Wells's short story "Walcote: A Christmas Tale," in *Separate Short Stories*. Whether or not the episode used by Wells took place here is unknown, but many of the names in the story are identical to those of local families. A year before the action of the story takes place Edwin murdered Sir Harry here. Playing cards with friends a year later on Christmas night, in the very room in which he committed the murder, Edwin is startled into a confession and then suicide by a parrot, which after a year's muteness suddenly shrieks out the dying man's final appeals.

WALESBY, Lincolnshire (pop. 279) A village discovered in the 19th century to have been the site of an extensive Roman villa, Walesby is a lovely old place on the edge of the Wolds, 3 miles northeast of Market Rasen. The village boasts two churches, one modern and one ancient; the latter, the Church of All Saints (restored), is perched high on a hill with a stunning view to Lincoln Cathedral. Around 1624 Robert Burton received the living here, but specific information about him is scanty at best. He obviously held Walesby in conjunction with livings in Oxford and Seagrave, Leicestershire, but the date when he gave up this post is unknown.

WALLINGTON DEMESNE, Northumberland (pop. 143) The little hamlet of Wallington Demesne, 10 miles west of Morpeth, contains the largest National Trust property in England, Wallington House; the "new" house was built in 1688 by Sir William Blackett on the site of an earlier manor. The house passed to the Trevelyans when the male Blackett line failed and the Blackett heiress married into the Cornish family. In the 1850s William Bell Scott, a native of Newcastle, was commissioned to paint the murals in the great Central Hall; a series of events in Northumbrian history, the murals are surmounted by portraits of the county's worthies. While Scott was at work in 1857, John Ruskin made one of his many visits to Wallington and with other guests painted flowers upon pillars in the hall. Ruskin first met Algernon Swinburne here on one of his trips; Swinburne was a close friend of Sir Walter and Lady Trevelyan and often stopped in on his way from his home in Capheaton to the rectory in Cambo where he was being tutored. The house, close to the Wansbeck River, was the inspiration for

> The Wansbeck sings with all her springs,
> The bents and braes give ear;
> But the wood that rings with the song she sings
> I may not see or hear;
> For far and far the blythe burns are,
> And strange is a' things here....

WALMER, Kent (pop. 25,240) A medieval village built away from the coast, Walmer has contained the official residence of the Lord Warden of the Cinque Ports since the 18th century. Only a mile south of Deal, it is a resort area with a shingle beach and an early-12th-century church with some wall paintings; indeed, the church was built originally as the chapel for the first Walmer Castle. The 16th-century Walmer Castle has a number of Georgian rooms appended to Henry VIII's massive fortification, and now picture windows have been cut into the original thick walls. The warden often does not live here (Sir Winston Churchill did not), but the Duke of Wellington did, and the room where he died in 1852 has been kept exactly as it was furnished, with a camp bed and the wing chair in which he collapsed; in the adjacent room is a pair of the original Wellington boots.

Walmer was the birthplace of Robert Seymour Bridges on October 23, 1844. The eighth of nine children, Bridges grew up at Roselands, an old family house here which was set in gardens and walks, and the boy's childhood here was extremely pleasant. The Bridges family attended the local church, where there was a family pew, and one of the poet's fond recollections was of the Duke of Wellington, who paused at the Bridges's pew every Sunday to bow to Mrs. Bridges. In September 1854 young Robert was sent to Eton, and with his mother's remarriage that year the family home was sold and turned into a convent. A number of poems in *Shorter Poems* draw on Bridges's childhood here, as does "Kate's Mother." Perhaps the most characteristic memoir of the poet's delight with the Kentish coast occurs in "Elegy" ("The Summer House on the Mound"):

> That sea is ever bright and blue, the sky
> Serene and blue, and ever white ships lie
> High on the horizon steadfast in full sail,
> Or nearer in the roads pass within hail,
> Of naked brigs and barques that windbound ride
> At their taut cables heading to the tide.

WALSALL, Staffordshire (pop. 107,300) While in two directions, north and east, Walsall looks to lovely unspoiled countryside, in the other two are all the reminders that the town is on the edge of the Black Country, 6 miles east of Wolverhampton. With both coal and iron in ample supply, Walsall has long been an industrial center; however, most of the early activity was in the saddlery trade, and Walsall is still England's capital for the manufacture of fine leather goods and saddles. Adapting to modern times, it also makes leather equipment for automobiles. William Camden commented on the town in his *Britannia* and cited John Leland as well:

> "At *Walleshall* be pittes of secole, pittes of lyme, that serve also *South town*, four miles off. There is also yren owre." ...
> Ther be many smithes and bytte makers in the towne.

Walsall was the birthplace of Jerome Klapka Jerome on May 2, 1859; the youngest son of a Nonconformist colliery owner, Jerome had a childhood of poverty. Flooding ruined his father's mine, and the family was forced to leave for London, where the elder Jerome set up as an ironmonger. The house on Bradford Street where Jerome was born has been swept away in a high tide of redevelopment, but a plaque on Belsize House marks the site.

WALTHAM CROSS, Hertfordshire (pop. 5,657)

On the south side of Cheshunt, Waltham Cross is included in the Cheshunt parish and is often considered part of the larger community; it is also often confused with Waltham Holy Cross, Essex, which is just 1 mile across the Lea River. Edward I raised a cross here to mark one of the resting places of Queen Eleanor's body on the journey from Lincoln to Westminster Abbey. The body rested in the abbey in Waltham Holy Cross; the cross here, perhaps the best of the twelve commemorative markers, is thought to be the work of William Tyrell, the goldsmith who made the Queen's tomb.

Waltham House (gone) was the home of Anthony Trollope from 1859 to 1871; the house

was a rickety old place, requiring much repair and not as weathertight as it should be. But for strawberries, asparagus, green peas, out-of-door peaches, for roses and such everyday luxuries, no place was ever more excellent.

Trollope first leased the property and, after spending £1,000 improving it, bought it. He kept himself on a rigid writing schedule here and was up and working at his desk at 5:30 every morning; by his own admission he used a watch to pace his writing at 250 words every quarter hour. Although Trollope was still holding down his administrative Post Office position and fitting his writing in around his office schedule, many of his best novels were written here: *Framley Parsonage, The Small House at Allington, The Claverings, Can You Forgive Her?, The Last Chronicle of Barset,* and *Phineas Finn, the Irish Member.* Trollope left Waltham House in 1871 and sold the house two years later at a loss of £800.

There is one other literary association with Waltham Cross; the old Four Crowns Inn was a favorite spot of Charles Lamb.

WALTHAM HOLY CROSS, Essex (pop. 7,164)

Almost no one uses the proper name of this town; generally it is called Waltham or Waltham Abbey, and part of the reason may be that there is a town called Waltham Cross just 1 mile across the Lea River in Hertfordshire. The tradition surrounding the naming of this Essex town, while no doubt apocryphal, is quite lovely. It is said that Tovi, the standard-bearer of King Cnut (Canute), found a rood (cross) on his land in Montacute, Somerset. Tovi placed the relic in an oxcart to be taken to Glastonbury, but the oxen refused to move. After several refusals the oxen accepted the choice of Waltham, where Tovi built a church for the cross. This church was rebuilt by Harold Godwinsson (who became King Harold II), who supposedly came here for prayer before the Battle of Hastings in 1066, and the rallying cry for the English troops in that battle was "Holy Rood." Tradition maintains that Harold's body was brought back here for burial after the battle and that a plain slab in the abbey marks his grave, but there are other claimants for his burial. At the dissolution of the monasteries in the 16th century Sir Anthony Denny, who acquired the grounds, destroyed the proportions of the place and used some of the stones for building materials,

but even so a third of the original structure remains. The nave of the abbey church was saved by the parish, which claimed it as their church, and the 13th-century Lady Chapel on the south side of the church is also a remnant of the original.

Waltham Holy Cross was the home of John Foxe, the martyrologist, in 1565, and the evidence suggests that he might have been here as early as 1561 when he was translating his *Actes and Monuments,* commonly known as *The Book of Martyrs,* from Latin. He settled in Waltham in 1563 after resigning his canonship at Salisbury in protest against some of the church practices. Two of his children were baptized in the church here in January 1569. Probably in the early 1570s Foxe left here for London, where he lived until his death in 1587.

Izaak Walton came to Waltham Holy Cross on a combined business and pleasure trip; he certainly did not pass up an opportunity to fish here, although the purpose of his visit was rather to obtain from Thomas Fuller information for his life of Richard Hooker. Fuller himself had been appointed to the rectory here around 1649, but this date is based wholly on circumstantial evidence. He found here "the quiet residence" he had long desired and was able to work on *The History of the Worthies of England* and *The Church-History of Britain.* He remarried during his tenure here, probably in late 1651, and a son, James, born in December 1652, was baptized on December 27 in the parish church. Both this child and a second, Anne, are buried in the abbey chancel. Fuller most likely resigned his curacy here in late 1658, but no document in existence gives the specific date. Walton's fishing in the area was quite good, and in *The Compleat Angler* Piscator mentions that he and a friend "will go down towards Waltham."

Richard Brinsley Sheridan, under painful circumstances, spent more than six months here beginning in August or September 1772. Having been apprehended by irate family members after eloping with Elizabeth Linley of Bath, Sheridan found himself engaged in two duels with Maj. Thomas Mathews who, the playwright thought, had defamed Miss Linley's character. Sheridan was injured in the second duel and was sent here by his father to recuperate. He stayed with good family friends, Mr. and Mrs. Parker, at Hill Farm, on the Epping Forest side of the abbey.

Alfred, Lord Tennyson, who lived at nearby High Beech, often attended church services here, and the pealing of the abbey bells on Christmas and New Year's Eves inspired:

Ring out the old, ring in the new,
  Ring, happy bells, across the snow:
  The year is going, let him go;
Ring out the false, ring in the true.

WALTHAM ST. LAWRENCE, Berkshire (pop. 960)

Situated 2½ miles east of Twyford in an area once covered by coniferous forests, Waltham St. Lawrence is a village of old houses, a timbered 17th-century inn, and a medieval church whose door is carved with St. Lawrence and the grid on which he was martyred and on which he is traditionally said to have made his macabre request to be turned since he was done on one side. The churchyard contains the grave of John Newbery, publisher and author of children's books and a friend of Oliver Goldsmith, Samuel Johnson, Christopher Smart, and Tobias Smollett, all of whom probably visited here. Newbery frequently came to Goldsmith's aid financially, and Goldsmith models his St. Paul's bookseller in *The Vicar of Wakefield* on Newbery.

WALTHAMSTOW, Essex (pop. 129,395)   Even though technically a part of the county of Essex, Walthamstow is at the same time a part of the metropolitan area of Greater London. A population explosion (in the last ten years an increase of more than 22,000) has helped to aggravate the discomforts of congestion; but once, because of easy access to the city and a location on the edge of Epping Forest, Walthamstow was a popular place for a country house. Roger Ascham spent a short time here at Salisbury Hall (Farm), granted to him by Queen Mary on January 22, 1557. The grant was to run for forty years, dating from March 25, 1564, and the rent was £22/12/6 for the large house, slightly more than 200 acres of land, and a fishery on the Lea River. Unfortunately Ascham had to sell the lease (Christmas 1561) before he could realize any income from it because of a severe financial strain produced partly by the desperate need of his recently widowed mother-in-law. It is most likely that Ascham knew both George Gascoigne and his stepson Nicholas Breton, for Gascoigne, after his marriage to the widow of William Breton, came here to live. His house here (gone) is where *Supposes*, the basis for William Shakespeare's *The Taming of the Shrew*, was written; *Jocasta* was probably written here as well. Sir Walter Ralegh was a frequent visitor to the Gascoigne home.

Another literary figure, Samuel Pepys, was often here as the guest of Sir William Batten. It might be suspected that part of Pepys's interest and enjoyment here was the wine for which Sir William's vineyard was renowned. Benjamin Disraeli, whose home was in Enfield, Middlesex, attended Cogan's School (Unitarian) here for four years from the age of thirteen. The school, which admitted Nonconformists and Jews as well as members of Church of England families, was then located at Higham Hall, an old manor house about 2 miles outside the town. Disraeli later uses Higham Hall in *Endymion* as Hainault House, a country mansion on the edge of a forest (Epping) within an hour's ride of Bishopsgate Street.

William Morris was born at Elm House (gone), Clay Hill, on March 24, 1834; it was a roomy Victorian house and had a large kitchen garden with a mulberry tree and an extensive shrub-surrounded front lawn. Because of his frail constitution Morris was unable to take part in normal childhood activities and turned to reading; by the age of four, it is said, he was reading Sir Walter Scott's Waverley novels. In 1840 Morris's family moved to Woodford, but they returned after his father's death in 1847 and settled at Water House (now Lloyd Park), whose name derives from a 40-foot moat surrounding an island of aspen trees. This became a perfect all-season playground for the children: in the summer they rowed around the island and fished in the moat; in the winter they skated on it. Much of Morris's work reflects this pleasant environment; poetic references, especially to the moat and the island, occur often:

> Many scarlet bricks there were
>   In its walls, and old grey stone,
>   Over which red apples shone,
> At the right time of the year. . . .
> Deep green water fill'd the moat. . . .

News from Nowhere is a somewhat inaccurate description of the countryside of his boyhood.

WALTON, Suffolk   On the crumbling coast of Suffolk near the relatively unpopulated Landguard area, Walton is actually part of the Felixstowe Urban District. Once a haunt of smugglers, it has an excellent relic of those times in the curiously constructed Dooley Inn, each room of which has multiple doors provided to foil the authorities and press-gangs. When Richard Steele, with the rank of captain, was posted to the bleak Landguard Fort with his men in 1702, he endured the deprivations of the coastal area for a few months and then moved into a farmhouse here. At that time he was working on his second play, *The Election of Gotham* (not completed).

WALTON-ON-THAMES, Surrey (pop. 14,644)   A heavily developed residential town on the Thames River 6 miles southwest of Kingston and 17 miles southwest of London, Walton-on-Thames has now become part of a township made up of Walton and Weybridge. Industry and urbanization have much changed the area, and even the famous view of the Walton Bridge painted by J. M. W. Turner is unrecognizable because of encroaching industries. The town's prize possession is the Church of St. Mary (restored), which contains a great deal of Saxon stonework; the massive tower is heavily buttressed, as is common in many Thames-side churches, to keep it from sinking into the soft subsoil. The 17th-century astrologer William Lilly is commemorated with a stone set near the north door by Elias Ashmole, the founder of Oxford's Ashmolean Museum. Lilly, who was suspected of causing the Great Fire of London owing to a remark in one of his tracts, is supposedly both Sidrophel and Erra Pater in Samuel Butler's *Hudibras*:

> That deals in destiny's dark counsels
> And sage opinions of the Moon sells.

In the churchyard is the grave of William Maginn, "brilliant bright Maginn," the Irish poet and journalist friend of Charles Dickens; Maginn is the original of Captain Shandon in William Makepeace Thackeray's *Pendennis;* Shandon is in Fleet Prison ("very much at home he is there, too") when Pen is taken to meet him. Maginn died in Walton, addicted to drink and much in debt.

William Congreve stayed at Ashley Park (gone) in 1717 and 1719, when it was the seat of Viscount Shannon. Edward Lear came to the Oatlands area (between Walton and Weybridge) in September 1860, settled into the Oatlands Hotel, and used the cedars at the hotel as the models for his *Cedars of Lebanon.* He thought the hotel

> a large & sumptiously commodious place, in a part of the old Oatlands Park—with nice broad terrace walks, & a wonderfully lovely view over the river Temms & the surrounding landskip.

And he breakfasted, he said, "audibly in the public coughy-room." Lear seems to have been well settled for a long stay when an extremely cold December and January caused the hotel pipes to burst. While his room was not touched by the water, he could not abide the workmen and so returned to London. Lear stayed a second time for a few days following the death of his sister in March 1870.

WALTON-ON-THE-HILL, Surrey (pop. 1,795) Walton stands 600 feet above sea level 3½ miles northwest of Reigate and clusters around its much-modernized church. Anne of Cleves, tradition says, lived at the 14th-century stone-built Walton Hall after she managed to be divorced from Henry VIII and retain her head. Far more recently Anthony Hope (Sir Anthony Hope Hawkins) lived at Heath Farm, Deans Lane; suffering from ill health, he leased and subsequently bought the farm after giving up his large London residence. At the outbreak of World War I, Hawkins joined the Editorial and Public Branch Department in London in 1918. He died here on July 8, 1933.

WANTAGE, Berkshire (pop. 4,260) Situated in a rich agricultural area in the Vale of the White Horse, Wantage is surrounded by numerous small villages on the old Roman road traversing the Berkshire Downs. The Church of SS. Peter and Paul, on the west side of the square, dates from the 13th century and contains some fine monuments to the Fitzwaryn family, into which Dick Whittington married. There are numerous cobbled streets, most of which are lined with 17th- and 18th-century houses; of special interest is the cobbled passageway from Newbury Street to some 17th-century almshouses. The cobbles are sheep's knucklebones.

The town's greatest claim is as the 849 birthplace of Alfred the Great, the fourth son of Aethelwulf of Essex. As many legends and traditions have grown up around Alfred as around Robin Hood or Arthur, no doubt with more justice. Much of what is known of Alfred has come from Asser's *Life*, and serious doubts have been raised as to its veracity; certainly, however, Alfred's reign was the turning point in early English history, politics, and the arts. There is a commemorative statue of Alfred by Count Ferdinand Victor Gleichen in the town square.

Wantage enters Thomas Hardy's *Jude the Obscure* as Alfredston. It is to Alfredston that Jude goes for a short time, first as an apprentice stonemason and then as a masonry restorer. Much later in the novel Sue hires a car at the Bear here to drive her back to Marygreen (Fawley) so that she can return to Phillotson.

WARE, Hertfordshire (pop. 8,100) On the Lea River 2 miles northeast of Hertford, Ware was used by the Danes on their journey up the river and has a fine medieval cruciform church. Ware first entered literature in medieval times: Geoffrey Chaucer mentions the town in the description of the Pardoner in the General Prologue to *The Canterbury Tales*:

> A voys he hadde as smal as hath a goot.
> No berd hadde he, ne nevere sholde have;
> As smothe it was as it were late shave.
> I trowe he were a geldyng or a mare.

> But of his craft, fro Berwyk into Ware,
> Ne was ther swich another pardoner
> For in his male he hadde a pilwe-beer,
> Which that he seyde was Oure Lady veyl. . . .

Ware also figures in William Cowper's "The Diverting History of John Gilpin," for it is the turning point of the ballad. Mounted on a speeding horse, Gilpin races by Edmonton, where his wife awaits him at the Bell:

> But yet his horse was not a whit
>   Inclined to tarry there;
> For why?—his owner had a house
>   Full ten miles off, at Ware.

The most consistent mention of Ware in literature concerns the Great Bed of Ware (now in the Victoria and Albert Museum in London); 10 feet wide, 11 feet long, and more than 7 feet high, it was at one time in Ware Park (now a sanatorium). In the early 18th century it was removed to the Crown Inn in Ware and eventually made its way to the Victoria and Albert in 1931. The bed has richly carved pillars and canopy and is probably Elizabethan despite an earlier date carved on it. William Shakespeare refers to it in *Twelfth Night;* Sir Toby urges Sir Andrew Aguecheek to write to Olivia:

> Go, write it in a martial hand; be curst and brief; it is no matter how witty, so it be eloquent and full of invention; taunt him with the licence of ink: if thou *thou'st* him some thrice, it shall not be amiss; and as many lies as will lie in thy sheet of paper, although the sheet were big enough for the bed of Ware in England, set 'em down; go about it.

Both Ben Jonson and George Farquhar mention the bed in their works.

WAREHORNE, Kent (pop. 383) A remote village clustered around a tiny green, 7 miles south of Ashford, Warehorne has a church which is much too large for its area but which has beautiful medallions more than 600 years old. The church tower was rebuilt after being struck by lightning in 1770, but otherwise the church is unchanged since Richard Harris Barham lived at the rectory (now Church Farm) from 1817 to 1824, when he took the combined living of Snargate and Warehorne. Here he did his first writing when he was housebound after an accident; however, *Baldwin* "fell dead from the press." Smuggling was once rampant in this part of Romney Marsh, and Barham was frequently challenged by smugglers while on his way from Snargate to Warehorne at night.

WARKWORTH, Northumberland (pop. 1,042) Located where the Coquet River, one of the most famous salmon-fishing reaches in Northumberland, flows into the North Sea, Warkworth with its 12th-century castle at the top of Castle Street, a magnificent coastal defense, was long one of the principal seats of the Percy family, whose history is intertwined with the history of England. Warkworth Castle, in existence in 1139, had no historical or literary importance until the 14th century, when it was granted to the 2d Baron Percy of Alnwick by Edward III. Henry Percy, who earned the sobriquet Hotspur at the 1378 siege of Berwick Castle (then a Scots stronghold), was born here on May 20, 1364. He was heavily involved in the area

ROMNEY MARSH Because of its remoteness and desolation, the eerie, unpopulated area of Romney Marsh, which Richard Harris Barham called the "lonely fifth quarter of the globe," was once popular with smugglers and the occasional pursuing law agents. Frequently Barham was forced, as Rudyard Kipling puts in in *Puck of Pook's Hill*, to "watch the wall, my darling, while the Gentlemen go by!"

conflict with the Scots Douglases and with the Battle of Otterburn, in which the 2d Earl of Douglas was slain and Hotspur, who should never have attacked the strong Scottish position, was taken prisoner. The Douglas-Percy feud continued until the decisive defeat of the 4th Earl of Douglas in 1402 at Homildon Hill. As a result of this success there followed the famous uprising of the Percys in 1403, the Battle of Shrewsbury, and the consequent death on July 21 of Hotspur, all of which William Shakespeare documents in *Henry IV*. Warkworth Castle is described as "this worm-eaten hold of rotten stone"; this was quite possibly the case in Shakespeare's day, but in Hotspur's time it was in fine condition. The castle is the setting in *Henry IV: Part I;* from a room here the events leading up to the departure of Hotspur are acted out. Two scenes in *Henry IV: Part II* take place before the great outer walls of the castle. With the return of the Percy family to Northumberland in the 18th century some renovation was undertaken on the keep, gatehouse, and great hall, and in the 20th century the Earl of Northumberland made family apartments in the tower habitable.

There is an intriguing cave dwelling in the sandstone above the river; in the 14th and 15th centuries the cave was hewn out for use as a hermitage-cum-chapel. Known officially as the Hermitage, it contains three rooms (a chapel, a confessional, and a dormitory) and is said to have been the home of Sir Bertram of Bothal, whom Bishop Thomas Percy's *Reliques of Ancient English Poetry* names as the Hermit of Warkworth. The female effigy in the chapel is said to represent Bertram's love Isabel Widdrington, whose accidental murder caused Bertram to live the rest of his life in penitence for his impulsive act.

WARNHAM, Sussex (pop. 1,237) A neatly kept village of houses roofed with Horsham stone, which gives a false sense of antiquity, Warnham is 2 miles northwest of Horsham. Near the 14th-century church, in a situation darkened by overhanging trees,

is Field Place, the birthplace of Percy Bysshe Shelley on August 4, 1792; the original 13th-century house was enlarged in 1680, and the pillared portico was added in the mid-19th century. One of seven children and the eldest son, Shelley was born in a room on the first floor directly above the "Confusion Hall"; his education began at the age of six when he was sent to learn Latin under the vicar, the Rev. Thomas Edwards. At ten he was removed and sent first to Sion House in Isleworth and then to Eton; from that point on he spent little time here except during the holidays. By the Christmas 1809 holidays, Shelley was considering a writing career, and by the midsummer 1810 holidays, when he enjoyed walks in the St. Irving's Hills, his "views on religion" were becoming well defined. Indeed, Timothy Shelley, later Sir Timothy, heard of his son's attitudes by Christmas from John Joseph Stockdale, a London bookdealer, and the father's immediate reaction was to blame the influence of Thomas Jefferson Hogg and to threaten Shelley's enforced withdrawal from Oxford. Shelley was again at home in May but because of the strained relationship was spending a great deal of time at Cuckfield Park in Cuckfield, the home of his uncle, Capt. John Pilfold. The father's attitude hardened, especially after his son's marriage to Harriet Westbrook in August 1811, and when Percy approached him on October 20, he was told to see the family attorney about his allowance. Relations were strained even more after Shelley, who had abandoned Harriet and was fleeing to the Continent with Mary Godwin, appeared at Field Place in January 1815 upon the death of his grandfather. Denied admission to the house, he sat on the doorstep, it is said, reading Milton's *Comus*. A slight turn of events occurred when Sir Timothy realized that his son could now encumber the estate; deciding that the best course of action was to come to terms with him, the elder Shelley settled £1,000 a year on him, £200 of which Percy settled on Harriet and the son she had borne in 1815.

After the poet's death in Italy on July 8, 1822,

Charles Bysshe Shelley, his son by Harriet, was placed in the care of his grandfather; the child, who was consumptive, died here on September 16, 1826, and is buried here. The church has on display a copy of the poet's baptismal entry from the parish register. There is no other monument. Field Place, which is not open to the public, has over the fireplace a brass commemorative tablet erected by Sir Percy Shelley, the poet's son by Mary Godwin:

> Shrine of the dawning speech and thought
>   Of Shelley! Sacred be
> To all who bow where Time has brought
>   Gifts to Eternity.

The quatrain was written by Dr. Richard Garnett.

WARNINGLID, Sussex Nearly one-quarter of Sussex is woodland, a legacy of the great primeval forest of Anderida, which in Roman times stretched more than 120 miles across southeastern England. The hamlet of Warninglid, 8 miles southeast of Horsham, is in the sort of quiet, undisturbed hinterland often left behind after the demise of much of the old forest. This hamlet was where in 1850 Alfred, Lord Tennyson and his new bride made their first home, and, as Tennyson wrote, "The full song of the birds delighted us as we drove up to the door." But a violent storm changed all that: part of the wall of their bedroom blew down, and the room was badly drenched. While some of their discoveries were interesting—their dining room and bedroom had been a Roman Catholic chapel; an infant had been buried on the premises; and one member of the notorious Cuckfield gang of thieves and murderers had lived here—some were not. Indeed, the postman never came, and the nearest market and doctor were at Horsham. Thus the Tennysons left, with the newly created Poet Laureate pushing his wife in a Bath chair over badly rutted roads to Cuckfield.

WARWICK, Warwickshire (pop. 18,289) The county town of Warwickshire, set spectacularly on the banks of the Avon River, Warwick lies almost in the center of England where the river has cut through an outcropping of hard rock. Part of the town is set on a steep cliff above the Avon, and the area has long had strategic importance. It is not known what the first defensive works were; legend has it that Ethelfleda (Aethelflaed), Alfred the Great's daughter, erected the first important works in 914, but some prior structure must have existed. At any rate, a mound at the southern end of the castle courtyard is said to be all that is left of her structure, a ditched and palisaded fortification. Probably, though, the work is Norman. The marauding Danes sacked the city on various occasions, and each time the fortification was renewed as part of the Mercian defense system; the outpost was guarded by men specially picked by Ethelfleda, it is maintained, and this is said to have been the beginning of the Saxon earldom of Warwick. Undoubtedly one of the earliest and by far the best known of the earls was Guy of Warwick, who acquired the title by marrying the daughter of Rohand, the first true Earl of Warwick. Whatever the actual story of Guy (and it is long vanished), his prowess was great. After slaying the cruel giant Amarant and

making a pilgrimage to the Holy Land, he returned to England, slew the Dane Colbrand, and, somehow keeping his return secret even from his wife, lived the rest of his life as a hermit in a local cave. The story is told in the early-14th-century *Guy of Warwick;* the tale of the encounter between Guy and Colbrand was picked up and used by Michael Drayton in *Poly-Olbion:*

> Thus stood those irefull Knights; till flying back, at length
> The Palmer, of the two the first recovering strength,
> Upon the left arme lend great *Colebrond* such a wound,
> That whilst his weapons poynt fell wel-neere to the ground
> And slowly he it rais'd, the valiant *Guy* againe
> Sent through his cloven scalpe his blade into his braine.
> When downeward went his head, and up his heeles he threw;
> As wanting hands to bid his Countrimen Adieu.

At the time of the Norman Conquest, Turchil was Earl of Warwick; known as the "Traitor Earl" because of his refusal to support Harold at Hastings, he did not do well under William, who stripped him of his title and his estate. Henry de Newburgh, created Earl of Warwick by William Rufus, began an extensive building program; the Newburghs died out after four generations, and the title went to William Mauduit. Mauduit's nephew, a Beauchamp (pronounced "bee'sham"), succeeded to the earldom; the Beauchamps, who held the title through six generations, were responsible for much of today's castle, including the 14th-century Caesar's Tower and Guy's Tower, examples of early military architecture.

The second Beauchamp earl was opposed to Edward II, and when Edward succeeded to the throne and recalled Piers Gaveston, his opposition increased. Called the "Black Hound of Warwick" by Gaveston, the earl was instrumental in bringing about the minion's execution; captured at Scarborough Castle, Gaveston was brought here, sentenced in the Great Hall on June 10, 1312, and beheaded on Blacklow Hill (a nearby wooded knoll) on June 19. A wooden cross (with an incorrect date) commemorates the execution. This is the story related in Christopher Marlowe's *Edward II;* however, Marlowe sets neither sentencing nor execution here. A later Earl of Warwick, Richard Neville, enters literature as the "Kingmaker"; he is William Shakespeare's "setter-up and puller-down of kings" and the hero of Edward Bulwer-Lytton's *The Last of the Barons.* With the death of Richard Neville at the Battle of Barnet in 1471, the earldom in effect ceased to exist until it was granted in 1493 to the son of George, Duke of Clarence, who had been drowned in the butt of malmsey on Richard III's orders.

Henry VIII gave the castle to John Dudley, one of the most unscrupulous men in England, and created him Earl of Warwick; the earldom again ceased to exist after Dudley's son Ambrose died without issue in 1590. Sixteen years later, James I gave Warwick Castle to Sir Fulke Greville, Baron Brooke, who lavished great sums in restoration. He renewed the domestic block, built the chapel, and added the eastern part of the castle adjoining the Great Hall. Greville, Sir Philip Sidney's friend, spent more than £20,000 in repairs and alterations to the estate, and his heirs have carried on his work; indeed, Warwick

Castle is still held by the Greville family, which in 1759 was granted the earldom of Warwick. "Iter Boreale," by a now-unknown poet-cleric, Richard Corbet, describes the castle:

> [I]t is a scholar's home;
> A place of strength and wealth: in the same fort
> You would conceive a castle and a court.
> The orchards, gardens, rivers, and the air,
> Do with the trenches, rampires, walls, compare:
> It seems not art nor force can intercept it,
> As if a lover built, a soldier kept it.
> Up to the tower, though it be steep and high,
> We do not climb, but walk; and though the eye
> Seems to be weary, yet our feet are still
> In the same posture cozen'd up the hill;
> And thus the workman's art deceives our sense,
> Making those rounds of pleasure a defence.

Fulke Greville spent most of the rest of his life here, but his death occurred in his London home in Holborn. Then aged seventy-four, Greville was stabbed by a servant, Ralph Haywood, who then killed himself. Greville lasted only a few weeks and died on September 30, 1628. His body was brought here for burial in St. Mary's Church on October 27 and placed in the chapter house (now a mausoleum). Greville himself chose both the monument (a ponderous thing of black stone built in two stages, the lower consisting of a sarcophagus on a raised base) and the epitaph. The castle today, complete with landscaping by Lancelot (Capability) Brown, contains an outstanding collection of paintings by Rubens, Raphael, Van Dyck, Dobson, Lely, and Holbein, among others, and armor.

WARWICK Near the West Gate Leycester Hospital (meaning "hospitality") was originally a religious house but was converted to a hospital in 1571 by Robert Dudley, Elizabeth's "sweet Robin" and Amy Robsart's husband. Now retired service pensioners live here in their own quarters under the hereditary patronage of Viscount De L'Isle, head of the Sidney family.

Most of the town grew up around the castle. While only fragments of the medieval walls exist, much of Warwick's medieval splendor survives in spite of a disastrous fire on September 5, 1694, which destroyed more than half the town. Leycester Hospital, a gabled black-and-white building, has the 15th-century Chapel of St. James above it. Originally the hall of two united guilds, the hospital was the idea of Robert Dudley, Earl of Leicester; he persuaded Elizabeth that providing a place where old soldiers could live out their lives would aid immensely in recruiting new soldiers to the ranks. She granted the charter in 1571, and the present hospital, which offers free lodging and a heating allowance to retired soldiers and their wives, is under the hereditary patronage of Viscount De L'Isle.

Most of the old Collegiate Church of St. Mary was destroyed by the 1694 fire, but its history by far predates that incident. A church existed here before the Domesday survey, and when it was rebuilt after the fire, most of the monuments had to be resited. The Beauchamp Chapel was built to the directions of Richard, Earl of Warwick, who died in Rouen in 1439; this is the Earl of Warwick who became lieutenant general of France and the Duchy of Normandy, who captured Joan of Arc, and who is portrayed vividly in George Bernard Shaw's *Saint Joan*. A second monument of interest is that of Robert Dudley, Earl of Leicester, the favorite of Elizabeth I; the husband of Amy Robsart, whose death at Cumnor Place in 1560 created rumors of murder, he is portrayed in Sir Walter Scott's *Kenilworth*.

Of Warwick itself much has been written; Daniel Defoe's impression of the town and its castle is contained in *A Tour thro' the Whole Island of Great Britain*:

> [I]t is really a fine Town, pleasantly situated on the Bank of the Avon.... *Warwick* was ever esteem'd a handsome, well-built Town, and there were several good Houses in it, but the Face of it is now quite alter'd; for having been almost wholly reduc'd to a Heap of Rubbish, by a terrible Fire about two and twenty Years ago, it is now rebuilt in so noble and so beautiful a Manner, that few Towns in *England* make so fine an Appearance.

He viewed the castle, "a fine Building . . . [which] overlooks a beautiful Country," and found "no Irregularity in the whole Place, not withstanding its ancient Plan, as it was a Castle not a Palace, and built for Strength rather than Pleasure"; from here he went on to visit Guy of Warwick's hermitage.

Walter Savage Landor was born at Ipsley Court on January 30, 1775, and baptized on February 26 in the parish church of St. Nicholas. His earliest years were spent here, and before he was five years of age, he was sent away to school at Knowle, about 9 miles northwest. From then on, he divided his family time between his maternal grandparents' home at Bishop's Tachbrook and Warwick. Landor left England in 1814 after a great deal of financial and legal difficulty and returned only occasionally until resettling in Bath in 1836. He paid his final visit to Warwick in August 1853. The house where Landor was born is now part of the Warwick High School for Girls, and the Queen Anne house now contains the headmistress' study.

Sir Walter Scott visited Warwick in the spring of

1828 on his way to London and observed that the castle was "still the noblest sight in England." The remark with which Scott is often credited, that the castle was "the fairest monument of ancient and chivalrous splendor . . . which yet remains uninjured by time," was made by Sir William Dugdale, the Warwickshire historian, in 1655. Ten years after Scott was here, Charles Dickens and Phiz (Halbot Knight Browne) came from Leamington to visit the castle, which Dickens said was "an ancient building, newly restored, and possessing no very great attraction beyond a fine view and some beautiful pictures." Dickens later used Warwick and its castle in *Dombey and Son;* Mr. Dombey, the Major, Mrs. Skewton, and Edith travel here in a barouche with Mr. Carker bringing up the rear on horseback:

> Mrs. Skewton was bent on taking charge of Mr. Carker herself, and showing him the beauties of the Castle. She was determined to have his arm, and the Major's too. It would do that incorrigible creature: who was the most barbarous infidel in point of poetry: good to be in such company. This chance arrangement left Mr. Dombey at liberty to escort Edith, which he did: stalking before them through the apartments with a gentlemanly solemnity.
>
> "Those darling bygone times, Mr. Carker," said Cleopatra, "with their delicious fortresses, and their dear old dungeons, and their delightful places of torture, and their romantic vengeances, and their picturesque assaults and sieges, and everything that makes life truly charming! How dreadfully we have degenerated!"

The lack of detail is evidence of Dickens's lack of interest in the great castle.

A more modern note should be made concerning the Poet Laureate John Masefield; born in Ledbury, Herefordshire, in 1878, he received his first schooling there before being sent to King's School in Warwick. Never a scholar and so much attracted to the sea that he ran off from the school on several occasions, he finally persuaded his father to apprentice him aboard a windjammer in 1892, at which time he left Warwick.

WASDALE, Cumberland   One of the best-known areas in the Lake District, Wasdale, or Wasdale Head, as it is sometimes called, is a climber's paradise; indeed, British rock climbing is said to have begun here, and the tiny churchyard contains the graves of a number of the victims of the sport. Wastwater Lake, whose overspill forms the Irt River, is the deepest of the district lakes (260 feet) and is half a mile wide and more than 3 miles long. The tiny village of Wasdale Head, in a hollow of the fells above the head of the lake, is typical of the region in its gray stone houses and narrow walled-in streets. Great Gable (2,949 feet) and Scafell (3,206 feet) tower over the village; a range of screes rises directly from the bed of the lake, a pertinent reminder that in some future time the lake will be filled in.

Wasdale Hall, at the end of the lake and well protected by a large stand of trees, belonged to Stansfeld Rawson in the 19th century. In June 1832, just a short time after his return from an eighteen-year self-exile, Walter Savage Landor came here from Moresby. Landor's appreciation of the dale and Rawson's hospitality are noted in "Written at Mr. Rawson's Wastwater Lake." William Wordsworth, who had also

WASTWATER   Called by Sir Hugh Walpole "the most awe-inspiring" of the lakes in the Lake District, Wastwater and the inn at Wasdale, a tiny village at the head of Wastwater, come into *Rogue Herries.* David Herries and Sarah escape across the pass from Scarf Hall with Captain Bann and Mr. Denburn in pursuit.

been in Moresby, visiting his son's family, came here at the same time.

In more recent years George Gissing uses Wastwater in *The Odd Women,* but the more famous association comes with Sir Hugh Walpole. Walpole's first encounter with the area occurred in September 1898; in a letter to Canon A. J. Mason, his godfather, the novelist comments that "Wastwater is the most awe-inspiring and Derwentwater the most beautiful" of the lakes and notes that Wastwater was "made lovely by the Screes descending straight into it." In *Rogue Herries* David Herries comes to Wasdale to buy sheep from "a man called Denburn" and falls in love with the young Sarah. He rides over the fells from Rosthwaite:

> It was dark when his horse (he was riding Deb's Appleseed) had picked its way to the bottom of Stye Head, and it was difficult to find his way. He found his path across Lingmell Beck, and then plunged into a black thicket of trees. Here he stumbled for a long while, hearing water tumbling all about him, and the wind roaring down the pass.
>
> He was not a man to mind wind and tumbling water, but he was uncomfortable nevertheless. This lake-end valley, cut off from the world, was an excellent rendezvous for smugglers from the seacoast, only a few miles away. The inn at that time, the Wasdale Inn, was a wretched place, as he well knew, both in accommodation and reputation, but it was there that he must pass the night.

WATCHET, Somerset (pop. 2,500)   The village of Watchet, because of its strategic position on the Bristol Channel almost 17 miles northwest of Taunton, has figured as an important port since 918, when the Danes attempted to plunder it and were defeated. In the 17th century the Royalists used Watchet to ship reinforcements and provisions from the loyal South Wales area; the village reached its peak in the Victorian era, when the harbor was enlarged and an eastern wharf added to deal with an extensive trade in timber and Welsh coal.

The 13th-century parish church is dedicated to St. Decuman, the subject of several local legends. In one, the Welsh saint, who is said to have been beheaded by the heathen natives, picked up his head and recrossed the channel. In another, he supposedly officiated at the marriage of King Arthur and Queen Guinevere.

In 1797 Samuel Taylor Coleridge and William Wordsworth frequently walked in the Watchet area from Alfoxden and Nether Stowey, discussed poetry, and worked jointly on a poem which ultimately Coleridge alone wrote, *The Rime of the Ancient Mariner*. Coleridge also designates Watchet as the mariner's port of embarkation: "Here is where he shall set out on his fateful voyage," he told Wordsworth. If this is the case, the kirk most likely is St. Decuman's, and the lighthouse is on the west breakwater:

> The ship was cheered, the harbor cleared
> Merrily did we drop
> Below the kirk, below the hill,
> Below the lighthouse top.

However, topographers disagree over this identification; some claim that the landscape at Clevedon is more fitting.

WATENDLATH, Cumberland Two miles south of Keswick a minor road turns off through lush green but dark hills and leads to the tiny valley hamlet of Watendlath, which is separated from Borrowdale by a low ridge. Watendlath, brooded over by Armboth Fell (1,588 feet), has its own tarn and is cut through by Lodore Stream. Sir Hugh Walpole uses the village throughout the "Herries" chronicle and especially in *Judith Paris*. This is the beloved home of Judith, and while local tradition has settled on a particular house—indeed, one farm displays a Judith Paris staircase (presumably the one that brings the end of George)—it seems that Walpole had no specific place in mind. He describes the area carefully at several points in the novel, capturing in each a different aspect of Watendlath; in one instance he writes:

> They left the little wood behind them and started to climb. They were now on the open moor. The Langdale Pikes, Fairfield, Helvellyn were beyond, and across Yewdale loomed the hump of the Old Man. The light about and around him was diffused as though shed by the multitude of stars. The pools of shadow, neither brown nor grey, lay below them like lakes of sleeping water. Fairfield and Helvellyn were marked with crags and precipices like the tearing made by some giant's fingers. How black, how black the hills against the luminous sky! A little higher on the moor and they were suddenly staring into the moon's face. . . .
>
> They sat down against a gigantic boulder; the stones around them rose in that moonshine like monolithic sacrificial monuments. As they sat in that stillness the hills seemed to approach them. Helvellyn, always a beneficent hill, leaned towards them, Fairfield embraced them, the pools below smiled at them.

WATER EATON, Oxfordshire (pop. 125) Three miles north of Oxford, on the west bank of the Cherwell (pronounced "char'well"), is a village that essentially no longer exists except for a Jacobean manor house and an old church. The three-gabled manor

house looks to the Cherwell and has a fine example of a priest's hiding hole over its porch. The house belonged to relatives of Richard Lovelace and in the poet's time was inhabited by the 2d Baron Lovelace, a staunch Royalist. It is to Lady Lovelace that the poet dedicates the volume of poems containing the lines

> I could not love thee (deare) so much,
> Lov'd I not Honour more.

While there is no clear proof that Lovelace visited his kinsman here, he is generally assumed to have done so.

WATER NEWTON, Huntingdonshire (pop. 105) The major north-south English road has always gone through the center of this small village and recently has threatened its very extinction. This is a busy transportation route, and the Nene River village, 5 miles west of Peterborough, has been able to regain some of its former beauty only since a bypass to the A1 was built. The houses are generally of typical Northamptonshire stone construction; Water Newton House is early-17th-century. Near the village is the Roman town of Durobrivae. John Clare, the Northamptonshire poet, helped to excavate some of the Roman villa.

WATERINGBURY, Kent (pop. 1,143) A Medway village 5 miles southwest of Maidstone, Wateringbury has a main street lined with Georgian houses and arcaded shops; over the door of the 13th-century church (reconstructed) is the Dum Borsholder of Chart, a staff of office dating to Saxon times and used here until 1748. Its keeper was elected annually and was permitted to collect a penny from every house in the hamlet of Pizein Wall. Halfway down the hill to the Medway is a Whitbread brewery, well situated since this is hop country.

In 1931 George Orwell (Eric Blair) left London in the company of two tramps whom he had met in a doss house to come here to work in the hop fields. He worked for almost three weeks at Home Farm and slept on straw in the barn, just as do the hop pickers in *A Clergyman's Daughter*:

> Seemingly there were women down among the straw. Dorothy burrowed forward more circumspectly, tripped over something, sank into the straw and in the same instant began to fall asleep. A rough-looking woman, partially undressed, popped up like a mermaid from the strawy sea.
>
> "'Ullo, mate!" she said. "Jest about all in, ain't you, mate?"
>
> "Yes, I'm tired—very tired."
>
> "Well, you'll bloody freeze in this straw with no bedclo'es on you. Ain't you got a blanket?"
>
> "No."
>
> "'Alf a mo, then. I got a poke 'ere."
>
> She dived down into the straw and re-emerged with a hop-poke seven feet long.

WAVERLEY ABBEY, Surrey Although Surrey is heavily populated, the North Downs retain much of their natural beauty; here there is extensive heathland, and much of the woodland is cut by small streams. On the Wey River, 2 miles southeast of Farnham, is Waverley Abbey; located at the base of the hill, the abbey is in a secluded and well-watered area, fitting the Cistercian rule that the foundation be "remote from the conversation of men" and near a stream. Founded in 1128 by William Giffard, Bishop of Winchester, it was the first Cistercian abbey to be established in England and became one of the order's most influential but not wealthy institutions. Waverley was among the first to succumb at the dissolution of the monasteries in the 16th century, and the buildings provided materials for the rebuilding of nearby Loseley.

Time has further destroyed the structures, and almost nothing remains above ground; the marvelous groined undercroft of the guesthouse and the transept of the second church are about all that are now visible. In John Aubrey's time more was standing, including the walls, which enclosed some 60 acres. Richard Gough notes in the additions to William Camden's *Britannia:*

> *Waverley* abbey, the first of the Cistercian order among us, is beautifully situated among sandy and heathy hills. A stream from the river Wye surrounds it on three sides coming close to the ruins. It has also three other rivers of less note, the *Wandle,* the *Mole,* and the *Wey....* At present only part of the fourth aile remains, with the corner stones of the chancel or tower. In the middle of the nave is a coffin-fashioned tomb covered with black and yellow tesselae. Further east another with a cross fleuri. Part of the refectory, dormitory, and cloisters are also standing, as was in the last century a large handsome chapel and the hall with a row of pillars in the middle.

William Cobbett came here with his son in October 1825 and notes in *Rural Rides:* "[A]ll the old monks' garden walls are totally gone, and the spot is become a sort of lawn." He goes on to point out to Richard

> the spot where the strawberry garden was, and where I, when sent to gather *hautboys,* used to eat every remarkably fine one, instead of letting it go to be eaten by Sir Robert Rich. I showed him a tree, close by the ruins of the Abbey, from a limb of which I once fell into the river, in an attempt to take the nest of a *crow....* I found the ruins not very greatly diminished; but it is strange how small the mansion, and ground, and everything but the trees, appeared to me.

This, of course, is the source of the title of Sir Walter Scott's novel *Waverley,* although the novel is not set here. Indeed, Scott notes:

> The title of this work has not been chosen without the grave and solid deliberation which matters of importance demand from the prudent. Even its first, or general denomination, was the result of no common research or selection, although, according to the example of my predecessors, I had only to seize upon the most sounding and euphonic surname that English history or topography affords, and elect it at once as the title of my work and the name of my hero.... I must modestly admit I am too diffident of my own merit to place it in unnecessary oppostion to preconceived associations; I have, therefore, like a maiden knight with his white shield, assumed for my hero, WAVERLEY, an uncontaminated name....

WEETING, Norfolk (pop. 312)   Possibly one of Norfolk's most interesting villages, Weeting (also known as Weeting-cum-Bromshill) is in the area known as Breckland, ancient tracts of heath once partly cultivated but now reverted to wilderness. The village itself is bounded on the west by the Devil's Dyke, which is probably part of a Saxon defense system.

More interesting is Grime's Graves, Neolithic flint mines to the east of the village, which were worked extensively around 2100 B.C. Almost 35 acres of land were mined, and just adjacent to the area are the knapping sites where the flints were worked into usable forms. Funnel-shaped shafts were employed, and radiating galleries were dug from their base. Two of the pits have been fully excavated and are open to the public.

Weeting once had a castle and a priory. The castle, now in ruins with a dry, square moat, dates from the 12th century, when the land came into the possession of a later member of the family which founded the Augustinian Bromshill Priory. Only a few of the buildings remain, and they have been incorporated into the farm on the site. William Camden wrote of Weeting and its buildings in his *Britannia:*

> At *Weting All Saints* are venerable ruins of a square castle of flint, moated, with a keep.... Two miles East of the town are certain pits inclosed in a semicircular intrenchment of 12 acres on the side of a hill, with a tumulus at the East end of the work called *Grimes Graves,* which is equivalent to *Graham's dyke* in Scotland.... In Weting parish was *Bromehill* priory founded by sir Hugh de Plaiz in the reign of John, or Henry III. for Austin canons, of which there now little remains. Thomas Shadwell the poet is reported to have been born about 1640 in the parish of Weting, whereof his family were lords.

Broomhill House, on the priory site, was the birthplace of the dramatist and Poet Laureate Thomas Shadwell in 1640 or 1642. Little is known of Shadwell's early life here, but he attended school in Bury St. Edmunds before going up to Caius College, Cambridge.

WELLINGTON, Shropshire (pop. 10,352)   Situated 10 miles east of Shrewsbury on Watling Street, an old Roman road, Wellington is the modern town of the ancient Wrekin, a cone-shaped hill rising 1,335 feet above sea level. The town is a fairly modern industrial center, but occasional half-timbered buildings remain. The Wrekin is the main attraction here, and from its summit the panorama is astounding: Snowdon, Brecon Beacons, the Peak Hills in Derbyshire, the Abberley Hills in Worcestershire, the Cotswolds in Gloucestershire, and the Hawkstone and Parkgate Hills in Cheshire are all visible. On a fine day even the Banbury Hills, 70 miles away, can be picked out. In prehistoric times the Wrekin was supposedly an active volcano, and in fairly recent times a hilltop beacon was lighted to alert the Marches country when the Spanish Armada was sighted. Thomas Babington Macaulay relates the scene in *The Armada;* he traces the hilltop blazes from southern England northward:

> Till twelve fair counties saw the blaze on Malvern's lonely height,
> Till streamed in crimson on the wind the Wrekin's crest of light,
> Till broad and fierce the star came forth on Ely's stately fane,
> And tower and hamlet rose in arms o'er all the boundless plain....

A. E. Housman includes the Wrekin beacon in the first poem in *A Shropshire Lad:*

> From Clee to heaven the beacon burns,

The shires have seen it plain,
From north and south the sign returns
    And beacons burn again.

Look left, look right, the hills are bright,
    The dales are light between,
Because 'tis fifty years to-night
    That God has saved the Queen.

WELLS, Somerset (pop. 7,000)   Wells is situated in one of the most attractive parts of Somerset, at the foot of the Mendip Hills between Bath and Glastonbury. The Mendips are limestone ridges covering a substructure of red sandstone which accounts for the large number of drystone walls, large caves such as Wookey Hole, and "swallet holes" (holes in the rock structure which swallow up streams). The reason for the name of the town is obvious: as John Leland, the antiquarian and library keeper to Henry VIII, notes in his *Itinerary*, "The toun of Welles is sette yn the roots of Mendepe Hille in a stony soile and full of springes, whereof it hath the name." In actual fact Wells consists of two towns, for inside the municipal division is the ecclesiastical city, enclosed by walls and containing the cathedral, Chapter House, Bishop's Palace, and Deanery. The heart of Wells is the cathedral, mainly 13th-century, with its renowned west front. The tradition is that the first church was founded here in 705 by the Wessex king Ine on the advice of St. Aldhelm, then Bishop of Sherborne, and in the early 10th century Edward the Elder, realizing that the existing bishoprics of Winchester and Sherborne could not administer ecclesiastical affairs in all of Wessex, created a new see. On the north side of the cathedral, begun between 1175 and 1185, is the Vicar's Close, a set of buildings unique in England: housing the Vicars Choral had been a problem for more than 100 years before Bishop Ralph began the construction of forty-two small row houses for this purpose. The early tranquility of the close has been preserved: there are no cars, and cats sun themselves on the garden walls. Even though the Cathedral School has existed here since at least 1140, its rather specialized emphasis on music and the training of choristers has resulted in a dearth of literary associations.

One erroneous literary association is the best known: Wells is frequently said to be the Barchester of Anthony Trollope's novels, especially because of the opening paragraph of *The Warden*, in which he writes:

The Rev. Septimus Harding was, a few years since, a beneficed clergyman residing in the cathedral town of——; let us call it Barchester. Were we to name Wells or Salisbury, Exeter, Hereford, or Gloucester, it might be presumed that something personal was intended.... Let us presume that Barchester is a quiet town in the West of England, more remarkable for the beauty of its cathedral and the antiquity of its monuments, than for any commercial prosperity; that the west end of Barchester is the cathedral close....

Trollope, however, maintained that Barchester was a composite and that Winchester was more nearly the model, especially for Hiram's Hospital.

From 1784 to 1790 William Beckford sat as the Member of Parliament for Wells, even though he was living mostly in Switzerland, and in 1792 Richard Brinsley Sheridan brought his wife's body here for burial from Bristol, where she had died. W. H. Hudson particularly liked the cathedral and close and usually visited them on his West Country jaunts. The most extensive use of Wells comes in Thomas Hardy's "A Tragedy of Two Ambitions" *(Life's Little Ironies)*, where the town masquerades under the name Fountall. Hardy describes Fountall Theological College, which Joshua attends, and the cathedral:

It was afternoon. All was as still in the Close as a cathedral-green can be between the Sunday services, and the incessant cawing of the rooks was the only sound. Joshua Halborough had finished his ascetic lunch, and had gone into the library, where he stood for a few moments looking out of the large window facing the green.

The town gets passing mention in H. G. Wells's *The Secret Places of the Heart* when Hardy, Miss Grammont, and Miss Seyffert put up at an unidentified inn.

On August 17, 1908, Virginia Woolf arrived in Wells for a working holiday and with two dogs took lodgings in the Vicar's Close with a Mrs. Wall, an elderly person with good but misplaced intentions. Mrs. Wall thought her lodger was a bit lonesome and provided company in the form of a timid theological student. The outcome was that Virginia Woolf promptly moved, this time to a verger's house on the Cathedral Green. But she found it difficult to work here and, after a few excursions to Bath and Glastonbury, left for Manorbier, Pembrokeshire.

WELWYN, Hertfordshire (pop. 1,762)   On the edge of the Maran Valley 4 miles north of Hatfield, Welwyn (pronounced "wel'lin") is now a dual community, a modern village (Welwyn Garden City) and an old village 1 mile away. The old village was settled by the Romans, and the Church of St. Mary, believed to stand on the site of an early temple, has incorporated numerous Roman bricks in its fabric. Welwyn was the living to which Edward Young, author of *Night Thoughts*, was presented in July 1730, and he served here until his death in 1765. Within a year of his preferment he married Lady Elizabeth Lee, daughter of the 1st Earl of Lichfield, and was settled in Guessons, opposite the church. His stepdaughter and her husband died in 1736 and 1740 respectively, and his wife died in 1741; thus, the reference to deaths "ere thrice yon moon had filled her horn" in *The Complaint, or Night-Thoughts on Life, Death, and Immortality* (June 1742). As popular as the poem made Young, it did nothing for his clerical career, and he stayed in relative retirement here. Young died in Welwyn on April 5, 1765, and was buried under the altar in the chancel of the church near his wife. A later rector of the community erected the memorial urn at the entrance to the avenue of lime trees in the garden; Young had planted the trees.

Young attempted to promote Welwyn as a spa and built the Assembly Rooms (now cottages on Mill Street) to that end. One of his frequent guests was Samuel Richardson, who published part of *Night Thoughts* and all the poet's succeeding pieces. Richardson was a poor traveler, so his visits here were somewhat of an event. On two of these trips, those in 1752 and 1754, he was ill here. Dr. Samuel Johnson, who had admired *Night Thoughts*, stopped in Welwyn with James Boswell in 1781; they both wanted to visit Young's home, which was then inhabited by the poet's son. Boswell had to resort to subterfuge to set up the visit, as his *Life of Samuel Johnson* relates:

I therefore concerted with Mr. Dilly, that I should steal away from Dr. Johnson and him, and try what reception I could procure from Mr. Young; if unfavourable, nothing was to be said; but if agreeable, I should return and notify it to them. . . . [Mr. Young] behaved very courteously, and answered, "By all means, Sir; we are just going to drink tea; will you sit down?" I thanked him, but said, that Dr. Johnson had come with me from London, and I must return to the inn to drink tea with him. . . ." "Sir, (said he,) I should think it a great honour to see Dr. Johnson here. Will you allow me to send for him?"

Boswell went back for Dr. Johnson himself so that the ruse would not be detected; they returned.

We went into the garden, where we found a gravel walk, on each side of which was a row of trees, planted by Dr. Young, which formed a handsome Gothick arch; Dr. Johnson called it a fine grove. I beheld it with reverence.

WEM, Shropshire (pop. 2,172)   Wem, a small market town 10½ miles north of Shrewsbury, goes back at least to the days of a substantial Norman castle (of which nothing remains) and a 14th-century church (of which the tower remains, incorporated in the present church). It was a bustling and prosperous market town, well stocked with half-timbered buildings and famous for its strong ale, until 1677, when a fire almost leveled it. On Noble Street is the childhood home of the essayist William Hazlitt, who came here with his family in 1787. (In 1783 the Rev. William Hazlitt had taken his family to the United States after an unhappy stay in Ireland.) Young William did not attend the local school but received most of his education at home from his father. Although he spent periods in London, studying portraiture with his older brother, who had been one of Sir Joshua Reynolds's pupils, and in Paris, in the winter of 1802–1803, Wem was his home until his marriage to Sarah Stoddart in 1808. Wem and his childhood are both recalled in the essay "Why Distant Objects Please":

All that I have observed since, of flowers and plants, and grass-plots, and of suburb delights, seems, to me, borrowed from "that first garden of my innocence"—to be slips and scions stolen from that bed of memory. . . . If I have pleasure in a flower-garden, I have in a kitchen-garden too, and for the same reason. If I see a row of cabbage-plants or of peas or beans coming up, I immediately think of those which I used so carefully to water of an evening at W-m, when my day's tasks were done. . . .

Hazlitt's first meeting with Samuel Taylor Coleridge occurred in January 1798, when Coleridge came to Shrewsbury as a candidate for a vacant Unitarian ministry post. Hazlitt walked the 12 miles to Shrewsbury even though an invitation had already been extended to Coleridge to visit the Hazlitts. Coleridge's sermon and the visit here are recalled in "My First Acquaintance with Poets":

Coleridge had agreed to come over to see my father, according to the courtesy of the country, as Mr. Rowe's probable successor; but in the meantime I had gone to hear him preach the Sunday after his arrival. A poet and a philosopher getting up into a Unitarian pulpit to preach the Gospel, was a romance in these degenerate days. . . .
Never, the longest day I have to live, shall I have such another walk as this cold, raw, comfortless one, in the

winter of the year 1798. . . . When I got there, the organ was playing the 100th psalm, and, when it was done, Mr Coleridge rose and gave out his text, "And he went up into the mountain to pray, HIMSELF, ALONE." As he gave out his text, his voice "rose like a steam of rich distilled perfumes," and when he came to the two last words, which he pronounced loud, deep, and distinct, it seemed to me, who was then young, as if the sounds had echoed from the bottom of the human heart, and as if that prayer might have floated in solemn silence through the universe.

Coleridge invited the young Hazlitt to visit him in Nether Stowey, a trip he undertook later that year.

WENDOVER, Buckinghamshire (pop. 2,366)   Nestled in one of the few gaps in the Chiltern Hills, 5 miles south of Aylesbury, Wendover is on the Icknield Way, an ancient track extending from East Anglia to southwest England over the Berkshire Downs and the Chilterns where for a few miles it divides into the Upper and Lower Icknield Way; the High Street here is, in fact, the old Lower Way. A number of the buildings are timber-fronted, and because of its position on the coaching route Wendover has a large stock of good old inns. On the High Street is the old Red Lion Inn, where Robert Louis Stevenson once stayed; Stevenson notes his impressions of the Wendover area in "An Autumn Effect":

The vale, as it opened out into the plain, was shallow, and a little bare, perhaps, but full of graceful convolutions. From the level to which I had now attained the fields were exposed before me like a map, and I could see all that bustle of autumn field-work which had been hid from me yesterday behind the hedgerows, or shown to me only for a moment as I followed the foot-path. Wendover lay well down in the midst, with mountains of foliage about it.

Stevenson calls Wendover "a straggling, purposeless sort of place" with the "look of an abortive watering-place," but he had real pleasure in the Red Lion:

The interior of the inn was answerable to the outside: indeed, I never saw any room much more to be admired than the low wainscoted parlour in which I spent the remainder of the evening. It was a short oblong in shape, save that the fireplace was built across one of the angles so as to cut it partially off, and the opposite angle was similarly truncated by a corner cupboard. The wainscot was white, and there was a Turkey carpet on the floor. . . . The furniture was old-fashioned and stiff. Everything was in keeping, down to the ponderous leaden inkstand on the round table. And you may fancy how pleasant it looked, all flushed and flickered over by the light of a brisk companionable fire. . . .

Daniel Defoe's accusation that the village was "a mean dirty corporate town" has no relevance today, as Wendover is now attractive. Richard Steele stood successfully for Parliament here in 1722.

WEST BRADENHAM, Norfolk (pop. 259)   West Bradenham and East Bradenham, half a mile to the northeast, are often confused, but they are distinct entities; West Bradenham, 5½ miles southwest of East Dereham, is a scattered village with the tiny Wissey River running through it. The village contains the 18th-century Bradenham Hall, once the home of Lord Nelson's sister. In the early 19th century the hall was sold to Henry Haggard and passed to his son William Meybohm Rider Haggard, and here (Sir) Henry Rider Haggard was born on June 22, 1856. The novelist spent almost all his childhood here and was privately tutored when he was not at the grammar school in Ipswich. Haggard left West Bradenham in 1875, when he went to South Africa, and soon after his marriage to Mariana Louisa Margitson he settled at Ditchingham House near Bungay.

WEST FIRLE, Sussex (pop. 480)   Situated 4½ miles southeast of Lewes with Firle Beacon rising 718 feet in the background, Firle (pronounced "furrell"), as the hamlet is popularly known, has a reputation all over England as the home of the greengage, which was introduced to the garden at the Tudor Firle Place by the botanist Sir William Gage. Sir John Gage, an uncompromising Catholic, was a friend of Henry VIII, who made him Constable of the Tower of London, and as such he was the jailer of Lady Jane Grey, over whose execution he presided, and of Princess Elizabeth. It is this Gage and his story that William Harrison Ainsworth uses in *The Constable of the Tower*. Later, Virginia Woolf, looking for a country house because London was thought to be particularly bad for her health, found a new villa here, into which she moved in early 1911. She renamed the red house Little Talland House and remained only a short time. One of her favorite pastimes was walking on the Downs.

WEST GRINSTEAD, Sussex (pop. 1,515)   The two Grinsteads, East and West, are 17 miles apart and totally unalike; East Grinstead is a thriving town, while West Grinstead, 6¾ miles south of Horsham, is hardly a village in size. But it is a lovely village with a remote, partly Norman church reached at the end of a back road near the old bridge across the Adur River. The broach spire is silver-shingled and appears to rise straight up from the Horsham slab roof, and some of the windows contain fragments of 14th-century glass. Nothing is left of the manor house of West Grinstead Park except the battlemented stables and the park itself.

The manor was once the home of John Caryll, friend of Alexander Pope and John Gay, and it was upon Caryll's instigation that Pope wrote *The Rape of the Lock*, in which Caryll is mentioned. Tradition maintains that the poet wrote the poem under an old oak in the park in 1712, and indeed Pope's Oak is still pointed out. Gay also visited Caryll on various occasions and explored the park thoroughly. In more recent times Sir Arthur Conan Doyle was frequently seen stalking through the village on his visits to his sister Connie and his brother-in-law, Ernest William Hornung, a minor novelist who died in 1921. There are also specific associations with Hilaire Belloc, who lived in nearby Shipley. He sometimes attended midnight mass here at Christmas, and when his wife Elodie died on February 2, 1914, she was buried here, as was their son Peter when he died in 1941. Belloc died in a nursing home in Guildford in July 1953 and was buried here on July 20; the monks from Downside Abbey chanted the requiem, and the Bishop of Southwark celebrated the mass. Finally, the church here was the scene of the marriage in October 1791 of Timothy Shelley and Elizabeth Pilfold, the parents of the poet Percy Bysshe Shelley.

WEST HORSLEY, Surrey (pop. 927)   The hamlet of West Horsley, 5½ miles southwest of Leatherhead, had a settlement before the Norman Conquest; its early greatness came when the manor and lands were held by the Berners family in the 13th century. Sir James Berners was executed after the barons rose against Richard II in 1388. His daughter is of special literary interest, for she was the Dame Juliana Berners who is believed to have been the prioress of Sopwell, Hertfordshire, and who allegedly wrote *The Boke of St. Albans*, a series of treatises on hawking, hunting, and heraldry. She grew up here, and if the compilation is her work, even in part, this area must be the one where she learned of outdoor life.

West Horsley Place eventually came into the hands of Sir Anthony Browne, who built the oldest (rear) portion of the house existing today. Sir Anthony eventually married Lady Elizabeth Fitzgerald, the Fair Geraldine of the poetry of Henry Howard, Earl of Surrey, but there is no evidence that Surrey was ever here. Indeed, he made her the idealized woman when she was nine and he was nineteen, married, and the father of a child. Later the estate passed to the Carews of Beddington and then to Sir Nicholas Throckmorton, who took the name Carew upon his inheritance; it was through Sir Nicholas that Carew Ralegh, son of Sir Walter, succeeded to the estate in 1643. Young Ralegh had also been granted lands in East Horsley by the Earl of Southampton. All this is by way of saying that the claim that the poet Thomas Carew, who was related to Ralegh, was a frequent guest of Sir Walter's son at West Horsley Place is not possible. The best estimate of Carew's death is about 1639, four years before Ralegh inherited the estate; either Carew visited Sir Nicholas, to whom he was also related, or he was the guest of Ralegh in East Horsley. One of Carew Ralegh's known guests here, though, was the diarist John Evelyn, who noted dining here on August 10, 1658; Evelyn also frequently visited other friends in West Horsley, including Arthur Onslow, whose house was "a pretty dry seate on the Downes."

West Horsley Church, just across from the house of West Horsley Place, has some traces of Saxon work and an extremely fine east window of 13th-century glass. According to Richard Gough, who enlarged William Camden's *Britannia*, Carew Ralegh is buried here:

> Tradition says, his mother, and afterwards he kept his father's head to be buried with him, and a skull was found in a small niche of the chalk rock by his coffin.

The tradition is that Ralegh's head was interred in the Nicolas Chapel and that a headless trunk was discovered there in 1703.

WEST LULWORTH, Dorset (pop. 797)   West Lulworth is a popular and attractive tourist spot in south Dorset, and Lulworth Cove, its main attraction, is where the chalk cliffs suddenly stop and two walls of Portland and Purbeck stone reach out like arms to protect the chalk from erosion and to encircle the bay. The Durdle Door is an arch in the Purbeck limestone which juts out to sea and through which waves crash. Lulworth Cove masquerades as Lulstead or Lulwind Cove in Thomas Hardy's Wessex and is mentioned in

Tess of the D'Urbervilles, Desperate Remedies, "A Tradition of 1804" (*Life's Little Ironies and a Few Crusted Characters*), "The Distracted Preacher" (*Wessex Tales*), and *Far from the Madding Crowd,* in which it becomes the scene of Troy's supposed drowning:

At last he reached the summit, and a wide and novel prospect burst upon him with an effect almost like that of the Pacific upon Balboa's gaze. . . . Nothing moved in sky, land, or sea, except a frill of milk-white foam along the nearer angles of the shore, shreds of which licked the contiguous stones like tongues.

He descended and came to a small basin of sea enclosed by the cliffs. . . . He undressed and plunged in. Inside the cove the water was uninteresting to a swimmer, being smooth as a pond, and to get a little of the ocean swell Troy presently swam between the two projecting spurs of rock which formed the pillars of Hercules to this miniature Mediterranean. Unfortunately for Troy a current unknown to him existed outside, which, unimportant to craft of any burden, was awkward for a swimmer who might be taken in it unawares. Troy found himself carried to the left and then round in a swoop out to sea.

In 1907, when Rupert Brooke selected this town for his summer vacation and took rooms above the post office upon his arrival from Grantchester, he lost the keys to his trunks and had to break them open with a pickax; subsequently, he ate something which made him extremely ill, "throwing up, indeed, all I had eaten for weeks, and also my immortal soul and several political convictions." These experiences did not keep him from returning. In late December 1910 he joined Ka Cox, Gwen Darwin (later Raverat, author of *A Period Piece*), and Jacques Raverat at Cove Cottage, and on New Year's Day wrote "Sonnet Reversed" while Raverat drew his portrait. In December of that year he had rooms at Churchill House with Lytton Strachey for their annual reading party, and the group was joined by the artist Augustus John.

WEST TANFIELD, Yorkshire (pop. 537) Situated on the Ure River 6½ miles northwest of Ripon, the small red-roofed village of West Tanfield, clustered above the riverbank, is dominated by a Perpendicular church which contains numerous tombs of the Marmion family. John Leland was impressed with the church and comments: "There be divers tombs in the chapell . . . of the Marmions . . . there lieth alone a lady in the apparel of vowes, and another lady with a coronet on her head." This was the hereditary home of the Marmion family, made famous by Sir Walter Scott in his tale of Flodden Field, *Marmion.* The 15th-century Marmion Tower, gatehouse to the original castle, is all that remains of the family home. Lord Marmion, Scott's hero, is purely imaginary.

WESTON-SUPER-MARE, Somerset (pop. 43,150) Well known since the late 18th century as a watering place on the Bristol Channel at the mouth of the Severn, Weston (as it is popularly called) is 19 miles southwest of Bristol. The populous seaside resort is a paradise for aficionados of Victorian architecture, just as Bath is for Georgian buffs. However, Weston never rivaled Bath until relatively recent times, and even in 1822, when the town's first guidebook appeared, Weston's attraction was noted as "health and not dissipation," and its public amusements (unlike now) were few. An early visitor was Alfred, Lord Tennyson, who came here with his new bride just after their marriage in June 1850; they did not stay long and went on to see Arthur Henry Hallam's grave in Clevedon.

More recently Mary Webb made her home at 6 Landemann Crescent after her marriage in 1912.

WESTON UNDERWOOD, Buckinghamshire (pop. 222) Weston Underwood, 1½ miles southwest of Olney, is located in the northern part of the shire, where the land is permeated with numerous small rivers, marshes, and streams and the terrain is either flat or gently rolling. William Cowper was a frequent visitor to Weston Hall (demolished in 1827); the Throckmorton residence was open to Cowper and Mrs. Morley Unwin after his initial visit in the summer of 1781, when Lady Austen first came to the hall. After Lady Austen's departure in the spring of 1784, Cowper frequently dined at the hall and eventually became an intimate of the family. His walk here from Olney is described in *The Task:*

WESTON-SUPER-MARE When the popular Bristol Channel resort town of Weston-super-Mare was attractive more for its "healthy atmosphere" than for its amusements, Alfred, Lord Tennyson and his new bride spent part of their honeymoon here.

> . . . far beyond, and overthwart the stream,
> That, as with molten glass, inlays the vale,
> The sloping land recedes into the clouds;
> Displaying on its varied side the grace
> Of hedge-row beauties numberless, square tower,
> Tall spire, from which the sound of cheerful bells
> Just undulates upon the listening ear;
> Groves, heaths, and smoking villages remote.
> Scenes must be beautiful which daily view'd,
> Please daily, and whose novelty survives
> Long knowledge and the scrutiny of years. . . .

In the autumn of 1786 Cowper and Mrs. Unwin moved here from Olney into Western Lodge, a plain stone house which stood opposite Weston Hall. Cowper was not happy, complaining mostly of a lack of privacy; and when Mrs. Unwin's son William died of typhus in Winchester in November, the strain began to show. Cowper twice tried to commit suicide. Unfortunately for the poet, Mrs. Unwin was seriously burned in a fire in her bedroom the next year, and Cowper nursed her throughout her recovery although the task was abhorrent to him. Within four years she suffered two paralytic strokes, and a third one, in April 1793, showed that Cowper could not deal with the crises. He and Mrs. Unwin were removed to North Tuddenham, Norfolk, in 1795. Before he left here, Cowper wrote on the bedroom shutter:

> Farewell, dear scenes, for ever closed to me;
>   Oh, for what sorrows must I now exchange ye!

The village inn, Cowper's Oak, is named after "The Yardley Oak."

WESTON ZOYLAND, Somerset (pop. 611)   The Levels, or Plain of Sedgemoor, in which Weston Zoyland is located, were once largely covered with water. The fame of Weston Zoyland rests on the Battle of Sedgemoor, which ended the Duke of Monmouth's rebellion against James II on the night of July 5, 1685. The topography of the field has changed since the battle, which has been called one of the most "fierce and bloody hand-to-hand struggles" on English soil; King's Sedgemoor Drain did not then exist, and the tactically vital Bussex Rhine (a drainage ditch) has been covered over. More than 1,500 men were killed, and the lovely little Weston Zoyland Church was used as a prison and was the place from which orders for execution went forth.

More than a century earlier, Weston Zoyland was the birthplace of Sir Edward Dyer, author of "My mind to me a kingdom is." In February 1540, his father, a gentleman steward in the service of Henry VIII, was granted the manor here, described as *unum mansum amplum et largum ac sumptuosum*. At the death of his father in June 1565, Edward Dyer inherited what has been put, no doubt with ample exaggeration, at £4,000 per year and "fourscore thousand pounds in money."

WESTWARD HO!, Devon   The most spectacular part of Devon's north coast, where high wooded cliffs often drop straight down to the sea, occurs between Welcombe and Trentishoe and includes Westward Ho! The association with Charles Kingsley seems obvious, but in fact something like a historical reversal has occurred, because Westward Ho! was an obscure village of another name until the publication of Kingsley's novel and the council's adoption of this name. Indeed, Kingsley deplored the council's action but was unable to do anything about it. At one time there was in the village a United Services College, a school established for the children of men in the services, civil, foreign, and military. Rudyard Kipling was sent to school here after the unhappy experience he had in Southsea, Hampshire. The headmaster, Cormell Price, who had founded the famous public school at Haileybury, took a row of a dozen "bleak houses by the shore" (now Kipling Terrace) for the school here and ran a sympathetic and understanding establishment. Kipling acquired his nicknames of Gig-lamps and Gigger at this time because of the heavy glasses he had to wear, and almost every character who appeared later in *Stalky and Co.* came from this school and this period of Kipling's life: Stalky was based on Lionel Dunsterville, M'Turk on George Beresford, Bettle on Kipling himself, Prout on M. H. Pugh, a pedantic housemaster who is described as "[a] suspicious, humourless well-meaning man," Hartopp on H. A. Evans, a rather sympathetic master, and Gillett on the Rev. O. Wiles, the second chaplain. Kipling was here from 1878 to 1882 and is commemorated by the nearby Kipling Tors, where he enjoyed walking.

WESTWELL, Kent (pop. 849)   Frequently characterized as a remote yet attractive village, Westwell is only 3 miles north of Ashford, but over a tortuous road which provides the source of its isolation. The church, 14th-century and later, is an external hodgepodge of brick buttresses, and its spire is awkwardly placed on a narrow tower. Richard Harris Barham was curate of this church from 1814 to 1817, and there is a memorial in the chancel to his infant son, who died here.

There is a second literary association with Westwell: William Shakespeare's *Henry VI: Part II* places Cade's death here in the garden of Alexander Iden's Ripley Court. However, it should be noted that some historians have placed Cade's death in Sussex.

WETHERINGSETT, Suffolk   The central plateau area of Suffolk often offers a bleak landscape; once rich forest land, it is now open farmland with very little shelter from trees or hedgerows. The hamlet of Wetheringsett, actually part of West cum Brockford (total population, 812), is 5 miles south of Eye and 3 miles northwest of Debenham, on a tributary of the Dove River. This is a hamlet with thatched houses, a 14th-century church with a carved nave roof, and an old rectory. Here Richard Hakluyt lived from April 1590 until his death in 1616; appointed to the living here, he had a choice of far more prestigious positions in reward for the publication of *The Principall Navigations, Voiages and Discoveries of the English Nation* (1589) but chose to come here. He revised and enlarged the *Navigations* in the first ten years here and married around 1594 and again in 1604 after he had been a widower for seven years. He died here on November 23, 1616, and was buried in Westminster Abbey, London.

WEYBRIDGE, Surrey (pop. 6,684)   At the influx of the Wey River into the Thames, 2½ miles southeast of Chertsey and within 20 miles of Waterloo Station in

London, Weybridge is now a modern suburb as well as part of the Greater London urban area. This was a natural and important settlement from early times on, but its low-lying position precluded Iron Age settlers, who generally preferred more upland situations (Monument Hill here was probably too isolated to counteract the basic flatness).

Weybridge became the home of the novelist George Meredith and his new wife, Mary Ellen Peacock Nicholls, the daughter of Thomas Love Peacock, a short time after their August 1849 marriage. Here the couple and Mrs. Meredith's daughter Edith Nicholls boarded at the Limes, a house run by a Mrs. Macirone, whose daughter became Meredith's model for Emilia. The novelist began work on *The Ordeal of Richard Feverel* and *Poems* in this period, but the struggle with poverty made it difficult for him to write. Nevertheless, he began working on *The Shaving of Shagpat,* which he tested on his stepdaughter; in 1853 Peacock invited his daughter and son-in-law to share his house in Lower Halliford, where Meredith's only child was born. One of the novelist's frequent guests here was Edward Bulwer-Lytton (Lord Lytton).

Oatlands Park here was the birthplace of the poet and novelist Maurice Hewlett on January 22, 1861. His family moved to Farningham, Kent, in 1872, when he was sent on to the grammar school in Sevenoaks.

There is a more recent association with H. G. Wells, who gives the town a major role in *The War of the Worlds;* headquarters were established here, but

> No one in Weybridge could tell us where the headquarters were established; the whole place was in such confusion as I had never seen in any town before. Carts, carriages everywhere, the most astonishing miscellany of conveyances and horseflesh. . . . In the midst of it all the worthy vicar was very pluckily holding an early celebration, and his bell was jangling out above the excitement.

The curate, driven mad by fright, thinks the coming of the Martians is a visitation of God upon the town:

> I began to explain my view of our position. He listened at first, but as I went on the dawning interest in his eyes gave place to their former stare, and his regard wandered from me.
> "This must be the beginning of the end," he said, interrupting me. "The end! The great and terrible day of the Lord! When men shall call upon the mountains and the rocks to fall upon them and hide them—hide them from the face of Him that sitteth upon the throne!"
> I began to understand the position. I ceased my laboured reasoning, struggled to my feet, and, standing over him, laid a hand on his shoulder.
> "Be a man!" said I. "You are scared out of your wits! What good is religion if it collapses under calamity? Think of what earthquakes and floods, wars and volcanoes, have done to men! Did you think God had exempted Weybridge? He is not an insurance agent."

WEYHILL, Hampshire   Weyhill does not exist as a separate entity: the village is contained in the parish of Penton Grafton (total population, 341), about 3 miles west of Andover. Since at least the 16th century Weyhill has been the location of a fair whose origins are lost in a babble of scholars' voices. Elizabeth I granted a charter for the express purpose of holding a Weyhill fair three times a year, but the fair itself must date from at least two centuries earlier. At present, the fair occurs once a year, with its principal day October 10, and deals notably in sheep. The earliest reference to the fair points out that it was already widely known by the late 14th century: William Langland's *Piers Plowman* has Avarice speak of the two most widely known medieval fairs, that at Winchester and the one here. "I learnt to lie in a small way to begin with," he says, "and my first lesson was in giving false weights. Then my master would send me to the fairs at Weyhill and at Winchester with all kinds of wares. . . . "

No doubt because everything seemed to be sold at the Weyhill Fair, Thomas Hardy turns Weyhill into Weydon Priors in Upper Wessex in *The Mayor of Casterbridge.* The novel opens in Weydon Priors

> itself at the top of an open down, bounded on one extreme by a plantation, and approached by a winding road. At the bottom stood the village which lent its name to the upland and the annual fair that was held thereon. The spot stretched downward into valleys, and onward to other uplands, dotted with barrows, and trenched with the remains of prehistoric forts.

Then, just as now, at least in spirit, the visitor will find "peep-shows, toy-stands, waxworks, inspired monsters, disinterested medical men who travelled for the public good, thimble-riggers, nick-nack vendors, and readers of Fate." Here is the site of Michael Henchard's selling his wife, the place to which he returns in search of his wife the next year, and the place to which Elizabeth-Jane and her mother return sixteen years later in search of Henchard. Hardy locates 3 or 4 miles away the church to which Henchard goes the morning after selling his wife and swears off drink for twenty-one years, but the church is not identifiable. Weydon Priors is also used in "The Lady Icenway" (*A Group of Noble Dames*).

WEYMOUTH, Dorset (pop. 32,810)   The modern borough of Weymouth and Melcombe Regis is an amalgamation of two older towns, Weymouth on the south side of the river and Melcombe Regis on the north, which were united in the 16th century. The Wey River, which separates the two districts, is crossed by an old stone bridge, and the town lies at the influx of the river into Weymouth Bay. Weymouth functioned as a port throughout its history, but not always happily. It was a supplier of men and ships for the siege of Calais in 1346 and a prime target for invading forces; further, Melcombe Regis has the dubious distinction of being the port which brought the plague to England.

From the 18th century on, thanks partly to a visit by George III, Weymouth became a fashionable resort; the lovely Georgian houses on the Esplanade date from this period, and Gloucester House (now a hotel) was where the King and his entourage stayed on their six or seven visits. Fanny Burney notes being here in the summer of 1789 with Queen Charlotte; she says, "Nothing but the sea at Weymouth affords any life or spirit" and comments on the King's "great success" at bathing:

> [A] machine follows the Royal one into the sea, filled with fiddlers, who play *God Save the King,* as his Majesty takes his plunge!

On the Esplanade the townspeople have erected an absolutely monstrous statue of George, and this is approximately the place where Dick Dewey meets

Fancy Day when he takes some swarms of bees into town for Mr. Maybold's mother in Thomas Hardy's *Under the Greenwood Tree*. Weymouth, as Budmouth or Budmouth Regis in Hardy's works, is extremely important in his Wessex topography, and the details are quite specific. Hardy knew the town very well: at the invitation of G. R. Crickmay, he came to 3 Wooperton Street in 1869 and explored the entire town.

Desperate Remedies, which was written here, includes a large number of local references: the Belvedere Hotel, where Miss Aldclyffe interviews Cytherea Graye; 3 Cross Street, where the Grayes lodge; the High Street; Mary Street; the post office; the harbor, Harbor Bridge, and the quay; King George's Esplanade and the Parade; and, of course, Weymouth Bay itself.

Another of Hardy's novels dealing with Budmouth in detail is *The Trumpet-Major*. The Old Rooms Inn on Cove Row, which Hardy mentions, was popular with the ladies and gentlemen who formed George III's court and was used for dances, dramatic entertainments, and the like. The Theatre Royal is where John Lovejoy takes his brother Bob and Anne Garland for a look at his nonexistent sweetheart and where the King interrupts the performance to announce "the capture of two Spanish line-of-battle ships, and the retreat of Villeneuve into Ferrol." The Nothe, or Look-Out Hill, is a small promontory now laid out as gardens and a parade. Other locations are equally easy to place: the quay; Gloucester Lodge; the Esplanade, down which Anne and Bob walk after the evening at the theater and where Festus Derriman and Matilda Johnson plot the means of Bob's impressment; and the bay, known to sailors as Deadman's Bay because of its treacherous banks. Stacie's Hotel, where the yeomanry officers eat, is unidentifiable.

Budmouth also appears in *A Laodician*, *The Mayor of Casterbridge*, *Far from the Madding Crowd* (Dr. Barker, who thinks he has witnessed Troy's drowning at Lulstead Cove, that is Lulworth Cove, is from Budmouth), *The Return of the Native*, *Two on a Tower*, *The Woodlanders*, *The Well-Beloved* (Jocelyn Pierston attends the local preparatory school), various of the *Wessex Tales* and *Life's Little Ironies and a Few Crusted Characters*, "Squire Petrick's Lady" in *A Group of Noble Dames*, and numerous poems. The location of Creston Shore in *Desperate Remedies* is most likely the portion of Weymouth Bay nearest to Preston. Even *The Dynasts*, in which most of the action takes place outside England, includes Weymouth: The Old Rooms Inn is where the Battle of Trafalgar is discussed.

A number of other authors are associated with Weymouth. Thomas Love Peacock was born here on October 18, 1785, and lived here until shortly after his father's death in 1788. Robert Southey spent his school holidays from William Williams's school in Bristol here at the home of his aunt and passed many hours sitting on the beach. William Makepeace Thackeray had a home here to which he came after leaving Cambridge, but its location is not known. George Eliot spent a holiday here in late August or early September 1859, probably at Gloucester House, and Jane Austen visited here, although the evidence consists of the fact that she used Weymouth as part of

the setting for *Emma*. The town becomes one of the "idlest haunts in the kingdom," the watering place to which Mr. Knightley refers when talking of Frank Churchill, and the scene of the October engagement between Jane Fairfax and Churchill. Finally, Francis Bacon was the Member of Parliament for Melcombe Regis in 1584.

WHALLEY, Lancashire (pop. 1,378) Deep in a vale of the Calder River 7½ miles northeast of Blackburn, the old village of Whalley draws many visitors because of its charm and its ruined Cistercian abbey. The church contains a magnificent display of woodwork, and the churchyard has three Saxon crosses, two stone coffins, and two gravestones with impossible dates, April 31, 1752, and February 30, 1819. The ruined abbey which stands nearby appears in William Harrison Ainsworth's *The Lancashire Witches*; Ainsworth visited the site from nearby Newchurch-in-Pendle in 1848, when he was staying at the vicarage with the incumbent.

WHARNCLIFFE SIDE, Yorkshire On the Don River high up in the Yorkshire moors, 6 miles northwest of Sheffield, Wharncliffe is an isolated area noted for its rocky crags, heather moorlands, and a dragon. The north of England seems to have been the home ground for horror stories of fiery dragons, maiden-killing worms, and "things that go bump in the night." The Worm of Sockburn and the Lambton Worm are only two of the many creatures which keep the famous Dragon of Wantley company (Wantley is a corruption of Wharncliffe). Below the Wharncliffe Crags is a spot pointed out as the den of the dragon, to which

> Houses and churches
> Were as geese and turkeys!
> He ate All, and left none behind—
> Save some stones, dear Jack, which he could not crack,
> Which on the hill you will find.

John Taylor was entertained here in 1639 by Sir Francis Wortley, whose home was Wharncliffe Lodge. Taylor, who left a rather glowing account of Wortley's generous hospitality and the bounty of his table, says nothing about the dragon. This was not the case in the next century, when Horace Walpole visited Edward Wortley Montagu; in fact, much had changed. Walpole wrote, "'Old Wortley Montagu' lives on the very spot where the Dragon of Wantley did, only I believe the latter was much better lodged." He comments, rather more graciously, about the scenery:

> The savageness of the scene would please your Alpine taste: it is tumbled with fragments of mountains that look ready laid for the building of a world. . . . I am persuaded it furnished Pope with this line, so exactly it answers to the picture—

> "On rifted rocks, the Dragon's late abode."

It is also thought that Alexander Pope visited Wharncliffe Side and Wharncliffe Lodge in 1716, when he traveled extensively in Yorkshire.

Sir Walter Scott opens *Ivanhoe* with a reference to the Dragon of Wantley, saying it is one of the ancient holdovers which gives character to "that pleasant district of merry England watered by the river Don."

It also appears that the Wharncliffe Crags area, dominated by gigantic oaks, may well have been the source of the forest scene when Gurth and Wamba are introduced. Finally, this is the scenery described by George Eliot when she writes:

The sun o'er purple moorland wide
Gilds Wharncliffe's wood, while Don is dark below.

WHEATHAMPSTEAD, Hertfordshire (pop. 2,870) Equidistant from St. Albans to the southwest and Hatfield to the southeast, Wheathampstead and this area were well known to Charles Lamb; as a child he lived in nearby Harpenden, at Mackery End, a place of which he later wrote in "Mackery End, in Hertfordshire." In that essay he notes that Mackery End is "delightfully situated within a gentle walk from Wheathampstead," and it is thought that in "Blakesmoor in H———shire" he refers to the Church of St. Helen here:

[G]o alone on some week-day, borrowing the keys of good Master Sexton, traverse the cool aisles of some country church: think of the piety that has kneeled there—the congregations, old and young, that have found consolation there—the meek pastor—the docile parishioner. With no disturbing emotions, no cross conflicting comparisons, drink in the tranquillity of the place, till thou thyself become as fixed and motionless as the marble effigies that kneel and weep around thee.

WHITBURN, County Durham (pop. 5,291) At one time known for its sandy beaches and good swimming, Whitburn is now becoming part of the larger industrial complex of Sunderland. But when Lewis Carroll (Charles Lutwidge Dodgson) visited here, the village was recognized as an especially pleasant place. Always extremely family-oriented, Carroll made frequent visits during the Oxford holidays to see his cousins, the Wilcoxes, some of whom were as interested in versification as the author. On one occasion while sitting around composing verses to while away time, Carroll contributed "Jabberwocky," which was to become an integral part of *Through the Looking-Glass.*

WHITBY, Yorkshire (pop. 11,690) A fishing port and resort town of great charm situated at the mouth of the Esk River and backed by extensive and lofty moorland, Whitby vies with Lindisfarne for the title Cradle of English Christianity. Whitby Abbey, a stark and impressive ruin which stands on the headland over the Esk, has especially dramatic views of the town and beaches. The Benedictine abbey founded in 657 by St. Hilda, as the Venerable Bede relates in his *Historia Ecclesiastica Gentis Anglorum,* was raised as a thanksgiving by Oswy, King of Northumbria, for his victory over Penda of Mercia in 655. The community here was unusual in its organization, not because both nuns and monks were cloistered together (a relatively common practice), but because the abbess was superior to the abbot. St. Hilda was well known for her miraculous powers, and stories of miracles are a part of the Whitby tradition which is enshrined in literature. The most famous miracle is that of ridding the headland of its snakes; through St. Hilda's prayers not only were all the snakes beheaded but they were fossilized. These fossils, properly termed ammonites, are still found. Both John Leland's *Itinerary* and William Camden's *Britannia* comment on these "snake stones," and Camden also relates the miracle of the wild geese, which, he says, he would not have believed "if I had not received it from several reliable men." These geese, flying to the unfrozen southern lakes in the winter, "to the great amazement of everyone, fall down suddenly upon the ground, when they are in their flight over certain neighbouring fields hereabouts. . . ." Michael Drayton comments on both these legends in *Poly-Olbion:*

Over this attractive earth there may no wild goose fly,
But presently they fall from off their wings to earth;
If this no wonder be, where is there wonder found?
Thereat may ye more behold
Snakes that in their natural gyves are up together rolled.

Shortly after the founding of Whitby, Caedmon, an uneducated herdsman whom Bede calls the first-known poet of the English language, entered the

WHITBY The stark and impressive ruins of Whitby Abbey and the Norman St. Mary's Church stand on the headland overlooking the Esk. Here Caedmon, called by the Venerable Bede the first known poet of the English language, composed "Caedmon's Hymn."

monastery of Streaneshalch, as Whitby was then called; all the information about Caedmon comes from Bede's *Historia*. Shortly after his entry, unable because of his illiteracy to take part in the normal procedure of entertaining the order in verse with the traditional harp accompaniment at a banquet, Caedmon fled from the abbey's hall. That night, in a vision, he learned the art of poetry and composed "Caedmon's Hymn." At the top of the 199 steps leading to the nearby St. Mary's Church, there is a commemorative cross unveiled in 1898 by the Poet Laureate Alfred Austin. The carved panels include Caedmon with his harp, St. Hilda treading on snakes, and two lines from the hymn:

> Now we must praise the Guardian of heaven's realm,
> The Creator's might and his mind's thought.

Caedmon died at the abbey in 679 or 680 and presumably was buried in the grounds.

It seems inevitable that the Robin Hood legend settled on Whitby, if only because Robin Hood's Bay, where the outlaw is said to have found refuge, is only 6 miles away. His association with Whitby dates from the days of Abbot Richard and his successor Peter at the end of the 12th century, when Robin, hiding at the abbey, indulged in longbow pulling that boggles the imagination. In the parish precincts are two fields, Robin-his-Field and John's Field, named after the event. Following dinner with the abbot, Robin Hood was asked for an example of the archery skills for which he was famous. He proposed mounting the abbey tower, and from there he and Little John would each shoot once. And so they did. Robin Hood's arrow fell near Whitby Lathes on one side of the land, and Little John's fell on the other side, more than 1½ miles away. The abbot's delight with the accomplishment caused him to erect two pillars to commemorate the feat; the commemorative stones were still there in the mid-19th century.

Sir Walter Scott tells another of the time-honored traditions associated with Whitby Abbey in *Marmion*. He refers to the ceremony known locally as Horn Garth or Penny Hedge, which was carried out in the bay on Ascension Day. This was a yearly penance imposed upon William de Bruce, Ralph de Percy, Allatson, and their families to retain their Whitby estates after their murder of a Whitby hermit who they felt interfered with their hunting wild boar. Instead of their deaths, the hermit on his deathbed requested that annually on Ascension Day they respond to the abbot's officer's horn, receive a bundle of stakes, proceed to the shore by 9:00 A.M., and drive the stakes so securely into the shore line at 1-yard intervals that they would withstand three tides. Failure to perform this service would render their lands confiscate to the abbey. This is the story alluded to in *Marmion* when the

> . . . Whitby nuns exulting told
> How to their house three barons bold
> Must menial service do,
> While horns blow out a note of shame,
> And monks cry, "Fye upon your name!
> In wrath, for loss of sylvan game,
> Saint Hilda's priest ye slew."—
> "This, on Ascension-day, each year
> While labouring on our harbour-pier,
> Must Herbert, Bruce, and Percy hear."—

Charles Dickens visited Whitby at Easter, 1844, from nearby Mulgrave Castle and had lunch at the sign of the White Horse and Griffin on Church Street; he wrote to Wilkie Collins about the lovely Pickering-Whitby railway line ride through Newton Dale (now defunct) and some rather remarkable oystershell grottoes (these have also disappeared). Years later Dickens's enthusiasm persuaded Collins that the area was pleasant and conducive to writing, and he spent most of the month of August 1861 here at the Royal Hotel on West Cliff. Collins had a private sitting room with three bow windows overlooking the harbor, but he was pestered by a brass band, by children in general, and by one family in particular: he wrote, "Among the British matrons established in the hotel is a Rabbit with *fourteen* young ones. She doesn't look at all ashamed of herself—nor her husband either." Lewis Carroll was another visitor to Whitby; he spent the long vacation of 1854 reading mathematics with Professor Bartholomew Price.

Almost the entire novel *Sylvia's Lovers* by Elizabeth Cleghorn Gaskell takes place here; the fishing village and port of Monkshaven is Whitby at the end of the 18th century. The accounts of the return of the whaling fleet and of the press gang are easy to document in general terms. The account of Daniel Robson's capture, trial, imprisonment, and hanging for taking part in an attack upon the press gang is based on the story of the Whitby execution of an innocent man for the murder of William Pickering. The steps to the parish church of St. Mary's are the ones Sylvia climbs, and at the shop near the bridge she buys the red duffel coat in defiance of Philip Hepburn's warning. It is to Whitby that Philip, badly disfigured after the Battle of Acre, returns to be reunited with Sylvia before he dies.

Bram Stoker uses Whitby in *Dracula* as the place where Lucy and her mother live; "the house at the Crescent" where they have rooms has been identified as 4 Crescent Terrace, where rooms were then rented out by a Mrs. Storm. Mina Murray writes:

> This is a lovely place. The little river, the Esk, runs through a deep valley, which broadens out as it comes near the harbour. . . . The valley is beautifully green, and it is so steep that when you are on the high land on either side you look right across it, unless you are near enough to see down. . . . Right over the town is the ruin of Whitby Abbey. . . . It is a most noble ruin, of immense size, and full of beautiful and romantic bits. . . .

WHITSTABLE, Kent (pop. 15,600) A Thames Estuary resort which for centuries was the port for Canterbury, 6 miles to the southeast, Whitstable has been famous since Roman times for its native oysters, but, as at Colchester, the native mollusk is now little more than a memory. On the quay here are the Walls, rows of weatherboarded fishermen's cottages; there is no planned waterside parade, and houses, boatsheds, ropes, and other paraphernalia litter the beach front.

The Old Vicarage on Canterbury Road became the home of W. Somerset Maugham in 1884; born in Paris in 1874, he was orphaned at the age of ten when his father died of cancer (his mother had died of tuberculosis in 1882). The boy was sent here to live with his uncle, the Rev. Henry Macdonald Maugham, vicar of the 13th-century All Saints'

Church. The Reverend and Mrs. Maugham were a middle-aged childless couple who believed in and led a severely quiet life, and the child's life was lonely and unhappy. The Reverend Mr. Maugham, unused to dealing with children, thought his nephew obstinate and uncooperative, but the vicar himself was unimaginative and selfish. *Of Human Bondage* deals with this period of Maugham's life, and Whitstable becomes Blackstable:

> [W]hen they reached it [the vicarage], Philip suddenly remembered the gate. It was red and five-barred: it swung both ways on easy hinges; and it was possible, though forbidden, to swing backwards and forwards on it. . . . It was a fairly large house of yellow brick, with a red roof, built about five and twenty years before in an ecclesiastical style. The front-door was like a church porch, and the drawing-room windows were gothic.

The interior of the Old Vicarage is minutely described: the hall

> was paved with red and yellow tiles, on which alternately were a Greek Cross and the Lamb of God.

And the polished pine staircase is "imposing . . . with a particular smell." Throughout even the descriptive passages concerning the house runs an undercurrent of the vicar's selfishness:

> The dining-room, large and well-proportioned, had windows on two sides of it, with heavy curtains of red rep; there was a big table in the middle; and at one end an imposing mahogany sideboard with a looking-glass in it. . . . On each side of the fireplace were chairs covered in stamped leather, each with an antimacassar; one had arms and was called the husband, and the other had none and was called the wife. Mrs. Carey never sat in the armchair: she said she preferred a chair that was not too comfortable. . . .

The large black stove in the hall "was only lighted if the weather was very bad and the Vicar had a cold . . . [but not] if Mrs. Carey had a cold. Coal was expensive."

The vicar, his wife, and Whitstable are portrayed with brutal frankness in *Of Human Bondage*, but the portrayal of the town, again under the name Blackstable, and of the vicar and his wife is far more sympathetic in *Cakes and Ale*. This is especially true in the case of Maugham's aunt:

> My aunt was a German. She came of a very noble but impoverished family. . . . She was a simple old lady, of a meek and Christian disposition, but she had not, though married for more than thirty years to a modest parson with very little income beyond his stipend, forgotten that she was *hochwohlgeboren*. When a rich banker from London, with a name that in these days is famous in financial circles, took a neighbouring house for the summer holidays, though my uncle called on him . . . she refused to do so because he was in trade. No one thought her a snob. It was accepted as perfectly reasonable.

Other parts of the town are described in this work as well:

> Blackstable consisted of a long winding street that led to the sea, with little two-story houses, many of them residential but with a good many shops; and from this ran a certain number of short streets, recently built, that ended on one side in the country and on the other in the marshes. Round about the harbour was a congeries of narrow winding alleys. Colliers brought coal from Newcastle to Blackstable and the harbour was animated.

One of the added notes in this novel is the description of the late-19th-century local feeling that Whitstable was being ruined by outsiders:

> The stranger nodded and smiled as we parted, but I gave him a stony stare. I supposed he was a summer visitor and in Blackstable we did not mix with the summer visitors. We thought London people vulgar. We said it was horrid to have all that rag-tag and bobtail down from town every year; but of course it was all right for the tradespeople. Even they, however, gave a faint sigh of relief when September came to an end and Blackstable sank back into its usual peace.

WICKHAM, Hampshire (pop. 1,146) This small Georgian town lies just west of the Forest of Bere, on the Meon River and about 5 miles north of Fareham. It was the birthplace, in 1324, of William of Wykeham, founder of Winchester College and New College, Oxford. William Leland, surveying the country for Henry VIII, comments in his *Itinerary* that Wickham is a "praty townlet" but says little else about the village. In 1783 Joseph Warton was given the living at Thorley, Hertfordshire, which he promptly exchanged for the one here. Having had an extremely unsuccessful headship at Winchester College (there were three separate student insurrections, the last of which brought about his resignation), he retired to this rectory in 1793; from 1790 he had held this living jointly with that at Upham. Warton died here on February 23, 1800, and was buried in Winchester Cathedral.

WICKHAMBROOK, Suffolk (pop. 846) A tiny Suffolk heathland village 6 miles north of Clare and 9 miles southwest of Bury St. Edmunds, Wickhambrook was the home of George Crabbe in 1768, when he was apprenticed to a local apothecary-surgeon, a Mr. Smith. He worked as a farm laborer and delivery boy until he changed his apprenticeship in 1771 to a surgeon in Woodbridge. The work here was pure drudgery and very unrewarding; as a consequence, Crabbe turned to writing verse, none of which survives.

WIDCOMBE, Somerset The Palladian mansion here, which belonged to Ralph Allen in the 18th century, has often been cited as an example *par excellence* of the "fashionable, metropolitan architecture of the Whig aristocrats who ruled England from their great country houses." Built in 1743, Prior Park, 1½ miles southeast of Bath, and Allen's generous hospitality became an attraction for many literary figures including Alexander Pope, who advised Allen on the gardens as well as on his paintings and sculpture. Pope was here frequently, and on a trip in the summer of 1742, when his health was declining, some sort of disagreement with Allen occurred after Teresa Blount arrived. Miss Blount, by no means an impartial observer, implies that the Allens treated Pope disgracefully, and some degree of coolness remained until Pope's death in 1744.

Another frequent guest was Henry Fielding, who often received Allen's benefactions; indeed, one tradition maintains that Allen and his sisters loaned Fielding their house in Twerton and that most of *Tom Jones* was written there. More probably, that novel was composed in London. Fielding had the greatest respect for Allen and refers to him in *Joseph Andrews* as

> a commoner, raised higher above the multitude by superior talents than is in the power of his prince to exalt him; whose behavior to those he hath obliged is more amiable than the obligation itself, and who is so great a master of affability, that, if he could divest himself of an inherent greatness in his manner, he would often make the lowest of his acquaintances forget who was the master of that palace in which they are so courteously entertained.

More important, Fielding based the character of Squire Allworthy in *Tom Jones* on Allen. Laurence Sterne visited in 1765, and in 1833 Thomas Moore visited Prior Park.

WIDFORD, Hertfordshire (pop. 436) Widford is on the Ash River, 4 miles northeast of Ware. The church mainly 14th- and 15th-century, is aisleless and has a green copper spire. The east window is a memorial to John Eliot, the 17th-century clergyman who first translated the Psalms and the Bible for his missionary work with American Indians. Nearby is Blakesware, built in 1878 on the site of the house described in the essay "Blakesmoor in H——shire," where Charles Lamb's maternal grandmother, Mary Field, was housekeeper; young Charles spent many of his holidays from Christ's Hospital, London, here. Staying at the Bell in Widford, Lamb revisited the area after the house was demolished in 1822 and recalled his childhood days:

> I was astonished at the indistinction of everything. Where had stood the great gates? What bounded the courtyard? Whereabout did the out-houses commence? a few bricks only lay as representatives of that which was so stately and so spacious. . . .
>
> Had I seen these brick-and-mortar knaves at their process of destruction, at the plucking of every panel I should have felt the varlets at my heart. I should have cried out to them to spare a plank at least out of the cheerful store-room, in whose hot window-seat I used to sit and read Cowley, with the grass-plot before. . . .
>
> Why, every plank and panel of that house for me had magic in it. . . .

The old estate was sold by Walter Plumer, and Lamb perhaps would have been secretly pleased to know that the place to which the Plumers moved was sold by the sheriff twenty-five years later because of Plumer's bankruptcy. Lamb knew everyone here, and the poems he gave to Coleridge in 1795 deal with the people here:

> Kindly hearts have I known,
> Kindly hearts they are flown.

In a poem later suppressed, he describes the wicked Dorrell, commenting that if Dorrell had changed his ways in life, he would not

> Have groaned in his coffin,
> While demons stood scoffing:
> You'd ha' thought him a coughing:
> My own father heard him.

Dorrell, who is buried in the churchyard here, is thought to have cheated Lamb's family out of some £2,000. On a hilltop in the churchyard is the grave of Mary Field, of whom he wrote in "The Grandame":

> She served her heavenly Master. I have seen
> That reverend form bent down with age and pain,

> And rankling malady. Yet not for this
> Ceased she to praise her Maker, or withdraw
> Her trust in Him, her faith, and humble hope. . . .

Another association with Lamb exists here. In Blenheim, a cottage in Widford village, lived Ann Simmons, with whom Lamb fell in love. There are references to her in two of Lamb's sonnets first published in Samuel Taylor Coleridge's first volume of poetry. Not much is known of the affair, and the reasons for Lamb's disappointment are not known.

WIGAN, Lancashire (pop. 82,954) One of the most important industrial towns in the shire, Wigan is more than a collection of slag heaps, cooling towers, and enormous rows of tenement houses, as it is normally pictured. The town is on the Douglas River almost equidistant from Preston and Lancaster. Two of the early industries here were bell founding and the manufacture of pewter ware, but the 19th century brought coal mining and textile manufacturing, and the 20th has seen diversification into iron forging, metal rolling, and extensive chemical works.

The church, which resembles a small cathedral, sits on the highest ground in town where a Saxon church stood, and may be on the site of the Roman fort. Much rebuilding has taken place since the first Saxon church. One of the most fascinating objects is a 14th-century altar tomb in the south side of the chancel; here lie Sir William Bradshaw and his wife Mabel, and the carving on the tomb portrays an incident described in Sir Walter Scott's *Waverly*. The carving shows Mabel Bradshaw, gowned in a long robe kneeling at the foot of a cross; at the other end of the tomb knights are fighting. The legend relates that Sir William's wife remarried when he had been away at the wars for years and that upon his return his wife did penance by walking barefoot to Wigan Cross. Scott relates the incident somewhat differently:

> The deeds of Wilibert of Waverley in the Holy Land, his long absence and perilous adventures, his supposed death, and his return on the evening when the betrothed of his heart had wedded the hero who had protected her from insult and oppression during his absence; the generosity with which the Crusader relinquished his claims, and sought in a neighbouring cloister that peace which passeth not away;—to these and similar tales he would hearken till his heart glowed and his eye glistened.

Wigan also appears in a modern work by George Orwell (Eric Blair). *The Road to Wigan Pier* (1937), commissioned by the Left Book Club, is "a documentary report on the conditions among the unemployed in the north of England." Since the book deals almost entirely with conditions in the coalmining industry in the 1930s, Orwell's choice of Wigan was obvious:

> As you walk through the industrial towns you lose yourself in labyrinths of little brick houses blackened by smoke, festering in planless chaos round miry alleys and little cindered yards where there are stinking dustbins and lines of grimy washing and half-ruinous w.c.'s. The interiors of these houses are always very much the same, though the number of rooms varies between two and five. All have an almost exactly similar living-room, ten or fifteen feet square, with an open kitchen range; in the larger ones there is a scullery as well, in the smaller ones the sink and copper are in the living-room. At the back there is the yard, or part of a yard shared by a number of houses, just big enough for the dustbin and the w.c. Not

a single one has hot water laid on. You might walk, I suppose, through literally hundreds of miles of streets inhabited by miners . . . without ever passing a house in which one could have a bath.

WILLENHALL, Staffordshire (pop. 28,500) A Black Country town with views to the north of an area unspoiled by heavy industrialization, Willenhall lies midway between Wolverhampton and Walsall, each 3 miles distant. The Black Country is a result of the industrial revolution, and reminders are scattered all about, especially when the economy is prospering. Then vast furnaces light up the sky at night; mines are in constant operation; and factories and rolling mills run day and night. Just north of the town is a piece of wasteland, Mumpers Dingle, which George Borrow uses in both *Lavengro* and *The Romany Rye*. Here Lavengro fights the Flaming Tinman:

> The battle during the next ten minutes raged with considerable fury, but it so happened that during this time I was never able to knock the Flaming Tinman down, but on the contrary received six knock-down blows myself. "I can never stand this," said I, as I sat on the knee of Belle, "I am afraid I must give in: the Flaming Tinman hits very hard," and I spat out a mouthful of blood.
> "Sure enough you'll never beat the Flaming Tinman in the way you fight—it's of no use flipping at the Flaming Tinman with your left hand; why don't you use your right?"

In *The Romany Rye* Lavengro and Isopel Berners camp at Mumpers Dingle.

WILLESDEN, Middlesex (pop. 209,230) Within 7 miles of St. Paul's Cathedral in northwest London and once a bustling rural area whose agricultural products were marketed in the city, Willesden is now part of Greater London, but under a 9th-century charter it was once wholly owned by St. Paul's Cathedral. Modern Willesden is overstocked with industries, and parts of the area are distinctly run down; yet the Neasden area has both the late-18th-century building known as the Grange and Oxgate Farm, the oldest relic of Willesden's agricultural past. Authorities differ as to the date of Oxgate Farm; the farmhouse itself has a plaque which claims 1483. The 13th- and 14th-century Church of St. Mary has records to 1181; its famous Black Virgin, to whom numerous miracles were ascribed, was destroyed by Thomas Cromwell's men in 1538. The major literary interest at St. Mary's is the tomb just in front of the church door; here Charles Reade was buried after his death in London on April 11, 1884. His longtime friend and eventual housekeeper, the actress Laura Seymour, was buried here in the autumn of 1879, and Reade wanted this to be his burial place as well.

William Harrison Ainsworth is often claimed as a resident, but that is untrue; the house on Kilburn Road and the nearby Kensal Lodge and Kensal Manor House with which he is associated are all actually in London. However, one Ainsworth association can be admitted; his novel *Jack Sheppard* has some of its more dramatic scenes placed in and around the old church here. Local legend maintains that Sheppard lived in a house near Dollis Mill, the site of the murder of the farmer's wife, and Sheppard is supposed to have waited in the area in seclusion following one of his numerous exploits. While it was once thought that Ainsworth actually drew on local legends, it is now conceded that he himself created them. A modern writer to include Willesden in his work is John Betjeman; Willesden is a rail junction, and at one time the trains into the Cricklewood area were especially noisy and smelly; the Cricklewood area was also one of two known as a laundering center:

> Come walk with me, my love, to Neasden Lane
> The chemicals from various factories
> Have bitten deep into the Portland stone
> And streaked the white Carrara of the graves
> Of many a Pooter and his Caroline,
> Long laid to rest among these dripping trees;
> . . . .
> And this, my love, is Laura Seymour's grave—
> "So long the loyal counsellor and friend"
> Of that Charles Reade whose coffin lies with hers.

WILLINGTON, Bedfordshire (pop. 432) An extremely old village 4 miles east of Bedford, Willington was an ancient ship-repairing site, but the river connection is gone. Danes settled here, and near the railway station is an earthwork which might have been part of a Danish harbor and ship-repairing area. On the other end of the village are a fine Tudor gabled dovecote and stable which belonged to the manor house of John Gostwick. In 1650 John Bunyan was here repairing the metalwork on one of the 100-year-old buildings, the cowhouse (what today is called the barn). It had a large open fireplace (still there) on the upper floor, and on the chimneypiece Bunyan carved:

> IOHN   BVN
>   YAN
>   1650

WILMCOTE, Warwickshire (pop. 438) Just 3 miles northwest of Stratford-on-Avon, Wilmcote is an attractive hamlet whose fame is assured because of its connection with William Shakespeare; this is the village where Mary Arden, his mother, lived. The Arden home, described as a cottage, is a substantial black-and-white timbered farmhouse; its ancient dovecote has nesting places for 650 doves. Inside the house is a huge fireplace with a great oven door, one of the few remaining specimens in England. It has been suggested by many Shakespearean scholars that Wilmcote is Wincot, the place of Christopher Sly's debauch in *The Taming of the Shrew*:

> What, would you make me mad? Am not I Christopher Sly, old Sly's son of Burton-heath; by birth a pedlar, by education a card-maker, by transmutation a bear-herd, and now by present profession a tinker? Ask Marian Hacket, the fat ale-wife of Wincot, if she know me not: if she say I am not fourteen-pence on the score for sheer ale, score me up for the lyingest knave in Christendom.

The same claim has been made for Wincot, about 4 miles south of Stratford, However, Wilmcote's ale appears to have been famous in Shakespeare's day and for long after if the lines written by Sir Aston Cokayne (Cockain) in 1658 are given credence:

> *Shakespeare* your *Wincott* ale hath much renown'd
> That fox'd a Beggar, so (by chance was found
> Sleeping), that there needed not many a word
> To make him believe he was a Lord:
> But you affirm (and in it seem most eager),
> 'Twill make a Lord as drunk as any Beggar,

Bid *Norton* brew such.Ale as *Shakespeare* fancies,
Did put *Kit Sly* into such Lordly trances;
And let us meet there (for a fit of Gladness),
And drink ourselves merry in sober Sadness.

WILTON, Wiltshire (pop. 2,232) At least in part because of its setting on a peninsula between the Wylye (Wiley) and Nadder Rivers before their confluence and against a bank of high downs immediately to the west, Wilton (from which it has been claimed the shire took its name) is 3 miles west of Salisbury. The town was the capital of the early kingdom of Wessex, and the Saxon palace is supposed to have stood on the present Kingsbury Square. A small Benedictine priory, founded here by Egbert after he defeated the Mercians and Northumbrians in 801, was refounded and enlarged as a nunnery by Alfred the Great after his victory over the Danes. It became one of the most important nunneries in the kingdom, its abbess being a peeress of the realm; and it educated, among others, Edith, the town's patron saint, and Matilda, the wife of William the Conqueror.

The pride of modern Wilton, besides a carpet industry initiated by the 8th Earl of Pembroke, is Wilton House, on the site of the old religious establishment. The abbey and its grounds were granted to the 1st Earl of Pembroke at the dissolution of the monasteries; the house was enlarged, enriched, and embellished by each succeeding earl until it became one of the outstanding homes in the nation. Inigo Jones is responsible for the front and many of the rooms, including the famous Double-Cube Room, designed especially for the Van Dycks it still contains. It is with Wilton House that all the literary associations exist.

Sir Philip Sidney came to Wilton first in 1577, after his sister married the 2d Earl of Pembroke (the present buildings are not those Sidney knew). When in disfavor at court, Sidney came here, and tradition holds that *Arcadia* was written under the lime trees in the garden; more realistically, it was probably composed in a small house in Ivy Church, virtually on the estate grounds. About 1591, when the 3d Earl-to-be was eleven years of age, the Countess of Pembroke engaged Samuel Daniel as a tutor for her son. Daniel later dedicated both *Delia* and *The Complaint of Rosamond* to the countess, but neither poem was written here. For some reason a breach between patroness and poet occurred, and Daniel was literally driven out of Wilton House in 1594; not until 1609 was the rift healed. Among the other literary figures of the time whom the countess and the 2d and 3d Earls patronized were Edmund Spenser, Nicholas Breton, and Ben Jonson, who were here on various occasions; Spenser makes the countess Urania in "Colin Clout's Come Home Again." William Browne, known as William of Tavistock, was also favored, and he is the one whose lines commemorating the countess have been placed on her memorial plaque in Salisbury Cathedral:

Underneath this sable hearse
Lies the subject of all verse:
Sidney's sister, Pembroke's mother.
Death, ere thou hast slain another
Fair and learned and good as she,
Time shall throw a dart at thee.

Philip Massinger, whose father was in Pembroke's household, spent a great deal of his boyhood here.

Another dramatist who quite possibly has an association with Wilton House is William Shakespeare, whose *As You Like It* was performed here before James I in 1603; it is usually assumed that the author was present. The claim of Shakespeare's presence also is made for a performance of *Twelfth Night*.

Both Izaak Walton and John Aubrey were visitors to Wilton House. The former states in his *Life of George Herbert* that Herbert journeyed to Wilton and

presented his thanks to the earl for his presentation to Bemerton, but had not yet resolved to accept it, and told him the reason why; but that night the earl acquainted Dr. Laud, then Bishop of London, and after Archbishop of Canterbury, with his kinsman's irresolution. And the bishop did the next day so convince Mr. Herbert that the refusal of it was a sin, that a tailor was sent for to come speedily from Salisbury to Wilton to take measure and make him canonical clothes against next day. . . .

However, the deed of presentation making Herbert rector of Bemerton is dated from Westminster on April 16, 1630. John Evelyn visited Wilton House in July 1654 and recorded his impressions in his diary:

In the afternoone we went to *Wilton*, a fine house of the E. of *Penbrochs*, in which the most observable are the Dining-roome in the modern built part towards the Garden, richly gilded, & painted with story by *De Creete*. . . . The Garden (heretofore esteem'd the noblest in all *England*) is a large handsome plaine, with a *Grotto* & Waterworks, which might be made much more pleasant were the *River* that passes through, clensed & rais'd, for all is effected by a meere force: It has a flower Garden not inelegant: But after all, that which to me renders the Seate delightfull, is its being so neere the downes & noble plaines about the Country & contiguous to it.

Daniel Defoe seemed to be even more greatly impressed with Wilton and its grounds in the next century; he salutes the 8th Earl as a "true Patriarchal Monarch" and catalogs his virtues. Defoe then goes on to describe "this noble Residence" and its works of art in great detail in *A Tour thro' the Whole Island of Great Britain;* he states in part:

When you are enter'd the Appartments, such Variety seizes you every way, that you scarce know which hand to turn your self: First, on one Side you see several Rooms fill'd with Paintings[;] . . . while looking another way, you are call'd off by a vast Collection of Busto's, and Peices of greatest Antiquity of the Kind, both *Greek,* and *Romans;* . . . I never saw anything like what Appears here, except in the Chamber of Rarieties at *Munick* in *Bavaria.*

Passing these, you come into several large Rooms, as if contriv'd for the Reception of the beautiful Guests that take them up; one of these is near 70 Foot long and the Ceiling 26 Foot high, with another adjoyning of the same Height, and Breadth, but not so long: Those together might be call'd the *Great Gallery* of *Wilton,* and might vie for Paintings with the Gallery of *Luxemburg* in the *Fauxbourg* of *Paris.*

Finally, in the late 19th century Thomas Hardy uses Wilton House as the home of the title character in "The Marchioness of Stonehenge" in *A Group of Noble Dames.*

WIMBORNE MINSTER, Dorset (pop. 4,100) Often called "the venerable town in the Stour Valley," Wimborne Minster (or Wimborne, as it is often known) is only 7 miles from the coastal towns of Poole and Bournemouth. There was a Roman town here, and the earliest dated find is a fragment of tesselated pavement in the nave of the minster, which is a rare example of a church built directly on the site of a pagan foundation. The Norman minster itself was founded by Edward the Confessor (r. 1042–1066), and the town and its environs formed part of the royal household of Wessex. Successive monarchs showed great interest in events here throughout the Middle Ages, and by the 13th century the minster was an entity of its own, thanks to Henry III, who gave it the free status of a royal chapel. At the beginning of the 14th century Edward II endowed it as a collegiate church (that is, endowed it for a chapter of canons but removed it from the jurisdiction of the see); it then became extremely powerful and, in time, especially wealthy.

By the 16th century the church had a grammar school, which, tradition says, Matthew Prior attended before going up to Cambridge in 1682. Prior's exact place of birth is often disputed, but it is known that he was born on July 21, 1664, in a Wimborne, although whether it is Wimborne Minster or Wimborne Came is in dispute; the former seems the most likely. A widely circulated story concerns Matthew Prior and a copy of Sir Walter Ralegh's *History of the World* in the chained library of the minster. More than 100 pages of the volume have been burned, supposedly by Prior, and subsequently mended, again by Prior. The damage to the book could not have been effected by a candle, the instrument Prior is alleged to have used, but most likely was done with a hot iron. Further, unless Prior returned from Cambridge to do the deed, it was impossible, for the chained library was not placed in the minster until 1686; there is no evidence of a return trip. Wimborne has named a passage leading from the East Borough to the West as Prior's Walk; a commemorative brass has been placed there.

Thomas Hardy lived in Wimborne from June 1881 until June 1883 in a house called Llaherne on the Avenue. Coming from London, he was looking for material for a new novel and found it in Wimborne. *Two on a Tower*, said to be based on ancient events in the town, was the result. Wimborne is Warborne in this novel and in "Barbara of the House of Grebe" (*A Group of Noble Dames*), and the grammar school where Swithin St. Cleve is educated is the Warborne (Wimborne) Grammar School. Hardy describes the town's churchyard in "The Levelled Churchyard" (*Poems of the Past and Present*), where a game of ducks and drakes is played with the headstones at the Restoration. His bantering tone in the first few verses describes the situation in the churchyard quite vividly:

> "We late-lamented, resting here,
>   Are mixed to human jam,
> And each to each exclaims in fear,
>   'I know not which I am!'

He then goes on to a final plea:

> "From restoration of Thy fane,
>   From smoothings of Thy sward,
> From zealous Churchmen's pick and plane
>   Deliver us, O Lord! Amen!"

WIMPOLE, Cambridgeshire (pop. 244) Located on the Roman Akeman Street, with Wimpole Park bounded on its other side by the Roman Ermine Street, Wimpole is 7 miles southwest of Cambridge. Wimpole Hall, which may be the finest house in the shire, was built by Sir Thomas Chicheley in the 17th century and was later enlarged extensively by the 1st Earl of Oxford and Philip Yorke, 1st Earl of Hardwicke. The mansion was in the hands of Edward, Lord Harley, later 2d Earl of Oxford, in the early 18th century; Harley, who was the patron of Matthew Prior, had an outstanding library which Prior found "a sort of earthly paradise." The poet frequently spent time here beginning in 1719, when he was here for nine months. Returning in March 1720, he wrote:

> My noble, lovely, little Peggy,
> Let this my first epistle beg ye
> At dawn of morn and close of even
> To lift your heart and hands to Heaven.
> In double beauty say your prayer,
> Our Father first, and then notre Père,
> And, dearest child, along the day,
> In everything you do or say
> Obey and please my Lord and Lady,
> So God shall love, and angels aid ye.
>
> If to these precepts you attend,
> No second letter need I send:
> And so I rest your constant friend.

It was largely due to Lord Harley that Down Hall, Essex, was secured for Prior in 1719. A July 1721 trip to Wimpole was Prior's last; he contracted a "lingering fever" in September and died on September 18. He was buried, according to his wishes, "at the feet of Spenser" in Westminster Abbey, London. Alexander Pope was another of Harley's guests.

A more recent resident of Wimpole Hall was Mrs. Elsie Bambridge, the only surviving daughter of Rudyard Kipling and the Una of *Puck of Pook's Hill*. She died in May 1976 and was buried in the Wimpole churchyard.

WINCHELSEA, Sussex (pop. 152) Winchelsea is properly Winchelsea, St. Thomas the Apostle; it is an orderly place, and the town's charm permeates everything about it. Its counterpart, Rye, 3 miles to the northeast and on the opposite hill, bustles with activity and tourists and appears to be ready to spill over its boundaries, but here red-brick and white weatherboarded buildings are easily contained within the town's ample grassy areas. Winchelsea was an early thriving seaport, but natural forces have taken a great toll. In an exposed area on a shingle spit which ran northeast from the cliffs near Fairlight, the town was constantly buffeted by the ocean and strong winds, and the spit gradually eroded through the mid-13th century; then, when two great storms struck in 1252 and 1287, the submerged town had the distinction of appearing on maps as "Old Winchelsey Drowned."

John Leland writes of the drowning and its consequences in his *Itinerary*:

> The olde toune of Winchelesey of a vi. or 7. yeres together felle to a very soore and manifest ruine, be reason of olde rages of the se, and totally in the tyme of the aforesayde vi. or 7 yeres.

Edward I came to the town's rescue, and because of the importance of its defensive position, no time was wasted in the rebuilding on a hill called Higham. Edward, himself Warden of the Cinque Ports, laid out the new town in a regular grid plan (this was England's first town planning), and as a result the usual narrow medieval streets are missing. Public buildings were erected, storage cellars were built, and wharves were constructed on the riverbanks. Winchelsea then suffered the raids of the French and Spanish, and during one of the French attacks the cathedral-like Church of St. Thomas was almost completely destroyed; all that remains are the choir and side chapels. For almost a century after its rebirth, Winchelsea rivaled the fame of the old town with a population reaching 6,000, and then disaster struck again: an alteration of the tide pattern left the town stranded 1 mile inland. This disaster was final. Daniel Defoe's *A Tour thro' the Whole Island of Great Britain* leaves a vivid impression of the town in the early 18th century:

> *Winchelsea,* a Town, if it deserves the Name of a Town, is rather the Skeleton of an Ancient City than a real Town, where the Antient Gates stand near Three Miles from one another over the Fields, and where the Ruins are so bur'd, that they have made good Corn Fields of the Streets, and the Plow goes over the Foundations, nay, over the first Floors of the Houses, and where nothing of a Town but the destruction of it seems to remain. . . .

Today much is different, and Winchelsea has not tried to take on a modern appearance. Architecturally the town with its many old and well-preserved buildings is of great interest; the interior of St. Thomas' Church is of great beauty with especially fine tombs in the north and south aisles, the two in the south aisle, of Gervase Alard and Stephen Alard, being richly canopied. Sir John Millais was so deeply impressed that he used Gervase Alard's tomb as the background for one canvas and the old pew by the door in another.

Millais liked Winchelsea so much that on one trip he brought William Makepeace Thackeray along, and the novelist later incorporated the town in the unfinished *Denis Duval.* In the novel Dr. Barnard, rector of St. Peter's Church, aids the French Protestants here and exerts a great deal of influence on the young Denis; in fact, the tomb Millais painted is incorporated in the novel. Madame de Saverne, having sought refuge in the Duval household, goes mad after the dueling death of her husband, the Comte de Saverne, and abandons her infant child on the shore:

> "You take her home, Mother," says I, all in a tremble. "You give me the lantern, and I'll go—I'll go"—I was off before I said where. Down I went, through Westgate; down I ran along the road towards the place I guessed at. . . .
>
> I got down to the shore, running, running, with all my little might. The moon had risen by this time, shining gloriously over a great silver sea. A tide of silver was pouring in over the sand. Yonder was that rock where we often had sat. The infant was sleeping on it under the stars unconscious. He, who loves little children, had watched over it. . . . I scarce can see the words as I write them down. My little baby was waking. She had known nothing of the awful sea coming nearer with each wave. . . .

Denis passes his boyhood here and becomes the devoted attendant of Agnes de Saverne; learning of his grandfather's smuggling, he also is involved in the trade. The Priory, the house near Winchelsea which is the Westons' home, was modeled on the Friers,

which had been occupied by the notorious Weston brothers, thieves and murderers.

Later, in October 1886, Dante Gabriel Rossetti was here on a walking tour; he was delighted by the old church and the ancient tombs and effigies. He stayed in an inn and attended the court sessions before leaving. John Ruskin also visited Winchelsea, and Joseph Conrad stayed at the Bungalow in June 1901.

WINCHESTER, Hampshire (pop. 31,041) Topographically, there are four distinct Hampshires: chalk downs, forest, water meadows, and what William Cobbett in *Rural Rides* terms "villinous heaths." Winchester, in fact, is mostly water meadows, but nearby there is a fair amount of heathland and forest. John Evelyn, who visited here on numerous occasions, surprisingly has left no real impression of the town and its environment and notes only that the cathedral is a "worthy antiquity." In Saxon England much of the area was predominantly farmland, and outside the town proper it is much the same today. The early growth of Winchester was quite natural; it lay on the access route to Southampton Water, and, in fact, the earliest-known settlement here dates from about 1800 B.C. However, there was no regular communal life until immediately prior to the invasion by the Belgae, in about 50 B.C. After the Roman conquest in the 1st century A.D., Winchester became Venta Belgarum, the commercial center for the area, with a wall (of which there are remains) and five straight roads leading away to other centers. From the time the Romans left until the reign (871–899) of the Wessex king Alfred, little is known of Winchester, although the Venerable Bede records the founding of a bishop's see, and the city obviously continued to grow. In a state of almost total ruin from a sacking by the Danes in 860, Winchester, with the Wessex kingdom, was led by Alfred to a position unequaled by any other city (or kingdom) in England. Here, under Alfred's enlightened rule, the codification of English law began, the precursors of modern schools were begun, and Anglo-Saxon replaced Latin as the official language. Under Alfred, Winchester became not only a city with immense commercial influence but one with perhaps the finest calligraphic and illuminating school in Europe.

The medieval period was the most glorious in the history of the city. Edward the Confessor was crowned here in 1043, and William the Conqueror (r. 1066–1087) had his capital here. The magnificent cathedral and castle were built then, and a prosperity based on the wool trade emerged. One of the earliest-known literary references to Winchester occurs in the early-14th-century *Sir Orfeo.* Thraciens or Thrace is said to be the old name for the town, and this is the location of Orfeo's court:

> Thrace they named his stout demesne,
>   Then the strongest of cities. . . .

Another early reference is found in William Langland's *Piers Plowman.* Avarice speaks:

> I learnt to lie in a small way to begin with, and my first lesson was in giving false weights. Then my master would send me to the fairs at Weyhill and at Winchester with all kinds of wares. . . .

An ancient one-day fair held on St. Giles's Hill (first

granted by William the Conqueror) was later extended to sixteen days, and by the 14th century the fame of the fair was kingdomwide. The medieval period also saw the arrival of pilgrims at the cathedral here, and St. Swithun's Shrine in the north transept became an important stopping point for pilgrims coming up from Southampton on their way to Canterbury. The Pilgrims' School in the southeast corner of the Cathedral Close contains the Pilgrims' Hall, where many of the travelers lodged; and the Pilgrims' Stables was located near the close gate. In modern times Hilaire Belloc, in the company of Harold Baker, sometime warden of Winchester College, and Philip Kershaw, re-created the medieval pilgrimage; in December 1902 they left from the Old North Gate on what was the most probable date of the first pilgrimage and aimed to reach Canterbury and St. Thomas à Becket's shrine at the same hour and on the same day as Becket's murder.

Inevitably, the town fell on bad times, and by Elizabeth's reign Winchester (the 1587 charter states) was in "great ruin, decay, and poverty."

Literature in Winchester begins with the cathedral. The library contains an outstanding collection of medieval and later manuscripts including the Winchester Vulgate, perhaps the best extant example of 12th-century English illumination, and a 10th-century copy of Bede's *Historia Ecclesiastica Gentis Anglorum.* The library also houses the famous Anglo-Saxon Heremod brooch, familiar to readers of *Beowulf.* The west side of the retro-choir contains the grave and effigy of a cross-legged knight, Arnoud de Gaveston, who almost without doubt is the father of Edward II's favorite, Piers Gaveston, made infamous in Christopher Marlowe's *Edward II.* William of Wykeham, founder of Winchester College and New College, Oxford, is buried in the south aisle of the nave. Aelfric, also known as Grammaticus, an early monk at Winchester, most probably began his *Homilies* and *Lives of the Saints* here. In 1618 Lancelot Andrewes became bishop of Winchester, a position he held until his death in 1626, and finished the well-known *Private Devotions* while in the post. There is also a commemorative monument to Dr. Joseph Warton, one-time master of Winchester College, in which he is represented as a schoolmaster with a group of his students before him. The cathedral also figures in the land of legend: King Utherpendragon, father of King Arthur, remembering Merlin's explanation of the bright star and beam of light spreading into a dragon, had two dragons fashioned in gold here and gave one (of which there is no trace) to the "cathedral church and see of Winchester," as Geoffrey of Monmouth relates in his *Historia Regum Britanniae.* And, naturally, Winchester figures heavily in Sir Thomas Malory's *Le Morte d'Arthur* and in Alfred, Lord Tennyson's *Idylls of the King.*

The cathedral also contains the graves of Izaak Walton and Jane Austen, both of whom lived in the city for a time. Walton's grave, in the Chapel of Prior Silkestede (the corner stone of the screen to the chapel is marked "Thomas S") on the east side of the south transept, carries an inscription believed to be by Thomas Ken, a distant relative:

Awake my Soul
Glory to Thee, my God, this Night.

WINCHESTER A window in Winchester Cathedral commemorates Izaak Walton, who spent the last years of his life at his son-in-law's home in the close. Walton, who fished in the Itchen River, is buried in the cathedral in the Chapel of Prior Silkestede.

The Walton memorial window, containing two corner pictures of the angler and biblical fishing scenes, is modern (1914) and was financed by worldwide subscriptions. Jane Austen's grave is in the floor of the north aisle, opposite the fifth arch from the west end of the building; on the wall nearby are a brass memorial tablet and a stained-glass commemorative window. One additional memorial is of literary interest: the Lady Chapel reredos was placed in memory of Charlotte Yonge, the novelist from nearby Otterbourne.

Westgate Museum, mostly of the 13th century, in one of the two remaining city gates, contains a relatively recent acquisition; cathedral excavations in 1965 revealed part of a frieze (most probably erected by King Cnut or Canute) which undoubtedly portrays the episode of Sigmund's escape from the wolf in the *Völsunga Saga.* Along the same lines, the castle, near Westgate, contains "King Arthur's Round Table," itself reasonable enough, although its known history dates it closer to the time of Malory than to that of Arthur. Hanging on the west wall of the Great Hall, the table is 17 feet in diameter and contains spaces for Arthur and twenty-four of his knights. To complete the anachronism, the center of the table is decorated with a Tudor rose. The table's earliest verifiable date is 1450, and it is known to have had its first repainting in 1522, when Emperor Charles V of Hapsburg was shown the table by Henry VIII. Less than a century later the castle became the scene of the sentencing of Sir Walter Ralegh, who had been tried for complicity in a plot to murder James I. He was brought for trial to nearby Wolvesey Palace in 1603; the prosecution, led by Sir Edward Coke, began its case on November 17 (an ironic date for Ralegh, for it was the anniversary of Elizabeth I's accession) and did its job well. Ralegh was transferred to the castle and sentenced to death, a penalty not carried out, and he was removed from here to the Tower of London.

Winchester College, founded by William of Wykeham, Bishop of Winchester, received its first group of scholars in 1394. It has had many literary figures in attendance: William Grocyn, Nicholas Udall, Sir Henry Wotton, Sir John Davies, Thomas Coryate, Sir Thomas Browne, Thomas Otway, Edward Young, William Whitehead, William Lisle Bowles, Joseph Warton, Thomas Warton, William Collins, Sydney Smith, Anthony Trollope, Thomas Arnold, Matthew Arnold, and Lionel Johnson. Nicholas Udall's entrance on the admission rolls of the college for 1517 is one of the earliest facts known of his life; he left Winchester in 1520 to go up to Corpus Christi College, Oxford, and later returned as a master. Joseph Warton was an usher here in 1755 and headmaster from 1766 to 1793. Most of these scholars had relatively uneventful careers here, but this was not the case with both Trollope and Matthew Arnold. Trollope's time was particularly bad; with both parents in the United States because of his father's inability to support the family, young Trollope, without money or a uniform, was held up to constant ridicule by both staff and fellow students. Matthew Arnold lasted only one year here, from August 1836 to July 1837, when his parents removed him to Rugby. His unpopularity, resulting from telling the headmaster that his work was much too light, brought on a pelting by his fellows with "pontos" (buckeyes) in a traditional ritual known as "cloister peelings."

Izaak Walton spent his last years in Winchester and is known to have been fond of fishing in the Itchen River, as was Charles Kingsley at a later date. Walton comments that the area "exceed[s] all England for swift, shallow, clear, pleasant brooks, and stores of trout." Coming here first in 1662, he lived with Bishop George Morley in Wolvesey Palace, where he may have been the Bishop's steward and where he wrote his lives of Richard Hooker and George Herbert. Later he moved to Western House, 7 Dome Alley, in the close, the residence of his son-in-law, Dr. William Hawkins. He died here in December 1683. Jane Austen also lived in Winchester, but for a very short time. She came to 8 College Street (the house is marked with a plaque) on May 24, 1817, from Chawton. To her correspondents she appeared hopeful, and she wrote until only a few days before her death, but she was obviously aware of her imminent death. Writing to her niece, she says:

> I am now out of bed from nine in the morning to ten at night; upon the sofa, it is true, but I eat my meals with Aunt Cassandra in a rational way, and can employ myself, and walk from one room to another. Mr. Lyford says he will cure me, and if he fails, I shall draw up a memorial and lay it before the Dean and Chapter, and have no doubt of redress from that pious, learned, and disinterested body.

Even though seriously ill (possibly with Addison's disease) when she arrived and under the care of Mr. Lyford, a well-known physician, she continued to work on *Persuasion*. Her sister Cassandra came to Winchester to care for her and remained until Miss Austen's death on July 18, 1817; only her family attended the funeral.

John Keats lived in Winchester for a time in the summer of 1819 after leaving the Isle of Wight. From August 12 to early October he had lodgings here; the exact location is not known, although two possibilities emerge from his letters. The most likely candidates are the High Street and the corner of Paternoster Row and Colebrook Street; the latter seems more probable from the description in a letter to his brother George:

> I go out at the back gate across one street; into the Cathedral yard, which is always interesting; then I pass under the trees along a paved path, past the beautiful stone front of the Cathedral, turn to the left under a stone doorway . . . which leaving behind me I pass on through two college-like squares. . . . Then I pass through one of the old city gates and then you are in College Street.

In these two months he worked on *Otho the Great, Lamia,* and *The Eve of St. Mark;* sent "To Autumn," a description of the town in the autumn, off to Richard Woodhouse; and composed the final version of "Ode of a Grecian Urn." His early opinion of Winchester never changed; to his sister he wrote, "[I]t is the pleasantest town I ever was in, and it has the most recommendations of any." He commented especially on the clear, shallow Itchen with its fat, speckled store of trout and on the old mill by the weirs. Of much the same opinion was William Cobbett; including Winchester in his *Rural Rides,* he writes:

> Here [most likely St. Giles's Hill] looking back at the city and at the fine valley above and below it, and at the smaller valleys that run down from the high ridges . . . I could not help admiring the taste of the ancient kings who made this city a chief place of residence. There are not many finer spots in England.

And presumably, somewhere near St. Giles's, King Arthur set the tournament scene in which Launcelot of the Lake secretly takes part wearing the sleeve of Elaine, the Fair Maid of Astolat.

Thomas Hardy uses Winchester extensively as Wintoncester in his Wessex novels; Winton is one of the old names for the city. *Tess of the D'Urbervilles* makes the most extensive use of Wintoncester. West Hill and the milestone, where Angel Clare and Liza-Lu stand to watch "in paralyzed suspense" for the final signal by the black flag of Tess's execution, is Roebuck Hill, just outside the city on the Stockbridge Road. And Hardy's description of the town lying "amidst its convex and concave downlands" with its "sloping High Street," its "West Gateway," its "medieval cross," St. Thomas' Church, St. Catherine's Hill, the college, and the cathedral is fairly accurate even today. Only the jail, where Tess is executed, cannot be seen from the hill; trees have obscured the view. In "Lady Mottisfont" (*A Group of Noble Dames*), the first scene is set in the cathedral, and Hardy's description of the interior is so realistic that the reader can easily visualize the exact spot where Sir Ashley Mottisfont proposes to Philippa. Hardy mentions Winchester by its real name in "On the Western Circuit" (*Life's Little Ironies*), and, finally, at the old George Inn he wrote "At an Inn" (*Wessex Poems*). William Makepeace Thackeray uses the cathedral in *The History of Henry Esmond, Esquire* as the place where the reconciliation between Lady Castlewood and Henry Esmond occurs.

George Borrow was a childhood visitor to the town; his father, a professional soldier, always took his wife and children with him when he was posted anywhere. Consequently, Borrow was at various undocumented times in almost every part of Great Britain. *Lavengro*, undoubtedly his best-known and wholly autobiographical work, mentions staying here, "looking out from our hostel-window upon the streets of old Winchester. . . ."

The Hospital of St. Cross, almshouses about 1½ miles south of the city center, was founded in 1136 by Henry of Blois, Bishop of Winchester. His original provision was for 13 poor men and dinner for 100 more daily. Today the pensioners still wear the traditional flowing claret gowns and ruffed hats and occasionally are seen in the town. Keats made the walk across the fields to St. Cross in the summer of 1819; whether or not he asked for the traditional wayfarer's dole of bread and ale, his letters do not say. Today an early-morning visitor may make the request, if he can find anyone about, and receive his portion. Trollope, too, was intrigued by the walk to St. Cross and by the hospital itself. Hiram's Hospital in *The Warden* is based on this almshouse; and, in fact, Trollope points out in his *Autobiography* that Winchester, not Salisbury, is the Barchester of *Barchester Towers*.

WINCHMORE HILL, Middlesex Once a village in its own right, Winchmore Hill (along with Southgate) is now incorporated into Enfield and is part of the Greater London borough consisting of Enfield, Edmonton, and Southgate. At one time Winchmore Hill Wood covered most of the hilly area, and even though this is no longer a village, it has retained its village green and a few old houses. In 1829, after he became editor of *Gem*, Thomas Hood took Rose Cottage, which, enlarged after Hood's time, stands a bit back from the road and was a quiet place to work. Few particulars are available about the two-year stay at Winchmore Hill; Hood's daughter Fanny was born here in 1830, and the period seems to have been one of health and prosperity for the poet, who was generally noted for his financial difficulties.

WINDERMERE, Westmorland Standing on the eastern shore of the biggest lake in England, from which it takes its name, Windermere is the major tourist town in the Lake District. Windermere officially took this name only with the arrival of the railway in 1847; earlier the proper name was Birthwaite. The houses of the town now extend south until they link up with the village of Bowness-on-Windermere, and both communities are now governed by the same urban council. The lake is 10½ miles long and 1¼ miles wide and extends from Waterhead in the north to Lake Side at the foot.

The Lakeland advantage of the town is easy access to beauty spots. From Orrest Head, just above the village, the panorama is striking and includes in the distance the Langdales, the Grasmere mountains, Coniston Fells, and Morecambe Bay.

One of the earliest visitors to the lake was John Leland, who comments on the lake in his *Itinerary*:

There is a very great lake, or mere, whereof part is

under the egge of Furnes Felles, cawlled Wynermerewath, wherein a straung fisch crawlled a chare, not sene els where in the cuntery as they say.

This fish seems to have been of general interest, for Daniel Defoe refers to it in *A Tour thro' the Whole Island of Great Britain:*

But I must not forget *Winander Meer,* which makes the utmost Northern Bounds of this Shire, which is famous for the *Char Fish* found here and hereabout, and no where else in *England*. . . . It is a curious Fish, and, as a Dainty, is Potted, and sent far and near, as Presents to the best Friends; but the Quantity they take also is not great. Mr. *Cambden's* Continuator calls it very happily the *Golden Alpine Trout.*

Fishing is still good in the lake. Michael Drayton also found Windermere beautiful, as he states in *Poly-Olbion:*

But to his inner earth, divert we from the deepe,
Where those two mightie Meres, out-stretch in length do wander,
The lesser *Thurstan* nam'd; the famouser *Wynander,*
So bounded with her Rocks, as Nature would descry,
By her how those great Seas *Mediterranean* lye.

For many years Windermere was the home of John Wilson (Christopher North); he bought Ellray Cottage in 1806 and built a house here later. Both buildings were pulled down in 1869, but the name has been perpetuated in a school on the site, and Wilson's favorite view from Orrest Head is preserved and under the care of the National Trust:

There is not such another splendid prospect in all England. The lake has much of the character of a river, without losing its own. The islands are seen almost all lying together in a cluster—below which all is loveliness and beauty—above, all majesty and grandeur. Bold or gentle promontories break all the banks into frequent bays, seldom without a cottage or cottages embowered in trees; and, whilst the whole landscape is of a sylvan kind, parts of it are so laden with woods that you see only here and there a wreath of smoke but no houses, and could almost believe that you were gazing on primeval forests.

Robert Southey, Thomas De Quincey, Hartley Coleridge, and William Wordsworth were among Wilson's numerous guests. This is a spot Wordsworth knew well, and in *The Prelude* he describes Windermere and its islands:

When summer came,
Our pastime was, on bright half-holidays,
To sweep along the plain of Windermere
With rival oars; and the selected bourne
Was now an Island musical with birds
That sang and ceased not; now a Sister Isle
Beneath the oaks' umbrageous covert, sown
With lilies of the valley like a field;
And now a third small Island, where survived
In solitude the ruins of a shrine
Once to Our Lady dedicate, and served
Daily with chaunted rites. In such a race
So ended, disappointment could be none,
Uneasiness, or paint, or jealousy:
We rested in the shade, all pleased alike,
Conquered and conqueror. . . .

The islands are easily identified: House Holme or Thomson's Holme (probably the former) is the one "musical with birds"; the sister sown "with lilies of the valley" is Belle Island; and Lady Holme has the shrine to Our Lady. Lady Holme was at one time the site of a hospital, founded in 1256, and later of a chantry which, though fallen into ruin during the reign of Henry VIII, was still standing in the 19th century. Other poems refer to Windermere; especially noteworthy is "There Was a Boy," which commemorates a schoolfellow, William Rayrigg, who died at the age of twelve.

Other Lake poets have come to Windermere: Samuel Taylor Coleridge knew the lake well and includes it in his catalog of the Lake District areas in "Christabel":

> And hence the custom and law began,
> That still at dawn the sacristan,
> Who duly pulls the heavy bell,
> Five and forty beads must tell
> Between each stroke—a warning knell,
> Which not a soul can choose but hear
> From Bratha Head to Wyndermere.

Percy Bysshe Shelley was here in the autumn of 1813, when he stayed at nearby Low Wood Inn; unable to find a suitable house to lease, he went on to Edinburgh. John Keats was here in June 1818 and, before going into Bowness, stopped to take in the full view. His first comment on the lakes, according to Charles Armitage Brown, his traveling companion, was:

> I cannot describe them ... they surpass my expectation—beautiful water—shores and islands green to the marge—mountains all round up to the clouds.

Keats maintained that no view in the world could exceed or even equal this view, and as he and Brown continued toward the end of the lake, he thought it more and more wonderfully beautiful.

Alfred, Lord Tennyson spent part of late May 1835 here with Edward FitzGerald; they were staying at Mire House in Bassenthwaite with James Spedding and took delight in rowing up and down the lake talking about poetry and reciting some. FitzGerald recalled the event later:

> Resting on our oars one calm day on Windermere, ... resting on our oars, and looking into the lake quite unruffled and clear, Alfred quoted from the lines he had lately read us from the MS of "Morte d'Arthur" about the lonely lady of the lake and Excalibur—
>
> Nine years she wrought it, sitting in the deeps
> Upon the hidden bases of the hills.
>
> "Not bad that, Fitz, is it?"

Charles Dickens was also here on various occasions after the annual sports day was initiated by John Wilson; the Ferry Inn was the scene of the festivities until about 1861, when they were transferred to Grasmere. The Ferry Sports of 1857 was described by Dickens in *Household Words*. Some years later, in July 1889, William Ernest Henley was at the Crown Hotel on a brief holiday from Edinburgh; "The Nocturn" was written at this time. Perhaps the reason why Windermere itself has always seemed attractive to visitors is summed up in Harriet Martineau's description of the town in *Guide to Windermere:* she notes that almost all of the houses are new and still have a feeling of "newness, but it is not the crude newness of bricks, but the fresh and attractive newness of grey stone against a charming background of trees and flowers."

WINDSOR, Berkshire (pop. 8,802; munic. bor. 20,122)
On the Thames River in the eastern part of Berkshire, Windsor is much more than a Victorian town with an immense castle. A settlement here predated the Norman Conquest, and both the ancient Britons and Julius Caesar knew fortifications at Old Windsor, 1½ miles to the southeast. The Saxon kings also had a seat here, and the remains of a building thought to have been Edward the Confessor's palace have been discovered on this hill location. But it was William the Conqueror who saw the strategic importance of Windsor and the attractiveness of its location, only 21 miles from London on the leafy upper Thames, and undertook the building of the castle on the chalk outcrop overlooking the river. Nothing of his structure remains, but the present Round Tower on a 50-foot-high mound is on the site of the original keep. The earliest architecturally identifiable portions of the present structure date from the reign (1154–1189) of Henry II; they have been added to by almost every monarch: indeed, Henry III added the Curfew Tower; Edward III, the canons' cloister; Edward IV, the church; Elizabeth I, the north terrace; and George III, the royal apartments. However, the castle never took on importance as a residence of the royal family until the time of Queen Victoria; it was the Prince Consort who brought about the first extensive use of Windsor as a refuge from a detested London.

St. George's Chapel, one of the most beautiful buildings in the country, was begun under Edward IV for the Knights of the Garter, but by the time of Christopher Wren the roof of the chapel was severely cracked. Repairs were undertaken, but in time additional cracks appeared. Only in the 20th century was it discovered that the roof beams merely rested against the walls with minimal support, that more than half of the flying buttresses of the choir aisle were purely ornamental, that the Beaufort Chapel had been erected over a rubbish-filled chalk pit, and that pieces of tracery were held together with a shallow cement overlay. The chapel was closed for ten years (1920–1930) for the necessary restoration work.

On February 26, 1666, Samuel Pepys came to Windsor and was taken to St. George's by Dr. William Child, the chapel organist, who

> came to us and carried us to St. George's Chapel, and there placed us among the Knights' stalls; and pretty the observation, that no man, but a woman, may sit in a Knight's place, where any brass plates are set, and hither come cushions to us, and a young singing-boy to bring us a copy of the anthem to be sung. And here, for our sakes, had this anthem and the great service sung extraordinary, only to entertain us. It is a noble place indeed, and a good choir of voices. . . . This being done, to the King's house, and to observe the neatness and contrivance of the house and gates: it is the most romantic castle that is in the world. But, Lord! the prospect that is in the balcony in the Queen's lodgings, and the terrace and walk, are strange things to consider, being the best in the world, sure.

Later in the century Daniel Defoe was in Windsor and describes it at length in *A Tour thro' the Whole Island of Great Britain;* he is at first concerned with William the Conqueror's castle and then dismisses as fabulous the "old Story, that *William* of *Wickham* [Wykehan] built this Castle. . . ." Among other places, he visited the royal chapel at this time; on one previous occasion he had been here in the company of a dissenting friend, and this former visit is recalled along with a more current discussion of the chapel:

At the *West* End of the Hall, is the Chapel Royal, the neatest and finest of the Kind in *England;* the carv'd Work is beyond any that can be seen in *England,* the Altar-Piece is that of the Institution, or, as we may call it, our Lord's first Supper. I remember, that going with some Friends to shew them this magnificent Palace, it chanced to be at the Time when the Dissenters were a little uneasy at being obliged to kneel at the Sacrament; one of my Friends, who, as I said, I carried to see *Windsor Castle,* was a Dissenter, and when he came into the Chapel, he fix'd his Eyes upon the Altar-Piece with such a fix'd, steady Posture, and held it so long, that I could not but take Notice of it, and asked him, Whether it was not a fine Piece? Yes, says he, it is; but, whispering to me, he added, How can your People prosecute us for refusing to kneel at the Sacrament? Don't you see there, that though our Saviour himself officiates, they are all sitting about the Table?

One of the earliest literary citations of Windsor and its surroundings occurs in Michael Drayton's *Poly-Olbion,* and the view is almost reverential:

Then, hand in hand, her *Tames* the Forrest softly
    brings,
To that supreamest place of the great English Kings,
ff The *Garters* Royall seate, from him who did advance
That Princely Order first, our first that conquered
    France:
The Temple of *Saint George,* whereas his honored
    Knights,
Upon his hallowed day, observe their ancient rites:
Where *Eaton* is at hand to nurse that learned brood,
To keepe the Muses still neere to this Princely Flood;
That nothing there may want, to beawtifie that seate,
With every pleasure stor'd. . . .

As John Evelyn visited Windsor, he consistently noted the building and decorating changes; under the date of June 8, 1654, he records a stop here:

The Church & Workmanship in stone (though *Gotic*) is admirable: The Castle it selfe, large in Circumference, but the roomes Melancholy & of antient magnificence: The keepe (or mount) hath besides its incomparable Prospect, a very profound Well, & the *Terrace* towards *Eaton,* with the Park, meandring *Thames,* swete Meadows yeilds one of the most delightfull prospects in the World. . . .

A later trip, on June 16, 1683, brings out dramatically the changes which occurred in the 17th century:

That which now at *Winsore* was new & surprizing to me since I was last there, was that incomparable fresca painting in St. *Georges Hall,* representing the Legend of St. *George,* & Triumph of the *black-Prince,* and his reception by *Edw:* the 4d, The *Volto* or roofe not totaly finished: Then the *Chapell* of the *Resurrection,* where the figure of the *Ascension,* is in my opinion comparable to any paintings of the most famous *Roman* Masters: The Last-Supper also over the *Altar* (I liked exceedingly the Contrivance of the unseene Organs behind the Altar) nor lesse the stupendious, & beyond all description, the incomparable Carving of our *Gibbons.* . . . There was now the *Terraces* almost brought round the old *Castle:* The Grafts made cleane, even, & curiously turf't, also the *Avenues* to the New-Park, & other Walkes planted with *Elmes* & limes, and a pretty Canale, & receptacle for fowle. . . .

James I of Scotland, captured on his way to France, was imprisoned in Windsor around 1406; he especially enjoyed walking in a garden around the area of the old moat. He received a solid education while in captivity and wrote *The Kingis Quair* during his enforced exile; the long poem (197 stanzas) is generally considered to be an allegorized account of his suit for the hand of Lady Jane Beaufort, Geoffrey Chaucer's grandniece and a cousin of Richard II. James I's marriage to her in 1424 and the payment of a large ransom from Scotland brought about his release.

Earlier Chaucer himself appears to have been in Windsor on at least two occasions; in 1357 he is said to have been in the Countess of Ulster's party when they were present for the feast of St. George. His later association is more definite; appointed Clerk of the Works around 1389, Chaucer had the responsibility of the first documented restoration of the Chapel of St. George. It is often claimed that he lived in Winchester Tower here while overseeing the work; he appears to have held the clerkship for only two years, and his accomplishments cannot have been especially great, for by the mid-15th century Edward IV, known for "the adauncement of vaine pompe," set about destroying the original chapel and building the present structure.

In the early 16th century Henry Howard, Earl of Surrey, spent a number of years here as a companion to Henry Fitzroy, Duke of Richmond, Henry VIII's illegitimate son. Howard arrived, most likely, on April 23, 1529, and remained here until the autumn of 1532, when both boys accompanied the King to France for a stay of a little more than a year in the French court. Even after their return and Howard's marriage in February 1532 to Lady Frances de Vere, daughter of the 15th Earl of Oxford, the Earl of Surrey remained in Windsor because he and his wife were thought too young to live together: Howard was no more than fifteen, and the Lady Frances was even younger. Some years later, in June 1537, Howard was confined to the grounds here by the Privy Council for striking Edward Seymour, and he began writing poetry during his short confinement. Most probably "Prisoned in Windsor, He Recounteth His Pleasure There Passed" was written at this time; in it he first recalls his youth:

So cruell prison how could betide, alas,
As proude Windsor? where I in lust and ioy,
With a kinges sonne, my childishe yeres did passe,
In greater feastes than Priams sonnes of Troy:
Where eche swete place returns a taste full sower.

He concludes with a lament of his present situation:

Thus I alone, where all my freedome grewe,
In prison pyne, with bondage and restraint,
And with remembrance of the greater griefe
To banish the lesse, I finde my chief reliefe.

"When Windsor Walles Susteyned My Weary Arme" is also thought to date to this period. Surrey was released in November 1537. His fortunes rose and fell with the Howard family; and when Catherine Howard, a cousin, married King Henry, Surrey held numerous important posts and was made a Knight of the Order of the Garter. He was formally initiated here on May 22, 1541, and given possession of his stall in St. George's Chapel, fifth on the sovereign's side.

Nicholas Udall, dramatist, educator, and cleric, was nominated to a canonship at St. George's Chapel in November 1551; Udall's life following his dismissal from Eton on a charge of buggery had become simultaneously more statesmanlike and more religious, and with Edward VI's favor the canonry here was considered his by right. Until recently Udall was thought never to have taken up actual residence here and, indeed, never to have appeared. The evidence now seems to point in a different direction; in fact, *Ralph Roister Doister,* which usually has been thought to have been written at Eton and first produced there, was more than likely first produced here with Udall in attendance in September 1552. By June 1554 he was replaced here and, indeed, in March 1553 had been given the living at Calbourne, on the Isle of Wight.

A little later Windsor Castle became a retreat for Queen Elizabeth I and her court from the plague in London; and because of their removal here in the late autumn of 1563, Roger Ascham undertook the writing of *The Scholemaster,* the first major treatise on the subject in England. Following dinner on December 10 in Sir William Cecil's chamber, Sir Richard Sackville pressed Ascham to express the gathering's views:

> "[A]t your leisure, put in some order of writing the chief points of this our talk, concerning the right order of teaching, and honesty of living, for the good bringing up of children and young men; and surely, beside contenting me, you shall both please and profit very many others."

WINDSOR   The castle at Windsor, with additions by almost every monarch from its original date in the reign of Henry II, overlooks the Thames River; the castle walls surround nearly 13 acres, and all around are parklands and forests. Here *The Merry Wives of Windsor* was first performed for Elizabeth I, who commanded a play of the "fat knight in love."

Ascham demurred, claiming "lack of ability and weakness of body." With some additional pressure from Elizabeth, Ascham produced the work.

Another early literary figure and statesman was frequently in attendance here with the royal entourage: Thomas Sackville, Earl of Dorset and Baron Buckhurst, held many posts under both Mary and Elizabeth and was, in fact, a valued member of the court. Both his Induction for *A Mirror for Magistrates* and *The Tragedy of Gorboduc* (written with Thomas Norton) predate his ambassadorial and parliamentary career. He was received into the Order of the Knights of the Garter on December 18, 1589, at St. George's Chapel.

One writer more than any other stands out in his association with Windsor during this period; indeed, while few existing sites outside of Stratford-on-Avon are firmly associated with William Shakespeare, Windsor is one of the chosen. Shakespeare makes some slight use of Windsor Castle in *The Tragedy of King Richard II;* here Aumerle's treason is discovered and confessed to, and his mother, the Duchess of York, successfully pleads for her son's life. More important is *The Merry Wives of Windsor;* it has long been maintained that Shakespeare's all-too-obvious haste in writing the play was probably the fault of Queen Elizabeth, who urgently wanted a play of the "fat knight in love," and it appears that the first performance of the play occurred here with the Queen in attendance and the choristers of the chapel as the actors. For a performance as important as this, the playwright would probably have overseen the rehearsals

and almost certainly would have been present for the actual production. The entire play takes place in Windsor and the surrounding area, but not one scene is set in the castle itself. Page's house cannot be definitely placed (it seems to be located on the edge of town, on the right side of the Long Walk looking away from the castle gates), and the houses belonging to Dr. Caius and Sir Hugh Evans are similarly difficult to pinpoint. The first is possibly in the Lower Ward of the castle, and the second is probably in the Horseshoe Cloisters. Close to the castle walls on the High Street is an inn with the name Ye Harte and Garter (at one time The Star and Garter), which may well be the Garter Inn referred to in the play. "The street in Windsor" is undoubtedly Thames Street. In Shakespeare's day as today, Windsor had only three important streets: Thames, High, and Peascod; and of these only the first has any pretension to being called *the* street. The scenes set in the surrounding area are generally easy to locate. The Windsor Park site where Caius awaits the duel is near the bank of the Thames on the west side of the castle; Sir Hugh's location, "a field near Frogmore," is in Home Park. The Windsor Park area where Page, Slender, and Shallow "crouch i' the castle-ditch till . . . [they] see the light of . . . [their] fairies" is the moat at the foot of the castle walls. The final scene, "another part of the park," would have been more aptly titled "Herne's oak"; this oak of enormous girth was eventually cut down during George III's reign.

In the 18th century Jonathan Swift was in Windsor on various occasions between the early summer of

1711 and September 1712. After taking lodgings in Chelsea, London, in April 1711, he frequently accompanied Her Majesty's ministers to Windsor. This is documented in his imitation of the sixth satire of the second book of Horace's *Sermones*. Four years earlier he had met Esther Vanhomrigh (pronounced "vanummry") and wrote of their love affair in *Cadenus and Vanessa*, composed here the first summer. In 1713 he wrote of the Windsor area:

> My Lord would carry on the jest,
> And down to Windsor take his guest.
> Swift much admires the place and air
> And longs to be a Canon there;
> In summer round the park to ride,
> In winter—never to reside.

But Swift's aspirations were never satisfied.

A few years later, in 1726, William Congreve spent some time in Windsor recuperating from an "attack of gout in the stomach" which very nearly killed him, as was reported to Swift by John Arbuthnot on July 26. One of Congreve's visitors during his illness was Alexander Pope. Later Frances Burney, subsequently Madame d'Arblay, lived at Windsor Castle as Second Keeper of the Robes to George III's Queen; persuaded to accept the appointment against many misgivings, she assumed her duties on July 17, 1786, and was unable to break her indenture until July 7, 1791. In fact, contrary to all she had been promised, she was given mainly menial duties; she attended the Queen's toilette three times a day and spent the rest of the time engaged in trivial tasks. She records life here and at other royal homes in her *Diary* and *Memoirs*. Miss Burney finished a draft of *Edwy and Elvina* here in August 1790; the play opened at Drury Lane on March 21, 1795, but was withdrawn after the first performance.

When Percy Bysshe Shelley and Mary Godwin lived in Bishop's Gate, Surrey, just on the edge of the great forest, for a few months in the summer of 1816, one of their favorite pastimes was walking the mile-long Rhododendron Walk from Bishop's Gate to Cumberland Lodge, the official residence of the ranger. Sir Walter Scott stopped here on at least two occasions; the first was in the spring of 1803, when he later recalled, he sat under an old and venerable oak in Windsor Forest reading a number of cantos of *The Lay of the Last Minstrel* to Mr. and Mrs. George Ellis. Another visit occurred in October 1826, when Sir Walter stayed in Cumberland Lodge as the guest of George IV; he also toured the castle at this time.

Much later in the 19th century Alfred, Lord Tennyson was a guest at the castle; first here on March 6, 1873, in obedience to a royal command, he records the experience in a letter to his wife:

> The visit to Windsor went off very well, and we were first ushered into a long corridor in the Castle. There the Queen came, and was very kindly, asking after all at home, pitying Lady Simeon (for the loss of Sir John). We talked too of Romanism and Protestantism. Then I walked with the Dean and Lady Augusta to Frogmore, and pottered about till the Queen and Princess Beatrice arrived. The Queen took me into the building and explained everything.

Soon after his return home, Tennyson received a telegram inquiring about the poet's acceptance of "some honour [if it] were offered...." Tennyson eventually explains his position to William Gladstone in a letter dated March 30:

> I speak frankly to you when I say that I had rather we should remain plain Mr. and Mrs, and that, if it were possible, the title should first be assumed by our son at any age it may be thought right to fix upon: but like enough this is against all precedent, and could not be managed: and on no account would I have suggested it, were there the least chance of the Queen's construing it into a slight of the proffered honour.

The possibility of vesting the title in Hallam seems to have been given some sort of initial vague approval, even though that action was most innovative; but, of course, Tennyson himself did assume the barony in 1884. The poet and Queen Victoria had great respect and admiration for each other, and Tennyson enjoyed numerous audiences with her here and at Osborne.

H. G. Wells uses the town and the river here in two of his novels; in *Tono-Bungay* Edward Ponderevo rows up the Thames after the bankruptcy of his uncle's firm. In *Joan and Peter* this is the site of High Cross Preparatory School, that "traditional, purposeless" establishment that Peter is forced to attend by Lady Charlotte Sydenham.

WINESTEAD, Yorkshire (pop. 154) The coastline of this part of the East Riding of Yorkshire is in constant flux. The North Sea annually takes from 2 to 7 feet off the cliff and coastline, sometimes depositing it elsewhere, and Spurn Head is one area where redeposited land causes annual growth and frequent change in configuration. Spurn Head is the location of Winestead, a tiny East Riding village, at present about 3½ miles and once more than 5 miles from the North Sea coast. On March 31, 1621, Andrew Marvell was born in Rectory House; his father was the vicar. Winestead is still famous for the roses to which Marvell alludes in his poetry, and the fruit trees are still mossy; it is also still possible

> Through the hazels thick [to] espy
> The hatching throstle's shining eye.

Marvell's early childhood here was brief. The family left for Hull in 1624, when the Reverend Mr. Marvell was made headmaster of the Hull Grammar School.

WINTERBOURNE ABBAS, Dorset (pop. 175) On the south side of a tiny stream known as the South Winterbourne is the hamlet of Winterbourne Abbas. Immediately to the west is Thomas Hardy's "Nine-Pillared Cromlech" of "My Cicely" (*Wessex Poems*). Often called "a kind of Stonehenge in miniature," this is a small circle, about 25 feet in diameter, of rough megaliths thought to date from approximately 1500 B.C.

WINTERBOURNE BISHOP, Wiltshire A village so small it is neither listed in gazetteers nor located on most maps, Winterbourne Bishop is one of a series of four small villages on the Bourne River, from which they take their names: Winterbournes Bishop, Dauntsey, Earls, and Gunner. They are from 3½ to 5 miles northeast of Salisbury. Winterbourne Bishop was W.

H. Hudson's favorite of the four, and he writes of it and the others in *A Shepherd's Life:*

> Placed high itself on a wide, unwooded valley or depression, with the low, sloping downs at some distance away, the village is about as cold a place to pass a winter in as one could find in this district. And, it may be added, the most inconvenient to live in at any time. . . .

WINTERBOURNE CAME, Dorset (pop. 101) The tiny village of Winterbourne Came, although less than 2 miles southeast of Dorchester, retains all the charm and beauty of the 18th- and 19th-century village; the church, too, has escaped tasteless renovation. Beside the Palladian-designed Came House, hidden in the woods, is the fine Decorated and late Perpendicular village church of which William Barnes, the Dorset poet, was rector from 1862 to 1886. The gray ashlar church contains a very fine Jacobean pulpit from which Barnes preached. He came here from Dorchester when he received the joint livings of Winterbourne Came and Whitcombe; the preceding ten years, following the death of his wife, had been spent in ever-increasing misery and poverty. Barnes moved into the thatched rectory near the church and immediately set to work turning the garden into a botanical paradise; from his upstairs study window he was able to look out at apricot trees and asparagus fern. Barnes was an active and well-liked parish priest, and until his death at the age of eighty-five, he called on each of his parishioners at least once a fortnight. Thomas Hardy and Edmund Gosse visited him shortly before his death on October 7, 1886. Barnes was buried in the churchyard here on October 11, and a Celtic cross marks his grave. Hardy walked to the funeral from Max Gate, Dorchester, and was greeted at the churchyard by sunlight reflected from the poet's coffin. Hardy describes his final farewell to the Dorset poet in "The Last Signal." He included a rather unusual local site in *The Trumpet-Major.* Near the church in Came Park is an ecclesiastical remnant known as Faringdon Ruin (Hardy uses the real name): it is this "gable" which Anne Garland and John Lovejoy pass on their walk back to Overcombe (Sutton Poyntz) after Bob's departure on the *Victory;* only the gable remains of the ancient settlement.

WINTERSLOW, Wiltshire (pop. 788) East of the Bourne River and 6 miles northeast of Salisbury, Winterslow, while set upon the vast Salisbury Plain, is not typical of plain villages. The area around the village is scraggly, and the stray fir trees are testimony to the village's position on the northernmost extremity of the Test Basin. In 1808, following their London marriage, William Hazlitt and his wife Sarah (Stoddart) settled here, where she owned Middleton Hut; so partial was Hazlitt to this area that even after he and his first wife had separated and were divorced (1822), he often returned to the village. He loved roaming in the woods and walking to Stonehenge (10 miles northwest) and frequented the Winterslow Hut (now the Pheasant Inn) as well.

Charles Lamb and his sister Mary, who had been Miss Stoddart's bridesmaid, came for a visit in late September (probably) 1809; they remained for a month, obviously enjoying themselves, as a letter to Samuel Taylor Coleridge indicates: "We have had nothing but sunshiny days and daily walks from eight to twenty miles a-day; have seen Wilton, Salisbury, Stonehenge, &c." The Lambs returned again in 1810. From 1819 on Hazlitt lived in the inn, and *Winterslow* is a result of this stay. Of Winterslow and the area Hazlitt's son writes in the Preface:

> But the chief happiness was the thorough quiet of the place, the sole interruption of which was the passage, to and fro, of the London mails. The Hut stands in a valley, equidistant about a mile from two tolerably high hills, at the summit of which, on their approach either way, the guards used to blow forth their admonition to the hostler. . . .

There is one other possible literary association: this village may be the one intended by Charles Dickens in *Martin Chuzzlewit* as the "little Wiltshire village, within an easy journey of the fair old town of Salisbury." Both Amesbury and Alderbury have made the same claim, but only in Winterslow are two important conditions met. Winterslow was indeed on the London coach road, and its Lion's Head Inn appears to have been properly located so that it matches the novel's description of the Blue Dragon Inn. Dickens writes:

> The vane upon the tapering spire of the old church glistened from its lofty station in sympathy with the general gladness; and from the ivy-shaded windows such gleams of light shone back upon the glowing sky, that it seemed as if the quiet buildings were the hoarding-place of twenty summers, and all their ruddiness and warmth were stored within.

WIRKSWORTH, Derbyshire (pop. 4,822) An ancient market town almost wholly stone-built with exceedingly narrow streets, Wirksworth is situated at the head of the Ecclesbourne Valley, a lovely hilly wooded area 14 miles northeast of Ashbourne. Wirksworth dates at least to Roman times, when it was an important lead-mining center, and some of the surrounding hills are still littered with Roman remains. The Saxons also worked the mines, and the entire district known as King's Field was famous for its deposits long before the Normans arrived. The cruciform church here is a gem; while the building itself dates from the 13th century, it has a sculpted Saxon stone coffin, and a Norman sculpted wall depicting a miner with pick and bucket.

The church is rich in monuments, especially in the chancel aisle, but an unmarked grave in the churchyard draws pilgrims; this is the grave of Elizabeth Evans, the Dinah Morris of *Adam Bede* by George Eliot (Mary Ann Evans). Wirksworth, which appears in the novel as Snowfield, was the home of Eliot's "Methodist Aunt Samuel," who gave the author the germ of the story used in *Adam Bede.* Eliot is supposed to have visited here in 1842, staying with her cousin; however, she never mentioned the visit. Elizabeth Evans commented:

> [S]he [George Eliot] gets me to tell her about my life and religious experience, and she puts it down in a little book. I can't make out what she wants it for.

The Wesleyan Chapel in Chapel Lane contains a marble tablet to the memories of Elizabeth and Samuel Evans on which she is mentioned as Dinah Bede. The cottage where the Evanses lived is on the road to Derby just opposite the Haarlam Tape Works, where Samuel was manager and where Elizabeth probably worked as well. On two occasions Snowfield comes into *Adam Bede*. When Hetty disappears from Hall Farm and Adam searches for her, he comes here to Dinah Morris's home:

> [T]he country grew barer and barer: no more rolling woods, no more wide-branching trees near frequent homesteads, no more bushy hedgerows; but gray stone walls intersecting the meagre pastures, and dismal wide-scattered gray stone houses on broken lands where mines had been and were no longer. "A hungry land," said Adam to himself. . . . And when at last he came in sight of Snowfield, he thought it looked like a town that was "fellow to the country." The town lay, grim, stony, and unsheltered, up the side of a steep hill, and Adam did not go forward to it at present, for Seth had told him where to find Dinah. It was at a thatched cottage outside the town, a little way from the mill—an old cottage, standing sideways towards the road, with a little bit of potato-ground before it.

The house is a stone-built four-room cottage which stands exactly as just described, with a bit of potato patch in front. The second mention of Snowfield comes later in the novel:

> It was more than two o'clock in the afternoon when Adam came in sight of the grey town on the hillside, and looked searchingly towards the green valley for the first glimpse of the old thatched roof near the ugly red mill. The scene looked less harsh in the soft October sunshine than it had done in the eager time of early spring. . . .

WISBECH, Cambridgeshire (pop. 15,670) Wisbech, 22 miles northeast of Petersborough, is probably the most satisfying town in the shire outside of Cambridge itself. Surrounded by bulb fields and orchards which are at their special best in spring, Wisbech is architecturally distinguished; North Brink, above the Nene River, is an outstanding series of Georgian houses, all different but complementary. Thomas Clarkson, who was born here in 1760, became one of the 18th century's most outspoken leaders for the suppression of the slave trade and a founder of the Anti-Slavery Society. A friend of William Wilberforce and Granville Sharp, he has a place of honor in William Wordsworth's poetry; Wordsworth addressed to him a sonnet, "On the Final Passing of the Bill, for the Abolition of the Slave Trade":

> Clarkson! it was an obstinate hill to climb;
> How toilsome—nay, how dire—it was, by thee
> Is known; by none, perhaps, so feelingly:
> But thou, who, starting in thy fervent prime,
> Didst first lead forth that enterprise sublime,
> Has heard the constant Voice its charge repeat,
> Which, out of thy young heart's oracular seat,
> First roused thee.

On the site of the old castle moat is the Wisbech and Fenland Museum, which also houses the Town Library; here among other items are "sundry very old abbey manuscripts" that Samuel Pepys looked at on his trip to this "pretty town," which he calls Wisbeach, on September 18, 1663. The library also contains the Charles Dickens manuscript of *Great Expectations* and the Matthew Lewis manuscript of *The Monk*. Finally, John Clare spent a brief period in his youth here at his uncle's home when trying to secure an apprenticeship in a lawyer's office.

WISTANSTOW, Shropshire (pop. 885) Wistanstow is a legendary town, for this is the holy place of St.

Wigstan or Wystan, the royal Mercian saint who was martyred here at a council of peace in 849, when Wiglaf, King of Mercia and uncle to Wigstan, pretending to embrace the heir to the throne, struck him down with a blow to the head. Legend states that for a full month after Wigstan's death a shaft of light rose from the ground where he fell and that for many years the hairs cut from his head grew on the spot like grass. The name of this village is the source of W. H. Auden's first name; Auden's uncle, an antiquarian, was the rector here, and the boy was a frequent visitor to Wistanstow.

WITHAM, Essex (pop. 7,162) Nine miles northeast of Chelmsford, on the busy A12, Witham is in many ways typical of Essex towns and villages; it has a history dating at least to the 10th century and a pride in its past, in this case its architectural past. The town has carefully preserved many Georgian and older houses, and the Spread Eagle Inn with its bow windows is an excellent example of effective restoration. Witham is traditionally held to be the birthplace of Thomas Campion in 1567. No facts support this claim; indeed, the facts of Campion's life are obscure until his matriculation at Cambridge. In modern times Dorothy Sayers made 24 Newland Street (marked with a plaque) her home from 1929 until her death here on December 17, 1957.

WITHYHAM, Sussex (pop. 2,498) A hamlet which has grown up around a village green and an ancient manor, Withyham, 7 miles southwest of Tunbridge Wells, is closely associated with Knole, Kent, largely because of its connections with the Sackvilles. Withyham is on the border of the Ashdown Forest with Buckhurst Park on one hill, an old inn, the Dorset Arms, in the hollow, and the partly Norman church on a second hill. The major attraction of the church is the Sackville Chapel, a veritable museum of funerary carving with commemorative work by Caius Gabriel Cibber, John Flaxman, Sir Francis Chantrey, and Joseph Nollekens. The history of the Sackvilles is portrayed in the windows.

Buckhurst Park came into the hands of the Sackvilles in 1200; the present house, built in the Tudor style about 1738, looks out over a sunken garden, a lake, and ancient beech trees. An older manor house was the birthplace of the poet and dramatist Thomas Sackville, 1st Earl of Dorset and Baron Buckhurst, in 1536. He was probably baptized in the church and most likely spent most of his childhood here before entering the grammar school at Sullington. Sackville died at the council table at Whitehall in London on April 19, 1608, and after funeral services held at Westminster Abbey, his body was brought back for burial in the Sackville Chapel. The commemorative tomb was one of those "turned to lime and ashes" by lightning and a fire in 1663. Charles Sackville, 6th Earl of Dorset, was a dissipated friend of Charles II, a patron of poets, and a minor poet in his own right. After his death in Bath in 1706, he was buried in the family chapel here; the epitaph, composed by Alexander Pope, reads in part:

> Dorset, the grace of Courts, the Muses Pride,
> Patron of Arts, and Judge of Nature dy'd!
> The Scourge of Pride, though sanctify'd or great,
> Of fops in learning, and of knaves in state:

Yet soft his nature, though severe his lay,
His angel moral, and his wisdom gay.

A modern member of the family, Victoria Sackville-West, is also buried here in the Sackville Chapel with a tablet which reads only "V. Sackville-West C.H., poet."

WITLEY, Surrey (pop. 4,289)   Somehow much of the county of Surrey has managed to absorb an enormous commuter population without sacrificing all its natural beauty, and Witley seems to be one of the places especially fortunate in this respect. Although it lies within a few miles of Godalming (3 miles to the north), itself in the shadow of Guildford, the surrounding district is beautifully wooded, and much of the old village itself has been well preserved. The land originally belonged to Earl Godwin, but whether the old church is his doing has not been discovered. That the basically 12th-century parish church dates from Saxon times is a fairly recent discovery. The windows of the south wall of the nave, the west gable, and the plaster on the nave walls are all Saxon. The village can claim one of the oldest pubs in England in the tile-hung White Hart, which dates to the 14th century; built onto a hunting lodge belonging to Richard II, it is a lovely old timbered building in very good repair.

Witley has long been attractive to literary figures. George Eliot (Mary Ann Evans) and George Henry Lewes bought the Heights (now Rosslyn Court), about a mile out of the village, in 1876 with the idea of settling here. On a small rise and within view of Black Down and Hindhead, the house had an especially fine location, and here George Eliot may have put the finishing touches on *Daniel Deronda,* which she started in 1874. Both Alfred, Lord Tennyson and Henry James visited the Leweses here. Lewes's death in 1878 was sudden, and for a time George Eliot would see no one and would neither read nor write but kept herself occupied by preparing Lewes's unfinished manuscripts for the press. In 1869, on a trip to Italy, George Eliot had met J. W. Cross (many years her junior), whose mother resided in Weybridge. An intimacy between the Leweses and the Crosses developed over the years, and Cross was especially supportive when Lewes died. Eliot and Cross were married on May 6, 1880, in London and came to Witley after a tour on the Continent. The English fogs bothered Mrs. Cross greatly, and in early December the couple moved to London, where she died on December 22.

Rudyard Kipling was also here, but the exact date of his visit is not certain; however, as a boy he spent a summer holiday here with his sister Trix (she was still at Southsea and he was in school at Westward Ho!) and was kept awake by the nightingales. It is thought that the most likely time for the trip was before 1880. Finally, Arnold Bennett took The Fowl House here around 1899, and his "appetite for the country" began at that time. The name of the house was later changed to Godspeace.

WODEN CROFT, Yorkshire   The scenery surrounding the Tees River, which forms much of the Yorkshire–County Durham boundary, is some of the best in northern England. The north Yorkshire moors, set on a high tableland, are bleak, windswept, and dangerous, especially in winter, when driving snowstorms sweep across the hills. With the rivers like the Tees running to the east coast, these areas were often explored by invaders, but because of the harshness of the environment no permanent communities seem to have evolved except around the Roman wall. Woden Croft, an area on the southern bank of the Tees near Egglestone Abbey, is a field thought to have been named by the Norse. In *Rokeby* Sir Walter Scott refers to a number of these valleys named by the invaders after their gods:

. . . the Norsemen came,
Fixed on each vale a Runic name,
Rear'd high their altar's rugged stone,
And gave their gods the land they won.
Then, Balder, one bleak garth was thine,
And one sweet brooklet's silver line,
And Woden's Croft did title gain,
From the stern Father of the Slain.

There used to be earthen mounds at Woden Croft marking the site of an old building traditionally thought to be a Norse temple.

WOKING, Surrey (pop. 75,771, including Woking Village)   Gazetteers normally describe Woking as situated on the Wey River, 6 miles north of Guildford and 24 miles southwest of London, in relatively barren heathland. In fact, Woking is not really on the river: the village of Old Woking is. A modern urban community on the periphery of London, Woking did not develop until after the 1838 railway link with the metropolis. Indeed, when the station was built in 1850, it stood in the middle of a heath with only an inn nearby. Woking has been a royal manor since the reign of Edward the Confessor, and after Henry VII granted it to Margaret Beaufort, his mother, she lived here until her death in 1509. Henry VIII and Cardinal Wolsey were frequently here, and, in fact, the news of Wolsey's appointment as a cardinal reached him here. Daniel Defoe visited Woking in 1724 and says in *A Tour thro' the Whole Island of Great Britain:*

'[T]is very little heard of in *England;* it claims however some Honour, from its being once the Residence of a Royal Branch of the Family of *Plantagenet,* the Old Countess of *Richmond,* Mother to King *Henry* VII, who made her last Retreat here, where the King her Son Built, or rather Repair'd, an Old Royal House, on purpose for her Residence, and where she ended her Days in much Honour and Peace. . . .

At the end of the 19th century, after his divorce from Isabel Mary Wells (his cousin), H. G. Wells turned respectable and married Amy Catherine Robbins, his student at the University Tutorial College in London, with whom he had run off in 1893. He rented Lynton on Maybury Road in September and married Amy in October; the semidetached villa remained their home for a few years, and at this time Wells began writing in earnest. The autobiographical work *The Wheels of Chance* was completed in 1896, *The Invisible Man* followed in 1897, and Wells began *The War of the Worlds.* For this he cycled around Surrey to find accurate topographical details for a novel, he said,

in which I completely wreck and sack Woking—killing

my neighbours in painful and eccentric ways—then proceed via Kingston and Richmond to London, which I sack, selecting South Kensington for feats of peculiar atrocity.

Wells and his family moved to Worcester Park in 1897.

A second major association with Woking concerns William Ernest Henley, who moved here in January or February 1902; he and his wife had finally found their "country home," Heather Brae on Maybury Hill, and they moved into the house in March. Shortly after, Henley was the victim of a stupid accident at the Coombe and Malden railway station; the train guard signaled the train to start before Henley had entered the carriage, and the poet was thrown from the train. He never really recovered from the accident, and although subsequently able to travel up to London, he did so infrequently. He died here on July 11, 1903, and was cremated; his ashes were interred at Cockayne Hatley, Bedfordshire, where his only child Margaret had been buried in 1894.

WOKINGHAM, Berkshire (pop. 7,506) An ancient market town 36 miles southwest of London and 7 miles southeast of Reading, Wokingham is an attractive blend of old and new; its narrow streets are lined with black-and-white cottages, some of them overhanging the way, old timbered houses, and mulberry trees, providing a reminder of the early silk industry here. The Olde Rose Inn on the marketplace has associations with John Gay, Jonathan Swift, and Alexander Pope. Here, on a wet afternoon in 1726, they met the innkeeper's daughter who, it is said, inspired the ballad Gay wrote to "Molly Mog, or The Fair Maid of the Inn":

Says my Uncle, I pray you discover
    What hath been the cause of your woes,
That you pine and you whine like a lover?
    —I have seen *Molly Mog* of the *Rose*.

The Rose in London makes the same claim.

WOLVERHAMPTON, Staffordshire (pop. 216,073) Usually called "The Capital of the Black Country," Wolverhampton is the largest city in the shire (although it is smaller than Stoke-on-Trent, the Potteries conglomerate) as well as part of the sprawling Birmingham urban mass. Its history dates at least to the 10th-century founding of the Church of St. Peter and an adjacent monastery, which was of great importance before the Norman Conquest. The present church, mainly 15th-century but with some 13th-century arches, stands high on a hill with the Dane's Cross nearby. Dating probably from the 9th century, this is an enormous carved churchyard cross. One of the memorial plaques in the porch of the church is to the 18th-century musician Charles Phillips, admired by all for his "absolute contempt of riches and inimitable performance upon the violin"; his epitaph, written by Dr. Wilkes of Trinity College, Oxford, was recited to Dr. Samuel Johnson by David Garrick, as James Boswell reports in *The Life of Samuel Johnson:*

"Exalted soul! whose harmony could please
The love-sick virgin, and the gouty ease;
Could jarring discord, like Amphion, move
To beauteous order and harmonious love;

Rest here in peace, till angels bid thee rise,
And meet thy blessed Savior in the skies."

Johnson shook his head at these common-place funeral lines, and said to Garrick, "I think, Davy, I can make a better." Then stirring about his tea for a little while, in a state of meditation, he almost extempore produced the following verses:

"Phillips, whose touch harmonious could remove
The pangs of guilty power or hapless love;
Rest here, distress'd by poverty no more,
Here find that calm thou gav'st so oft before;
Sleep, undisturb'd, within this peaceful shrine,
Till angels wake thee with a note like thine!"

In fact, Garrick misquoted the original lines.

An episode in Wolverhampton's history found its way into literature; the ironmaster William Wood, who began the smelting of iron ore with coal (instead of charcoal), was granted the monopoly to strike all halfpennies and farthings for Ireland for fourteen years. The English coinage of the time allowed 23 pence to be minted from 1 pound of copper, but Wood was allowed to get 30 pence to the pound for Ireland. Furthermore, he bribed the court to obtain a patent which George II had originally given to the Duchess of Kendal; Wood paid her £10,000. Wood was also authorized to supply £85,000 of small change in excess of the Irish need so that he could make an annual profit estimated at £4,000. The Irish Parliament denounced the operation; and various declarations were made, including the accusation that the currency was debased even beyond the specification of 30 pence to the pound. At this juncture Jonathan Swift entered the fray with *The Drapier's Letters:*

At last one Mr. WOODS *a mean ordinary Man, a Hard-Ware Dealer,* procured a *Patent* under His MAJESTIES BROAD SEAL to Coin FOUR-SCORE AND TEN THOUSAND POUNDS in *Copper* for this *Kingdom,* which Patent however did not oblige any one here to take them, unless they pleased. Now you must know, that the HALF-PENCE and FARTHINGS in *England* pass for very little more than they are worth. And if you should beat them to Pieces, and sell them to the *Brazier* you would not lose above a Penny in a Shilling. But Mr. WOODS made his HALF-PENCE of such *Base Metal,* and so much smaller than the *English* ones, that the *Brazier* would not give you above a *Penny* of good Money for a *Shilling* of his. . . .
Perhaps you will wonder how such *an ordinary* Fellow as this Mr. WOODS could have so much Interest as to get his MAJESTIES Broad Seal for so great a Sum of bad Money, to be sent to this Poor Country. . . . Now I will make that Matter very Plain. . . . [H]e is an ENGLISH MAN and had GREAT FRIENDS, and it seems knew very well *where to give Money,* to those that would speak to OTHERS that could speak to the KING and could tell A FAIR STORY.

The effect of the letters was enormous, and prosecution was instituted against Swift; however, the grand jury refused to indict him and instead returned a true bill against those persons accepting the coins. The protest became even more strident and finally brought with it the cancellation of Wood's license.

Wolverhampton was to turn up again in literature. Charles Dickens was here on various occasions, including a stop on his 1838 Midlands tour to Shrewsbury and Chester. He and Phiz (Hablot Knight Browne) left Birmingham via Wolverhampton,

> starting by eight o'clock through a cold, wet fog, and travelling, when the day had cleared up, through miles of cinder-paths, and blazing furnaces, and roaring steam-engines, and such a mass of dirt, gloom, and misery, as I never before witnessed.

Dickens's impressions of the Black Country were later used extensively in *The Old Curiosity Shop:*

> A long suburb of red-brick houses,—some with patches of garden-ground, where coal-dust and factory smoke darkened the shrinking leaves and coarse rank flowers, and where the struggling vegetation sickened and sank under the hot breath of kiln and furnace, making them by its presence seem yet more blighting and unwholesome than in the town itself,—a long, flat, straggling suburb passed, they came, by slow degrees, upon a cheerless region, where not a blade of grass was seen to grow, where not a bud put forth its promise in the spring, where nothing green could live but on the surface of the stagnant pools, which here and there lay sweltering by the black roadside. . . .
>
> Dismantled houses here and there appeared, tottering to the earth, propped up by fragments of others that had fallen down, unroofed, windowless, blackened, desolate, but yet inhabited.

The night, according to Dickens, was much worse; then

> the smoke was changed to fire; when every chimney spirted up its flame; and places, that had been dark vaults all day, now shone red-hot, with figures moving to and fro within their blazing jaws, and calling to one another with hoarse cries—night, when the noise of every strange machine was aggravated by the darkness; when the people near them looked wilder and more savage; when bands of unemployed labourers paraded the roads, or clustered by torch-light round their leaders, who told them, in stern language, of their wrongs, and urged them on to frightful cries and threats . . . night, when carts came rumbling by, filled with rude coffins (for contagious disease and death had been busy with the living crops . . .).

Indeed, this is where Little Nell faints in the street: "The child clapped her hands together, uttered a wild shriek, and fell senseless at his [the schoolmaster's] feet."

Dickens returned in the winter of 1853; and "Fire and Snow," which first appeared in *Household Words* (January 21, 1854), was the result. In 1858 he stayed at the Swan Hotel, where Lloyds Bank now stands, on Queen's Square; the sign of the Swan was later moved to the Peacock in Snow Hill.

The 20th-century saw J. B. Priestley here; he records his impressions in his *English Journey:*

> I remember noticing in Wolverhampton, after half an hour of dingy higgledy-piggledy, the new building of the *Midland Counties Dairy,* white and trim and with immense windows, and thinking how alien it looked there, like the outpost of a new civilisation. I remember arriving at the very end of the earth, where the land appeared to have been uprooted by a giant pig and where there were cottages so small and odd that they must have been built for gnomes. . . .

Finally, Wolverhampton can claim one famous native son: Alfred Noyes was born here on September 16, 1880. The son of a grocer who later became a teacher, Noyes lived here only a short time before his family left for Aberystwyth, Wales, where he received his early classical education.

WOODBRIDGE, Suffolk (pop. 5,010) Set on the slopes of the Deben River estuary 8 miles northeast of Ipswich, Woodbridge is now one of the loveliest towns in Suffolk. The town, whose name was once literal, dates to Saxon times, when the settlement was in the lower and shallower river valley; the movement up the slopes to form the present town probably began by the 11th century. Woodbridge has always enjoyed prosperity, but its base has shifted with the times; it has been variously a market town, a center of the wool trade, and a seaport. At present it is an official subport of Ipswich and a yachting and sailing center.

The town was a special favorite of Edward Fitz-Gerald, who lived almost his entire life in Suffolk. An undated letter concerning the town, which he loved but considered boring, noted, "I shall be at Woodbridge, but you know I don't advise anyone to go *there* unless on the road elsewhere." In 1853 he came here from nearby Boulge to escape the incursions of his family and moved to Farlingay Hall (gone), just outside the town, where he remained almost seven years; the hall was owned by the Smith family, and the son, Alfred, read for FitzGerald. During FitzGerald's residence here, in August 1855, he was visited by Thomas Carlyle, with whom he made numerous excursions in the area, visiting Aldeburgh, Dunwich, and Framlingham Castle. After a disconcerting six-month marriage (1859) to Lucy Barton, daughter of Bernard Barton, the Quaker poet and FitzGerald's friend, FitzGerald moved into lodgings on Market Hill over a gunsmith's shop owned by Sharman Berry. The building is marked with a plaque noting FitzGerald's thirteen-year residence. The poet's two rooms on the first floor were quite suitable, and his comfort seemed to be ensured until Berry decided to marry a local widow. In a moment of pique FitzGerald commented, "Now old Berry will have to be called Old Gooseberry!" Inevitably the remark filtered back to the new wife, who, seeing FitzGerald as a threat, insisted that he be disposed of. Berry was not the kind of man to discard years of friendship over a single comment, but he was forced into undertaking the eviction. As he went up the stairs to confront his paying guest, Mrs. Berry screeched, "Be firm, Berry! Remind him of what he called you!" But FitzGerald only moved next door. FitzGerald occasionally attended the local Church of St. George, but more regularly he frequented the Bull, also on Market Hill, where he enjoyed his Scotch ale. Responding to FitzGerald's letter and exhortations for a return visit ("I will do my best to entertain you, by giving you what food you will *at the inn* closest to my lodgings: taking you to Sea in my little Ship—and—leaving you alone"), Carlyle arrived on August 8, 1862, and stayed at the Bull Inn.

In 1873 FitzGerald left the town proper and moved to Grange Farm (renamed Little Grange), Pytches Road, just outside Woodbridge, where he lived until his death in Merton, Norfolk, on June 14, 1883. He had bought the property in 1865 and spent the intervening years enlarging and renovating it. The protracted and probably frustrating renovation period once prompted FitzGerald to muse, "I shall never live in it, but I shall die there"; he was wrong on both counts. Alfred, Lord Tennyson, visited Old Fitz at Little Grange and with his son Hallam had accommodations at the Bull Inn in September 1876. Arriving in provincial Woodbridge, Tennyson asked directions to Mr. FitzGerald's house and was sent to Seckford Street, the home of Police Inspector Fitz-Gerald. Tennyson enjoyed his two-day visit to the older poet; he remarked on his trip on the Orwell River, and "To E. FitzGerald" refers to FitzGerald's attempt to convert him to a vegetarian diet:

> . . . once for ten long weeks I tried
> Your table, of Pythagoras,
>   And seem'd at first "a thing enskied"
> (As Shakespeare has it) airy light
>   To float above the ways of men,
> Then fell from that half-spiritual height
>   Chill'd, till I tasted flesh again
> One night when earth was winter-black,
>   And all the heavens flash'd in frost. . . .

Old Fitz never saw these words, as his death occurred before the poem was published.

George Crabbe spent four years in Woodbridge, from 1771 to 1775, when he took up a surgeon's apprenticeship under the care of a Mr. Page. Crabbe undoubtedly lodged in Page's home, and it was here, probably in 1771, that he first met Sarah Elmy, whom he was to marry many years later.

WOODCROFT, Northamptonshire A tiny hamlet 5 miles northwest of Peterborough and 1 mile southeast of Helpston, Woodcroft holds the ruins of a 13th-century castle besieged by the Parliamentarians; the castle inspired John Clare's early poem, "Woodcroft Castle," which was written when he came here to work.

WOODFORD, Essex (pop. 21,236) Woodford is now a parish made up of three once-distinct Woodford villages: Woodford Bridge, Woodford Green, and Woodford Wells. Though partly surrounded by Epping Forest, most of which lies to the northwest, the Woodfords are essentially London suburbs, lying just north of the North Circular Road; Woodford Green is the most attractive. By the 17th century Woodford Green was a fashionable area to live in: close enough to the city for easy access and far enough removed to be natural. "About the year 1629," says Izaak Walton, ". . . Mr. Herbert was seized with a sharp quotidian ague, and thought to remove it by the change of air: to which end he went to Woodford in Essex. . . ." Indeed, George Herbert was quite ill and came here to the home of his brother Sir Henry Herbert to attempt a cure. He remained a full year, ministering to himself: he ate no meat or fowl unless it was salted and would drink nothing. Herbert did manage to cure his ague, but in the process he became consumptive; he left Woodford Green to attempt a second cure, at the Earl of Danby's home in Dauntsey, Wiltshire. Sydney Smith, the droll and witty canon of St. Paul's, cofounder of *The Edinburgh Review,* and author of *The Letters of Peter Plymley,* was born in Woodford in 1771. The house of his birth has not been identified, nor has the date of his leaving here been discovered, but the assumption is that this was his boyhood home. Also a native of Woodford was Coventry Pat-

more, who was born at the home of his great-uncle on July 23, 1823, but again the house cannot be identified. Patmore spent much of his childhood here and at the home of his uncle, Robert Stevens, in Epping Forest.

In 1840 William Morris's family moved here from Walthamstow, on the other side of Epping Forest. Their house, Woodford Hall, was a large Georgian mansion situated in about 50 acres of private parkland adjacent to the forest proper. It was here that Morris played in his toy suit of armor, among the hornbeams, that he created a woodland population of knights and ladies, and that he imagined medieval romance and adventure. "Shameful Death" contains a description of the hornbeams and re-creates some of his childhood fancies. The stocks and lock-up on the village green opposite Woodford Hall made so vivid an impression on the young boy that fifty years later he writes to his daughter:

> When we lived at Woodford there were stocks there on a little bit of wayside green in the middle of the village: beside them stood the cage, a small shanty some twelve feet square, and as it was built of brown brick roofed with blue slate, I suppose it had been quite recently in use, since its style was not earlier than the days of fat George. I remember I used to look at these two threats of law and order with considerable terror, and decidedly preferred to walk on the other side of the road. . . .

When aged nine, Morris began to attend a school in Walthamstow kept by the Misses Arundel, and he would ride the 2-mile distance on a pony; in 1845 the school moved to George Lane here.

Matthew Arnold came to Woodford in 1864, having already begun *Thyrsis,* the elegy for Arthur Hugh Clough, and here heard "the cuckoo I have brought in in Thyrsis":

> So have I heard the cuckoo's parting cry,
>   From the wet field, through the vexed garden-trees,
>   Come with the volleying rain and tossing breeze:
> The bloom is gone, and with the bloom go I!

WOODSTOCK, Oxfordshire (pop. 1,955) Woodstock, on the Glyme River 8 miles northwest of Oxford, has a history predating the Norman Conquest, although at the Domesday census of 1086 it was described as a royal forest. The town has a number of very good old houses, including one with a medieval chimney, a partly 13th-century church, and, formerly, a royal palace, which was torn down to build neighboring Blenheim Palace (where Sir Winston Churchill was born and where he is buried). Chaucer's House, which has never been shown to have a direct connection with Geoffrey Chaucer, was granted to Thomas Chaucer, Speaker of the House of Commons and the poet's putative son; traditionally, the old poet is supposed to have visited his son here. Henry I had a zoo here, but for centuries poets, dramatists, and romantics have made this site of a pilgrimage, for it was here that Henry II is supposed to have built the bower for Fair Rosamond. Rosamond Clifford, acknowledged as the King's mistress, is known to have died here; and, says legend, she was poisoned by Henry's Queen, Eleanor of Aquitaine. Henry and Fair Rosamond had met at Godstow, and, states the chronicler John Stow, Rosamond

dyed at Woodstocke where King Henry had made for her

a house of wonderful working, so that no man or woman might come to her but he that was instructed by the King. This house after some was named Labyrinthus, or Dedalus worke, wrought like unto a knot in a garden, called a maze; but it was commonly said that lastly the queene came to her by a clue of thridde of silke, and so dealt with her that she lived not long after. . . .

The story is told in numerous poems and ballads; one of the most explicit is Thomas Deloney's "A Mournfull Dittie, on the Death of *Rosamond*, King *Henry* the Seconds Concubine." He describes Woodstock:

Most curiously this Bower was built of stone and timber strong,
An hundred and fifty doores did to that bower belong.
And they so cunningly contriu'd with turnings round about,
That none but with a clew of threed, could enter in or out.

Deloney then describes the King's farewell when he leaves for France, his entrusting Rosamond to the care and safekeeping of Sir Thomas, and the Queen's securing of access to the King's mistress:

But when the Queene with stedfast eyes beheld her heauenly face:
She was amazed in her mind, at her exceeding grace.
Cast off thy Robes from thee, she said, that rich and costly be:
And drink thee vp this deadly draught which I haue brought for thee.

In 1592 Samuel Daniel published *The Complaint of Rosamond*, which describes the palace:

A stately Pallace he foorthwith did buylde,
Whose intricate innumerable wayes,
With such confused errors so beguil'd
Th' vnguided entrers with vncertaine strayes,
And doubtfull turnings kept them in delayes,
    With bootlesse labor leading them about,
    Able to finde no way, nor in, nor out.

Within the closed bosome of which frame,
That seru'd a Center to that goodly round:
Were lodgings, with a garden to the same,
With sweetest flowers that eu'r adorn'd the ground,
And all the pleasures that delight hath found,
    T' entertaine the sence of wanton eyes,
    Fuell of loue, from whence lusts flames arise.

A few years later Michael Drayton followed the lead and composed "The Complaint of Rosamund"; in 1707 Joseph Addison used the same story for his opera *Rosamond,* and Alfred, Lord Tennyson writes of it in *Becket.*

In 1570 Queen Elizabeth gave to Edward Dyer "in consideration of good and faithful service. . .the stewardship of the manor and woods of Woodstock, Oxford, and its members for life, and the rangership and portership of the park." At this time the estate contained the royal palace, several lodges, seven villages, and ample parks; in fact, it was larger than the present-day estate of Blenheim. A few years after Dyer took possession of Woodstock, Elizabeth paid a month's visit to the palace. At this time Dyer had completed "The Songe in the Oke" for her to regain her favor. Elizabeth paid another visit to the estate at the end of September 1600, on one of the very last extended trips she made before her death in March 1603. Dyer was

removed as steward by July 1604 after James I took the throne.

Later, Sir Walter Scott used the town in two of his historical novels. While the palace is mentioned in *Kenilworth* as one of the Queen's places, Woodstock's major use occurs in his novel of the same name. The action of *Woodstock* takes place during the Civil War, and the scene is set mostly in the Royal Lodge and park here. Scott describes it thus:

They stood accordingly in front of the old Gothic building, irregularly constructed, and at different times. . . .The oldest part[,]. . .Fair Rosamond's Tower[,]. . .was a small turret of great height, with narrow windows and walls of massive thickness. The tower had no opening to the ground, or means of descending, a great part of the lower portion being solid mason-work. It was traditionally said to have been accessible only by a sort of small drawbridge, which might be dropped at pleasure from a little portal near the summit of the turret, to the battlements of another tower of the same construction, but twenty feet lower, and containing only a winding staircase, called in Woodstock Love's Ladder; because it is said, that by ascending this staircase to the top of the tower and then making use of the drawbridge, Henry obtained access to the chamber of his paramour.

In the 17th century Woodstock had a strong association with the dissolute poet and courtier John Wilmot, 2d Earl of Rochester. After leaving Oxford and traveling abroad, Wilmot spent most of his rather licentious life in the service and court of Charles II, who made him ranger here. When he realized that he had not much longer to live, he asked that Gilbert Burnet, Bishop of Salisbury, minister to his soul. Growing progressively weaker, Wilmot went to High Lodge and requested that the bishop hear his final confession and repentance. Burnet was just in time, and the earl died on July 26, 1680, two days after the bishop's departure. He was buried in nearby Spelsbury. The bed in which he died is preserved in the modern Blenheim Park on the far side of the lake.

In the 18th century one of the century's arbiters of taste, Alexander Pope, arrived in the area after being in Oxford. Sir John Vanbrugh had finished the palace at Blenheim in 1704, and Lancelot (Capability) Brown designed the grounds; about these Pope made no comment, but he certainly disliked Vanbrugh's "little kingdom in stone":

I never saw so great a thing with so much littleness in it. . . . It is a house of entries and passages; among which there are three vistas through the whole, very uselessly handsome. . . . [The series of cupolas and turrets] make the building look at once finical and heavy. . . . In a word, the whole is a most expensive absurdity; and the Duke of Shrewsbury gave a true character of it, when he said, it was a great *quarry of stone above ground.*

WOOKEY, Somerset (pop. 869) Wookey is located 2 miles west of Bath at the edge of the Mendip Hills, an outcrop of limestone covering a substructure of red sandstone. It is the limestone which provides the famous caves of the area, as well as the notorious "swallet holes," holes which temporarily swallow up streams. The Axe River flows through the first three chambers of the great cave of Wookey Hole (northeast of the village) before broadening into a lake; underwater explorations have established that at least seventeen more chambers exist in the cave. The ancient tale of the Witch of Wookey Hole, for whom a giant stalagmite has been named, was given veracity in this century when excavations revealed a woman's skeleton, a dagger, a sacrificial knife, and a witch's crystal (a round stalagmite) under the floor of one chamber.

Wookey Hole has been an attraction for centuries. William Camden records a visit to the cave in his *Britannia* (he calls it Ochie), and Michael Drayton includes it in *Poly-Olbion* under the name Ochy:

> Yet *Ochyes* dreadfull Hole still held her selfe disgrac't,
> With th' wonders of this Ile that she should not be plac't:
> But that which vext her most, was, that the *Peakish* Cave
> Before her darkesome selfe such dignitie should have. . . .

Later, Daniel Defoe visited Wookey Hole, which he compared to Poole's Hole in Derbyshire. He was not impressed by the cave and wrote a curt passage concerning the "famous and so much talked of" cave, noting that there was "nothing of wonder or curiosity in it."

The village itself has associations with the young H. G. Wells, who came here in October 1880 with a distant relative, Alfred Williams, who was to be headmaster of the village school. Wells's place in the situation was that of an "improver," or pupil-teacher. The Wells family did not realize how much of a scoundrel "Uncle" Williams was, and H. G. Wells was put in a difficult position. Unknown to Wells, Williams had forged a complete set of documents to secure this job; Wells left Wookey in January 1881 for Surly Hall, Berkshire, and Alfred Williams, who was found out, was dismissed from his post in May.

WOOL, Dorset (pop. 2,290) Situated just west of Wareham on the Frome River, the village of Wool contains one of the best specimens of 17th-century bridgework in Dorset. At the northern end of the bridge is the Elizabethan Woolbridge Manor House,

WOOKEY HOLE The limestone outcropping of the Mendip Hills provides the swallet holes and famous caves of the area. Wookey Hole, undoubtedly the most famous of all, contains, at last count, no fewer than twenty chambers, but Daniel Defoe found nothing wondrous about the cave.

WOOL Here at Woolbridge Manor House Tess and Angel Clare spent their horrible wedding night, during which Tess forgives Angel his past transgressions but Angel finds he cannot forgive Tess's past with Alec D'Urberville.

Thomas Hardy's Wellbridge House, ancestral home of the D'Urberville family in *Tess of the D'Urbervilles*, where Angel Clare and Tess spend their terrifying wedding night.

> [R]eaching Wellbridge, [they] turned away from the village to the left, and over the great Elizabethan bridge which gave the place half its name. Immediately behind it stood the house in which they had engaged lodgings, whose exterior is so well known to all travellers through the Froom Valley; once portion of a fine manorial residence, the property and home of a D'Urberville, but since its partial demolition a farmhouse

The farmhouse, now a hotel, retains its original appearance with its tall fluted chimneys and stone-mullioned windows and courtyard of red brick. Inside on the staircase are the "two life-size portraits on panels built into the masonry." Now these portraits are only faint tracings, thanks to merciless soap-and-water scrubbings which were designed to make them cleaner. The legend which Hardy presents about the coach is now part of local folklore: when the family coach passes over the Elizabethan bridge and stops at the house on Christmas Eve, it presages death or disaster. According to both Hardy and legend, only the doomed can hear the coach.

Just east of the village, but farther away than Hardy places it, is Bindon Abbey, a Cistercian foundation moved here from Little Bindon in 1172 by the local lord, Robert de Newburgh. The dissolution of the monasteries in the 16th century almost totally ruined the abbey; as Hardy states, "The abbey had perished, creed being transient." Sleepwalking, Angel Clare carries Tess along the bank of the river and across to the abbey grounds until he

> reached the ruined choir of the Abbey church. Against the north wall was the empty stone coffin of an abbot, without a lid, in which every tourist with a turn for grim humour was accustomed to stretch himself. In this Clare carefully laid Tess.

The stone coffin has been carefully preserved as Hardy must have seen it. Wellbridge is mentioned in "The Withered Arm" (*Wessex Tales*), and the original of East Stoke Farm is located between Wool and Wareham.

WOOLBEDING, Sussex (pop. 314) A tiny hamlet 1 mile north of Midhurst, Woolbeding is reached down a rutted cart track so narrow that cars negotiate it with difficulty. The church has vertical stone strips protruding from the pebble-dash wall and a Norman font. The village rectory was the boyhood home of the dramatist Thomas Otway, whose father was presented with the living here around 1655. The Rev. Humphrey Otway probably held this post until his death in 1670, when Thomas was eighteen years of age. The young boy left a curious memorial, scribbled Latin quotations (with his signature) in his father's parish registers. Otway was sent to Winchester College in 1668 and spent only his holidays here from then on.

More recently, Charlotte Smith, the 18th-century novelist and poet, lived next to the church in the 17th-century Woolbeding Hall, whose garden contains a tulip tree 130 feet high that is supported by a trunk 20 feet around. She came here from a miserable sojourn in France around 1786 and is thought to have left four years later.

WORCESTER, Worcestershire (pop. 53,532) The first recorded history of Worcester, on the Severn River 22 miles southwest of Birmingham, occurred in the 7th century, when a new site was chosen above the flooding riverside lands. Curiously, there is no evidence of any pre-Saxon settlement, but Worcester did have a dragon, as attested by Geoffrey of Monmouth, who used (and possibly created) it in the prophecies of Merlin in his *Historia Regum Britanniae*:

> "Then indeed shall come a very Giant of Wickedness, who will terrify everyone with the piercing glance of his eyes. Against him will arise the Dragon of Worcester, which will do its best to destroy him; but when they come to grips the Dragon will be worsted and overwhelmed by its conqueror's wickedness. . . ."

What can be confirmed emerges in the 7th century, when the see of Worcester was founded for secular canons; they were constantly harassed by the marauding Danes, who were attracted to the wealthy town. A gruesome reminder of the times is preserved in the cathedral in the form of a piece of skin said to have been flayed from a Dane who was caught, chalice in hand, at the church door. St. Wulstan built the crypt and part of the nave and transept from 1084 to 1092, and when King John died in 1216, his will directed that he be buried here (he had paid no fewer than eleven visits to the city), and his tomb was placed about where the apse ended. At the same time the choir was rededicated after a serious fire, and the body of St. Wulfstan was moved to its present site. So great an attraction were the monument of the King and the shrine of the Archbishop that pilgrims came in droves to be cured and to leave their money in the town. Most of the cathedral was built from these proceeds; the whole would give quite a uniform impression if it were not for the west front, which suffered from an energetic 19th-century restoration.

Medieval Worcester was the fifth largest town in England, owing its importance especially to its wool and glove industries, and was the center of an enormous diocese. The crowded town was surrounded by a wall, 50 feet high in places, and a deep ditch, and was ¾ mile in length. This was a peaceful and prosperous town until 1651, when it became the site of the most decisive battle in the Civil War; as a consequence, the walls and most of the houses outside them were destroyed. The battle occurred when Charles II with his Scottish troops marched south into the city and secured the Commandery, as it is now known, for their headquarters. The Parliamentarians, far outnumbering the Royalists, attacked on two fronts and seized the city; Charles himself managed to escape, supposedly through a New Street house (now known as King Charles's House) built on the city wall with a door to the outer side.

Worcester has long been an interesting spot to visit. John Leland was here a century before the destructive Civil War and commented that it "is reasonably well waulyd and the waule is maynteynid," with six gates, but even then (ca. 1535–1543) Worcester Castle was not standing:

> It is now clene downe, and halfe the base courte or area of it is now within the waulle of the close of the cathedrall churche of Worcestar.

Daniel Defoe was in Worcester after the Parliamentarian destruction and states in *A Tour thro' the Whole Island of Great Britain*:

> *Worcester* is a large, populous, old, tho' not a very well built City; I say not well built because the Town is close and old, the Houses standing too thick. The North part of the Town is more extended and also better built.

He found the cathedral uninteresting and was especially curious about King John's entombment:

> The Cathedral of this City is an antient, and indeed, a decay'd Building; the Body of the Church is very mean in its Aspect, nor did I see the least Ornament about it, I mean in the out side. . . .
>
> The Inside of the Church has several very antient Monuments in it, particularly some Royal ones; as that of King *John*, who lyes Interr'd between two Sainted Bishops, namely, St. *Oswald*, and St. *Woolstan*. Whether he ordered his Interment in that manner, believing that they should help him *up* at the last call, and be serviceable to him for his Salvation I know not. . . .

Another writer in another century looked at the city differently; William Cobbett, in his *Rural Rides*, calls Worcester "one of the cleanest, neatest, and handsomest towns I ever saw; indeed, I do not recollect to have seen any one equal to it." He does, however, echo the earlier opinion of the cathedral:

> The *cathedral* is, indeed, a poor thing, compared with any of the others, except that of Hereford; . . . but the *town* is, I think, the very best I ever saw; and which is, indeed, the greatest of all recommendations, the *people* are, upon the whole, the most suitably dressed and most decent looking people. The town is precisely in character with the beautiful and rich country, in the midst of which it lies. Everything you see gives you the idea of real, solid wealth. . . .

There are several other literary associations, and one of the earliest and most interesting concerns William Shakespeare. In the archives of the diocese, at St. Helen's Church, is the bond, or obligation, for £40 signed by Fulk Sandells and John Richardson for the special license issued for the William Shakespeare–Anne Hathaway wedding. The bond, dated November 28, 1582, is the only record of the marriage; the men bound themselves in the surety so that William Shakespeare and Anne Hathaway might

> lawfully solemnize matrimony together, and in the same afterwardes remaine and continew like man and wiffe, according unto the lawes in that behalf provided; and, moreover, if there be not at this present time any action, sute, quarrell or demaund moved or depending before any judge, ecclesiasticall or temporall, for and concerning any suche lawfull lett or impediment; and, moreover, if the said William Shagspere do not proceed to solemnizacion of mariadg with the said Anne Hathwey without the consent of hir frindes; and also if the said William do, upon his owne proper costs and expenses, defend and save harmles the right reverend Father in God, Lord John Bushop of Worcester, and his offycers, for licencing them the said William and Anne to be married together with once asking of the bannes of matrimony betwene them, and for all other causes which may ensue by reason or occasion thereof, that then the said obligacion to be voyd and of none effect, or els to stand and abide in full force and vertue.

Also of interest is a register entry dated November 27, 1582, one day before the Shakespeare-Hathaway special license, for a license issued for the marriage of "William Shakespeare and Anna Whatley of Temple Grafton." This, though, is an entry and not a bond.

A second association existed in the 17th century, and of this too there is little information. Samuel Butler, the author of *Hudibras*, who was born in nearby Strensham, was educated at the Worcester Free Grammar School.

The 18th century saw William Wordsworth composing a sonnet about one of the most celebrated tombstones in England; a stone labeled simply "Miserrimus" stands in the cathedral cloisters. Possibly this is the grave of the Reverend Mr. Morris, who was deprived of his living after William III came to the throne and who lived the rest of his life in abject poverty. Wordsworth's description of the appearance and situation of the stone tallies today:

> Most wretched one,
> *Who* chose his epitaph?—Himself alone
> Could thus have dared the grave to agitate,
> And claim, among the dead, this awful crown;
> Nor doubt that He marked also for his own
> Close to these cloistral steps a burial-place,
> That every foot might fall with heavier tread,
> Trampling upon his vileness. Stranger, pass
> Softly!—To save the contrite, Jesus bled.

Wordsworth's association with the cathedral is not the most important one; that is Francis Brett Young's. Born in the shire, he said that he dreamed of it whenever he was away. Addressing the annual dinner of the Worcester Association in London in 1934, he expressed the hope that he would die in the shire,

> but not just yet. And if I come to you in the penitent guise of a prodigal returned I must ask you to accept me not merely as a sheep but as the whole hog.

He died, though, in a South African nursing home

on March 28, 1954, but his ashes were buried at Worcester Cathedral, where services were held on July 3, 1954. An appropriate quotation from Young's works was used for the service:

> "And when they asked him where he would lie, he bethought him of our Church of St. Mary at Worcester saying: '*I commend My body and soul to God and to St Wulston.*' So here we buried him. . . ."

A few other associations with Worcester are of passing interest. William Shenstone, who lived in nearby Halesowen, was a frequent visitor to the Worcester Music Festival, and Lewis Carroll (Charles Lutwidge Dodgson) spoke to the girls at the High School in 1892. Finally, William Makepeace Thackeray set part of *Catherine: A Story* here and created the Three Rooks, a mean public house frequented by criminals:

> It will be necessary to explain the reason of it. We gave the British public to understand that the landlady of the "Three Rooks," at Worcester, was a notorious fence, or banker of thieves; that is, a purchaser of their merchandise. In her hands Mr. Brock and his companions had left property to the amount of sixty or seventy pounds, which was secreted in a cunning recess in a chamber of the "Three Rooks," known only to the landlady and the gentlemen who banked with her. . . .

WORCESTER   Worcester Cathedral, now not the "decay'd Building" Daniel Defoe saw or the "poor thing" William Cobbett described, was originally a Benedictine foundation where the monk Florence of Worcester wrote *Chronicon ex chronicis* before his death here in 1118.

WORCESTER PARK, Surrey (pop. 502) Worcester Park, both a hamlet and a seat, was once known as Old Malden and today is most frequently referred to as Malden; it is now part of the borough of Malden and Coombe, which has been incorporated into the new London borough of Kingston-upon-Thames. Thus, although the hamlet and seat no longer exist, they once did and were located on the Hogsmill River 3 miles southeast of Kingston-upon-Thames; this was one of the parks surrounding the extravaganza known as Nonsuch, which was built by Henry VIII. Henry, though, died before this project was completed, and Worcester Park was sold to the 12th Earl of Arundel, who later sold it to Elizabeth. Eventually, during the plague, the Office of the Exchequer was moved to Nonsuch, and after the estate was given to the Countess of Castlemaine by Charles II, she sold it off piecemeal to satisfy her debts. Before that, John Evelyn visited and dined at his "good friends Mr. Packer"; he then toured the grounds:

> The Palace concists of two Courts, of which the first is of stone Castle like, . . . the other of Timber a Gotique fabric, but these walls incomparably beautified. . . . There stand in the Garden two handsome stone *Pyramids,* & the *avvenue* planted with rows of faire *Elmes,* but the rest of those goodly Trees both of this & of *Worcester*-Park adjoyning were fell'd by thos destructive & avaritious Rebells in the late Warr, which defac'd one of the stateliest seates his Majestie had.

In 1897 H. G. Wells moved into Hatherlea from his house in Woking; it was, said Wells, "a picturesque and insanitary house in the early Victorian style." A frequent guest was George Gissing, who lived in Dorking, and it was here at Hatherlea, in July or August 1898, that Gissing first met Gabrielle Fleury. She had approached Gissing about translating *New Grub Street,* and the initial talks on the project took place here.

WORTH, Sussex (pop. 4,568) With suburbia to the north and woodlands and lakes to the south, Worth has an almost perfect location $6\frac{1}{2}$ miles west of East Grinstead. Worth Abbey was not an abbey but rather the 19th-century fancy of a wealthy industrialist who bought Paddockhurst (its name then) and enlarged it. Fittingly, it is now a Roman Catholic public school and monastery. Crabbet Park, now a riding school, became the home of Wilfrid Scawen Blunt when he inherited the family estate after the death of his elder brother in 1872. His wide interests were given scope here, and he maintained a stud farm with the brood mares he acquired in Ha'il, Arabia, and persuaded Newmarket to include a July meet for Arabs. From 1881 on he rarely spent winters in England and in 1895 gave up Crabbet Park for Newbuildings Place in Southwater.

On his jaunts around the countryside William Cobbett frequently stayed at North Lodge (gone), the home of Samuel Brazier, who employed Cobbett's farming methods.

WORTHING, Sussex (pop. 67,500) Situated between the South Downs and the sea, Worthing is on the coast 11 miles west of Brighton and roughly halfway between Beachy Head and Selsey Bill. The town's history, though uneventful, can be traced to a pre-Roman settlement on the rounded height of Cissbury, a few miles north, and the Romans and the Saxons settled in successive waves. Its first charter, granting the right to hold a market, came from Edward III, but the town was never more than a fishing village and an appendage to nearby Broadwater.

There are two important literary links with the town; Oscar Wilde and his family took 5 Esplanade Terrace here in the summer of 1894, a year before his trial and sentencing to two years of hard labor. He was working on *The Importance of Being Earnest,* and much of the general attitude of the play is said to be a result of the good temper of Worthing. Of more significance is that the hero was named John Worthing in appreciation, Wilde claimed, of his pleasant experiences here. William Ernest Henley came to St. George's Lodge, Chesswood Road, in 1899 to recuperate from surgery and to escape from London. His time was spent working on *Hawthorne and Lavender;* in fact, he finished the book here, and the dedication is dated "Worthing, July 31, 1901." He left in 1901 for Battersea before going on to Woking.

WOTTON, Surrey (pop. 550) The Tillingbourne Valley is one of the most beautiful in Surrey; the "vale," says William Cobbett in his *Rural Rides,* "is skirted partly by woodlands and partly by sides of hills tilled as corn fields." He was then most concerned about the perversion of this "bountiful providence . . . one of the choicest retreats of man" into an area for the "execution [of] two of the most damnable inventions . . . of men . . . the making of *gunpowder* and of *banknotes!*"

> Here in this tranquil spot, where the nightingales are to be heard earlier and later in the year than in any other part of England; where the first bursting of the buds is seen in spring, where no rigour of seasons can ever be felt; where everything seems formed for precluding the very thought of wickedness; here has the devil fixed on as one of the seats of his grand manufactory; and perverse and ungrateful man not only lends him his aid, but lends it cheerfully! As to the gunpowder, indeed, we might get over that.

In fact, the paper mill burned down in 1896, and the gunpowder went with World War II; but Cobbett would probably still be disgruntled by the type of housing which presently spills over the landscape. Wotton, though, is one of the less changed places in the valley; $2\frac{1}{2}$ miles southwest of Dorking, it is just at the beginning of the rise to Leith Hill (965 feet), in a beautifully wooded area. The church, basically 13th-century, may be Saxon in part and has been fully restored.

The manor of Wotton House, bounded on the north by the Downs, was the birthplace of the diarist John Evelyn on October 31, 1620. Evelyn describes the house and its environs in great detail in his diary:

> It is situated in the most Sothern part of the Shire, and though in a Vally; yet realy upon a very greate rising, being on part of one of the most eminent hills in England for the prodigious prospect to be seen from its summit, though by few observed. . . .The house is large and antient, suitable to those hospitable times, and so sweetely environ'd with those delicious streames and venerable Woods, as in the judgment of strangers, as well as Englishmen, it may be compared to one of the most tempt-

ing and pleasant seates in the Nation . . . for it has risings, meadows, Woods & Water in aboundance; not destitute of the most noble and advantagious accommdations. . .

At the age of two weeks, Evelyn was baptized in the dining room of the house rather than in the parish church, a fact about which he later expressed great regret. His earliest schooling took place at the church, most likely in the porch under the tower:

I was not initiated into any rudiments till neere 4 yeares of age; and then one Frier taught us at the Church-porch of Wotton; and I do perfectly remember the greate talke and stirr about il Conde Gundamar, now Ambassador from Spaine. . . .

At an early age Evelyn went to reside with his maternal grandparents in Lewes, Sussex; being badly spoiled there, Evelyn refused to go to Eton, as his father wanted, and was allowed to return to Sussex. In the spring of 1636 he entered the Middle Temple in London, but his plans were never seriously to study law; his desire was only to acquire sufficient legal savoir-faire for a country gentleman. Evelyn continued to spend a great deal of time here, and when he was disturbed by the violence and confusion in London surrounding the Civil War, he escaped to Wotton, determined to find "some quiet if it might be." He busied himself in building a fishpond in the gardens and a study for himsel.

After his marriage in Paris to Mary Browne, aged twelve, in 1647, Evelyn returned to Wotton without her and remained in England for two years, often spending time here at the manor, which by then had passed to his eldest brother, George, upon the death of their father. After his return to England with his wife in 1652, the two stayed for a time at Wotton Hall, where their first daughter, Mary, was born on October 1, 1665; Mary was christened in the parish church. In 1691 Evelyn's nephew died, and he came into the estate:

So as now (there remaining onely Daughters, women grown, & of an Elder sons of my Bro:) according to the Intailement; I became the next heire to my Bro: & our Paternal Estate, exceedingly far from my least expectation, or desert: The Lord God render me & mine worthy of this Providence, & that I may be a comfort to my Bro: whose prosperity I did ever wish & pray for:

He and his family finally moved here in 1694, and Evelyn took over the management of the estate after the death of his brother George in 1699. The diarist spent much time, energy, and money in improving the estate, but the great storm of November 26, 1703, undid much of this work. It is easy to understand the feelings of this old man of eighty-three who wrote on November 26 and 27:

26 The dismall Effects of the Hurecan & Tempest of Wind, raine & lightning thro all the nation, especial⟨ly⟩ London, many houses demolished, many people killed: [27] & as to my owne losse, the subversion of Woods & Timber both left for Ornament, and Valuable materiall thro my whole Estate, & about my house, the Woods crowning the Garden Mount, & growing along the Park meadow; the damage to my owne dwelling, & Tennants farmes & Outhouses, is most Tragicall: not to be paralleled with any thing hapning in our Age or in any history almost. . . .

Evelyn died in London on February 27, 1706, and was buried here in a plain stone coffin in the chapel above the family vault on March 4. The epitaph reads, in part:

Living in an age of extraordinary events, & revolutions he learn't (as himself asserted) this truth which pursuant to his intention is here declared That all is vanity wch is not honest, & that there's no solid Wisdom but in real Piety.

His wife, who died in 1709, was also buried here. Much of the original house was destroyed by fire in 1800 and has since been greatly rebuilt and added to. The present house contains many treasures, including Evelyn's books and drawings, three portraits of the diarist, and the prayer book carried by Charles I at his execution.

A 19th-century visitor to Wotton House was Matthew Arnold, a friend of the owner, W. J. Evelyn; Arnold was especially interested in the herbarium collected by John Evelyn in Italy in the 17th century.

WRINGTON, Somerset (pop. 1,369) Wrington, on the north side of the valley of the same name, has become a popular residential village for commuters to Bristol, 12 miles away. The Yeo River flows nearby, and the village lies below the wooded slopes of Bull Wood and Wrington Hill. Here, in 1623, John Locke was born; the church, with an extremely fine Perpendicular tower, contains a commemorative bust in the south porch. The church also contains a monument, and the churchyard the grave, of Hannah More, who lived in the general area from 1785 until her death in 1833. In 1800 she built Barley Wood, half a mile northeast of the village, and she was living here when she "made a pet" of Thomas Babington Macaulay, whose mother she and her sisters had taught at Bristol. At Barley Wood as well, Hannah More met Thomas De Quincey first in 1809. De Quincey's mother had moved into nearby Westhay, and De Quincey made several visits here that year. He had read Miss More's *Coelebs*, which he called "trash," commenting, "I could not find a sentence with any thought in it; and the grossest errors in propriety and good sense in every page." Hannah More and her sisters were in daily touch with the De Quinceys. In a letter to William Wordsworth's wife, De Quincey described Miss More as "a horrid bigot—censorious—and greedy of flattery to any amount under cover of a frequent disclamation of all merit—and with all the forms and phrases of profound humility." Samuel Taylor Coleridge was a visitor in 1814. Cowslip Green, a hamlet half a mile southwest of Wrington, was Miss More's home before she built Barley Wood.

Following the death of his mother in July 1898, Francis Brett Young came with his father to an uncle's house in Wrington. The events are related in *The Young Physician*, in which Edwin and his father bicycle to Wringford; at this time Edwin is informed (as, indeed, was Francis) that there is no possibility of his attending Oxford and that he is to take a degree in medicine.

WYCOLLER, Lancashire   Near the Calder River and 3 miles east of Colne, Wycoller lies at the edge of the Trawden Forest, at the foot of the moorlands north of Burnley. The village is known for its seven bridges, including a 13th-century double-arched packhorse bridge and the Druid bridge, consisting of three monstrous boulder-supported stones. The 16th-century Wycoller Hall, now in ruins and once the rambling, spacious home of the Hartleys and the Cunliffes, was the original of Ferndean House in Charlotte Brontë's *Jane Eyre*. After the fire at Thornfield Hall and the death of his mad wife, Rochester retires to Ferndean, "a building of considerable antiquity, moderate size, and no architectural pretensions, deep buried in a wood," where Jane seeks him:

> Presently I beheld a railing, then the house—scarce, by this dim light, distinguishable from the trees; so dank and green were its decaying walls. Entering a portal, fastened only by a latch, I stood amidst a space of enclosed ground, from which the wood swept away in a semicircle. There were no flowers, no garden-beds; only a broad gravel walk girdling a grass-plat, and this set in the heavy frame of the forest. The house presented two pointed gables in its front; the windows were latticed and narrow: the front door was narrow too, one step led up to it. The whole looked, as the host of the Rochester Arms had said, "quite a desolate spot."

WYE, Kent (pop. 1,390)   Set between the Stour River and the escarpment of the Downs, 10 miles southwest of Canterbury and 4 miles northeast of Ashford, Wye is generally a quiet market town, but in the early spring the Wye Races draw thousands of visitors. The church here still has the nave and aisles of the original early-14th-century cruciform church, but the rest is later, with the buttressed tower dating from the 18th century. Wye was probably the birthplace of the dramatist and novelist Mrs. Aphra Behn in July 1640, and she was baptized in the Church of St. Gregory and St. Martin on July 10; little is known about her life here, and she left Wye as a child for Surinam. In early 1919 Joseph Conrad moved to Spring Grove here and finished *The Rescuer*, but he was in Wye for only few weeks before going on to Bishopsbourne.

WYTHBURN, Cumberland (pop. 60)   Wythburn has an especially attractive location in the Lake District lying under the shadow of Helvellyn on the southeast corner of Thirlmere, the highest lake in the area. Dunmail Raise, a pile of stone thought to commemorate the Saxon king Edmund I's victory over Dunmail, the last Cumbrian king, is just south of the village and is the meeting point of Cumberland and Westmorland. Some of the earlier beauty of Thirlmere was lost in the 19th century when the lake was dammed to form a reservoir; the level of the lake was raised 60 feet and with the accompanying flooding of part of the valley floor the old Cherry Tree Inn disappeared. This was the inn William Wordsworth describes in "The Waggoner":

> "Blithe souls and lightsome hearts have we
> Feasting at the CHERRY TREE!"
> This was the outside proclamation,
> This was the inside salutation;
> What bustling—jostling—high and low!
> A universal overflow!
> What tankards foaming from the tap!
> What store of cakes in every lap!
> What thumping—stumping—overhead!
> The thunder had not been more busy:
> With such a stir you would have said,
> This little place may well be dizzy!
> 'Tis who can dance with greatest vigour—
> 'Tis what can be most prompt and eager;
> As if it heard the fiddle's call,
> The pewter clatters on the wall;
> The very bacon shows its feeling,
> Swinging from the smoky ceiling!

Wythburn Church, a small building with a floor sloping upward to the altar, is now somewhat less simple than when Hartley Coleridge wrote of it:

> Humble it is, and meek, and very low,
> And speaks its purpose by a single bell;
> But God Himself, and He alone, can know
> If spiry temples please Him half so well.

Wordsworth also writes of the church in "The Waggoner."

There are two other literary associations with Wythburn: Dante Gabriel Rossetti completed his last volume of poems at nearby Fisher Place, and a stone seat has been erected here to the memory of Matthew Arnold.

YAFFORTH, Yorkshire A tiny North Riding village 1½ miles west of Northallerton, Yafforth has a lovely Tudor Old Hall (altered), the birthplace of Thomas Rymer in 1641. Rymer's father, an ardent Roundhead, was granted this estate (which he previously had rented) for his services during the Commonwealth, but he was compelled to return the holding at the Restoration. Thomas was educated at a nearby school in Danby Wiske by Thomas Smelt before going up to Sidney Sussex College, Cambridge.

YALDING, Kent (pop. 2,555) A perfect example of old England with cobbled walks, timber-fronted houses with tile and thatched roofs, and hop gardens and kilns, Yalding is 6½ miles southwest of Maidstone where the Beult and Teise join the Medway River. Two 15th-century bridges, scheduled as national monuments, span the rivers. Edmund Blunden was born in Yalding on November 1, 1896, and spent his childhood here; "Forefathers" presents this Kentish countryside:

> Here they went with smock and crook,
>   Toiled in the sun, lolled in the shade,
> Here they mudded out the brook
>   And here their hatchet cleared the glade:
> Harvest-supper woke their wit,
> Huntsman's moon their wooings.

YARDLEY HASTINGS, Northamptonshire (pop. 804) Eight miles southeast of Northampton, Yardley Hastings has a modest situation that belies its early importance; the avenue of beeches leading to Castle Ashby Park and the park itself, just north of the village, are all that remain of the early forest which once engulfed the whole countryside. The village church is Norman to 14th-century, and the south door, through which the church is entered, is 13th-century and still on its original iron hinges. Yardley Chase, still unspoiled and uncleared, was a favorite spot of William Cowper; an old giant of a tree, known as Cowper's Oak, is traditionally held to be the place where he wrote "Light Shining out of Darkness" ("God moves in a mysterious way. . . ."); and, it is said, the tree will never die because it sheltered the poet during a heavy thunderstorm as he wrote. Cowper also wrote of the oak; the unfinished work was found among his papers:

>   Time made thee what thou wast, king of the woods;
> And time hath made thee what thou art—a cave
> For owls to roost in. Once thy spreading boughs
> O'erhung the champaign; and the numerous flocks
> That grazed it, stood beneath that ample cope
> Uncrowded, yet safe shelter'd from the storm.
> No flock frequents thee now. Thou hast outlived
> Thy popularity, and art become
> (Unless verse rescue thee awhile) a thing
> Forgotten, as the foliage of thy youth.

YARMOUTH *See* GREAT YARMOUTH.

YATTENDON, Berkshire (pop. 283) A woodland setting in the Pang Valley complete with thatch-and-timber houses makes Yattendon an extremely desirable location; the village is, as well, only 10 miles west of Reading and has good access to both London and Oxford. The 15th-century church with its open timber roof has a good Jacobean pulpit and chest, and the church contrasts nicely with the modern Yattendon Court. For slightly more than twenty years Yattendon was the home of Robert Bridges. Returning from convalescence in Italy in 1882, Bridges and his widowed mother took the Manor House, and the poet found the ordered world he needed for his work. Two years later he married a local girl, Monica Waterhouse, the daughter of an architect, and their three children were born here. The house was a pleasant old red-brick building with a rook-haunted garden at the back. The period at the Manor House was one of the most productive in Bridges's life: *Eros and Psy-*

che, eight dramas, a semidrama, numerous critical essays, lyrics, and odes, and *The Yattendon Hymnal* all date from this time. The last-named work was a direct result of Bridges's lifelong love of music, which was underscored by his training the boys' choir in the local church. Gerard Manley Hopkins visited Bridges here twice, in May 1886 and August 1887, and the two poets talked extensively of Hopkins's work. It was while here, in 1895, that Bridges was invited to stand for the Chair of Poetry at Oxford, an invitation which he declined. In 1907 he settled at Chiswell House on Boar's Hill, Berkshire, where he died on April 21, 1930. Bridges was buried here, and the grave is marked by a cross.

YEALMPTON, Devon (pop. 878)   All too infrequently the literary origins of popular rhymes, especially children's nursery rhymes, cannot be traced, but Yealmpton (pronounced "yamp′ton"), located 10½ miles southeast of Plymouth, is one of the rare villages with specific information. Mother Hubbard's Cottage (now a café) is traditionally held to have been owned by a housekeeper at Kitley, a mile to the west. This was the home of the Pollexfen Bastards, into whose family Sarah Martin's sister married. Miss Martin, who wrote the Mother Hubbard rhyme, lived with her sister and brother-in-law for a time and wrote the rhyme here. The library at Kitley contains the only known first edition (1805) of *Mother Hubbard.*

YELDEN, Bedfordshire (pop. 160)   There are two spellings of the name of this village 3½ miles southeast of Higham Ferrers: Yelden and Yielding. To confuse matters further, the postal authorities have insisted on an amalgamation of the two: Yielden. The village proper is a combination of thatch-and-stone houses and some very modern, squat detached brick cottages. The 14th-century, mostly Decorated church has a squat little spire. It contains a number of notable old brasses and a 15th-century pulpit from which John Bunyan preached on Christmas Day, 1659.

YEOVIL, Somerset (pop. 19,078)   In England the term "border town" is almost never applied to any town outside the North, but the industrial town of Yeovil on the Yeo River, 19 miles northwest of Dorchester on the Somerset-Dorset border, is an exception. The town has been called Ivel, Gifle, Yoel, Yevel, and Iula, and some of these names have also been applied to the river. Medieval Yeovil was a rich town known for its cloth and glove-making trades; the Perpendicular church, the George Inn, Woborne's Almshouses, and the Three Choughs date from this period. These are the principal survivors of a series of early fires, the worst of which was the great fire of 1449. But the leather-glove industry survived, and by the time of Daniel Defoe's visit here the glove industry had become the economic basis of the community.

Yeovil was the home of Thomas Hardy and his wife for a short time in 1876; they came here from Swanage in March but remained only until May, when they took a holiday on the Rhine and in Holland before settling for a time at Sturminster Newton. The town becomes Ivell in Hardy's works,

in a shift to an older form of the name, and occurs principally in "A Tragedy of Two Ambitions" (*Life's Little Ironies and a Few Crusted Characters*). Many of the locations in the story are readily identifiable. After Joshua Halborough is released from jail, he requests his sons to meet him at the Castle Inn in Ivell "with a coach-and-pair, or some other such conveyance, that he might not disgrace them by arriving like a tramp" at Narrobourne (East Coker). Finding him gone from the inn, the sons realize they have already met him as "some one who was unsteady in his gait, under the trees on the other side of Hendford Hill, where it was too dark to see him." "For Conscience' Sake" in the same group of stories also uses Ivell: the Rev. Percival Cope, whom Frances Frankland marries, is the curate of St. John's Church here and has lodgings on St. Peter's Street. The town is also specifically mentioned in various other works: Ivell Church is noted in "The Homecoming" (*Time's Laughingstocks and Other Poems*); Ivel Road, that is, the road from Dorchester to Yeovil via Cerne Abbas, is mentioned in "At Casterbridge Fair" in the same volume; and in "San Sebastian" (*Wessex Poems*) Ivel Road is called Ivel Way. In the works of Thomas Coryate Yeovil becomes Evil.

YIELDEN or YIELDING   *See* YELDEN.

YORK, Yorkshire (pop. 100,800)   Situated ideally in the broad expanse of lowland known as the Vale of York, this town is often called the capital of the north and has always been part of the main north-south thoroughfare. York is located at the corner of the three ridings and belongs to none of them; it is a county borough and a city, administers its own affairs, and has both a lord mayor and a sheriff. Michael Drayton in *Poly-Olbion* praises York as the shire's "most-lov'd City" and enlivens his map of the area with "that great Forrest-Nymph fair *Gautresse,*" a personification of the ancient forest which bounded York on the north. The depiction of York Minster adroitly balanced on the head of a rather hefty young lady with outspread arms is probably one of the most delightful of his illustrations.

When the early Celts lived here, York was known as Ebrauc; in A.D. 71 Petillius Cerealis set up a camp here, and by the 3d century Ebracum (the Roman name for York) had become the capital of lower Britain. As a consequence of the town's important position, the Romans surrounded it with walls. A fragment of the original wall can still be seen from the street in the grounds of 9 St. Leonard's Place; right beyond Monk Bar the wall rises to a height of 16 feet. But most of the extensive remaining walls are medieval; stretching for 3 miles, they include a number of interesting gates. There are also extensive remains of a Roman bath complete with hypocaust (the brick hot-air ducting system) at the Roman Bath Inn on St. Sampson's Square. York has a unique place in Roman history, for it was here in A.D. 306 that Constantine the Great was proclaimed Emperor; during his reign the Christian Roman Empire began.

When the Romans left, York reverted to its Northumbrian natives and flourished until the Danish invasions. With its strategic location and easy accessibility, Jorvic, as York was now called, became a large

Danish community and the center of Danish trading. By the time of William the Conqueror (r. 1066–1087) the city was too important and prosperous not to be subjugated immediately; William added two enormous fortifications on the Ouse. One remnant of the Conqueror's period is the scanty remains of a Norman house reached through a small alley at 52A Stonegate.

With the prosperity of medieval York and its guilds the building of the great Cathedral of York was undertaken. It took more than two centuries to erect the cathedral, and although it is an architectural hodgepodge, it is extraordinarily interesting. The real highlight is the stained glass: the collection, which covers a period of 800 years, was removed during World War II for safekeeping. The enormity of that task becomes apparent if one realizes that the Great West Window (1405–1408) contains more than 2,700 square feet of glass. The cathedral was untouched by the Parliamentarians following the Battle of Marston Moor because of direct orders by Gen. Thomas Fairfax and thus, unlike the Cathedrals of Winchester and Salisbury, managed to retain its original fabric. The diarist John Evelyn visited York a few years after the Civil War and noted that the cathedral "which of all the greate churches in England had been best preserv'd from ye furie of ye sacrilegious . . . it is a most entire magnificent piece of Gotic architecture." The cathedral is represented by an archbishop, styled the Primate of England; the Archbishop of Canterbury is the Primate of all England. Richard Scrope, whose posthumous fame was enhanced by William Shakespeare in Parts I and II of *Henry IV*, was Archbishop when he was sentenced to death at Bishopthorpe. His plain table tomb is in the north choir aisle.

As the medieval guilds prospered, they began their production of the famous York Mystery Plays (a *mistery* is a trade). The recorded history of the Corpus Christi plays begins in the late 14th century, but a reference to the plays in the York Memorandum Book (1378) implies that they were ancient even by that date. The plays, originally performed in churches to dramatize the Bible for the illiterate, were moved outdoors when they began to take on a secular tone. It was natural to give to each of the guilds a play or the part of a play to produce, but exactly how the play and the guild were combined is not always known precisely. At York the Shipwrights Guild was concerned with *God Forewarning Noah to Make an Ark of Light Wood*, and the Goldsmiths, Goldbeaters, and Moneymakers with *The Three Kings*. In 1417 the objects and mode of the performances were defined, and each pageant was set to "be played at twelve stations." Each individual play was produced on a pageant wagon, paid for and maintained by a guild and drawn from station to station by a team of men hired for the purpose. Criticism of the congestion caused by the plays and of the "popularity" of the performances themselves was recorded even in the 15th century, and in 1561 a house book notes that the feast of Corpus Christi was no longer kept; the last-known performance of the cycle was in 1569. Not until 1951 were the plays revived; then the cycle was shortened, the texts amalgamated, and the whole made comprehensible for 20th-century audiences. The performance is now held mainly

YORK   The ruins of the 13th-century St. Mary's Abbey, a Benedictine house founded in the late 11th century, form an impressive backdrop for the modern revival of the medieval York Mystery Plays.

in one place, the 13th-century ruins of St. Mary's Abbey, a Benedictine house founded in 1083. The extensive ruins of this once-famous abbey make a particularly exciting backdrop for the modern cycle. Several of the individual plays are performed at two or more of the original medieval stations, usually the west front of the minster and King's Square. In addition, *The Flood*, produced in medieval times by the Fishers and Mariners Guild, takes place at two sites on the riverbank with cast and scenery arriving by boat.

As might be expected, York has a place in Arthurian tradition. Geoffrey of Monmouth's *Historia Regum Britanniae* states that Arthur defeated the pagan Saxons and Irish at Loch Lomond in A.D. 524 and came to York to hold the first Christmas celebrated in Britain. King Arthur's grief in seeing the pagan destruction of the churches and town led to his rebuilding of York and to the refounding of religious orders. It might also be expected that York would have many legends concerning Robin Hood, since his habitat was Yorkshire and Nottinghamshire, but the city plays almost no part in the lore. One stanza in "A Gest of Robyn Hode" mentions St. Mary's Abbey, but Robin Hood pays little attention to York or its immediate surroundings.

Twelfth-century York is well depicted in Sir Walter Scott's *Ivanhoe*, and although virtually none of the action takes place in the city, a very strong impression of the medieval English attitude toward Judaism is presented in the ill-treatment of Isaac of York. York, indeed, has its enduring memories of the medieval ghetto in the names Jewsbury (the site of the Jewish cemetery) and Jubbergate. Scott has the marriage between Wilfrid of Ivanhoe and Rowena take place in the cathedral, with King Richard in attendance. As Scott says, "The nuptials of our hero . . . were celebrated in the most august of temples, the noble Minster of York. The King himself attended. . . ." Earlier, York Castle is presented in all its splendor as the castle "to which Prince John had invited those nobles, prelates, and leaders by whose assistance he hoped to carry through his ambitious projects upon his brother's throne." Only Clifford's Tower, the keep of the castle, remains, and this medieval quatrefoil keep is the one referred to erroneously by Scott. The original tower and castle were built by William I and set on fire in 1190 during anti-Jewish riots; the stone structures referred to by Scott were not built until the 13th century. Scott visited the city a number of times, and on his July 1815 trip to York, following Napoleon's final retirement, he began "The Field of Waterloo." On this visit as well, he attended services in York Cathedral and was impressed with the beauty of the structure.

The use of the castle in literature is by no means confined to Scott. William Shakespeare, in *Henry VI: Part II*, has Queen Margaret welcome her husband to York with the sight of "the head of that archenemy," the Duke of York, above the gate. Act IV, scene vii of the same play is set here at Micklegate Bar, referred to as the Gate of Royalty. King Edward and his entourage find "[t]he gates made fast" and demand entry, which is denied by the mayor of York and his aldermen. Edward's admission to the town is effected by his assertion that he comes as the Duke of York and as "King Henry's friend." Once inside the city walls, Edward proclaims himself Edward IV. In *Henry IV: Part II* the overt setting of the Archbishop's Palace in York is misleading; the episcopal home was in the nearby village of Bishopthorpe. Thomas Heywood places the fourth act of *A Woman Killed with Kindness* in York; this is the scene of Sir Charles Mountford's imprisonment for nonpayment of debts and his subsequent release because of the good offices of Sir Francis Acton, the man who brought about his initial confinement.

Daniel Defoe knew York quite well and mentions it as a "pleasant and beautiful" town in *A Tour thro' the Whole Island of Great Britain*. At the very beginning of *The Life and Strange Surprizing Adventures of Robinson Crusoe* he takes some license with the actual history of Alexander Selkirk, upon whose experiences the book is based. Crusoe is said to be "of York, mariner. I was born in the year 1632, in the city of York of a good family, though not of that country." Defoe's prototype, Selkirk, was a native of Lower Largo, Fifeshire, Scotland, and the family still inhabits an old stone house on the waterfront there. William Beckford, like Defoe an inveterate traveler, toured England from August through October 1779 and visited York. His *Journal* contains a long description of York Minster. He gives his impression of the stained-glass window of the cathedral, which "filled him with religious feeling," and describes the windows as "magic," "enchantment," and "illusion." Horace Walpole, who visited York and the cathedral in 1722, was annoyed by the placement of the only royal tomb in the cathedral, that of Prince William of Hatfield, the younger brother of the Black Prince. Walpole describes the effigy in the north choir aisle as being "tossed aside into a corner." Percy Bysshe Shelley and his first wife, Harriet, were here shortly after their marriage in 1811. They arrived in York in October with Thomas Jefferson Hogg and found lodgings at a Miss Dancer's at 20 Coney Street but were unimpressed by the city. Indeed, the whole story was unhappy, for it was in their lodgings here, when Shelley was out, that Hogg declared his love for Harriet. Parrying his advances, she managed to get her sister Eliza to stay with her until Shelley returned. Shelley forgave Hogg but decided a move from York was necessary, and the group made its way to Keswick, Cumberland.

The real Eugene Aram was tried and executed for the murder of Daniel Clarke here, but neither Edward Bulwer-Lytton in *Eugene Aram* nor Thomas Hood in *The Dream of Eugene Aram* places the event here. William Wilkie Collins uses York in *No Name*, which depicts with extreme accuracy the old streets. One of these is Stonegate, on which is "At the Sign of the Bible," occupied from 1682 to 1873 by the booksellers who sold the first printing of Laurence Sterne's *Tristram Shandy*, and another is the Shambles, originally the Fleshammels, the street of butchers, one of the best-preserved medieval streets in England. An extremely good Grinling Gibbons monument in York Minster commemorates Archbishop Richard Sterne, the great-grandfather of Laurence Sterne. Sterne himself delivered his last sermon in this cathedral; he had acquired a prebendal stall in York when he was vicar of Sutton-on-the-Forest and occasionally preached here. However, he was not popular and gradually gave up preaching at the cathedral. Sterne spent a great deal of his childhood here; upon the death of his father he was removed from his school in Halifax and brought to York to live with a cousin who had a rather large estate. It was this cousin who provided the funds for Sterne's education at Jesus College, Cambridge, after he spent two years of absolute idleness at home. Dr. John Burton, a well-known 18th-century physician at York County Hospital, is lampooned under the name Dr. Slop in *Tristram Shandy*.

A 20th-century native of York was W. H. Auden, who was born at 54 Bootham on February 21, 1907; the Auden family was here only until 1908, when Dr. Auden took the post of medical officer and professor of medicine at the University of Birmingham.

The Bede window in All Saints' Church, North Street, which is usually associated with the Venerable Bede, has nothing to do with him. The window depicts events of the final fifteen days before the Last Judgment, which Bede did not describe (St. Jerome did); the window is called the Bede Window in the sense of a bede being a prayer; it is, indeed, a prayer for the donors of the window.

ZENNOR, Cornwall (pop. 298) In the westernmost area of Cornwall, only half a mile from the rock-strewn coast, Zennor is isolated and provincial. The name of the village is a corruption of the name of Senara, an obscure Cornish saint. The Norman church contains a remarkable bench carving of the Mermaid of Zennor, who sang so beautifully that she enticed a squire's son to live with her in her underwater cave; a well-preserved Norman window and font; and a commemorative plaque to John Davys, Sr., and John Davys, Jr., allegedly the last men to speak Cornish.

In early March 1916 D. H. Lawrence and his wife stayed at the Tunners' Arms before leasing Higher Tregerthen for £5 a year. Lawrence was fascinated by the location: "The place is rather splendid. It is just under the moors, on the edge of the few rough stony fields that go to the sea. It is quite alone, as a little colony." Katherine Mansfield and John Middleton Murry were persuaded to join Lawrence and his wife here in April, but they disliked the cottage and its situation from the first and stayed only a short time; Lawrence's frequently changing moods contributed to their unease. Lawrence was working on *Women in Love* and *The Rainbow* at the time; in a later work, *Kangaroo*, a chapter titled "The Nightmare" depicts Cornwall during World War I and indicates that the Lawrences were not happy in Zennor after all. Actually Lawrence's moods and Frieda's German ac-cent did not mix well with the villagers' suspicions of foreigners. Indeed, the Lawrences were suspected of spying and signaling German submarines. The end came one night when they were exuberantly singing Hebridean songs; the villagers thought these were German and reported the Lawrences to the appropriate officials. On October 12, 1917, the police descended on the cottage; finding nothing of significance, they nevertheless delivered orders expelling the Lawrences from Cornwall.

INDEX

NOTE: Page numbers in *italic* indicate that the entry appears in more than one article on the page.